Footage 89

Footage 89

North American
Film and Video Sources

Edited by
Richard Prelinger and Celeste R. Hoffnar

Index edited by
Tom Damrauer

Prelinger Associates, Inc.

Published by Prelinger Associates, Inc.
430 West 14th Street, Room 403
New York, NY 10014 (USA)
(800) 243-2252 or (212) 633-2134

Library of Congress Catalog Card Number 88-90769

ISBN 0-927347-01-6

Printed in USA

Information contained in *Footage 89* was supplied by the listees themselves.
Attempts were made to update all names, addresses, telephone and fax
numbers and contact names prior to publication. All listings and information
appear at the discretion of the publisher. Although every effort has been made
to make *Footage 89* as accurate and complete as possible, the publisher
disclaims any responsibility or liability for the inclusion or omission of any
source, for incorrect or incomplete information, and for typographical errors.

Table of Contents

The Voyager Company

THE CRITERION COLLECTION

THE FINEST VIDEO VERSIONS OF THE WORLD'S GREATEST FILMS

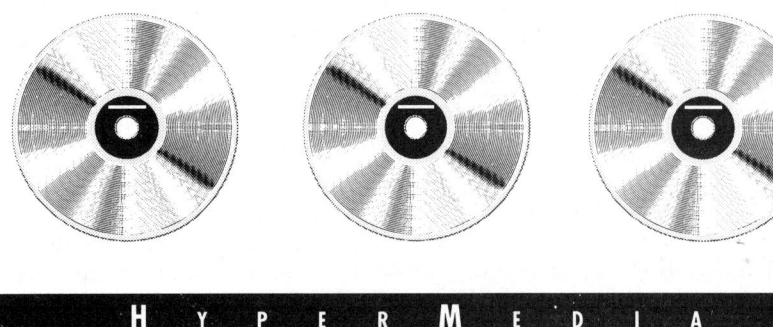

H Y P E R M E D I A

The Voyager VideoStack

HYPERCARD TOOLKIT FOR INTERACTIVE VIDEO

interactive discs

THE LOUVRE ❧ MUYBRIDGE ❧ BACHDISC

NATIONAL GALLERY OF ART

❧ AND NEARLY **100** MORE TITLES ❧

Call or write for free catalog or information:

The Voyager Company

1351 PACIFIC COAST HIGHWAY · SANTA MONICA, CALIFORNIA 90401
213.451.1383 · 800.446.2001 · CA ONLY 800.443.2001

The Voyager Company is a joint venture of Janus Films and Voyager Press

Publisher's Preface

by Richard Prelinger

Footage 89 is designed to facilitate access to moving image materials (film, videotape and computer graphics) for all potential users, whether their interests are academic, artistic, commercial, documentary, educational, historical, newsworthy or scientific. The many research leads contained in this book offer a wealth of entry points to the rich visual record held by North American repositories.

The first edition of *Footage 89* appears at a time when the number (and variety) of moving image collections, along with the demand for access to their holdings, is rapidly increasing. This edition lists 1,635 collections in North America, many which have only recently become accessible. We expect that subsequent editions will list many more.

Access to moving image material lags behind access to information in other media. This is due in part to complex ownership and rights situations, the fragility of the materials, and, in many cases, the lack of duplicate or viewable copies. Despite similar conditions, however, union catalogs of printed books, recorded sound collections, newspapers and periodicals have existed for some time, and several source directories facilitate access to still photographs and graphics. Until now, however, no systematic survey of North American film and video resources has been issued (although subsets such as educational films, sponsored films and videotapes and 16mm films in non-theatrical distribution are well documented). We feel that the time for such a survey is long overdue.

Much communication is rapidly shifting from print-based modes into what might be called a "moving mode." The often-noted shrinkage in the public's attention span and the proliferation of information competing for everyone's time have exerted pressure on communicators to make their messages quickly comprehensible and distinct from all others. Bearing this in mind, associations, corporations, educators, political organizations, institutions and independent media-makers of every type have turned to film and videotape, aided by increasingly simple and accessible production technology. With this growth in media production, the demand for ready-made footage has increased tremendously.

Influenced by considerations of cost and creativity, more producers are incorporating pre-existing footage into their programs than ever before. A few of the new applications for moving images that have emerged in the very recent past include: image modification using compositing and computer graphic techniques; the compilation of audiovisual encyclopedias and reference works on optical disc; hypermedia; interactive training and instructional materials; "desktop" presentations; and "architectural" uses of moving images, including videowalls and video billboards.

The commercial stock footage sector has experienced tremendous growth during the 1980s. From perhaps two dozen libraries at the beginning of the decade, the industry has grown to comprise over 160 companies today who characterize themselves as stock footage libraries, as well as hundreds of producers and other companies who license stock footage on an occasional basis. The stock footage business is also becoming increasingly marketing-oriented and competitive, and it would be fair to assume that it will see its share of mergers and acquisitions in the next few years.

The historical and analytical value of moving image records has also drawn increased recognition in recent years, as biases favoring print-based materials gradually disappear. Academic researchers and scholars have begun to engage in the analysis of images, and look to visual documentation for information unavailable elsewhere.

As the mass of moving image material retained by public and private repositories grows, these institutions face new challenges. Requests for research and access to collections often outpace the sources' ability to service them. Active discussion continues with regard to such problem areas as the state of preservation technology, sources of funding, evaluation of materials for continuing retention, the status of rights to archival materials, and expediting access to audiovisual materials through new technology. However, these knotty problems have not inhibited the formation of new collections or the continuing growth of existing ones. We hope to continue documenting this fascinating field and the changes that it undergoes over time.

Our experience in operating a commercial stock footage library has led us to include moving image sources of all kinds, regardless of their nature. *Footage 89* expresses no opinion as to the relative "value" of collections. Since film and videotape materials are held by a wide variety of public and private entities, researchers or potential users will find it difficult to limit a search either to public or private sources. In the same way, we list numerous sources for material on political and social issues of current interest, including many organizations that espouse currently "unpopular" causes. Though the nature of holdings and accessibility differs between sources, we feel that their commonality as moving image sources merits listing them in one sequence. The length and detail of each listing is determined both by the nature and quality of information supplied by the listees and by our editorial judgment. We actively seek additional information on all sources, whether listed or not, in order to complete our coverage in future editions.

We hope that users will feel free to offer their reactions, criticism and advice in order that *Footage 89* can evolve into a reference resource of continuing value.

Criteria for inclusion

All types of institutions, organizations and corporations holding moving image collections were encouraged to provide information in support of an entry. The decision whether or not to list individual sources was solely that of the editors. Since this is the first directory of its kind, we have avoided overly restrictive inclusion criteria; the user will therefore find a great variety of general and specialized collections listed with equal emphasis.

In general, sources were included if they held unique moving image material (or material not easily accessed through other sources), and indicated a willingness to serve either the general public or specific categories of users. Practically all sources, of course, regulate and/or limit access to and reuse of material in their collections. Subdistributors and educational media centers whose collections comprise materials acquired from commercial distributors were generally omitted, although there were certain exceptions to this rule. (We list, for instance, The New York Public Library, Donnell Media Center, as the size and breadth of its collection and its location in the nation's media capital render it an indispensable reference source for many researchers and producers. Certain specialized collections and collections located outside major metropolitan areas are also listed, even though they may primarily hold commercially acquired materials.)

Certain sources are omitted from this book due to lack of available information, our inability to reach individuals authorized to provide information, or their unwillingness to be represented. Three commercial stock footage libraries and two studio-based stock footage libraries, all in the Los Angeles area, declined our repeated invitations to supply information, generally out of reluctance to expand their customer base. A number of private or proprietary collections, including several corporate archives, musical film collections and a New York-based library of boxing films and African-American newsreels, have also declined representation. Several collections familiar to professional archivists and film researchers are also omitted due to their present inaccessibility.

No attempt has been made to describe still photograph, graphic, paper, book or recorded sound collections in detail, as other reference resources exist in these areas.

Authorized listings

Information contained in listings was solicited by questionnaires, telephone interviews and personal visits. All listings appear by authorization of the listees. Many of the more extensive entries (e.g., Library of Congress, National Archives, the major newsreel libraries, and the Mexican collections) were researched and written by qualified specialists. A number of entries reprint material supplied by the listees themselves (e.g., UCLA Film and Television Archive, the National Archives of Canada, and Petrified Films, Inc.). *Footage 89* does not contain information derived from secondary sources, other directories or compilations of information, unless such information was supplied to us expressly for publication and accompanied by reprint permission. The editors hope that listees will participate in improving the quality and depth of their listings in subsequent editions.

Geographical coverage

Collections in North America (United States, Canada, Mexico, and the Caribbean) are listed. Although we attempted to give equal weight to North American collections located outside the United States, we would appreciate assistance in making our coverage more complete. Coverage of collections outside North America in future editions is under study.

Guest articles

We are pleased to include articles relating to various aspects of moving image archives and preservation, stock footage, research, rights and clearances, and copyright. Each was written by an authority in the field.

Acknowledgements

The book you hold in your hands owes its existence to the labor and generosity of many people. Their support throughout *Footage 89*'s long gestation period and their unswerving belief in the importance of this book has been indispensable.

Footage 89 is not a new idea. Many have seen the need for a reference to moving image collections, and other books partially covering this territory have been published. I am especially indebted to Bonnie Rowan, whose *Scholars' Guide to Washington, D.C. Film and Video Collections* (1980; a revision is in preparation) inspired the publication of this book; and to David Thaxton, one of *Footage 89*'s earliest supporters.

This book would not exist in its present form without the efforts of Celeste R. Hoffnar, my co-editor and collaborator. Unfazed by austerity, recurrent delays and lack of air conditioning, she brought a sorely needed measure of organization to the project and imposed structure, coherence and consistency upon information emanating from many sources. She began working when the information base comprised a small box of file folders, and has become the person most responsible for shaping this mass information into a completed book. Her contributions are too numerous to count, but include the codification of *Footage 89*'s format and style, the supervision of employees, the invention of many productivity tricks, the design of an order-fulfillment system and the administration of a massive research undertaking. Her influence has affected every aspect of research, writing, editing and production, and the quality of the finished book is largely due to her efforts.

Information for the listings was gathered by questionnaires, telephone interviews and personal visits. In this process we were assisted by many capable researchers, including Richard Benz; Annik Brunet, whose bilingual capabilities were essential in questioning Francophone sources; Sarah Drury, who interviewed literally thousands of individuals in every kind of institution imaginable; Kathryn High, who researched and wrote the listings for media arts centers, public access television facilities, museums, video art and independent video collections, and Cuban archives; Celeste R. Hoffnar; Jeannie Hutchins, who verified names, addresses, telephone numbers and contact information prior to publication; Lewanne Jones, who visited the major newsreel collections and interviewed staff members; Lorena Parlee, who with Irma Avila researched and wrote the entire section on Mexico; Kate Ross, who, as *Footage 89*'s first employee, identified several thousand potential moving image sources; Cyndy Turnage, whose persistence and tenacity resulted in the inclusion of dozens of elusive collections; Jane White, who researched and wrote entries for the ABC Television Network; and Susan Zeig, responsible for the Puerto Rico listings.

Entries were written by L.K. Aubrey, Annik Brunet, Sarah Drury, Susan Emerling, Erika Gottfried, Susan Haven-Scheer and Dee Ann Dart, Kathryn High, Celeste R. Hoffnar, Barbara Humphrys, Lewanne Jones, Susan Lasher, Hillary Middlekauff, Lorena Parlee, Richard Prelinger, Bonnie G. Rowan, Lyrysa Smith and Jane White.

Our detailed subject index was edited by Tom Damrauer, who worked patiently for many months on the complex task of defining subject categories appropriate to a wide range of institutions and research needs. Thanks to his effort and rigorous insistence on accuracy and quality, researchers will find answers to many complex queries already present in the index. We have benefitted immensely from his advice and experience, and he has made many conceptual contributions to the book as a whole.

I am especially indebted to Barbara Humphrys for her article on the Library of Congress, Motion Picture, Broadcasting and Recorded Sound Division, a great leap forward in making the Library's vast collection known to researchers; to Bonnie G. Rowan for her lengthy description of the moving image collections of the National Archives and Records Administration, the most complete and accurate summary ever prepared; to Lewanne Jones for her articles on the major newsreel collections; and to Branda Miller, for the generous, long-term loan of a computer.

Richard Benz, Lorna Lentini and Sally Stark proofread over a million words.

Our cover was designed by Karen Kowles.

Advertising sales were handled by Cyndy Turnage on the West Coast and Lisa F. Overton on the East Coast.

Thanks are due to many others, including Prudence Arndt; L.K. Aubrey; Jules Backus, for cheerleading and extraordinary help; Leslie Belt; Jessica Berman-Bogdan; Diane Bertolo, for timely and inspired graphic assistance; Larry Bird; Michael Bogdan; Anne Bray; Eric Breitbart; Susan Caraher; Cathy Carapella; Nancy Casey; Russ Clower, for graphic assistance; Tony Conrad; Marcia DeSanctis; Mary Dore; David Dreyfuss; Keller A. Easterling, for her continuing support; Erik Feder; Robert Finehout; Jim Fleming; Teresa Fox; Linda Goldman; Jeffrey Goodman; Kevin P. Green; Howard Greenberg of Axiom Design; Maria Groumbos; Dee Dee Halleck; Howard Hays; Chris Hill; Robert Hoffnar; Mark Holechek, designer of the *Footage 89* mailer; Adriene Jenik; Laurie Kahn-Leavitt, who generously shared her research with us; Joel Kanoff; Dayna Kirk; Joel Kovel; Mary Lance; Alan Lewis; Linda Lilienfeld; David Loesch; Gregory Lukow; Paula Lumbard; Fred MacDonald; Libby McDonald; Martha Magill, for computer input; Tom Mann of Wickersham Printing Co.; Electra McDowell; Media Network; Kati Meister; Monica Melamed; Thad Meyerriecks; Philip Miller; John Minkowski; Susan Morris; Richard W. Morton; Roberta Oster; Rosanne Percivalle; the staff of Petrified Films, including Robert Cates, Lori Cheatle, Michael O'Callaghan and Marian Thatos; David Pierce; Richard Pieto, for proofreading and assistance on the index; Harold Potter; Jane Prelinger, who assisted in questionnaire processing; Polly Prelinger, for timely assistance; Dorothy, Elizabeth and Ernst Prelinger, for their patience and unfailing boosterism; Larry Racies; Karen Ranucci; Megan Ratner; Deborah Richardson; Karen Y. Rosen, who supplied valuable information on film distributors; David Rothkopf;

Keith Sanborn, for computer input; Richard Scheckman; Fay Schreibman; Anthony Slide; Aleen and Bob Stein, for their timely assistance; Bob Summers, for much information and support; Anne Sweeney; Renee Tajima; Ruth Tamura; Catherine Taylor; Richard Weiss; and Pamela Wintle.

We thank the archives, libraries, corporations and institutions profiled within for their efforts to provide information. It is our hope that *Footage 89* will serve their needs as well as the needs of researchers, scholars and producers.

Special thanks are due to our advertisers, who supported this book before it came into existence. Their assistance has been invaluable.

Many of you who are now using this book expressed your faith in its concept by ordering in advance of publication. We are extremely grateful for your patience.

Finally, my personal thanks to Pierce Rafferty, who has supported this endeavor in every conceivable way, and, most of all, to Kathy High, for her love, patience and support.

Richard Prelinger
New York, June 1989

Some Thoughts About Film and Video Research

by David Thaxton

For much of the past twenty years I have been involved with film and video research — as a teacher, archivist and filmmaker. During the past decade I have worked on many television documentaries and independent features as a "film researcher." And I have been asked many times: "What is film research? What does the film researcher actually do?"

First of all, "film research" usually means *film and video* research. For more than a decade, events around the world have been recorded primarily on videotape. And today, even events recorded originally on film are available for research and study only on reference videotape in many archival collections. But while technologies may change, the process remains much the same.

Film and video research usually involves locating images which, though shot for a particular project (or as film of record), can be acquired for inclusion in another production. It could mean finding color footage of robins and bluebirds building nests for a television commercial by a Hong Kong bank. It could mean finding newsreel footage of the bombing of Shanghai in 1937 for Bernardo Bertolucci's *The Last Emperor*. Or it could mean looking at hundreds of film reels shot by military cameramen for a documentary series on World War I or II, Korea or Vietnam.

Sometimes looking at film or video is the last thing one does. Simply finding the footage to view can occasionally become a process with many steps.

Recently, an Australian producer called me for help. He was making a documentary about the trial of General Yamashita, the Japanese general whose fanatical defense of the Philippines in 1945 left the city of Manila in ruins. Yamashita was convicted as a war criminal in a controversial trial and hanged in 1946.

The producer had located footage of the trial but was unable to find a related film that everyone he interviewed remembered. It was a short film produced in Hollywood and reportedly had a sensational, propagandistic tone. No one was sure of the film's title but its point was clearly remembered: that General Yamashita's troops had ravaged Manila and its civilian population under direct orders from Tokyo.

I had never come across the film in years of research in the newsreel and military collections from World War II. Archive colleagues I called were also unfamiliar with the film. But the copyright records at the Library of Congress revealed that Warner Brothers produced a 20-minute short in 1945 entitled *Orders From Tokyo*. The OSS [Office of Strategic Services] and the government of the Philippines were listed as co-producers. And the Warner Brothers release sheet synopsis I found in the copyright registration records indicated that the film would show how Manila was "systematically ruined by direct orders from Tokyo" with footage which "will be used to hang the Japanese war lords."

Unfortunately, there was no viewing print in the Library of Congress collection, but there was a Technicolor negative in the Library's storage vaults in Ohio. The archive staff at the Library was as intrigued as I was. But preservation work would have to be completed before the film could even be viewed. And copyright clearance was required before the footage could be included in the Australian documentary.

Knowing that the producer was working against deadlines which might not allow the time required to obtain the material from the Library of Congress, I began to search for a print elsewhere. None of the public or private collections I checked could locate a print of the film. The legal departments and film vaults at Warner Bros. (which produced the film) and MGM/UA/Turner Entertainment (which now owns much of Warner Bros. "product") could find no record of the film. Except for the Technicolor material in the Library's nitrate vaults, *Orders From Tokyo* seemed to have disappeared.

Several months later, with preservation work completed, I was finally able to view a video transfer of the film. *Orders From Tokyo* was what the synopsis had promised: "one of the bloodiest and most amazing sagas to come out of this war. Here it is in all its terrible glory."

Dramatic music introduced the title letters dripping in blood. And after an introduction by General Carlos Romulo, resident commissioner of the Philippines, there were grim scenes of the Battle of Manila with violent street fighting along with emotional scenes of suffering women and children, now homeless refugees.

And there was one scene (which every witness remembered) of an American GI searching the body of a dead Japanese soldier as the narrator intoned: "Then, the shocking discovery. On the Japanese dead was found proof of 'orders' — from the Japanese Supreme Command — for the systematic massacre of Manila's citizens and the complete destruction of the city."

The "proof" was never made visible in the film, but the narrator was so convincing that proof seemed hardly necessary at the time. Like many of the more well-known films of the period, *Orders From Tokyo* turned out to be a brilliant example of wartime propaganda — and in Technicolor!

The process of film and video research is not always so drawn out. But when the researcher is involved from the beginning of a project, there is often time to look for more important and unusual material which might require weeks or months to view and acquire. Often, the *early* involvement of a film and video researcher can help to shape a project as well as influence its budget.

Several years ago, I was called by a network producer then beginning work on a television documentary about the Vietnam War. It was the tenth anniversary of America's withdrawal. He was planning to focus on the origins of the war, specifically the Tonkin Gulf incident.

Aside from the expected television news stories filmed in

the days following the incident, I found eight reels of 35mm Ektachrome negative at the National Archives labelled: "Simulated Tonkin Gulf Incident." There were no viewing prints but the catalog cards noted that the footage was taken aboard the USS Ticonderoga, USS Maddox, USS Constellation and USS Turner Joy and "attempts to reconstruct the activities which actually took place aboard these ships during the period of the Tonkin Gulf incident."

A video transfer of the color negative confirmed our hopes. Within two weeks of the incident, the events had been re-staged for Navy cameras complete with aircraft, artillery, ships, commanders and crew.

The discovery would have a significant effect on the shape of the finished program. The details of the incident were complex and had been the subject of controversy since the mid-sixties. The interviews already planned with eyewitnesses could be intercut with the Navy material. And the audience would not have to visualize what had happened; the Navy had already done it on film.

The producer used the footage extensively. And the fact that the film was in the public domain meant significant savings to the budget. The finished documentary received critical praise as well as awards for television journalism.

Sometimes what is found through research can determine the style and substance of a film or video project. The style of *The Atomic Cafe,* for example, was determined in part by the footage Pierce and Kevin Rafferty and Jayne Loader found during their years of research. In similar fashion, the outtakes Kevin Brownlow and David Gill turned up in the Chaplin family archives revealed the methods Chaplin used in producing his films and thereby determined the story the producers were able to tell in their television series, *The Unknown Chaplin.*

Occasionally, the archival film and videotape elements of a documentary project are so complex that systems need to be devised simply to keep track of the material. Kenn Rabin designed a computer software program for the 13-hour *Vietnam: A Television History* (produced by WGBH/Boston) which enabled the producers to identify every frame of footage (by source, date, description and cost) and track the images from acquisition through editing and post-production. Similar applications of computer technology are now fairly common even on smaller documentary projects.

While archival collections are too varied and the uses of film and video too diverse to suggest a "best way" to proceed in every case, some general suggestions for anyone new to the business of moving image research might be helpful.

First, it is important to know the story to be told. This is especially critical when film or video of specific historical events is required. Nothing beats historical training and experience — except perhaps a few good books. While knowledge of history may not be essential, a sense of history is required. The more you know about what you are looking for, the more likely you are to recognize it when you see it.

It helps to know why particular images are needed and how they are going to be used. And the more the film and video researcher knows about the production and the production process, the better. The early involvement of a researcher as well as the integration of the research process into the production schedule can prove enormously important (if not essential) to any project with a significant archival dimension and a limited budget.

In order to make the best use of whatever time and money are available, it is especially important for the film and video researcher to be organized and to understand what a particular collection is likely to contain. Moreover, advance planning is required. Most public and private film and video collections require reservations to view. And while you must determine the costs of rights and duplication, you will also need to know if there are any special requirements or restrictions on usage.

Perhaps most importantly, never forget you are the eyes (and ears) of a production, something of a fourth-dimensional forward observer. You are likely to see more film and video than anyone else involved in a project. While you must find the needed images or suggest alternatives, you will most likely be the only person who can speak for the wonderful, unexpected images which you discover in the course of research. Never disregard the potential importance of such images found by accident and good fortune.

David Thaxton taught history at West Point, served as Associate Archivist of the American Film Institute and Assistant Director of the Woodrow Wilson International Center for Scholars prior to forming Thaxton Green Studios in 1980 with partner Kevin Green. Recent projects include Eyes on the Prize *(Blackside, Inc.),* War and Peace in the Nuclear Age *(WGBH) and* Reaching for the Skies *(BBC/CBS).*

Stock Footage Libraries: A Major Part of the Film Industry for More Than Seventy Years

by Anthony Slide

The use of stock footage in both film and television production can be traced back almost to the beginnings of both media. Today, although it is often overlooked and seldom discussed, stock footage continues to play an important role in the production of television programs and commercials, as well as a lesser part in independent feature film production.

The creation and use of stock footage illustrates how the efforts of one producer can benefit another. Studio libraries retain footage which they generate, not only for their own use, but also for the use of outside producers. Independent stock footage libraries generally acquire their holdings from consignees, producers who place film shot for but not utilized in a specific production with the library. In return for so doing, the consignees receive a portion of the license fees charged by the libraries for the use of such footage, have the film cataloged at no charge, and enjoy free access to it for future projects. Thanks to the foresight of the original producers, other filmmakers can use this footage at prices which are minimal compared to the cost of recreating the production shots they need.

Many freelance cinematographers also work in tandem with stock footage libraries, shooting film wherever they happen to be. Certainly, any library will welcome footage of exotic locations, but it also appreciates what might, at first, seem mundane: film of an Eastern home in the rain, for example, or a small American town with snow on the ground. For stock footage is far more than establishing shots of foreign cities. Producers are far more likely to ask for sample matching shots of homes at day and night or of an expensive East Coast restaurant. At the height of summer, they will need footage of snow scenes or Christmas decorations. Certainly, there will be calls for cars or helicopters exploding, but there will be a greater demand for a 747 jet flying by day or night, or a taxicab runby on a suburban street.

Among the footage licensed by Producers Library Service, one of the oldest and largest of the independent stock footage libraries, during the 1986-87 television season, was the mountain cabin in the snow, in which the heroes of *Perfect Strangers* were stranded for two episodes; a deserted carnival at night seen in an episode of *Stingray;* the fraternity lodge where Cliff went for his initiation in *Cheers;* B-52 bombers for *The Wizard;* aerials of Hawaii for *Magnum, P.I.;* aerials of the Pentagon for *Scarecrow and Mrs. King;* and the South American hotel where Bobby stayed as he tried to solve the mystery as to whether his father was really dead in *Dallas.*

Some television series, such as *McGyver* and *Stingray,* make heavy use of stock footage, while situation comedies, such as *Golden Girls* or *Cheers,* may use the odd shot in occasional episodes. Major feature films today seldom, if ever, utilize stock footage, while independent features still rely heavily on it.

It is always surprising to discover the use of stock footage rather than newly shot film by a major television series. Although it should have been obvious to the producers of *Mr. President* that the series would regularly need establishing shots of the White House, no effort was made to shoot such footage until the production went into its second season. The White House shots during the first year came from a number of stock footage libraries, notably Mike Cohen's EVCO. The opening sequence in *Newhart,* with the camera following a car through the New England countryside, is actually outtakes from *On Golden Pond,* provided by the Cameo Film Library. Every stock footage library dreams of providing main title footage for a television series. Each shot, each season, can bring in a revenue of $2,800.00 or more.

This is, perhaps, the time to explain what stock footage is and what it is not. In recent years, the term "stock footage" has been used to describe any piece of a film in a library, be it black and white or color, cut picture or an outtake. "Stock footage" should be used to refer only to trims and outs from productions or specially filmed color footage. It should never be used to describe clips from features or shorts in either black and white or color. Material which cannot be cut into another production without its use being apparent to the average viewer is not stock footage. *[Editor's Note:* Footage 89 *follows industry practice, employing a more liberal definition of the term "stock footage." Libraries are listed as "stock footage sales libraries" if they have designated themselves as such.]*

The earliest known stock footage library was created by Abram Stone in 1908, and remained in existence until World War II. Its card index has survived and is presently housed at the Library of Congress. Situated on the East Coast, The Film Library (as it was called) suffered from the westward migration of the film industry, and by the 1930s was more concerned with the production of series utilizing its own stock footage, notably *Flicker Frolics.*

Because The Film Library was some 3,000 miles removed from Los Angeles producers, a method had to be devised to provide viewing prints which could not be pirated. The answer was the "scratched print," which is still in use today. As Stone's daughter, Dorothy, recalled in a 1951 article in *Films in Review:*

"This was a print made from the negative, usually a selection of scenes, and much more footage than that required by a scenario. This work print was scratched from end to end through its middle, so it could not be used. The director or editor who needed footage had the privilege of using it as a rough work print in combination with his rushes and other material. When the final editing was finished, this scratched print was returned to the library with paper markers indicating the actual footage the director or editor wanted to buy. These lengths were then matched to the negative and a duplicating positive was delivered to the purchaser, who had a duplicate negative made and inserted it in the complete production negative."

Then, as now, prints and negatives were matched through the key numbers on the edge of the film. "Scratched prints" are generally utilized today if a producer needs a workprint to determine if a stock shot will work when cut into his or her production. However, most producers can decide if they need a specific shot by looking at a library's viewing print, and based on that they will order negative. Because it is industry practice for a library to charge a license fee once a negative is pulled and released to a client, "scratched prints" tend to be used less and less, and many laboratories today are unfamiliar with the term.

William K. Everson has written extensively — notably in the January 1953 and April 1955 issues of *Films in Review* — on films of the 1920s, 1930s and 1940s which have utilized scenes from other, earlier productions. However, it should be stressed here that stock footage is not film used in earlier productions but rather film shot for but *not* used in an earlier feature. Strictly speaking, films such as *Isle of Love* from 1922, which re-edits footage from a feature of two years earlier, *An Adventuress,* to emphasize the presence of Rudolph Valentino, is not an example of the use of stock footage. The most important criteria for film to be culled and used as stock footage is that it must not include actors or actresses in the scene. Any footage with recognizable individuals in the shot is deemed "production," and would not be acceptable to a stock shot library. Film in a stock shot library cannot generally be released for use until at least one year after release of the film from which it came or, in some cases, until the original production has been given a network television airing.

During the first half of this century, independent producers had only one major stock footage source, the General Film Library, operated by Sidney Kandel and Morris Landres. Because Landres had so much footage — some 20 million feet — available to the independent producer, he was dubbed by *Motion Picture Herald* "the Mayor of Poverty Row." Founded in 1920, with offices in both Los Angeles and New York, the General Film Library included two earlier libraries, Horsley and Dawes, as well as a complete run of the *Kinograms* newsreel.

In a 1941 interview with *The New York Times,* Sidney Kandel revealed that the most profitable film in his library was of the sinking of the Austrian battleship, St. Stephen, by an Italian torpedo boat during World War I. That one scene, showing hundreds of seamen swarming over the overturned hull of the boat, was licensed to First National for use in its 1927 feature, *Convoy,* for $10,000.

Aside from the General Film Library, the only major, independent stock footage library operating prior to the 1950s was the Elmer Dyer Film Library, founded in 1920 by the highly regarded aerial cinematographer. The Dyer Library was recently acquired by the New York-based Petrified Films, Inc.

For many years, the major studios did not want it known that stock footage libraries existed on their lots. There was a strong feeling that if the public became aware that a feature had utilized stock footage it would, in some way, diminish the film's production values. Nonetheless, several of the major studios did operate stock footage libraries, with one of the most important being on the Paramount lot under the guidance of Hazel Marshall.

Miss Marshall became Paramount's librarian in 1924, when she left the lab where she was working and went in to help the woman who was supposed to be in charge. When she joined the library the most recent can of cataloged film was numbered 173. When Hazel Marshall retired on June 15, 1975, there were more than ten thousand cans of film in the vaults. (Hazel Marshall was succeeded by Connie Bulmer, who remains the Paramount librarian.)

Hazel Marshall recalls that there was little restriction on the use of footage in a studio library. Any independent producer who had the money to pay the bills could have access to the footage (although certain Paramount producers did not permit the use of their outtakes for stock footage purposes). The one exception was in the use of process plates, which were strictly for internal use. Wherever a production crew was filming, it was expected to shoot many thousands of feet of process footage for use in later Paramount features.

It was Hazel Marshall who introduced the ten foot minimum charge per cut, which remains a standard in stock footage library practice to the present. Any client utilizing stock footage must pay a minimum fee for the use of ten feet of film per editorial cut, no matter how little film the client may actually use in that cut. As Hazel Marshall recalls, "Around 1940, I was feeling guilty about sending out such small bills for the use of two or three feet of film at $2.50 per foot. And the accounts department was raising Cain about paperwork involved costing more than the film was bringing in." Prior to the 1940s, there had been no standardized minimum cut charge within the industry, although Abram Stone's Library did, apparently, charge for a twenty-five foot minimum.

Studio stock shot libraries were also maintained at Republic, Walt Disney, M-G-M, Universal, Warner Bros., and Columbia; the last three remain active, under the guidance of Jack Rush, Martin Fox and Barbara Goetz. The Columbia stock footage library handles film only from the Columbia television series. Columbia features are nominally handled for stock by the Warner Bros. stock footage library — the two companies share studio space at the Burbank Studios — but no stock footage from Columbia features has actually been pulled or cataloged in recent years.

With the demise of Republic Pictures, its stock footage was handled for a number of years by the EVCO Film Library (founded in 1962), and subsequently taken over by the CBS/MTM Film Library when Janet Meyer became its librarian in the mid-1960s. CBS/MTM Film Library, now supervised by Phil Podley, also has the outtakes from two David O. Selznick productions, *A Star Is Born* and *Nothing Sacred.* With her husband Norman, Janet Meyer presently operates the Cameo Film Library, which represents stock from Tri Star, NBC Productions, Viacom and others.

Each of the studios and the two major independent libraries dating back to the 1950s used a different color to identify their film cans. Paramount's cans were (and still are) yellow; Warner Bros. orange; CBS blue; Sherman Grinberg green; and Producers Library Service pink.

Doris Dashiell began her career with Gene Autry's Flying A Company. She subsequently became a librarian at Columbia and Desilu, when Desilu took over RKO. The RKO stock footage was eventually acquired by Paramount, and in 1964 Dashiell founded her own library at 725 North Seward Street in Hollywood. "I had the benefit of working at a studio," she notes, "and I knew what the studios had, and, more importantly, I knew what they did not have." She also realized that

16mm was now viable for use as stock footage, and made it a point to acquire 16mm color footage from cinematographers around the world. When Doris Dashiell retired, the Dashiell Film Library was absorbed by Producers Library Service.

Hazel Marshall points out that stock footage libraries came into their own with World War II and the shortage of raw stock. "Anywhere you could save ten feet of negative stock by using somebody else's establishing shot of City Hall, say, you would go with it."

A further resurgence in the importance of stock footage libraries came in the 1950s with the ready availability of 16mm footage. Prior to that decade no one went out and shot film just for possible use as stock footage, but with 16mm that became a viable proposition. The Lem Bailey library, consisting entirely of 16mm film, was founded in 1953, and is now owned by White Janssen, Inc., of Evanston, Illinois. Actor Jon Hall founded his company, the Torrejon Film Library, three years later. Today, two major stock footage libraries continue to offer a substantial collection of footage which they have shot (in 35mm): Larry Dorn Associates and Carl Barth's The Stock House.

Nick Archer has never promoted his library of specially shot footage, Telecine International Productions Inc., and yet it is one of the most widely used by the Hollywood studios, and Nick's proud boast is that he has serviced and billed over 4,000 Hollywood and New York productions from *Studio One* and *Playhouse 90* in 1957 to *I'll Take Manhattan* and *The Two Mrs. Grenvilles* in 1987.

Three major producers of the television era, Stephen J. Cannell, Lorimar-Telepictures and Aaron Spelling, were quick to recognize their need for stock footage, and have established their own stock libraries, under the supervision of Richard Wiedner, Hal Nyborg and Wendy Carter respectively.

There were many stock footage libraries in the 1950s and 1950s which are totally forgotten today, including Cinerama, Inc. Film Library (established 1962); Seth Larson's Continental Film Library (founded 1964); Dynamic Films Inc. (founded 1948 and specializing in auto racing footage); Guy Haselton (with 16mm color footage of national parks); Arthur Lodge Productions (founded 1953); Marathon International Productions (established 1947); and Stock Shots To Order, Inc. (founded 1956).

Changes in the film industry led to the creation of other libraries. Reggie Lyons (son of the ASC cinematographer of the same name) and Jack Reilly, the respective librarians at RKO and M-G-M, decided to form their own company, Producers Library Service, in 1957. The Library was intended to represent stock footage from any number of independent producers, acting as a service to both the consignee and the buyer. It now represents stock footage from the Spelling-Goldberg television series, ABC Circle Films and Orion Pictures Corporation.

The man who more than anyone else made the public and the industry aware of the use and potential of stock footage was Sherman Grinberg, who had entered the film industry in the early 1950s and, in 1957, founded the Sherman Grinberg Film Libraries, which now represent the stock footage libraries of 20th Century-Fox, Allied Artists and M-G-M, the Pathé and Paramount Newsreels, and, since 1963, footage shot for ABC *World News Tonight*.

Grinberg utilized his black and white stock footage for television series, such as *Biography, Greatest Headlines of the Century, Sportfolio, Battleline,* and *Survival*. Strictly speaking, black and white film has ceased to have potential value as stock footage; indeed, in the 1950s, libraries were licensing its use at half the price of color stock footage. Grinberg developed additional uses for black and white stock footage, and with John E. Allen Inc. of New Jersey (founded 1950) remains a major source for such film.

Sherman Grinberg died at the relatively young age of 54, on January 6, 1982. Happily, his company continues to thrive, both in New York and Hollywood, under the guidance of his daughter Linda, librarian Nancy Casey and Bernie Chertok (who has been with Grinberg since 1959).

More than 75 years after the first stock footage library was established, stock shot libraries continue to assist, in a very unique way, in film and television production. The advent of new production technologies offers new challenges to the libraries, but there can be little question that these are challenges which the libraries are willing and able to meet.

As the author or editor of some 35 books on the history of popular entertainment, Anthony Slide has been described as "a one-man publishing phenomenon" by the Los Angeles Times. *He has held executive positions with both the American Film Institute and the Academy of Motion Picture Arts and Sciences, and is presently co-owner of Producers Library Service. This essay is a revised version of an article which first appeared in the February 1988 issue of* American Cinematographer.

This article copyright © 1988 by Anthony Slide

Industrial Archive Benefits Corporate Producers

by Libby McDonald and David Dreyfuss

Two hours before a client presentation, Broad Street Productions' Senior Editor Alan Cohn decided to change the first image of a ten-minute videotape. Cohn wanted to evoke a human quality in the initial shot of a program depicting the impact of creative financing on industrial America. Working "under the gun," he input the reference point FACTORY in Broad Street's computerized stock footage catalog and received a printout which included the subcategories "exteriors, interiors, time clock," and "workers." Then, by accessing "time clock," Cohn found his shot: lit from behind with breaking sun, the factory gates burst open and a stream of workers punch a time clock. In researching stock footage for a strong opening sequence, Cohn also found a corresponding image to effectively "bookend" the piece: the sun sets over the horizon as clusters of workers emerge from a factory, punch out and head home.

The floor of the New York Stock Exchange, the manufacturing of computer chips, and a concerned physician examining a patient — these are just three of millions of images contained in Broad Street Productions' stock footage library.

Specializing in corporate communications and home video, Broad Street Productions has been shooting footage for client productions since 1981 with the deliberate intention of capturing images generic enough to have "archival" value. Today, with more than 18,000 reels of business-related footage, Broad Street houses one of the largest industrial stock footage libraries in the nation. The library handles the needs of Broad Street's in-house producers as well as requests from dozens of outside clients at production houses across the United States.

The library has proven to be a vital resource for corporate producers. Using top quality stock footage not only decreases production costs, but also allows producers to experiment quickly and economically with different kinds of shots to produce the most sophisticated and dynamic programs possible.

The availability of a collection of easily accessible footage enables producers to give their clients quality productions more quickly and less expensively. With fewer hours spent research–ing, locating and acquiring stock footage, the production process is accelerated. These benefits, however, can only be maximized with an efficient system for cataloging materials. A sophisticated collection is often updated with computer soft–ware designed to meet specific archival needs. Broad Street's system has been developed to orient a search to four points of reference — subject, visual description, location and name(s) of identifiable individuals. In addition to the database, editors' log sheets are kept on file.

The economic benefits of a stock footage library go far beyond the saving of time. A large collection of images provides a producer with a substantial portion of the footage required to piece together a program. Therefore, it is no longer necessary to shoot all new footage. Consequently, a day of shooting, which can cost as much as $4,000, becomes a day of researching and screening footage, which generally amounts to about $200. Furthermore, when a producer uses footage from an in-house source, the expense of purchasing footage and buying stock footage rights is greatly decreased and may be entirely eliminated.

By multiplying the number of shots from which to choose, an in-house archive provides producers and editors with the materials they need to match a concept with the most appropriate images and consequently fulfill a client's needs with greater accuracy. If diverse shots, such as construction sites, medical laboratories, trading floors, skylines of various U.S. and international cities, and homes are easily available, an editor gains a wide array of choices to influence the look of a videotape, deliver a specific message, and add flare and impact. Also, editors are guaranteed the quantity of footage necessary to create a dynamic montage sequence.

Broad Street Productions' Senior Archivist Laurie Friedman explains, "The only drawback to a substantial stock footage library is that you continually have to redesign a facility to properly house the expanding archive." Indeed, to safely store its growing collection, Broad Street has recently expanded its facility for the fourth time in three years.

Libby McDonald is a writer for Broad Street Productions. David Dreyfuss is President of Broad Street Productions.

Antiquated Images and Modern Technology: Stock Footage at Charlex

by Electra McDowell

Charlex Productions is a commercial production facility in New York whose work involves special effects and video post-production for television commercials, network and cable show titles and openings, and music videos. In the 11 years of our existence, many of our productions have included stock footage (both old and new), used with varying degrees of complexity.

Stock footage can help a producer cover more territory in a commercial, where the production of *one second* of running time can consume up to 50 hours of labor involving as many as 30 people. It is also true that using pre-existing imagery, rather than hiring a production crew to get a perfect shot, helps keep costs down. But the real reason that Charlex uses stock footage is that it is a convenient excuse to use cool-looking stuff.

We use every kind of footage, including silent movies, newsreels, 1940s-vintage industrials, educational films from the 1950s, footage of wacky inventions, pristine scenics and all kinds of clouds. An image may appear as an entire frame or as a cutout matted against a contrasting sequence. We modify footage (whether newly shot or archival) by painting, tinting, colorizing, crispening, blurring, making grainy and adding scratch marks and pops. There are limitless creative possibilities.

Usage may involve the most simplistic combinations, such as matting one element into another (e.g., placing a train into contemporary stock footage of clouds to make it appear that the train is flying through them). Sometimes the combinations are more complex, with multiple layers from various sources used in an eclectic mix: the figure of a 1920s trapeze artist flying in front of a group of 1950s bystanders, who are set into a 1940s Times Square shot with a background of 1970s clouds matted in behind. Apart from cutting out and shuffling old and new footage, we also use it "straight" or as a base for rotoscoping.

One of our most comprehensive uses of archival footage occurred in *9012 Live,* a longform concert video produced several years ago for the band Yes. The footage combined through the vehicle of the concert ranged from industrial films, such as *Waters of the Commonwealth* and *How the Ear Functions,* to studio outtakes, all grouped in a zany mix and unified by performance footage. Each song explored a different way of using stock material. In one, a housewife in a 1950s kitchen pulled back a curtain over her sink to reveal a mortise outside the window, containing the band flying through outer space. In another, the teenage heroine of an old sex education film moved through the stock scenes in tinted color while all the other characters and backgrounds remain black and white. Throughout the video, the songs were tied together architecturally with other elements in the form of an arcade, through which the mortised clips of footage appeared and disappeared.

A different approach was used for the opening of *Later, With Bob Costas,* a late-night television show produced by Dick Ebersole. In this show, the host interviewed various celebrities and talked to them about their past. The look of the opening was inspired by home movie-type footage, generally 8mm films made by amateur filmmakers. We came up with copious amounts of footage from the 1950s and 1960s, some from the personal collections of people who work at Charlex and NBC. We looked for memorable moments of childhood in beautiful, rich colors, complete with the blurs, out-of-focus sections and camera mistakes that give home movies their distinctive look. We used a clock wipe as a device to move the footage selects forward in chronological time, and a moving graphic pattern that looked something like the cover of an old composition notebook colored in bright, saturated hues. The clash of the old, highly reminiscent imagery and the moving colors was both powerful and fun, and succeeded in communicating the cyclical theme of generation supplanting generation and being "eye candy" at the same time.

For an Amtrak campaign, we worked with footage from two distinct sources: stock footage from libraries specializing in contemporary nature footage and client-provided footage, shot over a 10-year period, that had a distinctly routine look to it. The challenge in both cases was to take good-looking, but somewhat dull footage, and jazz it up by enhancing it with the equipment available to us. We sifted through the footage, selected the best takes, and treated it in a multitude of ways. Much was altered in the Harry, a digital editing system that also allows the editor to alter material frame by frame in the Paintbox. Certain automatic functions that alter the timing and appearance of footage, when used in combination with each other, can create distinct identities for a client's campaign.

For example, in one spot we took a shot of a train rounding a bend and heading straight at the viewer, and put it through the Kaleidoscope to change the framing of the train. This brought the train into a tight closeup by the end of the move. To increase the dynamism of the shot even more, we altered the timing by eliminating certain frames so that the shot jumped towards the viewer in a staggered, forceful punch. Finally, the industrial look of the film was enhanced by adding a grainy texture over the footage and altering its color, again using the Harry.

However it is treated, the content of the footage must convey a strong idea. With so many collections to choose from, there is no shortage of great material. Often the weirdest shot will determine the course or the look of a portion of a spot. As long as the image is as strong as possible, and communicates clearly, it is suitable. If it's possible to integrate the product into wacky stock footage scenes, we'll try it. To sell rum, for example, why not take the strangest early flying machine and make its fuselage out of the bottle; or shoot a human cannon-ball out of it; or go boating in a canoe made from the product. These ideas are simple, funny and communicate with the audience. In this way, the contrast between different subjects can create the basis for an entire style or "look."

In a regional spot for Pepsi-Cola, we chose a shot from the black and white film *Knute Rockne* showing a football player running down the field, and cut him out of his background on the Harry. Then, again with the Harry, we matted in a background of bleachers filled with cheering 1980s fans, licensed from another stock footage source, behind the running football player. The third layer, added over these two, was the product, which replaced the football, and flew in to be caught by the football player in a touchdown pass.

An effective use of footage may simply be to put two diverse subjects next to each other. We chose, for example, to pair "Crunch Tator" Cajun-style potato chips with silent film footage, along with newly shot footage and animation. This product's package is colored purple-magenta and electric yellow, and we presented it with black and white footage of 1920s-era ladies at a fancy-dress party batting balloons (painted various colors on the Harry) to one another. We took the colors from the package and created an entire palette based on them, which when used on old and new footage elements helped to relate the two diverse worlds in a wacky way, as when the balloons were painted to resemble the yellows, pinks and purples of the package.

Traditionally, resistance to using stock footage is often based on the reluctance to lend an over-nostalgic tone to the image of a new product. However, the witty combinations that can be achieved when technology brings together a new product with old iconography soon eliminate any antiquated feeling. Instead, the antiquated feels funky and fresh.

Advertising clients can't help but like using older footage to make a memorable pitch. Though many events depicted in the stock footage are impossibly surreal or frequently staged, viewers accept them as facts and see them as charming historical truth, as revelations about where we have come from. Responding immediately to this imagery, audiences feel satisfied that civilization is progressing favorably, yet feel nostalgia and sentimentality for a former innocence and simplicity. What more could a client ask for, the past and future so inexorably intertwined, and cool-looking too?

Electra McDowell graduated with a B.A. in Art History from Stanford and is currently Head of the Art Department at Charlex Productions.

Licensing Footage: Copyright and Other Legal Considerations

by Philip Miller

When you "buy" film footage, you are usually not pur-chasing the footage itself — only a license to use the material in a defined manner for a limited period of time. To understand exactly what that license buys you, you need to be familiar with the fundamentals of copyright law. You also need to know about the various levels of rights present in much film and video footage, and the steps that you can take to ensure that the license you have negotiated contains all of the clearances necessary to cover your use of the materials.

Copyright

Copyright is actually a series of rights granted to the creators of literary, artistic, musical, dramatic and audiovisual works. Under U.S. and international law, copyright gives the creators of these "intellectual properties" the exclusive right to reproduce, distribute, and create derivative versions of their works. Significantly, copyright law also gives authors and artists the right to license others to copy, distribute and adapt their work. This happens all the time in the world of film and video production, where producers regularly assign publishers and distributors the right to reproduce and distribute copies of their productions. It also happens when the owners of film and video materials license their works to be used in other produc-tions, and when authors allow their works to be adapted for the stage, cinema or television.

Under the Copyright Act of 1976, the copyright on works created after December 31, 1977 extends for the life of the author (the creator of the work) plus 50 years. If the author is listed as a group or corporation, as is often the case for film and video productions, the term of copyright is 75 years from the date of publication (the date when the work was first distributed to the public) or 100 years from the date of creation, whichever comes first. For most works created before January 1, 1978, the Copyright Act of 1976 has changed the term to 75 years from the date that the original copyright went into effect — as long as the copyright is renewed before the original 28-year term that applied under the old law expires.

If you use a copyrighted work in a manner that violates the rights of the copyright owner, you are guilty of infringement. If convicted, infringers may be required to pay damages of up to $50,000 to the copyright owner. The copyright owner can also ask the court to confiscate all copies of the work that contain the unauthorized material. In some severe cases, convicted infringers may also face criminal penalties that include fines, imprisonment, or both.

The Myth of Fair Use

Some producers make the mistake of assuming that it is legal to incorporate copyright material in a production as long as they use only a brief excerpt, or as long as they acknowl-edge the source of the material in the production credits. Often, the assumption is that this sort of use is permissible under the "fair use" provisions of U.S. copyright law. However, as many producers have discovered during litigation, fair use applies almost exclusively to certain situations where the material is being added to productions that are newsworthy, educational or nonprofit in nature. If the material is being added instead to a production that will be sold or distributed for profit, the pro-ducer is almost always required to seek and receive permission from the copyright owner. In some cases, this simply involves having a staff member who specializes in clearances or "rights and permissions" contact the copyright owner, describe the intended use, and request and receive written permission to use the material in the manner described. More often than not, however, it also involves negotiating some sort of payment to the copyright owner. The copyright owner can be the indivi-dual or company that created the material or, as tends to be the case with film and video footage, the individual or company that has obtained the rights to license material.

Note that the copyright owner (or owner's estate, if the owner is deceased) always retains the right to refuse permis-sion to use copyright material.

Levels of Rights

Most film and video productions are actually a mix of materials that a producer has licensed from a variety of sources. For example, the producer of a feature film might purchase the movie rights to a bestselling novel from one source, existing songs or an original musical score from a second source, footage of remote locations from a third source, and so on. This can mean that, along with the copyright that protects the entire work, some or all of these component pieces are protected by separate copyright and licensing restrictions.

Most productions are also collaborative efforts that involve the services of many individual contributors: actors and actresses, writers, musicians, set designers, crew members, etc. In many cases, union contracts or the individual agree-ments between performers and the producer place additional restrictions on the distribution of the finished production. For example, an actor's contract might grant the producer unlimited rights to license the work containing the actor's performance for theatrical, cable and homevideo distribution. However, the same contract might stipulate that the actor's performance cannot be licensed for reuse in television commercials. In cases where deceased performers or individuals appear in film clips, clearances from their estates may be required.

If you are purchasing the rights to reuse or distribute film or video materials, you must make sure that there are no restrictions that will prevent you from using the material in the manner that you intend. In other words, you must define the rights that you need, and you must make sure that the license for the materials includes those rights. Just as important, you must make sure that the individual or company that is licensing the material has the authority to grant you those rights. The best way to secure these guarantees is through a carefully constructed legal agreement.

Grant of Rights and Warranties

Whenever you make a deal to use film or video footage, the terms of the deal should be spelled out in a written agreement. That legal agreement should specify:
- the materials that are included in the deal;
- the exact rights that you have to use the materials, including how long you will retain the rights and where you can distribute programs that contain the materials; and
- the rights you have to modify the materials.

Here is how these rights might be defined in a sample contract between a fictitious cable television network ("The Family Channel") and a stock footage company (the "Grantor") that is licensing film material to the network.

Grant of Rights
For each picture, Grantor hereby grants The Family Channel (TFC) the non-exclusive right and license to exhibit, distribute, transmit, and perform each Picture or part thereof on Cable Television as part of the TFC program on "Nature's Way" in the Territory an unlimited number of times on each Exhibition Day during the License Period, and in connection therewith to use and perform any and all music, lyrics and musical compositions contained in each Picture.

TFC shall have all editing rights with respect to each of the materials, including the right to cut and dub each Picture, to excerpt portions of each Picture, and to combine the excerpts with material from other pictures and programs, and to replace or superimpose matter over the music and sound effects track or over the full sound track of each Picture.

Definitions
1.1. "Picture" means any film material selected from the Grantor's library.

1.2. "Cable Television" means the medium in which exhibitions of audiovisual works are transmitted to subscribers who are not all assembled in a single location and who are obligated to pay for the privilege of receiving such exhibitions on a particular channel or station, it being understood that the license to the subscriber shall not entitle them to receive possession of physical materials embodying such audiovisual works.

1.3. "Exhibition Day" means any 24-hour period beginning at such time as TFC shall determine in each instance. Under this agreement, the number of Exhibition Days in the License Period will be unlimited.

1.4. "License Period" under the terms of this Agreement means the period from January 1, 1989 through December 31, 1994.

1.5. "Territory" means the United States, its territories and possessions, and Canada.

Along with defining and describing the rights that you are purchasing, the agreement should stipulate that the licensing

company has the authority to grant those rights. That is the purpose of a Warranties and Indemnity clause.

Warranties and Indemnity
Grantor hereby represents and warrants that it is free to enter into and fully perform this Agreement. Grantor also represents that it has the right to grant all rights granted herein with respect to the copies of the Pictures.

Grantor shall at all times indemnify and hold harmless TFC, its officers, employees, licensees, assignees, and affiliated companies against and from any and all claims, damages, liabilities, costs, and expenses arising out of any breach by Grantor of any representation, warranty or other provision hereof.

In a contractual agreement, the Warranty and Indemnify provisions work together. The Warranty clause states that the film library (the Grantor) has the legal authority to grant the rights described in the agreement. The Indemnity clause stipulates that any challenges over those rights will be resolved at the expense of the Grantor.

[*Editor's Note:* Many footage sources (including the major U.S. newsreel libraries, Hollywood motion picture studios, the three major television networks and numerous independent stock footage libraries) decline to make any warranties or representations with respect to the footage they furnish, other than that of title (i.e, that they legally possess and own the footage in its physical form). Generally, they require that users indemnify the source library against any claims, losses, demands and liabilities arising out of User's use of the provided footage. What explains this reluctance? Many collections legally hold footage (especially public domain and older footage) about which little is now known, or footage lacking documentation relating to releases, union or guild agreements, or underlying rights. Since these collections are unable to specify the status of all rights embodied in the footage, they prefer to shift the burden of risk to the user. Furthermore, libraries cannot effectively control the manner in which footage is used by their customers. Individuals appearing in old feature film clips might, for instance, find certain contemporary uses of footage to be derogatory or libelous. Bearing these reasons in mind, libraries limit their liability by requiring indemnification from users.]

Public Domain

Public domain works fall into three categories: works that were never copyrighted, works for which the copyright has expired, and works for which the copyright has been abandoned. Unfortunately, it is often not easy to determine whether a work was ever copyrighted, or whether the copyright on a work has expired or been abandoned. In particular, it is a mistake to assume that a work is in the public domain simply because it is missing a copyright notice.

If a work truly is in the public domain, you are free to use it without any obligation under the copyright law to pay royalties or usage fees. You can make and sell copies of public domain materials, and you can incorporate the materials into other works. But you cannot copyright public domain materials, even when those materials are being used as part of another work. In that case, you could copyright the part of the work that you created, but your copyright would not give you any right of ownership over the public domain portion.

Even though public domain materials are free for anyone to use, most producers choose to purchase public domain footage from suppliers that specialize in rights-free materials. There are two important advantages to this approach. First, because many suppliers stockpile and catalog large collections of materials, they can usually help you find the exact footage that you need quickly and efficiently. Second, because suppliers will certify that the footage is indeed free from copyright restrictions, you are freed from having to worry about infringement suits originated by irate copyright owners. Considering how difficult and time-consuming it can be to determine whether a work is truly in the public domain, this last advantage is especially significant.

If public domain materials truly are free for anyone to use, how can suppliers charge for the public domain footage that they license? In practical terms, a supplier does not charge for the program or film material itself, but rather for the service that it provides in stockpiling the footage and delivering it in the form that you require. That is why several suppliers can and often do carry the same public domain materials, and why the charges for the same footage might vary from one supplier to the next. That is also why your use of the material is governed entirely by your contractual agreement with the supplier, rather than by copyright law.

Contractual agreements governing the use of public domain material should always be placed in writing, and they should always contain "grant of rights" and "warranty and indemnity" clauses similar to those described earlier. In this case, the supplier should warrant that the materials are indeed in the public domain, and it should indemnify the purchaser against legal claims to the contrary. As always, the "grant of rights" clause should specify how and where you will be able to use the material — and for how long.

Note that public domain status has no bearing upon the status of rights other than copyright in and to the footage itself. If you use public domain footage in a production, you are still liable for securing all necessary clearances and permissions from talent, unions and guilds, and the owners of copyrighted musical or literary material that may appear within the footage.

Remember that your contract with a supplier of public domain footage is a voluntary agreement between two parties that have decided to do business together. In the contract, the supplier is free to place restrictions and conditions on your use of the materials. If a contract places unacceptable restrictions on your use of the public domain materials, you are free not to sign it. You are also free to look for the materials elsewhere.

International issues

Through international conventions and bilateral treaties, the United States has established formal copyright relationships with more than 80 nations. In most cases, this means that materials created by citizens of those countries are protected by U.S. law, and that those countries must reciprocate by extending copyright protection within their boundaries to works created by U.S. citizens. It also means that you should approach all foreign works with the same care and caution that you direct toward American works. In fact, foreign materials often require a closer examination. The exact copyright status of these works can be difficult to determine, and the copyright owners can be difficult to contact. With this in mind, you may want to work through a clearance specialist or copyright lawyer who is an expert in international copyright.

Summary

When you are licensing footage, you must make sure that the licensing agreement gives you the right to use the material in the manner that you intend. You also must make sure that the individual or company that is licensing the footage has the authority to grant you those rights. Begin by defining the rights that you need. Then enter into a legally binding licensing agreement that both grants and guarantees those rights. The guarantees are especially important when you are licensing material that may contain many levels of rights.

Philip Miller is Director of Product Development for the Software Division of Scholastic Inc. He is also a freelance writer and a member of the faculty at the New School for Social Research, where he teaches graduate courses in corporate communications and media law. His book Media Law for Producers *will be published this year by Knowledge Industry Publications, 701 Westchester Avenue, White Plains NY 10604.*

How to Investigate the Copyright Status of a Work

IN GENERAL

Methods of Approaching a Copyright Investigation

There are several ways to investigate whether a work is under copyright protection and, if so, the facts of the copyright. These are the main ones:

1. Examine a copy of the work (or, if the work is a sound recording, examine the disk, tape cartridge, or cassette in which the recorded sound is fixed, or the album cover, sleeve, or container in which the recording is sold) for such elements as a copyright notice, place and date of publication, author and publisher (for additional information, see "Copyright Notice");

2. Make a search of the Copyright Office catalogs and other records; or

3. Have the Copyright Office make a search for you.

A Few Words of Caution About Copyright Investigations

Copyright investigations often involve more than one of these methods. Even if you follow all three approaches, the results may not be completely conclusive. Moreover, as explained in this circular, the changes brought about under the Copyright Act of 1976 must be considered when investigating the copyright status of a work.

This circular offers some practical guidance on what to look for if you are making a copyright investigation. It is important to realize, however, that this circular contains only general information, and that there are a number of exceptions to the principles outlined here. In many cases it is important to consult a copyright attorney before reaching any conclusions regarding the copyright status of a work.

HOW TO GO ABOUT SEARCHING COPYRIGHT OFFICE CATALOGS AND RECORDS

Catalog of Copyright Entries

The Copyright Office publishes the *Catalog of Copyright Entries (CCE),* which is divided into parts according to the classes of works registered. The present categories include: "Nondramatic Literary Works," "Performing Arts," "Motion Pictures and Filmstrips," "Sound Recordings," "Serials and Periodicals," "Visual Arts," "Maps," and "Renewals." Effective with the Fourth Series, Volume 2, 1979 Catalogs, the CCE has been issued in microfiche form **only;** previously, each part of the *Catalog* was issued at regular intervals in book form. Each CCE segment covers all registrations made during a particular period of time. Renewals made for any class during a particular period can be found in Part 8, "Renewals."

Before 1978, the catalog parts reflected the classes that existed at that time. Renewals for a particular class are found in the back section of the catalog for the class of work renewed (for example, renewal registrations for music made in 1976 appear in the last section of the music catalog for 1976).

A number of libraries throughout the United States maintain copies of the *Catalog,* and this may provide a good starting point if you wish to make a search yourself. There are some cases, however, in which a search of the *Catalog* alone will not be sufficient to provide the needed information. For example:

• Since the *Catalog* does not include entries for assignments or other recorded documents, it cannot be used for searches involving the ownership of rights.

• There is usually a time lag of a year or more before the part of the *Catalog* covering a particular registration is published.

• The *Catalog* entry contains the essential facts concerning a registration, but it is not a verbatim transcript of the registration record.

Individual Searches of Copyright Records

The Copyright Office is located in the Library of Congress James Madison Memorial Building, 101 Independence Ave., S.E., Washington, D.C.

Most records of the Copyright Office are open to public inspection and searching from 8:30 a.m. to 5 p.m. Monday through Friday (except legal holidays). The various records freely available to the public include an extensive card catalog, an automated catalog containing records from 1978 forward, record books, and microfilm records of assignments and related documents. Other records, including correspondence files and deposit copies, are not open to the public for searching. However, they may be inspected upon request and payment of a $10-per hour search fee.

If you wish to do your own searching in the Copyright Office files open to the public, you will be given assistance in locating the records you need and in learning searching procedures. If the Copyright Office staff actually makes the search for you, a search fee must be charged.

SEARCHING BY THE COPYRIGHT OFFICE

In General

Upon request, the Copyright Office staff will search its records at the statutory rate of $10 for each hour or fraction of an hour consumed. Based on the information you furnish, they will provide an estimate of the total search fee. If you decide to have the Office staff conduct the search, you should send the estimated amount with your request. The Office will then proceed with the search and send you a typewritten report or, if you prefer, an oral report by telephone. If you request an oral report, please provide a telephone number where you can be reached during normal business hours (8:30-5:00).

Search reports can be certified on request, for an extra fee of $4. Certified searches are most frequently requested to meet the evidentiary requirements of litigation.

Your request, and any other correspondence, should be addressed to:

Reference and Bibliography Section, LM-451
Copyright Office
Library of Congress
Washington, D.C. 20559
(202) 707-6850

What the Fee Does Not Cover

Note that the search fee does *not* include the cost of additional certificates, photocopies of deposits, or copies of other office records. For information concerning these services, request Circular 6 from the Copyright Office.

Information Needed

The more detailed information you can furnish with your request, the less time-consuming and expensive the search will be. Please provide as much of the following information as possible:
• The title of the work, with any possible variants;
• The names of the authors, including possible pseudonyms;
• The name of the probable copyright owner, which may be the publisher or producer;
• The approximate year when the work was published or registered;
• The type of work involved (book, play, musical composition, sound recording, photograph, etc.);
• For a work originally published as a part of a periodical or collection, the title of that publication and any other information, such as the volume or issue number, to help identify it;
• Motion pictures are often based on other works such as books or serialized contributions to periodicals or other composite works. If you desire a search for an underlying work or for music from a motion picture, you must specifically request such a search. You must also identify the underlying works and music and furnish the specific titles, authors, and approximate dates of these works; and
• The registration number of any other copyright data.

Searches Involving Assignments and Other Documents Affecting Copyright Ownership

The Copyright Office staff will also, for the standard hourly search fee, search its indexes covering the records of assignments and other recorded documents concerning ownership of copyrights. The reports of searches in these cases will state the facts shown in the Office's indexes of the recorded documents, but will offer no interpretation of the content of the documents or their legal effect.

NOTE: Unless your request specifies otherwise, Copyright Office searches include records pertaining to registrations, renewals, assignments and other recorded documents concerning copyright ownership. If you want the office to search any other special records such as notices of use, or if you want to exclude specific records from your search, please make this clear in your request.

LIMITATIONS ON SEARCHES

In determining whether or not to have a search made, you should keep the following points in mind:

No Special Lists

The Copyright Office does not maintain any listings of works by subject, or any lists of works that are in the public domain.

Contributions

Individual works, such as stories, poems, articles, or musical compositions that were published as contributions to a copyrighted periodical or collection, are usually not listed separately by title in our records.

No Comparisons

The Copyright Office does not search or compare copies of works to determine questions of possible infringement or to determine how much two or more versions of a work have in common.

Titles and Names Not Copyrightable

Copyright does not protect names and titles, and our records list many different works identified by the same or similar titles. Some brand names, trade names, slogans, and phrases may be entitled to protection under the general rules of law relating to unfair competition, or to registration under the provisions of the trademark laws. Questions about the trademark laws should be addressed to the Commissioner of Patents and Trademarks, Washington, D.C. 20231. Possible protection of names and titles under common law principles of unfair competition is a question of state law.

No Legal Advice

The Copyright Office cannot express any opinion as to the legal significance or effect of the facts included in a search report.

SOME WORDS OF CAUTION

Searches Not Always Conclusive

Searches of the Copyright Office catalogs and records are useful in helping to determine the copyright status of a work, but they cannot be regarded as conclusive in all cases. The complete absence of any information about a work in the office records does not mean that the work is unprotected. The following are examples of cases in which information about a particular work may be incomplete or lacking entirely in the Copyright Office:
• Before 1978, unpublished works were entitled to protection at common law without the need of registration.
• Works published with notice prior to 1978 may be registered ay **any** time within the first 28-year term; to obtain renewal protection, however, the claimant must register and renew such work by the end of the 28th year.
• For works that came under copyright protection after 1978, registration may be made at any time during the term of protection; it is not generally required as condition of copyright protection (there are, however, certain definite advantages to registration; please call or write for Circular 1, "Copyright Basics").
• Since searches are ordinarily limited to registrations that have already been cataloged, a search report may not cover recent registrations for which catalog records are not yet available.
• The information in the search request may not have been complete or specific enough to identify the work.
• The work may have been registered under a different title or as part of a larger work.

Protection in Foreign Countries

Even if you conclude that a work is in the public domain in the United States, this does not necessarily mean that you are free to use it in other countries. Every nation has its own laws governing the length and scope of copyright protection, and these are applicable to uses of the work within that nation's borders. Thus, the expiration or loss of copyright protection in the United States may still leave the work fully protected against unauthorized use in other countries.

OTHER CIRCULARS

For further information, request Circulars 15, "Renewal of Copyright," 15a, "Duration of Copyright," 15t, "Extension of Copyright Terms," and 6, "Obtaining Copies of Copyright Office Records and Deposits," from:

Publications Section, LM-455
Copyright Office
Library of Congress
Washington, D.C. 20559
    OR

You may call 202/707-9100 at any time, day or night, to leave a request for forms or circulars as a recorded message on the Forms HOTLINE. Requests made on the HOTLINE number are filled and mailed promptly.

IMPACT OF COPYRIGHT ACT ON COPYRIGHT INVESTIGATIONS

On October 19, 1976, the President signed into law a complete revision of the copyright law of the United States (Title 17 of the United States Code). Most provisions of the new copyright statute came into force on **January 1, 1978,** superseding the previous copyright act of 1909, and made significant changes in the copyright law. If you need more information about the provisions of the 1976 Act, or if you want a copy of the revised statute, write or call the Copyright Office and request Circular 92.

For copyright investigations, the following are some of the main points to consider about the impact of the Copyright Act of 1976:

A Changed System of Copyright Formalities

Some of the most sweeping changes under the 1976 Act involve copyright formalities; that is, the procedural requirements for securing and maintaining full copyright protection. The old system of formalities involved copyright notice, deposit and registration, recordation of transfers and licenses of copyright ownership, and United States manufacture, among other things. In general, while retaining formalities the present law reduces the chance of mistakes, softens the consequences of errors and omissions, and allows for the correction of errors.

Automatic Copyright

Under the present copyright laws, copyright exists in original works of authorship created and fixed in any tangible medium of expression, now known or later developed, from which they can be perceived, reproduced, or otherwise communicated, either directly, or indirectly with the aid of a machine or device. In other words, copyright is an incident of creative authorship not dependent on statutory formalities. Thus, registration with the Copyright Office generally is not required, but there are certain advantages that arise from a timely registration. For further information on the advantages of registration, write or call the Copyright Office and request Circular 1, "Copyright Basics."

Copyright Notice

Both the 1909 and 1976 copyright acts require a notice of copyright on published works. For most works, a copyright notice consists of the symbol ©, the word "Copyright," or the abbreviation "Copr.," together with the name of the owner of copyright and the year of first publication; for example: "© Marion Crane 1987" or "Copyright 1987 by Milton Arbogast." The present law prescribes that all visually perceptible published copies of a work, or published phonorecords of a sound recording, shall bear a proper copyright notice. This requirement applies equally whether the work is published in the United States or elsewhere by authority of the copyright owner. Compliance with the statutory notice requirements is the responsibility of the copyright owner. Unauthorized publication without the copyright notice, or with a defective notice, does not affect the validity of the copyright in the work. Advance permission from, or registration with, the Copyright Office is not required before placing a copyright notice on copies of a work, or on phonorecords of a sound recording. Moreover, for works first published on or after January 1, 1978, omission of the required notice, or use of a defective notice, does not result in forfeiture or outright loss of copyright protection. Certain omissions of, or defects in the notice of copyright, however, may lead to loss of copyright protection is certain steps are not taken to correct or cure the omissions or defects. The Copyright Office has issued a final regulation (37 CFR 201.20) which suggests various acceptable positions for the notice of copyright. For further information, write to the Copyright Office and request Circular 3.

Works Already in the Public Domain

The 1976 Act does not restore protection to works that fell into the public domain before January 1, 1978. If copyright in a particular work has been lost, the work is permanently in the public domain in this country, and the 1976 Act will not revive protection. Under the copyright law in effect prior to January 1, 1978, copyright could be lost in several situations: the most common were publication without the required copyright notice, expiration of the first 28-year copyright term without renewal, or final expiration of the second copyright term.

Scope of Exclusive Rights Under Copyright

The present law has changed and enlarged, in some cases, the scope of the copyright owner's rights as against users of a work. The new rights apply to all uses of a work subject to protection by copyright after January 1, 1978, regardless of when the work was created.

DURATION OF COPYRIGHT PROTECTION

Works Originally Copyrighted On or After January 1, 1978

A work that is created and fixed in tangible form for the first time on or after January 1, 1978, is automatically protected from the moment of its creation, and is ordinarily given a term enduring for the author's life, plus an additional 50 years after the author's death. In the case of "a joint work prepared by two or more authors who did not work for hire," the term lasts for 50 years after the last surviving author's death. For works made for hire, and for anonymous and pseudonymous works (unless the author's identity is revealed in Copyright Office records), the duration of copyright will be 75 years from publication or 100 years from creation, whichever is less.

Works created before the 1976 law came into effect, but neither published nor registered for copyright before January 1, 1978, have been automatically brought under the statute and are now given Federal copyright protection. The duration of copyright in these works will generally be computed in the same way as for new works: the life-plus-50 or 75/100 year terms will apply. However, all works in this category are guaranteed at least 25 years of statutory protection.

Works Copyrighted Before January 1, 1978

Under the law in effect before 1978, copyright was secured either on the date a work was published with notice of copyright, or on the date of registration if the work was registered in unpublished form. In either case, copyright endured for a first term of 28 years from the date on which it was secured. During the last (28th) year of the first term, the copyright was eligible for renewal. The new copyright law has extended the renewal term from 28 to 47 years for copyrights in existence on January 1, 1978. However, the copyright still must be renewed in the 28th calendar year to receive the 47-year period of added protection. For more detailed information on the copyright term, write or call the Copyright Office and request Circulars 15a and 15t.

WORKS FIRST PUBLISHED BEFORE 1978: THE COPYRIGHT NOTICE

General Information About the Copyright Notice

In investigating the copyright status of works first published before January 1, 1978, the most important thing to look for is the notice of copyright. As a general rule under the previous law, copyright protection was lost permanently if the notice was omitted from the first authorized published edition of a work, or if it appeared in the wrong form or position. The form and position of the copyright notice for various types of works were specified in the copyright statute. Some courts were liberal in overlooking relatively minor departures from the statutory requirements, but a basic failure to comply with the notice provisions forfeited copyright protection and put the work into the public domain in this country.

Absence of Copyright Notice

For works first published before 1978, the complete absence of a copyright notice from a published copy generally indicates that the work is not protected by copyright. However, there are a number of exceptions and qualifications to this general rule. The following are some of them:

Unpublished Works. No notice of copyright was required on the copies of any unpublished work. The concept of "publication" is very technical, and it was possible for a number of copies lacking a copyright notice to be reproduced and distributed without affecting copyright protection.

Foreign Editions. Under certain circumstances, the law exempted copies of a copyrighted work from the notice requirements if they were first published outside the United States. Some copies of these foreign editions could find their way into the United States without impairing the copyright.

Accidental Omission. The 1909 statute preserved copyright protection if the notice was omitted by accident or mistake from a "particular copy or copies."

Unauthorized Publication. A valid copyright was not secured if someone deleted the notice and/or published the work without authorization from the copyright owner.

Sound Recordings. Reproductions of sound recordings usually contain two different types of creative works: the underlying musical, dramatic, or literary work that is being performed or read, and the fixation of the actual sounds embodying the performance or reading. For protection of the underlying musical or literary work embodied in a recording, it is not necessary that a copyright notice covering this material appear on the phonograph records or tapes in which the recording is reproduced. As noted above, a special notice is required for protection of the recording of a series of musical, spoken, or other sounds which were fixed on or after February 15, 1972. Sound recordings fixed before February 15, 1972, are not eligible for Federal copyright protection. Neither the Sound Recording Act of 1971 nor the present copyright law can be applied or be construed to provide any retroactive protection for sound recordings fixed before that date. Such works, however, may be protected by various state laws or doctrines of common law.

The Date in the Copyright Notice

If you find a copyright notice, the date it contains may be important in determining the copyright status of the work. In general, the notice on works published before 1978 must include the year in which copyright was secured by publication (or, if the work was first registered for copyright in unpublished form, the year in which registration was made). There are two main exceptions to this rule.

• For pictorial, graphic or sculptural works (Classes F through K under the 1909 law) the law permitted omission of the year date in the notice.

• For "new versions" or previously published or copyrighted works, the notice was not usually required to include more than the year of first publication of the new version itself. This is explained further under "Derivative Works" below.

The year in the notice usually (though not always) indicated when the copyright began. It is therefore significant in determining whether a copyright is still in effect; or, if the copyright has not yet run its course, the year date will help in deciding when the copyright is scheduled to expire. For further information on the duration of copyright, request Circular 15a.

In evaluating the meaning of the date in a notice, you should keep the following points in mind:

WORKS PUBLISHED AND COPYRIGHTED BEFORE JANUARY 1, 1978: A work published before January 1, 1978, and copyrighted within the past 75 years may still be protected by copyright in the United States if a valid renewal registration was made during the 28th year of the first term of the copyright. If renewed, and if still valid under the other provisions of the law, the copyright will expire 75 years from the end of the year in which it was first secured.

Therefore, with one exception, the United States copyright in any work published or copyrighted more than 75 years ago (75 years from January 1st in the present year) has expired by operation of law, and the work has permanently fallen into the public domain in the United States. For example, on January 1, 1989, copyright in works first published or copyrighted before January 1, 1914, will have expired; on January 1, 1990, copyright in works first published or copyrighted before

January 1, 1915, will have expired.

WORKS FIRST PUBLISHED OR COPYRIGHTED BETWEEN JANUARY 1, 1910, AND DECEMBER 31, 1949, BUT NOT RENEWED: If a work was first published or copyrighted between January 1, 1910, and December 31, 1949, it is important to determine whether the copyright was renewed during the last (28th) year of the first term of the copyright. This can be done by searching the Copyright Office records or catalogs, as explained above. If no renewal registration was made, copyright protection expired permanently on the 28th anniversary of the date it was first secured.

WORKS FIRST PUBLISHED OR COPYRIGHTED BETWEEN JANUARY 1, 1910 AND DECEMBER 31, 1949, AND REGISTERED FOR RENEWAL: When a valid renewal registration was made and copyright in the work was in its second term on December 31, 1977, the renewal copyright term was extended under the present act to 47 years. In these cases, copyright will last for a total of 75 years from the end of the year in which copyright was originally secured. Example: Copyright in a work first published in 1917, and renewed in 1945, will expire on December 31, 1992.

WORKS FIRST PUBLISHED OR COPYRIGHTED BETWEEN JANUARY 1, 1950, AND DECEMBER 31, 1977: If a work was in its first 28-year term of copyright protection on January 1, 1978, it must be renewed in a timely fashion to secure the maximum term of copyright protection provided by the present copyright law. If renewal registration is made during the 28th calendar year of its first term, copyright will endure for 75 years from the end of the year copyright was originally secured. If not renewed, the copyright expires at the end of its 28th calendar year.

UNPUBLISHED, UNREGISTERED WORKS: Before 1978, if a work had neither been "published" in the legal sense nor registered in the Copyright Office, it was subject to perpetual protection under the common law. On January 1, 1978, all works of this kind, subject to protection by copyright, were automatically brought under the new Federal copyright statute. The duration of these new Federal copyrights will vary, but none of them will expire before December 31, 2002.

Derivative Works

In examining a copy (or a record, tape, film or videotape) for copyright information, it is important to determine whether that particular version of the work is an original edition of the work or a "new version." New versions include musical arrangements, adaptations, revised or newly edited editions, translations, dramatizations, abridgments, compilations and works republished with new matter added. The law provides that derivative works are independently copyrightable and that the copyright in such a work does not affect or extend the protection, if any, in the underlying work. Under the 1909 law, courts have also held that the notice of copyright on a derivative work ordinarily need not include the dates or other information pertaining to the earlier works incorporated in it. This principle is specifically preserved in the present copyright law.

Thus, if the copy (or the record or tape) constitutes a derivative version of the work, these points should be kept in mind:

• The date in the copyright notice is not necessarily an indication of when copyright in all of the material in the work will expire. Some of the material may already be in the public domain, and some parts of the work may expire sooner than others.

• Even if some of the material in the derivative work is in the public domain and free for use, this does not mean that the "new" material added to it can be used without permission from the owner of copyright in the derivative work. It may be necessary to compare editions to determine what is free to use and what is not.

• Ownership of rights in the material included in a derivative work and in the preexisting book upon which it may be based may differ, and permission obtained from the owners of certain parts of the work may not authorize the work of other parts.

The Name in the Copyright Notice

Under the copyright status in effect before 1978, the notice was required to include "the name of the copyright proprietor." The present act requires that the notice include "the name of the owner of copyright in the work, or an abbreviation by which the name can be recognized, or a generally known alternative designation of the owner." The name in the notice (sometimes in combination with other statements on the copy, record, tape, container, or label) often gives persons wishing to use the work the information needed to identify the owner from whom licenses or permission can be sought. In other cases, the name provides a starting point for a search in the Copyright Office records or catalogs, as explained at the beginning in this circular.

In the case of works published before 1978, copyright registration is made in the name of the individual person or the entity identified as the copyright owner in the notice. For works published after 1978, registration is made in the name of the person or entity owning all the rights on the date the registration is made. This may or may not be the name appearing in the notice. In addition to its records of copyright registration, the Copyright Office maintains extensive records of assignments, exclusive licenses, and other documents dealing with copyright ownership.

(Reprinted in part from Circular R22, *How to Investigate the Copyright Status of a Work,* published by the Copyright Office, Library of Congress, Washington, DC 20559.)

Film and Videotape Preservation Factsheet

The information in this factsheet has been gathered from a variety of sources, including the experiences of archivists in the United States and abroad, as well as professional journals and industry product recommendations. It is intended as a brief summary of current understanding of preservation and storage for film and videotape. The standards outlined here are not intended as definitive, but as practical working guidelines.

MOTION PICTURE FILM

Nitrate

Prior to 1951, 35mm films for theatrical release were made on a film stock composed of nitrocellulose (or nitrate), a relative of guncotton which is used for explosives. Nitrate is highly flammable, and once ignited, cannot be extinguished. It deteriorates, giving off an acrid odor, becoming sticky with soft bubbles, and eventually disintegrating into a fine brown powder. In its final stage of decomposition, it can ignite spontaneously at a temperature as low as 106° F, a level often reached in attics or garages during the summer months. The degree and rate of deterioration depend on the conditions in which the film has been stored and the quality of its original processing and manufacture.

Besides 35mm films, 21mm, 11mm, and most 17mm films also were made on nitrate stock. Usually a nitrate film can be identified by the word "nitrate" on the edge of the film. When a nitrate film suffers advanced deterioration with no remaining image, it must be disposed of carefully, with assistance from the local fire department.

Safety

As early as 1912, safety (non-flammable) film stock was developed for non-theatrical use. This "diacetate" safety film was used extensively in educational, religious, and amateur films, and often gives off an odor of camphor.

Modern safety film bases usually are composed either of acetyl cellulose (triacetate) or polyester (product names "Estar" or "Cronar"). When exposed to a flame, modern safety film will curl and extinguish itself. While safety film must be stored properly to minimize shrinkage and brittleness, it does not decompose over time and is estimated to have a shelf life as long as that for good quality paper, approximately 200 to 300 years.

The most common gauges on safety stock are 70mm, 35mm, 16mm, 8mm, Super 8mm, and a number of early gauges which utilized diacetate safety, including 9.5mm, 22mm, 28mm, and some 17.5mm (positives only).

Preservation

Nitrate film is preserved by copying onto safety film stock. Using the best surviving material, a duplicate negative is made from a positive, or a fine grain master positive is made from a negative. In either case, the process is best carried out to the answer print stage to test the quality of the preprint. The print then may be used for viewing. Opinion is divided on what to do with the original nitrate after copying. Some suggest retention for as long as possible. Others propose junking once the preservation safety material has been checked thoroughly.

Black and white safety film which has been processed, used, and stored properly does not require preservation. It is important, however, where conditions have not been ideal, to safeguard original negatives, fine grains or positive reversals by making additional copies for printing and viewing, and properly storing originals. Safety films which have been damaged must be recopied onto new safety stock.

Color safety film. Color dyes in all monopack (single-strip emulsion/Eastman process) color films fade over time. The degree and rate of fading depend on conditions of use and storage, and original processing. Fading occurs in both negatives and positives. Color films made in the Technicolor process using black and white separation negatives and imbibition positives do not fade. However, this process is not often used today because of its considerable expense for processing, equipment, and storage. Currently, the only way to preserve a color film is to make black and white separation negatives. The only cost-effective means of dealing with color fading is to slow the rate of fade by storing color films in low temperature and humidity vaults. This is, however, only a stopgap method designed to safeguard the film.

Storage

Films for long-term storage should be checked, wound and rewound with a uniform tension periodically to optimize shelf life. Films should be stored in cans on cores. The cans should be kept horizontally, and not stacked more than six to eight high to allow "breathing" (the natural escape of gases given off by all films). Stability — even more than specific levels of temperature and humidity — is critical, since fluctuations can cause problems such as fading, extreme shrinkage, brittleness, fungal growth, emulsion flaking, and decomposition. It is recommended that preservation preprint and originals be stored separately under proper conditions while acceptable answer prints (used first to check preprint quality) be utilized for viewing.

Nitrate film should be copied onto safety film as soon as possible. Until that is done, nitrate should be stored in specially designed and constructed vaults at no more than 50° F and 40%-50% r.h.

Black and white safety film also should be stored at 50° F and 40%-50% r.h. It must not be stored with nitrate since the gases given off by nitrate will harm safety film.

Color safety film should be kept at 32° F and 30% r.h. to slow the rate of color fading. Film stored at such levels must be "staged" or "acclimatized" before use: the film must be allowed to adjust slowly to the ambient temperature in a staging room over a period of 24 hours. Failure to stage a film can result in problems with condensation.

It must be noted that some sources recommend below freezing temperature and relative humidity of 15%-30%. While such levels should, in fact, significantly retard the fading of color dyes, they also may contribute to other physical problems, such as brittleness and curling. Some have suggested, therefore, that to be safe, color films be stored just above freezing and in a moderately dry environment: 32°-40° F and 30%-50% r.h.

VIDEOTAPE

By means of a magnetic, mechanical, and/or electronic device, images and sounds can be recorded as electronic signals onto magnetic oxide particles which adhere via a binder to a polyester base. This is basically what happens when recordings are made onto videotape. There are many varieties of this medium, which came into existence in the 1950s. Since then, there have been numerous changes in tape technology both for hardware and tape itself. Some common reel-to-reel formats include 2" quadruplex, 2" helical, 1" helical, and 1/2" helical. There are also cassette formats such as 3/4" U-Matic, Betacam, 1/2" Beta, 1/2" VHS, Video 8, and 1/4".

Images and sounds on videotape can be affected by a number of problems. There is, of course, the loss of information on a tape by accidental erasure. Economic, rather than archival, considerations can force the intentional erasure of information as a tape is reused. Dropout — an impairment or loss of video information caused by a loss in the level of the recorded signal — normally results in a black or white horizontal line in the picture. Print-through can result from the magnetic field of one layer of oxide particles on a tape affecting the signal on an adjacent layer, and causes overlapping sound and sometimes picture. While these and other problems are inherent in the material itself, storage conditions — as with film — are a major factor in the long-term keeping characteristics of videotape.

Preservation

Many archivists do not consider magnetic tape to be an archival medium because the information recorded on it is not permanent and can be altered or removed. While there is evidence that tapes produced in recent years may retain an acceptable signal for at least 20 to 30 years and possibly for as long as 100 years, there does not yet exist a means to guarantee a shelf life equal at least to that of safety film. Research in videodiscs, laser and holographic storage media, and digital mass storage may provide a means to preserve information on videotape sometime in the near future, but for now safeguarding appears to be the most appropriate strategy.

The condition of a videotape depends on the quality of tape manufacture and conditions of use and storage. Poor or uneven tape batches, overuse, hot and humid conditions, and dirty tape player heads and transports all can severely shorten the life of a tape. As with safety film, making a copy of a tape for viewing while properly storing the original appears to be the best available means to safeguard a tape and still make the information it holds accessible. This arrangement also holds the promise that, when a truly archival means to preserve videotape is developed, the original material will still exist for preservation.

Because of the rapid development of videotape technology and the variety of tape formats, it has become apparent that in long-term archival storage, equipment for playing tapes (as well as spares for parts and manuals for operation) also must be safeguarded. There already are formats, such as 1/2" reel-to-reel, which are no longer actively used and for which playback equipment is hard to find.

Storage

Tape should be stored and used in a dust-free environment. Stability of the temperature and humidity levels is critical for proper storage of videotape. As for film, periodic checking, winding and rewinding of tape is recommended for long-term storage. Reel-to-reel tape should be kept in its original box or replacement container, and cassettes stored in original boxes or canisters which support the tape reel at its hub. For reel-to-reel tapes, the outer end of the tape should be secured with an adhesive tab which leaves no residue after it is removed.

There are two points of view on the need to keep the tape away from anything which may generate a magnetic field. Recently, there has been discussion that the danger of a loss of signal from exposure to equipment which may generate a magnetic field has been overestimated. There has also been the more conservative view, however, that to be safe, tapes should be stored away from such things as motors, transformers, electrical fixtures, and loudspeakers. In addition, if a metal rack is used for storage, it should be grounded as a further safeguard against damage to the signal from voltage fluctuations or lightning.

With regard to transporting tapes, there is no evidence that passing videotape through X-ray machines at security checkpoints in airports is damaging. The hand-held wands which may be passed around an individual, however, do generate a magnetic field; thus, tapes should be kept away from these.

Most sources recommend storage at 65°-70° F and 40%-50% r.h. Some archivists have recommended storage at 50° F and 40%-50% r.h. Recently, there has been some evidence to suggest that a low humidity environment of 25%-30% r.h. may be best for long-term storage of videotape.

Most sources recommend storing tapes — whether reel-to-reel or cassette — on end. Tape should be wound with proper tension and uniformity before storage. There is no agreement on the type or direction of wind, however. Some recommend a real-time winding of a tape back to start without stopping before storage, while others suggest simply a full fast rewind. Another point of view suggests that a tape be stored "tails out," since there may be less of a chance for print-through to occur. Whichever recommendation is followed, it is clear that a tape must not be put back on a shelf after use without a uniform winding, since the starts and stops of normal play can result in wide variations in tension and wrap that may damage a stored tape.

Prepared by Joseph G. Empsucha

The National Center for Film and Video Preservation at The American Film Institute works with the nation's public archives and the film and television industry to coordinate the preservation of our moving image heritage. Established in 1984 by the National Endowment for the Arts and the AFI, the Preservation Center serves as the central office for establishing and implementing preservation policies on a national scale.

For more information, contact:

National Center for Film and Video Preservation
The American Film Institute
P.O. Box 27999
2021 North Western Avenue
Los Angeles, CA 90027
(213) 856-7637

or:
National Center for Film and Video Preservation
The American Film Institute
2600 Virginia Avenue, NW
Washington, DC 20037
(202) 828-4070

(Reprinted by permission of The American Film Institute,
National Center for Film and Video Preservation)

Old Open-Reel Videotape Restoration

by Tony Conrad

As an impermanent storage medium, videotape presents special problems for librarians and archivists. These problems are especially acute with regard to 1/2" open reel videotape, the medium on which many early video works were recorded. Many 1/2" open reel videotapes are in jeopardy; others have been given up for lost. The restoration procedure outlined in this article is feasible for even the smallest collections, and may help save unique works.

Tony Conrad is currently perfecting a process for treatment of 3/4" videotapes. For consultation on 3/4" problems and a treatment service, contact him in care of the New York Media Decentralization Institute (see below).

Application. The videotape in question was a 1/2" Sony 60-minute reel, presumed to have been recorded in 1973. Upon playback, no image was produced. A professional transfer house had ascertained the videotape to be irreparable, and it had been given up for lost by the maker, although it was the sole copy of a significant video art work (recorded on black and white portapak).

Technical. When first put in play, the head of the videotape showed a hint of image, only momentarily. Presently the forward motion of the tape stalled, and when urged forward, it squeaked, stuttered, and stuck to the head drum. In fast forward no image appeared whatever. The tape would move only for a few moments in fast forward; then stuck fast. After several tries in fast forward, the tape moved about ten minutes, only to come jamming to a freeze against the head drum, causing permanent damage to a short section of the tape which was abraded against the audio heads and other tape guides. Playback was on a Sony AV-8650 deck.

Analysis. Close examination and cleaning of the deck revealed that deposits of backing material and (to a lesser degree) of magnetic oxide coating were scraping off and clotting on the tape guides, head drum, and (especially) the skew post. This accumulation of deposits significantly impeded the tape motion, caused the tape to stick to the metal surfaces, and threatened the mechanical stability of the tape (because of possible stretching or other damage caused by the high tension on, and irregular motion of, the tape).

Procedure. By means of an unorthodox tape handling procedure (outlined in detail below) the tape was lubricated with silicone. Simultaneously, the worst of the flaking coating material on the tape was wiped off. Following the procedure, the tape played normally for ten to fifteen minutes at a time — sufficient to re-record the program on a master, for editing to a final restoration master tape. Quality of the copy is comparable to playback quality when the tape was last seen here, about 1977.

After ten or fifteen minutes, the deposits seen originally again built up to a level sufficient to degrade the image quality, to cause image roll, to make the tape chatter and squeal, and

finally to stop the tape. However, a thorough cleaning of the heads, head drum, tape guides, and so forth immediately restored the ability of the tape to run for another segment.

Commentary. The field is full of stories circulating about old video art masters that have deteriorated, that have "lost their signal." *Before these tapes are discarded, the procedure here outlined must be tried.*

The tape treated in this instance was fully and dramatically recovered, the only damage being in handling prior to the lubrication of the tape. Given the age and diagnosis of this tape, it is conceivable that most, or even all, of the vintage videotapes which have "lost signal" (without having been erased by stray magnetic fields) have, in fact, only lost their binder and lubrication.

Restoration Lubrication of Vintage Open Reel Videotapes

Tools
Head cleaning fluid
Head cleaning chamois
Q-tips
Lint-free wipes (for photo or film use)
Strip of flannel or similar absorbent cloth, about 3/4" x 12"
Silicone lubricant spray
    (Union Carbide or equivalent; *not* with oil)
Phillips screwdriver
Empty reel for 1/4" audiotape
45 rpm record, 7"
Gaffer's tape

Procedure
Clean hands; you will handle the videotape. Don't touch the middle of the oxide coating side; try to carry it by the edges at all times.

Remove plastic cover from the head drum. Do not open the drum itself. On the Sony AV-8650, the cover lifts off. Use Phillips screwdriver to remove lower front shield (plastic) from the head drum. This will allow careful and complete cleaning of the head path, without damage to the plastic parts.

Assemble a rig which will elevate the right-hand (takeup) reel about 9/16" above its usual seating. Do this by gaffer's taping a 45 rpm 7" record together with an empty audiotape reel. They will fit on the takeup reel spindle, and the takeup reel for the videotape can ride atop them. It should then be very close to *level with the feed reel.* Use two or three small pieces of gaffer's tape, curled on themselves to make a loop, to affix the video takeup reel to the top of the audio reel and the 45.

Place the vintage tape on the feed reel spindle. It may now be wound *directly* across to the takeup reel, without threading it past the heads.

Spray enough silicone lubricant on a piece of the wipe material so that it is thoroughly dampened. The wipe will be folded over the tape, and the silicone-impregnated areas should contact both sides of the tape.

Let the wipe dry completely.

While holding the folded piece of wipe gently against both sides of the tape, in the space where it passes between the two reels, you will also need to hold the takeup reel, gently, so it does not move (or jump) when the machine is put in "Fast Forward."

Turn the machine to "Fast Forward." The automatic cutoff switch (next to the audio head) will turn the machine off. Use this switch to control the movement of the tape.

VERY CAREFULLY AND ATTENTIVELY fast forward the tape through the silicone wipe. Stop from time to time to change wipes, when the wipe becomes dirtied with rubbed-off oxide and backing material. When stopping the tape, BE CAREFUL TO BRAKE THE TAKEUP REEL, especially, and the feed reel, so that the tape does not snap itself or jerk itself into a crunched-up mess on the takeup reel. Should this happen, don't panic; stop and think about how to remove it gently.

After the tape has been wiped and cleaned to the end, run it back from the takeup reel to the feed reel, through the wipe. This time less material will be removed from the tape. Notice that more *backing* material is removed than oxide coating.

The tape is now ready to play.

Playing the Tape

Clean the tape path carefully, using Q-tips and head cleaning fluid. Clean the heads. Use a strip of flannel to clean the two posts on either side of the head drum: put cleaning fluid on the cloth, wrap it around the post, and pull the cloth back and forth in a shoe-shine motion to burnish. The posts collect the backing material, and get more than their share of dirt buildup.

Play the tape. When it begins to stall, chatter, or play a degraded or unstable image, stop immediately to re-clean the machine as above.

Remove the tape from the head drum, and pull it far enough out that it will not be accidentally wiped or dripped with cleaning fluid. Make sure to remember to remove the tape from the capstan and pinch roller, since you will want to put the machine in "Play" to clean the heads. When the machine is in "Play," you will have to *hold the takeup reel* from moving, and use the automatic cutoff switch to activate the mechanism. Turn the function switch back to "Stop" when you're done.

After cleaning, re-thread the tape and start playing again. Make sure to doublecheck the tape threading path before putting the machine in "Play," since (with the covers removed) the tape may tend to fall below the guides which direct it around the head drum properly.

General Precautions

Practice this whole procedure with a scratch tape before you risk a valuable original.

Don't lean on the metal head drum cover.

Maintain an attentive outlook throughout

Always *check for slack in the tape,* before putting the machine in motion.

Tony Conrad can be contacted in care of the New York Media Decentralization Institute, 129 Prospect Ave., Buffalo, NY 14201; (716) 856-8838.

Footage 89: North American Film and Video Sources

**Use this card
to order
*Footage 89.***

Footage 89: North American Film and Video Sources
430 West 14th Street, Room 403, New York, NY 10014 / (800) 243-2252 or (212) 633-2134

Rush me *Footage 89!*
❑ Bill us. **$95.00** per copy (plus tax and shipping). (Corporate and institutional orders only.)
❑ I'm enclosing payment. Send **only $89.00** per copy. (Make checks payable to Prelinger Associates, Inc.)
❑ Send me information about *Footage 89* on floppy disk (MS-DOS and Mac formats, $225.00)

_____ copies *Footage 89* @ $89.00 each *(Payment with order required for discount.)* _____
Sales tax: $7.34 (NY City) or $3.56 (NY State) _____
Shipping: ($4.00 in US; $7.50 in Canada; elsewhere $20 airmail, $8 seamail) _____
TOTAL ENCLOSED _____

Name _____ Company _____

Street Address _____

City/State/Zip _____ Telephone _____

TO ORDER BY PHONE CALL TOLL-FREE 1-800-243-2252

Please call for information on CODs, overnight delivery, foreign delivery and quantity discounts.

**Use this card to
register as a user
of *Footage 89.*
We'll let you
know about
revisions,
updates, and
new products.**

Footage 89: North American Film and Video Sources
430 West 14th Street, Room 403, New York, NY 10014 / (800) 243-2252 or (212) 633-2134

❑ **Please register me as a user of *Footage 89.* I want to receive the latest information about revisions, updates and new products.**

Name _____

Title _____

Company _____

Address_____

City/State/Zip _____

Telephone _____

Type of Company or Institution _____

**Use this card
to tell us
what you think.**

Footage 89: North American Film and Video Sources
430 West 14th Street, Room 403, New York, NY 10014 / (800) 243-2252 or (212) 633-2134

We'd like your feedback. What do you think of *Footage 89?* What changes would you like to see i
future editions? Have we left out any sources? Please use the space below for your comments.

Please supply your name, address and telephone number.

Name _____Company _____

Address _____

City/State/Zip _____

Telephone _____
❑ Y___ ___ ___ __ to discuss this comment   ❑ I'd prefer not to be contacted at this time

BUSINESS REPLY MAIL
FIRST CLASS MAIL   PERMIT NO. 1786   NEW YORK, NEW YORK

POSTAGE WILL BE PAID BY ADDRESSEE

Footage 89
Prelinger Associates, Inc.
430 West 14th St., Room 403
New York, NY 10014-9943

BUSINESS REPLY MAIL
FIRST CLASS MAIL   PERMIT NO. 1786   NEW YORK, NEW YORK

POSTAGE WILL BE PAID BY ADDRESSEE

Footage 89
Prelinger Associates, Inc.
430 West 14th St., Room 403
New York, NY 10014-9943

BUSINESS REPLY MAIL
FIRST CLASS MAIL   PERMIT NO. 1786   NEW YORK, NEW YORK

POSTAGE WILL BE PAID BY ADDRESSEE

Footage 89
Prelinger Associates, Inc.
430 West 14th St., Room 403
New York, NY 10014-9943

Using Consultants in Film/Video Archives

by Alan Lewis

Vast collections of moving image materials are housed in local and state historical societies, trade associations, libraries, arts organizations and other institutions that are not well organized to deal with them. Often institutional focus and priorities, operating and capital budgets, personnel expertise and a host of other reasons are given as to why materials are not well organized and stored, poorly preserved, inadequately described or indexed and thus inaccessible to academic researchers or prospective users. One step in dealing with these problems is to use a consultant with special knowledge to help.

A consultant is like a hired farmhand. He/she is an individual with special skills, training, knowledge, or time who is hired to do a job and then leave. This oversimplifies the relationship because there often needs to be a follow-up phase, but on the surface, this is an adequate description. A consultant may be a freelance entrepreneur, an individual who works with a firm of consultants or might be a fully employed individual who moonlights. The purpose of this brief article is to suggest some areas in which consultants work.

If you ask a consultant what s/he does, you might get a "What do you need done?" answer. That isn't necessarily a glib or opportunistic answer, but one based on the fact that a consultant is most often hired to perform some service or project that the host institution has decided needs to be done. Very often the institution's administration has a clear vision of the nature of the problem, defines it, quantifies it, plans the strategy to meet the goal and needs only to hire someone's "fingers and toes" to get the job done. That's OK and is clearly a situation we encounter, a case (Scenario 1) where the problem is defined by the client and the consultant enters the picture with a fixed target at which to shoot.

Scenario 2. Project design. Consider the case of the Local Historical Society (LHS), which has decided to accept the gift of WZZZ-TV's 30-year newsfilm collection. The collection is of obvious importance because it is a visual history of the locale, is within the collecting policy of the institution and is thus a gift that couldn't be refused. Because the Society was founded some time ago and its focus has been on paper materials with an occasional museum object accepted from time to time, it probably doesn't have staff audiovisual expertise. Panic hits the Board of Trustees and the senior staff; what do they do next?

The first answer is that they probably should have talked to a consultant *first,* before accepting the collection, in order to have an accurate sense of the size, complexity, special problems and cost of the undertaking. Given that they couldn't or didn't seek an opinion up front, now they need a consultant to help make the best of the situation.

Making the best of the situation means finding a consultant who can talk them through and develop a plan of attack for the legal, physical and intellectual control of the material. What's needed is someone with appropriate knowledge that can deal with the broad ramifications of this kind of collection as well as the details.

Scenario 3. Proposal writing. A consultant can assist in this work because the care and feeding of moving image materials is usually a foreign subject to most traditionally trained archivists and librarians. Proposals to funders, especially those who use peer panels to review applications, are quick to spot proposals that are not well founded in technical matters. They are equally quick to throw them out.

A well-chosen consultant will know the professional terminology, the concepts and the conventional (and some unconventional) ways to approach dealing with these collections. S/he may also have contacts at the funding agencies who can be of assistance in answering questions during the writing phase and smoothing the way for the proposal. But beware, hiring a consultant to write a proposal isn't a guarantee that it will be funded. Indeed, there are more requests for moving image preservation dollars at the Endowments and at the NHPRC (National Historical Publications and Records Commission) than they can possibly distribute in any given year. Sometimes, too, funds are granted at a lesser level than a project requests and an alternative plan of work needs to be developed. These lesser amounts might be granted for additional planning purposes, to encourage the project or as seed money to help the requestor gather funds from other sources.

Scenario 4. Money and development functions. To a certain extent, this overlaps with formal proposal writing but there are other ways of raising dollars through special community events, publications, travel programs, etc. In smaller institutions, the fundraiser might very well be an outside consultant who is hired to raise funds from a variety of sources in a variety of ways.

Scenario 5. Time. Projects sometimes get themselves into tight deadline situations where an extra pair of hands is necessary to complete a project, write a report, apply for a grant renewal or do some other function that the staff can't seem to get around to. A consultant who can devote a major time block to a specific task is often the answer to this kind of problem.

Scenario 6. The "Western Union Function." Administrators sometimes find themselves in situations where they prefer not to do or say certain things to certain people for a variety of reasons. A consultant can be used as a message carrier, either up or down the organization's chain of command, to carry these difficult messages or to bypass the usual channels that staff people go through. This kind of work requires a consultant with sensitivity, grace and tact, and an institutional situation that is set up to make it seem logical and reasonable that this outsider is doing what s/he is doing. This "good cop/bad cop" routine is usually submerged in some kind of research project, staff study or site inspection to explain the presence of the consultant.

Scenario 7. "The Validator." In lots of cases, the professional staff leader knows exactly what to do, when to do it and what resources are required. S/he actually doesn't need an outside expert to say the plan is OK; *but the boss does*. It is a sad fact that often administrators require the assurance and validation of an outside source, the hired consultant, to say that the staff people are on the right track. It's a simple case of the prophet being without honor in his own land and someone from outside these borders needs to come in and celebrate the local person's wisdom!

With those many and various functions behind us, I'd like to make one final point and answer your question as to why consultants *appear* to be so expensive. Assuming that the consultant in question is a freelance entrepreneur, s/he has a cost base that is composed of the market value of his/her time and expertise + the value of a benefits package that they must fund for themselves (retirement plan, insurance, self-employment tax, income for periods in which they are not working, etc.) + their overhead (the costs of doing business like office space rent, Xerox service, equipment rental or amortization [typewriters, computers, etc.], postage, printing, legal and accounting services, utilities, etc.). Add that all together and you have a fee structure akin to what any employee *really* costs his/her company, but because the consultant *is* his/her own company, the dollars look higher than for a staff member.

Consultants aren't the answer to all of "moving image humankind's" problems but they can be an effective way to provide a film/video collection with an additional brain, an additional set of hands, an outside opinion, an information conduit or a troubleshooter to help it through a time of need. What is important is to select the consultant carefully, to be clear about the work to be done and to follow up on the results of that work.

Alan Lewis is a consultant in the establishment and operation of film and videotape archives and libraries. He is founder and former director of the Public Television Archives and former director of the CBS Newsfilm and Videotape Archives.

How to Use This Book

Footage 89 contains 1,635 entries, each describing a source for moving image material (film, videotape or computer graphics). Listings include North American moving image sources of all kinds, whether they make material available for study, research, rental, purchase, licensing or reuse.

Users should note that *not all collections are available for all purposes;* that *many sources consider requests on a case-by-case basis;* and that *additional clearances are often necessary if material is to be reused.*

Organization

Sources and Collections Index (pages A-37 through A-81) lists names of moving image sources and collections held by these sources. The main source listings (pages 1-577) are arranged geographically. The fifty states, Puerto Rico and the Virgin Islands (listed in alphabetical order) are followed by the Canadian provinces, Mexico, the British Virgin Islands and Cuba. *Research and Resources* (pages 581-596) lists 142 individual researchers, research organizations and information resources. The main *Index* (pages 597-778) lists over 9,000 subjects, locations and individuals cited in the source listings. A *Television Series Index* (pages 779-787) lists television series appearing in the source listings. The *Glossary* (pages 789-795) defines certain terms used in this book.

Within each state, province, territory or country, entries are listed alphabetically by city and then by source name. When a personal name is part of a source name, the last name is used to determine alphabetical order.

Three major metropolitan areas (Los Angeles, the District of Columbia and New York City) house many moving image sources. Since researchers may not know the name of the city or suburb in which a source is located, *all entries within these three metropolitan areas are listed alphabetically by source or institution name, rather than the name of the city or town in which they reside.*

Source Listings

Source name. Names are shown as supplied by the sources themselves. In cases where information is lacking or contradictory, the name of the parent institution is generally given first. When a collection, division or activity within a larger institution is generally known by its own name (e.g., George Foster Peabody Collection, University of Georgia Library), this name is given first. Many variant source names are listed in the *Sources and Collections Index* to aid in finding sources whose exact name is not known.

Source address. Mailing address precedes street address (if different).

Telephone, fax and telex numbers. Direct lines are supplied whenever possible.

Chief official(s). Names are supplied by the sources themselves. Depending on the nature of the source, the name shown may relate to the parent institution or a collection, division or activity within the institution.

Contact(s). Names are supplied by the sources themselves. These individuals have been designated to receive and process outside requests and should be a first point of contact. Researchers should be aware that these names are subject to frequent change.

Services. Provides a brief summary of the services that each source is prepared to offer. Limitations and restrictions are often indicated and should be noted with care. *Many sources provide moving image material and associated research services on a limited and/or selective basis. Not every source is prepared to provide all kinds of footage to all requesters on an unrestricted basis. Please do not assume that every request for an "exception to the rule" will be honored.*

Note: Major studios and television production companies are generally not represented by detailed listings in this book. Though most permit clip licensing on a case-by-case basis, *casual inquiries are discouraged* due to the high volume of requests and the cost of legal research necessary to determine the availability of a given clip for licensing. Substantial license fees are generally charged, and the user is responsible for clearances and approvals by third parties, including talent, guilds and music publishers. Licensing requests must always be submitted in writing and designate the specific clip requested together with a description of the context, media, territory and term in which the clip will be used.

Description. Contains descriptions of moving image materials held by the source. The length and detail of each listing is determined by the nature and quality of the infor–mation supplied by listees. Large collections may be described in a generalized manner, while numerous smaller repositories are sometimes treated in greater detail. The descriptive infor–mation and sample titles in each listing were selected in order to characterize the nature of each collection and impart a sense of its particularity, strengths and research value. Since many larger collections (whether film archives, newsreel libraries or stock footage houses) defy brief description, they should be routinely consulted in the course of research.

Size & Elements. The accuracy of this information is determined by information supplied by the sources themselves. Many collections exist in an unprocessed or uncataloged state and counts are approximate. These figures are also subject to frequent change. When a collection is described as containing film or videotape, this refers to the nature of the material held, *not* to the availability of copies in a particular medium. For instance, most 35mm film can be copied to 16mm film; most 1" videotape to 3/4" or other formats; and most film can be transferred to videotape.

Cataloging. Describes systems of organization or cataloging relating to the collections. No attempt has been made to describe catalogs of non-moving image collections.

Access. Describes access conditions, policies and procedures. Many collections are open to researchers or prospective users on a case-by-case basis, rather than to all requesters. Other collections limit access due to staff and time limitations. Many require the payment of research fees. *Researchers should note carefully any applicable restrictions.* It is always best to contact the source for information prior to making a personal visit.

Rights. Derived from information supplied by the sources themselves. ***Due to the variety and quantity of material described in* Footage 89, *it is impossible to provide comprehensive rights information with regard to particular items or complete information on their availability for licensing or reuse. Therefore, the information shown should be regarded only as a general guide.*** "Licensability" rests, above all, on the willingness of an owner to license material, and many sources reserve the right to consider requests on a case-by-case basis. Please consult Philip Miller's article, "Licensing Footage: Copyright and Other Legal Considerations" (page A-19), for additional information.

Licensing. Describes the availability of material for licensing, whether or not license and usage fees are charged, and indicates whether restrictions apply. Since fees are often quoted on a per-job basis, and price schedules volatile, specific figures are not mentioned in *Footage 89.* Consult the source for current information.

Restrictions. Restrictions frequently apply to research or reuse. Many collections are maintained for research, scholarly or in-house use only, and are not equipped to respond to stock footage requests. Conversely, stock footage libraries, who depend on license fees for income, are generally unable to respond to "research-only" requests. Certain collections restrict the nature of reuse, or require that the intended context of use be established before any material is released. A few minutes spent noting the specific conditions that apply to each collec–tion will help to avoid unwanted or unnecessary inquiries.

Viewing Facilities. Refers to facilities maintained in-house. Occasionally outside facilities are described when these are the only ones available.

Duplication Facilities. Refers to facilities maintained in-house, although frequent reference is made to outside facilities if these are the only ones available.

Related Materials. Lists non-moving image collections (such as holdings of print and photograph materials) that relate directly to moving image collections held in the same institution.

Publications. Lists publications that relate directly to moving image collections. Distributors' catalogs, however, are generally listed under **Cataloging.**

Indexes

Sources and Collections Index (pages A-37 through A-81). Lists all sources appearing in the book alphabetically by their names (and variants). It also lists *(in italic)* all collections held by these sources, if known by a distinct name.

Index (pages 597-778). Contains over 36,000 subject references derived from listings in *Footage 89.* For further information, see "How to Use This Index" (page 599).

Television Series Index (pages 779-787). This finding aid lists television series cited in the source listings. Although it is by no means a complete list of all programs held by the sources in *Footage 89,* it acts as a reference to titles actually appearing in the book.

Sources and Collections Index

Names of moving image sources appear in roman type. *Names of collections held by those sources appear in italic type.* Names followed by (R&R) are found in the Research and Resources section (pages 581-596).

Names of moving image sources appear in roman type. *Names of collections held by those sources appear in italic type.* Names followed by (R&R) are found in the Research and Resources section (pages 581-596).

Names of moving image sources appear in roman type. *Names of collections held by those sources appear in italic type.* Names followed by (R&R) are found in the Research and Resources section (pages 581-596).

Names of moving image sources appear in roman type. *Names of collections held by those sources appear in italic type.* Names followed by (R&R) are found in the Research and Resources section (pages 581-596).

E

Names of moving image sources appear in roman type. *Names of collections held by those sources appear in italic type.* Names followed by (R&R) are found in the Research and Resources section (pages 581-596).

Moving Pictures.

Fabulous Footage – The Motion Picture Library.

A refreshing new resource of exciting, production-ready motion picture film that provides dynamic, cost-effective solutions for your television commercial, industrial, or music video productions.

Cities and landscapes, people and industry, historical footage and more. All mastered on 35mm motion picture negative and available on any format of film or tape.

The search is over. Fabulous Footage is here. Call us for a sample cassette.
12 Mercer Street, Toronto, Canada. M5V 1H3   (416) 591-6955, fax: (416) 591-1666

Names of moving image sources appear in roman type. *Names of collections held by those sources appear in italic type.* Names followed by (R&R) are found in the Research and Resources section (pages 581-596).

Names of moving image sources appear in roman type. *Names of collections held by those sources appear in italic type.* Names followed by (R&R) are found in the Research and Resources section (pages 581-596).

L

Names of moving image sources appear in roman type. *Names of collections held by those sources appear in italic type.* Names followed by (R&R) are found in the Research and Resources section (pages 581-596).

Names of moving image sources appear in roman type. *Names of collections held by those sources appear in italic type.* Names followed by (R&R) are found in the Research and Resources section (pages 581-596).

Names of moving image sources appear in roman type. *Names of collections held by those sources appear in italic type.* Names followed by (R&R) are found in the Research and Resources section (pages 581-596).

How To Find Footage Fast.
NBC News Video Archive.

You probably won't have to call anywhere else. The NBC News Archive is an incomparable resource. Miles of footage covering dozens of countries, from decades ago to today. Not only news events, but rich background material on every conceivable subject.

And vast as the Archive is, it's easy to find what you need. You'll work one-on-one with an expert researcher, right through to your final edit.

NBC News' commitment to its own on-air quality guarantees first-class, carefully preserved material. And a variable price structure guarantees lowest possible costs.

Call or write NBC News Video Archive
30 Rockefeller Plaza, New York, NY 10112/(212) 664-3797

FAX: 212-957-8917 • INTERNATIONAL TELEX: 232346 A • DOMESTIC TELEX: 12471

Names of moving image sources appear in roman type. *Names of collections held by those sources appear in italic type.* Names followed by (R&R) are found in the Research and Resources section (pages 581-596).

Names of moving image sources appear in roman type. *Names of collections held by those sources appear in italic type.* Names followed by (R&R) are found in the Research and Resources section (pages 581-596).

Names of moving image sources appear in roman type. *Names of collections held by those sources appear in italic type.* Names followed by (R&R) are found in the Research and Resources section (pages 581-596).

SO WHO HAS THE BEST CHOW FUN?

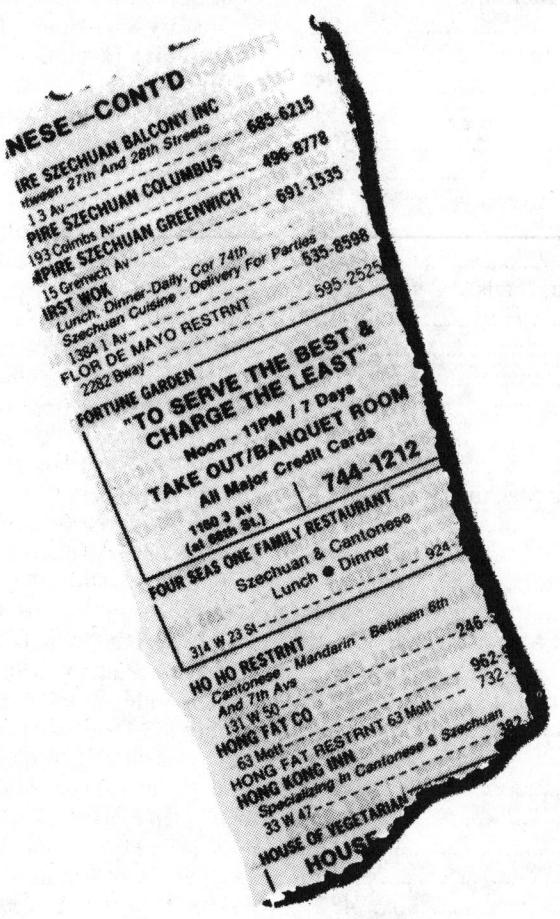

Choosing footage libraries is a little like choosing
restaurants. They all claim they have the best food…
Good Luck.
There are thousands of sources in this book…
Good Luck.

But if luck isn't enough, call **Second Line Search.**
We'll do the research, find the footage, obtain
all licensing agreements, clear talent, handle all
transfers and meet your deadline. One call, one bill.
Luckily, it's that simple…

At Second Line Search, we make stock footage easy.

330 West 42nd Street 29th floor
New York, New York 10036
New York (212) 594-5544
London (01) 259-6993

By the way, the best "chow fun" is at Sun Lok Kee . 13 Mott Street . New York City

Names of moving image sources appear in roman type. *Names of collections held by those sources appear in italic type.* Names followed by (R&R) are found in the Research and Resources section (pages 581-596).

Names of moving image sources appear in roman type. *Names of collections held by those sources appear in italic type.* Names followed by (R&R) are found in the Research and Resources section (pages 581-596).

Names of moving image sources appear in roman type. *Names of collections held by those sources appear in italic type.* Names followed by (R&R) are found in the Research and Resources section (pages 581-596).

Names of moving image sources appear in roman type. *Names of collections held by those sources appear in italic type.* Names followed by (R&R) are found in the Research and Resources section (pages 581-596).

Z

Names of moving image sources appear in roman type. *Names of collections held by those sources appear in italic type.* Names followed by (R&R) are found in the Research and Resources section (pages 581-596).

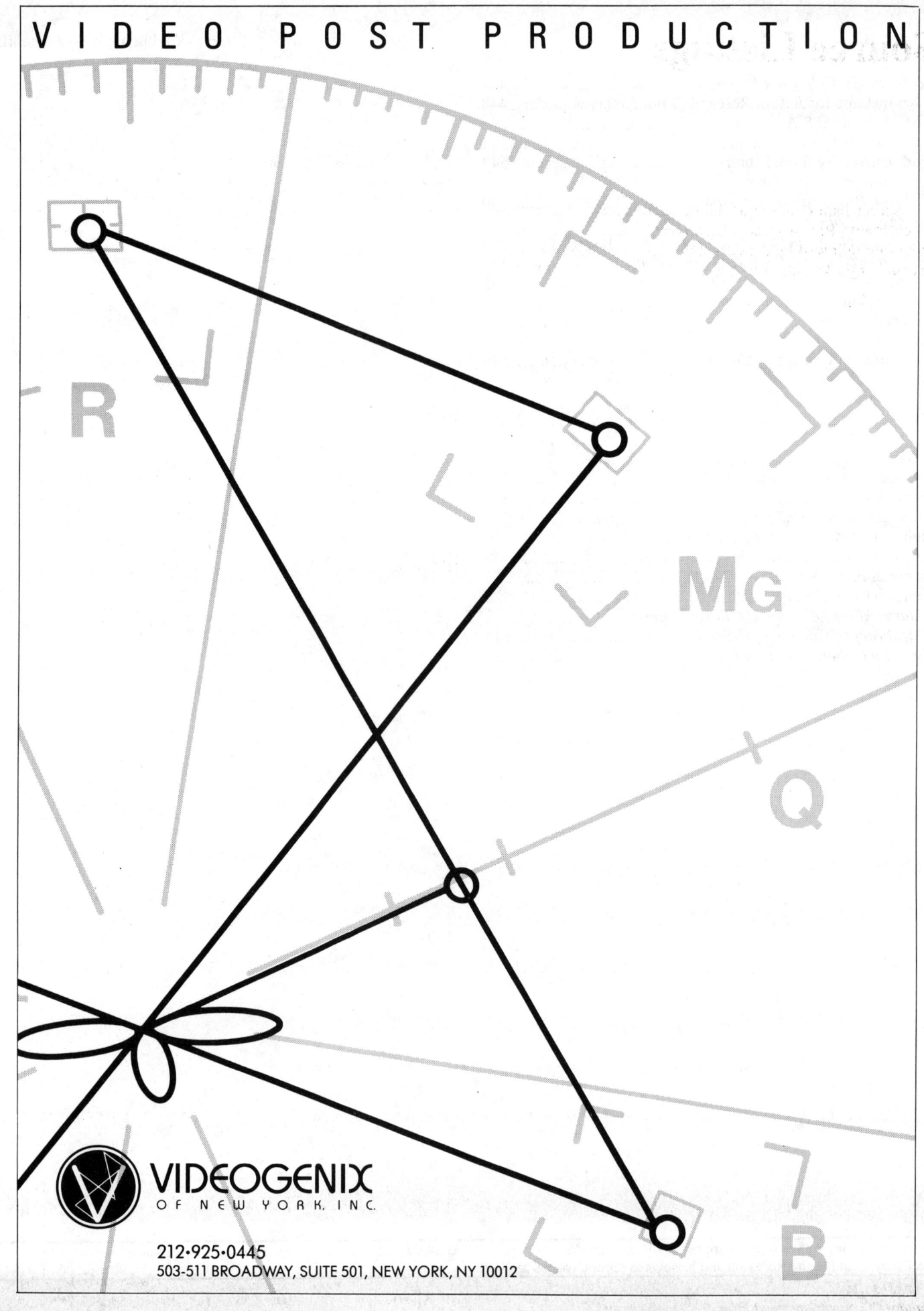

VIDEOGENIX
OF NEW YORK, INC.

212·925·0445
503-511 BROADWAY, SUITE 501, NEW YORK, NY 10012

Source Listings

Source listings are arranged geographically. The fifty states, Puerto Rico and the Virgin Islands (listed in alphabetical order) are followed by the Canadian provinces, Mexico, the British Virgin Islands and Cuba.

ALABAMA

ALABAMA (Auburn University)

AUBURN UNIVERSITY ARCHIVES
RALPH BROUN DRAUGHON LIBRARY
Room 143
Auburn University, AL 36849
(205) 826-4465

Dr. Dwayne Cox (University Archivist)

Contacts: David J. Rosenblatt (Archives Assistant); Beverley S. Powers (Reference Assistant)
Services: University archives. Film and videotape collection available for licensing, subject to restrictions.
Description: Begins 1930s. Majority of material is sports-related. Collections include: Alumni Association Athletic Films (1960s-present); Athletic Department (1930s-present); Educational TV (1950s-present); University Relations (1930s-present); football films and Bowl games (1930s-present); basketball films (1950s-present); track films (1930s-present); and general motion pictures (1930s-present). Other areas covered include: campus activities, students, schools and departments, politics, arts and sciences, entertainment, visiting dignitaries, space program and Alabama Cooperative Extension (agriculture).
Size & Elements: Film: 16mm (3,037 titles [2,000 Athletic Department, 1,037 other]; all positive). Videotape: 2", 3/4" and 1/2" (300 titles; masters).
Cataloging: Card catalogs; shot lists; dope sheets or release sheets; other finding aids.
Access: Open to the public with the permission of the creating agency. Limited to 24-hour on-campus use. Available for duplication. Research requests accepted by mail and telephone or in person (walk-in).
Rights: Full rights held to all material.
Licensing: Available for licensing, subject to restrictions. Usage fees charged.
Restrictions: Some access restrictions apply. Credit must be given to Archive for material used.
Viewing Facilities: Film (in Library Film Room); videotape (elsewhere on campus).
Duplication Facilities: Videotape (in University Relations Department).
Representative: Bill Battle, Collegiate Concepts, Inc., Cooperative Forum, 4501 Circle 75 Parkway, Suite E5180, Atlanta, GA 30339; (404) 956-0520.

ALABAMA (Birmingham)

AMERICAN TRUCK HISTORICAL SOCIETY
P.O. Box 59200
Birmingham, AL 35259
(205) 868-6566

Street address: 250 Office Park Drive, Birmingham, AL 35223

Zoe S. James (Executive Director)

Contact: Zoe S. James
Services: Historical society. Films and videotapes available for rental to society chapters and for reuse, subject to restrictions.
Description: Begins 1920s. Most items are safety and promotional films relating to trucking and transportation. *Ship by Truck* (1920) is the oldest film in the collection, a silent movie with sub-titles, showing advantages of trucks over rail transport. *Singing Wheels* (mid-1930s) shows that everything you need or want is delivered by truck. *Champions of the Highway* (early 1960s) shows a Mason & Dixon driver at home and at work, with the slogan: "If you've got it, a truck brought it." *The Case of Officer Hillerbrand* shows many vehicles of the late 1940s and early to mid-1950s. In *A Professional Portrait* (1952-54) a newspaper reporter, who is planning a series of articles against accident-causing trucks, winds up "a one-man cheering section for the trucking industry." *League of Frightened Men* (late 1950s) shows old war buddies meeting at a truck roadeo at which all receive safety awards; after the roadeo over coffee in a carnival tent, each tells what he was afraid might happen and how he prevented it from happening. *And There Were Four* (1950) is a safety thriller of sorts, moderated by Jimmy Stewart; featuring four characters — "each is shown starting home at the end of the day and arrives at the place where a fatal accident occurs. Suspense is built by showing those at the homes of each. At the end the police are shown requesting the next of kin to identify the victim." *They Drive the Long Haul* (1952) shows West Coast Fast Freight

routes between Arizona and Washington; *American Roadmaster* (1983) is a safety film narrated by actor and country music star Hoyt Axton; *Looking for Trouble* (1940s) shows vehicle inspection. *Tommy Looks at Trucking Careers* (mid-1960s) shows Tommy doing a trucking display for a school fair, covering the period from 1904 when there were only 700 trucks on the road, through the mid-1960s, highlighting the growth of trucking and the careers it has generated.

Other films include: National Truck Roadeo (1953); Kenworth factories and assembly line in Kansas City and Seattle (late 1960s); Pacific Intermountain Express (PIE) operations (early 1950s; updated 1968); A-P-A company history, sales presentation and roadeo (1976); a home movie of 1956 roadeo at Lansing (Mich.) Includes: airports; winter driving hazards; driver responsibility in freight deliveries; truck comparisons; hazards of tailgating; safety and its relationship to the center line of the highway; history of trucking in North Carolina; road damage in Maryland.
Size & Elements: Film: 35mm and 16mm (50 titles; 60 cans). Videotape: VHS (5 titles).
Cataloging: Title list.
Access: Available for rental to ATHS Chapters. Research fees charged. Research requests accepted by mail, telephone and in person (by appointment only).
Rights: Material in the public domain.
Licensing: Usage fees charged.
Restrictions: Only an officer or Chapter of ATHS may rent films or guarantee a film rental on behalf of a non-member.
Viewing Facilities: None.
Duplication Facilities: None.

ALABAMA (Birmingham)

BIRMINGHAM PUBLIC LIBRARY
DEPARTMENT OF ARCHIVES AND MANUSCRIPTS
LINN HENLEY RESEARCH LIBRARY
2100 Park Place
Birmingham, AL 35203
(205) 226-3645

George R. Stewart (Director, Birmingham Public Library)

Contact: Marvin Y. Whiting (Archivist)
Services: Public library. Film and videotape collection available for research and reuse.
Description: Local history and local television news. Includes all footage used in the preparation of the documentary film *Sacred Harp Singing in Alabama;* all footage used in the preparation of *Birmingham,* the history of the city of Birmingham; outtakes from WBCR-TV local nightly news; and two small collections of 8mm film relating to local events and organizations (1975-84).
Size & Elements: Film: 16mm (5 titles, 450 cans); 8mm (3 linear feet). Videotape: 3/4" (30 linear feet).
Cataloging: Card catalogs.
Access: Open to the public. For in-house use only.
Rights: Full rights held to all material.
Licensing: Available for reuse. Usage fees not charged.
Restrictions: None specified.
Viewing Facilities: Film (16mm and 8mm projectors); videotape.
Duplication Facilities: None.

ALABAMA (Birmingham)

BIRMINGHAM PUBLIC LIBRARY
MEDIA SERVICES DEPARTMENT
2100 Park Place
Birmingham, AL 35203
(205) 226-3656

George R. Stewart (Director, Birmingham Public Library)

Contact: Elna T. Allen (Media Services Librarian)
Services: Public library. Film and videotape collection open to the public for research.
Description: Library holds a general collection of children's films, documentaries and feature films.

Materials of special interest include four films: *Birmingham: A City Its People Changed* (WMTD, 1979) presenting a historical perspective of Birmingham, Alabama from its early beginnings as an industrial town, through the civil rights activities of the 1960s and the present, emphasizing beneficial

ALABAMA (Marshall Space Flight Center)

changes. *Lost in Time* (Auburn University, 1984), is a documentary on Southeastern prehistory. *The Lloyd Noland Story: The Boss* and *The Legacy* presents the history of Dr. Lloyd Noland, his medical work at the Panama Canal construction site, and in the hospital which bears his name. *Being Different* (Service Guild of Birmingham, 1982), is an educational film about the mentally retarded.
Size & Elements: Film: 16mm (2,500 titles); 8mm (approx. 1,000 titles). Videotape: VHS (1,500 titles).
Cataloging: Published catalogs; computerized cataloging for staff use only.
Access: Open to the public. Research fees not charged. Research requests accepted by mail, telephone and in person (walk-in).
Rights: Additional clearances may be necessary in some cases if material is to be reused.
Licensing: Apply for information.
Restrictions: None specified.
Viewing Facilities: Film and videotape (previews available upon request).
Duplication Facilities: None.

ALABAMA (Marshall Space Flight Center)

NATIONAL AERONAUTICS AND SPACE ADMINISTRATION (NASA)
GEORGE C. MARSHALL SPACE FLIGHT CENTER
REGIONAL FILM LIBRARY
Public Affairs Office, CA20
Marshall Space Flight Center, AL 35812
(205) 453-0040

Contact: Staff
Services: Government agency; circulating film and videotape library. Films and videotapes available for loan.
Description: Films and videotapes describing NASA research and development programs and achievements in space and aeronautics. Programs offered are similar to those available from other NASA Regional Film Libraries (q.v.).
Size & Elements: Film: 16mm. Videotape: 3/4". (Hundreds of titles total).
Cataloging: Published catalog.
Access: Available for loan to educational, civil, industrial, professional, youth and similar groups, and for unsponsored public service telecasts. Research and rental fees not charged. Requests accepted by mail.
Rights: Material is in the public domain. Additional clearances may be necessary in some cases if material is to be reused.
Licensing: Available for reuse, subject to restrictions.
Restrictions: Film material or footage of recognizable astronauts may not be reused for commercial purposes.
Viewing Facilities: None.
Duplication Facilities: None.

ALABAMA (Montgomery)

ALABAMA STATE DEPARTMENT OF ARCHIVES & HISTORY
ARCHIVAL SERVICES DIVISION
624 Washington Avenue
Montgomery, AL 36130
(205) 261-4361

Alden Monroe (Head of Division)

Contact: Alden Monroe
Services: State historical archives. Videotape material available for research, licensing and reuse, subject to restrictions.
Description: Alabama history, important political events and racial issues. Holdings include a film of the Selma to Montgomery March, produced by the Sovereignty Organization; the campaign of Governor Folsom (1948), the man who brought George Wallace into politics; material on Folsom's successor, Governor Patterson; and a "modern romance," (1914) using local people and Montgomery background shots. Additional videotape material documents various Alabama state functions.
Size & Elements: Videotape: 3/4" and 1/2" (4 titles; transfers from film).
Cataloging: None specified.
Access: Available to the public for research and reuse. Research requests accepted by mail and telephone. Uncataloged film holdings are strictly inaccessible at present.
Rights: Full rights held to all material.
Licensing: Available for licensing and reuse. Usage fees not charged.

Restrictions: Written requests required for licensing and reuse. Uncataloged film holdings are strictly inaccessible at present.
Viewing Facilities: None.
Duplication Facilities: None.

ALABAMA (Tuscaloosa)

UNIVERSITY OF ALABAMA
W. S. HOOLE SPECIAL COLLECTIONS LIBRARY
Box 870266
Tuscaloosa, AL 35487-0266
(205) 348-5512

Joyce Lamont (Assistant Dean for Special Collections and Preservation)

Contacts: Joyce Lamont; Joe Moudry (Technical Archivist); Clark Center (Reference Archivist)
Services: University library; special collections and archives. Film and videotape collection open to the public, subject to restrictions.
Description: Three collections contain film and videotape material. Subjects covered are: the people and activities of the University of Alabama; people, events, and places in the state of Alabama; ethnic and women's history; and videotaped oral history.
  Corry Family Collection (84 VHS videotapes; 1986-present). Includes a growing collection of videotaped histories: *Alabama: Her People and Their Proud Heritage;* material dealing with Alabama Representative Carl Elliott; and coal mining in Alabama.
  Archive of the American Minority Cultures (60 VHS videotapes and other formats; collected since 1979). Material deals with women's history, Black music and midwifery. Specializes in nonprint materials relating to ethnic, folk, minority, women's history and culture.
  University of Alabama Archives. Consists of the permanent records of the University. Includes approximately 300 16mm films generated by University Relations, relating to some aspect of the University. Notable among the VHS videotapes included in the Archives is a videotape of the 1981 Sesquicentennial Celebration, and one of the 1963 "stand" of George Wallace in the schoolhouse door. Also included is a growing selection of UA Television videotapes produced for public television. These (VHS; approx. 30) depict the people, places and events of the state of Alabama.
  Other collections containing assorted footage include: The John Sparkman Collection, Hudson Strode Collection, Carl Elliott Collection, and the Warner Film Collection (16mm, 3 titles; 8mm, 40 titles, all popular films).
Size & Elements: Film: 16mm (303 titles); 8mm (40 titles) (over 517 titles and 343 cans total; positive, originals and release prints). Videotape: VHS (over 174 titles; masters and viewing copies).
Cataloging: Card catalogs; finding aids; lists; records and surveys.
Access: Open to the public. Archives use requires permission of the office which generated the material. Research fees not charged. Research requests accepted by mail, telephone and in person (walk-in).
Rights: Full rights held to some material.
Licensing: Apply for information. License and usage fees generally not charged.
Restrictions: Permission must be obtained from from original donor if library is not assigned full rights.
Viewing Facilities: Videotape (VHS). Currently no viewing facilities for film, but special arrangements can be made.
Duplication Facilities: None. Duplication, when permissible, can be arranged with the Educational Media Office on campus.

ALASKA

ALASKA (Anchorage)

BRADLEY/McAFEE PUBLIC RELATIONS
1840 South Bragaw, Suite 201
Anchorage, AK 99508
(907) 274-9563
(907) 276-6353
Fax: (907) 276-1042

George Mason (Vice President)

Contacts: George Mason; Trisha Craig; Cherie Gojenola
Services: Public relations consultants. Film and videotape stock footage

available for research, licensing and reuse.
Description: Alaskan films and videotapes, including newsclips, scenic footage, wildlife, adventure, Eskimo culture, and outdoor activities. Also holds all recent footage produced by the Alaska Division of Tourism.
Size & Elements: Film and videotape (formats and amounts unspecified).
Cataloging: Limited card and computer cataloging available.
Access: Open to researchers and scholars. Available for reuse and resale. Research requests accepted by mail and telephone.
Rights: Some rights held to some material.
Licensing: Available for licensing and reuse.
Restrictions: None specified.
Viewing Facilities: None.
Duplication Facilities: None.

ALASKA (Anchorage)

NINE STAR PRODUCTIONS
P.O. Box 140088
Anchorage, AK 99514
(907) 276-5062
Fax: (907) 276-0573

Street address: 1840 South Bragaw, Suite 103, Anchorage, AK 99508

Red Bradley (Owner)

Contacts: Red Bradley; Bill Holden
Services: Film and videotape producer; stock footage sales library.
Description: Alaskan scenics include: major cities, villages, winter and summer scenes, skiing, water sports and mountain climbing. Industrial activities include: commercial fishing, construction, barge loading and unloading, airports and airplanes and oil-related activities. Animal life includes bears (fishing), moose and musk oxen. Aerial footage includes glaciers, ice, villages, and the city of Anchorage. Other materials include various locations around Alaska and the Alaska Railroad.
Size & Elements: Film: 35mm (5,000 feet; color negative); 16mm (2,000 feet; color negative). Videotape: Betacam and 3/4" (40 hours total; masters).
Cataloging: Computerized cataloging for staff use only.
Access: Available for duplication and reuse. Research requests accepted by telephone.
Rights: Full rights held to all material.
Licensing: Available for licensing and reuse. License fees charged.
Restrictions: None specified.
Viewing Facilities: Videotape (Betacam, 3/4" and VHS).
Duplication Facilities: Videotape.

ALASKA (Anchorage)

VISUART, INC.
5915 Doncaster Drive
Anchorage, AK 99504-3232
(907) 337-5006

Roger L. Miller (Owner)

Contacts: Roger L. Miller; Katherine M. Miller
Services: Film and videotape producer; stock footage sales library. Custom shooting services available.
Description: Alaskan subjects, including sportfishing, mushing (dog sled racing), winter sports, wildlife, reindeer herds and glaciers. Can shoot footage to order; 35mm and anamorphic camera equipment available.
Size & Elements: Film: 35mm and 16mm (10,000 feet; mostly 16mm; negative and workprint; color). Videotape: 1" (film-to-videotape transfers; masters); 3/4" (masters and time-coded viewing copies). Due to the lack of nearby film laboratory facilities, stock footage is available only in videotape form.
Cataloging: Cataloging in progress.
Access: Open to the public. Available for duplication, licensing and reuse. Due to the lack of nearby film laboratory facilities, stock footage is available only in videotape form. Research fees charged. Research requests accepted by mail and telephone.
Rights: Full rights held to all material.
Licensing: Available for licensing and reuse. License fees charged.
Restrictions: None specified.
Viewing Facilities: Videotape (3/4" and VHS).

Duplication Facilities: Videotape (3/4" and VHS).

ALASKA (Bethel)

KYUK-TV
Box 468
Bethel, AK 99559
(907) 543-3131

John McDonald (Producer)

Contact: John McDonald
Services: PBS station; film and videotape producer. Material available for purchase.
Description: Lifestyles and native culture of the Yukon-Kuskokwim Delta.
Traditional. Titles include: *Eyes of the Spirit* (masks made by Yup'ik Eskimo master carvers); *A Matter of Trust*, an analysis of the Alaska Native Claims Settlement Act; *Old Dances, New Dancers; A Dancing People; Russian Mission, Yukon; St. Mary's Potlatch* (1981 dance festival); *The Way We Live; Traditional Migration*, on traditional Eskimo subsistence practices and hunting; *They Never Asked Our Fathers*, about U.S. government policies concerning Yup'ik Eskimo communities of Nunivak Island, off Alaska's Bering Sea coastline; *Archaeology Series;* and *People of Kashunuk.*
Entertainment. Titles include: *Alaskan River; Parlez Vous Yup'ik,* an Alaskan theatrical group's performances in France and New York City; *Yup'ik Antigone (The Play); Somebody's Taking Pictures* (1950s), home movies of Joe Mendola, a long time resident of Southwest Alaska; and *Racing the Wind,* about the Kuskokwim 300 Sled Dog Race.
Topical. Titles include: *The Issue is Children: Child Sexual Abuse in Rural Alaska; Hard Time and Treatment: Child Molesters in Alaskan Prisons; Revved Up and Roughed Up: Three Wheelin' in Alaska; Just a Small Fishery,* on Eskimo villages establishing a commercial herring fishery at Cape Romanzof; and *Yup'ik Schoolroom.*
Other titles include: *We of the River,* about the history of Bethel, Alaska; *From Hand to Hand: Bethel Native Artist Profiles;* and *Let's Eat,* the effect of Western foods on the health of native Alaskans.
Size & Elements: Film: 16mm and regular 8mm (originals). Videotape: 1/2". (28 titles total).
Cataloging: Published catalogs.
Access: Available to the public for purchase. Orders and inquiries accepted by mail and telephone.
Rights: Full rights held to all material.
Licensing: Apply for information.
Restrictions: None specified.
Viewing Facilities: Videotape.
Duplication Facilities: None.

ALASKA (Fairbanks)

ALASKA NATIVE HERITAGE FILM PROJECT
Box 106
University of Alaska
Fairbanks, AK 99775
(907) 474-7437
(907) 455-6542

Sarah Elder; Leonard Kamerling (Co-Directors)

Contacts: Sarah Elder; Leonard Kamerling
Services: Educational institution. Films available for research, rental, licensing and reuse, subject to restrictions.
Description: Anthropological and sociological films concerning various native Alaskan cultures. *The Drums of Winter* (1988) presents the spiritual music and dance of the Yupik people and their struggle against the objections of Jesuit missionaries. *From the Elders: Three Films on the Eskimo Oral Tradition* (1987) documents the lives of a Siberian Yupik elder on St. Lawrence Island, an Inupiaq subsistence hunter/dog driver along the Kobuk river, and an elder who tells a traditional Siberian myth of "The Reindeer Thief." Aspects of contemporary life are presented in *Every Day Choices: Alcohol and an Alaska Town* (1985) and *Overture on Ice* (1985), which follows the Fairbanks Symphony Orchestra to the remote village of Savoonga. Films from the 1970s include *From the First People* (1977), showing the changing times for the rural Inupiaq people (filmed in minus 45-degree temperatures) and *Atka, An Aleutian Village* (1973), documenting spring subsistence activities. *On the Spring Ice* (1976), shows the Coast Guard helicopter rescue of walrus-hunters from

Gambell, St. Lawrence Island, and the next day's successful hunt; *At the Time of Whaling* (1974) documents the community activities of the whale-hunting season and follows an Eskimo party who strike a bowhead whale in the Bering Sea. *Tununerimiut (The People of Tununak)* (1972) presents four events: the village's evacuation during the Amchitka nuclear test; a disastrous fishing trip over the tundra; an ocean storm hitting the village; and a gathering in the community hall for traditional dancing.
Size & Elements: Film: (11 titles, each 18-90 min.).
Cataloging: Shot lists; logs; dope sheets.
Access: Open to researchers and scholars. Research requests accepted by mail, telephone or in person. Research fees charged for commercial users; waived for educational or academic researchers. Maintained for distribution or rental rather than research or reuse.
Rights: Full rights held to all material.
Licensing: Available for licensing and reuse. License fees charged for commercial use (price varies with material).
Restrictions: None specified.
Viewing Facilities: Film (16mm Steenbeck and projector); videotape (VHS).
Duplication Facilities: None.
Representative: Documentary Educational Resources (q.v.).

ALASKA (Fairbanks)

ALASKA VIDEO PRODUCTIONS
1449 Gillam Way
Fairbanks, AK 99701
(907) 452-6109

Garry Russell (President)

Contact: Garry Russell
Services: Videotape producer; stock footage sales library.
Description: "Every conceivable subject relating to Alaska (from Ketchikan to Barrow) and the Arctic" (1977-present).
Holds exclusive footage of the Yukon Quest (1985-88), a wilderness dog sled race from Whitehorse (Yukon Territory) to Fairbanks. This footage comprises 500 Betacam master videotapes and has been edited into several completed programs available for homevideo use.
Extensive collection of cross-cultural material, including six programs (each 30 min.) on the Arctic Winter Games, featuring children from Alaska, the Yukon Territory, Labrador and the Northwest Territories playing traditional White, Inuit, Eskimo and Aleut sports and games.
Other subjects include: Arctic beauty shots, caribou, Eskimo peoples, fishing, hunting, ice climbing in the Wrangell Mountains, oil and oil drilling, outdoor recreation, the petroleum industry, Prudhoe Bay, rock climbing, the trans-Alaska oil pipeline, wildlife and the "Yukon 800" (the world's longest riverboat race).
Size & Elements: Videotape: Betacam and other formats (2,500 videotapes total). 35 hours of selected stock shots are maintained on Betacam master videotapes for easy access.
Cataloging: Computerized cataloging in progress (for staff use only). A published catalog is planned.
Access: Open to the public. Available for duplication, reuse and resale. Research fees charged. Research requests accepted by mail, telephone and in person (by appointment only).
Rights: Full rights held to all material, including stock footage, completed shows, industrials and documentaries. Additional clearances may be necessary in some cases if material is to be reused, especially in the case of library music used in completed programs.
Licensing: Available for licensing. License fees charged.
Restrictions: None specified.
Viewing Facilities: Videotape (Betacam and 3/4").
Duplication Facilities: Videotape (Betacam and 3/4", between formats). Dubbing from Betacam and 3/4" to 1" available locally.
Representative: None, except for the 1987 Yukon Quest program, which is exclusively represented for broadcast sale.

ALASKA (Fairbanks)

UNIVERSITY OF ALASKA, FAIRBANKS
ALASKA MOTION PICTURE ARCHIVES
IMPACT DEPARTMENT, RASMUSON LIBRARY
Fairbanks, AK 99775-1120
(907) 474-7296
(907) 474-7023

Dr. Edmund S. Cridge (Dept. Head, IMPACT, Rasmuson Library)

Contact: Nat Good (Film Librarian, IMPACT)
Services: Educational institution. Film and videotape library available to researchers, scholars and the public for research and reuse, subject to restrictions.
Description: Collection focuses on the Circumpolar regions, with particular emphasis on Alaskan footage. Films and videotapes are acquired primarily through donations. However, some important footage has been purchased from the National Archives and commercial sources.
Footage (1914-present) depicts historical, cultural and natural subjects, including: exploration; cities, towns and villages; the Alaska Railroad; mining; dog mushing; clothing and ornamentation; Eskimo peoples; exploration; the Aleutian Islands; early aviation; hunting; missionaries; homes; Alaska business enterprises; and Arctic research conducted by the U.S. Navy. Also holds early home movies.
Much of the footage received must be restored before being made available to researchers. After restoration, films are transferred to videotape. The videotape copies are then available for study. The original film is not available for projection except under special circumstances. Unrestored materials are not normally available for viewing.
Size & Elements: Film: format unspecified (approx. 200,000 ft.). Videotape: format unspecified (approx. 200 to 250 titles).
Cataloging: Computerized cataloging for staff use only. Shot lists, abstracts of each item and shot subject index are available. Microfiche catalog available.
Access: Open to the public. Researchers and the public may use items from the collection with prior notice. Research requests accepted by mail, telephone and in person (walk-in and by appointment). "The Alaska Motion Picture Archives exists primarily for instructional and research purposes for the University of Alaska Fairbanks. An ancillary purpose is to make the materials accessible to the general public. It is not the intent of the University to engage in commercialization of these materials. Furthermore, there may be restrictions imposed by donors on certain footage. Patrons interested in using the collection for productions will be charged a fee based on staff time used to assist in research, and the amount of footage...needed for the production."
Rights: Full rights held to some material. Some rights held to some material.
Licensing: Available for licensing and reuse, subject to restrictions. License fees charged.
Restrictions: Donor and copyright restrictions may apply. Any reuse must be credited in final production. Permission for the use of any copyrighted materials is responsibility of the patron.
Viewing Facilities: Videotape (3/4" and 1/2").
Duplication Facilities: Film (16mm to 3/4" or VHS videotape); videotape.

ALASKA (Fairbanks)

UNIVERSITY OF ALASKA, FAIRBANKS
ALASKA NATIVE LANGUAGE CENTER
P.O. Box 900111
Fairbanks, AK 99775-0120
(907) 474-7874

Street address: 218 Eielson Building

Prof. Michael Krauss (Director, Alaska Native Language Center)

Contact: Helen M. Howard (Administrative Assistant)
Services: Educational institution. Videotape collection open to researchers and scholars only. One videotape available for rental and purchase.
Description: Established in 1972 by state legislation to document the 20 native (Indian, Aleut and Eskimo) languages of Alaska. Major center in the U.S. for the study of Eskimo and Northern Athabaskan languages.
One videotape is distributed: *Interethnic Communication,* part of the *Talking Alaska* series, which also includes videotapes on the Koyukon Athabaskan, Haida, Tanaina, Inupiaq Eskimo (North Slope), Inupiaq Eskimo (Bering Strait and Seward Peninsula) and Kutchin languages.
Size & Elements: Videotape: format unspecified (10 titles; viewing copies).
Cataloging: Research library.
Access: Open to researchers and scholars only. One videotape available for rental and purchase. Research fees not charged. Staff cannot offer research services for videotape material.
Rights: Some rights held to all material. Additional clearances may be necessary in some cases if material is to be reused.
Licensing: Material possibly available for licensing. License fees charged.
Restrictions: None specified.

Viewing Facilities: Videotape (3/4").
Duplication Facilities: Videotape (by arrangement with University Media Services through Center).
Related Materials: A booklet, *Interethnic Communication*, is often used in conjunction with videotape of the same name.

ALASKA (Juneau)

ALASKA STATE ARCHIVES
141 Willoughby Avenue
Juneau, AK 99801-1720
(907) 465-2270
Fax: (907) 465-2665

Virginia Newton (State Archivist)

Contact: Virginia Newton
Services: Government agency. Film and videotape material available for research, duplication, licensing and reuse, subject to restrictions.
Description: Videotapes from the Office of the Governor (1971-87) and the Legislative Impeachment Proceedings of Governor Sheffield (1985). Collection is located in Record Groups 01 and 401.
Size & Elements: Videotape: 3/4", VHS and Betamax (80 cubic feet).
Access: Open to the public for in-house use only. Research requests accepted by mail, telephone and in person. Research fees not charged. Available for duplication.
Rights: Full rights held to all material.
Licensing: Available for reuse, subject to restrictions. License and usage fees not charged.
Restrictions: Requests for licensing and reuse accepted on a case-by-case basis.
Viewing Facilities: Available at State Archives or State Film Library.
Duplication Facilities: Available at State Library.

ALASKA (Juneau)

JOEL BENNETT PRODUCTIONS
114 West Sixth Street
Juneau, AK 99801
(907) 586-1255

Joel Bennett (President)

Contact: Joel Bennett
Services: Film and videotape producer; photographer. Stock footage and still photographs available for licensing and reuse. Custom shooting services available.
Description: Natural history and environmental subjects (unedited footage). Material shot in Alaska, Canada, Japan and Scandinavia; covers national parks, wildlife refuges, various species of birds and mammals, and portraits of people in their environments, focusing on natural history. Much of the material was produced in association with various television production companies.
Size & Elements: Film: 16mm (approx. 20,000 feet; color negative and workprint). Videotape: various formats (amount unspecified; viewing copies of edited films).
Cataloging: None.
Access: Open to the public. Available for duplication, licensing and reuse. Research fees not charged. Research requests accepted by mail and telephone.
Rights: Full rights held to all unedited material. No rights held to completed films.
Licensing: Available for licensing and reuse. License fees charged.
Restrictions: None specified.
Viewing Facilities: None.
Duplication Facilities: None.
Related Materials: 10,000 still photographs on the above subjects, and a large body of material on Antarctica and other regions of the world.

ALASKA (Juneau)

HURLOCK CINE-WORLD, INC.
P.O. Box 34619
Juneau, AK 99803-4619
(907) 789-3995

Street address: 2858 Mendenhall Loop Road

Mary L. Hurlock (Vice President and Chief Operating Officer)

Contact: Mary L. Hurlock
Services: Distributor. Films available for rental only.
Description: Feature films for non-theatrical use. Strengths of the collection include:
Subtitled foreign films. Includes *La Femme Infidèle* (Claude Chabrol); *Diary of a Schizophrenic Girl* (Nelo Risi); *Black God, White Devil* and *Terra em Transe* (Glauber Rocha); *Grande Cidade* (Carlos Diegues); and *Matraga* (Roberto Santos).
"B" films. Produced by Monogram and Allied Artists, including *Attack of the 50-Foot Woman; Crime and Punishment USA* (Denis Sanders); *Crime in the Streets* (Don Siegel); *The Naked Kiss* (Samuel Fuller); *The Phenix City Story* (Phil Karlson); *Queen of Outer Space; Shock Corridor* (Samuel Fuller); *Teenage Doll* and *Little Shop of Horrors* (Roger Corman).
Also distributes horror, science fiction and Westerns.
Size & Elements: Film: 35mm and 16mm (several hundred titles; release prints). Most films in 16mm.
Cataloging: Published catalog.
Access: Available for rental.
Rights: Rights retained by original producers or copyright holders.
Licensing: Not available for licensing or reuse.
Restrictions: Footage not available for licensing or reuse.
Viewing Facilities: None.
Duplication Facilities: None.

ALASKA (Ketchikan)

CITY OF KETCHIKAN MUSEUM DEPARTMENT
629 Dock Street
Ketchikan, AK 99901
(907) 225-5600

Roxana Adams (Director)

Contact: Suellen Liljeblad (Curator of Collections)
Services: Municipal archives. Film and videotape material held primarily for research purposes; possibly available for licensing and reuse, subject to restrictions.
Description: Anthropological materials relating to Northwest Coast native cultures, pre-contact with Europeans to present; southern Southeast Alaska Euro-American cultures and history (1890-present).
Size & Elements: Film: 16mm (6 titles, each 30 min.). Videotape: format unspecified (5 titles, each 30 min.).
Cataloging: Research library; computerized cataloging for staff use only.
Access: Open to researchers by appointment only. Research fees are charged for staff work. Research requests accepted by mail, telephone and in person.
Rights: Full rights held to all material.
Licensing: Licensing may be negotiated by contract. License fees charged.
Restrictions: Some restrictions may apply.
Viewing Facilities: Film and videotape (viewing room).
Duplication Facilities: None.

ALASKA (Sitka)

SITKA NATIONAL HISTORICAL PARK
P.O. Box 738
Sitka, AK 99835
(907) 747-6281

Street address: 107 Metakatla Street

Ernest Suazo (Superintendent)

Contact: Ernest Suazo
Services: Government agency. Film collection available to the public; intended primarily for local use.
Description: Nature and native Alaskan (particularly Tlingit Indian) culture (mid-1800s to the present). Sample titles include: *Age of Alaska* (1977), an explanation of the Alaska Native Claims Settlement Act as it pertains to federal land selection for national parks, refuges and forests in Alaska; *Bentwood Box*, in which Mungo Martin carves a bentwood box by steaming and bending and tells of its use in native cultures; *Do We Want Us To?* (1978), the Tlingit Indian view of their past cultural heritage and their current cultural dilemma; *The Last*

Double Eagle, a history of Russian America describing the Russian discovery, the establishment of the Russian American Company, the eventual colonization of Alaska's southeast coast, and the establishment of Sitka as the capital of Russian America; *Tlingit-Ani,* a survey of Tlingit history and culture from the time preceding the arrival of Europeans to the present, with stories of and interviews with Tlingits living in southeastern Alaska; and *The Totem Pole,* in which Mungo Martin demonstrates carving totem poles and gives an overview of their history and meaning.
Size & Elements: Film: 16mm (14 titles, black and white and color).
Cataloging: Dope sheets or release sheets.
Access: Collection available to the public, but intended for local use only. Research requests accepted by mail, telephone and in person (walk-in and by appointment). Research fees not charged.
Rights: Rights status of material not known.
Licensing: Possibly available for reuse. Usage fees not charged.
Restrictions: None specified.
Viewing Facilities: Film (48-seat theater).
Duplication Facilities: None.

ARIZONA

ARIZONA (Phoenix)

ARIZONA HISTORICAL SOCIETY
1242 North Central
Phoenix, AZ 85004
(602) 255-4470

Andrew Masich (Director)

Contact: Janet Michaelieu (Librarian)
Services: Historical society. Film and videotape collection available for research, and in some cases for reuse, subject to restrictions.
Description: Arizona history. Films (mostly produced 1950s-60s) include *Days Remembered,* comprised of recollections of Arizona's early days; *Trip by Dons Club to Pueblo Grande* (1945-46); and a film relating to the 50th anniversary of Arizona's statehood (1962).
Videotapes include oral history interviews with long-time Arizona residents who describe their experiences living in the state.
Size & Elements: Film (23 titles, 18 cans; release prints). Videotape: VHS (5 titles; viewing copies).
Cataloging: None.
Access: Open to researchers and scholars only. Available for reuse or resale. Small research fee charged only to out-of-state residents. Research requests accepted by mail and telephone.
Rights: Full rights held to some material (statehood anniversary film). Additional clearances may be necessary in some cases if material is to reused.
Licensing: Available for reuse in some cases, subject to restrictions.
Restrictions: Additional clearances necessary in order to reuse material depicting individuals in oral history interviews; they can be contacted through the Glendale Historical Society. Society cannot make interlibrary loans.
Viewing Facilities: Videotape (VHS).
Duplication Facilities: None (outside arrangements can be made).

ARIZONA (Phoenix)

CITIZENS FOR DECENCY THROUGH LAW
2845 East Camelback Road, Suite 740
Phoenix, AZ 85016
(602) 381-1322
Fax: (602) 381-1613

William D. Swindell (President)

Contacts: Norma Moran; Camille Horn
Services: Legal advocacy organization. Distributes videotapes; maintains research collection. Some material possibly available for duplication and reuse.
Description: Holds two videotapes by Alan Sears. *The Attorney General's Commission on Pornography: An Overview* summarizes the conclusions contained in the Attorney General's Report, provides an introduction into the law of obscenity, and tells how citizens can put the Commission's recommendations to work in their communities. *The War We Are Winning* discusses the emerging issues in obscenity law, points out specific problem

areas and priorities, and describes the progress that has been made in this important fight.
Maintains research collection of materials videotaped off-air on issues relating to pornography and obscenity law. These are available to the public for in-house research.
Size & Elements: Videotape: VHS (2 titles; approx. 25 videotapes of broadcast television material).
Cataloging: None specified.
Access: Open to the public. Some material available for distribution. Some material maintained for research and duplication. Research requests accepted by mail and telephone. Research fees not charged.
Rights: Full rights held to some material. Additional clearances may be necessary if material is to be reused. No rights held to material videotaped off-air.
Licensing: Available for licensing and reuse, subject to restrictions.
Restrictions: Requests for reuse subject to acceptance and approval; reuse of some material is restricted due to rights status.
Viewing Facilities: Videotape (VHS).
Duplication Facilities: Videotape (VHS).

ARIZONA (Phoenix)

MILTON H. ERICKSON FOUNDATION, INC.
3606 North 24th Street
Phoenix, AZ 85016
(602) 956-6196

Jeffrey K. Zeig, Ph.D. (Director)

Contact: Jeffrey K. Zeig, Ph.D.
Services: Foundation. Videotape collection primarily for the use of scholars and researchers in the field of psychotherapy.
Description: Videotapes of the late Milton H. Erickson, M.D.; demonstrations of hypnosis and hypnotherapy; workshops on the topic of hypnotherapy conducted by renowned practitioners; lectures and demonstrations of psychotherapy by internationally renowned therapists.
Size & Elements: Videotape: 3/4" and 1/2" (400 hours).
Cataloging: None specified.
Access: Open to researchers and scholars. For in-house use only. Research fees charged. Research requests accepted by mail only.
Rights: Full rights held to all material.
Licensing: Apply for information.
Restrictions: None specified.
Viewing Facilities: Videotape (3/4" and 1/2").
Duplication Facilities: Videotape (3/4" and 1/2").

ARIZONA (Phoenix)

PHOENIX VIDEOFILMS/PAUL S. KARR PRODUCTIONS
P.O. Box 11711
Phoenix, AZ 85061
(602) 266-4198

Street address: 2949 West Indian School Road, Phoenix, AZ 85017

Paul Karr (Customer Service)

Contact: Paul Karr
Services: Film and videotape producer. Material available for duplication, licensing and reuse.
Description: Footage covering a wide variety of subjects, including the Grand Canyon, Monument Valley, recreation, scenic vistas, news events, historic material, and some California scenes (1950s-70s). Earlier historic materials include still photographs that have been transferred to film.
Size & Elements: Film: 16mm (over 500 cans; reversal, originals).
Cataloging: Shot lists; staff assistance required.
Access: Available for duplication and reuse. Research requests accepted by mail, telephone and in person (by appointment only). Research fees not charged unless extensive research is done.
Rights: Full rights held to some material. Some rights held to all material.
Licensing: Available for licensing. License fees negotiable.
Restrictions: None specified.
Viewing Facilities: Film and videotape.
Duplication Facilities: None (outside arrangements can be made).

ARIZONA (St. Michaels)

THE NAVAJO TRIBE
OFFICE OF BROADCAST SERVICES
P.O. Box 799
St. Michaels, AZ 86511
(602) 871-4941

Erwin Bowman (Director)

Contact: Philip Denny (Media Specialist)
Services: Videotape producer; media organization. Material maintained for distribution and rental rather than for research or reuse.
Description: Local news and scenic footage from the Navajo Reservation.

Subjects include: lifestyles; daily local news; the construction of a wind pump on the Reservation near Ganado; the construction of the Quartzsite Dam, built by the Navajo Tribal Utility Authority; Espel Ranch, featuring resources of the land, flora and fauna; Big Boquillas Ranch; Philippe Pettit's tightrope walk across a canyon on the Reservation; a John Wayne Film Festival and appreciation dinner; and the dedication of the "Margaret Arch," named for Margaret Goldwater.

Also produced a 28-minute television news program broadcast for 18 years on KOAT (Albuquerque) to southern Colorado, southeast Utah, northeast Arizona and all of New Mexico. This program is produced in the Navajo language and reaches a wide-ranging Navajo audience. Programs from 1984-88 have been saved; earlier programs were erased. The office also holds some materials for the Salt River Project, a production group in Phoenix, which has produced a series of videotapes focusing on cultural aspects of the Navajo.
Size & Elements: Videotape: 3/4" (900 videotapes, each 20 min.; masters).
Cataloging: None.
Access: Open to the public. Available for reuse and resale. Maintained for distribution and rental rather than for research or reuse. Research requests accepted by mail and telephone.
Rights: Full rights held to all material. Additional clearances may be necessary in some cases if material is to be reused (Salt River Project footage).
Licensing: Material possibly available for licensing and reuse. License fees generally not charged.
Restrictions: Credit (on-screen or otherwise) must be given for footage used.
Viewing Facilities: Videotape (3/4").
Duplication Facilities: Videotape.

ARIZONA (Tempe)

ARIZONA STATE UNIVERSITY
THE WAYNE KING COLLECTION
MUSIC LIBRARY — UNIVERSITY LIBRARIES
Tempe, AZ 85287
(602) 965-3513

Arlys L. McDonald (Head, Music Library)

Contact: Arlys L. McDonald
Services: University library. Film collection available for research.
Description: Kinescopes of *The Wayne King Show,* featuring Wayne King and his Orchestra. Featuring popular music of the period, the program was aired only over NBC's Midwest network on Thursday nights (October 1949-June 1952).
Size & Elements: Film: 16mm (115 kinescopes, each 30 min.).
Cataloging: Card catalogs.
Access: Open to the public. For in-house use only. Access by appointment only; apply in advance for appointment. Research fees not charged.
Rights: Some rights held to some material. Additional clearances may be necessary in some cases if material is to be used for any public viewing. Rights status of material has not been reviewed for any widespread dissemination.
Licensing: Apply for information.
Restrictions: None specified.
Viewing Facilities: Film (16mm projector, by arrangement through Special Collections Division).
Duplication Facilities: None.

ARIZONA (Tucson)

ARABIAN HORSE OWNERS FOUNDATION
W. R. BROWN MEMORIAL LIBRARY
P.O. Box 31391

Tucson, AZ 85751
(602) 326-1515

Street address: 4101 North Bear Canyon Road, Tucson, AZ 85749

Howard Shenk (Director)

Contact: Howard Shenk
Services: Association library. Films available for reuse, subject to restrictions.
Description: Silent and sound films (1920s-present) relating to horses, focusing on Arabian breeds. One finished production combines a film shot by Valentino about his horses with various horse footage; and another production (in progress) uses Ohio stud farm footage from the late 1930s-40s.
Size & Elements: Film: mostly 16mm (approx. 200-300 cans).
Cataloging: Mostly uncataloged at present; new catalog in progress.
Access: Available to the public for licensing and reuse. Research fees not charged. Research requests accepted by mail and telephone.
Rights: Full rights held to some material. Additional clearances may be necessary in some cases if material is to be reused.
Licensing: Available for licensing and reuse, subject to restrictions. License fees charged in some cases, depending on project.
Restrictions: Requests for reuse considered on a case-by-case basis.
Viewing Facilities: Film (16mm).
Duplication Facilities: None.

ARIZONA (Tucson)

CENTER FOR CREATIVE PHOTOGRAPHY
UNIVERSITY OF ARIZONA
Tucson, AZ 85721
(602) 621-7968

James L. Enyeart (Director)

Contact: Terence Pitts (Curator)
Services: Independent research institute affiliated with the University of Arizona; film and videotape archives. Material not available for loan but possibly available for reuse, subject to clearance and approval.
Description: Videotapes relating to 20th century photographers and photography. Most videotapes were produced by the Center and document lectures by or interviews with photographers. Other videotapes are commercially produced documentaries about photographers or videotapes made by photographers as works of art.
Size & Elements: Videotape: 3/4" and VHS (approx. 500 videotapes total).
Cataloging: Finding aids (lists).
Access: Open to the public. Videotapes may be viewed by individuals or groups at the Center but are not available for loan. Research fees not charged. Research requests accepted in person (walk-in).
Rights: Some rights held to all material. Some rights held to some material. Additional clearances may be necessary in some cases if material is to be reused.
Licensing: Material possibly available for reuse. Usage fees not charged.
Restrictions: None specified.
Viewing Facilities: Videotape (individual and group viewing stations for 3/4" and VHS).
Duplication Facilities: Videotape (duplication for in-house use only).

ARIZONA (Tucson)

GRAPEVINE PRODUCTIONS, LTD.
5055 East Broadway, Suite C214
Tucson, AZ 85711
(602) 747-3115
Fax: (602) 747-8226

Karl R. Morton (President)

Contacts: Karl R. Morton
Services: Film and videotape producer. Videotape material maintained for distribution and rental rather than for research or reuse.
Description: *Arizona Sonora Desert Museum — A Living Place* (25 min.), a videotape on the Desert Museum and the Sonora Desert.
Size & Elements: Videotape: 1" (1 title; master); also available in 3/4", VHS and Betamax.
Cataloging: None specified.

ARIZONA (Tucson)

Access: Maintained for distribution and rental rather than for research or reuse.
Rights: Full rights held to all material.
Licensing: Apply for information. License fees charged in some cases.
Restrictions: Apply for information regarding restrictions.
Viewing Facilities: Film (16mm); videotape (3/4" and VHS).
Duplication Facilities: Videotape (3/4" and VHS).

ARIZONA (Tucson)

THE SOURCE STOCK FOOTAGE LIBRARY, INC.
1709 South 29th Place
Tucson, AZ 85710
(602) 298-4810

Bill Briggs (President)

Contacts: Bill Briggs; Lynn Briggs; John Willwater
Services: Film and videotape producer; stock footage sales library.
Description: Stock shots (all originated on film). Most coverage (75%) from 1980s; 25% from 1970s. Special strengths include scenics, wildlife, time-lapse, heavy industry and environmental footage.

Subjects include: Acapulco, agriculture, airplanes, air shows, Alaska, animals, antique cars, balloons, baseball, beaches, the bizarre, blasts, bridges, Bryce Canyon, bullfights, cactus, cactus flowers, camping, canoes, Canyon de Chelly, Caribbean, carnivals, cattle, China, cliff divers, clouds (including time-lapse), coal mining, Coast Highway, Colorado, Colorado River, Colossal Caves, copper, cowboys, crafts, crowds, dams, deer, deserts, Desert Museum, Disneyland, dog racing, dynamite blasts, Egypt, elk, environmental footage, fall colors, falls, farming, fireworks, fishing, Flores, flowers, forests, geothermal energy, glaciers, gliders, gold bullion, Golden Gate, golf, Grand Canyon (including aerial views), Guanajuato, Guatemala, Guaymas, Havasu Falls, hiking, horseback riding, horse racing, hot air balloons, Indians, industrial, jungles, Kitt Peak, Lake Powell, Lake Tahoe, Las Vegas, lightning, London, luxury, medical footage, Mexico, Mexico City, mining, molten metal, Montezuma's Castle, Monument Valley, moon, mountains, museums, New York, New Zealand, North Slope (Alaska), nuclear plants, oceans, oil rigs, old stills, Old Faithful, old Tucson, open pits, parachutes, parasails, Park City, petroleum, pollution, prairies, pyramids, radiotelescopes, rafting, rain, Rainbow Bridge, rainbows, refineries, rodeos, Sabino Canyon, sailing, San Francisco, San Xavier, scenics, Sedona, sheep, ships, skylines, smelters, snow, snow skiing, space shuttles, spring, square dancing, streams, suburbia, sun, sunsets, surfing, swimming, Taxco, tennis, Tetons, time-lapse cinematography, Tokyo, tombstones, traffic, trucks, Tucson, underground footage, underwater footage, University of Arizona, Venice (California), Voladores, water skiing, welding, White Mountains, wind generators, workers, Xochimilco, Yellowstone and Yosemite National Parks.
Size & Elements: Film: 16mm (amount unspecified; negative and reversal). Videotape: 1" (transfers from film; masters; PAL and NTSC); 3/4" (masters and viewing copies with visible time code) and 1/2" (viewing copies with visible time code). (22 hours of selected and condensed scenes total). Entire library has been transferred from original film negatives to PAL format for foreign use.
Cataloging: Computerized cataloging for staff use only but available to researchers; shot lists; dope sheets; release sheets.
Access: Available to the public for licensing and reuse. Research fees not charged. Research requests accepted by mail and telephone. Screening videotapes loaned without charge.
Rights: Full rights held to all material.
Licensing: Available for licensing and reuse. License fees charged per scene; no "time" or "footage" charges apply.
Restrictions: None specified.
Viewing Facilities: None.
Duplication Facilities: None.

ARIZONA (Tucson)

TUCSON COMMUNITY CABLE CORPORATION
124 East Broadway
Tucson, AZ 85701
(602) 624-9833

Sam Behrend (Executive Director)

Contacts: Mark Taylor (Programming Director); Chris Wagganer (Cablecast Coordinator)

Services: Public access television facility. Videotape collection available for duplication and reuse, subject to restrictions.
Description: Community-oriented programming on local issues, health, religion, immigration, the arts, local music (jazz and rock) and locally produced video art. Also holds videotapes of the impeachment hearings in the historic case of former Arizona Gov. Evan Mecham, produced by the local public television station, and the (locally) controversial Frank Jarvis Atwood murder trial involving a missing girl.
Size & Elements: Videotape: 3/4" and VHS SP (approx. 1,800 videotapes).
Cataloging: Computerized cataloging for staff use only.
Access: Available for duplication with permission of original producers. Research fees not charged. Research requests accepted by mail, telephone and in person (walk-in).
Rights: Some rights held to some material. Additional clearances may be necessary in some cases if material is to be reused.
Licensing: Apply for information. License fees charged for profit-making use.
Restrictions: All public access videotapes restricted to nonprofit use. Any duplication or reuse requires permission of original producer.
Viewing Facilities: Videotape (3/4" and 1/2") (by appointment only).
Duplication Facilities: Videotape (3/4" and 1/2"; all formats to Betamax; time base correction available).

ARIZONA (Tucson)

UNIVERSITY OF ARIZONA
FILM COLLECTION
Audiovisual Building
1325 East Speedway Boulevard
Tucson, AZ 85721
(602) 621-3282

Carrie Russell (Media Librarian)

Contacts: Carrie Russell; Bonnie Travers (Head Media Librarian); Tod Gregoire (Library Assistant)
Services: University library. Film and videotape collection open to the public for in-house use only.
Description: In addition to an extensive collection of educational support materials and feature films, Instructional Media Services (IMS) has produced 23 titles.

Sample titles include: *Mirrors on the Universe,* on the Mount Hopkins multiple mirrors telescope; *Runaways from What to Where,* a dramatization of the actual court case of a young runaway girl in Pima County, filmed in Tucson and San Francisco; *Solar Powered Irrigation,* presenting possible approaches to solar-powered irrigation for the Southwest; *Journey Through Eden,* a panorama of East African life, filmed in Kenya and Tanzania; *Fever,* portraying Black African rituals at the Brazilian Carnival; *Fire on the Sea,* the volcanoes, history, atmosphere and beauty of Sicily; *American Realists,* documenting American painters Copley, Stuart, Homer, Eakins, Ryder, Inness, the Hudson River School, the Impressionists, Marin, Stuart Davis, Burchfield, Wyeth, Milton Avery, Ben Shahn and Walt Kuhn; *Bellota: A Story of Roundup,* on the disappearing traditions of the *vaquero* (cowboy); *DeGrazia,* in which the well-known Arizona artist discusses how his life among the Southwest Indians and Mexicans is reflected in his work; *Fantasmas (Ghosts),* on the cradle of Incan civilization, filmed in Cusco, the Urubamba Valley, Lake Titicaca and Machu Picchu, Peru.
Size & Elements: Film: 16mm (5,000 titles, 5,094,000 feet, 5,282 cans). Videotape: 3/4" and VHS (over 800 videotapes).
Cataloging: Published catalogs (dated); computerized cataloging for staff use only.
Access: Open to the public. For in-house use only. Research fees not charged. Research requests accepted at the Library Reference Service by mail, telephone and in person (walk-in).
Rights: Full rights held to all IMS-produced material.
Licensing: Apply for information.
Restrictions: None specified.
Viewing Facilities: Film (16mm); videotape (3/4" and VHS).
Duplication Facilities: None.

ARIZONA (Window Rock)

NAVAJO NATION LIBRARY SYSTEM
P.O. Drawer K
Window Rock, AZ 86515
(602) 871-6517

Irving Nelson (Program Manager)

Contact: Irving Nelson
Services: Library. Film collection available for in-house use and research.
Description: Films relating to the Navajo people, including ethnographic coverage and tourism promotionals. Approximately 20 to 30 of the films are inaccessible due to poor condition.
Size & Elements: Film: format unspecified (48 titles total).
Cataloging: Item-by-item search.
Access: Open to researchers and scholars only. For in-house use only. Research fees not charged. Research requests accepted by mail, telephone and in person.
Rights: Apply for information.
Licensing: Certain usage fees may be charged.
Restrictions: None specified.
Viewing Facilities: Film (children's room in library).
Duplication Facilities: None.

ARKANSAS

ARKANSAS (Little Rock)

ARKANSAS DEPARTMENT OF PARKS & TOURISM
One Capitol Mall
Little Rock, AR 72201
(501) 682-7609

Jo Luck Wilson (Executive Director)

Contact: Carol VanPelt (Photo Librarian)
Services: State government agency. Promotional film available for reuse.
Description: *Arkansas: A Land Where Dreams Come True* (22 min.) gives a comprehensive overview of the state from a tourist perspective.
Size & Elements: Film: 16mm. Videotape: 3/4" and 1/2". (1 title total).
Cataloging: None specified.
Access: Available to the public for duplication and reuse (apply for information).
Rights: Full rights held to all material.
Licensing: Available for licensing and reuse. License fees not charged.
Restrictions: None specified.
Viewing Facilities: None.
Duplication Facilities: None.

ARKANSAS (Little Rock)

ARKANSAS HISTORY COMMISSION
One Capitol Mall
Little Rock, AR 72201
(501) 371-2141

Dr. John L. Ferguson (State Historian)

Contact: Dr. John L. Ferguson
Services: State archives. Material available for licensing and reuse, subject to restrictions.
Description: Most items are Arkansas State promotional films (1950s-present) pertaining to Arkansas and its history.
Size & Elements: Film and videotape (less than 50 titles).
Cataloging: Material uncataloged.
Access: Open to researchers and scholars only. Research requests accepted in person (by appointment only).
Rights: Some rights held to some material.
Licensing: Available for licensing and reuse. License fees not charged.
Restrictions: None specified.
Viewing Facilities: Available by special arrangement.
Duplication Facilities: None.

ARKANSAS (Mountain View)

OZARK FOLK CENTER
Box 500
Mountain View, AR 72560
(501) 269-3851

Bob Von Kronemann (General Manager)

Contact: Bill McNeil (Folklorist)
Services: State park. Videotape collection available for licensing and reuse, subject to restrictions.
Description: Interviews with individuals about their lives in the Ozark Mountains. A variety of subjects are covered, including schooling, music and crafts, families and other aspects of Ozark life.
Size & Elements: Videotape: VHS (20 videotapes; masters and viewing copies; each 60 min.).
Cataloging: Shot lists.
Access: Open to the public for research. Requests accepted by mail, telephone and in person (walk-in).
Rights: Apply for information. Additional clearances may be necessary if material is to be reused.
Licensing: Available for licensing and reuse. License and usage fees not charged.
Restrictions: Requests for licensing and reuse subject to clearance and approval.
Viewing Facilities: None.
Duplication Facilities: None.

CALIFORNIA

CALIFORNIA (Acton)

JOYCE MEDIA, INC.
See **CALIFORNIA** (Los Angeles Metro)

CALIFORNIA (Agoura Hills)

VALLEY OF THE SUN PUBLISHING
See **CALIFORNIA** (Los Angeles Metro)

CALIFORNIA (Alameda)

THE LATHAM FOUNDATION
Latham Plaza
Clement and Schiller Streets
Alameda, CA 94501-1397
(415) 521-0920

Hugh H. Tebault (President)

Contact: Hugh H. Tebault
Services: Nonprofit foundation; film and videotape producer and distributor. Films and videotapes available for rental and possibly reuse, subject to approval.
Description: Wildlife and the environment; pet care; the use of animals in therapy programs for people in need (e.g. mentally or physically handicapped patients, the elderly, and children in foster care); animal welfare; human and animal interdependence and relationships.
Human-companion animal bond. Films documenting the mutually beneficial relationship between people and animals. Sample titles include *Ability, Not Disability,* in which physically and mentally impaired people learn horseback riding. This highly beneficial form of pet-facilitated therapy provides exercise, improves coordination, and builds self-esteem. *Dolphin...Swim* documents the therapeutic effects of swimming and associating with dolphins on autistic children. *Institution Without Walls,* in West Germany, houses over 9,000 residents, many severely mentally or physically handicapped; dogs, cats, horses, birds and other animals have played an important part in rehabilitating patients ever since the community was founded over 100 years ago.
Withit (33 programs, each 30 min.; many also available in Spanish). This family-oriented action and adventure series explores "the world looking at animals of all kinds — from honeybees to horses, peacocks to people." Titles include: *The Family Chooses a Pet; Strange and Unusual Animals; Training Your Dog; Birdwatch; Police Horses; What is a Cat?; Reptiles and Amphibians; Zoo Constant; Aquarium;* and *Relating to Chickens.*
General interest. Short educational documentaries about animals and pets. Titles include *Big Bad Wolf, Big Bad Lie,* documenting the plight of the wolf in the U.S. and examining widespread misunderstandings. *So Little Time* shows migratory waterfowl and their rapidly disappearing habitat, the marshland. *A World To Build* is a closeup look at the day-to-day activities of a modern animal shelter, including pet population control, pet care and selection, and finding homes for homeless animals.

Size & Elements: Film: 16mm (over 60 titles). Videotape: 3/4" and VHS (over 60 titles).
Cataloging: Published catalogs.
Access: Available to the public for rental and reuse, subject to approval. Research requests not accepted. Programs can be rented for preview.
Rights: Full rights held to all material.
Licensing: Apply for information regarding licensing policies.
Restrictions: None specified.
Viewing Facilities: None.
Duplication Facilities: Videotape (3/4" and VHS).
Related Materials: Study guides for *Withit* series. Scripts for translation, music and sound effects tapes are also available.

CALIFORNIA (Altadena)

GOAL PRODUCTIONS, INC.
TOURNAMENT OF ROSES FILM LIBRARY
See **CALIFORNIA** (Los Angeles Metro)

CALIFORNIA (Anaheim)

AMERICAN PORTRAIT FILMS
and
ENCORE ENTERTAINMENT
See **CALIFORNIA** (Los Angeles Metro)

CALIFORNIA (Belmont)

ELECTRIC AUTO ASSOCIATION
1249 Lane Street
Belmont, CA 94002
(415) 591-6698

Videotapes available for loan from:
Dr. John Reuyl
2050 Dartmouth Street
Palo Alto, CA 94301
(415) 857-9340

John B. Newell (Chairman of the Board) (415/322-8886)

Contact: Staff
Services: Nonprofit international association. Videotape collection available for duplication, licensing and reuse.
Description: Organization established 1967 to promote clean and quiet electric cars for personal transportation. Provides literature, education and technical aid for persons wanting to build or purchase electric vehicles.
   Footage includes electric passenger cars, rally coverage from Expo 1986 in Vancouver, B.C., General Motors Sun Racers, and *Running With The Sun: Stanford University Solar Car Project* (videotape, 20 min.).
Size & Elements: Videotape: 1/2" (amount unspecified; masters and viewing copies).
Cataloging: None specified.
Access: Available to the public for duplication, licensing and reuse.
Rights: Full rights held to all material. Some material in the public domain.
Licensing: Available for licensing and reuse.
Restrictions: None specified.
Viewing Facilities: None.
Duplication Facilities: None.

CALIFORNIA (Berkeley)

EAST WEST CLASSICS
1529 Acton Street
Berkeley, CA 94702
(415) 526-3611
Fax: (415) 526-3628

Contact: Audie Bock
Services: Distributor. Films available to the public and educational institutions for rental.
Description: Distributes feature-length foreign (especially Japanese) motion pictures.
   Selected titles include: *Ah Ying* (1984), about the real-life story of an aspiring young actress and her friendship with her teacher; *Father and Son* (Allen Fong, 1981), the bittersweet tale of a stormy relationship between father and son in contemporary Hong Kong; *The Pornographers* (Shohei Imamura, 1966), about a group of 8mm pornography filmmakers struggling against the high risks and low production values of Japan's booming underground X-rated industry; *No Regrets For Our Youth* (Akira Kurosawa, 1946), in which a vivacious but sheltered young woman falls in love with an outspoken left-wing law student; *Human Bullet* (Kihachi Okamoto, 1968), taking place in the last days of World War II, when a Japanese recruit learns that his glory will be a *kamikaze* mission, and spends his last 24 hours learning about life and love; *When a Woman Ascends the Stairs* (Mikio Naruse, 1960), a glimpse behind the scenes of the most expensive Tokyo "hostess" bars; *Chushingura (47 Ronin)* (Hiroshi Inagaki, 1962), a story of loyalty and revenge based on an actual incident of heroic mass suicide in 1748; *Onibaba* (Kaneto Shindo, 1963), a story of raw survival, lust and the supernatural with two women who eke out a living by stealing the armor from dead samurai and selling it; *Bastille* (Rudolf van den Berg, 1984), in which an Amsterdam Jew goes searching for his lost twin brother, convinced he has also survived the Holocaust; and *38: Vienna Before The Fall* (Wolfgang Glück, 1988).
Size & Elements: Film: 35mm (approx. 20 titles); 16mm (approx. 15 titles).
Cataloging: Published catalog.
Access: Available to educational institutions and the public for rental.
Rights: Apply for information.
Licensing: Apply for information.
Restrictions: None specified.
Viewing Facilities: None.
Duplication Facilities: None.

CALIFORNIA (Berkeley)

EDUCATIONAL FILM AND VIDEO PROJECT
1529 Josephine Street
Berkeley, CA 94703
(415) 849-1649

Ian Thiermann (Executive Director)

Contact: Ian Thiermann
Services: Foundation; media organization; television broadcaster; film and videotape producer and distributor. Film and videotape material available to the public for rental, purchase and reuse, subject to restrictions.
Description: Nuclear arms race, Central America, citizen diplomacy and environmental issues.
   Nuclear War. Titles include: *Women: For America, For The World; Star Wars: A Search for Security; In the Nuclear Shadow,* in which children of various races and backgrounds respond to the threat of nuclear war; *A Step Away From War; The Last Epidemic,* showing the effects of nuclear weapons on a civilian population; *Life on Earth Perhaps; A Question of Power; The Nuclear Winter,* featuring Carl Sagan; *Growing Up Nuclear,* shot in Hiroshima; *The Biology of Nuclear War; Faith, War and Peace in the Nuclear Age; Buster & Me; What Soviet Children Are Saying About Nuclear War;* and *Dark Circle.*
   Other films include: *Preparing for Peace: Economic Conversion Means Job Insurance; The Edge of History,* in which Admiral Noel Gayler and others stress the need for cooperation in international affairs; *What About the Russians?,* with comments by Robert McNamara, George Kennan, William Colby and John Marshall Lee; *Building a World Beyond War; Reliability and Risk,* exploring our increasing dependence upon computers to make crucial military decisions; *Gods of Metal,* analyzing the arms race from a Christian perspective; *Weapons in Space,* featuring Carl Sagan and Admiral Noel Gayler; *A Call for Peace,* with Harry Belafonte; and *The Need for Christian Peacemaking.*
   Central America. Titles include: *Destination Nicaragua; Nicaragua for the First Time,* examining the election process; *Face to Face: Teenagers Talk About Nicaragua; In the Shadow of War; Faces of War; Until it is Safe to Return,* on an El Salvadorean woman and child who found refuge in Ithaca, New York; *Neighbors to Nicaragua: The Story of Project Minnesota/Leon; Macmichael on Nicaragua.*
   Citizen diplomacy and responsibility. Titles include: *A Soviet School Day; Direct Connection; When the People Lead; People To People; No Frames. No Boundaries.; Beyond War: Spacebridge; How Then Shall We Live.*
   Environmental issues. Titles include: *Earth First!: The Struggle for the Australian Rainforest; A Thousand Cranes; The Global Brain.*
Size & Elements: Film: 16mm (over 40 titles). Videotape: 3/4", VHS and Betamax (over 40 titles).
Cataloging: Published catalogs.
Access: Available to the public for rental and purchase. Research requests

10

accepted by mail, telephone and in person (by appointment only).
Rights: Full rights held to some material. Additional clearances may be necessary in some cases if material is to be reused.
Licensing: Available for licensing and reuse, subject to restrictions. License fees charged.
Restrictions: Different fee scales apply to nonprofit and for-profit requests.
Viewing Facilities: Videotape.
Duplication Facilities: None.

CALIFORNIA (Berkeley)

GRADUATE THEOLOGICAL UNION LIBRARY
2400 Ridge Road
Berkeley, CA 94709
(415) 649-2400

John Baker-Batsel (Library Director)

Contact: Judy Clarence (Head of Reference)
Services: Religious educational institution; library. Videotape collection primarily available for in-house research.
Description: Theological topics including cults, new religious movements, pastoral counseling and logotherapy (Viktor Frankl).

Sample titles include: *Sun Myung Moon; The Heresy Trial of the Rev. Richard Lamm: Copernican Politics and Copernican Ethics; The Magnetism of Cults; God is Rice; Hare Krishna; Tantra of Gy'Uto; The Gospel According to St. Matthew; Constructing the Multi-Generational Family Genogram; Logotherapy; World Council of Churches 6th Assembly Highlights; Introduction to Scientology; Sin; Evolution of a Yogi;* and *Krishnamurti.*

Additional videotapes are held in the Starr King School for the Ministry collection.
Size & Elements: Videotape: VHS and Betamax (48 titles total).
Cataloging: Card catalogs; computerized cataloging for staff use only.
Access: Open to the public. For in-house use only.
Rights: Rights status of material not known.
Licensing: Apply for information.
Restrictions: Apply for information.
Viewing Facilities: Videotape (VHS and Betamax).
Duplication Facilities: None.

CALIFORNIA (Berkeley)

JUDAH L. MAGNES MUSEUM
BLUMENTHAL LIBRARY
2911 Russell Street
Berkeley, CA 94705
(415) 849-2710

Seymour Fromer (Director)

Contact: Jane Levy (Librarian)
Services: Library. Open to the public. Maintains film and videotape collection.
Description: Holds a large collection of recently acquired films on the Holocaust; one original film of a Bar Mitzvah ceremony in India (1940s, 16mm, made by a local University professor and donated to the Library); and some film documenting local Jewish theater productions.
Size & Elements: Film: 16mm (amount unspecified). Videotape (format and amount unspecified).
Cataloging: None specified.
Access: Open to the public. Research requests accepted by mail and telephone.
Rights: Full rights held to all material.
Licensing: Apply for information.
Restrictions: None specified.
Viewing Facilities: None.
Duplication Facilities: None.

CALIFORNIA (Berkeley)

PACIFIC FILM ARCHIVE
UNIVERSITY ART MUSEUM
UNIVERSITY OF CALIFORNIA, BERKELEY
2625 Durant Avenue
Berkeley, CA 94720
(415) 642-1412 (General)
(415) 642-1437 (Library)

Edith R. Kramer (Director and Curator of Film)

Contacts: Nancy Goldman (Head, Library and Public Service Program); Lee Amazonas (Assistant Film Consultant)
Services: University film archives. Materials available for in-house research use only.
Description: Japanese features (1950s-60s) produced by the Daiei, Shochiku, Toho and Nikkatsu studios; Soviet silent cinema; Soviet Georgian cinema (1970s); significant collection of West Coast avant-garde films (1960s); international contemporary animation; small collection of early silent cinema (1900-15); contemporary Chinese films (late 1970s-80s); and Nazi training films (duplicates of those in Library of Congress collection). Miscellaneous Northern California historical footage includes footage of Market Street (pre-1906) and the Pan-Pacific Exposition in San Francisco (1915).
Size & Elements: Film: 35mm and 16mm (6,000 titles; primarily release prints). Videotape: format and amount unspecified.
Cataloging: Card catalogs; finding aids; research library. Published catalog of Daiei Motion Picture Company films held in PFA's Japanese collection.
Access: Open to the public. For in-house use only. Research fees charged. Research requests accepted by mail, telephone and in person (walk-in). Screening time must be reserved at least two weeks in advance.
Rights: No rights held to any material. Additional clearances will be necessary in some cases if material is to be reused.
Licensing: Not available for licensing or reuse.
Restrictions: Films available for in-house research use only.
Viewing Facilities: Film (35mm, 16mm and Super 8mm single- or double-system; 35mm and 16mm flatbed viewing tables); videotape (3/4" NTSC; VHS multiformat).
Duplication Facilities: None.
Related Materials: Library with non-circulating collection of film books, periodicals, stills, posters, and clippings files on films, personalities, festivals and other film-related topics.

CALIFORNIA (Berkeley)

QUEST PRODUCTIONS INC.
2600 10th Street
Berkeley, CA 94710
(415) 548-0854
Fax: (415) 548-1824

Bill Jersey (President)

Contact: Joy Ramos (Director of Distribution)
Services: Film and videotape producer. Material available for duplication, licensing and reuse.
Description: Subjects covered include: U.S.-Soviet relations (1934-84); U.S.-Soviet propaganda cartoons (1930-86); Chicago riots (1968); youth gangs (1982); interview with a murderer (1986); interviews with President Richard M. Nixon and George Kennan (1984); interviews with the Christian far-right (1986); paintings, sculpture and city views of Florence, Italy (1987); and solar homes (1980).

Titles include: *The First Fifty Years* (1985), a comprehensive guide to relations between the United States and Soviet Union from the establishment of diplomatic ties in 1933 through the present; *Faces of the Enemy* (1987), a documentary film that examines the sociological, psychological, and political aspects of war to discover what drives nations and individuals to kill; *Children of Violence* (1982) guides the viewer through the lives of gang members of the Chicano community in Oakland, California.
Size & Elements: Film: 16mm (100,000 feet, 3 titles, 100 cans; positive, negative, originals and release prints). Videotape: 1" (10 hours; masters); 3/4" (50 hours; masters and viewing copies); and VHS (viewing copies).
Cataloging: Shot lists and transcripts.
Access: Available for duplication, licensing and reuse. Research fees charged (per hour). Research requests accepted by mail, telephone and in person (by appointment only).
Rights: Full rights held to all material.
Licensing: Available for licensing and reuse. License fees negotiable.
Restrictions: None specified.
Viewing Facilities: Film (16mm); videotape (3/4" and VHS).
Duplication Facilities: Videotape (3/4" to VHS only).

CALIFORNIA (Berkeley)

UNIVERSITY OF CALIFORNIA
EXTENSION MEDIA CENTER
2176 Shattuck Avenue
Berkeley, CA 94704
(415) 642-0460

Olga Knight (Director)

Contacts: Olga Knight (415/642-0618); Chip Taylor (National Sales Manager) (800/876-2447 or 603/434-9262); Barbara Gray (Customer Service) (415/642-5578); Dan Bickley (Marketing and Promotion Manager) (415/642-1340)
Services: Educational institution; film and videotape distributor. Materials available for rental and in some cases purchase.
Description: The Center is the sole distributor of over 400 titles on a wide range of subjects, including:

Social sciences. Includes American history, U.S. government and contemporary issues; ethnography and world cultures; physical anthropology and archaeology, Native Americans, Hispanic studies, Black studies, women's studies, family life and aging. Sample titles include: *Prophet of Peace: The Story of Dr. Martin Luther King, Jr.; The California Gold Mining Series; Water Wars: The Battle of Mono Lake; The Cities in China Series; Trobriand Cricket: An Ingenious Response to Colonialism; The Living Maya; The Movement Style and Culture Series;* and *Some Babies Die.*

Physical and biological sciences. Covers chemistry, physics, astronomy, biology, animal studies, environmental science and great scientists. Sample titles include: *Organic Chemistry Laboratory Techniques; Understanding Space and Time Series; The Baboon Social Life Series; Humboldt Bay;* and *Ecological Realities: Natural Laws at Work.*

Arts and humanities. Offers materials on film study, dance, theatrical arts, music, art and design, architecture, language arts, literature and philosophy. Sample titles include: *Film Graphics: Abstract Aspects of Editing; Mary Wigman: When the Fire Dances Between the Two Poles; Chiang Ching: A Dance Journey; The Theatrical Makeup Series; Living Music for Golden Mountains; Wearable Art from California;* and *Cities for People.*

Health and medical sciences. Subjects include parenting, medical sciences and issues, psychology and mental health, sex education and safety. Sample titles include: *Dirofilaria Immitis, Development and Transmission; The Attendant Care Training Series; The Microbiology Teaching Series; Dance Therapy: The Power of Movement;* and *Laser Safety.*

Includes two University-produced film series: The *American Indian* series, 15 films (1961-65). Titles include *Acorns: Staple Food of California Indians; Basketry of the Pomo: Forms and Ornamentation; Beautiful Tree: Chickkale; Calumet: Pipe of Peace; Dream Dances of the Kashia Pomo; Obsidian Point Making* and *Wooden Box: Made by Steaming and Bending.* In *The Great Scientists Speak Again* series, Prof. Richard M. Eakin depicts through impersonation the discoveries, methods of study, theories and personal philosophies of Charles Darwin, Gregor Mendel, Hans Spemann, Louis Pasteur, William Beaumont and William Harvey.

Also maintains a film and videotape rental library which includes approximately 4,000 titles purchased from other distributors.
Size & Elements: Film: 16mm (release prints). Videotape: 3/4", VHS, Betamax I and II (viewing copies). (Over 4,400 titles total).
Cataloging: Published catalogs.
Access: Available for rental (and in some cases purchase) rather than for research or reuse. Research fees not charged. Requests accepted by mail, telephone and in person.
Rights: Full rights held to some material. Some rights held to all material. Additional clearances may be necessary in some cases if material is to be reused.
Licensing: Available for licensing, subject to restrictions. License fees charged.
Restrictions: Restrictions may apply to reuse of some titles.
Viewing Facilities: Film and videotape (for preview toward purchase).
Duplication Facilities: None.

CALIFORNIA (Berkeley)

UNIVERSITY OF CALIFORNIA, BERKELEY
THE BANCROFT LIBRARY
Berkeley, CA 94720
(415) 642-8176

Contact: Vivian C. Fisher (Head, Microforms Division)

Services: University library. Film and videotape collection available for research and reuse on a case-by-case basis, subject to restrictions.
Description: [The following description was provided by The Bancroft Library, and is printed verbatim at their request.]

"The Bancroft Library has a small collection of motion pictures, relatively few of which are videotape. They relate primarily to the history of the University of California, California politics, the Sierra Club and conservation, and the Kaiser industries. Many of the motion pictures are in poor condition and cannot be screened. Bancroft has no screening or copying facilities. Arrangements for screening can be made with other University offices for those movies in good enough condition. There are no copying facilities on campus to dub onto 16mm film, but there are facilities to dub onto videotape. As some of the films are in remote storage, it is necessary to make arrangements for viewing at least a week in advance. All requests for information must be made in writing to: Head of Microforms Division, The Bancroft Library, University of California, Berkeley, California 94720."
Size & Elements: Film and videotape (formats and amounts unspecified).
Cataloging: Apply for information.
Access: See above.
Rights: Apply for information.
Licensing: Apply for information.
Restrictions: See above.
Viewing Facilities: None (arrangements can be made with other University offices to view films in good condition).
Duplication Facilities: None (film-to-videotape transfers available elsewhere on campus).
Related Materials: Rare books, manuscripts and photographs.

CALIFORNIA (Berkeley)

UNIVERSITY OF CALIFORNIA, BERKELEY
INSTITUTE OF INDUSTRIAL RELATIONS
LABOR OCCUPATIONAL HEALTH PROGRAM
2521 Channing Way
Berkeley, CA 94720
(415) 642-5507

Available for rental from:
LOHP FILMS
P.O. Box 315
Franklin Lakes, NJ 07417
(201) 891-8240

Robin Baker (Director, Labor Occupational Health Program)

Contact: Audiovisual Staff
Services: Educational institution. Films and videotapes available to the public for rental and purchase.
Description: Programs relating to occupational health and safety.

Titles include: *Working For Your Life,* focusing on the hazards faced by American working women and their fight to improve working conditions, including interviews with hairdressers, clerical workers, operating room nurses and smelter workers; *Another Day's Living,* filmed on location in the forest and sawmills of Washington and British Columbia, examining past and present hazards of the forest products industry; *Working Steel,* showing hazards in the steel foundry, one of the most dangerous workplaces today; and *Five Walnuts: The Health Effects of Asbestos.*
Size & Elements: Film: 16mm (3 titles; originals and release prints). Videotape: VHS (4 titles; masters and viewing copies).
Cataloging: Published catalogs.
Access: Open to the public. Available for rental and purchase. Rental and purchase fees charged. For sales, contact California office; rental requests handled by New Jersey office. Requests accepted by mail and telephone.
Rights: Full rights held to all material. Additional clearances may be necessary in some cases if material is to be reused.
Licensing: Apply for information. License and usage fees charged.
Restrictions: None specified.
Viewing Facilities: None.
Duplication Facilities: None (arrangements can be made to duplicate material at Educational Television Office on nearby University campus).

CALIFORNIA (Beverly Hills)

ACADEMY OF MOTION PICTURE ARTS AND SCIENCES
ACADEMY FILM ARCHIVE

and
DE LAURENTIIS ENTERTAINMENT GROUP, INC.
and
GOETHE INSTITUTE LOS ANGELES
and
MGM/UA COMMUNICATIONS COMPANY
and
QINTEX ENTERTAINMENT
and
TWENTIETH CENTURY FOX FILM CORPORATION
See CALIFORNIA (Los Angeles Metro)

CALIFORNIA (Bonita)

GERSON INSTITUTE
P.O. Box 430
Bonita, CA 92002
(619) 267-1150
Fax: (619) 267-6441

Street address: 5012 Central Avenue, Suite E

Charlotte Gerson (President)

Contacts: Charlotte Gerson; Norman Fritz (Executive Vice President)
Services: Educational organization. Videotapes available to the public for distribution.
Description: Material relating to Gerson Therapy, an alternative, nutritional cancer therapy. Videotapes include a lecture on Gerson Therapy; a presentation of 50 "cured incurables" healed on Gerson Therapy; and food preparation for Gerson Therapy patients.
Size & Elements: Videotape: VHS and Betamax (approx. 3 titles).
Cataloging: None specified.
Access: Available to the public for distribution.
Rights: Full rights held to all material.
Licensing: Apply for information.
Restrictions: None specified.
Viewing Facilities: None.
Duplication Facilities: Videotape.

CALIFORNIA (Burbank)

CARSON TONIGHT INC.
and
dick clark media archives, inc.
(Division of dick clark productions, inc.)
and
COLUMBIA ENTERTAINMENT CO.
and
COLUMBIA PICTURES TV/STOCK FILM LIBRARY
and
WALT DISNEY ARCHIVES
and
THE WALT DISNEY COMPANY
and
FILM BANK
and
INTER VIDEO/TTI
and
ROCK SOLID PRODUCTIONS
and
SPECTRAL COMMUNICATIONS
and
WARNER BROS. INC.
See CALIFORNIA (Los Angeles Metro)

CALIFORNIA (Calabasas)

AUDIENCE PLANNERS, INC.
See CALIFORNIA (Los Angeles Metro)

CALIFORNIA (Camarillo)

ERIN SHEFFIELD PRODUCTIONS
1174 Guinda Court

Camarillo, CA 93010
(805) 484-2618

Erin Sheffield (Producer)

Contact: Erin Sheffield
Services: Film and videotape producer. Material available for licensing and reuse.
Description: Footage shot on the island of Java (Indonesia), including: Taman Mini, Sunda Kelapa, sidewalk flower, bird and antiques markets, Komodo dragons, a zoo, the Ancol amusement park, native Javanese crafts, Bogor, mountain village, cowboy and an American Indian girl in a rice paddy.
Also holds footage of Buffalo Bill's Wild West Show as performed in an Indonesian arena, produced by Montie Montana, Jr. Footage includes trick riding, roping, knife throwing, American Indian dances, Argentine gauchos, Mexican charros, Roman riding, trick whip cracking, tent pegging, a parade of show performers down a street in Jakarta and a cowboy and American Indian princess in a Javanese village.
Size and Elements: Videotape: Betacam (amount unspecified; masters).
Cataloging: Logs.
Access: Available for duplication and reuse. Apply for information regarding research fees and procedures.
Rights: Full rights held to all material.
Licensing: Available for licensing and reuse. License fees charged.
Restrictions: None specified.
Viewing Facilities: Videotape (off premises). Can supply 1/2" viewing copies in response to serious inquiries.
Duplication Facilities: Videotape (off premises).

CALIFORNIA (Capitola)

ASBESTOS VICTIMS OF AMERICA
P.O. Box 559
Capitola, CA 95010
(408) 476-3646

Street address: 2715 Porter Street, Soquel, CA 95073

Heather Bechtel-Maurer (Executive Director)

Contact: Susan Bradley (Secretary)
Services: Nonprofit educational institution. Videotape collection maintained for educational purposes.
Description: Asbestos and asbestos victims. The *Asbestos Safety Workshop* series includes: *Type C Respirators Explained: Guide to Supplied Air; Guide to Negative Air Filtration Systems; Asbestos Abatement: Video Guide to the Process; Maintaining Asbestos-Covered Pipes and Surfaces; Testing Buildings for Asbestos Hazards;* and *Asbestos Safety in the Schools.*
Other materials include approximately 25 videotapes about asbestos victims and various newscasts relating to asbestos.
Size & Elements: Videotape: format unspecified (approx. 30 videotapes).
Cataloging: Lists.
Access: Apply for information.
Rights: Apply for information.
Licensing: Apply for information.
Restrictions: None specified.
Viewing Facilities: None.
Duplication Facilities: None.

CALIFORNIA (Carlsbad)

CRM FILMS L.P.
2233 Faraday Street, Suite F
Carlsbad, CA 92008
(619) 431-9800
(800) 421-0833
Fax: (619) 931-5792

Contact: Marilyn McKelvey
Services: Distributor. Films and videotapes available to the public for preview, rental and purchase.
Description: Films and videotapes on management and sales training.
Management. Titles include: *Communication: The Non-Verbal Agenda*

CALIFORNIA (Carpinteria)

(1975); *Creative Problem Solving* (1979); *Case of the Snarled Parking Lot* (1982); *Case of Working Smarter Not Harder* (1982); *Discipline Without Punishment* (1982); *Learning to Think Like a Manager* (1983); *Managing Stress (1979); Who Wants Unions?* (1983); *Women In Management* (1975); *Working With Difficult People* (1984); and *How to Influence Motivation* (1986).

Customer service and sales training. Titles include: *Closing the Sale* (1983); *Dealing With Difficult Customers* (1986); *Overcoming Objections* (1983); *Selling to Tough Customers* (1981); *Professional Communication on the Telephone;* and *Why People Buy* (1981).

Meeting openers. Animated films by Stephen Bosustow, used to launch programs, illustrate key topics, open meetings and start discussions. Titles include: *Advice Without Consent; Clear As Mud; Communication: Getting in Touch; The Divided Man: Commitment or Compromise; The Ego Trap; I Told 'Em Exactly How to Do It; Is It Always Right to be Right?;* and *Competition: Planning for Change.*
Size & Elements: Film: 16mm. Videotape: 3/4", VHS and Betamax. (Approx. 95 titles total).
Cataloging: Published catalog.
Access: Available to the public for rental, preview and purchase. Quantity and volume discounts may be available. Orders accepted by mail and telephone.
Rights: Apply for information.
Licensing: Apply for information.
Restrictions: No materials may be reproduced in whole or in part without the written consent of CRM Films.
Viewing Facilities: None.
Duplication Facilities: None.

CALIFORNIA (Carpinteria)

INNERQUEST COMMUNICATIONS CORPORATION
6383 Rose Lane
Carpinteria, CA 93013
(805) 684-9977
Telex: 6971013 AFC

Donald L. Higley (Principal)

Contact: Rogers V. Follansbee
Services: Film and videotape stock footage sales library.
Description: African nature, ethnographic and wildlife footage. Includes: Ituri Forest pygmies (activities and dancing); tribal dancing from East Africa, shot near Mombasa; Masai dancing; and animals (rhinoceros, elephant, buffalo and plains game).
Size & Elements: Film: 35mm (50,000 feet; color negative); 16mm (over 1,000,000 feet; reversal and color positive). Videotape: format unspecified (masters and viewing copies).
Cataloging: Computerized cataloging available to researchers.
Access: Available to the public for licensing and reuse. Research fees charged. Research requests accepted by mail.
Rights: Some rights held to all material.
Licensing: Available for licensing, subject to restrictions. License fees charged.
Restrictions: Requests for licensing and reuse considered on a case-by-case basis.
Viewing Facilities: Film and videotape.
Duplication Facilities: None.

CALIFORNIA (Carpinteria)

MERKEL FILMS
Box 722
Carpinteria, CA 93013
(805) 648-6448

East Coast contact:
SECOND LINE SEARCH
330 West 42nd Street, Room 2901
New York, NY 10036
(212) 594-5544

Dan Merkel (Owner, Merkel Films)

Contact: Dan Merkel
Services: Film and videotape producer; stock footage sales library.

Description: Action water sports cinematography (shot over the past twenty years) including: bodyboarding, hang-gliding, hot air ballooning, kayaking, motor bikes, ocean waves, river rafting, sailboarding, skateboarding, skimboarding, snowboarding, storm surf, sunsets, surfing, waterskiing and windsurfing.
Size & Elements: Film: 16mm (approx. 8-10 titles, including edited films and much unedited footage; negatives). Videotape: 1" (transfers from 16mm film).
Cataloging: Finding aids (unspecified).
Access: Available for licensing and reuse. Research fees charged.
Rights: Full rights held to all material. Additional clearances may be necessary in some cases if material is to be reused.
Licensing: License and usage fees charged.
Restrictions: None specified.
Viewing Facilities: Film (Kem flatbed); videotape (3/4" and 1/2").
Duplication Facilities: None (outside laboratory and videotape facility used).

CALIFORNIA (Chico)

TAMARELLE'S INTERNATIONAL FILMS, LTD.
110 Cohasset Stage Road
Chico, CA 95926
(800) 356-3577
(916) 895-3429

Claire Tamarelle (President)

Contact: Order Desk
Services: Distributor. Videotapes available for rental and purchase.
Description: Over 1,800 foreign feature films and short subjects on videotape are available for rental and purchase; 6,000 American films on videotape are available for purchase only. Special strengths include French, German and Spanish feature films, but films of all nations are offered. Short subjects include cultural films, documentaries, travel videotapes, children's programs, music and opera performances and films on art and artists.
Size & Elements: Film: 16mm (very limited collection of French films). Videotape: VHS and Betamax (approx. 7,800 titles; many transferred from film).
Cataloging: Published catalogs.
Access: Available to the public for rental and purchase. A membership program is offered to educational institutions, permitting exchange of videotapes over a period of time.
Rights: Distribution rights held to all titles. Some titles distributed on an exclusive basis.
Licensing: Not available for licensing or reuse.
Restrictions: None specified.
Viewing Facilities: None.
Duplication Facilities: None.

CALIFORNIA (Concord)

PRODUCTION HOUSE INC.
MOTION MEDIA PRODUCTIONS
2450 Whitman Road
Concord, CA 94518
(415) 680-8273

Hugh Churchill (President)

Contacts: Hugh Churchill; Bob Pruter (Vice President)
Services: Videotape producer; production and post-production house. Videotape collection available to the public for duplication and reuse. Custom shooting services available.
Description: Contemporary color videotape footage on various subjects, including the San Francisco Bay Area and the East Bay; farm animals; agriculture; scenics, including sunsets in San Francisco and the hills and bridges of the East Bay; and local architecture. Also holds footage of topical news subjects occurring in San Francisco and the East Bay.
Size & Elements: Videotape: 3/4" (masters); VHS (viewing copies) (approx. 150-200 items total).
Cataloging: Cataloging in progress.
Access: Available to the public for duplication and reuse. Research fees charged (rates negotiable). Research requests accepted by mail, telephone and in person (by appointment only).
Rights: Full rights held to all material. Additional clearances may be necessary in some cases if material is to be reused.

Licensing: Available for licensing and reuse. License fees charged.
Restrictions: Restrictions apply to reuse of some material.
Viewing Facilities: Videotape (3/4" and VHS).
Duplication Facilities: Videotape (3/4" and VHS; editorial facilities).
Related Materials: Extensive collection of 35mm slides animated onto videotape.

CALIFORNIA (Corona Del Mar)

PSYCHOLOGICAL AND EDUCATIONAL FILMS
3334 East Coast Highway, Suite 252
Corona Del Mar, CA 92625
(714) 494-5079

Everett L. Shostrom, Ph.D. (President)

Contact: Sharon Shostrom (Manager)
Services: Film and videotape distributor. Materials available for rental, preview and purchase.
Description: Films and videotapes intended for clinical psychologists, counseling psychologists, marriage counselors, social workers and psychiatrists.

Three Approaches series. Includes: *Three Approaches to Psychotherapy III,* with Drs. Hans Strupp, Donald Meichenbaum and Aaron T. Beck; *Three Approaches to Psychotherapy II,* with Drs. Carl Rogers, Everett Shostrom and Arnold Lazarus; and *Three Approaches to Psychotherapy I,* with Drs. Carl Rogers, Frederick Perls and Albert Ellis.

Other titles include: *Three Approaches to Group Therapy; Journey Into Self* (1968), a dramatic documentary of an intensive basic encounter group; *A Conversation With Carl Rogers* (1969); *Carl Rogers on Marriage* (1973, 4 titles); *B. F. Skinner on Education* (1972); *Frederick Perls and Gestalt Therapy* (1970); *Gestalt Dream Analysis; Albert Ellis: Rational Emotive Psychotherapy* (1970); *Rollo May on Existential Psychology* (1975); *Rollo May on Creativity and the Tragic* (1975); *Maslow and Self-Actualization* (1968), *The Humanistic Revolution: Pioneers in Perspective* (1971), *The Actualization Group* (1968, 7 films), showing authentic unrehearsed psychological group therapy, with Dr. Everett L. Shostrom and Nancy W. Ferry; *Between Man and Woman* (1973), an interview with Dr. Shostrom; *Touching* (1975), a conversation with Ashley Montagu; *Frankl and the Search for Meaning* (1973), with Dr. Viktor Frankl; *Lowen and Bioenergetic Therapy* (1973), with Dr. Alexander Lowen; *Encounter: To Make a Start* (1974), documenting a confrontation between police and young radicals, facilitated by Dr. Joel Fort; *The Inner Voice in Child Abuse* (1986), on the personality dynamics involved in the perpetuation of the damaging cycle, with Dr. Robert W. Firestone; and *Micro-Suicide — A Case Study* (1985), on a self-denial and self-destructive regression wherein a person gives up life-affirming activity and retreats from relationships.
Size & Elements: Film: 16mm. Videotape: 3/4". (86 titles total).
Cataloging: Published catalog.
Access: Available for rental, preview and purchase. Requests accepted by mail and telephone.
Rights: Apply for information.
Licensing: Apply for information.
Restrictions: All films and videotapes are licensed for the life of the film or videotape and shall not be duplicated, televised or broadcast in whole or in part or used in any showing for which admission is charged, nor edited, adapted or changed in any manner whatsoever without specific, prior written permission.
Viewing Facilities: None.
Duplication Facilities: None.

CALIFORNIA (Corte Madera)

GOLDEN GATERS PRODUCTIONS
400 Tamal Plaza
Corte Madera, CA 94925
(415) 924-7500
Fax: (415) 924-0264
TWX: (910) 384-2025

Robert Horowitz (General Manager)

Contact: Darrell Ewalt (Director of Operations)
Services: Television syndicator; production facility; videotape producer. Videotape collection available for duplication, licensing and reuse.
Description: Footage of sports and athletes (1978-88), including World Cup skiing (France, Italy, Austria, Colorado and Canada); college football (Pac-10

teams and other conferences, Stanford); professional tennis (Eckerd/FFTO, Wells Fargo Tennis Open, World Team Tennis); professional cycling (Giro D'Italia, Los Angeles, Philadelphia); professional football (NFL and USFL); horse racing (Triple Crown 1987); rodeo (Winston Pro Tour); boxing and various other sports.

Holds footage of actual competition (in all catagories listed above), B-roll and interviews with athletes, managers and coaches.
Size & Elements: Videotape: 1" (1,200 videotapes); 3/4" (4,000 videotapes).
Cataloging: Computerized cataloging for staff use only.
Access: Available to the public for duplication, licensing and reuse. Research requests accepted by mail, telephone and in person (walk-in). Research fees charged.
Rights: Some rights held to some material.
Licensing: Available for licensing and reuse. License fees charged.
Restrictions: None specified.
Viewing Facilities: Videotape.
Duplication Facilities: Videotape.

CALIFORNIA (Costa Mesa)

INSTITUTE FOR HISTORICAL REVIEW
and
STUART JEWELL PRODUCTIONS
See **CALIFORNIA** (Los Angeles Metro)

CALIFORNIA (Culver City)

LORIMAR TELEPICTURES
and
TURNER ENTERTAINMENT COMPANY
See **CALIFORNIA** (Los Angeles Metro)

CALIFORNIA (Davis)

UNIVERSITY OF CALIFORNIA, DAVIS
SHIELDS LIBRARY
DEPARTMENT OF SPECIAL COLLECTIONS
Davis, CA 95616
(916) 752-1621

Donald Kunitz (Department Head)

Contact: John Skarstad (Assistant Department Head)
Services: University archives. Film and videotape material available for in-house research only.
Description: *Alternative Theater.* Performances (1960s-present) by the San Francisco Mime Troupe, the Firehouse Theater, the Bread & Puppet Theater, El Teatro Campesino, the Living Theatre, and Squat Theatre. San Francisco Mime Troupe films include: *Ubu; Outside Agitators;* and *Have You Heard of the San Francisco Mime Troupe?*
A Man Says Goodbye to His Mother and *The King's Story, Laos* are Bread & Puppet Theatre performances in Washington Square Park, New York City (May 1972). *I* is a performance by the Theatre Laboratoire Vicinal at the San Francisco Museum of Modern Art (November 1976).
U. C. Davis Archives. Dating from 1914, sample titles include: *Clear Lake Historical Campus* (1941); *Picnic Day, Spring 1939; Military Day* (1941-42); *California Aggie Marching Band* (1949); *California Aggie Marching Band* (1962).
Avant-garde, etc. poetry. Includes "Recent poems and thoughts" by Gary Snyder.
Other materials include agricultural technology films by the Caterpillar Tractor Co. and *California's Liquid Gold,* a film about California wine.
Size & Elements: Film: format unspecified (30 titles, 30 cans). Videotape: format unspecified (27 titles).
Cataloging: Card catalogs.
Access: Open to the public. For in-house research only. Research fees not charged. Research requests accepted by mail, telephone and in person.
Rights: Rights status of material not known.
Licensing: Generally not available for licensing or reuse.
Restrictions: For in-house research only. Duplication may be possible in cases where written clearance has been obtained.
Viewing Facilities: Film (on campus); videotape (3/4" and VHS).
Duplication Facilities: Videotape.

CALIFORNIA (Del Mar)

FRONTLINE VIDEO, INC.
243 12th Street
Del Mar, CA 92014
(619) 481-5566

Ira Opper; James Marino (Producer/Directors)

Contacts: Ira Opper; James Marino
Services: Videotape producer. Footage available for licensing and reuse.
Description: Producer of *Surfer Magazine* for ESPN. Holds surf footage from many worldwide and exotic locations; surf footage (1950s-60s), some black and white, including a documentary on Malibu surfers and an interview with the original Gidget; and vintage striptease acts (1930s-50s), including a striptease by Mrs. John Barrymore. Now produces *Powder Magazine* (also for ESPN), and will be adding worldwide ski footage to library.
Size & Elements: Film: 16mm (amount unspecified; all transferred to videotape). Videotape: Betacam (over 100 hours; masters). Collection is constantly growing.
Cataloging: Staff assistance required; computerized cataloging and shot lists for staff use only.
Access: Open to the public. Available for duplication and reuse. Research fees charged in some cases. Research requests accepted by mail and telephone.
Rights: Full rights held to all material. Frontline will handle any additional clearances necessary for reuse.
Licensing: Available for licensing. License fees charged.
Restrictions: None specified.
Viewing Facilities: Videotape (by arrangement with individual clients only).
Duplication Facilities: Videotape (Betacam to 1", VHS or other formats).

CALIFORNIA (Edwards)

NATIONAL AERONAUTICS AND SPACE ADMINISTRATION (NASA)
AMES RESEARCH CENTER
DRYDEN FLIGHT RESEARCH FACILITY
PUBLIC AFFAIRS OFFICE
Edwards, CA 93523
(805) 258-3456

Ralph Jackson (Public Affairs)

Contacts: Public Affairs Office (for research requests); Robert Rhine (for information on films) (805/258-3646); George Finley (for information on videotapes) (805/258-3976)
Services: Government agency. Film and videotape material available to the public for duplication and reuse.
Description: Documentation of aircraft research projects and programs (ca. 1960-present) and aircraft flight tests. Footage includes aerial views, ground-based views of airplanes and air-to-air shots. Almost all footage is in film form; Dryden documents space shuttle landings on videotape but forwards master videotapes to NASA, Johnson Space Center, Stock Film Library (q.v.).
Dryden is in the process of reducing its film collection; most workprints and some originals have been donated to a historical society (apply for information).
Size & Elements: Film: 16mm (1,361 titles; originals). Videotape: format unspecified (negligible amount).
Cataloging: Various finding aids for staff use only; staff assistance required.
Access: Open to the public. Available for duplication and reuse. Research fees not charged. Research requests accepted by mail. All requests must be submitted in writing to the Public Affairs Office. Requests must be specific as to subject matter required, estimated length of shot desired, etc. Requesters generally required to view and select footage in person.
Rights: Material in the public domain. Additional clearances may be necessary in some cases if material is to be reused.
Licensing: Available for reuse. Usage fees not charged.
Restrictions: Material may not be used to promote commercial products or services.
Viewing Facilities: Film (16mm).
Duplication Facilities: None (outside arrangements can be made; duplication fees apply).
Related Materials: 190,000 still photographs documenting flight research (1949-present) housed in Photo Lab.

CALIFORNIA (El Cerrito)

FLOWER FILMS AND VIDEO
10341 San Pablo Avenue
El Cerrito, CA 94530
(415) 525-0942
Fax: (415) 525-1204

Les Blank (Director)

Contact: Toni Rosenberg (Distribution Manager)
Services: Independent film producer and distributor. Videotapes available to the public for purchase. Films and videotapes not available for use in classrooms, churches or other assemblies.
Description: Subjects and titles (by Les Blank and others) include:
Women/self-acceptance. Gap-Toothed Women interviews almost 100 gap-toothed women to find out their interests, beliefs and lifestyles and whether or not a space in one's teeth can make a difference.
Serbian Americans. Ziveli: Medicine for the Heart features the culture and music of the Serbian American communities of Chicago and California.
Fiction/dark humor. The Short Films of Pascal Aubier.
Adolescent relationships. In The Land of the Owl Turds looks at American youth.
Cuban Americans. Photo Album on the filmmaker's experiences as a young immigrant from Cuba.
Filmmaking/Peruvian Indians. Burden of Dreams is the account of German filmmaker Werner Herzog's obsession to complete the painfully plagued on-location jungle shooting of *Fitzcarraldo.*
Culinary arts. Titles include: *Garlic Is As Good as Ten Mothers,* about the history, consumption, cultivation, and culinary and curative powers of garlic; and *Werner Herzog Eats His Shoe,* showing Herzog honoring his vow to eat his shoe in the event Errol Morris ever actually made one of the films he was forever talking about.

Music. Titles include: *Always For Pleasure* and *Piano Players Rarely Ever Play Together* (both on New Orleans music); *Zydeco, Les Blues De Balfa Cajun Visits, Spend It All, Hot Pepper* and *Dry Wood* (all concerning Cajun, Zydeco and Creole music); *Chulas Fronteras* and *Del Mero Corazon: Love Songs of the Southwest* (Tex-Mex music); *The Blues Accordin' To Lightnin' Hopkins, The Sun's Gonna Shine* and *A Well Spent Life* (Texas blues); *Dizzy* and *Cigarette Blues* (jazz).

Asian studies. Titles include: *Perfumed Nightmare*, on a young Filipino and his reactions against American cultural colonialism; and *Turumba*, about a family in a tiny Philippine village and the loss of traditional ways of life.

Appalachia. Titles include: *Sprout Wings and Fly*, a film about fiddler Tommy Jarrell; *Stoney Knows How*, interview with a dwarf tattoo artist; and *Chicken Reel*, a documentary on an automated chicken-growing operation.

Polish American. In Heaven There is No Beer? features Polish American culture and polka dances.

Anthology videotapes. Two compilations: *A Blank Buffet* contains classic music scenes; and *The Best of Blank* contains highlights from 13 films (1967-87).

Size & Elements: Videotape: 1/2" (over 44 titles).
Cataloging: Published catalog available on request.
Access: Available to the public for purchase.
Rights: Apply for information.
Licensing: Apply for information.
Restrictions: Material cannot be used for classrooms, churches or other assemblies.
Viewing Facilities: None.
Duplication Facilities: None.

CALIFORNIA (El Toro)

WINGS WILDLIFE PRODUCTIONS INC.
WILDLIFE FILM LIBRARY
25191 Rivendell Drive
El Toro, CA 92630
(714) 830-7845

Gary Gero (2nd Unit Director, Cameraman)
Reg. Stark (Manager, Film Library)

Contacts: Gary Gero; Reg. Stark
Services: Film producer; stock footage sales library.
Description: Wildlife in North America and other continents.

Birds. Includes African birds, avocet, baby birds, bald eagle, wading birds, blackbirds and marsh hawk, boobies, cactus wren, cockatoo, coots and babies, sandhill crane, dove flying, ducks and shorebirds, Agoura golden eagle, golden finch, purple gallinule, geese and babies, grebe, hawk heads, hawk sitting, heron, hummingbird, killdeer, mockingbird and rattlesnake, nesting on odd eggs, osprey, ostrich, ouzel, owl, puffins, quail sitting, raven, vultures and woodpecker.

Insects. Includes ants and millipede, beetle, bugs flying and bird, cricket, scorpion, trapdoor spider, stinkbug, tarantula, termites, water bugs.

Mammals. Includes African scene, antelope, armadillo, black and brown bear, Cape buffalo and wart hog, chimp, coatimundi, cougar, coyote, elephant, fox, giraffe, gopher, hippopotamus, hyena, jackal, leopard and cubs, lions, mole, mouse, rabbit, raccoon, rat, rhinoceros, sea otter, shrew and centipede, skunk, grey squirrel, tiger blue, whales blowing, grey wolf, howling wolf.

Reptiles. Includes frog, Gila monster, lizard, salamander and blue tail skink.

Snakes. Includes cobra, rattlesnakes, king snake, rattlesnake and roadrunner, miscellaneous snakes.

Miscellaneous. Includes fiddler crabs, flowers (oceans and cliff), flying scenes, Indian dancers, Masai dance, ocean waves, ox wagon train, pollywog, salmon, sunset, African sunset, marshes, misty lake, moon and a Newfoundland town.

Size & Elements: Film: 35mm and 16mm (approx. 200 titles; negatives and release prints).
Cataloging: Published catalogs; shot lists.
Access: Available for duplication, licensing and reuse. Viewing prints will be sent within the United States upon request. Shipping fees are the responsibility of customer. Research fees not charged. Research requests accepted by telephone.
Rights: Full rights held to all material.
Licensing: Available for licensing and reuse. License fees charged.
Restrictions: None specified.
Viewing Facilities: None.

Duplication Facilities: None.

CALIFORNIA (Escondido)

DICK WALLEN PRODUCTIONS
P.O. Box 2261
Escondido, CA 92025
(619) 749-4406
(800) 992-8433 (orders only)

Dick Wallen (Owner)

Contact: Dick Wallen
Services: Film producer; stock footage sales library.
Description: Motor racing footage (1959-present); footage of U.S. cities.

Motor racing footage. Cars and races include Formula One, Indianapolis 500 cars, stock cars, sprint cars, sports cars, off-road vehicles, drag racers and destruction derbies. All racing footage is 16mm Ektachrome Commercial (color reversal).

U.S. cities (35mm color negative). Includes New York City; Washington, D.C.; Philadelphia; Hartford, Conn.; Honolulu; Las Vegas, Nev.; San Francisco; Des Moines, Iowa; Miami; and Atlanta. Coverage for each city includes establishing shots, landmarks and tourist sites, signs, people, airports, taxis, buildings and generic shots.

Size & Elements: Film: 35mm (color original negative and workprint); 16mm (color reversal [Ektachrome Commercial] and workprint) (3 million feet total).
Cataloging: Cities footage cataloged; staff assistance available with regard to motor racing footage.
Access: Not open to the public. Available for licensing, reuse and resale for commercial purposes (i.e., theatrical and television) only. Research fees charged. Research requests accepted by telephone and in person (by appointment only).
Rights: Full rights held to all material.
Licensing: Available for licensing. License fees charged.
Restrictions: None specified.
Viewing Facilities: Film (16mm).
Duplication Facilities: None (outside arrangements can be made).
Representative: Worldwide representative: Film Search, Inc. (q.v.).

CALIFORNIA (Gardena)

H. B. HALICKI PRODUCTIONS
and
NISSAN MOTOR CORPORATION OF THE UNITED STATES
and
RAINBOW VIDEO PRODUCTIONS
See **CALIFORNIA** (Los Angeles Metro)

CALIFORNIA (Graton)

WISHING WELL DISTRIBUTION
P.O. Box 529
Graton, CA 95444
(707) 823-9355

Debra Giusti (President)

Contact: Debra Giusti
Services: Distributor; film and videotape marketing and distribution consultant. Videotapes available to the public for rental, distribution and purchase. Can refer inquirers to stock footage sources.
Description: Videotape distributor specializing in New Age materials (broadly defined as "anything that improves the quality of life"), including documentaries and instructional videotapes on metaphysics, astrology, psychic development, channeling and futurism. Also distributes special interest, how-to, educational, instructional, music and documentary videotapes.

Some material is available for stock footage sale; can refer inquirers to original producers or sources. Consultants can also provide access to stock footage sources.

Size & Elements: Videotape: VHS (approx. 2,000 titles, 12 exclusively distributed).
Cataloging: Published catalogs.
Access: Open to the public. Available for rental, distribution and purchase. Some material available for duplication and reuse. Research fees charged. Research requests accepted by mail, telephone and in person (by appointment

CALIFORNIA (Hawthorne)

only).
Rights: Some rights held to all material. Additional clearances may be
necessary in some cases if material is to be reused (Wishing Well will handle
any necessary clearances).
Licensing: Available for licensing and reuse, subject to clearance. License fees
charged.
Restrictions: None specified.
Viewing Facilities: None.
Duplication Facilities: None.

CALIFORNIA (Hawthorne)

PHOTO-CHUTING ENTERPRISES
See **CALIFORNIA** (Los Angeles Metro)

CALIFORNIA (Helendale)

EXOTIC DANCERS LEAGUE OF NORTH AMERICA
EXOTIC WORLD MUSEUM AND HALL OF FAME
29053 Wild Road
Helendale, CA 92342
(619) 243-5261
(619) 948-1153

Jennie Lee (President and Founder)

Contact: Jennie Lee
Services: Museum. Film and videotape collection available for research,
licensing and reuse, subject to restrictions.
Description: Small collection of films and videotapes relating to striptease and
exotic dance.
Size & Elements: Film and videotape: formats unspecified ("two dozen"
titles).
Cataloging: Research library.
Access: Open to the public. Lifetime membership fee is $15. Research requests
accepted by mail only and with S.A.S.E. Material available for duplication to
members only. Videotape only available for reuse at this time.
Rights: Full rights held to all material.
Licensing: Apply for information. License and usage fees charged (apply for
rates).
Restrictions: Films not available for reuse at the present time.
Viewing Facilities: Videotape.
Duplication Facilities: None.
Related Materials: Photos, posters, books and magazines relating to striptease
and exotic dance.

CALIFORNIA (Hermosa Beach)

WARREN MILLER PRODUCTIONS, INC.
See **CALIFORNIA** (Los Angeles Metro)

CALIFORNIA (Hollywood)

DREAMLIGHT IMAGES, INC.
and
JAMES FORSHER PRODUCTIONS & ARCHIVES INC.
and
SHERMAN GRINBERG FILM LIBRARIES, INC. (WEST)
and
INTERNATIONAL GAY AND LESBIAN ARCHIVES
NATALIE BARNEY/EDWARD CARPENTER LIBRARY
and
MORCRAFT FILMS
and
PRODUCERS LIBRARY SERVICE
and
SHIELDS ARCHIVAL
and
RICK SPALLA VIDEO PRODUCTIONS
HOLLYWOOD NEWSREEL SYNDICATE, INC.
and
AARON SPELLING PRODUCTIONS
and
THE STOCK HOUSE
See **CALIFORNIA** (Los Angeles Metro)

CALIFORNIA (Huntington Beach)

ZIELINSKI PRODUCTIONS, INC.
See **CALIFORNIA** (Los Angeles Metro)

CALIFORNIA (Irwindale)

BARR FILMS
See **CALIFORNIA** (Los Angeles Metro)

CALIFORNIA (Keene)

UNITED FARM WORKERS OF AMERICA, AFL-CIO (UFW)
P.O. Box 62
La Paz, Keene, CA 93531
(805) 822-5571

Cesar E. Chavez (President)

Contact: Daniel Martin
Services: Labor union. Films and videotape collection available for rental,
purchase, licensing and reuse, subject to restrictions.
Description: Films and videotapes produced by the UFW and the National
Farm Workers Service Center about farm workers and the history and struggles
of the UFW.
   Titles include: *Huelga* (1966); *Viva La Causa* (1970); *Si Se Puede* (1972);
Fighting For Our Lives (1974); *Why We Boycott* (1974); and *The Wrath of
Grapes* (1986). Films portray the early organizing efforts of the Union under
farm labor leader Cesar Chavez; the international grape boycotts; the struggles
against agribusiness in Delano, California and the San Joaquin and Imperial
Valleys. Includes the formation and performances of El Teatro Campesino,
with Luis Valdez; labor union support and boycott activity throughout the U.S.
and Canada; support from Coretta King, Joseph Kennedy, Jr., Senator George
McGovern, Joan Baez and Taj Mahal; support of church leaders and members
and the California Migrant Ministry. Includes documentation of the living and
working conditions of farm workers and the dangers of pesticides.
   Collection also contains films produced by other film and television
producers relating to farm workers and migrant workers throughout the U.S.
(1950-73), and on the United Farm Workers Union (1967-78). Includes
material on farm workers in New Jersey, New York, Florida, and California.
Other films relating to the UFW feature Walter Reuther (United Auto
Workers); Robert F. Kennedy; the Senate Subcommittee hearings on migrant
labor (1966); El Teatro Campesino; Governor Ronald Reagan; and Dom
Helder Camera, Archbishop of Recife, Brazil.
Size & Elements: Film: 16mm (35 titles; positive). Videotape: 3/4" (1 title,
master; 20 titles, film transfers); VHS (20 titles; film transfers).
Cataloging: List of UFW and National Farm Workers Service Center films (6
titles) available on request. Staff assistance on other films.
Access: UFW and National Farm Workers Service Center films available for
rental, purchase, licensing and reuse. Research fees not charged. Staff
assistance necessary to locate producers of and obtain rights to other films.
Rights: Full rights held to all UFW and National Farm Workers Service Center
films. Additional clearances will be necessary if other films in collection are to
be reused.
Licensing: Available for licensing and reuse, subject to restrictions. License
fees charged depending upon nature of production and intended use.
Restrictions: Restrictions apply in some cases. All reuse must be approved by
UFW.
Viewing Facilities: None.
Duplication Facilities: None.
Related Materials: Thousands of still photographs documenting the history of
the United Farm Workers of America (1965-present); available for duplication.
Contact Victor Alemán.
Publications: *Food and Justice*, a monthly UFW publication, contains
materials about its current activities, which sometimes include videotape
production and distribution.

CALIFORNIA (Lake Elsinore)

NUCLEAR FREE ZONE REGISTRY
See **CALIFORNIA** (Los Angeles Metro)

CALIFORNIA (Lawndale)

APPLEGATE ENTERTAINMENT

See **CALIFORNIA** (Los Angeles Metro)

CALIFORNIA (Loma Linda)

LOMA LINDA UNIVERSITY
DEL E. WEBB MEMORIAL LIBRARY
DEPARTMENT OF ARCHIVES AND SPECIAL COLLECTIONS
See **CALIFORNIA** (Los Angeles Metro)

CALIFORNIA (Long Beach)

CENTER FOR MARITAL AND SEXUAL STUDIES
FILM LIBRARY
and
LONG BEACH MUSEUM OF ART
See **CALIFORNIA** (Los Angeles Metro)

CALIFORNIA (Los Angeles Metropolitan Area)

CALIFORNIA (Los Angeles Metro)

ABC VIDEO ENTERPRISES
2040 Avenue of the Stars
Los Angeles, CA 90067-4785
(213) 557-6343
Fax: (213) 557-7925
Telex: 234-337

Archie C. Purvis (Senior Vice President)

Contact: Marvinia Hunter (Director, Worldwide Cable/Cassette Marketing)
Services: Distributor and licensor of ABC-owned entertainment programs to
homevideo, theatrical, television, pay television and cable television markets.
Programs available for licensing and reuse, subject to restrictions.
Description: Miniseries, specials, animation, children's programs, made-for-
television movies and feature films. Some titles include: *Moonlighting;*

Amerika; Out On A Limb; Prizzi's Honor; Silkwood; Straw Dogs; Cabaret;
Duel in the Sun; Notorious; and *Shindig.*
Size & Elements: Film and videotape: all formats (approx. 500 titles in current
distribution).
Cataloging: Printed catalog available to distributors only.
Access: Not open to the public. Research fees not charged. Research requests
accepted by mail only.
Rights: Full rights held to all material.
Licensing: Available for licensing, subject to restrictions. License fees charged
depending on material and its intended use.
Restrictions: Restrictions may apply to licensing.
Viewing Facilities: None.
Duplication Facilities: None.

CALIFORNIA (Los Angeles Metro)

ACADEMY OF MOTION PICTURE ARTS AND SCIENCES
ACADEMY FILM ARCHIVE
8949 Wilshire Boulevard
Beverly Hills, CA 90211
(213) 278-8990
Fax: (213) 859-9351

Daniel Woodruff (Curator of Film)

Contact: Daniel Woodruff
Services: Film archives. Collection maintained primarily for research and
study purposes. Some material available for reuse, subject to restrictions.
Description: Films relating to the history and development of the motion
picture as an art form and an industry. Holds the most comprehensive
collection of motion picture primitives, including nearly all films registered for
copyright between 1894 and 1912; films by Thomas Edison, Georges Méliès,
D. W. Griffith, Lumière and Pathé. Holds films donated by Mary Pickford,
William S. Hart, Mack Sennett, Buster Keaton, Will Rogers, David O.
Selznick, John Huston, Cary Grant and Lewis Milestone. Of special note is the
Alfred Hitchcock collection which contains outtakes, home movies, screen tests
and 35mm release prints. The Academy recently acquired the Tom Tarr

Collection of Technicolor Specimens (1917-50). Also holds Academy Award films (winners and nominees) including documentaries, animated shorts, foreign films and Student Academy Award winners.
Size & Elements: Film and videotape: all formats (8,000 titles total).
Cataloging: Computerized cataloging for staff use only.
Access: Open to researchers and scholars only. For in-house use only. Research fees charged. Requests accepted in person by appointment only. *Most items in collection can be found at the Library of Congress and the National Archives, which are better able to handle research and reproduction requests.*
Rights: Full rights held to some material. Academy does not own rights to most material in collection; rights retained by owners and must be cleared with them. Some material in the public domain. Additional clearances may be necessary in some cases if material is to be reused.
Licensing: Available for licensing and reuse, subject to restrictions. License fees charged.
Restrictions: Restrictions apply to licensing and reuse with regard to rights status of specific material.
Viewing Facilities: Film (35mm and 16mm); videotape (3/4", VHS and Betamax).
Related Materials: 4 million film stills; 5,000 scripts; and extensive files on approximately 60,000 films and 50,000 film personalities.

CALIFORNIA (Los Angeles Metro)

AIMS MEDIA
6901 Woodley Avenue
Van Nuys, CA 91406-4878
(818) 785-4111
(800) 367-2467
Fax: (818) 376-6405
Telex: 494-8329

Jeff Sherman (Vice President)

Contact: Adrienne Milder
Services: Educational film and videotape producer and distributor. Most materials available for rental, purchase and licensing.
Description: General educational films and dramatic shorts. Categories include: language arts (children's literature, animated films, reading, grammar and language skills and language stimulus); English (library and study skills, drama and literature and poetry); social studies (American history, world history, geography, community studies and economics); science (life science, ecology, natural history, physical science, weather, energy and conservation, astronomy and space); mathematics; computer courseware; art and music (art media, artists, filmmaking and music); technology; vocational education; physical education (exercise, sports and games); health and nutrition (includes eating disorders); staff development; guidance (conduct and character development, dropping out, prejudice, careers, pets and their care, mental health and sex education); substance abuse (alcohol, alcohol and drugs, drugs and tobacco); driver education (drunk driving, driver training and school bus driver training); crime prevention (child abuse prevention, "McGruff the Crime Dog," rape prevention, youth crime deterrence and home and property protection); safety (home and school safety, babysitting safety, school bus passenger safety, pedestrian and bicycle safety, fire safety, emergency calls, emergency care, cardiopulmonary resuscitation [CPR] and the Heimlich Maneuver); training and development (occupational health and safety, human resource development, wellness and health promotion and security).
Size & Elements: Film: 16mm (1,200 titles). Videotape: 3/4", VHS and Betamax I, II and III (1,200 titles).
Cataloging: Published catalogs; release sheets.
Access: Available primarily for rental and purchase. Some material available for duplication, licensing and reuse. Orders accepted by mail and telephone. Shipping and handling fees charged. Rental fees may be applied toward purchase. Free previews available to authorized buyers.
Rights: Full rights held to all material.
Licensing: Television and duplication licenses available for most titles.
Restrictions: None specified.
Viewing Facilities: None.
Duplication Facilities: None.
Related Materials: Discussion guides available for most titles.
Representatives: Various representatives (apply for information).

CALIFORNIA (Los Angeles Metro)

AIRLINE FILM & TV PROMOTIONS

13246 Weidner Street
Pacoima, CA 91331
(818) 899-1151

Byron W. Schmidt (President)

Contact: Byron W. Schmidt
Services: Film stock footage sales library.
Description: Airplanes and establishing shots of airports, foreign and U.S. cities. Includes footage of passenger jet aircraft in flight, takeoff, landing, taxiing, etc. Cities include New York, San Francisco, Las Vegas, Los Angeles, Washington (D.C.), Miami, Hawaii and U.S. small towns; foreign cities in Europe, Asia and the Far East. Some of this footage is from the 1960s. Footage of old propeller aircraft, specifically Connies, DC-3s and Stratoliners, is also available.
Size & Elements: Film: 35mm (100,000 feet; color negative, CRI and interpositive); 16mm (5,000 feet; negative and positive).
Cataloging: Shot lists.
Access: Available for duplication. Research fees charged. Requests accepted by mail and in person (walk-in).
Rights: Full rights held to all material.
Licensing: Available for licensing and reuse, subject to restrictions. License fees charged.
Restrictions: Some restrictions apply to reuse. Requests for reuse considered on a case-by-case basis.
Viewing Facilities: Film (35mm Moviola).
Duplication Facilities: None.
Related Services: Maintains fleet of mock 747, DC-10, 727/737 and DC-9 bodies and cockpits, an airport terminal complete with ticket counter, customs and restrooms. Fleet also includes a 747 upstairs lounge and an executive private jet.

CALIFORNIA (Los Angeles Metro)

THE A. M. STOCK EXCHANGE, INC.
4741 Laurel Canyon Boulevard, Suite 207
North Hollywood, CA 91607
(818) 762-7865

Chris Angelich (Chief Executive Officer)

Contact: Chris Angelich
Services: Film and videotape producer; stock footage sales library.
Description: Company began operations in 1987. Has provided custom stock shots for 18 different prime-time television shows, feature films and "movies of the week." Subjects covered include: airports and office buildings (day and night), schools and public buildings.
Size & Elements: Film: 35mm (approx. 12,000 feet; positive, negative and original); 16mm (approx. 4,000 feet). Videotape: 1" (amount unspecified; masters).
Cataloging: Research library; card catalogs and computerized cataloging (for staff use only).
Access: Open to the public. Available for duplication, licensing and reuse. Research fees not charged. Research requests accepted by mail, telephone and in person (by appointment only).
Rights: Full rights held to all material.
Licensing: Available for licensing and reuse. License fees charged (apply for fee schedule).
Restrictions: None specified.
Viewing Facilities: Film (35mm and 16mm Moviolas).
Duplication Facilities: None.

CALIFORNIA (Los Angeles Metro)

AMATEUR ATHLETIC FOUNDATION LIBRARY
2141 West Adams Boulevard
Los Angeles, CA 90018
(213) 730-9600
Fax: (213) 730-9637
Telex: (910) 240-9846

Anita L. DeFrantz (President)

Contact: Wayne Wilson (Library Director)

Services: Foundation; library. *Policies regarding access to and usage of moving image holdings under development.*
Description: Historical and current films and videotapes relating to amateur athletics and the Olympic Games. Collection emphasizes track and field and football in Southern California (1930s-present) and the Olympic Games (1932-present). Also holds instructional videotapes on various sports (produced in the 1980s).
Size & Elements: Film: 35mm (16,761 feet, 31 titles); 16mm (178,266 feet, 356 titles). Videotape: VHS (approx. 250 titles).
Cataloging: Computerized cataloging available to researchers.
Access: Open to the public. Policies regarding access to and usage of moving image holdings under development. Research requests accepted by mail, telephone and in person (by appointment only).
Rights: Full rights held to some material. Rights status of some material not known. Additional clearances may be necessary in some cases if material is to be reused.
Licensing: Apply for information.
Restrictions: Policies regarding access to and usage of moving image holdings under development.
Viewing Facilities: Film and videotape.
Duplication Facilities: None.

CALIFORNIA (Los Angeles Metro)

AMERICAN PORTRAIT FILMS
1695 West Crescent Avenue, Suite 500
Anaheim, CA 92801
(714) 535-2189
Fax: (714) 535-3816

Donald S. Smith (President)

Contact: Gene Gatch (Director of Distribution)
Services: Film and videotape producer and distributor. Material available for purchase and broadcast.
Description: Promotional material relating to the pro-life side of the abortion controversy. *Assignment: Life* presents the dilemma of unwanted pregnancy and alternatives to abortion, showing actual suction and saline abortions and a live birth; *A Matter of Choice* is a shortened version of *Assignment: Life* with explicit religious references removed for screening in public schools; *Conceived in Liberty* shows "the problems abortion has created in society," including a sonogram of suction abortion and footage on fetal experimentation; *The Hidden Holocaust* is a version of *Conceived in Liberty* produced for evangelical Christian audiences; *The Silent Scream,* a presentation by Bernard Nathanson, M.D., of a 12-week suction abortion shown on an ultrasound screen, is available in English and seven foreign languages and bears the endorsement of President Ronald Reagan.
Pro-Life Video Library. Titles include: *Pro-Life Doctors Speak Out* with Surgeon General C. Everett Koop; *The Miracle of Ultrasound; Death on Demand: An Abortionist's Day; Living Experiments* "shows how living, unborn babies are used for scientific experimentation"; *Higher Laws,* featuring pro-life activist Randall Terry, discussing non-violent, direct action (civil disobedience); *Your Crisis Pregnancy* explaining "why abortion is not the right answer to a problem pregnancy." Some films are available in several foreign languages.
Size & Elements: Film: 16mm (5 titles). Videotape: 1", 3/4", VHS and Betamax (12 titles; NTSC, PAL and SECAM).
Cataloging: Published film list.
Access: Available to the public for purchase and broadcast. Requests accepted by mail and telephone.
Rights: Full rights held to all material.
Licensing: Available for licensing and reuse. License fees charged.
Restrictions: None specified.
Viewing Facilities: None.
Duplication Facilities: None.

CALIFORNIA (Los Angeles Metro)

APPLEGATE ENTERTAINMENT
15229 Fonthill Avenue
Lawndale, CA 90260
(213) 676-3262

Bob Applegate (President)

Contact: Bob Applegate
Services: Film and videotape producer. Material available for duplication, licensing and reuse.
Description: Data processing, personal computing and office activity showing people using computers; manufacturing environments (photocopiers being assembled); high-technology business scenes (foreign and domestic) and shop-floor scenes of heavy manufacturing (brass and automotive plants); Olympic torch runner on the beach at Los Angeles; street scenes and aerials of Minneapolis; sailboats; glamor photography instruction sessions; restaurants, including behind-the-scene shots, food preparation and people eating; wedding receptions; scenics of Santa Barbara, California; gospel music and Black choirs; generic footage of European cities and countryside. Also holds a quantity of Steadicam footage.
Size & Elements: Film: 16mm (amount unspecified; negative and videotape transfers). Videotape: 1", 3/4" and Betacam (masters) (approx. 400 videotapes).
Cataloging: None specified.
Access: Available to the public for duplication, licensing and reuse. Research fees not charged. Research requests accepted by mail and telephone.
Rights: Full rights held to some material. Some rights held to all material.
Licensing: Available for licensing and reuse. License fees charged.
Restrictions: None specified.
Viewing Facilities: Videotape (Betacam, 3/4" and VHS).
Duplication Facilities: Videotape (Betacam to 3/4").

CALIFORNIA (Los Angeles Metro)

ARMENIAN FILM FOUNDATION
580 East Thousand Oaks Boulevard, Suite 101
Thousand Oaks, CA 91360
(805) 495-0717

Dr. J. Michael Hagopian (Chairman)

Contact: Dr. J. Michael Hagopian
Services: Cultural foundation. Films and videotapes available to the public for purchase.
Description: Films and videotapes relating to Armenian people, history and culture.
Mandate for Armenia, produced by the U.S. Army, documents General James G. Harbord's mission to Turkey and the Republic of Armenia in 1919, covering the towns of Istanbul, Afion-Kharahissar, Adana, Sivas, Kharpert, Erzinjan, Diarbekir, Mardin, Erevan, Erzeroum, Tiflis and Trabizond. *Cilicia...Rebirth* provides an inspiring view of how the Armenian survivors of the Genocide established themselves in Syria. *California Armenians: The First Generation* tells the story of the original Armenians emigrating from Turkey to Fresno, California, and the establishment of Fresno as an Armenian center. *The Forgotten Genocide* is the classic documentary of the first genocide of the twentieth century, narrated by Mike Connors. *Supplement to The Forgotten Genocide* describes the post-genocide period, the establishment of the Armenian Republic, the Sovietization of Armenia, and the rebuilding of Armenian life in the Diaspora, narrated by Mike Connors.
Historical Armenia documents a journey through the ancient Armenian homeland, with sequences covering Istanbul, Ani, Ankara, Adana, Aintab, Kharpert, Akhtamar, Bitlis, Kars, Van and Soviet Armenia. *Soviet Armenia* presents the daily life of an Armenian boy in Erevan. *Strangers in a Promised Land,* narrated by California Governor George Deukmejian, tells the saga of the Armenians of Fresno, California (1879-present), depicting the universal experience of immigration and the overcoming of adversity and discrimination. *The Art of Traditional Armenian Cooking* is a step-by-step demonstration of diverse regional preparations.
Size & Elements: Videotape: VHS and Betamax (10 titles).
Cataloging: Brochure.
Access: Available to the public for purchase.
Rights: Apply for information.
Licensing: Apply for information.
Restrictions: None specified.
Viewing Facilities: None.
Duplication Facilities: None.
Related Materials: Cookbook for use with the videotape *The Art of Traditional Armenian Cooking.*

CALIFORNIA (Los Angeles Metro)

ATLANTIS PRODUCTIONS, INC.
1252 La Granada Drive

CALIFORNIA (Los Angeles Metro A)

Thousand Oaks, CA 91362
(805) 495-2790

Contact: J. Michael Hagopian
Services: Documentary/educational film and videotape producer and distributor; materials available to the public for rental and purchase.
Description: Ethnographic and cultural documentaries; educational classroom films (also available on videotape). Subjects covered include Mexican American and Native American peoples.

Titles include: *Africa is My Home; African Girl...Malobi; Ali and His Baby Camel; Ancient Phoenicia; The Arab-Israeli Conflict; Boat People of Vietnam; A Century of Silence: Problems of the American Indian; Hindu Village Boy; History of Southern California; Jerusalem: Center of Many Worlds; Jesus Garcia: Hero of Nacozari; Making a Piñata; A Mexican-American Family; Mexican or American; Negro Heroes from American History; Silkmaking in China; Winter on an Indian Reservation;* and *An Indian Summer.*
Size & Elements: Film: 16mm. Videotape: VHS and Betamax. (Approx. 50 titles total).
Cataloging: Published list.
Access: Available to the public for rental and purchase.
Rights: Apply for information.
Licensing: Apply for information.
Restrictions: None specified.
Viewing Facilities: None.
Duplication Facilities: None.

CALIFORNIA (Los Angeles Metro)

AUDIENCE PLANNERS, INC.
5107 Douglas Fir Road
Calabasas, CA 91302
(818) 884-3100
(312) 822-0892 (Chicago office)

Ralph Rafik (President)

Contact: Susan Rafik
Services: Distributor of sponsored films and videotapes. Material available for free loan. *Not a stock footage source.*
Description: Founded in 1970, AP provides film and videotape distribution services to sponsors (i.e, religious and special-interest organizations, corporations and foreign governments). Material also available to television broadcasters and cablecasters, the general public, the travel industry and church-related groups.

Research or rental requests are generally routed to AP by sponsors; AP holds no rights to any material and cannot itself furnish film or videotape for reuse or resale.

Sponsors using AP for distribution services include the British Tourist Authority, Children's Home Society of California, Concordia Publishing House, the Embassy of South Africa and Consulates General of South Africa in the United States, Maryknoll World Films, Norwegian Information Service, Paulist Productions, U.S. Dept. of Agriculture (Forest Service) and U.S. Environmental Protection Agency.
Size & Elements: Film and videotape: various formats (3,000 titles total).
Cataloging: Film lists and brochures (issued by sponsoring organizations).
Access: Available for free loan. Requests accepted by mail and telephone.
Rights: Rights retained by sponsors or original producers.
Licensing: Not available for licensing through AP. Arrangements must be made with sponsors or original producers.
Restrictions: Permission to reuse any material must be obtained directly from sponsors or original producers.
Viewing Facilities: None.
Duplication Facilities: None.

CALIFORNIA (Los Angeles Metro)

AZTECA FILMS
555 North LaBrea Avenue
Los Angeles, CA 90036
(213) 938-2413

Carlos Yates (President)

Contact: Juan L. Montezuma (Production Manager)
Services: Film and videotape distributor. Films available for rental and

purchase outside Mexico. Staff can assist in obtaining clip rights.
Description: Largest distributor of Mexican films outside Mexico with over 2,000 titles (1920-present). Library includes many classics of Mexican cinema, available for rental and purchase, mainly to television stations and theaters. Also sells videotape copies for home distribution.
Size & Elements: Film: 35mm and 16mm (2,000 titles; positive and negative). Videotape: 1", VHS and Betamax (transfers from film).
Cataloging: Catalog for staff use only; staff assistance available.
Access: Available for distribution, rental and purchase outside Mexico. Staff can assist in contacting producers to obtain rights for clips or stock footage. Research fees not charged. Requests for films and other services accepted by mail (direct request to president) and telephone (if followed by written request).
Rights: Distribution rights held to all material. Some clip or stock footage rights held.
Licensing: Staff can assist in obtaining clip rights. License fees charged.
Restrictions: None specified.
Viewing Facilities: Film (35mm and 16mm); videotape (1").
Duplication Facilities: Handled by laboratories through distributor.
Related Materials: Promotional materials for films.

CALIFORNIA (Los Angeles Metro)

FRED BAKER FILM & VIDEO COMPANY
6736 Cleon Avenue, Suite 55
North Hollywood, CA 91606
(818) 763-5510

Contact: Staff
Services: Independent film and videotape producer and distributor. Material available to the public for distribution, purchase and possibly reuse.
Description: Classical jazz videotape archives, including material on Billie Holiday and Charlie Parker. Political footage includes anti-Vietnam war and material relating to Central America.

Film titles include: *Vintage Getz*, four Stan Getz concert programs (each 30 min.); *Lenny Bruce Without Tears*, a documentary on the satirist featuring Steve Allen, Paul Krassner, Mort Sahl, Kenneth Tynan, Nat Hentoff, and Malcolm Muggeridge; *The Road to Liberty (El Camino de la Libertad)*, from El Salvador; *Rio San Juan, the Golden Door (A Este Lado de la Puerto)*, from Nicaragua; *Generous in Victory (Generosos en la Victoria)*, from Nicaragua; *Tales of Ordinary Madness* (Marco Ferreri); and *Garde à Vue* (France, 1982).
Size & Elements: Film: 35mm and 16mm. Videotape: 1" and 3/4" (masters); 1/2" (viewing copies). (Approx. 14 feature-length films; approx. 20 titles total)
Cataloging: Printed brochures.
Access: Available to the public for distribution and purchase.
Rights: Full distribution and clip rights held to all material. Additional clearances may be necessary in some cases if material is to be reused.
Licensing: Apply for information.
Restrictions: None specified.
Viewing Facilities: None.
Duplication Facilities: None.

CALIFORNIA (Los Angeles Metro)

BANKS FILM LIBRARY/
INTERNATIONAL NEWSREEL SERVICE
8966 Sunset Boulevard
Los Angeles, CA 90069
(213) 271-2840

Bill Banks (Owner and Archivist)

Contact: Bill Banks
Services: Film and videotape stock footage sales library. Research services available.
Description: Entertainment-oriented coverage of personalities and events, centered in Hollywood and the Los Angeles area (1948-80s). Footage was primarily shot to promote Twentieth Century-Fox stars and motion pictures, although some coverage of Paramount and MGM personalities and films is also held. Frequently, Fox stars "loaned out" to other studios are pictured.

Coverage includes film premieres; openings; costume parties; Christmas shows; Easter parades; award ceremonies (e.g., Emmys, Foreign Press Association, Globe, and Academy); imprint ceremonies at Grauman's Chinese Theatre in Hollywood; testimonial dinners and premiere breakfasts; publicity appearances; the inaugurations of Governors Edmund G. "Pat" Brown of California and Sawyer of Nevada (both 1959); visits of the Beatles to Los

Angeles in August 1964 and August-September 1965, including concerts at the Hollywood Bowl, coverage of fans, airport arrivals and press conferences; and material relating to Ronald and Nancy Reagan and their Hollywood careers (1958-64).

Other personalities pictured in the Library include (partial list covering cataloged material from 1958-65 only): Edie Adams, Gracie Allen, Steve Allen, June Allyson, Dana Andrews, Julie Andrews, Paul Anka, Ann-Margret, Michael Ansara, Louis Armstrong, Desi Arnaz, Fred Astaire, Gene Autry, Frankie Avalon, Jim Backus, Lucille Ball, Warren Beatty, the Bee Gees, Jack Benny, Candice Bergen, Edgar Bergen, Polly Bergen, Milton Berle, Joey Bishop, Bill Bixby, Sonny Bono, Debby Boone, Pat Boone, Ernest Borgnine, Eddie Bracken, Sybil Brand, Buddy Bregman, Walter Brennan, Lloyd Bridges, James Brown, Joe E. Brown, Les Brown, Peter Brown, Yul Brynner, Ed Burns, George Burns, Raymond Burr, Richard Burton, Francis X. Bushman, Red Buttons, James Cagney, Sammy Cahn, Rory Calhoun, Corinne Calvet, Eddie Cantor, Hoagy Carmichael, Vicki Carr, Diahann Carroll, Jack Cassidy, Fidel Castro, Sid Caesar, Jeff Chandler, Cyd Charisse, Chubby Checker, Cher, Maurice Chevalier, Van Cliburn, Imogene Coca, Mickey Cohen, Nat King Cole, Joan Collins, Sean Connery, Jackie Coogan, Gary Cooper, Jackie Cooper, Bing Crosby, Gary Crosby, Bob Cummings, Tony Curtis, Vic Damone, Rodney Dangerfield, Linda Darnell, Bobby Darin, Bette Davis, Sammy Davis Jr., Doris Day, Sandra Dee, Angie Dickinson, Troy Donahue, William O. Douglas, Kirk Douglas, Don Drysdale, Patty Duke, Nat Dumont, Jimmy Durante, Leo Durocher, Dan Duryea, Clint Eastwood, Buddy Ebsen, Vincent Edwards, Dwight D. Eisenhower, Queen Elizabeth II, Fabian, Peter Falk, Jose Ferrer, Mel Ferrer, Eddie Fisher, Ella Fitzgerald, Rhonda Flemming, Errol Flynn, Henry Fonda, Jane Fonda, Peter Fonda, Joan Fontaine, Glenn Ford, Tony Franciosa, Stan Freberg, Clark Gable, Eva Gabor, Zsa Zsa Gabor, Ava Gardner, Judy Garland, James Garner, Greer Garson, Jackie Gleason, Barry Goldwater, Eydie Gorme, Frank Gorshin, Robert Goulet, Cary Grant, Johnny Grant, Peter Graves, Lorne Greene, Buddy Hackett, Jack Haley Jr., Gus Hall, Brett Halsey, George Hamilton, Ty Hardin, Mickey Hargitay, Susan Hayward, Rita Hayworth, Tippi Hedren, Van Heflin, Hugh Hefner, Audrey Hepburn, Charlton Heston, Dwayne Hickman, Conrad Hilton, Alfred Hitchcock, Jimmy Hoffa, Bob Hope, Hedda Hopper, Lena Horne, Rock Hudson, Jeffrey Hunter, Sherry Jackson, Sam Jaffe, Dean Jagger, David Janssen, George Jessel, Lady Bird Johnson, Lyndon Baines Johnson, Van Johnson, Carolyn Jones, Jack Jones, Shirley Jones, Spike Jones, Buster Keaton, Gene Kelly, Grace Kelly, John F. Kennedy, Robert F. Kennedy, Deborah Kerr, Martin Luther King Jr., Eartha Kitt, Goodwin Knight, Don Knotts, Susan Kohner, Ernie Kovacs, Stanley Kramer, Burt Lancaster, Hope Lange, Charles Laughton, Peggy Lee, Janet Leigh, Jack Lemmon, the Lennon Sisters, Joseph E. Levine, Jerry Lewis, Joe E. Lewis, Liberace, Art Linkletter, Peter Lorre, Gina Lollobrigida, Trini Lopez, Sophia Loren, Bart Lytton, Shirley MacLaine, Fred MacMurray, Dorothy Malone, Jayne Mansfield, Ferdinand Marcos, Dean Martin, Freddy Martin, Tony Martin, Lee Marvin, Groucho Marx, Harpo Marx, Johnny Mathis, Willie Mays, Joel McCrea, Roddy McDowall, Darren McGavin, Steve McQueen, Audrey Meadows, Ethel Merman, Ann Miller, Vincente Minnelli, Sal Mineo, Robert Mitchum, Marilyn Monroe, Yves Montand, George Murphy, David Nelson, Paul Newman, David Niven, Richard Nixon, Kim Novak, Pat O'Brien, Maureen O'Hara, Walter O'Malley, Jack Oakie, Merle Oberon, Jack Palance, "Colonel" Tom Parker, Fess Parker, Louella O. Parsons, Gregory Peck, George Peppard, Mary Pickford, Suzanne Pleshette, Dick Powell, Otto Preminger, Elvis Presley, Dorothy Provine, Juliet Prowse, George Putnam, George Raft, Prince Rainier, Tony Randall, Martha Raye, Donna Reed, Lee Remick, Burt Reynolds, Debbie Reynolds, Don Rickles, Cliff Robertson, Edward G. Robinson, Sugar Ray Robinson, Buddy Rogers, Ginger Rogers, Roy Rogers, Cesar Romero, Mickey Rooney, Eleanor Roosevelt, James Roosevelt, Barbara Rush, Rosalind Russell, Pierre Salinger, Telly Savalas, Carl Sandburg, Tommy Sands, John Saxon, Gia Scala, Art Seidenbaum, Martin Sheen, Willie Shoemaker, Dinah Shore, Simone Signoret, Phil Silvers, Frank Sinatra, Nancy Sinatra, Red Skelton, Keely Smith, Robert Stack, Barbara Stanwyck, Casey Stengel, Connie Stevens, Inger Stevens, James Stewart, The Three Stooges, Gloria Swanson, Elizabeth Taylor, Rod Taylor, Danny Thomas, Sophie Tucker, Mamie Van Doren, Robert Wagner, Governor George C. Wallace, Jack L. Warner, John Wayne, Jack Webb, Johnny Weismuller, Tuesday Weld, Lawrence Welk, Richard Widmark, Andy Williams, Cara Williams, Chill Wills, Paul Winchell, Jonathan Winters, Shelley Winters, Natalie Wood, Joanne Woodward, Ed Wynn, Keenan Wynn, Sam Yorty, Gig Young and Loretta Young.

Film coverage extends into the 1970s and is largely exclusive. Videotape coverage spans 1970s-80s, is strongest from 1986-87, but is largely non-exclusive footage of events at which there were other camera crews.

Library also contains industrial footage featuring construction, manufacturing and other subjects.

Size & Elements: Film: 16mm (over 1 million feet; reversal original; black and white and color, silent). Videotape: format and amount unspecified.
Cataloging: Chronological catalog (beginning 1955); published catalog (covering 1958-65, indexing approx. 500,000 feet); computerized cataloging available to researchers. A large portion of material is uncataloged.
Access: Open to the public. Available for reuse and resale. Research fees charged. Research requests accepted by mail and telephone.
Rights: Full rights held to all material. Additional clearances may be necessary in some cases if material is to be reused. Personal releases from recognizable individuals are necessary for commercial use.
Licensing: Available for licensing. License fees charged.
Restrictions: None specified.
Viewing Facilities: Film; videotape (3/4" and VHS).
Duplication Facilities: Film (16mm to 3/4" or 1/2" videotape); videotape (3/4" to 1/2").
Related Materials: Still photographs.

CALIFORNIA (Los Angeles Metro)

BARR FILMS
12801 Schabarum Avenue
Irwindale, CA 91706
(818) 338-7878
Fax: (818) 814-2672

Allen Dohra (Chief Executive Officer)

Contact: George Holland (Vice President, Product Development & Acquisitions)
Services: Distributor. Films and videotapes available to the public for rental and purchase.
Description: Educational and training programs (kindergarten through college) covering various topics, including: English and language arts; literature into film; guidance; values clarification; *Fat Albert and the Cosby Kids;* library and study skills; oral and written expression; holiday films; communication; social studies; psychology; human behavior; career; business; history; citizenship; government; energy and ecology; geography; comparative cultures; world affairs; economics; consumer education; science; mathematics; health and safety; alcohol and drug education; mental health; nutrition; safety; physical education; music; art; Spanish-language films.

Adult training and management subjects include: termination skills; interviewing techniques; managerial skills; performance appraisal; listening skills; communication skills; negotiation skills; supervisory skills; conflict resolution; personal image; customer service; leadership styles; sales training; new employee orientation; motivation; equal employment opportunity guidelines; decision making; stress management; time management; and employee assistance.
Size & Elements: Film: 16mm. Videotape: 3/4" and VHS. (Over 400 titles total).
Cataloging: Published catalogs.
Access: Available to the public for rental and purchase. Requests accepted by mail. Preview requests by nonprofit organizations considering purchase accepted by telephone.
Rights: All television and reproduction rights to films and videotapes distributed are reserved. Rental or purchase price of a film or videotape does not include television, broadcast or duplication rights of any kind.
Licensing: Free three-year videotape duplication rights available with purchase of educational films; lease/warranty agreement available for training films.
Restrictions: Apply for information.
Viewing Facilities: None.
Duplication Facilities: None.
Distributors: Apply for information regarding international distributors and university rental libraries' arrangements with Barr Films.

CALIFORNIA (Los Angeles Metro)

BUDGET FILMS INC.
4590 Santa Monica Boulevard
Los Angeles, CA 90029
(213) 660-0187
(213) 660-0800
Fax: (213) 660-5571

Albert Drebin (President)

CALIFORNIA (Los Angeles Metro C)

Contact: Layne Drebin (Controller)
Services: Distributor; film and videotape stock footage sales library. Material available for rental, purchase, duplication and reuse, subject to restrictions.
Description: Thousands of obscure, camp, rare silent and foreign titles, and a large assortment of classic public domain feature films (late 1890s-early 1980s). Large library of short subjects, including documentaries, cartoons, comedies and newsreels.

Categories include: classic American features (silent and sound); classic foreign features; feature documentaries; all-Black cast films; literary classics; titles relating to filmmaking and film history; serials; religious shorts; war films; sports films; animation and cartoons; Christmas films; comedy shorts; motivational films; experimental shorts; horror condensations; musical shorts; spoofs, bloopers and satires; trailers and travel films. Authorized distributor of Columbia Pictures titles for non-theatrical rental only.

Budget Films differs from typical stock footage libraries in that materials exist within complete films and are not filed by specific shot.
Size & Elements: Film: 16mm (over 10,000 titles); other film elements (unspecified). Videotape: 3/4" (over 200 titles).
Cataloging: Published catalogs (available on request); research library.
Access: Not open to the public. Available for duplication and reuse, subject to restrictions. Research fees charged for each shot located (three-hour minimum research fee per shot). Film rental fees charged. Research requests accepted by mail or in person (walk-in). Videotape viewing copies with visible time code can be sent to clients.
Rights: Most material in the public domain. Full rights held to some material. Some rights held to some films (those that are available only for distribution). Additional clearances may be necessary in some cases if material is to be reused.
Licensing: Available for reuse, subject to restrictions. Film rental and research fees (three-hour fee per shot located) charged. Shots are not defined by length but merely as a continuous section of film; therefore length can be anywhere from five seconds to five minutes, depending on customer's specific need. License fees not charged.
Restrictions: Does not provide legal indemnification of any kind.
Viewing Facilities: Film and videotape (after Budget has performed research).
Duplication Facilities: Film and videotape. Films also rented to customers in order for them to arrange their own laboratory and/or transfer sessions.

CALIFORNIA (Los Angeles Metro)

CALIFORNIA INSTITUTE OF TECHNOLOGY
INSTITUTE ARCHIVES
Mail Stop 1-32
Pasadena, CA 91125
(818) 356-6433

Dr. Judith Goodstein (Institute Archivist)

Contact: Paula Hurwitz (Assistant Archivist)
Services: University archives. Film and videotape material intended primarily for research and scholarly use.
Description: Begins 1930s. Primarily comprised of interviews with and lectures by famous scientists, CIT events and site visits to various locations. Topics include: Albert Einstein and assorted footage shot at Caltech (1930s); construction, mirror casting, transport and miscellaneous scenes at Palomar Observatory; interview (1982) with Charles F. Richter (seismologist); Tacoma-Narrows Bridge failure and collapse (1940); space shuttle news conference (1986) with participation of Richard Feynman; Murray Gell-Mann interview for Radio Luxembourg (1985); Roger Sperry (*Science and Man* roundtable discussion); G. J. Wasserburg (interview for NBC-TV *Knowledge* series, 1979); John K. Fairbank lecturing about communist China (separate negative film and 1/4" audiotape elements); the sinking of the *Panay;* Robert A. Millikan's Cosmic Ray Expedition to Bangalore, India (1940); Edwin Hubble (aged 60) observing at the 200-inch telescope; aerial views of Mt. Wilson Observatory; Justice William O. Douglas with Caltech students (mid-1950s). Additional films and videotapes in the manuscript collections are not cataloged.
Size & Elements: Film: 16mm (8 titles). Videotape: 3/4" (13 titles).
Cataloging: Computerized cataloging for staff use only.
Access: Open to researchers and scholars only. Research requests accepted by mail. Research fees charged if search requires more than 30 minutes.
Rights: Full rights held to some material. Some rights held to other material. Rights status of some material not known. Additional clearances may be necessary in some cases if material is to be reused.
Licensing: Available for reuse, subject to restrictions. Usage fees charged.
Restrictions: Restrictions on reuse may apply based on discretion of the

archivist or donor restrictions.
Viewing Facilities: Videotape.
Duplication Facilities: None.

CALIFORNIA (Los Angeles Metro)

CALIFORNIA INSTITUTE OF TECHNOLOGY
JET PROPULSION LABORATORY
PUBLIC AFFAIRS OFFICE
Building 280, Room 201
Pasadena, CA 91109
(818) 354-5011

Jurrie van der Woude (Senior Public Information Officer)

Contact: Jurrie van der Woude
Services: University research laboratory; government agency. Film and videotape materials available for research, duplication and reuse, subject to restrictions.
Description: Jet Propulsion Laboratory, under NASA contract, supports all unmanned exploration of the solar system. As a by-product of unmanned missions and other research projects, JPL produces "wrap-up" summary films (generally 28 min. each) and many shorter scientific films made for professional use. Frequently, footage of special interest from shorter films is incorporated into longer films, which often are widely distributed.

Major wrap-up films produced by the JPL include *The JPL Story*, an orientation film (periodically updated); *Lunar Bridgehead; Planet Mars; Voyager: The Movies;* and *Mercury: Exploration of a Planet.* Numerous video news releases (VNRs) and press release or "handout" films are also produced.

Responds to specific requests for film or videotape material from professional and scientific users or the news media. Those seeking films or videotapes for public showings or broadcast are urged to contact the NASA Regional Film Libraries (q.v.) for information on free-loan distribution of NASA productions. All "wrap-up" films (see above) are available from NASA Regional Film Libraries.
Size & Elements: Film: 16mm (amount unspecified; negatives and release prints). Videotape: 1" (masters); 3/4" (masters and viewing copies) (amount unspecified). Major programs are available on videodisc for on-site viewing and reference.
Cataloging: Not specified. NASA publishes catalogs on films and videotapes available for public distribution (available from NASA Regional Film Libraries).
Access: Available for duplication and reuse. Research fees not charged. Research requests accepted by mail and telephone. Can respond to specific requests from professional and scientific users or the news media. Research cannot be performed for outside users. *Those seeking films or videotapes for public showings or broadcast are urged to contact the NASA Regional Film Libraries (q.v.) for information on free-loan distribution of NASA productions.*
Rights: Material in the public domain.
Licensing: Available for reuse. Usage fees not charged.
Restrictions: Footage cannot be used to endorse commercial products or services.
Viewing Facilities: Film and videotape.
Duplication Facilities: Videotape (duplication requests handled by outside contractors in the Los Angeles area, who hold all printing and master materials).
Related Materials: Still photographs.

CALIFORNIA (Los Angeles Metro)

CALIFORNIA INSTITUTE OF THE ARTS
LIBRARY
24700 McBean Parkway
Valencia, CA 91355
(805) 253-7887
Fax: (805) 254-8352

Fred Gardner (Dean of Library)

Contact: Margie Hanft (Reference and Film Librarian)
Services: Arts institute. Film and videotape library open to researchers and scholars for in-house use only.
Description: Video art, dance footage and experimental animation (international). Collection covers the visual arts, dance, music, theater and film; and includes work produced by CalArts students (1960s-present).

Size & Elements: Film: 16mm (800 titles, 1,600 cans; release prints).
Videotape: 3/4" (158 titles); VHS (34 titles); Betamax (300 titles) (all viewing copies). Videodisc: Laserdiscs (138 titles).
Cataloging: Card catalogs; computerized cataloging.
Access: Open to researchers and scholars only. For in-house use only. Research fees not charged. Research requests accepted in person (by appointment only).
Rights: No rights held to any material.
Licensing: Not available for licensing or reuse.
Restrictions: Reuse not permitted.
Viewing Facilities: Film (Moviola); videotape (3/4", VHS, Betamax); laserdisc.
Duplication Facilities: None.

CALIFORNIA (Los Angeles Metro)

CALIFORNIA STATE UNIVERSITY, NORTHRIDGE
URBAN ARCHIVES CENTER
South Library, Room 205
Northridge, CA 91330
(818) 885-2487

Contact: Robert Marshall (Archivist)
Services: University archives. Film and videotape material possibly available for reuse, subject to restrictions.
Description: Begins 1950s. Historical and biographical material relating to the San Fernando Valley area (generally part of the City of Los Angeles). Includes films concerning Congressman James C. Corman; films relating to the Los Angeles Herald-Examiner strike; and some U.S. Air Force and Army films. Collection includes some unseen footage, as yet uncataloged.
Size & Elements: Film: 16mm. Videotape. (Amounts unspecified).
Cataloging: Card catalogs; additional audiovisual material is indexed separately. Some material uncataloged.
Access: Open to the public for in-house use. Research fees not charged. Research requests accepted by mail and telephone. Material possibly available for duplication.
Rights: Rights status of most material not known.
Licensing: Possibly available for reuse. Fee policy not yet established (apply for information).
Restrictions: Copyright restrictions may apply.
Viewing Facilities: Film and videotape (available through library's multi-media center).
Duplication Facilities: None.

CALIFORNIA (Los Angeles Metro)

CAMEO FILM LIBRARY, INC.
10620 Burbank Boulevard
North Hollywood, CA 91601
(818) 980-8700

Janet Meyer (President)

Contacts: Marilyn Chielens (Vice President/Librarian); Steven Vrabel (Librarian)
Services: Film stock footage sales library.
Description: General stock footage library covering a wide range of subjects (late 1970s-present). Represents stock shots and outtakes from MGM/UA, NBC Productions, Tri-Star Pictures and Viacom Productions.
Special subjects covered include: rare footage of F-16 fighter planes and MIGs in flight, including air-to-air footage and stunts (from *Iron Eagle*); interior shots of formal audiences (*The Muppets Take Manhattan*); scenics and street scenes of North American cities, especially New York. Primarily covers North America, but includes some footage of Rome, Italy.
Size & Elements: Film: 35mm (over 20,000 stock shots; color negatives and viewing prints). Library is continuously expanding.
Cataloging: Card catalogs incorporating reference frames from stock shots. Dope sheets. Catalog notebooks arranged by subject matter and original production source, permitting access to all stock shots available from a given production.
Access: Available to the public for duplication, licensing and reuse. Research fees not charged, although a library charge is levied for in-house viewing. Research requests accepted by telephone.
Rights: Full rights held to all material.
Licensing: Available for licensing, subject to restrictions. License fees charged.

Restrictions: Talent clearances and payments are required for reuse of scenes containing stuntpersons.
Viewing Facilities: Film (35mm Moviola).
Duplication Facilities: None.

CALIFORNIA (Los Angeles Metro)

CAMINO FILM PROJECTS
P.O. Box 291575
Los Angeles, CA 90029
(213) 461-7305

Pamela Cohen (Project Director)

Contact: Pamela Cohen
Services: Film and videotape producer; media organization. Material available for purchase, distribution and reuse, subject to restrictions.
Description: Provides an alternative source of information about issues concerning the people of El Salvador and Central America, and the role of the United States in that region. Two films are available for rental and purchase:
In the Name of Democracy (1984), the first major collaborative effort between North American and Salvadoran filmmakers, details the events of one of the most controversial elections in recent years — the U.S.-sponsored Constituent Assembly elections in El Salvador (1982). It reveals the state of siege that accompanied the elections, government intimidation of voters and the repression of international journalists.
Dateline: San Salvador (1986) documents a march by 80,000 Salvadorans on May 1, 1986 through the streets of their capital, protesting the government's austerity measures and demanding an end to the seven-year-old civil war. It features a walking tour through the ruins of the national university, a visit to a refugee camp, and a look at a sack factory where workers are battling for the union and their own survival. Also featured are interviews with Salvadoran human rights and labor activists and testimony from U.S. human rights advocate Aryeh Neier (Americas Watch), U.S. State Department spokesman Elliott Abrams, and William Doherty (Director, American Institute for Free Labor Development).
Holds unedited videotape footage relating to various aspects of the civil war in El Salvador, including footage of the guerrilla army in action; life in guerrilla-controlled territories; civilian opposition in the countryside; labor unions; human rights organizations; university students; conditions in refugee camps; and historical footage (1932-present).
Size & Elements: Film: 16mm (2 titles; internegatives and release prints). Videotape: 3/4" (2 titles, 30 hours; masters) and 1/2" (2 titles; viewing copies).
Cataloging: Research library; release sheets for completed films.
Access: Not open to the public except by special request. Completed films available for distribution and purchase. Available for duplication and reuse, subject to restrictions.
Rights: Full rights held to some material. Additional clearances may be necessary in some cases if material is to be reused.
Licensing: Available for licensing and reuse, subject to restrictions. License fees charged.
Restrictions: Use of footage must be specified by contractual agreement.
Viewing Facilities: None.
Duplication Facilities: None.

CALIFORNIA (Los Angeles Metro)

STEPHEN J. CANNELL PRODUCTIONS, INC.
7083 Hollywood Boulevard
Los Angeles, CA 90028
(213) 856-7444

Richard Wiedner (Head Film Librarian)

Contact: Richard Wiedner
Services: Television production company; film and videotape stock footage sales library.
Description: Outtakes and unused material from all programs produced by Stephen J. Cannell Productions (1981-present), including *The A-Team, Hardcastle & McCormick* and *The Greatest American Hero* (on film) and *21 Jump Street* (on videotape).
Subjects represented include: automobile stunts; automobile and motor vehicle runbys; automobile accidents and crashes; limousines; buildings (especially in the Los Angeles area and on the West Coast); marinas (action and scenics); harbors and military vehicles (e.g., jeeps and military police cars).

CALIFORNIA (Los Angeles Metro C)

Size & Elements: Film: 35mm (approx. 10,000 shots, each 30 to 150 feet; color negative with matching workprint). Videotape: format and amount unspecified. Library continuously expanding.
Cataloging: Shot lists.
Access: Available to the public for duplication and reuse. Research fees not charged. Research requests accepted by telephone.
Rights: Full rights held to all material. Additional clearances may be necessary in some cases if material is to be reused.
Licensing: Available for licensing. License fees charged.
Restrictions: Reuse of scenes incorporating stuntpersons or recognizable talent will require talent payments.
Viewing Facilities: Film (Kem flatbed).
Duplication Facilities: None.

CALIFORNIA (Los Angeles Metro)

CANNON GROUP, INC.
640 South San Vicente Boulevard
Los Angeles, CA 90048
(213) 658-2100

Services: Motion picture producer and distributor.

CALIFORNIA (Los Angeles Metro)

CARSON TONIGHT INC.
c/o *Tonight Show*
3000 West Alameda
Burbank, CA 91523
(818) 840-3690
Fax: (818) 840-4157

Contact: Peter Steen (Programs Coordinator)
Services: Television production company. Film and videotape material available for licensing under very limited circumstances, subject to restrictions.
Description: Assorted show histories (copies of televised programs) of the *Tonight Show* (1962-present). A few shows (1962-73) are held, some on 2" videotape and miscellaneous segments in kinescope form. Complete show histories (1974-present) are held on videotape (2" and 1"). Also holds 3/4" videotapes (1976-77) transferred from original 2" format.
Size & Elements: Videotape: 2", 1" and 3/4" (amount unspecified). Film: kinescopes ("a few").
Cataloging: Cataloging for staff use only.
Access: Not available to the public. Copies of shows generally made available to guests and their representatives or agents. Occasional access given to feature film producers. Requests for film clips must be made in writing and will be considered on a case-by-case basis.
Rights: Full rights held to all shows produced after September 15, 1980. NBC holds full rights to all shows produced prior to that date.
Licensing: Available for licensing under certain circumstances (apply for information). License fees charged.
Restrictions: Prior approvals from NBC and Johnny Carson are necessary in some cases. Requests for reuse considered on a case-by-case basis and granted depending on intended use and content of production.
Viewing Facilities: None.
Duplication Facilities: None.

CALIFORNIA (Los Angeles Metro)

CENTER FOR MARITAL AND SEXUAL STUDIES FILM LIBRARY
1825 Ostrom Avenue
Long Beach, CA 90815
(213) 596-4691

Contact: James L. Young (Audio-Visual Coordinator)
Services: Educational center producing and distributing films limited to professional "applications in research, education, therapy or counseling by an agency, institution or professional person so engaged."
Description: Films on human sexuality produced for professional use in the treatment of sexual dysfunction or sex education. Sample films include: *Female Masturbation — Justine*, developed to help women use masturbation to experience orgasm; *Coital Positioning*, showing a couple who move very freely in a series of coital positions without disengaging; *Sex at Seventy; Sex Therapy for a Quadriplegic Couple; Transsexuality; Terri Jo*, two interviews

with a 74-year-old male-to-female transsexual; and *Research: Multiorgasmic Man.*
Size & Elements: Film: 16mm. Videotape: 3/4", Betamax I, Betamax II, and other 1/2" formats (NTSC, PAL, SECAM). (36 titles total).
Cataloging: Published catalogs.
Access: Maintained for distribution only. Films and videotapes for sale by special order; films for rental only. Orders accepted by mail. Contractual agreement covering professional use status of material required.
Rights: Full rights held to all material.
Licensing: Materials not generally available for licensing or reuse.
Restrictions: Use limited to professional applications in research, education, therapy or counselling by an agency, institution or professional person so engaged. Materials may not be used for public or commercial purposes or reproduced, copied or duplicated in any way. Transactions do not include television, broadcast, theatrical or export rights, unless acknowledged in writing by the Center. Attendance fees may not be charged without prior written permission.
Viewing Facilities: None.
Duplication Facilities: None.

CALIFORNIA (Los Angeles Metro)

CHURCHILL FILMS
662 North Robertson Boulevard
Los Angeles, CA 90069
(213) 657-5110
(800) 334-7830
Fax: (213) 652-9840

George McQuilkin (President)

Contact: Jim Churchill (Marketing Manager)
Services: Film and videotape producer and distributor. Materials available for rental, purchase and licensing, subject to restrictions.
Description: Distributes educational films and videotapes on various subjects, including: language arts; children's stories; communication skills; creative expression; folklore; English; humanities; social studies; contemporary issues; elementary science (animals, plants, earth science, physical science); biological science; health; adolescence; hygiene; nutrition; physiology; disorders; AIDS; sexually transmitted diseases; substance abuse; health for young people; birth control; childbirth and early infancy; parent and family education; first aid and safety; the elderly; stress; mental health; death and dying; health staff development; guidance; decisions about sex; values; careers; society and the law; computer literacy; mathematics; music; art; filmmaking; test preparation; critical thinking; staff development; and entertainment.
    Spanish and other foreign language versions are available for some titles.
Size & Elements: Film: 16mm. Videotape: 3/4", VHS, Betamax I, II and III. (Hundreds of titles total).
Cataloging: Published catalogs.
Access: Available to the public for rental, preview, purchase and possibly reuse. Requests accepted by mail. Available for rental through Audience Planners, Inc. (q.v.).
Rights: Full rights held to all material.
Licensing: License agreements for duplication or television broadcast are available. Apply for information regarding rates and clearances.
Restrictions: "Reproduction, duplication, transmission or re-transmission of Churchill Films by any means whatsoever, including by tape or by television, without the express written permission of Churchill Films is strictly prohibited."
Viewing Facilities: None.
Duplication Facilities: None.
Related Materials: Discussion guides available for all titles.

CALIFORNIA (Los Angeles Metro)

CINENET (CINEMA NETWORK)
2235 First Street, Suite 111
Simi Valley, CA 93065
(805) 527-0093
Fax: (805) 527-0305

Jim Jarrard; Robert Thompson (Partners)

Contact: Jim Jarrard
Services: Film and videotape producer; stock footage sales library.

Description: Specializes in time-lapse and high-speed cinematography. Library is comprised of premium, broadcast-quality images originally shot on film. In addition to filming on location, Cinenet is developing computer-controlled camera equipment in its studio to create unusual stock images. Custom filming of material at normal stock footage rates and library packages designed exclusively for television station promotional use are also available.

Subjects (most available both in real-time and time-lapse) include: amusement park rides; autumn colors; beaches, featuring Waikiki, Hawaii, California, rocky and sandy, with people, suns, boats and waves; bees; birds, including ducks, Canadian geese, blue jays, grey jays, myna, tropical birds and road runners; boats; burros; canyons; carnival rides; cities, including establishing and beauty shots, day and night, with sun and traffic shots, featuring Hawaii, Denver, Las Vegas, valley lights, mountain and valley towns; clouds, including blue skies with white clouds, skies with suns, with lightning flashes, with storm and twilight clouds, over cities, landscapes, glaciers, mountains and with shadow movements; clowns; cowboys; crabs; desert landscapes; driving (point-of-view scenes); elk; farms; fish, including koi and trout; fireworks; flowers; fog; forests; geese; glacier peaks; golf courses; harvesters; Hawaii, including beauty shots from Kona, Waikiki, Maui and Kauai; helicopters; horseback riding; Hoover Dam; lakes; landscapes, including deserts, valleys, forests and mountains; lighthouses; lightning flashes; meadows and fields; monster trucks; moons; mountains; observatories; oceans, including California, Hawaii, rocky and sandy beaches and sunsets; palm trees and coconuts; plants; people, including time-lapse crowd shots, sunbathing, walking and beach scenes; point-of-view scenes, including suburbia aerials, streets at night, Las Vegas streets at night, canyon driving and fall foliage driving; rainbows; rodeo, including bucking horses, bull riding and roping; sailboats; sand and surf; shadows on landscapes; snowy peaks; spiders; stars; storms, including lightning flash clouds, stormy seas and trees in harsh wind; streams; squirrels; suburbia; sunbathers; suns, including sunrises and sunsets; surfing; tidepools; tractor pull contests; traffic; trains; tropical scenes, including beauty shots, birds and foliage; waves; water scenes and waterfalls.
Size & Elements: Film: 35mm (amount unspecified; color negative). Videotape: 3/4" (amount unspecified; transfers from film).
Cataloging: Computerized cataloging for staff use only.
Access: Available for licensing and reuse. Research fees charged. Research requests accepted by mail and telephone. Custom demonstration videotapes can be prepared (charges apply). Offers an introductory music videotape containing examples of the types of images available within its library (available for a fee with written request on company letterhead). The contents of this cassette will be updated periodically to include new material.
Rights: Full rights held to all material. Additional clearances may be necessary in some cases if material is to be reused.
Licensing: Available for licensing and reuse. License fees charged.
Restrictions: None specified.
Viewing Facilities: Film (16mm); videotape.
Duplication Facilities: Videotape (3/4" and 1/2").

CALIFORNIA (Los Angeles Metro)

CINEPHILE AMALGAMATED PICTURES
Box 8054
Universal City, CA 91608
(213) 939-9042

Rick Mitchell (Owner)

Contact: Rick Mitchell
Services: Film stock footage sales library.
Description: General stock footage material; establishing shots, skylines, buildings and landmarks of Los Angeles and San Francisco; nondescript or anonymous buildings and houses.
Size & Elements: Film: 35mm (45,000 feet; negatives and viewing prints).
Cataloging: Shot lists.
Access: Available for licensing and reuse. Research fees not charged. Research requests accepted by mail and telephone.
Rights: Full rights held to some material.
Licensing: Available for licensing and reuse. License fees charged.
Restrictions: None specified.
Viewing Facilities: None.
Duplication Facilities: None.

CALIFORNIA (Los Angeles Metro)

dick clark media archives, inc.
(Division of dick clark productions, inc.)
3003 West Olive Avenue
Burbank, CA 91510-7811
(818) 841-3003
Fax: (818) 954-8609
Telex: 662708 (DICKCLARK BUBK)

Contact: Jeff Kopp (Operations Manager)
Services: Production company; film and videotape stock footage sales library. Exclusively represents several other libraries for stock footage sales.
Description: Largest popular music film library in the world. Currently represents over 20,000 different performance clips (1957-present) covering all forms of music, including rock and roll, country and soul/rhythm and blues. Virtually every major artist in popular music is represented by a film clip held in the archives. Also represented are many of the dances popular throughout the last three decades.

Library (established 1983) was formed originally to license film and videotape clips owned by the various Dick Clark corporate entities, and now also exclusively represents various other libraries.

Some of the more prominent Dick Clark-produced programs represented by the archives include *American Bandstand* (beginning 1957 and still currently in production); *The Dick Clark Show* (1958-60); *Where the Action Is* (1965-67); *It's Happening* (1968-69); *New Year's Rockin' Eve* (since 1973 and still an annual event); *The Academy of Country Music Awards* (since 1979) and numerous other variety specials and series produced by Dick Clark over the past thirty years.

Currently represents other libraries and programs, as follows:

The Arthur Murray Dance Party (1952-66). These dance instruction programs hosted by the famous duo of Arthur and Katherine Murray featured many performances and appearances by television, film and recording stars. Among the more notable appearances is one of only two existing filmed appearances of Buddy Holly performing *Peggy Sue*. Also featured are early performances by Johnny Carson, Jerry Lewis and Bob Hope.

The DEJ library (late 1970s-early 1980s). Consists of various live and lip-synch performances from Dutch television. Including by ABBA, David Bowie, Dire Straits, Foreigner, the Jacksons, Linda Ronstadt and many others.

Gene Weed/Film Factory library (late 1960s-early 1970s). One of the pioneers of early rock videos, Gene Weed produced a number of promotional films for various record labels in the late 1960s. Included are performances by Glen Campbell, Steppenwolf, Steve Miller, Lynyrd Skynyrd and many others.

The Hy Lit Show (1968-71). This local, Philadelphia-produced program featured live and lip synch performances by some of the great rock and roll stars of the 1960s. Included are performances by Marvin Gaye, the Four Tops, Joe Cocker, Otis Redding and many others.

The Murray The "K" Specials (1965-70). Murray "The K" Kauffman, famous throughout the world as the "Fifth Beatle," produced four specials for network television. Included are performances by the Doors, Aretha Franklin, Patti LaBelle, the Ronettes and many others.

The Nancy Carter Films (1968-70). Silent color films featuring rare footage of Jimi Hendrix, The Rolling Stones, The Who, Led Zeppelin and others. Also included is period footage of hippies, love-ins and various events associated with the late 1960s.

One Man's Challenge (1962). This short film was produced as a promotional effort for a Teen Club in Southern California. This film contains the earliest filmed performance of the Beach Boys, who sing *Surfin' Safari*.

The T.A.M.I. Show (1964). This classic movie was the first "rockumentary" ever produced. Features memorable performances by James Brown, Marvin Gaye, Smokey Robinson, the Supremes, The Rolling Stones and others.
Size & Elements: Film: 16mm. Videotape: 2", 1" and 3/4". (Amounts unspecified). 65% of materials originate on 16mm kinescopes. All have been transferred to 1" videotape. 15% of materials originate on 2" videotape; all has been transferred to 1" videotape. Remainder of library originates on 1" videotape. All footage has been transferred to 3/4" videotape with visible time code (available for reference and review purposes).
Cataloging: All footage completely cross-referenced in computerized database.
Access: Research requests accepted by telephone, letter, telex and fax. Research fee must be paid prior to assembly of a viewing videotape. This fee is non-refundable but is deductible from any license fee for usage of material contained within the videotape. Fee covers preparation of one 3/4" or 1/2" time-coded viewing videotape.

All performances contained on research videotapes have visible time code.

These numbers relate directly to the 1" master videotape sources. Research videotape should be used in the preparation of any off-line or rough-cut edit involving the footage to be licensed.
Rights: Full rights held to 95% of material. Exclusively represents rights to other 5%.
Licensing: Available for licensing and reuse. Signed license agreement and payment of license fee required prior to release of broadcast-quality material. Fee schedule available on request. "All footage licensed by dick clark media archives is delivered with the express understanding that we make no warranty, expressed or implied, except that we have title to the physical property of the footage licensed."
Restrictions: Licensee must obtain any and all necessary clearances and/or waivers that may be required for the usage of material. As with all programming that originated under the auspices of AFTRA (American Federation of Television and Radio Artists), licensee is responsible for clearing the talent and the music synchronization and master rights. Clearances, if applicable, must also be obtained from the director and writer of the original programming source.

It is the strict policy of dick clark media archives to never release the complete performance of a song when the client is licensing only a portion of that song.
Viewing Facilities: None.
Duplication Facilities: Videotape.

CALIFORNIA (Los Angeles Metro)

THE CLIP JOINT FOR FILM
5304 Agnes Avenue
North Hollywood, CA 91607
(818) 761-3228
Fax: (818) 980-2679

Ken Kramer (Owner and President)

Contact: Ken Kramer
Services: Film and videotape archives; producer; stock footage sales library. Research and clearance services available.
Description: Feature films and television programs (pre-1970). Can clear all third-party releases (except music), and handle indemnifications to ensure that producers' errors and omissions coverage remains in force.
Size & Elements: Film: format unspecified (1 million feet, thousands of titles; all elements).
Cataloging: None specified.
Access: Available for licensing and reuse. Research fees charged. Research requests accepted by telephone and in person (by appointment only). Can supply 1/2" viewing copies.
Rights: Full rights held to some material. Some rights held to all material. Additional clearances may be necessary in some cases if material is to be reused.
Licensing: Available for licensing and reuse. License fees charged.
Restrictions: None specified.
Viewing Facilities: Videotape.
Duplication Facilities: Film to videotape.

CALIFORNIA (Los Angeles Metro)

COLUMBIA ENTERTAINMENT CO.
Columbia Plaza
Burbank, CA 91505
(818) 954-6000

Services: Motion picture producer and distributor.

CALIFORNIA (Los Angeles Metro)

COLUMBIA PICTURES TV/
STOCK FILM LIBRARY
Room G, Producers Building 4
Columbia Plaza
Burbank, CA 91505
(818) 954-5139

Contact: Barbara Goetz (Head Librarian)
Services: Motion picture and television studio; film stock footage sales library.
Description: Extensive general stock footage collection includes outtakes from

current television programs (1973-present); stunts; animals (from *Born Free*); police car runbys (especially Los Angeles Police "black-and-whites"); battle scenes; scenic footage from around the world; famous architecture and buildings.

Size & Elements: Film: 35mm (19,000 individual stock shots; color negative and workprint).

Cataloging: Computerized cataloging for staff use only.

Access: Available to the public for duplication, licensing and reuse. Research requests accepted by telephone. Research fees not charged. Library reciprocates with all other studio stock libraries, and independent and commercial feature producers.

Rights: Full rights held to all material. Additional clearances may be necessary in some cases if material is to be reused.

Licensing: Available for licensing. License fees charged.

Restrictions: Some restrictions may apply to some shots. Stunts, battle scenes, or other material featuring recognizable talent may need further clearance.

Viewing Facilities: None.

Duplication Facilities: None.

CALIFORNIA (Los Angeles Metro)

CREATIVE FILM SOCIETY
8435 Geyser Avenue
Northridge, CA 91324
(818) 885-7288

Angeline Pike (Executive Director)

Contact: Angeline Pike

Services: Film archives; distributor. Films available for rental and purchase.

Description: Formed in 1957 by Robert Pike as an informal affiliation of West Coast "filmartists" dedicated to the promotion of film as an art form. The primary function was the rental and sale of 16mm films produced by members, but all types of creative short films and several historically important feature films have been added to the library.

Library includes 35mm and 16mm short subjects (1903-present), including: abstract and non-objective films, animation, avant-garde films, comedies, feature films, independent films, music films, serials and student films. Filmmakers whose work is distributed by CFS include: Kenneth Anger, Freude Bartlett, Scott Bartlett, Jordan Belson, Walerian Borowczyk, Charles Braverman, Luis Buñuel, Noel Burch, Mary Ellen Bute, Doris Chase, Emile Cohl, Bruce Conner, Carson Davidson, Marcel Duchamp, Charles and Ray Eames, Jerry Fairbanks, Hans Fischinger, Oskar Fischinger, Robert Florey, Red Grooms, Bert Haanstra, Curtis Harrington, Will Hindle, John Hubley, Larry Jordan, George Kuchar, Mike Kuchar, Evelyn Lambart, Jan Lenica, Howard Lester, Don Levy, Arthur Lipsett, Leonard Lipton, Len Lye, Winsor McCay, Norman McLaren, Dan McLaughlin, Georges Méliès, Jimmy Murakami, Robert Nelson, George Pal, Bob Pike, Ernest Pintoff, Edwin S. Porter, Kevin Rafferty, Tom Rettig, Hans Richter, Kathy Rose, Jules Schwerin, Mack Sennett, Frank Stauffacher, John Stehura, George C. Stoney, Chick Strand, Paul Strand, Joseph Strick, Francis Thompson, Stan Vanderbeek, Ben Van Meter, Slavko Vorkapich, Michael Wadleigh, James Whitney, John Whitney, Michael Whitney, Fred Wolf and Ferdinand Zecca.

Numerous titles are also of historical interest, including *N.Y., N.Y.* (Francis Thompson), using special lenses to transform the city of New York into a series of surrealistic images; *Notes on the Port of St. Francis* (Frank Stauffacher), a "City Symphony" cinepoem on San Francisco; *Peace Pickets Arrested for Disturbing the Peace* (Leonard Henny), on the October 1967 nonviolent anti-draft demonstration at the Oakland, Calif. induction center that led to the arrest of Joan Baez and 120 pacifists; and *What Really Happened at the East Los Angeles Chicano Riot* (Kevin Rafferty).

Size & Elements: Film: 35mm and 16mm (over 600 titles; negatives, reversal originals and release prints).

Cataloging: Published catalog.

Access: Available for rental and purchase. Requests accepted by telephone.

Rights: Some rights held to some material. Rights to some films held by original filmmakers or producers. Additional clearances (e.g., music) may be necessary in some cases if material is to be reused.

Licensing: Material available for licensing and reuse, subject to restrictions. License and usage fees charged.

Restrictions: All requests for licensing and reuse subject to clearance and approvals by original filmmaker or producer.

Viewing Facilities: Film.

Duplication Facilities: None.

Related Materials: Comprehensive still photograph archives containing stills

from both classic feature films and art film shorts.

CALIFORNIA (Los Angeles Metro)

DE LAURENTIIS ENTERTAINMENT GROUP, INC.
8670 Wilshire Boulevard
Beverly Hills, CA 90211
(213) 854-7000

Services: Motion picture producer and distributor.

CALIFORNIA (Los Angeles Metro)

DIAMOND P. SPORTS
21130 Costanso Street
Woodland Hills, CA 91364
(818) 702-9723

John B. Mullin (Vice President/General Manager)

Contact: Lulu Baskins-Leva

Services: Videotape stock footage sales library.

Description: Motor sports and action footage, including: NHRA Championship drag racing; "World of Outlaws" sprint cars; swamp buggies; Speedway and Motocross motorcycles; ISMA road racing; short track stock car racing; hydroplane boat racing; formula boat racing; tractor and truck pulling; monster truck racing; mud bog competition; jet dragsters; wheel standing exhibition vehicles; and miscellaneous motor sports.

Size & Elements: Videotape: 3/4" and VHS (amount unspecified).

Cataloging: None.

Access: Available for licensing and reuse. Research requests accepted by mail and telephone.

Rights: Full rights held to all material.

Licensing: Available for licensing and reuse, subject to restrictions. License fees charged.

Restrictions: Requests for reuse considered on a case-by-case basis.

Viewing Facilities: None.

Duplication Facilities: Videotape.

CALIFORNIA (Los Angeles Metro)

DIRECT CINEMA LIMITED
P.O. Box 69799
Los Angeles, CA 90069-9976
(213) 652-8000

Available for rental from:
DIRECT CINEMA LIMITED LIBRARY
P.O. Box 315
Franklin Lakes, NJ 07417
(201) 891-8240
(800) 345-6748

Mitchell Block (President)

Contacts: Mitchell Block (Los Angeles); Edie Terhune (New Jersey)
Services: Distributor. Films and videotapes available for rental and purchase.
Description: *Art.* Titles include: *DeKooning on DeKooning* (1982); *Arshile Gorky* (1982); and *Jackson Pollock: Portrait* (1984).
   Crafts. Titles include: *The Art of Chinese Cooking* (1983); and *The Stone Carvers* (1985).
   Dance. Titles include: *Flamenco at 5:15* (1984); *He Makes Me Feel Like Dancin'* (1984), a principal dancer with the New York City Ballet teaching school children to dance; *No Maps on My Taps* (1979), a unique insight into jazz tap dancing as a neglected Black American art form; and *Best of All a Dancer* (1983), on a man with Down's syndrome, his choreography and dance performances.
   Films as art and entertainment. Titles include: *Sundae in New York* (1984), clay animation extravaganza; and *LA LA: Making It in L.A.* (1979), a documentary providing the real lowdown on making it in showbiz.
   Films on filmmaking. Titles include: *The Making of Gandhi* (1983); and *Filmmaker: A Diary by George Lucas* (1982).
   History. Titles include: *America Lost and Found: The Depression Decade* (1980), a compilation of rare footage conveying the psychological impact of the economic and social collapse of America during the Depression years; *The Brooklyn Bridge* (1982); *The Trials of Alger Hiss* (1980); and *The Adirondacks,* on the history of this rare and rugged wilderness and the problem of acid rain.
   John F. Kennedy Series. Four documentaries by Drew Associates, filmmakers who had unprecedented access to both John and Robert Kennedy during the Kennedy administration. Titles include: *Being with John F. Kennedy; Crisis: Behind a Presidential Commitment; Faces of November;* and *Primary.*
   Literature and language arts. Titles based on short stories include: *Mr. Preble Gets Rid of his Wife* (1981); *A Shocking Accident* (1982); and *The Spice of Wickedness* (1984).
   Music. Titles include: *Jazz: The Intimate Art* (1980); and *The Wizard of Waukesha: The Film About Les Paul* (1981).
   Nuclear issues. Selected titles include: *If You Love This Planet: Dr. Helen Caldicott On Nuclear War* (1982); *The Atomic Cafe* (1982); *SL-1: America's First Fatal Nuclear Reactor Accident* (1984).
   Environmental Issues. Titles include: *The Garden of Eden* (1985), about the necessity to preserve the world's plant and animal life; and *Karl Hess: Toward Liberty* (1980), discussing the dangers of "bigness" and the logic in "appropriate technology."
   Films for young adults. Titles include: *Leaving Home: A Family in Transition* (1981); and *Feeling Good, Feeling Proud* (1981), on a member of a unique ensemble of disabled performers.
   Family life. Titles include: *Who Happen to be Gay* (1979), in which six professionals discuss their decisions to lead openly gay lives, and the effects on family and friends; *Marshall High Fights Back* (1985), showing a Chicago inner-city school making a crucial and dramatic turnaround against great odds; and *Making Points* (1981), a clever examination of sex-role stereotyping.
   Business. Titles include: *The American Entrepreneur Series: I Can Do It!* (1984-85), profiling three people and their businesses, with stories of the risks, determination, and creative thinking that led each to success; and *Urge to Build* (1981), about the risks involved with planning and building your own home.
   Inspirational. Titles include: *Hellfire* (1984), exploring the controversies of contemporary religion through a popular television evangelist; *A Lady Named Baybie* (1980), a portrait of two women friends of 50 years, both blind from birth, who sing on New York City sidewalks to support themselves; and *Number Our Days* (1977), on a community of elderly Eastern European Jews who sustain a vivid cultural heritage while contending with poverty and loneliness in modern America.

Films for children are also available.
Size & Elements: Film: 16mm. Videotape: 3/4", VHS and Betamax. (Approx. 120 titles total).
Cataloging: Published catalog.
Access: Available for rental and purchase. Rental requests accepted in writing only.
Rights: Apply for information.
Licensing: Apply for information.
Restrictions: Apply for information.
Viewing Facilities: None.
Duplication Facilities: None.
Related Materials: Selected titles have accompanying study guides.

CALIFORNIA (Los Angeles Metro)

MOE DI SESSO WILD LIFE FILM LIBRARY
24233 The Old Road
Newhall, CA 91321
(805) 255-7969

Moe Di Sesso (Owner)

Contact: Moe Di Sesso
Services: Film and videotape stock footage sales library. Trained birds and animals available.
Description: Wildlife footage and scenics from North America and Africa.
   African — jungle birds and animals. Touconette, red macaw, yellow head parrot, rhinoceros, elephants, cheetah, African lion, African buffalo, hyena, zebra, leopard, mixed herds (large), giraffe, hippopotamus, monkeys, jackal, African sunsets and landscapes.
   Animals. Wild rabbits, white rabbit, coyote, sheep, bobcat, baby opossum, squirrel, turtles, fawn, foxes, raccoon, jack rabbit, timber wolf (Northern Grey), deer, big horn mountain sheep, woodchuck, eagles, ringtail cats, moose, bison and elk.
   Birds. Mallard ducks, red tail hawks, linnet, buzzard, robin, screech owl, pigeons, Mexican caracara, wild canary, western oriole, raven and crow, hummingbird, blue jay, sea gulls, grey horned owl, dove and miscellaneous birds.
   Snakes. Indigo snake eating a young chicken, cobra snake (striking), lizards and rattlesnakes.
   Also has trained birds and animals that can be filmed for clients.
Size & Elements: Film: 35mm ("some"); 16mm ("quite a few thousand"). Videotape: format and amount unspecified.
Cataloging: Shot lists.
Access: Available for licensing and reuse. Research fees charged in some cases. Research requests accepted by telephone.
Rights: Full rights held to all material.
Licensing: Apply for information.
Restrictions: None specified.
Viewing Facilities: Film.
Duplication Facilities: None.

CALIFORNIA (Los Angeles Metro)

WALT DISNEY ARCHIVES
500 South Buena Vista Street
Burbank, CA 91521
(818) 560-5424

David R. Smith (Archivist)

Contact: David R. Smith
Services: Corporation; corporate archives. Film and videotape material available to researchers and scholars only. *Research collection only; copies of films and videotapes are not available.*
Description: Comprehensive archives relating to the history and productions of Walt Disney Studios (1923-present).
Size & Elements: Film: 16mm (500 titles). Videotape: 3/4" and VHS (1,200 titles; viewing copies).
Cataloging: Card catalogs; finding aids (lists).
Access: Open to researchers and scholars only. Materials not available for duplication. Research fees not charged. Research requests accepted by mail, telephone and in person (by appointment only).
Rights: Full rights held to all material.
Licensing: For information regarding clearances, contact: Helena Cardoza

(Legal Department, The Walt Disney Company [q.v.]).
Restrictions: Most films are not kept in Archives. Research collection only; not available for duplication.
Viewing Facilities: Videotape (3/4" and VHS).
Duplication Facilities: None.

CALIFORNIA (Los Angeles Metro)

THE WALT DISNEY COMPANY
500 South Buena Vista Street
Burbank, CA 91521
(818) 840-1000

Services: Motion picture producer and distributor.

CALIFORNIA (Los Angeles Metro)

SCOTT DITTRICH FILMS
P.O. Box 301
Malibu, CA 90265
(213) 459-2526
(213) 456-1743
Fax: (213) 451-5921

Scott Dittrich (President)

Contact: Derek von Briesen (Marketing Director)
Services: Film and videotape producer and distributor; stock footage sales library. Custom shooting services available.
Description: Specializes in sports cinematography, including surfing, windsurfing, skateboarding, snowboarding and tropical scenics. Available for second unit action sports cinematography (DGA member); can shoot in 35mm and 16mm.
Size & Elements: Film: 16mm (approx. 16 hours total, 10 completed films, each 80 min.; color negative and workprint). Videotape: 1" (masters, transfers from film).
Cataloging: Promotional material for completed films.
Access: Completed films available for rental and purchase. Stock footage available for licensing and reuse. VHS preview videotapes available. Research requests accepted by mail and telephone.
Rights: Full rights held to all material. Additional clearances may be necessary in some cases if material is to be reused.
Licensing: Available for licensing and reuse. License fees charged.
Restrictions: None specified.
Viewing Facilities: None.
Duplication Facilities: Videotape (1/2").

CALIFORNIA (Los Angeles Metro)

LARRY DORN ASSOCIATES/
TWA FILM LIBRARY/
WORLD BACKGROUNDS FILM LIBRARY
5550 Wilshire Boulevard, Suite 303
Los Angeles, CA 90036
(213) 935-6266
Fax: (213) 935-9523

Contacts: Linda Dorn; Larry Dorn
Services: Film and videotape stock footage sales library; airline archives.
Description: TWA airline footage, jet airplane stock footage (1940s-80s); airports; cities of the world; scenics; international sport; railroad trains (1900s-present); aerials; Africa; Switzerland; France; England; Scotland; Ireland; international airlines; point-of-view shots and process plates in different countries; space vehicles; galaxy shots; islands; Caribbean; sunrises and sunsets; generic hotels; buildings; apartments; castles; villas; lakes; countryside; Alps; desert; beaches; New York; Los Angeles; San Francisco; San Diego and the Grand Canyon.
  Has associate offices in London, Paris and Milan; can research various London libraries for vintage news footage and international World War I and World War II stock footage.
Size & Elements: Film: 35mm (over 50,000 feet; positive and original negative). Videotape: 3/4" (masters for some jet stock footage and viewing copies); 1/2" (viewing copies).
Cataloging: Card catalogs; published TWA catalogs; computerized cataloging; shot lists and dope sheets.

Access: Open to the public. Available for duplication and reuse. Research fees charged. Research requests accepted by mail, telephone and in person (by appointment only).
Rights: Full rights held to all material. Additional clearances may be necessary in some cases if material is to be reused in future or reedited for other usage.
Licensing: Available for licensing and reuse. License fees charged.
Restrictions: Reuse limited to one-time usage only (other than syndication).
Viewing Facilities: Film (35mm Moviola); videotape (3/4" and 1/2"; NTSC, PAL and SECAM).
Duplication Facilities: None.

CALIFORNIA (Los Angeles Metro)

DREAMLIGHT IMAGES, INC.
932 North La Brea Avenue, Suite C
Hollywood, CA 90038
(213) 850-1996
Fax: (213) 850-5318

Contacts: Marcie Alexander; Hilary Groner; Elon Yurwit
Services: Film and videotape stock footage sales library.
Description: In addition to shooting original 35mm film material and representing artists who create computer and video graphics and cel animation, Dreamlight also represents over fifty award-winning cinematographers and production companies with diverse specialties.
  Aerials. Point-of-view shots flying through, over and under clouds; fields, farming, landscapes and scenics; flying through canyons, rivers, mountains and waterfalls; sand dunes, snowy mountains and ski areas; the "Hollywood" sign; the Grand Canyon; cruise ships, sailboats and beaches; cities, including Los Angeles, New York, Dallas, Fort Worth, Hawaii, Seattle and London.
  Agriculture. Aerials over farms, irrigation, harvesting; tractors, machinery, laborers, packing and processing; fields of wheat; orchards.
  Airplanes. Time-lapse and real-time; air-to-air shots of Lear Jets; vintage airplane footage.
  Airports. Point-of-view landing and takeoff; airliner taxiing up to gate; establishing exterior shots; people checking baggage; day and night landings and takeoffs; control towers.
  Alaska. Time-lapse and real-time, including beauty shots; icebergs; cruise ships; waterways; pipeline; nature and mountains.
  American flag. Various shots; waving; against sky and at various monuments.
  Amphibians. Various shots include shovel nose frog; tree frog; bufo toad; desert spade-footed toad; wax frog; cocoon frog.
  Amusement Parks. Mostly time-lapse, including shots of rides and lights; point-of-view rides and rollercoasters; water rides.
  Animals (African). Cheetah with kittens; lions; gazelles; giraffes; wildebeest; gerenuk; baboons; elephants; hippopotamus; alligators.
  Animals (U.S.). Various types, including deer; moose; raccoons; elk; bears; mountain goats; horses; cattle; sheep; polar bears; horses.
  Automobiles. Various makes and models (vintage, color and black and white).
  Beaches. Real-time and time-lapse, including generic beach scenes; Waikiki; people on beach; women sunning on beach; surfing; swimming.
  Birds. African and United States; too numerous to list.
  Boats. Time-lapse and real-time, including barges; freighters; ocean liners; sailboats at sunset; catamarans; point-of-view shots of shorelines and cities.
  Bridges. Aerials over various bridges across the United States; London Bridge; exploding bridges and bridges with old cars.
  Business. Establishing exterior shots; banks; offices; interior scenes with people; meetings; interviews; aerials over industrial areas and cities; factory workers; bakery workers; fishermen.
  Butterfly. Emerges from a cocoon (total metamorphosis); flying around flowers; perching on flowers.
  Cities. New York; Washington, D.C.; Baltimore; San Francisco; Philadelphia; Memphis; Nashville; Los Angeles; Portland; Atlantic City; Dallas; Detroit; Seattle; Chicago; Houston; St. Louis; Paris; Rome; London; Tokyo.
  Clocks. Time-lapse and real-time, including hands moving fast; clock towers; Big Ben; old and new.
  Clouds. Time-lapse and real-time, including various colors and shapes, sizes and speeds; flying through, over and under clouds; over landscapes and oceanscapes; over cities; storm clouds with lightning; twilight clouds; and more.
  Crowds. Various modern and vintage; rock concerts; people clapping; sports crowds; people on city streets; etc.

Decomposition. Maggots eat a mouse; ants eating a grasshopper and fish; various rust and mold; decomposing food (time-lapse); oranges; bowl of fruit.

Dynamite explosions. Vintage and modern, including trains; cars; boats; buildings; bridges; warehouses; landmarks; graveyards exploding. Also "Secret Agent"-type bombs, devices and packages.

Eating. Various time-lapse and real-time, including modern and vintage; people in cafes; picnics; restaurants; hot dog stands.

Exercise. People with weights; bicycles; joggers; aerobics; track and field; sports.

Explosions. Nuclear; houses; buildings; light bulbs; match ignites.

Flowers. Extensive collection of time-lapse flowers blooming; wilting; fields of flowers; fruit and vegetable flowers blooming; cactus flowers blooming; vase of flowers dying.

Geese. In-flight goose footage; camera soars with Canadian geese as they fly; flocks of geese at sunset.

Graphics. Computer-generated and animated; backgrounds for titles and logos; custom footage available (apply for information and cost estimates).

Hallucinations. Custom-created tank effects, strange images, kaleidoscope.

Hang-gliding. Launches; point-of-view shots; air-to-air following one another.

Hawaii. Various shots, including aerials; clouds; beaches; dancers; sunrises; sunsets; sailboats; waterfalls.

High-speed photography. Drops of all types and speeds falling; splashes of various types, colors and sizes; water splashing on flowers; water drops hitting hot lava and evaporating; seeds blowing and floating in the wind; light bulbs exploding; dirt falling through frame; bees flying; hummingbirds feeding; leaves falling and blowing in the wind; match igniting.

Hollywood. Time-lapse, real-time and aerials, including "Hollywood" sign; Mann's Chinese Theater (formerly Grauman's), handprints on "walk of fame," billboards; Paramount Studios gate; Capitol Records building; various vintage Hollywood films and scenes.

Horses. Aerials following running horses; cowboys riding; riding on beach; vintage Western scenes; horses and grazing.

Insects. Various macro, time-lapse, real-time and high-speed shots, including activities; various phases of life; katydid; grasshopper; tomato worm; cabbage looper; millipede; mosquito; praying mantis; caterpillar; butterfly; aphid; ant; ladybug and dragonfly.

Landmarks. Various time-lapse, real-time and aerials, including Statue of Liberty; Washington Monument; New York scenes (e.g., World Trade Center, Radio City Music Hall and Empire State Building); Yosemite; Yellowstone; Hawaii; Cadillac Ranch; Iwo Jima; city skylines; "Hollywood" sign; bridges; Graceland gates; Paramount studio gates; Gateway Arch (St. Louis, Missouri); London Bridge; Big Ben; Piccadilly.

Microscopic photography. Organisms; blood vessels; crystals; diatoms; cells.

Nature. Real-time and time-lapse, including animals; plants; landscapes; forests; birds; reptiles; underwater; stars; moons; clouds; establishing shots; lakes; waterfalls.

Oceanscapes. Waves crashing against shoreline and rocks; aerials; seals; birds; otters; whales; sharks; underwater life and vegetation; surfing; sailing; windsurfing.

People. Time-lapse, real-time and high-speed, including air traffic control; utility companies; truck and bus drivers; office workers; stock exchange; fishermen; bicycle racers; crowds and concerts; eating; cooking; on streets; on trolleys; beaches; "slice of life"; punks; sports; erotic.

Planets. Zooms to and from Earth's surface; red planets; moon; starfields; novas; nebulae; clouds (video-generated).

Plants. Full life cycles from seed to flower or fruit; seeds germinate, sprout and grow; fruits and vegetables grow and ripen; carnivorous plants feeding; plants rotting and decomposing; ferns grow and unfold; pine cones mature and expand; high-speed dandelion seeds blow in the wind; pineapple fruit blooms, grows and ripens on plant.

Rain. Time-lapse, real-time and high-speed, including various shots, mist; hitting leaves, ponds and flowers; storms; tropical rain forests; water dripping; lightning against black, clouds, telephone poles.

Skylines. Real-time and time-lapse, including cities going from day into night; establishing shots; landmarks; people on streets; with sunrises, sunsets and clouds.

Sports. High-speed and real-time, including track and field (warmups, stretching, sprints, hurdles, javelin, discus, long jump, high jump, starting block, pole vault, cross country, running, races and coaching); indoor and gym (wrestling, referees, rubdowns, crowds, fencing, situps, exercise bicycles, gymnastics, rope climb, boxing and weightlifting) and outdoor (pistol shooting, rifle range, archery, bicycles, crowds, swimming, diving, hang-gliding, ultralight aircraft, water skiing, snow skiing, surfing, boats, rowing, jogging,

soccer, tennis, roller-skating and marathon running).

Statue of Liberty. 1986 Fourth of July celebration; fireworks; day-to-night; aerials; time-lapse and real-time; shots with and without the restoration scaffolding.

Underwater photography. Oceanscapes; divers; fish; coral; sea mammals; schools of fish; assorted sharks; manta rays; eels; humpback whales; dolphins; sea lions; otters; sunken shipwrecks; various ships; pillow lava forming; underwater time-lapse cinematography. The underwater library contains material shot by cinematographers Dr. Lee Tepley, Bill Lovin and Hardy Jones, among others.

Other subjects covered include: balloons (hot air); bees; cable cars; car crashes; cattle; children; Christmas scenes; churches; computers; construction; cows; dams; dancing; demolition; deserts; dew; driving; elevators; factories; fall leaves; fire; fireworks; fist fights; floods (vintage); food; fog; forests; freeways; gems; geysers; gold panning; golf; graffiti; hiking; holidays; hospitals; hot-air balloons; ice and snow; Indians; industrial scenes; jellyfish; jungle; keyboards; larvae; license plates; lighthouses; Maine; money; museums; mushrooms; national parks; neon; oil wells; palm trees; parasailing; petroleum; piers; pollution (including Los Angeles' finest smog); post office; Pope John Paul II; the *Queen Mary;* rafting; rainbows; reflection; religion; rural scenes; saloons; science; sea; seasons; signs; skateboarding; snow; snowmobiles; soap bubbles; space program; spiders; stadiums; streaking traffic; suburbia; subways; suns; telephone; television; temples (Japanese); traffic; trains; transportation; trees; trucks; the Vatican; vegetables; video pixillation; vintage film; volcanoes; water; welding; woodworking; workers; windsurfing; X-rated (topless beaches and swimming); yachts; zebras and zooms.

Size & Elements: Film: 35mm (approx. 250,000 feet); 16mm (approx. 1 million feet). Most film footage has been transferred to 1" and 3/4" videotape. Library has access to over 5 million feet of film footage from various sources which it represents for stock footage sale.

Cataloging: Published catalog (available on request). Computerized cataloging for staff use only.

Access: Available for duplication, licensing and reuse. Research fees charged. Research requests accepted by mail, telephone and in person (by appointment only). Clients can view material at the Hollywood office (by appointment only) or customized demonstration videotapes can be prepared and sent (research and assembly fees charged).

Rights: Full rights held to some material; some rights held to all material.

Licensing: Available for licensing and reuse, subject to restrictions. License fees charged (fee schedule available on request).

Restrictions: All images are supplied on a non-exclusive basis. For other restrictions, see published catalog.

Viewing Facilities: Videotape.

Duplication Facilities: Videotape (3/4" and 1/2").

CALIFORNIA (Los Angeles Metro)

KEVIN DUFFY PRODUCTIONS
19500 Strathern Street
Reseda, CA 91335
(818) 993-1244

Kevin Duffy (Producer)

Contact: Kevin Duffy

Services: Documentary producer; film and videotape stock footage sales library.

Description: Extensive collection, featuring anthropological and wildlife subjects from Africa, India and the Arctic. Includes footage from films produced for National Geographic, the PBS *Nova* series and the major networks. Especially strong in African subjects, as Mr. Duffy lived and worked on that continent for more than 20 years. Of notable interest is *BaMika BaHlula: Children of the Forest* (produced for *Nova*) about the Mbuti pygmies of the Ituri rain forest. Subsequent to its production, the government of Zaire banned photography of these people. Other strengths of the collection are African, Indian and Arctic wildlife, Indian religion and anthropological material from North Greenland and the Arctic.

Size & Elements: Film: 16mm (100,000 feet; negatives and originals). Videotape: format unspecified (amount unspecified; masters and viewing copies).

Cataloging: None specified.

Access: Available for duplication, licensing and reuse. Nominal research fee charged (apply for information). Research requests accepted by mail and telephone.

Rights: Full rights held to some material. Some rights held to all material.
Licensing: Available for licensing and reuse. License fees charged.
Restrictions: None specified.
Viewing Facilities: Film (16mm); videotape.
Duplication Facilities: Videotape.
Related Materials: Color transparencies of Africa and India.
Representative: Pyramid Film and Video Corp. (q.v.).

CALIFORNIA (Los Angeles Metro)

ELYSIUM ARCHIVES AND RESEARCH CENTER
5436 Fernwood Avenue
Los Angeles, CA 90027
(213) 465-7121

Ralph Gerowitz (Custodian)

Contact: Ralph Gerowitz
Services: Nudist organization. Videotapes available for purchase. Films available for research and possibly reuse, subject to clearance and approval.
Description: Nudity, nudism, naturism, naturist outings and the clothing-optional lifestyle (late 1950s-present). The *Nude Living Videotape Series* includes *Sailing Sea and Sand,* inviting the viewer to "...come with Fran and her carefree nudist friends...Leave your worries and cares behind while you share the pleasure of a nude vacation." *The Simple Pleasures* (15-min.) includes underwater nude action. *Educating Julie* is a dramatic "story of a college student who is given the assignment of researching 'Nudity in the 80s.' "
Size & Elements: Film: 16mm (10,000 feet; 12 titles). Videotape: VHS and Betamax (3 titles).
Cataloging: Research library; brochures available.
Access: Open to researchers only for viewing. Research fees charged. Research requests accepted in person (by arrangement only).
Rights: Full rights held to all material. Additional clearances may be necessary in some cases if material is to be reused.
Licensing: Available for licensing and reuse. License fees charged.
Restrictions: None specified.
Viewing Facilities: Film and videotape.

Duplication Facilities: None.
Representative: Videotapes available for purchase from Sun West, P.O. Box 85204, Los Angeles, CA 90072.

CALIFORNIA (Los Angeles Metro)

EM GEE FILM LIBRARY
6924 Canby Avenue, Suite 103
Reseda, CA 91335
(818) 981-5506
(818) 881-8110

Murray Glass (Owner/Manager)

Contact: Murray Glass
Services: Film and videotape distributor; stock footage sales library.
Description: Distributes over 3,000 films (1895-1970s), most available for stock footage sale. Strengths of collection include silent and sound features and shorts, including many works important to the history of the cinema; Westerns; early animation and documentary films.
   Feature films. Films directed by L. Frank Baum, Charles Chaplin, René Clair, Alexander Dovzhenko, Carl Th. Dreyer, Sergei Eisenstein, Louis Feuillade, Jacques Feyder, Dave Fleischer, Abel Gance, D. W. Griffith, Howard Hawks, Alfred Hitchcock, Buster Keaton, Lev Kuleshov, Fritz Lang, Oscar Micheaux, Kenji Mizoguchi, F. W. Murnau, G. W. Pabst, Jean Renoir, Leni Riefenstahl, Abram Room, Roberto Rossellini, Preston Sturges, Jacques Tati, Edgar G. Ulmer, Dziga Vertov, King Vidor, Jean Vigo, Josef von Sternberg, Erich von Stroheim, Edward D. Wood, Jr., Sam Wood and many others.
   Short subjects. D. W. Griffith (many films), Charles Chaplin (many films), Harold Lloyd, Stan Laurel and Oliver Hardy, Buster Keaton, Harry Langdon, Charley Chase, Mack Sennett, Hal Roach, *Little Rascals, Our Gang,* Will Rogers, Al Christie, Max Linder, Ben Turpin, Larry Semon, Vitagraph Company, Burns & Allen, W. C. Fields and Robert Benchley.
   Westerns. Films starring "Bronco Billy" Anderson, Tom Mix, William S. Hart, Buck Jones, Roy Rogers and Dale Evans.
   Historical and pioneer films. Films from early producers, including

Edison, Kalem, Biograph, Lubin, Selig, Vitagraph, Thomas Ince, Crystal, Essanay, Solax, Thanhauser and Universal Pictures Company. French primitive films, including films of the Lumières, Méliès and Pathé Frères.

History and documentary. Art, aviation, big bands, bloopers, British documentaries, dance, disasters, early sound, ecology, entertainment, Robert Flaherty, Hollywood, Joris Ivens, Pare Lorentz, musical films, musical novelties, newsreels, personalities, politics, railroads, rock and roll, "screen magazines," sports, theatrical events and personalities, travel, World War I and World War II.

Animation. Short subjects by Charles Bowers, Bray Studios, Emile Cohl, Walt Disney, Ted Eshbaugh, Oskar Fischinger, Max Fleischer, Hugh Harman and Rudolf Ising, International Film Service, Ub Iwerks, Walter Lantz, Len Lye, Winsor McCay, Norman McLaren, Otto Messmer, Willis O'Brien, George Pal, Lotte Reiniger, Ladislas Starevitch, Paul Terry, UPA, Van Beuren Studios and Warner Brothers.

Other areas covered by the collection include all-Black cast features (18 titles), antique "adult" films, avant-garde films (American, French and German), experimental films, fantasy, horror, outtakes, science fiction, screen tests, series and serials, Surrealist films and trailers.

Size & Elements: Film: 35mm and 16mm (3,000 titles; positives and some negatives, mostly 16mm). Videotape: 3/4" (masters); VHS and Betamax (viewing copies) (200 videotapes total).
Cataloging: Published catalog; data sheets on individual films.
Access: For in-house use only. Available for rental, purchase, licensing and reuse. Research requests accepted by mail, telephone and in person (walk-in).
Rights: Full rights held to some material. Some rights held to other material. Much material in the public domain. Additional clearances (especially for music) may be necessary in some cases if material is to be reused.
Licensing: Available for licensing and reuse, subject to restrictions. License fees charged.
Restrictions: Restrictions may apply in some cases.
Viewing Facilities: Film (16mm projector).
Duplication Facilities: None.

CALIFORNIA (Los Angeles Metro)

ENCORE ENTERTAINMENT
P.O. Box 3457
Anaheim, CA 92803
(714) 526-4392

Ronnie L. James (Owner/Proprietor)

Contact: Ronnie L. James
Services: Television archives; film stock footage sales library.
Description: Holds historic television programs (mostly U.S., 1948-65), including many rare kinescopes, pilots (with some versions never aired) and network versions with original commercials. Also holds an eclectic collection of thousands of short subjects, particularly motion picture shorts, outtakes, and trailers of coming attractions. Television collection entries are primarily 16mm black and white original prints (mostly 30 min.) filmed in the U.S.

Sample titles include: *The Adventures of Ozzie and Harriet,* with various episodes from the 1953-54 through 1965-66 seasons; *The Adventures of Rin-Tin-Tin; The Adventures of Superman; Around the Beatles* (1964, kinescope, 60 min.), a special starring The Beatles, with Cilla Black, Sounds Incorporated, Long John Baldry, The Vernons Girls, P. J. Proby and The Jets (dancers); *The Amos and Andy Show; The Alfred Hitchcock Hour; The Andy Griffith Show; Arthur Godfrey Time; Astro Boy; The Avengers; Bat Masterson; Beverly Hillbillies; Beat the Clock; The Bill Cullen Show; The Barbara Stanwyck Show; Buffalo Bill, Jr.; Candid Camera; Captain Midnight; Captain Z-ro; Case History Theatre; The Cisco Kid; The Colgate Comedy Hour; Danger Man; Death Valley Days; Dennis The Menace; The Detectives; The Dick Powell Show; Dangerous Assignment; The Danny Thomas Show; Dragnet; Do You Trust Your Wife?; The Ed Wynn Show; Flash Gordon; Ford Theatre; Foreign Intrigue; Fractured Flickers; Frontier; The George Burns and Gracie Allen Show; Gomer Pyle; Gumby; The Guns of Will Sonnet; The General Electric Theater; Get Set; Hollywood Premiere Theatre; The Hank McCune Show; The Joey Bishop Show; Jungle Jim; Lash of the West; The Liberace Show; The Life of Riley; Little Theatre; The Milton Berle Show; The Millionaire; My Three Sons; Naked City; The New Loretta Young Show; Our Miss Brooks; On Trial!; Panorama Pacific; The Ray Milland Show; The Red Skelton Show; Revlon Mirror Theater/America's Finest; Rocky Jones, Space Ranger; Route 66; The Roy Rogers Show; Schlitz Playhouse of Stars; Screen Directors Playhouse; Sea Hunt; Shirley Temple's Storybook; Sky King; So This Is Hollywood; Space Patrol; Stars of Jazz; The Steve Allen Show; Stump The Stars; Toast of the Town; Tom Corbett, Space Cadet; The Tonight Show—The Jack Paar Show; Treasure Isle; Treasury Men In Action; The Veil; Wanted Dead or Alive; Westinghouse Appliance Commercials; You Bet Your Life; You Can Do It Too;* and many more.
Size & Elements: Film: 35mm (450,000 feet, 500 titles); 16mm (10.8 million feet, 10,000 titles).
Cataloging: Approximately 50% of collection has been processed and cataloged. Computerized cataloging and simple listings of unchecked, unresearched holdings (in progress). Current cataloging includes shot lists, dope sheets, release sheets, research library, and *T.V. Guide* microfilm editions (Los Angeles and New York).
Access: Available for duplication, distribution and reuse. Research fees charged. Research requests accepted by mail, telephone and in person (by appointment only).
Rights: Some material in the public domain. Additional clearances may be necessary in some cases if material is to be reused. Some material copyrighted by producers.
Licensing: Available for reuse (usually in perpetuity, without restrictions). Usage fees charged depending on rarity, rights, type of duplication and intended use.
Restrictions: None specified.
Viewing Facilities: Film (35mm and 16mm); videotape (3/4", VHS and Betamax).
Duplication Facilities: Film (outside laboratories used); videotape (3/4", VHS and Betamax). Screening videotapes (non-broadcast quality) can be made in house from 35mm and 16mm film material.

CALIFORNIA (Los Angeles Metro)

ENERGY PRODUCTIONS
2690 Beachwood Drive
Los Angeles, CA 90068
(213) 462-3310
Fax: (213) 871-2763

Atlanta office:
ENERGY PRODUCTIONS
2433 Cedar Wood Court
Marietta, GA 30068
(404) 977-4324

Louis Schwartzberg (President)
Murray Okem (Sales Representative, Atlanta)

Contacts: Joan Sargent; Brian Van Beck; Jan Ross
Services: Film and videotape producer; stock footage sales library. Custom shooting services (director of photography and second unit) available.
Timescape™ Image Library (35mm, over one million feet). Time-lapse and real-time production-ready images, all shot pin-registered. Includes skyscapes, airscapes, cityscapes, landscapes, naturescapes, seascapes, people in motion, Americana, landmarks and special effects. General subjects include:
Aerials and airscapes. Aerials through and over cities; rural areas; landscapes; monuments; skylines; ocean and fresh water; traffic; architecture; mountains; forests, beaches; point-of-view takeoffs and landings; spins; air-to-air views of planes, helicopters and balloons.
Agriculture. Aerials over green crops; golden rows of grain; harvesters (combines); sunlit farmhouses; geometric fields.
Airports. Airplanes landing, taxiing and taking off; day and night shots; control towers; control panels; air traffic controllers; scopes; point-of-view shots from airplanes; landing gear opening and closing.
American cities. Skylines, aerials, landmarks and drive-throughs; day and night street scenes. Cities include New York City; Los Angeles, Chicago; Boston; San Francisco; Detroit; Washington, D.C.; Pittsburgh; Miami; Minneapolis/St. Paul; Seattle/Tacoma; Houston; Richmond, Va.; Tucson, Ariz.; Atlanta; Tampa/St. Petersburg, Fla.; St. Louis; Baltimore; Sacramento, Calif.; Indianapolis; Hartford, Conn.; Cincinnati, Ohio; Nashville, Tenn.; Memphis, Tenn.; Oklahoma City; Mobile, Ala.; Jacksonville, Fla.; New Orleans; Lake Tahoe, Nev.
American flag. Waving in blue sky; on Iwo Jima statue; and at various national monuments and landmarks.
Amusement parks. Point-of-view rides; lights; roller coasters; crowds; cotton candy; vendors; and Disneyland.
Animals. Alligators; bears; birds; bison, buffalo; cattle; chipmunks; coyote; deer; dogs; elk; insects; javelina; moose; prairie dogs; rabbits; raccoons; sheep; tortoises; reptiles, including snakes and lizards; species mating, eating, playing

and fighting.

Autumn colors. Fall in New England; blazing forests; falling leaves; rural areas.

Balloons. Hot air; released at festivals; rising over crowds.

Baseball. Time-lapse baseball game in sold-out stadium.

Beaches. Aerials; sunrises and sunsets; scenic coastline shots; waves rolling in; shells; people on beach; scuba lessons; water skiing lessons; girls in bikinis; East and West Coasts.

Big business. Aerials; factories; conveyor belts; workers; assembly lines; stock market and traders.

Birds. Eagles; hawks; sea gulls; swans; owls; woodpeckers; exotic birds, including macaws and flamingos; birds in the wild; generic birds in flight, in trees, in natural habitats, building nests and guarding their young.

Boats. New York City Circle Line; Staten Island Ferry; point-of-view shots on fresh and salt water; speedboats; sailboats; barges; freighters; "anything floats" races; pleasure boats; tankers; cruise ships; canoes; "Tall" ships; shrimp trawlers.

Bridges. Day and night; aerials; Golden Gate Bridge; Brooklyn Bridge; London Bridge; point-of-view shots over bridges; views from tops of various bridges.

Bullfights. Mexico (bull versus toreador); crowd shots.

Cactus. Flowering; silhouetted by setting sun.

Canoes. Paddling; on lakes; rapids; fishing from.

Carnivals. Point-of-view carnival rides; Ferris wheels; day and night; time-lapse; lights; Caribbean carnivals.

Cattle. Time-lapse cows on farm; grazing; long shots; cattle drive; herds; in pastures; calves; stockyard,; day and night; closeups.

Cells. Microscopic cell movement and formation.

Cities. Night and day aerials; skylines at magic hour; twinkling mid-city building lights; bright lights; skyscrapers; skylines with billowing clouds; skimming over tips of buildings looking down at city streets; sunrises and sunsets; moonrises.

Clocks. Time-lapse; "hours pass in seconds"; clock on building overlooking city streets; Chicago's Wrigley Tower (interior and exterior).

Clouds. Time-lapse and real-time; billowing; boiling; multi-directional; storm clouds; fluffy white; multicolored; layered; moving to and from camera; right and left; split-screen clouds; above-line clouds; airplane point of view.

Computer. Generated graphics and animation.

Construction. High-rise building construction; concrete pouring; bulldozers at work; welding; mining; dump trucks.

Countries. Egypt; China; Mexico; Canada; Caribbean; India.

Crystals. Time-lapse growth of crystals.

Dams. Landmarks; Glen Canyon Dam; turbines at work; power stations.

Dancing. Time-lapse; aerobic; ballet; water ballet; religious Voodoo rituals; tribal celebrations.

Deserts. Sand dunes; cracked earth; irrigation wheels; dunes forming and eroding; shadows across landscapes; clouds over; sun setting behind cacti; Indians on dunes; horseback riders; blowing tumbleweed; Joshua trees.

Dynamite blasts. Explosions; live and animated; industrial pit blasts.

Explosions. Live and animated.

Factories. Factory smokestacks; sun rising and setting in background; aerials; assorted machinery workers; automobile plant; copper factory; assembly lines; welding; generators.

Fall leaves. Aerials over autumn forests; point-of-view drives through forests and landscapes.

Falls. Waterfalls; time-lapse and real-time; mountain and rural landscapes.

Fantastic. Unusual shots, including slow-motion match head lighting; point-of-view fisheye on Ferris wheel; streaking lights; starfields; microscopic crystals; point-of-view subway rides; lightning over cities; clouds with lightning; surrealistic phenomena.

Farming. Aerials; point-of-view shots; geometric fields of agricultural products; harvesters, oxen with wooden plow; Egyptian and Mexican farmers; baling hay; grain sprouting; farm animals.

Fishing. People fishing on dock and pier; fish in nets; flyfishing; shrimp trawlers.

Fires. Burning buildings and cars.

Fireworks. Generic fireworks; fireworks over Statue of Liberty (Liberty Weekend, 1986); closeups and wide shots; multicolored.

Flowers. Asta Marias; tigerlilies; roses; poppies; cacti; camellias; exotic plants and flowers from bud to blossom.

Fog. Rural and city areas; oceans; valleys; forests.

Food. Time-lapse sequences in restaurants, at food markets, fish markets, fruit and vegetable stands.

Forests. Wide shots; closeups, points-of-view; aerials; seasonal; mossy trees; pine trees; snow; sun filtering through trees; rain; clouds.

Freeways. Large freeway overpasses; night and day aerials; rush hour traffic; red and white cars lights streak at night; multi-level freeways; cities in background; day-to-night transitions.

Fruits and vegetables. Time-lapse corn; okra; vegetables growing on stalks; strawberries; peppers; tomatoes; fruits and vegetables ripening; peapods; green beans; mushrooms and bean sprouts breaking through soil.

Geysers. Yellowstone and Hawaii.

Golf. Golfers; golf course skylines; golf carts; putting on green; sand trap shots; in Mexico; in Tucson, Ariz.

Grand Canyon. Aerials; sun rising and setting; cloud shadows moving across canyon floor; clouds moving overhead; rafting through on Colorado River; various angles in all seasons.

Graphics. Computer-generated and animated customization available.

Hang-gliding. Points-of-view, launching, over land and water.

Hawaii. Clouds; mountains; people on streets; beach resorts; sunrises and sunsets; Haleakula; Maui; Kauai; Hawaii; beach resorts; waterfalls; lava flows; scenics.

High-speed. Point-of-view drives; aerial footage over Indianapolis speedway; crowds; lights streaking at night; snow and rain falling; fireworks; waterfalls; sports; horseback riding; steeplechase.

Hiking. Back trails; desert hikes; mountains.

Holidays. Easter lilies blooming; Valentine's Day lovers; candy heart with time-lapse disappearing candies; time-lapse jack-o'-lantern; Washington's Birthday; Lincoln's Birthday; Veteran's Day celebrations at respective monuments in Washington, D.C.; parades; champagne bottle cork popping off; time-lapse Christmas tree; Statue of Liberty; fireworks.

Horse racing. Steeplechase, jumping.

Horseback. Riding on beaches; through snowy scenes and greenery; in streams; couples on beach; steeplechase; racing; silhouetted with Saguaros on the desert; Indian "cowboys."

Hospitals. Operating room; surgeons; infant in incubator; heart monitor; vital signs monitor; general equipment.

Hot-air ballooning. From the ground; air to air.

Ice and snow. Icicles; snow scenes in mountains; rural areas; cities; cabins; snow sports; skiing; snowmobiling.

Indians. Hopi; Apache; Navajo; ritual dances; tribal culture; children; elders; farmers; Indians in Monument Valley; on dunes; riding horses.

Industrial. Aerials; industrial complexes; smoking factories; nuclear power plants; large factory smokestacks; copper pits; workers shoveling coal into furnaces; drilling rigs in desert; pit blasts; conveyor belts; mills; bottle fabrication; nuclear plants; container ships; tankers; closeups of panel lights; warning lights; control panels; radiotelescopes.

Insects. Spiders; tarantulas; scorpions; wasps and bees; maggots; walking sticks; butterflies.

Jungles. Mossy streams; overgrown foliage; African; lush tropical scenics; exotic plants and flowers; birds; waterfalls; vegetation.

Lakes. Scenic aerials; static shots of mountain lakes; in national parks; seasonal; activities on lakes, including boating, water skiing and fishing.

Landmarks. Monuments and landmarks spanning the country, including: Detroit skyline; Chicago fountains, Wrigley Tower and skyline; French Quarter of New Orleans; New York City, including Times Square, Empire State Building, World Trade Center, Statue of Liberty, Chrysler Building, Wall Street and the Brooklyn Bridge; San Francisco, including the Golden Gate Bridge, Transamerica Pyramid, Lombard Street; the Gateway Arch in St. Louis; the "Hollywood" sign, Capitol Records tower, Cinerama domed theater and Hollywood Boulevard in Los Angeles; Seattle's Space Needle; monuments in Washington, D.C.; Monument Valley; Death Valley; Yosemite; and Yellowstone.

Landscapes. All geographic areas covered; mountains; deserts; cities; valleys; waterscapes; rural areas; seasons; clouds; suns.

Lava. Flowing; hardening; volcanic craters; Hawaii.

Lightning. Bolts over cities; skylines; landmarks; storm clouds; animated against black sky.

Microscopy. Organisms; microscopic crystal growth.

Monument Valley. Aerials, including shots passing by spires and scenics.

Moon. Full; half; quarter; large; medium; small; blue or black skies; a variety of color tints; rising or setting; different speeds; behind clouds, trees and mountains; over cities; time-lapse eclipse.

Mountains. Sun and moon rising and setting; clouds; point-of-view driving; flying over; stars moving overhead; day and night scenics.

Museums. Desert museums; interiors; Indian artifacts; sculptures; the Metropolitan Museum of Art (New York).

Mushrooms. Time-lapse mushroom breaking soil; growing to full size; nuclear mushroom cloud.

National parks. Big Sur; Bryce Canyon; Canyon de Chelly; Death Valley; Grand Tetons; Grand Canyon; Joshua Tree Desert; Lake Powell; Olympic

Peninsula; Monument Valley; Point Lobos; Yellowstone; Yosemite.

Nature. Aerials; above autumn woods; tree-lined riverbanks; sloping sand dunes; desert spires; national parks; waterfalls; oceans and lakes; springtime growth; winter scenes; animals; time-lapse plant and flower growth.

New England. Aerials and scenics; Cape Cod coast; autumn colors; seasons.

Neon. Las Vegas; details and medium shots; neon from various cities.

Nuclear. Power plants; suns setting; clouds moving over; time-lapse sequences; nuclear bomb explosions.

Oceanscapes. Aerials; over blue-dotted marinas; coastline; golden beaches; blue waves breaking on shore; sun setting over; low over sandy beaches.

Parachutes. Air shows; parachutists; crowds watching; USAF Thunderbirds; planes spinning.

Parasails. Point-of-view parasail rides; wide shots from beach; aerials; Hobie sailboats; Mexico; Hawaii.

People in motion. Waiting for and boarding subways and trains; walking on streets, with umbrellas and in generic crowds; in parks, playing games and participating in sports; assembling cars in plant; buying and trading in stock market; eating; up and down escalators; in Grand Central Station; through revolving doors; at carnivals; swimming; surfing; aerobics; horseback riding; on tractors; harvesting fields; on telephones; operating adding machines and conveyor belts.

Petroleum. Refinery workers; smokestacks; aerials; drilling rigs; pit blasts; Alaskan pipeline; storage tanks; oil tankers; loading oil tankers; flotation cells; propane tanks.

Plants. Growth stages of various types of domestic and exotic plants, flowers and vegetables.

Pollution. Air pollution; smoke billowing out of industrial stacks; pollution plants; stagnant water.

Pyramids. Egypt; Sphinx; Mexico; tourists and ruins; sunset time-lapse sequences.

Rafting. White water; rapids; point-of-view shots; Colorado River; through Grand Canyon.

Rain. Storms; raindrops in cities; rural areas; deserts; crowds with umbrellas; storm clouds forming.

Rainbows. Time-lapse; real-time; over various backgrounds, including "Hollywood" sign; mountains; clouds.

Refineries. Smokestacks billowing smoke; suns setting behind; spectrum skies; molten copper; ladling molten metals; dumping slag; smelter workers.

Reflections. Sunrises across building windows; cloud reflections; "magic hour" (sunrise and sunset colors); reflections on lakes.

Rivers. Aerials; points of view; scenic shots of meandering rivers through rural areas, monuments and national parks; seasonal; West to East coast.

Rodeos. Calf roping; steer wrestling; saddle broncing; rodeo parades; rodeo crowds.

Rural. Small towns; country; scenics; street scenes; aerials; traffic; people in motion.

Sailing. Parades; single boats; point-of-view shots; real-time and time-lapse.

Sea animals. Sharks; tropical fish; live sea plants; fish in markets; fishermen.

Seascapes. Time-lapse waves; mid-ocean and shoreline; sun setting and rising over crashing waves; magic hour; beaches; piers; sailboats; color tropical fish and sea creatures; water sports; people on beach.

Scenics. Wide variety of landscapes spanning the United States, including rural and manmade monuments; national parks; cities; aerials; points of view; time-lapse and real-time; day-to-night and night-to-day; China; Egypt; Mexico.

Science. Science fair; outer space photography and simulations; microscopic time-lapse crystal growth.

Skiing. Points-of-view downhill; cross-country; skiers on slopes; chairlifts; jumpers; falls; ski school; ski lodge.

Skylines. Cities at night and by day; cities with sunsets and sunrises in background; clouds passing over various cities; rural skylines; valleys and mountains with clouds.

Snow. Snow-covered mountains; streams with snowy banks; snow-covered cabins; snow-covered trees, bushes and plants; icicles melting; storm clouds over snowy landscapes, mountains and valleys.

Snowmobiling. Through snowy forest.

Space shuttle. Aerial over space shuttle on ground in New Orleans; point of view from Earth orbit.

Sports. Time-lapse baseball; real-time volleyball; sailing; skiing; horse racing; Olympic gymnastics; diving; swimming; aerobics; dancing; water ballet; golf; tennis; cliff diving.

Spring. Time-lapse flowers and plants blooming; vegetables growing; grass growing.

Stadiums. Day and night aerials; time-lapse baseball games; spectators.

Stars and starfields. Stars rising over mountains and rural areas; day to night sequences; animation.

Statue of Liberty. Extensive footage from Liberty Weekend (1986), featuring the statue as it will never be lit again; aerials; with fireworks; silhouettes; sunrises and sunsets in background; unveiling.

Stock market. High-speed stock market traders; on telephones; on trading floors; closeups; wide shots.

Storms. Dramatic storm fronts forming, passing and clearing; storm clouds; windy beach scenes; waves.

Streaking traffic. Day and night traffic streaks to and from camera; aerials; multi-lane freeways; country roads; high angles; wide angles; cities in background; pans; tilts; focussing in and out.

Suburbia. Skylines; aerials; traffic; houses; people in motion; inner city row houses; suburban tracts; rural neighborhoods.

Subways. Point-of-view shots from front and rear of subways in New York and Chicago; station time-lapse series.

Suns. Large; small; medium; setting; rising; behind clouds and mountains; over water; behind cities; trees; valleys; cities; aerials; behind manmade and natural monuments; night-to-day sequences.

Surfing. Slow-motion; real-time; Hawaiian waves; windsurfing; somersaults; boogieboarding.

Swimming. Water ballet; swimming in ponds; lakes and oceans; high-diving.

Television. Television sets; full-screen turn off receding to dot.

Tennis. Serve and volley sequences; tennis clubs; time-lapse and real-time.

Traffic. Night and day; four-way intersections; freeways; aerials; point-of-view; cities; suburbia; rural areas; streaking and slow-motion.

Trains. Aerials over and points of view from trains; trains to and from camera; through rural areas; cities; in stations; crossing bridges; subways; people waiting for trains.

Transportation. Cars; trucks; trains; airplanes; point-of-view drives through cities; rural areas; point-of-view train and subway rides; space shuttle landing and takeoff.

Trees. Bristlecones; forests; Joshua trees; giant sequoia; palm; pine; single silhouettes; springtime; autumnal blaze; snow-covered; dead branches.

Trucks. On freeways; streets; points of view from; monster trucks.

Underwater. Colorful tropical fish; sharks; sea creatures; scuba lessons.

Volcanoes. Lava; craters; Hawaii.

Water and waterfalls. Breakers crashing against rocky coast; 20-foot curls; full-frame; wide-angle shots; open shutter; tilts; rises; tropic and forest; greenery in background; icicles and snow; stormy swells.

Waves. Lapping calmly on beaches; breaking over rocky coastline; mid-ocean; 10-foot high swells; surfers.

Welding. Arc welding; cutting metal; closeups; industrial workers.

Windsurfing. Slow-motion and real-time; on oceans and lakes.

Winter scenes. Rural and city areas, including snow-capped mountains; valleys; frozen waterfalls; city streets; skylines; aerials; falling snow.

Workers. Time-lapse factory and assembly-line workers; blue- and white-collar; in offices and on streets.

Yellowstone National Park. Seasonal; winter and summer; day-to-night sequences; suns and moons rise over mountains; shadows move across valleys; show; steam; geysers; buffalo.

Yosemite. Waterfalls; scenics; moonlit shadows across valley floor; Half Dome; El Capitan.

Ron Hays Special Effects Library. Over 430 sophisticated, versatile computer graphic images to choose from. Includes raster scan motion graphics and electronic animation.

Size & Elements: Film: 70mm; 35mm and 16mm (color negative and workprint) (over 1.5 million feet total). Videotape: 1" (masters transferred directly from 35mm negative); 3/4" and VHS (viewing copies with visible time code).

Cataloging: Published catalog; computerized cataloging for staff use only; dope sheets.

Access: Available to the public for duplication, licensing and reuse. Research fees charged. Research requests accepted by mail, telephone, fax and in person (by appointment only). Apply for information regarding research and licensing procedures.

Rights: Full rights held to all material. Additional clearances may be necessary in some cases if material is to be reused.

Licensing: Available for licensing and reuse. License fees charged (rate sheet available upon request).

Restrictions: Licenses subject to territorial restrictions in some instances. Renewals apply on commercials.

Viewing Facilities: Film (35mm flatbed editor and projector); videotape (3/4"

and VHS).
Duplication Facilities: Videotape (3/4" and VHS).

CALIFORNIA (Los Angeles Metro)

EZTV
8547 Santa Monica Boulevard
West Hollywood, CA 90069
(213) 657-1532

John H. Dorr (Director)

Contact: John H. Dorr
Services: Videotape producer; homevideo distributor. Collection available for rental and purchase, and possibly duplication and reuse.
Description: Distributes independently produced videotapes (1982-present), including 100 hours of material produced through or in cooperation with EZTV.

Titles currently available: Eric Bogosian's *Fun House; Kay Baxter: Anatomy of a Bodybuilder; Trio* (Pat Barr); *Laughing Horse; Sometimes Jones': Basement Tape* (Larry Hankin); *Polly Perverse Strikes Again!* (Dan Sallitt); *Dorothy and Alan at Norma Place* and *Approaching Omega* (John Dorr); *Henry Miller* (John Hunt); *Lemuria* (Kim McKillip); and *Blonde Death* (James Dillinger).

Holds copies of many videotapes screened at EZTV (no formal access agreements apply to these materials and no rights are held); alternative fictional work, including early fiction video (1982-84); and archival documentation of recent performances, performance artists, painters and dance.

Currently producing a series of poetry videotapes (13 programs, each 60 min.) including readings by and interviews with local poets.
Size & Elements: Videotape: 3/4" (200 videotapes; submasters).
Cataloging: Published brochures.
Access: Available for rental and purchase. Research requests accepted by mail, telephone and in person (walk-in and by appointment). Screening fees charged.
Rights: Full rights held to some material. Additional clearances are necessary in some cases if material is to be reused.
Licensing: Material available for duplication and reuse, subject to restrictions. License fees charged in some cases.
Restrictions: Some restrictions may apply to reuse. Duplication, licensing or reuse requires permission of original producer.
Viewing Facilities: Videotape (3/4" and VHS).
Duplication Facilities: Videotape (3/4" and VHS).

CALIFORNIA (Los Angeles Metro)

FASHION INSTITUTE OF DESIGN & MERCHANDISING
818 West 7th Street
Los Angeles, CA 90017-3407
(213) 624-1200
Fax: (213) 895-0660

Toni Hohberg (President)

Contact: Gina Camacho (Special Collections Coordinator)
Services: Library. Videotape collection available for research and duplication.
Description: Fashion, fashion merchandising, apparel manufacturing, advertising and historic costumes. Includes interviews with fashion and design industry personalities from all areas of the business; business ethics and management; commercials; designer collections and shows; fabrics; fashion awards; FIDM functions; interior design; labor relations; retailers; and techniques of drafting, draping and construction.
Size & Elements: Videotape: 3/4" (542 titles; masters and viewing copies).
Cataloging: Card catalogs, title list and research library.
Access: Open to the public. For in-house use only. Available for duplication. Research fees not charged. Requests accepted by mail, telephone and in person (walk-in).
Rights: Full rights held to some material. Rights status of some material not known.
Licensing: Apply for information. License fees not charged.
Restrictions: None specified.
Viewing Facilities: Videotape (3/4").
Duplication Facilities: Videotape.

CALIFORNIA (Los Angeles Metro)

FILM BANK
3306 West Burbank Boulevard
Burbank, CA 91505
(818) 841-9176
Fax: (818) 567-4235

Paula Lumbard (Marketing)

Contacts: Paula Lumbard; Elizabeth Canelake (Librarian)
Services: Film and videotape stock footage sales library. Represents award-winning cinematographers and production companies. Research and custom shooting services available.
Description: Houses a broad-based collection ranging from historical (1903-present) to contemporary film and videotape images. Library comprises 19 major categories, as follows:

Aerials. Cities (Chicago, Detroit, Los Angeles, New York, San Francisco, Washington D.C., bridges, freeways, rural roads); foreign countries (African landscapes and wildlife, Israel, South Pacific Islands, New Zealand, Poland and Spain); historical views (air-to-air battles, air-to-air disasters, air-to-air stunts, atomic bombs, United States, Europe and Japan); natural phenomena (Big Sur and Carmel, beaches, cliffs, clouds, deserts, farmland, forests, glaciers, jungle terrain, mountains, oceans, rivers, seals, spins and turns, swamps, waterfalls); sports (hang-gliding, hot-air ballooning, skydiving, stunt planes).

Agriculture. Crops (grains, fruits, vegetables); equipment (1900s-present); farm scenics (animals, farmhouses and farm buildings, panoramas); farm workers (harvesting, packing and shipping); historical (cowboys, Dust Bowl and other weather conditions).

Animation. Cartoons (historical favorites); cel animation (many styles and subjects); computer animation (raster graphics, motion control); stop-motion animation (dinosaurs, dolls, people, pizzas, monsters and more).

Archival. Wars (World War II air-to-air battles, land encounters, troop landings, 1940s domestic factories and war efforts, reenactments of Vietnam battles); industry and production (automation, automobile production, assembly lines, early radio, television and film production, farming, factories, people relating to products); sociology (Mom, pop and the kids, amusement parks and fairs, animation, automobiles, beatniks, battles, fads, fashions, morality and propaganda, oddities, politics and politicians, sports, stunts and daredevils).

Cityscapes. Day and night matches and moves are available, covering many contemporary structures and neighborhoods. Airports (establishing shots, inside cockpit, radar screens in operation, runways with takeoffs and landings, terminals, towers); domestic skylines and streets (Chicago, Denver, Honolulu, Kansas City [Missouri], Los Angeles, New York City, Omaha, San Francisco, Venice Beach [California], Washington D.C., Wyoming, freeways, rural roads); foreign cities (Africa, Iran, Katmandu, London, Moscow, South Pacific, Toronto, Turkey and Warsaw); scenic city settings (amusement parks and fairs, apartments, churches, condominiums, coroners and mortuaries, courthouses and jails, hospitals, houses, libraries and museums, lofts, mansions, offices and store fronts, police and fire stations, schools and universities, urban parks and gymnasiums); signage and advertisements (assorted neon, including Times Square, Piccadilly Circus, bars, theaters, products, print and broadcast advertisements); urban problems (accidents, earthquakes, fires, floods, riots and marches; historical and contemporary).

Energy. Coal processing, dams and hydroelectric plants, nuclear power plants, oil rigs and tankers, solar energy panels and plants, strip mining, telecommunications, windmills and wind farms.

Humorous. A growing collection of historical and contemporary humor, including the episodic TV series *You Asked for It* and classic health, hygiene and social guidance films. *You Asked for It* episodes include: "The Human Rubber Band," "The Ducks Who Live Like Millionaires," "Acrobatic Waiters," "The Yo Yo Man," "Limbo Roller Skaters," "He Hangs From His Toes from a Helicopter," "He Takes a Bath While 3,000 Feet Above Los Angeles," "Cows Who Ski," "The Kissing Cobra" and "Samurai Warrior for a Day."

Landscape and nature. Generic beauty shots (deserts, flora and fauna, lakes, moon alone and in rural or urban settings, moonrises and moonsets, mountains, ponds and waterfalls, rivers, seascapes, suns, sunrises and sunsets, waves); foreign (African landscapes and wildlife, Easter Island, Israel, Mt. Everest, New Zealand, Poland, South Pacific, Spain, Turkey); natural disasters (avalanche, earthquakes, floods, forest fires, hurricanes, lava eruptions and tornadoes); United States (deserts, Hawaii, Pacific Coast scenics, national parks, New England in autumn, New Orleans swamps); weather (clouds, fog and mist, lightning, rain, seasons, smog, snow, weather maps); wildlife (assorted wild and domestic animals, microcinematography of insects and reptiles, land and sea birds).

Medical. Ambulances; equipment; hospitals and paramedics; microscopy (antibody molecules, bacteria, blood cells and veins, cell divisions and cell growth, electron micrographs, fungi [including time-lapse growth], molds, protozoa, tissue cultures, viral organisms); procedures (autopsy, birth, injuries, lab setups, patient care, surgery).

On-set playback. Entire collection is available for establishing authenticity or mood.

People and the things they do. Athletes and competition; children (at birth, at play, in school, with Mom and Dad); crowds (amusement parks, audiences, beaches, campuses, churches, dancing, downtown bustle, parades, parks); domestic and foreign rituals and customs; food (eating, drinking, food preparation); historical (70 years of Mom, Pop and the kids); stunts and oddities.

Physical effects. Explosions; fireworks; flames and fire; moire patterns; smoke; tank clouds; Tesla ball; time-lapse cinematography of cities, clouds and nature; wire scan.

Political. Atomic blasts; Winston Churchill; civil disobedience, riots and marches; Dwight D. Eisenhower; Queen Elizabeth II; Lyndon B. Johnson; Martin Luther King; John F. Kennedy; Douglas MacArthur; Franklin D. Roosevelt; Vietnam; and World War II.

Special visual effects. Animation (earth, satellites, space shuttle); computer graphics (city skylines, geometric patterns, world map); Earth; lightning; planets (flybys, orbiting and stationary, surface terrain); selected NASA footage (control center, moon and moonwalk, rocket lift-offs, satellites, space exploration, space shuttle); spaceships (multiple moves in flight, various models); star fields (moving, streaking, overhead point-of-view shots, stationary); stop-motion animation (dinosaurs, monsters).

Sports and action. Aerobatics; baseball; bicycling; BMX racing; boat racing; boogie boarding; bowling; boxing; drag racing; football; hang-gliding; historical sports footage; hockey; hot-air ballooning; jet skiing; motocross racing; ping-pong; precision flying; racquetball; river rafting; rock climbing; rodeo; rollerskating; sailing; skateboarding; spectators and ambience; sports humor; stock car driving; surfing; waterskiing; windsurfing; wrestling.

Stunts and daredevils. Car crashes (rural and urban settings, various cars); conflicts (battle footage, gangsters and shootouts, various theaters, Western gunfights and barroom brawls); explosions (against black for optical process, paint store, school); historical (*You Asked for It*, chock-full of breathtaking brushes with death).

Time-lapse and slow motion. Cities (Chicago, Detroit, New Orleans, New York, San Francisco, Washington, D.C.); natural phenomena (clouds, flowers, moon, moonrise, storm clouds, sunrise, sunset, swamp); science (cell division, fungus, tissue cultures, viral organisms); slow motion (birds in flight, butterflies, hummingbird, raindrops, various stunts and action); sociological (a man sleeps, a woman cleans her house); vehicles and transit systems (aerial highways, cars, city traffic, a drive through Los Angeles, pedestrians, subways, trains).

Vehicles, aircraft and transit systems. Air (commercial and private jets landing, commercial and private jets taking off, dirigibles [including the Hindenburg crash and the Goodyear blimp], helicopters over city terrain, helicopters over jungle terrain, helicopters taking off and landing, historical military and private planes [including Lindbergh's transatlantic flight], terminals and various locations, towers); land (buses and city transit systems, emergency medical vehicles, passenger cars, city traffic and highways); rail (freight and passenger trains, steam engines to modern railroading, train signage, stations, tunnels and track); sea (clipper ship, cruise ships, freighters, historical military, private boats and submarines, Staten Island Ferry); spaceships (miniatures, selected NASA footage); subways and streetcars (Chicago, historical, London, New York, Paris, San Francisco streetcars, San Francisco Bay Area Rapid Transit [BART], Washington, D.C.).

Size & Elements: Film: 35mm (75% of film library, amount unspecified); 16mm (25% of film library, amount unspecified). Majority of library backed by 35mm original color negative. Videotape: 1" (50% of film library; film transfer masters); 3/4" and 1/2" (screening copies). Growing collection of 1", 3/4" and Betacam master videotape footage.

Cataloging: Published catalog, containing information on products, services, policies and procedures; card catalogs and computerized cataloging available for staff use only; research library.

Access: Open to the public. Available for duplication, licensing and reuse. Research fees charged. Research requests accepted by mail, telephone and in person (by appointment only).

Rights: Full rights held to all material.

Licensing: Available for licensing and reuse, subject to restrictions. License fees charged (fee schedule available). All orders are COD unless otherwise arranged. Licensor is responsible for all laboratory fees and duplication costs.

Restrictions: Each usage must be individually licensed.

Viewing Facilities: Film (35mm and 16mm); videotape (3/4" and VHS).

Duplication Facilities: Videotape (3/4" and 1/2").

Research Services: Film Bank's staff of researchers can locate stock footage from unique and obscure sources as well as traditional libraries.
Camera Services: Film Bank offers camera services. "We will find a suitable location, submit Polaroids for your approval, and shoot to your specifications — in most cases, all in less than one week. Due to the many variables involved in production costs, it is necessary to quote prices on a per project basis."
Representative: Film Bank is represented by an agent for the territory of South America.

CALIFORNIA (Los Angeles Metro)

FILM PRESERVATION ASSOCIATES
8307 San Fernando Road
Sun Valley, CA 91352
(818) 768-5376

David Shepard; Kimberly Shepard (Owners)

Contacts: David Shepard; Kimberly Shepard
Services: Film laboratory; specialized film title service; distributor; stock footage sales library. Some films available for purchase.
Description: *Blackhawk Films Collection.* Comedies, historical railroad and aviation films, silent newsreels, animation and early dramatic films. Most titles are silent.
Hal Roach Studios. Distributes films (1927-53) from the Roach library for purchase only (no rights held for stock footage sale). Featured comedians include Laurel & Hardy (100 features and shorts); Our Gang (100 titles); and Charley Chase (65 titles). Other Roach films are also available.
Robert Youngson shorts. Short subjects edited from the Pathé News library. A list follows the entry for Sherman Grinberg Film Libraries, Inc. (West) (q.v.). Represents the series for worldwide distribution in all media, including the sale of excerpts.
Size & Elements: Film: 35mm and 16mm (2,000 titles; negatives and fine grain masters).
Cataloging: Title chronology and artist list for completed films; shot-by-shot lists for Youngson shorts.
Access: Open to the public. Available for licensing and reuse. Research fees charged in some cases. Research requests accepted by mail and telephone.
Rights: Full rights held to some material. Some rights held to some material. Some material in the public domain.
Licensing: Available for licensing and reuse, subject to restrictions. License and usage fees charged.
Restrictions: Some material may be subject to special restrictions. Material licensed for one-time use only.
Viewing Facilities: Film (35mm and 16mm flatbeds).
Duplication Facilities: Film (35mm and 16mm; can do blowups and reductions in house). Provides specialized film title services; can produce silent film intertitles matching original typography.

CALIFORNIA (Los Angeles Metro)

FILMFAIR COMMUNICATIONS
10621 Magnolia Boulevard
North Hollywood, CA 91601
(818) 985-0244
Fax: (818) 766-8786

Contact: Ethel Poirier (Marketing)
Services: Distributor. Films and videotapes available to the public for rental and purchase.
Description: General educational films and videotapes for all age groups.
Business education. Titles include: *It's A Matter of Pride,* vignettes of humorously portrayed job situations and the rewards of having pride in one's work; and *Business: What's It's All About.*
Career education. Titles include: *When You Grow Up; Free To Choose;* and *If At First You Don't Succeed.*
Fine Arts. Titles include: *Guitar Craft; Puppets: How They Happen;* and *Creative Hands,* on folk art and crafts.
Health. Titles include: *Drugs — Use Or Abuse?; Health Habits For A Healthy Life;* and *Coping With Depression (Suicide Prevention).*
Language arts. Titles include: *What Did You Say (Oral Communications); George Writes An Essay; Sound of Sunshine — Sound of Rain,* an animated film giving rare insights into the life of a blind boy and his world of sounds and touch; and *Paddington Bear Programs* (5 volumes, 56 episodes, each approx. 5 min.), showing the world famous Peruvian emigrant bear in England in dozens of delightful situations, growing up and dealing with the world.
Living and coping. Titles include: *That's Stealing; There's Nobody Else Like You; Coping With Parents; Acid Rain; Recycling in Action; Robin...A Runaway;* and *The Witness.*
Safety. Titles include: *Better Safe Than Sorry* (4 programs), directed at young people, dealing openly with the difficult subject of child sexual abuse; *Winter Safety; In Charge At Home (Latchkey Children);* and *Common Sense Self Defense.*
Science and math. Titles include: *Simply Metric; Coral Reef Community; The Apes; Seeds of Survival;* and *Winter In Nature.*
Social studies. Titles include: *Morning Zoo; American Indians: Yesterday and Today; Transportation in America's History; The Dancing Lion — An African Folktale; The Fastest Animal On Earth;* and *AmaZulu — People of the Sky.*
Size & Elements: Film: 16mm. Videotape: 3/4", VHS and Betamax. (250 titles total).
Cataloging: Published catalog.
Access: Available to the public for rental, preview and purchase. Requests accepted by mail and telephone.
Rights: Purchase, lease or rental of films and videotapes include television rights. All FFC films are available for use on television, but must first be cleared for televising and covered by a licensing agreement before broadcast. Apply for information regarding broadcast fees and permission.
Licensing: Available for licensing and reuse. License fees charged.
Restrictions: All FFC materials are protected by international copyright. Purchase, lease or rental includes only the right of direct optical projection to non-paying audiences.
Viewing Facilities: None.
Duplication Facilities: None.
Related Materials: Study guides available for selected titles.

CALIFORNIA (Los Angeles Metro)

FILMS OF INDIA
P.O. Box 48303
Los Angeles, CA 90048
(213) 383-9217

R. M. Bagai (President)

Contact: R. M. Bagai
Services: Distributor; film and videotape archives; film and videotape producer; private collection; stock footage sales library.
Description: Feature and documentary films relating to India and Mohandas K. Gandhi. Some films have been produced by FOI and others by Indian producers. Feature-length titles include: *The Dancing Ranee; Two Eyes, Twelve Hands* (based on a 1940s Indian experiment in nonviolence, it depicts an attempt to restore convicted murderers and criminals to society); *The King and the Maiden; Life of Mahatma Gandhi; Light of India;* and *Indian Bracelets.* Short subjects include *India's Dance Queens* (in golden sepia color); *Folk Songs of India; Village Life of India;* and *Dances of India.*
Size & Elements: Film: 35mm and 16mm (10 titles total, each 12 to 120 min.).
Cataloging: Printed brochure.
Access: Available for distribution and rental for commercial and educational use; available for reuse or resale. Requests accepted by mail and telephone. Research fees charged.
Rights: Full rights held to all material.
Licensing: Available for licensing and reuse, subject to restrictions. License fees charged.
Restrictions: Requests for licensing and reuse considered on a case-by-case basis.
Viewing Facilities: None.
Duplication Facilities: None.

CALIFORNIA (Los Angeles Metro)

ELFRIEDE FISCHINGER
8925 Wonderland Park Avenue
Los Angeles, CA 90046
(213) 656-3109

Contact: Elfriede Fischinger
Services: Private collection; film distributor. Films available for rental and purchase.
Description: Distributes films (1920-54) by the noted animator Oskar

Fischinger. Elfriede Fischinger, his widow, is available for lectures and film screenings.
Size & Elements: Film: 35mm (originals); 16mm (release prints). (25 titles total; each 3 to 10 min.).
Cataloging: Published catalog (from Creative Film Society [q.v.]).
Access: Open to the public. Available for rental, purchase and reuse. Research requests accepted by mail and telephone.
Rights: Full rights held to most material.
Licensing: Available for licensing and reuse. License fees charged.
Restrictions: None specified.
Viewing Facilities: None.
Duplication Facilities: None.
Distributors: Available for rental from Creative Film Society (q.v.) and The Museum of Modern Art, Circulating Film Library (q.v.). *The World of Oskar Fischinger*, a Pathfinder Series laser videodisc, has been released in Japan on the Pioneer label and is available in the U.S. as an import.

CALIFORNIA (Los Angeles Metro)

FISH FILMS, INC.
4548 Van Noord Avenue
Studio City, CA 91604
(818) 905-1071
Fax: (818) 905-0301

David Fishbein (President)

Contact: David Fishbein
Services: Videotape producer and distributor; videotape stock footage sales library.
Description: Subjects include: adventure, audience shots, automobiles, beauty (make-up, etc.), buildings, cartoons, celebrations, cities, dancing, eating, educational films, fashion, graphics, historical, Hollywood, industrial films, kids, kissing, lifestyles (1950s-60s), medical, military, newsreel footage, outer space, people, personalities, races, rock and roll, romantic couples, science fiction, slapstick, trains, transportation, western, World War I and World War II.

Also available are acrobats, aerial shots, airplanes, aliens, American flags, capitols and monuments, armies, atomic explosions, babies, balancing acts, ballroom dancing, bands, banquets, baseball (players and stadiums), bathing beauties, bathroom scenes (shower and shaving), birthday parties, blimps, boats, boxing, brawls, broadcast studios, cattle drives, chase scenes, chorus lines, Christmas, cigars (exploding, smoking, etc.), Civil War, clocks, clouds, clowns, communications, cops and robbers, cotton pickers, countdowns, courtrooms, cowboys, dance contests, death scenes, detectives, diabolical characters, diners, dinosaurs, dogs (including tricks), dope (marijuana and cocaine), drag races, driving, drums, electrical charges, elevators, Ellis Island, explosions, eyes (closeups), fires, flames, fireworks, fist fights, Foreign Legion, funeral processions, gambling, gas stations, ghosts, glamour, golf, grooming, gunfights, horse racing, hospitals, hot rods, hotel lobbies, immigrants, Indians, invasions, island natives, jitterbugging, juke boxes, juvenile delinquents, kings and queens, laborers, lightning bolts, love scenes, lovers, marching, monsters, moons, musicians, mystics and mind readers, native girls, nerds, New York City, New Year's Eve, newspaper headlines with presses rolling, nightclubs, nude dancers (ca. 1920s), office scenes, oil wells, Olympics, orchestras, palm trees, parades, parties, photographers, piano players, pie fights, presidents, protests, puppets, radio announcers, rainstorms, records spinning, rescues, restaurants, robots, rock and roll fans, rockets, roller-skating, royalty, sail boats, schools, screens, secretaries, signs and slates, silhouettes, skiing, smokers, stampede, Statue of Liberty, steamships, strippers, surfing, swimming, switchboard operators, television sets and screens, technicians, telephones (and conversations), theaters, Times Square, traffic, U.S. landmarks, villagers dancing, violinists, volcano erupting and wrestling.
Size & Elements: Videotape: 1" (amount unspecified; masters, all transferred from film); 3/4" and 1/2" (amount unspecified; viewing copies).
Cataloging: Computerized cataloging for staff use only; shot lists.
Access: Open to the public. Available for licensing and reuse. Research fees charged. Research requests accepted by telephone.
Rights: Full rights held to all material. Some material in the public domain.
Licensing: Available for licensing and reuse. License and usage fees charged.
Restrictions: None specified.
Viewing Facilities: None.
Duplication Facilities: None.

CALIFORNIA (Los Angeles Metro)

FLYING A PICTURES INC.
5858 Sunset Boulevard
Los Angeles, CA 90028
(213) 460-6616
(213) 460-5678

Alex Gordon (Vice President)

Contact: Alex Gordon
Services: Film and videotape producer, distributor and archive; foundation and museum.
Description: Films and television programs featuring Gene Autry; material relating to the Gene Autry Film and Television Archives, Gene Autry Foundation and Gene Autry Western Heritage Museum; other Western movies (silent and sound) and stars (1920-present).
Size & Elements: Film: 35mm and 16mm ("several million" feet; approx. 300 titles; "several thousand" cans). Videotape: all formats ("several hundred" videotapes).
Cataloging: Staff assistance required.
Access: Not open to the public. Maintained for distribution and rental rather than for research or reuse. Research fees not charged. Research requests accepted by mail and telephone.
Rights: Full rights held to all material.
Licensing: Apply for information.
Restrictions: None specified.
Viewing Facilities: None.
Duplication Facilities: Film and videotape.

CALIFORNIA (Los Angeles Metro)

JAMES FORSHER PRODUCTIONS & ARCHIVES INC.
953 North Highland
Hollywood, CA 90038
(213) 465-9527

James Forsher (President)

Contact: Michael Yakaitis
Services: Film and videotape archives; producer; stock footage sales library.
Description: Begins pre-1900. Strengths of collection include: old Hollywood, stars of silent and sound motion pictures, locations around the globe, newsreels, historical events, world war, comedy, censorship, serial and weekly magazines, bloopers, Kodascopes, outtakes and film trailers.
Animals. A wide assortment of animals, including dogs, peacocks, unicorns and dinosaurs.
Celebrities. Includes Theodore Roosevelt, Franklin D. Roosevelt, John F. Kennedy, William Randolph Hearst, Howard Hughes, Thomas Edison, Albert Einstein, the Wright Brothers, Babe Ruth, Knute Rockne, Amelia Earhart and Charles Lindbergh.
Industries. Farming, automobile, assembly lines, mines, and steel.
Locations. American and foreign cities, urban and rural homes, hospitals, police stations, college campuses, schools, amusement parks, nightclubs, restaurants, stadiums, courtrooms, harbors, bridges, beaches, deserts, oceans, rivers, mountains, caves, tropical jungles and forests (all in a variety of seasons).

Moments and milestones. 1906 San Francisco earthquake, Ohio floods, World War I and World War II, Depression (1930s), flapper era, civil rights movement, KKK, McCarthy and anti-Communist scare, Vietnam and Korea, 1900s operetta, swing, jazz, bebop, blues and rock and roll; disasters and calamities.

Personalities. Includes Charles Chaplin, Keystone Kops, Three Stooges, W. C. Fields, Benito Mussolini and Marie Curie.

Transportation. Horses and buggies, bicycles, airplanes, balloons, buses, sailboats, yachts, warships, tanks, jeeps, helicopters and roller skates.

Work and play. Picnics, concerts, theater and film openings, baseball, football, dancing, politicians, police officers, lifeguards, car and motorcycle stunts.

Size & Elements: Film: 35mm and 16mm (250,000 feet, 300 titles; positives, negatives and prints). Videotape: 1" and 3/4" (4,000 titles).
Cataloging: Computerized cataloging available to researchers; research library.
Access: Available to the public for duplication, licensing and reuse. Requests accepted by mail, telephone and in person (by appointment only).
Rights: Full rights held to some material. Most material in the public domain. Additional clearances may be necessary in some cases if material is to be reused.
Licensing: Available for licensing and reuse. License and usage fees charged (fee schedule available).
Restrictions: None specified.
Viewing Facilities: Videotape.
Duplication Facilities: Videotape.

CALIFORNIA (Los Angeles Metro)

FREELAND PRESS
Box 26044
Santa Ana, CA 92799
(714) 979-5737
Fax: (714) 979-5739

Street address: 2727 South Croddy Way, Suite J, Santa Ana, CA 92704

Lawrence Samuels (Executive Director)

Contact: Lawrence Samuels
Services: Political organization. Videotapes available for purchase.
Description: Libertarian perspective on politics, philosophy, natural rights, Freeland projects, and liberty. Videotapes from annual Future of Freedom Conferences, an individualist/decentralist/libertarian convention (1984 and 1985).

Freeland II (1984). Videotapes from this conference include: *How to Achieve a New World of Privacy* (Barry Reid), including tactics to deal with the threat of computerized data files and discussion of alternate identities — a must for anyone who wants to remain as free as possible; *A Realist's Plan for Building a Free Community in Space* (Terry Savage), an outline of a proposed space community, with a target deadline of 2025; *Where to Find Liberty Today: The Best Places to Live* (William R. Pozzi), a discussion of the best way to select a freer place to live, based on criteria such as climate, male/female ratio and political aspects; *Liberty from the Pacific Rim to Space* (Gary Hudson), an historical discussion of culture, of China and Japan's influence on our present society, and space as the ultimate and unlimited frontier; *Space Law: Real Property Rights in Outer Space* (Wayne White), a detailed description of property rights as they are applied in space.

The Future of Freedom Conference (1985). Videotapes from this convention include: *Natural Rights* (debate of George Smith vs. David Ramsey Steele); *Guardian Angels: Vigilantes or Protectors* (Scott McKeown); *A Revolting Proposal* (Robert LeFevre); *Guerrilla Capitalism* (Barry Reid); *Tales of the Dark Side of Prohibition and the Stupidity of Government* (Jeff Riggenbach), about inconsistencies in FDA drug policies; *Tribute Honoring Karl Hess and the H. L. Mencken Awards; Why Deregulate Public Utilities?* (Robert Poole); *History of Conscription* (Jeff Hummell); *Liberty's Lifestyles* (Karl Hess); *Medical Crisis in Afghanistan* (Dr. Robert Simon); *From Marxism to Liberty* (David Ramsey Steele); *Statebuster's Contest: Evils of the State; From Cop to Call Girl* (Norma Jean Almodovar), about corruption in the Los Angeles Police Department; *Freedom Afloat* (Walt Patrick), focusing on the ocean as a real estate development, suggesting that a tanker or other ship can be a site for manufacturing, living, and playing; and *Imagining Free Futures* (Victor Koman, Mike Grossberg and Samuel E. Konkin, III), exploring underground economies, science fiction situations and fantasy novels.
Size & Elements: Videotape: VHS and Betamax (24 videotapes, each 60 min.).

Cataloging: Published list.
Access: Available to the public for purchase. Research fees charged. Research requests accepted by mail.
Rights: Full rights held to all material.
Licensing: Material possibly available for licensing and reuse. License and usage fees charged, depending on use.
Restrictions: None specified.
Viewing Facilities: None.
Duplication Facilities: Videotape (1/2").
Representative: Footage originally shot by Liberty Audio & Film, 824 West Broad Street, Richmond, VA 23220; (804) 788-7008. Other related materials are available.

CALIFORNIA (Los Angeles Metro)

BUCKMINSTER FULLER INSTITUTE
1743 South La Cienega Boulevard
Los Angeles, CA 90035
(213) 837-7710

John Ferry (Operations Manager)

Contact: John Ferry
Services: Institute and information clearinghouse. One videotape available for purchase; archival films available for research, licensing and reuse on a case-by-case basis, subject to approval.
Description: The wacky scientific world of engineer, inventor, mathematician, architect, cartographer, philosopher, cosmologist, environmentalist, humanitarian, teacher, and genius Buckminster Fuller on videotape and film.

In 1975 Bucky Fuller said, "I can tell you everything I know in 40 to 50 hours." The result of that statement was 42 hours of film entitled *Everything I Know*, an extraordinary series of 12 consecutive "thinking out loud" sessions over a two-week period. In this series, which is partly autobiographical, he recounts his own personal history in the context of human evolution on Spaceship Earth. These sessions were recorded on videotape and audiotape at Bell Laboratories' studios.

Other footage held includes material on Fuller and his work (1950s-present). *The World of Buckminster Fuller* (Robert Snyder, 85 min.), a documentary that has been described as "the definitive, synthesized lecture by one of the great teachers and minds of our time, transcribed in sight and sound for the archives of posterity." Includes footage of the Dymaxion Car, Dymaxion House, the Expo dome and Fuller at his summer home in Maine.
Size & Elements: Film: 16mm. Videotape: 2", 1", 3/4" and VHS (approx. 100 hours total).
Cataloging: Published catalogs; detailed log of the *Everything I Know* sessions.
Access: Videotapes available to the public for purchase. Archival footage available for viewing by researchers and scholars. Research requests accepted by mail and telephone.
Rights: Full rights held to all material.
Licensing: Available for licensing and reuse, subject to restrictions. License fees charged.
Restrictions: Requests for reuse considered on a case-by-case basis.
Viewing Facilities: None.
Duplication Facilities: Videotape (3/4" to VHS).
Related Materials: Audiocassettes.

CALIFORNIA (Los Angeles Metro)

GAY MEDIA TASK FORCE
2172 Moreno Drive
Los Angeles, CA 90039
(213) 464-1376

Newton E. Deiter (Director)

Contact: Newton E. Deiter
Services: Media organization; image consulting service. Videotape collection available for in-house research only.
Description: Consultant to producers of television shows and motion pictures portraying lesbians and gay men. Collection includes videotapes of productions which have consulted with GMTF in creating gay or lesbian images and portrayals, whether positive or negative.

Titles of productions held include: *Gay* (an NBC documentary); *Medical Center*; *Baretta*; *The Users*; *Today's Gays on TV*; *Lou Grant*; *Just Friends*;

NYPD; *Dynasty* (20 episodes); *A Very Natural Thing*; and *Is School Out for Gays?*
Size & Elements: Videotape: 3/4" (82 titles, 164 hours; many videotapes include several parts or episodes).
Cataloging: Printed list.
Access: Available to the public for research. For in-house use only.
Rights: No rights held to any material.
Licensing: Material not available for duplication or reuse.
Restrictions: Material not available for duplication or reuse.
Viewing Facilities: Videotape (3/4").
Duplication Facilities: None.

CALIFORNIA (Los Angeles Metro)

GOAL PRODUCTIONS, INC.
TOURNAMENT OF ROSES FILM LIBRARY
2027 North Lake Avenue
Altadena, CA 91001
(818) 797-7668
Fax: (818) 797-7591

Jack Oswald (President)

Contacts: John Gura (Vice President); Rhonda Reyer (Production Assistant)
Services: Film and videotape producer; stock footage sales library.
Description: *Tournament of Roses Film Library.* Tournament of Roses parades (1898-present) and Rose Bowl football games (1916 and 1930-present); mostly highlights. Game footage includes some sideline, half time and crowd scenes. Some years of both the parades and the games are not available or are only partially covered.

Goal Productions footage. Hot-air ballooning in California, Austria, France and Switzerland; vineyards in California and France; and wine production, including labelling, bottling, corking and foil, crush and aging.
Size & Elements: Film: 16mm (amount unspecified). Videotape: Betacam and 3/4" (amount unspecified).
Cataloging: Computerized cataloging for staff use only.
Access: For in-house use only. Available for licensing and reuse. Research fees charged. Research requests accepted by mail, telephone and in person (by appointment only).
Rights: Full rights held to material produced by Goal Productions. Additional clearances may be necessary in some cases (Tournament of Roses Film Library) if material is to be reused.
Licensing: Available for licensing and reuse, subject to restrictions. License fees charged.
Restrictions: Requests for licensing subject to acceptance and approval.
Viewing Facilities: Film and videotape.
Duplication Facilities: Videotape.

CALIFORNIA (Los Angeles Metro)

GOETHE INSTITUTE LOS ANGELES
8501 Wilshire Boulevard, Suite 205
Beverly Hills, CA 90211
(213) 854-0993
Telex: 65031487068

Reinhard Dinkelmeyer (Director)

Contact: Marje Schuetze-Coburn (Librarian)
Services: Educational institution; library. Film and videotape collection maintained primarily for teaching and research purposes.
Description: German life and culture. Materials include serials on Germany, language instruction films, art, music, feature films, theater, dance, literature, authors, cities and regions of the Federal Republic, history, humor, and youth films.
Size & Elements: Film: mostly 16mm (8 films). Videotape: 3/4" (PAL and NTSC); VHS (PAL and NTSC) (approx. 220 titles, approx. 430 videotapes).
Cataloging: Published catalogs; computerized cataloging for staff use only.
Access: Open to the public. Research fees not charged. Research requests accepted by mail, telephone and in person (walk-in). Available for loan by written request for non-commercial purposes.
Rights: Apply for information.
Licensing: Apply for information.
Restrictions: It is illegal to copy any material borrowed from the Institute.
Viewing Facilities: Film (16mm projectors); videotape (3/4" and VHS; PAL,

SECAM and NTSC).
Duplication Facilities: Videotape.

CALIFORNIA (Los Angeles Metro)

THE SAMUEL GOLDWYN COMPANY
10203 Santa Monica Boulevard
Los Angeles, CA 90067
(213) 552-2255

Services: Motion picture producer and distributor.

CALIFORNIA (Los Angeles Metro)

GORNICK FILM PRODUCTIONS
4200 Camino Real
Los Angeles, CA 90065
(213) 223-8914

Contact: Al Gornick
Services: Film producer; photographer. Footage available for licensing and reuse.
Description: Underwater footage (1966-present), specializing in macro-cinematography (undersea substrata, tiny sea life, cherry anemones, etc.). Primarily shoots off the California coast and the Channel Islands, frequently documenting the research work of marine biologists. Other specialties include underwater wrecks and kelp ledges. Footage includes spherical and anamorphic film. Gornick is an IATSE signatory and director of photography for major motion picture film studios.
Size & Elements: Film: 35mm and 16mm (30,000 feet).
Cataloging: Computerized cataloging (for staff use only).
Access: Available for licensing and reuse. Research fees charged. Research requests accepted by mail and telephone. Workprints furnished to qualified clients.
Rights: Full rights held to all material.
Licensing: Available for licensing and reuse. License fees charged.
Restrictions: None specified.
Viewing Facilities: None.
Duplication Facilities: None.
Related Materials: Stock library of 40,000 still photographs.

CALIFORNIA (Los Angeles Metro)

GREAT AMERICAN STOCK
420 Bond Street
Redlands, CA 92373
(714) 793-1903
Fax: (714) 798-2896

Susan Haven Scheer (President)

Contacts: Susan Haven Scheer; Dee Ann Dart
Services: Film and videotape producer; private film and videotape collection. Material available for licensing and reuse on a case-by-case basis. Film and script research services available.
Description: Military, historical, newsreel and space stock footage (1940s-80s). Since footage is still being cataloged, its exact contents are not currently known.
Size & Elements: Film: 16mm (60,000 feet). Videotape: 3/4" (40 hours).
Cataloging: Computerized cataloging for staff use only. Most material has not yet been cataloged.
Access: Research fees charged. Research requests accepted by mail and telephone.
Rights: Apply for information.
Licensing: Available for licensing and reuse, subject to restrictions. License fees charged in some cases.
Restrictions: Requests for reuse considered on a case-by-case basis.
Viewing Facilities: None. Some 1/2" videotapes with visible time code are available for loan.
Duplication Facilities: None.
Please see the Research and Resources *section for further information on Great American Stock.*

CALIFORNIA (Los Angeles Metro)

GREAT WAVES/DELANEY FILMS
483 Mariposa Drive
Ventura, CA 93001
(805) 653-2699

Contact: Bill Delaney
Services: Film and videotape stock footage sales library.
Description: Contemporary ocean scenes, waves, surfing and windsurfing.
Size & Elements: Film: 16mm (20,000 feet). Videotape: 1", Betacam and 3/4" (15 hours; masters and film transfers).
Cataloging: Research library.
Access: Available for licensing and reuse. Research fees charged. Research requests accepted by telephone.
Rights: Full rights held to all material.
Licensing: Available for licensing and reuse. License fees charged.
Restrictions: None specified.
Viewing Facilities: Film (16mm); videotape (3/4").
Duplication Facilities: None.

CALIFORNIA (Los Angeles Metro)

SHERMAN GRINBERG FILM LIBRARIES, INC. (WEST)
1040 North McCadden Place
Hollywood, CA 90038-2486
(213) 464-7491
Fax: (213) 462-5352
Telex: 269950 SGFL LA

Linda Grinberg (Vice President)

Contacts: Bill Brewington (Librarian); Linda Grinberg (Librarian)
Services: Film and videotape stock footage sales library. See also Sherman Grinberg Film Libraries, Inc. (East).
Description: Represents film and videotape produced for ABC's *World News Tonight;* Paramount and Pathé Newsreels; production outtakes from just about every feature and television show ever produced by MGM, 20th Century-Fox, Allied Artists, HBO and ITC; stock footage from WGBH's *Nova;* Public Broadcasting Associates' *Odyssey;* ABC's *American Sportsman;* BBC Enterprises' *Wildstock* collection and a number of smaller collections.
Founded in 1957, Grinberg has offices in Hollywood and New York. One of the largest stock film collections in the country, the Grinberg library has supplied footage to many features, television shows, commercials, and documentaries. Woody Allen's *Zelig* production purchased nearly an hour's worth of material; *Midway* with Gregory Peck incorporated stock footage into the film's battle sequences. The television serials *The Fall Guy* and *Airwolf* each used stunt material from the production outtakes. Grinberg was the source of clips of the Concorde used in *Airplane* and the soaring clouds backdrop against which Superman flew in the original *Superman* movie.
The collection is physically divided between the offices on the East and West coasts, but research prior to screening can be done at either branch. For instance, while the studio production outtakes are stored in Hollywood, some production guides are available in New York. Similarly, while the ABC collection is physically in New York, there is an ABC computer terminal in the West Coast office.
Following are the major collections held in the Hollywood office:
Production outtakes. Grinberg (West) represents for stock footage sale the production outtakes from MGM, 20th Century-Fox, Allied Artists, HBO and ITC studios. Outtakes from all feature films and television shows are held. All outtakes used for stock footage are generic shots; recognizable performers never appear, for complex reasons relating to payments, copyrights and royalties. Frequently requested shots include exploding buildings, Western saloons, lightning and airplanes landing. The MGM and Fox outtakes date back to the silent film era, and material from nearly every one of their films is available. Production outtakes are often used in music videos, commercials, television shows and features. For example, if a producer wishes to recreate the flavor of Dust Bowl Oklahoma, he or she can investigate the hundreds of listings from *The Grapes of Wrath,* John Ford's 1940 film starring Henry Fonda. A sample description might read, "Shooting to highway — large truck parked by cafe — light traffic in b.g."
Frequently requested material such as footage of New York City, Paris and Rio de Janeiro street scenes and car stunts has been assembled into rolls, which are separated by studio (one each for Fox and MGM). Otherwise, the outtakes are on separate rolls, each one scene measuring generally 50 to 60 feet. All outtakes are 35mm negative and one-light workprint. The collection is accessed through typewritten production books, one set for the black and white material,

another for color (see Cataloging).

Pathé Newsreel. The Pathé Newsreel is the oldest American newsreel (1912-mid-1957). A small amount of material in the collection dates from 1896, some acquired from the Pathé's older foreign branches and the rest from outside sources. All material is 35mm negative; fine grain masters available on some rolls. Outtakes and unused material, as well as the edited newsreel issues, comprise the collection's 24 million feet.

Pathé covers all the major newsworthy and human interest stories during its period. Like the other major newsreels, the Pathé newsreel was produced in New York City and appeared in cinemas twice a week. Each issue was approximately 7-1/2 to 9 minutes in length.

Greatest Headlines of the Century (260 shorts, each 5 min.) were produced by Grinberg for syndication using material from the Pathé collection. Most of the main events of this century through 1960 are covered. These are available for viewing on 16mm and 3/4" videotape at the library.

The Pathé Short Subjects. In addition to the theatrical newsreel, Pathé News, Inc. produced a number of one- and two-reel short subjects. Written and produced by Robert Youngson, these are often referred to as the "Youngson shorts." Made from the original Pathé newsreel material, two of these shorts won Academy Awards, and three others received nominations. The Award winners, *This Mechanical Age* and *The World of Kids* have been sources of stock footage for many films. *This Mechanical Age* is a hilarious saga of flight; a review of crackpot inventions from the Parasol plane invented by the "Wrong" brothers to every conceivable kind of strange gadget and invention. Grinberg licenses clips only (as opposed to complete reels) from these subjects. (See end of this entry for list of Pathé short subjects.)

BBC Enterprises' Wildstock. This comprehensive natural history and wildlife collection is Grinberg's most recent addition. Printed catalogs and viewing videotapes are available in both the Hollywood and New York offices.

Miscellaneous newsreel collections. Other smaller collections include the Blackton collection, one of the library's "oddball" newsreel collections. This and other miscellaneous newsreel material are cataloged in a book which is organized by decade.

Industry on Parade. Industrial and promotional films (1940s-50s).

Caltex Petroleum. Footage of the Middle East.

Dickason Collection. The Dickasons were a husband/wife team who filmed such exotic subjects as tiger hunts in India.

David Frost interviews. Twenty-two hours of the Nixon interview from just after his resignation (1974), as well as the recently deposed Shah of Iran (1979).

Additionally, Grinberg represents the footage of some 50 filmmakers for stock sale.

Size & Elements: Film: 35mm and 16mm. Videotape: 1" and 3/4". Some material is available on both film and videotape. Some "highlight cassettes" are available, containing frequently requested material.

All studio production outtakes (approx. 200 million feet) are 35mm; negative and one-light workprint is available. Frequently requested material has been compiled into assembly rolls.

The Pathé newsreel collection contains approximately 24 million feet of 35mm black and white negative; positive fine grain masters are available on some rolls. Pre-1951 material is generally on nitrate-base film.

Greatest Headlines of the Century is available on 16mm, 35mm fine grain backing and videotape.

There are 38 Pathé short subjects, all 35mm one- or two-reel films.

Cataloging: All production outtakes are cataloged in typewritten books. One series details black and white material in one area of the library, another (93 volumes) describes color material. The black and white books catalog material from MGM and 20th Century-Fox separately; in the color catalog, all production facilities are cataloged together. Each set is extensively cross-referenced.

The catalog books are arranged into general subject areas as follows: miscellaneous subjects (arranged alphabetically), agriculture, amusement and recreation, animal kingdom, aviation, boats and ships, buildings, countries, industries and occupations, military, World War II, people, period, police, railroads, scenics, science fiction, sports, states, western, vehicles, moving process and stationary process.

The individual entries in the books give a brief description of the scene, indicate from which production it is taken, name the director, and provide key numbers, file numbers and footage counts. Some entries have a frame from the scene itself affixed to the sheet for reference.

The Pathé newsreel collection has a card catalog which is arranged by personality, chronology, geography and miscellaneous subjects. The collection is also accessed by roll number. There is a printed list with descriptions of all the Pathé short subjects.

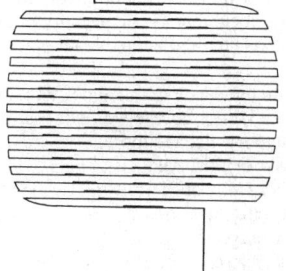

CALIFORNIA (Los Angeles Metro G)

Stock footage from the miscellaneous smaller collections described above has been incorporated into the production books which cover the studio material.

An ABC computer terminal is available for use by researchers, although the ABC News collection is physically located at Grinberg (East) in New York, N.Y.

Access: Open to producers, film researchers, and other bona fide stock footage users. Available for duplication, licensing and reuse. Hourly research fees charged for card and computer searches and for screening time (2-hour minimum). Research requests accepted by mail, telephone and in person.

The library recommends that, whenever possible, customers arrange to do their own research, as experience has proven that stock footage is a very subjective matter. The Grinberg librarians can do small amounts of very specific research or pre-screening research for clients. Librarians can also refer clients to experienced, local researchers who are familiar with the collection. Within the Los Angeles area, viewing prints may be borrowed to be screened at the client's production facility. Library material is not to be shipped out of town.

Experienced librarians are available to assist clients in finding their way through the collection. Library services are charged for by the hour with a two-hour minimum. It is necessary to make an appointment for computer and screening time as facilities are limited and sometimes heavily booked.

If required, the library will supply black and white contact reversal or color scratch prints at customer's expense. A minimum non-refundable service fee, applicable to final usage, will be charged.

Rights: Footage supplied is without representation or warranties other than that of title. The licensee shall be solely responsible for obtaining any and all necessary legal clearances or waivers.

Licensing: Available for licensing, subject to restrictions. Footage furnished is authorized for non-exclusive use only in the production specified on client's purchase order and library Licensing Agreement, and for that one production only. Footage may not be sold, rented, licensed, reused or recut into any other production. Material is not purchased from the Sherman Grinberg Film Libraries, Inc.; rather, a limited usage license is granted. Film is not authorized for use until a signed copy of the contract is returned to the library and is fully paid for.

License fees are determined by the amount of footage used and the rights required by the client. A rate card is available from the library. There is an overall minimum charge. When an order is placed for any film or videotape duplication, an advance against final usage is required. This deposit is in addition to the actual duplication costs. It is deductible from any final license fees, but is non-refundable in the event of non-use. All laboratory and transfer charges, shipping costs, wires, messengers, phone calls, photocopies, etc. will be paid by the customer. A copy of the completed production will be made available to the library if requested.

The rates for footage or videotape of "high production value" are slightly higher than the posted rate. In addition, there are special rates for use of process footage, main titles, and ancillary uses of stock in markets such as pay and cable television and homevideo cassette and disc.

Restrictions: It is important to understand the studios' policy with respect to licensing stock footage from any one particular production. The studios do not wish to license footage that can be identified as stock from any specific theatrical feature, without prior consent. Therefore, Grinberg reserves the right to limit the amount of stock licensed from any one particular production so that it cannot be identified. Under no circumstances will the studio permit any form of publicity which identifies the stock used with the name of the studio or the title of the picture. Use of any likenesses of principal actors or actresses in stock film is strictly prohibited.

Viewing Facilities: Film (35mm and 16mm); videotape (3/4").

Duplication Facilities: Arranged through outside facilities.

Duplication Procedure: It is most practical and economical to order work elements first (i.e., scratch prints or videotapes with exposed time codes). At this time an advance against final usage is required. All laboratory work must be paid for on a COD basis. After the edit, the client makes an order for masters. At this time the license fee is computed and the advance deducted. If it is decided that the work elements and masters are to be made at the same time, the client should expect the library to retain the master and release only the work elements. The masters are held until the final edit. The client then supplies the time codes or edge numbers and the library will supply the corresponding masters. The amount of footage released is based upon the footage report.

Customers should note that there is a per cut minimum which is 10 feet in 35mm and 4 feet in 16mm. Both of these are equivalent to 6.66 seconds running time. Customers should be aware that when a print is made from the library master for transfer to videotape, the print becomes the property of the library and must be returned following the transfer. All unused, unlicensed material must be returned to the library.

16mm customers should be aware that it is strictly prohibited to make a direct reduction from the 35mm nitrate negative. The library requires making a 35mm contact element first, from which the reduction will be made. These safety elements are then to be retained by the library.

No film or videotape is to be submitted directly by the customer to a laboratory or videotape transfer house for duplication without the written authorization of the library to that facility.

Pathé Short Subjects

Animals Have All the Fun. "Here the Animal Kingdom comes into its own. Not a human in sight."

A-Speed on the Deep. "This film recaptures the thrills of wind-blown sailing contests, surfboard riding, crew racing, shooting the rapids, motorboat racing, water skiing, and the never ending battle to skim over water at greater and greater speeds."

Batter Up. "Relive the excitement of baseball's golden age." With John McGraw, Babe Ruth, Tris Speaker, Kenesaw Mountain Landis, Lou Gehrig, Connie Mack, Carl Hubbell and Enos Slaughter.

Blaze Busters. "Gallant smoke eaters battle the fury of: a large building fire, the Morro Castle, the fabulous Normandie flaming in her berth, a Chicago grain holocaust, an oil field inferno, a raging forest fire."

Camera Hunting. With Florida's Everglades, mechanical miracles, how the Indians made the desert bloom, and the life and work of Thomas Alva Edison.

Cavalcade of Girls. "Girls — Girls — Girls — Well padded and corseted women in New York's Easter Parade in 1903. Women workers in World War I — Suffragettes, flappers of the 20s — girls of the turbulent thirties, fateful forties, and present day fantastic females — BLESS 'EM."

Daredevil Days. "Starting with the end of the First World War, a new era began. Crazy stunts of the 1920s, human flies, super strongmen, aerial stuntmen and barnstormers. The world was a carefree, mad, whirling, twirling, topsy-turvy place back in the Daredevil Days."

Disaster Fighters. "Here is a saga of the battle of man against storms."

Faster and Faster. Depicts the most exciting thrills and spills of boat racing from 1907 until today.

Fire, Wind and Flood. "In some of the most chilling scenes ever recorded, we witness the forces of nature on a rampage..."

Football Magic. "From the grime and sweat of the training field, on to professional football where they play rough! Next we see highlights of college and high school games..."

Gadgets Galore. "Here is the story of the once-fearsome monster, the automobile..."

The Glory Around Us. "Our world is full of glorious sights: glory of the plant world, the beauty beneath the sea, the wonders of the bird world, the fun of the Animal Kingdom, the splendor of Siam, the majestic falls of Yosemite." (2 reels)

Head Over Heels. "This is the story of the skier and bobsled enthusiast, as only the motion picture can record it. Plenty of spills, but we guarantee the spills won't hurt *you* a bit."

Horsehide Heroes. Baseball. With Rogers Hornsby, Jimmy Foxx, Ted Williams, Christy Mathewson, Ty Cobb, Honus Wagner, Pepper Martin, "Joltin' Joe" Di Maggio. Farewell speeches of "Iron Man" Gehrig and the "Bambino" Babe Ruth.

I Remember When. "From the Gay 90s, to the Twitching 20s. Lillian Russell, Buffalo Bill, Orville and Wilbur Wright, the San Francisco earthquake, Teddy Roosevelt, the Ohio Floods, fashions of the era, William Jennings Bryan."

It Happened To You. The story of America's participation in World War I.

Lighter Than Air. "An exciting filmed documentary on the story of the dirigibles, from the beginning of balloons to the flaming death of the *Hindenburg*..."

Looking At Life. "This film delves into the past, present and future: explosions on the face of the Sun, a rocket ride 135 miles up, the world beneath the earth, a miniature city, the coming of the automobile, and more."

No Adults Allowed. "This picture is about kids. All kind of kids."

The Picture Parade. Includes Oregon's Halls of Marble, the Castle in the Desert, Miniature Miniatures, and Animals in Closeup.

Pigskin Passes. With Harold "Red" Grange and Knute Rockne.

Roaring Wheels. "Starting with the Vanderbilt Cup Race of 1906, we see a half-century of the most thrilling races ever captured on film."

Say It With Spills. "This film is dedicated to those individuals who earn their living by risking their necks and their nerves. What happens in this film, shouldn't."

Shoot the Basket. Basketball thrills.

Ski Devils. "Whether you thrill to riding the wind on a magic carpet of hickory or not, this film will provide a never to be forgotten experience of watching those that do."

Spills and Chills. "An epic about barnstormers, those men and women who bet their limbs and lives on their own coordination and the infallibility of a throbbing machine." *The Swim Parade.* With Johnny Weismuller, Gertrude Ederle, Elinor Holm, and the Olympic Divers.

They Were Champions. Boxing's greats. With Johnson, Willard, Dempsey, Tunney, Baer, Carnera, Louis, Marciano, Walcott and Charles.

They're Off. Horse racing. Includes Man O'War vs. Sir Barton, War Admiral vs. Seabiscuit, Alsab vs. Whirlaway, The Kentucky Derby and England's Grand National. *This Mechanical Age.* "This Academy Award winner is a hilarious saga of flight. A review of crackpot inventions — starting from the Parasol Plane invented by the Wrong Brothers — to every conceivable strange-looking gadget from the minds of inventors who hoped to enhance *This Mechanical Age.*"

This Was Yesterday. "Historic motion pictures tell the exciting and interesting story of America during the fateful years before our entry into World War I."

Those Exciting Days. "The first three years of World War I, prior to America's entry. Scenes shown in this film for the first time in forty-five years! Nicholas, Czar of all the Russias, and his family, Kaiser Wilhelm, Franz Wilhelm, Lenin, Trotsky and many more..."

Through the Camera's Eye. "This film deals with three different worlds: the everyday world we know, the hidden world of microscopic life and the limitless world of outer space where our own earth is merely a speck among the stars."

Too Much Speed. "This is a tale of wheels that whirl too fast. Races featuring bicycles, motorcycles, autos, midget autos, and finally stock car races."

When Sports Were King. "Relive the period of Sportsdom's Golden Age. See the fabulous leaders of every branch of the sports world starting with the end of World War I."

The World of Kids. "Here's a film about kids. All kinds of kids. Beware! If you give them half a chance they'll take you back — back to the time when you belonged to *The World of Kids.*"

The preceding article was researched and written by Lewanne Jones, a film researcher working in New York City.

CALIFORNIA (Los Angeles Metro)

H. B. HALICKI PRODUCTIONS

P.O. Box 2123
Gardena, CA 90247
(213) 770-1744
(213) 327-1744
Fax: (213) 719-1990
Telex: 3786008 HBH

Street address: 17902 South Vermont Avenue, Gardena, CA 90248

Toby Halicki (Owner)

Contact: Toby Halicki
Services: Film and videotape stock footage sales library.
Description: Specializes in action footage. Holds all types of vehicles, auto stunts, chase scenes, explosions, point-of-view driving shots, city scenes, and stock shots of the sun and moon.
Size & Elements: Film: 35mm (300,000 feet). Videotape: 2", 1" and 3/4" (50,000 feet) (all elements available).
Cataloging: Research library.
Access: Available for licensing and reuse. Not open to the public. Research fees generally not charged. Research requests accepted by telephone and in person (by appointment only).
Rights: Full rights held to all material.
Licensing: Available for licensing and reuse. License fees charged.
Restrictions: None specified.
Viewing Facilities: Videotape.
Duplication Facilities: None.

CALIFORNIA (Los Angeles Metro)

ARMAND HAMMER PRODUCTIONS

10889 Wilshire Boulevard, Suite 970
Los Angeles, CA 90024
(213) 443-6155

Telex: 19-4970

Derek Hart (Executive Producer)

Contacts: Robert Bogdanoff (Post-Production Supervisor); David Fanti (Assistant Post-Production Supervisor)
Services: Corporation and corporate archives; film and videotape producer. Footage available for licensing and reuse, subject to restrictions.
Description: Film and videotape footage chronicling the life and activities of Dr. Armand Hammer and Occidental Petroleum. Also holds street scenes from around the world, including China, Pakistan, the Soviet Union, Colombia, Peru and Swaziland; footage of on- and offshore oil drilling operations in the United States, Peru, Colombia, Pakistan and the North Sea; footage of heavy industry, including chemical plant operations and pipeline construction; footage of Arabian horses and Arabian horse auctions; and footage documenting Dr. Hammer's art collection, its travels, and openings at museums around the world, including Beijing and Mexico City.
Size & Elements: Film: 16mm (approx. 50,000 to 350,000 feet; 98% color negative original, 2% color reversal original). Videotape: 1", Betacam and 3/4" (amount unspecified; masters and viewing copies). Approximately 25% of original negative has been transferred to videotape.
Cataloging: Computerized cataloging available to researchers; shot lists.
Access: Available for licensing and reuse, subject to restrictions. Research requests accepted by mail and telephone.
Rights: Full rights held to all material. Additional clearances may be necessary in some cases if material is to be reused.
Licensing: Available for licensing and reuse, subject to restrictions. License fees charged (fee schedule available).
Restrictions: Requests for reuse considered on a case-by-case basis, depending on intended use.
Viewing Facilities: Film (16mm Steenbeck flatbeds); videotape (Betacam, 3/4" and 1/2").
Duplication Facilities: Videotape (Betacam, 3/4", VHS and Betamax).

CALIFORNIA (Los Angeles Metro)

HANDEL FILM CORPORATION

8730 Sunset Boulevard, Suite 420
Los Angeles, CA 90069
(213) 657-8990

In Canada:
OMEGA FILMS LIMITED

70 Milner Avenue, Unit 5A
Scarborough, ON M1S 3P8

Contact: John McAlister
Services: Film and videotape producer and distributor. Materials available to the public for preview, rental and purchase.
Description: Primary school to adult programming. Topics include: art; career and guidance; environment; foreign language and captioned versions; health and safety; language arts; science and mathematics; social studies; American personalities; civics; map skills; discovery of America; nutrition; historical events; multicultural topics; presidents; U.S. and world geography.

Sample titles include: *The American Indian: Before the White Man* and *After the White Man*, narrated by Iron Eyes Cody; *Black American Odyssey; Map Reading; The Last of the Mayas; Food from A to Z Series; James Monroe: The Man and the Doctrine; Edgar Allan Poe: The Fever Called Living; Thomas Alva Edison: The Wizard of Menlo Park; Wagons West*, narrated by Will Geer; *A Light Beam Named Ray* (animated); *School Lab Safety; How to Make a Solar Heater; Moped Safety; Safety for Seniors; The Common Cold*, developed with the American Lung Association; *Art in America Series; The Magic of the Atom Series; Drop Out Now, Pay Later;* and *Police Dog.*
Size & Elements: Film: 16mm (release prints). Videotape: 3/4", VHS and Betamax. (Approx. 90 titles total).
Cataloging: Published catalog.
Access: Available to the public for preview, rental and purchase. Requests accepted by mail and telephone. Many titles also available for rental from several university media centers (apply for information).
Rights: Apply for information.
Licensing: Apply for information.
Restrictions: Material may not be transmitted by television, closed-circuit television, cable television or other devices or processes, nor copied or transferred or adapted in any manner in whole or in part without prior written

consent from Handel Film Corporation.
Viewing Facilities: None.
Duplication Facilities: None.

CALIFORNIA (Los Angeles Metro)

ALFRED HIGGINS PRODUCTIONS, INC.
6350 Laurel Canyon Boulevard
North Hollywood, CA 91606
(818) 762-3300

Alfred Higgins (President)

Contacts: Audrey Plant (Assistant to the President); Antoinette Montegrande (Sales Manager)
Services: Educational film and videotape producer. Material available for rental, purchase and, in some cases, television broadcast.
Description: Educational materials geared to elementary through high-school levels. Subjects include language arts, learning responsibility, social studies, mathematics, environment, safety, consumerism, science, health, nutrition, guidance, and the *Harv and Marv* health and safety film series.
   Sample titles include: *Study Skills: Note-Taking and Outlining; Newspapers: A Reading Adventure; The Good Manners Game; The Supermarket,* a behind-the-scenes look at the many people it takes to run a supermarket; *Where Does Food Come From?,* in which animated talking food items trace their journey to the kitchen; *The Litter Monster; Vandalism— Why?; Read the Label—and Live!; To a Babysitter; Soap, Scents, and the Hard, Hard Sell; What's So Bad About Drugs?; Smokeless Tobacco: It Can Snuff You Out; Scott Goes to the Hospital; Build a Better Bag Lunch; Posture Perfect with Harv and Marv; Sex Myths and Facts;* and *Teenage Parents: Their Lives Have Changed.*
Size & Elements: Film: 16mm (release prints). Videotape: 3/4" and 1/2" (transfers from film). (Approx. 85 titles total).
Cataloging: Published catalog.
Access: Available to the public for rental and purchase. Rental fees charged. Rental or preview-to-buy requests accepted by mail.
Rights: Full rights held to all material.
Licensing: Television broadcasting rights possibly available (apply for information).
Restrictions: Copyright restrictions apply. Duplication rights not included with sale or rental.
Viewing Facilities: None.
Duplication Facilities: None.
Related Materials: Study guides.
Representatives: Local sales representatives (apply for information).

CALIFORNIA (Los Angeles Metro)

HISTORIC THOROUGHBRED COLLECTIONS, INC.
P.O. Box 966
Sierra Madre, CA 91024
(818) 355-4361

Street address: 35 Monterey Lane

Joseph W. Burnham (President)

Contact: Joseph W. Burnham
Services: Film producer. Film and videotape available for licensing and reuse, subject to restrictions.
Description: Thoroughbred horse racing, including footage of almost all great horses, riders, and trainers of the past 50 years. Historic races photographed at many racetracks, including Aqueduct, Bay Meadows, Belmont Park, Churchill Downs, Del Mar, Delaware Park, Golden Gate, Hollywood Park, Keeneland, Monmouth Park, Oaklawn Park, Pimlico, Santa Anita, Saratoga and Sunland Park. Also holds exclusive Kentucky Derby coverage (1958-86). Although the emphasis of the collection is West Coast racing, it contains historic newsreel footage of many races elsewhere in the U.S. and exclusive films of many other historic events relating to thoroughbred racing.
   Also held are the only complete films of Secretariat running in the Triple Crown (1973); coverage of all Triple Crown winners through Affirmed in 1978; public relations films for many racetracks; personal films of famous horses (many of which have been transferred to videotape and can be purchased for research).
   In Pursuit of Greatness (1987, 60 min., videotape), co-produced with

Santa Anita Racetrack, covering 50 years of Santa Anita Handicap history. *Thoroughbred Horses* and other homevideo tapes are available for purchase.
   Has provided stock racing film to Hollywood studios, television producers and corporations for racing-related projects. Produced the annual ECLIPSE Award show (1971-87).
Size & Elements: Film: 35mm (amount unspecified; historic black and white material); 16mm (300,000 feet, Ektachrome color reversal original; 10,000 feet, black and white). Videotape: 3/4" (transfers from film).
Cataloging: Card catalogs; shot lists.
Access: Available to the public for licensing and reuse. Research fees charged in some cases. Research requests accepted by mail, telephone and in person (by appointment only).
Rights: Full rights held to all material. Additional clearances may be necessary in some cases if material is to be reused.
Licensing: Available for licensing and reuse. License fees charged.
Restrictions: Not available to projects damaging to thoroughbred racing.
Viewing Facilities: Film and videotape.
Duplication Facilities: None.

CALIFORNIA (Los Angeles Metro)

THE IMAGE BANK WEST, LOS ANGELES
8228 Sunset Boulevard, Suite 310
Los Angeles, CA 90046
(213) 656-9003
Fax: (213) 656-2726

Contact: Lilly Filipow
Territory: Alaska, Arizona, California, Colorado, Hawaii, Idaho, Montana, Nevada, Oregon, Utah, Washington and Wyoming.
Services: Exclusive marketing agent for Film Search, Inc. (q.v.).

CALIFORNIA (Los Angeles Metro)

INSTITUTE FOR HISTORICAL REVIEW
1822 1/2 Newport Boulevard, Suite 191
Costa Mesa, CA 92627
(714) 631-1490

Contact: Steve Scott
Services: Political organization. Videotapes available for purchase.
Description: "Revisionist history" videotapes relating to World War II, including: *Tour of Auschwitz Fakes,* "the undeniable proof that something is terribly wrong with the Establishment claims about Auschwitz"; *Epic: The Story of the Waffen SS,* "an unapologetic and moving memoir of the history, philosophy and ideals of the unprecedented, all-volunteer, pan-European fighting force"; and *Thies Christophersen,* in which a German agronomist "...refutes the wildly exaggerated tales of smoking furnaces and death-dealing poison gas chambers." These titles indicate the nature of the collection, which also includes a German version of the Polish conflict which precipitated World War II, a German film with English subtitles presenting "a dismal picture of the Soviet paradise," and various other versions of historic events.
Size & Elements: Videotape: VHS and Betamax (19 titles total).
Cataloging: Published list.
Access: Available to the public for purchase. Requests accepted by mail.
Rights: Apply for information.
Licensing: Apply for information.
Restrictions: None specified.
Viewing Facilities: None.
Duplication Facilities: None.

CALIFORNIA (Los Angeles Metro)

THE INSTITUTE OF THE AMERICAN MUSICAL, INC.
121 North Detroit Street
Los Angeles, CA 90036
(213) 934-1221

Miles M. Kreuger (President)

Contact: Miles M. Kreuger
Services: Historical society; archival film collection. Material for in-house research use only. *Not available for duplication, licensing or reuse under any circumstances.*
Description: World's largest collection of documentation relating to the history

of the American musical theater. The primary archival holding is a unique 16mm silent film collection of short segments from 175 Broadway musicals, filmed by Ray Knight (1931-75) during actual performances of virtually every Broadway show. Productions filmed include: Ethel Merman musicals (beginning with her third show); Gene Kelly in *Pal Joey;* Carol Channing in *Gentlemen Prefer Blondes* and *Hello Dolly;* Gertrude Lawrence in *The King and I* and virtually all Rogers and Hammerstein shows.

Size & Elements: Film: 16mm (175 shows, 16,000 feet; primarily color, originals and viewing copies). Film viewing prints are available; transfers to videotape for viewing purposes may be available in the future.

Cataloging: Printed list.

Access: Available to the public. For in-house use only. Open to researchers and scholars (by appointment only). Only films that have been duplicated are available for viewing. Research requests accepted by mail and telephone.

Rights: Full rights held to some material.

Licensing: Licensing and reuse not permitted under any circumstances.

Restrictions: Material not available for duplication, licensing or reuse.

Viewing Facilities: Film (16mm).

Duplication Facilities: None.

Related Materials: 200,000 motion picture stills (beginning 1914); 40,000 disc, cylinder and audiotape recordings (1890s-present); Vitaphone discs from *The Jazz Singer* and other early talkies; radio and television airchecks on audiotape; 16-inch transcriptions; Robert Lewis' world-famous collection of 78 rpm records; over 100,000 Broadway theater playbills; extensive collection of sheet music; librettos dating back to 1836; every script ever published of Broadway productions, including unpublished copies belonging to Cole Porter and Oscar Hammerstein.

CALIFORNIA (Los Angeles Metro)

INTER VIDEO/TTI
733 North Victory Boulevard
Burbank, CA 91502
(818) 569-4000
Fax: (818) 843-6884

Richard Clark (President)

Contact: Post-Production Manager

Services: Film and videotape stock footage sales library; production company; post-production facility; equipment rental house.

Description: Outtakes, alternate takes and unused material from live action, aircraft displays, radar displays, medical displays, computer graphics and computer animation. Specializes in videotape footage shot at 24 frames per second, produced for synchronized playback within a motion-picture scene.

Inter Video also represents several collectors of public domain film footage.

Size & Elements: Film: 35mm (color negative, some matching workprint). Videotape: 1" and Betacam (masters). All material available in 35mm, 16mm and any television standard (NTSC, PAL or SECAM).

Cataloging: Card catalogs; staff assistance.

Access: Open to the public. Available for duplication, licensing and reuse. Research fees not charged, although there is a charge to prepare preview videotapes. This charge is applied against license fees in the event that material is used. Research requests accepted by telephone.

Rights: Full rights held to all material. Some material in the public domain. Represents some material for other filmmakers.

Licensing: Available for licensing and reuse. License fees charged.

Restrictions: None specified.

Viewing Facilities: Videotape.

Duplication Facilities: Film to videotape (Bosch telecine with standards conversion; transfers to NTSC, PAL and SECAM television standards). A proprietary process enables transfer of videotape to film in any standard or format.

CALIFORNIA (Los Angeles Metro)

INTERNATIONAL FASHION VIDEO LIBRARY
110 East 9th Street, Suite C602
Los Angeles, CA 90079
(213) 627-5540

Frankie Gittleman (Coordinator)

Contacts: Frankie Gittleman; Lonnie Green (Assistant to the Coordinator)

Services: Videotape archives; library and museum. Material available for in-house use, research and reference only. Reuse permitted only with consent of copyright holders.

Description: Fashion industry and fashion design. Particular strengths include runway footage of fashion shows from around the world (1970s-present) and concept videos (1984-present).

Library includes apparel industry interviews; award shows; California Mart Fashion Shows; educational, training and how-to videotapes; demonstration reels; fashion-influenced music videos; Fashion Institute of Merchandising and Design shows; fashion videotapes; in-house retail production; magazine format videotapes; retrospective pieces (1910-present); specialized footage of furs, footwear and bridalwear; television commercials and programs; theatrical and cinematic costume research and video catalogs.

Size & Elements: Videotape: 3/4", VHS and Betamax (1,200 titles; viewing copies only).

Cataloging: Computerized cataloging planned.

Access: Open to the public. Available for in-house use, research and reference only. Research fees not charged.

Rights: No rights held to any material. Rights retained by copyright holders.

Licensing: Reuse permitted only with consent of copyright holders.

Restrictions: Restrictions apply to duplication, licensing and reuse. For in-house use only.

Viewing Facilities: Videotape (3/4", VHS and Betamax; monitors and group screening room with videotape projector).

Duplication Facilities: None.

Related Materials: International fashion periodicals collection; apparel industry reference books.

CALIFORNIA (Los Angeles Metro)

INTERNATIONAL GAY AND LESBIAN ARCHIVES
NATALIE BARNEY/EDWARD CARPENTER LIBRARY
P.O. Box 38100
Hollywood, CA 90038
(213) 662-9444

Jim Kepner (Curator)

Contact: Jim Kepner

Services: Library and archives. Film and videotape collection available to the public for in-house research. Some material available for reuse, subject to restrictions.

Description: Films and videotapes relating to gay and lesbian issues. Holdings include male hard- and softcore pornography (1945-74), donated by its producers; nonprofessional documentaries on the gay rights movement (early 1970s); cable television programs and interview shows on gay and lesbian issues; approximately 25-30 videotaped oral history interviews; and raw footage of the "Women Take Back the Night" march (1980).

Size & Elements: Film: 70mm, 35mm and 16mm (approx. 70-80 items; primarily release prints, some documentary originals). Videotape: format unspecified (approx. 120 videotapes; each 2 to 6 hours).

Cataloging: Card catalog; shelf list; other finding aids. Moving image collection only partially cataloged at this time.

Access: Open to the public. For in-house use only. Research fees charged in some cases. Research requests accepted by telephone and in person (by appointment only).

Rights: Some rights held to some material. Additional clearances may be necessary in some cases if material is to be reused (release forms for interviews are not held).

Licensing: Available for licensing and reuse, subject to restrictions.

Restrictions: Requests for reuse considered on a case-by-case basis.

Viewing Facilities: Videotape (VHS and Betamax).

Duplication Facilities: None.

Related Materials: 22,000 books; 100,000 periodicals; manuscripts and other items.

CALIFORNIA (Los Angeles Metro)

JESSIEFILM
3553 Willow Crest Avenue
Studio City, CA 91604
(213) 650-1844

Leonard Maltin (President)

CALIFORNIA (Los Angeles Metro J)

Contact: Leonard Maltin
Services: Film and videotape producer and archives; stock footage sales library.
Description: Specializes in vintage Hollywood footage (fictional and documentary). Holds many rare feature films and short subjects. Special strengths include: behind-the-scenes footage of Hollywood, especially covering the 1920s-30s; silent comedies; early animation; and Soundies. Rare and unusual sequences include a swimming lesson conducted by Johnny Weissmuller and a cigarette endorsement by Jesse Owens.
Size & Elements: Film: 16mm (several hundred titles). Videotape: 3/4" (masters, transfers from film).
Cataloging: Staff assistance required.
Access: Not open to the public. For in-house use only. Available for duplication, reuse, distribution and homevideo sale. Research fees charged. Research requests accepted by mail and telephone.
Rights: Material in the public domain. Additional clearances may be necessary in some cases if material is to be reused.
Licensing: Available for licensing and reuse. License fees charged.
Restrictions: None specified.
Viewing Facilities: None.
Duplication Facilities: None.

CALIFORNIA (Los Angeles Metro)

STUART JEWELL PRODUCTIONS
2040 Garden Lane
Costa Mesa, CA 92627
(714) 548-7234

Stuart Jewell (Owner)

Contact: Stuart Jewell
Services: Film producer; private collection; stock footage sales library.
Description: Footage shot by Stuart Jewell, veteran nature cinematographer and time-lapse photographer for feature films and television. In the 1950s, Jewell produced theatrical nature documentaries under an exclusive contract with Walt Disney Studios. Titles include: *The Living Desert; Nature's Half Acre; The Vanishing Prairie; Secrets of Life; Mysteries of the Deep;* and *Island of the Sea.* Jewell's television credits include: *Disneyland Today; Building Disneyland; Behind the True-Life Cameras; Following the Oregon Trail; Battle for Survival; Yellowstone Park; Jackson Hole; Rolling to Guatemala; Plant Reactions; Amphibian 17;* and *Flight of the Magellan.*
Film footage available for licensing and possible sale (95% never released) is all 16mm unless noted otherwise.
Time-lapse. "World's oldest and largest" time-lapse library, 39 years of production (50,000 feet), includes flowers blooming and growing, clouds and suns of all types in various settings.
Rolling to Guatemala. Following the Pan American highway from the U.S. to Guatemala in an ordinary automobile; driving through a terrific sandstorm; visit to the volcano, Parícutin, that emerged in a cornfield and the only sequence with its owner ("the only man in the world to own a volcano"); loading car onto a flatcar for a steam engine jungle ride to Guatemala City; the world's largest tree; Guatemala City churches, buildings, Indian crafts and merchants; secret pagan rites on a mountaintop; a ride on a narrow gauge steam train over sky-scraping jungle bridges; Antigua ("the city that nature destroyed three times"); how chicle (chewing gum) is hunted and prepared in the jungle; exploring Tikal, the ancient Mayan city; the first scenes of a newly discovered temple; and the aftermath of a killer earthquake.
Plant reactions. Time-lapse footage demonstrating the various reactions of plants to water, light and gravity.
World's greatest fishtrap. Air views of the mount and delta of the Colorado river; plane lands and bounces on a small dirt strip at a native fish camp; turtle fisherman with giant turtles; diving pelicans in slow motion; chasing sporting whales; and fishing. Filmed in Baja California.
Following the Oregon Trail. An 1,800-mile trek retracing the historic trail from Missouri to the Pacific coast; vital waterholes, trail campsites, and landmarks used by American pioneers; river fordings; famous buttes; battlegrounds; famous trees (that still stand); cliffs inscribed with carved names and messages; roadside graves.
Winter in Yellowstone, Teton and Mount Rainier National Parks. Winter sports; skiing; "Snocats"; snowstorms; coyotes scrounging in the snow for food; elk in snow; bison feeding; snowshoeing; birds tamed by winter; icehole fishing; snowplanes skimming the frozen lake; buildings, roads and trees under a 400-inch snowfall; rotary snowplows pluming high in the air; an expedition by Snocat into Yellowstone at 40 degrees below zero; steaming geysers (Old

Faithful); thermal features (hot pools and hot rivers); and animals.
Summer in the above National Parks. Mountain climbing in the Tetons: a ride down the Snake River in a giant rubber raft; fall colors of quaking Aspen trees; aerial scenes of mountain peaks; Yellowstone geysers, hot pools; encounters with bears; and stimulating a large hot pool geyser to boil over.
Oregon seascapes. Scenes along the rugged Oregon coast: monstrous killer waves; giant riptides; blowholes; scenics; and people washed off rocks.
The Great Aerial Odyssey. The adventures of 17 people retracing the old routes of history using a giant amphibian airplane, completely circling the globe, traveling east to west, 38,000 miles, 29 different countries, many times at tree-top levels. Footage includes: natives in remote spots; the search for the world's largest single piece of gold (a 5-1/2 ton Buddha); world's largest radishes ("large as a man's leg"); the cannibal isles and the braining pillar; "icing up" and a daring aerial repair in flight; the hunt for the world's largest bat; world's largest clams ("man-killers"); oil leak and losing an engine; stranded on a South Seas island; and "other episodes too numerous to mention."
Hummingbirds. Slow motion and close-ups on various flowers; mother pumping nectar into its nestlings; puncturing flower base to get nectar; and the life of a hummingbird from egg to the flyaway stage.
Spider. Weaving web from start to finish; catching insect and spinning its shroud; and eating.
Desert wildflowers. Vast wildflower fields; Joshua trees; yucca; getting water from a water barrel cactus; and sand storms. Wildflower fields in desert.
Alaska. Muddy Alaskan highway; grizzlies; caribou; aerials; glaciers; icebergs (some blue); lakes; spectacular narrow-gauge train ride; birth of icebergs; steam train ride in cab of giant locomotive; tunnels, curves and mountains; killer whales; and time-lapse sunsets.
Hawaii. Aerials; volcanoes; shore scenics; mountain scenics; green valleys; and cloud-filled dead volcanoes.
Borneo. Rivers, aerials, trek to cave source of nest for bird's nest soup; guano carriers; former head hunters; and native longhouses.
Thailand. Hill tribes; river life; temples; gold Buddhas; praying, chanting monks; threshing rice; embroidery by hill tribes; village life; elephant training in jungle for timber work; and elephant roundup.
African Animals. Lions; cubs sporting; giraffes; baboons; gazelles; dik diks; crocodiles; elephants; rare white rhinoceros; birds; largest concentration of birds on earth at a lake (over a million flamingos), malibu storks and white pelicans; slogging through 6,000-foot bamboo forests to film the extremely rare mountain gorilla ("one even tried to open our packsack while on our back").
Nile. Life along the Nile; watering methods and plowing; ruined temples; King Tut's tomb; a trek to a pyramid field of 40 pyramids (almost unknown, never before pictured); and the junction of White and Blue Niles where waters don't mix (extremely rare footage).
Egypt. Following Moses' route fleeing Egypt: campsites, oasis, wells, snowstorm, Hill of the Golden Calf, climbing Mt. Sinai (where Moses received the Ten Commandments), Plain of the Tribes campsite; St. Catherine's monastery; sandstorm at Great Pyramids and Sphinx: pyramids' interior, methods of construction and secrets exposed; temples along the Nile by boat; Karnak; Valley of the Kings (where Tut is buried); colossus of Memnon; Luxor; Thebes; Edfu; ancient quarries (source for Great Pyramids blocks), quarrier's marks, unfinished stelae.
Oshkosh air show (1985). Private airplanes, old military, stunt and experimental.
India. Taj Mahal; how and why it was built ("the world's greatest monument to love").
Steam train in American mountains. Old steam train in mountains: yellow cars, inching along cliffs, rivers, canyons and bridges; Canadian steam: big, black, fearsome and dashing; Australian steam: diesel and electric, 30-day tour; and Guatemala steam.
Nepal. Safari by elephant in tall grass; rhinoceros, crocodiles, valleys, rivers, peoples, temples, rivers, and the land of Shangri-la.
World's highest tide. A six-foot-high tidal bore sloshes upstream under bridges, tributaries and along banks for 27 miles.
Extensive and highly detailed narration available for all scenes. "No hotels, restaurants, shops or race tracks in any of this footage."
Size & Elements: Film: 35mm (50,000 feet); 16mm (50,000 feet) (some 16mm with double-system sound; 16mm and 35mm silent; all color).
Cataloging: Card catalogs; shot lists; research library; staff assistance.
Access: Available to the public for distribution, licensing and reuse. Research fees charged. Research requests accepted by mail, telephone and in person (by appointment only).
Rights: Full rights held to all material.
Licensing: Available for licensing and reuse. Sale of all or portions of camera original considered.

Restrictions: Material licensed for specific markets and territories.
Viewing Facilities: Film (projector and Moviola).
Duplication Facilities: Apply for information.
Related Materials: Still photographs; director's notes may be available.

CALIFORNIA (Los Angeles Metro)

JOYCE MEDIA, INC.
P.O. Box 57
Acton, CA 93510
(805) 269-1169

John Joyce (President)

Services: Film and videotape producer and distributor. Available to the public for rental and purchase.
Description: Collection specializes in sign language and education of the deaf. Topics include: sign language training; sign language for parents; Ameslan; Bible stories told in sign language; interpreter training; deaf history; sign language poetry, songs and children's stories.
 Also available on videotape are half-hour segments of *Off Hand!*, a sign language talk show simultaneously interpreted in voice and in sign.
 Some titles available for rental in 16mm.
Size & Elements: Film: 16mm (21 titles). Videotape: 3/4", VHS and Betamax (approx. 25 titles, 50 segments of *Off Hand!*).
Cataloging: Published catalog.
Access: Videotapes available to the public for purchase; films available to the public for rental.
Rights: Apply for information.
Licensing: Apply for information.
Restrictions: None specified.
Viewing Facilities: None.
Duplication Facilities: None.

CALIFORNIA (Los Angeles Metro)

LOMA LINDA UNIVERSITY
DEL E. WEBB MEMORIAL LIBRARY
DEPARTMENT OF ARCHIVES AND SPECIAL COLLECTIONS
Loma Linda, CA 92350
(714) 824-4581 (Library)
(714) 824-4942 (Archives)

James R. Nix (Chairman, Department of Archives and Special Collections)

Contact: Randall R. Butler (Acting Chairman, Department of Archives and Special Collections)
Services: University library; archives. Film and videotape collection available to the public for viewing; possibly available for duplication and reuse.
Description: *Film collection.* Topics include revival meetings; mission stations around the world; General Conference (denominational governing body) annual and five-year meetings; and University and community footage (primarily scenic views and construction projects). Guides are not available for this material, but it is open for public use.
 ABC (Ask/Believe/Claim) Prayer Crusade International Inc. collection. Contains Elder Glenn Coon's sermons on videotape (31 items). Videotaping began ca. 1978; many of these programs have been shown at over a thousand churches and schools across America. Series titles include: *Family Communications* (5 videotapes, 10 programs); *ABC's of Prayer* (10 videotapes); *Getting Acquainted with Jesus* (3 videotapes, 5 programs); *Lovely Lord of the Lord's Day* (5 videotapes, 10 programs); *Youth Asks — God Answers* (3 videotapes, 6 programs); and *An Amazing New Kind of Prayer* (5 videotapes, 10 programs). These represent six of the fourteen series titles that will be available on videotape.
 Dr. Bailey's Heart Transplant Case collection. Cases covered include: "Baby Fae" (with extensive coverage of the operation, interviews with participants, media coverage and press conferences); "Baby Moses"; "Baby Paul and Eve"; and "Baby Jesse." Over 70 VHS videotapes available for public viewing.
Size & Elements: Film: 16mm (approx. 30 linear feet). Videotape: 3/4" (31 titles); VHS (70 videotapes).
Cataloging: Finding aids (lists).
Access: Open to the public for viewing. Research requests accepted by mail and telephone.
Rights: Full rights held to all material.

Licensing: Possibly available for duplication and reuse. Duplication fees charged.
Restrictions: None specified.
Viewing Facilities: Film and videotape.
Duplication Facilities: None in library (arrangements can be made through Media Services).
Related Materials: Audiocassettes of radio programs aired on the Adventist Network and photographs of Elder Glenn Coon.

CALIFORNIA (Los Angeles Metro)

LONG BEACH MUSEUM OF ART
2300 East Ocean Boulevard
Long Beach, CA 90803
(213) 439-2119

Material housed at:
LBMA VIDEO ANNEX
5373 East Second Street
Long Beach, CA 90803
(213) 439-0751

Josine Ianco-Starrels (Acting Director)
Michael Nash (Video Curator)

Contact: Martha Chono (Assistant Manager, LBMA Video Annex)
Services: Museum. Videotape collection available to researchers, scholars and the public for in-house viewing; some material available for distribution. Videotape post-production services available.
Description: Video art (1968-present), primarily works by California artists, documenting the development of video as an art form on the West Coast. Many works were produced at LBMA's post-production facility, sponsored by or exhibited at LBMA; others were acquired through purchase or deposit. Also holds video documentation of LBMA exhibitions. Work by non-U.S. artists is well represented in the collection.
 Exhibition compilations. Some compilations are available for circulation through LBMA. Exhibitions include: *Americans in Florence: Europeans in Florence* (1975); *California Video* (1980); *California Video: 1984; Southland Video Anthology II* (1976-78); *30/60 TV Art* (1980); *French Video Art/Art Video Français* (1981); *Bruised TV Dinners* (1983); *Shared Realities: A Cultural Arts Cable Series* (1984, 12 programs); and *The Artist and the Computer* (1983, 4 programs).
 Video Resource Library. Artists represented in collection include Ruth Abbott, Karen Achenbach, Vito Acconci, Alan Ackoff, Chey Acuña, Moira Adams, Billy Adler, Edit deAk, Max Almy, Hanspeter Ammann, Dave Anderson, Nancy Angelo, Ant Farm, Eleanor Antin, Wendy Appel, Stephanie Arena, Juan Arkotxa, John Arvanites, Robert Ashley, David Askevold, Autobabies, Roland Baladi, John Baldessari, Wenden Baldwin, Joyce Wexler Ballard, Peter Barton, Baylin, Dede Bazyk, Stephen Beck, Dominique Belloir, Stuart Bender, Guila Benesty, Lynda Benglis, Ronald Benom, Joseph Beuys, Gary Beydler, Robert Biggs, Dara Birnbaum, Rabyn Blake, Wendy Blatt, Bob and Bob, Harris Boldt-Edelman, Dan Boord, Ed Bowes, Tom Bowes, Kevin Boyle, Ante Bozanich, Klaus vom Bruch, Nancy Buchanan, Peter Bull, Chris Burden, Donald Burgy, Thomas Burton, Jose Maria Bustos, Robert Cahen, John Caldwell, Pierpaolo Calzolari, Colin Campbell, Peter Campus, Alba Cane, Cecilia Ryan Cantania, Yreina Cervantez, Shelley Chamberlain, Ben Chase, Doris Chase, Giuseppe Chiari, Roman Cieslewicz, Ronald D. Clark, Maxi Cohen, Guy de Cointet, Candace Compton, Steve Conant, Cecelia Condit, Brian Connell, Bill Copley, Judith I. Corona, Linda Cossey, Nicole Croiset, Eric Crystal, Robert Cumming, Jack Cummins, Dorit Cypis, Peter D'Agostino, Lowell Darling, David Dashiell, Mary Daval, Jaime Davidovich, Susan Davis, Jonathan Dayton, Tom DeBiaso, Colette Deblé, Olivier Debré, Tom DeFanti, Helen DeMichiel, Tom DeWitt, Frank Dietrich, John H. Dorr, Paul Dougherty, Juan Downey, Hildegarde Duane, John Duncan, Tom Eatherton, Sarah Elgart, Salomon Emquies, Ed Emshwiller, Bill Etra, Louise Etra, Wylci Fables, Valerie Faris, Ken Feingold, Tom Finerty, Kit Fitzgerald, Rochelle Ford, Brian Forrest, Terry Fox, Christiano Toraldo di Francia, Piero Frassinelli, Charles Frazier, Freeway Productions, Vera Frenkel, Bart Friedman, Roberta Friedman, Captain Frith, Kit Galloway, Howard Ganz, Alex Gates, Cherie Gaulke, Edward Geis, Matthew Geller, Alex Gibney, Jo Ann Gillerman, Frank Gillette, Stan Gilula, Joel Glassman, Joel Gold, Robert Goldman, Paul Goldsmith, Neil Goldstein, Debbie Gorchos, John S. Gordon, Carey Gorney, Nicholas C. Gorski, John Goss, Raúl Guerrero, Howard Gutstadt, Diane Andrews Hall, Doug Hall, Noel Harding, William Gray Harris, Maren Hassinger, Ron Hays, Kevin Head, John Helmore, François Helt, Dale Herd, Joel Wm. Hermann,

Douglas Heubler, Gary Hill, Susan Sims Hillbrand, Jon Hilton, Louis Hock, Diane Holland, Nan Hoover, Jeffrey Hudson, Tony Humecke, Mako Idemitsu, Catherine Ikam, Elizabeth Ince, Peggy Ingalls, Jeffrey Isaak, Peter Ivers, Gary Jacobelly, Thomas Jancar, Ulysses Jenkins, Joan Jonas, Bryan Jones, Douglas Kagel, Rebecca Kalin, Kathryn Kanehiro, Allan Kaprow, Lou Katz, Larry Kaufman, Stanton Kaye, Ray Keating, Pat Kelley, Deans Keppel, Harry Kipper, Peter Kirby, Rodger Klein, Thomas Klein, Cindy Kleine, John Knight, Lisa Koper, Marlene Kos, Paul Kos, Jannis Kounellis, Bernd Kracke, Mitchell Kriegman, Richard Kriesche, Shigeko Kubota, Thierry Kuntzel, Bruce Kurtz, Robert Kushner, Tony Labat, Suzanne Lacy, David Lamelas, Alan Lande, Jacky K. Lavin, Sharon Lawson, William Leavitt, Joseph Leonardi, Gary Lloyd, Louise Lo, Jane Logemann, Joan Logue, Fred Lonidier, Chip Lord, Alvin Lucier, Urs Lüthi, Jay McCafferty, Claire McCance, Paul McCarthy, Carol Porter McClintock, Alan McGlade, Mickey McGowan, Ellen MacKinnon, Alessandro Magris, Roberto Magris, Andy Mann, Chris Marker, Hudson Marquez, Pier Marton, Artur Matuck, Cynthia Lee Maughan, Nelson Max, David Megill, Markar Melkonian, Edward Mellnick, Memory of Your Nose, Pete Mendez, Doug Michels, Branda Miller, Susan Mogul, Zsuzsa Molnar, Juliette Mondot, Linda Montano, Stephen Moore, Jac Mote, Unidas Mujeres, Mary Mullen, Antonio Muntadas, Marcy Muray, Thomas G. Musca, Rita Myers, Kou Nakajima, Maureen Nappi, Adolfo Natalini, Suzanne Nessim, Stephen Neumann, Hervé Nisic, Sumie Nobuhara, Art Nomura, Robert K. Olson, Ingrid Oppenheim, John Orentlicher, Mike Osterhout, Jean Otth, Tony Oursler, Tim Owens, Nam June Paik, François Pain, Slobodan Pajic, Charlemagne Palestine, Giulio Paolini, Jore Park, Jan Peacock, Lynn Phillips, Sheila Pinkel, Alberto Pirelli, Patti Podesta, Michael Portis, Bruce Postman, Patrick Prado, Jody Proctor, Aysha Quinn, Sherrie Rabinowitz, Tom Radloff, Scott Rankin, Esther Raucher, Joe Rees, Dan Reeves, Judy Rifka, Mike Robinson, Judson Rosebush, Alex Roshuk, Martha Rosler, Pierre Rovère, Denis Rubin, Allen Rucker, Allen Ruppersberg, Cynthia Rush, Nina R. Salerno, David Salle, John Sanborn, Dan Sandin, Jo Sandman, Norie Sato, Glen Scantlebury, Van Schley, Ira Schneider, Curtis Schreier, Patrick Scott, Michael Scroggins, Stephen Seemayer, Ilene Segalove, David Seidner, Allan Sekula, Michael Shamberg, Scott Shand, Celia (Sally) Shapiro, Mimi Shevitz, Judy Shoemaker, Javier Silva, Barry Singer, Barbara Smith, Bradford Smith, Michael Smith, Nina Sobel, Elon Soltes, Vibeke Sorensen, Arla Sorkin, Lisa Steele, Philip Steinmetz, Viola Stephan, Wolfgang Stoerchle, Sharon Stricker, John Sturgeon, Superstudio, Starr Steven Sutherland, Richard Swacus, Barbara Sykes, Mitchell Syrop, T. R. Uthco, Janice Tanaka, Target Video, Tava, Bart Thrall, TNR (The New Repertory), Claude Torey, Vincent Trasov, Mark Trezise, Pat Trimble, Michael Tucker, Phil Turvey, TVTV (Top Value Television), Vampire Video, Beth Van de Water, Steina Vasulka, Woody Vasulka, Glenda Vaughn, Jane Veeder, Videma Productions, Video Rouge, Videowest, Bill Viola, Dan Wagner, "Captain" Bruce E. Walker, George Waller, William Wegman, Tom Weinberg, Lawrence Weiner, Stephanie Weinshel, James Welling, Greeley Wells, Teresa Wennberg, John Whitney, Sr., Geoffrey Wickland, Arthur Wicks, Bob Wilhite, Megan Williams, Dean Winkler, Gene Wirth, Terry Wolverton, Yen Lu Wong, Daniel Wray, WTV, Nil Yalter, Bruce Yonemoto, Norman Yonemoto, Janice Yudell, Joey Zanotti, Karen Zaptiff, Connie Zehr, Bob Zimmerman and Zipcut Video.

Interviews. Holds videotaped interviews with artists, philosophers and others, including: Carlos Almarez (East Los Angeles artist, 1981); Max Almy (1982 and 1983); Jennifer Bartlett (Video Data Bank, 1976); Dara Birnbaum (1982); M. Alvarez Bravo (1980); Nancy Buchanan (1979 and 1983); David Em (1982); Paul Fairweather (1983); Michel Foucault (1982); Buckminster Fuller (1984); Charles Ginnevar (1978); Raúl Guerrero (1983); Noel Harding (1981); Joel Wm. Hermann (1977); Gary Hill (1981); Kathy Rae Huffman (1984); John Paul Jones (1979); Les Levine (1979); Stanley Marsh III (1977); Jay McCafferty (1984); Antonio Muntadas (1983); Nam June Paik (1975); Giuseppe Panza di Biumo (1975); Scott Rankin (1984); Susan Shore (1979); Ilene Segalove (1981); Joan Semmel (1974 and 1975); Silvia Salazar Simpson (1983); Matthew Thomas (1981); Vibeke Sorensen (1984); Barbara Sykes (1977); Bill Viola (1981 and 1982); Fred and Marcia Weisman (1977); and William T. Wiley (1982-83).

The LBMA Video Annex houses a screening room, production and post-production facilities.

Size & Elements: Videotape: 3/4" and 1/2" open reel (over 1,000 titles; mostly viewing copies, some masters and submasters).
Cataloging: Computerized cataloging in progress (staff use only); printouts available. LBMA has received a grant from the National Center for Film and Video Preservation, American Film Institute, to catalog its videotapes in MARC-compatible format.
Access: Open to researchers, scholars and the public. Available for viewing and duplication (with consent of artist). Research fees charged in some cases. Research requests accepted by mail, telephone and in person (by appointment only).
Rights: Rights retained by artists. LBMA holds limited distribution rights to videotapes in series distributed or funded by LBMA.
Licensing: Available for reuse, providing clearance of artist is obtained. License or usage fees charged under some conditions.
Restrictions: None specified.
Viewing Facilities: Videotape (3/4" and 1/2; NTSC, PAL and SECAM).
Duplication Facilities: Videotape (3/4").
Publications: *Video: A Retrospective, Long Beach Museum of Art 1974-1984,* by Kathy Rae Huffman. Lists and reviews video exhibitions at LBMA during this important period; contains lists of works held in Video Resource Library.

CALIFORNIA (Los Angeles Metro)

LORIMAR TELEPICTURES
10202 West Washington Boulevard
Culver City, CA 90232
(213) 202-2000

Services: Motion picture producer and distributor.

CALIFORNIA (Los Angeles Metro)

LOS ANGELES BLUES ARCHIVES
1251 14th Street, Suite 207
Santa Monica, CA 90404
(213) 395-4939

Alexia Baum (President)

Contact: Alexia Baum
Services: Tax-exempt organization, historical society and archives. It is planned that material will be made available for research, licensing and reuse, subject to restrictions.
Description: Begins 1980. "Personality pieces" including interviews and performance footage with Los Angeles and nationally renowned blues musicians; including Sam Taylor, John Juke Logan, Blind Joe Hill, Hollywood Fats, Johnny Otis, Richard Berry, Rockin' Dopsie, and others.

Some videotapes are part of a feature-length documentary (in progress, 1988) on the roots of rock and roll music (1940s-50s). The entire Los Angeles Blues Archives benefit show (September 1986) is held on film and includes performances by such artists as Coco Montoya, Maggie Mayall, Danny Krieger and others.

Holds primarily videotapes at present, although film will be held in the future. Presently engaged in consolidating and organizing material.
Size & Elements: Videotape: 3/4" (masters and viewing copies); VHS (viewing copies) (over 100 videotapes, ranging from 20 to 60 min.).
Cataloging: Card catalog, published catalog and computerized cataloging accessible to researchers (in process).
Access: Available to the public for duplication, licensing and reuse (pending completion of footage licensing contract). Research fees charged. Research requests accepted by mail and telephone.
Rights: Rights status of materials not known at this time.
Licensing: Intent is to make materials as accessible as legally possible, but availability of material for licensing is pending completion of footage licensing contract. Minimal license fees will probably be charged.
Restrictions: Restrictions may apply.
Viewing Facilities: Film (35mm and 16mm); videotape (3/4" and VHS).
Duplication Facilities: Videotape (VHS to VHS).
Related Materials: Still photographs.

CALIFORNIA (Los Angeles Metro)

LOS ANGELES CITY ARCHIVES
City Clerk's Office — Records Management Division
555 Ramirez Street, Space 320, Mail Stop 161
Los Angeles, CA 90012
(213) 485-3512

Elias Martinez (City Clerk)

Contacts: Hynda L. Rudd (City Records Management Officer); Robert B. Freeman (Administrative Assistant)
Services: Local government agency. Archival film collection available for research, duplication and licensing.

CALIFORNIA (Los Angeles Metro M)

Description: Los Angeles street scenes (1920-50). Film was shot by Public Works (Right of Way and Land Bureau). The small collection provides a perspective on street conditions and planning issues.
Size & Elements: Film: 16mm (1,000 feet, approx. 50 titles; original material). Videotape: VHS (10 videotapes, transfers from film).
Cataloging: Finding aids.
Access: Open to the public. Available for duplication. Requests accepted by mail, telephone and in person (walk-in).
Rights: Full rights held to all material.
Licensing: Available for licensing. License fees not charged.
Restrictions: None specified.
Viewing Facilities: Film and videotape (viewing arranged through Los Angeles Department of General Services; must be arranged in advance).
Duplication Facilities: Videotape (duplication fees charged).

CALIFORNIA (Los Angeles Metro)

LOS ANGELES CONTEMPORARY EXHIBITIONS (LACE)
1804 Industrial Street
Los Angeles, CA 90021
(213) 624-5650

Joy Silverman (Executive Director)

Contact: Video Coordinator
Services: Nonprofit organization. Videotape archives available to visiting curators for in-house viewing.
Description: Artist organization committed to the presentation and development of new art work. Maintains an exhibition gallery for all media; a performance space for new music, new dance and performance art; and a videotape screening room.

The archives contains recent video works by emerging and established Southern California artists which is available for viewing by visiting curators. Artists include: Max Almy, Skip Arnold, Stuart Bender, Susan Braig, Nancy Buchanan, David Bunn, John Caldwell, Fu-Ding Cheng, Hildegarde Duane and David Lamelas, Ed Emschwiller, Valerie Faris and Jonathan Dayton, Jeanne Finley, Wendy Geller, Shalom Gorewitz, John Goss, Ulysses Jenkins, Hilja Keading, Barnaby Levy and Wayne Reynolds, Chip Lord, Pier Marton, Donna Matorin, Branda Miller, Tony Oursler, Patti Podesta, Scott Rankin, Jonathan Reiss, Peter Rose, Erika Suderburg, Kathy Tanney, Marshall Weber and Bruce Yonemoto.

Also distributes curated exhibitions of video works (curated by Anne Bray, Branda Miller and others), including: *Baby Needs A Change; LA Video; Landscape Video: Works From the Seventies; Resolution: A Critique of Video Art; Surveillance;* and *Video and Language: Video As Language.*
Size & Elements: Videotape: 3/4" (mostly) and VHS (over 260 titles by 150 different artists).
Cataloging: Computerized cataloging available to researchers.
Access: Open to curators. For in-house use only. Research fees not charged. Research requests accepted in person (by appointment only).
Rights: No rights held to any material. All rights retained by artists.
Licensing: General collection not available for licensing or reuse. Curated exhibitions possibly available for rental and purchase.
Restrictions: All viewing, screening or reuse of videotapes outside LACE must be negotiated with individual artists.
Viewing Facilities: Videotape (3/4" and 1/2").
Duplication Facilities: None.
Related Materials: Bookstore containing magazines, books, records, audio and videotapes, postcards, art theory, criticism, documentation, artists' books, poetry and new writing; and symposiums on art related topics.
Publications: Catalogs and publications relating to curated exhibitions.

CALIFORNIA (Los Angeles Metro)

LOS ANGELES DEPARTMENT OF WATER AND POWER
111 North Hope Street, Room 1514
Los Angeles, CA 90051
(213) 481-6351
Fax: (213) 580-0739

Barry Tuller (Manager, Public and Employee Communications)

Contact: Valerie Gray
Services: Government agency. Videotape material available for distribution, licensing and reuse.

Description: Videotapes produced for customers and employees (1983-present) relating to water and power. Topics include conservation programs, new research, nuclear power stations, environmental conditions, safety campaigns and health issues. Titles include: *The Eastern Sierra — Land of Contrast; Mono Lake Status Update; Solar One Site Dedication 1980; Department of Water and Power Video News* (each episode approx. 10 min., covering three or four current projects and issues, produced several times a year); *I Love Me, I Buckle Up; Water For Los Angeles; Earthquake Do's and Don'ts; Total Health Expo Speaker* (3 segments, with well-known personalities discussing their experiences); and *It Couldn't Happen To Me.*

Over the past 20 years, DWP has produced many instructional films, most of which have been donated to the UCLA Film and Television Archive (q.v.).
Size & Elements: Videotape: format unspecified (over 40 titles).
Cataloging: Finding aids; printed title list with short film descriptions.
Access: Available for duplication. Research requests accepted by mail and telephone.
Rights: Full rights held to all material.
Licensing: Available for licensing. License fees not charged.
Restrictions: None specified.
Viewing Facilities: None.
Duplication Facilities: None.

CALIFORNIA (Los Angeles Metro)

LOS ANGELES NEWS SERVICE (LANS)
1341 Ocean Avenue, Suite 262
Santa Monica, CA 90401
(213) 398-3449

Robert Tur (President)

Contacts: Robert Tur; Judy Tur (Office Manager)
Services: Television news gathering organization. Videotape library available to the public for duplication. ENG/EFP production and post-production services available.
Description: Television news service active in greater Los Angeles and Southern California. Maintains videotape library (most footage produced 1984-present) comprising major and minor breaking news stories; some major stories also held for the period 1982-84. Stories are covered by ground and helicopter crews "24 hours a day, 365 days a year." All material originates on Betacam or 3/4" master videotape; all footage shot is saved.

Topics include celebrities and personalities, politicians, police activity, fires, disasters, scenics, traffic accidents, rescues, Edwards Air Force Base and aviation. Recent stories covered include: the Dorothy Mae Fire in a downtown Los Angeles tenement, which killed 25 people (1982); the Coalinga earthquake in central California (1983); the Paramount Studios fire (1983); Baby Fae's heart transplant (1984); *Twilight Zone: The Movie* helicopter accident (1984); Michael Jackson's freak accident during the filming of a Pepsi-Cola commercial (1984); Rock Hudson's last press conference and death from AIDS (1985); the weddings of Sylvester Stallone and Brigitte Nielsen, and Madonna and Sean Penn (1985); Sean Penn in court and in jail; and the PSA passenger air crash near Paso Robles, Calif., which killed 44 people (1987).
Size & Elements: Videotape: Betacam and 3/4" (over 3,000 videotapes, approx. 15,000 titles; masters).
Cataloging: Computerized cataloging for staff use only; shot lists.
Access: Open to the public. Available for duplication, licensing and reuse. Research fees charged in some cases. Research requests accepted by telephone and in person (by appointment only).
Rights: Full rights held to all material. Additional clearances may be necessary in some cases if material is to be reused.
Licensing: Available for licensing and reuse. License fees charged.
Restrictions: None specified.
Viewing Facilities: Videotape (Betacam and 3/4").
Duplication Facilities: Videotape (Betacam and 3/4").

CALIFORNIA (Los Angeles Metro)

MACGILLIVRAY FREEMAN FILMS
P.O. Box 205
South Laguna, CA 92677
(714) 494-1055
Fax: (714) 494-2079

Greg MacGillivray (President; Producer/Director)

Footage 89: North American Film & Video Sources

53

CALIFORNIA (Los Angeles Metro M)

Contact: Matthew Muller
Services: Film and videotape producer; stock footage sales library.
Description: Extensive collection of natural beauty scenic shots; especially strong in aerials, as well as aesthetic sports. Aerial views include national parks, coasts, clouds, rolling hills, Niagara Falls, major cities, Hawaii, Tahiti and the Bahamas. Beauty shots and scenics include sunrises and sunsets (both real-time and time-lapse), ocean waves, some national parks, sea gulls and wheat fields. Sports footage includes air-to-air hang-gliding, sailplaning and hot air balloons; also surfing, skiing, sailing and skateboarding. Also holds footage of fireworks, snow scenics, road point-of-views, national landmarks and an air show.
Size & Elements: Film: 35mm (approx. 70,000 feet; negative and occasional interpositive); 16mm (75,000 feet; Ektachrome Commercial) (approx. 120 titles total). Videotape: 1" (film-to-videotape transfers).
Cataloging: Library organized into subject reels. Information package available.
Access: Available to the public for licensing and reuse. Library does not conduct research. Demonstration reels on 3/4" videotape or film can be provided. Requests accepted by mail and telephone.
Rights: Full rights held to most material. Talent fees necessary in some cases.
Licensing: Available for licensing and reuse. License fees charged depending on intended use.
Restrictions: Additional clearances may be necessary in some cases if material is to be reused (e.g., talent fees).
Viewing Facilities: None.
Duplication Facilities: Videotape (3/4" and VHS).
Representative: Film Search, Inc. (q.v.) for East Coast stock footage sales (CT, DE, MA, ME, VT, NH, NY, NJ, RI, DC)

CALIFORNIA (Los Angeles Metro)

MCA INC./UNIVERSAL PICTURES
100 Universal City Plaza
Universal City, CA 91608
(818) 777-1000

Services: Motion picture producer and distributor.

CALIFORNIA (Los Angeles Metro)

MEXICAN AMERICAN LEGAL DEFENSE AND EDUCATIONAL FUND (MALDEF)
634 South Spring Street, 11th Floor
Los Angeles, CA 90014
(213) 629-2512
Fax: (213) 629-8016

Antonia Hernandez (President and General Counsel)

Contacts: Alicia Maldonado (Director of Communications); Diana Palmiotti (Communications Assistant)
Services: Legal organization. Videotape archives open to researchers and scholars only.
Description: Mexican Americans, education, employment, immigration, voting rights and women's rights are topics covered by *Informe MALDEF*, a weekly issue-oriented television show, produced in cooperation with KDTV, San Francisco. Segments held (October 1985-April 1987) include guests from the Mexican American community.

Specific programs include: *Women's Round Table; Hispanic Economic Development; Hispanics in Media; Higher Education: Community College Issues; Employment Discrimination; Welfare and Workfare; Housing Discrimination; MALDEF Dinner; Education: Universities and Minorities; Education: Bilingual Programs; Education: Issues in San Francisco; Stereotypes and Public Perception of Hispanic Culture; The Contributions of Hispanic Women; Hispanic Representation: Building Leaders; Hispanic Participation in the Electoral Process; The Future of the Hispanic Family; University Admissions Requirements; Passage of the Simpson-Rodino Bill; Election Analysis; The Homeless; Poverty and the Poor; Public Education; Women and Education; The Economic Future for Hispanics; Poverty and the Third World; The Changing Role of Women in Society; The Experience of the Undocumented;* and *The Impact of the Immigration Reform and Control Act of 1986.*
Size & Elements: Videotape (format and amount unspecified).
Cataloging: Listings available.
Access: Open to researchers and scholars only. Research fees generally not charged. Research requests accepted by telephone.
Rights: Some rights held to some material.
Licensing: Materials possibly available for licensing and reuse, subject to restrictions. License fees generally not charged; donations accepted (apply for information).
Restrictions: Any reuse must be credited.
Viewing Facilities: Videotape.
Duplication Facilities: None.

CALIFORNIA (Los Angeles Metro)

MGM/UA COMMUNICATIONS COMPANY
450 North Roxbury Drive
Beverly Hills, CA 90210
(213) 281-4000

Services: Motion picture producer and distributor.

CALIFORNIA (Los Angeles Metro)

MILITARY/COMBAT STOCK FOOTAGE
4091 Glencoe
Marina Del Rey, CA 90291
(213) 827-1168
Fax: (213) 301-0560

Joseph Dickstein (Manager)

Contacts: Joseph Dickstein
Services: Videotape producer and distributor; film and videotape stock footage sales library. Research and videotape duplication services available.
Description: Military, combat and aviation coverage (both stock footage and completed films) (1903-present).

Collection includes: Air Force (U.S.); Army (U.S.); aviation footage, from the Wright Brothers' flight at Kitty Hawk (1903) to the unveiling of the Stealth bomber (1988); combat footage; defense systems; Department of Defense footage; government-produced films and videotapes (World War I-present); Grenada (1983); historical features, including the *Why We Fight* series;

54

instructional films; Korean War; Lebanon (1980s); Marine Corps; Navy; the Soviet Union, including combat, military maneuvers and equipment; technology; Vietnam War; weapons; World War I; and World War II.

Distributes completed programs on military equipment and conflicts (World War I-present).

Size & Elements: Film: 35mm and 16mm (release prints and access to many originals). Videotape: 1" (transfers from film, masters); Betacam (masters and transfers from film); 3/4" (masters and viewing copies). (Thousands of hours total).

Cataloging: Staff assistance required for stock footage. Published catalog of completed programs.

Access: Open to the public. Available for duplication and reuse. Research fees charged. Research requests accepted by mail, telephone and in person (walk-in).

Rights: Full rights held to some material. Some material in the public domain.

Licensing: Available for licensing and reuse. License fees charged.

Restrictions: None specified.

Viewing Facilities: Videotape (3/4").

Duplication Facilities: Videotape (3/4" and 1/2").

CALIFORNIA (Los Angeles Metro)

DAVID LEE MILLER PRODUCTIONS
1388 Cheswick Place
Westlake Village, CA 91361
(805) 495-9709

David Lee Miller (Executive Producer)

Contact: David Lee Miller
Services: Film and videotape producer. Videotape footage available for distribution, licensing and reuse.
Description: Broadcast-quality footage picturing hundreds of different zoo animals without cages or bars. Includes many extreme closeups of every variety of animal. Animal shots include: giraffes with moving lips and tongues; hippopotamus; rhinoceros; elephants; reptiles; snakes eating mice; small mammals; exotic fishes; birds and performing birds (e.g. macaws); ostriches; rare storks; zebras; "big cats," including white tigers; polar bears diving and jumping; tarantulas on human arms; vultures tearing meat off bones; animals eating; zookeepers working with animals, demonstrating elephant care and hugging big cats; and interviews with zookeepers.
Size & Elements: Videotape: 3/4" (12 hours; masters and viewing copies).
Cataloging: Shot lists; dope sheets or release sheets.
Access: Available for duplication, licensing and reuse. Research fees charged. Research requests accepted by mail, telephone and in person (walk-in).
Rights: Full rights held to all material.
Licensing: Available for licensing and reuse. License fees charged.
Restrictions: None specified.
Viewing Facilities: Videotape (3/4").
Duplication Facilities: Videotape.

CALIFORNIA (Los Angeles Metro)

WARREN MILLER PRODUCTIONS, INC.
505 Pier Avenue
Hermosa Beach, CA 90254
(213) 376-2494
Fax: (213) 374-4042

Contact: Doug Kleist (Stock footage)
Services: Film producer; stock footage sales library.
Description: "Largest library of action sports footage in the world." Footage (1949-present) includes snow and skiing; European and U.S. scenics; snowboarding; crazy snow antics; bloopers; the funny side of all sports; windsurfing; off-road racing; horse racing; wine-making and vineyard cultivation. Productions (1978-present) have been transferred from 16mm film original to videotape (1" or 3/4").
Size & Elements: Film: 16mm (450 completed films, each 5 to 90 min.). Videotape: 1" and 3/4" (transfers from 16mm film).
Cataloging: None.
Access: Available to the public for licensing and reuse. Research fees charged. Minimum research charge applies to all requests. Research requests accepted by mail and telephone.
Rights: Full rights held to all material.
Licensing: Available for licensing and reuse. License fees charged.

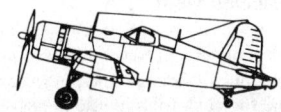
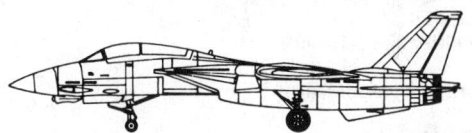
Restrictions: None specified.
Viewing Facilities: None.
Duplication Facilities: Videotape (3/4").

CALIFORNIA (Los Angeles Metro)

MOODY INSTITUTE OF SCIENCE
12000 East Washington Boulevard
Whittier, CA 90606
(213) 698-8256

Lad Allen (Director of Production)

Contacts: Wyona Starts (Librarian); Lad Allen
Services: Film and videotape producer. Collection open to the public. Programs available for broadcast, licensing and reuse. Stock footage also available.
Description: Program series available include *The Family: God's Pattern for Living* (6 parts, each 50 min.); *Help! Our Family Is Unraveling!* (2 parts); and *Building the Family of God: Spiritual Discipling* (4 films, each 44 min.).

Science Classics (15 films, each 28 min.). Titles include *Journey of Life,* relating the travels of a tiny seed to the journey of the living seed of God's Word; *City of the Bees,* contrasting bees' life with God's design for human relationships; *Dust or Destiny,* feats of animal behavior that reflect the infinite wonder and wisdom of God; *Signposts Aloft,* why man needs guidance from God, just as pilots need guidance from their instrument controls; *Facts of Faith,* showing laboratory experiments that demonstrate powerful spiritual truths relating to faith; *Red River of Life,* on blood, the lifeline through the human body and how the shed blood of Christ is the source of life in the Spirit; and *Where the Waters Run,* explaining how God provides for our spiritual needs with His supply of Living Water, just as He provides for our physical needs with H_2O.

The Hidden Holocaust (50 min.) presents the case against legalized abortion, with the participation of key leaders including Chuck Colson and Bernard Nathanson, M.D.

Also available for distribution are children's adventures (6 films, each 10 min.); and children's Bible adventures (17 films, each 13 min.).

CALIFORNIA (Los Angeles Metro M)

Stock footage. No stock footage will be sold from original material appearing in any Moody Institute of Science release. Material not used in completed films is available for stock footage sale in many cases.

Collection spans 40 years and was photographed around the world. Includes footage of objects, creatures and events in the world of natural science and related areas of interest. Strengths include animal and insect life with particularly good footage of honeybees, water, plant life, birds, and ecosystems (e.g., the Everglades); time-lapse and high-speed studies of clouds, plants, seed dispersal and the sun. There is extensive coverage of energy, its sources (e.g., geothermal, biogas) and its use (automobiles and appliances); also footage of general domestic life and scenery.
Size & Elements: Film: 16mm (unedited footage, approx. 100,000 feet, approx. 50 completed films; reversal original). Videotape (some completed films available in homevideo formats).
Cataloging: Card catalogs; stock footage indexed by subject; published catalog for programs in current distribution.
Access: Open to the public. Programs available for distribution and rental. Stock footage available for duplication and reuse. Research fees charged (search fee payable in advance for each and every subject or scene listing). Research requests accepted by mail, telephone and in person (by appointment only). Purchaser must describe in writing scenes desired, amount of footage needed, how footage will be used, and name of program.
Rights: Full rights held to most material. Footage not available for reuse if full rights not held.
Licensing: Available for licensing and reuse, subject to restrictions. License and usage fees charged.
Restrictions: No stock footage will be sold from original appearing in any Moody Institute of Science release.
Viewing Facilities: Film (16mm).
Duplication Facilities: Film (16mm).

CALIFORNIA (Los Angeles Metro)

MORCRAFT FILMS
837 North Cahuenga Boulevard
Hollywood, CA 90038
(213) 464-2009

Dermott Morgan (President)

Contact: Dermott Morgan
Services: Film and videotape archives; distributor. Collection available for rental, purchase, duplication and reuse.
Description: Holds public domain films (1894-1960), including features, short subjects and cartoons. Genres include comedy, drama, silents, mystery and suspense, horror, science fiction, adventure, musicals and Westerns. Also held are hand-colored films, newsreels (Fox Movietone, Hearst Metrotone, International News, and Pathé News), World War II propaganda films, various television series, and an extensive collection of trailers.

Access to the Blackhawk Films library and other collections is also available.
Size & Elements: Film: 16mm (over 1 million feet, over 2,000 titles). Videotape: 3/4" and 1/2" (over 2,700 videotapes).
Cataloging: Published catalogs.
Access: Available for rental, purchase, duplication and reuse. Research fees charged. Research requests accepted by mail and telephone.
Rights: Material in the public domain.
Licensing: Available for reuse. Usage fees charged.
Restrictions: None specified.
Viewing Facilities: Film (16mm); videotape (3/4" and 1/2").
Duplication Facilities: Film: (35mm to 16mm, 16mm to 16mm, 9.5 to 16mm blowup); videotape (1/2" to 1/2", 3/4" to 1/2").
Related Materials: Original collection of organ music and a sound recordings library.

CALIFORNIA (Los Angeles Metro)

JESS S. MORGAN & COMPANY, INC.
5750 Wilshire Boulevard, Suite 590
Los Angeles, CA 90036
(213) 937-1552
Fax: (213) 937-6532
Telex: 686-409 JSMCO

Contact: Office

Services: Business managers for Harriet H. Nelson, holder of rights to all episodes of the television series *The Adventures of Ozzie and Harriet.* Any requests or questions concerning reuse of material from the series should be directed to the above office.
Description: *The Adventures of Ozzie and Harriet,* a television situation comedy series (1952-66).
Size & Elements: Apply for information.
Cataloging: Apply for information.
Access: Apply for information.
Rights: Full rights held to all material.
Licensing: Material available for licensing and reuse, subject to restrictions.
Restrictions: Requests for licensing and reuse considered on case-by-case basis.
Viewing Facilities: None.
Duplication Facilities: None.

CALIFORNIA (Los Angeles Metro)

MORRIS VIDEO
2730 Monterey Street, Suite 105
Torrance, CA 90503
(213) 533-4800
Fax: (213) 533-1993

George Morris (Vice President)

Contacts: George Morris; Dawn Morris
Services: Videotape producer and distributor. Markets videotapes for retail sales. Material possibly available for licensing and reuse.
Description: Health and medical, travel and "leisure activities" programs for home viewing. General areas include: success, cooking, garden, fix-it and how-to, automotive, crafts, image, art and music, sports, boating and horses.

Sample titles include: *How to Buy a Home; Your Money Series,* including *Understanding the Business World and Stocks, The Marketplace,* and *Bonds; The One Minute Cook: Microwave Made Easy; Seafood Cookery; The Consumer's Guide to Meat; Food Drying and Storage; Making Your Own Wine; Design With Plants; Blue Ribbon Veggies; Ground Covers; Exclusive Lawns; Spectacular Roses; Pruning; Upholstering a Dining Room Chair; Be Your Own Plumber; Oil Change, Filters, and Lube; Detailing; Tune Up and Maintenance; Motorcycle Maintenance: EZ4U; Custom Tailored Skirts and Blouses; Decorate Your Home for Christmas; Contemporary Crochet Made Simple; Fun With Fabric; Silk Flower Making; Crafting With Discards; New Ideas for Crayons and Paints; Make a Puppet, Make a Friend; Lose Weight With Alf Fowles; Coping With Stress; Haircutting at Home for Boys and Men; Make-Up for Women; Landscape Painting with Harold Riley; Portrait Painting with Harold Riley; Tips for the Beginning French Horn Player; Beginning Trumpet Techniques; Golf the Miller Way with PGA Champ Johnny Miller; Football Series with Tom Landry; The Art of Hitting; Baserunning Basics with Maury Wills; How Tennis Pros Win; Bowling With Earl Anthony; Skiing With Gordy Skoog and Bill Johnson; Winning Softball; Secrets of Steelheading; Self Defense; Cheerleading Routines; Successful Duckhunting; Basic Guide to Shotguns; The Marathon Challenge; Boating: Basic Navigation; Small Boat Engine Maintenance;* and *Prepare Your Halter Horse for Show.*

Approximately 70% of the collection is comprised of in-house productions (1984-present).
Size & Elements: Videotape: 1" (1,200 hours; masters); VHS and Betamax (over 1,000 titles, some unreleased).
Cataloging: Published lists; shot lists.
Access: Videotapes available for sale by retailers and dealers. Footage available for duplication, licensing and reuse. Inquiries and orders accepted by mail, telephone and in person (by appointment only). Apply for information.
Rights: Full rights held to some material. Some rights held to all material.
Licensing: Apply for information.
Restrictions: None specified.
Viewing Facilities: Videotape.
Duplication Facilities: Videotape (3/4", VHS and Betamax).

CALIFORNIA (Los Angeles Metro)

MOTIVATIONAL MEDIA, INC.
12001 Ventura Place, Suite 202
Studio City, CA 91604
(818) 508-6553
(800) 331-8454

Fax: (818) 508-6572

Jeff Miller (Vice President)

Contact: Jeff Miller
Services: Videotape producer and distributor.
Description: Programs designed to assist in treating chemical dependency patients, hosted by well-known celebrities.
Titles include: *The Orientation Film; The Aftercare Film; AA & the Alcoholic; Pandora's Bottle; The Twenty Questions; The Bottom Line; Boozers and Users; Drugs and Alcohol* (3 parts); and three films on prejudice and human relations, designed for treatment facilities: *Beyond Black and White; Perceiving & Believing;* and *The Prejudice Film.*
Size & Elements: Videotape: 3/4" and VHS (15 titles, each approx. 30-45 min.).
Cataloging: Published catalog.
Access: Available to the public for purchase. Orders accepted by mail and telephone.
Rights: Apply for information.
Licensing: Apply for information.
Restrictions: Apply for information.
Viewing Facilities: None.
Duplication Facilities: None.

CALIFORNIA (Los Angeles Metro)

NEW WORLD PICTURES
1440 South Sepulveda Boulevard
Los Angeles, CA 90025
(213) 444-8100

Services: Motion picture producer and distributor.

CALIFORNIA (Los Angeles Metro)

NEWS ON FILM
1428 North Curson, Suite 6
Los Angeles, CA 90046
(213) 874-7471

Paul Hart (Director)

Contact: Paul Hart
Services: Film stock footage sales library.
Description: Small collection of unique footage of recent events, including the anti-nuclear movement, politicians and political activism, and foreign wars (El Salvador and Afghanistan). Additional material includes two speeches by Rev. Jesse Jackson, one shot at a Washington, D.C. rally (April 1986); the other at a high school in Michigan, during his Presidential campaign (1987-88).
Size & Elements: Film: 16mm (over 10,000 feet, 20 to 25 separate stories).
Cataloging: Published list.
Access: Available to the public for licensing and reuse. Research fees not charged. Research requests accepted by mail and telephone.
Rights: Full rights held to all material.
Licensing: Available for licensing and reuse. License fees charged.
Restrictions: None specified.
Viewing Facilities: None.
Duplication Facilities: None (outside arrangements can be made).

CALIFORNIA (Los Angeles Metro)

NEWSREEL VIDEO SERVICE
7329 Donna Avenue
Reseda, CA 91335
(818) 344-7107

Gary Arnote (Owner)

Contacts: Gary Arnote; Kim Arnote
Services: Videotape producer; ENG stringer service. Footage available for licensing and reuse. Custom shooting services available.
Description: Covers spot news stories throughout the greater Los Angeles area, emphasizing police- and fire-related incidents. Footage (ca. 1978-present) includes fires and flames; traffic accidents; paramedics and firefighters in action; dramatic physical rescues; air crashes; aerial views of Los Angeles shot from helicopters; brush fires; police pursuits; SWAT operations; and heavy coverage of gang activity. Events of special interest include the 1988 fire at the First Interstate Bank building in downtown Los Angeles and Little Richard's automobile accident.
Newsreel Video Service crews work the Los Angeles streets on a 24-hour basis, enabling them to respond quickly to custom shooting requests. Footage is also available for background use (e.g., for playback on television monitors within motion picture scenes).
Size & Elements: Videotape: 3/4" and Super VHS (approx. 2,000 hours).
Cataloging: Computerized cataloging (printouts) available to researchers; other finding aids. A demonstration reel is available on request.
Access: Open to the public. Available for duplication and reuse. Research fees charged. Research requests accepted by telephone and in person (by appointment only).
Rights: Full rights held to all material. Additional clearances may be necessary in some cases if material is to be reused.
Licensing: Available for licensing and reuse. License fees charged.
Restrictions: Since most footage is shot in the context of news events, releases are not obtained from individuals featured therein.
Viewing Facilities: Videotape (3/4", Super VHS and VHS).
Duplication Facilities: Videotape (3/4", Super VHS and VHS).

CALIFORNIA (Los Angeles Metro)

NISSAN MOTOR CORPORATION OF THE UNITED STATES
P.O. Box 191
Gardena, CA 90247-7638
(213) 532-3111
Fax: (213) 516-7967

Contact: Bill Pauli (Corporate Public Relations Manager)
Services: Corporation; corporate archives. Films and videotapes maintained for promotional use; possibly available for reuse by approved broadcasters and producers only.
Description: Film and videotape material is held both by Nissan and Bob Thomas & Associates, Inc., an advertising agency representing Nissan.
Coverage, all related to auto racing (1977-present), includes the Paul Newman car; the GTP (X-Turbo); the Stadium and Desert trucks; the Paul Newman television show (not available for reuse); the 300 CX "Road Atlanta" SECA Finals and the Mint 400 races. Nissan also holds instructional materials for in-house use.
Size & Elements: Film: 16mm (amount unspecified). Videotape: 1" and 3/4" (approx. 40 videotapes; transfers from film).
Cataloging: None specified.
Access: Not open to the public. Available for reuse by approved broadcasters and producers, subject to restrictions. Research fees not charged. Research requests accepted by telephone.
Rights: Full rights held to some material. Additional clearances may be necessary in some cases if material is to be reused.
Licensing: Materials available for licensing and reuse, subject to restrictions.
Restrictions: Requests for reuse considered on a case-by-case basis. Copyright clearance and project approval required. Name-identity credit generally required. Paul Newman's name and image may not be reused in any manner.
Viewing Facilities: None.
Duplication Facilities: Videotape.

CALIFORNIA (Los Angeles Metro)

NORTHROP UNIVERSITY
ALUMNI LIBRARY
AMERICAN HALL OF AVIATION HISTORY
5800 West Arbor Vitae
Los Angeles, CA 90045
(213) 337-4436

Dr. Jerome Halpin (Library Director)

Contact: Bradford S. Miller (Special Collections Librarian)
Services: Library. Film and videotape material available for in-house research, duplication and reuse on a case-by-case basis.
Description: History of aeronautics and aviation (late 1800s-1960). Holds approximately 500 newsreel clips (beginning 1940s, each 3-5 min.), covering aviation history from the beginning of powered flight; training films, primarily in the field of aeronautical engineering, including collections donated by TRW, Northrop and other corporations; and documentary films on aviation history

produced by aircraft manufacturers, television networks and individual production companies.
Size & Elements: Film: 16mm (1,200 films, each 3-40 min.; release prints, black and white and color). Videotape: VHS (75 videotapes; viewing copies). In process of transferring all films to videotape viewing copies.
Cataloging: Accession list of film and videotape titles. Computerized cataloging for staff use only (will be available to researchers when completed).
Access: Open to responsible users. For in-house use only. Available for duplication and reuse on a case-by-case basis. Collection does not circulate except by interlibrary loan. Private loans are considered on an individual basis, depending on intended use and uniqueness of film to collection. Research fees charged for work performed by staff. Research requests accepted by mail, telephone and in person (walk-in and by appointment).
Rights: Full rights held to some material (TRW and Northrop collections). Most material in the public domain. Additional clearances may be necessary in some cases (corporate collections) if material is to be reused.
Licensing: Available for licensing and reuse, subject to restrictions. License fees charged in some cases.
Restrictions: Requests for licensing and reuse considered on a case-by-case basis.
Viewing Facilities: Film (16mm projector); videotape (VHS).
Duplication Facilities: None.
Related Materials: Books, pamphlets, periodicals and 50,000 still photographs all relating to aviation history.

CALIFORNIA (Los Angeles Metro)

NUCLEAR FREE ZONE REGISTRY
28222 Stonehouse Road
Lake Elsinore, CA 92330
(714) 674-6576

Contact: Jeanne Tanase
Services: Political and educational organization. Videotapes available for distribution and rental.
Description: Grassroots group organizing nuclear-free zone (NFZ) declarations in opposition to the development, transport and use of nuclear weapons.

Titles (from various producers) available for rental: *Leading Double Lives*, on people in a small U.S. town who begin to act on their concerns about nuclear weapons; *A Good Planet is Hard to Find* (Marin Nuclear Freeze), a documentary on citizens in Mill Valley, California, who influenced the city council to pass an NFZ resolution; *Islands of the Empire*, a documentary on New Zealand's military relations with the U.S.; *Strategic Trust*, an award-winning documentary on Belau, and the "Palau Plebiscite of 1986"; *If the World Goes Away, Where Will the Children Play?*, featuring a mime showing children from around the world that peace is our only choice; *A Step Away From War* (Center for Defense Information), presenting arguments for a comprehensive nuclear test ban; *Sonia Johnson at Atomic Cafe*, presenting "Feminism: The Centerpiece of the Puzzle"; *Portraits of Peacemakers, Part II: The Women* (Marybeth Webster); *Peace Allelujah*, a visual music experience produced by Raphael Ornstein; *Express Nuclear Waste* (KQED), documenting a discussion and public hearing on nuclear waste transport; and *John Stockwell Talks About the C.I.A.*, a homemade videotape by an ex-intelligence officer.
Size & Elements: Videotape: VHS (11 titles).
Cataloging: Published brochures.
Access: Available to the public for 10-day rental. Postage fees apply. Orders and reservations accepted by mail.
Rights: Apply for information.
Licensing: Apply for information.
Restrictions: Apply for information.
Viewing Facilities: None.
Duplication Facilities: None.

CALIFORNIA (Los Angeles Metro)

OCCIDENTAL COLLEGE LIBRARY
1600 Campus Road
Los Angeles, CA 90041
(213) 259-2640

Michael C. Sutherland (Special Collections Librarian)

Contact: Michael C. Sutherland
Services: Library; educational institution. Film collection available for research

and reuse, subject to restrictions.
Description: Films relating to the history of Occidental College; athletic events.
Size & Elements: Not specified.
Cataloging: Films are in labeled cans but not cataloged.
Access: Open to researchers and scholars only. Available for duplication and reuse, subject to restrictions. Research fees not charged. Requests accepted by mail.
Rights: Rights status of material not known.
Licensing: Available for reuse, subject to restrictions. Usage fees not charged.
Restrictions: College must be credited if any material reused.
Viewing Facilities: None.
Duplication Facilities: None.

CALIFORNIA (Los Angeles Metro)

ONE, INC.
Blanche M. Baker Memorial Library
3340 Country Club Drive
Los Angeles, CA 90019
(213) 735-5252

Contact: Office Staff
Services: Educational institution; library. Material available to researchers and scholars for in-house use only.
Description: History of the gay movement; oral history interviews with early figures (1920s-present); and lectures by movement figures and professionals (e.g., Evelyn Hooker and Christopher Isherwood).
Size & Elements: Film and videotape (formats and amounts unspecified).
Cataloging: None.
Access: Open to researchers and scholars only. For in-house use only. Research requests accepted by telephone and in person (by appointment only).
Rights: Full rights held to all material.
Licensing: Apply for information. License or usage fees charged in some cases.
Restrictions: Apply for information.
Viewing Facilities: None.
Duplication Facilities: None.

CALIFORNIA (Los Angeles Metro)

ORION PICTURES CORP.
1888 Century Park East
Los Angeles, CA 90067
(213) 282-0550

Services: Motion picture producer and distributor.

CALIFORNIA (Los Angeles Metro)

PALISADES WILDLIFE FILM LIBRARY
PALISADES EDUCATIONAL PRODUCTIONS
1205 South Ogden Drive
Los Angeles, CA 90019
(213) 931-6186

Louis Kisner (Owner)

Contact: Louis Kisner
Services: Film and videotape producer; stock footage sales library.
Description: U.S. wildlife, habitats, scenics and ecology.

Holds edited wildlife "story films" (62 films, each 4 min.) showing animal encounters with scientifically accurate narration; and short films of songs and rhymes from classical children's literature, featuring mimes, clowns and magicians, originally produced for Paramount.
Size & Elements: Film: 16mm (100,000 feet). Videotape: 1", 3/4" and 1/2" (100 titles).
Cataloging: Card catalogs by subject; published catalogs; shot lists.
Access: Available for duplication, licensing and reuse. Requests accepted by mail, telephone and in person (by appointment only).
Rights: Full rights held to all material.
Licensing: Available for licensing and reuse. License fees charged.
Restrictions: None specified.
Viewing Facilities: Film and videotape.
Duplication Facilities: None.

CALIFORNIA (Los Angeles Metro)

PARAMOUNT PICTURES CORPORATION
5555 Melrose Avenue
Los Angeles, CA 90038
(213) 468-5000
(213) 468-5184 (Film Clip Licensing)
(213) 468-5520 (Screening Room Reservations)
Fax: (213) 468-8411
Telex: 882501 PARAMOUNT LSA

Contact: Diane Isaacs (Coordinator, Film Clip Licensing)
Services: Motion picture and television producer and distributor.
Description: Stock footage from Paramount feature films and television productions. Outtakes and unedited footage available from Paramount Pictures Stock Film Library (q.v.).
Size & Elements: Film: 35mm and 16mm (amount unspecified; feature motion pictures). Videotape: 1" and 3/4" (amount unspecified; television productions and feature films; masters and viewing copies).
Cataloging: Not available for public use.
Access: Not open to the public. Research requests not accepted. Only 16mm prints and 3/4" videotapes with visual time code are made available for off-lot viewing.
Rights: Apply for information. Additional clearances always necessary if material is to be reused.
Licensing: Contact Diane Isaacs (Film Clip Licensing) for information regarding licensing policies and procedures, legal affairs inquiries, and the availability of film and videotape viewing copies. License fees charged.

Licensing requests must be submitted in writing, and include a detailed description of clip required, specify the context in which clip will be used, the term of use, distribution territory and media exhibition. Storyboard required if clip intended for use in commercials. Allow three weeks (from receipt of request) for a reply. Requester is responsible for all clearances and approvals by third parties, guilds, music publishers, performing rights societies, etc.
Restrictions: No one scene licensed may exceed two minutes thirteen seconds (2:13); the aggregate of scenes from any single production may not exceed four minutes twenty-six seconds (4:26). Music and/or soundtrack must be cleared separately.
Viewing Facilities: Film (screening rooms, by reservation only). Screening fees charged.
Duplication Facilities: None.

CALIFORNIA (Los Angeles Metro)

PARAMOUNT PICTURES STOCK FILM LIBRARY
Hal Wallis Building
5555 Melrose Avenue
Los Angeles, CA 90038
(213) 468-5510

Connie Bulmer (Head Librarian)

Contact: Connie Bulmer
Services: Film stock footage sales library.
Description: One of Hollywood's largest stock footage libraries. Collection includes outtakes and unused footage from Paramount's features and television series, spanning over 50 years. Holds exclusively 35mm film, including three-strip Technicolor and many "miniature" scenes.
Size & Elements: Film: 35mm (black and white and color; safety and nitrate; negatives and workprints).
Cataloging: Production books organized by subject and production title. Eight-frame clips of each scene from every film in the collection are on file.
Access: Open to the public. Available for duplication, licensing and reuse. Research fees not charged. Research requests accepted by telephone. Library's services are restricted to Los Angeles-area producers only; no prints are sent out of town. Outside producers are serviced once they have established an account. Those without an account pay a nonrefundable minimum license fee if any negative is furnished.
Rights: Full rights held to all material.
Licensing: Available for licensing. License fees charged.
Restrictions: Cecil B. De Mille stock footage material is not available. Out-of-town producers not serviced unless they have established an account.
Viewing Facilities: None.
Duplication Facilities: None (film-to-videotape transfers may be made for account holders).

CALIFORNIA (Los Angeles Metro)

PARTIDO NACIONAL LA RAZA UNIDA
P.O. Box 13
San Fernando, CA 91340
(818) 365-6534

Street address: 483 5th Street

Xenaro G. Ayala (National Chair)

Contact: Xenaro G. Ayala
Services: Political party. Videotape collection for in-house use only.
Description: Independent Chicano Mexicano political party. Videotape collection documents La Raza Youth Conferences I-IV (1984-87); youth marches (1983, 1984); the 1984 Vecinos Youth Fair; the Chicano Park commemoration in San Diego, Calif. (1985); and the August 29th Commemoration in Los Angeles (1981, 1983, 1987).
Size & Elements: Videotape: format unspecified (9 titles; masters).
Cataloging: Computerized cataloging for staff use only.
Access: For in-house use only. Maintained for distribution or rental rather than for research or reuse. Research requests accepted by mail.
Rights: Full rights held to all material.
Licensing: Apply for information. License fees charged in some cases (depending on nature of request).
Restrictions: None specified.
Viewing Facilities: Videotape.
Duplication Facilities: None.

CALIFORNIA (Los Angeles Metro)

PATRICK MEDIA GROUP
1550 West Washington Boulevard
Los Angeles, CA 90007
(213) 731-5111
Fax: (213) 732-7736

CALIFORNIA (Los Angeles Metro P)

Gerald Joyce (President and Owner)

Contact: Joe Blackstock (Photography Department)
Services: Advertising corporation; media organization. Archival film collection available to researchers, scholars and the public primarily for in-house viewing.
Description: Films dating from the 1920s depicting outdoor advertising in Los Angeles, San Francisco and Seattle. All films were produced by Foster & Kleiser, predecessor to Patrick Media. Footage includes scenes of the Sunset Strip, billboards advertising various West Coast businesses, street scenes and cars driving by. Also holds one 8mm film (ca. 1940s-50s).
Size & Elements: Film: 16mm (12 films); 8mm (1 film).
Cataloging: None.
Access: Open to researchers, scholars and the public primarily for in-house viewing. Collection maintained for historical and archival purposes. Research fees not charged. Research requests accepted by mail, telephone and in person (by appointment only).
Rights: Full rights held to all material.
Licensing: Apply for information.
Restrictions: Material generally not available for loan. Other restrictions may apply depending on intended use.
Viewing Facilities: Film.
Duplication Facilities: None.

CALIFORNIA (Los Angeles Metro)

PAULIST PRODUCTIONS
P.O. Box 1057
Pacific Palisades, CA 90272
(213) 454-0688
(800) 624-8613 (orders)
(818) 884-3100 (in California)
Fax: (213) 459-6549

Street address: 17575 Pacific Coast Highway

Ellwood E. Kieser, C.S.P. (President/Executive Producer)

Contact: Paul A. Weber (General Manager)
Services: Media organization; film and television producer. Material available to the public for rental and purchase.
Description: Social-theme television shows collectively called *Insight* (1962-84). "These shows were done to dramatize the Judeo-Christian ethic that stresses the presence of God in all persons. This was done by presenting everyday situations wherein decisions had to be made as to how one was going to live one's life."

Sample titles include: *The Game Room,* an allegory of the nuclear arms race and a dramatization of the underlying message of the Catholic Bishops' Pastoral on war and peace. *She's Waiting For Us* follows a drunk man through a car crash that kills his girlfriend, and into an after-death experience, and his continuing growth as his soul is sent back to his body by the Light. *Butterfly* shows a couple whose new baby has died in delivery. The woman blames herself, her husband and God for the baby's death. A friend shares her faith in the Resurrection and helps create a hope for new birth in the woman.

Other series distributed include: *Reflections Film; Bloomin' Human Films* (elementary and junior high school); *Vignette Films;* and *Words of Jesus Films.*

Additional materials include extensive footage showing famine in Ethiopia and other African countries.
Size & Elements: Film: 16mm. Videotape: VHS. (300 titles total, each 30 min.).
Cataloging: Published catalogs.
Access: Available to the public for rental and purchase. Requests accepted by mail and telephone.
Rights: Some rights held to all material. Additional clearances may be necessary in some cases if material is to be reused.
Licensing: Available for licensing and reuse, subject to restrictions.
Restrictions: Requests for reuse considered on a case-by-case basis.
Viewing Facilities: Film (16mm); videotape (3/4" and VHS).
Duplication Facilities: None.
Related Materials: Study guides available for all productions.
Representative: Audience Planners, Inc. West Coast: 5107 Douglas Fir Road, Calabasas, CA 91302; (818) 884-3100. East and Midwest: The Merchandise Mart, Suite 1358, Chicago, IL 60654; (312) 822-0892.

CALIFORNIA (Los Angeles Metro)

PHOTO-CHUTING ENTERPRISES
12619 South Manor Drive
Hawthorne, CA 90250
(213) 678-0163

Jean Boenish (Owner)

Contact: Jean Boenish
Services: Film and videotape producer. Stock footage available for licensing and reuse. Videotape programs available to the public for purchase. Custom shooting services available.
Description: Sport skydiving and parachuting footage documenting the growth of and milestones in freefall skydiving and early canopy formation (early 1960s-early 1980s). Also holds footage of BASE jumping (i.e., skydiving or parachuting from fixed objects: Buildings, Antenna towers, Spans [bridges] and Earth [cliffs]) from its original popularization in 1978 through 1984.

A number of completed videotape programs are available for purchase, including *Filmpoems,* featuring skydiving, formation diving, skydiving from cliffs, star formations, sequential relative work, aerial gymnastics, the early development of hang-gliding, car towing, water and snow kiting, balloon launches, and comedy crashes. *Minifilms* feature BASE jumps, with jumps from a Texas skyscraper under construction; antennas; the New River Gorge Bridge (Charleston, W. Va.); Yosemite's El Capitan and Half Dome, the roof of the Houston Astrodome; and a tethered balloon anchored at 400 feet. Also featured is hang-gliding parachuting and practice flights with a hydrogen peroxide rocket belt.

Can shoot custom footage of skydiving or limited BASE jumping.
Size & Elements: Film: 16mm (approx. 250,000 feet, 291 cans; ECO color reversal; also 7 completed titles, release prints). Videotape: 3/4" (7 completed titles; transfers from 16mm release prints); VHS (preview cassettes available). BASE jumping footage is not available in release print form; rough cuts (approx. 120 min.) have been transferred to 1" and 3/4" videotape from 16mm workprints.
Cataloging: Shot lists (limited, for staff use only).
Access: For in-house use only. Research fees charged in some cases. Research requests accepted by mail, telephone and in person (by appointment only). Completed programs available to the public for purchase.
Rights: Full rights held to all material. Additional clearances may be necessary in some cases if material is to be reused (Astrodome and rocketbelt footage).
Licensing: Available for licensing and reuse. License fees charged (vary according to intended use and market).
Restrictions: Some footage restricted per individual contracts; most footage restricted to specific one-time use.
Viewing Facilities: Film (16mm); videotape (3/4", VHS and Betamax) (by appointment only).
Duplication Facilities: Videotape (3/4", VHS and Betamax).
Representative: Two titles (*Sky Dive!* and *Sky Capers*) distributed by Pyramid Film and Video Corp. (q.v.).

CALIFORNIA (Los Angeles Metro)

PLAYBOY PROGRAMS, INC.
8560 Sunset Boulevard
Los Angeles, CA 90069
(213) 659-4080
Fax: (213) 652-4481

Richard Sowa (President, Playboy Video Corp.)

Contact: Legal Affairs Department
Services: Corporation; film and videotape producer. Not open to the public. Material primarily available for broadcast and cablecast; available for licensing and reuse, subject to restrictions.
Description: Programs concerning nudity, sex, "adult entertainment" and censorship issues, produced by Playboy Programs (1950s-present). (Playboy Programs is distinct from Playboy Productions, which produced feature films in the 1970s.)

Early programs include *Playboy Penthouse* (black and white) and *Playboy in the Dark* (color). The Playboy Channel (carried on pay cable) features "adult viewing material" produced by Playboy Programs. Contemporary programs include: *Sexetra: The News According to Playboy,* a news magazine program focusing on sex, censorship, First Amendment freedoms in television and homevideo, current events and current media issues; the videotape version of

Playboy Magazine and interviews with film directors and stars; and *Women on Sex*, a panel-discussion show.

Size & Elements: Film: 35mm and 16mm. Videotape: 1" (masters); 3/4" (transfers from films; viewing copies). ("Thousands of hours" total).
Cataloging: None.
Access: Not open to the public. Research fees charged to cover costs. Research requests accepted by mail only.
Rights: Full rights held to all material.
Licensing: Materials available for licensing and reuse, subject to restrictions. Usage fees charged (fees determined on a individual basis).
Restrictions: Requests for licensing and reuse considered on a case-by-case basis.
Viewing Facilities: None.
Duplication Facilities: None.

CALIFORNIA (Los Angeles Metro)

POLITICAL ISSUE ARCHIVE
2923 Pearl Street
Santa Monica, CA 90405
(213) 453-8830
(213) 396-4959

Peter Broderick (Director)

Contact: Peter Broderick
Services: Private videotape collection. Available to researchers and scholars only for research, duplication and reuse.
Description: "Advocacy television" (spots and programs designed to persuade viewers on issues).

The core of the collection is made up of pro and con spots on a wide range of issues, including abortion, gun control, nuclear power, nuclear weapons, women's rights, smoking, gay rights, bottle bills and bills to tax big oil companies. There are also political spots created by parties, political action committees (PAC's) and candidates in opposition which are juxtaposed.

Includes *Point-Counterpoint: Controversy By Television*, a program produced by Peter Broderick, which provides a historical overview and tactical analysis of advocacy television.

Size & Elements: Videotape: 3/4" (amount unspecified).
Cataloging: Staff assistance required.
Access: Not open to the public. Open to researchers and scholars only. Available for duplication and reuse. Research fees charged. Research requests accepted by mail, telephone and in person (by appointment only).
Rights: No rights held to some material. Some material in the public domain. Additional clearances may be necessary in some cases if material is to be reused.
Licensing: Available for duplication and reuse. Usage fees charged.
Restrictions: None specified.
Viewing Facilities: Videotape (3/4") by appointment only.
Duplication Facilities: None.

CALIFORNIA (Los Angeles Metro)

PRODUCERS LIBRARY SERVICE
1051 North Cole Avenue
Hollywood, CA 90038
(213) 465-0572
Fax: (213) 465-1671

Jeffrey A. Goodman; Anthony Slide (Co-Owners)

Contacts: Jeffrey A. Goodman; Anthony Slide
Services: Film and videotape stock footage sales library; library of entertainment-oriented photographs; research services available.
Description: Founded in 1957, Producers Library Service is one of the two oldest and largest stock footage libraries in Los Angeles.

Holds 35mm color stock footage covering all subjects (mid-1950s-present). Special strengths include animals, buildings, cars, domestic and foreign cities, helicopters, military, planes, police, scenics, ships, sports, trains, volcanoes and westerns. Library represents stock footage outtakes from all productions of ABC Circle Films and Orion Pictures Corporation, including *Out on a Limb; Love Among the Ruins; Franklin and Eleanor; The Woman in Red; Code of Silence;* and *Desperately Seeking Susan.* 35mm color stock footage is also available from the films of many independent producers. Library also represents stock footage outtakes from all Spelling-Goldberg television series,

including *Hart to Hart, The Rookies, Mod Squad, Charlie's Angels, SWAT* and *Starsky and Hutch.*

Holds 35mm color recreations of historical events such as the Civil War, Western American history, 19th century railroads, World War II, the Korean War, and the Vietnam War.

Holdings of 16mm color footage (late 1940s-late 1950s) cover most American cities and all aspects of American life and society, at home, at play and in the workplace; also most foreign countries, including establishing shots of cities, industry, ethnic faces and cultures, and children.

35mm black and white footage (1910s-50s) includes more than 200 complete features and short subjects (dramas, comedies, slapstick, melodramas, musicals and cartoons). Most Hollywood personalities are represented, and the collection is particularly rich in "B" Westerns. Library also maintains a small black and white newsreel collection and a small collection of 16mm original archival prints.

Black and white feature films. James Cagney in *Great Guy* and *Something to Sing About* (1937); Bela Lugosi in *The Human Monster* (1940) and *Black Dragons* (1942); James Mason in *The Mill on the Floss* (1937); Paul Lukas in *Sing Sinner, Sing* (1933); Anna Sten in *Exile Express* (1939); Jack Oakie in *Uptown New York* (1932); Ilona Massey in *New Wine* (1941); Lum and Abner in *Two Weeks to Live* (1943); Douglass Montgomery and Evelyn Venable in *Harmony Lane* (1935); Richard Arlen in *Wildcat* (1942) Pinky Tomlin and Toby Wing in *Sing While You're Able* (1937); Thelma Todd in *You Made Me Love You* (1933); George O'Brien in *Daniel Boone* (1936).

Black and white exploitation features. *Damaged Lives* (1937) depicts the dangers of venereal disease; *Picture Brides* (1934) diamond miners order mail-order brides; *Rebellious Daughters* (1938) young girls in the wicked city; *Island Captives* (1937) lechery and murder in the South Seas; *City of Missing Girls* (1941) shows innocent girls lured to work in nightclubs; *Face on the Barroom Floor* (1932) extolls the perils of alcohol.

"B" Westerns. Johnny Mack Brown in *Between Men* (1936), *Desert Phantom* (1937) and *Rogue of the Range* (1937); Ray "Crash" Corrigan in *Kid's Last Ride* (1941), *The Range Busters* (1940), *Trail of the Silver Spurs* (1941); *Wrangler's Roost* (1941); Buster Crabbe in *Billy the Kid Trapped* (1942); Hoot Gibson in *Frontier Justice* (1936); Ken Maynard in *Six Shootin' Sheriff* (1938), *Whirlwind Horseman* (1933); Kermit Maynard in *Arizona Stagecoach* (1942), *His Fighting Blood* (1935), *Roaring Six Guns* (1937), *Song*

of the Trail (1936), *Whistling Bullets* (1937); Tim McCoy in *Roarin' Guns* (1936); Dave O'Brien in *Cowboy Millionaire* (1935), *Hollywood Cowboy* (1937), *Whispering Smith* (1936); Tex Ritter in *Arizona Days* (1937), *Rollin' Plains* (1938), *Sing, Cowboy Sing* (1937), *Tex Rides with the Boy Scouts* (1937); Bob Steele in *El Diablo Rides* (1940), *The Rider of the Law* (1935), *Riders of the Sage* (1939), *Sundown Saunders* (1937); Tom Tyler in *Santa Fe Bound* (1937).

Size & Elements: Film: 35mm (4.5 million feet); 16mm (1 million feet). Videotape: 1" (masters) and 3/4" (viewing copies) (all transfers from film).

All materials originate on film. Positive viewing prints and camera original negatives exist on all 35mm color items. All 16mm color footage consists of unique camera originals. All 35mm black and white footage is of the highest quality, primarily original nitrate elements. A small portion of collection has been transferred to 3/4" viewing videotapes, and some items also exist as 1" masters.

Cataloging: In-house catalogs (books arranged by subject and location) exist for all 35mm color materials, indicating the exact footage available on any shot. 16mm color and 35mm black and white footage is more generally cataloged by subject.

Access: Open to the public. Research fees charged for major projects, but most requests can be answered immediately at no charge. Screening fees charged. Clients in Los Angeles with 35mm viewing facilities are welcome to take 35mm color footage away for viewing at no charge. Any footage can be transferred to a 3/4" or VHS viewing videotape for a small service fee, plus laboratory charges. Research requests accepted by mail, telephone and in person (by appointment only).

Rights: Full rights held to all material. 35mm and 16mm color material can be licensed for worldwide use; 35mm black and white material can be licensed for U.S. use.

Licensing: Available for licensing and reuse. License fees charged on an individual basis, with a minimum fee applicable for all jobs. License fees are payable upon delivery of master elements and are not refundable.

Restrictions: License fees clear one-time footage use only. Talent clearances may be necessary if actors are visible in footage that is to be used for advertising purposes.

Viewing Facilities: Film (35mm and 16mm); videotape (3/4").

Duplication Facilities: None (outside duplication houses are used). All laboratory, film to videotape transfer, shipping and messenger fees are payable by the client.

Related Materials: 10,000 black and white photographs covering motion picture subjects, vaudeville, radio, television and Hollywood history.

Related Services: Offers a research service providing access to all other stock footage libraries in Los Angeles and all major motion picture studio libraries. Library also represents a number of private collectors with large public domain collections of early television programs, and films covering all aspects of Hollywood history.

CALIFORNIA (Los Angeles Metro)

PROTELE, INC.
9200 Sunset Boulevard, Suite 1024
Los Angeles, CA 90069
(213) 859-4788
Fax: (213) 859-7615
Telex: 691026 PROTELE

Marcele Vimay (President)

Contact: Belinda Menendez
Services: U.S. office of Protele, S.A. (q.v.). Handles international distribution and sales of television programs (except news) produced by Televisa.
Description: See Protele, S.A. (Mexico, D.F.)

CALIFORNIA (Los Angeles Metro)

PYRAMID FILM AND VIDEO CORPORATION
P.O. Box 1048
Santa Monica, CA 90406
(213) 828-7577
(800) 421-2304
Fax: (213) 453-9083
Telex: 678262 Pyrmidfv uq

David Adams (President)
Lynn Adams (Vice President)

Randy Wright (Vice President)
Denise Adams (General Manager)

Contacts: Jean Phillips (Marketing Director); Pat Hamada (Acquisitions); Penny Rembert (Stock Footage, Special Licenses, TV and Cable Broadcasts); Art Pasante (International Orders); Tami Arneson (International Assistant)
Services: Film and videotape producer and distributor; stock footage sales library. Collection maintained for distribution and rental rather than for research.
Description: Specializes in educational and safety and health films and videotapes. Other subject areas include literature and art, social science, science and mathematics, sports, and entertainment.

Alcohol, drugs and tobacco. Titles available: *Cocaine Blues: The Myth and Reality of Cocaine; Psychoactive; Promises: Profile of an Alcoholic; Drinking; Beating the Booze Blues; We Have an Addict in the House; The Alcoholic Within Us; Death in the West,* juxtaposing the healthy independent image of the Marlboro Man with the stark reality of six smoking cowboys; *Smokescreen; The Feminine Mistake,* showing what happens to women who smoke; *Smoking: How to Stop;* and *Why People Smoke.*

Artists. Films on Jacques Louis David, Gian-Battista Piranesi, Henry Fuseli, William Blake, Francisco Goya, Ingres, Gericault, John Constable, Joseph Mallord William Turner, Eugene Delacroix, Jean-Francois Millet, Auguste Rodin, Edgar Degas, Robert Gilbert and Henri Rousseau. Other topics include the beginnings of ancient civilization in Egypt, Romantic versus Classical art, highlights of western art, American quilts, Waterford crystal, and Black American art.

Entertainment. Titles include *Ballet Robotique* (Bob Rogers & Company); *Bambi Meets Godzilla* (Marv Newland); *Blaze Glory, Sergeant Swell* and *Vicious Cycles* (Chuck Menville and Len Janson); *Java Junkie* (Tom Schiller); *Why'd the Beetle Cross the Road?* (Jan Skrentry); *Closet Cases of the Nerd Kind* (Rick and Ann Harper); *Porklips Now* and *Hardware Wars* (Ernie Fosselius and Bill Couturie); *Fish Heads* (Barnes, Barnes, and Paxton); *The Killing of an Egg* (Paul Driessen); *Rendezvous* (Claude Lelouch); *The Great Cognito* (Will Vinton and Susan Shelburne) and *Recorded Live* (S. S. Wilson).

Film history and film as art. Features include *Birth of a Nation* and *The Battle at Elderbush Gulch* (D. W. Griffith); *Experiments in Motion Graphics* and *Arabesque* (John Whitney); *The City* (Willard Van Dyke and Ralph Steiner); *N.Y.N.Y.* (Francis Thompson); *The Big Bang and Other Myths, Sky Dance, Step by Step, Second Chance: Sea, W.O.W. (Women of the World), Hello, Starlore, Whither Weather, Enter Life,* and *Voyage to Next* (Faith Hubley). Also held are the films of Charles and Ray Eames, including *Alpha, The Black Ships, Clown Face, A Communications Primer, Computer Perspective, Copernicus, Daumier: Paris and the Spectator, Day of the Dead, Dead Sequence, Degas in the Metropolitan, DeGaulle Sketch, Design Q&A, Eames Lounge Chair, The Expanding Airport, Exponents, The Fiberglass Chairs, House, IBM at the Fair, Meet Me in St. Louis, Music Sequence, National Fisheries Center and Aquarium, Newton's Method, Soft Pad, Something About Photography, SX–70, Toccata for Toy Trains, Two Baroque Churches in Germany, Two Laws of Algebra, Two Puppet Shows* and *Westinghouse in Alphabetical Order.*

Geography. James Michener investigates Hawaii, Israel, Poland, Spain and the South Pacific. Other areas examined are Iran, Turkey and the Great Lakes.

Health education. Titles include the *I Am Joe* series, presenting information about essential body parts (e.g., *I Am Joe's Kidney, I Am Joe's Spine), Please Take Care of Your Teeth; Have a Heart;* and *A Change of Heart.*

History. The atomic bomb and J. Robert Oppenheimer; the turbulent 1960s; Edwardian England during World War I; the Battle of Little Big Horn; and Black American freedom fighters (Denmark Vesey, Harriet Tubman, Frederick Douglass and others).

The *In Search Of...* series hosted by Leonard Nimoy includes: Amelia Earhart, the Ice Age, Dead Sea Scrolls, hypnosis, life after death, strange visitors, the Bermuda Triangle, "Bigfoot," deadly ants, firewalkers, the Garden of Eden, hurricanes, immortality, Martians, Michael Rockefeller, Nazi plunder, swamp monsters, and psychic detectives.

Literature and language arts. Titles include: *The Open Window,* an adaptation of Saki's short story; *A Rose for Emily,* a dramatization of William Faulkner's first short story; *Young Goodman Brown,* Nathaniel Hawthorne's short story; *The Man and the Snake,* loosely based on Ambrose Bierce's short stories; *The Bet,* based on a Chekhov tale; *Notes on the Popular Arts,* how the popular arts serve as vehicles for self-projection and fantasy fulfillment; *Coleridge: The Fountain and the Cave; The Legend of Sleepy Hollow,* Washington Irving's classic; *Kudzu,* shows how Southern folk humor and traditions have grown up around a botanical past; *Paul Lawrence Dunbar; Mark Twain: Beneath the Laughter; The Happy Prince; The Legend of John

Henry; The Legend of Paul Bunyan; Gnomes; and *The Sorcerer's Apprentice.*

Media studies. Basic motion picture photography, editing, and lighting, animation techniques, Claymation (discussed by Will Vinton), television advertising, history and production. Highlights include Leonard Nimoy leading us through the world of television and a day in the life of the television newsman Bill Redeker.

Natural science and environment. Titles available: *Embryo; The Solar Film; Down to Earth: City Living; A Walk in the Forest,* chronicling the seasons with time-lapse photography; *Seashore; Spring; Ecology: Checks and Balances,* studying opposing forces in nature, such as the prey and the predator; *The Beginning of Life,* a study of conception and the embryo; *Miracle of Life,* showing both human and animal fetuses; *Dinosaur; Speaking of Harvey,* on the ethical issues of animal experimentation; and *Ant World.*

Nutrition and exercise. Titles include: *Total Fitness in 30 Minutes a Week* (based on Dr. Lawrence Morehouse's book); *The Target Zone: Aiming For Whole Body Fitness; The Caffeine File; Salt and Hypertension: How To Save Your Life; The Sugar Film;* and *I Am Wheat.*

Patient education and counseling. Titles available: *It Happens,* about the alternatives available to a 15-year-old pregnant girl; *Prenatal Care; Diabetes: Focus on Feeling; Children and Deafness;* and *Bypass: The Story of a Patient.*

Performing arts. Titles available: *The Bolero; Beethoven: Triumph Over Silence; Scott Joplin; All The World's A Stage,* showing an actor training at Juilliard School; *Ballet Adagio,* in which David and Anna Marie Holmes interpret Messerer's ballet *Spring Water; Paul Taylor and Company; Three By Martha Graham; All About Music; Peter and the Wolf; The Mourning Spider,* created by the Julian Chagrin mime troupe; *Mountain Music,* a commentary on electronic music, in which the sounds of nature are enhanced by folk music and eclipsed by hard rock; and *Monsieur Pointu.*

Physical science and mathematics. Topics include: the metric system; Buckminster Fuller's discoveries of nature's inherent geometry; the Chinese Tangram puzzle; the search for an antimatter universe; outer space (including rarely seen NASA film clips); cells, molecules and atoms.

Politicians. Profiled in the collection are Richard Nixon, Jimmy Carter, Benjamin Franklin, Teddy Roosevelt and Thomas Jefferson.

Psychology and human development. Titles include: *Everybody Rides a Carousel,* Faith Hubley's view of Erik Erikson's theory of personality development; *Oh Brother, My Brother,* on the conflicts of early childhood; *Windy Day,* a child's view of love, death, and marriage visualized through animation; the *Who We Are* series, six films that help children respect other races and cultures while learning to value their own individuality; *Bill Cosby on Prejudice; Get It Together,* on how Jeff Minnebraker achieved a happy life despite the loss of his legs in a car accident; and *Survival Run,* featuring blind marathon runner Harry Cordellos.

Religion and inspirational. Titles include: *The Silent Witness,* a documentary on the Shroud of Turin; *The Healing Ministry of the Church, He Restoreth My Soul,* the true story of Merrill Womach; *Though I Walk Through the Valley,* a statement on death and religious faith; *The Return,* investigating Old Testament predictions; *David and Goliath; The Walls of Time,* a documentary on the history of the English Bible; and *Mountain Tops,* the story of a paraplegic's climb up a 13,163-foot peak in the High Sierras.

Safety and health. Titles available: *CPR for Healthsavers; CPR for Citizens; CPR for Totsavers; New Pulse of Life; New Breath of Life; Eye Emergency; Emergency Obstetrics; The Trauma Patient; Bedside Cardiac Output; Going Into Shock; Burn Emergency; Hospitals Don't Burn Down; Motorcycle Safety Tips; Up To Code; Lady Beware; Safety Check Your Car; Water: Friend or Foe; Bleeding: What To Do; Everything About Bicycles; Bicycle Safety: You Can Prevent an Accident; Walk Safe! Young America; All About Pedestrian Safety; Skateboard Safety; Animals Can Bite;* and *All About Fire.*

Sociology and social issues. Titles available: *Scared Straight,* on the realities of prison life; *Just Another Missing Kid; Moonchild,* on entering the Unification Church; *Remember Me,* narrated by Dick Cavett, on Middle Eastern and Asian children; *Goodnight Miss Ann,* a portrait of a boxer; *Every Child,* an animated tale of an unwanted infant; *Football in America; Sports in America; The Black Athlete,* including interviews with O. J. Simpson and Harry Edwards; *Women in Sports,* with commentary by Chris Evert-Lloyd, Janet Guthrie and Nancy Lopez; *Children and Sports; Greenpeace: Voyages to Save the Whales; Kiss the Animals Goodbye; Leisure;* and *Man of Wheat,* on the life of a wheat farmer.

Sports. Row!; Dare the Wildest River, featuring the Colorado River and Arizona's Grand Canyon; *Tumbles, Mumbles and Bumbles,* bloopers by famous athletes; *If You Can Walk,* on the techniques of cross-country skiing; *Off the Wall,* a look at racquetball; *On the Run; On the Rocks,* highlighting rock gymnastics; *Americans on Everest; Solo,* a climber's quest toward the summit of his mountain; *Listen to the Mountain; First Ascent; Challenge Over the Atlantic,* in which three businessmen cross the Atlantic Ocean in a balloon; *Dawn Flight,* with stunning aerial maneuvers; *Fall Line,* featuring skiing in the upper regions of the Grand Tetons; *Ikaros,* showing skiers somersaulting through the air; *The Cutting Edge,* in which Yuichiro Miura skis down an Antarctic peak; *Up,* about hang-gliding; *Karate; A Sports Suite,* combining sports vignettes with classical music; *Angler's Autumn,* a portrait of a fisherman; *Seaflight,* on surfing; *Windflight; Moods of Surfing; Turned On,* a montage of dune buggies, speedboats, snowmobiles and motorcycles; *The Will to Win; Ski Wiz; Ski The Outer Limits; Sky Dive; Roller Skate Fever; Floating Free,* a glimpse of the World Frisbee Disc championship; *Catch the Joy,* on dune buggies; *Vrooom!,* on drag racing; *The Magic Rolling Board;* and *Gravity Never Sleeps,* on deep powder skiing.

Size & Elements: Film: 16mm (200 titles, 200 cans). Videotape: 3/4" and VHS (200 titles).
Cataloging: Published catalogs.
Access: Available for rental, purchase, licensing and reuse. Research requests accepted by mail and telephone.
Rights: Full rights held to most material. Additional clearances may be necessary in some cases if material is to be reused.
Licensing: Available for licensing and reuse. License fees charged.
Restrictions: None specified.
Viewing Facilities: Film and videotape.
Duplication Facilities: None.

CALIFORNIA (Los Angeles Metro)

QINTEX ENTERTAINMENT
345 North Maple Drive
Beverly Hills, CA 90210
(213) 281-2600

Services: Motion picture producer and distributor (formerly Hal Roach Studios).

CALIFORNIA (Los Angeles Metro)

RAINBOW VIDEO PRODUCTIONS
18321 Western Avenue, Suite K
Gardena, CA 90248
(213) 515-0706

Jon Sekiguchi (President)

Contact: Tom Kuwahara (Production Manager)
Services: Videotape producer. Collection available to the public for duplication, licensing and reuse.
Description: Traditional Asian cultural activities, events, exhibits, arts and crafts. Subjects include: parades; dance (Japanese, Korean, Filipino, Thai, Balinese and Chinese); arts and crafts exhibits; tea ceremonies; bonsai treemaking; dollmaking; sword displays; paintings; artifacts; Hawaiian scenics; shots of historical Ming Dynasty objects; clothing; and sports such as automobile and motorcycle racing.
Size & Elements: Videotape: Betacam and 3/4" (approx. 150 hours; masters and viewing copies); VHS and Betamax (viewing copies).
Cataloging: None specified.
Access: Available to the public for duplication and reuse.
Rights: Full rights held to all material.
Licensing: Available for licensing and reuse. License fees charged.
Restrictions: None.
Viewing Facilities: Videotape (Betacam, 3/4", VHS and Betamax).
Duplication Facilities: Videotape (Betacam, 3/4", VHS and Betamax).

CALIFORNIA (Los Angeles Metro)

REPUBLIC PICTURES CORPORATION
P.O. Box 66930
Los Angeles, CA 90066-0930
(213) 306-4040

Street address: 12636 Beatrice Street

Services: Motion picture producer and distributor.

CALIFORNIA (Los Angeles Metro)

RESEARCH VIDEO
4900 Vineland Avenue
North Hollywood, CA 91601
(818) 509-0506

Paul Surratt (Owner)

Contact: Paul Surratt
Services: Film and videotape stock footage sales library.
Description: Music clips of all kinds (1950s-80s). Genres include rock and roll, jazz, pop, folk, musicals, classical and opera. Holds both performances by and interviews with musicians.
Size & Elements: Film: 35mm and 16mm (original negatives and prints). Videotape: 2" and 1" (masters). (10,000 hours total).
Cataloging: Card catalogs.
Access: Not open to the public; open to business and industry only. Available for duplication, licensing and reuse, subject to clearance and restrictions. Research fees charged (rates negotiable). Research requests accepted by mail (preferred) and telephone.
Rights: Full rights held to some material. Some rights held to all material. Additional clearances may be necessary in some cases (from artists, directors and music publishers) if material is to be reused.
Licensing: Available for licensing and reuse, subject to restrictions. License and usage fees charged.
Restrictions: Restrictions apply on a case-by-case basis, depending on footage involved. Additional clearances are frequently necessary for reuse.
Viewing Facilities: Film and videotape (fees apply).
Duplication Facilities: Film (film-to-videotape planned); videotape (2" and 1").

CALIFORNIA (Los Angeles Metro)

RKO PICTURES
1900 Avenue of the Stars, Suite 1562

Los Angeles, CA 90067
(213) 277-3133

Services: Motion picture producer and distributor.

CALIFORNIA (Los Angeles Metro)

ROCK SOLID PRODUCTIONS
801 South Main Street
Burbank, CA 91506
(818) 841-8220
Fax: (818) 843-8099

Geoffrey Leighton (President)

Contact: Geoffrey Leighton
Services: Videotape producer. *Collection maintained for use of commercial facility clients only; footage not available to the public at present. Research requests not accepted.*
Description: Contemporary footage of most major U.S. cities, including scenics, beauty shots, landmarks, sights and attractions. Also holds recent footage of Nicaragua (approx. 50 hours), featuring scenics, general background shots, footage of cities and the countryside.
Size & Elements: Videotape: Betacam (approx. 600 hours; masters).
Cataloging: Partial computerized cataloging for staff use only.
Access: Not open to the public. Available to existing facility clients only. *Footage not available to the public at present. Research requests not accepted.*
Rights: Full rights held to all material. Additional clearances may be necessary in some cases if material is to be reused.
Licensing: Available for licensing and reuse, subject to restrictions. License fees charged.
Restrictions: Material not currently available to the public for research, duplication or reuse of any kind.
Viewing Facilities: None.
Duplication Facilities: None.

CALIFORNIA (Los Angeles Metro)

SALENGER FILMS, INC.
1635 12th Street
Santa Monica, CA 90404
(213) 450-1300

Contact: Distribution Staff
Services: Distributor. Films and videotapes available for rental and purchase.
Description: Sales and training films addressing management issues. Topics covered include: customer service, sales training, creativity, human behavior, communication, motivation, leadership, organization development, meeting planning (session starters), career and self-development, health and safety, management history and theory, lectures and seminars. Styles range from documentary and dramatization to animation and humor.
   Sample titles include: *Telephone Talk: How to Deal With People Over the Telephone; Dealing With Angry Customers; Skills for Successful Selling; The Egg: A Film About Resistance to Change; Communication and Management: A Conversation with Dr. Carl Rogers; Satisfaction: A Job Well Done; Case Studies in Leadership; So Who's Perfect? — How to Give and Receive Criticism; Japan Inc: Lessons for North America?;* and *Heart Attack: Tension! Overwork! Burnout!*
   Management Theory Classics. Frederick Taylor and Scientific Management explains industrial engineer Frederick Winslow Taylor's principles of scientific management and explores the relevance of Taylor's concepts for today's managers. *Henri Fayol: The Process Approach to Management* illustrates how today's managers can use Fayol's "process approach" to help improve their management skills. *Hawthorne Studies for Today's Managers: The People Factor* uses original footage from the 1920s to show some of the experiments conducted by Western Electric, designed to increase productivity by improving the work environment. *Maslow's Hierarchy of Needs* explores Dr. Abraham Maslow's answer to the question, "What motivates people?" Other films cover Douglas McGregor's work on democratic versus authoritarian management, expectancy theory and contingency approaches to management.
Size & Elements: Film: 16mm. Videotape: 3/4", VHS, Betamax I and II. (93 titles total)
Cataloging: Published catalog.
Access: Available for rental, preview and purchase. Requests and orders

accepted by mail and telephone.
Rights: Apply for information.
Licensing: Apply for information.
Restrictions: Apply for information.
Viewing Facilities: None.
Duplication Facilities: None.
Related Materials: Comprehensive support materials, including participants' workbooks and leaders' guides.

CALIFORNIA (Los Angeles Metro)

FULTON J. SHEEN COMMUNICATIONS LTD.
19355 Business Center Drive
Northridge, CA 91324
(818) 885-1044
Fax: (818) 885-1021

Edward Weston (Chairman)

Contacts: Ann Weston (President); Edward Weston
Services: Corporation; distributor; film and videotape producer; stock footage sales library. Collection available to libraries, educational institutions and the public for purchase, duplication, licensing and reuse, subject to restrictions.
Description: Television programs featuring the wit and wisdom of Bishop Fulton J. Sheen, speaking on a wide variety of subjects. The *Life Is Worth Living* series, featuring "timeless messages for all faiths" was first aired on the Dumont Television network (beginning in 1939 on WABD, New York) and later on ABC (1950s-60s).
   Programs include: *Are We More Neurotic These Days?; Birth Patrol; Three Kinds of College Students; Is Woman an It?; The Hell is There; Death of God; How to Talk; The Clown is Right; He Always Turns Me Out; The Alcoholic is No Pig; Morticians of God; Quo Vadis, America?; The Psychology of Temptation; Is Neurosis the Stepchild of American Culture?; Along the Freudian Way; How to Meet Communism; The Woman with Five Husbands; What Everyone Should Know About Communism; The Divine Sense of Humor; Have You Been Tempted More Lately?; Women Caught in Sin; Why the Gloom in Modern Literature?; The Kiss That Blistered; Are Human Relations Human?; What the Communists Mean by Truth; Fig Leaves and Fashions; Three Moments of Human Love; The Man Who Changed His Name; The Greeks Had Three Words for It; The Russian Lullaby of Co-Existence; Should Parents Obey Children?; Some Nice People Live in Alleys; Why Work is Boring; How to be Unpopular; How Mothers are Made; To Spank or Not to Spank; The Anatomy of Melancholy; Content with Sawdust Brains?; Marriage is Neither Heaven or Hell — But What is It?; Children: Burdens or Joys?; The Love Trilogy Set* and many more.
Size & Elements: Film: 16mm (100 titles). Videotape: 2" (100 black and white titles, 49 color titles); 1" (masters); 3/4", VHS and Betamax (10 titles, viewing copies).
Cataloging: Published list; brochure.
Access: Available to libraries, educational institutions and the public for purchase, duplication, licensing and reuse. Research fees charged. Research requests accepted by mail.
Rights: Full rights held to some material. Some rights held to other material.
Licensing: Available for licensing and reuse, subject to restrictions. License fees charged (rates vary according to nature of request).
Restrictions: Sponsorship is allowed, subject to approval.
Viewing Facilities: None.
Duplication Facilities: None (outside facilities used).
Related Materials: Audiotapes: *The Seven Program Library Audio Cassette Set; The Love Trilogy Audio Cassette Set.*

CALIFORNIA (Los Angeles Metro)

SHIELDS ARCHIVAL
6404 Hollywood Boulevard, Suite 216
Hollywood, CA 90028
(213) 962-1899

Mark Punswick (President)

Contact: Mark Punswick
Services: Stock footage sales library. Research services available.
Description: Library includes world events, disasters, wars, world leaders, celebrities, unusual events, cities (U.S. and foreign), industry, family life,

animal antics, classic films and television shows, cartoons, movie stars, sports figures and vintage commercials. Stock footage, complete motion pictures and short subjects are available.
Size & Elements: Film (format and amount unspecified). Videotape: 1" (masters); 3/4" (viewing copies).
Cataloging: Finding aids; computer database; listings and logs.
Access: Available for duplication and reuse. Research services available. Fees charged for creation of viewing cassettes.
Rights: Some material in the public domain. Other material represented for stock footage sale on behalf of the copyright owner.
Licensing: Available for licensing and reuse. License and usage fees charged.
Restrictions: None specified.
Viewing Facilities: Videotape (on and off-premises).
Duplication Facilities: Videotape (outside facility).

CALIFORNIA (Los Angeles Metro)

SHOKUS VIDEO
P.O. Box 8434
Van Nuys, CA 91409
(818) 704-0400

Stuart Shostak (President)

Contact: Stuart Shostak
Services: Film and videotape archives. Collection available for duplication and reuse, subject to restrictions.
Description: Vintage television material, mostly live kinescopes and "lost" series episodes (1948-present).
   Classic cartoons (1930s-40s). Betty Boop, Porky Pig, Bugs Bunny, Daffy Duck, Casper, Popeye, Bosko and Little Lulu.
   Television shows. Jack Benny and his regulars Dennis Day, Don Wilson, and Eddie "Rochester" Anderson; Milton Berle; George Burns and Gracie Allen; Bob Hope; Groucho Marx; *I Remember Mama,* with Peggy Wood, Dick Van Patten, and Judson Laire; *Make Room for Daddy,* starring Danny Thomas, Jean Hagen, Rusty Hamer, and Sherry Jackson.
   1950s situation comedies. The Life of Riley; My Little Margie; The People's Choice; The Ruggles; Life With Elizabeth; The Goldbergs; Duffy's Tavern; Hey Mulligan!; Let's Join Joanie; My Favorite Husband; Meet McNutley; Life With Luigi Pilot; Professional Father; I Married Joan; The Beulah Show; The Great Gildersleeve; and *Mr. Peepers.*
   Children's programs from the 1950s. Winky Dink Show; Carson's Cellar; Howdy Doody Show; Art Linkletter and the Kids; Andy's Gang; Saturday Night Revue; The Farmer Alfalfa Show; Life With Buster Keaton; Robin Hood; and *Captain Gallant of the Foreign Legion.*
   Network game shows. Do You Trust Your Wife?; You Bet Your Life; Play Your Hunch; People Are Funny; Take a Good Look; Concentration; I've Got a Secret; The Price is Right; Truth or Consequences; The Face is Familiar; PDQ; Bride and Groom; Beat the Clock; The $64,000 Question; Queen for a Day; The $64,000 Challenge; Dollar a Second; Place the Face; Two for the Money; and *What's My Line?*
   Variety shows. Arthur Godfrey's Talent Scouts; The Ed Sullivan Show; The Spike Jones Show; The Walter Winchell Show; Texaco Star Theater Starring Milton Berle; Person to Person; The Bob Hope Frigidaire Comedy Hour; Four Star Revue; The Perry Como Show; The Faye Emerson Show; The Frankie Laine Show; The Garry Moore Show; The Robert Q. Lewis Show; The Tennessee Ernie Ford Show; Dinner With the President; The Ed Wynn Show; The Easter Teleparade of Stars; The Jimmy Durante Show; Bulova Watch Time; The Edsel Show; The Colgate Comedy Hour; The Johnny Carson Show; The Cavalcade of Stars; The Red Skelton Show; The Dennis Day Show; Ernie Kovacs Special; The Scene Stealers; The Colgate Summer Comedy Hour; Strictly for Laffs; The Summer Chevy Show; The Dinah Shore Chevy Show; and *Your Hit Parade.*
   Miscellaneous programs. The Roy Rogers Show; Dragnet; soap operas from the 1950s (*The Guiding Light, Love of Life, Search for Tomorrow*); 1950s current events (Nixon's "Checkers Speech," *See It Now*); Christmas classics (*The Liberace 1953 Christmas Show, Racket Squad "The Christmas Caper"* and *Date with the Angels*).
   Animated and celebrity commercials (1950s-60s). Animated stars include The Flintstones, Bugs Bunny, and Bucky Beaver. Celebrities include Lucille Ball, Desi Arnaz, Dick Van Dyke, Mary Tyler Moore, Andy Griffith, Don Knotts, Danny Thomas, Jean Hagen, Phil Silvers, Groucho Marx, Joey Bishop, Dave Garroway, Buster Keaton, the Three Stooges, Jack Benny, Louise Lasser, Steve Allen, Jay North, Anita Bryant, Lucie Arnaz, Vivian Vance, Ernie Kovacs, John Cameron Swayze, Jack Somack, Andy Devine, Hilary Brooke,

CALIFORNIA (Los Angeles Metro S)

Dwayne Hickman, Danny Kaye, Hugh Downs, Tennessee Ernie Ford, Arthur Godfrey and Dick Powell. Spokespeople include Josephine the Plumber, Mr. Whipple, and Mrs. Olson. Jingles include "You'll wonder where the yellow went," "Nothin' says lovin' like something from the oven," "You get a lot to like with a Marlboro," "Ajax, the Blue-Dot Cleaner," "Chewy Chewy Tootsie Roll," "I've Got a Snickers," and "Captain Action."

Maps to Stars' Homes Video is a guided tour of mansions in Beverly Hills, Holmby Hills, and Bel Air, California. Featured are the homes of Elizabeth Taylor, Burt Reynolds, James Stewart, Peter Falk, Sammy Davis, Buddy Hackett, Faye Dunaway, Jack Benny, Walter Pidgeon, Laurel and Hardy, and Humphrey Bogart.

Size & Elements: Film and videotape: formats unspecified (over 3,000 items).
Cataloging: Published catalog; computerized cataloging for staff use only.
Access: For in-house use only. Available for duplication (videotape only) and reuse. Research requests accepted by mail and telephone. Research fees charged.
Rights: Some rights held to some material. Some material in the public domain. Additional clearances may be necessary if material is to be reused.
Licensing: Available for licensing and reuse, subject to restrictions. License fees charged per clip.
Restrictions: Only videotape material available for duplication.
Viewing Facilities: None.
Duplication Facilities: Film (film-to-videotape); videotape (3/4", VHS and Betamax).

CALIFORNIA (Los Angeles Metro)

SLINGSHOT PRODUCTIONS
8309 Ponce Avenue
West Hills, CA 91304
(818) 999-2539

Alessandro Machi (Projects Coordinator)

Contact: Alessandro Machi
Services: Camera service; custom shooting services available. Film and videotape stock footage available for licensing and reuse.
Description: Collection highlights time-lapse cinematography and special effects. Holds time-lapse, stop-motion, long time exposures and live action shots of landscapes, cityscapes and movement (people, automobiles, clouds, beach activity, etc.). Directors of photography are available for location work.
Size & Elements: Film: 35mm, 16mm and 8mm (approx. 3 hours; originals). Videotape: 1" and 3/4" (amount unspecified; masters transferred from film).
Cataloging: Staff assistance required; shot lists; other finding aids.
Access: Open to the public. Available for duplication and reuse. Research fees not charged. Research requests accepted by telephone.
Rights: Full rights held to all material.
Licensing: Available for licensing and reuse. License fees charged.
Restrictions: None specified.
Viewing Facilities: Videotape (3/4" and 1/2").
Duplication Facilities: None.

CALIFORNIA (Los Angeles Metro)

SOUTHERN CALIFORNIA BLUES SOCIETY
P.O. Box 59297
Los Angeles, CA 90059
(213) 591-6504

Contact: Clementine Bradley
Services: Videotape archives. Collection open to the public. Some material available for research, rental, licensing and reuse, subject to restrictions.
Description: Blues singers and nightclub performers; documentation of blues artists, including Big Mama Thornton, Big Joe Turner, Charles Brown, Joe Houston, Pee Wee Crayton and Bo Diddley, among others.
Size & Elements: Videotape: VHS and Betamax (approx. 30 videotapes total).
Cataloging: None.
Access: Open to the public. Available for research, rental, licensing and reuse, subject to restrictions. Research requests accepted by mail.
Rights: Full rights held to all material. Additional clearances may be necessary in some cases if material is to be reused.
Licensing: Available for licensing and reuse, subject to restrictions. License fees charged under some conditions.
Restrictions: All requests are subject to acceptance and approval of proposed project.

Viewing Facilities: Videotape.
Duplication Facilities: None.

CALIFORNIA (Los Angeles Metro)

SOUTHERN CALIFORNIA INSTITUTE OF ARCHITECTURE (SCI-ARC)
MEDIA CENTER
1800 Berkeley Street
Santa Monica, CA 90404
(213) 829-3485 (Ext. 22)
Fax: (213) 829-7518

Anna Krajewska-Wieczorek (Media Center Director)

Contact: Anna Krajewska-Wieczorek
Services: Educational institution. Videotape collection open to researchers and scholars for in-house use only.
Description: Videotaped public lectures and panel discussions on architecture and related subjects delivered at SCI-ARC (1974-present).

Architecture: design, history and theory. Lectures and discussions include: *On Technology* (C. Ellwood, D. Dworsky and J. Lomax); *Geometry and Architecture* (Robin Evans); *Architecture as a Stage* (Kurt Forster); *Neofuturism — On Architecture and Technology* (Hal Foster); *On Structures* (R. Snyder and R. Buckminster Fuller); *Modern Architecture of Los Angeles* (Frank Gehry); *Virtual Space: The Electronic Environment of Mobile Image* (Kit Galloway and Sherrie Rabinowitz); *On Vernacular Architecture* (J. B. Jackson); *Modernism, Freestyle, Classicism of 1980* (Charles Jencks); *Making Cities Work For People Series* (Jon A. Jerde); *KNXT Interviews — On Low-Cost Housing* (Raymond Kappe); *Planning* (Herb Kahn); *Downtown Los Angeles: Overview, Innerview and Outerview* (Kurt Meyer); *Residential Architecture of Japan* (Riichi Miyake); *Alternative Architecture — Panel Discussion* (Charles Moore); *Music and Architecture* (Doug Michels); *Friedrich Nietzsche's Philosophy* (Fritz Neumayer); *History and Theory* (Werner Oeschlin); *Architecture and Technology* (Eric Orr and Tony Longson); *Perspective in History* (Alberto Perez-Gomez); *Changing Concept of Space in Architecture and Art* (Jorge Silvetti); *Alternative Architecture Panel Discussion* (Glen Small); *Japanese Architecture* (Marc Treib); *Uses and Abuses of Architectural History* (Anthony Vidler); *Women In Architecture* (panel discussion); and *The World Through Child's Eye*, a student videotape.

Profiles and work of contemporary American architects and artists. Lecturers and subjects include: Vito Acconci; Steven Badanes; Dara Birnbaum; Alberto Bertoli; Bud Brown; William Bruder; James Burns; Roland Coate; Peter Cook; Christine Hawley; Peter Debrettville; Sheila Debrettville; Charles Gwathmey; Bud Goldstone; Lawrence Halprin; Daniel Herren; Ron Herron; Coy Howard; Jim Hull; *Work of Venturi and Rauch: Theory* (Steve Izenour); an interview with Philip Johnson; Louis Kahn; Fred Koetter; Peter Pearce; Whitney Smith; Glen Small; Bernard Tschumi; and Stanley Tigerman.

Contemporary foreign architects and architecture. Lecturers and subjects include: Augusto Alvarez (Mexico); Tadao Ando (Japan); Ian Athfield, N. John Blair, Rewi Thompson and Roger Walker (New Zealand); Gunnar Birkerts; Mario Botta; Marianne Burkhalter (Switzerland); Enrique Del Moral (Mexico); Marcelo D'Olivo (Italy); Charles and Ray Eames; Nader Khalili; Waquidi Falicoff; Zaha Hadid ("Hong Kong Peak" Competition Winner); Itsuko Hasegawa; Zvi Hecker (Israel); Augustin Hernandez (Mexico); Hans Hollein; Rem Koolhaas; Ricardo Legorreta (Mexico); *Team Zo* (Kinya Maruyama, Japan); *Coop Himmelblau — Architecture Is Now* (Wolf Prix); *Prefabricated Schools and Buildings* (Luigi Pelligrin); *Guatemalan Architecture* (Efrain Recinos); Minoru Takeyama (Japan); *Japanese Architecture* (Hiroshi Watanabe); *Australian Architecture* (Tony Wheeler); Abraham Zabludovsky (Mexico); and Teodoro Gonzales (Mexico).

Architectural lectures and documentaries. Titles include: *Le Corbusier — The Nature and Origin of Form* and *The White Cubic Architecture of the '20s* (Geoffrey Baker); *American Industrial Building, 1900-1925* and *The European Response — Fagus and Fiat Factories* (Reyner Banham); *A. Aalto and Beyond* (Reyner Banham and Paul David Pearson); *Nature and Tradition* (William Curtis, on Le Corbusier); *Germany — Dada* (film) from the *Museum Without Walls* series; *The Significance of Classic Structures* (Michael Graves); *Bruno Taut — Utopian Design and Urban Planning* (Rose-Marie Haag-Bletter); *G. L. Bernini — Theater and Its Architectural Double* (Richard Ingersoll); *On Geltaftan* (Nader Khalili); *Understanding a Vernacular in the Mud Dwellings of Northwest Morocco* (William Curtis); *Charles R. Mackintosh and the Glasgow School* (Andrew MacMillan); *Thomas McEvilley; Works of Mies Van Der Rohe* (Fritz Neumayer); *Building Mechanism, A Dutch Tradition* (Rijk Rietveld); *Le Corbusier and Chandigarh* (Mohan Sharma); *Architecture in*

Nepal (Katherine Blair); and *On Alvar Aalto* (Eric Vertainen).

Landscape architecture and environment. Lectures include: *Architecture as Landscape* (Mary Alice Dixon-Hinson); *Natural Process Design* and *Underwater Housing* (Carolyn Dry); *Music, Language and Environment* (David Dunn); *Biosphere II — A Blueprint for Survival* (Merle Jensen); *Solar Energy* (Raymond Kappe); *Earth, Water, Fire,* a film on the work of Nader Khalili; *Organic Architecture* (Ken Kellog); *Design Process, Product, Participation versus Commitment* (Paul Kennon); *Nuclear Arms,* a discussion at AIA Convention, San Francisco, Calif. (1985); *Urban Landscaping in Ancient Rome* (Diane Favro); *Architecture As Landscape* (Jay Fellows); *Environmental Issues* (Tom Hayden); *Solar Energy in Cuba* (Jerry Lax); a lecture by Mary Miss, sculptor and landscape designer; *Space Habitats* (Fritz Runge); *Human Factors in Space Station Architecture* (Marc Cohen); and *Ecology and Technology* (Ellen and Michael Jantzen).

Size & Elements: Videotape: VHS (330 videotapes, each 120 min.; viewing copies).
Cataloging: Computerized cataloging for staff use only; printed lists.
Access: Open to researchers and scholars. For in-house use only. Research requests accepted by mail and telephone. Screening fees charged for group viewing.
Rights: Some rights held to all material.
Licensing: Apply for information.
Restrictions: None specified.
Viewing Facilities: Videotape.
Duplication Facilities: Videotape (3/4", VHS and Betamax I).

CALIFORNIA (Los Angeles Metro)

SOUTHERN CALIFORNIA LIBRARY FOR SOCIAL STUDIES AND RESEARCH

6120 South Vermont Avenue
Los Angeles, CA 90044
(213) 759-6063

Sarah Cooper (Director)
Mary Tyler (Assistant Director)

Contacts: Sarah Cooper; Mary Tyler
Services: Library. Film and videotape collection available to the public for research, duplication, licensing and reuse, subject to restrictions.
Description: Labor, radical and progressive films (primarily 1930s-60s). Selected films include:

Berry Pickers' Strike, El Monte, California, 1933 (approx. 20 min., black and white, silent). Dramatization of the strike.

Kern County Cotton Strike, Kern County, California, 1937 (approx. 20 min., black and white, silent with titles). Shows conditions among agricultural workers in Kern cotton fields, conditions leading to the strike, workers' arrest and picket march. Shots of Communist Party speakers, including young Dorothy Healey (then Dorothy Ray).

San Pedro, California demonstration, 1934 (approx. 10 min., black and white, silent with titles). Includes police melee against demonstrators; Sam Darcy of *Western Worker* telling of vigilante terror in San Francisco; Paul Cline urging support for the Loyalists in Spain; W. Z. Foster and Earl Browder, speaking north of San Pedro in Los Angeles.

Free Tom Mooney rallies, 1938 (approx. 6 min., black and white, silent). Tom Mooney, San Francisco labor activist, was imprisoned 1919-38 on charges stemming from a bombing during a 1919 Preparedness Day Parade in San Francisco. Mooney, viewed as a political prisoner by the left and by organized labor, was pardoned in 1938 by California Governor Culbert Olson. Footage includes shots of Communist leader Ben Dobbs addressing Mooney supporters; and the demonstration at the 1932 Olympics in Los Angeles when Mooney supporters raced around the Coliseum track sporting "Free Tom Mooney" banners.

Tom Mooney following release from prison, ca. 1938 (approx. 15 min., black and white, silent). Mooney in San Francisco, alighting from car as flashbulbs pop, and waving to crowds; Gov. Culbert Olson conferring pardon on Mooney; Mooney waving the pardon; Mooney marching in a victory parade along Market Street in San Francisco; quick shots of speakers at his victory rally, including Longshoremen leader Harry Bridges; Mooney's arrival in Los Angeles; and his arrival at the Coliseum before 35,000 supporters.

The Chicago Memorial Day Massacre (1937, approx. 7 min., black and white, silent). The 1937 massacre of strikers by police during the Republic Steel strike.

The Modesto Case (1930s, approx. 30 min., black and white, sound).

Produced by Charles Haas. Dramatic reenactment of a frame-up of the leaders of a seamen's strike due to collusion between police and the Standard Oil Company. Leaders were convicted of plotting to dynamite oil depots. Actors include members of the Longshoremen's Union.

Scrap Iron (1930s, approx. 10 min., black and white, silent). Dramatization of how scrap iron from Los Angeles was used by Japanese to kill Chinese in the Manchurian war; and to line the pockets of local entrepreneurs.

Hollywood Lockout (1946, approx. 20 min., black and white, silent). 1946 Hollywood studio strike which shut down studios at Columbia, Republic, Warner Brothers and MGM. Includes the famous car blockade and melees between strikers and police.

Conditions in Los Angeles (1934, 15 min., black and white, silent with titles). Produced by C. Siminow, Los Angeles Film and Photo League. Shows shots of the new City Hall, construction sites and gracious houses contrasted with shacks, slums, row houses, "Hoovervilles," depression lines, people looking for food in garbage cans and sleeping in fields. Includes shots of a New Deal federal housing project.

Conditions in Chicago (1934, 15 min., black and white, silent with titles). Intersperses shots of the World's Fair with "Hoovervilles," bums, breadlines and towering skyscrapers.

Those Who Fought (ca. 1937, approx. 21 min., black and white, silent). Film of the Abraham Lincoln Brigade in Spain. Includes clips of Brigade members eating, making camp and fighting, and their welcome in New York City.

San Diego Youth Demonstration Day film (mid-1930s, 5 min., black and white, silent). Includes shots of Ben Dobbs addressing a rally, the rally turning into a melee and the police assault.

Camp Kinderland (mid-1930s, 25 min., black and white, silent). Film on a Communist Party camp for children and adults. Produced by C. Simonow and Leo Seltzer.

Chinese Revolutionaries, ca. 1934 (approx. 7 min., black and white, silent). Includes Battle of Pagoda Hill; single-engine airplanes taking off; shots of field commanders and mortar fire; dead and wounded carried off the field.

Deadline for Action (1946, 40 min., black and white, sound). Produced by the United Electrical Workers (UE). Expresses the need to project a strong union stance in the wake of World War II and the death of Franklin D. Roosevelt.

The Peace Candidate (1952, 30 min., black and white, sound). Election-year film made for the Progressive Party campaign in which Vincent Hallinan ran for President. Includes shots of Earl Robinson singing (*Join Your PPA*) and Paul Robeson.

Palestine Protest March (1940s, approx. 15 min., black and white, silent) Produced by Pioneer Films. Film of various groups marching in Philadelphia, apparently to rally support for the creation of a Jewish state.

Bridge to Yinshi (ca. 1950, 24 min., color, sound). Film which seeks to promote friendship between China and the United States by comparing Yinshi to Junction City, Kansas.

Peace Will Win (ca. 1951, 40 min., black and white, sound). Documentary by Joris Ivens and Jerzy Szelubski about the Second World Congress of Peace, held in Sheffield, England and then switched to Poland. Shows Polish workers erecting quarters on one week's notice, followed by film of the Congress, with delegates from various countries, including Poland, Italy, China, Korea and England. Includes some newsreel footage of the Korean War.

We'll Never Turn Back (ca. 1964, approx. 30 min., black and white, sound). Story of the civil rights movement in the South (early 1960s), told by SNCC workers, other activists and black residents who tell of being victimized by discrimination. Interview subjects include Fannie Lou Hamer and Julian Bond.

A Dream Deferred (ca. 1964, approx. 40 min., black and white, sound). Produced by SNCC. Focuses on personal accounts of frequently horrendous conditions afflicting Black tenant farmers in the South.

[UCLA campus protest] (1970, approx. 5 min., color, sound). Protest against the invasion of Cambodia. Includes shots of police beating marching students.

Winter Soldier (ca. 1971, approx. 25 min., black and white, sound). Testimony of soldiers about atrocities in Vietnam during the U.S. involvement in the war.

[Washington, D. C. peace demonstration] (approx. 35 min., black and white, sound). Film of the November 13-15, 1969 Moratorium as seen through the eyes of a family who lost their son in Vietnam.

Year of Decision (1964, 23:30 min., black and white, sound). California Democratic Council convention of 1964. Liberal goals and policies outlined. Speakers include Alan Cranston, then state controller, and Senator Eugene McCarthy.

Size & Elements: Film: 16mm (approx. 100 titles). Preservation negatives

(now stored at UCLA Film and Television Archive [q.v.]) and reference prints for many films have been made. Videotape: format unspecified (20 videotapes; primarily transfers from films).
Cataloging: Film list.
Access: Open to the public. Available for duplication. Research fees not charged for in-person screenings; charges apply for preparation of videotape reference copies supplied for out-of-town screenings. Research requests accepted by telephone and in person (by appointment only).
Rights: Rights status of most material not known. Additional clearances may be necessary in some cases if material is to be reused.
Licensing: Available for licensing and reuse, subject to restrictions. License and usage fees charged.
Restrictions: Restrictions may apply to some material.
Viewing Facilities: Videotape.
Duplication Facilities: None.
Related Materials: 16,000 volumes (U.S. and foreign); 21,000 pamphlets; 2,800 periodicals; 3,500 audiotape recordings; 2,000 photographs; 1,500 posters; and many manuscripts, all concerning political movements, labor, minorities, civil rights and civil liberties.

CALIFORNIA (Los Angeles Metro)

RICK SPALLA VIDEO PRODUCTIONS
HOLLYWOOD NEWSREEL SYNDICATE, INC.
1622 North Gower Street
Hollywood, CA 90028
(213) 469-7307

New York office:
301 West 45th Street
New York, NY 10036
(212) 765-4646
Contact: Tony Spalla

Rick Spalla (President)
Jeff Spalla (Vice President, Production)

Contacts: Rick Spalla; Jeff Spalla
Services: Film and videotape producer; stock footage sales library. Produces video news releases. Custom videotape shooting services available.
Description: News and stock footage collection specializing in entertainment-related material. General subject areas include: Hollywood; travel; adventure; news events; documentaries; film and television stars; entertainment industry and events; political figures; world news; beauty pageants; business and industry; sports, including baseball, football, basketball, track and field; special events; the Academy Awards; celebrities; and "footprint" ceremonies. Can shoot videotape stock shots to order.
Television news footage. News footage originally shot for KHJ-TV, Los Angeles (1958-62). Covers major news events in Southern California.
Hollywood Backstage (39 programs, each 30 min). Typical sequences include: *Elke Sommer "Bubble Bath"* (Show 1); *Paramount Set Party & Fire* (Show 1); *Frank Sinatra Footprint Ceremony* (Show 2); *Rock & Roll Wedding* (Show 3); *Jayne Mansfield Baby Christening* (Show 3); *Sonny & Cher* (Show 4); *Rock & Roll Date with April Stevens and Nino Tempo* (Show 5); *Dean Martin Roast* (Show 6); *How to Film a Massacre* (Show 6); *Liberace's Antique Shop* (Show 7); *Bob Hope Golf Classic* (Show 9); *Teen Night at "It's Boss"* (Show 10); *Tina Louise: Close-Up* (Show 14); *Richard Zanuck's Party at 20th Century-Fox* (Show 14); *Lunch with Zsa Zsa* (Show 15); *Prince Philip Visit* (Show 16); *Natalie Wood Party* (Show 17); *Sunset Strip* (Show 19); *Academy Award Night Special* (Show 20); *Sid Caesar Paramount Party* (Show 22); *On the Set with "The Munsters"* (Show 23); *Phyllis Diller — Den Mother* (Show 24); *Edie Adams Interview* (Show 24); *Century of Fashion in Movies* (Show 27); *Mr. Ed on Strike* (Show 29); *Mort Sahl Interview* (Show 30); *Governor's Party* (Show 31); *Herman's Hermits* (Show 33); *Carnaby Street, London* (Show 33); *Nancy Sinatra Date* (Show 36); *Belly Dancers on the Sunset Strip* (Show 37); and *Caesar's Palace Opening* (Show 38).
Hollywood Star Newsreel (26 programs, each 30 min.) Features on the behind-the-scenes world of the stars.
Guest Shot (26 programs, each 30 min.; 44 stars featured). Features on the hobbies of Hollywood stars. Typical shows feature Keenan Wynn and Lee Marvin racing motorcycles; Dan Dailey fox hunting and Jayne Mansfield bodybuilding; Jerry Lewis and electronics; Liberace designing; Fabian on a mountain lion hunt; Rory Calhoun boar hunting; Frankie Avalon playing stickball; Tony Curtis as an artist; Robert Stack trapshooting; Charlton Heston collecting souvenirs; and Lee Marvin deep sea fishing.

High Road to Danger (33 programs, each 30 min., black and white and color). True stories of danger and adventure, hosted by Steve Brodie. Subjects include shark hunting; white-water rafting on the Colorado River; Navy frogmen undergoing "Hell Week"; the Pan American Road Race; daredevils of yesteryear; buffalo hunting; the Hydroplane Gold Cup race at Lake Mead, Nevada; junior stunt kids (all under ten years of age); daredevil stock car drivers; tricks used in Western movies; 101st Airborne paratroopers in training at Fort Campbell, Kentucky; an expedition through the jungles to the estate of Nicaragua's former president William Walker; champion stuntman Harry Woolman, who blows himself up in a dynamite coffin; and expeditions in primitive Mexico.
Holiday on Wheels (6 programs, each 30 min.). Travel and adventure series highlighting tourist destinations reachable by recreational vehicles, including Monument Valley, the California coastline, Florida, New England and Hollywood.
Numerous other programs, especially relating to Hollywood and entertainment personalities, are available.
Size & Elements: Film: 16mm (2 million feet, 5,000 cans, 500 titles; color and black and white). Videotape: 1" and 3/4" (2,000 videotapes).
Cataloging: Card catalogs; computerized cataloging for staff use only; release sheets, storylines and synopses for program series.
Access: Available for duplication and reuse. Research fees charged. Research requests accepted by mail and telephone.
Rights: Full rights held to all material.
Licensing: Available for licensing. License fees charged. Custom-shot videotape stock footage available for normal stock footage rates (videotape production fees not charged).
Restrictions: Some restrictions may apply to reuse of footage depicting celebrities or other recognizable individuals.
Viewing Facilities: Film (16mm Moviola and Moviscop); videotape (3/4").
Duplication Facilities: Film (film-to-videotape transfers); videotape.
Related Materials: Background music libraries available for purchase.

CALIFORNIA (Los Angeles Metro)

SPECTRAL COMMUNICATIONS
178 South Victory, Suite 106
Burbank, CA 91502
(818) 840-0111

Michael Povar (Senior Partner)

Contact: Michael Povar
Services: Stock footage sales library.
Description: Videotape news footage of celebrities; establishing shots and general shots of Southern California.
Personalities featured include: Alan Alda, Steve Allen, Don Ameche, Julie Andrews, Rosanna Arquette, Ed Asner, Patty Duke Astin, René Auberjonois, Burt Bacharach, Barbara Bain, Anita Baker, Bananarama, Anne Bancroft, Rona Barrett, Bonnie Bartlett, Carole Bayer Sager, The Beastie Boys, Ed Begley Jr., Ralph Bellamy, Jim Belushi, Barbi Benton (pregnant), Milton Berle, Steven Bishop, Ruben Blades, Richard Boyle, Ray Bradbury, Tom Bradley, Jeff Bridges, Morgan Brittany, Matthew Broderick, Charles Bronson, Joel Brooks, Mel Brooks, George Stanford Brown, George Burns, Red Buttons, Mario Marino Cantinflas, Kim Carnes, David Carradine, Jack Carter, Helena Bonham Carter, Sid Caesar, Cyd Charisse, Chevy Chase, Dick Clark, James Coburn, "Iron Eyes" Cody, Joan Collins, Alex Cord, Ronny Cox, Alan Cranston, Richard Crenna, Cathy Lee Crosby, Billy Crystal, Willem Dafoe, Tyne Daly, Rodney Dangerfield, William Daniels, Ted Danson, Bill Davila, Bette Davis, Frederick DeCordova, Antonio DeMarco, Catherine Deneuve, William Devane, Danny DeVito, Angie Dickinson, Phyllis Diller, Placido Domingo, Phil Donahue, Eric Douglas, Kirk Douglas, Richard Dreyfuss, George Deukmejian, Shelly Duvall, Clint Eastwood, Jose Eber, Barbara Eden, Blake Edwards, Linda Evans, Don Everly, Phil Everly, Morgan Fairchild, Mike Farrell, John Ferraro, Sally Field, Jane Fonda, Betty Ford, John Forsythe, Michael J. Fox, Richard Frank, Charles Fries, Eva Gabor, Max Gale, Allen Garfield, Teri Garr, Sharon Gless, Whoopi Goldberg, Samuel Goldwyn Jr., Louis Gossett Jr., Robert Goulet, Johnny Grant, Merv Griffin, Charles Grodin, Dan Haggerty, Alan Hale, Jack Haley Jr., Armand Hammer, Herbie Hancock, Tom Hanks, Mariette Hartley, Goldie Hawn, Hugh Hefner, Howard Hesseman, Charlton Heston, Earl Holloman, Bruce Hornsby, Bob Hope, John Hurt, John Huston, Angelica Huston, Julio Iglesias, James Ingram, Michael Jackson, Janet Jackson, Jimmy Jam, Shirley Jones, John Karlen, Alex Karras, Jeff Katzenberg, Stacy Keach, Sally Kellerman, Gene Kelly, George Kennedy, Jane Kennedy, Coretta King, Kris Kristofferson, Laker Girls, Lambchop, Burt Lancaster,

Angela Lansbury, John Larroquette, Shari Lewis, Terry Lewis, John Lithgow, David Lynch, Shelley Long, Marilyn McCoo, Roddy McDowall, Malcolm McDowell, Bobby McFerran, Elizabeth McGovern, Mark McIntire, Nancy McKeon, Shirley MacLaine, Ed McMahon, Fred MacMurray, Kristy McNichol, Karl Malden, Henry Mancini, Howie Mandel, Ann-Margret, Cheech Marin, Penny Marshall, Pamela Sue Martin, Tony Martin, Marlee Matlin, Bette Midler, Ronnie Millsap, Lee Minnelli, Liza Minnelli, Minnie Mouse, Ricardo Montalban, Dudley Moore, Eddie Murphy, Brigitte Nielsen, Bob Newhart, Olivia Newton-John, Stevie Nicks, Hugh O'Brian, Carroll O'Connor, Sandi Patti, Gregory Peck, Anthony Perkins, Rhea Perlman, Bernadette Peters, Tom Petty, Joe Piscopo, Stefanie Powers, Jurgen Prochnow, Richard Pryor, Sarah Purcell, Anthony Quinn, John Randolph, Helen Reddy, Christopher Reeve, Sly Richardson, Don Rickles, Molly Ringwald, John Ritter, Lee Rocker, Sugar Ray Robinson, Kenny Rogers, Wayne Rogers, Cesar Romero, Kevin Russell, Kurt Russell, Jill St. John, Emma Sams, Roy Scheider, Arnold Schwarzenegger, Bob Seger, Tom Selleck, Brian Setzer, Jane Seymour, William Shatner, Ally Sheedy, Cybill Shepherd, Maria Shriver, Siegfried, Silver Bullet Band, Paul Simon, Red Skelton, Grace Slick, Slim Jim, Kevon Smith, Sissy Spacek, Steven Spielberg, Aaron Spelling, Robert Stack, Sly Stallone, Harry Dean Stanton, James Stewart, Barbra Streisand, Oliver Stone, Larry Storch, Sally Struthers, George Takai, Alan Thicke, Betty Thomas, Danny Thomas, Marlo Thomas, Lily Tomlin, Robert Townsend, Kathleen Turner, Ted Turner, Tina Turner, Fernando Valenzuela, Dick Van Dyke, Steven Van Zandt, Jon Voight, Robert Wagner, Robert Walden, Dennis Weaver, Sigourney Weaver, Tracy Wells, Bill Welsh, Adam West, Betty White, Bruce Willis, Oprah Winfrey, Henry Winkler, Steve Winwood, Bob Wise, Jane Withers, Michael Woo, James Woods, Moon Zappa, Dweezil Zappa, Efrem Zimbalist Jr., Stephanie Zimbalist, Don Zimmerman and Daphne Zuniga.

Celebrities featured are interviewed or shown speaking or in overheard conversation and in silent shots, at such public events as the Emmy Awards, the NOW Anniversary Celebration, the AFI awards, Alan Cranston's election and the Academy Awards.

Stock footage available includes: Academy Awards; aerobics; airplanes; airports; animals; apartments; aquariums; arenas; audiences; automobiles, including accidents, dealerships, limousines and sports cars; balloons; beaches; belly dancing; bikini contest; birds; blimps (McDonald's and Goodyear); boats, including sailboats, 12-meter boats, speedboats and yachts; bodybuilders; bridges; brush fires; buildings, including Art Deco, skyscrapers, under construction and dilapidated; buses; California desert scenes; celebrities (television, movie and music); children at play; childrens' zoo; city skylines, including Century City, Los Angeles, San Francisco, Santa Monica, Warner Center, Wilshire Corridor and at night; clouds; coastlines; computers; concerts (rock and jazz); condominiums; construction workers; conventions; crowds; cults; dams; dancing; emergency vehicles; Emmy Awards; entertainment; excavations (construction and fossils); exercise; factories, including high-technology, industrial shots and aerials; farms; firefighters; fires; fireworks; fishing; flowers; food festivals; forests; fountains; freeways, including traffic shots, aerials and interchanges; Hands Across America (1986), including ground and aerial shots; helicopters, including police, military, civilian, fire department and water drop; houses; humor; jet skiing; lifeguards, including stands, vehicles and contest; lightning; marathons; a Marilyn Monroe party; mini-malls; mountains; movie premieres; movie theaters; museums; neon; observatory; ocean; oil wells; palm trees; paramedics; parks; parties; pickets; piers; racing (car, offroad and truck); rain; recording studios; restaurants; sailing; ships, including automobile carriers and the Queen Mary; signs; skydiving; smog; sports, including volleyball, swimming, handicapped sports and track; stadiums; star ceremonies; statues; stores; street festivals; street scenes, including Beverly Hills, Chinatown, downtown Los Angeles, East Los Angeles, Hollywood and Melrose Avenue; sunset; surfers; theaters; traffic; trains (stations and miniature steam railroads); video games; waves; weather; and xylophones.
Size & Elements: Videotape: 3/4" (300 videotapes; masters).
Cataloging: Published catalog; computerized cataloging available to researchers; shot lists.
Access: Open to the public. Available for duplication and reuse.
Rights: Full rights held to all material.
Licensing: Available for licensing. License fees charged (fees depend on specific clip used).
Restrictions: None specified.
Viewing Facilities: Videotape (3/4").
Duplication Facilities: Videotape (3/4").

CALIFORNIA (Los Angeles Metro)

AARON SPELLING PRODUCTIONS
1041 North Formosa Avenue
Hollywood, CA 90046
(213) 850-3193
Fax: (213) 850-2839

Aaron Spelling (Chief Executive Officer)

Contact: Wendy Carter (Librarian)
Services: Film stock footage sales library.
Description: General stock footage library containing outtakes and unused footage from television series and "movies of the week" produced by Aaron Spelling Productions.
Size & Elements: Film: 35mm (over 20,000 stock shots; color negative, most with viewing prints).
Cataloging: Card catalogs.
Access: Available to the public for duplication, licensing and reuse. Research fees not charged. Research requests accepted by mail and telephone.
Rights: Full rights held to all material.
Licensing: Available for licensing and reuse, subject to restrictions. License fees charged (apply for information).
Restrictions: All stock footage requests are subject to acceptance and approval. Clearances and payments are required for reuse of scenes in which stuntpersons or recognizable talent appear.
Viewing Facilities: Film (35mm Moviola).
Duplication Facilities: None.

CALIFORNIA (Los Angeles Metro)

SPORTS CINEMATOGRAPHY GROUP
73 Market Street
Venice, CA 90291
(213) 785-9100
(212) 744-5333 (New York office)
Fax: (213) 450-4988

David Stoltz (Executive Producer)

Contact: David Stoltz
Services: Film producer. Footage available for duplication, licensing and reuse.
Description: Specialized footage of action and adventure sports (90% produced 1983-present). Represents footage of skydiving, rock climbing, white-water kayaking, surfing, windsurfing, sailing, waterskiing, ballooning, downhill skiing, snowmobiling, cross-country skiing and ski racing.
Size & Elements: Film: 35mm (5,000 feet); 16mm (10,000 feet).
Cataloging: Shot lists.
Access: Available for duplication, licensing and reuse. Research fees charged. Research requests accepted by mail and telephone.
Rights: Full rights held to some material.
Licensing: Available for licensing and reuse. License fees charged.
Restrictions: None specified.
Viewing Facilities: Videotape (3/4").
Duplication Facilities: None.

CALIFORNIA (Los Angeles Metro)

THE STOCK HOUSE
6922 Hollywood Boulevard, Suite 621
Hollywood, CA 90028
(213) 461-0061

Carl Barth (President and Owner)

Contacts: Juli Feldman; Vicki Siamas
Services: Corporation and corporate archives; library; stock footage sales library. Custom shooting services available.
Description: General stock footage library. Subjects include: airplanes; airports; buildings, featuring antique shops, book stores, offices, shopping malls and morgues; building demolition; car runbys; cities, including Boston, Chicago, London, Los Angeles, New York, San Diego and San Francisco; fireworks; government buildings; harbors; hospitals; hotels; motels; houses; industry; moons; suns; parks; police stations; prisons; process plates; restaurants; scenics; schools; small towns; sports, including crowds, arenas and stadiums; taxis; tenements; and trains.

Can provide photographic services for a wide range of needs. License or

production fees depend on requirements and labor contracts in force at the time. Represents a variety of producers for stock footage sales. Library is continually being updated.
Size & Elements: Film: 35mm (amount unspecified; color negative and workprint). Videotape: VHS (amount unspecified; viewing copies). Videotapes can be prepared for client viewing (fees apply).
Cataloging: Card catalogs.
Access: Open to the public. Available for licensing and reuse. Research fees charged for extensive research. Can provide positive prints for client viewing. Research requests accepted by mail, telephone and in person (by appointment).
Rights: Footage furnished by the Stock House is protected by copyright.
Licensing: Available for licensing and reuse. License fees charged.
Restrictions: Footage licensed for nonexclusive use in specific productions only. The Stock House warrants only its title to the actual footage. Licensee indemnifies the Stock House against any liability which may arise from licensee's use of the footage.
Viewing Facilities: Film (35mm); videotape (VHS).
Duplication Facilities: None (outside facilities used).

CALIFORNIA (Los Angeles Metro)

TRI-STAR PICTURES
1875 Century Park East
Los Angeles, CA 90067
(213) 201-2300

Services: Motion picture producer and distributor.

CALIFORNIA (Los Angeles Metro)

TURNER ENTERTAINMENT COMPANY
10100 Venice Boulevard
Culver City, CA 90232
(213) 558-7300

Services: Motion picture producer and distributor.

CALIFORNIA (Los Angeles Metro)

TWENTIETH CENTURY FOX FILM CORPORATION
P.O. Box 900
Beverly Hills, CA 90213
(213) 277-2211

Street address: 10201 West Pico Boulevard, Los Angeles, CA 90035

Services: Motion picture producer and distributor.

CALIFORNIA (Los Angeles Metro)

**UCLA BEHAVIORAL SCIENCES MEDIA LABORATORY
NEUROPSYCHIATRIC INSTITUTE AND HOSPITAL**
760 Westwood Plaza, Room 37-451
Los Angeles, CA 90024-1759
(213) 825-0448

Barnett Addis, Ph.D. (Director)

Contact: Celesta Billeci
Services: Laboratory; film and videotape producer and distributor. Selected titles available to the public for rental and purchase.
Description: Documentary films and videotapes on mental health and the biobehavioral sciences.
Titles include: *Actualization through Assertion; Doctor-Patient Interaction; Nurse-Patient Interaction; Impairment; Alcohol, the Brain, and Behavior; Alcohol and the Driving Task; Tolerance; Alcohol and Drug Interaction; Dystonia; Generative Graphics: Image Making in Psychotherapy; Haight-Ashbury: Summer of '68; The Hamilton Anxiety Scale; The Hamilton Depression Scale; Here Tomorrow,* on cystic fibrosis; *Infantile Autism: The Invisible Wall; Insomnia: In Search of Morpheus; July 19, 132,470 is a Saturday,* a film interview with idiot savant calendar-calculating twins; *King of the Minors; Medical Staff Conflicts; New Directions in Alcohol Research; Portrait of an Autistic Young Man; Suicides; Tarahumara: Racers Against Time; The Alcoholic: A Woman's Perspective;* and *Tourette Syndrome: The*

Sudden Intruder.
Size & Elements: Film: 16mm (19 titles). Videotape: 3/4" and VHS (21 titles).
Cataloging: Brochures.
Access: Selected titles available to the public for rental and purchase. Research requests not accepted. Orders accepted by mail.
Rights: Some rights held to some material.
Licensing: Material not available for reuse.
Restrictions: Material not available for reuse.
Viewing Facilities: None.
Duplication Facilities: None.

CALIFORNIA (Los Angeles Metro)

UCLA FILM AND TELEVISION ARCHIVE

For inquiries regarding scholarly and academic research:
1438 Melnitz Hall
University of California, Los Angeles
Los Angeles, CA 90024
(213) 206-8013

Robert Rosen (Director)
Edward Richmond (Curator)
Charles Hopkins (Motion Picture Archivist)
Daniel Einstein (Television Archivist)

For inquiries regarding footage licensing and reuse:
Commercial Services
1015 North Cahuenga Boulevard
Los Angeles, CA 90038
(213) 466-8559

Howard Hays (Manager, Commercial Services)

Contact: Appropriate personnel as listed above depending upon nature of inquiry.
Services: Film and television archives, study and preservation center. Archive's facilities are open for individual study to researchers and scholars. Some material, including the *Hearst Metrotone News* Film Library, available for duplication, licensing and reuse, subject to restrictions.
Description: The UCLA Film and Television Archive was founded in 1965 to fill the need for a film and television study and preservation center on the West Coast. Today, its collection totals over 200,000 titles, with an additional 27 million feet of newsreel footage — the largest university-based repository of film and broadcast materials in the world.
Film Collections. The Archive's film collection is strongest in the Hollywood sound cinema (1930s-50s), but also includes significant selections representing many other periods and aspects of filmmaking.
Holdings include major 35mm collections from Paramount Pictures, Twentieth Century-Fox, Warner Brothers, Columbia Pictures, New World Pictures, National Telefilm Associates, Orion Pictures and the Hearst Corporation. The *Harold Lloyd Memorial Collection* contains more than 1,500 16mm prints. In addition, films have been received from hundreds of individuals, including Tony Curtis, Stanley Kramer, George Pal, Rudy Vallee, King Vidor and William Wyler.
Archive facilities are open for individual study to researchers from around the world. The immediate needs of researchers are balanced with a long-term preservation program. Archive also exhibits hundreds of films each year for University and public viewing.
The following description indicates some special areas of interest within the collection.
Studio Prints. The Archive contains extensive 35mm studio print collections from Paramount (over 800 prints of films 1928-48), Twentieth Century-Fox (over 600 prints of films 1921-65), and Warner Brothers (over 600 prints of films from the 1930s-40s). Other important collections include Columbia, Orion and New World Pictures. In addition, the Archive holds sufficient examples of 35mm prints from other studios to provide the basis for comparative studies of studio styles.
Animation. The Archive works in close collaboration with the UCLA Animation Workshop in promoting the preservation and study of animated films. The animation collection includes hundreds of important films, mostly in original 35mm format. The *Animated Film Study Collection* consists of nearly 200 films on deposit from the Professional, Technical and Clerical Employees Union, Local 986. It contains works by such filmmakers as Tex Avery, Jiri Brdecka, Pete Burness, Robert Cannon, George Dunning, Witold Giersz, Bob

Godfrey, Paul Grimault, William Hanna and Joe Barbera (MGM), Hugh Harman, John and Faith Hubley, Ub Iwerks, Chuck Jones, Bob Kurtz, Jan Lenica, Winsor McCay, Norman McLaren, Otto Messmer, Jimmy Murakami, Barrie Nelson, Paul Terry, Bill Tytla, Richard Williams, Fred Wolf and dozens of others. The *George Pal Collection* contains a side selection of *Puppetoons*. A collection of Betty Boop cartoons, produced by Max Fleischer, includes many original negatives. Holdings include many Warner Brothers cartoons, negatives from the silent Paul Terry films and a collection of Walter Lantz films.

"B" Westerns. Collection is strong on "B" Westerns (1930s-40s). Produced by Grand National, Mascot, Monogram and PRC studios, these films feature such stars as Buck Jones, Ken Maynard, Tex Ritter, Bob Steele and John Wayne.

"Exploitation" Films. This unusual collection of 160 independently produced films (1930s-50s) deals with drugs, prostitution, variant sex and other topics avoided by the major studios. Titles of these films, collected and deposited by Sonney Amusement Enterprises, include *Slaves of Bondage*, *Souls in Pawn* and *The Virgin in Hollywood*.

Filmmakers. Substantial holdings by noted cinematographers, directors, performers and writers.

Directors represented include Dorothy Arzner, Frank Borzage, John Brahm, David Butler, Frank Capra, Charles Chaplin, Shirley Clarke, John Cromwell, George Cukor, Jules Dassin, Cecil B. DeMille, Edward Dmytryk, Allan Dwan, Blake Edwards, John Farrow, John Ford, Henry Hathaway, Howard Hawks, Alfred Hitchcock, Henry King, Stanley Kramer, Fritz Lang, Walter Lang, Mitchell Leisen, Ernst Lubitsch, Rouben Mamoulian, George Marshall, Leo McCarey, Lewis Milestone, F. W. Murnau, Otto Preminger, Robert Siodmak, Joseph Von Sternberg, Preston Sturges, King Vidor, Raoul Walsh, William Wellman, Billy Wilder and William Wyler.

Performers represented include Don Ameche, Jack Benny, Maurice Chevalier, Claudette Colbert, Gary Cooper, Bing Crosby, Tony Curtis, Marlene Dietrich, Alice Faye, W. C. Fields, Henry Fonda, Betty Grable, Bob Hope, Miriam Hopkins, the Marx Brothers, Alan Ladd, Jeannette MacDonald, Joel McCrea, Ray Milland, Tyrone Power, Barbara Stanwyck, Shirley Temple, Spencer Tracy, John Wayne, Mae West and Loretta Young.

Writers represented include Sidney Buchman, Raymond Chandler, Philip Dunne, Jules Furthman, Oliver H. P. Garrett, Nunnally Johnson, Joseph L. Mankiewicz, Herman J. Mankiewicz, Edwin Justus Mayer, Horace McCoy, Seton I. Miller, Samson Raphaelson, George Seaton, Lamar Trotti, Harry Tugend and Waldemar Young.

Cinematographers whose work is represented include Lee Garmes, James Wong Howe, Charles Lang, Jr., Ernest Laszlo, J. Peverell Marley, Arthur Muller, Victor Milner, Ray Rennahan, John Seitz, Leon Shamroy, Karl Struss and Gregg Toland.

Television Collections. With over 125,000 programs, the Archive maintains the most extensive television archive west of the Library of Congress. Collection contains examples of all types of broadcasting, representing every aspect of American television history (1947-present). The Archive also maintains a special collection of television technology, with hundreds of historical artifacts reflecting milestones in the development of broadcast equipment and home receivers.

The following sketch of Archive holdings gives some idea of the wealth of materials available.

Dramatic Programming. The *Hallmark Hall of Fame* series is represented by 163 programs (1951-72), studio versions of theater productions available to a mass audience. Programs include "Dial M For Murder," "Ah, Wilderness!," "Teahouse of the August Moon," "Pygmalion," "The Fantasticks," "Hamlet" and "Harvey." The series also dramatized the lives of historical figures such as Abraham Lincoln, Joan of Arc and Napoleon.

Three anthology series sponsored by the Alcoa Company comprise 222 dramatic titles. *The Alcoa Hour* (94 programs, 1956-59) features such stars as Charles Boyer, John Cassavetes, Lillian and Dorothy Gish, Cliff Robertson, Robert Ryan and Joanne Woodward. *Alcoa Presents One Step Beyond* (92 programs, 1959-61) dramatized accounts of psychic and occult phenomena. Fred Astaire hosted *Alcoa Premiere* (36 programs, 1961-63), and the Archive holds episodes featuring performers such as Charlton Heston and Lee Marvin. Of particular interest are two programs: "It Takes A Thief," written by Arthur Miller; and "Flashing Spikes," starring James Stewart and directed by John Ford, in one of his few excursions into television.

Story Theater (25 programs from the 1950 season) features adaptations of stories by Sir Arthur Conan Doyle, Charles Dickens, Victor Hugo, Guy de Maupassant, Robert Lewis Stevenson and Oscar Wilde. *Crossroads* (76 programs, 1953-56) offers religious dramas starring Lloyd Bridges, Pat O'Brien, Brian Donlevy, Edmund Lowe and Vincent Price.

Other dramatic anthologies include *Robert Montgomery Presents* and *The*

Loretta Young Show (the complete series, 1954-60).

Notable individual dramatic programs include the Emmy Award-winning "The Price of Tomatoes" (*Dick Powell Theater*, 1/16/62); the offbeat and compelling "Dangerous Games" (*Police Story*, 10/2/73); and the highly praised *The Autobiography of Miss Jane Pittman* (1/3/74).

Two of the first talents to emerge from television are Paddy Chayevsky, represented in the collection by "Holiday Song" (*Philco-Goodyear Playhouse*, 9/29/53); and Rod Serling, whose original "Requiem for a Heavyweight" (*Playhouse 90*, 10/11/56) was a milestone in dramatic programming.

In addition to anthologies, the collection holds episodes from continuing series, including: *Bonanza, The Defenders, The Fugitive, Ironsides, Naked City, Route 66, Run for Your Life, Slattery's People* and *Wagon Train*.

Comedy Programming. The Archive collection of television comedies highlights many notable personalities. One of the most popular and durable is Jack Benny, represented by 243 of his programs (1951-67) including his half-hour series, *The Jack Benny Show; The Jack Benny Hour;* appearances on other shows and specials, such as *Four Star Theater* (1955), *Easter Parade of Stars* (1955) and *Carnegie Hall Salutes Jack Benny* (9/27/61). Benny's guest stars include Humphrey Bogart, George Burns and Gracie Allen, Maurice Chevalier, Gary Cooper, Bob Hope, Ernie Kovacs, Frank Sinatra, Barbara Stanwyck and John Wayne, some of them making their sole television appearance.

Milton Berle, who brought vaudeville to television and became the medium's first major star, is represented by 46 programs. The majority of these are from *Texaco Star Theater* (1953). Among the guest stars appearing with Berle are Lon Chaney, Jr., Nat King Cole, Lena Horne and Peter Lorre. (Berle himself is featured in a rare dramatic role, the "Doyle Against the House" episode of *Dick Powell Theater*.)

Ernie Kovacs is featured on 10 programs from the 1955 television season. Kovacs' brand of offbeat humor and satire influenced numerous television comedians, including Tom and Dick Smothers. The 1969 season of *The Smothers Brothers Hour* is represented by 13 programs, excerpts from other seasons and by promotional spots.

The Archive holds 17 programs from Carol Burnett's comedy and variety series (1967-68). Guests include Lucille Ball, Ella Fitzgerald and Liza Minnelli. In addition, seven entertainment specials are included, notably the award-winning programs featuring Julie Andrews: *The Entertainers* (9/25/64), *Julie and Carol at Carnegie Hall* (6/11/62) and *Julie and Carol at Lincoln Center* (12/7/71).

Many other popular comic personalities are represented in the Archive. The *Colgate Comedy Hour* features Bud Abbott and Lou Costello, Eddie Cantor, Dean Martin and Jerry Lewis. Also featured are programs starring Danny Kaye, Martha Raye and Red Skelton. Johnny Carson's early show, *Carson's Cellar* (1953) is represented here, as is Steve Allen's syndicated show (1962-64) and episodes from his 1968 network series.

Rounding out the comedy collection are episodes from many continuing comedy series: *The Dick Van Dyke Show, Bewitched, Here's Lucy, The Lucy Show, The Adventures of Ozzie and Harriet, The Courtship of Eddie's Father, Hennesey, I Married Joan, The Mary Tyler Moore Show, Private Secretary, The Ann Sothern Show, You'll Never Get Rich, Mr. Ed, All In the Family* and *Happy Days*.

DuMont Television Network Collection (formerly the Peter Vest collection). Approximately 200 kinescopes of television shows produced for the DuMont network (1949-56), including episodes of *Captain Video*. Some 100 shows exist in positive print form; the remainder are in negative form with separate negative soundtrack. A significant portion (estimated to be 50%) of the collection is kinescopes of boxing matches from the St. Nicholas Arena in New York City.

Documentary and Historical Programming. The Archive has an outstanding collection of materials documenting John F. Kennedy's career. Documentaries, speeches, promotional messages and endorsements from his 1958 senatorial and 1960 presidential campaigns are included, as well as filmed highlights of the 1960 Democratic Convention, the Kennedy-Nixon debates, a Huntley-Brinkley interview and several important post-assassination documentaries.

Material from the 1952 and 1956 presidential campaigns of Adlai Stevenson include highlights of the 1956 Democratic convention. An interview with Senator Estes Kefauver and the documentaries *Campaigning with Stevenson* and *The Stevenson Story* are among the political events chronicled.

Other examples of political programming include a Winston Churchill speech to the United States Congress, the *See It Now* program featuring Edward R. Murrow's famous exposé of Senator Joseph McCarthy (3/9/54) and the controversial CBS program *The Selling of the Pentagon*. Ten other Murrow *You Are There* programs feature pre-stardom appearances by John Cassavetes, Robert Culp and Paul Newman in dramatizations of historical events within the format of news reporting.

The Archive has 35 specials produced by David L. Wolper. *Race for Space* (3/11/59), *China: The Roots of Madness* (3/11/59), *The Thin Blue Line* (1966; directed by William Friedkin) and three *Making of the President* programs from 1960, 1964 and 1968 form the backbone of this collection. 20 episodes of Wolper's *March of Time* series are also held.

Other documentary material includes the locally produced *The Negro in American Culture*, various examples of *NBC White Paper* and *Close-Up*. In addition to the other documentary and public affairs programs is an extensive collection of Los Angeles newscasts (1940s-50s) donated by newscaster Clete Roberts.

Cable Programming. In 1983, Home Box Office presented the Archive with a complete collection of original programs produced during its first decade of operation. Included are many award-winning specials, sports programs and documentaries, such as *She's Nobody's Baby: The American Woman in the 20th Century; Sports Illustrated: The First 25 Years; Standing Room Only: Diana Ross;* and *Remember When*. HBO is the first pay television service to have its programming represented in the Archive.

Hearst Metrotone News. Newsreels (so named because of their intent to portray news events and because they rarely ran longer than the 10-minute length of a single 35mm film reel) dominated the field of audiovisual journalism from the 1920s through the 1950s. Like most other major American newsreels, *Hearst Metrotone News* appeared in U.S. theaters biweekly. The Canadian and South American editions appeared once a week in separate editions, with appropriate translations.

Unlike the other major newsreels, which were affiliated with the major motion picture studios, the parent company of *Hearst Metrotone News* was a news organization. The Hearst Corporation sent cameramen to cover events of newsworthy, political, economic and social interest, along with its army of reporters and photographers.

Hearst launched a number of newsreels, beginning with *Hearst-Selig News Pictorial* (1914); then *Hearst-Vitagraph Weekly News* (1916); *Hearst-Pathé News* (1917); *The International Newsreel* (1919); and finally, *Hearst Metrotone News* (1929). In 1934, Metro-Goldwyn-Mayer, which had been distributing *Hearst Metrotone News* since its inception, became an equal partner in the venture. The library contains footage from all of these newsreels, comprising an immense pictorial record of 20th-century world events.

While MGM owned half of *Hearst Metrotone News,* it was responsible only for its distribution and release. It was produced solely by ex-newspapermen who had risen through the ranks of the Hearst organization. Although *News of the Day* was the official name of the newsreel, the competition always referred to it as "Hearst." An anecdote about the disappearance of "Hearst" from the newsreel masthead has it that during the Depression audiences booed when the Hearst name appeared on the screen.

In 1911, Edgar B. Hatrick, International News Service's chief of photographic services, urged William Randolph Hearst to begin motion picture news production. In March 1913, Hatrick produced a dramatic 10-minute news film on the inauguration of President Woodrow Wilson. This was distributed to theaters in association with Harry Warner, later one of the Warner Brothers founders.

Early in 1914, Hearst began a venture with the Selig Polyscope Company in Chicago. The *Hearst-Selig News Pictorial* was the first news film advertised to the public as a "newsreel." Two years later, under a new agreement with the Vitagraph Company, Hearst produced the *Hearst-Vitagraph Weekly News*. This was the first biweekly newsreel, "a film newspaper in the making," to quote one contemporary motion picture commentator. Unfortunately, state-of-the-art technology in 1916 could not support such an ambitious endeavor: camera equipment, laboratories, and freight shipping were insufficiently advanced, and the venture had to be abandoned. Yet another effort was launched by Hearst in 1919: the *International Newsreel*. Released through Pathé (then Universal Studios), this silent newsreel bore title captions and lasted for ten years, until the advent of sound. In 1929 it was replaced by the all-sound *Hearst Metrotone News*.

As a rule, the typical *News of the Day* story was somewhat shorter than those of its competitors. The editor-in-chief preferred to edit and score as many as 20 separate stories a day and make the final decision as to which 9 or 10 would be used in the newsreel as late as possible. Occasionally, when events of the day warranted, an issue consisted of only one story, as in the case of the abdication of Edward VIII or the inauguration of a U.S. president. Generally the newsreel included a couple of "hard news" items, a foreign story or two, a "lifestyle" item (such as a beauty contest or Harvest Moon Ball), and concluded with a sports story.

Hearst's highest weekly theatrical print release (1,150 per week) was in 1941. As the years passed and costs rose, the average length of each newsreel issue was reduced. By the late 1940s, they averaged slightly over 7 minutes per issue. Costs were also increased when newsreels switched from using nitrate to

acetate stock (also known as "safety film") in the early 1950s.

The Hearst collection at UCLA contains material from all of the various Hearst ventures into newsreel production. Additionally, there is material which predates the Hearst productions. Throughout their history, the Hearst newsreels acquired film from outside sources; the earliest material in the collection is of this nature and dates from the 1880s. The vast World War II holdings include material from the UFA newsreels (Germany), the *Nippon News* (Japan), and the British Gaumont newsreel. Acquisitions did not cease with the end of newsreel production in 1967. *Hearst Metrotone News* continued covering news events and producing *Screen News Digest,* primarily for educational use, until 1983. Much of this material is also part of the collection.

Wars and battles comprise one of the strongest areas in the Hearst collection. Coverage is vast and covers the Crimean War, World War I, World War II and the Arab-Israeli wars, and the film is of extremely high quality. The collection is also strong in domestic issues, including the civil rights movement. The Soviet Union is also well represented (Hearst set up an exchange arrangement with Sovexportfilm beginning in 1954, allowing for the exchange of newsreels with the Soviet Union).

Sports is also a strong category. The collection contains all film from the series *This Week in Sports* (1954-62, produced in 35mm for syndication and distributed in 16mm). There is ample coverage of baseball and the Kentucky Derby, as well as more obscure sports.

Entertainment figures covered include the Beatles and Marilyn Monroe. Hearst's association with MGM ensured good coverage of many MGM stars and events, including Mickey Rooney and Judy Garland, Clark Gable, personal appearance tours of the stars, the *Gone With the Wind* premiere in Atlanta, the *Lolita* premiere (with a young Stanley Kubrick, 1962), and Academy Awards ceremonies.

Most major "hard news" events of the century are covered. Because the collection contains "vault material" (material never used in a released issue), cuts and outs, there is often more coverage available than meets the eye. For example, the edited newsreel story on the Cuban missile crisis will contain excerpts from President Kennedy's press conference; but the "cuts and outs" contain most of the press conference.

In the 1950s, *Hearst Metrotone News* augmented its weekly theatrical newsreel with a daily television news service called *Telenews*. During the 1950s and 1960s, *Telenews* was distributed to over 100 television stations around the world, and to the CBS and ABC networks. *Telenews* film was produced and distributed by a number of U.S. and foreign bureaus, until production ended in 1963. As network television news operations rapidly expanded, the newsreel companies weakened and eventually stopped producing newsreels for movie theaters. Hearst Metrotone halted its releases to movie theaters in November 1967, but it continued other production operations through 1983.

While edited newsreels and the stock film library have been donated to UCLA (where it is physically housed), certain "derivative works" are still held by and available from Hearst Metrotone News (q.v.) in New York City.

The UCLA Film and Television Archive is involved with preserving the collection on an ongoing basis, transferring material from nitrate to safety film. Priority is given to the material which is most in danger of disintegration. Funding has sometimes permitted the preservation of certain subject areas within the collection, such as science and technology or the Japan-China war. The finest quality 35mm safety prints and preservation fine grain masters are made. Printing and film-to-videotape transfers from nitrate negatives is possible if their condition permits. Excellent videotape transfers may also be derived from 35mm preservation materials.

Size & Elements: Film and videotape (over 200,000 titles; all elements, nitrate and safety stock). The Hearst collection consists of approximately 27 million feet of both 35mm and 16mm film. Although the film is mostly 35mm, both 35mm and 16mm were in use simultaneously after 16mm production began in the 1950s. The choice of one format or another would largely be determined by the nature of the event (e.g., hand-held 16mm for action footage of demonstrations and riots). Original camera negative is held on most rolls of film. Original nitrate 35mm release prints are held for 1930s and 1940s newsreels; cut negatives, outtakes, cuts and unused vault material are also held. A small amount of color film is held, some produced by Hearst, the rest acquired from outside sources for incorporation into the newsreels in black and white form. Most color film is 16mm Kodachrome and relates to space, Vietnam, Presidential inaugurations, and major international events.

Cataloging: The Hearst collection is indexed by a cross-referenced card catalog. The original file cards fill twenty five-foot filing cabinets. Most of the cards were microfilmed, and the microfilm and reader are also available. Material added to the collection after the microfilming is cataloged only on file cards.

The filing system is divided into three large categories: "Personality,"

"Geography," and "Miscellaneous Subjects." Personalities are filed alphabetically by name; larger entries, such as Franklin Roosevelt, are subdivided by year. "Geography" is also divided alphabetically by country and city; large files are also subdivided by year. Within the United States, the files are alphabetical by state, and within each state by city. An alphabetical list of miscellaneous subjects, filed by title, runs 45 pages from "Abdication" to "Zoo."

Several separate subject indexes are maintained, including "Education," "War," "Military" and "Sports."

Both 35mm and 16mm are found in the same catalog, but a separate catalog exists for color material.

The library index cards contain a wealth of information about the film. Two slightly different formats are utilized, depending on whether the material was shot for *Telenews* or for the theatrical newsreel releases. Cards contain subject, title, description, and frequently, a complete cross-referenced shot list. The cards also indicate in which daily volume the material was used, the date the material was filed, the length of the roll, the elements, and whether or not there are cuts. Also on file at the Archive are the release sheets for each *News of the Day* issue. The contents of the release are described, newspaper-style, e.g., *The Front Page — Dramatic Highlights of the Czechoslovakian Crisis!*, *The Woman's Page — Unique School Trains Debutantes!*, or *The Sporting Page — New Football Razzle Dazzle for 1938*. Names of the commentators and a brief summary of each story are also given.

A duplicate microfiche catalog is available at Hearst in New York.

Access: Open to researchers and scholars. For in-house use only. Research and screening fees charged in some cases. Research fees not charged for using card or microfilm catalogs. Research requests accepted by mail, telephone and in person (by appointment only). Librarians can provide viewing videotapes and copies of file cards in response to specific requests for material from the Hearst collection.

Many items in collection are available for on-site viewing for research purposes. Demand for use of the collection is high, and appointments should be made as far in advance as possible.

Rights: Full rights held to *Hearst Metrotone News* collection. Rights to most other material retained by original producers or copyright holders. Additional clearances may be necessary in some cases if material is to be reused.

Licensing: Hearst Metrotone News material available for licensing and reuse through Commercial Services. License fees charged depending on intended use of material (apply for fee schedule and information). Minimum license fees are due and payable at the time footage is ordered from the Archive, and are nonrefundable in the event that footage is not used. Discounts for quantity usage are available.

Restrictions: Donor restrictions prohibit circulation of the collection. Some television programs are subject to special donor restrictions; in other instances, 2" videotapes and rare kinescopes must be transferred to smaller-format videotapes before they can be viewed for reference purposes.

Viewing Facilities: The Archive Study Center is equipped with 35mm Steenbeck viewing machines, 16mm Moviola viewing machines, videotape monitors and 3/4" and 1/2" videotape decks. A special room for viewing nitrate films is located at the Archive's storage facility in Hollywood. Screening fees may apply. Clients must screen film with the assistance of an Archive staffperson.

Duplication Facilities: None (outside film laboratories and videotape transfer facilities are used).

Related Materials: The Archive Collection of Television Technology and Design consists of over 300 historical artifacts, mostly broadcast equipment and home receivers dating back as far as the 1930s.

The collection encompasses all major lines of development in the history of television technology: black and white television system development; color television system development; live and film pickup camera and broadcast equipment development; receiver development; video recording systems; and industrial design.

Highlights from the collection include: two experimental receivers built in 1937 and 1938 by Los Angeles station W6XAO; an RR-359 receiver, one of only 100 sets originally built by RCA for field tests in New York in 1936-39; a TRK-12 receiver, RCA's first set sold to the public in 1939; a project block iconoscope camera used during World War II; a TK-10 image orthicon camera from 1946; a CBS-Columbia 12CC2 receiver from 1951, the only set sold for use with the CBS field sequential color broadcasts; an RCA CT-100 receiver from 1954, the first set mass produced for the NTSC color standard; several TK-41's, the first commercial NTSC color cameras; and an Ampex VR-1000, the first commercial videotape recorder, introduced in 1956.

In addition to historically significant equipment, the Archive also collects and preserves related documentation, such as manuals, drawings, technical reports and texts.

The Archive holds more than 50,000 radio broadcasts (early 1930s-present).

The UCLA Theater Arts Library (213/825-7253) contains a major, interdisciplinary research and reference collection in the fields of motion pictures, television and radio. The library contains over 12,000 books, 200 periodicals, thousands of original documents, screenplays, television scripts, portraits, production stills, storyboards, posters, lobby cards, pressbooks, clipping files, animation material, correspondence, business papers and production files. There is a strong collection of personal papers, correspondence, business records, production files, publicity, shooting schedules, various versions of scripts, and photographs of important directors, actors, screen writers and cinematographers.

Rare books, manuscripts, personal papers, business records, photographs and miscellaneous material relating to motion pictures, television and radio are held in the University Research Library, Department of Special Collections (213/825-4879 or 213/825-4988).

Preservation: The Archive's primary commitment is to the preservation of our film heritage. Tragically, over 50% of all films produced in the United States no longer exist in any form. The Archive's goal is to help save those that remain and those that are being produced today and tomorrow.

Nitrate Preservation. A major part of the Archive's effort involves the costly transfer of pre-1950 films from deteriorating nitrate stock to safety acetate stock. With the help of funding from governmental, corporate and private sources, the Archive has saved many last prints of films from destruction. A great deal of work remains to be done, however. The Archive holds more than 28 million feet of unpreserved nitrate — everything from unknown silent shorts to famous Hollywood features, and much of the historic newsreel footage in the *Hearst Metrotone News* collection. Current funding is not at all adequate to the task at hand, and contributions to the Archive's Preservation Fund are eagerly sought.

Paper Print Preservation. In 1983, the Archive assumed responsibility for preservation of the Library of Congress' paper print collection. This collection consists of thousands of early films on photographic paper rolls, originally deposited with the library as copyright records. Not only do the paper prints trace the development of cinema from a simple recording device to a complex and unique art form, but they also document the people and events from the period 1895-1915. To be viewable as films, the paper prints must be rephotographed a single frame at a time back onto celluloid. Kemp Niver, film historian and archivist, has donated to the Archive the special equipment which he developed for this project in the 1950s while working in conjunction with the Library of Congress and the Academy of Motion Picture Arts and Sciences. The Archive is carrying on Mr. Niver's work of nearly 30 years in preserving the earliest records of film history.

This article draws heavily on A Guide to Media Research Resources at UCLA, *prepared by the Media Study Group in association with the UCLA Film and Television Archive. We reprint information from the* Guide *by permission of the Archive. The description of the* Hearst Metrotone News *library was researched and written by Lewanne Jones, a film researcher working in New York City.*

CALIFORNIA (Los Angeles Metro)

U.S. DEPARTMENT OF DEFENSE
MOTION MEDIA RECORDS CENTER

Building 248
Norton Air Force Base, CA 92409-5996
(714) 382-2307
(714) 382-3826
AUTOVON: 876-2307 or 876-3826

Larry Wilson (Manager)

Contact: Robert Laur (Senior Researcher)
Services: Government agency; film and videotape archives; stock footage sales library. Material available for duplication and reuse, subject to restrictions.
Description: The Department of Defense (DOD) Central Motion Media Records Center, operated by the 1352d Audiovisual Squadron (AVS), is an official DOD archives for storage and preservation of motion picture and videotape products and their related materials used in visual information (VI) production and documentation media. This archives preserves, maintains, and makes final disposition of official VI materials in its possession, as long as the collection remains in active use for official DOD purposes. Research and duplication services for all material in its possession are provided by the 1352 AVS. Upon final disposition, materials having permanent historic value are offered to the National Archives and Records Administration (q.v.) for

permanent archival preservation as a national resource, and continued availability.

The following is a private researcher's analysis of the Motion Media Records Center and does not reflect the opinions or imply the endorsement of the Department of Defense.

The DOD Motion Media Records Center, the largest motion media collection within the DOD, houses film and videotape (1930s-present). Both documentary coverage of military events and exercises, plus edited informational and training films, are available to the public for use as stock footage.

The collection is divided into five parts, corresponding to the four branches of the Armed Services and the DOD as a whole. Each branch has a separate cataloging system, but all finding aids are accessible. Post-1981 service files are consolidated into one comprehensive cataloging system.

Air Force collection. Covers the beginning of aviation; the early space program; missile programs from the earliest days of testing; the space shuttle; and satellite programs. There are also air power films from World War II, Korea and Vietnam, and excellent footage of virtually every Air Force and Army Air Corps aircraft ever made. Holds all volumes of *The Air Force Story;* and trims and outtakes from such films as *Memphis Belle, Combat America* and *The Last Bomb.* The Air Force Collection is the largest collection housed at Norton.

Army collection. Holds the complete *Big Picture* series, covering the history of the Army's various regiments, programs and training, and also combat bulletins which detail World War II and Korea campaign-by-campaign and sometimes battle-by-battle. There is a strong emphasis on exercises and equipment inventory, as well as material on the early anti-ballistic missile program and the Army's participation in Vietnam.

Department of Defense collection. Holds many news releases (early 1950s through early 1980s; each 1-3 min.) showing noteworthy developments and events within all branches of the military.

Marine Corps and *Navy collections.* Primarily holds footage of these two services' participation in the Vietnam War and footage relating to their role as peacekeepers and protectors of the seas. There is strong documentation of modern equipment, including ships, aircraft and amphibious warfare exercises. Edited films from the Navy and Marine Corps offer an historical perspective of each service.

Size & Elements: Film: 35mm and 16mm (over 300 million feet; preprint material and viewing prints). Videotape: 1", Betacam and 3/4" (178,000 minutes; masters and viewing copies). Footage through World War II is primarily in 35mm form; from the Korean War through the early 1980s in 16mm; and from the early 1980s, on Betacam videotape.

Cataloging: Card catalogs; shot lists. *DOD Productions Cleared for Public Release,* a published catalog, available through Public Affairs Offices (see below).

Access: Open to the public. Available for duplication and reuse, subject to restrictions. Fees charged for staff assistance. Commercial (non-military) clients have the option of doing their own research while visiting Norton, or arranging for a freelance researcher to review and select material for them. Official customers and the public may view films in screening rooms or request that the Records Center research staff review required subjects for them. There is no charge if the customer screens films directly; however, a standard research fee is charged public customers if Records Center personnel perform this service. Prints or viewing cassettes are generally available for selection of scenes before preprint material is sent to the laboratory. Research requests accepted by mail, telephone, messages and in person.

Access to Norton's collection is through one or more of the military Public Affairs offices, usually located at the Pentagon. Use of Air Force footage, for example, requires Air Force approval; Navy footage requires Navy approval, and so on. All-service requests are coordinated through the Office of the Assistant Secretary of Defense, Public Affairs (OASD/PA) at the Pentagon. Some large cities also have local Public Affairs Offices, which can help in coordinating your request. Public Affairs Offices are listed below.

Requests for use of stock footage are usually submitted in writing, with an outline or script attached to clarify the nature of the project, the intended audience and the type of footage required. Once approval to access the collection and use the footage is granted, the user is informed and the request forwarded to Norton.

Research and duplication services for the DOD Motion Media Records Center collection are provided to both official DOD and other federal agencies as well as the general public; however, priority is given to official DOD requirements in preference to non-official requests. Official DOD requests either support government requirements or promote government business in accordance with established DOD and military sales directives. All DOD activities are considered official customers. Also considered official customers are other federal agencies, state, county and city governments. Television newscasters, newspaper reporters, veterans' organizations, scholars and individual citizens are considered public or non-official customers. Research and duplication services performed for these organizations and individuals are conducted on a cost-reimbursable basis.

The Records Center is prohibited by DOD regulation from selling, loaning for reproduction or renting complete copies of visual information productions. These can only be purchased from NARA, National Audiovisual Center (q.v.). Copies of DOD VI products are accountable and their use and reproduction is strictly controlled by the military services.

Rights: Material in the public domain. Additional clearances may be necessary in some cases if footage is to be reused.

Licensing: Available for reuse, subject to restrictions. Usage fees not charged.

Restrictions: Research and reuse requires approval by appropriate branch of the Armed Services. Requests must be submitted in writing and accompanied by scripts or project outlines. Some material is classified or designated for official use only.

Viewing Facilities: Film and videotape.

Duplication Facilities: None (arranged through user's facilities at user's expense). The Air Force is studying the possibility of in-house reproduction for commercial clients.

Public Affairs Offices — Army

Headquarters, Department of the Army
Office of The Chief of Public Affairs
Attn: SAPA-MRD
Washington, DC 20310-0001
(202) 695-3007
AUTOVON: 225-3007 or 225-9375

633 Fifth Avenue
New York, NY 10022-5309
(212) 688-7572
AUTOVON: 994-3466

11000 Wilshire Boulevard, Suite 10104
Los Angeles, CA 90024-3688
(213) 209-7621

Public Affairs Offices — Navy

Department of the Navy
Chief of Information
Code OI-220
Pentagon, Room 2D340
Washington, DC 20350-0001
(202) 697-0866
AUTOVON: 227-0866

Navy Office of Information
11000 Wilshire Boulevard, Suite 11100
Los Angeles, CA 90024-3688
(213) 209-7481

Public Affairs Offices — Air Force

Secretary of the Air Force
Office of Public Affairs
Pictorial/Broadcasting Branch
Washington, DC 20330-0001
(202) 695-9664
(202) 695-9665
AUTOVON: 225-9664 or 225-9657

11000 Wilshire Boulevard, Suite 10114
Los Angeles, CA 90024-3688
(213) 209-7511

663 Fifth Avenue
New York, NY 10022-5309
(212) 753-5609
AUTOVON: 938-3761 or 938-3762

Public Affairs Offices — Marine Corps
Commandant of the Marine Corps
Code PAM
Headquarters, U.S. Marine Corps
Washington, DC 20380-0001
(202) 694-1492
(202) 694-1493
AUTOVON: 224-1492 or 224-1493

United States Marine Corps
Public Affairs Office
11000 Wilshire Boulevard, Suite 10117
Los Angeles, CA 90024-3688
(213) 209-7272

CALIFORNIA (Los Angeles Metro)

**UNIVERSAL CITY STUDIOS
STOCK FILM LIBRARY**
100 Universal City Plaza, Building 99
Universal City, CA 91608
(818) 777-3674
Fax: (818) 777-6431

Jack Rush (Head Librarian)

Contact: Chris Soto (Librarian)
Services: Film stock footage sales library.
Description: Outtakes and unused material from Universal feature films and television programs (1946-present). Most general subjects are covered; over 5,000 categories of footage, most in color, are represented. Special coverage includes material from the television series *Galactica* and *Buck Rogers,* featuring special effects, rocket ships and spaceships.
    Black and white material (beginning 1931-32) is held in New Jersey and accessible only on a case-by-case basis.
Size & Elements: Film: 35mm (22 million feet; color negative; workprints held for most material).
Cataloging: Card catalogs incorporating cut frames from shots for reference.
Access: Available to producers with accounts or who have otherwise established credit with library. Research fees charged. Research requests accepted by telephone.
Rights: Full rights held to all material.
Licensing: Available for licensing and reuse, subject to restrictions. License fees charged.
Restrictions: Additional clearances must be obtained for reuse of some stunt footage.
Viewing Facilities: Film (Kem flatbed viewing tables); videotape (3/4").
Duplication Facilities: None.

CALIFORNIA (Los Angeles Metro)

**UNIVERSITY OF SOUTHERN CALIFORNIA
FILM AND VIDEO DISTRIBUTION CENTER**
School of Cinema-Television
University Park, MC 2212
Los Angeles, CA 90089-2212
(213) 743-2238
Fax: (213) 746-7838

Georges Webei (Director)

Contact: Georges Webei
Services: University film library; film and videotape producer. Collection maintained for rental, purchase and educational use.
Description: Films produced at the University of Southern California and by its students. Also holds an extensive general collection of educational support materials acquired from outside sources. University productions include:
    Contemporary drama. Titles include: *Baby Blue* (1966), about a young American woman's emotional conflict due to her infidelity while her husband is fighting in Vietnam; *Cocoon* (1968), presenting an excursion into the world of a young Black dishwasher, his frustration and his failure to communicate with the world around him; *Log 43* (1969), a re-enactment based on the Algiers Motel incident in which three people were killed during the Detroit riots of 1967; *Jazz* (1980), depicting the struggle of three Los Angeles jazz musicians to gain recognition in their field; *Passing Lane* (1969), a satire on the

"urbanization" which has created many social problems, not the least of which is the impersonal nature of the megalopolis; and *Viking Women Don't Care* (1968), in which hippies with a carload of marijuana meet a runaway bank robber in a car containing a dead body. Their confrontation satirizes the portrayal of violence in films.
    Science fiction and fantasy. Titles include: *The Bug* (1963), an experimental film offering a solution to the ills of the atomic age; *Daydreamer* (1981), the story of a 12-year-old boy who fantasizes about a forest paradise inhabited by forest children; *Inspiratio Diaboli,* presenting a scientific revolution caused by Satanic inspiration, where men worship science; *Morris* (1979), a humorous look at an undersea society; and *The Survivors* (1967), a dramatic confrontation between the last man and woman left on earth after an atomic war.
    American history. Titles include: *The American Love Affair* (1975), tracing the growth of Los Angeles from a dirt-street pueblo into today's metropolis and the innovations and displacements caused by various transportation systems; *After The Eagle,* telling the story of a young Indian who learns the importance of his heritage through a mystical revelation and the sacrifice of his father; and *Bird,* a quick succession of images and photographs satirizing President Lyndon Johnson.
    Drama and literature. Titles include: *The Black Cat* (1955), dramatizing Poe's tale; and *An Occurrence At Owl Creek Bridge* (1956; a USC Graduate Workshop Production), a dramatic adaptation of Ambrose Bierce's famous Civil War story.
    Documentary. Titles include: *Chabad Movement,* a glimpse into the alternative lifestyle of an orthodox Jewish group which believes in the combination of joy and ritual, not only in prayer but in all aspects of their lives; *Clowns* (1981), examining the present state of the art of clowning, with interviews, performances and historical information; *People's Temple* (1973), documenting the origins of the People's Temple Community in California, including interviews with Pastor Jim Jones, providing insight into his charismatic character and presenting case histories; and *Ritual* (1966), presenting a visual exploration of the ritual involved in the application of eye makeup and the elaborate materials used.
    Science. Titles include: *Neon* (1980), exploring the wonders of luminous tubes; *The Story of Dentistry* (1964), tracing the history of dentistry from ancient Egypt to the present; *The Thinnest Slice* (1949), in which tissue is sliced to one five hundred-thousandth of an inch on a microtome.
    Social issues. Titles include: *Two Steps at a Time* (1981), studying a young woman whose rehabilitation from an accident is complicated by the additional roles of mother and wife; *Aphasia In Childhood,* describing the communication problems of an aphasic 12-year-old girl; and *Amanda,* depicting the pain and frustration of a young woman as she tries to accept her mentally retarded sister.
Size & Elements: Film: 16mm (approx. 3,000 titles). Videotape: 3/4" (approx. 60 titles).
Cataloging: Published catalogs.
Access: Available for rental and purchase for educational use. The Library is unable to supply preview prints for rental titles or facilities for rental consideration. Preview prints are available for films sold by USC when the title is being considered for purchase by an authorized buyer. Requests accepted by mail and telephone.
Rights: Full rights held to some material. Some rights held to some material. Additional clearances may be necessary in some cases if material is to be reused.
Licensing: Apply for information.
Restrictions: None specified.
Viewing Facilities: None.
Duplication Facilities: None.

CALIFORNIA (Los Angeles Metro)

**UNIVERSITY OF SOUTHERN CALIFORNIA
ARNOLD SCHOENBERG INSTITUTE ARCHIVES**
University Park, MC 1101
Los Angeles, CA 90089-1101
(213) 743-5393

R. Wayne Shoaf (Archivist)

Contact: R. Wayne Shoaf
Services: Educational institution; archives. Film and videotape collection available solely to researchers and scholars for in-house use only.
Description: Material (produced 1940-87) relating to Arnold Schoenberg, 20th-century composer.
Size & Elements: Film: format unspecified (10 titles, 20 cans; positive).

CALIFORNIA (Los Angeles Metro U)

Videotape: 3/4" and VHS (5 videotapes; masters).
Cataloging: None specified.
Access: Available to researchers and scholars only. For in-house use only. Research fees not charged. Research requests accepted in person (by appointment only).
Rights: Some rights held to some material. Rights status of other material not known.
Licensing: Apply for information. Usage fees charged in some cases.
Restrictions: None specified.
Viewing Facilities: None.
Duplication Facilities: None.

CALIFORNIA (Los Angeles Metro)

UNIVISION TELEVISION NETWORK
9200 Sunset Boulevard, Suite 1100
Los Angeles, CA 90069
(213) 859-7200
(213) 859-0066
Fax: (213) 859-7454

Contacts: Rosita Peru; Vilma Ortiz (Cable Division, New York office, 212/826-5200).
Services: Television program producer and distributor. Programs available for broadcast and cable television distribution.
Description: Distributes a full range of Spanish-language programming, produced both in the U.S. and throughout the Spanish-speaking world. Founded in 1961 as SIN Television Network and renamed UNIVISION in 1987.

Programming is broadbased, family oriented and all originally produced in Spanish. Most programs are originated in Hispanic production centers throughout the world, although now increasingly produced by UNIVISION in the U.S., and include national, international and local news programs; specials; morning and late evening talk shows; *novelas;* variety, musical and comedy programs; movies; live sporting events; children's programs; and miniseries.

Programs offered include: *Noticiero UNIVISION,* a weekday evening news program; *América,* a bi-weekly news magazine reporting on various topics from the Hispanic point of view; *America En La Cultura,* a weekly magazine-style show focusing on music, dance, literature, fine arts and history of Latin culture in the Americas; *Para Gente Grande,* hosted by Ricardo Rocha, featuring news, features, business, show business, sports and celebrity interviews; *El Extraño Retorno de Diana Salazar,* a *novela* with a story line involving witchcraft and reincarnation; *Rosa Salvaje,* a rags-to-riches love story; *Desde Hollywood,* a weekly magazine-style show featuring celebrity interviews, the latest show business gossip, glamorous film previews and parties; *Especiales,* various specials highlighting well-known personalities, such as Carlos Gardel, the "King of Tango," with colorized segments of his most famous films, as well as other more contemporary figures and subjects; and *Sabado Gigante,* a Spanish-language potpourri of games, contests, talent searches and celebrity guest appearances.

Siempre En Domingo, which originates in Mexico City and elsewhere, is a musical entertainment show that has been running for 18 years and has featured such stars as Celia Cruz, José José, Tony Bennett, Emmanuel, Barry Manilow, Tina Turner, and host Raúl Velasco; *OTI Song Festival* brings amateur musicians annually from all areas of the U.S. to compete for the chance to be part of the spectacular followup in Argentina; *Topo Gigio* features the return of Italy's endearing puppet mouse, now speaking Spanish.

Children's programs include *Las Aventuras del Principe Pequeño; La Princesa Caballero; Remi; La Maquina del Tiempo.* Sports programming includes boxing, auto racing, soccer and various specials.
Size & Elements: Film and videotape (formats and amounts unspecified).
Cataloging: Published press releases.
Access: Available for broadcast or cable television distribution. Requests accepted by mail and telephone.
Rights: Full rights held to some material. Additional clearances may be necessary in some cases if material is to be reused.
Licensing: Apply for information.
Restrictions: Apply for information.
Viewing Facilities: None.
Duplication Facilities: None.

CALIFORNIA (Los Angeles Metro)

UPA PRODUCTIONS OF AMERICA
14101 Valleyheart Drive, Suite 200

Sherman Oaks, CA 91423
(818) 990-3800
Fax: (818) 990-4854

Henry G. Saperstein (President)

Contact: Patricia Saperstein (Marketing Director)
Services: Distributor; film and videotape producer. Material maintained for distribution and rental rather than for research or reuse.
Description: Holdings include: cartoon programs featuring characters such as Mr. Magoo, Dick Tracy, and Gerald McBoing Boing; *Godzilla* and other science fiction movies; Roy Rogers television shows; *The T.A.M.I. Show,* with The Rolling Stones, The Supremes, Marvin Gaye and other performers, and *The T.N.T. Show,* with Tina Turner, The Ronettes and more.
Size & Elements: Film and videotape: formats unspecified (100 titles total).
Cataloging: None specified.
Access: Maintained for distribution and rental rather than for research and reuse.
Rights: Full rights held to some material. Some rights held to all material. Some rights held to some material. Additional clearances may be necessary in some cases if material is to be reused.
Licensing: Apply for information. License fees charged.
Restrictions: None specified.
Viewing Facilities: None.
Duplication Facilities: None.

CALIFORNIA (Los Angeles Metro)

VALLEY OF THE SUN PUBLISHING
Box 3004
Agoura Hills, CA 91301
(818) 456-7361
Fax: (818) 706-3606

Contact: Dick Sutphen
Services: Videotape producer and distributor. Videotapes available to the public for purchase.
Description: New age videotape producer and distributor offering tools and teachings to create your own reality. Topics include: health improvement, higher-self, meditation, metaphysical, new age music, regression, ritual white magic, self-improvement, sexual self-help, subliminals, success and motivation.

Video-Hypnosis. Titles include: *Accelerated Learning; Attracting Love; Chakra Balance; Lose Weight Now; Develop Psychic Ability Now; Healing Acceleration; How To Create The Life You Want to Live; Incredible Self-Confidence; Intensifying Creative Ability; Master of Life; Sedona: Psychic Vortex Experience; Stop Smoking Forever; Ultra Monetary Success;* and *Un-Stress.*
Size & Elements: Videotape: VHS and Betamax (15 titles; viewing copies).
Cataloging: Published catalog.
Access: Available to the public for purchase.
Rights: Apply for information.
Licensing: Apply for information.
Restrictions: None specified.
Viewing Facilities: None.
Duplication Facilities: None.

CALIFORNIA (Los Angeles Metro)

VIDEO TAPE LIBRARY, LTD.
1509 North Crescent Heights Boulevard, Suite 2
Los Angeles, CA 90046
(213) 656-4330
Fax: (213) 656-8746

Stephanie Siebert (General Manager)

Contact: Melody Schock (Director of Sales and Marketing)
Services: Videotape stock footage sales library.
Description: A growing library drawing on 350 to 400 sources.
Sports. A large collection, including over 400 hours of *CBS Sports Spectacular* footage, featuring track and field, boxing, wrestling, gymnastics, diving, martial arts, skating, automobile racing, rodeo, swimming, equestrian, weightlifting, skiing, basketball, roller-skating, football, bowling, tennis, volleyball, surfing, the *Mr. America* contest, water polo, canoeing, water

skiing, skateboarding, hang-gliding, Frisbee championships, ski flying, landsailing, skateboarding, rugby and parachuting. Also holds footage from the United States Football League (USFL); and several full-length features on California water sports, such as surfing, windsurfing and windsailing. Other sports include aerobatics, aerobics, exercise, horse racing, jet skiing, motocross, video games and white-water rafting.

Other subjects include white-collar work situations, including people at computers and telephones, board meetings, office interiors, clerical workers and the stock exchange floor. Also holds footage of Thailand, Russia, political events from the 1960s, Adolf Hitler, frantic crowds, amusement park rides, parades, police, cults, chemical dumps, pollution, a water reclamation plant, prisons, punk clubs, Vietnam, wars, health foods, picket lines, wind generators, explosions, chemical explosions, aftermath of an earthquake, disasters, emergency vehicles, firefighters, hook-and-ladders, military vehicles, train derailments and air rescues.

Also holds airplanes, blimps, space exploration, satellites, helicopters, robotics, computer graphics, high technology, joggers, traffic, buses, automobiles, recreational vehicle (RV) activities, freeway aerials, city aerials, restaurants, cathedrals, churches, castles, villas, houses, laboratories, lighthouses, museums, stadiums, factories, construction workers, mud baths, mineral baths, mountains, rain forests, rainbows, rain, waves, rivers, whales, beaches, cliffs, lagoons, volcanoes (erupting and dormant), islands, flowers, foliage, glaciers, jungles, the moon, planets, spider webs, desert (sand dune aerials), sharks, snakes, tide pools, underwater scenes, African animals, aquariums, antiques, brownstones, casinos, farms, statues, fireworks, villages, mining towns, humor, gorges, geysers, forts, forests, orchestras, snow, lava and dancing.

Also holds a collection of black and white footage. Videographers in Paris and London can accommodate custom footage requests.
Size & Elements: Videotape: 1" and 3/4" (masters); 3/4" and VHS (viewing copies) (6,000 hours total).
Cataloging: Computerized cataloging for staff use only; published brochure.
Access: Available for duplication and reuse. Research fees not charged. Will assemble demonstration reels for out-of-state clients. Research requests accepted by mail and telephone.
Rights: Full rights held to all material (with very few exceptions).
Licensing: Available for licensing and reuse. License fees charged.
Restrictions: None specified.
Viewing Facilities: Videotape.
Duplication Facilities: Videotape.

CALIFORNIA (Los Angeles Metro)

VIDEOBRARY, INC.
6117 Carpenter Avenue
North Hollywood, CA 91606
(818) 761-5265

Contact: Paul Lisy
Services: Videotape distributor. Materials available to the public for purchase.
Description: Small company offering rare films to the homevideo market. The collection is intended for the avid film collector as well as the more casual movie buff.

Sound comedy shorts (1930s-40s). Extensive list of titles by Leon Errol, Edgar Kennedy and Andy Clyde, as well as shorts featuring George Beckel, Milton Berle, Billy Bevan, Walter Calett, Monty Collins, Joe Cook, Ray Cooke, Bing Crosby, The Easy Aces, Rita Flynn, Billy Gilbert, Charlotte Greenwood, Lloyd Hamilton, Bob Hope, Tom Howard, George Shelton, Willie Howard, Pert Kelton, Harry Langdon, Ida Lupino, Moran and Mack, Daphne Pollard, The Ritz Brothers, Larry Semon, Stoopnagle and Budd, Harry Von Zell, West and Patricola, York and King, Shirley Temple, Our Gang and Charlie Chaplin.

Feature films (late 1930s-early 1950s). Includes: *Boss of Big Town; The Contender; Hoosier Schoolboy; Inyaah (Jungle Goddess); L'il Abner; Machine Gun Mama; Nabonga (Gorilla); Stage Door Canteen; Wrong Number; Algiers; Baron of Arizona; Beyond Tomorrow; His Girl Friday; Made For Each Other; Scarlet Street; The Secret Weapon; That Uncertain Feeling; Things To Come; Topper Returns; The Woman In Green;* 15 films starring John Wayne; and other westerns, including *Navajo.*

Television. Includes an anthology show, *Trails West,* hosted by Ray Milland, with selected episodes; *Wind At Your Back,* starring June Dayton and Steve Terrell; *Death Ride,* written by Ernest Pascal; *A Bullet for the D.A.,* with Carole Mathews and Don Haggerty; *Money To Burn,* written by Norman Jacobs; and *Battle of Mokehume,* with Marcel Dalin and Diane Dubois.
Size & Elements: Videotape: VHS and Betamax (approx. 200 titles; film-to-

videotape transfers).
Cataloging: Printed catalog.
Access: Available to the public for purchase. Research requests accepted by mail and telephone.
Rights: No rights held to any material. Some material in the public domain.
Licensing: Material not available for licensing or reuse.
Restrictions: Material not available for licensing or reuse of any kind.
Viewing Facilities: None.
Duplication Facilities: None.

CALIFORNIA (Los Angeles Metro)

VISUAL COMMUNICATIONS
SOUTHERN CALIFORNIA ASIAN AMERICAN STUDIES CENTRAL, INC.
263 South Los Angeles Street, Suite 307
Los Angeles, CA 90012
(213) 680-4462

Linda Mabalot (Executive Director)

Contact: Archivist
Services: Distributor; nonprofit media arts center. Film and videotape collection available to the public for rental and purchase.
Description: Nonprofit Asian Pacific American Media Arts Center founded in 1970. Provides the Asian American community with film and videotape production services, technical instruction and audiovisual distribution and exhibition.

Sample titles include: *Chisai Samurai* (Chris Tashima); *Kusei: Endangered Species* (Karen Mayeda and Denise Okimoto), a futuristic spoof of modern-day Japanese American habits and tradition; *Renewal* (Kaz Takeuchi); *Harusame: Spring Rain* (José de Vega); *Little One Inch* (Kelly Takemura); *Mochi Monster* (Troi Pang); *Pak Bueng on Fire* (Supachai Surongsain); *Lotus* (Arthur Dong), a historical drama about how one woman in 1914 China decides whether she will bind her daughter's feet.

Also distributes many other films and videotapes on Asian American subjects, including the jazz/rock group *Hiroshima;* the Samoan community in

California; the struggles of Asian American farmers; the history of Japanese immigration through the accounts of three Issei; the "manong" (the first wave of Pilipinos to America); and Asian American actors.

Size & Elements: Film: 16mm and Super 8mm (approx. 24 titles; release prints, color). Videotape: 3/4" and VHS (4 titles originally in videotape; viewing copies of films).

Cataloging: Published brochures.

Access: Available to the public for rental and purchase. Requests accepted by mail and telephone. Preview prints and viewing copies of some titles available (fees apply).

Rights: Apply for information.

Licensing: Apply for information.

Restrictions: None specified.

Viewing Facilities: None.

Duplication Facilities: None.

Related Materials: Archives of historical photographs; print materials.

Publications: *In Focus,* published quarterly for the Friends of Visual Communications.

CALIFORNIA (Los Angeles Metro)

THE VOYAGER COMPANY
THE CRITERION COLLECTION
1351 Pacific Coast Highway
Santa Monica, CA 90401
(213) 451-1383
(800) 446-2001 (except California)
(800) 443-2001 (California only)
Fax: (213) 394-2156

Contacts: Bob Stein; Aleen Stein

Services: Videodisc and videotape distributor; hypermedia developer. Materials available to the public for purchase.

Description: Produces definitive editions of classic films on laser videodiscs, many in the CAV (full feature format). Many include extensive supplementary sections with both still frames and motion footage, and audio essays on a second soundtrack that may be listened to while watching the film. All widescreen films are shown in *Videoscope,™* which maintains their original aspect ratio.

The Criterion Collection. Titles include: *Adam's Rib; The Adventures of Robin Hood* (1938); *The Asphalt Jungle; L'Avventura; Black Narcissus; Black Orpheus; Blade Runner; The Blob* (1958); *Blow-Up; Breathless; Carnal Knowledge; Citizen Kane; Darling; Fellini Satyricon; Forbidden Games; Forbidden Planet; The Graduate; Grand Illusion; A Hard Day's Night; Help!; The Hidden Fortress; High Noon; The Horse's Mouth; Invasion of the Body Snatchers* (1956); *It's A Wonderful Life; The Killing; King Kong; The Lady Vanishes; La Strada; The Life and Death of Colonel Blimp; Lola Montes; The Magnificent Ambersons; The Man Who Knew Too Much* (1934); *Mr. Hulot's Holiday; Monterey Pop; A Night at the Opera; The Night of the Hunter; The Night Porter; North By Northwest; Paths of Glory; The Princess Bride; The Producers; Pygmalion; Rashomon; The Red Balloon; Rules of the Game; Sabotage; Scaramouche; The Secret Agent; The Seven Samurai; The Seventh Seal; Shoot the Piano Player; Show Boat; Singin' in the Rain; Swing Time; The Third Man; The 39 Steps; The Three Penny Opera; Tunes of Glory; 12 Angry Men; 2001: A Space Odyssey; Vengeance is Mine; West Side Story; The White Mane; The Wizard of Oz; Young and Innocent;* and *Zulu.*

Interactive videodiscs from The Voyager Company. Titles include:
Orson Welles Radio Disc (6 hours). Radio plays from the Mercury Theater.
Salamandre: Châteaux of the Loire (CAV; bilingual, English-French). An in-depth look at the architecture, art and history of 18 French châteaux in the scenic Loire Valley, with breathtaking aerial fly-bys and narrated walks through the majestic interiors. Also includes a computer-animated sequence on the construction of several châteaux, and over 750 photographs covering architectural details, furniture, paintings and tapestries, and more. Brief history of each château.

The Louvre (CAV). Videodisc catalog in three volumes: paintings and drawings, sculpture and objets d'art, and antiquities (Greek, Roman, Egyptian and Near Eastern). Contains 6,000 works of art, 35,000 images (including details) and video commentary on 75 selected works. Produced under the direction of the curators of the Louvre Museum. Also available are *The Louvre Laserguides,™* HyperCard software products running on a Macintosh computer. The Laserguides turn the still photos and motion pictures stored on videodiscs into vast visual databases that can be explored and used in innumerable ways. (Laserguides are also available for several videodiscs not produced by Voyager, including *The National Gallery of Art; Vincent: A*

Portrait in Two Parts, on Vincent van Gogh; and *The Bio Sci Videodisc.*

Dream Machine: The Visual Computer (1987, CAV). A definitive anthology of computer graphics. The 112 motion picture sequences on this videodisc explore one of the most profound developments in the history of human communication — the computer as a visual instrument that combines the objectivity of the photograph, the subjectivity of painting and the gravity-free motion of hand-drawn animation.

Dream Machine II (1988, CAV). A sequel to *Dream Machine: The Visual Computer.*

Videodiscs from Voyager Press. Titles include:
Salt of the Earth (1953); *Bill Viola: Selected Works; I Do Not Know What It Is I Am Like* (Bill Viola); *Bachdisc* (Juan Downey, 1988); *Power of the Myth* (3 discs, 6 programs), featuring interviews with mythologist Joseph Campbell; and *The Vancouver Disc,* an eclectic electronic archive of Vancouver, B.C. (1872-1983) consisting of 20,876 still pictures and 37 time-lapse sequences).

Persistence of Vision (3 videodiscs). An anthology of work by video artists, including Richard Serra, Ilene Segalove, Ant Farm, Bill Viola, William Wegman, Dan Reeves, Cecelia Condit, Branda Miller and Peter Campus.

To New Horizons: Ephemeral Films 1931-1945 (19 selections, 60 min.). An anthology of sponsored films from the collection of Prelinger Associates, Inc. depicting pre-World War II lifestyles and utopian dreams. Selections include: *In My Merry Oldsmobile* (1931); *Master Hands* (1936); *We Drivers* (1936); *Chevrolet Leader News* (1936); *Relax* (1937); *Precisely So* (1937); *Extra* (ca. 1938); *Breakfast Pals* (ca. 1938); *Three Smart Daughters* (ca. 1938); *Oxydol Goes Into High* (1938); *'Round and 'Round* (1939); *Back of the Mike* (1939); *Leave it to Roll-Oh* (1940); home movies of the New York World's Fair (1940); *To New Horizons* (1940); *Let Yourself Go* (1940); *Magic in the Air* (1941); *To Market, To Market* (1942); and *News Sketches by Max Fleischer* (ca. 1944-45).

You Can't Get There From Here: Ephemeral Films 1946-1960 (19 selections, 60 min.). An anthology of educational, industrial and sponsored films from the collection of Prelinger Associates, Inc. depicting postwar disappointments, anxieties and social control. Selections include: *Report to Home Builders* (1946); *Shy Guy* (1947); *Are You Popular?* (1947); *Technicolor for Industrial Films* (ca. 1949); *Meet King Joe* (1949); *Dating: Do's and Don'ts* (1949); *The Last Date* (1950); *A Date With Your Family* (1950); *Treasures for the Making* (1951); *What to Do on a Date* (1951); *A Young Man's Fancy* (1952); *Eisenhower for President* (1952); *Mother Takes a Holiday* (1952); *Sniffles and Sneezes* (1955); *Two-Ford Freedom* (1956); *Design for Dreaming* (1956); *The Relaxed Wife* (1957); *American Look* (1958); and *A Wonderful New World of Fords* (1960).

Size & Elements: Videotape: VHS and Betamax. Videodisc: CAV and CLV laserdisc formats. (Over 80 titles total; all available on videodisc, some available on videotape.)

Cataloging: Published catalogs; release sheets.

Access: Available to the public for purchase.

Rights: Full rights held to some material. Distribution rights held to other material. Additional clearances may be necessary in some cases if material is to be reused.

Licensing: Available for licensing and reuse in some cases. License fees charged.

Restrictions: Most material requires clearance for reuse from original producers or copyright owners.

Viewing Facilities: None.

Duplication Facilities: None.

CALIFORNIA (Los Angeles Metro)

WARNER BROS. INC.
4000 Warner Boulevard
Burbank, CA 91522
(818) 954-6000

Services: Motion picture producer and distributor.

CALIFORNIA (Los Angeles Metro)

WAYFARER PUBLICATIONS
P.O. Box 26156
Los Angeles, CA 90026
(213) 665-7773

Marvin Smalheiser (Director)

Contact: Marvin Smalheiser

Services: Foundation; videotape distributor. Videotapes available for purchase only.
Description: Instructional videotapes relating to T'ai Chi Chuan; Ch'i Kung (Qigong), an internal exercise system; and other health-related subjects.
Size & Elements: Videotape: VHS (approx. 25 videotapes, each 30 to 120 min.).
Cataloging: Published catalog.
Access: Available to the public for purchase. Orders accepted by mail and telephone.
Rights: No rights held to any material. Rights retained by original producers.
Licensing: Not available for licensing or reuse.
Restrictions: Videotapes available for purchase only.
Viewing Facilities: None.
Duplication Facilities: None.

CALIFORNIA (Los Angeles Metro)

WEINTRAUB SCREEN ENTERTAINMENT INC.
11111 Santa Monica Boulevard
Los Angeles, CA 90025
(213) 477-8900
Fax: (213) 478-5170
Telex: 170747

In Great Britain:
WEINTRAUB HOUSE
167-169 Wardour Street
London W1V 3TA, England
(01) 439-1790
Fax: (01) 734-1509
Telex: 269919

Jerry Weintraub (Chairman)

Contacts: Film Library; Richard Milnes (Managing Director, London)
Services: Film and videotape producer and distributor; stock footage sales library. Material available for licensing and reuse, subject to restrictions.
Description: *British Pathé News Film Library* (1896-1970; approx. 11 million feet). Comprehensive newreel coverage of news events ranging from the earliest moving images of Queen Victoria to the moon landing. Represented for U.S. stock footage sales by Worldwide Television News (q.v.).
Elstree Stock Shot Library. Over 20,000 stock shots from more than 2,000 feature films; all in 35mm, black and white and color. Comprises outtakes (1930-present) from feature films and television programs produced by Ealing Studios, Welwyn Studios, Elstree Studios, Associated British Picture Corporation, British International Pictures, Anglo-Amalgamated, Group 3, British Lion and others.
Feature films, television series and documentaries. Properties owned by Weintraub Screen Entertainment (over 1,500 titles), including the television series *The Avengers* (1966-69). Feature films in all genres.
Size & Elements: Film and videotape (formats and amounts unspecified).
Cataloging: Card catalogs; published catalog.
Access: Not open to the public. British Pathé News and Elstree stock shot libraries are equipped to handle requests for research, licensing and reuse. Other materials are maintained primarily for distribution and rental rather than for licensing or reuse. Research fees charged. Research requests accepted by mail, telephone and in person (by appointment only).
Rights: Full rights held to some material. Some rights held to all material. Additional clearances may be necessary in some cases if material is to be reused.
Licensing: Available for licensing and reuse. License and usage fees charged.
Restrictions: None specified.
Viewing Facilities: Film and videotape (all formats).
Duplication Facilities: None.
Representative: British Pathé News is represented in the U.S. for stock footage sales by Worldwide Television News (q.v.).

CALIFORNIA (Los Angeles Metro)

SIMON WIESENTHAL CENTER
9760 West Pico Boulevard
Los Angeles, CA 90035
(213) 553-9036
Fax: (213) 553-8007

Rabbi Marvin Hier (Dean)

Contact: Richard Trank (Director of Media)
Services: Foundation; archives; film and videotape producer and distributor. Some material available for rental and distribution; other material possibly available for reuse.
Description: Has produced one feature-length film, *Genocide* (by Rabbi Marvin Hier), a documentary incorporating interviews of Holocaust witnesses and scholars, narrated by Orson Welles and Elizabeth Taylor. Available with Spanish and German subtitles.
Distributes other Holocaust-related films for rental. Sample titles include: *Raoul Wallenberg: Between The Lines,* which examines the political background against which Wallenberg worked, including the failure and unwillingness of the U.S. to rescue Jews from German-occupied Europe; *The World At War,* a 26-hour series of documentary accounts of World War II, incorporating interviews with former soldiers, civilian accounts and actual newsreel footage from the war; *Forbidden,* the story of a handful of German Jews who actually lived underground throughout World War II; and *Shoah,* an epic documentary by Claude Lanzmann, featuring interviews with concentration camp witnesses.
Archives contains an unspecified amount of footage (predominantly 16mm) from World War II and continues to acquire new material. Includes: home movies taken by a German soldier during the capture of Paris; assorted German newsreel footage (1943-44); and an American GI's home movies of Paris after liberation; and footage of the concentration camps at the time of liberation.
Size & Elements: Film: 35mm and 16mm (23 titles, release prints; original footage, amount unspecified). Videotape: 1", 3/4", VHS and Betamax (viewing copies).
Cataloging: Published catalog.
Access: Open to the public. Some material maintained for rental and distribution. Some material possibly available for reuse. Research fees generally not charged. Research requests accepted by mail and telephone.
Rights: Full rights held to some material. Additional clearances will be necessary in some cases if material is to be reused.
Licensing: Available for licensing and reuse, subject to restrictions. License and usage fees charged.
Restrictions: Restrictions apply, depending on use.
Viewing Facilities: Film.
Duplication Facilities: None.

CALIFORNIA (Los Angeles Metro)

WINDSOR PRODUCTIONS
157 South Windsor Boulevard
Los Angeles, CA 90004
(213) 931-1188

Harry Mynatt (President)

Contact: Harry Mynatt
Services: Private videotape collection. Not open to the public.
Description: Holds episodes of *Queen For A Day,* a television show originally aired on NBC (January 3, 1956 to September 2, 1960) and ABC (September 28, 1960 to October 2, 1964). In this top-rated daytime show, hosted by Jack Bailey, female contestants told stories of the hardships of their lives, stating a "wish" and hoping to be chosen "queen" for a day by the studio audience, thereby winning the fulfillment of their wish and many other prizes.
Size & Elements: Videotape: VHS (15 videotapes, each 30 min.).
Cataloging: None specified.
Access: Not open to the public.
Rights: Full rights held to all material.
Licensing: Apply for information.
Restrictions: None specified.
Viewing Facilities: None.
Duplication Facilities: None.

CALIFORNIA (Los Angeles Metro)

ZIELINSKI PRODUCTIONS, INC.
7850 Slater Avenue, Suite 80
Huntington Beach, CA 92647
(714) 842-5050

Richard E. Zielinski (President)

CALIFORNIA (Malibu)

Contact: Richard E. Zielinski
Services: Videotape producer; stock footage sales library. Custom shooting services available.
Description: Has produced videotape stock footage since 1971. Extensive collection of sports footage covers children's, high-school, college and professional sports; men's and women's sports; football; basketball; Olympics; British sports; bloopers; and historical sports events (on black and white film). International footage covers cities around the world; underwater footage; aerial views from many locations; islands; native peoples, dancing and cannibals; sunrises and sunsets; boats. Holds coverage of approximately 50 U.S. cities, including landmarks, people, building exteriors, scenics and street scenes; high technology, including computer terminals, radar dishes and electronic equipment; crowds and audiences at sports events, the Live Aid concert, the Olympics and the Rose Bowl; and generic material, including point-of-view shots, beaches, scuba diving, animals, nature, fires and accidents.

Videotape crews on location in the U.S. and around the world can shoot specific footage on request; events can also be staged for shooting.
Size & Elements: Film: 35mm and 16mm (amount unspecified; all transferred to videotape). Videotape: 1", Betacam and 3/4" (10,000 videotapes; masters and viewing copies). (Videotape copies available in any format).
Cataloging: Computerized cataloging for staff use only.
Access: Available to the public for duplication, licensing and reuse. Research fees not charged. Research requests accepted by telephone. Viewing videotapes are supplied at no charge.
Rights: Full rights held to some material. Additional clearances may be necessary in some cases (for some sports footage) if material is to be reused.
Licensing: Available for licensing and reuse. License and usage fees charged.
Restrictions: None specified.
Viewing Facilities: Videotape (limited viewing facilities available).
Duplication Facilities: Videotape (1", Betacam, 3/4", 1/2" and Video 8).

CALIFORNIA (Malibu)

SCOTT DITTRICH FILMS
See **CALIFORNIA** (Los Angeles Metro)

CALIFORNIA (Marina Del Rey)

MILITARY/COMBAT STOCK FOOTAGE
See **CALIFORNIA** (Los Angeles Metro)

CALIFORNIA (Mill Valley)

GOLDEN GATE BAPTIST THEOLOGICAL SEMINARY LIBRARY
Strawberry Point
Mill Valley, CA 94941
(415) 388-8080 (Exts. 239, 284)

Street address: Seminary Drive

Bill Hair (Librarian)

Contact: Kevin Compton (Reader Services Librarian)
Services: Seminary library. Film and videotape collection available for licensing and reuse.
Description: Begins 1970. Baptist history, Baptist missions and missiology, Bible study and teaching, church history, biblical archeology, Greek and Hebrew language instruction. Other topics include 18 lessons on Genesis, 15 lessons on the Gospel according to Luke; 21 lessons from the Old Testament; family unity; marital crisis; missions to China, Japan, Indonesia, Israel, Thailand, Yemen, Brazil and Africa; religious liberty; Seminary events; and suicide prevention.
Size & Elements: Film: 16mm (70 titles). Videotape: 3/4" (400 titles).
Cataloging: Card catalogs; film list.
Access: For in-house use only. Requests accepted by mail, telephone and in person (by appointment only).
Rights: Full rights held to some material.
Licensing: Available for licensing and reuse. License fees not charged.
Restrictions: None specified.
Viewing Facilities: Videotape.
Duplication Facilities: Videotape (3/4" and VHS).

CALIFORNIA (Moffett Field)

NATIONAL AERONAUTICS AND SPACE ADMINISTRATION

(NASA)
AMES RESEARCH CENTER
HUMAN FACTORS RESEARCH CENTER
Mail Stop 239-21
Moffett Field, CA 94035
(415) 694-6599

David Nagel (Chief, Human Factors Research Center)
Bob Shiner (Head, Manned-Vehicle Systems Research Facility)

Contact: Mark Allard (Engineering Technician)
Services: Government agency; technical support facility. Videotape collection primarily for in-house use; available for outside use on a case-by-case basis, subject to restrictions.
Description: The Human Factors Research Center researches issues relating to human performance and man-machine interaction in aeronautics and space environments. Footage includes documentation of Center experiments, promotional materials and training programs.
Size & Elements: Videotape: VHS (approx. 60 to 100 hours).
Cataloging: None specified.
Access: For in-house use only. Available for outside use on a case-by-case basis, subject to restrictions. All requests for material must be made through the Phototechnology Branch (415/694-6218) at Ames. Research fees not charged.
Rights: Material in the public domain. Additional clearances may be necessary in some cases if material is to be reused.
Licensing: Available for reuse on a case-by-case basis. Usage fees charged under some conditions.
Restrictions: All requests for material must be made through the Phototechnology Branch. Some material may carry security restrictions. Permission of researchers may be required for reuse in some cases.
Viewing Facilities: None.
Duplication Facilities: None.

CALIFORNIA (Moffett Field)

NATIONAL AERONAUTICS AND SPACE ADMINISTRATION (NASA)
AMES RESEARCH CENTER
IMAGING TECHNOLOGY BRANCH
Mail Stop 203-6
Moffett Field, CA 94035
(415) 694-6218

Roland Michaelis (Branch Chief)

Contact: Lynn Albaugh (Head of the Repository)
Services: Government agency. Film and videotape collection available to the public for duplication and reuse, for nonprofit and noncommercial use only.
Description: The mission of the Imaging Technology Branch is to document the construction and tests of aircraft. The branch holds all official moving image and still photographic material produced at Ames, and coordinates outside duplication orders and activities.

Collection (1940-present) holds historical footage, including aircraft construction, tests of the space shuttle, the Apollo modules and other spacecraft, and test footage of all commercial and military aircraft; documentaries; documentation of research projects; public affairs programs; high-altitude aerial film and videotape footage shot from DC-8, C-130, U-2 and ER-2 aircraft; and technical presentations. Programs generally relate to aircraft, wind tunnel experiments, the life sciences, including documentation of an ozone project in Brazil and Antarctica, flight simulation (for state-of-the-art and developmental aircraft, including display screens, aircraft cabs, and computer generated scenes as viewed by pilots), computation, computer graphics and animal research (relating to animals traveling into space).

Aircraft types covered include helicopters; U-2 photographic surveillance aircraft; ER-2 (an updated version of the U-2); Lear jets; DC-8; C-141; C-130; Harriers (vertical takeoff and landing aircraft); QSRA; X-15 tilt rotor; and others.
Size & Elements: Film: 16mm (981 films, each 20 min.; negatives, originals and prints). Videotape: 3/4" (234 videotapes, each 2 to 120 min.; masters). Copies can be made in any format.
Cataloging: Computerized cataloging for staff use only.
Access: Open to the public. Available for duplication and reuse, subject to restrictions. Research fees not charged. Research requests accepted by mail, telephone and in person (walk-in and by appointment).
Rights: Material in the public domain. Additional clearances may be necessary

in some cases if material is to be reused (commercial use requires clearance through Public Affairs, 415/694-5091). Some material exempt from public release due to its classified or sensitive nature.
Licensing: Available for reuse. Usage fees not charged.
Restrictions: Available for nonprofit, noncommercial use only. Any commercial reuse requires clearance through Public Affairs.
Viewing Facilities: Film (16mm Moviola); videotape (3/4").
Duplication Facilities: Videotape (3/4" and VHS). Outside arrangements can be made for duplication of film and other videotape formats.
Related Materials: Still photographs.

CALIFORNIA (Moffett Field)

NATIONAL AERONAUTICS AND SPACE ADMINISTRATION (NASA)
AMES RESEARCH CENTER
REGIONAL FILM LIBRARY
Educational Programs 204-7
Moffett Field, CA 94035
(415) 694-6270

Contact: Sonya Cardenas (Film Librarian)
Services: Government agency; circulating film and videotape library. Films and videotapes available for loan. Serves California, Arizona, Idaho, Montana, Nevada, Oregon, Utah, Washington and Wyoming.
Description: Films and videotapes describing NASA research and development programs, and achievements in space and aeronautics. Programs offered are similar to those available from other NASA Regional Film Libraries (q.v.).
Size & Elements: Film: 16mm. Videotape: 3/4". (Hundreds of titles total).
Cataloging: Published catalog.
Access: Available for loan to educational, civil, industrial, professional, youth and similar groups, and for unsponsored public service telecasts. Research and rental fees not charged. Videotapes may be requested for duplication. Requests accepted by mail.
Rights: Material in the public domain. Additional clearances may be necessary in some cases if material is to be reused.
Licensing: Available for reuse, subject to restrictions.
Restrictions: Film material or footage of recognizable astronauts may not be reused for commercial purposes.
Viewing Facilities: None.
Duplication Facilities: None.

CALIFORNIA (Monterey)

KIT PARKER FILMS
1245 Tenth Street
Monterey, CA 93940
(408) 649-5573
Fax: (408) 649-8040

Kit Parker (President)

Contact: Distribution Staff
Services: Non-theatrical film distributor; film and videotape archives. Materials available for rental, licensing and reuse, subject to restrictions.
Description: Newsreels (1946-67), public domain features, and short subjects of all types, with an emphasis on classics.
Special releases. Titles include: *Becket; Art Pepper: Notes of A Jazz Survivor; The Love Goddesses; The Best New UCLA Films;* and *The Maya Deren Collection.*
General comedy, drama, and variety. Titles include: *The Whole Town's Talking; To Be or Not To Be; Beat the Devil; The Fortune; His Girl Friday; The Hungry i Reunion; A Run For Your Money; The Mouse That Roared; Cover Girl; Tommy; Cromwell; Fail Safe; The Leather Boys; Letter From An Unknown Woman; The Blue Gardenia; Repulsion; The Spiral Staircase; The Taming of the Shrew; One Day in the Life of Ivan Denisovich; As You Like It* (Paul Czinner); *A Raisin in the Sun; The Red Pony; From Here to Eternity; 3:10 to Yuma; Never Cry Wolf; Breaking the Sound Barrier; The Seventh Voyage of Sinbad; Stairway to Heaven; Something Wicked This Way Comes; Dark Star; The Amityville Horror;* and *The Phantom of the Opera.*
Foreign films. Titles include: *Three Strange Loves; Orpheus; Le Petit Théâtre de Jean Renoir; M; The Fiancés; Woman of the Dunes;* and *Potemkin.*
The "Overlooked Archive." Titles include: *A Chump at Oxford* (Laurel and Hardy); *The Freshman* (Harold Lloyd); *The Three Stooges in Orbit; Steamboat*

Bill, Jr.; Murder in Greenwich Village; Tawny Pipit; Meet John Doe; Glorifying the American Girl; Cream: The Farewell Concert; Don't Knock the Rock; Judge Horton and the Scottsboro Boys; Synanon; Women's Prison; The Strange Love of Martha Ivers; Dick Tracy Meets Gruesome; Bulldog Drummond's Revenge; Boston Blackie's Rendezvous; The Manxman; Valentino; The Guns of Navarone; They Came to Cordura; I Shot Jesse James; Hell's Angels on Wheels; Black Magic; The Man They Could Not Hang; Godzilla vs. Megalon; I Married a Witch; Dimenstoogia in 3-D; 13 Ghosts (1960, in "Illusion-O"); *80 Million Women Want?* (1913), on early feminist support for the suffrage movement; *The King of Kings* (1927); *The Adventures of Dollie* (1908, Biograph short directed by D. W. Griffith); *Arsenal* (Dovzhenko, 1929).
Non-fiction. Titles include: *Witchcraft Through the Ages* (Sweden, 1922); Frank Capra's *Why We Fight* (World War II series); Nazi propaganda films; Combat Bulletins; *What Soviet Children Are Saying About Nuclear War; Red Nightmare; What Is Communism?; The MacArthur Report; The Forgotten Village* (John Steinbeck), a docudrama; *Hands* (WPA production); *The March of Time* series; Fox Movietone News; Warner-Pathé Newsreels; *The News Parade; Ali vs. Spinks Fights;* and *Rodeo.*
Short subjects. Items include: Norman McLaren films; Andrew Lugg's postcard films; Arthur Lipsett films; literature on film; the *Fables* of Jean de la Fontaine; Mr. Magoo films; Hoffnung cartoons; Pink Panther cartoons; Paul Terry's *Aesop's Fables* cartoons (1920s); the Three Stooges; Abbott and Costello programs; and W. C. Fields.
"Campy" short subjects. Titles include: *Ambassador of Friendship: Richard Nixon* (1960), a campaign film highlighting Nixon's antics around the globe; *Candy is a Healthy Food* (1927), a tour of a candy factory; *Daily Beauty Rituals* (1937), a cosmetics promotion; *The Hippie Temptation* (1967), narrated by Harry Reasoner for CBS News; *Jimmy Durante NRA Trailer* (1931), a song-filled romp as Jimmy clowns around with pro-Roosevelt slogans; *La Folie Du Docteur Tube* (1915), a French spoof by Abel Gance featuring a crazy scientist who consumes so much cocaine it looks like it's snowing in the laboratory; and *The Living Picture* (1925), in which an artist fools customers by having a nude woman actually posing in his painting frame.
Film study collection. Complete early films include: *Kingdom of the Fairies* (Méliès, 1903); *A Trip to the Moon* (Méliès, 1902); and *Dream of a Rarebit Fiend* (Edwin M. Porter, 1906). Other titles include: *Abel Gance Interview; René Clair Interview; Edison Album;* and *The Great Primitives.*
Size & Elements: Film: 16mm (4 million feet, hundreds of titles). Videotape: 3/4" (24 hours).
Cataloging: Published catalogs.
Access: Available to the public for rental, licensing and reuse, subject to restrictions. Requests accepted by mail and telephone.
Rights: Full rights held to some material.
Licensing: Available for licensing and reuse, subject to restrictions.
Restrictions: Restrictions apply regarding reuse of some titles. Films may not be televised or videotaped or reproduced in any way, nor may they be re-rented, donated or loaned to anyone else without Kit Parker Films' written permission. Most films are restricted to non-theatrical use only, allowing no public advertising without written permission from Kit Parker Films.
Viewing Facilities: None.
Duplication Facilities: None.

CALIFORNIA (Mountain View)

MOONLIGHT PRODUCTIONS
2243 Old Middlefield Way
Mountain View, CA 94043
(415) 948-0199

Dr. Lee Tepley (Owner)

Contact: Dr. Lee Tepley
Services: Film and videotape producer and distributor; stock footage sales library.
Description: Underwater and related "topside" footage, mostly of marine life.
Anemones. Extensive footage, mostly filmed with underwater lights.
Basking sharks. Fierce-looking animals, some scenes with divers.
Blue whales. Surface shots of the world's largest animal and closeup scenes of its flukes.
California sea lions. Extensive footage on land and surface of water, including pups leaping and surfing; and underwater, including adults interacting with divers and charging at the camera.
Coral reefs and gardens. Extensive footage of the coral reef community, including many types of exotic corals, tropical fish and other animals. *Cloud*

Over the Coral Reef (27 min). shows how pollution is destroying coral reef communities.

Dolphins. Many different types on the surface showing acrobatics (riding bow wave, breaching, etc.). Underwater scenes of bottlenose and spinners. Closeup underwater shots of white-beaked and Pacific spotted dolphins. Topside shots of Risso's dolphins (grampuses) breaching and swimming belly-up near boat.

Elephant seals. Females and pups on land and underwater. Land footage of bulls, including bulls fighting and a humorous sequence of a small dog chasing a bull.

Finback whales. Aerial and surface shots; closeup scenes of diving and surfacing; and closeup underwater shot.

Garibaldis. Humorous scenes of Garibaldis (a very colorful ocean-going goldfish) interacting with photographer.

Gray whales. Surface behavior, including acrobatics (breaching, spy-hopping, etc.) and friendly whales (cow and calf being petted by people in small boat). Also holds closeup underwater scenes of cow and calf and aerial footage of migrating whales.

Harbor seals. Adults and pups underwater.

Humpback whales. Many behavioral activities of cows, calves and adult males in two educational films: *The Humpback Whale: Winter — A Time for Singing* and *Summer — A Time for Feeding.* Underwater activities include singing, feeding (including bubble-net) and interacting with divers. Surface activities include breaching, fluking, flipper-flopping, spy-hopping, etc. Videotape material of summertime behavioral activity in Alaska, including their rare and remarkable feeding songs.

Jellyfish. Extensive footage of many types, including dramatic scenes of very large (approx. 15 feet long) white jellyfish and closeups of stinging cells. Some of this footage is included in *Medusa.*

Kelp beds. Includes the giant kelp, and many other types of seaweeds, fish and other animals that make up the kelp bed community.

Killer whales. Surface behavior filmed in the wild, including acrobatics, breaching and spy-hopping. Closeup underwater scenes filmed at the Vancouver (B.C.) Aquarium. Closeup underwater shots of a false killer whale (pseudo-orca) apparently posing for the camera. Closeup underwater shots of pygmy killer whales.

Lava flows. Fire Under the Sea (20 min.) contains footage of undersea lava activity, showing undersea avalanches, implosions, explosions, red-hot lava flowing underwater and a diver being struck by hot lava. The film also includes a sequence of an erupting volcano and lava flows above water.

Manta rays. Daytime scenes of large manta rays, including one scene of an unusual green manta ray. Underwater nighttime shots filmed with artificial lights, including closeups of rays doing acrobatics, feeding on plankton and interacting with divers. Sequence of a diver riding a manta ray at night.

Melon head whales. Underwater shots of a large group swimming very slowly. Includes a nursing sequence and a scene of melon heads accompanied by an oceanic white tipped shark.

Oceanic white tipped sharks. Underwater shots, including extreme closeups; also scenes of sharks swimming with pilot and melon head whales and following a woman in a bikini.

Octopus. Many behavioral aspects, including color changes, male and female wrestling, mating, expelling ink and fighting with moray eels.

Pilot whales. Closeup underwater scenes of pilot whales in the open sea; and scenes of pilot whales accompanied by oceanic white tipped sharks.

Salmon. Videotape footage featuring extensive topside and underwater scenes of pre- and post-spawning activity of sockeye, chum (dog) and pink (humpy) salmon.

Sea cucumbers. Many different types.

Sea otters. Extensive footage both on the surface and underwater. Surface scenes include otters using tools, sleeping in kelp, tumbling, eating clams, abalone and crabs, interacting with people and mother carrying pup. Underwater activities include otters obtaining food, including crabs, abalone and sea urchins; using tools; and interacting with divers, including a comical sequence of otter taking food from a diver's mouth. Also holds a humorous sequence of an otter struggling to remove an abalone from a mirror.

Sharks and rays. Includes the blue shark, black tip shark, horned shark, dogfish, angel shark, guitar ray, bat ray and torpedo ray.

Squid. Footage of mating; also scenes of bottom covered with egg sacs.

Steller sea lions. On the surface and underwater, including growling and interacting aggressively with divers.

Starfish. Extensive footage of many different types, mostly filmed with underwater lights. Footage of the "Crown of Thorns" starfish, including a sequence of one being eaten by a Triton conch.

Tropical fish. Extensive footage of many different types, mostly filmed with the aid of an underwater lighting system to bring out colors.

Undersea pollution. Extensive footage of the effects of pollution in both tropical and temperate waters. Some of this footage is included in two educational films *Cloud Over the Coral Reef* and *The Poisoned Sea,* which consider the results of different types of pollution (mostly sewage and sedimentation) on the marine environment.

Size & Elements: Film: 16mm (approx. 100,000 feet; positive, negative, reversal, originals and release prints). Videotape: 3/4" (amount unspecified; masters and viewing copies); VHS (amount unspecified; masters and viewing copies). Five completed films are available in film and videotape form.

Cataloging: Shot lists; research library.

Access: Not open to the public. For in-house use only. Completed films available for rental, preview and resale. Research requests accepted by mail, telephone and in person (by appointment only).

Rights: Full rights held to all material.

Licensing: Available for licensing and reuse. License fees charged.

Restrictions: None specified.

Viewing Facilities: Film (16mm projector); videotape (3/4" and VHS).

Duplication Facilities: Videotape (3/4" and VHS).

CALIFORNIA (Mountain View)

TVA/TELEVISION ASSOCIATES
2410 Charleston Road
Mountain View, CA 94043
(415) 967-6040
Fax: (415) 964-2453

Ed Carlstone (President)

Contact: Peter Homer (Production Manager)

Services: Videotape producer; videotape production, post-production and duplication facility. Material available for duplication, licensing and reuse.

Description: Scenics and landscapes of the San Francisco Bay Area, including the Peninsula, forest land, suburbia and aerials of the San Andreas Fault area.

Size & Elements: Videotape: 1", Betacam and 3/4" (amount unspecified; masters).

Cataloging: Most material uncataloged at present.

Access: Available to the public for duplication, licensing and reuse. Research fees charged (fees negotiable). Research requests accepted by mail, telephone and in person (by appointment only).

Rights: Full rights held to all material available.

Licensing: Available for licensing. License fees charged.

Restrictions: None specified.

Viewing Facilities: Videotape (by prior arrangement only).

Duplication Facilities: Videotape (all formats available).

CALIFORNIA (Newhall)

MOE DI SESSO WILD LIFE FILM LIBRARY
See **CALIFORNIA** (Los Angeles Metro)

CALIFORNIA (North Hollywood)

THE A. M. STOCK EXCHANGE, INC.
and
FRED BAKER FILM & VIDEO COMPANY
and
CAMEO FILM LIBRARY, INC.
and
THE CLIP JOINT FOR FILM
and
FILMFAIR COMMUNICATIONS
and
ALFRED HIGGINS PRODUCTIONS, INC.
and
RESEARCH VIDEO
and
VIDEOBRARY, INC.
See **CALIFORNIA** (Los Angeles Metro)

CALIFORNIA (Northridge)

CALIFORNIA STATE UNIVERSITY, NORTHRIDGE
URBAN ARCHIVES CENTER
and

CREATIVE FILM SOCIETY
and
FULTON J. SHEEN COMMUNICATIONS LTD.
See **CALIFORNIA** (Los Angeles Metro)

CALIFORNIA (Norton Air Force Base)

**U.S. DEPARTMENT OF DEFENSE
MOTION MEDIA RECORDS CENTER**
See **CALIFORNIA** (Los Angeles Metro)

CALIFORNIA (Oakland)

ESTUARY PRESS
408 Thirteenth Street, Suite 279
Oakland, CA 94612
(415) 832-6603

Paul Richards (Owner)

Contact: Paul Richards
Services: Private collection. Material available for duplication, licensing and reuse.
Description: The Harvey Wilson Richards Film Collection consists of 19 of the filmmaker's productions (1960-78) relating to California farm workers (1958-70); the U.S. forestry industry and its practices (1960s); the civil rights movement and voter registration drives in California and the Southern U.S. (1960-63); and antiwar movement activities and demonstrations in California (1960-72).

The Harvesters (1960) documents farm labor conditions in California's fields during the late 1950s, when workers were paid 85 cents to one dollar per hour for 14- to 16-hour days. The film shows people working many different crops and exposes how the *bracero* program imported Mexican nationals at wages lower than the sub-minimum rates available to American workers. This film was used as an organizing film by the Agricultural Workers Organizing Committee (AWOC) and the United Packinghouse Workers Union.

Perch of the Devil (1960) concerns the hard rock miners of Butte, Montana and the 1960 copper miners' strike. It reviews the history of the Mine, Mill and Smelter Workers Local Union No. 1 and the many violent struggles that have rent the mining camps of the western Rockies. There are interviews with victims of silicosis, a fatal lung disease affecting miners, and footage of mining operations one mile below the surface.

Everyman (1962) is the name of a boat built in Sausalito, California by the San Francisco Bay Area peace movement with the intention of sailing into Pacific Ocean nuclear test zones to protest nuclear testing. The film shows *Everyman's* first and only voyage on May 27, 1962, when she sailed under the Golden Gate, only to be stopped twenty miles out by the U.S. Coast Guard, who arrested the crew and impounded the boat. Subsequent protests included sit-ins at the San Francisco U.S. Marshal's office, in which Joan Baez took part, singing "We Shall Overcome." Peace demonstrators conducted long vigils outside San Francisco courtrooms. The crew was eventually sentenced to 30 days in jail.

Uno Veintecinco (1962) documents the Agricultural Workers Organizing Committee (AWOC) drive to win an hourly wage of $1.25 for lettuce pickers in California. The film interviews organizers and workers and reviews 20th-century history of California farm labor organizing.

Women for Peace (1962) covers that organization's founding and the peace demonstrations that preceded it. With narration by Frances Herring, a founder of Women for Peace, the film shows anti-nuclear demonstrations in California and Nevada (1961-62).

Women of Russia (1962) was the product of a filmmaking tour of the Soviet Union that focused on the work, housing, education, child care and medical facilities available to women in Moscow.

Far From Moscow (1962) shows the conditions of women and children in Soviet areas outside Moscow, with emphasis on the towns of Sochi on the Black Sea; Tashkent; Uzbekistan; and Irkutsk, Siberia. The film shows work, housing, education, child care and medical facilities for women and children.

Freedom March (1963) focuses on the May 26, 1963 protest march sponsored by San Francisco Bay Area Black churches and the labor movement in the shocked aftermath of the Birmingham, Alabama bombing of a Black church and the deaths of five children. The film shows the march, rally and speakers.

We'll Never Turn Back (1963) is a Student Non-Violent Coordinating Committee (SNCC) organizing film shot by Richards in Mississippi, Alabama and Georgia in 1963 during the voter registration drives. It shows Julian Bond,

Bob Moses, Fannie Lou Hamer, Charles McLaurin and other local civil rights leaders. Black farmers and farm workers relate their experiences (often bloody) trying to register to vote.

Dream Deferred (1964) was also produced by the SNCC for its southern voter registration drive in 1964. It contains more interviews with activists, voter registrants and leaders, and features Fannie Lou Hamer's speech, including her famous line: "I'm sick and tired of being sick and tired."

The Wasted Woods (1964) shows wasteful forestry practices in the Western U.S. during the 1960s. Focusing on clear cutting and mechanized processing of the giant redwoods, the film reveals the rapid deterioration of the forest ecosystem and the disappearance of towns and businesses that once relied on these destructive forestry practices.

Decision in the Streets (1965) shows the tumultuous beginnings of the Bay Area civil rights and peace movements (1960-65). Segments include demonstrations protesting House Un-American Activities Committee (HUAC) investigations (1960); "hands-off Cuba" demonstrations during the Bay of Pigs invasion and Cuban missile crisis (1962-63); the march of 15,000 people protesting the Birmingham church bombings (1963); mass arrests of protesters sitting in at San Francisco's Sheraton Palace Hotel over racist hiring practices; the 1964 anti-Goldwater protests at the Republican Convention; the Free Speech Movement at Berkeley, California (1964) and others.

Hot Damn! (1965) is a power-packed short film with unique footage of the Bay Area peace movement at a time of rapid escalation of the Vietnam War. Segments include the Berkeley troop train demonstrations; marches from Berkeley to Oakland, ending in a massive confrontation with local police; the Oakland Army Induction Center protests; draft card burnings; and the sit-ins of 1964-65.

The Land is Rich (1965) documents the United Farm Workers' struggle to organize California farm workers, including their march from Delano to Sacramento in spring 1966. The film contrasts the economic strength of California agribusiness with the migrant workers' poverty, as reflected in breadlines, poor living conditions and the impact of extensive exposure to agricultural chemicals.

No Greater Cause (1968) chronicles the height of the anti-Vietnam War movement in the San Francisco Bay Area. Footage shows the massive confrontations between police and anti-draft protesters in 1967; the April 1967 Kezar Stadium antiwar rally (attendance 100,000); and other events.

Warning! Warning! (1970) focuses on environmental conditions in San Francisco Bay and threats to the Bay caused by dumping of municipal, farming and industrial wastes into its tributary rivers and the Bay itself.

Timber Tigers (1971) resulted from a national tour of U.S. forest areas. It shows giant forest-cutting machinery used to harvest trees across the country. The film exposes the forestry industry's approach to logging: "After us, the deluge and the desert."

Vanishing Redwoods (1975) depicts the delicate natural balance required for growth and survival of redwood forests. It shows how the logging industry's current practice of clear cutting threatens the very survival of redwood trees as a species.

Two Systems (1978) was the last film made by Richards. In it, he contrasts the "wasteful and destructive policies of raw materials acquisition and control pursued by Western capitalist nations with the self-sufficient, balanced approach of the socialist camp." The film offers viewers the chance to consider socialism as an alternative solution to the natural and social crises currently confronting developed nations of the "Free World."

Archives also holds unfinished footage of the Northern California flood (January 1965) (original film and workprint).
Size & Elements: Film: 16mm (19 titles; color and black and white; 19 titles total; some black and white raw footage). Archival holdings include various negatives, release prints, originals, duplicates and A&B rolls.
Cataloging: List available.
Access: Available to the public for duplication, licensing and reuse. Research fees charged. Research requests accepted by mail and telephone.
Rights: Full rights held to all material.
Licensing: Available for licensing and reuse. License fees charged.
Restrictions: None specified.
Viewing Facilities: Films are available for viewing at Estuary Press and at a local film laboratory.
Duplication Facilities: Film (at local laboratory).

CALIFORNIA (Oakland)

BERT GOULD/bay area archive
484 Lake Park Avenue, Box 170
Oakland, CA 94610
(415) 836-2378

CALIFORNIA (Oakland)

Contact: Bert Gould
Services: Film stock footage sales library; videotape program producer. Material available for licensing and reuse, subject to restrictions. *A high volume of requests restricts the archive's ability to provide research information and engage in speculative searches.* Operates film restoration laboratory.
Description: Newsreels and historical motion-picture footage of people and events in San Francisco, the Bay Area and Northern California (1900-40). Most items in this collection are available for licensing and reuse.

Archive also holds early advertising, animated, historical and documentary films. This material is available for research only.

Archive is currently producing a number of videotapes for the homevideo market which will feature historical footage from its own collection.
Size & Elements: Film: 35mm and 16mm (amount unspecified; transfers from nitrate film). Videotape: format and amount unspecified (viewing copies).
Cataloging: Published catalog (available on request). Some items listed in catalog are no longer available.
Access: Not open to the public. Available for duplication, licensing and reuse. Research fees charged. Research requests accepted by mail. Archive prefers to provide reference videotapes for preview purposes, rather than screening for researchers in person.
Rights: Full rights held to some material. Some material in the public domain.
Licensing: Available for licensing, subject to restrictions. License fees charged.
Restrictions: Material not available for licensing in certain situations.
Viewing Facilities: Film and videotape.
Duplication Facilities: Reference-quality film chain (film-to-videotape duplication) available. In-house black and white film laboratory can reduce 35mm to 16mm or duplicate 16mm to 16mm. Specially designed slow speed step printers handle old and shrunken original material.
Related Materials: Sound recordings and still photographs relating to history of the San Francisco Bay Area.

CALIFORNIA (Oakland)

OAKLAND PUBLIC LIBRARY
ASIAN BRANCH LIBRARY
449 Ninth Street
Oakland, CA 94607
(415) 273-3400

Suzanne Lo (Branch Librarian)

Contact: Suzanne Lo
Services: Public library. Film collection available for in-house viewing only.
Description: Extensive collection relating to Asia and Asian subjects.

Subjects covered include: art, Asia, Asian America, Bali, China, Chinese Americans, cultural, India, Japan, Japanese Americans, juvenile, historical, Korea, medicine, music, Philippines, religion, sports and Vietnam. The majority of the films are documentaries, but there are some narrative shorts and some feature films.
Size & Elements: Film: 16mm (approx. 100 films).
Cataloging: Published catalogs.
Access: Open to the public. For in-house use only. Research fees not charged.
Rights: Rights retained by original producers.
Licensing: Not available for licensing or reuse.
Restrictions: For in-house use only; not available for licensing or reuse.
Viewing Facilities: Film (16mm).
Duplication Facilities: None.

CALIFORNIA (Oakland)

OCEAN IMAGES
8001 Capwell Drive
Oakland, CA 94621
(415) 562-8000
Fax: (415) 562-8001

Al Giddings (President)

Contact: Terry Thompson (Vice President)
Services: Film and videotape producer; stock footage sales library.
Description: Underwater and above-water footage depicting all aspects of marine life, including shipwrecks, submersibles, sharks and whales. Highlights of the shark coverage include spectacular topside, underwater, and high speed feeding of Great Whites, white shark capture, gray reef/feeding frenzy, and divers wearing chain mail suits. Whale coverage consists of extraordinary group and individual feeding activity, topside and underwater behavior, calves, adults and shots of whales alone and with divers. An underwater whalebone "graveyard," an abandoned whaling station, the Newfoundland rescue program and killer whales are also available. Other footage includes Antarctica, marine life, scenics, kelp forests, diving, ships and submersibles, shipwrecks, treasure and dolphins.
Size & Elements: Film: 35mm and 16mm (800,000 feet; internegatives and interpositives). Videotape: 1" (amount unspecified).
Cataloging: Dailies/workprint logs.
Access: Available for duplication. Research fees charged. Research requests accepted by mail, telephone and in person (by appointment only).
Rights: Full rights held to all material.
Licensing: Available for licensing. License fees charged (rates determined on a case-by-case basis).
Restrictions: None specified.
Viewing Facilities: Film (35mm and 16mm flatbed viewers); videotape (3/4" and 1/2" decks and editing machines).
Duplication Facilities: Videotape (3/4" and 1/2" duplication for client preview).

CALIFORNIA (Oakland)

PERALTA COLLEGES TV
900 Fallon Street
Oakland, CA 94607
(415) 464-3253

Diane Nelson (Station Manager)

Contact: Lashaa Gatlin (Director of Scheduling and Traffic)
Services: Educational institution; videotape producer and distributor. Some videotape material available for rental, purchase, duplication and reuse, subject to restrictions.
Description: College district television station serving four community colleges. Produces and distributes a wide variety of programming, including telecourses, documentaries, music and theatrical performance programs, and how-to series ranging from cooking to yoga. Most material was produced by outside producers and other television facilities, but Peralta is an active program producer in all the above areas.

Telecourses. Distributes college-level courses for credit in the areas of history, sociology, psychology, foreign languages, set design, interior design, anthropology and G.E.D. courses.
Size & Elements: Videotape: 3/4" (masters and viewing copies); 1/2" (viewing copies). (Approx. 500 videotapes total).
Cataloging: Card catalogs in process; computerized cataloging in process (will be available to researchers). Staff assistance required as catalog updating is in process. Member of League Information Video Exchange (LIVE), a computerized database of community college videotape libraries throughout the United States.
Access: Open to the public. For in-house viewing only. Many programs available for rental, purchase, duplication or reuse, subject to restrictions on specific programs. Research fees not charged. Research requests accepted by telephone and in person (by appointment only).
Rights: Full rights held to in-house productions. Some rights held to outside-produced material. Additional clearances (copyright) may be necessary in some cases if material is to be reused.
Licensing: Available for licensing, subject to restrictions. License fees charged in some cases, depending on copyright owner and intended use.
Restrictions: Available for licensing on a case-by-case basis. Much material carries copyright restrictions. Use of videotapes other than for in-house viewing at facility is subject to approval of Station Manager or copyright owner.
Viewing Facilities: Videotape (3/4" and 1/2").
Duplication Facilities: Videotape (3/4" and 1/2"; duplication charges apply).

CALIFORNIA (Oakland)

SOBEK PRODUCTIONS
555 Mira Vista Avenue
Oakland, CA 94610
(415) 834-1166
Fax: (415) 834-1725
Telex: 3775709

Richard Bangs (President)

Contact: Leslie Jarvie (Director of Special Projects)
Services: Film and videotape producer; stock footage sales library. Collection available for rental, licensing and reuse, subject to restrictions.
Description: Adventure and travel films featuring white-water rafting. Films include information about the people, culture and wildlife indigenous to the areas filmed.

Subjects include: *Whitewater I,* rafting on the BioBio River, Chile (1980), Omo River, Ethiopia (1973), Rogue River, Oregon (1978), Tutshenshini River, Alaska (1978), and Colorado River, Grand Canyon, Arizona (1976); *Whitewater II,* rafting on the Watut River, Papau, New Guinea (1981), and San Juan River, Utah (1978); *River of the Ape* (1985), rafting on the Alas River (Sumatra, Indonesia), including shots of native peoples and orangutans; *Yangtze Expedition* (1987, 3 hours of unedited footage); *Awash River* (1973), on the first descent of the Awash River, including rafting, culture and wildlife.
Size & Elements: Film: format unspecified (5 titles; positive). Videotape: VHS (5 titles; masters and viewing copies).
Cataloging: Dope sheets or release sheets.
Access: Available for rental, licensing and reuse. Research fees not charged. Research requests accepted by mail and telephone.
Rights: Full rights held to some material. Additional clearances may be necessary in some cases if material is to be reused.
Licensing: Available for licensing and reuse, subject to restrictions. License fees charged (negotiable).
Restrictions: Additional clearances may be necessary for reuse of Awash River material.
Viewing Facilities: Videotape (3/4" and VHS).
Duplication Facilities: Videotape (3/4" and 1/2").

CALIFORNIA (Oakland)

SOCIETY FOR NUTRITION EDUCATION
1700 Broadway, Suite 300
Oakland, CA 94612
(415) 444-7133

Gwyneth Donchin (Managing Director)

Contact: Susan Reiter
Services: Association. Films and videotapes available for purchase.
Description: Distributes educational films and videotapes on nutrition, intended for children, pregnant women and older adults.

Titles include: *No Better Gift,* on children's eating habits; *First Foods,* about baby feeding; *Great Expectations,* on diet during pregnancy; *Nutritional Management of High Risk Pregnancy;* and *Help Yourself to Better Health,* about nutrition for older adults. Some titles also available in Spanish.
Size & Elements: Film: 16mm. Videotape: 3/4" (2 titles); VHS (5 titles). (5 titles total).
Cataloging: Brochures.
Access: Available to the public for purchase. Requests accepted by mail.
Rights: Some rights held to all material.
Licensing: Apply for information.
Restrictions: Apply for information.
Viewing Facilities: None.
Duplication Facilities: None.
Related Materials: Study guides available.
Distributor: For rental: SNE Resource Lending Service, 321 Wallace Avenue, Vallejo, CA 94590; (707) 557-1592.

CALIFORNIA (Ojai)

KRISHNAMURTI FOUNDATION OF AMERICA
P.O. Box 1560
Ojai, CA 93023
(805) 646-2726

R. E. Mark Lee (Administrative Officer)

Contact: Mark Lee
Services: Foundation and educational institution; videotape producer and distributor. Videotape material available for purchase. Film and videotape archives not open to the public.
Description: The life and ideas of Krishnamurti. Subjects include meditation, conditioning, the mind and brain, death, love, compassion and culture. Collection ranges from an early film of Krishnamurti in 1920 to his last talks in 1986.

Videotapes available for purchase include: *Krishnamurti and Ronald Eyre: The Element of Playfulness* (1984); *Krishnamurti and Iris Murdoch: The 'Who' Who Experiences* (1984); *Krishnamurti and Professor David Bohm: The Future of Man* (1983); *Krishnamurti and Pupul Jayakar: Is There An Eastern Mind and a Western Mind?* (1983); *Krishnamurti and Dr. Jonas Salk: Can We Uncondition Ourselves?* (1982); and *Krishnamurti and Philosopher Huston Smith* (1968). Various talks (1983-85) include: *Observation and Love; Beyond Thought and Time; To Be Deeply Honest; The Origin of Primal Energy; Responsibility in a Chaotic World; Why Human Beings Hurt Each Other; Freedom and the Sacred; Holistic Observation; What is Relationship?; Health and Conflict;* and *What is the Religious Brain?.*

Various *Questions and Answers* series also available.
Size & Elements: Film: gauge unspecified (approx. 500 cans; masters). Videotape: 1/2". (Approx. 300 titles total).
Cataloging: Published lists of videotapes for purchase; research library; computerized cataloging for staff use only.
Access: Some material available to the public for purchase, orders accepted by mail. Research requests accepted by mail and in person (by appointment only). The film masters in the archives collection are used only to make copies for sale. Some film and videotape material of poor quality is maintained for archival and preservation purposes only.
Rights: Full rights held to all material.
Licensing: Apply for information.
Restrictions: Archival material not accessible at present.
Viewing Facilities: Videotape (1/2").
Duplication Facilities: None.

CALIFORNIA (Pacific Palisades)

PAULIST PRODUCTIONS
See **CALIFORNIA** (Los Angeles Metro)

CALIFORNIA (Pacoima)

AIRLINE FILM & TV PROMOTIONS
See **CALIFORNIA** (Los Angeles Metro)

CALIFORNIA (Palo Alto)

ELECTRIC POWER RESEARCH INSTITUTE
3412 Hillview Avenue
Palo Alto, CA 94303
(415) 934-4212 (information on completed programs)
(415) 420-1713 (information on stock footage)

Floyd Culler (President)
Dennis Clinthorn (Manager, Video/Graphics/Photography) (415/855-2928)

Contact: Dennis Clinthorn
Services: Nonprofit research and development institute. Film and videotape material available for research, licensing and reuse, subject to restrictions.
Description: Electric power generation, transmission, distribution and end use; technology information for utility executives, planners and engineers; state-of-the-art reviews, summary of important research results, overview of program areas and technical lectures.

Topics include: computer model that quantifies factors of acid rain damage; adjustable speed drives; progress report on the Six Cities Study of effects of air pollution; application of systems technologies to nuclear power; emission control; battery systems; tracking air masses; gas turbines, acid rain concerns; JetMole cable follower; laser cutters; technical lecture on Chernobyl Nuclear Power Station accident; clean power from coal; coal analyzers; coal cleaning; coal waste artificial reef; transport of coal-water slurry; compressed-air energy storage; fuel contracts; cool storage technology; coal-gasification-combined-cycle system; demand-side management; coal liquefaction; control center computer screen displays; ecological effects of utility effluents; research into the health effects of power frequency electric and magnetic fields; electricity supply and demand; generating electricity with coal and wind; EPRI facilities and research projects; baghouses; computer model for transport options; commercial fuel cells; simulation of tornado-driven debris; turbine missile casing and concrete tests; geothermal energy overview; evaluation of seam-welded pipes; heat pumps; helical driver system; lake and watershed acidification; indoor air quality; acidic deposition effects on forest ecosystems; bonding tubes to tubesheets; lake liming; leaching and attenuation chemistry; LOADISM computer model; methanol; residential energy conservation; fuel inventory planning; modular generation; office lighting design; PCB risk assessment; photovoltaic power; pipe cracking in nuclear installations; plasma torch demonstration; plume modeling techniques; Polysil insulators; rock augering method; safety relief valve test; solid-waste management update; steam turbine blade reliability; subsynchronous resonance; Three Mile Island; EPRI's Technical Interest Profile system; TLWorkstation; TOMCAT; transmission lines; torsional vibration monitoring system; efforts to protect wild birds; visibility and air quality; power plant performance; underground cable testing; water saw; wet/dry cooling of power plants; energy R&D; turbine missile casing tests.

Size & Elements: Film: 16mm (100 titles, 25 cans). Videotape: Betacam, 3/4" and 1/2" (2,000 videotapes). All elements available.
Cataloging: Published catalogs; computerized cataloging available to researchers.
Access: Available for duplication, licensing and reuse. Research fees charged. Requests accepted by mail, telephone and in person (by appointment only).
Rights: Full rights held to some material. Some rights held to all material. Additional clearances may be necessary in some cases if material is to be reused.
Licensing: Available for licensing and reuse. License fees charged.
Restrictions: None specified.
Viewing Facilities: Film (16mm); videotape (3/4" and VHS).
Duplication Facilities: None.
Related Materials: Photograph and slide library.

CALIFORNIA (Palo Alto)

HEWLETT-PACKARD CO.
1819 Page Mill Road
Palo Alto, CA 94304
(415) 857-4193
Fax: (415) 857-7536

Contact: Monique McQuaid
Services: Corporation; corporate archives; videotape producer. Archival material for in-house use only; videotape programs available for purchase.
Description: Films and videotapes relating to electronic instruments, systems, computer products and technology.

Corporate archives. Holds training, documentary and marketing footage relating to electronic testing and instruments; medical diagnostic technology and instruments; analytical systems; and technology training materials related to electrical engineering.

Although Hewlett-Packard has on occasion released footage to news organizations, educational institutions, government agencies, and nonprofit organizations, the archives is generally closed to researchers and the public.

Videotape programs available for purchase. Educational and practical programs produced by the Hewlett-Packard Television Network. Tutorial titles include: *Why a Transistor Amplifies; Digital Building Blocks; Numbering Systems and Digital Devices; Binary Nature of Digital Circuits; Logic Gates and Symbols; Understanding Microprocessors; Analog vs. Digital Systems; Microprocessor Fundamentals; DMA and Handshaking; Using Interrupts; Silicon IC Technology Series; Chemical Vapor Disposition; Oxidation of Silicon; How to Use an Oscilloscope; How to Solder;* and *Fiber Optic Series.*

Other series include: *Electronic Instruments; IC Tester Series; Microwave Test Equipment; Computer Systems; Safety;* and *Disability.*
Size & Elements: Videotape: 3/4", VHS and Betamax I (over 700 titles).
Cataloging: None specified.
Access: Videotapes available to the public for purchase. Requests accepted by mail and telephone. Corporate archives not generally available to the public; for in-house use only.
Rights: Full rights held to all material.
Licensing: Material not generally available for licensing or reuse.
Restrictions: Material in corporate archives not available for viewing, duplication or reuse of any kind.
Viewing Facilities: None.
Duplication Facilities: None.

CALIFORNIA (Pasadena)

CALIFORNIA INSTITUTE OF TECHNOLOGY INSTITUTE ARCHIVES
and
CALIFORNIA INSTITUTE OF TECHNOLOGY JET PROPULSION LABORATORY PUBLIC AFFAIRS OFFICE
See CALIFORNIA (Los Angeles Metro)

CALIFORNIA (Placerville)

NATURAL REFLECTIONS VIDEO
2814 Hocking Street
Placerville, CA 95667
(916) 621-1771

Michael Dennis (President)

Contact: Michael Dennis
Services: Videotape producer; production and post-production facility. Material available to the public for duplication, licensing and reuse. Some completed programs available for distribution.
Description: *White-water rafting.* Holds the "largest white-water rafting library in the world," including footage shot from a boat and from land; interviews; rivers and wildlife; death-defying activities; and point-of-view footage. Rafting shots are categorized and can be retrieved by such characteristics as color of raft and the gender, number or ethnicity of the people thereon.

California Gold Rush and mining footage. Contemporary and historical documentation of the Gold Rush era and historical locations. Holds videotape copies of all relevant materials held by the National Archives and Records Administration (q.v.) and the [California] State Park Service.

World War II. Holds a small amount of footage relating to airport runway construction on Okinawa under combat conditions.
Size & Elements: Videotape: 3/4" (3,000 hours; masters).
Cataloging: Computerized cataloging for staff use only.
Access: Available to the public for duplication and reuse. Some completed programs available for distribution. Research fees charged. Research requests accepted by telephone.
Rights: Full rights held to all material.
Licensing: Available for licensing and reuse. License fees charged.
Restrictions: None specified.
Viewing Facilities: Videotape (3/4").
Duplication Facilities: Videotape.

CALIFORNIA (Redlands)

GREAT AMERICAN STOCK
See CALIFORNIA (Los Angeles Metro)

CALIFORNIA (Reseda)

KEVIN DUFFY PRODUCTIONS
and
EM GEE FILM LIBRARY
and
NEWSREEL VIDEO SERVICE
See CALIFORNIA (Los Angeles Metro)

CALIFORNIA (Sacramento)

ANIMAL PROTECTION INSTITUTE OF AMERICA
P.O. Box 22505
Sacramento, CA 95831
(916) 422-1921
Fax: (916) 731-4467
TWX 910 367 2375 API SAC

Street address: 2831 Fruitridge Road

Emily R. Baker (Librarian)

Contact: Bruce Webb (Vice President, Program/Wildlife)
Services: Technical library. Films and videotapes available for reuse, subject to restrictions.
Description: Animal protection, wildlife, endangered species, pet care, individual animal species and animal cruelty. Two titles are produced by Institute: *Empty Ark* and *9th Crusade.*
Size & Elements: Film (16mm). Videotape (VHS and Betamax) (2 titles).
Cataloging: Brochures (available on request); research library.
Access: Available to the public. Research requests accepted by mail, telephone and in person (by appointment only), although access is granted mainly to staff and members.
Rights: Full rights held to Institute productions. Some rights held to other material. Additional clearances may be necessary in order to reuse material

from films not produced by the Institute.
Licensing: Available for licensing and reuse, subject to restrictions. License fees charged in some cases.
Restrictions: Requests for licensing and reuse considered on a case-by-case basis. Contact Ted Crail (Public Relations) for information on clip usage and rights.
Viewing Facilities: None.
Duplication Facilities: None.
Distributor: Modern Talking Picture Service, Inc. (q.v.) handles sale of Institute productions.

CALIFORNIA (Sacramento)

CALIFORNIA DEPARTMENT OF TRANSPORTATION (CALTRANS) GRAPHIC SERVICES SECTION
P.O. Box 942874
Sacramento, CA 94274-0001
(916) 445-6675

Street address: 1120 "N" Street, Room 5125, Sacramento, CA 95814

Contact: David Douglas (Chief, Graphic Services)
Services: Government agency. Film and videotape library available for distribution or reuse, subject to restrictions.
Description: The Graphic Services Section of Caltrans produces and holds original film footage (mostly 1960s-present) relating to California transportation, engineering and energy. Some historical material dating from the 1920s is also available.
Sample titles include: *The Aerotrain* (1974), the story of the development of the Rohr System Aerotrain for final guideway high speed transportation; *Alternative Energy Expo* (1980), with exhibits on experimental transportation modes such as gasohol powered vehicles and a 2-rider bike which can travel at over 50 mph; *Bridging the Bay* (1937), tracing the planning and construction of the San Francisco-Oakland Bay Bridge from 1929 to its completion in 1936; *California Highways* (1936); *Carquinez Bridge Construction #1 & #2* (1957), showing construction of building piers and steel work; *Crash Tests With Lightweight Truck Mounted Attenuators* (1985); *Design Aesthetics* (1966), relating to highway engineering design; *Freeway Capacity and Congestion* (1985); *Hazardous Spills Dressing Exercise* (1985); *Let's Keep America Beautiful* (produced by Richfield Oil Company) showing the highway littering problem and pointing the finger of blame at the casual vacation traveler; *Pine Valley Bridge* (1974), with time-lapse footage of bridge construction using the cast-in-place cantilever method and *Soaring Sculptures* (1967), showing the daring design features of the Papago Freeway through Phoenix, Arizona.
Size & Elements: Film and videotape: formats unspecified (approx. 80 titles).
Cataloging: Lists available.
Access: Open to the public. Material available for distribution and reuse. Research requests accepted by mail. Research fees not charged.
Rights: Apply for information. Additional clearances may be necessary in some cases if material is to be reused.
Licensing: Available for reuse, subject to restrictions. Usage fees not charged.
Restrictions: Departmental approval required for footage reuse.
Viewing Facilities: None.
Duplication Facilities: None.

CALIFORNIA (Sacramento)

CALIFORNIA DEPARTMENT OF WATER RESOURCES
P.O. Box 942836
Sacramento, CA 95802
(916) 445-7595

Street address: 1416 Ninth Street, Sacramento, CA 95814

Larry Filby (Chief, Graphic Services)

Contact: Rex Dean (Film Library)
Services: Government agency. Film and videotape library available for purchase and free loan; material possibly available for reuse, subject to restrictions.
Description: Has documented various California water projects since 1950s. Subjects include historic footage of the construction of the largest aqueduct in the world, part of the California State Water Project (late 1950s-early 1960s) and the construction of the Oroville dam. Contemporary documentaries cover such topics as salmon swimming upstream; ecology; Mono Lake; droughts;

conservation; dams; hydraulic power; and irrigation techniques. A series of children's videotapes shows the water cycle and water-related activities, narrated by Dewey, the animated water droplet.
Size & Elements: Film: 16mm. Videotape: 3/4". (Approx. 30 titles). Some archival material has been transferred to videotape.
Cataloging: Brochure.
Access: Available to the public. Maintained primarily for distribution or rental rather than for research or reuse. Research requests accepted by mail and telephone. Research fees not charged.
Rights: Full rights held to all material.
Licensing: Available for reuse, subject to restrictions. Usage fees generally not charged.
Restrictions: Requests for reuse considered on a case-by-case basis.
Viewing Facilities: Film and videotape.
Duplication Facilities: Videotape.

CALIFORNIA (Sacramento)

CALIFORNIA STATE ARCHIVES
1020 "O" Street, Room 130
Sacramento, CA 95814
(916) 445-4293

John F. Burns (Chief of Archives)

Contact: Genevieve Troka (Reference Archivist)
Services: Government agency. Film and videotape material available for research and reuse.
Description: Films and videotapes from Jesse Unruh's gubernatorial campaign (1970); a film assembled by the Los Angeles Police Department during their investigation of the assassination of Robert F. Kennedy; and several films produced or collected by such state agencies as the Department of Forestry and the Health and Welfare Agency.
Size & Elements: Film and videotape: formats unspecified (approx. 50 titles).
Cataloging: Card catalogs, inventories, published catalogs and computerized cataloging for staff use only.
Access: Open to the public. Research requests accepted by mail, telephone and in person. Research fees not charged.
Rights: Material in the public domain.
Licensing: Available for reuse. Usage fees not charged.
Restrictions: None specified.
Viewing Facilities: None.
Duplication Facilities: None.

CALIFORNIA (Sacramento)

CALIFORNIA STATE RAILROAD MUSEUM LIBRARY
111 "I" Street
Sacramento, CA 95814
(916) 323-8073

Street address: 113 "I" Street

Stephen E. Drew (Curator)

Contacts: Ellen L. Schwartz (Librarian); Blaine P. Lamb (Archivist)
Services: Museum. Film collection maintained for reference use only; not available for licensing, duplication or reuse.
Description: Travelogues and documentaries produced by professional and amateur filmmakers on railroad history and operation; training and promotional footage released by railroads and railroad-related organizations; entertainment films.
Size & Elements: Film: 35mm, 16mm and 8mm (over 200 titles). Videotape: format and amount unspecified.
Cataloging: Largely uncataloged.
Access: Open to the public. For reference viewing only. Research fees not charged. Research requests accepted by mail, telephone and in person.
Rights: Apply for information.
Licensing: Material not available for duplication, licensing or reuse.
Restrictions: For reference use only. Not available for duplication, licensing or reuse.
Viewing Facilities: Film and videotape.
Duplication Facilities: None.

CALIFORNIA (Sacramento)

KCRA-TV
3 Television Circle
Sacramento, CA 95814-0794
(916) 444-7300 (switchboard)

Contact: Bob Jordan
Services: Television broadcaster; film and videotape archives. Material available for licensing and reuse, subject to restrictions.
Description: Television newsfilm and videotape collection (1976-present). KCRA-TV film footage from 1959 through January 1976 is held by the Museum and History Division, City of Sacramento (q.v.).

Newsfilm coverage begins June 1976 and ends June 30, 1982, at which time videotape completely replaced film. Videotape coverage covers 1980-present.

Both the film and videotape collections reflect local and regional news events in the Sacramento Valley and the San Francisco Bay Area, as well as events of statewide interest transpiring in and around Sacramento, the state capital. There is extensive footage of California state politics, including coverage of the State Assembly and Senate and Governors Edmund G. "Pat" Brown, Ronald Reagan, Jerry Brown and George Deukmejian.

On The Go, a series (938 episodes) profiling people, places and events in Northern California, is held primarily at KCRA-TV, although some episodes are held at the Museum and History Division. Other documentaries and special programs, although produced before 1976, are still held at KCRA-TV, including *Alien in the Midst* (1959, 60 min.), a documentary on redevelopment in Sacramento and the displacement of inner-city residents.

Major California news events such as the Free Speech Movement (University of California at Berkeley, 1964); the United Farm Workers and the agricultural labor movement and the kidnapping of Patricia Hearst by the Symbionese Liberation Army (1974) are covered at length. This coverage is held partly at KCRA-TV and partly at the Museum and History Division.
Size & Elements: Film: 16mm (over 5 million feet, 28,000 cans; negative and positive, black and white, silent and sound). Videotape: 3/4" (18,500 videotapes, each 20 min., 30 min. and 60 min.). *Figures relating to film collection reflect material held in part by the Museum and History Division.*
Cataloging: Card catalogs; computerized cataloging for staff use only.
Access: For in-house use only. Available for duplication, licensing and reuse, subject to restrictions. Research fees not charged.
Rights: Full rights held to some material. Some material in the public domain. Additional clearances may be necessary in some cases if material is to be reused.
Licensing: Available for licensing and reuse, subject to restrictions. License fees charged.
Restrictions: Newsfilm cannot be used for commercial purposes.
Viewing Facilities: Film (16mm RTI Cinescan); videotape (3/4").
Duplication Facilities: Film (16mm to 1", 3/4" and VHS); videotape (1", 3/4" and VHS).

CALIFORNIA (Sacramento)

MUSEUM AND HISTORY DIVISION/
CITY OF SACRAMENTO
551 Sequoia Pacific Boulevard
Sacramento, CA 95814
(916) 449-2072

Contact: Charlene Gilbert
Services: Museum; historical society. Newsfilm collection available for research, licensing and reuse, subject to clearance and approval.
Description: Television newsfilm and videotape (1959-76) originally produced by KCRA-TV (Sacramento). Film and videotape footage (January 1976-present) is still held by KCRA-TV (q.v.).

The film collection reflects local and regional news events in the Sacramento Valley and the San Francisco Bay Area, as well as events of statewide interest transpiring in and around Sacramento, the state capital of California. There is extensive footage of California state politics, including coverage of the State Assembly and Senate; Governors Earl Warren, Goodwin Knight, Edmund G. "Pat" Brown, Ronald Reagan, and Jerry Brown; and state and local political campaigns.

Holds extensive footage relating to issues and events surrounding the creation of the Old Sacramento Historic Area, including footage on the controversial relocation of the transient community that lived in the West End hotels, the project's continued progress and, its successes and failures. Other footage relates to the Oak Park (Sacramento) race riots of 1966, and to the needs and demands of Sacramento's ethnic and racial minorities. There is also coverage of the devastating floods which affected Northern California from Mt. Shasta to Marysville-Yuba City (1955-65).

Regional stories of national significance covered in the collection include Richard Nixon's 1962 gubernatorial campaign after his defeat in the 1960 presidential election; Robert F. Kennedy's Presidential primary campaign, victory and assassination on June 5, 1968; all Presidential primary campaigns in 1964; the farm labor movement and the rise of the United Farm Workers Union; the Symbionese Liberation Army and the kidnapping of Patricia Hearst. Also covered are all national political conventions (1964-76); the Johnson-Goldwater presidential race in 1964; the Free Speech Movement (1964) and antiwar activities at the University of California, Berkeley; and controversy surrounding the development of Alaskan oil reserves.

Additional footage reflects the station's in-depth features on the highly emotional social issues of rape; doctors and mercy killings; capital punishment; prison reform; women in prisons; crime victims; draft resistance; abortion; wiretapping and the FBI; the Pit River Indian sit-ins; and Channel 3 Reports and Camera 3 interviews with the celebrated, the notorious, the obscure and the unknown on virtually every contemporary subject and issue.
Size & Elements: Film: 16mm (over 5 million feet, 28,000 cans; negative and positive, black and white, silent and sound). *Figures reflect material held in part by KCRA-TV.*
Cataloging: Daily cameramens' logs; *TV Guides* (Sacramento edition, 1959-72).
Access: Available for research and reuse, subject to restrictions.
Rights: Full rights held to all material. Additional clearances may be necessary in some cases if material is to be reused.
Licensing: Available for licensing and reuse. License fees charged.
Restrictions: Apply for information.
Viewing Facilities: Film.
Duplication Facilities: None.

CALIFORNIA (Sacramento)

HARRY SWEET FILM COLLECTION
4305 Dennis Way
Sacramento, CA 95821
(916) 487-9827

Harry Sweet (Owner)

Contact: Harry Sweet
Services: Private film collection. Material available for research and reuse.
Description: Television news footage originally shot by Harry Sweet for a now-defunct station (KCCC-TV, the first television station in the Sacramento Valley) between June 1, 1953 and May 30, 1957. Contains general news stories, including the Marysville-Yuba City flood (Dec. 23, 1955); the construction of the Folsom Dam (dedicated 1956) and the Port of Sacramento; and general coverage of Mather Air Force Base, McClellan Air Force Base and Beale Air Force Base.
Size & Elements: Film: 16mm (5,000 feet; negative and positive, mostly black and white, some color, most silent).
Cataloging: Dope sheets.
Access: Open to researchers and scholars. Available for duplication, reuse and resale. Research fees charged. Research requests accepted by mail and telephone.
Rights: Material in the public domain.
Licensing: Available for reuse. Usage fees charged.
Restrictions: None specified.
Viewing Facilities: Film.
Duplication Facilities: None.

CALIFORNIA (San Diego)

AMERICA'S CUP ORGANIZING COMMITTEE
1660 Hotel Circle North, Suite 710
San Diego, CA 92108
(619) 296-9224
Fax: (619) 543-0836

Tom Ehman, Jr. (Chief Operating Officer, Executive Vice President)

Contact: Tom Mitchell (Vice President, Communications and Development)
Services: Foundation. Film and videotape library available for duplication,

licensing and reuse.

Description: Formerly known as Sail America Foundation. Holds the official and exclusive library of Dennis Conner's successful campaign to recapture the America's Cup (1984-87), including footage of the yacht *Stars and Stripes 1987* (testing, training, and racing); interviews with the crew and Dennis Conner; action sequences; the victory tour and behind-the-scenes events, shot on location in Hawaii and Australia; and the Louis Vuitton Challenger Series.
Size & Elements: Videotape: 1", Betacam (PAL masters; NTSC sub-masters), 3/4" and VHS (viewing copies with visible time code). (approx. 80 hours total).
Cataloging: Computerized cataloging for staff use only.
Access: Available to the public for duplication, licensing and reuse. Research fees charged. Research requests accepted by mail and telephone.
Rights: Full rights held to all material. Additional clearances may be necessary in some cases if material is to be reused.
Licensing: Available for licensing and reuse. License fees charged.
Restrictions: None specified.
Viewing Facilities: Videotape (through Mincey Productions, Inc. with prior access approval from Sail America).
Duplication Facilities: Videotape (through Mincey Productions, Inc.)

CALIFORNIA (San Diego)

CRYSTAL PYRAMID PRODUCTIONS
2336 Sumac Drive
San Diego, CA 92105
(619) 282-6126

Mark Schulze (President)

Contacts: Mark Schulze; Patricia Mooney
Services: Film and videotape producer; videotape distributor. Collection available for duplication, licensing and reuse. Custom videotape shooting services available.
Description: Holds contemporary color footage, all with sound, including: bicycling (mountain and general); helicopter shots of mountains; landscapes with mountains and oceans; massage; sailplanes; self defense, with karate demonstrations; anti-terrorism, with weapons and tactics training and explosives footage; male erotic dancers (no frontal nudity); downtown San Diego street scenes; and shots of people participating in various activities (working and construction).
Size & Elements: Film: 16mm (small amount; release prints). Videotape: 1", 3/4" and VHS (over 100 hours total).
Cataloging: Computerized cataloging for staff use only.
Access: Available to the public for duplication, licensing and reuse. Completed videotapes distributed through New and Unique Videos (see below).
Rights: Full rights held to all material.
Licensing: Available for licensing and reuse. License fees charged.
Restrictions: None specified.
Viewing Facilities: Videotape (3/4" and VHS).
Duplication Facilities: Videotape.
Related Materials: Still photographs.
Distributor: New and Unique Videos, 2336 Sumac Drive, San Diego, CA 92105; (619) 282-6126.

CALIFORNIA (San Diego)

INTERNATIONAL DANCE EXERCISE ASSOCIATION
6190 Cornerstone Court East, Suite 204
San Diego, CA 92121
(619) 535-8979
Fax: (619) 535-8234

Peter Davis (Chief Executive Officer)
Kathie Davis (Executive Director)

Contacts: Diana Page Wood (Public Relations Director); Patty Howard-Jones (Director of Event Operations)
Services: Professional fitness association. Videotape collection primarily available to the news media.
Description: Holds footage shot at the 1987 IDEA Industry Convention, an event hosting over 1,800 fitness instructors, club owners and manufacturers from North America and around the world at the Disneyland Hotel in Anaheim, California. Includes specialized aerobic classes (e.g., male and aqua), stretching, lectures, aerobic professionals, equipment and merchandise displays and manufacturer activity in the exhibit hall. There is also exclusive footage of

the Industry Awards Ceremony, featuring aerobic industry leaders such as Jane Fonda, Kirk Lawrence, Mary Manta, Sheila Cluff and many others.
Size & Elements: Videotape: Betacam (approx. 10 broadcast quality videotapes, each 20 min.); 3/4" (amount unspecified; raw footage).
Cataloging: Shot lists.
Access: Available primarily to the news media. Research requests accepted by mail.
Rights: Additional clearances may be necessary in some cases if material is to be reused.
Licensing: Available for licensing and reuse, subject to restrictions. License and usage fees charged under some conditions (media charged for costs only; others charged depending on project).
Restrictions: Requests for licensing and reuse subject to acceptance and approval.
Viewing Facilities: None.
Duplication Facilities: None.

CALIFORNIA (San Diego)

THE MEDIA GUILD
11722 Sorrento Valley Road, Suite E
San Diego, CA 92121
(619) 755-9191

Preston Holdner (President)

Contact: Scott Isenberg (National Sales Manager)
Services: Corporation; distributor. Films and videotapes available for rental, preview and purchase to educational institutions and libraries. Materials possibly available for duplication, licensing and reuse, subject to clearance and approval.
Description: Educational films and videotapes, particularly geared to secondary and college levels. Areas covered include: elementary computer science; elementary science; secondary science; energy education; life science and biology; chemistry; photochemistry; physical chemistry; physics; earth science; paleontology; the Earth's physical resources; ecology; mathematics and economics; statistics; crafts, design and technology; children's entertainment; elementary language arts; contemporary literature; literature; foreign languages; elementary music; general music; film; architectural history; drama and theater; music; dance; elementary social studies; American history; secondary social studies; modern history; South America; India; ancient history; social issues; ethics; guidance; family relationships; drugs and alcohol; suicide prevention; nuclear issues; counseling; depression; human abuse; health; safety; emergency childbirth; and teacher education.

Exclusive U.S. distributor for *Open University* (BBC-TV, approx. 100 titles) productions in the areas of secondary science, history, ecology, literature, social studies and teacher education. Non-theatrical North American distributor for Thames Television productions (approx. 135 titles) in the areas of science, foreign language, children's entertainment, language arts, music, literature, the humanities, social studies, technology, guidance and health. Also distributes materials from independent producers, including Paulist Productions and the National Film Board of Canada.
Size & Elements: Film: 16mm. Videotape: 3/4", VHS and Betamax. (Approx. 500 titles total).
Cataloging: Published catalogs.
Access: Available for rental, preview and purchase to schools, colleges and public libraries. Rental fees charged; a rent-to-own plan is available with minimum purchase. Rental bookings accepted by telephone; orders accepted by mail. Research fees depend upon type of request. Research requests accepted by mail and telephone.
Rights: Full rights held to some material. Some rights held to all material. Additional clearances may be necessary in some cases if material is to be reused.
Licensing: Materials protected by copyright. Purchasers of films or videotapes may request television broadcast licenses or duplication privileges. Apply for information regarding fees and details.
Restrictions: Restrictions apply depending on individual title; requests for reuse are individually negotiated.
Viewing Facilities: None.
Duplication Facilities: None.

CALIFORNIA (San Diego)

SAN DIEGO AEROSPACE MUSEUM
N. PAUL WHITTIER HISTORICAL AVIATION LIBRARY

CALIFORNIA (San Diego)

2001 Pan American Plaza
Balboa Park
San Diego, CA 92101
(619) 234-8291

Capt. Edwin McKellar (Director)

Contact: Ray Wagner (Archivist)
Services: Museum. Film and videotape collection open to members and the public.
Description: Aviation history and events. Materials include: *Air Power Series,* an Air Force broadcast (1950s); *Lindbergh in South Dakota* (1927); *The Dole Race* (California to Hawaii, late 1920s); *The Blue Angels* (produced by the U.S. Navy); *The Air Force Thunderbirds* (produced by General Dynamics); and other assorted materials.
Size & Elements: Film: 16mm (approx. 200 films). Videotape: VHS (one-third of the film collection has been transferred to videotape).
Cataloging: None.
Access: Maintained primarily for use by members. Open to the public. Research fees not charged; handling costs apply. Research requests accepted by mail and telephone.
Rights: Full rights held to some material. Additional clearances may be necessary in some cases if material is to be reused.
Licensing: Apply for information.
Restrictions: Restrictions apply to reuse.
Viewing Facilities: Film and videotape.
Duplication Facilities: None (outside arrangements can be made).

CALIFORNIA (San Diego)

SAN DIEGO STATE UNIVERSITY
SPECIAL COLLECTIONS
University Library
San Diego, CA 92182-0511
(619) 594-5831
(619) 594-6791

Ruth Leerhoff (Head, Special Collections)

Contacts: Ruth Leerhoff; Lyn Olsson (Archives Assistant, Special Collections)
Services: University library. Film collection open to the public for in-house use only.
Description: Majority of the film collection was donated by Desi Arnaz. Donated materials include various episodes from the television series:
The Mothers-In-Law. Includes: 56 television episodes (1967-69), accompanied by scripts, miscellaneous production material, and a documentary on the series (6 reels, silent). Episodes include: "Who's Afraid of Elizabeth Taylor"; "How You Moonlight A Meatball"; "The Not Cold Enough War"; "The Wig Story"; "I Haven't Got a Secret"; "Even Mothers-in-Law Have Mothers-in-Law"; "Haven't You Had That Baby Yet"; and "Show Business is No Business."
Desilu Playhouse. Episodes include: "Trial at Devil's Canyon" (1958); "Tender in the Night" (1959); and "So Tender, So Profane" (1959).
I Love Lucy. Episodes include: "Lucy Wins a Racehorse"; "The Benefit" (1952); and "Ricky Minds the Baby" (1954).
Lands End. Episodes include: "The Lone Survivor"; and "Filming of Lands End."
Arnaz personal. Home movie reels (16mm), including *Jitterrumba* (1947); *Star Party Test* (1960, black and white); *Las Cruces House and Fishing* (color, silent); and *Dapi Fishing* (color, silent).
Other items include several reels of *Washoe* (origin unknown), an American Indian coming-of-age ceremony; and *The Incredible Mr. Limpet* (3 reels) accompanied by 13 linear feet of production materials and original cartoon cels.
Size & Elements: Film: 16mm (7 titles, 103 cans; positive and negative).
Cataloging: Finding aids (inventories).
Access: Open to the public. For in-house use only. Research fees not charged. Research requests accepted by mail and telephone.
Rights: Rights status of material not known.
Licensing: Apply for information. Usage fees not charged.
Restrictions: None specified.
Viewing Facilities: Film.
Duplication Facilities: None.

CALIFORNIA (San Fernando)

PARTIDO NACIONAL LA RAZA UNIDA
See **CALIFORNIA** (Los Angeles Metro)

CALIFORNIA (San Francisco)

ADAIR FILMS
900 23rd Street
San Francisco, CA 94107
(415) 826-6500

Peter Adair (Producer)

Contact: Kevin Murphy (Office Manager)
Services: Distributor. Film and videotape collection available to the public for rental.
Description: Titles available: *Stopping History,* a documentary on responses to the threat of nuclear war; *Stories Everywhere,* featuring some of America's most renowned storytellers and chronicling four different kinds of storytelling; *The Word Is Out,* featuring gay men and lesbians who talk about their lives with disarming candor; *The AIDS Show: Artists Involved With Death And Survival,* dealing with the impact of the AIDS epidemic on the gay community, including both performance and documentary material; and *Teaching Adults To Read,* documenting the stories of five participants in San Francisco Public Library's "Project Read" literacy program.
Size & Elements: Film: 16mm (2 titles). Videotape: 3/4", Betamax and VHS (4 titles).
Cataloging: Published brochures.
Access: Available for distribution and rental. Requests accepted by mail and telephone.
Rights: Apply for information.
Licensing: Apply for information.
Restrictions: None specified.
Viewing Facilities: None.
Duplication Facilities: None.
Distributors: *The AIDS Show* is available from Direct Cinema Limited (q.v.); *Word Is Out* from New Yorker Films (q.v.).

CALIFORNIA (San Francisco)

ART COM/LA MAMELLE, INC.
P.O. Box 3123, Rincon Annex
San Francisco, CA 94119-3123
(415) 431-7524
(415) 431-7672
Fax: (415) 431-7841
Telex: 4946074 ART COM
WELL: artcomtv

Carl Loeffler (Executive Director)

Contact: Carl Loeffler
Services: Arts organization. Videotapes and videodiscs available to the public for rental and purchase. Some material available for broadcast.
Description: Artists' service organization for new art activities. Founded in 1975, Art Com publishes as well as distributes artworks and publications produced in a wide variety of formats, including print, video, audio, rubber stamp, online computer and other electronic formats. Art Com has always supported experimental forms of art, including performance, video and other crossover art activities, and continues to document and disseminate works which incorporate new ideas and technologies to broaden the base of art disseminated to the public.
Collections available for distribution (some for purchase) include: *Alive From Off Center* (Twin Cities Public Television [KTCA] [q.v.]), a public television series showcasing leading artists in the vanguard of dance, theater, music, comedy, video and film; *The Friday Club* (7 programs), a public access television series produced in the Chicago area, featuring music, video art, comedians, performers, artists and other political figures; *The Low Cal Show* (California Institute of the Arts, September 1987-March 1988, 8 programs); *Produced for Television* (Art Com/La Mamelle for KTSF-TV, 1979); *T.V.C.A.G.E.* (Cincinnati Artists Group Effort, 1987), a compilation of Ohio video art; *TV on TV* (Electronic Arts Archive and Research Institute of Texas Tech University), a series of broadcast-quality interstitial programs by performance-based artists, with work by Jaime Davidovich, Lynn Hershman, Michael Smith, Bruce and Norman Yonemoto; *TNT* (The Kitchen, 1982-87, 5 programs, each 60 min.), an overview of video art and its relationship to

television; and *Waveforms: Video/Japan* (1987, 2 programs), a selection of innovative video work from Japan, concerned with the persistence of tradition and the embracing of new technology.

Also distributes work by numerous individual artists. Some videotapes are available for purchase in VHS format.
Size & Elements: Videotape: 1", 3/4", VHS and 1/2" open reel (2,000 videotapes). Videodisc: Laserdiscs.
Cataloging: Published catalogs for library and distribution collection; computerized cataloging available to researchers (via modem and WELL).
Access: Open to researchers, scholars and the public. Research fees charged. Research requests accepted by mail, telephone and in person (by appointment only).
Rights: Full rights held to material produced by Art Com/La Mamelle, Inc. Additional clearances may be necessary in some cases if material is to be reused.
Licensing: Available for licensing and reuse. Some programs available for broadcast and closed-circuit presentations. License fees charged.
Restrictions: Apply for information.
Viewing Facilities: Videotape (3/4" and VHS).
Duplication Facilities: None.
Related Materials: Books; computer software.

CALIFORNIA (San Francisco)

ASSOCIATION OF INDEPENDENT COMMERCIAL PRODUCERS

1305 Stevenson
San Francisco, CA 94103
(415) 861-3100

Ronald K. Lakis (President)

Contacts: Ronald K. Lakis; Linda Jones (Production Coordinator); John Luce
Services: Association. Videotape collection available for research and reuse (subject to clearance).
Description: Over 100 public service announcements (PSAs) pertaining to AIDS, broadcast 1985-88, produced in the U.S. and abroad.
Size & Elements: Videotape: 3/4" (100 titles; viewing copies).
Cataloging: Computerized cataloging for staff use only.
Access: Available for research and reuse. Research fees "undetermined." Research requests accepted by mail, telephone and in person (walk-in).
Rights: Some rights held to all material. Additional clearances may be necessary in some cases if material is to be reused.
Licensing: Apply for information.
Restrictions: Clearances for reuse must be obtained from original producers; contact information is provided.
Viewing Facilities: Videotape (by appointment only).
Duplication Facilities: Videotape.

CALIFORNIA (San Francisco)

BAY AREA ELECTRIC RAILROAD ASSOCIATION, INC.
WESTERN RAILWAY MUSEUM

P.O. Box 3694
San Francisco, CA 94119
(707) 374-2978 (Museum)
(415) 534-0071 (Museum Curator)

Museum address: 1802 East 23rd Street, Oakland, CA 94606-3316

Vernon J. Sappers (Museum Curator)

Contact: Vernon J. Sappers
Services: Railroad museum, historical society and library. Film collection currently being cataloged; available for research, licensing and reuse.
Description: Railroads and railroad history (1929-50).
Size & Elements: Film: 16mm (amount unspecified).
Cataloging: Research library; cataloging in process.
Access: Open to researchers and scholars. Requests accepted by mail and in person (walk-in and by appointment). Museum open only on weekends.
Rights: Full rights held to all material.
Licensing: Available for licensing and reuse. License fees charged.
Restrictions: None specified.
Viewing Facilities: None.
Duplication Facilities: None.

CALIFORNIA (San Francisco)

BAY AREA VIDEO COALITION (BAVAC)

1111 17th Street
San Francisco, CA 94107
(415) 861-3282

David Bolt (Executive Director)

Contact: Merle Mason (Operations Supervisor)
Services: Nonprofit media arts center. Videotape collection for in-house viewing only.
Description: One of the Bay Area's first media art centers, offering state-of-the-art production and post-production facilities to artists. Facilities have been used by virtually every prominent video artist in America over the past twelve years in the creation of over 700 non-commercial programs.

Holds copies of programs that have been produced and subsidized by BAVAC's production and post-production access program. Collection reflects the nature of artists' and independent producers' interests over the past fifteen years. Subjects and length vary widely, from documentaries and public service announcements to narratives and experimental works.
Size & Elements: Videotape: 3/4" (250 titles).
Cataloging: Card catalogs.
Access: Open to the public for in-house viewing. Reservations necessary for use of screening room; hourly screening room fees charged. Research requests accepted by telephone.
Rights: Rights to all materials retained by artists; they must be contacted directly for permission to reuse.
Licensing: Not available for licensing or reuse.
Restrictions: Must contact producer directly for permission to reuse.
Viewing Facilities: Videotape (screening room with 19" monitor, various formats).
Duplication Facilities: Videotape (1", Betacam, 3/4" and VHS).
Publications: *Video Networks,* monthly journal devoted to keeping video artists informed about media arts.

CALIFORNIA (San Francisco)

CALIFORNIA COLLEGE OF PODIATRIC MEDICINE
PACIFIC COAST HOSPITAL & CLINICS

1210 Scott Street
San Francisco, CA 94115
(415) 563-8070 (Exts. 267 and 470)

Scott Ludwig (Director, Educational Media Services)

Contact: Scott Ludwig
Services: Educational institution. Videotapes available for purchase only.
Description: Instructional videotapes intended to supply accurate demonstrations of various podiatric techniques for practitioners and students desiring reinforcement and update of their skills. Collection is continually updated and revised.
Podiatric skills. Injection techniques for local anesthesia; the six most commonly used blocks of lower extremity for anesthesia; X-ray evaluation of bunions; radioscopic positioning in podiatry; evaluation of acute inversion sprain of ankle; soft tissue ankle injury series and proper scout X-rays to be taken and their evaluation; inversion stress and push-pull maneuvers; application and removal of below-the-knee walking cast; compression cast and posterior splint; how to tie a simple interrupted stitch; performing Gram's Stain; visual changes in normal locomotion with various types of neuromuscular pathology; osteosynthesis in forefoot surgery.
Surgical case reports. Excising neuroma through a plantar transverse incision; surgical approach and technique for freeing the posterior tibial nerve of fibrous attachments; Keller bunionectomy with total implant; McBride bunionectomy; Logroscino bunionectomy; retro-calcaneal exostectomy; skin graft from the thigh to the lateral posterior aspect of the ankle; excision of a soft tissue mass; intermediate phalangectomy; surgical matricectomy; four classical mechanism of fractures using Lauge-Hansen classification.
Biomechanics. Lower extremity musculoskeletal examination on an infant; neutral suspension casting techniques; fabrication of the positive cast; fabrication of functional orthoses.
Miscellaneous. Podiatry in the 1980s; preparing for oral exams.
Size & Elements: Videotape: 3/4", Betamax and VHS (approx. 45 titles).
Cataloging: Published catalog.
Access: Available to the public for purchase. Requests accepted by mail.

CALIFORNIA (San Francisco C)

Rights: Full rights held to all material.
Licensing: Not available for licensing or reuse.
Restrictions: Material not available for rental or loan.
Viewing Facilities: None.
Duplication Facilities: None.

CALIFORNIA (San Francisco)

CALIFORNIA NEWSREEL
630 Natoma Street
San Francisco, CA 94103
(415) 621-6196

Larry Adelman (Producer)

Contact: Sam Chong
Services: Film and videotape producer and distributor. Completed films and videotapes available for rental and purchase; stock footage available for licensing and reuse.
Description: Videotapes on important contemporary social issues. Subjects covered include Southern Africa, labor, the Japanese workplace, the steel industry, the airline industry, the 1960s and Vietnam.

Southern Africa Media Center. Films include: *Bound To Strike Back* (1987), showing the ruthless behavior of South African security forces in the current state of emergency, as well as how people sustain their struggle despite overwhelming repression; *Destructive Engagement* (1987) criss-crossing the frontline states — Zimbabwe, Mozambique, Botswana, Zambia and Angola — in an unprecedented investigation of South Africa's regional war; *Corridors of Freedom* (1987) on the initiation of the Southern African Development Coordination Conference (SADCC); *Winnie and Nelson Mandela* (1986, Peter Davis) presenting their story through Winnie's eyes; *Generations of Resistance* (1980, Peter Davis) combining testimony from survivors of earlier battles with rare archival footage; *Woza Albert!* (1982) the international hit play written and performed by two Black South Africans; *You Have Struck a Rock* (1981), on Black South African women, who have taken the lead in mobilizing mass opposition to apartheid despite the triple oppression of race, class and sex, featuring Lillian Ngoyi, Helen Josephs and others; *South Africa Belongs To Us* (1980), an intimate portrayal of five typical Black women describing how apartheid impoverishes, dehumanizes and ultimately enslaves; *Allan Boesak: Choosing For Justice* (Hugo Cassirer and Nadine Gordimer, 1984) tracing the religious and political odyssey of the first non-White head of the 70-million member World Alliance of Reformed Churches and founder of the United Democratic Front; *Namibia: Africa's Last Colony* (1984), in which members of the SWAPO liberation movement explain why, despite the terrorist policies of White rule, they are defying the South African authorities and speaking out to the world; *Moving On: The Hunger For Land In Zimbabwe* (1982) recounting the history of this rich agricultural land.

Women, work and technology. *Hired Hands* (1985) asks why it is almost impossible in this age of equality for most women to climb out of the "pink collar ghetto" onto the management ladder; *Terminal: VDTs And Women's Health* (1985) looks at the health hazards this new technology may pose for workers; *The Electronic Sweatshop* (Sophie Bissonette, 1985), on the millions of women who work each day on the frontlines of the computer revolution; *Collision Course: Labor and Management at the Crossroads* (1987) documents a test case for workplace cooperation in America, the dramatic story of the initial success and ultimate collapse of employee involvement at Eastern Airlines; *Manufacturing Miracles* (1987) shows how Mazda Motor Company became a remarkably flexible and intelligent industrial organism through the deliberate nurturing of a committed and resourceful workforce; *Final Offer* (1985) follows Bob White, the president of the Canadian United Auto Workers, through the landmark 1984 negotiations and 13-day auto strike at General Motors; *Clockwork* (Eric Breitbart, 1982) uses original archival footage to document and challenge the legacy of Frederick Taylor, a contemporary of the Gilbreths and proponent of "scientific management" in the modern American workplace, suggesting the need for more participative working conditions in today's global economy; *The Business of America* (California Newsreel, 1984), shows two Pittsburgh steelworkers' growing realization that increased profits won't necessarily "trickle down" to them, as well as interviews with the Chairman of U.S. Steel and a Harvard Business School professor; *The Wall Street Connection* (1985), in which some of Wall Street's most aggressive traders candidly reveal the speculative fever which governs how 98% of the nation's capital is bought and sold; *What's Good For GM...* (1981) is a dramatic case study of the escalating cost of corporate control over the vital processes of industrial change and urban development; *Controlling Interest* (California Newsreel, 1978), examines how the ever-increasing concentration and velocity of capital affects employment in the U.S., shapes patterns of development in the Third World and influences our nation's foreign policy.

Other titles include: *God & Money* (1986) which follows the vigorous dialogue among leading Catholic thinkers and a typical parish in response to the 1986 pastoral letter from the U.S. Catholic bishops which boldly questions fundamental American economic ideas; *The Willmar 8* (Lee Grant) tells the story of eight women in America's heartland who risked jobs, friends, family and the opposition of church and community to begin the longest bank strike in American history; *Ethnic Notions* (1987) takes the viewer on a disturbing voyage through American history and culture, examining racial stereotypes in detail (e.g., "loyal Toms," "carefree Sambos," "faithful Mammies," "grinning Coons," "savage Brutes" and "wide-eyed Pickaninnies") and interweaving minstrel shows, greeting cards, advertisements, popular songs, cartoons, films and household artifacts to link each stereotype to White society's shifting need to justify Black oppression; *Computers in Context* (1987) introduces Americans to a human-resource based computer design paradigm now emerging in Scandinavia which conceives of computers as part of larger organizational strategies to augment, not supplant, workers' skills, creativity and motivation; *The Fighting Ministers* (David Soul and Bill Jersey, 1986), tells the story of three clergymen and their wives and families who were galvanized by the Denominational Ministry Strategy, an ecumenical urban outreach to Pittsburgh's thousands of unemployed steelworkers, to confront the city's business leaders with the moral implications of their economic policies; *Mad River: Hard Times in Humboldt County* (1983), set in the redwood empire of Northern California, is a disturbing saga of a community torn asunder when its resource base is exhausted.

An outreach program is directed at labor unions, working class community groups, high schools, colleges, grassroots social service groups and the like. Has a flexible rental policy, making films and videotapes available on a sliding rental scale, based on the organization's ability to pay.
Size & Elements: Film: 16mm. Videotape: 1", 3/4" and VHS (viewing copies) (60 titles total).
Cataloging: Published catalogs; press materials.
Access: Films and videotapes available to the public for rental and purchase. Stock footage available for licensing and reuse. Research requests accepted by telephone and in person (by appointment only).
Rights: Full rights held to some material. Some rights held to some material.
Licensing: Some material available for licensing and reuse, subject to restrictions. License and usage fees charged.
Restrictions: Requests for reuse subject to acceptance and approval.
Viewing Facilities: Film (16mm); videotape (3/4" and VHS).
Duplication Facilities: Videotape (3/4" and VHS).
Representative: For stock footage sales: Petrified Films, Inc. (q.v.).

CALIFORNIA (San Francisco)

CANNED FRUIT PROMOTION SERVICE
P.O. Box 7111
San Francisco, CA 94120
(415) 541-0100
Fax: (415) 541-0296
Telex: 278724 Cling Ur

Street address: 160 Spear Street, Suite 1330, San Francisco, CA 94105

Thomas Krugman (General Manager, California Cling Peach Advisory Board)

Contact: Jan Barahona
Services: Trade association; state agency. Films available primarily for free loan.
Description: Small film library holds educational films describing the process of canning fruit "from orchards to table."
Size & Elements: Film: 16mm (amount unspecified). Videotape: VHS (3 titles from California Cling Peach Advisory Board).
Access: Not open to the public. Maintained for free-loan distribution rather than for research or reuse.
Rights: Some rights held to some material. Additional clearances may be necessary in some cases if material is to be reused.
Licensing: Apply for information. License fees not charged.
Restrictions: None specified.
Viewing Facilities: None.
Duplication Facilities: None.
Representative: Films distributed through Modern Talking Picture Service, Inc. (q.v.).

CALIFORNIA (San Francisco)

CANYON CINEMA, INC.
2325 Third Street, Suite 338
San Francisco, CA 94107
(415) 626-2255

Dominic Angerame (Administrative Director)

Contacts: Dominic Angerame; Wendy Blair
Services: Nonprofit cooperative distribution center for independent filmmakers. Films available for rental only; videotapes of some films in library available for purchase.
Description: Independently produced short films. Genres and subjects include: abstract, animation, assemblage and collage, autobiographical, avant-garde, children, comedy and satire, conceptual, dance, documentary, dramatic, ecology and environment, educational, erotic, ethnographic, fantasy, music, personal films, political and social commentary, portraits and biographies, psychology, religion, structural films, surrealism, "underground film," video and women's issues.
Size & Elements: Film: 16mm and Super 8mm (over 2,000 titles; release prints, sound and silent). Some titles available on videotape.
Cataloging: Published catalogs. Computerized cataloging for staff use only.
Access: For in-house use only. Available for rental. Some titles available for purchase on videotape. Rental fees charged. Rental inquiries accepted by mail, telephone and in person.
Rights: No rights held to any material. All rights retained by filmmakers.
Licensing: Prospective users must contact filmmakers regarding licensing or reuse.
Restrictions: None specified.
Viewing Facilities: Film.
Duplication Facilities: None.

CALIFORNIA (San Francisco)

ELFSTROM-HILMER PRODUCTIONS
4307 20th Street
San Francisco, CA 94114
(415) 821-0617

Robert Elfstrom; Lucy Hilmer (Producers)

Contacts: Michael Moore (Producer); Ray Day (Producer)
Services: Film producer. Material available for duplication, licensing and reuse.
Description: Contemporary footage of San Francisco, originally shot June 1988 for a promotional film sponsored by the San Francisco Convention and Visitors Bureau. Shots cover 24 hours in a "day-in-the-life of the City format." Both the completed film and outtakes are available for reuse.

Scenes available include: scenic footage of San Francisco; Chinatown and all tourist sites; aerial views; ethnic neighborhoods; the Golden Gate and San Francisco-Oakland Bay Bridges; downtown and skylines; Golden Gate Park; the Marina district; sailing; shots from boats and the oceanfront. Footage of the Napa Valley, Muir Woods and other outlying areas is also available.
Size & Elements: Film: 16mm (16 min. [completed film]; 8 hours [outtakes]; original negative and release prints).
Cataloging: Computerized cataloging for staff use only.
Access: Open to the public. Available for duplication and reuse. Research fees not charged. Research requests accepted by mail, telephone and in person (by appointment only).
Rights: Full rights held to all material.
Licensing: Available for licensing and reuse. License fees charged.
Restrictions: None specified.
Viewing Facilities: Film (16mm KEM flatbed).
Duplication Facilities: None (outside arrangements can be made).

CALIFORNIA (San Francisco)

THE EXODUS TRUST ARCHIVES OF EROTOLOGY INSTITUTE FOR ADVANCED STUDY OF HUMAN SEXUALITY RESEARCH LIBRARY
1523 Franklin Street
San Francisco, CA 94109
(415) 928-1133
Fax: (415) 928-8284

Ted McIlvenna, Ph.D. (President of the Institute)
Laird Sutton, Ph.D. (Chairman of the Department; Director of Instructional Media)

Contacts: Ted McIlvenna, Ph.D.; Laird Sutton, Ph.D.; Winnie McIlvenna (Business Manager)
Services: Educational institution; film and videotape archives, producer and distributor; historical society; library and museum. Film and videotape material primarily available to researchers and scholars only; possibly available for duplication and reuse, subject to restrictions.
Description: Human sexuality, sexual lifestyles and the gay and lesbian movement in the U.S. (1925-present). Includes sexually graphic material; videotapes of lectures given at IASHS; documentation of the San Francisco Gay and Lesbian Freedom Parade (ca. 1980-present); overall documentation of the "sexual movement" in the United States. All film and videotape materials at the Institute were either donated to or produced by the Institute.
Size & Elements: Film: 35mm (1 million feet); 16mm (5 million feet); 8mm (6 million feet). Videotape: 3/4" (3,800 videotapes); 1/2" (17,000 videotapes). Over 120,000 titles total are held on film and videotape.
Cataloging: Computerized cataloging for staff and student use only; card catalogs; other finding aids; research library.
Access: Not open to the public. Open to researchers and scholars only. For in-house use only. Research requests accepted by mail and telephone.
Rights: Full rights held to some material. Additional clearances may be necessary in some cases if material is to be reused.
Licensing: Material possibly available for licensing in some cases.
Restrictions: Restrictions apply to licensing and reuse.
Viewing Facilities: Film and videotape.
Duplication Facilities: None.
Related Materials: Photographs and 35mm slides.

CALIFORNIA (San Francisco)

FILM ARTS FOUNDATION
346 Ninth Street, 2nd Floor
San Francisco, CA 94103
(415) 552-8760

Gail Silva (Director)

Contact: Robert Hawk (Exhibition Coordinator)
Services: Media arts service organization; library. Maintains non-circulating videotape collection. Open to FAF members, researchers, scholars, media programmers and buyers.
Description: Works on videotape by Northern California independent film and videomakers. All genres are represented; approximately two-thirds are documentaries. Also provides general services, consultation and sponsorship to nonprofit film and videotape projects.
Size & Elements: Videotape: 3/4" and VHS (90 titles; viewing copies).
Cataloging: Research library; published catalogs.
Access: Open to FAF members, researchers, scholars, media programmers and buyers. For in-house use only. Research fees charged (for viewing). Consultation fees vary. Research requests accepted by mail, telephone and in person (by appointment only).
Rights: No rights held to any material.
Licensing: Apply for information.
Restrictions: Apply for information.
Viewing Facilities: Film (16mm and 8mm projectors); videotape (3/4" and VHS). (Viewing room).
Duplication Facilities: None.
Publications: *Media Catalog* of films and videotapes completed under FAF's sponsorship includes nearly 100 titles and contains information on funding, awards, screenings and distribution. *Release Print,* a members' newsletter, contains articles, announcements and classified advertisements.

CALIFORNIA (San Francisco)

GOETHE INSTITUTE SAN FRANCISCO LIBRARY
530 Bush Street
San Francisco, CA 94108-3689
(415) 391-0370
Fax: (415) 391-8715
Telex: 650 311 0267 MCI UW

CALIFORNIA (San Francisco H)

Dr. Barbara Bernhart (Librarian)

Contact: Librarian (415/391-0428)
Services: Government agency; library. Videotape collection maintained primarily for research purposes and free loan to educational institutions.
Description: German language and culture. Materials cover: German cities, customs and landscapes; social and historical topics; literature, art, music, and dance.
Size & Elements: Videotape: 3/4" and VHS (200 videotapes; NTSC and PAL).
Cataloging: Card catalogs; published catalogs; computerized cataloging in preparation; research library.
Access: Available to the public for viewing on a first-come, first-served basis, and to educational institutions for free loan (shipping fees charged). Loan requests must be submitted in writing on official stationery. Research fees not charged. Limited research requests accepted by mail, telephone and in person (walk-in).
Rights: Full rights held to some material.
Licensing: Apply for information.
Restrictions: Most material subject to copyright restrictions and cannot be duplicated.
Viewing Facilities: Videotape (3/4" and VHS; PAL, SECAM and NTSC) (on a first-come, first-served basis or by reservation).
Duplication Facilities: None.

CALIFORNIA (San Francisco)

HOLOCAUST CENTER OF NORTHERN CALIFORNIA
639 14th Avenue
San Francisco, CA 94118
(415) 751-6040

Joel Neuberg (Executive Director)

Contact: Jacob Boas (Associate Director); Joel Neuberg
Services: Library; research center. Videotape collection maintained primarily for research and study purposes.
Description: Movies, documentaries, and instructional videotapes pertaining to the Holocaust (primarily off-air copies of television broadcasts, 1983-present). Personal interviews, local lectures and events have also been videotaped.
Size & Elements: Videotape: VHS and Betamax (500 videotapes; masters and viewing copies).
Cataloging: Inventory sheets.
Access: Open to the public. Research fees not charged. Research requests accepted by mail, telephone and in person.
Rights: Some rights held to some material.
Licensing: Not available for licensing or reuse.
Restrictions: Material not available for reuse; primarily for research.
Viewing Facilities: Videotape.
Duplication Facilities: Videotape (VHS and Betamax).

CALIFORNIA (San Francisco)

THE IMAGE BANK, SAN FRANCISCO
22 Battery Street, Suite 202
San Francisco, CA 94111
(415) 788-2208
Fax: (415) 392-6637

Contact: Carol Campbell
Territory: San Francisco.
Services: Exclusive marketing agent for Film Search, Inc. (q.v.).

CALIFORNIA (San Francisco)

LABOR VIDEO PROJECT
P.O. Box 5584
San Francisco, CA 94101
(415) 641-4440
Fax: (415) 566-5160

Contacts: Steve Zeltzer or Lee Heller (Producers)
Services: Film and videotape producer and distributor. Produces monthly cable television program. Videotapes and some films available for rental, duplication and reuse.

Description: Material relating to labor and labor unions. Subjects covered include: immigration, including interviews with undocumented workers; unemployment; railroad workers; health care workers, including on-the-job interviews, working conditions and the crisis in health care for working people; labor in El Salvador, including interviews with trade union leaders and footage of workers; gay and lesbian workers, including footage of labor contingents at gay and lesbian demonstrations in San Francisco and interviews with members of the Lesbian and Gay Labor Alliance; labor and the law, including interviews with lawyers representing workers and employers; a cannery workers' strike (Watsonville, California, 1986), with footage and interviews; labor and anti-intervention, including interviews with trade unionists who have visited the Philippines, Israel, South Africa, Great Britain, Japan and Nicaragua; "witch-hunts" against labor, including interviews with victims; homelessness, featuring interviews with homeless people; the CIA and the AFL-CIO, including interviews with and debates between unionists on labor and foreign policy, footage of labor demonstrations against CIA and AFL-CIO connections, and a press conference with Tom Kahn (AFL-CIO International Affairs Director).

Other subjects include: maritime workers, including reports and interviews on a shipyard workers' strike and a tugboat workers' strike; labor and the presidential elections of 1984 and 1988, with interviews, press conferences and television appearances; union-busting in the construction trades, with footage of a large demonstration and interviews with workers at demonstration; the construction of the Golden Gate Bridge, featuring interviews with unionists who worked on the bridge, footage of its construction, and a history of the labor movement in the 1930s; Palestinian workers, including interviews with workers and lawyers, and footage of a demonstration in San Francisco protesting Israel's treatment of Palestinian workers; the Histadrut (Israeli Trade Union Federation), with interviews on its relations with the AFL-CIO and connections with South Africa (including footage of South Africa showing investments owned by Histadrut); a San Francisco longshore workers boycott of South African goods; and a janitors' demonstration in the San Francisco Bay Area, with interviews.

Forty completed programs are available for rental. Also distributes films and videotapes produced by other organizations relating to South Africa and other countries.
Size & Elements: Film: 16mm (small amount). Videotape: 3/4"; primarily 1/2" (masters and viewing copies; 150 hours unedited footage, 40 completed titles).
Cataloging: Published catalog of programs and titles. Stock footage uncataloged.
Access: Open to the public. Completed programs available for rental. Stock footage available for duplication and reuse. Research fees not charged. Research requests accepted by telephone.
Rights: Full rights held to some material. Some rights held to all material. Additional clearances may be necessary in some cases if material is to be reused.
Licensing: Available for licensing and reuse. License fees charged.
Restrictions: None specified.
Viewing Facilities: Videotape.
Duplication Facilities: Videotape (3/4" and 1/2").

CALIFORNIA (San Francisco)

THE FITZ HUGH LUDLOW MEMORIAL LIBRARY
P.O. Box 640346
San Francisco, CA 94164

Michael R. Aldrich, Ph.D. (Curator)

Contact: Michael R. Aldrich, Ph.D.
Services: Library; museum; private collection. Material available to qualified researchers for in-house use only.
Description: Feature films, music videos, documentaries and news footage on drug-related issues, videotaped off San Francisco cable television (January 1986-present). Covers most drug and AIDS-related issues (1986-present); includes drug-related excerpts from several dramatic films; news coverage of the "Drug War" (1986-87); drug movies (1960s-1980s); drug-related music videos and recent drug-related documentaries, with special attention given to films on musicians and drugs.

Of particular interest are archival movies beginning with the "cigarette" movies of 1897, including: *Rube in an Opium Joint* (1905); *Trip to Berkeley* (1906); *For His Son* (1912); *Mystery of Leaping Fish* (1916); *High on the Range* (1929); *Assassin of Youth* (1935); *The Cocaine Fiends* (1936); *Reefer Madness* (1936); *Marijuana, Weed with Roots in Hell* (1937); *Hemp for Victory* (1942); and *Somewhere in Dreamland* (1946).
Size & Elements: Videotape: format and amount unspecified (viewing copies).

Cataloging: Computerized cataloging; research library.
Access: Not open to the public. Open to researchers, scholars and journalists only. For in-house use only. Research fees charged. Research requests accepted by mail and in person (by appointment only).
Rights: Most rights retained by original producers. Some rights held to some material. Rights status of most material not known. Additional clearances may be necessary in some cases if material is to be reused.
Licensing: Apply for information. License fees charged on a case-by-case basis.
Restrictions: Most material has been videotaped off cable television and cannot be used for commercial purposes; rights retained by original producers.
Viewing Facilities: Videotape viewing can be arranged.
Duplication Facilities: None.
Related Materials: Extensive collection of drug literature, history, research papers, art, artifacts, drug-related illustrations and images.

CALIFORNIA (San Francisco)

MULTI-FOCUS, INC.
1525 Franklin Street
San Francisco, CA 94109
(415) 673-5100
(800) 821-0514 (orders)
Fax: (415) 928-8284

Winnie McIlvenna (Executive Director)

Contact: Renee Jone (Film Booking Department)
Services: Educational film and videotape distributor. Material available for rental and purchase for use in an educational context only. Selected titles are available for reuse and broadcast.
Description: Established ca. 1976. Distributes film, videotapes, slides and filmstrips on human sexuality to clinics, classrooms, community centers and medical facilities.

Subjects covered include abortion, AIDS, anatomy, bisexuality, childbirth, erotica, heterosexuality, homosexuality (male and female), humor and satire, incest, masturbation, multiple partners, physiology, prostitution, sex and disability, sex and later life, sex and pregnancy, sex roles, sex therapy, sexuality, teenage sexuality, touch and massage, vasectomy, and women's issues.
Size & Elements: Film: 16mm. Videotape: 3/4", VHS and Betamax (viewing copies, some transferred from film). (Approx. 300 titles total).
Cataloging: Published catalogs.
Access: Not open to the public. Open to researchers and scholars. Available for use in an educational context (i.e., clinics, classrooms, community centers and medical facilities). Maintained for distribution and rental rather than for research or reuse. Research requests accepted by mail and telephone.
Rights: Some rights held to some material. Additional clearances may be necessary in some cases if material is to be reused.
Licensing: Some titles available for reuse and broadcast. In cases where no rights are held to material, referrals to filmmaker or producer who holds the rights can be made. License fees charged.
Restrictions: Restrictions apply to certain titles.
Viewing Facilities: Videotape (VHS).
Duplication Facilities: None.

CALIFORNIA (San Francisco)

NAN HAI (U.S.A.) CO., INC.
644 Broadway, Suite 403
San Francisco, CA 94133
(415) 398-6671
Fax: (415) 433-4016
Telex: 880035 WE SFO

Shi Xu Dong (Chairman of the Board and President)

Contact: Jinglu Yu (Manager)
Services: Film and videotape distributor. Material available for rental and purchase.
Description: Films and videotapes produced or coproduced by Nan Hai Film Co., Beijing, China; television dramas; Chinese operas; variety shows; documentaries; and travelogues. Distributes "the most complete collection of videotapes from China in the United States."

Titles include: *New Year Sacrifice; The Lin Family Shop; Call of the Home Village; Xu Mao and His Daughters; Red Peony; Love on Lushan Mountain; The True Story of Ah Q; The Xi'an Incident; Along the Silk Road; The Family; Sunset Street; Qiu Jin — A Revolutionary; Regret for the Past; The Red Guards on Lake Hunghu; Hua Tuo and Cao Cao; Trouble Arises at Home; A Back-Lit Picture; The Undaunted Wu Dang; Bubbling Spring; Pride's Deadly Fury; Pomegranate Flower; My Memories of Old Beijing; The Unfinished Chess Game; The Tortuous Mountain Path; The Legend of "Clay-Figurine Chang"; Life; Yellow Earth; Women Generals of the Yang Family; Complaints at the Qing Count; The Presumptuous Mr. Nobody; Bi Sheng — The Inventor of Movable Type; Woman Basketball Player No. 5;* and *Ginseng Fruit.*

Other titles include: *The Last Emperor of China — Pu Yi* (Wang Xui Shan), a documentary on his life and times; *Amazing Marriage Customs,* on the traditions of China's different nationalities; *The Great Wall* (Peter Wang), on the reunion of a Chinese American family from California with their relatives from Beijing after a thirty-year separation; and *Spiritual Boxing,* on "hard" or "martial art" Qigong.
Size & Elements: Film: format and amount unspecified (release prints). Videotape: format and amount unspecified (masters and viewing copies).
Cataloging: Release sheets; brochures.
Access: Available for rental and purchase. Requests accepted by mail and telephone.
Rights: Full rights held to some material. Some rights held to all material. Some rights held to some material.
Licensing: Not available for licensing or reuse.
Restrictions: Not available for duplication, licensing or reuse.
Viewing Facilities: Videotape.
Duplication Facilities: Videotape (3/4" and 1/2").

CALIFORNIA (San Francisco)

NATIONAL ASIAN AMERICAN TELECOMMUNICATIONS ASSOCIATION
CROSSCURRENT MEDIA
346 Ninth Street, 2nd Floor
San Francisco, CA 94103
(415) 552-9550
(415) 863-0814

Contact: Chrys Fa (Distribution Coordinator)
Services: Media organization; videotape distributor. Videotapes available for rental, preview and purchase.
Description: CrossCurrent Media is a nonprofit educational service of the National Asian American Telecommunications Association (NAATA), a nationwide organization of professional and community media individuals and organizations. By assisting in the creation, production and distribution of media projects, NAATA provides resources and information on Asian American media and related issues for the general public.

Titles include: *A Dollar A Day, Ten Cents A Dance* (Geoffrey Dunn and Mark Schwartz), chronicling the history of the more than 100,000 "Pinoys" (Filipino Americans) who immigrated to California between 1924 and 1935 to work the state's farmlands; *East of Occidental* (Maria Gargiulo), on Seattle's International District, the home of Chinese, Japanese and Filipino Americans; *In No One's Shadow: Filipinos in America* (Naomi and Antonio De Castro); *Monterey's Boat People* (Spencer Nakasako and Vincent DiGirolamo), on the tensions between the established Italian fishing community and recently arrived Vietnamese fishermen on California's Monterey Peninsula; *The New Puritans: The Sikhs of Yuba City* (Ritu Sarin and Tenzing Sonam), on a Sikh community in northern California; *The Price You Pay* (Christine Keyser), on Southeast Asian refugees in the United States; *The Fall of the I-Hotel* (Curtis Choy), on the fight to save a hotel in Manilatown, San Francisco; *Survivors: 40 Years After Hiroshima* (Frances Politeo and Steven Okazaki), in which nuclear survivors speak for themselves about what happened on the day of the bombing; *Unfinished Business: The Japanese American Internment Camps* (Steven Okazaki); *Dim Sum Take-Out* (Wayne Wang), on one woman from Chinatown and her personal issues of independence and sexuality; *Q It Up* (Chinatown Youth Center), a drama about young people and drugs; *With Silk Wings: Asian American Women at Work* (Loni Ding and Spencer Nakasako), a four-part series; and *Slaying the Dragon* (Deborah Gee), on the roles and images of Asian women promulgated by the Hollywood film industry and network television over the past 50 years.
Size & Elements: Videotape: 3/4" and VHS (22 videotapes).
Cataloging: Published catalog.
Access: Available for rental, preview and purchase. Requests accepted by mail and telephone.
Rights: Apply for information.

CALIFORNIA (San Francisco N)

Licensing: Apply for information.
Restrictions: None specified.
Viewing Facilities: None.
Duplication Facilities: None.
Related Materials: Audiocassettes.

CALIFORNIA (San Francisco)

NATIONAL ASSOCIATION OF RADIATION SURVIVORS
942 Market Street, Suite 710
San Francisco, CA 94102
(415) 397-2001

T. Wade Randlett (Administrative Director)

Contact: T. Wade Randlett
Services: Nonprofit organization. Videotape library available to the public.
Description: Atomic test shots.
Size & Elements: Videotape: VHS (6 titles).
Cataloging: None specified.
Access: Available to the public; requests accepted by mail.
Rights: Full rights held to all material.
Licensing: License fees charged in some cases. Duplication and shipping fees charged.
Restrictions: None specified.
Viewing Facilities: None.
Duplication Facilities: None.

CALIFORNIA (San Francisco)

NEW AMERICAN MAKERS
442 Shotwell Street
San Francisco, CA 94110
(415) 695-2904

Joanne Kelly (Co-Director)

Contact: Joanne Kelly
Services: Videotape and public television producer; distributor; videotape archives. Open to the public. Material for in-house viewing only.
Description: Nonprofit organization maintaining the videotape archives originally collected by Video Free America, a pioneering independent West Coast video production, distribution and exhibition group. NAM now handles distribution, exhibition and archival activities; VFA, a separate organization, is now exclusively involved in production.

Collection primarily contains video works screened in the VFA exhibition series (1970-present). Most material is regional (West Coast) video art, but some documentary productions are held. Approximately 10% of the work in the collection was produced at VFA, the remainder elsewhere. Videotapes from three early San Francisco-based video collectives (TVTV, Ant Farm and Optic Nerve) are also held. Genres include: experimental television; dance video; documentation of performance art and theater; and video art.
Size & Elements: Videotape: 3/4" (approx. 250 titles). Some material was originated on 1/2" open reel and early 1" formats and has since been transferred to 3/4".
Cataloging: Card catalogs.
Access: Open to the public. For in-house viewing only. Research fees not charged. Research requests accepted by mail, telephone and in person (by appointment only).
Rights: Some rights held to some material. Most rights retained by original producers or artists. Can refer inquiries regarding reuse to original producers and artists.
Licensing: License fees charged in some cases (for material produced by VFA).
Restrictions: None specified.
Viewing Facilities: Videotape.
Duplication Facilities: Videotape (3/4", VHS, Betamax and 1/2" open reel).

CALIFORNIA (San Francisco)

NEW LANGTON ARTS
1246 Folsom Street
San Francisco, CA 94103
(415) 626-5416

Contacts: Shauna O'Donnell (Office Manager); Nayland Blake (Program Coordinator)
Services: Arts organization. Videotape collection open to researchers and scholars only; not available for reuse.
Description: Videotapes (1985-present) by established and emerging artists. These videotapes are featured in their video screening room for one month before becoming part of the permanent collection. Langton is also beginning to build a videotape archives documenting performances in its space.
Size & Elements: Videotape: 3/4" and 1/2" (20 videotapes; viewing copies).
Cataloging: List of videotapes.
Access: Open to researchers and scholars only. Research fees not charged. Research requests accepted by mail, telephone and in person (by appointment only).
Rights: Some rights held to some material.
Licensing: Not available for licensing or reuse.
Restrictions: Reuse not permitted.
Viewing Facilities: Videotape (3/4" and VHS; viewing room).
Duplication Facilities: None.
Related Materials: Audiotape archives of all writer-in-residency programs, new music concerts, lectures and occasional performances (1975-present).

CALIFORNIA (San Francisco)

POSTCARDS ASSOCIATES
350 Townsend Street, Suite 203
San Francisco, CA 94107
(415) 648-8942
(415) 495-3328 (messages only)

Dana W. Atchley (Director)

Contact: Dana W. Atchley
Services: Videotape archives; producer; stock footage sales library.
Description: Videotapes featuring American roadside attractions, scenic vistas, nostalgia, portraits of unusual people, strange events, art, architecture, signs, collections and museums, souvenirs, animals, plants, American myths and legends, and original comedy. Footage was shot primarily between 1980-87; some material was shot in the 1930s-40s and 1970-80.

Titles include: *Alligator Man; American Pet Motel; Bald Headed Men of America; Balloons; Big Chief Diner; Cadillac Ranch; Car Cancer; Christo's Surrounding Islands; Corn Palace; Dan Bailey's Fly Shop; Forest Queen Mine; Gator Wrestler; Hi Jolly's Tomb; House of Enchantment; IQ Zoo; Jello Wrestling; Love Motel; Police Hall of Fame; Randy's Donut; Rattlesnakes and Ashtrays; Stick Your Head Through Here; Teapot Gas; Turkey Races;* and *Suburban Theater.*
Size & Elements: Videotape: 3/4" (800 videotapes; averaging 1 min. in length).
Cataloging: Computerized cataloging available to researchers and staff; shot lists.
Access: Available to the public for duplication, licensing and reuse. For in-house use only. Research fees charged. Research requests accepted by mail, telephone and in person (by appointment only).
Rights: Full rights held to all material. Additional clearances may be necessary in some cases if material is to be reused.
Licensing: Available for licensing and reuse. License fees charged.
Restrictions: None specified.
Viewing Facilities: Videotape (1", Betacam, 3/4" and VHS).
Duplication Facilities: Videotape (1", Betacam, 3/4" and VHS).

CALIFORNIA (San Francisco)

PREVIEW MEDIA
1160 Battery Street, Suite 100
San Francisco, CA 94111
(800) 992-8439
(415) 397-2494
Fax: (415) 421-4982

Jim Hornthal (President)

Contacts: Daniel Young (Producer); Katie Walsh (Production Assistant)
Services: Videotape producer. Footage available to professional industry users for duplication, licensing and reuse. Travel videotapes available to the public for purchase.
Description: Large library of travel-related footage covering all areas of the

world. Areas of special strength include Hawaii, the Pacific area, the United States, Canada and Mexico (345 destinations total). Continuously growing collection emphasizes action, adventure, beauty shots, local culture, "mood" scenes, people, scenics and wildlife. Coverage includes lifestyles; honeymoons; sports; hotels; cruises; and specialty shots, including dude ranches, helicopter tours and houseboating.

International footage includes: Acapulco, the Amazon, Athens, Bahamas, Baja California (whale-watching); Barbados, Barcelona; Belize; Bermuda; Cabo San Lucas (Mexico); Cairo; Calgary; Canada (heli-hiking); Cancun (Mexico); Chile; China; China by train (the Dynasty Express); Costa del Sol; Costa Rica; Dominican Republic; Dublin; Egyptian Sinai; England (countryside); Fiji; Florence, French Riviera; France (wine country); Galapagos Islands; Greek islands (cruise); Grenada; Grenadines (cruise); Guadalajara; Hawaii (cruise); Hong Kong; Ireland (countryside); Israel; Ixtapa-Zihuatanejo; Jamaica; London; Mazatlan; Mexico City; Mexico (cruise); Netherlands Antilles; New Zealand (North and South Islands); Nile River (cruise); Norway (cruise); Panama Canal (cruise); Peru; Puerto Vallarta; Puerto Rico: Rhine (cruise); Rome and the wine region; St. Lucia; St. Moritz; St. Vincent; Singapore; Spain (Madrid and Seville); Tahiti; Taiwan; Toronto; Vancouver (B.C.); Venice (Italy); and Victoria (B.C.).

Domestic destinations include: Alaska (cruise); Alaska (wilderness); Amish country; Amtrak; Anchorage and the Kenai Peninsula (Alaska); antebellum plantations; Arizona (dude ranches); Aspen and Vail (Colorado); Atlanta; Atlantic City; Baltimore; Baton Rouge; Blue Ridge Mountains; Big Sur and Hearst Castle (California); California (gold country); Cape Cod (Mass.) and Newport (R.I.) bus tour; Carolina coast; Catalina and Long Beach (Calif.); Charleston (S.C.); Chicago; Chesapeake and Delmarva; Cochise County (Arizona); Colorado River (rafting); Colorado (spring skiing); Connecticut (winter); Dallas; Florida Panhandle coast; Grand Canyon (summer and winter); Great Smoky Mountains; Gulf Shores; Honolulu; Indiana (back roads); Jackson Hole (Wyoming); Jersey Shore; Key West; Knoxville; Kona Coast (Hawaii); Lahaina and Kaanapali (Hawaii); Lake Powell (houseboating); Lake Tahoe; Las Vegas; Louisiana (bayou country); Los Angeles and Hollywood; Mackinac Island (Michigan); Maui; Mendocino Coast (California); Miami Beach; Midwest ski vacations; Minnesota (lake country); Mississippi River (cruise); Monterey (California); Napa (wine region); Nashville; New England (fall colors); New Orleans; New Mexico (Albuquerque and Taos); New York City; Newport (Rhode Island); Niagara Falls; Northwest Oregon; Oahu; Orlando; Ozark Mountains; Palm Springs; Pennsylvania Dutch Country; Philadelphia; Phoenix and Scottsdale (Arizona); Poconos; Poipu; Reno; Salem (Mass.) on Halloween; San Antonio; San Diego; San Francisco; San Juan Islands; St. Augustine, Florida; St. Paul (Winter Carnival); Santa Barbara; Santa Fe and Taos (New Mexico); Savannah and Hilton Head Island; Seattle; South Padre Island (Texas); Southern California (deserts); Southwest Florida (Naples and Marcos Island); Sun Valley (Idaho); Tampa and St. Petersburg (Florida); Tucson; Utah (skiing); Vermont (skiing); Waikiki; Washington (D.C.); West Palm Beach; Williamsburg (Virginia); Wisconsin (Door County); Yellowstone National Park; and Yosemite National Park.

NTN Lifestyle Series includes adventure getaways; camping tips; family cruises; family theme parks; fishing getaways; gourmet getaways; guest ranches; health spas; honeymoon hot spots; horseback getaways; houseboat vacations; introduction to cruising; mini-cruises; national parks; recreational vehicle (RV) vacations; sailing adventures; tennis camps; and "yuppie tours."

Rendezvous Travel Videos (approx. 150 videotapes). Completed videotapes on destinations listed above, each 8 to 12 min. Available to the public for purchase.
Size & Elements: Videotape: 1", Betacam and 3/4" (1,800 hours; masters and viewing copies); VHS (approx. 150 completed videotapes; viewing copies).
Cataloging: Published catalog.
Access: Footage available to professional industry users for duplication and reuse. Completed videotapes available to the public for purchase. Research fees charged. Research requests accepted by telephone and in person (by appointment only).
Rights: Full rights held to all material.
Licensing: Available to professional industry users for licensing and reuse. License fees charged.
Restrictions: None specified.
Viewing Facilities: Videotape (3/4" and 1/2").
Duplication Facilities: Videotape (1", 3/4" and 1/2").

CALIFORNIA (San Francisco)

SAN FRANCISCO ACADEMY OF COMIC ART LIBRARY
2850 Ulloa
San Francisco, CA 94116

(415) 681-1737

Bill Blackbeard (Director)

Contact: Bill Blackbeard
Services: Library. Videotape collection available to the public for research and duplication, subject to restrictions.
Description: Reference collection contains animated cartoons (1920s-present) and examples of other kinds of dramatic and comic motion pictures; compiled by videotaping off-air.
Size & Elements: Videotape: VHS (several hundred videotapes).
Cataloging: Materials shelved according to subject area.
Access: Open to the public. Available for research. Research fees not charged. Research requests accepted by telephone and in person (walk-in).
Rights: No rights held to any material. All rights retained by original producers.
Licensing: Apply for information.
Restrictions: Not available for reuse.
Viewing Facilities: Videotape (VHS).
Duplication Facilities: None.

CALIFORNIA (San Francisco)

SAN FRANCISCO BAY AREA TELEVISION NEWS ARCHIVES
SAN FRANCISCO STATE UNIVERSITY
J. PAUL LEONARD LIBRARY
1630 Holloway Avenue
San Francisco, CA 94132
(415) 338-1856

Olive James (Library Director)
Helene Whitson (Special Collections Librarian/Archivist)

Contact: Helene Whitson
Services: University library; archives. Television newsfilm and documentary collection maintained primarily for research and scholarly use. Footage possibly available for licensing and reuse, subject to clearance by television stations.

Description: Archives is a unit of the J. Paul Leonard Library devoted to the identification, acquisition, organization, preservation and dissemination of film and videotape materials relating to the portrayal of San Francisco Bay Area life. Holds television news and documentary film and videotape from the San Francisco Bay Area. Two major collections are held:

KQED Film Archive. Approximately 1.8 million feet of 16mm news and documentary film produced by educational television station KQED (1967-80; some documentary film predates 1967). Collection is primarily outtakes and trims; some edited programs are held.

KQED's programs cover a broad spectrum of subject areas and include programs in the arts, the humanities, the social and natural sciences. Includes interviews with San Francisco Mayors Joseph Alioto, George Moscone and Dianne Feinstein; labor leader Harry Bridges; poets Allen Ginsberg and Charles Olson; dramatist Lillian Hellman; photographers Dorothea Lange and Edward Weston; and composer Darius Milhaud. Covers social and political issues, including California student uprisings in the 1960s; Patricia Hearst and the Symbionese Liberation Army; Cambodia; the Iran crisis; the Black Panther Party; gay rights and activities, including the assassinations of George Moscone and Harvey Milk; Cesar Chávez and the United Farm Workers; youth and drugs; droughts and water pollution. Artistic and cultural programming includes a concert by the Griller String Quartet, two programs on calligraphy and on Japanese brush painting, and science programs describing environmental problems in the modern world.

KPIX Library. Approximately 5 to 8 million feet of 16mm news and documentary film produced by KPIX, San Francisco's CBS affiliate and the oldest television station in Northern California (1948-80). Contains outtakes, trims and edited programs; not presently available to the public.

In addition to collecting local television news footage, the Archives plans to include production information from the stations, as well as other support materials documenting the creation of the news footage; locally produced film, materials from private collections, corporations, associations and clubs; and oral histories of filmmakers and television station personnel.

Size & Elements: Film: 16mm (approx. 10 million feet; 4,000 cans in KQED Film Archives). Videotape: 1/2" (over 60 videotapes, each 2 hours; transfers from film in KQED Film Archives).

Cataloging: KQED collection has subject card catalog prepared by television station and cross-reference date index prepared by Archives staff. KPIX collection has card catalog prepared by the station.

Access: For in-house use only. "Since we are an academic institution, our collection is mainly for faculty and students, but we welcome inquiries from researchers and scholars." Research fees not charged at this time, but will be charged in the future. Research requests accepted by mail, telephone and in person (walk-in and by appointment; appointments preferred). Archives lacks staff to do research for patrons.

Rights: No rights held to any material. All rights retained by television stations.

Licensing: Users who wish to reproduce material must make arrangements with television stations.

Restrictions: None specified.

Viewing Facilities: Film (Cinescan film viewer); videotape (VHS).

Duplication Facilities: None.

CALIFORNIA (San Francisco)

SAN FRANCISCO MARITIME NATIONAL HISTORICAL PARK
J. PORTER SHAW LIBRARY
Building E, 3rd Floor
Fort Mason
San Francisco, CA 94123
(415) 556-9870

David Hull (Principal Librarian)

Contact: Irene Stachura (Reference Librarian)
Services: National museum; library. Film and videotape material available for licensing and reuse, subject to restrictions.
Description: Collects and preserves films and videotapes about the people, ships and industries that helped shape the development of the Pacific Coast from California to Alaska. Collection holdings range from untitled footage to RKO theatrical short subjects and contemporary television documentaries.

Earliest material in the collection (1905) depicts a view of Market Street (San Francisco) from a moving trolley car. Six films deal with Alaskan packing vessels and canneries: *Ice Kist Treasures,* made for the Alaska Salmon Co. (ca. 1930-35) depicts a voyage on a cannery vessel; *Last of the Windships* (1934) chronicles the last voyage of the Packers Association's vessels; *Alaska Packers*

(1928), photographed by "Uncle Gus"; untitled footage from 1917 shows the fleet in both San Francisco and Alaska.

Another group of related titles concern the restoration of the museum ship Balclutha (*Saga of a Ship,* ca. 1955) and an interview with its captain, Fred Klebingat. *Around the Horn in a Square-Rigger,* shot by Alan Villiers of the four-masted bark Parma and *Bucking the Billows,* a race between a Gloucester fishing schooner and a Nova Scotian fishing schooner both show sailing in the 1930s. Other topics covered include: San Francisco Bay ferries (ca. 1935-50); films of other vessels such as steam tugs, full riggers, brigs and schooners; and a typical lumber operation on the Mendocino Coast (Caspar Lumber Co.).

Size & Elements: Film: 35mm (1 title); 16mm (31 titles). Videotape (3 titles). Films range from 3 to 60 min. in length.
Cataloging: Research library.
Access: Open to the public. Research fees not charged. Research requests accepted by mail, telephone and in person, on a limited-time basis.
Rights: Some rights held to some material.
Licensing: Available for licensing and reuse, subject to restrictions. License and usage fees charged in some cases.
Restrictions: Restrictions apply to licensing and reuse.
Viewing Facilities: None.
Duplication Facilities: None.

CALIFORNIA (San Francisco)

SHANTI PROJECT
PUBLIC EDUCATION PROGRAM
525 Howard Street
San Francisco, CA 94105
(415) 777-2273

Contact: Greg Day (Community Relations Director, Public Education Program)
Services: Nonprofit organization. Videotape material available for purchase.
Description: Provides support services to people with AIDS. Videotape collection consists of a 44-hour training program designed to instruct volunteers how to counsel people with AIDS and their loved ones. These videotapes are primarily sold to organizations who want to train volunteer groups in their own communities.
Size & Elements: Videotape: VHS (44 hours, 22 titles).
Cataloging: None.
Access: Available for purchase.
Rights: Full rights held to all material.
Licensing: Apply for information.
Restrictions: None specified.
Viewing Facilities: None.
Duplication Facilities: None.

CALIFORNIA (San Francisco)

STIMULUS
P.O. Box 11621
San Francisco, CA 94101
(415) 558-8339

Grant Johnson (General Manager)

Contact: Grant Johnson
Services: Videotape producer; commercial production house. Collection available to the public for duplication, licensing and reuse. Research services available.
Description: *Landscape-oriented footage.* Holds scenics and aerials of the Southwestern U.S., including Bryce Canyon, White Sands, Grand Canyon, most of the national parks in the area and Indian reservations; Hawaii; Europe, including France and Germany; and action footage of rafting.

Computer graphics. Includes LANDSAT (earth satellite) imagery, some processed by computer; computer terrain modeling (synthetic landscape models and computerized topographic maps); a computer-generated animated fly-through of Yosemite Valley; video effects generated with analog equipment, including decorative "video wallpaper" and various other types of computer-generated imagery.

Also produces educational and music programs.
Size & Elements: Videotape: Betacam and 3/4" (50 hours) (primarily 3/4", but currently shooting exclusively in Betacam).
Cataloging: Logs.
Access: Available to the public for duplication and reuse. Research fees not

charged. Research requests accepted by mail, telephone and in person (by appointment only).
Rights: Full rights held to all material. Additional clearances may be necessary in some cases (e.g., computer-generated imagery) if material is to be reused.
Licensing: Available for licensing and reuse, subject to restrictions. License fees charged.
Restrictions: Additional clearances may be necessary for reuse of computer-generated imagery.
Viewing Facilities: Videotape (Betacam, 3/4" and VHS).
Duplication Facilities: Videotape (Betacam, 3/4" and VHS).

CALIFORNIA (San Francisco)

SURVIVAL RESEARCH LABORATORIES
1458C San Bruno Avenue
San Francisco, CA 94110
(415) 821-4544

Contact: Jonathan Reiss (Producer)
Services: Film and videotape producer and distributor. Videotapes available for purchase; stock footage available for licensing and reuse.
Description: Conceived and founded by Mark Pauline in November, 1978. Matt Heckert joined as a full-time member in 1981; Eric Werner in 1982. Since its inception, SRL has served as a means to facilitate the staging of a unique type of performance event. The shows feature no human performers whatsoever, being organized entirely around the interactions of menacingly reconstructed industrial or scientific equipment and a wide variety of "special effects" devices. In each event a selection of these performance machines, accompanied by a suitable soundtrack, is actuated remotely through centralized control panels, acts autonomously, or is operated by assistants under the direction of the three SRL members, in order to develop themes of socio-political satire.

Examples of performances documented on videotape include: *Misfortunes of Desire: Enacted in an Imaginary Location Symbolizing Everything Worth Having* (Shea Stadium parking lot, Queens, N.Y., May 19, 1988); *Delusions of Expediency: How To Avoid Responsibility For Social Disintegration By Acting Without Principle Under the Pretences of Utility* (Lot, corner Townsend and Eighth Sts., San Francisco, Calif., January 30, 1987); and *Deliberately False Statements: A Combination of Tricks and Illusions Guaranteed to Expose Shrewd Manipulations of Fact* (Folsom and Main Sts., San Francisco, Calif., October 6, 1985).

Edited compilations include: *Virtues of Negative Fascination,* documenting five mechanized performances (1985-86); *A Scenic Harvest From the Kingdom of Pain,* with three performances (1983-84); and a third compilation, forthcoming. Also available is *A Bitter Message of Hopeless Grief* (Jonathan Reiss, 1988, 13 min., 16mm), a fractured narrative featuring large anthropomorphic robots constructed by SRL and the first film to exclusively feature SRL machines.
Size & Elements: Film: 16mm (1 title, 490 feet; release prints). Videotape: 1", Betacam and 3/4" (70 hours; 100 videotapes; masters and viewing copies). Three edited videotapes covering 18 performances are available.
Cataloging: Shot lists; release sheets.
Access: Not open to the public. Edited films and videotapes available for purchase. Footage available for duplication and reuse. Research fees charged in some cases. Research requests accepted by mail and telephone.
Rights: Full rights held to all material.
Licensing: Available for licensing and reuse. License fees charged.
Restrictions: None specified.
Viewing Facilities: Videotape (3/4" and VHS).
Duplication Facilities: Videotape (3/4" and VHS).
Related Materials: Photographic documentation.

CALIFORNIA (San Francisco)

TARGET VIDEO
(a subsidiary of Alpha, Inc.)
678 South Van Ness Avenue
San Francisco, CA 94110
(415) 863-0118
Fax: (415) 431-7595

Joe Rees (Director)

Contacts: Jon Rees; Petra Rees
Services: Videotape producer and distributor. Videotapes available for

purchase, licensing and reuse, subject to restrictions.
Description: Experimental, punk, new wave and avant-garde music and performance footage documenting events occurring chiefly in Northern California (1976-present). Holds edited shows, homevideo tapes (available for purchase) and thousands of hours of unedited footage. Homevideo releases include:

Performances. Dead Kennedys (Part I); Rank & File; Avengers (1978-79), with live performances of *We Are The One* and *Car Crash; Bauhaus: Live at the University of London* and *Chrome; Live 79,* with The Damned; *Hardcore Volume I,* with Black Flag, Code of Honor, Toxic Reasons, D.O.A., Flipper, M.D.C. and Sex Pistols; *Hardcore Volume II,* with Sleepers, Germs, Bad Brains, Circle Jerks and TSOL; *Hardcore Volume III,* with Negative Trend, the Avengers, Screamers, Weirdos and Dead Kennedys; *Screamers: Live in San Francisco, September 1978; Iggy Pop: Live in San Francisco, 81; Was Are/Will Be* (1985) and *Slow Fire* (1986), with the Paul Dresher Ensemble; *The Litanies of Satan,* featuring Diamanda Galas; *Throbbing Gristle: Live at Kezar; Toxic Reasons; Tuxedomoon: Four Major Events; Zev: Six Examples; Black Flag: T.V. Party; A Free Concert at the Napa State Hospital,* with the Cramps and Zev; *Crucifix and M.D.C. (Millions of Dead Cops): Compilation; Live at Target* (1980), with Factrix, Nervous Gender, Zev and Flipper; *A Scenic Harvest From the Kingdom of Pain* (1983-84), documenting three performances by Survival Research Laboratories (SRL); *Seven Machine Performances* (1979-82), documenting seven SRL performances (1979-82); *Virtues of Negative Fascination: Five Mechanized Performances by S.R.L. 1985-86;* and *Dash Thirty Dash,* with Penelope Houston.

Underground Forces 1. Contains an early public performance by Mark Pauline; the Dead Kennedys playing *California Über Alles* (1978); a performance by Johanna Went (1979); the Bush Tetras playing *Too Many Creeps* (1979); the New York band DNA in performance (1980); Devo videotaped live at the Phoenix Theater in Petaluma, Calif. (1981); the Mutants at Target Studios (1980); Bob, a San Francisco band, performing two songs; Teenage Jesus and the Jerks live at Max's Kansas City, New York (1979); an early rehearsal by Rank & File; and a performance by Tuxedomoon.

Underground Forces 2. Includes Siouxsie and the Banshees performing *Hong Kong Garden* (1980); footage from the Sex Pistols' last performance in San Francisco (1980); a performance by Judy Nylon at her home in London; and a live performance by Young Marble Giants.

Underground Forces 3. Includes performances by Germs; Screamers; John Cooper Clarke; The Raybeats, live in Berkeley, Calif.; Flipper, performing *Low Rider;* Gun Club, a San Francisco band, in performance; the Vancouver band D.O.A.; and Throbbing Gristle at their last performance in Kezar Stadium, San Francisco. Also includes a sequence of a punk skateboard team skating to the music of the Raybeats (1981).

Underground Forces 4. Includes performances by Dead Kennedys (1981); Cramps (1981); Black Flag performing *Rise Above* (1981); Mark Pauline (1981); Sick Pleasure (later to reform into the less violent Code of Honor); Gang of Four performing *Damaged Goods;* Bauhaus, performing at the University of London (1980); a press conference by Public Image Ltd. in San Francisco (1980); and a performance by the Bush Tetras at Tier 3 in New York (1980).

Underground Forces 5. Includes performances by Code of Honor (1982); Theater of Hate; D.A.F.; two songs by X, *White Girl* and *Your Phone Is Off the Hook;* two songs by Circle Jerks; T.S.O.L.; Bad Brains; Mark Pauline; Tuxedomoon; and a performance by and TV party with Black Flag (1982).

Underground Forces 6. Includes performances by Dead Kennedys (1982); Cramps; Iggy Pop; Rank and File; Flipper, performing *Nothing;* Appliances; The Avengers, performing *The American In Me;* and Iggy Pop.

Underground Forces 7. Includes a performance by Survival Research Laboratories (Nov. 13, 1982); and performances by Channel 3, Exploited, M.D.K., Minimal Man, and Crucifix.

Underground Forces 8. Includes performances by Zev; Mutants; Minimal Man; Mau Maus; Circle Jerks; and Toxic Reasons.

Memorable events include a performance by The Cramps at Napa State Hospital, a Northern California psychiatric facility; the punk group Crime at San Quentin Prison; an interview with Charles Manson; and many hours of performances by Survival Research Laboratories.

Performers, groups and acts include Abwarts, Ads, Alleycats, Appliances, Avengers, Bad Brains, Bags, Bauhaus, Bay of Pigs, Beauty Killers, Joseph Beuys, Before, Jello Biafra, Black Flag, Blessed, Blondie, Blurt, Bob, B-People, Brian Brain, James Brown, Bush Tetras, Jim Carroll, Castration Squad, Catholic Discipline, Cavellini, Chick A Diesels, James Chance, Christian Lunch, Chrome, Circle Jerks, City X, John Cooper Clarke, Clash, Code of Honor, Contortions, Contractions, Controllers, Cramps, Crime, Cripples, Crucifix, Damned, dBs, Dead Boys, Dead Kennedys, Death Review, Devo, D.A.F., Dickies, Dils, Dinettes, Dishrags, DNA, DOA, Paul Dresher, DV8,

Enemy, Erasers, Exploited, Eye Protection, Factrix, Feederz, Female Hands, Fleshapoids, Flesheaters, Flipper, Flyboys, Flying Lizards, Fuck Ups, Diamanda Galas, Gang of Four, Germs, Geza X, Geza X and the Mommymen, Go-Gos, Peter Gordon, Gun Club, Jacques Higelin, Humans, Hüsker Du, Iggy Pop, Il Ya Volkswagen, Impatient Youth, Imposters, Indoor Life, Insults, The Jam, Jane Doe, Jayne County, John Doe, Lenny Kaye, KGB, Killing Joke, K-Tels, Lewd, Liars, Local Color, Los Microwaves, Lounge Lizards, Lydia Lunch, Johnny Lydon, Madama La Rue, Mau Maus, Meat Puppets, Members, Mentors, Middle Class, Minimal Man, Magazzini Criminali, MDK, Minutemen, Millions of Dead Cops (M.D.C.); Mum Brothers, Mutants, MX-80, Naked City, Nash the Slash, Negative Trend, Nervous Gender, Nervous Surgeons, No Alternative, No Magazine, NOIA, No Sisters, Noh Mercy, Nuns, Judy Nylon, Offs, Panther Burns, Pink Section, Plastics, Plugz, Pointed Sticks, Public Image Ltd., Rad Command, RAF Punks, Ramones, Rank & File, Rats, Raybeats, Readymades, Rebels, Red Rockers, Rockabilly Rebels, Sapho, Saccharine Trust, Screamers, Seizure, Selecter, Sex Pistols, Sic Pleasure, Silence Hospital, Silvertone, Siouxsie & The Banshees, Sham 69, Situations, Sleepers, Sonic Youth, The Sound, Soul Rebels, SSI, SST, Karl Stewart, Stiff Little Fingers, Stingers, Stranglers, Subhumans, Suburban Lawns, Survival Research Laboratories (Mark Pauline, Matthew Heckart, Eric Werner), SVT, SWA, Symptoms, Talking Heads, Snuky Tate, Teen Idles, Teenage Fakes, Teenage Jesus & The Jerks, Theatre of Hate, Throbbing Gristle, Times 5, Tools, Touchtones, Toxic Reasons, Tubes, Tuff Darts, Tuxedomoon, Tredie Tilstand, T.S.O.L., Ultrasheen, UK Decay, Units, Uns, UXA, Silke Verlain, Michael Valeur, Sid Vicious, VIPs, VKTMS, VS., Weirdos, Wire, Johanna Went, Wolverines, Wounds, X, X-Mal Deutschland, Xiles, XTC, Yoel, Young Canadians, Young Marble Giants, Zeros, and Zev.

Film holdings document events from the mid-1970s. Until approximately 1984, all events were recorded on 3/4" videotape; since that time, Betacam has been the format of choice.
Size & Elements: Film: 16mm and Super 8mm (approx. 5 to 6 hours). Videotape: Betacam and 3/4" (400 events total, 38 hours edited shows, 24 homevideo tapes, thousands of hours unedited footage; masters and time-coded viewing copies).
Cataloging: Published catalog; press kit with list of events and performers.
Access: Not open to the public. Available for duplication and reuse, subject to restrictions. Research fees charged. Research requests accepted by mail and telephone. Viewing copies (1/2" formats) can be furnished to requesters at cost.
Rights: Full rights held to most material. Additional clearances may be necessary in some cases if material is to be reused.
Licensing: Most material available for licensing and reuse, subject to restrictions. License fees charged.
Restrictions: Some material (especially music) requires additional clearances for reuse.
Viewing Facilities: None.
Duplication Facilities: Videotape (all formats; PAL and SECAM standards conversion).

CALIFORNIA (San Francisco)

TRAILERS ON TAPE
1554 Grove Street
San Francisco, CA 94117
(415) 921-8273 (Mon.-Sat., 11am-2pm, PST)

Bill Longen (Owner and President)

Contact: Bill Longen
Services: Film and videotape archives; producer; distributor; private collection. Not open to the public. Videotapes available for purchase. Footage available for duplication, licensing and reuse.
Description: Approximately 4,000 classic movie trailers (previews of coming attractions) (1910s to late 1960s). Produces collections of trailers, grouped by specific genres. Materials available to the homevideo consumer comprise only a small portion of the total library. Some collections offered are:

Academy Awards: Oscar's Best. Trailers to Hollywood's award-winning "Best Pictures" from the true Golden Era of the movies, including: *Wings* (1927); *Ben-Hur* (1959); *Bridge on the River Kwai; On The Waterfront; The Greatest Show on Earth;* and *The Lost Weekend.*

A.I.P. Vol. II: The Cool and the Crazy. Includes tons of low-budget monsters and musicals, with juvenile delinquents tossed in, including trailers from: *Amazing Colossal Man; The Cool and the Crazy; Ghost of Dragstrip Hollow; The She-Creature; Pajama Party* (Cinemascope in letterbox format); *Horrors of the Black Museum;* and *War of the Colossal Beast.*

Horror Sci-Fi Vol. IV: Horrible Honeys. Trailers from B- to Z-grade

features (1950s to early 1960s) including: *Snake Woman; Wasp Woman; She-Freak; Teenage Gang Debs* and recently discovered 35mm prints of *Wild Women of Wongo* and *Sinderella and the Golden Bra.*

Hitchcock Collection. Including trailers from: *Rebecca; Suspicion; The Saboteur; Shadow of a Doubt; Spellbound; Notorious; The Paradine Case; Rope; Under Capricorn; Dial M for Murder; Rear Window; To Catch a Thief; The Man Who Knew Too Much; The Trouble with Harry; Vertigo; North by Northwest; Psycho; The Birds; Marnie;* and *Torn Curtain.*

1939 — The Vintage Year. A representative sampling of trailers from the year with the greatest number of film releases, including: *Gone With the Wind* (1953, 1974 and 1976); *The Light that Failed; Allegheny Uprising; Gulliver's Travels; Idiot's Delight; Another Thin Man; The Women; The Wizard of Oz; Dark Victory; The Roaring '20s; Marx Bros. At the Circus; Goodbye, Mr. Chips; Each Dawn I Die; Only Angels Have Wings; Union Pacific; Intermezzo; Juarez; King of the Underworld; Gunga Din; The Human Monster; Beware Spooks;* and *Wuthering Heights.*
Size & Elements: Film: 35mm and 16mm (approx. 4,000 titles; prints not available to the public under any circumstances). Videotape: 1", Betacam SP, 3/4", VHS and Betamax (viewing copies).
Cataloging: Published catalogs; computerized cataloging for staff use only.
Access: Not open to the public. Available for duplication and reuse.
Rights: Full rights held to catalog releases. Some material in the public domain. Additional clearances may be necessary in some cases if material is to be reused.
Licensing: Material possibly available for licensing and reuse. License fees charged in the case of catalog releases.
Restrictions: Purchaser accepts all responsibility for reuse of materials.
Viewing Facilities: None.
Duplication Facilities: Videotape (1", Betacam SP, 3/4", VHS and Betamax; all duplication done by designated laboratory).

CALIFORNIA (San Jose)

COMPUTER TELEVISION GROUP, INC.
1641 North First Street, Suite 160
San Jose, CA 95112
(408) 437-8990
Fax: (408) 437-9095

Peter Jacobus (President)

Contact: Richard Fisher (Vice President, Marketing and Sales)
Services: Videotape producer. Material available to the public for purchase, duplication and reuse.
Description: Produces videotapes and television programs relating to personal computers for broadcast and non-broadcast markets. Has produced *The Computer Show,* a nationally syndicated program, for four years. Both complete programs (each 60 or 30 min.) and excerpts from the programs are available.

Subjects covered include personal computers; personal computer software and hardware; product demonstrations; how-to tutorials on various subjects including desktop publishing; feature stories covering such subjects as children and computers, computer trade shows, computers in education, art and computers, computer games and computers in foreign countries. Also interviews with industry leaders and personalities, including Stephen Wozniak, Steven Jobs, Bill Gates and John Sculley.
Size & Elements: Videotape: 1", Betacam and 3/4" (over 300 hours; masters); VHS (viewing copies). Holds four years of completed programs and outtakes.
Cataloging: Published catalog of completed programs (approx. 1986-88); computerized cataloging of unedited footage in process (staff use only).
Access: Available to the public for purchase, duplication and reuse. Research fees not charged (fees apply for furnishing preview videotapes). Research requests accepted by mail, telephone and in person (by appointment only).
Rights: Full rights held to all material.
Licensing: Available for licensing and reuse. License fees charged.
Restrictions: None specified.
Viewing Facilities: Videotape (3/4" and VHS).
Duplication Facilities: Videotape (3/4" to VHS).

CALIFORNIA (San Jose)

SAN JOSE HISTORICAL MUSEUM
635 Phelan Avenue
San Jose, CA 95112
(408) 287-2290

Contact: Nancy Valby (Curator)
Services: Museum. Film and videotape collection open primarily to researchers and scholars. Requests for access and reuse considered on a case-by-case basis.
Description: Holds footage of local history and news events relating to San Jose and the Santa Clara Valley.

KNTV newsfilm collection (pre-1979). Material from this local television station collection is held in two lots.

The first lot (ca. 1964-69; black and white, silent) contains partial film production of the station during that period; it is supplemented by a set of scripts (also incomplete). The second lot (beginning 1969, skipping early 1970s, incomplete coverage of 1975-79) is in color and with sound. All film from these two lots is stored on small 100- or 400-foot reels. KNTV newsfilm (1969-79) not held in the Museum has been discarded or lost. Due to insufficient funding, there is limited access to the newsfilm collection; material has not yet been restored, preserved, transferred, properly stored, cataloged or viewed.

Home movies. Includes 35mm home movies (1930s); Chamber of Commerce footage (1950s); commercial (newsreel) footage of the San Jose Chamber of Commerce (1915); and *Delights of the Santa Clara Valley,* showing the construction of U.S. Highway 101, beginning with the pouring of concrete from a wheelbarrow and ending with the building of the Bayshore Freeway. This footage, copied from nitrate film to 35mm safety film and then transferred to VHS videotape, has also been used in a finished film, *The Valley of the Heart's Delight.* This is the only circulating film in the collection.
Size & Elements: Film: 35mm; 16mm (approx. 850,000 feet). Videotape: VHS (small amount).
Cataloging: Finding aids consist of outdated newsfilm index books (organized by date).
Access: Open primarily to researchers and scholars. Open to the public on a case-by-case basis. Access to newsfilm collection limited; access to home movie collection is not permitted. Requests for access considered on a case-by-case basis. Research fees generally not charged. Research requests accepted by mail and telephone. One film available for circulation.
Rights: Some rights held to all material. Additional clearances may be necessary in some cases if material is to be reused.
Licensing: Available for reuse, subject to restrictions. Usage fees charged depending on project.
Restrictions: Access to newsfilm collection limited; access to home movie collection not permitted. Requests for reuse considered on a case-by-case basis.
Viewing Facilities: None.
Duplication Facilities: None (outside arrangements can be made).

CALIFORNIA (San Jose)

STOCK SHOTS
1085 Louise Avenue
San Jose, CA 95125
(408) 971-1325
Fax: (408) 723-3846

Thomas Mertens (President)

Contact: Peggy Casey (Manager)
Services: Film and videotape producer; stock footage sales library.
Description: High technology; computers and computer applications; Silicon Valley (California); San Jose (California); sports; nature; scenics; vintage movies; aerials (San Francisco, San Diego and San Jose); medicine (operating rooms and recovery rooms, a pregnant woman undergoing fetal monitoring, an exercise/yoga class for expectant mothers, and shots of an infant in a nursery); Americana; transportation (mass transit, including new light rail operations in Portland and San Jose, construction, traffic diversion, and rush-hour automobile traffic); science; ships and construction (streets and light rail transit systems).

Vintage movies, old newsreels and historic footage are also available.
Size & Elements: Film: 16mm (12,000 feet). Videotape: 1" (50 hours); 3/4" (100 hours).
Cataloging: Computerized cataloging for staff use only; research library.
Access: Not open to the public. Available for licensing and reuse. Research fees charged. Research requests accepted by mail and telephone.
Rights: Full rights held to most material.
Licensing: Available for licensing and reuse. License fees charged. All fees clear one-time use only. Discounts available for quantity usage. All materials must be returned upon conclusion of production.
Restrictions: None specified.
Viewing Facilities: None.

Duplication Facilities: Videotape (duplication as necessary for clients).

CALIFORNIA (San Juan Bautista)

EL TEATRO CAMPESINO
P.O. Box 1240
San Juan Bautista, CA 95045
(408) 623-2444

Street address: 705 Fourth Street

Phillip Esparza (Producer, Administrative Director)

Contact: Robert Castro
Services: Nonprofit theater company. Film and videotape collection available for distribution and rental rather than for reuse or resale.
Description: Founded 1965; dedicated to the creation and advancement of Chicano culture through the performing arts. Holds five films documenting the social and historical realities of the culture through entertainment: *I Am Joaquin* (the film version of the epic poem by Corky Gonzales), an inspiring panoramic vision of Chicano culture from Tenochtitlan to the present; *NET: El Teatro Campesino,* a documentary of the first five years of El Teatro; *Los Vendidos,* a humorous and satiric special; a featured concert of the music and artistry of Daniel Valdez entitled *America de Los Indios;* and *El Corrido,* the Luis Valdez adaptation of *La Carpa de Los Rasquachis,* one of the most popular theater productions ever produced by El Teatro Campesino.

Also offers a *Film Festival,* which includes other films involving El Teatro Campesino, but is not available to the general public.
Size & Elements: Film: 16mm (5 titles; release prints). Videotape: VHS (5 titles; viewing copies).
Cataloging: Published catalogs.
Access: Maintained for distribution and rental rather than for reuse or resale.
Rights: Apply for information.
Licensing: Apply for information.
Restrictions: None specified.
Viewing Facilities: None.
Duplication Facilities: None.
Related Materials: Various publications and LP records.

CALIFORNIA (San Marcos)

UDS COMPANY
AVIATION FILM COLLECTION
P.O. Box 1945
San Marcos, CA 92069
(619) 471-1802

Adam Robbins (General Manager)

Contact: Adam Robbins
Services: Film and videotape archives; videotape distributor. Videotapes available for purchase.
Description: Films relating to aviation and its history, many produced by the U.S. armed services (1930s-40s); about 20% are feature films. Collection has two main purposes: to provide a wide selection of aviation-related films for sale to collectors, and to continue to locate and acquire aviation films.

Titles available range from silent films (1920s) to Mach 3+ documentaries (1970s-80s). Sample titles include: *Things To Come* (1936), an adaptation of an H. G. Wells story forecasting the beginning of World War II and describing the conflict and destruction which was to ensue; *Target for Tonight* (1941), an on-the-spot documentary produced in England, documenting the RAF's planning and execution of a bombing raid in Germany; *Hayabusa,* a compilation of rare film footage on one of the more famous Japanese Army Air Force fighters from the early years of World War II; *The Memphis Belle* (1944), one of the best-known aviation films from this period, following an actual combat mission from beginning to end; *Combat America* (1945), a documentary featurette produced for theatrical screening and morale-building during World War II; *RCAF Collection No. 1,* three films on the Royal Canadian Air Force, with *Wings of Youth* (1941), a rousing, patriotic short produced as part of the *Canada Carries On Series; It's Your Pigeon* (1942), describing the method of releasing homing pigeons in the event of emergency ditching of an aircraft; and *Target Berlin* (1944), the Avro Lancaster bombers, from production to a thousand-plane night raid on Berlin.
Size & Elements: Film: 35mm and 16mm (over 300 titles; originals and release prints). Videotape: VHS (same 300 titles; film-to-videotape transfers).

CALIFORNIA (Santa Ana)

Cataloging: Published catalog.
Access: Available for purchase rather than research or reuse. Requests accepted by mail.
Rights: Full rights held to some material. Some material in the public domain.
Licensing: Reuse generally not permitted.
Restrictions: Restrictions apply to licensing and reuse.
Viewing Facilities: None.
Duplication Facilities: None.
Related Materials: Related books, magazines and journals.

CALIFORNIA (Santa Ana)

FREELAND PRESS
See **CALIFORNIA** (Los Angeles Metro)

CALIFORNIA (Santa Barbara)

FMS PRODUCTIONS
P.O. Box 4428
Santa Barbara, CA 93140
(800) 421-4609
(805) 564-2488
Fax: (805) 965-5021

Street address: 520 East Montecito Street, Suite F, Santa Barbara, CA 93103

P. Randall Frederick (Executive Vice President)

Contact: Yvonne Parsons (Vice President/General Manager)
Services: Film and videotape producer and distributor. Collection available primarily for rental and purchase.
Description: Alcohol and drug abuse education films dealing with dependency and addiction at all ages and related problems.

Topics include: intervention; alcohol and drugs in industry and the workplace; sobriety; seniors and alcohol abuse; drinking and driving; cocaine and crack; women and alcoholism; celebrities and their personal struggles with alcohol; Father Joseph C. Martin's *Guidelines for Helping Alcoholics* and other films; children and parental alcoholism; the alcoholic and the family; co-dependency; medical aspects of alcoholism; mixing sedatives and alcohol; medical aspects of mind-altering drugs; effects on sexuality of alcohol and drugs; physical abuse and incest; family violence; child abuse; important figures and advances in the field; in- and out-patient treatment.

Some titles available in Spanish.
Size & Elements: Film and videotape: formats unspecified (approx. 100 titles total).
Cataloging: Published catalogs.
Access: Maintained for distribution or rental rather than reuse or resale.
Rights: Full rights held to some material. Additional clearances may be necessary if material is to be reused.
Licensing: Apply for information.
Restrictions: Material generally not available for reuse.
Viewing Facilities: None.
Duplication Facilities: None.

CALIFORNIA (Santa Barbara)

INTELLIMATION
ANNENBERG/CPB PROJECT
P.O. Box 1922
Santa Barbara, CA 93116-1922
(805) 968-2291
(800) 532-7637
Fax: (805) 966-4861

Street address: 130 Cremona, Santa Barbara, CA 93117

Marie S. Holmes (Director)

Contacts: Marie S. Holmes; Patti Young (Manager, Customer Service).
Services: Film and videotape distributor. Material available for rental, purchase, duplication, telecourse licensing and broadcast.
Description: Educational videotape programs aimed at expanding opportunities for individuals to acquire quality education. Each title may be used as a complete course for college credit or as a supplement to classroom teaching. Subjects include the humanities (modern poetry and writing); ethics;

the social sciences; biology; mathematics and computers. All are accompanied by texts and study guides.

Voices and Visions. Includes one-hour television programs about each of the following poets: Robert Frost, Ezra Pound, Langston Hughes, Walt Whitman, Hart Crane, William Carlos Williams, Emily Dickinson, Marianne Moore, T. S. Eliot, Wallace Stevens, Elizabeth Bishop, Robert Lowell and Sylvia Plath.

The Write Course: An Introduction to College Composition. 30 programs, each 30 min.

French in Action. 52 programs, each 60 min.

Ethics in America. 10 programs, each 60 min., including: *The Military: Under Orders; The Military: Confidential; American Journalism: Privacy and Politics; Government: Public Service, Private Interests; The Anatomy of a Corporate Takeover: Ethics on the Business Battlefield;* and *Autonomy vs. Paternalism: The Pregnant Cancer Patient and the Unborn Child.*

Congress: We The People. 26 programs (13 study units), each 30 min., including: *We The People (A Freshman Comes to Washington/The Two Houses of Congress); Who Serves in Congress? (A Variety of Voices) Congressional Elections ("...And If Elected."); Congress in Committee (Compromise in Congress);* and *Who Runs Congress? (Varieties of Leadership).*

The Constitution: That Delicate Balance. 13 programs, each 60 min., including: *The President versus Congress: Executive Privilege and Delegation of Power; The President versus Congress: War Powers and Covert Action; Nomination, Election and Succession of the President; Criminal Justice and a Defendant's Right to A Fair Trial;* and *Crime and Insanity.*

War and Peace in the Nuclear Age. 13 programs, each 60 min., including: *Dawn; The Weapon of Choice; A Bigger Bang for the Buck; Europe Goes Nuclear; At the Brink; The Education of Robert McNamara;* and *One Step Forward.*

The Brain. Eight programs, each 60 min., including: *The Enlightened Machine; Vision and Movement; Rhythms and Drives; Stress and Emotion; Learning and Memory;* and *The Two Brains.*

The New Literacy: An Introduction to Computers. 26 programs, each 30 min., including: *A Literate Society; The Computing Machine (Parts I and II); Communicating with a Computer; Data Representation; Putting Data In; Getting Information Out; Storing Data; Secondary Storage; Processors; Computer Operations; Personal Computing; Micros to Monsters; System Analysis and Design; Problem Solving and Design; Programming Languages; The Programming Environment; Operating Systems; Systems Options; Computer Files and Databases; Data Communications; Office Automation; Computing Services; Computing, Organization, and the Individual; Computer Security;* and *Issues and Trends in Computing.*

For All Practical Purposes: Introduction to Contemporary Mathematics. 26 programs, each 30 min.
Size & Elements: Videotape: 3/4", VHS and Betamax (10 program series, 8 more to be added in 1989).
Cataloging: Published catalogs; release sheets on each program.
Access: Available for rental and purchase, telecourse licensing, off-air recording and duplication, subject to appropriate licensing arrangements. Maintained for distribution rather than for research or reuse. Requests accepted by mail and telephone.
Rights: Rights retained by producers. Additional clearances may be necessary if material is to be reused.
Licensing: Available for telecourse licensing, off-air recording and duplication, subject to appropriate licensing arrangements. Duplication rights available (fees apply). License fees charged if material is used as a complete college credit course.
Restrictions: Apply for information.
Viewing Facilities: None.
Duplication Facilities: Videotape (3/4", VHS and Betamax).

CALIFORNIA (Santa Barbara)

SANTA BARBARA MUSEUM OF ART
1130 State Street
Santa Barbara, CA 93101
(805) 963-4364

Richard V. West (Director); Robert Henning (Chief Curator)

Contact: Deborah Tufts (Curator of Education)
Services: Museum. Videotape collection available to the public for viewing.
Description: The Education Department currently produces videotapes to supplement museum art exhibitions. Subjects include: techniques of Japanese woodblock printing; interviews with photographer Harry Callahan, artists

Nancy Graves and Augusto Torres; and overviews of the *Eye of the Child* exhibition and of the *Another Time, Another Face* doll collection.
Size & Elements: Videotape: format unspecified (7 videotapes; others in progress).
Cataloging: Card catalogs; published catalogs; computerized cataloging in process for staff use only; research library.
Access: Open to the public. Research fees not charged. Research requests accepted by mail and in person (walk-in).
Rights: Full rights held to all material. Rights status of some material "not fully codified."
Licensing: Apply for information.
Restrictions: Apply for information.
Viewing Facilities: Film (in-house auditorium); videotape.
Duplication Facilities: Videotape (can be arranged with Museum photographer).

CALIFORNIA (Santa Clara)

DE SAISSET MUSEUM
SANTA CLARA UNIVERSITY
Santa Clara, CA 95053
(408) 554-4528

Robert McDonald (Director)

Contact: Registrar (for inquiries regarding videotape collection).
Services: Art museum. Videotape collection available for in-house viewing by researchers and scholars only.
Description: *Video by and about artists and art work.* Documentation of art work exhibited at museum; documentation of performances; interviews with visiting or exhibiting artists and collection of artists' videotapes (1971-72). Videotapes are EIAJ-1 1/2" format; they are being stored for possible archival preservation, and are presently not viewable. Included are works by: John Baldessari, Lynda Benglis, George Bolling, Douglas Davis, Terry Fox, Videofreex, Howard Fried, Frank Gillette, Joel Glassman, Taka Iimura, Paul Kos, Shigeko Kubota, Nam June Paik, Keith Sonnier, Richard Serra, Joan Jonas, Rainbow Video, William Wegman, David Ross, Andy Warhol and Clear Blue Light.
New Deal Art documentation. Videotapes were produced jointly by Museum and Archives of American Art. Material consists of site visits and interviews with artists. Some, but not all, of collection is transferred to VHS (from masters held in EIAJ-1 1/2" format) and is viewable. Another set of copies is held at the De Young Museum in San Francisco. Includes interviews with: Belle Baranceanu, Edward Biberman, Helen and Margaret Bruton, Ralph Chesse, Joseph Danysh, Lorser Feitelson and Helen Lundeberg, Charles Kassler, Albert King and Jason Herron, Daniel Mendelowitz, Francis O'Connor, Richard and Anne O'Hanlon, Hilda Preibisius, Le Roy Robbins, Jacques Schnier, Gene Swigget, Hermann Volz, Glenn Wessels and Bernard Zakheim.
Some of the New Deal sites include: George Washington High School, by Victor Arnautoff; La Jolla Post Office, by Belle Baranceanu; Venice Post Office, by Edward Biberman; Modesto Post Office, by Ray Boynton; University of California at Berkeley, by Bruton and Swift; Sun Yat Sen Park, Maritime Museum, San Francisco, by Beniamino Bufano; Coit Tower (first floor); Piedmont High School, San Francisco, by Claire von Falkenstein; Los Angeles Federal Court House, by Archibald Garner; City of Hope, by Goldstein and Kadish; Ventura Post Office, by Gordon Grant; Los Angeles Federal Court House, by James Hansen; Maritime Museum, San Francisco, by Hilaire Hiler; Maiden of the Waters, San Diego, by Donald Hord; George Washington High School and Maritime Museum, San Francisco, by Sargent Johnson; Beverly Hills Post Office, by Charles Kassler; Beach Chalet, San Francisco, by Lucien Labaudt; Centinela Park, Los Angeles, by Helen Lundeberg; Santa Monica City Hall, by Stanton MacDonald-Wright; and Mother's House, San Francisco, by Piccinelli and Forbes.
Size & Elements: Videotape: 1/2" open reel (63 EIAJ-1 format masters, some transferred to VHS).
Cataloging: Card catalogs.
Access: Access restricted to researchers and scholars only; not open to the public. For in-house use only. Requests for viewing accepted by mail only. Open reel videotapes which are not transferred to VHS are not viewable.
Rights: Rights status of material unknown.
Licensing: Not available for licensing or reuse.
Restrictions: Restrictions apply regarding access and licensing.
Viewing Facilities: Videotape (VHS).
Duplication Facilities: None.

CALIFORNIA (Santa Cruz)

RESOURCE CENTER FOR NONVIOLENCE
515 Broadway
Santa Cruz, CA 95060
(408) 423-1626

Anita Heckman (Audiovisuals Coordinator)

Contact: Anita Heckman
Services: Educational institution; distributor. Films and videotapes available to the public for rental and purchase.
Description: Nuclear arms control, pacifism, nonviolence and global warfare issues.
Films include: *The Last Epidemic,* documenting a 1981 conference of the Physicians for Social Responsibility; *One Million Hiroshimas,* a conference of the International Physicians for the Prevention of Nuclear War (1982); *In the Nuclear Shadow,* in which children talk about nuclear war; *King: A Filmed Record, Montgomery to Memphis,* on Dr. Martin Luther King's activities (1955-68); *War Without Winners,* American and Russian people expressing their thoughts on an age of nuclear weapons (also available on videotape); and *Paul Jacobs and the Nuclear Gang,* documenting the activities of the political activist who sought to expose the U.S. government's suppression of information about radiation from nuclear power and weapons programs.
Videotapes include: *The Day After,* a dramatization of the effect of a nuclear attack on the U.S.; *The War Game,* dramatizing a nuclear attack on Britain; *Dr. Gene Sharp: June 1983; Helen Caldicott: April 1979 — UCLA; April 23, 1981 — Sandia Base, Albuquerque.*
Size & Elements: Film: 16mm. Videotape: 3/4", VHS and Betamax. (10 titles total).
Cataloging: Published lists.
Access: Open to the public for rental and purchase. Selected film titles available only for rental. Requests accepted by mail, telephone and in person.
Rights: Full rights held to some material. Additional clearances may be necessary in some cases if material is to be reused.
Licensing: Apply for information.
Restrictions: None specified.
Viewing Facilities: None.
Duplication Facilities: None.

CALIFORNIA (Santa Cruz)

SHIRE FILMS
P.O. Box 1728
Santa Cruz, CA 95061
(408) 425-0842

Contacts: Dan Bessie; Helen Garvy
Services: Film and videotape producer. Collection available for distribution, rental, licensing and reuse.
Description: *Heart of Spain* (ca. 1937, by Paul Strand), a description of battlefield medical practices during the Spanish Civil War; *Spanish Refugees* (ca. 1941), describing the plight of Spanish loyalists fleeing Franco forces; *Spain in Exile* (1946); and *The Hollywood 10* (1950), a film made in support of 10 screenwriters who were convicted of contempt of Congress in 1947, and later blacklisted.
Size & Elements: Film: 16mm (3 titles; black and white, positive). Videotape: 3/4" (1 title, black and white).
Cataloging: None specified.
Access: Available for distribution, rental, licensing and reuse. Research fees charged. Research requests accepted by mail and telephone.
Rights: Rights status of material unknown. Additional clearances may be necessary in some cases if material is to be reused.
Licensing: Available for licensing and reuse. License fees charged (fees determined on a case-by-case basis).
Restrictions: Restrictions may apply to some material.
Viewing Facilities: Film.
Duplication Facilities: None.

CALIFORNIA (Santa Monica)

LOS ANGELES BLUES ARCHIVES
and
LOS ANGELES NEWS SERVICE (LANS)
and

CALIFORNIA (Santa Rosa)

POLITICAL ISSUE ARCHIVE
and
PYRAMID FILM AND VIDEO CORPORATION
and
SALENGER FILMS, INC.
and
SOUTHERN CALIFORNIA INSTITUTE OF ARCHITECTURE (SCI-ARC)
MEDIA CENTER
and
THE VOYAGER COMPANY
THE CRITERION COLLECTION
See CALIFORNIA (Los Angeles Metro)

CALIFORNIA (Santa Rosa)

SONOMA VIDEO PRODUCTIONS
553 Mendocino Avenue
Santa Rosa, CA 95401
(707) 579-3902
Fax: (707) 527-0223

Michael Heumann (President)

Contact: Michael Heumann
Services: Film and videotape producer. Videotape footage available for licensing and reuse.
Description: Travel- and tourist-related footage of many areas throughout the world (ca. 1982-present). Coverage includes Alaska, Bali, Brazil, China, Hong Kong, Singapore, Germany, California, national parks throughout the U.S., Florida, the South Pacific, Mexico, Hawaii and the Caribbean. Holdings for each of these areas include extensive coverage of all tourist locations and attractions, people, wildlife, geographical features, food, cultural events, music and underwater footage.
    Also holds fishing footage, including sport fishing (especially fly-fishing); air racing footage, featuring all classes from ultralights to unlimited class; and scenes of wine and wineries.
Size & Elements: Videotape: Betacam and 3/4" (500 hours; masters); 3/4" and VHS (time-coded viewing copies). Collection is continuously growing.
Cataloging: Computerized cataloging available to researchers (searchable, indexed computer logs for Macintosh and other microcomputer systems).
Access: Open to the public. Available for duplication and reuse. Research fees charged in some cases. Research requests accepted by mail, telephone and in person (by appointment only).
Rights: Full rights held to all material.
Licensing: Available for licensing. License fees charged.
Restrictions: None specified.
Viewing Facilities: Videotape (3/4" and VHS).
Duplication Facilities: Videotape (Betacam, Betacam SP and 3/4").
Representative: Apply for information.

CALIFORNIA (Sherman Oaks)

UPA PRODUCTIONS OF AMERICA
See CALIFORNIA (Los Angeles Metro)

CALIFORNIA (Sierra Madre)

HISTORIC THOROUGHBRED COLLECTIONS, INC.
See CALIFORNIA (Los Angeles Metro)

CALIFORNIA (Simi Valley)

CINENET (CINEMA NETWORK)
See CALIFORNIA (Los Angeles Metro)

CALIFORNIA (Somis)

10TH FOOT ROYAL LINCOLNSHIRE REGIMENTAL ASSOCIATION — AMERICAN CONTINGENT
P.O. Box 850
Somis, CA 93066
(805) 388-1136

Col. Vincent J. R. Kehoe (Curator)

Contact: Col. Vincent J. R. Kehoe
Services: Association. Film and videotape collection open to researchers and scholars only.
Description: Documentation of the RLRAAC, including coverage of the Bicentennial Era (1968-78).
Size & Elements: Film: format unspecified (4,000 feet, 6 titles, 6 cans). Videotape: various formats (amount unspecified).
Cataloging: None specified.
Access: Open to researchers and scholars only. Research fees not charged. Research requests accepted by mail.
Rights: Full rights held to all material.
Licensing: Apply for information.
Restrictions: None specified.
Viewing Facilities: Film and videotape.
Duplication Facilities: Videotape.

CALIFORNIA (South Laguna)

MACGILLIVRAY FREEMAN FILMS
See CALIFORNIA (Los Angeles Metro)

CALIFORNIA (Stanford)

HOOVER INSTITUTION ON WAR, REVOLUTION AND PEACE
HOOVER INSTITUTION ARCHIVES
STANFORD UNIVERSITY
Stanford, CA 94305-6010
(415) 723-3563

Charles Palm (Archivist)

Contact: Sondra Bierre (Archival Specialist)
Services: Educational institution; film and videotape archive. Material available for research, duplication, licensing and reuse, subject to restrictions.
Description: Holds numerous collections which include moving image material. Particular strengths include: China (1930-45); Germany (1940-43); the camera original of the only film footage of Hiroshima and Nagasaki A-bomb explosions, shot for Harold Agnew of the Los Alamos Scientific Laboratory staff in 1945; Herbert Hoover (1916-64); Latvia (1939-50); Leon Trotsky (1938-39); Soviet Union (1900-72) and World War II (1939-45).
    Major collections incorporating moving image material include:
    Harold Agnew collection (1 reel). Depicting explosion of atom bombs over Hiroshima and Nagasaki, Japan (1945).
    Gvido Augusts collection (1940-72, 18 reels). Latvian motion pictures including dramas, documentaries and newsreels depicting daily life in Latvia, Latvian culture and postwar treatment of events in Latvia during World War II.
    Herman Axelbank collection. Pre-revolutionary and revolutionary political, military and cultural actuality footage (ca. 1900-72) (35mm and 16mm positive, 266 reels, approx. 250,000 feet). Some of collection closed for preservation at this time. Periods presently available are rolls 1-28 (1900-21); Lenin's funeral (roll 40) (1924); Red Army push to Berlin, concentration camp liberations (rolls 90, 93, 97 and 99) (1945); Jews in Russia and the Soviet Union and Jews under Nazism (rolls 118-123). Additional reels will be opened for use as funds become available to produce preservation masters and reference copies.
    Footage (1901-37) is extremely rare and some portions unique. Includes the Tsar, his family and associates in moments of relaxation, at official ceremonies in provincial towns, Moscow and St. Petersburg; the Civil War with good coverage of Siberia and the Far East; revolutionary and governmental leaders of the Tsarist, Provisional Government and Soviet periods; the Kronstadt Mutiny (March 1921); Trial of the Socialist Revolutionaries (1922); extensive coverage of World War II; ceremonial events; May Day and October revolution anniversaries and funerals of prominent figures, including Tolstoy and Lenin. Coverage extends into the 1970s. Includes some Soviet feature films, such as *Kombrig Ivanov* (1923). Rights status unknown.
    George B. Barbour collection. Includes a film relating to political and social conditions, missionary service and university education in China.
    Alexander Buchman collection. Contains film of Shanghai, China (ca. 1937-39), including bombing of Shanghai (1937) during Sino-Japanese War. Also holds a motion picture (1938, 2 reels) depicting Trotsky and members of his entourage with Diego Rivera and Frida Kahlo in Coyoacan, Mexico.
    John Caldwell collection. Contains film depicting life in China (1930-42).
    Joseph M. Cronin collection. Contains one film relating to various aspects of education in the U.S.

Czechoslovak subject collection (1 reel). Topic not listed.

Paul Domke collection (1936-45, 8 reels). Contains films depicting missionary schools in China (1936-37); effects of Japanese bombing in China (1939); the transport of a giant panda from China to the St. Louis Zoo (1939); scenes at Angkor Wat (1939); the U.S. Observer Mission to Yenan (1944-45); U.S. Army headquarters in Chungking (1945); and various other scenes in China (1936-45).

Steven Drewes collection. Contains two films: *Berlin im Olympiaschmuck* (1936) depicts the celebration of the 11th Olympic games, including scenes of flags, bringing of fire, Adolf Hitler and the Brandenburg Gate; a newsreel, *Degeto Weltspiegel* (1940) depicts the destruction of Rouen in World War II.

Educational Research Council of America collection (41 reels). Relating to elementary and secondary school education in the U.S. (1959-77).

Lawrence Fertig collection (2 reels). Relating to U.S. and international economic policy and laissez-faire economics.

Milton Friedman collection (10 reels). Relating to economic theory, economic conditions in the United States and governmental economic policy from the television series *Free to Choose.*

G. William Gahagan collection (8 reels). Relating to U.S. Office of War Information analysis of Japanese propaganda and preparation of U.S. propaganda during World War II, including a few examples of postwar U.S. anti-communist propaganda.

K. Hope Hamilton collection (4 reels). Relating to the activities of Inter-America House in providing entertainment for American and Allied junior officers during World War II.

Ivan Heisler collection (restricted) (1938, 2 reels). Depicts Leon Trotsky, his wife and members of his entourage, and the artists Diego Rivera and Frida Kahlo, in Coyoacan, Mexico.

Robert Hill collection (9 reels). Relating to conditions in and U.S. relations with Latin America and Spain, U.S. foreign policy and domestic politics and the Republican party.

Hiroshima-Nagasaki Publishing Committee collection (restricted) (1982, 2 reels) depicting atomic destruction of Hiroshima and Nagasaki, Japan (1945), and subsequent condition of survivors of the atomic bomb.

Herbert Hoover collection (160 reels). Relates to 20th century American policies and relief administration in World Wars I and II. Includes documentary and interview films and excerpts from newsreels (8,000 feet) regarding life and activities of Herbert Hoover (1916-64); rights held by various film and television companies. Also includes *This is Worth Remembering,* film of Hoover's 80th birthday celebration at West Branch, Iowa.

Charles F. Kettering Foundation collection (19 reels). Relates to research in the fields of international affairs, science, education and urban affairs.

Eduards Kraucs collection (3 reels). Relating to Latvian refugees in Germany and the U.S. (with translations) in the collection of Latvian-American photographer and TV cameraman.

Latviesu Centrala Komiteja. (1 reel). Produced by this Latvian emigre organization, relating to conditions in Latvia under Soviet and German occupation and to Latvian displaced persons during and after World War II.

Myers Lowman collection (3 reels). Relates to communism and other leftist movements, the civil rights movement, and anti-communism. Contents of films not specified.

Mildred Merland collection. Includes a film (1929, 2 reels) depicting the state burial of Sun Yat-sen, president of China, in Nanking.

William Miller collection (5 reels). Relating to U.S. Army Signal Corps operations in North Africa, Germany, Italy and France (1943-45).

National Broadcasting Company (NBC) collection. Documentary films depicting political events in Cuba (1958-63, 97 reels).

Pacific Gas & Electric Company collection (1960-70). Holds a series of 21 political education film programs (campaign presentations by major candidates for state political offices in California).

Boris T. Pash collection (62 reels). Relating to the life and activities of Colonel Boris T. Pash, military intelligence officer in the U.S. Army.

Wilbur Peterkin collection (4 reels). Relating to Chinese communist forces and the Japanese occupation in China during World War II.

Wanda Roehr Foundation motion picture (1939, 1 reel). Depicts the effects of the German bombing of Warsaw (September 1939).

Soviet Union. Film material includes: *The Frozen War: America Intervenes in Russia, 1918-20* (1973) relates to American intervention during the Russian Revolution; a film (ca. 1977) depicts Soviet sculptor E. I. Neizvestnyi; *The Right to Believe* (undated) relates to religion in the USSR and Eastern Europe; *Russia's Five Year Plan* (2 reels) relating to the first five-year plan (1928-32).

Charles Stuart collection. Soviet Russia through the Eyes of an American, documentary film (ca. 1932). Film shot 1920s, music and narration added later. 16mm amateur footage of mining in Soviet Union, (ca. 1926-32). Collection closed for preservation. Rights held by Hoover Institution.

Alexandre Tarsaidze collection (16 reels). Political and military actuality footage (ca. 1900-17) (16mm positive, approx. 1,500 ft.), including a documentary on Nicholas II. Rights status unknown.

Le Temps des Doryphores (5 reels). Depicts social and political conditions in German-occupied France (1940-44) including scenes of leading German political and military figures, German armed forces and daily life in French towns and villages.

United Nations Association of the United States of America, San Francisco Chapter collection (74 reels). Relates to the operations of United Nations organizations, world politics and international human rights.

Universal Newspaper Newsreel collection (2 reels). Depicting Japanese intervention in China and scenes of bombing of Shanghai (1931-32).

Universum-Film-Aktiengesellschaft (UFA) collection. Newsreels from the German *Tobis* and *Deutsche Wochenschau* series (ca. 1940-43) (442 newsreels, not a complete set, approx. 500,000 feet) depicting military campaigns and conditions in Germany in World War II. This collection is for in-house use only; rights held by Transit-Film GmbH, Munich, Germany.

Alonzo Walter collection (ca. 1938-43, 19 reels). Depicting German military and aerial operations and German political leaders in World War II.

The Warsaw Uprising (1 reel). Relating to the German occupation of Warsaw during World War II, and to the Warsaw uprising (1944).

Other materials of note. 2 films relating to the Nigerian Civil War (1967-70) in the American Committee to Keep Biafra Alive collection; 30 film reels relating to the activities of the Devin-Adair Publishing company in the Devin A. Garrity collection; *The Irish Rising, 1916* (produced for television) in the James Augustine Healy collection; a film of domesticated reindeer in Manchuria in the collection of British anthropologist Ethel John Lindgren (restricted); three film reels relating to Minutemen and other right-wing paramilitary groups in the U.S. and to the Irish republican movement in Northern Ireland in the Mark Monday collection. Warren Olney collection includes a silent film of ceremonies held in Hindenburg Park in Los Angeles on German Day (1936). 16 film reels and one videotape relating to Washington state politics and nuclear energy in the Dixy Lee Ray collection; a film relating to Aleksandr I. Solzhenitsyn and especially his visits to Hoover Institution (1975-76); 14 film reels relating to fuel industries in the U.S. and U.S.S.R. in the Charles Edward Stuart collection. Also, *Red Myth* (1961, 13 reels) a film relating to the history of communism, produced for television by KQED-TV (San Francisco) in cooperation with the Hoover Institute.

Size & Elements: Film: 35mm (450 cans, 500,000 feet); 16mm (1,000 cans, 750,000 feet). Videotape: 3/4" (100 videotapes); VHS (50 videotapes).

Cataloging: Card catalogs; guides, finding aids and lists; published catalogs; computerized cataloging available to researchers. Shot lists exist for part of the Axelbank Collection.

Access: Open to the public. For in-house use only. Available for duplication, licensing and reuse, with some exceptions. Research fees not charged. Limited research available for telephone and mail requests. A fee-based research assistance program available (apply for information). Research requests accepted by mail, telephone and in person (by appointment only).

Rights: Full rights held to some material. Some rights held to some material. Some material in the public domain. Rights status of some material not known. Additional clearances may be necessary in some cases if material is to be reused.

Licensing: License fees not charged. Duplication fees charged at twice actual cost; advance payment necessary.

Restrictions: No more than 15 minutes of film from any one collection may be ordered per academic year (September 1-August 31), subject to the discretion of archivist. Limit is waived on videotapes with visible time code.

Viewing Facilities: Film (35mm, 16mm and Super 8mm); videotape (3/4" and VHS).

Duplication Facilities: None (full laboratory services can be arranged with outside facilities).

Related Materials: Most collections contain related photographs, correspondence, newspaper clippings and ephemera.

CALIFORNIA (Stanford)

MULTI-MEDIA PRODUCTIONS, INC.

P.O. Box 5097
Stanford, CA 94305
(415) 327-0660

James P. Quinn (President)

Contact: James P. Quinn
Services: Educational videotape producer and distributor. Material available to

the public for purchase.
Description: The educational series *Telling It Like It Is* is directed at adolescents and features teen discussions and role-playing. Videotape program titles include: *Growing Up; Adolescent Suicide; Family Relations; Pressure; Drugs; The Opposite Sex; Friendship to Early Dating; Heavy Dating to Sex;* and *Choices.* Also: *AIDS: Fears and Facts.*

Archival and historical films include: *The Plow That Broke the Plains; Mirror of America; Eleanor Roosevelt — First Lady of the World; A Place in History (Eisenhower); Famous Generals — Patton; The MacArthur Story; Chester W. Nimitz — Honor Roll; Prelude to War; The Nazis Strike; December 7th* (Academy Award winner); *Appointment in Tokyo; Normandy Invasion; The True Glory* (1945 Academy Award winner for best documentary; includes battle footage and voices of soldiers); *The Battle of Midway; The Motion Picture History of the Korean War; Truman — A Self-Portrait; The Road to War; One Week in October; America in Space — The First Decade; Eagle Has Landed — The Flight of Apollo II; Skylab;* and *The Man From Deer Creek, The Story of Ishi.*
Size & Elements: Videotape: VHS and Betamax (approx. 35 titles total).
Cataloging: Published catalogs.
Access: Available to the public for purchase. Requests accepted by mail and telephone.
Rights: Some rights held to some material.
Licensing: Material possibly available for licensing. License fees generally not charged.
Restrictions: None specified.
Viewing Facilities: Videotape (VHS).
Duplication Facilities: Videotape (VHS).

CALIFORNIA (Stanford)

STANFORD UNIVERSITY LIBRARIES
DEPARTMENT OF SPECIAL COLLECTIONS
AND UNIVERSITY ARCHIVES
GREEN LIBRARY
Stanford, CA 94305-6004
(415) 723-4054

Michael Ryan (Department Chief and Curator of Special Collections)

Contacts: Roxanne Nilan (Assistant Chief and Curator of University Archives); Margaret Kimball (Archives and Manuscripts Librarian)
Services: University library. Film and videotape collection open to researchers and scholars only. Material available for licensing and reuse, subject to restrictions.
Description: Topics relating to Stanford University, including campus events, scientific research, athletic programs, student life, overseas studies, academics, alumni programs, buildings and grounds and interviews with distinguished faculty and staff. Also included are talks and seminars given by the Stanford Energy Information Center.
Size & Elements: Film: 16mm (153,800 feet, 321 titles, 391 cans; mostly positive originals and outtakes). Videotape: 1" (4 videotapes); 3/4" (28 videotapes); VHS (240 videotapes) (mostly viewing copies with visible time code).
Cataloging: Finding aids.
Access: Open to researchers and scholars only. Research fees not charged. Research requests accepted by mail, telephone and in person (by appointment only).
Rights: Full rights held to some material. Some rights held to all material. Additional clearances may be necessary in some cases if material is to be reused.
Licensing: Available for licensing and reuse, subject to restrictions. Usage fees charged.
Restrictions: Contract arrangement may require licensing through Stanford University.
Viewing Facilities: Film (16mm); videotape (3/4" and VHS).
Duplication Facilities: None (outside arrangements can be made).

CALIFORNIA (Studio City)

FISH FILMS, INC.
and
JESSIEFILM
and
MOTIVATIONAL MEDIA, INC.
See **CALIFORNIA** (Los Angeles Metro)

CALIFORNIA (Sun Valley)

FILM PRESERVATION ASSOCIATES
See **CALIFORNIA** (Los Angeles Metro)

CALIFORNIA (Sunnyvale)

THE FILM EDUCATION INSTITUTE
911 Suntree Court
Sunnyvale, CA 94086
(408) 246-8962

Donald N. Klipper (Director); George A. Russell (Owner)

Contact: Donald N. Klipper
Services: Historical film archives; stock footage sales library.
Description: Newsreels and reassembled newsreels (1897-1975), including footage of McKinley's inauguration, the Spanish-American War, the San Francisco earthquake, the search for Pancho Villa, World War I, 1920s newsreel and documentary footage.
Presidents and leaders. Theodore Roosevelt, Franklin D. Roosevelt, John F. Kennedy, Lyndon B. Johnson, Winston Churchill, Charles DeGaulle, Mohandas K. Gandhi, Jawarlahal Nehru, Juan and Evita Peron.
Aviation and space. Kitty Hawk, moonwalk, biplanes, blimps, boosters, Charles A. Lindbergh, Amelia Earhart, barnstormers, bombardiers, Jimmy Doolittle, John Glenn, "Spruce Goose" and space monkeys.
Sports. Babe Ruth, Knute Rockne, Babe Didrikson, Bobby Jones, Bill Tilden, Esther Williams, Johnny Weissmuller and Sonja Henie.
Fads and fashions. Human flies, flagpole sitters, goldfish swallowers, marathon dancers, fox trotters and jitterbuggers.
The "In" fashions. Mini, maxi, cloche, skimmer, Boyish Bob, Marcel wave, skirted and bikini swimsuits, corsets, trousers, pajamas for lounging, sleeping, and entertaining, gloves and spats.
Travel and ethnic films from 110 countries (1915-75). Among many subjects covered are families, including working, cooking, eating, sleeping, praying and playing; wedding ceremonies, including traditional, religious and civil, from the Arctic to Indonesia, Holland and India; dancers (international); and traditions, including Fiji firewalkers, Dutch cheese porters, carnivals, pilgrimages, boat trains on the Amazon and water elevators on the Nile.
Dramatic and comedy films (1895-1975) include Keystone Kops, Mack Sennett bathing beauties, slapstick, satire, Charles Chaplin, Charley Chase, Buster Keaton, Harry Langdon, Harold Lloyd and Abbott and Costello.
Size & Elements: Film: mostly 16mm (over 7,000 titles). Videotape: 3/4", Betamax and VHS (over 3,000; viewing copies).
Cataloging: Shot lists; research library.
Access: Open to researchers, scholars and the public. Available for duplication and reuse. Research fees charged. Research requests accepted by mail and telephone.
Rights: Full rights held to some material. Some rights held to all material. Some material in the public domain. Additional clearances may be necessary in some cases if material is to be reused for broadcast.
Licensing: Available for licensing and reuse. License fees charged in some cases.
Restrictions: None.
Viewing Facilities: Film and videotape.
Duplication Facilities: Film to videotape (3/4", Betamax and VHS).
Related Materials: Radio broadcasts.

CALIFORNIA (Sunnyvale)

VIDEO-SIG
1030-C East Duane Avenue
Sunnyvale, CA 94086
(408) 730-9291
(800) 245-6717 (orders, except California)
(800) 222-2996 (orders, California only)

Bruce Kent (Manager)

Contacts: Customer Service (for orders); Julia Hutton or Susan Powers (for information on distributing a videotape)
Services: Videotape distributor. Videotapes available to the public for purchase.
Description: Distributes inexpensive, independently produced videotapes on a non-exclusive basis. Considers submissions from independent producers in all

areas; actively markets programs through direct-mail catalogs. Collection includes independent productions (dramatic and documentary) as well as public domain film classics.

Subject areas include: business; cartoons; classic (public domain) feature films; foreign classic films; videotapes by Martin Moyer on art, travel and geography; NASA-produced films; classic television programs; the *Victory At Sea* series; educational and instructional videotapes; how-to videotapes; experimental videotapes; comedy; music; health and fitness; children's stories; exercises for mothers and children; mathematics education; religion; New Age videotapes on astrology, crystal consciousness, Kabbala, vibrations, yoga, acupressure and homeopathy; authors; documentary videotapes; economics; personal growth and development; sports documentaries; sports instruction; bicycling; travel and leisure.

Size & Elements: Videotape: VHS (approx. 1,000 videotapes; viewing copies).
Cataloging: Published catalogs.
Access: Available to the public for purchase (by mail). Quantity discounts available. Orders accepted by mail and telephone.
Rights: Non-exclusive distribution rights held to all material. Copyrights retained by original producers. Some material in the public domain.
Licensing: Not available for licensing or reuse.
Restrictions: Not available for licensing or reuse.
Viewing Facilities: None.
Duplication Facilities: Videotape (1", 3/4", and VHS).

CALIFORNIA (Thousand Oaks)

ARMENIAN FILM FOUNDATION
and
ATLANTIS PRODUCTIONS, INC.
See **CALIFORNIA** (Los Angeles Metro)

CALIFORNIA (Torrance)

MORRIS VIDEO
See **CALIFORNIA** (Los Angeles Metro)

CALIFORNIA (Universal City)

CINEPHILE AMALGAMATED PICTURES
and
MCA INC./UNIVERSAL PICTURES
and
UNIVERSAL CITY STUDIOS STOCK FILM LIBRARY
See **CALIFORNIA** (Los Angeles Metro)

CALIFORNIA (Valencia)

CALIFORNIA INSTITUTE OF THE ARTS LIBRARY
See **CALIFORNIA** (Los Angeles Metro)

CALIFORNIA (Van Nuys)

AIMS MEDIA
and
SHOKUS VIDEO
See **CALIFORNIA** (Los Angeles Metro)

CALIFORNIA (Venice)

SPORTS CINEMATOGRAPHY GROUP
See **CALIFORNIA** (Los Angeles Metro)

CALIFORNIA (Ventura)

GREAT WAVES/DELANEY FILMS
See **CALIFORNIA** (Los Angeles Metro)

CALIFORNIA (West Hills)

SLINGSHOT PRODUCTIONS
See **CALIFORNIA** (Los Angeles Metro)

CALIFORNIA (West Hollywood)

EZTV
See **CALIFORNIA** (Los Angeles Metro)

CALIFORNIA (West Sacramento)

CALIFORNIA HIGHWAY PATROL ACADEMY MEDIA CENTER
3500 Reed Avenue
West Sacramento, CA 95605
(916) 372-5620 (Ext. 248)

Contact: Sue Ketchingham
Services: Government agency library. Films available for free loan, subject to restrictions.
Description: Instructional films (safety and driver education; law enforcement and CHP training).

Topics include: alcohol and drugs (in particular "angel dust"/PCP), marijuana and DWI (driving while intoxicated); bad-weather driving; bicycle safety; commercial trucking (particularly air brake systems); hazardous materials transport and spills, truck accidents and tank vehicle inspections; first aid and emergency medical training, ambulance familiarization, emergency treatment (childbirth, multiple injury patients, shock, diabetes, heart attack, heat and cold, drowning, bleeding and bandaging, fractures and spinal injuries); freeway driving phobia; health, fitness, nutrition, hypertension and stress; management (hiring standards, positive reinforcement, sexual harassment in the workplace); moped and motorcycle safety; pedestrian safety; school bus safety; seat belts; special interest films (Diablo Canyon nuclear power plant and Lawrence Livermore Laboratory demonstrations, CH Patrolwomen), automotive maintenance and repair, skateboarding, highway flares; traffic safety (*Broken Glass,* children and infants in crashes, defensive driving, and *Red Asphalt II*), CHP training (accident investigation, body armor, problem drinkers in law enforcement, bomb scares, evacuation and disposal, civil liabilities, stolen vehicles, rape and occupational safety).
Size & Elements: Film: 16mm. Videotape: 3/4" and VHS. (Amounts unspecified).
Cataloging: Published catalogs.
Access: Open to the public. Materials available on a free-loan basis; requests accepted by mail on CHP 89 form, 10 to 30 days in advance. Telephone requests accepted only in emergencies. Maintained for distribution rather than research or reuse.
Rights: Some rights held to most material (apply for information).
Licensing: Apply for information.
Restrictions: Some material restricted to internal or law enforcement use only. No more than two films per school or organization may be booked at one time.
Viewing Facilities: None.
Duplication Facilities: None.
Related Materials: Sync-slide shows.

CALIFORNIA (Westlake Village)

DAVID LEE MILLER PRODUCTIONS
See **CALIFORNIA** (Los Angeles Metro)

CALIFORNIA (Whittier)

MOODY INSTITUTE OF SCIENCE
See **CALIFORNIA** (Los Angeles Metro)

CALIFORNIA (Woodland Hills)

DIAMOND P. SPORTS
See **CALIFORNIA** (Los Angeles Metro)

CALIFORNIA (Woodside)

THE GORILLA FOUNDATION
Box 620-530
Woodside, CA 94062
(415) 851-8505

Francine Patterson, Ph.D. (President)

Contact: Ronald Cohn, Ph.D. (Vice President)

Services: Foundation. Videotape material available for licensing and reuse, subject to restrictions.
Description: Research videotapes showing learning and use of sign language by gorillas; the interaction of gorillas with humans using sign language; gorillas interacting with pet kittens.
Size & Elements: Videotape: 1" (approx. 15 hours); 1/2" (approx. 150 hours; black and white).
Cataloging: Shot lists.
Access: Not open to the public. Open to researchers with permission of officers. Research fees not charged. Research requests accepted by mail.
Rights: Full rights held to all material.
Licensing: Available for licensing and reuse, subject to restrictions. License fees charged.
Restrictions: Requests for licensing and reuse subject to clearance and approval.
Viewing Facilities: None.
Duplication Facilities: None.

COLORADO

COLORADO (Aspen)

ASPEN HISTORICAL SOCIETY
620 West Bleeker Street
Aspen, CO 81611
(303) 925-3721

Virginia Haberman (Archivist)

Contact: Virginia Haberman
Services: Historical society. Film and videotape collection available for in-house viewing.
Description: Skiing and local personalities (1940s through mid-1970s); Aspen and the Aspen area in the summer months; Aspen Music Festival; recreational activities, including swimming, tennis, fishing, jeeping, horse jumping, rodeo, camping and skydiving.
Titles include: *Ski Trails* (1950s), on skiing in the Canadian Rockies and pre-helicopter skiing in Bugaboos, including footage of mountain climbs; *Snowmass Before The Lifts, Via Snowcat* (1967); *Crystal Palace* (1964), showing a dance party at the Palace and a slalom race in a snowstorm; *The Many Faces of Aspen* (1963), skiing, partying and Peter Green playing bongos; *It's Easy to Ski* (1940s or 1950s, silent); *Ski Colorado* (1950) showing Arapahoe with rope tows and single chair lifts; *Aspen Scenes* (1961, silent) containing ski school demonstrations and Snowcat grooming; *Until We Meet in Aspen* (1949), a promotional film; *Ski with Buick* (1958-59), featuring Stein Ericksen at the Aspen Highlands; *Little Skiers Big Day* (1956), about a little girl who skis to school; *Aspen Album* (1950s), the history of Aspen (1880s-1950s); *White Badge* (1958) showing a ski instructor's exam (1958); *Yoo Hoo! I'm a Bird* (1964), demonstrating freestyle skiing; *Ski Time in Aspen* (1955); *Aspen Winter Moods* (1961). Also held is an untitled film that includes footage of Aspen (1948-49) with very few buildings; exteriors of old public buildings and interior of the Hotel Jerome.
Size & Elements: Film: 16mm (approx. 20 titles). Videotape: 3/4" and VHS.
Cataloging: Computerized film lists.
Access: Open to the public. For in-house use only.
Rights: Rights retained by original producers.
Licensing: Apply for information.
Restrictions: Films are used strictly for viewing at Aspen Historical Society and cannot be reused or duplicated unless permission is obtained from original producer.
Viewing Facilities: Film (16mm); videotape.
Duplication Facilities: None.

COLORADO (Aspen)

ASPEN PHOTO & FILM AGENCY
P.O. Box 4063
Aspen, CO 81612
(303) 925-8280

Street address: 1225 Alta Vista, Aspen, CO 81611

Casey Clark (President)

Contact: Casey Clark
Services: Stock footage sales library and broker.
Description: Wildlife and action sports.
Size & Elements: Film and videotape (format and amount unspecified).
Cataloging: None specified.
Access: Available to the public for licensing and reuse. Research fees charged (reimbursable in the event of purchase) and must be paid in advance. Research requests accepted by telephone.
Rights: Full rights held to all material. Rights status of some material not known. Additional clearances may be necessary in some cases if material is to be reused.
Licensing: Available for licensing and reuse, subject to restrictions. License fees charged.
Restrictions: Minimum sale restrictions apply.
Viewing Facilities: None.
Duplication Facilities: Available.
Related Materials: Still photographs.

COLORADO (Aspen)

FREEWHEELIN' FILMS, LTD.
P.O. Box 599
Aspen, CO 81612
(303) 925-2640
Fax: (303) 925-9369
Telex: 955318 INTL. DIV. ATTEN. NEW VISIONS

Street address: 28075 East Highway 82

Rodney Jacobs (Director/Producer)

Contacts: John Baker (Production Manager); Reid Knowlton
Services: Film producer and distributor. Footage available for licensing and reuse, subject to restrictions.
Description: Sports productions, including auto racing (on- and off-road), skiing, soccer, football, hydroplane racing, triathlons, the XIII Winter Olympiad and the Leadville 100 ultra-marathon.
Documentary film titles include *Sacred Ground,* which examines the Native American's relationship with the earth; *Cowboy Up,* a rodeo film; and *All The King's Horses,* featuring Clydesdales.
Size & Elements: Film: 35mm (over 1 million feet, 45 titles, hundreds of cans).
Cataloging: Brochures.
Access: Access and distribution procedures vary, depending on materials.
Rights: Full rights held to some material. Some rights held to some material. Some material in the public domain.
Licensing: Available for licensing and reuse, subject to restrictions. License fees charged.
Restrictions: Restrictions may apply to some material.
Viewing Facilities: None.
Duplication Facilities: None.

COLORADO (Aspen)

MOVING MEDIA
Box 1329
Aspen, CO 81612
(303) 920-2354

Greg Poschman (Director)

Contact: Greg Poschman
Services: Film and videotape producer; stock footage sales library.
Description: Contemporary footage of Colorado recreation and cultural activities, including outdoor sports action (winter and summer), scenics, time-lapse, water sports, skiing, arts and human interest stories. Also holds historic skiing footage (1930s-60s). Some material was originally shot for television commercials, industrials, marketing and public relations films.
A Portrait of Aspen (1987) contains scenes of Aspen and vicinity, including: establishing shots of the town; mountain wildflowers; time-lapse cinematography of mountain peaks; lightning storms, clouds and the moon; aerial views; the July 4th parade through town; street scenes at sunset; a mountain sunset with rainbows; a hiker in a field of wildflowers; rock climbers; violinists; river scenics; a rugby tournament, rafting; kayaking; tennis, with John McEnroe, Vitas Gerulaitis and Howard Cosell; cowboys rounding up

horses; dude ranch scenes; mountains with new snow; a llama eating fruit; mountain bikers; autumn scenes; Victorian houses with fall colors; gliders and sailplanes; aerial over forest; horses in meadow; first snow falling; and winter scenes.
Size & Elements: Film: 16mm (over 10,000 feet, several completed films, each 30 min.; positives, negatives, originals and release prints). Videotape: 1" and 3/4" (amount unspecified; masters); VHS (approx. 6 programs; viewing copies with visible time code).
Cataloging: Shot lists; computerized cataloging for staff use only.
Access: Open to the public. Available for reuse. Research fees charged. Research requests accepted by mail and telephone.
Rights: Full rights held to some material. Some rights held to some material. Additional clearances may be necessary in some cases if material is to be reused (e.g., in the case of identifiable individuals).
Licensing: Available for licensing and reuse, subject to restrictions. License fees charged.
Restrictions: Additional clearances and/or fees may be necessary if images of identifiable individuals are used.
Viewing Facilities: Videotape.
Duplication Facilities: Videotape (outside arrangements can be made).

COLORADO (Aurora)

CIMARRON PRODUCTIONS
3131 South Vaughn Way, Suite 134
Aurora, CO 80014
(303) 368-0988

Don Cohen (President)

Contacts: Sam Brennan (Vice President, Production); Buddy Saper (Executive Producer)
Services: Videotape stock footage sales library.
Description: Small but growing collection of Colorado stock footage. Includes the Denver Capitol building, the front range of the Rocky Mountains, the farmlands of the Eastern Colorado plains, an older couple in a park in springtime, office workers working on IBM PC computers and using telephones, and an X-ray technician at a hospital.
Size & Elements: Videotape: Betacam and 3/4" (6 videotapes).
Cataloging: Card catalogs.
Access: Available for duplication, licensing and reuse.
Rights: Full rights held to some material.
Licensing: Available for licensing. License fees charged.
Restrictions: None specified.
Viewing Facilities: Videotape (3/4" and VHS).
Duplication Facilities: None.

COLORADO (Aurora)

Z-AXIS
10800 East Bethany Drive, Suite 500
Aurora, CO 80014
(303) 696-9608

Steve Cohen (President)

Contact: Ray Haushel (Vice President, Sales)
Services: Animation house. Videotape backgrounds and animated elements available to the public for duplication, licensing and reuse. Produces custom animation and special effects to order.
Description: Animated backgrounds, special effects, and objects. Holds backgrounds of all kinds, including simple, graded and animated starfields; moving plates and environment; special effects, including starbursts and laser effects; and miscellaneous objects, including two- and three-dimensional objects, airplanes, trees, buildings and graphic elements of all kinds.
   Also creates custom special effects and animation to order.
Size & Elements: Videotape: 1" (masters); 3/4" and VHS (viewing copies) (approx. 200-300 backgrounds; 500 animated elements total).
Cataloging: Staff assistance required.
Access: Available to the public for duplication, licensing and reuse. Research fees not charged. Research requests accepted by mail and telephone.
Rights: Full rights held to all material.
Licensing: Available for licensing. License fees charged.
Restrictions: None specified.
Viewing Facilities: Videotape (1", 3/4", VHS and MII).

Duplication Facilities: Videotape (1", 3/4", VHS and MII).

COLORADO (Boulder)

UNIVERSITY OF COLORADO, BOULDER
WESTERN HISTORICAL COLLECTIONS
NORLIN LIBRARY
Campus P.O. Box 184
Boulder, CO 80309
(303) 492-7242

Cassandra M. Volpe (Archivist and Acting Department Head)

Contact: Cassandra M. Volpe
Services: University library and archives. Film and videotape collection open to researchers and scholars for in-house use only.
Description: University football films (3,500 films, 1926-present). Also holds six videotapes: *We Were Never Supposed To Be Rich: The Story of Cripple Creek, CO*, a history of working class families from Cripple Creek Gold Mining District (1893-1978); *University History* (1950s), including academic and social aspects of the school and alumni; *Diffusion of Light* (1950s), on the history of higher education; *University History (1877-1985)*, highlights of events, academic programs and social aspects of student life; *As Far As the Eye Can See: A High Plains Documentary* (1976), describing the lives of the people who lived on the High Plains, including homesteading, farming, ranching, schooling; and *The Life of the Western Coal Miner*, three videotapes describing the history of coal mining, mining techniques and the lives of coal miners.
Size & Elements: Film: 16mm (3,698 cans). Videotape: format unspecified (6 titles).
Cataloging: Card catalogs; printed lists.
Access: Open to researchers and scholars. For in-house use only. Research fees not charged. Research requests accepted in person (walk-in).
Rights: Some rights held to some material. Additional clearances may be necessary in some cases if material is to be reused (football films).
Licensing: Material not available for reuse.
Restrictions: Material not available for duplication or reuse of any kind.
Viewing Facilities: Film and videotape.
Duplication Facilities: None.

COLORADO (Colorado Springs)

NATIONAL WHEELCHAIR ATHLETIC ASSOCIATION
1604 East Pikes Peak Avenue
Colorado Springs, CO 80909
(719) 635-9300

Contact: Patricia Long (Program Administrator)
Services: Association. Videotapes available to the public for rental.
Description: Wheelchair sports and competitions. Titles include: *Wheelin' Steel*, a motivational documentary of the 1981 National Wheelchair Games, featuring interviews with several top athletes; *1985 National Wheelchair Games*, dominated by track and weightlifting competitions; *Los Angeles Olympics Wheelchair Track Events*, ABC Sports' coverage of the historic wheelchair track exhibition events at the 1984 Olympic Games in Los Angeles; *1985 Boston Marathon*, with good coverage of the wheelchair division; *1984 NWAA Olympic Trials*; and *Pan American Wheelchair Games*, highlights of the 1982 Pan Am Games in Nova Scotia.
Size & Elements: Videotape: 3/4" and VHS (7 titles; masters and viewing copies).
Cataloging: Brochure.
Access: Available to the public for rental.
Rights: Full rights held to some material.
Licensing: License fees charged.
Restrictions: None specified.
Viewing Facilities: None.
Duplication Facilities: None.
Related Materials: Brochure includes information on additional films and videotapes available through other sources.

COLORADO (Colorado Springs)

UNITED STATES OLYMPIC COMMITTEE
1750 East Boulder Street
Colorado Springs, CO 80909-5746
(719) 632-5551

COLORADO (Colorado Springs)

Fax: (719) 578-4654
Telex: 45-2424

Patricia R. Olkiewicz (Film Library)

Contact: Patricia R. Olkiewicz
Services: National sports committee. Film library available to educational institutions and nonprofit organizations for loan; possibly available for reuse, subject to restrictions.
Description: Highlights of Olympic games (1972-84); history of the Olympics; Olympic athletes. Titles include:
Elements of Gold (1984 Summer Olympics); *Frozen in Time* (1984 Winter Olympics), highlighting figure skating and alpine skiing; *The Struggle and the Triumph* (1980), with former Olympians John Nabor and Harvey Glance and appearances by Eric Heiden and Jesse Owens; *Fire and Ice* (1980 Winter Olympics), featuring Eric Heiden and the United States hockey team; *Beginnings* (1979 National Sports Festival).
Best With the Best (1976 Summer Olympics), features track and field footage of Lasse Viren, Dwight Stones and Dave Roberts, and the race between Frank Shorter and Waldemar Cierpinski. *The Swift, The Strong, The Beautiful* (1976 Summer Olympics), highlights combat sports, featuring Leo Randolph, John-John Davis, Sugar Ray Leonard, and the Spinks brothers; swimming events with Shirley Babashoff, John Nabor, Bruce Furniss, and Jim Montgomery; gymnastics, with Nadia Comaneci, Nelli Kim, Olga Korbut, Shun Fujimoto, and Peter Kormann. *Higher, Faster, Stronger* (1976 Summer Olympics), features yachting, rowing, weightlifting, cycling, basketball, equestrian competition and Bruce Jenner's record-breaking decathlon win.
Innsbruck '76 (1976 Winter Olympics). With Dorothy Hamill and Linda Fratianne (figure skating); Sheila Young and Peter Mueller (speed skating); Cindy Nelson and Phil Mahre (giant slalom); Bill Koch (cross-country skiing); Tai Babilonia and Randy Gardner (ice dancing).
Also holds *Olympic Harmony* (1976 Summer and Winter Olympics), with skater Dorothy Hamill and gymnast Nelli Kim; *Munich '72-Part I, II* and *III* (1972 Summer Olympics); *Sapporo '72* (1972 Winter Olympics); and *Olympic Skates and Skis* (1968 Winter Olympics).
Listed with, but not available from the USOC film library, are the following titles: *Best You Can Be* (Levi Strauss & Company), which highlights the Pan-American Games held in San Juan, Puerto Rico (1972); *Ten For Gold* (General Mills), a motivational film on Bruce Jenner; *New Gold for Old Glory* (Amateur Hockey Assn. of the U.S.), documenting the 1980 U.S. hockey team. Apply for information regarding these films.
Size & Elements: Film: 16mm (11 films; color).
Cataloging: Published list. USOC also provides filmography of related film and videotape materials.
Access: Collection available to the public. Maintained for distribution and rental rather than for research or reuse. Research requests accepted by mail and telephone. Research fees not charged. Available on a free-loan basis to educational institutions and nonprofit organizations; shipping fees charged.
Rights: Some rights held to all material. Additional clearances may be necessary in some cases if material is to be reused.
Licensing: Available for licensing and reuse, subject to restrictions. License fees not charged.
Restrictions: Material may not be used for commercial purposes.
Viewing Facilities: None.
Duplication Facilities: None.
Distributor: Selected titles available only from Modern Talking Picture Service, Inc. (q.v.).

COLORADO (Colorado Springs)

UNITED STATES SOCCER FEDERATION
1750 East Boulder Street
Colorado Springs, CO 80909-5791
(719) 578-8300
Fax: (719) 578-8307
Telex: 450024 US SOCCER FED

Werner Fricker (President)

Contact: Doug Newman (Administrative Assistant, National Teams)
Services: United States governing body of soccer. Videotape collection available for licensing and reuse.
Description: International soccer matches, featuring United States national teams.
Size & Elements: Videotape: format unspecified (approx. 20 videotapes;

masters and viewing copies).
Cataloging: Dope sheets or release sheets.
Access: Available for duplication. Research requests accepted by mail and telephone.
Rights: Full rights held to all material.
Licensing: Available for licensing. License fees not charged.
Restrictions: None specified.
Viewing Facilities: Videotape (3/4" and VHS).
Duplication Facilities: Videotape.

COLORADO (Denver)

AMERICAN BISON ASSOCIATION
P.O. Box 16660, Stockyard Station
Denver, CO 80216
(303) 292-2833

Laurie Dineen (Executive Director)

Contact: Laurie Dineen
Services: Association. Videotape material available for reuse on a case-by-case basis.
Description: Formerly known as American Buffalo Association. Holds one videotape showing various buffalo herds around the United States.
Size & Elements: Videotape: format unspecified (1 title).
Cataloging: None specified.
Access: Available to the public. For in-house use only. Research fees not charged. Research requests accepted by mail and telephone.
Rights: Full rights held to all material.
Licensing: Apply for information.
Restrictions: Requests for reuse considered on a case-by-case basis.
Viewing Facilities: Videotape.
Duplication Facilities: None.

COLORADO (Denver)

AMERICAN HUMANE ASSOCIATION
9725 East Hampden Avenue
Denver, CO 80231
(303) 695-0811
Fax: (303) 695-6348

Larry Brown (Executive Director)

Contact: Carol Moulton (Information and Education Specialist)
Services: Association. Videotape material available for educational distribution and possibly reuse, subject to clearance and approval.
Description: Television documentary *Charlie, The Dog Nobody Wanted*, about the life of a dog abandoned on the streets and the saga of homeless pets.
Size & Elements: Videotape: 3/4" and 1/2" (1 title).
Cataloging: Brochure (available on request).
Access: Intended for educational distribution rather than for research or reuse. Requests are accepted by mail and in person. Rental fees charged.
Rights: Additional clearances may be necessary if material is to be reused.
Licensing: Available for licensing and reuse. License fees charged.
Restrictions: None specified.
Viewing Facilities: Film (16mm); videotape (1/2").
Duplication Facilities: None.
Distributor: Program also distributed by Focus on Animals (q.v.).

COLORADO (Denver)

COLORADO HISTORICAL SOCIETY
STEPHEN H. HART LIBRARY
1300 Broadway
Denver, CO 80203
(303) 866-2305

Katherine Kane (Director, Public Service and Access)

Contact: Katherine Kane
Services: Historical society. Film and videotape collection available for rental, research and duplication, subject to restrictions.
Description: History of Colorado. Particular strengths include Colorado resources and industry, railroads and educational films. Collections held

include: commercial and development films from State Division of Department of Commerce; films from Denver television stations (1960s); railroad films produced and/or distributed by Blackhawk Films (1960s); Sarochrome Film Co. promotional films for Colorado and the film production business in Colorado (1920s-70s); and educational films for student use.

Jean M. Dubois collection. Film relating to Colorado industries, tourist attractions and major events in Colorado history (1920s-50s). Dubois, a freelance newsreel cinematographer, filmed events throughout Colorado. Collection includes: the Cherry Creek flood in Denver (1933); the discovery of gold nuggets at the Lucky Charles Mine near Blackhawk (1934); martial law on Raton Pass (1936); testing of the new "M2-A2" tank for the Colorado National Guard (1937); the Canon City State Penitentiary and gas chamber; and Evelyn Walsh McLean wearing the Hope Diamond.

Colorado Ghost Towns relates Colorado's mining era from Pikes Peak Gold Rush (1859) to present day high-country ghost towns and mining camps. Includes scenic shots of early spring and the arrival of fall; Mesa Verde cliff dwellings; Rocky Mountain National Park and Blue Jeans Symphony.

Ballad of the Colorado Ute relates the ancient Ute Indian legends of youth versus age and war versus peace; *Colorado's Magic Wonderlands* shows four of Colorado's national monuments (Great Sand Dunes, Black Canyon of the Gunnison, Colorado National Monument, Dinosaur National Monument) and dude ranch life.

Size & Elements: Film: 16mm (50,000 feet); 8mm (5,000 feet) (500 items total; positive, negative, originals). Videotape: 1" (13 titles, 10 hours); 3/4" and 1/2" (6 titles, 5 hours; viewing copies).
Cataloging: Card catalogs for 8mm film; research library; cataloging of other materials in process.
Access: Open to the public. For in-house use only. Educational films available for rental. Research requests accepted by mail, telephone and in person (walk-in).
Rights: Rights status of material not known.
Licensing: Available for licensing and reuse, subject to restrictions. License fees charged (fees negotiated on an individual basis).
Restrictions: Restrictions depend on rights held by Society.
Viewing Facilities: Videotape (3/4" and VHS).
Duplication Facilities: None.
Related Materials: Photograph collection.

COLORADO (Denver)

DATURA PRODUCTIONS
3175 South Beeler Street
Denver, CO 80231
(303) 752-2511

Roger L. Dudley (President and Owner)

Contact: Roger L. Dudley
Services: Private collection. *Not open to the public.* Material available for licensing and reuse, subject to clearance and approval.
Description: Television newsfilm and television programs relating to the Denver area and the state of Colorado (1952 to the late 1970s). Subjects include Denver local news, transportation, television and cameras in Colorado courtrooms.
Size & Elements: Videotape: primarily 3/4" (600 videotapes; primarily masters, viewing copies not available).
Cataloging: Computerized cataloging for staff use only.
Access: Not open to the public. Available for licensing and reuse. Research requests accepted by mail and telephone.
Rights: Some rights held to some material.
Licensing: Available for licensing and reuse, subject to restrictions. License fees charged.
Restrictions: Licensing and reuse may be restricted.
Viewing Facilities: Videotape (3/4" and Betamax).
Duplication Facilities: None.

COLORADO (Denver)

DENVER PUBLIC LIBRARY
WESTERN HISTORY DEPARTMENT
1357 Broadway
Denver, CO 80203-2165
(303) 571-2009

Eleanor M. Gehres (Manager)

Contact: Eleanor M. Gehres
Services: Library. Videotape collection available for in-house research only.
Description: Recently produced videotapes relating to Western United States, Colorado and Denver local history; and Americana.

Sample titles include *Soldiers of the Summit* (10th Mt. Division activities during World War II and training activities in Washington and Colorado); *Colorado Getaways* (a travelogue of 40 scenic or historic Colorado locations); *The Challenge: Preserving Our Western Heritage; History Recovered* (a documentary on the 1984 archaeological survey of the site of the Battle of Little Big Horn with General Custer, narrated by Dick Cavett); *Denver: Emergence of a Great City; Science or Sacrilege: The Study of Native American Remains; Los Testamentos* (a documentary about Mexican American textile crafts and folk art); *Ute Indian Land;* and *Thomas Hornsby Ferril, One Mile Five Foot Ten* (featuring readings from the Denver poet's works).
Size & Elements: Videotape: 3/4" (67 titles).
Cataloging: Computerized cataloging; departmental general index.
Access: Open to the public. For in-house use only. Research fees not charged. Research requests accepted by mail, telephone and in person.
Rights: Some rights held to some material.
Licensing: Not available for licensing or reuse.
Restrictions: Duplication or reuse not permitted.
Viewing Facilities: Videotape (3/4").
Duplication Facilities: None.

COLORADO (Denver)

INTERNATIONAL ARABIAN HORSE ASSOCIATION
VIDEO LIBRARY
P.O. Box 33696
Denver, CO 80233
(303) 450-4774
Fax: (303) 450-5127

Street address: 12000 Zuni, Westminster, CO 80234

Contact: Tammie Utt (Merchandise Coordinator)
Services: Association. Videotapes available for rental and purchase. Material possibly available for licensing, subject to restrictions.
Description: Arabian horses; training, competitions, clinics and racing.

U.S. Nationals. Footage includes highlights (1982-86) and finals in various categories (since 1979).

Fair clinics. Dating from 1976, programs include: *Competitive Trail Ride Clinic; Dressage Demonstration; Endurance Ride Clinic; Hunter/Jumper Clinic; Park Horse/Working Cow Horse; Pleasure Driving Clinic; Stallion Management Lecture; Halter Clinic; Photo Clinic; Formal Driving Clinic; Round Ring and Leg Aids Clinic; Side Saddle Equitation Over Fences;* and *Trail Clinic (Showring).*

IAHA Arabian Horse Video Educational Library. Educational videotapes featuring top Arabian trainers include: *Cutting and Working Cow* (Don Ulmer); *English Pleasure* (Bob Battaglia); *Hunters and Jumpers* (Nikki McGinnis); *Halter Training and Conditioning* (Ron Palelek); and *Native Costume* (Rhita McNair).

Racing. Arabian racing (1979-80).

Miscellaneous. Titles include: *Drinkers of Wind; Kids and Kolts; The Proud Breed; Grooming Your Horse; Leading Your Horse; Nichols and Dimes; Preparing the Halter Horse for Show; Witez II;* and *Skowronek.*
Size & Elements: Videotape: VHS and Betamax (326 titles total).
Cataloging: Published catalogs.
Access: Open to the public. Research fees charged. Rental fees charged. Research requests and inquiries accepted by mail, telephone and in person.
Rights: Full rights held to some material. Some rights held to all material.
Licensing: Material possibly available for licensing. License fees charged (apply for information).
Restrictions: None specified.
Viewing Facilities: Videotape.
Duplication Facilities: Videotape.

COLORADO (Denver)

PASSAGE HOME COMMUNICATIONS
7800 East Iliff, Suite E
Denver, CO 80231
(303) 750-0055
Fax: (303) 750-0249

COLORADO (Englewood)

John Evans (President, Producer/Director)

Contact: Sales Representative
Services: Videotape producer. Videotapes available to the public for purchase and reuse, subject to restrictions.
Description: *SEA FANS, The Video Magazine of Planet Ocean* (quarterly programs, each 90 min.). Specializes in underwater photography, travel and diving footage. Each issue covers three diving travel destinations around the world, above and below water, and includes an underwater photo clinic with renowned photographers, equipment information, marine life closeups, and original music.

Subjects include: scuba diving, snorkeling, fish, blue sharks, manatee, corals, kelp, marine life, seaplane diving and exotic islands. Locations include: Micronesia, the Sea of Cortez, Bonaire, Kauai, Little Cayman, Grand Cayman, Palau, Truk, Ponape, British Virgin Islands, Belize, Cozumel, Andros, the Bahamas, Guanaja, Palm Beach, Saba, Maui and Key Largo.

Additional material includes underwater and sailing footage.
Size & Elements: Videotape: 1" (amount unspecified; unedited footage); VHS and Betamax (6 videotapes, each 90 min., NTSC, PAL and SECAM).
Cataloging: Footage logs.
Access: Available for purchase and reuse, subject to restrictions. Research fees charged, depending on intended use. Research requests accepted by mail and telephone.
Rights: Full rights held to all material. Additional clearances may be necessary in some cases if material is to be reused.
Licensing: Available for licensing and reuse, subject to restrictions. License fees charged, depending on intended use.
Restrictions: Reuse may be restricted, depending on intended use.
Viewing Facilities: Videotape (1/2").
Duplication Facilities: Videotape (none in-house, outside arrangements can be made).

COLORADO (Englewood)

H. M. EDWARDS
P.O. Box 3132
Denver Tech Center
Englewood, CO 80155
(303) 770-1971

Street address: 9059 East Chenango, Englewood, CO 80111

Contact: H. M. Edwards (Owner)
Services: Film and videotape producer; stock footage sales library.
Description: Horses and horsemanship, sports, vanishing Americana, historical documentary, auto racing; and camping (produced 1950s-present).

Sample titles include *Getting Ready to Jump; Showing and Judging the Saddlebred* and *Grand Prix Dressage.*
Size & Elements: Film: 16mm (59 titles, 250 cans, over 50,000 feet; positive, negative, reversal and original material). Videotape: 3/4" and VHS (59 titles, each 30 min.; masters and viewing copies).
Cataloging: Release sheets.
Access: Available for duplication, licensing and reuse. Research fees charged in some cases. Research requests accepted by mail, telephone and in person.
Rights: Some rights held to some material.
Licensing: Material available for licensing. License fees charged.
Restrictions: None specified.
Viewing Facilities: Film and videotape.
Duplication Facilities: Film (all formats); videotape.

COLORADO (Englewood)

NATIONAL CATTLEMEN'S ASSOCIATION
5420 South Quebec Street
Englewood, CO 80111
(303) 694-0305
Fax: (303) 694-0305 (Ext. 364)

John Meetz (Executive Vice President)

Contact: Jamie Kaestner (Manager, Broadcast Services)
Services: Industry association; videotape distributor. Material available primarily for distribution and rental.
Description: Videotapes in which Association leaders address policy issues. *Producing Wholesome Beef* deals with the use of growth-promoting hormones

in the beef supply. *The Story of Modern Beef* deals with modern production practices that enhance lean beef production.
Size & Elements: Videotape: 3/4" or VHS (2 videotapes).
Cataloging: None specified.
Access: Maintained for distribution and rental rather than for research or reuse.
Rights: Apply for information.
Licensing: Apply for information.
Restrictions: None specified.
Viewing Facilities: None.
Duplication Facilities: None.

COLORADO (Englewood)

SPORTS CAR CLUB OF AMERICA, INC.
P.O. Box 3278
Englewood, CO 80112-2105
(303) 694-7222
Fax: (303) 694-7391
Telex: 45-674 SCCA DVR

Street address: 9033 East Easter Place

Nicholas Craw (Chief Executive Officer and President)

Contact: Richard Smythe (Superintendent, Shipping and Receiving)
Services: Association; film rental library. Films available for rental to SCCA Regions only; some material possibly available to qualified requesters for duplication, licensing and reuse, subject to clearance and approval.
Description: Programs generally relating to sports cars, stock car racing, drag racing, Grand Prix and races at Daytona and Indianapolis.

Sample titles include: *LeMans, 1954,* showing the efforts of the Jaguar team; *A Month of Sundays,* following the 1981 NASCAR Grand National circuit; *Vroom at the Top; Men With Cars,* the 1958 running of the Sebring 12 Hour; *Zero to Sixty,* the history of the automobile and automobile racing in America from the late 1800s to 1960; *Mustang,* the history of Ford's revolutionary automobile; *Fastest Man on Wheels,* the thrilling saga of Mickey Thompson as he drives his 7,000-pound car to a new land-speed record.
Size & Elements: Film: 16mm. Videotape: VHS. (Over 100 titles total).
Cataloging: Published catalog (available to qualified parties on request).
Access: Available for rental to SCCA Regions (member clubs) only. Rental fees charged. Research requests accepted by mail and telephone.
Rights: Full rights held to some material. Additional clearances may be necessary in some cases if material is to be reused.
Licensing: Available for licensing and reuse, subject to restrictions.
Restrictions: Material available to qualified requesters for duplication, licensing and reuse in some cases.
Viewing Facilities: None.
Duplication Facilities: None.

COLORADO (Fort Collins)

COMMITTEE TO RESTORE THE CONSTITUTION
P.O. Box 986
Fort Collins, CO 80522
(303) 493-2408

Street address: 2218 West Prospect Road, Fort Collins, CO 80526

Archibald E. Roberts, Lt. Col., AUS (ret.) (Director)

Contact: Archibald E. Roberts
Services: Political organization. Videotape available for purchase.
Description: Organization specializing in political and economic publications. Has produced one videotape, *The Federal Reserve* (29 min.), an "interview with Col. Roberts, Mrs. Sofranko, Walter Robb. Facts behind national crisis. Identifies core problem. Explains county/state solution."
Size & Elements: Videotape: VHS (1 title).
Cataloging: Brochure.
Access: Available for purchase.
Rights: Full rights held to all material.
Licensing: Apply for information.
Restrictions: None specified.
Viewing Facilities: None.
Duplication Facilities: None.

COLORADO (Golden)

LEN AITKEN PRODUCTIONS, INC.
790 South Colorado Highway 74
Golden, CO 80401
(303) 526-1896

Leonard Aitken (President)

Contact: Leonard Aitken
Services: Film and videotape producer. Materials available for rental, purchase, licensing and reuse.
Description: Outdoor sports (rock climbing, skiing, ski touring and kayaking); nature (western rivers, reservoirs, lakes and dams); Colorado and the American West.

Titles include: *Good Time Skiing; Cross-Country Experience,* with Olympic Silver Medalist Bill Koch; *Winter Without Words; Cross-Country Ski Racing; Kayak; Break On Through,* on rock climbing at the Naked Edge; *Sky Sails,* on hang-gliding; *A River in the Desert,* on use of the Colorado River; and *A Divine Madness,* on performing arts in Colorado.
Size & Elements: Film: 16mm (10,000 feet; positive and negative); 8mm (1 title). Videotape: 3/4" (20 videotapes, each 10 min.); and VHS (9 titles, each 10-30 min.).
Cataloging: Brochures.
Access: Available to the public for rental and purchase. Orders accepted by mail. Inquiries and research requests accepted by telephone. Rental fee can be applied toward purchase.
Rights: Full rights held to all material. Additional clearances may be necessary in some cases if material is to be reused.
Licensing: Materials available for licensing and reuse, subject to clearance. License fees charged.
Restrictions: None specified.
Viewing Facilities: Film and videotape.
Duplication Facilities: None (outside arrangements can be made).

COLORADO (Gypsum)

SUMMIT FILMS, INC.
P.O. Box 420
Gypsum, CO 81637
(303) 524-9769

Street address: 1055 Cottonwood Pass Road

Roger C. Brown (President)

Contact: Rayl Zimmerman
Services: Film and videotape stock footage sales library.
Description: Sports, adventure, and travel films shot worldwide (1960-present). Specialized photography consists of travel shots and point-of-view (POV) shots from skis, kayaks, and hang gliders; 200 to 400 frame per second super slow motion shots of sports action, and traveling time-lapse shots (created by cinematographer Gordon Brown).

Action sports include: auto racing (Pike's Peak Hill Climb), biking (mountain and racing), climbing (mountain, rock, snow, ice, Yosemite), dog sledding, golf, hang-gliding (regular and stunt flying), hiking, horseback riding, hot air ballooning, ice skating (figure and speed), inner tubing (river and snow), kayaking (big water and rodeo), luge, parachuting, racewalking, rafting, rodeo (broncos and bulls), running, skiing (Alpine, cross-country, freestyle, glacier, skijoring, telemarking), snowmobiling, snowboarding, surfing (Hawaii North Shore, pipeline, Waimea Bay), swimming, tennis, trout fishing (lakes and streams), windsurfing.

Cities and towns include: Cambridge, Mass., Colorado Springs, Dar es Salaam, Denver, Gunnison, Lamu, Nairobi, Paris, San Francisco, Santa Fe, Sapporo, Washington, D.C., Zanzibar, mining towns (Aspen, Central City, Crested Butte, Leadville, Telluride and Ouray) and ski resorts.

Nature studies include aspens in the fall and spring, water (abstract reflections, brooks, drops, icicles, lakes, oceans, rivers, rivulets, streams, and waterfalls), snow (falling and on trees) and wildflowers from Africa and the desert.

Miscellaneous footage includes the Air Force Academy, Bent's Old Fort, Broadmoor, Chichen Itza, concerts (bluegrass, celebrity specials and classical), cowboys, ghost towns (Crystal River Mill, Red Mountain Pass, St. Elmo and others), the Masai Tribe, Mesa Verde, narrow gauge railroads (Georgetown Loop and Silverton-Durango), oil shale (Parachute Creek and Piance Basin),

Pike's Peak and the cog railway, Royal Gorge, Taos Pueblo and more.

Scenic footage includes canyon scenics (Black Canyon of the Gunnison, Dolores and the Grand Canyon), mountain aerials (summer and winter), ski resorts (Canada, Eastern and Western United States and Europe), mountains (El Capitan, Gore Range, Grand Tetons, Kilimanjaro, Maroon Bells, Mt. Rainier, Mt. Kenya, Mt. of the Holy Cross, Sentinel [the West Face], time-lapse cinematography (clouds, canyon walls and mountain landscapes), traveling time-lapse (cities, ski resorts and landscapes).

Wildlife (African) includes birds, buffalo, crocodiles, elephants, gazelles, giraffes, hartebeest, hippopotamus, Lake Naivasha flamingos, leopards, lions, monkeys, rhinoceros, wart hogs, wildebeests and zebras; (Colorado) butterflies, eagles, elk, deer, grouse, hawks, hummingbirds, ouzel; (Coral Reef) moray eels, sharks, turtles, and various fish; (Mexico) coyotes, sea gulls, ospreys, sea lions and sea turtles.
Size & Elements: Film: 16mm (1 to 2 million feet, over 100 titles; transferred to 1" videotape). Videotape: 1" (masters transferred from film); 3/4" and 1/2" (viewing copies with visible time code).
Cataloging: Subject catalog available upon request (no charge); computerized cataloging for staff use only; shot lists.
Access: Available for licensing and reuse. 3/4" or 1/2" videotape viewing copies with visible time code will be sent upon request. Research fees charged. Research requests accepted by mail and telephone.
Rights: Full rights held to some material. Shared rights held to some material. Additional clearances (extra talent releases) may be necessary in some cases if material is to be reused.
Licensing: Available for licensing and reuse. License fees charged. (Sponsor credits may be negotiated against cost in some cases.)
Restrictions: Restrictions apply.
Viewing Facilities: Film (16mm Steenbeck); videotape (3/4" and 1/2").
Duplication Facilities: Videotape (3/4" and 1/2").
Representative: Footage is sold or licensed through a representative acting on the corporation's behalf (apply for information).

COLORADO (Steamboat Springs)

SKI TV PRODUCTIONS INC./CHANNEL 24
P.O. Box 775048
Steamboat Springs, CO 80477
(303) 879-3724

Street address: Torian Broadcast Center, Torian Plum Plaza, Ski Time Square

Tom M. Greer (Director); C. J. Hall (Producer)

Contacts: Tom M. Greer; C. J. Hall
Services: Television broadcaster; film and videotape producer. Collection available for duplication, licensing and reuse.
Description: Stock footage and edited "recreational segments" (1982-present, mostly produced 1985-87) relating to summer and winter recreation, including skiing and ski racing; major U.S. resort destinations, including St. Thomas (U.S. Virgin Islands); senior citizens partaking in summertime activities; *Photographers' Eye* series, featuring interviews with 26 world-famous photographers; interviews with pioneers of the ski industry, famous skiers and ski racers. Thirteen episodes of the *Ski TV* series are available.
Size & Elements: Film: 35mm (15,000 feet; color negative). Videotape: 1" (amount unspecified; transfers from film and bump-ups of some 3/4" videotapes); 3/4" (approx. 5,000 hours; masters and viewing copies); 1/2" (amount unspecified; viewing copies).
Cataloging: Log sheets; computerized cataloging available to researchers; shot lists; research library.
Access: Available for duplication, licensing and reuse. Research requests accepted by mail, telephone and in person (by appointment only).
Rights: Full rights held to all material.
Licensing: Available for licensing and reuse, subject to restrictions. License fees charged.
Restrictions: Additional clearances may be necessary in some cases if material is to be reused. Some restrictions apply to series usage for broadcast, cable and educational purposes.
Viewing Facilities: Film (16mm) and videotape.
Duplication Facilities: Videotape (3/4" with timebase correction, 1/2" with or without time base correction). 1" bump-ups can be arranged out-of-house.

COLORADO (Westminster)

ARABIAN HORSE TRUST
12000 Zuni Street
Westminster, CO 80234
(303) 450-4710

Gary L. Carpenter (Executive Director)

Contacts: Deborah A. Wilson (Public Events Coordinator and Film Program Coordinator); Lori Grumet (Librarian/Archivist)
Services: Nonprofit charitable foundation. Film library maintained primarily for distribution or rental; material generally not available for reuse.
Description: Arabian horse breeding programs; the various breeds and pedigrees; attempts to breed the perfect Arabian horse on a number of different farms in the U.S. and Europe; films on individual Arabian stallions and mares; history of the Arabian horse and its uses (working, showing and racing).
To Fly Without Wings, narrated by Orson Welles, depicts the Imperial Egyptian Stud breeding program. *The Kellogg Dream*, a compilation film with footage dating from 1926, shows steam shovel and mule teams preparing land for the ranch, pictures of famous horses, an eight-horse liberty drill team, trick horses and several scenes showing W. K. Kellogg enjoying the farm and horses.
Size & Elements: Film: 16mm (13,000 feet); 8mm (3,000 feet) (50 titles total). Videotape: VHS and Betamax (32 titles total).
Cataloging: Computerized cataloging.
Access: Open to the public. Maintained for distribution or rental rather than for research or reuse. Research fees charged based upon the extent of the request; requests accepted by mail, telephone and in person (walk-in and by appointment).
Rights: Full rights held to the historical collection; no rights held to contemporary collection.
Licensing: Apply for information. License fees charged.
Restrictions: Historical footage is not available to the public.
Viewing Facilities: Film (16mm projector); videotape (VHS).
Duplication Facilities: None.

COLORADO (Winter Park)

PEAK PRODUCTIONS, INC.
P.O. Box 329
Winter Park, CO 80482
(303) 726-5881

Denver office:
13791 East Rice Place, Suite 110
Aurora, CO 80015
(303) 699-7067
Fax: (303) 680-8947

Brooke Johnson (Vice President, Winter Park office)
Jim Anderson (President, Denver office)

Contacts: Brooke Johnson; Jim Anderson
Services: Film and videotape producer. Material available to the public for duplication, licensing and reuse.
Description: Winter sports, summer sports, leisure activities, Western lifestyle, mountain and tropical scenes.
Summer. Subjects include: Alpine slide; bicycling; balloon flight (point-of-view and ground shots); backpacking and hiking; fishing (lakes and streams); golfing; glider flight (point-of-view and ground shots); horseback rides; horseshoes; jeeping; mountain scenery; old buildings and cabins; outdoor concerts; running race and trail run; rafting; railroad trains (Amtrak); sunsets; sailing; tennis; ultralight flight (point-of-view and ground shots); windsurfing; wildlife (deer, elk and birds); and wildflowers.
Winter. Subjects include: Alpine skiers (model and public); ballet-skiers (competition); deer and elk; dog weight pull competition; freestyle aerial competition; handicapped skiers (lessons and races); mountain scenery; mogul ski competition; Nordic ski race; old ski footage (1940s); overview ski parade; powder skiing; professional ski races (1979-87); ski school classes; skijoring (horse and skier); ski patrol accident scene; ski rodeo; torchlight ski parade; cross-country skiing and picnics.
Miscellaneous. Subjects include: cattle branding and ranching; condominiums and homes (interiors and exteriors); computer (ski area design); hot-air balloons; jazz and bluegrass festivals; Las Vegas (casino signs); restaurants and bars; ski fashion show (professional models); ski lift construction (with helicopters); and tropical scenes (beaches and palm trees).
Size & Elements: Film: format and amount unspecified (all film has been transferred to videotape). Videotape: 1" (small amount); 3/4" (180 videotapes; masters and viewing copies).
Cataloging: In-house logging system.
Access: Available to the public for duplication and reuse. Research fees charged for preparation of sample reels. Research requests accepted by mail, telephone and in person (walk-in).
Rights: Full rights held to all material.
Licensing: Available for licensing and reuse. License fees charged.
Restrictions: None.
Viewing Facilities: Videotape (3/4" and 1/2").
Duplication Facilities: Videotape (3/4" and 1/2").

CONNECTICUT

CONNECTICUT (Cos Cob)

HARTLEY FILM FOUNDATION, INC.
Cat Rock Road
Cos Cob, CT 06807
(203) 869-1818

Elda Hartley (Founder and President)

Contacts: Carol Grayson (Vice President and Business Manager); Jim Porter (Production)
Services: Film and videotape producer. Materials available for rental, purchase and possibly licensing, subject to approval.
Description: *Aging.* In *Green Winter,* filmmaker Elda Hartley addresses the eternal but intensely personal issues of old age and attitudes toward death, work and euthanasia.
Consciousness research. Life After Death brings into focus the question of the persistence of consciousness after biological death. *The Human Computer* takes the viewer on a visual tour through the various forms of consciousness

control, from biofeedback to self-hypnosis. *Expanding the Limits of Consciousness* shows doctors, educators, artists and psychics using peak experience states to effect changes in perception.

Eastern medicine. *Introduction to Acupuncture* and *Tibetan Medicine: A Buddhist Approach to Healing.*

Health and healing. Titles include: *The Therapeutic Touch: Healing in the New Age,* relating to research in paranormal healing; *Biofeedback: The Yoga of the West* and *Hypertension: The Mind/Body Connection,* showing techniques for control of hypertension through the use of biofeedback.

Holistic health. Titles include: *Holistic Health: The New Medicine,* showing leading doctors in the field at work; *Healing and Wholeness: Holistic Health in Practice;* and *Fitness in the New Age.*

Mythology. Joseph Campbell, an expert in world mythology, wrote the narration for *Stairways to the Mayan Gods,* a journey to the ceremonial centers of the Mayan Indians.

Psychic research. Four films on parapsychology, including: *Edgar Cayce* and *Psychics, Saints and Scientists, Inner Spaces* and *The Ultimate Mystery,* with Apollo 14 astronaut Edgar D. Mitchell, combine recent scientific findings with ancient religious and meditational practices.

Stress relaxation. *Healing Yourself* and *The Relaxation Tape* train viewers in self-directed techniques, including controlled breathing techniques, point by point relaxation, use of autogenic phrases, concentration on living in the moment and deep relaxation.

Visualization. *Inner Vision: Visualizing Super Health,* featuring the work of Dr. Bernie Siegel, illustrates the many uses and varied practice of visualization, from fighting cancer to improving reading skills, and concludes with an extended visualization exercise.

Alan Watts films, including: *Going With the Flow; What Makes Japan Work; Zen and Now; Flowing with the Tao; Mood of Zen; Buddhism, Man and Nature* and *The Flow of Zen.*

World religions. Films and videotapes on animism, Baha'i, Buddhism, Christian mysticism, Hinduism, Islam, Jainism, Sufism, Taoism and Yoga.

Other films and videotapes include *The Global Brain,* based on Peter Russell's highly acclaimed book. This videotape suggests that humanity stands on the threshold of a major leap in human evolution and that spiritual growth is no less than the force of evolution working through the human mind.

Size & Elements: Film: 16mm. Videotape: VHS and Betamax. (Approx. 60 titles total).
Cataloging: Published catalogs; brochures.
Access: Available to the public for rental and purchase. Requests accepted by mail and telephone. Foundation membership available; members receive discount on film and videotape purchases.
Rights: Full rights held to all films and videotapes produced by the Foundation. Additional clearances may be necessary for other material to be reused.
Licensing: Available for licensing and reuse in some cases. License fees charged.
Restrictions: None specified.
Viewing Facilities: None.
Duplication Facilities: None.

CONNECTICUT (Enfield)

CONSTITUTIONAL REVIVAL
29 Fairfield Road
Enfield, CT 06082
(203) 745-2221

Andrew J. Melechinsky (President)

Contact: Andrew J. Melechinsky
Services: Educational institution. Videotapes available for purchase.
Description: Three videotapes are available: *The Constitution* (70 min., color) ("a 'nutshell' lecture on many of the absolute guarantees of individual freedom mandated by the U.S. Constitution," with a question and answer period); *Harry's War* ("a hilarious, soul-stirring fiction story of defiance of the I.R.S., with a moving and dramatic climax"); and *Anarchy USA* ("insights into the civil riots of the 1960s").
Size & Elements: Videotape: VHS and Betamax (3 titles).
Cataloging: List of media materials (available on request).
Access: Apply for information.
Rights: Apply for information.
Licensing: Apply for information.
Restrictions: None specified.
Viewing Facilities: None.

Duplication Facilities: None.

CONNECTICUT (Greenwich)

ARTSAMERICA, INC.
12 Havemeyer Place
Greenwich, CT 06830
(203) 869-4693

Contact: Staff
Services: Film, videotape and videodisc distributor. Materials available to the public for purchase.
Description: Films, videotapes and laser videodiscs relating to the visual arts. A sampling of titles includes: *Salvador Dali: A Soft Self Portrait* (1969); *Philip Pearlstein Draws the Artist's Model* (1985, available on videotape and videodisc); *End of the Art World* (Alexis Krasilovsky, 1971); *Picasso: The Man and His Work; Andrew Wyeth: The Helga Pictures* (available on videotape and videodisc); three films on Christo by Maysles Films, Inc., *Christo's Valley Curtain* (1974), *Running Fence* (1978) and *Islands* (1986); *Art 21 Video Magazine* (1987), a review of current New York shows; and several videotapes on photographers and photography.
Size & Elements: Videotape: VHS and Betamax. Videodisc: Laserdiscs. (Approx. 54 titles total).
Cataloging: Published brochures.
Access: Available to the public for purchase.
Rights: Apply for information.
Licensing: Apply for information.
Restrictions: None specified.
Viewing Facilities: None.
Duplication Facilities: None.

CONNECTICUT (Hartford)

CONNECTICUT HISTORICAL SOCIETY
PRINT & PHOTOGRAPHS DEPARTMENT
One Elizabeth Street
Hartford, CT 06105
(203) 236-5621

Christopher P. Bickford (Director)

Contacts: Kate Steinway (Curator, Prints & Photographs); Paige Savery (Curatorial Assistant, Prints & Photographs)
Services: Historical archives. Film and videotape material held primarily for research purposes; possibly available for reuse on a case-by-case basis.
Description: Historical film footage includes: *Yale, Dauntless Club, Hartford* (football game) (1930-32); *Trip Abroad* (1933); *Aviation* (1926); *Hartford Flood* (1936); *Hurricane* (1938); *St. Joseph's Cathedral Fire* (Aetna Life Insurance Co., 1956); *1st Kodachrome Hartford/Maxim Boat* (1935, color); and *Tercentenary, Connecticut* (1935). Other footage covers topics such as housebuilding, bricklaying, Alaska and Hartford.

Archival material (ca. 1919-20s) includes: *Company B 307 Infantry; Hose Company Outing; East Hampton; Red Cross Parade;* and *Silk Pageant.*

Videotapes held include: the history of Hartford public schools; *Colt: The American Legend; Sam Daggetts House,* by the Edison Institute; Earl Ray Holmes; and Colchester Historical Society movies on videotape (1931-40).
Size & Elements: Film: 16mm (27 cans). Videotape: VHS (7 titles, each 20 to 120 min.).
Cataloging: List available.
Access: Available to researchers and scholars only. Research fees charged in some cases. Research requests accepted by mail and in person (by appointment only).
Rights: Some rights held to some material.
Licensing: Available for licensing and reuse on a case-by-case basis. License and usage fees charged.
Restrictions: None specified.
Viewing Facilities: None.
Duplication Facilities: None.

CONNECTICUT (Hartford)

CONNECTICUT STATE LIBRARY
231 Capitol Avenue
Hartford, CT 06106
(203) 566-3690

CONNECTICUT (Hartford)

(203) 566-3692
(203) 566-5650

Mark H. Jones (State Archivist)

Contact: Ted Wohlsen (Head of History and Genealogy Unit)
Services: State library; film and videotape archives. Collection available to the public. Material possibly available for reuse.
Description: Films and videotapes produced in and about Connecticut (1930s-present).

Film materials include: *Flight* (1933), produced by the State Commission on Aeronautics; films from the World War II era, such as *How To Plant a Victory Garden, Preserving the Victory Garden Crop* and *Highway Sabotage;* film documenting the tenure of Gov. Robert Hurley (1941-43); *The 2nd Battalion Connecticut Infantry Leaving Hartford for the Front; Danger: Men Working; Points for Peddlers,* a film on bicycle safety; *Connecticut Answers* (1946), a television program produced by Southern New England Telephone Company; *The American Colonies; American Heritage* (black and white); film produced during the tenure of Gov. Raymond Baldwin (35mm negative and 16mm positive print); weekly television shows produced by Sen. Prescott Bush (1956-59), including 11 reels of Senator Bush's visit to Fort Bragg, N.C.; and the Connecticut Constitutional Convention of 1965 (25 items).

Videotape materials include: *Cameras in the Courtroom* (1982), footage from the first videotaped sessions of the Connecticut Supreme Court; news and documentary coverage of the death of Gov. Ella T. Grasso in 1981 (3/4", 6 videotapes); and the 1983 dedication ceremony in commemoration of Gov. Raymond E. Baldwin (VHS).
Size & Elements: Film: 35mm and 16mm (approx. 60 titles; negatives, positives and release prints). Videotape: 3/4" and VHS (approx. 10 items).
Cataloging: Printed list.
Access: Available to the public. Research fees not charged. Research requests accepted by mail, telephone and in person (walk-in).
Rights: Full rights held to some material. Much material in the public domain. Rights status of some material not known. Additional clearances may be necessary in some cases if material is to be reused.
Licensing: Available for licensing and reuse, subject to restrictions. License and usage fees not charged.
Restrictions: Licensing and reuse subject to clearance and approval.
Viewing Facilities: Film (16mm); videotape (VHS).
Duplication Facilities: None.

CONNECTICUT (Hartford)

REAL ART WAYS
94 Allyn Street
Hartford, CT 06103
(203) 525-5521

Jill C. Stone (Interim Managing Director)

Contact: Victor Velt (Video Curator)
Services: Contemporary arts center. Videotape open to the public for in-house viewing.
Description: Provides emerging and established artists the resources needed to make and show art. Videotape library contains early videotapes by Nam June Paik (1969); works purchased for the collection from artists and distributors; and documentation of all concerts and performances presented at the Center (1986-present), produced in-house with a two-camera system.

Artists include: Ernest Gusella, Woody Vasulka, Nam June Paik, Ant Farm, Meredith Monk, Bill Viola and Robert Wilson. Documentation videotapes include performances by John Cage, Karen Finley, Ethyl Eichelberger, Michael Peppe and Susan Foster.
Size & Elements: Videotape: 3/4" (approx. 200 titles; masters and viewing copies); VHS (some).
Cataloging: Published catalogs.
Access: Open to the public. For in-house use only. Research fees not charged. Research requests accepted in person (walk-in).
Rights: Limited rights held for in-house screening only.
Licensing: Not available for licensing or reuse through Real Art Ways.
Restrictions: Not available for licensing or reuse through Real Art Ways.
Viewing Facilities: Videotape (3/4" and VHS).
Duplication Facilities: Videotape (3/4" and VHS; editing facilities).

CONNECTICUT (Hartford)

MARK TWAIN MEMORIAL
Nook Farm
351 Farmington Avenue
Hartford, CT 06105
(203) 247-0998

Nancy Grover (Acting Executive Director)

Contact: Laura Vassell (Photo Archivist)
Services: Museum. Film and videotape material available for research, licensing and reuse, subject to restrictions.
Description: Documentary film (videotape viewing copies available) produced during the restoration of Mark Twain's house, with outtakes; and a collection of seven 16mm home movies from Nina Clemens Gabrilowitsch (Mark Twain's only grandchild). These films were recently acquired and have not yet been cataloged.
Size & Elements: Film: 16mm (7 items). Videotape: 3/4" and VHS (1 title).
Cataloging: Published list.
Access: Not open to the public. Access limited due to fragile condition of the film. Open to serious researchers and scholars, subject to approval by a review committee. Research requests accepted by mail and telephone.
Rights: Full rights held to all material.
Licensing: Available for licensing and reuse, subject to restrictions.
Restrictions: Requests for access to and reuse of collection considered on a case-by-case basis.
Viewing Facilities: Videotape (VHS).
Duplication Facilities: None.

CONNECTICUT (Lakeville)

CAMPBELL NORSGAARD
P.O. Box 448
Lakeville, CT 06039
(203) 435-9457

Contacts: Campbell Norsgaard; Ernestine Norsgaard
Services: Film and videotape producer; private collection. Material available for licensing and reuse.
Description: Original nature footage filmed in the Norsgaard backyard and meadow in Connecticut over the last 35 years. Includes insect life cycles; birds and nesting habits; and originals, masters and internegatives of 50 short subjects (each 4 min.) formerly distributed to schools. Provided some of the footage featured in the National Geographic television special, *The Hidden World* and all the footage in *The Backyard Jungle* (ABC-TV).

Recently produced their first videotape (transferred from 16mm film), *Nature's Great Balancing Act* (approx. 26 min.), narrated by Meryl Streep.
Size & Elements: Film: 16mm (85,000 feet; original Ektachrome shot at sound speed). Videotape: format unspecified (1 title).
Cataloging: Shot lists.
Access: Not open to the public. For in-house use only. Available for licensing and reuse.
Rights: Full rights held to all material.
Licensing: Available for licensing and reuse. License and usage fees charged.
Restrictions: None specified.
Viewing Facilities: None.
Duplication Facilities: None.

CONNECTICUT (Middletown)

WESLEYAN UNIVERSITY
WESLEYAN CINEMA ARCHIVES
301 Washington Terrace
Middletown, CT 06457
(203) 347-9411 (Ext. 2259)

Prof. Jeanine Basinger (Curator, Wesleyan Cinema Archives)

Contacts: Prof. Jeanine Basinger; Candace Bothwell (Associate Curator) (Ext. 3101)
Services: Film and television archives. Open to researchers, teachers and scholars only. Material available for licensing and reuse, subject to restrictions.
Description: *Omnibus Collection.* 230 broadcast hours of the weekly television series *Omnibus,* aired on CBS, ABC and NBC (1952-61). Created by the Ford Foundation's TV-Radio Workshop and its executive producer Robert Saudek, the series was conceived as a forum for material which had no place in

commercially dictated television programming; an agreement was reached with its sponsors, barring them from any creative control.

The series is a compendium of the performing arts in the U.S., containing such performances as Gene Kelly's *Dancing: A Man's Game,* in which Kelly presents a history of tap and modern dance featuring famous athletes Mickey Mantle, Sugar Ray Robinson, Johnny Unitas and Bob Cousy, likening athletic movement to dance movement; *A Jury of Her Peers,* directed by Yul Brynner; *The Art of Ballet* and *The Art of Choreography,* two television essays choreographed by Agnes de Mille; Charlton Heston discussing the Renaissance; several programs by Leonard Bernstein designed to popularize classical music; a film written by E. B. White about a Maine lobsterman; Peter Ustinov's first appearance on American television, playing Dr. Samuel Johnson; and the television appearance which made Elaine May and Mike Nichols famous. Other television firsts include the first film of an X-ray, the first mini-series, the first dramatic plays written expressly for television, the first opera staged for television and the first presentation of a Jacques-Yves Cousteau film.

Size & Elements: Film: kinescopes, format unspecified (230 broadcast hours). Videotape: 3/4" (masters).
Cataloging: Staff assistance required. Organized by broadcast date. There are minimal cast credits; some indexing on personal names is available.
Access: Open to researchers, scholars, teachers and institutions. Material possibly available for duplication, licensing and reuse, subject to copyright clearance. Research fees charged in some cases. Research requests accepted by mail and telephone.
Rights: Screening rights held to all material. Broadcast rights retained by copyright owner. Additional clearances may be necessary in some cases if material is to be reused.
Licensing: Available for licensing and reuse, subject to restrictions. License fees charged in some cases.
Restrictions: Reuse and licensing restricted. Duplication requests must be initially approved by Archives. License fees negotiated on a case-by-case basis with copyright owner (not by Wesleyan University).
Viewing Facilities: Videotape (3/4").
Duplication Facilities: None.
Related Materials: Supporting paper documentation (scripts, contracts, etc.)

CONNECTICUT (Middletown)

WESLEYAN UNIVERSITY
WORLD MUSIC ARCHIVES
OLIN LIBRARY
Middletown, CT 06457
(203) 347-9411 (Ext. 2529)

James Farrington (Music Librarian)

Contact: James Farrington
Services: Library; videotape archives. Open to researchers and scholars only.
Description: Holds primarily ethnomusicological subject matter, such as field recordings and documentation of local productions by visiting artists. Includes films which accompany theses and dissertations.

Sample items include: *Extreme Close-Up* (John Rudel), the story of an Afro-Caribbean drumming ensemble created at Penfield House, a Montreal residential school for mentally handicapped students; a film made in Tashgurghan, Afghanistan, featuring a shamanistic ritual with gobuz fiddle, followed by shots of a garden in Kabul; an Uzbek male dance performed by a half-dressed female impersonator; several videotapes of Sioux Indians Bill Horncloud, vocalist, and Bill Powers, dancer (1970), including an interview with Bill Horncloud by David McAllester; Australian Aboriginal dances (1975) such as the Mosquito Dance, Fish Dance, Rope Dance, Devil Dance and Bubinda Dance; singers recorded on the island of Samothraki, Greece in 1968; *Ch'in* demonstration by Tong Kin-Woon, followed by demonstration of a tea ceremony; performance on the Javanese Gamelan, including the Flower Garden Scene from the Javanese opera *Ramajara* (1971); Balinese Dance and Balinese Wayang (1969); South Indian music, featuring the teaching of Karnatic Raga Bhairavi, with Barbara Benari and Lenore Smith (1969); Kathak dances performed by North Indian dancer Gopi Krishna and tabla player Sharda Sahai, with explanations in Hindi (1973).
Size & Elements: Videotape: VHS and other formats (approx. 125 videotapes).
Cataloging: Partial cataloging.
Access: Open to researchers and scholars only. Research fees not charged. Research requests accepted in person (by appointment only).
Rights: Rights status of most material not known.
Licensing: Apply for information.

Restrictions: None specified.
Viewing Facilities: Videotape (VHS).
Duplication Facilities: None.

CONNECTICUT (Mystic)

MYSTIC SEAPORT MUSEUM, INC.
MEDIA RESOURCE CENTER
FILM/VIDEO ARCHIVES
P.O. Box 6000, Route 27
Mystic, CT 06355-0990
(203) 572-0711 (Ext. 279 or 289)
Fax: (203) 572-8693 (office hours EST)
Telex: 5106014254 SEA VID UQ
Easylink: 62929838

Kenneth E. Mahler (Manager of Film/Video Archives)

Contacts: Kenneth E. Mahler; Suki Williams (Film/Video Promotion and Research Assistant)
Services: Museum; educational institution; film and videotape archives, producer and distributor; stock footage sales library. Open to researchers, scholars, producers and to the public by appointment only.
Description: Maritime subjects, scenes and events. Subjects covered include: square-rigged sailing passages; whaling footage; America's Cup races, including many hours of 1930 and 1937 footage of J boats and period spectator craft, early 12-meter racing, and 1983 footage of America's loss to the Australians; famous and historic ocean passages, often shot by notable amateurs and professionals; yacht races; ice boating; sand yachts; Off Soundings Club races (1937-present); boatbuilding and restoration footage; Gold Cup Motor Boat racers; SORC races (1983); footage of grounds, vessels and special events at the Mystic Seaport Museum; model testing; tank testing; swordfishing; oystering; hydrofoil boats; adverse weather footage, including a stormy passage around Cape Horn (1929); recreational sailing; and various sailing personalities.

Completed programs available for purchase include the *America's Cup Yachting Series* (6 videotapes), documenting the races of 1958, 1962, 1964, 1967, 1970, 1974, 1977, 1980 and 1983; *ARC Across the Atlantic,* on the Atlantic Rally for Cruisers (November, 1986); *Around Cape Horn,* on Captain Irving Johnson's round-the-world sail on 1929; *The Ways at Wallace and Sons,* on the building of the ill-fated coasting schooner *John F. Leavitt; The Bank Dory,* on the construction of a dory at Lunenburg, Nova Scotia; *Irving Johnson: High Seas Adventurer,* showing seven of his round-the-world voyages; *Yachting in the '30s,* featuring 45 minutes of newsreels and home movies; *Sail To Glory,* the development of the yacht *America* and its 1967 America's Cup victory; and *To Win At All Costs: The Story of the America's Cup,* an historical look at the race for the most prestigious trophy in yachting.
Size & Elements: Film: 16mm (700,000 feet; master negatives, interpositives, internegatives and prints). Videotape: 2" (amount unspecified); 1" (220 hours; masters); 3/4" (220 hours; masters and viewing copies); VHS (amount unspecified; viewing copies).
Cataloging: Card catalogs; computerized cataloging available to researchers; shot lists; research library.
Access: Open to researchers, scholars, producers and the public (by appointment only). For in-house use only. Available for duplication and reuse. Research fees charged. Research requests accepted by mail, telephone and in person (by appointment only). Preview videotapes available.
Rights: Full rights held to all material. Additional clearances may be necessary in some cases if material is to be reused (e.g., for spot commercial use).
Licensing: Available for licensing and reuse, subject to restrictions. License and usage fees charged (fee schedule available).
Restrictions: Maximum footage usage per production limited to 10 minutes screen time per 60-minute program.
Viewing Facilities: Film (16mm); videotape (3/4" and VHS).
Duplication Facilities: Film (16mm and 8mm to 1", 3/4" and 1/2" videotape); videotape (1", 3/4", VHS and Betamax).
Representatives: In Europe and Australia (apply for information).

CONNECTICUT (New Haven)

NEW HAVEN COLONY HISTORICAL SOCIETY
THE WHITNEY LIBRARY
114 Whitney Avenue
New Haven, CT 06510-1025
(203) 562-4183

CONNECTICUT (New Haven)

Arthur D. Reinhart (Librarian and Curator of Manuscripts)

Contact: James Campbell (Assistant Librarian)
Services: Historical society. Film collection available for research and possibly reuse.
Description: *Civil Defense Collection* (1940-47). Holds *The Warning; They're Dropping Incendiaries; Aerial Films of New Britain, Connecticut;* and *Aerial Films of Englewood, Colorado.*
Little Theater Guild of New Haven Collection (1935). Five reels of silent film from a Guild production of *Vanity Fair.*
Size & Elements: Film: 16mm (10 films).
Cataloging: Card catalogs.
Access: Available for research and reuse, subject to clearance. Research and viewing fees charged. Research requests accepted by mail.
Rights: Rights status of material unknown. Additional clearances may be necessary in some cases if material is to be reused.
Licensing: Apply for information.
Restrictions: None specified.
Viewing Facilities: None.
Duplication Facilities: None.

CONNECTICUT (New Haven)

SEA TV
1619 Chapel Street
New Haven, CT 06511
(203) 624-0470
(800) 323-7245

Charles Croft (President)

Contact: Charles Croft
Services: Videotape producer and distributor. Footage available to the public for licensing and reuse.
Description: Sailing and power boating footage, including racing, cruising, sailboats, general power boating footage and sailing conditions. Also holds footage of the Caribbean region from the Virgin Islands to Grenada, concentrating on scenics, shoreside footage, boats and boating; and polo footage shot at the Palm Beach (Fla.) Polo and Country Club.
Has access to, and in some cases represents for stock footage sale, other collections of historical and contemporary footage related to sailing, including collections owned by famous sailing personalities.
Produces and distributes approximately 120 videotapes to the homevideo market, all relating to sailing and boating.
Size & Elements: Videotape: 1" (20 hours; masters); 3/4" (50 hours; masters and viewing copies); VHS (viewing copies).
Cataloging: Staff assistance required.
Access: Available to the public for duplication and reuse. Research fees charged in some cases. Research requests accepted by mail and telephone.
Rights: Full rights held to all material, except for certain videotapes which are available for distribution only. Additional clearances may be necessary in some cases if material is to be reused.
Licensing: Available for licensing and reuse. License fees charged.
Restrictions: None specified.
Viewing Facilities: Videotape (3/4" and VHS).
Duplication Facilities: Videotape (3/4" and VHS; outside arrangements can be made for 1").

CONNECTICUT (New Haven)

YALE FILM STUDY CENTER
Box 174, Yale Station
New Haven, CT 06520
(203) 432-0148

Street address: 305 Crown Street, New Haven, CT 06510

Audrey Kupferberg (Director)

Contact: Sharon DellaCamera (Administrative Assistant)
Services: University film study center. Film and videotape collection open to researchers and scholars for in-house use only. Some material available for duplication and reuse, subject to restrictions.
Description: *Yale Film Collection* (16mm, Super 8mm and 8mm, approx. 2,000 titles). Classic American and European feature films, short subjects, documentaries and independent films from all periods.
Victor Cromwell Collection (1940s-60s). Various television programs, mostly aired on CBS. Consists of kinescopes and programs originally presented on film.
Hubley Studio Archive. Reference collection containing papers and films (prints and workprints) pertaining to the careers of animators John and Faith Hubley.
Herbert Brodkin Archive (primarily 35mm positive prints). Several hundred television shows, many originally produced by Plautus Productions and Titus Productions, including episodes from the series *The Defenders, Espionage* and *The Nurses.* Also contains kinescopes of early live television dramas, papers, scripts and production materials. No rights are held to this collection, which is available for research use only.
Columbia Pictures Deposit (16mm, approx. 200 titles; release prints). Feature films produced by Columbia. Available for research use only.
John Griggs Collection. Includes approximately 200 Kodascopes (ca. 1920s-30s), short subjects once distributed to amateurs and home users.
Archival material relating to the history of Yale University is to be transferred to the Center. Material relating to Yale athletics is held by the Athletic Department at the Ray Tompkins House.
Size & Elements: Film: 35mm, 16mm, Super 8mm and 8mm (approx. 2,000 titles). Videotape: format unspecified (1,000 videotapes). Videodisc (format and amount unspecified).
Cataloging: Computerized cataloging for staff use only.
Access: Open to researchers and scholars only. For in-house use only. Public domain material available for duplication and reuse, subject to restrictions. Research fees charged. Research requests accepted by mail, telephone and in person (by appointment only).
Rights: No rights held to most material. Some material in the public domain. Additional clearances may be necessary in some cases if material is to be reused.
Licensing: Available for reuse, subject to restrictions. Usage fees charged.
Restrictions: Copyright and donor restrictions apply to some material.
Viewing Facilities: Film (35mm [limited], 16mm and Super 8mm); videotape (3/4", VHS and Betamax); videodisc.
Duplication Facilities: None.
Related Materials: Movie memorabilia, including approximately 100,000 glossy film stills; one million posters and lobby cards (1945-70); and film scripts.

CONNECTICUT (Norwalk)

FRIENDS OF ANIMALS
30 Haviland Street
Norwalk, CT 06854
(800) 631-2212
(203) 866-5223
Fax: (203) 853-9102

Priscilla Feral (President)

Contact: Sara Seymour (Business Manager)
Services: Nonprofit animal rights organization. Films and videotapes available for rental and licensing, subject to restrictions.
Description: Two films are available: *Skins,* concerning the fur industry and *Seals,* relating to seal hunting in the U.S.
Size & Elements: Film: 16mm (2 titles; release prints). Videotape: 3/4" and VHS (viewing copies).
Access: Available to the public for loan, rental and reuse. Research and loan requests accepted by mail and telephone.
Rights: Full rights held to all material.
Licensing: Available for licensing, subject to restrictions. License fees charged.
Restrictions: Requests for licensing and reuse considered on a case-by-case basis.
Viewing Facilities: None.
Duplication Facilities: None.
Distributors: *Skins* is also available through Focus on Animals (q.v.) and International Society for Animal Rights, Film Library (q.v.).

CONNECTICUT (Sandy Hook)

VIDEO YESTERYEAR
Box C
Sandy Hook, CT 06482

(203) 426-2574
(800) 243-0987
Fax: (203) 797-0819

Jon Sonneborn (President)

Contact: Jon Sonneborn
Services: Film and videotape archives; stock footage sales library.
Description: Over 1,000 titles of "nostalgia" movies, featuring rare and unabridged versions of many films and early television programs.

Genres and collections include: comedy and cartoons; music and variety; drama and adventure; crime, mystery, suspense and horror; science fiction and fantasy; Westerns; serials; films from the National Film Board of Canada; documentary and propaganda; avant-garde; and the "Golden Age" of television.

Examples of the more unusual titles available include: *The Silent Enemy* (1930), with Chief Yellow Robe and his tribe of Ojibway Indians, in which the Chief calmly states that American civilization is ending his people's way of life, and that "soon we will be no more"; three films featuring Richard Nixon, *Checkers, Old Glory* and *Resignation;* Alain Resnais' *Night and Fog* (1955); *Die Deutsche Wochenschau #1 (The German Weekly Newsreel)* (1941), four Nazi newsreels for German homefront exhibition during the war; *Borneo* (1937, Martin and Osa Johnson); *Anarchy U.S.A.* (1966); and *Father Sergius* (1917, Yakov Protozanov), an adaptation of Leo Tolstoy's story and one of the rare surviving Russian films from the pre-Soviet era.
Size & Elements: Film: Super 8mm (some titles). Videotape: 3/4", VHS, Betamax I and II (1,000 titles; viewing copies; some in PAL).
Cataloging: Published catalogs; card catalogs.
Access: Available for rental and purchase. Stock footage available for duplication, licensing and reuse on a case-by-case basis. Research fees charged in some cases. Research requests accepted by mail and telephone.
Rights: Some rights held to some material. Some material in the public domain. Additional clearances may be necessary in some cases if material is to be reused. Can clear all necessary rights.
Licensing: Available for licensing and reuse, subject to restrictions. License and usage fees negotiated on a case-by-case basis.
Restrictions: All requests for licensing and reuse subject to acceptance and approval. Videotape titles in catalog are for sale to consumers; stock footage requests will be accepted and researched on a case-by-case basis.
Viewing Facilities: Videotape.
Duplication Facilities: Videotape.

CONNECTICUT (Stamford)

TITAN SPORTS, INC.
1055 Summer Street
Stamford, CT 06905
(203) 352-8703
Fax: (203) 352-8699
Telex: 643283 TITAN STM

Contact: Myrna Gardner (Manager, Marketing and Personal Appearances)
Services: Corporation; corporate archives; distributor; film and videotape producer and archives; television syndicator. Material available for syndication and possibly licensing, subject to restrictions.
Description: Complete footage of World Wrestling Federation television programs and specials (1973-present). Includes: Spanish language programs (122 shows); Arabic language programs (13 shows); French language programs (12 shows); *Wrestlemania I, II* and *III;* World Wrestling Federation music videos; action footage of the World Wrestling Federation; and archival footage of individual wrestlers in the ring with opponents and in interview situations.
Size & Elements: Film: 16mm (approx. 53 cans; original prints, not for release). Videotape: 1" (2,270 videotapes; masters and protection copies); 3/4" (3,600 videotapes; masters and protection copies).
Cataloging: Dope sheets and release sheets.
Access: Maintained for distribution and rental rather than for research or reuse. Research fees not charged. Research requests accepted by mail and telephone.
Rights: Full rights held to all material. Additional clearances may be necessary in some cases if material is to be reused.
Licensing: Available for licensing, subject to restrictions. License fees charged (payment required in advance).
Restrictions: Requests for licensing reviewed on a case-by-case basis.
Viewing Facilities: None.
Duplication Facilities: Videotape.

CONNECTICUT (Trumbull)

FOCUS ON ANIMALS
P.O. Box 150
Trumbull, CT 06611
(203) 377-1116
Fax: (203) 261-7423

Esther R. Mechler (Director)

Contact: Esther R. Mechler
Services: Foundation; film and videotape distributor. Collection maintained primarily for distribution.
Description: Materials relate to animal rights and animal welfare issues, including African wildlife, animal research, animal rights and the role of religion, extinction, fur production, Greenpeace's campaign to save the whales, hunting and trapping, pet surpluses and the need for spaying and neutering, vegetarianism, vivisection and wolves.
Size & Elements: Film: 16mm (amount unspecified). Videotape: 3/4" and VHS (16 titles).
Cataloging: Published catalogs; research library.
Access: Available to researchers, scholars and filmmakers only. Maintained primarily for distribution. Research fees not charged. Research requests accepted by mail.
Rights: Rights retained by original producers. Additional clearances from original producers may be necessary in some cases if material is to be reused.
Licensing: Apply for information. License fees charged.
Restrictions: None specified.
Viewing Facilities: Film (16mm); videotape.
Duplication Facilities: None.

CONNECTICUT (Weston)

WESTON WOODS
Weston, CT 06883-1199
(800) 243-5020
(203) 226-3355

Contact: Blanche Stout (Customer Service)
Services: Distributor. Films and videotapes available for rental and purchase.
Description: Children's films and videotapes.

Animated. Sample titles include: *In The Night Kitchen* (Maurice Sendak); *The Silver Cow,* a retelling of a traditional Welsh tale illustrated by Warwick Hutton; *The Most Wonderful Egg in the World,* in which Helme Heine's vivid watercolors set the stage for this tale of three hens, each determined to win the title of princess; *Harold and the Purple Crayon,* Crockett Johnson's story in which Harold decides to go for a walk in the moonlight, finds there isn't any moon and draws one with his purple crayon.

Iconographic. Productions based on non-animated illustrations. Titles include: *Frog Went A-Courtin',* a 400-year-old Scottish ballad which tells the tale of the courtship of Mr. Frog and Miss Mouse; *Stone Soup,* a witty vignette of French village life in which three soldiers encounter selfish townspeople, cook up a soup of stones and a clever way of tricking the villagers; set in Dreamtime, *The Rainbow Serpent,* an Aboriginal legend of the Creation, follows the serpent Goorialla on his journey across Australia, where he creates the birds, animals, plant life and geographical features present there today.

Live action. Titles include: *Sendak,* in which Maurice Sendak describes the significant events of his life and their impact on his work; *The Doughnuts,* based on Robert McCloskey's character Homer Price and his experiences with a doughnut machine gone berserk; *The Sorcerer's Apprentice,* set to Paul Dukas' symphony, demonstrates the relationship between the musical and the graphic arts, with illustrator Lisl Weil.

Selected titles are available in foreign language versions.
Size & Elements: Film: 16mm (132 titles; release prints). Videotape: VHS and Betamax (132 titles; viewing copies).
Cataloging: Published catalog.
Access: Available for rental and purchase. Research requests accepted by mail and telephone.
Rights: No rights held to any material. Additional clearances are necessary if material is to be reused.
Licensing: Apply for information.
Restrictions: None specified.
Viewing Facilities: None.
Duplication Facilities: None.

BRAY STUDIOS, INC.
P.O. Box 14
Westport, CT 06881
(203) 226-3777

Street address: 19 Ketchum Street, Westport, CT 06880

Paul Bray, Jr. (Producer)

Contact: Paul Bray, Jr.
Services: Film and videotape producer. Film material available for stock footage sale.
Description: All facets of aviation, especially accident reconstruction, pilot orientation, education and training, and historical footage. The accident reconstruction films contain radar plots and flight recordings, synchronized with air traffic control and cockpit voice recordings.
Size & Elements: Film: 35mm and 16mm (hundreds of titles; all elements; edited films and outtakes).
Cataloging: Production listings; staff assistance.
Access: For in-house use only. Available for licensing. Research fees charged in some cases. Research requests accepted by telephone.
Rights: Full rights held to all material.
Licensing: Available for licensing. License fees charged.
Restrictions: None specified.
Viewing Facilities: Film and videotape.
Duplication Facilities: None.

DELAWARE

DELAWARE (Dover)

DELAWARE STATE DIVISION OF HISTORICAL AND CULTURAL AFFAIRS
BUREAU OF ARCHIVES AND RECORDS MANAGEMENT
Hall of Records
Dover, DE 19901
(302) 736-5318

Street address: Legislative Avenue and Duke of York Street

Joanne Mattern (State Archivist)

Contact: Randy L. Goss (Photo Archivist)
Services: State agency. Historical film and videotape available for research and duplication; not available for reuse.
Description: Films relating to Delaware and its history (1922-present), especially from the 1940s-50s. Major topics include the National Guard, civil defense, World War II, local events and the Bicentennial (1976).

Sample titles include: *Fireman Parade* (1922); *Visit to Mt. Vernon* (1937); *Delaware Day, World's Fair* (1940); *Girl on Beach; Victory Gardens, World War II; Spinning Demonstration DuPont Exhibit* (1953); *Your Chicken Has Been to War; Wonderful Delaware* (1966, original print); *The Delaware Story* (1955; 1959 edition); and *The DuPont Story* (1956).

Recent videotape holdings consist of gubernatorial materials, including *Hats in the Ring.*
Size & Elements: Film: primarily 16mm (approx. 75 titles, 250 cans; positives, negatives, originals and release prints). Videotape: 3/4" and 1/2" (approx. 20 titles; mostly viewing copies).
Cataloging: Title list.
Access: Available to the public for research and duplication. Research fees not charged. Research requests accepted by mail, telephone and in person (by appointment only).
Rights: Some rights held to some material.
Licensing: Material not available for reuse.
Restrictions: Some material is restricted; material not available for reuse.
Viewing Facilities: None (equipment must be borrowed).
Duplication Facilities: None.

DELAWARE (Wilmington)

HAGLEY MUSEUM & LIBRARY
P.O. Box 3630

Wilmington, DE 19807
(302) 658-2400 (Ext. 276, Pictorial Collection)
Fax: (302) 658-0568

Street address: Buck Road

Dr. Glenn Porter (Director)

Contact: Jon Williams (Curator of Prints and Photographs)
Services: Museum. Films available to researchers, scholars and the public for in-house use only.
Description: Materials documenting the history of American business, technology and economy. Holds records of and works about business organizations and companies with national impact. Corporate archives containing film include:

Sperry Gyroscope Company (later Sperry Rand) *Collection.* Approximately 50 to 75 16mm films (1920s-60s), including: *Gunsight & Turret Testing 1943-1945; K-Sight Rolling Platform, 1943; Poland (W. L.) Various Devices, 1959; Construction of Sperry Plant, Lake Success, Great Neck; Talos Missile; Nike-Zeus Discrimination Radar Transmitter HV Power Supply; Test Flying with the Lockheed Hudson; Aerodynamics of the House Fly; One Second in the Life of a Hummingbird;* and various flight test films.

National Association of Manufacturers. Holds approximately 20 programs from the television series *Industry on Parade* (produced in the 1950s and early 1960s). Other episodes are held at the Smithsonian Institution and Library of Congress, Motion Picture, Broadcasting and Recorded Sound Division (q.v.).

Society of the Plastics Industry. Holds approximately 25 films from this trade association, located in Washington, D.C.
Size & Elements: Film: 16mm (approx. 125-150 titles).
Cataloging: Collection inventories.
Access: Open to researchers, scholars and the public. For in-house use only. (Pending capability for in-house transfer to videotape, Museum plans to make materials available for circulation). Research fees not charged. Research requests accepted by mail and telephone.
Rights: Full rights held to some material. Additional clearances may be necessary in some cases if material is to be reused.
Licensing: Material possibly available for licensing and reuse, depending on film and intended use.
Restrictions: Copyright restrictions may apply.
Viewing Facilities: Film; videotape (pending).
Duplication Facilities: Film (film to videotape; pending).

DISTRICT OF COLUMBIA METROPOLITAN AREA

DISTRICT OF COLUMBIA METRO

ACCURACY IN MEDIA, INC.
1275 K Street, NW, Suite 1150
Washington, DC 20005
(202) 371-6710
Fax: (202) 371-9054

Reed Irvine (Chairman of the Board)

Contact: Don Irvine (Executive Secretary)
Services: Organization. Videotapes available for purchase.
Description: Produced *Television's Vietnam; Part One: The Real Story* and *Part Two: The Impact of the Media* as a corrective response to PBS's 13-part series, *Vietnam: A Television History. Part One: The Real Story* explains: "Why the Communists who now rule Vietnam praised the airing of the PBS series as 'the great event of 1983.' Why it was absurd to describe the North Vietnamese Communist leader, Ho Chi Minh, as a great nationalist and patriot. How the PBS series insulted the Americans who fought in Vietnam. How the torture of American prisoners of war (POWs) by the Communists was justified. Why the PBS series shocked and saddened Vietnamese refugees. How the good news about our Vietnam veterans was covered up. How Congress foolishly sealed the fate of Vietnam, sacrificing all that 58,132 Americans and over 225,000 Vietnamese fighting men had given their lives to achieve." *Part Two: The Impact of the Media* explores how the absence of battlefield censorship "influenced the public opinion and official policy, focusing primarily on the media coverage of the 1968 Tet Offensive and siege of Khe Sanh, showing how badly flawed reporting helped erode support for the war."

Both parts are narrated by Charlton Heston.

Plans to produce a videotape documenting an AIM conference on what 1960s radicals now think of their actions and deeds.
Size & Elements: Videotape: VHS (amount unspecified).
Cataloging: None specified.
Access: Available to the public for purchase.
Rights: Full rights held to some material. Some rights held to some material. No rights held to other material.
Licensing: Apply for information.
Restrictions: Reuse of some material may be restricted.
Viewing Facilities: None.
Duplication Facilities: None.

DISTRICT OF COLUMBIA METRO

ALUMINUM ASSOCIATION
900 19th Street, NW
Washington, DC 20006
(202) 862-5162
Fax: (202) 862-5164
Telex: (710) 822-1129

John C. Bard (President)

Contact: Samuel J. McCracken (Director, Communications)
Services: Industry association. Film and videotape collection maintained primarily for distribution to engineering schools. Materials available for licensing and reuse, subject to restrictions.
Description: Aluminum fabrication, design and recycling.
General. Titles include: *Aluminum: An Element of Change* (with some mine-to-metal footage); *Recycling: A Way of Life; Nomenclature & Characteristics of Aluminum;* and *Structural Design with Aluminum.*
Mill products. Titles include: *Aluminum Foil; Aluminum Forgings* (features applications on the redesigned Chevrolet "Corvette"); *Aluminum Alloy Conductors; Extrusion: Process of Choice;* and *The Wondrous World of Extrusions.*
Processing. Titles include: *Aluminum Press Forming Processes; Leveling and Cutting-to-Length of Aluminum Coiled Sheet; Equipment for the Slitting Line; Slitter Tooling and Set-up;* and *Theory and Techniques of Aluminum Coil Slitting.*
Health, environment and safety. Titles include: *Guidelines for Handling Molten Aluminum; Molten Metal Explosions; Hazard Communication Core Training Program for Workers; Hearing Conservation: Training Aid;* and *Potroom Electrical Safety.*
Size & Elements: Videotape: 3/4", VHS and Betamax (NTSC, PAL and SECAM) (approx. 12 titles total).
Cataloging: Published lists.
Access: Available to the public for purchase. Orders accepted by mail. Certain videotape programs and 16mm films available on a free-loan basis to engineering colleges and universities
Rights: Full rights held to all material.
Licensing: Available for licensing, subject to restrictions.
Restrictions: Requests for licensing and reuse accepted on a case-by-case basis.
Viewing Facilities: None.
Duplication Facilities: None.
Distributor: Some materials available for free loan from Modern Talking Picture Service, Inc. (q.v.).

DISTRICT OF COLUMBIA METRO

AMERICAN ALLIANCE FOR HEALTH, PHYSICAL EDUCATION, RECREATION AND DANCE ARCHIVES
1900 Association Drive
Reston, VA 22091
(703) 476-3423
Fax: (703) 476-9527

Michael Everman (Archivist)

Contact: Michael Everman
Services: Association archives. Material available for research, duplication and reuse.
Description: Instructional films (produced or co-sponsored by the Alliance) for physical education, recreation, health and dance teachers at high-school and

college levels. Collection dates from the 1950s, with the exception of one film of playground activity in New York in the 1930s. In addition to teacher training films, the collection also includes some newsreel-style footage of conventions and conferences.
Size & Elements: Film: 35mm (1 reel); 16mm (40 reels, approx. 25 titles; positive).
Cataloging: Research library; no detailed film cataloging.
Access: Open to the public. Available for duplication. Research fees not charged. Requests accepted by mail, telephone and in person (by appointment only).
Rights: Full rights held to some material. Some rights held to some material. Additional clearances may be necessary in some cases if material is to be reused.
Licensing: Available for licensing and reuse. License fees not charged.
Restrictions: None specified.
Viewing Facilities: Film and videotape (must be scheduled in advance).
Duplication Facilities: None.

DISTRICT OF COLUMBIA METRO

AMERICAN-ARAB ANTI-DISCRIMINATION COMMITTEE
4201 Connecticut Avenue, NW, Suite 500
Washington, DC 20008
(202) 244-2990
Fax: (202) 244-3196

Abdeen Jabara (President)

Contact: Marvin Wingfield (Outreach Director)
Services: Association; civil rights organization. Film and videotape library available for rental and reuse, subject to clearance and availability of material.
Description: The Middle East, Arab culture and civilization. *The Traditional World of Islam* (6-part series) examines the heritage of Islamic civilization and its historical, religious and aesthetic influences.
The Arabs: A Living History (10-part series) explores Arab history, culture and society from within the lives of Arabs today. Subjects covered include: the geography and variety of the region known as the Arab world; the source of Arab identity, which crystallized early in the 20th century; modern business in the ancient city of Fez, Morocco; instilling the deep tradition of Arab family values in children raised in the modern world; a farmer's village life versus city life in Cairo; war-torn Lebanon as a meeting place, refuge and publishing center of contemporary intellectual thought in the Arab world; the origins of Arab theater and poetry and the Arab writers' response to modern world; how the oil-generated wealth of the last 20 years has changed Kuwait from a small community of traders, fishermen and pearl divers into a modern, technologically advanced city-state; guidance and blessing from elderly religious Sheikh in Umduban, central Sudan; the situation of Palestinians, traced by Edward Said; the course of European involvement in the Near East from the Crusades to Napoleon's campaign in Egypt, and the French and English entrepreneurs, adventurers and empire builders who came in his wake; Algeria since its independence in 1962; women in the Arab world; effects of the educational explosion; the huge labor migration; and the revolution in communications and its effect on Arabs and the Western world.
Report from Beirut: Summer of '82 interviews Beirut residents, portraying the terror of everyday life during the siege of Beirut; *Arabs in America* chronicles the simultaneous processes of assimilation and retention of their cultural, religious and intellectual traditions; *Native Sons* portrays three Palestinian families in the Badawi and Rashadiya camps in southern Lebanon, describing their lives as refugees living a few miles from their homeland; *Arab Stereotypes in America* details negative images of Arabs in the mass media, popular literature and textbooks; *Lebanon Fights for her Future* interviews Lebanese children and adults, describing life in shattered Lebanon; *The Massacre and The Masquerade* deals with the massacres in the Palestinian refugee camps of Sabra and Shatila (Beirut, 1982); and *Women of South Lebanon,* made by the Lebanese resistance movement against the Israeli occupation.
Size & Elements: Film: 16mm (7 titles). Videotape: VHS (16 titles).
Cataloging: None specified.
Access: Available to the public. Available for rental to organizations. Maintained for distribution and rental rather than for research or reuse.
Rights: Some rights held to some material. Rights status of other material not known.
Licensing: Apply for information. License fees charged.
Restrictions: None specified.
Viewing Facilities: None.
Duplication Facilities: None.

DISTRICT OF COLUMBIA METRO

AMERICAN ASSOCIATION FOR COUNSELING AND DEVELOPMENT
5999 Stevenson Avenue
Alexandria, VA 22304
(703) 823-9800
(800) 545-2223 (orders)

Patrick J. McDonough (Executive Director)

Contact: Debra Bass (Director of Marketing)
Services: Association. Films and videotapes available for rental and purchase.
Description: Counseling and human services for all ages. Films are directed both at those seeking counseling and professionals in the field, and include discussions of counseling issues, therapy demonstrations for counselors and stimulus vignette films.

Topics include: stress management; goal setting and risk-taking; life transitions; assertiveness training; emerging directions in counseling; professional counselors in schools and community settings; Carl Rogers on hurt and anger; B. F. Skinner on the crisis of American education; Aubry on the impact of high technology and social/environmental changes and their effects; marriage and family; parent effectiveness training; behavior problems in children; teenagers; family counseling; adolescent suicide; adulthood; child sexual abuse; children of divorce; career education and careers; career changes; life and work planning; confidentiality; group therapy; family therapy; rational-emotive therapy; the student personnel profession; blacks in higher education; student services; and nuclear defense.

Of special note are *Confidentiality: The Professional's Dilemma,* assisting professionals in ethical decisions involved in confidentiality issues, such as release of records, court-ordered information, incest, pregnancy of a minor and homicide; and *Great Minds in Counseling,* a historical series featuring interviews with major figures of the profession, including Albert Ellis, Rollo May, B. F. Skinner, Carl Rogers and Leona Tyler.
Size & Elements: Film (16mm). Videotape: 3/4", VHS and Betamax II. (50 titles total).
Cataloging: Published catalogs.
Access: Open to the public. Available for rental and purchase.
Rights: Full rights held to all material.
Licensing: Apply for information.
Restrictions: None specified.
Viewing Facilities: None.
Duplication Facilities: None.

DISTRICT OF COLUMBIA METRO

AMERICAN ASSOCIATION OF RETIRED PERSONS
1909 K Street, NW
Washington, DC 20049
(202) 872-4700
Fax: (202) 785-8526

Contacts: Steve Mehlman (Office of Communications); Wayne Moore (Director, Legal Counsel for the Elderly); George Selby (Manager, Resource Promotion Section, Program Resources Department)
Services: Association; film and videotape producer. Material available for licensing and reuse, subject to restrictions.
Description: Films and videotapes specifically relating to the elderly. Sample titles include: *Arthritis,* produced with the Arthritis Foundation, discussing the importance of proper diagnosis and treatment to minimize pain and disability; *Using Your Medicines Wisely,* demonstrating proper use of medication and ways to work with doctors and pharmacists for good health; *Pioneers in Community Television: Older Persons and Local Cable Television,* a motivational program aimed at getting seniors involved in all facets of cable television production, showing older people currently producing successful programming in local communities; *Mediation: The Win Win Solution,* describing alternative methods of resolving minor civil or neighborhood disputes through trained mediators at the local level.

The Constitution: That Delicate Balance (6-part series) explores controversial human rights questions and constitutional issues such as the right to die; covert and military action in the absence of a declaration of war; school prayer; immigration reform; affirmative action versus reverse discrimination; and violent and white collar crimes and their punishments.
Size & Elements: Film: 16mm (2 titles). Videotape: 3/4", VHS and Betamax (8 titles).

Cataloging: Published catalogs.
Access: Available for free loan only to nonprofit groups providing services to the elderly. Available for purchase and duplication. Permission to duplicate granted on a case-by-case basis. Research requests accepted by mail.
Rights: Full rights held to some material. Some rights held to some material. Additional clearances may be necessary in some cases if material is to be reused.
Licensing: Available for licensing and reuse, subject to restrictions.
Restrictions: Requests for duplication and reuse accepted on a case-by-case basis and subject to clearance and approval.
Viewing Facilities: None.
Duplication Facilities: Videotape (all formats).
Related Materials: Workbook publications designed to accompany certain films and videotapes.

DISTRICT OF COLUMBIA METRO

AMERICAN AUTOMOBILE ASSOCIATION FOUNDATION FOR TRAFFIC SAFETY
1730 M Street, NW, Suite 401
Washington, DC 20036
(202) 775-1456

Sam Yaksich (Executive Director)

Contact: Robert Stratton (Marketing Manager)
Services: Foundation; film and videotape distributor. Material available primarily for rental.
Description: Traffic safety educational films. The *Starting Early* series deals with dangers of alcohol and is targeted for kindergarten through 6th and/or upper grade levels.

Topics covered in the collection include: car care; single-vehicle accidents; adult and teenage drinking and driving; high-speed driving; marijuana; DWI reeducation; rehabilitation and counseling; bicycle safety; driver information and education; car-truck crash prevention; signs; signals and pavement markings; car size and occupant fatality risk; freeway driving; winter driving; visual perception; car driver's view of motorcycling; hydroplaning; night driving; hazardous materials accidents; role of fatigue in heavy truck accidents; deregulation of the trucking industry; older drivers; bridges; small cars; skidding accidents; pedestrian safety; school bus safety; and common driving errors.

Collection also includes television and radio public service announcements using Fred Flintstone and other Hanna-Barbera cartoon characters.
Size & Elements: Film: 16mm. Videotape: 3/4" and VHS. (Amounts unspecified).
Cataloging: Published catalogs (available on request).
Access: Maintained for distribution and rental rather than for research or reuse. Research fees charged. Research requests accepted by mail, telephone and in person (walk-in).
Rights: Full rights held to all material.
Licensing: Apply for information. License fees charged.
Restrictions: Material is not to be duplicated without written permission of Foundation.
Viewing Facilities: None.
Duplication Facilities: None.
Distributors: Many films distributed by local AAA clubs.

DISTRICT OF COLUMBIA METRO

AMERICAN BAKERS ASSOCIATION
1111 14th Street, NW, Suite 300
Washington, DC 20005
(202) 296-5800
Fax: (202) 371-0017

Paul Abenante (President)

Contact: Public Relations
Services: Trade association. Film and videotape collection intended primarily for distribution rather than research or reuse.
Description: Films produced for the customers, employees and consumers of commercial baked goods, particularly bread. Two films, one aimed at drivers and salesmen and the other at supermarkets and fast-food restaurant operators, outline ways to combat the "enormous container-loss problem affecting the baking industry." *Who Do You Think You Are?* is an award-winning musical

presentation promoting bread's nutritional values, geared to junior-high and high-school audiences (starring Hollywood actress Elizabeth Shue).
Size & Elements: Film: 16mm (3 titles). Videotape: 3/4", VHS and Betamax (3 titles).
Cataloging: Brochures available.
Access: Maintained for distribution and rental rather than reuse or resale. Requests accepted by mail.
Rights: Apply for information.
Licensing: Apply for information.
Restrictions: Additional clearances may be necessary for licensing or reuse.
Viewing Facilities: None.
Duplication Facilities: None.

DISTRICT OF COLUMBIA METRO

AMERICAN CHEMICAL SOCIETY
1155 Sixteenth Street, NW
Washington, DC 20036
(800) 227-5558
(202) 872-4600

Dr. John K. Crum (Executive Director)

Contact: ACS Distribution Office (to order videotapes).
Services: Association. Film and videotape collection available to researchers, scholars and the public. Some material available for duplication.
Description: Films and videotapes relating to chemistry and chemical scientists.
Eminent Chemists Programs. Color videotape programs produced by the American Chemical Society (available for rental only) featuring distinguished chemists discussing their achievements. Includes interviews with the following chemists: Hubert N. Alyea, acclaimed for his teaching demonstrations and the Tested Overhead Projection System (TOPS), discussing his early contributions to science and demonstrating the "lucky accidents" of science discoveries; Arnold O. Beckman, discussing his development of the world's first pH meter; Melvin Calvin, detailing his Nobel Prize-winning work on photosynthesis; John T. Edsall, recalling the "crash" programs of World War II, and the first manufacture and use of blood plasma; Ronald W. Estabrook, on the research events of the early 1960s leading to the discovery of the significance of cytachrome P-450 to chemical carcinogenesis; Paul J. Flory, recalling his early research work in polymer studies; Karl Folkers, discussing his contributions to the development of vitamins B-6, B-12 and penicillin; Louis P. Hammett, founding father of physical organic chemistry; Anna J. Harrison, reflecting on her career as a chemical educator and organizer, and discussing the influences affecting her during the Depression Era; Joel Hildebrand, discussing his work as an educator, and his research and contributions to the development of solution theory; Roald Hoffmann, reflecting on some of the key accomplishments that led to his receipt of the 1981 Nobel Prize; Izaak Kolthoff, reviewing the major influences in the development of his career, and his collaborations and contributions to analytical chemistry; Herman Mark, reviewing his contributions to the development of polymer chemistry; Carl S. ("Speed") Marvel, a leader in the field of polymer science; Glenn T. Seaborg, discussing his work with plutonium and atomic fission, the discovery of the transuranium elements, the Manhattan Project and the revision of the periodic table; Max Tishler, renowned industrial chemist, discussing his research and developments in the organic synthesis of vitamins; Rosalyn S. Yalow, Nobel laureate (1977) and Senior Medical Investigator for the Vietnam Veterans Association, co-author of the technique called radioimmunoassay; W. Lincoln Hawkins, discussing his work at AT&T Bell Laboratories and lectures on polymer degradation and stabilization; and Carl Djerassi, discussing the applications of computer artificial intelligence techniques in solving organic chemistry problems. Also included is a series called the *Perspectives Lectures,* lectures by prominent chemists.
Education Division. Provides videotape courses for purchase and rental only. Titles available from the Catalog of Continuing Education Courses include: *Chemical Engineering for Chemists; Chemical Laboratory Techniques; Chemical Toxicology; Chemists and Questions; Gas Chromatography; Interpretation of Infrared Spectra; Molecular Reactivity; Organic Chemistry Laboratory Techniques; Technical Writing* and *Techniques in Basic Infrared Spectrophotometry.*
On The Science Scene. 40 news features (each 2 min.) narrated by local anchorpersons, produced by the ACS, and supplied to approximately 125 television stations for possible on-air use in a news segment dealing with the same topic. Schools also use these features as "start-up pieces" to discussion sessions. Also holds approximately nine 30-second public service

announcements for television stations on various topics: poison prevention, science education, improving American productivity, drugs and alcohol in the workplace, and risks and benefits. All material provided to television stations and schools is broadcast-quality and free of charge.
Also holds one film *Chemistry: The Endless Frontier* (produced by ACS).
Size & Elements: Film: format unspecified (1 title). Videotape: 3/4", VHS and Betamax (over 100 items total).
Cataloging: Published catalogs available upon request.
Access: Available to researchers, scholars and the public. Maintained for distribution and rental rather than for research or reuse. Some material (e.g., *Eminent Chemists* programs) available for duplication free of charge. Requests accepted by mail and telephone.
Rights: Full rights held to all material.
Licensing: Apply for information. License fees charged.
Restrictions: None specified.
Viewing Facilities: None.
Duplication Facilities: None.
Related Materials: Produces three radio programs sent directly to 780 radio stations (available in open reel or in cassette form).

DISTRICT OF COLUMBIA METRO

AMERICAN CORRECTIONAL ASSOCIATION
TRAINING DIVISION
8025 Laurel Lakes Court
Laurel, MD 20707
(301) 206-5100
Fax: (301) 206-5061

Anthony P. Travisono (Executive Director)

Contact: John J. Greene III (Director, Membership, Training and Contracts)
Services: Association. Videotapes available for purchase to corrections-related organizations.
Description: Training materials relating to AIDS in the correctional setting. Two videotapes, *AIDS: Key Facts for Correctional Staff* and *AIDS: Key Facts for Inmates* are available in English and Spanish versions.
Size & Elements: Videotape: 3/4", VHS and Betamax (2 titles).
Cataloging: Brochure.
Access: Available for purchase to corrections-related organizations. Research fees not charged. Research requests not accepted.
Rights: Full rights held to all material.
Licensing: Apply for information.
Restrictions: Restrictions apply to licensing and reuse.
Viewing Facilities: Videotape.
Duplication Facilities: None (outside arrangements can be made).
Related Materials: Publications (study guides and lesson plans) relating to videotapes.

DISTRICT OF COLUMBIA METRO

AMERICAN DEFENSE PREPAREDNESS ASSOCIATION
1700 North Moore Street, Suite 900
Arlington, VA 22209
(703) 522-1820
Fax: (703) 522-1885

Lawrence F. Skibbie (President)

Contact: Cathy Vilga (Managerial Assistant)
Services: Association. Videotape available to the public for purchase.
Description: One title available: *S.D.I.: A Prospect for Peace* (28 min.).
Size & Elements: Videotape: 3/4" and VHS (1 title).
Cataloging: None specified.
Access: Available to the public for purchase.
Rights: Full rights held to all material.
Licensing: Apply for information.
Restrictions: None specified.
Viewing Facilities: None.
Duplication Facilities: None.

DISTRICT OF COLUMBIA METRO

AMERICAN DIABETES ASSOCIATION
NATIONAL SERVICE CENTER

DISTRICT OF COLUMBIA METRO A

1660 Duke Street
Alexandria, VA 22314
(703) 549-1500
(800) 232-3472
Fax: (703) 836-7439

Robert S. Boland, Ph.D. (Executive Vice President)

Contact: Amy Danzig (Director of Communications)
Services: Association. Film and videotape material available to the public. Maintained primarily for distribution and rental; possibly available for duplication, licensing and reuse.
Description: Educational material on diabetes and people with diabetes. Films include: *The Journey and the Dream,* a portrait of six people with diabetes; *Josh,* focusing on a seven-year old child with diabetes; *The Other Diabetes,* a series of vignettes; and *No Sugar Coating,* a group of teens with diabetes talk candidly about their lives.
Size & Elements: Film: 16mm (4 titles). Videotape: 3/4" and 1/2" (viewing copies transferred from films).
Access: Available to the public. Maintained for distribution and rental rather than research or reuse. Material available for duplication and licensing, subject to restrictions. Research requests accepted by mail.
Rights: Full rights held to all material.
Licensing: Available for licensing, subject to restrictions. License fees charged for commercial use.
Restrictions: Requests for licensing considered on a case-by-case basis.
Viewing Facilities: Videotape.
Duplication Facilities: None.

DISTRICT OF COLUMBIA METRO

AMERICAN DRIVER AND TRAFFIC SAFETY EDUCATION ASSOCIATION
239 Florida Avenue
Salisbury, MD 21801
(301) 860-0075

Jefferson D. Keith (Executive Director)

Contact: Jefferson D. Keith
Services: Association. Film and videotape library maintained primarily for rental purposes; possibly available for duplication, subject to restrictions.
Description: Driver education films. Most films date from the 1970s and are produced by automotive manufacturers.
Titles include: *Emotions and Driving,* produced in conjunction with Allstate Insurance Co.; *A Driver Education Series* (8 parts), produced on videotape in conjunction with Ford Motor Company, including: *It's a Matter of Attitude, On the Street, Taking Care of It, When the Sun Sets, When the Pavement's Slick, On the Freeway, The Little Things,* and *Prom Day.*
Size & Elements: Film: 16mm (3 titles). Videotape: VHS (8 titles).
Access: Open to researchers and scholars only. Maintained for distribution and rental rather than for research or reuse. Available for duplication, licensing and reuse. Requests accepted by mail and telephone. Research fees not charged.
Rights: Full rights held to some material. Additional clearances may be necessary in some cases if material is to be reused.
Licensing: Apply for information. License fees charged.
Restrictions: Requests considered on a case-by-case basis.
Viewing Facilities: None.
Duplication Facilities: None.

DISTRICT OF COLUMBIA METRO

AMERICAN ENTERPRISE INSTITUTE FOR PUBLIC POLICY RESEARCH
Public Relations Office
1150 17th Street, NW
Washington, DC 20036
(202) 862-5829
Fax: (202) 862-7178

Christopher C. DeMuth (President)

Contact: Pam Prothro (Manager of Public Relations)
Services: Association. *In-house videotape collection currently not open to the public or available to researchers.*

Description: Debate programs produced by AEI (1970-86, each 60 min.). Debates focus on public policy issues, featuring such public figures as Jeanne Kirkpatrick, Henry Kissinger, Gerald Ford, Ronald Reagan, Lawrence Tribe and various academics. Videotapes were often aired on network television.
Size & Elements: Videotape: 1" and 3/4" (150 titles).
Cataloging: Currently uncataloged; cataloging planned.
Access: *Collection currently not open to the public; not equipped to handle research inquiries.* Material may be reused if accessed through a channel other than AEI; much of their material is held by the National Archives and Records Administration (q.v.).
Rights: Full rights held to all material.
Licensing: Collection not presently available for licensing or reuse through AEI.
Restrictions: Access to, viewing of and reuse of material restricted.
Viewing Facilities: None.
Duplication Facilities: None.

DISTRICT OF COLUMBIA METRO

AMERICAN INSTITUTE OF ARCHITECTS AUDIO-VISUAL DEPARTMENT
1735 New York Avenue, NW
Washington, DC 20006
(202) 626-7495
Fax: (202) 783-8247

James Cramer (Executive Vice President)

Contact: Michelle A. Jones (Assistant Manager, Audio-Visual)
Services: Nonprofit membership organization. Film library maintained for distribution and rental.
Description: 20th century American architecture and urban planning. Topics include: architectural design and vocational opportunities, discussed by Warren Cox, George Hartman, Ulrich Franzen and Philip Johnson, with examples of their work; energy efficiency and the Brookhaven House; urban schools; the architect's role in society; American and European downtown areas from the pedestrian's viewpoint; Lafayette, Louisiana; community design centers in Cleveland, New Orleans, Philadelphia and San Francisco; Prince Charles' 1985 visit to AIA, the Octagon Museum, Savannah and Baltimore; careers as an architect in industry; architect's offices; how to prepare for appearance on broadcast, cable television or business video; team building; design and development of continuing care facilities.
Size & Elements: Film: 16mm. Videotape: 3/4" and VHS. (Amounts unspecified).
Cataloging: Card catalogs; audiovisual bibliography; research library.
Access: Available to the public. Some titles available for rental and purchase. Some titles for in-house use only. Research fees charged. Research requests accepted by mail and telephone.
Rights: Some rights held to all material. Additional clearances may be necessary in some cases if material is to be reused.
Licensing: Apply for information. Fees charged for purchase and rental.
Restrictions: None specified.
Viewing Facilities: Film and videotape (3/4" and VHS).
Duplication Facilities: Videotape (3/4" to VHS and VHS to VHS).
Publications: Institute publishes an audiovisual bibliography covering approximately 60 current film and videotape releases (1980-present) on architecture and related areas, available from a variety of sources.

DISTRICT OF COLUMBIA METRO

AMERICAN IRON AND STEEL INSTITUTE COMMUNICATIONS DEPARTMENT
1133 15th Street, NW
Washington, DC 20005
(202) 452-7114
Fax: (202) 463-6573

Milton Deaner (President)

Contact: Mary Jackson
Services: Association. Film and videotape material maintained primarily for educational purposes. Some material available for stock footage use.
Description: Steel manufacturing and the steel industry. *Steel: The Metal Giant* (1984, 18 min.) was produced for educational institutions and general audiences; two videotape clip reels showing current steelmaking processes

(each 28 min., color, silent) are available to television broadcasters for stock footage use.
Size & Elements: Film: 16mm (1 title). Videotape: format unspecified (2 videotapes).
Cataloging: Finding aids (list).
Access: Available to the public. Material primarily available to schools and the news media and for free loan (non-commercial use only). Limited research requests are accepted in person (walk-in).
Rights: Full rights held to all material. Additional clearances may be necessary in some cases if material is to be reused.
Licensing: For licensing requests, contact James J. Hughes (Vice President, Communications). Requests for licensing and reuse considered on a case-by-case basis. License fees not charged.
Restrictions: Material primarily distributed to schools, news media and for non-commercial use. Requests for licensing and reuse considered on a case-by-case basis.
Viewing Facilities: None.
Duplication Facilities: None.

DISTRICT OF COLUMBIA METRO

AMERICAN OCCUPATIONAL THERAPY ASSOCIATION
AOTA PRODUCTS
P.O. Box 1725
Rockville, MD 20850-4375
(301) 948-9626
Fax: (301) 948-5512

Street address: 1383 Piccard Drive

Jeanette Bair (Chief Executive Officer)

Contact: Order Department
Services: Association. Videotapes available primarily for rental and purchase.
Description: Practice and history of occupational therapy.

Topics include: elderly people; biofeedback; bioengineering; neurological injuries; cardiovascular and vascular disorders; occupational behavior; drug addiction; splints; prostheses; amputees; hand evaluation, edema and splinting; the supervision of occupational therapy students; Medicare Prospective Payment System and its implications for occupational therapy; behavioral sciences and their relationship to rehabilitation; the nervous system; the extrapyramidal system; the limbi system; diagnosing CNS lesions; learning and memory; home health services; case histories; sensorimotor processing in child development; spasticity; sensory integration; therapeutic clinics and equipment; magical illusions in treatment resulting from stroke, head injury and hand injuries; recruitment aids.

Visual History Series: The Early Years traces the history of the profession through World War I, with historical photos and interviews with some of the pioneers of the field (e.g., Dr. Sidney Licht, Beatrice Wade, Clare Spackman and Helen Willard).
Size & Elements: Videotape: 3/4" and VHS (27 hours; 34 titles).
Cataloging: Published catalogs.
Access: Available for rental and purchase.
Rights: Full rights held to all material.
Licensing: Apply for information. License fees charged in some cases.
Restrictions: None specified.
Viewing Facilities: None.
Duplication Facilities: None.

DISTRICT OF COLUMBIA METRO

AMERICAN PHYSICAL THERAPY ASSOCIATION
1111 North Fairfax Street
Alexandria, VA 22314
(703) 684-2782
Fax: (703) 684-7343

William D. Coughlan (Executive Vice President and Chief Executive Officer)

Contact: Alexis Waters
Services: Association. Films and videotapes available to APTA members and nonmembers for rental and purchase.
Description: Collection focuses on career opportunities in physical therapy, the growth of the profession, and public education.
Titles include: *Equal Opportunities in PT: Profiles from a Caring*

Profession (Office of Minority Affairs), examining the varied roles of physical therapists in the health care setting, with emphasis on minority therapists; and *Time for a Change: Physical Therapy Practice Without Physician Referral*, a documentary designed to support legislative efforts to remove statutory requirements for physician referral. Discusses cost-containment benefits of direct access, evolution of the practice, dangers and fears of direct access, ethical boundaries and the scope of physical therapy practice.
Size & Elements: Film: 16mm (amount unspecified). Videotape: 3/4", VHS and Betamax (4 titles).
Cataloging: Published catalog/brochure.
Access: Available to APTA members and nonmembers for rental and purchase.
Rights: Full rights held to all material.
Licensing: License fees charged.
Restrictions: None specified.
Viewing Facilities: None.
Duplication Facilities: None.

DISTRICT OF COLUMBIA METRO

AMERICAN POLITICAL SCIENCE ASSOCIATION
1527 New Hampshire Avenue, NW
Washington, DC 20036
(202) 483-2512
Fax: (202) 462-7849

Catherine E. Rudder (Executive Director)

Contact: Sheilah Mann (Director of Education Programs)
Services: Association. Videotapes available for rental and purchase. Some material possibly available for reuse, subject to clearance and approval.
Description: Videotapes co-produced by Project '87 (a joint effort of American Historical Association and American Political Science Association) in conjunction with the League of Women Voters Education Fund on the U.S. Constitution.

The Constitution and the Courts: Text, Original Intent and the Changing Social Order documents the Constitutional Forum in Philadelphia to commemorate the opening of the Constitutional Convention. Panelists include Robert H. Bork, Patricia M. Wald, Shirley S. Abrahamson and Dr. Jack W. Peltason.

This Constitution: A History (eight programs, each 30 min.) is a series designed for credit curricula in colleges and universities, emphasizing historical events and processes that have resulted in constitutionalism as we know it today. Topics include: *The Origins of American Constitutionalism, A New Constitutional Order; Political Parties and Democratic Politics; Political Parties and the Constitutional System; Implementing the Constitution as Law: Origins of Judicial Review and Establishment of Judicial Sovereignty; A Nation of States, 1775-1865: The Origins of American Federalism; A Nation of States since 1865; The Constitution and Political Power in Society and the Economy; Civil Rights and Liberties Before the Civil War; Civil Rights and Liberties From the Civil War; The Quest for Equality; The Origin of the American Presidency and the Rise of the Administrative State; Foreign Affairs and National Security; Constitutional Change: Objectives and Readings.*
Size & Elements: Videotape: format unspecified (9 videotapes, each 30-40 min.).
Cataloging: Descriptive sheet.
Access: Maintained for distribution and rental rather than for research or reuse. Available for purchase.
Rights: Full rights held to all material.
Licensing: Apply for information. License fees charged in some cases.
Restrictions: Permission required for reuse and licensing.
Viewing Facilities: None.
Duplication Facilities: None.

DISTRICT OF COLUMBIA METRO

AMERICAN PSYCHIATRIC ASSOCIATION
LIBRARY AND ARCHIVES
1400 K Street, NW
Washington, DC 20005
(202) 682-6059

Mrs. Zing Jung (Director of Library and Archives)

Contact: William Baxter (Archivist/Records Manager)
Services: Association. Film collection available for research and professional

use only.
Description: Small collection of historical films focusing on psychiatry. Contents include: the classic documentary film *Functions of the Brain,* depicting Pavlov's experiments; *Remotivation; Shock Therapies* (5 reels); a film entitled *Sigmund Freud; Frontiers of Psychiatry on Camera;* an interview with J. C. Whitehorn and one film showing U.S. psychiatrists at a Polynesian concert.
Size & Elements: Film: 16mm (11 titles; color and black and white).
Cataloging: Film list (apply for information).
Access: Available to researchers and scholars only. Research requests accepted by mail, telephone and in person (by appointment only).
Rights: Full rights held to all material.
Licensing: Apply for information. License fees not charged.
Restrictions: Available for professional use only (related to the teaching of psychiatry or historical research on the history of psychiatry). Films cannot be viewed at this time.
Viewing Facilities: Videotape (VHS).
Duplication Facilities: None.

DISTRICT OF COLUMBIA METRO

AMERICAN PUBLIC TRANSIT ASSOCIATION
1201 New York Avenue, NW, Suite 400
Washington, DC 20005
(202) 898-4000
Fax: (202) 898-4070

Jack R. Gilstrap (Executive Vice President)

Contact: Rose Gander (Manager, Information Center)
Services: Association. Videotape library maintained primarily for rental. Material available for licensing, subject to restrictions.
Description: Employee training programs for the mass transit industry in the fields of maintenance, management, operator training, "disability awareness" for the elderly and handicapped and meeting the mobility needs of the disabled.
    The Transit Renaissance (1987) gives general positive information about transit. Produced for use at local gatherings, the videotape has two alternate beginnings and endings, one alluding to National Transportation Week.
    Other topics include eliminating and controlling absenteeism, reducing job-related injuries and management and supervisory training. The AFL-CIO Transit Employee Training Project for Operator Training covers passenger relations; emergency and accident procedures; defensive driving and bus maneuvers; new employee orientation with a historical view of the transit industry and vehicles; and the evolution of the public transit industry in America.
Size & Elements: Film: 16mm. Videotape: 3/4". (Approx. 22 titles total).
Cataloging: Published catalogs.
Access: Open to the public. Available for rental, duplication and reuse. Research requests accepted by mail.
Rights: Full rights held to all material.
Licensing: Available for licensing, subject to restrictions. License fees not charged.
Restrictions: Requests for reuse subject to clearance and approval.
Viewing Facilities: None.
Duplication Facilities: None.

DISTRICT OF COLUMBIA METRO

AMERICAN PULPWOOD ASSOCIATION, INC.
1025 Vermont Avenue, NW, Suite 1020
Washington, DC 20005
(202) 347-2900

Kenneth S. Rolston (President)

Contact: Neil A. Ward (Administrative Assistant)
Services: Trade association. Film library maintained primarily for free-loan distribution; some material possibly available for licensing and reuse, subject to restrictions.
Description: Films and videotapes intended for the forest industry professional, emphasizing logging safety. Topics include: safe use of a chain saw; safe and improper felling procedures; logger safety; notching and felling; sitbacks; snags; interviews with injured workers; various cutting techniques; bucking techniques; bow saw safety; Swedish wood harvesting techniques; consumer wood harvesting techniques; limbing techniques; vibration syndrome

or "white finger" (a harmful condition resulting from too much contact with vibrating engine casings); safe manual felling; skidding; safe pulpwood loading; transport; fire prevention; and accident control.
Size & Elements: Film: 16mm. Videotape (VHS) (approx. 24 titles).
Cataloging: Published catalog.
Access: Available to the public. Research fees not charged. Research requests accepted by mail and telephone. Materials available on a free-loan basis but should be requested three to six months in advance and can be held for only a few days.
Rights: Full rights held to some material. Rights status of some material not known. Additional clearances may be necessary in some cases if material is to be reused.
Licensing: Available for licensing, subject to restrictions. License fees not charged.
Restrictions: Requests for reuse subject to clearance and approval.
Viewing Facilities: None.
Duplication Facilities: None.

DISTRICT OF COLUMBIA METRO

AMERICAN RED CROSS
AUDIOVISUAL DEPARTMENT
FRANK STANTON PRODUCTION CENTER
5816 Seminary Road
Falls Church, VA 22041
(703) 379-8160
Fax: (703) 820-1533

Available for rental from:
MODERN TALKING PICTURE SERVICE, INC. (q.v.)

Craig Reinertson (Audiovisual Coordinator)

Contact: Craig Reinertson
Services: Public health organization; film and videotape library. Material available for licensing and reuse.
Description: Contemporary Red Cross-produced films relating to such topics as blood donation, high blood pressure, epidemics, disaster relief, boating and water safety, handicapped people, medical emergencies and other public health concerns. Historical materials documenting Red Cross efforts from the 1940s and 1950s (notably in World War II and Korea) are currently inaccessible, but will soon be transferred to the National Archives.
Size & Elements: Film: 16mm. Videotape: 3/4" and VHS. (20 titles, each 8 to 40 min.).
Cataloging: Published catalogs.
Access: Available for distribution, rental and reuse, subject to restrictions. Research requests accepted by mail and telephone.
Rights: Full rights held to all material.
Licensing: Available for licensing and reuse, subject to restrictions.
Restrictions: No reuse of the material for profit is permitted. Reuse restricted based on footage-sensitive criteria, (e.g., material relating to AIDS, disability, etc.).
Viewing Facilities: Film (flatbed viewing table); videotape.
Duplication Facilities: None.

DISTRICT OF COLUMBIA METRO

AMERICAN TEXTILE MANUFACTURERS INSTITUTE
1801 K Street, NW
Washington, DC 20006
(202) 862-0550
Fax: (202) 862-0570

Carlos Moore (Executive Vice President)

Contacts: Jim Morrissey (Director of Communications)
Services: Trade association. Film and videotape available primarily for distribution.
Description: *America's Textiles: An Industry Fights Back* shows products of the U.S. textile industry, ranging from new fabrics to artificial arteries, and the dangers the industry faces from foreign imports.
Size & Elements: Film: 16mm (amount unspecified). Videotape: format and amount unspecified.
Cataloging: None specified.
Access: Apply for information.

Rights: Some rights held to some material.
Licensing: Apply for information. License fees not charged.
Restrictions: None specified.
Viewing Facilities: None.
Duplication Facilities: None.

DISTRICT OF COLUMBIA METRO

AMERICAN TRUCKING ASSOCIATION
2200 Mill Road
Alexandria, VA 22314
(703) 838-1700
Fax: (703) 684-5720

Contact: Jerry Buckman (Office of Public Affairs)
Services: Association. *Film collection unavailable for viewing or reuse.*
Description: Small collection of safety and training films (1940s-70s), produced by various truck and automotive manufacturers. Most historical materials have been transferred to the American Truck Historical Society (q.v.).
Size & Elements: Film: format unspecified (approx. 30 to 40 titles).
Cataloging: Materials uncataloged.
Access: Very limited accessibility; material unavailable for viewing and reuse (stored in warehouse). Association unable to handle research requests. Inquiries accepted by mail and telephone.
Rights: Some rights held to some material. Rights status of some material unknown.
Licensing: Apply for information. License fees charged in some cases.
Restrictions: Material unavailable for viewing or reuse.
Viewing Facilities: None.
Duplication Facilities: None.

DISTRICT OF COLUMBIA METRO

ANIMAL WELFARE INSTITUTE
P.O. Box 3650
Washington, DC 20007
(202) 337-2332
Fax: (202) 338-9478

Christine Stevens (President)

Contact: Laura Swedberg (Administrative Assistant)
Services: Humane society; film rental library. Material available for reuse, subject to clearance and restrictions.
Description: Films include: *Canada's Shame,* showing the suffering of fur-bearing animals caught in leghold traps; *Down on the Factory Farm* (BBC), examining the confinement of farm animals; *Laboratory Dogs,* showing the housing of dogs in a laboratory under humane conditions; *The Great Whales* (National Geographic Society); and *Last Day of the Dolphins?* narrated by Dick Cavett, with footage of dolphins killed in tuna fishing. A public service announcement (:30), produced by the Institute, relates to trapping.
Size & Elements: Film: 16mm (5 titles). Videotape: VHS (2 titles).
Cataloging: Brochure.
Access: Available to the public for rental.
Rights: No rights held to any material. Rights retained by original producers. Additional clearances necessary if material is to be reused.
Licensing: Apply for information.
Restrictions: Restrictions may apply to some titles. Permission of original producer required for reuse.
Viewing Facilities: None.
Duplication Facilities: None.

DISTRICT OF COLUMBIA METRO

ARISTOTLE INDUSTRIES
205 Pennsylvania Avenue, SE
Washington, DC 20003
(202) 543-8345
(800) 243-4401
Fax: (202) 543-6407

John Aristotle Phillips (President)

Contact: John Aristotle Phillips
Services: Videotape producer. Videotapes available for purchase.

Description: Political campaign consulting. *How to Win a Political Campaign* is a two and a half-hour videotape clinic featuring prominent political consultants. Each discusses his or her area of recognized expertise in a one-on-one format.

Participants include: Matt Reese (campaign management); Hugh Schwarz (strategic research); Stuart Spenser (campaign judgement); V. Lance Torrance, Jr. (polling); Frank Tobe (computer applications); Bob Nelson (campaign innovations); Chip Neilson and Barry Fadem (legal aspects); Charlotte Conway (Fundraising); Leslie Francis (campaign drganization); Martin Franks (issues); Dennis Holt (media buying); Hal Larson (advertising); and Joseph Canzeri (advance).

Other videotapes include: *The Best Campaign Commercials of 1984; The Best Campaign Commercials of 1986; The Best Campaign Commercials Ever Made; The Campaign Manager Video Tutorial;* and *The Get Out the Vote Video Tutorial.*
Size & Elements: Videotape: VHS and Betamax (9 titles total).
Cataloging: Published lists.
Access: Available to the public for purchase. Orders accepted by mail and telephone.
Rights: Apply for information.
Licensing: Apply for information.
Restrictions: None specified.
Viewing Facilities: None.
Duplication Facilities: None.

DISTRICT OF COLUMBIA METRO

ASSOCIATED GENERAL CONTRACTORS OF AMERICA
1957 E Street, NW
Washington, DC 20006
(202) 393-2040
Fax: (202) 347-4004

Contact: William Henry
Services: Association; videotape library. Videotapes available for distribution and reuse.
Description: Construction industry and construction techniques. Topics include: financial management for company executives and chief financial officers; an overview of the construction industry and its importance to the nation's economy; career opportunities in construction from the junior high-school level to civil engineers; drug abuse and substance control problems in the workplace; the Immigration Reform Legislation of 1986 and how it will be enforced by the federal government; theft and vandalism prevention.

Infrastructure uses news clips to document the deterioration of America's highways and bridges, water and sewerage systems and other elements of its infrastructure, ending with President Reagan signing the 1982 Surface Transportation Assistance Act. *Water: America's Most Vital Resource* uses news clips to show the results of underinvested water programs and inadequate water and sewerage systems, such as broken water mains, water pollution and stifled municipal growth. *Buildings: Our Vertical Infrastructure* relates to the maintenance of public buildings, particularly schools, hospitals, government buildings, prisons and public housing. *Infrastructure Newsreel* is a quick paced montage of infrastructure disasters.

Safety Training Series covers 20 different safety areas in building, highway, heavy and municipal/utilities construction operations and can help contractors meet OSHA's safety training requirements.
Size & Elements: Videotape: 3/4", VHS and Betamax (6 titles).
Cataloging: Published catalogs.
Access: Available to the public for distribution and reuse.
Rights: Full rights held to all material.
Licensing: Apply for information.
Restrictions: None specified.
Viewing Facilities: None.
Duplication Facilities: None.

DISTRICT OF COLUMBIA METRO

ASSOCIATION FOR UNMANNED VEHICLE SYSTEMS
1133 15th Street, NW, Suite 1000
Washington, DC 20005
(202) 429-9440
Fax: (202) 775-9631

John Siegel (Executive Director)

DISTRICT OF COLUMBIA METRO B

Contact: Daryl Davidson
Services: Association. One videotape available for viewing.
Description: *Unmanned Systems: The Future is Now* (23 min.), featuring RPVs (remotely piloted vehicles) and RDVs (remotely driven vehicles).
Size & Elements: Videotape: 3/4" and VHS (1 title).
Cataloging: None specified.
Access: Apply for information.
Rights: Apply for information.
Licensing: Apply for information.
Restrictions: None specified.
Viewing Facilities: None.
Duplication Facilities: None.

DISTRICT OF COLUMBIA METRO

ALEXANDER GRAHAM BELL ASSOCIATION FOR THE DEAF
3417 Volta Place, NW
Washington, DC 20007-2778
(202) 337-5220 (voice and TTY)

Distribution and rental inquiries:
ALEXANDER GRAHAM BELL FILM LIBRARY
445 West Main Street
Wyckoff, NJ 07481
(201) 891-8240

Donna McCord Dickman, Ph.D. (Executive Director)

Contacts: Judith A. Anderson (Librarian); Lucy Cuzon duRest (Director of Publications)
Services: Association for the deaf. Film and videotape library available for distribution and rental.
Description: Videotapes relating to the oral education of deaf and hearing-impaired persons (developed in 1970s-80s). Includes interviews with educators of the deaf and teaching programs. Additional films and videotapes held in the library are presently uncataloged.
Size & Elements: Film: 16mm. Videotape: 3/4" and VHS (9 titles).
Cataloging: Published catalogs.
Access: Maintained for distribution and rental rather than research or reuse.
Rights: Full rights held to all material.
Licensing: Apply for information.
Restrictions: None specified.
Viewing Facilities: Videotape (3/4" and VHS).
Duplication Facilities: None.

DISTRICT OF COLUMBIA METRO

BNA COMMUNICATIONS, INC.
(a subsidiary of THE BUREAU OF NATIONAL AFFAIRS, INC.)
9439 Key West Avenue
Rockville, MD 20850-3396
(800) 233-6067
(301) 948-0540
Fax: (301) 948-2085
Telex: 28-5656 Attn: BNAC

Robert L. Velte (President)

Contact: Sales and Training Department
Services: Film and videotape producer and distributor. Materials available for rental, preview and licensing.
Description: Since 1950, BNA Communications has provided state-of-the-art training materials and expertise for developing human resources in business, industry, education, health care, associations and government. BNAC was the first to present the views of top management authorities and leading behavioral scientists in films, and now offers programs in interactive videotape and videodisc formats. Many films are available in foreign-language versions, dubbed or subtitled.

Subject areas include: employee communications and development; management development; quality improvement; EEO compliance; labor relations; supervisory training; communication; computer literacy; sales training; case studies; management philosophy; delegation; motivation; arbitration; employee orientation; interviewing; meetings and public speaking; occupational health and safety; customer service; loss prevention; and product liability.

Many management authorities and behavioral scientists are featured in BNAC programs, including Joe Batten, Richard Beckhard, David Berlo, Robert Blake, Peter Drucker, Saul Gellerman, Frederick Herzberg, John Humble, Harry Levinson, Gordon Lippitt, Norman Maier, Alan Mogensen, Jane Mouton, M. Scott Myers, Dru Scott, David Sirota and Melvin Sorcher.
Size & Elements: Film: 16mm. Videotape: 3/4" and VHS (NTSC, PAL and SECAM). Videodisc. (Over 250 titles total).
Cataloging: Published catalogs.
Access: Open to the public. Research requests accepted by telephone.
Rights: Full rights held to all material.
Licensing: Available for licensing and reuse, subject to restrictions. License fees charged.
Restrictions: BNAC training programs, films and videotapes are not sold outright, but are licensed, rented or previewed. Materials furnished in any format, whether on a life-of-print license or on a daily or weekly rental, are licensed only for use by the person or organization acquiring them directly from BNAC. Without written permission of BNAC they may not be copied, duplicated or reproduced in any manner, shown at events for which a charge is made, or shown on television. Customers wishing to depart from the foregoing limitations should contact BNAC to discuss use under special contractual arrangements.
Viewing Facilities: Screening center in Atlanta, Chicago, Rockville, Md. and Toronto.
Duplication Facilities: None.

DISTRICT OF COLUMBIA METRO

B'NAI B'RITH INTERNATIONAL HEADQUARTERS
1640 Rhode Island Avenue, NW
Washington, DC 20036
(202) 857-6580
(202) 857-6588
Fax: (202) 857-1099

Thomas Newmann (Executive Vice President)

Contacts: Dr. Michael Neiditch (Director, Continuing Jewish Education) (Ext. 6580); Joshua Blinder (Director, Audiovisual Department of the Department of Communications)
Services: Religious organization. Film and videotape material available for distribution and rental.
Description: Titles include: *Making the Difference* (1984), an overview of the B'nai B'rith system; *The ARI Experience,* on the B'nai B'rith-Israel Commission for American retirees in Israel; *In a Time of Peril* (1987), interviews with B'nai B'rith members in Germany (1920s-30s); *Scroll of Fire,* made by the Israeli Production Company; and Abba Eban's series on Israel. Also includes different symposia on Israel-Diaspora relations and Jewish-Catholic relations. Subjects covered include: interviews, documentation of projects in action, community volunteer programs, Seder on the Mall, sporting events and camp programs.
Size & Elements: Film: 16mm (7 titles; originals). Videotape: 3/4" (7 titles; transferred from film originals); and VHS (viewing copies). (24 hours total).
Cataloging: None.
Access: Available to the public. Available for reuse and resale. Maintained for distribution and rental rather than for research and reuse. Research fees generally not charged. Research requests accepted by mail and telephone.
Rights: Full rights held to some material. Additional clearances may be necessary in some cases if material is to be reused.
Licensing: Available for licensing and reuse, subject to restrictions. License fees charged in some cases.
Restrictions: Research requests subject to acceptance and approval.
Viewing Facilities: None.
Duplication Facilities: None.

DISTRICT OF COLUMBIA METRO

BRAZILIAN-AMERICAN CULTURAL INSTITUTE, INC.
4103 Connecticut Avenue, NW
Washington, DC 20008
(202) 362-8334

Dr. José M. Neistein (Executive Director)

Contacts: Gil Raposo (Librarian), Giselle Müller (Public Relations)
Services: Educational institution. Film and videotape collection available for rental and reuse.

Description: Films on Brazil, its people, cities and culture. Most films are in Portuguese; some are available in English versions.

Film titles include: *The Last Paradise,* an ethnographic study of the Kamaiurás, an Indian tribe of the Brazilian Central Plateau in the Amazon region; *The Cities of Porcelain,* on northeastern Brazil, the flora, fauna and farm products of the Amazon region and the "quaint cities" of Northern Brazil (Manaus, Belém, São Lius, Alcântara and Recife); *Cities of Steel,* showing the industrial part of Southern Brazil, Belo Horizonte and São Paulo, the impressive Sete Quedas and Iguaçu Cataracts, the *gauchos* and their folk dances; *The Cities of Yesterday and Tomorrow,* contrasting Brasilia with ten colonial baroque cities; *Rio, Portrait of a City; Carnival in Rio;* and *Bahia: City of All Saints,* on Salvador, Brazil's most picturesque city.

Videotape titles include *Xingu* (120 min., Portuguese-language); *A Brazilian Song; A Video Portrait of Brazil; Carnaval 86;* and *Concert: Elizeth Cardoso/Radamés Gnatalli, Camerata Carioca.*
Size & Elements: Film: 16mm (7 titles). Videotapes: VHS (5 titles).
Cataloging: Title lists with descriptions.
Access: Available for rental and reuse. Requests accepted by telephone.
Rights: Some rights held to all material.
Licensing: Apply for information. License and usage fees charged.
Restrictions: None specified.
Viewing Facilities: Film (available under certain conditions); videotape.
Duplication Facilities: Videotape.

DISTRICT OF COLUMBIA METRO

BRICK INSTITUTE OF AMERICA
11490 Commerce Park Drive
Reston, VA 22091
(703) 620-0010
Fax: (703) 620-3928

Nelson J. Cooney (President)

Contact: Charles Farley
Services: Association. Film and videotape library available for rental and purchase.
Description: Technical and educational films relating to brick.

Sample titles include: *Basic Bricklaying,* a primer showing use of trowel, line, level, spacing rule, corner pole, jointing tools, hammer, spreading and furrowing, laying brick, laying trigs, jointing and keeping bond; *Brick Veneering,* showing techniques involved in house masonry; *Earth and Fire,* exploring the aesthetics of brick, with a music soundtrack; *Clay and Craftsmanship,* tracing masonry guilds which have built empires from Babylon to Colonial America; and *Concepts in Clay,* a history of architecture and design with brick.
Size & Elements: Film: 16mm (10 titles). Videotape: format unspecified (5 titles).
Cataloging: Published catalogs.
Access: Maintained primarily for distribution and rental; available for loan reservations (required). Research requests accepted by mail, telephone and in person.
Rights: Full rights held to all material.
Licensing: Apply for information.
Restrictions: None specified.
Viewing Facilities: None.
Duplication Facilities: None.

DISTRICT OF COLUMBIA METRO

CABLE SATELLITE PUBLIC AFFAIRS NETWORK (C-SPAN)
444 North Capitol Street, NW, Suite 412
Washington, DC 20001
(202) 737-3220

Contact: Matthew Moore (Program Services Coordinator)
Services: Cable news network. Videotapes available to regularly scheduled news or public affairs broadcasts for reuse.
Description: Holds programs televised by C-SPAN, although not all material covered is archived. The 24-hour network's collection includes live gavel-to-gavel coverage of Congress, including the House of Representatives on the original C-SPAN channel since 1979 and the Senate on the newer C-SPAN II, initiated in 1986. During the remaining hours of the day, C-SPAN covers subcommittee hearings, National Press Club addresses, the national party conventions, and other activities in Washington and on the campaign trail.

C-SPAN has granted a limited, non-exclusive license to the Purdue University Public Affairs Video Archive (q.v.) to record their signal off-air and make videotapes available to students and faculty for classroom use. Duplicate copies are available only for educational and research purposes. This collection was established in 1987 and is due to be cataloged in computer files. For further information, contact Robert Browning at 317/494-9630.

C-SPAN also has an agreement with the National Archives and Records Adminstration (q.v.) by which the Archives will receive, on an annual basis, programs from the C-SPAN collection. C-SPAN will retain all rights for 25 years from the record date, after which it will become a public document. NARA holds selected master videotapes with identifying titles for all speakers. Plans are to index the collection on INFOCEN, an audiovisual database cataloging system; indexing will be completed in the next five years. All questions regarding access to this collection should be directed to the National Archives at 202/523-3063. All inquiries regarding duplication and reuse must be directed to C-SPAN.
Size & Elements: Videotape: 3/4" (approx. 4,000 programs; masters, stored in-house). Duplicates can be made on either 3/4", consumer-grade VHS or Betamax formats.
Cataloging: All programs are cataloged by the record date. Cataloging is not yet computerized, so cross referencing by key speakers or subject headings is not possible. All requestors must supply library staff with a date before a search can be conducted.
Access: Collection available for reuse to regularly scheduled news or public affairs broadcasts.
Rights: Full rights held to all material.
Licensing: Licensing requests considered on a case-by-case basis. General usage fees not charged; duplication fees (per hour) apply for any material requested, whether actually broadcast or not. No clips or soundbites can be pulled from that one hour.

For news and public affairs programs, up to three minutes of material may be used within a particular news segment or program. An on-screen credit naming C-SPAN as the source of the material is required.
Restrictions: C-SPAN restricts the use of its product, for broadcast purposes, to regularly scheduled bona-fide news or public affairs broadcasts (i.e., nightly newscasts or weekly wrap-up shows). Documentaries or three-part "news specials" may not use C-SPAN material. Footage cannot be used for any commercial, political or promotional purposes. Limited licenses (non-broadcast) are available for certain public performances and related uses. Rates and restrictions vary (apply for information).
Viewing Facilities: None.
Duplication Facilities: None.
Representatives: Purdue University, Public Affairs Video Archive (q.v.); and National Archives and Records Administration (q.v.).

DISTRICT OF COLUMBIA METRO

CENTER FOR AUTO SAFETY
2001 S Street, NW, Suite 410
Washington, DC 20009
(202) 328-7700

Clarence Ditlow (Executive Director)

Contact: Debra Barclay (Editor)
Services: Nonprofit consumer organization. Videotape collection available to journalists and researchers only; material not available for reuse.
Description: Motor vehicle and automobile safety, including fires in Ford ambulances and vans, sudden acceleration problems in the Audi automobile, misleading automobile advertisements and recalls. Materials are primarily videotapes of television broadcast segments featuring or mentioning the Center and related issues.
Size & Elements: Videotape: 3/4" and 1/2" (amount unspecified; masters).
Cataloging: None specified.
Access: Available to journalists and researchers only. Material not available for duplication or reuse. Research requests accepted by telephone.
Rights: No rights held to any material. Additional clearances may be necessary in some cases if material is to be reused.
Licensing: Not available for licensing or reuse.
Restrictions: Not available for reuse without permission of original producers.
Viewing Facilities: None.
Duplication Facilities: None.

DISTRICT OF COLUMBIA METRO

CENTER FOR DEFENSE INFORMATION
1500 Massachusetts Avenue, NW
Washington, DC 20005
(202) 862-0700

Adm. Gene R. LaRocque, USN (ret.) (Director)

Contact: Daniel Sagalyn (Associate Producer)
Services: Media resource center; videotape library. Material not generally available for duplication or reuse; Center prefers to refer inquiries to other sources of related materials.
Description: Material relating to United States national defense. Produced *America's Defense Monitor* (26 completed programs) covering such issues and subjects as the Persian Gulf, nuclear testing, the Pentagon, military spending, covert action, U.S.-Soviet relations, U.S. forces in Asia, the Strategic Defense Initiative (SDI) and homeporting.
    Also holds a collection of stock footage, mostly of weapons system testing, and a large library of material relating to defense issues, videotaped off the air.
Size & Elements: Videotape: format unspecified (approx. 500 videotapes).
Cataloging: None at present.
Access: For in-house use only. Open only under special circumstances. *Center prefers to refer inquiries to other sources.* Research fees not charged. Research requests accepted by mail, telephone and in person.
Rights: Full rights held to *America's Defense Monitor.* Additional clearances may be necessary in some cases if other material (especially reference material videotaped off the air) is reused.
Licensing: Center-produced material available for licensing, if it cannot be found elsewhere. License fees not charged.
Restrictions: Collection not generally available for duplication, licensing or reuse. Much material copyrighted.
Viewing Facilities: None.
Duplication Facilities: None.

DISTRICT OF COLUMBIA METRO

CENTER FOR PUBLIC DIALOGUE
10615 Brunswick Avenue
Kensington, MD 20895
(301) 933-3535
(301) 933-0277

Walter Rybeck (Director)

Contact: Erika Rybeck (Executive Secretary)
Services: Research and public education organization. One film available for rental and purchase.
Description: Concerned with land economy and policy, the CPD sponsors various programs and research projects relating to land tenure, infrastructure finance, farmland protection, urban growth patterns and local property tax reform. Has produced one film, *A Tale of Five Cities — Tax Revolt Pennsylvania-Style,* presenting an overview of a two-rate property tax reform by which unused land is taxed at a much higher rate than improved land. Designed to spur constructive discussion of local finance, housing, and urban revitalization issues, the film details the successes and problems of a modified land tax adopted by Pennsylvania cities (Pittsburgh, Scranton, Harrisburg, McKeesport and New Castle).
Size & Elements: Film: 16mm. Videotape: 3/4", VHS and Betamax. (1 title, 26 min.).
Cataloging: Published brochure available upon request.
Access: Available for rental and purchase.
Rights: Full rights held to all material.
Licensing: Apply for information.
Restrictions: Some restrictions may apply.
Viewing Facilities: None.
Duplication Facilities: None.

DISTRICT OF COLUMBIA METRO

CIRCLE RELEASING CORPORATION
One Westin Center
2445 M Street, NW, Suite 225
Washington, DC 20037
(202) 331-3838

Fax: (202) 429-9043

Contact: Staff
Services: Distributor. Films and videotapes available to the public for non-theatrical rental and leasing.
Description: Holds international and American feature films.
    Titles include: *Distant Harmony, Pavarotti in China; The Houses Are Full of Smoke* (Allan Francovich), a documentary on Central America; *Blood Simple* (Joel and Ethan Coen); *The Family Game* (Yoshimitsu Morita); *No Surrender* (Peter Smith); *The Go Masters; Letter to Brezhnev* (Chris Bernard); *My Sweet Little Village* (Jiri Menzel); *Rouge Baiser* (Vera Belmont); *Salvation!* (Beth B); and *Thérèse* (Alain Cavalier).
Size & Elements: Film: 16mm. Videotape: 3/4". (11 titles total).
Cataloging: Published brochures.
Access: Available to the public for rental; print leases available to institutions and organizations. Apply for information regarding public performance. Orders and preview requests accepted by mail.
Rights: No rights held to any material.
Licensing: Apply for information.
Restrictions: Rentals and print leases are made subject to the condition that the films will not be altered, televised, videotaped or reproduced in any manner whatsoever without written permission from Circle Releasing.
Viewing Facilities: None.
Duplication Facilities: None.

DISTRICT OF COLUMBIA METRO

COMMITTEE IN SOLIDARITY WITH THE PEOPLE OF EL SALVADOR (CISPES)
P.O. Box 12056
Washington, DC 20005
(202) 265-0890

Street address: 1314 14th Street, NW

Angela San Grano (Executive Director)

Contact: Diane Greene (National Program Organizer)
Services: Political and human rights organization. Videotape available for purchase and cable television distribution.
Description: *Winning Democracy* (25 min.) is "an up-to-date videotape focusing on the growing grassroots movement working for a true democracy in El Salvador, and the Duarte government's attempts to destroy it through a brutal campaign of arrests and torture of its leaders. Military-controlled death squads assassinate human rights leaders and union workers in the streets of San Salvador. But repression cannot stop the people of El Salvador. With every blow they come back stronger." Includes recent interviews with labor leaders Julio Portillo and Febe Velazquez; Reynaldo Blanco of the non-governmental Human Rights Commission of El Salvador; footage of Herbert Anaya; the October rally (attended by 40,000) supporting the dialogue in San Salvador between the FMLN/FDR and President Duarte; and visits to repopulated villages in the countryside.
Size & Elements: Videotape: 1", 3/4", VHS and Betamax (1 title).
Cataloging: Brochure.
Access: Available for purchase and cable television distribution.
Rights: Full rights held to all material.
Licensing: Available for cable television distribution. License fees not charged. Apply for information regarding reuse in other situations.
Restrictions: None specified.
Viewing Facilities: None.
Duplication Facilities: None.

DISTRICT OF COLUMBIA METRO

COMPUTER & BUSINESS EQUIPMENT MANUFACTURERS ASSOCIATION
COMMUNICATIONS DEPARTMENT
311 First Street, NW, Suite 500
Washington, DC 20036
(202) 737-8888
Fax: (202) 638-4922
Telex: 270-0995

Oliver Smoot (Acting President)

Contact: Maryann Karinch (Director of Communications)
Services: Association. Videotapes available for rental and purchase.
Description: Materials relating to video display terminals (VDTs) in the workplace. *Setting the Record Straight: The Facts about VDT's* (13 min.) and *Visual Displays: Questions and Answers* (22 min.) discuss the health and safety aspects of VDTs, featuring the opinions of academic and scientific radiation experts.
Size & Elements: Videotape: 3/4", VHS and Betamax (2 titles).
Access: Maintained primarily for rental and purchase rather than for research or reuse.
Rights: Full rights held to all material.
Licensing: Apply for information. License fees charged.
Restrictions: None specified.
Viewing Facilities: Videotape (3/4").
Duplication Facilities: None.
Related Materials: The association also holds rights to a videotape, *Ergonomics of the VDT Workstation,* available from an outside distributor (apply for information).

DISTRICT OF COLUMBIA METRO

COUNCIL FOR EXCEPTIONAL CHILDREN
1920 Association Drive
Reston, VA 22091
(703) 620-3660
Fax: (703) 264-9494

Jeptha Greer (Executive Director)

Contact: Jean Nazzaro
Services: Association. Videotapes available for purchase only.
Description: Collection is aimed at teachers, school administrators, teacher educators and parents. Films relate to working with the exceptional child (i.e., the mentally gifted and retarded, the visually, auditorially and physically handicapped, and those with learning disabilities, behavioral disorders and speech defects) in the classroom environment.
   Topics include: teaching mildly handicapped students; identifying physically abused, neglected, sexually abused or emotionally maltreated children; meeting the needs of gifted and talented students; a historical overview of special education; individualized education programs for handicapped children; workshops for understanding the needs of the handicapped; video training; and understanding child variance.
Size & Elements: Videotape: VHS (19 titles).
Cataloging: Published catalogs.
Access: Available to the public for purchase. Requests accepted by mail.
Rights: Apply for information.
Licensing: Not available for licensing or reuse.
Restrictions: Available for purchase only; not available for rental or loan.
Viewing Facilities: None.
Duplication Facilities: None.

DISTRICT OF COLUMBIA METRO

CYSTIC FIBROSIS FOUNDATION
VIDEO COORDINATOR
6931 Arlington Road
Bethesda, MD 20814
(301) 951-4422
Fax: (301) 951-6378

Contact: Chris Lloyd
Services: Foundation. Films and videotapes available to the public for purchase.
Description: Materials relating to cystic fibrosis.
   Sample items include *Living With Cystic Fibrosis; Diary of a Disease: Cystic Fibrosis; Research That's Working;* several editions of *Intercom,* with news stories; several public service announcements; and a message from President Ronald W. Reagan.
Size & Elements: Film: 16mm. Videotape: 1", 3/4", VHS and Betamax. (14 titles total).
Cataloging: Computerized cataloging for staff use only.
Access: Available to the public for purchase (nominal duplicating fee applies). Research fees not charged. Requests accepted by mail only.
Rights: Full rights held to most material. Some rights held to material produced by outside producers. Additional clearances may be necessary in

some cases if material is to be reused.
Licensing: Apply for information. License fees not charged.
Restrictions: Reuse restricted in some cases.
Viewing Facilities: None.
Duplication Facilities: None.

DISTRICT OF COLUMBIA METRO

DEVELOPMENT COMMUNICATIONS INC.
815 North Royal Street
Alexandria, VA 22314
(703) 683-3100

Welby Smith (President)

Contacts: Welby Smith; Steve Woehrle (Production Manager)
Services: Videotape producer; television production and training facility. Material available for duplication, licensing and reuse. Custom shooting services available by request in the Washington, D.C. area.
Description: Footage of military and technical training, including weapons systems, aircraft and ships; and the Washington, D.C. area, including monuments, suburbs and aerials of outlying areas, sewage systems and construction.
Size & Elements: Videotape: 3/4" (approx. 200 hours; masters).
Cataloging: Staff assistance required.
Access: Available to the public for duplication, licensing and reuse. Research fees charged on an hourly basis (fees negotiable). Research requests accepted by mail, telephone and in person (by appointment only).
Rights: Full rights held to all material.
Licensing: Available for licensing and reuse. License fees charged.
Restrictions: None specified.
Viewing Facilities: Videotape (3/4", VHS and Betamax).
Duplication Facilities: Videotape (3/4", VHS and Betamax).

DISTRICT OF COLUMBIA METRO

DEVILLIER DONEGAN ENTERPRISES
1608 New Hampshire Avenue, NW
Washington, DC 20009
(202) 232-8200
Fax: (202) 232-5634
Telex: 248724 DDEI UR

Ron Devillier (President); Brian Donegan (Vice President)

Contact: Frank Liebert (Director of Domestic Sales)
Services: Distributor. Film and videotape programs maintained for television distribution and rental rather than for research and reuse.
Description: International television program distribution company with agents in Paris, Munich, Rome, Madrid, Athens, Sydney and the Middle East. Serves independent producers with quality distribution services. Distributes programs in North America for a diverse group of foreign producers. Among them are the following:
   NHK Enterprises of Japan. Special programs include: *Chernobyl — The Bitter Taste of Wormwood; These Things We Left — Hiroshima's Warning; Pursuit in the Wake of Nuclear Fuel Shipments; The Japan News: 1940-1945; The Miracle Planet; Japan as a Technological Power; Postwar Japan: 40 Years of Change; The Crash;* and *The Silk Road of the Sea.* Other documentary programs on Japan, China and Asia include: *Zen Training at Eiheiji; Bejart's Kabuki Ballet; Ceremony in the February Pavillion; Elegance in Architecture; Nozomi Is Now Five; What Has Mankind Been Eating?; The Yellow River; Up Stream on the Sino-Soviet Border; Elunchun: The Hunters; A New Look for Department Stores; The Home of Chinese Porcelain; The Market for Medicinal Plants; 3,000 Years of Traditional Medicine; Cambodia Now: A Great Expedition of Farmers; Micronesia: Flawed Paradise; Bhutan: A Kingdom in the Himalayas; Timber-Rafting in Burma;* and *At the Helm of Korean Business.* Dramatic programs include: *Benkei; Knave of Hearts; The Shirt Makers; Sanctuary in Space; The Sound of Cracking Ice;* and *Sakuma.*
   Channel Four, Great Britain. Dramas, documentaries and specials include: *The Disputation,* a historical piece on the medieval debate between Christians and Jews; *Sputniks, Bleeps and Mr. Perry,* a dramatized documentary; *Shattered Dreams: Picking Up the Pieces,* profiling the current Israeli struggles for social renewal; films on India (e.g., *Saving the Tiger, Elephant — Lord of the Jungle,* and *Man-eating Tiger*); *Born in the RSA,* an adaptation of the Market Theatre of Johannesburg's drama on the lives of seven South Africans

of different racial and social backgrounds; *Avoiding Armageddon;* and the *Animal Traffic* series on the illegal trade in live animals, including programs from around the world such as *31 Tigers, Taken From the Wild, A Taste of the Exotic* and *Skin.*

Film Australia. Titles include: *Uluru: An Anangu Story,* recording the history, spiritual meaning and impact of tourism on one of Australia's most famous landmarks (Ayers Rock) from the point of view of its Aboriginal owners; *What's A Jew To You?,* a personal film by Aviva Ziegler; *Mum, how do you spell Gorbatrof?,* a deeply moving film looking at the way one small boy pushes his capacity to speak up for himself in a world he sees careening towards destruction; *Sounds Like Australia,* on the sounds of the bush; *The Human Face of Russia,* visiting homes, schools, theaters and workplaces to present a series of portraits of people engaged in day-to-day living in the largest country in the world; *The Human Face of Hong Kong,* contrasting wealth and working conditions in Hong Kong, as the colony anticipates the 1997 expiration of the British colonial lease; and *The Human Face of China,* following a family in Shanghai, a traveling acrobatic troupe, barefoot doctors providing basic medical care for 80% of the population, a commune production team and a riverboat trip on the Yangtze.

Other sources represented include RKO Pictures; Monty Python; Belbo Films, the Netherlands; The National Film Board of Canada; and Keg Productions, Toronto.

Distribution of domestic programs outside North America is represented in *The American Collection,* a catalog featuring Academy Award-winning documentaries, a series of classic children's stories, a probing science series, contemporary dramas from the American Film Institute and revealing portraits of some of Hollywood's legendary stars. Sample titles include: *Werner Herzog Eats His Shoe; The Emperor's Nightingale; The Brain; Everly Brothers Rock 'N' Roll Odyssey; Virgil Thompson: Composer; The Weavers: Wasn't That A Time; Strange Fruit; America and Lewis Hine; Garlic Is As Good As Ten Mothers; The West of the Imagination; Zasu Pitts Memorial Orchestra;* and *The Joy That Kills.*

Also provides consultant services in programming and marketing for clients in cable, homevideo and broadcasting.
Size & Elements: Film and videotape: various formats (over 150 titles total).
Cataloging: Published catalogs.
Access: Maintained for distribution and rental rather than for research or reuse. Research requests accepted by mail and telephone. Videotape viewing copies (3/4" and VHS) are available for preview.
Rights: No rights held to any material. Additional clearances will be necessary in all cases if material is to be reused.
Licensing: Apply for information.
Restrictions: None specified.
Viewing Facilities: None.
Duplication Facilities: Film and videotape.

DISTRICT OF COLUMBIA METRO

EDISON ELECTRIC INSTITUTE
1111 19th Street, NW
Washington, DC 20036
(202) 778-6414
Fax: (202) 778-6673

Hal Dunham (Director, Special Projects and Member Services)

Contact: Hal Dunham
Services: Association operating audiovisual exchange network to connect those in need of stock footage with possible sources. Does not maintain its own film or slide library.
Description: Operates the EEI Audio-Visual Exchange Network. This network provides computerized descriptions of stock footage, slides, and other audiovisual materials available from electric companies across the nation. Participating companies report brief descriptions of their audiovisual productions. These are entered into the computer and indexed by subject matter, key words describing their content, and other descriptors. These reports initially are reproduced and distributed to the network for filing in a loose-leaf binder. This timely distribution means participants are up-to-date on new and planned productions. Periodically, as the number of collected reports warrants, EEI publishes them in the *Network Journal.*

Borrowers are put in contact with originators of the materials. EEI does not maintain a film and slide library of its own. Requests for footage not listed in existing catalogs may be filled by special alerts sent to the networking companies.

A recent *Network Journal* covered the following subjects: acid rain,

alternative energy sources, aquaculture, electric system design, electric utility plants, electric vehicles, electricity generation, electrostatic precipitators, emergency planning, emergency procedures, employee benefits, employee orientation, employee relations, endangered species, energy and agriculture, energy and development, energy and jobs, energy audit, energy conservation, energy future, energy independence, health insurance benefits, meteorology, meter reading, motivation, National Energy Conservation Policy Act, Natural Gas Policy Act, nuclear power, rate increases and transmission issues.
Size & Elements: Applicable to material requested.
Cataloging: Computerized cataloging available to researchers.
Access: Open to the public. Available for duplication, licensing and reuse through Exchange subscribers. Research requests accepted by mail, telephone and in person (walk-in). Research fees may be charged where extensive effort is required.
Rights: Full rights held to some material. Additional clearances may be necessary in some cases if material is to be reused.
Licensing: Available for licensing and reuse through Exchange subscribers. License fees charged in some cases (particularly in cases of extensive use for commercial purposes).
Related Services: Institute assists producers seeking locations or footage of electric utility facilities and operations; technical assistance (engineers, scientists, economists, botanists); technical expertise on any electricity-related subject; script reviews or research assistance; and experts for on-camera interviews.
Publications: *EEI Network Journal* updates list of audiovisual material in network.
A-V Exchange Subscribers:
Alabama Power Company
Alberta Power Limited
Baltimore Gas & Electric Company
Boston Edison Company
Breeder Reactor Corporation
Carolina Power & Light Company
Central Illinois Public Service Company
Consolidated Edison Company of New York
Consumers Power Company
Detroit Edison Company
Duke Power Company
Duquesne Light Company
Eastern Utilities Associates
El Paso Electric Company
Empire District Electric Company
Electric Power Research Institute (EPRI)
Florida Power & Light Company
Idaho Power Company
Lower Colorado River Authority
Montana-Dakota Utilities Company
Nevada Power Company
New York State Electric & Gas Company
Ohio Edison Company
Oklahoma Gas & Electric Company
Otter Tail Power Company
Pennsylvania Power & Light Company
Philadelphia Electric Company
Potomac Electric Power Company
Public Service Company of Colorado
Public Service Company of New Hampshire
Public Service Electric & Gas Company
Puget Sound Power & Light Company
Sierra Pacific Power Company
Southern California Edison Company
Toledo Edison Company
Union Electric Company
The United Illuminating Company
Virginia Electric & Power Company
Wisconsin Electric Power Company

DISTRICT OF COLUMBIA METRO

ELECTRONIC INDUSTRIES ASSOCIATION CONSUMER ELECTRONICS GROUP
1722 Eye Street, NW
Washington, DC 20006
(202) 457-4919
Fax: (202) 457-4901

TWX: 710-822-0148

Contact: Tom Lauterback (Vice President Communications, Consumer Electronics Group)
Services: Industry association. Film and videotape material available primarily for loan.
Description: *Parade* (29 min.) is "set in a typical American town showing how consumer electronics enrich our lives and help us communicate and create"; *Electronics...Your Bridge to Tomorrow* (17 min.) illustrates career opportunities in the field.
Size & Elements: Film: 16mm. Videotape: VHS and Betamax. (2 titles total).
Cataloging: None specified.
Access: Maintained for distribution and rental rather than for research or reuse.
Rights: Full rights held to all material.
Licensing: Apply for information.
Restrictions: None specified.
Viewing Facilities: None.
Duplication Facilities: None.

DISTRICT OF COLUMBIA METRO

FAMILY LIFE SEMINARS
370 L'Enfant Promenade SW, Suite 801
Washington, DC 20024
(202) 488-0700
Fax: (202) 488-0806

Dr. Tim La Haye (President)

Contact: Bill Lyons (Business Manager)
Services: Association; cable television program producer. Videotape material available for licensing, subject to restrictions.
Description: News commentaries by Dr. Tim La Haye. The program, aired daily on cable television, presents a conservative, religious viewpoint on current issues.
Size & Elements: Videotape: 3/4" (260 programs).
Cataloging: Program list.
Access: Available to the public. Research fees not charged. Research requests accepted by mail.
Rights: Full rights held to all material.
Licensing: Available for licensing, subject to restrictions. License fees generally not charged.
Restrictions: Requests for licensing considered on a case-by-case basis.
Viewing Facilities: None.
Duplication Facilities: None (outside arrangements can be made).

DISTRICT OF COLUMBIA METRO

STUART FINLEY, INC.
3428 Mansfield Road
Falls Church, VA 22041
(703) 820-7700

Stuart Finley (President)

Contact: Stuart Finley
Services: Distributor; film and videotape producer; stock footage sales library; television broadcaster.
Description: Extensive filming (1954-81; mostly color) throughout the U.S.; some overseas coverage. Primary coverage area is the environment; strengths include hard-to-find early material and specialized subjects. Films were originally produced for educational use.
   Energy (1974-80; all color). *Science of Energy* series (4 films) includes: *The Solar Generation,* showing how a solar-heated home works and illustrating some early industrial uses of the sun's heat; *Which Energy* (1976), a comparison of energy sources and conservation concepts; *The Breeder* (1978), the story of nuclear energy from uranium mining to the nuclear reactor; and *Energy Consequences* (1980), showing the consequences of burning coal and other fossil fuels. Also offers three films about natural gas, including: *A Well in West Virginia,* about a drilling crew and a geologist combining talents to locate natural gas.
   Environment (1956-81; mostly color). Titles and topics include: *The Green City* (1963), a documentary about the wholesale destruction of our natural open spaces; *Sewers; Where the Sewage Goes; A River Called Potomac; Landfill; Urban Sprawl vs. Planned Growth; City in Trouble* (1960), about city planning

and coordination, set in Southwest Washington, D.C. before urban renewal; *A City is People,* working to preserve and enhance downtown areas; *Environment: Friend or Foe?* and *Can We Survive?,* both featuring Dr. Abel Wolman.
   Mental retardation (5 films, 1967-72; color). Titles and topics include: *P.E. — Lever to Learning,* about the benefits of physical education activities and education of the mentally retarded; *Time is For Taking,* about a residential camp for the mentally retarded; *Becky,* on raising the mentally retarded at home versus institutional life; *I.Q. — Questionable Criterion,* on multiple testing techniques versus I.Q. testing for evaluation of a child's learning disabilities; and *Retardation Research,* describing a research program testing the controversial Dolman-Delacato theory of neuropsychology.
   Soil and water conservation (6 films, 1968-81). Titles and topics include: *Conservation Down on the Farm* (1981), about one farmer who created a conservation plan for his farm with the help of his Soil Conservation District and SCS District Conservationist; *The Land Lives On,* a positive look at soil and water conservation; *Mud,* illustrating methods of preventing erosion and sedimentation through the process of orderly urban development; *Brush Creek Bounces Back,* about the revitalization of Princeton, West Virginia due to the Brush Creek flood control project; and *Drip,* a water conservation film featuring "Miss Drip."
   Solid waste management (15 films, 1966-81; all color). Titles and topics include: *Recycling; The Stuff We Throw Away,* about solid waste management; *5,000 Dumps,* a visit to some of our ugliest dumps; *A Day at the Dump,* a visit to the notorious Kenilworth Dump, showing environmental pollution at its worst; *Burn, Bury or What?; What's New in Solid Waste Management?; The Green Box; The Realities of Recycling;* and *Ecology Lady,* about a recycling center.
   Water pollution (1954-79). General coverage, including historic footage of early water pollution; primary locations include the Potomac Valley, the Ohio River Valley, New York State and Pennsylvania. Titles and topics include: *Coal and Water,* a documentary about the fight against "black water" and mine-acid drainage; *One, Two, Three...Clean,* describing modern sewage treatment processes; *Oops!* on the prevention of stream-damaging industrial spills by in-plant surveillance and personnel training; *The Valley,* managing municipal and industrial wastes in a major industrialized valley; *Water Resourcefulness,* on how planning water resources can protect land and water by preventing floods, droughts and pollution; *Where the Sewage Goes;* and *Sewers.*
   Miscellaneous (1960-81). Titles and topics include: *Jobs; Language...the Social Arbiter,* a series on linguistics; *A Living Constitution; Mosquito Fighters,* on large-scale mosquito control; *Museum of the Solar System,* analyzing moon rocks and soil from the moon; *Physical Education in Elementary Schools; Tintypes;* and *Hey, Dad!,* a time-lapse study of stone carving. *Journey to Augustow* details Nazi brutality in a Polish town where the gravestones from the Jewish cemetery were used by the Nazis to build roads. Shows the erection of a memorial to the eradicated Jewish population, including the first public ceremony honoring Jewish victims of World War II.
Size & Elements: Film: 16mm (500,000 feet, 50 titles; release prints, A&B rolls, internegatives and soundtracks).
Cataloging: Film lists; brochures.
Access: Available for research and reuse, subject to restrictions. Research requests accepted by mail and telephone. Research fees charged in some cases.
Rights: Full rights held to all material.
Licensing: Available for licensing and reuse, subject to restrictions. License fees charged.
Restrictions: Requests for research, licensing and reuse considered on a case-by-case basis.
Viewing Facilities: None.
Duplication Facilities: None.

DISTRICT OF COLUMBIA METRO

FOLGER SHAKESPEARE LIBRARY
201 East Capitol Street, SE
Washington, DC 20003
(202) 544-4600

Werner Gundersheimer (Director)

Contacts: Karen Greene (Registrar; for permission to use collection and permission to view films and videotapes); Elizabeth Walsh (Reading Room Supervisor; for reservations to view films and videotapes)
Services: Private research library. Film and videotape collection open to researchers and scholars for in-house use only, subject to approval.

Description: Films and videotapes (1913-present) relating to William Shakespeare and his work, including: live performances of plays; motion pictures based on Shakespeare's plays, including adaptations such as *West Side Story* (1961); documentaries on the Folger Library; and educational films relating to Shakespeare. A few silent films are held.

Sample titles include: *Antony and Cleopatra* (Enrico Guazzoni, 1913); *As You Like It* (Paul Czinner, 1936), with Laurence Olivier, Elisabeth Bergner and Sophie Stewart; *Broken Lance* (Edward Dmytryk, 1954), an adaptation of *King Lear; Bromo and Juliet* (Leo McCarey, 1926), with Charley Chase and Oliver Hardy; *Falstaff (Chimes At Midnight)* (Orson Welles, 1965); *Hamlet* (Tony Richardson, 1969), with Nicol Williamson, Anthony Hopkins and Marianne Faithfull; and *Kiss Me Petruchio* (Wilford Leach, 1979), videotaped in Central Park, with Raul Julia and Meryl Streep.

Size & Elements: Film: 16mm (release prints). Videotape: VHS and Betamax (viewing copies). (Approx. 300-400 titles total).
Cataloging: Card catalogs; film list; research library.
Access: Open to researchers and scholars only. For in-house use only. Research fees not charged. Research requests accepted by mail. Prospective users must apply for permission to use collection and/or to view films and videotapes. Holders of a Ph.D. or individuals working on doctoral dissertations should apply directly through Karen Greene (Registrar). Others, including first-year Ph.D. students, holders of master's or bachelor's degrees and those with professional experience must apply to Philip Knachel (Associate Director). Applications for permission to use collection should include two letters of reference.
Rights: No rights held to any material.
Licensing: Not available for licensing or reuse.
Restrictions: All material for in-house use only. Access to collection is by permission only (see above).
Viewing Facilities: Film (16mm flatbed); videotape (VHS and Betamax). Facilities can accommodate a maximum of three people at one time.
Duplication Facilities: None.

DISTRICT OF COLUMBIA METRO

FOUNDATION FOR HANDGUN EDUCATION
100 Maryland Avenue, NE
Washington, DC 20002
(202) 544-7227

Contact: Marjolijn Belefeld
Services: Political lobbying organization. Videotape material available for distribution.
Description: *Handguns Are Not the Answer* (1984, 14 min.), an educational videotape, was produced in cooperation with the now-defunct National Alliance Against Violence. Hosted by Michael Douglas, the program depicts the dangers of keeping guns in the house (e.g., children find a gun under parents' bed while playing and accidentally shoot a playmate; a couple has an argument in which one shoots the other). Suggestions follow on ways to protect home and self.
Size & Elements: Videotape: VHS and Betamax (1 title).
Cataloging: None specified.
Access: Available to the public free of charge upon request. Requests accepted by mail, telephone and in person.
Rights: Full rights held to all material.
Licensing: Available for licensing and reuse, subject to restrictions.
Restrictions: Restrictions may apply to licensing and reuse. Requests subject to consideration on an individual basis.
Viewing Facilities: Videotape.
Duplication Facilities: None.

DISTRICT OF COLUMBIA METRO

FUTURE FARMERS OF AMERICA
NATIONAL FFA CENTER
P.O. Box 15160
Alexandria, VA 22309-0160
(703) 360-3600
Fax: (703) 360-5524
Telex: 899121
StarGram: FF100A

Street address: 5632 Mt. Vernon Memorial Highway

Contact: Jeri Mattics

Services: Association. Film and videotape collection available for distribution and purchase.
Description: Audiovisuals produced to assist FFA chapters with instructional programs, recruitment of students and "Food for America" activities. Primarily produced by outside sponsors. Historical films from FFA are held by Venard Films, Ltd. (q.v.).

Titles include: *America — We Are the FFA; Stars Over America; The Case of the Sneaky Snack; Be All You Can Dream,* aimed directly at young students considering enrollment in vocational agriculture programs and membership in the FFA; *Keeping America on the Grow,* on training for technological change and diversification in the agricultural field; *That Special Feeling,* a film on the National FFA Convention; *Choices, Challenges, Changes,* on FFA's efforts for building local communities; *Consider the Possibilities* (sponsored by U.S. Department of Agriculture, Farmers Home Administration); *Bridging The Gap* (sponsored by Ciba-Geigy); *Hometown America* (sponsored by RJR Nabisco, Inc.) explains how to tackle community development through the "Building Our American Communities" program; *The Learning and the Land* (sponsored by The Firestone Tire & Rubber Company) documents the history of the FFA since the 1920s and explains the contributions the FFA and vo-ag have made to American agriculture and society; and *Agriculture's New Generation,* in which FFA members from across the U.S. tell about their varied career goals in agriculture and agribusiness.

Size & Elements: Film: 16mm (approx. 13 titles). Videotape: 3/4", VHS and Betamax (viewing copies).
Cataloging: Published brochures.
Access: Available for distribution and purchase. Primarily intended for FFA chapters.
Rights: Apply for information.
Licensing: Apply for information.
Restrictions: None specified.
Viewing Facilities: None.
Duplication Facilities: None.
Related Materials: Filmstrips and audiotapes.

DISTRICT OF COLUMBIA METRO

FUTURE HOMEMAKERS OF AMERICA, INC.
1910 Association Drive
Reston, VA 22305
(703) 476-4900

Carol Ann Kiner (Executive Director)

Contact: Alicia Montecalvo; Loy McGaughy
Services: Student vocational organization. One film and one videotape available for purchase.
Description: *Skills for Life* (10 min.) stars Judy Woodruff, news commentator for PBS television, who was a member of Future Homemakers of America during her high-school years. This promotional film "shows what membership in this exciting organization has meant to three young people: Lily — a shy, attractive teenager who blossoms into a self-confident leader; Shelli — a dynamic, enthusiastic student who discovers the personal satisfaction of helping others; and Dustin — an accomplished athlete who explores a restaurant career through a challenging HERO project." *Stand Out from the Crowd* (10 min.) is a training and motivational videotape on public relations and chapter activities of the organization.
Size & Elements: Film: 16mm (1 title). Videotape: VHS (1 title).
Cataloging: Brochures.
Access: Available to the public for purchase.
Rights: Full rights held to all material.
Licensing: Apply for information.
Restrictions: None specified.
Viewing Facilities: None.
Duplication Facilities: None.

DISTRICT OF COLUMBIA METRO

GEORGETOWN UNIVERSITY
SPECIAL COLLECTIONS DIVISION
GEORGETOWN UNIVERSITY LIBRARY
Washington, DC 20057
(202) 687-7444

Street address: 37th and O Streets, NW

George M. Barringer (Special Collections Librarian)
Nicholas B. Scheetz (Manuscripts Librarian)

Contacts: George M. Barringer; Nicholas B. Scheetz
Services: University archives. Films and videotapes available for research and reuse, subject to restrictions.
Description: *McCarthy Historical Project Archive.* Approximately 500 cans and reels of film and videotape (1967-70). Created to document Senator Eugene J. McCarthy's 1968 campaign for the Democratic Presidential nomination, the Archive is among the largest collections of records of any American political primary campaign. It has since served as a model for chroniclers of the political efforts of others, notably George McGovern (1972). Records of the national campaign office are supplemented by selected records of state offices, paid television and radio advertising, speech and release files, and a wealth of written and oral history narratives by many of the most active participants in the campaign.
  Library also holds some films concerning the history of Georgetown University.
Size & Elements: Film: format unspecified (positives). Videotape: format unspecified (masters). (500 cans and reels total).
Cataloging: Research library.
Access: Available to the public primarily for research. Research fees generally not charged. Research requests accepted by mail.
Rights: Some rights held to some material.
Licensing: Available for licensing and reuse, subject to restrictions. License and usage fees charged in some cases.
Restrictions: Available primarily for research. Requests for licensing and reuse considered on a case-by-case basis.
Viewing Facilities: Film (limited).
Duplication Facilities: None.
Related Materials: McCarthy manuscript collection.

DISTRICT OF COLUMBIA METRO

GOODWILL INDUSTRIES OF AMERICA
9200 Wisconsin Avenue
Bethesda, MD 20814
(301) 869-6011

Admiral David M. Cooney (Chief Executive Officer)

Contact: Robin Star (Public Relations Director)
Services: Social service organization. Films available primarily for distribution and rental.
Description: Goodwill Industries produced four films on the organization's rehabilitation program for physically and mentally impaired persons in the 1950s-60s, hosted by celebrities. Films are narrated by Joe E. Brown (1952), Gene Raymond (1960s), Charlton Heston (1960s) and Goodwill workers (1960s).
Size & Elements: Film: format unspecified (4 films, each 25 to 30 min., color).
Cataloging: Finding aids; files.
Access: Available for in-house use, distribution and rental. Research requests accepted in person (apply for information).
Rights: Some rights held to some material.
Licensing: Apply for information.
Restrictions: None specified.
Viewing Facilities: None.
Duplication Facilities: None.

DISTRICT OF COLUMBIA METRO

GREENPEACE, U.S.A.
1436 U Street, NW
Washington, DC 20009
(202) 462-1177
Fax: (202) 462-4507
Telex: 89 23 59

Peter Bahouth (Executive Director)

Contact: Jay Townsend (Director, Film and Photo Division)
Services: International organization. Videotape materials maintained primarily for rental, and for licensing, subject to restrictions.
Description: Educational materials on environmental issues, including nuclear

power and energy, toxic waste, wildlife and ocean ecology. Footage documents Greenpeace activities (1975-present). Most of the collection is held in the London office. Finished productions held in Washington, D.C. include: *Voyage to Save the Whales; Desperate Measures,* on nuclear waste dumping; and *Bitter Harvest.* Other materials are held in Washington, D.C. for distribution to schools.
Size & Elements: Videotape: Betacam ("small amount"); 3/4" (primarily); 1/2" and 8mm (approx. 250-300 hours total).
Cataloging: Computerized cataloging and in-house list for staff use only.
Access: Available to the public for rental. Requests accepted by mail and telephone.
Rights: Full rights held to all material. Additional clearances may be necessary in some cases if material is to be reused.
Licensing: Available for licensing, subject to restrictions. License fees charged.
Restrictions: Requests for licensing considered on a case-by-case basis. Restrictions may apply, depending on footage requested and intended use. London office approval necessary.
Viewing Facilities: Videotape.
Duplication Facilities: Videotape.

DISTRICT OF COLUMBIA METRO

GUGGENHEIM PRODUCTIONS, INC.
3121 South Street, NW
Washington, DC 20007
(202) 337-6900
Fax: (202) 337-9639
Telex: 251668 GPIXUR

Charles Guggenheim (President)

Contacts: Nathan Antila (Production Manager); Donna Devereaux (Production Coordinator)
Services: Documentary and political campaign film producer. *Footage not available for licensing or reuse.* Some titles available to the public through the National Park Service.
Description: Political campaign advertising and promotional films, including films produced for Democratic candidates such as Robert F. Kennedy, John F. Kennedy, Edward Kennedy, George McGovern, Walter F. Mondale, Joseph Biden, Gary Hart, Albert Gore, Jr. and Ernest O. Hollings.
  Producer of award-winning documentaries, primarily concerning American history and themes (1950s-present). Sample titles include: *The Big City* (1956), depicting 24 hours in the life of the city of St. Louis, Missouri; *A City Decides* (1956), dramatizing the events surrounding the Supreme Court's *Brown vs. Board of Education* ruling in 1954; *Nine From Little Rock* (1964), the story of what happened to the nine high-school students who integrated Little Rock's Central High School in 1957; *Robert Kennedy Remembered; May Peace Begin With Me* (1973), tracing the journeys of four young men of diverse backgrounds leaving their Israel kibbutz for family holidays; *The Eye of Thomas Jefferson* (1977), the story of Jefferson's contribution to American art and architecture; *John F. Kennedy (1917-1963);* and *The Klan: A Legacy of Hate in America* (1982).
  Recent PBS television programs produced by Guggenheim include *The Making of Liberty,* about the Statue of Liberty, and *America by Design,* a series on U.S. architecture and design.
Size & Elements: Film and videotape (formats and amounts unspecified).
Cataloging: Lists available.
Access: Available for distribution only. Footage not available for licensing and reuse. John F. Kennedy materials held at the John F. Kennedy Library (q.v.)
Rights: Full rights held to some material. Some rights held to some material. Additional clearances may be necessary in some cases if material is to be reused.
Licensing: Not available for licensing or reuse.
Restrictions: Rights to political campaign material retained by campaign organizations.
Viewing Facilities: None.
Duplication Facilities: None.

DISTRICT OF COLUMBIA METRO

GYPSUM ASSOCIATION
1110 Fidler Lane, Suite 421
Silver Spring, MD 20910
(301) 587-7607

Jerry A. Walker (Executive Director)

Contact: Jerry A. Walker
Services: Association. Films and videotapes available primarily for free loan or purchase.
Description: Promotional and technical films and videotapes produced by the Gypsum Association. *Beauty With Safety* is a dramatic film which effectively demonstrates how fire-resistant gypsum board roof membrane reduces and restricts burning on combustible roofs. *Time to Live* demonstrates the fire resistance qualities of gypsum board products.

Building Opportunities for All of Us is a lively and informative film addressing the contributions and services the Gypsum Association provides to improve the business climate for contractors. *Alert* was filmed on location at various gypsum mines, quarries, mills, board plants and warehouses; covers attitude, rules and procedures, equipment, and recognition of hazards and offers a formula for a safe passage through the work day. *Don't Drop the Ball* is devoted to an important professional, the forklift truck operator. Filmed on location in gypsum plants where the lift truck is the heart of materials handling operations, this film compares the experienced fork truck operator to a professional sportsman.
Size & Elements: Film: 16mm. Videotape: VHS. (*Don't Drop the Ball* also available in 3/4" and *Time to Live* also available in Super 8mm).
Cataloging: Brochure.
Access: Available to the public for purchase or free loan for a one-time showing only. Available to researchers and scholars. Research fees not charged. Research requests accepted by mail, telephone and in person (by appointment only).
Rights: Full rights held to all material.
Licensing: Apply for information.
Restrictions: None specified.
Viewing Facilities: Film and videotape.
Duplication Facilities: None.

DISTRICT OF COLUMBIA METRO

HARRIMAN COMMUNICATIONS CENTER
430 South Capitol Street, SE
Washington, DC 20003
(202) 485-3400

Ginnie Kontnik (Director)

Contacts: David Potasznik (Operations Manager); Liz Moore (Director of Marketing)
Services: Videotape producer; audiovisual production and post-production facility. Material available for duplication, licensing and reuse.
Description: Democratic National Conventions (1984 and 1988), including gavel-to-gavel coverage; footage of Washington, D.C., including shots of the U.S. Capitol, various monuments and the cherry blossom trees on the Mall.
Size & Elements: Videotape: 1", Betacam and 3/4" (masters and viewing copies); VHS and Betamax (viewing copies). (Approx. 75 to 100 hours total).
Cataloging: Lists; staff assistance required.
Access: Available to the public for duplication, reuse and resale. Research fees charged in some cases (for unindexed footage). Research requests accepted by mail and telephone.
Rights: Full rights held to all material.
Licensing: Available for licensing. License fees charged.
Restrictions: The Democratic Party footage is not for political partisan use other than by the Democratic Party.
Viewing Facilities: None.
Duplication Facilities: Videotape (1", Betacam, 3/4", VHS and Betamax).

DISTRICT OF COLUMBIA METRO

HEALTH AND EDUCATION RESOURCES, INC.
ART PROJECT
4733 Bethesda Avenue, Suite 735
Bethesda, MD 20814
(301) 656-3178
Fax: (301) 656-3179

Dallas Johnson (President)

Contact: Dallas Johnson
Services: Educational institution. Videotape available for purchase, rental,

duplication, licensing and reuse.
Description: *Jenny Read, In Pursuit of Art and Life* (57 min.), a documentary portrait of Jenny Read, a young artist who lived, wrote and learned to be a sculptor in San Francisco in the 1970s. She was murdered in her studio in 1978 at the age of 29. Taken from her book, *Jenny Read,* the documentary visualizes life and art in a way that will inspire young creative persons and their parents who see it.
Size & Elements: Videotape: 3/4", VHS and Betamax (1 title; 57 min.).
Cataloging: None.
Access: Available for purchase, rental, duplication, licensing and reuse.
Rights: Full rights held to all material.
Licensing: Apply for information regarding licensing and reuse. License fees charged in some cases.
Restrictions: None specified.
Viewing Facilities: None.
Duplication Facilities: None.
Publications: The book, *Jenny Read,* is available in hardcover and paperback.

DISTRICT OF COLUMBIA METRO

HIGH FRONTIER
2800 Shirlington Road, Suite 405A
Arlington, VA 22206
(703) 671-4111
Fax: (703) 931-6432

Lt. General Daniel O. Graham, USA (Ret.) (President)

Contact: Jon Metrey (Director of Communications)
Services: Foundation. Film and videotape available for distribution.
Description: *A Defense That Defends* (13 min.), produced in support of the Strategic Defense Initiative (SDI). Discusses near-term deployment options for a strategic defense of the U.S.; argues in favor of a strategic defense and against mutually assured destruction.
Size & Elements: Film: 16mm. Videotape (format and amount unspecified).
Cataloging: None specified.
Access: Available to the public.
Rights: Full rights held to all material.
Licensing: Available for licensing, subject to restrictions. License fees charged.
Restrictions: Restrictions apply (apply for information).
Viewing Facilities: Videotape.
Duplication Facilities: None.

DISTRICT OF COLUMBIA METRO

IDEAL COMMUNICATIONS, INC.
1920 G Street, NW
Washington, DC 20006
(202) 833-4567

See NEW YORK METRO

DISTRICT OF COLUMBIA METRO

INSTITUTE FOR LOCAL SELF-RELIANCE
2425 18th Street, NW
Washington, DC 20009
(202) 232-4108

Neil Seldman (President)

Contact: Jan Simpson (Business Manager)
Services: Nonprofit educational institute. Videotapes available for rental and purchase.
Description: Energy conservation and economic development on a community scale. Topics include: *Building a Homegrown Economy,* examining the Homegrown Economy project in St. Paul, Minnesota and describing resource flows within the city; local enterprises; reasons to pursue local self-reliance; the 1987 citizens training conference, culminating 15 years of grassroots organizing, co-sponsored by the Institute; technical research and implementation of alternative systems to mass burn incineration.
Size & Elements: Videotape: format unspecified (2 videotapes; viewing copies).
Cataloging: Publication list.

Access: Maintained for distribution and rental rather than for research or reuse. Requests accepted by mail and in person (by appointment only).
Rights: Some rights held to all material.
Licensing: Apply for information.
Restrictions: None specified.
Viewing Facilities: None.
Duplication Facilities: None.

DISTRICT OF COLUMBIA METRO

INSTITUTE OF MAKERS OF EXPLOSIVES
1120 19th Street, NW, Suite 310
Washington, DC 20036-3605
(202) 429-9280
Fax: (202) 293-2420

Contact: Diane Wegener
Services: Association. Two videotapes available to the public; both available for purchase, one available for free loan.
Description: *Don't Touch* is a safety videotape and the centerpiece of a nationwide blasting cap safety education program which the IME has sponsored since 1926. The videotape is aimed at educating children to the dangers of commercial blasting caps or detonators and demonstrates the hazards of blasting caps and instructs children on what to do if a cap is found. Available for purchase and 30-day free loan.
   Emergency Instructions is a detailed view of how public safety personnel should respond to fires and accidents when commercial explosives-carrying vehicles are involved. There are step-by-step instructions on safe reactions to the four most common fire scenarios, accidents and disablements. Each situation is demonstrated with authentic, experienced participants. Videotape is copyrighted and available only through IME. Available for purchase only.
Size & Elements: Videotape: VHS (2 titles).
Cataloging: Brochures available upon request.
Access: Available to the public for purchase and 30-day free loan.
Rights: Full rights held to some material. In some instances, IME will authorize individuals and organizations to reproduce *Don't Touch* for nonprofit safety education purposes, provided IME's copyright is acknowledged in reproduced copies. Additional clearances may be necessary in some cases if *Emergency Instructions* is to be reused.
Licensing: Available for licensing and reuse, subject to restrictions. License fees charged in some cases.
Restrictions: Authorization for reuse and acknowledgement of copyright is required.
Viewing Facilities: None.
Duplication Facilities: None.

DISTRICT OF COLUMBIA METRO

INSURANCE INSTITUTE FOR HIGHWAY SAFETY
LIBRARY
1005 North Glebe Road, Suite 800
Arlington, VA 22201
(703) 247-1500
Fax: (703) 247-1678

John Cook (Executive Vice President)

Contact: Mark Andrich (Audiovisual Specialist)
Services: Research organization. Films and videotapes available for free loan and purchase.
Description: Nine documentaries on highway safety in current distribution; 12 older documentaries withdrawn from circulation (limited availability).
   Titles currently available include: *About Air Bags* (1985); *Antilock Brakes Make Sense* (1987); *The Automotive Answer* (1979); *Boobytrap!* (1972); *Cars that Crash and Burn* (1973); *Children in Crashes* (1981); *Crashing Cars: Testing for Safety* (1986); *Crashes That Need Not Kill* (1976); *Effects of Multipiece Truck Wheel Failure During Tire Inflation* (1978); *Faces in Crashes* (1981); *In the Crash* (1970); *Making the Law Work: Safety Belt Use in Elmira, New York* (1986); *Report on Bumpers* (1983); *Small Cars and Crashes* (1972); *When Teenagers Drive* (1985); *Vehicle Handling Test: AMC Jeep CJ-5* (1980); *Underride* (1978); and *Using the Passive Alcohol Sensor* (1985).
Size & Elements: Film: 16mm. Videotape: 3/4", VHS and Betamax. (12 titles total).
Cataloging: Printed lists.
Access: Films and videotapes available for purchase from the Institute and for

free loan on a first-come, first-served basis from Modern Talking Picture Service, Inc. (q.v.). Research fees not charged. Requests accepted by mail and telephone.
Rights: Full rights held to all material.
Licensing: Apply for information.
Restrictions: Prior written permission required for reuse of any kind.
Viewing Facilities: None.
Duplication Facilities: None.
Distributor: Modern Talking Picture Service, Inc. (q.v.) (for free loan).

DISTRICT OF COLUMBIA METRO

INTER-AMERICAN FOUNDATION
1515 Wilson Boulevard
Rosslyn, VA 22209
(703) 841-3800
Fax: (703) 841-0973

Available for free loan from:
MODERN TALKING PICTURE SERVICE, INC. (q.v.)

Available for purchase from:
WEST GLEN COMMUNICATIONS
1430 Broadway
New York, NY 10018
(212) 921-2800

Deborah Szekely (President, Inter-American Foundation)

Contact: Carol delCampo
Services: Foundation; videotape producer and distributor. Material possibly available for licensing and reuse, subject to restrictions.
Description: Economic development in Jamaica, Mexico and Peru. *The Grassroots Development Series* includes three productions: *The Women's Construction Collective of Jamaica,* "a fast-paced, upbeat motivational story about ten unemployed young Black women from the ghettos of Kingston who were trained in construction trade skills. They are currently operating their own construction and carpentry business and working on commercial construction sites." *Cooperative Without Borders: The First Step,* "depicts Mexican migrant workers' struggle for survival and new hope for the future. The cooperative's peasant members are working with U.S. citrus growers and funding organizations to improve economic conditions in rural Mexico as an alternative to migration." The most recent production covers Alpaca migration in Peru.
Size & Elements: Videotape: 3/4", VHS and Betamax (3 titles).
Cataloging: Order forms available.
Access: Available to the public for distribution. Videotapes are distributed free of charge by request only through Modern Talking Picture Service, Inc. (q.v.). Open to researchers and scholars, subject to clearance. Research fees not charged. Research requests accepted by mail and telephone.
Rights: Full rights held to all material. Additional clearances may be necessary in some cases if material is to be reused (must contact coproducer).
Licensing: Available for licensing and reuse, subject to restrictions.
Restrictions: Permission to reuse must be obtained from coproducer.
Viewing Facilities: Videotape.
Duplication Facilities: None.

DISTRICT OF COLUMBIA METRO

INTERFAITH ACTION FOR ECONOMIC JUSTICE
110 Maryland Avenue, NE
Washington, DC 20002
(202) 543-2800

Arthur B. Keys, Jr. (Executive Director)

Contact: Stephen Clapp (Communications Coordinator)
Services: Advocacy organization. Videotapes available for purchase.
Description: *Economic Justice Pastorals and Economic Justice Advocacy* (3 videotapes, each 120 min.) produced at a convocation of religious leaders concerned with hunger and poverty.
Size & Elements: Videotape: VHS (3 videotapes).
Cataloging: None specified.
Access: Available to researchers and scholars only. Maintained for distribution and rental rather than research or reuse. Research fees not charged. Requests accepted by mail, telephone and in person (by appointment only).

DISTRICT OF COLUMBIA METRO I

Rights: Rights status unknown. Additional clearances may be necessary in some cases if material is to be reused.
Licensing: Apply for information.
Restrictions: None specified.
Viewing Facilities: None.
Duplication Facilities: None.

DISTRICT OF COLUMBIA METRO

INTERNATIONAL ASSOCIATION OF INDEPENDENT PRODUCERS — LIBRARY
Box 2801
Washington, DC 20013
(202) 775-1113

Dr. Edward von Rothkirch (Director)

Contacts: Dr. Edward von Rothkirch; Leo Scanlon (Assistant Director); David Walsh (Assistant Director)
Services: Film and videotape archives. Material available to the public for licensing and reuse, subject to restrictions.
Description: Eclectic film library acquired through donation, auction, inheritance and trade.
  South America. Extensive holdings include silent films of jungle expeditions in Ecuador, Colombia, Brazil and the Amazon basin; and travel footage of Rio de Janeiro and other destinations, all produced in the 1950s.
  Other subjects. Includes prewar and postwar Berlin; a dramatic film, made in conjunction with Howard Hughes, about two young women traveling along the Pan American Highway in Mexico (1950s); a false tooth factory in Liechtenstein (early 1970s); footage relating to Korea and Malaysia; a government-produced travelogue from Canada; newsreels relating to Vietnam; footage depicting the end of World War II in the Soviet Union, shot covertly and smuggled out of the U.S.S.R.; 13 color vignettes (each 12:30 min.) photographed in Cuba (1954).
Size & Elements: Film: 35mm, 16mm and Super 8mm (200,000 feet). Videotape: 2", 1", 3/4", 1/2" and 1/4" (small amounts held).
Cataloging: Rough lists.
Access: Available to the public for reuse. Research fees generally not charged (depending on size of job). Research requests accepted by mail and telephone.
Rights: Full rights held to some material. Some rights held to all material. Some material in the public domain. Rights status of some material not known. Additional clearances may be necessary in some cases if material is to be reused.
Licensing: Available for licensing and reuse, subject to restrictions. License fees charged in some cases.
Restrictions: Requests for reuse will be considered on a case-by-case basis.
Viewing Facilities: Film (16mm).
Duplication Facilities: None.

DISTRICT OF COLUMBIA METRO

INTERNATIONAL FREEDOM FOUNDATION
200 G Street NE, Suite 300
Washington, DC 20002
(202) 546-5788
Fax: (202) 546-5488
Telex: 910 240 8891

Duncan Sellars (International Chairman)

Contact: Jeffrey L. Pandin (Executive Director)
Services: Political foundation. Videotape collection available to researchers and scholars for research and possibly reuse. One title available to the public for purchase.
Description: "[T]he Foundation's activities include programs that focus on: exposing the failures of totalitarian ideologies; rejecting the subjugation of the individual to the tyranny of the collective; highlighting the threat posed by totalitarian regimes to the Free World; [and] opposing international terrorism, because people who live in fear can never be truly free."
  Videotape materials include: combat footage inside Nicaragua; interviews with Nicaraguan refugees; documentaries on Nicaragua; documentaries on South Africa (in English- and Afrikaans-language versions); footage of South African terrorist attacks; Australian and U.S. television coverage of protests against the African National Congress. One program, *Telling It Like It Is,* features Lt. Col. Oliver North on the situation in Nicaragua: "Supporters of the

Contras need to act fast. To support this effort, the International Freedom Foundation has produced a thirty-minute homevideo version of the now-famous slide show which the congressional committee tried to cover up during the hearings. We've also added some additional materials never before released to the public."
Size & Elements: Videotape: 3/4" (NTSC, 10 videotapes, each 30 min.); VHS (PAL, 20 videotapes, each 30 to 60 min.; NTSC, 10 videotapes, each 30 to 60 min.). (40 videotapes total).
Cataloging: Card catalogs.
Access: Available to researchers and scholars for research and possibly reuse. *Telling It Like It Is* is available to the public for purchase. Research requests accepted by mail, telephone and in person (by appointment only).
Rights: Full rights held to some material. Some rights held to some material.
Licensing: Apply for information.
Restrictions: None specified.
Viewing Facilities: None.
Duplication Facilities: None.

DISTRICT OF COLUMBIA METRO

INTERNATIONAL TELECOMMUNICATIONS SATELLITE ORGANIZATION (INTELSAT)
3400 International Drive, NW
Washington, DC 20008-3098
(202) 944-6815

Dean Burch (Director General)

Contact: Jim Mattson
Services: Media organization. Videotape available for in-house use only.
Description: INTELSAT, an international organization of government telecommunications entities, maintains and operates the space segment of the world's communications satellite system.
  Beyond Horizons, produced by Hillmann and Carr for INTELSAT, portrays its role in developing and providing telecommunications around the world. Shots and sequences include: scenes of birds; discussion of the importance of telecommunications; cities and locations around the world (Stonehenge, a Chinese parade, Petropolis Hills, India and Africa); rocket launch; satellite in orbit; construction of satellite; INTELSAT V satellite; INTELSAT control center in Washington, D.C.; liftoff of INTELSAT V; various rocket stages in orbit; satellite in orbit "seeing" earth; various earth stations and satellite dish antennas located around the world; a businessman in New York calling his family in Stockholm; examples of business applications of satellites (e.g., computers); antennas on ship, showing INTELSAT's role in establishing a separate maritime communications system in conjunction with INMARSAT; London switching center; viewers watching a televised soccer game; engineers working at earth station in Senegal; people watching television in a Brazilian bar; and a satellite dish against the sunset.
Size & Elements: Videotape: format unspecified (1 title).
Access: For in-house use only.
Rights: Some rights held to some material. Additional clearances may be necessary in some cases if material is to be reused.
Licensing: Apply for information.
Restrictions: Apply for information.
Viewing Facilities: Apply for information.
Duplication Facilities: None.

DISTRICT OF COLUMBIA METRO

LABOR INSTITUTE OF PUBLIC AFFAIRS (AFL-CIO) (LIPA)
815 16th Street, NW, Suite 206
Washington, DC 20006
(202) 637-5334
Fax: (202) 637-5058

Larry Kirkman (Executive Director)

Contact: Karla Garland (Program Associate for Marketing and Distribution)
Services: Media organization for labor unions. Videotape library available for educational use; licensing and reuse permitted, subject to restrictions.
Description: Labor-oriented films and videotapes intended for use by affiliated unions, as well as for the education of nonmembers about labor history and issues. Programs are acquired both from outside sources and produced by LIPA. Sample titles include: *The Controlling Interest,* relating to multinational corporations; *No Easy Way; Parliamentary Procedure; Song of the Canary,* on

occupational health and safety; and *Eugene Debs and the American Movement.*
Size & Elements: Videotape: 1", 3/4", VHS and Betamax (115 titles, each 30 sec. to 60 min.; masters and viewing copies).
Cataloging: Published catalog.
Access: Available for rental. Most material available for duplication and distribution. Research requests accepted by mail and telephone. Research fees not charged.
Rights: Full rights held to all material.
Licensing: Available for licensing and reuse, subject to restrictions. License and usage fees charged.
Restrictions: Requests for licensing and reuse considered on a case-by-case basis. Some material restricted for use by labor organizations only; other material available for public television broadcast.
Viewing Facilities: Videotape.
Duplication Facilities: Videotape (3/4" and VHS).

DISTRICT OF COLUMBIA METRO

LANDSCAPE ARCHITECTURE FOUNDATION
1733 Connecticut Avenue, NW
Washington, DC 20009
(202) 223-6229

Tina Resnick (Executive Director)

Contact: Harriett James (Publications Coordinator)
Services: Foundation. Film and videotape material available to the public for distribution and rental.
Description: Three titles available: *Roberto Burle Marx,* showing the life and works of Burle Marx, including his presentation at the 1985 LAF Luncheon, slides and a full narrative of his many gardens and other projects; *Street Graphics,* a colorful narration detailing the life of commercial signs in the built environment; and *Designing Environments for Everyone,* a disabled person's view of Lawrence Halprin's Levi Strauss Plaza in San Francisco, showing how design barriers are encountered by the disabled and discussing the design of barrier-free environments.
Size & Elements: Film: 16mm. Videotape: 3/4" and VHS. (3 titles total).
Cataloging: List and order form.
Access: Open to the public. Maintained for distribution and rental rather than research and reuse. Research requests accepted by mail and telephone.
Rights: Full rights held to all material.
Licensing: Available for licensing. License fees charged in some cases.
Restrictions: Requests for licensing and reuse considered on a case-by-case basis; permission dependent on intended use.
Viewing Facilities: None.
Duplication Facilities: None (outside arrangements can be made).

DISTRICT OF COLUMBIA METRO

LEAGUE OF WOMEN VOTERS OF THE UNITED STATES PUBLICATION SALES
1730 M Street, NW
Washington, DC 20036
(202) 429-1965

Nancy M. Neuman (President)

Contact: Pat Lunenfeld
Services: Nonprofit organization. Videotapes available for purchase.
Description: The League promotes citizen education about political, social and international issues. Four videotapes are available for purchase. *SDI Debate Video* (Nov. 1985, available in 60 min. and 42 min. versions); *The Third World Challenge to U.S. Policy* (1985, 20 min.) contains "striking footage of developing countries, accompanied by expert commentary"; *The Constitution and the Courts* (1987, 41 min.), a panel discussion illustrating the ways judges interpret the Constitution in their decisions; and *Mr. Madison's Constitution and the Twenty-first Century* (1987, 33 min.) a panel discussion concerning the balance of powers between Congress and the White House.
Size & Elements: Videotape: 3/4" (3 programs); VHS (all 4 programs); and Betamax (1 program).
Cataloging: Published catalog.
Access: Available to League members and the public for purchase. Requests accepted by mail; prepayment required.
Rights: Full rights held to all material. Additional clearances may be necessary in some cases if material is to be reused.

Licensing: Apply for information. License fees charged in some cases (depending on type of usage and intended project).
Restrictions: Programs primarily available for purchase rather than research or reuse.
Viewing Facilities: None.
Duplication Facilities: None.
Related Materials: Each program (except *SDI Debate Video*) has an accompanying discussion guide containing fact sheets, statistics, charts, discussion questions, additional sources and other information.

DISTRICT OF COLUMBIA METRO

LIBERTARIAN PARTY
1528 Pennsylvania Avenue, SE
Washington, DC 20003
(202) 543-1988

Dave Walter (National Chairman)

Contact: Nick Dunbar
Services: Political party. One film available to the public for free loan.
Description: *We Hold These Truths* (1980) describes the Libertarian Party and its platform.
Size & Elements: Film: 16mm (1 title). Videotape: Betamax (same title).
Cataloging: None specified.
Access: Available to the public for free loan. Research fees not charged. Research requests accepted by mail and telephone.
Rights: Full rights held to all material.
Licensing: Apply for information.
Restrictions: None specified.
Viewing Facilities: None.
Duplication Facilities: None.

DISTRICT OF COLUMBIA METRO

LIBRARY OF CONGRESS (LC)
AMERICAN FOLKLIFE CENTER
ARCHIVE OF FOLK CULTURE
Thomas Jefferson Building, Room LJ G-152
Washington, DC 20540
(202) 707-5510

Joseph C. Hickerson (Head)

Contacts: Joseph C. Hickerson; Gerald E. Parsons (Reference Librarian); Marsha Maguire (Archivist)
Services: Library. Moving image collection open to the public by special arrangement; available for duplication and reuse on a case-by-case basis, subject to restrictions.
Description: The Archive contains field recordings and documentation relating to worldwide folklore and ethnomusicology. Film and videotape materials reside in a number of unprocessed collections, which are either inaccessible or available only by special arrangement. Cataloged moving image material includes:
Fahnestock South Sea Collection (16mm, 5 reels, color). Footage shot by brothers Bruce and Sheridan Fahnestock on two widely publicized ethnomusicological and intelligence-gathering expeditions to Oceania and Southeast Asia (1940 and 1941).
Paradise Valley Project (16mm film and videotape, approx. 10 hours). Documentation of an American Folklife Center field research project in Paradise Valley, a small community near Winnemucca, Nevada (1978-82). *The Ninety-Six: A Cattle Ranch in Northern Nevada,* a two-sided laser videodisc and accompanying 84-page booklet, contains motion picture and videotape footage, including: scenes from a fall cattle roundup, drive and branding; two animated maps; talks by ranch owner Les Stewart on the use of wattles to identify cattle; the protocol for sorting dry cows from the herd; and other topics. An archive of 2,400 still photographs documents ranches, churches, clubs and other sites in the Winnemucca area. The videodisc also presents anecdotal reminiscences of ranch workers; explores the role of Native Americans on the ranch; and includes a discussion of key parts of a cowboy's saddle, the method for tying a scarf and other aspects of the material culture of ranching. Also included are 20 minutes of footage excerpted from films about the Ninety-Six made by Les Stewart (1940s-50s), showing hog butchering, how a hay derrick works, and the ranch's annual home rodeo and barbecue.
Size & Elements: Film and videotape: formats and amounts unspecified.

Videodisc: combined CAV and CLV formats (1 Laserdisc).
Cataloging: Not specified.
Access: Open to the public by special arrangement. Research fees not charged. Research requests accepted by mail, telephone and in person (by appointment only). Many moving image items are physically in the custody of Library of Congress, Motion Picture, Broadcasting and Recorded Sound Division (q.v.).
Rights: No rights held to any material. Additional clearances may be necessary in some cases if material is to be reused.
Licensing: Available for reuse on a case-by-case basis, subject to restrictions. License fees not charged.
Restrictions: Donor and copyright restrictions apply to some collections.
Viewing Facilities: Available by special arrangement.
Duplication Facilities: Available by special arrangement.
Related Materials: Sound recordings.

DISTRICT OF COLUMBIA METRO

LIBRARY OF CONGRESS (LC)
MOTION PICTURE, BROADCASTING AND RECORDED SOUND DIVISION (M/B/RS)
Room 336, Madison Building
Washington, DC 20540
(202) 707-1000

Robert Saudek (Chief)
Paul Spehr (Assistant Chief)
Patrick Sheehan (Head, Documentation and Reference Section)
Katharine Loughney; Madeline Matz (Reference Staff)

Contact: Reference Staff
Services: Government agency; library. Film and videotape collections available for research, viewing, duplication and reuse on a case-by-case basis, subject to restrictions.
Description: The Library of Congress houses the largest and most diverse collection of moving images in North America. Though it serves film and video producers as well as scholarly researchers, those seeking to reuse footage should be well prepared. The collections are complex, as are the uses to which they may be put; and those uses are also generally more limited than the majority of the public may assume.

Introduction

It will be helpful for the footage researcher to understand the overriding mission of M/B/RS (often referred to by the film and television staff in the shorthand form, "Motion Picture Division"). Functioning as a unit of what amounts to the United States' national library, its primary purpose is to collect and preserve moving image materials and to make them available for scholarly research.

The emphasis in collecting over the years has been put upon theatrical features — largely because this has been the dominant form of production for most of the century and the one most in demand by Library patrons. However, the Library of Congress has never limited its acquisitions to features and in fact has, in general, a sizeable amount of probably all production forms: theatrical shorts; theatrical newsreels; "educational" films (used here in a broad sense to encompass virtually any nontheatrical, non-television industry production in any format); television entertainment programs; television documentaries; television news; and others.

Date of production ranges from 1894 to last month (or thereabouts); country of origin is almost exclusively the U.S., though there are notable exceptions (described below).

Having made such a sweeping description, it is important to note that all of these categories are represented in varying strengths, especially for different time periods. Access to them varies, but mostly due to factors other than their production forms. However, realizing the diversity of the collections is a major step toward understanding LC collections and their potential uses.

One important characteristic of almost all of the Library of Congress's moving image collections is that the holdings are comprised of complete productions. Although some titles may be incomplete, the Library has not collected outtakes or raw footage. (Exceptions exist: see the Margaret Mead Collection, described under *Non-Copyright, Non-AFI Collections.*)

Using the collections

An initial inquiry regarding purchase of footage is likely to receive this response in the form of a handout from the Motion Picture, Broadcasting and Recorded Sound Division:

Our Division is frequently asked whether we provide stock shots or newsreel footage. As an archive, we are primarily concerned with the preservation of our 100,000 motion pictures and television programs and with making them available in the Library for scholarly research. With the strictest attention to our legal and archival responsibilities, we may be able to copy certain items in our custody. Two basic conditions limit our usefulness to those seeking stock shots or newsreel footage: 1. we copy whole reels only; 2. most of our collection is accessible solely by title and we do not provide subject research.

We do not duplicate films acquired as copyright deposits. Most of our collection dating from 1942 to the present falls into this category. Films acquired through sources other than copyright may be purchased, although their availability depends on several factors, including their preservation status, restriction by copyright or donor, and the uniqueness of the Library's film material.

Duplication of these latter films, such as those acquired through the American Film Institute, requires written permission from the copyright owner or proof that no copyright owner exists. In some cases, permission from the film's donor may also be necessary. Potential purchasers are responsible for obtaining these permissions and for having copyright searches made. (Information on copyright searches may be obtained from the Copyright Office, Library of Congress, Washington, D.C. 20559; 202-707-8700.) If the Library's film material is unique, purchasers may also be required to pay for the making of printing material, to be retained by the Library, in order to protect preservation masters.

The American Film Institute has published a list of their acquisitions as of September 1977. *The Catalog of Holdings: The American Film Institute Collection and The United Artists Collection at the Library of Congress* may be purchased from the A.F.I., Archives Department, Kennedy Center, Washington, D.C. 20566; the price is $5.00 (prepaid).

Many historical films from the period ca. 1894-1915, including a wide range of fictional and actuality films, are the most accessible of the films that may be copied. Most are free of copyright restriction, and three catalogs describing these films are available, each with subject indexing:

Early Motion Pictures: The Paper Print Collection in the Library of Congress, by Kemp Niver. (Washington, D.C., Library of Congress, 1985). This catalog, which may be purchased from the Superintendent of Documents (Government Printing Office, Washington, D.C. 20402; order #030-001-00110-5; $24.00) or in person at the Library's Sales and Information Counter, Thomas Jefferson Building, describes some 3,000 films made between 1894 and 1915.

Some libraries may still have only the previous edition: *Motion Pictures From the Library of Congress Paper Print Collection, 1894-1912,* by Kemp Niver. (Berkeley, University of California Press, 1967.)

The George Kleine Collection of Early Motion Pictures in the Library of Congress: A Catalog. (Washington, D.C., Library of Congress, 1980). This catalog, which may be purchased from the Superintendent of Documents (Government Printing Office, Washington, D.C. 20402; order #030-001-00088-5; $15.00), describes 456 motion pictures produced between 1898 and 1926.

The Theodore Roosevelt Association Film Collection: A Catalog. (Washington, D.C., Library of Congress, 1986). This catalog describes 318 films relating to the life and career of Theodore Roosevelt and may be purchased by mail from the Government Printing Office (order #030-001-00113-0) or in person at the Library's Sales and Information Counter for $12.00.

We have no standard price list; costs are based on the charges made to the Library by commercial film labs. For information about the costs of specific items, contact the Public Services Coordinator, M/B/RS, Library of Congress, Washington, D.C. 20540; 202-707-5623. For further information about our holdings and to arrange screening appointments, contact a Reference Librarian, M/B/RS, Library of Congress, Washington, D.C. 20540; 202-707-1000.

Careful attention should be paid to this handout, especially to the sentences regarding copyright deposits. A telephone conversation is likely to supply the same information and may conclude with the offer to mail this handout. It is intended to apply to a wide variety of requests and attempts to strike a balance between brevity and necessary detail. Through experience the reference staff has learned that these aspects of the Library's policies and practices most affect patrons who wish to purchase stock footage.

Initial inquiries — by mail, telephone and in person — and research assistance are handled by a reference librarian in the Motion Picture and Television Reading Room.

Many inquiries receive a fairly quick, negative response because of the hurdles spelled out in the handout reprinted above. If, in the estimation of the reference librarian, there is some possibility of meeting the patron's requests, he or she is referred to an appropriate catalog or finding aid. The patron is then responsible for conducting the necessary research or for hiring a free-lance researcher to do it. Library staff will assist as much as possible with catalog research, but are unable to provide viewing lists for specific projects. (There are exceptions, of course; especially for topics of popular interest, such as the Statue of Liberty, for which M/B/RS has little readily available for reuse and can conveniently make up short lists of available holdings).

Once the patron has identified potential material from the catalogs, he or she can make an appointment for viewing with the reference librarian. Here are the ground rules, from a handout supplied by M/B/RS:

1. Viewing facilities, which are available without charge, are provided for those doing research of a specific nature leading toward a publicly available work such as a dissertation, publication, or film/television production. We regret that the facilities may not be used for purely personal study or appreciation, nor in ways — such as preview — that conflict with commercial distribution.

2. Graduate students and undergraduates in advanced classes wishing to screen films should first obtain letters from their professors endorsing their projects. The Motion Picture, Broadcasting, and Recorded Sound facilities may not be used to make up missed classroom screenings, or to complete class assignments.

3. Each film may be viewed once by any individual. Although our viewing machines have no fast forward/fast reverse capability, they may be stopped for notetaking.

4. We are unable to accommodate groups. Only the person for whom the appointment has been made may view films.

5. All viewing is by advance appointment. Waiting time varies, but those persons whose projects involve more than one or two feature films should expect a wait of one or two weeks.

6. Because many of our collections are stored in remote locations, viewing lists must be received at least three days in advance of appointments. Long lists require one week for preparation.

7. Viewing lists for films should be arranged in alphabetical order.

8. A maximum of three features, or their equivalent, may be viewed in one day. Three consecutive weeks of viewing time may be reserved.

9. Taping or photographing is permitted only with written permission of the copyright owners and/or donors. Any such activity disturbing to others in the viewing room will not be permitted. The Library does not provide equipment for these purposes.

10. Bear in mind that screening time is limited and must be scheduled. Cancellation without sufficient notice tends to prevent others from having access to the facilities. Please be considerate of others in this regard.

More flexibility in scheduling is possible than is implied in the two-week waiting period suggested by the Guidelines; the longest waits usually are experienced by scholars viewing 35mm features. Be warned that the advance notice requirement, especially for preparation, is quite necessary. A more serious barrier to quick access is the location of material. Large portions of the collections are stored in a suburban warehouse, and patrons should expect a three-day wait for this material. It can be longer or shorter, depending on such factors as the time of day, whether other viewing lists are being filled at the same time, and the running condition of transport trucks. The good news is that most of the footage that researchers want (or will settle for) is 16mm film stored on the premises. Still, researchers should be advised to expect a week's wait.

Once titles have been selected, the next stop is the Public Services office. Public Services staff handles, among other matters, all orders for duplication of M/B/RS motion picture and recorded sound holdings. It serves as LC's "publisher" and distributor of certain preselected sound recordings, but all film and videotape duplication orders are handled and priced individually. Copies to film are made by laboratories outside LC but in the Washington, D.C. area. LC's Preservation Laboratory in Dayton, Ohio, only makes preservation copies for LC collections. Film to videotape transfers and videotape copies are made primarily in LC's Recording Laboratory.

Rates vary according to specific laboratory fees and must be prepared for each specific order. Note: it is nearly impossible to get a preliminary budget estimate from Public Services without knowing the precise titles requested from LC collections.

Questions about rights will certainly have emerged while you worked with the reference librarian, and they may have been answered. But here is where you will finally have to face them. You may be told that an official copyright search is required, or be referred to a donor to obtain necessary permission. Expect full allegiance to the rights of copyright owners and observance of restrictions placed by donors.

Public Services staff also serve as liaison with appropriate administrative and curatorial staff to assure that LC meets its archival responsibilities regarding the material you wish to reproduce. *The one hard-and-fast rule which is never waived is the "whole reel minimum"* (see Restrictions).

The Collections

Contents of this section include:
I.   The Copyright Collection
    A. Paper Print Collection
    B. American Film Institute Collections
        i.   Black Films in the Library of Congress
        ii. DeForest Films (AFI/Zouary Collection)
        iii. Méliès Films (AFI/Academy Collection)

II. Non-Copyright, Non-AFI Collections
    A. George Kleine Collection
    B. Theodore Roosevelt Association Collection
    C. Captured Foreign Collections
        i.   German Collection
        ii. Italian Collection
        iii. Japanese Collection
    D. United Artists Collection
    E. Embassy of South Vietnam Collection
    F. Gatewood W. Dunston Collection
    G. Edison Laboratory Collection
    H. Harmon Foundation Collection
    I. Eastman Teaching Films Collection
    J. Margaret Mead Collection
    K. Public Archives of Canada/Dawson City Collection

III. Television Collections
    A. NBC Television Collection
    B. NET (National Educational Television) Programs

IV. U.S. Government Productions

The danger of creating misconceptions by taking a collection approach to describing LC's motion picture holdings is that, except for published catalogs, there is almost no way to search catalogs by collection name. Individual title access dominates, supplemented occasionally by subject and credit indexing (see Cataloging). In any case, the majority of collections are small, miscellaneous in content, and reveal little by their names. The following descriptive list of collections is intended not so much to itemize the most important films in M/B/RS as to suggest the range and types of material available.

Even though there is no collection index to these holdings, additional information on certain collections and other topics may be found in Reading Room Subject Files. (Specific references are made to these files in descriptions below.) The best way to search for material in M/B/RS is to describe your needs to a reference librarian, who will know whether M/B/RS is likely to have it and whether there is a way to search for it.

LC has acquired its moving image collections via copyright deposit, gift, exchange and purchase. Although very few items are purchased, this has been the case for individual works and a handful of entire collections. Exchange of material has occurred primarily in working with domestic and foreign film archives, and represents a relatively small amount of material. Gifts, ranging from one film to major studio deposits, have contributed enormously to M/B/RS collections and filled inevitable gaps.

I. *The Copyright Collection*

Copyright deposits comprise the largest, most visible portion of M/B/RS holdings, and are the materials most often used by M/B/RS patrons (virtually all copies are considered reference prints). *Duplication of copyright deposits is not permitted* (see Restrictions).

LC's holdings (in all forms) have been built by copyright regulations requiring deposit of works, usually in connection with copyright registration. M/B/RS's collections began similarly, but the collection process was not systematically maintained.

One of M/B/RS's earliest and most important collections, the Paper Print Collection (see below) is comprised of copyright deposits. Because there was no provision in the copyright law for registering a moving picture, these films were deposited as photographs printed on strips of paper. In 1912, new copyright legislation permitted the registration of motion pictures as a distinct form, but the Library chose not to house the inflammable nitrate film in use at the time and returned all works to their claimants.

This practice changed in 1942, when the Library began to request the return of *selected* works, and M/B/RS continues to do so to this day.

Selection of copyright deposits currently functions as the principal source of current acquisitions. (In fact, it is virtually the only such source, as funds for purchase are minuscule and become available only occasionally.) Some 7,000 to 8,000 titles have been added annually in recent years. Although the quantity and range of acquired works has expanded since 1942, the concept of selectivity remains, which makes the copyright catalog (issued by the Copyright Office) a list of possibilities, rather than a match to M/B/RS holdings.

The Copyright Collection therefore represents less a specific, definable collection than an ongoing process of acquisition. It continues to exemplify the wide range of U.S. film and video production and to reflect the diversity of American thought and experience. Remember, too, that external forces — especially the nature of the entertainment business and the technicalities of copyright regulation — have shaped the nature of the existing collection. For the footage researcher, the most important result is the predominant occurrence in the Copyright Collection of *complete* motion pictures produced and distributed in the U.S. (i.e., no raw footage, no outtakes and very little non-U.S.-productions).

A more specific description of the copyright deposits in M/B/RS would amount to a history of filmmaking in the U.S. These further observations, however, will benefit the footage researcher in search of actuality material.

1. *Copyright deposits may not be duplicated.* They are, however, available for viewing for research purposes and can provide useful information. M/B/RS catalogs provide almost no subject access to this material. (The reference staff does hand out a "Guide to Audiovisual Materials," a brief bibliography of publications that will help in subject searches.)

2. *The vast majority of LC's news programs (theatrical and television) are copyright deposits.* (These holdings, in fact, represent a rare, if incomplete, source of the release version of theatrical newsreels and complete broadcasts of television news programs.) There is *no* subject access to news footage in LC catalogs. Specific holdings are listed in M/B/RS catalogs by issue number or date; for convenience, here is a broad summary of news material in LC:

Theatrical Newsreels. As with other copyright deposits, very few issues were selected in the first few years, but their numbers increased in time. *Movietone News* holdings include scattered issues from 1942-45, 1950 and 1954-63 (12 issues are held for 1942-43; nearly complete holdings exist for the 1960s). *News of the Day* holdings include newsreels from 1941-49, 1952-53, 1956-57 and a complete run 1957-68 (3 to 6 issues exist for 1942 and 1952; heavier holdings exist for mid-1940s). Scattered issues of *Paramount News* for 1942-45 and 1955-57 are held. For *Universal Newsreel,* scattered issues are held for 1943-45; nearly complete runs for 1946-54, 1957-58 and 1960-67; none are held for 1955-56. (Coincident with the eventual holdings of *Universal Newsreel* in the National Archives, LC early on decided to collect heavily from one series and acquire samples from the rest. The choice of Universal now creates some confusion for inexperienced researchers as to the respective holdings and policies of the two archives.) Very scattered, mostly earlier issues of these newsreels occur throughout other collections in M/B/RS.

Television News. (This outline is limited to regularly scheduled news programs and does not include documentaries, special coverage and other productions of network news divisions, which are listed by title in M/B/RS catalogs.) All networks have used various titles for their series. M/B/RS organizes its television news catalogs by date and daypart. There is probably a six- to eight-month lag between broadcast and receipt in M/B/RS. Nearly complete weeknight broadcasts of ABC's *Evening News* (April 1977-present) and scattered issues of *Nightline* (beginning 1987) are held; nearly all CBS news programs have been registered since January 1975; and no NBC News programs are held. The only example of "early" television news in M/B/RS is a non-copyright deposit television news series, *Douglas Edwards With the News* (CBS) (40 issues, 26Sep–11Nov1960), comprised primarily of coverage of the Kennedy-Nixon presidential election campaign.

3. Television programs have been acquired by M/B/RS since 1949, primarily via copyright deposit. (Major exceptions, described below, include NBC and NET. Television holdings are also described below in connection with the expected publication of a catalog.) Copyright technicalities (especially the definition of "publication") have tended to emphasize the registration of primetime entertainment series, as opposed to such programs as musical variety specials or game shows.

4. One final note in connection with copyright: since 1912, copyright regulations have required deposit of written material for published motion pictures submitted for registration. All of these "copyright descriptions," which can range from one sentence to a full dialogue and cutting continuity, have been retained and may be consulted in the Motion Picture and Television Reading Room; they are arranged by copyright registration number.

(A) *Paper Print Collection.* Spanning 1894-1914 and containing approximately 3,000 titles, there is probably no more important single collection of motion picture film in LC. It is one of the largest collections of early productions available and encompasses all period genres. 16mm reference prints and printing negatives exist for all titles, and there are no copyright restrictions on duplication. For both scholars and footage researchers it has been, and remains, the most active of all collections in M/B/RS.

History. In fact, the original materials in this collection are not motion picture *films,* but rolls of paper strips, deposited in the Copyright Office as part of registration of motion picture productions. Prior to 1912 copyright law made no explicit provision for motion pictures, although some entrepreneurs in the burgeoning entertainment industry found a way to protect their properties by registering them as photographs, submitting contact prints on photographic paper. While the nitrate copies of so many of these films were scattered or self-destructed, the paper-based photographs survived in relatively good condition, patiently awaiting discovery and a rekindled interest in the history of our motion picture heritage.

Many of the earliest deposits (including the first: the famous "Fred Ott's Sneeze," registered as *Edison Kinetoscopic Record of a Sneeze*), were comprised of separate photographs (in standard sizes) of sample frames from each work. There are also many films from the period represented by strips of paper on which were printed samples of successive frames — ranging from a stack of short strips, each displaying three frames from a scene, to longer strips that would run several seconds if they could be projected.

The best-known materials among these copyright deposits are the full-length paper positive copies that have been restored to usefulness and are described in published catalogs of the Paper Print Collection. This restoration project, in which the printed-on-paper images (without perforations!) were rephotographed onto 16mm celluloid is an interesting story in itself, and garnered an Academy Award for Kemp Niver in 1955.

In fact, the restoration continues, although slowly: M/B/RS hopes to start over again with the paper originals, better equipment and techniques, and 35mm film. Test prints show remarkable improvement in picture quality. And some attention has finally been given to the (relatively) ignored shorter strips, which are in need of conservation and restoration. Most have recently been sorted and rehoused, and some have been copied onto 35mm film. (These excerpts are more likely to be of interest to scholars than footage researchers, however.)

Contents. The Paper Print Collection encompasses the full range of filmmaking activity during the early years of the industry. The first deposit was received in 1894; the practice ended rather quickly after a 1912 revision of copyright law expanded its protection to motion pictures in their own right. Notable latecomers were a number of 1914 and 1915 Keystone comedies.

Among the 3,000 titles one finds comedies, dramas and actualities (genuine and artificial) on a wide variety of topics. Period cameras recorded such historical events as the Spanish-American War, the Russo-Japanese War (watch out for "reconstructions"), and the Boxer Rebellion; international fairs and expositions in Buffalo, St. Louis and Paris; the America's Cup and automobile races; lots of fire departments; Union Pacific railroad trains; and urban mass transit in Boston. New York is most frequently represented among the urban street scenes. Historical figures include Admiral George Dewey, Prince Henry of Prussia, Jack Johnson and William McKinley.

There are a few early advertising films, vaudeville acts, "peep shows" and an animated spoof of Theodore Roosevelt. Also included are thirty works by Georges Méliès, one of the most inventive of all filmmakers.

Productions are primarily U.S. in origin. In fact, a considerable portion of the collection originated from two companies: the Thomas A. Edison Company and the American Mutoscope and Biograph Co. (later and more widely known as the Biograph Company.) A wide variety of smaller American companies are also represented: for example, Oklahoma Natural Mutoscene, responsible for a handful of unusual films shot in Oklahoma, including *The Bank Robbery,* a 1908 Western featuring ex-outlaw Al Jennings; and a few foreign producers of fictional works. The small number of valuable actuality films made in foreign locations, including Mexico, Cairo (Egypt) and the Philippines, were produced by U.S. companies.

Researchers interested in the history of the motion picture will find over 300 films supervised by D. W. Griffith and performances by the legendary actors Joseph Jefferson and Sarah Bernhardt. A great deal of effort was made to identify production and performance credits for publication in the new edition of the "paper print catalog."

Picture quality, as one might expect of films copied from paper, is not the best. There are additional problems with registration (jumpy image) and deterioration of some of the paper originals. (In fact, frequent use in compilation films — two short pieces showing the arrival of immigrants on Ellis Island being a recent, ubiquitous example — has led many viewers, even producers, to assume that *all* early films would look like these prints.) However, tests show that superior copies from the paper rolls are possible (with sufficient time and money) and the researcher can sometimes find another copy of a desirable title in LC or another archives.

Access. The films in the Paper Print Collection are probably the most thoroughly described of any in M/B/RS, and a published catalog is widely available: *Early Motion Pictures: The Paper Print Collection in the Library of Congress,* by Kemp Niver. Washington, D.C., Library of Congress, 1985. (Volume may be purchased from the Superintendent of Documents, Government Printing Office, Washington, D.C. 20402; order #030-001-00110-5; $24.00).

Kemp Niver, who was principally responsible for the actual copying of the paper rolls, has authored two editions of the "paper print catalog." Although the 1967 edition published by the University of California Press (*Motion Pictures From the Library of Congress Paper Print Collection, 1894-1912*) is out of print, it still may be the only edition available in some libraries. Researchers should try to obtain the 1985 edition, as it is much improved with the inclusion of the 1914-15 Keystone comedies, many additional credits and shooting locations, and an expanded index. Inclusion of shelf numbers (for negatives and prints) will save a trip to the Reading Room card catalog for this information. Lengths (in 16mm feet) and descriptions of contents have been retained. On the other hand, fans of the first catalog's organization (by genre) may want to hold on to their copies; the entries in the current catalog are arranged in straightforward alphabetical sequence.

Additional information. The riches of the Paper Print Collection have made it the Division's most popular subject for articles. In addition to introductory pieces in both editions of the catalog there are:

Niver, Kemp R. "From Film to Paper to Film," *The Quarterly Journal of the Library of Congress.* Vol. 21, no. 4, October 1964, pp. 248-64. The story of the LC paper print conversion program.

Spehr, Paul C. "Some Still Fragments of a Moving Past," *The Quarterly Journal of the Library of Congress.* Vol. 32, no. 1, January 1975, pp. 33-50. Edison films in LC.

(B) *American Film Institute Collections.* With the founding of the American Film Institute (AFI) in 1967, there was finally a national organization that could focus attention on film preservation and actively seek motion picture materials in need of preservation. "Nitrate won't wait!" became the rallying cry. Rather than create new physical facilities for film preservation, AFI assumed the role of catalyst and facilitator — soliciting material, working with collectors and seeking funds — while depositing collected films (now also television programs) in existing archives, primarily LC.

The AFI collections fill some of the gaps in LC's other acquisitions, primarily for the years 1912-42, when no copyright deposits were retained, and in holdings of preprint materials. Some 20,000 titles have come to LC (as gifts) from AFI, the majority of them original nitrate negatives and masters from major studios (Columbia, RKO and Universal). A wide variety of other films has been collected from individuals, corporations and historical organizations, mirroring M/B/RS's non-AFI collections. Almost all were produced prior to 1951, the period in which 35mm motion pictures were produced on nitrate-based stock and are, therefore, most in need of preservation.

Once received, the films collected by AFI are integrated into M/B/RS operations. Of concern to footage researchers is the fact of their integration into M/B/RS catalogs; there is no distinct listing of AFI materials in LC.

AFI's National Center for Film and Video Preservation (q.v.) does keep records of films it has collected and deposited in cooperating archives, and LC's holdings of AFI acquisitions as of September 1, 1977 are listed alphabetically in: *Catalog of Holdings; The American Film Institute Collection and the United Artists Collection at the Library of Congress.* Washington, D.C., American Film Institute, 1978. 214 pp. (available from AFI, National Center for Film and Video Preservation, John F. Kennedy Center for the Performing Arts, Washington, D.C., 20566; $5.00, prepaid).

For additional information on the AFI collections, see: Karr, Kathleen, ed. *The American Film Heritage; Impressions From the American Film Institute Archives.* Washington, D.C., Acropolis Books Ltd., 1972. 184 pp. Thirty-four articles by scholars, journalists and archivists demonstrate the wide range of the collections (e.g., "B" Westerns, early examples of non-Hollywood filmmaking and Hal Roach shorts) and provide details on individual films, including *Mission to Moscow, The Emperor Jones* and *Only Angels Have Wings.* An

index to filmmakers and titles is provided.

What follows are highlights among the AFI Collections in M/B/RS, with emphasis on those for which M/B/RS has created organized access.

(i) *Black Films in the Library of Congress.* The AFI has collected and deposited in LC several groups of films (from a variety of sources) documenting a particular corner of film history: the production of films with all-Black casts, originally intended for Black audiences. Because of a steady demand for such information, M/B/RS reference staff has compiled a brief list of its holdings in this area. (The list is quite narrowly defined and is by no means a comprehensive index of the Black-interest films in M/B/RS.)

These entertainment features and shorts (1918-55) range from drama to musical variety shows. Producing and performing credits include Oscar Micheaux, Nina Mae McKinney, Mantan Moreland, Spencer Williams and Louis Jordan.

Availability for duplication varies on the case-by-case basis typical of all non-copyright collections. Researchers should note that these films are not unique to LC's collections as they once were; having been collected, preserved and made known to an increasingly interested public, many of these films are back in theatrical, homevideo and television distribution.

(ii) *DeForest Films (AFI/Zouary Collection).* Researchers in quest of early sound films of musical performances (many were made) almost inevitably face disappointment. Even when a collection of Vitaphone pictures, for example, can be located (as in LC) it usually lacks sound elements. Exceptions to this rule are the Lee DeForest films in the Zouary Collection.

DeForest was one of the most important and successful experimenters with sound on film. His productions from the mid-1920s preserve a variety of spoken and musical performances — from DeWolfe Hopper's *Casey at the Bat* and Calvin Coolidge to Eubie Blake and opera, although most featured artists could be characterized as vaudeville performers. His system did not become the industry standard; therefore, current copies do not always have perfectly synchronized sound. Catalog entries warn researchers of this pitfall, but users have found most prints to have acceptable synchronization.

The Zouary Collection as a whole has yet to be completely sorted; however, a handy list of reference prints of DeForest films is available from Reading Room subject files. By digging in various files, staff may be able to locate other titles (usually a version of performer name) that have yet to be printed. There are no restrictions on duplication.

(iii) *Méliès Films (AFI/Academy Collection).* One of the earliest and most inventive of all filmmakers, Georges Méliès made films in France early in the century that continue to astound each new generation. They were imported to the U.S., distributed widely under new titles, imitated and even pirated. In recent years, scholars have made significant progress in sorting out the true identities of extant copies.

LC has a number of Méliès films in the Paper Print Collection, and scattered titles among other collections. A significant body of these films was acquired from the Academy of Motion Picture Arts and Sciences. This group is particularly noteworthy because it was acquired in nitrate and preserved by LC in 35mm. Individual title cards are filed in the Film and Television Catalog, but the most convenient source of information on these holdings is the Reading Room subject file for Georges Méliès.

II. *Non-Copyright, Non-AFI Collections*

A wide variety of other motion picture films and videotapes has been received by LC over the years, independent of copyright deposit and the American Film Institute. Collections range in size from one to many items. Most of them may be duplicated with permission.

Following are sample collections of interest. Non-copyright and non-AFI collections of television programs are described below under Television Collections.

(A) *George Kleine Collection* (1898-1926, 456 titles). One of the oldest collections of early films in M/B/RS was purchased in 1947 from the estate of George Kleine, a film industry pioneer who specialized in importing European productions. The films span all genres, including drama, comedy, educational and actuality films. The collection is probably most notable for its Italian epics, including *Cabiria* and *Quo Vadis,* but also such popular stock footage items as *Push Carts, Lower East Side.* The collection also includes *Deliverance* (1919), a biography of Helen Keller that includes appearances by Keller and her teacher, Anne Sullivan.

Reference prints and printing negatives (almost all 16mm) are available for the entire collection. (The absence of 35mm material provides a lesson instructive to archivists. The collection of 35mm nitrate was acquired in the division's infancy and copied onto safety film in its adolescence, before LC had its own preservation laboratory. For reasons of economy, 16mm reduction prints were made and the nitrate destroyed. That was not a shocking decision at the time, though it certainly is a sad one from today's perspective, when new 35mm prints in the Paper Print Collection and from nitrate holdings demonstrate the improvements a laboratory could make today).

An excellent published catalog describes the Kleine Collection films with credits, physical description, shelf numbers, summaries, notes on related materials (e.g., stills and scripts) purchased with the film and a subject index. *The George Kleine Collection of Early Motion Pictures in the Library of Congress, a Catalog.* Washington, D.C., U.S. Library of Congress. M/B/RS, 1980; prepared by Rita Horwitz and Harriet Harrison, with the assistance of Wendy White. (The volume may be purchased from the Superintendent of Documents, Government Printing Office, Washington, D.C., 20402; order #030-001-00088-5; $15.00.)

Title cards also are filed in the Film and Television Catalog. George Kleine's business correspondence and records are housed in LC's Manuscript Division.

(B) *Theodore Roosevelt Association Collection.* The only other collection of early film that can be researched through a published catalog is entirely actuality in nature and focused on a single theme: the life and times of Theodore Roosevelt. As the catalog introduction points out, "He was the first U.S. president whose life was extensively recorded and preserved in the motion picture format. The collection reveals that although Roosevelt obtained fame before the motion picture form was perfected, he was one of the most frequently photographed subjects among public men."

In 1967 the National Park Service transferred to the Library of Congress 381 early news films documenting the career of Theodore Roosevelt. Collected in the 1920s and 1930s by the Theodore Roosevelt Association, the films were first housed in the Association's library at the Roosevelt birthplace in New York City, then turned over to the National Park Service when the building was designated a national historic site in 1962. The collection covers Roosevelt's activities from his "Rough Riders" days through his later life, with the emphasis on the period 1909-19. Roosevelt, a favorite subject for newsmen, is shown at major political events of the day, as well as in the company of family members, friends and internationally famous celebrities. Also in the collection are films of Roosevelt's funeral and several posthumous tributes.

Reference prints and printing negatives are available for all titles. Unlike the Kleine Collection, much of the Roosevelt Collection has been preserved in 35mm, although many of the reference prints and some negatives are in 16mm. Another unusual aspect of the material in this collection is the existence of different versions — both in length and format — of several productions. The footage researcher should note these variations carefully; they can either complicate or ease research and pricing of copies.

The films are individually listed on cards in the Film and Television Catalog and described in a published catalog; the latter is also indexed by subject, date, place and name: *The Theodore Roosevelt Association Film Collection: A Catalog.* Washington, D.C., U.S. Library of Congress, M/B/RS, 1986; prepared by Wendy White-Henson and Veronica M. Gillespie, with the assistance of Harriet Harrison. (The volume may be purchased from the Superintendent of Documents, Government Printing Office, Washington, D.C., 20402; order #030-001-00113-0; $12.00.)

Additional information on the collection has been published in:
Gillespie, Veronica M., "T. R. on Film," *The Quarterly Journal of the Library of Congress.* Vol. 34, January 1977.

Theodore Roosevelt Association, "The Theodore Roosevelt Association and the T.R.A. Motion Picture Collection," *Theodore Roosevelt Association Journal.* Vol. 2, Winter/Spring 1976.

(C) *Captured Foreign Collections.* At the end of World War II a substantial number of films were confiscated in Germany, Italy and Japan and eventually transferred to repositories in the U.S. The films were deposited in the National Archives and Records Administration (q.v.) and LC. Although it has never been clear (nor, to our knowledge, has anyone tried to identify) how they were divided between the institutions, it can generally be assumed that — as with other collections — theatrical entertainment films are more likely to be found in LC, and actuality films are more likely to be available at the National Archives.

Public Laws 87-846 and 87-861 returned the film copyrights to their original owners (or successors) in 1963 and gave the Library screening privileges and permanent custody of the prints. LC has worked with film archives in West Germany, Italy and Japan to return the original nitrate prints in exchange for 16mm viewing copies, although in some instances LC has done the preservation work. The bottom-line consequence for footage researchers interested in purchasing copies from these collections is that M/B/RS will, in most cases, refer them to organizations in the country of origin to obtain material or (in limited cases) request permission to duplicate material in M/B/RS.

Almost all of these films are represented solely by 16mm prints (the major

exception being the Italian Collection features); titles and soundtracks have not been translated.

Title cards are filed alphabetically both in the Film and Television Catalog and separately in the German, Italian and Japanese Collection Catalogs. Newsreels are listed only by issue number, under each series title, in the Foreign Newsreels Catalog. Although there is *no subject index*, dedicated researchers may browse through data sheets containing brief descriptions of the shorts and newsreel issues. Feature films are included in the Directors File (see Cataloging).

(i) *German Collection.* This collection contains approximately 1,000 silent and sound features (1919-45); over 1,000 newsreels, including an extensive run of *Die Deutsche Wochenschau* (Sept. 1939-March 1945); and numerous educational, entertainment, documentary and propaganda shorts. Despite the barriers of language and inadequate cataloging, the German films have remained in active use, particularly by scholars who have studied such diverse topics as propaganda, musicals and the works of major directors (e.g., Fritz Lang) — evidence of both the rich variety and profound influence of German cinema.

(ii) *Italian Collection.* This is the smallest of the captured collections, containing 40 features (1934-40); 275 Istituto Luce newsreels (1938-43); and 100 Luce shorts (1930-43). Small, but mighty; the features (like the Italian spectacles in the Kleine Collection) have attracted the interest of scholars who find prints of these films difficult to locate. The preservation history of the Italian Collection is the source of its major distinction among the captured collections. LC assumed the responsibility for copying the nitrate originals, so that there are 35mm negatives and prints in M/B/RS for most of the feature titles. The original prints and the copyrights have, however, been returned to Italy.

(iii) *Japanese Collection.* As with the German and Italian Collections, the Japanese Collection contains a wide range of 200 features and 700 educational, documentary and propaganda shorts from the 1930s and early 1940s; and the newsreels *Asahi News* (1935-39), *Yomiuri News* (1936-40), and *Nippon News* (1940-45).

Although the Japanese Collection has by no means been neglected, the relative absence of fluency in Japanese among researchers has limited its use. There is an additional set of title cards for this collection, providing an alphabetical listing of English-translation titles. However, there is some evidence that the transliterated titles on which they are based are not always accurate.

Two very useful and unique reference aids have recently been acquired for Reading Room subject files: an issue-by-issue list of headlines in both Japanese characters and English translation for *Asahi News;* and English-language summaries of *Nippon News.*

(D) *United Artists Collection.* In 1969 the United Artists Corporation presented LC with its earliest surviving preprint material for approximately 3,000 motion pictures from the pre-1949 film library of Warner Bros. pictures. The collection contains 50 silent features (1913-30); 750 sound features (1927-48); 1800 sound short subjects (1926-48); and 400 cartoons, among them *Looney Tunes* and *Merrie Melodies.* The collection also includes nearly 200 sound features released by Monogram Pictures Corporation and a number of *Popeye* cartoons released by Fleischer Studios. There are no United Artists films in the United Artists Collection. The early synchronized sound Vitaphone shorts are lacking accompanying sound discs.

This is an enormous collection of nitrate negatives and masters, which are still undergoing transfer to acetate stock. Most of the safety film copies exist only in the preservation master stage, limiting accessibility for viewing and duplication. Some years ago, LC obtained 16mm prints (unfortunately, many are television prints, flat in picture quality and occasionally edited) for 70 well-known Warner Bros. features (among the most popular of all American films), including *The Jazz Singer* (1927); *Little Caesar* (1930); and *Knute Rockne, All American* (1940). Additional prints have been added to the collection, ranging from "reject fine grain master positives" (copies made for preservation but deemed inadequate) suitable for reference use, to sparkling 35mm prints reserved for theatrical projection.

United Artists also donated 16mm prints of most of the Warner Bros. and Monogram films to the Wisconsin Center for Film and Theater Research, Film and Photo Archive (q.v.).

Titles and holdings are listed in the various M/B/RS catalogs. There are a number of published reference books on Warner Bros. films. Film titles also are included (with asterisks) in the *Catalog of Holdings; the American Film Institute Collection and the United Artists Collection at the Library of Congress.* (Washington, D.C., American Film Institute, 1978. 214 pp.), available from the AFI Archives Department, John F. Kennedy Center for the Performing Arts, Washington, D.C., 20566; $5.00, prepaid.

Copyrights still are in effect for most of the films in this collection; a donor restriction also applies. United Artists has passed through various hands in recent years; ownership of this material currently resides with Turner Entertainment Co.

(E) *Embassy of South Vietnam Collection.* More recently, the consequences of war have provided another interesting collection of motion pictures to LC.

Shortly after the collapse of the South Vietnamese government in late April 1975, its embassy in Washington, D.C. was closed and emptied; some of its contents found a new home in LC. Among the hastily packed and transferred materials were 527 reels of 16mm film.

These films have been inventoried and partially cataloged. The inventory reveals a variety of documentaries, some in English and in multiple copies (presumably intended for distribution in the U.S.); and more than 400 reels of newsreels, probably all in Vietnamese. Production dates probably range from the late 1950s to the mid-1960s. Subject matter ranges from general human interest to "hard" war propaganda.

Viewing access to this collection is limited to the films for which M/B/RS has multiple copies and the videotape copies of selected other films held by M/B/RS as a by-product of WGBH-TV's research for the series *Vietnam: A Television History.*

Cataloged titles are listed in the Film and Television Catalog, but the best information on the collection can be found in Reading Room subject files: the collection inventory (based on can labels), a list of videotape copies, and an article by Sarah Rouse, "South Vietnam's Film Legacy," (*Historical Journal of Film, Radio and Television,* vol. 6, no. 2, 1986, pp. 211-222).

(F) *Gatewood W. Dunston Collection.* The Dunston Collection is both illustrative of the many named collections in M/B/RS (small in size and comprised of theatrical features from the 1910s-20s) and atypical in its method of acquisition and thematic focus (i.e., it *has* a focus).

Dunston was devoted to collecting material relating to the popular cowboy star William S. Hart. In 1957 he left his paper materials (scripts, scrapbooks, photographs and correspondence) to LC and the films to the Smithsonian Institution, which transferred them to LC in that same year. Of the approximately 40 titles (in nitrate), about half are 28mm; only a few of these "non-standard" reels have been converted to standard-gauge acetate and the rest remain unviewable. One particularly interesting item is a sound prologue Hart made for the 1939 reissue of *Tumbleweeds* (1925).

Researchers should be aware that there are non-Hart films in the Dunston Collection and Hart films scattered among other collections. The point is that film archives are grateful to individual collectors (such as Dunston) for saving most of what survives of American films made in the silent period; but taking a collection-name approach to M/B/RS catalogs will not be very helpful for most research projects.

Title cards are filed in the Film and Television Catalog.

Note. Other small but valuable (non-AFI) collections of silent films have been received from John Allen and Louise Ernst (the latter noted for animation films). There are no ready inventories for these collections.

(G) *Edison Laboratory Collection.* This small collection should not be confused with the many Edison Company films in the Paper Print Collection (so many, in fact, that some researchers refer to it as an Edison collection) and in several other collections. The Edison Laboratory Collection is the result of a 1965 cooperative agreement with the National Park Service, in which LC reproduced on safety film (mostly 16mm) the motion pictures found at the Edison Laboratory in West Orange, N.J., shortly after its designation as a national historic site.

The project preserved some of the Edison Company's early releases, promotional films for various Edison industries, and some Kinetophone productions (Edison's film-and-sound experiments; LC lacks the sound elements). An elderly Thomas Edison is also featured in several sound newsreel outtakes from the late 1920s. Reference prints and negatives are available for most of the 75 reels in the collection. Obtaining permission to copy the newsreels can be a problem, because many are unidentified as to source.

Title cards have not been integrated into the Film and Television Catalog, but reference staff can lead the researcher to a nearby Working File for cards listing holdings. (The researcher may also profit from browsing further in this drawer.)

(H) *Harmon Foundation Collection.* This small but interesting collection of early educational films is one of the few in M/B/RS to contain actuality footage from the late 1920s to the 1940s. The Harmon Foundation first produced films beginning in 1926 for use in church worship and later turned its attention to films on peoples of other lands for church mission study. Attracting the interest of educators, these films became the nucleus of a distribution library, to which the Harmon Foundation added new films in its other areas of interest, such as "Negro Art," but always focusing on youth, constructive

achievement and world understanding.

Users of the Harmon Collection should be aware of a counterpart Harmon Collection at the National Archives and Records Administration (q.v.), RG 200. Legend has it (the files provide no explanation as to why or how) that Harmon's library was divided between LC and NARA: prints in LC, and negatives in NARA. However, experience has shown that this is not always the case. There definitely are only prints at LC, but lists of titles have never been compared.

Title cards are filed in the Film and Television Catalog; the Dictionary Catalog also has individual subject entries and a full set of title cards filed under Harmon Foundation.

(I) *Eastman Teaching Films Collection.* Similar to the Harmon Collection, this collection is comprised of classroom films from the late 1920s and 1930s. LC has only an incomplete set of prints, many in poor condition; it is hoped that negatives and other prints exist somewhere. M/B/RS also has a complete set of study guides (unindexed), which demonstrate the wide variety of topics filmed. Cards are filed by title in the Film and Television Catalog, and subject and collection name in the Dictionary Catalog.

(J) *Margaret Mead Collection.* A sizable collection of 16mm films shot by Margaret Mead and Gregory Bateson as part of their anthropological field work has been in the possession of M/B/RS for just a few years, and it promises to provide a major cataloging challenge for many years to come.

Most of the footage is unedited, positive camera originals; either in small rolls or assembled on larger reels of varying lengths. There are some negatives and very few reference prints. During the 1940s and 1950s many of the originals were screened and even edited for teaching, lecture and study purposes. Using Mead's field notes and photographs (held by LC's Manuscript Division), the processing staff must sort through many tiny pieces to make the puzzle whole.

To date, two groups of Mead films have been inventoried and made available: films made during the 1938 expedition among the Iatmul people of New Guinea; and footage shot in Bali (1936-39). Cards in the Film and Television Catalog (and separate inventories) log originals, duplicate negatives and reference prints. Permission to duplicate films in this collection must be obtained from Margaret Mead's heirs.

(J) *Public Archives of Canada/Dawson City Collection.* This collection of early theatrical films, known more familiarly as the Dawson Collection, is most notable for its source: a Yukon swimming pool. During the summer of 1978, amid restoration of Dawson City (a gold rush era boom town in the Yukon Territory) workmen unearthed a cache of 35mm nitrate film. At the end of the distribution chain, some 500 reels had accumulated there, and in 1929 were dumped as fill in a swimming pool that had come to the end of its usefulness. The region's deep and abiding cold (still today the only known retardant of nitrate deterioration) contributed to a high survival rate of the buried treasure, although water damage took its toll, especially from the top layer. Quick, improvised action on the part of the Public Archives of Canada (now National Archives of Canada, Moving Image and Sound Archives [q.v.]), with the cooperation of LC and the American Film Institute, was necessary in order to salvage the survivors. See Sam Kula's "There's Film in Them Thar Hills!" (*American Film,* July/August 1979) for an action-packed account of the discovery and rescue.

LC has the U.S. productions (some 190 reels); all have been copied and most cataloged.

Although a number of important, and rare, early films (including *Polly of the Circus* [1917], with Mae Marsh and *Bliss* [1917], with Harold Lloyd) were unearthed in Dawson City, many survive only as incomplete copies. There are features, shorts, several serials and some news films. Title cards are filed in the Film and Television Catalog, and copies of these cards have been collected for a subject file in the Reading Room.

III. *Television Collections*

(A) *NBC Television Collection.* The NBC Television Collection was acquired by LC in July 1986. This is an historic collection of 18,000 television programs broadcast, preserved and for the most part produced by NBC. With programs dating from the beginning of network television in the United States (1948) through 1977, the NBC Television Collection includes not only performances by major actors and musical talents, but also numerous events featuring significant individuals in public affairs. This acquisition significantly increases M/B/RS's holdings of television programs *not* acquired via copyright deposit: programs from the late 1940s and early 1950s and genres such as sports, game shows, children's programs and daytime television. It should be noted that this acquisition does not include NBC's news archives (containing raw footage shot for news broadcasts) nor any post-1977 material.

Kinescopes may comprise as much as 50% of the NBC Television

Collection. The rest are programs produced on film prior to broadcast. M/B/RS holds mostly picture negatives with separate sound tracks. Viewing copies are presently available for only a few titles. Researchers with enough lead time for viewing copy preparation (8-12 weeks) may request 3/4" videotape viewing copies (for in-house use only), to be produced using LC's film-to-videotape transfer system. At the time of the transfer, a 1" videotape preservation master for LC will also be produced; the original negatives will be retained as film preservation material. (Requests for purchase or reuse of material in the NBC Collection must be made directly to NBC Television Network, Enterprises Department [q.v.], as NBC retains all rights to the material.)

At present, access to this collection is gained by consulting a photocopy of NBC's handwritten alphabetical packing list, arranged alphabetically by program or series title, primary performer or other key identification word; researchers knowing series title and date of broadcast enjoy speedier access to material. M/B/RS more recently received copies of the NBC Program Analysis File — a microfiche of 1.25 million cards, providing name, date and subject indexing to programs broadcast by NBC. Cross-checking of inventories and even containers on LC shelves will still be necessary, however, to determine LC's actual holdings. Clearly, much organization of the collection is required before it can be easily researched.

Documentary material in the NBC Television Collection, while temporarily retained by NBC in New York, may be identified using the packing lists; preparation of videotape copies will take longer for this material than for titles physically at the Library. Similarly, about 2,000 entertainment programs are also being withheld by the network while new masters are prepared for use by NBC.

Despite the rudimentary finding aids for this collection, sample titles indicate the collection's wide scope. These include: *Kraft Television Theatre; Miss America Pageant; Colgate Comedy Hour; Wide, Wide World; Your Hit Parade; Your Show of Shows; Hallmark Hall of Fame; Kraft Music Hall; The Jack Paar Show; Today; Mrs. [Franklin D.] Roosevelt Meets the Public; Meet the Press* (added to the Library's already extensive coverage); press conferences with Presidents Kennedy and Johnson; coverage of Martin Luther King; and the astronaut John Glenn at Cape Canaveral.

(B) *NET (National Educational Television) Programs.* NET programs held by LC probably total over 10,000 titles and date from 1955-69. (NET metamorphosed into PBS [Public Broadcasting Service] in 1969, and a few PBS programs from the early 1970s are included in this group of NET programs.) While cataloging of the majority of programs remains to be done, it is clear that collectively they represent an invaluable record of early non-commercial American television.

The material in the three separate collections comprising the collection of NET programs is largely preprint, and 2" videotape and 16mm film negatives predominate. Scholars needing access to programs should know that an 8- to 12-week period for preparation and videotape transfer may be required for titles requested. Further, researchers should be aware that for each of the three segments of this collection of programs, there is a separate finding aid.

Because the "collection's" three segments were acquired at different times and from different sources, strictly speaking they are not a single collection. Each, however, represents a facet of the large body of work generated for NET, naturally combining as a pseudo-collection. The most accessible portion of this "collection" is its first segment. All 550+ titles are 16mm prints, accessible by title through the Film and Television Catalog. The prints were acquired from NET's general distribution center in Michigan (1965-67). Programs are instructional or educational, including the series *Touristen-Deutsch* (WTTW Chicago, 1957, 14 programs), teaching elementary conversational German; *The Nature of Communism* (Vanderbilt and Notre Dame Universities, 1964, 60 programs); and *Two Centuries of Symphony* (WGBH Boston, 1960, 20 programs), teaching music appreciation.

The second segment, comprised of 1,019 titles, primarily instructional materials and all negatives, came to the Library in 1982 via Indiana University, which was a distribution center for NET programs broadcast for public schools, colleges and universities. Access is by title only using an inventory card file and list. Titles in this group include: *The Basic Issues of Man* (12 programs produced in the early 1960s by the Georgia Center for Continuing Education); *The Red Myth* (a series on the history of communism, produced ca. 1960 by San Francisco's KQED); and *Search for America* (a Washington University-produced series on American institutions and problems). There is likely to be an overlap between this collection and the first, resulting in both prints and negatives for some titles.

The third and largest group of NET titles at LC was acquired in 1984. Approximately 8,000 programs had been warehoused by PBS until their archives program was cut back. A preliminary inventory list of unverified titles made by LC staff reveals that this collection includes many series of international scope, including *Casals Master Class; Civilisation; Creative Person,* including such subjects as Nadia Boulanger, Georges Braque, Rudolf Bing and Satyajit Ray; and *Intertel,* as well as programs documenting the social revolution of the 1950s and 1960s. Examples of the last category are: *Escape from the Cage* (on mental illness); *History of the Negro; Jazz Meets the Classics; NET Festival;* and *NET Journal.* An NET Inventory — a title list of the second and third segments combined — is available at the Reference Desk for consultation.

Information on NET and PBS programming still held at PBS can be found under the entry for the Public Broadcasting System, Program Data and Analysis (q.v.).

There is no separate list or catalog of M/B/RS's total television holdings; individual program titles are scattered throughout most of the catalogs. However, M/B/RS expects to announce in mid-1989 the availability of a major published source of information on its holdings of television programs: *Three Decades of Television: a Catalog of Television Programs Acquired by the Library of Congress, 1949-1979,* compiled by Sarah Rouse and Katharine Loughney.

Intended originally (in 1978, as a six-month project!) to be a complete listing of LC's television programs, the catalog eventually was given an acquisition cutoff date of December 31, 1979 and excludes commercials and news programs. In identifying and compiling entries from other existing catalogs, it was discovered that the first LC television acquisition was received in 1949 (a "Hopalong Cassidy" feature edited for television broadcast).

Almost 20,000 entries will provide synopses of fiction and nonfiction programs, genre and broad subject terms, cast and production credits, and copyright and telecast information.

The vast majority of these programs were received as copyright deposits. Footage researchers are reminded once again of the consequent restrictions on duplication, but the copyright connection has also influenced the nature of the material. Primetime series predominate in this catalog. Also documented is an apparent reluctance to collect television programs in the early years; only 13 selections from copyright registrations were made in 1950, compared with over 3,000 in 1980.

The catalog *Three Decades of Television* includes these two major series received as gifts: *Meet the Press,* donated by Lawrence E. Spivak, producer of this long-running program (first broadcast on radio in 1945). Television programs (1949-present) exist mostly in 16mm kinescope negative, with videotape formats beginning in May 1974 (new programs continue to be received). Reference prints exist for about 100 of the pre-1978 shows. Card entries are filed in the Film and Television Catalog under *Meet the Press,* alphabetically by guest. Extensive documentation was also donated. The *Original Amateur Hour* (550 kinescopes, 16mm, November 1948 through 1968), a long-running radio and television series hosted by Ted Mack, was donated to LC in 1970 by Lloyd Marx. There are only eight pre-1951 programs. Card entries in the Film and Television Catalog list holdings chronologically but do not identify contestants.

IV. U.S. Government Productions

This heading was created as a distinct category only to remind the reader that LC is not the repository for U.S. government productions. Although there are a few titles scattered throughout M/B/RS collections, the National Archives and Records Administration (q.v.) is the appropriate institution to query for such works.

Size & Elements: Film and videotape: all formats (amounts unspecified). (Approx. 130,000 titles total).

Cataloging: *Published catalogs.*

The only published catalogs of LC's moving image collections (and the only ones available for perusal off premises) are those cited in collection descriptions above. Again, these include: *Early Motion Pictures: the Paper Print Collection in the Library of Congress; The George Kleine Collection of Early Motion Pictures in the Library of Congress;* and *The Theodore Roosevelt Association Film Collection.*

Fortunately, these collections are generally the most useful for footage researchers: they represent an unusually large assemblage of very early films; subject indexing is available; viewing copies are near at hand; printing material already exists; and the films are almost completely free of copyright and donor restrictions.

There is one additional published work that serves as a helpful finding aid to LC's collections: *Catalog of Holdings: The American Film Institute Collection and the United Artists Collection at the Library of Congress* (Washington, D.C.: The AFI Archives Dept., 1978). This title list of films transferred to LC by the AFI through 1977 also includes the United Artists Collection deposited in LC (the difference between the AFI and United Artists collections is an administrative distinction that will have little noticeable impact on the researcher). This material is described above and also in the entry for AFI's National Center for Film and Video Preservation (q.v.).

The only new catalog publishing project currently underway or planned is a listing of LC's television program holdings as of 1979. *Three Decades of Television* is expected to be issued by the Library in mid-1989.

The *most complete catalog* of LC's moving image collections is to be found only on the M/B/RS premises. Even so, there is no single catalog, but rather a "collection" of catalogs in a variety of formats, begun at different times to serve an array of purposes, and requiring various levels of assistance to use. Most are accessible to the public in the Motion Picture and Television Reading Room. Since late 1987 new inventory, accession and cataloging records have been created in automated systems, but the vast bulk of M/B/RS catalog records still remain on cards or other manual files.

The most important fact to remember about M/B/RS catalogs is that the only access point available for the vast majority of holdings is *by title*. Exceptions, including the published catalogs mentioned above, have been noted. Catalog records vary in detail, depending on the procedures in place at the time of cataloging. Many newer entries are actually inventory and accession records created by laboratory and technical staff, but in the absence of other records they become M/B/RS's de facto "catalog."

Footage researchers should note that catalog records do not indicate a work's availability for duplication.

Card catalogs in the Motion Picture and Television Reading Room

The Film and Television Catalog is the primary access to the motion picture and television collections, and most material available for viewing is represented in this catalog. (The Division has traditionally maintained separate catalogs to control its nitrate and safety [acetate] film collections, because the inflammability of nitrate film requires special storage and handling. See below for a description of the Nitrate Tracking System, an automated file that controls nitrate holdings.) Cards for materials in videotape formats are interfiled with those describing safety film in the Film and Television Catalog, which is sometimes called the "Safety Catalog" or the "Safety Shelf List."

Approximately 120,000 cards are arranged by title (the main entry) and also contain a shelf location number, basic physical description (length, gauge, color and sound) and archival control information (collection, source and date of acquisition, availability for viewing). Most cards also contain a variety of other filmographic data (dates, original copyright claimant, production credits, alternative and other related titles), more specific technical data and special notes. Cross references are made from other titles associated with the production, such as foreign release, reissue, or episode in television series.

No cards have been added to this catalog since late 1986, when M/B/RS's Processing Section began creating records on-line for A/V, an automated cataloging system (see below). This date should not be considered a cutoff date for receipts, however, as there is a sizeable backlog (copyright deposits received approximately 1983-87 and Library of Congress Preservation Laboratory products received approximately 1978-86) that remains accessible only through manual Working Files, with the assistance of reference librarians.

The Paper Print Catalog contains 3,000 cards describing the Paper Print Collection of early motion pictures (1894-1912) registered for copyright and deposited with the Library in the form of paper strips. (See above for additional information on the collection.) The cards are arranged by title, and contain information regarding copyright claimant and date, physical description and shelf location number. These title cards have never been interfiled into the main Film and Television Catalog. It was essential for its alphabetical order and shelf location numbers while the first published Paper Print catalog was in use; the current edition of the published catalog has shelf numbers, but only these cards have shelf numbers for the original paper rolls.

The Newsreel Catalog lists American Newsreels (primarily *Universal Newsreel* and *News of the Day*), which are copyright deposits selected during 1943-67, and Foreign Newsreels, which are part of the captured foreign collections of German, Japanese and Italian motion pictures confiscated at the end of World War II (see above). Designed simply as a location tool, some 5,500 cards are arranged by company, and then chronologically by volume and issue number.

The Dictionary Catalog contains printed cards created by LC's Processing Services Department (from data supplied by motion picture staff) for safety films held in its collections for approximately 1957-71. Most of these films are copyright deposits. These cards are duplicates of those filed by title in the Film and Television Catalog, but there are additional access points by added entry (mostly companies, series titles and literary source authors) and a limited number of subject headings for non-fiction films. Containing about 72,000 cards covering about 18,000 titles, the Dictionary Catalog is located outside the

Motion Picture and Television Reading Room, but reference staff will pull appropriate drawers when it seems likely to help researchers.

The Directors File lists directors whose feature films are available for viewing. Approximately 4,000 cards are arranged by director and list titles, distributing companies and release dates.

The German, Japanese, and Italian Collections Catalogs list (by original titles) films seized by the United States Government at the end of World War II. Included are features, short subjects, documentaries, newsreels, and educational films. Each collection is filed separately, and cards for safety copies are also filed in the Film and Television Catalog. In addition to Japanese titles in transliteration, an additional set of cards for the Japanese collection is arranged by English translation title.

Each card contains titles, production and release companies, release date, some individual credits, shelf location numbers and physical description. These catalogs contain approximately 5,500 cards, excluding newsreels (see above).

A limited number of films (about 3,000 in 16 drawers) are represented in the Silent Film Catalog by duplicates of cards in the Film and Television Catalog. There are three basic categories — Silent Features, Silent Shorts, and Silent Non-Fiction — with three sets of title cards arranged by subcategories of title, date of release and company. This project has been worked on intermittently since about 1973 and exists primarily for reporting to the International Federation of Film Archives' (FIAF) Embryo project (a union catalog of members' silent film holdings). [The current printed volume is restricted to administrative use, but FIAF intends to issue future volumes for public access. The Museum of Modern Art has a listing of short films in galley form, and the Cinémathèque Royale in Belgium is preparing a feature films volume.] The absence of any clear definition of date, collection, or any other parameter to define the Silent Films catalog can cause some frustration, but many footage researchers find the Non-Fiction/Date drawer to be helpful.

Most catalog entries include copyright information. This "filmographic" data should not be mistaken for official Copyright Office records. It is recorded frequently because so much material is acquired via copyright deposit procedures, and because other information sources in M/B/RS are also controlled by copyright registration number. Readers should note that the cards almost never provide any specific information on quality or availability for duplication.

Automated catalogs

Automation has come recently to M/B/RS collection control and cataloging, and there have been several transition and test periods in recent years into which holdings information may have fallen — to be retrieved only by a clever staff member. Currently, the framework appears to be in place.

M/B/RS automated data files have also been shaped by the organizational environment of its parent, the Library of Congress. They are adaptations of the Library's large and complex cataloging and operations systems, providing both advantages and disadvantages to the wide range of researchers visiting LC. At present (and for the foreseeable future) users unfamiliar with LC's internal online system will want assistance from the reference staff. (Patrons are encouraged to learn the system, however; no one is deterred from practicing on idle terminals, and training classes are offered through LC's general reading rooms.)

An introduction to M/B/RS automated, online catalogs requires some reference to LC's umbrella LOCIS system (Library of Congress Information Systems), which embraces MUMS (Multiple Use MARC System; MARC stands for MAchine Readable Cataloging) and SCORPIO. The two systems have different searching logic, commands and display formats.

MUMS was designed for the creation of cataloging records for books in the late 1960s, later extended to other materials, and now provides public access to this bibliographic information. SCORPIO, a system better known to many LC patrons because of its relative simplicity, was created primarily to serve the research needs of Congress, and also provides public access to some of its unique data files and many of the same files searchable through MUMS. This distinction is important, because A/V, the file discussed below, is available only through the MUMS system, while copyright registration records (see COHM below) are available only through SCORPIO.

All of the systems in this description are created and maintained through LC's mainframe, as opposed to smaller computers under M/B/RS control. The point is that M/B/RS automated catalogs are parts of larger "systems," which have their own sets of priorities. This will explain some of the limitations appearing below, or at the time a footage researcher actually sits down in front of a terminal. On the other hand, the structure has benefits for other types of patrons doing research elsewhere in LC, and for standardization of moving image cataloging records in the long run.

A/V; or Audiovisual Materials, or Visual Materials. Any of these names is likely to appear in published references to this file. All are, in effect, interchangeable; only A/V actually appears on terminal screens.

Some history of film cataloging in LC is in order, to be preceded by an important point: M/B/RS catalog records are *included* in this file; there is *no* distinct LOCIS file of M/B/RS holdings.

As a cataloging service to the nation, LC began issuing printed catalog cards for educational films and filmstrips in 1951, using data supplied primarily by producers and distributors. Coverage has been expanded to include transparencies, slides, kits and videorecordings. Since 1972 film cataloging records have been included in the Library's MARC data base (although not available online until recently).

In addition, book catalogs reproducing this information and including detailed subject indexes have been published in LC's *National Union Catalog* series under various titles, most recently as *Audiovisual Materials*. In January 1983 the publication format was changed to microfiche. (Details concerning subscriptions to the microfiche, printed cards or computer tapes may be obtained from: NUC Desk, Customer Services Section, Cataloging Distribution Service, Library of Congress, Washington, DC 20541; 202/707-6171.)

Researchers should be aware of this published series, because it is held by most large U.S. and some foreign libraries (though it may take some perseverance to locate it). The series functions as one of the few sources of subject indexing available for a wide variety of nontheatrical motion pictures.

In late 1985, all of the audiovisual cataloging records created by LC's Processing Services Department since 1972 were added to LC's online MUMS system, making them more readily available for searching at terminals in LC (depending on the type of search) and from additional access points.

Meanwhile, M/B/RS processing staff had been working to adapt LC cataloging rules — created for books, applied to audiovisual materials, and modified for automation and international standards — to its own specialized needs — i.e., a diverse collection of material actually held, multiple copies in varying formats and archival responsibilities (e.g., knowing the source of an item and where it is located). After years of struggling with these issues, M/B/RS had developed internal standards more compatible with those of its colleagues in the international community of film archives than with traditional library cataloging practice. Nevertheless, the puzzle pieces were made to fit, and in late 1986, M/B/RS catalogers began entering new records into LC's online system as part of the A/V File.

At this writing, M/B/RS processing staff are still working out kinks in the new system, and the rate at which records are created is slower than the manual system of several years ago. However, the rate of entry is increasing, and a large number of accession records (preliminary to full cataloging) have been entered into the A/V File since December 1987.

The A/V File also includes records created since 1986 by LC's Prints and Photographs Division for its own holdings of still images.

Notes regarding searching the A/V File: M/B/RS catalog records created since late 1986 are *included* in the A/V File (and the published microfiche); there is *no* distinct file of M/B/RS holdings. Furthermore, it is not even possible to sign on to A/V. However, a patron *may* sign on to a combination of files that *includes* A/V and restrict each individual search query to the A/V File.

Records are searchable by virtually any keyword in the entry, but access possibilities are limited to words already entered. Although no subject headings are established for any but the "Full Level" records, much can be done with keyword searching for informative terms. And a subject search of the A/V File will reveal non-M/B/RS records that can be cross-checked in M/B/RS manual files. (Once a search query reveals a list of "hits," one must learn to distinguish M/B/RS records from non-M/B/RS records, even for non-motion picture records. Reference librarians will assist in this process.)

NTS (Nitrate Tracking System). The Nitrate Tracking System (NTS) was created in 1984 to provide a means of controlling LC's nitrate holdings in detail through the steps of receipt, maintenance, and duplication or preservation. The system provides a unique informational link between M/B/RS in Washington, its nitrate vaults and its Preservation Laboratory locations in Maryland and Ohio.

In appearance and function NTS is very different from the bibliographical-style data files more common to LC, based as it is on an inventory control system, rather than a classic library cataloging system. In effect, NTS is "unfriendly" to unfamiliar users, but staff will do the searching when necessary. Because most of the recently made safety film copies, including reference prints, can be located only by searching NTS, it is mentioned here for the record.

NTS contains no subject headings; title is the most appropriate access point. Remember, this file was created to answer questions such as: for a given title, what reels exist in LC, where are they today and what was their condition at last inspection?

COHM. COHM (Copyright Office History Monograph file) is not an M/B/RS file, but it is used frequently by M/B/RS staff for clues as to receipt of a particular work. This file may be searched by the public throughout LC, including the Motion Picture and Television Reading Room. As a continuation of the Copyright Office's card catalog, it is a collection of bibliographic records of copyrighted works registered in the Copyright Office since January 1, 1978 (when the Copyright Act of 1976 went into effect).

COHM combines all works in a variety of media and classes — including literary works other than periodicals, works of the performing and visual arts, and sound recordings, as well as renewals of previously registered works — in one browsable, alphabetical list of titles, claimants and selected credits (mainly authors [a technical term in copyright parlance] and companies). Titles, claimants and selected credits, plus registration number, are also the specific access points. Note: no subjects, no keyword searching.

COHM is a SCORPIO-type file; see above for general information on LC online files. (Patrons familiar with LC files may spot an irony here; SCORPIO was created to provide subject access to MUMS files, but copyright catalog records have no subject headings.)

Unfortunately, it is not possible to isolate all the motion pictures in COHM. Additionally, the design of the system tends to emphasize the specific, which can make searches relating to series rather tedious. But the information provided in individual records can be very helpful, and COHM is the only current source of copyright cataloging information, as the published version is several years in arrears.

·*M/B/RS staff do not conduct copyright searches.* Researchers who require searches or further information and instruction on COHM and other automated copyright data files should contact the Copyright Office.

Access: Open to the public. Moving image collections available for research, viewing, duplication and reuse on a case-by-case basis, subject to restrictions. Research and screening fees not charged. Research requests accepted by mail, telephone and in person (by appointment only). (For further information, see Description above).

Rights: No rights held to any material. Some material in the public domain. Additional clearances are necessary in most cases if material is to be reused.

Licensing: Available for reuse on a case-by-case basis, subject to restrictions.

Restrictions: *The Library of Congress does not duplicate moving image works received as copyright deposits.* The only exception considered is a request from a copyright owner for a copy of its own production. Because the finality of this fact contradicts the assumptions of many patrons and only becomes clear after some possibly wasteful expense of time, it cannot be overemphasized. (In fact, this material is largely unsuitable for quality reproduction because it is comprised almost totally of single release prints [of varying quality when received] possibly damaged over the years due to prolonged research use.) The implications are enormous for the researcher in search of recent footage; almost all LC holdings 1942-present (and especially since 1951) have been received as copyright deposits.

However, copyright deposit material can be extremely useful to the footage researcher. Probably no other institution provides the opportunity to view such a wide range of films; a researcher thereby may be able to identify or eliminate potential (albeit scattered) original sources or discover an unexpected source, which he or she may then pursue directly.

Productions acquired by LC via channels other than copyright deposit may be under *copyright protection,* and permission for duplication must be obtained from the owner.

The Copyright Office, where official copyright records are kept and made available to the public, publishes several excellent booklets (free of charge) that provide basic information on copyright law and procedures. Titles of special interest to moving image researchers include:

Circular R1. *Copyright Basics*
Circular R2. *Publications on Copyright*
Circular R15. *Renewal of Copyright*
Circular R15a. *Duration of Copyright*
Circular R15t. *Extension of Copyright Terms*
Circular R22. *How To Investigate the Copyright Status of a Work*
Circular R45. *Copyright Registration for Motion Pictures Including Video Recordings*

To obtain these circulars, write to: Publications Section, LM-455, Copyright Office, Library of Congress, Washington, DC 20559, or telephone 202/707-9100. They may also be obtained at the Copyright Office's Public Information Office, Room 401, Madison Building (one floor above the Motion Picture and Television Reading Room).

Donor restrictions. Distinct from copyright restrictions (though often intertwined with them in LC) are donor restrictions — conditions under which the Library accepted a gift of motion picture materials. These restrictions typically require that written permission from the donor must be obtained for any duplication (other than by LC for preservation), even if it can be demonstrated that copyright ownership has expired. In general, researchers should expect to encounter donor restrictions on all of LC's major studio deposits (see above) and on scattered, smaller collections. There is no way to predict the existence of donor restrictions by date, genre or any other common denominator. In some cases, a researcher must obtain material directly from the donor.

Why these restrictions? The desire to control reuse of a product is a fact of economic life and a limitation LC found acceptable in order to preserve worthwhile material which otherwise might have been lost, destroyed, or remained inaccessible to the public.

Archival considerations also can come into play; LC takes seriously its responsibilities in this area. Details are as diverse as the collections, but a governing principle is that M/B/RS does not order material for a customer directly from a preservation master; some intervening printing master is required. On occasion (to suggest a worst-case situation) even a worn release print can fall into the category of preservation master (or "archival positive") if it has been determined that LC's copy is a rare item worth preserving.

Viewing Facilities: Film (35mm and 16mm); videotape (3/4", VHS and Betamax).
Duplication Facilities: Film (film-to-videotape transfers); videotape (videotape-to-videotape; all formats). Film-to-film duplication is handled by outside contractors. LC's Preservation Laboratory at Wright-Patterson AFB, Dayton, Ohio, only makes preservation copies for LC collections.
Related Materials: Audio recordings; still photographs; substantial reference holdings relating to motion pictures and television.

Our thanks to Sarah Rouse of M/B/RS for her substantial contribution to the information on the NBC and NET collections.

This entry copyright © 1988 by Barbara Humphrys

Barbara Humphrys was a reference librarian for many years in the Library of Congress, Motion Picture, Broadcasting, and Recorded Sound Division. She is currently Head, Audiovisual Collections, in the Archives Center of the Smithsonian Institution's National Museum of American History.

DISTRICT OF COLUMBIA METRO

MANKIND RESEARCH FOUNDATION INC.
1315 Apple Avenue
Silver Spring, MD 20910
(301) 587-8686
Fax: (301) 585-8959

Dr. Carl Schleicher (President)

Contact: Dr. Carl Schleicher
Services: Educational institution. Videotape library available primarily for distribution and rental; also available for licensing and reuse.
Description: Programs relating to accelerated learning and new educational methods, including demonstrations of biofeedback and Kirlian electrophotography, "Frontiers of Science" biotechnology program, and accelerated learning (Lozanov method) in the classroom.

Sample titles include: *Suggestopedic Teaching of Foreign Languages; Children's School Experiment,* showing a first grade class in Bulgaria being taught reading and other subjects in a few weeks with the Lozanov method; *Russian Soul,* a demonstration of the Lozanov method as used in teaching French at the Moscow State Pedagogical Institute; *High Tech Careers for the Blind,* showing blind people learning computer programming, computer operations and word processing using the Lozanov method.
Size & Elements: Videotape: 3/4", VHS and Betamax (12 titles).
Cataloging: None specified.
Access: Maintained primarily for distribution and rental rather than for research. Available for duplication, licensing and reuse. Research fees not charged. Research requests accepted by mail and telephone.
Rights: Full rights held to all material.
Licensing: Available for licensing and reuse. License and usage fees charged for commercial use.
Restrictions: None specified.
Viewing Facilities: None.
Duplication Facilities: None.

DISTRICT OF COLUMBIA METRO

GEORGE MASON UNIVERSITY
SPECIAL COLLECTIONS AND ARCHIVES
FENWICK LIBRARY
4400 University Drive
Fairfax, VA 22030
(703) 323-2251
Fax: (703) 323-3582

Charlene Hurt (Director of Libraries)

Contacts: Ruth Kerns (Archivist/Librarian, Special Collections and Archives); Josephine Pacheco (Director, Center for the Study of Constitutional Rights, GMU)
Services: University library. Public lecture series available on videotape for research, licensing and reuse, subject to restrictions.
Description: Materials focusing primarily on the United States Constitution. *The Legacy of George Mason* is a series of annual public lectures by distinguished scholars. Beginning in 1982, the series of four annual lectures follow a ten-year plan exploring the historical background, evolution and continuing impact of the ideas of Mason and other founding fathers. Annual themes are as follows: *The Legacy of George Mason* (1982); *The First Amendment* (1983); *Natural Law and Natural Rights* (1984); *Federalism* (1985); *The Will of the People* (1986); and *The Allocation of Powers in the Federal Government* (1987). The series is produced by George Mason Center for the Study of Constitutional Rights in cooperation with GMU Telecommunications and public service stations in Northern Virginia.
Size & Elements: Videotape: 3/4" (34 videotapes, approx. 28 hours); VHS (7 videotapes, approx. 7 hours). Viewing copies (1982-87) on 3/4"; 1982 and lectures 1, 3 and 4 of 1983 also available on VHS.
Cataloging: Finding aids.
Access: Open to the public. Available for research, duplication and possibly licensing and reuse, subject to restrictions. Research fees not charged. Research requests accepted by mail, telephone and in person (by appointment only).
Rights: Full rights held to some material. Authors hold copyright to some materials.
Licensing: Available for licensing and reuse, subject to restrictions.
Restrictions: Copyright restrictions may apply.
Viewing Facilities: Videotape (in audio-visual department).
Duplication Facilities: Videotape (fees apply).

DISTRICT OF COLUMBIA METRO

MATHEMATICAL ASSOCIATION OF AMERICA
1529 18th Street, NW
Washington, DC 20036
(202) 387-5200

Films available for rental from:
WARD'S MODERN LEARNING AIDS DIVISION
P.O. Box 92912
5100 West Henrietta Road
Rochester, NY 14692
(716) 359-2502

Alfred Wilcox (Executive Director, MAA)

Contacts: Sharon Ford; Alicia Bennett
Services: Association. Films and videotapes available for duplication, rental and free loan.
Description: Films are available from the following categories:

MAA Arithmetic. A total of 14 animated films designed for use in a college course for training elementary school teachers, and as part of actual classroom instruction in elementary school arithmetic. Titles include: *Mr. Simplex Saves the Aspidistra; What Is a Set?; Ordered Pairs and the Cartesian Product;* and *Counting.*

MAA General Mathematics. Includes three categories of films: basic, collegiate and advanced. Titles include: *Let Us Teach Guessing; The Kakeya Problem; Matching Theory and the Marriage Theorem; What Is an Integral?; Can You Hear the Shape of a Drum?;* and *Singular Perturbation Theory and Geophysics.*

MAA Calculus. This series of animated films is useful as an instructional aid for high-school courses, college-level calculus courses and mathematics clubs. Titles include: *Area Under A Curve; I Maximize; Newton's Method; The Theorem of the Mean;* and *What Is Area?.*

Allendoerfer Series. Includes two categories of films: arithmetic and set theory, and geometry. Titles include: *Binary Operations and the Commutative Property; Equivalent Sets; Area and Pi;* and *Geometric Transformations.*

Teaching Experimental Applied Mathematics (TEAM) is a videotape collection of learning modules featuring applied mathematics problems supplied by industry. These programs are aimed at college and university students and their instructors. Titles include: *Satellite Communications Subsystem; Loan Insurance Analysis; Highway Slope Design;* and *Aircraft Sidestep Maneuver.*
Size & Elements: Film: 16mm (approx. 70 titles). Videotape: VHS and Betamax (approx. 6 titles).
Cataloging: Published catalog; brochures.
Access: Available for duplication, rental and free loan. Films available for rental from Ward's Modern Learning Aids; videotapes available for free loan from MMA.
Rights: Apply for information.
Licensing: Apply for information.
Restrictions: None specified.
Viewing Facilities: None.
Duplication Facilities: None.

DISTRICT OF COLUMBIA METRO

THE MIDDLE EAST INSTITUTE
ISLAMIC AFFAIRS PROGRAMS
AUDIOVISUAL LIBRARY
1761 N Street, NW
Washington, DC 20036
(202) 785-1141
(202) 785-0196

Ambassador Christopher Van Hollen (Director)

Contact: Mary N. Sebold (Program Assistant)
Services: Association. Film and videotape collection maintained primarily for rental and purchase.
Description: Films and videotapes relating to Islam and the Middle East. Programs cover topics such as Islam for non-Muslims; and Middle Eastern history, politics, religions and cultures.

Sample titles include: *A Common Ground,* exploring the commonalities and differences of Judaism, Christianity and Islam; *Islam: An Introduction; The Arabs in America; Islam: A Pictorial History; Islamic Architecture of Bangladesh; Morocco in the Free Camp; The Oil Kingdoms; Berber Villages of Southern Tunisia; Closeup on Kuwait; Egypt: The Struggle For Stability; History and Culture of the Middle East* (in two parts); *Iran on the Move; Jackpot in Libya; Jerusalem: Prophets and Paratroopers; Jews and Their Worship; A Just Peace in the Middle East: How Can It Be Achieved?; Of Time, Tombs and Treasure: The Treasures of Tutankhamun; The River Nile; Saudi Arabia Today; Abu Dhabi: Land of the Gazelle;* and *Afghanistan: Land of Beauty and Hospitality.*
Size & Elements: Film: 16mm (approx. 45 titles). Videotape: 3/4" (4 titles); VHS (5 titles); Betamax (5 titles).
Cataloging: Published catalog.
Access: Available for rental and purchase. Rental fees charged. Requests accepted by mail.
Rights: Full rights held to some material.
Licensing: Apply for information.
Restrictions: Restrictions may apply to licensing and reuse.
Viewing Facilities: None.
Duplication Facilities: None.
Related Materials: Discussion guides for some programs; slides and filmstrips.

DISTRICT OF COLUMBIA METRO

MONTGOMERY COMMUNITY TELEVISION, INC.
7548 Standish Place
Rockville, MD 20855
(301) 424-1730

Ralph N. Malvik (Executive Director)

Contacts: Richard Turner (Operations Director); Stuart Garfinkle (Programming Director); Shelley Nemerofsky (Training Director); Don Katzen (Marketing Director); Beth Ross (News Director)
Services: Corporation; public access television facility. Videotape library

maintained primarily for cablecast.
Description: Local public affairs and community events, including informational programming, profiles and County Council coverage.
Size & Elements: Videotape: 3/4", Super VHS and VHS (400 titles; masters).
Cataloging: Computerized cataloging for staff use only.
Access: For in-house use only. Research fees not charged. Research requests accepted by mail.
Rights: Full rights held to some material. Some rights held to all material.
Licensing: Apply for information. License and usage fees not charged.
Restrictions: Reuse of most material is restricted.
Viewing Facilities: Videotape (limited equipment available; specific and prior arrangements must be made).
Duplication Facilities: Videotape (3/4", VHS and Betamax).

DISTRICT OF COLUMBIA METRO

MICHAEL MOSER/MEDIA
1429 21st Street, NW
Washington, DC 20036
(202) 293-1780

Michael Moser (President)

Contact: Michael Moser
Services: Videotape producer. Material available for duplication, licensing and reuse. Custom shooting services provided on request.
Description: Footage of Washington, D.C., including the U.S. Capitol, monuments and official buildings (in various weather conditions).
Size & Elements: Videotape: Betacam SP and 3/4" ("a few hours"; masters); VHS (viewing copies).
Cataloging: Shot lists.
Access: Available to the public for duplication, licensing and reuse. Research fees not charged. Research requests accepted by telephone.
Rights: Full rights held to all material.
Licensing: Available for licensing. License fees charged.
Restrictions: None specified.
Viewing Facilities: Videotape (3/4" and VHS).
Duplication Facilities: None.

DISTRICT OF COLUMBIA METRO

MUSEUM OF MODERN ART OF LATIN AMERICA/
AUDIO VISUAL PROGRAM
ORGANIZATION OF AMERICAN STATES
1889 F Street, NW
Washington, DC 20006
(202) 458-6021

Angel Hurtado (Chief of Audio/Visual)

Contact: Nicole Ober (Coordinator)
Services: Museum. Film and videotape producer. Material available to the public for purchase and reuse, subject to approval.
Description: Latin American and Caribbean art, artists, culture and history. Films and videotapes available include: *Manabu Mabe Paints a Picture; David Manzur Paints a Picture; Alejandro Obregon Paints a Fresco; Fernando De Szyszlo of Peru Paints a Picture; South Americans in Córdoba,* showing artists represented at the Córdoba Biennial in Argentina; *Esso Salon of Young Artists; Chancay, The Forgotten Art,* showing pre-Columbian ceramics from Peru; *Art of Central America and Panama,* showing artists with their paintings in their native environment; *Easter Island,* filmed on location; *Julio Rosado Del Valle,* a visit to the artist's studio in San Juan, Puerto Rico; *Nine Artists of Puerto Rico; The World of a Primitive Painter,* showing the works of the renowned Honduran primitive painter J. A. Velásquez; *Belize,* showing patterns of culture; *Barbados, A Culture in Progress; Vibrant Mirror of the Sun,* a kinetic work by Venezuelan artist Alejandro Otero; *Torres-Garcia and the Universal Constructivism; Jamaican Heritage; Honduras: A World Into Itself; Guatemala, Land of Color; Rhythms of Haiti; Dominican Republic, Cradle of the Americas; Grenada, Land of Spice; The Pyramids of the Sun and the Moon,* a comprehensive panorama of Teotihuacán and the Aztec art; *Caribbean Music and Dance; The Legend of El Dorado; Come to Saint Lucia;* and *The Rebellion of the Santos.*
Size & Elements: Film: 16mm (41 films). Videotape: 3/4", VHS and Betamax

(40 titles).
Cataloging: Published catalog.
Access: Available to the public for purchase. Requests accepted by mail, telephone and in person (walk-in and by appointment). Research fees not charged.
Rights: Full rights held to all material.
Licensing: Available for licensing and reuse. License fees charged in some cases.
Restrictions: None specified.
Viewing Facilities: Available by appointment only.
Duplication Facilities: Videotape (3/4", VHS and Betamax).

DISTRICT OF COLUMBIA METRO

NARCOTICS EDUCATION, INC.
6830 Laurel Street, NW
Washington, DC 20012-9979
(800) 548-8700
(202) 722-6740 (in Alaska)
Fax: (202) 722-6990

Contact: Leilani Proctor (Director of Marketing)
Services: Nonprofit organization; film and videotape producer and distributor. Material available to the public for distribution and rental only.
Description: Films and videotapes focusing on drug and alcohol abuse prevention, addiction, health promotion and AIDS education.
  Alcohol. Titles include: *Drinking,* describing the physical and behavioral changes caused by alcohol; and *All the Kids Do It,* warning of drinking and driving.
  Behavior change. Titles include: *The Wizard of No,* teaching young audiences to say no to peer pressure and the negative influences of advertising; *Psychology of Winning; Twelve Steps,* explaining the Twelve Step support group program for individuals and families plagued by alcoholism, drug addiction, overeating and gambling; and *You Pack Your Own Chute,* helping battle unrealistic fears.
  Drugs. Titles include: *How Do You Tell?,* using animation to deal with problems of drugs, alcohol, marijuana and cigarettes; *Why Say No to Drugs?; Epidemic! Kids, Drugs and Alcohol,* focusing on marijuana's detrimental effects on the lungs, memory and reproductive system; *Hazards of Drugged Driving;* and *Medical Aspects of Mind-Altering Drugs.*
  Cocaine. Titles include: *Cocaine and the Student Athlete;* and *The Haight-Ashbury Cocaine Film,* describing physical and behavioral changes and the process of cocaine addiction and recovery.
  Crack. Titles include: *Crack,* in which three teenage addicts present a firsthand look at the realities of crack addiction; and *Crack (Phil Donahue),* drawing on the experiences of crack users and experts to reveal destructive behavior and treatment for crack use.
  Health. Titles include: *Triangle of Health Series,* showing the physical, mental and social sides of health; *Steps Toward Maturity and Health; The Social Side of Health,* describing living with others while maintaining individuality; *Understanding Stresses and Strains,* showing negative effects of worrying that can be minimized by common sense; *Physical Fitness and Good Health; AIDS Alert,* using cartoons to give facts about AIDS in a non-threatening way; *The Sugar Film,* discouraging high-sugar consumption; *Exercises for Anyone, Anywhere, Anytime,* showing exercises that can be done routinely in spare moments to increase activity level; and *The First Step,* showing people with serious health problems taking the first step towards good health.
  Marijuana. Titles include: *Marijuana and Human Physiology,* testifying to the physical, psychological and emotional consequences of drug use; and *Waking Up From Dope,* describing the effects of drug abuse.
  Parents and teenagers. Titles include: *Sons and Daughters/Drugs and Booze,* showing parents' role in prevention and rehabilitation; and *New Parents' and Teachers' Guide to Drug Abuse,* providing information about drugs, recognition of paraphernalia, how to talk about drug abuse and its prevention.
  Peer pressure reversal. Titles include: *The Bizarre Trial of the Pressured Peer,* on conflicting parental norms and teenage peer pressure; and *Setting Norms for Refusal,* using interactive video techniques to encourage assertiveness.
  Tobacco. Titles include: *You've Come a Long Way, Rene,* showing a conflict between a girl who wants to be a championship runner and the pressure to smoke; *Breathing Easy,* educating young people on the hazards of smoking to health and appearance; *Feminine Mistake,* focusing on the female smoker and hazards to unborn children, beauty and health; *Secondhand Smoke,* telling of dangers of "side-stream" smoke; *Smokeless Tobacco: The Whole Truth,* showing hazards of snuff and chewing tobacco; *Smokeless Tobacco — It Can Snuff You Out,* discussing oral cancer, irreversible damage to teeth and gums and addictiveness; *Death in the West,* contrasting Marlboro ads with six cowboys dying of smoking-related diseases; *Cancers of the Head and Neck,* showing evidence that cancers of the head and neck almost always occur in tobacco and/or alcohol users; and *Smoking/Emphysema: A Fight for Breath.*
Size & Elements: Film: 16mm. Videotape: VHS and Betamax. (46 titles total).
Cataloging: Published catalogs.
Access: Available to the public for distribution and rental only. Research requests not accepted. Orders accepted by mail and telephone.
Rights: Full rights held to material produced by Narcotics Education. Additional clearances may be necessary for material distributed by NE if material is to be reused.
Licensing: Apply for information.
Restrictions: Clip reuse rarely permitted.
Viewing Facilities: None.
Duplication Facilities: None.
Related Materials: Publish two periodicals: *The Winner Magazine* and *Listen Magazine.* Teaching aids and audiovisual tools to help demonstrate health hazards are available.

DISTRICT OF COLUMBIA METRO

NATIONAL ABORTION RIGHTS ACTION LEAGUE
1101 14th Street, NW
Washington, DC 20005
(202) 371-0779
Fax: (202) 371-0756

Kate Michelman (Executive Director)

Contact: Renee Cravens (Media Coordinator)
Services: Association. Videotape collection available for research, licensing and reuse, subject to restrictions.
Description: Videotapes relating to the issue of abortion (1973-present). Includes videotapes of marches, speeches, news broadcasts, talk shows, conferences, demonstrations and films relating to abortion rights. Both pro-choice and pro-life viewpoints are represented. Other topics covered are reproductive health care, teenage pregnancy, politics and birth control.
Size & Elements: Videotape: 1" (20 videotapes); 3/4" (100 videotapes); VHS (250 videotapes).
Cataloging: None specified.
Access: Available to the public. Research requests accepted by mail and telephone.
Rights: Full rights held to some material. Additional clearances may be necessary in some cases if material is to be reused.
Licensing: Available for licensing and reuse, subject to restrictions. License fees not charged.
Restrictions: Reuse subject to clearance and approval.
Viewing Facilities: Videotape (3/4" and 1/2").
Duplication Facilities: None.

DISTRICT OF COLUMBIA METRO

NATIONAL AERONAUTICS AND SPACE ADMINISTRATION (NASA)
GODDARD SPACE FLIGHT CENTER
REGIONAL FILM LIBRARY
Public Affairs Office
Mail Code 130
Greenbelt, MD 20771
(301) 286-8101

Contact: Staff
Services: Government agency; circulating film library. Films available for loan.
Description: Films and videotapes describing NASA research and development programs and achievements in space and aeronautics. Programs offered are similar to those available from other NASA Regional Film Libraries (q.v.).
Size & Elements: Film: 16mm. Videotape: 3/4". (Hundreds of titles total).
Cataloging: Published catalog.
Access: Available for loan to educational, civil, industrial, professional, youth and similar groups, and for unsponsored public service telecasts. Research and rental fees not charged. Requests accepted by mail.

Rights: Material in the public domain. Additional clearances may be necessary in some cases if material is to be reused.
Licensing: Available for reuse, subject to restrictions.
Restrictions: Film material or footage of recognizable astronauts may not be reused for commercial purposes.
Viewing Facilities: None.
Duplication Facilities: None.

DISTRICT OF COLUMBIA METRO

NATIONAL AERONAUTICS AND SPACE ADMINISTRATION (NASA)
OFFICE OF COMMUNICATIONS
MEDIA SERVICES DIVISION
BROADCAST AND AUDIOVISUAL BRANCH
Mail Code LMD
Washington, DC 20546
(202) 453-8594
Fax: (202) 472-2309

Street address: 400 Maryland Avenue, SW

Joseph Headlee (Chief, Broadcast and Audiovisual Branch)

Contact: Joseph Headlee
Services: Government agency. Videotape footage available for duplication and reuse *to bona fide news media representatives only*. Requests from the general public are serviced by the NASA Regional Film Libraries (q.v.) (for loan and distribution) and by NARA, National Audiovisual Center (q.v.) (for purchase).
Description: NASA produces the *Aeronautics and Space Report* (ASR) program in a magazine format intended for use by the news media. This program, of which 246 episodes (each 15 min.) have so far been produced, contains highlights of NASA activities in all areas. From January 1965 through September 1984, the *Report* was issued monthly; since December 1984 to the present, every 90 days. Until 1983, all production was on film; since then, programs have been originated on videotape. Two distinct soundtracks are provided in videotape format: Channel 1 contains the full sound mix, with narration, sound effects and actualities; while Channel 2 contains a mix without narration, allowing users to insert their own voiceovers.

Some ASRs are available for free loan from NASA Regional Film Libraries throughout the United States (q.v.).

Members of the news media may find that these programs and the footage contained therein meet many of their needs. Although the collection begins some four years after the start of the United States manned space program, most, if not all manned space missions as well as significant unmanned missions and ground activity are covered in detail. A partial list of subjects covered includes the Gemini program; the X-15 experimental aircraft; simulators and wind tunnels; the Apollo lunar program; Tiros and other weather satellites; the Saturn rocket; early communications satellites; Surveyor (unmanned lunar landing); Apollo 11 (the moon landing); moon rocks; Skylab; the Earth Resources Technology Satellite (ERTS and LANDSAT) program; ocean research; Comet Kohoutek; the space shuttle program; zero gravity research; the NASA Tech House; the Voyager planetary probe to Jupiter, Saturn and Uranus; research relating to the volcano Mount St. Helens; a profile of Christa McAuliffe; the return of Halley's Comet; and space suit design and technology.
Size & Elements: Videotape: 3/4" (approx. 50 hours, 246 programs, each 5-15 min.; masters). Programs originally produced on film are now available on videotape.
Cataloging: Program lists and indexes maintained for internal use only; computerized cataloging for staff use only (in progress).
Access: Not open to the public. Available only to *bona fide* representatives of the news media. Available for duplication and reuse. Research fees not charged. Research requests accepted by mail and telephone. Requester must send new 3/4" videotape with list of scenes requested. NASA will dub scenes onto supplied videotape and return by overnight courier (Federal Express preferred). Paid return waybills must be supplied; no videotapes are shipped collect; requesters must supply valid courier service account numbers.
Rights: Most material in the public domain. A limited amount is copyrighted. Additional clearances may be necessary in some cases if material is to be reused.
Licensing: Available for reuse to *bona fide* news media representatives. Usage fees not charged.
Restrictions: Available for duplication and reuse to *bona fide* news media representatives only. As with all NASA material, no footage may be used to endorse a specific product, and no likenesses of any astronauts may be used for commercial purposes without express permission.
Viewing Facilities: None.
Duplication Facilities: Videotape (3/4" to 3/4").

DISTRICT OF COLUMBIA METRO

NATIONAL ARCHIVES AND RECORDS ADMINISTRATION (NARA)
MOTION PICTURE, SOUND AND VIDEO BRANCH
7th and Pennsylvania Avenue, NW, Room 2W
Washington, DC 20408
(202) 786-0041
(202) 786-0042

William Murphy (Branch Chief)
Les Waffen (Assistant Branch Chief)

Contacts: Donald Roe, Mark Meader, Herb Sumpter, Darlene McClurkin, Jill Abraham (Reference Staff)
Services: Government agency. Film and videotape material available for research, duplication and reuse, subject to restrictions.
Description: The primary mission of the National Archives and Records Administration (NARA) is the preservation of a permanent record of U.S. history for future generations. The collections include materials created for and acquired by the U.S. government, as well as gift materials from private sources that relate to the history of the United States.

The permanent collection is arranged by Record Group (RG). Each numbered group contains the records of a single government agency or subdivision. The National Archives Gift Collection (RG 200), contains non-government-produced material donated to the Archives, including newsreels, the *March of Time* and the Ford Collection. The Stock Film Collection, described after RG 452, contains additional footage available for viewing, duplication and reuse.

Permanent Collection

RG 4: U.S. Food Administration (1917-18, 2 items). Films of supporters of the Food Control Act, Senators George E. Chamberlain and Willard Saulsbury, Representatives Champ Clark and Asbury F. Lever, and Food Administrator Herbert C. Hoover. A film on wartime farming in France. Animated cartoons dramatizing the need to conserve food.

RG 7: Bureau of Entomology and Plant Quarantine (1930s, 1 item). A short film of insecticide use on an apple orchard by Purdue University scientists in Orleans, Indiana.

RG 9: National Recovery Administration (1933, 3 items). One short film produced by Warner Brothers for the NRA, *The Road Is Open Again*.

RG 12: Office of Education (1940-80, 59 items). *Fight for Life*, a 1940 documentary about obstetrical training and practice in the Chicago slums, written and directed by Pare Lorentz. Films (1944-45) intended for use in supervisory training and a film on the industrial skills of the blind. A filmed address of President Dwight D. Eisenhower to the White House Conference on Education (November 28-December 1, 1955). 33 films (1944-77) made under agency grants, on the changing role of technology in education, methods to combat illiteracy, improving communication, supervising and training the handicapped, supervising women employees, and various types of public service jobs. A film of a ceremony of the establishment of the Department of Education (1980).

RG 15: Veterans Administration (1919 and 1946, 27 items). Films pertaining to the work of the Bureau of War Risk Insurance (1919). A film explaining the organization of the Veterans Administration (1946). Several documentaries explaining and illustrating the educational, financial, medical and rehabilitation services of the Veterans Administration.

RG 16: Office of the Secretary of Agriculture (1928-79, 1,408 items). These films document the activity and projects of the various units within the Department of Agriculture, agriculture-related projects of state and other federal agencies and 20th century farm life. This RG includes some of the earliest motion pictures produced by a civilian agency: *Forest and Health* (1928); *Green Pastures* (1930); *Negro Soldier* (1936); and *Victory Harvest* (1945). Among the titles is the critically acclaimed documentary film *Power and the Land* (1940), directed by Joris Ivens for the Rural Electrification Administration. A color short with Stan Laurel and Oliver Hardy entitled *Tree in a Test Tube*. 27 selections from the USDA television programs *A Better Way* and *Down to Earth* which presented information to the general public on being an informed consumer; and information to rural and agricultural communities on topics such as the use of pesticides, improving dairy herds and farm loan programs.

RG 18: Army Air Forces (1912-49, 6,059 items). World War II training films illustrating the coordination of the various operational units of the American 8th Army Air Force, and the combined efforts of these units in preparing and completing a bombing mission; and World War II training films on flight and gunnery and the maintenance and use of planes, helicopters, airfield tractors, forklift trucks and spray painting equipment.

Air Transport Command briefing films consisting of aerial and ground views of terrain, flight routes and landing facilities in the South Atlantic, North Atlantic, Europe, India and China, the Caribbean, South America, Africa, the Pacific, the British Isles, Alaska, the Canal Zone and the United States. Animation for the briefing films shows particular flight routes, locations of landing strips, radio beams and the principal geographic configuration of specific areas.

Outtakes from *Thunderbolts,* a 1946 William Wyler production documenting activities of the 12th Army Air Force in Europe (June 1944-April 1945). Combat footage made in all theaters of operation in World War II concerning activities of the USAAF, and containing camera records on all other aspects of the war, including: land and sea battles; amphibious operations; civilian and military leaders of the Allied Powers attending conferences and visiting troops; entertainers; war correspondents; Red Cross activities; rest and recreation activities; native peoples and their customs and participation in the war; captured enemy spies and saboteurs; Allied and Axis prisoners of war and prisoner-of-war camps; internees and internee camps; concentration camps; Axis atrocities; V-E and V-J days; the occupation of Germany and Japan; atomic scientists; the A-bomb blast over Nagasaki; and damage to Nagasaki and Hiroshima.

Films concerning the development and use of lighter-than-air craft (1925-35). A film made by the Air Corps of the 1933 Arkansas flood. A Coast Guard training film on swimming through burning oil and in surf. A film entitled *Last Rites of the Battleship Maine* (1912), made by the Selig Corporation.

Color footage shot by the Army Air Force during the closing months of the war in France and Germany (March-June, 1945).

Paper files with digest sheets and caption sheets are available.

RG 21: District Courts of the United States (1903-34, 11 items). Films filed as plaintiff's exhibits in a copyright case brought before the U.S. Circuit Court for the Eastern District of Pennsylvania, *American Mutoscope and Biograph Company v. Sigmund Lubin* (October, 1903). Films from the records of the U.S. District Court for the Western District of Washington of the Dempsey-Tunney heavyweight boxing match held at Soldiers Field, Chicago (September 22, 1927), and of the Dempsey-Sharkey fight held at Yankee Stadium, New York City (July 21, 1927). Two films used as exhibits in *U.S. v. Bates, et. al.,* also known as the "Machine Gun Kelly Case," titled *The Retribution of Clyde Barrow and Bonnie Parker* (1934) and *The Visualization of the Urschel Kidnapping Showing the Federal Government's Determined Drive on Crime.*

RG 22: Fish and Wildlife Service (1915-27, 13 items). Films made by the Bureau of Fisheries (1920s) concerning cooperative fish culture in the United States and pearl culture in Japan. Film relating to an inspection trip to Alaska made by Bureau officials, including Commissioner Henry O'Malley (ca. 1929). Department of Agriculture films on the control of pests such as rats, prairie dogs, and porcupines (1915-16). A film on life in a Boy Scout camp (ca. 1937), and a film illustrating aerial bombing techniques of the Air Service (1921).

RG 24: Bureau of Naval Personnel (1917-27, 101 reels). Films made or collected by the Bureau of Naval Personnel or its predecessor, the Bureau of Navigation, relating to naval air activities during World War I in the Atlantic and at the Key West Naval Station, including submarine patrol, convoy escort, rescue operations and ground operations; ship launchings and maintenance at the Newport News Naval Shipyard; submarine maneuvers; Marine training; torpedo manufacturing and firing; and mine laying in the North Sea from a base in England.

Films of Liberty Loan Drive activities, patriotic celebrations, parades, ceremonies and armistice celebrations in New York City, Washington, D.C., Pittsburgh and London. Persons participating include President Woodrow Wilson, Secretary of the Navy Josephus Daniels, Secretary of War John Pershing, Alexander B. Dyer, Lt. John Philip Sousa, Gov. Charles S. Whitman of New York and Mayor John F. Hylan of New York City.

News coverage of President Wilson's second inaugural and films of his first visit to Europe following the armistice, including his departure aboard the transport *George Washington,* the arrival of the convoy in Brest, and the welcoming procession in the streets of Brest.

Films depicting war damage to Rheims, France, and Ostend, Belgium, and to other towns and the countryside of both France and Belgium.

Films of German prisoners of war, captured German armaments and a U-boat. Newsreel films of postwar Volendam, Holland and the gardens at Versailles.

Films of American leaders, including Secretary of the Navy Daniels, Secretary of State Robert Lansing, Admirals William S. Sims, William S. Benson, Roger Welles, Albert Gleaves and Hugh Rodman, with foreign dignitaries on visits to the United States and aboard U.S. Navy vessels. Dignitaries include Prince Exel of Denmark, King Alfonso and Queen Victoria of Spain, and King George V of Britain. Films of the dedication of an American Expeditionary Forces monument at St. Nazaire, France, with U.S. Ambassador Myron T. Herrick, Marshal Ferdinand Foch and General Pershing participating; and of President and Mrs. Warren G. Harding aboard the Presidential Yacht *Mayflower* (ca. 1921).

Films of the 1924 transatlantic flight of the airship *Los Angeles* (ZR-3), of rescue operations by lighter-than-air craft, and of a demonstration of aerial mapping techniques at Miami, Florida.

Films of postwar Navy training in seamanship, first aid, and the repair and maintenance of electrical equipment, machinery, dirigibles and airplanes aboard ships, at several Navy yards and bases, and at the Naval Academy and the Great Lakes Naval Training Station.

News coverage and Navy films of League of Nations, Red Cross, and U.S. Navy activities relating to the removal of Armenian and Greek refugees from Turkey to Greece (ca. 1921) and films of the rescue of personnel from grounded and burning ships.

Films of recreation aboard ships and of sightseeing all over the world. Many scenes of U.S. Navy ships in harbors, at sea and on maneuvers, and of ships of the Italian, British and Turkish Navies.

A film about the newly acquired Virgin Islands (ca. 1918).

RG 25: National Labor Relations Board (1938, 1 item). A film of the complete assembly of Ford automobiles.

RG 26: United States Coast Guard (1918-55, 84 items). Films (1918-38 and 1945-55) about the peacetime activities of the Coast Guard, including rescue work at sea and in inland disaster areas, cooperation with the Fish and Wildlife Service in the whaling and fur seal industries, waterfront and harbor protection and law enforcement, enforcement of ship safety regulations, beach and offshore patrols against smuggling, icebreaking and lighthouse duties in the Great Lakes, iceberg patrol, lighthouse and light buoy construction and maintenance, navigation assistance to ships in U.S. coastal waters and abroad, weather observation, training and education at the Coast Guard Academy and at other institutions, and recreation.

Films relating to domestic activities during World War II, including dock and harbor patrol, ship inspection, investigations of ship sinkings, firefighting, weather observation, and beach patrol (including a film showing FBI agents posing with German spies captured by the Coast Guard); and films concerning Coast Guard overseas activities during the war, such as amphibious operations in all theaters, transportation of troops and war materials, rescue at sea, submarine patrol, and convoy escort. Films of a yacht race and of activities of U.S. political and military leaders (ca. 1938).

RG 28: Post Office Department (1921-57, 77 items). Films depicting activities and facilities of the Department, including the Dead Letter Office; mail handling and delivery; transporting mail by air, land and water; parcel post; manufacturing and repairing mailbags; printing and issuing stamps; protecting the mails from fraudulent use; and post office buildings and the construction and dedication of the New Post Office, Washington, D.C. (1931-34). The films include footage of persons such as Presidents Herbert C. Hoover and Franklin D. Roosevelt, Postmasters General Harry S. New, Walter F. Brown and James A. Farley, and aviatrix Amelia Earhart.

A scenic film about Mount Rainier National Park.

German propaganda films (1939-40), including *Baptism of Fire,* which depicts the conquest of Belgium, Holland, France and Poland. Addressed to the German consul in New York, the films were impounded as undeliverable mail shortly after the United States entered the war.

RG 29: Bureau of the Census (1937-39 and 1960, 40 items). Films seeking public cooperation in the National Unemployment Census of 1937 and in the 1940 census. Training films for enumerators for the 1940 census. A National Educational Television series on the 1960 census illustrating the work of the Bureau, presenting the history of census-taking in the United States, and explaining the kind of information sought in the 1960 census and the uses to which it can be put. Short films in English and Spanish encouraging return of the 1960 census forms featuring celebrities such as Sugar Ray Robinson, Steve Allen and Chi Chi Rodriguez.

RG 31: Federal Housing Administration (1935-36, 10 items). Films of a series entitled *Better Housing News Flashes* relating to the construction, renovation and modernization of homes, farm buildings and commercial properties under the Administration and to the effect of the FHA and its government-insured loan program on the building industries. Also a film on the construction of low-cost housing in Bethesda, Maryland.

RG 33: Federal Extension Service (ca. 1913-70, 589 items). Films made or collected by the Department of Agriculture, relating chiefly to the educational activities of the Extension Service, including assisting and advising farmers and ranchers in methods of cultivation, soil conservation, the use of farm machinery, crop storage and marketing, plant and animal breeding, plant and animal pest and disease control, the care and feeding of animals, livestock butchering and marketing, farmyard sanitation, and home improvement and modernization; home economics instruction, including such topics as canning, nutrition, child care, housekeeping, sewing and bookkeeping; sponsorship of and cooperation with 4-H Clubs, American Farm Bureau Federations, the National Grange, and state farm organizations and extension services; work with the land-grant colleges in agricultural education; and cooperation with the Federal Emergency Relief Administration in establishing and operating cooperative farm communities.

Films (1913-47) on the history and organization of the Department of Agriculture; Department facilities, including the buildings in Washington, D.C., and the research center at Beltsville, Maryland; and secretaries, Department personnel and other prominent persons. Films on the role of the Department in enforcing the Pure Food and Drug Act (1920-32 and 1959), in conducting agricultural explorations of other lands for plants that could be grown in the United States (1928-32 and 1952) and in inspecting imported seeds and plants (1922 and 1932). Also the role of the Department in both World Wars and a 1924 film on its motion picture-making activities.

Films illustrating activities of the Forest Service, including the regulation of lumbering and grazing in national forests, fire prevention and fighting, pest and disease control and wildlife conservation. Films illustrating the work of the Bureau of Public Roads (1915-37). Films relating to national parks in all areas of the United States. Films explaining the work of the Weather Bureau. Films covering highlights of the Coolidge and Hoover administrations and depicting activities of well-known persons and news events (1925-39).

Paper records that are available include U.S. Department of Agriculture caption sheets.

RG 35: Civilian Conservation Corps (1933-43, 2 items). Motion pictures on the role of the CCC in erosion control and on work and recreation during one day in a CCC camp.

RG 38: Office of the Chief of Naval Operations (1941, 1 item). A film of the testing of Higgins amphibious tanks by the Board of Inspection and Survey.

RG 39: Bureau of Accounts (Treasury) (ca. 1935, 1 item). A film illustrating the accounting system of the Treasury Department and showing President Franklin D. Roosevelt addressing Congress on the public works program.

RG 40: Department of Commerce (1979, 1 item). A film on the importance of coastal sea life and salt marshes, funded by the Coastal Plains Regional Commission.

RG 43: International Conferences, Commissions and Expositions (1936-68, 4 items). A film illustrating power resources in the United States (1936). A 70mm film entitled *Us*, which was shown at the U.S. Federal Pavilion at the 1968 Hemisfair in San Antonio, Texas. Films used at the Seattle World's Fair (1962).

RG 46: United States Senate (1936-87, 244 items). Newsreel footage received from a subcommittee of the Senate Committee on Education and Labor of the 1936 San Francisco dock strike, the 1937 Republic Steel strike in Chicago and the 1938 Stockton, California cannery strike.

A complete set of recordings of the Iran-Contra Hearings of the Senate Select Committee on Secret Military Assistance to Iran and the Nicaraguan Opposition (1986-87).

RG 47: Social Security Administration (1936-66, 366 items). Films on procedures for obtaining old age and survivors insurance, disability insurance and unemployment benefits. Newsreel footage covering activities of President Franklin D. Roosevelt, Secretary of State Cordell Hull and Governor Alfred M. Landon, among others.

317 public service shorts (each 15 min.) made in Hollywood studios for the television series *Social Security in Action* (1958-66). Informal interviews feature film and television personalities and other public figures, predominantly older Americans, who talk about their lives, careers, special interests and future plans. Guests include Hollywood producer Cecil B. DeMille, writer Rod Serling, director George Cukor, cartoonist Dave Fleischer, prizefighter Archie Moore, entertainers Eddie Cantor, Danny Thomas, Jonathan Winters, Harold Lloyd, Jane Russell, Rudy Vallee, Francis X. Bushman and Rex Ingram.

RG 48: Office of the Secretary of the Interior (1929-62, 179 items). Films (1935-37) relating to the overall activities of the Department, including the activities of the Office of Indian Affairs, the Bureau of Reclamation, the National Park Service, the Division of Territories and Island Possessions, and the Bureau of Mines. Films of President Harry S Truman signing the Defense Production Act of 1950 and of Secretary of the Interior Oscar L. Chapman speaking (ca. 1950).

A film about the operation of the Alaska Railroad (1962).

Films made by or for the Office of Indian Affairs (1933-36) about the origin and history of American Indians and their contemporary customs and ways of life.

Films made or collected by the Bureau of Mines (ca. 1936) relating to volcanic action and resultant geological formations, mountain building and geological problems in mining and structural engineering, and to Texas, its industries and geography.

Films from the 1930s made by or relating to National Park Service activities, including films of scenery, work and recreation in national and state parks and at national monuments and national historic sites all over the United States and in the territories.

Films made by the Bureau of Reclamation or relating to Bureau activities (1934-38 and 1952), concerning conservation in general, the history of the westward expansion of the United States and the depletion of natural resources, activities of the General Land Office and the Geological Survey, activities of the Civilian Conservation Corps, and reclamation projects and their impact on communities.

Films made or collected by the Division of Territories and Island Possessions of the 1929 Carpenter-Whitney Expedition to Alaska and films about the Katmai National Monument (undated). Films concerned mainly with sugar cane growing and refining in Hawaii (1937), and films of scenery, tourist activities and agricultural and other work on St. Thomas, St. Johns and St. Croix Islands in the Virgin Islands (1935-36).

Films depicting activities of agencies other than the Department of the Interior, including a film made by the Public Buildings Administration of the Federal Works Agency of a housing project for married enlisted men at Fort Jackson, S.C. (1941); and a few films (1935-36) on the creation and development of the Tennessee Valley Authority.

RG 49: Bureau of Land Management (1956-67, 2 items). Films about the remaining public lands in the western U.S. and the work of the Bureau in improving these lands, especially the arid plateau of eastern Oregon.

RG 53: Bureau of the Public Debt (1914-18, 4 items). Films dramatizing several heroic acts of World War I infantrymen, produced by the Treasury Department to promote the fourth Liberty Loan Drive. Films of the Salvation Army Congress in London (1914).

RG 56: Department of the Treasury (1941-78, 307 items). Incentive films and advertising spots used in connection with defense and Victory Bond promotional drives by the Savings Bonds Division and covering aspects of World War II, Korea and Vietnam, as well as peacetime defense needs.

A promotional television spot for U.S. Savings Bonds entitled *The Uncle Sam Caper* (1975).

A set of 96 films explaining and promoting the sale of U.S. Savings Bonds (1954-78). Some feature celebrities such as Rock Hudson, Charlton Heston, Dean Martin, James Stewart, Jack Webb, Arthur Godfrey, General William Westmoreland, Hubert Humphrey and Elvis Presley. Others are information films which use the casts of popular television shows such as *The Odd Couple, Father Knows Best, Mister Ed, Superman* and *The Life of Riley*.

RG 58: Internal Revenue Service (1960-70, 4 items). Films produced by the Taxpayer Information and Education Branch which explain services available to taxpayers from the IRS, the administration of tax law, and tax questions of the elderly and disabled.

RG 59: Department of State (1911-66, 207 items). Films made by the Department, its subsidiary agencies, other government departments, and private companies reflecting Department of State activities and policies, and illustrating the history of the U.S. role in world affairs.

Films of the construction of the Panama Canal and views of the surrounding countryside and native life (1911-13).

News coverage of British Foreign Secretary Arthur J. Balfour's visit to Washington, D.C. (1917).

A film showing President Calvin Coolidge with members of his Cabinet (1925).

A 1926 film of the U.S. Legation in San Salvador and a 1929 film of La Paz, Bolivia, Bolivian cities and towns, the Bolivian countryside and U.S. Minister David E. Kaufman with Bolivian President Hernando Siles.

A Fourth of July celebration in Shanghai (1924).

The Notre Dame Boys Choir singing Christmas hymns (1933).

A 1938 film in the *March of Time* series entitled *Uncle Sam — The Good Neighbor*. The film illustrates U.S. Foreign Service activities, with several officials of the Service and the Department of State and several ambassadors participating. A film of discussion by Assistant Secretary of State Sumner Welles about Nazi infiltration in South America and of the Presidents of Brazil,

Argentina and Uruguay meeting to confer on the problem.

Films of activities aboard the Swedish Red Cross ship *Gripsholm* in New York Harbor as it prepares to repatriate Japanese citizens and to deliver packages to American prisoners of war in Japan (1943).

Documentaries and newsreels produced by the Office of War Information, reporting on World War II activities at home and in the combat theaters; covering a visit to the United States by Madame Chiang Kai-shek (1943); and reenacting the sinking of the freighter *Delia B* by a German submarine and the sinking of the submarine by a B-24. Documentaries about life in America from the *American Scene* series made during the war by the Office of War Information for distribution abroad.

A film illustrating Office of Strategic Services Operations during the Allied invasions of Sicily and Italy (1944).

A film made by the Foreign Liquidation Commission in Italy illustrating procedures for disposing of surplus property and reconstruction work (1946).

A film about the work of the United Nations Educational, Scientific and Cultural Organization (UNESCO) in assisting students from all over the world (1947).

A film showing a U.S. military cemetery in Margraten, Netherlands, and scenes and life in Limburg Province (ca. 1950), presented to the U.S. Ambassador to the Netherlands by the Association of Netherlands Coal Mines.

Films illustrating reconstruction and economic development made possible by Marshall Plan aid to Italy, Greece and Great Britain (1950-51); and films on efforts to improve the quality of life in Mexico and South America under the Point 4 Program (1951).

Films reviewing international events (1945-51); covering the proceedings of the Japanese peace treaty conference held in San Francisco (1951); depicting the plight of Arab refugees from Israel in the Gaza Strip and Jerusalem (1950); showing refugees from East Berlin (1951); covering the Korean War; and relating to youth activities in East and West Germany (1950-51).

A film biography of General Dwight D. Eisenhower to the time he was appointed commander of the North Atlantic Treaty Organization (NATO) (1951).

Films showing the construction of the U.S. pavilion at the Brussels World's Fair, the opening ceremonies of the fair, and films (known as the "loops" at the time they were produced) shown as exhibits in the U.S. pavilion (1958). These short films, all in color, depict various aspects of everyday life and culture in the United States, including supermarkets, gasoline stations, harbors, construction sites and drive-in restaurants; many were produced by distinguished filmmakers, including Francis Thompson, Wheaton Galentine and D. A. Pennebaker.

Films, mostly from television shows, of speeches, interviews and discussions featuring Secretaries and Assistant Secretaries of State and others, including Dean Acheson, Christian Herter, Dean Rusk, George Ball, Douglas Dillon and W. Averell Harriman (1950-65), relating to U.S. foreign policy and world conditions.

Two public affairs documentaries, one describing the work of the U.S. mission to the United Nations under Arthur Goldberg and the other a film about U.S. aid to Ecuador to combat communist ideology and insurgency. A 1966 UNESCO film on Abu Simbel (Egypt), Latin America and the Indian Ocean.

RG 60: Department of Justice (ca. 1986, 23 items). Exhibits from Attorney General's [Edwin Meese] Commission on Pornography include 15 videotapes, eight 8mm films, and audio tapes.

RG 64: National Archives and Records Service (1936-77, 70 items). Films of the first meeting of the National Archives Council (June 10, 1936) and of a luncheon meeting of the National Historical Publications Commission, (June 17, 1958). Films of ceremonies at the National Archives marking the opening of the exhibit of the Japanese surrender documents (1945); concerning historical documents in the Library of Congress; and of the transfer of the Declaration of Independence and the Constitution from the Library to the National Archives (1952). Films of tests conducted at the National Bureau of Standards on the burning characteristics of nitrate motion picture film (1936-38). A film entitled *Your National Archives* (1953). A film of the voyage of the *U.S.S. Skate* under the North Pole (1958).

And That's The Way It Was, T.V. News 1947-1968, a series of 19 programs that were shown at the Archives and then donated to the collection. Events include the Cuban missile crisis, the Bay of Pigs, the U-2 incident, civil rights, the Nixon-Khrushchev debate and many others.

RG 65: Federal Bureau of Investigation (1936, 3 items). A motion picture entitled *You Can't Get Away With It,* which portrays FBI activities in detecting and arresting criminals.

RG 69: Works Progress Administration (1931-39, 105 items). Films produced or distributed by the Motion Picture Record Division or its successors relating to WPA activities, including: flood, drought and hurricane relief and rehabilitation; dam, road, park, airport and public building construction; slum clearance; development of recreation facilities; projects for promoting children's welfare; public education; women's work projects; and "white collar" work projects, including the Federal Theater Project and the Federal Art Project (1935-39). Films illustrating WPA programs in particular areas of the country and in Alaska (1935-37).

Instructional films in the *Physical Science* and *Bringing the World to the Classroom* series (1931-36).

Films illustrating activities of the Civilian Conservation Corps (CCC) and the National Youth Administration (NYA) (1936).

RG 70: Bureau of Mines (1913-55, 270 items). Films relating to mining methods, processing, refining, manufacturing, and products; uses of nickel, silver, lead, iron, copper, aluminum, magnesium, sulfur, clay, asbestos, carborundum, and sillimanite (1919-38 and ca. 1943); coal mining methods (1919-38); drilling oil wells and quarrying sandstone, granite and limestone for Portland cement (1915-31); automobile manufacture and assembly, including explanations of the principle of the internal combustion engine and of the lubrication of a car (1926-36); manufacturing, testing and uses of dynamite, electric detonators, electric meters, safety glass, spark plugs, steel, storage batteries, valves and watches (1922-38); applications of steam, water and electric power (1922-38 and ca. 1943); and demonstrations of the uses of the oxyacetylene torch (1922 and 1938).

Films used in the Bureau's safety and health education programs (1913-17); gas, fires, dust explosions, equipment handling and digging in coal mines (1914-30); shoring, blasting equipment handling and ore loading in metal mines (1914-30); fires in oil wells and general safety in the oil industry (1923-24); carbon monoxide poisoning (1928); rescue and first aid (1915-31); traffic safety (1924 and 1937); and sanitation practices in mining towns.

Films on the natural resources and beauty of Arizona and Texas and films on the national parks, including Yellowstone, Yosemite, Grand Canyon, Rocky Mountain and Shenandoah (1925-55).

News coverage of the Royalton, Illinois mine disaster (1914); testing of railway guns at Fort Story, Virginia (1929); and the arrival of the *U.S.S. Houston* at Cartagena, Colombia with President Franklin D. Roosevelt aboard (1934).

RG 75: Bureau of Indian Affairs (1908-73, 38 items). Films made by the Rodman Wanamaker Historical Expeditions to the North American Indians (1908-20). The films depict the life, religious customs, dances and methods of warfare of North American Indians; the adoption of Marshall Ferdinand Foch by the Crow; the groundbreaking ceremony for an Indian memorial in New York State, with President William Howard Taft and his Cabinet in attendance; the declaration of allegiance made by the tribes on becoming American citizens; and the adoption of Joseph M. Dixon, leader of the expeditions, into the Wolf Clan of the Mohawk Nation, Iroquois Confederacy.

A film made by the Office of Indian Affairs during a trip by the revenue cutter *Bear* from the Aleutian Islands to Siberia showing many Arctic scenes, including icefields, Eskimos and their homes, and animals, especially reindeer (1921).

Training and information films produced or acquired (1941-73) by the Bureau. Subjects include educational options for Alaskan Natives; offender rehabilitation in Oklahoma; life of the Pueblos; a Zuñi comprehensive development plan; irrigation and water conservation; the Alaska Native Claims Settlement Act; relocation of the Hopi and Navajo to a reservation and farm once used as a War Relocation Authority Center; agricultural methods; and health services.

RG 77: Office of the Chief of Engineers (1940-63, 102 items). Footage (16mm, color) of construction and base life in the Aleutian Islands (1940-44), including detailed footage of construction projects on the islands of Attu, Umnak, Adak, Amchitka and Shemya; projects at Resurrection Bay, Whittier Tunnel, Ladd air field and Excursion Inlet.

Polar and cold regions experiments "Greenland" and "Cold Mission" (1947-63).

Color footage of preparations and blast of the so-called "Trinity test" of the Fat Man plutonium bomb (July 16, 1945).

RG 78: Naval Observatory (1930, 1 item). A film of an astronomical expedition to Samoa to study a solar eclipse.

RG 79: National Park Service (1930-36, 17 items). Scenes of the Mt. McKinley region (ca. 1925). Films (1930-36) illustrating tourist activities, Park Service work, park facilities and the people who lived in the Shenandoah and Great Smoky Mountains National Parks before the parks were dedicated. A film depicting a typical day at Camp Roosevelt, a Boy Scout camp at Willows, Maryland (ca. 1930).

RG 80: Department of the Navy (1925-65, 483 items). Films made or collected by the Navy and used in training during World War II relating to the

history of naval aviation, ships, submarines, airplanes, training of personnel and mail delivery; kamikaze attacks; the battles of Midway and the Marianas; invasions of the Solomon Islands, Eniwetok, Saipan and Guam; preparations for the invasions of the Ryukyus and Okinawa; bombing raids over Japan; and Japan and the Japanese people.

Outtakes and camera records (1942-65) from the central motion picture files of the Navy showing experimental equipment, aircraft in flight, aircraft crashes and flight deck operations; ship movements; Pacific engagements and landings during World War II and the Korean War; the Japanese surrender ceremonies; the Allied occupation of Japan; returning prisoners of war; and ceremonies, reviews and disasters at sea. News outtakes and clips relating to World War II and the Korean action.

A *Combat Bulletin* film on the Japanese surrender showing President Harry S Truman announcing the surrender, celebrations in the United States and the surrender ceremonies aboard the *U.S.S. Missouri* (1945).

Captured enemy films relating to naval activities during World War II. British and American films of the Atlantic Conference between President Roosevelt and Prime Minister Churchill aboard the *U.S.S. Augusta* (1941).

News coverage of the wreckage of the Navy dirigible *Shenandoah (ZR-1)* (1925). A *March of Time* film about medical training in the United States (1938).

RG 82: Federal Reserve System (1937, 1 item). A film made at the dedication ceremonies opening the Federal Reserve Building, Washington, D.C., with President Franklin D. Roosevelt making the dedicatory remarks.

RG 85: Immigration and Naturalization Service (1942-54, 2 items). Footage of the alien enemy detention facility at Crystal City, Texas, originally a migratory labor camp and later redesignated to house 3,600 as a family detention center for Japanese-Americans. Two edited films made in the 1950s use the footage.

RG 86: Women's Bureau (1928-38, 6 items). Dramas concerning the role of women in industry and the impact of labor laws and union activity on working conditions for women.

RG 87: United States Secret Service (1939, 2 items). A motion picture entitled *Know Your Money*, containing instructions on detecting counterfeit bills and coins and the action to be taken when counterfeit money is received.

RG 88: Food and Drug Administration (pre-1976, 4 items). Film of the effects of nuclear weapon residual radiation ("fallout") on various commodities; public service announcements on consumer fraud; and Betty Furness consumer announcements.

RG 90: Public Health Service (1924-77, 73 items). Films in a series entitled *Science of Life*, produced in 1924 and designed for use in the life sciences and personal hygiene instruction for young men and women. Films pertaining to the causes, treatment and control of malaria, syphilis, other communicable diseases and cancer (1924-50).

The *Distant Drummer* film series on drug abuse (1969) and films produced by the Emergency Health Services (1961-74).

RG 91: Inland Waterways Corporation (1932, 1 item). A film of the christening of the packet boat *Mark Twain* at Jeffersonville, Indiana, including film of an animated map of the inland waterways routes in the Mississippi River region from Minnesota and Lake Michigan to New Orleans.

RG 96: Farmers Home Administration (1936-37, 11 items). Documentaries produced by the Rural Settlement Administration and the Farm Security Administration under the direction of Pare Lorentz. The documentaries include *The Plow That Broke the Plains,* a film that illustrates the history of the Great Plains from the era of the open range through the coming of the "dirt farmer," the exploitation of the soil, and the drought and winds that stripped the topsoil from the area; and *The River,* a pictorial history of the role the Mississippi River played in the history of the United States from frontier days to the flood of 1937, emphasizing the erosion and floods that occur as a result of careless use of the land.

Miscellaneous films about migratory labor camps; agricultural and industrial cooperatives in Russia, England, Sweden, Finland and Scotland; and the construction of different types of houses and barns.

RG 100: Bureau of Labor Statistics (1938, 1 item). A film entitled *Stop Silicosis,* illustrating the causes and prevention of the disease.

RG 102: Children's Bureau (1919-26, 11 items). Films on prenatal, infant and child care and diseases.

RG 103: Farm Credit Administration (1936-37, 4 items). A film promoting the cooperative marketing of wool. Films of President Franklin D. Roosevelt at his desk in the White House, of Governor William I. Myers of the Farm Credit Administration in front of the FCA Building, and of several other buildings in Washington, D.C.

RG 104: Bureau of the Mint (1940, 1 item). A film dealing with minting coins and casting medals at the Philadelphia Mint.

RG 106: Smithsonian Institution (1903-49, 49 items). Films (1931-41) from Bureau of American Ethnology records illustrating the preparation of an anthropological exhibit at the Smithsonian and of the diggings and surrounding areas made in the course of archaeological explorations in New Mexico, Arizona, Tennessee, Colorado, Yucatan and Honduras. Films (ca. 1930) illustrating the making of a dictionary of intertribal sign language of the Great Plains Indians and depicting the theory, history and practice of their sign language.

Films (1929 and 1950) pertaining to the history of the planning and development of Washington, D.C.

Films pertaining to the history of flight (1903-27) and films (1927-32) of important events in the life of Charles A. Lindbergh, from his transatlantic flight to the kidnapping of the Lindbergh baby, and of a glider exhibition and contest.

RG 107: Office of the Secretary of War (1941-45, 191 items). Films from the Bureau of Public Relations documenting American military activities in all theaters of operation during World War II and activities of the Allied military governments in Europe and in the Far East. Some captured German films from the same period.

RG 111: Office of the Chief Signal Officer (1909-64, 22,437 items). Pre-World War I films concerning the development of flight, the construction of the Panama Canal (1910-14), President William Howard Taft on an inspection tour of the Canal (ca. 1912), and the Mexican Punitive Expedition (1916). Most of these are from the Historical (H) series.

Films of the World War I period depicting activities of the American Expeditionary Forces in France; homefront activities, such as mobilization and training and industrial production; U.S. Navy activities, submarine warfare and convoys carrying troops overseas; British, French, Russian and Italian participation in the war; the war in the Near East; peace celebrations in Paris and in America; and President Woodrow Wilson's two trips to France and the signing of the Treaty of Versailles. Most of these are from the H and Miscellaneous (M) series.

Films made between the wars relating to all phases of Regular Army, Army Reserves, ROTC, Citizens Military Training Corps, and West Point training, education, and maneuvers; Army activities in the territories and other countries; military medicine; ordnance manufacturing, testing and demonstrations; installing and maintaining communications systems; the history of flight, including Air Service activities, early parachute jumps and air races; civil projects of the Army, including river and harbor improvements and disaster relief; sports and recreation, including the Olympic games, national rifle matches and Army-Navy football games; and Army participation in parades and celebrations and in various funeral ceremonies, including the burial of the Unknown Soldier. Coverage of news events, such as Charles A. Lindbergh's transatlantic flight, President Franklin D. Roosevelt's first and second inaugurations, the *Hindenburg* disaster, and volcanic eruptions. These films are in the M series.

Films of the Second World War period relating to all aspects of the conflict, including the Allies and the Axis Powers and their conduct of the war in all theaters; the Italian invasion of Ethiopia (1935); the Spanish Civil War (1937); the Japanese invasion of China (1937); American homefront activities and war production; mobilization and training; the roles of women, Negroes, and Nisei in the war effort; entertainment for troops; the atom bomb; the end of the war; the Cairo, Teheran, Yalta, Quebec and San Francisco Conferences; Allied military governments in Germany and Japan; postwar problems in Europe and Asia; and war crimes trials in Germany and Japan. Films are from the M, Army Depository Copy (ADC), Training Films, Combat Reports, Engineering Board Film Digest, Educational Films, Film Bulletins, Historical Reports, Staff Film Reports, Orientation Films, Army-Navy Screen Magazine (SM), Special Bulletins, Team 21 and War Film series.

Films relating to the Korean action and covering all aspects of the conflict and the peace negotiations, drawn from the Combat Bulletins, ADC, Library Copy (LC), M and SM series.

Films of the inaugural ceremonies and parades of Presidents Harry S Truman (1949) and Dwight D. Eisenhower (1953) from the M series.

Films made by other government agencies, including the Navy Department, the Bureau of Mines and the War Relocation Authority. Films from private sources such as the Red Cross and newsreel companies, and films made in Germany, Japan, Italy, Finland, Great Britain, France, Russia and Canada.

There are 19 boxes of paper records for this group of films which include production files (1942-54) and training film digest sheets (1930-45).

RG 115: Bureau of Reclamation (1963, 1 item). *The Great River* documents the Columbia River system with its hydroelectric power, flood control and concern for fish and wildlife. Produced by the Bureau and the Bonneville Power Administration.

RG 116: Administrative Office of the U.S. Courts (1976, 4 items). *Equal Justice Under the Law* is a series of four one-hour dramatizations produced for television as part of the Courts' observance of the Bicentennial. They feature the historic decisions in *Aaron Burr, Marbury v. Madison, McCulloch v. Maryland* and *Gibbons v. Ogden.*

RG 117: American Battle Monuments Commission (1937, 8 items). A motion picture entitled *America Honors Her War Dead,* showing excerpts from dedication ceremonies of American war memorials and chapels in Europe (August and October 1937).

RG 119: National Youth Administration (1937-42, 56 items). Motion pictures illustrating the functions of the Adminstration, including the work and student programs, recreational activities, programs for Negroes and activities at resident centers; and dramatizations of the problems of unemployed youth and NYA assistance given them.

Two films made by NYA personnel: the visit of King George VI and Princess Elizabeth of England to Washington (1939), and the inauguration of President Franklin D. Roosevelt (1941).

RG 121: Public Buildings Service (1940-43, 2 items). Films of President Franklin D. Roosevelt speaking at the dedication of Washington National Airport (1940); and of the site clearance and construction of the War Department Building (the Pentagon) (1940-43).

RG 126: Office of Territories (1939-41, 97 items). Films covering all aspects of the Byrd Antarctic expedition (1939-41).

RG 127: United States Marine Corps (1914-78, 2,934 items). Training films used during World War II and films of combat in the South Pacific. Unedited footage shot by Marine Corps units in wars and conflicts ranging from World War I to Vietnam, with some footage of Marine Corps activities in the Caribbean. Includes Marine Corps aviation, amphibious landings and significant military leaders.

The Marine Corps Film Depository collection, formerly located at Quantico Marine Base in Quantico, Virginia, has become three collections: this one at the National Archives; another at the Motion Media Records Center, Norton Air Force Base in California [q.v.]; and a small collection at Quantico. Note: Other footage shot by Marine Corps units can be found in RG 428.

RG 128: Joint Committees of Congress (1965-81, 3 items). Films of the inaugurations of Presidents Lyndon B. Johnson (1965) and Richard M. Nixon (1969); and videotape of the inaugural address and ceremonies for President Ronald Reagan (1981), made under the direction and authority of the Joint Congressional Committee on Inaugural Ceremonies.

RG 129: Bureau of Prisons (undated, 1 item). A film entitled *Protecting the Public.*

RG 130: White House Office (ca. 1923-32, 5 items). Films relating to the informal activities of President Calvin Coolidge (ca. 1923-29), and activities of President Herbert C. Hoover (1929-32), including a fishing trip Hoover made and his plea to the nation for relief aid. Films of the 1932 Republican National Convention.

RG 131: Office of Alien Property (1930s, 56 items). Films from the records of the Hamburg-American Line — North German Lloyd concerning travel in Germany and other countries. Films collected or created by the German-American Vocational League, an organization of German immigrants in the U.S., affiliated with the state-run union in Nazi Germany. These films were seized from the group's national headquarters in 1942. The collection includes footage of Hitler; summer youth camp activities in Offenberg, Germany; Camp Bergwald in the Catskill Mountains, New York; and a youth vacation camp in St. Louis, Missouri. Japanese dramas from the records of Haruta & Co., Inc.

RG 142: Tennessee Valley Authority (1940, 2 items). *Spirit of the West* reviews the history of the TVA and illustrates the dramatic improvements brought about by the massive hydroelectric power and flood control project.

RG 145: Agricultural Stabilization and Conservation Service (1941, 5 items). A film entitled *The Land,* directed and photographed by Robert Flaherty for the Agricultural Adjustment Administration, concerned with the reclamation and conservation of farmland exhausted or eroded by poor agricultural practices.

RG 146: United States Civil Service Commission (1921-68, 34 items). A film illustrating the career possibilities offered by the merit system. Films of Commission conferences and events, documentaries and television programs.

RG 147: Selective Service System (1940-69, 4 items). Films of Gen. Lewis B. Hershey and the 1969 draft lottery.

RG 149: Government Printing Office (1930s, 3 items). Early films from the GPO explain the free distribution of government publications; *Bound to Last* documents the process of bookbinding used by the GPO.

RG 151: Foreign and Domestic Commerce and Successor Agencies (1974, 1 item). An IMAX film, *Man Belongs to the Earth,* about the need for protecting the environment. The film was prepared for the Expo 1974 World's Fair in Spokane, Washington.

RG 153: Office of the Judge Advocate General (Army) (undated, 1 item).

Rome March, presented in the case of *U.S. v. Kurt Maelzer (Lt. General).*

RG 170: Bureau of Narcotics and Dangerous Drugs (1928-37, 14 items). Films relating to drug traffic and the enforcement of narcotics laws in Egypt, China and the United States. A British instructional film on the cultivation of the poppy plant.

RG 171: Office of Civilian Defense (1941-45, 57 items). Films used in training civilian defense workers in mobilization, rescue, firefighting and prevention, child care, defense against poison gas attacks, smoke concealment, air raid defense operations and defense equipment and its use. Films of London under aerial attack. Films promoting victory gardens and food conservation.

RG 173: Federal Communications Commission (1930, 1 item). Promotional film about radio station WIBO in Chicago showing its history (1925-30), facilities and program segments.

RG 174: Department of Labor (1940-68, 100 items). Films the Labor Department made or collected relating to its history and its activities in areas such as discrimination in hiring, employment for youth and the elderly, enforcement of labor legislation and regulations, civil rights and foreign trade (1940-68).

Television documentaries, interviews and panel discussions (1960-68) aired by American Broadcasting Company (ABC) news. Columbia Broadcasting System (CBS) programs *Face the Nation* and *Washington Conversation*, National Broadcasting Company (NBC) programs *Today Show* and *Meet the Press*, and National Educational Television (NET) programs. The documentaries include *Harvest of Shame* (1960), a CBS documentary about the living conditions of migrant workers in the United States; *A View from the Cabinet*, featuring some of President John F. Kennedy's Cabinet members and President Lyndon B. Johnson discussing the Kennedy administration; and other films that present the Secretaries of Labor, other Cabinet members, the Vice Presidents and various Congressmen and labor leaders discussing labor and economic conditions and the labor policies of the Kennedy and Johnson administrations.

Television spot announcements in support of Labor Department policies, featuring such persons as Secretaries of Labor Willard Wirtz and Arthur Goldberg, and Vice President Hubert H. Humphrey.

RG 178: United States Maritime Commission (1924-45, 75 items). Films depicting the history of the merchant marine from Revolutionary times through World War II, including its activities during the Revolutionary War, the War of 1812, and the Civil War; peacetime shipping and passenger service on the Great Lakes and at sea; rescue work; and convoy duties in all theaters of operation during World War II.

Films illustrating recruiting, training, and other activities of the Maritime Commission at training schools and stations, at a convalescent center, and aboard sailing vessels and steamships (1938-44).

Films concerning the manufacture of all types of merchant vessels during World War II; and of President Franklin D. Roosevelt, Henry J. Kaiser, the Dionne quintuplets and others participating in ship launchings. Films illustrating the principles of the steam turbine engine; relating to the repair and renovation of ships for the Victory Fleet; and showing the manufacture of World War II materiel, including train axles and wheels, B-24 bombers and tanks.

Miscellaneous films of Richard E. Byrd and Clarence Chamberlin participating in an early airmail flight from the deck of a ship (1928); of the work of the Coast Guard in keeping shipping lanes open and safe (1929); and of British coastal fortifications (1940).

RG 179: War Production Board (1940-44, 15 items). Films produced to stimulate war production concerning the conduct of the war in several theaters. Films of Allied and Axis military and political leaders; films about the manufacture and transportation of war materiel and how war materiel is damaged and repaired.

Instructional films on good telephone manners.

RG 182: *War Trade Board* (ca. 1919, 1 item). A film of Board employees and of the War Trade Board building, with a large number of employees in front of the building.

RG 185: *Panama Canal* (1956-79, 30 items). Unedited footage produced and acquired by the Panama Canal Commission, including visits by Latin American presidents (1956); 1959 and 1964 riots; student demonstrations (1976-77); the 1968 inauguration of Arnulfo Aria as president of Panama; and the 1978 visit to Panama of President Jimmy Carter, Vice-President Walter Mondale and United Nations diplomats.

RG 188: *Office of Price Administration* (1943-46, 15 items). Films created to enlist the cooperation of the public in OPA programs, concerning the necessity for price controls and rationing both during and immediately following World War II, explaining the role of the consumer in enforcing regulations, and warning against participation in the black market because of the inflationary results.

RG 200: National Archives Gift Collection (1896-present, 56,539 items).
Newsreels (1919-67). Chiefly unbroken series of *Paramount News* (October 1941-March 1957); *Fox Movietone News* (January 1957-October 1963); *News of the Day* (October 1963-December 1967); and *Universal Newsreels*, both releases and outtakes (1919-48 and 1950-67).

A 1977 fire in the National Archives nitrate film vaults destroyed 75% (approximately 12.6 million feet) of the outtakes from *Universal Newsreels* from the 1930s and 1940s. A listing of nitrate-era outtakes that survived and were subsequently copied onto safety film is available in the research room. The safety-era outtakes (1951-67) were unaffected by the fire, but about 40% have been disposed of because they lacked sufficient research value. In 1981, 760,000 feet of outtakes from *Universal Newsreels*, all "Canadian locals" (material shot in Canada and intended for distribution in that country) were transferred to the National Archives of Canada, Moving Image and Sound Archives (q.v.).

In an economy measure, Universal unfortunately disposed of many separate music and narrative soundtracks before donating the library to the National Archives. Hence there is relatively little sound prior to 1957. The extant sound for the period 1929-56 consists mostly of lip-synchronized speeches or interviews. Fortunately, the narrative tracks are complete for the last ten years (1957-67) and the script files which contain the written commentaries are also complete.

The Library of Congress has many *Universal Newsreel* issues (1943-67). Since they are copyright deposit prints, they may only be copied and sold with the written permission of MCA-Universal Pictures, Inc.

Universal Newsreel releases and outtakes are in the public domain, although additional clearances may be necessary in order to reuse items containing certain personalities, performances or sports events. The donor, MCA-Universal Pictures, Inc., placed no restrictions on the use of the *Universal Newsreel* library given to the National Archives. However, neither the donor nor the National Archives guarantees the public domain status of sound or pictorial elements in the *Universal Newsreel* library, and it may therefore be necessary to obtain permission from owners of underlying rights before any commercial use or other use is made. (The National Football League, for example, has advised the National Archives of its rights to Universal's coverage of football games sponsored by the NFL.)

Newsreels produced by Movietone, Pathé, Fox, International, Paramount and Telenews covering selected news items, including the Big Four at the Paris Peace Conference (1919); the Navy's transatlantic flight from the Azores to Lisbon (1919); activities of Presidents Calvin Coolidge, Franklin D. Roosevelt, Harry S Truman and Dwight D. Eisenhower; the 1924 Republican National Convention; events leading to and occurring during World War II; and the 1959 swearing-in ceremonies of the first Senators from Alaska and the first Congressmen from Hawaii.

Changes in the newsreel collections include the addition of *Telepix Television Newsreels* (1948-53), which have a New York City orientation but include many national and world events. *Telepix* was the first newsreel made for television, and this collection shows the evolution of television news style as well as filling a gap in the National Archives newsreel collection. Other additions include a 1940 *News of the Day* on Wendell Willkie; a 1918 Hearst-Pathé Newsreel; six issues of Universal-International Newsreels (1920-21); and a short composite film of newsreel clips (1895-1975).

The March of Time (1935-51). These include documentary films relating to U.S. history, culture, social problems, science, education, mental health and international problems; to government agencies, such as the FBI, the Secret Service and the Post Office Department; to wartime and postwar activities of private institutions, such as the American Red Cross; and to the effect of World War II on one small American town. This monthly series, shown in movie theaters, differed from the newsreels in that it explored social issues. The releases used both actuality footage and staged sequences. *Time, Inc. retains copyright ownership of all edited stories. Therefore, requests for reproduction and sale of edited stories must be accompanied by the written authorization of SFM Media (q.v.), the agent for Time, Inc.*

The March of Time Stock Film Library (1935-51). 15,000 reels of unedited footage relating to the subjects listed above. In 1987, videotape viewing copies were added to the collection and the elaborate card file was made available on microfilm. All material in the Stock Film Library is in the public domain.

205 issues of the *March of Time* were produced between 1935 and 1951. Each issue was released once a month (to as many as 9,800 U.S. theaters) and ran approximately 20 minutes. Between February 1935 and May 1938, each issue was comprised of several "stories." After May 1938, each issue covered only one subject; in all, 290 subjects were produced. Though both the *March of Time* and the commercial newsreels presented events that had been staged or recreated for the camera, the *March of Time* acknowledged this while the newsreels did not. Many *March of Time* stories employ celebrity impersonators

to substitute for unavailable footage.

For a definitive history, see Raymond Fielding, *The March of Time, 1935-1951*, New York: Oxford University Press, 1958.

Following is a list of *March of Time* releases and subjects:

Vol. 1:1 (Feb. 1, 1935): *Saionji* (Premier of Japan), *Speakeasy Street; Belisha Beacons; Buchsbaum; Fred Perkins* (constitutionality of NRA); *Metropolitan Opera.*

Vol. 1:2 (March 8, 1935): *Germany; New York Daily News; Speed Camera; Mohawk Disaster; Leadbelly.*

Vol. 1:3 (April 19, 1935): *Trans-Pacific; Munitions; Huey Long; Mexico.*

Vol. 1:4 (May 31, 1935): *Navy War Games; Russia; Washington News.*

Vol. 1:5 (Aug. 16, 1935): *Army; Father Coughlin; Croix de Feu.*

Vol. 1:6 (Sept. 20, 1935): *Ethiopia; Bootleg Coal; CCC.*

Vol. 1:7 (Oct. 18, 1935): *Palestine; Neutrality; Summer Theaters; Safety.*

Vol. 1:8 (Nov. 13, 1935): *G.O.P.; Wild Ducks; Strikebreaking.*

Vol. 1:9 (Dec. 13, 1935): *Japan-China; Narcotics; Townsend Plan.*

Vol. 2:1 (Jan. 7, 1936): *Pacific Islands; TVA; Diebler* (France's official executioner).

Vol. 2:2 (Feb. 14, 1936): *Moscow, Hartman Discovery, Father Divine.*

Vol. 2:3 (March 13, 1936): *Tokyo, Japan; Devil's Island; Fisheries.*

Vol. 2:4 (April 17, 1936): *Veterans of Future Wars; Arson Squads in Action; Florida Canal; Field Trials* (dogs).

Vol. 2:5 (May 15, 1936): *League of Nations Union; Railroads, Relief.*

Vol. 2:6 (June 12, 1936): *Otto of Hapsburg; Texas Centennial; Crime School.*

Vol. 2:7 (July 10, 1936): *Revolt in France; An American Dictator* (Trujillo); *Jockey Club.*

Vol. 2:8 (Aug. 7, 1936): *Albania's King Zog; Highway Homes* (trailers and trailer camps); *King Cotton's Slaves.*

Vol. 3:1 (Sept. 2, 1936): *The "Lunatic Fringe"* (Gerald L. K. Smith, Dr. Francis Townsend, Reverend Charles E. Coughlin); *Passamaquoddy; U.S. Milky Way.*

Vol. 3:2 (Sept. 30, 1936): *Labor Versus Labor* (CIO); *England's Tithe War; The Football Business.*

Vol. 3:3 (Nov. 6, 1936): *The Presidency; New Schools for Old.*

Vol. 3:4 (Nov. 27, 1936): *A Soldier-King's Son* (Belgium's King Leopold); *St. Lawrence Seaway; "An Uncle Sam Production"* (the Federal Theatre).

Vol. 3:5 (Dec. 24, 1936): *China's Dictator Kidnaped; Business Girls in the Big City.*

Vol. 3:6 (Jan. 22, 1937): *Conquering Cancer; Mormonism — 1937; Midwinter Vacations.*

Vol. 3:7 (Feb. 19, 1937): *Father of All Turks* (Mustapha Kemal); *Birth of Swing; Enemies of Alcohol* (WCTU).

Vol. 3:8 (March 19, 1937): *Child Labor; Coronation Crisis; Harlem's Black Magic.*

Vol. 3:9 (April 16, 1937): *Britain's Food Defenses; The Supreme Court; Amateur Sleuths.*

Vol. 3:10 (May 14, 1937): *Irish Republic — 1937; U.S. Unemployment* (Workers' Alliance); *Puzzle Prizes.*

Vol. 3:11 (June 11, 1937): *Poland and War; Dust Bowl; Dogs for Sale.*

Vol. 3:12 (July 9, 1937): *The 49th State* (Hawaii); *Babies Wanted; Rockefeller Millions* (Rockefeller Center).

Vol. 3:13 (Aug. 6, 1937): *Rehearsal for War* (Spanish Civil War); *The Spoils System; Youth in Camps.*

Vol. 4:1 (Sept. 10, 1937): *War in China; Pests of 1937* (insects).

Vol. 4:2 (Oct. 1, 1937): *Junk and War; England's D.O.R.A.* (Defense of the Realm Act); *Fiorello LaGuardia.*

Vol. 4:3 (Oct. 29, 1937): *Crisis in Algeria; "Amoskeag" — Success Story* (recovery of cotton mill); *U.S. Secret Service.*

Vol. 4:4 (Nov. 26, 1937): *Alaska's Salmon War; Britain's Gambling Fever; The Human Heart.*

Vol. 4:5 (Dec. 23, 1937): *Finland's 20th Birthday; The Laugh Industry* (radio comedians); *Ships-Strikes-Seamen.*

Vol. 4:6 (Jan. 21, 1938): *Inside Nazi Germany — 1938.*

Vol. 4:7 (Feb. 18, 1938): *Russians in Exile; Old Dixie's New Bloom; One Million Missing.*

Vol. 4:8 (March 18, 1938): *Arms and the League; Brain Trust Island.*

Vol. 4:9 (April 15, 1938): *Nazi Conquest — No. 1; Crime and Prisons.*

Vol. 4:10 (May 13, 1938): *England's Bankrupt Peers; Racketeers vs. Housewives; "Friend of the People"* (a typical U.S. Congressman).

Vol. 4:11 (June 10, 1938): *Men of Medicine.*

Vol. 4:12 (July 8, 1938): *G-Men of the Sea* (U.S. Coast Guard).

Vol. 4:13 (Aug. 6, 1938): *Threat to Gibraltar, Man at the Wheel* (auto accident reduction).

Vol. 5:1 (Sept. 2, 1938): *Prelude to Conquest* (Hitler and Czechoslovakia); *Father Divine's Deal.*

Vol. 5:2 (Sept. 30, 1938): *The British Dilemma; U.S. Fire Fighters.*

Vol. 5:3 (Oct. 28, 1938): *Inside the Maginot Line.*

Vol. 5:4 (Nov. 25, 1938): *Uncle Sam: The Good Neighbor.*

Vol. 5:5 (Dec. 23, 1938): *The Refugee — Today and Tomorrow.*

Vol. 5:6 (Jan. 20, 1939): *State of the Nation — 1939.*

Vol. 5:7 (Feb. 1939): *Mexico's New Crisis; Young America* (Boy Scouts).

Vol. 5:8 (March 1939): *The Mediterranean — Background for War.*

Vol. 5:9 (April 1939): *Japan — Master of the Orient.*

Vol. 5:10 (May 1939): *Dixie — U.S.A.*

Vol. 5:11 (June 1939): *War, Peace & Propaganda.*

Vol. 5:12 (July 1939): *The Movies March On!*

Vol. 5:13 (Aug. 1939): *Metropolis — 1939* (New York city police).

Vol. 6:1 (Sept. 1939): *Soldiers With Wings* (U.S. Air Force).

Vol. 6:2 (Sept. 1939): *Battle Fleets of England.*

Vol. 6:3 (Oct. 1939): *Uncle Sam — The Farmer.*

Vol. 6:4 (Nov. 1939): *Newsfronts of War — 1940.*

Vol. 6:5 (Dec. 1939): *Crisis in the Pacific.*

Vol. 6:6 (Jan. 1940): *The Republic of Finland.*

Vol. 6:7 (Feb. 1940): *The Vatican of Pius XII.*

Vol. 6:8 (March 1940): *Canada At War.*

Vol. 6:9 (April 1940): *America's Youth — 1940.*

Vol. 6:10 (May 1940): *The Philippines: 1898-1946.*

Vol. 6:11 (June 1940): *The U.S. Navy — 1940.*

Full-length feature (July 1940): *The Ramparts We Watch* (story of U.S. growth and development from 1914 until 1918 when she emerged as a world power).

Vol. 6:12 (Aug. 1940): *Spoils of Conquest* (Dutch East Indies).

Vol. 6:13 (Aug. 1940): *Gateways to Panama.*

Vol. 7:1 (Sept. 1940): *On Foreign Newsfronts.*

Vol. 7:2 (Oct. 1940): *Britain's R.A.F.*

Vol. 7:3 (Oct. 1940): *Mexico — Good Neighbor's Dilemma.*

Vol. 7:4 (Nov. 1940): *Arms And The Men — U.S.A.*

Vol. 7:5 (Dec. 1940): *Labor and Defense.*

Vol. 7:6 (Jan. 1941): *Uncle Sam — The Non-Belligerent.*

Vol. 7:7 (Feb. 1941): *Americans All* (immigrants).

Vol. 7:8 (Mar. 1941): *Australia At War.*

Vol. 7:9 (April 1941): *Men of the F.B.I. — 1941.*

Vol. 7:10 (May 1941): *Crisis in the Atlantic.*

Vol. 7:11 (June 1941): *China Fights Back.*

Vol. 7:12 (July 1941): *New England's Eight Million Yankees.*

Vol. 7:13 (Aug. 1941): *Peace — By Adolf Hitler.*

Vol. 7 (Special Feature) (Aug. 1941): *The Story of the Vatican.*

Vol. 8:1 (Aug. 1941): *Thumbs Up, Texas!*

Vol. 8:2 (Sept. 1941): *Norway in Revolt.*

Vol. 8:3 (Oct. 1941): *Sailors With Wings* (U.S. Naval Air Force).

Vol. 8:4 (Nov. 1941): *Main Street — U.S.A.*

Vol. 8 (Special Issue) (Dec. 1941): *Battlefields of the Pacific.*

Vol. 8:5 (Dec. 1941): *Our America At War.*

Vol. 8:6 (Jan. 1942): *When Air Raids Strike.*

Vol. 8:7 (Feb. 1942): *Far East Command.*

Vol. 8:8 (March 1942): *The Argentine Question.*

Vol. 8:9 (April 1942): *America's New Army.*

Vol. 8:10 (May 1942): *India In Crisis.*

Vol. 8:11 (June 1942): *India At War.*

Vol. 8:12 (July 1942): *Men in Washington — 1942.*

Vol. 8:13 (July 1942): *Men of the Fleet* (U.S. Navy).

Vol. 9:1 (Sept. 1942): *The F.B.I. Front* (war against sabotage).

Vol. 9:2 (Oct. 1942): *The Fighting French.*

Vol. 9:3 (Nov. 1942): *Mr. and Mrs. America* (homefront).

Vol. 9:4 (Dec. 1942): *Prelude to Victory* (invasion of North Africa).

Vol. 9 (full-length feature) (Dec. 1942): *We Are the Marines.*

Vol. 9:5 (Dec. 1942): *The Navy and the Nation.*

Vol. 9:6 (Jan. 1943): *One Day of War — Russia, 1943.*

Vol. 9:7 (Feb. 1943): *The New Canada.*

Vol. 9:8 (March 1943): *America's Food Crisis.*

Vol. 9:9 (April 1943): *Inside Fascist Spain.*

Vol. 9:10 (May 1943): *Show Business At War.*

Vol. 9:11 (June 1943): *Invasion!* (preparation for U.S. invasion of Europe).

Vol. 9:12 (July 1943): *Bill Jack vs. Adolph Hitler!* (war production).

Vol. 9:13 (Aug. 1943): *...And Then Japan!*

Vol. 10:1 (Sept. 1943): *Airways to Peace* (U.S. Air Transport Command).

Vol. 10:2 (Oct. 1943): *Portugal — Europe's Crossroads.*

Vol. 10:3 (Nov. 1943): *Youth in Crisis.*

Vol. 10:4 (Dec. 1943): *Naval Log of Victory.*

Vol. 10:5 (Dec. 1943): *Upbeat in Music* (talent entertains troops).

Vol. 10:6 (Jan. 1944): *Sweden's Middle Road.*

Vol. 10:7 (Feb. 1944): *Post-War Jobs?*

Vol. 10:8 (March 1944): *South American Front.*
Vol. 10:9 (April 1944): *The Irish Question.*
Vol. 10:10 (May 1944): *Underground Report* (European resistance).
Vol. 10:11 (June 1944): *Back Door To Tokyo* (Stilwell's jungle march).
Vol. 10:12 (July 1944): *Americans All* (racial tolerance).
Vol. 10:13 (Aug. 1944): *British Imperialism — 1944.*
Vol. 11:1 (Sept. 1944): *Post-War Farms.*
Vol. 11:2 (Oct. 1944): *What to Do with Germany.*
Vol. 11:3 (Nov. 1944): *Uncle Sam, Mariner?*
Vol. 11:4 (Dec. 1944): *Inside China Today*
Vol. 11:5 (Dec. 1944): *The Unknown Battle* (8th & 15th U.S. Air Forces).
Vol. 11:6 (Jan. 1945): *Report of Italy.*
Vol. 11:7 (Feb. 1945): *The West Coast Question* (future of U.S. Pacific Coast region).
Vol. 11:8 (March 1945): *Memo from Britain.*
Vol. 11:9 (April 1945): *The Returning Veteran.*
Vol. 11:10 (May 1945): *Spotlight on Congress.*
Vol. 11:11 (June 15, 1945): *Teenage Girls.*
Vol. 11:12 (July 13, 1945): *Where's the Meat.*
Vol. 11:13 (Aug. 10, 1945): *The New U.S. Frontier* (U.S. in Guam).
Vol. 12:1 (Sept. 17, 1945): *Palestine Problem.*
Vol. 12:2 (Oct. 5, 1945): *American Beauty.*
Vol. 12:3 (Nov. 2, 1945): *18 Million Orphans* (MacArthur's Philippines).
Vol. 12:4 (Nov. 30, 1945): *Justice Comes to Germany.*
Vol. 12:5 (Dec. 28, 1945): *Challenge to Hollywood* (British film boom).
Vol. 12:6 (Jan. 25, 1946): *Life With Baby* (Dr. Arnold Gesell's experiments).
Vol. 12:7 (Feb. 22, 1946): *Report on Greece.*
Vol. 12:8 (March 22, 1946): *Night Club Boom.*
Vol. 12:9 (April 19, 1946): *Wanted — More Homes.*
Vol. 12:10 (May 17, 1946): *Tomorrow's Mexico.*
Vol. 12:11 (June 14, 1946): *Problem Drinkers.*
Vol. 12:12 (July 12, 1946): *The New France.*
Vol. 12:13 (August 9, 1946): *Atomic Power* (reenactment of A-bomb development in which actual scientists play their own roles).
Vol. 13:1 (Sept. 7, 1946): *Is Everybody Happy?*
Vol. 13:2 (Oct. 4, 1946): *World Food Problem.*
Vol. 13:3 (Nov. 1, 1946): *The Soviets' Neighbor — Czechoslovakia.*
Vol. 13:4 (Nov. 29, 1946): *The American Cop.*
Vol. 13:5 (Dec. 27, 1946): *Nobody's Children?* (adoption).
Vol. 13:6 (Jan. 24, 1947): *Germany — Handle With Care!*
Vol. 13:7 (Feb. 21, 1947): *Fashion Means Business!*
Vol. 13:8 (March 21, 1947): *The Teachers' Crisis.*
Vol. 13:9 (April 18, 1947): *Storm Over Britain.*
Vol. 13:10 (May 16, 1947): *The Russians Nobody Knows.*
Vol. 13:11 (June 13, 1947): *Your Doctors — 1947.*
Vol. 13:12 (July 11, 1947): *New Trains for Old.*
Vol. 13:13 (Aug. 8, 1947): *Turkey's 100 Million.*
Vol. 14:1 (Sept. 6, 1947): *Is Everybody Listening?* (radio entertainment).
Vol. 14:2 (Oct. 3, 1947): *T-Men In Action* (U.S. Treasury enforcement agents).
Vol. 14:3 (Oct. 31, 1947): *End of an Empire?* (Indonesia).
Vol. 14:4 (Nov. 28, 1947): *Public Relations...This Means You.*
Vol. 14:5 (Dec. 26, 1947): *The Presidential Year.*
Vol. 14:6 (Jan. 23, 1948): *The Cold War: Act I — France.*
Vol. 14:7 (Feb. 20, 1948): *Marriage and Divorce.*
Vol. 14:8 (Mar. 19, 1948): *Crisis in Italy (Act II: The Cold War).*
Vol. 14:9 (April 16, 1948): *Life With Junior.*
Vol. 14:10 (May 14, 1948): *Battle for Greece (Act III: The Cold War.*
Vol. 14:11 (June 11, 1948): *The Fight Game* (boxing).
Vol. 14:12 (July 9, 1948): *The Case of Mrs. Conrad* (comfort of modern surgery).
Vol. 14:13 (Aug. 6, 1948): *White Collar Girls.*
Vol. 14:14 (Sept. 3, 1948): *Life With Grandpa.*
Vol. 14:15 (Oct. 1, 1948): *Battle for Germany.*
Vol. 14:16 (Oct. 29, 1948): *America's New Air Power.*
Vol. 14:17 (Nov. 26, 1948): *Answer to Stalin.*
Vol. 14:18 (Dec. 24, 1948): *Watchdogs of the Mail* (U.S. Postal Inspectors).
Vol. 15:1 (Jan. 21, 1949): *On Stage* (New York theater).
Vol. 15:2 (Feb. 18, 1949): *Asia's New Voice* (India and Prime Minister Nehru).
Vol. 15:3 (March 18, 1949): *Wish You Were Here* (vacations).
Vol. 15:4 (April 15, 1949): *Report on the Atom.*
Vol. 15:5 (May 13, 1949): *Sweden Looks Ahead.*
Vol. 15:6 (June 10, 1949): *It's In the Groove* (recording industry).
Vol. 15:7 (July 8, 1949): *Stop — Heavy Traffic!*
Vol. 15:8 (Aug. 5, 1949): *Farming Pays Off.*
Vol. 15:9 (Sept. 2, 1949): *Policeman's Holiday* (Scotland Yard).

Vol. 15:10 (Sept. 30, 1949): *The Fight for Better Schools.*
Vol. 15:11 (Nov. 11, 1949): *MacArthur's Japan.*
Vol. 15:12 (Dec. 23, 1949): *A Chance to Live* (Italian Boys' Republic).
Vol. 16:1 (Feb. 3, 1950): *Mid-Century: Half Way to Where?*
Vol. 16:2 (March 17, 1950): *The Male Look* (fashions).
Vol. 16:3 (April 28, 1950): *Where's the Fire?* (N.J. volunteer fire department).
Vol. 16:4 (June 9, 1950): *Beauty at Work* (18-year-old New York City model).
Vol. 16:5 (Aug. 18, 1950): *As Russia Sees It.*
Vol. 16:6 (Sept. 29, 1950): *The Gathering Storm* (U.S. defense preparedness).
Vol. 16:7 (Nov. 10, 1950): *Schools March On!*
Vol. 16:8 (Dec. 1950): *Tito — New Ally?*
Vol. 17:1 (Feb. 1951): *Strategy for Victory* (Mutual Defense Assistance Program).
Vol. 17:2 (March 1951): *Flight Plan for Freedom* (Curtis LeMay and SAC).
Vol. 17:3 (April 1951): *The Nation's Mental Health.*
Vol. 17:4 (June 1951): *Moroccan Outpost.*
Vol. 17:5 (July 1951): *Crisis in Iran.*
Vol. 17:6 (Aug. 1951): *Formosa — Island of Promise.*

World War I films (1917-19). Films made behind German lines by Jacob Berkowitz; the *Official War Review* series on land and air battles, maneuvers and training, distributed by the Films Division of the U.S. Committee on Public Information; the National Aeronautics Committee's film on the celebration at Hollywood, California, of Air Memorial Day (1919); a documentary on World War I, produced in 1956 by the National Broadcasting Company and entitled *The Great War;* and a large quantity of footage collected by the Columbia Broadcasting System from sources all over the world in producing the documentary entitled *World War I.* A recent addition is a 1918 film on the training of soldiers, produced by the Committee on Public Information (George Creel, chairman).

World War II films (1940-45). Films produced by Warner Brothers, Paramount Pictures, Inc. and Columbia Pictures Corp., under the technical supervision of the armed services, and several films distributed by the War Activities Committee of the Motion Picture Industry. The films concern activities of the Army Air Corps, the Navy, the Marine Corps and the Coast Guard, including officer training programs and homefront aspects of the war effort. Also documentaries compiled from newsreels, one on events leading up to the war entitled *The World in Flames,* and another by Paramount, concerning resettlement of Jewish refugees in the Dominican Republic; a re-release by the National Film Board of Canada of a World War I Charlie Chaplin film promoting the sale of war bonds; pictures of German air raids on London, presented to the National Archives by the British Library of Information; a Finnish Relief Fund film about the Russo-Finnish war; films relating to the training of Dutch troops in exile and to the liberation of Greece; a collection of German newsreels covering the early stages of the war, presented to the National Archives by Lt. William F. Rope; and an Army Air Forces film of the ceremonies attending the placing of the German surrender documents on exhibit in the National Archives.

Additions include *The Negro Soldier,* produced by the Army; *You, John Jones,* produced by the War Activities Committee of the Motion Picture Industry; *Which Way This Time,* produced by the Office of Price Administration; an RKO-Pathé film, *Here Come the Yanks;* a NOVA program on Hitler's secret weapons (rockets); outtakes from films on the dropping of the atomic bomb and the surrender of Japan; and films which used materials from the National Archives Collection about German rocketry and the destruction of Dresden.

Ford collection (1914-56). 1,500 reels. The *Ford Animated Weekly* (1914-21), consisting of short news features, films about cities and general interest films; the *Ford Educational Weekly* and the *Ford Educational Library* (1916-25), consisting of short features and unedited film on agriculture, civics and citizenship, industrial geography, regional geography, history, nature study, recreation and sports, sanitation and health and technical subjects; the *Ford News,* a series of newsreels shown at Detroit area theaters during 1934; and films on agriculture and conservation, charities, education, geography, sports and recreation and presenting dramas and news. Films of the informal activities of the Ford family and family's philanthropies and films relating to personal projects of Henry Ford, including the *Dearborn Independent* newspaper, the Ford farm and the Henry Ford Museum and Greenfield Village. Films illustrating the activities of the Ford Motor Company, including activities of domestic and foreign branches (1928-54); nonmanufacturing activities (1914-54), and plants and the major manufacturing activities (1906-56); and war-related activities during both World Wars and the Korean action. Also several films made by producers other than the Ford Motion Picture Laboratories and not produced for the Ford Motor Company, including advertisements for companies other than Ford, newsreels, personal films, propaganda films, public service features, technical features and travelogues.

Harmon collection (1930-51). 1,400 reels. Films produced by the Harmon Foundation on many aspects of the history and accomplishments of minority cultures in the United States and on the cultures of Asia, Africa and other developing areas.

League of Nations collection (1920-46). 56 reels. This collection was presented to the National Archives by the United Nations. It consists of films of the first and last meetings of the League; of meetings and activities concerning such problems as the Greco-Bulgar incident (1925), the Sino-Japanese conflict (1932) and the Italo-Ethiopian conflict (1936); of health and disarmament conferences; and of League delegates and officials.

Washington Debates of the Seventies (1970-73). 40 reels. Filmed recordings of televised discussions and seminars relating to public affairs, including U.S. policy in the Middle East, the role of Congress in foreign policy, the Presidency, consumer protection, national health insurance, social security, defense, civil disobedience, tax reforms, Vietnam and the "Nixon Doctrine." Sponsored by the American Enterprise Institute.

National Councils of Churches (1970-72). 26 reels. Discussions and interviews with writers, theologians, scientists and public leaders about peace, violence, racism, justice and other issues that affect the moral life of the nation.

AFL-CIO collection (1952-71). 32 reels. A gift of the AFL-CIO, this collection includes films about public issues affecting the American worker. The films were produced or acquired by the AFL-CIO and used in its educational library loan service.

Other educational and documentary films (1915-76). A series by Eastman Teaching Films, Inc. (1927-35) on history, geography, industry, conservation, recreation, agriculture and sports; two series produced by Warner Brothers Pictures, Inc. (1934-35), entitled *See America First* and *Our Own United States,* concerning U.S. history, industry, occupations, recreation, scenery and ethnic groups; a series, *The Washington Parade,* by Columbia Pictures, Inc., on scenes and activities of various federal agencies, chiefly at Washington, D.C.; and a Columbia Broadcasting System series, *Eyewitness to History* (1959-60), with pictorial summaries of President Dwight D. Eisenhower's trips abroad, Nikita Khrushchev's visits to the United States in 1959 and to France in 1960, and Charles de Gaulle's visit to the United States in 1960; and a television series, *Longines Chronoscope,* on public affairs, with interviews and discussions (1951-55).

Also documentaries, dramas, television news specials and stock footage received from individuals, motion picture companies and other organizations. These films are on American history; political parties; the administrations of Presidents Calvin Coolidge, Franklin D. Roosevelt, Dwight D. Eisenhower and John F. Kennedy; the 1959 funeral services for John Foster Dulles and Adm. William F. Halsey; the development of motion picture equipment, radio broadcasting, the telephone, aviation, atomic energy and space flight from Robert H. Goddard's experiments (1920s-30s) to Col. John H. Glenn's orbital flight (1962); Donald McMillan's expedition to Greenland (1925); Sir Ernest Shackleton's 1922 Antarctic expedition, Adm. Richard E. Byrd's 1927 transatlantic flight and his Antarctic expeditions (1926, 1928-30, 1933 and 1947-48), and Lincoln Ellsworth's 1936 Antarctic expedition; a 1915 Congressional visit to the Philippines and Hawaii; the 1947 Texas City disaster; and activities of the American Red Cross and the National 4-H Club Foundation. The films also cover other topics as diverse as poverty in the Tennessee hill country, whaling and walrus and bear hunting in the Arctic, integration in Atlanta, Georgia, charting ocean winds and many other social problems, ranging from venereal diseases to the need for city planning. There are also films relating to events and conditions outside the United States and its territories, including life in East Africa (1924), the eruption of Paricutin in Mexico (1943), communism in Russia and Cuba, Nazism in Germany, the history of Austria from the Hapsburgs to the end of World War II, the National Archives of India, and the state funeral of Sir Winston Churchill (1965).

Recent additions include films of the nation's Bicentennial celebration; ABC News coverage of "Liberty Weekend" (July 3-5, 1986); a film about the Massachusetts District Court proceedings and events relating to the Sacco-Vanzetti case (1920-27); construction of the Detroit-Windsor Tunnel (1928-30); footage shot in Washington, D.C. (1940s and 1950s); Admiral Richard Byrd's second expedition to the South Pole and the condor plane (1933-35); documentaries from the U.S.S.R. in the 1950s about nuclear explosions; and *Reporters Roundup* television series, Washington, D.C. (1955-56).

This category also includes films from the 1920s on naval torpedoes, Hopi and Pueblo Indians and the swearing-in ceremony for President William Howard Taft. Recent documentaries include: *March on Washington,* about a 1969 anti-war demonstration; *No Vietnamese Ever Called Me Nigger;* and *The Unquiet Death of Julius and Ethel Rosenberg.* A group of films made by Congressman Richard H. Poff to communicate with his constituency. Films of national parks and Indians (1941-46). Also held are the first and second generation copies of the 8mm motion picture film taken by Abraham Zapruder

showing the assassination of President Kennedy (November 22, 1963).

Very recent additions include footage from Nanking, Shanghai, Canton and Hong Kong (1928-38); 15 reels of the Mexican Revolution (1914-16) which show combat, prisoners, Red Cross activities, Mexican military leaders Generals Huerta, Orozco, Carranza and Villa, and U.S. Generals Pershing and Funston; a film of the Wounded Knee incident (Spring, 1973) showing the activities of U.S. Marshals during the American Indian Movement occupation; and footage of the 1967 "Support Our Men in Vietnam" parade in New York City.

Historical commercial film productions (1896-1943). Prints of motion picture productions presented to the National Archives as having historical or research interest incidental to the dramatic presentation. Includes two collections presented by Thomas Armat, consisting of "penny-in-a-slot" and nickelodeon shows produced by the Edison, Pathé, Méliès and Urban companies (1896-1910); *The New York Hat* (1912) and *Birth of a Nation* (1916), both directed by D. W. Griffith; Paramount Pictures' *The Biscuit Eater;* Warner Brothers' *Mission to Moscow* and a shortened version of *Black Legion;* and Theatre-on-Film, Inc.'s *Journey to Jerusalem.* Also eight films (*The Man I Married, Man Hunt, They Dare Not Love, Night Train, Confessions of a Nazi Spy, Dispatch from Reuters, Underground* and *Foreign Correspondent)* that were studied by a subcommittee of the Senate Interstate Commerce Committee investigating the dissemination of anti-Nazi propaganda before the United States entered World War II.

Television Newscasts (April 1, 1974-present). CBS has deposited their evening, morning and midday news, daily, since April 1, 1974 (see RG 330 for television news excerpts). MacNeil/Lehrer reports (film masters only) (January 1976-September 1983) contain interviews, commentary and news analysis. Microfiche copies of the transcripts of CBS news broadcasts (January 1, 1974-March 31, 1984) are available.

Television News Specials (April 1, 1974-present). *CBS News Specials* (April 1, 1974-present) and selected specials from ABC and NBC (1976-present) are part of the National Archives collection. These include State of the Union addresses, the Nixon impeachment hearings, the Democratic and Republican conventions (1976, 1980 and 1984) and the Carter and Reagan inaugurations. Microfiche copies of the transcripts of *Face the Nation* and *60 Minutes* to 1984 are available.

Cable Satellite Public Affairs Network (C-SPAN), (1979-present). C-SPAN provides coverage of public affairs in Washington to cable stations nationwide. The National Archives holds C-SPAN deposits of telecasts of selected House and Senate committees and subcommittees, press conferences, briefings and remarks by members of Congress and Federal officials, and conferences of public policy organizations.

Additional televised news specials in this collection include PBS coverage of the Judiciary Committee hearings (July 24-30, 1974) and the Daniel Schorr controversy. Individual documentaries made for television may be found elsewhere in Record Group 200 and in other record groups.

RG 207: Department of Housing and Urban Development (1948-69, 165 items). Documentation of the creation of the Department, President Lyndon B. Johnson's appointment of Robert C. Weaver as its first Secretary, several ceremonies relating to the establishment of the Department, and early Department activities. Footage produced by the Department for use in the film *Open Space;* fair housing television spots; and "instant rehabilitation" renewal project materials. Completed films on urban and community planning, discrimination in housing, urban poverty, housing codes and home construction. A few films on housing and planning in the Soviet Union, Great Britain and Latin America. A group of films on housing and urban planning acquired by HUD.

RG 208: Office of War Information (1941-45, 660 items). Informational, propaganda and documentary films covering all phases of homefront activities, including farming, industry, housing, education, manpower needs, the roles of women and Negroes in the war effort and Japanese relocation; urging citizen support for and participation in the war effort on the homefront, including participation in conservation, preventing inflation, war bond drives and safeguarding military information; illustrating the Social Security System and its benefits to the working man; covering lend-lease activities; reporting on all aspects of the war, from training of the armed forces to the fighting fronts in all theaters; depicting the Allied peoples' customs and contributions to the war effort; and films concerning the Axis powers and their conduct of the war, military strength and ambitions.

A film, narrated in Chinese, of the Chungking memorial service for President Franklin D. Roosevelt (1945).

Newsreels, including OWI's own *United News* (mid-1941 through mid-1946), most narrated in English, with samples narrated in Portuguese, Arabic, French, Chinese, Afrikaans and Japanese; *Fox Movietone News* (1942-45); *News of the Day* (1937-43); Free French newsreels (1945); *Indian News,* released in India in 1945; *Russian News,* made in Russia (1942-45); and *War Pictorial News,* produced in England (1943).

RG 210: War Relocation Authority (1942-43, 7 items). Films about the activities of the WRA, life in relocation camps, and the training and record of Nisei soldiers in World War II. A recent addition is *Barriers and Passes,* a color film which documents living conditions of Japanese Americans in relocation camps.

RG 217: General Accounting Office (1971-75, 12 items). Videotapes of lectures presented by GAO on improving management for more effective government. Comments by government leaders, members of Congress and Ralph Nader are included.

RG 218: United States Joint Chiefs of Staff (1942-46, 9 items). Motion pictures relating to the development of radar, radio, guided missiles and other equipment.

RG 220: Presidential Committees, Commissions and Boards (1957-86, 175 items). Records of the President's Committee on Employment of the Handicapped, consisting of films of the 1957 annual meeting, the life story of Glen Cunningham, and training for the handicapped. Also one-minute television spots featuring President Dwight D. Eisenhower and Roy Campanella.

Records of the President's Commission on Campus Unrest, consisting of six films of Kent State University and the city of Kent, Ohio during the period of protest and shooting (May 1-4, 1970). Films were taken by NBC, CBS and private citizens.

Records of the President's Committee on Pension Policy (1979-81) and the Committee on Wartime Relocation and Internment of Civilians (1981-83); the latter consists of 73 items including *Sand Island Story,* about the eviction of native Hawaiians.

Records of the International Women's Year Commission, consisting of 7 items, including a summary of the National Women's Conference. *Is Anybody Listening?,* the official film of the White House Conference on Youth (1971). A summary statement by Sen. Gary Hart of the National Commission of Air Quality (1981). Several films including statements by President Jimmy Carter and President Ronald Reagan relating to the White House Conference on Small Business (1978). Four items from the White House Conference on Families, including a speech by President Carter.

Records of the President's Commission Investigating the Accident at Three Mile Island in 1979, including tapes of meetings, news coverage and recovery tapes.

Records of the President's Commission on the Space Shuttle *Challenger* accident (1986) include 101 videotapes of interviews, briefings, panel reports and commission hearings on the accident, investigation and salvage.

RG 223: Office of the Bituminous Coal Consumers Council (1943, 2 items). Films entitled *Coal for Victory* and *Know Your Coal,* illustrating methods of coal conservation.

RG 226: Office of Strategic Services (1941-45, 641 items). Films produced or acquired by the OSS include an assessment of Axis industrial, mineral and agricultural resources; sociological portraits of the Japanese people; military equipment, explosives, sabotage and training of OSS agents and commando units; operations in the Balkans; the Allied invasion of North Africa; the rescue of American POWs in Romania; diplomatic and military missions to the Communist Chinese in Yenan, with footage of Mao Zedong and Zhou En-lai; Yugoslav and Italian partisan activities; the training of Polish agents and Chinese Nationalist troops; films on the geography and wartime action in the China-Burma-India theater; and a documentary which recreates the Japanese attack on Pearl Harbor.

RG 227: Office of Scientific Research and Development (1943-44, 14 items). Films by Divisions 8, 9, 10, 11 and 12 of the Office as illustrations for reports on the development of high explosives and rocket propellants; insecticides and protective chemicals for clothing and equipment; aerosols, gas mask absorbents, filters and screen smoke; incendiary devices and hydraulic fluids; amphibious vehicles, AZON, RAZON and radar.

RG 229: Office of Inter-American Affairs (1941-45, 45 items). Informational and propaganda films dealing with the peoples and cultures of Latin America, inter-American cooperation, Latin American minerals and archaeological treasures, a study of an ancient Inca city, and war activities of the United States.

RG 233: U.S. House of Representatives (1953-86, 2,149 items). Videotapes from proceedings of the U.S. House of Representatives, recorded by the House Recording Unit and sent to the Archives at the end of each two-year session of Congress. (Videotapes of the proceedings of the current session of Congress are available from the U.S. House of Representatives, House Broadcasting System [q.v.]).

Videotapes of special events, e.g., speeches before a joint session of Congress, casting Electoral College ballots and the 100th birthday of Franklin Delano Roosevelt.

Film exhibits of John F. Kennedy and Martin Luther King, Jr. displayed at hearings of the House Select Committee on Assassinations.

Films of the Kersten Committee on the Baltic States investigation (1953-54).

Special restrictions apply to items in this Record Group.

RG 234: Reconstruction Finance Corporation (1943-47, 29 items). Films relating to a U.S. Commercial Company survey of the economy, geography and sociology of the Micronesian Islands (1945-47); and films of cinchona plantations, natives and the countryside of Guatemala, taken in connection with the activities of the U.S. Commercial Company in developing sources of quinine (1943-44).

Films of plantations, natives, cities and the countryside of Brazil made in connection with activities of the Rubber Development Corporation (1943-44).

RG 235: Department of Health, Education, and Welfare (1963-73, 28 items). A film illustrating language teaching techniques. A film about mobilizing hospitals for nuclear and other disasters. The *You* television series (1970-73) of interviews about health, education and welfare issues.

RG 237: Federal Aviation Administration (1957, 3 items). Films illustrating the functions and activities of the Administration.

RG 238: National Archives Collection of World War II War Crimes Records (1921-45, 76 items). Films used as evidence at the war crimes trials of Axis leaders before the International Military Tribunal, Nuremberg (1945-46) and before the International Military Tribunal for the Far East, Tokyo (1946-48) consisting of German films documenting the Nazi rise to power and triumphs in Europe (1921-44), the entry of Germany into Austria (1938), the political and industrial activities of the Krupp family and company officials (1930-40), the construction of the No. 1 Hermann Goering steel plant (1939-41), and the Nazi Supreme Court trial of the 20th July 1944 conspirators against Adolf Hitler. Films of concentration camps taken by American and Russian forces as they advanced through Germany (1945). Also a Japanese film entitled *Japan in Time of Emergency.*

35 frames of 8mm film, the only actuality footage shot by a German within a German concentration camp.

RG 242: National Archives Collection of Foreign Records Seized 194– (1916-51, 2,484 items). German documentaries and newsreels covering World War I land and sea battles and the life of Paul von Hindenburg. Leni Riefenstahl's film, *Triumph of the Will,* made at the 1934 Nazi Party rally at Nuremberg, and coverage of the 1936 Olympic riding competition from her film entitled *Olympiad.* A feature film that was used in anti-Semitic indoctrination entitled *Jüd Suss* (The Jew Süss). The personal film collection of Eva Braun (ca. 1939-40). German films on the history of the Nazi Party in Germany, many aspects of World War II on all fronts, war materiel manufacture and weapons development, German culture, and the training of Hitler Youth and of political leaders for administrative posts in occupied countries.

Italian documentaries and newsreels covering World War II on several fronts, including the Ethiopian and Greek invasions and the North African campaign.

Japanese documentaries and newsreels (1932-44) relating to the fishing industry, travel in Japan, the invasion of China and many aspects of the war in the Pacific.

French newsreels (1944) about World War II and films (ca. 1950) about the campaign against the Vietminh in Indochina.

Russian newsreels, educational films, documentaries and feature films on subjects such as the natural sciences, technology, agriculture, transportation, housing, travel in the Soviet Union, Soviet life, culture, music, drama and filmmaking (1946-51), and on Russian culture and history. Films on the death of Nikolai Lenin (1924); the fall of Berlin at the end of World War II and the meeting of Russian and Western Allied troops at the Elbe; Hungary; the sovietization of several republics of the Soviet Union; Soviet cooperation with other Communist countries; and on North Korea (1950). Also several anti-American dramas.

North Korean films about the 38th parallel and of American prisoners at Pyongyang.

Chinese Communist anti-Nationalist propaganda films made during the postwar period and before the removal of Chiang Kai-shek to Taiwan.

American films relating to civilian victims of war (1942) and to the escape of American prisoners of war from the Island of Palawan in the Philippines.

German films of rocket experiments at Peenemunde (1942-45) with some footage in Agfacolor.

RG 243: United States Strategic Bombing Survey (ca. 1944, 11 items). Captured German films relating to American incendiary bombs and bombing methods and to German war industries.

RG 252: Office of the Housing Expediter (1946, 1 item). A film about housing for veterans.

RG 255: National Aeronautics and Space Administration (1959-74, 52 items). Films produced and acquired by the Goddard Space Flight Center, including materials on vehicles and payloads for scientific applications and manned space flight, a global satellite tracking network, the Explorer program, orbiting observatories, weather and communications; satellites ECHO, RELAY, SYNCOM, TELSTAR and INTELSAT; visits by Richard M. Nixon and Hubert H. Humphrey to the Goddard Center.

Documentation on film of the investigation of the 1967 Apollo 204 accident that killed three astronauts.

NOTE: Check the Stock Film Collection, described after RG 452, which includes almost 10,000 items from NASA.

RG 263: Central Intelligence Agency (1952, 3 items). Films produced in China and Korea alleging U.S. use of germ warfare during the Korean War.

RG 267: Supreme Court of the United States (1939-66, 5 items). Films of the effects on wildlife and on shipbuilding of water diversion from Lake Michigan by the city of Chicago.

RG 269: General Services Administration (1971, 2 items). Films entitled *Partners in Progress,* about minority businesses, and *Clear Skies, Clean Air* on the use of natural gas-powered automobiles.

RG 272: President's Commission on the Assassination of President Kennedy (1963, 15 items). Films collected in the course of the Warren Commission investigation. These films are held by the Judicial and Fiscal Branch of NARA.

RG 274: National Archives Collection of Records of Inaugural Committees (1965-73, 8 items). Films entitled *1965 Inaugural Parade, The Inaugural Story 1973,* and *Inauguration Ceremony and Parade — 1973.* The 1969 inaugural concert at Constitution Hall is on videotape.

RG 277: Department of Commerce (1952, 1 item). A television production on the impact of a steel strike on the Korean War effort.

RG 286: Agency for International Development (1955–?, 241 items). Films of the International Cooperation Administration, including a report to the American people on technical cooperation. The films highlight U.S. assistance to India, Libya, Ecuador, Indochina, Sudan, Ethiopia, Paraguay, Thailand, Indonesia and Afghanistan. Topics include education, agriculture and medicine. Films chronicle U.S. military assistance programs and cooperation in RIO, NATO and SEATO.

Note: The AID collection of over 2,200 titles has been transferred to the National Archives and a few hundred have been accessioned. It is in the process of being cataloged.

RG 288: National Foundation on the Arts and Humanities (1965-75, 14 items). Interviews and discussions with artists, politicians and Endowment officials explain programs such as "Artists-in-the-Schools," Expansion Arts, Design Arts and Literature. A selection of films about artists and arts programs produced with grants from the National Endowments for the Arts and Humanities,

RG 291: Property Management and Disposal Service (GSA) (ca. 1957, 1 item). A film concerning the processing of nickel ore at the Defense Materials Service Nicaro Project in Cuba.

RG 304: Office of Civil Defense and Mobilization (1947-61, 66 items). Films produced by the Federal Civil Defense Administration include nuclear bomb explosions, flood damage, civil defense exercises and plans, and slow-motion footage of the 1955 Nevada atomic bomb tests.

RG 305: Bonneville Power Administration (1949, 2 items). *The Columbia* and *Hydro* were films made by the BPA in 1949 using the songs of Woody Guthrie for the soundtrack. The films described the benefits of public ownership of electric power facilities. All copies were ordered destroyed in the 1950s, but a janitor rescued prints. Additional prints were later located.

RG 306: United States Information Agency (1942-86, 16,376 items). Documentaries and television programs produced or acquired by the Agency for distribution abroad relating to many aspects of life in the United States; the lives of famous Americans; the history of aviation; World War II; peacetime uses of atomic energy; U.S. foreign relations, including treaties, the Marshall Plan and reconstruction in Europe, visits of foreign heads of state to the United States, cultural exchange, international trade, the Berlin airlift and international sporting events; life in South America, Europe, North Africa and the Soviet Union. Many instructional films that were used in technical assistance programs on such subjects as farming, poultry raising, swimming, child care, training of nurses and teachers, medicine, rehabilitation of the blind and of veterans, apprentice training, civilian defense and industry.

Materials on videotape include *World Net,* a daily feed of news via satellite (beginning April 22, 1985). This two-hour news and information package includes 30 minutes of hard news, features, cultural and leisure programs. Landmark telecasts include international satellite links for journalists, scientists and educators and an extraterrestrial news conference which linked the

astronauts on the Space Shuttle *Columbia* with President Ronald Reagan, West German Chancellor Helmut Kohl and journalists in eight countries.

Welt im Film, a German language newsreel which was produced jointly by the British and American military governments and shown in the British and American zones of Germany, Austria, Vienna and Berlin (1945-52). The newsreels were part of the "denazification" efforts.

NOTE: The U.S. Information Agency materials are in the public domain, but Congressional restrictions prevent all but a few titles from being shown to the American public. This means that copies cannot be made of these materials, cataloging has just begun and few reference prints are available. *World Net* is indexed, and there are USIA distribution catalogs. Exceptions may be made for those producing materials for foreign audiences. Some films have been made available to the public through NARA's National Audiovisual Center (q.v.). For further information on the status of USIA productions and for access to current materials, researchers should contact USIA's General Counsel at (202) 485-8501.

RG 307: National Science Foundation (1969-81, 25 items). Films and videotapes used to explain scientific and technological advances and to promote careers in science and technology. Subjects include oceanography, astronomers, the earth's magnetosphere, water, political and scientific problems, nutrition, information technology, carcinogens in the environment, archaeological dating of artifacts, samples of the educational television show *3-2-1 Contact,* the experimental vessel *Glomar Challenger,* Antarctica and television.

RG 310: Agricultural Research Service (1939-49, 11 items). Films illustrating methods of cultivating and harvesting sugar beets.

RG 311: Federal Emergency Management Agency (1956-70, 99 items). Films, television programs and television spots produced and acquired by the Agency. Topics include civil defense, disasters and relief efforts and the dangers of nuclear war, radiation and fallout.

RG 326: Atomic Energy Commission (ca. 1964, 255 items). Films about the AEC's contribution to the peaceful uses of atomic energy. 79 films produced by the atomic energy agencies of the USSR, France, Italy, India and Canada which were shown at the Third International Conference on Peaceful Uses of Atomic Energy, Geneva (1964). Both technical and public information films are included. Also holds 121 reels of unedited research film.

RG 330: Office of the Secretary of Defense (1961-85, 598 items). Films of the inaugural ceremony and parade of President John F. Kennedy. Kinescopes of excerpts from television newscasts (1965-75) which covered the Vietnam War and other stories of interest to the Department of Defense, such as arms limitation and foreign relations. The excerpts were taped off the air for internal use, but are now available to researchers. Some typewritten daily summaries are available.

Television spots broadcast over stations of the Armed Forces Radio and Television Service to announce policy changes and educational opportunities of interest to military personnel.

RG 331: Allied Operational and Occupation Headquarters, World War II (11 items). Films gathered as part of the preparation of the "MacArthur Histories," the history of the Southwest Pacific Area. Titles include *The Petroleum Story* and *POWs in the Philippines.*

RG 334: National Wartime Information Security Organization (1968, 9 items). Training films about censorship station administration and operations; practical demonstrations of censorship procedures for postal and travelers' censors in times of national emergency.

RG 337: Headquarters Army Ground Forces (1942, 2 items). A film entitled *Speed with Power and Traction,* demonstrating the uses of the MG-2 high-speed tractor.

RG 338: U.S. Army Commands (1942–, 1944-45, 51 items). Rolls of assembled footage of the Malmedy line during the Battle of the Bulge, and footage of the liberation of POW camps in relation to the War Crimes investigations into the Malmedy massacre and other atrocities against American POWs.

Headquarters United States Air Force (1950-67, 20 items). Films received by the USAF during the official investigation into the existence of unidentified flying objects, filmed by military personnel and civilians. Includes 11 16mm films and seven 8mm films of alleged unidentified flying objects photographed between August 1950 and November 1967. Two television documentaries about UFOs are included.

RG 342: United States Air Force Commands, Activities and Organizations (1900-73, 4,179 items). Films made or collected by the Air Force on the history of the development of flight, including: activities of the Wright brothers from 1900; e.g., their demonstration flights in France, Italy and the United States; and on the development of airplanes, gliders, balloons, dirigibles, autogiros, helicopters, rockets, jets, satellites, aeronautical oddities, parachutes dating from the 1930s, ballistic cameras and radar.

Films about early air races, air shows and distance and altitude records; the flight by Richard E. Byrd and Floyd Bennett to the North Pole (1926); the Hindenburg crash (1937); Finne Ronne's Antarctic Expedition (1946-48); the dedication of the New York International Airport (1948); and people prominent in the history of flight, including Wilbur and Orville Wright, Edward V. Rickenbacker, Billy Mitchell, Charles A. Lindbergh, Richard E. Byrd, Floyd Bennett, Igor Sikorsky and Wiley Post.

Films reflecting noncombat activities of the Air Force and its predecessors (1920s-1964), including the airmail service; rescue and assistance missions in natural disaster areas at home and abroad; hurricane hunting; the Berlin airlift; training and maneuvers; airbase construction; the opening of the Air Force Academy (1955); participation in the preparations for and activities of the International Geophysical Year (1953-59); atomic bomb tests in the Pacific and elsewhere; and research and development work in the fields of guided missiles, remote-control weapons, supersonic flight and space technology.

World War I films illustrating the activities of the Army Air Service in France. Films made in all theaters of operation during World War II, concerning the activities of the Army Air Forces and all other aspects of the war, including the AAF at home; women in the AAF; Axis concentration and prisoner-of-war camps and atrocities; Allied bombing missions over Europe and Africa and in the Pacific area; the defense of Britain and Moscow; the effects of bombing raids on Japan, including the atomic bombing of Hiroshima and Nagasaki; the surrender of Germany and Japan; and the customs, religion, industry, black market and Allied occupation of Japan.

Films on aerial aspects of the Korean action and the truce-signing ceremonies.

Television news release prints on the war in Vietnam.

Films on the inauguration of Presidents Franklin D. Roosevelt and Harry S Truman. Films relating to the presidency of John F. Kennedy, including his inauguration, his activities as President and worldwide memorial services and tributes to him. Films of the funeral of Gen. John J. Pershing (1948). Films of the 1952 Olympic games. Captured German films depicting the war in Poland and covering research and development of planes, gliders, helicopters, jets, rockets and ballistic missiles (1912-44). Captured Japanese films relating to preparations for the Pearl Harbor attack and World War II combat. A Russian film of the 1949 May Day celebration.

Many military and civilian leaders appear in these films, including Theodore Roosevelt, Dwight D. Eisenhower, Fiorello La Guardia, Winston Churchill, Richard M. Nixon, Chiang Kai-shek, Syngman Rhee, Paul von Hindenburg, Josef Stalin and Vyacheslav M. Molotov.

Unedited footage of the USAF Thunderbirds and their audiences in the U.S., Europe and Latin America (1958-67).

Training films with approved War Department and DOD doctrine showing Air Force procedures, equipment and World War II combat. These films were used between 1942 and 1963.

Footage from Bien Hoa Air Force Base, Vietnam (1963-70) including activities and personnel on the base, in the air and in surrounding villages; and visits by U.S. and South Vietnamese officials. Footage of psychological warfare activities (1971-73); and turnover of aircraft to the South Vietnamese Air Force.

An additional 500 titled film productions made by the Air Force (1946-64) have recently been added to the archival collection. Among the films is combat footage of World War II and Korea; Dachau concentration camp; experimental crash and other tests using live animals; footage of experimental flights of various aircraft; films of polar exploration; International Geophysical Year experiments and activities; air shows; Air Force missile-testing programs; pre-NASA space tests; footage showing the development of the airplane; the role of women in the Air Force; and a captured Russian-made film of the 32nd anniversary of the Bolshevik Revolution.

RG 362: Agencies for Voluntary Action Programs (1961-71, 144 items). Films created, commissioned, or acquired by the Peace Corps, VISTA, the Foster Grandparents Program and other voluntary action programs which document the work of these programs, show conditions in other countries, or prepare volunteers for their assignments. Films produced by the governments of Botswana, Mexico, India, Indonesia and others.

RG 374: Defense Atomic Support Agency (1954-62, 20 items). Classified and unclassified training films used by the Nuclear Weapons School to instruct in the care, handling, storage and operation of atomic weapons.

RG 378: Economic Development Administration (1961-65, 9 items). Films produced and acquired to explain or document the revitalization of areas and industries in the U.S. with severe chronic unemployment and low family income. Individual films feature New Bedford, Massachusetts; Wilkes-Barre, Pennsylvania; automation; and teenage employment.

From the EDA's Indian program there is a film on the San Carlos Indian tribe of Arizona.

RG 381: Office of Economic Opportunity (1964-72, 499 items). Films produced and acquired by OEO for its social welfare programs to combat poverty and racism. Films showing the OEO workers among Indians, Chicanos, blacks and whites.

Films and unedited footage from an experiment in police-community relations in Washington, D.C., which were never released because of the negative image they showed.

Unedited footage of the Cuban missile crisis, Lady Bird Johnson and Robert Kennedy.

Most of the 37 short films produced in Farmersville, California, for a project in self-help through visual communication patterned after the "Challenge for Change" project tried in Canada by its National Film Board.

Interviews and discussions with private citizens and community leaders on poverty and nutrition in various U.S. communities. Includes materials on the White House Conference on Food, Nutrition and Health (1970). These 65 videotapes were part of a program modeled after the Canadian "FOGO" project.

RG 389: Provost Marshall General (1941–, 1952, 1 item). Koje-do Prisoners of War is a record of a POW camp during the Korean War.

RG 397: Office of Civil Defense (1952-60, 66 items). Documentaries produced by predecessor agencies of the OCD depicting nuclear bomb explosions, flood damage and all phases of civil defense.

RG 398: Department of Transportation (1978-79, 27 items). Television coverage of Secretary of Transportation Brock Adams and President Jimmy Carter and their decisions concerning the Washington, D.C. subway system.

RG 406: Federal Highway Administration (1972-76, 9 items). Speeches, addresses, and press conferences by DOT Secretaries John Volpe, Claude S. Brinegar, William Coleman and other officials.

RG 412: Environmental Protection Agency (1969-71, 44 items). Films, television documentaries, information shorts and public service announcements about environmental pollution.

RG 416: National Highway Traffic Safety Administration (1979-81, 21 items). Films on fuel efficiency through lower speeds and driving techniques. Films and television spots on the 55 mph speed limit, crash test and impact studies, drunk driving and seat belt restraints.

RG 428: Department of the Navy (1941-65, 12,119 items). Primarily silent, unedited footage (formerly maintained by the Naval Photographic Center in Washington, D.C.), this collection includes comprehensive photographic coverage of World War II naval and aerial operations, amphibious landings, cruises, launchings and military leaders. There are acquired newsreel clips and captured films. Footage covers naval aviation, ships, ship operations, crash landings, sea rescues, submarines and the Korean War.

Note: This collection of stock footage is served by an elaborate subject card file which describes each piece of film scene-by-scene.

RG 434: Department of Energy (1948-78, 291 items). Produced and acquired by the Atomic Energy Commission, the Energy Research and Development Administration, and the Department of Energy, these films relate primarily to the peaceful uses of the atom in programs sponsored or endorsed by the federal government. Subjects include radiation safety, nuclear and auxiliary power, handling nuclear fuels, nuclear medicine, nuclear propulsion in space, controlled photosynthesis, Bikini Atoll and solar eclipse study expeditions.

RG 439: Office of the Assistant Secretary for Human Development (HHS) (1971, 7 items). Films produced for the 1971 White House Conference on Human Aging. Topics include aging and retirement living.

RG 441: Department of Education (1978, 1 item). A film explaining the mission of the newly created department. President Jimmy Carter and Secretary of Education Shirley Hufsteder are featured in the film.

RG 452: American Revolution Bicentennial Administration (1976, 36 items). Films produced for the Bicentennial, entitled Project Civic.

Stock Film Collection

Formerly called the Stock Film Library and located in a Virginia suburb of Washington, this collection is now kept with the permanent collection and serviced by the Motion Picture, Sound and Video branch reference staff. The more than 10,500 reels of stock film and videotape held here were produced or acquired by the federal government. It serves government as well as private film producers and scholars. The collection dates back to the 1940s, with 95% of the footage from the National Aeronautics and Space Administration (NASA).

Other U.S. government agencies which have contributed to the collection include: Agency for International Development; Department of Agriculture; Department of Commerce (U.S. Travel Service); Department of Energy (Atomic Energy Commission); Department of Health, Education and Welfare

(Administration on Aging); Department of the Interior (U.S. Fish and Wildlife Service); Department of State; Department of Transportation (Coast Guard, Federal Aviation Administration and Federal Highway Administration); Environmental Protection Agency; National Science Foundation (Antarctica); and the Postal Service.

The footage is mostly a combination of trims, outtakes and unedited footage that is unaccessioned and unappraised.

Size & Elements: Film: 70mm, 35mm, 16mm and 8mm (300 million feet). Videotape: 3/4" and 1/2" (10,000 videotapes). More unedited footage is held than completed productions.

Video viewing copies are available for *Universal Newsreel* releases and outtakes; *March of Time* outtakes; Navy World War II footage; the Ford Collection; C-SPAN coverage of the House of Representatives; the Harmon Foundation Collection; RG 330; RG 381; and about one-third of the material in the Main Catalog.

Cataloging: Card catalogs; other finding aids. Card catalog microfilm sets (available for purchase) have been completed for *March of Time* outtakes and for *Universal Newsreels.*

INFOCEN, a database system, is now used for cataloging and contains approximately 5,000 entries.

Eleven card catalogs are available for public use at the Motion Picture, Sound and Video Branch.

Main catalog. Entries describe both government and commercially produced newsreels, information and documentary films covering a wide range of subjects. Earliest film dates from 1894, but material generally covers the period from 1915-early 1970s. Cards are arranged numerically by Record Group (RG) with the bulk of the catalog made up of subject and title entries. Subject headings loosely based on Library of Congress scheme.

Ford Film Collection catalog. Both edited and unedited material covering a broad range of "Americana subjects," with particular emphasis on the development of the automobile and its impact on American life. Covers the period 1914-56. Card index of key words and phrases refers to scene descriptions contained in separate notebooks. *Guide to the Ford Film Collection* available which gives overview of the Collection, but does not always correspond with index. Screening prints available on most subjects.

Army Air Force Combat Subjects/Signal Corps Army Depository Film (RG 18CS/111 ADC) catalog. Unedited and camera record footage covering all theaters of military activity during World War II, the occupation of Germany and Japan, war crime trials and the Korean War. Cards arranged numerically and by subject, with headings loosely based on Library of Congress scheme.

Universal Newsreel catalog (RG 200 UN). Edited stories as well as outtakes giving worldwide coverage for the period 1929-67. Over 500,000 cards arranged in 13 broad categories (foreign locations, general, U.S. locations, conveyances, education, types of people, animals, sports and amusements, U.S. government, aviation, U.S. Army, U.S. Navy and personalities), each of which is subdivided more specifically. The cards under U.S. locations are the most inclusive because Universal routinely entered a card under each location or dateline. The cards from 1929-43 are not as detailed as the later ones, but generally they contain subject descriptions, dates, cameramen or source, release and outtake numbers, footage counts and designations whether sound or silent. There is also a chronological file of newsreel release sheets summarizing each issue stored in the research room, as well as cameramen's notes and production files stored in the stacks. A General Information Guide is available, which gives explanation of card format and summary of the 13 categories.

U.S. Air Force miscellaneous series. Numerical cards only (no subject index) for film covering early aviation and Air Force activities (1900-early 1960s).

U.S. Air Force (various series). Numerical cards only for a variety of Air Force series, including News Reviews, News Releases and film relating to International Geophysical Year. In addition, Air Force-produced catalogs to Strategic Bombing Survey film relating to Hiroshima and Nagasaki, and footage of Thunderbirds stunt flying.

Army Air Forces Special Film Project (18 SFP) catalog. Outtakes from the Army Air Forces production, *Thunderbolts,* covering activities of the 12th AAF in Europe (June 1944-April 1945). Numerical and subject arrangement.

Navy catalog (RG 428 NPC). Unedited and camera record footage covering Navy activities (World War II-1965).

Atomic Energy Commission catalog (RG 326). Unedited film covering testing and research procedures at various AEC field installations (1950-53). Numerically arranged cards, as well as an AEC-produced subject catalog.

Marine Corps catalog (RG 127). Unedited and camera record footage shot mostly by Marine Corps units (World War I-ca. 1960). Microfilm aperture card catalog available.

Stock film catalog. Cards describe unedited U.S. government film footage

that has been deposited by federal agencies with the National Archives. This catalog is divided into three major sections: Record Group (numerically arranged); Outtakes from Edited Titles; and two subject sections, NASA Project Subject Catalog and the General Subject Catalog.

Access: Open to the public. The National Archives does not offer the kind of quick research and duplication services found at commercial stock shot libraries. Appointments often must be made weeks in advance and duplication services can take from three to eight weeks. Research requests accepted by mail, telephone and in person. Initial inquiries can be handled by the knowledgeable and helpful reference staff and a videotape viewing station is available for one hour to those arriving without an appointment. However, most projects require that you make an appointment and come to Washington to do card searches and viewing. No research fees are charged by the Archives. Many producers, though, find it best to hire one of the freelance researchers who are familiar with the collection. A list of local researchers is available.

Rights: With some exceptions, government-produced edited films and stock film are in the public domain. Material available for reuse, subject to copyright restrictions. *Some government-produced films may contain shots, sequences, sound or music material acquired from copyright holders; therefore, some material within government-produced films may not be available for duplication.*

Gift items (RG 200) may require permission from copyright owner. *Universal Newsreel* releases and outtakes, *March of Time* outtakes, the Ford Collection and the Harmon Collection are large collections (all in RG 200) that are in the public domain.

Licensing: Available for reuse. License fees not charged.

Restrictions: USIA (RG 306) materials have special restrictions.

Viewing Facilities: Film (35mm and 16mm Steenbeck flatbed viewers; 16mm Cinescan); videotape (3/4" and 1/2" videotape machines).

Duplication Facilities: Duplication services are provided by contract with private labs. *With the exception of supervised film-to-videotape transfers, full reels only are copied from the permanent collection.* Many items, especially newsreels, have a number of unrelated stories on a single reel. Full reels or 100-foot excerpts can be copied from the stock film collection. All orders must be in writing and prepaid in U.S. dollars, except those from U.S. federal, state and local agencies, U.S. television or radio stations, or U.S. universities and libraries, which may submit authorized purchase orders. Duplication services can take from three to eight weeks. A price list for duplication services is available on request.

Materials with no copyright restrictions can be dubbed or recorded off the screen if researchers bring their own equipment and have an appointment. A copy made by these methods is generally less than broadcast quality.

Publications: Handouts include a brief overview of the collections, guides to the twelve card catalogs and finding aids, a sources and permission list, and a price and ordering guide. An informal list of Washington-based researchers can be requested.

Guide to the Ford Film Collection in the National Archives. Compiled by Mayfield Bray, 1970. 118 pages, 54 illustrations. This volume describes the contents of and imagery contained within the Ford Collection, and enables researchers to locate specific footage. Available for $20.00 from the National Archives Trust Fund, Dept. 420 (NEPS), Room G-1, Cashier's Office, Washington, D.C. 20408 (specify item number 100008).

Related Materials: Some textual records are available for about 50% of the collection. These include *Universal Newsreel* release folders and *March of Time* dope sheets.

This entry copyright © 1988 by Bonnie G. Rowan

Bonnie Rowan is a Washington-based film researcher. She is currently revising her 1980 Scholar's Guide to Washington, D.C. Film and Video Collections.

DISTRICT OF COLUMBIA METRO

NATIONAL ARCHIVES AND RECORDS ADMINISTRATION (NARA) NATIONAL AUDIOVISUAL CENTER

8700 Edgeworth Drive
Capitol Heights, MD 20743-3701
(301) 763-1891
(800) 638-1300 (credit card orders only)

R. Kevin Flood (Director)

Contact: Customer Service
Services: Government agency; film and videotape distributor. Audiovisual materials available for rental, preview and purchase. *As the U.S. government*

may not have full rights to the films and videotapes it produces, purchase or rental by the customer does not constitute authorization for reproduction, resale or showing for profit.

Description: National Audiovisual Center was established to serve as the central source for all federally produced audiovisual materials and to make them available to the public through information and distribution services. Through the Center's distribution program, the public has access to more than 8,000 titles covering a wide range of subjects.

Distribution services. The Center's audiovisual materials are available for sale (formats include films, videotapes, slide/tape sets, audiotapes and multimedia kits); rental (16mm films only) and preview (16mm films and 3/4" videotapes *not available in 16mm film format*).

Information services. The Center sponsors the following information services: customer services (staff responds to telephone and written inquiries about federal audiovisuals); printed materials (*Media Resource Catalog* and a wide selection of free brochures, each organized around a specific subject theme); and a master data file (the Center is responsible for maintaining a master catalog file on audiovisual materials produced by the U.S. government).

Major subject concentrations include: agriculture, anthropology, atomic energy, aviation, biology, business and economics, chemistry, civics and government, computer science, dentistry, education, electricity, electronics, engineering, fine arts, forestry, geography, health, history, humanities, industrial arts, languages, library science, mathematics, medicine, military science, natural resources, naval science, physical science, physics, pollution, recreation, rehabilitation, safety, science, sociology, space programs and surgery. Each subject area is itself subdivided, and researchers are urged to consult the Center's catalogs and brochures for information on its immense holdings.

Of particular interest to film researchers and producers is the collection of documentary film classics produced by the U.S. government. All are available for rental and purchase. Sample titles include:

The Army-Navy Screen Magazine (1943-45). *Screen Magazine* was a bi-weekly news and information subject shown before the feature film in all military motion picture theaters during World War II. Typically, each 20-minute episode consisted of four or five segments featuring stories about the homefront, news about major events of the war, an animated cartoon and a variety show. A selection of highlights is available from the Center; it includes *Hollywood Canteen* (April 1944), with Dinah Shore, Marlene Dietrich, Lana Turner, Hedy Lamarr, Red Skelton, Eddie Cantor, Jimmy Durante and others; *The Story of Cpl. Jolley* (July 1945), the story of the Bataan death march; *By Request* (January 1945), with homefront scenes; *Jubilee* (June 1944), featuring songs by Lena Horne and Eddie "Rochester" Anderson; *Spies* (July 1943), a cartoon in which Private Snafu learns that the slip of a lip can indeed sink a ship; *V-1!* (February 1945), in which the Germans use V-1 rockets to rain death and destruction upon the cities of Great Britain; and *Command Performance, U.S.A.* (January 1944), hosted by Bob Hope, featuring Betty Hutton, Judy Garland and Lana Turner.

The Autobiography of a Jeep (1943). A lighthearted look at that most "all-American" of vehicles.

The Battle of Midway (1942). Directed and written by John Ford. Contains color combat footage, largely shot by Ford himself.

The Battle of San Pietro (1945). Directed, written and narrated by John Huston. Chronicle of savage fighting between American and German forces for control of the Liri Valley in Italy. The taking of a small military objective here becomes an indictment of modern warfare in general, with its incredible cost in both military and civilian casualties.

The Cummington Story (1945). Directed by Helen Grayson and Larry Madison. The true story of a group of immigrants settling in a small New England town, featuring the participants reenacting their own experiences. The film touchingly shows how cultural assimilation is possible in America, although difficult at times.

December 7th (1943). Directed by John Ford. Record of the attack on Pearl Harbor, combining actual footage with dramatic reconstructions.

The Fight for Life (1940). Directed and written by Pare Lorentz. Shows the lack of adequate prenatal and obstetrical care for great numbers of American women; shot in part at the Chicago Maternity Center. The film presents images of an unemployed and undernourished America that Hollywood did not show. Floyd Crosby's harsh, gritty outdoor cinematography of hungry children and teeming slums has rarely been duplicated in American nonfiction film.

Hands (1934). This silent short subject, directed by Ralph Steiner and Willard Van Dyke, features a montage of hands: idle hands, hands at work, and finally hands putting earnings from WPA relief projects back into circulation.

Japanese Relocation (1943). An early attempt to provide an official explanation for the removal of 110,000 people of Japanese descent from the "potential combat zone" of the West Coast. These people (two-thirds of them U.S. citizens) were forced to leave their homes, farms and businesses to spend the duration of the war in "relocation" camps located in the American interior.

The Land (1942). Directed, written and narrated by Robert J. Flaherty. The pictorial record of an odyssey that took Flaherty to almost every part of America during the summer of 1939. He and his crew drove through the rural countryside, stopping to photograph whatever seemed of interest, including migrant workers, the unemployed and the distribution of surplus food.

Let There Be Light (1946). Directed by John Huston. To explore the rehabilitation of returning soldiers who had been victims of psychosomatic disabilities ("shell shock" and "battle fatigue"), Huston brought a team of Signal Corps cameramen to Mason General Hospital on Long Island, New York. Their cameras became the impartial observers of intensely personal moments of self-revelation vital to the slow process of psychological healing.

The Memphis Belle (1944). Directed by William Wyler. Records the final mission over Germany of the "flying fortress" *Memphis Belle* and her veteran crew.

Mirror of America (1964). Utilizing footage from the Ford Historical Film Collection at the National Archives, *Mirror of America* is a film portrait of America (1915-20). Shown at work and play are many of the famous figures of the day: Woodrow Wilson, Henry Ford, Thomas Edison and "Buffalo Bill" Cody. The film also features ordinary Americans in their daily activities.

Nazi Concentration Camps (1945). An official record of the Nazi death camps as photographed by Allied forces advancing into Germany.

The Negro Soldier (1944). Directed by Frank Capra and Stuart Heisler. Shows the contributions and sacrifices made by Black Americans in virtually all of our nation's armed conflicts — from Crispus Attucks and Peter Salem in the Revolutionary War to Robert Brooks, the first soldier in the armed forces to die in World War II.

Nuremberg (1946). Compiled by Pare Lorentz and Stuart Schulberg. A grim and unflinching account of the Nuremberg trials, told almost totally without editorial comment. Excerpts of films shown as evidence in the trials are intercut with trial sequences.

Origins of the Motion Picture (1955). The history of the technological development of motion pictures, from Leonardo da Vinci's *camera obscura* to Edison's Kinetoscope. Shows the actual functioning of early devices for the reproduction of motion, including the Zoetrope, Phenakistiscope, and Praxiniscope. Highlights shown of later technical developments include Muybridge's first projected photographic motion pictures, the first copyrighted motion picture (Edison's *The Sneeze*), and rare footage of American troops landing in Cuba.

The Plow That Broke the Plains (1936). Directed and written by Pare Lorentz for the Resettlement Administration. This classic film about the Dust Bowl has been one of the most widely praised and studied documentaries to be produced in America.

Power and the Land (1940). Directed by Joris Ivens. In 1939, three out of four American farms were without electricity because of the reluctance of large utility companies to extend their lines into low-profit rural areas. *Power and the Land* was intended to encourage farmers to form their own electrical cooperatives with the help of the Rural Electrification Administration. However, Ivens transcended this original purpose by providing us with a timeless portrait of American farm life, rich in pastoral beauty and its celebration of traditional American values.

The Red Nightmare (1962). The story of Jerry Donovan, a small-town American who takes his civil liberties for granted. One night, Jerry dreams that his community has been taken over by communists. His friends and family quickly turn against him, leading to his arrest and conviction for "subversive" activities. Upon awakening, Jerry has a new appreciation for America's freedoms and resolves to shoulder a greater portion of his civic responsibilities.

Report from the Aleutians (1943). Directed, written and narrated by John Huston. Portrays the lives of soldiers manning the most remote outpost of World War II, the Aleutian Islands in the North Pacific. Huston and his camera crew spent six months on the island of Adak, which was used as a bomber base for raids against Japanese-held Kiska Island.

Reunion (Le Retour) (1946). Directed by Henri Cartier-Bresson. The moving story of the liberation of prisoners from Nazi concentration camps. This is an edited version with English soundtrack.

The River (1937). Directed and written by Pare Lorentz. Documentary about the exploitation and misuse of the Mississippi River, from the time of the Civil War to the disastrous floods of the 1930s.

Seeds of Destiny (1946). Documents the plight of the millions of children left at the end of World War II without food, clothing or the most minimal medical attention. Under the sponsorship of the United Nations Relief and Rehabilitation Administration (UNRRA), a team of Signal Corps photographers was sent to fourteen countries to film children in bombed-out cities, refugee camps, makeshift hospitals and other locations.

Steel Town (1944). Directed by Willard Van Dyke. The lives of steel workers in Youngstown, Ohio are portrayed as they contribute to America's war effort on the homefront.

Thunderbolt (1945). Directed by William Wyler and John Sturges. Documentary about the air war over Italy shows the activities of the 57th Fighter Group during "Operation Strangle," which destroyed vital supply routes deep behind German lines.

The Town (1944). Directed by Josef von Sternberg. Explores the European cultural roots of an American small town — Madison, Indiana.

The True Glory (1945). Directed by Garson Kanin and Carol Reed. The story of the Normandy Landing to the eventual surrender of Germany.

Valley of the Tennessee (1944). Directed by Alexander Hammid. Explores the role of the Tennessee Valley Authority in reclaiming the ruined Tennessee Valley.

Why Vietnam? (1965). Offers the official United States policy for our involvement in Vietnam. The war is placed in the context of America's traditional willingness to assist free peoples in retaining their sovereignty. Historical hindsight gives many of the film's pronouncements ("We will not surrender and we will not retreat") particular irony.

"Why We Fight" series (1942-45). Directed by Frank Capra and Anatole Litvak. One of the first major film projects undertaken by the military during World War II was a group of seven "orientation" films. Their purpose was to explain to over nine million Americans in uniform the reason for our entry into the war. *Prelude to War* (1942) portrays the events leading up to the war: Japanese attacks on Manchuria, the rise of fascism in Germany and Italy, and the lack of preparedness in the United States. *The Nazis Strike* (1943) shows the Nazi conquest of Austria and Czechoslovakia and the invasion of Poland. *Divide and Conquer* (1943) shows Hitler's invasion of Belgium, Holland, Denmark and Norway. The British are driven into the sea at Dunkirk, and France belongs to the Germans. *The Battle of Russia* (1944) shows the Nazi armies halted at the gates of Moscow and Leningrad, and suffering a stunning defeat at the Battle of Stalingrad. In *The Battle of Britain* (1943), Britain stands alone through relentless air attacks by the Nazis, in her "finest hour." *The Battle of China* (1944) shows China during the Japanese invasion and the Chinese people's stubborn struggle to remain free. *War Comes to America* (1945) is an overview of U.S. history, with an "emphasis on the events that forced us to fight for our survival."

Other films in the documentary collection include *Here is Germany* (1945); *Hymn of the Nations* (1944); *Know Your Ally — Britain* (1943); *Know Your Enemy — Japan* (1945); *Our Job in Japan* (1946); *The Road to the Wall* (1962); *World at War* (1943); and *Your Job in Germany* (1945).

Descriptions of the documentary films above are largely taken from the NAVC catalog *Documentary Film Classics produced by the United States Government*, written and researched by William J. Blakefield. This booklet is available from the Center.

Size & Elements: Film: 16mm. Videotape: 3/4", VHS and Betamax. (8,000 titles total).

Cataloging: Published catalogs; computerized cataloging (apply for information).

Access: Available for rental, preview and purchase. Rental fees charged. Research requests accepted by mail and telephone.

Rights: Some rights held to some material. Much material in the public domain. Additional clearances may be necessary in some cases if material is to be reused.

Licensing: Footage from completed productions not available for licensing or reuse through the Center.

Restrictions: *As the U.S. government may not have full rights to the films and videotapes it produces; purchase or rental by the customer does not constitute authorization for reproduction, resale or showing for profit.*

Viewing Facilities: Film and videotape.

Duplication Facilities: None.

Related Materials: Slide shows, audiocassettes and multimedia kits.

DISTRICT OF COLUMBIA METRO

NATIONAL ARCHIVES AND RECORDS ADMINISTRATION (NARA) OFFICE OF PRESIDENTIAL LIBRARIES NIXON PRESIDENTIAL MATERIALS PROJECT
7th Street and Pennsylvania Avenue, NW
Washington, DC 20408
(703) 756-6498

Street address: 845 South Pickett Street, Alexandria, VA 22304

James J. Hastings (Deputy Director)

Contact: Richard E. McNeill (Audiovisual Archives Specialist)

Services: Government agency; presidential library facility. Film material available for unrestricted reuse and duplication; videotape available for research use only.

Description: Presidential library facility administered by the National Archives and Records Administration. Holds film and videotape records of the administration of President Richard M. Nixon (1969-74).

The motion picture film file was produced by the Navy Photographic Center White House film unit. This collection (1969-74) contains coverage of selected official activities of President Nixon, including diplomatic events, speeches, foreign and domestic trips and activities of the First Lady.

The videotape file was recorded off the air by the White House Communications Agency from televised broadcasts (1969-75). This collection is composed of recordings of public affairs broadcasts by the three commercial networks and PBS. Included are documentaries, weekly summaries of national morning and evening news telecasts, scheduled public affairs programs, actualities, Presidential speeches and press conferences.

Size & Elements: Film: 16mm (1.2 million feet with double system sound; 517 titles, 1,207 cans). For each 16mm production there is reversal original, a positive workprint, and where there is sound, a synchronized full-coat magnetic track. Videotape: 2" (4,087 reels, 3,900 hours) and 3/4" (reference copies of all 2" videotapes).

Cataloging: Card catalogs and shot lists available for 16mm film; chronological title listing for videotape file.

Access: Open to the public. Available for duplication. Research fees not charged. Research requests accepted by mail, telephone and in person.

Rights: Motion picture collection in the public domain; videotape collection copyrighted (rights retained by television networks).

Licensing: Available for reuse, subject to restrictions. Usage fees not charged.

Restrictions: Copyrights apply to videotape collection.

Viewing Facilities: Film (16mm Steenbeck); videotape (2", 3/4", VHS and Betamax).

Duplication Facilities: Videotape (2" to 3/4", VHS and Betamax).

DISTRICT OF COLUMBIA METRO

NATIONAL ASSOCIATION FOR SPORT & PHYSICAL EDUCATION
1900 Association Drive
Reston, VA 22091
(800) 782-8787
(703) 476-3460 (Virginia residents)

Ross Merrick (Executive Director)

Contact: Bill Denniston (Project Director)

Services: Association. Videotapes available to the public for purchase only; not for research use.

Description: *STEP (Sport Training Education Program)* (co-sponsored with WinMark Sports) is a unique approach to physical education instruction. *STEP* features the use of instructional videotapes and is a total physical education program that benefits student and teacher alike. Instructional videotapes include: *Basketball, Soccer, Tennis, Golf* and *Baseball*. Ten additional videotapes are being completed on archery, badminton, field hockey, fitness development, motor skill development, softball, track and field, basic gymnastics, volleyball and bowling.

Size & Elements: Videotape: format unspecified (5 titles; each 3 hours).

Cataloging: None specified.

Access: Available to the public for purchase only; not for research use. Requests accepted by mail and telephone.

Rights: Full rights held to all material.

Licensing: Apply for information. License and usage fees charged.

Restrictions: Material not available for research purposes.

Viewing Facilities: None.

Duplication Facilities: None.

Related Materials: 24-page student training booklets featuring tips from instructors, graphic demonstrations and a full glossary of sports terms.

DISTRICT OF COLUMBIA METRO

NATIONAL ASSOCIATION OF CONVENIENCE STORES
1605 King Street
Alexandria, VA 22314

(703) 684-3600
Fax: (703) 836-4564

Contact: Amy Deoboald (Education Sales Coordinator)
Services: Association. Films and videotapes available for rental and purchase.
Description: Training programs designed to provide new and established employees with an understanding of the key elements for success in the convenience store industry. Programs cover customer and food service, management, merchandising and security.

Titles include: *Selling and Customer Service; Cash In On Courtesy; You Make the Difference; Avoiding Customer Conflicts; Introduction to Food Service Merchandising; Deli Food Service; In-Store Cooking; Microwave Cooking; Beverage Food Service; Food Service Merchandising Kit; Product Ordering and Inventory Management; MFS Kit; Interviewing Skills Series* (5 parts); *It's About Time; The NACS (Knack) of Training; Fund Raising... It's More Than Money; Techniques of Alcohol Management; Merchandising for Success Overview; Soft Drink Merchandising; Beer Merchandising; Tobacco Merchandising; Candy Merchandising; Health and Beauty Aids and General Merchandise; Gasoline Merchandising Module* (5 parts); *Product Location and Display; Signage; Receiving, Pricing and Stocking; Once Upon A Robbery; Armed Robbery;* and *24 and a Whole Lot More* (1986), a history of the convenience store industry.
Size & Elements: Film: 16mm. Videotape: VHS; Betamax I and II (for purchase only). (30 titles total).
Cataloging: Published catalogs.
Access: Maintained for distribution and rental rather than for research or reuse. Non-members must prepay and add a 50% surcharge to their order. Requests accepted by mail and telephone.
Rights: Full rights held to all materials.
Licensing: Apply for information. License fees charged in some cases.
Restrictions: Express written permission of NACS required for licensing or reuse.
Viewing Facilities: None.
Duplication Facilities: None.

DISTRICT OF COLUMBIA METRO

NATIONAL ASSOCIATION OF HOME BUILDERS PUBLISHING SERVICES
15th and M Streets, NW
Washington, DC 20005
(202) 822-0200

Contact: Publishing Services
Services: Trade association. Videotapes available to NAHB members for rental and purchase; available to non-members for purchase only.
Description: NAHB (organized 1943) is an association of builders and related industry professionals in many allied fields, such as housing finance, the building supply industry, and home sales and marketing. Distributes videotapes on the contemporary housing industry and market. Topics include: marketing and sales, design, remodeling, development and financing, land use and development, and multifamily housing.

Titles include: *Aggressive Selling in a Defensive Market; Be Good or Be Great; How to Demonstrate a Model Home; Establishing a Builder/Realtor Co-op Program; Money-Making Models: Selling Through Design; Renting is Selling; The 7 Basics of Selling New Homes; Using a Host/Hostess in the Sales Office; Dynamics of New Home Promotion; An Introduction to Salesmanship; How to Become a Successful Sales Manager* (5 videotapes), including *Role of the Sales Manager, Get Ready to Manage, Selection and Recruitment of Sales Personnel,* and *Training Sales People and Prospecting; Business Basics for a Successful Remodeler; Land Development Alternatives: A Key to Affordable Housing* (3 videotapes); *Higher Density: Cost Effective and Affordable; Practical Stormwater Management; Street Design Alternatives; Low- and Moderate-Income Housing: Progress, Problems and Prospects; Making Density Work; Housing Affordability; Advertising Mortgage Credit; Concepts and Elements of Joint Venture;* and *100% Financing.*
The Public Affairs Department holds an historic 16mm film collection dating from the early 1960s, which is uncataloged and currently inaccessible.
Size & Elements: Film: 16mm (amount unspecified). Videotape: 3/4", VHS and Betamax (approx. 30 titles).
Cataloging: Published catalog for currently available material. 16mm film collection uncataloged at present.
Access: Videotapes available to NAHB members for rental and purchase; available to non-members for purchase only. Requests accepted by mail and telephone for catalog and order form.

Rights: Full rights held to some material. Additional clearances may be necessary in some cases if material is to be reused.
Licensing: Apply for information. License fees charged in some cases.
Restrictions: Restrictions apply in some cases.
Viewing Facilities: None.
Duplication Facilities: None.

DISTRICT OF COLUMBIA METRO

NATIONAL ASSOCIATION OF SECONDARY SCHOOL PRINCIPALS
1904 Association Drive
Reston, VA 22091
(703) 860-0200
Fax: (703) 476-5432

Scott Thomson (Executive Director)

Contact: Thomas F. Koerner (Editor and Director of Publications)
Services: Association. Films and videotapes available for rental and purchase.
Description: Videotapes of programs recorded at the annual convention.

Building Success series. Titles include: *A Tool for Staff Development,* assisting administrators in staff development; *The Substitute Connection,* enhancing the value of substitute teachers in schools; and *Discipline: Managing Student Behavior in the Classroom and in the School.*

Administrative leadership. Titles include: *Evaluation — Your Key to Improving Learning,* for effective teacher evaluation; *Motivation: Key to Success,* for motivating teachers, students and co-workers; *A Study of High Schools: A Report on "Horace's Compromise,"* a report on a 6-year study; and *What Are You Going to Do Now?,* on improving teacher morale.

College admissions. Titles include: *The Selective Public and Private Colleges — Who Gets In and Why,* featuring two admissions directors discussing factors in college admissions; and *Just a Little Help from Some Friends: Student Financial Aid Today.*

Community involvement and public relations. Titles include: *Greater Community Support — And Without More Time or Money; Parent Activism That Can Help You;* and *School Public Relations — It's Everyone's Job.*

Curriculum. Titles include: *Helping Students Toward Academic Achievement Through Mastery of Study Skills.*

Learning styles and evaluation. Titles include: *Brain Development as It Relates to Adolescent Needs and Program Implications; Time-on-Task — Research Results That Point the Way to Increased Student Learning;* and *Understanding Brain Dominance and Its Effect on Teaching and Learning.*

Middle school. Titles include: *Adolescence Is a Required Course,* exploring transitional years; *Discipline Is a Special Kind of Love; Encounters in Excellence: A New Approach to Educating Middle School Adolescents; Love Me When I'm Most Unlovable — The Middle School Years; A Notion at Risk,* the legacy of protective custody; *Providing High Quality Learning Time for Middle Level Students,* on improving use of classroom time; and *The School in the Middle, What's Special About It?.*

School improvement. Titles include: *The American High School: Dark Trends and Bright Hopes; Excellence in Schooling: Effective Styles for Effective Schools; School Climate: The Key to an Effective School;* and *What Research Tells the Principal About School Climate: An NASSP Task Force Report.*

Special programs. Titles include: *Managing Conflict — From the Inside Out; Opening Doors to Self-Awareness — A Peer Counseling Model* shows students working under supervision of staff to reach students that the guidance staff cannot reach; *Student Leadership Class — A Positive Program for Your School; Systematic Training for Effective Parenting — Working with the Problems and Issues of Teens,* nine sessions for parents to improve communication with young people; *Coming of Age: A Musical Drama About Being Thirteen;* and *The Educational Impact of "Coming of Age: A Musical Drama About Being Thirteen."*

Student council. Titles include: *Side by Side,* about student leaders' involvement in school; *Together,* stressing the importance of council members working jointly to attain goals; *We Are Many — We Are One,* about the importance of student council; *Where Do You Go from Here?,* on the duties and responsibilities of a Student Council Executive Committee.
Size & Elements: Film: 16mm. Videotape: 3/4", VHS, Betamax I and II. (Approx. 170 titles total).
Cataloging: Published catalogs.
Access: Available for rental and purchase.
Rights: Full rights held to some material. Additional clearances may be necessary in some cases if material is to be reused.
Licensing: Maintained for distribution rather than reuse.

Restrictions: None specified.
Viewing Facilities: None.
Duplication Facilities: None.
Related Materials: Audiotapes on related subjects from NASSP conventions.

DISTRICT OF COLUMBIA METRO

NATIONAL CATHOLIC EDUCATIONAL ASSOCIATION
1077 30th Street, NW, Suite 100
Washington, DC 20007-3852
(202) 337-6232

Sister Catherine McNamee (President)

Contact: Phyllis Kokus (Publication Sales Manager)
Services: Nonprofit educational association. Videotape collection available primarily for rental and purchase.
Description: Videotapes produced for Catholic school and religious education personnel, parent groups, students in undergraduate or graduate education, religious education courses and catechetical programs.
 Topics covered include: administration and planning, justice and peace, religious education, special education, divorce and parents, morality and teacher formation.
 Titles include: *Building a Foundation for the Future* (1986), relating to Catholic elementary and secondary education; *The Christian Formation of Catholic Educators; Mainstreaming: Responding to the Individual Needs of Children Within the Regular Classroom* (1983); *Jean Vanier: The Challenge and Response to Peace for Catholic Educators* (1984), a two-part program of Jean Vanier's keynote address at General Sessions of the 1984 NCEA Convention; *Divorce: Information and Implications for Catholic Educators* (1983); *How To Teach Christian Morality* (1978); and *Sharing The Light of Faith — The National Catechetical Directory* (1978). Also available is a videotape of Pope John Paul II's visit and address to Catholic educators in the New Orleans Superdome and at Xavier University (September 1987).
Size & Elements: Videotape: 3/4", VHS, Betamax I and II (8 titles, each 10 to 60 min.).
Cataloging: Published catalog.
Access: Available to the public for rental and purchase. Material may be viewed at NCEA at no charge. Requests accepted in person (by appointment only).
Rights: Full rights held to all material.
Licensing: Apply for information.
Restrictions: None specified.
Viewing Facilities: Videotape (by special arrangement).
Duplication Facilities: None.

DISTRICT OF COLUMBIA METRO

NATIONAL CENTER FOR FILM AND VIDEO PRESERVATION
THE AMERICAN FILM INSTITUTE
The John F. Kennedy Center
Washington, DC 20566
(202) 828-4070
Telex: 910 240 9077 afi uq

Contact: Susan Dalton (Archivist)
Services: Film and videotape archive. Material available for research and reuse, subject to certain restrictions.
Description: The American Film Institute (AFI) Collection at the Library of Congress includes over 21,000 titles and consists primarily of theatrical features and shorts (1894-present), as well as substantial numbers of newsreels, documentaries and television programs.
 Major collections include:
Hal Roach Studios Collection. Contains approximately 700 films.
Thomas Ince Collection. Contains 55 features.
Columbia Pictures Collection (1928-52). Consists of over 4,000 features and shorts.
 Paramount Collection (1914-37). Includes nearly 200 features.
 RKO Collection (1929-56). Holds 740 features and 900 shorts.
 Universal Collection. 600 features and shorts.
 United Artists Collection of Warner Brothers releases (1920-50). Contains approximately 1,175 features and 1,500 shorts.
 Black Films Collection. Over 100 films produced by or starring Black Americans.
 Additional films in the AFI Collection are held by over a dozen other archives, particularly UCLA Film and Television Archive; The Museum of Modern Art, Department of Film; and International Museum of Photography at George Eastman House (all q.v.).
Size & Elements: All types of film and videotape elements. Most films originally received on nitrate stock. In many cases, viewing copies are not yet available.
Cataloging: Cataloged by title only.
Access: The Center is not a custodial archive. While information about the AFI Collection may be obtained directly from the Center, information regarding access should be obtained from the Library of Congress, Motion Picture, Broadcasting and Recorded Sound Division (q.v.) and other appropriate archives.
Rights: Some material in the public domain. Rights generally retained by original source or producer.
Licensing: Not applicable.
Restrictions: Users must assume full responsibility for copyright search and/or securing any necessary clearances or authorizations required for reuse of the material.
Viewing Facilities: Contact appropriate archive.
Duplication Facilities: Contact appropriate archive.
Publications: A catalog of film holdings is not available at this time. The Center publishes *The AFI Catalog of Feature Films,* a comprehensive national filmography providing documentation on all feature films produced in the United States. Volumes for 1911-20, 1921-30 and 1961-70 have been published.

DISTRICT OF COLUMBIA METRO

NATIONAL CENTER FOR MISSING & EXPLOITED CHILDREN
1835 K Street, Suite 600
Washington, DC 20006
(202) 634-9821
Fax: (202) 634-6106

Ellis E. Meredith (President)

Contact: David L. Shapiro (Director, Development and Education)
Services: Association. Videotape available for loan and licensing, subject to restrictions.
Description: A videotape containing a brief history of the Center and some case studies. It is used mainly to introduce the Center to corporate sponsors; viewing copies are also loaned to other interested parties. Plans are to expand in the audiovisual field to help educate and train professionals and social service workers about missing and exploited children.
Size & Elements: Videotape: 3/4", VHS and Betamax (1 title, 12 min.).
Access: Available to the public and corporate sponsors. Research fees not charged. Research requests accepted by mail and telephone.
Rights: Full rights held to all material.
Licensing: Available for licensing and reuse, subject to restrictions. License fees not charged.
Restrictions: Licensing and reuse subject to clearance and approval.
Viewing Facilities: Videotape (VHS).
Duplication Facilities: Videotape (VHS).

DISTRICT OF COLUMBIA METRO

NATIONAL CONSERVATIVE FOUNDATION
1001 Prince Street
Alexandria, VA 22314
(703) 548-0900

Maiselle Dolan Shortly (Chairman)

Contact: Scott Belliveau (Editor of *Newswatch*)
Services: Association; foundation. Videotape collection for reference and research purposes only; available for duplication.
Description: Research collection containing television news programs videotaped off the air (June 1985-present). Holds news shows and news specials from all three major networks, and some from PBS.
Size & Elements: Videotape: VHS (7,200 hours).
Cataloging: Material arranged by date (not by subject).
Access: Available to researchers, scholars and the public. Available for duplication. Research fees not charged; VHS videotape stock must be provided by researcher for duplication purposes. Research requests accepted by mail and telephone only.

Rights: No rights held to any material. Rights retained by original broadcasters or producers. Additional clearances will be necessary if material is to be reused.
Licensing: Available for reuse, subject to restrictions.
Restrictions: Original source or producer must be contacted for information regarding reuse.
Viewing Facilities: None.
Duplication Facilities: Videotape (VHS to VHS).
Publications: *Newswatch,* a monthly report from the Media Research Center (a project of the NCF) critically discusses news media coverage.

DISTRICT OF COLUMBIA METRO

NATIONAL CRIME PREVENTION COUNCIL
733 15th Street, NW, Suite 540
Washington, DC 20005
(202) 393-7141
Fax: (202) 638-2928

Contact: Leonard A. Sipes, Jr. (Director of Information Services, Technical Assistance Center)
Services: Organization. Film and videotape library available for in-house use and reuse, subject to clearance and restrictions.
Description: Extensive library of public service announcements (PSAs) relating to crime prevention and related issues.

Subjects covered include crime prevention; protection of homes against vacation-time burglaries; Halloween safety tips; rape prevention; history of the Advertising Council and its campaigns; crime scenarios and deterrents to crime. Several PSAs use the character of McGruff the Dog and the slogan "Take A Bite Out of Crime."
Size & Elements: Film: 16mm (amount unspecified). Videotape: format and amount unspecified.
Cataloging: Film lists; computerized cataloging.
Access: Primarily for in-house use; not available for loan. Copies of videotapes can be made if item is not copyrighted; requester pays all duplication fees.
Rights: Some rights held to some material. Some material in the public domain.
Licensing: Apply for information.
Restrictions: Copyrights apply to some material.
Viewing Facilities: None.
Duplication Facilities: None.

DISTRICT OF COLUMBIA METRO

NATIONAL DANCE ASSOCIATION
1900 Association Drive
Reston, VA 22091
(703) 476-3436

Margie Hanson (Executive Director)

Contact: Margie Hanson
Services: Association; film library. Films available for rental and purchase.
Description: National Dance Association is a division of the American Alliance for Health, Physical Education, Recreation and Dance (q.v.).

Holds short instructional films and videotapes on dance and gymnastics, designed for teachers and students. Three series are available: *The Dance Experience; The Original Dance Instrument Series;* and *Gymnastics.*
Size & Elements: Film: 16mm. Videotape: VHS (less than a dozen titles).
Cataloging: Included in the American Alliance for Health, Physical Education, Recreation and Dance catalog.
Access: Available for rental and purchase. Requests accepted by mail.
Rights: Apply for information.
Licensing: Apply for information.
Restrictions: None specified.
Viewing Facilities: None.
Duplication Facilities: None.

DISTRICT OF COLUMBIA METRO

NATIONAL ENDOWMENT FOR THE ARTS
MEDIA ARTS PROGRAM
1100 Pennsylvania Avenue, NW
Washington, DC 20506
(202) 682-5452
Fax: (202) 682-5798

Brian O'Doherty (Program Director, Media Arts Program)

Contact: Maria R. Goodwin (Program Specialist, Final Reports/Research, Media Arts Program)
Services: Government agency. Film and videotape collection for in-house use only. *Not open to the public.*
Description: The Media Arts Program's Film/Video/Audio Library contains copies of independent and organizational programs funded by NEA that have been submitted as part of the recipients' final reports. Productions vary in topic and length, from major series (*Wonderworks, American Playhouse*) to independent productions (*Chan Is Missing, Ansel Adams: Photographer*) and film and video artworks. Genres include documentary; docudrama; the performing arts; children's programming; and experimental film and video.

Collection is for in-house use only and is not available to the public. When possible, distribution information can be supplied to persons wishing to purchase copies of works; but since grantees are not required to inform the Program of any changes in distribution, this information is not always current.
Size & Elements: Film: formats unspecified (approx. 200 cans). Videotape: 3/4" (approx. 1,620 videotapes; viewing copies); VHS (approx. 180 videotapes; viewing copies). The percentage of VHS relative to the whole is increasing; all videotape formats are accepted from grantees.
Cataloging: Card catalogs; computerized cataloging for staff use only.
Access: Not open to the public. For in-house use only.
Rights: No rights held to any material.
Licensing: Not available for licensing or reuse.
Restrictions: Not open to the public.
Viewing Facilities: None.
Duplication Facilities: None.

DISTRICT OF COLUMBIA METRO

NATIONAL GALLERY OF ART
DEPARTMENT OF EXTENSION PROGRAMS
Washington, DC 20565
(202) 842-6273

Ruth R. Perlin (Head, Department of Extension Programs)

Contact: Ruth R. Perlin
Services: Museum. Films and videotapes available to qualified organizations for extended free loan. Selected programs may be available to approved borrowers for broadcasting and/or duplication.
Description: Films and videotapes relating to painting and the fine arts.

Titles include: *In Search of Rembrandt,* narrated by James Mason; *Leonardo: To Know How To See,* narrated by Sir John Gielgud; *On Loan from Russia: Forty-one French Masterpieces,* including scenes of packing, shipping, installation and other aspects of the exhibit; *Treasures of Tutankhamun; The Eye of Thomas Jefferson; Ancient Moderns: Greek Island Art and Culture, 3000-2000 B.C.; Femme/Woman: A Tapestry* by Joan Miró, including footage of the weaving process; *Mobile, by Alexander Calder; Picasso: The Saltimbanques; David Smith, American Sculptor, 1906-1965; James McNeill Whistler: His Etchings;* and *John James Audubon: The Birds of America.*

Awareness Films. Short, evocative presentations of major artists, accompanied by music and only a minimum of narration. Artists include: Francisco Goya, Jean Honoré Fragonard, Edgar Degas, John Singleton Copley, El Greco, Rembrandt, Pierre Auguste Renoir, J. M. W. Turner, William Blake, Canaletto, Mary Cassatt, George Catlin, Paul Cézanne, Albrecht Dürer, Peter Paul Rubens, Monet, Paul Gauguin and Pablo Picasso.
Size & Elements: Film: 16mm. Videotape: 3/4" (masters and viewing copies); VHS and Betamax (viewing copies). (Approx. 45 titles total).
Cataloging: Published catalog.
Access: Available to the public for free loan, via approved, nonprofit organizations. Material possibly available to organizations with large audiences or their own distribution systems for extended (annual) periods. Requests accepted four months in advance by mail.
Rights: Full rights held to some material. Some rights held to all material. Additional clearances will be necessary in some cases if material is to be reused.
Licensing: Apply for information.
Restrictions: None specified.
Viewing Facilities: Film (auditorium).
Duplication Facilities: None.

DISTRICT OF COLUMBIA METRO

NATIONAL GEOGRAPHIC SOCIETY
STOCK FOOTAGE LIBRARY
1600 M Street, NW
Washington, DC 20036
(202) 857-7659
Fax: (202) 775-6141
Telex: 64194

Patricia Gang (Head Audiovisual Librarian)

Contacts: Catherine Yelloz (AV Library Coordinator); Robert Wolman (Film Librarian); Sue Tomlinson (Administrative Assistant)
Services: Educational institution; film and videotape producer; stock footage sales library.
Description: Outtakes from National Geographic Society film and television productions and presentations (1964-present).

Topics include geography (world and United States), natural phenomena, animals and animal behavior, outdoor recreation, architecture, transportation, science and scientific methods, exploration, lands and people of the world, adventure, history, the undersea world and wildlife.

Numerous educational films are available for distribution in film and videotape formats.
Size & Elements: Film: 16mm (8 million feet; original color negative and Ektachrome Commercial positive, matching workprint). Videotape: 1" (masters); 3/4" (viewing copies, transfers from film).
Cataloging: Card catalog of subjects; scene-by-scene indexing; computerized cataloging in progress; shot lists.
Access: Available for licensing and reuse. Research fees charged on an hourly basis. Research requests accepted by mail, telephone and in person (by appointment only). Preview videotapes available upon request (assembly fee applies).
Rights: Full rights held to all material.
Licensing: Available for licensing and reuse. License fees charged (fee schedule available on request).
Restrictions: None specified.
Viewing Facilities: Film (16mm Steenbeck flatbed viewing tables). Library normally makes preview videotapes which are sent to clients.
Duplication Facilities: Film (film-to-videotape transfers for preview only); videotape (for preview only).

DISTRICT OF COLUMBIA METRO

NATIONAL GLASS ASSOCIATION
VIDEO GLASS
NGA MEMBER SERVICES
8200 Greensboro Drive, Suite 302
McLean, VA 22102
(703) 442-4890
Fax: (703) 442-0630

Philip J. James (Executive Director)

Contact: Leo M. Cyr (Director of Member Services)
Services: Association. Videotapes available to NGA members and the public for purchase only.
Description: Training and instructional videotapes on the use and installation of automotive glass, door glass, mirrors and tempered glass; glass cutting; office procedures; and glass safety.

Automotive glass. Titles include: *Auto Glass-Butyl and Urethane; Butyl & Urethane Sealants: An Update; Flush Fit Windshields; Mercury Sable Installation — 1986 Model; Ford Taurus Installation — 1986 Model; Meeting Structural Strength; Problem Auto Glass Installations, Parts 1-3; New Tools for Problem Auto Glass Installation;* and *Three Vinyl Backlite Installations.*

Doors. Titles include: *All Glass Doors & Storefronts; Custom Shower Door Installation; Commercial Door Hardware & Locks;* and *Door Closers.*

Glass cutting. Titles include: *Basic Glass Cutting; Laminated Glass/Uses of;* and *Laminated Glass/Cutting & Handling.*

Mirrors. Titles include: *Mirror Processing & Fabrication;* and *Mirror Measuring & Installation.*

Miscellaneous. Titles include: *Basics of Glass Tempering; Glass Shop Customer Service/Telephone Techniques;* and *Glass Handling Safety: Manual Techniques.*
Size & Elements: Videotape: VHS and Betamax (24 titles).

Cataloging: Catalog/brochure.
Access: Available to NGA members and the public for purchase only.
Rights: Full rights held to all material.
Licensing: License fees charged.
Restrictions: None specified.
Viewing Facilities: None.
Duplication Facilities: None.

DISTRICT OF COLUMBIA METRO

NATIONAL LIBRARY OF MEDICINE
HISTORY OF MEDICINE DIVISION
HISTORICAL AUDIOVISUALS COLLECTION
Building 38, Room 1E21B
8600 Rockville Pike
Bethesda, MD 20894
(301) 496-8949

Sarah L. Richards (Motion Picture Archivist)

Contact: Sarah L. Richards
Services: Government agency; film and videotape archives; library. Material available for research, and in some cases duplication and reuse, subject to clearance and restrictions.
Description: Formerly known as the National Medical Historical Film Program. Holds films and videotapes (1917-80) relating to medicine, public health, clinical medical teaching, psychiatry and mental institutions. Though most titles are in English, some are in German, Russian and French.

Collection holds all pre-1970 audiovisual titles in the National Library of Medicine. Donations include films from the National Medical Audiovisual Center, American Medical Association, Mayo Clinic, Microcirculatory Society, Museum of Modern Art, Psychological Cinema Register of Pennsylvania State University, private persons, firms and other organizations.

Categories include: teaching films, made for medical and allied schools; documentation of experiments, including films of recorded research data or those used as part of a biomedical experiment; films made to promote or publicize preventive medicine or specific health agencies; films depicting significant persons, events, research methodology, facilities or equipment in the health sciences; and films showing the evolution or development of medical motion pictures.

Recent acquisitions include two unique films made in a tuberculosis sanatorium at South Mountain, Pa. One film (1926) shows children being institutionalized to prevent them from contracting the disease and unusual medical treatment of adult patients. Other acquisitions include *Birth of a Baby,* an early film sponsored by the medical profession and banned as pornographic in many states and *Fraud Fighters,* an early dramatic film about the U.S. Food and Drug Administration's efforts to prevent fraud in food and drug product labeling and sale.

Current medical-related films are also available through interlibrary loan from the National Library of Medicine.
Size & Elements: Film: 35mm (114,944 feet); 16mm (1,629,590 feet). Videotape: 1" (22 titles, 9 hours) and 3/4" (352 titles; 115 hours). (3,000 titles total). Each title represented by different elements. Library tries to acquire the highest generation possible from which to make printing masters; print and videotape loan copies are also made.
Cataloging: Card catalogs; computerized cataloging for staff and researchers' use.
Access: Open to the public. Material available for research, and in some cases duplication and reuse, subject to clearance. Research fees charged in some cases (depending on complexity of search). Research requests accepted by mail, telephone and in person (by appointment only).
Rights: No rights held to some material. Some material in the public domain. Rights status of some material not known.
Licensing: Available for reuse, subject to clearance and restrictions. Usage fees not charged.
Restrictions: Library must receive credit in final production. Users must complete forms indemnifying Library from liability if material is misused.
Viewing Facilities: Film (4 flatbed viewing tables); videotape (3/4").
Duplication Facilities: None.

DISTRICT OF COLUMBIA METRO

NATIONAL OCEANIC AND ATMOSPHERIC ADMINISTRATION (NOAA) STOCK FILM LIBRARY

NOAA Public Affairs, Room 6013
14th Street and Constitution Avenue, NW
Washington, DC 20230
(202) 377-8090

Robert Amdur (Director of Audiovisual Services)

Contact: Jay Tebeau (Public Affairs Specialist)
Services: Government agency; film producer. Collection available to the public on a free-loan basis for nonprofit use; some material available for reuse.
Description: Weather; floods; hurricanes; tornadoes; estuaries; climate; oceans and ocean life; sunken ships; underwater photography; sockeye salmon; fish and fishing; and cooking and culture in various U.S. regions.

Weather. Titles include: *Flash Flood* (1979), illustrating the dangers of flash flooding in mountainous terrain when a family camping near a quiet stream suddenly finds itself in deadly peril; *Flood* (1975), describing the manner in which flood predictions are made, portraying basic precautions against the dangers and hardships imposed by floods, and showing floods caused by seasonal snow melt, hurricanes and heavy rainstorms; *Global Weather Experiment* (1980), documenting the massive, planetary and intelligence-gathering operation by 149 nations (1979); *The Climate Factor* (1984), examining agricultural architecture, fuel supply demands and the greenhouse effect; *Hurricane* (1984), tracking an actual hurricane from its tame beginnings in the Atlantic to its deadly landfall at Galveston, Texas (August, 1983); *Terrible Tuesday* (1984), featuring the compelling stories of survivors from one of history's worst tornado outbreaks in Wichita Falls, Texas.

Oceans. Titles include: *Down to the Monitor* (1980), depicting a diving mission uncovering the Civil War vessel *U.S.S. Monitor; Boundary of Creation* (1975), documenting the French-American study of the mid-Atlantic ridge, using underwater photography to illustrate plate tectonics; *Estuary* (1976), describing estuaries, including bays, lagoons and ends of the rivers; and *First Dive, Last Dive* (1980), on scuba diving safety.

Ocean life. Titles include: *Sockeye Odyssey* (1971), examining the life cycle and conservation of the Alaskan sockeye salmon; *The Great American Fish Story* (1976), on the history of the U.S. commercial fishing industry. Four additional titles in the series concern *The West, The Northeast, The South* and *The Lakes and Rivers.*

Other films. Titles include: *Sentinels in Space* (1980), covering environmental satellites which provide information from space for agricultural applications, water temperature measurement for commercial fishing and solar flare measurements; and *The Seventh Service* (1978), depicting the NOAA Corps in action through the eyes of officer trainees.
Size & Elements: Film: 16mm (amount unspecified; "older material"). Videotape: 3/4" (approx. 25 titles).
Cataloging: Published lists.
Access: Available to the public for free loan for nonprofit use (return postage must be paid). Requests accepted by mail (apply three months in advance). Some material available for reuse. Research fees not charged. Research requests accepted by telephone.
Rights: Full rights held to some material. Additional clearances may be necessary in some cases if material is to be reused.
Licensing: Available for reuse, subject to restrictions. Usage fees charged.
Restrictions: Some titles may be restricted from reuse.
Viewing Facilities: None.
Duplication Facilities: None.
Distributor: Modern Talking Picture Service, Inc. (q.v.).

DISTRICT OF COLUMBIA METRO

NATIONAL ORGANIZATION FOR WOMEN (NOW)
1401 New York Avenue NW, Suite 800
Washington, DC 20005
(202) 347-2279
Fax: (202) 785-8576

Molly Yard (President)

Contact: Junior Bridge
Services: Nonprofit political organization. One videotape available for purchase.
Description: NOW's 20th Anniversary Show of 1986, filmed live at the Dorothy Chandler Pavilion in Los Angeles. Interspersed between celebrities describing landmark events is archival film; two major film essays narrated by Marlo Thomas (one on the Vermont state ERA campaign and one on Title IX);

a monologue by Lily Tomlin; a speech by NOW's president Eleanor Smeal; and six musical numbers. Cast includes: Alan Alda, Eve Arden, Edward Asner, Rene Auberjonois, Yvonne Burke, Patty Duke, Linda Ellerbee, Fionnula Flanagan, Betty Ford, Betty Friedan, Charles Haid, Buck Henry, Gloria Steinem, Jessica Walter, James Whitmore, Paul Winfield and many others.
Size & Elements: Videotape: VHS (1 title).
Cataloging: Brochure.
Access: Available to the public for purchase. Postage and handling fees charged. Orders accepted by mail and telephone. Orders should be directed to: Peg Yorkin Productions, 8105 West 3rd Street, Suite 1, Los Angeles, CA 90048; (213) 651-0491.
Rights: Apply for information.
Licensing: Not available for licensing or reuse.
Restrictions: Not available for licensing or reuse.
Viewing Facilities: None.
Duplication Facilities: None.

DISTRICT OF COLUMBIA METRO

NATIONAL PARKS AND CONSERVATION ASSOCIATION
1015 Thirty-First Street, NW
Washington, DC 20007
(202) 944-8530
Fax: (202) 944-8535

Paul C. Pritchard (President)

Contact: Elliot Gruber (Media Coordinator)
Services: Association. Videotapes available for purchase.
Description: Videotapes related to National Parks and nature conservation. Sample titles include: *Wild Alaska, Touring Alaska* and *Touring America's National Parks.*
Size & Elements: Videotape: 1/2" (6 titles).
Cataloging: None specified.
Access: Available to the public for purchase (apply for rates). Maintained for distribution or rental rather than for research or reuse. Requests accepted by mail and telephone.
Rights: Rights status of material not known. Additional clearances may be necessary in some cases if material is to be reused.
Licensing: Available for reuse, subject to restrictions.
Restrictions: Original producer of material must be contacted for information regarding rights and reuse.
Viewing Facilities: None.
Duplication Facilities: None.

DISTRICT OF COLUMBIA METRO

NATIONAL RAILWAY HISTORICAL SOCIETY
FILM LIBRARY
6504 Barnaby Street, NW
Washington, DC 20015
(202) 363-7827

William D. Gray (Director, Film Library)

Contact: William D. Gray
Services: Historical society; operates Harry P. Dodge Memorial Film Library. Films available for rental to groups and organizations.
Description: U.S. and European railroads and trolleys (1924-85).

Educational film documentaries. Sample titles include: *Golden Age of Railroading, Railway and Trolley Memories; Mainline USA;* and *The Great Steam Machine.*

Historic trains. Sample titles include: *The California Zephyr; The Flying Scotsman* (1929 feature), starring Ray Milland; *Zambezi Express;* and *Victoria Line Report,* about the London Underground. *GG-1: An American Classic* (1985) tells the history of the classic Pennsylvania Railroad electric engine, whose exterior was designed by Raymond Loewy.

Vintage promotional and industrial films. Films promoting railroad companies. Sample titles include: *Operation Reading* and *Your Track to Profit.*

Travelogues. New York Calling; Through the Rockies by Rail; Rails Across the Summit; Elizabethan Express, a "poetic" non-stop trip from London to Edinburgh; and *Coast to Coast in 48 Hours,* a rail and air journey in the early 1930s, featuring Charles Lindbergh.

Transit systems. Films showing interesting views of American urban transit systems (1920s-40s). Sample titles include: *Safe Highways* (1924), a Chicago

Surface Lines "safety" film with hilarious staged automobile and trolley crashes; *It's A Big Job* (1947), showing how to operate a Los Angeles streetcar; *Getting About* (1934), glorifying Detroit's vast streetcar system; *1945 on the North Shore Line,* following the suburban MU trains and Electroliners of the Chicago North Shore and Milwaukee; *March of Progress* (1946), a promotional film made by the Key System for their Bay Bridge trains between San Francisco and Oakland, including an artist's conception of futuristic trains and "on-line" footage shot on the Bay Bridge and from the motorman's cab.

Told through a series of interviews with former porters, archival film clips and Hollywood footage, *Miles of Smiles — Years of Struggle* tells the hundred-year history of Black Pullman porters.

Size & Elements: Film: 16mm (65 films; mostly sound, some silent, varying lengths). Videotape: VHS and Betamax (1 title).
Cataloging: Card catalogs.
Access: Available to the public. Maintained primarily for rental and distribution rather than for research or reuse. Requests accepted by mail and telephone. Research fees not charged.
Rights: Material in the public domain.
Licensing: Apply for information. Usage fees not charged.
Restrictions: None specified.
Viewing Facilities: None.
Duplication Facilities: None.

DISTRICT OF COLUMBIA METRO

NATIONAL RESTAURANT ASSOCIATION PUBLICATIONS
1200 17th Street, NW, 8th Floor
Washington, DC 20036-3097
(202) 331-5900
Fax: (202) 331-2429

William P. Fisher (Executive Vice President)

Contact: Publication Department
Services: Association. Maintains training videotape library as a service to its membership. Apply for information concerning access to nonmembers.
Description: The Association's Video Training series consists of ten videotapes which cover basic restaurant operations. The videotapes are produced on location in an actual food service operation, and are designed for table service restaurants, whether they are family-style or white-tablecloth establishments. Student exercises are included.

Waitstaff Training (4 videotapes) instructs waitstaff in preparing their stations, greeting customers, taking orders, serving meals, maintaining service, presenting the check and saying farewell. One videotape deals with "suggestive selling" techniques; examples show actual waiters and waitresses using these techniques which range from "menu knowledge" to "enthusiasm when communicating with customers." Another videotape deals with teamwork, using the analogy of a football team on the playing field.

Back-of-the-House Training (3 videotapes, also available in Spanish) follows the flow of food from loading dock through its preparation to the customer, stopping at each point where bacteria could infect food.

Wine Training (3 videotapes) focuses on "wine knowledge" and its tremendous profit potential for restaurant operators. Developed with the Winegrowers of California, this series demonstrates the importance of merchandising strategies to a profit-boosting wine sales program. Another videotape emphasizes the importance of knowing the wine list, discerning taste preferences and price ranges of customers, how and when to suggest appropriate wines and how to serve them. The third videotape explores the wine regions of the world, examines the subtleties of wine making and reviews the basics of food and wine pairing.
Size & Elements: Videotape: 3/4", VHS and Betamax (10 titles, each 10 to 20 min.).
Cataloging: Published catalogs.
Access: Available as a service to Association members. Apply for information regarding access to non-members.
Rights: Full rights held to all material.
Licensing: Apply for information. License fees not charged.
Restrictions: None specified.
Viewing Facilities: None.
Duplication Facilities: None.

DISTRICT OF COLUMBIA METRO

NATIONAL RIFLE ASSOCIATION

Sales Department
P.O. Box 96031
Washington, DC 20090-6031
(202) 828-6000
(800) 336-7402

Available for free loan from:
NRA FREE LOAN LIBRARY
c/o Karol Media
22 Riverview Drive
Wayne, NJ 07470-3191
(201) 628-9111

Contact: Cathy Coffin
Services: Association. Films and videotapes available for purchase or free loan for educational purposes.
Description: Firearms, hunting, shooting and outdoor sports. Titles include: *Sure as Shooting; The Kid Who Can't Miss; Firearms Safety: First and Foremost; Firearms Responsibility; It Can Happen to You; Wilderness Survival; The Champions; Olympic Shooting; At Home with Guns; Pistol Shooting Fundamentals; Shotgun Shooting Fundamentals; Firing the Shot; Kneeling and Sitting; Standing and Prone; Wild Heritage; The Great Tradition; Skeet Shooting with D. Lee Braun; A Question of Hunting; Trapshooting with Remington Pros; Olympic Archery: The Mind, Body and Spirit; Bowhunting, North America;* and *Fly Fishing in America*.
Size & Elements: Film: 16mm. Videotape: VHS and Betamax II. (Approx. 25 titles total).
Cataloging: Published brochures.
Access: Available to the public for purchase, and for free loan to schools, clubs and groups for educational purposes. Requests accepted by mail and telephone.
Rights: Apply for information.
Licensing: Apply for information.
Restrictions: None specified.
Viewing Facilities: None.
Duplication Facilities: None.

DISTRICT OF COLUMBIA METRO

NATIONAL RIGHT TO LIFE COMMITTEE
419 Seventh Street, NW, Suite 500
Washington, DC 20004
(202) 626-8800
Fax: (202) 737-9189

J. C. Willke, MD (President)

Contact: Dan Donehey (Public Relations Director)
Services: Political organization; videotape producer. Videotape material available for reuse, subject to restrictions.
Description: Television footage (videotaped off the air) relating to issues of abortion, infanticide and euthanasia; original footage of convention program speeches (75 videotapes); marches and documentary material (6 hours). Committee has produced 14 television commercials and plans to produce a 30 min. cable television program series on medical ethics.
Size & Elements: Videotape: 1", 3/4" and 1/2" (100 hours total).
Cataloging: Printed list.
Access: Available to the public for reuse and resale. Research fees not charged. Research requests accepted by mail and telephone.
Rights: Full rights held to some material.
Licensing: Available for reuse, subject to restrictions. Usage fees not charged.
Restrictions: Requests for licensing and reuse subject to acceptance and approval.
Viewing Facilities: Videotape (1/2").
Duplication Facilities: Videotape.

DISTRICT OF COLUMBIA METRO

NATIONAL SCHOOL BOARDS ASSOCIATION
1680 Duke Street
Alexandria, VA 22314
(703) 838-6722
Fax: (703) 683-7590

Dr. Thomas A. Shannon (Executive Director)

Contact: Dr. Jeremiah Floyd (Associate Executive Director)
Services: Association. Film and videotape material available to researchers and scholars only.
Description: Has produced two training films and one public service announcement (PSA) on the role of school boards.

Titles include: *All on Board* (1985), a training film, part of a training program designed to emphasize the roles and skills of effective boardmanship; *A Delicate Balance: School Board/Superintendent Relations* (1987), a customized training film, part of a training program emphasizing the distinct governance and management roles of elected and executive leaders; and *Your School Boards* (1986), a PSA videotape presentation on the role of school boards.
Size & Elements: Film: 16mm (2 titles, each approx. 30 min.). Videotape: 3/4" (1 title).
Cataloging: None specified.
Access: Available to researchers and scholars only. Research fees not charged. Research requests accepted by mail and in person (walk-in).
Rights: Full rights held to all material.
Licensing: Apply for information. License fees not charged.
Restrictions: None specified.
Viewing Facilities: Film and videotape.
Duplication Facilities: None.

DISTRICT OF COLUMBIA METRO

NATIONAL SCIENCE FOUNDATION
1800 G Street, NW, Room 527
Washington, DC 20550
(202) 357-9498
Fax: (202) 357-9869

Erich Bloch (Director)

Contact: Susan Bartlett (Audiovisual Officer)
Services: Government agency; film producer. Films available for distribution, broadcast and reuse, but must be obtained directly from various distributors.
Description: The Foundation is a government agency producing films for public distribution each year to report progress in scientific research and its applications. The films reflect important research and cover a large array of scientific disciplines supported by the Foundation. A few of the films document research results for a more narrowly focused, technical audience.

Major categories of available films are general science, astronomy, earth sciences, ecology and environment, education and learning, energy, engineering, ocean sciences, physics, polar research, research applications, and weather and climate. The majority of the films in the current catalog were produced in the 1970s.

One of the most recent listings, *Science: Woman's Work* (1982) addresses itself to the small proportion of women scientists in the U.S. workforce. Other titles include: *A Stranger Near the Sun,* on Comet Kohoutek; *That Very Special Ship,* showing the Glomar Challenger research ship; and *Rivers of the Sea,* relating to ocean chemistry. Other films concern experimental forests and undersea research. Many films have received numerous U.S. and international festival awards.
Size & Elements: Film: 16mm (approx. 50 titles; internegatives and original elements are held at film laboratories). Videotape: format unspecified (1 title; master).
Cataloging: Published catalogs.
Access: Available for rental, duplication and reuse. In some cases, television stations may show these films as unsponsored public service telecasts and transfer them to videotape for this purpose without prior permission. For stock footage requests, requester must obtain films from distributors, then deal directly with laboratory holding original film elements. Contact NSF for information on current distributors. Research requests are accepted by mail, telephone and in person (by appointment only).
Rights: Some rights held to some material. Most material in the public domain. Additional clearances may be necessary in some cases if material is to be reused.
Licensing: Footage requests must be cleared with the Foundation. Persons wishing to use footage from any of these films should contact the Public Affairs and Publications Group of the Foundation. License fees not charged.
Restrictions: Requests for reuse subject to clearance and approval.
Viewing Facilities: None.
Duplication Facilities: None.

DISTRICT OF COLUMBIA METRO

NATIONAL SUDDEN INFANT DEATH SYNDROME FOUNDATION
National Office
8200 Professional Place, Suite 104
Landover, MD 20785-2264
(301) 459-3388
(800) 221-7437

Mitch Stoller (Executive Director)

Contact: Edith McShane (Assistant Executive Director)
Services: Foundation. Film collection available to the public for rental; some material available to qualified broadcasters.
Description: Material relating to Sudden Infant Death Syndrome (SIDS). Holds three public service announcements (PSAs), produced by the Foundation, *The Falling Beef, A Bedtime Story,* and *Morning Light.* These target various groups including physicians, nurses, emergency medical technicians, police, clergy, funeral directors, professional counselors, babysitters and coroners.

Three films produced by the U.S. Department of Health and Human Services are available for rental through the Foundation and available for purchase from NARA, National Audiovisual Center (q.v.). *You Are Not Alone* looks at an infant's death through the eyes of families and relatives who must cope with a condition that is still unexplained and unpreventable. *After Our Baby Died* explores the importance of counseling SIDS parents at the time of the loss. *A Call For Help* is designed for emergency workers and stresses the need for a thoughtful and concerned approach at a time when the family is still in a state of shock and confusion.
Size & Elements: Film: 16mm (3 films). Videotape: 3/4" (3 videotapes).
Cataloging: Published list.
Access: Films available to the public for rental from the Foundation and for purchase from National Audiovisual Center. PSAs available to qualified broadcasters. Requests accepted by mail and telephone.
Rights: Full rights held to all material.
Licensing: Contact Edith McShane for information regarding reuse.
Restrictions: None specified.
Viewing Facilities: None.
Duplication Facilities: None.

DISTRICT OF COLUMBIA METRO

THE NATURE CONSERVANCY
1815 North Lynn Street
Arlington, VA 22209
(703) 841-5300
Fax: (703) 841-1283

Irmgard Hunt (Associate Director, Communications)

Contact: Communications Department
Services: Nonprofit environmental organization. Film and videotape library maintained primarily for distribution and rental. Most material available for reuse.
Description: The Conservancy is an environmental organization dedicated to the preservation of biological diversity by protecting endangered species in their natural habitat. It identifies ecologically significant lands and protects them through gift, purchase, and by assisting or advising government or private agencies.

The films in the collection show some of the Conservancy's individual projects and programs. *An Oasis in Time* explores the geology and life of the ecosystem of Southern California's Coachella Valley, home of the endangered fringe-toed lizard; *Atlantic's Last Frontier* demonstrates the economic, cultural, historical and environmental significance of the Virginia Barrier Islands; and *Garden of Eden* (Continental Group, Inc.) shows how corporate and conservation interests can be simultaneously pursued in protecting natural diversity. Other topics covered include the reserve in the Snake River Canyon, Idaho; the rivers and hardwood forests of the deep South; Santa Cruz Island, California; and the Alabama Gulf Coast preservation project.
Size & Elements: Film: 16mm (12 titles, 33 cans; originals and release prints). Videotape: 3/4" and VHS (approx. 100 items, 5 titles; viewing copies).
Cataloging: List with brief description.
Access: Open to the public. Maintained primarily for rental rather than for research or reuse. Some titles available for duplication. *Garden of Eden* is distributed for rental purposes through Direct Cinema Limited (q.v.).
Rights: Full rights held to all material (except *Birds of Prey*).
Licensing: Apply for information. License and usage fees not charged (except

for postage costs).
Restrictions: None specified.
Viewing Facilities: Film (in-house projector); videotape.
Duplication Facilities: None.

DISTRICT OF COLUMBIA METRO

THE NEW ZEALAND EMBASSY FILM LIBRARY
37 Observatory Circle, NW
Washington, DC 20008
(202) 328-4800
Fax: (202) 667-5227

Contact: Mei Taare (202/328-4861)
Services: Government agency. Films available for distribution and free loan. Some material possibly available for reuse, subject to restrictions.
Description: New Zealand culture, nature and tourism.
  Titles include: *Flare — A Ski Trip; Freshwater Dive,* at the Pupu Springs in Nelson province; *Here's New Zealand; New Zealand: Farm for the World; In the Powerhouse,* on rugby; *Another Time,* a history of Edwardian and Victorian New Zealand; *Atoll People,* on the Tokelu culture; *Children of the Mist,* on the Tuhoe people who live in the valleys of the North Island's east coast; *City of Birds,* the resettlement of pukeko, grey herons, swallows and pheasants in urban Auckland; *Coal Valley; Cows, Computers & Customers,* on New Zealand's dairy industry; *Destination Auckland — Christmas Under the Sun; Down Here Near the Bottom of the World; The Early Days; Adventure World of Sir Edmund Hillary: Gold Rivers; Kiwifruit; Made in New Zealand; Maori; Maori Arts and Culture; Ocean Frontiers,* showing efforts of the New Zealand government to enforce the 200-mile "Economic Zone"; *Primeval Survivors — Tuataras,* on the Tuataras culture on Stephen Island; *Rugby Highlights; Tonga Royal; Your Most Humble and Obedient Servant, James Cook,* a documentary commemorating Cook's bicentennial.
Size & Elements: Film: 16mm (approx. 100 titles).
Cataloging: Printed lists.
Access: Available for free loan. Requests accepted by mail and telephone.
Rights: Full rights held to some materials, including *New Zealand: Farm for the World* and *Here's New Zealand.* Additional clearances may be necessary in some cases if material is to be reused.
Licensing: Some material available for reuse, subject to restrictions. Usage fees not charged.
Restrictions: Restrictions apply to films whose rights are not held by Embassy.
Viewing Facilities: None.
Duplication Facilities: None.
Distributor: Films available for free loan from Modern Talking Picture Service, Inc. (q.v.).

DISTRICT OF COLUMBIA METRO

NORTHSTAR PRODUCTIONS
3003 O Street, NW
Washington, DC 20007
(202) 338-7337
Fax: (202) 333-8554

Don North (Producer/Director)

Contact: Don North
Services: Film and videotape producer. Footage available for licensing and reuse through authorized representative.
Description: Social and political issues, with particular emphasis on Central America, the Middle East, Vietnam and Afghanistan; coverage of anti-terrorist training in France, the Middle East and the United States; footage of scenic, industrial and cultural interest from various countries; conservation; and solar automobile racing. Personalities featured in footage include Canadian Prime Ministers Brian Mulroney and Joe Clark, President Ronald Reagan, Dr. Charlie Clements, "Papa Doc" Duvalier, Mexican President Miguel de la Madrid and President Sukarno of Indonesia.
  Completed films include: *Afghanistan: Seven Soviet Years* (1987); *Guazapa: The Face of War in El Salvador* (1984) and *The War in El Cedro* (1987), showing Vietnam veterans from the U.S. working in Nicaragua to repair and rebuild damage caused by "Contra" activity; patrolling with Sandinista troops; and helping civilian casualties of the war.
  Afghanistan (1980s). Mujahedeen activity in Kandahar region; combat and supply operations; Soviet military activity.
  Austria (1945, 1980s). Activities at the end of World War II; post-war

rebuilding; daily life. Cultural life (1980s), with emphasis on music, scenics and industrial footage.
  Canada (1980s). Scenics, tourism and industrial material; defense footage, including Army, Air Force and Arctic defenses (e.g., NORAD and the DEW Line); atomic energy development; the oil industry.
  Costa Rica (1982). Footage of San José and rural areas.
  Egypt (1970s), *Ethiopia,* and *El Salvador* (1984).
  Finland (1980s). Industrial footage with particular emphasis on the electronics industry and wood products; scenics; tourist-related footage.
  Grenada (1987). Scenic footage.
  Guatemala (1987). General city and country material.
  Haiti (1961-62); *Honduras* (1980s); *Hong Kong* (1980s), including scenics and footage of the garment industry; *Indonesia* (1967), black and white footage, especially of Bali; *Israel* (ca. 1973), including general footage of cities and countryside; *Jamaica* (1987).
  Korea. Korean War footage, originating with the U.S. Department of Defense.
  Lebanon (1982). Footage of the siege.
  Mexico (1987). General footage of daily life; Mexican army anti-narcotics operations; aftermath of earthquake and reconstruction; scenics and tourist-related footage.
  Nicaragua. Sandinista army and helicopter patrols; Contra patrols; interviews with Contras; civilian casualties of Contras.
  Syria (1970s). Miscellaneous footage.
  United States (1970s-80s). Scenics of Washington, D.C., including monuments, landmarks and memorials; the presidential yacht *Sequoia;* ecological concerns relating to the Chesapeake Bay, including wildlife and fishing; Ku Klux Klan activities, cross burnings and a routine KKK meeting.
  Vietnam (1960s-70s). Various footage.
Size & Elements: Film and videotape: elements unspecified (approx. 150 hours total).
Cataloging: None specified.
Access: Available for licensing and reuse through authorized representative. Research fees charged. Research requests accepted by mail, telephone and in person (by appointment only).
Rights: Full rights held to all material.
Licensing: Available for licensing and reuse through authorized representative. License fees charged.
Restrictions: None specified.
Viewing Facilities: Film and videotape (through Film/Audio Services, Inc.).
Duplication Facilities: Film and videotape (through Film/Audio Services, Inc.).
Representative: Film/Audio Services, Inc. (q.v.).

DISTRICT OF COLUMBIA METRO

OFFICE OF THE GAY & LESBIAN MARCH ON WASHINGTON
P.O. Box 7781
Washington, DC 20044
(202) 546-9282

Contact: Lee Bush (Interested volunteer)
Services: Association. Two videotapes available for free loan.
Description: *Greetings from DC* (30 min.), showing the 1979 march on Washington for gay and lesbian rights; another videotape documents the march of October 11, 1987 (30 min.).
Size & Elements: Videotape: VHS (2 titles).
Cataloging: None.
Access: Available to the public for free loan.
Rights: No rights held to any material. Additional clearances may be necessary if material is to be reused.
Licensing: Apply for information.
Restrictions: None specified.
Viewing Facilities: None.
Duplication Facilities: None.

DISTRICT OF COLUMBIA METRO

PALESTINIAN CONGRESS OF NORTH AMERICA
P.O. Box 9621
Washington, DC 20016
(301) 652-0052

Said Arikat (Executive Director)

Contact: Said Arikat
Services: Cultural and political organization. Film collection available for free loan and reuse, subject to restrictions.
Description: Two documentary films produced by the Palestinian Cinema Institute (ca. 1980), *The Key* and *The Day of the Land.*
Size & Elements: Film: 16mm (2 films).
Cataloging: None specified.
Access: Collection available to the public for free loan. Research requests accepted by mail and telephone.
Rights: No rights held to any material. Additional clearances may be necessary in some cases if material is to be reused.
Licensing: Available for reuse, subject to restrictions.
Restrictions: Requests for reuse subject to clearance and approval.
Viewing Facilities: None.
Duplication Facilities: None.

DISTRICT OF COLUMBIA METRO

PEACE CORPS
OFFICE OF PUBLIC AFFAIRS
1990 K Street, NW
Washington, DC 20526
(202) 254-8373
Fax: (202) 254-4010

Deedie Runkel (Director, Office of Public Affairs)

Contacts: Bill Strassberger (Audiovisual and Photo Specialist); Nikki Vanasse (Director, Creative Services Division)
Services: Government agency. Material available for duplication and reuse, subject to restrictions.
Description: Recruitment films for the Peace Corps, portraying life and work overseas and showing the efforts of Peace Corps volunteers.
Size & Elements: Film: 16mm (approx. 85 titles). Videotape: 3/4" and 1/2" (15 videotapes, each 10 to 25 min.).
Cataloging: Finding aids (lists).
Access: Available to the public for duplication and reuse.
Rights: Some rights held to all material. Most material in the public domain. Rights status of some material not known.
Licensing: Available for reuse, subject to restrictions. Usage fees not charged.
Restrictions: Requests for reuse subject to clearance and approval.
Viewing Facilities: Film and videotape (available by appointment on a limited basis).
Duplication Facilities: None.

DISTRICT OF COLUMBIA METRO

PEOPLE FOR THE AMERICAN WAY
2000 M Street, NW, Suite 400
Washington, DC 20036
(202) 467-4999
Fax: (202) 462-4198

Arthur Kropp (President)

Contacts: Deborah Russell (Research Assistant, Media Video); Carol Keys (Librarian)
Services: Nonprofit, nonpartisan constitutional liberties organization. Videotape collection available for in-house use only.
Description: Monitors religious broadcasting and televangelical programming in order to gather information about religious groups and their political activities. Collection houses videotapes of televangelists such as Jimmy Swaggart, John Ankerberg, Jerry Falwell, Pat Robertson, Jim and Tammy Bakker and James Kennedy. Also collects television news appearances of organization members and programs related to such issues as First Amendment rights and education.
Size & Elements: Videotape: 3/4" and 1/2" (1,000 videotapes total).
Cataloging: Computerized cataloging.
Access: For in-house use only. Research fees not charged. Research requests accepted by mail, telephone and in person (by appointment only).
Rights: Full rights held to some material.
Licensing: Apply for information.
Restrictions: None specified.

Viewing Facilities: Videotape (3/4" and 1/2").
Duplication Facilities: Videotape (limited).

DISTRICT OF COLUMBIA METRO

PEOPLE FOR THE ETHICAL TREATMENT OF ANIMALS
P.O. Box 42516
Washington, DC 20015
(301) 770-7444
Fax: (301) 770-8969

Alex Pacheco (Chairperson)

Contact: Luis Pacheco (Office Manager)
Services: Animal rights organization. Videotape collection maintained for distribution and rental rather than for research or reuse.
Description: Educational material relating to animal rights and animal abuse. Titles include *Breaking Barriers; Britches; Dog Lab; Silver Spring Monkey;* and *Unnecessary Fuss.* Also held is a Lynx anti-fur commercial and five public service announcements on various animal issues.
Size & Elements: Videotape: 3/4", VHS, Betamax and 8mm (7 titles).
Cataloging: None specified.
Access: Maintained for distribution and rental rather than research or reuse. Research fees not charged. Research requests accepted by mail, telephone and in person (walk-in).
Rights: Full rights held to all material.
Licensing: Available for licensing. License fees charged under some conditions.
Restrictions: None specified.
Viewing Facilities: Videotape.
Duplication Facilities: Videotape (3/4", VHS, Betamax and 8mm).

DISTRICT OF COLUMBIA METRO

PHYSICIANS FOR SOCIAL RESPONSIBILITY
1601 Connecticut Avenue, NW, Suite 800
Washington, DC 20009
(202) 785-3777

Maureen Thornton (Executive Director)

Contact: Audio Visual Department
Services: Association. Film and videotape collection available to association members and the public for rental and purchase.
Description: Educational films and videotapes pertaining to nuclear arms control and the medical and psychological consequences of nuclear weapons, nuclear war, and the nuclear arms race.
   Materials include: *We the People...Preventing Nuclear War,* a statement of PSR's goals and activities; *CTB: The Next Step Towards Peace,* an overview of the issues surrounding nuclear testing and the possibilities of a comprehensive test ban treaty; *The Arms Race: The Human Cost,* information on the health, economic, and social costs of the arms race; *SDI: Defense or Delusion?; The Risk of Accidental Nuclear War,* on the possibility of a nuclear war through human error; *The Last Epidemic: The Medical Consequences of Nuclear Weapons and Nuclear War,* based on the 1980 PSR symposium in San Francisco with Dr. H. Jack Geiger, Dr. Helen Caldicott, Ret. Admiral Noel Gaylor, and other scientists and physicians; and *The Edge of History,* a 1984 symposium serving as a sequel to *The Last Epidemic.*
Size & Elements: Film: format unspecified. Videotape: VHS. (7 titles total).
Cataloging: Published lists.
Access: Available to PSR members and the public for rental and purchase. Research requests accepted by mail, telephone and in person (walk-in).
Rights: Some rights held to some material.
Licensing: Available for reuse. Usage fees charged.
Restrictions: None specified.
Viewing Facilities: None.
Duplicating Facilities: None.
Related Materials: Slide shows; audiocassettes; television, radio, and print advertisements.

DISTRICT OF COLUMBIA METRO

POPULATION REFERENCE BUREAU, INC.
POPULATION — ENVIRONMENT FILM LIBRARY

777 14th Street, NW, Suite 800
Washington, DC 20005
(202) 639-8040
Fax: (202) 347-1690

Dr. Thomas Merrick (President)

Contact: Kimberly A. Crews (Director of Population Program)
Services: Educational institution. Film and videotape library available to the public for distribution and rental rather than for research or reuse.
Description: Population, population growth and control. Popular titles include: *Animal Populations: Nature's Checks and Balances; The Business of Hunger; The Cheerful Revolution; China's Only Child; The Invisible Laborers: Rural Women in World Cultures; Limits to Growth; Natural Resources; Population Change and Economic Development; The Silent Explosion; Tomorrow's World; Will the World Starve?;* and *World Population.*
Size & Elements: Film: 16mm (81 titles). Videotape: 3/4", VHS and Betamax (31 videotapes).
Cataloging: Published catalogs.
Access: Available to the public for distribution and rental rather than for research or reuse. Rental fees charged. Rental requests accepted by mail and telephone.
Rights: No rights held to any material.
Licensing: Available for reuse, subject to restrictions.
Restrictions: Original producer must be contacted for permission if material is to be reused.
Viewing Facilities: None.
Duplication Facilities: None.

DISTRICT OF COLUMBIA METRO

PROJECT VOTE!
1221 Massachusetts Avenue, NW
Washington, DC 20005
(202) 393-3933

Sanford Newman (Executive Director)

Contact: Sanford Newman
Services: Nonprofit organization. Videotape collection available to the public.
Description: *Making Democracy Work,* a series of three training videotapes on registering voters and recruiting, training and motivating volunteers.
Size & Elements: Videotape: 1/2" (3 videotapes).
Cataloging: None specified.
Access: Open to the public. Research requests accepted by mail.
Rights: Full rights held to all material.
Licensing: Apply for information. License fees not charged.
Restrictions: None specified.
Viewing Facilities: None.
Duplication Facilities: None.
Related Materials: Supplemental print materials.

DISTRICT OF COLUMBIA METRO

PUBLIC BROADCASTING SYSTEM (PBS)
PROGRAM DATA & ANALYSIS
1320 Braddock Place
Alexandria, VA 22314-1698
(703) 739-5000
Fax: (703) 739-0775

Glenn A. Clatworthy (Associate Director for Program Data & Analysis)

Contact: Thom Watson (Program Data Specialist) (703/739-5230)
Services: Educational television support facility. Film and videotape collection available for broadcast by PBS member stations. Material available for duplication and reuse subject to clearance and approval by copyright owner. *Research inquiries from the public and outside producers accepted on a case-by-case basis, due to limited personnel resources.*
Description: PBS retains master copies of all programs broadcast by the network (1970-present), as well as a collection of films and videotapes from the National Educational Television (NET) era (ca. 1953-70).

Archives holds film and videotape master materials received from originating producers, and backup copies of these programs made for distribution to PBS stations. Their primary responsibility is to PBS member

stations; *research inquiries from the general public and outside producers are accepted on a case-by-case basis.*

Encore! collection. Contains programs not more than four years old, all of which have been accepted by PBS's National Program Service. Distributes repeat programming to local stations when this programming is not intended for any further national broadcast. Generally programs are licensed to the National Program Service for two transmissions and subsequently distributed by Encore! to local stations by videotape or satellite.

The NET Collection, housed at the Library of Congress, Motion Picture, Broadcasting and Recorded Sound Division (q.v.) holds preprint and production elements for many programs held by PBS. In general, these elements consist of picture and soundtrack master materials. PBS holds videotape copies of the programs (mostly 2" and 1", some 3/4" copies), as well as film release prints, broadcast master copies and some kinescopes. A search for specific NET material should include both collections, as PBS and Library of Congress each hold some materials not housed elsewhere.
Size & Elements: Film and videotape (formats and amounts unspecified).
Cataloging: (For PBS programs) online title list (staff use only); notebook of subject cross-references. PBS online database with full subject listings (contemplated coverage 1985-present) in progress (staff use only). (For NET programs) title list only; computerized searching by words in titles possible; microfiche program descriptions.
Access: Programs available for rebroadcast by PBS member stations, by contractual agreement. Available for research, duplication and reuse, subject to clearance and approval by original producers. *Due to limited personnel resources, inquiries from the public and outside producers are accepted on a case-by-case basis.* Research fees not charged. Research requests accepted by mail and telephone.
Rights: Holds PBS broadcast rights only. All other rights retained by original producers. Can refer requesters to original producers of programs, subject to staff time and availability. NET programs owned by WNET (New York City) in most cases. Contact Holly Ware (Distribution Dept.) or Dorothy Pringle (Legal Dept.) at WNET for further information regarding NET programs.
Licensing: Available for licensing and reuse through original producers. License fees not charged.
Restrictions: Due to limited personnel resources, research requests accepted on a case-by-case basis. All rights other than PBS broadcast rights retained by original program producers. Copies of programs can be made at requester's expense with written permission of original producer.
Viewing Facilities: None.
Duplication Facilities: Film (none; outside facilities used for film-to-videotape transfer); videotape (2", 1", 3/4", VHS and Betamax). Duplication fees charged.

DISTRICT OF COLUMBIA METRO

PUBLIC INTEREST VIDEO NETWORK
1642 R Street, NW
Washington, DC 20009
(202) 797-8997
Fax: (202) 797-8304

Arlen Slobodow (Director)

Contact: Debra Murton
Services: Nonprofit media organization. Videotape collection available to the public for duplication, licensing and reuse. Research services available; can provide access to material held at National Archives.
Description: Wide coverage of public rallies and events in Washington, D.C. (1979-present). Footage relating to U.S. policy toward Central America (White House pool newsfeed).

Documentaries on energy, ground water, nuclear power and arms control. Titles include: *Living Double Lives,* on the psychological effects of living in the nuclear age; *Thinking Twice About Nuclear War; Over a Barrel: Energy in the 80s; PCP — Not For Me; Your Water, Your Life;* and *New Voices,* examining the use of electronic media by alternative groups. Unused footage from these documentaries (including interviews) and stock shots of Washington, D.C. are also available.

A small amount of footage from Third World nations is also held.
Size & Elements: Videotape: 3/4" (300 videotapes; masters).
Cataloging: Computerized cataloging for staff use only. Information on holdings may be obtained by telephone.
Access: Available to the public for duplication, licensing and reuse. Research fees charged. Research requests accepted by mail, telephone and in person (by appointment only).

Rights: Full rights held to some material. Some material in the public domain. Additional clearances may be necessary in some cases if material is to be reused.
Licensing: Available for licensing and reuse. License and usage fees charged in some cases.
Restrictions: None specified.
Viewing Facilities: Videotape.
Duplication Facilities: Videotape (3/4" and VHS).

DISTRICT OF COLUMBIA METRO

RELIGIOUS COALITION FOR ABORTION RIGHTS
100 Maryland Avenue, NE, Suite 307
Washington, DC 20002
(202) 543-7032

Contact: Sabrae Davis (Director, Women of Color Partnership Program)
Services: Association. Videotape available for licensing and reuse.
Description: Reproductive rights issues seen from the perspectives of Black, Hispanic, Asian American and Native American people. Holds videotapes of speakers from two all-day forums ("Between Ourselves") on reproductive rights, and people of color (held February 1986 in Washington, D.C. and October 1986, in Chicago, Illinois.
Size & Elements: Videotape: 3/4" (Chicago Forum, 15 items; unedited masters); VHS (D.C. Forum, 3 videotapes; viewing copies).
Cataloging: None.
Access: Available for viewing and reuse. Research fees not charged. Research requests accepted by mail, telephone and in person (by appointment only).
Rights: Full rights held to all material.
Licensing: Available for reuse, subject to restrictions. License fees charged (determined on a case-by-case basis).
Restrictions: Restrictions may apply in some cases.
Viewing Facilities: Videotape (VHS).
Duplication Facilities: None.

DISTRICT OF COLUMBIA METRO

REPUBLICAN NATIONAL COMMITTEE BROADCAST SERVICES
310 First Street, SE
Washington, DC 20003
(202) 863-8895
Fax: (202) 863-8820

Carlos Rojas (Director, Broadcast Services)

Contact: Carlos Rojas
Services: Political organization. Videotape library maintained for research purposes.
Description: Videotape library contains coverage of presidential speeches, press conferences and party conventions.
Size & Elements: Videotape: 3/4" (400 videotapes).
Cataloging: Computerized cataloging available for staff use and researchers; research library.
Access: Open to researchers and scholars only. Research fees charged. Research requests accepted by mail and in person (by appointment only).
Rights: Some rights held to some material. Some material in the public domain. Additional clearances may be necessary in some cases if material is to be reused.
Licensing: Apply for information.
Restrictions: Copyright restrictions apply.
Viewing Facilities: Videotape (3/4" and 1/2").
Duplication Facilities: Videotape (3/4" and 1/2").

DISTRICT OF COLUMBIA METRO

R5/S8 PRESENTS
1028 Poplar Drive
Falls Church, VA 22046
(703) 534-6320

Shipping address:
2100 M Street, NW, Suite 407
Washington, DC 20037
(202) 452-1717

(202) 452-1614
Fax: (202) 223-3363

Michael Jeck (Managing Partner)

Contact: Michael Jeck
Services: Film distributor. Films available for rental. Footage not available for licensing or reuse.
Description: Feature films, many from Japan. Library includes work by the following directors:
　　Kon Ichikawa. Tokyo Olympiad (1964), a documentary on the 1964 Olympic Games, now restored to its full-length version (154 min.); *Film Actress* (1988), the biography of actress Kinuyo Tanaka; *The Makioka Sisters* (1983).
　　Midori Kurisaki. Dark Hair; Love Suicides.
　　Akira Kurosawa. The Hidden Fortress (1958); *The Most Beautiful* (1944); *One Wonderful Sunday* (1947); *Sanshiro Sugata, Part 2* (1943).
　　Also available are Robert Mugge's *Cool Runnings* (1983), filmed at the 1983 Reggae Sunsplash Festival in Montego Bay, Jamaica; Margarethe von Trotta's *Sheer Madness* (1983); Ann and Jeanette Petrie's *Mother Teresa* (1986); Hideo Gosha's *Goyokin* (1969); Kihachi Okamoto's *Zatoichi Meets Yojimbo* (1970); and Hideko Takamine's *Horse* (1941).
Size & Elements: Film: 35mm and 16mm (17 titles; release prints). Videotape: format and amount unspecified (masters and viewing copies).
Cataloging: Published catalogs; press kits.
Access: Available for rental in theatrical and non-theatrical situations. Rental fees charged. Requests accepted by mail and telephone.
Rights: Full rights held to some material; distribution rights held to all material. Clip rights retained by original producers. Video rights held for several titles.
Licensing: Not available for licensing or reuse.
Restrictions: Footage not available for reuse.
Viewing Facilities: None.
Duplication Facilities: None.

DISTRICT OF COLUMBIA METRO

THE ROOSEVELT CENTER FOR AMERICAN POLICY STUDIES
316 Pennsylvania Avenue, SE, Suite 500
Washington, DC 20003
(202) 547-7227
Fax: (202) 544-5008

Roger Molander (President)

Contact: Library
Services: Educational institution. Videotapes available to the public.
Description: *The Other Nuclear Arms Race* (30 min.), on the history of nuclear proliferation, examines how countries can acquire nuclear weapons technology.
Size & Elements: Videotape: 3/4", VHS and Betamax (2 videotapes, each 30 min.).
Cataloging: Release sheets.
Access: Open to the public. Research fees not charged. Research requests accepted by mail.
Rights: Full rights held to some material.
Licensing: Apply for information. License fees charged.
Restrictions: None specified.
Viewing Facilities: None.
Duplication Facilities: None.

DISTRICT OF COLUMBIA METRO

SAFE ENERGY COMMUNICATION COUNCIL
1717 Massachusetts Avenue, NW, Suite LL215
Washington, DC 20036
(202) 483-8491

Scott Denman (Director)

Contact: Scott Denman
Services: Public interest energy and media organization. Videotape collection available for duplication.
Description: Television advertisements by utilities and consumer groups; and

documentaries, all relating to nuclear power.
Size & Elements: Videotape: 3/4" and VHS (100 titles total).
Cataloging: Finding aids.
Access: Available for duplication. Research requests accepted by telephone and in person.
Rights: Rights status of material not known.
Licensing: Available for reuse, subject to restrictions. License and usage fees generally not charged.
Restrictions: None specified.
Viewing Facilities: Videotape.
Duplication Facilities: None.

DISTRICT OF COLUMBIA METRO

SANE/FREEZE
711 G Street, SE
Washington, DC 20003
(202) 546-7100

Nick Carter (Director)

Contact: Kay Shaw (Director of Communications)
Services: Nonprofit peace group. Videotape collection available to the news media, producers, and researchers.
Description: Small videotape collection relating to nuclear disarmament activities. Currently available: *Within Our Reach,* a documentary on grassroots lobbying for a comprehensive nuclear test ban; and an untitled discussion piece containing people-on-the-street reactions on U.S.-Soviet relations.
Size & Elements: Videotape: VHS (5 videotapes, each 30 min.); other videotape formats (approx. 50 hours; masters and outtakes).
Cataloging: None specified.
Access: Open to the public. Available to the news media, producers, and researchers.
Rights: Some rights held to some material. Additional clearances may be necessary in some cases if material is to be reused.
Licensing: Available for licensing in some cases. License fees generally not charged.
Restrictions: None specified.
Viewing Facilities: None.
Duplication Facilities: None.

DISTRICT OF COLUMBIA METRO

SCREEN PRESENTATIONS, INC.
309 Massachusetts Avenue, NE
Washington, DC 20002
(202) 546-8900

David Gerber (President)

Contacts: David Gerber; Jim Reid
Services: Film and videotape producer. Stock footage and other material available for licensing and reuse.
Description: Produces films and videotapes for corporate, institutional, association, and government clients. Holds stock footage from the Soviet Union (approx. 15-20 hours), predominantly focusing on military subjects, although daily and political life is also covered. Also available is material from their own productions (1960s-present) on medicine, chemistry and other subjects. Library includes public domain material from the National Archives covering the same scientific topics.
Size & Elements: Film: 35mm (amount unspecified). Videotape: 1" and 3/4", NTSC and PAL (some transfers from film; amount unspecified).
Cataloging: None.
Access: Available to the public for licensing and reuse. Research fees charged but credited to purchase of footage. Research requests accepted by mail and telephone.
Rights: Full rights held to some material. Some material in the public domain.
Licensing: Apply for information.
Restrictions: None specified.
Viewing Facilities: Film and videotape (all formats).
Duplication Facilities: Videotape.

DISTRICT OF COLUMBIA METRO

SILVER IMAGE

11025 Seven Hill Lane
Potomac, MD 20854
(301) 983-3366

Jack Silver (President/Producer)

Contact: Jack Silver
Services: Film and videotape producer. Collection available to the public for licensing and reuse.
Description: Holds live footage (field- and studio-produced) and hybrid footage (combination of live footage and stills) covering such subjects as telecommunications, space, and the public sector (e.g., hospitals). Most footage was produced in the Washington, D.C. area.
Size & Elements: Videotape: 1" and Betamax (amount unspecified).
Cataloging: None specified.
Access: Available to the public for reuse. Research requests accepted by mail and telephone.
Rights: Full rights held to some material. Rights to most material retained by clients. Additional clearances may be necessary in some cases if material is to be reused.
Licensing: Available for licensing and reuse, subject to restrictions.
Restrictions: Most footage produced on behalf of clients, who retain rights.
Viewing Facilities: Videotape.
Duplication Facilities: None.

DISTRICT OF COLUMBIA METRO

SMITHSONIAN INSTITUTION
FREER GALLERY OF ART
ARTHUR M. SACKLER GALLERY
Washington, DC 20560
(202) 357-2091 (Library)
(202) 357-4880 (Film rentals and sales)

Contact: Colleen Hennessey
Services: Museum. One film available for rental and purchase.
Description: *The Art of the Hyogushi* (1971) depicts the restoration of Oriental paintings at the Freer Gallery and the work of master restorer Takashi Sugiura.
  Other films, mostly related to bronze-making and Asian art processes, are held, but are not presently available for loan or public viewing.
Size & Elements: Film: 16mm (1 title available; approx. 25 films held in total).
Cataloging: Brochure.
Access: One title available to the public for rental and purchase.
Rights: Apply for information.
Licensing: Apply for information.
Restrictions: None specified.
Viewing Facilities: None.
Duplication Facilities: None.
Related Materials: Still photographs.

DISTRICT OF COLUMBIA METRO

SMITHSONIAN INSTITUTION
HIRSHHORN MUSEUM LIBRARY
8th Street and Independence Avenue, SW
Washington, DC 20560
(202) 357-3222

Anna Brooke (Librarian)

Contact: Anna Brooke
Services: Government agency; library. Film and videotape collection open to researchers and scholars only.
Description: Historical documentation of the Hirshhorn Museum's art collection; interviews with the Museum's director; documentation of the collection's relocation from Greenwich, Conn.; press coverage of Museum exhibitions.
Size & Elements: Film: format unspecified (15 cans). Videotape: format unspecified (32 videotapes).
Cataloging: None specified.
Access: Open to researchers and scholars only (by appointment). Research fees not charged. Research requests accepted in person (by appointment only).

DISTRICT OF COLUMBIA METRO S

Rights: Rights status of material unknown.
Licensing: Apply for information.
Restrictions: None specified.
Viewing Facilities: None.
Duplication Facilities: None.

DISTRICT OF COLUMBIA METRO

**SMITHSONIAN INSTITUTION
MUSEUM OF NATURAL HISTORY
HUMAN STUDIES FILM ARCHIVES**
Room E307
Washington, DC 20560
(202) 357-3349
Fax: (202) 357-2208

Wendy Shay (Assistant Director)

Contact: Wendy Shay
Services: Government agency; museum; film and videotape archives. Collection open to researchers and scholars for in-house viewing only; available for duplication on a case-by-case basis, subject to restrictions.
Description: The Human Studies Film Archives was established in 1981 to collect, preserve and make available anthropological film and videotape records for research use at the Film Archives. The collection includes historic (dating from 1908) and contemporary edited and unedited film and videotape materials, documenting traditional cultures, capturing vanishing and changing ways of life around the world. All footage is actuality footage of general and specific anthropological interest. In addition to documenting traditional lifeways, there are a number of films of archaeological sites and excavation work.

These records were created by a diverse group of professionals and amateurs, including anthropologists, archaeologists, Peace Corps volunteers, missionaries, teachers, commercial and independent filmmakers, artists and travelers. Much of the films and footage were made by professional independent filmmakers, but collection also holds a number of early amateur travel films. A unique aspect of the collection is the emphasis placed on acquiring outtakes or uncut footage. For example, HSFA holds 700,000 feet of film shot by John Marshall in Namibia and Botswana, South Africa (1951-82) and 42,000 feet shot in 1975 recording Huichol life in northern Mexico.

Geographical regions covered include Africa, Asia, Oceania, North America, Central and South America, Europe, and world travel. The collection is most diverse in Africa and Asia and weakest in Europe.

Sample items and collections include:
Healing Ritual of the Twelve Apostles Church of Ghana (1975, 2,000 feet). Martha Breidenbach's full film record of a weekly two-day healing ritual in Elmina, Ghana which blends indigenous African healing practices and Christian elements.
[Herskovits' Film Study of Dahomey, 1931] (1,900 feet). Footage shot by anthropologist Melville Herskovits and his wife Frances during fieldwork in Dahomey and Nigeria. Includes footage of dance, traditional technology, village activities and agricultural practices.
[Jie Film Project, 1968] (14,807 feet). Outtakes from the film project about the Jie pastoralists of Uganda from which David and Judith MacDougall produced the edited films *To Live With Herds, Nawi* and *Under the Men's Trees.*
[Marshall !Kung Film Project, 1951-1982] (700,000 feet). Full film record shot by John Marshall on numerous expeditions to the !Kung and /Gwi San homeland in Namibia and Botswana.
Sons of the Moon (outtakes) (1984, 12,000 feet). Outtakes and edited film shot by Dierdre LaPin and Francis Speed. The film follows the Ngas of Nigeria's Jos Plateau through a single growing season, showing the influence of the moon on all aspects of Ngas life.
[Tangoma Graduation Ceremony, Lomahasha, Swaziland, 1980] (5,400 feet). Full film record depicting ceremonies surrounding the initiation and graduation of diviners in Lomahasha, Swaziland.
[Turkana Conversations Film Project, 1974] (38,485 feet). Full film record of the Turkana pastoralists by David and Judith MacDougall from which they produced the *Turkana Conversations Trilogy: Lorang's Way, The Wedding Camels* and *A Wife Among Wives.*
[AUFS Afghanistan Film Project, 1972] (48,000 feet). Full film record of traditional life in northern Afghanistan from the American Universities Field Staff "Faces of Change" film project co-directed by David Hancock and Herbert DiGioia.
Beautiful Japan (1917-18, 3,600 feet). Edited film made by Benjamin

Brodsky, a Hollywood-based, professional travel lecturer, of a trip through Japan. Includes scenes of daily life as well as natural and manmade attractions.
The Initiation Into the Kalachakra Tantra By His Holiness the Dalai Lama of Tibet (1981, 16-1/2 hours). Edited archival videotape series (produced by Edward Bastian) document the first Kalachakra Initiation to be conferred in America, includes rituals before and after the Initiation. The Dalai Lama conferred the Initiation in Deer Park, Wisconsin in July 1981.
[Liqvan, A Village in Iran, c. 1970-1978] (13,000 feet). Full film record shot by Fereydoun Safizadeh documenting the annual agricultural cycle in Liqvan, a small mountain village in northern Iran.
[Pashtoon Nomad Research Film Project, 1975-1976] (95,000 feet). Full film record by Asen Balikci, Timothy and Patsy Asch, and a crew from the National Film Board of Canada documenting daily life among the Pashtoon Nomads of northern Afghanistan. The National Film Board produced the edited film *Sons of Haji Omar* from this project.
[Tragada Bhavai: A Rural Theater Troupe of Gujerat] (1980-81, outtakes, 20,000 feet). Outtakes from the film by Roger Sandall and Jayasinhji Jhala about a traditional theater troupe traveling throughout rural Gujerat, India.
The Wild Mountain Tribes of Northern Luzon (ca. 1929, 900 feet). Footage shot by U.S. Army Captain Roger Hilsman of various tribal peoples including the Ifagao, Bontoc Igorots, Kalinga and Negrito Pygmies of northern Luzon, Philippines.
[Films from the Australian Institute of Aboriginal Studies, c. 1960-1975] (11,000 feet). Edited films about Aboriginal rituals.
[Kalman Muller's New Hebrides Film Project, 1973-1974] (20,000 feet). Full film record shot by Kalman Muller on south-central Malekula. Records traditional life among the Mbogate and the "toka" dances as performed by the Melanesians of Tanna Island.
[Scott Williams' Micronesian Film Project, 1975-1976] (28,500 feet). Full film record shot by Scott Williams of daily life, with emphasis on child behavior and social interaction on Ifaluk Atoll, Yap District, Western Caroline Islands.
[Benjamin Harrison Hay's Footage of a Pennsylvania Colliery, c. 1930-1940] (800 feet). Footage shot by B. H. Hay, manager of two Schuylkill County anthracite coal companies, documenting daily operations.
[Birdwhistell Film Collection, c. 1961-1972] (90,000 feet). Research footage made and used by Raymond L. Birdwhistell and colleagues for behavioral research and analysis.
[Brooklyn Giglio Festival, 1939, 1950 and c. 1955] (780 feet). Footage documenting three different annual Giglio Festivals in the Italian-American communities of Brooklyn, New York.
[Dixon-Wanamaker Expedition to Crow Agency, 1908] (440 feet). Outtakes of film shot by Joseph Dixon during an expedition to Crow Agency, Montana, sponsored by Rodman Wanamaker. Includes scenes of Crow Fair and a re-enactment of the Battle of the Little Big Horn.
[Georgia Shouters, ca. 1930] (900 feet). Footage probably shot by anthropologist Melville Herskovits of dances performed by members of the "shouter" churches of the Georgia coast and islands.
[Navajo Film Project, 1982-1986] (40,000 feet). The full film record from which *A Weave of Time: The Story of a Navajo Family, 1938-1986* was produced. The film by Susan Fanshel, based on John Adair's 1938 work among the Navajo, explores Navajo life and culture through four generations of a Navajo family.
[Sanderson's Northwest American Indian Footage, c. 1926-1932] (3,700 feet). Footage taken by Grover T. Sanderson of the Karuk, Yurok and Hupa tribes of the Western U.S. Also includes footage of the Navajo, Zuñi, Hopi, Chippewa and Sioux.
Single Parent (outtakes, 1975, 16,700 feet). Outtakes of the edited film by Hubert Smith documenting a lower middle income family of three children headed by a divorced woman.
[William Van Valin's Films of Pt. Barrow, Alaska, 1912-1918] (2,000 feet). Footage recording northern Alaskan Eskimo life.
[Kalmun Muller's Huichol Indian Film Project, 1975] (42,000 feet). Full film record shot by Kalmun Muller recording Huichol life with emphasis on the influence of peyote use on behavior patterns.
[Rastafari: Conversations Concerning Women Video Project, 1983] (12 hours). Full videotape record recorded by Eliot Leib and Renee Romano concerning women's position in Jamaican society and the Rastafari movement.
[Yanomamo Film Project, 1968 and 1971] (97,000 feet). Full film record of the Yanomamo Indians of the Amazon Basin of southern Venezuela and northern Brazil, produced by Timothy Asch and anthropologist Napolean Chagnon.
[Yucatec Maya Film Project, 1977] (150,000 feet). Full film record shot by Hubert Smith over one year, concentrating on a single Mayan family in the village of Chican, in the Yucatan.

Size & Elements: Film: 35mm, 16mm, Super 8mm and 8mm (approx. 4 million feet total; originals and other formats). Videotape: 3/4" and 1/2" (54 hours; masters and viewing copies).
Cataloging: Published *Guide to the Collections;* camera logs; computerized cataloging available to researchers.
Access: Open to researchers and scholars only. Available for duplication on a case-by-case basis. Research fees not charged. Research requests accepted by mail, telephone and in person (by appointment only).
Rights: Full rights held to some material. Some rights held to some material. Rights to some material retained by original producers or donors. Some material in the public domain. Rights status of some material not known.
Licensing: Available for licensing and reuse, subject to restrictions.
Restrictions: Material is duplicated for use only in project for which material is being requested. Some material restricted by original producers or donors.
Viewing Facilities: Film (16mm flatbed); videotape (3/4").
Duplication Facilities: Videotape (3/4").
Related Materials: Supplementary materials such as annotations, photographs, sound recordings, field notes and dissertations accompany many of the film projects.

DISTRICT OF COLUMBIA METRO

SMITHSONIAN INSTITUTION
NATIONAL AIR AND SPACE MUSEUM
FILM ARCHIVES
7th Street and Independence Avenue
Washington, DC 20560
(202) 357-4721
Fax: (202) 786-2262

Mark Taylor (Film Archivist)

Contact: Mark Taylor
Services: Museum. Film and videotape collection open to researchers and scholars for in-house use only; materials available for duplication and reuse, subject to restrictions.
Description: Aviation and space history (1908-present). Coverage begins with the Wright Brothers Military Flyer (1908) and includes contemporary footage, including the Space Shuttle. Holds almost 1,000 NASA documentaries; documentary film and videotapes from major defense contractors; and U.S. Air Force productions.
Size & Elements: Film: various formats (over 2,500 titles, 7,000 cans; mostly release prints). Videotape: various formats (over 1,000 videotapes).
Cataloging: Published catalogs; computerized cataloging for staff use only.
Access: Open to researchers and scholars only. For in-house use only. Available for duplication, subject to restrictions. Research fees charged. Research requests accepted by mail.
Rights: Rights status of material not known. Some material in the public domain.
Licensing: Available for reuse, subject to restrictions. License fees not charged for reuse of film material; license fees charged for reuse of some videotape material.
Restrictions: The Museum cannot assure copyright clearances for all films in collection. Users must sign and return *Stock Footage Agreement* to Museum.
Viewing Facilities: Film (35mm and 16mm Steenbeck); videotape (3/4", VHS and Betamax).
Duplication Facilities: Videotape (3/4", VHS and Betamax). Outside arrangements can be made to duplicate film at requester's expense. Preparation fees charged.

DISTRICT OF COLUMBIA METRO

SMITHSONIAN INSTITUTION
NATIONAL MUSEUM OF AMERICAN HISTORY
ARCHIVES CENTER
Washington, DC 20560
(202) 357-3270

Street address: 12th Street and Constitution Avenue, NW

John Fleckner (Archivist)
Barbara Humphrys (Head, Audiovisual Collections)

Contact: Barbara Humphrys
Services: Museum research center. Film and videotape collections available for

research, viewing, duplication and reuse on a case-by-case basis, subject to restrictions.
Description: Houses and provides access to a wide variety of archival and research sources relating to the collections and interests of the National Museum of American History, including a small number of films, videotapes and sound recordings. Collections include:
Medical Sciences. A diverse collection of film release prints gathered by the Museum's Division of Medical Sciences over the years and transferred to the Archives Center in 1986.
Groucho Marx. Marx's bequest to the Smithsonian included 16mm prints of a number of his feature films and television appearances.
United Shoe Machinery. This collection, which is only partially inventoried, probably is comprised of both research and promotional films from a major manufacturer of shoemaking machinery. Access to this collection is limited until it is processed.
Center for Advertising History. Conducts studies of numerous aspects of the history of advertising, with a special focus on the development of advertising in the age of electronic media. Current collections focus on historically significant modern ad campaigns, and include reference videotapes from Pepsi-Cola, Alka-Seltzer, Federal Express and Campbell Soup campaigns. For further information, contact Stacy Flaherty (CAH Coordinator).
Size & Elements: Film: 16mm (approx. 400 reels; release prints). Videotape: 3/4" and 1/2" (approx. 75 videotapes).
Cataloging: Cataloging in progress.
Access: Open to the public. For in-house research use only. Available for duplication. Research requests accepted in person (by appointment only).
Rights: No rights held by Smithsonian Institution. Additional clearances may be necessary in some cases if material is to be reused.
Licensing: Some material possibly available for licensing and reuse, subject to restrictions. License fees charged in some cases.
Restrictions: Material available for licensing and reuse on a case-by-case basis. Many items carry copyright restrictions.
Viewing Facilities: Film and videotape.
Duplication Facilities: Handled by outside contractors.
Related Materials: Manuscript collections; historical photographic collections; and Duke Ellington Collection. Center for Advertising History holds Warshaw Collection of business advertising ephemera, containing over one million 19th and 20th century items; the N W Ayer Advertising Agency Records and the Norcross Historical Greeting Card Collection.

DISTRICT OF COLUMBIA METRO

SMITHSONIAN INSTITUTION
NATIONAL MUSEUM OF AMERICAN HISTORY
DIVISION OF ENGINEERING AND INDUSTRY
Washington, DC 20560
(202) 357-2228

Contacts: William Worthington (Museum Specialist); David Shayt (Museum Specialist)
Services: Museum. Film and videotape collection available to researchers and scholars only for viewing and loan.
Description: Films (1905-60) relating to the history of industry; civil and mechanical engineering; construction, including bridge building; factories, manufacturing and assembly lines; and foundries, forges and steel furnaces. Many films show processes and activities of historical interest.
Size & Elements: Film: 16mm (positive). Videotape: format unspecified (viewing copies). (24 cans total).
Cataloging: None specified.
Access: Open to researchers and scholars only. Available for viewing and loan. Research fees not charged. Research requests accepted by mail, telephone and in person (walk-in and by appointment).
Rights: Some rights held to some material.
Licensing: Apply for information.
Restrictions: None specified.
Viewing Facilities: Film and videotape.
Duplication Facilities: None.

DISTRICT OF COLUMBIA METRO

SMITHSONIAN INSTITUTION
NATIONAL MUSEUM OF AMERICAN HISTORY
DIVISION OF MEDICAL SCIENCES

NMAH, Room 5000
Washington, DC 20560
(202) 357-2145

Ray Kondrates (Supervising Curator)

Contact: Michael Harris (Museum Specialist)
Services: Government agency; museum. Videotape collection open to researchers, scholars and the public; available for reuse on a case-by-case basis, subject to restrictions.
Description: Films formerly held by the Division have been transferred to the Smithsonian Institution, National Museum of American History, Archives Center (q.v.) or to the National Library of Medicine, History of Medicine Division, Historical Audiovisuals Collection (q.v.). Videotape copies of some titles have been retained by the Division, which also holds a film on homeopathy, produced by the Institution's Office of Telecommunications; copies of videotapes on drug abuse produced by the State Department; and two videotapes on AIDS, showing patients near death.
Size & Elements: Videotape: format unspecified (approx. 12 titles; viewing copies).
Cataloging: None.
Access: Open to the public. Some material (AIDS videotapes) restricted to use by researchers and scholars only. Research fees not charged. Research requests accepted by mail, telephone and in person (by appointment only).
Rights: Rights status of most material not known. Some material in the public domain. Additional clearances may be necessary in some cases if material is to be reused.
Licensing: Available for licensing and reuse on a case-by-case basis.
Restrictions: Available for licensing and reuse on a case-by-case basis. AIDS-related material restricted to use by researchers and scholars.
Viewing Facilities: Viewing is arranged elsewhere (by appointment only).
Duplication Facilities: None.

DISTRICT OF COLUMBIA METRO

SMITHSONIAN INSTITUTION
NATIONAL MUSEUM OF AMERICAN HISTORY
DIVISION OF POLITICAL HISTORY
Room 4108
Washington, DC 20560
(202) 357-2008

Larry Bird (Curator)

Contact: Larry Bird
Services: Museum. Videotape collection open to researchers, scholars and the public for in-house viewing only.
Description: Reference collection of political television advertising spots (1980-present).

Collection includes: commercials from local, state and national campaigns (primarily national); referenda, issue and institutional advertising for groups such as the American Association of Retired Persons (AARP) and the American Federation of State, County and Municipal Employees (AFSCME); and institutional advertising for corporations (especially oil companies), interest groups (e.g., People for the American Way and National Conservative Political Action Committee) and labor (including material from the Labor Institute for Public Affairs). Some compilation reels of material (1950s-present) are also held.

Subjects include: a pro-family rally in Houston, Texas with Phyllis Schlafly and others (1978); six spots urging freedom of religious expression, produced by People For the American Way (1981); Republican National Committee congressional campaign spots (1980); Edward Kennedy presidential primary campaign spots (1980); Mobil Oil spots relating to government intervention aimed at business (1982); *Help Pass ERA* celebrity endorsement and *Countdown* spots produced by the National Organization for Women (1982); three spots in the *Making Advanced Technology Work for America's Defense* series, produced by Northrop Corporation (1985); videotapes made for the 50th anniversary celebration of the United Auto Workers (1986); and a collection of videotapes containing political campaign television spots used in Campaigns & Elections' production *The Classics of Political Television Advertising* (1986), including those produced by Ailes Communications, Doyle Dane Bernbach, Zimmerman Galanty & Fiman, First Tuesday, Hayes Productions, Joe Slade White Communications, Ken Swope and Associates, Political Advertising & Consulting, Raymond D. Strother, Ringe Media, Sawyer/Miller Group, and others.

Size & Elements: Videotape: 3/4" (approx. 40 linear feet; viewing copies).
Cataloging: Computerized cataloging available to researchers.
Access: Open to researchers, scholars and the public. For in-house viewing only. Research fees not charged. Research requests accepted by mail, telephone and in person (by appointment only).
Rights: No rights held to any material.
Licensing: Not available for licensing or reuse. Can refer requesters to producers for possible access to original materials in some cases.
Restrictions: Not available for licensing or reuse.
Viewing Facilities: Videotape (3/4"; by appointment only).
Duplication Facilities: None.
Related Materials: Political ephemera (campaign buttons, posters, etc.).

DISTRICT OF COLUMBIA METRO

SMITHSONIAN INSTITUTION
OFFICE OF TELECOMMUNICATIONS
American History Building, Room BB40
Washington, DC 20560
(202) 357-2985

Paul Johnson (Director, Office of Telecommunications)

Contact: Staff
Services: Film and videotape production and distribution facility for the Smithsonian Institution. Programs available for distribution and broadcast.
Description: Produces television programs, videotape productions, documentaries and educational films on Institution-related topics such as history, science, art, culture and museum research projects. Many programs are broadcast nationally; the Office has recently begun to produce programs for the homevideo market as well. Although most programs are placed with outside distributors after their first broadcast, the Office will refer inquirers to the correct distributor. Fifteen titles are available to the public for purchase.

Here at the Smithsonian... (20 features, each 3 min.). A series of video features, available to all television stations, presenting the sights, sounds and behind-the-scenes activities of the Smithsonian Institution. Features include: the latest developments in gamma ray astronomy; America's first look at late 19th-century Russian art; a visit to the Smithsonian's "home" for rare and endangered animals; and highlights from the Festival of American Folklife.

Size & Elements: Film: 16mm (15 titles; originals and release prints). Videotape: 1" (masters); 3/4" and 1/2" (viewing copies).
Cataloging: Film and videotape listings.
Access: Available to television stations for distribution and broadcast. Some titles available to the public for purchase. Research requests not accepted. Orders accepted by mail and telephone.
Rights: Full rights held to all material.
Licensing: Available for distribution and broadcast, subject to restrictions. Distribution fees charged.
Restrictions: Programs must be shown in their entirety and cannot be excerpted or reused in any manner.
Viewing Facilities: None.
Duplication Facilities: None.
Related Materials: Radio programs.
Distributors: Several distributors handle Smithsonian-produced programs (apply for information).

DISTRICT OF COLUMBIA METRO

SPECIAL OLYMPICS INTERNATIONAL
1350 New York Avenue, NW, Suite 500
Washington, DC 20005-4709
(202) 628-3630
Fax: (202) 737-1937
Telex: 650-284-1739 MCI

Eunice Kennedy Shriver (Chairman of the Board)

Contact: Sheila Dunn (Public Affairs Assistant)
Services: Nonprofit organization. Film and videotape collection available to member organizations, sponsors and researchers. Material available for licensing and reuse, subject to restrictions.
Description: Documentaries, promotional and fundraising materials, including films and public service announcements (PSAs) relating to the training and

competition of developmentally disabled children and adults.

Sample titles include: *A Dream to Grow On* (1968), on the First International Special Olympics held in July, 1968 at Chicago's Soldiers Field; *Grow High on Love* (1978), showing Special Olympics Games and vignettes about the athletes, volunteers, and communities; *Spirit of Special Olympics* (1978), in which parents, coaches, and athletes narrate the stories of 11 award winners; *The Best I Can...The Special Olympics Story* (1980), the story of the first ten years of the Special Olympics, told by three athletes; *1987 International Summer Special Olympics Games: The Parade of Athletes,* with delegations from all fifty states, the District of Columbia, four U.S. territories and 69 countries; and *The Special Olympics Video PSA Reel* (1987), with seven Special Olympics television PSAs.

Size & Elements: Film: 16mm (21 titles). Videotape: 3/4" and 1/2" (21 titles).
Cataloging: Published catalogs.
Access: Available to member organizations, sponsors and researchers. Research requests accepted by mail. Research fees charged (fees vary according to the nature of request).
Rights: Full rights held to some material. Additional clearances may be necessary in some cases if material (network-produced broadcasts) is to be reused.
Licensing: Available for licensing and reuse. License fees charged in some cases.
Restrictions: None specified.
Viewing Facilities: Videotape (3/4" and 1/2").
Duplication Facilities: None.

DISTRICT OF COLUMBIA METRO

TIRE INDUSTRY SAFETY COUNCIL
844 National Press Building
Washington, DC 20045
(202) 783-1022

Available for rental from:
MODERN TALKING PICTURE SERVICE, INC. (q.v.)

Edward Lewis (Director, Tire Industry Safety Council)

Contact: Modern Talking Picture Service, Inc. (q.v.)
Services: Association. One film available for distribution to driver education classes and instructors only.
Description: *Making The Grade With Tires* (12 min., color), produced by TISC.
Size & Elements: Film: 16mm (1 title; release print). Videotape: VHS (viewing copy).
Cataloging: Dope sheets or release sheets.
Access: Maintained for distribution and rental rather than for research or reuse.
Rights: Full rights held to all material.
Licensing: Apply for information.
Restrictions: Distribution restricted to driver education classes and instructors.
Viewing Facilities: None.
Duplication Facilities: None.

DISTRICT OF COLUMBIA METRO

TRANSPORTATION RESEARCH BOARD/ NATIONAL RESEARCH COUNCIL
2101 Constitution Avenue, NW
Washington, DC 20418
(202) 334-2934
Fax: (202) 334-2003
Telex: 248664 NASWUR

Street address: 2001 Wisconsin Avenue, NW, Washington, DC 20007

Thomas B. Deen (Executive Director)

Contact: Jewelene Gaskins (Manager, AV Library)
Services: Nonprofit organization. Films and videotapes available for rental, purchase and reuse.
Description: The Transportation Board, a unit of the National Research Council, serves as an independent advisor to the federal government on scientific and technical questions of national importance.

Collection relates to transportation planning, design and development.
TRB: On the Move explains the Board's programs and services. Videotapes

discussing the Strategic Highway Research Program include *America's Highways: Accelerating the Search for Innovation* and *Strategic Highway Research Program.* The latter discusses study areas being developed by SHRP: asphalt, long-term pavement performance, maintenance cost-effectiveness, protection of concrete bridge components, cement and concrete in highway pavements and structures, and chemical control of snow and ice on highways.

AASHO Road Test — Pavement Research describes the methods and findings of the AASHO Road Test, which has become the basis for pavement design throughout the world. *Research: The Common Denominator* (1971) commemorates the 50th Anniversary of the Highway Research Board (now TRB), covering the use of holosigns and electronic route guidance systems; computers programmed to produce perspective sketches; the testing of crash barriers and sign supports; drunk driving; air and noise pollution; and features early films and photographs of unpaved roads and traffic congestion.

Other films available: *Relief for Tired Streets; Guardrail Performance and Design; Safety at Freeway Exits;* and *Quiet Highway Designs.*
Size & Elements: Film: 16mm (9 titles). Videotape: 3/4", VHS and Betamax (8 videotapes, not all available in every format).
Cataloging: Published list.
Access: Available to the public for duplication. Maintained primarily for rental and purchase rather than for research and reuse. Research fees not charged.
Rights: Material in the public domain.
Licensing: Apply for information. License fees not charged.
Restrictions: None specified.
Viewing Facilities: None.
Duplication Facilities: None.
Related Materials: Still photographs, slide shows and an audiotape *(Illustrative Recording of Traffic Noise)* are also available.

DISTRICT OF COLUMBIA METRO

UNICORN PROJECTS
c/o The Production Group
2121 Wisconsin Avenue, NW, Suite 470
Washington, DC 20007
(202) 337-3572

Larry Klein (Vice President)

Contact: Larry Klein
Services: Film and videotape producer. Footage available for licensing and reuse through authorized representative.
Description: Footage relating to castles, cathedrals, pyramids, architecture and urban planning.

Foreign locales. Egypt, France and Wales.

United States locales. Coverage of Baltimore; Berkeley, Calif.; Big Sur, Calif.; Boston; Chicago; Daly City, Calif.; Los Angeles; New York City; Palo Alto, Calif.; Pittsburgh; San Francisco; and Savannah, Ga.

Interviews with architects, critics and planners. Subjects include Edward Larrabee Barnes; Peter Blake; James Marston Fitch; Aaron Green; Patricia Harris; Henry Russell Hitchcock; Lewis Mumford; Nathaniel Owens; Kevin Roche; Paolo Soleri; Robert Summer; Wolf von Eckhardt; and Harry Weese.

Architectural works. Includes works by Green & Green; Bernard Maybeck; Mies van der Rohe; H. H. Richardson; Louis Sullivan; and Frank Lloyd Wright. Buildings covered include: Auditorium Building (Chicago); Christian Science Church (Oak Park, Ill.); tract houses in Daly City, Calif.; Empire State Building; David B. Gamble House (Pasadena, Calif., 1908); John Hancock Tower (Boston); Hanna House and other houses designed by Frank Lloyd Wright; Quincy Market (Boston); Richardson buildings at Harvard University; Robie House; Seagram Building (New York City); Sears Tower (Chicago); Sullivan Building (Chicago); Carson Pirie Scott (Chicago); Lever House (New York City); Transamerica Building (San Francisco); and Trinity Church (New York City).

Other architectural subjects. Includes New York City neighborhoods and aerial views; Golden Gate Park (San Francisco); urban and suburban sprawl; downtown Chicago; Oak Park, Ill.; Baltimore's Inner Harbor district; the Cold Springs development in Baltimore, designed by Moshe Safdie; public housing projects in San Francisco, St. Louis, New York City and Baltimore; the problems and potential of urban renewal; historic preservation projects; Old Sturbridge Village, Mass.; and Savannah, Ga.

Castles. Aerials, ground and landscape shots of Welsh castles, including Harlech, Conway, Beaumaris, Caernarvon (restored) and the Great Hall at Penshurst. Also covered are several medieval town structures located at Weld and Downland Outdoor Museum in Sussex, England.

French Gothic cathedrals. Includes Amiens, Reims, Chartres, Notre Dame de Paris, Laon and the Royal Abbey Church of St. Denis. Details covered include stained glass, ornamentation, structural elements, aerial views and stone sculpture restoration work. The French countryside and the towns of Laon, Amiens and Chartres are also covered.

Egyptian pyramids. Pyramids, temples, tombs and art objects of Egypt, including: the Giza pyramids and temples, with special attention to the Great Pyramid of Cheops; Sphinx and Sphinx Temple; the Valley Temple of Cephren; the Tomb of Mersayenkh; the Step Pyramid at Saqqara; the pyramid complex at Meidum; the Valley of the Kings and the Valley of the Nobles, including the tombs of Tutankhamen, Seti the First, Ramses the Sixth and others. Also covered are Luxor Temple; the Nile and feluccas at Luxor; and artifacts and objects at the Egyptian Museum in Cairo, including the mummified body of Ramses the Second and King Tutankhamen's golden mask.

Size & Elements: Film: 35mm (approx. 20,000 feet); 16mm (approx. 100,000 feet).
Cataloging: None specified.
Access: Available for licensing and reuse through authorized representative. Research fees charged. Research requests accepted by mail, telephone and in person (by appointment only).
Rights: Full rights held to all material.
Licensing: Available for licensing and reuse. License fees charged.
Restrictions: None specified.
Viewing Facilities: Film and videotape (through Film/Audio Services, Inc.).
Duplication Facilities: Film and videotape (through Film/Audio Services, Inc.).
Representative: Film/Audio Services, Inc. (q.v.).

DISTRICT OF COLUMBIA METRO

U.S. CHAMBER OF COMMERCE
SPECIAL PROJECTS DEPARTMENT
1615 H Street, NW
Washington, DC 20062
(202) 463-5435
Fax: (202) 463-5836

Dr. Richard L. Lesher (President)

Contact: Sally A. Ulrich (Manager, Educational Services, Special Projects Department.)
Services: Association. Films available for rental and purchase, and for licensing, subject to restrictions.
Description: Economic education; the workings of the American free enterprise system (1954-present).

In the futuristic animated short, *Freedom 2000,* the crew of the Galaxia Kentron spaceship reviews the history of America's free enterprise system as they approach Earth for an observation pass. In *The Incredible Voyage of Mark O'Gulliver,* a U.S. Congressman is shipwrecked on an animal-run island — the United States of Animalia — which resembles our own bureaucracy so closely that the animals experience many of the drawbacks of an overblown federal government. George Washington and Ben Franklin join in an exuberant mix of song and dialogue in *Let's Get It Back America.*
Size & Elements: Film: 16mm. Videotape: 3/4", VHS and Betamax (9 titles).
Cataloging: Published catalogs (available on request).
Access: Maintained primarily for distribution, rental and purchase rather than research or reuse.
Rights: Full rights held to all material.
Licensing: Available for licensing, subject to restrictions. License fees charged in some cases (apply for information).
Restrictions: Written authorization required for licensing or reuse.
Viewing Facilities: Videotape (upon request).
Duplication Facilities: None.

DISTRICT OF COLUMBIA METRO

UNITED STATES CONFERENCE OF MAYORS
MAYORS' MEDIA RESOURCE CENTER
1620 Eye Street, NW
Washington, DC 20006
(202) 293-7330
Fax: (202) 293-2352

J. Thomas Cochran (Executive Director)

Contact: Thomas L. McClimon (Director, Institute for Urban and Regional

Economic Analysis)
Services: Association. Videotape collection available to the public for distribution and rental rather than research or reuse.
Description: Videotapes relating to municipal finance, financial management and city government revenues. *User Fees: Towards Better Usage* identifies new user fee opportunities and examines their social, economic and political impacts. *Municipal Bond Ratings: What You Should Know* answers questions on how city bonds are rated, on bond presentations and on the key factors that a rating agency uses in assigning a bond rating. *Municipal Finance: An Introduction* addresses the issues of how city bonds are sold and traded, ways to take advantage of the latest financing tools, how tax reform affects a city's ability to borrow money and other questions of municipal debt.

More programs are in development.
Size & Elements: Videotape: VHS and Betamax (3 titles, each 20 min.).
Cataloging: Published brochure. *Local Government Video Catalogue* contains a listing of municipal videotapes.
Access: Open to the public. Maintained for distribution and rental rather than for research or reuse.
Rights: Full rights held to all material.
Licensing: Apply for information.
Restrictions: Copyright restrictions apply.
Viewing Facilities: None.
Duplication Facilities: None.

DISTRICT OF COLUMBIA METRO

U.S. COUNCIL FOR ENERGY AWARENESS
1776 Eye Street, NW, Suite 400
Washington, DC 20006
(202) 293-0770
Fax: (202) 785-4019
Telex: 7854113

Harold B. Finger (President and Chief Executive Officer)

Contact: Mary A. Carruthers (Manager, Audio Visual Services)
Services: Association. Films and videotapes maintained for distribution and rental. Material available for research, licensing and reuse, subject to restrictions.
Description: Formerly the Atomic Industrial Forum, a nuclear industry advocacy organization. Materials serve as adjuncts to USCEA's public and corporate communications programs, technical programs, conference program and the National Environmental Studies Project.

Titles include: *Coping with Crisis: Accident at Ginna,* on a nuclear power plant accident (1982); *Extending the Harvest,* on food irradiation; *Fitting the Pieces...Managing Nuclear Waste,* attempting to answer questions about high-level radioactive waste disposal; *Nuclear Electricity and You,* a 13-part series designed for cablecast; *Fact or Fake,* a response to criticisms made by the Greenpeace conservationist group of nuclear safety testing in Great Britain; *Radiation in Medicine and Industry,* in which Dr. Arnold Muller describes the misinformation disseminated at the time of the Three Mile Island nuclear accident; and *Radiation...Naturally,* comparing low-level radiation found in nature with industrially produced radiation.
Size & Elements: Film: 16mm (24 titles). Videotape: 3/4", VHS and Betamax (viewing copies).
Cataloging: Published catalogs; computerized cataloging for staff use only.
Access: Available to the public for distribution and rental. Research requests accepted by mail and telephone.
Rights: Full rights held to all material.
Licensing: Available for reuse, subject to restrictions. Usage fees charged in some cases.
Restrictions: Requests for reuse subject to acceptance and approval.
Viewing Facilities: None.
Duplication Facilities: None.

DISTRICT OF COLUMBIA METRO

U.S. DEFENSE NUCLEAR AGENCY
PUBLIC AFFAIRS OFFICE
Washington, DC 20305-1000
(703) 325-7095
Fax: (703) 325-7366

Contact: Cheri E. Abdelnour (Assistant Public Affairs Officer)
Services: Government agency. Film and videotape collection maintained for

free loan. Available for duplication and reuse, subject to clearance and restrictions.

Description: Scientific and technical films relating to the effects of nuclear weapons on structures, equipment and people, and documenting nuclear detonations (mid-1940s through late 1970s). Films were primarily produced during the atmospheric nuclear test era (1951-60) by DNA and its predecessors, the Defense Atomic Support Agency (DASA), the Armed Forces Special Weapons Project (AFSWP) and other organizations.

The users of these films are warned that many are dated and reflect the outlook of the era in which they were produced. They are by their very nature historical and do not necessarily reflect current DNA or Department of Defense doctrine. *Some titles may represent classified information.*

Subject categories and sample titles include:

Orientation films. Defense Nuclear Agency Documentary (1975); *Effects of the Atomic Bomb on Hiroshima and Nagasaki* (1949); *From Caveman to A-Bomb* (1952); *Atomic Weapons Orientation: Part I, Organization for Atomic Energy* (1961) and *Part II, Basic Atomic Weapons* (1965); *Effects of Nuclear Weapons: Introduction, The Air Burst, The Ground Burst, The Water Burst and Target Considerations* (1957); and *Bio-Effects of Radiation: Part 1, Basic Concepts and History* and *Part 2, Determinants of Radiation Injury and the Acute Radiation Syndrome* (1977).

Nuclear weapons testing. Sample titles: *Story of Five Atomic Bombs* (1946); *Operation CROSSROADS: Able-Baker* (1946); *Operation SANDSTONE* (1948); *X-ray, Yoke and Zebra Report* (1948); *Journey to Zero Point; Atomic Tests TRINITY through BUSTER JANGLE* (1952); *Atomic Support for the Soldier* (1951); and *Operation TINY TOT* (1965).

Effects simulations. Sample titles: *Research on Explosive Cratering* (1965); *Mono Lake: Wave Generation Tests* (1965); *Pre-Dice Throw* (1975); *FLATTOP (A Ground Shock and Cratering Series); Rocket Sounding in the Arctic Ionosphere* (1969); and *Project HEART.*

Nuclear weapons. Sample titles: *CROSSROADS ABLE DAY Weapons Assembly* (1956); *SCREAMER* (1965); *MIDI MIST Documentary Film Report; The MARK 28 Weapon Family* (1962); *POLARIS Reentry Body and Associated Support Equipment* (1967); *Living with Nuclear Weapons* (1963); *Meeting the Terrorists' Threat* (1975); and *One Man's Terrorist* (1979).

Miscellaneous productions. Hiroshima (1946); *A Present from Nicholas* (1961); *Weapons Effects Display System; Price of Peace and Freedom;* and *The PAC-3G Alpha Counter* (1960).

Technical footage and film clips. These are short films without sound. (Additional short films of nuclear test detonations and nuclear test activities are held in the DASIAC collection and the DNA Archive at Field Command, Kirtland Air Force Base, New Mexico.) Items are: *UPSHOT-KNOTHOLE; TEAPOT; WIGWAM; REDWING; HARDTACK; DOMINIC; DIAL TRAIN; DIAL FLOWER; GARZA; DICE GAME; Underground tests; Compilation — stock footage; HE simulations; Ship response experiments; Miscellaneous simulations;* and *Systems.*

DNA films cleared for public release are listed in Volume IV of the *Department of Defense Catalog of Audiovisual Productions.*

Size & Elements: Film: 16mm. Videotape: 3/4". (Approx. 100 items total).

Cataloging: Published catalog entitled *Department of Defense Productions Cleared for Public Release — Vol. IV* is distributed by the National Technical Information Service in Springfield, VA, and lists most of the films available from the Defense Nuclear Agency Public Relations Office. This catalog may be obtained in hard copy or microfiche from: U.S. Department of Commerce, National Technical Information Service, 5285 Port Royal Road, Springfield, VA 22161; (703) 487-4650. Order number: AD-A 148 714.

Access: Many DNA films are available for free loan upon request through NARA, National Audiovisual Center (q.v.) and the U.S. Department of Defense, Motion Media Records Center (q.v.). Material available for duplication and reuse, subject to restrictions. Research fees not charged. Research requests accepted by mail and telephone.

Rights: Material in the public domain.

Licensing: Available for reuse, subject to restrictions. Usage fees not charged.

Restrictions: Reuse subject to approval by appropriate public affairs office of Department of Defense. Some material is classified or otherwise exempt from public release.

Viewing Facilities: None.

Duplication Facilities: None.

DISTRICT OF COLUMBIA METRO

U.S. DEPARTMENT OF TRANSPORTATION/ NATIONAL HIGHWAY TRAFFIC SAFETY ADMINISTRATION TECHNICAL REFERENCE DIVISION
Room 5109
400 Seventh Street, SW
Washington, DC 20590
(202) 366-4949

Contact: Betrinere Stewart (Library Technician, Technical Reference Division)

Services: Government agency. Film and videotape material available for loan, duplication and reuse.

Description: Documentation of extensive automotive safety testing as performed by NHTSA. Includes the results of the New Car Assessment Program (NCAP) involving crash testing; rear and frontal barrier impact tests at various car speeds (e.g., 1982 Chevrolet Camaro/two-door Coupe, frontal test); footage of fuel tank testing for explosion during impact (e.g., 1979 Ford Pinto Sedan/three-door runabout, rear impact); safety belt and rollover testing.

Size & Elements: Film: 16mm (3,300 items). Videotape (format and amount unspecified).

Cataloging: Published catalog of films available for purchase. Computerized cataloging for staff use only (search by keyword, make or manufacturer of car is possible).

Access: Available to the public for loan and duplication. Up to five films can be borrowed for two weeks.

Rights: Material in the public domain.

Licensing: Available for duplication and reuse. Usage fees charged.

Restrictions: None specified.

Viewing Facilities: Film (16mm).

Duplication Facilities: Film and videotape.

DISTRICT OF COLUMBIA METRO

U.S. HIDE, SKIN & LEATHER ASSOCIATION
1707 N Street, NW
Washington, DC 20036
(202) 833-2405
Fax: (202) 785-3919

Jerome Breiter (President)

Contact: Jerome Breiter

Services: Association. One videotape available for purchase.

Description: *Modern Cattlehide Processing* (18 min.) takes the viewer through the complete hide processing operation from hide removal to shipping of product. Included are proper procedures for trimming, fleshing, preservation, grading and storage. Filmed in a number of locations, the presentation demonstrates hide pulling and knife removal as a means of removing the hide from the carcass. It shows raceway, mixer and salt pack curing, and demonstrates fleshing, trimming and grading techniques.

While primarily intended for use as an introduction to the USHSLA Hide Training School, the videotape is also valuable in other areas. Hide processors and tanners will find it a useful tool in training new employees or in familiarizing those outside the industry with its workings. Those selling hides will be able to use the videotape to demonstrate to customers the process by which their product is provided.

Size & Elements: Videotape: VHS and Betamax II (1 title). PAL standard also available at a slightly higher cost.

Cataloging: Published brochure.

Access: Available for purchase to hide processors, tanners and other interested parties. Requests accepted by mail and telephone.

Rights: Apply for information.

Licensing: Apply for information.

Restrictions: None specified.

Viewing Facilities: None.

Duplication Facilities: None.

DISTRICT OF COLUMBIA METRO

U.S. HOUSE OF REPRESENTATIVES HOUSE BROADCASTING SYSTEM
Office of Records and Registration
Longworth Building, Room 1036
Washington, DC 20515
(202) 225-1300

Patricia Bias (Director)

Contacts: Kimberly Boland

Services: Government agency. Videotape collection available to the public for duplication and reuse, subject to restrictions.
Description: Videotape coverage of U.S. House of Representatives floor proceedings. Coverage is produced by the House Recording Studio and available to the public through the Office of Records and Registration. Footage is held by the Studio and is publicly accessible for a 60-day period; thereafter, it is inaccessible until the end of the current session of Congress, at which time copies are deposited with the National Archives and Records Administration (q.v.) in Record Group 233, and the Library of Congress, Motion Picture, Broadcasting and Recorded Sound Division (q.v.).
Size & Elements: Videotape: 1" (amount unspecified; masters).
Cataloging: Daily issues of the *Congressional Record* contain transcripts of floor proceedings; time code cues are printed at regular intervals. *Users are urged to refer to the* Record *and these cues when ordering footage.*
Access: Available to the public for duplication and reuse. Research requests accepted by mail and telephone.
Rights: Material in the public domain.
Licensing: Available for reuse, subject to restrictions. Usage fees not charged (service and duplication fees charged).
Restrictions: Material available for non-political reuse. Clearance for reuse may be obtained through the House Administration; (202) 225-2061.
Viewing Facilities: Videotape (in-house viewing possible; facilities only available when Congress is not in session).
Duplication Facilities: Videotape (1", 3/4", VHS and Betamax; material is duplicated at the House Recording Studio). Duplication fees apply.

DISTRICT OF COLUMBIA METRO

UNITED STATES MARINE CORPS
HISTORICAL CENTER LIBRARY
Washington Navy Yard, Building 58
Washington, DC 20374-0580
(202) 433-4253

Contact: Bennis Frank (202/433-3841)
Services: Government agency; library. Film collection inaccessible for research or reuse.
Description: Training films and films relating to the Vietnam War.
Size & Elements: Film: format and amount unspecified.
Cataloging: Uncataloged and unaccessioned.
Access: Collection inaccessible for research and reuse.
Rights: Full rights held to all material.
Licensing: Not available for reuse.
Restrictions: Collection inaccessible to the public.
Viewing Facilities: None.
Duplication Facilities: None.

DISTRICT OF COLUMBIA METRO

UNITED WAY OF AMERICA
ARCHIVES
701 North Fairfax Street
Alexandria, VA 22314
(703) 836-7100
Fax: (703) 683-7840
Fax: (703) 683-7839

Patricia Cooper (Director)

Contacts: Patricia Cooper (Ext. 297); Ann Longmore (Assistant Archivist) (Ext. 544)
Services: Foundation. Film and videotape library available to the public for licensing and reuse.
Description: Films and videotapes produced by the UWA (late 1950s-present), including productions by the groups which formed The United Way in the 1970s (The Torch Fund, The United Drive, The Crusade of Mercy), and films produced annually for the Combined Federal Campaigns (early 1970s-present). Also holds television public service announcements produced by the UWA (1950s-present).
   Supplies footage to UWA productions and to related organizations such as the Red Cross, The Salvation Army, day care organizations and health services. Other organizations will be serviced on a case-by-case basis.
Size & Elements: Film: 35mm, 16mm and Super 8mm. Videotape: 1", 3/4" and VHS. (10 million feet total).
Cataloging: Dope sheets or release sheets; research library.

Access: Available to the public for licensing and reuse. Research fees charged. Research requests accepted by mail and telephone.
Rights: Full rights held to all material.
Licensing: Available for licensing and reuse, subject to restrictions. License fees charged.
Restrictions: All research requests subject to acceptance and approval on a case-by-case basis. Nonprofit use preferred.
Viewing Facilities: Film and videotape (access to facilities through Production Department).
Duplication Facilities: Film and videotape (access to facilities through Production Department).

DISTRICT OF COLUMBIA METRO

UNIVERSITY OF MARYLAND
McKELDIN LIBRARY
HISTORICAL MANUSCRIPTS AND ARCHIVES DEPARTMENT
College Park, MD 20742
(301) 454-2318

Lauren R. Brown (Curator of Historical Manuscripts and University Archivist)

Contact: Lauren R. Brown
Services: Educational institution. Film and videotape collection available to the public for duplication and reuse, subject to restrictions.
Description: Holds campaign films produced on behalf of local politicians; promotional films from women's organizations (e.g., American Association of University Women) and labor unions (e.g., Bakery, Confectionery, and Tobacco Workers International Union); and films of labor union conventions and speeches. Materials date from ca. 1960s-70s.
Size & Elements: Film: format unspecified (12,000 feet, 12 titles, 12 cans; positive originals and release prints). Videotape: VHS (2 videotapes; masters and viewing copies).
Cataloging: Guides to manuscript collections.
Access: Open to the public. Research fees not charged in most cases. Research requests accepted by mail, telephone and in person (walk-in and by appointment).
Rights: Some rights held to some material.
Licensing: Available for reuse, subject to restrictions. Usage fees not charged.
Restrictions: "Normal copyright restrictions" apply.
Viewing Facilities: Film and videotape (available at Library's Non-print Media Center).
Duplication Facilities: None.

DISTRICT OF COLUMBIA METRO

VIETNAM VETERANS OF AMERICA
2001 S Street, NW, Suite 700
Washington, DC 20009
(202) 332-2700
Fax: (202) 265-8019

Mary R. Stout (President)

Contact: Barry Kasinitz (Communication Coordinator)
Services: Association; videotape producer. Videotape collection available for in-house use. Some material available to local VVA chapters.
Description: Six videotapes covering congressional hearings (1985-present) on issues of specific interest to veterans. These videotapes are primarily for use by local chapters of the VVA. Also holds an in-house research collection of material videotaped off the air.
Size & Elements: Videotape: VHS (6 videotapes).
Cataloging: None specified.
Access: Available to the public. Some materials for in-house use only. Some materials maintained for distribution to local VVA chapters. Research fees not charged. Research requests accepted by mail and telephone.
Rights: Full rights held to some material. No rights held to other material.
Licensing: Available for licensing and reuse, subject to restrictions. License and usage fees not charged.
Restrictions: Requests for licensing and reuse considered on a case-by-case basis and are subject to acceptance, approval and copyright clearance.
Viewing Facilities: Videotape (VHS).
Duplication Facilities: None.

DISTRICT OF COLUMBIA METRO

THE WASHINGTON BROADCAST VIDEO LIBRARY
CREATIVE VIDEO OF WASHINGTON, INC.
1011 Arlington Boulevard, Room 320
Arlington, VA 22209
(703) 524-1820

Kirby Whyte (President)

Contact: Kirby Whyte
Services: Videotape producer; stock footage sales library.
Description: The *Washington Broadcast Video Library* (30 min.) contains footage of many famous and familiar Washington, D.C. subjects, excerpted from a 14-hour collection. Library begins Summer 1985 and is updated annually with broadcast-quality material. Intended for unlimited use by news, documentary, public service and post-production users. The library includes aerial scenes, closeup and angle shots, government buildings and familiar backgrounds.

Subjects covered: Lincoln Memorial; Washington Monument; Iwo Jima Memorial; White House; Russell, Dirksen, and Hart Senate Office Buildings; Cannon, Longworth and Rayburn House Office Buildings; U.S. Capitol and the Mall; Library of Congress; Supreme Court; Union Station; Departments of Agriculture, Commerce, Defense (Pentagon), Education, Health and Human Services, Housing and Urban Development, Interior, Justice, Labor, State, Treasury and Transportation; Old Executive Office Building; Environmental Protection Agency; FBI; Federal Reserve Bank; FTC; General Accounting Office; IRS; Interstate Commerce Commission; NASA; National Transportation Safety Board; Nuclear Regulatory Commission; Office of Management and Budget; U.S. Postal Service; Jefferson Memorial; Vietnam Memorial; Kennedy Center and the Watergate; helicopter shots of Capitol Hill, DOT, HUD and DOE; National and Dulles Airports; Georgetown; Old Town; the National Theater.

Each subject is frequently seen from several sides and angles; signs are sometimes shown. Seasonal footage is also included, with some monuments in knee-deep snow. Most views are exterior.
Size & Elements: Videotape: 1", Betacam and 3/4" (14 hours; masters). The *Washington Broadcast Video Library* is available in 2", 1", Betacam, 3/4" (masters); and VHS (viewing copies). (PAL and SECAM conversions and viewing copies available upon request).
Cataloging: Published catalog and list; computerized cataloging for staff use only.
Access: Not open to the public. Available for licensing and reuse. Research fees charged. Research requests accepted by mail and telephone.
Rights: Some rights held to all material.
Licensing: Available for licensing and reuse, subject to restrictions. License fees charged.
Restrictions: "The *Washington Broadcast Video Library* is for the unlimited use of purchasers and lessors in broadcast and non-broadcast applications in news, documentary, public service and post-production applications. The Library and its scenes are not for use in any commercial applications where, by its presence, the scene used constitutes a commercial endorsement. Duplication of the Library or any part of it for sale and/or distribution is strictly forbidden and constitutes a violation of Creative Video's copyright."
Viewing Facilities: Videotape (3/4").
Duplication Facilities: Videotape (1", Betacam, 3/4" SP and 3/4").

DISTRICT OF COLUMBIA METRO

WETA-TV
P.O. Box 2626
Washington, DC 20013
(703) 998-2671
Fax: (703) 824-8343

Ward Chamberlain (President)
Thomas Ingold (Director of Operations and Production)

Contacts: Tape Library (703/998-2671); Thomas Ingold (703/998-2780)
Services: Public television broadcaster. Videotape collection available to the public for duplication, licensing and reuse on a case-by-case basis; subject to restrictions.
Description: News, public affairs and cultural programming, especially pertaining to the Washington, D.C. area. Has produced many programs for the Public Broadcasting System (PBS). General topics include political affairs;

interviews with Congressional and other political figures; *In Performance At the White House,* a cultural series; and stock shots, scenics and beauty shots of Washington, D.C.

Holds the only complete collection of coverage of the Watergate hearings (1973, 2" videotape).
Size & Elements: Videotape: 2", 1" and 3/4" (amount unspecified; masters). Can supply viewing copies in any format, including 1/2".
Cataloging: Staff assistance required (contact Tape Library).
Access: Open to the public. Available for duplication, licensing and reuse on a case-by-case basis, subject to restrictions. Research and screening fees charged (negotiable). Research requests accepted by mail, telephone and in person (by appointment only).
Rights: Full rights held to all material. Additional clearances may be necessary in some cases if material (with artists, talent or interviewees) is to be reused.
Licensing: Available for licensing, subject to restrictions. License fees charged.
Restrictions: Requests for licensing and reuse accepted on a case-by-case basis.
Viewing Facilities: Videotape (2", 1" and 3/4") (screening fees charged).
Duplication Facilities: Videotape (fees charged).

FLORIDA

FLORIDA (Cape Canaveral)

COMMUNICATIONS CONCEPTS
7980 North Atlantic Avenue
Cape Canaveral, FL 32920
(407) 783-5232
Fax: (407) 783-7065

Jim Lewis (General Manager)

Contact: Eric Roberts (Production Assistant)
Services: Videotape producer; full-service videotape production facility. Material available for duplication, licensing and reuse.
Description: Footage of the Kennedy Space Center, including rocket launches, space shuttle launches and payload processing; Florida beaches, rivers and waterfronts; and generic resort footage.
Size & Elements: Videotape: 1" and 3/4" (10 hours; masters). Viewing copies available in any videotape format.
Cataloging: Computerized cataloging for staff use only.
Access: Available to the public for duplication, licensing and reuse. Research fees not charged. Research requests accepted by mail and telephone.
Rights: Full rights held to all material.
Licensing: Available for licensing and reuse. License fees charged.
Restrictions: None specified.
Viewing Facilities: Film; videotape (3/4" and 1/2"). Screening fees charged.
Duplication Facilities: Videotape (any format available).

FLORIDA (Coral Gables)

UNIVERSITY OF MIAMI
ARCHIVES AND SPECIAL COLLECTIONS DEPARTMENT
P.O. Box 248214
Coral Gables, FL 33124
(305) 284-3247

Street address: Richter Library

Helen Purdy (Head, Archives and Special Collections)

Contacts: Helen Purdy; Esperanza Varona (Assistant Head)
Services: University library. Film and videotape collection open to researchers and scholars only.
Description: Subject areas relevant to regional concerns, the University, Cuban exiles and other national and ethnic groups present in Miami.

Titles include: *El Archivo Del Exilio* (WLTV/Miami), showing the impact of Cuban exiles in South Florida, including 23 interviews with Cuban exiles living in Miami and other areas of Dade County; *Centenario del Bolero,* celebrating 100 years of the Cuban musical form comprised of European and African influences, and featuring composers Sindo Garay, Manuel Corona, Miguel Companioni, Eusebio Delfín, Rafael Gómez ("Teofilito") and others; *The Cuban Periodicals in Exile,* on the exhibit of Cuban Exile periodicals at the University, including an interview with Esperanza Varona concerning the collection; *The Levine Collection,* eight videotaped interviews with members of the Cuban Jewish Community (now residents of South Florida), focusing on Cuban life (1918-61); *Miami...The Magic City* (ca. 1975), a historical film by Arva Parks; *Special Voices: Two Florida Women,* a series of recollections by Marjory Stoneman Douglas and Marjorie Carr.

The Dennis Gaffney Collection (60 videotapes). Interviews by Gaffney with notable Miamians related to the University and University alumni, including historical footage of the University. Interviews include: Fernandao Belaúnde, former President of Peru; Harold Long, first president of the United Black Students; Dante Fascell, U.S. Congressman; Alvin Snyder, head of the U.S. Information Agency's Television Network; and Doris Kromer, University of Miami student in the 1930s.

Historical films transferred to videotape include: *The Five Worlds* (1954), a recruitment film; an old military film; the mid-year reception for the Class of 1931; *Learning for Life* (1960s); hurricane, war and sports footage (1920s); and footage relating to the Rosenstiel School of Atmospheric Sciences (RSMAS).
Size & Elements: Film: format unspecified (13 films). Videotape: 3/4" and VHS (approx. 80 videotapes).
Cataloging: Finding aids.
Access: Open to researchers and scholars only. Research requests accepted in person (by appointment only).
Rights: Some rights held to some material. Additional clearances may be necessary in some cases if material is to be reused.
Licensing: Material possibly available for licensing and reuse. License fees not charged.
Restrictions: None specified.
Viewing Facilities: Videotape.
Duplication Facilities: None.

FLORIDA (Crystal River)

COURTER FILMS & ASSOCIATES
121 North West Crystal Street
Crystal River, FL 32629
(904) 795-2156
Fax: (904) 563-0573

Philip Courter (President)

Contact: Mary Ann Boline (Distribution Manager)
Services: Film and videotape producer. Material available for purchase, licensing and reuse, subject to restrictions.
Description: Emergency-response field training and technique films, produced especially for firefighters.

The *Incident Control Series* includes: *Hazardous Materials/Incident Command; Protective Apparatus;* and *Evacuation.* Topics include: the Union Carbide toxic chemical leak in Bhopal, India; a hydrogen fire in Phoenix, Arizona; chemical, thermal, radiation, asphyxiation, etiologic and mechanical hazards; school evacuation plans; hospitals and brush fires. Other emergency-response films include: *Hazardous Materials/Emergency Response; Structural Fire Attack; Basic Search and Rescue; Breathing Apparatus — Why?;* and *The Foam Film.*

Parenting Pictures division produces films concerning childbirth and parenting. *Saturday's Children* contains birth footage and labor coaching techniques. *Tender Loving Care: Parenting the Newborn* illustrates routine baby care, such as breastfeeding, cord and circumcision care, and diapering. *Family-Centered Cesareans* shows two Caesarean births, one emergency and one planned. Other titles include *Family Birthing; The Bonding Birth Experience; The Cesarean Birth Experience; The Breastfeeding Experience;* and *The Teenage Pregnancy Experience.*
Size & Elements: Film: 16mm and Super 8mm. Videotape: format unspecified. (10 titles total).
Cataloging: Brochures available.
Access: Available to professional users and the public for rental and purchase. Preview requests accepted for emergency-response films.
Rights: Full rights held to all material. Additional clearances may be necessary for licensing (especially for television rebroadcast).
Licensing: Available for licensing, subject to clearance and restrictions. License fees charged.
Restrictions: Television reuse subject to certain restrictions.
Viewing Facilities: None.
Duplication Facilities: None.

FLORIDA (Daytona Beach)

NASCAR VIDEO
P.O. Box K
Daytona Beach, FL 32015-9947
(904) 253-0611
Fax: (904) 254-6796

Street address: 1801 Speedway Boulevard

Contact: Jim Foster (NASCAR Historical Video)
Services: Association. One videotape available for purchase.
Description: *History of NASCAR and the Winston Cup* (90 min.) shows the great moments of car racing action and stories (1947 through the record-setting 1987 Winston Cup season) that have made NASCAR the most successful sanctioning organization in motor sports. One-hour annual highlight videotapes of the Winston Cup season will be available at a later date.
Size & Elements: Videotape: VHS and Betamax (1 title).
Cataloging: Printed brochure and order form.
Access: Available to the public for purchase.
Rights: Apply for information.
Licensing: Apply for information.
Restrictions: None specified.
Viewing Facilities: None.
Duplication Facilities: None.

FLORIDA (Fort Lauderdale)

INTERNATIONAL GAME FISH ASSOCIATION
INTERNATIONAL LIBRARY OF FISHES
3000 East Las Olas Boulevard
Fort Lauderdale, FL 33316-1616
(305) 467-0161
Fax: (305) 467-0331
Cable: IGFA

Elwood K. Harry (President)

Contact: Michael Leech (Executive Director)
Services: Association. Maintains videotape collection for use by members only. *Not available for loan, rental, purchase or reuse.*
Description: Material relating to fishing. Extensive list of titles covering different tactics for a wide variety of fish, equipment and conditions.
Size & Elements: Videotape (over 200 titles).
Cataloging: Card catalogs; film list.
Access: Available to members only. For in-house use only. Not open to the public.
Rights: Not specified.
Licensing: Not available for licensing and reuse.
Restrictions: Material not available for loan, rental, purchase or reuse at present.
Viewing Facilities: Videotape (VHS).
Duplication Facilities: Videotape (VHS).

FLORIDA (Fort Lauderdale)

INTERNATIONAL SWIMMING HALL OF FAME
One Hall of Fame Drive
Fort Lauderdale, FL 33316
(305) 462-6536

Don De Bolt (Executive Director)

Contacts: Bob Duenkel (Managing Director and AV Director)
Services: Museum and hall of fame. Film and videotape collection open to the public for in-house use only and available for reuse, subject to clearance.
Description: Films and videotapes, many shot by amateurs, of swimming meets, diving competitions and competitive aquatics (1920s-present).
Size & Elements: Film: 16mm (400 items; various elements). Videotape: format unspecified (45 videotapes).
Cataloging: Card catalogs.
Access: Available to the public. For in-house use only. Research fees not charged. Museum admission fees charged. Research requests accepted by mail, telephone and in person (walk-in).
Rights: Full rights held to some material. Additional clearances may be necessary in some cases if material is to be reused.
Licensing: Available for reuse, subject to restrictions. Usage fees not charged.

Restrictions: Clearance to reuse material must be obtained from its donor.
Viewing Facilities: Film (16mm); videotape.
Duplication Facilities: Videotape.

FLORIDA (Highland Beach)

FILMTEL INTERNATIONAL CORP.
c/o Peter M. Piech
2565 South Ocean Boulevard, Suite 311N
Highland Beach, FL 33487
(407) 278-9812

Peter M. Piech (President); Charles Haydon (Vice President)

Contact: Peter M. Piech
Services: Television producer and distributor. Programs available for television distribution, reuse and licensing, subject to restrictions.
Description: Animated children's television programs. Complete series available include: *Rocky and His Friends* (52 programs); *The Bullwinkle Show* (52 programs); *Hoppity Hooper* (52 programs); *King Leonardo* (39 programs); *Tennessee Tuxedo* (70 programs); *Underdog* (32 programs); and *Go Go Gophers* (13 programs).
   Individual short episodes available from: *Rocky and His Friends; Fractured Fairy Tales; Aesop & Son; Peabody's Improbable History; Dudley Do-Right; Hoppity Hooper; King Leonardo; Tooter Turtle; Hunter; Tennessee Tuxedo; Underdog; Go Go Gophers; Klondike Kat; Bullwinkle Corner; Mr. Know It All; Commander McBragg;* and *Twinkles.*
   Series are also available in Spanish.
Size & Elements: Film: 35mm and 16mm (total amount unspecified, black and white and color). Videotape: all formats.
Cataloging: Lists available.
Access: Not available to the public; maintained for television distribution. Much of the material is available for public viewing at The Museum of Broadcasting (q.v.)
Rights: Full rights held to all material.
Licensing: Available for licensing, subject to restrictions. License fees charged.
Restrictions: Not available to the general public for viewing, rental or purchase.
Viewing Facilities: None.
Duplication Facilities: None.

FLORIDA (Marineland)

MARINELAND OF FLORIDA
9507 Ocean Shore Blvd.
Marineland, FL 32086
(904) 471-1111
Fax: (904) 461-0156

David Drysdale (President)
Bill Puckett (Public Relations Director)

Contacts: Bill Puckett; David Schmid (Photographer)
Services: Corporate archives. Some material available for distribution and rental; other material available for duplication, licensing and reuse.
Description: Completed episodes and unedited footage from the series *Wonders of The Sea,* including: *The Pink Porpoise* (Amazon dolphins); *Marine Life Preview; The Sea Turtle; Jellyfish and Their Relatives; The Coral Reef; Knights In Armor; Barracuda; The Terrible Octopus; Adelie Penguins; How Do Fish Swim; Looking Like What You're Not; Life Begins At Sea;* and *Designs For Living.* Most film held is original unedited footage relating to Marineland of Florida history, expeditions and wildlife.
Size & Elements: Film: 16mm (approx. 150,000 to 250,000 feet; 20 to 40 titles [release prints]; raw footage [original material]; approx. 400-500 cans total).
Cataloging: None specified.
Access: Open to researchers and scholars. Available for distribution or rental. Some material available for duplication. Research fees charged. Research requests accepted by mail, telephone and in person (by appointment only).
Rights: Full rights held to all material.
Licensing: Available for licensing, subject to restrictions. License fees charged to commercial organizations but not to educational or nonprofit organizations.
Restrictions: Requests for licensing accepted on a case-by-case basis.
Viewing Facilities: Film (16mm projector).

Duplication Facilities: None.

FLORIDA (Miami)

JOHN F. HOGG
3813 Matheson Avenue
Miami, FL 33133
(305) 666-0882

Contact: John F. Hogg
Services: Private collection. Material available for reuse, subject to restrictions.
Description: Two promotional films (color, each 30 min.) showing travel from Chicago, Illinois to Oakland, California on the famous "California Zephyr" (ca. 1950 and 1954/63). Shows external trackside and inside from top of train; train travel through Midwest plains, the heart of the Rockies, and down California's Feather River Canyon in the Sierra Nevada; details of passengers riding in "Vista Domes" and coaches, eating in coaches (with closeups); Pullman car service shown in daytime and nighttime; Pullman porters shown making beds in sleeping cars. These films offer a very detailed account of railroad travel at the height of the postwar period on the most scenic continental train ever run in the United States.
Size & Elements: Film: 16mm (2 titles; release prints, each 30 min.).
Access: Not open to the public. Available for reuse and resale. Research fees charged. Research requests accepted by mail and telephone.
Rights: Material in the public domain.
Licensing: Available for reuse, subject to restrictions. Usage fees charged in some cases.
Restrictions: Requests for reuse subject to clearance and approval.
Viewing Facilities: Film.
Duplication Facilities: Videotape (3/4" and VHS).

FLORIDA (Miami)

INSTANT REPLAY, INC.
2951 South Bayshore Drive
Miami, FL 33133
(305) 448-7088
Fax: (305) 445-1998

Charles Azar (President)

Contact: Denise Blanchette (Manager)
Services: Aircheck service. Videotape material currently available for in-house use only; stock footage sales planned.
Description: Videotapes (1974-present) include off-air recordings of documentaries, news programs and other television shows; music videos, concerts and interviews with various musicians (produced in-house); video and computer graphics.
Size & Elements: Videotape: 3/4" (approx. 15,000 hours).
Cataloging: Computerized cataloging for staff use only.
Access: Currently available for in-house use only; stock footage sales planned. Research requests accepted by mail and telephone.
Rights: Some rights held to some material. Some material in the public domain. Additional clearances may be necessary in some cases if material is to be reused.
Licensing: Apply for information.
Restrictions: Some restrictions may apply.
Viewing Facilities: Videotape (3/4" and 1/2"; PAL, SECAM and NTSC).
Duplication Facilities: Videotape (3/4", 1/2" and 8mm; standards conversions).

FLORIDA (Miami)

KESSER STOCK FOOTAGE LIBRARY
21 South West 15th Road
Miami, FL 33129
(305) 358-7900
Fax: (305) 358-2209

Carl Kesser (Owner)

Contacts: Charles Carrubba (Head Librarian)
Services: Film and videotape stock footage sales library.
Description: Concentrates on high-quality production footage that is compatible with footage shot for national commercials and feature films. Very

little of the library originates on videotape. Videotape is broadcast quality. No news footage or archival footage is available (except for some Miami and southern Florida footage and material from the space program). Specialties include the Southeastern United States, the Caribbean, "sun 'n fun" and underwater footage ("Aquacolor").

Inventory covers: airports (John F. Kennedy, Ft. Lauderdale International, Miami International, small airports, aerials, planes landing and taking off, interior and exterior terminals, buses, plane interiors, cockpits and controls, runways and interior of control tower); amusement parks (water flumes, carousel, ferris wheel, buckets and cable cars); Caribbean Islands (Puerto Rico, Martinique, Curaçao, St. Thomas and the Bahamas); cities (New York, Chicago, Miami, Miami Beach, Ft. Lauderdale, Paris, Dallas, Pittsburgh, London, Caracas, Quito and Nassau); game fishing (tarpon leaps, marlin leaps, rods and reels spinning); cruise ships (ships in port, day and night, aerials at sea, passengers boarding and shipboard activity); high technology (computers, operators, screens, buttons and tape punched); industry (factories, construction); plants and flowers (hyacinth, hammocks, bird-of-paradise, orchids, tropical foliage and mangrove); ports and harbors (docks loading and unloading, equipment); space (shuttle, rocket, launch, moon landing and earth from space); sports (dog racing, trotters, jai alai, soccer, polo, baseball, football, equestrian riders and cricket); sun and fun (boating, fishing, water skiing, beaches, jet skiing, windsurfing, restaurants, tennis, discos, casinos and golf); sunsets (ocean, lakes, skylines, houses, beaches and waterways); underwater (coral reefs, divers, colorful fish and wrecks); water (surf, ocean, waves, white water rapids, waterfalls, streams and lakes); wildlife (white tigers, Bengal tigers, lions, flamingos, cranes, egrets, monkeys, pelicans, sea gulls, alligators, impalas, lizards, tapirs, bears, elephants, seals, penguins, frigate birds, orangutans, gorillas, throat monkeys and antelopes).
Size & Elements: Film: 35mm and 16mm (amount unspecified). Videotape: 1" and 3/4" (masters and time-coded transfers from film; very little broadcast original).
Cataloging: Shot lists; computerized cataloging for staff use only.
Access: Open to the public. Available for licensing and reuse. Research fees charged. Research requests accepted by mail, telephone and in person (by appointment only).
Rights: Full rights held to some material. Some rights held to some material. Additional clearances from originators of material may be necessary in some cases if material is to be reused.
Licensing: Available for licensing and reuse, subject to restrictions. License fees charged per production and per licensee's cut or edit. When a customer requires volume footage, a contract may be negotiated.
Restrictions: In a few cases, originators of material restrict use to non-competing companies or other conflicting interests.
Viewing Facilities: Film (35mm and 16mm flatbed, 16mm projector); videotape (3/4" and VHS).
Duplication Facilities: Videotape (3/4" off-line and VHS).

FLORIDA (Miami)

JEFF SIMON PRODUCTIONS
9000 Southwest 61 Court
Miami, FL 33156
(305) 666-5565

Contact: Jeff Simon
Services: Film producer; archives; stock footage sales library.
Description: Film footage of nature; underwater scenes; major Florida cities; aerial views; events, including Liberty Weekend (1986, 65mm); people; North America; South America; the Caribbean; Florida; water sports; sailing; and boating.
Size & Elements: Film: 65mm, 35mm and 16mm (over 250,000 feet; currently increasing amount of 65mm footage).
Cataloging: Computerized cataloging for staff use only; research library.
Access: For in-house use only. Available for duplication, licensing and reuse. Research requests accepted by mail, telephone and in person.
Rights: Full rights held to all material.
Licensing: Available for licensing. License fees charged.
Restrictions: None specified.
Viewing Facilities: Film (35mm and 16mm); videotape (Betacam, 3/4" and VHS).
Duplication Facilities: Videotape (Betacam, 3/4" and VHS).
Related Materials: Approx. 80,000 to 100,000 still photographs of related subject matter.

FLORIDA (Miami)

VIDEO VENTURES PRODUCTIONS
16505 Northwest 13th Avenue
Miami, FL 33169
(305) 621-5266
Fax: (305) 621-0803

Jim Duffy (President)

Contacts: David Ungarait (Operations Manager); Jim Duffy
Services: Videotape producer. Material available for duplication, licensing and reuse.
Description: Florida scenics (including action shots and shots with people) of Key West, Miami and Dade County, Ft. Lauderdale and Broward County, and Palm Beach. Also holds Arabian horse footage, including raising of horses, with farm and pasture scenes; and some footage of London, England, including generic sites and scenics.
Size & Elements: Videotape: Betacam (approx. 10 hours; masters). Viewing copies available in any videotape format.
Cataloging: Computerized cataloging for staff use only (in process).
Access: Available to the public for duplication, licensing and reuse. Research fees charged (based on edit time spent to compile requested material). Research requests accepted by telephone.
Rights: Full rights held to all material.
Licensing: Available for licensing and reuse. License fees charged.
Restrictions: None specified.
Viewing Facilities: Videotape (Betacam).
Duplication Facilities: Videotape (1", Betacam, 3/4", VHS and Betamax).

FLORIDA (Miami)

LOUIS WOLFSON II MEDIA HISTORY CENTER
MIAMI-DADE PUBLIC LIBRARY
101 West Flagler Street
Miami, FL 33130
(305) 375-4527
Fax: (305) 374-1573

Steven Davidson (Director)

Contact: Steven Davidson
Services: Film and television archives. Collection currently available only to researchers and scholars; will be accessible to the public in the future.
Description: Holds television newsfilm donated by the NBC affiliate station in Miami, WTVJ (1949-80). Collection includes coverage of Southern Florida and major news stories.
The Center is planning to function as a repository for other historically significant audiovisual documents within several broad categories: film, television, radio, advertising and public relations material that has featured some aspect of Florida history or has been produced in Florida and been experienced by Floridians.
Size & Elements: Film: 16mm (5 million feet, black and white and color, silent and sound). Videotape (format and amount unspecified).
Cataloging: Card catalogs; finding aids.
Access: Currently open to researchers and scholars; will be accessible to the public in the future. Research fees charged. Research requests accepted by mail, telephone and in person (by appointment only).
Rights: Full rights held to all material.
Licensing: Apply for information. License fees charged in some cases.
Restrictions: Restrictions apply to licensing and reuse (apply for information). Collection currently open to researchers and scholars only.
Viewing Facilities: Film (16mm).
Duplication Facilities: Available, depending upon specific request (apply for information).

FLORIDA (Miami Springs)

ORION POST PRODUCTION
17 Palmetto Drive
Miami Springs, FL 33166
(305) 888-2481
Fax: (305) 888-0510

Contact: Joe DelSordo
Services: Film and videotape stock footage sales library; production and post-production services available.

Description: Southeastern U.S. wildlife footage (ospreys, eagles, alligators and sea turtles); Florida wilderness, including aerial shots; and aerial views of cruise ships in the Gulf of Mexico, the Alaskan Pacific and the Caribbean Atlantic. All footage covers the period 1960s-present.
Size & Elements: Film: 70mm, 35mm and 16mm (50,000 feet, 40 titles, 100 cans; positive, negative, reversal and originals). Videotape: Betacam, 1", 3/4", VHS and Betamax (transfers from film, masters, viewing copies and time-coded viewing copies).
Cataloging: Dope sheets; computerized cataloging for staff use only.
Access: Available for duplication, licensing and reuse. Research fees charged. Research requests accepted by mail, telephone and in person (by appointment only).
Rights: Full rights held to all material.
Licensing: Available for licensing and reuse. License fees charged.
Restrictions: None specified.
Viewing Facilities: Film (35mm and 16mm); videotape (Betacam, 3/4" and VHS).
Duplication Facilities: Videotape (3/4", VHS and Betamax).

FLORIDA (Naples)

THE IMAGE BANK, FLORIDA
5811 Pelican Bay Boulevard, Suite 302
Naples, FL 33963
(813) 566-3444
Fax: (813) 566-1346

Contacts: John Domenie; Mayda Domenie
Territory: Florida, Puerto Rico, Bahamas and Bermuda.
Services: Exclusive marketing agent for Film Search, Inc. (q.v.).

FLORIDA (North Palm Beach)

THE ATHLETIC INSTITUTE
200 Castlewood Drive
North Palm Beach, FL 33408
(407) 842-3600

John Riddle (President/Chief Executive Officer)

Contact: Jean Rowan (Media Services Counselor) (Ext. 250)
Services: Nonprofit association; film and videotape producer and distributor. Material available for purchase and possibly reuse, subject to clearance and approval.
Description: Sports and physical education programs for children, athletes, coaches, teachers and parents.
Topics include: air gun marksmanship and competition; aerobics (teaching, theory, training, use of light weights, basic exercises and a balanced workout); archery fundamentals, intermediate shooting technique, mastery of bow and arrow sports; badminton basics and techniques; billiards fundamentals and advanced skills; bowhunting; bowling fundamentals; cheerleading, including jumps, conditioning, partner stunts and tumbling; cross-country ski skating; diving fundamentals, optional dives and required dives; drugs; floor hockey; golf fundamentals and techniques; a series of 15 children's programs covering all aspects of health and fitness; ice hockey fundamentals and techniques; ice skating for beginners; preschool lessons in sports participation; racquetball fundamentals and techniques; rowing; running speed improvement for all sports and preparation for the novice runner; softball; sports injuries; squash fundamentals; strength and conditioning for basketball, football, gymnastics and shot and discus; umpiring for baseball and softball; power volleyball (individual defensive and offensive skills); U.S.A. volleyball.
Baseball. Titles include: *Coaching Psychology and How to Handle Parents; Bragg Stockton Skills and Drills Baseball Series*; a softball skills series; *Dick Houser's Baseball Workout;* and *The Dodgers Way to Play Baseball,* power basics of the sport taught by professional athletes.
Basketball. Titles include: *Techniques of Ball Handling; Techniques of Shooting;* and *Power Basics of Basketball.*
Dance and gymnastics. Titles include: *Compulsory Gymnastic Routines; Rhythmic Gymnastics; Foundation of Gymnastics Excellence; Strength and Conditioning for Gymnastics; Preparing to Dance; Dance Design* series (motion, shape, time and space); and *Sources of Dance.*
Football. Titles include: *A Safer Game — A Better Game; The Elements of Danger; Power Basics of Football; Strength and Conditioning for Football.* Covers prevention of heat illness; proper fitting of helmets and avoidance of head injury; and emergency field care.

Handicapped. Titles include: *Tennis in a Wheelchair;* and *Horseback Riding for the Handicapped.*
Injuries. Titles include: *Sports On Trial,* about sports injury lawsuits; *Player Down!,* a series on how to recognize and treat injuries to the ankle, shoulder, knee, head and neck; and *A Report on Serious Football Injuries.*
Psychology. Titles include: *Coaching Psychology; Sports Psychology for Youth Coaches; Conditioning the Young Athlete; Introduction to Coaching Kids;* and *Teaching Sports Skills to Young Athletes.*
Soccer. Titles include: *Basic Individual Skills; Offensive and Defensive Maneuvering;* and *The Art of Goal Keeping.* Covers ball handling and kicking skills; assisting coaches in developing and conducting quality practice sessions; and the power basics of the sport taught by professional athletes.
Swimming. Titles include: *Freestyle and Backstroke Techniques; Breaststroke and Butterfly Techniques;* and *Starts, Turns and Progressive Drills.* Covers relay starts; drills and turns for long and short courses; and low-stress water workout.
Tennis. Titles include: *Applying Forehand and Backhand Strokes; Net Play; Tennis in a Wheelchair; The Serve;* and *Tennis the Van Der Meer Way,* instructional videotapes covering all aspects of the game.
Wrestling. Titles include: *Pinning Combinations; Organizing a Kids Wrestling Club; The Keys to Fitness, Nutrition and Safety;* and *Basic Skills and Better Techniques.*
Also available are *Eyerobics* exercises and techniques, designed to improve visual skills and a videotape companion to a stationary rowing machine which puts the viewer on the Charles River as a member of the U.S. rowing team with the splashing of the oars as he/she strokes in rhythm with Olympic rowers.
Size & Elements: Film: 16mm (amount unspecified). Videotape: 3/4", VHS and Betamax (approx. 175 titles).
Cataloging: Published catalogs.
Access: Available to researchers, scholars and the public for rental and purchase. Orders accepted by mail and telephone.
Rights: Full rights held to Institute-produced material. Additional clearances may be necessary in some cases if material is to be reused (applies to material distributed through Institute).
Licensing: Contact Jean Rowan for information regarding licensing and reuse. License fees charged in some cases.
Restrictions: No restrictions apply to Institute-produced material.
Viewing Facilities: None.
Duplication Facilities: None.

FLORIDA (Pensacola)

THE UNIVERSITY OF WEST FLORIDA
DEPARTMENT OF SOCIAL WORK
HUMAN RESOURCES VIDEOTAPE LIBRARY
11000 University Parkway
Pensacola, FL 32514-5751
(904) 474-2381

Bonnie C. Bedics (Program Director)

Contact: Carol Rafalski (Administrative Assistant)
Services: Educational institution; videotape library. Material available to researchers, scholars and the public for duplication, licensing and reuse.
Description: Subjects relevant to mental health and social services, notably child welfare, drug and alcohol abuse and aging. Collection was originally initiated by the University of Wisconsin School of Social Work, the primary producer of the materials, with a grant from the U.S. Department of Health, Education and Welfare. It was created to develop and promote a national library of videotapes on mental health and social service topics and to locate, conserve, catalog, duplicate and distribute such tapes for use by institutions, agencies, schools and individuals upon request. The HRVL is continually reviewing high-quality videotapes free of copyright restrictions for inclusion in the collection.
Selected titles include: *Adoptive Families Supporting One Another; AIDS Hospital Interview with AIDS Patient; Breaking the Cycle of Abuse (Don't Give Up On Me); Casework: How Not To Do It; The Cheerleader; Coming Out Is Like Peeling An Onion; Communication and Stress In Dealing With the Frail Elderly; Communicating with Children: Gender and Gender Role as Presented in Traditional and Modern Children's Literature and on TV; A Cultural Approach to Working with Alaskan Indians; Cultural Awareness Series: The Indian Way; Family Art Therapy; Fate Better Than Death: Treatment of Severe Brain Injuries; The Group No One Claims: Three Transvestites; Health Care in Vietnam — Judy Ladinsky; Incest: Who and Why; Loneliness — Treatment of the At-Risk Adolescent (Methadone Training Series); Nonverbal*

Communication; Nutrition For The Elderly; Ohoyo: Indian Women Speak; The Overly Suspicious Patient; Sexuality and Sexual Issues for the Severely and Profoundly Retarded; Should We Legislate Sexual Behavior?; Wheelchair Group; Wisconsin: A Proud Heritage — The Menomonee People; and *Working Together For Action.*
Size & Elements: Videotape: 3/4" and VHS (210 titles, each 20 to 60 min.; masters and viewing copies).
Cataloging: Published catalog.
Access: Available to the public for duplication and reuse. Previews and rentals not available by mail. Copies of videotape masters are available at production cost. Research fees not charged. Research requests accepted by mail and telephone.
Rights: Material in the public domain.
Licensing: Available for reuse. Usage fees not charged.
Restrictions: None specified.
Viewing Facilities: Videotape (local users may view videotapes on UWF campus at no charge).
Duplication Facilities: Videotape (3/4" and VHS) (duplication costs charged).

FLORIDA (Pompano Beach)

INTERNATIONAL ADVERTISING CENTER
3261 Northeast 14th Avenue
Pompano Beach, FL 33064
(305) 785-6133

See **INTERNATIONAL AIR CHECK** (New York Metro)

FLORIDA (Port Orange)

POSTCARDS UNLIMITED
640-B Dunlawton Avenue
Port Orange, FL 32019
(904) 788-6922

Rodney Tolleson (President)

Contacts: Claudia Bartelmay; Greg Bartelmay
Services: Videotape producer. Material available for licensing and reuse on a case-by-case basis.
Description: Coverage of Hawaii; San Francisco, Los Angeles, San Diego, Monterey and Carmel (Calif.); Reno, Las Vegas (Nev.); Lake Tahoe; Dallas (Tex.); Orlando and Daytona Beach (Fla.).
   Footage covers outdoor scenes, scenics, city scenes, tourist and historical attractions, amusement parks, action shots, outdoor activities, recreational activities and people. Both ground and aerial footage is held.
Size & Elements: Videotape: Betacam and 3/4" (approx. 150-200 hours; masters); VHS (viewing copies with visible time code).
Cataloging: Shot lists.
Access: Open to the public. Available for duplication and reuse. Research fees charged in some cases. Research requests accepted by telephone and in person (by appointment only).
Rights: Full rights held to all material.
Licensing: Available for licensing and reuse on a case-by-case basis. License fees charged.
Restrictions: Requests for licensing and reuse considered on a case-by-case basis.
Viewing Facilities: Videotape (3/4" and VHS).
Duplication Facilities: Videotape (Betacam and VHS).

FLORIDA (St. Augustine)

ST. AUGUSTINE HISTORICAL SOCIETY
271 Charlotte Street
St. Augustine, FL 32084
(904) 824-2872

Page L. Edwards (Director)

Contact: Jacqueline Fretwell (Librarian)
Services: Historical society. Film and videotape material not available for research, licensing or reuse.
Description: Collection relating to the history of St. Augustine and its festivals. Films include the Ponce De Leon Celebration (late 1920s); a film showing St. Augustine personalities (late 1920s); the Blessing of the Fleet and Easter Festival (ca. 1960); and the Minorcan Day celebration (1966). *The Story of St. Augustine: 400 Years of America's Heritage* (1961) traces the history of St. Augustine (1565-1959). There is a small videotape collection on local historical subjects, all produced in the 1980s.
Size & Elements: Film: 16mm (2,700 feet) and 8mm (550 feet) (14 titles total; 14 cans total; originals). Videotape: format unspecified (3 videotapes; viewing copies).
Cataloging: None.
Access: Not open to the public. Research requests not accepted.
Rights: Full rights held to some material.
Licensing: Not available for licensing or reuse.
Restrictions: Collection not available for research, licensing or reuse.
Viewing Facilities: None.
Duplication Facilities: None.

FLORIDA (St. Petersburg)

CENTURY VIDEO SERVICES, INC.
6241 Second Avenue North
St. Petersburg, FL 33710
(813) 347-9997

Marshall Rotz (President)

Contact: Marshall Rotz
Services: Videotape producer. Material available for duplication, licensing, and reuse.
Description: Florida scenics, including aerial footage of the Bay Area and the Gulf of Mexico, animals, beaches, boating activities, Florida houses of all types, tourist and restaurant information, marine life and windsurfing.
Size & Elements: Videotape: 3/4" (approx. 30 to 40 hours).
Cataloging: Shot lists.
Access: Available to the public for duplication and reuse. Research fees not charged. Research requests accepted by telephone.
Rights: Full rights held to all material.
Licensing: Available for licensing and reuse. License fees charged.
Restrictions: None specified.
Viewing Facilities: Videotape (3/4" and 1/2").
Duplication Facilities: Videotape (3/4" and 1/2").

FLORIDA (St. Petersburg)

MODERN TALKING PICTURE SERVICE, INC.
5000 Park Street North
St. Petersburg, FL 33709
(813) 541-7571
Fax: (813) 544-4624
(813) 541-5763 (Scheduling Center/Educational and Non-Theatrical Film & Video)
(800) 237-8913 (Scheduling Center/Television and Theatrical)

Regional Offices:

New York Metropolitan area:
P.O. Box 950
Chatham, NJ 07928
(201) 635-6000
Street address: 71 North Passaic Avenue

Philadelphia area:
3520 Progress Drive, Suite C
Cornwells Heights, PA 19020
(215) 639-6540

Washington, D.C. area:
5750 General Washington Drive
Alexandria, VA 22312
(703) 354-9772

Atlanta area:
4705-F Bakers Ferry Road
Atlanta, GA 30336
(404) 696-2025

Chicago area:
161 Tower Drive
Burr Ridge, IL 60521
(312) 325-4580

Dallas area:
2564 West Commerce
Dallas, TX 75212
(214) 638-2363

Los Angeles area:
6735 San Fernando Road
Glendale, CA 91201
(818) 240-0519

Montreal area:
9575 Côte de Liesse
Dorval, PQ H9P 1A3
(514) 631-9010

Toronto area:
115 Torbay Road, Unit 9
Markham, ON L3R 2M9
(416) 475-3750

Vancouver area:
L. M. Media Marketing Service, Ltd.
2168 Willingdon Avenue
Burnaby, BC V5C 5Z9
(604) 294-6231

Contact: Distribution Staff
Services: Distributor of sponsored motion pictures and videotapes. Titles available for free loan to community organizations, schools and colleges, and for theatrical showings; also available for broadcast and cablecast. *Material not available for licensing or reuse. Not a stock footage source.*
Description: Modern is and has been for many years the largest distributor of sponsored films and program materials. Hundreds of companies, including many of the *Fortune* 500, use Modern to reach audiences in community organizations, schools and colleges, and through television, cable and motion picture theaters. Modern Satellite Services, a recently formed division, traffics sponsored films and videotapes, video news releases, public service announcements and other programming by satellite news and information feeds. MSS also provides daily programming to such cable television services as The Learning Channel. The company's more than 130,000 films and videotapes are distributed from 10 regional distribution centers.

To meet the increasing demand for videotape copies of sponsored films, Modern has installed state-of-the-art film-to-videotape transfer and duplicating equipment in St. Petersburg. Videotapes are produced at Modern's expense with client approval, and distributed on the same basis as 16mm prints. Sponsors pay for each booking that results in a video or film showing. Schools and groups receive films on a free-loan basis.

Modern does not make stock footage available from its sponsored film and video offerings. This material is the property of the corporate and other underwriters who use Modern for outreach. Modern can, however, refer prospective users to film or videotape sponsors. Modern does not hold copies of films no longer in distribution or maintain archives.
Size & Elements: Film: 35mm and 16mm. Videotape: 3/4" and VHS. (Not all titles available in all formats.)
Cataloging: Published catalogs.
Access: Available to community organizations, schools and colleges for free loan. Some titles available for theatrical showings. Many titles available for broadcast and cablecast. Not all titles available in Canada. *Not a stock footage source.* Booking requests accepted by mail and telephone; contact the Scheduling Center in St. Petersburg or regional offices.
Rights: No rights held to any material. Rights retained by corporate and institutional sponsors or original producers. Additional clearances are necessary in all cases for reuse of material.
Licensing: Not available for licensing or reuse. Modern can refer producers, researchers and scholars to sponsors for permission to reuse. Catalogs indicate program sponsors in all cases.
Restrictions: Films and videotapes available for loan to appropriate groups. Some titles carry geographical or other restrictions. Footage is not available for licensing or reuse through Modern. All rights retained by sponsors or original producers.

Viewing Facilities: None.
Duplication Facilities: None.

Portions of the above listing have been excerpted from an article by Robert M. Finehout (Vice President, Modern Talking Picture Service, Inc.)

FLORIDA (Sarasota)

HACK SWAIN PRODUCTIONS, INC.
1185 Cattlemen Road
Sarasota, FL 34232
(813) 371-2360

Tony Swain (President)

Contact: Tony Swain
Services: Film producer. Film collection available for distribution, duplication, licensing and reuse.
Description: Films on Florida regional history (produced 1960-80) incorporating archival still photographs (with motion effects), early motion picture footage and historical reenactments. Various regions of Florida are documented, including Sarasota, Venice, Manatee County, Clearwater, Polk County and Winter Haven. Audiotape interviews with many pioneers and relatives of pioneers are also held.
Size & Elements: Film: 16mm ("thousands of feet"; reversal originals, workprints, release prints and outtakes).
Cataloging: None.
Access: Available for distribution, duplication, licensing and reuse. Research fees charged. Research requests accepted by mail and telephone.
Rights: Full rights held to all material.
Licensing: Available for licensing and reuse. License fees charged.
Restrictions: None specified.
Viewing Facilities: Film (16mm).
Duplication Facilities: None.

FLORIDA (Tallahassee)

FLORIDA STATE ARCHIVES
PHOTOGRAPHIC COLLECTION
R. A. Gray Building
500 South Bronough
Tallahassee, FL 32399
(904) 487-2073

Joan Morris (Supervisor)

Contact: Joan Morris
Services: State government agency. *Film archives currently unavailable for public use.*
Description: Holds Florida Development Commission films (1950s-70s) produced to encourage the state's growth. The films document tourist attractions, beaches, cities, sports, industry and celebrations. Other films held feature Florida governors and U.S. Congressmen (ca. 1947-70s).

Pending funding, archives may be organized and opened to the public.
Size & Elements: Film: format unspecified (approx. 1,500-2,000 cans).
Cataloging: Card catalogs (partial).
Access: Not open to the public.
Rights: Full rights held to all material.
Licensing: Not currently available for reuse.
Restrictions: Access and reuse restricted at present.
Viewing Facilities: None.
Duplication Facilities: None.

FLORIDA (Tampa)

ASSOCIATION FOR MULTI-IMAGE INTERNATIONAL, INC.
AMI ARCHIVES & CLEARINGHOUSE
8019 North Himes Avenue, Suite 401
Tampa, FL 33614
(813) 932-1692
Fax: (813) 932-5738

Peter K. Ryan (President)
Marilyn Kulp (Executive Director)

FLORIDA (Tampa)

Contact: Helen Gerhardt (Secretary)
Services: Association archives. Videotape material available to AMI members for research and loan, subject to approval.
Description: The Archives is a collection of materials important to the history of the Association and the history of multi-image research and development. The Clearinghouse holds material intended for distribution, much of it duplicated in the Archives.

The Clearinghouse contains videotapes of AMI International Festival Award Winners (1983-present); all produced for corporations, organizations and institutions. Genres include public relations/image, sales, meetings, documentary, motivation and student. Both in-house productions and shows produced by outside companies are included.
Size & Elements: Videotape: format unspecified (over 100 videotapes).
Cataloging: Published catalog.
Access: Available to AMI members for research and possibly loan, subject to approval. Research requests accepted by mail, telephone and in person (walk-in and by appointment).
Rights: Full rights held to some material. Rights to most material retained by original producers or sponsors.
Licensing: Available for reuse in some cases. Usage fees not charged.
Restrictions: Apply for information.
Viewing Facilities: None.
Duplication Facilities: None.

FLORIDA (Tampa)

ATLANTIC PRODUCTIONS
1508 Park Circle
Tampa, FL 33610
(813) 238-0402

Charles Lyman (Director)

Contact: Charles Lyman
Services: Film and videotape producer; stock footage available for licensing and reuse.
Description: Film and videotape (1979-present) covers Florida's fantastic architecture, including Spanish forts, Victorian hotels, Art Deco resorts and contemporary constructions. Specialties also include footage of European and North American prehistoric standing stones, such as stone circles, dolmens, menhirs, mounds and hill figures.
Size & Elements: Film: 16mm (approx. 30,000 feet). Videotape: 3/4" (amount unspecified).
Cataloging: None.
Access: Available to the public for reuse and resale. Research requests accepted by mail and telephone.
Rights: Full rights held to all material.
Licensing: Available for licensing and reuse. License fees charged.
Restrictions: None specified.
Viewing Facilities: Film (Steenbeck); videotape (at nearby university facility).
Duplication Facilities: None.

FLORIDA (Tampa)

SF•V INTERNATIONAL
(STOCK FILM • VIDEO INTERNATIONAL CORPORATION)
7722 West Hiawatha Street
Tampa, FL 33615
(813) 884-5963

Mark Hallinan (Principal)

Contact: Mark Hallinan
Services: Film and videotape producer; stock footage sales library. Represents outside producers for stock footage sales. Research services available.
Description: Subjects include: aerials, wildlife, animation, sports, romance, people, pets, time-lapse, astronomy, feature films, lightning, government, military, science, deserts, cruise ships, fireworks, disasters, circuses, parades, atomic bombs, underwater, robots, daredevils, ghosts and treasures.

Also represents more than 300 independent producers' services and stock footage collections from around the world. Works with other libraries, government organizations (such as the U.S. military and the Library of Congress), professional sports organizations and news-gathering facilities.
Size & Elements: Film: 16mm (amount unspecified). Videotape: 1", 3/4" and VHS (amount unspecified).

Cataloging: Brochure.
Access: Open to the public. Available for reuse or resale. Research fees not charged for preliminary inquiries. Viewing fees charged. Research requests accepted by mail and telephone.
Rights: Full rights held to all material.
Licensing: Available for licensing and reuse. License fees charged.
Restrictions: None specified.
Viewing Facilities: Videotape (VHS).
Duplication Facilities: Videotape (1", 3/4" and VHS).

FLORIDA (Tampa)

UNIVERSITY OF TAMPA
MERL KELCE LIBRARY
401 West Kennedy Boulevard
Tampa, FL 33606
(813) 253-3333
Fax: (813) 251-0016

Lydia Acosta (Director of Library)

Contacts: Lydia Acosta; John Giancola (Associate Professor of Communication)
Services: University library. Videotape collection open to researchers and scholars for in-house use only.
Description: Independent video productions acquired from distributors, including documentary, image-processed work and video art. Artists represented in collection include Skip Blumberg, Jean-Luc Godard, Shalom Gorewitz, Doug Hall, Wendy Clarke, Maxi Cohen, Jon Alpert and Keiko Tsuno, John Reilly and Julie Gustafson, Juan Downey, Joan Logue, Nam June Paik and Shigeko Kubota, George Stoney, TVTV, Bill Viola, William Wegman, Robert Wilson, Dan Reeves, Martha Rosler and Klaus vom Bruch.
Size & Elements: Videotape: 3/4" (28 titles).
Cataloging: Card catalogs; computerized cataloging available to researchers (OCLC Data Base).
Access: Open to researchers and scholars. For in-house use only. Research fees not charged. Research requests accepted by mail and telephone.
Rights: Rights retained by videomakers. Additional clearances may be necessary in some cases if material is to be reused.
Licensing: Material not available for licensing or reuse.
Restrictions: Material not available for duplication, broadcast or reuse without further clearance. All rights retained by videomakers.
Viewing Facilities: Videotape (pending).
Duplication Facilities: None.

FLORIDA (West Palm Beach)

HISTORICAL SOCIETY OF PALM BEACH COUNTY
Palm Beach County Public Library
3650 Summit Boulevard
West Palm Beach, FL 33406
(407) 471-1492

Nan Dennison (Director)

Contact: Nan Dennison
Services: Historical society. Film collection available for duplication, licensing and reuse.
Description: History of Palm Beach County. Sample titles include: *1926 Hurricane; Mar-a-Lago,* about the home of Marjorie Merriweather Post (now owned by Donald Trump); *From These Roots,* the early history of Palm Beach County; and *Belle Glade Beauty Pageant* (1950s-60s).
Size & Elements: Not specified.
Cataloging: Card catalogs.
Access: Available for duplication, licensing and reuse. Research fees charged. Research requests accepted by mail, telephone and in person.
Rights: Full rights held to all material.
Licensing: Available for licensing and reuse. License fees charged.
Restrictions: None specified.
Viewing Facilities: None.
Duplication Facilities: None.

FLORIDA (White Springs)

BUREAU OF FLORIDA FOLKLIFE PROGRAMS
FLORIDA DEPARTMENT OF STATE
DIVISION OF HISTORICAL RESOURCES
P.O. Box 265
White Springs, FL 32096
(904) 397-2192
Fax: (904) 397-2915

Street address: Highway 41 North

Dr. Ormond Loomis (Chief)

Contact: Debbie Fant (Folklife Specialist)
Services: Folklife program. Videotapes available for rental and purchase.
Description: Three programs documenting and exploring various aspects of Florida folklife.
Four Corners of Earth. Seminole Indian women, their roles and culture; especially traditional values and changes brought about by the 20th century.
Fishing All My Days: Florida Shrimping Traditions. The story of shrimp fishermen whose traditional arts, crafts and beliefs continue to influence the state's folklife and culture.
Learned It in Back Days and Kept It. Examines the traditional craft of white oak basketmaking in perspective with the folk artist's views on family, foodways and religion.
Size & Elements: Videotape: 3/4" and 1/2" (3 programs, each 30 min.).
Cataloging: Brochures.
Access: Available to the public for rental and purchase.
Rights: Full rights held to all material.
Licensing: Apply for information. License fees charged.
Restrictions: None specified.
Viewing Facilities: None.
Duplication Facilities: None.

GEORGIA

GEORGIA (Athens)

GEORGE FOSTER PEABODY COLLECTION
UNIVERSITY OF GEORGIA LIBRARY
Athens, GA 30602
(404) 542-3785
Fax: (404) 542-0518

Dr. Worth McDougald (Director of Peabody Awards Program)

Contact: Dr. Worth McDougald
Services: Film and videotape collection. Material available for in-house research use only.
Description: Holds most Peabody Award-winning television and radio programs (1940-present).
Size & Elements: Film: 16mm (color and black and white, some kinescopes). Videotape: 2", 1", 3/4", VHS and Betamax (approx. 17,000 to 18,000 programs). Collection increases by 800 to 1,000 programs annually. Material 1974-present has been transferred to 3/4" videotape masters and 1/2" viewing copies. Only materials which have been transferred can be viewed; no original films or videotapes can be viewed.
Cataloging: Partially cataloged. While there is a record of all award-winning programs dating back to 1940, many videotapes collected between 1940-69 are missing or incompletely cataloged, and the state of this portion of the collection has not yet been clarified.
Access: Open to the public. For in-house use only. Research fees not charged. Research requests accepted by mail and telephone. Access limited to certain materials (see above).
Rights: No rights held to any material. All rights retained by original producers or copyright owners.
Licensing: Material not available for licensing or reuse.
Restrictions: Duplication requires clearance from original owner.
Viewing Facilities: Videotape (1/2").
Duplication Facilities: Videotape.

GEORGIA (Athens)

UNIVERSITY OF GEORGIA
WSB TELEVISION NEWS FILM ARCHIVE
INSTRUCTIONAL RESOURCE CENTER
South PJ Auditorium
Athens, GA 30602
(404) 542-1582
Fax: (404) 542-0518

John R. Stephens, Jr. (Director, IRC)

Contact: John R. Stephens, Jr.
Services: Educational institution. Film and videotape archives open to researchers and scholars. Material available for duplication, licensing and reuse, subject to restrictions.
Description: Historical television newsfilm (1948-present) produced by WSB-TV (Atlanta, Georgia), the South's first television station; oldest and most comprehensive collection of its type in the South.

Highlights include: day-by-day coverage of the civil rights movement from a local point of view, including a lengthy interview with Martin Luther King, Jr. on the day following the assassination of John F. Kennedy; news stories on key Southern personalities, such as Jimmy Carter's rise, first as a gubernatorial and then presidential candidate; coverage of development and social changes in the region, including Atlanta's growth from the capital of a rural state to a thriving international city and the election of a black mayor in Atlanta.

Sample items: *Hosea Williams denies charges of driving while drunk, tells press to keep quiet* (1974); *KKK members defend their right to demonstrate* (1981); *State Senator Bond called the Community Relations Service "a tool of the Klan," he wants an investigation* (1980); and *Alan Shepard boards space capsule, is rescued at sea, is presented with medal by JFK* (1961).
Size & Elements: Film: 16mm (approx. 5 million feet, 94,000 stories; reversal originals, color and black and white). Videotape: 3/4" (masters) and VHS (viewing copies) (2,200 hours total).
Cataloging: Computerized cataloging for staff use only. Database search will allow search by a person's name, descriptor, date or location. Additional searches may be made upon special request.
Access: Open to researchers and scholars. Available for duplication, licensing and reuse. Research fees charged. A deposit is required prior to staff research and prior to delivery of preview material. All deposits will be held against final bill. Research requests accepted by mail, telephone and in person (by appointment only).
Rights: Full rights held to all material. Additional clearances may be necessary in some cases if material is to be reused.
Licensing: Available for licensing and reuse, subject to restrictions. License fees charged.
Restrictions: Film or videotape materials not available for political use. The definition of "political use" rests solely with the Director, IRC.
Viewing Facilities: Videotape (preview room).
Duplication Facilities: Videotape: 2", 1", 3/4", VHS and Betamax (film-to-tape and tape-to-tape transfer).

GEORGIA (Atlanta)

AMERICAN CANCER SOCIETY INC.
AUDIOVISUAL DEPARTMENT
1599 Clifton Road
Atlanta, GA 30329
(404) 320-3333
Fax: (404) 329-7943
Fax: (404) 329-7987

Contact: Joni Zeccola (Project Coordinator) (404/329-7914)
Services: Health organization. Films and videotapes available for broadcast, educational and instructional purposes.
Description: Films and television public service announcements (PSAs) relating to all forms of cancer, cancer education and research, and ACS services. Materials available in English and Spanish.

Subjects include: anti-smoking; bone cancer; breast cancer; breast self-examination; cancer updates; checkups; colorectal cancer; education and careers; Hodgkin's disease; mammography; nutrition; oral cancer; the Pap test; research; service; skin cancer; uterine cancer; warning signals; women and smoking.

Titles include: *Let's Call It Quits; Who's in Charge Here?,* emphasizing the immediate physiological effects of cigarette smoking; *The Art of Self Preservation,* on breast examination and mammography in the detection of breast cancer; *For a Wonderful Life,* stressing the importance of the Pap test; *Women in Middle Years,* about endometrial cancer in menopause years; *The Best in People,* discussing the ACS's role in cancer prevention, public education and rehabilitation programs, and community organizing; *Keeping*

Fit; The Cancer That No One Talks About, on colorectal cancer; *Cancer Today '86; The Right Foods; Circle of Caring,* about surviving cancer; *The Courage to Win,* on a man who ran 3,200 miles with an artificial leg; *A Model Recovery: The Story of Ivy Gunter,* about a woman who overcomes cancer and the loss of part of her leg to return to her modeling career; *A Ray of Hope,* about two young patients successfully treated for Hodgkin's disease; *Unreasonable People,* covering the physiological and psychological problems of patients with osteogenic sarcoma; *Word of Mouth,* about oral cancer; *Check it Out,* a message about smokeless tobacco produced in cooperation with the American Dental Association; *Winners in the Sun,* about avoiding overexposure to the sun; *A Report on Skin Cancer; The Intricate Cell,* examining basic biological concepts of normal and abnormal cell growth as related to lifestyle; *Journey Into Darkness,* a group of people involved with cancer "quacks" and a worthless remedy; *National Cancer Quiz,* focusing on three cancer sites (lung, breast and colorectal); *Taking Control,* a science-fiction film about cancer prevention; *Testicular Self Examination,* illustrating self-examination to guard against a highly curable disease; and *Video News Release: Nutrition & Cancer,* a series of three short segments for news media use.

Cancer Update series (26 programs). Films designed to cover research and progress made in fighting cancer. Programs include: *Progress Against Cancer; Road To Recovery; Answering Media Criticism; Colorectal Exemplar Program; Smoke-Free Young America; Discrimination;* and *Public Issues Program.*

Size & Elements: Film: 16mm. Videotape: 2", 1" 3/4" and VHS. (Approx. 140 titles total).
Cataloging: Published catalog.
Access: Open to the public. Films and videotapes available for broadcast, educational and instructional purposes. Research requests accepted by mail.
Rights: Full rights held to some material. Some rights held to all material.
Licensing: Available for licensing, subject to restrictions. License fees not charged.
Restrictions: Some material not cleared for broadcast. Certain films may be used only in their entirety.
Viewing Facilities: Film and videotape.
Duplication Facilities: None.

GEORGIA (Atlanta)

**ATLANTA HISTORICAL SOCIETY
LIBRARY/ARCHIVES**
3101 Andrews Drive, NW
Atlanta, GA 30305
(404) 261-1837

Bill Richards (Director of Library/Archives)

Contacts: Bill Richards; Elaine Kirkland (Visual Arts Archivist)
Services: Historical society; film and videotape collection. Viewing and duplication opportunities are limited and subject to restrictions.
Description: Atlanta and Civil War history, including film series relating to the Civil War; films on the American South, including the CBS television special *Who Speaks for the South?,* narrated by Edward R. Murrow (broadcast May 27, 1960); original footage shot at the *Gone With the Wind* premiere and ball (December 1939); *Robert W. Woodruff: A Great Georgian; Giantmaker* (broadcast April 18, 1977). Also holds videotapes documenting educational events and events sponsored by the Historical Society.
Size & Elements: Film: 16mm (approx. 50,000 feet; various formats); 8mm (approx. 500 feet) (approx. 85 titles total, approx. 77 cans total). Videotape: 3/4" (6 titles; masters and viewing copies); VHS (2 titles).
Cataloging: Inventory.
Access: Viewing and duplication opportunities limited. Limited staff research available. Research fees not charged. Research requests accepted by mail, telephone and in person (walk-in and by appointment).
Rights: Full rights held to some material. Additional clearances may be necessary in some cases if material is to be reused.
Licensing: Available for licensing and reuse, subject to restrictions. License fees charged.
Restrictions: Reuse controlled by Atlanta Historical Society and permitted on a case-by-case basis.
Viewing Facilities: Film and videotape (limited).
Duplication Facilities: Film and videotape (limited).
Related Materials: Historic photographs; audio archives.

GEORGIA (Atlanta)

CABLE NEWS NETWORK LIBRARY
P.O. Box 105366
Atlanta, GA 30348
(404) 827-1335

Street address: One CNN Center, 4th Floor, Atlanta, GA 30303

Stephanie Johnson (Coordinator, Library Tape Sales)

Contact: Stephanie Johnson
Services: Television broadcaster; videotape stock footage sales library.
Description: General library containing news coverage on thousands of subjects (June 1980-present). Coverage is international, national, regional and local. Library selectively archives videotape from CNN's daily news coverage. Varied types of material are held, including edited segments (frequently two to three minutes in length); cut VO's (voiceovers); unedited videotape material (many lengths) and live coverage of news events (e.g., the Bork confirmation hearings). Library also holds selected CNN programs such as *Larry King Live; Crossfire; Week in Review;* and *Inside Business.* While the library primarily serves CNN and Headline News, it also supports the videotape and information needs of all companies under the parent corporation, Turner Broadcasting System.

Broad subject categories include, but are not limited to: agriculture, art, business and industry, crime, disasters, education, entertainment, health and medicine, military, politics and government, religion, social issues and technology.
Size & Elements: Videotape: 1" (8,600 reels, 575,000 minutes); Betacam (16,000 videotapes); 3/4" (4,000 videotapes). (11,000 hours total). Collection is continuously growing; as of December 1988, the database contained approximately 216,000 records.
Cataloging: Computerized cataloging (on minicomputer) for staff use only; shot lists.
Access: Not open to the public. For in-house use only. Available for duplication, licensing and reuse. Research fees charged. Research requests accepted by mail and telephone.
Rights: Full rights held to most material. Third-party clearances may be necessary in some cases if material is to be reused.
Licensing: Available for licensing and reuse. License fees charged.
Restrictions: Additional clearances may be necessary in some cases if material is to be reused.
Viewing Facilities: None available to outside users.
Duplication Facilities: Videotape (1", Betacam, 3/4" and VHS).

GEORGIA (Atlanta)

JIMMY CARTER LIBRARY
One Copenhill Avenue, NE
Atlanta, GA 30307
(404) 331-3942

Don Schewe (Director)

Contact: David Stanhope (Audio-Visual Specialist)
Services: Presidential library. Film and videotape collection open to the public; some material available for duplication and reuse, subject to copyright and other restrictions.
Description: Presidential library administered by the National Archives and Records Administration.

Film and videotape collection documents the tenure of President Jimmy Carter (1977-81). The film collection was produced by the Naval Photographic Center (NPC), whose crews covered most presidential events, including visits by foreign heads of state, addresses to Congress, speeches, legislative signing ceremonies, press conferences and presidential trips. The videotape collection, recorded by the White House Communications Agency (WHCA), documents presidential speeches, press conferences, press briefings, and televised programs (featuring President Carter, the First Family, and his White House staff). The videotape collection also includes network news reports.
Size & Elements: Film: 16mm (2 million feet; color, positive, some with magnetic soundtracks); videotape reference copies available for a small number of the films. Videotape: 3/4" (1,600 tapes, each 60 min.).
Cataloging: Computerized cataloging available to researchers; shot lists; inventory available at library.
Access: Open to the public. Most material available for duplication.
Rights: Full rights held to some material. Some rights held to some material.

NPC film is in the public domain. Additional clearances may be necessary in some cases if material is to be reused.
Licensing: Available for licensing and reuse, subject to restrictions. License fees not charged.
Restrictions: Much of the videotape collection is under copyright restriction.
Viewing Facilities: Videotape (viewing room).
Duplication Facilities: Videotape (3/4" and 1/2").

GEORGIA (Atlanta)

CENTERS FOR DISEASE CONTROL
Mail Stop A 09
1600 Clifton Road, NE
Atlanta, GA 30333
(404) 639-1746
Fax: (404) 639-3296

Street address: Building 2, Room B33

Paul Horton (Chief, Television and Industrial Development)

Contacts: Paul Horton; Charles P. Fallis (Public Information) (Ext. 3286)
Services: Government agency. Produces videotapes for in-house use and for distribution to specific audiences. A limited amount of stock footage is available, subject to clearance and approval.
Description: The Lab Training division has produced instructional videotapes on specific diseases and their treatments; these videotapes are generally available only to those in the health care field. One videotape has been made on sexually transmitted diseases, to be used in conjunction with health care training courses. One videotape of general laboratory background scenes has been produced for purchase as stock footage.

Holds other materials, including a production on the Asian Tiger Mosquito, one on the Western Blot AIDS test and one on the Nigerian Guinea Worm. These have been produced either by outside producers or co-sponsored by such organizations as the United Nations, the President Carter Center, and the AIDS Task Force.

Other materials are intended primarily for in-house use only, including training materials, employee award ceremonies and lectures given in conjunction with internal meetings.
Size & Elements: Videotape: format unspecified (approx. 30 to 40 titles).
Cataloging: None specified.
Access: Open to researchers and scholars. Some material available for rental and loan to specific audiences in the health care field. Other material for in-house use only. Some material available for licensing and reuse.
Rights: Full rights held to some material. Additional clearances may be necessary in some cases if material is to be reused.
Licensing: Apply for information. License and usage fees charged.
Restrictions: None specified.
Viewing Facilities: None.
Duplication Facilities: None.

GEORGIA (Atlanta)

THE COCA-COLA COMPANY
ARCHIVES DEPARTMENT
P.O. Drawer 1734
Atlanta, GA 30301
(404) 676-3491
Fax: (404) 676-5856

Contact: Philip F. Moomey (Manager, Archives Department)
Services: Corporation; corporate archives. Film and videotape material available for research and reuse on a case-by-case basis, subject to restrictions.
Description: Coca-Cola soft drink commercials and promotional films, including those produced by other companies (1950s-present). Archives holds both American and foreign television advertisements.
Size & Elements: Film: 16mm (amount unspecified). Videotape: format and amount unspecified.
Cataloging: Computerized cataloging for staff use only.
Access: Available to the public. Research requests are accepted by mail, telephone and in person (by appointment only). Research fees not charged.
Rights: Some rights held to some material. Additional clearances may be necessary in some cases if material is to be reused.
Licensing: Available for licensing and reuse, subject to restrictions.
Restrictions: Primarily maintained for internal purposes, but requests for

research and reuse will be considered on a case-by-case basis.
Viewing Facilities: None.
Duplication Facilities: None.

GEORGIA (Atlanta)

CREATIVE VIDEO, INC.
THE VIDEO LIBRARY
1465 Northside Drive, Suite 110
Atlanta, GA 30318
(404) 355-5800
Fax: (404) 350-9823

Jim Rocco (General Partner)

Contacts: Jim Rocco; Edie Hook
Services: Videotape producer; stock footage sales library.
Description: Travel footage (1979-present), including attractions, destinations and activities. Locations include: United States cities; scenics of Atlanta, Boston, Charleston, Cincinnati, Dallas, Fort Worth, Hilton Head Island, Hollywood, Los Angeles, Miami, Myrtle Beach, New England, New York, Orlando, Palm Springs, Phoenix, San Francisco, Savannah, South Florida, Tampa, Washington (D.C.), Williamsburg; farmland, desert, mountains, shorelines and skylines. Also holds footage of the Caribbean region, including Aruba, Bahamas, Bermuda, Jamaica and St. Lucia; Europe, including London, Paris and Germany; South Pacific, including Hawaii, Hong Kong and Singapore; Canada; Israel.

Subjects include aerials, all water sports, beaches, Broadway shows, casinos, cruise lines, entertainment, farming, general travel, golf, health spas, horses, hotels and resorts, industry, international resorts, medicine, monuments, restaurants, professional sports, sailing, scuba diving, shopping, space footage, sunrises, sunsets, tennis, tourist spots, underwater footage, Wall Street and windsurfing.
Size & Elements: Videotape: 1" (100 videotapes, over 50 hours; masters); Betacam (300 videotapes, 100 hours, each 20 min.; masters); 3/4" (700 videotapes, over 200 hours, each 20 min.; masters and viewing copies); VHS and Betamax (viewing copies).
Cataloging: Shot lists; computerized cataloging available to researchers.
Access: Available to the public for licensing and reuse. Research fees charged. Research requests accepted in person (by appointment only).
Rights: Full rights held to all material.
Licensing: Available for licensing and reuse, subject to restrictions. License fees charged.
Restrictions: License fee clears one-time use only.
Viewing Facilities: Videotape (3/4" and VHS).
Duplication Facilities: Videotape (1", 3/4" and Betamax).

GEORGIA (Atlanta)

EMORY MEDICAL TELEVISION NETWORK
69 Butler Street, SE, Room 7
Atlanta, GA 30303
(404) 589-3556
Telex: (810) 751-8512

Dan C. Joiner (Executive Director)

Contact: Julie M. Budnik (Marketing Manager/Producer)
Services: Educational institution. Videotapes available for rental and purchase.
Description: Function of Emory University School of Medicine, an organization accredited for continuing medical education. Programs may be used for various types of credit. Videotapes (1980-present) are intended for the use of health care professionals only.

Subjects include: aging, AIDS, anatomy, arthritis, biochemistry, the cardiovascular system, deficiency diseases, dermatology, diabetes mellitus, diagnosis, the endocrine system, epidemiology, the gastrointestinal system, genetics, genital diseases, health education, health manpower, the hemic and lymphatic systems, herpes, history of medicine, hospitals, hypertension, immunology, infectious diseases, medical ethics, medical profession, metabolic diseases, microbiology, musculoskeletal system, myocardial infarction, neoplasms, the nervous system, neurosurgery, nursing, opthalmology, orthopedics, pathology, patient education, pediatrics, pharmacology, pregnancy, preventive medicine, psychiatry, public health, radiology, the reproductive system, respiratory system, sex behavior, sports medicine, substance dependence, surgery, toxicology, the urogenital system and venereal diseases.

Size & Elements: Videotape: 3/4" and VHS (hundreds of videotapes; viewing copies).
Cataloging: Published catalog.
Access: Available for rental and purchase. Institutional, hospital and medical school memberships are available, entitling members to unlimited loan privileges and duplication of videotapes for use in their own institutions. Requests accepted by mail.
Rights: Full rights held to all material.
Licensing: Apply for information.
Restrictions: None specified.
Viewing Facilities: None.
Duplication Facilities: Videotape (3/4" and VHS).

EMORY UNIVERSITY
SPECIAL COLLECTIONS
ROBERT W. WOODRUFF LIBRARY
Atlanta, GA 30322
(404) 727-6887

Dr. Linda M. Matthews (Head, Special Collections)

Contact: Beverly D. Bishop (Reference Archivist)
Services: University archives. Film collection available for research and reuse, subject to clearance and approval.
Description: *Charles F. Palmer Films* (1930s-50s; 21 titles, 16mm, color and black and white, sound and silent). Relating to housing projects, from slum clearance to urban renewal, and the rebuilding of Britain after World War II.
   Robert Tyre Jones Collection. Professional golf films, including films of the Masters Tournaments (1965-69), with archival and newsreel footage of "Bobby" Jones playing (1930s).
   Robert W. Woodruff Collection. Includes *Robert W. Woodruff — A Great Georgian.*
   Miscellaneous. Includes: *Nikko,* an 8mm color film on Japan, by Ralph McGill (1962); two films of Jacob M. Rothschild, one of Israel (1950) and an interview (1958); two videotapes of interviews with Lt. Gen. William Quinn, a witness to the Holocaust (Dachau); videotapes of the WETV series *Southern Voice* and *Erskine Caldwell;* and the University Archives containing oral histories and footage of commencements, inaugurations and President Jimmy Carter.
Size & Elements: Film: 16mm and 8mm (approx. 50 reels). Videotape: format not specified (50 videotapes). Many 16mm films have been transferred to videotape for viewing purposes.
Cataloging: Card catalogs; registers.
Access: Open to the public. Available for duplication. Research fees not charged. Research requests accepted by mail, telephone and in person.
Rights: No rights held to any material. Rights status of some material not known.
Licensing: Available for licensing, subject to restrictions. License fees charged for commercial use (fees determined on a case-by-case basis).
Restrictions: Some restrictions may apply due to rights status.
Viewing Facilities: Film (projectors); videotape (videotape recorders) available at Candler Library, an adjacent facility.
Duplication Facilities: Film and videotape (available at AV Production Unit at Candler Library).

GOETHE INSTITUTE ATLANTA
German Cultural Center
400 Colony Square
Atlanta, GA 30361
(404) 892-2226

Henner Oeppert (Director)

Contact: Luise Von Löw (Librarian)
Services: Educational institution; library. Videotapes maintained primarily for research purposes and free loan.
Description: German cultural news, arts and language, including documentaries in German and English. Materials include *Deutschlandspiegel,* featuring news and reports from Germany (1983-present); *Prisma,* including portraits of artists, museums, theaters and exhibitions; biographies and portraits of cultural figures, including Böll, Beuys, Walser and Domin; geography

(Berlin, West Germany); and language programs.
   Additional films and videotapes sponsored by the Goethe Institute and Consulate General of the Federal Republic of Germany in Atlanta are available through the Atlanta office of Modern Talking Picture Service (q.v.). Topics covered include: German cities and landscapes, politics and history, America and Germany, industry and economy, urban planning and transportation, science and research, education, sports, professional life, festivals and customs, architecture, visual arts, literature, music, dance, theater, film, animated and children's films.
   Sample film titles include: *Albert Einstein; Albrecht Dürer; Bauhaus; Christmas in the Rhoen; Dachau — Must Dachau Mourn Forever?; The Educational System in the Federal Republic of Germany; From Weimar to Bonn; German Folk Dances; Hesse's Life and Works; Historical Pageants in Eastern Bavaria; The Iron Curtain; Mies van der Rohe; Prussia: A Retrospective; Traitors to Hitler; Wagner und Bayreuth;* and *Why the German Republic Built the Wall.*
   Sample videotape titles include: *Berlin Means Business; The Cologne Cathedral; Graffiti on the Berlin Wall; Martin Luther; Poor Hölderlin;* and *Resistance to Hitler.*
Size & Elements: Film: 16mm (amount unspecified). Videotape: 3/4" and VHS (approx. 90 videotapes).
Cataloging: Card catalogs.
Access: Open to the public for free loan. Research fees not charged. Research requests accepted in person (walk-in).
Rights: Full rights held to some material. Additional clearances may be necessary in some cases if material is to be reused.
Licensing: Apply for information.
Restrictions: None specified.
Viewing Facilities: None.
Duplication Facilities: None.
Distributor: Modern Talking Picture Service, Inc. (q.v.).

HIGH MUSEUM OF ART
1280 Peachtree Street
Atlanta, GA 30309
(404) 892-3600

Gudmund Vigtel (Director)

Contact: Paula M. Hancock (Curator for Research)
Services: Museum; videotape producer. Selected videotapes available for rental, loan and purchase.
Description: Videotapes on topics in art history, produced to correspond with museum exhibitions.
   Titles for rental or purchase include: *Carlton Garrett,* on a Georgia folk artist; *Of Sky and Earth,* on the art and culture of prehistoric Southeastern American Indians of the Mississippian era; and *The High Museum Story.*
   Titles available for loan include: *The Golden Age of Dutch Painting; The Advent of Modernism; Arts in America: The Colonies to the Early Republic; Arts in America: The Democracy; Arts in America: The Gilded Age; Dawn's Forest,* on Louise Nevelson; *Ed Moulthrop: Turned Wood Vessels;* and *Komar and Melamid,* on a team of Soviet-born artists and their collaborative paintings.
Size & Elements: Videotape: 3/4" and VHS (11 titles, each 5 to 18 min.).
Cataloging: Brochure.
Access: Available to the public for rental and purchase; some titles available for loan only. Handling fees charged.
Rights: Some rights held to all material.
Licensing: Not available for licensing or reuse.
Restrictions: Videotapes may not be duplicated or reused.
Viewing Facilities: None.
Duplication Facilities: None.

THE IMAGE BANK SOUTH, ATLANTA
3490 Piedmont Road, NE, Suite 1106
Atlanta, GA 30305
(404) 233-9920
Fax: (404) 231-9389

Contacts: Lynn Brantley; Marianne Hardeman

Territory: Alabama, Georgia, Kentucky, Mississippi, North Carolina, South Carolina and Tennessee.
Services: Exclusive marketing agent for Film Search, Inc. (q.v.).

GEORGIA (Atlanta)

IMAGE FILM AND VIDEO COLLECTION
IMAGE FILM/VIDEO CENTER
75 Bennett Street, Suite M-1
Atlanta, GA 30309
(404) 352-4225

Ruby Lerner (Executive Director)

Contacts: Ruby Lerner; Shellie Fleming (Program Director).
Services: Nonprofit media arts center. Film and videotape collection available for in-house viewing for members only.
Description: Holds films and videotapes by local, regional and national media artists. Now in a new space, IMAGE has been able to organize its holdings and to begin actively soliciting additional works.

Film holdings include Southern experimental, narrative and documentary works purchased as past festival awards by the Chatham Valley Foundation or acquired by donation from their makers. Included are early works by Victor Nuñez and Ross McElwee; documentaries on Southern culture, people and places; and films made by Southern artists.

The videotape collection is more extensive, and includes past winners of the Atlanta Film & Video Festivals; all works produced through IMAGE's ON-LINE program; and a wide selection of purchased works and videotapes donated by the artists. Also held are a growing number of videotapes documenting video installations, and videotapes made for the 1985 TELE-VISIONS video installations exhibition in Atlanta. The 1987 Ackerman Video Installation Competition finalists all donated sample videotapes, giving the viewer a rare glimpse of the amazing variety of installations made by video artists from across the country. Also included in the collection are a selection of Southern music videos and IMAGE public service announcements.

Sample film titles include: *Subway People* (Eloise Philpot-Black); *A Night in Tunisia* (Bryan Elson); *Watersmith* (Will Hindle); *Raylum* (Center for Southern Folklore); *Charleen* (Ross McElwee); *Man In A Tree* (Business Committee for the Arts); *Wa Mini* (Steve Walker); *La Cadie* (Robert Russett); *Bird* (Victor Beitzel); *Candler Park* (Gary Moss/Georgia State University); *Mexican Jail Footage* (Gordon Ball); *Momentum* (Ray Day); *Primer Rebus* (Dan Curry/Mimi White); *Pandora's Box* (Steve Segal); *Aqui Se Lo Halla* (Lee Sokol); *Taking Care of Mother Baldwin*, *The Fasola Folk* and *Circle in the Fire* (Victor Nuñez); *Alabama Departure* and *Give My Poor Heart Ease* (Peter Bundy).

Videotape collection includes: eight finalist videotapes from the 1987 Ackerman installation competition (Dara Birnbaum, Gary Hill, Norie Sato, Buky Schwartz, Mary Lucier, Judith Barry, Rita Myers and Wendy Clarke); *Best of the Fest,* a four-part series featuring winners from past Atlanta Film & Video Festivals; *5th* and *6th Atlanta Film & Video Travelling Show* (1981 and 1982); various public service announcements and promotional videotapes for IMAGE and the Festival; *Songs in Minto Life* (Curt Madison); *Television Believers* (Aron Ranen); *Bring Me Your Love* (Starr Sutherland); *Buzz Box* (David Daniels); *How High the Moon* (Paul Nichols); *Power Spot* (Michael Scroggins); *Little Men* (Jamie Charles); *Ascension* (Dominica Kriz); and *Other Prisoners* (Stephen Roszell).

Also includes: *Declarations of Independents* (Robin Reidy and Bill Thompson); *Watusi Rodeo* and *Rockumentary featuring "Cattle Prod"* (Guadalcanal Diary); *Chastity* (The Raves and Daniel Maughan); *Eh Wot's This,* a sampler from a local cable show (Daniel Maughan); *Bouton's Comeback* (Marivee Cade and James Jones); *Dream # 2* (William Oates); and *Was a Copyrighted Feature* (Jack Frost).

1981 Ithaca Video Festival and *1982 Ithaca Video Festival* (Ithaca, NY); *Disarmament Video Survey 1982; Hamper McBee — Raw Mash, Showdown at the Hoedown* and *Symphony #5* (Blaine Dunlap and Sol Korine); *Scarborough Fair* (The Coolies); *Haute Culture* (installation videotapes by Antonio Muntadas); *Figure and Ground* (installation videotapes by Bill Viola); *Calculated Movements* (Larry Cuba); *Conversations with Phreddy* (Paula Granger); *Dominique* (Arms Akimbo); *TV Spinoff* (Mark Rappaport); and *Low Blood Sugar Series* (Ed Clark). Other video artists represented in collection include: Robert Ashley, Skip Blumberg, Dan Boord, Gary Hill, Louis Hock, Chip Lord, Meredith Monk, Mary Perillo, Daniel Reeves, John Sanborn, Edin Velez, Video In/Western Front and Bill Viola.
Size & Elements: Film: 16mm (over 20 titles; release prints). Videotape: 3/4" and VHS (over 80 titles; viewing copies).

Cataloging: Computerized cataloging available to researchers.
Access: Open to IMAGE members. For in-house use only. Research fees not charged. Research requests accepted by telephone and in person (by appointment only).
Rights: No rights held to any material. All rights retained by artists.
Licensing: Not available for licensing or reuse.
Restrictions: Available to IMAGE members for in-house viewing only. Material not available for rental, purchase or reuse.
Viewing Facilities: Film (16mm); videotape (3/4" and VHS with 25" monitor).
Duplication Facilities: Videotape (3/4" to 1/2").
Related Materials: Catalogs of above-mentioned exhibitions and festivals.

GEORGIA (Atlanta)

MARTIN LUTHER KING, JR. CENTER FOR NONVIOLENT SOCIAL CHANGE, INC.
449 Auburn Avenue, NE
Atlanta, GA 30312
(404) 524-1956

Contacts: Stoney Johnson (Director, Media Services); Althea Sumpter (Assistant Director, Media Services)
Services: Private collection. Currently being organized to permit access to researchers and producers.
Description: The King Center's Media Services department holds nearly complete documentation of events sponsored by or occurring at the Center (mid-1970s to the present). While pre-1986 material is presently being cataloged, events from 1986 and 1987 include complete coverage of King Week — the holiday celebration commemorating the birth of Dr. Martin Luther King, Jr. — including speeches, activities and appearances by dignitaries. There are interviews with Coretta Scott King, Christine King Farris, Edward Kennedy, Congressman John Lewis, Bishop Desmond Tutu, Rev. Jesse Jackson, Bernice King, Bill Cosby, Ryochi Sasakawa, Dick Gregory, Ralph David Abernathy, Sr., and many others. (3/4" videotape, approx. 160 hours).

Also holds documentation of the January 24, 1987 civil rights march in Forsyth County, Georgia (3/4" videotape, 22 hours). This material also includes interviews.

The collection also holds uncataloged film footage.
Size & Elements: Film: format and amount unspecified. Videotape: 3/4" (masters); VHS and Betamax (viewing copies); 1/2" open reel (hundreds of hours).
Cataloging: Inventory sheets. Organizing and cataloging of the collection is in process; a complete list of the Center's materials will ultimately be available.
Access: Open to researchers and scholars. Materials available for licensing and reuse. Research fees charged. Research requests accepted by telephone.
Rights: Full rights held to some material.
Licensing: Available for licensing and reuse, subject to restrictions. License fees charged.
Restrictions: Material not available for use in commercials.
Viewing Facilities: Videotape (3/4" and VHS).
Duplication Facilities: Videotape (3/4" and VHS).

GEORGIA (Atlanta)

PRIDE (NATIONAL PARENTS' RESOURCE INSTITUTE FOR DRUG EDUCATION, INC.)
The Hurt Building
50 Hurt Plaza, Suite 210
Atlanta, GA 30303
(404) 651-2548
Fax: (404) 688-6937
Telex: 543348 UD

Thomas J. Gleaton, Ed.D. (President)

Contact: Charles Ditto (Resource Specialist)
Services: Information, education and referral organization. Film and videotape collection available for distribution.
Description: Films addressing drug and alcohol problems among young people.

Titles include: *America Hurts,* showing individuals, families, communities, and nations destroyed by drug problems; *Breaking Free,* showing young people freeing themselves from harmful drugs; *Epidemic I: Kids and Alcohol; Epidemic II: America Fights Back — Community Action Plan; Epidemic II:*

GEORGIA (Atlanta)

America Fights Back — Business and Industry Plan; Epidemic III: Deadliest Weapon in America, a look at driving while intoxicated; *How Do You Tell?; Say No! to Drugs; Wasted: A True Story;* and *Why Say No to Drugs.*
Size & Elements: Film: 16mm (9 titles). Videotape (10 titles).
Cataloging: Published catalogs.
Access: Available for distribution.
Rights: Apply for information.
Licensing: Apply for information.
Restrictions: None specified.
Viewing Facilities: None.
Duplication Facilities: None.

GEORGIA (Atlanta)

SOUTHERN CHRISTIAN LEADERSHIP CONFERENCE
334 Auburn Avenue, NE
Atlanta, GA 30312
(404) 522-1420

Dr. Joseph E. Lowery (President)

Contact: Rev. E. Randall Osburn
Services: Civil rights organization; videotape producer. Collection available to the public for in-house viewing only. Some material possibly available for reuse, subject to consideration on a case-by-case basis.
Description: Videotapes on civil rights issues, the Black community, AIDS and poverty.
Holds one completed production on the Forsyth County March and Movement; documentation of conferences about the implications of AIDS in the Black community, and the April 4, 1988 pilgrimage from Memphis to Atlanta commemorating the anniversary of Dr. King's assassination (the latter to be edited into a finished videotape for distribution). Also holds footage of an ongoing project to document hearings on poverty in major U.S. cities, a reinstatement of Martin Luther King's campaign against poverty ("The Poor People's Crusade") begun in 1968.
SCLC productions may contain footage from television network news and other sources.
Size & Elements: Videotape (format and amount unspecified).
Cataloging: None specified.
Access: Available to the public. Some material currently available for in-house viewing only. Research requests accepted by mail and telephone.
Rights: Full rights held to some material. Additional clearances may be necessary in some cases if material is to be reused.
Licensing: Available for licensing and reuse, subject to restrictions. License and usage fees charged in some cases.
Restrictions: Some material available for in-house viewing only. Requests for reuse considered on a case-by-case basis.
Viewing Facilities: Videotape (VHS).
Duplication Facilities: Outside arrangements can be made.

GEORGIA (Marietta)

ENERGY PRODUCTIONS
2433 Cedar Wood Court
Marietta, GA 30068
(404) 977-4324

See **CALIFORNIA** (Los Angeles Metro)

GEORGIA (Norcross)

OMEGA FILMS
3100 Medlock Bridge Road, Suite 100
Norcross, GA 30071
(404) 449-8870

Cefus McRae (President)

Contacts: Cefus McRae; John Derck (Operations Manager)
Services: Film and videotape producer; stock footage sales library. Collection available to the public for duplication and reuse, subject to acceptance and approval.
Description: Footage of the Southeastern U.S., featuring urban and suburban Atlanta, including aerial views and morning, noon and night shots; mountain views, including aerial, ground and level shots, fishing, waterfalls, water sports

and snow skiing; sailboats; Louisville, Kentucky; Nashville, Tennessee; and horse farms, with static and travelling shots.
Also holds three hours of high quality 16mm black and white film (early 1900s) possibly shot by George Eastman, featuring New York City, New York Harbor and the Adirondacks (family vacation footage, harbor scenes, views from on deck, carriages, swimming and barbecues).
Size & Elements: Film: 16mm (over 50 hours; all transferred to 1").
Videotape: 1", Betacam and 3/4" (over 50 hours; transfers from film; masters).
Cataloging: Staff assistance required.
Access: Available to the public for duplication and reuse. Research fees not charged. Research requests accepted by telephone and in person (by appointment).
Rights: Full rights held to all material.
Licensing: Available for licensing, subject to restrictions. License fees charged.
Restrictions: All licensing requests subject to acceptance and approval.
Viewing Facilities: Videotape (1", Betacam, 3/4" and VHS).
Duplication Facilities: Videotape (1", Betacam, 3/4" and VHS).

GEORGIA (Savannah)

JULIETTE GORDON LOW GIRL SCOUT NATIONAL CENTER
142 Bull Street
Savannah, GA 31401
(912) 233-4501

Fran Powell (Director)

Contact: Katherine Keena (Program Director)
Services: Museum; Girl Scout National Program Center. Film collection available for research and reuse, subject to clearance and approval.
Description: Three films held, including *The Golden Eaglet* (1918, 20 min.), a recruitment film for Girl Scout leaders, with live footage of Girl Scouts. The Center will soon acquire a videotape copy of a 1937 film showing girls from an international Girl Scout camp.
Size & Elements: Film: format unspecified (3 titles).
Cataloging: None specified.
Access: Open to the public. Research fees not charged. Research requests accepted by mail, telephone and in person (if time is available).
Rights: Full rights held to all material.
Licensing: Apply for information.
Restrictions: None specified.
Viewing Facilities: Film.
Duplication Facilities: None.

HAWAII

HAWAII (Honolulu)

BISHOP MUSEUM
VISUAL COLLECTION
P.O. Box 19000-A
Honolulu, HI 96817-0916
(808) 848-4182
(808) 848-4183

Street address: 1525 Bernice Street

Lynn Davis (Chairperson of Visual Collection)

Contact: DeSoto Brown (Collection Manager, Moving Images)
Services: Museum. A small percentage of the moving image collection is presently available for research, duplication and reuse, subject to restrictions. Cataloging is currently in process; plans are to open entire collection both to the public and commercial users when cataloging is completed.
Description: Material from the Pacific region with particular emphasis on Hawaii, Hawaiian culture and industry (1898-present; most items from 1920-present). Special strengths include history, natural history, ethnology, anthropology and Hawaiian dance (hula). Coverage of Hawaii includes geography, scenics, volcanoes, surfing and the sugar, pineapple and tourism industries.
Size & Elements: Film: 35mm (14,200 feet); 16mm (268,800 feet); 8mm (7,000 feet) (760 titles, 803 cans total). Videotape: VHS (6 videotapes); Betamax (7 videotapes) (all viewing copies of television broadcasts).

Cataloging: Card catalog; cataloging of entire collection in progress.
Access: Some material available for research, duplication and reuse. Limited research requests accepted at this time. Research fees charged.
Rights: Full rights held to some material. Some rights held to other material. Rights status unknown for other items in the collection.
Licensing: Available for licensing and reuse, subject to restrictions. License fees charged (negotiated on an individual basis).
Restrictions: Restrictions apply to some items in collection. Limited research requests accepted at this time.
Viewing Facilities: Videotape (VHS and Betamax).
Duplication Facilities: None.

BREKKE TELEVISION PRODUCTIONS (BTV)
1140-A Kona
Honolulu, HI 96814
(808) 522-2200

Jon Brekke (President)

Contacts: Tom Wilson (Associate Producer); Susan Bilek (Production Coordinator)
Services: Stock footage sales library; film and videotape producer.
Description: Extensive library (1983-present) of Hawaiian scenery, volcanoes, palm trees, beaches, aerials, underwater scenes, whales, windsurfing, surfing, sailing, golfing, tennis, snorkeling, tourists, hotel and restaurant commercials.
Size & Elements: Videotape: 1" and Betacam (masters); 3/4" (masters and viewing copies); 1/2" (viewing copies) (amounts unspecified).
Cataloging: Shot lists; computerized cataloging for staff use only.
Access: Available for duplication, licensing and reuse. Research fees charged. Research requests accepted by mail and telephone.
Rights: Some rights held to some material.
Licensing: Available for licensing and reuse, subject to restrictions. License fees charged.
Restrictions: Some footage not available for reuse.
Viewing Facilities: Videotape (3/4" and 1/2").
Duplication Facilities: Videotape (3/4" to 3/4"; 3/4" to 1/2").

CHANNEL SEA TELEVISION
1750 Kalakaua Avenue, Suite 3-757
Honolulu, HI 96826
(808) 947-4460
Fax: (808) 941-9959
Telex: 294979 MAKAI HR (RCA) or 6502465719 (MCI)

Phil Uhl (President, Honolulu)
Leslie DeMeuse (President, Orange County, California) (714) 495-3320
Kaoru Soehata (Tokyo, Japan) (03) 404-0249

Contacts: Phil Uhl; Leslie DeMeuse; Kaoru Soehata
Services: Videotape producer; stock footage sales library.
Description: Yacht racing in California and Hawaii; Hawaiian scenics.
Size & Elements: Videotape: 3/4" (200 videotapes); also available in 1", 1/2" and 8mm formats.
Cataloging: Shot lists.
Access: Available for duplication and reuse. Some films maintained for distribution and rental rather than research or reuse. Research fees charged. Research requests accepted by mail, telephone and in person (by appointment only).
Rights: Full rights held to some material. Additional clearances may be necessary in some cases if material is to be reused.
Licensing: Available for licensing and reuse, subject to restrictions. License fees charged.
Restrictions: Some restrictions apply to licensing and reuse (apply for information).
Viewing Facilities: Videotape.
Duplication Facilities: Videotape (3/4" and 1/2").
Related Materials: Over 100,000 35mm transparencies of yacht racing in Hawaii, California, Australia, Italy, England, Great Lakes, Florida and other locations.

DOBOVAN PRODUCTIONS, INC.
1575 South Beretania, Suite 105
Honolulu, HI 96826
(808) 941-3399
Fax: (808) 943-0360

John Dobovan (President)

Contact: John Dobovan
Services: Videotape producer; stock footage sales library.
Description: Hawaiian scenics (1979-present). Includes natural beauty shots, Honolulu and its people, volcanic eruptions, snow on Mauna Kea, surfing and windsurfing, waterfalls, flowers, beaches, remote valleys, aerials, whales, hula dancing and Waikiki Beach.
Size & Elements: Videotape: Betacam (masters); 3/4" and Betamax (viewing copies) (500 videotapes, each 20 min.).
Cataloging: Computerized cataloging for staff use only; staff assistance required.
Access: Available for licensing and reuse. All research performed by in-house staff only. Research fees charged. Research requests accepted by mail, telephone and in person (by appointment only).
Rights: Full rights held to all material.
Licensing: Available for licensing and reuse. License fees charged.
Restrictions: None specified.
Viewing Facilities: Videotape (1", Betacam, 3/4", VHS, Betamax and 8mm).
Duplication Facilities: Videotape (1", Betacam, 3/4", VHS, Betamax and 8mm).

EAST-WEST CENTER
INSTITUTE OF CULTURE AND COMMUNICATION
RESOURCE MATERIAL COLLECTION
John A. Burns Hall, Room 4063
1777 East-West Road
Honolulu, HI 96848
(808) 944-7345
Fax: (808) 944-7670
Cable: EASWESCEN
Telex: 743-0331

Sumi Konoshima (Librarian)

Contacts: Sumi Konoshima; Polly Chan (Junior Librarian)
Services: Educational institution; film and videotape archives. Materials available for research and nonprofit reuse, subject to clearance and approval.
Description: Hawaii, the Pacific Basin region, Eastern and Southeastern Asia. Collection includes a substantial amount of NHK (Japanese television) footage, as well as various international and UNICEF productions. Sample subjects include: population planning and analysis in Korea and in the Pacific Basin; Japanese industry and culture (noodles, steel, silk, electronics, terminal care facilities, space program, weather forecasting, shoyu production, etc.); rural development in Haiti; Maori art; Korean dancing; the Solomon Islands; Micronesia; radioactive waste disposal in the Pacific Islands; toxic waste disposal in Norfolk, Virginia; Polish wildlife; the Sahara; history; civilization; antiquities and archaeology of Fiji; nutrition in El Salvador; Tunisia; Thai dance; Korean women; Chinese opera and Native American culture.

Videotape productions which the East-West Center has been involved with or produced include: *Change in the Pacific; China After Mao; Telecommunications in the Pacific;* and *The Trial of Worker Guo.* Other videotape footage includes: three Korean dances; documentation of a performance of Nigerian drumming; Ilokano immigrants in Hawaiian secondary schools; traditional and new communication in Fiji; Mela or folk festivals of Bangladesh; a lecture given by Margaret Mead in 1975 at the University of Hawaii at Manoa; the Hula; Paraguayan weaving; Sinhalese songs; Torres Strait Cultural Dance Troupe; Mexican culture; and various lectures.
Size & Elements: Film: 16mm. Videotape: 3/4" and VHS. (Approx. 300 titles total).
Cataloging: Card catalogs.
Access: Open to the public. Research fees generally not charged. Research requests accepted by mail and telephone.
Rights: Full rights held to some material. Some rights held to some material. Additional clearances may be necessary in some cases if material is to be reused.

Licensing: Available for licensing and reuse, subject to restrictions. License fees charged in some cases (apply for information).
Restrictions: Requests for reuse considered on a case-by-case basis, with permission of the Director.
Viewing Facilities: Videotape (3/4", VHS and Betamax).
Duplication Facilities: Arrangements can be made at the Logistics Department of the University of Hawaii.

HAWAII (Honolulu)

HAWAII PUBLIC BROADCASTING AUTHORITY
HAWAII PUBLIC TELEVISION
2350 Dole Street
Honolulu, HI 96822
(808) 955-7878
Fax: (808) 949-7289

James B. Young (Executive Director, General Manager)

Contact: James B. Young
Services: Film and videotape producer; government agency and television broadcaster. Material possibly available for licensing or reuse, subject to restrictions of each individual department.
Description: Hawaii and Hawaiian-based material, including all the different cultures resident in the state; outtakes of sites, people and events (1983-present); location shots of Tahiti, the Cook Islands, New Zealand and other Pacific islands. Also held are newsreels, scenics, cultural documentation, music performances, documentaries, and oral histories, including interviews with 75 Pearl Harbor survivors from all over the U.S.
Size & Elements: Film: 16mm (approx. 600 cans). Videotape: 1", 3/4" and 1/2" (approx. 10,000 videotapes total).
Cataloging: Finding aids (log sheets developed by individual producers); shot lists; dope sheets; release sheets.
Access: Available to researchers and scholars only. Each department has own policy regarding access to material it has produced. Research requests accepted in person (by appointment only).
Rights: Full rights held to all material. Additional clearances may be necessary in some cases if material is to be reused.
Licensing: Material available for licensing and reuse, subject to restrictions.
Restrictions: Restrictions apply, depending on intended use and type of production. Requests for research and reuse accepted on a case-by-case basis. Each department has own policy regarding access to material.
Viewing Facilities: Available (limited by in-house programming and production needs).
Duplication Facilities: Available on a limited basis.

HAWAII (Honolulu)

PACIFIC FOCUS INC.
1013 Kawaiahao Street
Honolulu, HI 96814
(808) 536-3848
Fax: (808) 537-6438

Dennis Burns (President)

Contact: Ted Jung (Production Manager)
Services: Film and videotape producer. Collection available for duplication, licensing and reuse.
Description: Color beauty and action shots of the Hawaiian Islands, including "everything on the islands."
Size & Elements: Film: format and amount unspecified. Videotape: 1", Betacam and 3/4". Collection is "quite large and expanding" (exact size unspecified; mostly videotape).
Cataloging: Computerized cataloging for staff use only.
Access: Available to the public for duplication, licensing and reuse. Research fees not charged. Research requests accepted by telephone.
Rights: Full rights held to some material. Some rights held to all material.
Licensing: Available for licensing and reuse. License fees charged.
Restrictions: None specified.
Viewing Facilities: Videotape (on-line and off-line, all formats).
Duplication Facilities: Videotape.

HAWAII (Honolulu)

PACIFIC PRODUCTIONS
P.O. Box 2881
Honolulu, HI 96802
(808) 531-1560
(808) 732-1232

Street address: 700 Richards Street, Suite 2710, Honolulu, HI 96813

Robert B. Ebert (President)

Contact: Bill Bennett (Manager)
Services: Film and videotape producer. Material available for duplication, licensing and reuse.
Description: Areas covered include: Hawaiiana (1880-1988); Japan (1945-present); Alaska (1964-present); Korea (1962-present); Thailand; and Pacific Islands.
Size & Elements: Film: format unspecified (500-600 titles). Videotape: 3/4" and 1/2" (over 700 videotapes).
Cataloging: Computerized cataloging for staff use only.
Access: Available for duplication, licensing and reuse. Research fees not charged. Research requests accepted by mail and in person (by appointment only).
Rights: Full rights held to some material. Some rights held to all material. Additional clearances may be necessary in some cases if material is to be reused.
Licensing: Available for licensing and reuse. License fees charged.
Restrictions: None specified.
Viewing Facilities: Film and videotape.
Duplication Facilities: Videotape.
Related Materials: Still photographs and 35mm slides (color and black and white).

HAWAII (Honolulu)

PEOPLE'S FUND
2252 Puna Street
Honolulu, HI 96817
(808) 595-7362

John Witeck (Coordinator)

Contact: John Witeck
Services: Educational funding organization. Film and videotape collection held primarily for educational and research purposes.
Description: Hawaiian social and political struggles, the movement for a nuclear-free and independent Pacific, the Philippines, and a few antiwar films.
   Hawaiian struggles. The Hawaiian Movement (1985); *Sand Island struggle* (1983); *Kahoolawe Island struggle* (1980); *Nuclear Free Independent Pacific (NFIP) Conference in Vanuatu* (1983); *West Beach struggle* (1986-87); *Waimanalo Eviction* (1986).
   Philippine struggles. Negros — Social Volcano (1986); *Pain is the Price of Freedom* (1986); *Breaking Ground for Freedom* (1985).
   Antiwar films. Oliver Lee Tenure Case (1968, 65 min.) documents a sit-in at the University of Hawaii in support of an antiwar professor. Also holds various other anti-Vietnam War and draft resistance films.
Size & Elements: Film: 16mm and 8mm (amounts unspecified). Videotape: VHS and Betamax (over 12 titles, each 30 min. to 60 min.).
Cataloging: None specified.
Access: Available to researchers, scholars and the public primarily for educational purposes. Research fees not charged. Research requests accepted by mail and telephone.
Rights: Full rights held to some material. Additional clearances may be necessary in some cases if material is to be reused.
Licensing: Available for licensing and reuse, subject to restrictions. License fees generally not charged.
Restrictions: Material used primarily for educational purposes. Requests for licensing and reuse are considered on a case-by-case basis and depend on intended use.
Viewing Facilities: Videotape (VHS).
Duplication Facilities: None (outside arrangements can be made).

HAWAII (Honolulu)

QUENZER DRISCOLL DAWSON, INC.
816 Queen Street

Honolulu, HI 96813
(808) 521-6961
Fax: (808) 545-3519

Tim Bradley (Managing Director)

Contact: Tim Bradley
Services: Film and videotape production company; stock footage sales library.
Description: Beauty shots of Hawaii, covering all major islands. Subjects include waterfalls, beaches, flowers, boating, surfing and volcanoes. One edited videotape, *Sea Life Park* (1987, 30 min.), captures behind-the-scenes activities and training at Sea Life Park; it is available there and at bookstores on Oahu and neighboring islands. This videotape includes ground and ocean shots of the outlying area, such as the Koolau Mountain Range, Manana Island, the landmark known as Rabbit Island, bird sanctuaries and scenic Makapuu Point.
Size & Elements: Videotape: Betacam (amount unspecified; unedited footage, masters); 1/2" (1 title).
Cataloging: Shot lists.
Access: Available for purchase, licensing and reuse. Research fees charged. Research requests accepted by mail, telephone and in person (walk-in).
Rights: Full rights held to some material.
Licensing: Available for licensing and reuse. License fees charged (fees negotiable).
Restrictions: None specified.
Viewing Facilities: Videotape (Betacam and 3/4" playback).
Duplication Facilities: Videotape (Betacam to Betacam, 1", 3/4" and VHS).

HAWAII (Honolulu)

UNIVERSITY OF HAWAII AT MANOA
WONG AUDIOVISUAL CENTER
SINCLAIR LIBRARY
Honolulu, HI 96822
(808) 948-8009

Linda Engelberg (Audiovisual Librarian)

Contacts: Linda Engelberg; Lorraine Thorne (Library Technician)
Services: Audiovisual center. Film and videotape available for University research, loan and rental. Material possibly available for duplication and reuse.
Description: Materials on a broad range of subjects supporting the undergraduate and graduate curricula at the Manoa campus. Most titles are in English; some items are in Samoan, Japanese, French, Russian and Spanish. Center holds some duplicates of materials from library's Department of Special Collections. Subject areas most thoroughly covered by the collection include Hawaiiana, Asian cultures, Pacific cultures, social sciences, general science, music, Shakespearean drama and feature films.
Size & Elements: Film: format unspecified (3,000 titles, 4,000 cans). Videotape: 3/4", Betamax and VHS (1,000 titles).
Cataloging: Published catalogs; on-line microfiche cataloging available to researchers.
Access: Open to the public. Maintained primarily for student and faculty use. Materials cannot be transported off Oahu, but are otherwise available for loan. Research fees not charged; handling and service fees apply. Research requests accepted by telephone and in person (walk-in).
Rights: Rights status of material not known.
Licensing: Apply for information.
Restrictions: None specified.
Viewing Facilities: Film (16mm); videotape (3/4", VHS and Betamax).
Duplication Facilities: None.

HAWAII (Honolulu)

VIDEO-DOCUMENTARY CLEARINGHOUSE
Harbor Square, Suite 2201
700 Richards Street
Honolulu, HI 96813
(808) 523-2882

Morgan Cotlar (Executive Director)

Contact: Morgan Cotlar
Services: Videotape archives. Maintained primarily for distribution and rental. Material possibly available for duplication, licensing and reuse.
Description: Videotaped interviews with major authorities in the areas of

management, marketing, personnel, accounting, finance, economics and administration. Intended for use in colleges, non-credit seminars and organizational interventions.

Interviews and dialogues include: C. West Churchman, the originator of "operations research"; Harold Koontz, proponent of the "functional approach"; Edward W. Cundiff, widely known for his contributions to marketing thought; Charles T. Horngren, a leading academic in accounting theory, and a proponent of improved standards in accounting; Keith Davis, who talks with students about organizational communication, the importance of leadership behavior and the strong effect of environmental elements on organizations; and John Mee, who discusses "the importance of human asset accounting as a segment of human audits."
Size & Elements: Videotape: 3/4", VHS, Betamax and 1/2" EIAJ (over 12 titles total).
Cataloging: Published catalogs; viewer's guides.
Access: Available for rental, purchasing, duplication, licensing and reuse.
Rights: Full rights held to all material. Additional clearances may be necessary in some cases if material is to be reused.
Licensing: Material possibly available for licensing. License fees charged in some cases.
Restrictions: None specified.
Viewing Facilities: None.
Duplication Facilities: Videotape.

HAWAII (Kapaa)

DANE WARNER PHOTOGRAPHY/VIDEO PRODUCTION
P.O. Box 658
Kapaa, HI 96746
(808) 828-1900

Contacts: Dane Warner; John Young
Services: Videotape producer; location scouting service; stock footage sales library.
Description: Scenics and action footage of Kauai and other Hawaiian islands.
Size & Elements: Videotape: 3/4" (75 hours).
Cataloging: Shot lists.
Access: Available for duplication, licensing and reuse. Research requests accepted by mail and telephone.
Rights: Full rights held to all material.
Licensing: Available for licensing. License fees charged.
Restrictions: None specified.
Viewing Facilities: Videotape (3/4").
Duplication Facilities: Videotape (3/4" to VHS).

HAWAII (Kealakekua)

ACKERMAN-BLACK PRODUCTIONS, INC.
P.O. Box 715
Kealakekua, HI 96750
(808) 322-3672

Contacts: A. D. Ackerman; Noël Black
Services: Videotape stock footage sales library.
Description: Extensive stock footage of Hawaii, including flowers, Hawaiian culture and people, Hawaiian industries (e.g., coffee, macadamia nut and sugar), surfing, waterfalls, hula dancing, hotels, historical sites, diving, snorkeling, tourism and romantic shots. Special strengths include coverage of volcanoes, deep-sea fishing, scenics and sunsets.
Size & Elements: Videotape: 3/4" (amount unspecified; masters); 1/2" (viewing copies).
Cataloging: None specified.
Access: Available for licensing and reuse. Research fees charged in some cases.
Rights: Full rights held to all material.
Licensing: Available for licensing, subject to restrictions. License fees charged.
Restrictions: Some restrictions apply if material used commercially or for financial gain.
Viewing Facilities: Videotape (3/4").
Duplication Facilities: Videotape (3/4" and 1/2").

HAWAII (Kihei)

VIDEO CONCEPTS, INC.

HAWAII (Koloa)

1325 South Kihei Road, Suite 215
Kihei, HI 96753
(808) 879-1965

Bob Ramacher (Owner)

Contacts: Bob Ramacher; Kevin Harrington
Services: Videotape producer; production facility; stock footage sales library.
Description: Has been producing stock footage since 1983. Holds aerials and underwater footage of Maui.
Size & Elements: Videotape: Betacam (8 hours) and 3/4" (100 hours).
Cataloging: None.
Access: Available to the public for licensing and reuse. Research fees charged in some cases. Research requests accepted by mail and telephone.
Rights: Full rights held to all material.
Licensing: Available for licensing and reuse. License fees charged.
Restrictions: None specified.
Viewing Facilities: Videotape.
Duplication Facilities: Videotape.

HAWAII (Koloa)

TV-3
P.O. Box 879
Koloa, HI 96756
(808) 332-8348

Street address: 3580 Koloa Road, Lawai, Kauai, HI 96765

Jim Holbrook (Owner)

Contact: Jim Holbrook
Services: Videotape producer; stock footage sales library.
Description: Scenic nature shots of Hawaii, including birds, mountains, flowers, waterfalls, the ocean and the Napali Coast.
Size & Elements: Videotape: 3/4" (100 videotapes, each 20 min.; masters); VHS (viewing copies).
Cataloging: Shot lists.
Access: Available for licensing and reuse. Research fees not charged. Research requests accepted by mail, telephone and in person (walk-in).
Rights: Full rights held to all material.
Licensing: Available for licensing. License fees charged.
Restrictions: None.
Viewing Facilities: None.
Duplication Facilities: Videotape (3/4" to 3/4" and 3/4" to VHS).

IDAHO

IDAHO (Boise)

ECHO FILM PRODUCTIONS INC.
407 West Bannock
Boise, ID 83702
(208) 336-0349

Norman W. Nelson (President/Director)
Tyler S. Nelson (Vice President/Producer)

Contacts: Norman Nelson (Director); Suzanne Nelson (Production Coordinator)
Services: Film and videotape producer; stock footage sales library.
Description: Wildlife, particularly North American birds of prey and falconry. Specializes in slow motion footage of bald eagles, golden eagles, peregrine falcons and prairie falcons.

Wildlife. Golden eagle portraits, flight action and nesting; bald eagle flight action, roosting and aerial flight shots; prairie falcon kill strikes, portraits, flight action and nesting; peregrine falcon kill strikes, Canadian nesting and closeups; hawks and owls flight action, kills and portraits; sandhill cranes in flight, groups and portraits; wild horses running in slow motion and in scenic group shots; cougar, kittens and adult scenic establishing shots; moose browsing, winter shots and scenics; elk summer herd; deer portraits, running, browsing and winter starvation; osprey flight, portraits and nesting; salmon and trout underwater.

North American birdlife, waterfowl, geese and cranes in marsh and

wetland habitats across the country; work with various endangered hawk and eagle species at a center for birds of prey; footage of endangered species, including manatee, whooping crane, desert bighorn sheep, various endangered turtles and reptiles; people working with wildlife, habitat and wildlife management practices and results; forest management practices in Idaho.

Journey of the Kings discusses the environmental status of salmon runs in the Columbia River Basin; *Peregrine* shows captive breeding and other efforts to preserve the endangered Peregrine Falcon; *Golden Eagles* shows life cycle of the breed; *Silver Wires Golden Wings* documents efforts to prevent electrocution of eagles and other large birds on power lines.

Sports action. Powder skiing, including jumping, bumps, scenic groups, slow motion and tracking; surfing on Hawaii's North Shore, including waves, beach activity and wipeouts; kayaking, including expert white-water action, rolls and slow motion coverage; rodeo, including slow motion bronco riding, steer roping and horse riding; fly fishing; steelhead and bass fishing; salmon, trout and underwater fishing. Other topics include biking, hunting, water skiing and windsurfing.

Scenics. Helicopter point-of-view shots of winter rivers, mountains, summer wilderness and deserts; forest management practices, tree cutting and planting operations; time-lapse footage of clouds on mountains and a scenic white cloud building; desert and sand dune scenic coverage; fall leaves, mountains and streams; spring flowers; melting snows; scenic landscapes; winter scenics; streams; wildlife in winter backgrounds; Craters of the Moon National Monument and sunset scenics.

Cultural subjects. Mexico, including landscapes, birdlife, ocean wildlife and coastlines; Arabian falconry, oil lines, people working, landscapes and palaces; migrant field workers and their children at Cinco de Mayo Festival; Northwest Indian artwork and craftspeople; Navajo senior citizens arts and crafts; Indian artists painting and sculpting; historical Indian material; Indians on horseback; general farm cultivation and land-use activity. *In Quest of a Vision* examines Indian artists of the Northwest and their Vision Quest ritual.

Electric power company sponsored material. Power production; environmental management; power company personnel at work; power line construction; hydroelectric power dams; other subjects related to power production; several films on power company efforts to preserve wildlife habitats and help wildlife survive.
Size & Elements: Film: 16mm (300,000 feet, 18 edited titles). Videotape: format and amount unspecified.
Cataloging: Shot lists; dope sheets and release sheets.
Access: Available to the public for duplication, licensing and reuse. Research fees charged. Research requests accepted by mail and telephone.
Rights: Full rights held to most material. Some rights held to some material. Releases may be necessary in some cases if material is to be reused.
Licensing: Available for licensing and reuse, subject to restrictions. License fees charged (based on amount used and market).
Restrictions: Limited to one-time use only.
Viewing Facilities: Film (16mm); videotape (3/4" and VHS).
Duplication Facilities: Videotape (VHS).
Representative: For stock footage sales: Film Search, Inc. (q.v.)
Related Materials: Still photographs relating to above subjects.

IDAHO (Boise)

IDAHO STATE LIBRARY
FILM DEPARTMENT
325 West State Street
Boise, ID 83702
(208) 334-2152

Charles A. Bolles (State Librarian)

Contact: Dottie Burdiss (Clerical Specialist)
Services: State agency; library. Films and videotapes available for research and free loan. Some material possibly available for reuse, subject to clearance and approval.
Description: Collection consists primarily of educational and children's films and videotapes on all topics.

Idaho films. Approximately 15 films made by local producers (16mm, 1950s-70s). Subjects include Idaho, wildlife and travel.
Size & Elements: Film: 16mm (Idaho films: 15 titles, negatives and release prints; other films: 1,201 titles, 1,391 cans, release prints). Videotape: 3/4", VHS and Betamax (130 videotapes).
Cataloging: Published catalogs; card catalogs.
Access: Open to the public. Research fees not charged. Research facilities in library.

Rights: Full rights held to some material. Additional clearances will be necessary in most cases if material is to be reused. Rights to Idaho films retained by original producers.
Licensing: Apply for information.
Restrictions: Some restrictions may apply to reuse.
Viewing Facilities: Film (16mm); videotape (3/4" and 1/2").
Duplication Facilities: None.

IDAHO (Moscow)

APPALOOSA HORSE CLUB, INC.
P.O. Box 8403
Moscow, ID 83843
(208) 882-5578
Fax: (208) 882-8150

Darrell Dodds (Executive Secretary)

Contact: Don Pierce
Services: National breed registry; museum. Film and videotape material available for free loan to members only.
Description: Films and videotapes relating to Appaloosa horses. Titles include: *1987 Appaloosa World Stallion Avenue,* with videotapes from all Appaloosa ranches and farms that exhibited at the 1987 Stallion Avenue Show; *1988 American Classic Video,* a promotional film; and *Chief Joseph Trail Ride* (1973), including footage from the historic Chief Joseph Trail Ride, an annual Appaloosa event following the same trail the Nez Perce Indians followed (riding through Idaho, Oregon, Washington, Montana, and Wyoming).
Size & Elements: Apply for information.
Cataloging: None specified.
Access: Available to Club members free of charge. Research requests not accepted.
Rights: Full rights held to all material.
Licensing: Not available for licensing or reuse.
Restrictions: Reuse not permitted.
Viewing Facilities: None.
Duplication Facilities: None.

IDAHO (Spalding)

NEZ PERCÉ NATIONAL HISTORICAL PARK
P.O. Box 93
Spalding, ID 83551
(208) 843-2261

Roy W. Weaver (Superintendent)

Contact: Karen Bizak (Park Ranger/Interpretation)
Services: Government agency. Film and videotape collection open to the public.
Description: Four films and one videotape relating to Nez Percé National Historical Park.
Size & Elements: Film: format unspecified (4 titles, 4 cans; release prints). Videotape: VHS (1 videotape; viewing copy).
Cataloging: Research library.
Access: Open to the public. Research fees not charged. Research requests accepted by mail and in person (by appointment only).
Rights: Material is in the public domain.
Licensing: Material possibly available for reuse. Usage fees not charged.
Restrictions: None specified.
Viewing Facilities: Film and videotape.
Duplication Facilities: None.

ILLINOIS

ILLINOIS (Arlington Heights)

AMERICAN SOCIETY OF PLASTIC AND RECONSTRUCTIVE SURGEONS, INC.
PLASTIC SURGERY EDUCATIONAL FOUNDATION
COMMUNICATIONS DEPARTMENT
444 East Algonquin Road
Arlington Heights, IL 60005

(312) 228-9900
Fax: (312) 228-9131

Pamela Rasmussen (Director of Communications)

Contact: Cathy Coyne (Media Relations Coordinator)
Services: National medical society. Audiovisual library available to members of ASPRS and the media; not open to the public.
Description: *Operative procedures for the prospective patient.* Five-minute videotapes explaining what patients might expect in the initial consultation and during the post-operative recovery period. Titles include: *Rhinoplasty; Rhytidectomy; Blepharoplasty; Chemical Peel; Suction Assisted Lipectomy; Breast Augmentation; Cleft Lip and Palate; Post-Mastectomy Reconstruction; Breast Reduction; Abdominoplasty; Genioplasty;* and *Mastopexy.*
   Physician Education Materials — PSEF videotapes:
   Aesthetic. Titles include: *The Septum in Rhinoplasty; Rhinoplasty — "Bugs Bunny Syndrome"; Skin Muscle Flap Blepharoplasty; Corrective Makeup Techniques Following Cosmetic Surgery; Dermabrasion for Perioral Wrinkles;* and *Ancillary Procedures in the Aging Face.*
   Breast. Titles include: *Nipple-Areolar Reconstruction; Reduction Mammoplasty; Breast Ptosis Treatment; Rectus Abdominis Breast Reconstruction;* and *The Soft Breast.*
   Hand. Titles include: *Thumb Reconstruction with Great Toe Flap; Surgery of the Carpel Tunnel; Primary Tenorrhaphy in No Man's Land;* and *Flexor Tendon Grafting.*
   Head and neck. Titles include: *Anatomy of the Eyelid and Orbital Adnexa; The Role of Three-Dimensional Computer Imaging in a Craniofacial Center: Custom Editing and Processing of Pathology; Tissue Expansion for Scalp Reconstruction; Jaws IV; Parotidectomy; Repair of the Unilateral Cleft Lip Nose Deformity; Treatment of Facial Fractures; Nasal Reconstruction;* and *Otoplasty for Prominent Ears.*
   Flaps. Titles include: *Extended TLF Musculocutaneous Neurosensory Muscle Flap; The Deltoid Free Flap (Foot Reconstruction);* and *Island Flap Techniques.*
   Reconstruction. Titles include: *The Inner Limits — Techniques of Microsurgery; Thermal Injury — Closure of the Burn Wound;* and *Hypospadias.*
   EF Teleplast Videoteleconference Videotapes. PSEF and Hospital Satellite Network present the most current procedures in plastic surgery.
Size & Elements: Videotape: 3/4", 1/2" and Betamax (14 titles, viewing copies available for media use; 130 titles, viewing copies available to members only).
Cataloging: Published catalog available to physicians upon request.
Access: Not open to the public. Some material available for media use. Other videotapes available to active and life members, and applicants and candidates for membership in ASPRS. Some material possibly available to researchers and scholars. Research fees not charged. Research requests accepted by telephone.
Rights: Full rights held to all material.
Licensing: Available for licensing and reuse, subject to restrictions. License fees charged in some cases.
Restrictions: Collection maintained primarily for use by ASPRS members. Some material may be available for media use.
Viewing Facilities: None.
Duplication Facilities: None.
Related Materials: Patient education brochures corresponding with operative procedure videotapes.

ILLINOIS (Berwyn)

CZECHOSLOVAK HERITAGE MUSEUM LIBRARY AND ARCHIVES
CSA Fraternal Life
2701 South Harlem Avenue
Berwyn, IL 60402
(312) 795-5800
(800) 543-3272

George Vytlacil (President)

Contact: Lillian K. Chorvat (Museum Curator and Librarian)
Services: Fraternal organization. Films collection available for research, licensing and reuse.
Description: Film biographies of Czechoslovakian President Edward Benes (1936-46) and Jan Masaryk (1920s-48).
Size & Elements: Film: 16mm (2 titles).
Cataloging: Research library.
Access: Open to the public. For in-house use only. Available for duplication.

Research fees not charged. Research requests accepted by mail, telephone and in person.
Rights: Full rights held to all material.
Licensing: Available for licensing and reuse, subject to restrictions.
Restrictions: Requests for licensing and reuse considered on a case-by-case basis.
Viewing Facilities: None.
Duplication Facilities: Film.

ILLINOIS (Champaign)

RESEARCH PRESS
P.O. Box 3177
Champaign, IL 61821
(217) 352-3273

Street address: 2612 North Mattis

In Canada:
RESEARCH PRESS OF CANADA
123 Bridgeport Road East
Waterloo, ON N2J 2K3
(519) 743-3811

Contact: Distribution Staff
Services: Distributor. Film and videotape materials available for rental and purchase.
Description: Films and videotapes on social services and psychology.

Sample titles include: *A Family in Grief: The Ameche Story,* the account of a family's efforts to deal with the death of their 22-year-old son; *The Skillstreaming Video: How to Teach Students Prosocial Skills,* with Dr. Arnold P. Goldstein and Dr. Ellen McGinnis illustrating the concepts of modeling, role playing, performance feedback and transfer training; *Education for All Children: The Challenge of the Eighties,* examining traditional attitudes toward individuals with developmental disabilities and the future of the "Right to Education Movement"; *What's the Difference Being Different?,* demonstrating how a multicultural program can be implemented in a school system; *Catch 'em Being Good: Approaches to Motivation and Discipline,* contrasting the use of positive discipline with traditional, but often less effective methods; *The Bizarre Trial of the Pressured Peer,* illustrating the potentially negative consequences of peer pressure in an extraordinary dream sequence; *Bulimia,* illustrating the classic chain of events that may lead young women into the serious problem of binge-purge behavior; *Looking for the Words: Teaching Functional Language Strategies,* showing how individuals with severe language deficiencies are able to learn functional verbal responses and language strategies; *Three Styles of Marital Conflict,* true-to-life vignettes depicting three common styles of marital conflict; *Progressive Relaxation Training: A Clinical Demonstration,* featuring the late Dr. Donald T. Shannon directing a client through the stages of relaxation; and *B. F. Skinner and Behavior Change: Research, Practice and Promise,* featuring on-site interventions with patients, clients and students in a variety of settings.
Size & Elements: Film: 16mm. Videotape: 3/4", VHS and Betamax. (30 titles total).
Cataloging: Published catalog.
Access: Available for rental and purchase. Requests accepted by mail and telephone.
Rights: Apply for information.
Licensing: Apply for information.
Restrictions: Apply for information.
Viewing Facilities: None.
Duplication Facilities: None.

ILLINOIS (Chicago)

ALZHEIMER'S DISEASE AND RELATED DISORDERS ASSOCIATION, INC.
National Headquarters
70 East Lake Street
Chicago, IL 60601-0379
(312) 853-3060
Fax: (312) 853-3660

Mr. Edward Truschke (President)

Contact: Barbara Leutz (Coordinator of Education Services)

Services: Association. Film and videotape library available for distribution.
Description: Alzheimer's disease and care for its victims.
Size & Elements: Film: format unspecified (1 title). Videotape: format unspecified (10 titles).
Cataloging: None specified.
Access: Available for in-house use, to association chapters and the public, subject to clearance and approval. Research requests accepted by mail.
Rights: Some rights held to all material.
Licensing: Apply for information. License fees charged.
Restrictions: None specified.
Viewing Facilities: None.
Duplication Facilities: None.

ILLINOIS (Chicago)

AMERICAN DENTAL ASSOCIATION
211 East Chicago Avenue
Chicago, IL 60611
(312) 440-2808
Fax: (312) 440-7494

Available for rental from:
**AMERICAN DENTAL ASSOCIATION AUDIOVISUAL LIBRARY
c/o MODERN TALKING PICTURE SERVICE, INC.** (q.v.).

Jay Danielian (Director, A/V Services, Chicago)

Contact: Donna Burton (Staff Associate, Chicago)
Services: Association. Films available for rental only; not available for duplication, licensing or reuse.
Description: Educational films produced for the general public on the importance of dental health, brushing, flossing and regular dental visits; an extensive collection of films geared towards the dental professional, including clinical procedure and dental technique programs. Some films are available in Spanish-language versions.

Topics relating to patient education include: dental health basics, periodontal health, smokeless tobacco, fluoridation, preventive dentistry, nutrition, geriatric dentistry, consumerism and how to pick a dentist, dental care for the handicapped, endodontics (root canal therapy), prosthodontics, orthodontics, history of dentistry, dental training and education and careers in dentistry.

Topics for professional audiences include: anesthesia and analgesia, auxiliary personnel, chemical dependency and the dentist, cleft lip and palate, dental materials and equipment, emergencies, endodontics, hospital dentistry, implantodontics, operative dentistry, oral anatomy and physiology, oral diagnosis, oral pathology, oral radiology, oral surgery, orthodontics, pedodontics, periodontics, practice management, prosthodontics (complete, fixed partial, maxillofacial, removable partial) and research.

Material of historical value is now held by the National Library of Medicine, History of Medicine Division, Historical Audiovisuals Collection (q.v.).
Size & Elements: Film: 16mm (300 titles). Videotape: 3/4", VHS and Betamax (quantity unspecified; masters and viewing copies). Master elements for ADA-produced films and videotapes are housed in Chicago; viewing copies of programs produced by other sources have been purchased for library.
Cataloging: Published catalogs.
Access: Available to the public for rental. Requests accepted by mail and telephone.
Rights: Full rights held to some material. Rights to some material retained by original producers.
Licensing: Not available for licensing or reuse.
Restrictions: All materials are protected by copyright. This is a lending library only; footage cannot be reused or excerpted.
Viewing Facilities: Available (apply for information).
Duplication Facilities: None.
Representatives: In Canada: LM Media Marketing Services, Ltd., 115 Torbay Road (Unit 9) Markham, Ontario, L3R 2M9 Canada; (416) 475-3750.

ILLINOIS (Chicago)

**AMERICAN MEDICAL ASSOCIATION
SPECIAL COLLECTIONS DEPARTMENT**
535 North Dearborn Street
Chicago, IL 60610
(312) 645-5000

Fax: (312) 645-4184
TWX: (910) 221-0300

Victoria Davis (Director of Archives, History and Policy Information)

Contact: Marguerite Fallucco; Victoria Davis (312/645-4846)
Services: Association. Film and videotape collection open to researchers and scholars only; available for duplication, subject to restrictions.
Description: History of the AMA (1935-70), including films and videotapes documenting meetings and conventions. This material shows past presidents of the AMA and organizational activities.

Holds a series of AMA-produced health education spots, originally made for sponsored film and television distribution, including one to two-minute segments on such subjects as sunbathing, artificial respiration, emergency hints for babysitters, health and money, home accidents, venereal disease, childrens' safety on the way to school, colds, measles and influenza. These spots were originally distributed through AMA's film distribution library, which is now defunct.

A number of AMA-produced films of historical interest are held by the American Archives of The Factual Film, Iowa State University (q.v.).
Size & Elements: Film: 16mm (approx. 350 titles).
Cataloging: Inventory list (staff use only).
Access: Open to researchers and scholars only. For in-house use only. Available for duplication. Research requests accepted by mail.
Rights: Apply for information.
Licensing: Apply for information.
Restrictions: All requests for licensing and reuse subject to clearance and approval.
Viewing Facilities: Film and videotape.
Duplication Facilities: None.

ILLINOIS (Chicago)

AMERICAN OSTEOPATHIC ASSOCIATION
DEPARTMENT OF COMMUNICATIONS
142 East Ontario Street
Chicago, IL 60611
(312) 280-5800
Fax: (312) 280-5893

Al Boeck (Director of Communications)

Contact: Al Boeck
Services: Association. One film available to Association members for rental.
Description: *Touch of Health* (approx. 17 min.) is designed to increase public understanding and acceptance of osteopathic medicine, presenting the philosophy of osteopathic medicine and discussing the education and training of osteopathic physicians.
Size & Elements: Film: 16mm (1 title).
Access: Available to Association members for screening to general public audiences.
Rights: Apply for information.
Licensing: Apply for information.
Restrictions: None specified.
Viewing Facilities: None.
Duplication Facilities: None.
Distributor: Available for rental from Film Repository, 399 Gundersen Drive, Carol Stream, IL 60188; (800) 345-6522.

ILLINOIS (Chicago)

AMERICAN SOCIETY OF CLINICAL PATHOLOGISTS PRESS
2100 West Harrison Street
Chicago, IL 60612
(312) 738-4866
(800) 621-4142

Joyce Nuzzo (Vice President for Educational Publications)

Contact: Barbara J. Gardetto (Director)
Services: Medical pathology society press. Videotapes available for purchase.
Description: Medical pathology seen from diagnostic, technical, prognostic and histologic points of view. Videotapes are designed for professionals in the field with the exception of *Careers in Laboratory Medicine: The Medical Technologist,* which is designed for public relations use in schools, laboratories

and training programs.

Categories include anatomic pathology, body fluids, clinical chemistry, education, forensic pathology, hematology, immunohematology, immunopathology and microbiology. Subjects covered under these categories are benign and malignant breast diseases, renal biopsy, endometrial carcinoma, malignant melanoma, mediastal tumors, Hodgkin's Disease and non-Hodgkin's lymphomas, chronic and acute viral hepatitis, liver biopsy, urinalysis, blood gases, radioimmunoassay, digoxin assay, investigation of suspicious death, automobile accidents, occupant and pedestrian injuries, asphyxial deaths, handgun wounds, identification of human remains, death from natural causes, toxicology, rape investigation, bone marrow sections, cytochemistry of acute and hairy cell leukemia, anemia, platelets, T & B lymphocytes, autoimmune diseases, cellular immunity and immune deficiency diseases, immunology, antimicrobial susceptibility testing and anaerobic bacteriology.
Size & Elements: Videotape: 3/4", VHS, Betamax I and II (40 titles).
Cataloging: Published catalogs.
Access: Available for purchase.
Rights: Full rights held to all material. Authors' permission may be necessary in some cases if material is to be reused.
Licensing: Apply for information.
Restrictions: None specified.
Viewing Facilities: None.
Duplication Facilities: None.

ILLINOIS (Chicago)

BALZEKAS MUSEUM OF LITHUANIAN CULTURE
6500 South Pulaski Road
Chicago, IL 60629
(312) 582-6500

David Fainhauz (Chief Librarian)

Contacts: David Fainhauz; Val Ramonis (Director); Edward Mankus (Audiovisual Director)
Services: Museum. Film and videotape collection available to researchers and scholars only.
Description: Videotapes on Lithuanian culture include: *Traditional Song, Dance, Wedding and High Mass; 20 Lithuanian Women; St. Kasimir's 500th Anniversary;* and *Lithuanian Textiles.* One film about Lithuania is also available.
Size & Elements: Film: 16mm (1 title). Videotape: VHS (4 titles).
Cataloging: Card catalogs; computerized cataloging available to researchers.
Access: Open to researchers and scholars only. Research requests accepted by mail, telephone and in person. Research fees charged.
Rights: Full rights held to all material.
Licensing: Apply for information. License fees charged in some cases.
Restrictions: None specified.
Viewing Facilities: Viewing room (format unspecified).
Duplication Facilities: None.

ILLINOIS (Chicago)

BRITANNICA FILMS & VIDEO
ENCYCLOPAEDIA BRITANNICA EDUCATIONAL CORPORATION
310 South Michigan Avenue, 6th Floor
Chicago, IL 60604
(800) 554-9862 (Ext. 6515) (For stock footage inquiries)
(312) 347-7400 (Ext. 6515) (For stock footage inquiries)
(800) 554-9862 (Exts. 6517 or 6508) (For rental, preview or purchase)
Fax: (312) 347-7903
Telex: (910) 221-5573
Cable Address: ENCYFILMS — CHICAGO

Joseph Elliott (President)

Contacts: Sherry Ostrowski (Domestic Sales); Neici Zeller (International Sales) (Ext. 7958)
Services: Film and videotape producer and distributor; stock footage sales library.
Description: Produces and distributes educational films. Stock footage from films produced by EBEC and its predecessor companies is also available. The footage library consists primarily of material used in completed productions; its strengths are those of the films (geography, history, biology, nature, science, animals and plants).

Educational films and videotapes are targeted at age groups from kindergarten to adult. Curriculum groups covered include language arts, literature and the humanities, history, geography, government and citizenship, economics, guidance, life science, earth science, physical science, mathematics and computers, healthy lifestyles, foreign languages, staff development and business education.

Size & Elements: Film: 16mm (over 1,100 titles; color and black and white, negatives and release prints). Videotape: 1", 3/4" and 1/2" (hundreds of titles). Stock footage requests can, in most cases, be fulfilled in either film or videotape formats. Generally, EBEC provides a quality 16mm positive print from which footage may be dubbed onto videotape or processed into another format.

Cataloging: Computerized cataloging (shot lists on IBM PC) for staff use only; published catalog of current films; film lists (staff use only).

ENCYCLOVIDEO is a computer-arranged microfiche index for over 1,100 films produced worldwide over more than 50 years by Encyclopaedia Britannica Educational Corporation and its predecessor companies. Footage from each of these films is indexed by shot list, by category, by "action statement" (short description of scenes in terms of action and camera movement) and by location. Over 70,000 scene descriptions are listed alphabetically in up to three categories. Indexing productions through 1983, ENCYCLOVIDEO is available for purchase or can be consulted by contacting staff librarians.

Access: Available to the public for preview, rental, purchase, licensing and reuse. Research and preview fees charged. Research requests accepted by mail and telephone; telephone requests must be followed by confirming letter. Preview material available on videocassette.

Rights: Full rights held to most material. Additional clearances may be necessary in some cases if material is to be reused.

Licensing: Available for licensing, subject to restrictions. License fees charged. Fee schedule available. Higher rates apply to licensing of animated footage. Entire EBEC stock footage library is available for purchase on a worldwide basis; negotiated buyouts are available, permitting unlimited reuse.

Restrictions: EBEC retains the right to limit the amount of footage selected from a particular film. Licensee shall provide screen credit where appropriate for any EBEC film.

Viewing Facilities: None.

Duplication Facilities: None.

Related Materials: Filmstrips, computer software, books, training and development materials.

ILLINOIS (Chicago)

THE CENTER FOR NEW TELEVISION
912 South Wabash Avenue
Chicago, IL 60605
(312) 427-5446

Joyce Bollinger (Executive Director)

Contact: Madonna Gauding (Program Director)
Services: Nonprofit media arts organization. Videotape collection available for in-house viewing only.
Description: Facility was founded (ca. 1978) to give artists and independent producers access to editing and production facilities. It offers technical production and post-production workshops; cosponsors the "Women in the Director's Chair" annual festival; has an ongoing video exhibitions program; and sponsors regional fellowships for the National Endowment for the Arts.

The collection has been built over the years through the donations of videotapes from visiting artists, and includes performance, documentary, experimental, comedy and installation works (1978-88). It is especially strong in works by Chicago artists and nationally known video artists.
Size & Elements: Videotape: 3/4" and 1/2" (550 titles).
Cataloging: Card catalog; computerized cataloging for staff use only.
Access: Available to the public. For in-house use only.
Rights: No rights held to any material. All rights retained by original producers.
Licensing: Not available for licensing or reuse.
Restrictions: Videotapes restricted to in-house viewing only. Not available for distribution, reuse or exhibition.
Viewing Facilities: Videotape.
Duplication Facilities: None.
Publications: *SCAN*, a quarterly membership newsletter published by the Center, reporting information relating to independent video producers.

ILLINOIS (Chicago)

CHICAGO ACCESS CORPORATION
322 South Green Street
Chicago, IL 60607
(312) 738-1400

Sherry Goodman (President)

Contact: Barbara Popovic (Program Director)
Services: Public access television facility. Videotapes available for reuse in some cases, subject to restrictions.
Description: Videotapes produced by individuals and nonprofit organizations in Chicago. Topics include issues of concern to a particular population segment (e.g., the elderly, women or veterans) and entertainment programming.

Series exist on the following topics: labor (*Labor Beat*); peace efforts (*Freeze Frame*); veterans' issues (*Veterans' Forum*); Muslims (*Sadaga*); teenagers (*Hard Cover* and *Putting Your Life Together*); motorsports (*Motorsports Unlimited*); local and national authors (*Book Break*); baseball (*The Baseball Show*); drugs and alcohol (*Chemically Independent*); entertainment (*L Stop* and *Gordon Lake Presents*); and the elderly (*Seniors Network*).
Size & Elements: Videotape: 3/4" (748 videotapes; 220 60 min., 440 30 min., 88 20 min.).
Cataloging: Card catalog.
Access: Not open to the public.
Rights: Some rights held to some material. Producers retain rights to most programs.
Licensing: Apply for information.
Restrictions: Clearances must be obtained from producers if material is to be reused or duplicated.
Viewing Facilities: Videotape.
Duplication Facilities: Videotape (duplication fees charged).

ILLINOIS (Chicago)

CHICAGO A/V, INC.
215 West Ohio Street, 6th Floor
Chicago, IL 60610
(312) 645-8309
Fax: (312) 645-9462

Jan Silver (President)

Contact: Vicky Mann (Director of Client Operations)
Services: Videotape studio; editing facility; stock footage sales library.
Description: Chicago footage (1983-present). Holds year-round coverage of the city, historical landmarks and cover shots.
Size & Elements: Videotape: 1" and 3/4" (approx. 20 hours; masters and viewing copies).
Cataloging: Computerized cataloging available for staff use only.
Access: Available for duplication. Research fees charged. Research requests accepted by mail, telephone and in person (by appointment only).
Rights: Full rights held to all material.
Licensing: Available for licensing. License fees charged (rate sheet available).
Restrictions: None specified.
Viewing Facilities: Videotape (3/4").
Duplication Facilities: Videotape.

ILLINOIS (Chicago)

CHICAGO COMMITTEE TO DEFEND THE BILL OF RIGHTS
220 South State Street, Suite 1400
Chicago, IL 60604
(312) 939-0675

Rachel Rosen DeGolia (Director)

Contact: Rachel Rosen DeGolia
Services: Grassroots advocacy and educational organization. Films and videotapes available for research and free loan, subject to restrictions.
Description: *The Intelligence Network* reveals the extent of political surveillance by more than 100 government agencies in the United States and abroad, including: J. Edgar Hoover's "vendetta" against Martin Luther King, Jr.; the infiltration of the Methodist Church; the Chicago police attack on Fred

Hampton; the CIA's role in Chile and around the world; the infiltration of the American Indian Movement; surveillance of nuclear power opponents; the Law Enforcement Intelligence Unit (LEIU); a lengthy interview with an FBI informant, an account of the assassination of Orlando Letelier; and statements by political activists who have been wiretapped, spied on, monitored and physically attacked.

Also holds *Surveillance, Who's Watching* (1971), produced for public television; and *Operation Abolition,* produced by the House Un-American Activities Committee (mid-1960s).

Size & Elements: Film: 16mm. Videotape: format unspecified. (3 titles total).
Access: Available to the public for free loan. Requests accepted by mail, telephone and in person (by appointment only).
Rights: Some rights held to some material.
Licensing: Apply for information.
Restrictions: None specified.
Viewing Facilities: None.
Duplication Facilities: None.

ILLINOIS (Chicago)

CHICAGO HISTORICAL SOCIETY
PRINTS AND PHOTOGRAPHS COLLECTION
Clark Street at North Avenue
Chicago, IL 60614-6099
(312) 642-4600

Larry A. Viskochil (Curator of Prints and Photographs)

Contact: Linda Ziemer (Assistant Curator of Prints and Photographs)
Services: Historical society. Collection of film and television material available for research, duplication and reuse, subject to restrictions. *As Society is presently relocating its facilities and cataloging of moving image materials is in progress, casual inquiries are discouraged at present.*
Description: *WGN-TV newsfilm* (1948-77, 9,400 reels). News footage from the Chicago independent television station. An arrangement is being made with WTTW-TV, Chicago's public television station, to clean, catalog, and transfer the WGN-TV collection to videotape.

Burr Tillstrom Collection. 750 reels of kinescopes (each 30 min.) of the Chicago-produced television series *Kukla, Fran and Ollie* (1949-57), from the collection of its creator.

Documentary film, home movies, and industrial films relating to Chicago and Illinois history (530 reels).
Size & Elements: Film: 16mm (12,000 cans; positive originals). Videotape: format unspecified (masters and viewing copies).
Cataloging: Card catalogs; other finding aids. Cataloging of moving image materials in progress.
Access: Available to the public. Although collection is maintained primarily for research use, it is available for duplication, subject to restrictions.
Rights: Full rights held to some material. Some rights held to all material.
Licensing: Available for licensing and reuse, subject to restrictions. License and usage fees charged.
Restrictions: Restrictions apply to licensing and reuse (apply for information). Additional clearances may be necessary for reuse of WGN-TV newsfilm.
Viewing Facilities: Film (16mm Cinescan); videotape (3/4" and VHS).
Duplication Facilities: None.
Related Materials: Burr Tillstrom Collection includes all the puppets, stage sets and props, cue cards, music, audiotapes, and photographs from the *Kukla, Fran and Ollie* television series.

ILLINOIS (Chicago)

CHICAGO PUBLIC LIBRARY
VISUAL & PERFORMING ARTS
78 East Washington
Chicago, IL 60602
(312) 269-2858 (Art Information Center)
(312) 269-2886 (Music Information Center)

Contacts: Yvonne Brown (Head, Art Information Center); Richard Schwegal (Head, Music Information Center); Rosalinda Hack (Head, Visual & Performing Arts)
Services: Library. Videotape collection open to researchers and scholars for in-house use only.
Description: Special collections at the Chicago Public Library include:
Dance Video Collection. The Art Information Center maintains a collection of 130 dance videotapes with a particular emphasis on the work of Chicago dancers and choreographers, including Carol Bobrow, Jan Erkert, Jackie Radis, Gus Giordano and Ruth Page. Collection documents dance history, style and techniques ranging from classical ballet to modern, jazz, tap and ethnic dance. Dance companies and choreographers include Jan Bartoszek, Chicago Dance Medium (Fred Devore), Chicago Moving Company (Nana Solbrig), Chicago Repertory Dance Ensemble (Tara Mitton), Concert Dance (Venetia Chakos Stifler), Dancycle, Isadora Guggenheim, Julian Swain Dance Theater, Maggie Kast, Jill Kellner, Marvin Kravitz, Kate Kuper, Lynda Martha Dance Company, Moksha Dance (Pat Fischer Selby), Judith Ragir and Lin Shook.

Chicago Blues Archives. The Music Information Center maintains an archives that holds videotapes, photographs and documentary materials, in addition to many recordings charting the history of the art that makes Chicago its home. Titles include: *Blues at the Cultural Center; Blues on Chicago's South Side; Soundstage #101, Blues Summit* (WTTW/Chicago); *Soundstage #309, B. B. King* (WTTW/Chicago); and *Sweet Home Chicago* (WLS/Chicago).
Size & Elements: Videotape: 3/4" (89 titles); VHS (378 titles).
Cataloging: Finding aids (staff-generated lists).
Access: Open to researchers and scholars only. For in-house use only. Research fees not charged. Research requests accepted in person (walk-in and by appointment).
Rights: Apply for information.
Licensing: Most material not available for reuse (apply for information). Usage fees not charged.
Restrictions: Collection available for in-house use only. Most material not available for reuse.
Viewing Facilities: Videotape (3/4", VHS and Betamax).
Duplication Facilities: None.
Related Materials: Sound recordings, photographs and documentary material in the Chicago Blues Archives.

ILLINOIS (Chicago)

CHICAGO VIDEO TRANSFER
230 North Michigan Avenue, Suite 1518
Chicago, IL 60601
(312) 236-2600

Brian Bundesen (President)

Contact: Brian Bundesen
Services: Videotape producer; duplication, editing and film transfers available. Material available for licensing.
Description: Footage of Chicago, including aerials, architecture, the Board of Trade, buildings, businesses, the lakefront, manufacturing, parks, people, recreation (e.g., biking, running and tennis) and sculptures.
Size & Elements: Videotape: 3/4" (14 hours; masters) and VHS (viewing copies).
Cataloging: General subject listing available. Computerized cataloging in progress; will be available to researchers for a fee.
Access: Available to the public for duplication, licensing and reuse. Research fees generally not charged for material that is listed in their general subjects list; fees charged for special requests. Duplication fees also charged. Research requests accepted by mail, telephone and in person (by appointment only).
Rights: Full rights held to all material.
Licensing: Available for licensing, subject to restrictions. License fees charged.
Restrictions: Some restrictions may apply, depending on footage requested.
Viewing Facilities: Videotape (VHS).
Duplication Facilities: Film (16mm to 3/4", VHS and Betamax videotape). Fees apply.

ILLINOIS (Chicago)

CINE-MARK
(Division of Krebs Productions, Inc.)
10 East Ontario Street, Suite 1303
Chicago, IL 60611
(312) 337-3303

Clyde L. Krebs (President)

Contact: Clyde L. Krebs
Services: Film and videotape producer; stock footage sales library.
Description: Promotional films and videotapes produced for many large corporate clients, including films relating to the history of Arizona; attractions of the city of Chicago; tourism in Florida, Arizona, New Mexico and Texas; scenics of the Grand Canyon; and "off-the-mainstream" vacation areas of the United States. *Discover America* (1967), filmed entirely from a helicopter in *Aeroscope* — "a revolutionary new 'floating camera' process" — follows a 22,000 mile route from Boston to Honolulu, with an original musical score developed from the works of Igor Stravinsky and recorded by a 65-piece orchestra and the Mormon Tabernacle Choir.
Size & Elements: Apply for information.
Cataloging: None specified.
Access: Available for licensing and reuse. Research fees not charged. Research requests accepted by mail, telephone and in person (by appointment only).
Rights: Full rights held to some material. Some rights held to all material.
Licensing: Available for licensing and reuse. License fees charged.
Restrictions: None specified.
Viewing Facilities: Film (16mm); videotape (VHS).
Duplication Facilities: None.

ILLINOIS (Chicago)

CINEMA MEDICA
6652 North Western Avenue
Chicago, IL 60645
(312) 973-2297
(800) 621-5147

Services: Film and videotape producer. Materials available for rental and purchase.
Description: Childbirth, prenatal nutrition, infant feeding, family planning and social issues in family health care. Titles include: *Midwife,* a documentary about midwives and home births; *The First Days of Life,* where, through fiberoptic photography, the viewer is transported inside the womb to see life develop, from conception to natural childbirth; *Nutrition in Pregnancy; Breastfeeding: For the Joy of It; Caesarean Childbirth; Birth Centers; Children at Birth; Primum Non Nocere ("above all do no harm"); Alternative Childbirth; Pregnancy in Motion; Obstetrical Intervention; Natural Family Planning; Injections,* on insulin; and *Abortion — A Woman's Decision.*

Important titles include: *The Fight for Life* (U.S. Office of Education, 1940), concerning the Chicago Maternity Center. The film presents a bitter indictment of slum conditions and pleads for better and safer obstetrical care. *Bottle Babies* criticizes multinational corporations who aggressively promote infant formulas in Third World nations.
Size & Elements: Film: 16mm and Super 8mm. Videotape: 3/4", VHS, Betamax I and II. (Approx. 25 titles total).
Cataloging: Published catalogs.
Access: Available to the public for rental and purchase. Orders accepted by mail. Videotape previews available.
Rights: Rights retained by Cinema Medica or filmmakers.
Licensing: Apply for information.
Restrictions: Materials are copyrighted and may not be duplicated, reproduced (by videotape or any other means), televised or transmitted, in whole or in part, without specific written authorization from Cinema Medica.
Viewing Facilities: None.
Duplication Facilities: None.

ILLINOIS (Chicago)

COMMITTEE FOR LABOR ACCESS
P.O. Box 477178
Chicago, IL 60647
(312) 226-3330

Contacts: Larry Duncan; Virginia Keller
Services: Cable television producer; videotape distributor. Completed programs available for distribution; footage available for duplication and reuse on a case-by-case basis.
Description: Documentaries (approx. 30 programs, each 30 min.) relating to labor issues and events in the Chicago area, and to national and international issues.

Labor-related programs cover such issues as: union organizing; organizing clerical workers; strikes; flight attendants; United Farm Workers (UFW); National Association of Broadcast and Electronic Technicians (NABET); a union of the homeless; rank-and-file movements within unions; labor movements in Central America and South Africa; *The Road to Haymarket,* a documentary and dramatic reenactment of the Haymarket affair (1886); and the strike at Iowa Beef Packers. Other programs cover Vietnam veterans; the Strategic Defense Initiative ("Star Wars"); and a referendum on whether the National Guard should be sent to Honduras.

Stock footage covers the same areas as completed programs, but available footage is generally limited to Chicago-area subjects.
Size & Elements: Videotape: 3/4" (30 programs, each 30 min., 90 hours of stock footage; masters and viewing copies); 1/2" (viewing copies).
Cataloging: Published catalog of programs for distribution. Staff assistance required for access to stock footage.
Access: Completed programs available for public distribution. Footage available for duplication and reuse on a case-by-case basis. Research fees charged in some cases. Research requests accepted by mail.
Rights: Full rights held to some material. Some rights held to other material. Additional clearances may be necessary in some cases if material is to be reused.
Licensing: Available for licensing and reuse, subject to restrictions.
Restrictions: Restrictions apply to some material; requests for licensing and reuse considered on a case-by-case basis.
Viewing Facilities: Videotape (3/4" and 1/2").
Duplication Facilities: Videotape (3/4" and 1/2").

ILLINOIS (Chicago)

CULT AWARENESS NETWORK
National Office
2421 West Pratt Boulevard, Suite 1173
Chicago, IL 60645
(312) 267-7777

Cynthia S. Kisser (Executive Director)

Contact: Cynthia S. Kisser
Services: Nonprofit educational organization. Videotape collection available to researchers and scholars only.
Description: National nonprofit educational organization dedicated to promoting public awareness of the harmful effects of mind control. Collection includes videotapes on aspects of destructive cults, videotape copies of newscasts, documentaries and conference speeches.
Size & Elements: Videotape: format unspecified (60 videotapes).
Cataloging: None specified.
Access: Not open to the public. Open to researchers and scholars only. Research fees not charged. Research requests accepted by telephone.
Rights: Some rights held to some material.
Licensing: Apply for information.
Restrictions: Apply for information.
Viewing Facilities: None.
Duplication Facilities: None.

ILLINOIS (Chicago)

DARTNELL
4660 Ravenswood Avenue
Chicago, Illinois 60640-4595
(312) 561-4000
(800) 621-5463
(800) 441-7878 (for Canadian customers)
Fax: (312) 561-3801

Contact: Chuck Pearl (Sales Manager of Films)
Services: Film and videotape producer and distributor. Material available for preview, rental and purchase.
Description: Business training films and videotapes on salesmanship, supervisory, foreman and employee development.
    Sales training. Titles include: *Keep Climbing*, giving a new outlook to the age-old selling problem of complacency; *Dealing with Price Resistance*, to help all salespeople overcome the biggest obstacle in selling — objection to price; *How to Close the Sale*, instruction on how to be positive and close early and often; and *When You're Turned Down — Turn On*.
    Sales management. Titles include: *Managing Salesmen;* and *Training Salesmen On the Job*.
    Sales motivation. Titles include: *Second Effort*, starring Vince Lombardi as a living demonstration of the principles and ideas that inspire victory and winning attitudes; and *Put It All Together*, revealing how three famous people created success for themselves with a similar basic formula.
    Personal training and advancement. A series of more than 20 programs produced by Video Education Network (VEN) with some of the most distinguished educators in business and industry teaching advanced management, negotiating and leadership.
    Supervisory training and motivation. Titles include: *The Troubled Employee; Firm...But Fair;* and *Take Charge of Your Life*.
    Health Care and Safety. Titles include: *Crossroads: A Nurse's Story*, the frustrations and satisfactions of being a dedicated nurse; and *Who Cares?*, helping hospital employees look at their jobs through the eyes and ears of the patient.
Size & Elements: Film: 16mm. Videotape: 3/4", VHS and Betamax. (Approx. 70 titles total).
Cataloging: Published catalog.
Access: Available for preview, rental and purchase. Requests accepted by mail and telephone.
Rights: Full rights held to all material in programs produced by Dartnell. Rights to other programs held by original producers.
Licensing: Available for licensing and reuse, subject to restrictions.
Restrictions: Available for licensing and reuse on a case-by-case basis, subject to approval, clearance and authorization from Dartnell. All material fully protected by copyright laws and may not be copied, recast, duplicated or transformed in any manner without prior consent of the copyright owner. Films are not licensed for television broadcast or any other exhibition in which a charge is made without prior consent of the copyright holder.
Viewing Facilities: Film (16mm); videotape.
Duplication Facilities: None.
Related Materials: Meeting leader guides available for selected titles.

ILLINOIS (Chicago)

DEPARTURES, INC.
142 East Ontario

Chicago, IL 60611
(312) 337-6700
Fax: (312) 337-0500

David Prescott (Chief Executive Officer)

Contact: Brian Peters
Services: Videotape producer and distributor; videotape stock footage sales library. Research and custom shooting services available.
Description: Specializes in production, distribution and marketing of videotape programs for the travel and hospitality industries. Holds contemporary videotape footage, including U.S. cities (Chicago, New Orleans, Nashville, Las Vegas and Honolulu); extensive footage of Canada (Vancouver, Calgary, Toronto, Montréal, Ottawa and the Canadian Rockies [winter and summer]); Hawaii; Italy; Austria; and Jamaica. Crews available for custom shooting assignments.
Size & Elements: Videotape: 1", Betacam and 3/4" (amount unspecified).
Cataloging: Time code listings.
Access: Available for duplication, licensing and reuse.
Rights: Full rights held to all material.
Licensing: Available for licensing and reuse.
Restrictions: None specified.
Viewing Facilities: Videotape.
Duplication Facilities: Videotape.

ILLINOIS (Chicago)

**EVANGELICAL COVENANT CHURCH OF AMERICA
COVENANT ARCHIVES AND HISTORICAL LIBRARY/
SWEDISH AMERICAN ARCHIVES OF GREATER CHICAGO**
3225 West Foster
Chicago, IL 60625
(312) 583-2700 (Ext. 5267)
Fax: (312) 267-2362

Timothy J. Johnson (Director of Archives)

Contact: Timothy J. Johnson
Services: Church archives. Films and videotapes available for research and in-house use only; available for reuse, subject to restrictions.
Description: History of the Evangelical Covenant Church of America; history of Swedish immigrants in Chicago.
Size & Elements: Film: 16mm (positives). Videotape: VHS (viewing copies). (19 titles total).
Cataloging: Card catalogs.
Access: Available to the public. For in-house use only. Research fees generally not charged. Research requests accepted by mail, telephone and in person.
Rights: Full rights held to some material. Rights status of some material not known. Additional clearances may be necessary in some cases if material is to be reused.
Licensing: Available for licensing and reuse, subject to restrictions. License fees charged in some cases.
Restrictions: Restrictions may apply to some material. Requests for licensing or reuse considered on a case-by-case basis.
Viewing Facilities: Film (16mm); videotape (VHS) (in college library).
Duplication Facilities: Videotape (VHS).

ILLINOIS (Chicago)

**EVANGELICAL LUTHERAN CHURCH IN AMERICA
MEDIA SERVICES CENTER**
8765 West Higgins Road
Chicago, IL 60631
(312) 380-2700

Contact: Lowell Almen (Secretary)
Services: Church archives. Consolidation of film and videotape collection is currently in progress. Apply for information regarding access.
Description: Films and videotapes produced by all Lutheran churches in the U.S. except those affiliated with the Missouri Synod. Holds all material produced by The American Lutheran Church (1960-87), the Lutheran Church in America (1962-87), and their respective antecedents. Archival materials cover Lutheran World Action work (1948-present) and films produced by Lutheran Film Associates during the same period. Since the church administration (as well as the archives) has recently reorganized, consolidation

of the collection is currently in progress. Inquiries for further information are welcome.
Size & Elements: When complete, the collection will consist primarily of 16mm film (approx. 800 to 900 cans).
Cataloging: Card catalogs.
Access: Apply for information.
Rights: Apply for information.
Licensing: Apply for information.
Restrictions: Apply for information.
Viewing Facilities: None.
Duplication Facilities: None.

ILLINOIS (Chicago)

FACETS MULTIMEDIA, INC.
1517 West Fullerton Avenue
Chicago, IL 60614
(312) 281-9075
(800) 331-6197
Fax: (312) 929-5437
Telex: 20-6701

Milos Stehlik (Co-Director)
Nicole Dreiske (Co-Director)

Contact: Milos Stehlik (Video Sales)
Services: Nonprofit media organization; videotape distributor. Videotapes available for rental and purchase.
Description: Founded 1975, Facets is a unique, Chicago-based nonprofit arts membership organization. Facets distributes over 5,000 videotapes by film and videomakers from all over the world; presents daily screenings of foreign, independent American and classic films at Facets Multimedia Center and other locations; and presents the annual Chicago International Festival of Children's Films, which screens hundreds of new films for children.

Facets distributes the Amnesty Film and Human Rights Library, a collection of films and videotapes related to human rights issues. In cooperation with Hungaro-film, Facets also distributes the Hungarian Cinema touring program, a collection of sixteen recent Hungarian feature films. Through the Chicago Children's Film Distribution Network, Facets provides films particularly suited for minorities and young children to schools, day care centers and children's institutions at low cost.

Facets Multimedia Video Library distributes selections from international cinema, including works from Australia, Brazil, Canada, Czechoslovakia, Denmark, France, Germany, Great Britain, Greece, Holland, Hungary, India, Israel, Italy, Japan, Poland, the Soviet Union, Spain, Sweden, the United States, and Yugoslavia.

American independent films. Includes works by Kevin Rafferty, Pierce Rafferty and Jayne Loader, John Sayles, Susan Seidelman, Spike Lee, Jim Jarmusch, Charlie Ahearn, Peter Wang, Jill Godmilow, Alvin Goldstein, Woody Vasulka, Emile de Antonio, Danny Lyon and Les Blank.

Also available are documentary films; experimental film and video, including works by Nam June Paik, Bill Viola, Ant Farm, Carolee Schneemann, Brian Eno, Richard Foreman and Zbigniew Rybczynski; animation; cult films; comedy acts; musicals; television shows; science fiction; opera, theater, music, dance and art; language instruction; nature; travel; and children's films.
Size & Elements: Videotape: VHS and Betamax (5,500 titles total).
Cataloging: Published catalog.
Access: Available to the public for rental and purchase. Videotapes can be rented by mail. Requests accepted by mail, telephone and in person (walk-in).
Rights: Rights generally retained by original producers or distributors. Full rights held to some material. Some material in the public domain. Rights status of some material not known. Additional clearances may be necessary in some cases if material is to be reused.
Licensing: Available for rental and purchase.
Restrictions: None specified.
Viewing Facilities: None.
Duplication Facilities: None.
Publications: *Images at the Horizon: A Workshop with Werner Herzog; The Human Rights Film Guide; The Application of Theater Research to Life and Education; The Creation of the Book of Lear* and *Hispanic Children's Film: Towards a Viewer-Responsive Media.*

ILLINOIS (Chicago)

FILE TAPE COMPANY
210 East Pearson, Suite 14-C
Chicago, IL 60611
(800) 637-8273
(312) 649-0599 (Illinois only)

Susan Caraher (President)

Contact: Susan Caraher
Services: Videotape stock footage sales library. Research and custom shooting services available.
Description: Contemporary videotape footage, including U.S. cities (Chicago, New York City, St. Louis, and Washington, D.C.); Canada, Europe and the Soviet Union (cities, contemporary life, and culture); medicine; babies.

Can research and locate historical and contemporary footage of news events and topical subjects, including personalities, disasters and scenics. Crews available for custom shooting assignments.
Size & Elements: Videotape: Betacam and 3/4" (amount unspecified).
Cataloging: Finding aids; dope sheets; logs (staff use only).
Access: Available for duplication, licensing and reuse. Research services available. Research fees charged. Research requests accepted by mail and telephone.
Rights: Full rights held to all material.
Licensing: Available for licensing and reuse. License fees charged.
Restrictions: None specified.
Viewing Facilities: Videotape (off-premises).
Duplication Facilities: Videotape (outside facility).

ILLINOIS (Chicago)

FILMACK STUDIOS
1327 South Wabash Avenue
Chicago, IL 60605
(312) 427-3395
Fax: (312) 427-4866

Joseph R. Mack (President)

Contact: Joseph R. Mack
Services: Film, videotape and animation producer. Stock footage available for licensing and reuse.
Description: Begins 1930. Collection includes motion picture theater trailers, notably the famous *Let's Go To the Lobby* intermission trailer; the "clock" trailers, (15-second animated "countdowns" produced to be shown during intermissions at drive-in theatres); and an unnamed trailer admonishing teenagers to behave correctly during the show.

Has supplied vintage theater trailers to *Grease* and *It Came From Hollywood,* among other films.
Size & Elements: Film: 35mm (amount unspecified; color and black and white; negatives and prints). Some trailers have been transferred to videotape.
Cataloging: Card catalog.
Access: For in-house use only. Available for licensing and reuse. Research requests accepted by mail and telephone.
Rights: Full rights held to all material.
Licensing: Available for licensing and reuse. License fees charged depending on intended use (apply for information).
Restrictions: None specified.
Viewing Facilities: None.
Duplication Facilities: None.

ILLINOIS (Chicago)

FILMS INCORPORATED
5547 North Ravenswood Avenue
Chicago, IL 60640-1199
(800) 323-4222

For rental inquiries in the Central, Southern, Western U.S. and Alaska:
(800) 323-4222
(312) 878-2600 (Ext. 43) (Illinois only)

For rental inquiries in the Northeast:
35 South West Street
Mount Vernon, NY 10550
(800) 223-6246
(914) 667-0800 (New York State only)

Services: Distributor of entertainment, educational and training films and videotapes. Available for rental (and purchase, in some cases); *not available for duplication, licensing or reuse.*
Description: The world's largest distributor of 16mm films; distributes films and videotapes through several divisions.

Entertainment Division. Represents about half of the major Hollywood studios and many foreign and independent distributors for non-theatrical 16mm film distribution in the U.S. Theatrical distributors represented include: Paramount, MGM/United Artists, Twentieth Century-Fox, Orion, Tri-Star Pictures, Walt Disney Productions, Touchstone Films, Cineplex Odeon, Warner Bros., Columbia, RKO, New Horizons, ABC, Atlantic Releasing, David L. Wolper, BBC, Pathe Cinema, Universal, Toho Company Ltd., Miramax, American Film Theater, Selznick, Republic, New Line Cinema and others.

At present, represents over 5,000 feature films and short subjects (for each there is at least one projectable print). It is the primary U.S. rental source for historical and classic motion pictures, and in many instances the best source of viewing prints for research and reference purposes.

Films Incorporated *rents* prints and *cannot grant rights of any kind* to prospective users, including the right to duplicate, copy, excerpt or reuse the films, nor can it grant permission for their "background" use in other films or television programs. It can only act to refer inquiries to the copyright holder.

Training films and videotapes. Distributes and sells films and videotapes in a variety of subject areas, including quality and customer service, sales training, retail training, quality and productivity, meeting openers and closers, management training and leadership, equal opportunity, motivation and communication, creativity, personal computer training, foreign language training and continuing education.

Educational films and videotapes. Wide range of subject matter.

Home Vision Collection. Art, music, opera, dance and literature programs offered *for purchase only.* Public performance rights are available for most titles.
Size & Elements: Film: 35mm and 16mm. Videotape: 3/4", VHS and Betamax. Most films available primarily in 16mm.
Cataloging: Published catalogs (available on request).
Access: Maintained for rental and purchase rather than research or reuse. Rental fees charged. Rental requests accepted by mail and telephone.
Rights: No rights, other than non-theatrical distribution rights, held to any material.
Licensing: Not available for licensing or reuse. Can refer prospective users to copyright holders.
Restrictions: "Use of these films is limited to direct projection devices in the immediate presence of viewers. Any duplication, transmission, or television broadcast whether open or closed circuit, pay, or community television, or by means of any and all devices or systems now in existence or hereafter invented or discovered is strictly prohibited without written permission. Any violation of the copyright laws may subject the infringer to both civil and criminal damages."
Viewing Facilities: None.
Duplication Facilities: None.

ILLINOIS (Chicago)

GOETHE INSTITUTE CHICAGO
GERMAN CULTURAL CENTER, LIBRARY
401 North Michigan Avenue
Chicago, IL 60611
(312) 329-0915
Fax: (312) 329-2487

Dr. Walter Breuer (Director)

Contacts: Angela Greiner; Elisabeth Angele
Services: Library and educational institution. Videotapes available primarily for loan to library members; some videotapes produced by the Institute may be copied for non-commercial reuse.
Description: Videotapes relating to German history, society, politics, art, architecture, film and theater. Collection is strong in the area of art and artists, including "portraits" of Gropius, Beuys, Beckmann, Köllwitz and Moholy-Nagy. The feature films available include a few "classics" as well as films by Werner Herzog and Rainer Werner Fassbinder. Also available are German language instruction videotapes.
Size & Elements: Videotape: 3/4" and VHS (280 titles; NTSC and PAL).
Cataloging: Published catalogs (available on request).
Access: Open to the public. Research fees not charged. Requests accepted by mail, telephone and in person. Videotapes may be borrowed for two weeks or viewed at the Institute during library hours.
Rights: Full rights held to some material.
Licensing: Apply for information. License fees not charged for Institute-produced videotapes.
Restrictions: Copyright restrictions apply to materials not produced by the Institute. Some videotapes are for in-house use only.
Viewing Facilities: Videotape (multistandard videotape recorders).
Duplication Facilities: None.

ILLINOIS (Chicago)

ILLINOIS LABOR HISTORY SOCIETY
28 East Jackson, Suite 1012
Chicago, IL 60604
(312) 663-4107

Contact: Mr. Leslie Orear
Services: Voluntary nonprofit educational organization. Two titles available for rental and purchase.
Description: "The intent of the ILHS is to promote the study and appreciation of the profound contribution made by working people to the improvement of life and liberty in a democratic society."

Titles available: *Palace Cars & Paradise: Pullman's Model Town* (produced by Martin Buechley) is about the 19th century experiment in corporate paternalism that erupted in the famous Pullman Strike (1894); and *Memorial Day Massacre of 1937,* with the uncut, unedited newsreel film of the tragic event, supplemented with commentary and brief introduction.
Size & Elements: Film: gauge unspecified. Videotape: 3/4" and 1/2" (2 titles total).
Cataloging: Published brochure.
Access: Available to the public for rental and purchase (apply for rates). Requests accepted by mail and telephone.
Rights: Apply for information.
Licensing: Apply for information.
Restrictions: None specified.
Viewing Facilities: None.
Duplication Facilities: None.

ILLINOIS (Chicago)

THE IMAGE BANK, CHICAGO
510 North Dearborn Street, Suite 930
Chicago, IL 60610
(312) 329-1817
Fax: (312) 329-1029

Contacts: Claudette Mostyn; Jim Mostyn; Michael Jungert (Manager)
Territory: Illinois, Indiana, Iowa, Kansas, Michigan, Missouri, Nebraska and Wisconsin.
Services: Exclusive marketing agent for Film Search, Inc. (q.v.).

ILLINOIS (Chicago)

INSTITUTE FOR PSYCHOANALYSIS
GITELSON FILM LIBRARY
180 North Michigan Avenue
Chicago, IL 60601
(312) 726-6300

Henry Seidenberg (Director)

Contact: Glenn Miller (Librarian)
Services: Library. Films and videotapes available for distribution to academic and professional audiences; some material possibly available for licensing and reuse.
Description: Psychoanalysis, psychiatry, psychology and mental health.
Topics include:

Animal behavior. Sifaka in arid forests of southern Madagascar; behavior and ecology of free-ranging vervet monkeys in Masai-Amboseli Game Reserve of Kenya; sound signals used by chimpanzees in Tanzania's Bombe National Park.

Freud. Freud's theories are analyzed in *Freud: The Hidden Nature of Man; Freud: Office and Home, Vienna, 1938,* narrated by Eli Wallach, surveys Freud's Viennese quarters; and *The Rat Man,* based on Freud's case study of a case of obsessional neurosis.

Infants and children. Subjects and titles include: the life history and emotional problems of a child reared in a neurotic environment; the behavior of regressed psychotic children; *Birth and the First Fifteen Minutes of Life,* showing the birth of a baby and reactions to stimuli up to its first feeding; autistic children; clinical aspects of childhood psychosis; perceptual stimuli response in eight infants; mother-infant interaction; the genesis of emotion; children and hospitalization; grasping patterns; infant grief; the effects of prolonged absence of mother; *Growing Up Without Sight,* made in collaboration with Anna Freud, examining blind children; handicapped infants; young children during short stays in foster care; maternal deprivation in young children; the therapeutic benefits of patterned movement; *Mother-Infant Interaction,* a series of six films covering interaction at six weeks, six months and one year; nursery school child-mother interaction; the nature-nurture controversy; *Piaget's Developmental Theory,* five films relating to classification, conservation, formal thought, growth, memory and intelligence.

Where is Dead? depicts a close relationship between a young brother and sister and how the sister copes with her brother's death in a car accident; *Natural History of Psychotic Illness in Childhood* shows the gradual unfolding of the psychotic process in childhood, aided by an extremely complete family photograph album, home movies and a detailed and objective diary by the mother; childhood in Israel; a nursery school for blind children; sensorimotor development, causality, object permanence and spatial relationships; the smiling response; oral behavior in small infants.

Interviews. Abraham Maslow; B. F. Skinner; Dr. Rene Spitz, describing his analysis with Sigmund Freud; Carl G. Jung; Dr. Rudolf Ekstein; Erik Erikson (1966); Dr. Ernest R. Hilgard; Ernest Jones; Dr. Gardner Murphy; Dr. Merton Gill; Dr. Gordon Allport; Dr. Henry Murray; a four-part interview with Konrad Lorenz covering his research into animal behavior, ethology and imprinting, motivation and aggression, his reactions to his colleagues and reflections; Jean Piaget and Barbel Inhelder; *Psychology and Arthur Miller,* in which the playwright discusses the concept of motivation and reaction to psychoanalysis of an author through his works; Raymond Cattell; Dr. John Spiegel; Therese Benedek; Edwin Eisler; Helen McLean; Fritz Moellenhoff; Helen Ross and Louis B. Shapiro.

Additional topics. Character disorders; holiday depression; depressive states; socialization of the American woman; the psychoanalyst; psychotoxic diseases; psychology of creativity; *Everybody Rides the Carousel,* illustrating Erikson's personality development theory; *Mental Symptom Series,* a nine-part series covering depressive states, folie à deux or induced insanity, manic state, organic mental disorders, senile psychosis, paranoid conditions, catatonic, hebephrenic and chronic simple schizophrenia. In *To Die Today* Dr. Elizabeth Kubler-Ross interviews a 30-year old with Hodgkins' disease and life expectancy of no more than five years; in *Tolstoy Remembers,* Alexandria Tolstoy, age 86, reminisces about her famous father; *Secrets of the Soul,* directed by G. W. Pabst from Samuel Goldwyn's 1925 screenplay, deals with an obsessive-compulsive disorder, for which Goldwyn sought Freud's professional advice.

Size & Elements: Film: 16mm (100 titles). Videotape: format unspecified (200 titles).
Cataloging: Computerized cataloging available to researchers.
Access: Available for rental to academic institutions and mental health facilities. Telephone requests must be confirmed in writing on institution letterhead.
Rights: Full rights held to some material. Some rights held to some material.
Licensing: Apply for information. License fees charged.
Restrictions: None specified.
Viewing Facilities: Film and videotape.
Duplication Facilities: None.

ILLINOIS (Chicago)

INSTITUTE OF FINANCIAL EDUCATION
111 East Wacker Drive
Chicago, IL 60601
(312) 644-3100
Fax: (312) 938-2541

Dale C. Bottom (President)

Contact: Mary Gail Bennett (Manager of Training Services)
Services: Vocational training institution. Videotape programs available for purchase.
Description: Savings and loan industry training programs on videotape include: *Sales Skills for Financial Professionals; Teller Compliance and the*

Bank Secrecy Act; A Banker's Guide to Self-Defense; Exempting Transactions under the Bank Secrecy Act; Today's Professional Teller; Handling Money; Checking Deposits and Savings Transactions; Making the Check-Cashing Decision; Other Negotiable Instruments and Miscellaneous Transactions; Balancing Out; Forgery and Signature Verification; Detecting Counterfeits; Fraud; Building Savings Institution Business; You Make It Happen: An Overview of the Savings Institutions Business; and *Secrets of Career Success.*
Size & Elements: Videotape: format unspecified (16 titles).
Cataloging: Published catalog.
Access: Available to the public for purchase.
Rights: Full rights held to some material. Some rights held to all material. Some rights held to some material.
Licensing: Videotapes available primarily for purchase.
Restrictions: None specified.
Viewing Facilities: None.
Duplication Facilities: None.
Related Materials: Full training programs corresponding to videotapes including instructor's guides, manuals and workbooks.

ILLINOIS (Chicago)

INTERNATIONAL FILM BUREAU INC.
332 South Michigan Avenue
Chicago, IL 60604-4382
(312) 427-4545

Contact: Ben Hodge
Services: Distributor. Films and videotapes available to the public for rental and purchase. Material possibly available for reuse, subject to copyright clearance.
Description: Educational film and videotape distributor representing over 100 international producers.

Areas covered: stories for young people and all ages; cultural travelogues; history; social sciences; history and geography of Europe; tools and technologies in Europe and America; the Americas; Asia; ancient Egypt, Greece and Rome; archaeology; anthropology; ecology; environmental studies; American, English and Irish literature; Latin, Italian, Spanish, Portuguese, French, German and Russian language study; mathematics; algebra; geometry; topology; the sciences; animal life; human physiology; botany and horticulture; ecology; the environment; seasons; solar system; oceans; foundations and history of science; physics; chemistry; health; sex education; art history; artists; art theory and application; architecture; music; dance; filmmaking; recreation; safety; first aid; driver education; alphabet skills; teacher training; special education; career education; values clarification; business and office management. Animated films include work from Norman McLaren, Raoul Servais, the Zagreb School and the National Film Board of Canada.

Producers and other distributors represented include: ABC; Association for Educational Communications and Technology; Associated Electrical Industries; BBC; Commonwealth Scientific and Industrial Research Organization, Australia; Educational Foundation for Visual Aids; International Council for Educational Media; International Film Bureau; Mental Health Film Board; National Education Association; National Film Board of Canada; L'Office de Radiodiffusion-Télévision Français; State University of New York; and Visual Education Films.
Size & Elements: Film: 16mm. Videotape: various formats. (Over 800 titles total).
Cataloging: Published catalogs.
Access: Films available to the public for rental; films and videotapes available for purchase. Individual titles may be available for rental at no charge from local or state sources. Preview prints of films available to organizations who cannot accept new prints on approval. Requests accepted by mail and telephone.
Rights: Apply for information.
Licensing: Some materials possibly available for licensing and reuse. For clearance and fees for television use and duplication rights, apply for information.
Restrictions: Rental and purchase of IFB films and videotapes from any source does not include authorization for television use or duplication. Transmission by television or copying in any manner by any means is prohibited without prior written permission from International Film Bureau, Inc.
Viewing Facilities: None.
Duplication Facilities: None.
Distributors: For rental: Titles are available from many film rental libraries located throughout the United States.

For purchase: (In Canada): Marlin Motion Pictures, Ltd., 211 Watline

Ave., Suite 200, Mississauga, ON LAZ IP3; (416) 890-1500. (In the United Kingdom): Edward Patterson Associates Limited, Treetops–Cannongate Road, Hythe, Kent, England CT21 5PT; 0303-64195. (In Australia): Educational Media Australia, 7 Martin Street, South Melbourne, Vic., Australia 3205; 699-7144.

ILLINOIS (Chicago)

INTERNATIONAL HISTORIC FILMS, INC.
P.O. Box 29035
Chicago, IL 60629
(312) 436-0038
Telex: 4946408

Street address: 3015 West 59th Street

Peter Bernotas (Director)

Contact: Peter Bernotas
Services: Film and videotape distributor; stock footage sales library.
Description: Military, political and social history, especially documentary films. Special strengths include: German documentary and feature films from the Third Reich period; Russian, German, Eastern European and Allied newsreels and documentaries from World War II; original color footage of pre-World War II Eastern European cities; Vietnam-era films from North Vietnam, the Soviet Union and the United States; weapons and self-defense; aviation history; naval history; the Cold War and 1950s; Korean War; and classic Soviet feature films.
    Sample titles include: *Mussolini Visits Hitler* (Germany, 1937); *Der Marsch Zum Führer* (Germany, 1940); *Victory in the West* (Germany, 1940); the *Why We Fight Series* (U.S., 1942-45); *Franklin Delano Roosevelt: State of the Union Message, January 6th, 1942; Japanese Relocation* (1943); *Identification of the Japanese Zero* (1942, with Ronald Reagan); *Inside Russia* (USSR, 1941); *Kolberg* (Germany, 1945); *The Private Film Collection of Eva Braun* (1936-43); and *Marquette Park* (1975-78), on American Nazi demonstrations in the Chicago area.
Size & Elements: Film: 35mm (1,200,000 feet); and 16mm (600,000 feet). Videotape: 1" (70 videotapes; masters); 3/4" (1,000 videotapes; masters); VHS (viewing copies); Betamax II (viewing copies). All films are available in PAL standard.
Cataloging: Published catalog.
Access: Available for purchase, licensing and reuse. Research fees charged. Research requests accepted by telephone.
Rights: Full rights held to some material. Some rights held to all material. Some material is in public domain. Additional clearances may be necessary in some cases if material is to be reused.
Licensing: Available for licensing and reuse. License fees charged.
Restrictions: None specified.
Viewing Facilities: Videotape.
Duplication Facilities: Videotape (duplication services and standards conversion available though IHF Productions, 3533 S. Archer Ave., Chicago, IL 60609; 312/927-2900).

ILLINOIS (Chicago)

KARTEMQUIN FILMS
1901 West Wellington
Chicago, IL 60657
(312) 472-4366

Gordon Quinn (Producer); Jerry Blumenthal (Producer)

Contact: Stephanie Wertlake
Services: Film and videotape producer and distributor. Material available for research, licensing and reuse.
Description: Completed films, outtakes and unedited footage relating to the city of Chicago, labor issues, racism, urban affairs and women's issues.
    Civil rights and urban affairs. Unedited footage, especially concerned with civil rights activism (late 1960s-70s).
    Families. Now We Live On Clifton (1974) shows gentrification and the relocation of families caused by the building of a university campus in Chicago. *Winnie Wright, Age 11* (1974) portrays a young Chicago working-class girl. *Thumbs Down* (1968) pertains to the Vietnam War and its effect on families and includes antiwar discussions among members of a Catholic youth group.
    Racism. Racism in Chicago is the subject of *Trick Bag* (1975).
    Sociology. Maxwell Street (1964) is a cinema-verité account of Chicago's flea market. *Home for Life* (1967) follows an elderly man and woman during their first several months in a home for senior citizens. *Viva La Causa* (1974) documents Hispanic murals in Chicago.
    Students and education. The College (ca. 1968) documents life at the University of Chicago, showing the campus, students and classes. *Shulie* (1967) documents the experiences of a painting student at the School of the Art Institute of Chicago. *What the Fuck are These Red Squares?* (1970) discusses post-modernism and revolutionary art in the United States, with the participation of art students.
    Women's issues. Marco (1970) shows natural childbirth. *All of Us Stronger* (1975) is about women's self-defense training.
    Several Kartemquin films are currently available for distribution through New Day Films (q.v.). These titles include *Women's Voices: The Gender Gap Movie; The Last Pullman Car; Taylor Chain I: A Story of a Union Local; Taylor Chain II: A Story of Collective Bargaining;* and *The Chicago Maternity Center Story.*
Size & Elements: Film: 16mm (amount unspecified, various formats, originals and release prints). Videotape: various formats (amount unspecified; film-to-videotape transfers).
Cataloging: None specified.
Access: Open to researchers and scholars only. Available for licensing and reuse. Research fees charged in some cases. Research requests accepted by mail and telephone.
Rights: Full rights held to all material.
Licensing: Available for licensing and reuse. License fees charged (fees negotiable).
Restrictions: None specified.
Viewing Facilities: Film (16mm flatbed and projector); videotape (3/4" and 1/2").
Duplication Facilities: Videotape (3/4" and 1/2").

ILLINOIS (Chicago)

J. FRED MACDONALD, Ph.D.
MACDONALD & ASSOCIATES
2744 West Rascher Avenue
Chicago, IL 60625
(312) 878-4799

Contact: Dr. J. Fred MacDonald
Services: Private collection; film stock footage sales library.
Description: Collection contains television programs of historic interest (beginning June 1948); documentary and fiction films; and historic news footage from television and theatrical sources. Since this collection serves as a source for academic research and teaching, it contains materials of special interest to documentarians and nonfiction filmmakers in general. Approximately 60% of the collection's 2,600 titles are television programs or broadcast advertising; 40% are non-television.
    Major subject areas include: propaganda; television commercials; soap operas; political television commercials (especially from presidential campaigns); anti-communism and the Cold War; entertainment television; music on film; films concerning Blacks (both television shows and non-television footage); network news documentaries and newsreels; non-television newsreels; social movements of the 1960s; radio broadcasting; educational films produced for children and youth; "Golden Age" television dramas; and kinescopes. Many programs held are not available for research or viewing from any other source.
    Television news and documentaries. Sample programs include: *Vietnam Reports* (Armed Forces Radio and Television Service, 1967-68, three programs); *Teenage Revolution* (ABC-TV, 1965); *New York Illustrated: Oh, Woodstock!* (1969), on the Woodstock music festival; *Television Today* (CBS-TV, 1949); *This Is the BBC* (BBC, early 1960s); *LSD — The Trip to Where?* (WABC-TV, 1968); *The Young Set: Automobile Safety* (1965), a discussion with Ralph Nader the day after the publication of his book *Unsafe at Any Speed; What Everyone Should Know About Communism* (ca. 1964), hosted by Garry Moore; *Sex in the Sixties* (ABC, 1967), a documentary; *Television and the World* (BBC, 1961), on the stages of television development in Italy, Egypt, Thailand, Japan, the United States, Brazil, the Soviet Union, Poland, the United Kingdom and Nigeria; *Of Black America* (1968, five episodes), on Black history, Black soldiers, Blacks around the world, and the sentiments of Blacks and Whites; *Pull the House Down* (WCAU-TV, 1968), in which Harry and Stuart Reasoner discuss the "generation gap" and youth culture; *This Is Marshall McLuhan: The Medium Is the Message* (NBC, 1967); *The Meaning of*

Communism (Group W, ca. 1960s, in 6 parts); outtakes from Martin Luther King's march on Philadelphia, Miss. (July 1964); *Confidential File: The Business of Beauty* (1955), with Paul Coates; *Star Spangled Extremists* (mid-1960s), a lecture program on the radical right, with Alan Westin; *The Topeka Tornado Story* (WIBU-TV, 1966); *Your Senators Report,* featuring an interview with Leon Sullivan by Sen. Richard Schweiker; and nine episodes of *International Zone,* on the United Nations and its activities around the world.

1968 Democratic National Convention. Twelve reels of news outtakes from the street disturbances during the convention in Chicago.

John F. Kennedy Assassination Archive. Contains a television documentary produced in Dallas and news outtakes filmed during President Kennedy's fatal visit to Texas (November 22-26, 1963).

Independent television newsreels. Holds various daily and weekly stories from *Telenews* (1948-49); miscellaneous news footage (1950s-60s); United Press International newsfilm clips (1953-56); *The Texas News* (fall 1952-summer 1953), produced by WBAP-TV (Fort Worth), containing highlights of local news coverage, including footage of Dwight D. Eisenhower, Richard M. Nixon, Adlai Stevenson and Alben W. Barkley from the 1952 Presidential campaign; and nine episodes of *Texas in Review* (1953-54), a weekly summary of statewide Texas news.

Telenews Daily (March 1956 through early 1960, 16mm, 160 hours, approx. 640 newscasts, each 15 min.). Nearly complete set of syndicated television newsreels for this period, featuring coverage of all major national and international events. Although the programs are mostly silent and were intended to be accompanied by a reading of the day's news, there is sound-on-film coverage of speeches, press conferences, and other similar events.

Educational television documentaries. Approximately 24 programs (ca. 1957-65) produced by National Educational Television (NET) on such subjects as the political cartoons of editorial cartoonist Fitzpatrick; Sir Edmund Hillary; riverboats on the Mississippi; Kingsley Amis; modern Israel; Algeria; the history of printing; spiders; and Black history.

Political television advertising and programming. Items include: a kinescope of the network pool feed of the inauguration of President Harry S Truman (January 20, 1949); 33 political campaign spots from the 1952 Eisenhower campaign; *Campaigning With Stevenson* (1952), produced by the Democratic National Committee; *Year of Big Decision* (1954), produced to support the election of Republican candidates to the House and Senate; films from Texas gubernatorial candidates W. Lee O'Daniel and Price Daniel (1956); a five-minute campaign spot for Adlai Stevenson, featuring Dr. Benjamin Spock (1956); eight television spots from Lyndon B. Johnson's 1964 presidential campaign; and television spots from the 1968 presidential campaigns of Richard M. Nixon, George C. Wallace and Hubert H. Humphrey.

Network news and documentary programs. Holds over 250 programs, many now unavailable elsewhere. Sample programs include *Brink in Vietnam?* (ABC, August 6, 1964), on reactions during the first days after the Tonkin Gulf incident; *President Johnson and the Challenge* (ABC, December 1, 1963), on the implications of Lyndon B. Johnson's succession to the Presidency; *Big Brother Is Listening* (ABC, May 21, 1964), a prophetic report on electronic snooping on private citizens; *Howard K. Smith with News and Comment* (September 30, 1962), an analysis of U.S. relations with Cuba two weeks before the Cuban missile crisis; *ABC Scope: The Class of '65 — An American Dream* (June 13, 1965), probing campus discontent on issues ranging from overcrowding of universities to the Vietnam War, and featuring a performance by Phil Ochs; *ABC News Reports: World's Fair — Preview of Tomorrow* (May 2, 1964), on the New York World's Fair, with clips from earlier fairs; *Meet Comrade Student* (ABC, 1962), an analysis of the Soviet educational system in the wake of the Sputnik scare; *Walk in My Shoes* (ABC, 1961), one of the first important documentaries on civil rights problems; CBS News election night coverage (November 4, 1958), including a victory speech by Governor Nelson Rockefeller of New York; *ABC Scope: How Much Dissent?* (January 20, 1968), examining the extremes of Vietnam War dissent in the United States, from Jerry Rubin to George C. Wallace; *ABC Scope: The Wild World of Discotheque* (December 31, 1964), on adults dancing to rock and roll records at expensive New York City nightspots; various issues of *Longines Chronoscope* (1952-55); *A Tour of the White House with Mrs. John F. Kennedy* (CBS, February 14, 1962); *The Hippie Temptation* (1967), in which Harry Reasoner explores the world of drugs and the youth culture in San Francisco; *ABC Scope: Howard K. Smith — One Man's Opinion* (July 16, 1966), a spirited defense of U.S. involvement in the Vietnam War; *Republican Convention of 1956,* tracing events of the San Francisco convention in chronological order; and numerous episodes of *The Twentieth Century* and *CBS Reports.*

Situation comedies. Holds episodes from numerous series, including: *Amos 'n Andy; Bob Cummings Show; George Burns and Gracie Allen Show; The Adventures of Ozzie and Harriet; Father Knows Best; The Danny Thomas Show; Trouble With Father; My Little Margie; The Dennis O'Keefe Show*

(1950s); *The Addams Family; The Monkees; Mr. Deeds Goes to Town; He and She; I Dream of Jeannie; Bewitched; Happy Days; The Partridge Family; Maude; Love American Style; Mary Tyler Moore Show; Barney Miller; The Don Rickles Show* and *Sanford and Son.*

Non-situational comedies. Holds episodes from *The Smothers Brothers Comedy Hour; The Great American Dream Machine; Rowan and Martin's Laugh-In; The Colgate Comedy Hour; Timex All-Star Comedy Show* (1962); *The Milton Berle Show;* and *The Burns and Schreiber Comedy Hour.*

Crime and law enforcement programs. Holds episodes from *Adam-12; Dragnet 69; Armchair Detective; The Lawbreakers; N.Y.P.D.; The Public Defender; San Francisco Beat; Naked City; Racket Squad; Rocky King, Detective; Code 3; 21st Precinct; The Plainclothesman; The New Breed; 87th Precinct; 77 Sunset Strip; Peter Gunn; Meet McGraw; Bourbon Street Beat; Mr. Lucky; The Lone Wolf; Hollywood Off Beat; Perry Mason; They Stand Accused; The Defenders; Public Prosecutor; Follow That Man;* and *Honey West.*

Espionage programs. Holds episodes from *I Led Three Lives; China Smith; I Spy; The Man Called X; Foreign Intrigue; Biff Baker, U.S.A.; Passport to Danger;* and *It Takes a Thief.*

Westerns. Holds episodes from *Zorro; The Cisco Kid; Cheyenne; The Lone Ranger; Have Gun, Will Travel; Gunsmoke; Challenge of the Yukon; The Adventures of Wild Bill Hickok; Broken Arrow; The Rifleman; The Outcasts; Wanted: Dead or Alive; Johnny Ringo; The Roy Rogers Show; Bat Masterson; Frontier; Gunslinger;* and *Hopalong Cassidy.*

Medical programs. Holds episodes from *Medic, Dr. Hudson's Secret Journal; Ben Casey; Pulse of the City; Young Doctor Kildare;* and *Dr. Kildare.*

Variety programs. Includes *Toast of the Town (The Ed Sullivan Show)* (1948); *The Gay Nineties Revue* (1948); *The Tonight Show; The Now Generation; Arthur Godfrey's Talent Scouts; Art Linkletter and the Kids; The Smothers Brothers Comedy Hour; The Jack Paar Show* (1952); *The Garry Moore Show; The Ken Murray Show; Meet Betty Furness; The Jackie Gleason Show; KTTV Television Tape* (1960), a demonstration film intended for potential advertisers, showing the technical tricks made possible by the invention of videotape; *You Asked For It;* and *We The People* (1948), a kinescope of the first regularly-scheduled simulcast in television history (CBS, June 1, 1948).

Children's programs. Holds episodes from *Circus Boy; Space Patrol; The Mickey Mouse Club; Lassie* (premiere program, September 12, 1954); *Rocky Jones, Space Ranger; Captain Midnight; Crusader Rabbit; Diver Dan; Howdy Doody; Commander Cody, Sky Marshal of the Universe* (series finale, 1955); *Meet Mr. Wizard; The Magic Land of Alakazam; The Bullwinkle Show; Ding Dong School;* and *Young People's Concert,* with Leonard Bernstein conducting the New York Philharmonic.

Military programs. Holds episodes from *Crusade in Europe* and *Crusade in the Pacific* (produced 1949), on events and battles of World War II; *Court Martial; 12 O'Clock High; The Rat Patrol; Behind Closed Doors; Secret File U.S.A.; The Big Picture,* a U.S. Army production; *The Gallant Men; Navy Log; Victory at Sea;* and *Combat.*

Quiz, panel and audience participation programs. Holds episodes from *You Bet Your Life,* which include DeSoto automobile commercials; *The $64,000 Question; The $64,000 Challenge; Twenty Questions; Beat the Clock; Masquerade Party; Mike Stokey's Pantomime Quiz Time; Do You Trust Your Wife?; Meet Your Neighbors; Bride and Groom; Strike It Rich; Tic Tac Dough; It Pays to Be Ignorant;* and *Dr. I.Q., Jr.*

Adventure programs. Holds episodes from *The Twilight Zone; Star Trek; Sheena, Queen of the Jungle; Robin Hood; You Are There; The New People; Batman; The Beachcomber; Whirlybirds; Mr. Lucky; Coronet Blue; The Buccaneers; Circus Boy; Space Patrol; Rocky Jones, Space Ranger;* and *Captain Midnight.*

Drama programs. Holds episodes from *Alfred Hitchcock Presents; Playhouse 15; Playhouse 90; Cavalcade of America; The Millionaire; Slattery's People; Studio One; East Side, West Side; Telephone Time; The Diplomat; Bob Hope Presents the Chrysler Theater; Revlon Mirror Theater; Alcoa Premiere Theater; Profiles in Courage; Schlitz Playhouse of Stars; TV Reader's Digest; The Elgin Hour* (near complete collection of this ABC show, produced 1954-55); *Shower of Stars; Award Theater* (an episode starring Ernie Kovacs, 1960); and *The Loretta Young Show.*

Music programs. Holds episodes from *Coke Time (The Eddie Fisher Show),* with Morton Downey, Sr.; *American Bandstand; The Rainbow Quest* (1965), with Pete Seeger; *The Monkees; The Partridge Family; Your Hit Parade; Where the Action Is; The Patti Page Show; Town and Country Time; The Perry Como Show; Eddy Arnold Time; The Ezio Pinza Show; Variety, U.S.A.; The Lawrence Welk Show;* and *Showtime at the Apollo.*

Sports programs. Includes episodes from *The Jack LaLanne Show; Roller Derby; Surf's Up;* numerous bowling programs; *The Big Playback; Top Views in Sports;* and *Telesports Digest.*

Soap operas. Includes episodes from *Search for Tomorrow* (CBS); *Days of Our Lives* (NBC); *Hawkins Falls* (NBC); *The Guiding Light* (CBS); *Love of Life* (CBS); *Dark Shadows* (ABC); *The Secret Storm* (CBS); *Morning Star* (NBC); *The Road of Life* (CBS); *General Hospital; The Young Marrieds* (ABC); *Peyton Place* (ABC); and other series.

Religious programs. Includes episodes from *The Christophers; Life Is Worth Living,* with Bishop Fulton J. Sheen; *Look Up and Live; The Hour of Decision,* with the Rev. Billy Graham; *The Hour of St. Francis* (an episode entitled *Pages of Death,* on the story of a young woman raped and murdered by a boy under the influence of pornographic magazines); and *The Sacred Heart Program.*

Commercials and public service announcements. Holds approximately 3,000 spots in all product and service areas. Also holds commercials produced for charities which feature celebrities, including Adlai Stevenson, Jerry Lewis, Tommy Rettig and Jan Clayton, Phil Silvers, Walt Disney, George Burns, Lou "The Toe" Grozza, Jackie Robinson, Danny Kaye, Tommy and Jimmy Dorsey, Zachary Scott and Florian Zabach.

Non-television news and documentary films. Titles include *The City* (1939), the classic documentary on urbanism presented at the New York World's Fair; *The Plow That Broke the Plains; The River; Years of Lightning, Day of Drums* (1964), on the life and death of John F. Kennedy; *A Time For Freedom,* on a civil rights march on Washington (May 17, 1957); *Chicago World's Fair of 1933; News in the Air* (1938), on radio news, teletype and wire services; *The Baltimore Plan* (1953), on urban renewal; and *From One John Atanosoff,* on the development of the mechanical computer invented by Atanosoff at Iowa State University.

March of Time. Holds numerous episodes (1937-51).

News Magazine of the Screen, produced by Warner-Pathé News. Holds 16 issues (1952-58), each featuring national and international news events of the period. *The World in the Camera,* produced by Warner-Pathé News. Holds four issues (1954).

Screen News Digest, produced by Hearst Metrotone News. Holds numerous issues (1950s-70s).

Civil defense films. World War II-era films include: *Farming for Victory* (Sinclair Oil Co., 1943); *What To Do in an Air Raid; All Out for Victory* (Firestone Rubber); *The Arm Behind the Army,* designed to build morale in the civilian labor force; *Out of the Frying Pan* (produced by Walt Disney Productions); *Silence,* produced for the 6th War Loan drive; and *An Air Raid Warden's Report.*

Cold War-era civil defense films include: *Our Cities Must Fight* (1951); *This Is Civil Defense; Duck and Cover* (1951); *Survival Under Atomic Attack* (1951); *Disaster On Main Street; What You Should Know About Bacteriological Warfare; How to Beat the Bomb* (RKO); *Operation Ivy* (1954), on the 1952 H-bomb detonation at Eniwetok; *Sonic Boom* (1959), explaining that sonic booms are a sign that the United States is being protected against attack; *The House in the Middle* (ca. 1954), on A-bomb tests and their effect on sample houses; *Pattern for Survival; A Town of the Times* (1963), on the necessity to maintain bomb shelters in public buildings; *Let's Face It* (1954); *The Medical Effects of the Atomic Bomb;* and *Fallout and Agriculture* (ca. 1960s).

Propaganda and patriotic films. Titles include *The Price of Freedom* (1949), an anti-socialist film from the National Association of Manufacturers; *Freedom Rings* (ca. 1940); *New Deal Rhythm* (Paramount, 1934), supporting the National Recovery Act; *The Road Is Open Again* (Warner Brothers, ca. 1933), a pro-New Deal short subject with Dick Powell; *Backfire* (American Economic Foundation, 1940), an anti-New Deal film; *Wake Up America!* (1940), also in opposition to the New Deal; *How to Travel Abroad* (ca. 1950s), a military film produced to train servicemen to face rebuke in potentially hostile foreign situations; and *Keeper of the Lions* (U.S. Navy, 1950), on remaining sexually faithful while in the armed forces.

World War II-era propaganda and patriotic films. Titles include *The Price of Victory* (1942), in which Vice President Henry A. Wallace rereads his anti-fascist speech of 1942; *The Price of a Minute,* on efficiency; *Our Enemy* (U.S. Office of War Information, 1942), an anti-Japanese film; *My Japan* (U.S. Treasury, 1945), purporting to offer a cynical Japanese viewpoint on the war; *It's Everybody's War* (20th Century-Fox, 1943); *Scrap for Victory* (1942); *Three Cities* (1942), showing how people come to grips with war in Norfolk, Detroit and Cash Valley, Utah; *Mr. and Mrs. America* (ca. 1944), with Franklin D. Roosevelt, Henry Morgenthau, Eddie Albert and others; *Prices Unlimited* (Universal, 1942), on the bad dreams that come to women who buy black market meat; *Voyage to Recovery,* on the rehabilitation of injured soldiers; *This Could Be America,* a war bond film showing the bombing of Japan and suggesting that it could be the Japanese bombing the United States; *The Army Nurse* (1945), lauding the role of women nurses in the war; *Soldiers of the Soil*

(DuPont, 1943), praising farmers as war heroes; *One World or None* (National Committee on Information of the Federation of American Scientists, 1946), on the necessity of international cooperation to forestall atomic warfare; *The American Way* (1945), praising the United States electoral system, with footage of the 1944 election; *Campus on the March* (1942), on U.S. colleges educating students for the war effort; *Voice of Truth* (1945), on "Tokyo Rose" and her picture of a demoralized America; *Freedom Comes High* (U. S. Navy, 1942), on the seriousness of the war, shown through the experience of a young wife whose husband is lost in action; and *Avoid Unnecessary Trips* (1942), urging fuel conservation by avoiding driving in this pre-rationing period.

Anti-communist propaganda. Titles include: *Why Korea?* (20th Century-Fox, 1951); *Korea Reports* (1951), produced by the U.S. Armed Forces; *The Ultimate Weapon* (ca. 1960s), a dramatization of the treatment of American POWs by North Korean captors, narrated by Ronald Reagan; *Red Nightmare* (1961), with Jack Webb; *What Price Freedom?* (Church of Christ, ca. 1956), on an American visitor to East Berlin and the woman he meets; *Your Crusade for Freedom* (Radio Free Europe, ca. 1953); *Anarchy, U.S.A.* (ca. early 1960s), an anti-Communist, anti-civil rights and anti-Black film; *Espionage Target: You,* produced for businessmen traveling abroad; *The Price of Liberty* (ca. 1952), an anti-communist film praising the role of women in the U.S. military; *Communism* (U.S. Army, 1950), featuring a puppet on a string; *Operation: Abolition* (1960), an anti-communist documentary on the San Francisco demonstrations against the House Committee on Un-American Activities; *Operation: Truth* (ca. 1962), answering the distortions of *Operation: Abolition; Yankee, Go Home* (U.S. Department of Defense, 1957), with excerpts from Soviet propaganda films; *Crossroads for America [The American Communist]* (Research Institute of America, 1947), on Communists in our midst; *Something to Think About* (ca. 1970), on a fundamentalist minister's transition from campus radicalism to fundamentalist Protestantism; *Tragedy or Hope?* (National Education Program, late 1960s), an anti-communist and anti-counterculture film with Dr. George S. Benson, Harding College president; *A Letter From America* (early 1950s), in which a refugee in the United States writes patriotic letters to his sister behind the Iron Curtain; *The Whites of Their Eyes* (U.S. Army Reserves, ca. 1950), with Edward R. Murrow, on the need to be vigilant against enemy aggressors; and *This Is Reality* (U.S. Army Reserves, ca. 1962), a comparison of wars, rebellions and Communism as shown in movies and real life, hosted by Jack Warner, Jr.

Propaganda on presidential and political matters. Titles include *Let's Look at the Record* (1936), produced for the Alfred M. Landon presidential campaign; *Spokesman for the Future* (1944), from the Thomas E. Dewey campaign; *They Said Labor Didn't Count* (United Packinghouse Workers of America, 1948), from a campaign against open shop legislation in the state of Iowa; and *People's Political Poll* (CIO, 1952), in which men and women on the streets voice their opinions about Eisenhower and Stevenson.

Civil rights movement. Titles include *A Time for Freedom* (1957), showing a civil rights march on Washington; *Black Panthers* (late 1960s); *Black Power* (1967); *From the Inside Out* (mid-1960s), produced by Black teenagers in North Richmond, California; and *I'm A Man* (Peter Rosen, 1970), on John Barber, a Black activist from New Haven.

Vietnam War. Titles include *Name, Rank, and Service Number* (U.S. Army, ca. 1964-65), on the Military Code of Conduct; *Vietnam, Vietnam* (USIA, 1970), directed by John Ford; *In Search of Peace* (U.S. State Department, ca. 1966), on U.S. foreign policy; *Vietnam: Why?* (1964), produced after the Tonkin Gulf resolution; *America's Pledge: "We Seek No Wider War,"* produced after the Pleiku incident; *Why Vietnam?* (U.S. State Department, 1965), justifying the American combat role in Southeast Asia; *Where the Girls Are* (U.S. Army), on venereal diseases in Vietnam; and *The Full Blade*, on the U.S. Marines Civic Action Program in the Con Bien district.

Women's movement. Titles include *Women: The Hand That Cradles the Rock* (1975); *Women in Defense* (1941), written by Eleanor Roosevelt and narrated by Katharine Hepburn; and *Fashion Right Summer: Burlington* (1970), tying their product line to the women's movement.

Educational films. Titles include: *Shy Guy; Understand Your Emotions; Control Your Emotions; Going Steady; How Do You Know It's Love?; The Meaning of Engagement; Are You Popular?; The Meaning of Patriotism; Dating: Do's and Don'ts* (1949); *Good Grooming for Girls; Preparing for the Prom; Drug Addiction* (1952); *A Time and a Place* (Avon Products, 1967), on youth culture; *Social-Sex Attitudes in Adolescence* (1953); *Weapons Concealment* (FBI, late 1930s); *Boy With a Knife* (1955), on juvenile delinquency; two episodes of the *[Yale] Chronicles of America* (1924), with historical reconstructions; *Your Junior High Days* (1963); *Last Date* (1950); *Marriage Today* (ca. 1946); *Our Basic Civil Rights* (1950); *The Human Potential Movement* (late 1970s); *So You Want to Be a Cheerleader* (1968); *The Hickory Stick* (National Education Association, mid-1950s), on disciplining 5th graders; *Our Constitution* (1940); *Land of Liberty;* and *Our Bill of Rights* (1940).

Business films. Titles include *Hamburger U* (McDonald's, 1963), a management training film; *Image of a Man* (Esquire magazine, 1958), on motivational research; *This Is the Way* (Westinghouse, ca. 1949), a promotional film for washers and dryers; *Petticoats on Parade* (ca. 1947), two films (each 5 min.) promoting the Iron-rite automatic iron; *Fog Over Portland* (1952), on UHF television and the entry of Zenith TV into Portland, Oregon; *Uranium — A New American Frontier* (Precision Radiation Instruments, ca. early 1950s), on prospecting; *The Story of Lucky Strike* (1940); *Life Magazine* (1960), a film intended for advertising agencies, focusing on the 1950s and how the 1960s may turn out; *Behind Your Radio Dial* (1948), a tour of NBC's New York radio and television studio facilities; *A Great New Star* (Chevrolet, 1953), featuring Dinah Shore singing "See the U.S.A."; *Hall of Wonders* (1953), on the newly-introduced Corvette; *How to Buy a Car* (Chevrolet, 1953); *Key to Our Horizons* (1952), on the importance of the automobile in American life; *Tomorrow's Drivers* (1954), on driver education in the Phoenix schools; *How to Go Places* (1954), in which Gale Storm and family drive over good and bad roads; *Television Today* (CBS-TV, June 1949); and *Voice of the City* (Western Electric, 1937), on telephone equipment used in New York City.

Religious films. Holds two films from the 1980s: *A Christian Critique of Cults* and *A Christian Critique of Satanism and the Occult.*

Canadiana. Titles include *The New Nova Scotia*, a business development film; *The People of Blue Rock* (ca. 1940, Technicolor), on fishing life in Nova Scotia; *Democracy At Work*, on Canada during World War II; *Main Street Canada*, on the Depression, World War II and their effect on average Canadians; *Wartime Capital Ottawa;* and *Inner City* (ca. 1962), on urban problems in Hamilton, Ontario.

Radio- and television-related films. Titles include *News in the Air; Radio Broadcasting Today* (March of Time, 1947); *Behind Your Radio Dial* (1948); *Television Today* (CBS, June 1949); *The Wonderful World of Color* (NBC), celebrating the fifth anniversary of its color television broadcasts; *Television* (1939), a promotional film from RCA/NBC; *America Takes to the Air* (1943), on the place of radio in American life; *1949 TV Promotional Film*, for potential set buyers; and a variety of newsreel segments.

Numerous feature and short films are also held.

Size & Elements: Film: 16mm (2 million feet; 2,600 titles).

Cataloging: Computerized cataloging available to researchers.
Access: Available for duplication and reuse. Research fees charged. Research requests accepted by mail and telephone.
Rights: No rights held to any material. Some material in the public domain. Rights status of some material not known. Additional clearances may be necessary in some cases if material is to be reused.
Licensing: Available for reuse. Usage fees charged.
Restrictions: None specified.
Viewing Facilities: None specified (apply for information).
Duplication Facilities: Videotape (film-to-videotape transfers; all formats).
Related Materials: 4,700 reels (30,000 hours) of radio and audio recordings, including old programs, interviews, voice recordings, popular music and historic events (1930-80s).

ILLINOIS (Chicago)

MUSEUM OF BROADCAST COMMUNICATIONS

800 South Wells Street
Chicago, IL 60607
(312) 987-1500

Lilly Eide (Executive Director)
Mike Mertz (Archivist)

Contacts: Lilly Eide (museum business); Lauren Hassel (special events); Mike Mertz (collection inquiries)
Services: Museum. Videotape collection available to the public for in-house viewing and research purposes only. *Collection not available for distribution, licensing or reuse.*
Description: Television programs, ranging from the pilot of the George Burns & Gracie Allen Show to Peabody Award-winning documentaries on the Vietnam War. Collection is national in scope, with special emphasis on Midwest and Chicago. Museum has acquired a large collection of material from Steve Allen; Kraft and Johnson's Wax Company have also donated many programs they sponsored (1950s-60s). Other programs include *Kukla, Fran and Ollie* (donated by Burr Tillstrom); *Howdy Doody* (from Roger Muir); and materials made available by Professor J. Fred MacDonald, the Museum's curator for television. Holds the complete *NBC Tomorrow Show with Tom Snyder* collection.

The Museum has a substantial collection of television commercials, including the winners of the Mobius and Ad Age Awards, samples from the major Chicago agencies, special reels compiled by the museum staff with celebrities, and vintage commercials, such as cigarette advertising.

Entertainment programs. The David Susskind collection of early television dramas (1950s); situation comedies (1950s-60s); comedy and variety shows, including *Texaco Star Theatre*, and *Kraft Music Hall;* Westerns (1950s-60s); and American Children's Television Festival Winners (1984-88).

News and documentary materials. Nightly newscasts from local stations (beginning January 4, 1987); local Emmy Award winners and nominees; Scott Craig documentaries; and documentaries on the Vietnam war.

Sports programs. Highlights of Chicago sports history (1983-present); Chicago Bears at the Super Bowl; documentaries on Bill Veeck of the White Sox, Ernie Banks of the Cubs, and others; and a collection of the best of *ABC's Wide World of Sports.*

Size & Elements: Videotape: 3/4" (masters); VHS (viewing copies) (1,600 titles total).
Cataloging: Card catalogs, shot lists and dope sheets; computerized cataloging in progress.
Access: Open to the public. For in-house use only. Research fees not charged. Due to small staff, only limited research requests accepted. Research requests accepted by mail, telephone and in person (by appointment only).
Rights: No rights held to any material. Some material in the public domain. Rights status of some material not known.
Licensing: Not available for licensing or reuse.
Restrictions: VHS viewing copies available to the public for in-house research and viewing. 3/4" videotape masters not available to the public. The museum does not provide copies of their material to anyone for any purpose.
Viewing Facilities: Videotape (3/4" and VHS).
Duplication Facilities: None.
Related Materials: Radio collection containing 45,000 hours of programming (1920s-50s), including some Chicago local programming (early 1960s). Approximately 900 titles are currently available to the public for in-house use.

ILLINOIS (Chicago)

MUSEUM OF CONTEMPORARY ART
237 East Ontario Street
Chicago, IL 60611
(312) 280-2660
Fax: (312) 280-2687

Contacts: Alice Piron (Director of Education); Dennis O'Shea (Audio/Visual Technician)
Services: Museum; videotape producer and distributor. Videotapes available for preview and purchase for educational purposes.
Description: Conversations with or discussions about contemporary visual artists.

Highlights include: *Dennis Adrian Discusses His Collection* and *Dennis Adrian on Artists He Has Known,* conversations with the noted Chicago art critic and collector (1982); *Panel Discussion: Architects Talk About Late Entries to the Tribune Tower Competition* (1980), with Thomas Beeby, Stuart Cohen, Cesar Pelli and Stanley Tigerman; and *German Newsreels of the 1920s* (1981), a collection of newsreels, animated political cartoons and propaganda films from Germany's chaotic post-World War I period.

Also holds interviews with 19 different contemporary visual artists on their lives and art, including: *Magdalena Abakanowicz* (1982), a portrait of the Polish fiber artist discussing the organic sources of her inspiration, with footage showing her sculpture and clay work from 1957-82; *Melvin Charney* (1982), Canadian architect and sculptor commenting on the way his work reflects the socioeconomic history of particular sites; *Chuck Close* (1981), a review of the photorealist portrait painter's career and painstaking technique; *Leon Golub* (1985), discussing his visual influences and psychological insights into the causes of violence; and *Michiko Itatani: Spirit Taming* (1983), the Japanese-born painter speaks about her childhood fantasies and their influence on her stories and paintings. Other artists interviewed include Alice Aycock, Roger Brown, George Costakis, Jon Kessler, Sol Lewitt, Ed Paschke, Eric Fischl, David Gremp, Kenneth Josephson, Margaret Wharton, Anne Wilson and Donald Sultan.

All original videotape footage used in these productions is stored at the Archives of American Art Midwest Regional Center in Detroit, Mich.
Size & Elements: Videotape: 3/4", VHS and Betamax (22 titles).
Cataloging: Card catalogs; computerized cataloging available to researchers.
Access: Open to the public. Videotapes available for purchase for educational purposes. Material may be previewed at the Museum prior to purchase.
Rights: Full rights held to all material.
Licensing: Apply for information.
Restrictions: Museum videotapes may be used for direct playback and for educational purposes only. Any duplication or reuse requires the specific prior approval of the Museum of Contemporary Art.
Viewing Facilities: Videotape.
Duplication Facilities: Videotape.

ILLINOIS (Chicago)

NATIONAL EASTER SEAL SOCIETY
70 East Lake Street
Chicago, IL 60601
(312) 726-6200
Fax: (312) 726-1494

John R. Garrison (Executive Director)

Contact: Ann Saul (Director of Public Relations)
Services: Association. Apply for information concerning access and rights to videotape material.
Description: *Reality Rag,* a comedy revue commissioned by the Society, was produced in cooperation with Unicorn Theatre in Kansas City, Missouri. It deals with disability issues and has a cast of both able-bodied and disabled people.
Size & Elements: Videotape: 3/4 and VHS (1 title).
Cataloging: None specified.
Access: Apply for information.
Rights: Apply for information.
Licensing: Apply for information.
Restrictions: None specified.
Viewing Facilities: None.
Duplication Facilities: None.

ILLINOIS (Chicago)

NATIONAL SAFETY COUNCIL
444 North Michigan Avenue
Chicago, IL 60611
(312) 527-4800
Fax: (312) 527-9381

Available for rental from:
MODERN TALKING PICTURE SERVICE, INC. (q.v.)

In Canada:
WESTWOOD SCREEN
211 Watline Avenue
Mississauga, Ontario, Canada L42 1P3
(416) 890-1500

Contact: Audiovisual library
Services: Organization. Film and videotape programs maintained for institutional rental and purchase.
Description: Health, safety and employee assistance programs. Titles include: *Listening Skills; Handling Stress; Proper Lifting; Personal Protective Equipment; How to Prevent Falls; Fire Emergencies; Alcohol and Other Drugs; Communication Skills; Off-The-Job Safety; Crime Prevention; Physical Fitness and Health; Staying Afloat; Monday Night and Tuesday Morning* (on hangovers); *So You Think You Can Drink and Drive; Big Blind Spot* (for professional drivers); *Magic Circles of Defensive Driving; Surviving Winter Driving; Iron Graveyard; Think Snow!; Preventable — Yes or No?; Above All...Keep Your Head* (accident protection); *On Every Hand* (occupational hand injuries); *On the Road Again* (road construction crew safety); *A New Way to Lift;* and *Stop a Fire Before It Starts.*

Other materials cover topics including: manager and supervisor instruction, job safety analysis, low voltage safety, video display terminals, bus drivers and employee assistance programs.
Size & Elements: Film: 16mm. Videotape: several formats available. (Approx. 40 titles total, approx. 10 minutes each).
Cataloging: Published catalogs.
Access: Available to the public for rental and purchase.
Rights: All material protected by copyright.
Licensing: Apply for information.
Restrictions: None specified.
Viewing Facilities: None.
Duplication Facilities: None.
Related Materials: Guides and manuals available for some programs.

ILLINOIS (Chicago)

NIGHTINGALE-CONANT CORPORATION
7300 North Lehigh Avenue
Chicago, IL 60648
(312) 647-0300
(800) 323-5552
Fax: (312) 647-7145

Contact: Candy Edelson (Ext. 527)
Services: Videotape producer and distributor. Programs available for purchase to corporate users and the public.
Description: Collection covers self-improvement; personal and business management; and winning strategies.

Videotape programs include: *How to Be a Winner; What Do You Really Want For Your Children?; How to Speak With Confidence; 10 Keys to a More Powerful Personality; Five Steps to Successful Selling; Guide to Everyday Negotiating; Guide to Business Negotiating; How to Be A No-Limit Person; The Strangest Secret; Selling: A Great Way to Reach the Top; Winning in Life* (Walter Payton); *Politics of Love; Seven Keys to Greater Success; Goals: Setting and Achieving Them on Schedule; Peak Performance and the Peak Performers; The Psychology of Winning in Action; The Greater Golfer in You; 24 Techniques for Closing the Sale;* and *The Boss.*
Size & Elements: Videotape: VHS and Betamax (approx. 18 titles).
Cataloging: Published catalogs.
Access: Available to the public for purchase. Requests accepted by mail and telephone (for credit card orders). Quantity discounts available.
Rights: Apply for information.
Licensing: Apply for information.
Restrictions: None specified.
Viewing Facilities: None.
Duplication Facilities: None.

ILLINOIS (Chicago P)

ILLINOIS (Chicago)

PICTURE START, INC.
221 East Cullerton, 6th Floor
Chicago, IL 60616
(312) 326-6233

Contact: Ron Epple
Services: Film and videotape distributor. Collection available for rental.
Description: International collection of independently produced films and videotapes. Categories include animation, children's films, comedy, documentary, drama, experimental and music.

Animation. A sampling of titles from the huge animation collection includes: *Suspicious Circumstances* (Jim Blashfield); *Rapid Eye Movement* (Jeff Carpenter and Mary Lambert); *Swiss Army Knife with Rats and Pigeons* (Robert Breer); *Quasi at the Quackadero* (Sally Cruikshank); *Bus Stop* (Andrea Gomez); It's An *O.K. Life* (George Griffin); *Asparagus* (Suzan Pitt); and *The Doodlers* (Kathy Rose).

Comedies. Titles include: *Going Shopping* (Andy Aaron); *Murder in the Mist* (Lisa Gottlieb); *The Plight of the Headless* (David Reinisch); and *Juggling* (Elizabeth Sher).

Documentaries. Titles include: *Natural Habitat* and *An Acquired Taste* (Ralph Arlyck); *Sweet Sal* and *Washing Walls with Mrs. G.* (Toby Buba); *Clotheslines* (Roberta Cantow); *Right Out of History: The Making of Judy Chicago's Dinner Party* (Johanna Demetrakas); *George Kuchar: The Comedy of the Underground* (David Hallinger); *Ricky and Rocky and Jerry's* (Tom Palazzolo); and *Car of Your Dreams* (Bob Roger).

Experimental filmmakers. Work by Kenneth Anger, Scott Bartlett, Paul Brekke, Gary Beydler, James Broughton, William A. Brown, Tony Buba, Luis Bunuel and Salvador Dali (*Un Chien Andalou*), Molly Burgess, Doris Chase, Ronald Chase, Maya Deren, Dan Curry, Mary Cybulski and John Tintori, Michael Emery, Myron Emery, Ed Emshwiller, William Farley, Sal Giammona, Hilary Harris, Daina Krumins, Standish Lawder, Christine Loizeaux, Dana Hodgdon, Owen Land (George Landow), Andrew Lugg, John McClintock, David McCullough, David Michalak, Franklin Miller, J. J. Murphy, Robert Nelson, Pat O'Neill, Gunvor Nelson, Debrah Pearson, Mark Rappaport, J. Leighton Pierce, Peter Rose, C. Larry Roberts, Michael Rudnick, Robert Schiappacasse, Anita Thacher, Chel White and D. White.

Music. Includes *Honky Tonk Bud*, a jazz/rap music video in the Black oral tradition of the "jailhouse toast"; *Genius of Love* (Cucumber Studios), with the Tom Tom Club; *Accidents Will Happen*, with Elvis Costello; four videos from Ralph Records, including the Residents' *Hello Skinny* and *One Minute Movies; Apeman* and *Joe Bagodonutz* (Paul Tassie).

Video. Includes: *Rock 'N' Roll Disciples* (Tom Corboy), examining the most obsessive forms of Presley fanaticism; *Blind Date* (Jane Brackman and Joyce Weisiger), showing the point of view of a person on the receiving end of a blind date; *Norman Mailer: The Sanction to Write* and *James Jones: Reveille to Taps* (Jeffrey Van Davis); and *You Can't Print That: Conversations with George Seldes* (Robert Gershon and B. Marquand).
Size & Elements: Film: 16mm. Videotape: 3/4" and 1/2". (Over 550 titles total).
Cataloging: Published catalog.
Access: Maintained for distribution and rental rather than for research or reuse.
Rights: Apply for information.
Licensing: Apply for information.
Restrictions: None specified.
Viewing Facilities: None.
Duplication Facilities: None.

ILLINOIS (Chicago)

PRO-LIFE ACTION LEAGUE
6160 North Cicero Avenue, Suite 210
Chicago, IL 60646
(312) 777-2900

Joseph M. Scheidler (Executive Director)

Contacts: Joseph M. Scheidler; Ann Scheidler; Tommie Romano
Services: Social action and public interest group. Videotape collection available to researchers and scholars only.
Description: Television interview programs featuring pro-life leaders, particularly Joseph Scheidler. Subjects include anti-abortion activism, picketing, demonstrations, debates and speeches, and a conference (November 1987) with former pro-choice physicians who are now pro-life.

Size & Elements: Videotape: VHS (viewing copies).
Cataloging: None specified.
Access: Available to researchers and scholars only. Research fees not charged. Research requests accepted in person (by appointment only).
Rights: Some rights held to some material.
Licensing: Available for reuse. Usage fees not charged.
Restrictions: None specified.
Viewing Facilities: Videotape (VHS).
Duplication Facilities: None.

ILLINOIS (Chicago)

REHABILITATION INSTITUTE OF CHICAGO RESEARCH DISSEMINATION
345 East Superior
Chicago, IL 60611
(312) 908-6184
Fax: (312) 908-6181

Dr. Henry B. Betts (Medical Director and Chief Executive Officer)

Contact: Ellie Wydeven (Coordinator, Research Dissemination)
Services: Hospital; film and videotape producer. Collection open to the public. Maintained for distribution and rental rather than for research and reuse.
Description: Rehabilitation of the physically disabled individual (produced 1977-present). Certain programs are aimed at educating clinicians, while others are intended for use by the patient, family members and the general public.

Sample titles include: *Beginning Prosthetic Training for the Above-Knee Amputee; Bilingual Augmentative Communication by Cerebral-Palsied Adolescent; Application of Neurodevelopment Treatment Principles to Occupational Therapy Management of Adult Hemiplegia; Upper Extremity Orthotic Systems for Patients with Quadriplegia; Evaluation of Postural Reflex Mechanisms Necessary for Balance; Nursing Management Issues in Right and Left Stroke; Mechanisms of Impairment in Spinal Cord Injury; Video Feedback as a Treatment Modality for Persons with Low Back Pain;* and *Touchdown.*
Size & Elements: Film: 16mm (2 titles). Videotape: 3/4", VHS and Betamax I (23 titles; masters and viewing copies).
Cataloging: Published catalog; descriptive flyers.
Access: Open to the public. Available for distribution and rental rather than for research or reuse. Rental fees charged (prepayment required). Requests accepted by mail, telephone and in person (walk-in and by appointment).
Rights: Full rights held to some material. Additional clearances may be necessary in some cases if material is to be reused.
Licensing: Apply for information.
Restrictions: Material protected by copyright.
Viewing Facilities: Film and videotape.
Duplication Facilities: Videotape.
Distributor: One title is distributed by Aspen Systems Corporation (apply for information).

ILLINOIS (Chicago)

RENAISSANCE VIDEO CORP.
130 South Jefferson
Chicago, IL 60606
(312) 930-5005
Fax: (312) 930-9030

Eric Thurman (President)

Contact: Ted Ericson
Services: Videotape producer; production and post-production facility; special effects and computer animation producer. Custom shooting services available. Material available for licensing.
Description: Wide variety of Chicago footage, including street scenes, aerials, beauty shots, landmarks and buildings. Also holds some footage of Haiti, including people, landmarks and scenics.
Size & Elements: Videotape: 1" and 3/4" (approx. 10 hours; masters); VHS (viewing copies).
Cataloging: Staff assistance required.
Access: Available to the public for duplication, licensing and reuse. Research fees charged (fees negotiable). Research requests accepted by telephone.
Rights: Full rights held to all material.
Licensing: Available for licensing. License fees charged.
Restrictions: None specified.

Viewing Facilities: Videotape (VHS).
Duplication Facilities: Videotape (1", Betacam, 3/4", VHS and Betamax).

ILLINOIS (Chicago)

THE SCHOOL OF THE ART INSTITUTE OF CHICAGO
JOHN M. FLAXMAN MEMORIAL LIBRARY
37 South Wabash
Chicago, IL 60603
(312) 443-3700

Nadene Byrne (Director, Library)

Contact: Roland C. Hansen (Reader Services Librarian)
Services: Library. Film collection available for in-house use by researchers and scholars only. Regular film screenings open to the public.
Description: The *Film Study Collection* includes student and faculty films (1970s-present) and many classic and art films. Regular film screenings are open to the public. Membership is encouraged.
Size & Elements: Film: 16mm and Super 8mm (amount unspecified).
Cataloging: Card catalogs arranged by title and filmmaker.
Access: Open to researchers and scholars only. Research requests accepted by mail and telephone.
Rights: Apply for information.
Licensing: Apply for information.
Restrictions: Collection is primarily non-circulating.
Viewing Facilities: None (arrangements can be made).
Duplication Facilities: None.
Publications: *The Film Center Gazette,* a newsletter and film program schedule published by the Film Center at the Art Institute.

ILLINOIS (Chicago)

TRANS-WORLD FILMS, INC.
332 South Michigan Avenue
Chicago, IL 60604
(312) 922-1530

Rich Green (General Manager)

Contact: Staff
Services: Distributor. Films available for rental and lease.
Description: Distributes foreign feature films (especially French and German classics) and educational films (all subjects and grade levels).
Size & Elements: Film: 16mm (approx. 100 titles; release prints).
Cataloging: Published catalog.
Access: Available to the public for rental and lease. Requests accepted by mail and telephone.
Rights: Distribution rights held to all material. Rights retained by copyright owners.
Licensing: Not available for licensing or reuse.
Restrictions: Most films restricted to educational rental and lease only.
Viewing Facilities: None.
Duplication Facilities: None.

ILLINOIS (Chicago)

UNITED AIRLINES
CREATIVE SERVICES
Dept. EXOAL
P.O. Box 66100
Chicago, IL 60666
(312) 952-6734

Contact: Sue Moss (Editorial Assistant)
Services: Corporation. Film and videotape material available to legitimate users for licensing and reuse, subject to restrictions.
Description: Airplanes and airline industry-related activities. Footage includes aircraft (all with United logos) in flight, takeoffs and landings; United Airlines historical material (primarily film with some videotape transfers); footage of United Airlines destinations (primarily film original), including the Orient, Hawaii and certain U.S. cities (coverage not necessarily current). Holds a small amount of footage relating to airline activities, including agents, terminals and passenger services.

United is presently assembling a collection of film and videotape footage relating to corporate history and present-day activities, and plans to add outtakes from its television commercials to this collection.
Size & Elements: Film: 35mm and 16mm (amount unspecified; original negatives and workprints). Videotape: 1" (masters); 3/4" (viewing copies) (amount unspecified; some transfers from film).
Cataloging: Published catalog covering one part of collection; computerized cataloging planned.
Access: Available to the public for duplication and reuse. Nominal research fees charged. Research requests accepted by mail and telephone. Film stored at outside facility; videotape kept at United Airlines. Viewing facilities available at both locations.
Rights: Full rights held to all material.
Licensing: Available for licensing and reuse, subject to restrictions. License fees charged. License fees may be waived if United Airlines logo is visible in final production (apply for information).
Restrictions: Corporate Relations Dept. must clear and approve script of proposed production. Footage made available to legitimate users, subject to corporate approval. Some advertising material may carry restrictions.
Viewing Facilities: Film and videotape.
Duplication Facilities: None.

ILLINOIS (Chicago)

UNIVERSITY OF CHICAGO LIBRARY
DEPARTMENT OF SPECIAL COLLECTIONS
1100 East 57th Street
Chicago, IL 60637
(312) 702-8705

Robert Rosenthal (Curator)

Contacts: Daniel Meyer (University Archivist; Assistant Curator for Manuscripts and Archives); Richard Popp (Archives Assistant)
Services: Educational institution; library. Videotape collection open to researchers and scholars only.
Description: Promotional films produced by the University (1930s-present) relating to the undergraduate college and various research programs; news broadcasts concerning University events, research and faculty members; interviews with faculty members and administrators.
Size & Elements: Videotape: 3/4" (100 videotapes) and VHS (20 videotapes).
Cataloging: Title lists.
Access: Open to researchers and scholars only. Research fees not charged. Research requests accepted by mail, telephone and in person (walk-in).
Rights: Some rights held to some material. Rights status of some material not known. Additional clearances may be necessary in some cases if material is to be reused.
Licensing: Apply for information. Usage fees not charged.
Restrictions: None specified.
Viewing Facilities: None.
Duplication Facilities: None.

ILLINOIS (Chicago)

VIDEO DATA BANK
THE SCHOOL OF THE ART INSTITUTE OF CHICAGO
Columbus Drive at Jackson Boulevard
Chicago, IL 60603
(312) 443-3793
Fax: (312) 263-0141

Kate Horsfield (Executive Director)

Contacts: Mindy Faber (Assistant Director); Gail Sax (Director of Distribution)
Services: Videotape archives and distributor. Material available for rental, purchase, and for licensing and reuse, subject to restrictions.
Description: Research archives and distribution center. Collection comprises video works by artists, cataloged in *Video Tape Review,* and interviews with artists, cataloged in *On Art and Artists.* Genres and issues represented include painting, sculpture, video, performance, photography, music, computer graphics, criticism and theory.

Series and collections distributed include:

Castelli/Sonnabend Videotapes. Preserves 45 programs initially collected by Castelli/Sonnabend Tapes & Films (q.v.), which was at the forefront in supporting experimental video art. This program represents some of the most important video works (1965-73), including: *Left Side/Right Side* (Joan Jonas); *Association Area* (Vito Acconci); *Solo # 1* (Simone Forti); *To and Fro and Fro and To and To And Fro and Fro and To* (Lawrence Weiner); *Female Sensibility* (Lynda Benglis); *East Coast, West Coast* (Robert Smithson and Nancy Holt); *Animation I* and *Animation II* (Keith Sonnier); *Television Delivers People* (Richard Serra); *Art Herstory* (Hermine Freed); and *Reels 1-5* (William Wegman).

The C.A.T. Fund. The Contemporary Art Television Fund (q.v.) is an important and unique collaboration between the Institute for Contemporary Art (ICA) and the WGBH New Television Workshop, both located in Boston. Primary objectives are to commission and co-produce video works with artists who are breaking new ground with television as a creative medium and to perpetuate the creation of significant new work in video art. Titles include: *More TV Stories* (Ilene Segalove); *Damnation of Faust: Will-O'-The-Wisp (A Deceitful Goal)* (Dara Birnbaum); *EVOL* (Tony Oursler); *Execution of Clouds* (Dan Reeves); *Irony* (Ken Feingold); *Double Lunar Dogs* (Joan Jonas); *Easy Living* (Chip Lord and Mickey McGowan); and *The Water Catalogue* (Bill Seaman).

Paper Tiger Television (q.v.). New York-based cable access programming which tackles the communications industry from a radical perspective. Titles include: *Myrna Bain Reads Ebony; William Boddy Reminds the FCC of the 1934 Communications Act; Joan Braderman Reads the National Enquirer; Varda Burstyn Reads Playboy; Eva Cockcroft Reads Artforum; Martha Rosler Reads Vogue; Pelicula a las Once — Sandinista TV News; Sol Yurick Reads The New Criterion; Herb Schiller Reads The New York Times;* and *Brian Winston Reads TV Guide.*

The Artists Television Network. Two alternative arts programs: *Soho Television,* a showcase for alternative television, video art and performance, with programs containing the work and ideas of artists including John Cage, Vito Acconci, Les Levine, Richard Foreman, Julia Heyward, Laurie Anderson, Terry Fox and Juan Downey. *The Live! Show* is "a variety show featuring real and invented personalities from the art world, with interviews, opinions, art performances, live call-ins, art lessons and much more, all in a half-hour of lively entertainment." For further information on the original series, see Artists' Television Project, Special Collections Department, University of Iowa Libraries.

Out There Productions, Inc. Founded in 1975 to provide writers and poets with the opportunity and environment to collaborate on various types of artistic projects, establishing the *Words Into Film/Video Project* in 1979, and the first poetry video documentaries, *Poets In Performance,* in 1980. Poets featured are Allen Ginsberg, Anne Waldman, Bob Holman, Ted Berrigan, Maureen Owen, Barbara Barg and John Giorno.

Series. Various series provide contexts to better explore and analyze issues raised in the individual videotapes. Within each series, programs have been selected to provide suggestive contrasts in work, ideas and historical placement. The topics arising from these differences will encourage discussion about ideas and problems important to anyone interested in contemporary art. The fifteen series described represent the stages, both ideological and technical, within the history of experimental video. Series include:

Minding Media. Focuses on the political import of broadcasting as corporate monopoly and "imperialism of the air." Includes: *Kiss the Girls: Make Them Cry* (Dara Birnbaum); *Social Studies, Part II: The Academy* (Lyn Blumenthal); *The Fifth Republic: An Interview with Michel Foucault* (Branda Miller, Patti Podesta and Jim Czarnecki); *Watch It Think It* (Mitchell Syrop); *Media Ecology Ads: Slow Down* (Antonio Muntadas); *Brian Winston Reads TV Guide* (Paper Tiger Television); *Secrets From the Street: No Disclosure* (Martha Rosler); and *Television Delivers People* (Richard Serra).

Inventing the Everyday. These videotapes showcase a fascination with and desire for the allure and glamour that the media promise, while recognizing that these promises leech meaning. Titles featured include: *Perfect Leader* (Max Almy); *Arcade* (Lyn Blumenthal and Carol Ann Klonarides); *Call It Sleep* (Isaac Cronin and Terrel Seltzer); *The Eternal Frame* (Doug Hall, T. R. Uthco and Ant Farm); *Hell* (Ardele Lister); *Unity Through Strength* (Pier Marton); and *Political Advertisement* (Antonio Muntadas and Marshall Reese).

New Narrative Strategies. From fairy tales to political history, the story is a most efficient method for translating ideas into communicable narrative. The works featured in this series are: *The Little Match Girl Ballet* (Eleanor Antin); *Oued Nefifik: A Foreign Movie* (Liza Bear); *My Neighborhood* (Mitchell Kriegman); *Ellis Island* (Meredith Monk and Bob Rosen); *S.HE* (Bill Seaman); and *The Mom Tapes* (Ilene Segalove).

Body Politic. "Upon self-reflection we rarely equate ourselves with our bodies; our dreams, thoughts, virtues and desires far exceed corporeality. When considering others, however, we quite routinely assign primary exchange value to physical appearance. This, of course, is the essential mode of narrative viewing pleasure — in order to leave our own bodies, we "credit" mere pictures

with physicality. We of superior emotion and intellect fill up characters with ourselves, taking over their pleasure and pain as we visually consume their bodies. Similarly, we reduce other persons to pictures (as they do us), preparing them for the same cycle. Of course, the neutrality/reciprocity of this scheme has been contested in contemporary theory concerned with sexual difference. At a societal level, the ego-body split positions man with the ego and woman with the body." Videotapes in this series, some of which draw on contemporary theory to contest this scheme, include: *Open Book* (Vito Acconci); *Deadline* (Max Almy); *Mixed Emotions* (Annette Barbier); *You Too Can Win Over Depression* (John Caldwell); *Learn Where the Meat Comes From* (Hildegard Duane); *Out With the Girls* (Carol Porter and Joan Merrill); *Losing: A Conversation with the Parents* (Martha Rosler); *Selected Body Works: Crooked Finger; Cartoon Faces; Born With No Mouth; Deodorant* and *Bubble Up* (William Wegman).

The Progressive Text. "The videotapes in this series consider the apparatus through which meaning is deciphered; how we view ourselves and other people; how the terms of similarity and difference create the signposts by which cultures — and people — are linked and separated. These videotapes show that the changes brought on by the communications revolution are not simple, that human works are inextricable from human lives and must be understood beyond determinist equations." Titles include: *It's A Dictatorship, Eat!* (Carlos Anzaldua); *Social Studies, Part I: Horizontes* (Lyn Blumenthal); *Sign on a Truck* (Jenny Holzer); *Smothering Dreams* (Dan Reeves); *A Simple Case for Torture, or How to sleep at night* (Martha Rosler); and *Race Against Prime Time* (David Shulman).

Modern Life. "New forms for portraying modern life are being developed which borrow and build from fictional narrative, music television, surveillance, informational processing systems, advertising and sundry other sources. The seven videotapes in this series provide a diverse cross-section of approaches, both to videomaking and to modern living." Includes: *Go For It Mike* (Michael Smith and Mark Fischer); *Modern Times: Modern Marriage* (Max Almy); *Casual Shopper* (Judith Barry); *The Double* (Ken Feingold); *Windfalls or New Thoughts on Thinking* (Matthew Geller); *Easy Living* (Chip Lord and Mickey McGowan); and *L.A. Nickel* (Branda Miller).

Ritual (and Utterings and Chants). "The function of ritual is to make, to highlight or to pinpoint in personally experienced time, a transition from one defined position to another that is equally well-defined." Works which examine the consequences of this transition to both the individual and the societal order include: *Damnation of Faust: Evocation* (Dara Birnbaum); *I Want To Live In The Country (And Other Romances)* (Joan Jonas); *My Father* (Shigeko Kubota); *Mitchell's Death* (Linda Montano); *EVOL* (Tony Oursler); *Polish Dance* (Miroslaw Rogala); and *Shapes From the Bone Change* (John Sturgeon).

Video Noir. This series investigates the darker side of life and articulates the primary question — What do we fear, the past or the present? Includes *Beneath the Skin* (Cecelia Condit); *Human Skeleton* (Wayne Fielding); *Double Lunar Dogs* (Joan Jonas); *Naked Doom* (Edward Rankus); *Lines of Force* (Bob Snyder); and *The Commission* (Woody Vasulka).

Performing the Eighties. Examining the overlapping development of video and performance art. Features *The KCPT Tapes* (Teddy Dibble); *Songs of the 80's* (Doug Hall); *Manhattan Poetry Video Project* (Out There Productions); *30 Second Spots* (Joan Logue); *Spine/Time* (John Sturgeon); and *Spalding Gray's Map of L.A.* (Bruce and Norman Yonemoto).

Formal Investigations. The formal development of video art from the low-tech, unedited, marginal experimentation of the late 1960s, to contemporary uses of advanced technology. Includes *Prying* (Vito Acconci); *Left Side Right Side* and *Vertical Roll* (Joan Jonas); *30 Second Spots: Philip Glass; Steve Reich* (Joan Logue); *Lip Sync* and *Stamping in the Studio* (Bruce Nauman); *Spiral PTL* (Dan Sandin, Tom DeFanti and Mimi Shevets); *On Edge* (Norie Sato); *Boomerang* (Richard Serra); *Trim Subdivisions* (Bob Snyder); *Summer Salt: Photographic Memory* (Steina Vasulka); and *Selected Body Works: Stomach; Deodorant* (William Wegman).

Classics. "Six videotapes from different genres of video work as examples that offer the best of their type." Includes: *Leaving the 20th Century* (Max Almy); *Baldessari Sings LeWitt* (John Baldessari); *The Loner* (Tony Oursler); *AlienNATION* (Edward Rankus, John Manning and Barbara Latham); *Vital Statistics of a Citizen, Simply Obtained* (Martha Rosler); and *It Starts At Home* (Michael Smith and Mark Fischer).

Double Features. The Red Tapes (Vito Acconci); *The Nurse And The Hijackers* (Eleanor Antin); *A Coupla White Faggots Sitting Around Talking* (Michel Auder); *Virtual Play: the double direct monkey wrench in Black's machinery* (Steve Fagin); *Everglades City* (Matthew Geller); *Between the Frames, Eight Chapters: The Dealers, The Collectors, The Gallery, The Museum, The Docents, The Critics, The Media, The Epilogue* (Antonio Muntadas); *Piano Players Rarely Ever Play Together* (Stevenson Palfi); and

Green Card: An American Romance (Bruce and Norman Yonemoto).

Roles, Representations, Sexuality. Modern Times, Modern Love (Max Almy); *Seduction of Patrick* (Michel Auder); *Acts* (Beth Berolzheimer); *Sons and Fathers* (Daniel Klepper); *Thats It Forget It* (Branda Miller); *Exchange* (Robert Morris); *Beaver Valley* (Janice Tanaka); and *Vault* (Bruce and Norman Yonemoto).

The Science of Fiction/The Fiction of Science. A touring series, with a special emphasis on the early phases of video and television. Highlights include: *Dating in America* (1954, Sid Caesar); a Remington commercial (1960); *Lip Sync* (Bruce Nauman); *The Manhattan Poetry Video Project: Bob Holman's Rapp It Up;* McCarthy-era automobile ads; *Trim Subdivisions* (Bob Snyder); *R.M. Fischer — An Industrial* (Carole Ann Klonarides and Michael Owen); and *L.A. Nickel* (Branda Miller).

What Does She Want? is a new homevideo library series (six programs, each 90 min.) produced by Lyn Blumenthal. Organizes 30 of the most innovative women working in film, video and the performing arts into one collection. Six programs: *We are not sugar and spice and everything nice,* presenting a video album neatly countering the 19th-century family photo album in which family members stare out with fixed expressions; *Bad Attitude,* looking at politics in its various manifestations; *Fact Is Stranger than Fiction,* anthologizing seven videotapes which comprise worlds made up of Fantasy, Illusion, Fact and Speculation, all of which address the sticky questions of what and how we believe; *A Crack in the Tube,* looking closely at our TV dreams, with the underlying suggestion that a greater variety of visions ought to be possible; *Variety is the Spice of Life,* imagining a more generous world in which a variety of love and lovers is not only permitted, but welcomed; and *Women With A Past,* interviewing artists Christine Choy, Yvonne Rainer, Martha Rosler and Nancy Spero, each discussing aspects of her past which she finds relevant to her work. The series includes videotapes by Max Almy, Camille Billops and James Hatch, Dara Birnbaum, Lyn Blumenthal, Joan Braderman, Laurel Chiten, Cecelia Condit, Julie Dash, Valie Export, Mindy Faber, Jill Kroesen, Ardele Lister, Linda Look, Ann Magnuson and Tom Rubnitz, Mary McFerran, MICA-TV, Branda Miller, Linda Montano, Martha Rosler, Ilene Segalove, Sistema Sandinista de Television, Anne Waldman, Fronza Woods, and archival films from Prelinger Associates, Inc.

Video Against AIDS (2 programs, each 120 min., organized by Bill Horrigan and John Greyson). Compilations highlighting the efforts of activists and media artists to visualize the terms for a counter-representation of the AIDS crisis.

Other work by video artists. Videotapes by Nancy Angelo, Avalanche Video, D. L. Bean, David Belle, Mary Ida Bonadio, Drew Browning, California Institute of the Arts, Doris Chase, Candace Compton, Arturo Cubacub, Christine De Ligniéres, Jane Fay, Hermine Freed, Frank Gillette, Copper Giloth, Bob Harris, Bernard Hasken, Kate Horsfield, Tehching Hsieh, Peter Keenan, Paul Kos, Margia Kramer, Suzanne Lacy, Richard Landry, Long Beach Museum of Art, Andy Mann, Jeanine Mellinger, Susan Mogul, Robert Morris, John Orentlicher, Michael Owen, Aysha Quinn, Candace Reckinger, Robert Roesler, Susan Rogers, Nigel Rolfe, Jesse Rosser, Dan Sandin, Nina Sobel, Stedelijk Museum, Lisa Steele, Barbara Sykes and Christine Tamblyn.

On Art and Artists. A series of interviews with artists, made as an effort to create an interface between subjective knowledge and critical subject matter. Includes interviews with Vito Acconci, Chantal Akerman, Max Almy, Laurie Anderson, Carl Andre, Eleanor Antin, Betty Asher, Alice Aycock, John Baldessari, Jennifer Bartlett, Gregory Battcock, Romare Bearden, Billy Al Bengston, Joseph Beuys, Dara Birnbaum, Louise Bourgeois, Stan Brakhage, Phyllis Bramson, Joan Brown, Roger Brown, Rudy Burckhardt, John Button, John Cage, Sarah Canright, Cynthia Carlson, Louisa Chase, Judy Chicago, Christo, Chuck Close, A. D. Coleman, Lia Cook, Isaac Cronin, Robert Cumming, Brad Davis, Frank Dietrich, Jim Dine, Rackstraw Downes, Lauren Ewing, Eric Fischl, Louise Fishman, Audrey Flack, Edward Flood, Hermine Ford, Llyn Foulkes, Hollis Frampton, Benno Friedman, Buckminster Fuller, Sam Gilliam, Marna Goldstein, Leon Golub, Rob Gorchov, Nancy Graves, Nancy Grossman, Hans Haacke, Susan Hall, Jan Hashey, Robert Heineken, Gary Hill, James Hill, Doug Hollis, Richard Hunt, Robert Irwin, Miyoko Ito, Diane Itter, Yvonne Jacquette, Estelle Jussim, Allan Kaprow, Alex Katz, Jane Kaufman, Gerhardt Knodel, Lee Krasner, Barbara Kruger, Peter Kubelka, Shigeko Kubota, Syl Labrot, Ellen Lanyon, Thomas Lawson, June Leaf, Les Levine, Sol LeWitt, Lucy Lippard, Joan Livingstone, Chip Lord, Nathan Lyons, Mike Mandel and Larry Sultan, Stanley Marsh, Agnes Martin, Annette Michelson, Mary Miss, Joan Mitchell, Meredith Monk, Linda Montano, Ree Morton, Antonio Muntadas, Elizabeth Murray, Alice Neel, Louise Nevelson, Barbara Novak, Nance O'Banion, Pat Oleszko, Dennis Oppenheim, Craig Owens, Bill Parker, Betty Parsons, Ed Paschke, Philip Pearlstein, Richard Prince, Martin Puryear, Yvonne Rainer, Arlene Raven, Marcia Resnick, Rodney Ripps, Martha Rosler, Susan Rothenberg, Robert Ryman, Dan Sandin,

Arturo Sandoval, Miriam Schapiro, Peter Schjeldahl, Hanna Schygulla, Richard Serra, Joel Shapiro, Cindy Sherman, Hollis Sigler, Laurie Simmons, Charles Simonds, Ingrid Sischy, Neal Slavin, Keith Smith, Jenny Snider, Nancy Spero, Robert Stackhouse, Pat Steir, Evon Streetman, Michelle Stuart, John Sturgeon, Marcia Tucker, Jack Tworkov, Bill Viola, Dorothy and Herbert Vogel, William Wegman, Fred and Marcia Weisman, William T. Wiley, Jackie Winsor, John Wood, Claire Zeisler and Barbara Zucker.

Video Data Bank New Listings Supplement. Acquires new videotapes on a consistent basis. Includes recent works of most artists previously represented, as well as many titles by new artists. Sample titles include: *What You Mean, We?* (Laurie Anderson); *Forced Perspective* and *Table of Silence* (Annette Barbier); *some aspect of a shared lifestyle* (Gregg Bordowitz); works by Nancy Buchanan, including *The Work of Art in the Age of Electronic Reproduction* (1984), *Tech-knowledge* (1984), *These Creatures* (1969), *Primary and Secondary Spectres* (1979), *An End To All Our Dreams* (1982), *Webs* (1983) and *California Stories* (1983); *The Trial of Tilted Arc* (Shu Lea Cheang); *Orbit* (Arturo Cubacub); *And One And One And One* and *Consider Anything, Only Don't Cry*; *Las Mujeres Del Mercado (Women of the Market)* (Annie Goldson); *Wild Life* and *He's Like* (John Goss); *Rock My Religion* (Dan Graham); *The Kipling Trilogy (The Perils of Pedagogy, The Jungle Boy* and *Kipling Meets the Cowboys), Moscow Does Not Believe in Queers, You Taste American* and *The Ads Epidemic* (John Greyson); *Storm and Stress* (Doug Hall); *Spalding Gray: A Life in Progress* (Robby Henson); Carl Heyward's Artspeak series of interviews and performances, focusing on artists Brian Eno, John Giorno, Gronk, Idris Ackamoor, Rhodessa Jones, Paul Kwan and Ellen Sebastian; *The Mexican Tapes: A Chronicle of Life Outside the Law* (Louis Hock), a narrative series about three undocumented Mexican families living in San Diego; *Fuego De Tierra* (Kate Horsfield and Nereyda Garcia-Ferraz in collaboration with Branda Miller), a videotape on the life and work of Ana Mendieta; *Observer/Observed/Observer* (1976), *Moments At The Rock,* and *Arakawa: Atmospheric Resemblances (A Life of Blank)* (Taka Imura); *Ecstacy Unlimited, Your Money or Your Life* and *A Man's Woman* (Laura Kipnis); *Flaubert Dreams Of Travel But The Illness Of His Mother Prevents It* (Ken Kobland/The Wooster Group); *Video Album 5: The Thursday People* (George Kuchar); *The Circle of Charmion Von Wiegand* (Fay Lansner); *Las Nicas* and *Home Life* (Julia Lesage); *The Willie Walker Show, Bi-Coastal, Three Drugs, The Executive Air Traveler, Abscam (Framed), Auto Fire Life* and *Ballplayer* (Chip Lord); *The Art of Haiti* (Mark Mamalakis); *(are we and/or do we) Like Men?* (Pier Marton); *Bright Eyes* (Stuart Marshall); *Homage to May 19th* (Mary McFerran); *Womb with a View, Scenes from the Micro-War* and *Out of the Mouths of Babes,* with Ernie Larsen (Sherry Millner); *As If Memories Could Deceive Me* (Marcel Odenbach).

Also, Public Art Fund's messages screened over Times Square, produced annually since 1982 by such artists as Rebecca Howland, Catalina Parra, Chris Bratton, Kiki Smith, David Wojanarowicz, Ida Applebroog, Edgar Heap-of-Birds and Jane Dickson; *Fugue, Synchronicity, French Performance, Carousel, Simultaneous, Magic* and *This and That* (Scott Rankin); *She Heard Voices* (Edward Rankus); *Questions to Another Nation, Love Among Machines* and *Nature Is Leaving Us* (Miroslaw Rogala); *KabbaLAmobile* (Rachel Rosenthal); *Eloy* (Michael Rubenstein); *Here in the Southwest* (Joyan Saunders); *Telling Motions* (Bill Seaman); *Production Notes: Fast Food For Thought* (Jason Simon); *See Evil, White Dawn* and *Private Eyes* (Lisa Steele and Kim Tomczak); *Kaliyan* (Barbara Sykes); *Spin Off, Out Damn Spot* and *Stars In Her Eyes* (Kathy Tanney); *Testing the Limits* (a project by the Testing The Limits Collective, an organizing tool for AIDS activism); *There Was An Unseen Cloud Moving* (Leslie Thornton); *Jonas Mekas* (Jordi Torrent); *Sandino Vive — Fifty Years Later — Sandino Lives, Que Pasó Con El Paper Nigiénico? (What Happened to the Toilet Paper?), Testimonio: Así Avanzamos (Testimony: And So We Proceed)* and *Socio Drama* (X-CHANGE TV); and *Hey Bud* (Julie Zando).

Size & Elements: Videotape: 3/4", Betamax and VHS (approx. 3,000 titles; masters and viewing copies; PAL copies available).
Cataloging: Published catalogs; release sheets; research library.
Access: Available to the public for research, rental and life-of-tape purchase. Requests accepted by mail and telephone.
Rights: Full rights held to some material. Some rights held to some material. Rights to artist-produced works retained by original artists or producers. Additional clearances are necessary in many cases if material is to be reused.
Licensing: Material possibly available for licensing and reuse, subject to restrictions. Requests considered on a case-by-case basis.
Restrictions: All requests for reuse subject to acceptance and approval on a case-by-case basis.
Viewing Facilities: Videotape (3/4").
Duplication Facilities: Videotape.

ILLINOIS (Chicago)

VIETNAM VETERANS AGAINST THE WAR
P.O. Box 408594
Chicago, IL 60640
(312) 327-5756

Contact: Barry Romo; Pete Zastrow
Services: Association; film and videotape archives; distributor. Material possibly available for licensing and reuse, subject to restrictions.
Description: Distributes several finished productions: *Dewey Canyon* (1971), featuring Vietnam veterans at an antiwar demonstration in Washington, D.C., throwing their medals into a coffin; *Only the Beginning,* including footage from the Winter Soldier Tribunal, where veterans delivered testimony on U.S. atrocities in Southeast Asia; *Winter Soldier,* a feature-length film incorporating footage from the Winter Soldier Tribunal footage, emphasizing Black and Native American points of view; and *I'll Never Do That Again* (1986), an award-winning videotape produced for public access cable television featuring a "rap" with predominantly Black high-school students in Detroit talking about their feelings on war, the draft, military and U.S. intervention in foreign conflicts.

Also holds 20 hours of unedited footage from these and other productions, including Betacam footage of a Vietnam veteran's trip to Nicaragua.
Size & Elements: Film: 16mm (originals). Videotape: Betacam, 3/4", VHS and Betamax (masters and viewing copies).
Cataloging: None.
Access: Available to the public for research, rental and possibly reuse, subject to restrictions. Research fees generally not charged. Research requests accepted by mail and telephone.
Rights: Full rights held to some material. Additional clearances may be necessary in some cases if material is to be reused.
Licensing: Available for licensing and reuse, subject to restrictions. License fees charged in some cases.
Restrictions: Requests for reuse considered on a case-by-case basis and are subject to acceptance, approval and copyright clearance.
Viewing Facilities: Videotape.
Duplication Facilities: None.

ILLINOIS (Deerfield)

CORONET/MTI FILM & VIDEO
(Division of the Simon & Schuster School Group)
108 Wilmot Road
Deerfield, IL 60015
(800) 621-2131
(312) 940-1260
Fax: (312) 940-3600
Telex: 4330243 COROF

Wendell Shackelford (President)

Contacts: For general information, contact Marketing Staff. For print sales, contact Regional Sales Managers.
Services: Film and videotape distributor. Programs available for rental and purchase, and in some cases broadcast and cable television transmission. *Material not available for licensing or reuse as stock footage.*
Description: Distributes and sells film and videotape programs for use in educational and training situations.

Subject areas include: aging; AIDS; alcohol and drug abuse; animals; the arts; biology; birds; birth and early childhood; chemistry; child abuse; child development; communication skills; computer security; consumer education; corporate training; counterterrorism and hostage response; crime prevention and law enforcement; the criminal justice system; death and dying; diet and appearance; divorce; earth science; energy; environment and ecology; executive development; fables, fairy tales and folklore; families and communities; family living; film studies; fire safety; firearm safety; first aid; fitness and exercise; geography; global studies; government; guidance; handicaps; health; history; holidays; home economics; the human body; insects; job skills; language arts; law enforcement training; life sciences; literature; management and organizational development; marine biology; mathematics; matter and energy; music; Native Americans; organizational development; photography; physical science; plants; police-community relations; police tactical and skill training; rape prevention; reading and writing skills; rhymes and poetry; safety; science; security training; self-esteem; sex education; sexuality; shoplifting; social studies; space science; stress

management; study and test-taking skills; substance abuse; suicide prevention; teenage sexuality; vocational awareness; and world history.
Size & Elements: Film: 16mm. Videotape: 3/4", VHS and Betamax (NTSC, PAL and SECAM). (Over 1,000 titles total).
Cataloging: Published catalogs.
Access: Available for rental and purchase. *Coronet/MTI does not license or sell stock footage or film excerpts under any circumstances.*
Rights: Some rights held to all material. Rights retained by original producers in some cases. Broadcast and cable television rights available for many titles (apply for information regarding licensing and costs).
Licensing: Not available for licensing or reuse as stock footage.
Restrictions: Not available for stock footage use.
Viewing Facilities: None.
Duplication Facilities: None.
Representatives: Network of sales representatives throughout the U.S. (apply for information).

ILLINOIS (DeKalb)

NORTHERN ILLINOIS UNIVERSITY
REGIONAL HISTORY CENTER
155 Swen Parson Hall
DeKalb, IL 60115
(815) 753-1779

Glen Gildemeister (Director and University Archivist)

Contacts: Glen Gildemeister
Services: University and regional archives. Open to the public.
Description: *Northern Illinois University's Archives* (16mm, 227 reels; 1945-73; 1980-84). Consists mainly of documentation of athletic events, especially football and basketball games. Also covers the NIU band and other campus events such as alumni weekends, presidential inaugurations and homecoming parades.

Regional History Center's Collection (16mm, 88 reels; 61 videotapes). Material from People for Public Access, Inc. Films were produced as local programming for the community cable station (1973-85). Videotapes vary in length and the Center does not have facilities available for viewing.

Titles include: *Care of the Family Dog* (5 videotapes); *Our Town Series* (11 videotapes); *Realities of Life and Death* (Carol Troescher, 7 videotapes); *Bowen Tapes* (7 videotapes); *DeKalb Book Review Series* (14 reels); *Community Mental Health Series* (6 reels); *DeKalb Landfill — How the Dump Operates; Police Service Promo Tape; DeKalb Landmarks; Dauntless Women in Childhood Education; Kishwaukee Hospital — Make Your Spare Time Count; How About Those Huskies; Streets are Neat and the Truth About Country Music; Dixieland Jazz; Bicycling Through China;* and *Kishwaukee Barbershoppers.*

General subjects include: basketball, book reviews, cable television, community health and services, DeKalb, Ill., football, grief counseling, intercollegiate athletics, local history interviews and historic sites, marching band, Northern Illinois University, Star Trek Convention and Sycamore, Ill.
Size & Elements: Film: 16mm (315 reels). Videotape: 3/4" and 1/2" (61 videotapes).
Cataloging: Inventory.
Access: Open to the public. Research fees not charged. Research requests accepted by mail, telephone and in person (walk-in).
Rights: Full rights held to all material.
Licensing: Apply for information. License fees charged in some cases. Duplication fees charged.
Restrictions: None specified.
Viewing Facilities: Special arrangements must be made in advance to obtain the necessary equipment from the Audio-Visual Equipment/Media Pool in the Technical Services Department of the University.
Duplication Facilities: By special arrangement only.
Related Materials: Paper records of grant applications, programming schedules and production notes provide background information on the Regional History Center's Collection. Extensive photographs of campus life held in University Archives.

ILLINOIS (Evanston)

THE ALTSCHUL GROUP
930 Pitner Avenue
Evanston, IL 60202
(312) 328-6700

(800) 323-9084
Fax: (312) 328-6706

Joel Altschul (Chairman)

Contact: Bob Battista
Services: Distributor. Film and videotape programs available to the public for rental and purchase.
Description: The Altschul Group, composed of seven separate companies, markets and distributes educational and professional film and videotape programs in various areas.

Professional Research, Inc. Markets health care and patient education programs to hospitals, clinics, HMOs, government agencies, health departments and private physicians. Subject areas include: health promotion and wellness; diabetes education; dietary; general medicine; coronary care; obstetrics and gynecology; child health; opthalmology; surgery; and dentistry.

Perennial Education, Inc. Markets sex education, reproductive health, family planning, and personal and societal values programs to health departments, planned parenthood organizations, schools, libraries, hospitals and government agencies.

Teaching Films, Inc. Markets specialized medical teaching programs, nursing education, allied health, and staff training films and videotapes to medical facilities worldwide. Topics include: dissection; anatomy; skull anatomy; neuroanatomy; brain; human embryology; placenta and foetal membranes; bone development; the human eye; physical respiratory therapy; immunology; trauma; radiation therapy counseling; surgical skin preparation; handwashing and surgical scrub; gowning and closed gloving; the nursing home volunteer; disease-specific precautions; changing dry sterile dressings; and breastfeeding of the premature infant.

Journal Films, Inc. Markets curriculum-based and informational programs to schools (kindergarten through university level), libraries and instructional television systems. Topics include: business education; consumer education; guidance education; health and nutrition; home economics; language arts; grammar; reading; spelling; mathematics; science; social studies; and special education.

Lawren Productions, Inc. (q.v.). Markets educational films concerning special education, health education, child development, parenting, mental retardation, child abuse prevention and teacher training.

Medical Electronic Educational Services, Inc. Markets hospital staff training and nursing education programs, including: infection control, medical and surgical, maternity nursing, fracture therapy, psychiatric nursing, and the widely used comprehensive *Patient Assessment Series.*

Gilbert Altschul Productions, Inc. Produces film and videotape programs for all the Altschul Group companies; also performs outside contract work.
Size & Elements: Film: 16mm (approx. 1,000 titles, approx. 500,000 feet; release prints). Videotape: 3/4", VHS and Betamax (approx. 1,000 videotapes; viewing copies).
Cataloging: Published catalogs.
Access: Available to the public for rental and purchase. Orders accepted by mail; inquiries accepted by telephone.
Rights: Full rights held to some material. Some rights held to all material.
Licensing: Selected materials possibly available for licensing and reuse in some cases. License fees charged.
Restrictions: None specified.
Viewing Facilities: None.
Duplication Facilities: None.

ILLINOIS (Evanston)

FOREIGN IMAGES
1213 Maple Avenue
Evanston, IL 60202
(312) 869-0543

Contact: Gretchen Elsner-Sommer
Services: Film and videotape distributor. Films available for rental; videotapes available for rental and purchase.
Description: *Feminist experimental films.* Distributes *Syntagma* (Valie Export, 1985), a short film playing with visual sign systems, striving to release women's bodies from the historical restrictions of female representation; *Invisible Adversaries* (Valie Export, 1978), on one woman's internal struggle to overcome the invasion of alien and alienating forces; and *The Trouble With Love* (Helke Sander, 1984).

Videotapes. Distributes *Postcards from Nicaragua* (Chuck Kleinhans, 1984), showing arts and crafts, skills and labor, ceremonies and public statements, concentrating on the words and images of ordinary people; and *El Crucero* (Julia Lesage, 1984), an in-depth picture of a Nicaraguan coffee plantation, organized in four "movements," each in a different documentary style.
Size & Elements: Film: 16mm (3 titles; release prints). Videotape: 3/4", VHS and Betamax (2 videotapes; masters and viewing copies).
Cataloging: Published catalog sheets.
Access: Films available for rental; videotapes available for rental and purchase. Research fees not charged. Research requests accepted by mail and telephone.
Rights: American distribution rights held to all material. Can refer requests to film and videomakers.
Licensing: Not available for reuse.
Restrictions: Not available for reuse.
Viewing Facilities: None.
Duplication Facilities: None.

ILLINOIS (Evanston)

LAWREN PRODUCTIONS, INC.
930 Pitner Avenue
Evanston, IL 60202
(312) 328-6700
(800) 323-9084
Fax: (312) 328-6706

Joe Farragher (President)

Contact: Margaret Dugan
Services: Film and videotape producer and distributor. Material available to the public for rental, purchase, licensing and reuse, subject to restrictions.
Description: Educational programs relating to health, mental and physical disabilities and parent/child relationships.

Health education. Titles include: *Making a Difference: Living With a Congenital Heart Defect,* the story of a six-year-old boy with a cardiac pacemaker; *Living Every Minute: Coping With a Life-Threatening Illness,* on a terminally ill patient who works with handicapped children and gives comfort and aid in a hospice while studying for an advanced degree; and *Suicide at 17,* examining the current wave of adolescent suicides.

Child development. Titles include: *Infant Reflexes* (videotape only); *A Young Child Is...,* showing how young children learn, and demonstrating the importance of parental love and support; and *Child Check,* enlisting parents in the early detection of possible developmental problems.

Parenting. Titles include: *Adaptation to the Initial Crisis,* showing a couple learning to accept and adjust to their handicapped baby; and *A Very Important Person,* in which a mother has nightmares and is estranged from the rest of her family after an accident leaves one of her sons brain-injured.

Mental retardation. Titles include: *Unknown Genius,* examining three mentally retarded people (a sculptor, a "calendar mind" and a pianist) possessing skills that demand extraordinary complex mental and physical coordination; and *Exploding the Myth,* demolishing misconceptions about developmental disabilities.

Prevention of child abuse. Titles include: *If A Tell You A Secret...,* a training film demonstrating gentle and considerate treatment of children in order to elicit information that will hold up in court; and *A Time For Caring,* designed to alert teachers and administrators to behavioral indicators of possible sexual abuse.

Special education. Titles include: *The Reluctant Delinquent,* a teenager's delinquency is replaced by eagerness to learn when teachers solve his learning problems; and *The Blackboard Jumble,* on Los Angeles County's program for finding and correcting learning disabilities in delinquent youths.

History. Titles include: *A Brief Visit to the Hsin Hua School in Peking,* made during near the end of the Mao Zedong regime in China, emphasizing art, friendships, exercise, work and education; and *Afghan Ways* (1971), produced during the last monarchy, showing work, culture, foods, religions and music.

Curriculum programs. Titles include: *Building a Dream,* showing how 14 urban families built their own homes; *Homemade American Music,* in which six well-known folk musicians provide inspiration to younger musicians; and *Sonny Terry: Shoutin' The Blues,* on a talented blind man who brings exciting music out of his harmonica.

In-service training. Titles include: *Confident Teaching: Enhancing Self-Concept; Training the School Bus Driver* and *Discipline and the School Bus Passenger.*
Size & Elements: Film: 16mm (approx. 75 titles). Videotape: 3/4", VHS and Betamax (approx. 75 titles).
Cataloging: Published catalog.

ILLINOIS (Evanston)

Access: Open to the public. Programs available for rental and purchase. Requests accepted by mail and telephone.
Rights: Full rights held to some material. Some rights held to all material. Additional clearances may be necessary in some cases if material is to be reused.
Licensing: Available for licensing and reuse, subject to restrictions. License and usage fees charged.
Restrictions: Requests for licensing and reuse subject to approval on a case-by-case basis and must be cleared for copyright through Lawren offices.
Viewing Facilities: None.
Duplication Facilities: Apply for information.
Related Materials: Some programs have accompanying study guides.

ILLINOIS (Evanston)

SIGNAL PRESS
1730 Chicago Avenue
Evanston, IL 60201-4585
(312) 864-1322

Rachel Kelly (President, National Women's Christian Temperance Union)

Contact: Cara Tschanz (Manager, Signal Press)
Services: Distributor. Films and videotapes available to the public for purchase. Rentals available through local WCTU chapters only.
Description: Films and videotapes, sponsored by the National Women's Christian Temperance Union (WCTU), relating to the effects of alcoholic beverages and drugs, and the dangers of substance abuse.

Titles include *Theobald Faces the Facts*, for elementary grades; *Alcohol Abuse and Teens: The Turning Point; Alcohol and Drugs: Know What You're Doing; Alcohol and Human Physiology; Cocaine and Human Physiology; Choice Is Yours; Crack: Dead at 17; Dead Is Dead*, on heroin use; *Feelin' Good: Alternatives to Drug Abuse*, narrated by Rev. Jesse Jackson; *Just One; Marijuana and Human Physiology; One For My Baby*, on fetal alcohol syndrome; *Short Distance Runner*, on teenage drinking; *Smokeless Tobacco — It Can Snuff You Out; Verdict at 1:32*, on the effect of alcohol on the brain; and *What About Alcohol?*
Size & Elements: Film: 16mm (17 titles). Videotape: VHS (amount unspecified).
Cataloging: Published catalog.
Access: Available to the public for purchase. Orders accepted by mail and telephone.
Rights: Full rights held to some material. Additional clearances may be necessary in some cases if material is to be reused.
Licensing: Apply for information. Licensing inquiries should be directed to Mrs. Rachel Kelly.
Restrictions: None specified.
Viewing Facilities: Film (16mm).
Duplication Facilities: None.

ILLINOIS (Evanston)

WHITE JANSSEN, INC.
604 Davis Street
Evanston, IL 60201
(312) 328-2221
(800) 777-2223

Matthew White; Stefaan Janssen (Principals)

Contacts: Matthew White; Stefaan Janssen; Sharon Sandusky
Services: Film and videotape producer; stock footage sales library.
Description: Has acquired and now operates stock footage sales library formerly operated by Lem Bailey (beginning 1950s) under the name "Color Stock Library."

Holds outtakes and original film material from at least 40 different filmmakers (1900-present; mostly color footage 1950s-70s), including F. K. Rockett, Noble Trenham, Guy Haselton, Commodore Films, E. B. Brink, Tom McHugh, Bernie Howard, C. E. Talbot, Fort Pearson, Jacques Chatain, Frank Peiler, W. Tompkins, R. C. Bartlett, Martin Murray, R. Gilliam and Al Chambers. Special strengths include:

Americana (1945-65, 35mm and 16mm, color). Footage culled primarily from industrial and corporate films, including cutting grass; driving cars; drinking martinis; watching television; squinting eyes; going to the theater; attending school; reading the newspaper; fighting; football; travel; marriage; farming; and modeling.

Automobiles (1940s-50s, 35mm and 16mm). Virtually every model is represented, including: pink 1957 Thunderbirds; the 400,000th assembly-line model of the 1959 Rambler Rebel; the bubble-topped, wide-winged, futuristic Ford Futura; and the three-wheeled Davis car. Holds over 30 hours of Chrysler in-house 35mm film materials; 1953 DeSoto commercials; and a special collection of 1950s automobile "insert shots," including speedometers, gas pedals, taillights, road signs, stop lights, power windows, service stations, gas pumps and repair shops.

Beauty contests (1940s-60s). Color footage of beauty queens, contestants and judges.

Color footage from the 1950s. All subjects, including music, sports, lifestyles, small town life, rodeos, county fairs, Holiday Inns, agriculture, people, institutions, cities and celebrities.

Dance around the world. Footage from Yugoslavia, Thailand, Greece, Portugal, Nepal, Austria, Hawaii, Peru and other countries.

Fashions of the 1950s. Color footage originally shot for the fashion and textile industries, featuring models in the newest outfits.

Israel (1948-75). Film documentation on the creation and early years of Israel, including footage shot by and for B'nai B'rith. Topics include: refugees, settlements, political personalities, scenics, establishing shots, interiors and military demonstrations.

Lyndon Baines Johnson (1965-67, 16mm, color reversal). Closeups of Johnson at play (and on display) with his family and at work with his entourage. Also holds coverage of Lady Bird Johnson and Luci Baines Johnson's wedding.

Missionary films (1950s-78). Shot throughout the Third World, this unusual collection contains subjects such as natives of the African and South American jungles; bizarre rites, customs and rituals of New Guinea's headhunters; early attempts to Christianize Japan; and penitents throughout Mexico.

Native Americans (1975-81, 16mm, original film and audio materials). Coverage of two dozen native cultures, documenting all aspects of reservation life, originally designed to document the ways in which government monies were used on reservations.

Petroleum industry. Documentation on the history of oil production, including footage of early wooden oil rigs in production; and footage on gas station protocol and management.

F. K. Rockett collection (16mm, original elements). Cultural oddities, including: a pin-up girl in shorts and suspenders holding a spaghetti squash (ca. 1956); a short-order cook at a 1950s diner entitled Joe's Cafe; and much more.

Rose Parade (1957-64). Official footage of Rose Parades and associated activities, including the daily activities of a Rose Parade Queen, behind-the-scenes looks at the creation of a float, and footage of celebrities, including Dwight D. Eisenhower.

Tobacco industry. Extensive collection of tobacco-related programming, including commercials, government films, industrial programs and educational materials.

Vietnam. Collection of footage shot during the U.S. involvement in the Vietnam War. Although library holds relatively little combat footage, it is strong in ambient materials, including Saigon nightclubs; daily market activities; and the original footage from *The 5 Faces of Madame Ky,* a film about South Vietnamese Vice President Nguyen Cao Ky and family.

Miscellaneous subjects. San Francisco (1940s); small town beauty contests; a series of equestrian films; cultural and political films relating to Yugoslavia, India, Haiti (during François Duvalier's regime), Iran (under the Shah), Ireland, Spain, Switzerland, Norway and Third World countries; color footage of Lyndon B. Johnson's inauguration; Willie Mays breaking into baseball's major leagues; and scenes of hippies from San Francisco's Haight-Ashbury district; scenics, travel and transportation, including vintage automobiles; nature and wildlife, including wildflowers, birds and national parks.
Size & Elements: Film: 35mm (150,000 feet; elements unspecified) and 16mm (2 million feet; mostly original reversal positive).
Cataloging: Computerized cataloging in progress (Macintosh HyperCard stacks).
Access: Open to the public. Available for duplication, licensing and reuse. Research fees charged. Research requests accepted by mail, telephone and in person (by appointment only). Preview cassettes can be prepared for customers (research fees charged).
Rights: Full rights held to all material.
Licensing: Available for licensing and reuse. License fees charged.
Restrictions: None specified.
Viewing Facilities: Videotape.
Duplication Facilities: None.

ILLINOIS (LaGrange Park)

AMERICAN NUCLEAR SOCIETY
555 North Kensington Avenue
LaGrange Park, IL 60525
(312) 352-6611
Fax: (312) 352-0499
Telex: 4972673

Octave J. DuTemple (Executive Director)

Contact: V. Gay Easly (Manager, Public Communications Department)
Services: Not-for-profit society; audiovisual lending library. Films and videotapes available for loan.
Description: Producer and distributor of films and videotapes on a variety of topics relating to nuclear technology. Many of the films were produced by or for the electric power industry.

Accidents and drills. Coping with Crisis: Accident at Ginna (Rochester Gas & Electric Corp.) shows the handling of communications in an actual crisis. *Diablo Canyon Field Exercise* (Pacific Gas & Electric Co.) and *VEPCO Emergency Drill Exercise* (Virginia Electric & Power Co.) simulate a drill scenario.

Breeder reactors. Clinch River Breeder Reactor Plant Project: Progress Report '83 (Breeder Reactor Corp.) on the breeder's contributions and goals.

Careers in nuclear technology. Various one-minute public service announcements encouraging students to pursue careers in science and engineering, all produced by ANS:

Energy (general). It's An Electric Life (Edison Electric Institute) dramatizes the vital role electricity plays in modern life. *Just How Do We Make Electricity?* (Portland General Electric Co.) features Izard the Wizard teaching a group of children about electricity. *Voices of Energy* (New Hampshire Voice of Energy) profiles the pro-energy citizen's advocacy movement.

Energy (nuclear). The Atom: A Closer Look (American Nuclear Society, for grades 6-12) discusses nuclear power, atomic structure, radiation and waste. *Energy 101* (Westinghouse Electric Corp.) shows how a reactor works, demonstrating chain reactions with stacked tennis balls in a "Mr. Wizard"-style presentation. *Living in a Nuclear Age: Power from the Atom* (National 4-H Council) includes a short tour inside a nuclear plant, compares nuclear and other energy sources and guides a group of students around a fusion demonstration reactor. *Campus Energy Forum Excerpts* features Edward Teller, Miro Todorovich and others at a 1979 forum arranged by Scientists and Engineers for Secure Energy.

History. Energy: Need for a New Beginning and *A Play Half Written: The Energy Adventure* (Atomic Industrial Forum, Inc.) show the development of new energy sources and how each person's life will be altered by these changes.

Jobs. Electricity: America's Vanishing Power (Bechtel Power Corp.), *The Energy and Jobs Connection,* and *We're On Our Way* (U.S. Committee for Energy Awareness) emphasize how America's continuing industrial growth relies upon a constant supply of energy.

Radiation. This collection of films is designed to dispel "popular myths" about radiation. *Living in a Nuclear Age: Radiation and Living Things* (National 4-H Council) discusses dosages and beneficial effects of radiation in humans and animals. *Radiation Demonstration* (General Electric Co.) demonstrates radioactivity in common items with the aid of a radiation counter. *Radiation...Naturally* (Atomic Industrial Forum, Inc.) guides viewers through the basics (radiation sources, applications, effects, benefits and risks). *Radiation: The Health Effects of Radiation from Natural, Industrial and Medical Sources* (Louisiana Power & Light Co.) features three scientists in a panel discussion answering key nuclear questions.

Transportation. Accident Testing (Sandia National Laboratories) and *Operation Smash Hit* (Central Electricity Generating Board of the United Kingdom) show spent nuclear fuel shipping casks involved in dramatic crashes; in the second film, a cask is struck by a diesel locomotive moving at 100 mph. *Spent Nuclear Fuel* (Sandia) shows how fuel is made, placed in rods, loaded into a reactor, and later placed into shipping casks, transported and unloaded, and placed in storage pools.

Waste. Nuclear Waste Isolation: A Progress Report (Battelle Memorial Institute) examines the progress being made toward a safe nuclear waste disposal system not needing maintenance by future generations. *The Barnwell Site* shows the operation of a low-level waste disposal site in South Carolina.

Miscellaneous. Nuclear Medicine (American College of Nuclear Physicians) discusses medical uses of nuclear materials and disposal of the resulting low-level wastes. *Uranium: Fact or Fiction* (Americans for Rational Energy Alternatives) is a response to ABC's documentary *The Uranium Factor,* which criticized the uranium industry.

ILLINOIS (Long Grove)

Size & Elements: Film: 16mm (15 films). Videotape: format unspecified (24 videotapes).
Cataloging: Brochure (available on request).
Access: Available to the public on a two-week free-loan basis for screening purposes only. Requests accepted by mail and telephone. Only one item can be furnished per request.
Rights: Rights retained by original producers in most cases. Some rights held to some material.
Licensing: Apply for information.
Restrictions: Films may not be shown where admission is charged.
Viewing Facilities: None.
Duplication Facilities: None.

ILLINOIS (Long Grove)

DUCKS UNLIMITED, INC.
One Waterfowl Way
Long Grove, IL 60047
(312) 438-4300
Fax: (312) 438-9236

Matthew B. Connolly, Jr. (Executive Vice President)

Contact: Charlotte Rush (Director, Communications)
Services: Nonprofit conservation organization. Films and videotapes available for rental, purchase and licensing, subject to restrictions.
Description: Migration, habitat and life cycle of waterfowl; Ducks Unlimited's marsh and prairie habitat conservation projects in North America; hunting and conservation.

Films include *The Canada Goose* (1953); *Canvasback* (1969), portraying its life cycle; *Decisions* (1974), the history of Ducks Unlimited; *Ducks on the Wing* (1978), a waterfowl identification film; *A Place for Wildlife* (1985), on the building of DU's Kitsim wildlife habitat project in Alberta; *A Matter of Perspective* (1980), showing the key role played by wetlands in maintaining ecological balance in North America; *Mike — A Labrador Retriever,* a dog who learns his responsibilities in helping to conserve waterfowl; *A Question of Hunting* (1975), produced by the Remington Arms Company, examining the positions of those who do and those who don't hunt; *The Wetlanders* (1970), a documentary on the how, when, where, what and why of DU and its work in Canada; and *The Wood Duck's World* (1966), a life story.

Marshwalker (1987), available for purchase, is a commemorative videotape tribute to DU's fifty years of wetland conservation.
Size & Elements: Film: 16mm (23 titles; masters and release prints). Videotape: VHS (1 title).
Cataloging: Brochures.
Access: Available for rental and purchase (in some cases). Rental fees charged. Requests accepted by mail.
Rights: Full rights held to all material.
Licensing: Available for licensing and reuse, subject to restrictions.
Restrictions: Requests for licensing and reuse considered on a case-by-case basis.
Viewing Facilities: None.
Duplication Facilities: None.

ILLINOIS (Niles)

UNITED TRAINING MEDIA
6633 West Howard Street
Niles, IL 60648
(312) 647-0600
(800) 558-9015
Fax: (312) 657-0600 (Ext. 794)

Terry Nindl (Manager)

Contact: Terry Nindl
Services: Film and videotape distributor. Programs available for rental and purchase.
Description: Distributes over 300 programs. Subjects include: general management; interviewing; performance appraisal; training; negotiation; problem solving; stress; substance abuse; drugs and alcohol; sexual harassment; equal opportunity; time management; safety managers, directors and supervisors; hospital management, supervisors and service; employee theft; banks; computers; general motivation; sports themes; fitness, food and attitude; communications; telemarketing; telephone courtesy and retail sales.

Sample titles include: *Advice Without Consent; The One Minute Management System; What Went Wrong?; The Cocaine Trap; Sexual Harassment: Shades of Gray; Don't Lose Your Patients on the Phone; Crossroads: A Nurse's Story; Keeping F-I-T at Your CRT; The Muppet Meeting Films; Norman Krasner...Beloved Husband of Irma; Caffeine Capers; Change Your Mind: Inner Training for Women in Business;* and *Sports Bloopers.*

UTM also distributes training programs from Video Arts Inc. (q.v.).
Size & Elements: Film: 16mm. Videotape: 3/4", VHS, Betamax I, II and III. (Over 300 titles total).
Cataloging: Published catalog.
Access: Available for rental and purchase rather than for research and reuse. Films and videotapes that can be purchased are available for one-day preview for evaluation purposes only. Preview charge may be applied against the purchase or rental price. Requests accepted by telephone.
Rights: Full rights held to some material. Additional clearances are necessary in some cases if material is to be reused.
Licensing: Apply for information.
Restrictions: None specified.
Viewing Facilities: None.
Duplication Facilities: None.

ILLINOIS (Northbrook)

VIDEO ARTS INC.
4088 Commercial
Northbrook, IL 60062-1829
(312) 291-1008
(800) 553-0091
Fax: (312) 291-9469
Telex: 269-341

Ann Boland (General Manager)

Contact: Matthew Yates (Sales Manager)
Services: Film and videotape producer and distributor. Collection available for rental and long-term license.
Description: Videotapes and films for management, sales and employee development (1972-present). Materials, many starring British actor John Cleese, combine entertainment and training. Programs aim to change the attitudes, open the minds or remove the prejudices of the audience for which they have been produced, based on the practical advice of experienced professionals. Also produces commissioned films.

Programs available: *The Unorganized Manager,* a film in four parts, including *Damnation, Salvation, Lamentations* and *Revelations;* four films on employee interviewing, including *Man Hunt, How Am I Doing?, I'd Like A Word With You* and *Can You Spare A Moment?.* Other titles include *Meetings, Bloody Meetings* and *Decisions, Decisions.*
Size & Elements: Film: 16mm (release prints). Videotape: 3/4", 1/2" and Betamax (viewing copies). (80 titles total).
Cataloging: Published catalog.
Access: Available for rental and long-term license. Preview copies available (preview fees charged, can be credited toward rental). Requests accepted by mail, telephone and in person (by appointment only).
Rights: Full rights held to all material.
Licensing: Apply for information.
Restrictions: All requests for reuse subject to acceptance and approval.
Viewing Facilities: Film and videotape.
Duplication Facilities: None.

ILLINOIS (Oak Brook)

MCDONALD'S CORPORATION
McDonald's Plaza
Oak Brook, IL 60521
(312) 575-3000

Films and videotapes available for purchase and rental from:
MEDIATECH
Attn: McDonald's Broadcast
110 West Hubbard Street
Chicago, IL 60610
(312) 828-1146
Fax: (312) 828-9874

Contact: McDonald's Broadcast (Mediatech)
Services: Corporation. Films and videotapes available for rental and purchase.
Description: Educational films produced for school-age and young adult audiences.

Titles include: *Get It Straight,* on the dangers of drug abuse and the positive aspects of a drug-free lifestyle; *Happy Birthday, Dr. King!,* celebrating the life and message of Dr. Martin Luther King, Jr. in a contemporary, upbeat manner, using historical civil rights footage; and *Eating Right, Feeling Fit,* a comprehensive fitness and nutrition program featuring Mary Lou Retton and Bruce Jenner.

Two films are in production: one on safety rules for elementary school-age children; and another, produced with the U.S. Olympic Committee, offers an inside look into the process of becoming an Olympian athlete.
Size & Elements: Film: 16mm (2 titles; release prints). Videotape: 3/4" and 1/2" (3 titles; viewing copies).
Cataloging: Published catalog.
Access: Available to the public for rental (five-day loan period) and purchase from Mediatech. Requests accepted by mail.
Rights: Apply for information.
Licensing: Apply for information.
Restrictions: None specified.
Viewing Facilities: None.
Duplication Facilities: None.
Related Materials: Each program has an accompanying educator's guide.

ILLINOIS (Orland Park)

MOVIECRAFT, INC.
13916 Charleston
Orland Park, IL 60462
(312) 460-9082

Larry Urbanski (President)

Contact: Larry Urbanski
Services: Television syndicator and producer; stock footage sales library. Material available for syndication and licensing. Videotapes available for purchase.
Description: Extensive archives of films and television programs. Special strengths include early television programs, feature films, serials, cartoons, silent films, industrial films, newsreel footage, films produced by the U.S. government, vintage travel and educational films, and films on transportation. Also produces a weekly professional wrestling television show, from which stock footage is available.

TV's Magic Memories (52 shows, each 30 min.). Sample titles include: *The Jack Paar Show* (1953); *Take A Good Look* (1959), with Ernie Kovacs and Edie Adams; *You Bet Your Life* (1952); *Johnny Jupiter* (1953), a whimsical look at Planet Earth through the eyes of Johnny and his robot pal B-12, who make their judgments based on the television programs they see; *The Ted Mack Amateur Hour* (1951); *The Howdy Doody Show* (1948); *Gangbusters* (1952); *I Remember Mama* (1949); *Big Town* (1952); and *It's A Great Life* (1954).

Hollywood Dreams. Nostalgic trailers from feature films, with hundreds of well-known stars. Genres include action/adventure, comedy, drama, horror, musicals, mystery, romance, science fiction, serials and Westerns.

Silver Screen Movie Shorts (13 programs). Comedies from Al Christie, Three Stooges, Harry Langdon, Bert Lahr, and others.

The War Time Years (13 programs, each 30 min.). World War II battle films, including captured Nazi films, staff reports and Allied battle propaganda.

The Trouble With Father (78 episodes, each 30 min.). Classic television series starring Stu Erwin.

The Big Attack (39 episodes, each 30 min.). Series, filmed on location in Germany, using actual GI's as actors, dealing with the exploits of American and Allied troops in World War II.

Many films and television programs are also available for purchase.
Size & Elements: Film: 16mm. Videotape: 1" and 3/4". (Amounts unspecified).
Cataloging: Staff assistance required. Published catalog of videotapes available for purchase.
Access: Available for licensing and reuse. Many videotapes available for purchase. Research fees charged. Research requests accepted by mail and telephone. Screening cassettes and rush service available.
Rights: Apply for information.
Licensing: Available for licensing and reuse. License fees charged.
Restrictions: None specified.
Viewing Facilities: None.

Duplication Facilities: Film and videotape.

ILLINOIS (Park Ridge)

JACK HANSEN
1612 South Prospect
Park Ridge, IL 60068
(312) 692-2183

Contact: Jack Hansen
Services: Private collection.
Description: World War II footage, some in color, of the capture of the *Tasa Bana Maru,* a Japanese hospital ship used as a troop and arms transport, in the Banda Sea (1945); the landing of 3,500 soldiers and armaments in the Philippines; and Allied troops occupying T'singtao, China (1945).
Size & Elements: Film: format unspecified (2 cans). Videotape: format unspecified (1 videotape).
Cataloging: None.
Access: Apply for information.
Rights: Full rights held to all material.
Licensing: Apply for information. License fees charged in some cases.
Restrictions: None.
Viewing Facilities: None.
Duplication Facilities: None.

ILLINOIS (Pekin)

THE EVERETT McKINLEY DIRKSEN CONGRESSIONAL LEADERSHIP RESEARCH CENTER
Broadway and 4th Street
Pekin, IL 61554
(309) 347-7113

Dr. John Kornacki (Executive Director)

Contact: Janet Lange (Program Specialist)
Services: Manuscript repository; educational institution. Film and videotape possibly available for research, duplication and reuse, subject to restrictions.
Description: Films (1951-69) concerning former Republican Senate Minority Leader Everett McKinley Dirksen (1896-1969). Most of the material consists of Dirksen's weekly television program, *Your Senator Reports.* Produced in the Senate Recording Studio, these brief programs (each 7 to 15 min.) were distributed to various Illinois television stations.

Other films include *Everett Dirksen's Washington* (1968), a tour of the Capitol Building; *Everett Dirksen: A Self-Portrait* (1965), an interview with Roger Mudd; and *A Day in the Life of Your Senator* (1956), a film portraying Dirksen's typical working day.
Size & Elements: Film: format unspecified (944 titles, 681 unique; mostly black and white, duplicate negatives, masters and projection prints). Videotape: 2" (1 title).
Cataloging: Research library; finding aids.
Access: Open to the public. Many films unavailable for viewing. Available for duplication and reuse, subject to restrictions. Research fees not charged. Research fees accepted by mail, telephone and in person (by appointment only).
Rights: Full rights held to some material.
Licensing: Available for licensing and reuse, subject to restrictions. License fees not charged.
Restrictions: Viewing of many items is restricted. Other restrictions may apply.
Viewing Facilities: Film (restricted).
Duplication Facilities: None.
Related Materials: Transcripts for television programs available in the Remarks and Releases series of the Dirksen papers.

ILLINOIS (Peoria)

**BOARD OF TRADE OF THE CITY OF CHICAGO
c/o VENARD FILMS, LTD.**
P.O. Box 1332
Peoria, IL 61654
(309) 699-3911

Contact: For permission to reuse: Laura LaBarbera (312/435-3500)
Services: Commodities exchange. Films and videotapes available for rental,

purchase and reuse, subject to restrictions.

Description: Films and videotapes relating to commodities and the Board of Trade. Titles available include: *Where the World's Market Forces Converge; Agriculture Futures: The Stabilizing Force in World Agriculture; Financial Futures: The Stabilizing Force in Effective Money Management; Hedging: The Business of Risk Management; Options: A Positive Choice for Risk Management; Speculating: The Business of Risk Transference;* and *Futures in Your Life.*

Size & Elements: Film and videotape: various formats (7 titles).

Access: Open to the public. Available for rental and purchase from Venard Films, Ltd. and for free loan from Modern Talking Picture Service, Inc. (q.v.). Requests accepted by mail and telephone.

Rights: Full rights held to all material.

Licensing: Available for licensing and reuse, subject to restrictions. License fees charged, depending on intended use of material.

Restrictions: Restrictions may apply to reuse of some material.

Viewing Facilities: None.

Duplication Facilities: None.

ILLINOIS (Peoria)

VENARD FILMS, LTD.
P.O. Box 1332
Peoria, IL 61654
(309) 699-3911

Gary Smith (President)

Contact: Gary Smith

Services: Film and videotape producer and distributor.

Description: Producer and distributor of agricultural films since 1917. Represents 52 agricultural organizations and corporations, including livestock breed associations, Future Farmers of America, DuPont, Cyanamid, Ciba-Geigy and producers of agricultural products. Has recently acquired the collection of the Grange-Farm Film Foundation library.

Older materials from the Farm Film Foundation and many other films related to agriculture are held at the American Archives of the Factual Film, Iowa State University (q.v.).

Size & Elements: Film: 16mm (3,500 titles; release prints). Videotape: VHS. (110 titles total).

Cataloging: Published catalog.

Access: Maintained for distribution and rental primarily to individuals and organizations within the agricultural industry. Requests accepted by mail and telephone.

Rights: No rights held to any material. Rights retained by sponsors. Additional clearances are necessary if material is to be reused.

Licensing: Apply for information.

Restrictions: Requests for reuse subject to clearance by film sponsors. Terms negotiated on a case-by-case basis with sponsors.

Viewing Facilities: None.

Duplication Facilities: None.

ILLINOIS (Rosemont)

NATIONAL DAIRY COUNCIL
6300 North River Road
Rosemont, IL 60018-4233
(312) 696-1860 (Ext. 220)

Contacts: Marge Blahut

Services: Nonprofit scientific and educational organization. Films and videotapes primarily available for purchase.

Description: Dairy products and nutritional education. Titles include: *Wholly Cow,* showing how cows digest feed, absorb nutrients and use these nutrients to make milk; *Milk...in the Computer Age,* following a sixth-grade class on a tour through a modern dairy farm and a milk-processing plant, emphasizing the steps taken to protect the quality, safety and good flavor of milk; *Uncle Jim's Dairy Farm,* a short drama about a city boy who visits his cousin's family on their modern dairy farm; *Spice of Life,* teaching basic principles of healthful eating and gives practical suggestions for meal planning, grocery shopping, food storage and preparation; *Osteoporosis, Are You at Risk for Bone Disease?,* designed for adults (especially women), teenagers and health professionals, addressing risk factors, symptoms and prevention; and *Your Body, Your Diet and Cholesterol.*

Additional materials available as part of the *Lifesteps* adult weight and health management program include: *Such a Pretty Face; Monitoring: I Hardly Ate a Thing All Day; Chaining: One Thing Leads to Another;* and *Dealing with Others: The Diet Saboteurs; Osteoporosis and You;* and *Nutrition and Your Busy Lifestyle.*

Many titles are available in both film and videotape versions.

Size & Elements: Film: 16mm (release prints). Videotape: 3/4", VHS and Betamax II. (10 titles total).

Cataloging: Published catalogs.

Access: Contact national office or local affiliates (Order Department). Available to the public for purchase. Orders accepted by mail and telephone.

Rights: Full rights held to all material.

Licensing: Contact Gloria Kristopek, M.S., R.D. for copyright information or permission to reprint. Materials possibly available for licensing; some titles approved for use on educational, closed-circuit, nonprofit cable and/or network television.

Restrictions: Materials protected by copyright; permission required for any reuse.

Viewing Facilities: None.

Duplication Facilities: None.

Related Materials: Teacher guides available for some titles.

ILLINOIS (Schaumburg)

AMERICAN VETERINARY MEDICAL ASSOCIATION
930 North Meacham Road
Schaumburg, IL 60196-1074
(312) 605-8070
Fax: (312) 330-2862

Available for rental from:
MODERN TALKING PICTURE SERVICE, INC. (q.v.)

A. Roland Dommert (Executive Vice President)

Contacts: Sharon Curtis (Public Information Assistant); Jean L. Spears (Public Information Assistant)

Services: Membership association. *Film and videotape material restricted for use by association members and closely related groups only; not available to the general public.*

Description: Veterinary medicine and animal health. Includes titles suitable for public presentations to school groups, agricultural organizations, pet owners and others interested in veterinary medicine and animal health; other technical and semi-technical titles are primarily for use in colleges of veterinary medicine and for continuing education of graduate veterinarians, although some can be used for programs involving knowledgeable livestock producers, including 4-H and FFA members, Explorer Scouts in veterinary science posts, and other special interest groups.

General interest titles include: *Animals Can Bite; A Day in the Life of a Large Animal Practitioner; The Deadly Sting; The Extension Veterinarian; Furred, Feathered and Finned; A Horse of Her Own; I've Got to See the Doctor; Laboratory Animal Medicine; Planned Pethood; The Public Service Veterinarian; Rabies; The Small Animal Practitioner; Today's Veterinarian; Tomorrow's Veterinarian; Use of Animals for Research; Veal Farming is Special; Welcome Neighbor;* and *The Zoo Veterinarian.*

Collection also includes hundreds of technical and semi-technical films and videotapes covering such subject areas as: avian, bovine, canine, diagnostic, equine, feline, laboratory animals, porcine, sheep/goat and llama, surgery and wildlife.

Size & Elements: Film: 16mm. Videotape: 3/4" and VHS. (Over 300 titles total).

Cataloging: Published catalogs; card catalogs.

Access: Not available to the general public. Available for free loan or purchase to AVMA members only. Modern Talking Picture Service, Inc. (q.v.) distributes AVMA films and videotapes for free loan to AVMA and student AVMA members, constituent associations, veterinary medical associations, auxiliaries, colleges and departments of veterinary medicine, animal technician training programs and armed forces veterinary medical units in the United States. Research requests accepted by mail and telephone.

Rights: Full rights held to material produced by AVMA. Additional clearances may be necessary for reuse of material produced by others.

Licensing: Available for licensing and reuse, subject to restrictions. License fees charged in some cases, depending on intended use of material.

Restrictions: Requests for licensing or reuse considered on a case-by-case basis. Limited reuse of material permitted. Duplication of programs is prohibited without specific written permission from the producer and/or

sponsor.
Viewing Facilities: None.
Duplication Facilities: None.

ILLINOIS (Schaumburg)

NATIONAL SOCIETY TO PREVENT BLINDNESS
500 East Remington Road
Schaumburg, IL 60173
(312) 843-2020

Michael L. Weamer (Executive Director)

Contacts: Linda Shaub (Director, Marketing and Communications); Suzanne Gedance
Services: Voluntary health agency; film and videotape producer. Media library maintained for rental, purchase and reuse, subject to restrictions.
Description: Devoted to the prevention of blindness through public education, the Society maintains a film and videotape library. Subjects covered include eye safety and protective eyewear, preschool vision screening, glaucoma education, blindness, cataracts, lazy eye, and the effect of diabetes on the eyes.
  Medical. Titles include: *Glaucoma, A Silent Threat to Sight; Seeing,* a drama on glaucoma starring Helen Hayes, emphasizing the importance of sight to the fullest enjoyment of life and the world around us; *Small Surprises,* an animated film showing how glaucoma can gradually cause loss of sight; *Vision Loss: Focus on Feelings,* in which six people with different types of eye problems discuss their common fears and concerns; *Before We Are Six,* preparing professionals and volunteers to screen the vision of preschool children; *Crossroads at Four,* dramatizing the discovery of a young boy's unrecognized amblyopia; *Johnny's New World,* showing the need for early detection and treatment of children's eye problems; and *The Lazy Eye,* a documentary emphasizing the importance of early eye care for children.
  Safety. Titles include: *An Option to See,* encouraging students to use safety eyewear in labs and shops; *Don't Push Your Luck,* vividly depicting a eye-blinding accident in an industrial plant; *Eye and Face Protection in Chemical Laboratories,* showing the violence of chemical explosions, their danger to person and property and how the laboratory can be made safe; *Eye on the Home,* describing the most common eye hazards faced in and around the house; *For the Rest of Your Life,* demonstrating the inherently dangerous properties of anhydrous ammonia fertilizer, and how careless use can have blinding effects; *It's Still Up to You,* a forceful eye safety message, including an eye surgery sequence; *Protect Your Eyes on the Job,* featuring famous sight crusader Bill Frank, blinded in an industrial accident, telling why employees must wear safety glasses "every second, every minute, every hour on the job"; and *The Eyes Have It,* in which marionettes demonstrate eye safety at home and at school.
Size & Elements: Film: 16mm (18 titles). Videotape: 3/4", VHS and Betamax (sale copies transferred from film).
Cataloging: Published catalog (available upon request).
Access: Available to the public for rental, purchase and reuse, subject to approval. Requests accepted by mail and telephone.
Rights: Full rights held to most material. Most titles copyrighted by Society. Additional clearances may be necessary in some cases if material is to be reused.
Licensing: Available for licensing and reuse, subject to restrictions. License fees charged in some cases.
Restrictions: Written permission required for reuse. Requests for reuse subject to acceptance and approval.
Viewing Facilities: None.
Duplication Facilities: None.

ILLINOIS (Springfield)

ILLINOIS STATE HISTORICAL LIBRARY
PRINTS AND PHOTOGRAPHS
Old State Capitol
Springfield, IL 62701
(217) 785-7955

Contact: Mary Michals (Iconographer)
Services: Historical library. Film and videotape collection maintained for research purposes; material available for licensing and reuse, subject to restrictions.
Description: Illinois governors and public figures; Illinois history; regional politics; American history and politics.

Adlai Stevenson Collection. Documentary materials dating from the 1940s, including footage of Stevenson's governorship and presidential campaign; campaign speeches; television debates; and advertising.
  Sample footage includes President Harry S Truman's arrival in Chicago, a parade to Soldiers' Field, Governor Stevenson's and President Truman's speeches at the convention; ceremonies at Lincoln's Tomb, with laying of wreaths and several speakers, including Stevenson; Governor Stevenson's party at the State Fair on opening day; Stevenson and his sons in the stands at the Harvard-Princeton football game; a biographical narrative with still photographs of Stevenson, including pictures with Truman, John F. Kennedy, Nikita Khrushchev and Dwight D. Eisenhower; Stevenson playing disc jockey at a local radio station to benefit the March of Dimes; an informal debate between Stevenson and Estes Kefauver on defense, the hydrogen bomb, peaceful use of atomic energy, foreign policy and segregation (1956). Also holds promotional materials, including *Three Strangers,* a short film in which a woman elevator operator and her two male passengers are stuck in an elevator during an air-raid warning system test. One man is for Stevenson; the other is for Eisenhower; they discuss the merits of their candidates and each tries to convince the woman to vote for his favorite.
  Illinois Information Service Collection. Films cover Governor William G. Stratton; Illinois State Fair; highways and state buildings; conferences and banquets. Titles include *American Governors in the Soviet Union* (1959); *King Hussein Visits Springfield;* and *President Eisenhower's Address at Peoria* (1956).
  Also held are films on Monticello college student life; the Illinois Sesquicentennial; Carl Sandburg; Illinois Constitutional Convention (1970); Illinois Bicentennial Commission; state fairs; tourist attractions; and Abraham Lincoln.
  Sample films documenting the history of the state include *First Motion Pictures of Chicago from a Flying Machine,* with footage from old 35mm local newsfilms; *From Genesis to Jones,* depicting the Black struggle for freedom from slavery in Illinois; *It's All Yours, Vet,* on World War II veterans; and *Our Struggle in the South,* produced by the AFL-CIO.
  Public figures represented in film collections include Governor Ogilvie, Justice John Paul Stevens, Senator Ralph T. Smith; Representatives Springer, Kent Keller, Scott Lucas, Paul Powell and Luther Hodges.
Size & Elements: Film: 35mm and 16mm (over 200 titles). Videotape: format unspecified (approx. 20 videotapes).
Cataloging: Inventory listings.
Access: Open to researchers, scholars and the public. Research fees not charged. Research requests accepted by mail, telephone and in person (walk-in).
Rights: Full rights held to some material. Some rights held to all material.
Licensing: Available for licensing and reuse, subject to restrictions. License fees generally not charged.
Restrictions: All requests for licensing and reuse subject to approval on a case-by-case basis.
Viewing Facilities: Film and videotape.
Duplication Facilities: None.

ILLINOIS (Urbana)

UNIVERSITY OF ILLINOIS AT URBANA-CHAMPAIGN
UNIVERSITY ARCHIVES
19 Main Library
1408 West Gregory Drive
Urbana, IL 61801
(217) 333-0798

Maynard Brichford (University Archivist)

Contacts: Maynard Brichford; Robert Chapel
Services: University archives. Film and videotape collection open to researchers, scholars and the public for in-house use. Material available for licensing and reuse, subject to restrictions.
Description: Advertising Council public service advertising spots; campaign advertisements (1983-present); materials relating to education; footage of the 3rd Armored Division in World War II; extensive holdings of instructional and educational broadcasting productions; and University athletic events.
  Advertising Council videotapes. Includes: *Finding Solutions* (Dec. 20, 1983, 24 min.), a piece on the Ad Council, public service advertising and the *Take A Bite Out Of Crime* campaign; historical spots (each 10-20 seconds) of television film used in campaigns.
  Band films. 31 reels (16mm) of University Band performances, including High School Band Day performances, with three film clips of the University

band on tour at the inauguration in Washington, D.C. (1957), and films of football band formations (1934-47).

Third Armored Division Association. Motion pictures, some relating to World War II (1936, 1940-45).

University film clips. Includes 44 clips (1-5 min.) on University news subjects: football band, Block I, sports, student activities, University buildings and the Chicago medical campus; East and Central Illinois-area news relating to the University; the University team's appearance on *G.E. College Bowl* (1960), Krannert Center for the Performing Arts (ca. 1965), David D. Henry Centennial Address (1968), University Christmas shows (1970-79); John E. Corbally's addresses on the state of the University (1971-77); various departmental productions, e.g., *Feeding The Nation* (Agriculture Department), *Anthropology Field Trips, Art Extension, Olympic Gymnastics* (exercise on saddle) and *Physical Education for Men* (Navy Pier); *Art film: man walking on campus* (Abraham Rattner); retarded children's activities; *Tau Kappa Epsilon Initiation; The Story of the UI Airport; Rose Bowl Parade and Games* (1953 and 1964); installations of Presidents David Henry (1956) and George Stoddard (1946); Morning Star Free Will Baptist Church; interviews with agriculturists Orville Freeman and William Kuhfuss; Illinois politicians, including Otto Kerner and Adlai Stevenson; newsreel and documentary footage (ca. 1960-72).

WILL-TV documentaries. Videotapes produced by WILL-TV concerning human and race relations issues in Decatur, Springfield, Danville and Champaign-Urbana, including: *Justice: Color Blind or Just Blind; Black and Proud,* an interview with the Smiths, the first Black family in Champaign County; *This Bus Stops,* on equal educational opportunity in universities, elementary and high schools; and *Once A Ghetto.*

CBS Newsfilm (1957-61). News stories concerned with world affairs, politics, civil rights, natural disasters, fires, labor relations, fashions, scientific achievements, sports and holidays. Prominent individuals covered include Dwight D. Eisenhower, Harry S Truman, Richard M. Nixon, Jimmy Hoffa, Robert Kennedy, Nelson Rockefeller, W. Averell Harriman, Charles de Gaulle, John Foster Dulles, Pope Pius XII, Pope John XXIII, Orval Faubus, Adlai Stevenson, Lyndon B. Johnson, Queen Elizabeth and Winston Churchill.

Miscellaneous newsfilm. Includes items from: The French Ministry of Foreign Affairs (ca. 1967); The British Information Service (1961, 1964-66); National Television News (1963-69) on sports, economic outlooks and the automobile industry; Mercury Newsfilm (ca. 1964-68) on fashions, technical advances and commerce; Krosney Productions on Israel; Telenews (1967) on social security; News-screen on health care and appliances; Colorfilm on the small farm; Reader's Digest on school dropouts; and films on the Gizz Kids, a Champaign sports car rally, hunting wild turkeys and the College All Star Game (1959).

Illinois Constitution. A series of 19 videotaped programs (1975) concerning the Illinois Constitution, produced by Harrison K. Cornell and hosted by Edward Cade and Henry Lippold (UI Television News Director). Programs include: *Rules from Yesterday's Society; A Matter of Reapportionment; Home Rule for Chicago; Innovation and Obsolescence; To Revise, Amend or Abolish.*

Size & Elements: Film: 16mm (600 cans; 84.7 cubic feet in 19 records series; positive). Videotape: 2", 3/4" and VHS (60 videotapes; 20.6 cubic feet in 12 records series; viewing copies).
Cataloging: Card catalogs; finding aids; published catalogs; computerized cataloging available to researchers; research library.
Access: Open to researchers, scholars and the public. For in-house use only. Research fees not charged. Available for duplication, subject to restrictions. Research requests accepted by mail, telephone and in person (walk-in).
Rights: Some rights held to some material. Some material in the public domain. Additional clearances may be necessary in some cases if material is to be reused.
Licensing: Available for licensing and reuse, subject to restrictions. License fees not charged.
Restrictions: "Whenever a film or videotape is used in a public performance or broadcast, credit should be given to the University of Illinois Archives. Where necessary, the name of the record series or collection should be cited. Permission to use film or videotape is granted for research or single educational usage. Before public performance or broadcast, users must obtain advice as to its availability for performance. The Archives assumes no responsibility for the infringement of copyrights held by the original producers of films or videotapes."
Viewing Facilities: Film (16mm); videotape (3/4").
Duplication Facilities: "Persons wishing to obtain copies of films and videotapes may either bring their own equipment to the Archives or request that the Archives staff take the desired film or videotape to the Division of Broadcasting or a local vendor, who will make the necessary copies and bill the requester."
Related Materials: Still photographs, audiotapes, print materials, clippings, scrapbooks, artifacts, diaries, military Christmas cards, maps and travel literature.

ILLINOIS (Washington)

VIDEO I-D, INC.
105 Muller Road
Washington, IL 61571
(309) 444-4323
(309) 637-3131

Sam Wagner (President)

Contacts: Rick Holman (Production Chief); Stan Ellwood (Sales Representative); Sam Wagner
Services: Videotape producer. Material available for duplication, licensing and reuse.
Description: Scenics and wildlife footage of Canada (including backwoods areas); Florida (including the Florida Keys); Georgia; the Great Lakes, Illinois, Louisiana, and Minnesota; nature scenes and wildlife, including various U.S. wildlife and birds (e.g., eagles and loons); fishing scenes (sportfishing); bird hunting, including ducks, dogs working, puppies and upland game; agriculture, including fields, farming, plowing, harvesting, corn and soybeans; industrial shots; limited skylines and traffic scenes of Peoria, Chicago, Boston and Washington, D.C.
Size & Elements: Videotape: 3/4" (approx. 120 hours; broadcast-quality masters). Viewing copies available in any videotape format.
Cataloging: Computerized cataloging for staff use only (in process).
Access: Available to the public for duplication, licensing and reuse. Research fees not charged. Research requests accepted by mail, telephone and in person (walk-in and by appointment).
Rights: Full rights held to all material.
Licensing: Available for licensing. License fees charged.
Restrictions: None specified.
Viewing Facilities: Videotape (3/4" and VHS).
Duplication Facilities: Videotape (1", 3/4" and VHS).

ILLINOIS (Westchester)

NATIONAL INDUSTRIAL BELTING ASSOCIATION
2400 South Downing Street
Westchester, IL 60154
(312) 562-9063
Fax: (312) 562-8436

Charles J. Blanchard (Executive Vice President)

Contact: Sue Smith (Coordinator)
Services: Association. Videotapes available to the public and NIBA members for distribution.
Description: Holds a series of three videotape lessons designed for the entry-level employee for the purposes of acquainting the employee with the products, terms, and identification of products distributed by NIBA members.
Light Weight Conveyor Belt covers typical applications, roller support/slider bed, carcass construction, cover compounds, cover combinations, incline service belts, cleats, pegs and lugs, edge flanges and tracking guides. *Heavy Belt* explains typical applications, carcass construction, cover compounds, cover combinations and loading cycles. *Mechanical Belt Fasteners* covers the advantages, materials of construction, factors determining selection, solid plate fastener types, hinged fastener types, hinge pin types, installation tools and proper squaring of belt ends.
Size & Elements: Videotape: VHS, Betamax, and other formats (3 titles).
Cataloging: Printed lists available upon request.
Access: Available to the public and NIBA members for distribution. Maintained for distribution and rental rather than for research or reuse. Requests accepted by mail and telephone.
Rights: Full rights held to all material.
Licensing: Apply for information.
Restrictions: None specified.
Viewing Facilities: None.
Duplication Facilities: None.
Related Materials: Administrative guides designed to accompany videotape lessons.

ILLINOIS (Wheaton)

WHEATON COLLEGE
BILLY GRAHAM CENTER
ARCHIVES
Wheaton, IL 60187
(312) 260-5910

Robert Shuster (Director)

Contact: Lannae Graham (Reference Archivist)
Services: Educational institution. Film and videotape archives open to the public for in-house use only; availability for duplication is limited.
Description: Footage (1928-86) generally documenting the preaching component of evangelistic work. Collection touches on a wide range of topics, including the evangelistic use of dramatic film and television productions. Important items include kinescopes of Percy Crawford's *Youth on the March* television program (1949-54); footage of Salvation Army founder William Booth; evangelist Daniel Paul Rader; preacher and evangelist Billy Sunday; evangelist Aimee Semple McPherson; preacher Harry Ironside. Also available is footage of missionary life and indigenous cultures, usually shot as home movies by missionaries, notably in India, Tibet and several African countries.

Baptista Film Mission Records (1939-59). Over 65 16mm films and 10 3/4" videotapes documenting BFM's production of evangelistic films, including *The Story of a Fountain Pen* (1939) and information on the beginnings of the Christian film industry.

Billy Graham Center Records (1980-81). Documentation of various events at the Center, ranging from its opening to addresses and panels featured at its conferences (25 videotapes, 3/4" and VHS).

Billy Graham Evangelistic Association (BGEA) Records (1957-79). Graham's and BGEA's evangelistic crusades. (190 16mm films, 1957-75; 110 3/4" videotapes, 1969-79). Also includes news interviews with Graham, television specials and copies of several films.

World Wide Pictures. 363 films and 112 videotapes.

Leighton Ford Crusade Office (1964-1973). 21 16mm films and two 2" videotapes directed by Norman Pell and Irv Chambers, relating to crusades preached by Leighton Ford and other associate evangelists.

Walter F. Bennett and Company Records (1943-77). Films and videotapes produced under the direction of the advertising firm Bennett and Company for the Billy Graham Evangelistic Association. Includes 120 16mm films (1951-54) of the television program *Hour of Decision* and BGEA crusades; films of BGEA crusades (1950, 1957-62); and over 40 3/4" crusade videotapes (1974-79). Also a number of 3/4" videotape viewing copies of films (1950-58).

William Booth (1829-1912). One videotape containing black and white photographs and filmed segments of Salvation Army activities, including Booth's funeral.

William Marrion Branham (1905-65). Two 16mm films, two 3/4" videotapes and other materials containing sermons preached by charismatic-healing evangelist William Branham, including the healing portions of services.

Christian Films and Videotapes (1980-85). Topics related to mission and evangelism. (22 videotapes, 3/4" and 1/2").

Percy Crawford Ephemera (1949-54). Crawford's half-hour television program *Youth On The March,* one of the first evangelical television programs. (51 16mm films transferred to 3/4" videotape).

Silas Fowler Fox. Six 8mm films documenting Fox's career as an independent missionary in the Telugu-speaking area of India. The collection also holds information on indigenous Indian evangelists.

William Franklin "Billy" Graham Jr. (1949-83). Gathered from various sources, material relates to Graham's family history, his work as an evangelist and his public image. Includes videotapes of television programs about Graham, as well as information on his television work. (77 films, 18 3/4" videotapes).

Kathryn Kuhlman Foundation Records (1950s-75). 37 16mm films and 1,108 2" and 3/4" videotapes documenting Kuhlman's evangelistic and healing ministry. Beginning with her early life and ranging from her first years of ministry to the establishment of her work in Franklin (Pa.), Pittsburgh (Pa.) and Los Angeles (Calif.), materials document her ministry to the time of her death and eventual closing of the Foundation (1982).

Aimee Semple McPherson (1890-1944). Two films and one VHS videotape relating to McPherson's career as evangelist, radio speaker and church founder.

Pioneer Ministries Records (1939-present). Relating to the work of the Pioneer Ministries (formerly Pioneer Girls) in North American Churches, these describe origins, philosophy and ministry; work with sister movements in other countries; and the framework of the organization's program.

Victor Guy Plymire (1881-1956). Two 3/4" videotapes pertaining to the career of the Assemblies of God missionary. Documents evangelistic work among various strata of Tibetan society and also his evangelistic and exploratory expedition through Tibet (1927-28).

Prison Ministry Videotapes (1985-present). 11 3/4" videotapes.

Slavic Gospel Association Records (1930s-68). 72 films and one VHS videotape dealing with the early career of Peter Deyneka Sr., the work of individual missionaries, and evangelism in Europe, North America and South America.

William Ashley "Billy" Sunday (1862-1935). One 16mm film relating to Sunday's ministry as an evangelist.

Herbert John Taylor (1893-1978). Five 16mm films documenting BGEA's 1962 Chicago crusade.
Size & Elements: Film: 16mm and 8mm (approx. 750,000 feet, approx. 600 titles, 1,000 cans; primarily release prints, a few originals). Videotape: 2" (approx. 800 videotapes; some masters); 3/4" (approx. 400 videotapes; viewing copies) and VHS (80 videotapes; viewing copies).
Cataloging: Computerized catalog for staff use only; unpublished guides to individual collections; microfiche catalog.
Access: Open to the public. For in-house use only. Limited availability for duplication. Research fees not charged. Research requests accepted by mail, telephone and in person (walk-in).
Rights: Some rights held to some material.
Licensing: Apply for information. License fees not charged.
Restrictions: Material available for duplication on a limited basis.
Viewing Facilities: Film (16mm RTI previewer); videotape (3/4" and VHS).
Duplication Facilities: Film (16mm film chain in College Media Services Department); videotape (3/4" and VHS).
Related Materials: Still photographs and negatives, audiotapes, phonograph records, slide transparencies, print materials, microfilm and oversize materials.

ILLINOIS (Wheaton)

WHEATON COLLEGE
THE MARION E. WADE CENTER
Wheaton, IL 60187
(312) 260-5908

Dr. Lyle W. Dorsett (Director)

Contact: Virginia Kolb (Assistant Archivist)
Services: Library; research center; special collection. Videotape collection open to the public for in-house use only. Material available for licensing and reuse, subject to restrictions.
Description: Oral history interviews with Owen Barfield, G. K. Chesterton, C. S. Lewis, Dorothy L. Sayers, J. R. R. Tolkien and Charles Williams, including lectures on these authors and on George MacDonald. Center is also in the process of building a major videotaped oral history record of the reminiscences of these authors' relatives, friends and associates.
Size & Elements: Videotape: format unspecified (approx. 50 videotapes; masters and viewing copies).
Cataloging: Research library.
Access: Open to the public. For in-house use only. Research requests accepted by mail, telephone and in person (walk-in).
Rights: Full rights held to some material. Some rights held to some material. Additional clearances may be necessary in some cases if material is to be reused.
Licensing: Available for licensing, subject to restrictions. License fees charged in some cases.
Restrictions: Licensing and reuse subject to clearance and approval.
Viewing Facilities: Videotape.
Duplication Facilities: None.
Related Materials: "Several hundred" audiotapes, authors' published works, letters, manuscripts and literary ephemera.

INDIANA

INDIANA (Auburn)

AUBURN-CORD-DUESENBERG MUSEUM
TRI-KAPPA COLLECTION OF AUBURN AUTOMOTIVE
LITERATURE
P.O. Box 271
Auburn, IN 46706

INDIANA (Bloomington)

(219) 925-1444

Street address: 1600 South Wayne Street

Skip Marketti (Director)

Contact: Lee Beck (Staff Archivist)
Services: Museum. Archival film and videotape collection not currently accessible.
Description: Films relating to the Auburn automotive heritage, all produced in Indiana (1930s). Many are industrial films produced by the Auburn Automobile Company; others are unique to the collection. Topics include land speed records being set at Bonneville (Utah), footage showing the manufacturing of the 1927 Auburn, and Ab Jenkins' speed record (1935).
Size & Elements: Film and videotape: formats unspecified (approx. 20-25 titles). Nitrate film has been transferred to videotape.
Cataloging: Presently undergoing cataloging and reorganization.
Access: Currently not open to the public. When archives is ready for operation material will be available for research, duplication and reuse.
Rights: Full rights held to all material.
Licensing: When archives is in operation, license fees will be charged for use of material.
Restrictions: Collection currently not accessible.
Viewing Facilities: None.
Duplication Facilities: None.

INDIANA (Bloomington)

INDIANA UNIVERSITY
AUDIO-VISUAL CENTER
Bloomington, IN 47405-5901
(812) 335-2103 (for rental)
(812) 855-8087 (for purchase)

Thomas Schwen (Executive Director)

Contact: Martha Harsanyi (Reference Librarian) (812/335-8065); Chris Wagner (Field Services; for purchase inquiries)
Services: Educational institution; film and videotape distributor. Materials available for rental and purchase. *Not a stock footage source.*
Description: One of the oldest, largest and most comprehensive educational film libraries in the United States, the Center has distributed films since ca. 1940. The Rental Library loans films to universities and educational institutions, and rents films to the general public. The collection holds approximately 14,000 titles (late 1930s-present), but the current catalog lists approximately 7,500 (now in circulation). Most titles originate from outside sources; a smaller number are distributed by the Center; some were produced by the Center itself.

Within the Rental Library, some films are available for rental and purchase. These films originate primarily from local (mostly nonprofit) sources, but a few commercial sources do provide materials for sale and rental. Rights to some of this material are controlled by the Center. Sources of these films include: A-V Center productions; public television stations, including WTIU (Bloomington), WTTW (Chicago), WNET (New York), WQED (Pittsburgh) and KQED (San Francisco); independent filmmakers or filmmaking organizations; National Film Board of Canada; and a few commercial distributors.

National Educational Television (NET) collection (ca. 1955-72, approx. 10,000 titles). Center is exclusive distributor of this collection and holds programming ranging from early "chalk-talks" to sophisticated experimental programming. Although many titles in this collection have been withdrawn from sale, they can still be rented or loaned (unless withdrawn from circulation due to the delicate physical condition of the material, or if material is outdated or offensive in content). There is no published catalog for this material. Restricted items are not available to the general public, but can be made available to qualified film researchers with credentials (for on-premises viewing only).
Size & Elements: Film: 16mm (approx. 14,000 titles; mostly release prints). Videotape: 3/4" and VHS (viewing copies). Originals held for locally produced materials. Sales collection holds internegatives and master videotapes for each title.
Cataloging: Published catalog of current holdings (approx. 7,500 titles). Computerized cataloging for staff use only (includes a percentage of noncurrent holdings); staff assistance required.
Access: Available to the public for rental and purchase. Circulating collection

open to researchers, scholars and the public for on-premises viewing. Restricted items available to qualified researchers and scholars only. Research fees not charged. Research requests accepted by mail.
Rights: Full rights held to some material. Some rights held to some material. No rights held to some material. Additional clearances may be necessary in some cases if material is to be reused.
Licensing: Some material (Center-controlled titles) available for reuse, subject to availability and restrictions. All requests for licensing and reuse considered on a case-by-case basis.
Restrictions: *Not a stock footage source.* Most material unavailable for reuse. All requests for licensing and reuse considered on a case-by-case basis. Rental materials cannot be shown where there is an admission charge; no broadcast or duplication of any kind is permitted.
Viewing Facilities: Film (16mm projector); videotape (3/4" and 1/2").
Duplication Facilities: Reference-quality duplication facilities (apply for information).
Distributors: Many titles are distributed through other university media center libraries.

INDIANA (Bloomington)

INDIANA UNIVERSITY
BLACK FILM CENTER/ARCHIVE
Department of Afro-American Studies
Memorial Hall East
Bloomington, IN 47405
(812) 855-2684
(812) 855-6041

Dr. Phyllis R. Klotman (Director)

Contact: Dr. Gloria Gibson-Hudson (Assistant Director)
Services: Film and videotape archives. Material available to students, researchers, scholars and the public for in-house use only; not available for licensing or reuse.
Description: Repository of "Black films" and related materials. Black films include those which have substantial participation by Afro-Americans as writers, actors, producers, directors, musicians and consultants, as well as those which depict some aspect of the Black experience. Archives contains features, documentaries, dramatic and musical short subjects, comedy shorts, newsreels and animation in many film and videotape formats. Also holds videotaped interviews with filmmakers.

General collection. Includes important films made by independent Black and White filmmakers, including *Scar of Shame* (1927), a silent dramatic film produced by Colored Players Film Corporation, directed by Frank Perugini, starring Harry Henderson and Lucia Lynn Moses; *God's Step Children* (Oscar Micheaux, 1938); *The Blood of Jesus* (1941) and *Go Down Death* (1944), two religious folk dramas by Spencer Williams. Contemporary dramatic films by Black independents include *Bush Mama* (Haile Gerima, 1976); *A Place in Time* (Charles Lane, 1976); *Passing Through* (Larry Clark, 1977); *Killer of Sheep* (Charles Burnett, 1977); *A Different Image* (Alile Sharon Larkin, 1981); *Illusions* (Julie Dash, 1982); *Losing Ground* (Kathleen Collins, 1982); *Bless Their Little Hearts* (Billy Woodberry, 1984); and *Hair Piece: A Film for Nappy Headed People* (1984), an animated short by Ayoka Chenzira.

Norman Motion Picture Collection. From 1920 to 1928, Richard E. Norman, a White entrepreneur, produced seven all-Black cast films. Archive holds the only surviving film, *The Flying Ace,* a 1920s-style melodrama. Paper records are also available.

The Major Motion Picture Collection includes films produced by Hollywood studios (1929-75) including: *Hallelujah!* (MGM, 1929), the second musical sound film starring Blacks, directed by King Vidor; *The Green Pastures* (Warner Brothers, 1936), directed by William Keighley; *Cabin in the Sky* (MGM, 1943), an all-Black cast musical directed by Vincente Minnelli, starring Lena Horne, Ethel Waters and Eddie Anderson; *Intruder in the Dust* (MGM, 1949), directed by Clarence Brown, an adaptation of Faulkner's novel, exploring lynch law mentality in a small Southern town; *The Defiant Ones* (United Artists, 1967), directed by Stanley Kramer, starring Sidney Poitier and Tony Curtis as escapees from a chain gang; *In The Heat of the Night* (United Artists, 1967), directed by Norman Jewison, starring Sidney Poitier as a northern detective helping a southern sheriff solve a crime; *Cotton Comes to Harlem* (United Artists, 1970), directed by Ossie Davis, starring Raymond St. Jacques and Godfrey Cambridge as two Harlem detectives; *The Learning Tree* (Warner Brothers, 1969), directed by Gordon Parks, an adaptation of his autobiographical novel; *Shaft* (MGM, 1971), directed by Gordon Parks, starring Richard Roundtree as a street-smart detective; and *Lady Sings the*

Blues (Paramount, 1972), an adaptation of Billie Holliday's autobiography, directed by Sidney J. Furie, starring Diana Ross and Billy Dee Williams.

Size & Elements: Film: 16mm (approx. 150 titles; release prints). Videotape: 3/4" and 1/2" (100 videotapes; masters and viewing copies).

Cataloging: Card catalogs; computerized cataloging available to staff and researchers.

Access: Open to the public. For in-house use only. Research requests accepted by mail, telephone and in person (by appointment only). Research fees charged in some cases, depending on extent of request.

Rights: Full rights held to some material. Some rights held to some material. Some material in the public domain. Rights status to some material unknown.

Licensing: Material not available for licensing or reuse.

Restrictions: None specified.

Viewing Facilities: Film (16mm Cinescan and Moviola flatbed viewing equipment); videotape (VHS).

Duplication Facilities: None.

Related Materials: Materials relating to the film collection, including articles, stills and publicity photographs. Printouts can be made available of new material not yet included in second edition of *Frame by Frame: A Black Filmography,* by Phyllis R. Klotman (minimal fee charged).

INDIANA (Bloomington)

INDIANA UNIVERSITY FOLKLORE ARCHIVES
504 North Fess
Bloomington, IN 47405
(812) 855-0043

Archivist (appointed annually)

Contact: Inta Carpenter (Special Projects)

Services: Educational institution. Film and videotape archives maintained for research purposes; open to researchers and scholars only.

Description: Regional folklore of the Gary, Indiana area. During the early 1980s a group of folklorists from Indiana University conducted a local field study; many of the unedited videotapes of performances, interviews, steel mill workers, ethnic lore and music are now housed in the Folklore Archives.

Two films have also been produced by the Folklore Institute: *Classic Cars,* a study of the Auburn-Duesenberg automobiles once manufactured in northern Indiana; and *Joy Unspeakable,* documenting a study of Pentecostal religion in southern Indiana.

Size & Elements: Videotape: format unspecified (2 completed titles; viewing copies); other unedited videotape footage.

Cataloging: None.

Access: Open to researchers and scholars only. Research fees not charged. Research requests accepted in person (walk-in and by appointment).

Rights: Some rights held to all material. Additional clearances may be necessary in some cases if material is to be reused.

Licensing: Apply for information. License fees not charged.

Restrictions: None specified.

Viewing Facilities: None.

Duplication Facilities: None.

INDIANA (Bloomington)

THE KINSEY INSTITUTE FOR RESEARCH IN SEX, GENDER AND REPRODUCTION
INDIANA UNIVERSITY
Morrison Hall 313
Bloomington, IN 47405
(812) 335-7686

June Machover Reinisch, Ph.D. (Director)

Contact: Stephanie Sanders, Ph.D.

Services: Library; film and videotape producer. Film and videotape collection open to researchers and scholars only, subject to restrictions.

Description: Covers a wide variety of topics relating to sex and gender, dating from 1911 (the earliest film is entitled *El Satirio*) to the present. Consists largely of stag films, but includes other genres such as documentaries, narratives, experimental films, animation, educational and medical films; and a growing collection of videotapes. Original producers range from major studios to independents, artists, students and makers of home movies.

Films produced by the Kinsey Institute (all 16mm, black and white, silent;

available for rental). Titles include: *Mammalian Sexual Behavior: Reel #1* (15 min.) incorporating various segments (with commentaries) showing copulation in frogs, lizards, pigeons, sage grouse, rats, hamsters, guinea pigs, chinchillas, porcupines, rabbits, skunks and minks; *Mammalian Sexual Behavior: Reel #2* (15 min.) showing sheep, hogs, cattle, horses, elephants and chimpanzees; *Homosexual Animal Composite* (15 min.) on female homosexual behavior in rats, guinea pigs, cats, sheep, cattle and dogs; and male homosexual behavior in rats, guinea pigs, porcupines, rabbits cats, cattle and chimpanzees; and *Ponytail* (3 min., also available in 8mm), a home movie depicting a middle-aged married couple, very affectionate and unstaged.

Stag films. Sample titles include: *The Casting Couch; The Pick-Up;* and *Buried Treasure* (an animated cartoon from the 1920s).

Experimental. Sample titles include: *The Bed* (James Broughton, 1978); *Blue White, Blood's Tone and Vein* (Stan Brakhage, 1965); *Loving* (Brakhage, 1957); *Bodies* (students at Rutgers University, 1975); *Un Chant d'Amour* (Jean Genet); *Christmas On Earth* (Barbara Rubin, 1966); *Deep Donut* (Sweet Relish Films, 1977); *Fireworks* (Kenneth Anger, 1947); *Scorpio Rising* (Anger, 1964); *Flaming Creatures* (Jack Smith, 1963); *Noviciat (NOVICIA)* (Noel Burch, ca. 1964); and *Onan* (Takahiko Iimura, 1965).

Clinical. Sample titles include: *Physiological Responses of the Sexually Stimulated Female in the Laboratory* and *Physiological Responses of the Sexually Stimulated Male in the Laboratory* (Dr. Gorm Wagner, 1973), analyzing female and male sexual responses including sex flush and changes in pupils, clitoral enlargement, heart rate, vaginal sweating, tenting, and erection; and *Treatment of Erectile Impotence With an Inflatable Hydraulic Penile Prosthesis* (American Medical Systems, 1975).

Sex therapy and development. Sample titles include: *Imagery* (Edcoa, 1974), in which a sex therapist helps a young woman to express feelings about her body, sexuality and relationships; *Close-up* (Edcoa, 1975), with close-ups illustrating mutual giving in heterosexual intercourse; *The Erogenists* (Laird Sutton, 1971), showing a man giving a woman a full-body massage leading to orgasm; *Give To Get* (Laird Sutton, 1971), a woman massages a man leading to intercourse on a waterbed; *Heterosexual Intercourse* (Edcoa, 1971); *Holding* (Constance Beeson, 1970), depicting a relationship between two women through surrealistic flashbacks, montages and overlays; *A Look of Love* (Dick Kornbacher, 1974) showing a sexual relationship between two young people in a sensitive, explicitly erotic manner; *Sexuality and Communication* (Mobius Productions, 1974), presenting biomedical and emotional aspects of sexuality and emphasizing the importance of communication; *Touching* (Laird Sutton, 1972), in which a 34-year-old male paraplegic with a C-6 spinal cord injury participates in sexual activity with his female partner of three years; and *Vir Amat* (Laird Sutton, 1971), in which two young men who live together are shown preparing dinner, kissing, flirting and having sex relations.

Sexual techniques. Titles include: *An Experiment in the Teaching Methodology of Sensate Focus* (Edcoa, ca. 1974), in which a young couple discusses and demonstrates their techniques for teaching sexually dysfunctional couples the sensate focus exercises first described by Masters and Johnson; *Male Masturbation* (Focus International, 1975); *Relax and Enjoy It* (Behavioral Alternatives, ca. 1974), about masturbation therapy for pre-orgasmic females; and *Susan* (Laird Sutton, 1971), in which a woman explores several masturbatory techniques.

Self-help. Self-Health (1974) demonstrates breast self-examination, use of the speculum and the bi-manual exam; women discuss feelings about physicians' examinations.

Documentaries. Sample titles include: *I'm Something Else* (CTV, 1973), showing three male-to-female transsexuals in various stages of sex change discussing their feelings, prior histories, motivations for change and problems; *Kinsey Television Test* (NBC *Today,* 1956) with footage of Jordan Hall, the Institute offices and several takes of Alfred C. Kinsey being interviewed by Arlene Francis; *Mrs. Kinsey Interview* (WTIU-TV, 1975); *Lavender* (1972), a warm and revealing discussion by a lesbian couple; *Like Other People* (1973), about sexual and emotional relationships of handicapped people; *Sexual Freedom in Denmark* (1970), a commercial film comparing sexual behavior and social attitudes in Denmark with other countries; *This Nudist Life of Ours* (American Sunbathing Association, 1950); *A Three Letter Word for Love* (1969), a group of Puerto Rican inner-city teenagers discuss sexuality and emotions; and *New Guinea Dances* (1962), a documentary featuring male dancers wearing gourd penis sheaths.

History. Sample titles include: *Object Collection* (Dick Kornbacher, 1975), showing erotic objects of various eras and cultures, mostly from Kinsey Institute collections; and *Women and Sexuality: A Century of Change* (Dan Klugherz and Arthur Zitrin, M.D., 1982), depicts 19th-century woman and social attitudes relating to her sexuality, using pictorial materials from several archival sources, including the Kinsey Institute.

Videotape collection. This collection is fairly new and continues to grow

on a weekly basis. The major part of the collection is made up of X-rated videotapes, including some soft-core material (e.g., Russ Meyer productions).
Size & Elements: Film: 35mm, 16mm and 8mm (over 6,500 titles). Videotape (format and amount unspecified).
Cataloging: Approximately 1,000 films have been cataloged. Uncataloged materials are inaccessible to researchers.
Access: Use of collections is limited by law to qualified scholars, scientists, professionals or media representatives with a demonstrable research need. Research requests must be in writing; verifiable academic or professional credentials are required. A basic user fee is charged for profit-making organizations, nonresidents of Indiana, or students not enrolled in an Indiana university or college. Special consultation with staff, use of film archives or access to materials when Institute is normally closed necessitates payment of additional fees. Advance notice of preferred dates of access should be given.
Rights: Apply for information.
Licensing: Apply for information.
Restrictions: Requests for research, viewing and reuse of all materials considered on a case-by-case basis. Uncataloged materials are inaccessible to researchers.
Viewing Facilities: Film.
Duplication Facilities: None.

INDIANA (Elkhart)

MILES INCORPORATED
MILES CORPORATE ARCHIVE
P.O. Box 40
Elkhart, IN 46515
(219) 262-7966
Fax: (219) 262-7209
Telex: 258 450 MILES LAB EKR

Street address: 701 West Randolph Street, Elkhart, IN 46514

Contact: Donald N. Yates
Services: Corporate archives. Not generally open to the public. Research permitted on a case-by-case basis; all material for in-house use only. Film and videotape material possibly available for licensing, subject to restrictions.
Description: Alka-Seltzer's classic television commercials, diabetes education, industrial safety, and pharmaceutical manufacturing and research. Archives maintains commercials and news footage, coordinated with other in-house collections in the Media Arts Department; Health and Safety Videotape Library; and Ames Center for Diabetes Education.
Size & Elements: Film: gauge unspecified (120,000 feet, 2,000 titles, 4,000 cans; release prints). Videotape: 3/4" (200 videotapes; edited masters); 3/4" and 1/2" (500 videotapes; viewing copies).
Cataloging: Internal program guide.
Access: Not generally open to the public. For in-house use only. Materials possibly available for researchers. Research fees not charged. Research requests accepted by mail, telephone and in person (by appointment only).
Rights: Full rights held to some material. Some rights held to some material.
Licensing: Materials available for licensing, subject to restrictions. License fees charged for homevideo productions.
Restrictions: Viewing and licensing restrictions apply.
Viewing Facilities: Film (theater); videotape (numerous monitors, including multisystem).
Duplication Facilities: Film (transfer to videotape); videotape (transfer between formats).

INDIANA (Gary)

INDIANA UNIVERSITY NORTHWEST LIBRARY
CALUMET REGIONAL ARCHIVES
3400 Broadway
Gary, IN 46408
(219) 980-6628

Robert Moran (Director of Library Services)

Contact: Stephen McShane (Archives)
Services: Library. Videotape collection possibly available for research and reuse, subject to restrictions.
Description: Videotapes primarily produced at the University, including a videotape on the Bailley nuclear power plant project, which failed after meeting organized community opposition; interviews with local Vietnam

veterans; and a memorial tribute to Joseph Novick, a local left-wing labor organizer.
Other materials held include corporate promotional videotapes produced by U.S. Steel, Bethlehem Steel, and the City of Gary (early history). Also holds a videotape about the archives, produced by local cable television.
Size & Elements: Videotape: 3/4", VHS and Betamax (approx. 8 videotapes).
Cataloging: None.
Access: Open to the public. Available for research and reuse, subject to clearance and approval. Research fees not charged. Research requests accepted by mail, telephone and in person (walk-in).
Rights: Full rights held to material produced at University. No rights held to other material. Additional clearances may be necessary in some cases if material is to be reused.
Licensing: Available for licensing and reuse, subject to restrictions.
Restrictions: Restrictions may apply, depending on intended usage. All requests for research and reuse subject to clearance and approval.
Viewing Facilities: None (all videotape formats available elsewhere at the University).
Duplication Facilities: None (available elsewhere at the University).

INDIANA (Goshen)

ARCHIVES OF THE MENNONITE CHURCH
1700 South Main Street
Goshen, IN 46526
(219) 535-7477

Dr. Leonard Gross (Archivist)

Contacts: J. Kevin Miller (Assistant Archivist); Leonard Gross
Services: Corporation and corporate archives. Films and videotapes available to the public for in-house use only; apply for information regarding duplication and reuse.
Description: Completed films and unedited footage produced by Mennonite organizations, including the Mennonite Board of Missions; the Inter-Board, Mennonite Church; the Inter-Mennonite Media Group; and the Mennonite Central Committee (1940s-present). Subjects covered include Mennonite missionary and relief work in many countries around the world; documentaries and short films on the Mennonites; inspirational and educational short programs; and television spots.
Topics and titles include: *The Search* (1965), on the Mennonite Church; *Mennonites: The Peaceful Revolution* (CBS, 1967); *Africa in Three Dimensions* (1967); *Latin America: The Church Alive* (1971); *Bangladesh Plowman; Manana is Today; You Make the Difference; Wide is the River; Caring is Sharing; Call of the African Church; Mennonite World Conference in Switzerland* (1952); *City Poverty; Give Us Daily Bread; Straight Talk* (1981); *Hutterite Miller Colony, Montana; News: Chinese Visitors;* and *Mennonites and The Bible* (1986).
Size & Elements: Film: 16mm (approx. 275 titles; various elements). Videotape: 3/4" (4 videotapes; masters); VHS (1 videotape; master).
Cataloging: Card catalogs; inventory list.
Access: Open to the public. For in-house use only. Research fees not charged. Research requests accepted by mail, telephone and in person (walk-in).
Rights: Full rights held to some material. Some rights held to all material. Additional clearances may be necessary in some cases if material is to be reused.
Licensing: Available for licensing and reuse, subject to restrictions.
Restrictions: Restrictions apply to some material; additional clearances may be necessary for reuse in cases where only partial rights are held. All requests for reuse subject to clearance and approval.
Viewing Facilities: Film (16mm, can be arranged at nearby location); videotape (3/4", can be arranged at nearby location).
Duplication Facilities: Possibly available at another nearby location.

INDIANA (Greencastle)

DePAUW UNIVERSITY
ARCHIVES AND SPECIAL COLLECTIONS
ROY O. WEST LIBRARY
Greencastle, IN 46135
(317) 658-4500

Wesley W. Wilson (Coordinator of Archives and Special Services)

Contacts: Joan Cunningham (Archives Associate); Susie Moore (Archives

Assistant)
Services: University archives. Film and videotape materials available for research and reuse, subject to approval.
Description: Films relating to DePauw University, United Methodist Church, and local Indianapolis events.

Local television footage includes television shorts hosted by local Congressman Joseph Barr; commissioning ceremonies for ROTC graduates at DePauw (1962); and DePauw basketball and football. Historical film footage covers the crowning of Miss Marilyn L. Schaaf as "Miss DePauw" (1963), including an interview with Miss Schaaf by former motion picture star Frances Farmer; the Methodist Youth Camp at Bishop Roberts Park near Mitchell, Indiana; and various DePauw convocations and commencements.

Sample videotapes include: *From the Word Go*, history and information about the United Methodist Church in the United States; *Ground Breaking of DPU Athletic Complex; Ambassador from Sierra Leone to the USSR;* and various university lectures.
Size & Elements: Film: 16mm (amount unspecified; mostly positive, a few negatives) and 8mm. Videotape: 3/4", VHS (most material) and 1/2" open reel.
Cataloging: Card catalogs; inventories.
Access: Open to the public for research, duplication and reuse. Research fees charged for staff research. Research requests accepted by mail, telephone and in person.
Rights: Full rights held to some material. Additional clearances may be necessary in some cases if material is to be reused.
Licensing: Available for reuse, subject to restrictions. License fees charged for profit-related use.
Restrictions: Credit must be given to DePauw University.
Viewing Facilities: Film (projectors); videotape (all formats).
Duplication Facilities: Videotape (all formats).

INDIANA (Indianapolis)

AMATEUR ATHLETIC UNION
Box 68207
Indianapolis, IN 46268
(317) 872-2900
Fax: (317) 875-0548

Street address: AAU House, 3400 West 86th Street

J. William Kleindorfer (Executive Director)

Contact: Chip Powers (Assistant Communications Director)
Services: Sports organization; videotape rental library. Material available for rental, research and reuse.
Description: Holds promotional films presenting the AAU's programs, including awards ceremonies and the USA Junior Olympics.
Size & Elements: Film: 16mm (5 titles). Videotape: 3/4" and VHS (5 titles).
Cataloging: Card catalog; film list.
Access: Open to the public. Rental or research requests accepted by mail, telephone and in person. Research fees not charged.
Rights: Full rights held to all material.
Licensing: Apply for information. License fees not charged.
Restrictions: None specified.
Viewing Facilities: None.
Duplication Facilities: None.

INDIANA (Indianapolis)

THE AMERICAN LEGION
PUBLIC RELATIONS DIVISION
National Headquarters
700 North Pennsylvania Street
Indianapolis, IN 46204
(317) 635-8411

H. F. Gierke (National Commander)
Robert W. Spanogle (National Adjutant, Chief Administrative Officer)

Contacts: Lee Harris (Deputy Director of National Public Relations) (for rental); National Emblem Sales at National Headquarters (for sale)
Services: Organization. Film and videotape material available for loan and purchase. Historical and archival materials not currently available for research or reuse.
Description: Holds recent videotapes relating to political issues and patriotic

themes, including *Strategic Defense Initiative* (1985); *The American Legion and the Nuclear Freeze* (BBC, 1982); *The Challenge and The Response,* a State Department briefing on Central America; *Flag Etiquette* (1985); *Marching Along Together Again* (1983), a documentary of the National Salute to Vietnam Veterans, with highlights of performances by Jimmy Stewart, Wolfman Jack and Wayne Newton, as well as the dedication of the memorial.

Veterans' issues are addressed in *What to Do Before a Veteran Dies* (1987); *We Chose to Serve* (1985); and *We All Came Home* (1985), the story of Army and Navy Nurse prisoners of war in World War II.

The Legion's emphasis on motivation, character and youth activities is represented in videotapes such as *Motivation* (1983); *PR Workshop* (1985); and *Talk Your Way to College* (1984).

The film collection also contains short subjects, including *Above the Crowd,* using footage of the U.S. Air Force Thunderbirds as a background for a discussion of sales and professional goal achievement; and *American Legacy,* a brief history of the United States as seen through the eyes of the Statue of Liberty. Other titles concern the Special Olympics, bicycle safety, Reyes' Syndrome, the Navy, and baseball umpiring.

Historical and archival materials held by the Legion are not currently available for research, licensing or reuse.
Size & Elements: Film: 16mm (22 titles). Videotape: 3/4" and VHS (16 titles).
Cataloging: Audiovisual products catalog.
Access: Available to the public. Maintained for distribution and rental rather than research or reuse. Research requests accepted by mail and telephone.
Rights: Full rights held to some material. Additional clearances may be necessary in some cases if material is to be reused.
Licensing: Available for licensing and reuse, subject to restrictions.
Restrictions: Restrictions may apply to licensing and reuse of certain material.
Viewing Facilities: None.
Duplication Facilities: None.

INDIANA (Indianapolis)

GERMAN LANGUAGE VIDEO CENTER
(Division of Heidelberg Haus Imports)
7625 Pendleton Pike
Indianapolis, IN 46226
(317) 547-1257
Fax: (317) 547-1263

Gabi Jungbauer; Juergen L. Jungbauer (Owners)

Contacts: Gabi Jungbauer; Juergen L. Jungbauer
Services: Distributor. Videotapes available for rental and purchase.
Description: German language, German produced and German culture videotapes on a variety of subjects and from a wide range of time periods, usually with original German dialogue and/or English subtitles.

Genres include musical, comedy and Heimat films (all in German language); detective, drama and adventure; travel; German films dubbed into English; cartoons, puppet shows and videotapes for children; silent classics with music scores; and documentaries.

Notable fiction titles include: *Diesel* (1942), a drama about the difficulties, problems and intrigues the inventor Rudolf Diesel encounters as he develops and markets his engine; *Flüchtlinge (Refugees)* (1933); *Morgenrot (Dawn)* (1933); *Paracelsus* (G. W. Pabst, 1943); *Titanic* (1943); *Wunder Des Fliegens (Miracle of Flight)* (1935), starring stunt pilot Ernst Udet; *Zu Neuen Ufern (To New Shores)* (Douglas Sirk, 1937); *An Orphan Boy of Vienna* (1937), with the Vienna Choir Boys; *Baron Münchhausen* (1943), the spectacle created in honor of UFA Studio's 25th anniversary; *Berlin Alexanderplatz* (R. W. Fassbinder, 1983); *The Blue Angel* (Josef Von Sternberg, 1930); *The Blue Light* (Leni Riefenstahl, 1932); *Kameradschaft* (Pabst, 1931); *Kolberg* (Veit Harlan, 1945), an epic film produced during the collapse of the Third Reich; *M* (Fritz Lang, 1931); *Mädchen in Uniform* (1931); *Taxi Zum Klo* (1981); *Tiefland* (Leni Riefenstahl, 1945); *Männer (Men)* (Doris Dorrie, 1986); *Pandora's Box* (Pabst, 1928) and *Diary of a Lost Girl* (Pabst, 1929), both with Louise Brooks; *Faust* (F. W. Murnau, 1926); *The Golem* (1920); *Metropolis* (Fritz Lang, 1927); *Die Nibelungen* (Lang, 1924); and *Spies* (Lang, 1928).

Documentary titles include numerous films from the Third Reich (1933-45) and a few postwar films. Titles (1933-45) include *The Afrika Korps* (1942); *March to the Führer* (1943); eight prewar German propaganda short films; *The Private Film Collection of Eva Braun; The Fall of Berlin* (Yuri Raizman, 1945, USSR); *Feldzug in Polen* (1940); *Sieg im Westen* (Victory in the West) (1941); and *Triumph of the Will* (1934). Postwar films include *The California Reich* (1977), on Nazi groups in the United States; and *The Secret Life of Adolf Hitler* (Paul Rotha, 1958).

Directors represented in the collection include Doris Dorrie; Rainer Werner Fassbinder, Veit Harlan, Karl Hartl, Werner Herzog, Leopold Jessner, Fritz Lang, Johannes Meyer, Egon Monk, F. W. Murnau, G. W. Pabst, Wolfgang Petersen, Leni Riefenstahl; Herbert Selpin, Douglas Sirk, Luis Trenker, Gustav Ucicky; Josef Von Sternberg; and Wim Wenders.
Size & Elements: Videotape: VHS and Betamax II (approx. 400 titles total).
Cataloging: Published catalog.
Access: Available to the public for rental and purchase. Orders accepted by mail and telephone.
Rights: Rights retained by original producers.
Licensing: Apply for information.
Restrictions: None specified.
Viewing Facilities: None.
Duplication Facilities: None.

INDIANA (Indianapolis)

GIRLS CLUBS OF AMERICA
NATIONAL RESOURCE CENTER
441 West Michigan Street
Indianapolis, IN 46202
(317) 634-7546

Heather Johnston Nicholson (Director)

Contact: Susan L. Ellis (Assistant Director)
Services: Nonprofit organization. Produces and distributes videotapes available for rental through outside distributor.
Description: Videotapes relating to Girls Club of America programs. *In Video,* filmed at the Schenectady (N.Y.) Girls Club and the General Electric Research Center, is a colorful videotape which depicts GCA programs and the philosophy behind the Operation SMART project.

Other materials are held for in-house use only and are not available to the public.
Size & Elements: Film: format and amount unspecified. Videotape: VHS (approx. 13 titles; viewing copies).
Cataloging: Card catalog; printed brochure.
Access: Available to the public for rental through outside distributor (apply for information). Some materials are held for in-house use only and are not available to the public. Research requests accepted by mail, telephone and in person (by appointment only). Research fees charged in some cases.
Rights: Full rights held to some material.
Licensing: Material not generally available for licensing or reuse. Usage fees charged.
Restrictions: Reuse generally not permitted.
Viewing Facilities: None.
Duplication Facilities: None.

INDIANA (Indianapolis)

INDIANA HISTORICAL SOCIETY
WILLIAM HENRY SMITH MEMORIAL LIBRARY
315 West Ohio Street
Indianapolis, IN 46202
(317) 232-1879

Dr. Bruce Johnson (Director)

Contact: Stephen Fletcher (Curator of Visual Collections)
Services: Historical society. Film archives open to the public by special arrangement only. Some material available for licensing and reuse, subject to clearance and approval.
Description: Collection maintained in conjunction with the Indiana State Library, Indiana Division (q.v.), which holds half of the film. Includes local (Indiana and Indianapolis) newsreel footage from stations WRTV and WFBM dating from the 1940s-60s (15-min. to 60-min. reels).

Holds over 4,000 feet of 16mm film documenting aspects of Hoosier and national politics, made by former State Senator R. Hoyt Moore, Sr., dealing with Republican Party conventions, campaigns, and inaugurations (1952-69). Other footage covers Richard M. Nixon's visit to Indianapolis stumping for the Indiana governor. One film (1929) documents local history with vignettes of a neighborhood, construction of a church, etc.

With the State Library, the Historical Society is working to fund the transfer to videotape and cataloging of the film collection, which at present is inaccessible to researchers and the public. Specific requests will be accepted

under certain circumstances.
Size & Elements: Film: 16mm (480 cans).
Cataloging: Not yet cataloged.
Access: Generally not open to the public or to researchers. Specific research requests accepted by mail or telephone.
Rights: Full rights held to some material. Additional clearances may be necessary in some cases if material is to be reused.
Licensing: Available for licensing and reuse, subject to restrictions. License fees not charged.
Restrictions: Collection inaccessible at present. Requests for licensing and reuse subject to acceptance and approval. Restrictions may apply, depending on rights status of materials.
Viewing Facilities: None in-house; facilities available at Indiana State University. Viewing requests subject to acceptance and approval.
Duplication Facilities: Apply for information.

INDIANA (Indianapolis)

INDIANA STATE COMMISSION ON PUBLIC RECORDS
ARCHIVES DIVISION
140 North Senate Avenue
Indianapolis, IN 46204
(317) 232-3737

F. Gerald Handfield (Director)

Contact: Lawrie G. Meldrum
Services: Government agency and state archives. Material available for licensing and reuse, subject to restrictions.
Description: Films produced by the Public Information Division of the the Indiana State Department of Natural Resources (1930s-60s), deposited in 1981-82. Subjects include wildlife (birds, fish, mammals, insects), hunting, fishing, forestry and forest fires, outdoor safety, natural resources, water and rivers, Indiana parks and highways.

Titles include: *Ain't God Good To Indiana; Smokey the Bear; This Is Your Indiana; Angel Mounds; Bald Eagle; Bobwhite Quail; Fun With Pheasants; Mourning Dove; A Wild Turkey; This Is the Mallard; Indiana Trout; Fun With the Bluegills; White-Tail Deer; Meditations on Hunting; Deer Releasing in Indiana; Deer with Bow and Arrow; Shooting Safety; Better Pond Fishing; Cry of the Marsh; More Than Trees; Trees for Tomorrow; The Farm; Volunteer Firemen; Water vs. Fire; Fire Lane Instruction on Fighting Forest Fires; Frying Pan and the Fire; Forest Fire Fighting in the South, Part 1; Water Pollution; Flood Waters; Seal Island; Wild Rivers; Oil for Tomorrow; More Oil and Gas; Pipeline to the Clouds; Old State Park Film (1948); Indiana Scenic State Parks; State Beneath Us; Fur and Feathers in Alaska; Vacation to the Adirondack Mountains; Frontier Days Rodeo in Cheyenne; Salt Water Rodeo; George Rogers Clark; Design for Disaster; The Careless Crime;* and a set of 11 television spots on forest fire dangers.
Size & Elements: Film: 16mm (147 items).
Cataloging: Card catalogs; accession register.
Access: Open to the public. Research fees not charged. Research requests accepted by mail and telephone.
Rights: Full rights held to all material.
Licensing: Available for licensing and reuse, subject to restrictions. License fees charged in some cases.
Restrictions: Restrictions apply in some cases depending on intended use.
Viewing Facilities: Film.
Duplication Facilities: None.

INDIANA (Indianapolis)

INDIANA STATE LIBRARY
INDIANA DIVISION
140 North Senate Avenue
Indianapolis, IN 46204
(317) 232-3671
Fax: (317) 232-3728

C. Ray Ewick (Director)

Contact: Marybelle Burch (Manuscripts Librarian)
Services: Library. Films available for research and possibly duplication and reuse, subject to restrictions; some films and videotapes available for free loan.
Description: Films relating to Indiana, state politicians and public figures of Indiana; and locally shot home movies.

Political and public figures represented include: E. Ross Adair (U.S. House of Representatives); John V. Beamer (U.S. House of Representatives, 1950s); Governor Otis Ray Bowen, M.D. (1973); Donald C. Bruce (U.S. House of Representatives, 1960-64); Homer Capehart (U.S. Senate, 1950s-60s); William M. Chaney (former Grand Dragon of the Indiana Ku Klux Klan); Governor Harold Handley (1960); Will H. Hays (1941); Indiana Republican State Central Committee (1955-66); Hugh J. O'Donnel (home movies, 1940s-50s); Governor Matthew E. Welsh and Governor Edgar D. Whitcomb (1968).

WRTV/WFBM Collections. Television news footage from Indianapolis station WRTV and its predecessor WFBM. Holds almost all daily shows (1972-75) as well as scripts (1976-?). Other footage from this station is held by Indiana Historical Society, William Henry Smith Memorial Library (q.v.).

Harry Coburn Collection holds newsreel footage (1910s-20s), including the first Indianapolis 500 race and President Benjamin Harrison's funeral. Material has been transferred from nitrate to safety film and videotape. Rights held by the library; collection available to the public.

Recently produced films and videotapes, available for free loan. Sample titles include: *The Automobile: Born in Indiana; The Hoosier Poet,* on James Whitcomb Riley; *Indiana Avenue: Street of Dreams; Indiana Aviation History; Indiana Dunes; The Janet Guthrie Story; Mud, Sweat and Tears: A Community Remembers the Flood,* the story of the 1937 Ohio River flood; *Tough, Pretty, or Smart,* on the Patoka Valley Boys, a bluegrass music group from southern Indiana; and *Family Relatives & Friends of Foster P. Johnson* (1930, home movies).

Size & Elements: Film: 16mm (approx. 200 reels). Videotape: format and amount unspecified.
Cataloging: Published lists.
Access: Some parts of the collection available to the public; other parts available to researchers and scholars only. Some material is deteriorated and/or inaccessible. Research fees not charged. Research requests accepted by mail, telephone and in person (walk-in).
Rights: Full rights held to some material. WRTV/WFBM collection available for unrestricted public use (in part), but rights status is not currently clear. Permission to reuse this material must be obtained from WRTV.
Licensing: Available for licensing and reuse, subject to restrictions.
Restrictions: Requests for licensing and reuse considered on a case-by-case basis. Material in Congressional collections is accessible with special permission only. Special restrictions apply to the reuse of television news footage.
Viewing Facilities: Film and videotape (no sound equipment on premises, but films can be taken to another facility).
Duplication Facilities: None.

INDIANA (Indianapolis)

INDIANAPOLIS MOTOR SPEEDWAY CORPORATION
4790 West 16th Street
Indianapolis, IN 46222
(317) 248-6750
Fax: (317) 248-6750 (by arrangement)

Kurt Hunt (Special Projects Coordinator, Indy 500 Films)

Contact: Kurt Hunt
Services: Corporation and corporate archives; museum. Videotapes available to the public for purchase; archival films and videotapes available to researchers and scholars only and for reuse, subject to restrictions.
Description: A detailed description of collection is not available at this time. Holds archival footage of Indianapolis 500 mile automobile races (1911-present; collection strongest 1956-present). Also holds footage from various Pikes Peak Races and other early races (1950-60s).

32 titles are available on videotape for public purchase. Archives is pleased to answer any inquiries relating to the availability of footage for Indy 500 races or other materials contained in collection.
Size & Elements: Film: format and amount unspecified (negative and reversal). Videotape: 3/4" and 1/2" (amount unspecified; masters and viewing copies).
Cataloging: Card catalogs; computerized cataloging, to be available to researchers, is planned.
Access: Public access to collection limited. Open to researchers and scholars. Research fees charged. Research requests accepted by mail and telephone.
Rights: Full rights held to all material.
Licensing: Material possibly available for licensing, subject to restrictions. License fees charged.
Restrictions: Public access to collection limited. Reuse of material permitted

on a case-by-case basis.
Viewing Facilities: Videotape.
Duplication Facilities: None.

INDIANA (Indianapolis)

INTERNATIONAL HUMAN POWERED VEHICLE ASSOCIATION
P.O. Box 51255
Indianapolis, IN 46251
(317) 876-9478

Marti Daily (President)

Contact: Blake Davis (Secretary)
Services: Association. Small videotape library maintained primarily for reference purposes.
Description: Includes footage of land, air and water human-powered vehicles (1978-present). Some material has been videotaped off the air.
Size & Elements: Videotape: VHS (amount unspecified).
Cataloging: None specified.
Access: Not open to the public. Research requests accepted by mail.
Rights: Rights status of material not known.
Licensing: Available for licensing and reuse, subject to restrictions. License fees charged under some conditions.
Restrictions: Some material may not be copied or broadcast.
Viewing Facilities: None.
Duplication Facilities: None.
Related Materials: A videotape program (30 min.) on the Association and its championships is available through Video Management Systems (q.v.).

INDIANA (Indianapolis)

ELI LILLY AND COMPANY
LILLY ARCHIVES
Lilly Corporate Center
Indianapolis, IN 46285
(317) 276-2173

Richard D. Wood (Chairman of the Board and President)

Contact: Anita Martin (Archivist)
Services: Corporation; corporate archives. Moving image materials reserved for internal use only and not available to the public.
Description: Informational productions relating to Lilly products, past and present; a series of annual newsreels (produced 1950s) spanning a 10-year period.
Size & Elements: Not specified.
Cataloging: None specified.
Access: Not open to the public. For in-house use only.
Rights: Apply for information.
Licensing: Apply for information.
Restrictions: Reserved for internal use only.
Viewing Facilities: None.
Duplication Facilities: None.

INDIANA (Indianapolis)

VIDEO MANAGEMENT SYSTEMS
1004 East Washington Street
Indianapolis, IN 46202
(317) 639-6163

Contacts: Dan Hall; Denise Reiter
Services: Videotape producer. Material possibly available for licensing and reuse.
Description: *Haiti.* Views of the countryside, people, interviews and the city of Port-Au-Prince (footage shot in 1986).

International Human Powered Vehicle Association (q.v.). Has produced a 30-minute program on the Association and its championships, featuring land, air and water human-powered vehicles (footage shot in 1983).

Underwater. Various subjects, including manatees, some videotaped at Crystal River, Florida.

Also holds some political interviews, as well as contemporary footage of downtown Indianapolis.
Size & Elements: Videotape: MII and 3/4" (approx. 8 hours; masters); VHS

(viewing copies).
Cataloging: None specified.
Access: Possibly available for licensing and reuse. Research requests accepted by mail and telephone.
Rights: Full rights held to some material.
Licensing: Material possibly available for licensing and reuse. License fees charged in most cases.
Restrictions: None specified.
Viewing Facilities: Videotape (MII, 3/4" and VHS).
Duplication Facilities: Videotape (MII, 3/4" and VHS).

INDIANA (Muncie)

BALL STATE UNIVERSITY
MIDDLETOWN STUDIES COLLECTION
SPECIAL COLLECTIONS
Bracken Library
2000 University
Muncie, IN 47306
(317) 285-5078

Dr. Michael Wood (Dean of University Libraries)
David C. Tambo (Head, Special Collections)

Contact: David C. Tambo
Services: University; special collection. *Film and videotape collection has not been processed and is not available for viewing.*
Description: *Middletown Studies Collection.* Outtakes and project materials from the television series by Peter Davis entitled *Middletown* (made possible by grants from the National Endowment for the Humanities and Xerox Corporation). The series, first shown in 1982, was inspired by the classic community studies work of Robert and Helen Lynd. The Lynds went to Muncie, Indiana in the 1920s and again in the 1930s to probe the basic structures and values of American life. The television series spotlights the same six areas researched by the Lynds (politics, leisure, religion, work, marriage and education).
    Titles in the series: *The Campaign, The Big Game, Community of Praise, Family Business* and *Second Time Around.* Project materials for the sixth program in the series (*Seventeen*) are not available.
Size & Elements: Film and videotape: formats unspecified (500,000 feet).
Cataloging: None specified.
Access: Collection has not been processed and is not available for viewing.
Rights: Apply for information.
Licensing: Apply for information.
Restrictions: Material not available for viewing.
Viewing Facilities: None.
Duplication Facilities: None.

INDIANA (Notre Dame)

UNIVERSITY OF NOTRE DAME
EDMUND P. JOYCE, C.S.C. SPORTS RESEARCH COLLECTION
102 Hesburgh Library
Notre Dame, IN 46556
(219) 239-6506
Fax: (219) 239-6772

Jethrow D. Kyles (Curator)

Contact: Jethrow D. Kyles
Services: Educational institution. Film and videotape collection available to researchers, scholars and the media.
Description: The Sports Research Collection was established in 1968 at the suggestion of Victor Schaefer, then Director of Libraries, and the late Francis Wallace (Class of 1923) of Sewickley, Pennsylvania, a sportswriter and member of the Library Advisory Council.
    The Collection covers athletic sports and includes games and amusements (e.g., chess and other board games). It is comprised of printed books, journals, yearbooks, programs and other records of athletic teams and leagues, clippings and scrapbooks, motion picture film, microfilm, still photographs, videotapes and audiotapes, posters and sports memorabilia (artifacts). Emphasis is on the modern (post-1800) period, although some earlier materials are held. Works published in the United States and Canada are the focus, with materials acquired from other countries only if they are related to Notre Dame sports, the Olympics, or are of major scholarly importance. English-language materials

predominate.
    Other collections within the Sports Research Collection include: the Jack Level Collection (golf); the Richard L. Sutton Collection (billiards and golf); and the Goodwin Goldfadden Collection (general sports). All were acquired in the early 1970s.
    The film holdings of the Collection feature athletics footage generated by Notre Dame University (1920s-present) and serve as an "athletic archive" of the University. Additional areas covered include National Basketball Association footage (Converse, 1946-67); Professional Golfers Association Championships; and miscellaneous clips of boxing, auto racing, horse racing, tennis, speedboat competition, etc.
    Over 5,000 film reels have been contributed. An attempt is being made to collect appropriate print and non-print materials from all Notre Dame sports, including major and minor varsity sports and intramural activities.
Size & Elements: Film: 35mm and 16mm (5.5 million feet, over 5,000 cans; positive and negative). Videotape: 1", 3/4" and VHS (300 items total).
Cataloging: Research library.
Access: Open to researchers, scholars and the media. Research fees charged (for duplication requests only). Research requests accepted by mail, telephone and in person (walk-in).
Rights: Full rights held to all material.
Licensing: Available for licensing and reuse. License and usage fees charged in some cases (fees not charged if authorized by the University Office of Information Services).
Restrictions: None specified.
Viewing Facilities: Film and videotape.
Duplication Facilities: Film (film-to-film, film-to-videotape); videotape (3/4" and 1/2").
Related Materials: Books and journals; over 500,000 pieces of rare, specialized ephemeral print and non-print materials housed in the Department of Special Collections.

INDIANA (Rochester)

FULTON COUNTY HISTORICAL SOCIETY, INC.
Route 3, Box 89
Rochester, IN 46975
(219) 223-4436

Shirley Willard (President)

Contact: Shirley Willard
Services: Historical society; museum. Film and videotape available to the public for research and reuse, subject to restrictions.
Description: Fulton County history, including Elmo Lincoln, the first man to play Tarzan in the 1918 silent film; a film (1937) of Cole Brothers Circus which had its winter quarters in Rochester between 1935-40; a festival commemorating the Potawatomi Indians, who were removed from the territory in 1838; the Potawatomi Pow Wow in Shawnee, Oklahoma; other local festivals and the construction of local public facilities. Each year the society makes a videotape of its two living-history festivals: *Civil War Re-Enactment* and *Trail of Courage.*
Size & Elements: Film: 16mm (2 titles). Videotape: Betamax and VHS (8 titles).
Cataloging: Card catalogs; research library.
Access: Open to the public. For in-house use only. Research requests accepted by mail, telephone and in person (walk-in).
Rights: Full rights held to some material. No rights held to other material.
Licensing: Available for licensing and reuse, subject to restrictions. License fees charged.
Restrictions: Requests for reuse subject to clearance and approval.
Viewing Facilities: Film (16mm); videotape (by appointment only).
Duplication Facilities: Videotape.
Related Materials: Collection of photographs and slides (1880s-present).

INDIANA (South Bend)

STUDEBAKER NATIONAL MUSEUM
120 South St. Joseph Street
South Bend, IN 46601
(219) 284-9714

Thomas Brubaker (Director)

Contacts: Tom Appel; Edna Kaeppler

Services: Museum. Film collection open to researchers and scholars only; available for licensing and reuse.
Description: Collection is almost totally devoted to the Studebaker Corporation. It contains many commercials and films dating from the early years of television.

Titles include: *Ahead of the Parade* (1939), introducing the 1939 Champion, designed by Raymond Loewy; *Answer to the Axis* (ca. 1944), describing Studebaker production for World War II, including aircraft engines, the Weasel and trucks; *Desert Destiny* (1951), about Studebaker vehicles especially designed for desert use; *Different by Design* (1962), a promotional piece about Studebaker vehicles, emphasizing their difference from the Detroit product; *Safe Road Ahead* (1957), a promotional film about Studebaker trucks; *Beyond a Promise,* a fictionalized story of a young man, son of a Studebaker dealer, attending service school at the Studebaker factory ("The man is impressed, not only by the product, but by company virtues"); *Family of Craftsmen,* the story of the Bokons, a family of Studebaker workers; *First Hundred Years; Studebaker Story,* a Hollywood version of the Studebaker family, their success at making wagons and the company's venture into automobiles; *Avanti At Pikes Peak* (1963), an independent road test; *Model X* (1959), preview film of the "Model X" program; *Spot Commercials* (1963), a composite film of Studebaker Lark commercials; *Studebaker Commercials* (1962), a composite film of television commercials used on the television series *Mr. Ed; Lark* (1961), personal testimonials to the Lark's qualities; *Introductory Driveaway,* footage of Studebakers and Packard 1958 model lines; *Studebaker on Safari,* travelogue of a motorized photography expedition using Studebaker trucks and Commander V-8s; *1960 Press Review,* the press examining 1960 model lines; *Astral Car of Future,* footage of a "super futuristic" car; *Studebaker Theatre Ad* (1952), a composite of short ads for 1953 Studebakers; *Studebaker Spot,* films of the 1961 Auto Show; *Operation Success,* documentary-type film; *Classic Car Club* (August 1955), film of the Classic Car Club rally held at Packard's proving ground; *1960 Mobilgas Economy Run,* footage of Larks during a 5,000 mile run; *1952 Mobilgas Economy Run,* coverage of victorious Studebakers in the run; *Avanti Commercial* (4/27/62), a television commercial presenting the 1963 Avanti; *Studebaker Footage* (1962), racetrack, footage of early Studebaker racecars and the new Avanti; and *Studebaker Today* (1963), opening on the proving grounds with the new president of Studebaker.
Size & Elements: Film: format unspecified (approx. 300 titles, approx. 400 cans). Videotapes: format unspecified (69 videotapes; masters).
Cataloging: Card catalogs; research library.
Access: Open to researchers and scholars only. Research fees charged. Research requests accepted by mail, telephone and in person (walk-in and by appointment).
Rights: Full rights held to all material.
Licensing: Available for licensing and reuse. License fees charged.
Restrictions: None specified.
Viewing Facilities: Film and videotape.
Duplication Facilities: None.
Related Materials: Over 24,000 Studebaker- and South Bend-related photographs. Paper records in the collection include board minutes, company correspondence, scrapbooks, Studebaker magazines, magazine and newspaper advertisements, posters and shop manuals. Holds over 500 book titles and many periodicals about Studebaker, vintage cars and public history.

INDIANA (West Lafayette)

PURDUE UNIVERSITY
PUBLIC AFFAIRS VIDEO ARCHIVES
Stewart Center, G-39
West Lafayette, IN 47907
(317) 494-9630
Fax: (317) 494-9007
BITNET address: PAVA@PURCCVM

Robert X. Browning (Director)

Contact: Robert X. Browning
Services: University archives. Videotape available for public access viewing. Available to educators only for duplication; in-house viewing available for researchers and scholars.
Description: Public Affairs Video Archives, established in 1987, records and preserves all programming carried on both channels of the Cable-Satellite Public Affairs Network (C-SPAN). Archives is licensed to distribute duplicate recordings of all C-SPAN programming to users in educational institutions. In addition, researchers can view the archived recordings at facilities on the

Purdue University campus.

Archives will preserve the videotape record of the U.S. Congress and the extensive public affairs programming of C-SPAN, and will compile its own index of C-SPAN programming to assist teachers and researchers in using the collection.

Archives began recording twelve hours per day on September 15, 1987. Maintains a complete record of the Robert H. Bork confirmation hearings and many other speeches, press conferences, and hearings telecast since that date. Daily 24-hour videotaping on both channels began when the U.S. Senate took up the Bork nomination for Supreme Court justice on October 21, 1987.

Footage includes: U.S. Congress, House and Senate floor action; U.S. congressional hearings; presidential campaigns; presidential speeches and news conferences; public policy conferences; Supreme Court case discussions; judicial conferences and speeches; university conferences; campaign seminars; and C-SPAN call-in programs. Recent acquisitions include convention speeches from NBC News Archives (1948-80) aired on C-SPAN in 1988; 30 hours of C-SPAN telecasts in London, including the Queen's speech to Parliament and footage from the House of Lords, BBC and ITN News with discussion of televised coverage of Parliament; coverage of the 1988 Democratic and Republican conventions and all 1988 presidential and vice-presidential debates.
Size & Elements: Videotape: VHS (4,000 items annually, each 2 hours; masters).
Cataloging: Computerized cataloging for staff use only; additional cataloging in development; published catalogs.
Access: Available for public access viewing; duplication available for educators only. Research requests accepted by mail, telephone and in person (by appointment only).
Rights: No rights held to any material.
Licensing: Not available for licensing or reuse.
Restrictions: Not available for political or commercial use. Reuse, transfer or duplication not permitted.
Viewing Facilities: Videotape.
Duplication Facilities: Videotape (all NTSC formats).
Publications: Catalogs of C-SPAN programming (available for purchase; apply for information).

IOWA

IOWA (Ames)

AMERICAN ARCHIVES OF THE FACTUAL FILM
IOWA STATE UNIVERSITY
The Parks Library
Ames, IA 50011
(515) 294-6672

Dr. Stanley Yates (Curator)

Contact: Dr. Stanley Yates
Services: Film archives. Collection maintained primarily for research; material possibly available for reuse, subject to restrictions.
Description: All areas of "factual film" — educational, sponsored and industrial motion pictures (1930s-present). The impetus for collection came from a donation of films and other materials by Ott Coelln, a founder of the Industrial Audio-Visual Association and editor of *Business Screen* magazine for over 30 years.

Donors include: American Telephone & Telegraph (AT&T); Allis-Chalmers; American Automobile Association; American Cast Iron Pipe Association; American Dental Association; American Iron & Steel Institute; American Meat Institute; American Medical Association; American National Red Cross; American Sheep Producers Council; Benchmark Films; Bob Jones University; Caterpillar Tractor; Consolidated Edison; Delta Air Lines; Encyclopedia Britannica Educational Corporation; Equitable of Iowa; Exxon Company; Farm Film Foundation; Ford Motor Company; General Motors; Gulf Oil; Hughes Aircraft; Illinois Central; Inland Steel; International Film Foundation; International Harvester; Iowa Dept. of Public Instruction; Iowa Farm Bureau; Jam Handy Organization; Kimberly-Clark Co.; Walter J. Klein Co.; Pathescope Pictures; McGraw-Hill; Modern Talking Picture Service; NASA; National Film Board of Canada; New York Stock Exchange; North Dakota State University; Phillips Petroleum; Pioneer Hi-Bred; Planned Parenthood of Iowa; Provincial Archives of British Columbia; Prudential; Rocket Pictures; Shell Oil; Smith Kline & French; Sturgis-Grant Productions; 3M; U.S. Department of Energy; Union Pacific Railroad; United Technologies;

University of Iowa; Virginia Dept. of Education and the Wine Institute.

Strengths of the collection include agriculture, World War II, the Marshall Plan, social mores, safety and aeronautics. Very little newsreel material is held.

Size & Elements: Film: 35mm (a few titles); 16mm (12,000 cans; release prints). Videotape: VHS (viewing copies of some titles).

Cataloging: Computerized cataloging available to researchers. Printed catalog available for sale (see Publications).

Access: Available to researchers, scholars and the public. For in-house use only. Research fees not charged. Requests accepted by mail, telephone and in person (walk-in or by appointment). Archive will make VHS videotapes available with written permission from the copyright holder; they will then sell the videotape to the person requesting it.

Rights: No rights held to any material. Additional clearances are necessary if material is to be reused. Rights status of some material not known.

Licensing: Available for licensing and reuse, subject to restrictions. License fees not charged.

Restrictions: Duplication and reuse permitted only by approval of copyright holder.

Viewing Facilities: Film (16mm Moviola); videotape.

Duplication Facilities: Videotape (VHS). Duplication charges determined according to intended use (profit or nonprofit).

Related Materials: Books, journals, correspondence, newspaper articles and related ephemera, all relating to the history of the factual film.

Publications: *AAFF Film Index* (1988) lists approximately 8,077 titles in the Archives by title, producer and sponsor; *Films of the AAFF* provides information in longer form for a sampling of the collection. *Three Pioneers of the Documentary Film* features short biographies of Robert Flaherty, Julien Bryan and John Grierson.

ARTISTS' TELEVISION PROJECT
SPECIAL COLLECTIONS DEPARTMENT
UNIVERSITY OF IOWA LIBRARIES
Iowa City, IA 52242
(319) 335-5921
Telex: SAN 341-9193

Project office:
ARTISTS' TELEVISION PROJECT OF THE UNIVERSITY OF IOWA
International Center
Iowa City, IA 52242

Sheila D. Creth (University Librarian)

Contacts: Robert A. McCown (Head, Special Collections Department, University Libraries, 319/335-5921); Catherine A. Larson (Media Bibliographer, University Libraries, 319/335-5017 or 319/335-5884); Wallace J. Tomasini (Chairman of the Board of Directors, Artists' Television Project, School of Art and Art History, 319/335-1769)

Services: Educational institution; library. Videotape collection available to researchers, scholars and the general public for in-house viewing; not available for licensing or reuse.

Description: The Artists' Television Project (ATP) directs the academic and public use of the Artists' Television Network (ATN) videotape collection. The Project is committed to (1) public access to the ATP Video Archive and supporting documents for the purpose of study and research; (2) the collection and preservation of video art and other documents and recordings related to the development of alternative television, public access television and artistic uses of satellite communication; (3) the study and production of video pieces; (4) the interdisciplinary study of the history, cultural significance and production of video art; and (5) the support of artists and scholars through ATP Fellowships in Residence at the University of Iowa.

The ATN videotape collection consists of original video works produced by individual artists in conjunction with ATN of New York (mid-1970s through mid-1980s). The Network assisted video artists with their productions by providing studio space, equipment, technical and editing assistance, broadcasting and, occasionally, production funds. Videotapes represent some of the most important works of experimental video art, especially relating to dance, theater, music and the visual arts. While primarily a collection of video art, it is also of potential research value to studies in contemporary art, cable and alternative television, broadcasting history and communication studies. The collection was donated to the Libraries by Jaime Davidovich, a founder of ATN.

Highlights of the collection include original video works by and/or interviews with Vito Acconci, Laurie Anderson, Gregory Battcock, John Cage, Douglas Davis, Jean Dupuy, Les Levine and Dennis Oppenheim.

The Live! Show (ca. 1978-84). A series produced by Jaime Davidovich and ATN, featuring performances, art news, live phone-ins, guest appearances, and interviews with video and other contemporary artists.

Size & Elements: Videotape: 3/4" (375 masters and original recordings, 84 dubs, 459 videotapes total).

Cataloging: When cataloged, individual works will be accessible through the Libraries' online public catalog and the national bibliographic database, RLIN. A finding aid is planned as part of a special project, depending upon funding.

Access: The Libraries are currently seeking a means to make the collection accessible through the provision of viewing copies for the general public, students and interested scholars. The Special Collections Department should be contacted for further information. Research fees not charged. Research requests accepted by mail and in person (walk-in and by appointment).

Rights: Rights status of material not known; under investigation by the Libraries.

Licensing: Not available for licensing or reuse.

Restrictions: Restrictions apply to reuse.

Viewing Facilities: Videotape (3/4", VHS and Betamax).

Duplication Facilities: None.

Related Materials: Documents relating to the history of ATN.

STATE HISTORICAL SOCIETY OF IOWA
402 Iowa Avenue
Iowa City, IA 52240
(319) 335-3916

David Crosson (Administrator)

Contact: Mary Bennett (Special Collections Librarian)

Services: Historical society. Film and videotape collection available for duplication, licensing and reuse, subject to restrictions.

Description: Founded in 1857, the State Historical Society of Iowa serves as the major repository in the state for published and unpublished historical materials. Many special collections contain (or are comprised of) film and videotape materials, as follows:

KCRG-TV Collection. (2,699 3/4" videotapes and reels of film). Material (ca. 1969-82) from the ABC affiliate station in Cedar Rapids, Iowa. (The earlier years, ca. 1965-69, are held by Linn County [Iowa] Historical Society.) This material represents the original story videotapes or field cassettes, rather than edited newscasts. Also held are scripts for daily news broadcasts (1974-75 and 1979-82). Includes coverage of Eastern Iowa and rural issues, including the farming crisis; municipal government in Cedar Rapids, Iowa City; sporting events, including those of University of Iowa and University of Northern Iowa; nursing homes; traffic; toxic waste; schools, snowstorms, soil conservation; Rock Island Railroad and trains; airports; labor demonstrations. (This is a random sample of headings in a card catalog arranged alphabetically by topic covering the years 1977-81). Includes events in nearly every sphere of activity as covered by local news. There is also local coverage of nuclear power issues after the accident at Three Mile Island, including footage of the nuclear plant at Palo, Iowa.

Iowa City Community Access (Heritage Cablevision) Collection. 100 3/4" videotapes produced by local videotape producers in Iowa City (ca. 1980-87). The State Historical Society will serve as the archive for the master videotapes and the Iowa City Public Library will have a VHS copy available for circulation. Collection includes locally produced programs such as the National Issues Forum, dealing with current political issues (e.g., the farm crisis and taxes), and creative productions of video art, dance, comedy, etc. Public affairs issues are often documented through the recording of lectures by visitors to Iowa City and the University of Iowa. Subsequent donations will be made in the future.

Donald E. Johnson (Director of the Veterans Administration under President Nixon) *Collection* (restricted access). 12 reels of videotaped television spots (ca. 1970-72).

Roger Jepsen (U.S. Senator from Iowa) *Collection* (restricted access). 7 cubic feet of videotapes, including master films and videotapes from the 1978 campaign.

Jack Miller (U.S. Senator from Iowa) *Collection* (restricted access). 96 reels of film, 20 videotapes. Includes opinion statements on the Vietnam War.

Iowa Federation of Labor Collection (restricted access). Over 77 reels of film and over 146 videotapes.

United Packinghouse Workers of America, Local 46 (Waterloo) Collection.

4 reels of film.

The Homefront in Iowa During World War II Collection. (8 hours of Betacam videotape with VHS viewing copies). Four Iowa women tell their own stories of the homefront war effort in Iowa. Unedited footage used in the production of *It's A Woman's War Too* (1986, 60 min.).

Holds a few older films created by the State Historical Society to commemorate historic events: examples include film taken on the anniversary of the Lewis & Clark expedition with footage of river trips on the Missouri River (ca. 1950s); film showing cradling of grain as done in the pioneer period; a cruise on the Mississippi River (ca. 1950s); and the Iowa City Centennial Celebration (1939).

In addition to the above-mentioned material, miscellaneous film materials held include a number of home movies showing Iowa family life and places (1937-73); a Boy Scout Jamboree (1937); *Stone City: A Study of a Community* (concerning the artist Grant Wood); the 80th birthday celebration of former president Herbert Hoover; a John F. Kennedy Presidential campaign film (1960); and additional labor-oriented films.

Size & Elements: Film: 16mm (231 reels or titles; color and black and white, sound and silent); and some 8mm (silent). Videotape: 3/4" and VHS (approx. 2,998 items total).

Cataloging: Card catalogs; shot lists.

Access: Open to the public. For in-house use only. Available for duplication. Research fees not charged. Research requests accepted by mail, telephone and in person (walk-in).

Rights: Full rights held to some material. Additional clearances may be necessary in some cases if material is to be reused. Some materials require special permission for duplication or reuse.

Licensing: Most material available for licensing and reuse. License and usage fees not generally charged; a few films require usage charges.

Restrictions: Most holdings carry no restrictions.

Viewing Facilities: Film and videotape facilities available at University of Iowa (across the street). Videotape facilities also available at Public Library.

Duplication Facilities: None available in-house; facilities for film and videotape available at University of Iowa (across the street).

IOWA (Muscatine)

STANLEY CONSULTANTS
Stanley Building
Library
Muscatine, IA 52761
(319) 264-6600
Fax: (319) 264-6658
Telex: 468402 STANLEY MUSC

Street address: 225 Iowa Avenue

Gregs Thomopulos (President)

Contact: Marlys Grete (Librarian)

Services: Consulting engineers. Videotape collection maintained for in-house use only.

Description: Material relating to engineering management and practices.

Size & Elements: Videotape: format unspecified (approx. 120 items).

Cataloging: Card catalogs.

Access: For in-house use only. Research requests accepted in person (by appointment only).

Rights: Full rights held to some material.

Licensing: Apply for information.

Restrictions: None specified.

Viewing Facilities: Videotape.

Duplication Facilities: None.

IOWA (West Branch)

HERBERT HOOVER PRESIDENTIAL LIBRARY
Box 488
West Branch, IA 52358
(319) 643-5301

Street address: Parkside Drive

Richard N. Smith (Director)

Contact: J. Patrick Wildenberg (Audiovisual Archivist)

Services: Government agency. Film collection open to the public; available for duplication and reuse, subject to restrictions.

Description: Presidential library administered by the National Archives and Records Administration.

Professionally produced footage. Consists mainly of newsreels produced in the early years and television specials relating to the latter portion of Herbert Hoover's presidency. Most of this material is copyrighted by the original producers.

Hoover home movies. Film footage (17,000 feet) shot by the Hoover family (1924-43) (Most was photographed by Mrs. Hoover).

Lewis L. Strauss and *Bourke B. Hickenlooper Collections.* These donated collections contain films relating to atomic energy. The footage focuses on early atomic reactors and "Atoms for Peace" projects rather than nuclear testing.

Size & Elements: Film: 16mm (150,000 feet, 570 titles, 1,000 cans).

Cataloging: Research library; finding aids (chronological list).

Access: Open to the public. Available for duplication. Research fees not charged. Research requests accepted by mail, telephone and in person (walk-in).

Rights: A small amount of material is in the public domain. Additional clearances may be necessary in some cases if material is to be reused.

Licensing: Available for reuse, subject to restrictions. Usage fees not charged.

Restrictions: Copyright clearance required for reuse of most materials.

Viewing Facilities: Film (small viewer).

Duplication Facilities: None.

Related Materials: Presidential notes, papers, sound recordings and photographs.

KANSAS

KANSAS (Abilene)

DWIGHT D. EISENHOWER LIBRARY
Abilene, KS 67410
(913) 263-4751

Dr. John E. Wickman (Director)

Contact: Reference Section

Services: Government agency. Film and videotape material available for duplication and reuse, subject to restrictions.

Description: Presidential library administered by the National Archives and Records Administration.

Holds film and videotape materials documenting the life and tenure of President Dwight D. Eisenhower (1953-61). The largest portion of the motion picture holdings covers the presidential years and was given to the President by CBS; other holdings include a number of documentary films relating to World War II.

Subjects include: Presidential inaugurations; campaign speeches; political television commercials, campaign films and television programs (1952 and 1956); documentation of official visits; Eisenhower's military career; Eisenhower at West Point; at Columbia University; reviewing the armed services; the Allied Chiefs of Staff in World War II; Presidential press conferences, including the first to be televised (Jan. 19, 1955); State of the Union addresses, including Jan. 10, 1957, Jan. 9, 1958 and Jan. 9, 1959; other speeches and addresses; the President and his Cabinet; official visits around the world; Eisenhower family activities, birthday parties and celebrations; and Milton Eisenhower home movies (1932-58).

Key items held include *Eisenhower for President* (1952), an animated cartoon selling "Ike for President"; *Peace, Progress and Prosperity: A Report to the People* (1956), a political campaign film summarizing the accomplishments of the Eisenhower administration; *Highlights of the 1956 Republican Convention* (CBS, 1956); *Eisenhower Speaks in Abilene* (June 6, 1952), his first major address since leaving the military; Eisenhower's Republican convention acceptance speech (July 11, 1952); Eisenhower's radio and television address to the American people following his decision to seek a second term (Feb. 29, 1956); Eisenhower's pre-election speech, filmed on the eve of the 1952 election; and various campaign commercials from the 1956 campaign.

Size & Elements: Film: 35mm (251,620 feet, 78 titles); 16mm (497,630 feet, 505 titles); 8mm (1,000 feet, 8 titles). (All positives and release prints).
Videotape: 3/4" (51 videotapes, 2,737 minutes; viewing copies).

Cataloging: Card catalogs; research library.

Access: Open to the public. Available for duplication and reuse, subject to restrictions. Research requests accepted by mail, telephone and in person (walk-in).

Rights: No rights held to most material. Rights to most material retained by original producers. Some material in the public domain. Additional clearances may be necessary in some cases if material is to be reused.

Licensing: Available for licensing and reuse, subject to restrictions. License and usage fees not charged.

Restrictions: Many items in collection were produced by television networks and commercial producers, who retain rights.

Viewing Facilities: Film and videotape.

Duplication Facilities: None.

KANSAS (Chanute)

THE MARTIN AND OSA JOHNSON SAFARI MUSEUM
16 South Grant
Chanute, KS 66720
(316) 431-2730

Contact: Audiovisual Staff

Services: Museum. Film and videotape material available for licensing and reuse, subject to restrictions.

Description: Historic ethnographic films (1917-36) taken by Martin and Osa Johnson. "The Johnsons were a husband and wife team who financed their adventuresome trips by writing, lecturing, and releasing commercial movies. Martin was a professional photographer who carefully developed and cared for his film despite the difficult physical conditions. Osa was a full partner, taking care of the details of the trip and standing by Martin, gun in hand, when he photographed. She was an expert shot.

"The Martin Johnsons made two expeditions to the South Seas in 1917 and 1919 (Martin had visited the Solomons and New Hebrides with Jack London, 1907-09), two to Borneo in 1920 and 1935-36, and five extended trips to Africa...between 1921 and 1934. Although their South Seas films brought them global fame at the time, it is the five African expeditions for which they are best remembered."

Collection holds ethnographic films from the Solomon Island group, Vanuatu (includes 1917 and 1919 scenes from the Big Nambas), Malaysia (formerly British North Borneo) (1920, 1934-35) and East Africa (primarily Kenya, Tanzania and Zaire, 1921-34). African footage covers the Masai, the Samburu, Kikuyu and the pygmies, among other subjects.

Wildlife includes the common and uncommon animals of Africa and North Borneo. Footage covers all four species of ape, the white rhinoceros, shots of massive herds of elephants, the capture of a wild orangutan, and a lion hunt by spear-carrying natives.

The Museum also holds some ethnographic film and a collection of various videotapes on similar ethnological subjects, not made by the Johnsons.

Size & Elements: Film and videotape: formats and amounts unspecified.

Cataloging: Shot lists.

Access: Open to researchers and scholars only. Research requests accepted by mail, telephone and in person (by appointment only).

Rights: Full rights held to some material.

Licensing: Available for licensing and reuse, subject to restrictions.

Restrictions: Museum board must approve projects for licensing and reuse.

Viewing Facilities: Film and videotape.

Duplication Facilities: None.

KANSAS (Emporia)

EMPORIA STATE UNIVERSITY
SPECIAL COLLECTIONS/NONPRINT
WILLIAM ALLEN WHITE LIBRARY
1200 Commercial
Emporia, KS 66801
(316) 343-1200 (Ext. 5047)

Henry Stewart (Director, Library Services)

Contacts: Florence Haskett (Clerk); Mary Bogan (Head, Special Collections)

Services: University library. Film collection available for research and duplication.

Description: Silent and sound films produced, directed and filmed by University personnel (1950s-60s), featuring campus life.

Footage includes college football games, parades, tap dancing, homecomings, speeches, Master Teacher Award ceremonies, Band Day activities, commencements, the 50th Anniversary, construction of the Science

Hall and aerial views of campus (1950s-60s).

Titles include: *Citizenship Education in School; Decision for Joe; Sunken Garden Construction* (1964); *Harry, Ricky & Gail; Miss Emporia State* (1957 and 1967); *Look Who's Talking* (1964), the story of two students competing for the same Speech Department scholarship; and *Freshman Boy with Problems,* the story of a freshman trying to live down his older brother's football playing record.

Size & Elements: Film: 16mm (76 titles).

Cataloging: Title list.

Access: Not open to the public. Available for duplication. Research fees not charged. Research requests accepted by mail and telephone.

Rights: Full rights held to all material.

Licensing: Apply for information.

Restrictions: None specified.

Viewing Facilities: Film (16mm).

Duplication Facilities: Videotape.

KANSAS (Lawrence)

UNIVERSITY OF KANSAS
UNIVERSITY ARCHIVES
Lawrence, KS 66045
(913) 864-4188

John Nugent (Archivist)

Contacts: John Nugent; Barry Bunch; Ned Kehde

Services: University archives; film and videotape archives. Material available to the public for duplication and reuse, subject to restrictions.

Description: College football, basketball and track films (1929-present); other University-related footage (1932-present); KU-produced instructional materials in the liberal arts, especially history and psychology; and videotapes relating to child behavior, produced by Wayne State University. Athletic material is deposited in the Archives on an annual basis.

Size & Elements: Film: 16mm (3,000 cans). Videotape: 3/4" (2,600 videotapes).

Cataloging: Athletic films uncatalogued, but filed chronologically by sport and assigned accession numbers. Subject card index for 16mm films.

Access: Open to the public. Available for duplication and reuse, subject to restrictions. Research fees not charged.

Rights: Full rights held to all material.

Licensing: Available for licensing and reuse, subject to restrictions. License and usage fees charged.

Restrictions: Duplication and reuse requires permission of donor or office of origin. Athletic events must be cleared for reuse by Athletic Department. All reuse must be credited.

Viewing Facilities: Film and videotape.

Duplication Facilities: None.

KANSAS (Manhattan)

AMERICAN INSTITUTE OF BAKING
1213 Bakers Way
Manhattan, KS 66502
(913) 537-4750
Fax: (913) 537-1493
Telex: 881039 AIB MAN UD

William J. Hoover (President)

Contact: Bill Lockhart (Communications Coordinator)

Services: Educational research institution. Videotape library available primarily for rental and purchase.

Description: Instructional films for the commercial baking industry. *Sanitation Series* (9 programs) focuses on sanitation, pest control, personnel management, cleaning practices and preventive maintenance of wholesale production equipment. *Industry Series* demonstrates the proper usage and maintenance of bakery production equipment, including automatic pan greaser, depanner, bun slab slicer, divider, twist tie machine, band slicer, bread bagger, dough pump and cross grain moulder. *In-Store and Retail Series* (10 programs) covers working with frozen dough, yeast raised donut production, merchandising and decorating, roll and bread production and cake decorating.

Size & Elements: Videotape: format unspecified (39 titles).

Cataloging: Published catalogs.

Access: Open to the public. Available for rental and purchase. Requests

accepted by mail, telephone and in person (walk-in).
Rights: Full rights held to all material.
Licensing: Apply for information.
Restrictions: Written permission required for reuse.
Viewing Facilities: Videotape.
Duplication Facilities: Videotape.

KANSAS (Mission)

NCAA PRODUCTIONS
P.O. Box 1906
Mission, KS 66201
(913) 384-3220
Fax: (913) 831-8425
Telex: (910) 743-4169

Street address: 6300 Nall Avenue, Mission, KS 66202

Richard D. Schultz (Executive Director)

Contacts: Gina L. McNeal (Production Coordinator); James A. Marchiony (Director of Media Services)
Services: Association. Film and videotape collection available for licensing and reuse, subject to restrictions. Some programs available for rental and purchase.
Description: National Council of Amateur Athletics footage of various sporting events, primarily college basketball (1939-87). Other sports footage includes football, baseball, soccer, gymnastics, volleyball, track and field, lacrosse, ice hockey, swimming and diving, golf and wrestling. Footage from 1939-67 is 16mm film; from 1968-87 is 16mm film, 2" and 3/4" videotape.
NCAA Instructional Videotapes. Features top-flight college coaches of baseball, basketball, crew, fencing, football, golf, gymnastics, ice hockey, lacrosse, soccer, softball, swimming and diving, tennis, track and field, volleyball, water polo, women's basketball, and wrestling.
NCAA Video Library. Available for rental and purchase in film and videotape form. Includes highlights of College World Series baseball (1981-87); Men's Final Four basketball (1968-87); Women's Final Four (1984-87); college football season previews (1983-87); golf (1975-79); gymnastics (1972-85); ice hockey (1970-81); lacrosse (1975-81); soccer (1971-80); swimming (1970-81); track and field (1971-81); volleyball (1974-84) and wrestling (1970-81).
Size & Elements: Film: 16mm (amount unspecified; negatives and release prints). Videotape: 2", 1" and 3/4" (amount unspecified; masters).
Cataloging: Computerized cataloging for staff use only.
Access: Available for licensing and reuse. Research fees charged. Research requests accepted by mail and telephone. Some material available for rental and purchase.
Rights: Some rights held to all material. Additional clearances may be necessary in some cases if material is to be reused.
Licensing: Available for licensing and reuse, subject to restrictions. License fees charged according to intended use.
Restrictions: Requests for reuse considered on a case-by-case basis.
Viewing Facilities: None.
Duplication Facilities: None.
Distributor: NCAA Instructional Videotapes available for purchase from Karol Media, 22 Riverview Drive, Wayne, NJ 07470; (201) 628-9111.

KANSAS (North Newton)

BETHEL COLLEGE
MENNONITE LIBRARY AND ARCHIVES
North Newton, KS 67117
(316) 283-2500

David A. Haury (Director)

Contact: David A. Haury
Services: Historical society. Film and videotape collection available for research and reuse, subject to restrictions.
Description: Films and videotapes by and about Mennonites and the Amish. Various subjects are covered, including missions, relief work, church conferences and conventions, and general background information and documentaries relating to Mennonites and the Amish.
Size & Elements: Film: 16mm (100 titles; release prints). Videotape: VHS (50 titles; viewing copies).

Cataloging: Title lists.
Access: Available to the public. Research fees not charged. Research requests accepted by mail, telephone and in person (walk-in).
Rights: Some rights held to some material.
Licensing: Apply for information. License fees not charged.
Restrictions: Requests for licensing or reuse subject to approval.
Viewing Facilities: Film (16mm); videotape (VHS) (in Audio-Visual Department).
Duplication Facilities: Videotape.
Related Materials: Papers of Mennonite filmmaker William Zehr.

KANSAS (Topeka)

KANSAS STATE HISTORICAL SOCIETY
PHOTOGRAPH DIVISION
MANUSCRIPTS DEPARTMENT
120 West 10th Street
Topeka, KS 66612
(913) 296-3165

Nancy Sherbert (Photograph Curator)

Contact: Darrell D. Garwood (Photo Archivist)
Services: Historical society; film and videotape archives. Material available for licensing and reuse, subject to restrictions.
Description: Film and videotape archives relating to the history of Kansas.
Film collections. Includes the newsfilm collections of CBS affiliate WIBW-TV and NBC affiliate KSNT-TV (both of Topeka). These two collections consist of approximately 300,000 feet of raw film footage, primarily color positive prints, many with magnetic sound. Subjects cover local affairs (mid-1960s-80s). Film collection also includes approximately 100 feature films (1922-75). Subjects include Kansas, World War II, and the activities of the Atchison, Topeka and Santa Fe Railroad.
Videotape collections. Nightly newscasts of ABC affiliate KTKA-TV (1987-present); material from Kansas Association of Broadcasters representing annual awards (copyright restrictions limit use of this material to research at the Society); and topical programs donated by PBS station KTWU-TV relating to Kansas and its people.
Some of the film (KSNT collection) is in good physical shape, while other footage (WIBW collection) is in poor physical condition and not easily accessible to the public for research.
Size & Elements: Film: 16mm (over 500,000 feet). Videotape: 2", 3/4" and 1/2" (22 cubic feet; masters and viewing copies).
Cataloging: Card catalogs; dope sheets.
Access: Open to the public. Selected material for in-house research only. Available for duplication, subject to restrictions. Research requests accepted by mail, telephone and in person.
Rights: Full rights held to some material. Some rights held to some material. Some material in the public domain. Rights status of some material not known. Additional clearances may be necessary for newsfilm if material is to be reused.
Licensing: Available for licensing, subject to restrictions. License fees generally not charged.
Restrictions: Requests for licensing and reuse considered on a case-by-case basis. Some donors restrict reproductions.
Viewing Facilities: Film and videotape.
Duplication Facilities: Videotape (3/4" and 1/2"; 8mm and Betamax available).

KENTUCKY

KENTUCKY (Bowling Green)

WESTERN KENTUCKY UNIVERSITY
FOLKLIFE ARCHIVES
DEPARTMENT OF LIBRARY SPECIAL COLLECTIONS
Kentucky Building
Bowling Green, KY 42101
(502) 745-6086

Patricia M. Hodges (Manuscripts and Archives Supervisor)

Contact: Sue Lynn Stone (Manuscripts Librarian)
Services: Educational institution; research library. Film and videotape

collection available to the public for in-house use only. Most material available for duplication.

Description: Repository for unpublished holdings of materials donated, collected or produced for research purposes since the 1950s by the faculty and students of the Folk Studies Program. Most materials have been generated as projects for Folk Study classes and focus on the history, customs, speech and everyday life of South Central Kentuckians.

Collection includes videotapes on Warren County, Kentucky, such as *A Man and His Barn*, an interview with William Harrison Willis (early 1970s); *Lone Oak Restaurant* (1976); *A Message Through Song* (1983), an interview with minister James Fishback, with the music of the United Brotherhood Men's Choir of the Mt. Union Church, a Black gospel group; *Mt. Union Church Choir and Service of Loven CME Church* (1983); *Hunt's Garage Sale, Parts I, II and III* (1980), set in Glasgow, Kentucky; *Hand Rhymes and Actions of Children at Potter's Children's Home* (1976); *Fiddling* (1977), with Sammy Walker and his family of Summer Shade, Kentucky; *Clog Dancing* (1976), featuring the Tennessee Love Vine Squaredancers of Westmoreland and Lafayette, Tennessee, of whom it is said, "They just get it in their feet and want to go"; *Interview With Gladys Pace* (1978), regarding her memories of earlier times, conducted at her home near Antioch Church in Barren County; *The Survival of the Bell Witch* (1979, 8mm), set in Robertson County, Tennessee; and *Square Dances* at Pickett State Park and Cookeville, Tennessee (1984).

Size & Elements: Film: 8mm (1 title). Videotape: 3/4" (3 titles, 4 videotapes) and 1/2" open reel (10 titles, 14 reels; raw masters and master edits).

Cataloging: Research library; card catalogs; printed list.

Access: Open to the public. For in-house use only. Most material available for duplication. Research fees not charged. Research requests accepted by mail, telephone and in person (preferably by appointment).

Rights: Full rights held to some material. Some rights held to some material. Rights status of some material unknown. Additional clearances may be necessary in some cases if material is to be reused.

Licensing: Available for duplication, licensing and reuse, subject to restrictions. License and usage fees not charged.

Restrictions: Some material cannot be used for commercial purposes.

Viewing Facilities: Film (8mm); videotape (3/4" only).

Duplication Facilities: None (outside duplication may be arranged).

Related Materials: Printed matter, ephemera, still photographs, audiocassettes, slide transparencies and phonograph records.

KENTUCKY (Danville)

KENTUCKY SCHOOL FOR THE DEAF
LEARNING RESOURCE CENTER
Danville, KY 40422
(606) 236-5132 (Ext. 291)

George R. Benson (Director of Media Services)

Contacts: Stephen Bruce (videotapes); Genny Lyman (films)

Services: Educational institution; government agency. Some titles in film collection available for duplication.

Description: Sign language and manual communication.

Size & Elements: Film: 16mm (approx. 1,000 titles). Videotape: 3/4" and VHS (approx. 700 titles).

Cataloging: Published catalogs (available on request).

Access: For in-house use only. Some titles available for duplication. Research requests accepted in person (by appointment only).

Rights: Some rights held to some material.

Licensing: Apply for information. License fees not charged.

Restrictions: None specified.

Viewing Facilities: Film (16mm); videotape (3/4" and VHS).

Duplication Facilities: Videotape (3/4" and VHS).

KENTUCKY (Frankfort)

KENTUCKY DEPARTMENT OF LIBRARIES & ARCHIVES
PUBLIC RECORDS DIVISION, RESEARCH ROOM
P.O. Box 537
Frankfort, KY 40602-0537
(502) 875-7000

Street address: 300 Coffee Tree Road

Richard Belding (Director, Public Records Division and State Archivist)

Contacts: Jim Prichard (Research Room Supervisor); Charles Robb (Senior Archivist)

Services: State archives. Film and videotape collection available to the public for in-house use only.

Description: Central depository for the permanent public records of Kentucky state government and many of the Commonwealth's local governments.

Kentucky Educational Assistance Authority. Videotapes (1978-85, 35 cubic feet) covering highlights of the daily proceedings of the General Assembly's regular and special sessions, produced by Kentucky Educational Television. Miscellaneous legislative and education events are also covered, including the inaugural parade of Governor Carroll (1975), interviews with candidates for primary elections (1979) and various legislative reports and hearings. Videotapes of *This Other Eden* (1980), a documentary series concerning the religious, social and historical development of Kentucky, are also held.

Department of Agriculture. Three promotional films produced by the Governor's Council on Agriculture (1960-65), suggesting ways for Kentucky farmers to improve production.

Governor's Office. Videotapes from the Julian Carroll Administration (1975-78, 39 videotapes, 10 reels of 16mm film) include Inauguration Day activities, political debates, State of the Commonwealth messages, press conferences, national television network interviews and miscellaneous events, all featuring the Governor. Reels of film are silent and cover Bicentennial events, press conferences, presentations and addresses.

Department of Education. Three films relate to education in Kentucky: *The Last Generation; In Search of Innovation;* and *Fair Chance for Kentucky.*

Department of Public Information (1950-66, 16mm, six cubic feet). Films designed to highlight noteworthy events and aspects of the state of Kentucky. Films cover various subjects, including public safety, travel and tourism, fairs, bookmobiles, Boy Scouts, the Frankfort flood (1962), Shakertown, strip mines, construction, agriculture, fishing and political events.

Department of Health. One videotape transferred from seven 35mm nitrate films (originals were destroyed); some films are silent. The *1937 Flood Films* were produced by the Kentucky State Department of Health, U.S. Army Corps of Engineers and Movietone News. These films document the flooding of the Ohio, Monongahela and Mississippi Rivers (1937). Topics range from news coverage surveying flood damage to the technique of setting up local emergency centers. Most footage focuses on the effects of the flood in Kentucky, particularly the cities of Louisville and Frankfort.

Size & Elements: Film: 16mm (19 reels, plus 6 cubic feet; release prints). Videotape: format unspecified (42 videotapes, plus 40.4 cubic feet).

Cataloging: Published lists and descriptions.

Access: Available to the public. For in-house use only. Materials not available for loan. Limited reference service provided by mail and in person. Research Room staff does not perform detailed research for individual patrons; a list of persons willing to do research (fees apply) is available on request.

Rights: Apply for information.

Licensing: Apply for information.

Restrictions: None specified.

Viewing Facilities: Apply for information.

Duplication Facilities: None.

Related Materials: Microfilm (22,000 rolls), state publications, county histories, maps, newspapers and family files and genealogy publications.

KENTUCKY (Lexington)

AMERICAN SADDLEBRED HORSE ASSOCIATION
Kentucky Horse Park
4093 Iron Works Pike
Lexington, KY 40511
(606) 259-2742
Fax: (606) 259-1628

Patricia G. Nichols (Director of Administration)

Contact: Ellen Melcher (Special Events)

Services: Association; museum. Film and videotape library maintained primarily for distribution and rental.

Description: History and development of the American saddlebred horse, showing procedures in hand, in harness and under saddle. One title deals with preparation for the World Grand Championship five-gaited stake.

Size & Elements: Film: 16mm (2 titles). Videotape: VHS and Betamax (9 titles).

Cataloging: Published catalogs (available on request).

Access: Open to the public. Maintained for distribution and rental rather than for research or reuse. Research requests accepted by mail, telephone and in

person (walk-in).
Rights: Full rights held to all material. Additional clearances for reuse may be necessary in some cases (if material is co-owned by Association and another party).
Licensing: Apply for information.
Restrictions: None specified.
Viewing Facilities: Videotape (VHS).
Duplication Facilities: None.

KENTUCKY (Lexington)

UNIVERSITY OF KENTUCKY
AUDIOVISUAL ARCHIVES
SPECIAL COLLECTIONS AND ARCHIVES
111 King Library North
Lexington, KY 40506-0039
(606) 257-8634

Paul Willis (Director of Libraries)

Contact: Tom House (Audiovisual Archivist)
Services: University library; archives. Film and videotape archives open to the public for in-house use only. Material available for duplication, licensing and reuse, subject to restrictions.
Description: Although archives as a whole is international in scope, most of the collections emphasize aspects of Kentucky, Kentuckians, Appalachia and the University. Film and videotape preservation activity is focused on local television news programming and on collecting and preserving the works of Kentucky-related independent filmmakers. Aims to establish the Audiovisual Archives as a resource center for independent filmmakers and a regional repository for their works. Independently produced collections contain over 1.3 million feet of film, including such items as the production log, workprints and outtakes from Barbara Kopple's *Harlan County, USA.*
   WAVE Television Collection. Louisville-based television station (NBC affiliate) deposits its newsfilm, videotapes and news scripts with the University Audiovisual Archives. Collection currently contains over two million feet of film, over 500 videotapes and over 1,500 news scripts (all 1964-present). A three-year backlog is maintained by WAVE in its own archives.
   WLKY Television Collection. Louisville-based television station (ABC affiliate) has deposited one million feet of local newsfilm (1972-present).
   WKYT Television Collection. Lexington-based CBS affiliate has deposited newsfilm and scripts (1972-80).
Size & Elements: Film: 16mm (5,954,650 feet, 9,759 titles, 13,279 cans; mostly originals). Videotape: 2" (750 items); 3/4" (600 titles, 669 videotapes); 1/2" open reel (5 titles, 8 reels); and VHS (52 videotapes) (Total: 1,200 programs, 1,407 hours, 1,479 reels and cassettes, archival viewing copies).
Cataloging: Card catalogs; collection inventories; computerized cataloging for staff use only.
Access: Available to the public. For in-house use only. Available for duplication. Research requests accepted by mail (preferred), telephone and in person (by appointment).
Rights: Some rights held to some material. Additional clearances necessary in some cases if material is to be reused.
Licensing: Available for licensing and reuse, subject to restrictions. License fees charged in some cases.
Restrictions: Research requests subject to acceptance and approval, depending upon restrictions pertinent to each collection.
Viewing Facilities: Videotape (3/4" and VHS; facilities on campus or at television stations).
Duplication Facilities: Videotape (3/4" and VHS; facilities on campus or at television stations).
Related Materials: History of Broadcasting in Kentucky Oral History Project includes 171 recordings of early broadcasts from WHAS, Kentucky's first radio station. These recordings date from the early 1930s and include speeches by prominent Kentucky political figures, general news accounts and special public affairs programming.

KENTUCKY (Murray)

NATIONAL MUSEUM OF THE BOY SCOUTS OF AMERICA
MURRAY STATE UNIVERSITY
Murray, KY 42071
(502) 762-3383

Darwin Kelsey (Director)

Contact: David Conzett (Curator of Collection)
Services: Museum; film and videotape archives. Access to collection currently limited; material generally restricted to in-house use only.
Description: One of the largest film collections of material relating to the Boy Scouts of America (1920s-present), including Scouting history (e.g., the 1929 World Jamboree and National Jamboree); local, national and international Scouting activities and "the outdoor experience."
Size & Elements: Film: 16mm (approx. 600-700 titles; 95% originals and release prints, some transferred to videotape). Videotape: format and amount unspecified.
Cataloging: Cataloging in progress. Cataloging and accessibility will be greatly improved upon completion of the Research Center on Boy, Girl and World Scouting in 1989.
Access: Open to the public. Access to collection currently limited. Material available for in-house use only, although material may sometimes be accessed through local libraries. Research fees not charged. Research requests accepted by mail and telephone. With the completion of the new Research Center, materials will be more accessible. Much of the film will be transferred to videotape and some will be available for purchase.
Rights: Full rights held to some material. Some rights held to other material. Additional clearances may be necessary in some cases if material is to be reused.
Licensing: Available for licensing and reuse, subject to restrictions. License fees charged in some cases.
Restrictions: Requests for licensing and reuse considered on a case-by-case basis.
Viewing Facilities: Film (16mm); videotape (1/2").
Duplication Facilities: None.

KENTUCKY (Richmond)

EASTERN KENTUCKY UNIVERSITY
UNIVERSITY ARCHIVES
Cammack Building, Room 26
Richmond, KY 40475
(606) 622-2820

Charles Hay (Archivist)

Contact: Charles Hay
Services: University archives. Film and videotape collection available for research, licensing and reuse, subject to restrictions.
Description: Eastern Kentucky University football games (1938-present); basketball (1953-present); halftime band films (1968-78). Kentucky High School Athletic Association films and videotapes documenting football (1965-present), boys' basketball (1955-present) and girls' basketball (1975-present). High School Athletic Association collection also contains a few films and videotapes relating to wrestling, baseball, and swimming.
Size & Elements: Film: 16mm (5,000 feet). Videotape: 3/4" and VHS (150 videotapes, 3,000 hours). (Approx. 300 titles total).
Cataloging: Card catalogs.
Access: Open to the public. For in-house use only. Available for duplication. Research fees not charged. Requests accepted by mail, telephone and in person.
Rights: Full rights held to some material. Some material in the public domain.
Licensing: Apply for information.
Restrictions: If material from the High School collection is to be reused, additional clearances may be necessary from the Kentucky High School Athletic Association Films & Tapes.
Viewing Facilities: Film and videotape (VHS).
Duplication Facilities: Film-to-videotape; videotape-to-videotape (at University Radio/TV Center on campus). Film-to-film duplication must be done commercially.

KENTUCKY (Whitesburg)

APPALSHOP FILMS, INC.
306 Madison Street
Whitesburg, KY 41858
(606) 633-0108 (Kentucky)
(800) 545-7467 (outside Kentucky)

Dee Davis (Executive Producer)
Scot Oliver (Director of Distribution)

Contacts: Scot Oliver; Dee Davis

Services: Educational film and videotape producer and distributor; media arts center. Completed productions available for rental and purchase. Stock footage available for licensing and reuse.

Description: Appalachian issues and events; films about the history, culture and social issues of rural America (1969-present). Includes regional industries; labor and ecological conflicts; coal mining; tobacco farming; traditional farming; moonshining; local crafts and musical traditions; community events; local and national political figures; herbal medicine and midwifery; education and religion. Some titles in collection were produced by Headwaters Television (HTV).

Appalachian culture (general). Strangers & Kin: A History of the Hillbilly Image traces Appalachian stereotypes in popular culture. *Tomorrow's People* is a sight-and-sound experience of mountain music and culture, mixing archival photos and current footage.

Coal mining. Conflicts between coal miners and mining companies are documented in *Buffalo Creek Revisited* and *The Buffalo Creek Flood: An Act of Man. UMWA: A House Divided* and *Coal Miner: Frank Jackson* are portraits of the United Mine Workers of America and of a life-time miner. *Mine War on Blackberry Creek* (HTV, 1986) is a modern scenario of the ongoing strike of union miners against the A.T. Massey Co., chronicling the United Mine Workers of America's first confrontation with a multinational corporation. *Coalmining Women* (1982) covers social conditions and economic pressures facing women in nontraditional roles. *Woman Miners Conference* documents the June 1984 convention in Charleston, West Virginia. *Strip Mining: Energy, Environment and Economics* and *Strip Mining in Appalachia* show the beginnings, growth and consequences of this method of mining, which accounts for 50% of the coal produced in the Appalachian region.

Community events. Ramsey Trade Fair depicts the flea market as a center of rural living and shows the nearly lost art of barter, including a performance by blind musician Bill Denham, an early influence on Bob Dylan. *Judge Wooton and Coon-on-a-Log* is a portrait of a Leslie County, Kentucky judge against the background of a coon-on-a-log contest. *One-Ring Circus* (HTV) is a behind-the-tents look at one of the last small traveling circuses. *Feathered Warrior* documents the illegal sport of cockfighting, with a winning cockfighter outlining the rules of the game, and includes a slow-motion sequence of birds fighting.

Education. The struggles and pleasures of rural education are detailed in *The Kingdom Come School,* one of the last remaining one-room schools in rural Kentucky; and *The Struggle of Coon Branch Mountain. Appalachian Genesis* expresses the frustration of the Appalachian man and the need for change in the process of formal education. *In Ya Blood* concerns a young man who must decide whether to work in the coal mines or attend college. *I'm What This Is All About* (HTV) concerns West Virginia Supreme Court Judge Recht's 1982 decision to restructure West Virginia's school system. *Mabel Parker Hardison Smith* is about a woman who taught school for over 35 years in the coalfields of eastern Kentucky.

Electoral politics. The Big Lever: Party Politics in Leslie County, Kentucky concerns the Republican stronghold where Richard Nixon made his first post-resignation public appearance in 1978. Residents here have been pulling the "big lever" for the Republicans since the Civil War. *A Tribute to Carl D. Perkins* (HTV) shows the funeral of Congressman Carl D. Perkins, a 40-year veteran of the House of Representatives.

Farming. Lord and Father documents father-son conflicts over the morality and profitability of tobacco farming, providing an overview of the economic history of tobacco growing, sharecropping and the associated social system. *Waterground* shows one of the last remaining water-powered grist mills and its operator; *Mountain Farmer* and *Woodrow Cornett: Letcher County Butcher* also examine a traditional agricultural community.

Handcrafts. Several films (*Hand Carved, Chairmaker, Oaksie* and *Quilting Women*) explore the arts of chair making, carving, basket weaving and quiltmaking. *Millstone Sewing Center* employs elderly local seamstresses, gives clothing to the needy, operates a lunch program, provides productive employment for the community's elderly and a resource for its poor. *Sarah Bailey* (HTV) is about a folk artist from Harlan County, Kentucky.

Medicine. Nature's Way shows home-based medicine, including a midwife who has delivered more than 5,000 babies discussing her work as she delivers twins. *Catfish: Man of the Woods* concerns an herbalist, his skills and remedies. *Frontier Nursing Service* shows a pioneer nurse/midwifery service in a rural setting, including excerpts from Marvin Breckenridge Patterson's film *The Forgotten Frontier* (1929). The film shows a unique kind of medical service as well as glimpses of Eastern Kentucky mountain towns in the late 1920s. *Mud Creek Clinic* (HTV) shows the accomplishment of a community in organizing and maintaining health care for all its people.

Moonshining. Tradition is concerned with moonshining, illegal since the tax laws passed at the end of the 18th century, and the legendary conflict between the revenue agent and the moonshiner. One moonshiner "sent up" four times would "rather make whiskey than to get on welfare."

Music. Sunny Side of Life documents the old-time Southwestern Virginia country music tradition. *Nimrod Workman: To Fit My Own Category* is a portrait of a ballad singer and composer of traditional music, now in his eighties, who was also a coal miner and an early union organizer. *John Jacob Niles* is a portrait of the folk musician who played an important part in the revival of Appalachian music during the 1920s and 1930s. *Sourwood Mountain Dulcimers* shows musical instrument making and the origins of various instruments. *Artus Moser of Buckeye Cove* (HTV) details the life of this multi-talented singer, storyteller, actor, painter and naturalist who, among other talents, was an early collector of ballads for the Library of Congress.

Religion. In The Good Old Fashioned Way shows the Old Regular Baptist Church, one of the oldest denominations in the mountains.

Theater, storytelling and literature. Fixin' To Tell About Jack retells traditional folktales. *Ourselves and That Promise* interviews Kentuckians James Still, Robert Penn Warren, Ronnie Criswell and Billy Davis. *Tell Me a Story, Sing Me a Song* (HTV) shows the work of three independent theater companies that come together annually as the Three-Way Tour. Members of A Free Southern Theater, A Traveling Jewish Theater, and Appalshop's Roadside Theater, are seen in performance excerpts and interviews, offering a look at issues relating to Black, Jewish, and Appalachian theater in the U.S.

Toxic waste. Yellow Creek, Kentucky Part I (HTV) shows a Southeast Kentucky community's efforts to stop a commercial tannery from dumping toxic waste in the water.

Headwaters Television (HTV) Collection (1984-present). Extensive collection of videotapes originally broadcast over the Kentucky Educational Television network and public television stations in West Virginia, Virginia and Tennessee.

Size & Elements: Film: 16mm (37 films currently in distribution). Videotape: 3/4" (14 titles currently in distribution). Other material available; archival footage vaulted on premises. All films available on videotape. Film outtakes from completed productions are held with matching workprint.

Cataloging: Published catalog.

Access: Open to the public. Available for rental, purchase, licensing and reuse, subject to restrictions.

Rights: Full rights held to all material. Additional clearances may be necessary in some cases if material is to be reused.

Licensing: Available for licensing and reuse, subject to restrictions. License fees charged (fees negotiated individually).

Restrictions: Requests for licensing and reuse subject to clearance and approval.

Viewing Facilities: Film (16mm); videotape (3/4" and 1/2").

Duplication Facilities: Videotape (3/4" and 1/2").

LOUISIANA

LOUISIANA (Baton Rouge)

BROOKS READ & ASSOCIATES
P.O. Box 2345
Baton Rouge, LA 70821
(504) 343-1715

Street address: 236 Napoleon Street, Baton Rouge, LA 70802

W. B. Read (President)

Contact: W. B. Read

Services: Production company. Film and videotape material available for stock footage sale.

Description: Holds Louisiana-oriented footage (1950s-present), including television commercials, industrials, industrial training films, and political television spots for governors and local officials. Archives of television news footage includes newsreel coverage and stories shot for Fox Movietone News, UPI and Italian network television. Includes an interview with Robert Kennedy and filming of the Chafalaya Swamps. Pending funding, Louisiana State Archives has proposed joint holding and cataloging of collection.

Size & Elements: Film: 16mm. Videotape: 2", 1" and 3/4". (Amounts unspecified).

Cataloging: Cataloging in progress.

Access: Available to the public. Research requests accepted by mail and telephone. Research fees charged in some cases.

Rights: Full rights held to all news material. Additional clearances may be

necessary in some cases if material is to be reused; some material is client-sponsored.
Licensing: Apply for information.
Restrictions: None specified.
Viewing Facilities: None.
Duplication Facilities: Videotape (3/4").

LOUISIANA (Baton Rouge)

LOUISIANA STATE OFFICE OF THE SECRETARY OF STATE DEPARTMENT OF ARCHIVES, RECORDS MANAGEMENT AND HISTORY
P.O. Box 94125
Baton Rouge, LA 70804-9125
(504) 922-1206

Street address: 3851 Essen Lane

Dr. Donald J. Lemieux (State Archivist)

Contacts: Richard Holloway; Randall Perry
Services: Government agency. Videotape material available for research and reuse on a case-by-case basis.
Description: Videotapes pertaining to the 1984 New Orleans World's Fair (95% of library); nature of the remaining 5% unspecified. While the World's Fair videotapes have not been inventoried, they consist primarily of materials used for auditions.
Size & Elements: Videotape: format unspecified (approx. 30 cubic feet).
Cataloging: Inventory and indexing in progress but unavailable at this time.
Access: Not open to the public. Research requests accepted by mail and in person (appointments preferred). Research fees not charged.
Rights: Some rights held to all material.
Licensing: Available for licensing and reuse, subject to restrictions. License and usage fees not charged.
Restrictions: Requests for licensing and reuse considered on a case-by-case basis.
Viewing Facilities: None.
Duplication Facilities: None (outside arrangements can be made).

LOUISIANA (Baton Rouge)

LOUISIANA STATE UNIVERSITY LIBRARIES SPECIAL COLLECTIONS LOUISIANA AND LOWER MISSISSIPPI VALLEY COLLECTIONS
Hill Memorial Library
Baton Rouge, LA 70803
(504) 388-6568

Robert Martin (Assistant Director of Libraries for Special Collections)

Contact: Faye Phillips (Head, Louisiana and Lower Mississippi Valley Collections)
Services: University library. Film and videotape collection open to the public; available for licensing and reuse, subject to restrictions.
Description: *Earl K. Long Papers.* Includes silent color film of the inauguration of Governor Long (1956), depicting daylong ceremonies and activities, local surroundings and personalities. Also holds *Louisiana, The First Chapter* (ca. 1950) narrated by John Carroll, speaking in the role of Sieur de Bienville, discussing the State's history (1699-1950) "from A(rchitecture) to Z(est for Living)."
  Senator Russell B. Long Papers. Film (16mm) and videotape (2" and VHS) (1950-80s) covering the Senator's press conferences, television messages, speeches presented to various organizations and *Meet the Press* appearances.
  Professor T. Harry Williams Civil War Lectures. University classes conducted by the late renowned historian (1978, 63 VHS videotapes).
  Louisiana State University Archives. Recruiting films produced by the Public Relations Department (1960s, 5 films); the 1985 basketball team (8 films); and LSU Tigers Marching Band performances at football games, filmed by the Music Department (1958-82, 200 films, 16mm).
Size & Elements: Film: 16mm (approx. 250 films). Videotape: 2" (16 videotapes); VHS (approx. 71 videotapes).
Cataloging: Computerized cataloging for staff use only; card catalogs and inventories.
Access: Open to the public, subject to restrictions. Research requests accepted

by mail and in person (walk-in). Research fees not charged.
Rights: Some rights held to some material.
Licensing: Available for licensing and reuse, subject to restrictions. License fees not charged.
Restrictions: Requests for research and reuse considered on a case-by-case basis.
Viewing Facilities: Film and videotape (on campus).
Duplication Facilities: None.

LOUISIANA (Bossier City)

HOMOSEXUAL INFORMATION CENTER
115 Monroe Street
Bossier City, LA 71111
(318) 742-4709

Contact: Leslie Colfax (Librarian)
Services: Research library. Film and videotape collection available for research and reuse, subject to restrictions.
Description: Collection was gathered by individuals active in the U.S. homosexual movement beginning in the early 1950s. Over the years, it has developed into a special research collection containing many films and videotapes. Particularly noteworthy is one film (16mm, approx. 15 min., color, sound) documenting the first public demonstration on behalf of gay rights in Los Angeles — a motorcade through Los Angeles streets on Memorial Day 1966 — protesting the exclusion of homosexuals from the armed services.
Size & Elements: Film: 16mm (amount unspecified). Videotape: format and amount unspecified.
Cataloging: Research library.
Access: Open to the public. For in-house use only. Research fees not charged. Research requests accepted by mail, telephone and in person (walk-in and by appointment).
Rights: Apply for information.
Licensing: Apply for information. License fees not charged.
Restrictions: Requests for research and reuse considered on a case-by-case basis.
Viewing Facilities: Film (16mm).
Duplication Facilities: None.

LOUISIANA (New Orleans)

HISTORIC NEW ORLEANS COLLECTION
533 Royal Street
New Orleans, LA 70130
(504) 523-4662

Mrs. Ralph V. Platou (Director)

Contact: John H. Lawrence (Curator of Photographs)
Services: Privately funded history museum. Film and videotape collection available for duplication, licensing and reuse.
Description: Collection relating to New Orleans, Louisiana and Mardi Gras (1948-present). There is also one film on cypress logging in Louisiana (ca. 1930s, 2 reels).
Size & Elements: Film: 16mm (approx. 100 cans; silent and sound, release prints). Videotape: assorted formats from 2" to VHS (approx. 50-60 videotapes; viewing copies).
Cataloging: Computerized cataloging for staff use; also available to researchers.
Access: Available to the public. Available for duplication, licensing and reuse. Research fees not charged. Research requests accepted by mail, telephone and in person (by appointment only).
Rights: Full rights held to some material. Additional clearances may be necessary in some cases if material is to be reused.
Licensing: Available for duplication, licensing and reuse, subject to restrictions. Usage fees charged for commercial use.
Restrictions: Requests for reuse subject to acceptance and approval, depending on type of project and physical condition of film requested.
Viewing Facilities: Film and videotape viewing can be arranged with advance notice.
Duplication Facilities: None; outside arrangements can be made (fees charged).
Related Materials: 200,000 photographs (prints and negatives, mainly black and white) depicting New Orleans architecture, scenics, local street scenes and Mardi Gras.

LOUISIANA (New Orleans)

NEW ORLEANS PUBLIC LIBRARY
LOUISIANA DIVISION
219 Loyola Avenue
New Orleans, LA 70140
(504) 596-2614

Collin B. Hamer, Jr. (Head, Louisiana Division)

Contact: Collin B. Hamer, Jr.
Services: Library; film and videotape archives. Material available for in-house use by researchers and scholars only and for duplication, subject to restrictions.
Description: *WVUE-TV newsfilm* (1969-79). Daily news segments (excluding network feeds) from the New Orleans ABC affiliate station.
   Footage of municipal interest. New Orleans Mayor's Office, Police Department and other agency footage. Includes coverage of governmental activities, civic affairs, Mardi Gras parades, and mayoral trips (1955-75). Holds videotapes of City Council meetings (1983-88) produced for the city by the local cable television system; videotaped interviews with Mayor Ernest N. "Dutch" Morial; special news programs and segments relating to New Orleans; promotional and public service announcements produced for the city; and scattered local and national news programs monitored by the Mayor's Office (1978-86).
Size & Elements: Film: 16mm (6,800 cans [6,300 WVUE-TV; 500 Mayor's Office]; positives, originals). Videotape: VHS (35 videotapes; masters); Betamax (328 videotapes; masters); other formats (5 videotapes).
Cataloging: Card catalogs; finding aids; research library.
Access: Open to researchers and scholars only. For in-house use only. Available for duplication, subject to restrictions. Research requests accepted in person (by appointment only).
Rights: Some rights held to some material. Additional clearances may be necessary if material (especially WVUE-TV footage) is to be reused.
Licensing: Available for licensing and reuse, subject to restrictions. License fees not charged.
Restrictions: Use of material from the WVUE-TV collection requires approval of station management.
Viewing Facilities: Film (16mm); videotape.
Duplication Facilities: None.

LOUISIANA (New Orleans)

NEW ORLEANS VIDEO ACCESS CENTER (NOVAC)
2010 Magazine Street
New Orleans, LA 70130
(504) 524-8626

Julianna Padgett (President of Board)

Contact: Karen Kern (Director)
Services: Media organization; public access television facility. Videotape collection available for in-house research, rental and purchase.
Description: Videotape library holds videotapes produced by NOVAC staff (1972-present). Most videotapes were produced in the 1970s and early 1980s, when a larger staff permitted a greater focus on in-house production projects. The library holds videotapes relating to community issues, "survival" information and the culture of New Orleans, especially relating to the low-income community.
   Two compilation videotapes from NOVAC's Survival Information Project (each 60 min.) include many short, lively programs on health care, employment opportunities, social history, parenting and housing. These videotapes were designed to be shown to low-income "waiting-room" audiences at state offices and received national recognition.
   Other videotapes in NOVAC's library include those produced by NOVAC workshop participants (1972-present); videotapes of local political events and forums; videotapes about public access television; NOVAC-produced public service announcements for local arts and social service organizations; and national samplers of programs produced for public access television (such as the *Deep Dish* series).
   Titles include: *This Cat Can Play Anything,* on Emmanuel "Manny" Sayles, one of New Orleans' greatest banjo and guitar jazzmen; *Cheap and Greasy,* a documentary on the Hummingbird Hotel and Grill, located in the middle of skid row; *Changing the Channel: The Renovation Question,* on the effects of the renovation movement on the future of New Orleans; *High Blood Pressure,* a videotape directed at the Black community; *The Clarks,* on a single

mother with ten children, and their lives in a New Orleans housing project; and *Ain't Nobody's Business,* on battered women.
Size & Elements: Videotape: 2" (1 title; master); 3/4" (approx. 50 titles; masters and viewing copies); VHS (viewing copies).
Cataloging: Published lists.
Access: Available to members and the public for in-house research, rental and purchase. Membership required for out-of-house use. Research requests accepted by mail (for rental) and in person (by appointment only).
Rights: Full rights held to some material.
Licensing: Apply for information. Usage fees charged in some cases.
Restrictions: None specified.
Viewing Facilities: Videotape (3/4" and VHS).
Duplication Facilities: Videotape (3/4", VHS, Betamax I and II).

LOUISIANA (New Orleans)

TULANE UNIVERSITY
AMISTAD RESEARCH CENTER
6823 St. Charles Avenue
New Orleans, LA 70118
(504) 865-5535

Dr. Clifton H. Johnson (Executive Director)

Contact: Florence E. Borders (Senior Archivist)
Services: University library and archives. Film and videotape material available to the public for research and reuse, subject to restrictions.
Description: The Center is the largest archives of Black and ethnic history in the United States.
   Film material held includes *Yes Ma'am* (1982), concerning Black household workers in New Orleans. Raw footage and interviews are held as well as a completed print.
   Videotapes held include: *Blind Tom,* about Thomas Greene Bethune (1849-1908), a composer-pianist prodigy who was born a slave; *Charles Ziwi's Journal* (1980), telling the Amistad story; *The Battle of Liberty Place: Reconstruction* (1982), relating to an 1874 attempt by Whites to overthrow the existing government, which included Blacks among the officeholders; *History of Paul Breaux High School: Desegregation in Lafayette* (1982); *A House Divided* (1987), a documentary about the civil rights movement in New Orleans; *Jacob Lawrence Interview* (1986), with the Afro-American artist and teacher; *Liberty Street Blues* (1988), about New Orleans jazz and the Afro-Louisiana culture that produced it; *Proud Free Men* (1976), about the *gens de couleur libres* of Louisiana and their contributions to the culture and heritage of the state and nation; *St. Mark's Ethnic Heritage Project and Treme/7th Ward Griots* (1982), a two-part oral history of New Orleans's oldest and most diverse Black community (raw footage and interviews are also held); and *Zarico* (1986) about the music of Black Creoles of Southwest Louisiana (also known as "zydeco"), featuring Canray Fontenot, Alphonse Ardoin and Rockin' Dopsie.
Size & Elements: Film: various elements (1 title). Videotape: VHS (21 videotapes, various lengths).
Cataloging: Card catalogs; published catalogs; finding aids.
Access: Open to the public. Research fees charged when staff research time exceeds two hours on any single project. Research requests accepted by mail, telephone and in person (walk-in).
Rights: Full rights held to some material. Rights to most videotapes retained by original producers.
Licensing: Available for licensing and reuse in some cases. License and usage fees charged in some cases.
Restrictions: Standard copyright restrictions apply for reuse.
Viewing Facilities: Videotape.
Duplication Facilities: None.

LOUISIANA (New Orleans)

TULANE UNIVERSITY
HOWARD-TILTON MEMORIAL LIBRARY
WILLIAM RANSOM HOGAN JAZZ ARCHIVE
New Orleans, LA 70118
(504) 865-5688

Street address: 7001 Freret Street

Bruce Raeburn (Curator)

Contacts: Bruce Raeburn; Alma D. Williams (Associate Curator of Graphic

Materials)
Services: Library. Film and videotape collection open to the public for in-house research only.
Description: Historic and current footage relating to jazz, New Orleans music, funerals and parades. Footage is held in the Dominic LaRocca Collection and the William Russell Collection.
Size & Elements: Film: 35mm (1 reel); 16mm (18 reels); 8mm (3 reels) (33 titles, 15 cans total). Videotape: VHS and Betamax (77 videotapes).
Cataloging: Card catalogs.
Access: Open to the public. For in-house research only. Research fees charged. Research requests accepted by mail and in person (walk-in).
Rights: Full rights held to some material. Additional clearances may be necessary in some cases if material is to be reused.
Licensing: Available for licensing and reuse, subject to restrictions. License and usage fees charged.
Restrictions: Restrictions apply (apply for information).
Viewing Facilities: Film and videotape (by reservation).
Duplication Facilities: None.
Related Materials: Sound recordings; audiotaped oral histories.

LOUISIANA (Ruston)

LOUISIANA TECH UNIVERSITY ENGINEERING FILM RESEARCH CENTER
College of Engineering
P.O. Box 10348, Tech Station
Ruston, LA 71272-0046
(318) 257-2852
(318) 257-3176

Jack T. Painter; Leslie Guice (Co-Directors)

Contacts: Jack T. Painter; Leslie Guice
Services: Educational institution. Access policy and procedures regarding film collection currently being established.
Description: The purpose of the Center is to identify, locate, acquire, catalog and preserve records of engineering activities which have been documented on film and videotape. The Center's first major effort, currently in progress, focuses on obtaining films documenting landmark achievements in the engineering profession. Instructional and historical documentary films are also being sought.

Sample titles held include: *Building the Golden Gate Bridge* (Bethlehem Steel); *The Story of the Tacoma Narrows Bridge; The Brooklyn Bridge* (American Society of Civil Engineers); *The Story of Hoover Dam* (U.S. Dept. of the Interior); *Steel Spans the Chesapeake* (Bethlehem Steel); *Turnpike* (Asphalt Institute); *Concrete's Finest Fifty Years* (Portland Cement Association); *Lasers in the Real Production World* (Society of Manufacturing Engineers); *Designs in Energy* (Aries Films); *Approaching the Speed of Sound* (Shell Oil); *The Fluid Dynamics of Drag* (Encyclopedia Britannica); *Speaking of Models* (U.S. Army Corps of Engineers); *From Brimstone to Bread* (Freeport Sulphur Co.); and *Beginnings* (American Society of Civil Engineers).
Size & Elements: Film: format unspecified (40,000 feet, 16 titles, 16 cans). Videotape: VHS (20 videotapes, 22 hours).
Cataloging: In progress; currently unavailable.
Access: Access policy and procedure for reuse being established. Center will be open to educators and researchers.
Rights: Some rights held to some material. Rights status of some material not known.
Licensing: Apply for information.
Restrictions: Access policy and procedure for reuse being established.
Viewing Facilities: None.
Duplication Facilities: None.

LOUISIANA (Shreveport)

LOUISIANA STATE UNIVERSITY, SHREVEPORT ARCHIVES
8515 Youree Drive
Shreveport, LA 71115
(318) 797-5226

Patricia L. Meador (Archivist/Associate Librarian)

Contact: Patricia L. Meador
Services: Educational institution. Film and videotape collection possibly

available for reuse, subject to restrictions. *Licensing policies and fees not established at this time.*
Description: Film (1959-77) donated by KSLA-TV, the local CBS affiliate in Shreveport, and videotape (1980-84) donated by the local Cablevision station, covering a broad range of local news topics relating to Northwest Louisiana, Northeast Texas and Southwest Arkansas. Primary focus is the Shreveport-Bossier City metropolitan area. Topics covered extensively include Louisiana state politics, education, economy and local governments. There is also coverage of the Red River Valley Association, Louisiana Legislature, Barksdale Air Force Base, regional social events, "Holiday-in-Dixie," and visiting national celebrities.

The archives has an agreement with the Cablevision station to receive future programs, and agreements for the acquisition of videotapes of news and special programming from the local ABC and NBC affiliate stations are now in negotiation. Subject to these agreements, the archive will receive the earliest videotapes retained by the stations (all except those produced in the past 3 to 5 years).
Size & Elements: Film: 16mm (350,000 feet, 9,000 cans). Videotape: 3/4" (150 videotapes, 60 min. and 30 min.; masters and viewing copies). Additional videotapes are rapidly being acquired. Future plans include the transfer of film to videotape viewing copies.
Cataloging: Card catalog; computerized index planned for the near future.
Access: Open to the public. Research requests accepted by mail and telephone. Research fees not yet established.
Rights: Some rights held to all material. Additional clearances may be necessary in some cases if material is to be reused.
Licensing: Available for licensing and reuse, subject to restrictions.
Restrictions: Policies for research, licensing and reuse have not yet been established.
Viewing Facilities: None (videotape equipment planned).
Duplication Facilities: None (videotape equipment planned).

MAINE

MAINE (Bangor)

BANGOR HISTORICAL SOCIETY
159 Union Street
Bangor, ME 04401
(207) 942-5766

Abigail Ewing (Curator)

Contact: Abigail Ewing
Services: Historical society. Film and videotape material available for licensing and reuse, subject to restrictions.
Description: WABI-TV (Bangor, Maine) television newsfilm collection (1953-74, 16mm) on deposit with Northeast Historic Film (q.v.); an ice-harvesting film (1936, 8mm film and VHS videotape); a videotape of a Bangor bridge dedication (1986); and an unidentified reel of 35mm film.
Size & Elements: Film: 35mm (1 reel); 8mm film (1 reel). Videotape: VHS (1 videotape).
Cataloging: None specified.
Access: Available to the public. Research fees not charged. Research requests accepted by mail and telephone. (WABI-TV collection held by Northeast Historic Film [q.v.]).
Rights: Full rights held to all material.
Licensing: Available for licensing and reuse, subject to restrictions. License fees not charged.
Restrictions: Requests for licensing and reuse considered on a case-by-case basis.
Viewing Facilities: Videotape (VHS).
Duplication Facilities: None.

MAINE (Bar Harbor)

JEFF DOBBS PRODUCTIONS
Box 541
Bar Harbor, ME 04609
(207) 288-4354

Street address: 93 Cottage Street

Contact: Jeff Dobbs

Services: Videotape producer; stock footage sales library.
Description: Maine scenic footage, including coastal scenes, Acadia National Park area, Mt. Desert Island, birds and animals (eagles and puffins), boats, rock climbing, cross-country skiing and dog sledding.

Also produces cable television programming for the summer tourist trade.
Size & Elements: Videotape: 3/4" (approx. 100 hours; masters); 1/2" (viewing copies).
Cataloging: None specified.
Access: Available to the public for licensing and reuse. Research fees charged. Research requests accepted by mail and telephone.
Rights: Full rights held to all material.
Licensing: Available for licensing and reuse. License fees charged.
Restrictions: None specified.
Viewing Facilities: Videotape.
Duplication Facilities: Videotape (3/4" and 1/2").

MAINE (Blue Hill Falls)

NORTHEAST HISTORIC FILM
Blue Hill Falls, ME 04615
(207) 374-2736

David S. Weiss (Executive Director and Vice President)
Karan Sheldon (Vice President)

Contacts: David S. Weiss; Karan Sheldon
Services: Film and videotape archives. Material available for research, licensing and reuse, subject to restrictions.
Description: Established to preserve and make available to the public film and videotape of the region (Northern New England, particularly Maine and Canada's Maritime Provinces). Holds a wide range of materials including amateur films, industrials, news, the work of regionally based independents, and the dramatic pictures that were produced in New England from the early days of the cinema.

Bangor Historical Society/WABI Newsfilm Collection (1953-74). (16mm, approx. 600,000 feet; black and white). Newsfilm collection from Maine's oldest television station, affiliated with NBC (1953-57) and CBS thereafter. NHF holds collection on a five-year renewable deposit, and owns catalog materials and reference videotape copies that it produces; the Bangor Historical Society (q.v.) holds copyright.

Sample items include: spring fashions being modeled in Waterville, Maine (March 14, 1956); a demonstration of the "Gadget Master" food slicer, juicer, garnish maker, trimmer, safety grater and towel (April 19, 1955); civil defense evacuation scenes in Bangor, Maine (June 15, 1955); New England Basketball Tourney at the Boston Garden (1955); an airport interview with Hume Cronyn (1960); downtown Bangor during the Christmas shopping season (December 8, 1959); the Queen City Time Capsule, Bangor, Maine (December 31, 1959); and an interview with Maine Governor Haskell (December 30, 1959).

Daniel M. Maher Collection. Footage produced by one of Maine's newsreel pioneers (1919-33) (approx. 6 items).

Philip J. Abbott Collection. 16mm family films (1926-28) picturing summer colony life in Harpswell.

Robert M. Hume, Sr. Memorial Collection (1930-50, 16mm, 23 reels). Depicts early logging technology.

Walter Mitton Collection. Actuality footage and home movies relating to Maine, its occupations and local events.

Other items held include footage of indigenous activities, especially ice cutting and fishing; two dramas made in Maine, *The Knight of the Pines* and *Cupid, Registered Guide* (1921), by Holman Francis Day, a nationally popular novelist; a film of Cherryfield, Maine in 1938; the only known surviving copy of a 1915 Hearst-Selig newsreel story showing a saboteur's attempt to blow up the Vanceboro Bridge connecting the United States and Canada; film of Mt. Desert Island activities, winter and summer 1926; reference copies of paper print material in the Library of Congress, Motion Picture, Broadcasting and Recorded Sound Division (q.v.) relating to Maine; copies of films relating to Maine held in the National Archives and Records Administration (q.v.); and footage of the Maine Centennial (1920), with Penobscot and Passamaquoddy Indians in Portland.
Size & Elements: Film: 35mm (amount unspecified); 16mm (750,000 feet; primarily black and white negative).
Cataloging: Computerized cataloging for staff use only (in progress).
Access: Open to the public. Research fees charged. Research requests accepted by mail, telephone and in person (by appointment only).
Rights: Full rights held to some material. Bangor Historical Society owns copyright to WABI collection. Additional clearances may be necessary in some

cases if material is to be reused.
Licensing: Available for licensing and reuse, subject to restrictions. License fees charged.
Restrictions: Requests for licensing and reuse considered on a case-by-case basis.
Viewing Facilities: Film (35mm, 16mm, Super 8mm and 8mm); videotape (3/4" and VHS).
Duplication Facilities: Videotape (3/4" and VHS).

MAINE (Brunswick)

THE PEARY-MACMILLAN ARCTIC MUSEUM AND ARCTIC STUDIES CENTER
BOWDOIN COLLEGE
Brunswick, ME 04011
(207) 725-3062

Dr. Susan A. Kaplan (Director)

Contact: Dr. Gerald F. Bigelow (Curator)
Services: Museum; archival film collection. *Entire collection temporarily closed; not available for use for at least two years in order to facilitate inventory and conservation.*
Description: Holds footage shot on Arctic expeditions (1920-50) by two explorers, Donald B. MacMillan and Robert Bartlett. Both collections record the environments and peoples of Newfoundland, Labrador, Baffin Island, Ellesmere Island, Northwestern Greenland, Southern Greenland, East Greenland, and Iceland. In addition, Museum holds smaller collections that were donated by members of MacMillan's expeditions, covering the same areas. Some subjects include maritime history, Inuit culture, and Arctic fauna.
Size & Elements: Film: 35mm (70,000 feet safety stock, approx. 200,000 feet nitrate stock, awaiting preservation); 16mm (approx. 75,000 to 100,000 feet).
Cataloging: In process. Collections are largely uninventoried; a major portion consists of nitrate film awaiting conversion to safety stock.
Access: Temporarily closed in order to facilitate inventory and conservation. When reopened, the collection will be available for use in research and education.
Rights: Full rights held to all material.
Licensing: Possibly available for licensing and reuse. Policies and license fee schedule being determined.
Restrictions: Collection temporarily closed in order to facilitate inventory and conservation.
Viewing Facilities: None at present.
Duplication Facilities: None.

MAINE (Camden)

VARIED DIRECTIONS, INC.
69 Elm Street
Camden, ME 04843
(207) 236-8506
(800) 888-5236 (orders)
Fax: (207) 236-4512

David Hoffman (President)

Contacts: Andrée Duggan (Film Production); Curtis MacDonald (Marketing); Joyce Boaz (Marketing)
Services: Film and videotape producer; distributor. Material maintained for distribution, rental, purchase and possibly licensing and reuse, subject to restrictions.
Description: Produces programs on educational and health-related subjects for broadcast on PBS and for sale through direct distribution networks.

Current productions include *The Tony Schwartz Series,* including *If You Love Someone Who Smokes,* the story of Schwartz, his friend Ken McFeeley, a smoker who has contracted lung cancer, and their advertising campaign to raise consciousness about smoking; *Dirty Business,* an edited version of the above-mentioned film designed to discourage teenagers from smoking; *Guerrilla Media,* teaching nonprofit, corporate and community groups how to use electronic media to produce their own low-budget radio commercials; *How I Use Media in Politics,* aimed at school and corporate audiences; *Secrets of Effective Radio Advertising,* for university radio stations; and *The Journey Back,* made with the Sunny von Bulow Coma Research Foundation, telling the stories of coma survivors in order to increase awareness in high-school students about drinking and driving.

Other titles include *Fight For Your Life*, with Dr. Bernie Siegel, on survival techniques for living with cancer (e.g., meditation and exercise); *The Other Side of the Fence*, made with the ASPCA, contrasting the veal calf industry with family farming; *Black Magic*, a motivational film for inner-city physical education classes, showing "Double-Dutch" competition winners and their trip to London; *Why God — Why Me?* (made with the Knox County, Maine Child Abuse and Neglect Council) relating to sexual abuse of children; and *Showdown on Tobacco Road*, showing both sides of the tobacco industry, the advertising campaigns designed to lure teenage consumers and the efforts of anti-smoking groups to ban smoking.

Size & Elements: Film: 16mm (4 titles; originals and release prints). Videotape: 1", 3/4" and VHS (masters and viewing copies) (approx. 15 titles total).
Cataloging: Published brochures; educational catalog in progress.
Access: Completed films available for rental and purchase. Material possibly available for licensing and reuse. Research fees not charged. Requests accepted by mail and telephone.
Rights: Full rights held to most material. Additional clearances may be necessary in some cases if material is to be reused.
Licensing: Available for licensing and reuse, subject to restrictions. License fees charged under some conditions (fees negotiated).
Restrictions: Requests for licensing and reuse considered on a case-by-case basis. All requests subject to acceptance and approval.
Viewing Facilities: Videotape (3/4" and VHS).
Duplication Facilities: Videotape (3/4" and VHS; primarily for in-house use).

MAINE (Skowhegan)

MARGARET CHASE SMITH LIBRARY CENTER
P.O. Box 366
Skowhegan, ME 04976
(207) 474-7133
Fax: (207) 474-8878

Street address: Neil Hill

Gregory P. Gallant (Director)

Contact: Gregory P. Gallant
Services: Private collection. Videotape collection available to researchers and scholars only.
Description: Videotapes covering various aspects of Sen. Margaret Chase Smith's career (1954-88). Of note are interviews conducted by Senator Smith during her 1954-55 world tour and filmed by Edward R. Murrow's *See It Now* film crew. Among those interviewed are Gamal Abdel Nasser, Jawaharlal Nehru, Francisco Franco, Unu, Ramon Magsaysay, Pierre Mendes-France, Malcolm Muggeridge, Aneurin Bevan, Arnold Joseph Toynbee and Konrad Adenauer. The collection also includes a tour of Berlin; a *Face the Nation* debate (1956) between Senator Smith and Eleanor Roosevelt; an appearance on the same show during her 1964 presidential campaign; and a compilation of various campaign spots and several interviews with Senator Smith by various local journalists and friends. Many of the items are outtakes.

Also held are several videotapes concerning the history of the Library Center.
Size & Elements: Videotape: format unspecified (approx. 55 videotapes).
Cataloging: Card catalogs; computerized cataloging for staff use only.
Access: Open to researchers and scholars only. Research fees not charged. Research requests accepted by mail, telephone and in person (walk-in).
Rights: Full rights held to all material.
Licensing: Apply for information.
Restrictions: None specified.
Viewing Facilities: Videotape.
Duplication Facilities: None.
Related Materials: Audiotapes and photographs.

MARYLAND

MARYLAND (Baltimore)

BALTIMORE MUSEUM OF INDUSTRY
1415 Key Highway
Baltimore, MD 21230
(301) 727-4808

Dennis Zembala (Director)

Contact: Ann Steele (Assistant Director)
Services: Museum. Film and videotape archives available for research, licensing and reuse, subject to restrictions.
Description: Industrial films (1930s-60s) including footage of a tour of the S. K. Meatpacking Plant, Westinghouse Electric Company films (1940s-60s), and a film of the Allied Chemical Company's employee parking lot in the 1930s.
Size & Elements: Film: 16mm (approx. 35 titles, some transferred to videotape).
Cataloging: None specified.
Access: Open to the public. Research requests accepted by mail and telephone. Research fees not charged.
Rights: Full rights held to all material.
Licensing: Apply for information.
Restrictions: Requests for licensing and reuse considered on a case-by-case basis.
Viewing Facilities: Videotape.
Duplication Facilities: None.

MARYLAND (Baltimore)

JOHNS HOPKINS UNIVERSITY/ POPULATION COMMUNICATION SERVICES MEDIA/MATERIALS COLLECTION
527 St. Paul Place
Baltimore, MD 21202
(301) 955-7666
Fax: (301) 659-6266
Telex: 240430

Available for purchase and rental from:
JOHN HOPKINS UNIVERSITY
POPULATION INFORMATION PROGRAM
527 St. Paul Place
Baltimore, MD 21202
(301) 955-8200
Contact: Ann Simmons

Patrick L. Coleman (Project Director, Population Communications Services)

Contact: Susan Liebtag (Librarian, Population Communications Services)
Services: Educational institution; distributor. Film and videotape collection available to the public for rental, purchase and duplication.
Description: Films relating to family planning and population control communication in developing countries, all produced by The George Washington University Airlie Center with funding from the U.S. Agency for International Development. They are now distributed through the Population Communications Services, administered through the Population Information Program of The John Hopkins University.

The City: Implications for the Future (1977), discussing the reasons for rural-to-urban migration and its consequences, using Bogota, Colombia as an example; *Communicating Family Planning: Speak — They are Listening* (1974), case studies in family planning communication from Costa Rica, El Salvador, Hawaii, Indonesia, Kenya, Korea, Pakistan, Philippines, Tunisia, and Vietnam; *Choice Not Chance* (1973), exploring men's attitudes toward family planning, using narration and discussion by urban Jamaican men; *Indonesia: Family Planning First* (1978), showing how a rural, traditional, and relatively poor society in Java used family planning as an integral part of village life; *Mexico in the Year 2000* (1979), proposing family planning as a solution to uncontrolled development and growth, focusing on heavy industry and crowded cities.

To the People (1977) demonstrates successful household delivery of oral contraceptives in Bangladesh, Egypt and Tunisia; *(Two Roads) Dos caminos* (1979) shows problems caused by ignorance about human sexuality and by the myths about how a woman can become pregnant. *Technique of Laparoscopy* (1979), a medical training film, shows female sterilization by laparoscopy under local anesthesia in an outpatient clinic; preoperative evaluation, operative technique, and postoperative procedures are demonstrated. *A Question of Choice* (1978) shows voluntary sterilization programs in Bangladesh, El Salvador, the Philippines, Thailand, and the United States. *Social Marketing* (1978) demonstrates the delivery of condoms and oral contraceptives through social marketing and commercial retail sales programs, using as examples projects in Jamaica, El Salvador, and Bangladesh; *(Sowing the Seeds of Health)* *Sembrando salud* (1979) shows how trained women in Mexico help to change attitudes about health care practices, offering guidance in maternal, childcare, and family planning.

Many films are available in various language versions.

Size & Elements: Film: 16mm (18 titles; positive and release prints). Videotape: format unspecified (viewing copies).

Cataloging: Film list.

Access: Available to the public for rental, purchase and duplication. Family planning, health and population agencies in developing countries may receive films to add to their collections free of charge. Commercial institutions in developing countries and public and private organizations in developed countries may purchase films. Research fees not charged.

Rights: Full rights held to all material.

Licensing: Apply for information. License fees not charged.

Restrictions: None specified.

Viewing Facilities: Film (16mm projector); videotape (3/4", VHS and Betamax).

Duplication Facilities: None.

MARYLAND (Baltimore)

JOHNS HOPKINS UNIVERSITY
SCHOOL OF MEDICINE
MOTION PICTURE AND TV PRODUCTION

1721 East Madison Street
Baltimore, MD 21205
(301) 955-3562

Dale Roth Levitz (Chief, Motion Pictures and Production)

Contact: Dale Roth Levitz

Services: Educational institution; medical school. Film and videotape collection available for licensing and reuse. License and fee policies not yet determined. Can shoot specific footage upon request.

Description: *Historical.* Film and videotape footage dating back to the 1920s, covering all medical subjects. Included are early sound films of Dr. William Welch and Dr. John Able; leaders in medical science; unique footage (90 min.) of the Johns Hopkins Hospital in the 1930s, showing the day-to-day operation of each department (e.g., milk being pasteurized, cotton being made, old X-ray machines, iron lungs, methods of treatment in use at that time); footage of the Blalock-Taussig Blue Baby operation; other medical firsts and landmark procedures.

Current. Videotapes showing separation of Siamese twins, heart and lung transplants, state-of-the-art surgical procedures and educational programs on various subjects. Plans are to assemble a reel of stock hospital shots for use by the media. Footage can be shot upon request (fees charged).

Size & Elements: Film: format unspecified ("hundreds"; mostly reversal, originals, workprints and outtakes). Videotape: mostly 3/4" ("thousands"; originals, masters, duplicates and outtakes). Specific amounts are difficult to estimate at this time, but over 50 years of material is held.

Cataloging: Card catalogs; limited shot lists; computerized cataloging for staff use only. Plans are to catalog and inventory holdings pending funding.

Access: Available for licensing and reuse. Policy undetermined as to whether research fees will be charged. Research requests accepted by mail, telephone and in person (by appointment only).

Rights: Full rights held to some material. Some rights held to all material. Additional clearances may be necessary in some cases if material is to be reused.

Licensing: Licensing and fee policies not yet determined.

Restrictions: Policies on licensing not yet determined.

Viewing Facilities: Film (Steenbeck); videotape (3/4" and 1/2").

Duplication Facilities: Film (local laboratory used); videotape (3/4" and 1/2"); local facility used for 1".

MARYLAND (Baltimore)

MASS MEDIA MINISTRIES

2116 North Charles Street
Baltimore, MD 21218
(301) 727-3270

Contact: Janice York

Services: Distributor. Films and videotapes available to the public for rental and purchase.

Description: Religious and inspirational films offering "informative programs on issues of crucial concern to communities, challenging discussion films, film parables and profiles that inspire and teach important spiritual truths, fantasy and adventure films that enrich and entertain."

Subject areas include: adolescence; aging; alienation; Black history; capital punishment; celebration; censorship; coping with change; charismatic renewal; child abuse and neglect; children and their problems; Christian education; Christian living; church history; the church's mission and purpose; commitment; communication; community; compassion; confirmation; courage; creativity; crime; death; decision-making; divorce and separation; domestic issues and problems; drug abuse; emotional development; ethics and morality; faith; family relationships; forgiveness; freedom and justice; friendship; growth; the handicapped; healing; the Holocaust; honesty; hunger; identity; individual rights; Judaeo-Christian history; leadership; the mystery and meaning of life; love; Christian loyalty; marriage; materialism; nature appreciation; New and Old Testament study; the nuclear threat; parables for today; peace; perseverance; political activism; poverty; power and authority; prayer; prejudice; reproduction; self-awareness; sexual roles and mores; suicide; technology and modern life; theological issues; Third World issues; values; violence; wholeness; winning attitudes; Lenten programs; films for worship; and films for children.

Size & Elements: Film: 16mm (approx. 300 titles). Videotape: VHS and Betamax.

Cataloging: Published catalogs.

Access: Available to the public for rental and purchase. Inquiries accepted by mail and telephone.

Rights: All programs protected by copyright and all rights thereunder are reserved.

Licensing: Apply for information.

Restrictions: None specified.

Viewing Facilities: None.

Duplication Facilities: None.

Related Materials: Study and discussion guides for most programs.

MARYLAND (Baltimore)

NATIONAL ASSOCIATION FOR THE ADVANCEMENT OF COLORED PEOPLE (NAACP)

National Headquarters
4805 Mt. Hope Drive
Baltimore, MD 21215
(301) 358-8900
Fax: (301) 358-2332

Dr. Benjamin L. Hooks (Executive Director)
James Williams (Director, Department of Public Relations) (301/486-9141)

Contact: James Williams

Services: Civil rights organization. Videotapes available to the public for rental and purchase.

Description: Videotapes on the Association's history and activities.

The Longest Struggle: NAACP in Historical Perspective (four-part series) chronicles the oppressive and violent era following Reconstruction; the birth of the NAACP; and its accomplishments in providing equal opportunity in housing, employment, education and voter participation. In tracing the history of the NAACP, the series outlines the history of the struggle of Black Americans for full citizenship. Available on VHS videotape from: Tony Brown Productions, c/o George Martin, 1501 Broadway, Suite 2014, New York, NY 10036; (212/575-0878 or 212/247-4545).

The Challenge (17 min.), narrated by Virna Canson (NAACP Region I Director), gives an overview of NAACP programs and provides important historical information. Available on 3/4" and VHS videotape from: Virna Canson, NAACP Region I Director, 2480 Sutter Street, San Francisco, CA 94115; (415/931-3242).

NAACP Building Dedication Week. Videotapes highlight the activities which took place during the NAACP's Dedication Week Ceremonies, celebrating the NAACP's first year in Baltimore and its new ownership of a five-story building. They feature the Rev. Jesse Jackson, Alex Haley, Dr. Benjamin Hooks, Dorothy Heights, Reverend Joseph Lowery, Martin Luther King, Jr., Rosa Parks, Daisy Bates, Myrlie Evers and Dick Gregory. Available in videotape from: Ted Deveaux, TSCD Sight & Sound Productions, 6006 Greenbelt Road, Suite 165, Greenbelt, MD 20770; (301/982-0612).

NAACP 78th Annual Convention. Highlights of the NAACP's 78th Annual Convention in New York City (1987), featuring the Rev. Jesse Jackson, John Jacob, Dr. Benjamin L. Hooks, Chicago Mayor Harold Washington, Julius "Dr. J" Erving, White House Chief of Staff Howard Baker, New York Gov. Mario Cuomo, Sen. Albert Gore (D-Tennessee), former Arizona Gov. Bruce Babbitt,

Coretta Scott King, U.S. Surgeon General C. Everett Koop, Carl Rowan and others. Available from Ted Deveaux (see above).
Size & Elements: Videotape: 3/4" and VHS (approx. 4 titles).
Cataloging: List available.
Access: Available to the public for rental and purchase. Requests accepted by mail and telephone.
Rights: Full rights held to some material.
Licensing: Apply for information.
Restrictions: None specified.
Viewing Facilities: None.
Duplication Facilities: None.
Distributors: Various (see above).

MARYLAND (Baltimore)

UNIVERSITY OF BALTIMORE
A. S. ABELL TELEVISION NEWSFILM ARCHIVE
Langsdale Library, Special Collections Department
1420 Maryland Avenue
Baltimore, MD 21201
(301) 625-3135

Gerry Yeager (Head of Special Collections)

Contact: Gerry Yeager
Services: University film and videotape archives. Available to the public for in-house use only, and for duplication and reuse, subject to restrictions.
Description: WMAR-TV (Baltimore) news footage (1947-87), including daily local news coverage, comprising approx. 70 to 80% of collection, and documentaries (edited programs and unedited footage) arranged by subject. Collection emphasizes Baltimore history, politics and development, the Baltimore riots (late 1960s) and sports. Videotaped daily news programs (1980-87) are also held.
Size & Elements: Film: 16mm (7 million feet; positive). Videotape: 2" ("very few"); other videotapes in unspecified formats.
Cataloging: Computerized cataloging for staff use only; research library. Only a very rough catalog of material exists, arranged in chronological order under a few broad subject areas. Archive plans to produce an extensive and detailed catalog.
Access: Available to the public. For in-house use only. Staff will research and select footage for specific requests; research fees charged for more time-consuming requests. Research requests accepted by mail, telephone and in person (by appointment only).
Rights: WMAR-TV holds full rights to all material.
Licensing: Available for licensing and reuse, subject to restrictions. License fees usually not charged.
Restrictions: All requests for duplication, licensing and reuse subject to acceptance and approval by WMAR-TV.
Viewing Facilities: Film (limited viewing facilities; staff assistance preferred).
Duplication Facilities: Researchers are expected to cover the costs of duplication by outside facilities. Many users who have made videotape copies of material have provided an extra copy for the Library (which intends to transfer its film to videotape).
Related Materials: The Steamship Historical Society of America (still photograph collection).

MARYLAND (Bethesda)

CYSTIC FIBROSIS FOUNDATION
VIDEO COORDINATOR
and
GOODWILL INDUSTRIES OF AMERICA
and
HEALTH AND EDUCATION RESOURCES, INC.
ART PROJECT
and
NATIONAL LIBRARY OF MEDICINE
HISTORY OF MEDICINE DIVISION
HISTORICAL AUDIOVISUALS COLLECTION
See DISTRICT OF COLUMBIA METRO

MARYLAND (Capitol Heights)

NATIONAL ARCHIVES AND RECORDS ADMINISTRATION (NARA)
NATIONAL AUDIOVISUAL CENTER

See DISTRICT OF COLUMBIA METRO

MARYLAND (Chesapeake Beach)

INSTITUTE FOR SPACE & SECURITY STUDIES
7833 C Street
Chesapeake Beach, MD 20732
(301) 855-4600
(301) 855-4608
Telex: 3791342-ISSS

Dr. Robert M. Bowman (President and Director of Research)

Contact: Joan Luton (Director of Administration and Public Relations)
Services: Independent, nonprofit educational and research institution. Two videotapes available for purchase and broadcast.
Description: Headed by Dr. Robert Bowman, pre-eminent scientist and opponent of the "Star Wars" program, the Institute conducts research and educational activities in science and strategy relating to space and other high-technology areas important to national security and the maintenance of peace. "The overall goal of the Institute is to prevent nuclear war. It is our judgment that an arms race in space greatly increases the danger that such a war will occur."
Star Wars: Fact or Fiction (28 min.) is a television program featuring Carl Sagan, Dick Garwin, Admiral Gene Carroll, Carol Rosin, and Dr. Anne Cahn, narrated by Dr. Robert Bowman. *Star Wars and Security* (56 min.) is a presentation based on a lecture by Dr. Bowman.
Size & Elements: Videotape: 3/4" and VHS (2 titles).
Cataloging: Printed lists.
Access: Available to the public for purchase. Also available for broadcast. Fees charged (apply for information).
Rights: Apply for information.
Licensing: Broadcast rights available (apply for information).
Restrictions: None specified.
Viewing Facilities: None.
Duplication Facilities: None.

MARYLAND (College Park)

UNIVERSITY OF MARYLAND
McKELDIN LIBRARY
HISTORICAL MANUSCRIPTS AND ARCHIVES DEPARTMENT
See DISTRICT OF COLUMBIA METRO

MARYLAND (Greenbelt)

NATIONAL AERONAUTICS AND SPACE ADMINISTRATION
GODDARD SPACE FLIGHT CENTER
REGIONAL FILM LIBRARY
See DISTRICT OF COLUMBIA METRO

MARYLAND (Hagerstown)

AMERICAN JAIL ASSOCIATION
1000 Day Road, Suite 100
Hagerstown, MD 21740
(301) 790-3930
Fax: (301) 790-2941

Dick Ford (Executive Director)

Contact: Dick Ford
Services: Association. Videotapes available for purchase.
Description: Training programs for correctional facilities produced in cooperation with Instructional Video Productions, Inc. Titles include: *Intoxicated Inmates: What Can Happen?*, discussing specific guidelines for care and supervision of intoxicated prisoners and situations in which improper handling may result in serious illness, injury, or death for which jail personnel may be held personally liable. *Sticky Situations: True-Life Training Scenarios* includes role-playing by actual inmates and jail personnel. Topics include: sexism (What frictions are there between female officers and male inmates? Between male officers and female superiors?); cutting corners ("Going by the book" can be slow and frustrating. Should administrators ever relax the rules for the sake of efficiency?); and pulling rank (How do you respond when a superior officer does something you know is wrong?). *Suicide: The Silent*

MARYLAND (Kensington)

Signals is a guide to prevention of inmate suicide, stressing each officer's legal responsibility to keep suicidal inmates alive.
Size & Elements: Videotape: 3/4" and VHS (3 titles total).
Cataloging: Brochures.
Access: Available for purchase. Orders accepted by mail.
Rights: Apply for information.
Licensing: Apply for information.
Restrictions: None specified.
Viewing Facilities: None.
Duplication Facilities: None.
Related Materials: Study guides corresponding to programs available.

MARYLAND (Kensington)

CENTER FOR PUBLIC DIALOGUE
See **DISTRICT OF COLUMBIA METRO**

MARYLAND (Landover)

NATIONAL SUDDEN INFANT DEATH SYNDROME FOUNDATION
See **DISTRICT OF COLUMBIA METRO**

MARYLAND (Laurel)

AMERICAN CORRECTIONAL ASSOCIATION
TRAINING DIVISION
See **DISTRICT OF COLUMBIA METRO**

MARYLAND (Lutherville)

FIRE MUSEUM OF MARYLAND
1301 York Road
Lutherville, MD 21093
(301) 321-7500

Stephen J. Heaver, Jr. (Curator and President)

Contact: Stephen J. Heaver, Jr.
Services: Museum. One film available for in-house screening.
Description: Museum-produced film showing their antique firefighting equipment, including an 1897 steamer and a 1905 water tower, both horse-drawn and fully operational.
Size & Elements: Film: 16mm (700 feet, 1 title, 1 can).
Cataloging: None specified.
Access: Screened every Sunday along with other historical films at the Museum (apply for information).
Rights: Full rights held to some material.
Licensing: Apply for information.
Restrictions: None specified.
Viewing Facilities: Film (35-seat theater).
Duplication Facilities: None.

MARYLAND (Potomac)

SILVER IMAGE
See **DISTRICT OF COLUMBIA METRO**

MARYLAND (Rockville)

AMERICAN OCCUPATIONAL THERAPY ASSOCIATION
AOTA PRODUCTS
and
BNA COMMUNICATIONS, INC.
a subsidiary of THE BUREAU OF NATIONAL AFFAIRS, INC.
and
MONTGOMERY COMMUNITY TELEVISION, INC.
See **DISTRICT OF COLUMBIA METRO**

MARYLAND (Salisbury)

AMERICAN DRIVER AND TRAFFIC SAFETY EDUCATION ASSOCIATION
See **DISTRICT OF COLUMBIA METRO**

MARYLAND (Silver Spring)

GYPSUM ASSOCIATION
and
MANKIND RESEARCH FOUNDATION INC.
See **DISTRICT OF COLUMBIA METRO**

MARYLAND (Timonium)

MILNER-FENWICK, INC.
2125 Greenspring Drive
Timonium, MD 21093-9989
(800) 432-8433 (outside Maryland)
(301) 252-1700 (Maryland)
Fax: (301) 252-6316

Contact: Customer Representatives
Services: Film and videotape producer and distributor. Materials available for purchase, broadcast, duplication and possibly reuse, subject to restrictions.
Description: *Patientvision Education programs.* Designed for use by physicians, hospitals, clinics, health maintenance organizations, public health departments, volunteer health agencies, corporate health programs and libraries, these programs educate patients on a variety of health problems and treatments. Over 200 programs are available in the following fields: health promotion, coronary disease, weight control, gastroenterology, aging, pain management, diabetes, rheumatology, respiratory, orthopedics, general surgery, otolaryngology, urology, ophthalmology, pediatrics, obstetrics, genetic counseling, sexually transmitted diseases, contraception, gynecology, sexual counseling and dental health.
  Parentvision programs. Designed to be shown by physicians to parents at "well-baby" visits or after hearing a particular parental concern. The films speak directly to the parent's need for basic child care information, and provide this information in an interesting format. Titles include: *Well Child Care* series; *First Days of Parenthood; Child Safety; When Your Baby Is Sick;* and related titles.
  Informed consent videotapes. Consists of 12 videotapes that provide the information patients need to know to make informed decisions about specific procedures, treatment and recovery. Videotape content is reinforced and patient understanding confirmed by written guidebooks, quizzes and documentation forms. Subjects covered include cardiology, pulmonary, gastroenterology, and obstetrics and gynecology.
  Here's to Your Health series. Produced by KERA-TV (Dallas, Texas), these 23 programs focus on self-care for consumers, major health concerns and what kind of help is available. Episodes available include *Why We're Killing Ourselves,* relating to the factors in our lifestyles placing us at risk of developing cancer and heart disease; *Things That Go Bump...In Your GI Tract,* about the digestive system, its most common problems and the new techniques available for dealing with them; and *"Sexy" Transmitted Diseases,* a medical discussion of the facts about sexually transmitted diseases.
  Risk Management videotapes. Four videotapes on nursing liability and four on medical recordkeeping use realistic dramatizations of everyday risk situations to illustrate how efficient operational procedures, sound decision-making skills and effective communication can prevent injury and protect against legal liability.
Size & Elements: Film: 16mm and Super 8mm (Fairchild or Technicolor cassettes). Videotape: 3/4", VHS and Betamax. (Over 200 titles total; most available in Spanish-language versions, some with dual-language soundtracks).
Cataloging: Published catalogs.
Access: Available for preview, purchase, closed-circuit television use, broadcast and duplication. Preview fees charged.
Rights: Apply for information.
Licensing: Apply for information.
Restrictions: Shipment of videotape programs subject to the execution of standard licensing or non-duplication agreements.
Viewing Facilities: None.
Duplication Facilities: None.
Representatives: Programs available from international representatives in some countries outside the United States (apply for information).

MASSACHUSETTS

MASSACHUSETTS (Amherst)

UNIVERSITY OF MASSACHUSETTS
UNION VIDEO CENTER
216 Student Union Building

Amherst, MA 01003
(413) 545-1336

Contact: Coordinator
Services: University videotape production facility. Videotape collection open to the public for research and possibly reuse.
Description: Documentation of speeches given at the University by distinguished statesmen, politicians, academics and entertainers. Also holds documentation of cultural and political activities at the University.
Size & Elements: Videotape: VHS and Betamax (over 200 videotapes; masters and viewing copies).
Cataloging: None.
Access: Open to the public. Research fees negotiable. Research requests accepted by telephone and in person (walk-in).
Rights: Full rights held to some material. Additional clearances may be necessary in some cases if material is to be reused.
Licensing: Possibly available for licensing and reuse. License fees charged in some cases.
Restrictions: None specified.
Viewing Facilities: Videotape (by special arrangement).
Duplication Facilities: Videotape (3/4", VHS and Betamax).

MASSACHUSETTS (Arlington)

THE NEW FILM CO., INC.
7 Mystic Street, Suite 321
Arlington, MA 02174
(617) 641-2580

Christopher Knight (President)

Contacts: Christopher Knight; Joyce Zinno (Distribution Manager)
Services: Film and videotape producer and distributor. Material available to the public for distribution, licensing and reuse; subject to clearance in some cases.
Description: Completed films and unedited stock footage relating to sailing, environmental issues, Native Americans and other subjects.
   Sailing. Six completed films (each 60 min.); and footage relating to a modern-day retracing of Captain Cook's journey from San Francisco to Hawaii.
   Environmental issues. Three completed films (each 30 min.). Subjects include striped bass and eagles. One documentary film covers the decision whether or not to build an oil refinery off the coast of Maine, and includes footage of Maine's seacoast.
   Native Americans. Two anthropological films on prehistoric rock art (Mojave Desert, California); and another on the Pueblo Indian ruins of New Mexico.
   Miscellaneous. One film follows a solo canoeist through Canada's Northwest Territories; another relates to elderly Black people. *Carry It On* follows singer Joan Baez on tour and includes footage of the Woodstock Festival (1969).
Size & Elements: Film: 16mm (6 completed films, each 60 min., 20 hours of stock footage; negatives and prints). Videotape: 3/4" and 1/2" (quantity unspecified; viewing copies).
Cataloging: Printed brochures on completed films; staff assistance (for stock shots).
Access: Open to the public. Available for duplication, licensing and reuse. Research fees not charged. Research requests accepted by mail and telephone.
Rights: Full rights held to all material. Additional clearances may be necessary in some cases if material is to be reused (for shots in completed films obtained from outside sources).
Licensing: Available for licensing and reuse. License fees charged.
Restrictions: None specified.
Viewing Facilities: Film (16mm flatbed); videotape (3/4" and 1/2").
Duplication Facilities: None (outside arrangements can be made).

MASSACHUSETTS (Belmont)

JOHN BIRCH SOCIETY
395 Concord Avenue
Belmont, MA 02178
(617) 489-0600

G. Allen Bubolz (Chief Executive Officer)

Contact: Richard McKinney (Wholesale Book Division)
Services: Political and patriotic association; videotape producer. Videotapes

available for purchase.
Description: Videotape productions include: *An Overview of Our World,* about the growth of communism in the world; *Why Weren't We Told?,* an analysis of news and the growth of communism; *The John Birch Society Speaks,* a public relations videotape incorporating an interview with John McManus and Charles R. Armour; *Soviet Russia Inside and Out,* an interview with Avraham Shifrin and his wife on the situation of Soviet Jews; *Education is the Key,* in which the late Congressman Larry McDonald speaks on education; *A Program for Responsible Citizens,* about what it means to be an American; *Keeping Faith with America,* an inspirational videotape; *Welcome to Membership,* a Birch Society promotional film; *Who Shall Teach: The Case for Separation of School and State,* on parents' rights; and *Today's Youth: America's Future.*
Size & Elements: Videotape: VHS and Betamax (12 titles, each 60 min.).
Cataloging: None specified.
Access: Available to the public for purchase. Requests accepted by mail and telephone.
Rights: Full rights held to all material.
Licensing: All inquiries regarding reuse should be directed to: Herb Joiner, The John Birch Society, 2650 Mission Street, San Marino, CA 91108; (818) 799-0876.
Restrictions: Apply for information.
Viewing Facilities: None.
Duplication Facilities: None.

MASSACHUSETTS (Boston)

ASIAN AMERICAN RESOURCE WORKSHOP
27 Beach Street, 3rd Floor
Boston, MA 02111
(617) 426-5313

Fred Dow (Executive Director); Carlton Sagara (Administrative Director)

Contact: Helen Liu (Media Director)
Services: Educational institution; library; media organization; private collection. Film and videotape library open to members and the public.
Description: Nonprofit community arts, educational and advocacy organization whose purpose is to promote pride and respect in the history, culture and experiences of Asians in America. Provides a wide range of programs and services designed to increase public awareness and develop a sense of community among the diverse Asian American population. Includes the most extensive collection of written and audiovisual materials in New England on historical and contemporary experiences of Asians in America. Maintains a collection of educational films, slide shows and other Asian American media, some produced by members and staff.
   Chinese Americans. Film titles include: *The Chinese Americans: The Early Immigrants* (1973), telling the history of the first Chinese to come to the United States and their role in the Gold Rush, the building of the transcontinental railroad, their savage persecution and eventual unjust exclusion; *The Chinese Americans: The 20th Century* (1973), viewing changing roles from the turn of the century to the present, particularly in the labor force; *The Golden Mountain on Mott Street* (CBS, 1975), exploring the lives of Chinese immigrants in various American Chinatowns who experience the many problems of urban life in the United States; *I'm Going to be the Lion's Head,* in which a Chinese youth hopes to perform the part of the lion's head in the spectacular San Francisco Chinese New Year's Parade. Videotapes include: *Gum Saan Haak, Parts 1-6* (KRON-TV, English and Cantonese), a series examining in detail the history of Chinese in America.
   Exercises. Karate explains the origin of karate and then looks at the process of training a student.
   Immigration. To Be Me: Tony Quon is an account of an active ten-year-old Chinese immigrant who is learning how to adjust as a non-English speaker in an American elementary school.
   Asian American experience. Videotape (3/4" and VHS) titles include: *Asian Images in the Media: Those Lemon Colored Characters* (Asian American Resource Workshop, 1986), a detailed history of the stereotypical images of Asians portrayed in the media and the racial discrimination faced by Asian American actors and actresses who have tried to break out of Suzie Wong/Fu Manchu roles; *East + West = Music,* a variety of musical performances by Asian American musicians, including: Chris and Joanne with Charlie Chin (a folk trio), the Afro-Asian soul band "Sand," Mandarin folk songs sung by Wilma Pang, the San Francisco Chinese Chorus, and the Chinese Classical Music Club; *Pel Lee: Portrait of an Asian American Teenager* (Asian American Resource Workshop, 1984), documents the feelings and thoughts of an Asian American teenage girl living in Boston's Chinatown.

Asian communities. Videotape titles include: *Boston Chinatown History* (Asian American Resource Workshop and Chinatown Cable Council, 1983), presents an overview of Boston Chinatown's history from its development into a Chinese community to present-day struggles as it continues to exist as a residential and commercial neighborhood; *Chinatown, Our Home* (Chinese Media Committee), a realistic Cantonese-language drama with English subtitles, about the life and conflicts of a Chinatown immigrant family; *The Last Temple* (Chinese Media Committee), the history of a Taoist temple in Hanford, California that faces the threat of destruction.

Japanese Americans in concentration camps. Videotape titles include: *Boston Hearings* (1981, 6 videotapes), complete testimony of the Boston Hearings, focusing on legal and constitutional aspects of the camps and possible reparations; *Los Angeles Hearings* (1981, 2 videotapes), excerpts from the moving testimony of former internees; *New York Hearings: Artists Speak* (Renee Tajima, Asian Cine Vision), testimony by Japanese American artists who were interned and the impact of the camps on their work.

Social issues. Videotape titles include: *Against the Zone* (Asian American Resource Workshop, 1986), documenting the community organizing that resulted from the common goal to preserve Boston's Chinatown as a residential community and not as a "red light" district for prostitutes and pimps; *Long Road to Justice* (Asian American Resource Workshop), documents the case of Long Guang Huang, who was falsely arrested and beaten by a Boston plainclothes police detective on May 1, 1985.

Taiwan. Titles include: *Thunderstorm* (4 parts), a four-act drama about a bourgeois Taiwanese family.

Size & Elements: Film: 16mm (approx. 6 titles). Videotape: 3/4" and VHS (approx. 21 titles).
Cataloging: Published catalog.
Access: Available to the public, schools and communities for viewing and rental. Material also circulated to members. Research fees not charged (except for slides and photographs). Research requests accepted by mail, telephone and in person (walk-in); an appointment is necessary to preview material.
Rights: Full rights held to most material. Additional clearances may be necessary in some cases if material is to be reused.
Licensing: Apply for information. License fees charged.
Restrictions: None specified.
Viewing Facilities: Film (16mm); videotape (3/4" and VHS).
Duplication Facilities: Videotape (3/4" and VHS).

MASSACHUSETTS (Boston)

BOSTON COMMUNITY ACCESS AND PROGRAMMING FOUNDATION
BOSTON NEIGHBORHOOD NETWORK VIDEOTAPE LIBRARY
25 Huntington Avenue, Room 406
Boston, MA 02116
(617) 424-7292

Hubert Jessup (General Manager)

Contact: Hubert Jessup
Services: Public access television facility. Videotape library available primarily for in-house use only; possibly available for reuse, subject to restrictions.
Description: Nonprofit media foundation offering public access television facilities in the city of Boston. As part of their cable television franchise contract with the City of Boston, Cablevision of Boston provides core funding, channels on the system, production studios and a production van for the Boston Community Access and Programming Foundation.

Collection includes the best of Boston public access production (1984-present), consisting primarily of documentaries produced by Boston residents, many of a working-class background, who have been trained by Boston Neighborhood Network staff; funding for the programs has been provided by Cablevision. Some strengths of the collection are: drug education programs; ethnic language programs, including Creole, Spanish (mostly Puerto Rican), Irish, Italian, and Chinese (Mandarin and Cantonese); gay, lesbian and feminist programs; documentaries by producers of color, including Latino and Haitian productions; and daily local news programs (including all field reports) produced since 1984.
Size & Elements: Videotape: 3/4" (approx. 100 titles, varying from 5 to 120 min., masters and viewing copies); VHS (viewing copies).
Cataloging: Card catalog.
Access: For in-house use only. Available for duplication and reuse, subject to restrictions. Research requests accepted by mail and telephone.
Rights: Full rights held to some material. Additional clearances may be necessary in some cases if material is to be reused; rights to most material

retained by individual producers.
Licensing: Apply for information. License fees not charged at present.
Restrictions: Requests for licensing and reuse considered on a case-by-case basis.
Viewing Facilities: Available upon request.
Duplication Facilities: None.

MASSACHUSETTS (Boston)

BOSTON FAMILY INSTITUTE
315 Dartmouth Street
Boston, MA 02116
(617) 262-8651

Frederick J. Duhl, M.D. (Director)

Contact: Kate Schildhauer (Administrative Consultant)
Services: Educational institution. Videotapes available for rental and purchase for use in training only.
Description: The *Perceptions* collection, designed for the training of family therapists, comprises two distinct but integrated videotape series.

Interventions in Family Therapy (15 programs, each 60 min.). Well-known therapists interview real families and couples. Case histories include such subjects as couples, the family in socio-economic context, the isolated father in the family, the family interview, a single parent struggle, the family facing death, co-therapy with a family, suicide and anorexia.

Dialogues With Family Therapists (17 programs, each 60 min.). Discussions between individual therapists and Frederick J. Duhl, M.D., or between co-therapists and Dr. Duhl and his wife and co-therapist, Bunny S. Duhl, M.Ed. Therapists include Virginia Satir, James Framo, Carolyn Attneave, Leonard Unterberger, Carl Whitaker, Frederick J. and Bunny S. Duhl, Robert and Mary MacGregor, Lois Jaffe, David Rubinstein, Charles and Jan Kramer, Alberto Serrano, Yetta Bernhard, Vincent Sweeney, Jane Donner, Norman Paul, Salvador Minuchin and John Howells.
Size & Elements: Videotape: 3/4" and 1/2" open reel (40 titles).
Cataloging: Brochure.
Access: Available for rental and purchase. For use in training only.
Rights: Full rights held to all material.
Licensing: Apply for information.
Restrictions: Restricted to use in training only; written approval must be obtained for screenings where admission is charged.
Viewing Facilities: None.
Duplication Facilities: None.

MASSACHUSETTS (Boston)

BOSTON UNIVERSITY
DEPARTMENT OF SPECIAL COLLECTIONS
MUGAR MEMORIAL LIBRARY
771 Commonwealth Avenue
Boston, MA 02215
(617) 353-3696
Fax: (617) 353-5553

Dr. Howard B. Gotlieb (Director of Special Collections)

Contacts: Dr. Howard B. Gotlieb; Margaret R. Goostray (Assistant Director)
Services: University archives. Open to researchers and scholars only. Film and videotape material possibly available for research and duplication, subject to restrictions.
Description: The majority of film and videotape is held within individual collections of papers (manuscripts, diaries, correspondence, etc.). This material illustrates the careers of various actors, actresses, journalists, writers and public figures (1920s-80s). Although some home movies are included, material is largely positive release prints of commercial films.
Size & Elements: Film: 35mm; mostly 16mm (over 500,000 feet, approx. 450 titles, over 1,000 cans; mostly positive, small amount of negative). Videotape: format unspecified (approx. 200 titles; viewing copies).
Cataloging: Various finding aids.
Access: Open to researchers and scholars only. Research fees charged depending upon purpose of request. Research requests accepted in person (by appointment only).
Rights: Some rights held to some material. Some material in public domain. Rights status of some material not known. Additional clearances may be necessary in some cases if material is to be reused.

Licensing: Available for duplication and reuse, subject to restrictions.
Restrictions: Most material carries donor restrictions. Duplication of selected material is permitted for research purposes only.
Viewing Facilities: At University but not in Library (special arrangements must be made in advance). Equipment rental fee charged.
Duplication Facilities: Videotape (elsewhere at University).
Related Materials: Extensive manuscript collections.

MASSACHUSETTS (Boston)

BOSTON UNIVERSITY FILM ARCHIVE
COLLEGE OF COMMUNICATIONS
640 Commonwealth Avenue
Boston, MA 02215
(617) 353-3498

Jim Kent (Executive Director)

Contact: Jim Kent
Services: Film archives. Open to researchers and scholars only. Material available for in-house use, duplication, licensing and reuse.
Description: WNAC-TV (Boston) television newsfilm collection (1958-69, with some gaps). Coverage is sparse for 1958-60. All footage is "B-roll" (mostly silent footage lacking narration or commentary). The majority of footage was aired as part of daily news programs; there are some outtakes.

Collection is limited to events occurring in the Boston area. Special strengths include election coverage throughout the 1960s, with footage of many national political candidates in and around Boston, including Lyndon B. Johnson, Hubert H. Humphrey and George Wallace. Most footage of John F. Kennedy is missing from the collection.
Size & Elements: Film: 16mm (approx. 750,000 feet; mostly black and white, some color, positive).
Cataloging: Computerized cataloging available to researchers (in progress). Cataloging consists of a computerized chronological list and a computerized database searchable by name, location, date and subject. Presently, material from 1958 through mid-1965 is cataloged.
Access: Open to researchers and scholars only. For in-house use only. Available for duplication, licensing and reuse. Collection is presently in the process of formation and organization; plans are to make material accessible to College of Communications students. Research fees charged. Research requests accepted by mail and telephone.
Rights: Full rights held to all material. Additional clearances may be necessary in some cases if material is to be reused.
Licensing: Available for licensing and reuse. License fees charged.
Restrictions: None specified.
Viewing Facilities: Film (Steenbeck flatbed); videotape (elsewhere in building).
Duplication Facilities: None.

MASSACHUSETTS (Boston)

CHILDREN'S MUSEUM RESOURCE CENTER
Museum Wharf
300 Congress Street
Boston, MA 02210
(617) 426-6500 (Ext. 206)
Fax: (617) 426-1944

Peter Fekety (Senior Librarian)

Contact: Peter Fekety
Services: Museum. Videotape collection available to the public primarily for in-house use only.
Description: Holds 3/4" videotapes produced in-house documenting various science workshops (1983-present) by science developer Bernie Zubrowski. Material focuses on physical science for children. Also holds VHS videotapes dealing primarily with ethnic and Native American studies.
Size & Elements: Videotape: 3/4" (100 videotapes); VHS (25 videotapes) (all viewing copies).
Cataloging: Typed list.
Access: Open to the public. Primarily for in-house use only. Research fees not charged. Requests accepted by mail, telephone and in person (walk-in).
Rights: Some rights held to some material.
Licensing: Apply for information. License or usage fees not charged.
Restrictions: None specified.

Viewing Facilities: Videotape (3/4" and VHS; reservations must be made in advance.
Duplication Facilities: None.

MASSACHUSETTS (Boston)

THE COMPUTER MUSEUM
300 Congress Street
Boston, MA 02210
(617) 426-2800

Joe Cashen (Executive Director)

Contact: Allison Stelling (Registrar)
Services: Museum. Film and videotape collection available for in-house viewing, duplication, licensing and reuse, subject to restrictions.
Description: Museum is dedicated to public education in the field of computer technology, its social and scientific impact, and the preservation of its history. It is the only computer museum in the world.

Collection contains early historical films of computers, including some films showing old two- to three-story-high computers in operation before they were decommissioned. Some of these films have been produced by the museum, others have been donated. Collection also includes a lecture series on computer pioneers; and a series on computer-aided manufacturing and engineering, showing more recent technology (both on 3/4" and VHS videotape).
Size & Elements: Film: 16mm (40 films; positive and negative, mostly transferred to videotape). Videotape: 3/4" (180 videotapes; masters and viewing copies).
Cataloging: Finding aids (lists).
Access: Museum membership is encouraged to facilitate access to the collection. Open to researchers, scholars and members. For in-house use only. Available for duplication (fees charged). Research fees charged after the first hour. Research requests accepted by telephone and in person (by appointment only).
Rights: Full rights held to some material (films and videotapes that the museum has produced, including the lecture and technology series). Some rights held to other material. Additional clearances may be necessary in some cases if material is to be reused. Rights status of some material not known.
Licensing: Available for licensing and reuse, subject to restrictions. Loan and duplication fees charged.
Restrictions: Requests for reuse are considered on a case-by-case basis.
Viewing Facilities: Videotape (3/4" and VHS).
Duplication Facilities: None (outside arrangements can be made).

MASSACHUSETTS (Boston)

THE CONTEMPORARY ART TELEVISION (CAT) FUND
955 Boylston Street
Boston, MA 02115
(617) 266-5152

Kathy Rae Huffman (Curator/Producer)

Contact: Kathy Rae Huffman
Services: Coproduces and commissions television art works. Videotapes and videodiscs available to the public for rental, purchase, broadcast and licensing through authorized distributors. Handles national television and cable television sales only.
Description: "In 1983 The Institute of Contemporary Art (ICA), Boston and the WGBH New Television Workshop forged a unique collaboration through the creation of The CAT Fund.... This project's objective includes the development and coordination of effective and ongoing financial, administrative and creative mechanisms for the production of new works of art in television. Since its inception, The CAT Fund has strategically built on the strength of its alliances with the contemporary art world through The ICA, and with public broadcasting through WGBH. Its goals have always been and continue to be: to foster the highest level of excellence in the exploration of television as a creative medium; to broaden video art's international audience by local, national and international venues such as broadcast, home video distribution and gallery exhibition; and to substantially increase revenues for artists from the distribution of their works.... In four years, The CAT Fund has coproduced or commissioned seventeen videotapes. All have enjoyed public broadcast airings and have appeared in festivals worldwide."

Videotapes coproduced or commissioned by The CAT Fund include: *As If*

Memories Could Deceive Me (Marcel Odenbach, 1986); *Double Lunar Dogs* (Joan Jonas, 1984); *Easy Living* (Chip Lord and Mickey McGowan, 1984); *Evol* (Tony Oursler, 1984); *Ganapati/A Spirit in the Bush* (Daniel Reeves, 1986); *I Do Not Know What It Is I Am Like* (Bill Viola, 1986); *L'Image* (Jacques Louis and Danièle Nyst, 1987); *Irony* (Ken Feingold, 1985); *More TV Stories* (Ilene Segalove, 1985); *New England Fishermen: Spots* (Joan Logue, 1985); *O Panama* (James Benning and Burt Barr, 1985); *Storm and Stress* (Doug Hall, 1986); *The Watch Detail* (Bill Seaman, 1989, interactive videodisc installation); *The Water Catalogue* (Bill Seaman, 1984); *What You Mean We?* (Laurie Anderson, 1986); *Will-O'-The-Wisp (A Deceitful Goal)* (Dara Birnbaum, 1985); and *The World of Photography* (Michael Smith and William Wegman, 1986). The CAT Fund has also coproduced *TIME CODE* (1987), an international coproduction among television stations, artists and independent producers from seven countries, including the following works: *Lucksmith* (Gusztáv Hámos); *House* (Bernar Hébert); *Heart Beat* (Marty St. James and Anne Wilson); *Montenvers et Mer de Glace* (Robert Cahen and Stephane Hunter); *Sterd Am Am* (Jaap Drupsteen); *Time Squared* (Branda Miller); and *Whiplash* (Xavier F. Villaverde).
Size & Elements: Videotape and videodisc: various formats (17 works).
Cataloging: Published catalog.
Access: Available to the public for rental, purchase, broadcast and licensing through authorized distributors. The CAT Fund handles national television and cable television sales only.
Rights: Rights retained by individual artists and videomakers.
Licensing: Apply for information.
Restrictions: Permission of artist or videomaker is required for any licensing or reuse.
Viewing Facilities: None.
Duplication Facilities: None.
Distributors: Electronic Arts Intermix (q.v.); The Kitchen (q.v.); Le Vidéographe, Inc. (q.v.); Video Data Bank (q.v.).
Representative: For international television sales: Producer Services Group, Inc., 9230 Swallow Drive, Los Angeles, CA 90069; (213) 278-0501.

MASSACHUSETTS (Boston)

COUNCIL FOR A LIVABLE WORLD EDUCATION FUND
20 Park Plaza
Boston, MA 02116
(617) 542-2282

Jerome Grossman (President)

Contact: Amy Close
Services: Educational institution; videotape loan library. Material available for loan and possibly reuse, subject to clearance and approval.
Description: Arms control, the arms race, nuclear war and nuclear winter. Videotapes include: *In The Nuclear Shadow: What Can The Children Tell Us?; Race To Oblivion; The Eighth Day; The Last Epidemic: The Medical Consequences of Nuclear Weapons and Nuclear War; What About the Russians?;* and *Hiroshima and Nagasaki.* A few Congressional hearings on arms control are also available.
Size & Elements: Videotape: VHS (23 titles; viewing copies).
Cataloging: List.
Access: Available for loan. Loan requests accepted by mail, telephone and in person.
Rights: Some rights held to some material. Additional clearances may be necessary in some cases if material is to be reused.
Licensing: Apply for information. License fees charged (apply for information).
Restrictions: None specified.
Viewing Facilities: None.
Duplication Facilities: None.

MASSACHUSETTS (Boston)

EDITEL/BOSTON
651 Beacon Street
Boston, MA 02215
(617) 267-6400
Fax: (617) 421-1883

Don Berman (President)

Contact: Lee Rubenstein (Vice President, Sales)

Services: Videotape producer; teleproduction facility. Material available to the public for duplication, licensing and reuse. Custom shooting services available.
Description: Formerly Century III Teleproductions. Distributes syndicated graphic packages including starfields, logos and titles; animation (3D, Bosch and Wavefront).
Size & Elements: Videotape: 1" (approx. 30 syndicated packages, each one containing several hundred elements; masters). Viewing copies available in any videotape format.
Cataloging: Written descriptions for staff use only.
Access: Available to the public for duplication and reuse. Research fees not charged. Research requests accepted by mail and telephone.
Rights: Full rights held to all material.
Licensing: Available for licensing, subject to restrictions. License fees charged.
Restrictions: Material may be aired only in markets for which it is licensed.
Viewing Facilities: Videotape (all formats).
Duplication Facilities: Videotape (all formats).

MASSACHUSETTS (Boston)

FANLIGHT PRODUCTIONS
47 Halifax Street
Boston, MA 02130
(617) 524-0980

Contact: Staff
Services: Distributor. Films and videotapes available to the public for rental, preview and purchase.
Description: Health, education, work and family life.
Selected titles include: *Too Little, Too Late,* portraits of the families of AIDS patients; *A Different Heart,* on young children with heart defects; *Code Gray: Ethical Dilemmas in Nursing; Men & Women: After the Revolution; Frank: A Vietnam Veteran; First Dance,* dramatizing the court case which arose when a Rhode Island high-school senior was refused the right to attend the senior prom with his male date; *Doctor Woman,* one of Canada's first women physicians and her historic role in bringing women into medicine on equal terms; *The Pitch of Grief,* a look at the emotional process of grieving; *Nursing: The Politics of Caring; Abortion Clinic; New Relations,* about a new generation of fathers and sons; *I Don't Have to Hide,* an attempt to understand the feelings that lead some women to anorexia and bulimia; *Not Crazy Like You Think,* exploring the definitions of mental illness from the patients' perspective; *Significant Hazards: The Somerville DNA Debate,* in which residents and public officials evaluate the pros and cons of developing technologies in their community; and *A Perspective of Hope: Scenes from the Teaching Nursing Home.*
Size & Elements: Film: 16mm (approx. 16 titles). Videotape: 3/4" and VHS (approx. 30 titles).
Cataloging: Published catalog.
Access: Available to the public for rental, preview and purchase.
Rights: Film and videotapes protected by copyright.
Licensing: Apply for information.
Restrictions: None specified.
Viewing Facilities: None.
Duplication Facilities: None.

MASSACHUSETTS (Boston)

THE FRENCH LIBRARY IN BOSTON
53 Marlborough Street
Boston, MA 02116
(617) 266-4351

Vera Lee (Director)

Contacts: Persheng Vaziri (Director of Media); Michael Phillips (Media Specialist)
Services: Library. Films and videotapes available for rental to Library members only.
Description: Holds French feature films (mostly from 1930s-40s) and a few documentaries; most are in French, some with English subtitles. Also holds videotapes, mostly feature films (1970s-80s); and several educational and instructional programs.
The Marcel Carné Collection. The Library was chosen by the director Marcel Carné, as the main repository for his papers and memorabilia. Films in the collection include: *Jenny* (1936); *Les Enfants du Paradis (Children of*

Paradise, 1945); *L'air de Paris* (1954); and *Terrain Vague* (1960).

Feature films. Titles include: *A Nous La Liberté* (*Liberty For Us*, 1931); *Les Diaboliques* (1955); *Sang d'un Poete* (*Blood of a Poet*, 1930); *À Bout De Souffle* (*Breathless*, 1959); *Ascenseur Pour L'Echafaud* (*Elevator to the Scaffold*, 1958); *La Grande Illusion* (1937); *Les Vacances De M. Hulot* (*Mr. Hulot's Holiday*, 1953); *Tirez Sur Le Pianiste* (*Shoot The Piano Player*, 1960); and Marcel Pagnol's trilogy, *Marius* (1931), *Fanny* (1932) and *César* (1936).

Documentaries on videotape. Titles include: *The Sun King* (1984), portrait of the powerful and vain King Louis XIV; *40th Anniversary of D-Day* (1984); and *François Mitterrand* (1982).

Narrative videotapes. Titles include: *Danton* (1983), on the charismatic leader and his struggles with Robespierre in the chaotic years following the French Revolution; *Phèdre* (1968), Racine's famous tragedy of a queen's fatal passion for her stepson; and *La Nuit de Varennes* (1982), on the flight of Louis XVI and his wife Marie Antoinette at the outbreak of the French Revolution.

Also available are classic shorts; children's cartoons and animated films; puppet shows; lectures and pedagogical tools for all levels of French language instruction.

Size & Elements: Film: 16mm (75 titles, approx. 150 cans; release prints). Videotape: 3/4" (production masters held for Library productions); VHS (approx. 140 titles, various lengths; viewing copies of 100 feature films).
Cataloging: Published catalogs.
Access: Available for rental to Library members only. For in-house use only. Research requests accepted by mail, telephone and in person (walk-in and by appointment).
Rights: Full rights held to some material. Some rights held to all material. Some material in the public domain. Rights to some films retained by original filmmakers or producers.
Licensing: Apply for information.
Restrictions: Material available to Library members only.
Viewing Facilities: Videotape (VHS).
Duplication Facilities: Videotape (VHS).
Related Materials: Extensive collection of French slide shows, audiocassettes, record albums, books and periodicals.

MASSACHUSETTS (Boston)

THE IMAGE BANK, BOSTON

500 Boylston Street
Boston, MA 02116
(617) 267-8866
Fax: (617) 267-4685

Contact: Judith Salucci
Territory: Massachusetts (satellite office of TIB New York).
Services: Exclusive marketing agent for Film Search, Inc. (q.v.).

MASSACHUSETTS (Boston)

THE INTERNATIONAL WOMEN'S DAY VIDEO FESTIVAL

P.O. Box 176
Boston, MA 02130
(617) 522-7330

Contact: Janet Doherty (617/569-3670)
Services: Public access videotape programming. Available for distribution and cablecast.
Description: Annually compiled videotape program produced by women in the U.S. for distribution to cable access programmers. Subjects include militarism, health, sexuality, intervention in Central America, music, sexual assault and domestic violence, poverty and labor.

Titles in the Third IWDVF (1987) include: *Gigi's Flying Saucers* (Cindy Marshall); *Traditional Medicine of the 1980s* (Amy Meblin); *Las Nicas/La Historia dy Reyna Flores/Enfentando Escaseces* (Julia Lesage); *Ladies Against Women* (Lauren Lazin and Plutonium Play); *Japanese Women in the U.S.* (T. Koehn and Helen Fife); *All Our Lives* (Lisa Berger and Carol Mazer), interviews with women who participated in the Spanish anarchist movement in 1936 during the Spanish Civil War; *The Blooms of Banjeli* (Carlyn Saltman), documenting research on techniques, rituals and sexual prohibitions relating to iron smelting in Togo; *Have You Seen La Nueva Mujer Revolucionaria?* (Lisa L. Rudman), a visit with four Puerto Rican women prisoners of war; *Nuns* (Barbara Ulrich), an upbeat satire of convent life; *Private Lives* (Barbara Ulrich), a comic overview of the lesbian women's movement seen through "home movies" and quotes from Louisa May Alcott's *Little Women;* *Representation of Women in the Media* (Marisela R. Graham); *Steppin Razor*

(Sandy Zurowski), an all-women's reggae band; *Teaching Native Style* (Mary Alexander), on teaching in Alaska; *The Ultimate Test Animal*, examining the birth control injection Depo Provera and the international controversy over its use; *What's the Difference Between a Country and a House?* (M. J. Sullivan and Laura Flanders), a documentary about domestic violence within the nationalist movement in Northern Ireland; and *Women's Motorcycle Festival* (Michelle Gisser).
Size & Elements: Videotape: 3/4" and VHS (over 60 titles; some materials transferred from film).
Cataloging: Scripts and title lists with abstracts.
Access: Available for distribution and cablecast. Research requests accepted by mail and telephone.
Rights: No rights held to any material. Rights retained by original producers. Additional clearances will be necessary if material is to be reused.
Licensing: Apply for information.
Restrictions: None specified.
Viewing Facilities: None.
Duplication Facilities: None.

MASSACHUSETTS (Boston)

JOHN F. KENNEDY LIBRARY

Columbia Point
Boston, MA 02125
(617) 929-4500
Fax: (617) 929-4538

Charles Daley (Director)

Contact: Allan Goodrich (Supervisory Archivist) (617/929-4530)
Services: Library. Film collection open to the public. Material is available for in-house research, duplication and reuse, subject to restrictions.
Description: Presidential library administered by the National Archives and Records Administration. Materials, all donated, document the life and career of John F. Kennedy (1917-63). Footage is largely television newsfilm produced by government agencies and independent producers. Collections include:

White House Collection (1961-63, 87 reels). Film shot by White House staff cameramen covering President Kennedy's official activities, ceremonies at the White House, trips, vacations and leisure activities with his family and friends.

U.S. Government Agencies Collection (1961-65, 164 reels). Film of President Kennedy's activities, particularly as they related to the activities of various donor agencies such as the U.S. Information Agency, the U.S. Air Force and others. Includes memorial films produced or acquired by different agencies.

Television Networks Collection (1951-83, 877 reels). Newsfilm donated to the Library by the major American and foreign television networks. Includes stock footage of Kennedy's public appearances; documentaries and special reports on events and issues during his public career; and broadcasts of memorial services and documentaries on his life (aired after his assassination).

Robert F. Kennedy Collection (600 reels). Political campaign films created during the course of his campaigns for the Senate (1964) and the presidency (1968).

Victoria Schuck Collection (1948-68, 1,250 reels). Film of political speeches, rallies, campaign spot advertisements and other footage from state and national campaigns, such as Stevenson versus Eisenhower (1956).

Guggenheim Productions Collection (1956-83, 2,500 reels; collection closed). Political campaign film produced by Charles Guggenheim for numerous candidates, including Adlai Stevenson (1956); Robert F. Kennedy (1964 and 1968); George McGovern (1972); Edward M. Kennedy (1976 and 1980). Also includes documentaries, such as *RFK Remembered* (1968) and public service announcements for various organizations.

Miscellaneous Films Collection (1910-64, 253 reels). Film of Kennedy, his family and others, produced and donated by independent television stations, newsreel companies, filmmakers and individuals.
Size & Elements: Film: 16mm (1.5 million feet; 5,732 reels).
Cataloging: Published catalog; card catalogs.
Access: Open to the public. Available for in-house research. Some material available for duplication and reuse. Research fees not charged. Research requests accepted by mail and telephone.
Rights: Full rights held to some material. Some material in the public domain. Additional clearances may be necessary in some cases if material is to be reused.
Licensing: Available for licensing and reuse, subject to restrictions.
Restrictions: Materials held are donations which were privately owned, have

been deposited in the Kennedy Library under terms and conditions accepted by the Archivist of the United States, and are being preserved and administered by Library staff. Terms and conditions of access are specified by each donor in a formal deed of gift or deposit agreement. The Television Networks Collection, the Robert F. Kennedy Collection, the Victoria Schuck Collection and the Miscellaneous Films Collection require special permission for duplication. The Guggenheim Productions Collection is closed.

Viewing Facilities: Film (16mm Steenbeck); videotape (3/4").
Duplication Facilities: Film (film-to-videotape); videotape (3/4").
Related Materials: Still photographs, manuscripts and oral history audiotape collection. Many collections have been donated by Massachusetts residents, including Franklin D. Roosevelt short campaign films, Eisenhower films, Jack Benny programs, 800 glass photographic plates of mid-19th-century Bostonians and Vietnam photographs.

MASSACHUSETTS (Boston)

MASSACHUSETTS ARCHIVES
220 Morrissey Boulevard
Boston, MA 02125
(617) 727-2816

Dr. Albert H. Whitaker (State Archivist)

Contacts: William Milhomme (Reference Supervisor); Nancy Richard (Curator)
Services: State government archives. Film and videotape collection maintained for record and research purposes.
Description: *Massachusetts Department of Public Works Collection* (1936-38). Collection documents bridges and construction; heavy equipment; flooding; quarries; railroad construction; roadbuilding; sidewalk construction; opening ceremonies led by Governor Curley; DPW headquarters; a sign shop; and equipment conversion. Collection consists of 35mm nitrate film currently being converted to 16mm by John E. Allen, Inc. (q.v.) in New Jersey. Portions become available as preservation is completed; access to other material may be possible through John E. Allen, Inc.

Newsreels include 35mm footage of Governor Endicott Peabody (1963-64) and unindexed footage (approx. 100,000 feet) of Massachusetts political figures, such as John F. Kennedy and Edward M. Kennedy; and national figures such as Lyndon B. Johnson.

Also holds a videotape on correspondence courses as adult education, produced by the Bureau of Adult Services, Massachusetts Department of Education.
Size & Elements: Film: 35mm (nitrate, amount unspecified; acetate, over 100,000 feet); and 16mm (amount unspecified). Videotape: 1/2" open reel (2 titles).
Cataloging: Finding aids available.
Access: Open to the public. Research fees not charged. Research requests ("for minimal research" only) accepted by mail, telephone and in person.
Rights: Material in the public domain.
Licensing: Material possibly available for licensing and reuse. License and usage fees not charged. Duplication fees charged (apply for information).
Restrictions: None specified.
Viewing Facilities: Videotape (by appointment only).
Duplication Facilities: None.

MASSACHUSETTS (Boston)

OXFAM AMERICA
115 Broadway
Boston, MA 02116
(617) 728-2500
Fax: (617) 338-0187

John Hammoch (Executive Director)

Contact: Janet Green (Audiovisual Coordinator)
Services: Nonprofit international development agency. Films and videotapes distributed for educational purposes.
Description: World hunger and the Third World. Sample titles include: *Beginning Changes,* on Oxfam projects; *The Business of Hunger,* on land tenure in four countries; *Underdevelopment and the Dispossessed; Taking Charge,* on the negative effects of multinational corporations on Third World economies; *Hunger Hotline Revisited; Hamburger USA,* examining the production of its ingredients; *Habbanaae,* on the interaction between

development assistance project and nomadic culture in the Niger; *South Africa Belongs to Us!; Roots of Hunger, Roots of Change,* in Senegal; *Moving On: The Hunger for Land in Zimbabwe; Man-Made Famine; My Friend Jomo,* in Uganda; *Roots of Rebellion: Land and Hunger in Central America; With Oscar in Peru; Opening New Trails,* on the lives of cane and cotton workers in Bolivia; *Guatemala, I Carry Your Name; El Salvador: Nowhere to Run; Guazapa; Kampuchea After Pol Pot;* and *Sarvodaya Shramadana,* on the Sri Lankan grassroots movement.
Size & Elements: Film: 16mm (100 titles). Videotape: VHS (30 videotapes).
Cataloging: Published catalogs and brochures.
Access: Available to the public for rental. Reservations accepted by telephone; orders accepted by mail. Fees not charged for Oxfam America fund-raising events.
Rights: Full rights held to some material.
Licensing: Apply for information.
Restrictions: None specified.
Viewing Facilities: Film and videotape.
Duplication Facilities: None.

MASSACHUSETTS (Boston)

POLYMORPH FILMS, INC.
118 South Street
Boston, MA 02111
(617) 542-2004
(800) 223-5107 (outside of Mass.)
Fax: (617) 542-4957

Alvin Fiering (President and Founder)

Contact: Jay Kaufman (Sales and Marketing Director)
Services: Film and videotape producer and distributor. Films designed for patient and in-service education; available to professional groups only.
Description: Educational films specializing in birth and infant care.

Titles include: *Perinatal AIDS: Infection Control for Hospital Personnel; Through a Father's Eyes: A Birth Film for Both Parents; Infection Control in the Hospital; Infertility; Hospital Fire Safety; Alternatives to Infertility; Diabetes in Pregnancy: Caring for the Childbearing Woman; Obstetrical Emergency!; New Baby Care; New Mother Care; Labors of Love; Beginning Breastfeeding; Amazing Newborn; Prenatal Care; Teens Having Babies; What Guys Want; When Teens Get Pregnant; Your Baby's First Days; Now That You're Not Postpartum; Not Me Alone; Deliverance: A Family's Cesarean Experience; Having a Section is Having a Baby; Drugs; Smoking and Alcohol During Pregnancy; Learning to Breastfeed; Having Twins; Dubowitz Assessment of Newborn Gestational Age; The Ties That Bind; Death of a Newborn; Birth in the Squatting Position; Adapting to Parenthood; When a Child Enters the Hospital; Stepparenting; Gentle Birth; Essential Exercises for the Childbearing Year; Day Care Today; Not Together Now; Discussions with Parents of a Malformed Baby; To Have and Not to Hold; Prematurely Yours;* and *The Sensational Baby.*
Size & Elements: Film: 16mm (39 titles). Videotape: 3/4" and VHS (39 titles).
Cataloging: Published catalog.
Access: Films designed for patient and in-service education; available to professional groups only.
Rights: Full rights held to all material.
Licensing: Apply for information.
Restrictions: Apply for information.
Viewing Facilities: None.
Duplication Facilities: None.

MASSACHUSETTS (Boston)

SITE PRODUCTIONS
30 Worthington Street
Boston, MA 02120
(617) 277-7633

Dan Jones (President)

Contact: Dan Jones
Services: Videotape producer. Material available to the public for duplication, licensing and reuse.
Description: Footage originally shot for tourist- and travel-oriented videotapes, featuring scenics and tourist attractions around Boston, Cape Cod, and coastal Maine.

Boston. Footage includes historical sites, historic neighborhoods, tourist attractions, boats, scenics, cityscapes and panoramas.

Cape Cod and islands. Includes scenics, Cape Cod National Seashore, Provincetown, whale watching, fishing, antique architecture, beach scenes, Martha's Vineyard and Nantucket Islands.

Coastal Maine. Includes scenics, lighthouses, lobstering, sailing (including windjammers), "tall ships," Acadia National Park and fall foliage.

Size & Elements: Videotape: 3/4" (over 35 hours; masters); 1/2" (viewing copies).

Cataloging: Staff assistance.

Access: Open to the public. Available for duplication, licensing and reuse. Research fees charged (negotiable). Research requests accepted by mail and telephone. 1/2" viewing copies with visible time code are available for preview purposes.

Rights: Full rights held to all material.

Licensing: Available for licensing. License fees charged.

Restrictions: None specified.

Viewing Facilities: Videotape (1/2").

Duplication Facilities: None (outside arrangements can be made).

MASSACHUSETTS (Boston)

THE SPORTS MUSEUM OF NEW ENGLAND

1175 Soldiers Field Road
Boston, MA 02134
(617) 787-7678

Jim Blake (Executive Director); Dick Johnson (Associate Director/Curator)

Contacts: Dick Johnson; Steve Garabedian (Curatorial Assistant)

Services: Museum; film and videotape archives. Material possibly available for reuse.

Description: Boston area professional and college sports events, including Red Sox baseball (1964-71); Bruins hockey (1968-72); Patriots football (1960-87); the Boston Marathon (1985-87); other New England sports, events, teams, and athletes. Collection includes the WHDH-TV archives of sports footage.

Holds the Gillette Company (the first sponsor of television sports) collection of commercials (1940s-60s) featuring athletes, especially baseball players. Also holds videotapes and audiotapes (200 boxes, all formats) of many games, including some World Series games. Cataloging is in progress.

Size & Elements: Film: 16mm. Videotape: 2", 3/4" and VHS (50% masters, 50% viewing copies). (300 titles total; approx. 1,000 hours total).

Cataloging: Computerized cataloging; more detailed cataloging information available by telephone.

Access: Open to the public. Research requests accepted by mail.

Rights: Some rights held to some material. Rights status of Gillette Company material undetermined; Gillette Company may have to be contacted for any requests regarding commercial use of collection.

Licensing: Policy currently being decided.

Restrictions: Policy currently being decided.

Viewing Facilities: Videotape.

Duplication Facilities: Videotape (3/4" and VHS).

MASSACHUSETTS (Boston)

WGBH EDUCATIONAL FOUNDATION

125 Western Avenue
Boston, MA 02134
(617) 492-2777
Fax: (617) 787-0714
Telex: (710) 330-6887

Joe Anderson (Manager for Production Services)
Lynn Farnell (Director of Production Support)

Contact: Carl Piermarini (Archivist) (Ext. 4206)

Services: Film and videotape producer; television broadcaster. Collection open to researchers and scholars only; available for distribution, licensing and reuse on a case-by-case basis, subject to restrictions.

Description: WGBH Educational Foundation Archives was organized in 1979 to store and preserve permanently all of the program materials produced by WGBH, the award-winning PBS affiliate in Boston. Since its inception, the Archives has grown to become one of the largest collections of public television programming in the United States. WGBH currently produces one-third of all programs on prime time public television.

Archives currently contains WGBH television and radio programs (1956-present). Included in the collection are programs from the following series: *The Advocates; Rebop; NOVA; Frontline; Enterprise; The French Chef; Julia Child & Company; Crockett's (Victory Garden); Evening at Pops; New Voice; Evening at Symphony; Jean Shepard's America; Religious America; In Search of the Real America; Zoom; This Old House; Say Brother; La Plaza; Vietnam: A Television History; Bodywatch; Great Outdoors; Elliot Norton Reviews; World; Maggie and the Beautiful Machine; Making Things Work (Grow); New Television Workshop; Photo Show;* and *The Reporters.*

Significant individual television programs held include: *Scarlet Letter; Lemon Sky; Billy in the Lowlands; The Director — Marcel Ophüls; Concealed Enemies; Bennet & Basie; James Michael Curley — He Did It for Friends;* and *Mr. Speaker — Tip O'Neill.*

Size & Elements: Film: 16mm (15,000 reels, including kinescopes). Videotape: 2" (7,000 programs); 1" (6,500 programs); 3/4" (3,000 programs).

Cataloging: Computerized cataloging (VAX mainframe).

Access: Open to researchers and scholars only. Fees charged for use of viewing equipment (no fees charged for access to materials). Research requests accepted by mail.

Rights: Full rights held to some material. Some rights held to all material. Additional clearances may be necessary in some cases if material is to be reused.

Licensing: Available for licensing, subject to restrictions. License fees charged. Footage is licensed through WGBH's Distribution Office.

Restrictions: Reuse of material subject to clearance of various rights, which differ with individual programs.

Viewing Facilities: Film (Steenbeck flatbed viewing table; projector); videotape (2" and 1" [public viewing areas]; 3/4" [private rooms]).

Duplication Facilities: Videotape (2" and 1" to 3/4").

MASSACHUSETTS (Boston)

WORLD MONITOR

One Norway Street (C-22)
Boston, MA 02115
(617) 450-2000
Fax: (617) 450-2283
Telex: 174188

Annette Robertson (General Manager, Broadcasting)

Contact: Nancy McCann (Director of Communication)

Services: Television broadcaster; stock footage sales library. Videotape collection not presently available for licensing or reuse.

Description: Material produced by The Christian Science Monitor. Consists of footage originated from the news and public affairs documentary series *Christian Science Monitor Reports* which was nationally syndicated from July 1985 to August 1988. The series was produced once per month from its inception through June 1986, at which time it became a weekly. The collection also contains 1" recordings of the 112 episodes. The collection has increased with the addition of similar material videotaped for *World Monitor,* "a nightly news journal with a global perspective," (Sept. 12, 1988-present) and other videotape footage. The footage is international in scope and covers a wide variety of subjects, including wildlife, environment, technology, arts, politics, culture and society.

Locations and topics. Scenics and events shot overseas in the Middle East (Iran, Iraq, Israel and Egypt); Africa (Libya, Mozambique, Ethiopia and Zimbabwe); Central and South America (Mexico, Costa Rica, Nicaragua, El Salvador, Brazil and Chile); Europe (France, Great Britain and West Germany); Asia (Japan, Korea and Philippines); Caribbean (Jamaica and Haiti); and North America (United States and Canada). Topics covered with regard to these locations include: manufacturing, economics, civil disturbances, warfare, refugees, famine, agriculture, nuclear energy, drought, free trade, poverty, computers, oil, missiles, space exploration, pollution, values, air traffic, lotteries, women's issues, immigration, education, peace, terrorism, homelessness and corporate takeovers.

Size & Elements: Videotape: 1" (112 videotapes); Betacam and Betacam SP (approx. 4,000 videotapes); and 3/4" (500 videotapes).

Cataloging: Computerized cataloging for staff use only.

Access: Videotape collection not presently available for licensing or reuse. For in-house stock footage use only.

Rights: Full rights held to some material. Some rights held to some material. Additional clearances may be necessary in some cases if material is to be reused.

Licensing: Material not presently available for duplication, licensing or reuse.

MASSACHUSETTS (Brighton)

Restrictions: Videotape collection not presently available for licensing or reuse.
Viewing Facilities: None.
Duplication Facilities: Videotape (1", Betacam and 3/4"). Duplication fees charged. Other formats and standards available by special arrangement with outside sources.

MASSACHUSETTS (Brighton)

ARCHDIOCESE OF BOSTON ARCHIVES
2121 Commonwealth Avenue
Brighton, MA 02135
(617) 254-0100 (Ext. 108)

Ron Patkus (Archivist)

Contact: Ron Patkus
Description: Activities of the Archdiocese of Boston (1940s-present). Subjects include installations of archbishops, activities of Holy Name Societies, Catholic Youth Organization parades, and a papal visit to Boston. Collection is strong in ceremonial events involving Boston's Roman Catholic archbishops and activities of lay Catholic groups.
Size & Elements: Film: format unspecified (approx. 6 linear shelf-feet). Videotape: format unspecified (approx. 15 videotapes).
Access: Available to the public. Research requests accepted by mail and telephone. Donations accepted in lieu of research fees.
Rights: Rights status of material not known.
Licensing: Apply for information.
Restrictions: None specified.
Viewing Facilities: Archives must borrow equipment.
Duplication Facilities: None.

MASSACHUSETTS (Brookline)

HELLENIC COLLEGE & HOLY CROSS GREEK ORTHODOX SCHOOL OF THEOLOGY COTSIDAS-TONNA LIBRARY
50 Goddard Avenue
Brookline, MA 02146
(617) 731-3500 (Ext. 243)

Rev. Dr. George C. Papademetriou (Director of the Library)

Contact: Rev. Dr. George C. Papademetriou
Services: Library. Videotape collection available to researchers and scholars for in-house use only.
Description: Orthodox Christian religion and culture; explanations of major feasts; other Orthodox world centers (e.g., Jerusalem and Constantinople); Greek life, including ancient dress and modern Greek folkways; and Greek language. Some material has been acquired from the Greek Archdiocese of New York.
Size & Elements: Videotape: format unspecified (75 videotapes, 30 and 60 min.).
Cataloging: Descriptive lists.
Access: Open to researchers and scholars. For in-house use only. Research fees not charged. Research requests accepted in person (by appointment only).
Rights: Apply for information.
Licensing: Apply for information.
Restrictions: None specified.
Viewing Facilities: Videotape.
Duplication Facilities: None.

MASSACHUSETTS (Brookline)

VIZ WIZ, INC.
115 Dummer Street
Brookline, MA 02146
(617) 739-6400
Fax: (617) 277-0449

Peter Fasciano (President)

Contacts: Richard Reilly (Account Executive); Brian Baslik (Account Executive); Malcolm Tinkham (Senior Accountant Executive)

Services: Film and videotape producer. Material available for duplication, licensing and reuse.
Description: Boston scenics, historical landmarks and aerial views (contemporary color footage).
Size & Elements: Film: 35mm (transferred to 1" videotape). Videotape: 3/4", VHS and Betamax (viewing copies). (Approx. 2 hours total).
Cataloging: Staff assistance required.
Access: Available for duplication, licensing and reuse. Research fees not charged. Research requests accepted by mail, telephone and in person (walk-in and by appointment).
Rights: Full rights held to all material.
Licensing: Available for licensing and reuse. License fees charged.
Restrictions: None specified.
Viewing Facilities: Videotape (1", 3/4" and 1/2").
Duplication Facilities: Videotape (1" to 1", 3/4" and 1/2").

MASSACHUSETTS (Cambridge)

CAMBRIDGE DOCUMENTARY FILMS, INC.
P.O. Box 385
Cambridge, MA 02139
(617) 354-3677

Contact: Margaret Lazarus
Services: Film and videotape producer and distributor. Material available for rental and purchase.
Description: Documentary films and videotapes relating to social issues.

The Last Empire: Intervention and Nuclear War relates U.S. intervention in the Third World to the increasing danger of nuclear war arising from U.S. foreign policy strategies. Includes interviews with Noam Chomsky, Helen Caldicott, Admiral Gene LaRocque, Kosta Tsipis and Howard Zinn; and historical clips of Harry S Truman, John F. Kennedy, Lyndon B. Johnson, Richard M. Nixon and Ronald Reagan. *Eugene Debs and the American Movement* is a biography of the labor leader and founder of the Socialist Party of America.

Still Killing Us Softly: Advertising's Image of Women presents examples of advertisements from magazines, newspapers, album covers and billboards. It explores the relationship of media images and social problems, such as the channeling of men and women into traditional sex roles, economic discrimination against women, child and sexual abuse, rape, pornography, teenage pregnancy and eating disorders. *Calling the Shots: The Advertising of Alcohol* examines the images used by advertisers to sell alcohol.

Pink Triangles is a study of prejudice against lesbians and gay men, examining both historical and contemporary patterns of persecution. Film includes the research of a German-born historian who escaped Nazi imprisonment; a discussion with mental health and health care providers; historical material from the McCarthy hearings and "the pontifications of the so-called Christian right and the Moral Majority"; perspectives from parents of gays; and individual stories of the struggle against homophobia. *Choosing Children: A Film About Lesbians Becoming Parents* addresses new options in reproduction, donor insemination, non-biological mothers, biological fathers, adoption, male role models and homophobia.

Rape Culture examines popular films, advertising, music and "adult entertainment," and records the insights of rape crisis workers and prisoners working against rape. Includes footage of a prison self-help group at Lorton, Virginia, organized to eliminate rape both inside and outside the prison; a rape crisis center worker; authors Mary Daly and Emily Culpepper on the concept of phallocentric morality; and an interview with a convicted multiple rapist. *Taking Our Bodies Back: The Women's Health Movement* covers self-help, birth at home, abortion, high-school women, breast cancer, controversial research, the gynecological exam, drug company attitudes, hysterectomy and health care for women of color. *The Barefoot Doctors of Rural China* is a film made by Americans of Chinese descent, examining China's innovative efforts to provide adequate health care services for its agrarian population; discussing the "barefoot doctors'" role in the current family planning campaign; and the importance of jobs for women to the success of the program.
Size & Elements: Film: 16mm. Videotape: all formats. (9 titles total).
Cataloging: Published catalog.
Access: Available to the public for rental, preview and purchase. Rental fees charged. Requests accepted by mail and telephone. Preview fees deducted from purchase price.
Rights: Full rights held to most material.
Licensing: Apply for information.
Restrictions: None specified.
Viewing Facilities: None.

Duplication Facilities: None.
Related Materials: Study guides available for some films.

EDUCATORS FOR SOCIAL RESPONSIBILITY
23 Garden Street
Cambridge, MA 02138
(617) 492-1764

Susan Alexander (Executive Director)

Contact: Richard Bolton (Publications Director)
Services: Educational institution; educational videotape producer. Material maintained primarily for distribution and rental for educational purposes.
Description: Videotapes designed to present an alternative view on subjects such as nuclear technology and the representation of the Soviet Union in the American news media.

Titles available include *A Day at School in Moscow: A Videotape and Study Guide,* a view of Soviet schools without American commentary; *A Place to Begin: An Approach to Nuclear Age Education,* helping teachers deal with nuclear age issues through teaching critical thinking skills, examining students' concerns and reflective writing; *There's a Nuclear War Going On Inside Me,* in which adult leaders explore students' thoughts about nuclear war and weapons; and *What Soviet Children Are Saying About Nuclear Weapons,* an excellent discussion starter.
Size & Elements: Videotape: 3/4", VHS and Betamax (4 titles, each 20 to 30 min.; viewing copies).
Cataloging: Published catalog.
Access: Material intended for classroom distribution. Available to the public for distribution and rental rather than for reuse. Requests accepted by mail only.
Rights: Full rights held to some material.
Licensing: Apply for information.
Restrictions: None specified.
Viewing Facilities: None.
Duplication Facilities: None.

HARVARD-SMITHSONIAN CENTER FOR ASTROPHYSICS
60 Garden Street
Cambridge, MA 02138
(617) 495-7461

Irwin Shapiro (Director)

Contact: James Cornell (Publications Manager)
Services: Scientific research facility. Films and videotapes available to researchers, scholars, educational or academic users and filmmakers for distribution, licensing and reuse on a case-by-case basis, subject to restrictions.
Description: Distributes several films relating to astrophysics, astronomy and the space sciences, including *Mirrors on the Universe: The MMT Story* (1979), on the Multiple Mirror Telescope; *The Search for the Tunguska Meteorite* (Soviet Union, ca. 1968, English narration); *Welcome to Whipple Observatory* (1988), an introduction to the field facility located at Mt. Hopkins, Ariz.; and *A Slice of the Universe* (1988, 2 min.), a short introduction to cosmology.

Also holds unedited research footage, film, computer graphics and computer-generated videotape footage of astrophysical phenomena.
Size & Elements: Film (16mm; originals). Videotape: 3/4" (masters); 1/2" (viewing copies). (6 completed films; unspecified amount of unedited footage).
Cataloging: Staff assistance required.
Access: Open to researchers and scholars only. Footage available to educational or academic filmmakers for duplication, licensing and reuse on a case-by-case basis, subject to restrictions. Research fees charged in some cases. Research requests accepted by mail and telephone.
Rights: Full rights held to most material. Additional clearances may be necessary in some cases if material is to be reused.
Licensing: Available for licensing and reuse, subject to restrictions. License fees charged in some cases.
Restrictions: Requests for licensing and reuse considered on a case-by-case basis. Reuse restricted to educational and academic filmmakers; commercial reuse seldom permitted.
Viewing Facilities: Videotape (1/2"; by appointment only).
Duplication Facilities: Videotape (3/4" and 1/2").

HARVARD UNIVERSITY
GRADUATE SCHOOL OF EDUCATION
ACTION FOR CHILDREN'S TELEVISION LIBRARY COLLECTION
Monroe C. Gutman Library
Appian Way
Cambridge, MA 02138
(617) 495-4225

John W. Collins, III (Librarian)

Contact: Doris H. Christo (Special Projects Coordinator)
Services: Library. Videotape collection maintained primarily for research.
Description: Action for Children's Television (ACT) is a national grassroots organization advocating quality and diversity in television for children and adolescents. It maintains a collection of materials supporting its cause, now held by Harvard University, Graduate School of Education.

Collection consists of material both generated and collected by ACT (dating back to 1968). Topics covered in the collection include: children and television; advertising and children; violence and television; sex; social and cultural roles on television; the commercial networks; public television; cable television; and radio. Videotape materials include television shows submitted for ACT awards.
Size & Elements: Videotape: format unspecified (approx. 1,000 items, approx. 360 linear feet).
Cataloging: Computerized cataloging available to researchers; research library.
Access: Open to the public. Research requests accepted by mail and in person (by appointment only).
Rights: Apply for information.
Licensing: Apply for information.
Restrictions: Apply for information.
Viewing Facilities: Film and videotape.
Duplication Facilities: None.
Related Materials: General materials include speeches and published articles by staff members; legal documents (petitions and complaints) filed before the Federal Communications Commission and the Federal Trade Commission; reports from studies commissioned by ACT; completed forms for monitoring commercials; press releases and clippings; books and periodicals; still photographs from television programs; cartoons and quotes about television.

INTERLOCK MEDIA ASSOCIATES
P.O. Box 619
Harvard Square Station
Cambridge, MA 02238
(617) 491-3111

Street address: 21 Notre Dame Avenue, Suite 213-214, Cambridge, MA 02140

Jonathan Schwartz (Producer)

Contact: Ricardo Wray (Associate Producer)
Services: Nonprofit documentary film and videotape producer and distributor. Collection open to the public for distribution, duplication and possibly licensing and reuse.
Description: Film documentaries exploring the impact of economic development on human rights and the environment, with an emphasis on land rights of indigenous peoples in the Third World and specialized films on rain forests and their peoples. Interlock filmmakers have backgrounds in anthropological and feature filmmaking, international development and scientific journalism. Productions include commissioned pieces (for clients such as UNESCO, CBS Television, PBS Television, the Audubon Society, and Center for Development Policy) and media works of Interlock's own design.

Recent productions include: *Save the Rainforest: Support Tribal People — Video Segments* (in progress) a series of videotape vignettes produced for the SRSTP Campaign on the destruction of rain forests and the consequent threat to tribal peoples; *Irrigation in Somalia: Pragmatic Rehabilitation Along the Shabelle River* (1986), a multi-image videotape program for the U.S. Agency for International Development's Water Management Synthesis II Project underscoring the need for village level irrigation management by highlighting a model project in the Horn of Africa; *One County's Water* (1984), a multi-image videotape for the Massachusetts Audubon Society on water quality management in Essex County; and *Risk and Reliability: Computers in the*

Nuclear Age (1986), a multi-image videotape on the role of computers in life-critical situations and the Strategic Defense Initiative (made for Computer Professionals for Social Responsibility).

Also has produced or is able to locate various footage in topics including: topographical, biological and anthropological aspects of rain forests; native peoples; ethnomusicology; and the impact of war on rural populations, high-technology warfare and interviews with community leaders of the Third World. Will provide contacts for national and international footage sources.

Also maintains an extensive collection of films by outside producers relating to indigenous peoples, and welcomes proposals from independent producers for collaborative projects.

Size & Elements: Film: 35mm and 16mm. Videotape: 1", Betacam, 3/4" and VHS (approx. 50 titles total; NTSC, PAL and PAL-M versions).
Cataloging: Card catalogs; published catalogs; computerized cataloging for staff use only; research library; staff assistance.
Access: Available to the public for distribution, duplication and possibly reuse. Research requests accepted by mail, telephone and in person (by appointment only). Research fees charged in most cases, depending on project.
Rights: Full rights held to most material. Additional clearances may be necessary in some cases if material is to be reused.
Licensing: Apply for information.
Restrictions: None specified.
Viewing Facilities: Videotape (3/4").
Duplication Facilities: Videotape (3/4").

**MASSACHUSETTS INSTITUTE OF TECHNOLOGY
THE MIT MUSEUM**
N52-2nd
265 Massachusetts Avenue
Cambridge, MA 02139
(617) 253-4440
Telex: 92-1473

Warren A. Seamans (Director)

Contact: Michael Yeates (Assistant Director for Collections)
Services: Museum. Film and videotape collection open to the public for duplication and possibly reuse; some materials available for loan.
Description: Primarily MIT-related activities (education, research and social) and some related science and technological developments.

MIT history. Titles include: *Class of '22,* documenting the activities of the MIT Class of 1922 at their "Senior Week" and subsequent five-year reunions; *Class of '26 — Tenth Reunion* (1936), activities of the Class at their tenth-year reunion; *Class of '88* (1928), a short view of the 40th reunion of the Class of 1888; *Impressions: The Arts at MIT* (1978), a film done by the MIT Film Section on the various projects of the MIT Council for the Arts; *Men of Science* (1952), a brief survey of the accomplishments of the Institute and the men who made them happen (including Alfred P. Sloan, Vannevar Bush, Warren K. Lewis, James Rhyne Killian and others); *MIT: Progressions* (1969), shows the reorganization of the Institute in the late 1960s from a student's eye view; *Phi Beta Epsilon* (1927), antics and general life at the Institute in the Roaring '20s; *Victory and Science Show* (1945), a display of the weapons and instrumentation developed at MIT's labs during World War II; *They Were There: The Suffrage Movement and MIT* (1976), Florence Luscomb (Class of 1909) describing MIT in the 'teens and her involvement in the women's suffrage movement.

Technology. Titles include: *The Airplane at Play* (1932), Charles S. Draper and Robert M. Love performing aerial acrobatics and filming them from both the ground and the cockpit; *Camp Technology* (1936), showing the work and antics of the students at MIT's Civil Engineering Camp; *Clean Air Car Race* (1970), a documentary of the cross-country race of student-designed cars from all over the U.S.; and *Technology 1934* (1934), a recruitment film for high-school students.

Computers. Titles include: *Making Electrons Count* (1951), on the digital computer lab and Whirlwind I (interesting as a comparison of computing techniques then and now); *Automatically Programmed Machine Tool* (1959), part of the *WGBH Science Reporter* series with John T. Fitch; *Kludge* (1966), showing computer-generated graphic displays; and *Solving Computer Bottlenecks.*

Harold E. Edgerton Films. Titles include: *High Speed Motion Pictures: 1936* (1936), a collection of his best footage (e.g., cat, milk drops and hummingbird); *Quickern' a Wink* (1936, MGM), an award-winning film incorporating slow-motion footage; and *Underwater Photography* (1967), a

WGBH Science Reporter episode, with Edgerton and John T. Fitch.

Lectures and interviews. Titles include: *Churchill and Compton* (1949), the entire speech given by Sir Winston Churchill at the MIT Mid-Century Convocation; *MIT Lecture Series on World Peace: R. Buckminister Fuller* (1972), "Fuller speaks on anything and everything"; *Person to Person with Vannevar Bush* (1956), where Edward R. Murrow interviews the famous scientist and his wife at home; and *The Significance of Science* (1972), a Victor Weiskopf lecture.

Size & Elements: Film: 16mm (800 films). Videotape: 2", 1", 3/4" and 1/2" (510 videotapes total).
Cataloging: Card catalogs; dope sheets or release sheets.
Access: Open to the public. Some materials available for loan. Research fees charged. Research requests accepted by mail, telephone and in person (by appointment only).
Rights: Full rights held to some material. Additional clearances may be necessary in some cases if material is to be reused.
Licensing: Apply for information. License fees charged.
Restrictions: None specified.
Viewing Facilities: Film (16mm); videotape (VHS).
Duplication Facilities: None (original materials handled by Museum staff only; duplication can be arranged at an outside facility).

**MASSACHUSETTS INSTITUTE OF TECHNOLOGY
THE MIT MUSEUM
HART NAUTICAL COLLECTION**
N52-2nd
265 Massachusetts Avenue
Cambridge, MA 02139
(617) 253-5942

Warren A. Seamans (Director, MIT Museum)

Contact: John G. Arrison (Curator, Hart Nautical Collection)
Services: Special collection. *Limited access to film material. Currently being organized and cataloged. Clearance restrictions may apply.*
Description: Holds a small collection of black and white films from Bethlehem Steel, relating to shipbuilding in the Fore River Shipyard at Braintree, Massachusetts; and uncataloged corporate films (over 200) on shipyards (limited access to this material).
Size & Elements: Film: 35mm and 16mm (over 200 films total).
Cataloging: None (material currently being organized and cataloged).
Access: Limited access to material. *Written requests only.*
Rights: Material presently not available for licensing or reuse.
Licensing: Not available for licensing or reuse.
Restrictions: Use of material is restricted (apply for information).
Viewing Facilities: None.
Duplication Facilities: None.
Related Materials: 60,000 still images from Bethlehem Steel relating to shipyards.

**RADCLIFFE COLLEGE
ARTHUR AND ELIZABETH SCHLESINGER LIBRARY ON THE
HISTORY OF WOMEN IN AMERICA**
10 Garden Street
Cambridge, MA 02138
(617) 495-8647

Street address: 3 James Street

Patricia M. King (Director)

Contacts: Barbara Haber (Curator of Printed Books); Eva S. Moseley (Curator of Manuscripts)
Services: Educational institution; library. Film and videotape collection open to the public; available for duplication and reuse under certain conditions.
Description: History of women in the United States, primarily in the nineteenth and twentieth centuries.

Major subject areas include: women's rights, suffrage and feminism; social welfare, social settlements, reform movements, and voluntary organizations; women in the professions, politics and government services; working women and labor organizations; medicine, health, birth control and abortion;

education; prisons; family history, domestic life, household management and cooking; and women in sciences and the arts.

Twenty-one manuscript collections contain motion pictures; 33 collections contain videotapes. Examples of films and videotapes in manuscript collections and topics covered include: abortion rights (National Abortion Rights Action League); battered women (Transition House); birth control (Mary S. Calderone, Edna R. McKinnon, Barbara Seaman); Black women (Pauli Murray, Dorothy West); clerical workers (9 to 5); cookery (Julia Child, M. F. K. Fisher); feminism (Betty Friedan, National Organization for Women); and politics (Frances "Sissy" Farenthold, Anna Rosenberg Hoffman, Elizabeth Holtzman, Jeannette Rankin and Edith Nourse Rogers). Titles include: *She's Nobody's Baby; Woman Alive!;* and *Woman to Woman.*

Also holds commercially acquired videotapes (many transferred from film), mostly documentaries, all on the social history of women in the United States.

Size & Elements: Film: 16mm (60 cans); 8mm (10 cans). Videotape: 2", 1", 3/4" (ca. 180 videotapes); 1/2" (ca. 20 videotapes); format unspecified (ca. 95 videotapes).
Cataloging: Card catalogs; inventories.
Access: Open to the public. For in-house use only. Available for duplication, subject to restrictions. Research requests accepted by mail, telephone and in person (walk-in). Research fees charged according to staff time required.
Rights: Some rights held to some material. Rights status of some material not known. Additional clearances may be necessary in some cases if material is to be reused.
Licensing: Available for reuse, subject to restrictions. Licensing policies and fees currently undergoing revision.
Restrictions: Some material may carry certain restrictions.
Viewing Facilities: Film (16mm); videotape (3/4" and 1/2") (by appointment only).
Duplication Facilities: None.

MASSACHUSETTS (Cambridge)

RUDRA PRESS
P.O. Box 1973
Cambridge, MA 02238
(617) 576-3394

Nanette Redmond (Director)

Contact: Sarah Fahey (Marketing Director)
Services: Publisher. Videotapes available to the public for purchase only; stock footage possibly available for licensing and reuse on a case-by-case basis.
Description: Coproducer of two instructional videotapes on yoga exercise.
Size & Elements: Videotape: VHS or Betamax (2 videotapes, each 60 min.).
Cataloging: Brochure.
Access: Available to the public for purchase. Possibly available for duplication and reuse. Research fees not charged. Requests accepted by mail and telephone.
Rights: Full rights held to all material.
Licensing: Possibly available for licensing. License fees charged.
Restrictions: None specified.
Viewing Facilities: None.
Duplication Facilities: None.

MASSACHUSETTS (Cambridge)

UNION OF CONCERNED SCIENTISTS
26 Church Street
Cambridge, MA 02238
(617) 547-5552
Fax: (617) 864-9405
Telex: 294116 BOSTLXUR

Howard Ris (Executive Director)

Contact: Jan Wager
Services: Foundation; film and videotape producer. Films and videotapes available for distribution and rental; and possibly for duplication and reuse, subject to restrictions.
Description: Materials on nuclear arms control, the Strategic Defense Initiative, the arms race, science, technology and defense policy. Has sponsored a film entitled *No First Use: Preventing Nuclear War,* which includes candid commentary from military and political figures on both sides of the Atlantic,

and reviews the history of America's postwar defense strategy (distributed by the University of California, Extension Media Center [q.v.]). Also produces documentation of Union teleconferences.

Titles distributed include: *The False Frontier, Weapons in Space; First Strike, Last Strike; Satellite Summit: A Trans-Atlantic Dialogue on Nuclear Arms Issues;* and *The Threat of Nuclear War.*
Size & Elements: Film: 16mm (approx. 10 titles; release prints). Videotape: 3/4", VHS and Betamax (viewing copies).
Cataloging: Published catalog.
Access: Available for distribution and rental. Material available for duplication and reuse, subject to restrictions (provided free to the media). Research fees not charged. Research requests accepted by mail and telephone.
Rights: Full rights held to all material.
Licensing: Material available for duplication, licensing and reuse, subject to restrictions. License fees not charged.
Restrictions: On-air credit *must* be given for material reused.
Viewing Facilities: Videotape (by appointment only).
Duplication Facilities: None.

MASSACHUSETTS (Cambridge)

ZIPPORAH FILMS
1 Richdale Avenue, Unit 4
Cambridge, MA 02140
(617) 576-3603

Karen Konicek (Director of Distribution and Executive Director)

Contact: Karen Konicek
Services: Distributor. Films not available for duplication, licensing, or reuse of any kind.
Description: Sole distributor of documentary films directed by Frederick Wiseman. Titles include: *Titicut Follies; High School; Hospital; Law and Order; Basic Training; Essene; Juvenile Court; Welfare; Meat; Primate; Canal Zone; Sinai Field Mission; Manoeuvre; Model; The Store; Racetrack; Blind, Deaf, Adjustment and Work; Multi-Handicapped;* and *Missile.*
Size & Elements: Film: 16mm (21 titles).
Cataloging: None specified.
Access: Available for research, rental and educational use (rental fee applies).
Rights: Full rights held to all material.
Licensing: Material not available for licensing or reuse.
Restrictions: Material not available for licensing, reuse or duplication of any kind.
Viewing Facilities: None.
Duplication Facilities: None.

MASSACHUSETTS (Chestnut Hill)

BOSTON COLLEGE
UNIVERSITY ARCHIVES
JOHN J. BURNS LIBRARY
Chestnut Hill, MA 02167
(617) 552-3698

Joseph W. Constance, Jr. (Head, Archives and Manuscripts)

Contacts: Joseph Constance; Aimee Felker
Services: University archives. Film and videotape material available for duplication, research and nonprofit reuse.
Description: Boston College football films (1937-81) tracing the history of the Eagles on the field. Nearly every year is represented, and often several games from a single year are included. Collection includes games from the "bowl years" of the early 1940s and the "Mike Holovak years" of the 1950s. Not only talented teams but significant moments have also been preserved (e.g., Boston College-Holy Cross contests, the 1976 upset over Texas and Doug Flutie's first outing in 1981).

Videotapes of college events, such as speeches by the Rev. Jesse Jackson and others will soon be available.
Size & Elements: Film: 16mm (color, black and white). Videotape: 1" and VHS. (70 linear feet total).
Cataloging: Computerized cataloging available to researchers; finding aids.
Access: Open to the public. Available for duplication. Research fees not charged. Research requests accepted by mail, telephone and in person.
Rights: Apply for information. Additional clearances may be necessary in some cases if material is to be reused.

MASSACHUSETTS (Fall River)

Licensing: Apply for information. License fees not charged.
Restrictions: Materials available for research and nonprofit use only.
Viewing Facilities: Film and videotape (at Burns Library).
Duplication Facilities: Available at audiovisual center.

MASSACHUSETTS (Fall River)

BATTLESHIP COVE
EDUCATION OFFICE
Fall River, MA 02721
(508) 678-1905

Paul S. Vaitses, Jr. (Executive Vice President)

Contact: Mark Newton (Educational Coordinator/Curator)
Services: State park; maritime museum. Videotape collection held primarily for research purposes.
Description: Documentaries relating to naval and maritime affairs. World War II films include land, air and sea material, emphasizing the U.S. Navy. Unique to the collection is footage of the launching of the battleship *Massachusetts;* a Bethlehem Steel documentary, *Ship Ways* (1946), relating to shipbuilding around the U.S.; and Chrysler's *Water World* (1970s), a maritime news series with James Franciscus. Television specials include *World War II* and *Vietnam with Walter Cronkite.*
Size & Elements: Videotape: VHS (approx. 60 titles, various lengths)
Cataloging: Research library.
Access: Open to the public. Available for loan. Research requests accepted by mail and in person.
Rights: Some rights held to some material. Clearances from original producers will be necessary in most cases if material is to be reused.
Licensing: Apply for information.
Restrictions: None specified.
Viewing Facilities: Film and videotape.
Duplication Facilities: None.
Related Materials: Holds 1,200 35mm slides.

MASSACHUSETTS (Great Barrington)

ALBERT SCHWEITZER CENTER
Hurlburt Road
RD 1, Box 7
Great Barrington, MA 01230
(413) 528-3124

France Daniels-Thompson (Program Director)

Contact: Dr. Kathleen Collins (Director of Collections)
Services: Library; museum; archives; educational center. Film material available to the public for research, duplication and reuse on a case-by-case basis.
Description: Holds films made by Erica Anderson, who emigrated from Vienna to the U.S. in the late 1930s, becoming an American citizen and filmmaker. During her career, she made documentaries on Grandma Moses, Henry Moore and French tapestries, as well as sponsored films for the Girl Scouts of America, the Red Cross, humane societies and corporations. In 1951, she began to film Albert Schweitzer in and around his hospital in Lambaréné (Gabon) and in Europe, particularly in his hometown in the Alsace region of France. The resulting film, *Albert Schweitzer,* made with producer Jerome Hill, won the 1957 Academy Award for Best Documentary Film. *Schweitzer and Bach,* also produced with Hill, depicts Schweitzer playing the organ at his hometown church. Anderson went on to make several other films about Schweitzer and films about Schweitzer-inspired medical projects in various countries. She also directed *No Man Is a Stranger,* a documentary film on a mental hospital in Haiti where new drugs to treat manic depression were tested.

Footage covers many subjects, including Albert Schweitzer, Africa, African costumes, African flora and fauna, Europe, the Alsace region, Mexico, Peru, Haiti, medical footage, music and musicology, the music of Johann Sebastian Bach and organs. Complete copies, outtakes and unedited footage for many of Anderson's films are held.
Size & Elements: Film: 16mm (460 cans; originals and some release prints).
Cataloging: Catalog will be available to researchers (in progress). Will publish a guide to collection when completed. Research library.
Access: Open to the public. Available for duplication and reuse on a case-by-case basis. Since cataloging and processing is in progress, collection is presently accessible only in part.

Rights: Full rights held to all footage, including shots used in completed films. Distribution rights only held to some completed films. No rights held to some completed films.
Licensing: Available for licensing and reuse on a case-by-case basis. License fees charged.
Restrictions: Available for licensing and reuse on a case-by-case basis. Collection partially accessible to researchers at present.
Viewing Facilities: Planned.
Duplication Facilities: None (outside arrangements can be made).
Related Materials: Approximately 400-500 sound recordings and 49,000 still photographs; books, artifacts and clippings; two- and three-dimensional art work.

MASSACHUSETTS (Haydenville)

FLORENTINE FILMS
20 Kingsley Avenue
Haydenville, MA 01039
(413) 268-7934

Larry Hott and Diane Garey (Partners)

Contacts: Larry Hott; Diane Garey
Services: Film and videotape producer. Footage available for licensing and reuse through authorized representative.
Description: Films relating to ecology, logging, the wilderness idea, and the Northeast United States. Historical and contemporary coverage of the Adirondack Mountains, Niagara Falls, Quabbin Valley (Mass.) and reservoir, the Midwest, Yosemite National Park and Wisconsin; the semi-tropical bird life of Florida; nurses and nursing (World War I-present), with particular emphasis on World War I, public health nurses and nurses serving in the Vietnam War.

Personalities covered include wilderness writers Roderick Nash and Wallace Stegner, and wildlife ecologists Hugh Iltis and Thomas Eisner.

Selected film titles include: *The Old Quabbin Valley* (1980), on the history and construction of the Quabbin Valley reservoir (Mass.), with rural scenics and footage of Boston and Springfield, Mass.; *The Wilderness Idea,* a work in progress, focusing on Yosemite and Wisconsin; and *Garden of Eden* (1983), on endangered species and habitats, with emphasis on Florida and the Midwest.
Size & Elements: Film and videotape (formats and amounts unspecified).
Cataloging: None specified.
Access: Available to the public for rental and purchase, and for licensing and reuse through authorized representative. Research fees charged. Research requests accepted by mail and telephone.
Rights: Full rights held to all material. Additional clearances may be necessary in some cases if material is to be reused.
Licensing: Available for licensing and reuse (through authorized representative). License fees charged.
Restrictions: None specified.
Viewing Facilities: Film and videotape (through authorized representative).
Duplication Facilities: Film and videotape (through authorized representative).
Representative: Film/Audio Services, Inc. (q.v.).

MASSACHUSETTS (Leominster)

CENTRAL NEW ENGLAND FILM ARCHIVES, INC.
90 Overlook Drive
Leominster, MA 01453
(508) 840-1288
(617) 492-2777 (Ext. 4206) (Executive Director)

Carl Piermarini (Executive Director)

Contacts: Carl Piermarini; Jack Celli (Assistant Director)
Services: Private collection. Open to the public. Film available for duplication, licensing and reuse.
Description: Interviews with citizens of central New England, primarily Massachusetts, filmed ca. 1983-84, relating to their participation in the historical football rivalry between Fitchburg and Leominster High Schools. Also holds performance footage of tour and marching bands from the region.

Archives (formed in 1988) plans to locate and collect other historical film footage relating to Central New England.
Size & Elements: Film: 16mm (12 hours; originals and workprints). Currently securing grant to transfer film to videotape.
Cataloging: Uncataloged.

Access: Open to the public. Available for duplication and reuse. Research fees charged (negotiable). Research requests accepted by mail and telephone.
Rights: Full rights held to all material. Signed releases held for interview subjects.
Licensing: Available for licensing and reuse. License fees charged.
Restrictions: None specified.
Viewing Facilities: Film (planned).
Duplication Facilities: None (outside arrangements available).

MASSACHUSETTS (Lexington)

SULLIVAN VIDEO SERVICES
341 Marrett Road
Lexington, MA 02173
(617) 277-1710

John Sullivan (President)

Contact: John Sullivan
Services: Videotape producer. Provides network news production crews; produces segments for national television. Material available for duplication, licensing and reuse. Custom shooting service available.
Description: Collection begins ca. 1978. Contains footage of New England, including beauty shots and scenics of cities and the ocean; the *Queen Elizabeth II* ocean liner and fireworks; news footage shot for television news shows; China, including Beijing and the Great Wall; Ireland; music, including symphonies, rock groups and Tanglewood Music Festival (at Lenox, Mass.); tall ships; model ships and corporate scenes, including manufacturing, production and high technology. A wide variety of generic footage is also available.
Size & Elements: Videotape: 1", Betacam and 3/4" (approx. 1,200 to 1,300 videotapes; masters); VHS (viewing copies).
Cataloging: Card catalogs.
Access: Available to the public for duplication, licensing and reuse. Research fees charged on an individual basis. Research requests accepted by telephone.
Rights: Full rights held to some material. Some rights held to some material. Additional clearances may be necessary in some cases if material is to be reused.
Licensing: Available for licensing and reuse. License fees charged.
Restrictions: None specified.
Viewing Facilities: Videotape (3/4").
Duplication Facilities: Videotape (1", Betacam, 3/4" and VHS).

MASSACHUSETTS (Lincoln)

MASSACHUSETTS AUDUBON SOCIETY
HATHEWAY ENVIRONMENTAL RESOURCE CENTER
South Great Road
Lincoln, MA 01773
(617) 259-9500 (Ext. 7250)
Fax: (617) 259-8899

Jerry Bertrand (President)

Contacts: Douglas Fine (Public Information Officer); Peg Mariner (Public Information Assistant)
Services: Nonprofit environmental organization. Film library primarily maintained for rental; some material available for licensing and reuse.
Description: Films and videotapes relating to natural history, water resources, energy and land use. The Society's general natural history selection includes films on Florida wildlife, wolves, the albatross, the shrew, the bowhead whale, the Greater Sand Hill Crane, Kirtland's warbler and sea swallows. *Audubon's Shore Birds,* a film researched and edited by Society staff, is the first of a series and represents what John James Audubon first saw and painted, using his own observations to describe ornithological adaptations and behavior. *Home Free,* the story of Massachusetts "eagle man" Jack Swedberg (q.v.), was produced for the society and contains excellent footage of the reintroduction of bald eagles to Massachusetts.

Another group of films focus on the theme of conservation: *A Matter of Time,* on the destruction of the environment; *Paradise Polluted,* about air and water pollution; *So Little Time,* relating to endangered species; and *Tragedy of the Commons,* on overpopulation and the finitude of the earth's resources. Additional films relating to energy and water issues are available from the Liberty Council Conservation Education Center.
Size & Elements: Film: 16mm (30 films). Videotape: 3/4" and VHS (6 videotapes).
Cataloging: List with brief description of each title and rental information is available from the Society.
Access: Open to the public. Available primarily for rental rather than for research or reuse. Some titles available for reuse and resale.
Rights: Full rights held to some material.
Licensing: Apply for information.
Restrictions: None specified.
Viewing Facilities: None.
Duplication Facilities: None.

MASSACHUSETTS (Lynn)

REDDEN ARCHIVES
18 Lambert Avenue
Lynn, MA 01902
(617) 592-3390

Contact: Robert Redden
Services: Private collection; film and videotape producer. Material available for purchase.
Description: Historical and contemporary footage of buses and aviation.
Titles include: *History of Buses; To Catch an Eagle (Bus); Bussin' Round I* and *II* (video magazine, ongoing); *Logan: The Movie,* on the history of Boston's Logan Airport; and *Buzzin' Round I,* a video magazine featuring military and civil aviation coverage.
Size & Elements: Videotape (format and amount unspecified; each 90 to 120 min.).
Cataloging: Apply for information.
Access: Apply for information.
Rights: Full rights held to all material.
Licensing: Apply for information.
Restrictions: None specified.
Viewing Facilities: None.
Duplication Facilities: None.
Publications: *Redden's World Aircraft and Airport Journal* and *International Bus Collector* magazines.

MASSACHUSETTS (Nantucket)

NANTUCKET HISTORICAL ASSOCIATION
PETER FOULGER MUSEUM
RESEARCH CENTER, AUDIO-VISUAL SECTION
Box 1016
Nantucket, MA 02554
(508) 228-1655

Street Address: Broad Street

Mrs. Jacqueline Haring (Curator of Research Materials)
Peter MacGlashan (Audio-Visual Librarian)

Contacts: Mrs. Jacqueline Haring; Peter MacGlashan
Services: Historical society. Films and videotapes not currently accessible to the public.
Description: History of Nantucket Island and its people, emphasizing maritime history. Holds records of local lectures, interviews, oral histories and special events (1944-present).
Size & Elements: Film: 16mm (23 titles). Videotapes: 1/2" open reel (119 videotapes); other formats (30 videotapes).
Cataloging: Card catalogs; research library.
Access: Open to researchers and scholars only. Nominal research fees charged. Research requests accepted by mail, telephone and in person (walk-in).
Rights: Apply for information.
Licensing: Apply for information.
Restrictions: None specified.
Viewing Facilities: None.
Duplication Facilities: None.

MASSACHUSETTS (Needham)

THE BOSTON STOCK MARKET
399 Chestnut Street
Needham, MA 02192
(617) 455-8177

MASSACHUSETTS (Needham)

David L. Melpignano (President)

Contact: Judith Warren (Production Manager)
Services: Videotape stock footage sales library; private collection.
Description: Stock footage, including New England scenics, Boston aerials and scenics, high technology B-roll material, medical footage, general city and country shots, establishing shots of various U.S. cities, manufacturing, business and retail industry. Also includes NASA space shots, Boston and New York City (1930s-40s), some newsreel footage, political conventions, black and white "archival" and classic comedy material and raw field footage collected from national videotape producers.

Library footage is divided into two cost categories: "Blue Chip Stock" (high-quality or unusual footage or footage brokered from other collections, generally mastered on 1" videotape, 35mm or 16mm film); and "Penny Stock" (footage of varying quality, licensed at lower prices, generally available on 3/4" videotape).
Size & Elements: Videotape: 1", Betacam and 3/4" (1,250 hours; masters); 3/4" (viewing copies). Private collection contains 250 hours of videotape; brokered collection holds 1,000 hours originating from other producers and private collections. Some of the collection has been transferred from film.
Cataloging: Computerized cataloging for staff use only. Footage is indexed by subject, location, source, length and format.
Access: Available to the public for duplication, licensing and reuse. Research fees charged. Research requests accepted by telephone and in person (by appointment only).

Producers wishing to use footage should provide brief description of needs. Staff will search through computer listing for any and all shots fitting description. Shots may be viewed at library or library will compile preview reel and ship to producer. Master (broadcast-quality) material may be ordered using SMPTE time codes.
Rights: Full rights held to some material. Some material in public domain. Additional clearances may be necessary in some cases if material is to be reused.
Licensing: Available for licensing and reuse. License fees charged. Customers must complete licensing agreement. Rate sheet available.
Restrictions: Footage may not be modified by electronic paint systems without a license from BSM.
Viewing Facilities: Videotape (3/4"; viewing available on site, but assembly of custom preview videotapes preferred).
Duplication Facilities: Videotape (1", 3/4" and 1/2").

MASSACHUSETTS (Needham)

THE TV COLLECTOR
P.O. Box 188
Needham, MA 02192
(508) 238-1179

Street address: 69 South Street, Easton, MA 02375

Diane Albert (Editor and Manager)

Contacts: Diane Albert; Steve Albert
Services: Television magazine publisher; private film and videotape collection. Material available for rental and possibly for duplication and reuse. Research and consulting services available.
Description: Collection of television shows and footage (1949-present), specializing in unsold pilots, non-syndicated shows, public domain television shows, old soap operas, old kinescopes, old game shows, old commercials, complete runs of certain series, large collections of performances by selected actors and short-lived serials.
Size & Elements: Film: 16mm (400 shows, each 30 min.; 75 shows, each 1 hour). Videotape: 3/4" (100 hours); VHS (6,000 hours); Betamax (over 1,500 hours).
Cataloging: Published catalogs.
Access: Not open to the public. Available for rental. Some material possibly available for duplication and reuse, subject to restrictions. Research requests accepted by mail and telephone.
Rights: No rights held to any material. Some material in the public domain (broadcast rights may still apply). Rights status of some material not known. Additional clearances may be necessary in some cases if material is to be reused.
Licensing: Some material available for reuse, subject to restrictions. Usage fees charged (apply for rates).
Restrictions: Restrictions may apply, subject to specific material and

intended use.
Viewing Facilities: Film and videotape (screening room).
Duplication Facilities: Film (film-to-VHS videotape transfers).
Publications: *The TV Collector,* a bi-monthly television nostalgia publication for collectors of television materials.
Related Services: Consulting service available, offering start-to-finish assistance on any television-related project (fees charged).

MASSACHUSETTS (Newton)

EDUCATION DEVELOPMENT CENTER, INC.
55 Chapel Street, Suite 24
Newton, MA 02160
(617) 969-7100
(800) 225-4276 (outside Massachusetts)
Fax: (617) 332-6405

Contact: Millie LeBlanc
Services: Distributor. Films and videotapes available for rental and purchase.
Description: Nonprofit, publicly supported corporation engaged in educational research and development. Films and videotapes cover topics such as: childbirth, early childhood, parenting, adolescent health, youth development, teaching and education, aging, women's educational equity and anthropological studies.

Titles include: *Philosophy and Concepts of Newborn Assessment With T. Berry Brazelton, M.D.,* discussing his development of the "neonatal behavioral assessment scale"; *Violence Prevention Curriculum for Adolescents; Tools for Teaching the Case Method; Math Anxiety: We Beat It, So Can You!,* a motivational program documenting the progress made by an adult group enrolled in a course for the "math anxious"; *Where Do We Go From Here?,* about the elderly and the families who care for them, offering strategies for dealing with difficulties; *China: A Land Transformed; People of the Seal: Eskimo Summer; The Eskimo: Fight For Life* (1971), a portrait of the Netsilik Eskimos, their daily activities and last migration before their lives were transformed by modern technology; and *I Shall Moulder Before I Shall Be Taken* (1978), on an expedition to Surinam's interior jungles to study the Djuka tribes.
Size & Elements: Film: 16mm (12 titles). Videotape: 3/4" (15 titles); and VHS (2 titles).
Cataloging: Brochures.
Access: Available for rental and purchase. Requests accepted by mail and telephone.
Rights: Apply for information.
Licensing: Apply for information.
Restrictions: None specified.
Viewing Facilities: None.
Duplication Facilities: None.
Related Materials: Teacher guides and student study guides available for selected programs.

MASSACHUSETTS (Newton Highlands)

FIRE PREVENTION THROUGH FILMS, INC.
P.O. Box 11
Newton Highlands, MA 02161
(617) 965-4444

Julian Olansky (General Manager)

Contact: Julian Olansky
Services: Corporation; film and videotape producer and distributor. Material available for rental, purchase, duplication, licensing and reuse.
Description: Material relating to fire prevention and safety training. Subjects include: fire safety for children; safety for baby sitters; school fire safety; fire safety in the home; safety in health care facilities, including relocation and evacuation of patients; portable fire extinguishers; laboratory safety; fire problems in high-rise buildings; industrial safety and fire prevention in the workplace.

Also holds footage of fires, firefighting and rescues, primarily from the New England area.
Size & Elements: Film: 16mm (19 titles, 12,000 feet unedited footage; positive, reversal, originals and release prints). Videotape: various formats available on request.
Cataloging: Shot lists; release sheets; brochure.
Access: Available for rental, purchase, duplication, licensing and reuse.

Research fees charged. Research requests accepted by mail and telephone.
Rights: Full rights held to all material.
Licensing: Available for licensing. License fees charged.
Restrictions: None specified.
Viewing Facilities: Film and videotape.
Duplication Facilities: None.

MASSACHUSETTS (Northampton)

COUNTRY DANCE AND SONG SOCIETY OF AMERICA
17 New South Street
Northampton, MA 01060
(413) 584-9913

Brad Foster (Executive Director)

Contact: Brad Foster (Curator, Library and Archives)
Services: Association archives; film and videotape collection. Apply for information regarding research and reuse.
Description: Traditional, ritual and ceremonial dance from the Anglo-American folk tradition. Holdings include a morris dance film (1952), a film documenting Southern mountain square dancing (1929) and a jig competition (1982). The collection holds both edited and unedited footage.
Size & Elements: Film and videotape (approx. 25 titles).
Cataloging: Computerized cataloging available to researchers; research library.
Access: Open to the public. Research fees not charged. Research requests accepted in person (by appointment only).
Rights: Full rights held to some material. Some rights held to other material. Rights status of some material unknown. Additional clearances may be necessary in some cases if material is to be reused.
Licensing: Apply for information.
Restrictions: None specified.
Viewing Facilities: Videotape.
Duplication Facilities: None.

MASSACHUSETTS (Northampton)

SMITH COLLEGE
COLLEGE ARCHIVES
Northampton, MA 01063
(413) 584-2700 (Ext. 2972)

Susan Grigg (Director)

Contacts: Margery Sly (College Archivist); Maida Goodwin (Archives Specialist)
Services: Educational institution. Film and videotape collection open to the public for in-house use only; material available for reuse, subject to restrictions.
Description: Documentation of events, performances, programs, ceremonies, campus and buildings; items produced as public relations tools for prospective students, the general public, information for alumnae and aids to fund raising; home movies made by students, faculty and staff; instructional aids; and copies of national television coverage of the College, or appearances of people related to the College (collected as records of Public Relations Office). "These resources document local manifestations of national developments and institutional history."
Size & Elements: Film: format unspecified (approx. 150 cans; positive). Videotape: format unspecified (17 videotapes; viewing copies).
Cataloging: Card catalogs; finding aids (title list).
Access: Open to the public. For in-house use only. Material not available for loan. Research fees not charged. Research requests accepted by mail, telephone and in person (appointments preferred).
Rights: Some rights held to all material.
Licensing: Apply for information. License fees charged (fees vary according to intended use).
Restrictions: Apply to Director for permission for one-time use.
Viewing Facilities: Film and videotape (available for some formats in separate department located in the same building).
Duplication Facilities: Videotape.

MASSACHUSETTS (Quincy)

NATIONAL FIRE PROTECTION ASSOCIATION
Batterymarch Park
Quincy, MA 02269

(617) 770-3000
(800) 344-3555
Fax: (617) 770-0700

Robert S. Grant (President)

Contact: Harry Abraham (Manager, Film & AV Department)
Services: Association. Films and videotapes available for purchase. Licensing requests granted on a case-by-case basis, subject to restrictions.
Description: Films and videotapes relating to fire protection, intended for the general public (all ages) and fire safety personnel. Subject areas include fire service training, fire suppression, public relations, fire safety education, fire protection in hotels and motels, hazardous materials and petroleum fires.
Fire In America, produced for community awareness and public relations programs, traces four centuries of historic incidents, from the 1621 Plymouth Plantation fire to the recent catastrophe at the MGM Grand Hotel in Las Vegas. The film shows famous fire scenes in American history, in hospitals, schools, factories, prisons, shops, aircraft and hotels, while the narrative explains the causes of the disasters and their tragic results.
Size & Elements: Film: 16mm. Videotape: 3/4", VHS, Betamax I and II. (48 titles total).
Cataloging: Morgan Technical Library of the NFPA holds a complete list of films held in the Film Department.
Access: Not open to the public. Available for purchase, licensing and reuse. Research requests accepted by mail and telephone.
Rights: Full rights held to all material.
Licensing: Available for licensing, subject to restrictions. License fees charged.
Restrictions: Written requests for permission to use films or parts thereof should be directed to the Legal Department. It is best to request material from a specific film and explain the need for the material and its intended use. Permission to reuse is granted in some circumstances and is determined on a case-by-case basis. NFPA is not able to fulfill general, nonspecific stock footage requests and is not a stock footage house.
Viewing Facilities: None.
Duplication Facilities: None.
Related Materials: Publications and study guides related to films; training manuals; fire codes.

MASSACHUSETTS (Roxbury)

METROPOLITAN COUNCIL FOR EDUCATIONAL OPPORTUNITY, INC. (METCO)
55 Dimock Street
Roxbury, MA 02119
(617) 427-1545

Jean McGuire (Executive Director)
J. Marcus Mitchell (Public Relations Officer)

Contact: J. Marcus Mitchell
Services: Educational institution. Holds small videotape collection.
Description: Organization working to ensure equality in education. Holds several videotapes about the Council and its work.
Titles include: *METCO: A Model For Reducing Racial Isolation* (1979); *Interview With Jean McGuire on WGBH-TV* (1982); plus other interviews with Ms. McGuire about her being the first Black woman elected to the Boston School Committee (1982-present).
Size & Elements: Videotape: 3/4" (over 2 titles).
Cataloging: None specified.
Access: Research fees not charged. Research requests accepted by mail.
Rights: Some rights held to all material.
Licensing: Apply for information. License and usage fees not charged.
Restrictions: None specified.
Viewing Facilities: Videotape (3/4").
Duplication Facilities: None.

MASSACHUSETTS (Springfield)

NAISMITH MEMORIAL BASKETBALL HALL OF FAME
P.O. Box 179
Springfield, MA 01101-0179
(413) 781-6500

Street address: 1150 West Columbus Avenue

Joseph O'Brien (Executive Director)

Contact: Wayne Patterson (Research Specialist)
Services: Museum. Film and videotape library maintained primarily for archival and research purposes; available to researchers and scholars for in-house use only.
Description: Professional, college, high-school, amateur (AAU), international and Olympic basketball (1947-present). Coverage includes specific games and players, All Star teams, championships, training and miscellaneous films.
All American Teams. Covers the seasons 1960-61; 1962-63; 1963-64; 1964-65.
AAU. Includes AAU vs. Russia (1963); AAU Championship (1960); Finals (1958).
Boston Celtics. Highlights of 1966, with the Original Celtics demonstrating shot making, offense, defense and ball handling.
Converse season highlights. Covers the seasons 1947-48 through 1984-85. Includes NCAA Championships and Finals; NAIA Finals; NIT Championships and Finals; NBA All Star Games, Finals and Old Timers Games; Olympic Trials and Finals; Harlem Globetrotters and Harlem Magicians Exhibitions; and many other events.
Coach Ed Hickey Film Collection. Various instructional films; college games (1940s-60s).
NBA. Includes NBA on CBS (1974); NBA Playoffs (1969); All-Star Game (1971); Playoffs (1970 and 1971); 1968 Finals (Boston Celtics vs. L.A. Lakers); 25 Years: The NBA Story; Schoolyard Dreams: 35th Anniversary; Championship (1979); NBA Hot Shot 1977 Kids Competition.
NCAA. Highlights of 1960s-70s, including playoff and final games.
Olympics. Olympic tryouts (1952).
Skills. Titles include *1973 Sears Skills Film: Jack Twyman; Winning Ways; Basketball By the Rules; Basketball Today; 1977 Pepsi Cola Hot Shot Contest; Basketball Officials; Basketball Fundamentals; Basketball for Millions* (1957); *King Basketball (Jim Pollard);* and *Better Basketball* (1955).
Miscellaneous. Princeton (1964-65); Bill Bradley's last home game; Princeton losing in NCAA finals; *The Reach Film: On Making a Basketball;* Dean Smith and John Wooden; Hall of Fame materials; Olympic basketball (with Curt Gowdy); National Invitational Finals (1942); and Wheaties All Americans (1967-68 and 1969-70).
Size & Elements: Film: 16mm (positive, originals and release prints). Videotape: format unspecified (masters and viewing copies). (Approx. 1,025 titles total).
Cataloging: Printed lists; shot lists; research library. Videotapes currently being cataloged.
Access: Not open to the public. Available to researchers and scholars for in-house use only. Research fees charged. Research requests accepted by mail, telephone and in person (by appointment only).
Rights: Full rights held to some material. Some rights held to some material.
Licensing: Apply for information.
Restrictions: None specified.
Viewing Facilities: Film and videotape.
Duplication Facilities: Videotape.

MASSACHUSETTS (Turners Falls)

GREEN MOUNTAIN POST FILMS
P.O. Box 229
Turners Falls, MA 01376
(413) 863-4754
(413) 863-8248

Street address: 37 Ferry Road

Daniel Keller (President)

Contact: Charles Light (Producer/Research Director)
Services: Film and videotape producer and distributor. Films and videotapes available for rental and purchase; footage available for licensing and reuse on a case-by-case basis.
Description: Documentaries on environmental and nuclear issues.
GMP-produced titles include: *The Secret Agent* (Jacki Ochs, 1983), a comprehensive investigation of the herbicide Agent Orange and the health dilemma now faced by Vietnam veterans and other exposed Americans, with interviews with veterans, scientists, attorneys, and representatives of the U.S. Air Force, Veterans Administration and Dow Chemical Company; *Ecocide: A Strategy of War* (1982), an eyewitness portrayal of the war against the trees and crops of Vietnam; *Save the Planet* (1979), a history of the atomic age and the

debate over nuclear power, first produced for the Musicians United for Safe Energy (MUSE) benefit concerts at Madison Square Garden; *Lovejoy's Nuclear War* (1975), a documentary on the story of the earliest major act of civil disobedience against atomic power, presenting a cross-section of opinions on nuclear power, civil disobedience and the politics of energy; *Radiation and Health* (1978), an engaging debate between Dr. Helen Caldicott, pediatrician and anti-nuclear activist, and Reginald Rodgers, a nuclear supporter and Director of Radiological Assessment for Northeast Utilities, on the danger posed to workers and to the public by low-level radiation.
Also available: *The Last Resort* (1978), a chronicle of the roots of the dispute over the Seabrook (New Hampshire) nuclear plant and the first mass actions against nuclear plant construction; *Nuclear Reaction in Wyhl* (1976), documenting mass occupations of nuclear plant sites across Europe (1975), including some of the first reports of these spontaneous and exuberant actions originally filmed in 8mm by participants; *Early Warnings* (1981), featuring an on-site rally against the Seabrook atomic plant, with appearances by Jackson Browne, Sarah Nelson, Dr. John Gofman, Dick Gregory, Amory Lovins, Dr. Benjamin Spock and Pete Seeger; *Training for Nonviolence* (1978), documenting preparations for peaceful direct action through civil disobedience and the views of some long-time activists on the philosophy and historic framework of this practice; *A Solar Program for New England* (1980, 15 min.), an optimistic view of New England's solar future showing the results of a project to install low-cost, passive solar heating systems on weatherized homes; *Different Places Different People* (Daniel Keller, 1969), a sympathetic look at a rural New Hampshire home for mentally retarded children and adults; *Voices of Spirit* (1975), about a farmer living deep in the hills of Western Massachusetts who is also a trance medium; and *Vietnam Experience* (1987), combining the music of Country Joe McDonald with archival footage of the Vietnam War.
Size & Elements: Film: 35mm (10,000 feet; negatives and release prints); 16mm (200,000 feet; negatives, masters and release prints). Videotape: 1" and 3/4" (most titles available). (38 titles total).
Cataloging: Published catalog.
Access: Open to the public. Available for rental, purchase, licensing and reuse, subject to restrictions. Research fees charged. Research requests accepted by mail, telephone and in person (by appointment only).
Rights: Full rights held to some material. Some rights held to all material.
Licensing: Available for licensing and reuse on a case-by-case basis. License fees charged.
Restrictions: Requests for licensing and reuse considered on a case-by-case basis.
Viewing Facilities: Film.
Duplication Facilities: None.

MASSACHUSETTS (Waltham)

AMERICAN JEWISH HISTORICAL SOCIETY
2 Thornton Road
Waltham, MA 02154
(617) 891-8110

Bernard Wax (Director)

Contact: Nathan M. Kaganoff (Librarian)
Services: Historical society. Videotapes available for research, rental and duplication on a case-by-case basis.
Description: American Jewish history, particularly relating to the Boston area. Titles include: *American Jew; Haym Salomon: Gentleman of Precision and Integrity; On Common Ground: Boston Jewish Community 1649-1980; A Precious Heritage: American Jewish Historical Society.*
Size & Elements: Videotape: VHS (4 titles; viewing copies).
Cataloging: Card catalogs; research library.
Access: Open to researchers and scholars. Available for rental and duplication. Requests accepted by mail and telephone.
Rights: Full rights held to all material.
Licensing: Apply for information. Rental and license fees set on an individual basis.
Restrictions: None specified.
Viewing Facilities: Videotape (VHS).
Duplication Facilities: Videotape (VHS).

MASSACHUSETTS (Waltham)

BRANDEIS UNIVERSITY LIBRARY
ABRAHAM LINCOLN BRIGADE ARCHIVES
415 South Street

Waltham, MA 02254
(617) 736-4682

Dr. Charles Cutter (Acting Head, Special Collections)

Contact: Victor A. Berch (Curator, Abraham Lincoln Brigade Archives)
Services: Educational institution; library. Film and videotape collection available for research and for duplication and reuse in some cases, subject to clearance and restriction.
Description: Holds small collection of documentary and propaganda films and videotapes, largely focusing on the Spanish Civil War. Includes material relating to American participation in the Spanish Civil War; original footage and videotaped interviews with survivors of the Abraham Lincoln Brigade and their family members.
Size & Elements: Film: 35mm and 16mm (6 titles). Videotapes: format unspecified (over 230 videotapes).
Cataloging: Inventory of available materials.
Access: Open to the public. For in-house use only. Available for duplication on a limited basis. Research fees charged in some cases. Research requests accepted by mail, telephone and in person (by appointment only).
Rights: Full rights held to some material. Additional clearances may be necessary in some cases if material is to be reused.
Licensing: Apply for information. License fees charged.
Restrictions: Some restrictions may apply to reuse.
Viewing Facilities: Film and videotape (available by special arrangement).
Duplication Facilities: None.

MASSACHUSETTS (Waltham)

NATIONAL CENTER FOR JEWISH FILM
BRANDEIS UNIVERSITY
Lown Building, Room 102
Waltham, MA 02254
(617) 899-7044

Sharon Pucker Rivo (Executive Director)

Contacts: Miriam Krant (Associate Director); Sharon Rivo
Services: Film archives; library; distributor; stock footage sales library. Open to researchers and scholars only. Materials available for research, distribution, duplication, licensing and reuse, subject to restrictions.
Description: Founded in 1976 with the acquisition of 30 Yiddish-language features, the National Center for Jewish Film was established to gather, preserve and disseminate relevant film materials. Center holds the archival film collections of Organization for Rehabilitation through Training (ORT), Jewish National Fund, Joint Distribution Committee, Jewish Defense Committee, United Jewish Appeal and other organizations.

Holds films relating to the Jewish experience, including Yiddish films; early American silent short films; features on Jewish subjects; European, American and Soviet Jewry; Israel; anti-Semitic propaganda; and Holocaust materials.

Center has entered into an agreement with the Bundesarchiv-Film Archiv and other archival groups in the Federal Republic of Germany to acquire, subtitle and supervise the use of Nazi-produced anti-Semitic films. These extremely sensitive materials will be available strictly for educational use, and include such titles as *Der Ewige Jude, Jud Süss* and *Der Führer Schenkt den Juden eine Stadt.*

The Rutenberg and Everett Yiddish Film Library includes feature-length films produced in Europe and the United States (1930s-40s). Restored with complete English subtitles, this collection is available for public exhibition.

Films in distribution include: *Agro Joint* (USSR, 1936, 32 min., silent with English titles; documentary); *American Shadchen* (1940, 90 min., Yiddish with English titles; feature); *An Appeal to Jews of the World* (USSR, 1941, 6 min., Russian with English titles; documentary); *Auschwitz (Osweichim)* (USSR, 1945, 20 min.; documentary); *The Bells* (1926, 60 min., silent; documentary); *Bound for Nowhere: The St. Louis Episode* (1939, 106 min.; Yiddish feature); *Brivele der Maman (A Letter to Mother)* (Poland, 1939, 106 min., Yiddish with English titles; feature); *Camps of the Dead* (France, 1945, 19 min.; documentary); *Cantor on Trial* (1931, 10 min.; Yiddish fiction); *Carpathian Mountains, Jewish Farmers* (Hungary, ca. 1936, 17 min., silent; documentary); *Catskill Honeymoon* (1949, 90 min.; Yiddish feature); *Child of the Ghetto* (1910, 10 min., silent with English titles; fiction); *Children Must Laugh* (Poland, 1936, 63 min., Yiddish; documentary); *Cohen on the Telephone* (1929, 9 min.; fiction); *Cohen Saves the Flag* (1913, 10 min., silent with English titles; fiction); *Cohen's Advertising Scheme* (1904, 1 min., silent; fiction); *Cohen's*

Fire Sale (1907, 10 min., silent with English titles; fiction); *Dachau* (Germany, 1945, 12 min., silent with English titles; documentary); *Davidoff Newsreel* (Palestine, 1934, 10 min., Hebrew; documentary).

Additional titles include: *A Day In Warsaw* (Poland, 1939, 9 min., Yiddish travelogue); *Death Mills* (1946, 20 min.; documentary); *East and West* (Austria, 1923, 61 min., silent with English titles; Yiddish fiction); *Ebensee* (Austria, 1945, 11 min.; documentary); *Ellis Island* (1903, 1 min., silent; documentary); *Ellis Island* (1906, silent; documentary); *Feast of Passover* (1931, 15 min., Yiddish fiction); *Freylekhe Kabtsonim (Jolly Paupers)* (Poland, 1937; Yiddish feature with English titles); *The Fuhrer Gives a City to the Jews* (Germany, 1944, 16 min., English titles; Nazi propaganda); *Germany Awake* (Germany, 1968, 90 min.; documentary); *Ghetto Fish Market* (1903, 1 min., silent; documentary); *God, Man & Devil* (1949, 100 min.; Yiddish feature with English titles); *Green Fields* (1937, 95 min.; Yiddish feature with English titles); *Hatikvah: The Hope* (Germany, 1936, 48 min., silent with German titles; documentary); *His People* (1925, 91 min.; silent with English titles); *The Holy Land* (1917, approx. 5 min.; silent with English titles; documentary); *Horodok* (Poland, 1930, 11 min., silent; documentary); *How Mosha Came Back* (1914, 10 min., silent with English titles; fiction); *I Want to Be a Boarder* (1937, 15 min., Yiddish fiction with English titles); *The Illegals* (Israel, 1947, 56 min.; docudrama); *Immigrant Life Compilation* (1903-06, 4 min., silent; documentary); *Jewish Dance in Jerusalem* (1902, 1 min., silent; documentary).

Additional titles include: *Jewish Life in: Bialystok, Cracow, Lwow, Vilna* (Poland, 1939, each 9 min., Yiddish travelogues); *Jews, Lice & Bedbugs* (Poland, 1941, 10 min., silent; Nazi propaganda); *Jews in Dabrowa* (Germany, ca. 1940, 11 min., Nazi propaganda); *Jews Through Nazi Eyes* (Poland, 1939-41, 9 min., Nazi propaganda); *Kurow* (Poland, 1932, 10 min., silent; documentary); *Levi & Cohen: The Irish Comedians* (1903, 1 min., silent; fiction); *The Light Ahead* (1939, 94 min., Yiddish feature with English titles); *Long Fliv the King* (1926, 25 min., silent with English titles; fiction); *Lower East Side, NYC* (ca. 1934-35, 9 min., silent with English titles; fiction); *Mamele (Little Mother)* (Poland, 1938, 90 min., Yiddish with English titles; feature); *My Father's House* (Palestine, 1946, 85 min.; feature); *Nazi Concentration Camps* (1945, 59 min.; documentary); *Nowogrodek* (Poland, 1930, 26 min., silent with English and Yiddish titles; documentary); *Nuremberg* (1946, 76 min.; fiction); *Old Isaac, The Pawnbroker* (1908, 10 min., silent with English titles; fiction); *The Singing Blacksmith* (1938, 95 min., Yiddish feature with English titles); *Stuttgart Transport* (Germany, 1941, 3 min.; Nazi propaganda); *A Vilna Legend* (Poland, 1924 and 1933, 60 min., Yiddish with English titles; feature); and *Yidl mitn Fiddle* (Poland, 1937, 90 min., Yiddish with English titles; feature).

NCJF has entered into a non-theatrical sub-distribution agreement with Films Incorporated (q.v.) to distribute some 30 feature films for rental to institutions and organizations throughout the United States.

Four titles are available for purchase on videotape: *The Jews of San'a — Scenes of Daily Life; The Community of Salonika; The Community of Fez;* and *Chinese Jews on the Banks of the Yellow River.*

Size & Elements: Film: 35mm and 16mm (approx. 3,000 films). Videotape: VHS and Betamax (4 titles; film transfers).
Cataloging: Card catalogs; shot lists; staff assistance.
Access: Open to researchers and scholars only (by appointment). Some material possibly available for reuse. Research fees charged. Research requests accepted by mail, telephone and in person (by appointment only).
Rights: Full rights held to most material. Additional clearances may be necessary in some cases if material is to be reused.
Licensing: Available for licensing and reuse, subject to restrictions. Usage fees charged.
Restrictions: Restrictions may apply to reuse of certain material.
Viewing Facilities: Film (35mm and 16mm Steenbeck).
Duplication Facilities: None.
Related Materials: Still photograph collection.

MASSACHUSETTS (Watertown)

AMA FILM/VIDEO
AMERICAN MANAGEMENT ASSOCIATION
9 Galen Street
Watertown, MA 02172
(617) 926-4600
(800) 225-3215
Fax: (617) 923-1875

John Doerr (Vice President)

Contact: Fran Bloomfield (Customer Service Manager)

Services: Film and videotape producer. Material available for rental, purchase and possibly reuse, subject to restrictions.
Description: Management training films for employees, covering issues of quality, improving sales techniques, seeing the customer's point of view, innovation, identifying customer needs, handling objections, sales support and customer service skills, telephone selling and techniques, career management, time management and supervisory skills.
Size & Elements: Videotape: 3/4" and 1/2" (30 titles, each 10 to 30 min.).
Cataloging: Published catalogs (available on request).
Access: Open to the public. Available for rental and purchase. Requests accepted by telephone.
Rights: Some rights held to some material.
Licensing: Apply for information.
Restrictions: Restrictions apply to some uses.
Viewing Facilities: Videotape.
Duplication Facilities: Videotape.
Representatives: Extensive list of distributors in the U.S., Canada, United Kingdom, New Zealand and Australia (apply for information).

MASSACHUSETTS (Watertown)

DOCUMENTARY EDUCATIONAL RESOURCES
101 Morse Street
Watertown, MA 02172
(617) 926-0491
Fax: (617) 926-9519

Sue Marshall Cabezas (Executive Vice President)

Contact: Sue Marshall Cabezas
Services: Nonprofit organization; documentary film and videotape producer. Material available for rental, purchase, licensing and reuse, subject to restrictions.
Description: Ethnographic and anthropological documentary films (1971-present).
John Marshall films. A series produced in the early 1970s about the San, or Bushmen, of the Kalahari Desert in Namibia (South West Africa). Segments include: *An Argument About a Marriage; Baobab Play; Bitter Melons; Children Throw Toy Assegais; A Curing Ceremony; Debe's Tantrum; A Group of Women; A Joking Relationship; !Kung Bushmen Hunting Equipment; Lion Game; The Meat Fight; The Melon Tossing Game; Men Bathing; N!ai, The Story of a !Kung Woman; N!um Tchai; Playing with Scorpions; A Rite of Passage; Tug-of-War, Bushmen;* and *The Wasp Nest.*
Yanomamo Indian films. Based on a collaboration between filmmaker Timothy Asch and anthropologist Napoleon Chagnon, these segments were filmed in southern Venezuela: *Arrows; The Ax Fight; Bride Service; Children's Magical Death; Climbing the Peach Palm; A Father Washes His Children; The Feast; Firewood; Jaguar: A Yanomamo Twin Cycle Myth; Magical Death; A Man and His Wife Weave a Hammock; A Man Called "Bee"; Studying the Yanomamo; Moonblood: A Yanomamo Creation Myth; Myth of Naro as Told by Dedeheiwa; Myth of Naro as Told by Kaobawa; New Tribes Mission; Ocamo is My Town; Tapir Distribution; Tug-of-War, Yanomamo; Weeding the Garden;* and *Yanomamo: A Multidisciplinary Study.*
Other films held include Jean Rouch's classic series on West Africa (*Jaguar, Les Maitres Fous* and *The Lion Hunters*); *Las Hurdes (Land Without Bread)* (Luis Buñuel, 1932), a documentary on poverty in rural Spain; a recent exploration of Balinese trance and healing; BBC-produced films on the Masai; a variety of films relating to American life and heritage, from New England fiddlers to Aroostook micmac basketmakers; *The Past That Lives,* a biographical portrait of Dutch historian Jacob Presser who became fascinated with socialist ideology, Germany, and the Renaissance after his ghetto childhood and the devastation of Amsterdam's Jews during the Holocaust; and *A Week of Sweet Water,* about the condition of the residents of the Sahel region of West Africa, along the southern edge of the Sahara Desert, where over 200,000 slowly starved to death during the Great Sahel Drought (1973-74).
Areas covered include Namibia, Botswana, West Africa, Nigeria, Niger, Venezuela, Brazil, Argentina, Colombia, Mexico, Guatemala, Alaska, the United States, Pittsburgh, Indonesia, Papua New Guinea, China and Spain.
Size & Elements: Film: 16mm (150 titles; black and white and color). Videotape: format unspecified (some titles available).
Cataloging: Published catalogs.
Access: Available to the public for rental and purchase; and for reuse, subject to restrictions. Rental fee charged for research use of material. Research requests accepted by mail and telephone.
Rights: Full rights held to some material. Some rights held to all material.

Additional clearances may be necessary in some cases if material is to be reused.
Licensing: Available for licensing and reuse, subject to restrictions. License fees charged.
Restrictions: Restrictions may apply, depending on material used. Clearances and script approvals may be necessary for licensing and reuse.
Viewing Facilities: Film (16mm); videotape (3/4" and 1/2") (by special arrangement only).
Duplication Facilities: None.
Related Materials: Study guides for some titles.

MASSACHUSETTS (Watertown)

PERKINS SCHOOL FOR THE BLIND
SAMUEL P. HAYES RESEARCH LIBRARY
175 North Beacon Street
Watertown, MA 02172
(617) 924-3434 (Ext. 250) (Library)
(617) 924-3434 (Ext. 291) (Instructional Materials Center)
(800) 852-3133

Kevin Lessard (Director, Perkins School for the Blind)
Pat Kirk (Director, Library)

Contacts: Kenneth A. Stuckey (Research Librarian); Skip Schiel (Instructional Materials Coordinator)
Services: Educational institution. Film and videotape collection available to the public for in-house use only and for duplication, subject to restrictions.
Description: Informational films and videotapes relating to blindness, the education of the blind, deaf-blindness, the Perkins School for the Blind, Helen Keller and Anne Sullivan.
Archival titles include: *Children of the Silent Night* (1961), a documentary showing methods employed in the Perkins Deaf-Blind program; *Helen Keller Dedicates Keller-Macy Cottage* (1956); *Legacy of Anne Sullivan* (1968), a biography; *Light for All* (1920s), the first of the Perkins movies, in which a mother enrolls her blind child in Perkins; and *Perkins Institution* (1933), silent films of school activities.
Instructional titles include: *Communicating with Deaf-Blind People; Speech Instruction with a Deaf-Blind Person, The World of Deaf-Blind Children: How They Communicate;* and *The World of Deaf-Blind Children: Deaf-Blind Circus.*
Size & Elements: Film: 16mm (30 titles, 35 cans; negative). Videotape: VHS (12 videotapes; masters and viewing copies).
Cataloging: Research library; dope sheets and release sheets.
Access: Available to the public. For in-house use only. Available for duplication. Research fees not charged. Research requests accepted by mail, telephone and in person (walk-in).
Rights: Full rights held to all material.
Licensing: Apply for information.
Restrictions: Due to the films' age and fragile condition, videotape loans are preferred.
Viewing Facilities: Film and videotape.
Duplication Facilities: Film and videotape.

MASSACHUSETTS (West Millbury)

JACK SWEDBERG
P.O. Box 34
West Millbury, MA 01586-0034
(508) 865-4559

Contact: Jack Swedberg
Services: Film producer; private collection. Film footage available to the public for duplication, licensing and reuse.
Description: Footage of wildlife (1950-present) shot in Central Massachusetts, Alaska, Alabama, Virginia, New Jersey and national wildlife refuges up and down the East Coast. Subjects include beaver, deer, eagles (extensive coverage), shore birds, waterfowl and flowers.
Size & Elements: Film: 16mm (approx. 20,000 feet; originals and workprints).
Cataloging: Staff assistance required.
Access: Available to the public for duplication and reuse. Research fees not charged. Research requests accepted by mail. Will send workprints for viewing purposes.
Rights: Full rights held to all material.
Licensing: Available for licensing and reuse. License fees charged.

Restrictions: None specified.
Viewing Facilities: None (workprints can be sent for preview).
Duplication Facilities: None.

MICHIGAN

MICHIGAN (Ann Arbor)

GERALD R. FORD LIBRARY
1000 Beal Avenue
Ann Arbor, MI 48109
(313) 668-2218

Don W. Wilson (Director)

Contact: Richard L. Holzhausen (Archivist)
Services: Government agency. Film and videotape material available for research, duplication and reuse, subject to restrictions.
Description: Presidential library administered by the National Archives and Records Administration.

Film and videotape records of the administration of President Gerald R. Ford (1974-77). Materials were donated by President Ford's associates in government and politics, government agencies and private individuals. Although materials document many aspects of Mr. Ford's public and private life, most items relate to his term as President.

Naval Photographic Center (NPC) Collection. Film shot by Navy film crews assigned to cover the President. (16mm, 710,000 feet, color).

White House Communications Agency (WHCA) Collection. This office produced audiotapes and videotapes documenting Mr. Ford's activities as President. Videotapes include Presidential speeches, press conferences, television programs featuring Administration officials and Presidential advisers, and daily news reports from all three major television networks. Collection also includes a few items from his term as Vice President.
Size & Elements: Film: 16mm (approx. 710,000 feet, color, some with magnetic sound track); Videotape: format unspecified (765 videotapes).
Cataloging: Cross-reference index and shot cards available for each roll of film. Finding aids available at library.
Access: Open to the public. Research fees not charged. Research requests accepted by mail and telephone. All new researchers must complete an application and participate in an orientation interview with a reference archivist. Archivist will explain basic procedures and services and provide advice on specific Library holdings.
Rights: NPC Collection in the public domain. WHCA Collection contains copyrighted material; rights retained by original producers and networks.
Licensing: Available for reuse, subject to restrictions.
Restrictions: WHCA Collection may be used at Library for reference purposes but may not be reproduced, due to copyright restrictions.
Viewing Facilities: Film and videotape.
Duplication Facilities: None; outside videotape duplication services available (apply for rates).
Related Materials: Numerous audiotape recordings and still photographs.

MICHIGAN (Ann Arbor)

HISTORICAL HEALTH FILM COLLECTION
c/o Dr. Martin S. Pernick
Department of History
University of Michigan
Ann Arbor, MI 48109
(313) 747-4876
(313) 764-6408

Dr. Martin S. Pernick (Associate Professor of History)

Contact: Dr. Martin S. Pernick
Services: Specialized film collection. Maintained for research purposes; available to researchers and scholars and possibly for reuse, subject to restrictions.
Description: Films made for lay audiences (1900-50, concentrated in 1910-30 period) dealing with many aspects of medicine and health. Representative subjects include: abortion, anesthesia, bacteria, cancer, childbirth, clinical medicine, clinics, corruption, death, dentists, diphtheria, drug abuse, epidemics, eugenics, faith healers and faith healing, flu, hookworm, human reproduction, immigrants, immunization, insanity, insects, insurance, malaria, microphotography, nursing, oral hygiene, physiology, polio, prostitution, psychiatry, quackery, Red Cross, safety, sanatoriums, sanitation, sex, sex roles, smoking, surgery, typhoid, vectors, venereal disease, veterinary medicine, women doctors, x-rays and yellow fever.

Collection was assembled by Professor Pernick as part of the research for his forthcoming book, *Bringing Medicine to the Masses: Motion Pictures and the Revolution in Public Health 1910-1927.*
Size & Elements: Film: 16mm (approx. 32,000 feet, 15 titles, positive). Videotape: 3/4" (43 hours, 149 titles; viewing copies); VHS (approx. 24 hours, 94 titles). (Approx. 49 hours, 162 titles total).
Cataloging: Card catalogs and computerized cataloging for staff use only.
Access: Available to researchers and scholars only. For in-house use only. Research fees not charged to nonprofit users; fees charged to profit-making users. Research requests accepted by mail, telephone and in person (by appointment only).
Rights: Some rights held to all material. Additional clearances will be necessary if material is to be reused; some rights retained by filmmakers.
Licensing: Available for reuse, subject to restrictions.
Restrictions: Collection is for research use only. All other uses require permission of original owners or producers.
Viewing Facilities: None.
Duplication Facilities: None.

MICHIGAN (Ann Arbor)

ROBOTIC INDUSTRIES ASSOCIATION
P.O. Box 3724
Ann Arbor, MI 48106
(313) 994-6088
Fax: (313) 994-3338

Street address: 900 Victors Way

Donald A. Vincent (Executive Vice President)

Contact: Jeffrey A. Burnstein (Director, Marketing and Public Relations)
Services: Association. Film and videotape collection available for rental and purchase; and for reuse on a case-by-case basis.
Description: Films and videotapes promoting the use and development of robotics and machine vision technology.

Titles include: *Commitment to Robotics* (1987, narrated by William Shatner), in which executives from Alcoa, Corning Glass, Chrysler and Xebec describe how to successfully implement robotics; *Robotics: The Future is Now* (1984), showing a demonstration of robotics capabilities filmed at the Chrysler Minivan Plant and the National Bureau of Standards; *The Robot Safety Show* (1985); *The Story of MAP and TOP* (1986), examining manufacturing automation protocol (MAP) and technical office protocol (TOP); *Vision. Now.* (1987), a discussion of how to successfully apply machine vision technology; and *Machine Vision* (1985), presenting five case studies of machine vision use at GM's Orion Assembly plant, Zapata Industries, the Kearfott Division of Singer, and the Seaboard Lemon Association.
Size & Elements: Film: 16mm (6 titles). Videotape: 3/4" and 1/2" (6 titles).
Cataloging: Published catalog.
Access: Available for rental and purchase. Requests accepted by mail and telephone.
Rights: Some rights held to all material.
Licensing: Selected titles (*Vision. Now.*) available for reuse, subject to restrictions. Usage fees charged.
Restrictions: Requests for reuse considered on a case-by-case basis.
Viewing Facilities: None.
Duplication Facilities: None.

MICHIGAN (Ann Arbor)

THE UNIVERSITY OF MICHIGAN
MICHIGAN HISTORICAL COLLECTIONS
BENTLEY HISTORICAL LIBRARY
1150 Beal Avenue
Ann Arbor, MI 48109-2113
(313) 764-3482

Dr. Francis X. Blouin, Jr. (Director)

Contact: Nancy R. Bartlett (Reference Archivist)
Services: Historical library; public archives. Films and videotapes available to

the public for in-house viewing and duplication, subject to restrictions.

Description: Michigan history, people and events (1918-present). Manuscript and other collections containing moving image material include:

Robert D. Aldrich. Films showing various aspects of life in Concord, Jackson County, Michigan.

Ann Arbor Women's Christian Temperance Union. Educational and promotional films (4 titles; ca. 1940-50) on alcohol education, used by national and local WCTU organizations.

Julius A. Clauss. Films (ca. 1920-54) relating to the family of Julius Clauss and the development of the steel industry. Clauss was employed by the Great Lakes Steel Corporation of Ecorse, Michigan.

Elzada Urseba Clover. Film (1938), with a later copy, of an exploratory trip down the Colorado River Canyon. Elzada Clover and Lois Jotter were the first women to make the trip.

Mary S. Coleman. Videotape of a television interview with Coleman, Chief Justice of the Michigan Supreme Court.

Henry Hitt Crane. Film (ca. 1955) of a speech by Rev. Henry Hitt Crane, pacifist social reformer and pastor of Detroit Central Methodist Church, on pacifism and the Cold War period of the 1950s.

Detroit & Canada Tunnel Corporation. A film, *The Detroit-Windsor Tunnel* (Jack Kausch, 1980), showing tunnel construction.

Detroit Urban League. Films (1930s-76) relating to organization activities.

Wilma Thompson Donahue. Videotapes of papers presented at a 1979 symposium, "White House Conferences as Agents of Social Change."

Christian T. Feddersen. Film (1938) accumulated by Feddersen, relating to Scandinavian-American activities and organizations.

Harold Studley Gray. Six films (ca. 1932-48) and one videotape copy of films relating to the Saline Valley Farms cooperative, all made by Gray, the founder of the cooperative, as a continuing history and showing all aspects of the farms' activity.

Martha Wright Griffiths. Films (1961-63) from the collection of the Democratic congresswoman from Michigan.

Lucia Voorhees Grimes. From Rebel to Reformer (1962, videotape copy made 1978), on women's and reform organizations, including the WCTU and the women's suffrage movement; records an interview with Grimes, leader in the early women's movement.

Philip Aloysius Hart. Films and videotapes (ca. 1953-76) accumulated by the U.S. senator from Michigan.

Edward N. Hartwick. Films (ca. 1950-70) of individuals and groups active in Republican politics in Michigan and the U.S.

Joseph Ralston Hayden. Films (with VHS videotape copies) of travels in the Philippines during the 1930s.

Woodrow W. Hunter. Films (8 titles) from the University of Michigan film series *Preparation for Retirement.*

Milton G. Kendrick. Videotape and script of a "Salute to Michigan" broadcast on *Perry Como's Kraft Music Hall* (May 23, 1962), with guest Anne Bancroft; and a film containing outtakes of scenes during Michigan Day at the Seattle World's Fair (1962), with John B. Swainson and Adlai Stevenson.

Harry G. Kipke. Films of University of Michigan football games (ca. 1940s).

Justin W. Leonard. Films (1970) related to the life and career of the conservationist and professor of natural resources.

George Meader. Films (1962) accumulated by the Republican U.S. congressman from Michigan. Includes discussion of issues of foreign and domestic policy.

Michigan Abortion Referendum Committee. Film of interview with Marion Dreyfuss, chair of the Abortion Action Committee of the National Council of Jewish Women, discussing abortion legislation in the Michigan Legislature; and videotape (1972). (Limited access.)

Michigan. University. Affirmative Action Office. Videotapes (ca. 1974-83) accumulated by the Office; 3/4" videotapes of an appearance by Betty Friedan during an International Women's Year observance at the University.

Michigan. University. Department of Physical Education. A film (June 2, 1936) and videotape copy of *Oz University,* produced by the Freshman Women and presented by the Michigan League for Lantern Night ceremonies; scenes include registration, a lecture by "Professor Wagglebug" and a blue book exam.

Michigan. University. National Archive on Sino-American Relations. Films and videotapes collected for the Archive, relating especially to China.

Michigan. University. Professional Theatre Program. Films (1965-72) of classical drama programs for schools.

Blair Moody. Films relating to the career and family of the correspondent for the Detroit *News* and U.S. senator from Michigan.

Frank Murphy. Films relating to the life and activities of the Michigan governor.

National Music Camp, Interlochen, Michigan. Films relating to camp

activities, students, faculty and guest conductors.

Stella (Brunt) Osborn. Videotape (1981) relating to her life and activities.

Charles E. Potter. Films (ca. 1946-59) relating to the career of the Republican congressman from Lapeer, Mich. and U.S. senator.

Prohibition Party. National Committee. Three films on alcoholism and a Party convention.

Carmen A. Roberts. Film (8mm) of a 1976 anti-busing rally in Detroit.

George Wilcken Romney. Films and videotapes (ca. 1962-68) relating to his political career, including campaign spots, news features, speeches and television appearances.

Ralph Alanson Sawyer. One 16mm film of atomic bomb testing at Bikini Atoll (1946).

Charles Althen Simpson. Film containing miscellaneous scenes of American soldiers in Archangel, U.S.S.R. (1918-19).

Charles Robert Sligh, Jr. Films (ca. 1950-55) of the furniture manufacturer and president of the National Association of Manufacturers; including interviews, television appearances, debates with Walter P. Reuther and others, and footage of factory production.

Ansel Brooks Smith. Films (ca. 1930-31) of Dr. A. B. Smith of Grand Rapids, Mich., including scenes of family recreational activities and trips; also scenes of Arthur H. Vandenberg and family.

Gerald Lyman Kenneth Smith. Films (1960s) accumulated by the right-wing political and religious activist, organizer of the America First Party, and founder and publisher of *The Cross and the Flag.*

John Burley Swainson. Films relating primarily to economic and social services programs during his gubernatorial administration (1961-63).

Charles W. Ungerman, Jr. Film of the Soap Box Derby races at Akron, Ohio (1946).

Arthur Hendrick Vandenberg. Film and videotape copy about the United Nations Conference in San Francisco (1945).

Gordon Webber. Films (1939-60s) of the writer for radio and television programs and advertising executive; concerning in part advertising and his opposition to the Vietnam War.

Gerhard Mennen Williams. Films and videotapes relating to his gubernatorial, political and diplomatic activities.

Robert Franklin Williams. 3 videotapes (ca. 1963-69) concerning the civil rights activist and Black militant; his life in and travels to China, Cuba, Africa and Vietnam.

Size & Elements: Film: 16mm (approx. 150 films); 8mm (approx. 1 film). Videotape: assorted formats (approx. 80 videotapes).

Cataloging: Card catalogs; contents lists.

Access: Available to the public for in-house viewing and duplication, subject to restrictions. Research fees not charged. Research requests accepted in person (walk-in).

Rights: Some rights held to some material. Rights status of some material not known. Additional clearances may be necessary in some cases if material is to be reused.

Licensing: Apply for information. License and usage fees not charged.

Restrictions: Some material carries donor restrictions.

Viewing Facilities: Film and videotape.

Duplication Facilities: None.

Related Materials: Many collections also include photographs, filmstrips and audiotapes.

MICHIGAN (Bloomfield Hills)

CRANBROOK ACADEMY OF ARTS
ARCHIVE AND HISTORICAL COLLECTION
P.O. Box 801
Bloomfield Hills, MI 48013
(313) 645-3154

Street address: 191 Brady Lane

Mark Coir (Archivist)

Contact: Mark Coir

Services: Institute. Film and videotape archives available for research and reuse, subject to approval.

Description: Film and videotape (1920s-70s) relating to Cranbrook, a center of the Arts and Crafts movement in American design.

Film holdings include historical news footage of Detroit (1920s). Other materials relate to the Booth family, who founded the institute in 1908; Eliel Saarinen, the renowned architect affiliated with Cranbrook, at home in Finland; the construction of Cranbrook's unique buildings; and activities of the boys' school and Kingswood School for Girls. Other footage includes work in campus studios by artists such as Richard Thomas, metalsmith and theatrical productions at the institute. General footage shows Cranbrook's 315 acres.

Videotape material includes outtakes from the PBS series *Pride of Place* (1985), originally shot at Cranbrook, and interviews with individuals associated with the school and its founders.
Size & Elements: Film: 16mm (50 titles). Videotape: VHS (approx. 35 titles).
Cataloging: None.
Access: Open to the public. Research requests accepted by mail and telephone; one-month notice requested. Research fees not charged.
Rights: Full rights held to all material.
Licensing: Available for licensing, subject to restrictions.
Restrictions: Restrictions may apply to reuse of certain material.
Viewing Facilities: Film and videotape.
Duplication Facilities: None.
Related Materials: Unique still photographs dating from the 1840s.

MICHIGAN (Dearborn)

HENRY FORD MUSEUM AND GREENFIELD VILLAGE ARCHIVES
P.O. Box 1970
Dearborn, MI 48121-1970
(313) 271-1620

Street address: 20900 Oakwood Boulevard

Cynthia Read-Miller (Curator, Prints and Photographs)

Contact: Cynthia Read-Miller
Services: Museum. Film and videotape collection available for research, duplication, licensing and reuse, subject to restrictions.
Description: Ford Motor Company promotional films, television commercials and news releases (1950s). Includes footage of Edsel, Thunderbird, Lincoln Continental and other Ford automobiles. Also holds footage relating to company activities, including newsreel footage (1950s).

Researchers should note that the Ford Film Collection at the National Archives and Records Administration (q.v.) contains 1,500 reels on many subjects, including films illustrating the activities of the Ford Motor Company (1914-56). This collection, donated by the Ford Motor Company to the National Archives, is all in the public domain.
Size & Elements: Film: 35mm and 16mm (250 titles). Videotape: 1" and 3/4" (25 masters); VHS (25 viewing copies).
Cataloging: Catalog sheets arranged by film number. A subject index is planned, when staff time and funding permits.
Access: Available to researchers, scholars and the public for research and reuse. Research fees not charged, but staff is unable to conduct lengthy searches. Research requests accepted by mail and in person (by appointment only).
Rights: Full rights held to some material.
Licensing: Available for licensing and reuse, subject to restrictions. License fees charged. Duplication fees charged.
Restrictions: Material is licensed for one-time use only.
Viewing Facilities: Film (hand-operated viewer); videotape (VHS).
Duplication Facilities: Film (35mm to VHS); videotape (VHS to VHS).
Related Materials: Extensive collection of still photographs.

MICHIGAN (Dearborn)

SOCIETY OF MANUFACTURING ENGINEERS VIDEO COMMUNICATIONS DEPARTMENT
1 SME Drive
Dearborn, MI 48121
(313) 271-1500
Fax: (313) 271-2861
Telex: 297742

Tim Savage (Manager, Video Communications Department)

Contact: Steven Bollinger (Assistant Manager of Video Production)
Services: Association. Videotape collection available to the public for licensing and reuse.
Description: Educational materials for professionals and the public relating to various applications of manufacturing automation, including robotics; CAD/CAM; machine vision; lasers; personal computers; machining centers;

automated guided vehicles; and computer simulation.
Size & Elements: Videotape: 3/4" (200 videotapes, each 20 min.; masters); VHS (viewing copies).
Cataloging: Shot lists.
Access: Open to the public. Research requests accepted in person (by appointment only).
Rights: Full rights held to some material.
Licensing: Available for licensing and reuse. License and usage fees charged.
Restrictions: None specified.
Viewing Facilities: Videotape (3/4").
Duplication Facilities: None.

MICHIGAN (Detroit)

AMERICAN CONCRETE INSTITUTE
P.O. Box 19150
Detroit, MI 48219-0150
(313) 532-2600
Fax: (313) 538-0655
Telex: (810) 221-1454

Street address: 22400 West Seven Mile Road, Detroit, MI 48219-1849

George F. Leyh (Executive Vice President)

Contacts: Betty Borschell (Librarian); Michael A. Clark (Manager of Certification)
Services: Trade association. Videotape library available primarily for rental; available for licensing, subject to restrictions.
Description: Training videotapes covering topics such as concrete field testing, concrete laboratory testing and concrete finishing.
Size & Elements: Videotape: 3/4", VHS, Betamax I and II (5 titles).
Cataloging: Published catalog.
Access: Available for distribution and rental rather than for research or reuse.
Rights: Full rights held to all material. Additional clearances may be necessary in some cases if material is to be reused.
Licensing: Apply for information. Rental and license fees charged (price depends on amount of material used).
Restrictions: None specified.
Viewing Facilities: Videotape (VHS).
Duplication Facilities: None.

MICHIGAN (Detroit)

GENERAL MOTORS CORPORATION
3044 West Grand Boulevard
Detroit, MI 48202
(313) 556-5000
Fax: (313) 974-8266

Material housed at:
GM VIDEO
465 West Milwaukee Avenue
Detroit, MI 48202

Contacts: Public Relations Department: S. Allan Csiky (313/556-2011); Len Marsico (313/556-1139).
Services: Corporation; corporate archives. Film and videotape materials available for research, duplication, licensing and reuse, subject to restrictions.
Description: Historical and current films and videotapes produced by, for and about the various divisions of the General Motors Corporation.

The historical collection contains several hundred films (all release prints). Major subjects include:
Automobile design and styling. Body Bountiful (1955) pictures the conception, design, testing and production of an automobile body. *Modes and Motors* (1938) shows the process of designing a new car, and the "seven basic shapes of beauty." *Styling the Motor Car* (1949) dramatizes the contribution of applied art to the evolution and basic improvement of the automobile.
Automobiles and their operation. Numerous films, including the *ABC of the Automobile* series, showing the operation of the chassis, engine, catalytic converter, the Diesel engine, the high-energy ignition system and internal combustion engine.
Diesel engines. More Power For You (1956), a visit to the GM "Powerama" in Chicago (the largest industrial show ever staged) shows the GM "Aerotrain," a vertical takeoff plane, a cotton gin, a sawmill, and an outdoor

musical show featuring dancing bulldozers intermingled with trapeze artists and trained elephants.

Economics. The *Bird's Eye View of Economics* series (produced in 1951) was designed to promote the American free market economic system, and includes four films: *Joe Learns a Thing or Two, Where Joe's Living Comes From, How Joe Gets His Living* and *Joe and His Government. Fences and Gates* brings economic theory into perspective by an examination of the efforts of a young jazz-rock band to "turn a profit."

Environmental concerns. Air Pollution and Cars (1969), "a layman's look at the causes of smog and what is being done to reduce it." *The Answer is Clear* (1968) discusses air pollution from the viewpoint of a bus driver, played by Wally Cox.

Futurism. Caravan (1941), the story of the GM "Parade of Progress" caravan, which traveled throughout the United States, Canada, Cuba and Mexico, exhibiting homes of the past, present and future; the story of the evolution of power; and a kitchen unit that freezes and fries at the same time. *Easy Street* shows the Firebird III "dream car" and future innovations, such as automatic guidance, the electronic highway, the "Unicontrol" (concentrating all driving controls into a single fingertip knob) and highway information delivered to the driver by radio. *Fair Today...Futurama Tomorrow* pictures the GM pavilion at the 1964-65 New York World's Fair. *Firebird II* demonstrates the gas turbine-powered dream car of 1956, with an all-titanium body. *Futurama '64* shows the planning and design of the GM exhibit at the New York World's Fair. *Living Unlimited* (1956) is an animated film on the "kitchen of tomorrow." *On To Jupiter* (1939) "shows how science is continually pushing back the horizon and leading America toward finer things and a better life." *Out Of This World* (1964) shows kitchens exhibited at the GM Futurama in New York. *Tomorrow and Today in Kitchens* (1955) documents the "Frigidaire Kitchen of Tomorrow," a major exhibit of the GM Motorama.

General Motors history. Achievement USA (1955) pictures the celebration in Flint, Michigan (November 21, 1954) marking the production of the 50 millionth automobile by GM.

The *Close-Ups* (1938-40) show GM executives; a preview of the New York World's Fair of 1939; a Diesel-powered New York-Los Angeles "streamliner"; the construction and completion of the GM exhibit at the New York World's Fair; the monopoly investigation in Washington; tests at the GM proving ground in Phoenix, Arizona; the San Francisco World's Fair of 1939; the first automobile ride of the Dionne quintuplets (in a new Buick); North American Aviation in Inglewood, California; and the 25 millionth GM automobile.

From Fields to Wheels (1967) shows the effects of a large industrial plant — the Chevrolet assembly plant in Lordstown, Ohio — on a rural community.

The *GM Club* series (1941-76) includes plans for postwar car pricing and styling (1941); war production (1944); victory gardens (1944); automotive design (1953); Parade of Progress launching in Detroit (1953); Motoramas (1953-56); the inaugural run of the Aerotrain (1956); safety demonstrations (1956); the dedication of the new GM Technical Center (1956); an automatically-guided car (1958); the Firebird III "dream car" (1958); preparations for and exhibits at the New York World's Fair (1964); labor negotiations (1964); and miscellaneous coverage of GM executives (1940s-70s).

Also holds filmed coverage of various GM annual meetings and speeches by executives.

Highways. Freeway and highway construction is pictured in several films, including *Anatomy of a Road* (1969). *Let's Get Out of the Muddle* (1951), featuring TV commentator John Daly, points out America's need for a first-class road network.

Home appliances. A Crown for Catherine (1960) "shows how an industry teams with homemakers to create appliances that can transform dreams into reality." *How To Get the Most Out of Your Refrigerator* (1952) offers ideas on conserving and preparing foods. *A Kitchen Is a Feminine Thing* (1960) relates to the transition from the traditional kitchen to the "home operations center."

Motoramas. These traveling shows served as the occasion for new product announcements and presented prototype "dream" cars to the public. *A Date at the Waldorf* presents the 1950 Motorama. *Design for Dreaming* shows highlights of the 1956 Motorama; *Going Places* the 1954 Motorama; and *Transportation Unlimited* the 1949 Motorama.

Public relations. Industry and the News (1941) "deals with the philosophy of the relationships which should exist between business and the press" and features GM Chairman Alfred P. Sloan, Jr., and Roy Howard, President of Scripps-Howard Newspapers. *What Is Public Relations?* (1939) gives examples of "how GM goes about making friends."

Railroads. Several films show Diesel-electric locomotives (1938-60s).

Safety and courtesy. Behind the Wheel (1946), photographed from the driver's viewpoint, stresses the importance of the driver's attitude as well as the actual techniques of motor car operation. *Drinking Drivers* (1969) shows

inebriated volunteers at the GM proving ground. *Home at the Wheel* (1953) "dramatizes the very qualities women possess which can make them the most gracious and skillful drivers on the road. They don't have to learn anything complicated or mechanical, nor do they have to adopt any masculine traits...all they need is confidence. For when they take driving in their stride with the same poise and assurance with which they keep the home-fires burning, women drivers find that running errands in the family car actually becomes a pleasure rather than being a chore." *On Two Wheels* (1940) shows a bicycle traffic court run by youngsters. *Unrestrained Flying Objects* (1968) shows unbelted dummies in automobile accidents. *We Drivers* (produced in various versions) is a classic driving safety "attitude" film.

Sales training. Various films produced for GM internal groups and dealers' organizations, including *The Boss Takes His Coat Off* (1942).

Soap Box Derby. Various films (1930s-70s) on the Soap Box Derby, showing the national finals at the Derby Downs course in Akron, Ohio, construction of home-built coasters, and tributes to the hobby.

World War II. Several films made to inspire civilians and war workers to greater production, including *America Can Give It* (1942) and *Communique from Middletown* (1943). *Around the World With G.M.* shows GM war products serving throughout the world. *Highballing to Victory* presents scenes of trucks at work under fire in the European theater of operations (the "Red Ball Express") and in the China-Burma-India theater (the "Stilwell Road"). *It's Up To Us* (1941) shows motorists how to make their automobile last longer under wartime conditions. *Now Is the Time* (1941) "dramatically portrays the might of American Industry as it is being geared to the task of building an impregnable defense of America." *Victory News Parades* contain short newsreel-style clips on GM wartime activities, including submarine building, "E" awards and camouflaging.

Unedited film footage. Various television news clips produced in the mid-1950s on GM automobiles and other company activities. Record photography of GM company and UAW officials, automobiles, manufacturing and equipment.

More recent activities of the corporation are documented in the videotape collection, numbering approximately 2,000 titles, most produced internally. Subjects covered include high technology (e.g., robotic welding, robotic painting and "CAD/CAM" systems); solar-powered racing cars; and recent automobile manufacturing and models.

Size & Elements: Film: 35mm (several titles); 16mm (approx. 300 titles; release prints). Some film has been transferred to 1" videotape masters. Videotape: 1", Betacam and 3/4" (approx. 2,000 titles).

Cataloging: Title list (films only); staff assistance; computerized videotape cataloging for staff use only.

Access: Open to researchers and scholars only. Available for duplication, licensing and reuse, subject to restrictions. Research fees charged. Research requests accepted by mail and telephone.

Rights: Full rights held to all material.

Licensing: Available for licensing, subject to restrictions. Flat license fees charged (apply for information).

Restrictions: All requests for research and reuse subject to acceptance and approval by the Public Relations Department.

Viewing Facilities: Film and videotape.

Duplication Facilities: Videotape (1", Betacam and 3/4"). Film-to-videotape transfers performed by outside facilities.

MOTOR VEHICLE MANUFACTURERS ASSOCIATION COMMUNICATIONS DEPARTMENT

7430 Second Avenue, Suite 300
Albert Kahn Building
Detroit, MI 48202
(313) 872-4311
Fax: (313) 872-5400
Telex: (313) 872-4311-260

Thomas H. Hanna (President)

Contact: Gene McKinney (Director of Communications)
Services: Association. Film and videotape material available for duplication and reuse.
Description: Association is a research, statistics and information source for and about the motor vehicle industry.

Collection deals with safety issues and drinking and driving, including: several educational films and videotapes on the automobile industry; public service announcements (PSAs); and a presentation on occupant protection, side-impact crash testing and seat belt safety.

Also holds one "B" roll videotape on automotive design, manufacturing and testing (10 min.), available for stock footage use. Contents include: automotive engineers using computers to assist with designing cars; computer-guided robot draws blueprint; automotive craftsmen working with wood, clay and plastic models; futuristic car undergoes wind tunnel test, then runs on highway; testing windshield wipers, doors, seat cushions and window mechanisms; manual welding and sheet metal preparation; robot welders and transfer machines moving body components throughout plant; stamping presses; automated welding and transfer machines and operations; hand-finishing car bodies and dipping in rustproofing bath; robot paint sprayers in action; various final assembly scenes; automated engine and transmission machining and handling operations, ending with transmission being joined to engine; sewing upholstery, fabricating seats and seat installation in car. Also includes various proving ground tests, including car through splash test, brake test, car impacts barrier, running shots on proving ground roads; salt water spray; car off-road in mud, car up steep grade; electronic instrumentation on instrument panel; car zigzags through traffic cones; car in test cell; and other shots of proving grounds.
Size & Elements: Film: 16mm (1 film). Videotape: 3/4" (2 videotapes). PSAs (approx. 12) are mainly film with some 3/4" videotape.
Cataloging: None specified.
Access: Available to the public. Research fees not charged. Research requests accepted by mail, telephone and in person (by appointment only).
Rights: Full rights held to all material. Additional clearances may be necessary if side-impact footage is to be reused.
Licensing: Available for licensing and reuse. License and usage fees not charged.
Restrictions: None specified.
Viewing Facilities: None.
Duplication Facilities: None.

MICHIGAN (Detroit)

WAYNE STATE UNIVERSITY
ARCHIVES OF LABOR AND URBAN AFFAIRS
Walter Reuther Library
Detroit, MI 48202
(313) 577-4024

Street address: 5401 Cass Avenue

Dr. Philip P. Mason (Director)

Contacts: Margery Long; Thomas Featherstone (Archivists)
Services: Library and archives. Film and videotape collection available to researchers and scholars only for research, duplication, licensing and reuse, subject to restrictions.
Description: Labor and local history. Four major collections are held:
United Automobile Workers (UAW) Collection. 1,500 films; mostly 16mm; some videotape material. Begins late 1930s, but majority of material dates from late 1940s-early 1980s. Contains completed films (generally release prints withdrawn from the UAW film distribution library) and outtakes and stock footage from UAW productions (various elements, including negatives, workprints and A&B rolls). Most films were originally produced either for showing to UAW members or as public relations films intended for a broader audience. An inventory is available for examination by researchers on the premises.
WDIV-TV Collection. 1,000 rolls of film (lengths vary). Daily newsfilm and some stock footage shot in the Detroit metropolitan area (1973-78). The majority of this material was aired; there are some outtakes. All film is 16mm color reversal positive with magnetic soundtrack. Reuse of this collection is subject to special restrictions.
American Federation of Labor-Congress of Industrial Organizations (AFL-CIO) Collection. Approximately 400 titles. Films on labor unions, labor organizing, labor history, economics and other subjects. All are 16mm release prints withdrawn from the AFL-CIO distribution library; most films were originally intended for showing to union members and, in some cases, to general audiences.
Wayne State University Historical Collection. A small number of films (1930s-70s), mostly produced within the University, and some unedited footage. All relate in some way to the history of Wayne State University.
Size & Elements: Film: 35mm and 16mm (over 2,900 items total, primarily 16mm). Videotape: various formats (approx. 200 videotapes).
Cataloging: Inventories are maintained for specific collections and are

available for reference upon request. Archivists can assist in locating specific subjects of interest within the collection. There are no published finding aids. A small percentage of the material has been formally cataloged; cataloging continues as time permits.
Access: Open to researchers and scholars only. Persons wishing to use collection must be engaged in legitimate research projects. Available for duplication and reuse. If material is to be reused, a written description of intended use is required. Research assistance provided free for one hour; thereafter, research fees are charged. Research requests accepted by mail, telephone and in person (by appointment only).
Rights: Full rights held to some material. Additional clearances may be necessary in some cases if material is to be reused. In general, the Archives is free to make material available for reuse, subject to donor and copyright restrictions.
Licensing: Available for licensing and reuse, subject to restrictions. License and usage fees charged.
Restrictions: Copyright and donor restrictions apply. If material is to be reused, a written description of intended use is required.
Viewing Facilities: Film (16mm flatbed viewing table and projector).
Duplication Facilities: Film can be transferred to videotape elsewhere within the University.

MICHIGAN (Detroit)

WAYNE STATE UNIVERSITY
DIRECTIONS FOR EDUCATION IN NURSING VIA TECHNOLOGY
COLLEGE OF NURSING
Cohn Building, Room 15
5557 Cass Avenue
Detroit, MI 48202
(313) 577-4086

For rental inquiries:
AMERICAN JOURNAL OF NURSING COMPANY
VIDEOTAPE LIBRARY
c/o USCAN International
110 West Hubbard Street
Chicago, IL 60610
(312) 828-1146

For sales inquiries:
AMERICAN JOURNAL OF NURSING COMPANY
EDUCATIONAL SERVICES DIVISION
555 West 57th Street
New York, NY 10019
(212) 582-8820

In Canada:
INTERNATIONAL TELE-FILM ENTERPRISES, LTD.
47 Densley Avenue
Toronto, ON M6M 5A8
(416) 241-4483

Contact: Gerald Otzman (at Wayne State University)
Services: University-based production center. Educational videotapes available for rental and purchase.
Description: Lessons relating to generic nursing education, staff development and continuing education programs.
Over one hundred lesson titles, including: *Giving a Bed Bath; Surgical Asepsis; Dynamics of Fluid Exchange; Diuretics; Nursing Responsibilities in the Care of the Patient on a Circoelectric Bed; Principles of Administration of Medications; Equipment used in Gastric and Intestinal Decompression; A Means of Assistance to Ambulation: Crutch Walking; Intravenous Therapy: Basic Concepts; Care of the Patient in Traction; Care of the Patient with Endotracheal Intubation or a Tracheostomy; Clinical Application of Fluid & Electrolyte Imbalance: Deficits/Excesses; Human Sexuality III: Sexual Health Care in the Nursing Process;* and *Emotional Adaptation to Physical Illness: Crisis Intervention.*
Size & Elements: Film: 16mm. Videotape: 3/4". (21 lessons in color; 107 lessons in black and white, each approx. 30 min.).
Cataloging: Published catalog.
Access: Available to the public for rental and purchase.
Rights: Wayne State University holds full rights to all material.
Licensing: Apply for information.
Restrictions: None specified.

MICHIGAN (Detroit)

Viewing Facilities: None.
Duplication Facilities: None.
Related Materials: Study guides correlating to lesson videotapes.

MICHIGAN (Detroit)

**WAYNE STATE UNIVERSITY
FOLKLORE ARCHIVE**
448 Purdy Library
Detroit, MI 48202
(313) 577-4053

Dr. Janet L. Langlois (Director, Folklore Archives)

Contacts: Dr. Janet Langlois; Suzanne Kent
Services: Educational institution. Videotape collection open to the public for in-house use only.
Description: *English American and Finnish: Charles Tapola Interview,* an interview with a Finnish couple (the Tapolas) in Princeton, Michigan (November 19, 1973). Videotape covers the oral history of Market County, its mining industry and the local Finnish community. Charles Tapola lives in a log house built by his father in 1908. He is a miner, a well-known local craftsman and the last blacksmith in Market County to be employed by the Cleveland Cliffs Iron Co.
  Free Play — Program 21, a television program for Detroit Public TV, WTVS Channel 56 (recorded February 21, 1969). Shows two musicians, one from Texas and the other from from West Virginia, who perform their folk songs in a bar in Detroit. They are interviewed about their personal backgrounds and discuss issues including "Southern Hill" country song (Kentucky and Tennessee), "White Blues" song, the difference between life in the cities and the Hills, and folk music values.
Size & Elements: Videotape: 2" and 1/2" (2 titles).
Cataloging: None specified.
Access: Available to the public. For in-house use only.
Rights: Full rights held to all material.
Licensing: Apply for information.
Restrictions: None specified.
Viewing Facilities: Film and videotape.
Duplication Facilities: None.

MICHIGAN (East Lansing)

THE EDUCATIONAL INSTITUTE OF THE AMERICAN HOTEL & MOTEL ASSOCIATION
P.O. Box 1240
East Lansing, MI 48826
(517) 353-5500
Fax: (517) 353-5527
Telex: (810) 251-0701

Street address: 1407 South Harrison Road, East Lansing, MI 48823

E. Ray Swan (Executive Director)

Contact: Robert Page (Director of Telecommunications) (517/372-8370)
Services: Association; educational division. Videotapes available for purchase.
Description: Hotel and motel service, management and careers.
  Titles include: *Professional Dining Room Service,* training food and beverage servers to use proper serving procedures and techniques throughout all phases of the dining experience; *Hotel/Motel Careers: Check In Today!,* a look at the variety of choices, opportunities and rewards that can come from a career in the hospitality industry; *Front Office,* a series covering service strategies, including tips on how to handle an irate guest; *Housekeeping: Professional Guestroom Cleaning,* demonstrating how to clean in a professional, logical and thorough manner; *Housekeeping: Communications and Motivation,* stressing guest and fellow-employee relations, professionalism and the importance of housekeeping; *Hotel Security on Trial,* sensitizing Chief Executive Officers, hotel and motel managers, owners, and top-level supervisors to the issue of security in the hospitality industry, and dramatizing a hotel/motel security case that has gone to court; *Serving Alcohol with Care,* dramatically illustrating the "do's and don'ts" of serving alcohol and sensitizing managers and servers to the potential liabilities associated with alcohol service.
  Videotapes soon to be available cover courtesy van driver safety, security, personal computer applications for the lodging industry and sales.
Size & Elements: Videotape: VHS (9 titles).

Cataloging: Brochure.
Access: Available for purchase.
Rights: Apply for information.
Licensing: Apply for information.
Restrictions: None specified.
Viewing Facilities: None.
Duplication Facilities: None.

MICHIGAN (East Lansing)

**MICHIGAN STATE UNIVERSITY
ARCHIVES AND HISTORICAL COLLECTIONS**
EG-13 Library
East Lansing, MI 48824-1046
(517) 355-2330

Dr. Frederick L. Honhart (Director)

Contacts: John Sanford; Dorothy Frye (Archival Specialists).
Services: University archives. Material available for licensing and reuse, subject to restrictions.
Description: Films documenting the history and activities of Michigan State University, as well as a variety of other subjects. Major strengths of the collection are Big Ten football films (1949-present), other intercollegiate athletics, agricultural education (1940-80), and South Vietnam (1954-62).
Size & Elements: Film: various formats (approx. 2,000 films; black and white and color). Videotape: format unspecified (small collection).
Cataloging: Card catalogs; inventory book; computerized cataloging for staff use.
Access: Open to the public. Available for duplication. Research fees not charged. Requests accepted by mail, telephone and in person.
Rights: Full rights held to some material. Some rights held to all material. Rights status of some material not known. Additional clearances may be necessary in some cases if material is to be reused.
Licensing: Apply for information. License and usage fees charged under some conditions.
Restrictions: Restrictions may apply to some materials.
Viewing Facilities: Film.
Duplication Facilities: Reproduction available, in most cases, through the University Archives and Historical Collections.

MICHIGAN (Flint)

**MERLE G. PERRY ARCHIVES
ALFRED P. SLOAN MUSEUM**
1221 East Kearsley Street
Flint, MI 48503
(313) 762-1415

Street address: 303 Walnut Street

David C. White (Curator)

Contacts: David C. White; Carol deKalands (Assistant Curator)
Services: Museum. Film collection open to researchers, scholars and the public. Material possibly available for licensing and reuse.
Description: Local history museum dedicated to Flint and Genesee County, Michigan. Collection includes 16mm news footage from Flint television station WGRT (1958-72) and approximately six films relating to the automobile industry, produced by General Motors Corporation and Buick Motor Company.
Size & Elements: Film: 16mm (250 cans).
Cataloging: Computerized cataloging for staff use only.
Access: Open to the public. For in-house use only. Research fees not charged. Research requests accepted by mail.
Rights: Some rights held to all material.
Licensing: Possibly available for licensing and reuse (apply for information). License and usage fees charged for profit-making projects.
Restrictions: None specified.
Viewing Facilities: Film.
Duplication Facilities: None.

MICHIGAN (Grand Rapids)

GRTV — ARCHIVES
50 Library Plaza, NE

Grand Rapids, MI 49503
(616) 459-4788

Dirk Koning (Executive Director)

Contact: Judy Crandall (Programming Coordinator)
Services: Public access television facility. Videotape collection maintained primarily for in-house use.
Description: Videotapes relating to local history, world peace issues and veterans' issues, all produced through the public access center.
Size & Elements: Videotape: 3/4" and 1/2" (amount unspecified).
Cataloging: Computerized cataloging for staff use only.
Access: For in-house use only. Research fees not charged. Research requests accepted in person (by appointment only).
Rights: Material in the public domain.
Licensing: Apply for information. License fees not charged.
Restrictions: None specified.
Viewing Facilities: Videotape (3/4" and 1/2").
Duplication Facilities: Film (16mm and 8mm); videotape (3/4" and 1/2").

MICHIGAN (Highland Park)

**CHRYSLER MOTORS CORPORATION
PHOTOGRAPHIC SERVICES**
12800 Oakland Avenue
Highland Park, MI 48288
(313) 956-4111
Fax: (313) 252-7363

Manfred H. Strobel (Manager, Photographic Services)

Contact: Manfred H. Strobel
Services: Corporate archives. Film and videotape available for reuse, subject to restrictions.
Description: Historical and promotional films and videotapes from Chrysler Corporation and its subsidiaries. Holdings include product films (1914-present); travelogues (1930s); racing films (1960s); dealer introduction and promotion films; racing shots; safety and economy tips; stunt driving; and *The Story of Jeep*.
Size & Elements: Film: 16mm (300 titles). Videotape: 3/4" and VHS (500 titles).
Cataloging: Card catalogs; computerized cataloging available to researchers.
Access: Not open to the public. Available for duplication. Research fees not charged. Research requests accepted by mail and telephone.
Rights: Some rights held to some material.
Licensing: Available for licensing and reuse, subject to restrictions. License fees not charged.
Restrictions: Restrictions may apply to reuse of some material.
Viewing Facilities: Film and videotape.
Duplication Facilities: Videotape (3/4", VHS and Betamax; limited facilities).
Related Materials: The Chrysler Historical Collection consists of photographs, shop manuals, owners' manuals, brochures, sales literature and dealer books.

MICHIGAN (Lansing)

WHITE STAR PROFESSIONAL FILM SERVICES, INC.
16641 Airport Road
Lansing, MI 48906
(517) 321-4889
(517) 321-1776

Richard G. Cole (President)
Dean R. Olson, Jr. (Vice President)

Contacts: Richard G. Cole; Dean R. Olson
Services: Film and videotape producer; stock footage sales library.
Description: Subjects and locations pertaining to Michigan (1948-87) such as medicine, education, wildlife, travel, people, various commercial products, the State Capitol, Michigan State University, highway construction and usage, state police activities and seasonal views of Michigan.
Size & Elements: Film: format unspecified (originals and release prints). Videotape: various formats (masters and viewing copies). (600 titles, 1,800 items total).
Cataloging: Card catalogs.

Access: Available for licensing and reuse. Research requests accepted by mail, telephone and in person (by appointment only).
Rights: Full rights held to all material. Additional clearances may be necessary in some cases if material is to be reused.
Licensing: Available for licensing and reuse. License fees charged.
Restrictions: None specified.
Viewing Facilities: Film (flatbed, viewers and projector).
Duplication Facilities: Film and videotape.

MICHIGAN (Rochester)

SINGER-SHARRETTE TRADITIONAL HEALING FILMS
52370 Dequindre
Rochester, MI 48063
(313) 731-5199

or contact:
c/o Dr. Philip Singer
2810 Indian Lake Road
Oxford, MI 48051
(313) 693-9447

Bill Sharrette; Dr. Philip Singer (Principals)

Contacts: Dr. Philip Singer; Bill Sharrette
Services: Film and videotape producer and distributor. Completed films available for rental and purchase. Stock footage available to the public for duplication, licensing and reuse; subject to restrictions.
Description: Films relating to traditional healing practices around the world, studied from scientific and medical viewpoints. Exclusive U.S. distributor of World Health Organization films. Titles and subjects include:
Traditional healing series. Seven films on healing practices in Nigeria, including rural and urban specialists; positive and negative aspects of traditional healing; a Lagos male "gynecologist/midwife"; the African way of conceiving mental illness; the initiation of candidates into the secret lineage of healers; and the use of hallucinogenic herbs for "fourth eye" altered states of consciousness.
Israel. Cupping For Pain Control shows the ancient practice and demonstrates the importance of the healer-patient relationship.
Guyana. Trance, Dance and Healing in Guyana shows healers and patients "playing" the Big and Little Traditional Gods of India after achieving altered states of consciousness, and the treatment of mental illnesses.
Philippines. Two films on psychic surgery and paranormal healing practices demonstrate the treatment of patient conditions in European, American and Philippine patients, showing such techniques as incisions at a distance, massage, cupping, eye surgery, automatic writing and trance.
"Psychic Surgery": A Case History of Shamanic Sleight-of-Hand (1988, videotape) shows the subtleties of deception that creep into demonstrations of paranormal healing.
India. In *Hindu Loaves and Fishes — India,* a holy man appears to materialize sacred Indian food (Prasad) and transport objects from a distance (telekinesis).
Montana. Water Witching (Dowsing) in Middle America (1987, videotape) visits an annual gathering of dowsers in Montana, showing equipment, experiences and techniques. Though it presents no real test of validity, the anthropological analysis stresses the normal rather than the magical definition of the practice.
Medicine Woman/Medicine Man: Traditional Holistic Medicine in Middle America employs two magico-religious practitioners and shows that traditional holistic medicine can transcend specific cultural boundaries, creating a non-specific placebo that permits subjective relief.
World Health Organization films. Films on primary health care in Mexico, Benin, Thailand, Finland, Ghana, Kenya, Mozambique and Vietnam.
Size & Elements: Film: 16mm (approx. 27 titles, each 6 to 60 min.; originals and release prints). Videotape: Betacam, 3/4" and VHS (masters and viewing copies; most transferred from film).
Cataloging: Published catalog sheets.
Access: Available to the public for rental and purchase. Footage available for duplication, licensing and reuse on a case-by-case basis, subject to restrictions. Research fees charged in some cases. Research requests accepted by mail and telephone.
Rights: Full rights held to all material. Additional clearances may be necessary in some cases if material is to be reused (Singer-Sharrette will handle any needed clearances).
Licensing: Available for licensing and reuse, subject to restrictions. License

fees charged.
Restrictions: Requests for reuse considered on a case-by-case basis, depending on intended use.
Viewing Facilities: Film and videotape (by special arrangement).
Duplication Facilities: None.
Related Services: Dr. Philip Singer can also provide access to individuals with knowledge in all areas of traditional healing.

MICHIGAN (Troy)

MVP COMMUNICATIONS
1075 Rankin
Troy, MI 48083
(313) 588-7600
Fax: (313) 588-1899

Dick Hanson (President)

Contact: Staff
Services: Videotape producer. Material available to the public for duplication, licensing and reuse, subject to restrictions.
Description: Contemporary color footage, featuring a substantial amount of automotive material, including manufacturing, automobile racing, engineering, automotive products and beauty shots of cars; and scenics of all areas of the U.S., including coastal, aerial, urban and landscape shots.
Size & Elements: Videotape: Betacam and 3/4" (6,000 videotapes, each 20 min.).
Cataloging: Computerized cataloging for staff use only.
Access: Some material available to the public for duplication and reuse. Research fees charged.
Rights: Full rights held to some material. Some rights held to all material. Additional clearances will be necessary in some cases if material is to be reused.
Licensing: Available for licensing, subject to restrictions. License fees charged.
Restrictions: Requests for reuse of certain material subject to client approval; some material not available for broadcast use.
Viewing Facilities: Videotape (1", Betacam, 3/4" and VHS).
Duplication Facilities: Videotape (1", Betacam, 3/4" and VHS).

MICHIGAN (Troy)

VOLKSWAGEN OF AMERICA, INC.
888 West Big Beaver Road
Troy, MI 48007-3951
(313) 362-6122
Fax: (313) 362-6732

Contact: Camille Paluscio (Public Relations Services)
Services: Corporation; corporate archives. Film and videotape material available for distribution, licensing and reuse, subject to restrictions.
Description: Film and some videotape relating to Volkswagen history and products (1960s-present).
     In addition to archival material, there are three productions in current distribution: *Race to the Clouds* (1985, 30 min.), a travelogue featuring Audi automobiles in a race to the summit of Pike's Peak, featuring driver Michelle Mouton; *Think Fast* (1986, 23 min.), featuring a husband/wife team in the Volkswagen Cup Race, rallying and Super-V driving; and *King of the Hill* (1986).
     Archives plans to publish a catalog in the future and establish a stock film operation.
Size & Elements: Film: 16mm (originals). Videotape: 3/4" (originals and transfers from film).
Cataloging: None.
Access: Available to the public for rental and licensing, subject to restrictions.
Rights: Full rights held to all material. Research requests accepted by mail and telephone.
Licensing: Available for licensing, subject to restrictions. License fees charged (apply for information).
Restrictions: Requests for licensing considered on a case-by-case basis.
Viewing Facilities: Videotape.
Duplication Facilities: None.

MICHIGAN (West Bloomfield)

CHIAPPETTA PRODUCTIONS, INC.
4241 Cherry Hill Drive
West Bloomfield, MI 48033
(313) 682-0506

Jerry Chiappetta (President)

Contacts: Jerry Chiappetta; Rita Chiappetta
Services: Stock footage sales library.
Description: Wildlife and outdoor activity in the U.S. and Canada. Extensive coverage of outdoor recreational activities, including fishing, hunting, snowmobiling, skiing, ski jumping, dog sledding, canoeing and sport aviation.
Size & Elements: Film: 16mm (color negative and reversal). Videotape: 1" (masters).
Cataloging: Shot lists.
Access: Available to the public. Available for duplication, licensing and reuse. Research fees charged. Research requests accepted by mail, telephone and in person (by appointment only). A deposit is required in order to begin a search.
Rights: Full rights held to all material.
Licensing: Available for licensing and reuse. License fees charged.
Restrictions: None specified.
Viewing Facilities: Film and videotape.
Duplication Facilities: Available on request.

MICHIGAN (Ypsilanti)

HIGH/SCOPE EDUCATIONAL RESEARCH FOUNDATION
600 North River Street
Ypsilanti, MI 48198
(313) 485-2000

Contact: Consultants
Services: Alternative educational organization; film and videotape distributor.
Description: Materials relating to the High/Scope Cognitively Oriented Preschool Curriculum, an early childhood alternative education system developed in the 1960s.
     Sample film titles include the *Helping Children Make Choices and Decisions* series, produced in several Head Start centers; *Key Experiences for Intellectual Development During the Preschool Years; Learning About Time in the Preschool Years; Observing Role Play; Learning Through Problems: A Baby's Point of View;* and *Learning to Talk: An Introduction to Language Development in Infancy.*
     Videotapes in the *Small-Group Time Video Series* include: *Counting With Bears; Plan-Do-Review With Found Materials; Working With Staplers; Representing With Sticks & Balls;* and *Exploring With Paint & Corks.*
Size & Elements: Film: 16mm. Videotape: format unspecified. (Approx. 50 titles total).
Cataloging: Published catalog.
Access: Available to the public for rental and purchase. Rental fees charged. Rental requests accepted by mail. Inquiries accepted by telephone; ask switchboard for consultants.
Rights: Full rights held to most material.
Licensing: Apply for information. Fees for reuse must be individually negotiated.
Restrictions: None specified.
Viewing Facilities: None.
Duplication Facilities: None.

MINNESOTA

MINNESOTA (Apple Valley)

MINNESOTA ZOO
CREATIVE SERVICES DEPARTMENT
12101 Johnnycake Road
Apple Valley, MN 55124
(612) 431-9237

Don Strand (Creative Services Manager)

Contacts: Don Strand; Dennis Bergman (A/V Technician)
Services: Zoological garden; stock footage sales library. Can shoot broadcast quality videotape upon request.
Description: Wild and domestic animals (all residents of the Minnesota Zoo)

featuring hundreds of species in natural settings and foliage, both native Minnesotan and Southeast Asian. Also available are award-winning multi-image and videotape programs which provide an educational and entertaining look at nature and a modern zoo.

Species featured on videotape include: alligators, Asian wild horses, bactrian camels, beavers, beluga whales, bison, boa constrictors, Canadian lynx, Celebes apes, chevrotain, dolphins, ducks, egrets, elk, ermine, fisher, fjord horse, flamingoes, fox, geese, greater Indian hornbill, hawk, loon, lion-tailed macaque, moose, muntjac, musk oxen, otters, owls, parrots, porcupine, prairie dogs, pronghorn antelope, puma, pythons, rattlesnakes, raven, red panda, reindeer, Siberian tigers, sloth bears, snow monkeys, striped and spotted skunks, swans, Tahr goats, tarantula, wallabies, weasel, white-cheeked gibbon, wolverine and woodchuck.

Collection also includes many varieties of waterfowl, fishes and tropical birds, as well as crowd shots, behind-the-scenes zoo activities, veterinary procedures, keeper activities, zoo classes, foliage and scenery shots.
Size & Elements: Videotape: 3/4" (300 videotapes; each 20 to 30 min.).
Cataloging: Computerized cataloging for staff use only.
Access: Open to the public. Available for licensing and reuse. Research fees charged. Research requests accepted by mail, telephone and in person (walk-in).
Rights: Full rights held to all material.
Licensing: Available for licensing and reuse. License fees charged.
Restrictions: None specified.
Viewing Facilities: Videotape (3/4" and VHS).
Duplication Facilities: Videotape (3/4" and VHS).
Related Materials: Audiotapes and photographs.

MINNESOTA (Center City)

HAZELDEN FOUNDATION EDUCATIONAL MATERIALS
Pleasant Valley Road, Box 176
Center City, MN 55012
(800) 328-9000 (U.S. only)
(800) 257-0700 (Minnesota only)
(612) 257-4010 (Alaska and outside U.S.)

Karen Elliott (Director of Educational Materials)

Contact: Kerry Finn (Staff Film and Video Producer)
Services: Drug treatment center; film and videotape producer and distributor. Material available for rental and purchase, and for licensing and reuse on a case-by-case basis, subject to restrictions.
Description: Educational materials on drug addiction, alcoholism, eating disorders, psychological disorders and mental health. Some are in-house productions to which Hazelden holds rights; most are outside productions available for distribution only.

Hazelden-produced titles include: *Crack,* a documentary on crack addiction and social problems relating to the drug, filmed on location in New York City; *Cocaine: Beyond the Looking Glass; Falling Back: The Dry Drunk Syndrome; The Physiological Effects of Cocaine: Comprehensive Facts about Cocaine for Professionals; Hooked: The Psychology of Intoxication; Dark Secrets, Bright Victory: One Woman's Recovery from Bulimia; Family Matters,* a film about five families' struggles with addiction; and *Denial: The Inside Story.*

Hazelden Video Lecture Series. Topics include: *A.A. and the Self-Help Group Movement; Coping with Unmanageability; Denial; Diagnosis of Drug Dependency; Group Dynamics; The Nature of Drug Dependency; Shame and Guilt; Spiritual Awakening; Use of Time;* and a series in which Hazelden counselors discuss the first five steps of Alcoholics Anonymous.

Hazelden also produces a series, *Employee Assistance Program.* Other films by various producers cover such topics as adult children of alcoholics, physical abuse, Overeaters Anonymous, teenage substance abuse, and fetal alcohol syndrome.
Size & Elements: Film: 16mm. Videotape: 3/4" and VHS. (Approx. 50 titles total).
Cataloging: Published catalog.
Access: Available to the public for rental and purchase. Rental fees charged. Orders and inquiries accepted by mail and telephone.
Rights: Full rights held to some material. Additional clearances (from original producers) may be necessary for most material to be reused.
Licensing: Available for licensing and reuse, subject to restrictions.
Restrictions: Requests for licensing and reuse considered on a case-by-case basis, depending on usage and amount of footage requested.
Viewing Facilities: Film (16mm); videotape (3/4" and VHS).
Duplication Facilities: None (outside arrangements can be made).

MINNESOTA (Chisholm)

IRON RANGE RESEARCH CENTER
P.O. Box 392
Chisholm, MN 55719
(218) 254-3321

Street address: Highway 169 West

Dana Miller (Director)

Contacts: Edward Nelson (Archivist); Elizabeth Bright (Librarian)
Services: Government agency; library. Films and videotapes available to the public through interlibrary loan.
Description: Archival collection includes a silent film of early mining on the Mesabi Iron Range and a film relating to underground mining on the Vermilion Iron Range. Also holds unedited footage shot at the Tower-Soudan mine (1960s) and commercially acquired films.
Size & Elements: Film: 16mm (12 titles, 13 cans; positive). Videotape: format unspecified (16 videotapes).
Cataloging: Card catalogs; computerized cataloging available to researchers; other finding aids.
Access: Available to the public through interlibrary loan. Apply for information on research procedures.
Rights: Full rights held to some material.
Licensing: Apply for information.
Restrictions: None specified.
Viewing Facilities: Film and videotape.
Duplication Facilities: None.

MINNESOTA (Edina)

TIMOTHY D. KEHR ADVERTISING
6008 Saxony Road
Edina, MN 55436-1238
(612) 935-7347

Contact: Timothy D. Kehr
Services: Private film collection. Material available for duplication and reuse.
Description: Public domain feature films on film and videotape and collection of 16mm television shows from the 1950s.
Size & Elements: Film: 16mm. Videotape: 3/4" (masters). (400 titles total).
Cataloging: None specified.
Access: Available to the public. Available for duplication and reuse. Research requests accepted by telephone and in person (by appointment only).
Rights: Material in the public domain.
Licensing: Available for reuse. Usage fees charged.
Restrictions: None specified.
Viewing Facilities: Videotape.
Duplication Facilities: Videotape.

MINNESOTA (Eveleth)

U.S. HOCKEY HALL OF FAME LIBRARY
Hat Trick Avenue
Eveleth, MN 55734
(218) 744-5167

Archie Rauzi (Director)

Contact: Archie Rauzi
Services: Museum. Videotape collection open to the public.
Description: Documentation of enshrinement ceremonies of inductees into the Hockey Hall of Fame and enshrinement hockey games.

Inductees represented include: John Kirrane, Bill Cleary, John Magasich, Bill Christian, John Mariucci, Frank Brimsek, Sam Lopresti and George Bush. Material was produced locally by independent producers.
Size & Elements: Videotape: VHS (approx. 9 videotapes; masters and viewing copies).
Cataloging: None.
Access: Open to the public. Research fees not charged. Research requests accepted by mail and telephone.
Rights: Full rights held to all material. Additional clearances may be necessary in some cases if material is to be reused.
Licensing: Apply for information. License fees generally not charged;

handling costs apply.
Restrictions: Clearance must be obtained from featured hockey players if material is to be reused.
Viewing Facilities: Videotape (VHS).
Duplication Facilities: None.

MINNESOTA (Excelsior)

**TOM TALBERT PRODUCTIONS
c/o AMERICAN CITIZENS CONCERNED FOR LIFE
COMMUNICATIONS CENTER**
Box 179
Excelsior, MN 55331
(612) 474-0885

Street address: Leslie Curve

Jan Wilkins (President, Talbert Productions)

Contact: Jan Wilkins (612/777-8836)
Services: Film and videotape producer. Videotape available for rental, purchase and broadcast.
Description: *Who Broke the Baby,* a pro-life videotape narrated by teenager Casey Ivey, explores the meaning of pro-choice slogans such as "every woman has the right to control her own body" and "the fetus is not a person." The videotape is based on Dr. Jean Garton's book of the same name.
Size & Elements: Videotape: 3/4", VHS and Betamax (1 title; 28 min.).
Cataloging: Brochure available.
Access: Available for rental, purchase and broadcast through American Citizens Concerned for Life Communications Center.
Rights: Full rights held to all material.
Licensing: Available for rental, purchase and broadcast.
Restrictions: None specified.
Viewing Facilities: None.
Duplication Facilities: None.

MINNESOTA (Fridley)

ANOKA COUNTY COMMUNICATIONS WORKSHOP, INC.
350 63rd Avenue, Northeast
Fridley, MN 55432
(612) 571-9144

Michelle K. Glynn (Access Director of Operations)

Contact: Michelle K. Glynn
Services: Public access television facility. Videotape programs available for research, licensing and reuse, subject to restrictions.
Description: Videotapes produced for cablecast over Everyone's Television Channel 12 (ETC. 12). Subjects covered include music (contemporary to "extreme"); locally produced video art; the history of Fridley, Minnesota; and the "Willies Awards," administered by ACCW.
    Sample titles include: *Dick Lockman: Fridley Private Investigator; Inner Tube; Golda, a Dog Story; Channel 12 vs. Channel 3 Softball; This Isn't Cleveland;* and *The Swarm That Ate Minneapolis.*
Size & Elements: Videotape: VHS (101 videotapes).
Cataloging: Card catalogs.
Access: Open to the public. Available for research and duplication, subject to restrictions. Research fees not charged. Research requests accepted by mail, telephone and in person (by appointment only).
Rights: Rights retained by original producers.
Licensing: Available for licensing and reuse, subject to restrictions. Usage fees not charged (minimal duplication fees apply).
Restrictions: Duplication or reuse requires clearance from original producer.
Viewing Facilities: Videotape (3/4" and VHS; by appointment only).
Duplication Facilities: Videotape (3/4" and VHS).

MINNESOTA (Minneapolis)

CONUS COMMUNICATIONS
3415 University Avenue
Minneapolis, MN 55414
(612) 642-4645
Fax: (612) 642-4680

Charles H. Dutcher III (Vice President and General Manager)

Contact: Steve Cope
Services: Satellite news gathering service. Videotape material available for licensing and reuse, subject to restrictions.
Description: CONUS Communications gathers television news footage of national interest shot by approximately 80 local affiliate stations throughout the United States, and several (non-network) television news organizations in the United States, Japan and Australia. The footage is then distributed by satellite to the affiliates. Footage from affiliate stations (1984-present) is archived indefinitely. Stories from sources other than CONUS affiliates are not retained.
Size & Elements: Videotape: all formats, primarily MII and 3/4" (266 videotapes, each 60 to 90 min.; masters). Collection is constantly growing.
Cataloging: Computerized cataloging for staff use only; notebooks; staff assistance required. Material cataloged by broadcast date (date required for footage retrieval).
Access: Available to the public for reuse, subject to restrictions. Research fees included in cost of licensing. Research requests accepted by telephone.
Rights: Full rights held to all material for use in news programming only.
Licensing: Available for licensing and reuse, subject to restrictions. License and usage fees charged.
Restrictions: Requests for licensing and reuse considered on a case-by-case basis. Material cleared for use in news programming only; all other use requires clearance.
Viewing Facilities: None.
Duplication Facilities: Videotape (Betacam, MII, 3/4" and VHS; 2" and 1" duplication available for an additional charge).

MINNESOTA (Minneapolis)

FOOTAGE INC.
500 South 6th Street
Minneapolis, MN 55415
(612) 334-5905
Fax: (612) 334-5907

Richard Diercks (President)

Contact: Richard Diercks
Services: Film archives; producer; stock footage sales library.
Description: Holds archival news footage; historical jazz and music film collection; musical films (1930s-52); short subjects; "B" Westerns; World War II subjects; travelogues (1947-54, color), featuring Europe, Mexico, Costa Rica, Austria, Germany, Japan and Sweden; Hollywood; Minnesota; safari footage; rodeo footage; famous people; feature films; and documentaries.
Size & Elements: Film: 16mm (1.5 million feet; release prints, mostly black and white, 10% color). Videotape: 1" (10,000 minutes; transfers from film).
Cataloging: Card catalogs; information sheets; data retrieval cataloging system (in process).
Access: Open for viewing for specific projects only (by appointment). Research fees not charged. Research requests accepted by mail and telephone.
Rights: Some rights held to some material. Approximately 50% of material in the public domain.
Licensing: Available for licensing and reuse, subject to restrictions. License and usage fees charged in some cases.
Restrictions: Restrictions apply to some material.
Viewing Facilities: Film and videotape.
Duplication Facilities: Videotape (2", 1", 3/4", VHS and Betamax).

MINNESOTA (Minneapolis)

GENERAL MILLS, INC.
P.O. Box 1113
Minneapolis, MN 55440
(612) 540-2311

Street address: One General Mills Boulevard, Minneapolis, MN 55426

Contact: Kurt Steensland (Manager, Audiovisual Operations)
Services: Corporation; corporate archives. Film and videotape material available for in-house use only.
Description: Film and videotape material is held in two separate divisions.
    Corporate archives. Holds television commercials of every General Mills product (1940s-present); special promotional projects; and documentation of corporate events and meetings. Most material is 16mm film. *Not currently*

cataloged or accessible.

Audiovisual Department. Holds current television commercials on 1" videotape. Much of this material is also held by General Mills' advertising agencies.
Size & Elements: Film: 16mm (amount unspecified). Videotape: 1" (amount unspecified).
Cataloging: Cataloging in progress. Television commercials will be cataloged chronologically (according to product).
Access: Archives not open to the public. Audiovisual Department open to the public for inquiries. Research requests accepted by mail and telephone.
Rights: Full rights held to all material.
Licensing: Apply for information.
Restrictions: All requests for research and reuse considered on a case-by-case basis and must be directed to the Audiovisual Department.
Viewing Facilities: None.
Duplication Facilities: None.

MINNESOTA (Minneapolis)

THE IMAGE BANK, MINNEAPOLIS
822 Marquette Avenue
Minneapolis, MN 55402
(612) 332-8935
Fax: (612) 344-1717

Contact: Lora Iverson
Territory: Minnesota, North Dakota and South Dakota (Satellite office of TIB Chicago).
Services: Exclusive marketing agent for Film Search, Inc. (q.v.).

MINNESOTA (Minneapolis)

INTERMEDIA ARTS MINNESOTA
425 Ontario Street, SE
Minneapolis, MN 55414
(612) 627-4444

Tom Borrup (Executive Director)

Contact: Tom Borrup
Services: Nonprofit media arts organization. Videotape collection open to researchers and scholars for in-house viewing only. Some videotapes available for rental and purchase.
Description: Founded 1973, Intermedia Video's (formerly UCVideo) goal is to foster and advance artistic and cultural expression through new forms, mediums and technologies; and to further public appreciation, understanding and involvement in these arts. Has developed programming for broadcast and cable television, including the *Changing Channels* series (Twin Cities Public Television, 1974-78) and the Minneapolis MTN Cable Channel.

Distributes programs (1973-present) on adolescent issues; literature and fine arts; government and politics; Native American issues; performing arts; comedy; the handicapped; women's issues; and rural and agricultural issues. Produced mainly by upper Midwest and Minnesota producers. Also holds a large non-circulating videotape collection.

Adolescent issues. Titles include: *Red Light/Green Light* (1986), a videotape adaptation of a play about growing up female in the 1980s; *A Mother Is a Mother* (1982), examining teenage parenting through a discussion with young Black teenage mothers; *Just Blurt It Out!* (1980), addressing teenage sexuality, pregnancy and how to responsibly handle choices.

Literature and fine arts. Titles include: *American Grizzly* (Frederick Manfred, 1983), a portrait of an author from Siouxland who has adopted the grizzly bear as his totem animal; *The Movie at the End of the World* (1981), a portrait of the writer Tom McGrath; *A Man Writes to Part of Himself* (1978), a portrait of poet Robert Bly; *Prairie School Architecture* (1983), a lyrical look at the first truly American architecture, and its buildings throughout the Midwestern heartland.

Government and politics. Titles include: *Ashes, Ashes, We All Fall Down* (1983), an adaptation of Martha Boesing's stage play on our present nuclear predicament; *Subversive?* (1983), a biography of Terry Pettus, convicted in the 1950s under the Smith Act; *Stay With Me* (1982), about lesbian Karen Clark, who ran for state representative in Minneapolis; *A Common Man's Courage* (1977), a biography of John T. Bernard, an immigrant laborer who rose to become a U.S. congressman from Minnesota's Iron Range; *Pesticide Politics* (1976), on 2-4-5-T herbicide spraying near Britt, Minnesota; *Mother of the Year* (1984), the story of Ruth Youngdahl Nelson, an 80-year-old anti-nuclear

activist; *Labor's Turning Point* (1981), a documentary on the Minneapolis Teamsters strike of 1934, depicting its impact on Minnesota workers, and on business and political figures.

Native American issues. Titles include: *Great Spirit Within the Hole* (1983), on Indian people in U.S. prisons and how freedom of Indian religious practices aids in their rehabilitation; *Our Sacred Land* (1984), on the Oglala Sioux' fight for their legal and moral land rights; *Celebration* (1979) and *The Pipe is the Altar* (1980), on powwows and the ceremonial pipe as part of a daily prayer ritual; *Troubled Waters* (1986), about Norwegian Americans and Chippewa Indian commercial fishermen in a time of crisis, when state and federal agents entrapped them into selling illegal fish; *Clouded Land* (1986), exploring the "clouded title" of land ownership on the White Earth Ojibwe Reservation in Minnesota.

Performing arts. Titles include: *Art on Parade* (1985), documenting a gala arts parade through the streets of Minneapolis; *And One, And One, And One* (1984), an adaptation of three early plays by Gertrude Stein; *Break* (1983), a performance by Bill T. Jones; *Paris* (1982), Meredith Monk's nostalgic evocation of a Parisian bohemia; *Tympani* (1980), choreographed by Laura Dean; and *What You Just Did* (1981), on contact improvisation.

Women's issues. The Fear That Binds Us: Violence Against Women (1982) explores the history and underlying reasons for violence against women.

Handicapped issues. The Good Life (1977) is a true story of a young woman with cerebral palsy, inviting us to examine our feelings toward the handicapped.

Miscellaneous subjects. Say "I'm a Jew" (Pier Marton, 1985) is a chorus of voices of the post-Holocaust generation (born 1946-57), who inherited the legacy of terror which their parents somehow survived.

Non-circulating collection. Holds approximately 500 videotapes, primarily documentaries, many produced for public access cable television by UCVideo, and other access facilities and producers throughout the U.S. Topics include: abortion; the Abraham Lincoln Brigade; a speech by Bella Abzug; access video, including videotapes produced 1973-81; an interview with Margie Adam; advertising; Afro Americans; aging; agriculture; the American Indian Movement; amnesty; animation; art; baton twirling; Eddie Berger; biofeedback; Robert Bly; boxing; cable television and access issues; John Cage; Judy Chicago; children; civil rights; community issues, especially relating to the the Minneapolis area; consumer protection; criminal justice; dance, including videotapes on the James Cunningham Dance Workshop, the Minnesota Dance Theater, Pilobolus and the Twyla Tharp Teaching Project; an interview with Bernadette Devlin; documentaries; economics; education; energy and appropriate technology; environmental pollution; the Federal Bureau of Investigation; films from Film in the Cities; folklore; food and food issues; a performance by Al Franken and Tom Davis; freedom of speech; gay and lesbian issues; handicapped people; health; history, notably Minneapolis and St. Paul local history; housing; humor; journalism; labor issues; Latin American issues; marijuana; Minneapolis, including community issues, history, housing and urban issues; Minnesota; music; Native American issues; nuclear power and antinuclear activism; the Ozone Dance Company; Leonard Peltier; poetry; politics and government; pornography; pregnancy; prisons and prisoners; psychology; public utilities; religion; sampler videotapes from numerous public and community access television facilities; Sonia Sanchez; the San Francisco Mime Troupe in performance; E. F. Schumacher; sexuality; space exploration; theater; video art; the Vietnam war; violence against women; Wendy Waldman; welfare; Barb With; women's issues; Wounded Knee; and zoning.
Size & Elements: Videotape: 3/4" and 1/2" open reel (500 titles).
Cataloging: Published catalog (1973-82); dope sheets (1983-present).
Access: Open to researchers and scholars. Primarily available for rental; some videotapes available for purchase. Membership fees charged for viewing materials. Viewing requests accepted in person (by appointment only). Distribution collection available for free preview to libraries, schools, reviewers and broadcasters.
Rights: Full rights held to some material. Some rights held to all material. Additional clearances will be necessary in some cases if material is to be reused.
Licensing: Apply for information. License fees charged in some cases.
Restrictions: Material not available for licensing or reuse.
Viewing Facilities: Videotape (3/4" and 1/2").
Duplication Facilities: Videotape (all formats).

MINNESOTA (Minneapolis)

MINNESOTA CITIZENS COUNCIL ON CRIME AND JUSTICE
822 South 3rd Street, Suite 100
Minneapolis, MN 55415
(612) 340-5432

Richard C. Ericson (President)

Contact: Geraldine Graham (Educational Materials Coordinator)
Services: Nonprofit criminal justice organization. Film library available for rental and purchase primarily to community groups and educational institutions; material not available for licensing or reuse.
Description: Extensive collection of films and videotapes examining a wide range of issues and subjects concerning crime and justice. The films are aimed primarily at secondary school and adult audiences.

Topics include the courts and citizens' rights under the Constitution, juvenile delinquency, bomb threats, check fraud, hostage survival, shoplifting, loss prevention and risk management, training techniques for security officers, and the prison system. Most films examine topics through dramatized situations and the personal experiences of the participants.
Size & Elements: Film: 16mm (43 titles, 128 prints). Videotape: 3/4" and VHS (some titles available).
Cataloging: Published catalogs.
Access: Available for rental and purchase. Requests accepted by mail and telephone.
Rights: No rights held to any material.
Licensing: Council has no information on the reuse of material from the films.
Restrictions: Not available for licensing or reuse.
Viewing Facilities: Films may be previewed before rental in the Council's film library only.
Duplication Facilities: None.
Related Materials: Audiocassettes on the same topics also available for rental.

MINNESOTA (Minneapolis)

WALKER ART CENTER
FILM AND VIDEO STUDY COLLECTION
Vineland Place
Minneapolis, MN 55403
(612) 375-7600
Fax: (612) 375-7618

Bruce Jenkins (Director, Film Department)

Contact: Nancy Robinson (Assistant Director, Film Department)
Services: Museum. Film and videotape collection open to researchers and scholars only; available for duplication and reuse on a case-by-case basis, subject to clearance.
Description: Holds material on art and artists, independent films and videotapes, classic feature films and short subjects, and documentaries. Almost all films are commercially acquired from distributors.

Audio/Video Archive (approx. 600 3/4" videotapes). Holds documentation (generally unedited) of artists' visits and performances at the Walker Art Center (1968-present). Also held are extended interviews with artists and filmmakers, and documentation of dance, music and performance art events. Artists include: Merce Cunningham and John Cage (1981); Jean-Luc Godard (1981); Nancy Graves (1981); Dusan Makavejev (1981); Charles Simonds (1981); Isamu Noguchi (1982); Michael Powell (1982); Frank Stella (1982); Alice Aycock (1983); Lynda Benglis (1983); Jim Dine (1983); David Hockney (1983); Claes Oldenburg (1983); Jennifer Bartlett (1985); Jonathan Borofsky (1985); and Alan Shields (1985).
Size & Elements: Film: 16mm (amount unspecified). Videotape: 3/4" (approx. 600 videotapes; masters).
Cataloging: Inventory of videotapes; film title list.
Access: Open to researchers and scholars. Available for duplication and reuse, subject to clearance. Films are frequently shown at public screenings. Research fees not charged. Research requests accepted by mail (three weeks advance notice required).
Rights: Full rights held to most material. Additional clearances may be necessary in some cases (e.g., music) if material is to be reused.
Licensing: Available for licensing and reuse on a case-by-case basis, subject to clearance. License fees charged in some cases.
Restrictions: Copyright restrictions apply to most material; permission of artists and performers required in most cases.
Viewing Facilities: Film (35mm and 16mm); videotape (3/4" and 1/2"; NTSC and PAL).
Duplication Facilities: Videotape (3/4" and 1/2").

MINNESOTA (Minneapolis)

WORLD WIDE PICTURES, INC.
THE BILLY GRAHAM FILM MINISTRY
1201 Hennepin Avenue
Minneapolis, MN 55403
(612) 338-3335
(800) 328-4318
(204) 943-8963 (in Canada)
Fax: (612) 338-3029

Contact: Distribution Staff
Services: Film and videotape producer and distributor. Films available for rental; videotapes available for purchase and public performance.
Description: Has produced over 100 Christian films since 1952. Historical materials are held at Wheaton College, Billy Graham Center, Archives (q.v.).

Recent productions include: *Joni* (1979), the true story of a young woman left paralyzed from a freak accident who pieces her life back together with God's help; *By Love Set Free* (1982), about a young man held in a South American prison on drug charges, and the renewal of his faith; *The Hiding Place* (1975) based on the life of Corrie ten Boom, a Dutch woman who worked to help save the lives of countless Jewish families during World War II; *The Gospel Road* (1974), a musical account of the life of Jesus Christ filmed entirely in Israel, with Johnny and June Carter Cash; and *The Restless Ones* (1965), taking the viewer inside the turbulent world of teenagers.

Distributes the *Billy Graham Crusade Films,* featuring crusades in various American cities from the early 1970s. Also distributes many inspirational feature films such as *Chariots of Fire; Cry From The Mountain; The Blessings Of Brokenness; The Living Word; Then Sings My Soul; Souls in Conflict;* and *Oiltown, U.S.A.*
Size & Elements: Film: 16mm (approx. 40 titles; release prints). Videotape: VHS (viewing copies).
Cataloging: Published catalogs.
Access: Available for rental and purchase. Research requests accepted by telephone.
Rights: Full rights held to some material.
Licensing: Apply for information.
Restrictions: None specified.
Viewing Facilities: None.
Duplication Facilities: None.

MINNESOTA (Moorhead)

PLAINS ART MUSEUM LIBRARY
PLAINS ART MUSEUM EXTENSION PROGRAMS
521 Main Avenue, Box 37
Moorhead, MN 56560
(218) 236-7171

Roger Sherman (Curator)

Contacts: Jody Lirljequist (Curatorial Assistant); Ann Braaten (Educational Service Coordinator)
Services: Museum; library; distributor. Films and videotapes available to educational institutions and other interested groups for free loan.
Description: Art and artists; video arts; literary arts; cultural; and historical programs.

Portraits of artists. Includes one film copyrighted by the Museum, *Earl Linderman: The True & Incredible Adventures of Doktor Thrill,* which documents a project series created by artist Earl Linderman. Filmed at the Plains Art Museum during his retrospective exhibition (1982), this program looks at the gradual development of the *Dr. Thrill* series over a ten-year span. Also includes: *Interview with James Rosenquist; Georgia O'Keefe; Everything Is Photograph: Andre Kertesz; American Indian Artists: Fritz Scholder;* and *Fritz Scholder: An American Portrait.*

Video art. Titles include: *The Antenna Project; Star Awards;* and *Billy Curmano Performance Sampler.*

Cultural and historical programs. Titles include: *Lifeways: A Celebration of the Indian* and *Visible Target,* documenting Japanese American internment during World War II on Bainbridge Island.

The Plains Art Museum also distributes National Gallery of Art Extension Programs on art and artists, including *Treasures of Tutankhamun* and *Monet.*
Size & Elements: Film: 16mm (approx. 45 titles available from the National Gallery of Art Extension Programs). Videotape: 3/4" and 1/2" (approx. 35 titles available from the Plains Art Museum Extension Program and the National Gallery of Art Extension Programs).
Cataloging: Published brochures.

Access: Available to the public for free loan (approved groups only). Requests accepted by mail. Handling fees charged.
Rights: Some rights held to all material.
Licensing: Apply for information.
Restrictions: None specified.
Viewing Facilities: Film and videotape.
Duplication Facilities: None.

MINNESOTA (Richfield)

BOB DeFLORES
Film Consultant/Archivist
7507 Blaisdell Avenue South
Richfield, MN 55423
(612) 866-3186

Contact: Bob DeFlores
Services: Private film and videotape collection; archives. Material available for research and reuse.
Description: Holds 6,000 films (1900-late 1950s). Includes: musical films (over 300 hours of jazz and 300 hours of big bands); newsreels; historical and comedy short subjects; feature films; documentaries; sports; personalities; cartoons. 98% of the collection is black and white; silent and sound films are held.

2,000 of these films have been restored by Bob DeFlores through the years. Others (some the only copies in existence) have been sent to the American Film Institute for preservation.
Size & Elements: Film: format unspecified (6,000 titles, 6,000 cans). Videotape: 3/4" (approx. 3,000 titles transferred from film; masters); and VHS (viewing and research copies).
Cataloging: Personal assistance provided.
Access: Available for research and reuse. Research fees charged. Research requests accepted by phone only ("on a one-to-one basis").
Rights: Material in the public domain. Music clearances are necessary if music is to be reused.
Licensing: Available for reuse. Usage fees charged (prices set according to client budget; "clients big or small" are served).
Restrictions: None specified.
Viewing Facilities: Videotape (VHS viewing copies can be sent; fees charged).
Duplication Facilities: Videotape (3/4").

MINNESOTA (St. James)

RED BADGE OF COURAGE, INC.
1023 5th Avenue South
St. James, MN 56081
(507) 375-5435

Adrian Fisch (Director)

Contact: Adrian Fisch
Services: Private film and videotape collection. Materials maintained for reference purposes. Collection open to approved researchers.
Description: Prisoner-of-war and missing-in-action issues, consisting of videotaped and television documentation relating to POWs and MIAs (1969-present). Materials include television broadcasts, interviews and "healing tributes." Also holds a few U.S. Department of Defense films (black and white), on POWs and MIAs, which the DOD discontinued immediately after release.
Size & Elements: Film: format unspecified (approx. 2 titles). Videotape: format unspecified (approx. 75 videotapes).
Cataloging: None specified.
Access: Open to approved researchers. Research requests accepted by mail.
Rights: Rights status of material not known. Additional clearances may be necessary in some cases if material is to be reused.
Licensing: Apply for information.
Restrictions: None specified.
Viewing Facilities: None.
Duplication Facilities: Videotape (VHS).

MINNESOTA (St. Paul)

MINNESOTA DEPARTMENT OF PUBLIC SAFETY FILM LIBRARY
1821 University Avenue, Room 180 South
St. Paul, MN 55104-1897

(612) 297-3939

Janet Weber (Librarian)

Contact: Library staff
Services: State government agency. Educational film and videotape collection available to the public for rental and loan.
Description: Subjects covered include public safety, traffic safety, driver education, professional driving, motorcycle safety, bicycle safety, pedestrian safety, neighborhood crime watch, crime prevention, police training, emergency services, first aid, child guidance, winter safety, fire safety, safety restraints, alcohol and drugs, civil defense, basic life saving, car care and operation, disaster training, hospital preparedness, natural disasters, nuclear radiation, school bus safety, school bus drivers, vandalism, shoplifting and personal assault.
Size & Elements: Film: 16mm (color and black and white). Videotape: 3/4" and VHS. (Over 870 titles total; over 4,500 items total).
Cataloging: Published catalogs, research library.
Access: Open to the public. Research fees not charged. Research requests accepted by telephone. Orders accepted by mail. Rental fees charged only for traffic safety films.
Rights: No rights held to any material. Some material in the public domain.
Licensing: Materials not generally available for licensing or reuse.
Restrictions: Apply for information.
Viewing Facilities: None.
Duplication Facilities: None.
Related Materials: Slides, filmstrips and audiocassettes.

MINNESOTA (St. Paul)

MINNESOTA HISTORICAL SOCIETY
SOUND AND VISUAL COLLECTIONS
690 Cedar Street
St. Paul, MN 55101
(612) 296-2489

Bonnie Wilson (Curator of Sound and Visual Collections)

Contacts: Bonnie Wilson; Tracey Baker (Reference Librarian)
Services: Historical society. Film and videotape collection available to researchers, scholars and the public for research and reuse.
Description: Minnesota history and politics, personalities, places, customs, industries and Native Americans (1920-present). A wide variety of local film and videomakers is represented in the collection. Amateur, artistic, educational and commercial works are available for viewing, but not for circulation.

Hubert H. Humphrey Collection. 445 items relating to the life and political career of the Minneapolis mayor, U.S. senator and vice president.
Size & Elements: Film: 16mm (450 titles). Videotape: 3/4" and 1/2" (150 videotapes). The Hubert H. Humphrey collection, a separate entity, contains 445 titles (format unspecified).
Cataloging: Card catalogs.
Access: Open to researchers, scholars and the public. Research requests accepted by mail, telephone and in person.
Rights: Some rights held to all material.
Licensing: Apply for information. License fees charged (fees determined on a case-by-case basis).
Restrictions: None specified.
Viewing Facilities: Film (16mm Cinescan); videotape (3/4" and 1/2").
Duplication Facilities: None.

MINNESOTA (St. Paul)

NORTH CENTRAL FOREST EXPERIMENT STATION
1992 Folwell
St. Paul, MN 55108
(612) 649-5000
Fax: (612) 649-5285

Allan Taylor (Communications Department)

Contact: Allan Taylor
Services: Government agency. Videotape collection open to the public and available for duplication.
Description: Topics include natural resources, personal development and Eastern Europe and Soviet issues.

Natural resources. Forest management and projects undertaken by the U.S. Forest Service. Titles include *New Concepts in Managing 2nd Growth Northern Hardwoods; Wood Use and Competitive Technology; Integrated Strategies for Gene Conservation; Breeding;* and *Take Pride in America.*

Eastern European and Soviet issues. Titles include *Soviet Build-up in the Baltic Sea* and *Propaganda and Reality.*

Self-help and personal development. Titles include *What You Are Is What You See* and *Passion for Excellence.*

Size & Elements: Videotape: VHS (15 titles).
Cataloging: Research library.
Access: Available to the public for duplication. Research requests accepted by mail, telephone and in person (walk-in and by appointment). Research fees not charged.
Rights: No rights held to any material.
Licensing: Apply for information. Usage fees not charged.
Restrictions: None specified.
Viewing Facilities: Videotape (VHS).
Duplication Facilities: Videotape.

MINNESOTA (St. Paul)

**ST. PAUL PUBLIC LIBRARY
FILM AND VIDEO CENTER**
90 West 4 Street
St. Paul, MN 55102
(612) 292-6179

Marti Lybeck (Librarian)

Contact: Marti Lybeck
Services: Library. Open to the public. Videotape collection available for loan.
Description: Holds general collection of commercially acquired videotapes which are eclectic and popular in nature. Film collection is primarily for use by organizations, with an emphasis on children's films, adventure, travel, animals, short story adaptations, art music history, social issues, personnel training, health and classic comedy.

Some videotapes of local interest (25-30 titles) originate from various sources. Subjects include: local personalities (e.g., Les Blacklock, nature photographer and Justine Kerfoot); documentation of local theaters and locations, such as Carver's Cave. Also holds coverage of local events and issues, including a videotape on the local Viking heritage, a documentary on farm women entitled *Dairy Queen,* a videotaped performance of the American Ballet Theater, documentation of the Women Take Back the Night March, a documentary on the Picasso exhibition at the Walker Art Center and footage on the local Hispanic community.

Size & Elements: Film: 16mm (amount unspecified). Videotape: 3/4" (100 titles) and VHS (1,200 titles).
Cataloging: Published catalogs; computerized cataloging for staff use only; finding aids.
Access: Open to the public. Videotapes available for loan.
Rights: No rights held to any material.
Licensing: Apply for information.
Restrictions: Apply for information.
Viewing Facilities: Videotape (3/4").
Duplication Facilities: None.

MINNESOTA (St. Paul)

TWIN CITIES PUBLIC TELEVISION (KTCA)
1640 Como Avenue
St. Paul, MN 55108
(612) 646-4611
Fax: (612) 647-4502

Richard O. Moore (General Manager)

Contacts: Denis LaComb (Distribution Manager, *Alive From Off Center*); John Schott (Executive Producer, *Alive From Off Center*)
Services: Television broadcaster. Programs available for rental, purchase, licensing and reuse, subject to restrictions.
Description: Producer of the series *Alive From Off Center,* carried on PBS (1985-present), a showcase of new video works in dance, music, theater, performance and video art. Acquires works from artists and commissions artists to produce original works. The series is international in scope and includes works from England, the Netherlands, Japan, France, Canada and the U.S.

Size & Elements: Videotape: 1" (masters); 3/4" and VHS (viewing copies). (28 programs total, incorporating 76 works).
Cataloging: Computerized cataloging for staff use only; promotional brochures.
Access: Open to the public. Available for rental, purchase, duplication and reuse. Research fees not charged. Research requests accepted by mail and telephone.
Rights: Full rights held to some material. Some rights held to some material. Rights to some material retained by artists. Additional clearances may be necessary in some cases if material is to be reused.
Licensing: Available for licensing and reuse, subject to restrictions. License and usage fees charged. Inquiries should be directed to Distribution Dept.
Restrictions: Restrictions vary depending on individual works.
Viewing Facilities: Videotape (informal facility, by appointment only).
Duplication Facilities: Videotape.

MINNESOTA (St. Paul)

**UNIVERSITY OF MINNESOTA LIBRARIES
MANUSCRIPTS DIVISION**
826 Berry Street
St. Paul, MN 55114
(612) 627-4199

Alan K. Lathrop (Professor and Curator)

Contacts: Alan K. Lathrop; Vivian Newbold (Library Assistant)
Services: University library. Film and videotape collection open to the public.
Description: Architecture, engineering and the performing arts (1925-80). Selected holdings include: 11 reels of film (8mm) of prewar German hydrological installations (dams and waterworks); color footage of Prairie School-style homes by Purcell & Elmslie, Minneapolis architects (ca. 1950); speeches by Arthur Motley (Chairman of the Board, Parade Publications); and videotaped portions of Guthrie Theater productions.
Size & Elements: Film: format unspecified (approx. 198 titles, 26 cans; positive). Videotape: open reel and cassette (151 videotapes; viewing copies).
Cataloging: Inventories.
Access: Open to the public. Research fees not charged. Research requests accepted by mail, telephone and in person (walk-in and by appointment).
Rights: Full rights held to some material. Additional clearances may be necessary in some cases if material is to be reused.
Licensing: Apply for information. License fees not charged.
Restrictions: None specified.
Viewing Facilities: Film and videotape (at the Film and Video Department of the University).
Duplication Facilities: Film and videotape (at the Film and Video Department of the University).

MINNESOTA (St. Paul)

YMCA OF THE U.S.A. ARCHIVES
c/o University of Minnesota
2642 University Avenue
St. Paul, MN 55114
(612) 627-4632

Andrea Hinding (YMCA Archivist)

Contact: Andrea Hinding
Services: Association; film and videotape archives. Archives not currently open to the public for research of any kind. Cataloging and expansion currently in process.
Description: Archives currently in the process of organization and material is not accessible for research of any kind. Plans are to continue acquiring materials from other branches of the YMCA, and to open to the public in 1989. Current holdings include educational and inspirational films (1950s-70s).
Size & Elements: Film: 16mm (approx. 40 reels).
Cataloging: None.
Access: Not currently open to the public.
Rights: Apply for information.
Licensing: Material not currently available for licensing or reuse.
Restrictions: Material currently unavailable for research, reuse or duplication of any kind.
Viewing Facilities: None.
Duplication Facilities: None.

MISSISSIPPI

MISSISSIPPI (Jackson)

CITIZENS' COUNCILS OF AMERICA
666 North Street, Suite 102-A
Jackson, MS 39202
(601) 969-1500

Wm. J. Simmons (President)

Contact: Wm. J. Simmons
Services: Political organization. Films available to researchers, scholars and the public for in-house use only.
Description: The Citizens' Councils hold "a conservative view of the Civil Rights revolution." From April 1957 to November 1967, the Citizens' Council Forum produced a weekly television series in Washington, D.C., featuring interviews with U.S. congressmen and senators on a wide range of "conservative" subject matters. These programs (each 15 min.) were produced by Wm. J. Simmons (current President).

All programs from the television series are now held at the Mississippi Department of Archives and History (q.v.), and clearance through the CCA is not necessary for access to material.

Currently holds two films: a interview with Wm. J. Simmons (1959), conducted by Dr. Houston Smith as part of the national television series *Search for America,* and an interview with Ian Smith shortly after he became president of Southern Rhodesia (now Zimbabwe), conducted by Wm. J. Simmons and filmed by the Ministry of Education in Salisbury, Southern Rhodesia in 1966.
Size & Elements: Film: 16mm (2 titles).
Cataloging: None.
Access: Available to researchers, scholars and the public. For in-house use only. Research fees not charged. Research requests accepted by mail and telephone.
Rights: Material in the public domain.
Licensing: Apply for information. License fees not charged.
Restrictions: None specified.
Viewing Facilities: None available (films can be viewed in-house if researcher supplies own projector).
Duplication Facilities: None.

MISSISSIPPI (Jackson)

FREEDOM INFORMATION SERVICE
P.O. Box 3568
Jackson, MS 39207-3568
(601) 969-2269

Jan Hillegas (Treasurer)

Contact: Ken Lawrence (Research Director)
Services: Organization. Film and videotape collection available to researchers and scholars by appointment only.
Description: A small collection of full-length feature films, videotapes, and slide presentations relating to government surveillance, political repression, fascism, Nazism and the Holocaust.
Size & Elements: Film: 16mm ("a few"). Videotape: format unspecified ("a few").
Cataloging: Research library.
Access: Open to researchers and scholars (by appointment only). Research fees charged. Research requests accepted by mail, telephone and in person (by appointment only).
Rights: Some rights held to some material.
Licensing: Apply for information. License fees charged.
Restrictions: Restrictions apply to licensing and reuse.
Viewing Facilities: Film and videotape (by appointment only).
Duplication Facilities: None.

MISSISSIPPI (Jackson)

MISSISSIPPI DEPARTMENT OF ARCHIVES AND HISTORY
P.O. Box 571
Jackson, MI 39205
(601) 359-1424

Street address: 100 South State Street

Elbert R. Hilliard (Director)

Contact: Dan Den Bleyker (Audio Visual Records Curator)
Services: State archives. Film and videotape collection open to the public for research; materials available for licensing and reuse, subject to restrictions.
Description: Mississippi history and culture; the civil rights movement.
Highsaw Film Collection (1934, 450 feet, 16mm, black and white, silent). Shots of railroad stations along Columbus and Greenville railroad line; activity in Columbus rail yards; railroad employees; company picnic.
B. F. Jackson Film Collection (ca. 1945-50, 800 feet, 16mm, black and white and color, silent). Delta plantation scenes at Mattson; Moterry jailbreak and capture at Greenwood; White and Black individuals in downtown Ruleville; Ruleville business and town scenes.
Key Brothers Films (ca. 1935, 700 feet, 16mm, black and white, silent). Airport; helicopter; endurance flight; refueling in air; family shots; Key Brothers "Learn to Fly" booth; shots of "Ole Miss" (airplane); freight train pulled by steam engine.
Newsfilm Collection (ca. 1954-71, 550,000 feet, 16mm, black and white and color, silent and sound, original, positive, optical and magnetic sound). A Mississippi television station's coverage of the civil rights movement and other local events.
WAPT-TV Newsfilm Collection (ca. 1971-77, 225,000 feet, 16mm, color, silent and magnetic sound, original, positive).
WLBT-TV-3 Newsfilm Collection (1974-81, 500,000 feet, 16mm, color, silent and magnetic sound, original, positive).
Citizens' Council Forum Film Collection (1955-66, 90,000 feet, 133 films, 16mm, black and white and color, silent and optical sound, original and dupe, negative and positive). Discussions with leading "conservatives" about race, communism, the Supreme Court, religion, and other issues.
Natchez, The March of Time Collection (ca. 1939, 272 feet, 1 reel, 16mm, black and white, silent). Scenes of Natchez homes and the Armstrong Tire and Rubber plant. *Natchez Pilgrimage* (ca. 1930s, 250 feet, 16mm, color, silent). The Natchez pilgrimage at the Elms, Natchez, Mississippi.
Size & Elements: Film: 16mm (1.3 million feet, 3,700 cans). Videotape: 3/4", VHS and Video 8 (approx. 200 videotapes, masters and viewing copies).
Cataloging: Computerized cataloging for staff use only. Indices are being prepared for the collection. Published catalog to one television newsfilm collection.
Access: Available to the public for research, licensing and reuse. Research requests accepted by mail, telephone and in person (by appointment only). Research fees charged.
Rights: Full rights held to some material. Additional clearances may be necessary in some cases if material is to be reused.
Licensing: Available for licensing and reuse, subject to restrictions. License and usage fees charged.
Restrictions: Some collections carry donor and other restrictions.
Viewing Facilities: Film (Steenbeck); videotape (VHS; Video 8 in preparation).
Duplication Facilities: None.
Publications: *Newsfilm Index* (1985), an index to the largest television newsfilm collection held by Department.

MISSISSIPPI (University)

UNIVERSITY OF MISSISSIPPI
BLUES ARCHIVE
Farley Hall
University, MS 38677
(601) 232-7753
Fax: (601) 232-5453

Suzanne Flandreau Steel (Librarian and Assistant Professor)

Contacts: Suzanne Flandreau Steel; Walter Liniger (Research Associate)
Services: University library and archives. Videotape collection open to researchers, scholars and the public; available for duplication and reuse, subject to restrictions.
Description: Original footage of the Delta Blues Festival and the Chunky Rhythm and Blues Festival (1985), featuring various blues and gospel performances and interviews with performers. Also holds research collection of numerous finished productions provided by outside producers.
Size & Elements: Videotape: 3/4" (38 videotapes, each 30 min.; masters), VHS (32 masters; 43 viewing copies) and 1/2" open reel (18 videotapes; masters).
Cataloging: Card catalogs; logs. Cataloging not complete at present.

MISSISSIPPI (University)

Access: Open to researchers, scholars and the public. Research fees not charged. Research requests accepted by mail, telephone and in person (by appointment only).
Rights: No rights held to any material. Permission of copyright holder is necessary in all cases if material is to be reused.
Licensing: Available for licensing and reuse, subject to restrictions. License fees charged at direction of owner.
Restrictions: Duplication is not possible without clearance from copyright holder.
Viewing Facilities: Videotape (VHS only).
Duplication Facilities: Videotape (all duplication is done at the University's Communication and Resource Center).

MISSISSIPPI (University)

UNIVERSITY OF MISSISSIPPI
CENTER FOR THE STUDY OF SOUTHERN CULTURE
University, MS 38677
(601) 232-5993

William Ferris (Director)

Contact: William Ferris
Services: University research center. Films and videotapes available for rental and purchase.
Description: Distributes four films produced by Yale University Films in association with the Center for Southern Folklore (q.v.). Titles include: *Give My Poor Heart Ease,* with interviews and performances by B. B. King and James "Son" Thomas, Parchman Penitentiary work chants, and Wade Walton's barbershop boogie-woogie; *Two Black Churches,* documenting dramatic church services at Rose Hill Baptist Church near Vicksburg, Miss. and St. James Church in New Haven, Conn., and showing sermons, gospel choirs, faith healing and spirit possession; *Made in Mississippi,* showing intimate portraits of Black folk artists and their works, featuring James "Son" Thomas (clay sculptures), Amanda and Mary Gordon (quilts), Othar Thomas (cane fifes), Luster Willis (paintings and sculpted canes) and Leon Clark (white oak baskets); and *I Ain't Lyin',* folktales narrated by James "Son" Thomas, Shelby "Pappa Jazz" Brown, Mary Gordan and others, featuring preacher tales, toasts and dozens (available in adult and censored versions).
   The Center is also developing a catalog of films and videotapes on the American South which it plans to make available for distribution.
Size & Elements: Videotape: 3/4", VHS and Betamax (4 titles, each 20 min.).
Cataloging: Release sheet.
Access: Available for rental and purchase.
Rights: Apply for information.
Licensing: Apply for information.
Restrictions: None specified.
Viewing Facilities: None.
Duplication Facilities: None.

MISSOURI

MISSOURI (Columbia)

BLUE SKY COMMUNICATIONS INC.
P.O. Box 1522
Columbia, MO 65205
(314) 874-2253

David McAllister (President and Executive Producer)

Contacts: David McAllister; Sherri Griggs (Producer)
Services: Film and videotape producer. Material available for duplication, licensing and reuse, subject to restrictions.
Description: Agriculture, including footage of soybean planting and harvesting; Angus cattle grazing, being herded and auctioned; and medical footage, including hospitals, operating rooms, surgery, inpatient and outpatient procedures, physical therapy and doctors. All footage is in color.
Size & Elements: Film: 16mm (camera negative, workprints and release prints). Videotape: 1" (masters and viewing copies); Betacam (masters and viewing copies); 3/4" (viewing copies). (Approx. 50 hours total).
Cataloging: Computerized cataloging for staff use only (in process); shot lists.
Access: Available to the public for duplication, licensing and reuse, subject to restrictions. Research fees charged (fees negotiable). Research requests

accepted by mail and telephone.
Rights: Full rights held to some material. Additional clearances may be necessary in some cases if material is to be reused (permission of client and/or owners necessary in some cases).
Licensing: Available for licensing and reuse, subject to restrictions. License and usage fees charged.
Restrictions: Permission of client and/or copyright owners may be required for reuse in some cases. Some restrictions may apply to specific material; some material may be restricted if already used by local producers.
Viewing Facilities: Film (16mm); videotape (Betacam and 3/4").
Duplication Facilities: Videotape (Betacam, 3/4" and 1/2").

MISSOURI (Fulton)

WINSTON CHURCHILL MEMORIAL AND LIBRARY
WESTMINSTER COLLEGE
Fulton, MO 65251-1299
(314) 642-3361

Street address: 7th and Westminster Avenues

Dr. J. Harvey Saunders (President of the College)
Jane Flink (Director of External Relations)
Warren M. Hollrah (Museum Manager and College Archivist)

Contact: Warren M. Hollrah (314/642-6648)
Services: Memorial library and museum affiliated with Westminster College. Maintains film and videotape archive primarily for research and educational purposes.
Description: From the podium of the John Findley Green Lecture at Westminster College (March 5, 1946), Winston S. Churchill delivered his famous Iron Curtain Speech, originally titled "Sinews of Peace." The Memorial holds materials relating to this speech, Winston Churchill, England, World War II, and the dedication of the Churchill Memorial at Westminster College. Some of the most important documentary films in the collection include: *World Spotlight Turns on Westminster* (the "Iron Curtain Speech"; Pathe News); *Arrival Ceremony of Winston Churchill at Westminster College* (Emma Coultas, gift to the college); *Sinews of Peace* (Churchill's speech at Westminster, by the College Development Office); and *Churchill at Westminster* (John Frier, 8mm, color).
   The Library also has videotapes of selected speakers at the Churchill Memorial. The John Findley Green Lecture Series includes: Caspar L. Weinberger (1983); William J. Casey (1983); George Bush (1986); and Paul Ricoeur (1987). The Kemper Lecture Series includes: Professor J. H. Plumb of Cambridge University (1983); Sir William Deakin, Research Assistant to W. S. Churchill (1984); Sir John Colville, Principal Private Secretary to Churchill (1985); the Honorable Robert Rhodes James, Member of the English Parliament (1986); and the Honorable Lord Blake, Provost, Queen's College, Oxford (1987).
Size & Elements: Film: 16mm (42 films); 8mm (3 films). Videotape: format unspecified.
Cataloging: Dope sheets.
Access: Open to the public. Research fees not charged. Research requests accepted by mail, telephone and in person (by appointment only). Possibly available for duplication (apply for information).
Rights: Some rights held to some material (apply for further information).
Licensing: Available for licensing and reuse, subject to restrictions.
Restrictions: Requests for licensing and reuse considered on a case-by-case basis.
Viewing Facilities: Film and videotape.
Duplication Facilities: None.

MISSOURI (Independence)

REORGANIZED CHURCH OF JESUS CHRIST OF LATTER DAY SAINTS
LIBRARY AND ARCHIVES
RLDS Auditorium
Box 1059
Independence, MO 64051
(816) 833-1000
Fax: (816) 833-1000 (Ext. 218)

Tom Peterman (Commissioner of Communications)

Contacts: Betti Jo Kirk (for rentals); Tom Peterman (Ext. 349)
Services: Religious organization; film and videotape producer. Material available for distribution and rental.
Description: Produces three programs annually, all relating to the subject "restoration today and tomorrow." The series *In the Forefront* reports on activities of the church around the world. Subjects covered include earthquake relief, summer camp for handicapped children and a thrift store benefit for senior citizens.

Holds a Church-produced film on the history of RLDS expansion (1958-78) into over 30 different countries and documentation of the activities of the World Conference (an event attended by 10,000 people). Also included in the library are internal training program materials and television commercials.

Prior to 1978, all programs were produced on film; since 1978, all productions have originated on videotape. All archival material (including local and international church activities) is held in storage in Kansas City.
Size & Elements: Film: (16mm). Videotape: (3/4"). (Amounts unspecified).
Cataloging: None.
Access: Open to the public. Maintained for distribution and rental rather than for research. Research requests accepted by mail, telephone and in person (walk-in).
Rights: Full rights held to all material.
Licensing: Apply for information.
Restrictions: None specified.
Viewing Facilities: Videotape (available in Resource Center).
Duplication Facilities: None (outside arrangements can be made).
Distributor: Videotapes distributed by Herald House, Independence, Mo.; (816) 932-7812.

MISSOURI (Independence)

HARRY S TRUMAN LIBRARY
AUDIOVISUAL COLLECTION
U.S. Highway 24 and Delaware Street
Independence, MO 64050
(816) 833-1400

Benedict K. Zobrist (Director)

Contact: Pauline Testerman (Archives Technician)
Services: Presidential library. Film and videotape collection open to the public for in-house use only. Some material available for duplication and reuse.
Description: Presidential library administered by the National Archives and Records Administration. Collection relates to the life, career and administration (1945-52) of President Harry S Truman. Material on prominent events and individuals during his presidency are also included.

Film selections in the library include newsreels from Truman's presidency; the 1948 presidential campaign; and various materials from 1952, 1953 and 1956; an episode of *Person To Person*, hosted by Margaret Truman, in which she interviews her parents, broadcast from Independence, Missouri (1955); copies of the 26 half-hour episodes of *Decision: The Conflicts of Harry S Truman* (1964; copyrighted); and the films *The Man from Independence* and *The Truman Library Orientation Film.*

Videotapes in the collection are mainly copies of documentaries on Truman and related subjects, in addition to locally produced Truman-related films.
Size & Elements: Film: 16mm (325,604 feet). Videotape: 3/4" (73 hours) and VHS.
Cataloging: Film cataloged by subject in chronological order in a card file. The card file supplies a numerical file number corresponding to entries on pages in a 3-ring binder. The binder contains very detailed descriptions, sometimes shot-by-shot. Videotapes are arranged by title only and not otherwise cataloged.
Access: Open to the public. For in-house research only. Films do not circulate; some are available for purchase through the National Archives and Records Administration (q.v.). Research fees not charged. *Research requests accepted in person only after an application form has been completed on the premises.*
Rights: Full rights held to some material (2 titles). Some rights held to some material. Much of the material is in the public domain and is not restricted. Additional clearances may be necessary in some cases if material is to be reused. The Library will assist in finding the copyright holder when the information is available or known to them. Apply for more detailed information concerning copyrights.
Licensing: Some material available for duplication and reuse (apply for information). Duplication fees and expenses must be paid by researcher.
Restrictions: Most material not available for licensing or reuse.

Viewing Facilities: Film (viewer/editor); videotape (3/4").
Duplication Facilities: None on premises or in Independence; usually done at National Archives (arrangements must be made through the Library).

MISSOURI (Kansas City)

AMERICAN NURSES' ASSOCIATION
2420 Pershing Road
Kansas City, Missouri 64108
(816) 474-5720
(800) 821-5834

Contact: Nancy Perrin (Publications Manager)
Services: Association. Films and videotapes available for purchase and reuse on a case-by case basis, subject to restrictions.
Description: Material relating to the nursing profession, its goals and educational needs, the protection and advancement of nurses' welfare, conditions of employment and nursing care. *Nurses, Politics, and Public Policy* provides basic direction to professional nurses who are ready to become political activists.
Size & Elements: Film: 16mm (2 titles). Videotape: 3/4", VHS and Betamax (4 titles).
Cataloging: Published catalog.
Access: Available to researchers, scholars and the public. Materials primarily intended as educational tools for Association members. Research requests accepted by mail and telephone.
Rights: Full rights held to all material.
Licensing: Available for licensing and reuse on a case-by-case basis, subject to restrictions. License fees charged under some conditions.
Restrictions: Restrictions may apply in some cases; requests for licensing and reuse are evaluated on an individual basis.
Viewing Facilities: None.
Duplication Facilities: None.

MISSOURI (Kansas City)

FELLOWSHIP OF CHRISTIAN ATHLETES
8701 Leeds Road
Kansas City, MO 64129
(800) 289-0909
(816) 921-0909
Fax: (816) 921-8755

Richard Abel (President)

Contact: Kim Mangels
Services: Organization. Videotapes available to the public for purchase. Some archival material presently inaccessible.
Description: Inspirational videotapes concerned with sports and religion, hosted by well-known Christian athletes and coaches.

Sports figures in the series include: *Ken Hatfield,* University of Arkansas football coach, talking about courage as a means of overcoming failure; *Maryalyce Jeremiah,* women's basketball coach at Cal State Fullerton, discussing "Second Wind" in her coaching and faith; *Bill McCartney,* Colorado football coach, reflecting on his struggles and successes in rebuilding the Buff's program; *Wes Neal,* President of Christlike Living Ministries, sharing biblical principles for motivating athletes; *Tom Osborne,* Cornhuskers head man, focusing on the three "building blocks" necessary for strong character; *Ed Rush,* one of the NBA's top three referees, recapping his career and the importance of building one's life on a firm foundation; *Les Steckel,* former Minnesota Vikings head coach and now an assistant at New England, reflecting on "reordering your priorities"; *Grant Teaff,* Baylor's popular football coach, discussing "the victory business" at a Colorado coaches conference; *Kay Yow,* women's basketball coach at North Carolina State and coach of the 1988 Olympic women's team, talking about true riches and "first things first"; *Gary Bender,* ABC sportscaster sharing anecdotes and his faith; *Tanya Crevier,* nationally known basketball handling whiz, motivating, entertaining and sharing her faith at a FCA Girls Camp; *Tom Landry* and *Bill Yeoman,* two veteran Texas football coaches, offering pointers on how to be successful on and off the field; and *Donn Moomaw,* the dynamic California pastor and former UCLA All-American linebacker, riveting his audience with "Mountaintops and Valleys."

Approximately six films (16mm, black and white) show the early days of the Fellowship of Christian Athletes movement and some sports figures, but these do not circulate and are presently inaccessible.

MISSOURI (Kansas City)

Size & Elements: Film: 16mm (approx. 6 titles; black and white, presently inaccessible). Videotape: VHS (15 titles).
Cataloging: Published brochure.
Access: Open to researchers and scholars. Videotapes available to the public for purchase. Requests accepted by mail (preferred) and telephone (use toll-free number).
Rights: Full rights held to all material. Additional clearances may be necessary in some cases if material is to be reused.
Licensing: Material generally not available for licensing or reuse.
Restrictions: None specified.
Viewing Facilities: None.
Duplication Facilities: None.
Related Materials: Audiotapes on similar themes.

MISSOURI (Kansas City)

KANSAS CITY FILM ARCHIVE
JAZZ FILM COLLECTION
Grant Hall
4420 Warwick
Kansas City, MO 64110
(816) 531-6327

Carolyn Stockwell (Archivist)

Contact: Carolyn Stockwell
Services: Film archives. Collection currently being processed; not presently available for research or reuse.
Description: The Jazz Film Collection, a joint project of the City of Kansas City, Missouri and the University of Missouri-Kansas City, was purchased from the well-known collector John Baker. It includes full-length features, shorts, Soundies and kinescopes of rare material, plus miscellaneous books, magazines and other memorabilia — all relating to jazz.

The films are not limited to musical performances but chronicle American life in a very broad sense, providing insight into period customs, social stereotypes, language usage, dances, cinematography and scriptwriting.

The City of Kansas City recently signed a cooperative agreement with the University of Missouri-Kansas City (through the Institute for Studies in American Music, the Conservatory of Music) for the care, maintenance and cataloging of the collection. The collection is not yet available for research or reuse.
Size & Elements: Film: format unspecified (1 million feet, 500 hours, approx. 3,000 titles).
Cataloging: Computerized cataloging in progress.
Access: Not currently accessible for research or reuse.
Rights: Apply for information.
Licensing: Not currently available for licensing and reuse (apply for information).
Restrictions: None specified.
Viewing Facilities: None.
Duplication Facilities: None.

MISSOURI (Kansas City)

WADE WILLIAMS PRODUCTIONS
5500 Ward Parkway
Kansas City, MO 64113
(816) 523-2699

Contact: Wade Williams III
Services: Distributor; stock footage sales library. Films and videotapes available for licensing, reuse and theatrical distribution.
Description: "World's largest" proprietor of science fiction film copyrights. Principal holdings are science fiction and horror films (1950s-60s), and three major science fiction television series from the same period. Holdings also include over 4,000 35mm trailers on all subjects (produced 1930s-60s).

Titles include: *Destination: Moon* (1950), George Pal's Academy Award-winning film about man's first trip to the moon; *Rocketship X-M* (1950), a classic film starring Lloyd Bridges on man's first flight to Mars; *Plan Nine From Outer Space* (1959), starring Bela Lugosi and Tor Johnson, voted the Golden Turkey Award as the worst film ever made; *Mr. Krane* (1962), starring Sir Cedric Hardwicke, in which a visitor from outer space warns the world of doom; *Kronos* (1957), in which aliens in a giant energy cube rob the earth of its power; *Stranger From Venus* (1954), starring Patricia Neal and Helmet Dantine, in which a man from Venus arrives in a flying saucer to warn Earth

against testing atomic bombs; *Mr. Peek-A-Boo* (1951), the story of a man who can walk through walls until he falls in love; *Missile to the Moon* (1958), starring Richard Travis, Michael Whalen and Cathy Downs as astronauts on an expedition to the moon, only to discover a race of women guarded by a big spider and rock people; and *Cosmic Man* (1959), starring John Carradine and Bruce Bennett in the story of an invisible man from another planet who lands in California.

Also holds *Things To Come* (1936), starring Raymond Massey and Ralph Richardson, an H. G. Wells story of the future, ending with a trip to the moon; *Woman In The Moon* (1926), Fritz Lang's silent film about a trip to the moon; *Tales of Tomorrow* (60 shows, each 30 min.), starring James Dean and Paul Newman, who deal with monsters, flying saucers and science gone wild; *Midnight Movie Massacre* (1986), in which a group of kids go to the midnight show in 1956 and a monster eats them one at a time; *Repeat Performance*, starring Joan Leslie, playing a woman who gets the chance to relive a year of her life; and *Hideous Sun Demon* (1959), starring Robert Clarke as a man who turns into a lizard in the sunlight.
Size & Elements: Film: 35mm and 16mm (amount unspecified). Videotape: format and amount unspecified.
Cataloging: Printed lists.
Access: Available for distribution, licensing and reuse. Research requests accepted by mail and telephone.
Rights: Full rights held to some material. Additional clearances may be necessary in some cases if material is to be reused.
Licensing: Available for theatrical and non-theatrical distribution, broadcast, licensing and reuse, subject to clearance. License fees charged.
Restrictions: None specified.
Viewing Facilities: None.
Duplication Facilities: None.

MISSOURI (St. Louis)

AMERICAN SOYBEAN ASSOCIATION
Box 27300
St. Louis, MO 63141
(314) 432-1600
Fax: (314) 567-7642
Telex: AMSOY 4312061

Street address: 777 Craig Road

Kenneth L. Bader (Chief Executive Officer)

Contact: Dan Reuwee (Director of Communications)
Services: Association. Film and videotape collection maintained primarily for internal use.
Description: Several films relating to the soybean industry.
Size & Elements: Film: 16mm ("several titles"). Videotape: VHS.
Cataloging: None specified.
Access: Not open to the public. Primarily for internal use.
Rights: Apply for information.
Licensing: Apply for information.
Restrictions: Material not generally available for research or reuse.
Viewing Facilities: None.
Duplication Facilities: None.
Related Services: Can provide color or black and white still photographs relating to the soybean industry; can work with film producers to find filming locations related to soybean production and marketing.

MISSOURI (St. Louis)

ANHEUSER-BUSCH COMPANIES, INC.
CORPORATE ARCHIVES
Executive Offices
One Busch Place
St. Louis, MO 63118-1852
(314) 577-2179
Telex: 447 117 ANBUSCH STL

William J. Vollmar, Ph.D. (Manager, Archives & Records Administration)

Contact: Dr. William J. Vollmar
Services: Corporate archives. Closed to the public.
Description: Archival copies of Anheuser-Busch training films, television commercials and films featuring the Clydesdale horses.

Size & Elements: Formats and amounts unspecified.
Cataloging: None specified.
Access: Archives closed to the public. Access granted on a case-by-case basis.
Rights: Apply for information.
Licensing: Apply for information.
Restrictions: Material not generally available to the public or outside organizations.
Viewing Facilities: None.
Duplication Facilities: None.

MISSOURI (St. Louis)

CONCORDIA PUBLISHING HOUSE
3558 South Jefferson Avenue
St. Louis, MO 63118
(314) 664-7000
(800) 325-3391
(800) 392-9031 (in Missouri)
Fax: (314) 664-1492

Contact: Sales Department
Services: Videotape producer and distributor. Material available to the public for rental and purchase.
Description: Christian films and videotapes, directed towards children, teenagers, and the church population at large. Topics include: Bible stories; Christian living; the pressures of fitting into social peer groups; dating and depression; sexual education; communication between teenagers and parents; family relationships; Christian marriages; incorporating religion into everyday life; Sunday school teaching; Martin Luther; discipleship and stewardship; aging; loneliness; grief; and fear of death. Also available are a selection of programs appropriate for Christmas and Easter.
   Titles include: *Devil at the Wheel; I Wonder Why; How You Got To Be You; The New You; Lord of Life, Lord of Me;* and *Sexuality: God's Precious Gift to Parents and Children.* Titles from Family Films include: *Jimmy and the White Lie; Little Visits with God; Welcome the Stranger; Life in the Herd; There's More to Life Than the Weekend!; Building a Christian Marriage; Premarriage Counseling; Martin Luther — Heretic; Sing and Rejoice — Guiding Young Singers; I Will Take You to the Christ Child; No Escape from Christmas; An Interview with Pontius Pilate;* and *Topic: Fear of Death.*
Size & Elements: Videotape: 3/4", VHS and Betamax (approx. 70 titles).
Cataloging: Published catalog.
Access: Available to the public for rental and purchase. Requests accepted by mail and telephone.
Rights: Full rights held to all material.
Licensing: Possibly available for licensing and reuse, subject to approval and prior written permission from Family Films.
Restrictions: Videotapes may be used for home or public viewing by church groups or individuals. Videotapes may not be copied or reproduced in any form by any method without prior written permission.
Viewing Facilities: None.
Duplication Facilities: None.
Related Materials: Accompanying study guides, leaders' guides and participant guides available for some programs.

MISSOURI (St. Louis)

INTERNATIONAL LUTHERAN LAYMAN'S LEAGUE
LUTHERAN TELEVISION
2185 Hampton Avenue
St. Louis, MO 63139
(314) 647-4900
(314) 647-6923

In Canada:
LUTHERAN LAYMEN'S LEAGUE OF CANADA
Box 481
Kitchener, ON N2G 4A2
(519) 578-7420
Street address: 270 Lawrence Avenue

John Schoedel (Executive Director)
Janet R. Meyer (Director of Media)
Bill Jackson (Manager, Media Marketing & Promotions)

Contact: Linda L. Hirschbuehler (Audiovisual Sales)

Services: Television producer and program distributor. Material available for syndication, rental, licensing and reuse, subject to approval.
Description: Lutheran Television produces *This is the Life,* the longest running dramatic syndicated program in television history (1952-present).
   This Christian evangelistic program covers a variety of topics, including abortion, acceptance, aging, business ethics, chemical dependency, child abuse, Christian love, conscience, dishonesty, euthanasia, facing death, facing death on a child's level, faith, family, forgiveness, foster care, guilt, hope in adversity, human dignity, living together, love, lying, marriage, mastectomy, mental health, occult, power of prayer, prejudice, purpose in life, revenge, sexual sins, social concern, suicide, witnessing and world hunger.
   Tension Point Films (each 10 min.) present dramatic portrayals of human problems, including family problems, teenage sex, mental retardation, abortion, marital problems, adjusting to retirement, race relations, physical beauty, idolatry of self, premarital sex, respecting individual differences, stepchildren and stepparents, suicide, eternal life, caring for the elderly, child abuse, obscenity of death in American culture, world hunger, jealousy and Christian concern, forgiveness and justice.
   Lutheran Television Specials are also available.
Size & Elements: Film: 16mm (approx. 2,000 episodes). Videotape: current titles available for distribution in VHS format.
Cataloging: Published catalogs available on request.
Access: Maintained for distribution and rental rather than for research or reuse. Research requests accepted by telephone. Research (audition) fees charged.
Rights: Full rights held to most material.
Licensing: Available for licensing and reuse, subject to restrictions. License fees charged. For licensing inquiries, call (314) 647-4900 (Ext. 48).
Restrictions: Some restrictions apply. Requests for licensing and reuse considered on a case-by-case basis.
Viewing Facilities: None.
Duplication Facilities: None.

MISSOURI (St. Louis)

MISSOURI HISTORICAL SOCIETY
Jefferson Memorial Building
Forest Park
St. Louis, MO 63112
(314) 361-1424

Robert Archibald (Acting Executive Director)

Contact: Duane R. Sneddeker (Curator of Photographs and Prints)
Services: Historical society. Open to the public. Film and videotape collection possibly available for licensing and reuse.
Description: Historical footage relating to Missouri and St. Louis (beginning 1920s).
   Early black and white films include *St. Louis Scenes* (1926-27, silent, also available on 1" master and 3/4" videotape), with scenes of the St. Louis Zoo, streetcars, cars and double-deck buses in midtown, automobile parade, a children's auto safety parade, country roads seen from a moving car, hot-air balloon and a dirigible; *St. Louis Tornado* (1927); a film on the Mississippi River highwater and flood (1927); *Lindbergh: The Epic American Hero* (1927); *Lindbergh: The Lone Eagle* (1927); a film on Lindbergh's flight (1927) and one showing his welcoming back to St. Louis (1927).
   Other subjects covered include construction in St. Louis (1930s); an air show at Lambert Field (1930s); air races in St. Louis (1930s); Veiled Prophet Parade (1931); and a Chamber of Commerce film, *Spirit of St. Louis* (1950s, color), with aerial views of downtown St. Louis, a Constellation airliner at Lambert Airport, suburbia (St. Louis County), the Pruitt-Igoe housing project, St. Louis University, Washington University, a Braille reading at Missouri School for the Blind, the construction of interstate highways, towboats on the Mississippi River, Southwestern Bell long-distance calling center, and the S.S. Admiral (excursion steamboat).
Size & Elements: Film: format unspecified (approx. 5,000 feet; positive prints). Videotape: 1" (1 item, approx. 10 min.; transfer from film, master); 3/4" (1 item, approx. 10 min.; transfer from film, viewing copy); VHS (film transfers, viewing copies).
Cataloging: Card catalogs; rough shot lists.
Access: Open to the public by appointment. Research fees not charged. Research requests accepted by mail, telephone and in person (by appointment only).
Rights: Full rights held to some material.
Licensing: Apply for information. License and usage fees charged.
Restrictions: None specified.

MISSOURI (St. Louis)

Viewing Facilities: Videotape (3/4" and VHS).
Duplication Facilities: None.

MISSOURI (St. Louis)

NATIONAL ASSOCIATION OF CIVILIAN CONSERVATION CORPS ALUMNI (NACCCA)
Jefferson Barracks
16 Hancock Avenue
St. Louis, MO 63125
(314) 487-8666
Fax: (314) 487-9488

John J. Britton (National Executive Director)

Contact: John J. Britton
Services: Association; museum. Holds films and videotapes.
Description: History, activities and accomplishments of the Civilian Conservation Corps in the U.S. (April 1933-June 1942; August 1977-present).
Size & Elements: Film: 35mm (1 can; original); 16mm (4 cans; originals). Videotape: format and amount unspecified (masters).
Cataloging: Card catalogs; more extensive cataloging in progress.
Access: Open to the public. Research requests accepted by mail and in person (walk-in).
Rights: Full rights held to all material.
Licensing: Apply for information. License fees charged in some cases.
Restrictions: None specified.
Viewing Facilities: None.
Duplication Facilities: None.

MISSOURI (St. Louis)

OFF-BROADWAY VIDEO PRODUCTIONS
8319 Halls Ferry Road
St. Louis, MO 63147
(314) 389-9711

Clint Crandall (President)

Contact: Brian Cunningham (Director)
Services: Videotape producer. Material available for duplication, licensing and reuse, subject to restrictions. Collection maintained primarily for convenience of clients.
Description: Police, fire and action footage (e.g., emergency and accident response); television newsreel footage (shot over many years); locations; helicopter and aerial shots.
Size & Elements: Film: 16mm (over 200,000 feet; uncataloged). Videotape: 3/4" (over 100 hours; masters).
Cataloging: Shot lists available for videotape material; film is uncataloged.
Access: Available for duplication, licensing and reuse for business and industrial use only. Research fees negotiable. Research requests accepted by mail.
Rights: Full rights held to all material. Additional clearances may be necessary in some cases if material is to be reused (releases required for some individuals visible in shots).
Licensing: Available for licensing and reuse, subject to restrictions. License fees charged.
Restrictions: Some restrictions may apply depending on footage and client.
Viewing Facilities: Videotape (3/4").
Duplication Facilities: Film (16mm); videotape (2", 1", 3/4", VHS and Betamax).

MISSOURI (St. Louis)

SWANK MOTION PICTURES, INC.
P.O. Box 231
St. Louis, MO 63166
(800) 876-5577
(314) 534-6300 (Missouri only)
Fax: (314) 289-2172

Street address: 201 South Jefferson Avenue

East Coast rental inquiries:
SWANK MOTION PICTURES, INC.
350 Vanderbilt Motor Parkway
Hauppauge, NY 11787
(800) 876-3344
(516) 434-1560
Fax: (516) 434-1574

Contact: Brian Fox
Services: Distributor. Film and videotape collection available to schools, colleges and universities, and organizations for non-theatrical rental.
Description: Feature films from major motion picture studios, including AFD, Cannon, Cinema Center, Columbia, Crown International, Walt Disney, The Ladd Company, Metro-Goldwyn-Mayer, Mulberry Square, New Century/Vista, New World, Pacific International, Touchstone, Universal, and Warner Bros.

Collection covers a wide range of genres, including recent releases, featured attractions, animation, fantasy, comedy, adventure and drama, animal stories, film classics, curriculum movies, horror, Halloween packages, slapstick comedy shorts and color cartoon festivals. The *Cinematheque* series has a large selection of titles under such subject headings as foreign films, literature, popular classics, and montage.
Size & Elements: Film: 16mm (over 2,000 titles; release prints). Videotape: 3/4", VHS and Betamax (most film titles available on videotape).
Cataloging: Published catalogs.
Access: Available for non-theatrical distribution and rental to schools, colleges and universities, and organizations. Requests accepted by mail and telephone.
Rights: Films are copyrighted works protected under Federal law. No film or any portion thereof may be copied, duplicated, broadcast or televised in any manner.
Licensing: Not available for licensing or reuse through Swank.
Restrictions: Motion pictures are specifically licensed for non-theatrical showings only.
Viewing Facilities: None.
Duplication Facilities: None.

MISSOURI (St. Louis)

UNIVERSITY OF MISSOURI, ST. LOUIS
WESTERN HISTORICAL MANUSCRIPT COLLECTION
Thomas Jefferson Library
8001 Natural Bridge Road
St. Louis, MO 63121
(314) 553-5143

Contact: Ken Thomas
Services: University manuscript collection; film and videotape archives.
Description: *Thomas A. Dooley Collection.* Collected by a medical missionary to Southeast Asia, including such titles as: *This is Your Life* (Nov. 17, 1959), featuring Tom Dooley; *Dr. America in Laos; Parade in Downtown St. Louis Celebrating the Anniversary of Women's Suffrage (NOW); Platform For A Man, His Ideas and Convictions; Biography of a Cancer; Lamp Unto My Feet,* with Tom Dooley Memorial: *"Before I Sleep";* and *The Crisis Award — Tom Dooley Tells His Story.* All titles are 3/4" videotape transferred from film. Collection restricted (apply for information).

Charlotte Peters Papers. 16mm film and 3/4" videotape. Some titles include: *Charlotte Peters in Rome; Nobody Wants a Fairy When She's Old; Catalytic Music.*

James W. Symington Papers (1968-76). Documentation, television coverage and television commercials relating to Congressional campaigns and events in Missouri's 2nd District.

Harriett Woods Papers (1982-86). 188 videotapes from Senatorial campaigns, 1982 (against Danforth) and 1986 (against Bond).

Paul Preisler Papers. 16mm film. *May Day* (1934), with outtakes; *May Day* (1938); *Auto Workers; I.L.G.W.U. Picnic; Banquet Speakers.*
Size & Elements: Film: 16mm and 8mm (31 titles; positives and originals). Videotape: 2", 3/4" and VHS (214 videotapes; masters and viewing copies).
Cataloging: Card catalogs.
Access: Available to the public for research and possibly reuse. Research fees not charged. Research requests accepted by mail, telephone and in person (walk-in).
Rights: Some rights held to some material.
Licensing: Apply for information. Usage fees charged.
Restrictions: None specified.
Viewing Facilities: Film (16mm and 8mm, at Audiovisual Center); videotape

(VHS, in-house).
Duplication Facilities: None.

MISSOURI (St. Louis)

WASHINGTON UNIVERSITY
GEORGE W. BROWN SCHOOL OF SOCIAL WORK
VIDEO CENTER
P.O. Box 1196
St. Louis, MO 63130
(314) 889-6612

Street address: 1 Brookings Drive

Shanti Khinduka (Dean)

Contact: Liz Peterson (Assistant Director)
Services: Educational institution; videotape production facility. Material available for rental and purchase for nonprofit educational use.
Description: Videotapes "produced to meet the social work training needs of professional groups or the information needs of particular at-risk groups." Subjects cover children, health care, management, mental health, sex role issues, social work education and social action.
　Titles include: *My Parent's Divorce: I Wish It Never Happened; Foster Care Remembered — A Personal Story: Barbara Woods; Kids Pay Adult Prices: The Story of Runaway Youth; Elderly Eye Patient; "I Try A Little Harder Now,"* in which a 57-year-old, low-income Black woman shares her experiences living with diabetes; *Living is Just Being Me: A Portrait of David Bruce,* the story of a blind, insulin-dependent kidney recipient, musician and songwriter who attempts to overcome his burdens and get on with his life; *Sudden Infant Death Syndrome Autopsy Examiner; Men and Masculinity Conference,* presenting the highlights of the Fourth National Men's Conference on Men and Masculinity at Washington University; *The Crisis Shelter Alternative,* in which three women at a crisis shelter in Belleville, Illinois share their experiences with sexual abuse, emotional abuse and violence.
Size & Elements: Videotape: 3/4" and VHS (39 titles, 150 videotapes, each 20 to 120 min.).
Cataloging: Published catalog.
Access: Available for rental and purchase at low cost to educational, professional and self-help groups.
Rights: Full rights held to all material.
Licensing: Apply for information.
Restrictions: Materials available for educational and nonprofit use only. All other uses prohibited, including public broadcast or cablecast.
Viewing Facilities: Film (16mm); videotape (3/4", VHS and Betamax).
Duplication Facilities: Videotape (3/4" to VHS and VHS to 3/4").

MISSOURI (St. Louis)

WASHINGTON UNIVERSITY
OLIN LIBRARY
SPECIAL COLLECTIONS
Campus Box 1061
St. Louis, MO 63130
(314) 889-5495

Holly Hall (Head, Special Collections)

Contact: Kevin Ray (Curator of Manuscripts)
Services: University library. Videotape collection not available for duplication, licensing or reuse.
Description: Outtakes from *Closing Sentences* (1981), a PBS documentary on the poet Howard Nemerov, produced by KETC-TV, St. Louis. Videotapes are housed with the Modern Literature Collection.
Size & Elements: Videotape: VHS (1 title; 4 segments, 60 min. each; viewing copies).
Cataloging: Card catalogs; finding aids.
Access: Open to the public. Research fees not charged. Research requests accepted by mail, telephone and in person (walk-in).
Rights: No rights held to any material. Additional clearances from KETC-TV are necessary if material is to be reused.
Licensing: Not available for licensing or reuse without additional clearances.
Restrictions: Duplication, licensing or reuse not permitted without additional clearances.
Viewing Facilities: Videotape (VHS) (available in Audiovisual Department).

Duplication Facilities: None.
Related Materials: Script and transcript.

MISSOURI (Springfield)

INTERNATIONAL ASSOCIATION OF FAIRS AND EXPOSITIONS
M.P.O. Box 985
Springfield, MO 65801
(417) 862-5771
Fax: (417) 862-0156

Street address: 3040 East Cairo, Springfield, MO 65802

Lewis Miller (Executive Vice President)

Contact: Lewis Miller
Services: Association. Videotapes available to members only; possibly available for reuse, subject to restrictions.
Description: Videotapes pertaining to the fair industry and the history of expositions, including productions documenting individual fairs and award-winning television commercials. Material has been collected since 1980.
Size & Elements: Videotape: 3/4" and VHS (approx. 10 titles).
Cataloging: Card catalogs.
Access: Available to members only. Membership fees charged. Research requests accepted by mail.
Rights: Some rights held to some material. Additional clearances may be necessary for reuse of television commercials.
Licensing: Apply for information.
Restrictions: Requests for licensing and reuse considered on a case-by-case basis. Television commercials are not owned by the association.
Viewing Facilities: None.
Duplication Facilities: None.

MONTANA

MONTANA (Great Falls)

NORTH COUNTRY MEDIA GROUP
P.O. Box 2244
Great Falls, MT 59403
(406) 761-7877
Fax: (406) 761-2029

Margaret Kochman (President)

Contact: Brenda Peterson (Production Coordinator)
Services: Film and videotape producer. Material available to the public for duplication, licensing and reuse.
Description: Montana-related subjects. Industrial and agricultural footage includes hay and wheat production; harvesting; food processing; farming; ranching; a gasohol plant; and outfitters (guides) for rafting and fishing trips. Parks and wilderness footage includes Glacier National Park, shown in fall, winter and summer; bald eagles flocking around a glacier and feeding on salmon; Yellowstone National Park; wildflowers; and wildlife, including elk, moose and deer. Recreational footage includes water and snow skiing; white-water rafting (action footage); windsurfing; sailing and canoeing; fly-fishing; horseback riding; golfing in Hawaii; and rodeos. Also holds footage relating to Native American culture, focusing on Crow and Blackfoot dancers.
Size & Elements: Film: 16mm. Videotape: 1" (masters; transfers from film); 3/4" (viewing copies). (500 hours total).
Cataloging: Computerized cataloging in progress.
Access: Available to the public for duplication and reuse. Research fees charged. Research requests accepted by mail and telephone.
Rights: Full rights held to all material.
Licensing: Available for licensing and reuse. License fees charged.
Restrictions: None specified.
Viewing Facilities: Videotape (all formats).
Duplication Facilities: Videotape (2", 1", 3/4" and VHS).

MONTANA (Helena)

MONTANA DEPARTMENT OF COMMERCE
MONTANA TRAVEL PROMOTION DIVISION
1424 9th Avenue

NEBRASKA (Hastings)

Helena, MT 59620
(406) 444-2654
(800) 548-3390
Telex: 295708 MONTCOMM

John Wilson (Travel Director for the State of Montana)

Contact: Sherryl Vaughn (Film Librarian)
Services: Government agency. Films available to the public for free loan and duplication.
Description: Promotional films on Montana's history, seasonal and recreational activities, and tourist attractions.
Sample titles include: *Montana Revisited Along the Lewis and Clark Trail; Red Sunday* (1975), a documentary on the battle of Little Big Horn and General Custer; *Ghost Town, Montana* (1963); *Four Seasons of the Yellowstone; Montana: Big Sky, Big Snow* (1968); *Escape to Montana's Glacier National Park* (1972); *Travel: Montana's Beautiful Industry;* and *Tour Montana: Last of the Big Time Splendors.*
Size & Elements: Film: 16mm (15 titles; release prints).
Cataloging: Shot lists; research library.
Access: Available to the public for free loan and duplication. Research fees not charged. Research requests accepted by mail, telephone and in person (walk-in and by appointment).
Rights: Full rights held to all material.
Licensing: Apply for information.
Restrictions: None specified.
Viewing Facilities: Film.
Duplication Facilities: None.

NEBRASKA

NEBRASKA (Hastings)

ADAMS COUNTY HISTORICAL SOCIETY
Box 102
Hastings, NE 68902
(402) 463-5838

Street address: 1330 North Burlington Avenue

Catherine Renschler (Executive Director)

Contact: Catherine Renschler
Services: Historical society. Film and videotape materials available for in-house use only, with the exception of one film series which is available for rental and purchase.
Description: Adams County, Nebraska and Great Plains history. Holdings include *The Great Plains,* a film in six parts; various untitled newsreels; and videotapes relating to historic subjects.
Size & Elements: Film: 16mm (50 cans, 10 titles; originals and prints). Videotape: format unspecified (19 titles).
Cataloging: Card catalogs.
Access: Open to researchers and scholars. For in-house use only. Research requests accepted in person (by appointment only). *The Great Plains* is available for rental and purchase.
Rights: Full rights held to all material.
Licensing: Apply for information.
Restrictions: Collection maintained primarily for in-house use only.
Viewing Facilities: Viewing arrangements must be made in advance.
Duplication Facilities: None.

NEBRASKA (Lincoln)

GPN
P.O. Box 80669
Lincoln, NE 68501
(402) 472-2007
(800) 228-4630
Fax: (402) 472-1785

Street address: 1800 North 33rd, Lincoln, NE 68583

Lee Rockwell (Director)

Contact: Stephen C. Lenzen (Associate Director)
Services: Distributor of instructional television programming. Videotapes available for purchase, rental, preview and broadcast. Stock footage not available for licensing or reuse.
Description: The Great Plains National Instructional Television Library (GPN) (founded 1962), is a self-supporting agency of the University of Nebraska-Lincoln. It distributes quality videotaped instructional courses and programs, plus videodiscs and specialized slides, to educational institutions and public broadcasting stations across the United States. GPN also engages in the preparation of new and original materials for educational media users, and provides library and distribution services for a number of agencies, including the Central Educational Network, the Pacific Mountain Network and the U.S. Department of Education's Division of Educational Technology.
Programming is available for all grade levels from elementary through adult. Subjects covered include: alcohol education, art, artistic awareness, Asian studies, astronomy, business, career education, communications, computer literacy, consumer economics, cultural arts, documentaries, driver education, drug education, economics, educational in-service, environmental studies, family studies, foreign languages, foreign studies, forestry, geography, grantsmanship, handwriting, health and safety, history, job hunting, journalism, language arts, law education, management, mathematics, medical training, metric education, music, Native Americans, nutritional health, parenting, photography, physical education, psychology, reading, rhetoric, safety, science, self-awareness, semantics, sex education, social studies, sociology, study skills, testing, theater arts, video production and writing skills.
Size & Elements: Film: 16mm. Videotape: 3/4", VHS and Betamax II. Over 160 series, plus approx. 30 single programs (2,365 programs, 960 hours total).
Cataloging: Published catalogs.
Access: Available for rental and purchase for educational use, cablecast and broadcast. Preview and rental fees charged. Requests accepted by mail and telephone.
Rights: Rights retained by original producers.
Licensing: Not available for licensing or reuse.
Restrictions: Stock footage from GPN-distributed programs is not available.
Viewing Facilities: None.
Duplication Facilities: Videotape (2", 1", 3/4", VHS and Betamax) (available in NTSC, PAL and SECAM formats).
Related Materials: Telecourse teacher guides to be used in conjunction with GPN-distributed videotape series.

NEBRASKA (Lincoln)

NATIVE AMERICAN PUBLIC BROADCASTING CONSORTIUM
P.O. Box 83111
Lincoln, NE 68501
(402) 472-3522
Fax: (402) 472-2410

Frank Blythe (Executive Director)

Contact: Matthew L. Jones (Program and Project Coordinator)
Services: Distributor; nonprofit organization. Videotape programs available for broadcast and non-broadcast use.
Description: Founded 1977. A nonprofit organization encouraging the creation, production, promotion and distribution of quality programming by, for and about Native Americans. NAPBC first grew out of public broadcasting's need for a national resource center to hold and distribute Native American programming, and has since earned a reputation as a dependable membership organization that provides programming as well as extensive telecommunications services on a national level.
Offers services in program development, production and library distribution for public broadcast and for Native American and public education. Expert consulting is offered for Native American media production and distribution; can also assist in locating Native American professionals for film, video and radio productions and will serve as a liaison for all broadcast media in regard to Native American programming.
Programs relate to Native American arts, ceremony, culture and folklore, education, economy, family, food, Indian-white relations, health and history.
Arts. The American As Artist: Portrait of Bob Penn; Amiotte, profiling Sioux painter Arthur Amiotte; *Herman Red Elk: A Sioux Indian Artist,* on a Yankton Sioux artist best known for his skin paintings; *John Kim Bell,* the first Native American pursuing a career as a symphony conductor; *Oscar Howe: The Sioux Painter; 1,000 Years of Muscogee (Creek) Art,* developing Creek art forms from the prehistoric period of the mound-builders to the present; *Strength of Life — Knokovtee Scott,* in which an Indian artist describes his

shellwork jewelry and the authentic art of Creek and Cherokee ancestors. *American Indian Artists — A Series* (9 programs, each 30 min.) profiles seven contemporary Native American artists who fuse tradition with personal innovation; featured are potters, jewelers, a sculptor and a painter. *Indian Arts At the Phoenix Heard Museum — A Series* (6 programs, each 30 min.) explores six major areas of Southwest Native American art: basketry painting, pottery, textiles, silversmithing and Kachina doll sculpting.

Ceremony. Angoon One Hundred Years Later recalls the destruction (1882) of the Tlingit Indian village of Angoon, Alaska on October 26, 1882 by U.S. naval forces. Through ceremonies, the surviving Tlingit culture commemorates the destruction of Angoon's great tribal houses, the loss of canoes, food supplies and ceremonial objects, and the deaths of six children. *Children of the Long-Beaked Bird* follows a contemporary 12-year-old Crow Indian through his daily activities. *Huteetl: Koyukon Memorial Potlatch* presents the final death rites for a young couple, one year after their death, following the Koyukon tradition. *I Am Different From My Brother: Dakota Name-Giving* depicts the name-giving ceremony, in which three young Flandreau Dakota Sioux children come of age by receiving their traditional Indian names from their grandparents, and the ceremonial blessing of The Keeper of The Pipe. *Miss Indian American* documents the 20th annual pageant (1973), attended by representatives of 30 American Indian tribes from all over the United States. *Mother Corn* examines the historical significance of various types of corn among Hopi and Pueblo cultures and traces the symbolism of corn across the generations. *Ni'bthaska of the Umonhon* (3 programs, each 30 min.), set in the year 1800, is about a 13-year-old boy from the Omaha tribe in the first summer of his manhood. *Songs in Minto Life* is the first documentary to present traditional Athabaskan music from interior Alaska. Each song contributes to the survival of the community, is made by one person and cannot be sung without community approval.

Culture and folklore. Ancient Spirit, Living Word: The Oral Tradition shows how the traditional knowledge of Native Americans, spanning hundreds of years, is passed by word of mouth from one generation to the next. *Folklore of the Muscogee (Creek) People* describes the nature of folklore within Creek culture, breaking it down into three categories: legends, myths and fables, illustrating each with a traditional Creek tale. *Forgotten Frontier* documents the architectural, political, social and religious history of the Spanish mission settlements of southern Arizona and their conversion of the Indian population; *Four Corners of Earth* explores the roles and culture of Seminole women, including the clan system, legends, medical practices, foods, traditional clothing, crafts and education; *The Good Mind* explores similarities between Christian and Native American beliefs; *Navajo* shows two youngsters who leave their modern way of life behind to learn the ways of their traditional Navajo grandparents on a visit to the Navajo reservation; *Navajo Code Talkers* uses 1940s archival footage to show the vital role a small group of Navajo Marines played in the South Pacific during World War II; *Red Road: Toward the Techno-Tribal* presents contemporary views of Native American philosophy, spirituality and prophecy; *The Sun Dagger* explores the Anasazi culture that thrived over 1,000 years ago in the harsh Chaco Canyon environment, whose people produced a rock formation that marks solstices, equinoxes and the 19-year lunar cycle. *Tales of Wesakechak — A Series* (13 programs) is based on well-known Canadian Cree legends dramatized with an oral storyteller and shadow puppets. *We Are One — A Series* (8 programs) concerns the life and culture of a Native American family in early 19th-century Nebraska, in particular the Omaha culture, focusing on a 13-year-old boy and his young sister, their daily rituals and rites of passage.

Economy. Aboriginal Rights: I Can Get It for You Wholesale presents the concept of aboriginal rights in its various interpretations since the 16th century, traced through historical photographs and on-site footage throughout North America, from the Spanish conquest to modern times. Explores European immigration from an economic perspective, the differences between European and Native American values and attitudes toward land ownership, the Black Hills land dispute and how the land grab was handled in the U.S. and Canada. *Dineh: The People* focuses on the impending relocation of several thousand Navajo from a joint-use land area surrounding the Hopi Reservation, suggesting that a politically motivated interest in strip-mining has encouraged this land dispute. Portrays the cultural and economic conditions under which the Navajo attempt to survive while striving to preserve their traditional values, and examines a broad range of reservation concerns including unemployment, malnutrition, alcoholism, abuse by traders and health care.

Minorities in Agriculture: The Winnebago documents the economic development programs of Nebraska's Winnebago tribe, with a description of their food self-sufficiency program. *On the Path to Self-Reliance* concerns Seminole tribal history and their current state of economic development, covering thriving cattle operations, agriculture and aquaculture programs, and

how proceeds from bingo repay federal monies. *Pride, Purpose and Promise: Paiutes of the Southwest* shows how the Paiutes have struggled against disease, loss of land and economic deprivation in search of self-sufficiency. *The Probable Passing of Elk Creek* focuses on the controversy between the Grindstone Indian Reservation in Northern California and the state government, which plans to build a reservoir over the valley that will force both whites and Native Americans to leave their homelands. *Tomorrow's Yesterday* shows how the Pueblo people adapt to the challenges of modern civilization.

Education. Woonspe (Education and the Sioux) explores the problem of Native American education and the historical significance, advantages and disadvantages of the four school systems available to Native Americans: BIA boarding schools, public schools, tribal contract schools and mission schools.

Health. Health Care Crisis at Rosebud explores possible solutions to a serious shortage of physicians on the Rosebud Reservation in 1973.

History. Art of Being Indian: Filmed Aspects of the Culture of the Sioux presents the Sioux cultural heritage, beginning with their early days in the northeast, to the "Golden Age" of adaptation to the Dakota plains, and their present status and future hopes. *Canada's Original Peoples: Then and Now* contrasts the life of native Canadians before the arrival of Europeans with contemporary native life. Explores pre-European times, examines native artifacts and documents the contemporary life of three native communities, observing a logging operation, a potter and a snowshoe factory. *The Eagle and the Condor* examines interaction between the Native American cultures of North and South America.

Forest Spirits — A Series (7 programs, each 30 min.) was filmed on location in Wisconsin. The first three programs relate to the Oneida Nation and the last four with the Menominee people. Topics range from heritage, education and people's relationship to the land to the Native American's dreams for the future. *To Keep a Heritage Alive* shows how the Oneida heritage was almost obliterated when a generation was sent to boarding school at the turn of the century. The Oneida are reversing the erosion by teaching their children the native tongue, about artifacts and mementoes, moral ethics, respect for elders and regard for the land. *The Learning Path* focuses on the confrontation between the Oneida and the Green Bay Curriculum Committee over the introduction of an Indian history and culture course in the city's high schools. *Land is Life* covers the Oneida's journey from New York to Wisconsin and the allotment and subsequent loss of most of their land in Wisconsin. Oneida who now wish to return cannot do so because of the lack of land for building. *Ancestors of Those Yet Unborn* focuses on the lives, lifestyles and personal feelings of the Menominee tribe. *Living with Tradition* shows the Menominee people and their traditions. Under a federal process called "termination," the government ended the protected status of the Menominee as an Indian tribe and their reservation became a county; forced to live like white people, they strive to keep their culture alive. *Dreamers with Power* shows the Menominee tradition of dreaming; members of the tribe would fast, have visions, interpret them and use them to guide their decisions and actions.

Journey to the Sky: A History of the Alabama Coushatta Indians chronicles the passage of a hunting and gathering culture that flourished in the Southeastern forests of central Alabama, through their first contacts with Europeans and their migration to East Texas. *Menominee* documents the many social and political problems faced by the Menominee Indians of northwestern Wisconsin, which led them successfully to seek reversal of a federal government decision to terminate their status as an Indian reservation.

North of 60: Destiny Uncertain — A Series (5 programs, each 30 min.) was filmed on location in Canada's Northwest Territories, the Yukon and Alaska, exploring a part of the earth once shrouded in mystery, myth and fable, rich in minerals, oil and natural gas, now ruled by the vagaries of high-tech fortunetelling. *They Came to Stay* follows the growth of the fur trade and the whaling industry, the role of federal government and changes to the region; *The Alaska Experience* explores the building of the Alaska pipeline, settlement of Alaskan Native land claims and transition from territorial status to statehood; *Tell Me Who I Am* investigates the dilemma resulting from the recent attempt to provide relevant and useful educational opportunities to an ethnically diverse population in Canada's Northland; *New Way of Knowing* documents the clash between the traditional technologies of the North and modern scientific methods imported from the South; *Mending Bodies and Souls* examines how rapid change and acculturation have increased the stress in the lives of Canada's northern inhabitants, examining the effects of stress, altered eating habits and alcohol on the physical and mental health of the people.

People of the First Light — A Series shows how Native Americans in southern New England have maintained their cultural identity through dance, art, family and community. *Indians in Southern New England (The Survivors)* shows how Native Americans in Massachusetts, Connecticut and Rhode Island maintain tribal lifestyles and strive to preserve and transmit their cultures; *The*

Wampanoags of Gay Head (Community Spirit and Island Life) shows how three generations of Wampanoag Indians live and maintain traditional values on the island of Martha's Vineyard; *The Boston Indian Community (Change and Identity)* focuses on ways in which today's city-dwelling Native Americans maintain the essence of their culture and how they are able to aid other Native Americans who have migrated to Boston; *The Narragansetts (Tradition)* shows the ways Narragansetts strive to maintain their traditional heritage and to pass traditions from one generation to the next; *Indians of Connecticut (The Importance of Land)* discusses the five indigenous Indian tribes in Connecticut today (Eastern and Western Pequots, Paugausetts, Mohegans and Schaghticokes), and discusses the importance of maintaining a land base for preservation of the Native American culture; *The Indian Experience: Urban and Rural (Survival)* discusses how ancient traditions conflict with contemporary conformity; *The Mashpee Wampanoags (Tribal Identity)* discusses how the tribe live, work and maintain the long-standing culture of their ancestors on the same lands they have inhabited for thousands of years.

The Real People — A Series is the first television series made by and about American Indians, highlighting past and current life on and off reservations. *A Season of Grandmothers* emphasizes the revival of traditional Indian education, reverence for elders and yearning for the "old ways" through the use of traditional teachers, the Grandmothers; *Circle of Song Parts 1* and *2* focuses on traditional songs and dances; *Mainstream* examines the recollections of a Coeur d'Alene woman who lives in mainstream society; *Awakening* focuses on the spiritual rebirth of the American Indian, ending in a "sweat-house" and at an Indian wake; *Spirit of the Wind* emphasizes the place of the horse in the Plateau Tribes, featuring the recollections of two retired rodeo riders about their life on the rodeo circuit, enhanced by tribal footage shot in the 1930s; *Buffalo, Blood, Salmon and Roots* looks at old ways of gathering and preserving food, tribal values connected with roots and food, and the medicinal use of roots; *Legend of the Stick Game* recreates how the "stick game" came to be; *Word of Life — People of Rivers* serves as an introduction to the seven tribes and a map for future growth.

Return of the Raven, The Edison Chiloquin Story tells how Edison Chiloquin refused government payments in 1961 in compensation for the termination of federal recognition of his land claims, and later became the first individual Native American to have his land returned by Congress. *White Man's Way* recalls an experiment, beginning in the late 1800s, that endeavored to transform the American Indian "from savagery to civilization." The U.S. Indian School was built in the heart of what was once Pawnee Indian country (Genoa, Nebraska). In this government-supported military-style school for Indian children from more than 20 tribes, they were taught the white man's language, traditions and lifestyle and were forbidden to practice their own.
Size & Elements: Videotape: 1", 3/4" and VHS (approx. 120 titles; masters and viewing copies).
Cataloging: Published catalogs.
Access: Available for broadcast to NAPBC members (free or at reduced rates), public television stations, educators and organizations. Maintained for distribution and rental rather than for research or reuse.
Rights: Full rights held to some material. Some rights held to all material. Rights retained by original producers in most cases.
Licensing: Apply for information.
Restrictions: Most programs are available for both broadcast and non-broadcast use; some programs are available for non-broadcast use only.
Viewing Facilities: Videotape.
Duplication Facilities: Videotape.
Related Materials: Teaching guides accompany some programs.

NEBRASKA (Lincoln)

NEBRASKA STATE HISTORICAL SOCIETY
P.O. Box 82554
Lincoln, NE 68501
(402) 471-3270

Street address: 1500 R Street, Lincoln, NE 68508

James A. Hanson (Director)

Contacts: Sherrill F. Daniels (Director of Reference Services); Andrea I. Paul (Assistant State Archivist)
Services: Educational institution; government agency; historical society; library; museum. Open to researchers and scholars only. Film collection available for licensing and reuse, subject to restrictions.
Description: Holds daily news broadcasts (1958-81) donated by local Lincoln television station KOLN-TV. Material pertains to Nebraska history, local news,

events and politics.
Size & Elements: Film: 16mm (approx. 800 cans). More details available when collection is completely inventoried and cataloged.
Cataloging: Currently not inventoried or cataloged. Plans to inventory and catalog collection in future.
Access: Open to researchers and scholars only. Written permission must be obtained from KOLN-TV explaining research project and proposed use of footage before the Society can grant access to footage. Apply for information on processing research requests and fees.
Rights: Apply for information. Additional clearances necessary if material is to be reused.
Licensing: Apply for information. License fees charged in some cases; contact KOLN-TV for details.
Restrictions: Written permission must be obtained from KOLN-TV for access to and use of footage.
Viewing Facilities: Apply for information.
Duplication Facilities: Apply for information.

NEBRASKA (Lincoln)

NSDAP/AO
P.O. Box 6414
Lincoln, NE 68506

Services: Political organization. Videotapes available for purchase.
Description: Newsreels, documentary and propaganda films produced in Nazi Germany (1933-45). Includes films on World War II battles seen from the Nazi perspective; *Triumph of the Will*, Leni Riefenstahl's film of the Sixth Nazi Party Congress; *Germany Celebrates Hitler's Birthday* (1939); assorted Nazi political films (1932-43); *Germany Awake*, with excerpts from fiction films produced during the Third Reich; and *Jud Süss*, the notorious anti-Semitic film. All videotapes have English subtitles.
Size & Elements: Videotape: VHS and Betamax; NTSC and PAL (15 videotapes).
Cataloging: Published list.
Access: Available to the public for purchase.
Rights: Apply for information.
Licensing: Apply for information.
Restrictions: None specified.
Viewing Facilities: None.
Duplication Facilities: None.
Related Materials: Audiocassettes of German Army, Navy and Storm Trooper marches.

NEBRASKA (Omaha)

UNION PACIFIC RAILROAD AUDIOVISUAL SERVICES
1416 Dodge
Omaha, NE 68179
(402) 271-3857

M. A. Bieker (Director of Archives)

Contact: M. A. Bieker; Don Snoddy (402/271-3305)
Services: Museum; film and videotape archives. Open to the public. Material available for licensing and reuse, subject to restrictions.
Description: Industrial and educational films focusing on railroads (most produced 1940s-present). Some concentrate on subjects such as agriculture, aerials and landscapes, and contain incidental footage of trains.

Popular titles include: *Last of the Giants,* on the world's largest locomotive, detailing its operation and steam power; *The 8444,* on the most popular steam locomotive (still in operation); *Lucky You,* a safety film designed to prevent juveniles from trespassing in railroad yards; *Rails Across America,* on the combined histories of the Union Pacific and the Missouri Pacific Railroads, which merged in 1982; and *Trails of the Iron Horse* (1968), made for Union Pacific's centennial (1969), containing stock footage from other sources. One early film (1934) features the first streamlined train.

The archives makes use of these six titles on a regular basis, although the general collection contains other films. Research requests which cannot be fulfilled by these materials are accepted on a case-by-case basis.
Size & Elements: Film: 16mm (amount unspecified). Videotape: VHS (amount unspecified; film-to-videotape transfers and viewing copies).
Cataloging: None.
Access: Open to the public. Available for reuse. Research fees not generally

charged. Research requests accepted by mail and telephone.
Rights: Full rights held to some material. Some rights held to all material. Additional clearances may be necessary in some cases if material is to be reused.
Licensing: Available for licensing, subject to restrictions. License fees charged in some cases.
Restrictions: Requests for reuse accepted on a case-by-case basis.
Viewing Facilities: Videotape.
Duplication Facilities: None.

NEVADA

NEVADA (Incline Village)

KD ENTERPRISES PRODUCTIONS
P.O. Box 8321
Incline Village, NV 89450
(702) 831-8178
(702) 827-3821
Fax: (702) 827-3872

Caroline DiDiego (President)

Contact: Caroline DiDiego
Services: Film and videotape producer; stock footage sales library.
Description: Footage from environmental documentary films (1983-present). Material shot in the Western United States includes: aerial footage of Western rivers; the Grand Canyon; Great Basin flora and fauna; Great Basin birds (200 species, including hurons, red-tailed hawks, Western bluebirds, red-wing blackbirds, yellow-headed blackbirds and marsh birds); some Great Basin mammals; underwater footage shot in Lake Tahoe; and sub-Alpine (Sierra Nevada) environmental material. "Western nostalgia," in the style of Ansel Adams, includes footage of ghost towns.
  Coverage of East Coast waterfowl includes migration and nesting footage of ducks, geese and Eastern Goshawks shot in New England and on the Chesapeake Bay.
Size & Elements: Film: 16mm (200 cans, "steadily increasing"). Videotape: Betacam (transfers from film).
Cataloging: Computerized cataloging (shot lists) in progress.
Access: Open to researchers and scholars. Available for reuse. Research fees charged in some cases. Research requests accepted by mail, telephone and in person (by appointment only).
Rights: Full rights held to some material. Additional clearances may be necessary in some cases if material is to be reused.
Licensing: Available for licensing and reuse, subject to restrictions. License fees charged (fee scale varies depending on usage and size of job).
Restrictions: Licensing requests subject to approval and acceptance by library. Screen credit required if material is used.
Viewing Facilities: Videotape (Betacam) (by appointment only).
Duplication Facilities: Videotape (Betacam to VHS; in-house) (all formats available via outside facility).

NEVADA (Las Vegas)

AMERICAN SCIENCE FICTION ASSOCIATION
421 East Carson, Suite 95
Las Vegas, NV 89101
(702) 644-8085

P. G. Silvers (Executive Vice President)

Contact: P. G. Silvers
Services: Association. Film and videotape collection primarily maintained for use by ASFA members and for research and scholarly purposes.
Description: Full-length motion pictures, videotapes and other audiovisual materials concerning science fiction and fantasy themes.
Size & Elements: Film: format unspecified (over 400 titles). Videotape: format unspecified (2,000 videotapes). All elements available.
Cataloging: Card catalogs; published catalogs; research library.
Access: Primarily restricted to ASFA members. Open to researchers and scholars. Research fees not charged. Research requests accepted by mail and in person (by appointment only).
Rights: Full rights held to some material. Some rights held to some material. Additional clearances may be necessary in some cases if material is to be

reused.
Licensing: Apply for information. License fees charged for nonmembers.
Restrictions: Some restrictions may apply.
Viewing Facilities: Film and videotape.
Duplication Facilities: Videotape.

NEVADA (Las Vegas)

NORMAN BEERGER PRODUCTIONS
3217 South Arville Street
Las Vegas, NV 89102-7612
(702) 876-2328

Norman Beerger (Owner)

Contact: Norman Beerger
Services: Videotape distributor; film and videotape producer; stock footage sales library. Videotapes available to the public for purchase, duplication and possibly reuse.
Description: Geography and nature; travel; U.S. national parks; American heritage and adventure; space exploration; and aerial photography.
  Holiday Video Library. Titles from the *National Park and Monument Series* include: *Mount Rainier; Giant Sequoias; Death Valley; Yellowstone & Grand Teton; Denali Wilderness Alaska;* and *National Monuments of Southern Arizona.* Titles from the *Space and Science Series* include: *Universe; History of the Apollo Program; Jupiter & Saturn; Air War Over Europe: World War II;* and *The Return of Halley's Comet.* Titles from the *American Adventure Series* include: *Scenic Seattle; Las Vegas & Hoover Dam; Israel — This Land is Yours!; Howard Hughes and the Spruce Goose;* and *Eruption of Mount St. Helens.*
  Chronicle Videocassettes. Titles include: *America's Secret Places; Alaska; Trout Fishing: Northern California; Hong Kong; England; Rome;* and *Paris and the Seine.*
  National Geographic Series. Titles include: *The Sharks; Land of the Tiger;* and *Iceland River Challenge.*
  Other productions distributed. Titles include: *The Grand Canyon* (Norman Beerger Productions), an aerial journey of the entire canyon (shot before

NEVADA (Las Vegas)

current flight restrictions) showing the natural wonder of narrow gorges, chasms, water rapids and natural scenics; *Surf* (Larry Wood Productions), capturing ocean waves of the rugged California and Oregon coastlines; *Loon Country By Canoe* (Dan Gibson); *Kilauea Volcano* (Lee Productions), showing the volcano in full eruption; *Clouds* (Pinnacle Productions); and *Water Journey* (Natural Source Media).
Size & Elements: Videotape: 1", 3/4", VHS and Betamax (100 videotapes; masters and viewing copies).
Cataloging: Research library.
Access: Available to the public for purchase, duplication and possibly reuse. Research fees charged. Research requests accepted by mail and telephone.
Rights: Full rights held to some material (*The Grand Canyon*). Additional clearances may be necessary in some cases if material is to be reused.
Licensing: Apply for information. License fees charged for commercial use; fees depend on final amount used.
Restrictions: Apply for information.
Viewing Facilities: Videotape (1/2").
Duplication Facilities: Videotape.

NEVADA (Las Vegas)

LAS VEGAS NEWS BUREAU
Convention Center
Las Vegas, NV 89109
(702) 735-3611
Fax: (702) 457-3906

Don Payne (Bureau Manager)

Contact: John Reible (Assistant Manager)
Services: Nonprofit media organization. Film and videotape collection available to the public for duplication and reuse.
Description: Newsworthy events occurring in Las Vegas (mid-1950s through mid-1970s). The film was originally produced for syndication to television broadcasters in the West. Subjects covered include entertainers; social events at casinos, nightclubs and country clubs; promotional films produced for the city of Las Vegas; scenes of hotels and resorts and coverage of atomic tests. Most material is silent.

Some highlights of the collection include the "Sands Summit" (January 28, 1960), with Frank Sinatra, Sammy Davis Jr., Joey Bishop, Dean Martin and Peter Lawford; *Playground* (1965), a short promotional film produced by the Las Vegas Chamber of Commerce; Vice President Richard M. Nixon at the Sahara Hotel and the Last Frontier (1954); the "Mint 400" automobile race (1975); the Helldorado Parade (1954); Tallulah Bankhead, Cab Calloway, Mae West and Marlene Dietrich opening at the Sahara Hotel (all 1950s); an air show at McCarran Field, featuring jets (1950s); the Tournament of Champions (1954) with Bob Hope, Jack Benny and others; the Sands Time Capsule (1953); the crowning of "Miss Sonic Boom" at Nellis Air Force Base (ca. 1954); the *Blue Bird* setting the world speed record (October 1955); Frank Sinatra opening at the Dunes, seen on stage sitting on a camel (ca. 1955); and "cheesecake" footage of Christine Jorgensen, who underwent the first successful sex-change operation (November 1953).

Other material includes performances staged for the entertainment of soldiers in Las Vegas to participate in atomic tests; an "atomic hairstyle"; Joan Crawford's wedding; Judy Garland at the Frontier (July 17, 1956); Liberace and Vampira appearing at the Riviera; birthday celebrations for Sophie Tucker (1950s); Hoover Dam (1958); atomic test footage (1957), including footage of the trenches at the proving grounds; Sonny Liston in training (July 16, 1963); Orson Welles opening at the Riviera (February 23, 1956); a ceremony honoring the nine millionth visitor to Hoover Dam (October, 1962); Liberace and Elvis Presley (November 14, 1956); the wedding of Tommy Sands and Nancy Sinatra (September, 1960); the arrival of Lyndon B. Johnson on a campaign tour (April 25, 1960); a bed-pushing contest (March 20, 1961); Elvis Presley greeted at the airport (1969) and the PLUMBBOB atomic test (1957).
Size & Elements: Film: 16mm (amount unspecified; black and white and color, mostly silent). Videotape: 1" (masters transferred from 16mm film) and 3/4" (viewing copies).
Cataloging: Card catalogs; videotape logs.
Access: Available to the public for duplication and reuse. Research requests accepted by mail, telephone and in person (walk-in). Research fees charged only to cover costs.
Rights: Material in the public domain.
Licensing: Generally available for reuse. Usage fees charged only to cover costs.
Restrictions: None specified.

Viewing Facilities: Videotape (3/4").
Duplication Facilities: None (outside arrangements can be made).

NEVADA (Las Vegas)

NETWORK PRODUCTIONS
3900 Paradise Road, Suite 265
Las Vegas, NV 89109
(702) 734-3990

Contact: Michael Fawcett (Production Manager)
Services: Videotape producer; stock footage sales library.
Description: Videotape footage (1982-present) of Nevada locations and activities.

Coverage of Nevada includes all locations; day and night interior and exterior footage of hotels; Las Vegas; aerial and views of the Las Vegas Strip; Hoover Dam; casinos; state parks; mountain areas; ski resorts; Lake Mead; water skiing; scenics; and beauty shots. Also holds coverage of boxing, including interviews and press conferences; hydroplane races; interviews with celebrities and sports figures; kick boxing; karate; Grand Prix automobile racing; rodeos; and golf tournaments.
Size & Elements: Videotape: Betacam SP (700 hours; masters); VHS (viewing copies).
Cataloging: Brochure; computerized cataloging for staff use only.
Access: Open to the public. Available for duplication and reuse. Research fees not charged. Research requests accepted by telephone.
Rights: Full rights held to all material. Additional clearances may be necessary in some cases (footage showing celebrities and sports figures) if material is to be reused.
Licensing: Available for licensing and reuse, subject to restrictions. License fees charged. No minimum "cut" requirement.
Restrictions: Footage depicting celebrities and sports figures may carry special restrictions.
Viewing Facilities: Videotape (Betacam).
Duplication Facilities: Videotape (Betacam SP to 1", Betacam, 3/4" or VHS).

NEVADA (Reno)

NATIONAL COUNCIL OF JUVENILE AND FAMILY COURT JUDGES
P.O. Box 8970
Reno, NV 89507
(702) 784-6012
Fax: (702) 784-6628

Louis W. McHardy (Executive Director and Dean, National College of Juvenile Justice and Family Law)

Contact: Rene Chilton (702/784-6139)
Services: Nonprofit organization. Videotapes available for purchase by local communities as part of a training program.
Description: Training program designed for judges, prosecutors, defense attorneys and other juvenile justice professionals wishing to reduce trauma to and assist in the treatment of sexually abused children.

Program titles include: *A Judge's Overview on the Judicial Response to Sexual Cases; Pros and Cons of Videotaping Child Victims; The Intake Interview; Child Credibility;* and *Treatment and Sentencing.*
Size & Elements: Videotape: format unspecified (5 titles).
Cataloging: Catalog available from the Training Department.
Access: Available for purchase by local communities as part of a training program. Requests accepted by mail and telephone.
Rights: Apply for information.
Licensing: Apply for information.
Restrictions: Apply for information.
Viewing Facilities: None.
Duplication Facilities: None.
Related Materials: Audiotapes; manuals; journals; periodicals; textbooks.

NEW HAMPSHIRE

NEW HAMPSHIRE (Greenland)

CINEWORKS PRODUCTIONS INC.
124 Great Bay Road

Greenland, NH 03840
(603) 431-4241
Fax: (603) 433-5362

Gary Anderson (President)

Contact: Gary Anderson
Services: Film and videotape producer. Material available for duplication, licensing and reuse.
Description: Footage of Northern New England, including recreation (water and snow skiing, bicycling); tourist attractions and resorts (historical, cruise ships and water slides); environment (scenics, shot in all seasons with and without people, town squares and foliage); wildlife (birds and small animals); seacoasts and aerials (Maine and New Hampshire); and industrial scenes (generic, corporate, heavy and light assembly and electronics).
Size & Elements: Film: 16mm (approx. 400,000 to 500,000 feet; originals, reversal and negative). Videotape: Betacam and 3/4" (100 hours; masters).
Cataloging: Internal filing system; staff assistance required.
Access: Available to the public for duplication and reuse. Research fees not charged (fees charged for viewing cassettes). Previews required; can furnish time-coded viewing cassettes to customers.
Rights: Full rights held to all material.
Licensing: Available for licensing. License fees charged.
Restrictions: None specified.
Viewing Facilities: Film (full A/B editing suite); videotape (Betacam, 3/4" and 1/2")
Duplication Facilities: Film (film to videotape); videotape (Betacam, 3/4" and 1/2").

NEW HAMPSHIRE (Manchester)

ASSOCIATION CANADO-AMÉRICAINE
P.O. Box 989
Manchester, NH 03105
(800) 222-8577
(603) 625-8577
Fax: (603) 625-1214

Street address: 52 Concord Street

Eugène A. Lemieux (Président Général)

Contacts: Dr. Robert Beaudoin; Julien Olivier; Tom Dwyer
Services: Fraternal benefit society; cable television program producer. Videotapes available for duplication, purchase, cablecast, licensing and reuse.
Description: *Bonjour*, a French-language television magazine program (March 1987-present, each episode 27 min.), is co-produced by the Association and United Cable-8 (Manchester, N.H.). *Bonjour* features segments on history, personalities and other items of interest to Franco-Americans. Produced weekly, it is the only French-language program originating in New England.
Size & Elements: Videotape: VHS (amount unspecified).
Cataloging: None specified.
Access: Available for duplication, purchase, cablecast and reuse. Research requests accepted by mail, telephone and in person (walk-in).
Rights: Full rights held to all material (copyright is jointly owned by the Association and United Cable-8).
Licensing: Available for licensing and reuse. License fees charged.
Restrictions: None specified.
Viewing Facilities: None.
Duplication Facilities: Videotape.

NEW HAMPSHIRE (Orford)

APERTURA
P.O. Box 12
Orford, NH 03777
(603) 353-9067

Street address: Main Street

John Karol (Producer)

Contact: John Karol
Services: Film and videotape producer. Stock footage available for licensing and reuse.

Description: Environmental, historic preservation and educational films, as well as a variety of other subjects, including educationally disadvantaged students; New Hampshire's environmental crisis; television spots for the 1970 U.S. Senate campaign of former Vermont Governor Philip Hoff; and television spots on environmental issues.
Footage relating to drug use and abuse includes local citizens in a role-playing simulation of a community drug crisis; drug use from the point of view of high-school students; prison inmates; a Boston defense lawyer on the legal-judicial process as it applies to drug use and abuse; and the conflicts between a storefront counseling center and the local police.
Other films concern the National Championship of Exhibition Skiing at Waterville Valley, New Hampshire; problems of changing land use in Vermont; Environmental Planning Information Center television spots; gravedigging; the preservation of the American industrial heritage through adaptive reuse of obsolete industrial buildings; the status of women; bodybuilding; logging; financing of public education; ethics of tax policy; television advertising spots for local businesses and Chinese calligraphy. *Ben Thresher's Mill* (an Academy Award nominee) explores the workings of a 19th century water turbine-powered woodworking mill and forge, and its operator.
Size & Elements: Film: 35mm and 16mm (approx. 400,000 feet). Videotape: format and amount unspecified.
Access: Stock footage available for reuse. Completed films available for rental and purchase. Research requests accepted by mail, telephone and in person (by appointment only).
Rights: Additional clearances may be necessary in some cases if material is to be reused.
Licensing: Available for licensing and reuse. License and usage fees charged.
Restrictions: None specified.
Viewing Facilities: Film and videotape.
Duplication Facilities: None.

NEW HAMPSHIRE (Seabrook)

CHANNELL ONE VIDEO
P.O. Box 1437
Seabrook, NH 03874
(603) 474-5046

Street address: 459 Lafayette Road

Bill Channell (President)

Contact: Bill Channell
Services: Television and videotape producer. Stock footage available for licensing and reuse.
Description: *Ski Week*, an award-winning weekly television series, includes ski footage from the United States, Canada, and Europe; ski tips from top skiers Jim Redmond and Billy Kidd; behind-the-scenes views of the industry, from snow grooming to ski fashions; historical "flashbacks" of skiing (1930s-50s); and film clips shot by leading cinematographers, such as Warren Miller. Seven years' worth of episodes are held.
Other materials include: footage of humpback whales off the coast of New England; stock car racing from the weekly show *Speedway;* power boat racing from the Littleton, New Hampshire International Regatta (1980); mud football as seen on NBC's *Real People;* rock climbing; New England scenics; extensive auto racing coverage; and miscellaneous stock footage.
Size & Elements: Videotape: 3/4" (hundreds of titles). Material available in any format.
Cataloging: Listings available.
Access: Available to the public for duplication and reuse. Research fees charged. Research requests accepted by mail, telephone and in person (by appointment only).
Rights: Full rights held to most material. Some rights held to some material.
Licensing: Available for licensing and reuse. License fees charged.
Restrictions: None specified.
Viewing Facilities: Videotape.
Duplication Facilities: Videotape (3/4" and VHS).

NEW HAMPSHIRE (Windham)

VIDEOTROUPE
3 Industrial Drive
Windham, NH 03087
(603) 893-4554
Fax: (603) 893-9717

NEW JERSEY (Asbury Park)

Fred Conners (President)

Contact: John Conners (Vice President of Operations)
Services: Videotape producer. Material available for licensing and reuse, subject to restrictions.
Description: Contemporary footage of high technology industrial and manufacturing scenes; all in color.
Size & Elements: Videotape: 1" and Betacam (masters); 3/4" (masters and viewing copies); 1/2" (viewing copies). (Approximately 20 hours total).
Cataloging: Shot lists.
Access: Apply for information. Research fees charged (fees negotiable). Research requests accepted by telephone.
Rights: Full rights held to some material. Some rights held to all material. Additional clearances may be necessary in some cases if material is to be reused (client approval required in some cases).
Licensing: Available for licensing and reuse, subject to restrictions.
Restrictions: Requests for licensing and reuse considered on a case-by-case basis.
Viewing Facilities: Videotape (1", 3/4" and 1/2").
Duplication Facilities: Videotape (1", 3/4" and 1/2").

NEW JERSEY

NEW JERSEY (Asbury Park)

BILL QUINN PRODUCTIONS
710 Cookman Avenue
Asbury Park, NJ 07712
(201) 775-0500
Fax: (201) 774-9416

Bill Quinn (President)

Contacts: Bill Newman (Production Manager); Bill Quinn
Services: Film and videotape producer. Material available for duplication, licensing and reuse.
Description: Wild animals (many species) in natural habitats and in a Safari Park, including elephants, giraffes and rhinoceros; seashore scenes, including beach activities, water sports and activities, including windsurfing; amusement parks, including rides and point-of-view shots; hot air ballooning; and kite footage from kite festivals, including exotic kites and kites flying. A wide variety of generic footage is also available.
Size & Elements: Film: 16mm (negative, 90% of film transferred to videotape). Videotape: 1", Betacam and 3/4" (masters); 3/4" and VHS (viewing copies). (Over 1,000 hours total).
Cataloging: Shot lists.
Access: Available to the public for duplication, licensing and reuse. Research fees not charged; fee charged for preview reel (deductible from purchase). Research requests accepted by mail, telephone and in person (by appointment only).
Rights: Full rights held to all material.
Licensing: Available for licensing. License fees charged.
Restrictions: None specified.
Viewing Facilities: Videotape (3/4" and VHS).
Duplication Facilities: Videotape (3/4" and VHS).

NEW JERSEY (Atlantic City)

FAA TECHNICAL CENTER
ACM-411
Atlantic City International Airport, NJ 08405
(609) 484-4140
Fax: (609) 484-5126

Robert B. Marks (Manager, Visuals and Publications Section)

Contacts: Ann Kertz (TV Production Specialist) (Ext. 4058); Jim Valleley (TV Production Specialist) (Ext. 4102); Ron Meilicke (TV Specialist) (Ext. 4102); Joe Cox (Supervisor, A/V Unit–Film) (Ext. 4061)
Services: Government agency. Videotape material available for duplication and reuse, subject to restrictions.
Description: The FAA Technical Center (a unit of the U.S. Department of Transportation, Federal Aviation Admistration) conducts aviation research and development, testing and evaluation, and accident investigation. Collection covers all aspects of aviation including radar, aircraft, navigation, avionics, electronics and systems; also holds historical aviation footage.
Size & Elements: Videotape: 3/4" (3,000 videotapes, each 30 min.).
Cataloging: Computerized cataloging for staff use only.
Access: Available to the public. Permission must be obtained from FAA Public Affairs office in advance. Research fees not charged. Research requests accepted by mail, telephone and in person (by appointment only).
Rights: Apply for information. Additional clearances may be necessary in some cases if material is to be reused.
Licensing: Available for reuse, subject to restrictions. Usage fees not charged.
Restrictions: On-screen credit must be given if material is reused.
Viewing Facilities: Film (16mm); videotape (3/4", VHS and Betamax).
Duplication Facilities: Videotape (3/4", VHS and Betamax).

NEW JERSEY (Atlantic City)

THE MISS AMERICA PAGEANT
1325 Boardwalk
Atlantic City, NJ 08401
(609) 345-7571
Fax: (609) 347-6079

Videotapes available from:
SHORE PRODUCTIONS, INC.
P.O. Box 174
Mays Landing, NJ 08330
(609) 625-4614

Contact: Robert Marks (Shore Productions, Inc.)
Services: Shore Productions, Inc. is franchised by The Miss America Pageant and authorized to duplicate annual pageant coverage for sale in videotape format to the media and individuals. Material available for purchase. licensing and reuse, subject to restrictions.
Description: *Pageant Telecasts (1957-72)*. Complete programs as seen on network television. Transferred from the original kinescopes provided to the Miss America Pageant by television networks. All shows are approximately 120 min. each, except for 1961 and 1962 which are 150 min. each. Shows generally contain all original commercials; pre-1966 telecasts are in black and white.
Pageant Telecasts (1973-87). Complete shows as telecast on network television. Transferred from the original master videotapes provided to the Miss America Pageant by the network. All shows are approximately 120 min. in length. Some shows contain original commercials.
Miss America Newsreels. Videotape (approx. 90 min.) contains highlights of each of the events comprising The Miss America Pageants (1944-51, color, silent). Highlights include the Boardwalk Parade, swimsuit photo sessions, contestants walking down the runway, Miss America and other activities from each year.
Miss America Boardwalk Parades. Each show is 60 minutes, depicting all of the contestants, bands and floats that participated in that year's Boardwalk Parade.
Crowning Segments. These are the final moments of each show just before the Top Ten are narrowed down and the judges' decision for the new Miss America is announced. Each segment generally contains the last 10 or 15 min. of the telecast. Each videotape is approximately 100 min.
Preliminary Competitions. The Talent Preliminary Competitions from each year contain all contestants displaying their individual talents as seen during Wednesday, Thursday and Friday evenings in Convention Hall. Videotapes can also be purchased by individual night at reduced cost. Each evening's videotape is in color and approximately 50 min. in length; the entire series is approximately 150 min. in length. The Evening Gown and Swimsuit Preliminary Competitions contain all contestants in each of the three preliminary evenings. Each videotape is approximately 60 minutes in length.
Past Miss America Winners. Marilyn Van Derbur (1958); Mary Ann Mobley (1959); Lynda Lee Mead (1960); Nancy Ann Fleming (1961); Maria Beale Fletcher (1962); Jackie Mayer (1963); Donna Axum (1964); Vonda Kay Van Dyke (1965); Deborah Bryant (1966); Jane Jayroe (1967); Debra Barnes (1968); Judi Ford (1969); Pam Eldred (1970); Phyllis George (1971); Laurie Lea Schaefer (1972); Terry Meeuwsen (1973); Rebecca King (1974); Shirley Cothran (1975); Tawney Godin (1976); Dorothy Benham (1977); Susan Perkins (1978); Kylene Barker (1979); Cheryl Prewitt (1980); Susan Powell (1981); Elizabeth Ward (1982); Debbie Maffett (1983); Vanessa Williams and Suzette Charles (1984); Sharlene Wells (1985); Susan Akin (1986); Kellye Cash (1987); and Kaye Lani Rae Rafko (1988).
Size & Elements: Videotape: VHS and Betamax (covering 1957-88; viewing

copies).
Cataloging: Printed lists available upon request from Shore Productions, Inc.
Access: Available to the media and the public for purchase. Requests accepted by mail and telephone.
Rights: The Miss America Pageant holds full rights to all material. Additional clearances may be necessary in some cases if material is to be reused.
Licensing: Available for licensing and reuse, subject to restrictions. Must contact Leonard Horn at The Miss America Pageant (609/345-7571) for permission to reuse or rebroadcast.
Restrictions: Permission for reuse must be obtained through The Miss America Pageant.
Viewing Facilities: None.
Duplication Facilities: None.

NEW JERSEY (Belmar)

NEI-ALI PRODUCTIONS
214 19th Avenue
Belmar, NJ 07719
(201) 280-9442

Cliff Hores (President)

Contact: Cliff Hores
Services: Videotape producer. Material available for duplication, licensing and reuse, subject to restrictions.
Description: Coastal, forest and ocean scenics; urban and highway traffic; air shows and contemporary footage of antique airplanes.
Size & Elements: Videotape: 3/4" (approx. 3 to 4 hours; masters); 3/4" and VHS (viewing copies).
Cataloging: Shot lists.
Access: Available to the public for duplication, licensing and reuse. Research fees negotiable. Research requests accepted by mail.
Rights: Full rights held to some material. Some rights held to all material.
Licensing: Available for licensing, subject to restrictions. License fees charged.
Restrictions: Some restrictions may apply to licensing and reuse.
Viewing Facilities: None.
Duplication Facilities: Videotape (3/4" and VHS).

NEW JERSEY (Blackwood)

CABSCOTT BROADCAST PRODUCTIONS, INC.
One Broadcast Center
Blackwood, NJ 08012
(609) 228-3600
Fax: (609) 227-9624

Larry Scott (President)

Contacts: Larry Scott; Kim Davis (Operations Manager)
Services: Videotape producer; television production facility. Material available for duplication, licensing and reuse, subject to restrictions.
Description: Fireworks in different cities at various events and occasions (e.g., U.S. Bicentennial); city streets in Philadelphia, New York City and Southern California; people on the street (candid footage) and professionals at work (e.g., lawyers and doctors); a large variety of occupations from oil rigging to hospital work.
Size & Elements: Videotape: 1", Betacam (masters); 1", Betacam and 3/4" (viewing copies). (Approximately 250 subjects total).
Cataloging: Computerized cataloging for staff use only (in process).
Access: Available to the public for duplication, licensing and reuse. Research fees not charged. Research requests accepted by telephone and in person (by appointment only).
Rights: Full rights held to all material.
Licensing: Available for licensing, subject to restrictions. License fees charged.
Restrictions: Some restrictions apply based on proprietary interests.
Viewing Facilities: Videotape (1", Betacam, 3/4", VHS, Betamax and 8mm).
Duplication Facilities: Videotape (1", Betacam, 3/4", VHS, Betamax and 8mm).

NEW JERSEY (Clarksburg)

ALDEN FILMS

P.O. Box 449
Clarksburg, NJ 08510
(201) 462-3522
(800) 327-1960

Paul Weinberg (President)

Contact: Paul Weinberg
Services: Distributor. Films and videotapes available to the public for rental and purchase.
Description: Distributes non-theatrical films relating to Israel, Jewish history, religion, culture and customs.

Subjects include agriculture and reclamation; Aliyah; American-Jewish life; anti-Semitism; Arab and international relations; Arab-Jewish relations; Arab Jewry; archaeology; armed forces; art, music and theater; Black-Jewish relations; children's films; Christianity; coins and stamps; development in Israel; education; festivals and holidays; geography and nature; Hasidic life; health and science; Hebrew language and script; historical films; history (ancient and modern); the Holocaust; immigration; industry; inter-group relations; *Israel Reports;* Israeli life; Jerusalem; Jewish concepts and values; Jewish family; Jewish literature; Jews in other lands; Kashruth; kibbutz and settlement life; Middle East conflict; religion and tradition; Soviet Jewry; Spanish Jewry; special films; sports; synagogues; terrorism; travel; youth and Zionism.
Size & Elements: Film: 16mm (approx. 500 titles). Videotape: VHS (viewing copies). (3/4", Betamax I and II, PAL and SECAM available on special order).
Cataloging: Published catalogs.
Access: Available to the public for rental and purchase. Maintained for distribution rather than for research or reuse. Films can be previewed for purchase consideration at no cost other than return postage. Requests accepted by mail and telephone.
Rights: No rights held to any material. Additional clearances will be necessary if material is to be duplicated or reused.
Licensing: Material not available for licensing or reuse without further clearance.
Restrictions: None specified.
Viewing Facilities: None.
Duplication Facilities: None.

NEW JERSEY (Elmwood Park)

HOBBY INDUSTRIES OF AMERICA
VIDEO & AUDIO TAPE LIBRARY
See NEW YORK METRO

NEW JERSEY (Far Hills)

UNITED STATES GOLF ASSOCIATION
COMMUNICATIONS DEPARTMENT
Far Hills, NJ 07931
(201) 234-2300

John Morris (Director of Communications)

Contacts: John Morris; Karen Bednarski
Services: Association; library; museum. Film and videotape collection not open to the public. Some footage possibly available for use by written request.
Description: Golfers and golf events (1914-present). Most golf tournament footage is from the U.S. Open (assorted footage pre-1962, complete coverage 1962-present). The Senior's Open, Women's Open, and National and Amateur Championships comprise the rest of the tournament coverage. Also holds several donated films on golf and famous golfers.
Size & Elements: Film: 16mm (approx. 500 to 600 titles). Videotape: 1", 3/4" and VHS (amount unspecified; masters and viewing copies, all transferred from 16mm film).
Cataloging: Film log for staff use only. Collection partially cataloged at present.
Access: Not open to the public. Research requests accepted on a limited basis. Some footage possibly available for use by written request. Research requests accepted by mail. Research fees charged.
Rights: Full rights held to coverage of the U.S. Open, Senior's Open, Women's Open and National and Amateur Championships. Additional clearances may be necessary for other material to be reused.
Licensing: Available for licensing and reuse, subject to restrictions. License fees charged.

Restrictions: Additional clearances may be necessary for reuse of selected materials.
Viewing Facilities: None.
Duplication Facilities: Videotape (3/4" and 1/2").

NEW JERSEY (Garfield)

MOVIETIME, INC. ARCHIVES
See **NEW YORK METRO**

NEW JERSEY (Livingston)

MOTION PICTURE SERVICES
See **NEW YORK METRO**

NEW JERSEY (Madison)

FAIRLEIGH DICKINSON UNIVERSITY LIBRARY
OUTDOOR ADVERTISING ASSOCIATION OF AMERICA ARCHIVE
285 Madison Avenue
Madison, NJ 07940
(201) 593-8531

James Fraser (Library Director)

Contact: Renée Webber (Curator)
Services: Library. Film and videotape archives available to researchers, scholars and the public for duplication, licensing and reuse, subject to restrictions.
Description: Promotional and commercial footage (1940s-present) relating to the outdoor advertising industry. Many products and locations throughout the United States are shown.
Size & Elements: Film: 16mm and 8mm (approx. 200 items). Videotape: 1", 3/4" and VHS (approx. 100 videotapes).
Cataloging: Currently uncataloged.
Access: Open to researchers, scholars and the public for duplication, licensing and reuse. Research fees charged for commercial projects. Research requests accepted by mail, telephone and in person (by appointment only).
Rights: Full rights held to all material.
Licensing: Available for licensing and reuse, subject to restrictions. License fees charged.
Restrictions: Restrictions apply to use of materials in fragile condition.
Viewing Facilities: Film and videotape (limited facilities; advance arrangements must be made).
Duplication Facilities: Videotape (advance arrangements must be made).
Related Materials: Extensive collection of still photographs and transparencies.

NEW JERSEY (Madison)

THE UNITED METHODIST CHURCHES
THE ARCHIVES AND HISTORY CENTER
P.O. Box 127
Madison, NJ 07940
(201) 822-2826

Street address: Drew University Campus, 36 Madison Avenue

Arthur Swarthout (Assistant General Secretary)

Contact: Arthur Swarthout
Services: Religious organization; library. Film and videotape collection available to the public for research, duplication, licensing and reuse, subject to restrictions.
Description: Central archives for all branches of the Methodist Church. Holds film and videotape productions by various agencies of the denomination (1900-present). Holds world service films from 100 countries, mostly produced in Nashville at United Methodist Communications or in New York, documentation of historical figures, mission projects, church school curricula and promotional films for special days.

Collection receives all new productions, including *Catch the Spirit,* a weekly public broadcast. The Center is currently producing, in conjunction with United Methodist Communications, *History of the Church* (to be distributed by EcuFilm).
Size & Elements: Film: 16mm. Videotape: VHS (film-to-videotape transfers).

(Amounts unspecified).
Cataloging: Material is partially and inconsistently cataloged.
Access: Available to the public for research and duplication. Address research requests should be addressed to Assistant General Secretary, who will then direct researchers to the appropriate authorities. Research requests accepted by mail (must be made in writing).
Rights: Full rights held to some material. Additional clearances may be necessary in some cases if material is to be reused.
Licensing: Available for licensing and reuse, subject to restrictions. License and usage fees charged in some cases.
Restrictions: Requests for research and reuse subject to acceptance and approval. Restrictions may apply to commercial use of footage.
Viewing Facilities: Film and videotape (facilities available at nearby Drew University).
Duplication Facilities: None.

NEW JERSEY (Mahwah)

LATIN AMERICAN VIDEO ARCHIVES (LAVA)
SCHOOL OF CONTEMPORARY ARTS
RAMAPO COLLEGE OF NEW JERSEY
See **NEW YORK METRO**

NEW JERSEY (Mt. Laurel)

NFL FILMS, INC.
330 Fellowship Road
Mt. Laurel, NJ 08054
(609) 778-1600
Fax: (609) 722-6779

Steven D. Sabol (President)
Edwin M. Sabol (Chairman of the Board)

Contacts: Sheila Bumgarner (Director of Sales [footage for television commercials and home video projects]) Jeanne Costanzo (Sales Representative [footage for television sports and news related programs, corporate and educational use])
Services: Film and videotape archives; producer; distributor; stock footage sales library. Some programs available to the public for purchase.
Description: Footage from every NFL game (1965-present). Prior to 1965, limited footage exists, comprised mostly of championship games. Included in the collection are half-hour highlights of each Super Bowl; half-hour highlights on each team (28 teams in all); features on Hall of Fame players, coaches, and teams; documentaries on football; bloopers; historical highlights; and team histories.

A selection of homevideo titles available for purchase include *The NFL TV Follies,* a parody of television football programming, starring Jonathan Winters; *Strange but True Football Stories,* hosted by Vincent Price; *The History of the Super Bowl: Super Sunday; The Greatest Moments in Chicago Sports History; Learning Football the NFL Way: Defense; NFL Crunch Course,* showing high impact collisions and the players that cause them; *NFL Head Coach: A Self Portrait; Football Follies; The NFL's Best Ever Quarterbacks,* featuring Baugh, Graham, Unitas, Tarkenton, Namath, Bradshaw, Staubach, Montana, and Marino; *Big Game America,* a chronicle of the first fifty years of NFL history; and *Lombardi.*
Size & Elements: Film: 16mm (negative, positive, reversal, and release prints). Videotape: 1" (selected scenes originating on 3/4"); 3/4" (time-coded viewing copies); VHS and Betamax.
Cataloging: Research library.
Access: Available for duplication, licensing and reuse. Research fees charged. Research requests accepted by telephone.
Rights: Full rights held to all material. Additional clearances may be necessary in some cases if material is to be reused.
Licensing: Available for licensing and reuse, subject to restrictions. License fees charged.
Restrictions: Client must specify exact usage in advance and cannot deviate from that usage without prior consent.
Viewing Facilities: None.
Duplication Facilities: Film and videotape.

NEW JERSEY (Newark)

NEW JERSEY HISTORICAL SOCIETY
and

**RUTGERS, THE STATE UNIVERSITY OF NEW JERSEY
INSTITUTE OF JAZZ STUDIES**
See **NEW YORK METRO**

NEW JERSEY (North Haledon)

KEEP THE FAITH, INC.
See **NEW YORK METRO**

NEW JERSEY (Park Ridge)

ALLEN (JOHN E.) INC.
See **NEW YORK METRO**

NEW JERSEY (Plainfield)

**INTERNATIONAL MEDIA SERVICES, INC.
STUART ALLEN PRODUCTIONS**
See **NEW YORK METRO**

NEW JERSEY (Princeton)

BELOVE, LAISERIN & WALSH
301 North Harrison Street, Building B, Suite 351
Princeton, NJ 08540
(800) 527-8256
(609) 683-5615

John Friedman (Executive Producer)
Eric Walters-Belove (Writer/Director)
Jerry Albert Laiserin (Writer/Producer)

Contact: Jerry Albert Laiserin
Services: Distributor. Videotapes available to the public for purchase.
Description: Exclusive distributor of *AT&T Bell Laboratories Technical Briefings on Software Technology,* a videotape series designed for managers, software developers, and educators. Videotapes combine computer-generated animation and documentary-style interviews with noted AT&T Bell Laboratories computer scientists to present technical material on computer systems training. The first five *Technical Briefings* are: *Software Quality: What is it? Why is it important? What are its benefits? How do you get it?; A Guided Tour of Program Design Methodologies; Expert Systems: Knowledge Representation in Artificial Intelligence; The UNIX® System: Making Computers Easier to Use; The UNIX® System: Making Computers More Productive.*
Size & Elements: Videotape: 3/4", VHS and Betamax (5 programs).
Cataloging: Brochures.
Access: Available to the public for purchase. Preview service available for qualified educational institutions. Orders accepted by mail and telephone.
Rights: Apply for information.
Licensing: Apply for information.
Restrictions: None specified.
Viewing Facilities: None.
Duplication Facilities: None.
Related Materials: User guides and books related to programs.

NEW JERSEY (Princeton)

FILMS FOR THE HUMANITIES AND SCIENCES, INC.
P.O. Box 2053
Princeton, NJ 08543
(609) 452-1128
Fax: (609) 452-1602
Telex: 4945174 FFHCO

Harold Mantell (President)

Contact: Jeff Morris (Vice President, Marketing and Sales)
Services: Distributor of educational films and videotapes. Materials available for rental and purchase.
Description: Extensive library of educational programs.
  Biology. The Living Body series, biology, biology experiments and evolution.
  Children's programs. American history, friendship, handicaps, holidays, family relationships, social studies, values, object lessons, folk tales, Indian legends and international children.
  Classics. Classical drama and classical civilization.
  Drama. Shakespeare, playing Shakespeare, the history of drama, dramatic works, dramatists and directors.
  English and American literature. Survey of English and American poetry, Old and Middle English, author biographies, English fiction and American fiction.
  Fine art and architecture. Pride of Place television series on American architecture, fine art and painting masterpieces.
  Foreign languages. French culture, French literature, Spanish culture, Spanish authors, Peninsular literature, Latin-American fiction, *Spain in the New World* series, Espana Estuvo Alli, Aztec and Quechua myths, German literature and Russian culture.
  Health education. AIDS, sex education, pregnancy and childbirth, psychology, *The Human Animal* television series, substance abuse, diseases and disorders, emergency medicine, fitness and nutrition, aging, reconstructive surgery and health issues.
  Music. Beethoven by Barenboim series, music, early musical instruments, biographies in music and music in performance.
  Sciences. Chemistry, ecology, geology, astronomy and physics.
  Social studies. Economics, history, ancient Egypt, the world of Islam, American history, North American Indians, the West, military history, World War I, the period between the wars, World War II, the Vietnam conflict, Soviet studies, urban studies, Black studies and women's studies.
  Sports. Sports and sports medicine.
Size & Elements: Film: 16mm. Videotape: 3/4", VHS and Betamax. (Amounts unspecified).
Cataloging: Published catalog.
Access: Available to the public for rental and purchase only.
Rights: Rights generally retained by original producers. Full rights held to some material. Some rights held to all material. Some rights held to some material.
Licensing: Material generally not available for licensing or reuse.
Restrictions: None specified.
Viewing Facilities: None.
Duplication Facilities: None.

NEW JERSEY (Princeton)

DAVID SARNOFF RESEARCH CENTER LIBRARY
CN-5300
Princeton, NJ 08540
(609) 734-2507

Contact: Julie Maddocks (Public Affairs)
Services: Corporation; corporate archives. Film and videotape maintained for distribution and rental rather than for research or reuse.
Description: Research subsidiary of SRI International (formerly part of RCA). Library holds two moving image items: a short historical film featuring a demonstration of the first color television at the 1939 New York's World Fair (unavailable for research and reuse); and *Centers of Excellence,* a ten-minute videotape about the David Sarnoff Research Center (available as a promotional piece).
Size & Elements: Film: 16mm (1 film). Videotape: VHS (1 videotape).
Cataloging: None.
Access: Collection maintained for distribution and rental rather than for research or reuse. Requests accepted by telephone only.
Rights: Full rights held to all material.
Licensing: Apply for information.
Restrictions: Some material is restricted.
Viewing Facilities: None.
Duplication Facilities: None.

NEW JERSEY (Princeton)

**UNITED STATES TENNIS ASSOCIATION
CENTER FOR EDUCATION AND RECREATIONAL TENNIS**
707 Alexander Road
Princeton, NJ 08540
(609) 452-2580
Fax: (609) 452-2265

Ronald Woods (Associate Director)
Eve Kraft (Associate Director)

Contact: Claire Baxter (Head of Audio/Visual Department)
Services: Association. Film and videotape collection available to the public for rental, licensing and reuse, subject to restrictions.
Description: Tennis instruction; history; match highlights, including the U.S. Open (1975-present), Wimbledon (1975-present) and the World Championship of Tennis (WCT); clay court championships; professional profiles; court maintenance; court etiquette and injuries.

Sample titles include: *The Winner's Edge*, with Dennis Ralston, teaching the fundamentals of the game; *Forehand, Backhand and Serve*, with Vic Braden, teaching these elementary strokes; *How Tennis Pros Win*, with Trish Bostrum analyzing Tracy Austin, Rosie Casals, Andrea Jaeger, and Virginia Wade; *How to Beat a Better Player; Tennis: The Nasty Way*, a demonstration of tennis basics with Ilie Nastase; *Women's Tennis; You've Come a Long Way Baby!*, the changing face of women's tennis; *Billie Jean King*, including match play with Chris Evert-Lloyd; *Cocaine and the Student Athlete; First Game, First Set*, the origins of lawn tennis; *Great Moments in the History of Tennis; Hana Mandlikova; Ivan Lendl; Jimmy Connors; The John McEnroe Story; John Newcombe; Martina at Roland Garros; Tennis Balls*, how tennis balls are made; *USTA: The First Hundred Years.*

Match highlights include: the 1971 Wimbledon Championship final between John Newcombe and Stan Smith; the 1969 Davis Cup matches between Ilie Nastase, Ion Tiriac, Stan Smith, Bob Lutz, and Arthur Ashe; the 1971 WCT final between Rod Laver and Ken Rosewall; the 1979 Clay Court championships, featuring Evonne Goolagong Cawley, Chris Evert-Lloyd, Jimmy Connors, John McEnroe, and Guillermo Vilas; the 1983 Wimbledon finals match between Chris Lewis and John McEnroe; the 1984 United States Clay Court Championship women's finals between Manuela Maleeva and Lisa Bonder; the 1985 Wimbledon women's finals between Chris Evert-Lloyd and Martina Navratilova; and the 1986 Wimbledon match between Ivan Lendl and Boris Becker.
Size & Elements: Film: 16mm (approx. 100 films; release prints). Videotape: 3/4" (15 videotapes; masters and viewing copies); VHS (85 videotapes; masters and viewing copies).
Cataloging: Published index to materials, incorporating list of other distributors of related films and videotapes.
Access: Available to the public for rental, licensing and reuse, subject to restrictions. Research requests accepted by mail, telephone and in person (by appointment only). Research fees charged in some cases. Rental fee reductions for USTA members; selected titles available for free loan to organizations (shipping fees charged). Not all titles are available from the USTA; the index lists section and district branches.
Rights: Full rights held to some material. Additional clearances may be necessary for reuse of player clips. USTA owns rights to some of the U.S. Open matches; Wimbledon matches are owned by Rolex and donated to the USTA.
Licensing: Available for licensing and reuse, subject to restrictions. License and usage fees charged (determined on a case-by-case basis).
Restrictions: Permission from players and/or their managers may be necessary to reuse player clips. Other restrictions determined on a case-by-case basis.
Viewing Facilities: Film (16mm); videotape (VHS).
Duplication Facilities: None.

NEW JERSEY (Secaucus)

VISUAL INFORMATION SYSTEMS
See **NEW YORK METRO**

NEW JERSEY (Teaneck)

AMERICAN ANOREXIA/BULIMIA ASSOCIATION INC.
and
ERGO MEDIA
See **NEW YORK METRO**

NEW JERSEY (Trenton)

NEW JERSEY NETWORK
PROGRAM CATALOG DEPARTMENT
1573 Parkside Avenue
Trenton, NJ 08625
(609) 530-5180

Lou Pugliese (Manager Broadcast Operations)

Contact: Dawn Mackay (Coordinator of Project TAPE)

Services: Media organization; distributor; film and videotape archives; stock footage sales library.
Description: Distributes programs produced by NJN relating to New Jersey's history, culture, land and people.

Arts and performances. Titles include: *Christmas with the Westminster Choir*, a concert of Christmas carols performed in the Bristol Chapel on the campus of the Westminster Choir College in Princeton, New Jersey; *Image/Imagenes: Cuban Charanga Music*, featuring music performed by the New Jersey-based Charanga Casino; *Image/Imagenes: Hispanic Arts Magazine*, highlighting the work of major artists in the New York-New Jersey metropolitan area; *State of the Arts Groovin': A Jersey Jazz Special;* and *The Tropicana Music Bowl III*, on the talented high-school marching bands of New Jersey.

Biographical. Titles include: *Cards & Cigars: The Trenton in Ernie Kovacs*, presenting a look at the classic comedian, and the start of his career on State and Broad Streets in Trenton, where he sold cigars and held court to any available audience; *Gomberg at 82*, the life story of an elderly Jewish immigrant born in Russia and living in New Jersey; *In Saner Hours*, a visual essay on the works of Walt Whitman, including historic sites, New Jersey towns, present-day ghettos and rural scenes; *Mrs. Edge*, about Mrs. Walter Edge, the First Lady of New Jersey to live at Morven, the home of the New Jersey governors; *Night with the Champs*, featuring Rocky Graziano, Willy Pep, Jersey Joe Walcott and Joey Giardello; and *A Particular Sound: The Turner Organ*, on the building of the 4,400-pipe organ at the First Presbyterian Church of Trenton.

Documentary. Titles include: *Atlantic City: The Queen Takes a Chance*, tracing the city's history and looking at its future; *Battered Wives, Shattered Wives; Breaking Up Is Hard to Do*, an attempt to chronicle the divestiture of the largest corporation in the world, AT&T; *Cloth by the Yard*, a film tour of the Klopman Mills, a division of Burlington Industries; *Cocaine Kids; Cross Country Skiing*, set in the Poconos; *Departed This Life*, on the art and craft of gravestone rubbing, featuring New Jersey cemeteries; *Domestic Violence Help Line; Farmer's Spring*, examining the pressures causing the decline of small farms in the Garden State; *Images/Imagenes: Auto Safety; Images/Imagenes: Colombians In New Jersey; Images/Imagenes: Latinos in the Media; In Black & White: Civil Rights Organizations; Italians In Newark; Issei, Nisei, Sansei*, on the residents of the Japanese community in Seabrook, New Jersey; *No Place to Call Home*, about three homeless women living on the streets of New Jersey; *Pinelands Sketches*, featuring railbird hunting, cranberry growing, garvey boat building, fox hunting and cedarwood farming in New Jersey's Pinelands National Reserve; *Special Olympics; Steelmakers*, examining the struggle of Roebling, New Jersey, a once-thriving steel company town in Burlington County on the Delaware River; *They Don't Laugh at Hoboken Anymore*, about the development and rehabilitation programs underway in Hoboken; *Unions in New Jersey; The Vanishing Family Farm; What's Really Coming Down*, teenagers examining life in suburbia, filmed in Willingboro Township; *The Writing on the Wall*, a glimpse inside the graffiti subculture in Newark; and *Women, Power & Politics.*

Historical. Titles include: *Crossroads to Victory*, a dramatization of New Jersey's contribution to the American Revolution; *The D & R Canal*, a historical look at the Delaware and Raritan Canal; *Fare You Well Old House: Dutch Houses of the Hackensack River Valley; Fare You Well Federal Period Houses; The Great Batsto Furnace*, looking back to the 1770s when Batsto was the site of a raging iron furnace; *Greenwich Tea Party 1974*, on the anniversary of the tea-burning incident that occurred in Greenwich, New Jersey; *McKonkey's Ferry*, a re-creation of the events surrounding and including the Battle of Trenton; *To Grandfather's House We Go*, featuring the Victorian Era and its architecture; *Treasures of the Past*, archaeologists exploring the world of colonial Indians on Tock's Island; and the *World and Time* series, including *Islam & Politics, War In Lebanon, The Soviet Invasion of Afghanistan* and *South Africa Is Making Headlines.*

Outdoors and nature. Titles include: *Endangered Species of New Jersey; A Few Miles of History*, following the Appalachian Trail through New Jersey; *Fields of Gold*, examining possible uses of the New Jersey wetlands; *The Osprey: A New Jersey Success Story; Return of the Peregrine Falcon;* and *Three Days on Big City Water*, describing a scenic canoe trip over the 1975 Labor Day weekend.

Also maintains a limited stock footage library consisting primarily of nature footage and other items related to New Jersey.
Size & Elements: Film: 16mm. Videotape: 3/4" and 1/2". (Over 100 titles available).
Cataloging: Published catalog, *NJN Program Catalog.*
Access: Completed programs available for rental, preview and purchase to schools, colleges, public libraries, hospitals, community organizations or for broadcast. Some material (nature stock footage) possibly available for reuse.

Research requests accepted by telephone.
Rights: Full rights held to some material. Some rights held to all material. Additional clearances may be necessary in some cases if material is to be reused.
Licensing: Apply for information.
Restrictions: Completed programs not available for reuse as stock footage.
Viewing Facilities: None.
Duplication Facilities: Videotape.

NEW JERSEY (Union)

BRUCE RICCITELLI PRODUCTIONS
See **NEW YORK METRO**

NEW JERSEY (Verona)

SALVATION ARMY
NATIONAL COMMUNICATIONS DEPARTMENT
See **NEW YORK METRO**

NEW JERSEY (Warren)

AT&T ARCHIVES AND RECORDS MANAGEMENT SERVICES
5 Reinman Road
Warren, NJ 07060
(201) 756-1585
Fax: (201) 756-2105

Dr. Marcy Goldstein (AT&T Corporate Archivist)

Contacts: Joy Perillo (ARMS Public Information Office) (201/564-4247); Tim Newton (AT&T Video Resource) (201/234-5299)
Services: Corporate archives. Film and videotape material available for research, licensing and reuse, subject to restrictions.
Description: Current and historical footage of telecommunications development at AT&T; research at Bell Laboratories; and activities of the former Western Electric Company. All archival and film materials formerly held by various divisions of AT&T have now been consolidated in this collection.
Size & Elements: Film and videotape: formats unspecified (over 500 titles).
Cataloging: Computerized cataloging for staff use only.
Access: Available to the public, subject to clearance. Written research requests required. Research fees charged.
Rights: Full rights held to all material.
Licensing: Available for licensing and reuse, subject to restrictions. License fees charged.
Restrictions: Requests for licensing and reuse considered on a case-by-case basis. Material may not be used for advertising purposes. Additional clearances may be necessary in some cases if material is to be reused.
Viewing Facilities: None.
Duplication Facilities: Available with clearance.

NEW JERSEY (West Orange)

EDISON NATIONAL HISTORIC SITE
and
TIMESTEPS PRODUCTIONS, INC.
See **NEW YORK METRO**

NEW JERSEY (West Trenton)

MOTOR BUS SOCIETY LIBRARY
P.O. Box 7058
West Trenton, NJ 08628

John P. Hoschek (Vice President, Library and Research)

Contact: John P. Hoschek
Services: Historical society; library. Films available to the public.
Description: Buses; Greyhound Lines.
Size & Elements: Film: 16mm (approx. 5 to 6 titles).
Cataloging: Research library.
Access: Open to the public by appointment only. Research fees not charged. Research requests accepted by mail.
Rights: Apply for information.

Licensing: Apply for information.
Restrictions: Library open only by prior arrangement.
Viewing Facilities: None.
Duplication Facilities: None.

NEW JERSEY (Wyckoff)

AMERICAN SOCIAL HISTORY PROJECT FILM LIBRARY
See **NEW YORK METRO**

NEW MEXICO

NEW MEXICO (Alamogordo)

DANIEL W. FRY
P.O. Box 614
Alamogordo, NM 88311
(505) 434-2832

Contact: Daniel Fry
Services: Personal collection. Material available for licensing and reuse, subject to restrictions.
Description: Unidentified flying objects (UFOs) in flight (short clips, each approx. 8 to 10 feet); Giant Rock Conventions (meetings of an organization dedicated to the investigation of personal contacts with UFOs, 1960-73); and foreign travel, including documentation of visits to sites of UFO appearances and people who have been contacted by UFOs.
Size & Elements: Film: 16mm (several films, each 8 to 10 feet; 13 completed documentaries).
Cataloging: None.
Access: Available to researchers, scholars and interested individuals only.
Rights: Full rights held to some material. Additional clearances may be necessary in some cases if material is to be reused.
Licensing: Available for licensing and reuse, subject to restrictions. Usage fees generally not charged, except for cost of handling.
Restrictions: Requests for licensing and reuse considered on a case-by-case basis and subject to acceptance and approval.
Viewing Facilities: Film (16mm).
Duplication Facilities: None.

NEW MEXICO (Albuquerque)

LA LECHE LEAGUE OF NEW MEXICO FILM DEPOT
9505 Presley, NE
Albuquerque, NM 87111
(505) 294-7876

Jacie Coryell (Administrator)

Contact: Jacie Coryell
Services: Nonprofit organization. Film and videotape material available to the public for rental.
Description: Educational programs relating to pregnancy and breastfeeding (1962-present). Subjects covered include breastfeeding, pregnancy and childbirth, child care, parenting, and nutrition.
   Titles include: *The Bond of Breastfeeding* (1978); *First Attachment: Breastfeeding Techniques That Work, Vol. 1* (1987); *Lactating Mother; Childbirth: The Great Adventure* (1962); *A Story About Childbirth* (1966); *Childbirth For The Joy of It* (1968); and *First Foods* (1978). Some programs available in Spanish.
Size & Elements: Film: 16mm (approx. 26 titles). Videotape: VHS (3 titles; viewing copies).
Cataloging: Published catalog.
Access: Available to the public for rental. Requests accepted by mail and telephone. Rental fees charged.
Rights: Some rights held to some material.
Licensing: Apply for information. License and usage fees charged.
Restrictions: None specified.
Viewing Facilities: None.
Duplication Facilities: None.

NEW MEXICO (Albuquerque)

SOUTHWEST PRODUCTIONS, INC.

NEW MEXICO (Los Alamos)

812 Gold SW
Albuquerque, NM 87102
(505) 247-3300

David O. Roberts (President)

Contacts: Barry Kirk (Cinematographer); Peggy Durkin (Producer)
Services: Film and videotape producer. Videotape collection available for duplication, licensing and reuse.
Description: *Arabian Horses,* featuring U.S. Nationals, Arabian and Half-Arabian Championship competition (1983-87); *Uranium Mill Tailings,* showing cleanup sites in Utah, New Mexico, Oregon, and Colorado (1986-87); and *Southwest Scenics,* with vistas and panoramas of New Mexico, Arizona and Utah, including sunsets, landmarks, forests and Indians (1985-87).
Size & Elements: Videotape: Betacam and 3/4" (3 edited titles, 275 hours unedited footage; masters).
Cataloging: Shot lists.
Access: Available for duplication and reuse. Research requests accepted by telephone.
Rights: Some rights held to all material. Additional clearances may be necessary in some cases if material is to be reused.
Licensing: Available for licensing and reuse. License and usage fees charged.
Restrictions: None specified.
Viewing Facilities: Videotape (1", Betacam and 3/4").
Duplication Facilities: Videotape (1", Betacam, 3/4", VHS and Betamax).

NEW MEXICO (Los Alamos)

LOS ALAMOS COUNTY HISTORICAL MUSEUM ARCHIVES
P.O. Box 43
Los Alamos, NM 87544
(505) 662-6272

Hedy Dunn (Museum Director)

Contact: Hedy Dunn
Services: Museum and library. Film and videotape collection open to the public. Available for loan, licensing and reuse, subject to restrictions.
Description: History, life and culture of Los Alamos and New Mexico (1918-80s). Three films relate to the history of the Los Alamos Ranch School, where J. Robert Oppenheimer boarded as a student. Its land and buildings formed the center of the secret "atomic city" at the inception of the Manhattan Project. Held are *Ranch School Days* (1920s, 45 min.), *Ranch School Summer Camp* (1938, 20 min.) and *Ranch School Graduation* (1941, 5 min.). Also held is a film (60 min.) made during World War II showing recreation, a wedding and other scenes at Los Alamos National Laboratory.

Other items held include a film of Museum officials teaching docents about Indian petroglyphs (8mm, 200 feet); scenes of a local elementary school filmed by a teacher (1950, 350 feet); *The Last Run of the Chili Line* (1930s), about the last run of a Santa Fe train; *The First 25 Years,* on the history of the Los Alamos National Laboratory (1943-68); *The Town That Never Was,* on the history of the Laboratory; and *Recreating the Anasazi Turkey Feather Blankets* (1983), produced by Southwest Productions for Bandolier National Monument.
Size & Elements: Film: 16mm, Super 8 and regular 8mm (amount unspecified). Videotape: VHS (transfers from film).
Cataloging: Card catalogs.
Access: Open to the public. Since museum is understaffed, research service may be limited. Under certain circumstances, VHS videotapes may be loaned for circulation. Apply for information regarding research fees. Requests by mail preferred.
Rights: Full rights held to some material. Additional clearances may be necessary in some cases if material is to be reused.
Licensing: Available for licensing and reuse, subject to restrictions.
Restrictions: Requests for licensing and reuse considered on a case-by-case basis.
Viewing Facilities: None (VHS viewing possible at Library next door).
Duplication Facilities: None.

NEW MEXICO (Los Alamos)

LOS ALAMOS NATIONAL LABORATORY
FILM LIBRARY
P.O. Box 1663, MS P364
Los Alamos, NM 87545
(505) 667-4446

Fax: (505) 665-2948
Telex: 660495

J. Arthur Freed (Head Librarian) (Ext. 4448)

Contact: Dan Baca (Report Librarian)
Services: Government agency; film and videotape distribution library.
Description: Biosciences, chemistry, earth sciences, engineering, mathematics and computers, materials science, physics, military and peaceful uses of nuclear energy.
Size & Elements: Film and videotape: formats unspecified (285 titles total).
Cataloging: Card catalogs; computerized cataloging for staff use only.
Access: Maintained for distribution and rental rather than for research and reuse. Research fees charged. Research requests accepted by mail and telephone.
Rights: Some rights held to some material. Additional clearances may be necessary in some cases if material is to be reused.
Licensing: Apply for information.
Restrictions: None specified.
Viewing Facilities: None.
Duplication Facilities: Film (film-to-videotape); videotape (videotape and videotape-to-film).

NEW MEXICO (Santa Fe)

ANTHROPOLOGY FILM CENTER FOUNDATION
1626 Canyon Road
Santa Fe, NM 87501
(505) 983-4127

Joan Williams (Director)

Contact: Joan Williams
Services: Foundation; educational institution. Film collection open to researchers and scholars only; available for licensing and reuse, subject to restrictions.
Description: *Locations and subjects.* Southwest United States (Indian and Hispanic cultures); American Southwest (Pueblo Indians in the 1940s); Guatemala (Mayan Indian daily life and ritual life); Ixil Calendrical Divination; and a film about a Mayan village in the Guatemalan highlands (1967).

Documentaries. "Early Southwest" titles include: *And Now Miguel* and *Hopi Horizons;* documentaries produced by and about American Indians (1940-70); and PBS-produced documentaries (1960s).
Size & Elements: Film: 16mm (amount unspecified; mostly release prints).
Cataloging: Finding aids (lists).
Access: Open to researchers and scholars only. Research fees charged. Research requests accepted by mail, telephone and in person (by appointment only).
Rights: Full rights held to some material. Additional clearances may be necessary in some cases if material is to be reused.
Licensing: Apply for information. License fees charged for commercial use.
Restrictions: Requests for reuse subject to acceptance and approval (Foundation must see script and approve use and editing).
Viewing Facilities: Film and videotape.
Duplication Facilities: None.
Related Materials: Audiotapes and audiocassettes of conferences and meetings relating to visual anthropology.

NEW MEXICO (Santa Fe)

LISA LAW PRODUCTIONS
1624 Ben Hur Drive
Santa Fe, NM 87501
(505) 988-2917
Fax: (505) 988-1648

Lisa Law (Owner and Manager)

Contacts: Lisa Law; Elaine Mikels (Assistant Manager)
Services: Private collection. Film and videotape material available to the public for licensing and reuse.
Description: Films shot at the Woodstock Festival and the Dallas Pop Festival (both 1969).

Titles include: *Hog Farmer's Point of View of the Woodstock Festival* (1969, 1 hr., 8mm), showing behind-the-scenes preparation and how people entertained themselves at campgrounds away from the stage area: set-up, preparation of campgrounds and playground; food purchasing, set-up of food kitchen and food-serving booths and food preparation, volunteers working together, people in lines for food and eating; construction of stage area, group participation, children's activities, views from stage, aerial views from helicopter and plane of concert grounds and roadways, crowd shots; work with drug and alcohol users, aid being given at medical tents showing doctors working and massage techniques, festival goers helping save medical tent from collapsing during rainstorm; musicians (including Joan Baez) playing at free stage; post-concert activities, cleanup, "balloon making with giant tubes of plastic filled with notes sent aloft"; and groups of Hog Farmers working together to clean up the grounds.

Hog Farmer's Point of View of the Dallas Pop Festival (1969, 30 min., 8mm), similar to the above but without aerial shots and rainstorm.
Size & Elements: Film: 8mm (2 titles; originals and release prints). Videotape: 3/4" and VHS (90 min., 2 titles; viewing copies).
Cataloging: None specified.
Access: Available to the public for licensing and reuse. Research fees charged. Research requests accepted by mail and telephone.
Rights: Full rights held to all material.
Licensing: Available for licensing and reuse, subject to restrictions.
Restrictions: For one-time use only; on-screen credit required; copy of completed production must be sent to copyright holder.
Viewing Facilities: Film (8mm); videotape (3/4" and VHS).
Duplication Facilities: None.

NEW MEXICO STATE RECORDS CENTER & ARCHIVES HISTORICAL FILM COLLECTION
404 Montezuma
Santa Fe, NM 87503
(505) 827-8860

J. Richard Salazar (Chief, Archival Services Division)

Contact: Ron X. Montoya (Archivist)
Services: State government agency. Archival film and videotape collection possibly available for reuse.
Description: Historical and contemporary films concerning New Mexico, the Southwest and other subjects. Material dates from 1898 and covers historical subjects from the early 1900s.

Historical films. Sample titles include: *Santa Fe & Albuquerque* (1914); *West Side* (1914); *Adventures in Kit Carson Land* (1917); *Dawson* (1917); *Pueblo Legend* (1912); *Tourist* (1912); *Rattlesnake* (1913); *Scenes at the New Mexico State Fair* (1914); *East Side* (1914); *Local Color* (1916); *Indian Day School* (1897); *Pueblo Indians of Taos, N.M.* (1921); *Pueblo Indian Pottery Making* (1924); *San Ildefonso Dances* (1929); *Navajo Fair at Shiprock* (1939); *Indians on Parade* (1942); *Indian Ceremonials* (1952); *Denver and Rio Grande Railroad Chile Club* (1939); *Last Run of the Chili Line* (1941); *Spur Ranch-Tannehill Brothers* (1912); *Ridin', Ropin' and Rodeo* (1941); and *Ernie Pyle's New Mexico* (1945).

New Mexico Department of Game and Fish films. Titles include: *Vermejo Elk Hunt; Pheasant Fever; Fishing the High Country; Desert Flowers & Sand Dunes; Kenai Big Game; Spawn Talking; Duck Hunt; Antelope & Deer Hunting; Game Farm; El Vado Lake Survey; Beaver Trapping; Hen Trapping; Red River, Hondo & Chama; Elk & Buffalo on Philmont Ranch; Wild Fowl in Slow Motion; Trout Fishing on the Chama; Clayton Dam; Jackrabbit, Beaver & Marmot; Game and Fish; New Animals in New Mexico; Speckled Trout Across Canada; Atlantic Salmon; Prairie Chicken in Missouri; Big Horn Sheep; Fiesta & Flowers;* and *Elephant Butte.*

Tourism films (*Touring in the Land of Enchantment* series). Titles include: *Albuquerque Old Town; Carlsbad; Columbus; Conchas Lake; Eastern New Mexico; Elephant Butte; Fort Union; Las Cruces; Navajo Land; Old Lincoln County, Fort Stanton, Santa Rita; Red River & White Sands; Roswell Area; Santa Cruz; Santa Fe; Sunland Park;* and *Taos.*

Other archival films. Titles include: *Medical Effects of the Atomic Bomb; Operation Public Welfare, Oklahoma Dept. of Public Welfare; A Birth Certificate Tells the Fact; Individual Protection From Chemical Warfare; Handling of P.O.W.s; Baptism of Fire; Basic Map Reading; Highway Salvage; Javeline Hunt Check Station; Prairie Chicken Project; Exotic Birds in Pens at Bird Farm; La Cueva Goose Banding; Lion Trapping, Coyote Trapping; Desert Bighorn Hunt; Deer Hunting* (1940s); *Vintage Antelope Trap; Mule Riding; Rattlesnake — Killed Bird; State Fish Hatcheries & Fish Spawning Operations; Line From Yucatan; To Build a Road; Highway 180-45 Meeting in*

Juarez; Los Alamos Ranch School; Malaria in New Mexico; Materials Carried in the New Mexico Public Health Nurse's Bag; and *New Mexico Civil Air Patrol.*

Collection also includes film clips from local Albuquerque television stations KGGM and KOAT.
Size & Elements: Film: 16mm (approx. 600 titles, each approx. 20 min.). Videotape: format and amount unspecified.
Cataloging: Card catalogs and lists.
Access: Open to the public. Available for duplication. Research fees not charged. Research requests accepted by mail, telephone and in person.
Rights: Full rights held to some material. Some rights held to some material.
Licensing: Available for licensing and reuse, subject to restrictions. License fees not charged.
Restrictions: Requests for licensing and reuse considered on a case-by-case basis.
Viewing Facilities: Film (small viewing room).
Duplication Facilities: None.

WHEELWRIGHT MUSEUM OF THE AMERICAN INDIAN
P.O. Box 5153
Santa Fe, NM 87502
(505) 982-4636

Street address: 704 Camino Lejo

J. Edson Way (Director)

Contact: Steve Rogers (Curator)
Services: Museum. Film and videotape collection available to the public for research. Videotapes available for rental and purchase.
Description: Native American life and artistry; exhibit installations; artists at work; and scenes of Native Americans in their everyday life (all 1940s-present).

Films include: *The Mountain Chant* (1940s), on a curing ceremony based on myth and ritual, performed through herbal purification, sweating, sand paintings and prayers; *Family Life of the North American Indian, Part IV* (1940s), studying aspects of a Native American child's behavior in contrast to the Anglo-American world, depicting relationships between babies, children and their parents; *Tradition is the Enemy of Progress* (1950s), showing the changing social order of the Navajo people, their departure from traditional healing and curing ceremonies and the negative impact of influences from the Anglo world; *The Navajo People* (Mary Cabot Wheelwright, 1920s) shows a montage of Navajo life including sheepherding, horse races, school games and an early ceremonial exhibit at Gallup, New Mexico; and *Navajo Sandpainters* (1950s), the preparation of a sand painting for a Navajo patient.

Original videotape productions include *Akome, The Pottery of Acoma Pueblo* (1981), a profile of contemporary potters Marie Z. Chino and Lucy M. Lewis of Acoma Pueblo, set against the background of the spectacular Acoma village, inhabited since 1606; and *Looking at the Sun, He Dances* (1981), the contemporary pictographic tradition interpreted by the Brule-French artist, Randy Lee Whitehorse.

Many videotape titles are transfers from films in the Wheelwright film collection.
Size & Elements: Film: 16mm (approx. 20 titles; 31 cans). Videotape: 3/4" and VHS (46 titles).
Cataloging: Research library with accession files.
Access: Open to the public for research (by appointment only). Research fees charged upon extensive use of staff resources. Research requests accepted by mail, telephone and in person (by appointment only).
Rights: Full rights held to some material. Some rights held to some material. Some material in the public domain. Rights status of some material not known. Additional clearances may be necessary in some cases if material is to be reused.
Licensing: Available for licensing and reuse, subject to restrictions. License fees charged.
Restrictions: All reuse subject to clearance and approval.
Viewing Facilities: Videotape.
Duplication Facilities: None.

NEW YORK

NEW YORK (Albany)

NEW YORK STATE ARCHIVES AND RECORDS ADMINISTRATION
STATE ARCHIVAL SERVICES BUREAU
Cultural Education Center 11D40
Albany, NY 12230
(518) 474-8955

Larry J. Hackman (State Archivist)

Contact: William Evans (Head of Reference Services Unit)
Services: State government agency. Film and videotape archives available to the public for research and reuse, although limited access and reproduction services restrict use of holdings.
Description: Documentation of New York State government and public events.
Executive Chamber films (1954-77). Covers newsworthy events in the Thomas E. Dewey, Nelson A. Rockefeller and Malcolm Wilson administrations, including inaugurations; legislative sessions; and openings of New York State Thruway, the St. Lawrence Seaway, Adirondack Northway, the Saratoga Performing Arts Center and Empire State Plaza.
Executive Chamber videotapes (1975-82). Covers news conferences and other events during the Hugh Carey administration, including inaugurations; addresses to the legislature; production of "I Love New York" commercials; budget presentations; state and overseas tours; *Inside Albany* broadcasts on WMHT-TV; the Carey-Gouletas wedding; promotion of the Lake Placid Winter Olympics; and the dedication of Empire State Plaza.
Size & Elements: Film: 35mm (19 titles, 38 reels; negative and reversal original). Videotape: 3/4" (222 videotapes; masters).
Cataloging: Title lists.
Access: Available to the public for research and reuse. Limited access and reproduction services restrict use of holdings. Research requests accepted by mail, telephone and in person (walk-in).
Rights: Material in the public domain.
Licensing: Available for reuse, subject to restrictions. Usage fees not charged.
Restrictions: Limitations and restrictions apply regarding physical access to collection and duplication services.
Viewing Facilities: Videotape (1/2").
Duplication Facilities: Videotape (1/2"); materials reproduced at cost. Arrangements for film-to-videotape transfers and film duplication negotiated on a case-by-case basis.

NEW YORK STATE DEPARTMENT OF ECONOMIC
DEVELOPMENT
AUDIO-VISUAL UNIT
One Commerce Plaza
Albany, NY 12245
(518) 474-8486
Fax: (518) 474-1512

Bern Rotman (Director of Media Services)

Contact: Joan Lapp (Audio-Visual Manager)
Services: Government agency; film and videotape library. Complete productions available for loan to qualified groups and individuals. Materials, including stock footage, possibly available for reuse, subject to clearance and approval.
Description: The Department collection is primarily available to the tourism industry for use in promoting travel to and within New York State; and for other purposes relating to economic development.
Events. Documentation of selective events of importance to the economy of New York State (1979-present). These are for in-house use only.
Films and features. Several completed productions are available on film and videotape. Topics include: the Hudson River; the making of *The Godfather*; the Statue of Liberty; Bear Mountain State Park; Erie Canal; Lake Placid Winter Olympics; the Adirondack Railway; Harlem; the George Washington Bridge; New York City; Lake Champlain; and New York City subways.
Hi-tech/"Made in New York." A series of videotapes shot in factories throughout New York State for use at trade shows.
"I Love New York" television commercials. The Department holds the complete library, for archival use only. Spots are available for reuse only with payment of full residuals to talent and musicians through Wells, Rich and Greene, Inc., the advertising agency for the campaign.
Scenes and stock footage. Unedited footage of locations throughout the state. The stock footage library is divided into the eleven tourism regions designated by the "I Love New York" campaign: New York City, Capital District, Hudson Valley, Finger Lakes, Long Island, Chautauqua/Allegheny, Niagara Frontier, Central/Leatherstocking, Adirondacks, Catskills and Thousand Islands/Seaway regions.
Size & Elements: Film: 16mm (5 films; release prints). Videotape: 3/4" (1,000 videotapes; masters and viewing copies).
Cataloging: Partially computerized cataloging for staff use only; title logs.
Access: Programs and footage are made available to any group or individual demonstrating work on a project with economic benefits to New York State. (Travel presentations to tour groups or videotapes on worker recruitment for a New York State company are examples of appropriate projects). Requests for reuse accepted on a limited basis; most are individually evaluated. Research and loan fees not charged. Research requests accepted by mail and telephone. A letter describing intended use is required in order to obtain footage.
Rights: Full rights held to some material. Some rights held to some material. Additional clearances may be necessary in some cases if material is to be reused.
Licensing: Available for licensing and reuse, subject to restrictions. License and loan fees not charged.
Restrictions: Many restrictions apply to licensing and reuse (apply for information).
Viewing Facilities: Videotape (3/4" and 1/2").
Duplication Facilities: Videotape (3/4" and 1/2") (1" videotape duplicates are produced at the New York Network, a state production facility; charges for duplication and stock apply).

NEW YORK STATE DEPARTMENT OF ENVIRONMENTAL
CONSERVATION
AUDIO VISUAL SERVICES
FILM LOAN LIBRARY
50 Wolf Road, Room 516
Albany, NY 12233-4501
(518) 457-0858

Clark Pell (Chief, Audio Visual Services)

Contacts: For information: Rich Clauss (Photographer II); for booking: Maria Lamb (Keyboard Specialist); Tim Minch
Services: Government agency. Films available for free loan to responsible New York State organizations.
Description: *Outdoor safety.* Titles include: *Firearms Safety and the Hunter; First Aid in the Wilderness; Shoot, Don't Shoot;* and *Survival.*
Hunting and fishing. Titles include: *Bass Anglers 1980 Classic; Before You Hunt; Bigmouth; Bowhunting in North America; Ethics Afield; Feeding Habits of the Bass; Return of the Wild Turkey; The Right to Hunt; Smallmouth Bass; The Sportsman; The Way of the Trout; Wildlife Habitat and the Hunter;* and *World's Biggest Fish Bowl.*
Nature and wildlife. Titles include: *Bluebirds: Bring Them Back!; Ducks on the Wing; Legacy for a Loon; Osprey; Redtail: Story of a Hawk; Reproduction of Brook Trout; Sand County Almanac; Story of the Mourning Dove; A Trout Stream in Winter; Two Little Owls; Watching Wild Wings;* and *The Wood Duck's World.*
Environment and ecology. Titles include: *Acid Rain: Requiem or Recovery; The Adirondacks: The Land Nobody Knows; America's Wetlands; The Garden of Eden; Nuclear Energy; Riches from the Sea; Trapping: Modern Day Necessity; A Way of Life;* and *Wildlife and the Farm.*
Size & Elements: Film: 16mm (38 titles, 148 cans).
Cataloging: Brochure.
Access: Available for free loan to responsible organizations in New York State; not available to individuals. Requests accepted by mail and may be made up to three months in advance.
Rights: No rights held to any material. Rights retained by original producers or other copyright holders.
Licensing: Apply for information.
Restrictions: Films may not be used for commercial purposes, nor may admission be charged. Material is copyrighted and may not be broadcast or duplicated without permission from copyright holders.
Viewing Facilities: None.

Duplication Facilities: None.

LONG ISLAND STATE PARK COMMISSION
See **NEW YORK METRO**

NEW YORK (Bellvale)

WOODS N' WATER TELEVISION SERIES
P.O. Box 65
Bellvale, NY 10912
(914) 986-0326

Peter J. Fiduccia (President)

Contact: Kate Fiduccia (Assistant Producer)
Services: Videotape producer and distributor. Material available for duplication and reuse.
Description: Educational and entertaining outdoor videotapes. Titles include: *Bucks, Bucks and More Bucks,* showing mature, big-racked whitetail bucks in their natural habitat, "guaranteed to keep the adrenalin flowing until next deer season"; *How To Call and Hunt the Spring Gobbler,* featuring Peter J. Fiduccia and champion turkey callers Frank Dayon and Paul Butski, in which an eleven and one-half-inch bearded gobbler is bagged; *Best Of The Woods N' Water T.V. Show* (Vols. 1, 2 and 3); *How To Use Scents, Camouflage and Blinds Effectively While Hunting Whitetail Deer* teaches you how to become "invisible" while hunting.
Size & Elements: Videotape: format unspecified (13 titles).
Cataloging: Shot lists.
Access: Maintained for distribution and purchase. Available for duplication, licensing and reuse. Requests accepted by mail.
Rights: Full rights held to all material.
Licensing: Apply for information. License fees charged.
Restrictions: None specified.
Viewing Facilities: None.
Duplication Facilities: None.

NEW YORK (Binghamton)

**LINK FLIGHT SIMULATION DIVISION
OF CAE-LINK CORPORATION**
Corporate Drive
Binghamton, NY 13902-1237
(607) 721-6117

Paul Redfern (Manager, Marketing Communications)

Contact: Paul Redfern
Services: Film and videotape producer. Footage available for licensing and reuse, subject to restrictions.
Description: Computer-generated images of flight simulation and ground vehicle simulators, produced primarily for military and commercial airline training programs. Flight simulation imagery includes a wide variety of ground scenery and weather conditions, out-the-window views, over-pilot's-shoulder views with control panel and window as well as interior and exterior views of simulators and actual aircraft.

Numerous videotapes have been produced for marketing support purposes. Major customer areas are *Air Force/Navy Marketing, Army/Space Marketing* and *International/Commercial Marketing.*

Air Force/Navy Marketing. Titles include *Link General Capabilities* (1985), a marketing promo covering Link's role in the history of simulation up to current simulation programs; *B-52 Weapon Systems Trainer* (1984); *Esprit Briefing* (1985), demonstrating Link's helmet occulometer eye-tracking system and microprocessor-controlled servo projector; *Fixed Wing Dig* (1984), in which Digital Image Generation (DIG) visual system scenes show a representative response to a hostile attack; various videotapes showing dedications of B-52, C-130 and C-130H simulators and media coverage of flight simulation and other Link activities; *Visual Systems Presentation Support* (1986), consisting of excerpts from videotapes demonstrating the components of simulation and visual systems; various videotapes relating to the A-10 Thunderbolt II, B-1B, C-130, F-4, F-14, F-16, F-111, KC-10 and P-3C Orion aircraft. A number of videotapes explain Link's systems, divisions and capabilities. Historical material (1977-86) is comprised of dated videotapes, reviewing Link's achievements, dedications, trade shows and other news events.

Army/Space Marketing. Titles include *Space Programs Briefing* (1985), reviewing the simulators provided by Link to NASA since 1962, including Apollo 11, Gemini, SpaceLab and the Space Shuttle; a number of videotapes produced for trade show support, including *AH-1S Cobra ATACDIG: I/ITEC 1984,* demonstrating a typical U.S. Army aviation combat skills scenario; media coverage of the space program, from NASA and commercial television sources; helicopter simulators; espionage in the high-technology industry; videotapes on visual/sensor programs; videotapes relating to the AH-64 Apache, Black Hawk, AVC, XB-15, UH-1H Huey, CH-47 Chinook, AH-1 Cobra, LHX (light) and OH-58D Aeroscout helicopters. Historical material (1979-86) reviews achievements, trade shows, presentations and news events. *Singer-Link 50th Anniversary* (1978) reviews Link's accomplishments and simulators produced (1928-78).

International/Commercial Marketing. Titles include *Motion Systems and Image III-T Visual System: China Briefing* (1985), demonstrating Link's 6-degree-of-freedom motion system on a variety of simulators, as well as its IMAGE III-T visual system; *MST: Link-Binghamton 1985 Paris Air Show Promo* (1985), in which commercial simulation users discuss how they see simulation technology today and what they would like to see tomorrow; *C-130 Simulator International Briefing* and other simulator sales promotions; trade show footage and media coverage. Various videotapes (with and without audio) show commercial aircraft in flight, taking off and landing. *767 Moods in Flight* (1982), produced by Boeing, shows the complete production of a 767 aircraft in 16 minutes.

Unedited footage. Includes aircraft, interviews and presentations, simulators, visual/sensor footage and tanks (relating to all three markets as above).
Size & Elements: Film: 35mm ("some recent footage") and 16mm (60 reels, each 100 feet; positive, negative, reversal, originals and release prints). All post-1985 footage is in 16mm film form; all 16mm film has been transferred to 1" videotape and 3/4" videotape viewing copies. Videotape: 1" (all transferred from 16mm film), 3/4" (200 videotapes, as well as all footage produced pre-1985, and viewing copies of 16mm film-to-videotape transfers).
Cataloging: Published catalog.
Access: Available to the public for reuse. Research requests accepted by telephone. Research fees usually not charged.
Rights: Full rights held to some material. Additional clearances may be necessary in some cases if material is to be reused.
Licensing: Footage generally available for licensing and reuse without restrictions. Additional clearances may be necessary in some cases. License and usage fees charged.
Restrictions: Some programs have been produced by local and network television news organizations, public television stations, private producers, and government agencies; additional clearances may be necessary for reuse of this material.
Viewing Facilities: Videotape (3/4").
Duplication Facilities: Videotape (3/4").

NEW YORK (Briarcliff Manor)

BENCHMARK FILMS, INC.
See **NEW YORK METRO**

NEW YORK (Bronx)

BRONX COUNTY HISTORICAL SOCIETY
and
MILADY PUBLISHING CORPORATION
and
NEW YORK ZOOLOGICAL SOCIETY
See **NEW YORK METRO**

NEW YORK (Brooklyn)

**CATHERINE BENAMOU/
LATIN AMERICAN WOMEN ARTISTS SERIES (LAWAS)**
and
BROOKLYN BOTANIC GARDEN
and
**BROOKLYN COLLEGE OF THE CITY UNIVERSITY OF NEW YORK
CELIA NACHATOVITZ DIAMANT MEMORIAL LIBRARY OF
CLASSIC TELEVISION COMMERCIALS
DEPARTMENT OF TELEVISION AND RADIO**
and
CENTER FOR HOLOCAUST STUDIES
See **NEW YORK METRO**

NEW YORK (Buffalo)

ALBRIGHT-KNOX ART GALLERY
1285 Elmwood Avenue
Buffalo, NY 14222
(716) 882-8700

Douglas Schultz (Director)

Contacts: Judy Beecher; Tom Loonan
Services: Museum. Videotape collection maintained primarily for distribution and rental; some material available for research and scholarly use only.
Description: *Video Vasari* collection (1975-present) comprises interviews with artists exhibiting at the Gallery in one-person or group shows; also interviews with influential art dealers and writers. Interviews are conducted by curators and scholars. The majority of the videotapes relate to a single artist, although there are anthology videotapes and installation documentations.

Artists and personalities interviewed include: Carl Andre, Arman, Kenneth Armitage, Richard Artschwager, Milton Avery, John Baldessari, Ilya Bolotowsky, Cynthia Carlson, Anthony Caro, Leo Castelli, Lynn Chadwick, Charles Clough, Sonia Delaunay, Jim Dine, Piero Dorazio, Mary Beth Edelson, Richard Estes, Herbert Ferber, Helen Frankenthaler, Nancy Graves, Alan Green, Grace Hartigan, Hans Hartung, Douglas Hollis, John Hoyland, Sheila Isham, Alfred Jensen, Allen Jones, Anish Kapoor, Phillip King, Lee Krasner, Ibram Lassaw, Roy Lichtenstein, Robert Mangold, Melissa Miller, Henry Moore, François Morellet, Robert Motherwell, Isamu Noguchi, Nathan Oliviera, Judy Pfaff, Bridget Riley, Alain Robbe-Grillet, Milton Rogovin, James Rosenquist, Amy Ryan, Nicolas Schöffer, William Scott, George Segal, Tony Smith, Kenneth Snelson, Alan Sonfist, Frank Stella, Graham Sutherland, William Turnbull, Victor Vasarely and Jack Youngerman.

Anthologies include: *Speaking of Tomlin...; A New Heritage: Contemporary American Painting; Working in Great Britain; Working in France.* Installations include: *Jean Dubuffet; Rafael Ferrer; Joel Shapiro;* and *Hannah Wilke/Jackie Winsor.*
Size & Elements: Videotape: 3/4" (300 videotapes).
Cataloging: Cataloging in progress.
Access: Available to the public. Maintained for distribution and rental rather than for research or reuse. Research requests accepted by mail.
Rights: Full rights held to all material.
Licensing: Apply for information.
Restrictions: Older material not available for distribution, but accessible to scholars for in-house use only.
Viewing Facilities: Videotape.
Duplication Facilities: Videotape.

BUFFALO AND ERIE COUNTY HISTORICAL SOCIETY
25 Nottingham Court
Buffalo, NY 14216
(716) 873-9644

Dr. William Siener (Executive Director)

Contacts: Mary Bell (Director of Library and Archives); Yvonne Foote (Library Assistant)
Services: Historical society. Film collection available for research and reuse, subject to restrictions.
Description: Television newsfilm footage broadcast on Buffalo stations. All material was aired as part of the 6 pm or 11 pm news; no outtakes are held.
WGR-TV Collection (1970-78). All footage uncataloged and presently in storage.
WIVB-TV Collection (1963-80). Footage from 1963-75 haphazardly cataloged and stored on 120 feet reels; 1976-80 presently in storage.
WKBW-TV Collection (1962-80). Footage from 1962-75 cataloged; 1976-80 presently in storage.
Size & Elements: Film: 16mm (amount unspecified; originals).
Cataloging: Indexed by subject and dates.
Access: Not open to the public. Available to researchers, scholars and television stations, subject to approval.
Rights: No rights held to any material. Rights retained by television stations.
Licensing: Available for reuse, subject to restrictions. Usage fees charged in some cases.
Restrictions: Approval of originating stations required for reuse.
Viewing Facilities: Film (editor/viewer available at Resource Center).

Duplication Facilities: None.

4•6•8 PRODUCTIONS, INC.
1552 Hertel Avenue, Box 225
Buffalo, NY 14216
(716) 833-0468

Peter K. O'Connell (President and Chief Executive Officer)

Contact: Peter K. O'Connell
Services: Film and videotape producer. Footage available for licensing and reuse on a case-by-case basis, subject to clearance.
Description: Stock footage of scenics and landmarks in the Buffalo area, western New York State and southern Ontario, shot in all seasons; Buffalo Bisons (baseball); Buffalo Sabres (hockey); Buffalo Bills (football); mayors, county executives and other political figures; and generic industrial, manufacturing and office scenes.
Size & Elements: Film: 16mm and 8mm (originals and prints). Videotape: 3/4" (masters); 1/2" (viewing copies). (Approx. 300 hours total).
Cataloging: Staff assistance required.
Access: Open to the public. For in-house use only. Available for duplication and reuse. Research fees charged in some cases. Research requests accepted by mail and telephone.
Rights: Full rights held to most material. Additional clearances, obtainable through 4•6•8 Productions, may be necessary in some cases if material is to be reused.
Licensing: Available for licensing and reuse on a case-by-case basis, subject to clearance. License fees charged.
Restrictions: None specified.
Viewing Facilities: Videotape (3/4" and 1/2"; by appointment only).
Duplication Facilities: Videotape (1", 3/4" and 1/2").

HALLWALLS CONTEMPORARY ARTS CENTER
700 Main Street
Buffalo, NY 14202
(716) 854-5828

Christine Tebes (Executive Director)

Contacts: Barbara Lattanzi (Video Curator); Chris Hill (Video Curator); Ron Ehmke (Performance Curator)
Services: Nonprofit media organization and multi-arts center. Videotape collection open to the public for in-house viewing only.
Description: Devoted to the exhibition of multiple art forms, including film, video, performance, music, literature and the plastic arts. Founded in 1976 by artists Robert Longo, Cindy Sherman, Charles Clough and others, as an adjunct to their studios. Artists from a variety of disciplines were brought first from New York and later from throughout the U.S. and Canada to perform, exhibit and discuss personal theories pertaining to the making of art. In time, it became a place for artists to examine their own values and ideas by engaging in dialogue with one another, and an exhibition site for innovative and experimental work.

Events occurring at the gallery in each of the six exhibition areas are documented by photography, audiotape or videotape. Almost all documentation is unedited and the condition of the videotapes varies. An archival remastering project is planned to preserve the 1/2" open reel material.

Videotape collection documents live performances by artists (most from New York City) who appeared at Hallwalls (1978-present). Many of these artists have gone on to develop successful careers in the publishing, movie or recording industries. Collection also documents work by many Western New York performance artists during this same period.

Performance highlights (unless noted otherwise) include: Constance DeJong (literature, 1978); Michael Smith (1978); Laurie Anderson (1978); Kathy Acker (literature, 1979); David Van Tieghem (1979); Carolee Schneeman (1979); Jennifer Bartlett (literature, 1979); John Lurie (1980); Paul McMahon (1981); Winston Tong (1981); Karen Finley (1982); Kipper Kids (1982); Colab (video program, 1982); Mike Kelley (1982); Louis Grenier (1982); Cookie Mueller (1983); Ann Magnuson (1983); Tony Billoni (1983); Yoshiko Chuma and the School of Hard Knocks (1984); John Jesurun (1984); Ethyl Eichelberger (1984); Mike Osterhout (1986); Tony Conrad and Joe Gibbons (1986); Ann Carlson (1987); Robbie McCauley (1987); WOW Cafe

(1987); and DanceNoise (1988).

Size & Elements: Videotape: 3/4", 1/2", Betamax I, 8mm and 1/2" open reel (approx. 90 titles, ranging from 30 to 75 min.; most unedited).

Cataloging: Computerized cataloging for staff use only. A comprehensive catalog listing (including assessments of the condition of the videotapes) is currently being compiled. When this listing is completed, and as viewing copies of endangered videotapes are prepared, the archives will become accessible to the public.

Access: Open to the public. For in-house screening only. Research fees charged in some cases (depending upon the staff time necessary to fulfill request). Research requests accepted by mail, telephone and in person (by appointment only). Researchers will be assisted by a staff member.

Rights: Some rights held to some material. Additional clearances (i.e., consent of artist or performer) will be necessary if material is to be reused. Rights to most material retained by artists.

Licensing: Available for reuse, subject to restrictions. License fees not charged.

Restrictions: Reuse requires consent of artist or performer in all cases. At present Hallwalls has no contracts with artists to release or duplicate material.

Viewing Facilities: Videotape (3/4", VHS, Betamax I and 1/2" open reel).

Duplication Facilities: Videotape (3/4", VHS, Betamax I and 1/2" open reel).

Related Materials: Audio documentation of music and fiction reading events (1979-present); quarterly event schedule listing performing artists with exhibition descriptions. Also holds listings of past events, together with program notes.

Publications: Published catalogs for many exhibitions; film, video and performance programs.

NEW YORK (Buffalo)

SQUEAKY WHEEL
585 Potomac Avenue
Buffalo, NY 14222
(716) 884-7172

Julie Zando (Director)

Contact: Julie Zando (716/882-8761)

Services: Media organization. Videotape collection open to the public for in-house use only.

Description: Maintains a videotape library containing 150 titles by local film, video and audio artists. The library reflects two concurrent strengths of the Buffalo media community: a growing amount of work produced at the Center for Media Study (SUNY Buffalo), featuring image processing with Fairlight and Amiga computers; and performative and personal work, often using narrative content in experimental structures. This second group uses a "cheap and dirty" approach to video production that reflects the unavailability of media-making tools to the non-student community.

Also holds two compilation videotapes of Buffalo work produced for exhibition. *Video Girls* (1987) features two hours of video made by women in the Buffalo area, including Anita Bebe, Heather Connor, Lynn Devlin, Liz Evans, Joyce Gates, Chris Hill, Cheryl Jackson, Donna Kapa, Bethann Levin, Lisa Marchese, Pam Orcutt, Ellen Spiro, Lois Thompson, Maria Venuto, Patty Wallace and Julie Zando. *Waterfront Video* (1988) is a show of Buffalo video curated by Stefan Horner, with work by Tony Conrad, Lynn Devlin, Mark Frischman, Armin Heurich, Chris Hill, Judy LaFond, Barbara Lattanzi, Jimi Lyons, Alex Meyer, Ken Rowe, Paul Sharits, Ellen Spiro, Peter Weibel and Julie Zando.

Size & Elements: Videotape: 3/4" (30 videotapes, each 20 min.); VHS (30 videotapes). Some videotapes are transferred from film.

Cataloging: Program notes for videotapes included in exhibitions.

Access: Open to the public. For in-house use only. Research fees not charged. Research requests accepted by telephone and in person (by appointment only).

Rights: Some rights held to some material. Most rights retained by artists.

Licensing: Not available for licensing or reuse. All exhibition and distribution must be cleared with individual artists.

Restrictions: Not available for duplication, licensing or reuse.

Viewing Facilities: Videotape (3/4" and VHS).

Duplication Facilities: None.

NEW YORK (Cooperstown)

NEW YORK STATE HISTORICAL ASSOCIATION
P.O. Box 800
Cooperstown, NY 13326

(607) 547-2533

Street address: Lake Road

Dan Porter (Director)

Contact: Milo V. Stewart (Associate Director/Curator of Iconography)

Services: Historical society; videotape producer.

Description: In cooperation with Monadnock Media of Shutesbury, Massachusetts, the Association is in the process of producing videotape programs using the mid-19th-century diary of a ten-year-old girl who lived in Canandaigua, New York, and the extensive visual resources of the Association archives. The series (30 min. total) will be implemented as part of the fourth-grade social studies curriculum in New York State.

Size & Elements: Not yet determined.

Cataloging: None.

Access: Production will be made available to schools. Inquiries accepted by mail and telephone.

Rights: Full rights held to all material.

Licensing: Apply for information.

Restrictions: Apply for information.

Viewing Facilities: None.

Duplication Facilities: None.

Related Materials: Extensive still photograph collection.

NEW YORK (Corning)

THE CORNING MUSEUM OF GLASS
THE RAKOW LIBRARY
One Museum Way
Corning, NY 14830-2253
(607) 937-5371
Fax: (607) 974-8150
Fax: (607) 974-8250
Telex: 932498
Cable: CORNGLAS CORN U.S.A.

Dwight Lanmon (Museum Director)
Norma Jenkins (Head Librarian)

Contact: Gail Bardhan (Audiovisual Librarian)

Services: Museum. Videotape library available for in-house viewing only. Research requests not accepted. Can refer prospective users to copyright owners.

Description: Films and videotapes relating to the art and history of glass (1921-present), produced in Europe, Japan and the United States. Commercial and non-professional films (such as those featuring glass artists at work) are held as well as television programs. Topics include decorative, tableware, sculpture, studio, and stained glass (3000 B.C.-present), as well as commercial production and technique.

Rare materials include *Un Grand Verrier: Maurice Marinot*; and *Glas* (1958), an impressionistic treatment of glassblowing by hand and machine at the Royal Leerdam Factory in the Netherlands.

Other titles include *Chartres Cathedral, Broad Daylight,* produced for Patent Glazing Conference; *Cameo Glass, Conquest of Light,* showing how Waterford Crystal is handblown and cut in the Cork, Ireland factory; *Core Forming of an Amphoriskos*; *For Eyes to See,* produced for Bausch and Lomb, relating to eyes, optical glasses, vision and lenses; *Ford Has a Way with Glass,* showing Ford's Glass Division manufacturing flat glass for cars and windshields; *GAS II & III,* informal recordings of the Glass Art Society meetings; *Genii of the Glass,* depicting the intertwined professional and personal lives of Muhamid Gzazz, a traditional Arab glassblower living and working in Jerusalem; *Glasmacher von Bida,* showing Nigerian glassmakers who use open pot furnaces to make beads; *Glass,* showing the use of glass in England as seen through the eyes of a Roman glassmaker; *Glittering Song,* an animated fairytale using broken glass; *Grandma's Bottle Village,* showing a woman who has used bottles from the county dump to make 15 buildings and gardens in Simi Valley, California; and *The Great Paperweight Show.*

Size & Elements: Videotape: 3/4" and VHS (approx. 250 titles).

Cataloging: Published catalog.

Access: Available to the public. For in-house use only. Research requests not accepted. Can refer prospective users to copyright owners.

Rights: No rights held to any material. Rights retained by original producers.

Licensing: Material possibly available for licensing through original producers or distributors.

NEW YORK (Elmira)

Restrictions: Library available for in-house viewing only.
Viewing Facilities: Videotape (3/4" and VHS).
Duplication Facilities: None.

NEW YORK (Elmira)

EDUCATIONAL IMAGES, LTD.
P.O. Box 3456, West Side Station
Elmira, NY 14905
(607) 732-1090
(800) 527-4264 (orders only)

Street address: 306 Academy Place, Elmira, NY 14901

Dr. Charles Belinky, Ph.D (Executive Director)

Contact: Elizabeth Sill (Editorial Assistant)
Services: Distributor. Videotape material available for purchase and reuse.
Description: A wide variety of videotapes on science and natural history topics, including many award-winning programs.

Subjects covered include: anatomy; physiology; genetics; the human cell; biochemistry; cytology and histology; environmental hazards; methods of science; aquatic environment; terrestrial biomes; career planning; entomology; animal adaptation, classification and evolution; radiation and its effects; meteorology; geology and earth sciences; physics, chemistry, science and technology; botany; culture; and science.
Size & Elements: Film: format unspecified (release prints). Videotape: 3/4", VHS and Betamax (viewing copies). (Over 100 titles total).
Cataloging: Published catalog.
Access: Available for purchase and reuse. Research fees charged in some cases. Research requests accepted by mail; orders accepted by telephone.
Rights: Full rights held to some material. Some rights held to all material. Additional clearances may be necessary in some cases if material is to be reused.
Licensing: Apply for information. License fees charged (negotiable).
Restrictions: Numerous restrictions apply to licensing and reuse.
Viewing Facilities: None.
Duplication Facilities: Videotape.

NEW YORK (Garden City)

NASSAU COMMUNITY COLLEGE LIBRARY
NEW YORK STATE HEALTH FILM COLLECTION
See **NEW YORK METRO**

NEW YORK (Goshen)

TROTTING HORSE MUSEUM
PETER D. HAUGHTON MEMORIAL LIBRARY
240 Main Street
Goshen, NY 10924
(914) 294-6330

Philip A. Pines (Director); Gail Cunard (Administrator)

Contact: Walter Latzko (Registrar)
Services: Museum. Film and videotape collection open to researchers and scholars for in-house use only; available for duplication.
Description: Footage of harness racing, including newsreels (1930s), films (1950s-60s), full-length television productions, and a silent film (1910) of the pacer Dan Patch.

Titles include: *The Titan; Gait of Champions; Sulkies and Silks; Born to Pace; Harness Racing Driver (Bill Haughton); Evolution of the American Horse; Queen Bea; Trottown, U.S.A.; Hambletonian;* and *The Great Green Wave.*
Size & Elements: Film: 16mm (64 titles, 72 cans; release prints). Videotape: format unspecified (200 videotapes; viewing copies).
Cataloging: Computerized cataloging available to researchers.
Access: Open to researchers and scholars. For in-house use only. Available for duplication. Research requests accepted by mail, telephone and in person (walk-in). Research donations requested.
Rights: Material in the public domain.
Licensing: Apply for information.
Restrictions: Collection available for in-house use only.
Viewing Facilities: Film and videotape.

Duplication Facilities: Videotape.

NEW YORK (Hempstead)

BILL BAIRD INSTITUTE
PARENTS AID SOCIETY
See **NEW YORK METRO**

NEW YORK (Hempstead)

NASSAU COUNTY MUSEUM
REFERENCE LIBRARY
See **NEW YORK METRO**

NEW YORK (Hogansburg)

AKWESASNE LIBRARY CULTURAL CENTER
Hogansburg, NY 13655
(518) 358-2240

Margaret Jacobs (Director)

Contact: Beatrice Cole
Services: Library. Film and videotape collection maintained primarily for loan to researchers and scholars.
Description: Native American history, culture, arts and crafts, myths and legends.

Film titles include: *Age of the Buffalo; As Long as the River Shall Run; Cree Hunters of the Mistassini* (2 parts); *Cry of the Marsh; God Help the Man Who Would Part with His Land; Joseph Brant and the Six Nations; Longhouse People; High Steel; Mission of Fear* (3 parts); *Mohawk Basketing Making; More Than Bows and Arrows; The Ballad of Crowfoot; The American Indian Influence on the United States; The Dawn Riders; These are My People; The Long Road Home; Indian Arts and Crafts; Village in the Dust; Walk the High Iron* (a training program for ironworkers); *You Are On Indian Land; The Indian Speaks;* and *The Indians of Canada.*
Videotape titles include: *Portrait of a Reservation; Iroquois Myths and Legends; The Good Mind;* and *Mohawk Indian Crafts.*
Size & Elements: Film: 16mm (22 titles). Videotape: 3/4" (4 titles; viewing copies).
Cataloging: Lists available.
Access: Open to researchers, scholars and the public. Available for loan. Research fees not charged. Requests accepted by mail, telephone and in person.
Rights: Full rights held to some material. Additional clearances may be necessary in some cases if material is to be reused.
Licensing: Apply for information.
Restrictions: None specified.
Viewing Facilities: Film (16mm); videotape (3/4").
Duplication Facilities: None.

NEW YORK (Holcomb)

ANTIQUE WIRELESS ASSOCIATION, INC.
LIBRARY
Main Street, R.D. 3
Holcomb, NY 14469
(716) 657-7489

Bruce Kelley (Director/Archivist)

Contact: Bruce Kelley
Services: Library. Film and videotape collection not available for research or reuse except by special permission.
Description: History of radio and communications (beginning 1930s).
Titles include: *The Manufacturing of the All-Metal Radio Tube* (ca. 1930); *A Transatlantic Submarine Cable;* and *The Large Transatlantic Communications Stations.* Also holds videotapes of Association conferences.
Size & Elements: Film: 16mm (approx. 10 titles). Videotape: 1/2" open reel (amount unspecified).
Cataloging: None specified.
Access: Open by appointment only. Unable to accommodate research requests, except under certain circumstances and only when application is made in writing.
Rights: Full rights held to all material.
Licensing: Apply for information.

Restrictions: Special permission required for any research or reuse.
Viewing Facilities: Film and videotape.
Duplication Facilities: None.

NEW YORK (Huntington)

JALBERT PRODUCTIONS
See **NEW YORK METRO**

NEW YORK (Huntington Station)

FOCUS INTERNATIONAL, INC.
See **NEW YORK METRO**

NEW YORK (Hurleyville)

VILLON FILMS
Brophy Road
Hurleyville, NY 12747
(914) 434-5579

Contact: Peter Davis
Services: Film and videotape producer. Stock footage available for duplication, licensing and reuse through authorized representative.
Description: Footage relating to cultural, political and social issues (1920s-present).

Subjects include: American Indian life; antiwar movement in the U.S. (1960s); apartheid and resistance; the Catskill mountains and their summer culture; Cuban culture (1960s); education and school classrooms (late 1960s); espionage, including the Office of Strategic Services (OSS) and the Francis Gary Powers U-2 affair; international relations, with regard to Africa, Central America, Middle East, Philippines, Soviet Union and the United States; military activity in World War I, World War II, Korean War and in West Germany; National Council of Negro Women; naval activity, especially U.S. and Soviet; nuclear power; Watergate hearings; weaving; and youth culture in Britain, including motorcycle gangs, pubs, public schools, Soho scenes and striptease.

Foreign locations include: British Honduras (1960s); China (1940s); Cuba (pre- and post-revolution); Egypt (1960s-70s); England (1960s-70s); Jamaica (1960s); Middle East (1960s-70s), including Petra, Jordan (early 1970s), Palestinians and the West Bank (1983); Norway (World War II and ca. 1980); South Africa (1920s-80s); Southern Africa (1970s-80s).

United States locations include: Catskill Mountains, New York State ("Borscht Belt"); Miami, Florida (Cuban exiles); Providence, Rhode Island (Brown University); Southwestern and Midwestern U.S. (Navajo and Crow Indians).

Personalities include: interviews with Ronald Biggs ("Great Train" robber); Steve Biko (sound only); Athol Fugard, Martha Gellhorn, Jean Genet, Joris Ivens, R. D. Laing, Nelson and Winnie Mandela, Herbert Marcuse, Francis Gary Powers, George Seldes and Helen van Dongen. Other footage pictures Joan Baez, Stokely Carmichael, Ossie Davis, Ruby Dee, Allen Ginsberg, Abbie Hoffman, Julie Nixon, Richard M. Nixon, Valery and Galina Panov (Russian dancers), Jerry Rubin, Bobby Seale and Margaret Thatcher.
Size & Elements: Film: 35mm and 16mm (over 500,000 feet; mostly 16mm).
Cataloging: Shot lists; cataloging in progress.
Access: Available for duplication, licensing and reuse through authorized representative. Research fees charged. Research requests accepted by mail, telephone and in person (by appointment only).
Rights: Full rights held to most material. Additional clearances may be necessary in some cases if material is to be reused.
Licensing: Available for licensing and reuse through authorized representative. License fees charged.
Restrictions: None specified.
Viewing Facilities: Film and videotape (through Film/Audio Services, Inc.).
Duplication Facilities: Film and videotape (through Film/Audio Services, Inc.).
Representative: Film/Audio Services, Inc. (q.v.).

NEW YORK (Hyde Park)

THE CULINARY INSTITUTE OF AMERICA
North Road
Hyde Park, NY 12538
(914) 452-9600

Ferdinand Metz (President)

Contact: Lori Rudolph (Marketing Coordinator)
Services: Educational institution. Videotape library maintained primarily for distribution; possibly available for reuse, subject to restrictions.
Description: Culinary school videotapes, covering topics such as soups and stocks, meats and fish, *garde-manger,* basic cooking techniques, kitchen sanitation and international cuisine. Some historical and archival material may be available.
Size & Elements: Videotape: 3/4", VHS and Betamax (100 titles, each 10 to 25 min.).
Cataloging: Published catalog.
Access: Maintained primarily for distribution. Available to the public for research. Research fees charged. Research requests accepted by mail, telephone and in person.
Rights: Full rights held to all material.
Licensing: Available for licensing and reuse, subject to restrictions.
Restrictions: Clearance and approval required for licensing or reuse.
Viewing Facilities: Videotape.
Duplication Facilities: Videotape (VHS, 3/4" and Betamax).

NEW YORK (Hyde Park)

FRANKLIN D. ROOSEVELT LIBRARY
259 Albany Post Road
Hyde Park, NY 12538
(914) 229-8114

William Emerson (Director)

Contact: Mark Renovitch (Audiovisual Archivist)
Services: Government agency. Film and videotape collection open to researchers and scholars only. Material available for duplication.
Description: Presidential library administered by the National Archives and Records Administration. Holds films donated by President Roosevelt, his estate, Eleanor Roosevelt, other members of the Roosevelt family and various individuals and organizations. Recent acquisitions include videotapes of television programs about the Roosevelts. Most of the films are in black and white; approximately 15% are in color. All 35mm nitrate films have been converted to 16mm safety stock as part of the Library's ongoing preservation program. 85 reels of original color film have been placed in the cold storage vault of the John F. Kennedy Library (q.v.).

Franklin D. Roosevelt Collection. The core of the collection consists of newsreels produced by Fox Movietone News, Paramount, Pathé, Hearst and Universal that trace activities from FDR's 1932 presidential campaign until his death. The newsreels show FDR campaigning, delivering public addresses and "fireside chats," meeting with administration officials and foreign leaders, attending wartime conferences and vacationing at Hyde Park, Warm Springs and other locations with family and friends.

Color films on FDR produced by government agencies cover such topics as the visit to the United States (1939) by King George VI of Great Britain, FDR's third inauguration (1941), FDR's wartime inspection trips and overseas conferences (1940-45) and the Casablanca conference (1943).

Amateur films in the Collection provide informal glimpses of FDR taken by speechwriter Samuel I. Rosenman, John Boettiger (FDR's son-in-law) and Nancy Cook. Roosevelt is viewed at Warm Springs, sailing on the yacht *Sequoia,* in Yellowstone National Park, visiting Winston Churchill and the Duke of Windsor at Hyde Park (1944), with family and friends at Campobello (1930s-40s), dedicating public buildings and on political trips.

The Collection also includes commercial motion pictures, television documentaries, news programs and movies, including: *President Roosevelt's Message to Congress, December 8, 1941; The Inauguration of Franklin D. Roosevelt, 1933;* the 26-part documentary *FDR,* produced by ABC-TV; two programs produced by CBS-TV, *Roosevelt, the Man and the Politician* (1962) and *FDR Remembered* (1965); *Eleanor and Franklin* (1975 ABC television movie); *FDR, the Man Who Changed America* (1975); and *FDR: The Last Year* (1980).

Mr. W. H. Utterback, Jr. is in the process of restoring selected public addresses of President Roosevelt from the Universal Newsreel Collection at the National Archives and Records Administration (q.v.). The following speeches have been reconstructed on film: State of the Union Address (January 6, 1942); Navy and Total Defense Day Address (October 27, 1941); and the address at Chautauqua, New York (August 14, 1936).

Eleanor Roosevelt Films. Documentation of Eleanor Roosevelt's career from the 1932 presidential campaign until her death in November, 1962, including appearances with FDR and their children during the 1920 campaign. The newsreels cover not only FDR, but also focus on Eleanor Roosevelt's activities, including her trips to Puerto Rico, the Virgin Islands and Great Britain (1942); and to the Pacific Islands (1943). General film coverage of her post-1945 activities includes a portion of her address to the United Nations; speeches before the AFL-CIO merger meeting (December, 1955) and at the Democratic National Convention (1956); appearances on television discussion and interview programs, including *Face the Nation* (1956), *Citizen's Forum* (1958) and *Prospects of Mankind* (1959-62); traveling to Israel (1959); and making campaign announcements on behalf of John F. Kennedy (1960). Amateur films taken by John Boettiger, Nancy Cook and Victor Hammer show her touring the Caribbean (1934); visiting with family and friends at Campobello, Hyde Park (1930-60); and visiting Japan, France and Morocco (1950s). The Library also holds the Academy Award-winning film, *The Eleanor Roosevelt Story;* news coverage by NBC and CBS following Mrs. Roosevelt's death; a series of CBS film clips showing her activities during the post-White House years; and *Thinking Things Through,* the pilot for a weekly discussion program.

General subjects. Coverage of personalities, institutions, places, social conditions and events of the Roosevelt era. Personalities include Winston Churchill, Thomas E. Dewey and Harry S Truman. Institutional films include: *Lest We Forget* (1944); *Pursuit of Happiness* (1956); *Youth Visits Our Nation's Capitol* (1939); *Training Women for War Production;* and *The 1940 Census.* Films about places include *Dynamic New York* (1939) and *Washington, The Nation's Capital.* Social conditions are depicted in *The Plow That Broke the Plains* and *The River.* Major events of World War II are covered in *Countdown to World War II;* the *Why We Fight* series, including *Prelude to War, The Nazi Strike* and *The Battle of Britain;* and in *The Negro Soldier* and *Washington in Wartime.* A series compiled by Castle Films from newsreel footage shows combat action in the various theaters of the war.

Size & Elements: Film: 16mm (285,000 feet, 680 cans; release prints; negatives held at National Archives and Records Administration [q.v.]). Videotape: format and amount unspecified (viewing copies).
Cataloging: Card catalogs; shelf list. Library has a general guide to the newsreels and has begun preparing detailed descriptions of the contents of each newsreel. It has prepared a card index and typed listing of FDR, Eleanor Roosevelt and others speaking on film. It is also preparing a film subject index to the many films on FDR, Eleanor Roosevelt and to general topics that are not part of the newsreel collection. All of these finding aids are available to researchers.
Access: Open to researchers and scholars only. Available for duplication, subject to restrictions. Research fees not charged. Research requests accepted by mail, telephone and in person (walk-in).
Rights: Some rights held to some material.
Licensing: Apply for information.
Restrictions: Films may be viewed in the Library, but are not loaned out or rented. Library will gladly provide a list of distributors who rent and sell materials in the collection. Films in the public domain, such as those made by government agencies, may be duplicated without restriction. Copyrighted materials, such as newsreels and television programs, may not be reproduced without permission of the copyright holder. Videotapes of recent television programs on the Roosevelts may be viewed in the Library; they cannot be reproduced. Researchers requesting copies of these programs must contact the television network that produced the specific program.
Viewing Facilities: Film (16mm, Steenbeck); videotape.
Duplication Facilities: None.

NEW YORK (Ithaca)

CORNELL UNIVERSITY
MEDIA SERVICES
NB 13 MVR Hall
Ithaca, NY 14853-4401
(607) 255-5431
Fax: (607) 255-1533

David Watkins (Director of Media Services)

Contact: Glen Palmer (Customer Service Representative)
Services: Educational institution; videotape producer. Material available for duplication, licensing and reuse.
Description: Footage relating to Cornell University, including campus scenes, buildings, people, classrooms, football and graduation. Also holds agricultural footage, including cattle, hogs, crops (planting and harvesting) and farm implements and machinery.

Size & Elements: Videotape: 1" and Betacam (5 hours; masters). Viewing copies available in any videotape format. Other material is uncataloged and unavailable at present.
Cataloging: Compilation reels are available on videotape. Other material is uncataloged and unavailable at present.
Access: Available to the public for duplication, licensing and reuse. Research and duplication fees charged (based on length of viewing copy ordered). Research requests accepted by mail, telephone and in person (by appointment only).
Rights: Full rights held to all material.
Licensing: Available for licensing. License fees charged.
Restrictions: None specified.
Viewing Facilities: Videotape (any format).
Duplication Facilities: Videotape (2", 1", 3/4", VHS and Betamax).

NEW YORK (Jamaica)

ST. JOHN'S UNIVERSITY
SPECIAL COLLECTIONS
See **NEW YORK METRO**

NEW YORK (Jamestown)

CHAUTAUQUA-CATTARAUGUS LIBRARY SYSTEM
106 West 5th Street
Jamestown, NY 14702
(716) 484-7135

Murray L. Bob (Director)

Contacts: Alberta Pike (Film Department); Jean Haynes (Film/Video Librarian)
Services: Library. Film and videotape collection open to the public. Materials available for individual and interlibrary loan by special arrangement.
Description: Large collection of circulating motion picture materials on a wide range of subjects, including abortion, adolescence, aeronautics, Afro-Americans, America (discovery and exploration), animals, animation, art and artisans, avant-garde films, birds, blindness, Buddhism, Chile, civil rights, communism, fantasy, gliding and soaring, homosexuality, Mexican Americans, natural history, prejudice and antipathies, Protestantism, radio, resuscitation, rivers, satire, Scotland, spy stories, solar energy, surfing, U.S. history, venereal disease, water supply, Western states, biographies of women, World War II and zoological gardens.

Also holds locally produced videotapes, including documentaries on Jamestown and *Survival Arts Media* (1975-78), a videotape series on arts and crafts (8 titles).
Size & Elements: Film: 16mm (1,500 films). Videotape: 3/4" and VHS (1,500 titles).
Cataloging: Published catalogs.
Access: Open to the public. Films and videotapes available for individual and interlibrary loan by special arrangement. Research requests accepted by mail and in person (walk-in). Service fees charged for research requests from outside Chautauqua and Cattaraugus Counties.
Rights: Rights retained by original producers.
Licensing: Apply for information.
Restrictions: Special arrangements required for individual and interlibrary loan.
Viewing Facilities: Film (16mm); videotape (3/4" and VHS).
Duplication Facilities: None.

NEW YORK (Lake Success)

THOROUGHBRED RACING ASSOCIATIONS
See **NEW YORK METRO**

NEW YORK (Lockport)

LOCKPORT COMMUNITY CABLE COMMISSION
One Locks Plaza
Lockport, NY 14094
(716) 434-1733

Street address: 293 Niagara Street

Michael Drake (Access Manager)

Contact: Richard Zapp (Studio Supervisor)
Services: Public access television facility. Videotape program library open to the public for in-house use only; available for reuse, subject to restrictions.
Description: Local cable television programming on videotape. Subjects include Western New York community events, local entertainers, local sports, local entertainment events (1984-present); weekly and monthly series produced for airing over local public access channels, including shows relating to religious matters, animal care, talk shows (live and videotaped), financial planning programs and a live call-in sports show.
Size & Elements: Videotape: 3/4" (approx. 100 programs, each averaging 30 min.; masters).
Cataloging: Finding aids (notebook).
Access: Open to the public. For in-house use only. Research fees not charged. Research requests accepted by mail, telephone and in person (walk-in and by appointment).
Rights: Some rights held to all material (videotapes are owned by Lockport Cable and may not leave the facility; shows are copyrighted by the producer). Additional clearances from producer will be necessary if material is to be reused.
Licensing: Available for licensing and reuse, subject to restrictions. No charge for reuse of footage with permission of producer.
Restrictions: Master videotapes of programs must remain at facility. Duplicates may only be made with the approval of producer. Complete shows or footage from them may not be used in commercial projects (available for nonprofit use only).
Viewing Facilities: Videotape (3/4" and Betamax I). Viewing arrangements must be made in advance.
Duplication Facilities: Videotape (3/4" and VHS); fees apply.

NEW YORK (Maryknoll)

**MARYKNOLL FATHERS AND BROTHERS/
CATHOLIC FOREIGN MISSION SOCIETY OF AMERICA
THE MARYKNOLL WORLD VIDEO AND FILM LIBRARY**
Gonzaga Building
Maryknoll, NY 10545-0307
(800) 227-8523
(914) 941-7590 (Ext. 308 or 577)
Fax: (914) 762-0316
Telex: 240-025

Contact: Ronald E. Hines (Promotions Coordinator, Media Relations)
Services: Religious organization; film and videotape producer and distributor. Film and videotape collection available to the public primarily for rental and purchase.
Description: Films and videotapes designed to promote global awareness about human issues around the world, especially in Africa, Asia and Latin America (1970-present). Programs cover topics such as the arms race, culture, education, health, hunger, missionaries, peace, politics, religion and youth.
General programs. Titles include: *The Business of Hunger,* examining how in many Third World countries cash crops are exported while the poor go hungry and how this distribution problem is one of the major causes of world hunger; *Appalachia: No Man's Land,* an account of the effects of coal mining on several communities with economic and environmental hardships; *Samoa: Culture in Crisis,* on the threat that modernization poses to traditional values; *Kenyan Youth: Preparing For the Future; The New Zimbabwe,* showing Blacks and Whites who once lived in separate societies in colonial Rhodesia working together; and *El Salvador: The Seeds of Liberty,* an examination of the conflicts in this embattled land. *Consuming Hunger* (3 parts, each 29 min.) analyzes how television images of the starvation in Ethiopia superseded reality; asking why it took so long for Western television to cover the famine, what happened to the images of starving Africans once they became part of our television culture, and what the "Hands Across America" mega-event told us about hunger in America and how the images of our own homeless and hungry were used.
Common Table Series (an ongoing series of 21 programs, each 30 min.). Titles include: *A World of Refugees; Religion and Culture in China; Working for Peace: The Nuclear Issue; The Many Faces of Homelessness; Workers in the World; Women in Tanzania;* and *Education: The Hope of the Developing World.*
Size & Elements: Film: 16mm (27 titles). Videotape: VHS (approx. 50 titles).
Cataloging: Published catalogs.
Access: Open to researchers, scholars and the public. Available primarily for educational distribution and rental rather than for research or reuse. Requests accepted by mail, telephone and in person (walk-in).

Rights: Full rights held to all material.
Licensing: Apply for information. License fees charged under some conditions depending on intended use.
Restrictions: None specified.
Viewing Facilities: None.
Duplication Facilities: None.
Related Materials: Many programs have accompanying study guides.

NEW YORK (Mount Kisco)

**THE CENTER FOR HUMANITIES, INC.
GUIDANCE ASSOCIATES**
See **NEW YORK METRO**

NEW YORK (Mount Vernon)

**CONSUMERS UNION OF THE U.S.
ARCHIVES**
See **NEW YORK METRO**

NEW YORK CITY METROPOLITAN AREA

NEW YORK METRO

ABC DISTRIBUTION (EDUCATION)
825 Seventh Avenue
New York, NY 10019
(212) 887-1725
(212) 887-1731
Telex: 234-337 ABCWC

Jack Healy (President)

Contact: Patricia E. Vance (Director, Ancillary Market Sales)
Services: Videotape distributor. Television programs available for purchase. ABC-owned programs and segments available for licensing and reuse, subject to restrictions. Stock footage sales are handled through Sherman Grinberg Film Libraries, Inc. (q.v.).
Description: ABC Distribution sells programs directly on a custom-order basis for personal, educational and/or training use. While the focus is on news, cultural, children's and some sports programs are also available. Some complete news programs and segments originally produced for *World News Tonight, 20/20, Closeup, Nightline* and other news programs are available for purchase. Programs date from early 1970s, although most programs are current.
Programs cover a wide range of subjects, including health, safety, social issues, family, politics, law, crime, business, children and substance abuse. Several current titles are: *To Die For Ireland; To Catch A Rapist; When Mom Has to Work;* and *War on Cancer.* Many programs have been licensed to non-theatrical distributors (e.g., Coronet/MTI Film & Video and CRM Films L.P. [q.v.]).
Size & Elements: Videotape: available on 3/4" and 1/2" (currently 450 programs in catalog).
Cataloging: Printed catalog of programs currently in circulation.
Access: ABC Distribution's archives maintained for distribution and sales purposes; not open to the public. Programs and segments available for purchase; rentals not available. Research fees not charged. Research requests accepted by mail only.
Rights: Full rights held to all material available.
Licensing: Stock footage licensed through Sherman Grinberg Film Libraries, Inc. (q.v.). Segments and other programs marketed through ABC Distribution. License fees charged depending on material and its intended use.
Restrictions: Programs not available for rental. Programs cannot be used for sales and/or marketing purposes. Programs cannot be edited, duplicated or used for theatrical purposes.
Viewing Facilities: None.
Duplication Facilities: None.

NEW YORK METRO

ABC NEWS
47 West 66th Street
New York, NY 10023
(212) 456-7777
Fax: (212) 887-4968

Robert Siegenthaler (Vice President)

Contact: David Sternlicht (Legal Department) (212/887-4865)
Services: Television network division. Completed news programs not available for outside use except by special authorization. Some show segments may be available for purchase through ABC Distribution (Education) (q.v.). Outtakes from *World News Tonight* available for licensing and reuse through Sherman Grinberg Film Libraries, Inc. (q.v.).
Description: The News Division holds show histories (copies of televised programs) representing many news programs (1963-present). They include *World News Tonight; Nightline; Viewpoint; Closeup* (documentaries); *Discovery; Directions; Now; ABCScope; Special Reports* and *Special Events.* These show histories are not for public use or screening except for those handled through ABC Distribution (Education) (q.v.).

Topics covered by the various ABC News programs include a wide range of public issues: abortion, civil rights, drugs, ecology, fads, religion, war, and more.
Size & Elements: Film: 16mm (600 films). Videotape: 2" (2,000 videotapes, in process of being transferred to 3/4"); 3/4" (10,000 videotapes).
Cataloging: ABC News Operations has printed a summary of each years' news and special events programs. This summary is currently in the process of being computerized for internal use only. ABC News is currently being indexed by Research Publications (Woodbridge, Connecticut). Indexing has begun with the most current programs and is working backwards. Presently, the completed index covers 1985-present.
Access: Outtakes from ABC News' *World News Tonight* are available through Sherman Grinberg Film Libraries, Inc. (q.v.). Some show segments may be available for purchase through ABC Distribution (Education) (q.v.). ABC does not sell or license news programs except for those programs handled through ABC Distribution (Education). Depending on the purpose of the request some duplicates of show histories may be provided for screening. These requests are subject to approval and require a fee for duplication costs and research.
Rights: Full ownership rights held to all programs. Some material within programs has been licensed from outside sources and therefore is not available for resale.
Licensing: Outtakes from ABC World News Tonight are available through Sherman Grinberg Film Libraries, Inc. (q.v.). Some show segments may be available through ABC Distribution (Education). Show histories and documentaries are not available for outside use except by authorization from the Legal Department.
Restrictions: Show histories and documentaries not available for outside distribution. Licensing or reuse requires authorization from the Legal Department.
Viewing Facilities: None.
Duplication Facilities: None.

NEW YORK METRO

ABC NEWS INTERACTIVE
7 West 66th Street, 4th Floor
New York, NY 10023
(212) 887-4060
Fax: (212) 887-2305

William Lord (Vice President and Executive Producer)

Contact: Jane White (Director, Educational Services)
Services: Educational videodisc producer. Videodiscs available to educational institutions for purchase.
Description: ABC News Interactive is a service of ABC News, providing the educational community with a series of laser videodiscs focused on "instant replays of history." Materials will be produced using moving image material drawn from ABC's film and videotape libraries. Images will be retrievable from the videodiscs either by computer (using Macintosh interface) or through the disc player's remote controller. Study guides will be supplied with the videodiscs. The first disc, *The '88 Vote: Campaign for the White House* was released in January 1989; further titles are due for release.
Size & Elements: Videodisc (CAV format).
Cataloging: To be provided as collection develops.
Access: Available to educational institutions for purchase.
Rights: Full rights held to all videodiscs and to ABC-generated material located therein. Rights to some material on discs may be retained by outside suppliers.
Licensing: Apply for information. License fees charged, depending on material used and purpose of use. Educational institutions will be charged a flat fee for

purchase of disc.
Restrictions: Material can be used for internal, school-related activities. Material cannot be reused or resold for commercial use.
Viewing Facilities: None.
Duplication Facilities: None.
Related Materials: Study guides.
Distributor: Optical Data Corporation; (800) 524-2481.

NEW YORK METRO

ABC SPORTS, INC.
1330 Avenue of the Americas
New York, NY 10019
(212) 887-6446
Fax: (212) 887-6202
Telex (domestic): 649-511
Telex (international): 234-723 ABC VR

Dennis Swanson (President)

Contact: Louise Argianas (Manager, Rights and Clearances and Contract Administration)
Services: Television network division. Film and videotape available for licensing and reuse on a case-by-case basis, subject to restrictions.
Description: Licenses a wide spectrum of sports activities and events covered by ABC Sports, including excerpts from *Wide World of Sports* and other ABC Sports programs. The Sports archives (1966-present) includes auto racing, arm wrestling, bowling, college football, cycling, diving, golf, gymnastics, horseback riding, Little League, Olympics, rodeos, skiing, Special Olympics, swimming, surfing and weightlifting.
Size & Elements: Film: format and amount unspecified. Videotape: 2", 1" and 3/4" (over 10,000 events). Material available in all videotape formats.
Cataloging: Program material filed by date and event. Program logs are the only available means of locating material.
Access: Not open to the public. Available for licensing and reuse, subject to restrictions. Research requests accepted by mail. Limited research services available.
Rights: Full rights held to some material. Additional clearances may be necessary in some cases if material is to be reused.
Licensing: Excerpts of material available for licensing and reuse on a case-by-case basis. Written requests required and must specify the event in which the excerpt requested is located, the amount to be used and the intended use (e.g., broadcast, local, national, worldwide, syndicated non-broadcast, trade show or in-house). License fees charged.
Restrictions: Restrictions may apply; reuse requests accepted on a case-by-case basis.
Viewing Facilities: None.
Duplication Facilities: None.

NEW YORK METRO

ADBANK
49 East 21st Street
New York, NY 10010
(212) 460-5155
Fax: (212) 254-5204

Contact: Margaret Shiverick (Managing Director)
Services: Monitors and catalogs television broadcasts primarily for advertisers and advertising agencies. Provides custom-edited videotapes of television commercials. Material not available for reuse or resale.
Description: Commercials, political campaign and public service announcements. Coverage includes program segments from network broadcasts as well as regional, spot and cable television (1981-present). Categories include: travel, leisure and amusements; home furnishings, appliances and home entertainment; automotive; beverages; cosmetics and personal care; financial and business services; food; snack foods, food preparation and pet products; laundry and paper products; medicines; retail and apparel; toys and games.

Titles include: *The Best 100 Commercials Ever,* a compilation of vintage commercials (1960s-70s) and more recent ads. Nominations solicited from "top creatives in the U.S. and the U.K." Some of the footage is so rare that only "fragile 16mm versions" remain. Spots include: Alka-Seltzer, Benson & Hedges, Clairol, Mobil, Braniff, Fiat, Volvo, and Volkswagen. *The British Design & Art Directors 1987 Showreel* received England's prestigious Design

& Art Directors Award competition (38 commercials in 12 different categories).

Services include: spots on demand (custom-edited videotapes of television commercials, arranged by product segment or advertiser); segment spots subscription (new television commercials aired in a specific product segment requested by client, delivered monthly); segment or brand retrospective (custom-edited three- and six-month recaps of product segments or brands); *Adweek's Best Spots* (featuring 40 of the most significant television commercials of the month as chosen by *Adweek* editors), available on a monthly basis or by annual subscription; and *Best Spots of The Year,* available (1986-present).
Size & Elements: Videotape: 3/4", VHS and Betamax (amount unspecified).
Cataloging: Library organized by product segment, brand and advertiser.
Access: Open to the public. Primarily serves advertising agencies and corporations engaged in television advertising. Requests accepted by mail and telephone.
Rights: No rights held to any material. Additional clearances are necessary if material is to be reused.
Licensing: Not available through AdBank.
Restrictions: Material is for research and reference use only; no reuse permitted.
Viewing Facilities: None specified.
Duplication Facilities: Videotape (3/4", VHS and Betamax).

NEW YORK METRO

ADVERTISING INFORMATION SERVICES, INC.
353 Lexington Avenue
New York, NY 10016
(212) 683-9113
Fax: (212) 889-4098

Jack Safirstein (President)

Contacts: Dana Davis; Ryan Smith; Lucille Vitale
Services: Aircheck service; television commercial library. Videotape collection maintained for advertising research purposes.
Description: Library holds over 60,000 television commercials recorded off network and independent television in New York City (1976-present; library updated daily). Also maintains off-air recording facility providing public relations firms, advertising agencies and corporations with videotaped program segments. In New York City, continuous coverage includes ABC, CBS, NBC, PBS, CNN, ESPN, USA, WTBS, WNYW, WWOR and WPIX. Coverage of other stations and continuous coverage of other markets are also available.
Size & Elements: Videotape: 3/4", Betamax and VHS (5,000 videotapes, over 60,000 commercials total).
Cataloging: In-house cataloging.
Access: Apply for information.
Rights: Apply for information.
Licensing: Not available for reuse.
Restrictions: Materials may be used for internal research purposes only; not available for reuse.
Viewing Facilities: None.
Duplication Facilities: None.

NEW YORK METRO

AIDSFILMS
50 West 34th Street, Suite 6B6
New York, NY 10001
(212) 629-6288

John Hoffman (Executive Director)

Contact: John Hoffman
Services: Videotape producer and distributor. Videotape available for purchase, licensing and reuse.
Description: Distributes *AIDS: Changing the Rules* (26 min.), hosted by Ron Reagan, Jr., Beverly Johnson and Ruben Blades. This award-winning film targets adult heterosexuals and promotes the use of condoms and safer sex practices.
Size & Elements: Videotape: 3/4" and 1/2" (1 title, 26 min.).
Cataloging: None specified.
Access: Available for purchase, licensing and reuse.
Rights: Full rights held to all material.
Licensing: Available for licensing and reuse. License fees charged.

Restrictions: None specified.
Viewing Facilities: None.
Duplication Facilities: None.

NEW YORK METRO

AIRSHIP INDUSTRIES (USA), INC.
650 Fifth Avenue, 22nd Floor
New York, NY 10019
(212) 262-7230
Fax: (212) 262-7249
Telex: 981024 AIR NYK

George A. Spyrou (Executive Vice President)

Contacts: Alix Cochrane (Vice President, Marketing); Mary Lee Dickson (Marketing)
Services: Corporation and corporate archives. Videotape collection maintained for public relations purposes and client use.
Description: Aerial shots of and from a blimp over San Francisco, New York and Los Angeles. Holds two completed programs, including *Battle of the Blimps.*
Size & Elements: Videotape: 3/4" and 1/2" (2 titles; viewing copies).
Cataloging: None specified.
Access: Maintained for public relations purposes and client use. Research fees not charged. Research requests accepted by mail, telephone and in person (walk-in).
Rights: Full rights held to some material.
Licensing: Apply for information. License fees not charged.
Restrictions: None specified.
Viewing Facilities: None.
Duplication Facilities: None.

NEW YORK METRO

AL-ANON FAMILY GROUP HEADQUARTERS, INC.
P.O. Box 862, Midtown Station
New York, NY 10018-0862
(212) 302-7240
Fax: (212) 869-3757

Street address: 1372 Broadway, 7th Floor, New York, NY 10018-6106

Myrna S. Hammersley (Executive Director/General Secretary)

Contact: Ellen Duffy (CPC Coordinator)
Services: Educational institution; nonprofit organization. Film and videotape material available for purchase and licensing.
Description: Films directed towards Al-Anon members (people whose lives have been affected by alcoholics) and public service announcements (PSAs) for broadcast. *Lois' Story* is a history of Al-Anon. In *Al-Anon Speaks for Itself* Al-Anon/Alateen members share their experiences; this videotape is provided with closed captions for the hearing impaired.
Size & Elements: Film: 16mm. Videotape: 2" (PSAs only); 3/4", VHS and Betamax II (transfers from film).
Cataloging: Published catalog.
Access: Films and videotapes available for purchase; PSAs available for broadcast.
Rights: Full rights held to all material.
Licensing: Apply for information. License fees charged.
Restrictions: None specified.
Viewing Facilities: None.
Duplication Facilities: None.
Distributors: Al-Anon Literature Centers (apply for information).

NEW YORK METRO

ALLEN (JOHN E.) INC.
116 North Avenue
Park Ridge, NJ 07656
(201) 391-3299
Fax: (201) 391-6335

John E. Allen (President)

Contact: John E. Allen
Services: Stock footage sales library. Full-service in-house film and sound laboratory; broadcast-quality film-to-videotape transfer capability.
Description: Covers 1896-1955; especially strong in pre-1940 subjects.

General subjects. Agriculture (1910-50s) worldwide, all types; Americana (1900-50s) including small town life, American culture, car culture, patriotic celebrations and social life; American Legion; amusement parks; animals (1900-55), including newsreels, educational films, nature films, zoos, working circuses and comedies; audiences; bathing beauties (1905-50s) with beauty contests, feature clips and publicity shots.

Blacks (1915-50s) featuring especially strong coverage of rural life (1920-30s), Harlem (late 1920s-30s), middle-class life (1950s) and various work situations.

Boy Scouts; canals; celebrations; ceremonies; circuses; colleges; construction (1910-55), including bridges, canals, dams, housing, railroads and skyscrapers; conventions (1910-50s), both private and political; conferences (1915-50).

Dance (1900-50) featuring dances from cakewalk to jitterbug, classical ballet to nightclub adagio; and examples of ethnic dancing from all over the world.

Demonstrations (1910-50), including good labor and Communist demonstrations from between the wars, in U.S. and abroad, with especially rare footage from the Depression and late 1920s Weimar Germany; extensive footage of soup lines, dust bowls, jobless people, Hoovervilles, headlines, recovery programs and speeches.

Dictators; diplomats; earthquakes (1906-53) with coverage of major earthquakes in San Francisco, Japan and Mexico; ethnographic footage (1910-50s), showing peoples and cultures from all over the world; expeditions (1910-50) to Africa, Arctic, Antarctic, Asia, Central America and South America.

Fairs (1910-50), featuring major exhibits, Pan American Exposition, Chicago World's Fair (1933) and New York World's Fair (1939-40); flappers; floods; gags and silent film clips of a variety of humorous situations, routines, falls and chases; gambling; gangsters; Girl Scouts; government; governors; harbors; holidays; home movies and hurricanes.

Immigrants arriving at Ellis Island; shots of New York's Lower East Side (1910s); industry; inventions; Jazz Age; Ku Klux Klan; mayors; medical footage (1912-50s) including medical education films, news coverage of public health campaigns and public education films.

Military footage (1898-1950s) featuring all branches of the military, training, troop reviews, maneuvers, in action, U.S. and foreign; mining.

Motion picture personalities (1896-1950) shown in news footage, feature clips and publicity stories, strong in the silent period; motion picture production (1910-40) showing studios, filming, premieres and laboratories; motion picture trailers; national parks (1910-50), particularly strong in 1910s and 1920s (footage often includes tourists, some in stencil color); newspapers (1910-50s) showing presses, offices and distribution; Olympic games (1908-52).

Parades, including ticker tape, fraternal organizations, small town, circus and St. Patrick's Day; primitive films; prohibition, including speeches for and against, still-smashing and speakeasies; presidents; royalty; rural life; small town life; snow storms; strikes; suffragettes; telephone; television; tourists; vaudeville.

Western sequences (1905-40) including actuality and fiction, rodeos, wild West shows, gunfights, brawls, cowboys, cattle and buffalo herds, among other subjects.

World War I newsreels and documentaries covering various aspects and views of war, U.S. and European titles: *The German Side of the War, On the Italian Battlefront, France in Arms;* World War II newsreels, some Wochenschau and Soviet films; workers (1910-50s) men and women, showing many types of work.

Kinograms (1915-31). Original negatives, prints, trims and outtakes of a major newsreel whose camera crews covered news in the United States and abroad.

Sports (1910-50s). All types, especially strong for the periods 1915-35 and 1947-53; baseball, football (college and professional), golf, tennis, auto racing, horse racing and boxing.

Telenews (1947-53). Original negatives, prints, trims and outtakes. A syndicated film series for television news programs, patterned after theatrical newsreels. Coverage is worldwide.

Transportation. Automobiles (early cars, comedies, roadside attractions, manufacture, service stations and touring); aviation (experimental, barnstormers, record flights, air shows, commercial airlines, air mail, military, lighter-than-air ships, balloons, Zeppelins, blimps); railroads (primitive track laying, steam trains, streamliners, views from trains, railroad workers); ships (freighters, liners, sailing ships, sports, commercial and exhibition [including 35mm color of 1976 Operation Sail], shipbuilding); trucks (manufacturing,

maintenance, in use).

Travelogues and exploration (1895-1950s). Footage from virtually every region of world; particularly strong 1915-40. Extensive holdings from Argentina, Brazil, Chile, China, Egypt, Finland, France, Germany, India, Italy, Japan, Mexico, Poland, Russia/Soviet Union, Spain, Turkey, United Kingdom, Indochina, Venezuela and the South Seas.

United States (1900-50s). Footage from throughout the country; extensive coverage of New York City; and strong coverage of Los Angeles and Hollywood, Chicago and Washington, D.C.
Size & Elements: Film: 35mm, 28mm and 16mm (28 million feet; although elements exist in all formats, largest percentage of material is 35mm). Videotape: 1" and 3/4" (film-to-videotape transfers of some material).
Cataloging: Card catalogs; computerized cataloging for staff use only; shot lists; logs and records (internal use only); other finding aids; research library.
Access: Available to the public for licensing and reuse. Research fees charged. Research requests accepted by mail, telephone and in person (by appointment only).
Rights: Full rights held to some material. Some rights held to all material. Some material in the public domain.
Licensing: Available for licensing and reuse, subject to restrictions. License fees charged, depending on intended market for production (apply for fee schedule).
Restrictions: Restrictions may apply in some cases.
Viewing Facilities: Film (35mm and 16mm viewers, librarian assistance required); videotape (1", 3/4" [NTSC, Low Band PAL and SECAM], VHS and Betamax [NTSC, PAL, SECAM]).
Duplication Facilities: Film (full service 35mm and 16mm film and videotape lab in-house, including liquid gate contact and optical blowups and reductions); videotape (Rank Cintel MK III transfers from film to 1", 3/4", VHS and Betamax formats, including NTSC, low band PAL and SECAM; transfers available at 18, 24 and 30 frames per second).
Related Materials: Over one million stills, posters and lobby cards pertaining to feature films and the motion picture industry.

NEW YORK METRO

AMERICAN ALPINE CLUB, INC.
113 East 90th Street
New York, NY 10128-1589
(212) 722-1628

Franc de la Vega (Executive Secretary)

Contact: Patricia A. Fletcher (Librarian)
Services: Organization; library. Videotape collection maintained for viewing purposes only.
Description: Alpine, mountaineering and rock climbing films, either transferred to or originating on videotape.

Topics include alpinism, mountaineering, rock climbing, mountains and polar regions. Older films (beginning 1920s) will be transferred to videotape as they are found or acquired. Plans are to build a videotape collection of every film or videotape, including those in foreign languages, known to exist on these subjects. Collection began in June 1987.
Size & Elements: Videotape: VHS (20 videotapes). Acquisitions ongoing.
Cataloging: Card catalogs; computerized cataloging for staff use only.
Access: Open to the public. For in-house use only. Research or screening fees not charged. Research requests are accepted in person (by appointment only).
Rights: No rights held to any material.
Licensing: Material not available for reuse.
Restrictions: Collection maintained for viewing purposes only.
Viewing Facilities: Videotape.
Duplication Facilities: None.

NEW YORK METRO

AMERICAN ANOREXIA/BULIMIA ASSOCIATION INC.
133 Cedar Lane
Teaneck, NJ 07666
(201) 836-1800

Caaron Willinger (Executive Director)

Contact: Staff
Services: Information and referral organization. Holds film and videotape collection.

Description: Small collection relating to anorexia and bulimia. Titles include: *Wasting Away*, a videotape from the Guidance Association Center for Humanities; and *Anorexia & Bulimia*, a film from Career Aids.
Size & Elements: Film and videotape (formats and amounts unspecified).
Cataloging: None specified.
Access: Apply for information.
Rights: Apply for information.
Licensing: Apply for information.
Restrictions: Apply for information.
Viewing Facilities: None.
Duplication Facilities: None.
Related Materials: Filmstrips.

NEW YORK METRO

**AMERICAN CRAFT COUNCIL
SLIDE/FILM SERVICE**
45 West 45th Street
New York, NY 10036
(212) 869-9422
Fax: (212) 354-5287

Nancy Libas (Manager, Slide/Film Service)

Contact: Nancy Libas
Services: Educational institution and museum. Film and videotape library available for rental and purchase.
Description: Films relating to crafts and artisans. Coverage is international and highlights specific artists at work in a variety of media. *Mashiko Village Pottery* (1937), the earliest film in the collection, features the legendary teapot painter Minagawa. *Peruvian Weaving: A Continuous Warp for 5000 Years* portrays the weavers of Q'eros, including footage from Dr. Junius Bird's excavation of Huaca Prieta on the northwest coast of Peru (1946). Other, more recent, films cover such subjects as: a blacksmithing workshop at Southern Illinois University; self-employment as an artisan; pottery making; fiber artist Gerhardt Knodel; woodworking; mokume-gane (wood grained metal); glassmaking; enameling; textile manufacture and design; shoemaker Gaza Bowen, who employs 18th century techniques; and leather working.

Size & Elements: Film: 16mm. Videotape: VHS. (21 titles total).
Cataloging: Brochure (available on request).
Access: Available to the public for rental and purchase.
Rights: Some rights held to some material.
Licensing: Apply for information.
Restrictions: Visual material may not be reproduced for any reason without written consent of the ACC.
Viewing Facilities: None.
Duplication Facilities: None.

NEW YORK METRO

**AMERICAN FEDERATION OF THE ARTS
FILM PROGRAM**
41 East 65th Street
New York, NY 10021
(212) 988-7700
Fax: (212) 861-2487

Sam McElfresh (Film Program Director)

Contacts: Bill O'Donnell; Tom Smith (Assistant Director, Film Program)
Services: Film distributor; nonprofit organization. Films available for distribution and rental rather than for research or reuse.
Description: "Films as art" (animation, experimental narrative, lyrical documentary, abstract film) and "films on art" (documentaries on the lives and works of artists and on historical and contemporary art movements). Collection holds documentaries about the arts (175); experimental films (200); experimental videotapes (100); early American archival films (65).

Exhibitions include: *A History of the American Avant-Garde Cinema* (34 films). Produced 1943-72, including work by Maya Deren, Kenneth Anger, Stan Brakhage, Ian Hugo, Ken Jacobs, Shirley Clarke, Robert Breer, Tony Conrad, Jonas Mekas, Michael Snow, Hollis Frampton, Ernie Gehr and Paul Sharits.

The Originals: Women in Art (7 films). Series originally presented on public television, profiling Mary Cassatt, Georgia O'Keeffe, Louise Nevelson, Alice Neel, Helen Frankenthaler and Betye Saar.

Revising Romance: New Feminist Video (11 videotapes). Produced by video artists, including Deans Keppel, Ann-Sargent Wooster, Barbara Broughel, Bruce and Norman Yonemoto, Ilene Segalove, Cecelia Condit and Eleanor Antin.

1985 Whitney Biennial Film/Video Exhibition (14 films). Includes Lizzie Borden's *Born in Flames*, Sheila McLaughlin and Lynne Tillman's *Committed*, and films by Ken Kobland, Holly Fisher, Ericka Beckman, Elisabeth Ross and Pooh Kaye, Jane Aaron, Robert Breer, Morgan Fisher, Douglas Davis, Warren Sonbert, Sandy Moore and Larry Gottheim, and an anthology of video art divided into eight programs, including work by Charles Atlas, Dara Birnbaum, Bill Viola, Dan Reeves, Lyn Blumenthal, Doug Hall, Joan Jonas and Robert Ashley.

1983 Whitney Biennial Film/Video Exhibition (19 films). Includes work by Sandy Moore, Stuart Sherman, David Haxton, Barry Gerson, Dan Walworth, Martha Haslanger, Robert Breer, Bruce Conner, Warren Sonbert, James Herbert, Ericka Beckman, Vivienne Dick, Ernie Gehr, Ken Kobland and James Benning, and an anthology of video art divided into seven programs, including work by Juan Downey, Bruce Charlesworth, Ken Feingold, Edin Velez, Shalom Gorewitz, Stan Vanderbeek, Bill Viola, Matthew Geller, Doug Hall, Howard Fried, Barbara Buckner, Gary Hill, Bob Snyder, Nam June Paik and Shigeto Kubota, and Martha Rosler.

Before Hollywood: Turn-of-the-Century American Film from the American Archives. Films from the first two decades of cinema (1895-1915); 5 programs, each 90 min.

BBS Budapest: Twenty Years of Hungarian Experimental Film (18 films). Hungarian films from the Bela Balazs studio.

Also, *Video Art: Three Installations*, by Mary Lucier, Nam June Paik and Bill Viola; *Japanese Experimental Film 1960-80* (20 films); *Kenneth Anger's Magick Lantern Cycle* (9 films); *By Brakhage: Three Decades of Personal Cinema* (26 films) by Stan Brakhage; *The Ruckus Films of Red Grooms* (10 films); *Canadian Experimental Film in the Seventies* (7 films) short formalist experimental films; *The Other Side: European Avant-Garde Cinema 1960-80*; *Superfilmshow! Film as Art for Kids* (30 films), a selection of experimental films curated for a young audience; *Synthetic Movements* (22 films), a showcase of films by independent American animators (1974-80); and *Unreal Time: Animation and Film Graphics* (33 films), short animated films covering a broad spectrum of technique and style.

The extensive collection of art documentaries (available in film and videotape) cover artists and art-related subjects, including: Francis Bacon, Constantin Brancusi, "Buffalo Soldier" ballet, Noel Burch, Rudy Burckhardt, Edward Burra, Paul Cadmus, Harry Callahan, Michael Cardew, Judy Chicago, Joseph Cornell, Imogen Cunningham, Merce Cunningham, George Curtis, Dada and Surrealist masters, Piero della Francesca, Sari Dienes, Mark di Suvero, Marcel Duchamp, Alfred Eisenstaedt, Minnie Evans, Antonio Frasconi, Yoshiko Fujimoto, Alberto Giacometti, John Glick, Martha Graham, Michael Hall, Richard Hamilton, John Heartfield, Barbara Hepworth, Nancy Holt, Edward Hopper, Manji Inoue, Yvonne Jacquete, Linton Kwesi Johnson, Alex Katz, R. B. Kitaj, Gerhardt Knodel, Lee Krasner, Malcolm Le Grice, Roy Lichtenstein, Harry Lieberman, Maurice Lipscomb, Claude Lorrain, René Magritte, Kasimir Malevich, Andrea Mantegna, Brice Marden, Maria Martinez, Henri Matisse, Duane Michals, Claude Monet, Henry Moore, Barbara Morgan, Carole Morisseau and the Detroit City Dance Company, David Nash, Paul Nash, Alice Neel, Jim Pallas, The Phantom Captain, Tom Phillips, Pablo Picasso, Rolanda Polonsky, Popovich Brothers, Nicolas Poussin, Tressa Prisbrey, Odilon Redon, Rembrandt van Rijn, Malvina Reynolds, Bridget Riley, Anthony Rooley, Kay Sage, Charles Simonds, Aaron Siskind, Sam Smith, Robert Smithson, Michael Snow, Anna Sokolow, Alfred Stieglitz, Jim Stirling, Louis Sullivan, Joseph Mallord William Turner, Boaz Vaadia, Vorticist movement, Alfred Wallis, Neil Welliver, Mike Westbrook, Adolf Wolfi, Frank Lloyd Wright and the Prairie School, and Kes Zapkus.

Size & Elements: Film: 35mm and 16mm (over 400 titles). Videotape: 3/4" (approx. 275 titles).

Cataloging: Published catalogs.

Access: Maintained for distribution and rental rather than for research or reuse. Research requests accepted by mail. Screening fees charged.

Rights: Some rights held to all material. Additional clearances are necessary in almost all cases if material is to be reused.

Licensing: Apply for information.

Restrictions: Exhibitors must be or become members of the AFA and maintain their membership throughout the period of the exhibition.

Viewing Facilities: Film (16mm); videotape (3/4").

Duplication Facilities: None.

Publications: *A History of the American Avant-Garde Cinema; Japanese Experimental Film 1960-1980; The Other Side: European Avant-Garde Cinema 1960-1980; BBS Budapest: Twenty Years of Hungarian Experimental*

Film; New Video: Japan; Before Hollywood: Turn-of-the-Century Film from American Archives (1987).

NEW YORK METRO

AMERICAN FOUNDATION FOR THE BLIND
15 West 16th Street
New York, NY 10011
(212) 620-2024

Available for rental and purchase from:
PHOENIX FILMS & VIDEO
468 Park Avenue South
New York, NY 10016
(212) 684-5910
(800) 221-1274

Contact: Terry Allen (Audio Visual Coordinator, AFB)
Services: Foundation. Films and videotapes available to the public for rental and purchase.
Description: Films demonstrating the capabilities of the blind and visually impaired persons, and their ability to live their lives to the fullest.

Titles include: *Aging and Vision: Declarations of Independence*, on five senior citizens who have overcome recent vision loss; *As a Blind Person*, illustrating how a blind person can work at a difficult job; *Blindness: A Family Matter*, a documentary on the family's role during rehabilitation of a newly blinded person; *Communicating With Deaf-Blind People*, showing various methods of communication with the blind, such as printing in the palm, an alphabet glove and a one-hand manual; *Employed Ability: Blind Persons on the Job; Helen Keller in Her Story*, a documentary using still photographs and early movies of Helen Keller, her teacher Anne Sullivan and companion Polly Thompson; *No Two Alike*, showing how teachers use available support services and special aids to provide the best education possible for all students; *Not Without Sight*, depicting the major types of visual impairment, how they affect vision, and how affected people use their remaining vision; *Out of Left Field*, demonstrating how blind and visually impaired youths can be integrated with their sighted peers; *The Seven Minute Lesson*, a short lesson on how to be a sighted guide for a blind or visually impaired person; *What Do You See When You See a Blind Person?*, about the misconceptions concerning blind and visually impaired people; *To Climb A Mountain*, showing the Braille Institute's first mountain climbing expedition for students; and *To Share a Vision*, showing the main character's gradual acceptance of his loss of vision.
Size & Elements: Film: 16mm. Videotape: format unspecified. (14 titles total).
Cataloging: Published catalog.
Access: Films available to the public for rental and purchase; videotapes available for purchase only. Requests accepted by mail and telephone through Phoenix Films & Video.
Rights: Full rights held to all material. Additional clearances may be necessary in some cases if material is to be reused.
Licensing: Contact AFB regarding reuse. Available for licensing and reuse, subject to restrictions. License fees charged depending on intended use.
Restrictions: Requests for licensing and reuse considered on a case-by-case basis. Permission must be granted for reuse of any kind.
Viewing Facilities: None.
Duplication Facilities: None.

NEW YORK METRO

AMERICAN FUND FOR ALTERNATIVES TO ANIMAL RESEARCH
175 West 12th Street, Suite 16-G
New York, NY 10011
(212) 989-8073

Dr. Ethel Thurston (Trustee)

Contact: Dr. Ethel Thurston
Services: Association. Film and videotape library maintained primarily for distribution and rental.
Description: Association seeks "to speed up development, validation and use of non-animal substitutes for animals now used in research, testing and education."

Titles include *The Curiosity that Kills the Cat*, showing scenes of animal experimentation, breeding farms and the capture of primates in the wild; *Quantum Pharmacology*, a technical film explaining a mathematical model substitute for animals, designed for scientists and graduate students; and *We*

are all Noah, exploring the ethical teachings of Judaism and Christianity as they apply to human-animal interaction. Other films discuss alternatives to using animals in research. Most films are designed for non-scientific audiences.
Size & Elements: Film: 16mm. Videotape: VHS. (7 titles total).
Cataloging: Film list (available on request).
Access: Available to the public for distribution and rental.
Rights: Some rights held to some material.
Licensing: Apply for information.
Restrictions: None specified.
Viewing Facilities: None.
Duplication Facilities: None.

NEW YORK METRO

AMERICAN JOURNAL OF NURSING CO.
EDUCATIONAL SERVICES DIVISION
555 West 57th Street
New York, NY 10019
(212) 582-8820
Fax: (212) 586-5462

Thelma Schorr (President and Publisher)

Contacts: Judith Nierenberg; Judy Meyer
Services: Distributor. Videotapes available for rental and purchase.
Description: Nursing care videotapes. Topics include general medical and surgical; operating room and recovery room; orthopedics; infection control; neurological and rehabilitation; physical assessment; geriatric nursing; patient and health education; interpersonal relations; psychiatric nursing; management; leadership; legal issues; community health; maternity nursing; pediatrics; death and dying; and basic skills.

Sample titles include: *Administration of IV Medications; The Breast Exam; Cardiac Examination; Common Patient Problems — Alterations in Comfort; Disinfection: The War Against Infection; Draining Wound Management; Examination of the Peripheral Pulses; The Hospital Experience; Medicating Children; My CAT Scan; Pain Management Series;* and *Scrubbing, Gowning and Gloving.*
Size & Elements: Videotape: 3/4" and 1/2" (200 titles total).
Cataloging: Published catalogs.
Access: Available for rental and purchase. Orders and research requests accepted by mail.
Rights: Full rights held to some material. Some rights held to all material. Additional clearances may be necessary in some cases if material is to be reused.
Licensing: Apply for information.
Restrictions: Restrictions may apply in some cases.
Viewing Facilities: Videotape (by appointment only).
Duplication Facilities: None.

NEW YORK METRO

AMERICAN KENNEL CLUB LIBRARY
51 Madison Avenue
New York, NY 10010
(212) 696-8245

Roberta Vesley (Library Director)

Contact: Paula Spector (Circulation Director, AV Program) (212/696-8389)
Services: Association library. Film and videotape library available for rental and purchase.
Description: Material relating to dogs (1953-present) produced by AKC and others, including breed profiles, grooming, training and dog shows.

AKC-produced programs include the *AKC Breed Standard Series,* which will eventually cover all 130 breeds. Other films and videotapes include *In the Ring with Mr. Wrong,* a humorous film on dog show judging techniques; *Gait: Observing Dogs in Motion; AKC and the Sport of Dogs; The Quest for a Quality Dog Show; With Courage and Style: The Field Trial Retriever;* and *Inside AKC.*

Other videotapes include: *The Golden Retriever; Gun Dog Training Spaniels; A Veterinarian's Guide to the Care of Your Dog; B. J. Andrews Presents the Akita; Living with Animals; The Miniature Schnauzer; Poodles: Standards, Personality and Grooming; Puppy's First Year;* and *The Komondor.*
Size & Elements: Film: 16mm (11 titles). Videotape (37 titles, each 18 to 30 min.)

Cataloging: Card catalogs; film and videotape list (available on request).
Access: Available to the public. Many titles available for purchase. Research fees charged. Requests accepted by mail, telephone and in person (walk-in and by appointment).
Rights: Apply for information.
Licensing: Apply for information.
Restrictions: None specified.
Viewing Facilities: Videotape.
Duplication Facilities: None.

NEW YORK METRO

AMERICAN MUSEUM OF NATURAL HISTORY
FILM ARCHIVES
Central Park West and 79th Street
New York, NY 10024
(212) 769-5419
Fax: (212) 769-5233

Contact: Andrea LaSala
Services: Museum-based film archive. Material available for research, licensing and reuse, subject to restrictions.
Description: Begins 1908-13. Genres and subjects include: anthropology; archaeology; ethnography; expeditions; geology; museology; oceanography; paleontology; travel; zoology; expedition and travel films made by Museum staff members; scientists and explorers documenting unusual natural occurrences and phenomena; extinct and endangered species; societies that have irrevocably changed; historical record of natural history museums; scientific exploration and research; use of motion pictures in process of scientific documentation.

Rare and important films include: footage taken during Morden-Clark Asiatic expedition (1926) showing difficulties encountered in crossing the Himalayas; film from the Burden East India expedition (1926) recording Komodo dragons, including a scene of dragons feeding; five films made during Central Asiatic Expeditions (1921-30) on the fauna of Mongolia; dinosaur egg discovery in the Gobi Desert; expedition transportation; details of Mongol life and scenes of Beijing.
Size & Elements: Film: 35mm and 16mm (1 million feet, 400 titles; all elements). Videotape: 3/4" (masters and viewing copies).
Cataloging: Published catalog (see Publications).
Access: Open to the public. For in-house use only. Fees charged for in-depth research. Standard reference requests accepted by mail, telephone and in person (walk-in).
Rights: Full rights held to some material. Some material in the public domain. Additional clearances may be necessary in some cases if material is to be reused.
Licensing: Available for licensing and reuse, subject to restrictions. License fees charged (according to standard fee schedule; fees vary according to intended use).
Restrictions: A maximum of three minutes of film footage can be purchased for production purposes, provided approval is granted by the Department of Library Services; additional use may be negotiated.
Viewing Facilities: Videotape (3/4").
Duplication Facilities: Videotape.
Related Materials: 500,000 still photographs, covering many of the same topics, dating back to the 1800s.
Publications: *Catalog of the American Museum of Natural History Film Archives* (New York & London: Garland Publishing, Inc., 1987). Illustrated catalog describes holdings in detail; includes a list of titles by genre, a chronological list of titles and index.

NEW YORK METRO

AMERICAN ORT FEDERATION
PUBLIC RELATIONS DEPARTMENT
817 Broadway
New York, NY 10003
(212) 677-4400
Fax: (212) 979-9545

Donald H. Klein (Executive Vice President)

Contact: Avi Feinglass (Director of Public Relations)
Services: Association. Videotape collection available for distribution and broadcast.

Description: Material relating to the international operations and membership of the Organization for Rehabilitation through Training (ORT).

Topics include: international schools and programs; School of Engineering in Jerusalem; a solicitation training videotape for membership; ORT Israel network; Los Angeles Technical Institute; students and graduates of the Josephtal Technical High School in Herzlia, Israel; portraits of distinguished members.
Size & Elements: Videotape: 3/4", VHS and Betamax (amount unspecified).
Cataloging: Published catalogs.
Access: Research fees not charged.
Rights: Full rights held to all material.
Licensing: Apply for information. License fees charged in some cases.
Restrictions: None specified.
Viewing Facilities: Videotape.
Duplication Facilities: None.

NEW YORK METRO

AN AMERICAN PORTRAIT
305 West 21st Street
New York, NY 10011
(212) 924-1960

Contact: Lance Bird
Services: Film and videotape producer; stock footage sales library.
Description: American history, life and culture (1930s-50s and the fallout shelter era of the early 1960s). Special strengths include: events of the 1930s; Chicago World's Fair (Century of Progress Exposition, 1933); New York World's Fair (1939-40); World War II in Europe and the Pacific; Pearl Harbor and U.S. Government-produced films of the fallout shelter era.
Size & Elements: Film: 35mm (250,000 feet); 16mm (300,000 feet) (20 intact films, 500 cans total). Videotape: 1" (masters); 3/4" (masters and viewing copies) and VHS.
Cataloging: Computerized cataloging for staff use only.
Access: Available to the public for duplication. Research fees generally charged. Research requests accepted by telephone.
Rights: Full rights held to some material. Additional clearances may be necessary in some cases if material is to be reused.
Licensing: Available for licensing and reuse, subject to restrictions. License fees charged in some cases.
Restrictions: Collection is maintained primarily for in-house productions; inquiries are handled on an individual basis and many are turned down. A minimum, non-refundable fee is charged at rates generally above the industry norm. Although outside requests are often refused, will undertake research projects and supply stock footage.
Viewing Facilities: Film (35mm viewers; 16mm Steenbeck); videotape (3/4" and 1/2").
Duplication Facilities: Videotape (3/4", VHS and Betamax).

NEW YORK METRO

AMERICAN SOCIAL HISTORY PROJECT FILM LIBRARY
445 West Main Street
Wyckoff, NJ 07481
(201) 891-8240 (for orders and shipping)
(212) 944-8695 (for information, access and rights requests)

Steve Brier (Project Director)

Contact: Steve Brier (212/944-8695)
Services: Educational curriculum developer; videotape distributor. Material available for purchase, licensing and reuse on a case-by-case basis.
Description: *Who Built America?* (15 parts, each 30 min.) presents United States social history from Colonial times to the present. Based on the latest historical scholarship, each program dramatizes the work and family experience of "ordinary" Americans in the past: artisans, slaves, farmers, immigrants, women working at home, laborers, factory and white-collar workers. The behavior and beliefs of working Americans shed new light on key events and developments in the nation's first century, including the Revolution, early industrialization, the expansion of slavery, immigration and urbanization, the Civil War and Reconstruction, and industrial conflict. Programs employ many historical graphics and photographs.

Videotape programs include: *The Big H,* in the style of a *film noir* detective story, on the importance of studying U.S. history and the dangers of its misinterpretation; *Tea Party Etiquette,* on the life of a poor shoemaker active in

the struggle for American independence; *Daughters of Free Man,* on a young woman working in the textile mills of Lowell, Mass. who becomes a striker; *Doing As They Can,* on life, work and day-to-day resistance to slavery on a cotton plantation in the 1840s-50s; *Five Points,* a view of New York City and its immigrant poor in the 1850s; *Dr. Toer's Amazing Magic Lantern Show,* on the meanings of freedom for slaves freed after the Civil War; and *1877: The Grand Army of Starvation* (also available in 16mm film) on the massive nationwide industrial conflict sparked by a railroad strike and four years of economic depression. Eight other programs relating to more recent periods of U.S. history are also available.
Size & Elements: Film: 16mm (1 title). Videotape: 3/4" and VHS (15 programs; masters and viewing copies; 1 program transferred from film).
Cataloging: Published catalog of videotapes available for purchase.
Access: Available to the public for purchase. 16mm film available for rental. Research requests accepted by mail and telephone.
Rights: Full rights held to all material.
Licensing: Available for licensing and reuse, subject to restrictions.
Restrictions: Requests for licensing and reuse considered on a case-by-case basis. Some material within programs cleared for educational or public television broadcast only.
Viewing Facilities: None.
Duplication Facilities: None (outside arrangements can be made).
Related Materials: Study guides accompany videotapes.

NEW YORK METRO

AMERICAN STOCK EXCHANGE
86 Trinity Place
New York, NY 10006
(212) 306-1631
Fax: (212) 306-1488

Arthur Levitt, Jr. (Chairman)

Contact: Keith Silverman (Manager, Broadcast Services)
Services: Corporation; corporate archives. Material not available for duplication or reuse.
Description: Covers the history and overall workings of the American Stock Exchange; and describes technology used in today's market.
Size & Elements: Videotape: 3/4" and 1/2" (2 titles).
Cataloging: None specified.
Access: Open to the public. Research fees not charged. Research requests accepted by telephone.
Rights: Full rights held to all material.
Licensing: Apply for information. License fees not charged.
Restrictions: Duplication or reuse of material not permitted.
Viewing Facilities: None.
Duplication Facilities: Videotape (VHS).

NEW YORK METRO

AMERICAN ZIONIST YOUTH FOUNDATION
515 Park Avenue
New York, NY 10022-1144
(212) 751-6070

Ruth Kastner (Executive Director)
Leon Levy (Chairman)

Contact: Eric Zimmerman (Educational Resource Coordinator)
Services: Foundation. Film collection maintained primarily for distribution and rental; some material available for reuse.
Description: Israel, Jewish identity and Zionism; films in English and Hebrew.

Vistas and people. Tal Brodi, Israel's most famous basketball player; Maccabia games in Israel; kibbutz life; 26th anniversary of the State of Israel; Golan Heights; Jerusalem's past and present; the National Geographic Series *Families of the World: Israel,* a tour of Jerusalem with Mayor Teddy Kollek.

History. Sand Curtain, shot before the Six Day War, shows Jerusalem and its dividing wall; *Return to Gush Etzion* shows the return to Etzion Block, following the Six Day War; establishment of Israel; archaeological sites; J.N.F. during the founding and early years of State of Israel; Herzl and establishment of the State; Chaim Weitzmann; and a historical account of the Galil area; *Heritage: Civilization and the Jews; Pillar of Fire,* 19-hour television history of rebirth of Israel (1896-1948); David Ben-Gurion; Weizmann Institute; a tour of Israel with archaeologist, Walter Zanger.

Aliya and Jewish identity. Making Aliya; the connection between Zionism and Jewish identity; Jewish life in Israel; tent cities housing new immigrants (early 1950s); Israel during Purim; *Rachel,* about a father preparing to sit shiva as his daughter marries a non-Jew; Dimona; Aliya movement from Yemen; a Soviet Jewish scientist denied permission to emigrate to Israel; anti-Semitism in America; Soviet family making Aliya; Americans making Aliya; settlement of the Shaphir region; history of Israel in British Mandate period; history of the Jewish people; North Americans in Israel; five trends in Judaism.

Wars. A Letter From the Front, from a soldier to his wife; Yom Kippur War; volunteerism; story of a war widow; Israeli reaction to volunteers.

Israel programs. Olim and volunteers working in Kiryat Shmona and a Druze village on Golan Heights; long term programs in Israel.

Shoah and illegal immigration. The Holocaust; ship of illegal immigrants; Bergen-Belsen survivors return to Germany in 1965; *Voyage of the Unafraid,* describing Illegal Immigration Movement centered around the ship, *The Unafraid; The 81st Blow,* about the Holocaust; *Shoah,* Claude Landsman's 9-1/2 hour documentary; *Anne Frank's Diary; Genocide.*

Political topics. Titles include: *Beyond the Mirage,* discussing whether Arabs and Jews can live in peace; *P.L.O.;* peace conflict; the "Left" point of view regarding the peace conflict; *Kuneitra,* a non-Israeli film about the non-Israeli viewpoint; the history of the Jordanian border with maps and aerial photographs of region; a chronology of terrorist acts in the last years, focusing on Lebanon as hub of world terror; *Beyond the Walls,* on Jewish and Arab prisoners; *El Kaladieh Street,* about the climate between Arab and Jew in Jerusalem after the murder of a Yeshiva student.

Jews in other countries. The slow process of annihilation of Syrian Jewry; Jews in Arab countries; American Jews; and the acceptance of Israel into the U.N. and its role in assisting Third World nations.

Art and folklore. Chaim Topol reads from Yehuda Amichai; pantomime; Yeminite wedding; life and art of Herman Shtruck; stamp collecting; artists; fashion.

Religion and holidays. Shabbat in Israel; *The Life of Rav Uziel,* telling the life of the Chief Rabbi; life of Rav Kook; *39 Types of Work Forbidden on the Shabbat; Jerusalem Within these Walls,* describing the importance of Jerusalem for three monotheistic religions; and Chanukah.

Newsreels and reports. Includes *Geva News — The Six Day Way; Vistas of Israel,* covering the Druz in Israel, the Olive Tree, the Yarkon Negev Water Works, the opening of Maccabia, the Christian church in Nazareth; and Maskit.

Size & Elements: Film: 16mm (90 titles). Videotape: VHS (50 titles).
Cataloging: Published catalogs.
Access: Open to researchers and scholars only. Not open to the public. Maintained (although not exclusively) for distribution and rental rather than for research or reuse. Research requests accepted by mail.
Rights: Full rights held to some material.
Licensing: Apply for information.
Restrictions: Available to researchers and scholars only.
Viewing Facilities: None.
Duplication Facilities: None.

NEW YORK METRO

AMERICAS IN TRANSITION/FOSSIL FILMS, INC.
401 West Broadway
New York, NY 10012
(212) 226-2465

Obie Benz (Producer)

Contact: Obie Benz
Services: Film and television producer. Material available for licensing and reuse, subject to restrictions.
Description: *Americas in Transition* (1982) is a documentary film tracing United States involvement in Latin American affairs during this century. The film concentrates on the roots of dictatorship, attempts at democracy, communist influences and the role of the United States. It states that social problems, such as poverty, illiteracy and government repression are the primary causes of social unrest in the Americas, and that the revolutions in Latin America are not substantially different from our own past.

Outtakes from *Americas in Transition* are also held.
Size & Elements: Film: 16mm (1 film; original and outtakes). Videotape: 3/4" and VHS.
Cataloging: Editing logs.
Access: Available for duplication and reuse. Research fees charged. Research requests accepted by telephone.
Rights: Full rights held to some material.

Licensing: Available for licensing and reuse, subject to restrictions. License fees charged.
Restrictions: Some material may not be available for commercial use.
Viewing Facilities: Videotape (3/4" and VHS).
Duplication Facilities: None.

NEW YORK METRO

AMNESTY INTERNATIONAL USA
322 Eighth Avenue
New York, NY 10001
(212) 807-8400
Fax: (212) 463-9193
Telex: 666628

John G. Healey (Executive Director)

Contacts: Lisa Berg (Publications Manager); Helen Garrett (Communications Officer)
Services: International human rights organization. Videotapes available for distribution and purchase rather than for research or reuse.
Description: Titles currently available: *Colors of Hope* (1985), the story of a released Argentine prisoner and his family; *Amnesty International Report on Iran,* a documentary on human rights abuses occurring in Iran today, with commentary on the domestic and international legal standards contravened by these abuses; *Torture in the Eighties* (1985), an overview of torture by governments; *Free At Last* (1986), on the worldwide struggle to protect human rights; *US: Campaign Against the Death Penalty,* a look at the historical background and current use of the death penalty in the U.S.; and *Sri Lanka: A Nation In Anguish,* a presentation on "disappearances" and other human rights violations committed by the Sri Lankan government, and discussion of ways to stop the abuse.

Additional material in collection includes news footage, speeches and other films on country-specific human rights. Material is roughly cataloged and accessibility is very limited. This portion of the collection is currently being organized; viewing requests will not be accepted.

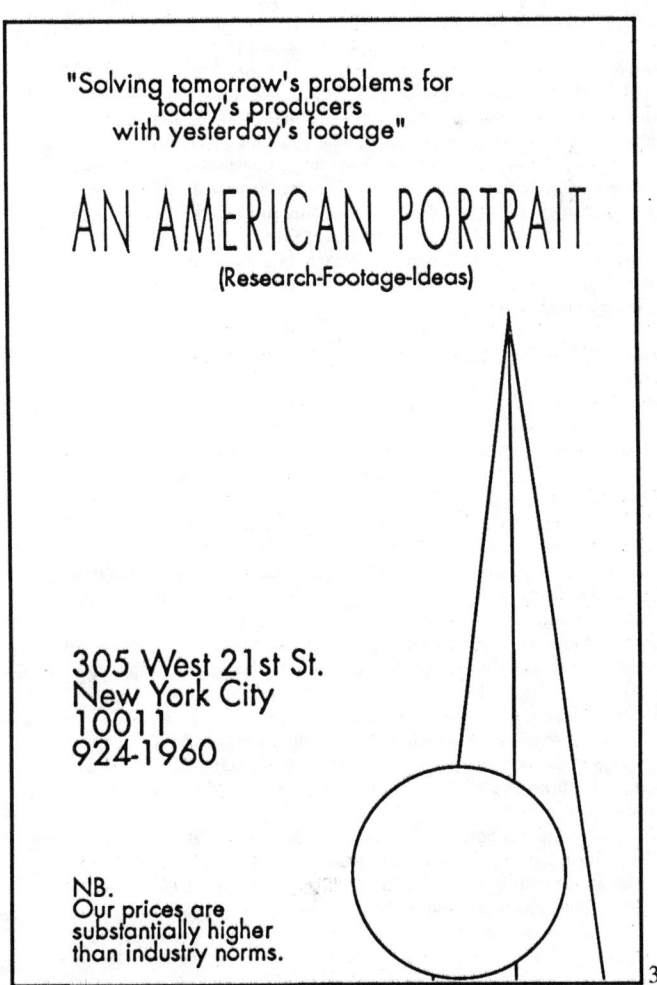

Size & Elements: Videotape: VHS (6 titles).
Cataloging: Published catalog of available videotapes; other material roughly cataloged.
Access: Open to the public. Available for distribution and purchase rather than for reuse. Other materials restricted to in-house viewing only.
Rights: Full rights held to all material. Additional clearances may be necessary in some cases if material is to be reused.
Licensing: Available for licensing and reuse, subject to restrictions. License fees generally not charged.
Restrictions: Uncataloged material not available for viewing or distribution.
Viewing Facilities: None.
Duplication Facilities: None.

NEW YORK METRO

ANTHOLOGY FILM ARCHIVES
32-34 Second Avenue
New York, NY 10003
(212) 505-5181

Jonas Mekas (Director)

Contact: Rick Stanbery (Archivist)
Services: Film and videotape archives. Collection open to researchers and scholars for research and viewing. Maintains regular schedule of public screenings.
Description: Major center for the preservation, study and exhibition of the essential works of alternative, avant-garde and independent film and video. In addition to its film preservation program and the daily repertory and informational film and video screenings, Anthology offers seminars and lectures on the theory and history of film and video; publishes scholarly and research works; and maintains an extensive reference library. Anthology has been engaged in the preservation of independent, non-industrial varieties of film and video since 1971, and has preserved over 300 different titles.

Film holdings at Anthology Film Archives include:

Essential Cinema Repertory Collection (500 cans; approx. 330 titles). Prints constituting Anthology's classic cinema repertory, projected on a repeated basis; struck from original materials, in original formats. Foreign language films carry no subtitles. Collection was assembled 1970-75 by the Film Selection Committee (James Broughton, Ken Kelman, Peter Kubelka, Jonas Mekas and P. Adams Sitney) and is devoted exclusively to film as an art with no consideration paid to a film's genre, length, format, production costs or public success. Additional titles will be added to the collection in the future. However, since the new additions will be selected by a different Committee and will represent different aesthetic views from those of the 1970-75 Committee, they will be presented as a separate, supplementary collection.

Study Collection (1,300 cans; approx. 1,000 titles). Films, mostly independently produced, which either relate to or complement the Essential Cinema Repertory Collection. Screened for researchers and students, and occasionally during special informational shows.

Preservation Collection. Includes: negatives, masters and prints (400 cans) produced by Anthology's Independent Film Preservation Program, all kept in cold storage and never touched unless needed to generate new printing materials; negatives and masters (250 cans) produced by Anthology, used to generate new prints; and original negatives, masters and prints (2,000 cans) which cannot be projected, as they are valuable towards the preservation of some of the films (e.g., unique prints of different versions and prints of films where the existence of other prints is not yet determined).

Storage Service for Filmmakers Collection (approx. 1,000 cans). Deposited by independent filmmakers for temporary or long-term storage.

Educational Film Collection (750 titles). Educational, art and children's films entrusted to Anthology by Films Inc., to be screened for the community, schools and children.

Out-Of-Business Film Laboratories Collection (2,000 cans). Primarily original negatives entrusted to Anthology by film laboratories going bankrupt. Material belongs mostly to independent film producers.

Special collections. Includes: *Joseph Cornell Collection* (approx. 400 cans); *Maya Deren Collection* (approx. 200 cans); *Jerome Hill Collection* (approx. 1,000 cans); *Contemporary Films Collection* (approx. 200 cans); and collections featuring the work of Hans Richter, George Maciunas (Fluxus), and Carl Linder.

Video Collection (approx. 1,250 videotapes). 1,000 videotapes are working videotapes from the now-defunct Experimental TV Lab/WNET-13; the remainder are uncataloged, though known to contain a significant number of very early artists' videotapes, some unique.

Size & Elements: Film and videotape: various elements (several thousand titles).
Cataloging: Card catalogs (for in-house use only).
Access: Open to researchers and scholars only. For in-house use only. Research fees charged for commercial purposes only. Research requests accepted by mail, telephone and in person (walk-in). Maintains regular schedule of public screenings.
Rights: Some rights held to some material.
Licensing: Apply for information.
Restrictions: Apply for information.
Viewing Facilities: Film and videotape.
Duplication Facilities: None.
Related Materials: The world's largest collection of materials documenting the history of American and international independent and avant-garde film and video. Holdings include books, periodicals, photographs, posters, videotapes of lectures and interviews, distribution and festival catalogs, and files on individual film and videomakers and organizations active in independent film and video.
Publications: *Film Culture* magazine; books on independent film and video.

NEW YORK METRO

ANTI-DEFAMATION LEAGUE OF B'NAI B'RITH
National Office
823 United Nations Plaza
New York, NY 10017
(212) 490-2525
Fax: (212) 867-0779
Cable: ANTIDEFAME
Telex: 649278

Contact: Audrey Merwin
Services: Educational organization. Film and videotape materials available for rental.
Description: Material relating to human relations. Topics covered include: anti-Semitism; the Holocaust; Israel and the Middle East; Jewish-Christian relations; Jews and Judaism; multicultural education; prejudice and discrimination and intergroup relations; philosophy in the classroom; political and social issues; and Soviet Jewry.

Prejudice and discrimination and intergroup relations. Includes 30- and 60-second public service announcements available free to television stations or for use in the classroom. These include several celebrity statements against prejudice, featuring Larry Hagman, Angela Lansbury and Carroll O'Connor. Films available include: *Behind the Mask; One People; What Color Are You?; You've Got to Be Taught to Hate;* and *Rumor.*

Multicultural education. Topics include: early American immigration, Asian Americans, American Blacks, Native Americans, Hispanic Americans, Italian Americans and American women. Sample titles include: *Birds of Passage,* which portrays three West Coast Japanese Americans — a gardener, a tuna fisherman and the widow of a farmer — all of whom came to the United States in the decade before World War I. The film follows their lives through the World War II internment of Japanese Americans. Also held: *Cubans in America; Slavery and Slave Resistance;* and *The Black Cowboy.*

Philosophy in the classroom. Titles include: *Klan Youth Corps; The Ku Klux Klan: An American Paradox; Ku Klux Klan: The Invisible Empire;* and *Vandals!.*

Jews and Judaism. Titles include: *Maimonides: Torah and the Philosophic Quest; Jewish Presence in Civilization; Bikel on Bikel;* and *Prayer and the Jewish People.*

Israel and the Middle East. Titles include: *Between North and South: Israel and Africa; The Healing of Jerusalem; Israel and the Palestinians: The Continuing Conflict; Masada; A Promise Shared: Women in Israeli Society; Zubin and the IPO* (Israel Philharmonic Orchestra); and *Uprooting Terror.*

Jewish-Christian relations. The Indiana University *Discussion Series* of 30-minute programs includes: *Jesus in Jewish and Christian Literature; The Messianic Idea in Jewish History;* and *Christian Theology in Israel.* Also available is *Oberammergau: The Passion Story and the Jews.*

The Holocaust. Materials include: *Genocide; To Bear Witness; The Camera of My Family: Four Generations in Germany, 1845-1945; The Rise and Fall of the Third Reich; Night and Fog; Scenes from the Holocaust; Father's Return to Auschwitz; Survivors of the Holocaust; Joseph Schultz; The Courage to Care; The Demjanjuk Trial: A Moment in History;* and *The World of Anne Frank.*

In addition to the circulating materials, the ADL library maintains a small collection of videotapes focusing on Jewish and minority issues, largely videotaped from television. Holdings also include a 30-minute videotape produced at North High School in Minneapolis (March 1987) featuring a presentation by two Israeli high-school students on a U.S. tour.

Size & Elements: Film: 16mm. Videotape: 3/4", VHS and Betamax. (Approx. 125 titles total).

Cataloging: Published catalogs.

Access: Films available to the public for purchase and rental; videotapes available for purchase only. Some material available for television broadcast. Materials also available from regional offices in the United States, Canada and abroad.

Rights: Additional clearances are necessary if material is to be reused.

Licensing: Apply for information.

Restrictions: Materials may not be duplicated without prior permission.

Viewing Facilities: None.

Duplication Facilities: None.

Related Materials: Study guides available for some titles.

NEW YORK METRO

ARC VIDEODANCE COLLECTION AND THE EYE ON DANCE COLLECTION

88 Lexington Avenue, Suite 3K
New York, NY 10016
(212) 725-5530

Celia Ipiotis (Director)

Contacts: Celia Ipiotis; Jeff Bush

Services: Videotape production company; media organization. Distributes library of programs; offers videotaping services to dance companies and performing artists. Some material available for rental and loan through public libraries; possibly available for reuse, subject to restrictions.

Description: Dance performance, choreography, music, history and sociology of dance, Third World dance and Black studies. The *Eye On Dance* collection (1981-present, each 30 min.), a series of discussions with prominent dancers and choreographers, is an issue-oriented interview series incorporating videotape dance excerpts.

Topics include: artistic freedom in South Africa, dance photography, athleticism in dance, athletes and dancers and religion and ritual in dance. Other materials held include educational and dance performance videotapes.

Size & Elements: Videotape: 3/4" (250 weekly *Eye on Dance* programs held at present); 3/4" and VHS (14 assorted dance videotapes).

Cataloging: Published catalog. *Eye On Dance* is organized chronologically; other videotapes cataloged by title.

Access: Research requests not accepted. Some videotapes may be available for distribution and rental. Some videotapes available for loan through some public libraries; request catalog for these listings.

Rights: Full rights held to all material.

Licensing: Available for licensing, subject to restrictions. License fees charged.

Restrictions: Some restrictions may apply.

Viewing Facilities: None.

Duplication Facilities: Videotape (VHS).

NEW YORK METRO

ARCHIVE FILM PRODUCTIONS, INC. STOCK FOOTAGE LIBRARY

530 West 25th Street
New York, NY 10001
(212) 620-3955
Fax: (212) 645-2137
Telex: 822023 AFP

Patrick Montgomery (President)

Contacts: Joseph Lauro (Library Director); Eileen Straussman (Foreign Sales)

Services: Film and videotape stock footage sales library; film producer; research and clearance service.

Description: All types of historical footage (1896-1960s) including footage from newsreels, silent films, sports films, cartoons, historical films, Hollywood features, documentaries, industrial films, educational films and television programs. Approximately 90% of the collection is black and white; 10% color. Collection does not include modern color stock shots or beauty shots.

Includes music footage of all types, especially rock and roll, jazz, folk, big

band, swing, blues and country. Material is largely drawn from television, feature films, live appearances and newsreels. Represents several large European collections of music footage. In addition to music-oriented material, library also includes associated dances, fads, fashions and frenzies. Library has compiled complete filmographies of many popular performers, allowing access in some cases to numerous versions of the same song.

Newsreel footage features Presidents, stunts, sports, fads, wars and disasters (1900-65).

Holds over 300 Hollywood and European features, including dramas, comedies, horror, science fiction, westerns and historical epics (1920s-50s) in both black and white and color, covering nearly every major Hollywood star from Chaplin to Bogart to John Wayne. Slapstick comedy trademarks — pie fights, car chases, collapsing buildings — from silent comedies are all represented.

Library holds numerous industrial and educational films which depict day-to-day happenings in the 20th century, notably technological advances, social customs and juvenile behavior. Footage from the 1940s and 1950s, much of it in color, illustrates design and fashion trends, some of which are re-emerging in contemporary styles. The first airlines, televisions, computers, household appliances, superhighways and more are all portrayed.

In addition to its own holdings, Archive represents the following collections for stock footage sales:

The March of Time. Newsreel series produced by the editors of *Time* magazine (1935-51). Includes news and documentary footage from over 300 episodes (each 20 min.) covering international politics, social problems, industry, science, the arts and important personalities of the 1930s and 1940s. For a complete list of *March of Time* episodes, see the entry for National Archives and Records Administration (RG 200).

Julien Bryan (International Film Foundation) collection. Extensive collection of uncensored 35mm black and white footage shot by cameraman Julien Bryan (1931-45) in Stalinist Russia, Imperial Japan, occupied Manchuria and Nazi Germany. Collection also includes coverage of prewar Poland, Italy, Turkey, China, Finland, Mexico and much of South America.

Flying A Productions Stock Footage Library. Archive has recently acquired exclusive rights to this library (approx. 100 hours of 35mm black and white outtakes from television series produced in the 1950s, notably the *Gene Autry Show, The Range Rider* series, *Death Valley Days* and *The Adventures of Champion*). Included in the footage are examples of typical Western scenes and situations, including horse chases and stunts, wagon chases, fist fights, cattle, western landscapes, etc. Rights were acquired from the Southwest Film/Video Archives, Southern Methodist University (q.v.), to which Gene Autry donated the library in 1987.

United States Football League (USFL) footage. Archive now holds exclusive stock shot rights to the Halcyon Days Productions collection of USFL footage of all games (1983-85, approx. 1,000 hours of 3/4" videotape footage). There is coverage of almost every imaginable football play from any angle, plus clips of all the trappings of a football game, such as crowds, empty stands, cheerleaders, coaches, locker room speeches, practices, different colored uniforms, play on Astroturf or grass. All material is cleared for general use, and much of the footage is available with audio. Many USFL players have since become stars, including Herschel Walker, Doug Flutie, Mike Rozier, Ricky Sanders, Kelvin Bryant, Reggie White, Jim Kelly and Irv Eatman.

TV House/Swedish Television. This library, shot-listed on computer for fast and easy access, contains an exciting range of seldom-seen performances of many American rock and roll stars and groups (1960s-70s). Performances include The Rolling Stones, Eric Burdon and the Animals, Creedence Clearwater Revival, The Everly Brothers, Fleetwood Mac, Herman's Hermits, The Hollies, Jethro Tull, The Who, Otis Redding, ABBA, Marianne Faithfull, Cliff Richard, Lonnie Donegan, Phil Collins, and Blood, Sweat and Tears. Also includes performances from jazz greats such as Sarah Vaughan, Miles Davis, Gerry Mulligan, Muddy Waters, Ella Fitzgerald, Count Basie and Duke Ellington. Archive represents this library exclusively in the United States.

Harold Baim Productions. Library of 35mm Technicolor footage (some in Cinemascope) shot around the world by British producer Harold Baim (1950s-60s). Includes footage of England, France, Italy, the Far East, Africa, animals, circuses, ships, and performers. The collection contains many high-quality color establishing shots from this period.

Size & Elements: Film: 35mm (20% of library; positive and negative) and 16mm (80% of library; positive and negative). Videotape: 1" (10% of film collection mastered); 3/4" (thousands of hours; masters and viewing copies). Most materials originate on film. Approximately 90% of the collection is black and white; 10% color. All footage has been transferred to videotape for easy access and viewing and may be screened on the premises.

Cataloging: Computerized cataloging available to researchers (extensive shot listings retrievable by keyword searches). Catalog listings are available on

CineScan, published by Newsreel Access Systems, Inc. (q.v.).
Access: Available to the public for duplication, licensing and reuse. Research requests accepted by mail, telephone and in person (by appointment only). Research fees charged; fees depend on the complexity of the job. All footage can be viewed on time-coded VHS screening videotapes. Customers may make VHS or 3/4" dubs of shots desired, for screening purposes only. If client is unable to screen material in person, a videotape with a variety of selections can be sent.
Rights: Full rights held to all material. Talent clearances may be necessary in some cases if material is to be reused for advertising purposes.
Licensing: License fees charged on a per-job basis, depending on distribution of finished production, based on footage used. Minimum license fee will be charged upon delivery of master materials, whether or not footage is actually used.
Restrictions: None specified.
Viewing Facilities: Videotape.
Duplication Facilities: None. All laboratory, videotape transfer, shipping and messenger charges are billed to client at cost.
Representatives: Toronto: Fabulous Footage, Inc. (q.v.) (416) 591-6955; London: Kobal Archive Films (01-240-9565); Stockholm: TV House (86630-320); Tokyo: American Video Library (3-561-2391); Rome: Moby Dick/Archive Films (6-359-5056); Melbourne: Archive Films Australia (3-836-1977); Amsterdam: Piet's Post Production (20-275711).
Related Services: Can locate and clear footage from features and television shows owned by other companies.
Production Credits: Since 1979 Archive has also produced a number of historical documentary films, including: *The Man You Love to Hate: Erich Von Stroheim* (1980); *The Compleat Beatles* (1982); *Rock and Roll: The Early Days* (1984); *British Rock: The First Wave* (1985); *The National Geographic Great Explorer Series* (1986). Archive also produces corporate histories, television commercials, industrial films and sales presentations using historical footage.

NEW YORK METRO

THE ARCHIVE OF CONTEMPORARY MUSIC (ARC)
110 Chambers Street
New York, NY 10007
(212) 964-2296
(212) 619-3503
Fax: (212) 529-5882
Telex: 650 335 6669

B. George (Director)

Contact: James Linderman (Archivist)
Services: Not-for-profit music library and research center. Videotape collection available for in-house research only.
Description: Commercially released popular music videos (1970s-80s); some outtakes (supplementing the archive's rock and roll music materials from the 1950s-60s and multicultural music holdings. Currently restricted to in-house research only, the videotape archive's ultimate goal is to facilitate duplication with the permission of copyright holders.
Size & Elements: Videotape: 3/4" (3,000 videotapes); VHS (500 videotapes).
Cataloging: Not cataloged.
Access: Open to the public for telephone inquiries and in-house use only. Nothing available for duplication at the present time.
Rights: No rights held to any material.
Licensing: Material not available for licensing or reuse at present.
Restrictions: Copyright restrictions apply to all material.
Viewing Facilities: None.
Duplication Facilities: None.
Related Materials: Large rock and roll phonograph record and audiotape collection; still photographs; other music resources.

NEW YORK METRO

THE ASIA SOCIETY
725 Park Avenue
New York, NY 10021
(212) 288-6400
Fax: (212) 517-7246
Telex: 22 49 53 ASIA UR

Timothy Plummer (Director, Education and Communications Department)

Contact: Sherrill Davis (Education and Communications Department)
Services: Educational institution; videotape producer and distributor. Collection available for rental and purchase.
Description: Educational videotape series designed to acquaint children and teenagers with the lifestyles and customs of Japan. *Video Letter from Japan, Part I* is a six-part series (12 programs, each 30 min.) providing a comprehensive view of Japanese life as seen through the eyes of Japanese school children. *Video Letter from Japan, Part II* is directed to high-school and early college levels and covers aspects of teenage lifestyles, university life, etc. Future series will include *Discover Korea Series* and *Indian Culture Series*.
Size & Elements: Videotape: VHS (most material); Betamax (1 title).
Cataloging: Materials list and brochures.
Access: Maintained for distribution rather than for research or reuse. *Video Letter from Japan* series is available for purchase, individually or as a set.
Rights: Apply for information.
Licensing: Apply for information.
Restrictions: Videotapes not available for duplication.
Viewing Facilities: None.
Duplication Facilities: None.

NEW YORK METRO

ASIAN CINE-VISION
32 East Broadway, Room 402
New York, NY 10002
(212) 925-8685

Peter Chow (Executive Director)

Contact: Marlina Gonzalez
Services: Media arts organization. Sponsors film and videotape research and production. Film and videotape archives open to researchers, scholars and the public. Material available for in-house research and viewing; not available for reuse.
Description: The Media Archive/Library houses one of the nation's most comprehensive collections of written and moving image material on the Asian American experience. Topics range from Asian American history to media stereotyping. A substantial portion of the library consists of film and video works by Asian American filmmakers (mostly shown at the ACV Film/Video Festival) spanning an 11-year period. Featured artists and documentarians include Wayne Wang, Steven Okazaki, Christine Choy, Lisa Shia, Nam June Paik, Arthur Dong, Bruce and Norman Yonemoto, Mako Idemitsu, Shigeko Kubota and Ping Chong.

Asian Cine-Video Production Services are open to the general public with fees charged on a sliding scale. The Media Information Service acts as a clearinghouse for information and referrals related to Asian American media arts. ACV also sponsors residencies, film festivals and discussions.
Size & Elements: Videotape: 3/4", VHS and Betamax (approx. 400 titles; viewing copies).
Cataloging: Computerized cataloging for staff use only.
Access: Available to researchers, scholars and the public. For in-house use only. Viewing fees charged. Research requests accepted in person (by appointment only).
Rights: No rights held to any material. Some material in the public domain.
Licensing: Material not available for reuse.
Restrictions: Material not available for reuse.
Viewing Facilities: Videotape.
Duplication Facilities: None.
Related Materials: *The Asian American Media Reference Guide* is a comprehensive, annotated resource catalog of film and videotape programs by, for and about Asian Americans; it lists over 570 works and is cross-referenced. *CineVue* magazine, published five times a year, provides in-depth reporting, exclusive interviews, work-in-progress updates, and new writing by prominent critics, film and videomakers.

NEW YORK METRO

BILL BAIRD INSTITUTE
PARENTS AID SOCIETY
131 Fulton Avenue
Hempstead, NY 11550
(516) 538-2626

Bill Baird (Director)

Contact: Patty Rosen
Services: Educational institution; private collection. Videotape collection available to the public for duplication.
Description: Videotapes of historical events relating to the reproductive rights movement (1963-present). Includes demonstrations and debates on the issues of birth control and abortion.
Size & Elements: Videotape: format and amount unspecified.
Cataloging: None specified.
Access: Open to the public. Available for duplication. Research requests accepted by mail and telephone. Research fees not charged.
Rights: No rights held to any material.
Licensing: Apply for information. License and usage fees not charged.
Restrictions: None specified.
Viewing Facilities: None.
Duplication Facilities: None.

NEW YORK METRO

BBC/LIONHEART TELEVISION

630 Fifth Avenue, Suite 2220
New York, NY 10111
(212) 541-7342
Fax: (212) 956-2399

Contact: Paula Hawes
Services: Distributor. Programs primarily marketed to independent public television stations, cable and commercial networks. *Not available for research or reuse; clip rights retained by BBC.*
Description: Sole U.S. distributor of BBC television programs. Over 150 shows available.

Comedy series. Titles include: *Are You Being Served?* (56 episodes); *It Ain't Half Hot, Mum* (54 episodes); *Wodehouse Playhouse* (20 episodes); *Stand Up!* (66 episodes).

Mini-series. Titles include: *Shackleton* (4 hrs.); *Murder Most English: Lord Peter Wimsey* (5 episodes); *Six Wives of Henry VIII* (6 episodes).

Drama. Titles include: *All Creatures Great and Small* (54 episodes), *War and Peace* (19 episodes); *Eastenders* (139 episodes); *Duchess of Duke Street* (31 episodes).

Australian prime time features. Titles include: *Crime of the Decade; Every Move She Makes; Natural Causes; Pokerface; Time's Raging;* and *White Man's Legend.*

Animal and nature. Titles include: *Great Zoos of the World* (8 episodes); *Great Parks of the World* (6 episodes); *Wild Side* (60 episodes).

Documentary series. Titles include: *The Ascent of Man* (13 hrs.); *Great Railway Journeys of the World* (7 hrs.); *Triumph of the West* (13 hrs.).

Documentaries. Titles include: *Auschwitz and the Allies* (2 hrs.); *MIA: We Can Keep You Forever* (90 min.); *Brasil Brasil* (4 hrs.); *Who Built Stonehenge* (1 hr.).

Science fiction/action-drama. Titles include: *Blake's 7* (52 hrs.); *Great Detectives* (52 hrs.); *Hitchhiker's Guide to the Galaxy* (6 1/2 hrs.).

Family classics. Titles include: *Alice in Wonderland* (4 1/2 hrs.); *Ivanhoe* (10 1/2 hrs.); *The Legend of King Arthur* (8 1/2 hrs.); *Robin Hood* (12 1/2 hrs.).

Cooking series. Titles include: *Floyd on Fish* (7 1/2 hrs.); *Ken Hom's Chinese Cooking* (8 1/2 hrs.); *Madhur Jaffrey's Indian Cooking Course* (8 1/2 hrs.).

Children's programming. Titles include: *Box of Delights* (3 hrs.); *Colour in the Creek* (10 1/2 hrs.); *Golden Pennies* (8 1/2 hrs.); *Thundersub* (27 1/2 hrs.).

Catalog. Titles include: *Europe The Mighty Continent* (13 hrs.); *Ireland: A Television History* (13 hrs.); *Window on the World* (9 hrs.); *Wilderness* (8 hrs.).
Size & Elements: Apply for information.
Cataloging: Published program catalog.
Access: Maintained for distribution and rental rather than for research or reuse. Requests accepted by mail and telephone.
Rights: Full rights held to all material.
Licensing: Apply for information.
Restrictions: Sales are primarily to television stations. Not available for research or reuse (clip rights are generally retained by BBC).
Viewing Facilities: None.
Duplication Facilities: None.

NEW YORK METRO

BELKA INTERNATIONAL INC.

515 Madison Avenue, Suite 2100
New York, NY 10022

(212) 371-2335
Fax: (212) 421-4036
Telex: 493-8010

Ken Schaffer (President)

Contacts: Ken Schaffer; Marina Albee; Karen Yaplater
Services: Corporation. Film and videotape material available for reuse.
Description: Formerly Orbita Technologies Corporation. Holds North American rights to all Soviet television broadcasts and some films. Collection includes daily Soviet television broadcasts, collected and recorded via satellite. Programs include newscasts, documentaries, science shows and cartoons. Other materials include videotapes of Soviet rock and roll music, and the only existing videotapes of the Matthias Rust trial.
Size & Elements: Film: 35mm ("uncounted cans"; positive). Videotape: 3/4" and 1/2" (over 100 videotapes).
Cataloging: Computerized cataloging for staff use only.
Access: Available for licensing and reuse. Research requests accepted by mail, telephone and in person (walk-in).
Rights: Full rights held to all material.
Licensing: Available for licensing and reuse, subject to restrictions. License fees charged.
Restrictions: Distribution into U.S.S.R. territory is restricted.
Viewing Facilities: Film.
Duplication Facilities: Videotape (VHS and Super VHS).

NEW YORK METRO

CATHERINE BENAMOU/
LATIN AMERICAN WOMEN ARTISTS SERIES (LAWAS)

291 Devoe Street
Brooklyn, NY 11211
(718) 782-6219
Telex: Latin American Women Artists Series 177368 IEBUT

Contact: Catherine Benamou
Services: Private collection. Videotapes available to researchers and scholars for research, and in some cases rental. Material not available for licensing or reuse.
Description: Holds documentaries (all produced in Brazil) relating to women's issues; ethnic commentaries on various cultures (Amazon Indians, Japanese and Afro-Brazilian); and popular music. One short documentary on the poetry of Aimé Césaire (Haiti). Nearly all videotapes have English narration or are subtitled in English.
Size & Elements: Videotape: 3/4" (5 titles, each 10-90 min.; NTSC standard) and VHS (4 titles, each 12-100 min.).
Cataloging: None specified.
Access: Open to researchers and scholars. Some material for use by researchers only; other material available for rental and distribution. Minimal research fee charged. Research requests accepted by mail and telephone.
Rights: Some rights held to all material.
Licensing: Not available for licensing or reuse.
Restrictions: Collection maintained primarily for distribution and research purposes; not available for reuse.
Viewing Facilities: None.
Duplication Facilities: None.

NEW YORK METRO

BENCHMARK FILMS, INC.

145 Scarborough Road
Briarcliff Manor, NY 10510
(914) 762-3838

Myron Solin (President)

Contact: Hildy Stein (Regional Sales Manager)
Services: Film and videotape producer and distributor. Educational materials maintained for purchase and rental primarily to schools and libraries.
Description: Biology, science, sociology and other educational topics. Some films contain color cinemicrography.

Modern Biology Series. Titles include: *Genetic Engineering and Protein Synthesis; Simple Multicellular Animals: Sponges, Coelenterates, and Flatworms; Protista: Protozoa and Algae; Fungi; Fungi and Man; The Paramecium; Mollusks: The Mussel, Respiration and Digestion; From*

Protistans to First Multicellular Animals; The Five Kingdom Classification; and *The Immune Response and Immunization.*

Science. Titles include: *Baobab: Portrait of a Tree; The Year of the Wildebeest; Mzima: Portrait of a Spring; Amate: The Great Fig Tree; The Rains Came; Birds of a Feather;* and *The Solar House.*

Other subjects include: anthropology, sociology, animal life, art, African studies, and fairy tales.

Size & Elements: Film: 16mm. Videotape: format unspecified. (100 titles total).
Cataloging: Published catalogs.
Access: Maintained for distribution and rental rather than for research and reuse. Orders accepted by mail.
Rights: Full rights held to some material. Some rights held to all material.
Licensing: Apply for information.
Restrictions: None specified.
Viewing Facilities: None.
Duplication Facilities: None.
Related Materials: Teachers' guides available for some films.

NEW YORK METRO

BLACK FILMMAKER FOUNDATION
80 Eighth Avenue, Suite 1704
New York, NY 10011
(212) 924-1198

Contact: Foundation office
Services: Foundation; distributor. Film and videotape material available for rental and purchase.
Description: Established in 1978 to provide institutional support services to Black independent film and videotape producers and to build audiences for their work. Services provided include: the Distribution Service, which represents over 70 Black directors, producers and writers from across the United States and makes their work available for rental and purchase; programming assistance and services to institutions and groups seeking to organize local Black film series or festivals; maintenance of a videotape reference library to assist scholars, critics and programmers of Black cinema; and production of *Black Film Focus,* a weekly television talk show that features interviews with directors and showcases their work.

Some film titles (and producers) available from Distribution Services include: *The Answer* (Spike Lee); *Babies Making Babies* (Carl Clay); *Black at Yale* (Warrington Hudlin); *Booker T. Washington* (William Greaves); *Death of a Prophet* (Woodie L. King); *Dark Exodus* (Iverson White); *Four Women* (Julie Dash); *From Harlem to Harvard* (Marco Williams); *From These Roots* (William Greaves); *Killer of Sheep* (Charles Burnett); *The Kold Waves* (Reginald Hudlin); *Kwanzaa* (Ablodun Khaliz); *A Minor Altercation* (Jacqueline Shearer); *The Nightmare* (John Perry III); and *Sarah* (Spike Lee); and *A Sense of Pride* (Monica Freeman).

Some videotape titles (and producers) available from Distribution Service include: *Bass Raves* (Anthony Wisdom); *Bucket Dance Video* (Warrington Hudlin); *The Devil is a Condition* (Carlos DeJesus); *Five Days in July* (Spencer Moon); *Long Train Running* (Marion Riggs); *Musica* (Gustavo Paredes); *Sky Captain* (Mary Neema Barnette); *Thurgood Marshall: Portrait of an American Hero* (Wayne Sharpe, Jesse Martin, Dexter Reed); *Return of the Saturnites* (S. Torriano Berry); *Shanty Town* (Charles Butler Nuckolls III); *Tambia Bourri* (Evelyn Fields Updite); and *Until the Last Stroke* (Joy Shannon).
Size & Elements: Film: 16mm (approx. 51 titles). Videotape: 3/4" (approx. 30 titles).
Cataloging: Published catalog.
Access: Open to the public, media organizations, programmers, and educators and schools. Preview copies available for librarians and media organizers living outside the New York area (shipping and handling costs apply). Requests accepted by mail and telephone (must be followed with an official written request).
Rights: Distribution rights held by the BFF Distribution Service. Copyrights on material retained by filmmakers and original producers.
Licensing: Apply for information.
Restrictions: Rentals and leases are for educational and non-theatrical 16mm optical projection and videotape playback only.
Viewing Facilities: Screening room open to educators and programmers interested in previewing works for classroom, festival or broadcast use.
Duplication Facilities: Apply for information.
Related Events: Annual film and videotape exhibition entitled "Dialogues with Black Filmmakers"; periodic seminars on important information and issues affecting Black cinema; annual benefit film premiere to support the Foundation's activities (Spike Lee's *She's Gotta Have It* premiered in 1986 and Robert Townsend's *Hollywood Shuffle* in 1987).

NEW YORK METRO

CHRISTIAN BLACKWOOD PRODUCTIONS, INC.
115 Bank Street
New York, NY 10014
(212) 242-6260
Telex: 755643

Christian Blackwood (Producer and Director)

Contact: Christian Blackwood
Services: Film producer. Film and videotape material available for distribution and possibly reuse, subject to acceptance and approval.
Description: Films produced and directed by Christian Blackwood.

Titles include: *Signed: Lino Brocka* (1987), the story of the Filipino film director's personal struggle in an environment where personal visions are not tolerated; *Nik and Murray* (1986), portraying the artistic collaboration and personal relationship between the two modern dance choreographers Alwin Nikolais and Murray Louis; *Private Conversations: On the Set of "Death of a Salesman"* (1985); *My Life For Zarah Leander* (1985), a musical film on the diva of Nazi Germany; *Observations Under the Volcano* (1984) observes John Huston directing the film version of Malcolm Lowry's classic novel, *Under the Volcano; Charles Aznavour: Breaking America* (1983); *All By Myself* (1982), with Eartha Kitt; *Sam Fuller* (1981), showing the director on the set of *White Dog; Edith Head* (1981), the life and work of the Academy Award-winning film fashion designer; *Tapdancin'* (1980), featuring performances, film clips and talks; *Memoirs of a Movie Palace* (1980), a portrait of the Loews Kings Theatre in New York; and *Cousins* (1979), the extended Vaughn family, now numbering over two thousand, who trace their history back through slavery in South Carolina to Nigeria.

Other titles include *Roger Corman: Hollywood's Wild Angel* (1978), showing the achievements of the notorious genius of grade "B" movies; *To Be a Man* (1977), a film about the changing roles and values of the American male, from the frontier through the age of Women's Liberation and beyond; *Rock: USA* (1976), with the bands Blondie, the Dead Boys, Heart, Mother's Finest, and Southside Johnny and the Asbury Jukes; *Living With Fear* (1974), an investigation of how fear affects the lives and lifestyles of Americans; *Yesterday's Witness: A Tribute to the American Newsreel* (1974), a chronicle of the newsreels; *Hollywood's Musical Moods* (1973), the music composed and arranged for silent films and music of the sound film era; *Kentucky Kith and Kin* (1972), on the roots and branches of an Appalachian family; *Juilliard* (1971), on New York's renowned music conservatory; *Eliot Feld: Artistic Director* (1970), an account of the founding and early performances of Feld's American Ballet Company; *Japan: The New Art* (1970); *Scenes Seen With Allen Jones* (1969), showing the artist's graphics, painting and costume design; *David Hockney's Diaries* (1969); *Richard Lindner* (1969), a portrait of the artist; *Christo: Wrapped Coast* (1969), depicting the artist's project-in-progress at Little Bay, Australia; *Summer in the City* (1968), interwoven episodes that investigate aspects of Manhattan's Upper West Side during the course of one summer; *Harlem Theater* (1968), a film about the new Lafayette Theatre, an all-Black troupe in Harlem; and *Spoleto: Festival of Two Worlds* (1967).
Size & Elements: Film and videotape: formats unspecified (approx. 34 titles total).
Cataloging: Staff assistance required.
Access: Available for distribution, broadcast, licensing and reuse, subject to restrictions. Research fees charged.
Rights: Full rights held to all material. Additional clearances may be necessary in some cases if material is to be reused.
Licensing: Available for licensing, subject to restrictions. License fees charged.
Restrictions: Requests for licensing and reuse subject to acceptance and approval.
Viewing Facilities: None.
Duplication Facilities: None.

NEW YORK METRO

BLACKWOOD PRODUCTIONS, INC.
251 West 57th Street
New York, NY 10019
(212) 247-4710
Fax: (212) 247-4713

Michael Blackwood (Director)

Contact: Signe Taylor (Director of Distribution)
Services: Film producer and distributor. Collection available for rental and purchase.
Description: Documentaries on contemporary art and artists; contemporary architecture; performing arts; Hollywood; social and political issues.

Individual artists' portraits (most narrated by featured artists). Titles include: *Christo: Ten Works in Progress; Christo: Wrapped Coast; Christo: Wrapped Walk Ways; Jim Dine, London; Sam Francis; Philip Guston; David Hockney's Diaries; Jasper Johns: Decoy; Scenes Seen With Allen Jones; Roy Lichtenstein; Robert Motherwell; Motherwell/Alberti: A La Pintura; Isamu Noguchi; Claes Oldenburg; Robert Rauschenberg: Retrospective; Larry Rivers; George Segal; Andy Warhol; Pablo Picasso: The Legacy of a Genius; The Artist's Studio: Meyer Schapiro Visits George Segal;* and *Francis Bacon and the Brutality of Fact.*

Surveys of art. Masters of Modern Sculpture, Part One: The Pioneers, featuring Auguste Rodin, Edgar Degas, Medardo Rosso, Antoine Bourdelle, Aristide Maillol, Wilhelm Lehmbruck, Henri Matisse, Pablo Picasso, Jacques Lipschitz, Henri Laurens, Jacob Epstein, Umberto Boccioni, Raymond Duchamp-Villon, Julio Gonzales and Constantin Brancusi; *Masters of Modern Sculpture, Part Two: Beyond Cubism,* featuring Vladimir Tatlin, Naum Gabo, Antoine Pevsner, Marcel Duchamp, the Dadaists, Man Ray, Joan Miro, Jean Arp, Max Ernst, Alexander Calder, Alberto Giacometti, Henry Moore, Barbara Hepworth, Germaine Richier, César, Gunther Uecker, Heinz Mack, Otto Piene, Joseph Beuys, Arman, Yves Klein, Daniel Spoerri, Jean Tinguely, Anthony Caro, and Gilbert & George. *Masters of Modern Sculpture, Part Three: The New World* features David Smith, Louise Nevelson, David Hare, Ibram Lassaw, Theodore Roszak, Herbert Ferber, Louise Bourgeois, John Chamberlain, Mark Di Suvero, Isamu Noguchi, George Rickey, Barnett Newman, Tony Smith, George Segal, Donald Judd, Claes Oldenburg, Robert Morris, Richard Serra, Carl Andre, Edward Kienholz, Christo, Michael Heizer and Robert Smithson.

Fourteen Americans: Directions of the 1970s features Vito Acconci, Laurie Anderson, Alice Aycock, Scott Burton, Peter Campus, Chuck Close, Nancy Graves, Joseph Kosuth, Gordon Matta-Clark, Mary Miss, Elizabeth Murray, Dennis Oppenheim, Dorothea Rockburne and Joel Shapiro. *American Art in the Sixties* features Carl Andre, Ron Davis, Dan Flavin, Sam Francis, Helen Frankenthaler, Ed Kienholz, Robert Irwin, Jasper Johns, Donald Judd, Ellsworth Kelly, Roy Lichtenstein, Morris Louis, Robert Morris, Kenneth Noland, Claes Oldenburg, Jules Olitsky, Robert Rauschenberg, Larry Rivers, Ed Ruscha, George Segal, Frank Stella, Andy Warhol, Jack Youngerman, John Cage, Leo Castelli and Clement Greenberg. *The New York School* features Arshile Gorky, Adolph Gottlieb, Philip Guston, Al Held, Hans Hofmann, Franz Kline, Willem de Kooning, Lee Krasner, Joan Mitchell, Robert Motherwell, Barnett Newman, Jackson Pollock, Ad Reinhardt, Mark Rothko, Clyfford Still, Jack Tworkov, and critics Clement Greenberg and Harold Rosenberg.

Photographers of the American Frontier: 1860-1880 features Carleton Watkins, Eadweard Muybridge, A. J. Russell, William Henry Jackson and T. H. O'Sullivan. *Artpark People* features Lynda Benglis, Charles Fahlen, Richard Fleischner, Lloyd Hamrol, Mary Miss, Ree Morton, Pat Oleszko, Sig Rennels, Jim Roche, Abe Rothblatt, James Surls, George Trakas and Connie Zehr. *Japan: The New Art* features Jiro Yoshihara and the Gutai group, Nobuo Sekine, Jiro Takamatzu, Ree Woo Fon and Katsuhiku Narita. *A New Spirit in Painting: Six Painters of the 1980s* features George Baselitz, Markus Lupertz, Sandro Chia, Francesco Clemente, David Salle, Julian Schnabel. Also available is *Four Artists: Robert Ryman, Eva Hesse, Bruce Nauman,* and *Susan Rothenberg.*

Contemporary architecture and architects. Beyond Utopia: Changing Attitudes in American Architecture; Mies; Arata Isozaki; Richard Meier; Ralph Erskine; O.M. Ungers; Frank Gehry; and *James Stirling.*

Performing arts. A Composer's Notes: Philip Glass and the Making of an Opera; Making Dances: Seven Post-Modern Choreographers; Colin McPhee: The Lure of Asian Music; Eliot Feld; The Third Generation: Trisha Brown, Lucinda Childs, Douglass Dunn, David Gordon, Kenneth King, Meredith Monk and Sara Rudner; Tap Dancin'; Juilliard; Rock USA; and *Spoleto USA: A Festival Discovers America.*

Hollywood. Roger Corman: Hollywood's Wild Angel; Hollywood's Musical Moods; Memoirs of a Movie Palace; and *Yesterday's Witness: A Tribute to the American Newsreel.*

Miscellaneous subjects. Kentucky: Kith and Kin; Cousins; Living With Fear; Hans Bethe: Prophet of Energy; Einstein; Empire City; George Kennan: A Critical Voice; The German-Americans: Three Hundred Years in the New Land; To Be a Man; and *We Were German Jews.*
Size & Elements: Film: 16mm. Videotape: 3/4", VHS and Betamax (transfers from film). (Approx. 56 titles total).
Cataloging: Published catalogs.
Access: Films available to the public for rental; films and videotapes available to the public for purchase. Requests accepted by mail and telephone (confirming purchase orders required).
Rights: Full rights held to all material.
Licensing: Apply for information.
Restrictions: Release prints are licensed for use only by the acquiring institution and may not be copied, reproduced or transferred to another audio-visual medium. Material may not be leased, loaned or rented to another institution or licensed for television broadcast; no parts may be excerpted.
Viewing Facilities: None.
Duplication Facilities: None.

NEW YORK METRO

BOROUGH OF MANHATTAN COMMUNITY COLLEGE MEDIA CENTER
199 Chambers Street
New York, NY 10007
(212) 618-1666

Robin Schanzenbach (Director)

Contact: Robin Schanzenbach
Services: Educational institution. Videotape collection intended primarily for in-house use; possibly available for licensing and reuse, subject to restrictions. Selected programs available for rental and purchase.
Description: One of the most sophisticated media facilities located in a Manhattan educational institution, teaching video production and post-production and collaborating to produce videotapes for outside clients such as the Office of Academic Affairs of the City University of New York.

Strengths include: footage of lower Manhattan (skylines, buildings and street scenes) and college life (student activities, classroom settings, teachers and instructional scenes).

Adult Literacy Teacher Training (ALTT) is a 12-part series instructing "teachers how to teach" adult literacy and English as a second language, showing actual classroom methods. The series is coproduced and distributed by the Office of Academic Affairs/CUNY and BMCC/CUNY.
Size & Elements: Videotape: 3/4" (250 videotapes, each 20 min.).
Cataloging: Shot lists available for most videotapes (for in-house use only).
Access: Open to researchers and scholars. ALTT series available through the Media Center for rental and purchase. Other footage possibly available for licensing and reuse on a case-by-case basis. Requests accepted by mail and telephone. Research fees charged in some cases.
Rights: Rights status of material not currently known.
Licensing: Available for licensing and reuse, subject to restrictions.
Restrictions: Requests for licensing and reuse considered on a case-by-case basis. Most material presently limited to in-house use. License policies and procedures not yet determined. Any reuse of material must be individually negotiated.
Viewing Facilities: Videotape (3/4" and 1/2").
Duplication Facilities: Videotape (1", 3/4" and 1/2").

NEW YORK METRO

BOYS CLUB OF AMERICA
771 First Avenue
New York, NY 10017
(212) 351-5900
Fax: (212) 351-5972

Thomas Garth (National Director)

Contact: Mark Lutin (Manager, Public Relations)
Services: Youth development organization. Films and videotapes available for licensing and reuse, subject to restrictions.
Description: Promotional films on the Boys Club movement, showing young people in positive activities, emphasizing youth sports and athletics.
Size & Elements: Film and videotape: formats unspecified (2 titles).
Cataloging: None specified.
Access: Available for licensing and reuse, subject to restrictions. Research requests accepted by mail.
Rights: Full rights held to all material.
Licensing: Available for licensing and reuse, subject to restrictions.

Restrictions: Requests for licensing and reuse subject to acceptance and approval.
Viewing Facilities: None.
Duplication Facilities: None.

NEW YORK METRO

JOHN BRANSBY PRODUCTIONS, LTD.
221 West 57th Street
New York, NY 10019
(212) 333-5656
Fax: (212) 333-7748

David Jacobson (President)

Contact: David Jacobson
Services: Film and videotape producer; stock footage sales library.
Description: "Postcard-type" color scenes of 18 Northeastern states (ca. 1946-56).
Size & Elements: Film: 16mm (18 titles, each 30 min.; negative). Videotape: all formats (amount unspecified).
Cataloging: Card catalogs; computerized cataloging for staff use only.
Access: Available for duplication. Research fees charged. Research requests accepted by mail and telephone.
Rights: Full rights held to all material.
Licensing: Available for licensing and reuse. License fees charged (negotiable).
Restrictions: None specified.
Viewing Facilities: Film (KEM flatbed); videotape (3/4" and 1/2").
Duplication Facilities: Videotape (3/4" and 1/2").

NEW YORK METRO

BRITISH INFORMATION SERVICES
RADIO AND TELEVISION DIVISION
845 Third Avenue, 9th Floor
New York, NY 10022
(212) 752-8400
Fax: (212) 758-5395

David Snoxell (Executive Director)

Contact: Mark Hopkinson (Head of Radio and Television)
Services: Government agency; film and videotape distributor. Material available for licensing and reuse.
Description: The British Information Services Library is a liaison with the British Central Office of Information (COI) and acts to locate television and radio materials, especially news footage, about current events, commercial and scientific developments in Britain. They also help radio and television producers on assignment in Britain with location services, obtaining footage and passes, and arranging access to ministers and officials.
Film and Video Stock Shot Library. Based in London. Contains extensive archive film footage from the Crown Film Unit and the Ministry of Information (late 1930s-present), covering a wide range of subjects including World War II. Footage is also drawn from recent documentaries on science and technology. Subjects include aircraft, Royal Air Force, airports, army, Aswan Dam, Australia, bacteria, barley, beaches, Big Ben, birds, blizzards, bridges, cattle, cliffs, coastlines, coffee crop, computers, Concorde, container transport, countryside, crops, crowds, dairy farming, deserts, diesel trains, diving, docks, drilling rigs, Egypt, electric trains, electricity, elephants, factories, the Far East, farming, fire, fireworks, fish, forestry, fungi, Ganges, Gambia, gas, Ghana, Guatemala, gulls, Hadrian's Wall, hang-gliding, Harrier STOL aircraft, harvests, helicopters, high speed train, Hong Kong, hospitals, Hovercraft, ice floes, India, industries, insects, Japan, Jodrell Bank telescope, jungles, Kariba Dam, Kashmir, Kathmandu (Nepal), lambs, lasers, leprosy, London, the Middle East, minerals, mining, missiles, mosques, navy, Nepal, Norway, nuclear power, oil, paddy fields, pollution, power stations, railways, red arrows, rivers, rockets, rough seas, royalty, safety, sailing boats, science, Scotland, seas, Seychelles, sheep, shipping, Singapore, snow, steel, submarines, tanks, temples, tigers, timber, tower castle, towns, traffic, trees, Turkey, United Arab Emirates, underground trains, Victoria Falls, war, water, welding, West Indies, Westminster, wheat, and windmills.
Finished productions of the COI include: *Afghanistan,* an eight-part series; *AIDS: The British Approach;* and *Falkland Islands Conversation Zone* (also available in Spanish).

Size & Elements: Film: mostly 16mm (amount unspecified). Videotape: 3/4" and VHS (viewing copies).
Cataloging: Film and Video Stock Shot Library cataloged by UDC (Universal Decimal Classification) system.
Access: Available to the public. Research fees charged by COI. Research requests accepted by mail and telephone.
Rights: Full rights held to all material.
Licensing: Available for licensing and reuse. Some material may be provided free of charge, but commercial projects will be charged for reuse of material.
Restrictions: None specified.
Viewing Facilities: Videotape (3/4" and VHS).
Duplication Facilities: Duplication performed in Britain.

NEW YORK METRO

BROAD STREET PRODUCTIONS
50 Broad Street, 20th Floor
New York, NY 10004
(212) 232-8031
Fax: (212) 797-9081

David Dreyfuss (President)

Contact: Laurie Friedman (Senior Archivist)
Services: Videotape producer; stock footage sales library.
Description: Urban, business and industrial stock footage; specializing in Wall Street and the financial sector.
Wall Street and finance. New York Stock Exchange, American Stock Exchange, Chicago Mercantile Exchange, London Stock Exchange, Federal Hall, Trinity Church, general Wall Street, bank exteriors, investment banking, trading floor shots, brokers and clients, computer activity, aerials and landmarks from various cities, including Washington, D.C.
Industrial. Construction, assembly line production, architectural drawing, oil rigs, loading docks, aircraft takeoffs and landings, ticket counters, fashion industry (modeling and runways), laboratory research, satellite dishes, video production equipment, homevideo store interiors, Western Union offices.
Miscellaneous. Hollywood behind-the-scenes, MGM (now Turner Entertainment) studios, 20th Century-Fox Studios, Universal Studios, casino interiors, gambling, suburban homes, nursing homes, senior citizens, day care, handicapped children, exercising, shopping malls, yachting, fireworks, Hard Rock Cafes in various cities, sunrises and sunsets, New York City scenes (streets, theaters, stores and restaurants).
Size & Elements: Videotape: 1", Betacam and 3/4" (masters); 3/4" (time-coded viewing copies).
Cataloging: Computerized cataloging for staff use only; logs; shot lists.
Access: Some material available for stock footage sale. Material not available for rental. Research requests accepted by mail and telephone.
Rights: Full rights held to some material.
Licensing: Available for licensing and reuse, subject to restrictions. License fees charged.
Restrictions: Some restrictions may apply, depending on material requested and its intended use.
Viewing Facilities: Videotape (Betacam, 3/4", VHS and Betamax).
Duplication Facilities: Videotape (3/4" to VHS, Betacam or Betamax).

NEW YORK METRO

BRONX COUNTY HISTORICAL SOCIETY
3309 Bainbridge Avenue
Bronx, NY 10467
(212) 881-8900

Dr. Gary Hermalyn (Director)

Contacts: Dr. Gary Hermalyn; Laura Tosi (Associate Librarian)
Services: Historical society. Videotape material available for research and reuse, subject to restrictions.
Description: Society lectures, forums and walking tours (1985-present). Collection also includes a special series of Bronx history, *Bronx Faces and Places,* produced for WNYE-TV (New York City).
Topics and titles include: Van Cortlandt Park; women's role in Bronx history; Marble Hill; the early history of Westchester Square; Bronx Historical Society Annual Dinner and Annual Auction (1985); *Pelham Bay, Freedomland and Co-op City* (slide lecture); Edgar Allan Poe; a Fordham University walking tour; a discussion with Kenneth T. Jackson, author of *Crabgrass Frontier,* a

study of suburbia; Robert Moses (slide lecture); Intervale Avenue; a debate between Assemblyman Jose Serrano and Borough President Stanley Simon (March 1986); Spuyten Duyvil and Inwood; architectural tour of the Bronx; urban women in health and health care; Morris Park; Mott Haven; history of Bronx street and place names; Bronx Zoo; the moving of the Valentine-Varian House; Fordham Archaeological Dig; Narcotics Task Force (six anti-crack commercials filmed in 1986); General Slocum disaster; *African Continuity in the Americas;* Jessie Tarbox Beals (photographer); New York City Water Systems; *Afro-American Slave Narratives; Puerto Rican Community in New York.*

Size & Elements: Videotape: format unspecified (45 videotapes; masters and viewing copies).
Cataloging: Card catalogs; research library.
Access: Open to the public. For in-house use only. Duplicate copies can be obtained for a fee. Research fees not charged. Research requests accepted by mail, telephone and in person.
Rights: Full rights held to all material.
Licensing: Apply for information. License fees charged.
Restrictions: Restrictions apply to licensing and reuse.
Viewing Facilities: Videotape.
Duplication Facilities: None.

NEW YORK METRO

BROOKLYN BOTANIC GARDEN
1000 Washington Avenue
Brooklyn, NY 11225
(718) 622-4433

Audre Meltzer (Vice President, Marketing)

Contact: Susan Moran (Marketing Manager)
Services: Botanic garden. Films and videotapes available for rental and purchase.
Description: Titles include: *Herbs — Use and Tradition; Pruning Practices at the Brooklyn Botanic Garden; Nature's Colors — The Craft of Dyeing With Plants; Planting and Transplanting; Bonsai — The Art of Training Dwarf*

Potted Trees; Dried Flowers and Plants; Get Ready, Get Set, Grow!, designed to accompany a "video kit" for children, parents and teachers on vegetable and flower gardening; *Romancing the Seed;* and *For the Love of Roses.*
Size & Elements: Film: 16mm (7 titles; release prints). Videotape: VHS (3 titles; viewing copies).
Cataloging: Published brochure; release sheets.
Access: Available for rental, purchase and reuse. Research requests accepted by telephone.
Rights: Full rights held to some material.
Licensing: Available for licensing and reuse. License fees charged.
Restrictions: None specified.
Viewing Facilities: None.
Duplication Facilities: None.

NEW YORK METRO

BROOKLYN COLLEGE OF THE CITY UNIVERSITY OF NEW YORK
CELIA NACHATOVITZ DIAMANT MEMORIAL LIBRARY OF
CLASSIC TELEVISION COMMERCIALS
DEPARTMENT OF TELEVISION AND RADIO
Bedford Avenue and Avenue H
Brooklyn, NY 11210-2816
(718) 780-5585

Robert C. Williams (Chairman)

Contact: Robert C. Williams
Services: College. Videotape collection available to schools, qualified researchers and nonprofit agencies for viewing and study.
Description: Collection of classic television commercials was donated to Brooklyn College by Lincoln Diamant, an independent producer and consultant (Spots Alive Agency, New York) in memory of his late wife, Celia Nachatovitz Diamant, who graduated from Brooklyn College in 1942.

Although the original spots were produced on film, Brooklyn College holds collection on videotape.

A list of the spots follows:
1. Lucky Strike (LSMFT): Square-dancing cigarettes (:60).

2. Old Gold with Dennis James. Dancing Old Gold pack. (:60).

3. Muriel cigars (dancing) (:60).

4. Kool cigarettes with singing penguin ("snow-fresh coolness") (:60).

5. Marlboro cigarettes (the type of man who smokes Marlboro) (:60).

6. Robert Burns cigars (memories make him smoke Burns cigars) (:60).

7. Winston cigarettes (animated musical notes play theme) (:30).

8. Chesterfield (smoked by the men of America; "tops in friendly satisfaction") (:60).

9. Ajax (the foaming cleanser, animated) (1:10).

10. SOS soap suds (live commercial with Durward Kirby and unknown lady; Garry Moore in drag; Garry thanks McCann-Erickson for the funny spot that they wrote) (3:00).

11. Raid commercial (animated; bugs are killed dead with a little bit of Raid) (:60).

12. Kleenex (Manners the butler saves the day) (:60).

13. Mr. Clean (animated, with original theme song) (:60).

14. Tide ("the cleanest clean under the sun") (:60).

15. Bufferin (with diagrams, to show that it's better than aspirin) (:60).

16. Alka-Seltzer (classic "Speedy" commercial) (:60).

17. Band-Aid (slow-motion as well as live-action) (:60).

18. Band-Aid (special effects used, including multiple images) (:60).

19. Gillette Blue Blades (:30).

20. Remington Shaver (shaving a peach) (:60).

21. Gillette (with Pee Wee Reese, of the Brooklyn Dodgers) (:60).

22. Mum deodorant (with "secret agent" flavor) (:60).

23. Pepsodent (animated; "you'll wonder where the yellow went") (:60).

24. Clairol (hair coloring; "only her hairdresser knows for sure") (:60).

25. Crest toothpaste ("Look Ma, no cavities!") (:60).

26. Live commercial featuring Arthur Godfrey, for Lipton's chicken noodle soup. He jokes about props, reads his script. Searches for the chicken in the soup (4:15).

27. Ritz crackers (still-frame action) (:20).

28. Heinz Worcestershire sauce (animated studio set; announcer has trouble with his mouth) (:60).

29. Skippy peanut butter (animated commercial tracing the history of peanut butter) (1:30).

30. E-Z Pop popcorn (animated commercial with jingle) (:60).

31. Jell-O (animated; housewife with busy day has trouble with dessert until she finds out how easy Jell-O is to make) (:60).

32. Kroger (animated; eggs with the perfect shape) (:60).

33. Pet Evaporated milk (lullaby with mother and baby) (1:30).

34. Snowdrift Wesson oil (shortening commercial that uses only three words: "John", "Marcis" and "Snowdrift") (1:30).

35. Nestle's Quik (with Jimmy Nelson and Danny O'Day (dummy) and Farfel (dog). Includes Nestle's jingle) (:60).

36. Maypo (animated; "I want my Maypo") (:60).

37. Anderson pea soup (animated, with Robert P. Soup Anderson) (:60).

38. Jell-O (Chinese animated commercial) (:60).

39. Instant Maxwell House coffee (with Rex Marshall, magnified coffee grains shown) (1:30).

40. Tea ("calms your stomach, relaxes your nerves." "Take tea and see...")

41. Wilkens coffee (with puppets) (:10).

42. Hamms Beer (animated, with live action. "The land of sky blue water...") (1:20).

43. Carling Black Label Beer (:60).

44. Piel's beer (with Bert and Harry Piel. Live and animated) (:60).

45. Schweppes tonic water (dignified woman and man trying to find out where they met one another) (:60).

46. Rheingold Beer (with parade of marching bottles, cans and toy trains) (:60).

47. Budweiser ("Where there's life, there's Bud"; by seashore) (:60).

48. Ballantine Beer (with marionettes) (:60).

49. Gallo wine (jazz music in background) (:60).

50. Bardahl (Bardahl solves the case; mimics *Dragnet*) (:60).

51. Delco (Air Force plane travelling through dangerous territory and weather is helped by Delco battery during a power failure) (3:00).

52. Speedway 79 Power Fuel (animated, with jingle) (:60).

53. Esso (animated; "Stalling is eliminated by using Esso") (:60).

54. Chevron Supreme (animated, with slogan) (:60).

55. Bank of America ("Instant Money") (:20).

56. Yellow Pages (animated) (:60).

57. Robert Hall (blackbirds singing) (:30).

58. Keds (with Keso the clown and the "Keds" theme song) (:58).

59. Chemstrand Corporation (nylon stockings; still frame action) (:58).

60. RCA Victor (portable radio, famous dog logo "Nipper") (:58).

61. Bulova watches (endorsement by newsman and action of watch surviving

Niagara Falls) (:55).

62. Westinghouse refrigerators (live commercial with Betty Furness. She is unable to open door of refrigerator. Camera dollies in so that floor manager can open door for Furness. As he does this, Furness is out of the light; and once again, she has trouble with the door) (2:20).

63. Westinghouse washing machines (live test. Part I: clothes being put into washer. Part II: clothes being taken out of machine) (6:10 total).

64. Dodge (factory commercial showing how cars are assembled) (2:00).

65. Chevrolet trucks (1957 models conquering the Alcan Highway run, as certified by the AAA) (3:40).

66. Renault Dauphine (with fast action; "A better way to get around") (:60).

67. Chevrolet (1959; Pat Boone and Dinah Shore sing. Cars only shown for fraction of a second) (1:40).

68. Chevrolet (convertibles) (2:15).

69. Chevrolet (1959; takes place in car showroom) (2:00).

Size & Elements: Videotape: 2" and 1" (69 commercials, approx. 120 min.).

Cataloging: Title sheet (all titles are listed in this entry, see above).

Access: Copies of videotape available to qualified researchers, nonprofit organizations and schools (duplication fee charged).

Rights: No rights held to any material.

Licensing: Not available for licensing or reuse; supplied for research and screening purposes only.

Restrictions: Additional clearances may be necessary in some cases if material is to be reused.

Viewing Facilities: None.

Duplication Facilities: Videotape (2", 3/4", VHS and 1/2" open reel). Fees must be prepaid and videotape stock supplied for duplication. Allow four to six weeks.

Related Materials: Mr. Diamant has written a companion book to this collection, *Television's Classic Commercials* (Hastings House) which contains scripts and background information on all 69 commercials.

NEW YORK METRO

BUND ARCHIVES OF THE JEWISH LABOR MOVEMENT
25 East 21st Street
New York, NY 10010
(212) 473-5101

Dr. Benjamin Nadel (Executive Director)

Contact: Dr. Benjamin Nadel

Services: Library; private collection. Films and videotapes available to researchers and scholars only.

Description: Material focusing on the history of Jewish Labor Bund and Jewish revolutionary movements.

Films include: *Mir Kumen On*, on the Medem Sanatorium in prewar Poland (1930s, in Yiddish); and *Revolutionnaires de Yiddishland* (1984, Kuiv Productions, in French). Also holds one videotape on the history of the Jewish Labor Movement.

Size & Elements: Film: format unspecified (2 titles). Videotape: format unspecified (1 item).

Cataloging: None specified.

Access: Available to researchers and scholars only. Research requests accepted by telephone and in person (by appointment only).

Rights: Full rights held to some material.

Licensing: Apply for information.

Restrictions: Apply for information.

Viewing Facilities: None.

Duplication Facilities: None.

NEW YORK METRO

CAMERA THREE PRODUCTIONS, INC.
One Madison Avenue
New York, NY 10010
(212) 685-7880

Contact: Archives Manager

Services: Film and videotape producer. Material available for stock footage sale.

Description: Archives contains documentaries and performance specials (1950s-present). Covers the history of the arts, profiles of creative individuals, ethnic dance, origins of contemporary theater and dance, cartooning, animation, photography, architecture, sculpture, writers and African arts. Holds many early or rare interviews with pioneers in the arts and sciences.

Examples of people and subjects covered include: Leni Riefenstahl, Buster Keaton, François Truffaut, Cambodian palace dance, Nigerian folk play, Bunraku puppet theater, Shodo, Kendo, reggae music, Andre Kertesz, Diane Arbus, Basil Bunting, George Dunning, Hans Richter, Paolo Soleri, Isamu Noguchi, Ravi Shankar, Stephen Sondheim, Noel Coward, Chester Himes, Stan Vanderbeek, Sylvia Plath, the Centre Pompidou, the Louvre, Tatyana Grossman, Philip Johnson, Henry Moore, Josef Albers, Norman McLaren, John Whitney, James Galway, The Chieftains, Canadian Brass, Bernard Herrmann, Kabuki theater, Zen Buddhism, Modern Jazz Quartet, Scott Joplin, Jean Gabin, Andre Serban, Gisela May, Alberta Hunter, Fats Waller, Anais Nin, Immanuel Velikovsky, tap dance, Maurice Bejart, Arturo Toscanini, Theater of the Deaf, Jerzy Grotowski, Pierre Boulez, Marc Blitzstein, R. D. Laing, Irving Berlin, John Wayne, Lawrence Welk, Alan Jay Lerner and Frederick Loewe.

Size & Elements: Videotape: Betacam and 3/4" (500 items).
Cataloging: Apply for information.
Access: Requests must be made in writing, specifying subjects needed.
Rights: Apply for information.
Licensing: Available for licensing and reuse. License fees charged.
Restrictions: None specified.
Viewing Facilities: None.
Duplication Facilities: None.

NEW YORK METRO

ARTHUR CANTOR, INC.

2112 Broadway, Suite 400
New York, NY 10023
(212) 496-5710

Arthur Cantor (Producer)

Contact: Film Department
Services: Distributor. Films available for rental and purchase.
Description: Documentary films on Jewish history and culture; New York City history; European history; theater, actors and directors; visual artists; authors and playwrights; ballet; the making of films and plays; architecture; opera and composers; and unusual people.

Jewish history and culture. Titles include: *The Golden Age of Second Avenue* (1968), tracing the history of the Yiddish theater in America, incorporating unique film footage of early Second Avenue and scenes from plays and movies, featuring Paul Muni, Maurice Schwartz, Menasha Skulnik, Molly Picon and Celia Adler. *Now...After All These Years* (1981) focuses on Rhina, a German village once predominantly Jewish, and the different memories of its German and Jewish residents. *Exile* (Alexis Krasilovsky, 1983) follows a young Jewish filmmaker who searches for the meaning of her existence, and her journey to the places of her ancestry in Czechoslovakia and Austria. *Brighton Beach* (1980) is a look at the current residents of Brooklyn's "poor man's paradise by the sea."

Theater. Titles include: *Joe Chaikin — Going On* (1983); a portrait of the founder of the Open Theatre; *The Serpent* (1970), a record of the Open Theatre production; *Akropolis* (1968), documentation of a performance by Jerzy Grotowski's Polish Laboratory Theatre; *Emlyn Williams As Charles Dickens* (1977); *Dame Edith Evans: I Caught Acting Like the Measles* (1978); and *Signals Through the Flames* (Sheldon Rochlin and Maxine Harris, 1984), on Julian Beck and Judith Malina's Living Theatre.

Art and photography. Titles include: *Ansel Adams: Photographer* (1981); *L.A. — As Suggested by the Work of Edward Ruscha* (1980); *Käthe Kollwitz* (1981), a documentary drama focusing on the final months of the artist's life in 1945; *Memories of Berlin: Twilight of Weimar Culture* (1977), with Christopher Isherwood, Louise Brooks, Elisabeth Bergner, Arthur Koestler, Carl Zuckmayer, Francis Lederer and Herbert Bayer, among others; *Tinguely: A Kinetic Cosmos* (1981); *Niki* (1982), on sculptor Niki de Saint Phalle; and *Robert Indiana Portrait* (1973).

Dance. Titles include: *Beginnings* (1976), on the School of American Ballet; and *American Ballet Theatre: A Close-up in Time* (1973), a compilation of six major dance pieces and interviews with choreographers.

Motion pictures. Titles include: *Storyville Story* (1977), a behind-the-scenes look at the making of Louis Malle's *Pretty Baby;* and *The Honeymoon Killers* (1970).

Architecture. Titles include: *Beaubourg* (1980), a guided tour through the Centre d'Art et Culture Georges Pompidou; *Triumph in Stone* (1979), on Gothic cathedrals in France; *Imperial City* (1980), on the design and building of New Delhi; and *The World of Buckminster Fuller* (1972).

Literature. Titles include: *Christopher Isherwood: Over There on a Visit* (1977), an interview; *Anaïs Observed* (1973), on Anaïs Nin; and *The Henry Miller Odyssey* (1969).
Size & Elements: Film: 35mm and 16mm (approx. 51 titles).
Cataloging: Published catalog.
Access: Maintained for rental and purchase rather than for research or reuse. Rental fees charged. Orders accepted by mail and telephone.
Rights: Apply for information.
Licensing: Apply for information.
Restrictions: Apply for information.
Viewing Facilities: None.
Duplication Facilities: None.

NEW YORK METRO

CAPPY PRODUCTIONS, INC.

33 East 68th Street
New York, NY 10021
(212) 249-1800
Fax: (212) 439-9165

Bud Greenspan (President)

Contact: Sidney Thayer (Producer)
Services: Film producer. Film and videotape footage available for licensing and reuse, subject to restrictions.
Description: Footage from the 1984 Olympic Games (Los Angeles) and the 1988 Winter Olympics (Calgary).
Size & Elements: Film: 35mm (Los Angeles 1984, 1 million feet); 16mm (Calgary 1988, 4 million feet). Videotape: 3/4" (transfers from film).
Cataloging: None specified.
Access: Available to the public for licensing and reuse. Research fees charged. Research requests accepted by mail and telephone.
Rights: Full rights held to all material. Additional clearances may be necessary if material is to be reused. Use of Olympic footage for any commercial or public purpose must first be cleared with Howard Stupp at the International Olympic Games Central Information Bureau, Lausanne, Switzerland.
Licensing: Available for licensing and reuse, subject to restrictions. License fees charged.
Restrictions: All reuse of footage subject to clearance and approval on a case-by-case basis.
Viewing Facilities: None.
Duplication Facilities: Videotape (3/4").

NEW YORK METRO

CARE
COMMUNICATIONS DEPARTMENT

660 First Avenue
New York, NY 10016
(212) 686-3110
Cable: PARCELUS NY

Contact: Pedro Soto (A/V Technician)
Services: International humanitarian relief organization. Films and videotapes available to the public primarily for fundraising presentations, and possibly for reuse, subject to approval.
Description: Films and videotapes documenting and promoting CARE and its projects. *People of CARE* tells the story of CARE (1946-81) using historical footage. *Eduardo of Ichu,* filmed in the Peruvian Andes mountains, tells of a shepherd boy whose sheep were killed by a speeding car, and how he received help from CARE. *The Business of America* covers projects in Latin America supported by such corporations as Gulf & Western, Chase Manhattan Bank, Nationwide Insurance Companies and IBM, including school gardens, beekeeping and honey production, nutrition centers, school construction and food production. Noted economist and management expert Peter Drucker provides a running commentary.

Crisis in Africa is an overview of the current situation in East Africa, focusing on drought and famine in Ethiopia and its ramifications in Somalia and the Sudan. The film shows refugee camps in the Sudan and the ongoing relief efforts in Somalia, including food delivery, logistics and distribution. Long-term development projects shown include tree nurseries and reforestation in Somalia and a community water project in Kenya.

Other videotapes documenting post-World War II history of CARE's international development programs include *Fighting Famine in Africa, A*

Bigger Package for a Smaller World, and *40 Years of Caring.*
Size & Elements: Film: 16mm (4 titles). Videotape: 3/4" and VHS (4 titles).
Cataloging: Brochure.
Access: Material "available to the public to help the CARE organization in its fundraising activities." Research requests accepted by mail.
Rights: Full rights held to all material.
Licensing: Apply for information.
Restrictions: Written permission required for duplication or reuse of materials.
Viewing Facilities: None.
Duplication Facilities: None.

NEW YORK METRO

CAROUSEL FILM AND VIDEO
260 Fifth Avenue, Room 705
New York, NY 10001
(212) 683-1660

For rental or purchase in Canada:
MARLIN MOTION PICTURES
211 Watline Avenue, Suite 200
Mississauga, ON L4Z 1P3
(416) 272-4100

Contact: Staff
Services: Distributor. Films and videotapes available to the public for purchase, and for rental through various rental libraries.
Description: Films and videotapes (many originally produced by CBS) relating to contemporary affairs, social studies, general instruction, and business.
   Categories include: Africa; aging; Americana; animation; art; automotive mechanics; biographies; Black studies; business and industry; career guidance; *60 Minutes* programs (CBS); child development; children's stories; computers and technology; consumer education; death education; drama; ecology and energy conservation; economics; education; ethnic studies; family life; film study; government; the handicapped; health and medicine; the Holocaust; humor and satire; international affairs; journalism; language arts; literature; mental health; motivational programs; music; nursing; photography; poetry; political science; poverty; prejudice; prison reform; psychology; religion; sex education; science; social studies; sociology; substance abuse; teacher training; theater arts; urban studies; U.S. history; values; and women's studies.
   Sample titles include: *Anyplace But Here,* examining the dilemmas facing the mentally ill in America and the people who try to help them; *China: A Hole in the Bamboo Curtain,* exploring lifestyles, children, handicrafts, medicine, industry, history and the future of the masses; *The CIA's Secret Army,* focusing on its secret operations and activities; *Days of Thrills and Laughter,* Robert Youngson's history of Hollywood's silent-screen era, emphasizing the "adventure" film; *Dreams On Hold,* on the growing gap between America's rich and poor and the nation's shrinking middle class; *Hunger In America; Is Anyone Out There Learning?,* an analysis of the weaknesses and strengths of public schools; *Ku Klux Klan: The Invisible Empire; Malcolm X,* a biography of the Black activist; *The Selling of the Pentagon,* a controversial examination of costly public relations activities and questionable practices at the Pentagon; *What's Communism All About?;* and *Women In Prison,* documenting the process of dehumanization and proposing alternatives to incarceration.
Size & Elements: Film: 16mm (approx. 143 titles). Videotape: 3/4" and VHS (approx. 168 titles).
Cataloging: Published catalog.
Access: Available to the public for preview and purchase. Available for rental from various rental libraries (apply for information). Requests accepted by mail and telephone.
Rights: Rights retained by original producers.
Licensing: Apply for information.
Restrictions: "All materials are protected by copyright laws and purchase or rental does not include the right to televise, videotape or reproduce by any or all technical or electronic processes in whole or in part. Any reproduction is in violation of the copyright law."
Viewing Facilities: None.
Duplication Facilities: None.

NEW YORK METRO

CASTELLI/SONNABEND TAPES & FILMS
578 Broadway
New York, NY 10012

(212) 431-6279

Michael Ortoleva (Director)

Contact: Michael Ortoleva
Services: Art gallery; film and videotape distributor. Open to researchers and scholars only for viewing; available to the public for rental, purchase, duplication and reuse.
Description: Distributes films and videotapes for those artists represented by Leo Castelli Gallery, Inc., including Robert Morris, Bruce Nauman, Claes Oldenburg, Robert Rauschenberg, Edward Ruscha, Richard Serra, Keith Sonnier and Lawrence Weiner.
   Important works by these artists from the years 1965-73 have been given to the Video Data Bank/The School of the Art Institute of Chicago (q.v.) to be remastered on 1" videotape and then copied to 3/4" videotape for distribution.
   Also holds videotapes produced as part of installations by artists, including Bruce Nauman, and a small collection of films and videotapes produced by outside producers, all relating to the Leo Castelli Gallery and its artists.
Size & Elements: Film: format unspecified (approx. 51 titles). Videotape: 3/4" (approx. 17 titles available; approx. 22 additional titles available from Video Data Bank).
Cataloging: Published catalog.
Access: Open to researchers and scholars only. Available to the public for rental, purchase, duplication and reuse. Research fees not charged; rental fees apply. Research requests accepted by mail, telephone and in person (by appointment only).
Rights: All rights retained by original artists.
Licensing: Available for reuse, subject to restrictions. Usage fees charged on a case-by-case basis.
Restrictions: Permission of individual artist required for reuse of material.
Viewing Facilities: Videotape (3/4").
Duplication Facilities: None.

NEW YORK METRO

CATHOLIC RELIEF SERVICES
FILM LIBRARY
1011 First Avenue
New York, NY 10022
(212) 838-4700 (Ext. 460)
Fax: (212) 838-4624

Contact: Paul Capcara
Services: Overseas relief and development agency. Films and videotapes available for free loan and purchase.
Description: Films and videotapes for general audiences, showing humanitarian assistance programs in Asia, Europe, the Middle East, Africa, and Latin America. Two films, *People First* and *In Our Name,* describe the philosophy and extent of the CRS program.
Size & Elements: Film (16mm). Videotape: 3/4" and VHS. (14 titles total). Not all titles available in all formats.
Cataloging: Brochure.
Access: Available for free loan (through Karol Media) and purchase (through Catholic Relief Services).
Rights: Apply for information.
Licensing: Apply for information regarding research, duplication, licensing and reuse.
Restrictions: None specified.
Viewing Facilities: None.
Duplication Facilities: None.

NEW YORK METRO

CBS ENTERTAINMENT
51 West 52nd Street
New York, NY 10019
(212) 975-1556

Contact: Virginia Frey (Manager of Business Affairs)
Services: Television broadcaster. Programs available for licensing and reuse on a case-by-case basis, subject to restrictions.
Description: Non-news programs owned and/or broadcast by the CBS Television Network.
Size & Elements: Film and videotape (format and amount unspecified).
Cataloging: Apply for information.

Access: Apply for information.
Rights: Apply for information. Additional clearances are necessary in most cases if material is to be reused.
Licensing: Available for licensing and reuse on a case-by-case basis, subject to restrictions. License fees charged.
Restrictions: Reuse of many programs carries specific restrictions.
Viewing Facilities: Film and videotape.
Duplication Facilities: None.

NEW YORK METRO

CBS NEWS ARCHIVES
524 West 57th Street
New York, NY 10019
(212) 975-2875
(212) 975-2876
Fax: (212) 315-2494
Telex: 234190 BCND-UR

Neil Waldman (Director of Archives Development)

Contact: Neil Waldman
Services: Television network archives; film and videotape stock footage sales library.
Description: Archives contains all film and videotape shot for regular CBS News programs, excluding *60 Minutes* and documentary programs.

Newsfilm and videotape library. Begins 1954. Comprehensive collection of local, national and international events and feature stories. Footage from 1954-67 is all 16mm original black and white film, mostly reversal positive, some negative, much sound on film. 1967-74 footage is all 16mm color reversal positive film, with some negative. Material 1975-present is all 3/4" videotape, with some Betacam from recent years. There is videotape (all formats) held on some older news events that were covered live (e.g., political conventions and space stories) Includes both aired and unaired footage, but unaired footage may be subject to various restrictions with respect to sales (see restrictions below).

Entire newscasts. All newscasts 1975-present have been kept in their entirety, in videotape form. Prior to 1975, some newscasts exist in various videotape formats and in kinescope form, but coverage is spotty. Many newscasts are available for reference at the National Archives and Records Administration (q.v.).

Documentary library. Begins 1951. Broadcast documentaries, including *CBS Reports, Face the Nation, In the News, Magazine, 60 Minutes, West 57th Street* and various *CBS News Specials* and *Special Reports.* Outtakes and unused footage from documentary productions are also held, but are generally unavailable for licensing.

Size & Elements: Film: format unspecified (hundreds of millions of feet). Videotape: format unspecified (hundreds of thousands of videotapes).

Cataloging: Newsfilm and videotape is cataloged in a card catalog (covering the period 1954-75) and by computerized database (1975-present). The card catalog, accessible to outside researchers, primarily indexes newsfilm (both aired stories and outtakes not broadcast) and is organized by subjects, personalities, locations and stock shots. FRIC (Film Retrieval and Inventory Control), the computer database, is not currently accessible to outside researchers, although Archives staff can perform searches and provide printouts for a fee. The database supports searches by subject, personality and location.

Various lists of documentary productions are maintained for staff use only; later documentary material is indexed on FRIC, though limitations on the sale of this material restrict these searches to reference use only. A research library is available for staff use only.

CBS Television News Broadcasts, a collection of microfilm transcripts of regular news programs, was compiled and published for the years 1975-86; it is no longer published. Regular broadcasts were also indexed in the *CBS News Index* covering the same period. Retrospective sets of these publications are available from University Microfilms International, 300 North Zeeb Road, Ann Arbor, MI 48106.

Transcripts of the current programs *60 Minutes* and *West 57th Street* are available from Journal Graphics, Inc., 267 Broadway, New York, NY 10007.
Access: Open to the public. Research fees charged. Research requests accepted by mail, telephone and in person (by appointment only). A letter of intent from the prospective user or researcher is required, specifying the material desired, how it is to be used and its intended distribution and format. Upon approval of the project by the Archives, a librarian will be assigned to research the subject or personality. Depending upon the results of this research, copies of catalog cards or computer printouts will be supplied. At that time, a viewing appointment may be made. It is suggested that research involving a great deal

of catalog or computer searching be performed directly at CBS News by the intended user or their representative. All material is for in-house use only; available for duplication, licensing and reuse, subject to restrictions.

Although Archives exists primarily to serve the internal needs of CBS and secondarily to license stock footage to outside producers on a fee-for-use basis, limited provisions can be made to accommodate academic and/or scholarly researchers who do not intend to purchase material for reuse. Research and screening fees are charged. It should be noted that many CBS News regular newscasts are available for reference at the National Archives and Records Administration (q.v.).
Rights: Full rights held to all material. Additional clearances may be necessary in some cases if material is to be reused.
Licensing: Available for licensing and reuse, subject to restrictions. License fees charged depending upon intended usage (apply for rate schedule).

Normal CBS News policy prohibits the sale and/or reuse of excerpts or clips from documentaries and news specials. Copies of some programs (*60 Minutes, 48 Hours, West 57th Street* and *CBS Reports*) may be purchased for educational or private use only from Holt, Rinehart & Winston in Austin, Texas (contact Debbie Wilcox at 512/440-5774).
Restrictions: Outtakes from interviews and any interviews featuring CBS correspondents are never licensed for outside use; occasionally, generic stock shots from documentaries may be approved for reuse and licensing upon written request. All other material is available for sale. *The voice and/or likeness of any CBS correspondent or reporter may not be used.* Clients are encouraged to avoid using closeups of recognizable individuals, and must indemnify and hold CBS News harmless from any claims, damages, liabilities, costs and expenses arising out of their reuse of footage.
Viewing Facilities: Film (16mm flatbeds); videotape (3/4").
Duplication Facilities: Film (16mm to 3/4" and 1/2" videotape); videotape (3/4" to 3/4" and 1/2" videotape). Film laboratory work and videotape duplication involving standards conversion is handled by outside facilities.

NEW YORK METRO

CEL EDUCATIONAL RESOURCES
(a division of CEL Communications, Inc.)
515 Madison Avenue
New York, NY 10022
(212) 421-4030
(800) 235-3339
Fax: (212) 752-2756

Contact: Lauren Snyder
Services: Producer and distributor of *The Video Encyclopedia of the 20th Century.* The *Encyclopedia* is available for purchase by libraries and educational institutions. Footage from the *Encyclopedia* is not available for licensing, reuse or resale.
Description: *The Video Encyclopedia of the 20th Century* consists of 75 hours of easy-to-access primary source material — the original sights and sounds of the past as recorded by motion picture and television news cameras. The basic set includes 75 one-hour 3/4", VHS or Betamax videotapes, or 38 laser videodiscs (CLV format), containing 2,217 individual historical units covering the years 1893-1965. Nothing stands between the student and the event or person on the screen because the *Video Encyclopedia* is unbiased and unencumbered by added commentary, music or sound effects.

The *Video Encyclopedia* is designed to illustrate and augment classroom lectures; bring textbooks to life; stimulate non-readers to read; encourage students to produce videotape term papers; use the daily index to develop an "on this day in history" lesson; use excerpts of famous speeches to illustrate communications skills and techniques; use individual units as subjects for debates, writing assignments, discussions and group projects; use as a resource library for in-school documentary filmmaking; use personalities and athletic events to provide inspiration; teach new research skills; create role models for non-motivated students; and to prove that history did not begin yesterday.

Examples of units included in the *Video Encyclopedia* are: Thomas Edison's turn-of-the-century film studio; the San Francisco earthquake (1906); the Russian Revolution; William Jennings Bryan and Clarence Darrow at the Scopes trial; the soup kitchens of the Depression years; the contributions of Helen Keller; Franklin Roosevelt's "Nothing to Fear" address; the rise and fall of Adolf Hitler; Japan's attack on Pearl Harbor; Mahatma Gandhi leading India to independence; Ralph Bunche negotiating the Middle East Armistice; the Army-McCarthy hearings; every 20th-century presidential campaign; Dr. Jonas Salk announcing the first polio vaccine; John Glenn orbiting the Earth; Dr. Martin Luther King, Jr., leading the march to Montgomery; Hank Aaron breaking Babe Ruth's home-run record; the Iranian hostage crisis; Sandra Day

O'Connor becoming the first woman Supreme Court Justice; and Gorbachev succeeding Chernenko in the Soviet Union.

Companion print material includes a User's Guide and Master Index, a comprehensive index system featuring both an Alphabetical Index listing people, subjects and categories, and a separate Daily Index listing the significant events for each day of the year. Also provided are four volumes of carefully researched printed background material on each of the 2,217 units, including detailed "shot lists" identifying the important people and places in each scene.

Annual updates and enrichment supplements will be issued periodically.

Size & Elements: Videotape: 3/4", VHS or Betamax (75 videotapes, each 60 min.). Videodisc: CLV format (38 laser videodiscs). (2,217 individual historical units total).

Cataloging: Indexes (see above).

Access: Preview videotapes available. Available for purchase (apply for information). Quantity discounts available.

Rights: Cable television, broadcast or ITFS broadcast rights are available by written permission only.

Licensing: Purchase price includes the right to copy individual units or segments of units within a videotape or videodisc for use within the purchasing institution only. Any other duplication or copying requires express written permission from CEL Educational Resources.

Restrictions: User-created programs, documentaries or video presentations containing material from the *Video Encyclopedia* can be broadcast or transmitted internally within the purchasing institution. Any other broadcast, transmission, distribution or sale is strictly prohibited without express written permission from CEL Educational Resources.

Viewing Facilities: None.

Duplication Facilities: None.

NEW YORK METRO

CENTER FOR BIOMEDICAL COMMUNICATIONS
COLLEGE OF PHYSICIANS AND SURGEONS
COLUMBIA UNIVERSITY
630 West 168th Street
New York, NY 10032
(212) 305-4101

Bob Demarest (Director, Center for Biomedical Communications)

Contact: Jeff Szmulewicz (Assistant Director)

Services: Educational institution; videotape producer. Material available for duplication, licensing and reuse, subject to restrictions.

Description: Contemporary color footage relating to biomedical topics. Includes operating rooms; open-heart surgery and other operations; hospitals, including nurses and doctors at work; and patients receiving tests and treatments of all kinds.

Size & Elements: Videotape: 3/4" ("several hundred hours of unedited footage").

Cataloging: Staff assistance required.

Access: Available to the public for duplication and reuse (depending on subject matter). Research fees not charged. Research requests accepted by mail, telephone and in person (by appointment only)

Rights: Full rights held to all material.

Licensing: Available for licensing, subject to restrictions. License fees charged.

Restrictions: Permission for reuse dependent on subject matter of footage requested.

Viewing Facilities: Videotape (3/4").

Duplication Facilities: Videotape (3/4", VHS and Betamax).

NEW YORK METRO

CENTER FOR CUBAN STUDIES
124 West 23rd Street
New York, NY 10011
(212) 242-0559

Sandra Levinson (Executive Director)

Contact: Irving Kessler (Distribution)

Services: Library; videotape distributor. Videotapes available for purchase.

Description: The Center for Cuban Studies opened in 1972 to bring to the U.S. public and to many educational and cultural institutions a wide range of Cuban resource material. Distributes Cuban-produced films and videotapes (1962-present).

Feature films (in Spanish with English subtitles). Titles include: *Death of a Bureaucrat* (Tomás Gutiérrez Alea, 1968); *A Girlfriend for David* (Orlando Rojas, 1985); *House for Swap* (Juan Carlos Tabio, 1984); *The Last Supper* (Tomás Gutiérrez Alea, 1976); *Lucia* (Humberto Solas, 1968); *Memories of Underdevelopment* (Tomás Gutiérrez Alea, 1968); *One Way or Another* (Sara Gómez, 1974); *Parting of the Ways* (Jesús Díaz, 1985); *Portrait of Teresa* (Pastor Vega, 1979); *Sometimes I Look at My Life* (Orlando Rojas, 1982); *A Successful Man* (Humberto Solas, 1986); *Tables Turned* (Rolando Díaz, 1984); *Underground* (Fernando Pérez, 1987); and *Wild Dogs* (Daniel Díaz Torres, 1985).

Feature films (in Spanish only). Titles include: *Aventures a de Juan Quin Quin* (Julio García Espinosa, 1967); *Habanera* (Pastor Vega, 1984); *El corazón sobre la tierra* (Constante Diego, 1985); *El hombre de Maisinicú* (Manuel Pérez, 1973); *Patakín* (Manuel Octavio Gómez, 1984); and *La primera carga al machéte* (Manuel Octavio Gómez, 1969).

Documentaries (in Spanish only). Includes five documentaries on Ernesto "Che" Guevara; *La guerra de la CIA contra Cuba* (1987, 6 hours of Cuban television), including interviews with many double agents; *La Habana te espera* (1986), on the tourist's Cuba, available in "macho" and "less macho" versions; four documentaries on the rumba and Cuban dances; documentaries on ballet; six documentaries on contemporary Cuban music; and *Fidel Castro: La impagable deuda externa de América Latina y el Tercer Mundo* (1985), with Castro's speech at the closing of the July 1985 Debt Conference in Havana.

Size & Elements: Videotape: 3/4" (masters); VHS and Betamax (viewing copies). (54 titles total).

Cataloging: Published catalog.

Access: Open to the public. Available for purchase. Research fees charged. Research requests accepted by telephone and in person (walk-in and by appointment).

Rights: Rights retained by original producers. Center can sometimes assist in arranging clearance for duplication and reuse of material.

Licensing: Not available for licensing or reuse.

Restrictions: Not available for licensing or reuse.

Viewing Facilities: Videotape (VHS and Betamax).

Duplication Facilities: Videotape (3/4", VHS and Betamax).

Related Materials: Books, magazines and newspapers; graphics and photographic archives; audiocassettes; slide shows.

Distributor: Many films distributed through New Yorker Films (q.v.) and The Cinema Guild (q.v.).

NEW YORK METRO

CENTER FOR HOLOCAUST STUDIES
1609 Avenue J
Brooklyn, NY 11230
(718) 338-6494
Fax: (718) 692-2168

Professor Yaffa Eliach (Founder and Director)

Contacts: Bonnie Gurewitsch (Librarian/Archivist); Gloria Waksman (Administrator)

Services: Documentation and research center. Films and videotapes available for rental. Material not available for duplication, licensing or reuse. Research requests considered on a case-by-case basis.

Description: Films and videotapes dealing with the Holocaust period, Jewish history and literature.

Sample titles include *Warsaw Ghetto* (Alexander Bernfes, 1966); *Night and Fog* (Alain Resnais, 1955); *K/Z Dachau Concentration Camp* (from U.S. Army footage); *Nightmare; Ambulance; The Holocaust; The Shtetl Kolbuszowa* (original footage, 1929); *To Bear Witness; Genocide; The Story of the Jews in Hungary;* and *The Jewish Community of Salonika.*

Size & Elements: Film: 16mm (approx. 7 titles; release prints). Videotape: VHS (14 titles; viewing copies).

Cataloging: Film list (available on request).

Access: Films and videotapes available for rental. Research requests considered on a case-by-case basis; research fees charged in some cases. No fees charged for on-premises research. Research requests accepted by mail, telephone and in person (by appointment only).

Rights: Some rights held to all material.

Licensing: Material not available for duplication, licensing or reuse.

Restrictions: Material available for rental only, not for purchase. Material not

available for duplication, licensing or reuse.
Viewing Facilities: None.
Duplication Facilities: None.
Related Materials: Slide shows (available for purchase).

NEW YORK METRO

THE CENTER FOR HUMANITIES, INC.
GUIDANCE ASSOCIATES
Communications Park
Box 1000
Mount Kisco, NY 10549-9989
(914) 666-4100
(800) 431-1242 (orders)
(800) 431-2266 (customer service)
Fax: (914) 666-0172

Contact: Maryann Valencourt
Services: Educational videotape producer and distributor. Materials available for purchase.
Description: Educational films for classroom use. Categories include: language skills, thinking skills, library skills, study skills, grammar skills, writing skills, reading skills, literature, criticism and analysis, American literature, English literature, mythology, communications and media, photography, history of art, social studies, history, government, humanities and values, science, physics, chemistry, physiology, biology, ecology, energy, earth science, astronomy, general science, computer literacy, mathematics, business mathematics, career skills, decision-making skills, drug prevention education, family life, sex education, psychology and human behavior, nutrition and fitness, first aid and safety, and the *Films-on-Video* programs.
Size & Elements: Videotape: 3/4", VHS and Betamax II (hundreds of titles).
Cataloging: Published catalogs.
Access: Available to the public for purchase.
Rights: Copyrights apply to all material.
Licensing: Apply for information.
Restrictions: None specified.
Viewing Facilities: None.
Duplication Facilities: None.

NEW YORK METRO

CENTER FOR NEW AMERICAN MEDIA
524 Broadway, 2nd Floor
New York, NY 10012-4408
(212) 925-5665

Andrew Kolker (President)

Contacts: Andrew Kolker; Louis Alvarez (Producer)
Services: Film and videotape producer. Material available for duplication, licensing and reuse, subject to restrictions.
Description: Videotape drawn primarily from two different productions:
American Tongues Collection. Material gathered for a PBS documentary on American speech. Includes footage of people speaking with each other in different parts of the country, upper-class to working-class speakers, from Boston to the West. Comprises conversations, interviews, and linguistic surveys. Shot in 1983, 1985 and 1986.
New Orleans Collection. Material on New Orleans speechways and culture. Conversation is highlighted, with some additional material on New Orleans cultural life (Mardi Gras, black street culture, music and food).
Size & Elements: Videotape: Betacam (250 videotapes); 3/4" (250 videotapes).
Cataloging: Shot lists available.
Access: Available for duplication and reuse. Research fees charged. Research requests accepted by mail, telephone and in person (by appointment only).
Rights: Full rights held to all material.
Licensing: Apply for information. License fees charged in some cases.
Restrictions: Requests for licensing and reuse subject to acceptance and approval.
Viewing Facilities: Videotape (3/4").
Duplication Facilities: Videotape (3/4" and VHS).

NEW YORK METRO

CHANNEL L WORKING GROUP
51 Chambers Street, Room 532
New York, NY 10007
(212) 964-2960

Susan Stone Shapiro (Executive Director)

Contact: Susan Stone Shapiro
Services: Cable television broadcaster; videotape producer. Collection available for research, rental, licensing and reuse, subject to restrictions.
Description: Holds over 1,500 archive videotapes (1978-present) in talk-show format, relating to issues of zoning, city planning, homeless, youth (jobs, education, special programs), women, discrimination (human rights), gentrification, small business, co-op ownership, tenants rights and environmental architecture. Although discussions relate to Manhattan issues, most apply nationally. Issues are discussed by community boards, City Council members, State Assembly members, State Senators and experts in particular fields.
Documentaries. Has produced mini-documentaries for many not-for-profit agencies, highlighting their community services in the fields of aging, community outreach, drug addiction and services for the handicapped.
Training videotapes. Visions, a videotape training volunteers to work with blind people. *UNITAS* and *Ties That Bind* relate to working with disadvantaged youth. *Correctional Association of New York* is a panel discussion, including videotape inserts of interviews with former inmates.
Arts programming. Museum Mile (1982); *Circle Repertory Theatre* (1982); *Cunningham Dance Foundation* (1982); *Art Across the Park* (1982); *Metropolitan Repertory Company.*
Architecture and city planning videotapes (produced with the Municipal Art Society). *The Upper West Side: Preserving its Past, Planning its Future* (1983); *The Future of 5th Avenue* (1984); *Adopt a Monument* (1987); *On Broadway* (1984); *Landmark Churches* (1985); *East River Gateway* (1985); *42nd Street: Keep It Alive* (1985); *A Better Way Than Westway* (1986); *The Coliseum Impact* (1987); *Municipal Arts Society 1987 Awards* (1987); *Upper West Side Historic District* (1988).
Also serves the independent video art community by airing videotapes which deal with social and political themes. *Video Spectrum* is a video exhibition series highlighting the works of award-winning and emerging artists involved in the visual arts, film, dance and theater. Copies of aired videotapes are retained by CLWG and available for duplication and purchase.
Size & Elements: Videotape: 3/4" and 1/2" (over 2,000 titles total).
Cataloging: Card catalog; numerical logging of videotapes.
Access: Open to researchers and scholars. Available for duplication, rental, licensing and reuse, subject to restrictions. Research requests accepted by mail and telephone.
Rights: Full rights held to some materials. Some rights held to other materials.
Licensing: Available for licensing and reuse, subject to restrictions. License fees charged.
Restrictions: Requests for licensing and reuse subject to clearance and approval.
Viewing Facilities: Videotape (3/4" and VHS); hourly fees charged.
Duplication Facilities: Videotape (3/4" and 1/2").
Publications: *Cutting Through,* bimonthly newsletter relating to activities of CLWG, including program and series schedules.

NEW YORK METRO

CHARISMA PRODUCTIONS, LTD./VISUAL MOTION
32 East 57th Street, 20th Floor
New York, NY 10022
(212) 832-3020

James Grau (President)

Contact: James Grau
Services: Film and videotape producer and distributor. Videotape material maintained primarily for distribution and rental; also available for licensing and reuse.
Description: Programs on the entertainment and music industries; cooking; sewing; situation comedies; teamwork; greatest moments in sports; and a variety of computer-generated special effects.
Entertainment series. Titles include: *The American Times* (26 episodes, each 30 min.), docudramas recreating the lives of entrepreneurial giants; *The Melting Pot* (130 programs, each 30 min.), cooking up ethnic foods with celebrity guest hosts and cooks; *Eat Yourself Healthy* (78 programs, each 30 min.), in which various panels of experts discuss questions about dietary habits and trends; *Sew What's New!* (78 programs, each 30 min.), colorful instruction

from an authority on pattern sewing; *The Fabulous Follies* (36 episodes, each 30 min.), a situation comedy set in a "big city nightclub," following the backstage lives of the performers; *Backstage on Broadway* (39 programs, each 30 min.), backstage interviews with actors, directors, costumers, composers, designers, writers and critics; and *Down Home USA* (52 episodes, each 30 min.), with performances from country, folk and bluegrass musicians.

Sports. Titles include: *Teamwork* (36 programs, each 30 min.), in which coaches and players discuss their working relationship, including film highlights from the career of each guest; *Of Sports & Man* (4 programs), a history and collection of greatest moments in hockey, tennis, soccer and polo; *World Cup Taekwondo '86* (41 programs), individual matches in all eight weight categories with competitors from 13 different countries; and *Sports Scrapbook* (78 episodes, each 30 min.), historic moments, memories and interviews with many great athletes.

Special effects. Computer-generated special effects by Visual Motion Corporation. Demonstration reel contains various special effects, including wave patterns; zodiac effects; the heavens with planets emerging from center screen; musical notes moving left to right; tunnel effects; snowflakes; oak leaves falling; atom nucleus; robot face; human eye; sky with pulsating sunbeams emanating from sun; starfields and starbursts; leaves; rain ripples; fog; earth globes; meteorites; nebular swirl; abstract effects and textures; searchlight beams at a movie opening; explosions; rain ripples; horse profiles; sunsets; winter scenes; eagle in flight; wireframe Christmas tree with star at top; and dancing neon palm trees. Also available are a variety of sports-related effects, including spinning hockey sticks, ice sprays, shots of hockey pucks, helmets, skates, backgrounds; animated boxers and tennis players.
Size & Elements: Videotape: all formats (amount unspecified).
Cataloging: Release sheets and shot lists.
Access: Available for distribution, licensing and reuse. Research requests not accepted; rental and purchase requests accepted by mail and telephone.
Rights: Some rights held to all material. Additional clearances may be necessary in some cases if material is to be reused.
Licensing: Available for licensing and reuse, subject to restrictions. License fees charged.
Restrictions: Apply for information.
Viewing Facilities: None.
Duplication Facilities: Videotape.

NEW YORK METRO

CHERTOK ASSOCIATES INC.
185 West End Avenue, Suite 8F
New York, NY 10023
(212) 874-0797

Michael Chertok (Vice President)

Contact: Michael Chertok
Services: Film and videotape stock footage sales library. Open to researchers and scholars only.
Description: Jazz (1929-present). Includes all of the great jazz figures ever filmed, including Louis Armstrong, Count Basie, Nat King Cole, John Coltrane, Miles Davis, Duke Ellington, Ella Fitzgerald, Dizzy Gillespie, Benny Goodman, Lionel Hampton, Coleman Hawkins, Billie Holliday, Charlie Parker, Art Tatum, Sarah Vaughan, Fats Waller and many more. Performers include big bands, small groups, soloists and vocalists. Collection also includes pop music artists, rhythm and blues, tap dance, rock and roll and blues musicians.

Material originates in the form of feature films (U.S. and foreign), television (U.S. and foreign, especially early programs), Soundies, newsreels, film shorts, private archives, kinescopes, etc.

Owners, in addition to providing stock footage, are also available for lectures and presentations.
Size & Elements: Film: 16mm (approx. 600 hours; mostly black and white composite prints, some negatives, separate optical and magnetic tracks). Videotape: 3/4" and VHS (approx. 400 hours).
Cataloging: Computerized cataloging for staff use only.
Access: Not open to the public. Open to researchers and scholars only. Available for licensing and reuse. Research fees charged in some cases (if extensive screening involved); refundable in case of purchase. Research requests accepted by mail, telephone and in person (by appointment only).
Rights: Some material in the public domain. Rights status of some material not known. Additional clearances may be necessary in some cases if material is to be reused.
Licensing: Available for licensing and reuse. License and usage fees charged

(apply for information).
Restrictions: None specified.
Viewing Facilities: Film and videotape.
Duplication Facilities: Videotape (3/4" and 1/2" viewing copies can be made for editing purposes).

NEW YORK METRO

CHILDREN'S TELEVISION WORKSHOP
One Lincoln Plaza
New York, NY 10023
(212) 595-3456
Fax: (212) 580-3845
RCA Telex: 236168

Gail Y. Miyasaki (Director, Corporate Relations)

Contact: Gail Y. Miyasaki
Services: Educational television producer. Material primarily available to schools for instructional and educational purposes. Can provide videotape clips of programs to other parties on a case-by-case basis, subject to restrictions.
Description: Has produced the following program series: *Sesame Street* (1969-present); *The Electric Company* (1970-present); *3-2-1 Contact* (1980-present); and *Square One TV* (1986-present).
Size & Elements: Format and amount unspecified.
Cataloging: Release sheets. CTW prepares television listings as part of promoting initial PBS broadcasts. Cataloging information and storylines are not furnished to outside entities.
Access: Not open to the public. For in-house use only. Available for licensing and reuse, subject to restrictions. Research fees not charged. Research requests accepted by mail and telephone.
Rights: Full rights held to all material. Additional clearances may be necessary in some cases if material is to be reused.
Licensing: "[W]e do not actively solicit ancillary use of our materials. For instructional and research use, we grant liberal three-year tape and erase rights for in-school use of our current broadcast materials." License fees charged.
Restrictions: Videotape clips are provided to outside qualified producers on a case-by-case basis. Only completed programs or entire segments of programs (not outtakes) are made available. Provision of clips to outside users is subject to script review, legal review and any necessary third-party clearances (e.g., talent releases).
Viewing Facilities: None.
Duplication Facilities: None.

NEW YORK METRO

CHRISTOPHER CLOSEUP
12 East 48th Street
New York, NY 10017
(212) 759-4050
Fax: (212) 838-5073

Rev. John T. Catoir (Director, The Christophers, Inc.)

Contact: Alma Stark (Distribution Manager)
Services: Catholic media organization; television producer. Program library available for distribution, licensing and reuse, subject to approval.
Description: The Christophers, Inc., a Catholic media organization, has produced *Christopher Closeup*, a weekly television program (1951-present).

Many Hollywood stars appeared in early broadcasts of this nationally syndicated program. Jack Benny, William Holden, Loretta Young, Bob Hope and Irene Dunne all starred in the very first Christopher film, *You Can Change the World*. More recent guests have included Doug Henning, Polly Holliday, Jane Alexander, Arlo Guthrie, and Steve Allen. Programs vary widely, ranging from performances by noted jazz pianist Dave Brubeck, to conversations with broadcaster Hugh Downs, to a moving account by a survivor of Hitler's death camps. The focus is always on the person stressing the Christopher motto: "It is better to light one candle than curse the darkness."
Size & Elements: Film: 35mm and 16mm (original materials); 16mm (release prints for screening). Videotape: 2", 1", 3/4" and VHS (masters); 3/4" and 1/2" (screening copies). (2,500 program segments total, each 1, 14, or 28 min.).
Cataloging: Card catalogs; dope sheets; release sheets; staff assistance.
Access: Series is primarily intended for distribution to television stations and cable systems. However, the series is available for research by scholars and students, and sold to individuals in videotape format (VHS). Available for

licensing and reuse. Research requests accepted by mail.
Rights: Full rights held to all material.
Licensing: Permission to screen, broadcast or reuse material must be obtained from The Christophers, Inc. License or usage fees not charged.
Restrictions: None specified.
Viewing Facilities: Film (16mm); videotape (3/4" and VHS).
Duplication Facilities: None.

NEW YORK METRO

CINECOM ENTERTAINMENT GROUP
1250 Broadway
New York, NY 10001
(212) 239-8360
Fax: (212) 947-7095

Contact: Staff
Services: Distributor. Films available for distribution. Videotapes available for public performance, classroom use and lease.
Description: Independent feature films and short subjects.
Titles include: *Swimming To Cambodia* (Jonathan Demme, 1987); *Metropolis* (Fritz Lang, 1926); *Native Son* (Jerry Freedman, 1987); *The Brother From Another Planet* (John Sayles, 1984); *Matewan* (John Sayles, 1987); *Return of The Secaucus 7* (John Sayles, 1980); *El Norte* (Gregory Nava, 1983); *Latino* (Haskell Wexler, 1985); *Salvador* (Oliver Stone, 1986); *Sammy and Rosie Get Laid* (Stephen Frears, 1987); *A Room With A View* (James Ivory, 1986); *Winter Flight* (Roy Battersby); *Forever Young* (David Drury); *The Revolt of Job* (Imre Gyongyossy and Barna Kabay, 1984); and *Starstruck* (Gillian Armstrong, 1982). Also distributes *The Times of Harvey Milk* (Robert Epstein, 1984), a documentary about the San Francisco gay rights activist and political leader who was assassinated in office; *Secret Honor* (Robert Altman, 1984), a dynamic and often scathing mythical portrait of former President Richard Nixon during his last days in the White House; and *Burroughs* (Howard Brookner, 1984), an intimate and revealing look at the highly controversial man often called the literary dean of the American avant-garde and the "father of Beat."
Size & Elements: Film: 35mm and 16mm (37 titles total). Videotape: VHS.
Cataloging: Published catalog.
Access: Films available for distribution. Videotapes available for public performance, classroom use and lease. Requests accepted by mail and telephone.
Rights: All films available for distribution exclusively from Cinecom.
Licensing: Apply for information.
Restrictions: Videotaping or copying a film by any other means is prohibited by law.
Viewing Facilities: None.
Duplication Facilities: None.
Related Materials: Trailers are available for some films for a nominal fee.

NEW YORK METRO

CINEMA ARTS ASSOCIATES
333 West 52nd Street
New York, NY 10019
(212) 246-2860
(212) 246-2865

Hans Dudelheim (President)

Contact: Hans Dudelheim
Services: Film and videotape producer; editorial house. Material available for duplication, licensing and reuse.
Description: Contemporary color footage of wildlife, including seals, birds and squirrels; aerial landscapes of New York City, Washington, D.C. and other East Coast cities; feature films (black and white); Hollywood short subjects and trailers (1930s-40s); historic "newsreel type" footage including Presidents Roosevelt, Kennedy and Johnson; action and people shots including roller-skating, jogging, Wall Street, crowds and various locations along the East Coast. Other varied footage is available, including cities, dripping water and an exploding clock.
Size & Elements: Film: 16mm (20,000 to 30,000 feet; originals, negative and positive). Videotape: 1" and 3/4" (4-5 hours; masters).
Cataloging: Staff assistance required.
Access: Available to the public for duplication and reuse. Research fees charged (fees negotiable). Research requests accepted by mail and telephone.

Rights: Full rights held to all material.
Licensing: Available for licensing. License fees charged.
Restrictions: None specified.
Viewing Facilities: Film (16mm); videotape (3/4").
Duplication Facilities: Film (film to videotape); videotape (any format).

NEW YORK METRO

THE CINEMA GUILD
1697 Broadway, Room 802
New York, NY 10019
(212) 246-5522
Fax: (212) 246-5525
Telex: 238790 NYK

Philip S. Hobel (President)

Contact: Gary Crowdus (General Manager)
Services: Film and videotape distributor. Material available for rental.
Description: Documentaries, dramas and docudramas; particularly strong in social issue documentaries. Some films in foreign languages with English subtitles. Topics include:
Anthropology. Titles include: *The Primal Mind* (1984), narrated by Jamake Highwater from his book *The Primal Mind: Vision and Reality in Indian America,* explores the basic differences between Native American and Western culture. *The Probable Passing of Elk Creek* (1983) focuses on the controversy between the town of Elk Creek, California (pop. 400) and the Grindstone Indian Reservation. *Mosquitoes and High Water* (1983) examines the history and culture of Spanish-speaking Islenos of St. Bernard Parish, Louisiana whose ancestors came over 200 years ago from the Canary Islands. *Man of Leather* (1979) depicts the life of the Brazilian cowboys. *The Witchy Weed* (1970) traces the development of the tobacco industry in Brazil. *The Brick-Makers* (1972) documents poverty in Latin America. *The Flour Mill* (1970) documents the transformation of the Brazilian manioc plant into flour. *Peruvian Weaving: A Continuous Warp for 5,000 Years* (1980) shows Andean Indian weaving in Peru, with archival footage of Dr. Junius Bird's archaeological excavation (1946). *Vision of Juazeiro* (1970) is about the transformation of the Brazilian small town of Jazeiro de Norte into a religious shrine, showing the pilgrimage as a religious experience for some and an economic and political opportunity for others. *The Sugar Mill* (1970) documents traditional sugar production in Brazil.
Arts. I Promise to Remember: The Story of Frankie Lymon and the Teenagers (1983) chronicles the meteoric success and catastrophic fall from grace of one of the first black rock and roll groups to cross the color barrier. *St. Louis Blues* (1929) contains Bessie Smith's only screen appearance. *Creation of the World: A Samba-Opera* (1978) documents the Carnival in Rio with performance by the Beija Flor Samba School; lithography and identification of original prints. *The High Lonesome Sound* (1962) documents Appalachian music in Kentucky. *Musical Holdouts* (1976) is about the music of communities who have resisted becoming part of America's melting pot, from the Carolina Sea Islands to Appalachia to Cheyenne and Comanche Indians. *Post Industrial Fiddle* (1982) examines Gerry Down's Down East style of fiddling. *Sara and Maybelle* (1981) is about the Carter family, whose recordings helped found the country music industry. The dance films of J Marks-Highwater (1962-74) include *Fire Sermon* (1965), *Kama Sutras* (1965), *Oracle of the Branch* (1965), *The Dance* (1960), *Choreography* (1964), *Art and the Technique of the Ballet* (1967), *Ballet in Jazz* (1962) and *Plasmasis* (1974). Other titles include: *It's a Rock and Roll World* (1976); *The Complete Pierre Cardin* (1970); *Mountain Music of Peru* (1984); *The Ballad and The Source* (1983); *The Music Films of John Cohen* (from 1958-79); *Fifty Miles From Time Square* (1972).
Biology. Titles include: *Learning To Live With Stress* (1973); *The Brain* (1970); *Genetics: Man The Creator* (1970); *Evolution by DNA* (1970); *Sociobiology* (1970); *Aging* (1970); *Longevity* (1973); *Medicine: Living to Be 100* (1970); *To Make Man Immune from Disease* (1970); *To Make Man Into Superman* (1970); *Biofeedback* (1970); and *To Discover Our Body's Clocks* (1973).
Black studies. Titles include: *Cimarrrones* (1983), about runaway African slaves in Latin America. *Angola: A Victory of Hope* (1976) traces the history of Angola from "discovery" to independence in 1976. *A Minor Altercation* (1976) investigates the racial conflicts in our public schools. *Iawo* (1978) examines the Cult of the Orisha brought to the New World by African slaves and still practiced today. *Finally Got The News* (1970) documents the League of Revolutionary Black Workers and their efforts to build an independent black labor union in the automobile industry. *You Hide Me* examines the cultural

aggression of European colonial regimes in Africa, revealing rarely seen works of African art stored in the basement of the British museum in London. *No Vietnamese Ever Called Me Nigger* (1967) discusses racism in the U.S. and abroad, interviewing black Vietnam veterans about racism on the battlefield.

Business. Human Resources and Organizational Behavior (1978) is a 13-part series examining important issues in the behavioral sciences with emphasis on management techniques, including an episode documenting the economic turnaround of Jamestown, New York. Other topics include operating a small, self-managed business and an interview with John Kenneth Galbraith.

Chicano studies. Yo Soy Chicano (1972) portrays the Chicano experience from its roots in 14th century Aztec civilization and the arrival of Cortez to the present. *Homeboys* (1978) is a more intimate look at the *vatos* (gang members) of the Cuatro flats in East Los Angeles, showing gang warfare, graffiti, low-riding, low wages and police harassment.

Conservation and environmental studies. Titles include: *The Four Seasons* (1970); *Organic Farming* (1970); *Food: Surviving The Chemical Feast* (1970); *To Save The Amazon's Green Hell* (1973); *To Defeat The Doomsday Doctrine* (1970); *The Cost of Cotton* (1979); *Air Pollution* (1970); *Water: The Effluent Society* (1970); *Waste: The Recycling World* (1970); *Sound/Noise* (1970); and *Earth: No Vacancy* (1970).

Criminal justice. Titles include: *Rape/Crisis* (1982); *Doing Justice* (1984); *Criminology* (1970); *Presumed Innocent* (1979); *Penology* (1970); *Doin' Life* (1980); *The Grand Jury* (1979); *To Humanize Our Police* (1970); *License To Kill* (1984); *Frame-up!: The Imprisonment of Martin Sostre* (1974). *Voices From Within* (1977) was written and acted by The Long-Termers Committee, a group of women serving sentences of four years to life at Bedford Hills Correctional Facility in New York; the film dramatizes the loneliness and desperation of long-term prisoners who are denied benefits enjoyed by short-term prisoners.

Economics. Five Billion People (1979-80), a 13-part series, explores the social and political implications of different economic issues. Series titles include: *A Golden Opportunity; The Organizations; The Gears; Unfair Exchange; The Conspiracy; To Work!; The New Order; The Dispossessed; and Who Helps Who?* Other films include *On The Line* (1977), relating to poverty in America and contemporary problems of the American economy.

Film, photography and media studies. Communications: The Wired World (1970) interviews Marshall McLuhan, Bell Laboratories scientists and communications experts regarding new communications technologies. *Six O'Clock and All's Well* (1980) is a behind-the-scenes look at a nightly news show. *Media: The Massaging The Mind* (1970) explores communications technology and the mass media. *America and Lewis Hine* (1984) is a portrait of America's pioneer social photographer. *Conversations with Willard Van Dyke* (1981) is a portrait of the filmmaker and photographer, with rare footage of Edward Weston. *John Hoagland: Frontline Photographer* (1985) examines the life and work of a leading photojournalist, killed in 1984 by a U.S.-made bullet in El Salvador. *Lyman H. Howe's High Class Moving Pictures* (1983) examines the life and career of the traveling motion picture exhibitor (1880-1920) who introduced rural America to the motion picture. *For the First Time* (1967) shows a film screening in the Cuban mountains, where peasants see movies for the first time.

Health. Titles include: *The Cancer War* (1983); *Cancer: The Wayward Cell* (1970); *Consumerism in Medicine* (1970); *Medical Careers* (1978); *Hard Drugs* (1976); *A Fat-Free Society* (1973); *Nutrition* (1975); *Smoking* (1975); *Acne* (1975); and *Alcoholism* (1975). Filmed in New York City's Lower East Side, *Skezag* (1970) is a particularly powerful and harsh portrait of a drug addict and hustler; in an epilogue filmed months later, the effects of the drugs are evident.

History. Roosevelt, New Jersey: Visions of Utopia (1983) is about a Jewish cooperative community established during the Depression. *Witness to the Holocaust* (1983-84, 7 parts) interviews survivors and uses archival materials to document the rise of the Nazis, ghetto life, deportations, resistance, the final solution, and the liberation of the concentration camps. *The Story of Chaim Rumkowski* documents how the Chairman of the Lodz Jewish Council organized and administered social services to the Lodz ghetto under the Nazi occupation of Poland, his illusory triumphs and the ultimate destruction of the ghetto and its people. *Before Stonewall: The Making of a Gay and Lesbian Community* (1984) documents the history of gays and lesbians in the United States before 1969. *San Francisco Good Times* (1973), shot between 1968 and 1972, provides a portrait of the lifestyle and culture of the era, including interviews with Timothy Leary, Bill Graham, Pete Townshend and the Black Panthers. *Last Summer Won't Happen* (1968) documents a group of activists on New York City's Lower East Side. *The History Book* (1974) is a series of nine animated films on Western civilization from the Middle Ages to the present day. *Crossroads of Civilization* (1978) explores Middle Eastern history and culture from Cyrus the Great to the present day. *Pompeii, A.D.79* (1979) recalls the volcanic eruption of Mount Vesuvius.

Labor studies. Brass Valley, a three-part series, covers the rise and fall of the brass producers in Connecticut's Naugatuck Valley; European immigration and development of an urban working class in late 19th century Brazil; closing of steel plants in Youngstown, Ohio (1976-80); assembly line production; how the computer will change the meaning of work; the U.S. garment industry; American working class consciousness; the plight of undocumented Mexican workers and the employers who are dependent upon them; and labor unions.

Latin American studies. Particular strengths: Haiti, El Salvador, Nicaragua, Chile and Mexican Revolution. *Bitter Cane* (1983), filmed clandestinely in Haiti, documents the history and culture of the Caribbean's oldest nation. *El Salvador: The People will Win* is the first documentary produced by the Film Institute of Revolutionary El Salvador, telling of 500 years of struggle against colonial invasions and providing an extensive look at the one-third of El Salvador that is controlled by the FMLN. *Bay of Pigs,* produced by the Cuban Film Institute, reconstructs the American invasion using actual documentary footage; *Grenada: The Future is Coming Toward Us* is a history of Grenada and Maurice Bishop's New Jewel Movement, completed just months prior to the U.S. invasion in Fall 1983. *Last of the Karaphuna* is the first filmed record of the Carib Indians. *Avenue of the Americas* focuses on the 1973 coup which overthrew Salvador Allende's Popular Unity government, with dramatic footage of the coup, including the aerial bombing of the Moneda Palace and the bloody aftermath. Other films relate to Colombia; Tupamaros; Mexican Revolution; Indian and peasant life in Argentina; Brazilian economic crisis; people of the Amazon basin; and ecology and industrial development projects.

Native American studies. Films on the Q'eros Indians of Peru; Shuar Indians; Yecuana Chaman of the Amazon; and the struggles of the Shoshone Indians of Nevada. *Noel Nutels* documents the life of a Jewish immigrant physician who dedicated himself to the health of the Indians in the Brazilian jungles, with footage shot by Nutels and rare footage of the Kwarip ritual. *Crow Dog* portrays Sioux medicine man Leonard Crow Dog, spiritual leader of 89 American Indian tribes. *The Native Americans* is a ten-part series covering the complete history of the North American Indian.

Physical science. Films on Albert A. Michelson; superconductors; fusion; robotics; space; weather; Albert Szent-Gyorgyi; energy; technology; computers; solar energy and tidal power; earthquakes and oceans. *The Physicists* covers some of the major issues, personalities and facilities in contemporary physics.

Political science. Kennedys Don't Cry is a history of the family's power and tragedies. Other films concern political activism in the 1960s; the Cold War and the Army-McCarthy hearings; Allard K. Lowenstein; the Jewish anarchist movement and a history of anarchism in America. *Red Squad* documents the New York City Police Department's Bureau of Special Services and their intelligence-gathering activities; *The Mercenary Game* documents the role of mercenaries in international politics, including interviews and profiles; and *The Ends of the Earth: Plaquemines Parish, Louisiana* documents the control exercised by the Perez family in that region.

Psychology. An overview of new concepts and treatments in the field of mental health; primal therapy; the Human Potential Movement; *I'm OK, You're OK* (from the book); behavior modification; post-Vietnam syndrome and the plight of the Vietnam veteran; depression and suicide; meditation; psychokinesis; and E.S.P. *Breaking the Silence: The Generation after the Holocaust* discusses the unique problems between the children of Holocaust victims and their parents.

Puerto Rican studies. Manos a la Obra: The Story of Operation Bootstrap chronicles the economic development plan of Puerto Rico undertaken in the 1950s and where it stands today, including archival photos and footage. Other films concern New York's Puerto Rican communities; Puerto Rico's relationship to the U.S.; its economy and culture.

Sex education. Some films are directed at young adults beginning to deal with sexuality. Topics include the social construction of sexuality; homosexuality and lesbianism; and interviews with Masters and Johnson.

Social studies. Child abuse; violence; urban crime; U.S. immigration policy (1983); *Time of the Locust,* a compilation film (1968) about the Vietnam War, with suppressed footage shot by Japanese television; animal rights; Palau, the Micronesian republic which has adopted the first nuclear-free constitution; anti-nuclear movement; arms race; the military budget; "Star Wars" defense program; interview with Alvin Toffler; intellectual think tanks; geopolitics; privacy; and consumerism.

Urban studies. Los Sures chronicles the plight of the residents of one of New York City's poorest Hispanic neighborhoods, Williamsburg, Brooklyn. *Squatters: The Other Philadelphia Story* shows urban squatters and the national Tent City in Washington, D.C. Other films concern gentrification in Park Slope, Brooklyn; skyscrapers; Paolo Soleri's concept of arcology; mass transit; mobility; New York City's garbage crisis; New York's Lower East Side

Tenants' Associations and residents; and political turmoil in the 1960s.

Women's studies. Films on abortion; *La Operacion,* documenting Puerto Rico as the country with the highest incidence of female sterilization in the world; post-hysterectomy syndrome; women's roles; the family; history of women in the U.S.; and working women in Latin America. *The Plan* documents the life of Michele Meservy, voted Utah's "Young Mother of the Year" in 1978 as she raises five children under the age of 5. *With Babies and Banners: The Story of the Women's Emergency Brigade* shows women's participation in the General Motors sit-down strike of 1937, with archival footage.
Size & Elements: Film: 16mm (400 titles). Videotape: 3/4", VHS, Betamax I and II (most titles).
Cataloging: Published catalogs.
Access: Maintained for distribution and rental rather than for research or reuse. Requests accepted by mail and by telephone with written confirmation.
Rights: Some rights held to all material.
Licensing: Apply for information. License fees charged.
Restrictions: All material is covered by U.S. Copyright Act and may not be copied, transformed, broadcast or commercially exhibited or subdistributed without the express written permission of the Guild.
Viewing Facilities: None.
Duplication Facilities: None.

NEW YORK METRO

CINEMA VERITÉ INTERNATIONAL, INC.
444 East 86th Street, Suite 21-J
New York, NY 10028
(212) 628-0226

Dr. Mildred Pollner (President)

Contact: Dr. Mildred Pollner
Services: Videotape producer and distributor. Material available primarily for purchase.
Description: Educational programs emphasizing women's issues, gender roles, and alternative lifestyles. Titles include *Sexuality in Advertising; Tomboys are Great!; Single Parent; You Can Be; Act Like a Man; Women Leaders;* and *Sari Dienes: 87 Years Young* (all videotapes were produced in 1986-87).
Size & Elements: Videotape: format unspecified (approx. 7 titles; each 15 to 30 min.).
Cataloging: Brochure available.
Access: Videotapes available for purchase.
Rights: Full rights held to all material.
Licensing: Apply for information. License fees charged.
Restrictions: None specified.
Viewing Facilities: None.
Duplication Facilities: None.

NEW YORK METRO

CITY UNIVERSITY OF NEW YORK
THE CITY COLLEGE ARCHIVES
THE LIBRARY
North Academic Center
Convent Avenue at 137th Street
New York, NY 10031
(212) 690-5367

Ann K. Randall (Chief Librarian)

Contact: Barbara J. Dunlap (Chief, Archives and Special Collections)
Services: University archives. Holds small film collection.
Description: Historical films relating to City College, including *Charter Day* (1925, 35mm); *Foremost Institutions of Higher Learning: City College* (Pathé News Service, 1926, Pathécolour); and the Art Department's *Demonstration of Drawing and Painting by Aba Vilmos Novak, Hungarian Painter,* filmed in the art class of Professor George Eggers (1939, 16mm).
Size & Elements: Film: 35mm and 16mm (3 titles).
Cataloging: List available.
Access: Apply for information at library.
Rights: Material in the public domain. Rights status of Pathé film not known.
Licensing: Apply for information. License fees not charged.
Restrictions: None specified.
Viewing Facilities: Film and videotape (in audiovisual division).

Duplication Facilities: None.

NEW YORK METRO

CLIO AWARDS
336 East 59th Street
New York, NY 10022
(212) 593-1900
Fax: (212) 754-0581
Telex: 62549
Cable: CLIOFEST

Michael Demetriades (Senior Vice President/International)

Contact: Michelle LaForey
Services: Library. Films available for rental and lease for educational purposes only; not available for reproduction.
Description: Award-winning television commercials. Awards have recognized creative excellence in advertising since 1959. Library retains 16mm reels of the annual CLIO winners (1960-present). Ranging from 30-45 min., these reels represent a special selection of each year's U.S. and international winners.
Size & Elements: Film: 16mm (one program per year, 1960-present; release prints).
Cataloging: None specified.
Access: Available for rental. Winners' reels (1980-present) available for lease. Rental requests accepted by mail; telephone orders not accepted.
Rights: Rights retained by advertisers and agencies.
Licensing: Rights retained by advertisers and agencies; requests for potential reuse must be negotiated with them.
Restrictions: "The CLIO Awards have obtained clearance from the advertisers and their agencies for this material to be used only for educational purposes with the intent of furthering the exchange of ideas in communications and advertising techniques. CLIO does not grant the rights for the use of this material for any part of a commercial or profit-making venture. They may not be reproduced, broadcasted, published, or shown on television, or as any part of any program inconsistent with the goals of the CLIO Awards. Furthermore, CLIO retains the right to repossess all material in the event of their misuse."
Viewing Facilities: None.
Duplication Facilities: None.

NEW YORK METRO

COE FILM ASSOCIATES, INC.
65 East 96th Street
New York, NY 10128
(212) 831-5355
Fax: (212) 996-6728

Bernice Coe (President)

Contact: Arlene Gross
Services: Distributor of short films and documentaries to television markets; stock footage available for television use only.
Description: Program categories include: abstract, Academy Award winners, adventure, aging, animals, animation, anthropology, archaeology, architecture, art, arts and crafts, biography, Black studies, careers, children's programs (animated, nonverbal and live), children's books, controversial issues (for adults and children), consumer, dance, discussion, documentary, dramatic, ecology and environment, essays, fairy tales, family, features, film and television, French, guidance, handicapped, health, history, holidays, how-to and training, humor, language, late night, legends, lifestyles, literature, management, mathematics, minorities, music, nature, nothing, old-time, performing arts, poetry, politics, psychology, religion, safety, science, science fiction, series, shorts collections, short stories, social studies, Spanish, spectacular footage, sports, teacher education, teenage, travel, U.S. geography and women.

The Shorts Collection. Over 2,000 shorts for use in family viewing hours, many of them Academy Award winners.

The Children's Package. More than 4,000 titles covering a wide variety of subjects appealing to all age levels (story films, live and animated, how-to, nature and science).

Children's specials. Titles include: *My Lady of Milk and Wafers; Voyage of the Courageous; The Strongest Man; The Magic Treasure; Voyage of the Barba Negra; Fish; L.A. Above & Below; The Sorcerer's Apprentice; Little Friend; Tuck Everlasting.*

Christmas films. Titles include: *The Great Toy Robbery; The Bear's Christmas; Tomorrow is New Year's; Ziggy's Gift.*

Dramatic short stories. Based on original plots or famous short stories, including: *The Cafeteria; Blind Date; The Horse Dealer's Daughter; The Silver Crown.*

Educational. Over 50 series including: *19th Century Literary Biography; American History; Family Life Around the World; Black Studies; Fairy Tales; Basic Grammar; Exploring Math.*

Features and dramas. Titles include: *The Sand Castle; Nuda di Dona*a; *Bellissima; Nose Job; Unfinished Business.*

The Nature Package. Titles include: *Cry of the Condor; The Harp Seal; Living with Reindeer; Project Puffin.*

Performing arts specials. Titles include: *The Baroque Invention; Homage to Verdi; Paul Horn in China; It's All Jazz; The Making of a Ballet; Les Ballets Trockadero de Monte Carlo.*

Sci-fi stories (macabre moments). Titles include: *Panic; The Contraption; Cry Wolf.*

Specials. Titles include: *Before the Nickelodeon; Otto: Zoo Gorilla; Leopards of Kora; In the Beginning God Created the Swimsuit; Before Mickey Mouse; Vincent Van Gogh; Devil at Your Heels; Ape and Super Ape.*

Sports specials. Over 50 titles including: *The Contender; Psychling; Escape Under Sail.*
Size & Elements: Film: 16mm. Videotape: 1" (masters); 3/4" (preview videotapes).
Cataloging: Various cataloging resources available.
Access: Open to the public. Research requests accepted by mail and telephone. Research fees charged depending on complexity of requirements.
Rights: Television rights held to all materials.
Licensing: Granted for television use only. License fees charged on a per-job basis, depending on market of finished production and footage used.
Restrictions: None specified.
Viewing Facilities: None.
Duplication Facilities: None.

NEW YORK METRO

COLUMBIA UNIVERSITY
TEACHERS COLLEGE
MILBANK MEMORIAL LIBRARY
RESOURCE CENTER
New York, NY 10027
(212) 678-3033

Contact: Jane Franck (Director)
Services: Library. Film and videotape collection available to researchers and scholars for in-house use only.
Description: *The Black Heritage Film Collection.* An award-winning television series entitled *Black Heritage: A History of the Afro Americans* (100 programs, 16mm, each 30 min., black and white). Series aired on CBS (summer 1969) and was later donated by the network to the Library. Programs are arranged by subject matter (e.g., slave trading, Africa, various lectures) and historical time period.

Educational films. Collection covers general subjects, including psychology and educational training films for teachers (685 films, 16mm).
Size & Elements: Film: 16mm (785 films; positive). Videotape: 3/4" and VHS (approx. 180-200 videotapes; viewing copies).
Cataloging: Card catalogs. The *Black Heritage* collection is arranged by subject matter and historical time period.
Access: Open to researchers and scholars. For in-house use only. The *Black Heritage* collection is available for use at no charge (except for a small deposit and shipping charges) on a 48-hour loan basis. Research fees charged. Research requests accepted in person (by appointment only).
Rights: Some rights held to some material.
Licensing: Not available for licensing or reuse.
Restrictions: For internal use only.
Viewing Facilities: Film and videotape (for internal use only).
Duplication Facilities: For internal use only.

NEW YORK METRO

COMMUNIST PARTY USA
VIDEO DEPARTMENT
235 West 23rd Street, 5th Floor
New York, NY 10011
(212) 989-4994

Gus Hall (National Chairman)

Contact: Pamela Mincey (Director of Video Productions)
Services: Political organization. Videotape and film material available for research, licensing and reuse, subject to clearance and approval.
Description: Communist Party activities, conventions and leaders. Includes videotape footage of Party conventions (1983-87); Gus Hall, Henry Winston and Angela Davis; some topical footage of demonstrations and strikes; and some independent productions. There is historical film material on similar subjects (1960s-70s); some of this material has soundtracks in various languages.
Size & Elements: Film: 16mm (amount unspecified; release prints, some with separate soundtracks). Videotape: 3/4" and VHS (approx. 250 videotapes; edited and unedited).
Cataloging: Computerized cataloging for staff use only; other finding aids.
Access: Not open to the public. Available for duplication and reuse. Research requests accepted by mail; follow-up telephone call and appointment are required.
Rights: Full rights held to some material.
Licensing: Available for licensing and reuse, subject to restrictions. License fees charged in some cases.
Restrictions: Requests for licensing and reuse subject to acceptance and approval.
Viewing Facilities: Videotape (3/4" and VHS) (by appointment only).
Duplication Facilities: Videotape (3/4" and VHS).

NEW YORK METRO

CONSULATE GENERAL OF JAPAN
299 Park Avenue
New York, NY 10171
(212) 371-8222
Fax: (212) 751-8344

Masamichi Hanabusa (Consulate General/Ambassador)

Contact: Wajima (Archives Director) (Ext. 457)
Services: Japanese government agency. Holds videotape collection.
Description: Promotional videotapes relating to Japan (all videotapes produced in Japan).
Size & Elements: Videotape: format unspecified (over 50 items).
Cataloging: Apply for information.
Access: Apply for information.
Rights: Apply for information.
Licensing: Apply for information.
Restrictions: None specified.
Viewing Facilities: None.
Duplication Facilities: None.

NEW YORK METRO

CONSUMERS UNION OF THE U.S.
ARCHIVES
256 Washington Street
Mount Vernon, NY 10553
(914) 667-9400

Rhoda Karpatkin (Executive Director)

Contact: Elizabeth Hamilton (Research Librarian) (Ext. 263)
Services: Publisher. *Film library currently inaccessible to the public.*
Description: Collection includes a one-hour documentary on the history of the consumer movement (producer and date unknown); six one-hour homevideo productions produced by Lorimar; and other unspecified items.
Size & Elements: Film: 16mm (approx. 10 titles). Videotape: format and amount unspecified.
Cataloging: Computerized cataloging for staff use only.
Access: *Film library currently inaccessible to the public.* Research fees not charged. Research requests accepted by mail, telephone and in person (by appointment only).
Rights: Full rights held to all material.
Licensing: License policy not yet determined (apply for information).
Restrictions: *Film library currently inaccessible to the public.*
Viewing Facilities: Film and videotape.
Duplication Facilities: None.

NEW YORK METRO

CORINTH FILMS/CORINTH VIDEO
34 Gansevoort Street
New York, NY 10014
(212) 463-0305
(800) 221-4720 (orders)

Peter Meyer (Executive Vice President)

Contact: Valerie Griggs
Services: Film and videotape distributor. Material available to the public for purchase.
Description: Opera, theater, ballet, dance, classic films and television series on videotape. Exclusive distributor for the Bolshoi Opera productions of *Boris Godunov, Eugene Onegin, Khovanshchina, Queen of Spades,* and *The Tsar's Bride; Parsifal* (Syberberg); and *Prince Igor* (Kirov). Theater programs distributed exclusively include: *Cyrano de Bergerac* (Ferrer); *Oedipus Rex* (Tyrone Guthrie); and *Unfinished Piece for Player Piano* (Platonov). Dance exclusives include: *Anna Karenina* (Plisetskaya); *Cinderella* (Berlin); *Carmen* (Plisetskaya); *Plisetskaya Dances; Romeo and Juliet* (Ulanova); *Spartacus* (Bolshoi); *Stars of the Russian Ballet;* and *Swan Lake* (Plisetskaya).

Classic television series include: *The Best of Upstairs Downstairs; Monty Python's Flying Circus* (volumes 1-7) and *Fawlty Towers.* Feature films include: *L'Age D'Or; Alexander Nevsky; Bartleby; The Bicycle Thief; Don Quixote* (Russian); *Ivan the Terrible* (Parts I and II); *Peter the First* (Parts I and II); *Potemkin; Quatermass 2; The Sleeping Tiger; St. Martin's Lane; A Time for Dying; I Vitelloni;* and *Woman in the Dunes.*
Size & Elements: Film: 35mm and 16mm (approx. 500 titles). Videotape: VHS and Betamax (approx. 200 titles).
Cataloging: Published lists.
Access: Available to the public for purchase. Shipping and handling fees charged. Special title requests accepted.
Rights: Rights retained by original producers.
Licensing: Materials available for distribution only.
Restrictions: None specified.
Viewing Facilities: None.
Duplication Facilities: None.

NEW YORK METRO

THE COUNCIL ON ECONOMIC PRIORITIES
30 Irving Place
New York, NY 10003
(212) 420-1133
Fax: (212) 420-0988

Alice Tepper Marlin (Executive Director)

Contact: Alice Tepper Marlin
Services: Nonprofit organization. Videotape library open to researchers, scholars and the news media. Material generally not available for reuse.
Description: Footage from television appearances by members of Council on Economic Priorities.
Size & Elements: Videotape: format unspecified (15 segments).
Cataloging: None specified.
Access: Open to researchers, scholars and the news media. For in-house use only.
Rights: Some rights held to some material.
Licensing: Apply for information. License fees charged.
Restrictions: None specified.
Viewing Facilities: None.
Duplication Facilities: None.

NEW YORK METRO

CUNNINGHAM DANCE FOUNDATION
463 West Street
New York, NY 10014
(212) 255-3130
Fax: (212) 633-2453

Street address: 55 Bethune Street, 2nd Floor

Merce Cunningham (Artistic Director)

Art Becofsky (Executive Director)
Michael Bloom (Education and Media Director)
Elliot Caplan (Filmmaker in Residence)

Contact: Michael F. Stier (Film and Video Distribution Coordinator)
Services: Dance institute; film and videotape producer. Material available for research, distribution, rental, licensing and reuse, subject to restrictions.
Description: Working with dance particularly from the point of view of the camera, under the direction of dancer and choreographer Merce Cunningham, the Foundation holds rare archival programs and adaptations, as well as choreography for television and expository, documentary and instructional programs.

The research archives includes both domestic and foreign productions; interviews with Merce Cunningham and collaborators, including John Cage and Robert Rauschenberg.

The sale and rental collection includes *Walkaround Time* (1973), an homage to the work of Marcel Duchamp, directed by Charles Atlas, with decor by Jasper Johns; *Event for Television* (1977), produced for the PBS *Dance in America* series; *Merce by Merce by Paik* (1978), using materials by Nam June Paik; *Channels/Inserts* (1982), with music by David Tudor; and *Points in Space* (1986), produced with BBC Television, with music by John Cage.

Also holds instructional videotapes produced by the foundation demonstrating technique.

Approximately 30 works existing only in 1/2" open reel videotape format are currently being restored for future access.
Size & Elements: Film: 16mm (15 titles available for rental and purchase; 14 for research). Videotape: 3/4" and 1/2" (22 titles available for rental and purchase; 70 for research).
Cataloging: Published catalogs.
Access: Available to researchers, scholars and the public. Maintained for research, distribution and rental rather than reuse or resale. Research requests considered by mail and telephone. Research fees not charged.
Rights: Full rights held to some material. Some rights held to some material. Additional clearances may be necessary in some cases if material is to be reused.
Licensing: Apply for public performance clearance (lease agreements). License fees charged.
Restrictions: Requests for research and reuse considered on a case-by-case basis.
Viewing Facilities: Videotape.
Duplication Facilities: Videotape (3/4", Super VHS and VHS).

NEW YORK METRO

DANCE THEATER OF HARLEM
466 West 152nd Street
New York, NY 10031
(212) 690-2800
Fax: (212) 690-8736

Arthur Mitchell (Executive Director)

Contact: Michael Sherker (Archivist)
Services: Arts organization; film and videotape archives. Material possibly available for licensing and reuse, subject to restrictions.
Description: Holds Dance Theater of Harlem performances on videotape. Includes rehearsals, special events, promotional materials, school recitals and television appearances (1973-present).

A small portion of the collection is comprised of dance-related materials from other sources (some videotaped off the air). Choreographers featured include: Arthur Mitchell, George Balanchine, Jerome Robbins, Frederic Franklin, and Geoffrey Holder. Dancers featured include Virginia Johnson, Hinton Battle and Donald Williams.
Size & Elements: Film: 16mm (50 reels). Videotape: 3/4", VHS, Betamax and 1/2" open reel (500 items total).
Cataloging: Card catalogs.
Access: Some videotapes available to the public for rental and purchase (22 titles). For in-house use only, except in the case of film researchers and producers. Research fees not charged. Research requests accepted by mail, telephone and in person (by appointment only).
Rights: Full rights held to some material. Additional clearances may be necessary in some cases if material is to be reused.
Licensing: Possibly available for licensing, subject to restrictions.
Restrictions: Fees and/or royalties will be charged under some conditions. Some choreographers may require additional clearances. Fees apply for any

usage over 60 seconds.
Viewing Facilities: Videotape (3/4" and 1/2").
Duplication Facilities: Videotape (3/4" and 1/2").

NEW YORK METRO

**DANCE THEATER WORKSHOP/
THE BESSIE SCHONBERG THEATER**
219 West 19th Street
New York, NY 10011
(212) 691-6500

Collection held by:
VIDEO D STUDIOS
29 West 21st Street
New York, NY 10010
(212) 242-3345

Contact: Dennis Diamond (Video D Studios)
Services: Video D Studios is a private company retained by Dance Theater Workshop to record and document their performances; it presently holds their collection. Material accessible under limited circumstances; possibly available for licensing or reuse, subject to restrictions.
Description: Videotape documentation of Dance Theater Workshop's performances and concerts (1979-present).
Size & Elements: Videotape: 3/4" (approx. 500 videotapes); 1/2" open reel (amount unspecified).
Cataloging: None specified.
Access: Access to collection limited. Available only to researchers who have obtained permission in advance from choreographer to view material or to presenters contemplating booking an act. Research requests accepted on a very limited basis by mail and telephone. Material made available on a case-by-case basis.
Rights: Additional clearances from individual choreographers will be necessary if material is to be reused.
Licensing: Possibly available for reuse, subject to restrictions.
Restrictions: Permission is needed from individual choreographer to gain access to or to reuse material.
Viewing Facilities: None.
Duplication Facilities: None.

NEW YORK METRO

DAPHNE PRODUCTIONS, INC.
1 West 67th Street, Suite 204
New York, NY 10023
(212) 769-4060

Dick Cavett (President)

Contact: Judy Englander
Services: Television production company. Videotape material available for licensing and reuse.
Description: *The Dick Cavett Show,* containing talk show programming (interviews from 1969-86). Aired on ABC (1969-75), PBS (1977-82), USA Cable Network (1985-86) and ABC Network (1986).

Guests interviewed include (partial list): F. Lee Bailey, Lucille Ball, Warren Beatty, Ruben Blades, David Bowie, Jimmy Breslin, Nicholas Cage, Cher, Shirley Chisholm, Rae Dawn Chong, Dick Clark, John Cleese, David Allen Coe, Quentin Crisp, Walter Cronkite, Salvador Dali, Sammy Davis, Jr., John DeLorean, Brian DePalma, Angie Dickinson, Sam Donaldson, Phil Donohue, Hugh Downs, Michael Dukakis, Perry Ellis, Julius Erving, Federico Fellini, Jane Fonda, Gerald Ford, Whitey Ford, Bob Fosse, Redd Foxx, Stan Getz, Lillian Gish, Jean-Luc Godard, Whoopi Goldberg, Benny Goodman, Cynthia Gregory, Roger Grimsby, Tom Hanks, George Harrison, Helen Hayes, Jimi Hendrix, Keith Hernandez, Charlton Heston, Alfred Hitchcock, David Hockney, Jimmy Hoffa, Abbie Hoffman, Celeste Holm, Lena Horne, Bob Hope, John Huston, Sen. Daniel Inouye, John Irving, Christopher Isherwood, Jesse Jackson, Bianca Jagger, Sen. Edward Kennedy, Joseph Kennedy III, Rose Kennedy, B. B. King, Billy Jean King, Stephen King, Henry Kissinger, Eartha Kitt, Robert Klein, Evel Knievel, Edward Koch, Ted Koppel, Kathryn Kuhlman, Louise Lasser, Norman Lear, Jack Lemmon, John Lennon, G. Gordon Liddy, Gina Lollobrigida, Trini Lopez, Sophia Loren, the Loud family, Sidney Lumet, Norman Mailer, Natalia Makarova, Louis Malle, Mickey Mantle, Lee Marvin, Groucho Marx, Sen. George McGovern, Margaret Mead,

Ethel Merman, Arthur Miller, "Miss Universe contestants," Mary Tyler Moore, Roger Moore, Agnes Moorehead, Eddie Murphy, Patricia Neal, Edwin Newman, Agnes Nixon, Dr. Thomas Noguchi, Rudolph Nureyev, Joyce Carol Oates, Laurence Olivier, Yoko Ono, Marina Oswald, Jack Paar, Roman Polanski, Dr. Wardell Pomeroy, Anthony Quinn, "radicals," Gov. Ronald Reagan, Harry Reasoner, Ginger Rogers, The Rolling Stones, Linda Ronstadt, Dr. Lee Salk, Martin Scorsese, Pete Seeger, Rod Serling, Ravi Shankar, Dinah Shore, Sivuca, Buffalo Bob Smith, Sly and The Family Stone, Stephen Spielberg, Mickey Spillane, Gloria Steinem, The Supremes, David Susskind, Donald Sutherland, Gloria Swanson, Fran Tarkenton, Twyla Tharp, Tiny Tim, Mel Torme, Mike Tyson, Ike and Tina Turner, Liv Ullmann, Peter Ustinov, Dick Van Dyke, Gore Vidal, "Vietnam veterans," Werner von Braun, Mike Wallace, Raquel Welch, Lina Wertmuller, Tennessee Williams, Shelley Winters, Frank Zappa and many more.
Size & Elements: Videotape: 2" and 1" (over 1,400 programs; masters); 3/4" ("a few" transferred from originals; viewing copies).
Cataloging: Catalog with guest interviews listed alphabetically and corresponding to videotape numbers (for staff use only).
Access: Available for licensing and reuse. Research requests accepted by mail and telephone.
Rights: Additional clearances may be necessary in some cases if material is to be reused.
Licensing: Available for licensing and reuse. License fees charged.
Restrictions: None specified.
Viewing Facilities: None.
Duplication Facilities: None.

NEW YORK METRO

DEEP DISH TV
339 Lafayette Street
New York, NY 10012
(212) 420-9045

Contact: Martha Wallner
Services: First national public access satellite network; nonprofit media organization; producer and distributor. Videotape material available for research, rental, cablecast and reuse, subject to clearance and approval.
Description: Alternative television network connecting public access cable television stations by satellite in order to distribute independently produced and public access programming. The idea of using satellite distribution for access programming evolved from discussions between Paper Tiger Television (q.v.) and other like-minded groups who wanted to share programming. Working with Public Interest Video Network (q.v.), DDTV developed a proposal for a series which would highlight nationwide community concerns and social issues, while involving as many producers as possible (including women and people of color) and emphasizing regional diversity.

DDTV has excerpted the work of grassroots and independent video producers and packaged it into thematically organized programs (each 60 min.). Although programs were collected for satellite distribution via DDTV, they are also available for exhibition to community groups and educational institutions.

Many videotapes show the potential of community-based and low-budget video production as an activist tool.

AIDS. Angry Initiatives/Defiant Strategies (John Greyson, Toronto, Ont.).

Age. Agewise (Senior Independence Project, Portland, Oreg.), including: *Senior Beat* (Madison, Wis.); *Agewise* (Portland, Oreg.).

Agriculture. People and the Land: Farming and Agriculture (Wade Britzius, Whitehall, Wis.).

Borders. The Border: Where Do You Draw the Line (Dee Dee Halleck and Dan Martin).

Central America. Central America Comes to Middle America, series produced by Martha Wallner, including: *Notes from Nicaragua* (George King and Elise Witt, Atlanta, Ga.); *Breaking Ground* (Pamela Cohen, Camino Film Projects; Nest & Film Institute of El Salvador, Los Angeles, Calif.); and *A Dish of Central America* (prepared by Michael Murphy and Danielle Villegas of the Empowerment Project, a producing group and distribution clearinghouse for documentaries about Central America).

Farm workers. This Land Is Our Land: The Farm Crisis in America, produced by Joan Jubela and Dan Marcus, including: *Killing the Golden Goose* (Jon Alpert, Downtown Community TV, New York City) and *Another Family Farm* (Charles Kanten, Lutheran Church in America, Minneapolis, Minn.).

Labor. Is This Working? — Labor in the Eighties (Committee for Labor Access, Chicago, Ill.); *Labor Produces: Access to Solidarity* produced by Pat Keeton, Pennee Bender, Ken Nash and Carol Anshien, including: *On the Job:*

Watsonville Strike (Steve Zeltzer, Labor Video Project, San Francisco, Calif.) and *Tennessee Heavy Metal* (Tobe Carey, Willow Mixed Media, Glenford, N.Y.).

Latin American. Sopade Videos: Selections from the Latin American Video Archives, produced at Ramapo College, N.J.

Latino images. Latino Images (Latino Collaborative, New York City).

Housing. Home Sweet Homefront: Fighting for a Decent Place to Live (Louis Massiah, Philadelphia, Pa.); *There's No Place Like Home: Housing Crisis USA,* produced by Fiona Boneham and Pamela Hoelscher, including: *Take Back the Hill: The Rebirth of a Neighborhood* (Kendall Hall, Roxbury, Mass.) and *Gentrification on the Lower East Side* (Scott Sinkler and Sachiko Hamada, Brooklyn, N.Y.).

Militarism. About Face: Soldiers, Refugees & Other Victims of War (We Are the City [WAC]-TV, Boston, Mass.).

Peace. Give Peace a Channel, produced by Caryn Rogoff and Kirk Ruebenson, including *Scenes from a Micro-War* (Sherry Millner, Los Angeles, Calif.) and *Disarmament Video Survey* (Skip Blumberg, Wendy Clarke, Dee Dee Halleck, Karen Ranucci, and Sandy Tolan, New York City).

Political humor. Biting the Hand That Leads Us: Humor and Social Change (Jesse Drew and Alan Steinheimer, San Francisco, Calif.).

Popular culture. Mediums Well Done: Re-Making Pop Culture, produced by William Boddy and Marisa Bowe, including: *I Like My TV* (Diane Allen Groenert, Home Baked TV, Fort Wayne, Ind.) and *Ronald Reagan Goes to Hell* (Fritz Bacher, Buffalo, N.Y.).

Public access. Getting a Grip on Access, produced by Diana Agosta, Andrew Blau and David Shulman, including interviews with: Trisha Dair, National Federation of Local Cable Programmers; Dee Dee Halleck, Paper Tiger TV/DEEP DISH TV and George Stoney, Film and Television Dept., New York University.

Racism. Racism on Main Street: A Look Around the Corner, produced by Shu Lea Cheang and Roy Wilson, including: *Racism in Somerville* (Somerville Producers Group, Somerville, Mass.) and *The Day the Klan Marched* (Paula Manley and Jim Cullers, ACTV, Austin, Texas).

Women. The Fourth International Women's Day Video Festival, produced by Janet Doherty, Susan Fleischmann, Ellen Hendrix, Robin Mide and Veda Reilly, Boston, Mass.; *That's Woman's Work!!* produced by Martha Wallner and Adriene Jenik, including: *The Maids!: A Documentary* (Muriel Jackson, Atlanta, Ga.) and *Women of Steel* (Mon Valley Media, Pittsburgh, Pa.).

Youth. Good Things Come From Small Packages: Video By & For Young People (Laura Tierney, Katho Kampfe and Emmaria Gilmore, Tampa, Fla.); *Kids Playback: TV Made By Children,* produced by Karen Einstein and Dee Dee Halleck, including: *Kids Alive Composit* (Kids Stuff, Monroe County Public Library, Bloomington, Ind.) and *Whiz Kids* (Donna Dager, Video for Kids, Mountain View, Calif.).

Size & Elements: Videotape: 3/4" and VHS (28 hours of compilation videotapes).

Cataloging: Published catalog.

Access: Available to researchers and scholars. Available for rental, purchase and duplication. Available primarily, although not exclusively, for cablecast.

Rights: Some rights held to some material.

Licensing: Apply for information.

Restrictions: None specified.

Viewing Facilities: Videotape (3/4" and VHS).

Duplication Facilities: Videotape (3/4" and VHS).

Publications: *Deep Dish Directory* (1986), a resource guide for grassroots television producers, programmers, activists and cultural workers.

NEW YORK METRO

DEMOCRACY IN COMMUNICATION
124 Washington Place
New York, NY 10014
(212) 463-0108

Contact: Karen Ranucci (Project Coordinator)

Services: Distributor. Videotapes available for rental, purchase, licensing and reuse.

Description: *Democracy In Communication — Popular Video and Film in Latin America* is a collection of works made by independent Latin American media producers.

"Many countries in Latin America have a long history of cinema production. However, the financial crisis which has wracked the continent has made it nearly impossible for independent filmmakers to work. The video revolution, which began in the U.S. more than a decade ago, is now reaching Latin America. Many filmmakers have transferred their skills to video

production and are creatively experimenting in a variety of community television projects. Television is one of the strongest forces in forming the ideas and opinions of a population. Control of it means power. In most Latin American countries access to the airwaves for independents is nonexistent. To sidestep the influence of broadcast TV, many communities produce their own television and show it in closed-circuit settings. Popular video is like an octopus reaching out in many different directions. In contexts where political repression has closed the channels of mass communication to democratic expression, alternative movements have arisen. In recent years, these isolated independent community groups have begun to share their experiences and create an alternative media network."

Videotapes available include:

Mexico. Cross Section One Afternoon of Mexican TV (1985) shows a sample of programming from state and privately owned channels, much of which is imported; *Lugares Communes (Common Places)* (Lillian Liberman, 1983), examines the reality of life for Mexican women by contrasting the stories of two women from different social classes; *Amas De Casa (Housewives)* (Colectivo Cine Mujer, 1984), an organizing tool made to prevent evictions in Mexico City's "cardboard villages"; *Nuestro Tequio (Our Tequio)* (1984), produced by a Zapoteca group from the state of Oaxaca, on the Indian custom of joining together to work on community projects; *El Triunfo (The Triumph)* (1985), on the destruction of the jungles; and *Video Road* (Sarah Minter, 1985), an independent video documenting a cross-country journey.

Brazil. Marley Normal (1985) condenses a day in the life of an urban working woman into five minutes; *Varela in Serra Pelada* (1984) is a satirical report from Brazil's gold-mining area, on prospectors' quest for fortune; *Valera in Xingu* (1985) documents the inauguration of a new tribal chief on the Xingu Indian reserve in the Amazon jungle, poking fun at the network news crews and White society; *Sound On/Vision On* (1985) contrasts Afro-Brazilian sounds and images with economic development projects that destroy Indian lands; and *Beijo Ardente: Overdose* (1984) documents the struggle by a group of artists to build a cultural center in Porto Alegre.

Chile. News Clips by Teleanalisis (1984), documenting the events leading to demonstrations against the military government; and *Chile's Forbidden Dream* (1983), on Chile's recent history and the work of ICTUS, a theater company; *Hasta Vencer (Until Victory)* (1984), on the housing crisis; and *Blanca Azucena (White Lily)* (1985), on a popular education experiment in rural Chile.

Peru. Miss Universe in Peru (1984), a behind-the-scenes look at the contest and its relationship to Peruvian womens' real lives; *Gregorio* (1983), a feature film on the disintegration of a rural family who migrates to Lima; and *Desparecidos (The Disappeared Ones)* (1985), a music video of Ruben Blades' song documenting the guerrilla war in the state of Ayacucho.

Panama. Algo De Ti (Something of You) (1985), a surrealistic music video speaking of the horrors of living under a military government.

Bolivia. Lucho: Que Vive En El Pueblo (Lucho: You Live Within the People) (1985), a documentary on the life and death of Father Luis Espinal, a leader in the movement for democratic communication.

Uruguay. Senal De Ajuste (Signal To Adjust) (1984), a comic adaptation of a short story in which a couple's relationship is ruined by their television set; and *El Sol Del Juez (The Judge's Coin)* (1983), an adaptation of an historical incident which led to the largest peasant uprising in Bolivia.

El Salvador. Atlacatl (1983), a publicity videotape made by the El Salvadoran military about the special forces brigade which was trained in the United States; *Los Refugiados (The Refugees)* (1985), produced in the United States, in which illegal Salvadoran refugees on Long Island explain why they left their country and discuss their "underground" lives; and *Tiempo De Audacia (Time of Daring)* (1983), on the guerrillas and their means of public communication.

Nicaragua. La Virgen Que Suda (The Sweating Virgin) (1983), a made-for-TV drama highlighting the uneasy relationship between Nicaragua and the U.S.; *Testimonios (Testimonies)* (1982), on the effects of contra raids on the lives of Nicaraguans; *Las Mujeres (The Women)* (1985), on the disparity in pay between men and women on cooperative farms; *Aqui En Este Esquina (Here On This Corner)* (1985), a traveling game show produced by Nicaraguan government television; and *Que Pasa Con El Papel Higenico (What Happened to the Toilet Paper)* (1983), an investigative report on the shortage of toilet paper in Nicaragua.

Size & Elements: Videotape: Betacam, 3/4", VHS and Betamax (9 hours; 35 titles).

Cataloging: Published catalog.

Access: Open to the public. Available for rental, purchase and reuse, subject to restrictions. Research fees not charged. Research requests accepted by mail and telephone.

Rights: Some rights held to all material. Most rights retained by original producers.
Licensing: Available for licensing and reuse, subject to restrictions. License fees charged (fees vary depending on intended use).
Restrictions: Duplication, licensing and reuse are subject to clearance and approval of original producers.
Viewing Facilities: Videotape (3/4" and VHS).
Duplication Facilities: Videotape (1", Betacam, 3/4", VHS and Betamax).

NEW YORK METRO

DOWNTOWN COMMUNITY TELEVISION CENTER (DCTV)
87 Lafayette Street
New York, NY 10013
(212) 966-4510

Jon Alpert and Keiko Tsuno (Directors)

Contact: Hye June Park (Community Projects Director)
Services: Nonprofit media organization; videotape producer and distributor. Completed videotapes available to the public for rental and purchase. Footage available for licensing and reuse, subject to restrictions.
Description: Founded in 1972. Provides free media services to individual producers, local artists and performers and community organizations (e.g., tenants' associations, day care centers, community theaters, dance companies, educational institutions, legal aid services, unions, student groups and health clinics). Over 200 programs (in 15 languages) are produced annually through DCTV on subjects such as community art, culture, local news and community issues. DCTV works to preserve the rich culture of the community it serves and to promote exchanges among different ethnic groups; at the same time working to create a new kind of television with solid community roots. Starting with its production *Cuba: The People* (1974), DCTV has helped open broadcast television to independent producers.

Sample titles include: *Cuba: The People,* a comprehensive look at life in communist Cuba, focusing on average people, problems of housing, medical care and education; *Cuba: Part II,* investigating places never visited by Western journalists — prisons, courtrooms, sugar factories, the Communist Party Congress, Havana's Chinatown and the Marriage Palace — and containing an interview with Fidel Castro; *Chinatown: Immigrants in America,* on the problems faced by immigrants, including sweatshops, crowded schools, poor housing and low-wage jobs; *Health Care: Your Money or Your Life,* a comprehensive look at America's medical system, exploring the role of government, health insurance, Medicaid and the health-product industry; *Vietnam: Picking Up the Pieces* (begun 1977), the first look at Vietnam since the end of the war; *Third Avenue: Only the Strong Survive,* profiling six people who live or work on a street that runs through Manhattan and the Bronx; *Southeast Asia,* a series of reports made during the Vietnam-China border war, and the first postwar look inside Cambodia by a Western television crew; *The War in Nicaragua,* exclusive reports videotaped with the Sandinistas during their revolution; *Nicaragua: The Revolution Continued,* containing footage of a five-day battle between the Sandinista Army and the contras; *Glasnost and Perestroika,* on the campaign to open up and restructure many aspects of Soviet society; *Fidel Comes to New York,* on Fidel Castro's visit to the United Nations; *Iran,* an examination of life in Iran after the fall of the Shah; and *Afghanistan,* on the guerrilla war.

Other programs include: *Homeless in New York; Hunger in the Suburbs; Housing in America,* on housing shortages and speculation in Hoboken, N.J. and Philadelphia, Pa.; *Junkie Junior — Life in the South Bronx; Home on the Range,* about a South Dakota rancher and his battle against agribusiness; *South Dakota Gold Miners,* on the history of labor unrest at the Homestake gold mine; *Urban Indians,* an account of Indian life in the cities and on the reservation, following an Oglala Sioux as he searches for his identity; *Invisible Citizens — Japanese Americans,* examining the lives of six Japanese Americans and how they have been affected by the wartime internment; *Killing the Golden Goose: The Poisoning of America's Farms and Foods; Toxic Waste in America; Migrant Farmworkers; How to Make Community TV: A Portrait of DCTV* (produced by the BBC); and *What A Way to Make A Living,* featuring Isreal Crespo (a breakdancer), Rib Tech (Kansas City's "College of Barbecue Knowledge"), Joe Barcelo (the fastest gun in the West), Bobby Chacon (a flyweight boxer from Los Angeles) and Ben Lee (the world's greatest turkey caller).

In addition to the distribution collection, DCTV holds many videotapes produced at the facility, including hundreds relating to community interests (1972-present). Several hundred videotapes (not used in completed productions) are of special interest, containing footage gathered during many trips to Cuba and Central America.
Size & Elements: Videotape: 3/4" (over 3,000 videotapes; masters and viewing copies); 1/2" (viewing copies). (Approx. 600-1,000 videotapes are completed productions; approx. 2,000-3,000 are outtakes and raw footage.)
Cataloging: Published catalogs describing distribution collection; release sheets; research library.
Access: Open to the public. Some completed productions available for rental and purchase. Footage available for licensing and reuse on a case-by-case basis, subject to restrictions. Research fees not charged for in-house viewing. Research requests accepted by mail, telephone and in person (by appointment only).
Rights: Full rights held to all material.
Licensing: Available for licensing and reuse, subject to restrictions. License fees charged in some cases.
Restrictions: Requests for reuse are considered on a case-by-case basis and depend upon intended use.
Viewing Facilities: Videotape (3/4" and 1/2").
Duplication Facilities: Videotape (1", 3/4", VHS and Betamax).

NEW YORK METRO

JACKSON DUBE (JED PRODUCTIONS) CORPORATION
140 East 56th Street, Suite 11E
New York, NY 10022
(212) 826-1221
Telex: 234134

Jackson E. Dube (President/Owner)

Contact: Jackson E. Dube
Services: Distributor. Films available for distribution, and in some cases for licensing and reuse. Collection not available for research or in-house viewing.
Description: Feature films (1930s-50s).
Size & Elements: Film: 35mm and 16mm (approx. 200 titles total).
Cataloging: Title list.
Access: Available for distribution, and in some cases for licensing and reuse. Not available for research and in-house viewing. Particular films may be viewed in connection with stock footage requests, but no in-house viewing facilities are available. Research requests accepted by mail and telephone.
Rights: Full rights held to some material. Additional clearances may be necessary in some cases if material is to be reused.
Licensing: Available for licensing and reuse, subject to restrictions. License fees charged.
Restrictions: Requests for licensing and reuse considered on a case-by-case basis. Restrictions apply in many cases.
Viewing Facilities: None.
Duplication Facilities: None.

NEW YORK METRO

ALFRED I. DUPONT CENTER FOR BROADCAST JOURNALISM AT THE GRADUATE SCHOOL OF JOURNALISM, COLUMBIA UNIVERSITY
701 Journalism
Columbia University
New York, NY 10027
(212) 854-5047

Contact: Jonnet Abeles; Lesley Kuchek
Services: Educational institution; archives. Videotape collection open to researchers and scholars for in-house use only.
Description: In 1942 Mrs. Jessie Ball duPont established the Alfred I. duPont Awards for excellence in public affairs radio programming, as a memorial to her husband. Rapid advances in broadcast technology soon caused the Awards to be extended to television. The Awards are given annually for excellence in broadcast journalism, honoring "distinguished and meritorious performance of public service by aggressive and accurate gathering and reporting of news."

Holds over 900 programs received for consideration (1968-present), covering a wide range of social, political and scientific issues, including: civil rights; crime; student rebellion; assassinations; the Vietnam War; genetic research; money and the effects of affluence; Third World countries; pollution's impact on the planet; and historical studies of people and events.

Sample award winners and program titles include: KQED-TV, San Francisco, Calif., for outstanding coverage of the 1968 political campaigns (1968); Fred Freed and NBC News, *Pollution is a Matter of Choice* (1969);

John Sharnik and CBS News, *Justice in America* (1970); Arthur Holch and ABC News, *Chile: Experiment in Red* (1972); WGBH-TV, Boston, Mass., *Arabs and Israelis* (1974); WQED-TV and The National Geographic Society, Pittsburgh, Pa., *The Living Sands of Namib* (1977); Perry Miller Adato and WNET-TV, New York, N.Y., *Picasso: A Painter's Diary* (1979); Robert Richter and WNET-TV, New York, N.Y., *For Export Only: Pesticides and Pills* (1981); WGBH-TV and PBS, *Vietnam: A Television History* (1983); DesertWest News, Tucson, Ariz., a series of reports on the American sanctuary movement (1984); ABC News, *45/85* (1985); WPLG-TV, Miami, Florida, *Florida: State of Neglect* (1986); and Blackside, Inc., *Eyes On the Prize: America's Civil Rights Years, 1954-1965* (1986).

Size & Elements: Videotape: 3/4" (approx. 1,200 videotapes, 919 titles; viewing copies).

Cataloging: Computerized cataloging (list with synopses and cross references) available to researchers; brochure listing award recipients.

Access: Open to researchers and scholars only. For in-house use and viewing only. Research fees not charged. Research requests accepted by mail and telephone.

Rights: No rights held to any material. All rights retained by original filmmakers or producers.

Licensing: Not available for licensing or reuse.

Restrictions: All rights held by original filmmakers or producers. Material restricted to in-house use and viewing only.

Viewing Facilities: Videotape.

Duplication Facilities: Videotape (3/4" to VHS).

NEW YORK METRO

EDEN ENTERTAINMENT, INC.
265 Cherry Street, Apartment 5-A
New York, NY 10002
(212) 964-3753

Tom Toth (President)

Contact: Tom Toth

Services: Private collection; film and videotape stock footage sales library. Research and historical consultation available.

Description: Feature films and short subjects relating to Hollywood and its history (through 1940).

Holds 300 feature films, including many rare public domain titles such as *Anna Karenina* (1947, with Vivien Leigh); *Marie Galante* (1934, with Spencer Tracy and Helen Morgan); *I Take This Woman* (1931, with Carole Lombard and Gary Cooper); *Common Law* (1931, with Constance Bennett and Joel McCrea); *Behind Office Doors* (1931, with Mary Astor); and *Millie* (1931, with Helen Twelvetrees).

Also holds 2,000 short subjects (many animated), including animation from Fleischer Studios, MGM, Paramount, Iwerks and Van Beuren.

Size & Elements: Film: 35mm and 16mm (mostly 16mm, approx. 2,300 titles; release prints). Videotape: 1" (masters; transfers from 35mm); VHS (several thousand titles; reference and viewing copies).

Cataloging: Clip reel in progress; staff assistance required.

Access: Open to the public. For in-house use only. Available for duplication and reuse. Research fees charged. Research requests accepted by mail, telephone and in person (by appointment only).

Rights: Apply for information. Additional clearances may be necessary in some cases if material is to be reused.

Licensing: Available for licensing and reuse. License and usage fees charged.

Restrictions: None specified.

Viewing Facilities: Film (16mm; 35mm can be arranged); videotape (3/4", VHS and Betamax).

Duplication Facilities: Film (16mm to 3/4", VHS and Betamax); videotape (3/4", VHS and Betamax).

NEW YORK METRO

EDISON NATIONAL HISTORIC SITE
Main Street and Lakeside Avenue
West Orange, NJ 07052
(201) 736-0550

Fahy C. Whitaker (Superintendent)

Contacts: Mary B. Bowling (Archivist); Lou Venuto (Chief of Visitor Services) or Supervisory Museum Curator (position presently vacant)

Services: Museum. Film collection available for research, duplication and reuse, subject to clearance and approval.

Description: Archives contain original material documenting the life, work and enterprises of Thomas Alva Edison (1847-1931). The Archives were acquired in 1954 by the U.S. Department of the Interior, National Park Service, along with the site of Edison's West Orange laboratory.

Collection (spanning approx. 1893-1954) contains newsreels, promotional and documentary films, and features made by Edison's motion picture companies (including copies of Edison Kinetoscopes, 1890s-1910s) and other producers. Most of the films relate to Edison himself, showing him at work, at numerous commemorative celebrations and in other settings. There are some variant versions of some titles.

Originals of the Edison films are held at Library of Congress, Motion Picture, Broadcasting and Recorded Sound Division (q.v.).

Size & Elements: Film: 35mm, 16mm and 8mm (mostly 16mm, approx. 195 titles, approx. 272 cans; mostly black and white positive, sound and silent). Videotape: VHS (11 videotapes, each containing copies of several films).

Cataloging: Computerized cataloging for staff use only. A printed guide is currently being prepared.

Access: Open to the public. Available for duplication and reuse. Research fees not charged. Research requests accepted by mail, telephone and in person (by appointment only). Persons wishing to examine materials should contact the Archivist or Supervisory Museum Curator at least two weeks in advance of their expected visits.

Rights: No rights held to any material. Some material in the public domain. Rights status of some material unknown. Determination of copyright is responsibility of researcher.

Licensing: Available for reuse, subject to restrictions. Usage fees not charged.

Restrictions: Reuse of material is restricted depending on rights status.

Viewing Facilities: Film (16mm); videotape (VHS and Betamax).

Duplication Facilities: None.

Related Materials: 60,000 photographs.

NEW YORK METRO

EDUCATIONAL VIDEO CENTER (EVC)
87 Lafayette Street
New York, NY 10013
(212) 219-8129

Steven S. Goodman (Executive Director)

Contacts: David Murdock (Assistant Director); Angela Rose (Distribution Manager).

Services: Nonprofit community-based educational media organization; videotape distributor. Videotapes available for rental and purchase.

Description: Promotes the educational use of video in schools and youth programs across the country. Has offered documentary workshops for students since 1981, providing teenagers the equipment and training needed to produce their own documentaries. Also works with teachers, training them to operate video equipment and to integrate video into their subject areas.

For years, EVC has been teaching video production classes in high schools across the country. Many impressive and award-winning social documentary videotapes have been produced in these workshops.

Titles include: *Shotgun,* a gripping story of a teenage gang member in the Bronx before and after he commits a brutal murder and is sentenced to life in prison; *Artie: Down and Out On the Bowery,* a moving portrait of a homeless alcoholic who lives in an abandoned truck; *Black History Month: A Chance to Reflect,* exploring the meaning of Black History Month and the challenges facing Blacks today; *Between C and D: Drugs on the Lower East Side,* a disturbing look at the world of junkies and street hustlers; *Looking for Shelter,* in which a homeless mother and her retarded daughter roam the streets of New York City looking for a place to live; *Youth Crime and Its Effect On the Family,* in which a South Bronx teenager talks with her family about her brother, who was recently sent to jail; *Making a Home on Roses Creek,* examining problems of rural housing in an Appalachian community in Tennessee; *Letta's Family,* a portrait of an Appalachian woman and her two sons who struggle to survive without running water, electricity or adequate food; *2371 Second Avenue: An East Harlem Story,* in which a teenager leads her family and neighbors in a struggle to improve the conditions in their rat-infested tenement building; *Teen Fashion: What's Your Favorite Style?,* an upbeat look at the latest New York teenage styles; *Dreams of the Future,* in which teenagers dramatize visions of their lives ten years in the future; *Hungry to Learn,* exploring the tough decision many Appalachian women are forced to make between food stamps or school because of Virginia's social services laws;

Young Parents: Ready or Not, a discussion with rural youth about what it is like to be parents; *Teen Suicide: No Way Out,* a talk with young people who have attempted suicide and with professionals who explain the warning signs and how to get help; *The Living Dictionary,* where language comes alive as students act out hilarious definitions of vocabulary words; *Truancy: Where are the Students?,* on the causes of and solutions to this growing problem; *Living With Illiteracy; Trends at Pacific High,* in which Brooklyn teenagers interview each other about the most recent trends and why they follow them; and *The Prostitutes of Forsyth Street,* interviews with three young women.

Size and Elements: Videotape: 1" and 3/4" (masters); 3/4", VHS and Betamax (viewing copies; approx. 40 titles, each 6 to 22 min.).
Cataloging: Published catalog.
Access: Open to the public. Available for rental and purchase. Requests accepted by mail and telephone.
Rights: Full rights held to all material.
Licensing: Apply for information. License fees charged.
Restrictions: None specified.
Viewing Facilities: Videotape (3/4" and 1/2"; for individuals and small groups).
Duplication Facilities: Videotape (3/4", VHS and Betamax).
Related Materials: Curriculum packages produced to accompany documentary videotapes.

NEW YORK METRO

EL SALVADOR MEDIA PROJECT
335 West 38th Street, 5th Floor
New York, NY 10018
(212) 714-9118

Tony Avalos (Director)

Contact: Tony Avalos
Services: Post-production, distribution, information and media resource center. Films and videotapes available for research, rental, purchase, duplication, licensing and reuse.
Description: Media organization devoted to the promotion, distribution and production of media by and about Central Americans. Since its founding in 1982, ESMP has translated 14 films and videotapes made by Salvadoran producers into English; participated in numerous festivals, conferences and tours; organized premieres and public presentations of Salvadoran media, and has created a network to distribute these works to community groups, universities, cable public access stations and other audiences. ESMP is currently producing its first feature-length documentary.

The film and videotape library represents all films and videotapes produced (1980-present) by the film collectives *Cero A La Izquierda* (Zero to the Left), *Sistema Radio Venceremos* (Venceremos Communications System), *Instituto de Cine Salvadoreno* (Film Institute of El Salvador), and the independent productions of various humanitarian and religious organizations. Ranging from an intimate look at the people and the culture of El Salvador in *Decision to Win* to the comprehensive historical and political documentary *Central America: A Defiant Volcano,* the material is a source of historical information and a tool to communicate the evolving reality of El Salvador and the growing intervention of the U.S. in the social and military conflicts in Central America.

Other titles include: *Morazan* (1980), depicting the formation of the Popular Army and military training in an FMLN-controlled zone; *Sowing Hope* (1983), on the Catholic Church's active stance in defending basic rights; *Time of Daring* (1983), a visual essay and montage of contrasts and a warning about U.S. intervention against a popular army; and *Two Types of Peace* (1984), a glimpse of two types of women who seek two types of peace: the women of the oligarchy and the women of the Mother's Committee of the Disappeared. Two documentaries produced by Honduran filmmakers are also available.

The videotape archives contain an ever-expanding collection of raw footage on El Salvador unavailable elsewhere; research services available.
Size & Elements: Film: 16mm (12 titles; release prints). Videotape: 3/4" (20 titles; viewing copies); VHS and Betamax (20 titles; viewing copies).
Cataloging: Brochure.
Access: Open to researchers and scholars. Completed films and videotapes available for research, rental and purchase. All material available for licensing and reuse. Research requests accepted by mail.
Rights: Full rights held to some material.
Licensing: Available for licensing and reuse. License fees charged.
Restrictions: None specified.
Viewing Facilities: Videotape.

Duplication Facilities: Videotape.

NEW YORK METRO

ELECTRONIC ARTS INTERMIX (EAI)
536 Broadway, 9th Floor
New York, NY 10012
(212) 966-4605

Lori Zippay (Director)

Contacts: Robert Beck (Assistant Director); Janice Young (Distribution Coordinator).
Services: Nonprofit media arts organization; videotape distributor. Videotapes available for in-house viewing, rental and purchase.
Description: EAI was founded in 1971 by Howard Wise, after his landmark exhibition "TV As A Creative Medium" (1969), which presented the potential for television as an art form. In 1972, editing and post-production services were introduced for use by the video arts community, and in 1973 EAI began to distribute video art to educational and cultural institutions.

Currently distributes an international and historic collection of over 800 independently produced videotapes (1968-present) by more than 125 major American and European artists. Works include video art and documentaries, including dance, performance and body art, experimental, image processing, "new narratives," video installations, music, media, theater, humor and comedy. EAI also maintains an archival videotape collection.

Artists and producers include: Marina Abramovic and Ulay, Vito Acconci, John Adams, Merrill Aldighieri and Joe Tripician, Max Almy, Marie Andre, Ant Farm (Chip Lord, Doug Michels and Curtis Schreier), Charles Atlas, Ros Barron, Stephen Beck, Raymond Bellour and Philippe Venault, Dara Birnbaum, Skip Blumberg, Ante Branovich, Barbara Buckner, Chris Burden, James Byrne, John Cage, Robert Cahen, Peter Campus, Frank and Laura Cavestani, Shirley Clarke, Wendy Clarke, Maxi Cohen, Cecelia Condit, David Cort, Peter Crown and Bill Etra, Merce Cunningham, Peter D'Agostino, Crane Davis, Douglas Davis, Cara DeVito, Dimitri Devyatkin, Tom DeWitt, Juan Downey, Downtown Community Television Center (DCTV), Jody Eisemann, Ed Emshwiller, Ken Feingold, Kit Fitzgerald and John Sanborn, Richard Foreman, Terry Fox, Paul Garrin, Matthew Geller, Davidson Gigliotti, Frank Gillette, Arthur Ginsberg, Jean-Luc Godard and Anne-Marie Miéville, Shalom Gorewitz, Dan Graham, Julie Gustafson, William Gwin, Doug Hall, Don Hallock, Gusztav Hamos, Ron Hays, Gary Hill, Nan Hoover, Mako Idemitsu, Image Union, Joan Jonas, John Keeler and Ruth Rotko, Laura Kipnis, Sol Korine and Blaine Dunlap, Shigeko Kubota, Tony Labat, Joan Logue, Chip Lord, Mary Lucier, Eva Maier, Christa Maiwald, Esti Galili Marpet, Pier Marton, Mickey McGowan, Media Bus, MICA-TV (Carole Ann Klonarides and Michael Owen), Branda Miller, Stefan Moore, Antonio Muntadas, Rita Myers, Jacques-Louis Nyst, Marcel Odenbach, Optic Nerve, Tony Oursler, Nam June Paik, Charlemagne Palestine, Mary Perillo, Jody Proctor, Raindance, Tony Ramos, Daniel Reeves, John Reilly and Julie Gustafson, Wiliam Roarty, Ulrike Rosenbach, Willard Rosenquist, Martha Rosler, Paul Ryan, John Sanborn, Dan Sandin, Ira Schneider and Beryl Korot, Bill Seaman, Willoughby Sharp, Eric Siegel, Michael Smith, Ellin Stein and Betsy Newman, George Stoney, Skip Sweeney, Barbara Sykes, Janice Tanaka, Suzanne Tedesko, Anita Thacher, T. R. Uthco (Doug Hall, Jody Proctor and Diane Hall), TVTV (Top Value Television), Twin Art (Ellen and Lynda Kahn), Stan Vanderbeek, Steina and Woody Vasulka, Edin Velez, Bill Viola, Klaus Vom Bruch, Willie Boy Walker, William Wegman, Robert Wilson, Dean Winkler, WTV (Tom DeWitt, Vibeke Sorensen and Dean Winkler), Jud Yalkut, and Bruce and Norman Yonemoto.

Artists' portraits. Includes *Marcel Breuer* (1973-74); *Marcel Duchamp: Interviewed by Russell Connor* (1964); *Alfred Jensen* (1973); *Jack Tworkov* (1974); *Joseph Beuys: Videoviewed by Willoughby Sharp* (1972); *Vito Acconci: Videoviewed by Willoughby Sharp* (1973); and *Chris Burden: Videoviewed by Willoughby Sharp* (1973).

TVTV (Top Value Television) videotapes include: *Four More Years* (1972), unusual coverage of the 1972 Republican Convention; *The World's Largest TV Studio* (1972), on the Democratic National Convention in Miami Beach; *Adland* (1973), on the advertising industry and the production of television commercials; and *Lord of the Universe* (1974), on the national gathering of Guru Mahara Ji's followers in the Houston Astrodome.
Size & Elements: Videotape: 3/4" (over 3,200 videotapes) and VHS. (Over 800 titles). Houses three videotape libraries: masters, distribution/circulating, and in-house/screening.
Cataloging: Published illustrated catalogs; card catalogs.
Access: Open to the public. Available for in-house viewing, duplication, rental

and purchase. Research and screening fees not charged. Rental and purchase fees charged. Research requests accepted by telephone and in person (walk-in).
Rights: Some rights held to all material. Copyrights retained by original artists or producers. EAI acts as distribution agent for producers who hold copyrights to materials.
Licensing: Rental and purchase fees charged per videotape (prices vary according to length). License fees for programs are for the physical life of the videotape. Rental fees are for a specific time period. Apply for information regarding reuse or broadcast.
Restrictions: Certain restrictions apply in commercial, for-profit or broadcast situations. The video program may not be duplicated, copied and reproduced in whole or in part; may not be exhibited commercially or theatrically; may not be broadcast or cablecast; and may not be sold, lent or transferred to any other institution and individual.
Viewing Facilities: Videotape (3/4" and VHS; NTSC and PAL).
Duplication Facilities: Videotape (3/4", VHS and Betamax).

NEW YORK METRO

ENGINEERING SOCIETIES LIBRARY
345 East 47th Street
New York, NY 10017
(212) 705-7611
Fax: (212) 486-1086

Francis J. Bohan (Manager)

Contact: Francis J. Bohan (212/705-7605)
Services: Library. Film collection maintained primarily for rental and purchase.
Description: Many fluid flow systems involve complex, time dependent phenomena that are most readily recorded by motion pictures. Over the years a considerable body of such motion pictures has been accumulated by research workers, but no organized channel for dissemination or location of these often important data existed.

Motion pictures are stocked for loan and purchase by the Library upon technical approval by the Fluid Mechanics Committee or the Heat Transfer Committee of the American Society of Mechanical Engineers (ASME). Only films relating to research data or teaching films on fluid mechanics or heat transfer are included.

Sample titles include: *Acoustic Tripping of the Flow Around a Sphere; Observation of Boiling by Schlieren; Bubble Behavior in Froth Rotation;* and *Film Boiling on a Horizontal Plate.*
Size & Elements: Film: 16mm (150 titles, 145 cans).
Cataloging: *Catalog of Motion Pictures of Research Data in Fluid Mechanics and Heat Transfer* (available for purchase).
Access: Open to the public. Maintained for distribution and rental rather than research or reuse. Research fees charged. Requests accepted by mail, telephone and in person (walk-in).
Rights: Rights status of material unknown.
Licensing: Apply for information.
Restrictions: None specified.
Viewing Facilities: None.
Duplication Facilities: None.

NEW YORK METRO

ENVIRONMENTAL ACTION COALITION
625 Broadway
New York, NY 10012
(212) 677-1601

Nancy A. Wolf (Executive Director)

Contact: Lori Klamner (Librarian)
Services: Nonprofit environmental group; educational film library. Material available to the public for rental.
Description: Environment, pollution, ecology and conservation.

Sample titles include: *A Land Betrayed,* showing visual pollution; *Birds in the City; Bulldozed America* (CBS News, 1965), a depiction of asphalt and concrete wastelands, narrated by Charles Kuralt; *City Tree; Cycles,* relating to glass recycling; *Ecology Brand Papers; Fuel Cell; Hydrasposal Fibreclaim; Portrait of a San-Man,* a description of a New York City sanitation worker's job, showing changes since horse-drawn trucks; *The Proud New Yorkers,* a children's clean-up project; *Sanitary Landfill — One Part Earth to 4 Parts*

Refuse; The Trouble with Trash; and *Long Island Duckling.*
Size & Elements: Film: 16mm (approx. 35 titles).
Cataloging: List available.
Access: Available to the public for rental.
Rights: Full rights held to some material; rights to most material retained by original producers.
Licensing: Generally not available for licensing or reuse.
Restrictions: None specified.
Viewing Facilities: Film (16mm).
Duplication Facilities: None.

NEW YORK METRO

ERGO MEDIA
P.O. Box 2037
Teaneck, NJ 07666
(201) 692-0404

Dr. Eric Goldman (President)

Contact: Dr. Eric Goldman
Services: Film and videotape distributor. Material available for purchase and rental only. Can refer licensing inquiries to original media producers.
Description: Videotapes relating to Jewish life and culture. Subject areas include the American Jewish experience, the Holocaust, Jewish life around the world, Jewish food and holidays, the arts, classics of the Israeli screen, and contemporary Israel.

Sample titles include: *The Golden Age of Second Avenue,* recalling the history of the Yiddish theater in America; *Rise and Fall of the Borscht Belt,* on the history of the Catskill resort hotels and the evolution of "Borscht Belt" humor; *The Miracle of Intervale Avenue,* on the survival of a Jewish community in New York's South Bronx despite the surrounding decay; *The Falashas,* Meyer Levin's 1973 film study of Ethiopian Jewry; *The Eighty-First Blow,* an historical document comprised of footage and stills shot by the Nazis; *Flames in the Ashes,* about Jewish resistance during the Holocaust; *The World of Anne Frank,* a documentary highlighted by dramatic recreations from Anne's diary; *A. M. Klein: The Poet as Landscape,* a film portrait of this century's leading Anglo-Jewish poet; *The Jewish Mothers Video Cookbook,* and *Hot Bagels: The Hole Story.*

A selection of 16mm feature films is also available for non-theatrical rental.
Size & Elements: Videotape: VHS (approx. 60 titles).
Cataloging: Published catalog.
Access: Available for purchase only. Feature films available for non-theatrical rental.
Rights: No rights held to any material. Can assist in tracing the owner of rights in some cases regarding reuse of material.
Licensing: Must apply to original producers.
Restrictions: Licensing and reuse of material is restricted; rights retained by original producers.
Viewing Facilities: None.
Duplication Facilities: None.

NEW YORK METRO

THE ESTATE OF ANDY WARHOL
19 East 32nd Street
New York, NY 10016
(212) 683-5300

Vincent Fremont (Executive Manager)

Contact: Vincent Fremont
Services: Artist's estate; film and videotape collection.
Description: Film collection holds works by Andy Warhol (1962-76). Videotape collection covers 1979-87, and includes *Andy Warhol's TV.* The entire collection is currently being organized, inventoried and cataloged.
Size & Elements: Film: 35mm (some); 16mm (most of collection). Videotape: assorted formats (amount unspecified; masters and transfers from film).
Cataloging: Material currently being organized, inventoried and cataloged.
Access: Apply for information.
Rights: Full rights held to all material. Additional clearances may be necessary in some cases if material is to be reused.
Licensing: Apply for information. License fees charged.
Restrictions: Requests for licensing and reuse considered on a case-by-case

basis, subject to acceptance and approval.
Viewing Facilities: None.
Duplication Facilities: None.

NEW YORK METRO

ETHNIC FOLK ARTS CENTER
325 Spring Street, Room 314
New York, NY 10013
(212) 691-9510

Martin Koenig; Ethel Raim (Co-Directors)

Contact: Howard Weiss (Director of Special Projects)
Services: Folk arts organization. Films and videotapes available for rental and reuse, subject to restrictions.
Description: International folk arts documentaries (mid-1970s-present) representing more than 30 ethnic groups. Includes traditional dance and music films, incorporating performance footage and interviews with artists, such as Dave Tarras (famous Klezmer musician) in a comeback concert. Material was filmed in U.S. immigrant communities as well as abroad; some 1970s footage was shot in Yugoslavia and Bulgaria.
   One completed film is available for rental: *The Popovich Brothers of South Chicago*, a portrait of a Serbian American musical family. For rental inquiries, contact Ethnic Folk Arts Center, P.O. Box 315, Franklin Lakes, NJ 07417; 201/891-8240.
Size & Elements: Film: 16mm (approx. 80 hrs.; negative and positive, some release prints). Videotape: Betacam (175 titles, each 20 min.); 3/4" (50 titles); 1/2" open reel (25 titles, each 30 min.); VHS (amount unspecified; viewing copies).
Cataloging: Card catalogs; shot lists.
Access: Open to the public. Research fees charged. Research requests accepted by mail, telephone and in person (by appointment only).
Rights: Full rights held to all material. Additional clearances by artists may be necessary in some cases if material is to be reused.
Licensing: Some material possibly available for licensing, subject to restrictions. License fees charged.
Restrictions: Performer or artist approval necessary for reuse in some cases.
Viewing Facilities: Videotape (VHS).
Duplication Facilities: None.

NEW YORK METRO

EXPERIMENTAL INTERMEDIA FOUNDATION (EIF)
224 Centre Street
New York, NY 10013
(212) 431-5127

Phill Niblock (Director)

Contacts: Lona Foote (Administrator); Stella Varveris (Video Director)
Services: Nonprofit arts presentation and service organization. Videotapes available for viewing by researchers and scholars only; selected material available for rental and purchase.
Description: Founded in 1968 to support the creation and presentation of multimedia and intermedia artworks. Presents annual series of intermedia and new music concerts, and radio and video projects. In two decades, EIF has sponsored over a thousand presentations, including solo and small group concerts of dance, music, film, holography and video.
   Documentation of EIF performance events (1984-present; approx. 50 events per year; approx. 200 events total). Includes: *Concerts by Composers* (30 concerts per year), featuring new and experimental music, using traditional instruments, sound sources created in performance, computer-generated music; and *Intermedia Presentations* series (20 performances per year) by intermedia artists, comprised of combinations of film, video, dance, theater, audio art, slides and performance art. Approximately 15 to 20 minutes of each performance is documented on videotape.
   Concerts by Composers (1986-88, 60 min.). Compilation reel of excerpts (each 2 to 4 min.) from fifteen composers performing their work at EIF.
   Produced by Experimental Intermedia Foundation at 224 Centre Street, New York 10013 (1986-88, 60 min.). Contains samples (each 2 to 4 min.) of the work of nineteen composers: Warren Burt, Joseph Celli, Nicolas Collins, David First, Ellen Fullman, Malcolm Goldstein, Daniel Goode, Shelley Hirsch with David Weinstein, Earle Howard, The Hub (Chris Brown, John Bischoff, Mark Trayle, Tim Perkis, Scott Gresham-Lancaster and Phil Stone), Petr Kotik, Guy

Klucevsek, Ron Kuivila, Mary Jane Leach with Camilla Hoitenga, Christian Marclay, Phill Niblock, Ned Rothenberg, Elliot Sharp and Susan Stenger.
   Art works by Phill Niblock. Titles include: *Terrace of Unintelligibility*, with music by Arthur Russell; *Yvonne Grant, Negril, Jamaica*; *Veronica "Sweetie" Campbell, Cousins Cove, Jamaica*; *Ellen Band on P.N.'s Chart*; *Dagmar Apel on Bodies*; *Earl Niblock Recounts*; *Audiobiography, in Three Parts*; and *Erica Hunt Reads from Evidence*. 16mm films transferred to videotape (each approx. 45 min., 3/4" and VHS) include: *Lesotho*; *Hong Kong*; *Tres Familias (Essex & La Purificacion)*; *Brasil 83*; *Brasil 84 #1 and #2*; *Sur Dos & Trabajando Dos*; *Arctic*; *Hungary*; *Ten Hundred Inch Radii*; *Tres Familias (Alpatlahua)*; *Portugal*; *Morning, Magic Sun, Dog Track*; and *Annie, Max, Raoul*. Two films, *Hannah Weiner* and *Armand Schwerner*, document poets reading from their work.
Size & Elements: Videotape: 3/4", Super VHS, VHS and Betamax (approx. 55 hours total).
Cataloging: Computerized list of concerts (videotape and audiotape).
Access: Open to researchers and scholars. Research fees charged. Research requests accepted by mail, telephone and in person (by appointment only).
Rights: Some rights held to some material (Phill Niblock videotapes). Rights to other material retained by performing artists. Additional clearances will be necessary if material is to be reused.
Licensing: Most archival materials not currently available for licensing or reuse. Some material (Niblock videotapes and compilation videotapes) available for rental and purchase.
Restrictions: Most rights retained by artists. Material generally not available for licensing or reuse.
Viewing Facilities: Videotape (3/4", Super VHS and Betamax).
Duplication Facilities: Videotape (3/4", Super VHS and Betamax).
Related Materials: Audiotape collection (1/4" stereo, 325 titles, 52 hours of programming), comprising a complete set of archival recordings of performances at EIF (1978-present), featuring works of audio art, music and literature (300 titles); and music produced by Phill Niblock (25 titles).

NEW YORK METRO

THE EXPLORERS CLUB
46 East 70th Street
New York, NY 10021
(212) 628-8383

John C. D. Bruno (President)

Contact: Rita W. Mathews, Ph.D. (Archivist)
Services: Educational institution. Film collection open to researchers and scholars only. Material possibly available for licensing, subject to clearance and approval.
Description: Small film collection relating to various explorers and their explorations, expeditions and travels throughout the world; and Club activities.
   Titles include: *From New Lands to Old* (1940, Humble Oil & Refining Co.); *Africa School*; *Djuka* (produced by Morton Kahn under the auspices of the American Museum of Natural History); *Antarctica Here We Come* (Lewis Cotlow); *2nd Byrd Expedition to Little America, Antarctica, 1933-35*; *Jambo Porini — The Cleveland Zoo East Africa Expedition*; *Explorers Club Oldtymers Film 1963*; *Riddle of a Mayan Cave*; *A Story of the Tropics*; *Arctic Survey Course 52*; *Alaska Dogs, Bear Cubs*; *Lewis Cotlow: In Search of the Primitive*; *Lewis Cotlow: High Arctic*; *Dr. Tom Gilliard and Quentin Keynes* (1940); *Sir Charles Wright: Scott's Race to the South Pole*; *Ethiopian Jubilee*; and *Pageant in Paradise — Ceylon*.
Size & Elements: Film: 16mm (17,600 feet, 20 titles; black and white and color, some magnetic sound).
Cataloging: Film list; other material uncataloged.
Access: Primarily available to researchers and scholars only. Research fees not charged. Research requests accepted in person (by appointment only).
Rights: Full rights held to all material. Additional clearances may be necessary in some cases if material is to be reused.
Licensing: Possibly available for licensing. License fees not charged.
Restrictions: None specified.
Viewing Facilities: Very limited (available by appointment only).
Duplication Facilities: None.

NEW YORK METRO

FARKAS STUDIOS, LTD.
386 Park Avenue South, Suite 903
New York, NY 10016

(212) 679-4300

Marvin Farkas (Owner)

Contact: Marvin Farkas
Services: Film and videotape producer. Videotape stock footage available for licensing and reuse through authorized representative.
Description: Contemporary and historical footage of Asian and Australasian locations.

Australia (4 hours). Coverage of Melbourne, including trolley cars; Australian rules football; Sydney, including Bondi Beach in the winter with surfers, street scenes, shopping arcades, shops, buildings, Sydney Harbor Bridge, Opera House, skyline and the Centre Point Tower; and Perth, including aerial views, golfing, Swan River, a black swan and the Swan Brewery. Other footage shows kangaroos, koala bears, the emu (a bird) and an Australian bar with beer drinkers.

China (6 hours). Footage of Canton (Kwangtung Province), including bicycles over the Pearl River Bridge, firecrackers exploding at a shop dedication, the interior of a tobacco store, rural scenes and farming villages; Shanghai; Beijing; Harbin (Manchuria), with railroads, street scenes, Russian Christian churches, Russian structures and an outdoor furniture market; and Xian, including landmarks, temples and the Great Wall of China.

Hong Kong (6 hours). Includes landmarks, temples, tourist attractions, businesses, stock market, street scenes, subway scenes, night shots, the airport, Chinese graves (with mausoleums and urns), pagodas, a gold-plated monk, the Dragon Boat Festival and the Bun Festival.

Indonesia (5 hours, silent). Footage of Bali, including folklore and dancing.

Japan (3 hours). Includes Ginza street scenes, the high-speed "bullet" train, traffic and schoolchildren.

Korea (3 hours). Footage of Seoul street scenes and markets, children playing, telephone factories, historical footage of Suwon (a very old walled city), the Daewoo Shipyards, building construction, oil rig manufacturing and rural scenes (including plowing and rice planting).

Malaysia (4 hours). Includes Moorish government buildings, scenes of Kuala Lumpur, Portuguese settlements in Malacca, Penang and its beaches (with luxury hotels), recreation, a cog railroad, the rubber harvest, a snake temple and industrial laboratories.

Philippines (3 hours). Footage of jeepneys (small buses), factories, churches, Santo Thomas University, Bacolod Island, Manila, a shrimp farm and sugar cane farming.

Singapore (4 hours). Includes street scenes, stock market interiors, the airport, river life, stewardess classes, food stalls at Newton's Circus night market and horse racing.

Taiwan (3 hours). Footage of Taipei, including street scenes, railroad tracks through the city center, the North Gate district, exteriors of the Chiang Kai-shek Memorial and military facilities.

Thailand (4 hours). Coverage of Bangkok, including temples, Buddhist monks, bar girls dancing, cooking shrimp chips, royal barges, farming, rivers, canals and canal life, barges and towboats, the petrochemical industry, refineries, textile mills and a Coca-Cola bottling plant.

Vietnam. A small amount of footage from the war era.
Size & Elements: Videotape: 3/4" (75 hours; masters and some transfers from film). All videotape has ambient sound.
Cataloging: Apply for information.
Access: Available for duplication, licensing and reuse through authorized representative. Research fees charged. Research requests accepted by mail, telephone and in person (by appointment only).
Rights: Full rights held to all material.
Licensing: Available for licensing and reuse through authorized representative. License fees charged.
Restrictions: None specified.
Viewing Facilities: Film and videotape (through Film/Audio Services, Inc.).
Duplication Facilities: Film and videotape (through Film/Audio Services, Inc.).
Representative: Film/Audio Services, Inc. (q.v.).

NEW YORK METRO

FEMME DISTRIBUTION, INC.
588 Broadway, Suite 1110
New York, NY 10012
(212) 226-9330

Candida Royalle (President)

Contacts: Candida Royalle; Vivian Forlander (Vice President)
Services: Film and videotape producer and distributor. Videotapes available for rental, purchase and licensing.
Description: Sexually explicit erotica from a woman's point of view. Material is shot softly and elegantly rather than pornographically. The sexual activity depicted is egalitarian and erotic. Videotapes have storylines and strong production values, with original music recorded in stereo.
Size & Elements: Videotape: 1" (edit masters); Betacam (7 videotapes, each 70 to 108 min.; camera masters).
Cataloging: Release sheets.
Access: Available for rental, purchase and licensing. Research fees charged in some cases. Research requests accepted by mail and telephone.
Rights: Full rights held to all material.
Licensing: Available for licensing. License fees charged in some cases.
Restrictions: Apply for information.
Viewing Facilities: Videotape (VHS editing system).
Duplication Facilities: Videotape (VHS).

NEW YORK METRO

FILMAKERS LIBRARY
133 East 58th Street
New York, NY 10022
(212) 355-6545

Contact: Library Staff
Services: Distributor. Film and videotape material available for rental and purchase.
Description: *International issues.* Titles include: *Maids and Madams* (Mira Hamermesh), examining apartheid through the complex relationship between a Black household worker and a White employer; *Chela: Love, Dreams and Struggle in Chile* (Lars Palmgren, Goran Gester and Lars Bildt), a portrait of a politically active teenager who has grown up under Pinochet's dictatorship; *Frontline: An Eyewitness Account of the Vietnam War* (David Bradbury), focusing on a news cameraman who spent 11 years in the combat zone of Vietnam.

Religion and society. Titles include: *The Mormons, Missionaries to The World* (Bobbie Birleffi), which suggests that the church's emphasis on obedience, discipline, sexual restraint and conformity not only affects its members, but has broader social and political implications; *The Family Album* (Alan Berliner), using a vast collection of rare home movies from the 1920s-50s to create an intimate composite portrait of American family life.

Arts and humanities. Titles include: *Made in China* (Lisa Hsia) in which a Chinese American woman journeys to China to learn about her background and discover some truths about herself; *Southern Voices* (George Stoney) follows the process of distilling the sounds and rhythms of Southern speech into an experimental musical work with composer Doris Hays; and *Uncommon Images* (Evelyn Barron) creates a portrait of Black photographer James Van Der Zee.

Anthropology. Titles include: *First Contact* (Bob Connolly and Robin Anderson), with newly recovered footage of the Leahy brothers' penetration into New Guinea's interior in 1930, and interviews fifty years later with some of the Papuans who vividly recall their first encounter with White culture; *Witchcraft among the Azande;* and *The Kwegu.*

Social issues. Titles include: *Not Just Garbage* (Julie Akeret); *Incest: The Family Secret* (CBC), which examines the role of the mother in an incestuous family, and one father's recollection of his own refusal to acknowledge his daughter's anguish; *Cowboys's Claim* (Miranda Smith), in which cattle ranchers near Florida's Disney World are determined to hold onto their land despite falling beef prices and real estate encroachment.

Nature and science, sports and health, rehabilitation. Titles include: *The Family of Chimps* (Bert Haanstra); *Health Care on The Critical List* (Roger Weisberg); *Allergies; Pre-Natal Diagnosis: To Be Or Not To Be; The Story of Susan McKellar* (CBC).

Women's issues. Titles include: *The Women of Summer* (Suzanne Bauman and Rita Heller) documenting the controversial and inspired educational experiment known as The Bryn Mawr Summer School for Women Workers, 1921-38; *Return to Appalachia* (Constance A. Marks); *In A Jazz Way: A Portrait of Mura Dehn* (Louise Ghertler and Pamela Katz); *Waiting Tables* (Linda Chapman, Pam LeBlanc, Freddi Stevens Jacobi).

Human sexuality, psychology and aging. Titles include: *AIDS: No Sad Songs* (Nick Sheehan); *Keltie's Beard* (Barbara Martineau), in which a woman challenges the stereotypical image of womanhood; *39, Single and Pregnant* (Christine Wynne); *Good Girl* (Phyllis Chinlund), a re-enactment of a diary kept by the filmmaker during her thirteenth year; *Back Wards to Back Streets* (Roger Weisberg), on the deinstitutionalization of mental patients; *Love Tapes*

(Wendy Clarke), in which diverse people speak candidly to the video camera about love; *Dreamspeaker* (Claude Jutra) portrays the interaction of a troubled youth and a sage old man, the latter played by an authentic Nootka Indian Shaman; *An Alzheimer's Story* (Kenneth Paul Rosenberg, M.D. and Ruth Neuwald); *The More We Get Together* (Edward and Naomi Feil), a documentary giving insight into working with old, disoriented nursing home residents; *Aging in Soviet Georgia: A Toast to Sweet Old Age* (Richard Breyer); *Women of Hodson* (Josephine Hayes Dean), in which septuagenarians at a local senior citizens center form a drama group and create theater pieces from their own life experiences.

Speech and hearing, developmental disabilities, death and dying. Titles include: *See What I Say,* featuring singer Holly Near; *The First Step* (Barbara Chobocky), on early socialization for retarded children; *Wall to Wall* (Peter Smilsky), in which prison inmates in British Columbia spend time with severely mentally retarded persons; *Little People* (Jan Krawitz and Thomas Ott), a moving and sometimes funny documentary on the experience of being a dwarf; *Essie* (Gerald Wenner); *Last Rites* (Joan Vail Thorne and Anne Macksoud), a drama about death and its incomprehensibility to a child; *Dax's Case* (Unicorn Media, Inc.), spanning a ten-year period in the life of a severely burned man who asserts his right to choose death.
Size & Elements: Film: 16mm (release prints). Videotape: format unspecified (film transfers and viewing copies). (231 titles total).
Cataloging: Published catalog.
Access: Available for rental and purchase rather than for research or reuse.
Rights: No rights held to any material. Additional clearances are necessary if material is to be reused.
Licensing: Apply to individual producers for further information.
Restrictions: Material may not be duplicated without additional clearances.
Viewing Facilities: None.
Duplication Facilities: None.

NEW YORK METRO

FILM/AUDIO SERVICES, INC.
430 West 14th Street, Room 402
New York, NY 10014
(212) 645-2112
Fax: (212) 691-8347

Bob Summers (President)

Contact: Bob Summers
Services: Film and videotape stock footage sales library; research service.
Description: Collection spans the entire 20th century, although the bulk of the material is from 1925-70. It is worldwide in scope, including rare footage of the U.S.S.R., Africa, Japan, Poland, Central and South America. Much of the collection is unedited original camera footage, although series and individual cut films are also represented. Research and consulting services available.

Particular strengths include: over 350 feature fiction films (ca. 1910-70); 150 short fiction films (ca. 1900-70); the Adirondacks; Africa; agriculture; Alaska; Americana (1895-present); animation (approx. 100 films); anthropology; anti-terrorism training; apartheid resistance; archaeology; architecture; the "Borscht Belt"; buildings; camping vacations; castles; cathedrals; the Catskills; Central America; documentaries; Eastern Europe; ecology; entertainers; ethnography; Florida bird life; home movies; interviews; landscapes; Lebanon siege (1982); logging (modern and historical); Mexican Indian rituals; the Middle East; military; music; Native Americans; newsreels (selected); Niagara Falls; nuclear energy; nurses and nursing; Poland (including the fall of Warsaw in World War II); political demonstrations (1960s); political movements and personalities; politics; popular culture (1960s); power plants; pyramids; recreation; refugees; religion; rituals; scenics; solar automobiles; the Soviet Union; tattooing; travel; urban studies; veterans; water and water resources; World War I; World War II; world's fairs; and worldwide travel (1925-80).

Important personalities include: President Kemal Ataturk (Turkey); Ethel Barrymore; Jack Benny; Stokely Carmichael; Ernesto Cardenal; Fidel Castro; Charles Chaplin; Dr. Charlie Clements; "Papa Doc" Duvalier; Thomas Eisner; Douglas Fairbanks; Carlos Fuentes; Athol Fugard; Jean Genet; Maxim Gorky; Manfred Henninger; Adolf Hitler; Abbie Hoffman; Bob Hope; Hugh Iltis; Buster Keaton; Francis Langford; President Miguel de la Madrid; Nelson and Winnie Mandela (1955, 1961); Canadian Prime Minister Brian Mulroney; Lewis Mumford; President Mohammed Najibullah (Afghanistan); Roderick Nash; President Daniel Ortega; Ivan Pavlov; Mary Pickford; President Ronald Reagan; Jerry Rubin; Wallace Stegner; President Sukarno; British Prime Minister Margaret Thatcher; Marshal Josip Broz Tito; and T-Bone Walker.

Videotape library includes: *Universal Newsreel* cut stories; *Universal Newsreel* outtakes; Ford Film Collection; *March of Time* outtakes; Harmon Foundation films; Army-Navy Screen Magazines; Signal Corps films; films from U.S. Departments of Agriculture, Interior, and Post Office; U.S. Bureau of Mines and Bureau of Public Roads films.

Specific film and videotape represented by Film/Audio Services, Inc.: Afghanistan (1926-27, 1960s, 1980-87); Australia (1926-27, 1975-87); Austria (1945, 1980s); British Honduras (1960s); Canada (1980s); Chile (1940-70, 1988); China (1926-27, 1930s-40s, 1975-87, including Peking, Shanghai, Canton, Harbin and Xian); Costa Rica (1982); Cuba (1926-27, 1930s, 1950s-60s); Dominican Republic (1920s, 1988); Egypt (1926-27, 1950s-70s); England (1930s-40s; color footage 1940-80); Ethiopia; Fiji (1926-27); Germany (1930s-40s, 1960s); Grenada (1987); Guatemala (1930s-60, color footage 1980s); Haiti (1915-35, 1961-62); Honduras (1930s-60; color footage 1980s); Hong Kong (1926-27, 1975-87); India (1926-27, 1960s); Indonesia (Bali: 1967, 1975-87); Iran (1970s); Israel (1926-27, 1950s-80s); Jamaica (1960s, 1987); Japan (1926-27, 1930s, color footage 1950-87); Jordan (early 1970s); Korea (1926-27, ca. 1950-55, 1975-87); Lebanon (1970s-80s); Malaysia (1926-27, 1975-87); Mexico (color footage 1930s-present); Middle East (1950s-70s); Nicaragua (1980s); Norway (World War II and 1980); Peru (1940s-80s); Philippines (1898-1902, 1926-27, 1960-present; approx. 60 hours total); Poland (1930s-1960s; color footage 1946-60; approx. 12 hours total); Sabah (formerly British North Borneo); Samoa (1926-27); Singapore (1975-87); South Africa (1920s-80s); South America (1930s-present); South Pacific (1926-27, 1940s); Southern Africa (1970s-80s); Syria (1970s); Taiwan (1975-87); Thailand (1926-27, 1975-87); Turkey (1930-60); United States (1900-present; with particular emphasis on Florida, New England and the Pacific Northwest); U.S.S.R. (1900-80; color footage 1947-80; approx. 100 hours); Venezuela (1960s); Vietnam (1960s-70s); West Bank (1980s); Yugoslavia (1950-60s).
Size & Elements: Film: 35mm and 16mm (50% 16mm, 20% 35mm). Videotape: formats unspecified (30% of collection). (Approximately 1,500 hours available for purchase as of August 1988; collection is expanding at a rate of 40 hours/month).
Cataloging: Card catalogs; shot lists; research library; computerized cataloging for staff use only.
Access: Open to researchers and scholars only. Available for duplication, licensing and reuse. Research fees charged. Requests accepted by mail, telephone and in person (by appointment only). Preview videotapes with visible time code will be provided for a charge.
Rights: Full rights held to some material. Some rights held to some material. Some material in the public domain.
Licensing: Available for licensing and reuse. License fees charged.
Viewing Facilities: Videotape (VHS, with high-speed search).
Duplication Facilities: Film (16mm film to 3/4" and VHS videotape for reference purposes).
Representatives: European outlets (apply for information).

NEW YORK METRO

FILM-MAKERS' COOPERATIVE
175 Lexington Avenue
New York, NY 10016
(212) 889-3820

Contact: Office Manager
Services: Distributor. Films available for rental only.
Description: Holds works variously described as independent, avant-garde, personal or underground films. Collection includes films made over the past four decades (1950s-present), all produced or made by individuals wishing to control their own distribution. Membership is open to any filmmaker placing a print on deposit, specifying the basic rental charge to be made for non-theatrical distribution. There is no selection process; any film offered by its maker is automatically accepted.

Current new work is constantly added to collection by both long-time members and by recent members. Includes work by North American filmmakers and by artists living and working on other continents.
Size & Elements: Film: 35mm, 16mm, Super 8mm and regular 8mm (over 3,000 titles, primarily 16mm; release prints, sound and silent).
Cataloging: Published catalog (donation requested).
Access: Open to the public. Collection maintained for rental only. Rental fees charged; set by filmmakers. Rental requests accepted by mail and in person.
Rights: No rights held to any material; all rights retained by filmmakers.
Licensing: Prospective users must contact filmmakers.
Restrictions: Set and controlled by each filmmaker.

Viewing Facilities: None.
Duplication Facilities: None.

NEW YORK METRO

FILM SEARCH, INC.
111 Fifth Avenue, 9th Floor
New York, NY 10003
(212) 532-0600
Fax: (212) 779-9732
Telex: FILMS 4973657

FILM SEARCH WEST
8228 Sunset Boulevard, Suite 310
Los Angeles, CA 90046
(213) 656-9003
Fax: (213) 656-2726

Henri Ehrlich (President)

Exclusively available worldwide from The Image Bank at the following
locations:

United States:
THE IMAGE BANK NEW YORK
111 Fifth Avenue, 9th Floor
New York, NY 10003
(212) 529-6793
Fax: (212) 529-8886
Telex: 429380 IMAGE
Contacts: Ellen Factor; Robin Parkinson

THE IMAGE BANK BOSTON
500 Boylston Street, Suite 260
Boston, MA 02116
(617) 267-8866
Fax: (617) 267-4685
Contact: Judy Galucci

THE IMAGE BANK CHICAGO
510 North Dearborn Street, Suite 930
Chicago, IL 60610
(312) 329-1817
Fax: (312) 329-1029
Contacts: Claudette Mostyn; Jim Mostyn; Michael Jungert (Manager)

THE IMAGE BANK TEXAS
1336 Conant Street
Dallas, TX 75207
(214) 631-3808
Fax: (214) 951-0278
Contacts: Rex Jobe; Lynn Martin (Manager)

THE IMAGE BANK HOUSTON
10377 Stella Link, Suite B
Houston, TX 77025
(713) 668-0066
Contact: Lynn Martin

THE IMAGE BANK WEST
4526 Wilshire Boulevard
Los Angeles, CA 90010
(213) 930-0797
Fax: (213) 930-1089
Contact: Lilly Filipow

THE IMAGE BANK FLORIDA
5811 Pelican Bay Boulevard, Suite 302
Naples, FL 33963
(813) 566-3444
Fax: (813) 566-1346
Contacts: John Domenie; Mayda Domenie

THE IMAGE BANK MINNEAPOLIS
822 Marquette Avenue
Minneapolis, MN 55402
(612) 332-8935
Fax: (612) 344-1717
Contact: Lora Iverson

THE IMAGE BANK SOUTH
3490 Piedmont Road, NE, Suite 1106
Atlanta, GA 30305
(404) 233-9920
Fax: (404) 231-9389
Contact: Lynn Brantley

THE IMAGE BANK SAN FRANCISCO
22 Battery Street, Suite 202
San Francisco, CA 94111
(415) 788-2208
Fax: (415) 392-6637
Contact: Carol Campbell

Canada:
THE IMAGE BANK CANADA
550 Queen Street East, Suite 300
Toronto, ON M5A 1V2
(416) 362-6931
Fax: (416) 362-4144
Contact: Julie Kovacs

Mexico:
THE IMAGE BANK MEXICO
Oso. No. 41
Col. del Valle
Deleg. B. Juarez
03100 Mexico, D.F.
(905) 524-4644 (Where area code 905 is not valid, dial [52] plus [5].)
(905) 660-1528
(905) 534-6200
(905) 534-4581
Telex: 1760718
Contacts: Juan Carlos Pulido; Teresa Robert (Manager)

South America:
THE IMAGE BANK ARGENTINA
Alsina 943
3er Piso, Oficina 3
1088 Buenos Aires
Argentina
(54) (1) 334-8121/4099
(54) (1) 334-0955/1906
(54) (1) 334-1817/1287
Telex: 17199 TIB AR
Contact: Jorge Fisbein

THE IMAGE BANK BRASIL
Rua Visconde de Piraje, 433/5
22410 Rio de Janeiro, RJ
Brasil
(55) (21) 267-1643
Telex: 2130577 TRAV BR
Contact: Jean Claude Lozouet

THE IMAGE BANK BRASIL
Rua Augusta, 2529/21
01413 Sao Paulo, SP
Brasil
(55) (11) 852-3466
Telex: 1132439 TRAV BR
Contact: Jean Claude Lozouet

THE IMAGE BANK BRASIL
Rua Coronel Bordini, 249
90420 Porto Alegre, RS
Brasil
(55) (512) 43-30-23
Telex: 520304 FBPF BR
Contact: Fernando Bueno

THE IMAGE BANK CHILE
Santa Beatriz 125
Providencia — Santiago
Chile
(56) (2) 225-5189
Fax: (56) (2) 429-49
Telex: 645129 CMTX CT
Telex: 340151 DIGITA CK
Contact: Eduardo Kawas, Jr.

THE IMAGE BANK COLOMBIA
Carrera 14, No. 85-24
Bogota
Colombia
(57) (1) 257-9674
Fax: (57) (1) 211-4598
Telex: 45351 CARMA CO
Telex: 44970 CXBOICO
Contacts: Maria Victoria de Mazuera; Felipe Mazuera

THE IMAGE BANK URUGUAY
Ituzaingo 1318
Montevideo
Uruguay
(598) (2) 95-73-04
Telex: 901 BOOTH UY
Contact: Oscar Bonino

THE IMAGE BANK VENEZUELA
Calle Orinoco Con Veracruz
Torre Orinoco, Oficina 1-E
Las Mercedes Caracas
Venezuela
(58) (2) 928619
Fax: (58) (2) 922714
Contact: Heberto Galicia Vargas

Europe:
THE IMAGE BANK BENELUX
60 Avenue de Mars
1200 Brussels
Belgium
(32) (2) 735-6762
Fax: (32) (2) 734-7171
Telex: 64509 IMAGE B
Contact: Marc Tielemans

THE IMAGE BANK LONDON
7 Langley Street
Covent Garden
London WC2H 9JA
England
(44) (1) 240-9621
(44) (1) 240-9627
Fax: (44) (1) 831-1489
Telex: 894839 TIB G
Contacts: Wilfred Cass; Pat Eaton (Manager)

THE IMAGE BANK ESPANA
Manuel Silvela, 7
28010 Madrid
Spain
(34) (1) 446-9061
(34) (1) 446-9362
Fax: (34) (1) 446-7706
Telex: 43060 RA E
Contact: Annick de Lara

THE IMAGE BANK ESPANA
Muntaner 244-5-1
08021 Barcelona
Spain
(34) (3) 209-3544
(34) (3) 209-3611
Contact: Domingo Garzagall

THE IMAGE BANK FINLAND
Keskuskatu 1
00100 Helsinki 10
Finland
(358) (0) 17.40.66
Telex: 124910 ULLA SF
Contacts: Ulla Danielson; Olle Danielson

THE IMAGE BANK FRANCE
130 Rue Reaumur
75002 Paris
France
(33) (1) 45.08.86.98
Fax: (33) (14) 0.13.02.54
Telex: 212687 TIB F
Contacts: Patrice Fury; Ronaldo Severo; Gilles Devicq

THE IMAGE BANK BILDAGENTUR GMBH
Prinzregentenstrasse 89
8000 München 80
West Germany
(49) (89) 470.20.68
Fax: (49) (89) 470.67.66
Telex: 5214832 TIB D
Contacts: Joachim Soyka; Sabine Hoffman

HELLAS PRESS SERVICE
(THE IMAGE BANK GREECE)
103 Kefallinias Street
112 51 Athens
Greece
(30) (1) 867-5386
(30) (1) 867-6611
Fax: (30) (1) 865-5989
Telex: 214925 HPSE GR
Contacts: Cathrin Sgoura; George Sgoura

THE IMAGE BANK ITALIA
Via Terraggio 17
20123 Milano
Italy
(39) (2) 86.93.964
Fax: (39) (2) 879-109
Telex: 315149 ACPRES I
Contact: Guido Rossi

THE IMAGE BANK ROME
Via Dei Cappuccini, 6
00100 Roma
Italy
(39) (06) 483607
Contact: Guido Rossi

THE IMAGE BANK NORWAY
Radhusgatan 9D
0151 Oslo 1
Norway
(47) (2) 33.06.50
Fax: (47) (2) 33.25.81
Contacts: Yngve Rakke; Aslak Poppe

THE IMAGE BANK SWEDEN
Kungsgatan 62
S-111 22 Stockholm
Sweden
(46) (8) 10.17.70
Fax: (46) (8) 11.04.25
Telex: 16895 IMSCAN
Contact: Inger Treff

THE IMAGE BANK SWITZERLAND
Dufourstrasse 56
P.O. Box 156
CH-8034 Zurich
Switzerland

(41) (1) 69.11.60
Fax: (41) (1) 69.19.40
Telex: 816300 WKR CH
Contacts: Aldo Depuoz; Jeannette Burgherr

THE IMAGE BANK DENMARK
Nyhavn 31C
DK-1051 Copenhagen
Denmark
(45) (1) 15.15.24
Fax: (45) (1) 15.72.15
Contact: Marianne Monrad

Africa/Middle East:
THE IMAGE BANK SOUTH AFRICA
P.O. Box 783277
Sandton 2146
South Africa
(27) (11) 883-7825
(27) (11) 883-7826
Fax: (27) (11) 884-1581
Telex: 427226 SA
Contact: Laurence Hughes
Street address: 79-12 Street, Parkmore, Sandton 2196

THE IMAGE BANK SOUTH AFRICA
Alianz Building
52 St. George Street
Capetown
South Africa
(27) (21) 24-4830
Contact: Laurence Hughes

THE IMAGE BANK ISRAEL
Image Mar'ot Ltd.
2 Koifman Street
Tel-Aviv 68012
Israel
(972) (3) 662-588
(972) (3) 664-308
Fax: (972) (3) 660-896
Telex: 361561 UMAR IL
Contact: Aviva Weinman

Australia/Asia:
THE IMAGE BANK AUSTRALIA
256 Albert Road
South Melbourne 3205
Australia
(61) (3) 699-7833
Fax: (61) (3) 699-6777
Contacts: Peter Hendrie; Bea Bisits (Manager)

THE IMAGE BANK NORTH SYDNEY
131 Blues Point Road
McMahons Point
Sydney 2060 NSW
Australia
(61) (2) 927-158
(61) (2) 954-4255
Fax: (61) (2) 922-6373
Contact: Sharon Stroud

THE IMAGE BANK HONG KONG
Room 1703, 17th Floor, Capitol Centre
5-19 Jardine's Bazaar
Causeway Bay
Hong Kong
(852) (5) 76.20.22
Fax: (852) (5) 76.59.90
Telex: 61373 TIBHK HX
Contact: Bill Sargent

THE IMAGE BANK JAPAN
Sekiguchi Building 2F

1-2-6, Shibadaimon
Minato-ku Tokyo
Japan 105
(81) (3) 435-8360
Fax: (81) (3) 435-8370
Telex: 2523193 IMAGE J
Contact: Shigemitsu Haga

THE IMAGE BANK OSAKA
Kouyou Building, 5th Floor
5-62 Minamikyuhougi-Cho
Higashi-ku
Osaka
Japan 541
(81) (6) 243-0300
Fax: (81) (6) 243-3200
Contact: Shigemitsu Haga

THE IMAGE BANK KOREA
Room 401, Kum-Poong Building
48-27 Jeo-Dong 2KA, Chung-Ku
Seoul
Korea
(82) (2) 273.27.92
Fax: (82) (2) 277.70.64
Telex: 32644 IMAGE
Contact: Dong Hoon Han

IMAGE SHOWCASE SDN BHD
19B Jalan 20/14
46300 Petaling Jaya
Selangor
Malaysia
(60) (3) 776-8136
(60) (3) 776-8549
Fax: (60) (3) 717-2110
Telex: 36800 WINGS MA
Contacts: Dato' Lim Kok Wing; Datin Tessie Lim (Manager)

Services: Film and videotape stock footage sales library and agency. Represents over 50 filmmakers and production companies. Research services, custom shooting and production services available.
Description: Founded in 1980, Film Search was the first company to specialize in providing film and videotape images to commercial producers. Its footage has been used in thousands of productions. In-house library is complemented by a full range of research and production services. Research staffers have over 15 years of experience locating and clearing footage from around the world. Contacts with every major government, sports, archival and institutional collection, as well as with film and television studios, provide comprehensive coverage. Releases for individuals appearing in footage either exist or can in most instances be obtained. Exclusive rights and other customized marketing packages can be negotiated.

Network of cinematographers is available for shooting assignments in most parts of the world. Film Search exclusively represents commercial, documentary and feature cinematographers and directors with Oscars, Clios and other top awards to their credit.

The Image Bank is an international marketing network of almost 50 offices in all major markets throughout the world. To further expand and to better service its clientele, it has acquired Film Search and is offering their footage through its network.

Editors are culling the most saleable original 35mm and 16mm footage from the collection of Film Search. From this material, an opening package of over 40 hours of quality film imagery will be mastered on film and on digital and analog videotape. Clients around the world will thus be able to quickly receive film elements and NTSC or PAL videotape copies of the highest quality from any office in The Image Bank network. This library of mastered footage will be continously augmented, insuring a constantly increasing supply of the newest footage.

General description of collection. Comprehensive assortment of footage including sports, wildlife, landmarks, scenics and cultures from around the world; aerials; Americana; time-lapse; industry; and vintage black and white. Library includes documentaries, features, television programs, outtakes and footage shot specifically for marketing by Film Search and The Image Bank.

Sports footage ranges from action and adventure sports (e.g., surfing, automobile racing and skiing) to professional sports (e.g., golf, tennis, hockey and baseball). The images of many athletes appearing in footage have been cleared for reuse; library can obtain clearances where necessary. Holds an assortment of unusual or daredevil stunts, e.g., water skiing through a hoop of fire and base jumping from tall buildings. Much footage in 35mm.

Wildlife footage ranges from the rare and exotic (e.g., sharks, whales and eagles) to everyday pets (cats and dogs). Animal species from around world are available (Africa, North and South America, Asia, Europe and the Arctic). Much footage in 35mm.

Represents extensive travel collections covering all continents (1920s-present). Subjects covered range from the coronation of Haile Selassie to beauty shots of Paris and New York City (1920s-30s). The majority of this material is shot in 35mm.

Industry and technology footage includes, among other subjects, steelmaking, assembly lines, robots, microchips and building demolitions. Every form of transportation is available, from high-speed trains to spaceships.

Represents large collections of 35mm black and white vintage footage from silent features and early newsreels. Some features and animation (1930s-40s) also available.

Represents 35mm collections of aerials covering scenic locations (rivers and lakes), U.S. cities and landmarks (e.g., the Statue of Liberty and the Golden Gate Bridge) and foreign locations (e.g., Tahiti and Indonesia).

The Americana collection shows current American life and culture from coast to coast, ranging from urban and rural lifestyles to natural scenic beauty. Much material in 35mm.

Represents precision-registered 35mm time-lapse collections. Has footage of natural phenomena (e.g., flowers opening, suns, clouds and moons) and city scenes (e.g. skylines, traffic and crowds).

Following is a sampling of the types of collections and cinematographers represented exclusively by Film Search:

Koyaanisqatsi (feature film plus 20 hours of outtakes). A feature-length tone poem that takes an intense view of modern life. Extraordinary aerials, time-lapse and slow-motion cinematography are used to contrast the natural beauty of the United States with the dehumanizing effect of technology on our big cities. The film and outtakes combine to form an incredible collection of 35mm shots ranging from generic natural scenics (including clouds, waves, mountains, canyons and deserts) to harshly beautiful cityscapes (skylines, traffic and factories) and classic Americana (Las Vegas casinos, New York City subways, fast-food stands and taxiing jets that take on a life of their own).

Powaqqatsi (feature film plus 80 hours of outtakes). A portrait of primitive lifestyles and rituals. The common experiences of living, whether people are dancing, working or praying, and the timeless expression of children's faces mirrored in a blaze of color and movement. The focus is the Third World, featuring universal aspects of life in 11 countries, including Peru, India, Egypt, Kenya and Brazil. The film and outtakes cover a wide assortment of subjects, including aerials of Sao Paulo, Katmandu, Hong Kong and volcanoes; scenics of reed boats, ancient sailing vessels and Mayan farmlands; exotic wildlife; and people chopping coconuts, twining ropes and marketing.

Ocean Images. For the past 25 years, this company has been creating some of the most innovative undersea and water-action films in the industry. Includes over 800 hours of 35mm and 16mm footage covering a wide assortment of marine subjects, from the most generic underwater views to such rare items as great white sharks and humpback whales.

Steve Marts. An award-winning documentary filmmaker, Steve Marts has traveled the world shooting exciting and exotic subjects. His footage embodies true "Americana" (scenic views, sports, wheat farming, dazzling sunsets and small towns) as well as the exotic and unusual.

Robin Lehman. The subjects of his films and outtakes range from East African wildlife to surreal impressions of Yellowstone National Park, exotic underwater locations, action sports and children's stories. Footage from this considerable library was all shot in 35mm negative.

Spectrum Associates has been shooting award-winning travel documentaries around the world for over 20 years. Its library covers every major location in the United States, Europe, the Middle East, South America and Asia. Besides including landmarks and cities around the world, the library also covers subjects ranging from sports and leisure activities to fashion, food, art and industry.

Size & Elements: Film: 35mm (amount unspecified, approx. 50% of library; negatives and workprints); 16mm (amount unspecified; negatives and workprints). Videotape: D-1 (digital) and 1"; NTSC and PAL (hundreds of hours total; masters); 3/4" (1,000 hours; viewing copies).

Core library contains 1,000 hours with access to thousands of hours of outtakes; videotape viewing copies available. Negative available for 95% of material in library. 50 hours of the best footage has been mastered on 35mm film and digital and analog videotape (D-1, 1"; NTSC and PAL). This initial mastered inventory will be supplemented on a continuous basis, ensuring

quality control and fast delivery of editing elements. Currently acquiring footage originally shot on videotape for use in videotape productions.

Cataloging: All mastered footage, selected outtakes and research information (including production sources, releases and distribution data) fully cross-referenced on computerized database and accessible at TIB offices. Videotape catalogs available. Much of library organized thematically.

Access: Open to the public. Requests accepted by mail, telephone and telex. TIB offices can organize screenings or send out selected material in film or videotape formats. Screenings by appointment only. Research fees charged, depending on complexity of job. Demonstration reel and brochure available on request.

Rights: Exclusive rights held to majority of material. Represents producers and other owners of footage, and has full rights to license all footage in its collection. Talent releases exist or are being obtained as mastered inventory is produced. TIB works with cinematographers to obtain all necessary releases and permissions at the time of shoot.

Licensing: License fees billed and payable when completion air-quality elements are ordered. Rates depend on footage being licensed, type of production and market. Marketing packages, exclusive rights and other options available.

Restrictions: None specified.

Viewing Facilities: Film (16mm and 35mm) at certain locations; videotape (3/4" and VHS) at all TIB offices.

Duplication Facilities: Videotape (3/4" and VHS).

Related Services: Cinematographers represented exclusively by Film Search are available to shoot for specific projects. Demonstration reels available on request.

NEW YORK METRO

FILM/VIDEO ARTS, INC.
817 Broadway, 2nd Floor
New York, NY 10003-4797
(212) 673-9361

Rodger Larson (Director)

Contact: Rodger Larson

Services: Media arts organization. Film and videotape collection available to researchers and scholars for research, duplication and possibly reuse, subject to restrictions.

Description: Collection includes short 16mm sound films (1964-74), created entirely by young people, ages 14-18, under the supervision and direction of Rodger Larson, co-founder of Film/Video Arts, Inc. (formerly Young Filmmakers, Inc.).

In 1966, educators Rodger Larson and Lynne Hofer, in collaboration with filmmaker Jaime Barrios, introduced 16mm motion picture equipment to a small group of New York City's Lower East Side youth from the University Settlement House. The teenagers were soon making highly personal films, primarily concerned with growing up in the neighborhood.

Topics include: death; oppression; drug-induced fantasies; heroes; social-sexual frustrations; growing up and aging; the Vietnam War; and science fiction. Films were created using a variety of techniques, including animation, documentary, montage editing, experimental shooting and film manipulation (e.g., scratching on film surface and hand-painting film). Filmmakers include Alex Roschuk, Linda Rivera, Orinne Takagi, Peter Wallach and Jane Warrenbrand, among others.

These movies were shown to enthusiastic street audiences on a "Moviebus" throughout the five New York City boroughs. Film production continued to increase in 1967 when a nearby storefront at 11 Rivington Street was acquired. Named "Film Club 16mm" by its members, this workshop was the first to enable young people to make their own movies by providing them with materials and instruction on a year-round basis.

Now in its twentieth year, Film/Video Arts is the New York metropolitan region's largest nonprofit media arts center, and its services are critical to the active, local independent media arts community.

Size & Elements: Film: 16mm (approx. 125 titles, approx. 400 cans; reversal originals and release prints). Videotape: 3/4" (approx. one-third of film collection transferred to videotape for viewing purposes).

Cataloging: Published catalog.

Access: Open to researchers and scholars only. Available for duplication. Research fees charged in some cases (negotiable). Research requests accepted by mail and telephone.

Rights: Full rights held to some material.

Licensing: Available for reuse. Usage fees negotiated on a case-by-case basis.

Restrictions: Requests for licensing and reuse subject to clearance and approval.
Viewing Facilities: Videotape (3/4"; hourly fee charged).
Duplication Facilities: Film (16mm to 3/4" or 1/2" videotape).

NEW YORK METRO

FIRST RUN/ICARUS FILMS, INC.
200 Park Avenue South, Suite 1319
New York, NY 10003
(212) 674-3375
Fax: (212) 477-2753
Telex: 6502733717

Jonathan Miller (President)

Contact: Lyna Shirley (Distribution Manager)
Services: Film and videotape distributor. Material available for rental, purchase and reuse, subject to restrictions.
Description: The combined collections of Icarus Films and First Run Features total over 275 titles, primarily documentaries. The main focus of the company is non-theatrical distribution. Collection is particularly strong in the areas of political and social issues, Latin America, South Africa, the Middle East, labor, women's issues, Jewish history, cultural issues and Asian issues. Most films have been produced and released since 1979.

Africa. Blood and Sand: The War in the Sahara examines the conflict between the Polisario guerrillas, native people of the Western Sahara fighting for the liberation of their land; and the Kingdom of Morocco, which now occupies the territory.

Animation. Four films by the American twins Timothy and Stephen Quay.

Asia. Back to Kampuchea concerns an exiled Cambodian's return to his native land in search of his family. *Survivors* examines the physical, emotional and financial hardships that characterize the lives of Japanese Americans trapped in Japan during the war who suffered the tragedy of the Hiroshima and Nagasaki atomic bombings.

Central America. American Journey follows a Vermont Witness for Peace group to the combat zone on Nicaragua's northern border. *Nicaragua: Report from the Front* provides an in-depth look at U.S. foreign policy in Central America as it is being played out along Nicaragua's borders. *Roses in December* chronicles the brief life of an American woman volunteer with the Maryknolls in El Salvador, murdered by Salvadoran security forces. *Witness to War* tells the story of Dr. Charlie Clements' journey from pilot in Vietnam to doctor behind rebel lines in El Salvador. Several films produced by the Farabundo Marti Front for National Liberation (FMLN) in El Salvador, showing life in guerrilla-controlled areas. *El Salvador: Another Vietnam,* the most comprehensive film introduction to that country, examines the civil war in light of the Reagan Administration's decision to "draw the line" against "communist interference" in Central America. *Americas in Transition* provides a concise introduction to the history of and forces at work in Central America. Distributes five films produced by the Nicaraguan Film Institute, including *Banana Company,* a tour of Nicaragua's large banana plantations; *History of a Committed Cinema,* a critique of Western cinema; and *These People May Pass,* recording the impressions of visitors to Nicaragua. Videotapes produced by the Popular Video Workshop "Timoteo Velasquez" in Nicaragua. *Waiting for the Invasion* explores the lives and work of the U.S. community residing in Managua, Nicaragua.

Civil rights. Fundi views history from the perspective of Ella Baker, a dynamic 79-year-old activist.

Culture and society. Herr Puntila in Sri Lanka (1985) records a traveling show of Brecht's play; *A Jumpin' Night in the Garden of Eden* (1987) shows the revival of klezmer music; *Painted Landscapes of the Times* (1987) introduces the politically inspired work of painter Sue Coe. The films of Ross McElwee, including *Sherman's March, Space Coast, Backyard, Charleen* and *Resident Exile. The Highly Exalted,* on the last true cowboys in America. *Minnie the Moocher and Many, Many More* is a nostalgic tour of Harlem jazz clubs of the 1930s and 1940s, led by musician Cab Calloway. *28 Up* follows British seven-year-olds from a variety of economic and social backgrounds, watching them grow from childhood to adolescence and young adulthood. *Seventeen,* originally part of a documentary series updating the Lynd's sociological study *Middletown,* uncovers the turmoil brewing beneath a seemingly placid working class community — reckless parties, drugs, interracial relationships and tensions, apathy in the classroom and teenage pregnancy. The film was never aired on PBS because of its explosive content. *Troupers* traces the history and development of the San Francisco Mime Troupe.

Economics. Free Markets for Free Men; Grow or Die; and *Time Is Money* (1986), on the world commodity markets.

Fiction films. Work by Lizzie Borden (*Born in Flames*), Sara Driver, Marleen Gorris, Suzanne Osten, Yvonne Rainer (*Film About a Woman Who...; Journeys from Berlin/1971;* and *The Man Who Envied Women*), Mark Rappaport (*Chain Letters*) and Rosa von Praunheim (*A Virus Knows No Morals*).

Gay issues. Track Two, on the evolution of Toronto's gay community.

History and politics. Are We Winning, Mommy? America and the Cold War, directed by Barbara Margolis (1986), explores the Cold War and its effect on American life. *Euskadi: The Stateless Nation* (1984) is the first definitive film treatment of the Basque-Spanish conflict. *The Good Fight* tells the story of the Abraham Lincoln Brigade, United States volunteers in the Spanish Civil War. *A Painful Reminder* (1985) records the moments of liberation of the Nazi concentration camps. This film, on which Alfred Hitchcock worked, was suppressed for 40 years. *Resurgence: The Movement for Equality vs. the Ku Klux Klan* examines how racism functions within the context of increased industrialization in the South. *The Secret Agent* documents the use of Agent Orange in the Vietnam War and the effects of dioxin on veterans and the environment. *Underground,* on the Weather Underground Organization. *The Unquiet Death of Julius and Ethel Rosenberg* examines the arrest, trial and execution of the "atom bomb spies" and the climate of the early 1950s in the U.S. *The War At Home* chronicles the antiwar protest movement of the 1960s and 1970s in Madison, Wisconsin.

Labor. Between a Rock and a Hard Place profiles three generations of Appalachian coal miners. *The Great Weirton Ste(a)l* analyzes worker ownership of industry through employee stock ownership plans, and tells the story of the experiment at Weirton Steel. *I Am Somebody* (1970) presents the story of a 113-day strike by Black women hospital workers in Charleston, South Carolina. *Pregnant But Equal* shows how pregnant women workers can gain the equal rights they are entitled to by highlighting the story of one group of factory workers and their fight for maternity benefits. *What Could You Do With a Nickel?* tells the story of 200 Black and Hispanic women employed by the City of New York who joined together to form the first domestic workers union in the United States. *The Wobblies* documents the history of the Industrial Workers of the World with photographs, archival footage, interviews and songs.

The Middle East. Routes of Exile: A Moroccan Jewish Odyssey reconstructs the history of Moroccan Jews and their struggle for equality in Israel. Also distributes films from Iran, Israel and Palestine.

Motion pictures. Before the Nickelodeon follows the history of filmmaking (1896-1909), focusing on Edwin S. Porter, the first great American filmmaker who directed such seminal works as *The Great Train Robbery* and *Life of an American Fireman. A Crime to Fit the Punishment* chronicles the making of the controversial labor film *Salt of the Earth.*

Southern Africa. Killing A Dream (1986) shows the war of terror waged inside Mozambique by a South Africa-sponsored guerrilla group, the MNR. *The Ribbon* (1987) tells the story of the Peace Ribbon, made by Black and White South African women. *South Africa Belongs to Us,* a film about the impact of apartheid on Black women and the Black family. *Passing the Message,* about the struggle to organize trade unions for Black workers.

Women. Chicken Ranch profiles the women of a Nevada brothel and examines the social, economic and emotional complexities of legalized prostitution. *The Dozens* examines the inadequacies of a prison system unable to prepare inmates for reentry into the "outside" world, and offers a provocative analysis of a society that ignores its working class women and prolongs the feminization of poverty.

Size & Elements: Film: 16mm. Videotape: various formats. (Approx. 275 titles total).
Cataloging: Published catalogs; computerized cataloging for staff use only; release sheets for individual titles.
Access: Available for rental and purchase. Some titles available to the public for purchase. Limited access available for preview. Apply for information regarding licensing and reuse. Research fees charged in some cases. Research requests accepted by mail, telephone and in person (by appointment only).
Rights: Full rights held to some material; non-theatrical distribution rights held to all material. Additional clearances may be necessary in some cases if material is to be reused.
Licensing: Available for licensing and reuse, subject to restrictions. License fees charged.
Restrictions: Apply for information.
Viewing Facilities: Film and videotape (small screening room, available by appointment only).
Duplication Facilities: None.

NEW YORK METRO

FOCUS
2567 Columbus Avenue
Oceanside, NY 11572
(516) 764-4584

Carol Giambalvo (National Coordinator)

Contacts: Carol Giambalvo; David Clark
Services: Nonprofit organization. Videotape available for duplication, subject to restrictions.
Description: Materials relating to various cults, including interviews with former cult members, conference workshop footage, cult-related movies and television interviews.
Size & Elements: Videotape: VHS (approx. 250 items).
Cataloging: Research library.
Access: Available to the public for research and duplication. Research fees not charged. Research requests accepted by mail, telephone and in person (by appointment only).
Rights: Rights status of material not known.
Licensing: Apply for information.
Restrictions: Copyright restrictions may apply to television programs. Permission from interviewees may be necessary in some cases if material is to be reused.
Viewing Facilities: None.
Duplication Facilities: Videotape (fees charged).

NEW YORK METRO

FOCUS INTERNATIONAL, INC.
14 Oregon Drive
Huntington Station, NY 11746
(516) 549-5320
(800) 843-0305

Mark Schoen, Ph.D. (President)

Contact: Mark Schoen
Services: Educational film and videotape producer and distributor. Materials available for rental and purchase.
Description: Sex education films and videotapes. Topics include aging and sexuality, AIDS, anatomy and physiology, assessment tools, birth, birth control, bisexuality, breast cancer, Chlamydia, condoms, contraception, disability, erotica, female orgasmic dysfunction, gender identity, heterosexuality, homosexuality and lesbianism, impotence, masturbation, reproductive technology, sex education, sex research, sex roles, sex therapy, sexual abuse, sexual history, sexually transmitted diseases, vaginismus and women's issues.

Sample titles include: *Exhibition: The Male Genitals; Grand Opening: The Female Genitalia; Loving Better; Oral Sex; Watching Stump-tailed Macaques; Teenage Birth Control: Why Doesn't it Work?; Bellybuttons are Navels; A Crime of Violence; Dressing Up: An Overview of Cross Dressing; Female Masturbation; Male Masturbation; AIDS Alert; How a Child Grows;* and *Love in Later Life.*
Size & Elements: Film: 16mm. Videotape: 3/4", VHS and Betamax. (Over 100 titles total).
Cataloging: Published catalog.
Access: Open to the public for rental and purchase, for educational and non-theatrical purposes only. Orders accepted by mail and telephone.
Rights: Full rights held to some material.
Licensing: Not available for licensing or reuse.
Restrictions: Material protected by copyright. Available for educational and non-theatrical purposes only.
Viewing Facilities: None.
Duplication Facilities: None.

NEW YORK METRO

FRANKLIN FURNACE ARCHIVE, INC.
112 Franklin Street
New York, NY 10013
(212) 925-4671

Martha Wilson (Founder/Director)

Contact: Martha Wilson
Services: Museum. Videotape collection open to researchers and scholars only.
Description: Documentation of various performance events occurring at Franklin Furnace (late 1970s-80s). Videotapes are copies which have been donated to archive; originals belong to featured artists.
Size & Elements: Videotape: format unspecified (approx. 15 to 25 videotapes).
Cataloging: Card catalog.
Access: Open to researchers and scholars only. Research fees not charged but membership encouraged. Research requests accepted in person (by appointment only).
Rights: No rights held to any material. Additional clearances are necessary if material is to be reused. All rights retained by artists, who must be contacted directly with requests regarding reuse.
Licensing: Apply for information.
Restrictions: Clearance for reuse must be obtained from artists.
Viewing Facilities: None.
Duplication Facilities: None.

NEW YORK METRO

FREMANTLE INTERNATIONAL, INC.
660 Madison Avenue
New York, NY 10021
(212) 421-4530
Fax: (212) 207-8357
Telex: 423459

Paul Talbot (President)

Contact: Josh Braun
Services: Television distributor; series, specials and features available for distribution primarily in foreign markets. *Material not generally available to the public for licensing or reuse.*
Description: *Game shows.* Titles include: *The Price is Right; Card Sharks (Play Your Cards Right); I've Got a Secret (Top Secret); Super Password; Family Feud (Family Fortunes); Blockbusters; Beat the Clock; To Tell the Truth; Match Game (Blankety Blank); Now You See It; Hollywood Squares; Satellite Bingo; Wordplay* (Canada only); *Second Guess* (Australia); *Child's Play; Concentration; The Better Sex; Tattletales; What's My Line?; Break the Bank; Quandaries; Strike it Rich; Babble; Go; Star Connection; The Dating Game; The Newlywed Game; Every Second Counts; Hot Potato; $25,000 Pyramid* (Canada only); *Press Your Luck.*

Specials. Sample titles include: *An All-Star Celebration Honoring Martin Luther King, Jr.* (NBC, 2 hours); *Tony Awards* (CBS, annual shows including 1987); *The Magic of David Copperfield* (7 specials, each 60 min.); *Elvis Memories* (60 min.); *The Johnny Cash Specials* (10 specials, each 60 min.); *Barbara Mandrell and the Mandrell Sisters* (32 programs, each 60 min.).

Paul Killiam Collection of Film Classics. 76 films (silent, restored, tinted; musical tracks added).

Daytime drama. Series include: *Ryan's Hope* (ABC, 30 min. programs, 11 years of production); *Loving* (ABC, 30 min. programs, 4 years of production); *Divorce Court* (130 programs, each 30 min., U.K. and Europe, except for Spain and France).

Comedy series. Series include: *Second City Television* (NBC, 156 programs, each 30 min., U.K. and Europe, except for Spain and France); *Candid Camera* (CBS, 140 programs, 70 in color); *The New Candid Camera* (130 programs, each 30 min.).

Children's programming. Series include *Romper Room* and *Mr. Wizard's World* (52 hours of practical science for young people).

Other programs held include television movies and features, animated series and specials, music and dance programs, comedy specials and documentaries.
Size & Elements: Videotape (all distribution formats).
Cataloging: Published lists.
Access: Material available for distribution primarily in foreign markets. *Footage generally not available to the public for research or reuse.*
Rights: Some rights held to all material. Additional clearances may be necessary in some cases if material is to be reused. *Clip rights generally retained by producer or copyright holder.*
Licensing: Most shows available only for foreign distribution. Domestic rights not held except in a few cases. *Footage generally not available for reuse* (apply to producer or U.S. copyright holder for information).
Restrictions: Restrictions may apply to some programs.
Viewing Facilities: None.

Duplication Facilities: None.

NEW YORK METRO

THE FUND FOR HUMAN DIGNITY, INC.
NATIONAL GAY AND LESBIAN RESOURCE CENTER
666 Broadway, Suite 410
New York, NY 10012
(212) 529-1600

Contact: Abby Tallmer (Coordinator, Resource Center)
Services: Educational and informational organization. Videotape material maintained for broadcast distribution to organizations.
Description: Public service announcements (PSAs) promoting healthy lesbian and gay self-images.
    Items include: *#1* (:30), columnist Abigail ("Dear Abby") Van Buren reads a letter from a mother who is distraught because one of her daughters is a lesbian; *#2* (:60), a collage of people of varying age, race and gender, each of whom introduces himself or herself by occupation; *#3* (:30), actor Mike Farrell introduces a picnic for families which include gay or lesbian members; *#4* (:30), the late actor Jack Albertson introduces a social event for older gays and lesbians, emphasizing the lesbian and gay presence among America's older population; *#5* (:30), lesbians and gay men talk about the challenges of being differently abled and gay or lesbian.
    Each PSA ends with the address and telephone number of The Fund for Human Dignity. Interested organizations may choose to leave this section blank, or insert their own names and addresses.
Size & Elements: Videotape: 3/4", VHS and Betamax (5 PSAs).
Cataloging: Published list and brochures.
Access: Available to organizations and broadcasters. Contact the Fund to request videotapes or for more information. Materials available for cost of duplication plus postage and handling.
Rights: Rights retained by original producers or filmmakers.
Licensing: Apply for information.
Restrictions: Apply for information.
Viewing Facilities: None.
Duplication Facilities: Material can be duplicated for distribution; duplication fees charged. Voiceover fee extra. Choice of graphics includes: National Gay Task Force graphic, no graphic (no extra charge), or new graphic (fees apply).

NEW YORK METRO

GAY CABLE NETWORK
32 Union Square East, Suite 1217
New York, NY 10003
(212) 477-4220

Louis P. Maletta (Producer)

Contact: Louis P. Maletta
Services: Media organization; videotape library. Material available for licensing and reuse.
Description: Begins 1982. Gay writers, playwrights, actors, plays and theater pieces; gay-oriented news coverage and events, including footage from 1984 Republican and Democratic Conventions and complete material on AIDS; extensive film reviews ranging from *Big Men on Campus* to *Taxi Zum Klo* and *Victor/Victoria;* interviews, including Frank Ripplof, Harvey Fierstein and Dietor Schidor.
Size & Elements: Videotape: 3/4" (768 videotapes); VHS (200 videotapes). Material added on a weekly basis.
Cataloging: Computerized cataloging for staff use only.
Access: Available for licensing and reuse. Research fees charged. Requests accepted by mail.
Rights: Full rights held to all material.
Licensing: Available for licensing and reuse. License fees charged.
Restrictions: None specified.
Viewing Facilities: Videotape (3/4" and VHS).
Duplication Facilities: Videotape (3/4" and VHS).

NEW YORK METRO

GAY MEN'S HEALTH CRISIS
129 West 20th Street
New York, NY 10011
(212) 807-7517

Fax: (212) 337-3656

Richard Dunne (Executive Director)

Contact: Jean Carlomusto (Audiovisual Coordinator, Education Department)
Services: Nonprofit association. Videotape collection maintained for distribution and rental.
Description: Currently producing *Living with AIDS* (over 50 programs produced to date, each 30 min.), aired weekly on cable television. The program concentrates on various political, psycho-social and health-related issues surrounding the AIDS crisis. Two segments from this show are in wider distribution: *Women and AIDS* (Jean Carlomusto and Alexandra Juhasz, 1987) covers issues relevant to women and AIDS, including safe sex and the portrayal of women in the mass media (as being responsible for birth control, for controlling men's sexual appetites and for the prevention of AIDS). *Doctors, Liars and Women* (Jean Carlomusto and Maria Maggenti, 1988) is a response to a *Cosmopolitan* article (January 1988) that stated that heterosexual women were not at high risk of contracting AIDS. This videotape explodes this myth, and offers how-to information on consciousness-raising organizing.
Size & Elements: Videotape: 3/4" and 1/2" (over 50 videotapes, each 30 min.; masters and viewing copies).
Cataloging: In progress.
Access: Maintained for distribution and rental rather than research and reuse. Fees charged for rental and purchase. Requests accepted by mail.
Rights: Full rights held to all material.
Licensing: Available for licensing, subject to restrictions. License fees charged (to cover costs).
Restrictions: Requests for licensing considered on a case-by-case basis.
Viewing Facilities: None.
Duplication Facilities: None.

NEW YORK METRO

GERMAN INFORMATION CENTER
FILM LIBRARY
950 Third Avenue, 24th Floor
New York, NY 10022
(212) 888-9840
Fax: (212) 752-6691

Hennecke Graf von Bassewitz (Director)

Contact: Peggy Reichert (Film Librarian)
Services: Government agency. Films available to the public on a free-loan basis for informational and educational purposes, and for educational broadcast.
Description: Recent documentaries on German history and culture. Primary topics include: Germany, its people, lifestyles, cities and regions; Berlin; sociology, education, work and careers, people and society; economy, business and industry; science and technology; environmental protection and agriculture; urban planning and living; transportation; communications and the media; the arts; politics and history; Germany and America; and sports.
    Sample films include: *The German Scene,* a monthly newsreel; *Along the Romantic Road* (1969), on the socio-historic background of the picturesque towns of Nördlingen, Dinkelsbühl and Rothenburg and their struggle to balance the old and new Franconia; *John F. Kennedy Speaks to the People of Berlin* (1963), a film record of his historic visit; *A Berlin Lost* (1983-84), a documentary on Western Europe's largest Jewish cemetery in Berlin-Weissensee, with commentary provided by (mostly emigrant) Jewish citizens of Berlin; *Everyday Student Life in Germany* (1980); *The Miracle that Wasn't One — Key Words to the Social Market Economy,* on the German economy, addressing post-World War II reconstruction and the Marshall Plan; *Mies van der Rohe* (1980), reminiscences of the architect, filmed by his daughter a year before his death; *Charlemagne — Builder of Europe* (1966); and *Speech by Richard von Weizsacker, President of the Federal Republic of Germany, in the Bundestag during the ceremony commemorating the 40th Anniversary of the End of the War in Europe and of National Socialist Tyranny — May 8, 1985.*
Size & Elements: Film: 16mm (amount unspecified). Videotape: 3/4" (some films available). (English and German soundtracks).
Cataloging: Published lists.
Access: Available to the public for loan (free of charge for informational and educational purposes). Available free of charge to television and cable television stations for educational broadcast.
Rights: Full rights held to some material. Some material in the public domain.
Licensing: Apply for information.

Restrictions: Some restrictions apply.
Viewing Facilities: Limited.
Duplication Facilities: None.
Distributor: Selected films available from West Glen Films, 1430 Broadway, 9th Floor, New York, NY 10018; (212) 921-0966. Contact regional Goethe Institutes (q.v.) for additional film and videotape materials.

NEW YORK METRO

GIORNO POETRY SYSTEMS INSTITUTE, INC.
222 Bowery
New York, NY 10012
(212) 925-6372

John Giorno (President)

Contact: John Giorno
Services: Film and videotape producer; foundation; media organization. Material available for research and possibly reuse. Completed videotapes available for purchase.
Description: Videotapes on poetry, music and performance.
   Poetry in Motion (Ron Mann). Features Jim Carroll, Charles Bukowski, Amiri Baraka, William Burroughs, Helen Adam, Jayne Cortez, Ted Berrigan, Robert Creeley, Tom Waits, Ed Sanders, John Cage, Miguel Algarin, Michael McClure, Four Horsemen, Christopher Dewdney, Ted Milton, Diane DiPrima, Michael Ondaatje, Kenward Elmslie, Gary Snyder, Anne Waldman, Ntozake Shange, Allen Ginsberg and John Giorno.
   Giorno Video Pak 1. With William Burroughs, the Lenny Kaye Connection and John Giorno.
   Giorno Video Pak 2. Burroughs, The Movie (Howard Brookner, 1983). Documentary film featuring William S. Burroughs, Patti Smith, Lauren Hutton, Allen Ginsberg, Jackie Curtis, Terry Southern, Brion Gysin, John Giorno and Francis Bacon. Holds all original film footage and outtakes.
   Giorno Video Pak 3. It's Clean, It Just Looks Dirty (1987). With Cabaret Voltaire, Hüsker Du, Diamanda Galas, Einsturzende Neubaten, Robert Frank/Rudy Wurlitzer/Gary Hill, John Giorno Band, David Johansen, Swans, Psychic TV, John Waters, and an excerpt from *Robert Wilson and the Civil warS.*
   Giorno Video Pak 4. With Tom Waits, Jim Jarmusch, Coil, and others.
Size & Elements: Film (format and amount unspecified). Videotape: VHS and Betamax (5 completed videotapes; viewing copies).
Cataloging: None specified.
Access: Open to researchers and scholars. Available to the public for purchase. Research fees not charged. Research requests accepted by mail.
Rights: Full rights held to some material. Some rights held to all material.
Licensing: Apply for information.
Restrictions: None specified.
Viewing Facilities: None.
Duplication Facilities: None.

NEW YORK METRO

GIRL SCOUTS OF THE U.S.A.
830 Third Avenue
New York, NY 10022
(212) 940-7800
Fax: (212) 940-7859

Bonnie McEwan (Director of Media)

Contact: Jamie Mollot (Audiovisual Producer/Media Services)
Services: Association. Producer of film and videotape materials primarily for in-house use. Currently planning to develop archives. Materials not available to the public for research, distribution or reuse at this time.
Description: Produces and holds public service announcements, promotional and training films. Plans are to collect and catalog material in an archives that will be accessible to the public.
Size & Elements: Apply for information.
Cataloging: Currently uncataloged.
Access: For in-house use only. Material not accessible to the public for research or reuse.
Rights: Apply for information.
Licensing: Not available for licensing or reuse.
Restrictions: Material not available for research, duplication or reuse of any kind.

Viewing Facilities: None.
Duplication Facilities: None.

NEW YORK METRO

GOETHE HOUSE, NEW YORK LIBRARY
1014 Fifth Avenue
New York, NY 10028
(212) 744-8310
Fax: (212) 988-0235
Telex: WUI 666701

Dr. Jürgen Uwe Ohlau (Director of Goethe House)
Gesine Worm (Head Librarian)

Contacts: Gesine Worm (Library); Freya Jeschke (Library); Marlis Arboleda (Teachers' Lending Library)
Services: Educational institution; library. Films and videotapes available to the public primarily for teaching and research purposes.
Description: German language and culture. Materials held in two separate libraries:
   Library (93 videotapes; in German and English, available to the public). Documentaries on German culture, art, literature and the contemporary scene.
   Teachers' Lending Library (564 films, 301 videotapes; generally available only to teachers). Documentaries on German culture and films for teaching German language. Sample title include: *Ich Bin Etwas Schief Ins Leben Gebaut; Carl Spitzweg; Traditional Wooden Toys Under The Christmas Tree; Walter Gropius;* and *Widerstand gegan Hitler — 20. Juni 1944.*
Size & Elements: Film: amount unspecified (564 titles total). Videotape: 3/4" (PAL) and VHS (NTSC) (394 videotapes total, both libraries; viewing copies).
Cataloging: Card catalogs of Library material; published catalogs of Teachers' Lending Library material.
Access: Library collection available to the public. 3/4" (PAL) videotapes held in the Library are for in-house use only; VHS (NTSC) videotapes available for free loan. Films and videotapes in Teachers' Lending Library available primarily to teachers for free loan by mail only. Research fees not charged. Research requests accepted by mail, telephone and in person (walk-in).
Rights: Some rights held to some material.
Licensing: Apply for information.
Restrictions: Copyright restrictions apply.
Viewing Facilities: Videotape (by appointment).
Duplication Facilities: None.

NEW YORK METRO

GORDON FILMS, INC.
119 West 57th Street, Suite 319
New York, NY 10019
(212) 757-9390
Fax: (212) 757-9392
Telex: 422142 GRDN UI

Richard Gordon (President)

Contact: Richard Gordon
Services: Distributor; film producer. Films and videotapes maintained for distribution and rental rather than for research or reuse. Material available for licensing as stock footage, subject to restrictions.
Description: Holds feature films produced for theatrical release (1957-87). Materials are in active worldwide theatrical distribution, on television and on videotape. Includes both color and black and white features ranging from classic material to horror, science fiction and other genre categories.
   Titles available: *The Atomic Submarine* ("Tomorrow's battle to save the world explodes under the Arctic ice"); *Corridors of Blood* ("See the blood-curdling experiments of Doctor Bolton") (played by Boris Karloff); *The Curious Female* ("It's erotic pandemonium...the oddest dating service in town!"); *Curse of the Voodoo* ("Blood sacrifice of the Simbazi"); *Days of Thrills and Laughter* ("An experience in comedy"); *Devil Doll* ("What is the terrifying evil secret of the dummy? And why is it locked in a cage every night?"); *Fiend Without a Face* ("...a monstrous army of mental vampires that feed on the brains and spines of human beings"); *First Man into Space* ("Warning! Not responsible if you look too long at the Gamma Ray monster!"); *The Gay Deceivers* ("They had to keep their hands off girls in order to keep the Army's hands off them"); *The Haunted Strangler* ("Their wild beauty marked

them for death!"); *Hell's Angels on Wheels* ("The shattering true story of the Hell's Angels of Northern California"); *Horror Hospital* ("The operation is a success...when the patient dies"); *Girls on the Road* ("Looking for men...looking for trouble...and finding both!"); *I Crossed the Color Line* ("A story packed with melodramatic action...with blood and sin...with treachery, sex and murder!"); *The Losers* ("Killers by instinct...mercenaries by profession!"); *Run, Angel, Run!* ("for those who like their action...rough, raw and real!"); *Secrets of Sex (Tales of the Bizarre)* ("Dead for 1000 years...he rose from the crypt to reveal strange and sinister passions!"); *Simon — King of the Witches* ("The evil spirit must choose evil...the black mass...the spells...the incantations...the curses...the ceremonial sex"); *This is a Hijack* ("It's timely...the thrill story of terror in the skies!"); *Top of the Heap* ("He was a violent man...trouble was he also was a cop"); *Tower of Evil* ("It was a night of terror with a fiendish creature on the prowl!"); and *Werewolves on Wheels* ("The gang thought it was tough 'til it found a new type of hell...the bride of Satan!").

Size & Elements: Film and videotape: all formats available (approx. 25 films; viewing copies available on videotape).
Cataloging: Release sheets.
Access: Maintained for distribution and rental rather than for research and reuse. Research requests accepted by mail.
Rights: Full rights held to all material.
Licensing: Available for licensing. License fees charged.
Restrictions: Requests for licensing and reuse accepted on a case-by-case basis and must be individually negotiated.
Viewing Facilities: Videotape (available upon request).
Duplication Facilities: Can be arranged as required.

NEW YORK METRO

GRAY CITY INC.
853 Broadway, Room 1711
New York, NY 10003
(212) 473-3600
Fax: (212) 420-9528
Telex: 669192 GCTY UW

Contact: Lilyan Sievernich (President)
Services: Corporation; corporate archives. One film and outtakes available for distribution, licensing and reuse.
Description: *John Huston and the Dubliners* (1987, 60 min., color) was produced and directed by documentary filmmaker Lilyan Sievernich. Shot on the set of the movie *The Dead* (based on James Joyce's novella), this documentary film provides an insider's account of its production and shows the artistry of film director John Huston at work. It features John Huston, Angelica Huston (daughter), Tony Huston (son) and Irish actor Donal McCann.
Size & Elements: Film: 16mm (1 completed film; 200,000 feet outtakes; positives). Videotape: 1" (1 videotape; film transfer master); 3/4" and VHS (viewing copies).
Cataloging: Printed brochure; finding aids (written logs).
Access: Completed film maintained for distribution and rental rather than for research or reuse. Outtakes available for licensing and reuse.
Rights: Full rights held to all material.
Licensing: Available for licensing. License fees charged.
Restrictions: Apply for information.
Viewing Facilities: Videotape.
Duplication Facilities: None.

NEW YORK METRO

SHERMAN GRINBERG FILM LIBRARIES, INC. (EAST)
630 Ninth Avenue
New York, NY 10036-3787
(212) 765-5170
Fax: (212) 262-1532
Telex: 265823 SGFL NY

Bernard Chertok (President)

Contacts: Nancy Casey (Chief Librarian); Michael Miller (Librarian); Andrew Noren (Librarian); Bill Hennessy (ABC Librarian)
Services: Film and videotape stock footage sales library. See also Sherman Grinberg Film Libraries, Inc. (West).
Description: Represents film and videotape produced for ABC's *World News Tonight;* Paramount and Pathé Newsreels; production outtakes from just about

every feature and television show ever produced by MGM, 20th Century-Fox, Allied Artists, HBO and ITC; stock footage from WGBH's *Nova;* Public Broadcasting Associates' *Odyssey;* ABC's *American Sportsman;* BBC Enterprises' *Wildstock* collection and a number of smaller collections.

Founded in 1957, Grinberg has offices in Hollywood and New York. One of the largest stock film collections in the country, the library has supplied footage to many features, television shows, commercials and documentaries. Woody Allen's *Zelig* production purchased nearly an hour's worth of material; *Midway* with Gregory Peck incorporated stock footage into the film's battle sequences. The television serials *The Fall Guy* and *Airwolf* each used stunt material from the production outtakes. Grinberg was the source of clips of the Concorde used in *Airplane* and the soaring clouds backdrop against which Superman flew in the original *Superman* movie.

The collection is physically divided between offices on the East and West coasts, but research prior to screening can be done at either branch. For instance, while the studio production outtakes are stored in Hollywood, some production guides are available in New York. Similarly, while the ABC collection is physically in New York, there is an ABC computer terminal in the West Coast office.

Following are the major collections held in the New York office:
ABC World News Tonight. Coverage began October 1, 1963; prior to this time the ABC news operation was serviced by the Fox/UPI Telenews service. As detailed below, the entire collection is indexed through the ABC computer, making this the only network news operation which is fully accessible by computer. Users can expect to find coverage of nearly all of the major news stories of the past 25 years. Because of the convenience afforded by computerization, this collection can also meet many stock footage needs. Certain frequently requested subjects (e.g., Liberty Weekend coverage and the attempted assassination of Ronald Reagan) have been compiled into highlight cassettes for ready accessibility. Videotape is housed on the premises and may be requested for same-day screening. 16mm material is stored in vaults in Fort Lee, N.J. and must be ordered by the librarians before 3pm at least one day prior to the screening appointment.

The World News Tonight library represented by Grinberg does not hold footage originated by other ABC News units, such as *20/20* and *Nightline.* Any requests for licensing or reuse of other ABC News materials should be directed to ABC News (q.v.).

Paramount Newsreels. The Paramount Newsreel began operation in 1927 and produced two issues per week through 1957. In 1963, the library was purchased by Grinberg. The original film for the issues from 1940-57 was given to the National Archives and Records Administration (q.v.), where safety negatives and prints are currently available. 1" master videotapes and 3/4" viewing copies are available in New York and Hollywood. Although little material survives from 1927, nearly all the original stories exist from 1928 on. Almost all material (1927-54) is available on original nitrate negative (with the exception of the material transferred to safety film at the National Archives); the Paramount newsreel was produced on nitrate film until 1954. (Though the major studios discontinued the use of nitrate as early as 1947-48, the newsreels continued using it into the mid-1950s.)

1930s Paramount newsreels typically ran from 7 to 9 min., with the average story running from 40 to 90 seconds. When the news warranted, as in the case of the bombing of Pearl Harbor, the entire issue was devoted to one major story. A typical issue began with a "hard" news item and was followed by increasingly "softer" news items: fashion, human interest, personality stories and sports.

Paramount News comprises approximately 80% domestic and 20% foreign stories. While most major news stories were covered by all the newsreel companies, there was occasionally exclusive coverage of an event. One well-known example, when Paramount had the only camera on the scene, was the Memorial Day Massacre of 1937, during which police opened fire on striking workers outside the Republic Steel plant near Chicago. Naturally, there is coverage of Paramount premieres and stars, including Bob Hope; Bing Crosby; Frank Sinatra at New York's Paramount Theater (1944) with throngs of bobby-soxers swooning; and W. C. Fields on a Paramount set when the 1933 Los Angeles earthquake hit.

Screen Souvenirs. A collection of Paramount short subjects. Approximately 70 reels, the earliest of which predates World War I, are available on film and 3/4" videotape.

Greatest Headlines of the Century (260 shorts, each 5 min.). This series was produced by Grinberg for syndication using material from the Pathé newsreel collection. Most major events (1900-60) are covered. These are available for viewing on 3/4" videotape at the library.

Nova and Odyssey. Collection of stock film from *Nova,* the popular science series produced by WGBH. Also holds stock film from the PBS *Odyssey* series.

ABC's American Sportsman. Series of wildlife programs produced over the last twenty years.

Wide Wide World of Animals (65 programs, each 30 min.) Produced by Time-Life.

BBC Enterprises' Wildstock. The most recent addition to the Library is this comprehensive natural history and wildlife collection, featuring extensive footage of birds, insects, mammals and fish. Printed catalogs and viewing cassettes are available in both the New York and Hollywood offices.

Also holds a number of small miscellaneous collections, including one reel of time-lapse nature photography; and the Greg Hudlin collection, featuring sports and windsurfing footage.

Size & Elements: Film: 35mm and 16mm. Videotape: 1" and 3/4". The ABC collection comprises both 16mm film and videotape. 16mm film predominates (1963-77); approximately 50 to 60 million feet of black and white and color footage are held. ABC shot black and white negative from 1963 through January 1967, switching at that point to Ektachrome color reversal with magnetic sound on film. Although these formats predominate, other formats (silent, optical sound, double-system and others) will occasionally be encountered. During 1976-77, ABC News phased out film in favor of videotape. Library houses approximately 250,000 3/4" videotapes; an additional 4,000 cassettes (each 20 min., 30 min., or 60 min.) are added to the collection every month.

The Paramount newsreel collection comprises approximately 15 to 20 million feet of 35mm film. Issues released between mid-1940 and 1957 are available on 1" master videotape and 3/4" viewing copies. The original 35mm nitrate negative (without music or narration) backs up this portion of the collection as well. (Safety negatives and prints of issues [mid-1940 through 1957] are available at the National Archives and Records Administration [q.v.].). Pre-1940 issues, added scenes (outtakes) and unused material are available on 35mm original nitrate negative.

Wide Wide World of Animals is held on 16mm film.

Cataloging: The ABC collection is accessed through the ABC computer. The computer can search a word, phrase or combination of words, and will supply the number of occurrences of the combination queried. The result can then be sorted or further selected for specific dates or time periods. Each computer record contains a fairly detailed description of the film or videotape, other pertinent information about the film or videotape and cross references. Using a nearby printer, hard copies of entries may be made on the spot. Although librarians can supply a handout on the use of the computer, they can also be most helpful with advice on its idiosyncrasies. For instance, stories about Viet Nam may be found not only under "Viet Nam" but also under "Vietnam"; "anti-ballistic missiles" will also be found under "A.B.M."

The Paramount collection is accessed through a cross-referenced card catalog system, comprising a personality file, a geography file and a miscellaneous subjects file. A catalog breakdown sheet is available. File cards have descriptions, pertinent information about the film (including its length and elements) and lists of cross-references. Cards indicate whether the material was used in an issue or unused. Release or "tear" sheets produced for each issue (1927-57) are also available. These sheets, filed by date, briefly describe the contents of each issue, but do not indicate anything about outtakes or unused material.

A microfilm copy of the Pathé Newsreel card catalog is available for research in the New York office (the actual films are housed at the Grinberg Library in Hollywood).

Access: Open to producers, film researchers and other bona fide stock footage users. Available for duplication, licensing and reuse. Hourly research fees charged for card and computer searches and for screening time (2-hour minimum). Research requests accepted by mail, telephone and in person.

The library recommends that, whenever possible, customers arrange to do their own research, as experience has proven that stock footage is a very subjective matter. The Grinberg librarians can do small amounts of very specific research or pre-screening research for clients. Librarians can also refer clients to experienced local researchers who are familiar with the collection.

Experienced librarians are available to assist clients in finding their way through the collection. Library services are charged for by the hour with a two-hour minimum. Charges for the use of library facilities must be paid at the time they are incurred, by cash or check. It is necessary to make an appointment for computer and screening time, as facilities are limited and sometimes heavily booked.

If required, library will supply black and white contact reversal or color scratch prints at customer's expense. A minimum non-refundable service fee, applicable to final usage, will be charged.

Rights: Footage supplied is without representation or warranties other than that of title. The licensee shall be solely responsible for obtaining any and all necessary legal clearances or waivers.

Licensing: Footage furnished is authorized for non-exclusive use only in the production specified on the client's purchase order and Library's Licensing Agreement, and for that one production only. Footage may not be sold, rented, licensed, reused or recut into any other production. Material is not purchased from the Sherman Grinberg Film Libraries, Inc.; rather, a limited usage license is granted. Film is not authorized for use until a signed copy of the contract is returned to the Library and is fully paid for.

License fees are determined by the amount of footage used and the rights required by the client (rate card available). There is an overall minimum charge. When an order is placed for any film or videotape duplication, an advance against final usage is required. This deposit is in addition to the actual duplication costs. It is deductible from any final license fees, but is non-refundable in the event of non-use. All laboratory and transfer charges, shipping costs, wires, messengers, phone calls, photocopies, etc. will be paid by the customer. A copy of the completed production will be made available to the Library if requested.

The rates for footage or videotape of "high production value" are slightly higher than the posted rate. In addition, there are special rates for use of process footage, main titles and ancillary uses of stock in markets such as pay and cable television and homevideo cassette and videodisc.

Restrictions: Reuse of any film or videotape showing ABC News personnel, such as reporters, interviewers, cameramen, etc. is strictly forbidden.

It is important to understand the studios' policy with respect to licensing stock footage from any one particular production. The studios do not wish to license footage that can be identified as stock from any specific theatrical feature without prior consent. Therefore, Grinberg reserves the right to limit the amount of stock licensed from any one particular production so that it cannot be identified. Under no circumstances will the studio permit any form of publicity which identifies the stock used with the name of the studio or the title of the motion picture. Use of any likenesses of principal actors or actresses in stock film is strictly prohibited.

Viewing Facilities: Film (35mm and 16mm flatbeds); videotape (3/4").
Duplication Facilities: Arranged through outside facilities.
Duplication Procedure: It is most practical and economical to order work elements first (i.e., scratch prints or videotapes with exposed time codes). At this time an advance against final usage is required. All laboratory work must be paid for on a COD basis. After the edit, the client makes an order for masters. At this time the license fee is computed and the advance deducted. If it is decided that the work elements and masters are to be made at the same time, the client should expect the Library to retain the master and release only the work elements. The masters are held until the final edit. The client then supplies the time codes or edge numbers and the Library will supply the corresponding masters. The amount of footage released is based upon the footage report.

Customers should note that there is a per-cut minimum (10 feet in 35mm and 4 feet in 16mm; both equivalent to 6.66 seconds running time). Customers should be aware that when a print is made from the Library master for transfer to videotape, the print becomes the property of the Library and must be returned following the transfer. All unused, unlicensed material must be returned to the Library.

16mm customers should be aware that it is strictly prohibited to make a direct reduction from the 35mm nitrate negative. The Library requires making a 35mm contact element first, from which the reduction will be made. These safety elements are then to be retained by the Library.

No film or videotape is to be submitted directly by the customer to a laboratory or videotape transfer house for duplication without the written authorization of the Library to that facility.

NEW YORK METRO

HALCYON DAYS PRODUCTIONS
12 West End Avenue, 5th Floor
New York, NY 10023
(212) 397-8785
Fax: (212) 397-2669

Gary Cohen (President)

Contact: Michelle Sinisgalli (Office Manager)
Services: Film and videotape producer; stock footage sales library.
Description: Collection focuses on newsreels, politics and wartime propaganda material.

John F. Kennedy (1951-67). In addition to coverage in the Universal Newsreel Library (see below), holds Kennedy family home movies.

United News. Government-sponsored newsreels (June 1942-June 1946, weekly releases, each approx. 10 min.) covering all aspects of World War II.

Includes: comprehensive coverage of fighting in Europe, Asia and the Pacific; the Nuremberg war crimes trials; and the last stages of the war in the Pacific.

Universal Newsreel Library (complete coverage December 1951-October 1967, 2 weekly releases, each approx. 7 min., over 200 hours total). Covers major world events, including World War II, the Korean and Vietnam Wars; important political figures, including U.S. presidents Theodore Roosevelt, Harry S Truman, Dwight D. Eisenhower, John F. Kennedy (1951-67, including home movies), Lyndon B. Johnson and Richard Nixon; U.S. news events, including the Rosenberg trial, the inauguration of John F. Kennedy (in color) and his assassination, the McCarthy hearings, disasters, accession of Alaska and Hawaii and the space program; fads and trends, including hula hoops, the Twist, fashions, dance crazes and high-wire stunts; fashions and technological innovations; and "goofy" Americana (e.g., animal tricks, triplet conventions and human dartboards).

Also includes celebrity public service announcements for cancer research and government bonds. Collection includes celebrities and world leaders, including: Spencer Tracy, Humphrey Bogart, Rock Hudson, Jimmy Durante, Barbara Stanwyck, the Smothers Brothers, Marilyn Monroe, Jimmy Stewart, Ronald Reagan, Doris Day, Jackie Onassis, Elizabeth Taylor, Elvis Presley, Queen Elizabeth, Princes Charles and Andrew (as boys), Charles de Gaulle, Francisco Franco, Mohandas K. Gandhi, Neville Chamberlain, Josip Broz Tito, Jawalarhal Nehru, Anwar Sadat, Shah Mohammad Reza Pahlavi, Winston S. Churchill, Josef Stalin, Nikita Khrushchev and Fidel Castro.

Other short films. Limited but growing collection of industrial films (1940s-50s); World War II-era propaganda; civil defense films; commercials; and short films (1930s-50s). Some material is in the process of being transferred to videotape and cataloged.

Size & Elements: Film: 16mm. Videotape: 3/4" (masters; transfers from film). (Approx. 700 hours total).

Cataloging: Shot lists; dope sheets or release sheets.

Access: Available for reuse. Research fees negotiated on an individual basis. Research requests accepted by telephone.

Rights: Full rights held to some material. Additional clearances may be necessary in some cases if material is to be reused. Some material in the public domain.

Licensing: Available for reuse, subject to restrictions. Usage fees charged (negotiated on an individual basis).

Restrictions: Restrictions may apply in some cases.

Viewing Facilities: Videotape.

Duplication Facilities: Videotape (3/4" and 1/2").

NEW YORK METRO

HATCH-BILLOPS COLLECTION, INC.
491 Broadway, 7th Floor
New York, NY 10012
(212) 966-3231

Contacts: James Hatch; Camille Billops

Services: Film producers; research library. Films primarily available for rental through outside distributors; available for purchase directly.

Description: Research library and archives of Black American cultural history. Produced two films, *Suzanne, Suzanne* and *Older Women and Love.* Camille Billops is available to accompany film showings as a lecturer.

Size & Elements: Film: 16mm (2 titles).

Cataloging: Published brochure.

Access: Research library open to the public. Films available for rental through authorized distributors; available for purchase directly (apply for information).

Rights: Apply for information.

Licensing: Apply for information.

Restrictions: None specified.

Viewing Facilities: None.

Duplication Facilities: None.

Related Materials: Extensive slide collection, oral history audiotapes and photographs.

Distributors: Women Make Movies, Inc. (q.v.); Third World Newsreel (q.v.).

NEW YORK METRO

HEARST METROTONE NEWS
235 East 45th Street, 11th Floor
New York, NY 10017
(212) 682-5600
Fax: (212) 687-8673

Ted Troll (Chief Librarian)

Contact: Ted Troll

Services: Film and videotape stock footage sales library.

Description: While the Hearst Metrotone News stock film library has been donated to the UCLA Film and Television Archive (q.v.), "duplicate footage used in derivative works" is still available from Hearst in New York. In the last few years of its operation, Hearst Metrotone News produced a number of derivative works using material drawn from the theatrical newsreel releases and the *Telenews* collections.

Telenews Weekly (1954 through April 1963, 35mm and 16mm, 52 issues per year). *Telenews Weekly* was produced in 35mm and distributed to television subscribers in 16mm. Although the *Weekly* used some of the same stories as the *Telenews* daily syndication service (now housed at UCLA), the two services were edited separately and often provided different coverage. Typical issues covered a major lead story, national news, world news, a personality-oriented story, a science story and sports highlights.

Hearst Almanac (35mm, 365 stories, each 3 min.). The *Almanac* series comprises a story corresponding to each day of the year. Examples include: *The Opening of the Burma Road* (January 28, 1945); *North Atlantic Storms and Floods* (February 5, 1953); and *Salk Vaccine to School Children* (February 23, 1954). Appropriately dated stories commemorate the birthdays of George Washington, Abraham Lincoln, Franklin D. Roosevelt, Thomas Edison and Babe Ruth. Narration tracks have been destroyed; episodes can be used for stock footage only. A typed list of all dates and subjects is available.

Hearst Reports (formerly *Screen News Digest*) (1958-83, most episodes approx. 14 min.). Film magazines produced for an educational market. *Screen News Digest* was produced by Hearst (1958-83) and later by Allegro Productions under the title *Hearst Reports.* Production was in 35mm black and white until 1972, then 16mm color until 1983, at which time all episodes were transferred to videotape. *Digests* varied in length, depending on the subject. An episode concerned with Adolf Hitler ran 14 minutes; one about George Eastman and the development of cameras and film, *World in Camera,* was a 24-minute double issue; while *China Today* (1982) ran 25 minutes. Such recent topics as the end of the Vietnam War, the return of the hostages from Iran, and the inauguration of President Reagan have all been covered. Although there is no catalog, a series of mimeographed sheets describes the stories in each volume.

Time Capsules (16mm film, 2" and 1" videotape; 2,000 stories, each 1 min.). Produced in the mid-1970s, the *Time Capsules* cover a wide variety of subjects, including serious and humorous stories, news, sports, human interest, animals and aviation. Covering ca. 1896-1970, the *Time Capsules* are broken down into sections: sports, war stories, oddities and trivia, humor, crime, disasters, space, aviation, women, show business and politics. Sample stories include: *Sharecroppers Protest Evictions* (1939); *The Discovery of Safety Glass* (1939); *Totalitarian Takeover in Small-Town America* (1941 and 1950); *Atomic Energy for Food Preservation* (1960s); *Contrast in Youth Cultures: United States and Japan* (1932); *Giant Panda Bears: Endangered Species* (1939); and *John F. Kennedy Runs On the Record* and *Jackie Helps J.F.K.'s Campaign* (1960). The *Time Capsules* are often licensed to television stations as a complete library; contracts permit use of footage for news purposes, but not for documentaries (apply for further information). Card and microfilm catalogs are available.

Time Out for Sports and *Big Moments in Sports.* *Time Out for Sports* (produced early 1960s, 26 programs, each 30 min.) is a series of programs featuring memorable moments in sports. *Big Moments in Sports* (150 segments, each 3 to 5 min.) covers similar, but not identical events. Both series were originally produced for television syndication.

Farm Newsreel (late 1950s, 24 issues). Produced for the American Cyanamid Company, Farm and Home Division, mainly for syndication in the Midwestern U.S., this series features farm-related stories such as *Farmer of the Week!; Ike Hails 4-H Winners!; Semi-Dwarf Type Wheat on Way;* and *Turkey Research at Beltsville.*

Perspective on Greatness (produced early 1960s, 35mm and videotape; 26 programs, each 50 min.). "Reality-based stud[ies] of some great people, times and places." Programs cover Harry S Truman; Douglas MacArthur (*The General*); Dwight D. Eisenhower; Helen Keller (*The World I See*); Charles A. Lindbergh (*The Crowded Idol*); Alfred E. Smith (*The Man from Oliver Street*); and Franklin D. Roosevelt, in two parts (*The Voice of Change* and *The Prince of Peace*); Mohandas K. Gandhi; and Hirohito. Some programs focus on historical events rather than on individuals, including *Crown in Crisis,* on the history of British royalty; and *All the King's Horses* and *All the King's Men,* on the history of the atomic bomb.

History Makers (produced late 1960s-early 1970s, approx. 12 titles). Produced for the educational market, programs include two films on Dwight D.

Eisenhower, *From Soldier to President* and *The Presidential Years;* and two on John F. Kennedy, *The New Generation* and *Challenges and Tragedy.*

American Insight (each 30 min.). The *Insights* series combines footage from *Hearst Reports, Perspectives on Greatness* and the stock library. Each program covers a topic such as *America Goes to War, The Space Age* (Dr. Goddard), *How America Elects a President, Women's Rights, The Vice Presidency* and *Henry Ford.*

Campaigns: U. S. Presidential Elections, 1928-1968. Series assembled from the Hearst library highlighting the problems, politics and issues of the day.

Size & Elements: Film: 35mm and 16mm (approx. 1 to 2 million feet; various elements, some footage on both 35mm and 16mm). Videotape: 2", 1" and 3/4" (approx. 50% of collection).

Cataloging: Microfiche copy of Hearst Metrotone News Card Index. Microfilm catalogs for *Almanacs, Time Capsules* and *Telenews Weekly.* Finding aids (lists and mimeographed sheets with descriptions) are available for the other series.

Access: Open to researchers, scholars and producers. Research fees charged. Research requests accepted by mail and telephone.

Rights: Full rights held to all material. Additional clearances may be necessary in some cases if material is to be reused.

Licensing: Available for licensing and reuse, subject to restrictions. License fees charged, depending on intended market for production. Clients must sign standard licensing contract.

Restrictions: Material may not be used in any context in which it is to the detriment of any individual.

Viewing Facilities: Film (35mm and 16mm Ace viewers); videotape.

Duplication Facilities: None (outside arrangements can be made).

NEW YORK METRO

HOBBY INDUSTRIES OF AMERICA
VIDEO & AUDIO TAPE LIBRARY
P.O. Box 348
Elmwood Park, NJ 07407
(201) 794-1133
Fax: (201) 797-0657

Street address: 319 East 54th Street

Walter Caddell (Executive Director)

Contact: Michelle Degrace (Director of Marketing)

Services: Association. Videotape library maintained for rental and distribution to retailer trade members.

Description: Videotapes promoting hobbies and the hobby industry, produced by the association and manufacturers to promote specific industries and to assist retailers with new product information, while entertaining customers with the fun and excitement of involvement in hobbies. Includes videotapes demonstrating models, miniatures, and home decor hobbies.

Sample titles include: *Aleene's Super Scrap Crafts; Kazari Punch Embroidery; Bunka with an American Flair; A Plane, a Place, a Perfect Day;* and *Wired for Excitement.* Some titles are dated.

Size & Elements: Videotape: VHS (30 videotapes; viewing copies).

Cataloging: Published catalog; release sheets.

Access: Maintained for distribution and rental rather than for research or reuse.

Rights: Full rights held to some material. Rights retained by original producers or sponsors. Additional clearances may be necessary in some cases if material is to be reused.

Licensing: Apply for information.

Restrictions: Videotapes not available for purchase or duplication.

Viewing Facilities: None.

Duplication Facilities: None.

NEW YORK METRO

HOLOCAUST SURVIVORS MEMORIAL FOUNDATION
350 Fifth Avenue, Suite 3508
New York, NY 10118
(212) 594-8765
Fax: (212) 868-8285

Jack P. Eisner (President)

Contact: Robert Gibson (Director)

Services: Foundation; film producer. Produced two films which are available from outside distributors.

Description: World War II and the Holocaust. Produced and holds rights to *War and Love* (1985, 35mm, distributed by Cannon Films) a feature-length film by Jack Eisner; and *Children in the Holocaust* (1981, 55 min., distributed by MGM), a documentary narrated by Liv Ullmann.

Size & Elements: Film: 35mm (1 title); 16mm (1 title). Both titles also available on videotape.

Cataloging: None specified.

Access: Not open to the public. Films available from authorized distributors. Requests accepted by mail and telephone.

Rights: Full rights held to all material.

Licensing: Apply for information.

Restrictions: Apply for information.

Viewing Facilities: None.

Duplication Facilities: None.

Distributors: Cannon Films; MGM.

NEW YORK METRO

THE HOUSE FOUNDATION FOR THE ARTS, INC.
325 Spring Street, Suite 352
New York, NY 10013
(212) 206-1440
Fax: (212) 727-2535

Meredith Monk (Artistic Director)
Barbara Dufty (Managing Director)

Contact: Sue Latham (Company Manager)

Services: Foundation. Film and videotape collection available partly for distribution and partly for in-house research only.

Description: Performance documentation of Meredith Monk's works.

Films and videotapes available for distribution. Titles include: *Quarry* (1975, 5.3 min., 16mm, black and white, silent), designed to be projected into the performance space during the opera of the same name; *Quarry* (1978, 86 min., 16mm, color, sound), a documentary record of the opera itself; *Ellis Island* (1979, 7 min., 16mm or 3/4" videotape, black and white), designed to be screened during a performance of *Recent Ruins; Ellis Island* (1981, 28 min., 35mm, 16mm and 3/4" videotape, black and white and color, sound), directed by Meredith Monk and Bob Rosen, on the experiences of immigrants entering America at the turn of the century; *16 Millimeter Earrings* (1980, 25 min., 16mm, color, sound), originally performed in 1966; *Paris* (1982, 26 min., 3/4" videotape, color, sound), a musical theater piece about "a place with a unique and formative role in history and in our consciousness"; and *Turtle Dreams (Waltz)* (1983, 27 min., 3/4" videotape, color, sound), a music piece with movement for four voices and two organs.

Private in-house videotape collection. Performance documentation made specifically for archival use; available only to researchers and scholars. Titles include: *Acts From Under and Above; Book of Days Concert; The Travelogue Series (Paris; Venice-Milan* and *Chacon); Education of the Girlchild; Ellis Island; The Games; Greenaway Film,* a documentary by Peter Greenaway; *Meredith Monk with Nurit Tilles; Meredith Monk Solo Concert; Paris, Plateau Series, Quarry, Specimen Days* and *Turtle Dreams (Waltz).*

Size & Elements: Film: 35mm (1 title); 16mm (5 titles). Videotape: 3/4" (12 titles); VHS (13 titles); and Betamax (1 title).

Cataloging: Card catalogs; printed lists.

Access: Open to researchers and scholars. For in-house use only. Some material maintained for distribution and rental (apply for rental contacts). Research fees not charged. Research requests accepted by mail, telephone and in person (by appointment only).

Rights: Full rights held to some material. Additional clearances may be necessary if material is to be reused.

Licensing: Apply for information.

Restrictions: In-house collection open to researchers and scholars for in-house viewing only.

Viewing Facilities: Videotape.

Duplication Facilities: None.

NEW YORK METRO

IBM CORPORATION
400 Columbus Avenue
Valhalla, NY 10595
(914) 749-3144

John Maloney (Program Manager, IBM Archives)

Contact: John Maloney
Services: Corporation; corporate archives. Film and videotape archives for in-house use only.
Description: Films and videotapes relating to the evolution of computers and technology at IBM, including product announcements, commercials and customer applications.
Size & Elements: Film: 16mm (2,100 titles, 3,900 cans; film elements available on certain titles only). Videotape: 3/4" (800 titles; viewing copies).
Cataloging: Computerized cataloging for staff use only.
Access: For in-house use only. Research requests accepted by mail only.
Rights: Full rights held to some material. Some rights held to some material. Additional clearances may be necessary in some cases if material is to be reused. Rights status of some material not known.
Licensing: Apply for information. License fees generally not charged.
Restrictions: Certain titles carry restrictions.
Viewing Facilities: Film (16mm projector).
Duplication Facilities: Videotape.

NEW YORK METRO

ICARUS FILMS INTERNATIONAL, INC.
200 Park Avenue South, Suite 1319
New York, NY 10003
(212) 674-3375
Fax: (212) 477-2753
Telex: 6502733717

Jonathan Miller (President)

Contact: Jonathan Miller; Lyna Shirley
Services: Television distribution company. Film and videotape material available for distribution and broadcast; reuse subject to restrictions.
Description: Comprehensive television distribution company with offices in London, New York and Sydney, representing leading independent television producers around the world. Collection includes documentaries on political and social issues, as well as shorter topical reports for current affairs and magazine programs; and cultural programs featuring animation, the arts, music and fiction.

Subjects covered include: the Miskito Indians of Nicaragua; military rule in Guatemala; the Philippines under the Aquino administration; Chile; the history of racial stereotypes in the United States; the story of police violence in Philadelphia; officers' and inmates' stories about the Kentucky State Reformatory; the international fast-food industry; Western media coverage of the famine in Africa; aboriginal Australia; armed Jewish resistance against the Nazis; the American tour of a Soviet "free" jazz group; the life and work of the Black poet Nikki Giovanni; a film workshop in a Santiago, Chile shantytown; graffiti on New York's subway trains; the sugar industry and the Philippines; the Communist Party of the Philippines and its military arm, the New People's Army; and reflections of Nazism in contemporary media.
Size & Elements: Videotape: various formats and standards (48 programs).
Cataloging: Storylines and synopses; published catalog; computerized cataloging for staff use only.
Access: Available for television broadcast and syndication. Research fees charged in some cases. Research requests accepted by mail, telephone and in person (by appointment only).
Rights: Full rights held to some material. Distribution rights held to some material. Additional clearances may be necessary in some cases if material is to be reused.
Licensing: Available for licensing and reuse, subject to restrictions. License fees charged.
Restrictions: Requests for licensing and reuse subject to clearance and approval.
Viewing Facilities: Film and videotape (small screening room, available by appointment only).
Duplication Facilities: None.
Representative: Offices in London, England and Sydney, Australia.

NEW YORK METRO

ICARUS-TAMOUZ MEDIA, INC.
123 West 93rd Street, Suite 4-B
New York, NY 10025
(212) 864-7603

Ilan Ziv (Producer)

Contact: Ilan Ziv
Services: Videotape producer. Stock footage available for licensing and reuse through authorized representative.
Description: Production company producing several feature-length documentaries annually, as well as a variety of magazine news reports. Holds footage relating to social change and the political process, with particularly strong coverage of Central America, Latin America and the Philippines.

Chile. Preparation of the non-violent opposition for the plebiscite and its aftermath (1988).

Dominican Republic. Footage (1988) relating to sugar production, Haitian migrant workers, working conditions, factories, cane cutting and mill processing. Also held is an interview with the head of the national sugar agency.

Guatemala. Extensive coverage (1982-83) of refugee centers near the Mexican border, and witnesses testifying to the atrocities then being committed. Coverage (1985) of refugee camps, tracing the origins of the refugees, and viewing the effects of the insurgency (including model villages and re-education camps run by the army). (Approx. 10 hours coverage).

Peru. Footage (1985-86) documenting human rights violations in the Ayacucho region of the Andes Mountains, birthplace of the "Shining Path" guerrilla movement. Videotapes include the only known footage of Shining Path guerrillas who were interviewed on camera when they stopped a journalist's car. Footage follows the aftermath and effect of the human rights violations involved in the killing of eight journalists. (Approx. 10 hours coverage).

Philippines. Thorough documentation covering all aspects of the country's life (1983-present). Coverage includes the pre- and post-revolution periods, but not the actual revolution. Special strengths include politicians, guerrillas, political movements, social turmoil, the countryside and the role of the Catholic Church in the life of the people. (Approx. 60 hours coverage).

South Lebanon. Filming during the Israeli invasion of South Lebanon.

West Bank. Footage (1980) including settlements; interviews with settlers; West Bank events; extensive interviews with political leaders, including the deposed West Bank mayor. (Approx. 30 hours coverage). Footage (1988) documenting the Israeli peace movement; a portrait of a West Bank village.
Size & Elements: Videotape: format unspecified (over 100 hours).
Cataloging: None specified.
Access: Available to the public for licensing and reuse. Research fees charged. Research requests accepted by mail, telephone and in person (by appointment only).
Rights: Full rights held to all material.
Licensing: Available for licensing and reuse. License fees charged.
Restrictions: None specified.
Viewing Facilities: Film and videotape (through Film/Audio Services, Inc.).
Duplication Facilities: Film and videotape (through Film/Audio Services, Inc.).
Representative: Film/Audio Services, Inc. (q.v.).

NEW YORK METRO

IDEAL COMMUNICATIONS, INC.
1026 Avenue of the Americas
New York, NY 10018
(212) 768-1600

1920 G Street, NW
Washington, DC 20006
(202) 833-4567

Gary Krane (Executive Director)

Contact: Gary Krane
Services: Videotape producer. Material available to the public for licensing and reuse.
Description: Extensive library of stock footage in the following areas: U.S. and Soviet military operations (approx. 30 hours); Middle East conflicts (approx. 3 hours); animation of weapons systems and command, control and communications; military history; history of arms control (from the first nuclear test ban to the present); grassroots political activity; political lobbying; congressional hearings on many subjects; high technology; computers; communications; and nature, including scenes of Arizona, Minnesota and canoeing.

Also holds interviews with military and foreign policy experts (100 hours), including Robert McNamara, Senator Sam Nunn, Rep. Patricia Schroeder, Admiral William Ramsey, management consultant Tom Peters, Soviet General Millstein, Daniel Ellsberg, Randall Forsberg and various computer scientists. An archive of interviews with "politically courageous" people (e.g., nuclear plant "whistleblowers") is in formation.

Size & Elements: Videotape: Betacam and 3/4" (approx. 140 hours; masters).
Cataloging: Partially cataloged; staff assistance required.
Access: Available to the public for licensing and reuse. Research fees charged. Research requests accepted by mail and telephone.
Rights: Full rights held to some material (approx. 80% of collection). No rights held to some material. Some material in the public domain.
Licensing: Available for licensing and reuse. License fees charged in some cases (exchange of footage encouraged).
Restrictions: None specified.
Viewing Facilities: Videotape (3/4" and VHS).
Duplication Facilities: Videotape (3/4").

NEW YORK METRO

IEA PRODUCTIONS, INC.
500 East 77th Street
New York, NY 10021
(212) 988-9244

Contact: Staff
Services: Videotape producer and distributor. Materials available to the public for rental and purchase.
Description: Professional educational materials. Family therapy training videotapes featuring live documentary counseling sessions, role-playing, demonstrations and discussions with professional psychotherapists.

Titles include: *The Process of Family Therapy; Initial Family Interview; Family Therapy Consultation; Three Generational Family Consultation; Assessment and Intervention Strategies in Family Therapy; The Family Consultation Interview: When an Impasse Develops in Therapy; Closing the Gap — Family Therapy Supervision; Family Consultation Assessment and Intervention; Family Circle; Marital Crisis; "King" or "Crazy" — Family Therapy and Supervision: Parallel Processes; "Puppets" — A Model of Live Supervision; Videotape in Couples Group Therapy; Multiple Couple Therapy; Time-Mirror,* demonstrating applications of video replay techniques in psychotherapy; *A Personal Experience with Cancer; Metalogue On Healing and Cancer; The New Epistemology;* and *Management and Treatment of the Violent Patient.*
Size & Elements: Videotape: 3/4", VHS and Betamax (19 titles).
Cataloging: Brochure.
Access: Available to the public for rental. Rental is for three-day period; orders must be received three weeks prior to showing date. Requests accepted by mail.
Rights: All IEA videotapes are copyrighted. Any reproduction of material contained within (including soundtrack and written transcript), is a violation of the copyright law.
Licensing: Apply for information.
Restrictions: Some materials restricted to professional audiences.
Viewing Facilities: None.
Duplication Facilities: None.

NEW YORK METRO

IFEX FILMS
201 West 52nd Street
New York, NY 10019
(212) 582-4318
Fax: (212) 956-2257
Telex: 420748 RAPP UI

Gerald J. Rappoport (President)

Contacts: Stephanie Holm; Alan Sherman
Services: Film and videotape distributor. Materials available for rental and purchase.
Description: International feature film releases, especially from the Soviet Union. Exclusive videotape distributor for more than 20 Russian-language feature films with English subtitles.

Titles from the U.S.S.R. include: *Incident at Map Grid 36-80,* dramatizing an encounter between the Soviet naval squadron and an American nuclear submarine; *Come and See,* a documentary on the destruction of a Byelorussian village during World War II; *Is It Easy To Be Young?,* about Soviet youth in

1987; *Kindergarten,* poet Yevgeny Yevtushenko's recollections of his World War II-era boyhood; *Mirror* (Andrei Tarkovsky); *Oblomov,* Goncharov's classic novel of the bourgeoisie; *¡Qué Viva México!,* Sergei Eisenstein's "lost" masterpiece; *Rasputin,* including rare newsreel footage; and *Siberiade.*

Films from the U.S., Denmark, Italy, Canada, the Netherlands, Argentina, Hungary, Czechoslovakia and Poland include features, World War II classics, political satire, biographies and punk "rockumentaries." Also holds a collection of short animated films from around the world.
Size & Elements: Film: 35mm and 16mm (80 titles). Videotape: 3/4", VHS and Betamax (25 titles).
Cataloging: Published catalogs.
Access: Films and videotapes available for purchase; videotapes also available for rental. Classroom rates available.
Rights: Apply for information.
Licensing: Apply for information.
Restrictions: None specified.
Viewing Facilities: None.
Duplication Facilities: Film (35mm and 16mm); videotape (3/4", VHS and Betamax).

NEW YORK METRO

THE IMAGE BANK, NEW YORK
111 Fifth Avenue, 12th Floor
New York, NY 10003
(212) 529-6700
(212) 532-0600
Fax: (212) 529-8886
Telex: 429380 IMAGE

Contacts: Ellen Factor; Robin Parkinson
Territory: Connecticut, Delaware, Maine, Maryland, New Hampshire, New Jersey, New York, Ohio, Pennsylvania, Rhode Island and Vermont.
Services: Exclusive marketing agent for Film Search, Inc. (q.v.).

NEW YORK METRO

IMAGEWAYS, INC.
440 West 47th Street, Suite 4-G
New York, NY 10036
(212) 265-1287
Fax: (212) 586-0339

Adam I. Sargis (President)

Contacts: Adam I. Sargis; Kenny Powell
Services: Stock footage sales library; film and videotape producer; research and clearance services available.
Description: All types of historical footage (1905-88), including footage from newsreels, silent films, cartoons, historical films, Hollywood features, documentaries, industrial films, educational films, television programs and original stock shot material. Collection includes some modern color stock shots and beauty shots.

More than 500 Hollywood and European features are represented, including dramas, comedies, horror, science fiction, war and epics (1920s-70s). All genres and nearly every major Hollywood star are represented.

Library holds over 2,000 cartoons and short subjects (75% color). All major studios and many noted animators represented. Short subjects include industrial and educational films depicting the array of possible human activities. Technological advances, such as new airplanes, machines and inventions are well-documented (many in color).
Size & Elements: Film and videotape (80% of collection mastered on 1" videotape; 3/4" viewing copies available) (approx. 40% color; 60% black and white).
Cataloging: Computerized lists available to the public; computerized cataloging for staff use only.
Access: Available for duplication and reuse. Screening copies of various selections can be assembled by request. Research and videotape editing fees charged. Research requests accepted by mail, telephone and in person (by appointment only).
Rights: Full rights held to some material. Partial rights held to some material. Some material in the public domain. Additional clearances may be necessary in some cases if material is to be reused.
Licensing: Available for licensing and reuse. License fees charged on a case-by-case basis, depending on distribution of finished production and based on

footage used. Minimum license fee will be charged upon delivery of master materials.
Restrictions: None specified.
Viewing Facilities: None. Clients are provided with 3/4" or 1/2" time-coded viewing copies, suitable for offline editing.
Duplication Facilities: None. Third-party laboratory and production arrangements can be arranged.
Related Services: Can clear footage from features and television shows owned by other collectors and companies. Also produces original programming incorporating library resources and production materials.

NEW YORK METRO

INDEPENDENT NETWORK NEWS (INN)
220 East 42nd Street
New York, NY 10017
(212) 210-2400
Fax: (212) 210-2590
Telex: 200392 INN UR

John Corporon, Sr. (President, INN and Senior Vice President for News, WPIX-TV)

Contact: Edith Rivera
Services: Television news broadcaster. Film and videotape material available for licensing and reuse.
Description: Holds news coverage of national and New York metropolitan area news events (1948-present).
Independent Network News. Coverage of recent national news events (1975-present, primarily videotape).
WPIX-TV newsfilm. Coverage of news events in the New York City area (1948-51; scattered coverage 1951-77). Holds primarily edited news broadcasts, all 16mm, most silent, black and white and color, optical and magnetic sound.
Videotape coverage (approx. 1978-present), combining local (WPIX-originated) and national (INN-originated) footage, consists of airchecks and selected field footage. Footage was originated on Betacam and 3/4" and is

generally archived on Betacam. Selected material is held in the News Department; other footage is stored off-premises.
Size & Elements: Film: 16mm (amount unspecified; black and white and color, silent and magnetic and optical sound). Videotape: Betacam and 3/4" (amount unspecified).
Cataloging: Computerized cataloging for staff use only. Staff assistance required.
Access: For in-house use only. Available for licensing and reuse. Research fees charged. Research requests accepted by mail and telephone.
Rights: Full rights held to INN-produced and WPIX-produced material.
Licensing: Available for licensing and reuse, subject to restrictions.
Restrictions: Requests for licensing and reuse accepted on a case-by-case basis.
Viewing Facilities: Videotape.
Duplication Facilities: Videotape (1", Betacam, 3/4" and VHS).

NEW YORK METRO

THE INSTITUTE OF ELECTRICAL AND ELECTRONICS ENGINEERS, INC.
345 East 47th Street
New York, NY 10017-2394
(212) 705-7369
Fax: (212) 752-4929
Telex: 236411

Dr. Harry W. Mergler (Vice President, Educational Activities)
Joyce Bedi (Acting Director, Center for the History of Electrical Engineering)

Contacts: Joyce Bedi; Julie Stern (Administrator, Public Information)
Services: Association; film and videotape producer. Films and videotapes available to the public and the industry for free-loan distribution, telecast and instructional use.
Description: Films and videotapes relating to electrical engineering, electronics and electrotechnology for educational use.
Videoconferences. Continuing education seminars including *Robot Dynamics and Control; Design for Manufacturability; Fiber Optics—*

Technology and Applications; and *Expert Systems and Prolog.*

Frontiers of High Technology. A two-hour cable television program on the impact and pervasiveness of high technology on people and the environment. Features five segments: *Automotive Electronics,* demonstrating head-up displays, automotive computers, navigational aids, multiplexing and collision avoidance systems; *Solid State,* on the continuing evolution of micron and submicron line technology and its use; *Computers,* a discussion about artificial intelligence computers; *Communications,* fiber-optic communications and the discovery, invention and development of materials, techniques and configurations for glass fiber waveguides; and *Power and Energy,* on alternative energy sources, environmental research, development of biomass energy systems and renewable energy technologies.

Miscellaneous materials. Titles available on a free-loan basis include: *The Miracle Force,* illustrating the contributions of electrical and electronics engineering to the welfare of humankind; *Generations of Giants,* dramatizing the major characters and events leading to the foundation of electrotechnology; and *The Second Century Begins,* documenting the IEEE Centennial Technical Convocation, featuring presentations by some of today's leading engineers and scientists.

A list of films on historical topics relating to electricity and electronics, all available from other distributors, is available through the Institute's Center for the History of Electrical Engineering.
Size & Elements: Film: 16mm (2 titles; release prints). Videotape: VHS and Betamax (5 titles; viewing copies).
Cataloging: Brochures; lists.
Access: Material available to the public and the industry for free-loan distribution, telecast and instructional use. Requests accepted by mail and telephone.
Rights: Some rights held to all material.
Licensing: Apply for information.
Restrictions: Some programs not cleared for broadcast.
Viewing Facilities: None.
Duplication Facilities: None.

NEW YORK METRO

INSTITUTE OF OUTDOOR ADVERTISING
342 Madison Avenue, Room 702
New York, NY 10173
(212) 986-5920
Fax: (212) 983-9808

Andrea MacDonald (Director of Marketing)

Contact: Catherine Holliday
Services: Industry association. Film and videotape material available for promotional use.
Description: Marketing presentations on the benefits of outdoor advertising (defined as poster panels and painted bulletins).

Gannett Creative Series. A four-segment videotape overview of the basics of outdoor advertising, including perspectives from practicing professionals in the media, research and creative fields. Produced by the Gannett Foundation. Segments include: *Larger Than Life,* a history of outdoor signs and development as a mass medium; *Masterwork,* the idiosyncrasies of good outdoor design; *The Effect,* the value of pre-testing copy; *Signs of the Times,* recent changes and prospects for outdoor advertising via backlights, electronic signs, inflatables, solar- or wind-powered boards and talking boards.

Mixed Media Marriages II. Presents case histories of television, radio and print campaigns in conjunction with outdoor advertising. Campaigns include Chiquita Banana, San Diego Zoo, Las Vegas Hilton and Samsung Electronics.

Other videotapes include: *The New Messenger,* in which narrator Hugh Downs makes a case for outdoor advertising; *A.D.,* a joint NBC-TV/IOA promotion study to gain awareness for the epic miniseries "A.D."; *1985* and *1986 Obie Awards Presentations,* videotapes of multi-image slide presentations shown at awards luncheons; *But Nobody Knew Her Name (Miss America 1985);* and *The Sights and Sounds of Outdoor Advertising.*
Size & Elements: Videotape: 3/4" and 1/2" (12 titles).
Cataloging: Published lists.
Access: Open to the public. Available for licensing and reuse. Research fees charged. Research requests accepted by mail and telephone.
Rights: Full rights held to all material.
Licensing: Available for licensing. License fees charged (apply for rates).
Restrictions: None specified.
Viewing Facilities: None.
Duplication Facilities: None.

Related Materials: Script available for *Mixed Media Marriages.*

NEW YORK METRO

INTERAMA
301 West 53rd Street, Suite 19E
New York, NY 10019
(212) 977-4830
Fax: (212) 581-6582

Contact: Eva Jakubawski
Services: Film distributor. Films available for rental only.
Description: French classic films; some international titles. Almost all films in French with English subtitles.

Jean Renoir films. Titles include: *Elena et les Hommes; French Can Can; The Crime of Monsieur Lange; La Marseillaise; The Lower Depths (Les Bas-Fonds); Toni; Little Theater of Jean Renoir; Le Dejeuner Sur l'herbe; Testament of Dr. Cordelier; Elusive Corporal (Le Caporal Epingle); Nana; The Little Match Girl (La Petite Marchande d'allumettes; People of France (La Vie est à Nous); La Fille de l'eau; Charleston; La Chienne; A Day in the Country;* and *Direction d'acteur de Jean Renoir.*

Raymond Depardon films. Titles include: *Empty Quarter (Une Femme en Afrique); Reporters; Les Annees Declic; San Clemente;* and *Faits Divers.*

Marcel Pagnol films. Titles include: *The Fanny Trilogy; The Baker's Wife (La Femme du Boulanger; Harvest (Regain); Topaze; The Well Digger's Daughter (La Fille du Puisatier); Letters From My Windmill (Les Lettres de Mon Moulin);* and *Angele.*

The International Collection. Titles include: *Rate It X* (Lucy Winer and Paula de Koenigsberg); *Espoir* (André Malraux); *My Name is Anna Magnani* (Chris Vermocken); *Raoni* (Jean-Pierre Dutilleux); *Cria Cuervos* (Carlos Saura); *Elisa Vide Mia* (Carlos Saura); *Mama Turns 100* (Carlos Saura); *Alyam, Alyam* (Ahmed El Maanouni); *Transes (*Ahmed El Maanouni); *Prix de Beauté (Miss Europa 1930)* (Augusto Genina); *Dream of Wild Horses* (Denys Colomb de Daunant); and *Willie* (Ghasem Ebrahimian).

Other titles include: *The Horse of Pride (Le Cheval d'orgueil)* (Claude Chabrol); *Bizarre, Bizarre (Drole de Drame)* (Marcel Carné); *L'affaire est dans le sac* (Pierre Prévert); *Diary of a Country Priest (Le Journal d'un Curée de Campagne)* (Robert Bresson); *Sartre Par Lui-Même (Sartre by Himself)* (Alexandre Astruc and Michel Contat); *Simone de Beauvoir* (Malka Robowska and Joseé Dayan); *Lola* (Jacques Demy); *A Woman is a Woman (Une Femme est une Femme)* (Jean-Luc Godard); *Lovers of Teruel (Les Amants de Teruel)* (Raymond Rouleau); *Le Beau Serge* (Claude Chabrol); *Le Doulos (The Finger Man)* (Jean-Pierre Melville); *Le Corbeau (The Raven)* (Henri-Georges Clouzot); *Voyage Surprise* (Pierre Prévert); *Un Chien Andalou* (Luis Buñuel and Salvador Dali); *Crazy Rays (Paris qui Dort)* (René Clair); and *My Night at Maud's (Ma Nuit Chez Maud)* (Eric Rohmer).
Size & Elements: Film: 16mm (amount unspecified). Videotape: format and amount unspecified.
Cataloging: Published brochures.
Access: Available to the public for rental. Inquire for rates for classroom and campus showings, and theatrical use. Rental fees charged. Inquiries accepted by mail and telephone. Some titles available for homevideo sale through Interama Video Classics.
Rights: No rights held to any material (other than distribution rights).
Licensing: Material generally not available for licensing or reuse.
Restrictions: None specified.
Viewing Facilities: None.
Duplication Facilities: None.
Related Materials: Press kits, stills and posters available for many titles.

NEW YORK METRO

INTERNATIONAL AIR CHECK
200 West 58th Street
New York, NY 10019
(212) 246-1446
Telex: 238557 IAC UR

Florida office:
INTERNATIONAL ADVERTISING CENTER
3261 Northeast 14th Avenue
Pompano Beach, FL 33064
(305) 785-6133

Bill Klokow (President)

Contacts: Bill Klokow; Keith Bunker (Coordinator)
Services: Videotape archives. Videotape material available for purchase; additional clearances may be necessary if material is to be reused.
Description: International videotape library of current and historic television commercials (1975-present). Offers (primarily to advertising agencies) annual subscriptions (4 one-hour international reviews), product category and made-to-order videotapes, "Competitive Updates" (3 one-hour videotapes per year, six product choices) and the annual "Reviews of TV Advertising" (60 min.).

Product and service categories include: air conditioners, airlines, amusements, anti-freeze, armed services, automobiles, automobile service, baby foods, plastic bags, baking products, bandages, banks, batteries, beer, beverages, bicycles, bleaches, bread, breakfast foods, bus lines, cake mixes, cakes, cameras, candy, canned goods, car rentals, cat food, cheese, chewing gum, cigars, cleansers, clothes dryers, clothes washers, clothing, cold remedies, colognes and after-shaves, computers, condensed milk, condiments, cookies, crackers, corporate, cosmetics, cough syrups and lozenges, credit cards and travelers' checks, dairy products, deodorants, deodorizers, department stores, desserts, detergents, dishwashing soaps, disinfectants, dog foods, dolls, drain cleaners, drugs, eyeglasses, express companies, fabric softeners, fertilizers, flashlights, flour, fast food, frozen food, forwarding agents, fruit, furniture, games, garden supplies, gasoline, gelatin, girdles, golf supplies, greeting cards, grocery stores, hair tonics and hair sprays, headache remedies, health and beauty aids, health foods, hotels, ice cream, insecticides, insurance, investment companies, jeans, jellies, juices, lawn mowers, laxatives, light bulbs, lingerie, liniments, lipsticks, logos, lubricants, luggage, magazines, margarines, mattresses, meats and chickens, motorcycles, mufflers, nail polish, newspapers, nuts, cooking oil, motor oil, oven cleaners, ovens and stoves, paints, perfumes, hair permanents, pet foods, petroleum corporations, photography supplies, polishes, political, publications, public service, radio stations, razor blades, refrigerators, resorts, restaurants, retail, salad dressings, savings and loan associations, schools, sewing machines, shampoos, shaving accessories, shock absorbers and transmissions, shoes, snack foods, soap, soft drinks, spark plugs, sporting goods, stereo equipment, stomach upset remedies, telephone, television sets, tires, toilet creams, toilet tissue, towels, toothpastes, tourism, toys, transportation, trucks, television stations, underwear, utilities, vacuum cleaners, videotape equipment, vitamins, watches and wines. (Research compilations available or made to order from the Advertising Library Service).

Compiled 30-minute videotape programs on advertising techniques cover: animals, animation, celebrities, children, demonstrations, graphics, humor, music, production techniques, retail, special effects, simplicity spokesmen and testimonials.

Subscriptions available to the quarterly videotape package, *Worldwide Television Advertising Update;* each installment contains 90 new commercials aired internationally.
Size & Elements: Videotape: 3/4", VHS, Betamax and 8mm (PAL or NTSC) (400,000 television commercials total).
Cataloging: Computerized cataloging for staff use only.
Access: Available for reuse. Research fees charged. Research requests accepted by mail, telephone and telex.
Rights: Some material in the public domain. Additional clearances necessary in some cases if material is to be reused.
Licensing: Available for reuse. Usage fees charged in some cases.
Restrictions: None specified.
Viewing Facilities: Videotape (NTSC, PAL and SECAM).
Duplication Facilities: Videotape (all international standards).
Related Materials: Television advertising reviews, updates and "critic's choice award" videotape viewing copies available.
Representatives: Located in London, Brussels, Madrid, Germany, Japan, Brazil, Argentina and Australia (apply for information).

NEW YORK METRO

INTERNATIONAL CENTER FOR THE DISABLED
340 East 24th Street
New York, NY 10010
(212) 679-0100

Ann M. Brancato (Director, External Affairs)

Contact: Ann Brancato
Services: Rehabilitation institution. Videotapes available for distribution; some material available for duplication.
Description: *Industrial quality ICD-produced videotapes.* Topics covered include stress management, and accommodating and supervising the disabled employee.

In-house videotape and audiotape file. Focuses on seminars conducted over the last five years, geared primarily for the rehabilitation community and related fields.
Size & Elements: Videotape: 3/4", VHS and 1/2" open reel (approx. 100 titles).
Cataloging: Published catalogs.
Access: Industrial ICD videotapes available for distribution and rental rather than for research or reuse. In-house videotapes available for duplication. Research fees charged in some cases. Research requests accepted by mail and in person (by appointment only).
Rights: Full rights held to some material. Some rights held to some material. Additional clearances may be necessary in some cases if material is to be reused.
Licensing: Apply for information. License fees charged in some cases.
Restrictions: None specified.
Viewing Facilities: Film (16mm); videotape (3/4", VHS and 1/2" open reel) (by appointment).
Duplication Facilities: Videotape (3/4", VHS and 1/2" open reel).
Related Materials: 5,000 photographs; 100 audiotapes.

NEW YORK METRO

INTERNATIONAL CENTER OF PHOTOGRAPHY
ARCHIVES AND COLLECTIONS
1130 Fifth Avenue
New York, NY 10128
(212) 860-1750
Fax: (212) 360-6490
Telex: ICPNY 420752

Miles Barth (Curator)

Contact: Miles Barth
Services: Museum. Film and videotape archives maintained for research purposes.
Description: Photography, history of photography, and technical issues related to the medium. Museum also collects films and videotapes made by recognized photographers who have worked in media other than still photography. Other materials include films donated by the Time-Life, Inc. Archives and promotional film material on Margaret Bourke-White.
Size & Elements: Film: 16mm. Videotape: 3/4", VHS and Betamax. (Amounts unspecified).
Cataloging: Card catalog; published catalogs.
Access: Not open to the public. For in-house use only. Videotape collection available to qualified scholars or individuals who have obtained permission to view specific videotapes from their producers. Research requests accepted by mail. Appointments necessary for research.
Rights: Rights generally not held.
Licensing: Materials generally not available for licensing.
Restrictions: In most cases, the ICP does not have permission to lend or copy its holdings.
Viewing Facilities: Film (16mm); videotape (3/4", VHS and Betamax).
Duplication Facilities: None.
Related Materials: Photograph archives; resource library.

NEW YORK METRO

INTERNATIONAL FILM FOUNDATION
155 West 72nd Street
New York, NY 10023
(212) 580-1111

Sam Bryan (Executive Director)

Contact: Sam Bryan
Services: Foundation; distributor; film and videotape producer. Film stock footage available for licensing and reuse through authorized representatives.
Description: Footage shot by Julien and Sam Bryan for incorporation into lectures, presentations and educational films. Rather than concentrating on current events, the footage covers everyday life in depth, showing people at work and play, urban and rural life, recreation, dance, theater, schools, factories, farms, households, worship and other activities. Both interiors and exteriors are covered; most post-1950 footage is in color. While virtually no sound exists before 1960, wild sound exists post-1960 for most locations.
Countries and subjects covered include: Africa (1960s and 1980s); China

(1934, 1946 and 1987); Egypt (1950s-60s and 1974), including monuments, the Nile Valley, Aswan Dam and everyday life; England and Scotland (ca. 1949, Kodachrome), with factories, mining, Oxford, Sadlers Wells Ballet, etc.; Germany (1930s), showing everyday life during the rise of Nazism, including the Decadent Art Show, the Anti-Bolshevik Exhibition, Adolf Hitler, and persecution of the Jews; Iran (mid-1970s); Israel (1979); Japan (1934, 1950s and 1970s); Lebanon (1970s); Mexico (1937); Middle East (1950s-70s); Peru (1940s and 1960s); Poland (mid-1930s-60s; Kodachrome 1946-60s), including prewar Jewish life, Catholic church activities, the investiture of Rydz-Smigly, the German invasion of Warsaw (September 1939); South America (1940s, 1960s and 1970s); South Pacific (1940s); Soviet Union (1930-62), including general footage of daily life throughout the country, Maxim Gorky, Ivan Pavlov, Habema players, avant-garde theater (1930s), dam and building construction, recreation parks, collective farms and approximately 40,000 feet of Kodachrome (1947-62 and 1970s) documenting postwar recovery, various Imperial palaces and museums; Turkey (1930s and 1960-61), with footage of Kemal Ataturk (1930s); United States (1940s-50s); and Yugoslavia (1950s-60s), including footage of Tito (ca. 1952).
Size & Elements: Film: 35mm (1 million feet); 16mm (3 million feet).
Cataloging: Staff assistance required.
Access: Available for duplication, licensing and reuse through authorized representatives. Research fees charged. Research requests accepted by mail and telephone.
Rights: Full rights held to all material.
Licensing: Available for licensing and reuse through authorized representatives. License fees charged.
Restrictions: None specified.
Viewing Facilities: Film and videotape (through authorized representatives).
Duplication Facilities: Film and videotape (through authorized representatives).
Representatives: For 16mm footage: Film/Audio Services, Inc. (q.v.). For 35mm footage: Archive Film Productions, Inc./Stock Footage Library (q.v.).

NEW YORK METRO

INTERNATIONAL MEDIA SERVICES, INC.
STUART ALLEN PRODUCTIONS
718 Sherman Avenue
Plainfield, NJ 07060
(201) 756-4060

Stuart Allen (President and Chief Executive Officer)

Contacts: Stuart Allen; C. A. Terminelli
Services: Film and videotape producer and distributor. Material available for rental, duplication, licensing and reuse, subject to restrictions.
Description: Maritime footage, sailing ships, automobile racing, tall ships, crossing the Atlantic under sail, environment, East Africa (people, places and wildlife), medical, pharmaceutical, the performing arts, scenics and scenes of New Jersey.
Size & Elements: Film: format unspecified (approx. 50,000 feet, over 100 titles, over 100 cans). Videotape: 2", 1" and 3/4" (approx. 50 to 100 videotapes). Most film and slide materials have been transferred to 3/4" videotape for cataloging purposes.
Cataloging: Computerized cataloging for staff use only; shot lists; dope sheets or release sheets.
Access: Not open to the public. Available for rental, duplication, licensing and reuse. Research fees charged. Research requests accepted by mail, telephone and in person (by appointment only).
Rights: Full rights held to some material. Some rights held to all material.
Licensing: Available for licensing and reuse, subject to restrictions. License and usage fees charged (depending on usage and costs of duplication).
Restrictions: Restrictions determined on an individual basis per usage or license agreement.
Viewing Facilities: Film and videotape (screening room).
Duplication Facilities: Film (16mm to 3/4"); videotape (3/4" and VHS).
Related Materials: Slide and print collection (70mm and 35mm, over 35,000 images).

NEW YORK METRO

INTERNATIONAL TENNIS HALL OF FAME AND TENNIS MUSEUM
100 Park Avenue, 2nd Floor
New York, NY 10017
(212) 878-2335

Col. Wm. F. Long, Jr. (Executive Director)

Contact: Christine Guarnaccia (Video Operations)
Services: Library; museum. Film collection available for duplication, licensing and reuse on a case-by-case basis.
Description: Holds historic films and footage relating to tennis, including films acquired by a predecessor organization, the International Lawn Tennis Association.

Holds various tennis teaching films (1930s, each 10 min.); the *Analysis of Motion Series* (20 titles, silent), featuring closeups of eminent players including Bill Tilden, Lacoste and Helen Wills Moody; a program on Maureen Connolly (60 min.); and *Great Moments in the History of Tennis* (45 min.). Examples of tennis contests held on film include the 1926 match between Helen Wills Moody and Suzanne Longlong and the 1936-37 Davis Cup.
Size & Elements: Film: 16mm (amount unspecified; positive prints, black and white and color).
Cataloging: In progress; staff assistance required.
Access: Open to the public. Available for duplication and reuse. Preview cassettes with visible time code can be supplied. Research fees charged in some cases. Research requests accepted by mail, telephone and in person (by appointment only).
Rights: Full rights held to most material. Some rights held to some material. Additional clearances may be necessary in some cases if material is to be reused.
Licensing: Available for licensing and reuse, subject to restrictions. License fees charged.
Restrictions: Requests for reuse considered on a case-by-case basis.
Viewing Facilities: Videotape (3/4").
Duplication Facilities: None.

NEW YORK METRO

ISLAND CINEMA RESOURCES
135 St. Pauls Avenue
Staten Island, NY 10301
(718) 727-5593

Robert A. Haller (President)

Contact: Robert A. Haller
Services: Nonprofit media organization. Film and videotape archives preserved and maintained for research and exhibition.
Description: Avant-garde and experimental film and videotape research collection includes: French and German avant-garde films (1920s-30s); American independent and avant-garde films (1920s-30s); independent and avant-garde films made in the U.S. (especially Pittsburgh) in the 1970s; and films by Stan Brakhage, Bruce Conner and Amy Greenfield.

ICR (founded in 1985) presents, preserves, and sponsors productions in and criticism about avant-garde film, videotape, dance and photography. Activities include: programs at the Museum of Staten Island Institute of Arts and Sciences and the Snug Harbor Cultural Center; and the preservation of rare films and videotapes.

Preservation collection includes the "lost" film *Four American Artists* by Ben Moore and Willard Maas and 3/4" videotapes by Steina and Joanne Kelly.
Size & Elements: Film: 16mm (24,000 feet, 175 titles, 175 cans); regular and Super 8mm. Videotape: VHS (30 videotapes).
Cataloging: None specified.
Access: Open to researchers and scholars only. Research requests accepted in person (by appointment only).
Rights: Rights status of material not known.
Licensing: Apply for information. License fees not charged.
Restrictions: None specified.
Viewing Facilities: Film.
Duplication Facilities: None.
Publications: Annual journal, *Field of Vision*.

NEW YORK METRO

ISLAND RECORDS, INC.
14 East 4th Street, 3rd Floor
New York, NY 10012
(212) 477-8000
Fax: (212) 477-5918
Telex: (710) 581-5293

Lou Maglia (President)

Contact: Janet Kleinbaum (Video Promotions)
Services: Record company; music video producer and distributor. Material for promotional use only; not available to the general public.
Description: Music videos by Island Records artists, dating back to the early days of music video production. Genres include rock, pop, jazz, rhythm and blues.
Size & Elements: Videotape: 1" and 3/4" (approx. 350 videotapes).
Cataloging: None.
Access: Not available to the public. Distributed for promotional use in nightclubs and for broadcast use only. Inquiries accepted by mail.
Rights: Full rights held to all material.
Licensing: Available for licensing, subject to restrictions. License fees charged.
Restrictions: Licensing requests considered on a case-by-case basis and subject to clearance and approval.
Viewing Facilities: None.
Duplication Facilities: None.

NEW YORK METRO

ISLAND VIDEO
182 Fairchild Avenue
Plainview, NY 11803
(516) 349-0333

John Lombardi (President)

Contact: John Lombardi
Services: Videotape producer; standards conversion work for European television; archival research service. Material available for duplication, licensing and reuse.
Description: General scenes relating to Long Island, New York, including Jones Beach, Fire Island, the Hamptons and historical sites.

Archival research service maintains collection of television programs (1950s-60s, over 200 reels, 16mm kinescopes and release prints); commercials (early 1950s); and some motion pictures.
Size & Elements: Film: 16mm (release prints and kinescopes, transferred to 1" master videotape for viewing or use). Videotape: 1", 3/4", Betacam, VHS and Betamax (viewing copies). (Amounts unspecified).
Cataloging: Computerized cataloging available to researchers.
Access: Available to bona fide producers and production companies for duplication and reuse. Research fees charged (based on the cost of transfer with time code). Research requests accepted by mail, telephone and in person (by appointment only).
Rights: Full rights held to some material (Long Island footage). Additional clearances may be necessary in some cases if material is to be reused (archival material).
Licensing: Some material available for licensing. License fees charged in some cases.
Restrictions: None, unless copyright holders place restrictions.
Viewing Facilities: Videotape (all formats).
Duplication Facilities: None (outside arrangements can be made).

NEW YORK METRO

ISRAEL BROADCASTING SERVICE
800 Second Avenue
New York, NY 10017
(212) 867-7584

Myra Cohen (Director)
Robert Socolof (Assistant to the Director)

Contacts: Myra Cohen; Robert Socolof
Services: Television broadcaster. Provides free-loan films and stock footage to broadcasters, community organizations and the general public.
Description: Collection is a resource for any organization or individual seeking programs or stock footage on any aspect of Israel. Holds many completed programs and some unedited footage. Though all programs were shot in Israel, some were produced in the United States. Can also direct researchers toward sources of needed material, especially in cases where desired shots are located in completed programs.

Free-loan films and videotapes for television (28 titles). All but one title is clear for use in whole or in part by broadcasters, who are also permitted to videotape or copy for future use. Subject areas covered include:

Agriculture. Titles include: *Every Drop Counts,* about water resources management; *Israel: The 20th Century Miracle; Hands Off,* on fruit harvesting; *Family of the Earth,* showing agriculture in the Negev Desert; *The Agricultural Miracle in the Negev;* and *Israel Review of Agriculture.*

Current events. Titles include: *The Cameras Are There: Israel and the Press,* how the news is made, reported and censored in Israel; *Nine Narrow Miles,* on the disputed area containing Israel's infrastructure and 80 percent of its population; *A Perspective on Israel with Barbara Tuchman* (not cleared for television use); and *Israel Review — Arabs and Jews Together.*

Energy and Science. Titles include: *The Eternal Light* and *Race for the Sun,* on solar energy); *Israel Review of Energy and Technology* and *Israel Review of Medical Science.*

The Holocaust. Titles include: *The Bird Man,* about concentration camp survivor Eitan Porat and his aviary; and *The Little Soldiers,* the story of the Jewish resistance fighters in World War II, showing their reunion forty years later.

Jerusalem. Titles include: *Jerusalem Jerusalem,* a history of the city from ancient times to present day; *Teddy Kollek's Jerusalem,* a portrait of the Mayor; *Jerusalem: A Cultural Profile; Spring in Jerusalem* and *Don McLean in Jerusalem.*

Nature. The Ibex of Ein Gedi shows the desert, its seasons and wildlife.

Religion. The Story of the Prophets, The Heart of a Stranger looks at Christian worship in the Jewish State.

Travel and archaeology. Titles include: *A Sea Called Galilee; Touring Israel with Walter Zanger; Secrets of Jerusalem,* about the life and times of the First and Second Temple periods; and *Shiloh.*

Free-loan video news features. Available to bona-fide broadcasters free of charge on 3/4" videotape with isolated audio.

Agriculture. Mobile Grain Silo, Minimum Tillage Tractor and *Automatic Turkey Egg Collector.*

Holidays. Easter in Jerusalem, Bethlehem's Three Christmases and *Bethlehem Celebrates Christmas.*

The Holocaust. Jewish Resistance Fighters of World War II and *Yad Vashem.*

Technology. Sabra Anti-Auto Theft System; On Guard Glasses, a computer device attached to the frames of ordinary glasses that sounds an alarm if the wearer's eyes close longer than it takes to blink; and *What's Cooking in Solar Energy.*

Travel. Dig for a Day, in which tourists of all ages become archaeologists for a day.
Size & Elements: Film: 16mm (amount unspecified; release prints). Videotape: 3/4" (substantial amount of material; masters and viewing copies).
Cataloging: Title list for in-house use; list of free-loan films available to the public. Consult staff for information regarding specific scenes or subjects desired.
Access: Available to the public for duplication and reuse. Research fees not charged. Research requests accepted by mail and telephone. Written requests preferred from organizations, broadcasters or producers. Films and videotapes are rented to individuals for the cost of duplicating the material onto videotape, and provided without charge to bona fide broadcasters.
Rights: Television rights held to most material. Additional clearances may be necessary in some cases if material is to be reused.
Licensing: Most programs carry no restrictions limiting licensing or reuse. License fees not charged.
Restrictions: None specified.
Viewing Facilities: Film (16mm projector); videotape. Viewing facilities not open to public except by special arrangement.
Duplication Facilities: Videotape (3/4" to 1/2").

NEW YORK METRO

ITALIAN CULTURAL INSTITUTE (ISTITUTO ITALIANO DI CULTURA)
686 Park Avenue
New York, NY 10021
(212) 879-4242

Prof. Gianclaudio Macchierella (Acting Director)

Contact: Dr. Amelia Antonucci (Cultural Assistant)
Services: Government agency. Films loaned for educational and scholastic purposes. Material may not be reproduced in any medium.
Description: Documentaries, travelogues, Italian language instruction films

and feature films in Italian (some with English subtitles) and English.

Archaeology, architecture, city planning, arts and crafts. All films in Italian and English, covering the Appian Way, artistic techniques, the Baroque period, Byzantine art in Southern Italy, Borromini and Guarini, Burchiello, Burri, Calamatta, Casorati, Leonardo da Vinci, De Pisis, Piero Dorazio, the Doric city, the Emilia, Etruscan civilization, Fontanesi, Futurism, Giotto, Guttuso, landscape gardening, Ligabue, Macchiaioli, Modigliani, Giacomo Manzu, Masaccio, Mastroianni, Michetti, Morandi, Naples, Palladio, Parma, Gio Pomodoro, Pompei, Portoghesi, Prampolini, Raffaello, Roman civilization in Tuscany, Pre-Roman Italy, underground Rome, the origins of Rome, the horses of San Marco, Raffaello Sanzio, Savinio, Sicilian castles, Siena, Tancredi, Titian and El Greco, Ernesto Treccani, Giulio Turcato, Paolo Uccello, the Uffizi, Venice, The Venice Biennale and Renzo Vespignani.

Cinema, theater and television. Italian feature films, performance films and television productions in Italian (some with English subtitles) and English. Represented are films by Antonioni, Bellocchio, Bene, Cardinale, De Filippo, De Santis, De Sica, Fellini, Ferreri, Goldoni, Lattuada, Macchiavelli, Magnani, Pasolini, Petrolini, Pirandello, Pontecorvo, Rosi, Rossellini, Salce, Scola, the Taviani brothers, Tosi, Verdi, Visconti and Wertmuller.

Economics, science, technology and industry. Subjects include Alitalia, aluminum, anesthesia in pediatric surgery, antibiotics, boat building, dragonflies, electric power, embryology, FIAT and the jet airplane, heredity, hydrobiology for electricity, insects, information processing, Italian design, Italian steel industry, Lancia, laser, liquid crystals, locomotives, mechanical fruit harvesting, meteorology, natural gas, nicotinic acid, off-season agricultural production, pharmacology, radiology in pediatrics, rodents, solar cells, technical achievements by Italian workers in Africa, thermal energy, traffic decongestion in Turin, underwater electric cables, uranium, viaducts and weather forecasting.

Geography, tourism, landscape and folklore. Visiting the Abruzzo, Admello-Brenta National Park, Aosta, Apulia, Assisi, Basilicata, Calabria, Capri, Elba, Etna, Florence and Tuscany, the Italian Alps, Montevergine, Palermo, Ravello and Sorrento, Sicily, Siena, la Festa del Taratata, Tyrrenian Isles, Umbria, Ustica, Verona and Vicenza.

History and politics. The Senate, Fascism, Mussolini, the Left in power, the 1976 Friuli earthquake, Garibaldi, the Italian Resistance, Mazzini, Naples, Norman Sicily, St. Benedict (the site of the most important school of surgery in the Middle Ages), St. Francis and Siracusa.

History and sociology. The Medicis and 16th century Florence, Sandro Pertini, Venice and the Plague, *Australia, the Promised Land,* and *The Italians and the Creating of America.*

Italian language. All films in Italian except *Basic Italian by Video.* Also available are films on the language and style of contemporary Italian poetry and language and culture courses focusing on Lazio, Sardegna and Sicily.

Juvenile. Christmas tales, the birth of a giraffe in captivity, and a silent film production of *Otello* from 1914 (all in Italian).

Literature. Most films are from the RAI series, *An Author and a City;* films are in Italian, covering Ungaretti, Bevilacqua, Bassani, Bernari, Moravia, Savinio, Testori, and Volponi. Holds *Il Futurismo,* an episode from the series *Enciclopedia dell'Arte Italiana.* Also represented are Pirandello; Cardarelli and Dante in exile.

Music and dance. This category is dominated by opera, but also covers contemporary composers and conductors, popular songs, contemporary dance and music and dance academies in Italy. Subjects include: Luciano Berio, Franco Corelli, Fiorenza Cossotto, Riccardo Muti, Neapolitan songs, Puccini's *Madame Butterfly,* Respighi, Rossini's *The Barber of Seville,* Giulietta Simionato, the Spoleto festival, Verdi, Vivaldi, the bicentennial of La Scala and the academies.

Miscellaneous. Furniture, jewels, fashion, restoration, artisan trade and modern techniques, silk, wine, antiques. Also available are two collections of Italian newsreels *Panorama Italiano* and *Presenza Italiana,* from the mid-1970s, in Italian.

Size & Elements: Film: 16mm (152 films). Videotape: format unspecified (250 videotapes; 142 titles; 84 NTSC, 166 PAL).
Cataloging: Card catalogs; *Audiovisual Aids* catalog.
Access: Open to researchers and scholars only. Maintained for distribution rather than for research or reuse. Research fees not charged. Requests accepted by mail on the letterhead of an academic institution or in person (by appointment only).
Rights: Some rights held to some material. Additional clearances may be necessary in some cases if material is to be reused. (Can duplicate videotapes to which they own the copyright.)
Licensing: Apply for information.
Restrictions: Material can be borrowed only for educational and scholastic purposes. It may not be reproduced in any medium.

Viewing Facilities: Film (16mm); videotape (viewing only if necessary and by appointment only).
Duplication Facilities: Videotape (3/4" to VHS; NTSC).

NEW YORK METRO

IVY FILM
165 West 46th Street, Suite 414
New York, NY 10036
(212) 382-0111
Fax: (212) 840-6182
Telex: 620852

Joshua Tager (Vice President)

Contacts: Larry Chadbourne (Sales Director); Joshua Tager
Services: Distributor. Film and videotape materials available for duplication, rental, licensing and reuse. Research services available for hard-to-find and lost titles.
Description: Holds classic and foreign features; animated and live-action short subjects; and newsreels (primarily 1930-50, black and white). Includes comedy, drama, mystery, animation, classics, television serials and children's films.

Sample titles distributed include: *What's Up Tiger Lily?* (1967); *Alice In Wonderland; Hound of the Baskervilles; Night of the Living Dead* (1968); *Nosferatu; It's A Wonderful Life* (1946); *Breathless* (1959); *The Third Man* (1950); *Naked City* (1948); *The African Queen* (1951); *Plan Nine From Outer Space* (1959); *Of Mice and Men* (1940); *The Red Balloon* (1951); and *The Gold Rush* (1925).
Size & Elements: Film: 35mm and 16mm (masters and viewing prints available for all films, but not in all formats; original negatives available for many titles). Videotape: 1" (100 videotapes); 3/4" (250 videotapes); 1/2" (75 videotapes). (800 titles total).
Cataloging: Card catalogs; published catalogs.
Access: Available to the public for duplication, rental, licensing and reuse. Research fees charged (for rush requests only). Research requests accepted by mail and telephone.
Rights: Full rights held to some material. Some rights held to all material. Some material in the public domain.
Licensing: Available for licensing and reuse.
Restrictions: None specified.
Viewing Facilities: None.
Duplication Facilities: None.

NEW YORK METRO

JALBERT PRODUCTIONS
775 Park Avenue, Suite 230
Huntington, NY 11743
(516) 351-5878
Fax: (516) 351-5875
Telex: 420 758 JALBERT

Joe Jay Jalbert (President)

Contact: Dan Schreiber (Production Coordinator)
Services: Film producer; stock footage sales library.
Description: Competitive and recreational sports footage, especially winter sports. Winter Olympics footage (1936-84) covers downhill skiing, slalom and giant slalom, ski jumping, cross-country skiing, figure skating and hockey, bobsled and luge. Featured athletes include Jean-Claude Killy, Peggy Fleming, Eric Heiden, Scott Hamilton, Franz Klammer, Bill Johnson and Bill Koch.

Other sports footage includes: World Cup ski racing; freestyle "hot dog" skiing (aerials, moguls and ballet); extreme skiing; windsurfing; hang-gliding; outrigger canoeing; kayaking; track and field; and tennis.

Library also contains winter and summer scenics, aerial photography, skylines and travelogue shots from around the world.
Size & Elements: Film: format unspecified (over 4 million feet). Videotape: various formats (viewing copies).
Cataloging: Shot lists.
Access: Available to the public for duplication and reuse. Research fees charged. Research requests accepted by telephone. Commercial demonstration reel available for screening on request.
Rights: Full rights held to all material.
Licensing: Available for licensing. License fees charged.

Restrictions: None specified.
Viewing Facilities: None.
Duplication Facilities: Videotape (3/4" and 1/2").

NEW YORK METRO

JANUS FILMS
888 Seventh Avenue, 4th Floor
New York, NY 10106
(212) 753-7100
Fax: (212) 956-5719
Telex: 236725

A. William J. Becker III (Partner)
Jonathan B. Turell (Managing Director)

Contacts: Jonathan B. Turell; Karen Y. Rosen (Director of Master Materials)
Services: Distributor. Collection available for rental, purchase, licensing and reuse; stock footage available, subject to restrictions.
Description: Foreign feature films and short subjects (1919-present), mainly from Rank and EMI Libraries.

Feature films. Titles include: *Aku Aku* (1959); *Androcles and the Lion* (G. B. Shaw, 1953); *Ashes and Diamonds* (Wajda, 1958); *L'Avventura* (Antonioni, 1960); *Ballad of Narayama* (Imamura, 1983); *Beauty and the Beast* (Cocteau, 1946); *Becket* (Glenville, 1964); *Belles of St. Trinians* (1954); *Billy Liar* (1963); *Black Narcissus* (Powell and Pressburger, 1947); *Black Orpheus* (Camus, 1959); *Blithe Spirit* (Lean, 1945); *Blood Wedding* (Saura, 1981); *The Blue Angel* (von Sternberg, 1930); *Blue Murder at St. Trinians* (Cole, 1954); *Le Bonheur* (Varda, 1965); *Breaking the Sound Barrier* (Richardson, 1952); *The Cabinet of Dr. Caligari* (Wiene, 1919); *Caesar and Cleopatra* (G. B. Shaw, 1945); *The Captain's Paradise* (1953); *Closely Watched Trains* (Menzel, 1966); *The Clouded Yellow* (1951); *The Dambusters* (1955); *Dead of Night* (1945); *The Devil and Daniel Webster* (1941); *Dodes' ka-den* (Kurosawa, 1970); *The Emperor Jones* (1933); *The Elusive Pimpernel* (1950); *Evergreen* (Rodgers and Hart, 1934); *The Fallen Idol* (1948); *Floating Weeds* (Ozu, 1959); *Forbidden Games* (1952); *Gate of Hell* (Kinugasa, 1953); *Grand Illusion* (Renoir, 1937); *The Great Chase* (1962); *Green Grow the Rushes* (1952); *The Happiest Days of Your Life* (1950); *Heavens Above* (Sellers, 1962); *Hidden Fortress* (Kurosawa, 1956); *High Noon* (Zinnemann, 1952); *Hobson's Choice* (Laughton, 1954); *The Horse's Mouth* (Guinness, 1958); *Ikiru* (Kurosawa, 1952); *Illicit Interlude* (Bergman, 1950); *I'm All Right, Jack* (Sellers, 1959); *The Importance of Being Earnest* (1952); *Invasion of the Body Snatchers* (Siegel, 1956); *In Which We Serve* (1942); *I Was Monty's Double* (1958); *Jour de Fete* (Tati, 1948); *Kanal* (Wajda, 1957); *Kameradschaft* (Pabst, 1931); *A Kid for Two Farthings* (Reed, 1955); *Kind Hearts and Coronets* (1949); *King Solomon's Mines* (1937); *Knife in the Water* (Polanski, 1962); *Kon-Tiki* (1951); *The Lady Vanishes* (Hitchcock, 1938); *The Ladykillers* (1955); *Last Holiday* (1950); *The Lavender Hill Mob* (1951); *The Legend of Valentino* (1959); *The Little Theatre of Jean Renoir* (1971); *Lola Montes* (Ophuls, 1955); *The Love Goddesses* (1974); *Loves of a Blonde* (Forman, 1965); *M* (Lang, 1930); *Maedchen in Uniform* (1931); *The Magician* (Bergman, 1958); *Major Barbara* (1941); *The Man in the White Suit* (1952); *Man of Aran* (1934); *The Man Who Knew Too Much* (Hitchcock, 1934); *Metropolis* (Lang, 1926); *Miss Julie* (Sjoberg, 1950); *Mon Oncle* (Tati, 1958); *Mon Oncle Antoine* (Jutra, 1971); *Mondo Cane* (1963); *Monika* (Bergman, 1952); *Monsieur Hulot's Holiday* (Tati, 1953); *The Most Dangerous Game* (1932); *Nicholas Nickelby* (1947); *Nosferatu* (Murnau, 1922); *Notorious Gentleman* (1946); *Odd Man Out* (1947); *Oliver Twist* (Lean, 1947); *Orpheus* (Cocteau, 1949); *Our Daily Bread* (Vidor, 1934); *Pandora's Box* (Pabst, 1928); *Playtime* (Tati, 1967); *Poetry in Motion* (Mann, 1982); *The Promoter* (1952); *Pygmalion* (1938); *The Railway Children* (1970); *Rashomon* (Kurosawa, 1950); *Rattle of a Simple Man* (1964); *Red Beard* (Kurosawa, 1965); *Richard III* (1955); *Rocking Horse Winner* (1950); *La Ronde* (Ophuls, 1950); *Rules of the Game* (Renoir, 1939); *Sabotage* (Hitchcock, 1936); *Salt of the Earth* (1954); *Sanjuro* (Kurosawa, 1962); *Sawdust and Tinsel* (Bergman, 1953); *Secret Agent* (Hitchcock, 1936); *Seven Samurai* (Kurosawa, 1954); *Seven Days to Noon* (1950); *The Seventh Seal* (Bergman, 1957); *Shadows of Forgotten Ancestors* (1964); *Shoot the Piano Player* (Truffaut, 1960); *The Shop on Main Street* (Kadar, 1965); *The Silence* (Bergman, 1963); *Smiles of A Summer Night* (Bergman, 1955); *So Long at the Fair* (1950); *The Spirit of the Beehive* (1974); *State Secret* (1950); *La Strada* (Fellini, 1954); *Summertime* (1955); *Tales of Beatrix Potter* (1971); *Tales of Hoffman* (1951); *That Obscure Object of Desire* (Bunuel, 1977); *The Third Man* (1949); *The 39 Steps* (Hitchcock, 1935); *This Happy Breed* (1947); *This Sporting Life* (1963); *The Threepenny Opera* (Pabst, 1931); *Three Cases of Murder* (Welles, 1955); *Throne of Blood* (Kurosawa,

1957); *Through a Glass Darkly* (Bergman, 1961); *Tunes of Glory* (1960); *Ugetsu* (Mizoguchi, 1953); *Umberto D* (de Sica, 1952); *The Virgin Spring* (Bergman, 1959); *Waltz of the Toreadors* (Sellers, 1962); *Westfront 1918* (Pabst, 1930); *Whistle Down the Wind* (Bates, 1962); *Wild Strawberries* (Bergman, 1957); *The Winslow Boy* (Donat, 1952); *Winter Light* (Bergman, 1962); *Yojimbo* (Kurosawa, 1961); *Young and Innocent* (Hitchcock, 1937); *Paul Robeson: Tribute to an Artist; The Bulldog Drummond Series* (10 films).

Children's films. The films of Albert Lamorisse: *Red Balloon* (1956); *White Mane/Bim the Little Donkey* (1953); *Stowaway in the Sky* (1962); *The Circus Angel* (1965); *Paddle to the Sea* (1966); *The Unicorn* (1983); *Rubber Tarzan* (1981); *Who Has Seen the Wind* (1977); *Lone Wolf* (1973); *A Boy and His Elephant* (1984); *Grandfather Frost* (1985); *My Home is Copacabana* (1965).

Short films. Titles include: *Labyrinth; Papageno; Renaissance; Ersatz; La Jetée; Do-It-Yourself Cartoon Kit; Enter Hamlet; The Fly; Corrida Interdite; The Magician; Two Men and a Wardrobe; The Stranger Left No Card; Bags; The Bespoke Overcoat; The Fat and The Lean; Games of Angels; Un Chien Andalou; The Stringbean; Acts Without Words;* and *Blood of a Poet.*
Size & Elements: Film: 35mm and 16mm (over 100 titles; original negatives, color reversal, internegatives, release prints). Videotape: masters of film transfers. Videodiscs.
Cataloging: Published catalogs.
Access: Not open to the public. Films available for rental, purchase, licensing and reuse. Requests accepted by mail and telephone.
Rights: Full rights held to some material. Some rights held to some material. Additional clearances may be necessary in some cases if material is to be reused.
Licensing: Available for licensing and reuse, subject to restrictions. License and usage fees charged.
Restrictions: Certain titles may carry specific restrictions.
Viewing Facilities: None. Can loan prints and videotapes (3/4" and VHS).
Duplication Facilities: None.
Distributor: For videodiscs and videotapes: The Voyager Company, The Criterion Collection (q.v.).
Related Materials: Extensive background information on films.

NEW YORK METRO

JAPAN EXTERNAL TRADE ORGANIZATION (JETRO)
1221 Avenue of the Americas
New York, NY 10020
(212) 997-0400
Fax: (212) 997-0464

Available for rental from:
MODERN TALKING PICTURE SERVICE, INC. (q.v.).

Yukimasa Kitagawa (President, JETRO)

Contact: Sarah Ressinger (Public Relations, JETRO)
Services: Trade organization. Films and videotapes available for rental through outside distributor.
Description: Japanese industry, trade and trade relations (primarily produced in the 1980s).

Film titles include: *Bridges and Barriers: Americans in Japan; Energy Conservation in Japan* (e.g., nuclear, solar, geothermal, hydraulic and tidal wave power generation); *A Department Store Looks Abroad,* filmed at a leading department store which employs 13,000 people, showing buyers working to find and import attractive products from other countries; *The Music Maker,* about a maker of a violins who used timber from the foothills of the Japanese Alps to start his manufacturing business of violins and later electric guitars; *A Report From Tokyo; Human Age and Robots in Japan; New Technology in Japan* (e.g., robotics, high-speed railway, time-piece and motor industries, medicine and optical fibers); *Past Meets Present in Mindani Hamlet; Four Women, Four Choices* focuses on four Tokyo suburban housewives; *Urikomi: Entering the Japanese Market; The Japanese Consumer News Needs & Diversified Tastes* analyzes consumption patterns; *Decision Making in Japan* deals with consensus and group thinking; *Kacho: A Section Chief and His Day; Understanding Japan; Japan is Your Market* "belies the myth that Japan is an impenetrable market"; and *The Door is Open.*
Size & Elements: Videotape (format and amount unspecified).
Cataloging: Published lists.
Access: Available to the public for rental from Modern Talking Picture Service, Inc. (q.v.).
Rights: Apply for information.

Licensing: Clearances may be necessary if material is to be reused.
Restrictions: None specified.
Viewing Facilities: None.
Duplication Facilities: None.

NEW YORK METRO

JAPAN NATIONAL TOURIST ORGANIZATION
630 Fifth Avenue, Suite 2101
New York, NY 10111
(212) 757-5640
Fax: (212) 307-6754

Kazunari Taguchi (Deputy Director, in charge of film)

Contact: Martha Fulton (Film Librarian)
Services: Government agency of Japan. Film and videotape library maintained for loan, solely for educational or promotional purposes.
Description: Japan, Japanese culture and tourism.
General. Titles include: *Holiday in Japan; Japan, Journey of Discovery; Japan, Land of Enchantment; A Cultural Journey into Japan; Destination Japan; This Year We Went to Japan; The Shimmering Inland Sea; Shinkansen Super Express Tokyo-Hakata; Japan, Season by Season; Portrait in Sound;* and *Encounter with Japan.*
Tourist resorts. Titles include: *Tokyo; Nara, A Stroll Through History; Osaka, The Dynamic City;* and *Southern Kyushu.*
Seasonal attractions. Titles include: *The Four Seasons in Japan; Japan in the Winter; Spring in Japan;* and *Summertime in Japan.*
Special interest films. Titles include: *Japanese Gardens; Japanese Handmade Paper; Bamboo; Invitation to Tea; Sports in Japan;* and *Japanese Handmade Toys.*
Films without narration. Titles include: *Handicrafts in Japan; Yuzen-Kimono;* and *Women in Kimono.*
Size & Elements: Film: 16mm. Videotape: VHS and Betamax (28 titles total).
Cataloging: Published lists.
Access: Open to the public for educational or promotional purposes only; for use by schools, libraries and travel agents. Loan requests accepted by mail and telephone.
Rights: Full rights held to all material.
Licensing: Not available for licensing or reuse.
Restrictions: Films must be shown in their entirety; titles and credits must be shown. Restricted to nonprofit showing. Not available for duplication.
Viewing Facilities: Film (16mm).
Duplication Facilities: None.

NEW YORK METRO

JAPAN SOCIETY, INC.
FILM CENTER
333 East 47th Street
New York, NY 10017
(212) 832-1155
Fax: (212) 755-6752
Telex: 234450

Professor John Gillespie (Director, Film and Performing Arts)

Contacts: Merle Okada; Kyoko Hirano (Film Program Coordinator)
Services: Nonprofit cultural and educational institution. Films available for rental and purchase; videotape research library for use by members only.
Description: Japan and Japanese culture. Four films are currently in distribution:
Shinto: Nature Gods and Man in Japan, filmed by Peter Grilli at the Shinto Art Exhibition at Japan House in New York City and on location in Japan at the Shinto shrines. Footage includes procession of Ise priests in which a ritual meal is carried into the shrine and offered to the gods; the massive buildings of the Izumo Shrine; the Chief Priest of the Munakata Shrine reciting a prayer before a simple outdoor altar; and the island of Okinoshima.
Full Moon Lunch (John Nathan) shows the everyday life of a downtown Tokyo family who caters elaborate box lunches for memorial services and other formal occasions at nearby Buddhist temples.
The Blind Swordsman (John Nathan) is a portrait of superstar Shintaro Katsu, actor, director and producer of the *Zatoichi* films.
Farm Song (John Nathan) documents four generations of a rural Japanese family speaking frankly about their labor, their relationships with each other,
and the seasonal celebrations that enliven their world.
Also in the process of launching *Japanese Society Through Film,* a series of modules that will reproduce Japanese theatrical films in videotape format (three full-length films per module, subtitled in English, with teaching guides). The first module concerns the Japanese family.
Size & Elements: Film: 16mm. Videotape: 3/4", VHS and Betamax. (4 titles total).
Cataloging: Published brochures.
Access: Open to the public. Films available for rental and purchase; videotape research library for use by members only.
Rights: Full rights held to some material. Additional clearances may be necessary if material is to be reused.
Licensing: Apply for information.
Restrictions: None specified.
Viewing Facilities: Film (247-seat theater; rarely used for private screenings); videotape (3/4", VHS and Betamax, for staff and authorized visitors only).
Duplication Facilities: None.
Publications: Grilli, Peter, ed. *Japan in Film: A Comprehensive Annotated Catalogue of Documentary and Theatrical Films on Japan Available in the United States.* New York: Japan Society, 1984.

NEW YORK METRO

THE JUILLIARD SCHOOL
LILA ACHESON WALLACE LIBRARY
Lincoln Center
New York, NY 10023
(212) 799-5000 (Ext. 265)
Fax: (212) 724-0263

Jane Gottlieb (Head Librarian)

Contact: Jane Gottlieb
Services: Educational institution; library. Film and videotape collection not open to the public; for in-house use only.
Description: Film and videotapes of Juilliard Dance Department performances (1952-present).
Size & Elements: Film: 16mm (72 films). Videotape: 3/4" and VHS (39 videotapes; viewing copies).
Cataloging: Finding aids (list).
Access: Not open to the public. For in-house use only. Research requests not accepted.
Rights: Full rights held to some material. Rights retained by choreographers in some cases. Rights status of some material not known.
Licensing: Apply for information.
Restrictions: Not open to the public. For in-house use only. Not available for reuse. Viewing Facilities: None.
Duplication Facilities: None.

NEW YORK METRO

C. G. JUNG FOUNDATION FOR ANALYTICAL PSYCHOLOGY, INC.
28 East 39th Street
New York, NY 10016
(212) 697-6430

Dr. Aryeh Maidenbaum (Executive Director)

Contact: Paul Levy (Book Service Manager) (212/697-6433)
Services: Foundation. Videotapes available for rental and possibly available for reuse, subject to clearance and approval.
Description: The life and work of Dr. Carl Gustav Jung.
Face to Face (BBC). Shortly before his death, Jung granted an interview with BBC television in the warmth and privacy of his home on the shores of Lake Zurich. In this definitive summing up he conversationally touched upon many aspects of his life and work, speaking of his parents, childhood, medicine, psychiatry and Freud.
The Story of Carl Gustav Jung (a Van Der Post film in three parts, 90 min. total), includes rare photos from the family album and footage from Jung's 1926 safari (with an examination of his thoughts and paintings in the "Red Book"). Part One: *In Search of the Soul* is about Jung's childhood and student years, a dream and a vision, his work with mental patients, his relations with Freud and the Red Book. Part Two: *67,000 Dreams* on Jung's work as a psychiatrist, Philemon, the building of Bollingen, travels, mythology, alchemy and dreams, the collective unconscious, and psyche in time and space. Part

Three: *The Mystery That Heals* about Jung in his old age, the shadow, Christianity, the death of Mrs. Jung, silence and the silence broken, and the final dream.
Size & Elements: Videotape: VHS (2 titles).
Cataloging: List.
Access: Available to the public for distribution or rental rather than for research or reuse. Rental fees must be prepaid. Orders accepted by mail and telephone (call for availability).
Rights: Some rights held to some material. Additional clearances may be necessary in some cases if material is to be reused.
Licensing: Apply for information. License or usage fees charged in some cases.
Restrictions: Letter of intent and purpose must be sent to the Executive Director. Requests for licensing and reuse considered on a case-by-case basis.
Viewing Facilities: None.
Duplication Facilities: None.

NEW YORK METRO

JAMES KARNBACH
7 East 14th Street
New York, NY 10003
(212) 929-3116

Contact: James Karnbach
Services: Videotape archives; private collection. Research services available.
Description: Rock and roll and popular music performances (1950s-70s).
Size & Elements: Videotape (format and amount unspecified).
Cataloging: Computerized cataloging for staff use only.
Access: For in-house use only. Research fees charged. Research requests accepted by mail and telephone.
Rights: No rights held to any material. Some material in the public domain. Rights status of some material not known. Additional clearances may be necessary in some cases if material is to be reused.
Licensing: Available for reuse, subject to clearance and approval.
Restrictions: Some restrictions may apply.
Viewing Facilities: Film and videotape.
Duplication Facilities: Videotape (3/4"; NTSC and PAL).

NEW YORK METRO

KEEP THE FAITH, INC.
P.O. Box 8261
North Haledon, NJ 07508
(201) 423-5395
(800) 221-1564 (orders)

Street address: 810 Belmont Avenue

Howard Walsh (Director)

Contact: Jack Hofbauer (Sales)
Services: Religious media organization; videotape distributor. Material available to the public for purchase.
Description: Christian topics on videotape. Recent titles include: *The Homosexual Today: A Catholic Response; Journey to the Forbidden China & Abortion; The Catholic Church in Nicaragua; Modern Attacks on the Family; The Life of St. Bernadette; Women, Hope of the World* (with Phyllis Schlafly); *Liberation Theology; The 1987 Vatican Instruction on Test-Tube Babies and Surrogate Mothers;* and *The AIDS Epidemic.*
Abortion. Titles include: *Mother Teresa; Politics of the Pro-Life Movement* (with Republican Senator Jesse Helms of North Carolina); *Congressman Henry Hyde Belts Liberal Establishment with Deadly Humor;* and *An Historical View of Abortion Around the World.*
Apologetics. Titles include: *The Antichrist; What Does It Mean to Be a Catholic Today?;* and *A Catholic Response to Human Secularism.*
The Bible. Titles include: *Joseph and His Brethren; Jacob, the Man Who Fought With God;* and *Where Jesus Walked* (filmed on location in Israel).
Blessed Virgin Mary. Titles include: *Satan's Head and Mary's Heel; Once on a Barren Hill: The True Story of Our Lady of Guadalupe; Our Lady of Czestochowa;* and *Our Lady of the Apocalypse.*
Church history. Titles include: *Fidelity to the Magisterium; Nicaragua — Model for Latin America; The Suffering Church Under Communism.*
Communism. Titles include: *The Communist Propaganda Machine and Its Victims; The Pope, Catholicism and Communism;* and *Patricia Hurley Attacks*

Our Foreign Policy As a Design for Defeat.
Occults and cults. Titles include: *Human Life International Conference: Sex Education in the Catholic Schools; Hinduism: Father of the New Age Movement; Religion Versus Cults; Hypnotizing Dick and Jane Into the New Age Movement;* and *Zen Buddhism.*
Other areas covered include: education, evolution, family life, family movies, modernism, the Mass, the papacy, philosophy, psychology, lives of the saints, spiritual life, theology, vocations and "Family Retreat" lectures by Bishop Fulton J. Sheen.
Size & Elements: Videotape: format unspecified (approx. 200 titles).
Cataloging: Published catalogs.
Access: Available to the public for purchase. Maintained for distribution and rental rather than for research and resale. Requests accepted by mail and telephone.
Rights: Full rights held to some material. Additional clearances may be necessary in some cases if material is to be reused.
Licensing: Apply for information.
Restrictions: None specified.
Viewing Facilities: In-house viewing not easily accommodated.
Duplication Facilities: None.

NEW YORK METRO

KILLIAM SHOWS, INC.
6 East 39th Street, Suite 502
New York, NY 10016
(212) 679-8230

John Rogers (Vice President)

Contact: Robert D. Bomersbach
Services: Film and videotape distributor; stock footage sales library.
Description: Feature films and newsreel "actuality" footage dating from the beginning of moving pictures (ca. 1896) to ca. 1940. Dramatic and comic footage covers the "Golden Era," silent films, etc.
Size & Elements: Film: 35mm and 16mm (positive, negative, reversal, originals and release prints). Videotape: 1" (masters). (5,000 titles total). Videotape transfers available in all formats.
Cataloging: Research index; card catalogs.
Access: Open to the public for consultation. Available for licensing. Research fees charged. Research requests accepted by mail and telephone.
Rights: Full rights held to all material. Additional clearances may be necessary in some cases if material is to be reused.
Licensing: Available for licensing, subject to restrictions. License fees charged.
Restrictions: Some restrictions apply to non-U.S. footage and to certain celebrities (e.g. Charles Chaplin).
Viewing Facilities: Film (16mm); videotape (3/4" and 1/2").
Duplication Facilities: Videotape (3/4" and 1/2").

NEW YORK METRO

KINO INTERNATIONAL CORPORATION
333 West 39th Street, Suite 503
New York, NY 10018
(212) 629-6880

Contact: Donald Krim
Services: Film and videotape distributor. Material available for rental, purchase and lease.
Description: Domestic and international features available to colleges, museums, libraries, film societies, community centers and nonprofit groups. Some titles available for theatrical distribution.
Titles for non-theatrical distribution include: *The Dead; Caravaggio* (Great Britain); *The Wolf at the Door* (Denmark/France); *Scene of the Crime* (France); *Vera* (Brazil); *Hour of the Star* (Brazil); *A Year of the Quiet Sun* (Poland); *Utu* (New Zealand); and *The Horse* (Turkey). All foreign films are in the original language with English subtitles. Also distributes Spanish-language films, American independent films, the films of Raoul Walsh and Gloria Swanson, Erich von Stroheim, G. W. Pabst and Louise Brooks, Harold Lloyd, Judaica, documentaries, Black history, epics and short films.
Classic films for theatrical exhibition include: *The Janus Festival,* international classics (1940s-present); silent movies with musical scores; and films by Charlie Chaplin, Alfred Hitchcock, Ingmar Bergman and David O. Selznick.

Short subjects include: *Hardware Wars; Naughty Nurse; The Only Forgotten Take of Casablanca; Romance With a Double Bass; Stranger Than Hoboken; Thank You, Masked Man;* and *The Big Tomato.*
Size & Elements: Film: 35mm and 16mm (hundreds of titles). Videotape: VHS and Betamax (some film titles available on videotape).
Cataloging: Published catalogs.
Access: Films available to the public for rental and lease. Videotapes available for purchase. Requests accepted by mail (credit card orders by telephone). Classroom rental rates available. Selected titles available on videotape for purchase by schools and libraries; available with full non-theatrical public performance rights. Apply for information regarding theatrical use.
Rights: No rights held to any material.
Licensing: Apply for information.
Restrictions: All prints and materials furnished the customer remain the property of Kino International Corporation subject to the right of the customer to make use of such material in accordance with the terms under which the picture is licensed. Violation of any of the restrictions of use are subject to penalties set forth in Section 101 of the U.S. Copyright Law. Licensee shall exhibit each picture in its entirety and shall not copy, duplicate, subrent, or part with possession of any print thereof, nor shall the licensee cut or alter same.
Viewing Facilities: None.
Duplication Facilities: None.

NEW YORK METRO

THE KITCHEN CENTER
FOR VIDEO, MUSIC, DANCE, PERFORMANCE AND FILM
(HALEAKALA, INC.)
512 West 19th Street
New York, NY 10011
(212) 255-5793

Barbara Tsumagari (Executive Director)

Contacts: Eileen Clancy (Director of Distribution); Daniel Minahan (Video Curator)
Services: Nonprofit performing arts institution; videotape archives. Videotape collection open to the public for viewing; some videotapes available for rental and purchase.
Description: The Kitchen was founded in 1971 by Woody and Steina Vasulka, pioneering video artists, who invited some friends to view work at the unused kitchen of the old Mercer Art Center (New York City). Since then, it has moved to larger spaces so as to present interdisciplinary exhibition programs to larger audiences and promote works resting outside traditional realms of artmaking.
The Kitchen presents over 100 events a year, and provides a range of programs and services that assist artists in further exhibiting, performing and producing their work. It maintains an extensive Video Archive that is a major resource for broadcasters, curators, producers and writers throughout the world. The Archive forms the nucleus of The Kitchen's Video Distribution Program, which promotes and licenses independently produced video works to galleries, museums, festivals, educational institutions, and for broadcast and cablecast.
Video Archive (over 2,000 videotapes, early 1970s-present). The archival videotapes have been remastered from 1/2" open reel and preserved on 3/4". Documentation of dance, performance events and exhibitions at The Kitchen. Includes documentation of artists such as *Primary Accumulation* (Trisha Brown); *Grand Union Tapes* (Yvonne Rainer, Steve Paxton, Douglass Dunn, David Gordon and Trisha Brown's collaborative company); Laurie Anderson; Simone Forti; and documentation of numerous dance works.
Media Productions. Consists videotapes produced by The Kitchen, including *Perfect Lives* (Robert Ashley and John Sanborn); *30 Second Spots: TV Commercials Artists* (Joan Logue); *The Kitchen Presents: Two Moon July* (directed by Tom Bowes), a compilation of performance artists such as Laurie Anderson, David Byrne and others; and *Totally New Television (TNT),* a compilation of video art works curated by Amy Taubin.
Video Distribution Program. Includes videotapes that reflect the curatorial decisions of the video exhibition programmers (the Vasulkas, Carlotta Schoolman, Tom Bowes, Amy Taubin and Dan Minahan) over the past 17 years. Currently represents over 125 artists and 250 independently produced works, including work by: Vito Acconci, Peggy Ahwesh, Max Almy, Laurie Anderson, Emily Armstrong, Robert Ashley, Charles Atlas, Michel Auder, Burt Barr, Martine Barrat, Judith Barry, M. J. Becker, Ken Beckman, Joe Beirne, Karen Bell, Dara Birnbaum, David Blair, Joan Blair, David Boatwright, David Boone, Jonathan Borofsky, Ed Bowes, Tom Bowes, Barbara Buckner, Robert Cahen, David Cale, Abigail Child, James Chressanthis, Tony Cokes,

Peter D'Agostino, David Daniels, Michael D'Elia, Dimitri Devyatkin, Vivienne Dick, Kristine Diekmen, Paul Dougherty, Steve Fagin, Ken Feingold, Karen Finley, Kit Fitzgerald, Richard Foreman, Howard Fried, Paul Garrin, Matthew Geller, Gisela Getty, Gary Glassman, Annie Goldson, Shalom Gorewitz, John Greyson, Joe Gibbons, Lisa Guido, Pat Hearn, Julia Heyward, Gary Hill, Louis Hock, Nancy Holt, Sara Hornbacher, Dale Hoyt, Intentional Acts, Pat Ivers, John Jesurun, Joan Jonas, The Judson Project Tapes, Hildja Keating, Deans Keppel, Cambiz Khosravi, Michael Klier, Ken Kobland, Mitchell Kriegman, George Kuchar, Shelley Lake, Owen Land (George Landow), Ardele Lister, Joan Logue, John Lurie and the Lounge Lizards, Maitres du Monde, Christian Marclay, Michael Marton, Bruce Mau, Debra McCall, Kevin McMahon, Dan Minahan, Annabella Miscuglio, Gordon Monahan, Laura Mulvey, James Nares, John Orentlicher, Tony Oursler, Nam June Paik, People for the Ethical Treatment of Animals, Mary Perillo, Paulette Phillips, David Plakke, Scott Rankin, Alan and Susan Raymond, Ishmael Reed, Dan Reeves, Peter Reich, The Residents, Judy Rifka, Martha Rosler, Ed Rudolph, Zbigniew Rybczynski, John Sanborn, Santos and Nascimento, Michael Scroggins, Ilene Segalove, Richard Serra, Renee Shafransky, Michael Smith, Squat Theatre, Carol Steinberg, Survival Research Laboratories, Elizabeth Streb, Skip Sweeney, Bruce Tovsky, "Blue" Gene Tyranny, Bill Viola, Frank Vitale, Kirk Von Heflin, Reynold Weidenaar, Robert Wilson, Dean Winkler, Peter Wollen, The Wooster Group, Bruce and Norman Yonemoto and Julie Zando.
Size & Elements: Videotape: 1" (some Media Productions; masters), 3/4" (archives: 2,000 videotapes; distribution collection: 250 titles, each 2 to 420 min.).
Cataloging: Title lists; card catalogs (staff use only); research library.
Access: Open to researchers, scholars, critics and the public. Research fees not charged. Research requests accepted by mail, telephone and in person (walk-in and by appointment). Archival videotapes for in-house screening only; distribution collection available for rental and purchase.
Rights: Some rights held to material produced by The Kitchen. Rights to other material retained by artists or producers. Additional clearances are necessary if material is to be reused.
Licensing: Videotapes available for rental and purchase. Some programs available for broadcast.
Restrictions: Archival videotapes are available to researchers, scholars and critics for in-house screening only. Videotapes in the distribution collection may not be subdistributed.
Viewing Facilities: Videotape (3/4"; NTSC, PAL and SECAM).
Duplication Facilities: Videotape (3/4").
Publications: Quarterly event schedule.
Related Materials: Files of past quarterly event schedules; program notes pertaining to specific events.

NEW YORK METRO

KOREAN CULTURAL SERVICE
CONSULATE GENERAL OF THE REPUBLIC OF KOREA
460 Park Avenue, 6th Floor
New York, NY 10022
(212) 759-9550
Fax: (212) 688-8640

Chan Yong Lee (Director)

Contact: Mrs. Park
Services: Government agency. Films and videotapes available for loan.
Description: Korea, Korean culture and peoples. Almost all materials are in English; some are Korean-language with English subtitles or in Korean only.
Sample films include: *The Korean War,* a documentary about the Korean War (1950-53); *Korean Ginseng,* an introduction to the cultivation, processing and history of ginseng; *The Lost 33 Years,* about the bitter experiences of families separated for 33 years as a result of the division of Korea; *Seoul; Korea-U.S.A. Centennial Friendship; Korean Farm; The Choice of a Certain Family,* a record of the defection of Kim Man Chul and his eleven-member family who fled North Korea, showing the warm welcome they received from the South and the first few days of their freedom in South Korea; *The Harvest Moon Festival; Oriental Medicine in Korea; The Neolithic Relics at Amsadong; The Bongson Mask-Dance Drama; Korean Painting; A Korean Shoemaker; Korean Ornamental Knots; Mt. Sorak; Traditional Martial Arts of Korea;* and *Religions of Korea.* Many film titles are also available on videotape.
Videotapes include: *Korean Traditional House; Pansori: Korea's Intangible Cultural Property;* and *Seoul 1988.*
Size & Elements: Film: 16mm. Videotape: 3/4", VHS and Betamax. (Approx.

170 titles total; many film titles on videotape; some titles on videotape only).
Cataloging: Published lists.
Access: Library and gallery open to the public. Materials available for free loan. Reservations must be made by mail in advance.
Rights: Apply for information.
Licensing: Apply for information.
Restrictions: None specified.
Viewing Facilities: None.
Duplication Facilities: None.

NEW YORK METRO

LAMBDA LEGAL DEFENSE AND EDUCATION FUND, INC.
666 Broadway
New York, NY 10012
(212) 995-8585
Fax: (212) 995-2306

Contact: Jerl Surratt (Associate Director)
Services: Organization.
Description: Legal defense fund dedicated to protecting the rights of people with AIDS; won the first AIDS-related suit ever filed in the United States. Holds rights to two AIDS-related public service announcements, originally produced and aired on Manhattan Cable TV, featuring Jeff Daniels and Julie Hagerty.
Size & Elements: Videotape (format and amount unspecified).
Cataloging: None.
Access: Apply for information.
Rights: Full rights held to all material.
Licensing: Apply for information.
Restrictions: None specified.
Viewing Facilities: None.
Duplication Facilities: None.

NEW YORK METRO

LATIN AMERICAN VIDEO ARCHIVES (LAVA)
SCHOOL OF CONTEMPORARY ARTS
RAMAPO COLLEGE OF NEW JERSEY
Mahwah, NJ 07430-1680
(201) 529-7368

Pat Keeton (Project Director and Assistant Professor of Communications)

Contact: Pat Keeton (201/529-7399)
Services: Educational institution. Open to researchers, scholars and the public. Available for non-commercial duplication and use by New Jersey educational and community groups.
Description: Established 1987 with grant support from the New Jersey Department of Higher Education. The goal of the Archives is to support Ramapo College's commitment to international and multicultural awareness and education.

Archives holds more than 40 different videotapes produced by Latin Americans, which cover a striking range of subjects and genres, including theater dramas, news shows, documentaries, experimental video, visual poems, satire and fiction. Topics covered include women's studies, housing, immigration, media, social class, Indians, war, environmental issues, propaganda, agrarian reform, music, poverty, labor, television, advertising, language, multicultural awareness, race, ethnicity, comparative politics, history, journalism, Latin American and international studies. At present, Archives holds videotapes from Bolivia, Brazil, Chile, El Salvador, Guatemala, Mexico, Nicaragua, Panama, Peru and Uruguay.

All videotapes are Spanish-language with English subtitles.
Size & Elements: Videotape: 3/4" (13 hours, 43 videotapes, most under 15 min.; submasters and viewing copies); VHS (viewing copies).
Cataloging: Brochure; title list.
Access: Open to researchers, scholars and the public. Available for non-commercial use and duplication by New Jersey educational and community groups. Apply for information regarding research fees and procedures.
Rights: Some rights held to some material (educational and non-commercial use by New Jersey schools and community groups only). Additional clearances may be necessary in some cases if material is to be reused.
Licensing: Not available for licensing or reuse.
Restrictions: Not available for licensing or reuse. Use of collection restricted to New Jersey educational and community groups only.

Viewing Facilities: Videotape (in Art Gallery and Library, by appointment).
Duplication Facilities: Videotape (3/4" and 1/2"; copies can be made on a limited basis for New Jersey institutions only).
Related Materials: Files of articles relating to individual videotapes and their producers.

NEW YORK METRO

LEUKEMIA SOCIETY OF AMERICA
733 Third Avenue
New York, NY 10017
(212) 573-8484

Peter N. Cakridas (Chief Executive Officer)

Contact: Marty Siederer (Assistant Director, Communications)
Services: Association. Film and videotape library available to the public for free loan, purchase, duplication and reuse.
Description: *Educational programs* (16mm film and 3/4" videotape). Titles include: *The Story of Walter,* a look at current research on feline leukemia; *A Sense of Hope,* featuring a young boy with leukemia; *Research: The Challenge of Survival,* spotlighting the work of four Society-sponsored researchers and offering a positive approach to fighting both childhood and adult leukemia; *Faces of Medicine: The Last Hope,* exploring bone marrow transplantation work; and *You're Not Alone,* tracing the experiences of a leukemia patient and the support that she receives from her family and treatment team of medical professionals.

Public service announcements (3/4" and VHS videotape only). *Town PSA Series* (two 30 sec. and one 10 sec., Spanish and English), uses everyday activities to dramatize the advances made in the survival rates for leukemia and related diseases.
Size & Elements: Film: 35mm and 16mm (7 titles, 100 cans). Videotape: 1" (masters); 3/4" and VHS (7 titles, each 10 to 30 min.; viewing copies).
Cataloging: Published catalog.
Access: Open to the public. Maintained primarily for educational distribution and research; available for duplication and reuse. Research and rental fees not charged.
Rights: Some rights held to all material.
Licensing: Apply for information. License and usage fees not charged.
Restrictions: None specified.
Viewing Facilities: Film (16mm); videotape (3/4" and VHS).
Duplication Facilities: Videotape (VHS).

NEW YORK METRO

VICKI GOLD LEVI
211 Central Park West
New York, NY 10024
(212) 724-1133

Contact: Vicki Gold Levi
Services: Private collection. Film and videotape material available for rental. Research and consultation services available.
Description: Historical archives of film and videotape relating to Atlantic City, N.J. (1917-64); also holds documentaries produced in recent years. Can provide access to other private collections of Atlantic City historical material.
Size & Elements: Apply for information.
Cataloging: Staff assistance required.
Access: Available for rental only. Research and consultation services available. Research fees charged. Research requests accepted by telephone. Some material available for viewing (appointments required).
Rights: Apply for information.
Licensing: Apply for information. License and usage fees charged.
Restrictions: Some restrictions may apply, depending on nature of project.
Viewing Facilities: None.
Duplication Facilities: None (outside arrangements can be made).
Publications: *Atlantic City: 125 Years of Ocean Madness* (co-author).
Related Materials: Large still photograph archives.

NEW YORK METRO

THE LIBRARY OF SPECIAL VISUAL EFFECTS/
DARINO FILMS
222 Park Avenue South, Suite 2
New York, NY 10003

(212) 228-4024
Telex: 4940255 DARINOUI

Ed Darino (Creative Director)

Contacts: Ed Darino
Services: Library of computerized animation and electronic visual effects. Syndicated packages on videotape available for purchase only; rights to unlimited reuse included. Custom design and production of computerized graphics and animation available.
Description: Collection of computerized animation and electronic visual effects, backgrounds, borders, generics, tags, wipes, motion graphics and opticals. The effects are created on film and videotape using state-of-the-art technology: animation (cel, computer-controlled and generated); opticals; wireframe digitals; 3-D solids; streaks; slit-scans and lasers. Effects are frequently enhanced with ADO, DVE and Mirage.
    Collection classified by sections, including: sports, news, health, Olympics, safety, religion, military, music, weather, movies, high technology, backgrounds, borders, bumpers and transitions. Specific elements include: ID logos, openings and closings, trailers, teasers, feature special effects, television spots, combinations of live action or 3-D objects with animation, days of the week, holidays, fireworks, explosions, rainbows, sunsets, traveling patterns, background loops, moving grids, marquees, spaceships, starfields and "stars that scintillate."
    The complete library includes five one-hour collections and is available in 1" or 3/4" videotape format.
Size & Elements: Film: 35mm and 16mm. Videotape: 1" and 3/4" (5 hours; masters and viewing copies, NTSC and PAL). (Syndicated packages contain approx. 2,000-3,000 effects, each 10 sec. to 3 min. in length).
Cataloging: Computerized cataloging for staff use only; published catalog and brochures; shot list. VHS preview videotape available (preview charge applies).
Access: Available for distribution and syndication. Research fees normally not charged. Requests accepted by mail, telephone and in person (by appointment only).
Rights: Full rights held to all material.
Licensing: Purchaser of library is granted licensing and usage without restrictions, permitting unlimited internal, commercial or broadcast use. Purchase fees charged. Discounts apply when entire library package is purchased at one time.
Restrictions: None specified.
Viewing Facilities: Film (35mm and 16mm); videotape (3/4" and VHS).
Duplication Facilities: Film (35mm and 16mm); videotape (1", 3/4" and VHS; NTSC and PAL).

NEW YORK METRO

LOCUS COMMUNICATIONS
151 West 25th Street, Suite 3F
New York, NY 10001
(212) 242-0281

Gerald Pallor (Executive Director)

Contact: Gerald Pallor
Services: Media arts center. Videotapes available to researchers and scholars only for in-house screening; and for loan, duplication and reuse subject to restrictions.
Description: Locus Communications provides access to equipment and production services for independent videomakers, and presents programs of artists' and independent videotapes throughout New York City (*Video in the Boroughs*) and on cable television (*LocusFocus,* aired weekly, September 1983-present).
    Holds programs of video art (1980-present), documentaries, community-produced and independent videotapes, all consisting of short subjects. Very few programs are unique. Also holds copies of programs produced at Locus.
Size & Elements: Videotape: 3/4" (approx. 40 hours; submasters and viewing copies); VHS (viewing copies).
Cataloging: Release sheets; exhibition programs.
Access: Open to researchers and scholars only. For in-house use only. Research and screening fees charged in some cases. Research requests accepted by mail, telephone and in person (by appointment only).
Rights: Some rights held to some material. Rights to most videotapes retained by artists or original producers.
Licensing: Available for licensing and reuse, subject to restrictions.
Restrictions: Reuse must be negotiated on a case-by-case basis and requires

approval of artist or original producer.
Viewing Facilities: Videotape.
Duplication Facilities: Videotape (3/4" and VHS).

NEW YORK METRO

LONG ISLAND STATE PARK COMMISSION
P.O. Box 247
Belmont Lake
Babylon, NY 11702
(516) 669-1000
Fax: (516) 669-1775

Ronald F. Foley (Regional Commissioner)

Contact: Ronald F. Foley
Services: Government agency. Film and videotape collection available to the public for distribution.
Description: Recently uncovered collection of 16mm films (1930s-40s). Subjects include: Jones Beach (1930s); Long Island State Parks (1930s-40s); New York state parkways (1935); New York City Expressways; Gowanus Bridge; Niagara Power Dam; and the Grand Central Parkway. There are plans to show portions of these films on Long Island Cablevision and in many of the state parks, and to make them available to the general public and school systems through mail distribution and in-house viewing.
Size & Elements: Film: 16mm (40 reels). Videotape: VHS (15 videotapes, each 60 min.; transfers from film).
Cataloging: Currently being inventoried; brochure will be available.
Access: Available to the public for distribution and rental rather than for research. Research fees not charged. Research requests accepted by mail and telephone.
Rights: Full rights held to all material.
Licensing: Apply for information. License fees generally not charged.
Restrictions: None specified.
Viewing Facilities: Videotape (VHS).
Duplication Facilities: None.

NEW YORK METRO

MANHATTAN MOVIETIME
15 Vandam Street
New York, NY 10013
(212) 675-0498

Contact: Jim Poling
Services: Film producer; private collection. Material available to the public for reuse, subject to restrictions.
Description: Holds public domain features, all-Black cast films, Hollywood-oriented short subjects, and other footage.
Size & Elements: Film: various formats (500 titles; negatives and positive prints).
Cataloging: Film list.
Access: Available to the public for reuse, subject to restrictions. Research fees charged in some cases. Research requests accepted by mail and telephone.
Rights: Some material in the public domain. Rights status of some material not known.
Licensing: Available for reuse, subject to restrictions. Usage fees charged.
Restrictions: Some restrictions apply, depending on intended use.
Viewing Facilities: None.
Duplication Facilities: None.

NEW YORK METRO

MARCH OF DIMES BIRTH DEFECTS FOUNDATION
1275 Mamaroneck Avenue
White Plains, NY 10605
(914) 428-7100
Fax: (914) 428-9515

Contact: Richard DelPrete (Archivist)
Services: Foundation. Film and videotape library open to researchers and producers. Material available for licensing and reuse on a case-by-case basis.
Description: Current programs pertaining to birth defects and fifty years of related historical material. Most programs available on film or videotape.
    Historical. Titles include: *A Dream Come True* (1955), showing the March

of Dimes' successful battle against polio and the development of the Salk vaccine; and *To Save a Child*, including historical footage.

Birth defects: causes and prevention. Titles include: *Time Against The Future*, an informative report on the growing problem of battered pregnant women and resulting birth defects; *Cocaine's Children*, showing the effects of cocaine use during pregnancy on newborn babies; *Environmental Risks and Pregnancy*, featuring documentary inserts and discussion by an expert panel; and *Healthier Babies: The Genetic Era*, showing how genetic counseling gives parents a better chance of preventing or lessening the effects of birth defects.

Prenatal care, health and nutrition. Titles include: *It's Up To Me*, on the importance of good prenatal care as shown through portraits of three mothers; *Unfinished Child*, a documentary on the importance of proper prenatal nutrition; *Woman-Child*, the consequences of adolescent pregnancy as seen through the eyes of six teenagers; and *Alcohol: Crisis For the Unborn*, on babies born with fetal alcohol syndrome.

Fund-raising activities and volunteer work. Titles include: *Mothers March Training Video; Walk With Us; Bid For Bachelors Auctions; Golf, Golf, Golf*, showing celebrity golf tournaments; and *A Winning Combination*, on youth volunteers around the country; and *National Ambassador Tradition*, on the history of March of Dimes poster children.

Research programs. Titles include: *Miracle Babies*, telling the stories of five miracle babies saved by March of Dimes research; *The Researchers*, highlighting various research programs to prevent birth defects; *RDS/Surfactant*, on recent progress in surfactant therapy to help premature infant victims of respiratory distress syndrome; and *Dyslexia*, reporting on studies indicating the problem is inherited.
Size & Elements: Film: format unspecified (approx. 30 titles). Videotape: 3/4" and VHS (approx. 60 titles).
Cataloging: Title list with descriptions.
Access: Open to researchers, producers and the public. Foundation prefers to work with major networks but is willing to consider any requests for access. Research fees not charged. Research requests accepted by telephone.
Rights: Full rights held to historical material. Foundation can assist in locating holders of rights to other material.
Licensing: Available for licensing and reuse, subject to restrictions. License and usage fees not charged; donations requested to cover costs in some cases.
Restrictions: All requests for access, research, licensing and reuse evaluated on a case-by-case basis.
Viewing Facilities: Film and videotape.
Duplication Facilities: None (outside facilities used).

NEW YORK METRO

MERRILL LYNCH PIERCE FENNER & SMITH
VIDEO NETWORK
One Liberty Plaza, 30th Floor
New York, NY 10080
(212) 637-4759

Marilyn Reed (Vice President and Manager)

Contact: Judy Noble (Marketing Manager)
Services: Corporation; media organization. Film and videotape material available for licensing and reuse on a case-by-case basis. *Not a stock footage library; has limited capacity to handle research requests.*
Description: Holds 700 completed productions (1976-present). Currently compiling a stock footage reel that will include shots relating to financial subjects (e.g., views of the New York Stock Exchange and Wall Street). This reel is intended to represent the collection and to fulfill the most common footage requests received by Video Network. Research requests that cannot be satisfied by shots contained on this reel will be accepted on a case-by-case basis.
Size & Elements: Film: format and amount unspecified. Videotape: 1" and Betacam (approx. 700 titles; substantial amount of stock footage).
Cataloging: None specified.
Access: Available for reuse. Research fees charged in some cases. Research requests accepted by mail and telephone. Research services are offered free of charge to news facilities; fees charged to individuals and groups requesting demonstration reel or research services.
Rights: Full rights held to some material. Additional clearances may be necessary in some cases if material is to be reused.
Licensing: Available for licensing and reuse, subject to restrictions. License fees charged.
Restrictions: Requests for research and reuse accepted on a case-by-case basis.
Viewing Facilities: Videotape (in-house viewing available only under certain circumstances).
Duplication Facilities: None.

NEW YORK METRO

METROPOLITAN MUSEUM OF ART
URIS CENTER FOR EDUCATION
THE MEDIA CENTER
Fifth Avenue and 82nd Street
New York, NY 10028
(212) 879-5500 (Ext. 2032)

Contacts: John Ross (Ext. 3442) (Public Information); Wendy Williams (Ext. 2032), Henriette Montgomery (Ext. 2035), Robin Schwalb (Ext. 3728) (Media Center); Karl Katz (for clearances to reuse material)
Services: Museum. Film and videotape collection open to staff, researchers and scholars for use in Museum programs and for study purposes.
Description: The Media Center is designed as a film and videotape resource facility for the Museum staff and for qualified researchers and scholars. The Center functions as the Museum's archives of videotape programs and documentary films on art, both Museum-produced and those produced by commercial and independent filmmakers.

Collection covers a broad range of topics, including programs about artists, art history, artistic techniques and processes, archaeology and culture. Films and videotapes relate to all the Museum's collections and curatorial departments, as well as to Conservation and Education Services.

Some highlights and titles include: original footage from the Museum's Egyptian expeditions (1920s, 35mm); 120 short films (mostly animated) for children and families, relating to art history, artistic processes and the Museum's collections; *Süleyman the Magnificent* (1987); *Edouard Manet: Painter of Modern Life*; and *A Day on The Grand Canal With The Emperor of China or Surface is Illusion But So Is Depth* (1988), a discussion with Philip Haas and David Hockney on the differences between Eastern and Western artistic perspectives.
Size & Elements: Film: 35mm (20 titles, 50 cans; about one-third unedited archival footage); 16mm (900 titles, 1,300 cans). Videotape: 3/4" (approx. 153 videotapes); VHS (approx. 20 videotapes); Betamax (2 videotapes); 1/2" open reel (approx. 250 videotapes; unedited in-house documentation).
Cataloging: Card catalogs; computerized cataloging for staff use only.
Access: Open to staff, researchers and scholars for use in Museum programs and for study (by appointment, Tuesdays, Wednesdays and Thursdays). For in-house use only. Research requests accepted by mail, telephone and in person (by appointment only). Requests for viewing or use of any equipment must be made at least 24 hours in advance.
Rights: Full rights held to some material (a few items). Some rights held to some material (a few items). No rights held to most material ("virtually entire collection"); rights retained by original producers or filmmakers.
Licensing: Available for licensing and reuse, subject to restrictions. License and usage fees charged in some cases.
Restrictions: Requests for licensing and reuse accepted on a case-by-case basis. Restrictions apply to most material.
Viewing Facilities: Film (16mm); videotape (3/4", VHS and Betamax).
Duplication Facilities: Videotape (3/4").

NEW YORK METRO

METROPOLITAN OPERA HOUSE
Lincoln Center
New York, NY 10023
(212) 799-3100 (Ext. 2228)
Fax: (212) 870-4520

Bruce Crawford (General Manager)

Contact: Ellen Rudolph (Media Department)
Services: Opera company; archives. Videotape collection maintained primarily for in-house reference, and special or educational viewing on a limited basis. *Collection not open to the public.*
Description: Grand opera and concert performances videotaped at The Metropolitan Opera (1977-present); interviews with artists, directors, and designers; short documentaries on The Metropolitan Opera, its history and activities.

Live From The Met telecasts (in chronological order by videotaping date): *La Boheme* (Scotto, Pavarotti, March 15, 1977); *Rigoletto* (MacNeil, Domingo, Cotrubus, Nov. 7, 1977); *Don Giovanni* (March 16, 1978);

Cavalleria Rusticana/Pagliacci (April 5, 1978); *Otello* (Vickers, Scotto, MacNeil, Sept. 25, 1978); *The Bartered Bride* (Nov. 21, 1978); *Tosca* (Pavarotti, Verrett, Dec. 19, 1978); *Don Pasquale* (Jan. 11, 1979); *Luisa Miller* (Jan. 20, 1979); *Otello* (Domingo, Cruz-Romo, Milnes, Sept. 24, 1979); *Mahagonny* (Nov. 27, 1979); *Un Ballo in Maschera* (Feb. 16, 1980); *Elektra* (Feb. 16, 1980); *Don Carlo* (Moldoveanu, Scotto, Feb. 21, 1980); *Manon Lescaut* (March 29, 1980); *Lulu* (Dec. 20, 1980); *L'Elisir D'Amore* (March 2, 1981); *La Traviata* (March 28, 1981); *Il Trittico* (Nov. 14, 1981); *Rigoletto* (Quilico, Pavarotti, Eda-Pierre, Dec. 15, 1981); *La Boheme* (Stratas, Carreras, Zeffirelli, Jan. 16, 1982); *Troyanos/Domingo Concert* (Feb. 28, 1982); *Price/Horne Concert* (March 28, 1982); *Der Rosenkavalier* (Oct. 7, 1982); *Idomeneo* (Nov. 6, 1982); *Lucia di Lammermoor* (Nov. 13, 1982); *Tannhäuser* (Dec. 20, 1982); *Hansel and Gretel* (Dec. 25, 1982); *Domingo/Milnes Concert* (Jan. 30, 1983); *Don Carlo* (Domingo, Freni, March 26, 1983); *Les Troyens* (Oct. 8, 1983); *Met Centennial Gala* (Oct. 22, 1983); *Ernani* (Dec. 17, 1983); *La Forza del Destino* (March 24, 1984); *Francesca da Rimini* (April 7, 1984); *Spring Gala* (May 13, 1984); *Simon Boccanegra* (Dec. 29, 1984); *Aida* (Jan. 3, 1985); *Tosca* (Domingo, Behrens, Zeffirelli, March 27, 1985); *Le Nozze di Figaro* (Dec. 14, 1985); *Lohengrin* (Jan. 10, 1986); *L'Italiana in Algeri* (Jan. 11, 1986); *Die Fledermaus* (Dec. 31, 1986); *Sutherland/Pavarotti Gala* (Jan. 11, 1987); *Carmen* (Feb. 28, 1987); *Dialogues of the Carmelites* (April 4, 1987); *Turandot* (April 4, 1987); *Tales of Hoffman* (Jan. 8, 1988); *Ariadne auf Naxos* (March 12, 1988).
Size & Elements: Videotape: 1" (49 titles; masters); 3/4" (49 titles; screening copies).
Cataloging: Card catalogs and computerized cataloging (for staff use only).
Access: Not open to the public. For in-house use only. Screening (by appointment) may possibly be available if deemed appropriate by The Metropolitan Opera and, even then, on a very limited basis. Research fees not charged. Research requests accepted by mail and telephone.
Rights: Full rights held to all material.
Licensing: Apply for information.
Restrictions: Not a public viewing facility; collection has limited access and licensing availability.
Viewing Facilities: Videotape (3/4") (by appointment only).
Duplication Facilities: None.
Representative: Apply for information.

NEW YORK METRO

MILADY PUBLISHING CORPORATION
3839 White Plains Road
Bronx, NY 10467-5394
(212) 881-3000
(800) 223-8055

Contact: Marketing Manager
Services: Distributor. Videotapes available to the public for purchase.
Description: Audiovisual aids on many aspects of cosmetology and hairstyling, produced for student and professional cosmetologists.
    Titles include: *Manicuring; The Skin; The Nature and Structure of the Hair; Changing the Form of Hair — Straightening, Waving, Curling; For the Love of Hair; Single Process Tint Application; Theory of Restructuring Over-Curly Hair; The Facial Technique; Acne...It's Not Your Fault; Permanent Wave Blocking; Blow Waving For Varied Loveliness; Male Makeover; Styling for Magazines and Television;* and *Makeup Techniques for Video by GiGi Coker.*
Size & Elements: Videotape: 3/4", VHS, Betamax I and II (50 titles).
Cataloging: Published catalog.
Access: Available to the public for purchase. Orders accepted by mail and telephone.
Rights: Apply for information.
Licensing: Apply for information.
Restrictions: Apply for information.
Viewing Facilities: None.
Duplication Facilities: None.
Related Materials: Program guides; slide shows; filmstrips with audiocassettes.

NEW YORK METRO

MILES EDUCATIONAL FILM PRODUCTIONS
P.O. Box 814, Lincolnton Station
New York, NY 10037
(212) 560-6916

William Miles (President)

Contact: William Miles
Services: Film and videotape producer. Collection available for reuse and resale.
Description: Programs about Black history and culture, and "Black-oriented footage" (covering events from 1898-present).
    Titles include: *The Different Drummer: Blacks in the Military* (3 hrs.), a three-part series tracing the history of Black participation in the U.S. armed forces (1776-present), distributed by Films Incorporated (q.v.); *Men of Bronze,* on the Black American combat regiment that served under the Fourth French Army in World War I, distributed by Killiam Shows, Inc. (q.v.); *Preaching The Word,* on the history and tradition of the Black church; *Black Champions,* a three-part series on the history of Black athletes (1920s-present); *I Remember Harlem — Part One: The Early Years 1600-1930, Part Two: The Depression Years 1930-1940, Part Three: Toward Freedom 1940-1965,* and *Part Four: Toward a New Day 1965-1980* (total 4 hrs.).
Size & Elements: Film: 35mm (4,000 feet; positive, negative, reversal, originals and release prints); 16mm (100,000 feet; positive, negative, reversal, originals and release prints).
Cataloging: Card catalogs.
Access: Available for licensing and reuse. Research requests accepted by mail, telephone and in person (by appointment only). Some titles available for rental through distributors (apply for information).
Rights: Full rights held to some material. Some material in the public domain. Additional clearances may be necessary in some cases if material is to be reused.
Licensing: Available for licensing and reuse, subject to clearance and approval. License fees charged.
Restrictions: None specified.
Viewing Facilities: Film and videotape.
Duplication Facilities: None.

NEW YORK METRO

MONDAY, WEDNESDAY, FRIDAY VIDEO CLUB
c/o Alan Moore
73 East Houston Street
New York, NY 10012
(212) 219-0765
Fax: (212) 475-1404 (c/o SST)

Contact: Alan Moore (Manager)
Services: Nonprofit media organization; film and videotape archives and producer; stock footage sales library. Videotapes available for rental and purchase.
Description: Represents video and film artists for rentals and purchase, emphasizing sales to the homevideo market. Since all videotapes consigned have been accepted, the collection is open to include donations from artists, and is not limited to the curatorial judgment of one person. Includes video artworks, underground cinema, documentary producers and television by artists. Many works are experimental in nature, documenting an art subculture of New York City, and are not available from other sources. The Club is an affiliated project of Collaborative Projects, Inc. (established 1978), a nonprofit artists organization.
    Titles include: *Open Mike* (ABC No Rio, 1985), documenting a reading by young poets and musicians at a Lower East Side gallery; *Twins* (Charlie Ahearn, 1980), a feature film starring performance artist Michael Smith; *Sampler* (All Color News, 1978), a collection of clips from a cable television news program, produced by John Ahearn, Tom Otterness, Scott and Beth B, and Charlie Ahearn; *Brian Eno: At a Distance* (Artspeak, 1986), a California lecture by the English musician; *John Giorno* (Artspeak, 1986), an interview with and performance by the poet; *3 Films by Beth B and Scott B* (1979-80), including *G-Man, Letters to Dad* and *Black Box;* five works by David Blair; *The Date* and *Glances,* both by Caterina Borelli; *Cave Girls* (Kiki Smith, Cara Brownell and Ellen Cooper, 1982), a fantasy of a prehistoric women's culture; *God's Police* (Robert Cooney, 1980), an Australian artist's indictment of religious bigotry; *Nazareth in August* (Damian and Walworth Cowie, 1985), the history of Palestinian Arabs living in Israel; two works by Jaime Davidovich; *Ena's Adventures, Part I* (Lee Eiferman and Kathy High, 1986), the story of a WPA-era photographer in a small desert town who discovers disturbing secrets through the lens of her portrait camera; *Everyone Sings/Cantemos Todos!* (Doug Eisenstark, 1986), documenting Carlos Meija Godoy's *Misa Campesina* as performed at the Cathedral of St. John the Divine in New York City; *Italy Wins World War III: 1990 Summit* (Peter Fend, 1983),

a live cable colloquium on the shape of the world and nation-states as they might look from space after a series of "ecological wars"; *X & Y Natural Disasters — Safety First* (Colen Fitzgibbon and Robin Winters, 1978); *Brunch* (Carol and Jill Fleishman, 1986); *Long Island Four* (Andres Grafstrom, 1980, originally produced in Super 8mm), a feature film about four Nazi saboteurs who landed in the U.S. in 1942 and are captivated by New York's decadent night life. Also distributes four works by Franck Goldberg, including *Red Souvenir* (1987), a verité look at kids in New York City; *No Sellout* (1986), a rap music video based on the speeches of Malcolm X; *Lynch: The Murder of Michael Stewart* (1985), a documentary on the police killing of a young graffiti artist in the New York subway; and *Promised Land* (1986), on the purposeless violence of the U.S.A.

Other titles include: *Doomed Love* (Andrew Horn, 1983); *Early Works* (Sara Hornbacher); *Fifth, Park & Madison* (Dragan Ilic, 1987), on the 1987 bicycle messengers' strike in New York; *An Evening at No Se No* (Ray Kelly, 1984), documentation of performance events outside the Lower East Side gallery; *The Chelsea Tapes* (Paul Lamarre, 1984-85); *Barbie* and *Snakewoman* (Tina Lhotsky, 1977); *Works 1978-83* (Hank Linhart); *11th & B* (Marie Martine, 1985), a rapid montage of people on the street and wall painting in the East Village; *Red Italy* (1979) and *Kidnapped* (1978), two feature films by Eric Mitchell; *Beehive* (Frank Moore and Jim Self, 1985), the story of a bumbling drone bee who unwittingly causes the transformation of a worker into a queen; *Raptures of the Deep* (1981) and *The Reptile Mind* (1982), both by Alan Moore; *When Things Get Rough on Easy Street* and *Ovid* (Joseph Nechvatal); *Debate of the Dead* (Betsy Newman with Ellin Stein); and *Streetwise* (Betsy Newman), a portrait of her Lower East Side neighborhood.

Also, *TV Party* (Glenn O'Brien, 1980-82), a sampler of a late-night talk show with David Byrne, Debbie Harry, Jean-Michel Basquiat and other "downtown" celebrities; *Short Pieces* (Virge Piersol, 1978), a documentary of musical performances at Jeffrey Lohn's loft, featuring Laurie Anderson, Rhys Chatham and Glenn Branca; three samplers from *Potato Wolf* (1979-84), an artists' cable television show, featuring work by Wolfgang Staehle, Christy Rupp, Cara Perlman, Kiki Smith, Ellen Cooper and Alan Moore; *City Wildlife: Mice, Rats & Roaches* (Christy Rupp, 1980), a television show containing science-oriented information about "vermin," a subject of her artwork; *Dialectics of Romance* (Ann Sargent-Wooster, 1985), a structuralist look at formula romance writing; *Willoughby Sharp's Downtown New York* (1986), a sampler of his cable television show, with appearances by Kathy Acker, Laurie Anderson, Rebecca Howland, the Kipper Kids, Gracie Mansion, Michael Smith, Cookie Mueller, Carlo McCormick, Amy Downs, Spada and Boris Policeband; *Ecstatic Stigmatic* (Gordon Stevenson, 1978), with Mary-Anne Cervenka, Arto Lindsay and Brenda Bergman; *Drug Bust on Eldridge Street* (Mindy Stevenson and Jim Sutcliffe, 1982), out-of-the-window footage of a major police arrest of scores of heroin dealers; *Virtues of Negative Fascination* (Survival Research Laboratories, 1985-86), documenting five SRL performances; *Tripe* (Betsy Sussler, 1980); *Interview with Jonas Mekas* (Jordi Torrent, 1986); *Art/New York: N.Y./New Wave at P.S. 1* (Paul Tschinkel, 1980), a look at the seminal show that marked the convergence of art and music in the late 1970s New York scene; *War Dance* (Video Band, 1986), a collection of music video art from the San Francisco band; two films by Penelope Wehrli; *Dr. Jekyll & Ms. Hyde* (J. Kathleen White, 1980); *Musica Para Hot Sundays* (Yomoma Arts, 1985), a document of a summer musical series in New York City parks; *They Eat Scum* (Nick Zedd, 1979); *Geek Maggot Bingo* (Nick Zedd, 1983); and a sampler of work by Neil Zusman (1982-86). Also available is *The Cinema of Transgression*, an anthology of shocking underground films by Nick Zedd, John Spencer, Lung Leg, Richard Klemann, Erotic Psyche, Tommy Turner, Richard Kern, Michael Wolfe and Manuel DeLanda.
Size & Elements: Film: 16mm and 8mm (amount unspecified). Videotape: 3/4" and VHS (150 videotapes; masters and viewing copies).
Cataloging: Published catalog.
Access: Open to the public. For in-house use only. Available for rental, purchase and reuse. Screening and nominal rental fees charged. Research requests accepted in person (by appointment only).
Rights: Some rights held to some material. Additional clearances may be necessary in some cases if material is to be reused.
Licensing: Available for licensing and reuse, subject to decision of producer or videomaker in consultation with Club. License and usage fees charged in some cases.
Restrictions: Restrictions apply to reuse or broadcast of some videotapes (negotiations with individual videomakers required).
Viewing Facilities: Videotape (VHS).
Duplication Facilities: Videotape (3/4" to VHS).

NEW YORK METRO

MORALITY IN MEDIA
475 Riverside Drive, Suite 239
New York, NY 10115
(212) 870-3222

Evelyn Dukovic (Executive Vice President)

Contact: Evelyn Dukovic
Services: Nonprofit organization; film and videotape rental library.
Description: National organization working to stop the illegal traffic in pornography using constitutional means, through vigorous enforcement of obscenity laws. *Pornography: You Are Its Victim* (30 min., available in 16mm film or 3/4" videotape) is a documentary on the pornography industry and its victims. *The People Vs. Pornography* (60 min.) is a videotape designed to educate audiences about the problems of pornography and to offer solutions. Films are designed primarily for group meetings. Also available are video and audiotapes on the 1985 and 1986 National Conference on Pornography.
Size & Elements: Film: 16mm (1 title, 60 min., also available in 3/4" videotape). Videotape: 3/4", VHS and Betamax (1 title).
Cataloging: None specified.
Access: Available for rental rather than for research or reuse. Research requests not accepted.
Rights: Some rights held to all material.
Licensing: Apply for information. License fees charged.
Restrictions: *The People Vs. Pornography* is not available for broadcast or cable use.
Viewing Facilities: None.
Duplication Facilities: None.

NEW YORK METRO

MOTION PICTURE SERVICES
P.O. Box 252
Livingston, NJ 07039
(201) 992-8194

Gloria Mankowitz (President)

Contact: Gloria Mankowitz
Services: Distributor. Films available for free loan in New Jersey.
Description: Safety, eye care and steel production. Holds films produced by the New Jersey American Automobile Association, the Steel Plate Fabricators Association, the New Jersey Optometric Association and The Seeing Eye, Inc.
Size & Elements: Film: 16mm (approx. 150 titles).
Cataloging: Brochures.
Access: Available for free-loan distribution in New Jersey. Out-of-state requesters apply for information. Requests accepted by mail and telephone.
Rights: No rights held to any material.
Licensing: Apply for information.
Restrictions: None specified.
Viewing Facilities: None.
Duplication Facilities: None.

NEW YORK METRO

MOVIETIME, INC. ARCHIVES
Box 216
Garfield, NJ 07026
(201) 478-7848

Sandy Oliveri (Producer)

Contact: Sandy Oliveri
Services: Film producer. Private film and videotape collection and archives. Material available for licensing and reuse. Specializing in low budget home video compilations using pre-existing footage.
Description: Since the 1960s, Movietime has been acquiring and merchandising non-copyrighted motion pictures, television shows, bloopers, movie trailers and television commercials. Maintains music clips from all years, especially rock and roll (1950s-60s). Archives include: motion picture features (1920s-60s); television shows (1949-60s); movie preview trailers (all years); cartoons, all types of studios and characters, (1920s-60s); bloopers and outtakes from movies and television (all years); newsreel footage and complete newsreels; educational, school, and safety films (1940s-60s); television commercials (1950s-60s); World War II combat footage and training films;

movie shorts (all years); car commercials (1950s-60s) and wrestling matches (1940s-60s).

Size & Elements: Film: 35mm (quantity unspecified; positives); 16mm (quantity unspecified; positives and negatives). Videotape: 1" and 3/4" (masters and some viewing copies).

Cataloging: Partial listing available; most orders are by specific request.

Access: Available to the public for licensing and reuse. Research fees charged. Research requests accepted by telephone and in person (by appointment only).

Rights: No rights held to any material. No registered U.S. copyrights on material. Additional clearances may be necessary in some cases if material is to be reused.

Licensing: Available for licensing and reuse. License fees charged.

Restrictions: None specified.

Viewing Facilities: Film (16mm); videotape (3/4").

Duplication Facilities: Videotape (3/4").

NEW YORK METRO

MTV NETWORKS
1775 Broadway, 10th Floor
New York, NY 10019
(212) 713-6780
Fax: (212) 713-6708
Fax: (212) 713-6599

Contacts: Abigail Kende (Rights and Clearances); Rick Austin (Librarian)

Services: Television cablecaster; videotape library not open to the public. Available for duplication, licensing and reuse, subject to clearance and approval.

Description: The MTV (Music Television) and VH-1 (Video Hits One) libraries contain material relating to musicians, music events, film and sports personalities (1981-present). Requests for footage from Nickelodeon and Nick at Nite, MTV-owned networks, are also handled through this office.

Size & Elements: Videotape: 1" and 3/4" (3,000 videotapes).

Cataloging: Card catalogs.

Access: Not open to the public. For in-house use only. Available for duplication, licensing and reuse. Research fees charged. Research requests accepted by mail only.

Rights: Some rights held to some material. Additional clearances may be necessary in some cases if material is to be reused.

Licensing: Available for licensing and reuse, subject to restrictions. License or usage fees charged.

Restrictions: Requests for licensing and reuse accepted on a case-by-case basis.

Viewing Facilities: Videotape (by special arrangement only).

Duplication Facilities: None.

NEW YORK METRO

MUSEUM AT LARGE, LTD.
20 West 22nd Street
New York, NY 10010
(212) 691-2977

Available for rental or preview from:
MUSEUM AT LARGE, LTD.
P.O. Box 315
Franklin Lakes, NJ 07417
(201) 891-8240

Hans Namuth (President)

Contact: Hans Namuth

Services: Film and videotape producer. Material available for rental and purchase.

Description: Documentary films produced by Hans Namuth and Paul Falkenberg, on 20th century artists and architects.

Balthus at the Pompidou (1984, narrated by Michael Peppiatt) was shot on location in Paris at the Musée National d'Art Moderne, Centre Georges Pompidou. It documents the first major retrospective (since 1956) of the works of the painter Balthus; presents a selection of the key works exhibited and revealing portraits of the artist; and introduces comparative material (e.g., photographs of the landscapes Balthus painted).

Alfred Stieglitz, Photographer. Through images of Stieglitz himself, his works and the works of the photographers he encouraged, the film reveals the importance of the artist. The narrative counterpoint is drawn from Stieglitz's observations and the reminiscences of various people who knew him well (Ansel Adams, Mary Steichen Calderone, Harold Clurman, Aaron Copland, Arnold Newman, Isamu Noguchi, Dorothy Norman and Mary Rapp).

Alexander Calder: Calder's Universe (narrated by Louisa Calder, the artist's widow, and Tom Armstrong, Director of the Whitney Museum) shows the cosmic universe of Calder's rotating spheres, spinning mobiles, animated wire sculpture, toys, prints, jewelry, tapestries, paintings and theater sets as displayed in 1976-77 at the Whitney Museum in New York City. Calder is shown discovering an old spoon and transforming it into a mobile; at work and at play.

Louis I. Kahn: Architect (written and narrated by Vincent Scully and Peter Blake). Made shortly before his death, the film describes Kahn's early rebellion against the Bauhaus and the classical clarity of his later works. Projects photographed in detail include: the Yale University Art Gallery; the Salk Institute in San Diego; the Olivetti plant in Pennsylvania; and the Kimball Art Museum in Texas.

Willem de Kooning at the Modern (narrated by Barbara Novak) portrays de Kooning at work on his sculpture in 1972. Covers his retrospective exhibition at the Museum of Modern Art in New York City (1969) and traces 35 years of his work in painting (1930s-60s).

Matisse Centennial at the Grand Palais (narrated by Pierre Schneider) is the only film record of the historic exhibition in Paris in 1970. It covers practically all of Matisse's oeuvre, including important loans from Moscow's Pushkin Museum and Leningrad's Hermitage.

Brancusi Retrospective at the Solomon R. Guggenheim Museum (written and narrated by Sidney Geist) gives an overall view of the exhibition at the Guggenheim Museum in New York City. Includes a tour of the sculptor's Paris studio as it was reconstructed in the Musée National d'Art Moderne, now housed in the Centre Pompidou.

Josef Albers: Homage to the Square shows Albers explaining his technique to the viewer who becomes his pupil, with the tools of his trade set out before him. Two of his former students, Richard Anuszkiewicz and Robert Rauschenberg, discuss Albers' theories and his influence on them.

Jackson Pollock was filmed during the late summer and fall of 1950, with Pollock's narration and Morton Feldman's score added in 1951. Pollock is shown working outdoors, first on canvas, later on glass, discussing his technique as he works. The viewer is made aware of the continuity of his method. In the final scene, Pollock is filmed through a glass on which a painting is slowly taking shape.

Size & Elements: Film: 16mm. Videotape: all formats. (9 titles total).

Cataloging: Published list.

Access: Available for rental and purchase.

Rights: Full rights held to all material.

Licensing: Apply for information.

Restrictions: None specified.

Viewing Facilities: None.

Duplication Facilities: None.

NEW YORK METRO

MUSEUM OF ADVERTISING AND COMMUNICATIONS DESIGN
ART DIRECTORS CLUB OF NEW YORK
250 Park Avenue South
New York, NY 10003
(212) 674-0500

Karl Steinbrenner (President)

Contact: Dan Forte (Manager of Public Relations and Media)

Services: Nonprofit museum, not yet open to the public. Film and videotape collection currently unavailable for research or reuse. Certain material available for rental, subject to restrictions.

Description: ADC has sponsored advertising competitions since 1921. Collection includes television commercials entered in the competitions (early 1960s-present); and commercials and other materials donated by various organizations, including advertising agencies, the Advertising Council, corporations and advertisers, and public service groups.

ADC TV. The videotape counterpart to the Club's *Print Annual;* an annual compendium of every commercial accepted in the Art Directors' competition every year. Available for purchase in 3/4" and 1/2" versions.

Collections of award-winning commercials are also available for rental; these collections are restricted to private viewing and/or research purposes.

Size & Elements: Film: 16mm (45 hours). Videotape: 3/4" (amount unspecified; submasters; 5 most recent years of competition entries).

Cataloging: Uncataloged at present.
Access: Museum not currently open to the public. Access policies currently being formulated. Collection will probably be restricted to in-house viewing and research only.
Rights: Rights retained by sponsors or advertising agencies. Additional clearances would be necessary in cases where material was to be reused.
Licensing: Collection will probably not be available for licensing or reuse.
Restrictions: Any reuse of television commercials, if permitted, requires payment of talent royalties and residuals.
Viewing Facilities: Film and videotape (planned).
Duplication Facilities: None.
Publications: *Print Annual* (1921-present).

NEW YORK METRO

THE MUSEUM OF BROADCASTING
1 East 53rd Street
New York, NY 10022
(212) 752-4690

Dr. Robert M. Batscha (President)

Contacts: Letty Aronson (Vice President, Public Relations); Ron Simon (Curator, Television Collection); Carol Shapiro (Associate Curator, Radio Collection)
Services: Nonprofit institution. Open to the public for in-house viewing only. *No program may be loaned or reproduced in whole or in part.*
Description: Collects, preserves, interprets and exhibits radio and television programs for broadcasting professionals, students, scholars and the public. While other archives amass radio and television programs on film, kinescope, audiotape, videotape and in script form, the Museum's collection is the only one which is accessible to the general public.

Collection grows annually through regular contributions from the three commercial networks, the Public Broadcasting Service, corporations, individuals and foreign and domestic producers. The Museum's operations are supported by the networks, foundations, corporations and members.

Television collection. Holds, with a few exceptions, at least one sample of almost every program ever aired on broadcast television, with 3,000 hours of programming added to the collection every year. Early items include an excerpt from a drama called *Poverty Is Not a Crime* (1936) and a rare segment of the drama *The Streets of New York* (NBC, 1939). It also holds segments of many television series, including *Mama, The Goldbergs, Naked City, The Honeymooners, I Love Lucy, The Ed Sullivan Show, Hill Street Blues, Cheers* and *The Cosby Show;* dramas from the "golden age of television," including *Marty* and *Requiem for a Heavyweight;* dozens of *Hallmark Hall of Fame* episodes; game shows; children's shows; news programs; collections of foreign programming from Ireland, Great Britain and West Germany; broadcasts of news events, including moon shots and moon walks, assassinations, inaugurations, fireside chats and Watergate hearings; cultural and educational programs, including *The Shakespeare Plays, Civilisation* and *The Ascent of Man;* dance programs featuring George Balanchine and Fred Astaire; televised jazz sessions with Billie Holiday, Duke Ellington, Louis Armstrong and Benny Goodman; concert performances by Judy Garland, Frank Sinatra and Barbra Streisand; comedy by Ernie Kovacs, Milton Berle, Jack Benny, Red Skelton and Jackie Gleason; sports coverage of Olympic Games, Super Bowls and World Series; and more than 25 years of political commercials.

The Museum has received a grant to acquire, preserve and catalog television and radio commercials. These will be incorporated into the program collection.

The Museum's new building, designed by Philip Johnson and located at 23 West 52nd Street (New York City), is currently under construction.
Size & Elements: Videotape: 3/4" (over 25,000 titles; masters); Betamax (over 25,000 titles; viewing copies). 3/4" masters are used for exhibitions and public screenings; Betamax copies are for use in viewing consoles. Beginning in 1988, television programs are being archived on digital (D-1) videotape masters.
Cataloging: Computer-generated card catalog, cross-referenced 25 ways by title, subject, date, network and significant cast and production credits.
Access: Open to the public for viewing (Tuesday-Saturday, 12 noon to 5 pm; Tuesdays until 8 pm). Research requests accepted by mail and telephone (Tuesday-Friday, 3:30 to 5:30 pm). Research fees charged during "scholar hours" (time booked for viewing in the morning, outside of normal viewing hours).
Rights: No rights held to any material.
Licensing: Not available for licensing or reuse through the Museum. Requests

for licensing or reuse must be directed to copyright holders. License and usage fees charged pursuant to arrangements with copyright holders, not by the Museum.
Restrictions: Collection maintained for research and viewing purposes only. Duplication of programs is rarely permitted and requires written approval of copyright holder.
Viewing Facilities: Videotape: 3/4" and Betamax (63-seat theater with video projector; 23 custom-built viewing consoles for Betamax; video projection systems).
Duplication Facilities: Videotape (3/4", VHS and Betamax).
Related Materials: Over 10,000 radio programs (1918-present); *NBC Radio Archive* (1927-69), comprised of 175,000 disc recordings; and 2,400 radio production scripts.

NEW YORK METRO

MUSEUM OF JEWISH HERITAGE
342 Madison Avenue, Suite 717
New York, NY 10173
(212) 687-9141
Fax: (212) 573-9847

David Altshuler (Museum Director)
Fay C. Schreibman (Project Coordinator, Learning Center)

Contact: Fay C. Schreibman
Services: *Museum opening to the public in 1990.* Currently collecting historic and documentary films for archival, research and media distribution purposes.
Description: Extensive newsreel and stock footage documentary collection is currently in formation. Materials being collected relate to pre-World War II Eastern and Western Europe (emphasizing Jewish life); the Holocaust; Jewish immigration to America; the creation of the state of Israel; and the aftermath of World War II, including displaced persons camps.

The Museum intends to collect documentary materials about Jewish life and culture before, during and after the Holocaust to be used in permanent exhibitions and in a publicly accessible Learning Center. Stock footage and outtakes from newsreels will be used mainly in the exhibitions. Documentaries, newsreels and features will be available to the public in the Learning Center. Materials will be for use within the institution only, but the Museum will try to acquire rights for media distribution. Film researchers will be accommodated in a separate area. "We do not see ourselves at this time being a stock footage sales agency."
Size & Elements: Film: 16mm (initial goal: 1,500 films; positive). Videotape: 3/4" (masters); and 1/2" (viewing copies) (initial goal: 500 videotapes).
Cataloging: Planned cataloging includes published catalogs; computerized cataloging for staff use only, possibly available to researchers; some shot lists; and a research library.
Access: Documentaries and newsreels will be available to the public. Stock footage and outtakes will be available to researchers and scholars for in-house use only. Policies regarding research fees and requests not yet determined.
Rights: Some rights held to some material. No rights held to some material. Some material in the public domain.
Licensing: Apply for information.
Restrictions: Museum not open at present.
Viewing Facilities: Videotape (not yet specified).
Duplication Facilities: Film (16mm film-to-videotape); videotape (all formats except 2", 1", Betacam and 1/2" open reel).

NEW YORK METRO

THE MUSEUM OF MODERN ART
CIRCULATING FILM LIBRARY
11 West 53rd Street
New York, NY 10019
(212) 708-9530
Fax: (212) 708-9889
Telex: 62370 MODART

William Sloan (Librarian)

Contact: Marilyn Mancino (Circulating Film Assistant)
Services: Museum; film and videotape distributor. Material available for educational rental, preview-for-purchase, purchase, print lease, licensing and reuse, subject to restrictions.
Description: Silent, documentary, experimental and independent films and

videotapes. Subjects, genres and producers include: animation; art and artists; avant-garde films from the United States and Europe; Biograph films; British independent films; Charles Chaplin; Directors Guild of America films, including *Precious Images;* early cinema; film history; films directed by D. W. Griffith; films from the National Film Board of Canada; primitive films; Soviet films; Surrealism; video art; and World War II.

Size & Elements: Film: 35mm and 16mm (approx. 1,000 titles; release prints). Videotape: format unspecified (approx. 50 titles).

Cataloging: Published catalog; release sheets.

Access: Open to researchers and scholars only. Available for educational rental, preview-for-purchase, purchase and print lease. Some titles available for television broadcast.

Rights: Full rights held to some material. Rights to some material retained by original producers. Additional clearances may be necessary in some cases if material is to be reused.

Licensing: Available for licensing and reuse, subject to restrictions. License fees charged.

Restrictions: Restrictions apply to some titles. Written requests for reuse are required and must indicate how footage will be used.

Viewing Facilities: Film.

Duplication Facilities: None.

Related Materials: Film stills (available through the Museum's Film Stills Archive).

NEW YORK METRO

THE MUSEUM OF MODERN ART
DEPARTMENT OF FILM

11 West 53rd Street
New York, NY 10019-5486
(212) 708-9400
(212) 708-9613 (for viewing requests)

Mary Lea Bandy (Director)
Barbara London (Assistant Curator, Video)

Contact: See Access (below).

Services: Museum; film and videotape archives. Open to researchers and scholars for in-house research and viewing; material available for reuse on a case-by-case basis, subject to restrictions. *Not a stock footage source.*

Description: The Museum of Modern Art Department of Film was founded in 1935 and became a founding member of FIAF (International Federation of Film Archives) in 1938. The archives collects representative works of international cinema, with an emphasis on the art and history of the medium. The collection presently contains approximately 9,000 films and over 500 videotape titles, from all countries of production and all time periods, including feature films, shorts, documentaries, animation and others.

Working in cooperation with other American film archives, the Department of Film collects selectively, not comprehensively. Preservation of the collection is the highest priority, and since the early 1950s the copying of its nitrate films to safety stock has been the major task of the archives. As part of an art museum, the archives is concerned above all with the best possible quality of image and sound. The Department also places emphasis on access to the collection through daily public screenings in its two theaters, a circulating film library for film study in schools and universities, and the Film Study Center, where films and written materials are available for scholarly research.

Among the special film collections held are: *The Biograph Collection; The Edison Collection; The D. W. Griffith Collection; The Twentieth Century-Fox Collection; The David O. Selznick Collection; Douglas Fairbanks Collection; Clint Eastwood Cinema Collection;* and *The Thomas Brandon Collection.*

The *Video Study Collection* consists of works produced internationally, largely by independent videomakers working on the fringes of the art world and the broadcast industry. In developing and preserving this unique archives, the Museum has sought works that have a strong idea, integrity and an engaging spirit. The works on view, made with consumer or more sophisticated commercial equipment, affirm the viability of video as a contemporary art form uniquely capable of reflecting the social and technological changes of modern society.

Size & Elements: Film: all formats (approx. 9,000 titles). Videotape: 2", 1", 3/4" and 1/2" (approx. 550 titles).

Cataloging: Computerized cataloging for staff use only. Published catalog: *The Film Catalog: A List of Holdings in The Museum of Modern Art,* edited by Jon Gartenberg. Boston and New York: G. K. Hall & Co./The Museum of Modern Art, 1985. Available for $60.00 (North American), $70.00 (foreign) from G. K. Hall, 70 Lincoln Street, Boston, MA 02111; (800) 343-2806. The

catalog lists approximately 5,500 films in the collection. Entries are arranged alphabetically by original title. Other information included for each film is alternate title, date, type (fiction feature, nonfiction short, animation short, etc.), country, producer and director. An index of producers and directors lists each of their films held by MOMA.

Access: The following is reproduced from a Museum publication entitled *Procedures For Access to the Film Collection (Commercial Use):*

The Department of Film collects motion pictures as works of art and for the study of the history of cinema. It is not a stock footage source and has no subject listings. Users are requested to apply to the stock footage suppliers or directly to the production companies for specific films. In most cases the Museum does not own the rights to the films in its collection. However, when the Department holds material not available elsewhere, it may be made available to commercial users under the following conditions:

1. The first step to access is to write the Curator describing the project and the kinds of films wanted, or, preferably, with a list of the specific titles wanted. The curatorial staff will do its best to give guidance as to our holdings and the names and addresses of copyright owners and/or donors. If the request requires extensive research, the user will be advised and asked to pay a research fee.

2. The permission of the owner and/or depositor for the requested use must be addressed in writing to the Curator. It is the responsibility of the user to obtain such permission. In the case of the films the Department believes to be in the public domain, the user must supply a letter of indemnity to the Museum. Many films in the public domain are still subject to depositor agreements. The Curator has the sole responsibility to determine when a film can be made available.

3. The Museum's archive prints may not be shown in commercial theaters or on television. After the permission has been obtained, the user must pay for new prints or videotapes to be made for any such purpose. (In a few cases, the department's Circulating Film Library is able to lend 16mm circulating prints for videotaping or television use, after rights have been obtained and a fee is paid. For information, call 212/708-9530.)

4. An order on the letterhead of the company is required, containing specific instructions as to the kind of material wanted, before the Department places an order with a laboratory. Outside laboratory orders cannot be permitted to interfere with the orderly progression of our Film Preservation Program, which has our highest priority. No rush orders can be handled. The Museum's printing materials remain at all times in the control of the Department of Film and will be handled only in the laboratories selected by the Department.

5. No cording off for excerpt footage is permitted. In order to protect the Museum's preservation materials, whole reels must be printed, including double reels when the material is so mounted.

6. No silent film material will be supplied unless the user has guaranteed that it will be projected or broadcast at the correct original speed, in keeping with the Department of Film's purposes to promote the art of the film.

7. When a film has not yet been preserved, the Department may require the user to pay the costs of preprint materials. When the Department determines that its materials are in danger of damage from overprinting, the user may be required to pay the costs of an additional negative or master. In such cases, the service fee is usually waived.

8. The costs to the user will be double the laboratory costs. One half of the amount is the Department's service fee and will be added to the Film Preservation Fund. Exceptions will be made only in cases where there are pre-existing agreements with depositors wanting access to the material they have deposited. Offers to donate films in lieu of a service fee will be given serious consideration.

9. Users must return all unused material, unless the Department has agreed to a deposit in another archive or to destruction, in which case a destruction certificate will be required.

10. Should the Department request it, the user will deposit at the user's expense one copy of the film or videotape produced with the help of the Department's material, in the same gauge as the original production.

11. Should the Department request it, a credit to The Museum of Modern Art for its assistance shall be put on the completed production. However, the Museum's name is not to be used without the permission of the Museum.

12. The Museum can make no guarantee of the quality of all its printing materials. Defective material that can be proved to be the result of incorrect laboratory work done at the user's order will not be charged for, but if the laboratory can show that the defect existed in the Museum's materials, the user will be obliged to pay for it. Advance viewing of the

Museum's answer prints, when they are available, will help to avoid such problems.

13. To select footage or to check in advance the quality of the materials available, it may be possible in some cases to view a 16mm print on the flatbed viewers of the Film Study Center. The amount of time available for this viewing service is quite limited, however, by other demands on the facilities. Call 212/708-9613 for an appointment. When selecting footage, it is important to measure the footage from the beginning of the film (from the first frame after the Museum's own head title) and stopping before the tail leader appears, adding on the footage for each additional reel of the same film viewed. This will make it possible for the staff to determine the equivalent reels wanted in the 35mm printing materials.

For additional information about access for commercial use, call 212/708-9605. However, our small staff is unable to handle extensive research by telephone. Requests should be in writing.

Rights: No rights held to most material. Additional clearances are usually necessary if material is to be reused.
Licensing: Available for licensing and reuse on a case-by-case basis, subject to conditions (see Access).
Restrictions: A signed copy of the conditions for access (reprinted above) is required with each duplication order.
Viewing Facilities: Film and videotape.
Duplication Facilities: None (outside arrangements are made with laboratories servicing Department).
Related Materials: Motion picture stills (approx. 3 million); posters; scripts; production records; advertising records; newspaper and periodical clippings.
Publications: *The Film Catalog: A List of Holdings in The Museum of Modern Art* (see Cataloging).

NEW YORK METRO

MUSEUM OF THE AMERICAN INDIAN
FILM AND VIDEO CENTER
Broadway at 155th Street
New York, NY 10032
(212) 283-2420
Fax: (212) 491-9302

Elizabeth Weatherford (Associate Curator)

Contact: Emelia Seubert (Assistant Curator)
Services: Museum; film and video center. Research and consulting services available. Film and videotape collection open to the public by appointment only.
Description: Serves as a national center for information on films and videotapes concerned with the native peoples of North, Central and South America. Museum exhibitions, publications, information services, symposia and consultancies serve a large public. Users of the Center include film and videomakers, programmers, researchers, television producers, educators and tribal organizations.

The Study Collection contains recent works by award-winning independent film and videomakers; material relating to native community media; and copies of productions shown at the Center.

The Archives consists of films made prior to 1930, incorporating historical material relating to Native Americans.
Size & Elements: Film: 16mm (approx. 30 titles; positive, negative, reversal and originals). Videotape: 3/4" and VHS (amount unspecified; masters and viewing copies). Collection is continually growing as the Center acquires study materials, and as film and videotape donations are made to the Center.
Cataloging: None specified.
Access: Open to the public by appointment only; primarily available to researchers, scholars and filmmakers. For in-house use only. Research fees not charged. Research requests accepted by mail, telephone and in person (by appointment only).
Rights: Some rights held to some material. Additional clearances may be necessary in some cases if material is to be reused.
Licensing: Available for licensing and reuse, subject to restrictions. License and usage fees charged.
Restrictions: Many films produced by television stations and independent producers; additional clearances may be necessary if this material is to be reused.
Viewing Facilities: Film (16mm); videotape (3/4" and VHS) (by appointment only).
Duplication Facilities: None (outside arrangements can be made).
Related Materials: Many programs have accompanying study guides.

Publications: *Native Americans On Film and Videotape, Volume I* (1981) describes approximately 400 films and videotapes made since 1970, with sections on archives and Native American media resources. *Native Americans On Film and Videotape, Volume II* (1987) describes approximately 200 films and videotapes made since 1980, with an up-to-date distributor index for Volumes I and II.

NEW YORK METRO

MYRIN INSTITUTE
COUNCIL FOR INTERNATIONAL UNDERSTANDING
136 East 64th Street
New York, NY 10021
(212) 832-2931
Fax: (212) 758-6498

Moorhead Kennedy (Executive Director)

Contact: Moorhead Kennedy
Services: Nonprofit educational organization. Videotapes available for purchase and reuse, subject to approval.
Description: Maintains educational programs designed to help Americans overcome psychological and cultural barriers to an understanding of foreign affairs.

Christianity and Terrorism series (1986, Episcopal Radio/TV Foundation and the Myrin Institute; 6 videotapes, each 12 min.) features Moorhead Kennedy delivering lectures and sermons. Topics include: the Middle East, terrorism, Christianity, faith and foreign policy, and terrorism as a teaching tool.
Size & Elements: Videotape: VHS (6 titles; viewing copies).
Cataloging: Research library.
Access: Available for purchase and reuse, subject to approval. Research requests accepted by mail and telephone.
Rights: Full rights held to some material.
Licensing: Apply for information. License fees charged.
Restrictions: None specified.
Viewing Facilities: None.
Duplication Facilities: Videotape (VHS).
Related Materials: Study guide to accompany series; publications.

NEW YORK METRO

NASSAU COMMUNITY COLLEGE LIBRARY
NEW YORK STATE HEALTH FILM COLLECTION
Garden City, NY 11530
(516) 222-7406

Prof. Arthur L. Friedman (Chairman, Library)

Contact: Prof. Arthur L. Friedman
Services: Educational institution. Films available for educational use by any individual, organization or group in New York State.
Description: The Professional Film Library was established in 1949 as a joint project of the Department of Health, Medical Society of the State of New York, and the Medical Film Institute of the Association of American Medical Colleges.

Films (1945-77) in the collection have been selected by professional film panels. Nursing films are reviewed by representatives of schools of nursing, the New York State Department of Education and the Department of Health. Cancer films are provided by the American Cancer Society.

Titles include: *Check the Neck* (1969); *Eating For Two* (1969); *First Steps* (1949); *Food As Children See It* (1952); *Foxgloves in Medicine* (1952); *Giving an Enema* (1955); *Glaucoma: Sneak Thief of Sight* (1965); *Heart Disease: Its Major Causes* (1955); *Injuries of the Peripheral Nerves* (1949); *Innovations in Transfusion Therapy* (1964); *An Introduction to Arthropod-Borne Encephalitis* (1958); *Lung Cancer: Early Diagnosis and Management* (1969); *The Nose, Throat and Ears* (1949); *A Paranoid-Schizophrenic* (1964); *Regulation of Atomic Radiation* (1964); *To Serve the Mind* (1956); *A Study in Maternal Attitudes* (1960); *Subject: Narcotics* (1954); *Teaching Crutch Walking* (1946); *Triumph Over Deafness* (1948); *Obstetrical Maneuvers on the Ayers Manikin* (1943); *The Otoneurological Examination for Vestibulocerebellar Function* (1966); and *The Treatment of Acute Drug Overdose* (1973).

Subjects include: anatomy, cardiology, clinical pathology, communicable diseases, communication skills, dentistry, embryology, endocrinology, endoscopy, fundamentals of nursing, gynecology, health facilities, hematology, maternal and child health, medicine, mental health and psychiatry, neurology, neurosurgery, nutrition, obstetrics, ophthalmology, orthopedics, otorhinolaryngology, pathology, pediatrics, pharmacology, physical and biological sciences, physical diagnosis, preventive medicine, psychiatry, public health, radiology, recruitment, rehabilitation, respiratory diseases, resuscitation, surgery, tumors and urology.

Size & Elements: Film: 16mm (860 titles, over 2,500 cans).
Cataloging: Published catalog.
Access: Open to the public. Research fees not charged. Requests accepted by mail, telephone (on a limited basis) and in person (walk-in and by appointment). A minimum of three weeks should be allowed to properly process request.
Rights: Some rights held to all material.
Licensing: Apply for information.
Restrictions: None specified.
Viewing Facilities: Film (16mm); videotape (3/4" and VHS); videodisc.
Duplication Facilities: None.
Related Materials: 35mm filmstrips; slides; overhead transparencies.

NEW YORK METRO

NASSAU COUNTY MUSEUM
REFERENCE LIBRARY
Hofstra University Library, 9th Floor
Hempstead, NY 11550
(516) 560-5162

Contact: Gary Hammond
Services: Educational institution; library. Film archives currently inaccessible to the public.
Description: Holds the aviation film collection of the Fairchild Republic Aviation Company (1940s-87). Pending transfer and cataloging, this material will be included in the future Cradle of Aviation Museum. Also holds film produced by Nassau County agencies (mid-1940s through 1960s) documenting Nassau County road maintenance, county development and public works projects.
Size & Elements: Film: 35mm and 16mm. Videotape (format unspecified). (68 cartons total).
Cataloging: Uncataloged.
Access: Materials currently inaccessible to the public. Research requests accepted by mail and telephone. Research fees not charged.
Rights: Full rights held to some material. Additional clearances may be necessary in some cases if material is to be reused.
Licensing: Apply for information.
Restrictions: None specified.
Viewing Facilities: None.
Duplication Facilities: None.

NEW YORK METRO

NATIONAL COUNCIL OF AMERICAN-SOVIET FRIENDSHIP, INC.
EDUCATIONAL SERVICES
85 East 4th Street
New York, NY 10003
(212) 254-6606

Alan Thomson (Executive Director)

Contact: Judith Solis
Services: Peace organization. Films available to the public for rental.
Description: Films on Soviet daily life, work, education, sport, industry, culture, economy, international relations, war and peace.
   Titles include: *Agriculture in the U.S.S.R.* (1974); *All About Moscow* (1975); *Anton Chekhov* (1977); *Around the Soviet Union* (1970s, 21 programs); *The Atom at Work; Comrade Woman* (1976); *A Day in the Life of A Director* (1967); *Let's Dance the Charkhuduzonu* (1971); *The Life of Lenin* (1967); *The Life of Muslims in the U.S.S.R.; My Poltava* (1973); *National Folk Art; National School Games* (1967); *October Days* (1958); *On Guard for Health* (1975); *On the Road to Berlin* (1969); *Readings From the Life of Lev Tolstoy* (1976); *Red Army Chorus Sings and Dances; Red Square* (1976); *The Rights and Duties of Soviet Citizens; The Russian Winter* (1971); *Social Security in the U.S.S.R.; Siberia Invites You; Soviet Culture; A Soviet Family* (1979); *Soviet Folk Talent; Soviet Industry; Soviet Medical Advances* (1973); *Soviet Theatre Today* (1975); *The Soviet Union By Car* (1978); *Stronger Soviet-Arab Friendship; Subways in Five Soviet Cities* (1971); *They Work at the Factory*

(Electrocila-Lenigrad) (1969); *Unbreakable Union of Free Born Republics* (1972); *Victorious Stalingrad; We Invite You, Olympiad* (1975); *With Leninism in My Heart* (1976); and *Years of Severe Trial: The Civil War 1918-1920* (1966).
Size & Elements: Film: 16mm (500 titles, 800 cans).
Cataloging: Card catalogs; computerized cataloging for staff use only.
Access: Open to the public. Research fees not charged. Research requests accepted by mail, telephone and in person (by appointment only).
Rights: Full rights held to all material.
Licensing: Apply for information. License fees charged.
Restrictions: None specified.
Viewing Facilities: None.
Duplication Facilities: None.

NEW YORK METRO

NATIONAL FILM BOARD OF CANADA
1251 Avenue of the Americas, 16th Floor
New York, NY 10020-1173
(212) 586-5131

See **QUEBEC** (Montreal)

NEW YORK METRO

NATIONAL JEWISH ARCHIVE OF BROADCASTING (NJAB)
THE JEWISH MUSEUM
1109 Fifth Avenue
New York, NY 10128
(212) 860-1886

Margo Bloom (Director)

Contacts: Ronnie W. Parker (Archive Coordinator); Peter Block (Cataloger/Programmer)
Services: Film and videotape archives; museum. Collection open to researchers and scholars only.
Description: Collects, catalogs and preserves television and radio programs pertaining to Jewish culture. Founded 1981, it is the first institutional subject-oriented broadcast collection. Approximately 2,240 items have been acquired from NBC, CBS, ABC, PBS, independent television stations, production companies and individual contributors. Programs are also being collected from sources abroad, including Israel, Great Britain, the Netherlands, Germany and Canada.
   Collection includes news reports and documentaries; religious programs; a representative selection of both dramatic and comic entertainment programs; educational series; public service announcements and commercials that use Jewish characterizations or advertise kosher products; and historical documentation.
   Highlights include two early episodes of *The Goldbergs;* the entire week of *Nightline in the Holy Land;* the *David Susskind Show* episode entitled "How to Be a Jewish Son"; a *Little House on the Prairie* episode, "Come Let Us Reason Together," highlighting issues relating to anti-Semitism and intermarriage; a recent Channel Four documentary entitled *Sabbath Bride;* ten episodes of *Bridget Loves Bernie,* as well as episodes of shows including *thirtysomething, A Year in the Life, L.A. Law, The Days and Nights of Molly Dodd, Kojak, M.A.S.H.* and *Dr. Kildare* that focus on Jewish culture or religion.
   Houses the 170 extant hours of videotape coverage of the trial of Adolf Eichmann, produced originally by Capital Cities in 1961. The 3/4" videotapes are arranged by session number and are available to researchers by appointment. Transcripts of the trial are also available.
   Heritage: Civilization and the Jews (outtakes; 200 hours, 500,000 feet). Holds unused archival footage and photographs from the public television series. On-location footage and animation produced for the series is co-owned by the Archive and WNET/13. Twenty logbooks and complete production notebooks include shot listings and other information.
   The Museum also presents regular public programs.
Size & Elements: Film: 16mm (originals and kinescopes). Videotape: 3/4" (masters); VHS (masters); 1/2" (viewing copies); Betamax. (2,240 items, each 30 to 60 min.).
Cataloging: Computerized cataloging for staff use only; published catalog listing titles of approximately 33% of collection by Library of Congress subject headings.
Access: Open to researchers and scholars only. Research requests accepted by mail, telephone and in person (by appointment only).

Rights: No rights held to any material.
Licensing: Apply for information.
Restrictions: None specified.
Viewing Facilities: Film (16mm); videotape.
Duplication Facilities: None.

NEW YORK METRO

NATIONAL KIDNEY FOUNDATION, INC.
30 East 33rd Street, 11th Floor
New York, NY 10016
(212) 889-2210
(800) 622-9010
Fax: (212) 689-9261

John Davis (Executive Director)

Contact: Gigi Politoski (Communications Director)
Services: Foundation. Films and videotapes available for distribution and rental rather than for research and reuse.
Description: Kidney disease and its treatments; organ transplantation; patient and professional education.

Titles include: *The Sweetest Thing*, highlights from the NKF summer camp program for children on dialysis and transplantation; *Bridging the Gap*, portraying four people with chronic kidney problems and the vital choice of therapy (kidney transplantation or dialysis), stressing the importance of organ donation; *An Equation for Living (Part 1: Emotional Impact)*, focusing on psychosocial issues and adjustments of in-center and home dialysis clients; and *Kidney Transplant: A New Lease on Life*.

Meeting the Challenge of Kidney Disease and Treatment is a six-part series including: *An Introduction to Treatment*, providing responses to most often asked questions; *Hemodialysis*, discussing access, treatment procedure at home and in center, functions of the kidney, medications and participation in one's own care; *Peritoneal Dialysis; Transplantation*, on the donor and recipient evaluation process, cadaver transplant waiting list, hospitalization and surgery, medications and post-hospital care; *Diet: An Essential Part of Treatment;* and *Coping Effectively*.
Size & Elements: Film: 16mm (1 title). Videotape: VHS (11 titles).
Cataloging: Published catalogs.
Access: Open to the public. Maintained for distribution and rental rather than research or reuse. Research fees not charged. Requests accepted by mail.
Rights: Full rights held to all material.
Licensing: Apply for information. License fees not charged.
Restrictions: Restrictions apply to reuse.
Viewing Facilities: None.
Duplication Facilities: None.
Related Materials: 38 public education brochures.

NEW YORK METRO

NBA ENTERTAINMENT, INC.
38 East 32nd Street, 4th Floor
New York, NY 10016-5507
(212) 532-6223
Fax: (212) 689-5527

Don Sperling (Executive Producer)

Contact: Leah Wilcox (Unit Manager)
Services: Film and videotape producer; film and videotape archives; stock footage sales library. *Collection not open to the general public; material available only to sports-related shows, television stations and motion picture or television producers.*
Description: National Basketball Association footage (1946-present), including game footage, off-court footage, teams and players.
Size & Elements: Film: 16mm (1.3 million feet; negatives, originals and prints). Videotape: 3/4" (50,000 hours).
Cataloging: Computerized cataloging for staff use only. General editors can locate specific shots in computer and then pull actual footage.
Access: Not open to the general public. Available only to sports-related shows, television stations, motion picture and television producers. An hourly "search and edit" fee is charged, in addition to the cost of the videotape stock. Research requests accepted by mail, telephone and in person (by appointment only).
Rights: Full rights held to all material.
Licensing: Available for licensing and reuse, subject to restrictions. License

fees charged.
Restrictions: Permission from teams and/or players may be necessary in some cases, depending on intended reuse of material.
Viewing Facilities: Videotape (by appointment only).
Duplication Facilities: Videotape (3/4" to 1/2"); other formats can be arranged.

NEW YORK METRO

NBC NEWS VIDEO ARCHIVES
30 Rockefeller Plaza, Room 922
New York, NY 10112
(212) 664-3797
Fax: (212) 957-8917
Telex: (USA) 12471
Telex: (International) 232346A

Michael Sosler (Director News Archives and External Sales)

Contact: Yuien Chin
Services: Television broadcaster; film and videotape stock footage sales library.
Description: The NBC News Video Archives (established mid-1930s) was set up to provide a central, well cataloged source of film material on a wide variety of subject matter that could be found and made available for immediate use. Most major news events were captured on film by the NBC Network News staff and its contingent of freelance cameramen. Today the collection consists of generic stock shot material, major news events and documentary and magazine show footage. Collection is added to on a daily basis with the most recent footage shot by NBC News' domestic and foreign bureaus located in major cities throughout the world.

All NBC News footage is available through the library, including documentaries, magazine shows, daily news shows and specials. Material is available for stock footage sale, with some exceptions. Unaired footage and outtakes are generally not available for reuse, but generic material (i.e., footage of public press conferences) or stock shots may be released on a case-by-case basis, subject to approval.

Film collection. Coverage begins sporadically in the mid-1930s, and increases dramatically beginning in the late 1950s and early 1960s. The film collection consists primarily of what was formerly known as the "Stock Shot Library," and is primarily 16mm material, with limited holdings in 35mm. Some newscasts predating the videotape period (prior to the mid-1970s) are held in kinescope form.

Videotape collection. Holds complete newscasts (mid-1970s to present) and aired news and documentary programs (for the previous five years; some earlier programs are held). Holds approximately 13,000 2" and 1" videotapes, primarily show histories (videotaped versions of complete programs as aired); and approximately 250,000 3/4" field cassettes (raw news footage; generated mid-1970s to mid-1987). All are stored in Fort Lee, New Jersey, except for videotapes generated during the most recent four to six months. Over the longer term, approximately 70% of field cassettes are retained. Also holds one year's coverage of the *Skypath* network newsfeed, which comprises footage from NBC network affiliates.

In mid-1987, NBC News switched from 3/4" videotape to the relatively new 1/2" MII format. Approximately 20,000 videotapes in this format are presently held; all news programs are currently recorded on MII.

Documentaries and other programs. Holds most episodes of *The Huntley-Brinkley Report* in kinescope form; kinescopes and videotapes of many *Today Show* episodes (in many cases, live and in-studio segments of *Today* may not have been recorded). Also holds videotaped episodes of *Prime Time; Weekend; First Tuesday; Chronolog; White Papers* (episodes exist both on film and videotape); *First Camera; Monitor; American Almanac;* and *1996*.

Archives holdings exist on kinescopes (many early programs), 35mm and 16mm film, 2" videotape (1959-82) and 3/4" videotape (1970s-present), depending on the origination date.

Archives has started to acquire or represent material from outside sources for internal use and stock footage sale. It represents exclusively a large collection of underwater footage, shot in the Caribbean region and available on Betacam videotape.

NBC programs produced by NBC Entertainment may be accessed and cleared through NBC Television Network, Enterprises Department (q.v.).
Size & Elements: Film: 35mm and 16mm (approx. 100 million feet). Videotape: 2" and 3/4" (approx. 250,000 videotapes; masters); MII (approx. 20,000 videotapes; masters); Betacam (amount unspecified; masters).
Cataloging: Computerized cataloging for staff use only (Honeywell "Ultimate"

computer system with proprietary software, for material originated mid-1970s to present). Almost all aired material in this time period has been screened and abstracts entered into the computer. Material is cross-referenced by a variety of searchable fields (subject, date of event, location and personality). Keyword-type searching is available.

Special cataloging projects have been undertaken which may assist researchers in locating specialized footage. Approximately 90% of the Archive's footage relating to the Vietnam War (both aired and unaired) has been screened and abstracted, as has footage relating to the Iranian hostage crisis. Most footage originated for *Nightly News* special segments is also fully indexed.

Since not all field cassettes (raw, unedited videotapes originated by news and documentary crews) are indexed by computer, staff assistance will be necessary to locate logs.

Access to the film library and other footage not indexed by computer is by means of *Film Library Abstracts,* encompassing a variety of logs, shot lists and camerapersons' dope sheets. The NBC Program Analysis Department maintains a complete index of all programs ever aired on the NBC television and radio networks (1920s-present), which includes a complete list of all guests appearing on news programs (such as *Today*); Archives holds a microfiche copy of this index (staff use only). Outside researchers with specific queries may contact Program Analysis directly (Betty Jane Reed, 212/664-5301).

A reference library is available for in-house use by researchers and staff; contents include almanacs (1946-present); *The New York Times Index* (1950-present); *Current Biography* (1946-present); and other print resources.
Access: For in-house use only. Available for duplication, licensing and reuse. Research fees charged. Research requests accepted by mail, telephone and in person (by appointment only). Staff assistance required for film screening; videotape may be screened by researchers and clients.
Rights: Full rights held to all material available for sale. Some rights held to other material in library (e.g., "handout" footage or footage originated by other networks or producers). Additional clearances may be necessary in some cases if material is to be reused.
Licensing: Available for licensing and reuse, subject to restrictions. License fees charged.
Restrictions: All footage is licensed on a nonexclusive basis only. Unaired footage and outtakes are not generally available for reuse, but generic material or stock shots may be released on a case-by-case basis, subject to approval. Images or voices of reporters or other on-air talent are ordinarily not available for reuse. Some exclusive interviews may be restricted from reuse. Footage visibly depicting the NBC Television Network, NBC graphics or NBC's corporate image may be reused only by specific permission.
Viewing Facilities: Film (flatbed viewing tables); videotape (3/4" and MII in-house; 2" and 1" available elsewhere in building).
Duplication Facilities: Film (dedicated in-house Rank Cintel film-to-videotape transfer facility with wet gate; film-to-film laboratory work performed by outside facilities); videotape (all formats). Film preparation fees charged.

NEW YORK METRO

NBC TELEVISION NETWORK
ENTERPRISES DEPARTMENT
30 Rockefeller Plaza
New York, NY 10112
(212) 664-5031
Fax: (212) 333-7546
Telex: 662 131 NBC INTL

Jan Kreher (Director of Enterprises)

Contact: Lisa Hackett (Coordinator) (212/664-5673)
Services: Television broadcaster. Film and videotape programs available for distribution, syndication, ancillary market sales, licensing and reuse, subject to clearance and approval.
Description: Entertainment and sports programs owned, produced or broadcast by NBC Television Network. Handles distribution, syndication and all ancillary market sales, as well as requests for licensing and reuse. Licenses current product (e.g., *Saturday Night Live, Late Night with David Letterman* and sports programs), as well as archival material.

Although NBC holds physical copies of many of its programs, much of its television program library was donated to the Library of Congress, Motion Picture, Broadcasting and Recorded Sound Division (q.v.). Many programs are also held at the UCLA Film and Television Archive (q.v.); The Museum of Broadcasting (q.v.) (for reference only); and the Museum of Broadcast Communications (q.v.) (for reference only). The Museum of Broadcast

Communications will house all NBC *Tomorrow* shows (3/4" videotape copies will also be retained by NBC in New York).

A clip reel of NBC properties, containing approx. 60 programming samples, is available to researchers.
Size & Elements: Film: format unspecfied (over 10,000 reels). Videotape (format and amount unspecified).
Cataloging: Computerized cataloging for staff use only. Microfiche of radio and television Program Analysis files (1920s-present) is available. These files list programs, air dates, sponsors and names of personalities and guests appearing.
Access: Open to researchers, scholars and the public. For in-house use only. Available for duplication, licensing and reuse. Research fees charged. Research requests accepted by mail and telephone.
Rights: Full rights held to some material; some rights held to some material. Additional clearances may be necessary in some cases if material is to be reused. Since ownership of rights to many NBC television programs is distinct from ownership of the physical material, clearances may be necessary both from NBC Enterprises and the rights holder.
Licensing: Available for licensing and reuse, subject to restrictions. License fees charged.
Restrictions: Requests for licensing and reuse subject to clearance and approval. Licensee is responsible for obtaining any additional clearances or releases that may be required for its reuse of material, including but not limited to union and guild clearances, music clearances and talent releases.
Viewing Facilities: Film (through duplication facility); videotape.
Duplication Facilities: Film (film to videotape); videotape (all formats).
Related Materials: Radio programs owned, produced or broadcast by the NBC Radio Network.

NEW YORK METRO

NEMIROFF PRODUCTIONS, INC.
152 Cold Spring Road
Syosset, NY 11791
(212) 832-7600

Paul Nemiroff (President)

Contact: Paul Nemiroff
Services: Film producer. Outtakes from industrial films available for stock footage sale on a case-by-case basis.
Description: Producer of industrial films and commercials. Holds contemporary color footage of a roller coaster (approx. 4,000 feet) shot with various lenses and effects, including high-speed material (500 frames per second); a sailing ketch shot from on board and from a camera boat (approx. 2,000 feet); motocross biking (approx. 1,000 feet); and skiing Rothorn in the Swiss Alps (1,000 feet). Also holds small amounts of footage of high-school football, cheerleading and band practices (approx. 4,500 feet each).
Size & Elements: Film: 16mm (8,000 feet; 18 titles).
Cataloging: Apply for information.
Access: Outtakes from some industrial films available for reuse on a case-by-case basis. Requests accepted by telephone.
Rights: Full rights held to all material.
Licensing: Available for licensing and reuse on a case-by-case basis. License fees charged.
Restrictions: None specified.
Viewing Facilities: None.
Duplication Facilities: None.

NEW YORK METRO

NEW DAY FILMS
853 Broadway, Suite 1210
New York, NY 10003
(212) 477-4604
Fax: (212) 505-1567

Contact: Cara Saposnik (Film Booker)
Services: Film and videotape distributor. Materials available for rental, preview and purchase.
Description: *International concerns.* Titles include: three films by Carma Hinton and Richard Gordon, *All Under Heaven: Life in a Chinese Village, Small Happiness: Women of a Chinese Village* and *To Taste a Hundred Herbs: Gods, Ancestors and Medicine in a Chinese Village; The Global Assembly Line* (Lorraine Gray with Anne Bohlen and Maria Patricia Fernandez Kelly), on the

lives of working men and women in the "free trade zones" of developing countries and North America; and *Becoming American* (Ken and Ivory Waterworth Levine), the story of a Hmong refugee family from highland Laos and their resettlement in the U.S.

Urban America. Titles include: *Metropolitan Avenue* (Christine Noschese), on a Brooklyn community's fight for survival in the face of racial tensions and cutbacks in municipal services; *Voices from a Steeltown* (Tony Buba), on the rise and fall of Braddock, Pa.; *Poletown Lives!* (George Corsetti, Jeanie Wylie and Richard Wieske), on the organizing attempts of elderly Polish and Black residents as they resist demolition of their neighborhood for a new automobile plant in Detroit; *Style Wars!* (Tony Silver and Henry Chalfant), a portrait of New York's subculture of graffiti artists; and *Murray Avenue* (Sheila Chamovitz), on the personal and cultural survival of Pittsburgh's Jewish community.

Historical perspectives. Titles include: *Seeing Red* (Jim Klein and Julia Reichert), on the individuals who made up the American Communist Party from the 1930s through the 1950s; *Union Maids* (Julia Reichert, Jim Klein and Miles Mogulescu), an oral history of women in the 1930s labor movement; *With Babies and Banners* (Lorraine Gray with Anne Bohlen and Lyn Goldfarb), the story of the Women's Emergency Brigade during the General Motors sitdown strike in Flint, Michigan (1937); and *Artists at Work* (Mary Lance), on the New Deal art projects supported by the Works Progress Administration.

Cultural studies. Titles include: *Godzilla Meets Mona Lisa* (Ralph Arlyck), reflections on Paris' Centre Pompidou versus the Louvre; *Quilts in Women's Lives* (Pat Ferrero), portraits of seven traditional quiltmakers; *Hopi: Songs of the Fourth World* (Pat Ferrero), on Hopi spirituality and their integration of art with daily life; and *Summer of the Loucheux*, showing how four generations of an Athabaskan family maintain traditional skills despite contact with modern civilization.

Young adult issues. Titles include: *The AIDS Movie* (Ginny Durrin), focusing on AIDS prevention; *Kevin's Story* (Ginny Durrin), a peer-to-peer film on teenage drinking and driving; *Am I Normal?* and *Dear Diary* (Debra Franco and David Shepard), two films for teenagers about puberty; *Once Upon a Choice* (Liane Brandon), a humorous fairy tale on sex-role stereotypes; *The Flashettes* (Bonnie Friedman), on young urban women and the positive effects of sports; and *Coming of Age* (Josh Hanig), in which a group of teenagers at a summer retreat express their most intimate feelings about race, class, family and sexuality.

Birth, parenting and the family. Titles include: *2 A.M. Feeding* (Kristine Samuelson), a realistic look at parenting during the first few months after birth; *Joint Custody: A New Kind of Family* (Josephine Hayes Dean), on the rewards, difficulties and mechanics of this increasingly popular custody choice; *Daughters of Time* (Ginny Durrin), portraits of three American nurse-midwives; and *Heroes and Strangers* (Lorna Rasmussen and Tony Heriza with Andy Garrison), on men, emotions and the family.

Men and women in transition. Titles include: *An Acquired Taste* (Ralph Arlyck), on the American obsession with success; *To Have and to Hold* (Mark Lipman), on the problem of male abuse of women seen through the abuser's experience; *Men's Lives* (Josh Hanig and Will Roberts), on the pressure, competition and conditioning of American men and the male mystique; and *Growing Up Female* (Julia Reichert and James Klein), showing the socialization of the American woman through a personal look into the lives of six women ranging in age from four to 35.

Social perspectives. Titles include: *Skokie: Right or Wrong* (Sheila Chamovitz), on the legal and ethical crisis posed when the American Nazi Party chose to demonstrate in Skokie, Ill., home to many Holocaust survivors; *Women's Voices: The Gender Gap Movie* (Kartemquin Films), on the impact of Reaganomics on the political thinking of many American women; *Where I Want to Be* (Ginny Durrin), a portrayal of six mentally disabled young adults living together in a group home; and *The Outskirts of Hope* (David Davis), on America's poor in the 1980s, the successes and the failures of the "war on poverty."

Labor films. Titles include: *The Last Pullman Car* (Kartemquin Films), on the Pullman strike of 1894 and the efforts of modern Pullman workers to save their jobs; *Taylor Chain I* and *Taylor Chain II*, documenting respectively a seven-week strike at a small Indiana chain factory and a closed-door contract negotiation.

Health and the environment. Titles include: *Song of the Canary* (Josh Hanig and David Davis), on occupational health and safety in the U.S.; *The Last to Know* (Bonnie Friedman), on the special problems faced by women alcoholics; and *In Our Water* (Meg Switzgable), on chemical waste pollution.

New Day classics. Titles include: *Anything You Want to Be* (Liane Brandon), a teenager's humorous collision with sex-role stereotypes; *Betty Tells Her Story* (Liane Brandon), an exploration of beauty and self-image; *Not So*

Young Now as Then (Liane Brandon), a poignant look at the filmmaker's 15th high-school reunion; *Sometimes I Wonder Who I Am* (Liane Brandon), on the conflicts felt by a young housewife; *Beauty in the Bricks* (Allen Mondell and Cynthia Salzman Mondell), on Black teenage girls growing up in a housing project; *Who Remembers Mama?* (Cynthia Salzman Mondell and Allen Mondell), on the plight of the divorced middle-aged homemaker; *It Happens to Us* (Amalie Rothschild), in which women speak candidly about their abortion experiences; *Nana, Mom and Me* (Amalie Rothschild), a portrait of three generations of women; *Woo Who? May Wilson* (Amalie Rothschild), in which a grandmother begins a new life as an underground artist; *They Are Their Own Gifts: A Trilogy* (Lucille Rhodes and Margaret Murphy), on the lives of artists Muriel Rukeyser, Alice Neel and Anna Sokolow; *Joyce at 34* (Joyce Chopra and Claudia Weill), in which a woman faces the conflict of work versus family; *A Wedding in the Family* (Debra Franco), on young women, marriage and career decisions; *Chris and Bernie* (Bonnie Friedman and Deborah Shaffer), on two single mothers sharing the responsibilities of family and career; *The Other Half of the Sky: A China Memoir* (Claudia Weill and Shirley MacLaine), an intimate dialogue between Chinese and American women; *Love It Like a Fool* (Susan Wengraf), an inspirational glimpse of the life of Malvina Reynolds; *Yudie* (Mirra Bank), on independence, aging and the immigrant experience; *Possum Living* (Nancy Schreiber), exploring creative living in the 1980s on a tight budget; and *The Chicago Maternity Center* (Kartemquin Films), on the fight for survival of a patient-oriented homebirth center.

Size & Elements: Film: 16mm. Videotape: 3/4", VHS and Betamax. (60 titles total; not all titles available in all videotape formats).
Cataloging: Published catalog.
Access: Available for rental, preview-for-purchase evaluation and purchase.
Rights: Apply for information.
Licensing: Apply for information.
Restrictions: Films and videotapes may not be altered, duplicated, reproduced by videotape or other means, televised or electronically transmitted in whole or in part without specific written authorization from New Day Films and the individual filmmaker.
Viewing Facilities: None.
Duplication Facilities: None.
Related Materials: Study guides, reviews and other materials available for many titles.

NEW YORK METRO

NEW JERSEY HISTORICAL SOCIETY
230 Broadway
Newark, NJ 07104
(201) 483-3939

Wilson E. O'Donnell (Acting Executive Director)

Contacts: Sarah Collins (Library Director)
Services: State historical society. Films maintained primarily for archival and research purposes.
Description: History of the state of New Jersey. Selected titles focus on histories of large New Jersey corporations and historic New Jersey sites.
Size & Elements: Film: format unspecified (20 titles, 20 cans; positive).
Cataloging: None.
Access: Open to researchers and scholars primarily; open to others by written request only. Research requests accepted in person (by appointment only).
Rights: No rights to any material.
Licensing: Apply for information. Usage fees charged, but may be waived in some cases.
Restrictions: None specified.
Viewing Facilities: None.
Duplication Facilities: None.

NEW YORK METRO

NEW TIME FILMS, INC.
P.O. Box 502, Village Station
New York, NY 10014
(212) 929-0022

Contact: Penny Bernstein
Services: Distributor. Films and videotapes available to the public for purchase; films available for rental.
Description: Contemporary political and social issue films by independent documentary film producers.

Titles include: *And That is Why the State is to Blame*, on the murder of Marianella Garcia Villas, president of the Human Rights Commission of El Salvador; *Paul Jacobs and the Nuclear Gang*; *Gaza Ghetto*, a portrait of a Palestinian refugee family (1948-84); *Report from Beirut: Summer of '82*; *Target Nicaragua — 1983*; *Nicaragua, September 1978*; *Counterpoint: The Case for the Sandinistas*; *Who Shot Alexander Hamilton* (1973), on the U.S. Congress during the Nixon administration; *Quest for Power: Sketches on the American New Right*; *September Wheat*, about hunger in industrialized and Third World countries; *Hard Times in the Country*, food production and distribution; *Fidel* [Castro]; *The Dead Are Not Silent*, on Chile; *Que Hacer*, on the 1970 elections in Chile; *An Interview With Salvador Allende*; *El Salvador: Revolution or Death*; *Brazil: A Report on Torture*; *The Long Chain*, a case study in imperialism; *Portrait of Nelson Mandela*; *Appalachia: Rich Land, Poor People*; *A Song For Dead Warriors*, on American Indian affairs; *Bottle Babies*; *Lay My Burden Down*, on civil rights; *Streets of Greenwood*, on civil rights in Mississippi; *CIA Case Officer* (with John Stockwell); *The Swine Flu Caper*, on the relationship between science and government; *Courage to Live*, on a cancer victim; and *Maurice Bishop Speaks*, with the Grenadan Prime Minister.
Size & Elements: Film: 16mm. Videotape: 3/4" and 1/2". (28 titles total).
Cataloging: Published catalogs.
Access: Films and videotapes available to the public for purchase; films available for rental. Reservations accepted by telephone, but orders accepted by mail only. Apply for information regarding exhibition rates and multiple screening rates.
Rights: Apply for information.
Licensing: Apply for information.
Restrictions: Films are rented and sold with the understanding that films will not be altered, videotaped or reproduced in any manner.
Viewing Facilities: None.
Duplication Facilities: None.

NEW YORK METRO

NEW YORK CHINATOWN HISTORY PROJECT
70 Mulberry Street, Room 2H
New York, NY 10013
(212) 619-4785

Charles Lai (Executive Director)

Contacts: Mei-Li Lin (Administrator); Dorothy Rony (Program Director)
Services: Nonprofit community education organization and historical society. One videotape available for rental; film archives in process of formation.
Description: The Chinese experience in the United States. *Eight Pound Livelihood* (30 min. color), produced by the Chinatown History Project in conjunction with public television station WNYC-TV, documents the history of Chinese laundry workers in the U.S. The videotape utilizes historical narrative, still photographs, folk music and oral history interviews to trace the profession from its earliest days of Chinese involvement in the West to scenes of contemporary laundry businesses in New York City.

Additionally, the Chinatown History Project is assembling a documentary collection of home movies shot by the U.S. Chinese community (1940s-present).
Size & Elements: Videotape: 3/4" and VHS (1 title).
Cataloging: Published catalogs.
Access: Available to the public for rental. Rental fees charged.
Rights: Full rights held to all material.
Licensing: Apply for information.
Restrictions: None specified.
Viewing Facilities: None.
Duplication Facilities: None.

NEW YORK METRO

NEW YORK CITY DEPARTMENT OF RECORDS AND INFORMATION SERVICES
DIVISION OF THE MUNICIPAL ARCHIVES
31 Chambers Street, Room 101
New York, NY 10007
(212) 566-5292

Eugene J. Bockman (Commissioner)

Contacts: Idilio Gracia-Pena (Director, Municipal Archives); Kenneth R. Cobb

(Deputy Director, Municipal Archives)
Services: Government agency; archives. Film and videotape collection currently closed, but will eventually be open to the public.
Description: Collection received from municipally owned radio and television broadcast stations, WNYC and WNYC-TV (1949-81; two-thirds of titles produced 1966-81).

Coverage from the 1950s consists of films produced by the WNYC Film Unit for various city agencies and departments (1950s), including training films (e.g., *On the Witness Stand*, for the New York City Police Department); and documentaries or educational films intended for a wider audience (e.g., *The Big City* and *New York — City of Magic*).

Footage (1966-81) consists primarily of news coverage of the Mayor, City Council members and New York City representatives to state and federal legislatures. Material covers press conferences, statements, interviews, speeches, ceremonies and dedications.

Special strengths include footage of New York City municipal government, news and cultural events, speeches, parades, people, places and issues (primarily of local significance, although some material is of national or international interest, such as *Truman Laying Cornerstone at the U.N.*).
Size & Elements: Film: 35mm and 16mm (5,300 cans; primarily 16mm, original and duplicate negatives, master composite prints, release prints, workprints, original reversal film, track negatives, magnetic and optical sound, black and white and color). Videotape: 2" (amount unspecified).
Cataloging: Shelf list.
Access: Collection currently closed, but will eventually be open to the public. Research requests not accepted at this time.
Rights: The City of New York holds full rights to all materials produced by its employees, contractors and sub-contractors, with the exception of any material that makes use of copyrighted or privately owned footage. Rights status of some material not known.
Licensing: Public domain license fees will be charged when collection is made available for reuse.
Restrictions: Collection currently closed, but will eventually be open to the public. Research requests not accepted at this time.
Viewing Facilities: None.
Duplication Facilities: None.
Related Materials: Extensive still photograph archives covering all facets of New York City life, including street scenes from the turn of the century; photograph collection of the Dept. of Bridges and Tunnels (1920s); WPA-New York City material not included in Library of Congress; papers and documents relating to New York City; glass plate negatives of Borough Presidents of Manhattan and Queens; 1/4" audiotapes (in WNYC collection).

NEW YORK METRO

NEW YORK CITY LABOR FILM CLUB
178 East 7th Street
New York, NY 10009
(212) 533-6515

Contact: Ken Nash
Services: Media organization. Videotapes available for distribution, rental and reuse, subject to restrictions.
Description: *Labor Journal*, a series of magazine-format programs produced for cable television (1984-86). Some programs contain various segments on labor-related issues; others focus on a single issue, using interviews and documentary footage.

Coverage includes: nurses in the New York City area; a white-collar organizing drive at Columbia University; Transport Workers Union Local 100 (New York City), including an interview with union official John Lowe; El Salvador (partly composed of footage from outside sources); a program on labor produced in collaboration with Paper Tiger Television (q.v.) for distribution by the Deep Dish TV (q.v.) satellite project; the Greyhound strike; and an organizing drive targeting the Marriott Corporation.
Size & Elements: Videotape: 3/4" (approx. 8 videotapes, each 30 min.; masters and viewing copies); 1/2" (viewing copies).
Cataloging: None.
Access: Maintained for distribution and rental rather than for research or reuse. Access is negotiable, depending on intended use. Research fees charged in some cases. Research requests accepted by mail and telephone.
Rights: Full rights held to some material (in-studio segments and documentary material shot specifically for *Labor Journal*). Additional clearances may be necessary in some cases (for subjects of interviews and documentary footage from outside sources) if material is to be reused.
Licensing: Available for licensing and reuse, subject to restrictions. License

fees charged in some cases (depending on intended use).
Restrictions: Requests for licensing and reuse considered on a case-by-case basis. Restrictions may apply. Interview subjects and documentary footage obtained from other sources cannot be reused without obtaining proper clearances.
Viewing Facilities: None.
Duplication Facilities: None.

NEW YORK METRO

THE NEW YORK HOSPITAL — CORNELL MEDICAL CENTER MEDICAL ARCHIVES
1300 York Avenue
New York, NY 10021
(212) 746-6072
Fax: (212) 746-6494

Adele A. Lerner (Archivist)

Contact: Adele Lerner
Services: Medical center; film and videotape archives. Collection available to the public for research and reuse.
Description: Productions of the Medical Center (1930s-present), primarily produced in the 1940s-50s. The "Hospital Without Walls" produced many of these films as training tools for nurses and other staff personnel.
Sample titles include: *Mealtime for John Henry; New Year's Babies; No Less Than Life; Right From the Start,* a film on high-risk pregnancy; and *Sugar.*
Of particular interest is footage of Dr. Ida Scudder receiving an award in Vellore, India; a film depicting women nurses in a coal mining area; a history of the hospital (1972); a videotape profiling Dr. George Papanicolaou (the creator of the Pap Smear); a film on burn treatment (1986); a film on premature birth (1987); and a film on the construction of the Medical Center.
Size & Elements: Film: 35mm, 16mm and 8mm (125 titles; majority are 16mm). Videotape: VHS (approx. 10-15 videotapes).
Cataloging: Finding aids.
Access: Available to the public for research and reuse. Research requests accepted by telephone.
Rights: Full rights held to some material. Additional clearances may be necessary in some cases if material is to be reused.
Licensing: Available for licensing and reuse. License fees charged.
Restrictions: None specified.
Viewing Facilities: Videotape.
Duplication Facilities: None.
Related Materials: Scripts and still photographs.

NEW YORK METRO

THE NEW YORK PUBLIC LIBRARY DONNELL MEDIA CENTER
20 West 53rd Street
New York, NY 10019
(212) 621-0609

Marie Nesthus (Principal Film Librarian)

Contact: Reference Desk
Services: Public library. Film and videotape collection maintained for in-house viewing and free loan to Library cardholders.
Description: Extensive film and videotape collections are maintained for public access and loan.
Videotape library. Contains feature films on videotape, artists' videotapes and documentaries. An "exemplary television" category contains made-for-television movies, generally in series (e.g., *Berlin Alexanderplatz*), and a separate children's section.
Film library. Particularly strong in social documentaries, covering foreign cultures, politics, geology, religion, anthropology, ethnography, current medical issues, sexually transmitted diseases and AIDS. Also holds a large collection of feature films (1900-present), including films by D. W. Griffith, Orson Welles, Luis Buñuel, Werner Herzog and R. W. Fassbinder. Other material includes dance films, humor films, films for children and young adults and experimental films by such contemporary filmmakers as Abigail Child and Ericka Beckman.
Size & Elements: Film: 16mm (5,500 titles; release prints). Videotape: 3/4", VHS and 1/2" open reel (1,500 titles; viewing copies, mostly VHS).

Cataloging: Published catalogs (periodically updated).
Access: Open to the public. Available for in-house viewing and free loan. Collection circulates to cardholders. A library card is required to reserve materials for loan. Materials must be reserved two weeks in advance; confirmation of reservations by mail is required. Research fees not charged. Research requests accepted by telephone and in person (by appointment only).
Rights: No rights held to any material.
Licensing: Material not available for licensing or reuse.
Restrictions: Material not available for licensing or reuse.
Viewing Facilities: Film (16mm); videotape (3/4", VHS and 1/2" open reel). Films or videotapes may be brought from outside for viewing on library equipment.
Duplication Facilities: None.

NEW YORK METRO

THE NEW YORK PUBLIC LIBRARY
EARLY CHILDHOOD RESOURCE AND INFORMATION CENTER
66 Leroy Street
New York, NY 10014
(212) 929-0815

Hannah Nuba (Director)

Contact: Hannah Nuba
Services: Library. Film and videotape collection open to the public for research and viewing.
Description: Parenthood, child development (psychological and physical), and educational tools and concepts (1970-present).
Film titles include: *Adjusting to Parenthood; Asthma and Your Child; Child Abuse and the Law; Child Care in China; Infant Development in the Kibbutz; Play and Cultural Continuity Parts 1-4 (Appalachian children, Southern Black Children, Mexican American children,* and *Montana Indian children); Single Parents and Their Children;* and *What's So Great About Books?.* Videotape titles include: *Brianna: A Two-Year-Old in a Group Setting; Lunch Time with Babies;* and *Child Abuse.*
Size & Elements: Film: format unspecified (51 titles). Videotape: format unspecified (9 titles).
Cataloging: None specified.
Access: Collection open to the public. Research requests accepted by telephone.
Rights: No rights held to any material.
Licensing: Apply for information.
Restrictions: None specified.
Viewing Facilities: Film and videotape.
Duplication Facilities: None.

NEW YORK METRO

THE NEW YORK PUBLIC LIBRARY AT LINCOLN CENTER
PERFORMING ARTS RESEARCH CENTER
JEROME ROBBINS ARCHIVE OF THE RECORDED MOVING IMAGE
DANCE COLLECTION
111 Amsterdam Avenue
New York, NY 10023
(212) 870-1659 (Film and Videotape Archive)
(212) 870-1657 (Reference)

Madeleine Nichols (Curator)

Contacts: Ellie Peck (Film Coordinator); Mary McFerran (Film/Video Specialist)
Services: Research library; film and videotape archives; producer. Collection available to the public for research and in-house viewing only. *Material not available for loan, duplication or reuse.*
Description: The film and videotape archives of the Dance Collection operates to acquire, preserve and centralize film and videotape records of choreography and dance performances. Archive staff locate and acquire extant films and videotapes on dance; other staff members are involved in the preservation of acquired work. Archive has arranged to act as the repository for current film and videotape documentation from many dance companies and dance showcases that are now documenting their repertories.
In addition, the Archive annually produces several original film and videotape records of current dance works. With the aid of a committee of dance

critics, choreography deemed most in need of documentation is selected. Over 350 films have been produced to date.

Collection begins with rare Biograph footage (1908) and continues to the present. Highlights include footage of Leonide Massine's work for the Ballet Russe de Monte Carlo; excerpts of Massine, Alexandra Danilova and Frederic Franklin in *Petrouchka* and Tamara Toumanova in *Three Cornered Hat;* footage of the Kirov Ballet School in Leningrad; a film of Rudolf Nureyev's graduation exercises, completed just before he went on to become a featured soloist with the Kirov; Anthony Tudor's *Pillar of Fire* with Nora Kaye; Jerome Robbins' *Fancy Free,* performed by John Kriza, Janet Reed and Robbins; *Giselle,* starring Cuban ballerina Alicia Alonso; Ruth St. Denis in *Red and Gold Sari; Three Virgins and a Devil,* with Agnes DeMille; an excerpt from *Septet,* by Merce Cunningham (1955); excerpts of Meredith Monk's *Juice;* Yvonne Rainer's *Continuous Project Daily,* performed by The Grand Union; Mura Dehn's *The Spirit Moves;* and documentation of Brooklyn Academy of Music's *Next Wave* performances.

Holdings include material from the Ballet Theater (now the American Ballet Theater), the Ann Barzel Collection, and the Jacob's Pillow Collection.
Size & Elements: Film: 16mm (2,509 titles). Videotape: 3/4", VHS and Betamax; NTSC, PAL and SECAM (4,903 titles).
Cataloging: Published catalog; computerized cataloging (in progress); research library.
Access: *Available to the public for in-house research and viewing only. Not available for loan, duplication or reuse.* Because of the rarity of much of the Dance Collection's film and videotape holdings and because of its heavy use by viewers, preservation is one of the most important aspects of the Collection's activities. Film master negatives are kept in off-site storage facilities and reference copies of videotape masters are maintained for public service use, while master videotapes are kept in archival storage. Material can be viewed six days a week in the Dance Collection reading room. Research fees not charged. Research requests accepted by mail, telephone (brief requests only) and in person (walk-in).
Rights: Rights to most material retained by choreographers or producers.
Licensing: Not available for licensing or reuse.
Restrictions: Not available for loan, duplication, licensing or reuse.
Viewing Facilities: Film (16mm Steenbeck); videotape (3/4", VHS and Betamax; NTSC, PAL and SECAM).
Duplication Facilities: None.
Related Materials: Study materials include books, periodicals, reviews, programs, photographs, original stage and costume designs and manuscripts.

NEW YORK METRO

THE NEW YORK PUBLIC LIBRARY AT LINCOLN CENTER PERFORMING ARTS RESEARCH CENTER THE BILLY ROSE THEATRE COLLECTION THEATRE ON FILM AND TAPE
111 Amsterdam Avenue
New York, NY 10023
(212) 870-1641

Betty Corwin (Director)

Contact: Betty Corwin; Victoria Kummer (Production Supervisor); Bonnie Metzgar
Services: Library; film and videotape archives. Not open to the public. Open to qualified researchers and scholars for in-house use only.
Description: Film and videotape documentation of theatrical performances. Comprises productions from Broadway (620 items), Off-Broadway, Off-Off Broadway, regional theater and theater from abroad (1970-present). Dialogues with notable theater personalities (66 items) and theater-related film and television programs (451 items) are included. Although the archives has been videotaping shows for less than two decades, several donated items in the collection are older.

In 1969, Betty Corwin proposed that Broadway and Off-Broadway shows be videotaped for an archives. *The Golden Bat,* a Japanese rock musical, was the first show recorded for the Collection, in 1970 at the Sheridan Square Playhouse.

Productions chosen to be recorded are based on guidelines that seek to preserve the unique, selected from a representative spectrum of contemporary theater. Elements taken into consideration include: outstanding quality, uniqueness, balance among types and styles of theater, representation from ethnic and minority theater groups, mime and choreography, special attractions, efforts of major figures and further documentation of artists who have already deposited their archives with the Theater Collection.

Drama. Expanded material on the careers of the following playwrights:
Edward Albee. Eight One Act Plays, written and directed by Albee for performance at Columbia University (1979); the Hartford Stage Company's production of *All Over* (1975); American Film Theatre's version of *A Delicate Balance,* starring Katherine Hepburn and Paul Scofield (1973); and a videotaped dialogue with Albee and Jack MacGowran (on Samuel Beckett, 1975).

Samuel Beckett. Two versions of *Waiting For Godot* (the 1971 production with Henderson Forsythe and a 1961 television "play of the week," starring Zero Mostel and Burgess Meredith); *Jack MacGowran in the Works of Beckett* (New York Shakespeare Festival, 1971); Mabou Mines' production of the *The Lost Ones* (1976); Joseph Chaikin's production of *Endgame* (Manhattan Theater Club, 1980).

Eugene O'Neill. Long Day's Journey Into Night, a version starring Robert Ryan and Geraldine Fitzgerald (1971) and the all-Black production directed by Ms. Fitzgerald for television (1982); two versions of *Ah, Wilderness;* AFT's television adaptation of *The Iceman Cometh,* directed by Sidney Lumet (1961); and *A Moon for the Misbegotten,* starring Colleen Dewhurst and Jason Robards (directed for television by Jose Quintero, 1975).

Other dramatic productions of note include: John Guare's *The House of Blue Leaves* (1971 and 1986 versions); Kaufman and Ferber's *The Royal Family,* starring Eva LeGallienne (1976); Chekhov's *Uncle Vanya,* starring Laurence Olivier, Michael Redgrave and Rosemary Harris (1963); Preston Jones' *A Texas Trilogy,* starring the author (Dallas Theatre Centre, 1978); *Torch Song Trilogy,* original production by and starring Harvey Fierstein (Actors Playhouse, 1980); David Hare's *Plenty,* starring Kate Nelligan and directed by the playwright (1982); Lanford Wilson's *Balm in Gilead,* directed by John Malkovich (Steppenwolf Theatre Company, 1984); JoAnne Akalaitis' *Dead End Kids* (Mabou Mines, 1982); Caryl Churchill's *Cloud Nine* (1981); Athol Fugard's *Blood Knot* (1986); Robinson Jeffers' adaptation of *Medea,* starring Zoe Caldwell and Judith Anderson (1981); *Ten by Tennessee,* ten one-act plays by Tennessee Williams (videotaped at the Lucille Lortel Theatre, 1986); Alfred Uhry's *Driving Miss Daisy* (1987); Mbongeni Ngema's *Asinamali* (1987); and most of New York Shakespeare Festival's open-air *Shakespeare in the Park* series.

Also held are dialogues with influential theatrical luminaries, including Stella Adler, Boris Aronson, Brooks Atkinson, Michael Bennett, Cheryl Crawford, Dame Edith Evans, Spalding Gray, Garson Kanin, Eva LeGallienne, Lucille Lortel, Al Hirschfeld, Arthur Miller, Joseph Papp and Neil Simon.

Musicals. Black and white silent footage (original home movies shot by Richard Rodgers) of the original Rodgers, Hart and Hammerstein shows: *Jumbo; I Married an Angel; Too Many Girls; By Jupiter; No Strings; I'd Rather Be Right; Pal Joey; A Connecticut Yankee; Allegro; Oklahoma!;* and *The King and I.*

Works by major artists include: Stephen Sondheim's *Merrily We Roll Along;* Betty Comden and Adolph Green's *A Doll's Life;* Charles Strouse, Joseph Stein and Stephen Schwartz' *Rags,* Marvin Hamlisch and Howard Ashman's *Smile;* and David Hare's *The Knife.*

Other musicals held include: *Floradora,* revival of the Gay 90's production (1981); *Follies,* excerpts from the original Broadway show (1971); *On Your Toes,* a revival starring Natalia Makarova (1983); *Sunday in the Park With George* (the first act of the workshop production at Playrights Horizons, 1983); *A Chorus Line Celebration,* the 3,389th performance of the musical, commemorating its becoming the longest-running show in Broadway history (September 29, 1983); *Pacific Overtures* (1985 revival); Brooklyn Academy of Music's production of *The Gospel at Colonus,* adapted and directed by Lee Breuer (1983) and Robert Wilson's *Einstein on the Beach,* Philip Glass, composer; an adaptation of *All the King's Men* (Trinity Theatre production, Providence, Rhode Island, 1987); Douglas J. Cohen's *No Way To Treat A Lady* (1987); and a "Gershwin Celebration" (presented at the Brooklyn Academy of Music) featuring George and Ira Gershwin's *Of Thee I Sing* and *Let 'em Eat Cake* (1978).

Vaudeville and burlesque. Items include: Joe Smith, of the vaudeville team Smith & Dale, recreating one of his famous routines with actor Ted Erwin; *Tangentally* (WNET/13), a documentary on "the Great Radio Comedians" (all of whom worked in vaudeville), preserves appearances by Edgar Bergen and Charlie McCarthy; George Burns and Gracie Allen; Jack Benny; Fibber McGee and Molly; Fred Allen; Eddie Cantor and Fanny Brice (1979). Also held is a videotape of the Broadway production *Sugar Babies,* and a television interview with its stars Ann Miller and Mickey Rooney; a videotaped interview with drummer Charles de Milt discussing "Music in Burlesque" (1979); and videotapes of comic Joey Faye and producer Morton Minsky discussing burlesque.

Avant-garde. Items include: *Empress of China* (Tina Chang's Pan Asian Repertory Company, 1984); Martha Clarke's *Garden of Earthly Delights,* based on a painting by Hieronymus Bosch (1984), *Vienna: Lusthaus* (1986), and *The Hunger Artist* (1987), her adaptation of the works of Franz Kafka; Richard Foreman's *Pandering to the Masses: a misrepresentation* (1975); Elizabeth Swados' *Fragments of a Trilogy: Medea, The Trojan Women & Electra* (La Mama, 1976); and the Wooster Group, performing at the American Place Theatre in *The Rumstick Road.*

Ethnic and minority theatrical heritage. Yiddish theater titles include: Shalom Yiddish Theatre's *Rebecca the Rabbi's Daughter* (1979); *An Afternoon with Molly Picon* (1979); a television documentary, *The Golden Age of Second Avenue,* featuring scenes from films and plays with Paul Muni, Maurice Schwartz, Menasha Skulnik, Molly Picon and Celia Adler; Joseph Chaikin's staging of *The Dybbuk* (1978); and *The World of Sholom Aleichem,* starring Jack Gilford (1982).

Black and Hispanic theater titles include: Miguel Pinero's *Short Eyes* (1974); Samm-Art Williams' *Home* (Negro Ensemble Company, 1980); *The Me Nobody Knows* (1970 television production); Lorraine Hansberry's *To Be Young, Gifted and Black* (WNET, 1971); and *A Colored Girl-Ntozake Shange* (WGBH, 1970).

Oriental theater is represented in live performance with the Korean National Theatre's *Chun-Hyang-Jeon;* Cao Yu's *Peking Man;* and Wakoko Yamaguchi's *And the Soul Shall Dance.*

Mime, dance and marionettes. Included in this collection are works by the American Mime Theatre; Claude Kipnis Mime Theatre; Bill Irwin's *In Regard of Flight;* and Valerie Bettis' *Adam and Eve.* Many videotapes of Bill Baird's marionettes are part of the permanent collection; and a documentary (1976) on the Lovelace Marionette Theatre demonstrating the creation of puppet and marionette production from concept to performance.

One-person shows. Includes *Emlyn Williams as Charles Dickens; Paul Shyre as H. L. Mencken;* and *Liza Minnelli at the Winter Garden.*

Television and motion picture productions. Included is a series entitled *Emerging Playwrights,* with interviews and excerpts from plays. Series features: *Kennedy's Children* (Robert Patrick); *The Rimers of Eldritch* (Lanford Wilson); *Duck Variations* (David Mamet); *Gemini* (Albert Innaurato); *A History of the American Film* (Christopher Durang); and *On Golden Pond* (Ernest Thompson). Filmed or videotaped presentations and special events include: *Happy End,* the 1929 Weill-Brecht opera (produced by the Arena Theatre of Washington, D.C., 1983); *Treemonisha,* a production of the Scott Joplin opera (1981); *Bernstein Conducts West Side Story; Lena Horne: The Lady and Her Music;* and *Sweeney Todd: The Demon Barber of Fleet Street.* *Wonderful Town* is a videotape transfer from a kinescope of the 1953 Broadway production starring Rosalind Russell; *Joseph Papp and the Public* (1979); *Steambath* (produced by Hollywood Television Theatre, 1971); and various Outer Critics Circle, Obie and Tony Awards presentations. Of special interest is Groucho Marx hosting the 1971-72 Obie Awards at the Village Gate Theatre.

Size & Elements: Film: 16mm (131,936 feet). Videotape: 1" (masters); 3/4" and 1/2" (viewing copies) (2,655 videotapes, 99,321 minutes total). (1,177 titles total).
Cataloging: Card catalogs; research library.
Access: Not open to the public. For in-house use only. Material must remain on premises. Collection open to qualified researchers and scholars, and theater professionals only (by appointment only). Research fees not charged. Research requests accepted by mail, telephone and in person (walk-in and by appointment).
Rights: Full rights held to some material. Some rights held to some material. Additional clearances may be necessary in some cases if material is to be reused.
Licensing: Not available for licensing or reuse.
Restrictions: Material is "highly restricted." Access to Archives is limited due to negotiated agreements with various theatrical unions. No videotapes may be copied or removed from the premises for any reason whatsoever.
Viewing Facilities: Videotape (3/4", VHS and Betamax; monitors and screenings rooms can be arranged for approved groups).
Duplication Facilities: None (materials must remain on premises).

NEW YORK METRO

THE NEW YORK PUBLIC LIBRARY
RARE BOOKS AND MANUSCRIPTS DIVISION
Fifth Avenue and 42nd Street
New York, NY 10018
(212) 930-0804
Fax: (212) 268-9129

Robert Sink (Archivist/Records Manager)

Contact: Robert Sink
Services: Library. Film and videotape materials available to the public for valid research purposes; available for duplication and reuse on a case-by-case basis, subject to restrictions.
Description: Several manuscript collections contain films and videotapes. Donor or copyright restrictions apply in some cases. Key collections include:
Citizens for a Quieter City, Inc. Collection (1966-74) (24 items). Organization founded by Robert A. Baron to reduce urban noise. Contains videotapes of conferences, television shows and public events sponsored by CQC or in which CQC participated, and videotapes on noise produced by other organizations.
Charles Ellsworth Goodell Papers. 27 videotapes, probably relating to his 1970 campaign for U.S. Senate.
Fran Lee Collection. Fran Lee (1910–), a New York-based actress and consumer advocate ("Mrs. Fixit"), who has made regular appearances on local television. Collection ("12 boxes" of 16mm film and 2" videotapes, 1949-79) comprises shows and segments in which she appeared, including *Skitch's New York, New Yorker Show, Mitchell Krause Show, Joe Franklin's Memory Lane, Tonight Show, Steve Allen Show, Girl Talk,* and *The Shari Lewis Show.* Subjects covered include poisoned and adulterated foods, dogs and the "pooper scooper" law, cyclamates, dog bites, menopause, fur buying, frozen foods, poisons, pantyhose, tie-dyeing and streaking.
Vito Marcantonio. American Labor Party member of Congress from Manhattan. One film documenting a Spanish-language campaign speech delivered by Marcantonio on behalf of Henry Wallace during his 1948 Presidential campaign.
Herbert Mitgang Papers. (16mm films, 17 titles). Documentaries (1963-65), probably *CBS Reports.*
New York World's Fair, 1964-65, Inc. Collection. Various 35mm and 16mm films. Production elements, including original negatives, soundtracks, outtakes and trims (173 cans total) from *Come to the Fair,* produced by Francis Thompson, Inc. Material produced by John Campbell Films, Inc. (120 cans), including completed films and unedited footage shot prior to the Fair's opening; material relating to labor issues; a *World's Fair Report;* and other material. *WNYC World's Fair Reports* (25 cans). *World's Fair Report with Lowell Thomas* (14 cans). Miscellaneous films, including 7 films relating to Robert Moses; *Great Fair Fun* (5 cans); various news clips including *President Kennedy at Fair, Mayor Wagner at Fair,* and *Hall of Free Enterprise Pillar Planting; World's Fair Progress Report,* narrated by H. V. Kaltenborn; and *New York: The World's Fair State.*
Size & Elements: Film and videotape: various formats (amount unspecified).
Cataloging: Accession sheets for each collection, listing partial inventories.
Access: Open to the public for valid research purposes. Undergraduate college students admitted only by special permission. For in-house use only. The collections are housed in the Annex storage facility and require advance notice for use. Available for duplication and reuse; requests for reuse evaluated on a case-by-case basis. Research fees charged in some cases; screening and service fees charged. Research requests accepted by mail, telephone and in person (by appointment only).
A card of admission to the Manuscripts and Archives Section may be requested by making written application to the Office of Special Collections, Room 316.
Rights: Rights status of material varies. Additional clearances may be necessary in some cases if material is to be reused.
Licensing: Available for licensing and reuse, subject to restrictions. License and usage fees charged.
Restrictions: Copyright and donor restrictions apply to some collections.
Viewing Facilities: None at division. Arrangements can be made on a case-by-case basis to view material at other New York Public Library facilities.
Duplication Facilities: None.
Related Materials: Still photographs and manuscripts.

NEW YORK METRO

NEW YORK STATE COUNCIL ON THE ARTS
915 Broadway
New York, NY 10010
(212) 614-2900

Contact: Sarah Zimmerman (Media Secretary)
Services: Government agency. Videotape collection open to researchers and scholars for in-house viewing only.
Description: Video art and independent documentary productions on videotape (1970-88). Many productions of historical and/or artistic significance are held. A sampling of producers represented in the extensive collection

includes: Alliance of Women on Architecture; Artists' Television Network (see Artists' Television Project, Special Collections Department, University of Iowa); Cable Arts; Cast Iron T.V.; Cathode Ray Theatre; Center for Non-Broadcast TV; Downtown Community Television Center (q.v.); Earthscore Foundation; Electronic Arts Intermix (q.v.); Electronic Body Arts; Experimental Television Center (q.v.); Global Village; Intermedia Arts Center; Ithaca Video Project, Inc.; The Kitchen Center for Video, Music, Dance, Performance and Film (q.v.); Locus Communications (q.v.); Media Bus (q.v.); Media Study/Buffalo; National Center for Experiments in Television; Paper Tiger Television (q.v.); Peoples' Video Theatre; Portable Channel; The Raindance Foundation (q.v.); Survival Arts Media; Synapse Video Center; Syracuse University Video Series; Video Repertorie; Women's Interart Center; Woodstock Community Video; WCNY-TV; WGBH Educational Foundation (q.v.); WNET-TV Lab; WXXI-TV; and Young Filmmakers/Video Artists (now Film/Video Arts, Inc. [q.v.]).

Size & Elements: Videotape: 3/4" (662 videotapes; viewing copies); 1/2" (251 videotapes; viewing copies; figure includes both open reel and cassette formats).
Cataloging: Computerized cataloging available to researchers; title list.
Access: Open to researchers and scholars only. Research fees not charged. Research requests accepted by mail, telephone and in person (by appointment only).
Rights: No rights held to any material.
Licensing: Not available for duplication, licensing or reuse.
Restrictions: Not available for duplication, licensing or reuse.
Viewing Facilities: Videotape (by appointment only).
Duplication Facilities: None.

NEW YORK METRO

NEW YORK STOCK EXCHANGE
COMMUNICATIONS DEPARTMENT
11 Wall Street
New York, NY 10005
(212) 656-3000

Richard Torrenzano (Senior Vice President)

Contact: Gary Miller (Manager, Broadcast Services) (Ext. 6626)
Services: Corporation; corporate archives. Videotape stock footage available for reuse to the news media only.
Description: One videotape containing B-roll footage of the New York Stock Exchange and Wall Street. Currently working on a five-part video news release which will explain the operations of the New York Stock Exchange and Wall Street.
Size & Elements: Videotape: format unspecified (1 videotape; 15 min.).
Cataloging: None.
Access: Not open to the public. Available for licensing. Circulated free of charge to television news producers. Other requests subject to acceptance and approval. Research fees not charged. Research requests accepted by mail and telephone.
Rights: Full rights held to all material.
Licensing: Available for licensing, subject to restrictions. License fees not charged.
Restrictions: Requests for licensing considered on a case-by-case basis and are subject to acceptance and approval.
Viewing Facilities: None.
Duplication Facilities: Videotape.

NEW YORK METRO

NEW YORK ZOOLOGICAL SOCIETY
Bronx Zoo
185th Street and Southern Boulevard
Bronx, NY 10460
(212) 220-5134
Fax: (212) 220-7114
Telex: 428279 NYZWCI

Contact: Thomas Veltre (Audio Visual Office)
Services: In-house production unit; film archives. Film, videotape and audio materials available to qualified individuals and agencies for research, licensing and reuse, subject to restrictions. Access restricted.
Description: Production unit and film archives for the Bronx Zoo, Central Park Zoo and New York Aquarium. Collection relates to animals and wildlife field research (1910-present). Most footage was shot inside exhibits at the Bronx Zoo and New York Aquarium, and features closeups of baby animals, openings of new exhibits and notable endangered species. Footage shot in the wild includes Argentine wildlife (50,000 feet); East African wildlife and Masai people (100,000 feet); and material from Wyoming, Alberta, Antarctica, Alaska, Southeast Asia and South America.

Rare footage includes panda collecting in China (1941); kouprey, the wild cattle of Cambodia (1953); blind cave fish in Mexico (1939); and William Beebe's historic bathysphere dives (1934).

Footage from 1910-36 is 35mm black and white (some transferred to 1" videotape); from 1936-40, 16mm black and white; from 1941-78, 16mm color reversal (Kodachrome and Ektachrome); from 1978-present, 16mm negative, 1" and 3/4" videotape.
Size & Elements: Film: 35mm and 16mm (approx. 2 million feet).
Cataloging: Card index; staff assistance required. Animal footage cataloged by species; scenic material by region, expedition or name of field researcher/photographer.
Access: Available to qualified individuals and agencies for research and educational production (by appointment only). Research and viewing fees charged (may be applied to license fee). Research requests accepted in writing only; must state proposed use for footage, including funding of production and distribution plans.
Rights: Full rights held to most material. Rights to some material retained by original photographers.
Licensing: Available for licensing and reuse, subject to restrictions.
Restrictions: Available for licensing and reuse primarily to educational productions. Limited commercial use is permitted with script approval. Written application required to view material. Rush service not available.
Viewing Facilities: Film (16mm); videotape (3/4" and VHS).
Duplication Facilities: None.
Related Materials: Audio collection, including the *Songs of the Humpback Whale* recordings; large slide library (contact Cathy Boldt, 212/220-5181).

NEW YORK METRO

NEW YORKER FILMS
16 West 61st Street
New York, NY 10023
(212) 247-6110
Fax: (212) 307-7855

Contact: Mario Ortiz
Services: Distributor. Films available for distribution and rental.
Description: Distributes domestic and international feature films, documentaries and short subjects.

Sample titles include: *Amadeus* (Milos Forman); *The Atomic Café* (Kevin Rafferty, Jayne Loader and Pierce Rafferty); *Faces of Women* (Désiré Ecaré); *The Funeral* (Juzo Itami); *A Great Wall* (Peter Wang); *Kiss of the Spider Woman* (Hector Babenco); *Law of Desire* (Pedro Almodóvar); *Liquid Sky* (Slava Tsukerman); *Marlene* (Maximilian Schell); *Men* (Doris Dörrie); *My Life As A Dog* (Lasse Hallstrom); *Police* (Maurice Pialat); *Rockers* (Theodoros Bafaloukos); *Rosa Luxemburg* (Margarethe von Trotta); *The Sacrifice* (Andrei Tarkovsky); *She's Gotta Have It* (Spike Lee); *Shoah* (Claude Lanzmann); *Sugar Cane Alley* (Euzhan Palcy); *El Sur* (Victor Erice); *Tampopo* (Juzo Itami); *Tasio* (Montxo Armendariz); and *Where the Heart Roams* (George Paul Csicsery).

Great directors. Films by Robert Bresson, Luis Buñuel, Rainer Werner Fassbinder, Jean-Luc Godard, Werner Herzog, Louis Malle, Ismael Merchant and James Ivory, Nagisa Oshima, Yasujiro Ozu, Ousmane Sembene, and Jean-Marie Straub and Danièle Huillet.

Africa and Australia. Includes films by Ababacar Samb, Sarah Maldoror, Paul Cox, David Bradbury and Fred Schepisi.

Belgium and France. Includes films by Chantal Akerman, François Truffaut, Joseph Losey, Jacques Rivette, Claude Chabrol, Maurice Pialat, Chris Marker, Jean Cocteau, Marcel Carné, René Clement and Alain Resnais.

Eastern Europe. Includes films by Gyula Gazdag, Pál Gábor, Krzysztof Kieslowski, Wojciech Marczewski, Andrzej Wajda and Krzysztof Zanussi.

Germany. Films by R.W. Fassbinder, Werner Herzog, Jean-Marie Straub and Danièle Huillet, Volker Schlöndorff, Reinhard Hauff, Wim Wenders, Wolfgang Petersen, Christian Weisenborn and Erwin Keusch, Peter Handke, Helma Sanders-Brahms, S. M. Horowitz, Percy Adlon, Dieter Schidor, Margarethe von Trotta and Doris Dörrie.

Great Britain. Includes Malcolm Mowbray, Nicolas Roeg and Stephen Frears.

Italy. Includes Ermanno Olmi, Michelangelo Antonioni, Bernardo

Bertolucci, Federico Fellini, Giuseppe di Santis, Cesare Zavattini, Dino Risi, Alberto Lattuada, Francesco Maselli, Luchino Visconti, Mario Monicelli and Roberto Rossellini.

Japan. Films by directors Yoshimitsu Morita, Yoshishigue Yoshida, Kaizo Hayashi, Sogo Ishii, Kohei Oguri, Masashiro Shinoda and Kenji Mizoguchi.

Latin America. Includes films by Fernando Solanas and Octavio Getino, Antonio Eguino, Hector Babenco, Bruno Baretto, Leon Hirszman, Ana Carolina, Tizuka Tamasaki, Carlos Diegues, Patricio Guzman, Pastor Vega, Humberto Solas and Tomas Gutierrez Alea.

The Netherlands, Mexico and Switzerland. Includes films by Paul Verhoeven, Ruy Guerra and Alain Tanner.

United States. Films directed by Pamela Yates and Thomas Sigel, Richard Lerner and Lewis MacAdams, Leon Ichaso and Orlando Jiménez-Leal, Allan Francovich, the Mariposa Film Group, Errol Morris and Wayne Wang.
Size & Elements: Film: 35mm and 16mm (approx. 400 titles; release prints).
Cataloging: Published catalogs.
Access: Available for distribution and rental. Requests accepted by mail and telephone.
Rights: Apply for information.
Licensing: Apply for information.
Restrictions: None specified.
Viewing Facilities: None.
Duplication Facilities: None.

NEW YORK METRO

92ND STREET YOUNG MEN'S AND YOUNG WOMEN'S HEBREW ASSOCIATION ARCHIVES
1395 Lexington Avenue
New York, NY 10128
(212) 427-6000 (Ext. 542)

Steven W. Siegel (Archivist)

Contact: Steven W. Siegel (212/415-5544)
Services: Association archives. Film and videotape collection open to the public for research.
Description: History and program activities of the 92nd Street Y, which sponsors Jewish, educational, music, poetry and other cultural programs.
Size & Elements: Film: 16mm (amount unspecified). Videotape: 3/4" and VHS (amount unspecified).
Cataloging: None specified.
Access: Open to the public. Research fees not charged. Research requests accepted by mail, telephone and in person (by appointment only).
Rights: Apply for information.
Licensing: Apply for information.
Restrictions: None specified.
Viewing Facilities: Film and videotape (by appointment).
Duplication Facilities: None.

NEW YORK METRO

OCEAN EARTH CONSTRUCTION AND DEVELOPMENT CORPORATION
P.O. Box 1138, Canal Street Station
New York, NY 10013
(212) 473-6778
(212) 533-7053

Street address: 217 Bowery, New York, NY 10002

Peter Fend (President)

Contact: Peter Fend
Services: Videotape producer and distributor. Material possibly available for reuse, subject to restrictions.
Description: Videotapes derived from satellite monitoring of major world news sites. Imagery is originated by U.S., French and other civil satellites and covers multiple dates over time periods (1973-present). Videotapes include, among other elements: charts and maps, narration, roam and zoom through the sites and three-dimensional fly-through models. Primary areas covered include:

Iran-Iraq war zone. Pictures the mouth of the Tigris and Euphrates Rivers, the site of a vast Soviet-Iraqi civil engineering project.

Sirte and Benghazi, Libya. Imagery of the two primary Libyan coastal military installations.

Chernobyl. Multi-date comparisons showing changes at the nuclear accident site — and 100 miles up and downstream — from 1985, March and April 29, 1986 (the date of the accident), and May 8, 31, July and August 1986.

Soviet mobile-missile bases. Yur'ya, Kirov and Kopu. This material, produced as part of a project commissioned by Dutch television starting in 1985, establishes that citizens can verify — on television and in photos — key elements of arms-control agreements.

Soviet naval bases. Severomorsk, Murmansk, Polyarny. The largest single concentration of Soviet nuclear submarine and sea-launched missile power.

Video-monitored sites from Ocean Earth. Includes: Falkland Islands (1982), showing the invasion routes, and evidence of their chief economic resource, kelp; Beirut (1982), showing Israeli attack strategy, and long-term implications for urban breakdown in Beirut; San Francisco Bay pollution and infrastructure; Pamlico Sound pollution and fisheries; Mississippi Delta, showing outflow and multispectral analysis, with further studies of agricultural runoff upstream; and comparison of Peking and Washington.
Size & Elements: Videotape: format unspecified (30 videotapes, each up to 60 min.).
Cataloging: Shot lists.
Access: Available for distribution and possibly reuse. Research and screening fees charged in some cases. Research requests accepted by mail and telephone.
Rights: Some rights held to all material. Additional clearances may be necessary in some cases if material is to be reused.
Licensing: Available for licensing and reuse, subject to restrictions. License fees charged depending on client and market.
Restrictions: All material copyrighted by Ocean Earth and the originating space-data agencies; appropriate clearances may be necessary for reuse.
Viewing Facilities: Videotape (by appointment).
Duplication Facilities: None.

NEW YORK METRO

O.D.N. PRODUCTIONS, INC.
74 Varick Street, Room 304
New York, NY 10013
(212) 431-8923

Contact: Beth Wachter
Services: Nonprofit educational media producer and distributor. Educational films and videotapes available for rental and purchase.
Description: Founded in 1974, O.D.N. produces and distributes films and videotapes on sensitive and critical issues, including: AIDS, child sexual abuse, date rape, family violence and teenage pregnancy.

Titles include: *Sex, Drugs and AIDS; No Time Soon; In Due Time; The Party Game; The Date; Just One of the Boys; End of the Road; Time Out Series; My Husband Hit Me; In Need of Special Attention; No More Secrets; Talking Helps; A Touchy Subject; The Subject is: AIDS;* and *Dropping In...A Film about Dropping Out.*
Size & Elements: Film: 16mm. Videotape: 3/4" and 1/2". (Approx. 15 titles available).
Cataloging: Published catalog (available on request).
Access: Available for rental and purchase to schools, libraries, hospitals, universities, community groups, social service agencies and individuals.
Rights: All materials protected by copyright.
Licensing: Apply for information.
Restrictions: Permission for reproduction, duplication or transmission is required.
Viewing Facilities: None.
Duplication Facilities: None.
Related Materials: Audiocassettes, study guides and training materials.
Distributor: For preview and rental information contact Karol Media (800/526-4773).

NEW YORK METRO

THE OFFICE OF TIBET
107 East 31st Street, 4th Floor
New York, NY 10016
(212) 213-5010
Fax: (212) 779-9245

Contact: Tinley Nyandak
Services: Association. Film and videotape material maintained primarily for distribution and rental rather than for research or reuse.
Description: Films and videotapes relating to Tibet. Titles include: *The*

Religious Investiture of His Holiness the Dalai Lama (1958-59); *Requiem for a Faith; Tibetan Story* (1965); *Untitled Documentary of a German Expedition to Tibet in 1939; Raid Into Tibet; The OSS Mission to Tibet: 1942-1943; Tibetan Folk Dance Performances Parts I* and *II* (1975); *Tibetan Medicine* (1982); *Dalai Lama UCSC* (1979); and *Ocean of Wisdom*.

Size & Elements: Film: 16mm (8 titles). Videotape: 3/4" (13 titles); VHS (1 title).

Cataloging: Lists (available on request).

Access: Open to the public. Maintained for distribution and rental rather than for research or reuse. Research requests accepted by mail and telephone.

Rights: Full rights held to some material (full rights held to *Ocean of Wisdom*, distribution rights held to other titles). Additional clearances may be necessary in some cases if material is to be reused.

Licensing: Apply for information. License fees charged in some cases and depend on intended use and length of clip requested.

Restrictions: Restrictions may apply to licensing and reuse.

Viewing Facilities: None.

Duplication Facilities: None.

NEW YORK METRO

PALLADIUM ENTERTAINMENT INC.
444 Madison Avenue, 26th Floor
New York, NY 10022
(212) 355-7070
Fax: (212) 319-4829
Telex: 147088

Contact: Ginny Wood

Services: Distributor. Films and television programs available for distribution, licensing and reuse, subject to restrictions. Material not available to the public.

Description: Holds feature films, television movies, and television series episodes.

Titles include: *Lassie* (192 episodes); *Jeff's Collie* (143 episodes); *Timmy and Lassie* (199 episodes); *Lassie TV Movies* (15 feature films); *The Magic of Lassie; Lassie: The New Beginning* (feature film); *The Lone Ranger* (feature film); *The Lone Ranger* (182 episodes); *The Adventures of the Lone Ranger* (13 feature-length programs); *The Lone Ranger and the Lost City of Gold; Lone Ranger Cartoons* (26 programs); and *Sgt. Preston of the Yukon* (78 episodes).

Also available: *Deadly Harvest; Face of Fear; Goodbye Raggedy Ann; The Family Rico; Death of Innocence; The Migrants; Hunter; Crime Club; Dr. Max; America at the Movies; Aunt Mary; City in Fear; Coffee, Tea or Me?; Crisis in Mid-Air; Cutter's Trail; Escape; The Four Feathers; The Horror at 37,000 Feet; I Want to Keep My Baby; Mongo's Back in Town; Orphan Train; Something Evil; An American Christmas Carol; The Bushido Blade; Chu Chu and the Philly Flash; Daddy I Don't Like It Like This; Graduation Day; Legend of Walks Far Woman; Mother & Daughter; My Bodyguard; Nightmare; Seduction of Miss Leona; Thaddeus Rose and Eddie; That Lucky Touch; Travis Logan, D.A.; Visions of Death; Agatha; Consenting Adult;* and *When She Was Bad*.

Size & Elements: Film: format unspecified (over 60 titles).

Cataloging: Release sheets.

Access: Available for distribution, licensing and reuse, subject to restrictions. Research requests accepted by mail and telephone on a selective basis. Research fees charged.

Rights: Some rights held to all material.

Licensing: Available for licensing and reuse, subject to restrictions. License and usage fees charged.

Restrictions: Research and licensing requests considered on a case-by-case basis and subject to clearance and approval.

Viewing Facilities: None.

Duplication Facilities: None.

NEW YORK METRO

PAN AMERICAN AIRLINES FILM LIBRARY
c/o The Negative Matchers, Inc.
10 Prince Lane
Westbury, NY 11590
(212) 354-4180
(516) 334-0227

Jay Wander (President)

Contact: Jay Wander

Services: Stock footage sales library.

Description: The Library consists of three separate units.

Historic Aviation Library. Footage of historic commercial planes, including the Sikorsky Flying Boats; Pacific Clippers (China Clipper); Trans-Atlantic Clippers (Yankee Clipper); the first double-decked Stratocruisers; DC-6; and DC-7.

Current Aviation Library. Footage of current commercial planes, including DC-8, 707, 727, 747 and 747SP.

World Locations Library. Covers most European countries, including Germany, France, Italy, Spain, the Low Countries, Romania, the Soviet Union, Czechoslovakia and Yugoslavia. Also includes footage covering most of South America, the South Pacific, Australia, New Zealand, Hong Kong, Japan, the Philippines, India, Pakistan, Central America, Mexico and the Caribbean Islands.

Size & Elements: Apply for information.

Cataloging: Card catalogs; shot lists; dope sheets.

Access: Apply for information. Research requests accepted by mail and telephone.

Rights: Full rights held to all material. Additional clearances may be necessary in some cases if material is to be reused.

Licensing: Available for licensing and reuse. License fees charged in some cases.

Restrictions: None specified.

Viewing Facilities: None.

Duplication Facilities: None.

NEW YORK METRO

PAPER TIGER TELEVISION
339 Lafayette Street, Suite 6
New York, NY 10012
(212) 420-9045

Contacts: Simone Farkhondeh; Daniel Marcus

Services: Collective; media organization; videotape archives; distributor. Videotapes available for rental, purchase and cablecast.

Description: Founded in 1981 as an ad hoc group of producers in New York City, PTTV has grown into a 150-videotape collection of critiques of the mainstream media (television, newspapers, magazines, motion pictures, and advertisements) with the participation of a wide range of scholars, critics, journalists, artists, performers and activists. "In each videotape, a publication, television show or some aspect of the communications industry is critically examined, uncovering the media's social/political role and the constraints and assumptions that have shaped it as a media product. Although most people are cynical about the media and are aware of being manipulated, most are unaware of how this manipulation is worked out issue by issue, ad by ad. By going over a publication or other media product in detail, by examining how it is enmeshed in the transnational corporate world and by pointing out exactly how and why certain information appears, a good critical reading forms the basis of an increased awareness. It gives the reader/viewer a foothold in what is too often seen as the hegemonic power of the media message.

"If there is a specific look to the show it is handmade, comfortable, non-technocratic; a look that says friendly and low-budget. Humorous backdrops, interviews, skits and 'anti-commercials' of background information enhance the speaker's presentation, forming a cartoony collage that pokes fun at television conventions."

Mainstream U.S. publications. Programs include: *Eva Cockcroft reads* Artforum: *Art and Language and Money; Renee Tajima reads* Asian Images in American Film: *Charlie Chan Go Home!; Teresa Costa reads* Biker Lifestyle: *What I Like About Biker Magazines; Harry Magdoff reads* Business Week; *Myrna Bain reads* Ebony: *Put Your Money Where Your Soul Is; Joan Braderman reads* The National Enquirer; *Sol Yurick reads* The New Criterion: *The Search for Quality After the Revolution; Stuart Ewen reads* The New York Post: *Fantasy, Morality and Authority; Noam Chomsky reads* The New York Times (2 videotapes); *Herb Schiller Reads* The New York Times (7 videotapes); *Varda Burstyn reads* Playboy: *Doing the Bunny-Hop the All-American Way; Joel Kovel reads* Psychology Today: *Technocracy/Consumerism/Psychology; Tuli Kupferberg reads* Rolling Stone: *Always Smile When You Give 'em the Shaft; David Avalos reads* The San Diego Union: *Border Crossing the News; Jill Macoska Dissects* Popular Science Magazines and Beyond: *Omni, Discover* and *Other Specimens; How to Marry a Millionaire: Tami Gold reads* Self-Help Booklets; *Ynestra King reads* Seventeen: *Selling the All-American Girl; Murray Bookchin reads* Time: *History as a Television Series; Patty Zimmerman reads* Variety; *Hooray for*

Hollywood?; Lauren Glenn-Davitian reads Fashions of the Times; *Gloria House reads* The Detroit Free Press; *Martha Rosler reads* Vogue: Wishing, Dreaming, Winning, Spending; *and Serafina Bathrick reads* Working Woman: Women in Grey Flannel Stifle Their Rage.

Foreign press. Titles include: *Michele Mattelart reads the Chilean Press Avant-Coup: "Every Day It Gets Harder to be a Good Housewife"; Michelle Gibbs reads* The Free West Indian: Inside Grenada; *and Sheila Rowbotham reads* The Star.

Television. Titles include: *Joel Kovel on the Shrinking of* AMERIKA: *a Psychoanalytic Interpretation of Anti-Communism; Joan Does* Dynasty, with Joan Braderman; *Sandinista TV; and* TV and Our Self Image: The Underseen Overweight, *produced by local critics in Lockport, New York.*

Film. Titles include: *Pearl Bowser Looks at Early Black Cinema: The Legacy of Oscar Micheaux; Richie Perez Watches* Fort Apache: The Bronx; and *Not Top Gun*, by Chip Lord.

Advertising. Titles include: *Kathleen Hulser Debones the Poultry Industry; Marc Crispin Miller reads Cigarette Ads: Lots More Ifs, Ands, and Butts!; and Judith Williamson Consumes Passionately in Southern California.*

Government policy and resistance. Titles include: *Ann Mari Buitrago reads Agents Names Censored by the U.S. Congress; Artist's Call to Central America: Lucy Lippard and Art for a Cause; Bill Boddy Reminds the FCC of the 1934 Communications Act; The Columbia Divestment Struggle: Paper Tiger at Mandela Hall; Thulani Davis asks Why Howard Beach?: Racial Violence and the Media; and The Trial of* Tilted Arc, with Richard Serra, other artists, politicians and community members.

Alternative media. Titles include: *Joel Kovel reads* Covert Action: A Salute to the Scourge of the CIA; Red Ink: Rebecca Zurier reads The Masses; *Paper Tiger Celebrates 100 Shows!!!; and Processed World reads* Processed World.

Other programs. Titles include: *Molly Kovel reads Kiddy Books: That Old German Classic — Der Struwwelpeter; Paper Tiger Scans The (Inter) National Audio/Video Fe$tival; Herb Schiller on The Selling of the New Technologies; Born to be Sold: Martha Rosler Reads the Strange Case of Baby M; and Nolan Bowie on High Tech Snooping: Government to Share Deadbeat List.*
Size & Elements: Videotape: 3/4" (masters); VHS (viewing copies). (152 titles; 400 videotapes total).
Cataloging: Card catalogs; published catalog; computerized cataloging for staff use only.
Access: Open to the public. Available for rental and purchase. Research fees not charged. Research requests accepted by mail, telephone and in person (by appointment only).
Rights: Apply for information.
Licensing: Available for broadcast or public access cablecast (license fees not charged).
Restrictions: None specified.
Viewing Facilities: Videotape (limited facilities; by appointment only).
Duplication Facilities: Videotape (3/4" and VHS).

NEW YORK METRO

PATHÉ PICTURES, INC.
161 West 54th Street
New York, NY 10019
(212) 247-4767
Fax: (212) 265-1956

Joseph P. Smith (President)

Contact: Joseph P. Smith
Services: Film and videotape distributor; stock footage sales library.
Description: Popular music (1940s-50s). Three program series are available; *Snader Telescriptions, Showtime at the Apollo,* and *Showtime.*

Snader Telescriptions (approx. 1,100 clips, each 3-1/2 min.) were produced in the mid-1950s for distribution to local television stations, which then assembled these clips into localized variety shows. Genres and styles include country and western, male and female "pop" singers, folk, polka, combos and jazz. Includes performances by Nat King Cole, Mel Torme, Joe Turner, Herb Jeffries, Lanny Ross, Peggy Lee, Teresa Brewer, Connie Boswell, Martha Davis, Gale Storm, Bonnie Baker, June Christy, Sarah Vaughan, Tex Ritter, Bob Wills, Westle Tuttle, Tex Williams, the Cass County Boys, and Tennessee Ernie Ford.

Showtime at the Apollo (13 half-hour episodes) was produced in 1955 and features Black jazz, big band, rhythm and blues and comedy performers, including Count Basie, Nat King Cole, Duke Ellington, Lionel Hampton, and many more.

Showtime (13 half-hour episodes) was also produced in 1955 as a white counterpart to the *Showtime at the Apollo* series. This music and variety show, with Frank Fontaine as master of ceremonies, features White artists such as Peggy Lee, Mel Torme and Teresa Brewer.
Size & Elements: Film: 35mm and 16mm (approx. 1,500 titles; negatives and release prints). Videotape: 3/4" (many titles; masters and viewing copies).
Cataloging: Printed catalogs; release sheets.
Access: Available for duplication, licensing and reuse. Research fees generally not charged, although there is a service charge when prints are sent to prospective users. This charge can be credited against a purchase. Research requests accepted by mail and telephone.
Rights: Full rights held to some material. Additional clearances may be necessary in some cases if material is to be reused.
Licensing: Available for licensing and reuse. License and usage fees charged.
Restrictions: None specified.
Viewing Facilities: Videotape (3/4").
Duplication Facilities: None.

NEW YORK METRO

PENNEBAKER ASSOCIATES, INC.
21 West 86th Street
New York, NY 10024
(212) 496-9195
Fax: (212) 496-9197

D. A. Pennebaker (Director)

Contact: Frazer Pennebaker
Services: Film and videotape producer and distributor. Completed films available for rental and purchase; footage available for licensing and reuse on a case-by-case basis.
Description: Documentary films directed by Donn Alan Pennebaker and others.

Selected titles include: *Alice Cooper* (1969), on his first performance at the Toronto Rock and Roll Revival; *The Anatomy of Cindy Fink* (Richard Leacock, Patricia Jaffe and Paul Leaf, mid-1960s), a portrait of a 17-year-old girl undergoing her first jazz dance audition in a Greenwich Village studio; *Breaking It Up At the Museum* (1960), documenting Jean Tinguely's "self-constructing and self-destroying machine" (Homage to New York) destroying itself at the Museum of Modern Art; *Campaign Manager* (Richard Leacock and Noel E. Parmentel, Jr. 1964), on the grueling day-to-day activities of John Grenier, executive director of the Republican National Committee during the 1964 Goldwater presidential campaign; *Chiefs* (Richard Leacock and Noel E. Parmentel, Jr., 1968), a visit to a 1968 convention of police chiefs and their wives at Waikiki, with discussions of the Black Panthers, the Chicago Democratic Convention and the latest weaponry; *The Children's Theater of John Donahue* (1971); *Dancers in School* (1971), on professional dancers-in-residence working in public schools under the Artists-in-Schools program; *Daybreak Express* (1953), Pennebaker's first film, a subway ride on the last days of New York's Third Avenue "L" with music by Duke Ellington; *DeLorean* (D. A. Pennebaker and Chris Hegedus, 1981), an inside view of John DeLorean and team from the boardroom to the assembly line as they design and produce his stainless steel, gull-winged door dream car in Belfast, Northern Ireland; *Don't Look Back* (1966), a cinema verité study of Bob Dylan, his poetry, personality and philosophy during a concert tour of England in 1965; *Elliott Carter at Buffalo* (1980), on the making of a concert performance of Carter's *Double Concerto; The Energy War* (D. A. Pennebaker, Pat Powell and Chris Hegedus, 1979, 5 hours), on the 18-month congressional battle over President Carter's natural gas bill; *Happy Mother's Day* (Richard Leacock and Joyce Chopra, 1963), on how the birth of the Fischer quints affected their hometown (Aberdeen, S.D.) and above all, Mrs. Fischer; *Hickory Hill* (Richard Leacock with George Plimpton, 1968), on the annual spring pet show at the Robert F. Kennedy estate in Virginia, emceed by Art Buchwald; *Jingle Bells* (1964), in which Robert F. Kennedy, his family and Sammy Davis, Jr. celebrate Christmas 1964 with New York City school children; *Keep on Rockin'* (formerly *Sweet Toronto*, 1969), with Chuck Berry, Little Richard, Jerry Lee Lewis and Bo Diddley at the Toronto Rock and Roll Revival concert in 1969; *Krapp's Last Tape* (1971), a television version directed by Alan Schneider, with the late Jack McGowran; *Lambert & Co.* (1964), in which Dave Lambert auditions for RCA with his new quintet, just before his untimely death; *Monterey Pop* (1968), with Jimi Hendrix, Janis Joplin with Big Brother and the Holding Company, Otis Redding, Jefferson Airplane, Ravi Shankar, The Who, Country Joe and the Fish, Scott McKenzie, The Mamas and The Papas, Hugh Masekela, Canned Heat, Eric Burdon and the Animals; *One PM* (D. A. Pennebaker with Jean-Luc Godard and Richard Leacock, 1968),

Godard's never-completed *One American Movie (One AM)*, compiled with additional film notes by Pennebaker, with Rip Torn, Jefferson Airplane, LeRoi Jones, Tom Hayden and Eldridge Cleaver; *Opening in Moscow* (1959), impressions of Moscow and its citizens under the Khrushchev regime, centered around the opening of the 1959 American Exhibition; *Queen of Apollo* (Richard Leacock, 1970), showing a debutante at an exclusive New Orleans Mardi Gras ball on her big night; *Rainforest* (Richard Leacock and D. A. Pennebaker, 1968), on the premiere performance of Merce Cunningham's ballet with music by John Cage; *Rockaby* (D. A. Pennebaker and Chris Hegedus, 1982), based on a play by Samuel Beckett; *Stravinsky* (Richard Leacock and Rolf Lieberman, 1965); *Town Bloody Hall* (Chris Hegedus and D. A. Pennebaker, 1971), on the Great Debate on Women's Liberation at Town Hall, New York City, with Norman Mailer, Germaine Greer, Jill Johnston, Diana Trilling, Elizabeth Hartwick and Anatole Broyard; *Two American Audiences* (Mark Woodcock, 1968), a discussion between Jean-Luc Godard and New York University graduate students on filmmaking and politics, intercut with scenes from Godard's *La Chinoise;* and *You're Nobody Till Somebody Loves You* (1964), on the wedding of Timothy Leary, featuring hairdresser Monte Rock III.

Size & Elements: Film: 16mm (29 titles; release prints). Some titles available for theatrical booking in 35mm. Videotape (format and amount unspecified).
Cataloging: Published catalog sheets.
Access: Completed films available for rental and purchase; footage available for licensing and reuse on a case-by-case basis.
Rights: Full rights held to some material. Additional clearances may be necessary in some cases if material is to be reused.
Licensing: Available for licensing and reuse, subject to restrictions.
Restrictions: Requests for licensing and reuse considered on a case-by-case basis.
Viewing Facilities: None.
Duplication Facilities: None.

NEW YORK METRO

ALVIN H. PERLMUTTER, INC.
45 West 45th Street, 15th Floor
New York, NY 10036
(212) 221-6310
Fax: (212) 302-1854
Telex: 4945297 (AHP)

Alvin H. Perlmutter (President)

Contact: Nancy Pelz-Paget (Director of Special Projects)
Services: Television and videotape producer. Videotape collection maintained primarily for in-house use only. Some material possibly available for licensing and reuse, subject to rights availability and clearance.
Description: *Public affairs and cultural programs.* Television programs include: *Moyers: Report From Philadelphia,* 90 video-essays (each 3 min.) on the Constitutional Convention of 1787; *The Secret Government — A Bill Moyers Special; The World of Joseph Campbell; The Primal Mind; Native Land; America at Risk: A History of Consumer Protest; Cover Story; The Priceless Treasures of Dresden; On Loan from Russia; Consumer Reports Presents;* and *The Great American Dream Machine.*

Business and financial programs. Titles include: *Adam Smith's Money World; The Eagle and the Dragons: The U.S. and the Challenge of the Pacific Rim Nations; Thunder From the East: The U.S./Japan Trade Wars; The Newest Japanese Export: Money; Adam Smith and the New China: From Marx to Mastercard?; The Business of Glamour;* and *Money Matters.*

Health and medical programs. Titles include: *Speaking From the Heart,* commercials on prevention of heart disease; *Healthcost Journal; The Nutrition Minutes,* one-minute nutritional messages for commercial syndication; *MD Report/Medical Journal; Nurseweek; One Measure of Freedom — A History of Medicare;* and *Moodswings.*

Corporate and how-to videotapes. Programs include: *Family Computing; Sylvia Porter's Personal Finance; The Joy of Stocks: Forbes Guide to the Stock Market;* and *Callanetics, The Video.*

Also produces popular homevideos and sales and training productions.
Size & Elements: Videotape (format and amount unspecified).
Cataloging: None specified.
Access: Maintained primarily for in-house use. Research requests accepted by mail.
Rights: Some rights held to some material. Some material in the public domain. Additional clearances may be necessary in some cases if material is to be reused (e.g., music for commercial use).

Licensing: Available for licensing and reuse, subject to restrictions. License and usage fees charged.
Restrictions: Requests for licensing and reuse subject to rights availability, clearance and approval.
Viewing Facilities: Videotape (3/4").
Duplication Facilities: Videotape (3/4" and 1/2").

NEW YORK METRO

PETRIFIED FILMS, INC.
430 West 14th Street, Rooms 411 and 404
New York, NY 10014
(212) 242-5461
Fax: (212) 691-8347

Pierce Rafferty (President)
Margie Crimmins (Vice President)

Contacts: Robert Cates (Film Librarian); Lori Cheatle (Film Librarian); Michael O'Callaghan (Film Librarian); Marian Thatos (Still Photographic Librarian)
Services: Film and videotape stock footage sales library; still photograph archives.
Description: Collection features material shot specifically for use as "stock footage" in all its manifestations: travel footage, beauty shots, inserts, establishing shots, scenics, aerials, title backgrounds and process plates for rear projection. Although there are over 1,000 completed films in the library, the emphasis is on the single shot; holdings total over 150,000 separate rolls of stock material.

Holds coverage of major 20th century events but the majority of footage depicts daily life, culture, industry, transportation and fads, predominantly in the United States, with some foreign coverage.

The collection spans the period 1910s-present, with holdings strongest from 1950 to 1970. Recent acquisitions of current material include a collection of Betacam videotape footage (100 hours) and 35mm color time-lapse urban coverage.

The listing that follows is by no means complete, but does indicate the strengths of the library and the variety of subject areas covered.

Academy Awards (1950s-60s, 35mm, color and black and white). Includes: establishing shots of ceremony locations with crowds; closeups of Award marquees at Grauman's Chinese Theater and Pantages Theater; celebrities exiting limousines and moving through fans and press; reporters, film crews and paparazzi; police and ushers controlling the crowds; fans in the stands (including autograph-seeking teenagers); closeups and long shots of rotating searchlights and criss-crossing light beams over Hollywood; and miscellaneous social events connected with the Awards.

Acapulco, Mexico (primarily 1950s-60s, 35mm, color and black and white). Featuring aerials, high shots and general coverage of streets, plazas, swimming pools, beaches, houses, churches, markets and cantinas. Includes calypso singers, cliff divers, tourists and jai alai stadiums (interior and exterior views). Establishing shots of numerous hotels, restaurants, bars and nightclubs. Closeups of period neon signs and billboards.

Accidents. Includes automobile accidents (1950s-60s), with smashed and overturned cars, crash victims, ambulances, police and medical emergency personnel; staged scenes of "fender benders" and cars going over cliffs (1930s); demolition derby crashes and crack-ups. Railroad accidents include wrecks, both actual and staged. Air accidents include 35mm color footage of a "barnstorming" monoplane crashing at an air show (1950s); miniature model World War I biplanes colliding in midair; and numerous biplanes crash landing on decks of early U.S. Navy aircraft carriers (1920s). Footage of some shipwrecks is also held.

Advertising. Holds miscellaneous historical television commercials. Additional clearances may be necessary for reuse of this material. See also *Billboards; Neon; Nightclubs;* and *Signs.*

Aerials (various decades, primarily pre-1970, some current; 35mm and 16mm, color and black and white; Betacam videotape).

Urban and suburban aerials include miscellaneous coverage of major and minor cities, towns and suburbs (primarily U.S., some foreign). Locations include Honolulu, Las Vegas, Levittown, Los Angeles, Miami Beach, New York City, San Francisco, San Diego and Washington, D.C. Extensive Los Angeles aerial footage includes low-flying shots over major Hollywood studios and other landmarks (ca. 1935). Betacam aerials include New York City; Washington, D.C.; and Sydney, Australia.

Aerial views of land and ocean cover the Arctic, beaches, canyons (including the Grand Canyon), mountains, countrysides, deserts, farmland, jungles and oceans. See also *Aviation; Clouds;* and *New York City.*

Africa (primarily 35mm, black and white and some color). Footage shot during expeditions (1920s-30s), featuring tribal musicians, chiefs, warriors, dancers, nomads, river workers and wildlife. Footage of bush children listening to a Victrola on a table in a clearing. Also holds "B" movie-type footage of African villages with Hollywood "natives," explorers, rampaging lions, tigers and elephants. Color footage of wildlife. See also *Animals.*

Agriculture (1920s-70, some current). General coverage of farms and agricultural activity around the world, focusing on the United States (1950s-60s). Establishing shots of farm buildings, fields, animals, farmers and farm laborers (including migratory workers). Coverage ranges from small family farms to large corporate holdings.

Farm activities depicted include plowing, sowing, spraying of herbicides and insecticides, cropdusting, irrigation, harvesting, crating produce, milking cows and goats, herding and shearing sheep, judging livestock at county fairs, repairing farm equipment, gathering maple syrup and turpentine sap, planting and felling trees.

Numerous scenes of both handpicking and mechanized harvesting. Crops include wheat, corn (maize), rice, cotton, tobacco, oranges, sugar cane, pumpkins, grapes, coconuts, apples, peaches and pineapples.

Agricultural equipment, both historical and modern, from animal-drawn plows and carts to gasoline-powered combine harvesters, corn pickers, orchard sprayers, cultivators, disc plows, wheat threshers, hay bailers and tractors.

Current footage includes beauty shots and aerials of farmlands and vineyards in the "greenbelt" surrounding San Francisco (with scenes of encroaching urbanization); extensive recent footage of traditional farming methods and lifestyle of the Amish in Pennsylvania. See also *Amish.*

Foreign locations include Canada, England, France, Greece, Holland, India, Ireland, Mexico, Philippines, Spain, Switzerland and Trinidad.

AIDS (35mm, color). Represents footage of AIDS candlelight vigil near the White House (October 15, 1986); and extensive coverage of The Names Project quilt on the Mall, Washington, D.C. (October, 1987), including high down and wide shots of the entire quilt and the Reflecting Pool with demonstrators.

Airports (primarily 1950s-70, 35mm, color and black and white). Coverage of large and small airports worldwide, including interiors and exteriors of main terminals, passengers boarding and disembarking, takeoffs and landings by day and night, wind socks, ticket counters, baggage handlers, and a point-of-view shot of an airliner landing at Los Angeles International. Detailed period coverage of airports at Los Angeles, Miami and New York (Idlewild, renamed Kennedy, and La Guardia). Other U.S. airports covered include those in Honolulu, Las Vegas, San Francisco, Washington, D.C., St. Louis, Pittsburgh and New Orleans. Foreign airports include those serving Paris (Orly), Salzburg, Acapulco, Mazatlan, Rio de Janeiro, Sydney, Hong Kong, Bangkok and Tokyo. See also *Aviation.*

Ambulances. Both staged and actuality scenes of ambulances in action (primarily 1950s-60s). Includes runbys, accident pickups and hospital deliveries, and an ambulance chase scene through Hollywood (1940s). See also *Accidents.*

Amish (16mm, color). Recent footage of the Amish community in the U.S. Includes horse-drawn buggies, farming methods, auctions, cheese production and scenes contrasting the Amish lifestyle with that of modern America.

Amsterdam, Holland (1950s). Views of the harbor, canals, buildings, streets and airport.

Amusement parks (principally 1946-70, 35mm and some 16mm, color and black and white). Extensive coverage of U.S. amusement parks and county fairs, identified and unidentified, including day and night establishing shots and general atmosphere. Features rides of all types, including merry-go-rounds, Ferris wheels, parachute jumps, kiddie trains, bumper cars, and roller coasters (with point-of-view shots). Includes coverage of barkers and booths, concession stands, penny arcades, rifle ranges, cotton candy machines, wheels of fortune, haunted houses, fireworks, and swirling neon signs. Identifiable locations include Coney Island, Long Beach, Ocean Park, Pomona, Susanville and Whitney Park.

Also holds in-depth coverage (16mm, color and black and white) of performers at Atlantic City's Steel Pier (1930-52). Includes aerialists, vaudeville performers, animal acts, water stunts, clowns and backstage scenes. Additional clearances may be necessary in some cases if this footage is reused.

Anatomy. Closeups of eyes staring, blinking, darting and crying; faces expressing shock, horror and worry; feet stepping on car brakes and accelerator pedals, parading in rows, pacing back and forth, walking in crowds, staggering across the desert and tapping to a beat. Closeups of hands reaching for doorknobs and bells, dialing phones, voting, turning on light switches, televisions and radios; drumming, praying, bound by rope, being fingerprinted and pulling triggers. Numerous closeups of hands working in factories and offices, filing and typing. Includes bathing beauty, perfect back, bald head and "Muscle Beach" contests featuring the human form.

Animals (various decades, 35mm and 16mm, color and black and white; Betacam videotape). Miscellaneous stock shots of domesticated and wild animals, including some microphotography of bacteria and protozoa.

African animals include antelope, chimpanzees, elephants, hippopotamus, hyenas, gazelles, giraffes, gorillas, leopards, lions, monkeys, rhinoceros, tigers, and zebras in their natural habitat, in captivity and roaming through Hollywood sets.

Animal oddities include a dog performing with hula hoop before an all-animal audience; X-ray footage of animals eating; an Indian elephant tug-of-war; a kangaroo versus human boxing match; an elephant riding a tricycle; an elephant smoking a hookah; shark versus octopus combat; Western stunts with horses going over cliffs into water and down ravines; performing bears, seals and other circus acts; horses high-diving into water tank; poodles with bizarre hairdos; alligators down slides; little girl rides alligator; kangaroos on a golf course; and lions attacking natives.

Arctic animals include walruses; whales; polar bears; Eskimo hunting scenes (ca. 1930); dog sled teams handled by Eskimos and U.S. explorers; and closeups of dog teams in action.

Birds are represented by various stock shots, ranging from pigeons to eagles. Footage includes blue jays, buzzards, crows, doves, ducks, eagles, flamingos, geese, grouse, hawks, hummingbirds, love birds, mallards, ostriches, owls, pheasants, roosters (crowing), sea gulls, swans and pigeons. Exotic birds of Australia are covered on Betacam videotape.

Coverage of domestic animals, with footage of people and their pets over the years. Includes puppies and kittens in pet store windows, and establishing shots of a pet hospital (1950s).

Farm animals include cattle, cows, oxen, water buffalo and yaks; horses, donkeys and mules; sheep and goats; hogs, pigs, sows and their litters; dogs; chickens and roosters.

Insects and spiders include bees, butterflies, mosquitoes, spiders and tarantulae, ants and anthills.

Reptiles and amphibians include alligators, crocodiles, frogs, lizards, pythons and rattlesnakes. X-ray footage of a snake eating. Footage of a 1950s roadside attraction featuring "World's Largest Alligator." Closeups of teeming alligators. Some footage shows an alligator being shot and killed, then used for fake wrestling scenes.

Research footage shows animals in research laboratories and vivisection.

Underwater footage includes crabs, fish, moray eels, octopus, sea horses, sharks, sea turtles and squid. There are some beauty shots and "B" movie-type scenes. Locations include the Great Barrier Reef off Australia (Betacam videotape).

Western footage includes buffalo herds, stampedes; horses of all kinds, both wild and broken; wolves; coyotes; cattle drives and stampedes. See also *Westerns.*

Other mammals include bats, bears, bulls, cats, chipmunks, deer, desert rats, dolphins, elk, foxes, giant pandas, hogs, jaguars, kangaroos, koala bears, monkeys, orangutans, panthers, penguins, ponies, pumas, rats, rabbits, seals, skunks, sloths, squirrels, walruses, wapitis, whales and wolves. See also *Zoos.*

Animation (16mm, color and black and white). Primarily U.S. Government-sponsored animation stereotyping "the enemy" during the World War II and Cold War periods. Also holds animation promoting U.S. civil defense and illustrating the "Red Menace" (1950s-60s). Holds miscellaneous animation from NASA and educational films.

Anti-communism (16mm, black and white and some color). A wide range of newsreel and U.S. Government films relating to the threat of communism in the United States and abroad (1946-early 1960s). Includes speeches, loyalty day parades and the staged takeover of a U.S. town by actors portraying communists. See also *Animation.*

Appliances (primarily 1940s-60s, 35mm black and white, some color). Classic product shots; stereotypical housewives using vacuum cleaners, hair dryers, irons, toasters, sewing machines, freezers, refrigerators, dishwashers, washing machines, stoves and television sets; men and boys raiding the refrigerator, using lawn mowers and electric razors; factory scenes of appliances being produced in the United States and Mexico (1950s). See also *Communications; Telephone;* and *Television.*

Architecture (primarily 1950s-present, 35mm and 16mm, color and black and white). Exterior and interior views of buildings, mostly in the United States, some foreign (especially India and Australia, and tourist attractions in Europe). Includes a wide range of building types, from igloos and adobe huts to skyscrapers and corporate headquarters. Footage of various building elements, including details, fixtures, furniture, gardens and swimming pools. See also *Buildings.*

Arctic (various decades, 35mm, black and white and some color). Includes a collection of expedition footage (ca. 1930), with extensive coverage of Eskimo life, hunting, igloos, dog sled teams, ice floes, icebergs, whales and aerial views of Arctic landscapes. Color views of U.S. military cargo planes landing on ice and dropping supplies.

Asia (various decades, primarily 1950s-60s, 35mm and 16mm, color and black and white). Urban and rural locations, including Bali, Burma, Hong Kong, India, Japan, Korea, Nepal, Philippines, Polynesia, Singapore and Vietnam. Cities include Bangkok, Bombay, Calcutta, Hong Kong, Seoul, Singapore, Manila and Tokyo. Holds footage of Mount Everest expedition with Sherpas (1930s, 35mm, black and white); glaciers; Buddhist monasteries; lama dances; Thai temple with dancing girls; Bali and temples (1930s); ritual dance performances; gamelan orchestra; funeral procession; and burial of ashes at sea. See also *India*.

Astronomy (various decades, 35mm, black and white and color). Miscellaneous views of observatories and telescopes (1930s and 1950s), including interior shots of Mount Palomar observatory and an unidentified observatory in the Swiss Alps. Celestial objects include starfields, a simulated Earth spinning in space, asteroids zooming to camera, comets and planetary landings. See also *Moon;* and *Sun, sunrises and sunsets.*

Atlantic City, New Jersey (1930-50s). General coverage (1940s-50s) and excellent Steel Pier coverage (1930-52). See also *Amusement parks.*

Audiences (various decades, 35mm, color and black and white, some 16mm). Television and radio studio audiences, featuring reaction shots, laughter and applause. Also holds footage of audiences at nightclubs, dance contests, rock concerts and sporting events of all kinds. Includes an audience of children at a marionette show. See also *Crowds.*

Australia (current Betacam videotape). Extensive coverage of tourist attractions; urban nightlife; famous buildings; beaches; scenic locations; sports, including skiing, golf, Australian rules football, windsurfing, lawn bowling, indoor cricket, surfing and horse racing; skylines; beauty shots; sunrises and sunsets. Locations include Sydney, Melbourne, Brisbane, Perth, Fremantle, Canberra and the aboriginal sacred ground at Uluru (Ayers Rock). Scenic areas include the Blue Mountains, the Snowy Mountains and the Olgas Range. Coverage of large gold mining operations at Kalgoorlie and ghost mining towns at Coolgardie; major gardens in Sydney and Perth with exotic flowers; wildlife, including koala bears and kangaroos; and scenic views of the desolate outback.

Automobiles (early 1900s-present, primarily 1930s-70, 35mm and 16mm, color and black and white). Large collection of automobilia on film, covering classic car makes and models and footage relating to car culture. Covers design, production, marketing and enjoyment of the automobile. Beauty shots of cars, both stationary and moving, manufactured by Buick, Cadillac, Chevrolet, Chrysler, Dodge, Ford, La Salle, Nash, Oldsmobile, Packard, Pontiac, Studebaker and Stutz. Coverage of dozens of different models, including Edsels, Corvairs, Corvettes and Thunderbirds. Miscellaneous foreign cars include Rolls Royce and Volkswagen.

Footage includes families driving (1920s-60s, some current); American teenagers being served by carhops and cruising in their convertibles; accidents; advertising; border inspections (U.S.-Mexico); car chases; car crushers; convertibles; comedies; crashes; dealerships; demolition derbies; design; diners; drive-in theaters and restaurants; experimental vehicles; factories; freeways; freeway construction; garages; gas stations; Grand Prix racing; hot rods; jalopies; junkyards; parking lots; racing cars; roadside attractions; showrooms; signals and road signs; sports cars; street scenes; stunts; time-lapse traffic (1988); traffic jams; traffic lights; and used car lots.

Closeups of car parts include car radios, classic 1950s tailfins, hood ornaments, brakes and accelerators, license plates, rearview mirrors, steering wheels, tires and windshield wipers.

Other ground vehicles include agricultural vehicles; ambulances; bicycles; buses; double-decker buses (New York and London); dune buggies; dump trucks; fire trucks; hearses; limousines; military vehicles (tanks, armored cars, missile launchers, etc.); motorcycles; newspaper trucks; police cars; road construction vehicles; sanitation trucks; streetcars; snowplows; tractor-trailers; trucks and taxis.

Hundreds of car process plates of locations throughout the U.S. (and some cities worldwide) shot from the point of view of a rider in a moving car. These were originally created for feature films and used for background rear-screen projection to simulate (in a studio) the moving scenery outside the car. Today they provide an invaluable historical record of major cities, small towns and business districts whose appearances have long since changed.

Process plates include extensive coverage of many identifiable locations, especially in Los Angeles and New York City, but also Las Vegas, San Francisco (including a point-of-view shot over the Golden Gate Bridge), Washington, D.C., Boulder Dam, Santa Barbara (Calif.), Pasadena, Miami and Palm Springs. Overseas coverage includes London (Trafalgar Square and over the Thames); Darmstadt (Germany); Paris (past the Champs Elysées, the Opéra, the Madeleine, the Tuileries district, the Place de la Concorde and the Eiffel Tower); and Tokyo's Ginza.

Rural process plates feature farmlands, mountains, forests, prairies, deserts, ocean and harbor areas.

Automobile racing (various decades, 35mm, color and black and white). Grand Prix races (1960s and 1980s). Major and minor hot rod and jalopy races, including on-track point-of-view coverage. Organized drag races and associated track activity, including tinkering with engines and awarding of trophies. Midget car races, demolition derbies, soap box derbies, various crashes, spills and thrills.

Avalanches (35mm, black and white). Long shots of avalanches in the Rocky Mountains. Includes footage of skiers schussing below falling avalanche.

Aviation. Extensive collection of aviation footage from the first flimsy flying machines to the jets of the modern era. Coverage includes pioneer experimental craft, Wright Brothers and early European flights, World War I dogfights, the *Spirit of St. Louis,* early air-mail planes, the first round-the-world flight, gliders, monoplanes, biplanes, triplanes, racers, balloons, Zeppelins, ambulance planes, autogiros, air circuses, air races, barnstorming stunt planes, formation flying, *Flying Clippers* and other commercial seaplanes, military craft (from World War I through the Vietnam War), helicopters and various private and commercial aircraft (1920s-70). Collection includes takeoffs, landings and many ground-to-air and air-to-air shots of these craft over different landscapes in various kinds of weather. Also held is footage of rockets and fake flying saucers.

Stunts, air races and air shows (primarily 1930s-50s) include: civilian and military air shows, air races, air circuses and glider meets; numerous daredevil stalls, spins, belly rolls and loops (shot from the ground and air-to-air); barnstorming; intentional and accidental stunt plane crashes; parachute exhibitions, vapor trails and crazy flyers; planes taking off from automobile roofs; biplane-to-biplane rope ladder stunts, wing-walkers (1920s) and other daredevil aviation acts.

Commercial airliners include Douglas aircraft from DC-3s through DC-10s; Boeing planes from the 1947 Stratocruiser through the 727 series; and extensive coverage of the Lockheed Electra, Constellation and Super Constellation.

Identifiable airlines include Air France, American, Aramco, BOAC, Braniff, Capitol, Central, De Holland, Eastern, Iberia, Japan, Lufthansa, Mexicana, Mid-Continent, National, Northwestern, Pan American, Pax, Sabena, SAS, Seaboard, Slick Airways, Swissair, Trans Canada, TWA, United, Western and World Airways.

Substantial coverage of military aircraft from World War I to the Vietnam War era.

Extensive coverage of World War I planes in the air, in dogfights and on the ground (though there is some actuality footage, most is comprised of recreations shot 1920s-30s). Classic shots of early aviators in goggles and scarves shooting down enemy planes, including closeups of cockpits, grinning pilots, point-of-view shots through propeller and spinning down-to-earth shots with streaking cloud backgrounds. World War I observation balloons under attack by biplanes and in flames. Dozens of miniature World War I airplane model shots with spins, loops, flaming dives and crashes. Identifiable planes include Curtiss JN-4 (the "Jenny"), the RAF Se-5 fighter, and various Sopwith, Fokker, Spad and Nieuport craft.

Footage from between the wars includes in-depth air-to-air and ground-to-air coverage of pre-World War II fighters, bombers, reconnaissance aircraft and trainers (primarily U.S.), including takeoffs and landings, test-dives and formation flying. Identifiable planes include Boeing P-12, F-4 and B-4; Curtiss F-9; Grumman F-3; Curtiss Shrike; Curtiss Goshawk; Keystone B-4; Stearman reconnaissance planes; Douglas Devastator; Consolidated PBY Catalina; Fairey Gordons; and Avro Tutors. Many other planes have not yet been identified.

Strong coverage of World War II aircraft, including bombers, fighters, reconnaissance and transport planes, comprised primarily of takeoffs, landings and air-to-air beauty shots. Bombers include B-17, B-24, B-25, B-26 and B-29; Consolidated PBY Catalina; Grumman Avenger; Douglas Dauntless; and RAF twin-engine bombers. Fighters include P-38, P-39, P-40 and P-51; Vought Corsair; Grumman Hellcat; and others. Transports include C-47, C-54 and C-59. Combat footage from most theaters, with special emphasis on the war in the Pacific, including extensive aircraft carrier and island combat scenes, Japanese kamikaze attacks and captured Japanese footage of fighters, bombers and seaplanes. Luftwaffe gun camera scenes of Allied bombers being shot down over Europe. Edited films on the following subjects: aircraft identification, aircraft production, the Battle of Britain, the bombing of Hiroshima and Nagasaki, civil defense, pilot training and photo reconnaissance.

Post-World War II aircraft include bombers, such as B-29, B-36, B-47, B

402

50 and B-52; fighters, including Ryan Fireball, North American F-86 Sabre, F-100 Super Sabre (with rocket sled takeoff), Convair F-102 Delta Dagger, Lockheed F-104 Starfighter, McDonnell F-2H Banshee, F-3H Demon and F-101 Voodoo; transports and tankers, including C-47, C-69, C-97A, KB-50, C-119, C-124 Globemaster and C-130; and helicopters, from the 1940s through the Vietnam era.

For the Korean and Vietnam Wars, miscellaneous coverage of helicopters, fighters and bombers; footage of the first use of helicopters in combat (the Sikorsky, in Korea); napalm strikes, bombing runs and helicopter jungle canopy rescue scenes; and North Vietnamese anti-aircraft emplacements in action.

See also *Rockets and spacecraft.*

Babies. U.S. baby boomers in maternity wards, cribs and high chairs and taking their first steps (1940s-50s). Numerous shots of infants and babies playing, smiling, crying, screaming, feeding and drooling. Includes babies alone and with parents and nurses. See also *Birth.*

Backgrounds, wipes and montage devices (primarily 1930s-70, 35mm, color and black and white). Hundreds of rolls shot for background "out the window" process plates for trains, planes, stagecoaches, cars, boats and stationary points of view. The transportation plates frequently have side, front and rear perspectives. In addition, there are smoke wipes, streaking oil wipes, swish pans, calendar pages (flipping, receding into space and falling through space), streaking cloud backgrounds (for Superman-style travel), closeups of spinning train wheels and a vortex of swirling water. See also *Automobiles; Aviation;* and *Trains.*

Bangkok, Thailand (1950s, 35mm, color). Establishing shots of the city, canals, street scenes, rickshaws, temples, University of Bangkok and the airport.

Banks (1930s-present). Establishing shots of U.S. banks in large cities and small towns; generic signs for "People's Bank," "National Bank" and various specific banks; and customer transactions at drive-in tellers and interior tellers.

Bars. See *Nightclubs, restaurants and bars.*

Baseball. Miscellaneous sandlot, family, Little League and high-school games. Interior and exterior coverage of Candlestick Park, Ebbets Field, Dodger Stadium, Wrigley Field, Giants Stadium (New York), a Kansas City stadium and Yankee Stadium. Crowd coverage, reaction shots and ballpark atmosphere, including lines, ticket takers and souvenir vendors. Color coverage of President Truman enjoying a game. President Kennedy throwing out the first ball.

Basketball. Assorted 1950s-era games, with high-school cheerleaders, pom-pom girls and school bands; closeups of ball action on backboard and rim; and some college coverage.

Beaches and beach activity (1920s-present, 35mm and 16mm, color and black and white; Betacam videotape). Footage of beaches with and without people. Activities include surfing, wading, swimming, boating, building sand castles, sunbathing, volleyball, and riding in dune buggies. Footage of "Muscle Beach" at Venice, California (1940s-50s), with male and female handstand stunts; bathing beauty contests from different decades; and period aerials of Miami Beach and various California beaches. Locations include Hawaii, Miami, Chicago, Acapulco, Rio de Janeiro, the California coast and various beaches in Australia. See also *Surfing.*

Beauty salons. Views of manicures, hairstyling, women under old-fashioned hairdryers and closeups of hairspray being applied. Some exteriors.

Bells. Closeups of church bells ringing with clappers visible; long shots of bells in a variety of church steeples; and insert shots of prize-fight bells.

Beverly Hills, California (1950s-60s, 35mm, color and black and white). General coverage of palm-lined streets, homes and commercial establishments. Period views of the Beverly Hilton, the Brown Derby, the Chateau Marmont and the Beverly Wilshire Hotel. Includes car process plates of residential streets. See also *Los Angeles, California.*

Billboards (primarily 1950s). In major cities and along roads and highways.

Birth. Standard Obstetrical Routine (1937, 35mm), a film which chronicles hospital procedures for human birth and includes a birth sequence. Staged scenes of an anxious father in a waiting room (ca. 1948); parents with newborn babies; and nurses wheeling infants down corridors.

Blacks (35mm, color and black and white). Primarily shots of U.S. automobile workers (various decades); cotton and sugar cane field workers (1930s and 1950s); loggers and lumber mill workers (1950s); and dockworkers in New Orleans and other locations. Miscellaneous depictions of Black workers (1930s) in Civilian Conservation Corps (CCC) and Works Progress Administration (WPA) films. Incidental coverage of Blacks in major urban areas of the United States (1950s-60s) with views of pedestrians, shoppers and predominantly Black neighborhoods. Miscellaneous coverage of the Black Panthers, civil rights and antiwar activists (1960s-early 1970s). See also *Civil*

rights; and *Music.*

Boats (various decades, most 1950s-60s, 35mm and some 16mm, color and black and white; Betacam videotape). Includes craft being used for pleasure, sport, travel, trade and war; craft at anchor and moving on all types of bodies of water from bayous to the high seas; commercial freighters and passenger ships, including ocean liners departing, at sea and arriving at various ports; a large variety of recreational and commercial boats (1920s-60s); some launchings, shipwrecks and "B" movie-type pirate ships; various kinds of boat races; and mothballed fleet in San Diego (35mm color). Extensive coverage of squareriggers (ca. 1931).

Boat types include aircraft carriers, barges, battleships, cabin cruisers, canoes, catamarans, Coast Guard cutters, destroyers, dhows, dugouts, ferry boats, firefighting boats, freighters, gondolas, hydroplanes, ice boats, kayaks, liners, motor launches, lobster boats, oil tankers, outriggers, paddle-wheeled steamers, riverboats, rowboats, seaplanes, schooners, shrimp boats, speedboats, square riggers, tugboats, tuna clippers, water taxis, whaling ships and yachts. Weather conditions range from becalmed moonlit seas to gale-force storms and hurricanes. See also *Ports and harbors.*

Boston, Massachusetts (1950s, 35mm, color and black and white). Views of landmarks and tourist attractions, including Boston Common, Harvard University, Old North Church and produce vendors in the old Haymarket.

Bowling (some 1930s coverage, mostly 1950s-60s). Families and teenagers bowling; interior and exterior shots of bowling alleys; closeups of strikes and spares; and pins being reset by hand and automatically. Lawn bowling in Australia (Betacam videotape).

Boxing. General coverage of boxing rings and atmosphere, including fights, lights, fans, announcers and referees. Insert shot closeups of punches, punching bags, bells, knockouts and countdowns. Mass blindfolded boxing by hundreds of U.S. Marines in boot camp (1940s). Man boxing with kangaroo.

Boy Scouts. Holds *The Scoutmaster* (1930s), an educational film on the function of Scouting, structured as a "poetic ode." Sequences include lighting fire with sticks; first aid; and campfire camaraderie.

Bridges (primarily 1930s-70, 35mm and 16mm, color and black and white; Betacam videotape). Period views of many famous and lesser-known bridges, mostly U.S., some foreign; establishing shots, aerials and car process plates of major and minor spans; and strong holdings in color beauty shots of bridges in San Francisco and New York City (1950s-60s), featuring period skylines. Major spans include the Golden Gate Bridge and the Bay Bridge in San Francisco; the George Washington, Brooklyn and Manhattan Bridges in New York; the Ponte Vecchio in Florence; Tower Bridge in London; bridges over the Seine in Paris; and the Harbour Bridge, Sydney, Australia.

Buildings (various decades, primarily 1930s-70, 35mm, color and black and white). Extensive stock shots of famous and generic buildings; primarily exteriors with some interiors (day and night); including airports, apartments, art galleries, bakeries, banks, barns, breweries, bridges, bunkers, bus stations, camps, casinos, castles, churches, colleges, concert halls, courthouses, dams, diners, embassies, factories, farms, firehouses, gas stations, government buildings, grain elevators, gymnasiums, homes, hospitals, hotels, igloos, laboratories, libraries, lighthouses, mausoleums, monuments, mosques, motels, museums, nuclear power plants, observatories, offices, opera houses, palaces, paper mills, primitive dwellings of various kinds, prisons, pyramids, schools, skyscrapers, stadiums, stores, supermarkets, temples, theaters, train stations, U.S. state capitols, universities, warehouses, water mills, water towers and windmills. Includes some closeups of various architectural elements and details, such as elevators, chimneys and plumbing systems. Some of the above categories are listed separately. See also *Architecture; Churches; Construction; Dams;* and *Monuments.*

Bullfights. Spanish and Mexican bullfights with stadium atmosphere. Includes color coverage.

Buses and bus stations (various decades, primarily 1950s-60s). Bus runbys in both urban and rural settings. Period establishing shots of bus depots, especially in New York City and Los Angeles; also generic small town stations. Greyhound bus logos and signs. School bus interior; exteriors with children boarding, traveling in, and exiting from school buses.

Cabins. Isolated cabins, shacks and lodges in mountain locations, by rivers and surrounded by snow.

Canyons (primarily 1950s-60s, 35mm, color). Aerials, high-down shots and process plates of U.S. canyons, including Grand Canyon, Bryce Canyon and Topanga Canyon. Some tourist scenes with period cars and closeups of rock formations.

Carson City, Nevada. Mark Twain's house, the Capitol Building, courthouse, mines and scenes of the pioneer town.

Castles. In France (including the Loire Valley), Ireland (including Blarney Castle), England, Holland, Germany, Switzerland (in the upper Rhône Valley) and miscellaneous unidentified castles.

Celebrations and holidays (35mm, color and black and white). Various holidays, festivals and celebrations, including New Year's Eve, Mardi Gras, Easter, Independence Day, Thanksgiving, Halloween and Christmas. Coverage of birthdays, weddings and funerals; and religious rituals and celebrations from various cultures. Wide range of processions, parades, dancing, decorations, fireworks and general revelry worldwide.

Christmas scenes were shot primarily in New York and Los Angeles (1940s-50s). They include public Christmas decorations, street scenes with window displays, Christmas shoppers, large Santa Clauses, reindeer, and Rockefeller Center (New York City), its Christmas tree and ice-skating rink.

Strong coverage of Mardi Gras in New Orleans and Carnival in Rio de Janeiro (primarily 1940s-50s), with street dancing, floats, costume balls and wild nightclub activity.

See also *War* (for World War I and II victory celebrations); *Hippies; Parades;* and *Religion.*

Cemeteries and tombs (35mm, color and black and white; Betacam videotape). Includes well-known and unidentified cemeteries with tombstones, grave markers and crypts. Panoramic views of Arlington National Cemetery with closeups of specific graves (including those of President John F. Kennedy, President Harrison, Robert F. Kennedy and Pierre L'Enfant) and the Tomb of the Unknown Soldier with changing of the guard. New Orleans cemeteries, showing old and unusual crypts and tombstones. Miscellaneous cemeteries in Philadelphia, New York City and San Francisco; military graveyards in the Pacific, Korea and Europe; Grant's Tomb in New York City; extensive coverage of the Taj Mahal in India; the Tomb of the Unknown Soldier under the Arc de Triomphe in Paris; and the Pyramid of Giza, Egypt.

Cheerleaders and majorettes (various decades, 35mm and 16mm, color and black and white). Cheerleaders (male and female), exhorting crowds at U.S. sporting events (1950s-60s); majorettes practicing, performing and leading parades; and majorette school (1930s).

Chicago, Illinois (1918-70, primarily 1950s-60s). Skylines, high shots, harbor views and general coverage of streets, neighborhoods, tenements, commercial districts and the stockyards. Includes a central railroad station, the airport and elevated trains. Dozens of establishing shots of restaurants, nightclubs, bars, department stores and hotels, including nighttime neon shots.

Children (various decades). Alone and in groups; with parents and pets, eating, going to school, playing, on amusement park rides, in sandboxes, on paper routes, at Soap Box Derbies, at Little League baseball games, in Boy Scout camps, on picnics, road trips and family excursions. Variety of urban, suburban and beach locations. Emotions displayed in closeup reaction shots. Primarily U.S., some foreign. See also *Babies.*

Chinatowns (1930s-70s, 35mm, color and black and white; Betacam videotape). Extensive collection of Chinatown footage shot primarily in Los Angeles, San Francisco and New York City. Includes neon signs; pagodas; street activity; shops; restaurants; and Chinese New Year's parades, with floats, dragons and firecrackers.

Christmas. See *Celebrations and holidays.*

Churches (primarily 1950-70, 35mm, color and black and white; Betacam videotape). Primarily Christian churches, cathedrals, chapels and shrines; mostly exteriors, some interiors. Hundreds of typical small-town churches across the United States, including Spanish missions in California and Mexico, colonial churches in New England and Virginia and wedding chapels in Las Vegas. Christian denominations include Catholic, Episcopalian, Baptist, Greek Orthodox and Russian Orthodox. Some Jewish synagogues, Tibetan Buddhist monasteries and stupas, Japanese pagodas and Islamic mosques; and Buddhist temples in Thailand. Includes numerous scenes of people entering and leaving churches.

Identifiable churches and temples include: St. Peter's in the Vatican, Rome; Notre Dame in Paris; St. Patrick's Cathedral in New York City; West Arun Temple of Dawn in Bangkok, Thailand; Old Mission San Fernando Rey de España (California); Mormon Temple and Brigham Young statue in Salt Lake City, Utah; wedding chapels in Las Vegas with signs advertising prices; various missions on the Camino Real in California; various churches in Chicago, Boston, New Orleans, San Antonio, Santa Barbara and Hawaii; Grosse Pointe (Michigan) Memorial Church; a Methodist church in Franklin Village, Michigan; historic Bruton Episcopal Church in Williamsburg, Virginia; Chapel of the Holy Cross, Sedona, Arizona; St. Louis Cathedral in New Orleans; and various shrines in San Diego and elsewhere in California. See also *Bells;* and *Religion.*

Circuses (35mm and some 16mm, color and black and white). Establishing shots and general coverage of large and small U.S. circuses. Footage includes audiences, clowns, animal trainers, midgets, lions jumping through fire hoops, bears on bicycles, high-wire and trapeze acts, tightrope walkers, parades, acrobats, bareback riders, dancers, "Indians," girls on ropes, jugglers, vendors, ushers and closeups of animals being fed and groomed. Additional clearances

may be necessary in some cases if this material is to be reused. See also *Amusement parks.*

Cities (various decades, primarily 1950s-60s, 35mm, color and black and white; Betacam videotape). General coverage of major and minor cities and towns, largely U.S. but also worldwide. Footage includes aerials, high shots, skylines, process plate travel shots, main avenues and business districts, skid rows, nightlife, transportation systems; and famous and generic buildings and landmarks, including numerous bars, hotels, restaurants and nightclubs.

Includes identifiable footage of the following cities and towns (not a complete list; coverage ranges from single shots to extensive holdings), some of which are also listed alphabetically by city name with highlights noted: Acapulco (Mexico); Agra (India); Ajanta (India); Amsterdam; Ann Arbor (Mich.); Aspen (Colo.); Athens (Greece); Atlanta; Aurangabad (India); Baltimore (Md.); Beverly Hills (Calif.); Bakersfield (Calif.); Benares (India); Bombay (India); Boston; Brisbane (Australia); Brussels (Belgium); Buffalo; Cairo (Egypt); Calcutta (India); Canberra (Australia); Cannes (France); Carmel (Calif.); Carson City (Nev.); Chicago; Cincinnati; Cleveland; Colorado Springs; Dallas; Darmstadt (West Germany); Dayton (Ohio); Denver; Detroit; Dillon (S.C.); Duluth (Minn.); El Paso (Tex.); Fatepur Sikri (India); Flint (Mich.); Fort Lauderdale (Fla.); Fort Worth (Tex.); Frankfurt (Germany); Fremantle (Australia); Gardena (Calif.); Geneva (Utah); Gulmarg (Kashmir, India); Harrisburg (Pa.); Hartford (Conn.); Havana; Henderson (Tex.); Hibbing (Minn.); Holland (Mich.); Hong Kong; Honolulu; Houston; Jaipur (Rajastan, India); Kansas City (Mo.); Key West (Fla.); Khajaraho (India); Lexington (Ky.); Laguna Beach (Calif.); Las Vegas (Nev.); London; Los Angeles; Long Beach (Calif.); Manila (Philippines); Mazatlan (Mexico); Melbourne (Australia); Mexico City; Miami; Milford (Mich.); Minneapolis; Monaco; Monterey (Calif.); Munich; Muncie (Ind.); New Delhi (India); New Orleans; Newport Beach (Calif.); New York City; Niagara Falls (N.Y.); Oak Creek Canyon (old abandoned mining town in Western U.S.); Old Delhi (India); Palm Beach (Fla.); Palmdale (Calif.); Palm Springs (Calif.); Pasadena (Calif.); Paris; Perth (Australia); Philadelphia; Pittsburgh; Pontiac (Mich.); Port of Spain (Trinidad); Reno (Nev.); Richmond (Va.); Rio de Janeiro; Rochester (Mich.); Rochester (N.Y.); Rome; Sacramento (Calif.); St. Augustine (Fla.); St. Louis; St. Paul (Minn.); Salt Lake City; San Antonio (Tex.); San Diego (Calif.); Santa Fe (N.M.); San Francisco; San Juan Capistrano (Calif.); San Luis Obispo (Calif.); San Pedro (Calif.); Santa Ana (Calif.); Santa Barbara (Calif.); Santa Monica (Calif.); Sausalito (Calif.); Savannah (Ga.); Scranton (Pa.); Schenectady (N.Y.); Seattle (Wash.); Singapore; Sonora (Calif.); Spokane (Wash.); Srinagar (Kashmir, India); Stockholm; Sydney (Australia); Tokyo; Tulsa (Okla.); Udaipur (India); Varanasi (India); Venice (Calif.); Venice (Italy); Virginia City (Nev.); Washington (D.C.); Williamsburg (Va.); Wilmington (N.C.); Windsor (Ont.); and Yonkers (N.Y.).

Civil defense (16mm, color and black and white). Coverage of U.S. civil defense program (World War II-1960s). Includes nuclear bomb and fallout shelters; school air-raid drills, including the legendary *Duck and Cover* sequence; Geiger counters; emergency supplies; and test evacuations of cities.

Civil rights movement. U.S. newsreel coverage of marches at Selma and Montgomery (Alabama), New York City and other locations (1960s). The March on Washington (1963), with crowds and speakers including Dr. Martin Luther King. A protest for racial justice in Pasadena, California (1964).

Clocks and watches. A variety of stock shots, including alarm clocks, watches, clocks in towers and on school walls. Includes some views of internal mechanisms. Also holds sundials, hourglasses with flowing sand, cuckoo clocks, stopwatches and water clocks.

Clothes, costumes and jewelry. Clothing (mostly 20th-century American and European); period costumes, including Early American, Roman, and Egyptian; and miscellaneous jewelry, diamonds, decorations and medals. Miscellaneous coverage of Native American, Asian, North and South American traditional dress.

Clouds (1920s-70s, some current; 35mm, color and black and white). A substantial collection of real-time and time-lapse cloud footage, including both ground-to-air and air-to-air coverage. Clouds of all types, shapes and sizes; alone in the sky; over urban and rural landscapes; and over bodies of water ranging from tropical lagoons and stormy oceans to the icebergs of the Arctic sea. Air-to-air scenes showing planes flying in clouds; and dive background plates of streaking clouds (à la Superman). Extensive thunderstorm clouds, but lightning shots are studio-produced.

Coastlines (35mm, color and black and white; Betacam videotape). Coastlines with cliffs, rocks, bays, estuaries, beaches, coves and waves.

Identifiable Pacific Ocean locations include: the California coast (Marin Headlands, San Francisco Bay, Monterey, Carmel, Big Sur, Santa Barbara, Santa Monica, Los Angeles, Long Beach, Newport Beach, San Juan Capistrano, La Jolla and San Diego); the Pacific coast of Mexico (e.g., Tijuana and Acapulco); Waikiki Beach and Diamond Head on Oahu, Hawaii; hidden coves in the South Sea Islands; and coastlines in the Philippines, Korea, Japan, Brazil and Australia.

Atlantic Ocean locations include the cliffs of Dover, England; the coast of Maine; New York Harbor; and the East Coast of Florida around Miami and Key West. Caribbean coastlines include Cuba and Trinidad. Mediterranean locations include the Côte d'Azur (including Monaco and Cannes, France) and some coastlines in Italy and Greece. Also holds footage of frozen Arctic coastlines in Alaska and Canada.

Colleges. See *Schools, colleges and universities.*

Communications (various decades, 35mm, color and black and white). Wide range of stock shots, including: air-raid sirens, antennas, billboards, books, cameras, computers, theater screens, Gutenberg's printing press, newspaper headlines, juke boxes, Klieg lights, loudspeakers, magazines, megaphones, microphones, motion picture equipment, "on the air" signs, newspapers, newspaper presses, pamphlets, paparazzi, phonographs, photographs, photocopy machines, Pony Express, postal service, posters, printing presses, projectors, quill pens, radar, radar screens, radios, radio broadcasting equipment, record players, smoke signals, tape recorders, telegraphs, telephones, telephone switchboards, telephone poles and wires, teletype machines, television sets, television cameras and broadcast equipment, typewriters, Victrolas and walkie-talkies.

See also *Motion pictures; Newspapers; Postal service; Radar; Radio;* and *Television.*

Computers. Miscellaneous stock shots of computers (1940s-60s).

Construction (various decades). Footage includes construction of stadiums, dams, bridges, roads, highways, homes, skyscrapers and other buildings. Also site-surveying, tree and stump removal, terracing, grading, laying underground pipes and lines and carpentry work. Equipment includes concrete mixers, steam shovels and rollers, bulldozers, scrapers, graders, cranes, pneumatic drills and pile drivers. See also *Freeways.*

Consumerism (various decades, primarily 1930s-70, 35mm, color and black and white; Betacam videotape). Footage of Americans buying and utilizing products, especially automobiles and appliances, but also food, household goods, gasoline and clothing. Window shoppers and displays; Christmas shopping crowds; showroom scenes; fashion shows; supermarkets; department stores; checkout lines; vending machines; drive-in restaurants; and automobiles on display. See also *Stores.*

Courthouses (35mm, color and black and white). Primarily exterior views of identifiable and generic courthouses in towns and cities across the U.S. and in some foreign countries. Includes the U.S. Supreme Court building in Washington, D.C.

Countries (various decades, primarily 1950s-60s and 1980s, 35mm and 16mm, color and black and white; Betacam videotape). Includes footage of Argentina, Australia, Belgium, Brazil, Canada, Cuba, Egypt, England, France, Germany, Greece, Hawaii, Holland, Hong Kong, India, Indonesia, Ireland, Italy, Japan, Korea, Malaysia, Mexico, Monaco, Nepal, Singapore, the Soviet Union, Spain, Sweden, Switzerland, Thailand, Trinidad, the United States, Vatican City and Vietnam. Some footage of unidentified countries in Africa, Asia and South America.

Crime. See *Police; Prisons;* and *Juvenile delinquency.*

Crowds (various decades). At sporting events of all kinds, movie premieres, Academy Award ceremonies, beaches, circuses, demonstrations and on the street.

Dallas, Texas (primarily 1950s-60s). Establishing shots, skylines, government buildings, police, banks, clubs and hotels.

Dams. Establishing shots of various hydroelectric dams, including Baldwin Hill Dam, Bonneville Dam, Boulder Dam, Coolidge Dam and Tainter Dam. Includes aerial views of Bonneville Dam under construction. Miscellaneous high-tension wires, transformers and towers. For dam disasters, see *Floods.*

Dancing. Assorted dance footage (U.S. and foreign). Includes popular American dances such as the Charleston, foxtrot, jitterbug, twist, Watusi, country swing and Western square dances. Also includes Hawaiian hula, Irish jigs and Native American dances (North and South America); African tribal dances (1930s); Mardi Gras street dancing in Rio de Janeiro and New Orleans; native dancers in Bali and Thailand; flamenco dancers in Spain; California hippies dancing at a love-in; dancing at proms and weddings, in recreation rooms and ballrooms, at nightclubs and in juke joints. Some exterior views of burlesque and strip-tease joints and nightclubs that feature dancing. Neon signs flashing "Dance, Dance, Dance." See also *Music and musical instruments.*

Demolition. Miscellaneous scenes of building demolition. Includes views of cranes with closeups of steel balls hitting walls and post-demolition rubble.

Demonstrations (various decades, primarily 1960s-70s). Includes anti-nuclear, anti-war, anti-Soviet, anti-Castro, anti-communist, pro-United States (Loyalty Day), pro-ecology, pro-marijuana, pro-civil rights and pro-peace demonstrations. Anti-Vietnam War demonstrations in New Haven,

Connecticut; New York City; Berkeley, Los Angeles and Santa Barbara, California; Chicago; Washington, D.C.; and Fort Dix, New Jersey. Includes street battles, draft card burnings, civil disobedience, crowds marching with signs, tear gas, riot troops and motorcycle police. Extensive coverage of the campaign to shut down the Diablo Canyon nuclear power plant in California; including protesters arriving by sea, blockading of roads and nonviolence training groups. See also *Civil rights.*

Depression era. Coverage includes the Wall Street crash (1929); Hoovervilles and other shanty towns; the Bonus Army march on Washington, D.C.; soup lines, "Work Wanted" signs; and some footage of strikes and protests.

Deserts. Desert landscapes; some barren, others with yucca plants, sagebrush, cacti, tumbleweed, Joshua trees and sand dunes. Specific deserts include the Sahara, the Mojave and Death Valley. Footage of miscellaneous desert towns in Nevada, Arizona and California. Car, stagecoach and train process plates of deserts (including footage with no visible paved roads, telephone poles or wire fences; suitable for period pieces). Current Betacam coverage of the Australian outback, including Uluru (Ayers Rock).

Detroit, Michigan (1920s-60s). Collection of footage covering the city and outlying residential areas. Establishing shots, skylines (including 1930s-50s), the harbor, buildings, factories, slums and streets. Identifiable locations include the Penobscot, Guardian and Buhl buildings; the Civic Center (during and after construction); the Ambassador Bridge; the Prime, Cadillac and Barnum Hotels; Dick de Graffe's Cocktail Lounge; the Burlesque and Michigan Theaters; the Carmel Hall marquee; the Ford Auditorium; the People's National Bank, Bank of Montreal and Bank of Nova Scotia; the Greyhound bus station; the City-County building; the municipal building; an old courthouse; a police station; crowds shopping on Woodward and Grand River Avenues; buses and street cars; and aerial views of Grand Circus Park.

Disasters. See *Accidents; Avalanches; Fires; Floods; Hurricanes;* and *Volcanoes.*

Drive-in restaurants (1950s). Exterior establishing shots with and without American teenagers and adults eating meals delivered by carhops.

Drive-in theaters (1950s-60s, 35mm, color and black and white). Primarily in the Los Angeles area. Day, dusk and night views of drive-in theater marquees and signs, cars at entrances and screens. Films advertised on marquees include *Psycho, Paths of Glory* and *Written on the Wind.* Pixillated night shot with freeway traffic streaming behind screen. Identifiable theaters include the Olympic, Gilmore, El Monte and Studio Drive-Ins.

Drugs (primarily 1960s, primarily 1" videotape). Pro-marijuana demonstrations; people smoking marijuana; Haight-Ashbury street scenes; closeups of marijuana plants; and a 1968 love-in (35mm, color). An Indian elephant smoking a hookah.

Dust storms. In desert and rural locations.

Egypt (various decades, primarily 1950s). Miscellaneous stock shots of the Sphinx, the Pyramids and the Nile River.

Electricity. General coverage of hydroelectric dams, nuclear and fossil fuel electrical power plants, generators, power transmission lines, dynamos, wires and plugs. "Mad scientist's" electrical contraption with high-voltage sparks and smoke. Electrical appliances of all kinds. Fake lightning bolts. Dramatizations of Thomas A. Edison in his laboratory. See also *Appliances; Dams;* and *Nuclear energy.*

El Paso, Texas. Street scenes, the town plaza and the Hilton Hotel.

Embassies (current footage, Betacam videotape). Coverage of embassies in Washington, D.C.; including those of Australia, Canada, Holland, Pakistan, the Philippines, Peru and Trinidad. Footage features architectural details, national flags and miscellaneous statues.

England (primarily 1950s-60s, 35mm, color and black and white). Primarily London, but also countryside views, country mansions, various train stations, and the cliffs of Dover. See also *London, England.*

Equestrian events. Footage shot at the 1932 Olympics in Los Angeles. Miscellaneous horse shows (1920s).

Erotica. Miscellaneous "smokers" and nudie shorts from the 1930s, including one with a Western theme.

Europe (various decades, 35mm and 16mm, color and black and white). Aerials, establishing shots and general coverage of urban centers and rural landscapes in Belgium, England, France, Greece, Germany, Holland, Ireland, Italy, Monaco, Spain, Sweden, Switzerland and the Vatican. See also *Cities; Churches; Monuments; Palaces;* and some specific cities and countries by name.

Explosions (16mm, black and white). Buildings exploding and collapsing; towers toppling; church mission steeple falling.

Factories (various decades, primarily 1930s-70, 35mm, color and black and white). Establishing shots, interiors and exteriors of factories, especially those producing automobiles, car parts and steel. Numerous views of workers entering and leaving plants; assembly line action; conveyor belts; and inspection of finished products. Types of factories include steel mills (with interior views of foundries, forges, coke ovens, vats of liquid metal and steel being rolled); beer bottling (U.S. and Mexico, 1940s-50s); on- and offshore oil rigs and refineries; lumber mills; sash and door mills; old and modern mills for grain, flour, sorghum and sugar; and factories for the production of automobiles, aircraft, electronics, jet engines, corrugated pipe, vending machines, newsprint, chemical fertilizers, ceramics, home appliances, paint, greeting cards, sugar cane and pineapple products. Identifiable factories include DuPont, Ford, Hughes, Goodyear, National Cash Register, National Carbon Company, Frigidaire, Fisher Body, General Motors and U.S. Steel. Identifiable locations include New York City, Detroit, Pittsburgh, Connecticut, Maine, Hawaii, New England, San Francisco and Kansas City, Missouri (not a total list).

Fads (various decades, 16mm, black and white). General coverage of twentieth century fads, including marathon dancing, flagpole sitting, yo-yos, jigsaw puzzles, hand-painted stockings, hula hoops, telephone booth and car stuffing, fatness competitions, baldness contests, outlandish hairdos, his-and-hers clothing and miniskirts. See also *Dancing.*

Farms (35mm, color and black and white). Various farm types, including wheat farms, vegetable farms, vineyards, orchards, cattle ranches, dude ranches and stud farms, forestries, coffee plantations, sugar cane fields, rice paddies and old rundown farms. See also *Agriculture.*

Fashion shows (various decades, primarily 1950s-60s). Variety of fashion shows displaying designers' wares and oddball fashions, including bizarre hats and sunglasses, fishnet mod dresses, "his and her" matching outfits, and period swimsuits.

Fields (35mm and 16mm, color). Establishing and beauty shots of meadows, prairies, pastures, cornfields, orchards, gardens, vegetable fields, pumpkin patches, pepper fields, corrals, vineyards, paddy fields and ranch grazing lands; irrigation ditches, furrows, and closeups of plowed earth; rolling fields of young corn; grain waving in the breeze; and haystacks.

Fires and firefighting (various decades, primarily 1950s-60s, 35mm and 16mm, color and black and white). Wide variety of homes and buildings on fire. Strong action coverage (1950s-60s) of firefighters and equipment in major and minor U.S. cities, especially New York, Los Angeles and Kansas City. Fire rescues (both staged and real). Numerous fire truck and ambulance runbys. Extensive color footage of oil refinery fires (primarily Signal Hill, California). Includes full-screen closeups of flames and billowing smoke. Miscellaneous forest and brush fires, including shacks and log cabins in flames. Forest firefighting by ground and by air, showing tree blasting for firebreaks and borate being dropped from planes. Fire created by military flamethrowers, napalm and hydrogen bombs. Numerous Western scenes featuring fires, including mobs with torches, flaming arrows; and burning teepees and forts. Fires and their aftermath in wartime include burning battleships in Pearl Harbor after the Japanese attack, Berlin after the Allied bombing in World War II (smoldering buildings, bucket brigades and rubble); Hiroshima and Nagasaki after the U.S. nuclear attack.

Fireworks (35mm, color and black and white). A variety of fireworks displays with and without ground visible. Single burst and superimposed layers of fireworks exploding.

Fishing. Recreational fishing in lakes, streams, rivers and the sea. Commercial fishing, including views of fishing fleets at sea and in harbors. Native fishermen in Trinidad and other foreign locations working with both nets and spears.

Flags (various decades, 35mm, color and black and white; Betacam videotape). Primarily U.S., some foreign. Includes flags atop ship masts, on buildings and embassies, in homes and offices, outside the United Nations building in New York, at half-mast and being lowered from flagpoles. Closeups of flags waving.

Floods (various decades, 35mm, color and black and white). Swollen and raging rivers; rampaging pack ice and ice floes; submerged streets; cars and homes; stranded people in canoes and rowboats; floating dead animals; and clean-up crews. Identifiable floods include the Connecticut flood (1936); the aftermath of the burst dam in Baldwin Hills (California), with destroyed homes and overturned cars; dike breaks in Holland, with flooded windmills and sandbags being stacked; and major Kansas City floods of the 1950s, with extensive cleanup and rescue operations depicted.

Flowers (35mm, color and black and white; Betacam videotape). Real-time and time-lapse footage, including sunflowers, cacti, tulips, roses, birds-of-paradise, daisies, gladiolas, poppies, gardenias, water lilies, irises, orchids and hothouse plants. Bees and butterflies pollinating flowers. Long shots of flowery meadows. Botanical gardens in Australia.

Food (various decades). Stock shots and newsreel stories focusing on the preparation and consumption of food. Period views of shopping in grocery

stores and supermarkets; cooking scenes in model "modern" kitchens of the 1940s and 1950s; Mom, Dad and the kids at breakfast, lunch and dinner; spaghetti-eating contests; waiter's races with tumbling food trays; and picnics and backyard barbecues. See also *Nightclubs, restaurants and bars.*

Football. High-school and college games and practices; also half-time activities, strutting majorettes and marching bands. Includes closeups of scoreboards, penalty flags and referees' signals. Interior and exterior views of stadiums across the U.S., both empty and full.

Fort Lauderdale, Florida. The Bay, homes, marinas, boats and bayous.

France (various decades, primarily 1950s-70; 35mm, color and black and white). Period views of the French Riviera. Travel shots through the French countryside. Small town and village scenes. Train stations and train runbys. For Paris coverage see *Paris, France.*

Freeways (1946-present, 35mm, color and black and white). Generic and identifiable U.S. freeways with light and bumper-to-bumper traffic (day and night views). Includes high-down shots, car runbys and moving point-of-view shots. Extensive coverage of freeway construction in California, Michigan and other, unidentifiable locations (1950s-60s). Numerous cloverleafs, on- and off-ramps and beauty shots of individual cars on freeways.

Gambling (primarily 1950s-60s, some current Betacam videotape of Australian casinos). Extensive coverage of gambling casinos in Las Vegas and Reno, Nevada. Includes slot machines, roulette wheels, neon, poker and crap games. Large collection of U.S. racetrack activity. See also *Horse racing; Las Vegas;* and *Reno.*

Gas stations (various decades, primarily 1950s-60s, 35mm and 16mm, color and black and white). Exterior views, with and without service activity. Period cars pulling in and out of stations. Interior scenes include auto body repairs.

Gay culture (35mm, 16mm and Video 8). Miscellaneous establishing shots of discos, bars and burlesque houses, primarily shot in New York City during the 1970s; men in drag at Mardi Gras (New Orleans, 1959); the 1987 march on Washington; various AIDS-related demonstrations (1987-88); and Gay Pride parades in San Francisco and New York City (1987-88). Represents footage of a candlelight vigil near the White House (October 15, 1986); and The Names Project quilt on the Mall in Washington, D.C. (1987).

Globes (35mm, color and black and white). Spinning and stationary Earth globes, appearing to be in "space" but actually shot in the studio, with surreal cloud and starfield backgrounds. Zooms into and pans over the continents.

Golf. Americans enjoying Ike's favorite sport; some tournaments; and establishing shots of various country clubs and courses across the U.S. Kangaroos on a golf course in Australia.

Graduation scenes. High-school and college graduation scenes with students and parents, award ceremonies, caps and gowns and diplomas being handed out. Includes West Point cadets celebrating with mass cap toss.

Havana, Cuba (1950s, 35mm and 16mm, color and black and white). Establishing shots of the city and harbor, buildings, streets, traffic and Old Havana, including musicians serenading on a veranda overlooking Morro Castle and the sea. Miscellaneous newsreel coverage of Castro and the revolution.

Haunted houses. Stock shots of houses and mansions chosen for their spooky exteriors.

Hippies (35mm and 16mm, color and black and white). 35mm color footage of a "love-in" in a Los Angeles Park (1968); views of "freaks" with tie-dyed clothes, beads and bangles; unidentified rock and roll band with wild dancing on-and off-stage. Also newsreel and other documentary coverage of hippies at concerts and other counterculture events (1960s-early 1970s).

Hollywood, California (various decades, primarily 1940s-70, 35mm and 16mm, color and black and white). Substantial collection documenting Hollywood streets, bars, restaurants, hotels and tourist attractions. Numerous process plate travel shots. Automobile chase through Hollywood streets. Dawn, day, dusk and night high shots. Movie premieres and Academy Award ceremonies with searchlights and crowds. Closeups of period neon signs. See also *Academy Awards; Motion Picture Studios;* and *Premieres.*

Homes. Establishing shots, interiors and exteriors of generic and identifiable types of homes from hovels to palaces, worldwide. Includes barrios, shanty towns, slums and a range of apartments and houses from the poverty-stricken to the palatial. Footage of American homes (1930s-70s) with and without their inhabitants. Some historical homes. Footage includes driveways, exterior views, gardens, aerials and swimming pools; and interior shots of entrances, living rooms, dining rooms, bedrooms, kitchens, bathrooms, laundry rooms, utility rooms, basements, attics and garages. Also holds footage of a two-story house being moved down a highway (1950s, 16mm, color).

Hong Kong (primarily 1950s, 35mm, color and black and white). Establishing shots of the city, the harbor and various buildings, street scenes with rickshaws and laborers. Kowloon waterfront with junks and other boats.

Kowloon Railroad Station and Hong Kong Airport scenes.

Honolulu, Hawaii (various decades, primarily 1950s-60s, 35mm, color and black and white). Aerials, establishing shots and general atmosphere. Includes coverage of hotels, nightclubs, old tropical homes, native huts, lanais, the airport, Chinese bazaars, the old town, a police station and a pineapple canning factory. Beach and harbor scenes with swimming, surfing and sailing. Hula dancers spelling out "Hawaii," greeting liner passengers and teaching overweight tourists how to dance. Harbor views, featuring ocean liner arrivals and departures. See also *Surfing.*

Horse racing and equestrian sports (primarily 1930s-60s). Extensive coverage of horse races at various major tracks in the U.S. Includes establishing shots and track atmosphere, with paddocks, starting gates, race action, finish lines, jockeys, winners' circle, grandstands and crowds. Miscellaneous polo matches, sulky races and steeplechases. For show jumping, see *Olympic games.*

Hospitals (various decades, primarily 1950s-60s). Wide selection of exterior establishing shots of large and small hospitals and sanitariums; some interiors of waiting rooms, corridors and operating rooms; nurses and doctors alone and with patients; and ambulance arrivals and departures. Closeups of individual hospital signs, and generic signs, including "Sanitarium," "Emergency" and "24 Hour Medical Service." Strong period coverage of Los Angeles and New York City hospitals. Other locations include New Orleans, San Diego, Miami, Montreal and San Francisco.

Houston, Texas (primarily 1940s-60s, 35mm, color and black and white). Includes oil industry (derricks and refineries), establishing shots, skylines, bridges, parks, a courthouse, warehouses and riverside shacks. Identifiable buildings include Farmer's Merchant Bank, Majestic Theater, Sam Houston Hotel, Hotel Cortez, Knight's Food Store and the Obelisk.

Hunting. Primarily game bird hunting, featuring hunters and dogs.

Hurricanes (35mm, black and white; 16mm, color). Florida hurricane stock footage, including palm trees bent to the ground, huge waves crashing over breakwalls and signs spinning. Includes footage of the U.S. East Coast hurricane (1938) and the Atlantic City hurricane (1962) with wreckage of the Steel Pier and coastline homes.

Ice skating (1950s, 35mm, color). Recreational ice skating at outdoor locations, including the Rockefeller Center rink in New York City. Miscellaneous ice shows and competitions.

India (various decades, some 35mm, color and black and white; mostly current Betacam videotape). Extensive collection documenting Indian daily life, religion and culture, with numerous views of cities, villages, methods of transportation and architecture. Animals depicted include camels, elephants, oxen, monkeys, buzzards, cobras and cows. Occupations include artisans; cotton workers; dancers (Hindu, Tibetan and Chinese); farmers; fishermen; merchants selling chai, spices, vegetables, peanuts, pottery and rugs; monks; musicians; pilgrims; puppeteers; sadhus; soldiers; snake charmers; tailors; children playing cricket; and old men smoking hookahs. Exterior and interior views of Buddhist, Hindu and Baha'i temples; palaces with gardens and lakes; stupas; ghats; mosques; ruined cities; hotels; stores; bazaars; graveyards; and ruins. Details of sculptures, bas-reliefs, erotic carvings, mosaics, frescoes and paintings.

Identifiable locations include Agra; Ajanta (including the caves); Aurangabad; Benares/Varanasi (with scenes of burning ghats and people bathing in the Ganges); Bombay (including beach and harbor scenes, India Gate, Victoria Station and the production of an Indian feature film); Calcutta; Ellora Caves; Fatepur Sikri; Jaipur; Kashmir; Khajaraho; New Delhi; Old Delhi; and Udaipur. Identifiable buildings and locations include the Taj Mahal in Agra; Qutab Tower, Humayun's Tomb, the Red Fort and Chadni Chook in Old Delhi; the erotic temples at Khajuraho; the Gandhi Memorial, the Parliament building, the Presidential Palace and India Gate in New Delhi; the Amber Palace, Palace of the Wind and the sundial at Jaipur in Rajasthan; the birthplace of Buddhism at Sarnath; and various palaces in Udaipur (exterior and interior views). Kashmiri footage includes Srinagar; Lake Nagin; street scenes; rug factory interior; exterior and interior views of houseboats; houses and villages in the Zaskar mountains; Gulmarg; winter scenes; people in traditional costumes; women with veils; barbers; butchers; shepherds; and people washing clothes in river, riding on horseback and making papier-maché handicrafts, rugs and woodcarvings.

Indians. See *Native Americans;and Westerns.*

Jai alai (1950s). Interior and exterior views of a jai alai stadium in Acapulco, Mexico.

Japan. See *Tokyo, Japan.*

Jungles. Stock shots of jungle locations in Africa, Hawaii and South America. Includes Hollywood "jungles" with wildlife and "natives."

Junkyards (1960s, 35mm, color and black and white). Full coverage of the operations of a large auto junkyard, showing: cars lifted by crane into crusher; closeups of crusher in operation; crushed cars on conveyors into freight train; and pan views and long shots of entire junkyard.

Juvenile delinquency (1950s). Staged scenes of juvenile delinquents stealing cars, mugging passersby and breaking bottles.

Key West, Florida. Includes 35mm color point-of-view travel shot across Key West Causeway and views of U.S. Naval Station.

Korean War. See *War.*

Lakes. Includes scenic shots of lakes with and without people. Recreational activity includes boating, swimming, water skiing and fishing. Identifiable lakes include Lake Arrowhead, Lake Mead, Lake Tahoe, Donner Lake, Mirror Lake, Lake Washington, the Salton Sea and some lakes in Yosemite and on the Rio Grande. Numerous unidentified ponds and lakes.

Landscapes (various decades, mostly 1940s-70, some current, 35mm and 16mm, color and black and white; Betacam videotape). World coverage, primarily U.S. Footage includes aerials, panoramic views, high shots, process plates and other footage (both moving and stationary) of generic and identifiable scenic locations. Current Betacam of Indian and Australian landscapes (including the outback).

Las Vegas, Nevada (1940s-70, 35mm, color and black and white). Extensive coverage. Aerials, high shots, process plates, and general views of neon-illuminated streets, gambling casinos, hotels, nightclubs and wedding chapels (including the "Little Church of the West"). Strong collection of famous and obscure neon signs over a 30-year period (mostly 35mm color). Footage includes: McCarran Field (airport) with "Welcome to Fabulous Las Vegas" sign; a streamliner at Las Vegas railroad station; convention center; television station; and the Las Vegas Country Club. Also coverage of rodeos; tourist attractions; the Western Day Parade with cowboys and stagecoaches; the Last Frontier Village; streetcars; and some sporting events, including the 1963 Las Vegas Golf Championships.

Identifiable casinos and nightspots include: Caesar's, Golden Nugget, Mint (including a "go-go" dancer on roof), Stardust, Silver Palace, Tropicana, Last Frontier, Flamingo, Desert Inn, Tower, Riviera, Fremont, Aladdin, Dunes, Four Queens, Motel 400 Imperial and Gaslight Hotels; the Moulin Rouge, Pussy Cat A Go Go, Horseshoe Casino, Bonanza, Town Club, Oxford Club, Al Maika and the Sahara.

Logging (various decades). Extensive coverage from the first cut through the milling process. See also *Trees.*

London, England (various decades, some period views; 35mm, color and black and white). Establishing shots and coverage of famous buildings and tourist attractions; street scenes with traffic, pedestrians, men in bowler hats, schoolboys, nannies with perambulators, red double-decker buses, fog, drizzle and rain. Identifiable landmarks include Buckingham Palace (with the Changing of the Guard), the Houses of Parliament, Westminster Abbey, the Tower of London, Big Ben, Thames river, Tower Bridge, Piccadilly Circus (with color neon), Oxford Street, Trafalgar Square, 10 Downing Street, Waterloo and Paddington Stations, Barclay's Bank, Grosvenor House, Scotland Yard, Nelson's Pillar and Heathrow Airport.

Los Angeles, California (this entry encompasses the metropolitan area, including Hollywood, Beverly Hills and Santa Monica) (some coverage 1910-40s, strong 1950s-70; 35mm, color and black and white). Extremely strong coverage of Los Angeles and outlying areas, including period aerials, process plate travel shots, skid rows, neighborhood views, streets and freeways; and famous and obscure nightclubs, bars, hotels, diners and restaurants (featuring neon signs). Establishing shots of television stations, motion picture studios and theaters (including drive-ins); sports stadiums and events; star-studded movie premieres and Academy Award nights; and Hollywood signs, sights, theaters and streets.

Identifiable areas include (partial list): Beverly Hills, Santa Monica, Hollywood, downtown Los Angeles, East Los Angeles, Venice, Watts, Sunset Strip and Bunker Hill. Numerous period process plate travel shots cover the commercial and residential areas and the various freeways of greater Los Angeles.

Low aerial views from the 1930s feature the Los Angeles Marina, Warner Brothers, Fox, Western and MGM Studios. 1950s and 1960s aerials cover the entire city with its landmark buildings, parks, freeways and its beach-studded coastline. High shots feature the skyline and shape of Los Angeles (1930s-70s).

Period establishing shots depict hundreds of famous and obscure Los Angeles buildings, including: Pan Pacific Auditorium, Civic Center, Hollywood Bowl, Griffith Park Observatory; Time, Capitol, Taft, American Airlines and *Los Angeles Times* buildings; and various schools, colleges, hospitals and prisons.

Hotels include: the Beverly Hilton, Statler, Hollywood, Chateau Marmont, Roosevelt, Chapman Park, Knickerbocker, Wilcox, Plantation, Gaylord, Belair, Miramar and the Beverly Wilshire. Restaurants, bars and clubs include: Perino's, Cinegrill, Seven Seas, Lindy's and Hody's restaurants; Leaping Liz's,

Jerry Lewis's, the Gold Cup, the Roaring Twenties, the Gay Nineties and Melody Lane; the Broadway, Ciro's and the Millionaire's Club; the Sinbad in Santa Monica; and, on Sunset Strip, establishing shots of various cafés and of Romanoff's, Scandia, Jack's, Largo and Dino's Clubs.

Signs include the famous "Hollywood" sign on the ridge; "Hollywood Bowl" neon; and restaurants, bars and clubs, including "Ciro's," "Cinegrill," "Macambo," "Earl Carroll's," "Crescendo," "Egyptian," "Roxie," "McGoo's," "Gold Cup," "Leaping Liz's," "Movie Land," "Dance Studio," "Melody Lane of Hollywood," "Players," "Follies," "El Rancho Burlesque" and "Strip City." See also *Academy Awards; Motion picture studios; Movie stars;* and *Schools, colleges and universities.*

Mardi Gras. See *Celebrations and holidays.*

Marquees. Numerous marquees of stage and motion picture theaters, including drive-ins and burlesque theaters.

Mexico (primarily 1950s-60s, 35mm, color and black and white). Strong collection covering Mexico City, Acapulco and Tijuana, with lesser coverage of Mazatlan, Xochimilco and other locations. Includes U.S. border scenes, bullfights, nightclubs, hotels, beaches, airports, industry, housing, daily life and musicians. See also *Acapulco;* and *Mexico City.*

Mexico City, Mexico (1950s-60s). Miscellaneous coverage of street scenes, parks, famous buildings and hotels. Includes a nightclub performance of the "Aztec Sacrificial Dance," featuring the staged "sacrifice" of a bare-breasted young woman; and establishing shots, buildings, the Presidential Palace, Avenue Juarez, streets, parks, people, traffic police, churches, theaters, a stadium, Xochimilco floating gardens, melon stands, a church wedding and an old mission.

Miami, Florida (1950s-60s). Strong coverage, including airport scenes, hotels, nightclubs, streets, beaches and aerial shots over Miami Beach and its hotels.

Mines and mining (primarily 1930s-50s). Establishing shots of mines; and coverage of miners entering shafts, drilling, blasting and operating huge power shovels. Types of mines include coal, copper, gold and iron; some stone quarries. Aerial shots of strip mining. See also *Australia.*

Monuments and memorials (35mm, color and black and white; Betacam videotape). Memorials, monuments and statues around the world. Includes current and historical coverage of memorials in the Washington, D.C., area, including: Jefferson and Lincoln Memorials; Tomb of the Unknown Soldier (with changing of the guard); the Kennedy Memorial and its eternal flame; the Iwo Jima Memorial; the Vietnam Veterans Memorial; and the Challenger Monument. Other memorials include the Arc de Triomphe in Paris and Mount Rushmore, South Dakota. Various war memorials in Australia honoring veterans of World War I and World War II, Korean and Vietnam Wars.

Moon (35mm, color and black and white). Beauty shots of the moon over urban, tropical and western settings; shots of moon alone in the sky; phases of the moon from crescent to full; and a wolf howling at the moon. Some "B" movie-type fake moon landings.

Monterey, California. Establishing shots, coastline, beach, town, streets, harbor and marina.

Motion pictures. See *Academy awards; Hollywood; Motion picture equipment; Motion picture studios* and *Premieres.*

Motion picture equipment. Closeups of cameras and projectors in operation. Miscellaneous sound and film editing equipment.

Motion picture studios (primarily 1950s-60s, 35mm, color and black and white). Period establishing shots of the Warner Brothers, Paramount, MGM, Universal, Four Star, Desilu and Selznick studios. Low aerials over Hollywood studios (ca. 1935). Includes footage of the 1967 fire at Universal Studios, with smoke, firefighters and smoldering ruins (including the European sets). Scenes of motion pictures being filmed and stuntmen warming up for action. Test proofs from *Gone With the Wind* (1939) that reveal the Cosgrove plate process (this footage available only after 1991 by agreement with copyright holder. Certain restrictions apply).

Motorcycles (various decades). Extensive coverage of motorcycle police. Some motorcycle stunts and dirt bike racing.

Mountains. Identifiable and generic mountain scenes, mostly in the Rocky Mountains; and some footage of the Alps and Himalayas. Identifiable summits include various peaks in Yellowstone and Yosemite National Parks, San Simeon, the California Sierras, Singing Hills, near Donner Pass, Grand Tetons, Canadian Rockies, the Cascade Range, Cedar Peaks and the Maricopa Mountains in Arizona. Alpine footage includes the Aiguille du Midi (Mont Blanc) and the Mer de Glace glacier in France, and the Matterhorn in Switzerland. Himalayan footage includes Mount Everest in Nepal. Scenes of trekking, mountain climbing, ski process plates and avalanches. See also *Australia.*

Movie stars (primarily 1950s-60s, 35mm, color and black and white). Closeups of numerous stars arriving at premieres and Academy Award

ceremonies. Includes Humphrey Bogart, Lauren Bacall, Julie Andrews, Audrey Hepburn, Jayne Mansfield, Angela Lansbury, George C. Scott, Steve McQueen, Ann-Margret, Sandra Dee, Ronald Reagan and many more. Also handprints and footprints of celebrities in front of Grauman's Chinese Theater in Hollywood, and Marcello Mastroianni in the act of sticking his feet into the wet cement.

Music and musical instruments (various decades, primarily 1940s-60s). Varied collection of music-related footage with miscellaneous country and western, rock and roll, jazz, brass bands, big band and Latin musicians. Includes musicians at Love-Ins; the Grateful Dead performing for the strikers at Columbia University (1968); newsreel coverage of Frank Sinatra, Duke Ellington, Art Tatum, Benny Goodman and the Beatles with screaming fans. Miscellaneous historical African, Cuban, Native American (North and South), Balinese, Indonesian, Mexican and Tibetan musicians. Some current Betacam videotape of Indian musicians.

Native Americans (1920s-60s). Coverage of village scenes, tribal dances, musicians, baking, weaving, basketmaking, sports (including lacrosse, tug-of-war and horse races with potatoes being scooped up by riders). A Wampanoag marriage ceremony. Other tribes depicted include Hopi, Navajo, Pueblo, Zuñi, Sioux and Yaquis. See also *Arctic; South and Central America;* and *Westerns.*

Neon (extensive coverage, various decades; 35mm, color and black and white). Hundreds of neon advertising signs and marquees in major cities, small towns and along roads (worldwide). Most footage covers New York, Las Vegas, Los Angeles, San Francisco, New Orleans and various Chinatowns. Foreign footage includes neon in London, Tokyo, Rome, Paris and Hong Kong (1950s). Process plates through neon-illuminated districts. Closeups and medium shots of specific signs. See also *Signs.*

New Orleans, Louisiana. Extensive footage of historic New Orleans, including establishing shots, period skylines, the French Quarter, old buildings with balconies and wrought-iron grillwork, cemeteries, waterfront scenes and dozens of jazz clubs, bars and hotels (exterior views only). Nighttime neon and scenes of Bourbon, Burgundy and Canal Streets are also featured. See also *Celebrations* for *Mardi Gras.*

Newspapers (various decades). Newspaper building interiors; printing presses in action; vendors and newsstands; boys selling newspapers on the street; closeups of headlines announcing major events of the 20th century; and spinning newspaper headlines.

New York City (various decades, primarily 1950s-60s and current, 35mm, color and black and white, 16mm, Betacam videotape). A major collection of footage documenting New York City life and structure. Includes aerials; high shots; process plates; skylines and general coverage of bridges, tunnels, airports, train stations, bus terminals, fire and police stations; famous and obscure buildings; and views of neighborhoods and commercial areas.

Commercial areas include: Orchard Street, Fulton Fish Market, South Street Seaport, Wall Street area and Fifth Avenue; and the diamond, garment and theater districts (including off-Broadway).

Manhattan neighborhood coverage includes: Upper West Side, Soho, Chinatown, Little Italy, Greenwich Village, Times Square, Upper East Side, Lower East Side and the Bowery. Minor period coverage of the other boroughs.

Greenwich Village locations include the Washington Square monument and park, sidewalk artists and ice cream vendors, as well as generic and identifiable sidewalk cafes, restaurants, bars, theaters, nightclubs and the Earle Hotel.

Brooklyn locations include Flatbush Avenue, the Municipal Building, warehouses, the Brooklyn Navy Yard, Brooklyn College, Brooklyn Public Library, Soldiers' and Sailors' Memorial and car process plates through residential areas.

Especially strong collection covering Times Square area (1928-present, primarily 1950s-60s and current). Extensive views of the streets, structure, stores, clubs and neon of this illuminated "crossroads of the world."

Aerials (1930s-60s) feature Manhattan, Brooklyn, Staten Island, New York harbor, and the Statue of Liberty. Aerial beauty shots of TWA Constellation over Manhattan. Aerials (current Betacam videotape) feature Ellis Island, Statue of Liberty, Verrazano-Narrows Bridge, Liberty Island, Financial District (bird's eye view); Greenwich Village, Central Park, Harlem, the Bronx, Yankee Stadium, United Nations Building, Hudson River and various landmark buildings. Manhattan aerials include views from 3,000 feet.

Skyline footage includes both period views (35mm color) and current Betacam videotape footage of Manhattan shot from New Jersey, Brooklyn and boats in the harbor. Some current time-lapse footage (35mm color) of the Manhattan skyline is held.

Period process plates (1950s-60s, 35mm, color and black and white) include Central Park; Fifth Avenue; Grand Central Terminal; Times Square; Pennsylvania Station; Wall Street; Broadway; George Washington Bridge;

Brooklyn Bridge; Triborough Bridge and the East River Drive.

Coverage includes period and/or current views of museums; corporate buildings; numerous bars, nightclubs, theaters and hotels. Tourist attractions include: Lincoln Center, Museum of Modern Art, Metropolitan Museum of Art, Museum of Broadcasting, Natural History Museum, Radio City Music Hall, Carnegie Hall, Rockefeller Center (with NBC tour and ice-skating rink), American Craft Museum, St. Patrick's Cathedral, Trinity Church, Intrepid Museum, World Trade Center, Trump Tower; Chrysler, Woolworth and Empire State Buildings, Grants Tomb, City Hall, etc.

Also held are establishing shots (primarily 1950s-60s) of federal and municipal buildings, hospitals, prisons, police precinct headquarters and courthouses.

Identifiable nightclubs include El Morocco, Embers, Stork Club, Moulin Rouge, Copacabana, Pendulum Club, Jimmy Ryan's, Sardi's, Diamond Jim's, Roseland Dance Hall, Golden Slipper, Brass Rail, Playland, Girls, Pigalle, 21 Club, Tango Palace and the "The Original Village Nut Club" (partial sign showing only).

Identifiable hotels include The Plaza, Waldorf-Astoria, Sherry-Netherland, St. Moritz, Astor, Holland, Barbizon Plaza, Victoria, Park Sheraton, George Washington, International, St. George, Commodore Vanderbilt, New Yorker, Taft, Penn View, the Earle and the Buckingham.

New York harbor footage includes views of the George Washington, Brooklyn and Manhattan Bridges; Governor's Island; Brooklyn Navy Yard; reflections of Manhattan in the water; also a variety of boats, barges, pleasure craft, ferries, tugs and liners, including the *Queen Mary* and the *Queen Elizabeth* docked, the *City of New York*, the *America* and the Staten Island Ferry (interior and exterior shots); and the Statue of Liberty.

Niagara Falls, New York (35mm and 16mm, color and black and white). Period skylines, street scenes and town hall. Numerous views of the waterfall. Includes shots of the *Maid of the Mist* tourist boat.

Nightclubs, restaurants and bars (1920s-70s, 35mm, color and black and white). Numerous generic exterior views and identifiable nightclubs, restaurants and bars; primarily U.S., some foreign. Long shots, medium shots and closeups of buildings, signs and windows. Interior views of nightclubs with celebrations in progress, chorus lines and bartenders in action (1930s-40s). For identifiable nightclubs and bars, see listing by city location. See also *New York City;* and *Los Angeles.*

Nuclear energy (35mm and 16mm, color and black and white). Completed films and stock shots chronicling the history of the U.S. atomic energy program. Includes period films of the often-overrated promise of atomic energy; stock footage of uranium and plutonium refining; radioactive waste disposal; and nuclear energy and/or weapons facilities including Oak Ridge (Tennessee); Shippingport (Pennsylvania); Rocky Flats (Colorado); Three Mile Island (Pennsylvania); and Diablo Canyon (California). See also *Demonstrations.*

Nuclear weapons (35mm and 16mm, color and black and white). Coverage of the history of the U.S. nuclear weapons program from Alamogordo to the Cuban missile crisis. Includes footage of the *Trinity* test (1945); the bombings of Hiroshima and Nagasaki; nuclear weapons tests in the Pacific Ocean and in the continental U.S.; radiation victims in the U.S., Marshall Islands and Japan; the U.S. civil defense program; bomb and fallout shelters; and numerous views of nuclear explosions.

Occupations (various decades). Footage documenting the full range of human labor. Categories include acrobats, aerialists, airplane pilots, architects, artists, bankers, bakers, ballerinas on stage, barbers, blacksmiths, brewers, bricklayers, barmaids, cab drivers, captains, carpenters, cash register operators, cavemen, chefs, city planners, clergy, clowns, coal miners, cooks, comedians, congresspeople, construction workers, cowboys, dancers, dentists, designers, dictators, ditchdiggers, divers, doctors, draftsmen, elevator attendants, explorers, factory workers, farmers, film cutters, film projectionists, firemen, fishermen, flower salesmen, fruit pickers, fashion models, fools, gangsters, garage attendants, gardeners, gas station attendants, glass blowers, housewives, ice cream salesmen, iron miners, laboratory technicians, librarians, lumberjacks, machinists, magicians, mailmen, mechanics, medical researchers, metermen, milkmen, miners, mountain climbers, musicians, newsboys, newspaper vendors, nuns, nurses, officers, office workers, oil drilling engineers and workers, painters, parachutists, photographers, plasterers, plumbers, policemen, priests (Catholic), printers, projectionists, prospectors, puppeteers, rabbis, radio announcers, radio operators, rickshaw drivers, sailors, salesmen, sculptors, seamstresses, secretaries, service station attendants, shepherds, shoemakers, soldiers, stagecoach drivers, steelworkers, stockbrokers, street peddlers, students, surgeons, surveyors, teachers, telegraph operators, telephone operators, thieves, tourists, traders, the unemployed, weavers, welders and woodcarvers.

Ocean liners (primarily 1950s-60s, 35mm, color and black and white).

Numerous views of ocean liners arriving, departing and at sea. Includes the *Queen Elizabeth, Queen Mary* and *Lurline.*

Oceans (35mm, color and black and white; Betacam videotape). Seen from shore, from the air, through portholes, from outriggers and from the decks of yachts and liners. Coverage of the Atlantic, Pacific, Arctic and Indian Oceans; the Mediterranean, China and Caribbean Seas; and the Bay of Bengal. Holds day and night shots, with sunrises, sunsets, moonlight and reflections.

Oddities (various decades). Wide range of human and animal oddities. See also *Animals.*

Offices and office buildings (1930s-70, 35mm, color and black and white). Primarily U.S. Establishing shots, interiors and exteriors of large and small office buildings. Includes interior shots of office activity: typing, phoning, filing, taking dictation, etc. A "gag" story showing the boss blowing smoke at a long-suffering secretary.

Oil industry (1930s-60s, 35mm, color and black and white). Establishing shots and closeups of on- and offshore oil rigs, with workers drilling and pumping. Footage of early oil fields and derricks in California, Oklahoma and Texas (includes aerials). Refineries, pipelines and oil fires. Numerous exterior and interior views of gasoline stations. Housewives using gas cookers. See also *Fires.*

Olympics (Los Angeles, 1932). Footage includes swimming, equestrian and track events; flags of different countries; the Olympic torch burning; scoreboards; grandstands; crowds; and identifiable winners. Signs: "Olympiad L.A. 1932," "Olympiad Athens 1896," and "Olympiad Berlin 1936."

Palaces. Buckingham Palace, London; the Palais des Elysées, Paris; the Doge's Palace and various lesser *palazzi* in Venice, Italy; and an unidentified Arab palace with golden cupolas.

Palm Beach, Florida (1950s, color and black and white). Establishing shots, harbor and street views, hotels and golf course.

Palm Springs, California. Aerials, Main Street views, golf course, pool scenes, homes, date farms and gas stations. Sign: "Palm Springs — 20,000 population." Numerous hotels, cafes and bars.

Parades (various decades, 35mm and 16mm, color and black and white). Extensive coverage of big city and small town parades, with floats, marching bands, musicians, majorettes, auto cavalcades and crowds. Parades celebrating holidays, sporting events and returned heroes. Specific parades include the Easter Parade (New York City); the Rose Parade (Pasadena); May Day (Moscow); Mardi Gras (New Orleans and Rio); Tulip Festival (Holland, Michigan); and miscellaneous ticker-tape parades, including those welcoming Amelia Earhart and General Douglas MacArthur.

Paris, France (various decades, some 1920s, mostly 1950s-60s, 35mm, color and black and white). Establishing shots, high shots, car process plates and views of most of the city's major landmarks. Includes numerous shots of cathedrals, churches, cafes and nightclubs. Process plates of the city shot from a moving elevator in the Eiffel Tower.

Streets and locations include panoramic high shots of the city (shot from the top of the Eiffel Tower); and rooftop and ground-level scenes, including the Champs Élysées, Place de la Concorde, the Tuileries, Rue du Faubourg St. Honoré, Avenue de l'Opéra, Ile St. Louis, various bridges and barges on the Seine, Montmartre (including artists and easels on the sidewalk), Place de l'Opéra, Trocadéro and the Madeleine, along with their respective statues and fountains.

Buildings include government buildings, monuments, museums, churches, bridges, apartments, hotels, cafés and nightclubs. Identifiable buildings include the Eiffel Tower (with process plate of an ascending elevator point of view over the rooftops), Arc de Triomphe, Notre Dame cathedral, Palais du Louvre, Hotel de Ville, Hotel Georges V, Hotel Royal Pigalle, Galeries Lafayette, Ministère des Finances, Sacré-Coeur, Conseil d'État, the American Express building, an Au Printemps department store and interiors and exteriors of the Gare de Lyon and the Gare St. Lazare.

Identifiable cafés and nightclubs include Café aux Deux Magots, Café de la Paix, Café du Palace and some unidentified sidewalk cafés on the Champs-Élysées; and various nightspots, including the Moulin Rouge, Charley's Bar, the Schéhérazade, Pigalle, Casino and Sphinx-Narcisse.

Parks (various decades). Large and small parks in cities and towns (mostly U.S., some around the world). Coverage of picnics, pigeon feeding and other typical park activities. Includes Central Park (New York City); Griffith Park (Los Angeles); Golden Gate Park (San Francisco); and numerous unidentified parks. National and state parks, forests and monuments include Yosemite, Yellowstone, Olympic, Cedar Breaks, Mt. Rushmore and the Petrified Forest.

Personalities (various decades). Miscellaneous coverage of politicians, presidents, heads of state, activists and entertainers. Includes celebrities at movie premieres and Academy Award ceremonies. Some dramatic portrayals of historical figures. Political personalities include Czar Nicholas, Kaiser Wilhelm, Emperor Franz Josef, Josef Stalin, the Shah of Iran, Prince Rainier and Princess Grace of Monaco, Indira Gandhi, Hideki Tojo, Benito Mussolini, Adolf Hitler, General Douglas MacArthur, J. Edgar Hoover, Martin Luther King, Queen Elizabeth, Jerry Rubin, Tom Hayden, Abbie Hoffman and Angela Davis.

U.S. presidents held include Theodore Roosevelt, Herbert Hoover, Franklin D. Roosevelt, Harry S Truman, Dwight D. Eisenhower, John F. Kennedy, Lyndon Baines Johnson and Richard M. Nixon.

Actors and actresses include Charlie Chaplin, Buster Keaton, Lillian Russell, Sandra Dee, Rock Hudson, Elizabeth Taylor, Douglas Fairbanks, Mary Pickford, Jerry Lewis, Bing Crosby and Bob Hope.

Other personalities include Andrew Carnegie, "Buffalo Bill" Cody, Enrico Caruso, Amelia Earhart, the Wright Brothers, Marie Curie, Thomas A. Edison, Babe Ruth and Margaret Bourke-White.

Philadelphia, Pennsylvania. Establishing shots, street scenes and process plates covering famous buildings, Independence Hall, Constitution Hall, City Hall, Philadelphia Art Museum, Liberty Bell and the homes of Betsy Ross and Benjamin Franklin.

Philippines (35mm and 16mm). Miscellaneous stock shots of Manila and countryside locations (1950s-60s). Some aerials, high shots and harbor views. Street scenes include rickshaws and period traffic.

Pocket billiards (primarily 1950s). Establishing shots of pool halls in Los Angeles and New York City. Some flashing "Pool" and "Snooker" neon signs. Closeups of trick shots.

Police (various decades, 35mm, color and black and white). Footage includes staged and actuality scenes of U.S. police pounding the beat, in squad cars and on horseback. Police directing traffic and at fires, roadblocks and accident scenes. Police chase scenes from the silent film era (Keystone Kops), the 1930s ("B" movie gangsters) and the 1950s. Closeups of the fingerprinting process.

Police oddities include a camera/gun that fires bullets and shoots film at the same time; FBI agents firing on a test-range "building" until it collapses; and hilarious Mexican police motorcycle stunts in a bullfight arena. Police buildings include identifiable and generic establishing shots of police stations in New York, Los Angeles, Chicago, Detroit, San Francisco, San Diego, La Jolla and Malibu (Los Angeles) and various small town stations across the U.S. There is some footage of foreign police (mostly directing traffic). Closeups of various "Police" and police station signs; interior shots with doors marked "Police"; and closeups of hands pulling callbox switches.

Police vehicles include police cars; paddy wagons; and motorcycles pulling out of stations, patrolling streets and freeways, waiting at curbside and speeding in pursuit of criminals.

Politics (various decades, 35mm and 16mm, color and black and white). Miscellaneous newsreel and documentary coverage of key events of the 20th century, including Prohibition, the Depression, wars, demonstrations, conventions, politicians, headlines, civil defense, the space race and others. See also *Anti-communism; Demonstrations; Personalities* and *War.*

Port of Spain, Trinidad (mostly 1950s). Street life and harbor atmosphere. Numerous views of local inhabitants and tourists. Includes the Hotel de Ville; and miscellaneous church, restaurant, patio and poolside locations.

Ports and harbors. Identifiable harbors and docks include those of Acapulco, Amsterdam, Balboa, Bangkok, Bombay, Calcutta, Catalina, Chicago, Havana, Hawaii, Hong Kong, Los Angeles, London, Long Beach, Newhaven (England), Newport Beach, New York, Perth, Polynesia, Rio de Janeiro, San Diego (with mothballed Navy fleet), San Francisco, San Pedro, Santa Barbara, Singapore, Stockholm, Sydney, Trinidad, Venice (Italy) and Washington D.C., as well as resorts on the Riviera in the South of France.

Footage includes scenes of buoys, docks, fishing villages, lighthouses, marinas, piers, sailors, stevedores, warehouses, wharfs and yacht clubs.

Postal service (various decades). Miscellaneous scenes of the U.S. Postal Service, including staged views of the Pony Express, actuality footage of early airmail planes, closeups of mailboxes with and without people depositing mail, exteriors of various post offices and postal employees on their rounds.

Premieres (primarily 1950s-60s, 35mm, color and black and white). Crowds and celebrities at movie premieres and Academy Awards ceremonies (1950s-60s). Includes the premieres of *Cleopatra, Giant, The Good Widow, The Great Race, The Robe, On The Beach, Ten Commandments, The Sound of Music* and *It's a Mad, Mad, Mad, Mad World.* Unidentifiable premieres and generic shots of crowds, ushers, film and television crews, paparazzi, Klieg lights and light beams criss-crossing in the sky. See also *Academy Awards.*

Presidents (U.S.). See *Personalities.*

Prisons (primarily 1950s-60s, 35mm, color and black and white). Establishing shots, exteriors and interiors of generic and identifiable United States prisons. Includes various state penitentiaries, county jails, honor farms, reformatories, an old New England stone jail and an adobe prison. Details include guard towers, barbed wire fences, cell windows and doors with bars,

cell blocks, sirens, and guards in towers and patrolling on walls. Prison signs include "State Penitentiary," "State Prison," "Honor Farm," "Sheriff's Honor Farm" and "New York State Property — Private." Interior scenes of prisoners marching en masse into the yard entering cells and mess halls. Identifiable locations in California include San Quentin and Alcatraz (San Francisco), Lincoln Heights Prison (Los Angeles), Folsom Penitentiary (Represa, California), Union Penitentiary, the Mojave County Jail and the Orange County Jail (Santa Ana, California). Also Yuma Territorial Prison (Yuma, Arizona), Joliet State Penitentiary (Joliet, Illinois), Sing Sing (Ossining, N.Y.) and the Tombs in New York City.

Process plates (35mm, color and black and white). Numerous moving and stationary process plates shot with a lock-down camera for rear projection for use as backgrounds. Includes backgrounds for automobiles, buses, stagecoaches, airplanes, trains, boats and skiing, featuring various locations worldwide (primarily U.S.). See also *Automobiles; Aviation; Backgrounds, wipes and montage devices; Clouds; Mountains;* and *Trains.*

Prohibition. Coverage includes scenes of raids on warehouses filled with illegal beer and liquor. Suds flow as axes smash barrels of illicit brew.

Propaganda. See *Anti-communism.*

Radar. Large and small military and scientific radar antennae, both turning and stationary. Radar scopes with blips.

Radio. Radios (1930s-60s) with and without people listening. Includes car radios, tabletop models, transistor sets, ham radios, walkie-talkies, portable radios in the battlefield and radios in aircraft. Exterior and interior views of radio stations with "On The Air" and "Quiet Please" signs and studio audiences. A variety of radio towers (1930s-50s). People listening to broadcasts: families, housewives, teenagers, workers, soldiers, and children, all in a variety of situations, with some dramatic reaction shots. Closeups of hands turning radios on and tuning dials. Radio station interiors (1931).

Rain and rainbows. Rain falling in urban, rural and jungle locations. Closeups of rain hitting the ground and falling on leaves. A background plate of rain falling. Some rainbows.

Religion (35mm and 16mm, color and black and white). Christian ceremonies of various denominations. Footage includes priests celebrating mass, rosaries, choirs, people going to confession, passing the collection plate, weddings, funerals, congregations, people kneeling, church bells ringing and candles being lit. Other subjects include the Muezzin calling the faithful to the mosque; a Tibetan Buddhist masked lama dance in a monastery near Mount Everest in Nepal; Balinese sacred dance performance with masked dancers and gamelan orchestra; an elaborate Balinese funeral procession with disposal of ashes at sea; and a Thai temple with dancing girls.

Religious artifacts include closeups of statues of Buddha, Jesus Christ, the Virgin Mary and various gods and goddesses from Asia; frescoes; Thangka paintings; stained glass windows; mandalas; icons; altars; pulpits; pews; confessionals; bells; crucifixes; Stars of David; candlesticks; cruets for water and wine; chalices; Bibles and other religious texts.

See also *Churches.*

Reno, Nevada (1950s-60s, 35mm, color and black and white). General coverage of the "Biggest Little City in the World," with establishing shots of casinos and hotels and period nighttime neon footage. Nightspots include Harrah's, Nevada Club, Horseshoe Club, Primadonna Casino, Harold's Club and Ground Cow; and signs, including one advertising "Free Nylons With Jackpot."

Rio de Janeiro, Brazil. Establishing shots, aerials, beach and street scenes, hotels and the airport. For Carnival scenes, see *Celebrations and holidays.*

Riots. See *Demonstrations.*

Rivers (various decades, 35mm, color and black and white, also Betacam videotape). Identifiable footage of the Nile, Ganges, Amazon, Mississippi, Volga, Rhône, Rhine, Loire, Tiber, Seine, Thames, Hudson, Rio Grande, Colorado, Potomac and New York's East River; Louisiana bayous; canals in Venice, Holland and Bangkok; majestic waterfalls at Yosemite, Potomac, Niagara Falls, and Multnomah Falls, Oregon; and streams, brooks, rapids, cascades, torrents and floods. Includes beauty shots; travel process plates; general coverage of recreational and commercial activity (including fishing and logging); and various craft, including paddleboats and steamers.

Robots (16mm, color). "Electro the Robot" performs at the New York World's Fair (1939-40); he walks, talks, counts and smokes a cigarette before an admiring crowd.

Rockets and spacecraft. Test footage from the German rocket factory at Peenemünde (World War II). Assembly of the (U.S.) V-2 rocket. Miscellaneous coverage of the U.S. space program. Various shots of launchings, misfires and explosions. Closeup of the X-15 being launched from a B-52. Interior of U.S. rocket factory. See also *UFOs.*

Rodeo (1930-70, 35mm, color and black and white). Bronco busting, steer roping, trick riding and parades; in small towns and at large state fairs.

Rome, Italy (primarily 1950s-60s, 35mm, color and black and white). Establishing shots, including the Vatican, St. Peter's, the Coliseum, the Piazza della Republica, the Spanish Steps, the Continental Hotel, the Ciampino Ovest airport, the Parliament building, the Castle of San Angelo and interiors and exteriors of the main railway station; piazzas, fountains, statues and ruins; and streets, traffic, streetcars, markets, buildings and neon signs.

Sacramento, California. The State Capitol building, main street and stores.

San Antonio, Texas. The Davy Crockett Monument and the Alamo Mission.

San Diego, California (1950s-60s, 35mm, color and black and white). Aerials and establishing shots of the shoreline, harbor and downtown area. Covers diners, cocktail lounges, the zoo, the "Mothball Fleet" and numerous buildings and homes. Period aerials include views of subdivisions, the harbor and business district.

San Francisco, California (1930s-present, 35mm, color and black and white). Extensive collection of footage of San Francisco and the Bay Area, including aerials, high shots, skylines and process plates. Coverage includes the Golden Gate and Bay Bridges, Golden Gate Park, harbor views, major buildings, skyscrapers, tourist attractions, all kinds of architecture, hotels, restaurants, nightclubs and Skid Row. Neighborhoods featured are Nob Hill, North Beach, Pacific Heights and Chinatown (including closeups of Chinese establishments and neon signs and a Chinese New Year Parade with dragons and fireworks). There is also coverage of the transportation system (airports, cable cars, trains and ferries) and footage of the 1939 Golden Gate International Exposition on Treasure Island.

Identifiable buildings include Coit Tower, the Shell Building, Cow Palace, the Courthouse and the Opera House, the Rescue Mission, a General Motors factory and the Legion of Honor building; the Golden Gate, San Francisco and Bay Bridges; the University of California, Berkeley; the Palace of Fine Arts and the Presidio; Alcatraz and San Quentin prisons; and the St. Francis Yacht Club.

Other locations include the Golden Gate Park, Market Street, the downtown business district and Haight-Ashbury; Treasure Island and Goat Island; Seal Rock, the Embarcadero, Fisherman's Wharf, the Marina, ferry boats and docks; Emperor Norton's statue; Tanforan racetrack, Golden Gate Fields Race Track, and a cemetery. Various scenes and process plates (including car chase shots) across the Golden Gate and around Sausalito.

Holds aerial footage of San Francisco and the Bay Area; flying over and under the Golden Gate Bridge, over the Bay Bridge, along rugged coastlines and over the harbor and its various islands, including Alcatraz Prison. See also *Drugs.*

Schools, colleges and universities (various decades, primarily 1950s-60s). General coverage of U.S. grade school, high-school and college students entering and leaving school, attending classes, playing sports and engaging in recreational activities. Numerous views of teachers and students in classrooms. High-school and college graduation scenes with caps, gowns and diplomas. Establishing shots of school buildings, campuses, libraries and fraternities. Includes some identifiable high schools (mostly in California) and many identifiable colleges and universities across the U.S. Also miscellaneous nursery schools, kindergartens, prep schools, boarding schools, orphanages, convents, Catholic schools and night schools.

Identifiable schools include the Little Red Schoolhouse in New York City; Beverly Hills High, Los Angeles High, Fairfax High, John Burroughs Junior High, Le Conte Junior High and Colfax Grammar School in California. Identifiable colleges and universities include Harvard; University of California, Los Angeles; Georgetown; University of Southern California; Northwestern; Stanford; Berkeley; Duke; California Institute of Technology; the Universities of Pennsylvania, Maryland, Oklahoma, Vermont, New Mexico, Virginia, North Carolina, Wisconsin and Hawaii; Arizona State University; Iowa State University; Michigan State University; Purdue University; Kansas University; Los Angeles City College; San Fernando State Junior College; Sul Ross State College (New Mexico); Tulane University; College of the Pacific; West Point; Rice Institute; McGill University; the University of Mexico; and the University of Bangkok.

Science. Primarily generic stock shots of unidentified laboratories filled with bubbling beakers, glass tubes and other scientific paraphernalia. Also holds footage of scientists and teachers at work on experiments, staring into microscopes.

Seattle, Washington. Establishing shots, skyline, bridges, freeways, downtown area, business district, Smith Tower and the totem pole in Pioneer Square. Extensive coverage of the Seattle Sea Fair (1949).

Sex roles (various decades). Men and women in stereotypical sex roles at work, home and play. See also *Homes;* and *Appliances.*

Signs (various decades, primarily 1950s-present, 35mm and some 16mm, color and black and white). Hundreds of famous and obscure signs, billboards and marquees promoting commercial establishments, including coffee shops, diners, hotels, restaurants, strip joints, bars, nightclubs, gambling casinos, roadside attractions, amusement parks, theaters, pawn shops and Skid Row missions. Closeups of classic product billboards (e.g., the Camel sign blowing smoke in Times square and the giant Pepsi-Cola bottle). Closeups of generic signs, both neon and painted: "Vacancy," "We Believe," "Money," "Massage," etc. Strong coverage of neon-illuminated commercial districts, especially Times Square, Las Vegas, Los Angeles and various Chinatowns in the U.S. Signs promoting specific cities and attractions, including the giant "Hollywood" sign, "Welcome to..." and city limit billboards. Company signs and logos on buildings and factories. Some sandwich boards and skywriting. See also *Neon.*

Sirens. Closeups of air-raid sirens (1950s-60s).

Skid rows and slums (primarily 1950s-60s, some current, 35mm and 16mm, color and black and white; also Betacam videotape). Street life, storefronts, bars, soup lines and rescue missions, mostly shot in New York City, Los Angeles, San Francisco and Chicago. Recent footage of New York's Lower East Side, with graffiti, homeless people and abandoned buildings. Videotape footage of homeless people on park benches near the White House in Washington, D.C. Also holds scenes of shantytowns and barrios in Rio de Janeiro and other Third World locations.

Skiing. See *Winter sports.*

Skylines (various decades, primarily 1950s-60s, some current, 35mm, color and black and white). Skyline views (day and night) of major and minor U.S. and some foreign cities. Extensive coverage of New York City, San Francisco and Los Angeles. Lesser coverage of Chicago, Dallas, Detroit, Houston, Miami, New Orleans and other cities. See also *New York City.*

Small towns, U.S.A. (various decades, primarily 1950-70, 35mm, color and black and white). Establishing shots, aerials, process plate run-throughs and high-down views of numerous small towns. Typical all-American main streets, gas stations, department and drugstores, post offices, churches, schoolhouses, courthouses, police stations, diners and parking lots. See also *Villages.*

Snow (35mm and 16mm, color and black and white). Generic and identifiable scenes of snow-blanketed mountains, plains, Arctic regions, rural landscapes, forests, farms, highways, cities, towns, villages, homes, cabins, lodges and igloos; airplane landings, horse-drawn sleds and Eskimo dog teams; avalanches, blizzards and snowdrifts; cars stalled, snowplows, pedestrians, snowball fights and skiers; winter sports in the U.S.A. (Rockies) and in St. Moritz and Zermatt (Swiss Alps); and a 1931 British expedition to Mount Everest (Himalayas). Includes 1940s studio shots of white snow on black background; and various scenes of Americans coping with snow, including stuck cars and spinning wheels. See also *Winter sports;* and *Avalanches.*

South America and Central America (35mm, color and black and white). Footage of various locations including the Amazon rain forest, Argentina, Cuba, Mexico, Trinidad and Brazil (including Carnival in Rio de Janeiro). Also holds footage of tribal people of the Amazon.

Sports. Organized, amateur and oddball sports of the 20th century, with special emphasis on the 1950s-60s. Includes establishing shots of sports stadiums and arenas (interior and exterior), crowd reaction shots and general coverage of Americans engaging in recreational sports. Some specific sports are listed by individual heading. See also *Water sports* and *Winter sports.*

Stadiums. Includes establishing shots of sports stadiums and arenas (interior and exterior), crowd reaction shots and general coverage of stadium activities.

Footage of baseball stadiums includes establishing shots, interior and exterior, of Candlestick Park, Ebbets Field, Dodger Stadium, Wrigley Field, the Polo Grounds (New York), a Kansas City stadium and Yankee Stadium. Coverage includes various crowd coverage and reaction shots and ball park atmosphere (e.g., lines, ticket takers and vendors). Football coverage includes various stadiums across the U.S., both empty and full. See also *Sports.*

Statues (35mm, color and black and white; also Betacam videotape). Statues in squares, parks and other locations, honoring heroes, religious and political figures. War memorials and statues honoring U.S. heroes, generals and fallen soldiers from the Revolutionary War through Vietnam. Famous statues include the Statue of Liberty in New York City; Christ of the Andes in Rio de Janeiro; statues at the Lincoln Memorial and the Iwo Jima Memorial; and the Vietnam Veterans Memorial in Washington, D.C. Also holds various religious and artistic statues and sculptures; Native American totem poles, and miscellaneous foreign statues, including the Sphinx in Egypt, and numerous Australian statues.

Stockholm, Sweden. High shots, the port area, docks, ferries, yachts, main street, Grande Hotel, trams and cafés and children playing in a housing project swimming pool.

Stores (various decades, 35mm, color and black and white). Primarily exterior views of a wide variety of commercial establishments. Interior shots of small shops and large department stores (1930s-60s). Includes shopping plazas and parking lots, shopping malls, supermarkets, department stores, showrooms, markets, bakeries, delicatessens, malt shops, florists, pharmacies, dry cleaners, laundromats, hairdressers, haberdasheries, beauty parlors, steam baths, dog grooming salons, art galleries, boutiques, newspaper stands, cabinetmakers, lumberyards, builders and general contractors, realtors, gas stations and a car wash. Also stores that sell groceries, liquor, drugs, shoes, clothing, sporting goods, jewelry, pets, books, antiques, furniture and pianos.

Streetcars, cable cars and trolleys (various decades, 35mm and 16mm, color and black and white). Primarily exterior views, some interiors. Locations include San Francisco (1905 and 1940s-60s); Los Angeles (1930s-40s); Detroit (1937); Chicago; Rome (1950s-60s); Paris (1960s); and Rio de Janeiro.

Stunts (various decades). Wide range of human and animal stunts, including car, plane, train, motorcycle and circus stunts. See also *Aviation, Animals* and *Fads.*

Suburbia (various decades, primarily 1950s-60s). Extensive collection of classic suburban views with numerous drive-bys and stationary shots featuring the streets and houses of the suburban United States. Footage includes archetypal nuclear families around the home; watering and mowing the lawn, washing the car, playing with the kids, hanging out laundry and enjoying backyard barbecues. Includes aerial views of Levittown (Long Island, N.Y.) and high-down shots of Daly City, California.

Sun, sunrises and sunsets (some current, mostly shot 1930s-70, 35mm, color and black and white). Various sunrises, sunsets and sun-in-sky shots. Sun over cities and landscapes, and sun alone in sky. Includes closeups of a hot, blazing sun.

Surfing (primarily 1950s-60s, 35mm, color and black and white; Betacam videotape, Australian). Hawaiian and Californian surfing. Includes side shots filmed from a moving outrigger off Diamond Head, Hawaii. Crowds watching surfing competitions and awards ceremonies.

Swamps. Miscellaneous swamps and bayous, mostly in Louisiana, with Spanish moss and mangroves.

Teenagers (various decades, especially 1940s-60s, 35mm and 16mm, color and black and white, primarily U.S.). Teenagers out for rides in convertibles; eating at drive-ins; watching football, baseball and basketball games; dancing in clubs; in classrooms and schoolyards; with families; engaging in sports activities; and cheerleading. Some footage is held of teenage gangs.

Telephones (various decades, 35mm and 16mm, color and black and white). A wide variety of telephone styles, from early to modern. Closeups of hands dialing; women operators and switchboards; pay phones; automobile phones (1950s); office workers and executives using phones; telephone wires and poles; and a montage of angry office workers slamming phones down.

Television (1940s-60s, primarily 16mm, color and black and white, some 35mm, black and white). Various stock shots of television sets, with and without people watching; primarily living room locations, with some shots in bars, studios, and classrooms. Shots of children and classic nuclear families staring at television sets. Closeups of dials being turned on and off. Television demonstration at the New York World's Fair (1939); television screen exploding in slow motion after being hit by swinging steel ball; television studio interiors with audiences and early cameras; and television antennas on homes and trailers. Establishing shots of television stations and studios (1950s-60s), including ABC, CBS, NBC and stations KTLA and KTTV (Los Angeles).

Theaters (various decades, primarily 1940s-70, 35mm, color and black and white). Mostly exteriors, with some interiors of U.S. stage and motion picture theaters. Includes drive-in theaters and burlesque houses; and miscellaneous marquees, box offices, ticket booths, lines and lobbies. There are scenes of people entering and exiting and closeups of tickets being taken by an usher. Many theaters are identifiable, especially in the Los Angeles and New York areas, including the Pantages, Grauman's Chinese, the Roxy, Winter Garden, Carnegie Hall and Radio City Music Hall.

Time-lapse (35mm, color). Includes a current collection of time-lapse footage shot in New York City (covering traffic, crowds of pedestrians, the Staten Island Ferry, dawn over Manhattan, Central Park, subway train runbys and much more); time-lapse clouds; and a large collection of time-lapse views of flowers blossoming. See also *Clouds;* and *Flowers.*

Tokyo, Japan (ca. 1957, 35mm, color and black and white). Establishing shots, high shots and street views with rickshaws, bicycle traffic, crowds, cars and workers. Numerous early neon signs. Shopping district with plazas and stores, including the Ginza. Various buildings, including the Imperial Palace, airport, Imperial Hotel, Takashima department store, Atago police station, Kokusai Kanko Hotel and miscellaneous pagodas and shrines. See also *War: World War II.*

Tourism and tourist attractions (various decades, primarily 1950s-60s, 35mm and 16mm, color and black and white; also Betacam videotape). Major and minor tourist attractions, both U.S. and foreign. Includes period views of such attractions as Niagara Falls, the Grand Canyon, Statue of Liberty, Empire State Building, Eiffel Tower, Piccadilly Circus, Mount Rushmore and Big Ben. Includes classic shots of American tourists on vacation in the U.S. and around the world. There is extensive current coverage of tourist attractions in Washington, D.C., New York City, Australia and India (including the Taj Mahal).

Traffic signals. Various traffic and pedestrian signs and signals. Includes closeups of "Walk" and "Dont Walk" signs from different decades.

Trains and train stations (1900-70, 35mm, color and black and white). Primarily U.S., some foreign. Freight and passenger trains, including vintage wooden, period steam, modern diesel and electric trains, as well as subways and streetcars. Hundreds of runbys, pit shots, beauty shots and numerous classic montage devices, including closeups of churning wheels, receding tracks and whistles blowing. Also holds catastrophic train wrecks, both real and staged; Western outlaw and Indian attacks; death-defying stunts from the silent era; and train personnel, porters and passengers.

Cut films include *New York Calling,* which celebrates the joys of the New York Central System (circa 1950); *Right of Way,* about U.S. train travel during World War II; and *The Great Train Robbery* and other early silent films.

Dozens of process plate "out the window" backgrounds covering period Western landscapes, postwar suburban and urban scenes and a broad variety of rural, desert, mountain and wilderness regions.

Identifiable and generic shots (interior and exterior) of railroad stations in big cities, small towns and remote locations worldwide. Especially strong coverage (primarily 1950s and 1960s) of major American stations, including New York City's Grand Central Terminal and Pennsylvania Station and stations in Los Angeles, San Francisco and Washington, D.C. Overseas coverage includes the Gare de Lyon and Gare St. Lazare in Paris; Waterloo and Marylebone stations in London; Vienna's Westbahnhof; the Stazione Termini in Rome; and stations in Frankfurt, Darmstadt, Hong Kong (Kowloon), Singapore and Tokyo.

Trees (35mm and 16mm, color and black and white). Various species of trees growing wild, cultivated, single, in stands, groves, orchards, woods, forests and jungles. Trees being planted; and being felled by atomic bomb blasts, burned in forest fires, chain-sawed, bulldozed, axed, dragged by elephants, climbed upon by snakes and monkeys, floated downriver, milled, stacked in lumberyards; and being turned into sawdust, pulp and cardboard. Includes extensive coverage of logging, lumber mills, forest management and roadbuilding.

Tropical islands (35mm, color and black and white). Footage of palm trees, idyllic lagoons, moonlit nights and village scenes. Includes the evacuation of natives from Bikini Atoll by the U.S. Army prior to the 1946 atomic bomb tests. See also *Havana, Cuba; Honolulu, Hawaii;* and *Trinidad.*

Tulsa, Oklahoma. Oil fields, oil refineries, courthouse, church and the Tulsa Hotel.

Unidentified flying objects (UFOs) (1950s, 35mm, black and white). "B" movie-style flying saucers flying in formation.

U.S. government buildings. Numerous stock shots of identifiable and generic U.S. government buildings, including state capitols, courthouses, post offices, county and municipal buildings. Extensive coverage of government buildings in Washington, D.C. See also *Washington, D.C.*

Vatican City (35mm, 1950s). Process plate travel shot past St. Peter's Basilica with the Vatican in the background. Miscellaneous newsreels of Papal processions.

Venice, Italy. Establishing shots of the Grand Canal, San Marco and the Doge's Palace; and gondola point-of-view process plates through canals and under bridges.

Villages (various decades, 35mm, color and black and white). Villages and small towns around the world. Includes locations in Trinidad, the Amazon basin, the Philippines, Hawaii, Polynesia, Vietnam, France, Burma and Africa. Includes scenes of native inhabitants, local technology and tourists. See also *Small towns, U.S.A.*

Virginia City, Nevada. Aerials and high shots; Piper's Opera House and the Gold Field Hotel; an old church; abandoned buildings; a cemetery; mines; silver-mine shafts; miners; and a sign saying "Virginia City, Queen of the Comstock."

Volcanoes (16mm, color). Spectacular Hawaiian eruptions, lava flows and burning palm trees. Day and night views.

War (various decades). Includes staged scenes of the U.S. Revolutionary War, the Civil War and United States campaigns against Native Americans in the 19th century. Some actuality footage of Teddy Roosevelt and the Rough Riders.

World War I: Headlines announcing the beginning and end of World War I. U.S. Bond rallies with troops and equipment on parade. Tanks in trials over steep hills and rough forests. Some trench warfare and actual combat.

Numerous World War I aircraft (see *Aviation*). Armistice Day. Celebrations at war's end with cheering civilians and soldiers.

World War II: Primarily U.S. government and newsreel footage. U.S. propaganda films exhorting factory workers to increase production. Training films on hand-to-hand combat, aircraft identification and civilian defense. Substantive coverage of the war in the Pacific, with lesser coverage of European and other theaters of action. Headlines announcing the outbreak and conclusion of hostilities in Europe and Asia. Strong holding of footage on World War II aircraft (see *Aviation*). Holds footage of other war materiel, including aircraft carriers, destroyers, frigates, tanks and landing craft. Color footage of homefront activities in New Jersey (1943). V-E and V-J Day footage includes scenes of crowds celebrating the war's end in New York, San Francisco and other cities, with cheering, confetti, banners and signs.

Korean War: Miscellaneous coverage of war and materiel, soldiers in and after battle, prisoners of war, destroyed towns and tanks, military ceremonies and funerals.

Vietnam War: General coverage of both the French and U.S. involvement in Vietnam. Includes combat footage, aerial bombing, napalm strikes, the spraying of Agent Orange, helicopter gunships in action and a rescue mission for downed pilots. Color footage of crowds in San Diego greeting returning veterans (1968). Dockside reunion scenes. See also *Demonstrations*.

The Cold War: Numerous cut films and newsreel stories on the struggle between the United States and the Soviet Union in the post-World War II period. See also *Anti-communism*.

Warehouses. Deserted warehouses, loading docks with trucks and high-down shots over warehouse districts.

Washington, D.C. (various decades, 1930-present, 35mm, color and black and white; also Betacam videotape). Extensive holdings covering the U.S. capital. Includes car process plates, aerials and high shots. Numerous establishing shots with some interiors of government buildings, landmarks, transportation centers, tourist attractions and monuments. Identifiable landmarks include the Brookings Institution; Capitol; Constitution Hall; Departments of Agriculture, the Interior, Justice and Treasury; various embassies; Internal Revenue Service; Federal Bureau of Investigation; Iwo Jima Memorial; Jefferson Memorial; Kennedy Center for the Performing Arts; Library of Congress; Lincoln Memorial; National Airport; National Archives (including interior views with the Declaration of Independence and the U.S. Constitution on display); National Gallery; National Zoo; Old Executive Office Building; Pentagon; Smithsonian Institution (including the Air and Space Museum); Supreme Court; Union Station; Veterans Administration; Vietnam Veterans Memorial; Washington Monument; the Watergate complex; and the White House. Current Betacam videotapes of the Capitol. Cherry blossoms in the spring. See also *Monuments and Memorials*.

Waterfalls. Miscellaneous stock shots of Yosemite, Potomac, Multnomah and Niagara Falls. Period cars visible in some shots. Also some unidentified falls in the tropics.

Water sports. Miscellaneous coverage of both recreational and exhibition water sports, from competitive swimming to California beach culture. Cliff-diving in Acapulco, Mexico; high diving; surfing in California, Hawaii and Australia (including point-of-view footage shot from an outrigger off Diamond Head in the 1960s); daredevil aqua stunts; and waterskiing by pros and amateurs. Beach bathing through the decades. Hydroplane races, yachting regattas and crew races. Various scenes of lake, river and ocean fishing.

Westerns (1920s-50s). A large selection of cowboy and Indian "B" movie stock shots. Covers every cliché under the Western (and Hollywood) sun, including: whooping Indian war dances; Indian raids on white settlements; U.S. cavalry charges; pitched battles; besieged forts; flaming arrows; lone sentries; dastardly ambushes; daring rescues; pioneer covered wagons rolling and being attacked by Indians; prairie fires; holdups of all kinds; gunfights and duels; barroom brawls; and the torching of everything from tepees to whole towns. There are mobs and posses and hangman's nooses; chases and stunts of all types, including stagecoaches going through fire, crashing down steep ravines and falling over cliffs with horses; "Wanted Dead or Alive!" posters; sheriffs with badges; and powder kegs and TNT fuses burning. See also *Native Americans*.

Western process plates include "Out the window" shots from early steam trains and stage coaches, providing a moving film background of typical Western locations.

Footage of Western wildlife includes buffalo grazing and stampeding; cattle doing everything cattle do (including stampeding); wild horses alone and in herds; stallions fighting and being chased by wolves; wolves howling at the moon; and various shots of mountain lions, coyotes, rattlesnakes and tarantulas.

Western activities includes cowboys (actual and actors) getting drunk, singing, lassoing, practicing whip and rope tricks, playing poker, flirting, square dancing, herding cattle and sheep, performing at rodeos (1930s-50s) and

prospecting and panning for gold.

Western locations include Western and ghost towns, forts, teepee camps, saloons, jails, adobe houses, haciendas, gold mines and ranches (1940s-50s). For typical Western landscapes, see also *Landscapes*.

Williamsburg, Va. Residential streets, churches and tourist attractions from the 1950s.

Winter sports. Downhill skiing (including a lone skier pursued by an avalanche); ice luge (Cresta Run, St. Moritz, Switzerland); tobogganing; ski jumping; ice hockey; ice skating; and figure skating.

World's Fairs. The New York World's Fair (1939-40) is represented by *The Middleton Family,* produced for Westinghouse to tout capitalism over communism. The film includes sequences featuring "Electro the Robot," the "Kitchen of Tomorrow," the Westinghouse time capsule and a dishwashing contest pitting a harried housewife ("Mrs. Drudge") against a washing machine (Mrs. Modern). Includes exterior establishing shots of the Fair. There is minor coverage of the Unisphere at the New York World's Fair (1964-65) and coverage of the Chicago World's Fair (1933).

Zoos (35mm, color and black and white; also Betacam videotape). Miscellaneous historical coverage of zoos, their inhabitants and visitors. Various zoo-oddity stories, including Salvador Dali painting a hippopotamus. Includes current views of the National Zoo in Washington, D.C., with tigers, gorillas, orangutans, sloths, monkeys and a giant panda ("Ling Ling").

Size & Elements: Film: 35mm (approx. 13,000 cans); 16mm (approx. 3,000 cans); 8mm (approx. 20 cans). Videotape: 1" (approx. 110 hours; 100 hours transfers from film, 10 hours originating on videotape); Betacam (100 hours; masters); 3/4" (masters and viewing copies); VHS (viewing copies).
Cataloging: Finding aids and catalogs for many portions of collection; card catalogs; videotape inventories and logs; reference library.
Access: Available to the public for licensing and reuse. Research fees charged. Research requests accepted by telephone and in person (by appointment only).
Rights: Full rights held to most material. Additional clearances may be necessary in some cases if material is to be reused.
Licensing: Available for licensing and reuse, subject to restrictions. License fees charged (rates depend on intended markets for production). Minimum project fees (non-refundable) charged upon shipment of broadcast-quality film or videotape masters. Discounts for quantity usage negotiable.
Restrictions: Clients must indemnify and hold library harmless from any and all claims, losses, demands and liabilities arising out of client's use of footage.
Viewing Facilities: Film (35mm Steenbeck, 16mm viewer); videotape (3/4", VHS and 8mm).
Duplication Facilities: Film (reference-quality film-to-videotape transfers); videotape (3/4" and VHS).
Related Materials: 400,000 still photographs on similar subjects; 50,000 postcards.

NEW YORK METRO

THE PHOENIX COMMUNICATIONS GROUP, INC.

1212 Avenue of the Americas
New York, NY 10036
(212) 921-8100
Fax: (212) 719-0614

Joseph L. Podesta (Chairman)
James E. Holland (President)
Geoff Belinfante (Senior Vice President, Executive Producer)
Terry Kassel (Senior Vice President, Sales and Syndication)

Contact: Peggy White (Director of Sales and Syndication)
Services: Film and videotape producer; stock footage sales library.
Description: *Major League Baseball Productions.* Operates Major League Baseball Productions under license from Major League Baseball and serves as their exclusive agent for the licensing of game highlights.

National Hockey League. Licensed by the National Hockey League as its Official Production Company, and serves as the NHL's exclusive agent for the licensing of game highlights.
Size & Elements: Apply for information.
Cataloging: Apply for information.
Access: Apply for information.
Rights: Apply for information.
Licensing: Apply for information.
Restrictions: Apply for information.
Viewing Facilities: None.
Duplication Facilities: None.

NEW YORK METRO

PHOENIX FILMS AND VIDEO
470 Park Avenue South
New York, NY 10016
(212) 684-5910
Fax: (212) 779-7493

Heinz Gelles (President)
Barbara Bryant (Executive Vice President)

Contact: Lizabeth K. McGraw (Promotions Advertising)
Services: Film and videotape producer and distributor. Material available to the public for rental, lease and purchase.
Description: Educational films and videotapes covering the following subject areas: adolescence; advertising; African studies; aging; alcoholism and addiction; Americana; animal life; animation; anthropology; architecture; art and art appreciation; art of film; authors; biography and profiles; biology; birds; birth; Black filmmakers; Black studies; boys' lives; business and industry; career education; child development; children's films; children's literature; choral music; cities and communities; comparative cultures; consumer education; crafts; criminology; dance; death and dying; drama; earth sciences; ecology; economics; education; energy; English; environmental studies; European studies; experimental films; family life; feature-length films; featurettes; fiction; film study; folktales and fables; foreign language films; future studies; geography; geology; girls' lives; government, economics and politics; guidance; health and safety; history; holidays; human relations; humor and satire; Indians (North American); interdependence; jazz; Jewish studies; language arts; Latin and South American studies; law enforcement; literature; management and management training; marine biology; men's concerns; mental health; Middle Eastern studies; motivational films; mountain climbing; music; Native Americans; nonverbal films; nutrition; opera; painting; parenting; people at work; performing arts; pets; philosophy; photography; physical education; physically and mentally handicapped; poetry and poets; political issues; political science; pottery; prejudice; psychology; reading motivation; religion and mysticism; rhythm and blues; science; sculpture; sex education; short stories; silent classics; social issues; social studies; sociology; Spanish-language films; special education; sports and recreation; teacher training; theater arts; time-lapse photography; travel; values; warfare; women filmmakers; women's studies; and young adults.
Size & Elements: Film: 16mm. Videotape: 3/4", VHS and Betamax. (Approx. 2,500 titles total).
Cataloging: Published catalogs.
Access: Available to the public for rental, preview and purchase. Selected titles available for leasing. Requests accepted by mail.
Rights: Rights retained by original producers or filmmakers. Videotape duplication rights possibly available.
Licensing: Apply for information.
Restrictions: Copyright restrictions apply.
Viewing Facilities: None.
Duplication Facilities: None.

NEW YORK METRO

J. PILSUDSKI INSTITUTE OF AMERICA FOR RESEARCH IN THE MODERN HISTORY OF POLAND, INC.
381 Park Avenue South
New York, NY 10016
(212) 683-4342

Stanislaw Jordanowski (President)

Contact: Woytek Dodzynski (Executive Director)
Services: Educational institution. Film and videotape collection available to researchers, scholars and the public.
Description: Records relating to the history of Poland (1863-present) and the Polish-American community. The majority of documentaries and feature films are in the Polish language and directed by Poles. Included in the collection is *Katyn,* a documentary on family events in World War II Russia and *Life of J. Pilsudski,* a feature film depicting Polish political events (1905-35).
Size & Elements: Film: 16mm (8,500 feet, 7 titles). Videotape: VHS (7 videotapes).
Cataloging: Card catalogs.
Access: Available to researchers, scholars and the public. Research requests accepted by mail. Research fees not charged.

Rights: Full rights held to all material.
Licensing: Apply for information. License fees charged (determined on a case-by-case basis).
Restrictions: None specified.
Viewing Facilities: None.
Duplication Facilities: None.

NEW YORK METRO

PISCATOR MEMORIAL FOUNDATION
17 East 76th Street
New York, NY 10021
(212) 737-4202

Contact: Dr. Maria Piscator
Services: Private foundation. Holds one film (on deposit at The Museum of Modern Art, Department of Film [q.v.]).
Description: *Fishermen of Santa Barbara* (original title), more commonly known by the title *The Revolt of the Fishermen* (USSR, 1934), was written, produced and directed by Erwin Piscator.
Size & Elements: Film: format unspecified (1 title).
Cataloging: None.
Access: Available to researchers and scholars only. Research requests accepted by mail and telephone. The Museum of Modern Art owns a copy of the film and shows it periodically when they have a retrospective on the filmmaker.
Rights: Full rights held to all material.
Licensing: Contact Dr. Maria Piscator regarding rights and reuse.
Restrictions: Permission must be obtained through Dr. Maria Piscator to gain access to film or for viewing outside of the Museum of Modern Art.
Viewing Facilities: None.
Duplication Facilities: None.

NEW YORK METRO

PLANNED PARENTHOOD FEDERATION OF AMERICA, INC. EDUCATIONAL DEPARTMENT
810 Seventh Avenue
New York, NY 10019
(212) 603-4632
(212) 603-4629
Fax: (212) 245-1845

Contact: Maria E. Matthews (Associate Director of Education)
Services: Nonprofit organization. Educational videotape available to the public for distribution.
Description: Topics relevant to human sexuality and reproductive health. Materials are produced and distributed by various affiliates of Planned Parenthood Federation.
  Sample titles include: *Birth Control: The Movie,* designed for teenagers and adults; *Breast Exam For Professionals,* teaching doctors and nurse practitioners how to do breast examinations using the guidelines of the American Cancer Society; *Margaret Sanger,* a documentary on the life and influence of the founder of the American birth control movement, narrated by Katharine Hepburn; *New Image Teen Theater,* featuring a teenage theater group performing skits and songs on incest and peer pressure; *Swept Away Is Not OK,* a videotape by and for teenagers, saying "protect yourself even if it's difficult"; *Teenage Mothers: Beyond The Baby Showers,* interviews with three teenage mothers; *Personal Decisions* showing the stories of four women who have had abortions: one who was raped and had a "back-alley" abortion before 1976, one concerned about her family's future, and two who are economically unable to become parents.
Size & Elements: Videotape: VHS (13 titles; viewing copies).
Cataloging: Computerized cataloging available to researchers.
Access: Available to the public for distribution from local affiliates. Requests accepted by mail, telephone and in person (by appointment only).
Rights: Apply to local affiliates for information.
Licensing: Apply for information.
Restrictions: None specified.
Viewing Facilities: None.
Duplication Facilities: None.

NEW YORK METRO

PORT AUTHORITY OF NEW YORK AND NEW JERSEY COMMUNICATIONS SERVICES

One World Trade Center, 86th Floor
New York, NY 10048
(212) 466-7000
Telex: 424 747 PANYNJ

Bernard J. Shusman (Executive Producer)

Contact: Bernard J. Shusman
Services: Government agency. Film and videotape library material available for duplication, licensing and reuse, subject to restrictions.
Description: Historical and current footage of Port Authority facilities and activities. Includes: historical footage of bridge and tunnel construction; early ferry service across the Hudson River before the construction of bridges and tunnels; a film of existing Port Authority facilities (early 1950s); a documentary film (late 1950s) of New York and Port Authority facilities; considerable footage (shot 1960s) of the PATH (Port Authority Trans-Hudson) rail line between New York City and New Jersey, the construction of the World Trade Center (in minute detail), lower Manhattan scenes and scenes of New Jersey, especially Jersey City; film coverage of Port Authority facilities in the 1970s, including upgrading of facilities, new rail trains, and the completion of the World Trade Center; considerable coverage (1980s) of airports, bus terminals, train stations, and the New York City skyline.

Special strengths include shots of the New York City skyline and airports (1960s-present); historical footage of PATH rail line (from its early days as the Hudson & Manhattan Railroad in the 1920s to the present); Port Authority Bus Terminal (1960s-80s); tunnels and bridges (including beauty shots of the George Washington Bridge, 1930s-present); Lincoln and Holland Tunnels from early days of construction to the present; recent shots of Port Newark and Port Elizabeth (N.J.) including containerized loading and unloading, cars unloading and loading of scrap iron; early pier shots in New York Harbor, and many shots of the Statue of Liberty.

Videotape footage is constantly being shot and added to library, with coverage of airports, new Port Authority construction sites at airports, PATH rail stations in New Jersey, and skylines of New York City and Jersey City.
Size & Elements: Film (format and amount unspecified). Videotape: 3/4" and VHS (amount unspecified). Almost all film in library is in the process of being transferred to videotape.
Cataloging: Finding aids; computerized cataloging in process.
Access: Available for duplication and reuse. Apply for information on current access policy and research fees. Research requests accepted by telephone.
Rights: Full rights held to all material.
Licensing: Available for licensing, subject to restrictions. License fees charged.
Restrictions: Written requests for reuse of footage stating purpose are required.
Viewing Facilities: None.
Duplication Facilities: Videotape (Betacam, 3/4" and 1/2").

NEW YORK METRO

PORT WASHINGTON PUBLIC LIBRARY
One Library Drive
Port Washington, NY 11050
(516) 883-4400 (Ext. 140)

Lillian R. Katz (Head of Media Services)

Contact: Media Services
Services: Public library. Videotape collection available to the public for in-house viewing only.
Description: Video art (late 1960s-present); documentary videotapes; videotapes on photography; interviews with photographers, filmmakers and videomakers.

Video art. Artists and videomakers featured in collection include Max Almy, Claude Beller, Dara Birnbaum, Carol Parrott Blue, Skip Blumberg, Barbara Buckner, James Byrne, Doris Chase, Steve Christiansen, Wendy Clarke, Tony Cokes, Lynn Corcoran, Peter D'Agostino, Cara Devito, Dimitri Devyatkin, Tom DeWitt, Nell Dorr, Juan Downey, Downtown Community Television Center, Ed Emshwiller, Fred Finkelstein, Kit Fitzgerald, Davidson Gigliotti, Shalom Gorewitz, Julie Gustafson, Gary Hill, Warrington Hudlin, Deanna Kamiel, Margia Kramer, Joan Logue, Chip Lord, Mary Lucier, Gunilla and Phillip Mallory-Jones, Bill and Esti Marpet, Branda Miller, Stefan Moore, Antonio Muntadas, Cynthia Neal, Nam June Paik, Susan and Alan Raymond, Dan Reeves, John Reilly, Bruce Ricker, Peter Rose, John Sanborn, Steina, Dore Steinberg, Martha Stuart, Skip Sweeney, Edin Velez, Bill Viola and William Wegman.

Photography. Documentation of interviews with and gallery talks given by photographers in conjunction with exhibitions; some videotapes were acquired from other sources. Photographers include: Berenice Abbott (talk by Hank O'Neal), Ansel Adams, Diane Arbus, Eugene Atget, Rudy Burkhardt, Bill Brandt (talk by Maria Morris Hambourg), Harry Callahan, Robert Capa, Lois Conner, Roy DeCarava, George DeVincent, Donald Dietz, Russell Drisch, El Salvador photographers, Mitch Epstein, Sandi Fellman, Jill Freedman, Roland Freeman, Laura Gilpin, Betty Hahn, Joan Harrison, Rick Horton, Lotte Jacobi, Barbara Kasten, Henri Lartigue, Arthur Leipzig, Scott MacLeay, Alen MacWeeny, Elliott McDowell, Sheila Metzner, Gjon Mili, Margarette Mitchell, Lisette Model, Robert Monroe, Barbara Morgan, Claus Mroczynski, Joan Myers, Bea Nettles, Anne Noggle, Starr Ockenga, Arthur Ollman, Olivia Parker, Photography Club of Long Island, John Pinderhughes, Bernard Plossu, Philip Pocock, Rosamond Purcell, Marc Riboud, Walter and Naomi Rosenblum, August Sander, Judy Seigel, Wayne Sorce, Edward Steichen, George Tice, Jerry Uelsmann (talk by Lee Battaglia), Tony Velez, Weegee (talk by Lee Sievan), Edward Weston (talk by Willard Van Dyke) and Minor White (talk by Peter C. Bunnell).

Cinema art documentation. Discussions with filmmakers about their works. Filmmakers include Perry Miller Adato, Eric Barnouw, Lance Bird, Les Blank, Barry Braverman, Jim Brown, John Canemaker, Sally Cruikshank, Ed Cullen, Connie Devilbiss, Kathleen Dowdey, Connie Field, Debra Franco, Richard Gordon, Emily and Faith Hubley, Tom Johnson, Miroslaw Kijowicz, Peter Kinoy, Caroline Leaf, William Miles, Kevin Rafferty, Amalie Rothschild, Charles Samu, Martha Sandlin, Victoria Schultz, Veronica Soul, George Stoney, Meg Switzgable, Amos Vogel, Paul Wagner, John Waletzky, Martha Wheelock, Paul Winkler and Ira Wohl.

Video art documentation. Discussions with videomakers about their work. Videomakers include: Diana Agosta, Robert Ashley, Claude Beller, Dara Birnbaum, Skip Blumberg, Barbara Buckner, Doris Chase, Lynn Corcoran, Peter D'Agostino, Cara Devito, Ed Emshwiller, Fred Finkelstein, Dee Dee Halleck, Margia Kramer, Shigeko Kubota, Mary Lucier, Phillip Mallory-Jones, Stefan Moore, Nam June Paik, Karen Ranucci, Dan Reeves, Caryn Rogoff, John Sanborn, Edin Velez and Bill Viola.
Size & Elements: Videotape: 3/4" (approx. 300 videotapes; masters and viewing copies).
Cataloging: Card catalogs; title lists.
Access: Open to the public. For in-house use only. Research fees not charged. Research requests accepted by mail, telephone and in person (walk-in and by appointment).
Rights: No rights held to any material.
Licensing: Not available for licensing or reuse.
Restrictions: Videotape collection available for in-house viewing only.
Viewing Facilities: Videotape (3/4" and VHS).
Duplication Facilities: None.

NEW YORK METRO

PRELINGER ASSOCIATES, INC.
430 West 14th Street, Room 403
New York, NY 10014
(212) 255-8866
Fax: (212) 691-8347

For stock footage requests:
PETRIFIED FILMS, INC.
430 West 14th Street, Rooms 411 and 404
New York, NY 10014
(212) 242-5461
Fax: (212) 691-8347

Richard Prelinger (President)

Contacts: Robert Cates (Film Librarian); Lori Cheatle (Film Librarian); Michael O'Callaghan (Film Librarian)
Services: Publisher of *Footage 89: North American Film & Video Sources;* film archives; film and video stock footage sales library. Most material available for research, licensing and reuse, subject to restrictions.
Description: American life, culture, industry and institutions (1915-70). Collection concentrates on everyday life and imagery not documented by newsreels or Hollywood films, and is strongest for the period 1935-65.

Special strengths include: educational and guidance films from all eras; promotional, advertising and industrial films; sponsored films; television commercials; home movies; everyday life and culture; families; labor; leisure;

recreation; industrial design; 20th-century science and technology; business history; sales training (many vintage films); sex roles; "smokestack" industries (steel and coal mining); suburbia; postwar prosperity; consumerism; regional Americana; automobile industry; car culture; animation; humor; food; "camp"; houses and homes; rural life; agriculture; immigration to the United States (1980s); communications; radio and television, energy and electricity.

Majority of collection consists of films produced by major and minor non-theatrical producers (1926-present). Among production companies represented by numerous films are: Audio Productions (New York); Calvin (Kansas City); Caravel Films (New York); Coronet; Encyclopedia Britannica; Frith Films (California); Jam Handy Organization (Detroit); Jerry Fairbanks Productions (Hollywood); William Matthews Co. (Pittsburgh); McGraw-Hill; Mode-Art Pictures (Pittsburgh); Wilding Picture Productions (Chicago); and Young America (New York). Some of this material is available for reference use only due to copyright or other restrictions. Numerous films produced by small or infrequent producers are also held.

Holds a substantial amount of color footage (1935-88), much of it reversal or negative original; many color films are held in original or preprint form.

The collection holds relatively few (approx. 200) government or Hollywood-produced films; no feature films; a handful of television programs; and relatively few educational or industrial films produced outside North America.

The summary that follows lists subjects and films of special interest. It should be noted, however, that roughly 85% of the collection has not been viewed and 60% is yet to be inventoried. Therefore, it should be regarded as suggestive, and readers should assume that additional material in most subject areas will also be available. As the nature of further material becomes known, it is expected that holdings will increase in the areas of advertising, sponsored films of the late 1930s, 1960s and 1970s, home movies, and educational films produced on the West Coast.

Subject coverage includes, but is not limited to, the following areas:

Adolescence. See *Social guidance.*

Advertising. Thousands of "sponsored" films (1925-70), produced for showing in theaters, to community groups and in schools. The films, running from 10 to 45 min., are partly "institutional" (promoting a company or an industry rather than a specific product or product line) and partly "industrial" (showing a process or product). PAI holds one of the largest historical collections of sponsored films in the U.S.

Hundreds of television commercials, primarily for automobiles, appliances, and health aids (1948-70). Some of this material requires additional clearances for reuse. A few historic commercials are held, such as the 1948 American To-bacco Co. commercials for Lucky Strike, *Marching Cigarettes* and *Barn Dance.*

20 "Minute Movies" or "screen ads" produced for showing in motion picture theaters (1934-41). These advertisements, precursors of the familiar television commercial, attempted to tell an interesting story (frequently a testimonial) in no more than 45-60 seconds. Products represented by screen ads include Esso Extra (gasoline); Dreft (detergent); instant starch; Whiz (candy bars); Nonesuch (coffee); Eveready (flashlight batteries); Chevrolet; Singer Sewing Centers; Kellogg's Rice Krispies and Oldsmobile (a series of minute movies featuring the last prewar 1942 models is held).

Several films, produced by makers of consumer goods for showing to retailers, demonstrate their support of product lines by showing advertising and publicity campaigns. Films of this type include: *It Takes Two To Make a Champ* (1938), concerning the advertising of reformulated Crisco shortening; *Oxydol Goes Into High* (1938), about the laundry soap; *1935 Pontiac Advertising;* and *Chevrolet Advertising Rings the Bell* (1950).

Africa. *Martin Johnson's African Expedition* (ca. 1930s) follows noted explorers Martin and Osa Johnson on a motor safari and features a rhinoceros kill. *Wheels Across Africa* (ca. 1935), photographed by Armand Davis for the Dodge Division of Chrysler Corporation, documents adventures including hunting and an encounter with a snake charmer.

Agriculture. Films produced by the seed industry, including *Background for Beauty* and *Bountiful Heritage. Waves of Green* (1950), a Technicolor film on the history of the land-grant college system in the United States and its role in agricultural research. Films about herbicides and pesticides, including *Death to Weeds* (1948), introducing the chemical 2-4-D to the agricultural market. Films produced by major corporations in the food industry, including Campbell Soup, Heinz, Beatrice Foods, General Mills, Meadow Gold Dairies and Swift and Co. Black workers picking cotton in Southern fields (shot ca. 1938); and other footage of the cotton and textile industry. *The Modern Trend in Swine Production* and *Saving Little Pigs,* both produced for farm audiences, promote new agricultural technology. Several films were produced for the poultry industry by feed and pharmaceutical suppliers, including *Protecting Poultry Profits* and *The Chicken of Tomorrow. Romance of a Lemon* (ca. 1927, silent)

shows lemon farming and processing in California. The uses of the tart fruit are not neglected — a woman is pictured rubbing her face with a lemon for beauty's sake.

There is spotty coverage of agriculture (1900-20), mostly derived from the Ford Film Collection.

Amusements. A film about Coney Island (1940s) showing amusements, rides, sideshows, food (hotdogs and cotton candy), a roller coaster sequence and Luna Park by night. Other coverage of Coney Island (1920s) includes novelty rides (some quite unusual) and the boardwalk. Isolated shots in other films feature roller coasters, sword swallowers and "wheels of fortune".

Animals. All In One (1937) compares the quest for the perfect dog to the quest for the perfect automobile. Films on elephants in captivity. Films on dog training, including *Partners* and *Training You to Train Your Dog. Mother Mack's Puppies Find Happy Homes* (1952) is the story of how Don and Doug Dowell give away six Scotty puppies to families of different races and nationalities; this educational film was produced partly to increase understanding between different ethnic groups.

A number of films depict various sorts of animal abuse. This ranges from anthrocentrism, in which, for example, monkeys are dressed in human costumes and their faces made up with human cosmetics, to laboratory animal experimentation undertaken as a part of medical research. One roll of untitled agricultural footage shows physical abuse of sick hogs.

Animation. A Is For Atom (1953), featuring an "Element Town" sequence; *Aluminum on the March,* containing a stop-motion animation sequence of aluminum shapes and products; *Auto-Lite on Parade* (1940) and *Motors on Parade* (1951), stop-motion product parades; *A Coach for Cinderella* (1937), the first Technicolor industrial film, influenced in part by George Pal's advertising films for Philips; *Down the Gasoline Trail* (1935) picturing the journey of a drop of gasoline from pump to carburetor, where it explodes and becomes a winged angel, flying out the auto exhaust pipe; and *Drawing Account* (1941) showing the technical work of the studio animator.

In My Merry Oldsmobile (1931, 35mm, original nitrate print), a classic promotional film produced by the Fleischer Studios for the Olds Motor Works, is full of sexual innuendos and risqué interludes. *Just Imagine* (1947) shows parts reassembling themselves into a complete telephone (in stop-motion). *Marching Cigarettes* and *Barn Dance* (1948), produced by Jam Handy Organization for the American Tobacco Co., are two award-winning commercials for Lucky Strike cigarettes, featuring stop-motion animation. *News Sketches* (1944-45), in the manner of the *Out of the Inkwell* series, produced by Max Fleischer. *Precisely So* (1937) includes a sequence of stop-motion animation featuring precision measuring tools. *The Princess and the Pauper* (1938) is a Technicolor cartoon featuring Arab princes and princesses, genies, jewels, magic carpets, chases and Chevrolets. *Rudolph, the Red-Nosed Reindeer* (1948, 35mm, directed by Max Fleischer, sponsored by Montgomery Ward) is a classic Technicolor rendition of the Christmas story.

Something for Nothing (1940), produced for Chevrolet, discusses the economical aspects of the internal-combustion engine. The teaching is done by animation and presented by Rube Goldberg in his Hollywood studio. There are scenes in which Goldberg is seen drawing still photographs, which are animated at the end of the film. *The Tip-Tops in Peppyland* (1934) includes a primitive (and occasionally surreal) animation sequence relating to the beneficial effects of different vitamins. *We Drivers* (produced in several versions, 1936, 1955 and 1962) mixes animation and live-action (see *Safety,* below).

Anti-communism. Films produced by private industry and U.S. government agencies, including the military. Numerous Cold War-era films promote the virtues of the American economic system in an affirmative manner, without mentioning socialism or communism, including the animated Technicolor cartoons *Meet King Joe, Going Places* and *Why Play Leapfrog? A Day of Thanksgiving* (1952) celebrates what an American family should be thankful for, whether or not it can afford a turkey dinner. *Priceless Heritage* (1952), produced by the Superior Coach Company (a school bus manufacturer) compares the free American system of education with the totalitarianism of the French Revolution, integrating school buses into the democratic tradition. *The Challenge of Ideas* (produced by the U.S. Defense Department) and *The War We Are In: Communism vs. Capitalism* (produced by Harding College) counterpose the American way of life to Communist threats emanating from other quarters. *A Welcome Guest in the House* (National Assn. of Broadcasters, ca. 1959) praises television for showing youngsters the "nature of evil" in the persons of Soviet leaders. *What You Should Know About Biological Warfare* (1951), though not mentioning communism explicitly, shows a fifth columnist in a trenchcoat poisoning public water supplies, and civil defense measures against biological weapons.

Appliances. Many films about home appliances (1925-75), including refrigerators, ovens and stoves, washing machines, dryers, irons and electric ironers, vacuum cleaners and toasters. *Fortress of Steel* (1936) shows the strength of a Frigidaire refrigerator with an elephant standing on top of one. *Grandma Goes to School* and *Grandma Goes to Town* (see below, under *Home economics*) convince homemakers of the virtues of electric kitchen appliances. Six television commercials (1954) promote the Frigidaire refrigerator. Four films introduce the new Frigidaire range and refrigerator models for 1957, and show their (mostly stylistic) innovations. There is excellent prewar footage of small appliances, notably irons. *The Last Word in Automatic Dishwashing* (1951) shows Mullins dishwashing machines, with their exclusive "Jet Tower" feature.

Mother Takes a Holiday (1952), produced by Whirlpool Corporation, begins in a kitchen where a teenage girl tries to write a theme on women's emancipation. Her two friends look on as she relates liberation to time-saving electrical appliances, and decide to trick their fathers into buying electric laundries for their long-suffering wives. *Norge News* (ca. 1936) introduces the new ironers and washing machines, some available with gasoline-powered motors for homes without electrical service.

Young Man's Fancy (1952), produced by Edison Electric Institute, is the story of Judy, a happy-go-lucky teenager, and Alex, a college student apparently interested only in engineering and time study. Throughout the film, in which every scene begins with a plug for one or another electric appliance, Judy struggles to get Alex's attention, finally hooking him with a home-cooked meal (made possible by electricity), after which he gives away his tickets to the lecture on mushroom growing and invites her to go dancing.

Architecture. Most films in this category relate to building materials and construction practices. *Imagination Unlimited* (1961) demonstrates the creative potential of concrete blocks for architects and builders. *Skylines Unlimited* and *Touch and Go* (both early 1950s), both produced by Otis Elevator Co., show how automatic elevator control adds to the efficiency and amenities of office buildings.

The Arctic. Alaska's Silver Millions (1936) pictures the commercial fishing industry, with excellent footage of salmon migration and processing. Some footage of Eskimo life and dog sledding is included.

Atomic energy. A Is For Atom (1953), the classic cartoon produced by General Electric, providing basic scientific background on nuclear energy and promoting peaceful uses of atomic power; and *Atomic Energy: A Force For Good* (1955) promoting the atom as a lifesaving tool of medical science. Several films on nuclear medicine (all mid-1950s) show radioisotopes and their administration to patients. *Taking the "X" Out of X-Rays,* produced by General Electric, recreates Röntgen's discovery.

Atomic weapons. Damaging Effects of the Atomic Bomb Compared to Conventional Weapons (color) pictures several blasts and contains scientific animation relating to nuclear weapons effects. The Trinity test (1945) is pictured in *Atomic Energy: A Force For Good. Survival Under Atomic Attack* (1951), produced by the Federal Civil Defense Administration, trains families in survival methods around the home.

Automobiles. Substantial coverage of automobiles, including films produced for showing to the public and to train workers in the automobile industry.

Advertising material includes *1955 Chevrolet Screen Ads,* a series of one-minute movies produced for showing in theaters; material from the Buick, Chevrolet, GMC Truck, Oakland, Oldsmobile and Pontiac divisions of General Motors; television commercials and promotional films (in black and white and color) from Nash, Dodge, and Ford Motor Company.

Assembly lines: Chevrolet (1927, 1936, 1951, 1955, 1956 and 1960).

Chevrolet: general coverage (1935-65); advertising films (1952-61); coverage of the Corvair from its introduction (1960); the introduction of the Corvette (1953); and a promotional film, *How To Go Places* (1954), with Gale Storm and family.

Chrysler-Plymouth: promotional films (late 1960s-early 1970s).

Ford: the introduction of the Falcon, Ford's first compact car (1960); Thunderbirds (1958-61); introduction of the Ford V-8 engine (1930s); various material drawn from the Ford Film Collection, picturing Ford automobiles, assembly lines, plants and workers (approx. 1908-20); and Ford commercials for the 1956 model year, showing safety devices included with the new cars, hosted by Joie Chitwood (noted stunt driver) among others.

Institutional films, promoting industries and corporations rather than specific products, include: *American Engineer* (Chevrolet, 1955); *American Harvest* (Chevrolet, 1951 and 1955); *American Look* (Chevrolet, 1958); *American Maker* (Chevrolet, 1960); *The American Road* (Ford, 1955); *American Thrift* (Chevrolet, 1962); *Chevrolet Leader News* (1935-39, 16 issues); *Roads to Romance* series (Chevrolet, 1950s); *From Dawn to Sunset* (Chevrolet, 1937). *Key To Our Horizons* (Chevrolet, 1952) demonstrates the centrality of the automobile in American life by explaining that one out of every seven Americans is employed in some area of the automotive industry.

Of *American Harvest,* General Motors had this to say: "America, the birthplace of plenty, is superbly photographed in full color in this pictorial story of how raw materials are fashioned by men and machines into usable wealth. Across fertile plains to breath-taking mountains, from majestic forests to rich oil fields, camera crews traveled over 35 states to bring us magnificent scenes of our natural resources. The camera also takes us into busy factories. Roaring blast furnaces, humming machines, and skillful men transform these bounties of nature into entirely new forms. We see rusty red earth becoming steel, sand becoming glass, corn becoming man-made leather. We see how gears, paint, tires, windshields and upholstery are made. And when we finally see new cars and trucks rolling off assembly lines by the millions to be delivered to the farmers, miners, factory workers, and all the others who helped make them, we begin to understand how all of us are interdependent upon one another in our American enterprises that have made us the most prosperous people on earth."

Master Hands (1936, 40 min.) shows every detail of Chevrolet assembly from the foundry and rolling mill to the finished vehicle. Set to dramatic music without any voiceover or narration, it was designed to ennoble the process of mass production and contains excellent footage of automobile workers, assembly lines and machines in the year immediately preceding the sitdown strikes that led to General Motors' recognition of the United Auto Workers.

Nash: one 1953 promotional film (negative only).

Oldsmobile: a series of "minute movies" produced for theatrical release (1942), promoting the last motor vehicles produced for civilian use on the eve of the United States' entry into World War II. These shorts stress the durability of the Oldsmobile. Various promotional films from the postwar period, including *The Car of Tomorrow, Today* (1948), relating to the first, and one of the most advanced, true postwar cars. Four "minute movies" from the same year advertise the "Futuramic" features of the new models. Several promotional films showing Oldsmobiles from the early 1950s are also held.

In My Merry Oldsmobile (1931), sponsored by the Olds Motor Works and produced by the Fleischer Studios, was certainly one of the oddest and most sexually explicit films ever sponsored by a major corporation in this country. It features a "bouncing ball" rendition of the 1908 song, from which the film takes its name.

Parts and accessories: films produced by manufacturers, including *Champions At Work* (Champion Spark Plugs, 1933) and *Under the Tread* (Brunswick Tire Corp., 1934).

Pontiac: various color announcement and promotional films, containing running shots, beauty shots and footage relating to design and styling (1952-56). One film features a striking parade of 1952 Pontiacs driving in circular formation.

Product announcement films, made to introduce new models to the consumer market. *Design for Dreaming* (General Motors, 1956) introduces the new cars, the kitchen of tomorrow, and the electronic highways of the future. Several of the "dream cars" of the 1950s, including the Oldsmobile *Golden Rocket* and the Pontiac *Firebird II,* are featured.

Service stations and garages: coverage (1933-63), including Sinclair and Esso stations.

Training films produced for in-house orientation and indoctrination, especially directed to salesmen (1927-68). The earliest, *The Story of a Wonderful Dealer* (1927), shows the "do's and don'ts" of running a dealership.

Aviation. Harnessed Lightning (1951), a film explaining the principles of the jet engine and turbo-prop. *New Power For Flight* (1955), an explanation and demonstration of the turbo-prop engine. *6-1/2 Magic Hours* (Pan American World Airways, ca. 1956), shows passenger services on a commercial flight from Europe to the United States; *Aviation: The Career for Marc* is a simply constructed vocational film. Two educational films (1950s) introduce helicopters, with many color shots of early production rotorcraft. Vintage aviation material from the Ford Film Collection pictures Col. Charles A. Lindbergh on tour after his transatlantic flight in 1927; civil aircraft (1920s); and World War I aviation. *Look to Lockheed for Leadership* (ca. 1947) depicts the history of the Lockheed Co. and its aircraft production. Holds several training films used in World War II-vintage flight simulators, including *Multiple Attacks on the Tail Cone. On Guard* (ca. 1957) is an introduction to the SAGE (Semi-Automatic Ground Environment) air-defense system and shows large radar screens, computers that fill large rooms and the command center located at Owego, New York.

One film, *Riding the Skies With Amelia Earhart* (ca. 1935) intercuts library footage of Earhart with original aerial views of cities along the Northeast Corridor, including New York, Newark, Philadelphia and Camden, Baltimore and Washington. Although the footage of Earhart is of little use, the urban aerials are of excellent quality. *Sky Billboards* (1935) pictures skywriting equipment and maneuvers; the diminutive biplanes write Chevrolet slogans in the sky.

Baby Boom. The post-World War II baby boom is depicted in such films as *Baby Goes Home* (1955), a training film for new parents; *Lucky Junior* (1949), which shows obstetricians, post-natal care, incubators and a parade of nurses wheeling bassinets through a hospital corridor.

Beauty pageants. Little footage is held. Although it emphasizes that the Junior Miss competition is not a beauty pageant, *That Junior Miss Spirit* (1965) shows teenage girls competing for national awards.

Black culture and history. Relatively little material is held, although there is good footage of Black laundry workers in *Protecting Your Profits* (1946); agricultural workers picking cotton (1938); and minor coverage of Black workers in the steel and automobile industry (1930s-50s). Though there are a few examples of overt racism in the collection, what is more revealing is the almost total absence of nonwhite faces in all sponsored and educational films until the 1960s.

Business. Because of its concentration on sponsored and industrial films, this collection is strong in the documentation of American business history and practice. Holds films produced by hundreds of major and minor American corporations; management and sales training films; and educational films relating to business, e.g., *What Is a Contract?*, *What Is a Corporation?*, and *What Is Business?* Although numerous exceptions exist, the collection is at its best when revealing general business trends or practices, rather than historical or economic information relating to specific corporations.

Central America. Relatively little material is held, but there are several films of interest, including *Jack's Visit to Costa Rica* (1947), in which Jack (from Chicago) visits a young boy whose father manages a plantation and *Our Monroe Doctrine*, an introduction to American interventionism.

Chemistry. A variety of educational films relating to different aspects of experimental chemistry are held. *Test Tube Tale* (1938) shows the beneficial effects of industrial chemistry, especially in the field of synthetic compounds, with early footage of nylon stockings and consumer goods made from plastic. *What's It To You* (1955), produced by DuPont, introduces Mylar and its industrial uses, and includes several unusual experiments designed to confirm Mylar's strength and stability.

Children. Chevrolet's *The All-American Soap Box Derby* (1936) is an homage to the American boy, his ingenuity and his sportsmanship. There are additional Soap Box Derby films in the library, and coverage of the first Derby in 1934. *Bill Garman, 12-Year-Old Businessman* is the story of a young rabbit entrepreneur who employs some of his friends on his farm. *Priceless Cargo* (1947) shows children leaving for school (including a sequence in which a mother tells her daughter to behave well during the day) and riding the school bus.

Cities. Material from the Ford Film Collection pictures a number of cities (especially New York) in the 1910s and 1920s. Pictured are the Lower East Side and its immigrant population; skylines; Central Park and bridges. *From Dawn to Sunset* (1937) shows skylines, street scenes, markets and homes in various cities, including Detroit, Baltimore, Buffalo, Atlanta, Cincinnati, St. Louis, Kansas City, San Francisco and Oakland. *The City* (1939), the classic documentary film produced by Willard Van Dyke and Ralph Steiner, shows first a small New England country town, the effects of uncontrolled industrialization in Pittsburgh and Homestead (Pennsylvania), then the chaos, crowding and noise of New York City life, and finally the promise of the planned community, as exemplified by Greenbelt (Maryland) and Radburn (New Jersey), among others.

A 1941 amateur Kodachrome film documents the city of San Francisco, showing the airport, aerial views of the Sunset and Richmond districts, hilltop views of other neighborhoods, street scenes, cable cars and trolleys, Chinatown, the Fisherman's Wharf area, Market Street, the Ferry Building, the Transbay Transit Terminal, Key System interurban trains, the Golden Gate Bridge, Treasure Island and its seaplane base serving the Pan American "Clipper" flying boats, and the arrival of the Southern Pacific "Coast Daylight" train at Oakland.

To Market, To Market (1942) was produced by the General Outdoor Advertising Co. and shows how the city of Chicago is covered by "scientifically planned poster showings" enabling an advertiser to reach any kind of specialized audience with his billboards. The film contains excellent color footage of Chicago neighborhoods, people and transit facilities, all showing outdoor advertising of the time.

Several films produced by an electric utility company in Rochester, New York are held, showing the city, its industry, and cultural and social amenities; similar films cover Detroit, Cleveland, and Providence, R.I. Educational and industrial films from all periods show glimpses of many cities, especially Chicago, Los Angeles and New York City.

Civics. Numerous educational films (1941-60) on city, state and Federal government functions and agencies. Many, such as *A Citizen Participates* and *A Citizen Makes A Decision,* contain dramatized sequences, and many others,

such as *Our Living Constitution* and *How A Bill Becomes a Law,* include animated diagrams of governmental structure and function. In general, these films view American politics and government uncritically, and are striking evidence of a kind of consensus between government and governed that is all but invisible today.

Colleges and universities. *Postmark East Lansing* (1951), a recruiting film produced by Michigan State University, is introduced by President John C. Hannah, and goes on to depict the University campus, student activities, recreation (including dancing and canoeing), and Quonset huts for married students attending college on the G.I. bill. The film takes the form of a letter sent by a student to a prospective applicant.

Color. Numerous films in Technicolor (1937-69), Kodachrome (1938-70), Anscochrome and Ektachrome Commercial (all of which are relatively dye-stable). Many original Eastmancolor negatives of varying color stability are held. *Color Harmony* (1938), explains how we perceive color, and contains an unusual animated sequence. *Color Harmony for Your Home* (1956), concerns the choice of colors for do-it-yourself home decorators.

Communications and the mass media. Subjects pictured include newspapers, magazines, outdoor advertising and billboards, printing, radio, television and phonograph records. *Seventeen Days: The Story of Newspaper History in the Making* covers the New York City newspaper strike of 1945; *1935 Pontiac Advertising* shows newspapers, magazines, radio and other media of the period; *Billions for Millions* (ca. 1947) has various shots of mass media; *Chevrolet Advertising Rings the Bell* (1950) includes shots of a family watching television, listening to the radio, reading newspapers, at the movies, and more.

Spot News (1935) shows how wirephotos are made and sent over telephone lines, with scenes of a crowded newspaper office, inside the mobile photo unit, at the newspaper pressroom, newsboys on the street selling papers, and a customer opening a newspaper to read an article. The news event pictured is a stunt in which an airplane takes off from the roof of a moving automobile. *Telegram for America* (late 1940s) pictures all aspects of the commercial telegraph industry.

A film on the making of phonograph records (1942) shows all phases of the production process, from performance and recording through pressing (of 78 rpm records) and distribution. A film promoting the Zenith "Cobra-matic" 78 rpm record-changer system (1949). Another film (1956) shows the making of LPs. One film (1962) shows an animated stereo LP groove from the point of view of the stylus. Several educational films relate to sound waves, motion picture soundtracks, sound recording and reproduction; each contains animated footage of sound waves and electrons.

From Trees to Tribunes (1927), produced by the *Chicago Tribune,* shows the process of putting out a daily newspaper, beginning with the forest and ending with the delivery of finished papers to readers. Included are shots of lumbering; papermaking; printing presses; the Tribune Tower in Chicago; and columnists and cartoonists of the time. Another film (1944) pictures behind-the-scenes activity at the Minneapolis (Minnesota) *Star-Tribune. Journalism* (1940) shows careers in newspaper and magazine work. *Printing* (1946) shows job and newspaper printing shops, typesetting and press procedures. *Radio and Television* (1940), a vocational guidance film for students, shows prewar studios, technicians and equipment.

Several films on the U.S. Post Office Department, primarily produced for educational use in the 1940s and 1950s, are held. These picture mailmen and letter carriers, mail sorting and other postal procedures. *The Twenty-Six Old Characters* (1947) traces the history of writing from the ancient scribes to the modern fountain pen.

Consumerism. Many films, especially from the post-World War II period, feature the new products of the time. *The Best Made Plans* (1956), produced by the Dow Chemical Company, shows the many uses of plastic wrap in the home and on the road (items in a suitcase, including the baby's cup and diapers, are all safely wrapped in Saran Wrap). *Dateline Tomorrow* (1946) shows new products made of aluminum. *Engagement Party* (1957) is a drama about love, the generation gap and trading stamps.

International Moves the Browns to Sterling Street (1941, color) was made for jewelers and other dealers of International Silver Co. products. The film describes a marketing campaign in which silver was first made available to working-class and middle-class families on the installment plan. *It Takes Two to Make a Champ* (1938), aimed at Crisco retailers, details Procter & Gamble's marketing plan for shortening. *Quality Control in Modern Merchandising* (1952) shows internal testing and Q.C. procedures as practiced by J. C. Penney & Co.; there is footage of laboratories, department stores, shoppers and customers.

Crime and criminals. Boy in Court (1940) shows juvenile delinquents and their rehabilitation; *Boy With a Knife* (1956) the roots of delinquency and a social worker's attempts to work with youthful offenders. A 1956 film contains frightening footage of state prisons and juvenile institutions, including cells, dining rooms, showers and other public areas, armories, guards, observation towers, and more.

Dancing. Though the collection has only incidental holdings relating to entertainment and performance, there is a great deal of dance footage available, including: social dancing (1930s-50s); proms (1946, 1953 and 1962); teenagers slow-dancing; burlesque dancers; ethnic and folk dancing, shot in the United States and abroad; stylized Latin dancing, mostly from 1940s-vintage musical short films; ethnographic footage of Native Americans, Africans, peoples of the Soviet Union and others; Philippine stick dancing; ballet (especially dances of Russian origin);

Most of the dance material has been assembled onto select reels.

Dating. Many of the classic educational and instructional films on teenage dating and social behavior (1946-58), including *Are You Popular?* (1947), a treatise on teenage popularity, in which Caroline brings Wally home to introduce him to her parents properly; *Dating: Do's and Don'ts* (1949), the classic "how-to" film that explains how to say goodnight; *Junior Prom* (1946); and *What To Do On a Date* (1951), suggesting such activities as weenie roasts and taffy pull.

Design. Many films in the collection contain rare or unusual imagery depicting graphic, industrial and product design trends from the periods in which they were produced. *American Look* (1958), a "tribute to the American stylist," shows home interiors, furniture, kitchens and kitchen equipment, packaging, appliances, textiles, offices and office furniture, office machines, industrial machines, lawn mowers and sprinklers, architecture, automobile styling and design and the work of the design staff at the General Motors Technical Center in Warren, Michigan. *Aluminum on the March* (1956) depicts numerous domestic and industrial design innovations, all made from aluminum. *The Refreshing Look* (1957), made to promote a line of Coca-Cola vending machines, begins with a summary and statement relating to the "new look" in American industrial design. *The Golden Years* (1960) introduces "the American Way of life on the threshold of the 'Golden Sixties,'" showing design-related elements. *Streamlines* (1937), though primarily oriented towards a technical view of streamlining, contains shots of streamlined trains and automobiles, animation of air currents and one animated sequence depicting a fanciful city and traffic, all designed so as to expedite motion. *Taking the Air* (1941), also technically oriented, shows how engineers design aerodynamically efficient automobiles.

Disasters. A film depicting the eruption of Mt. Vesuvius and other films showing volcano eruptions. Films depicting the aftermath of floods (1930s).

Drugs. Several anti-drug films are held, including *Subject Narcotics* (1951), a semi-documentary treatment of the criminal drug subculture in downtown Los Angeles (made for police use) and *The Terrible Truth* (1948), recounting the (drug-induced) unhappy experiences and premature aging of a teenage girl, once a beauty. *Saint Paul Police Detectives and Their Work* (1941) shows laboratory samples of various illegal substances; a pile of marijuana mysteriously appears in the image.

Early cinema. Films by Edison, Méliès, Porter, Biograph, and others; all are release prints only. Scattered newsreel footage (1900-20) is available.

Economics. Several films (1940s-50s) on the workings of the stock exchange; the banking system, including *Using the Bank* and *Pay to the Order Of;* careers in banking and accountancy; a film attempting to show the superiority of large enterprises over small businesses; *Bill Bailey and the Four Pillars,* a story of a small-town banker and his rescue of a depressed community; *Destination Earth,* an animated cartoon expressing the superiority of the American system over a centralized economy, set on the planet Mars; *It's Everybody's Business* (1954), a cartoon on American enterprise and its blessings, produced by the U.S. Chamber of Commerce. *Meet King Joe, Going Places* and *Why Play Leapfrog?* (all 1949) are cartoons produced to promote the American free enterprise system.

Films produced by multinational corporations, including Coca-Cola, General Motors and Parke-Davis. *Round and Round* (General Motors Public Relations, 1939) uses a team of puppets to explain the interdependence of labor, manufacturing and agriculture within the system of free enterprise.

Education. Numerous films relating directly to teaching and learning techniques in all subject areas (late 1930s-1965), including *Successful Scholarship, Making Yourself Understood* and *Maintaining Classroom Discipline.* Many films incorporate shots of teachers, students, schools, school buses, classrooms and laboratories. *The Sixth Chair* (1947) shows crowded schools, inadequate facilities and poor student-teacher interaction, and argues for more and better schools.

Educational films. (Begins 1920s, strong coverage 1945-70; approx. 6,000 titles). Comprehensive collection of educational films, many produced by defunct companies, most considered outdated and no longer in circulation. Includes substantial holdings on social guidance, sex education, vocational education, geography, science, biology, social studies, schools and education, and in many other subject areas.

Electricity. Many educational films on the theory of electricity, magnetism and electrodynamics (1920s-60s). Films on electric power generation and transmission, mostly promoting public utilities, include *The Power to Serve* (Cleveland Electric Illuminating Co., 1957); *Rochester: A City of Quality* (Rochester Gas & Electric, 1962); *Take It For Granted* (New England Electric System, 1946); *What Is Electricity?* (Westinghouse Electric Co., 1953); *Sun to Sun* (Duquesne Light Co., 1937); and *My Dad's Company* (Detroit Edison Co., 1946). Many of these films show consumer appliances in use in the home. *Power By Which We Live* (General Electric Co., 1949), depicts turbine generators.

Indiana Public Service TV Spots (1954) were produced to be part of the "Live Better Electrically" campaign.

Electronics. Numerous films picturing electronic engineering and inventions in the fields of radio, telephony, television, radar and digital computers. Several films introduce stereophonic sound equipment in the late 1950s and early 1960s. Two World War II-era training films concern radar equipment, and were classified at the time of their initial release.

Energy. See also descriptions under *Atomic Energy* and *Electricity.* The critical post-World War II period (when energy demand exceeded supply) is portrayed in *Pipe of Plenty* (1946), on the construction of a natural gas pipeline to help supply the energy needs of the Detroit metropolitan area. The film includes shots of domestic and industrial energy use, including hair dryers, gas stoves, bakeries and foundries. *This Nation's Power* (1941) deals with energy use in the United States, showing steam-powered equipment, internal combustion engines, automobiles, highways, airplanes, industrial plants and motors, railroads, and many more examples. Characterizing the United States as the world leader in available power, the film itself is more than a faint indication of military readiness.

Engineering. Many engineering innovations (1910s-20s) including early footage of Ford assembly lines, are shown in material originating in the Ford Film Collection. There is some footage of older industries, including wheelmaking, blacksmithing, cooperage, lumber milling and woodworking in several films. *American Engineer* (1956) is an homage to American skill and know-how, depicting breakthrough technology at mid-century. Several films, mostly dramatized discussions, relate to time and motion study.

Fashion. Relatively little footage relating to fashion *per se* is held in the library, but many films do depict clothing (especially everyday wear). *Fashions on the Ice and Snow* (1940, part color) depicts winter fashions, skiing and snow trains. *How To Be Well Groomed* (ca. 1951) bypasses fashion for propriety, teaching a teenage boy and girl how to wash, dress and style themselves. *The Story of a Star* (1956) promotes the synthetic yarn Agilon (used in hosiery) and contains a television commercial which incorporates a jingle. *The Story of Leather* (ca. 1946) shows leather processing and manufacturing at great length, ending with a color sequence of fashionable shoes, handbags, belts and other accessories. *The Well-Mannered Look* (1963) pictures well-dressed and well-behaved teenagers in and out of school, wearing the latest in synthetic fabrics. *The Wonderful World of Wash and Wear* (1958) demonstrates the variety of synthetic fabrics and the ease they bring to daily life.

Food. A film depicting industrial baking (1946). *Breakfast Pals* (1938), a one-minute color advertising cartoon produced for the Kellogg Company, featuring "Snap," "Crackle" and "Pop." Numerous films produced by and for the dairy industry, including: *Butter Is Made This Way; It's All In Knowing How; Triple Goodness; Our Foster Mother: The Cow; A Brighter Day; Food for America; Make Mine Ice Cream; Of Town and Country;* and *The Miracle of Milk.* Coverage of supermarkets (1938-present), including color footage from 1941, 1948, 1950s and 1960s. Automated food-packaging machinery (including bread baking and the filling of mayonnaise jars) (1948, color). *Food For Thought* (1940), a film about cellophane and its use as a packaging material. *Thought for Food* (1933) is a guided tour through the Kroger Food Foundation and its research laboratories at Cincinnati, Ohio.

The Magic Shelf (1952), produced for Campbell Soup Co., presents recipe ideas, all employing soup as their major ingredient, showing people in different walks of life enjoying soup at home, in restaurants and luncheonettes, and on the job. The film begins with a series of magic tricks. *The Miracle of the Can,* an industrial film with a self-explanatory title. *White Wonder,* a film about salt, "the indispensable crystals of life."

Numerous films on nutrition, including films promoting the four basic food groups, the five basic food groups and the seven basic food groups.

Frith Films collection. Begins 1940s. 85 films (16mm Kodachrome and Anscochrome originals and release prints). Series of educational films produced for primary school students, widely distributed through the 1970s. Frith films were produced at low cost and offer an (unintentionally) humorous view of family life, farm life in the San Fernando Valley prior to its urbanization, European cities, American institutions, and domestic and farm animals. Selected titles include: *Bill Garman: 12-Year-Old Businessman; Our Foster Mother: The Cow; Family Teamwork; Patty Learns to Stop, Look and Listen; Fire: Patty Learns What To Do; The U.S. Customs Safeguards Our Foreign Trade; What It Means To Be An American* and *Mother Mack's Puppies Find Happy Homes.*

Futurism. Films produced by industrial corporations to promote their view of technological progress, including *Streamlines* (1936); *To New Horizons* (1940) (see *World's Fairs,* below); *Leave It To Roll-Oh* (1940), picturing a domestic robot; *Design for Dreaming* (1956); and *American Look* (1958).

Geography. Numerous educational films cover all regions of the United States and all countries of the world. *Caught Mapping* (1940) dramatizes the production of gasoline company road maps.

Health and hygiene. A film on body care and grooming, showing good and bad examples on the college campus; a film on caring for the skin; films on cleanliness, the common cold, germs, good eating habits, immune system, infectious viruses and illness and posture habits; numerous films on dentistry, especially those produced for children; a film on the therapeutic effects of ultraviolet light; and several films on the medical profession, including how to choose a doctor.

Films on exercise and calisthenics include *Getting Ready Physically* (1952), produced to prepare young men for military service in the Korean War era. Films on shoes and feet, including *Experience Points the Way* (Dr. Scholl's Co., 1937). *Forty Billion Enemies* (Westinghouse, 1941) promotes refrigeration as a defense against the multiplication of life-threatening bacteria. *Insomnia,* produced by the U.S. Navy (1945) and starring Dick York, demonstrates defenses against insomnia and shows how to relax into sleep. *Personal Hygiene,* produced for the U.S. Army (World War II-vintage) is a long-winded drama (with songs) in which barracks residents teach one of their buddies the elements of cleanliness. *Physical and Mental Fitness* (1920s, silent), a drama showing adolescents and exercise. *Rest and Health,* with Dick York, shows the physical difficulties that can beset a teenager who fails to get enough sleep at night.

Sniffles and Sneezes (1955), a health film for children of junior high-school age, exploits the fear of epidemics while admonishing children to avoid behavior patterns that tend to spread disease. Animated dark spots on hands, plates, doorknobs, mouths and pencils are used to show the spreading of germs; human carelessness is, of course, to blame. *Told By A Tooth* (ca. 1930s, part animated) speaks to children in the voice of a tooth. In one scene, a young girl dumps a plate of food into a huge model tooth. *Weight Reduction Through Diet* (1951) shows obese adults and their treatment at Michigan State University. A fantasy sequence at the start shows an overweight woman reclining on the couch eating chocolates and imagining a dance at which she is not present.

Highways. Conquering Roads (1938) glamorizes the United States highway system, showing construction in progress. Several films show futuristic highways, including *To New Horizons* (1940) and *Design For Dreaming* (1956). *Give Yourself the Green Light* (1954) was produced by General Motors as part of its lobbying campaign for the construction of the Interstate Highway System, and features crowded cities and freeways, poor rural roads, traffic jams, new urban expressways and a Robert Moses speech. "Superb color photography and dramatic aerial views of expressways through crowded cities, parking facilities, cross-country super-highways, and cloverleafs already completed and now in use in many sections of the country give a thrilling preview of what motoring will be like tomorrow."

There is some coverage of 1920s highways, originally from the Ford Film Collection and in home movies (1927). *Seeing Green* (1938, partly in Technicolor) outlines the theory, history and operation of the traffic light, showing scenes of traffic control in different countries, odd mechanical and electrical variations on the standard red-amber-green pattern, and stop-motion animation of model cars on a model street pattern to show the theory of traffic signal synchronization.

Home economics. Films on cooking, food, home appliances, budgeting, housework, nutrition and shopping. *400 Years in 4 Minutes* (baking); *American Thrift* (1962), a "tribute to the woman American" and her money-management ability, showing shopping, supermarkets, clothing stores, freeways, homes and more; *Easy Does It* (1940) compares men's and women's work, arguing that women's work in the home is really too difficult for men. *Frozen Freshness* (1946) was produced to capitalize on postwar affluence, and promotes home freezing.

Grandma Goes to School (1952), produced for home economics students by Frigidaire, was described in this way when it was released: "In this warmly human photoplay, photographed in full color, a school principal has difficulty convincing the school board of the need for modern equipment to help home economics students prepare for careers as wives and homemakers. His task is further complicated by the illness of the regular teacher and the fact that her

post is filled by Grandma who has come out of retirement with some rather quaint ideas on kitchen arts. Because Grandma is so well-loved and highly respected in the community, the school board decides to base its decisions on her recommendations. The amusing situations that develop when the principal tries to modernize Grandma's thinking lend humor to the story. In the climax, however, Grandma out-foxes everyone. With a surprise party, she subtly demonstrates that only with the best of equipment can the girls learn to make proper use of electric ranges, ironers, refrigerators and home freezers, and thus be prepared for their own homemaking."

Grandma Goes to Town (1949), also produced by Frigidaire, attempts to convince reluctant adults of the ease of electric cooking. "Cooking is one of the homemaker's main responsibilities in the home. Every woman has her favorite recipes — her individual cooking procedures — her personal short cuts. In coming to her son's home to take over the cooking chore for the family while his wife is away, Grandma is confronted for the first time with an electric range. She is not only unfamiliar with electric cooking, but has numerous reservations concerning it. In the process of preparing foods, however, she learns — with the help of a granddaughter — and a next door neighbor, a former economist, that cooking with electricity is safe, economical, fast, clean and flexible. Along with this, she also learns many new fascinating food ideas, using simple, inexpensive foods. Grandma's moment of triumph comes when she prepares a lavish dinner for an important guest — an executive in her son's business."

The Home Economics Story (produced by Iowa State College, 1951) follows three young Iowa women through their college career; all are majors in home economics. Their training in fashion and textile design, food preparation and institution management is shown in great detail; physics class is devoted to reverse-engineering the electrical system of a toaster, while chemistry involves analyzing the preparation of tomato soup.

A film on Hoover floor polishers (1960). *Let's Make a Meal in 20 Minutes* (1951), sponsored by the American Gas Association, shows how a teenager (by the name of Sally Gasco) can rapidly "fix" a complete meal with the help of a gas range. *More Food For Your Money* and *The Most For Your Money* (both 1955) are both consumer education films. *Thought For Food* (1933) begins with an argument at the breakfast table between wife and husband, in which the husband criticizes his wife for insufficient meal planning. At the end of the meal she turns to the television set to watch a program presented by the Kroger Food Foundation.

Treasures For the Making (1951), produced by the Certo and Sure-Jell divisions of General Foods, argues that "it's not just making jelly, it's making a home."

Home movies. A large collection is held, generally picturing middle- and upper-class life in East and West Coast communities (1927-63). None of the individuals appearing in these movies has been cleared for public showings, although many now are probably deceased. Among subjects pictured are the Arctic and Arctic cruises; Argentina (Buenos Aires); Arizona; automobile travel, motoring and vacations; backyards; Cairo; Carthage; Crater Lake; Egypt; European, Asian and Middle Eastern travel; Florida, especially Miami, Miami Beach and the Miami Zoo (1930s-50s); France; the Grand Canyon (1953); Greece; Italy, including color footage of a 1937 Fascist party rally in Naples, with long shots of Hermann Goering; Los Angeles (1940s); Malta; a New Orleans-San Francisco railroad journey (1941), featuring bridges over Lake Pontchartrain and a grade crossing accident involving a private automobile somewhere in Mississippi; New York City (Times Square); the New York World's Fair (1939-40); San Francisco (1941); the Soviet Union (1931-33), with footage of Leningrad, Red Army soldiers marching, Orthodox churches, street vendors, banners, and workers in parks on their day of rest); Norway; Trinidad and Tunis.

Housing. Films, primarily produced by various sectors of the building industry, showing building materials, construction, financing and suburbia. *According to Plan* (1952) pictures asbestos sidewalls, suburban tract homes, Levittown (Long Island) and a young couple planning their first home. *New Neighbor* (1953) depicts the construction of U.S. Steel's Fairless Works near Philadelphia, and shows how a nearby Levitt development met the need for workers' housing. *Power By Which We Live* (1949) and *The Power to Serve* (1957) picture early mornings in suburbia. *Problems of Housing* (1946) discusses the poor condition of America's housing stock, and offers hints to homeowners on remodeling their houses for greater efficiency. *A Report to Home Builders* (1946) promotes steel as a modern building material for postwar mass-produced homes. *The Road to Better Living* (mortgage bankers Association of America, 1959) shows the contributions of mortgage bankers to the well-being of our country, emphasizing the influence that they have exerted towards the goal of more and better housing for all.

Humor. Many films mentioned elsewhere also fall into this category. Genres and styles include: films depicting gags and stunts, many of them involving automobiles; animal-related humor, from monkeys dressed in human costumes to boxing cats; social guidance films depicting dated social mores and funny situations; poorly acted dramatic films; industrial or advertising films for products that no longer exist; naive films using strange or exaggerated images to make their point; films including surreal or surprising moments; films with images which, when taken out of context, are humorous (many industrial films fall into this category); and educational films tending to oversimplify their subject matter, e.g., *Mother Mack's Puppies Find Happy Homes.*

Several sponsored films in dramatic form, including *Yeggs Aren't Safe* (1937), *Penny Turns Pro* (1935), *Holiday For Bill* (Dearborn Motors, 1951) and *Young Man's Fancy* (Edison Electric Institute, 1952) contain numerous jokes, gags, puns and reaction shots.

Immigration. Unedited film footage (1986) shows new immigrants to the United States from Asia, Latin America and the Middle East. Footage shot along the United States-Mexico border showing illegal immigration and the efforts of the U.S. Border Patrol to prevent illegal entry into this country. Footage of garment workers and sweatshops in Chinatown, New York City. Footage of farm workers in southern California and Texas. Footage of New York City schoolchildren representing many different ethnic groups.

Insects. Films on ants, beetles (including giant beetles), cockroaches, insecticides lice and pesticides. Two films, *Goodbye Mr. Roach* and *Goodbye Mrs. Ant,* show the generous use of chlordane as a pest control agent.

Insurance. In addition to numerous safety films produced by or in consultation with the insurance industry, several films, including *Life Insurance Occupations* and *Sharing Economic Risks,* show the day-to-day activities of insurance agents and home office workers.

Juvenile delinquency. A number of films show juvenile delinquency in the 1950s, picturing misbehavior in the high-school classroom, muggings, stealing, fighting and boys with knives. None feature well-known actors.

Korean War. Little is held on the war itself. The *Are You Ready For Service?* series (1951-52), intended for boys of high-school age, offers information on preparing for military service. Areas covered include citizenship, educational preparation and physical fitness. One television commercial produced for Eisenhower's 1956 campaign is targeted at the Korean War veteran.

Labor. Material on workers in many industries (1927-70). Almost all of the material held in the library was produced by or in association with corporate management, rather than by labor unions or groups. Footage of Chinese women garment workers and sweatshops in Chinatown, New York City (1986). *Deadline for Action* and *The Great Swindle,* two films produced by the United Electrical, Radio and Machine Workers of America (UE) in the late 1940s, explain inflation, monopolies, political action and strikes from a left-wing perspective. *Protecting Your Profits* (1946), promoting industrial laundry equipment, is a color film showing laundry workers, especially Black men and women, on the job.

From Dawn to Sunset (1937) shows the daily lives of Chevrolet assembly-line and white-collar workers in eleven cities, with scenes of waking up; morning ablutions; walking or driving to work; large crowds assembling and filing into factories; a day's work (both production and office workers are shown); many scenes of receiving paychecks; the trip home in the evening; evening recreation (bowling, dancing and playing cards); and getting in bed for a night's sleep. Shots of downtown skylines, landmarks, and food markets in each of these cities: Tarrytown and Buffalo, N.Y.; St. Louis and Kansas City, Mo.; Detroit and Flint, Mich.; Baltimore, Md.; Norwood (Cincinnati), Ohio; Atlanta, Ga.; Oakland, Calif. and Janesville, Wis.

Several others show white-collar and office workers (1927-65), including: *General Motors Around the World* (1927), *Life Insurance Occupations* (1946); *I Want to Be a Secretary* (1941); *Office Etiquette* and *Office Courtesy* (1952); *The National Post-Tronic* (1957); and *The Power to Serve* (1957).

Lilliputians. A Great Car (1936) follows the journey of three miniaturized explorers through the engine of an impossibly large automobile.

Literacy. Numerous films in the field of language arts, literature and librarianship. *How to Read a Book,* starring Dick York, covers basic skills. *How to Remember, How We Learn* and *How To Write a Term Paper* relate to school study skills.

Machinery and machine shops. Coverage begins mid-1930s. Typical titles include: *How To Machine Aluminum* (1943), produced to train World War II aircraft workers; *The Machinist and Tool Maker* (1940), a vocational film; and *More Than Machines* (1941), produced by the Micromatic Honing Corp., emphasizing the need for precision machining.

Magic. Films by Georges Méliès (all in 16mm) embody some of the earliest motion picture trickery. A travelogue shows Indian magicians, fakirs and snake charmers. *The Magic Shelf* features a magician performing disappearing tricks with various foods; this film was produced in 16mm Kodachrome and the splices separating each scene (which make the tricks

possible) are clearly visible.

Management. Numerous films on personnel and industrial management (1930s-60s). *Experiment* (1947), "combines live-action photography with cartoon animation to convey a real understanding of a fundamental principle in getting along with people. This principle is that people can't be 'socked' into acting or thinking the way we want them to, but, like a heavy cannon ball pendulum, they will respond to a series of gentle pushes — 'not too fast — not too slow — and keep on doing it.' The moral is so clear that no one could miss the point that gentle persuasion is oftentimes more effective than brute force." *The Open Door* (1943), a famous General Motors training film for line management, tells the story of foreman Jim Baxter and his family.

Manufacturing. All industries, from steel mills to the Fuller Brush Co. Three films on watch and clock manufacturing, produced by the Hamilton Watch Co.

Medicine. Numerous educational films and a few sponsored by pharmaceutical companies on subjects including: circulation of the blood; the common cold; germs, the heart; heredity; the immune system; infectious viruses; illnesses; muscles and muscle strain. There are numerous films on dentistry, many produced for children. Several films treat the medical and nursing professions, including *Choosing a Doctor* and *Nursing.* First aid techniques are shown in a number of films (1943-70), including *Help Wanted,* produced by Johnson and Johnson and shown widely during World War II. *March of Dimes 1954* was produced as part of the organization's annual fundraising campaign. Several educational films from the 1930s and 1940s depict the processes of normal birth and Caesarean sections. *The Pharmacist* (1946) is a vocational guidance film. Two films (produced mid-1950s) relating to radioisotopes show radiation therapy operators and equipment and the oral administration of nuclear medicines. *Sucking Wounds of the Chest* (1952), a U.S. Navy training film, shows techniques of emergency treatment.

Metallurgy, mining and metalworking. Films on aluminum, brass, copper, iron and steel, many in color. Mining, ore processing, fabrication and finished products are shown. *Iron Country,* a color film (1952) on the Mesabi Iron Range and the surrounding territory. *South Dakota Saga* (ca. 1940), produced for Homestake Mining Company, details that company's history and operations. Many films are held on steelmaking and specialty steel production, including *The Open Hearth Furnace, Something More Than Steel, Walls Without Welds* (on seamless tubing) and more.

Military training films. Subjects covered include insomnia (starring Dick York, later known for his work in the television series *Bewitched*); nursing; personal hygiene; learning from training films; swimming; the operation of the breeches buoy; malaria; aircraft identification; emergency treatment of sucking chest wounds; aircraft automatic pilots; correctional treatment of military prisoners and land mines. Although most films were produced by or for the United States armed services, several films from the British military establishment and one Indian army training film are held.

Psychological Operations in Support of Internal Defense and Development Assistance Programs (1968), a U.S. Army training film, portrays a mythical Latin American country plagued by guerrilla warfare and insurgency. The U.S. Army "psywar" team assists the indigenous military forces in winning the loyalty of the population by setting the mass media in motion, printing leaflets, posters and newspapers and using other means to influence popular opinion. *Safeguarding Military Information* (see Safety, below) dramatizes the saying that "loose lips sink ships."

Mode-Art Collection: Begins 1937. Strong coverage 1948-82. Subjects covered include: Pittsburgh (city and environs); urban redevelopment; the construction of the Gateway Arch in St. Louis, Mo.; mining industry; steel industry, especially specialty milling and manufacturing; electrical industry, from switches and connectors to nuclear power plants; early nuclear power plant construction and testing; rivers and maritime commerce; beer and brewing, notably in the form of television commercials, including "Olde Frothing Slosh" seasonal beer spots; education and social services. Some coverage of the 1937 Pittsburgh flood. Approximately 1,800 cans, mostly 16mm color reversal original and workprint. Inventoried by card catalog.

Mortuary science. A Monument to the Living, produced by Gupton-Jones College of Mortuary Science, documents the Episcopal funeral service. *Burr-Davis Funeral Home* (1949) tours all public rooms and work areas of the mortician by the same name, located at Mount Vernon, N.Y.

Motion pictures and the film industry. Several movie trailers, including a Christmas holiday trailer (1949), suitable for generic use in any year; two generic "creepshow" trailers once used to introduce horror or science-fiction films; and fifty "minute movies" (1934-55), each presenting commercial advertising in an entertaining form to appeal to a paying audience. *Behind the Lens: The Camera Goes to College* (1940) shows infrared, slow-motion and Schlieren photography, and various applications of cinematography in scientific research, as well as a Hollywood premiere with searchlights, crowds, and audiences inside theaters. *The Movies and You* series, produced by the Academy of Motion Picture Arts and Sciences in cooperation with the major studios (early 1950s) includes *The Art Director, The Screen Actor, The Screen Writer* and *The Sound Man.* One trailer features Olivia deHavilland speaking about her upcoming picture, *A Midsummer Night's Dream.*

How You See It (1936), produced by the Chevrolet Motor Company, uses scientific animation and live action to explain the principle of persistence of vision and how it makes motion pictures possible. This film includes scenes of patrons at the box office, movie theater audiences, motion picture projectors and film being wound onto a reel out of a trash can.

Film Tactics, a training film, shows how to use motion pictures in the training process. *Let Yourself Go* (1940) shows a family looking at 16mm home movies in their living room. *Making Films That Teach* (1954), produced by Encyclopedia Britannica Films to commemorate its 25th anniversary, takes viewers behind the scenes to show the process of educational film production, including scriptwriting, research, shooting, editing, animation and post-production. *Technicolor For Industrial Films* (1949), produced by the Technicolor Corporation, promotes the use of color in industrial films with many examples, including beauty shots, product shots, footage of people interacting with products, interiors and exteriors.

Musical shorts. Soundies and other musical variety shorts (1940s), featuring talent of the times, novelty acts and classical music performances.

Newsreels. Chevrolet Leader News (16 issues released from 1935 to 1939) contains informational and entertaining newsreel-type stories, all featuring Chevrolet automobiles. Subjects covered include: animal stunts and gags; the Tennessee Valley Authority; the Soap Box Derby; fashions; futuristic house trailers; trailer camps; the construction of U.S. Highway 1 to Key West, Florida; combination rail and highway vehicles built to reach remote locations; a chimpanzee driving a car; driver education; the introduction of the parking meter; a dog birthday party; boxing cats; a firefighting cat; model airplanes; the opening of the Golden Gate Bridge; a drive-in bank in California; a Boy Scout Jamboree; a story on the Dust Bowl; a mobile barber; the New Jersey State Police and their aviation unit; a circus with performing rats; railroad buffs on a photo tour of a roundhouse; a deer that lives with a family in New Jersey; surfing on the Pacific Coast in California; a cow smoking a pipe and dancing; bathing beauties practicing archery; women fencing in the sand; and the transportation of baby chicks to South America by air freight.

New York City. The City (1939) shows Wall Street; midtown Manhattan; various neighborhoods, including Little Italy and Hell's Kitchen; crowded access roads just outside the city; and restaurants and eating. Many of these shots are part of a montage showing the stresses of urban life. A film depicting Coney Island (1940s). A film depicting traffic and transportation facilities of New York City (1941). Footage depicting the seven daily newspapers and their buildings during a newspaper strike, in *Seventeen Days,* produced by the (New York) *Daily News* (1945). Color footage (1941) of Times Square movie marquees, Fifth Avenue traffic and sidewalk scenes, in *International Moves the Browns to Sterling Street.*

Offices and office workers. Numerous industrial and advertising films contain footage of offices, white-collar workers and secretaries in various situations, e.g. meetings, boardrooms, reception areas, operating business machines and using telephones. *Picture of Comfort,* produced by the Harter Chair Co., promotes executive-style chairs. Several films, notably *Office Courtesy* and *Office Etiquette* (both 1952), were designed to train office workers in the rules of proper business conduct.

Perception and vision. Films on the eye, including: *How The Eye Functions* (1941); visual perception; light; photography; color and color vision; and the X-ray as an aid to ordinary perception. There are a number of films about sound, sound waves, hearing and the functions of the ear. Several films introduce stereophonic sound equipment (1957-62), including *New Dimensions in Sound, Living Stereo* and others. *Wonderland of Vision* (1947), produced by the Better Vision Institute, extols the benefits of eyeglasses, saying that "nothing gives you so much and costs you so little."

Photography. Several films on the workings of cameras and lenses; light and optics and careers in photography (ca. 1940). *The Girl on the Magazine Cover* (1940), concerns the work of the magazine photographer and professional model, as well as the representation of women from a male viewpoint.

Physical sciences. Solar and Terrestrial Radiation (1951) shows how different radiation sources reach the earth, concentrating on their absorption by our atmosphere and the results of this process. The film contains excellent scientific animation and still drawings.

Plastics. Looking Ahead Through Rohm & Haas Plexiglas (1947) shows production technology and new products, including hammerproof helmets, knicknacks and furniture. The film ends with a color sequence picturing the "Dream Suite," a bedroom and bathroom combination in which everything is constructed from Plexiglas. *American Look* (1958) pictures new plastic products for the home and office, many in extreme closeup, including housewares, appliances, knives and pencil sharpeners. *Color Harmony for Your Home* (1956) pictures new plastic products, including polyethylene pitchers, new colored telephones and Melmac dinnerware. *Plastics,* produced by the General Electric Company (1940s) is a general introduction to technology and design. *Test Tube Tale* (1938) shows the benefits of industrial chemistry, with footage of many consumer items made from plastics.

Politics and elections. Various civics and social studies films are held, bearing titles such as *Political Parties* and *Politics and Elections.* Television commercials from the Eisenhower presidential campaigns of 1952 and 1956 (each 1 to 4 min.), include "man in the street" interviews on women's issues, war and peace and the economy. Two films from the Republican National Committee are held, *We The People* and *The Truth About Taxes,* both produced on behalf of 1940 presidential candidate Wendell Willkie. The latter film contains animation ridiculing the proliferation of "alphabetic" New Deal agencies, showing letters blowing out the top of the U.S. Capitol building.

Presidents. A small amount of footage (none unique) is held on each of the following U.S. Presidents: Theodore Roosevelt, William Howard Taft, Woodrow Wilson, Warren G. Harding, Calvin Coolidge, Herbert Hoover, Franklin D. Roosevelt, Harry S Truman, Dwight D. Eisenhower and John F. Kennedy.

Primitive films. Films by Méliès, Edison, Porter and early newsreel cameramen are held, all in 16mm release print form.

Psychology. Attitudes and Health (1955) is a simplified explanation of psychosomatic disease; *Don't Be Afraid,* made for children; *Let Yourself Go* (1940), featuring Dr. Donald A. Laird (director, Colgate University Psychology Laboratory) gives tips on relaxation in a stressful age; and *Preventive Psychiatry in the Navy* (ca. 1951) depicts the mental stresses and strains of military life, with animation showing the forces that cause men to go off the beam. *The Relaxed Wife* (1957) depicts a man in a state of extreme anxiety and insomnia, and the attempts of his relaxed wife to calm him down. Proposing that "some folks aren't helped by relaxing exercises," the film suggests that doctors prescribe "ataraxic" (relaxing) medication so as to make room "to relish the joys of life." *Understand Your Emotions* (1952) uses a psychology class as a background for an explanation of the three basic emotions: fear, anger and love.

Radio. Back of the Mike (1937) depicts behind-the-scenes activity in a studio during the broadcast of a Western drama show, with actors, technicians and sound effects men. Various animated radio waves, including a map of the United States with many animated emitters (1935); and animation of radio waves (1927). *Hear and Now* (1958) shows studios, facilities, radios and people listening to the radio, as well as examples of various kinds of programming. Color footage (1941) of announcers, studios, and listeners at home (*International Moves the Browns to Sterling Street*). *Into All the World* shows footage of announcers, transmitting towers, and listeners at home (ca. 1935-50). Films promoting table and portable radios (1960). Films relating to industrial design, showing modern plastic radios (1955 and 1958). *On The Air* (1938) shows the behind-the-scenes labor that results in the broadcast of a musical radio show, including studio activity and sign language. *Voices of Victory* (1944) shows the contributions of Hallicrafters radio equipment to the war effort.

Railroads. Modern railroading is shown in *At This Moment* (1956), which contains excellent footage of freight and passenger service, including Vista-Dome observation cars. A 1942 film contains complete coverage of all divisions of the New York, New Haven and Hartford Railroad, showing: train operations (freight and passenger); dining cars; stations; train runbys; steam engines; and shops and workers in all departments. *New England: Yesterday and Today* (1938), also produced by the New Haven Railroad to promote tourism in its territory, contains a few shots of passenger train operation. *Safe Roads* (1938) compares driving an automobile to running a railroad engine, and contains excellent footage of steam-powered passenger trains. The film begins with a montage of well-known named trains (along with their distinctive logo signs) running on railroads all over the U.S.

Religious films. Numerous religious films relating to tithing; evangelism; youth and the church; music and hymns; religious radio broadcasting; and more. *A Note of Praise* animates the musical notes of a hymn. *The Beatnik and Christianity* (1964) poses faith against nihilism.

Robots. Leave It to Roll-Oh (1940) shows a chromium-plated domestic robot in the home performing ordinary housework; following this fanciful example, it shows how switches and relays are already making life easier for human beings.

Rural America. Unedited footage (1985) showing small-town and rural life in the state of Minnesota. *Waves of Green* (1950), a dramatized history of the American farm and farm family.

Safety. Dramatic safety films, using a variety of storylines and devices to influence audiences toward safe behavior, include *Anatomy of an Accident* (1961); *And Then There Were Four* (1950); *Jimmy of the Safety Patrol* (ca. 1952), a tale of a boy's redemption; *The Last Clear Chance* (1960), in which two teenagers die in a railroad grade crossing accident; *The Last Date* (1949), a classic safety film intended for those of high-school age which uses facial disfigurement, rather than death, to shock its audience; and *None for the Road* (1957), blending a tragic story of teenage drunken driving with scientific footage of the effects of alcohol injections in rats. *Octopus in the House* (1953), based on a play, is a living-room comedy dramatizing the dangers of inadequate household wiring. *Safe As You Think* (1947) tells the story of a man who trusted too long in his good luck, and is maintained in an uninjured state long enough for his guardian angel to make the lesson hit home. Contained in the film is a "wheel of fortune" sequence and an elevator ride into a bureaucratic heaven where divine actuaries keep accident scores. *The Terrifying Tale of Tizzie Gooch* (ca. 1954) shows the plight of an uncoordinated woman. *X Marks the Spot* (1942) shows the death of Joe Doaks, a reckless driver, and his rise to a heavenly traffic court, where his "guardian angel" presents his driving record to a judge. This film was designed to prevent unnecessary deaths of workers useful to the war effort.

Safeguarding Military Information (1942), though not strictly a safety film, dramatizes the military proverb that "loose lips sink ships." A train wreck, the torpedoing of a troop transport and the explosion of a ship are all brought about through the unintentional revelation of military secrets. The film was produced in Hollywood (with Hollywood talent) as a contribution to the war effort, and was scripted by Preston Sturges.

Cautionary safety films intended for children, including *Live and Learn* (1951), which shows shocking accidents caused when youngsters take risks, e.g., tripping onto scissors held with points up and falling over cliffs at the Palisades in Santa Monica, California. *Safe Use of Tools* (1941) avoids shock and contains excellent color footage of prewar family life and leisure.

Driving safety films without storylines, such as *An Honorary Doctor's Degree in Driving* (1952) and *Mickey's Big Chance* (1953), in which Mickey's elder brother, home on leave from the armed forces, teaches him the elements of safe and sane driving. *The Safest Place* (Chevrolet, 1935) compares the hazards of home life with the relative safety of the modern automobile, unsurprisingly concluding that the car is the safer place. *Safety Patrol* (1955) presents ten safety rules for children and adults in the form of a discussion between a young patrol member and a policeman. *Tomorrow's Drivers* (1955) documents driver training in the Phoenix, Arizona public schools, which starts at a very young age and includes ample practice in pedal-powered "kiddie cars." The film also shows teenagers tinkering with and driving hot rods under police supervision, driver training in high schools and a car being stopped by police. *We Drivers* (produced 1936, revised 1955 and 1962) dramatizes the struggle between the two sides of a driver's personality, counterposing "Reckless Rudolph" against "Sensible Sam." While one side (shown as an animated character) seeks to draw the driver into unsafe behavior, the other side yanks him back — and ultimately prevails — in a prize fight. *When You Are a Pedestrian* (1948), shot on the streets of Oakland, California, shows safe and unsafe conduct, with numerous simulated accidents, near-misses and feltboard animation of automobiles and pedestrians. *Your Permit To Drive* (1952) is narrated by a talking driver's license.

Films on fire safety and firefighting, including *Crusaders Against Fire* (1952); *How To Call the Fire Department* (1951); *Modern Magic in Fire Control* (1941), showing up-to-date sprinkler systems; *Not Too Hot To Handle* (1952), produced by the Kidde Co., promoting hand-held fire extinguishers and *Too Young To Burn* (1951), which argues that children should experience the pain of a burn just once so as to learn the need for caution.

Several films showing automobile crash research and crash tests, including *Crash and Live* and *Crash Research* (both produced by Ford Motor Company, 1955), illustrating efforts to develop a safer car for the 1956 model year. There are also a few Ford television commercials from 1956 which, in contrast to those of other manufacturers, stress safety. *Safety Belt for Susie* (1962) shows crash tests conducted by the Institute of Traffic and Transportation Engineering at the University of California, Los Angeles; these tests employed dolls to assess crash injuries inflicted on unrestrained children and infants. A film of Chevrolet's Corvair (1960) showing its handling and maneuverability on test tracks in Michigan and Connecticut. *Priceless Cargo* (1947), which won the coveted "Best Safety Film of the Year" award when released, concerns school bus safety.

A film on the dangers of hot-water heater explosions, with many tests and examples (1949).

Industrial safety films, such as *Factory Safety* (1937) and *Days of Our Years* (Union Pacific Railroad, 1955), featuring three tear-jerking stories of carelessness, injury and death.

Sales training. Many films (1935-65); some made with general appeal, others concerned with specific lines or industries. There are a few classic titles in this genre, such as *Beware of Mental-itis* (1937); *Selling America* (1938), ostensibly hosted by Benjamin Franklin; *The Face In The Mirror* (1938) and *The Things People Want* (1948). *Selling As a Career* (ca. 1953), a vocational guidance film, shows a day in the life of a sporting goods salesman, who, in order to prove that his shoes are watertight, fills one with a glass of water. *The Things People Want* (1948), starring John Forsythe, encourages salesmen to consider the role of deep-seated human wants in influencing buying decisions. While seated in his office at night, Forsythe is visited by the voice of his alter ego, who "walks him through" the necessary thought process.

Scientists and scientific experiments. Experimental subjects in difficult situations include: a test pilot on a giant centrifuge; a typist subjected to noise while wearing a gas mask; and a man sweating in a steam bath. Many films contain shots of researchers and scientists, occasionally with large or mysterious machinery. Dramatizations of Alessandro Volta, Benjamin Franklin, Samuel F. B. Morse and Alexander Graham Bell. Footage of Thomas Edison (with Henry Ford), originally from the Ford Film Collection at the National Archives and Records Administration.

Sex education. Until the 1960s, relatively few sex education films were produced, with the prominent exception of films (mostly produced by the Army and Navy) relating to venereal disease. Many of the "classic" sex education films are held in the collection, including *Human Beginnings; Human Growth; Human Reproduction*, seen by millions of adolescents in darkened classrooms; *Physical Aspects of Puberty*; and *Your Body During Adolescence*. *In The Beginning* (1938), produced by the U.S. Department of Agriculture, shows the process of mammalian reproduction, including microphotography of egg and sperm cells in the human. Another "scientific" film, *Reproduction Among Mammals*, uses rabbit cells and embryos to explain fertilization, cell division and growth of the fetus.

A number of films were produced for showing to teenage women and explain the menstrual cycle. Some of these films are still being shown in schools and may be currently protected by copyright. Titles include: *It's Wonderful Being A Girl; Molly Grows Up* (1953); and *Naturally A Girl*.

Social guidance. *Act Your Age* shows a troubled teenager's path to maturity; *Age of Turmoil* (adolescence); *Am I Trustworthy?; Appreciating Our Parents; Are Manners Important?; Are You Popular?* (1947), in which teenagers are taught to avoid petting, going steady and "parking in cars with the boys at night"; *Are You Ready for Marriage?*, in which a boy and girl contemplating marriage are advised that there is more to marriage than mutual sexual attraction; *As Others See Us* (1955), shot in Webster Groves, Missouri, trains teenagers in good manners and social courtesy; and *The Benefits of Looking Ahead*, designed to teach teenagers the importance of planning for the future. *Cheating* shows the effects of dishonesty on the career of a student who was once a student council member; *Choosing for Happiness, Marriage Today* and *This Charming Couple* (1950-51) are marriage training films produced in response to the increase in the divorce rate after World War II. *Cindy Goes to a Party* employs Cindy's dream as a device to impart a lesson in manners and acceptable behavior; *Control Your Emotions*, in which an overwrought teenage boy and a psychologist explain the interaction of love, fear and anger; *A Date With Your Family* suggests that you behave with your family as you would in the company of someone you really wanted to be with.

Going Steady (1952) marshals parental arguments against premature pairing; *How Do You Do?* (1946) instructs teenagers in rather stiff behavior; *How Do You Know It's Love?* (1950) helps college-age men and women decide whether they are ready for marriage; *How Friendly Are You?; How Much Affection?* (1957) discusses how far teenagers can take petting before the risks outweigh the pleasures. *How To Be Well Groomed* (ca. 1951) shows a teenage boy and girl, their ablutions and preparation for the school day, linking grooming to popularity.

How To Say No: Moral Maturity (1951) was designed to help teenagers avoid dangerous or undesirable situations. It shows models for possible behavior at difficult moments, e.g., how to turn down an alcoholic drink or refuse a cigarette gracefully and how to deal with the sorts of situations that lead to petting. There is a discussion of the differing responsibilities of boys and girls in sexual situations.

Junior Prom (1946, color) provides behavioral guidance for high-school age boys and girls on the occasion of their first prom. The story is told using two couples. *The Meaning of Adolescence, Meeting the Needs of Adolescents* and *Social-Sex Attitudes in Adolescence* (all ca. 1953) were produced to familiarize adults with common behavioral and developmental teenage traits. They contain excellent footage of teenagers arguing with their parents, partying, dancing, driving, drinking, petting and making out. *Mental Health* (1953) presents several hints on how children and teenagers can maintain good mental health, and is narrated by an elderly general practitioner. *Mind Your*

Manners (1951) was produced for elementary school students.

More Dates For Kay (1952, not available for reuse), presents the story of a teenage girl suffering from "dating slumps" and her attempts to become more popular.

O'Mara's Chain Miracle (1952), a rare example of a social guidance film directed at adults, stars Victor McLaglen. "McLaglen plays the archetype of [a] gruff traffic cop on a busy street intersection in a typical small community. One of the passing motorists encroaches too far on the crosswalk when he stops on signal. Breathing the fire of righteous indignation, the policeman strides toward the unhappy victim who slumps in his seat with resignation. But for some inexplicable reason, the officer can't seem to find words vitriolic enough and finally waves him on with a rueful caricature of a grin. The astonished driver perks up and drives off with a thoughtful expression. From then on the infectiousness of a smile spreads throughout the town like an epidemic...it just serves to prove that a little kindness goes a long way!"

Office Courtesy and *Office Etiquette* (both 1952) train secretaries and white-collar employees in proper on-the-job conduct, incorporating guilt-ridden dreams of incompetence and hilarious "do's and don'ts" sequences.

One Thousand Hours (1935) responds to widespread adolescent disillusionment during the Depression, advising children to complete their education so that they will be ready for the "world of tomorrow." Narrated by a passenger airline pilot, it demonstrates how education (especially in the fields of science and engineering) is necessary in order to fly an airplane. *Other People's Property* explains the importance of respecting the property of others. *Overcoming Fear* uses a boy's reluctance to swim as a vehicle for explaining the nature of phobias. *Responsibility* (1952) is directed at teenagers and approaches the concept of responsibility by showing the necessity to complete homework assignments on time. *School Rules: How They Help Us* (1955, color) shows a student-directed effort to regulate behavior, including the setting up of "up" and "down" staircases. *Self-Conscious Guy* (1951) and *Shy Guy* (1947, starring Dick York), explore two common adolescent behavior syndromes. In *Shy Guy*, York wonders how his overall shyness and solitary interest in radios, coupled with his being new at school, will ever result in acceptance by his peers. His problem is resolved by advice from his father, himself a victim of corporate relocation. *Shyness*, produced in Canada, is a study of a young teenage woman and her efforts (especially at school) to conquer diffidence. *Social Acceptability* (1957) shows a shy teenage girl's excitement after being asked to a party by another girl who enjoys the esteem of her classmates. She waits all evening for a telephoned invitation that never comes. *Social-Sex Attitudes in Adolescence* (1953) traces the stages of sexual development in boys and girls, from pre-pubescent stages to adulthood; this film contains excellent footage of necking, making out, teenage drinking and driving and relaxed intimacy.

A series of educational films on speech (early 1950s) contains episodes including *Function of Gestures, Platform Posture and Appearance, Stage Fright and What To Do About It* and *Using Your Voice*. Each uses animation, surrealism, point-of-view shots and other such devices to make a point.

Toward Emotional Maturity (1955) shows a female teenager's coming of emotional age, picturing mood swings, mob psychology and the decision of whether or not to drive to a secluded place for necking and petting. *What About Drinking* (1959) and *What About Juvenile Delinquency?* (1955) pose problems for group discussion by teenagers. The latter film ends with a sequence in which the "straight" teens race the delinquent teens to the city hall in order to defend their good intentions at an emergency city council meeting. *What Makes A Good Party?* (1951) offers social and behavioral rules for success, and presents the improbable picture of high-school seniors singing *Jimmy Crack Corn* around the piano. *What To Do On a Date* (1951) eases fears of embarrassment and boredom, proposing skating parties, weenie roasts and miniature golf. *Writing Better Social Letters* and its companion film *Writing Better Business Letters* (both early 1950s) are aimed at teenagers. *You And Your Family* (1946) relates to conflicts between parents and teens over such topics as permission to date on school nights.

Soviet Union. Approximately 80 documentaries, travelogues and promotional films produced in the Soviet Union for international distribution (ca. 1970s).

Space exploration. Numerous films, all produced originally by NASA. Subjects include: the first moon landing (1969); the space shuttle; satellites of various types (with satellite animation); Skylab; early manned spaceflight; human engineering in space; and civilian technological spinoffs from the government space program. Several advertising and business films attest to the high level of space consciousness in early-1960s America, showing rockets, launches, observatories, stars and space-oriented toys.

Sports and recreation. Collection generally avoids professional or spectator sports, concentrating instead on amateur sports (e.g., bowling and sandlot baseball) and more informal leisure pursuits. Almost all material is

historical. One film, *Fashions on the Ice and Snow* (1940, part color) depicts prewar skiing, ski jumping and snow trains. A sequence in *Chevrolet Leader News* shows prewar surfing on the California coast. A number of films show cheerleaders and pep activities (1950-64). Numerous films show school sports in the United States, especially with children of high-school age. Two films (1959-61) show modern bowling alleys and pocket billiard (pool) parlors playing host to idealized, all-American families. An early tinted film shows bobsledding. *Park Conscious* (1930s), produced for the Minnesota state park system, shows hiking, riding, canoeing, swimming and other activities.

A newsreel on the 1936 Olympic games in Berlin contains footage of many noted athletes, including Jesse Owens.

Steel. Numerous films produced by the steel industry, including: *Behind the Annual Report* (U.S. Steel, 1945), relating to wartime production; a German documentary showing steel production (ca. 1930); a newsreel showing Pittsburgh steel mills (ca. late 1920s); and *Steel: Symphony of Industry* (1936), produced for the American Iron and Steel Institute, which boasts of the many parking places provided for steelworkers, characterizing this as an index of mass prosperity. *Unfinished Business* (U.S. Steel, 1948) shows how U.S. Steel retrains World War II veterans as they return to claim their prewar jobs.

Stunts. Group motorcycle riding stunts (*Around the Corner*, 1937); various stunts in different issues of *Chevrolet Leader News* (1935-39).

Surrealism. Aluminum on the March, a surreal stop-motion march of modern metal products; *Another Cup of Coffee*, in which a man sees an image of himself in his coffee cup; *Auto-Lite on Parade*, stop-motion animation; *Back of the Mike*, behind the scenes at a radio studio during the production of a Western show; *Beware of Mental-itis*, a 1937 sales training film purporting to show the inside of a man's brain; *A Case of Spring Fever*, in which a man's wish (that all springs were to disappear) is granted, resulting in chaos and inefficiency; *Design for Dreaming* (1956), a musical showing a woman's romp through the General Motors Motorama, the kitchen of the future, and the electronic highways of tomorrow. *Diana Lives* (1951), made for the Mullins Manufacturing Co., shows the strange meeting of a sales manager with the company logotype (the goddess Diana), who comes to life as a real, full-sized woman, and their ensuing cross-country journey. *Once Upon A Honeymoon* (1956), produced for the Bell System, is a 15-minute musical in which a guardian angel effects the modernization of a old home, redecorating rooms past their prime, updating kitchen appliances and installing new color-coordinated telephones.

Precisely So (1937) tells the story of measurement beginning in Babylonian times, ending with a stop-motion animated march of precision measuring tools, including compasses, slide rules, gauge blocks and micrometers. *The Relaxed Wife* (1957) contains an extraordinary sequence intended to symbolize the process of tranquilization. *Saint Paul Police Detectives and Their Work* (1941) portrays the activities of different police divisions in three-dimensional stop-motion animation. Noteworthy sequences include robbery, homicide, morals and sex crimes. *Speech: Stage Fright and What To Do About It* (1951) visualizes the fears of an unwilling public speaker, including snakes, gunshots and falls off the platform. Also included are scenes of animated question marks rapidly superimposing themselves over a man's image. *The Things People Want* (1948) shows John Forsythe (as a puzzled sales trainee) encountering the voice of his alter ego, who helps him understand the true role of human motivations.

A film on evacuation of patients from hospitals in emergencies shows nurses wrestling patients out of their hospital beds, bringing them down fire escapes and depositing them on floors.

Also holds numerous sequences of odd clocks, timepieces and pendulums; films with montages of eyes, ears and animated question marks; animated sound, radio and television waves; and globes floating in space.

Teenagers. Extensive coverage of teenagers in the post-World War II era (color and black and white). Films (primarily described in *Social guidance*) portray teens at home, at school, at soda shops, in automobiles, dancing, on the street and in other environments. Almost all teenagers represented in the collection are middle-class and upper-middle-class whites.

Telephones and telephony. Telephones and telephone conversations (especially in business contexts) are shown in many films. *Just Imagine* (1947) shows the different parts of a standard desk telephone set assembling themselves in stop-motion animation. *A Nation At Your Fingertips* (1951) introduces direct distance dialing and recaps telephone history in the United States, with excellent shots of old-time operators using outdated equipment. *Once Upon A Honeymoon* (1956), a musical, promotes the new color telephones. *Story Without End* (1952) shows the continuing efforts on the part of the Bell System to modernize and upgrade its plant and transmission systems. Transcontinental telephone lines from copper wire to the then-new microwave radio relay system are shown. *Telephone and Telegraph* (1940) is a vocational guidance film, showing equipment and workers in all sectors of the industry. *Thanks for Listening* (ca. 1950) relates to the development of good telephone manners for executives.

Television. Numerous shots and scenes relating to television (1933-60) in various films, including: television studios and transmission; men, women, children, couples and families watching television; cameras; transmission towers; television at sports events; demonstrations of television sets that fold into a piece of furniture; early UHF converters; early remote-control devices; and devices to program television viewing ahead of time (1960). *The Reasons Why* (1959) shows the engineering, manufacture and testing of new television sets in the laboratory and at the factory. There are a number of shots of television screens suitable for compositing new visual imagery. *A Welcome Guest in the House* (National Assn. of Broadcasters, ca. 1959) is a tribute to television's public role, with excerpts of news and public affairs programs.

Magic in the Air (initially produced December 1941, revised 1955) follows television from the studio into the home, showing men watching early television sets; remote production units at Ebbets Field (Brooklyn, N.Y.); studio scenes; cameras; an explanation of the scanning process; and the Empire State Building in New York City transmitting an animated television wave. It ends with a fantasy of the future, as an actress (previously shown in the studio) materializes in the male viewer's home through the television screen and freshens up his drink.

Thought for Food (1933) contains a fanciful scene of a housewife watching a home economics program on television in her living room.

Holdings of television commercials are indicated above under *Advertising*.

Very few television programs are held in the collection; none are available for reuse or resale, as rights are retained by original producers.

Time and motion study. The Easier Way (1947) "shows how the science of motion study makes a worker's job easier and more productive." Of this film, the sponsor said: "The picture opens in the home of Bob Mills, a motion study man. Stop-watch in hand, Bob times himself as he tries to develop easier methods of setting the table. Dick Gardner, a foreman, and his wife are coming for dinner. After dinner Bob and Dick get into a discussion about the merits of motion study. Before long they are busy testing themselves with the pegboard device Bob uses to illustrate the principles of motion study. The men's wives are intrigued by this method and Dick is amazed to see that by using the proper method his wife can work the pegs as well as he can. Later, as the discussion continues, flashback scenes in a plant illustrate how improved methods of job operation have made various jobs more productive and easier to handle. The picture ends as the two men are marched off to work out a better method of dishwashing at the kitchen sink."

Transportation. Arteries of New York City (1941) shows urban transportation, including trucks, automobiles, tunnels, streets, trains, subways, railroads and streetcars. *The Bus Driver* (1948) shows intercity bus transportation. See *Automobiles, Cities* and *Railroads* for numerous other films.

Travel and travelogues. Several films in the *Roads to Romance* series (each approx. 3 min.), produced for Chevrolet in the early 1950s, show a touristic perspective on North American landmarks and historic sites, including: Coral Gables, Florida; the Santa Cruz Trail and land of the giant cactuses; Arizona; and the Adirondacks. *Midwest Holiday* (early 1950s) follows a man and woman on a journey to various tourist attractions in the central United States, as their romance develops at a glacial pace. *New England: Yesterday and Today* (1938) shows modern tourist spots and the historical events that occurred in these places, counterposing travelogue-type shots with the "ghostly" past. *Sapphire Lake* (ca. 1949), produced for Evinrude, traces the comic misadventures of a family on vacation at a Tennessee lake.

United States history. Stock shots of U.S. Presidents William McKinley, Theodore Roosevelt, Woodrow Wilson, Warren Harding, Calvin Coolidge, Herbert Hoover, Franklin D. Roosevelt, Harry Truman, Dwight D. Eisenhower and John F. Kennedy. Television campaign commercials from the 1952 and 1956 campaigns of Dwight D. Eisenhower. Dramatized reenactments of many famous personalities, eras and events in American history, including the life and works of George Washington; Peter Stuyvesant; the building of the transcontinental railroad; the Revolutionary War; the Monroe Doctrine; the Civil War; the signing of the Constitution and the Declaration of Independence; the drafting of the Bill of Rights; Abraham Lincoln; the Pilgrims and early settlement in New England; and more.

The Story of Our Flag (1941) shows the history of United States expansion (both within and outside its present borders) from 1776, with recreations of historical events and animation of historical flags. *Territorial Possessions of the United States* (1939) contains animated maps and historical footage of U.S. possessions throughout the world.

Vocational guidance. Numerous films held, including *Choosing Your Occupation; Diversified Occupations;* and *Finding Your Life Work* (1940), containing interesting animation relating to a young person's occupational choices and alternatives.

Washington, D.C. A film depicting tourist highlights of Washington (1954, color) and various shots of Washington (1920s-60s) included in various educational and advertising films.

Western Americana. The American Cowboy, Ford Motor Company's classic institutional film. Also holds some "cowboy" and musical shorts.

Wildlife. Arthur C. Twomey Collection. Represents for stock sale this collection of natural history footage, some 300,000 feet, most in color (1935-80). Covers the peoples, flora and fauna of Africa, Asia, Latin America, the Arctic, Soviet Union, Mongolia and China. Includes footage from numerous expeditions showing animals, birds, fish, scenics and landscapes of all kinds.

Women. See also *Home economics,* above. Numerous films depicting sex roles in the United States, especially in relation to consumerism and the home. Titles of interest include: *The Best Made Plans; Cooking: Terms and Their Meaning; Easy Does It* (1940), which compares ironing to bricklaying and concludes that the "little woman" really works very hard; and *The Girl on the Magazine Cover* (1940), ostensibly about the work of models who pose for magazine photographers, but most revealing as an example of how woman's image is often constituted from a male viewpoint.

In *Mother Takes A Holiday* (1952), two teenage women trick their fathers into buying electric home laundries for their wives, believing that women's emancipation is directly related to the acquisition of labor-saving devices. *Three Smart Daughters* (1938), a one-minute advertisement produced for Singer Sewing Centers, shows how three unmarried sisters make their own fashionable dresses to attract men at a dance.

Several films train women for office or secretarial work, including *Help Wanted: Secretary; Office Courtesy; Office Etiquette* and *I Want To Be A Secretary* (1941). Many of these films feature "do's and don'ts" sequences.

World War II. Numerous newsreels, most incorporating U.S. military footage, of Pearl Harbor, battles and bombings in Europe and Asia and the events of 1944-45. *Postwar Germany* (40 min., color, original) shows ruined cities, devastated industry and the effects of the American bombing. War production is shown in a number of films, including *An American Miracle* (1945), "a comprehensive back-stage glimpse of all the many steps necessary to mass-produce a simple product," in this case a 3-inch artillery shell; and *Behind the Annual Report* (1945). *Close Harmony* (1942) uses a barbershop as a location for a discussion on how cooperation between labor and management and among different industries can hasten our winning the war. *Pearl Harbor* (1942), a short film without narration produced for theatrical showings, includes newsreel clips of Japanese atrocities in an attempt to stimulate national solidarity. Two films, one with a short color sequence (1946) and another containing a black and white sequence (1948), dramatize the return of two veterans and their reunions with their wives. In the second film, the veteran distributes souvenirs from Europe to his family.

All-Star Bond Rally records the promotional efforts of Hollywood and radio personalities on behalf of the U.S. Treasury Department.

Several films picture wartime industrial production on the homefront, including *These Are The People* (Kimberly-Clark Co., 1944), showing workers riding bicycles to work and women operating large paper manufacturing machinery; and *These People* (Frigidaire Division of General Motors Corp., 1944), showing how a Dayton, Ohio refrigerator plant converted itself into a propeller plant in record time. Newsreels from General Motors (1944) show Army-Navy "E" award ceremonies and aircraft production in the Midwest. *The Town* (1944), produced by the U.S. Office of War Information, shows everyday life during wartime in an Indiana town. *When Work Is Done,* another U.S. government-produced film, shows how the residents of Sylacauga, Alabama welcomed an influx of war workers from other parts of the country.

World's Fairs. Material held on the San Francisco World's Fair (1939-40), including its opening: views of some pavilions and scenes after its closing, when it became an air terminal for Pan American Airways' *China Clippers;* on the New York World's Fair (1939-40), with various films, including Kodachrome home movies, the General Motors exhibit and Futurama, Billy Rose's *Aquacade,* and miscellaneous day and night scenes; on the Seattle World's Fair (1962), featuring technology exhibits; and on the New York World's Fair (1964-65), featuring views of many pavilions and attractions.

To New Horizons (1940), an homage to technological progress and an evocation of an abundant future, documents the General Motors "Highways and Horizons" exhibit at the New York World's Fair. "Popularly called the Futurama, it is credited with being the most popular and most impressive exhibit ever shown at a World's Fair. To capture in this moving picture the thrilling beauty, the wizardry and the inspirational appeal of that very unique and tremendously popular exhibit, all available modern techniques of motion picture color photography were drawn upon. Valleys, lakes, mountains, rivers and plains, great industrial cities, residential communities, intercommunicating highway systems with their bridges, hydroelectric plants, dams, airfields, canals and locks are shown as they are envisaged by Norman Bel Geddes for the world of tomorrow."

Size & Elements: Materials held on over 15,000 completed productions (60% preprint elements, 40% release prints); approx. 35,000 cans outtakes and unedited footage. Film: 35mm (approx. 7 million feet; color and black and white, negatives, fine grain masters and release prints); 16mm (approx. 23 million feet; color and black and white, all elements); 9.5mm (300 feet); 8mm (5,000 feet). Videotape: 1", Betacam and 3/4" (masters, approx. 150 hours); 3/4" and VHS (viewing copies and reference cassettes, approx. 800 hours). All videotape material is transferred from film.

Many frequently requested stock shots are available on 1" broadcast-quality master and matching 3/4" viewing copies with visible time code. Most stock material of immediate interest is available on reference-quality cassettes for quick screening.

Cataloging: Finding aids and catalogs for many portions of collection; computerized cataloging in progress (staff use only); card catalogs for some collections; videotape inventories and logs; reference library.

Access: Available to researchers, scholars and the public. Research fees charged for commercial users. Scholarly and historical researchers accommodated within limits of staff and equipment necessary to process requests. Research requests accepted by mail and telephone (appointments always necessary). Viewing cassettes furnished to prospective stock footage researchers upon request, but screening in person is recommended for complex projects.

Rights: Full rights owned to some material. Most material in the public domain and furnished in return for payment of access fees. Rights to some material retained by copyright holders or original producers; any reuse requires their permission. Users must assume full responsibility for securing any necessary clearances or authorizations required for reuse of the materials.

Licensing: Available for licensing and reuse, subject to restrictions. License and usage fees charged depending on intended markets for production. Fees computed on amount of footage actually used in final cut. Minimum project fees (non-refundable) charged upon shipment of broadcast-quality film or videotape masters. Discounts for quantity usage negotiable. Clients responsible for all videotape transfer, laboratory, messenger and shipping costs.

Restrictions: Clients must indemnify and hold library harmless from any and all claims, losses, demands and liabilities arising out of client's use of footage. Some material available for reference or research use only; any reuse requires clearance from copyright owner.

Viewing Facilities: Film (35mm Steenbeck; 16mm projector and hand viewers); videotape (3/4", VHS and 8mm).

Duplication Facilities: Film (reference-quality 16mm film-to-videotape transfers); videotape (3/4" and VHS; Sony UP-701 video graphics printer).

Related Materials: Books, catalogs, directories and ephemera on the history of the non-theatrical film industry in the United States. Reference sets of *Business Screen* (1938-76), *Educational Screen* (1922-75) and *Journal of the Society of Motion Picture and Television Engineers* (1930-present).

Publications: *Footage 89: North American Film & Video Sources; To New Horizons: Ephemeral Films 1931-45* and *You Can't Get There From Here: Ephemeral Films 1945-60* (key selections from archives, available on CAV laser videodiscs and VHS videotapes).

Distributor: *To New Horizons* and *You Can't Get There From Here* are distributed by The Voyager Company (q.v.).

Representative: Petrified Films, Inc. (q.v.).

NEW YORK METRO

PRESTIGE FILM CORPORATION
18 East 48th Street, Suite 1601
New York, NY 10017
(212) 826-3112
Fax: (212) 308-2995

Contact: David Dinnerstein
Services: Non-theatrical film distributor. Films available to the public for rental and long-term lease; videotapes available for purchase.
Description: International feature films and documentaries (mostly art or non-mainstream titles). Exclusive non-theatrical distributor of Almi Pictures Inc. film library and Miramax Films.

Features. Titles include: *I've Heard the Mermaids Singing; Twist and Shout* (Denmark); *Working Girls; The Official Story* (Argentina); *The American Way; Escalier C* (France); *When Father Was Away on Business* (Yugoslavia); *Taxi Zum Klo* (Germany); *What Have I Done to Deserve This?* (Spain); *Alsino and the Condor* (Nicaragua/Cuba/Mexico/Costa Rica); *The Last Movie; Monty Python and the Holy Grail* (Great Britain); *The Crazies; Outrageous* (Canada); *Heartland Reggae* (Bob Marley and the Wailers); *Love*

and Anarchy (Italy); *Hester Street; Iphegenia* (Greece); *A Slave of Love* (U.S.S.R.); *In the Realm of the Senses* (Japan); and *The Consequence* (Germany).

Documentaries. Titles include: *Harlan County, U.S.A.,* on the struggles of coal miners in Kentucky; *Poetry in Motion,* a spoken poetry anthology; *Image Before My Eyes,* on Jewish life in pre-World War II Poland; *Idi Amin Dada* (1976), profile of the Uganda dictator; and *Pumping Iron,* about bodybuilding.

Miscellaneous. Titles include: *South Beach,* about the everyday life of retirees living in South Miami Beach, Florida; and *Trial of the Catonsville Nine,* on the 1968 federal prosecution of the Berrigan brothers and seven others who napalmed draft board files.

J. Arthur Rank Film Collection. Titles include: *All Cops Are?,* showing 48 hours in the life of a young policeman; *Children Galore; No, My Darling Daughter; Rentadick; The Seekers; Up to His Neck;* and *Woman Hater.*

Films in 35mm only include: *The Adventures of Picasso,* a history of Picasso's career from his birth to his death; *Ashram,* a documentary on Bhagwan Shree Rajneesh, the "Free Sex Guru"; *Irezumi; Sebastiane;* and *Tales from the Vienna Woods.* Films are in original languages with English subtitles.

Size & Elements: Film: 35mm and 16mm (amount unspecified). Videotape: VHS (amounts unspecified).
Cataloging: Published catalogs.
Access: Films available to the public for rental and long-term lease; videotapes available for purchase. Requests accepted by mail and telephone. Package discounts available.
Rights: Rights retained by original filmmakers or producers.
Licensing: Apply for information. Public performance licenses available.
Restrictions: Apply for information.
Viewing Facilities: None.
Duplication Facilities: None.
Related Materials: Promotional materials available for most films at no charge. Trailers and radio spots available at nominal charge for some titles.

NEW YORK METRO

RADIO CITY MUSIC HALL PRODUCTIONS ARCHIVES
1260 Avenue of the Americas
New York, NY 10020
(212) 246-4600 (Ext. 310)
Telex: 126547

James A. McManus (President and Chairman of the Board)

Contact: Jamie Ramos (Archivist)
Services: Film and videotape archives. Available to the public for reuse, subject to restrictions.
Description: Holds approximately 150 reels of special effects (e.g. waves of grain, skies and lightning bolts) made for use in Radio City Music Hall productions; approximately 400 commercials (1979-present); approximately 25 productions carried on Home Box Office (1979-present); and approximately 10 specials produced for television broadcast.

Leon Leonidoff Collection. Contains personal films documenting musical productions (1930s-40s).

Also holds Fox Movietone and Pathé News short subjects, copies of network news coverage relating to Radio City Music Hall, and promotional videotapes by featured concert artists.
Size & Elements: Film: 35mm and 16mm (200 cans; originals). Videotape: 3/4" and VHS (approx. 475 items; masters and viewing copies).
Cataloging: Card catalogs.
Access: Available to the public for research, duplication and reuse. Research and licensing fees will be charged in the case of commercial productions.
Rights: Full rights held to some material. Rights to Fox Movietone and Pathé News shorts, network news coverage and promotional videotapes retained by original sources or producers. Additional clearances may be necessary in some cases if material is to be reused.
Licensing: Some material available for licensing, subject to restrictions.
Restrictions: Rights not held to all material. License fees charged for commercial productions.
Viewing Facilities: Film (must rent projector); videotape (by appointment only).
Duplication Facilities: Videotape.
Related Materials: Extensive collection of scripts and other related materials.

NEW YORK METRO

THE RAINDANCE FOUNDATION

51 Fifth Avenue
New York, NY 10003
(212) 807-9566

Ira Schneider (President)

Contact: Ira Schneider
Services: Nonprofit foundation; media organization. Film and videotape collection available to researchers, scholars and the public for rental and reuse.
Description: Incorporated 1971. Holds many key works produced by early independent videomakers (1969 through mid-1970s). Many of these videotapes depict cultural and political events of the era.

Videotapes (some of which may be damaged, or salvageable but in need of preservation) include: *Antioch Tapes* (1969), documenting midwestern American subcultures with interviews and experimental video entertainments; *TV as a Creative Medium* (1969), composite videotapes assembled for the pioneering show at the Howard Wise Gallery; documentation of the Wise Gallery show (1969); *Flash Pasteurized or Song of Redcheek* (1969), an assemblage of lifestyle videotapes made during the very early days of portable video; *Tony Barsha Bathtub Sequences* (1969); *Woodstock Tapes* (1969); *Abbie Hoffman Tape at Conspiracy Office, NYC* (1969); *Altamont Tapes* (1969); *Urban Ecology Tapes: City Mix 1, 2 and 3* (1970); *Earth People's Park Meeting — Electric Circus* (1970); *Locusts Attack Chicago* (1970); *California Trip* (1970), including *The Rays*, a video acid trip on a California beach, *Supermarket*, and other videotapes; *Earth Day in New York* (1970); *Interview with R. Buckminster Fuller, NYC* (1970); *Post-Kent State — Washington, D.C. Peace Demonstration* (1970); *City Hall Labor and Student Anti-Administration Demonstration* (1970); *Alternate Education* (1971), a distillation of a conference held at the Metropolitan Museum in New York; *Weekend at White Tank* (ca. 1970), a two-part videotape documenting a meeting of videomakers; *Double Feedback #2*, a pioneering exploration of video environments; *Loop Sketch*, an abstract videotape composed of feedback patterns; *Vietnam*, the first porta-pak footage from Vietnam, recording GI life on a fire base north of Saigon; *Computer*, a document on the home computer; *Keep*, a composition for four synchronized screens; *Clinton Project* videotapes, produced by high-school students; *Tender is the Tape II*, a basic exercise in the grammar of video; and *Knowledge and Industry III: Raindance Media Primer*.

Unedited film and videotape. Footage on the late 1960s, including rock and roll stars; video art; alternative cultures; Woodstock; images and sounds from around the world, many in collage form; and television news clips (1969-74).

Night Light TV (1984-present, each 60 min.). Weekly cable television program carried in Manhattan, showcasing the video work of artists, documentarians and performers. Holds completed programs and works aired as parts of programs.
Size & Elements: Film: 16mm (approx. 50 hours). Videotape: 3/4" (200 hours); 1/2" open reel CV (100 hours); 1/2" open reel AV (150 hours).
Cataloging: Coded catalog for staff use only.
Access: Available for rental and reuse. Research fees charged. Research requests accepted in person (by appointment only).
Rights: Most rights held to all material.
Licensing: Available for licensing in most cases. License fees charged (fees vary depending on intended use).
Restrictions: None specified.
Viewing Facilities: Film and videotape.
Duplication Facilities: Videotape (3/4").

NEW YORK METRO

A. PHILIP RANDOLPH EDUCATIONAL FUND

260 Park Avenue South, 6th Floor
New York, NY 10010
(212) 533-8000

Norman Hill (Executive Director)

Contacts: Norman Hill; Mary E. Pearce (Administrative Director); Walter Naegle
Services: Nonprofit civil rights and labor organization. One videotape available to the public for duplication and reuse.
Description: Eighty-minute videotape covering the memorial service held for civil rights leader Bayard Rustin at Community Church in New York City (October 1, 1987). Featured speakers include Lane Kirkland, Vernon Jordan, Congressman John Lewis, Liv Ullmann, Rev. Donald Harrington, Rev. Thomas Kilgore, Rabbi Marc Tannenbaum, Norman Hill, Charles Bloomstein,

Piroshaw Camay and DeWitt Luff. Also included are performances by the Carr-Hill Singers and three songs from Bayard Rustin's recordings.
Size & Elements: Videotape: VHS (1 videotape).
Cataloging: None.
Access: Available to the public for duplication and reuse. Research requests accepted by telephone and in person (by appointment only).
Rights: Rights status of material not known.
Licensing: Available for reuse.
Restrictions: None specified.
Viewing Facilities: None.
Duplication Facilities: None.

NEW YORK METRO

REGIONAL PLAN ASSOCIATION

1040 Avenue of the Americas
New York, NY 10018
(212) 398-1140

John P. Keith (President)

Contact: Mary Rivers
Services: Association. Videotapes available for free loan and purchase.
Description: New York metropolitan area housing, cities and suburbs, poverty, transportation, and environment. Titles available are *New Jersey Cities* (1979); *Bridgeport: It's All There* (1981); *Downtown Brooklyn* (1983); *Getting There* (1985), proposing long-term public transit improvements in the MTA district; *Westchester 2000* (1986), the final summary report of a project in Westchester County, New York; and *Fairfield 2000*, a report on a public participation project.
Size & Elements: Videotape: format unspecified (6 titles, 9 videotapes).
Cataloging: None specified.
Access: Apply for information.
Rights: Apply for information.
Licensing: Apply for information.
Restrictions: None specified.
Viewing Facilities: None.
Duplication Facilities: None.

NEW YORK METRO

RHAPSODY FILMS, INC.

P.O. Box 179
New York, NY 10014
(212) 243-0152

Bruce Ricker (President)

Contact: Bruce Ricker
Services: Distributor. Film and videotape collection available for rental, purchase, licensing and reuse.
Description: Jazz and blues films and videotapes, including: *Jazz is My Native Language*, a look at Toshiko Akiyoshi; *Big City Blues*, a musical documentary filmed in Chicago featuring Jim Brewer, Son Seals, Queen Sylvia Embry, and Billy Branch; *Anything for Jazz*, a view of pianist Jaki Byard and his band the Apollo Stompers, with commentary by Ron Carter and Bill Evans; *Blues Like Showers of Rain*, an introduction to country blues with Otis Spann, J. B. Lenoir, Little Brother Montgomery, Willie Thomas, Sunnyland Slim, Robert Lockwood, Lightnin' Hopkins and Speckled Red; *Born to Swing*, celebrating Dickie Wells, Buck Clayton, Buddy Tate, Earl Warren, Jo Jones and Count Basie. Eddie Durham, Snub Mosley, Gene Ramey, Tommy Flanagan and Joe Newman are also featured.

The New Music, profiling John Carter and Bobby Bradford; *Chicago Blues*, featuring Johnnie Lewis, Muddy Waters, Floyd Jones, Buddy Guy, Junior Wells, and J. B. Hutto; *Bill Evans; Talmage Farlow; Hampton Hawes All Stars*, with Leroy Vinnegar, Bobby Thompson, Joe Turner, Sweets Edison, Sonny Criss, and Teddy Edwards; *Barry Harris*, with Red Rodney, Clifford Jordan, and Pepper Adams; *After Hours*, with Coleman Hawkins, Roy Eldridge, Milt Hinton, Johnny Guarnieri, and Cozy Cole; *Jazz*, filmed in the studios of Earl Hines and Coleman Hawkins; *An American Songster*, a musical portrait of John Jackson; *Different Drummer*, a study of Elvin Jones; *Jazz in Exile*, explaining why some of the finest American musicians have been drawn to live and work in Europe; *Jazz is Our Religion*, a look at the lifestyles and attitudes of Jo Jones, Dizzy Gillespie and Sunny Murray; *Jazz Shorts; Lift the Bandstand*, featuring Steve Lacy; *The Last of the Blue Devils*, with Count

Basie and his orchestra, Big Joe Turner, and Jay McShann; *Jazz Hoofer,* recording the bebop dance style and the life of Baby Laurence; *Shelly Manne Quartet; Les McCann Trio; Jackie McLean on Mars,* with Woody Shaw and the Jackie McLean Septet; *New Orleans,* with Kid Punch Miller and Bobby Hacket; *Outside in Sight,* a portrait of United Front, the San Franciscan jazz quartet; *Sonny Rollins Live; Zoot Sims Quartet; Sun Ra: A Joyful Noise;* and *Sippie,* the life and music of Sippie Wallace.
Size & Elements: Film: 16mm (33 titles). Videotape: VHS and Betamax (33 titles).
Cataloging: Published catalogs.
Access: Available for rental, purchase, licensing and reuse. Research fees not charged. Research requests accepted by mail and telephone.
Rights: Full rights held to all material.
Licensing: Available for licensing. License fees charged.
Restrictions: None specified.
Viewing Facilities: None.
Duplication Facilities: Videotape.

NEW YORK METRO

BRUCE RICCITELLI PRODUCTIONS
P.O. Box 1387
Union, NJ 07083
(201) 688-2129

Bruce Riccitelli (President)

Contact: Bruce Riccitelli
Services: Videotape producer; still photographer. Material available for duplication, licensing and reuse. Custom shooting service available.
Description: Industrial machinery, including people working, factory interiors and exteriors and the plastics industry; refineries, container shipping and freighters in ports; ocean scenes, including commercial fishing, lighthouses, pleasure boats, beaches and people; general urban shots of New York City; highways, including New Jersey, Pennsylvania and rural areas; and airplanes, including airlines, the Air Force, the military; footage of aircraft, shot from the ground and taking off.
Size & Elements: Videotape: 3/4" (approx. 15 to 20 hours; masters); VHS (viewing copies).
Cataloging: Shot lists.
Access: Available to the public for duplication and reuse.
Rights: Full rights held to all material.
Licensing: Available for licensing. License fees charged.
Restrictions: None specified.
Viewing Facilities: None.
Duplication Facilities: Videotape (3/4" and VHS) (on a limited basis).

NEW YORK METRO

RICHTER PRODUCTIONS
330 West 42nd Street, Room 2410
New York, NY 10036
(212) 947-1395
Fax: (212) 643-1208 (shared; must specify for Richter)

Robert Richter (President)

Contact: Robert Richter
Services: Film and videotape producer. Material available for distribution and rental. Stock footage can be furnished from completed productions.
Description: Films and videotapes on public interest issues, addressing topics such as acid rain, air pollution, American history, the automobile industry, business ethics, chemistry, civil liberties, the coal industry, consumer issues, economics, the environment, foreign policy, forestry, industrial relations, international relations, labor, nuclear arms, occupational health and safety, pesticides, the petrochemical industry, political science, public administration, public health, Southeast Asia, the steel industry, the Vietnam War, war and peace studies and water pollution.

Titles include: *Vietnam: An American Journey,* including an interview with the sole survivor of the My Lai massacre; *Incident at Brown's Ferry,* an investigation of nuclear energy and nuclear plant safety; *The Visa War Against Ideas,* an examination of the U.S. law barring visas for ideological reasons, featuring Hortensia Allende, Tomas Borge, Carlos Fuentes, Dario Fo and Franca Rame, Gabriel Garciá Márquez, and others; *Asbestos Alert; Hungry for Profit,* exploring the connection between corporate motives and Third World

hunger; *Linus Pauling, Crusading Scientist; What Price Clean Air?,* filmed in England, Japan, Sweden, and the United States; and *A Plague on Our Children,* on the controversy over man-made poisons and their safe disposal.

In Our Hands covers the June 12, 1982 disarmament march and rally in New York City. 41 separate film crews donated their time and equipment to cover the demonstration; 60 hours of footage was edited down to 90 minutes.
Size & Elements: Film: (approx. 15 titles; release prints). Videotape: 3/4", VHS and Betamax (approx. 15 titles; masters and viewing copies).
Cataloging: Shot lists.
Access: Not open to the public. Available for distribution and rental. Stock footage can be furnished from completed productions. Research fees charged in some cases. Research requests accepted by mail.
Rights: Full rights held to all material.
Licensing: Available for licensing. License fees negotiable.
Restrictions: None specified.
Viewing Facilities: Film and videotape.
Duplication Facilities: Videotape.

NEW YORK METRO

RK EDITIONS
P.O. Box 444, Prince Street Station
New York, NY 10012
(212) 982-3099

Contact: Richard Kostelanetz
Services: Independent filmmaker; private film and videotape collection. Open to researchers and scholars only. Materials available for duplication and reuse, subject to approval.
Description: Rare film footage of the Jewish cemetery at Berlin-Weissensee. Also holds language-oriented videotape, film and holographic artworks.
Size & Elements: Film: 16mm (amount unspecified); videotape (format and amount unspecified).
Cataloging: None specified.
Access: Open to researchers and scholars only. Available for duplication and reuse.
Rights: Full rights held to all material.
Licensing: Available for duplication, licensing and reuse. License fees charged (rates negotiable).
Restrictions: None specified.
Viewing Facilities: Videotape (3/4" and VHS).
Duplication Facilities: Videotape (3/4" to VHS).

NEW YORK METRO

WILL ROGERS INSTITUTE
785 Mamaroneck Avenue
White Plains, NY 10605
(914) 761-5550
Fax: (914) 761-1513

Martin H. Newman (Executive Director)

Contact: Kathleen Adams (Director of Public Relations)
Services: Nonprofit health education institution. Not open to the public. Film and videotape holdings maintained for distribution and rental rather than for research or reuse.
Description: Largest supplier of health and safety-related public service announcements (PSAs) for broadcast and cable television. PSAs, usually 30-60 seconds in length, cover a wide variety of subjects including AIDS, blood donation, cholesterol, drinking and driving, choking rescue, Fetal Alcohol Syndrome, burn prevention and treatment, prevention of falls, stress, drug abuse, "crack," diving safety, immunizations and nutrition for children, child safety seats, seat belts, high blood pressure and fitness.

Note: No footage of Will Rogers is available from the Institute.
Size & Elements: Film and videotape (formats and amounts unspecified).
Cataloging: Computerized cataloging for staff use only.
Access: Not open to the public. Collection maintained for distribution and rental rather than for research or reuse. Research fees not generally charged. Research requests accepted only by mail.
Rights: Full rights held to all material.
Licensing: Apply for information. License fees not charged.
Restrictions: Requests for licensing and reuse considered on a case-by-case basis. The Institute's logo must remain intact on all PSAs.
Viewing Facilities: None.

Duplication Facilities: None.

NEW YORK METRO

ROSEBUSH VISIONS CORPORATION
25 West 45th Street
New York, NY 10036-4902
(212) 398-6600

Judson Rosebush (President)

Contact: Gwen Sylvan (Director of Research)
Services: Film and videotape producer; computer animator; stock footage sales library.
Description: Computer animation (1970-present), all originating on 35mm film. Holds a wide variety of animation styles, both low- and high-tech. Major areas of the collection include architecture, cellular biology, communications and information, logos and planetary systems.

Subjects include: airplanes, including airplane cockpit and joysticks; alphabets and letters, including full-screen, tumbling, exploding and other types of motion; architecture; atoms; automobiles; automobile tires; binary numbers; birds; blueprints; boxes and cans; buildings; buttons; cameras; cartoon-type characters (computer-generated); charts; chips; clouds; communications; computer rooms; computers, including insides of computers, computer screens, personal computers and circuit boards; consumer products; diagrams; diamonds and jewels; Egyptian masks; explosions; eyes; fireworks; flames; flamingoes; four-dimensional space; geography, including maps, planets and solar systems; geometric environments; geometric shapes and forms, including fractals, polyhedrons and spheres; golf clubs; Halley's Comet, Earth, Venus, Jupiter, Saturn, galaxies and starfields; geometric backgrounds; graphs, including contour graphs; grids, including perspective grids; industry and manufacturing processes; information themes; lips; logos; medical, including parts of the body, heart, lungs, skin, viruses, cells, cell walls, heads, hands, feet, skeletons and brain; molecules; motion-picture projectors; nuclear bombs; numbers; pyramids of Giza; ribbons; robots; room interiors; satellites; shoes; telephone networks; telephone switching exchanges; textured surfaces; three-dimensional forms and abstract structures; Times Square; tomography (similar to CAT scans); two-dimensional abstract scenes; video art, including abstract video; water, including ripple effects; wavy grid backgrounds; and X-ray vision.

The entire collection is available for purchase on eight videotapes, each one hour.

Represents the *Digital Effects Collection* (1978-84) and the *Judson Rosebush Collection.*
Size & Elements: Film: 35mm (6 hours; original color negatives, interpositives and prints); 16mm (prints). Videotape: 1" (6 hours; masters; NTSC, PAL and SECAM); 3/4", VHS and Betamax.
Cataloging: Staff assistance required.
Access: Open to the public. Available for purchase, duplication, reuse and resale. Research fees charged. Research requests accepted by mail and telephone.
Rights: Full rights held to all material. Additional clearances may be necessary in some (rare) cases if material is to be reused.
Licensing: Available for licensing and reuse. License fees charged.
Restrictions: No exclusives are offered on any material. A few pieces carry special restrictions.
Viewing Facilities: Film (35mm); videotape (3/4") (by appointment only).
Duplication Facilities: Film and videotape (by contractors).

NEW YORK METRO

RUTGERS, THE STATE UNIVERSITY OF NEW JERSEY
INSTITUTE OF JAZZ STUDIES
135 Bradley Hall
Newark, NJ 07102
(201) 648-5595

Dan Morgenstern (Director)

Contact: Vincent Pelote
Services: Historical society; library; film and videotape archives. Open to the public. Available for reuse or resale.
Description: Small collection of jazz-related films and videotapes, including unique footage of Eubie Blake at the Third Annual Discographic Research Conference held at Rutgers (1970). Also holds outtakes from the film *The Last of the Blue Devils.*

Size & Elements: Film: 16mm (4 large reels). Videotape: VHS (46 videotapes).
Cataloging: None.
Access: Open to the public. Available for licensing and reuse. Research fees generally not charged. Research requests accepted by telephone.
Rights: Full rights held to some material. Additional clearances may be necessary in some cases if material is to be reused.
Licensing: Apply for information. License fees charged in some cases.
Restrictions: None specified.
Viewing Facilities: Videotape (VHS).
Duplication Facilities: None.
Related Materials: Audio recordings.

NEW YORK METRO

SAATCHI & SAATCHI DFS COMPTON
375 Hudson Street, 17th Floor
New York, NY 10014
(212) 463-2693

Contact: Janine Gordon
Services: Corporation; corporate archives. Collection for use by agency personnel only. *Material unavailable to the public for research or reuse of any kind.*
Description: Holds the archives of Dancer Fitzgerald Sample (DFS), containing television commercials produced for agency clients (1940s-80s). These materials are currently held in underground vaults in lower Manhattan and in New Jersey. This collection does not include the archives of Saatchi & Saatchi, the agency with which DFS recently merged.
Size & Elements: Not specified.
Cataloging: Uncataloged.
Access: For use by agency personnel only. Not available to the public for research or reuse of any kind.
Rights: Not specified.
Licensing: Not available for licensing.
Restrictions: Not available for research, licensing or reuse.
Viewing Facilities: None.
Duplication Facilities: None.

NEW YORK METRO

ST. JOHN'S UNIVERSITY
SPECIAL COLLECTIONS
Grand Central and Utopia Parkways
Jamaica, NY 11439
(718) 990-6161 (Ext. 6737)
Fax: (718) 380-0353

Sister Marie Melton (Director of University Libraries)

Contact: Szilvia E. Szmuk (Special Collections Librarian)
Services: Educational institution and library. Film and videotape collection available to researchers and scholars for in-house use only.
Description: Material relating to New York State political figures, including campaign television commercials and films from James Buckley's senatorial race (1970), news conferences with Governor Hugh Carey (1982), and the Evangeline Gouletas/Carey wedding (April 11, 1981).
Size & Elements: Information not currently available.
Cataloging: Not presently cataloged.
Access: Open to researchers and scholars. For in-house use only. Policy regarding research fees undetermined at present. Research requests accepted in person (by appointment only).
Rights: Rights status of material not known.
Licensing: Apply for information.
Restrictions: None specified.
Viewing Facilities: Apply for information.
Duplication Facilities: None.

NEW YORK METRO

SALVATION ARMY ARCHIVES AND RESEARCH CENTER
145 West 15th Street
New York, NY 10011
(212) 337-7428

NEW YORK METRO S

Thomas Wilsted (Archivist/Administrator)

Contact: Judith Johnson (Archivist)
Services: Religious archives. Film and videotape collection open to the public; available for research, licensing and reuse, subject to copyright clearance.
Description: Current and historical activities of The Salvation Army. Holds films profiling General Evangeline Booth (commander of The Salvation Army in the United States for thirty years), and a nearly complete set of episodes from *The Living Word,* a television series (1950s-60s). Some films are made by Salvationists Edward J. Parker and Paul Parker, who pioneered the Salvation Army's use of photography and film.
Size & Elements: Film: 16mm (300 titles, 350 cans; positives, originals and release prints). Videotape: VHS (38 videotapes; viewing copies).
Cataloging: Card catalogs.
Access: Open to the public. Research fees not charged. Research requests accepted by mail, telephone and in person (walk-in).
Rights: Some rights held to some material. Rights status of some material not known.
Licensing: Apply for information. Usage fees not charged.
Restrictions: Reuse of material subject to copyright clearance.
Viewing Facilities: Videotape.
Duplication Facilities: None.

NEW YORK METRO

SALVATION ARMY
NATIONAL COMMUNICATIONS DEPARTMENT
799 Bloomfield Avenue
Verona, NJ 07044
(201) 239-0606
Fax: (201) 239-8441
Telex: 133-129

Commissioner Andrew S. Miller (National Commander)

Contact: Lt. Colonel Leon Ferraez (Director, National Communications Department)
Services: Nonprofit religious organization. Film and videotape collection available to the public for free loan, licensing and reuse, subject to project approval.
Description: Documentaries and public service announcements profiling The Salvation Army's tradition of "helping others to help themselves."

Sample titles, available in 16mm film and 3/4" videotape, include: *A Home for Osmar,* showing the rebuilding of a Guatemalan home and village after the 1976 earthquake; *¡Terremoto!,* about the courage and invincibility of the Guatemalan people and Salvation Army volunteers in the aftermath of an earthquake; *The Tragic Comic,* a revealing portrait of alcohol abuse; *The Descendants,* a celebration of The Salvation Army's 100 years of service in America; *The Uprooted,* filming Salvation Army refugee and relief operations on location in Africa and Asia, featuring Uganda, Zambia, Thailand, and Hong Kong; *Los Damnificados,* showing The Salvation Army's work after the 1985 Mexican earthquake; and *On Solid Ground,* about the Salvation Army's adult rehabilitation centers.

Blood and Fire tells the life story of William Booth, the history of the movement he founded, and offers documentary glimpses of The Salvation Army's present day activities in America and some of the more than eighty other countries where the Salvationists are serving.

Public service announcements are also available on videotape.
Size & Elements: Film: 16mm (10 titles). Videotape: 2", 1", 3/4" and 1/2" (masters and viewing copies).
Cataloging: Published catalog.
Access: Available to the public for free loan, licensing and reuse. Research fees not charged. Research requests accepted by mail and telephone.
Rights: Full rights held to all material.
Licensing: Available for licensing, subject to restrictions. License fees charged in some cases.
Restrictions: Project approval mandatory for licensing and reuse.
Viewing Facilities: None.
Duplication Facilities: None.
Distributor: Films and 3/4" videotapes are distributed on a free-loan basis by Modern Talking Picture Service, Inc. (q.v.). Films also available from The Salvation Army Community Relations and Development Department regional offices. Some material available in videotape format from the Salvation Army, Office of Media Ministries (q.v.).

NEW YORK METRO

SAMAYA FOUNDATION
75 Leonard Street
New York, NY 10013
(212) 925-9763

Barry Bryant (Director)

Contact: Gregory Durgin
Services: Arts foundation. Videotape collection available to the public for research, and possibly licensing and reuse, subject to restrictions.
Description: Asian and North American culture, including documentation of Tibetan folk dance, ritual art and ceremonies, and Japanese culture (800 hours) and North American documentaries and artists' videotapes (400 hours).
Size & Elements: Videotape: format unspecified (1,200 hours).
Cataloging: Lists.
Access: Open to the public. Research requests accepted by mail and telephone.
Rights: Full rights held to all material. Additional clearances may be necessary in some cases if material is to be reused.
Licensing: Available for licensing and reuse, subject to restrictions. License fees charged.
Restrictions: Requests for licensing and reuse considered on a case-by-case basis.
Viewing Facilities: Videotape.
Duplication Facilities: Videotape (VHS and Betamax).

NEW YORK METRO

SCHOMBURG CENTER FOR RESEARCH IN BLACK CULTURE
NEW YORK PUBLIC LIBRARY
515 Malcolm X Boulevard (formerly Lenox Avenue)
New York, NY 10037
(212) 491-2236
Fax: (212) 491-6761

Howard Dodson (Chief)

Contact: James Briggs Murray (Head, Moving Image and Recorded Sound Department)
Services: Library; film and videotape archives. Open to researchers, scholars and the public for research, duplication and reuse, subject to restrictions.
Description: Films and videotapes, primarily documentaries, on many aspects of Black history and culture throughout the world. Collection concentrates on film as a means of interpreting history and culture rather than film as an art form. Both commercially acquired and historical and archival materials are held; archival materials were generally acquired as part of manuscript or other collections donated to the Center.

Special strengths of collection include jazz films; films relating to South Africa; African-based religions; anthropology; travel films relating to Africa, Haiti and other areas; Black dance film footage, including social dancing, tap, and some modern dance; oral history and videotape documentation; and public affairs television programming.

Oral History/Video Documentation Project. Founded 1980 by J. B. Murray; now consists of over 100 videotaped interviews (200 hours). Consists of oral history interviews and documentation of personal appearances relating to individuals in a variety of fields. Some subjects include: Katherine Dunham, dancer, choreographer and anthropologist, who incorporated African movement into modern dance; Lillian Roberts, former New York State Commissioner of Labor; Dr. June Christmas, psychiatrist; Dr. J. D. Elder, Trinidadian anthropologist; Wallace Muhammad, son of Elijah Muhammad; Pappa Susso, a *griot* from West Africa; Michael Manley, former prime minister of Jamaica; Susan Taylor, editor-in-chief of *Essence* magazine; various physicians and staff of Harlem Hospital; and Elizabeth Cotten, folksinger.

The Project also encompasses documentation of personal appearances and events occurring at the Center and elsewhere, including appearances by Ella Fitzgerald, Bishop Desmond Tutu and James Baldwin.

CEBA Awards (2,000 videotapes). CEBA, standing for "Communication Excellence to Black Audiences," recognizes special achievement in television production. Collection, including awards entries produced by stations throughout the United States, includes talk shows, specials, local programming, commercials and public affairs television programs on Black-related topics.

Other videotape footage held includes independent productions, especially those produced by PBS (1976-present); television commercials representing Blacks, deposited by the World Institute of Black Communications; and conference series, including the *Oritia* conference held at the Caribbean Cultural Center (1988) and the Black Folk Arts Festival, held at the Schomburg Center.

Some films in collection, originally distributed commercially, are no longer available through normal channels and are possibly unique to Schomburg, including *I Owe It All to the Songs I Sing,* on the Fisk Jubilee Singers and *The Shape of Darkness* (late 1950s), relating to African art.

Size & Elements: Film: 16mm (300 films; 85% commercially acquired, 15% archival). Videotape: 3/4" (3,000 videotapes; masters and viewing copies) and VHS (viewing copies only).

Cataloging: Published catalog in progress. Computerized cataloging (local database) in progress; subject-oriented searches will be supported. Some material cataloged through RLIN (Research Libraries Information Network).

Access: Open to researchers, scholars and the public. For in-house use only. Available for duplication, licensing and reuse, subject to restrictions. Research fees not charged. Research requests accepted by telephone and in person (by appointment only).

Rights: Full rights held to Center-produced material (interviews). No rights held to most material. Additional clearances may be necessary in some cases if material is to be reused.

Licensing: Available for licensing and reuse, subject to restrictions.

Restrictions: Center principally functions as a research institution. Requests for licensing and reuse considered on a case-by-case basis. Much of collection is subject to special restrictions (donor restrictions, requirement for permission of interviewees, etc.).

Viewing Facilities: Film and videotape (3/4", 1/2", PAL and NTSC) (by appointment only).

Duplication Facilities: Film (16mm to 3/4", VHS and Betamax); videotape (3/4", VHS and Betamax).

Related Materials: Phonograph records (12,000 LPs, 5,000 78s); photographs, audiotapes, manuscripts and other archival material.

NEW YORK METRO

JULES SCHWERIN
317 West 83rd Street
New York, NY 10024
(212) 724-2997

Contact: Jules Schwerin

Services: Film producer. Holds rights to three films, which are available for viewing at the Museum of Modern Art, Department of Film (q.v.).

Description: Holds rights to three films: *Loves of Franistan; A Publisher Is Known By The Company He Keeps* (1974); and *Dialogue With the Knopfs.* Also produced by Schwerin: *Got To Tell It* (1974), a documentary on Mahalia Jackson; *Indian Summer,* on Pete Seeger; and *Salt of the Earth* (1954), a feature film.

Size & Elements: Film: format unspecified (6 titles).

Cataloging: Research library.

Access: Viewing copies of some films available through the Museum of Modern Art, Department of Film (q.v.).

Rights: Full rights held to some material.

Licensing: Apply for information.

Restrictions: Apply for information.

Viewing Facilities: None.

Duplication Facilities: None.

NEW YORK METRO

SECOND LINE SEARCH
330 West 42nd Street, Suite 2901
New York, NY 10036
(212) 594-5544
Fax: (212) 594-5213

Rick Gell (President)

Contacts: Rick Gell; Todd Pavlin

Services: Research organization; film and videotape stock·footage sales library.

Description: Supplies stock film, videotape and still photographs; and specializes in research, budgets, contracts and clearances. In addition to its own footage, Second Line can quickly and easily access highlight material from other stock libraries, feature film companies, music video producers, independent documentaries, cinematographers and other sources. Specializes in footage with "clearable" talent, and is frequently employed by advertising

agencies to handle negotiations with celebrities, sports figures, feature film companies and sports organizations.

Can handle footage-related projects from start to finish — developing a budget, locating the footage, compiling time-coded screening videotapes, negotiating licensing fees and talent agreements, and supervising all transfers and final contracts.

Represents Merkel Films (q.v.), well-known watersports cinematographer, whose footage library includes surfing, windsurfing, boogie boarding, waterskiing, catamarans, jet skiing and power boating. Also holds championship diving and swimming footage (real-time and slow-motion), featuring gold medalist Greg Louganis and other Olympic divers and swimmers; waterskiing footage featuring world champion freestyle waterskier Corey Picos; extensive collection of sports footage (early 1970s), featuring hockey, basketball and selected material from other sports; production-quality NASA footage, with astronauts, payloads, Earth views, launches and the space shuttle; and point-of-view footage, including flyovers of mountains, forests, lakes, rivers, vineyards and other locations.

Particular strengths include high-action sports, including kayaking, rock climbing, rodeo, hang-gliding and skiing (competitive and stunt); professional sports, including the Indianapolis 500, football, baseball, basketball, golf and tennis; Olympic footage; commercial-quality footage of national and international travel destinations; newsreels and contemporary news footage; black and white (including public domain) footage; classic Americana; and time-lapse footage of cities, locations and natural phenomena.

Size & Elements: All footage originates on either 16mm or 35mm film, and is available in any format. Can obtain requested production elements for final edits.

Cataloging: None specified.

Access: Open to researchers and producers. Available for reuse. Research fees charged. Research requests accepted by telephone and fax. Depending on the specific nature of each request, Second Line will begin researching or screening of footage. Screening material is then provided to the client; clients make final footage selections through the use of individually time-coded videotapes. Arranges all necessary transfers, organization and shipping of final elements.

Rights: Holds title to some footage featured in its collection. Rights to other materials are obtained through individual filmmakers, cinematographers or footage owners.

Licensing: Available for licensing and reuse. License fees charged (fees vary depending on intended use of footage and market of production). Minimums and kill fees are sometimes charged.

Restrictions: None specified.

Viewing Facilities: Not available for public screening.

Duplication Facilities: Videotape (3/4", Super VHS and VHS).

NEW YORK METRO

SFM MEDIA
c/o Pavia & Harcourt
600 Madison Avenue, 12th Floor
New York, NY 10022
(212) 980-3500
Fax: (212) 980-3185
Telex: 66146

Contact: Nancy Otero

Services: Represents owners of the *March of Time* for distribution, licensing and film clip rights. Material available for licensing and reuse. The actual physical film materials for *March of Time* are held at the National Archives and Records Administration (q.v.) and are available for viewing there.

Description: See National Archives and Records Administration (RG 200) for a complete list of titles, episodes, release dates, and volume and issue numbers.

Size & Elements: Film (all material held at the National Archives in Washington, D.C.). Copies of many episodes are also held at the National Film Archive, London (England).

Cataloging: Filmography (chronological list and synopsis of titles, episodes and feature films) available upon request. For a list of titles and episodes, see National Archives and Records Administration (RG 200).

Access: Available for duplication and reuse. Research requests accepted by mail and telephone. *Pavia & Harcourt does not hold viewing copies; researchers must view material at the National Archives.* Selected episodes of *March of Time* are now distributed by Embassy Home Entertainment, and are available for rental and purchase in VHS videotape format only. Some of these videotapes, made for the homevideo market, have been reedited or condensed.

Outtakes from *March of Time* are also held at the National Archives, and

are in the public domain. For further information, consult the entry for National Archives and Records Administration.
Rights: Full rights held to all material on behalf of copyright owner (Time, Inc.).
Licensing: Available for licensing and reuse, subject to restrictions. License fees charged. Material will be released from the National Archives upon the authorization of Pavia and Harcourt. This authorization is provided upon completion of a standard license agreement. A standard minimum license fee applies to each issue, regardless of the length of the clip used. The license fee clears usage in all media throughout the world in perpetuity.
Restrictions: Aggregate duration of footage used from any one issue may not exceed 3 minutes, and if any issue is comprised of more than one episode, the aggregate duration of footage used from any episode may not exceed 1-1/2 minutes.
Viewing Facilities: None.
Duplication Facilities: None.
Representative: Archive Film Productions, Inc./Stock Footage Library (q.v.) for stock footage sales.

NEW YORK METRO

SIGGRAPH
ASSOCIATION FOR COMPUTING MACHINERY
11 West 42nd Street
New York, NY 10036
(212) 869-7440
Fax: (212) 869-0481

Videotapes available for purchase from:
ACM ORDER DEPARTMENT
P.O. Box 64145
Baltimore, MD 21264
(800) 342-6626
(301) 528-4261 (Maryland, Alaska, Hawaii and outside U.S.)

Contact: Order Department
Services: Association; videotape producer. Videotapes available for purchase.
Description: Produces *SIGGRAPH Video Review,* the world's only computer graphics publication on videotape. The *Review* is a collection of artistic, commercial, scientific and applications-oriented motion computer graphics, illustrating current concepts in computer graphics and interactive techniques. Videotapes (32 issues, each 60 or 120 min.) provide an opportunity to study advanced computer graphics ideas and applications.

Recent issues contain segments on real-time digital image processing from the National Bureau of Standards; a walk through the Ohio State animation system; the University of Illinois at Chicago's "Interactive Image" show which premiered at the Museum of Science and Industry, Chicago; commentary of 17 top computer graphic experts; hardware, software and tools; supercomputing and the need for graphics in scientific visualization; NASA's work on intuitive virtual workstation environments; graphics workstations; visualization systems, including work at the Jet Propulsion Laboratory; the Pixar Image Computer; synthetic holography; electronic theater, including television commercial production, human interaction research and animation projects; and many projects, experiments and systems now of historic interest.
Size & Elements: Videotape: 3/4" and VHS (32 videotapes, approx. 45 hours).
Cataloging: Brochure.
Access: Available for purchase. Requests accepted by mail and telephone.
Rights: Apply for information.
Licensing: Apply for information.
Restrictions: Apply for information.
Viewing Facilities: None.
Duplication Facilities: None.

NEW YORK METRO

SIMON & GOODMAN PICTURE COMPANY
107 West 70th Street, Penthouse 1
New York, NY 10023
(212) 873-6531

Karen Goodman; Kirk Simon (Partners)

Contacts: Karen Goodman; Kirk Simon
Services: Film and videotape producer. Material available for licensing and reuse.

Description: Current footage of New York City street scenes, Harlem and general cityscapes; street performers in New York City; Indonesia, including children, the arts and performance; Christmas in New York City; scenics and landscape footage of the U.S.
Size & Elements: Film: 16mm (amount unspecified; color negative and workprint). Videotape: 1" and 3/4" (masters and viewing copies).
Cataloging: Staff assistance required.
Access: Available for licensing and reuse. Research fees charged. Research requests considered on a case-by-case basis.
Rights: Full rights held to all material. Additional clearances may be necessary in some cases (e.g., street performers) if material is to be reused.
Licensing: Available for licensing and reuse. License fees charged.
Restrictions: Requests for research, licensing and reuse considered on a case-by-case basis.
Viewing Facilities: Film (16mm); videotape (3/4").
Duplication Facilities: Videotape (3/4" and 1/2").
Related Materials: Still photographs and music on similar subjects; collection of Indonesian gamelan music.

NEW YORK METRO

SKYLIGHT PICTURES
330 West 42nd Street, 24th Floor
New York, NY 10036
(212) 947-5333

Contacts: Pam Yates; Tom Sigel; Peter Kinoy
Services: Film producer. Films available to the public for rental and distribution. Stock footage available for licensing and reuse on a case-by-case basis.
Description: Films primarily address Central American politics and culture, as well as other contemporary political issues.

Productions available for distribution include: *When The Mountains Tremble,* a story told by exiled Guatemalan Indian Rigoberta Menchú, as history transforms her from a migratory peasant to a leading voice shaping the destiny of her people; *Witness To War: An American Doctor In El Salvador,* following the activities of Dr. Charlie Clements, a career military pilot whose dedication to nonviolence led him to refuse to serve in Vietnam and later to practice medicine among El Salvadorean peasants; *Nicaragua: Report From The Front,* an in-depth, firsthand look at United States policy toward Nicaragua as it is being played out along the border between Nicaragua and Honduras, including the first footage of the secret counterrevolutionary base camps in Honduras; *Resurgence: The Movement for Equality vs. the Ku Klux Klan,* focusing on a lengthy strike of chicken processing plant workers in Laurel, Mississippi, and the Ku Klux Klan/Nazi hate campaign in North Carolina.

Stock footage on these subjects is also available for licensing.
Size & Elements: Film: 16mm (over 4 titles). Videotape: 1" and 3/4" (over 4 titles).
Cataloging: Published brochures.
Access: Available for distribution and rental. Stock footage material available for licensing and reuse. Research fees charged. Research generally done in-house. Research requests accepted by mail and telephone.
Rights: Full rights held to all material. Additional clearances may be necessary if material from *Witness to War* is to be duplicated or reused.
Licensing: Available for licensing and reuse, subject to restrictions. License fees charged.
Restrictions: Requests for duplication or reuse are subject to acceptance and approval on a case-by-case basis.
Viewing Facilities: Film (16mm); videotape (3/4" and VHS).
Duplication Facilities: Videotape (3/4").

NEW YORK METRO

SOCIAL PSYCHIATRY RESEARCH INSTITUTE, INC.
150 East 69th Street
New York, NY 10021
(212) 628-4842

Ari Kiev, M.D. (Director)

Contacts: Elaine Neese (Administrative Assistant); Dona Lopez
Services: Association. Videotape collection maintained primarily for distribution and rental rather than for reuse or resale.
Description: Videotapes examining mental health and psychiatric issues.
Topics covered include hypnosis; manic depressive illness and lithium

therapy; interpersonal communication patterns; the new sex therapy; psychoanalysis of depression; territoriality; dream appreciation; genetic and environmental factors in schizophrenia; strategies of psychotherapy; family therapy; communication theory and behavior; transcultural psychiatry; faith healing; traditional Chinese medicine, including acupuncture and bone setting; psychological issues and the modern woman; psychological dimensions of plastic surgery; prediction of suicide; profiles and treatment of suicidal patients; the effect of lithium on manic depressive illness; electroconvulsive therapy; alcoholism; existential psychiatry; biofeedback in psychiatry; male and female homosexuality; anorexia nervosa; masked depression; chronic physical illness; therapeutic work with adolescent prostitutes; biochemical aspects of depression and afflective disorders; forensic psychiatry; transactional analysis; paradox therapy; group psychotherapy; psychodrama; hypnosis; rational-emotive therapy; group therapy for sexual dysfunction; and gerontology.

Size & Elements: Videotape: 3/4" and 1/2" (51 titles).
Cataloging: Published catalog.
Access: For in-house use only. Maintained for distribution and rental rather than for research or reuse.
Rights: No rights held to any material.
Licensing: Apply for information.
Restrictions: None specified.
Viewing Facilities: None.
Duplication Facilities: Videotape (3/4").

NEW YORK METRO

SOCIETY FOR FRENCH AMERICAN CULTURAL SERVICES AND EDUCATIONAL AID (FACSEA)
972 Fifth Avenue
New York, NY 10021
(212) 439-1400
Fax: (212) 439-1455

Anne Marie Morotte (Executive Director)

Contacts: Cathy Gottlieb (Film Librarian) (212/439-1439 or 212/439-1449); Eva Bessenyey (Film Librarian)
Services: Educational foundation. Films and videotapes available for non-theatrical distribution to schools, colleges, universities, cine-clubs and French clubs.
Description: Feature films and documentaries in French, English and subtitled versions. Most items are documentary films on France and French subjects. Strengths are history, literature, sociology, language and culinary instruction courses.

Feature films. Extensive list of feature-length and hour-long films; films based on plays; biographies of authors and artists; and *Histoire du Cinema,* a 13-part series produced for French television with extensive excerpts from French films (beginning 1895). Directors include: Claude Chabrol, Marguerite Duras, Jean-Luc Godard, Alain Resnais, Jacques Rivette, Eric Rohmer and Agnès Varda.

Shorts and documentaries. Many topics are covered, including:
Civilization and contemporary life in France. Regional culture, celebrities, French institutions and museums, Christmas celebrations, sociology, sheep farming, industrial areas and workers, scouting, a small-village letter writer for the illiterate, Black culture in France, government and general elections.

Paris. Paris landmarks; aerial views; the Metro; bistros; public transportation; and *Paris La Belle,* narrated by Jacques Prevert, showing Paris seen through the photographs of Man Ray (1928) and Sacha Vierny (1959).

Versailles. Louis XIV; tours in and around the castle; and restoration of the castle.

Geography. Films covering the different regions, including: the Alps, Alsace, Aquitaine, Auvergne, Bourgogne, Bretagne, Champagne, Corse, Ile-de-France, Languedoc-Roussillon, Pays de la Loire, Lorraine, Nord, Normandie, Picardie, Poitou-Charentes, Provence/la Côte d'Azur, the Pyrenees, France-Overseas (Martinique, Guadeloupe and Tahiti) and France in general.

History: Prehistory to the Middle Ages. The Megaliths, Mother-Goddess, bronze, the Celts, Gaul, the Roman conquest, the Barbarian conquest, tapestries at Bayeux cathedral, La Basilique Saint Denis, the Abbey of Fontenay, University of Paris and Joan of Arc. *Le Temps des Cathedrales* is a series of nine films exploring Western Christian civilization, shot on location in France, Italy and Spain, covering the events surrounding the building of the great cathedrals. Also covered: monasteries, religious quests, knights, saints, assertion of nations, artworks, ars morendi, and the philosophical views and major events of the times.

Renaissance. Louis XI, Jean and François Clouet, François I, Henri II, Catherine de Médicis and Diane de Poitiers arguing over the ownership of the Château de Chenonceaux at the death of Henri II.

17th Century. Mazarin, Louis XIV, Jean Fouquet, Sébastien Le Prestre, Hotel des Invalides and Richelieu.

18th Century. Saint-Simon, Louis XV ("Le Bien Aimé"), Thomas Jefferson, the French Revolution, revolutionary songs, music, engravings and paintings, André Chénier and Michelet.

19th Century. Several films on Napoléon, Georges Cadoudal, the Prince de Talleyrand, the Revolution of 1848, Napoléon III and the Second Empire, industrial growth and the Commune de Paris.

20th Century. Georges Clémenceau, World War I, the German occupation of Paris, the Normandy invasion; and *Nuit et Brouillard,* Alain Resnais' documentary on Nazi concentration camps.

Literature. Authors include: Guillaume Apollinaire, Louis Aragon, Honoré de Balzac, Baudelaire and Delacroix, Joachim du Bellay, Camus, Chateaubriand, Paul Claudel interview, Colette (including rare footage of Colette in her early youth, at the height of her fame, and at her apartment at the Palais Royal in the company of Jean Cocteau), Descartes, Robert Desnos, Diderot, Dumas (père and fils), Paul Eluard, Fénelon, Jean de la Fontaine, André Gide, Giono, Victor Hugo, Lamartine, Lautréamont, Malraux, Guy de Maupassant, Andre Maurois, Nerval, Marcel Pagnol, Blaise Pascal, Péguy, François Ponge, Vladimir Pozner, Jacques Prévert, Marcel Proust, Rabelais, Rimbaud, Romain Rolland, Pierre de Ronsard, Edmond Rostand, Jean-Jacques Rousseau, Antoine de Saint-Exupéry, George Sand, Madame de Sévigné, Madame de Staël, Michel Tournier, Paul Valéry, Jules Verne, Voltaire and Emile Zola. Includes philosophers: Philippe Ariés, Vladimir Jankelevitch, Jacques Lacan, Claude Lèvi-Strauss and Pierre Teilhard de Chardin. Also, Gallimard, Bibliobus, the Académie Française, Saint-Germain des Prés and the television series *Apostrophes,* with interviews of major figures of current literary production in France.

Art history. Covers the Middle Ages and the Renaissance: French Romanesque painting, illuminated manuscripts of the Duc de Berry, medieval illuminated manuscripts, the Primitives, Fontainebleau, Jehan Fouquet. From the 17th century: Le Brun, Philippe de Champaigne, Claude Gellée and Le Nain brothers, Nicolas Poussin and Georges de la Tour. From the 18th century: François Boucher, Courbet, Daumier, Delacroix, Géricault, Antoine Gros, Ingres, Millet and the rococo style. From the 19th century: impressionists and neo-impressionists, Bazille, Cezanne, Degas, Manet, Monet, Pissarro and Renoir. From the 20th century: Chagall, Cézanne, Cocteau, Derain, Dunoyer de Segonzac, Gauguin, Lacourière's print shop, Manessier, Masson, Matisse, Michaux, Mirò, Picasso, Pignon, Rouault, le douanier Rousseau, Van Gogh, Vasarély, the Fauves, Cubists, abstract art and surrealism.

Museums and archives. Le Musée D'Orsay, Bibliothèque Nationale de Paris, L'Orangèrie, the Louvre, Mobilier National, Musée des Arts et Traditions Populaires, Le Musée de L'Homme, Centre Georges Pompidou, Aimé Maeght, Musée Leon Alegre, Museum of Saint Martin. Also art collections, including: the Maeght collections, Matisse Museum, Jacqueline Picasso's collection on display at the Marais Cultural Center.

Architecture. Hardouin Mansart (architect of Versailles), Viollet-le-Duc, Paris Opera House, Gustave Eiffel, Le Corbusier, Charlotte Perriaud and urban planning.

Sculpture. Brancusi, Giacometti, Ipoustéguy, Maillol and Rodin.

Arts, crafts and techniques. Glass blowing, pottery, porcelain, Limoges china, French crystal, Sèvres porcelain works, cloisonné, restoration of paintings on wood and canvas, Jean Després (goldsmith), wood carving and tapestry.

Music. French folkloric music and ballads; "France Musique" radio network, composers including: Debussy, Ravel and Rameau; and Bach illustrated by Braque, Ravel by Chagall, Satie/Cocteau, Stravinsky/Picasso, Debussy/Monet, Lancret, Corot and Degas. Also, the organ at Notre Dame and at the cathedral of Poitiers.

Theater. Classic and modern theater directed in France, Avignon Theatre Festival, Comedia del Arte, Comédie Française and Molière.

Dance. Alwin Nikolais Dance School, Paris National Opera House, *Le Jeune Homme et La Mort* (performed by Rudolf Nureyev and Zizi Jeanmaire, written by Jean Cocteau and choreographed by Roland Petit), Maurice Bejart, The Marseilles Ballet and Maia Plissetskaia.

Mime. Marcel Marceau in performance and at home surrounded by documents detailing the history of pantomime; and the Grand Magic Circus.

Popular entertainment. French rock, including Bernard Lavilliers, Jacques Higelin, Johnny Hallyday, Mr. Dupont, Telephone; cabaret incudes: Rufus, Frères Jacques, Amiel, Farid Chopel, Jacques Villeret; and Festival à Nancy; Georges Brassens; theater and music festivals; Michel Jonasz, Edith Piaf, Josephine Baker and Charles Aznavour. Jazz, including Henri Texier, Christian Escoudé and Michel Petrucciani.

Photography. Daguerre; Robert Doisneau; beginnings of photography in France (1875-1900); a four-part film series on Jacques-Henri Lartigue (interviewed by François Reichenbach), beginning with Lartique's first photograph at the turn of the century when he was six years old. Also, Jean Dieuzaide, Gisèle Freund, André Kertész, Willy Ronis, Jean-Loup Sieff and Bruno Barbey.

Cinema. Covers the history of cinema in the 19th century, the Lumière brothers, the Cinémathèque Française, Georges Méliès, French silent films (1920s), Abel Gance, René Clair, Volker Schlöndorff, François Truffaut, Jean-Luc Godard, Claude Lelouch, Bertrand Tavernier, Joris Ivens; a group of shorts by directors of the New Wave, including Godard and Rivette; and French television commercials (1978-79).

Winemaking. Champagne, wine harvest in Beaujolais, Chateau Lafite, the Baron Philippe de Rothschild at Château Mouton, and the Bordeaux region and its wines.

Technology. Automobiles, robotics, high-speed runway tractor, microlight aircraft, nuclear energy, electronic telephone directory, high-speed train, space, aeronautics, textiles and glass.

Sciences. Marine biology; excavating the Grand Louvre; reproductions of the Lascaux caves; the eruption of Martinique's Mount Pelée; archaeological expeditions; the image of the child from 16th century to the dawn of the 20th century; geology, neurophysiology; biologist-writer Jean Rostand; Louis Pasteur; Champollion, who discovered the key to the translation of hieroglyphics in 1822; the Curies; African animals; the expedition of Paul-Émile Victor to Terre Adélie (South Pole); and penguins.

Ecology. French natural treasures and parks, pollution, the biosphere, the Seine, natural resources and the energy crisis.

Fashion. Lyon, the silk capital and its museum of fabrics; haute-couture and prêt-à-porter collections (1974); Jean-Charles de Castelbajac; Marc Bohan, Emanuel Ungaro, Montana, Beretta; International Contemporary Art Fair art and fashion show; and fashion photography.

Gastronomy. 13 films in the *Tour de France* series, each relating a particular event to a famous dish (with recipes). Also, Alpine cooking, bouillabaisse, foie gras and cheeses.

Sports. Baron de Coubertin and the restoration of the Olympics, mountaineering, sailing, horseback riding, cycling, Le Mans, Roland Garros Tennis International, boxing, skiing, Tour de France, gymnastics, long-distance running, mountain climbing, winter Olympics at Grenoble (1968) with Jean-Claude Killy and sports car racing.

Fiction. Short fiction films by a variety of directors, including: Marguerite Duras' *Aurelia Steiner;* and a 14-episode series directed by Marcel Camus.

Children's films. An animated version of Saint-Exupéry's *Le Petit Prince;* a 12-film series about children around the globe; and fables animated by marionettes.

Mysteries. 9 episodes from the *Arsène Lupin* series; 13 episodes from the *Schulmeister* series; 13 episodes of the *Belphegor* series (inside the Louvre); and 13 episodes of the *Le Trésor des Hollandais,* inside the Paris Opera House.
Size & Elements: Film: 16mm (140 features, 781 documentaries, 3,236 cans total). Videotape: format unspecified (1,700 titles, each 30 to 60 min.; viewing copies).
Cataloging: Published catalogs.
Access: Available for non-theatrical distribution to high schools, colleges, universities, cine-clubs and French clubs. Requests accepted by telephone, but must be confirmed in writing.
Rights: Some rights held to some material. Additional clearances may be necessary in some cases if material is to be reused.
Licensing: Apply for information.
Restrictions: Films may not be screened commercially. Transfer of films to videotape is strictly prohibited by law.
Viewing Facilities: None.
Duplication Facilities: Film and videotape.
Related Materials: Posters and slide shows.

NEW YORK METRO

SOCIETY OF MOTION PICTURE AND TV ENGINEERS (SMPTE)
595 West Hartsdale Avenue
White Plains, NY 10607
(914) 761-1100
Fax: (914) 761-3115
Telex: 4995348

Lynette Robinson (Executive Director)

Contact: Lynette Robinson

Services: Association. Films and videotapes available for purchase.
Description: Test films and videotapes designed to provide motion picture and television equipment performance checks.
Projection Performance Test Films. Titles include: *The Jiffy 16mm Projector Evaluation Film; Projector Alignment and Image Quality Films; 35mm Anamorphic Projector Alignment; Universal Jitter, Weave and Travel Ghost;* and *35mm Theater Sound Test Film.*
Laboratory Test Films. Titles: *Registration Test Films* and *Universal Leader.*
Magnetic Sound Test Films. Titles include: *Multifrequency Test Films; Flutter Test Films; Signal Level Test Films; Channel Four (Switching Channel) Test Films;* and *Azimuth Alignment Test Films.*
Photographic (Optical) Sound Test Films. Titles include: *Multifrequency Test Films; Buzz Track Test Films; Sound Focus and Azimuth Alignment Test; Signal Level Test Films; Flutter Test Films;* and *Scanning Beam Test Films.*
Television Test Materials. Titles include: *Video Cassette for Receiver/Monitor Setup; Subjective Color Reference Films/Slides TV; Television Operation Alignment Test Pattern; Television Alignment and Resolution Test Pattern; Television Operational Registration Test Pattern; Television Mid-Frequency Response Test Pattern; Television Safe Action; Safe Title Area Test Pattern;* and *Television Deflection Linearity Test Pattern.*
Size & Elements: Film: 70mm, 35mm, 16mm and 8mm (approx. 100 titles; various format options available). Videotape: 3/4", VHS and Betamax (4 titles).
Cataloging: Published catalogs; brochures.
Access: Available for purchase.
Rights: Full rights held to all material.
Licensing: Apply for information.
Restrictions: None specified.
Viewing Facilities: None.
Duplication Facilities: None.

NEW YORK METRO

SOLARIS DANCE/THEATRE/VIDEO
264 West 19th Street
New York, NY 10011
(212) 741-0778

Henry C. Smith (Artistic Director)

Contacts: Henry C. Smith; Shelley Latham; Catharine Holmes (Video Projects Coordinator)
Services: Dance theater videotape company, film archives and producer; media organization; distributor. Videotapes available for distribution and rental rather than for research or reuse.
Description: Videotapes, produced and directed by Henry C. Smith, include: *Cerberus* (1978), an innovative union of dance, music and video, shot on location in Northern California; *Vision Dance* (1982), a cross-cultural dance theater piece interpreting Lakota Sioux legends, myths and spirit qualities, shot entirely on location in the Black Hills, the Badlands and Rosebud Reservation; *Life in the Dust/Fragments of African Voyages,* coproduced with Congolese National TV, featuring the Congolese National Ballet and SOLARIS performing along the Congo River, in tribal villages and in the rain forest; *Live and Remember,* an intimate discussion with Lakota elders, medicine men and traditional dancers about their sacred traditions and the challenge of keeping them alive today, featuring footage of a sweat lodge ceremony and traditional dance performances; and *You Have Another Chance,* a performance video and documentary based on the real-life experience of five Rikers Island inmates.

Also holds extensive Lakota Indian interview footage with tribal elders, medicine men, traditional dancers and Indian educators; and footage of locations on the Rosebud Reservation.
Size & Elements: Videotape: 1" (masters); 3/4" and VHS (viewing copies) (6 titles).
Cataloging: Apply for information.
Access: Not open to the public. Maintained for distribution and rental rather than for research or reuse. Research fees charged. Research requests accepted by mail and telephone.
Rights: Full rights held to all material.
Licensing: Available for licensing and reuse. License fees charged.
Restrictions: None specified.
Viewing Facilities: Videotape (3/4" and VHS).
Duplication Facilities: Videotape (VHS planned).

NEW YORK METRO

RICK SPALLA VIDEO PRODUCTIONS
HOLLYWOOD NEWSREEL SYNDICATE, INC.
301 West 45th Street
New York, NY 10036
(212) 765-4646
Contact: Tony Spalla

See **CALIFORNIA** (Los Angeles Metro)

NEW YORK METRO

SPECTACOLOR, INC.
One Times Square
New York, NY 10036
(212) 221-6938
Fax: (212) 221-7051
Telex: 428209 SPCL
Cable: WORLDSIGNS NEW YORK

George Stonbely (President)

Contact: George Stonbely
Services: Film and videotape producer. Collection available to the public for licensing and reuse.
Description: Spectacolor, Inc. operates the computer-controlled multicolored lighted sign in Times Square (New York City), which displays animation, advertising, public service announcements and public artworks. Holds footage of the digital marquee above Times Square and of the surrounding area. Also available are edited forms for use in television commercials.
Size & Elements: Film: 16mm. Videotape: 3/4". (Amounts unspecified).
Cataloging: Published brochure.
Access: Available to the public for licensing and reuse. Research requests accepted by telephone.
Rights: Full rights held to all material.
Licensing: Available for licensing. License fees charged.
Restrictions: None specified.
Viewing Facilities: None.
Duplication Facilities: None.

NEW YORK METRO

CECILE STARR
50 West 96th Street, Apartment 8A
New York, NY 10025
(212) 749-1250

Contact: Cecile Starr
Services: Film distributor. Films available for rental and purchase, and for reuse on a case-by-case basis.
Description: Distributes avant-garde and early experimental animation of historical and artistic significance. Has restored original negatives of some films and often has the best available copies.
  Filmmakers include: Alexander Alexeieff and Claire Parker (8 films), Robert Ascher, Diana Barrie (5 films), Berthold Bartosch, Mary Ellen Bute with Ted Nemeth (12 films), Douglas Crockwell (2 films), Carmen D'Avino, Storm De Hirsch (3 films), Viking Eggeling, Oskar Fischinger (18 films), Dwinell Grant (4 films), Maxine Haleff, Drew Klausner, Linda Klosky (2 films), Alfred Kouzel, Francis Lee (3 films), Helen Levitt with Janice Loeb and James Agee, Len Lye (8 films), Donn Alan Pennebaker, Dennis Pies (9 films), Lotte Reiniger (3 films), Hans Richter (7 films) and Walter Ruttmann (4 films).
  Special programs present film without sound, music on film, animation on serious themes, women animators (1930s-80s) and films for children and adults.
Size & Elements: Film: 16mm (approx. 100 titles; release prints). Videotape: VHS (approx. 3 titles; transferred from films).
Cataloging: Published catalog sheets.
Access: Films available to museums, universities, libraries, researchers and film specialists for rental and purchase. Not open to the public. Open to researchers and scholars only. Research fees not charged. Research requests accepted by mail and telephone.
Rights: Non-theatrical and non-commercial distribution rights held to all material. Can refer inquiries regarding copyright clearance to filmmakers or heirs.
Licensing: Available for licensing and reuse, subject to restrictions. License and usage fees charged.

Restrictions: Requests for licensing and reuse considered on a case-by-case basis.
Viewing Facilities: Film (16mm projector and editing table; by appointment only).
Duplication Facilities: None.

NEW YORK METRO

GENE STAVIS
10 Waterside Plaza
New York, NY 10010
(212) 746-5454

Contact: Gene Stavis
Services: Film and videotape stock footage sales library.
Description: Public domain theatrical films and documentaries (1900-40s). Most titles are 16mm and in black and white.
Size & Elements: Film: 16mm. Videotape: format unspecified. (Several hundred titles total).
Cataloging: None specified.
Access: Available to the public for viewing, research and reuse. For in-house use only. Research fees charged in some cases. Research requests accepted by mail and telephone.
Rights: Material in the public domain.
Licensing: Apply for information.
Restrictions: None specified.
Viewing Facilities: Film (16mm); videotape.
Duplication Facilities: None.

NEW YORK METRO

THE STEPFAMILY FOUNDATION, INC.
National Headquarters
333 West End Avenue, Suite 11C
New York, NY 10023
(212) 877-3244

Jeannette Lofas (Founder and President)

Contact: Kathleen Drohan (Director of Programming)
Services: Foundation. Videotapes available for duplication and purchase.
Description: Titles available include: *Step Relationships: The New American Family,* a compilation of television interviews on the concept of step relationships in our society; and *Fighting Fair!,* a technique for resolving conflicts for helping professionals and "steps" as well, presenting actual "Fight Fair" sessions in which disagreements between participants are presented and then resolved.
Size & Elements: Videotape: format unspecified (10 videotapes).
Cataloging: Brochure/order form.
Access: Available for duplication and purchase. Research fees charged. Research requests accepted by mail and telephone.
Rights: Full rights held to some material.
Licensing: Apply for information.
Restrictions: Apply for information.
Viewing Facilities: None.
Duplication Facilities: Videotape.
Related Materials: Audiotapes, books and publications.

NEW YORK METRO

STREAMLINE FILM ARCHIVES, INC.
109 East 29th Street
New York, NY 10016
(212) 696-2616
(212) 696-2617

Mark Trost (President)

Contacts: Mark Trost; Mark Heller (Vice President)
Services: Film and videotape producer; stock footage sales library.
Description: Library includes newsreels, corporate films, feature films (Westerns, musicals, adventures, science fiction and horror), silent and sound short subjects, silent features, educational films, nature films, medical films, films on and about Hollywood and Broadway, sports films, theatrical cartoons, contemporary news video (1986-present), commercials, television shows

(kinescopes and filmed programs), theatrical trailers, serials (silent and sound cliffhangers), travelogues, home movies (amateur and semi-professional) and government films.

Features material (1896-present) in black and white (60%) and color (40%). Highlights include material on virtually every Hollywood star and personality; behind-the-scenes Hollywood footage; documentaries on filmmaking, television and radio broadcasting; "B" Westerns (featuring Gene Autry, Roy Rogers, et al.); educational and etiquette films with substantial camp appeal (e.g., *Dating: Do's and Don'ts* and *Are Manners Important?*); U.S. government films (restricted and unrestricted, documentaries and dramatizations, campy and powerful) covering World War II, the Korean conflict, the Cold War, Vietnam, soldier indoctrination and training; the New York World's Fair (color and black and white on the 1939-40 and 1964-65 Fairs); major events (newsreel coverage of virtually every major newsmaker, politician and newsworthy story since 1898); and general campy footage culled from newsreels, silent film comedies and industrials (obese men dancing, human flies, cats fighting in the boxing ring, aircraft that never get off the ground, women praising sludge, etc.).

Federal Follies. Include government-produced films made for general civilian consumption and servicemen's use only, many no longer available from government sources. Collection includes the *Fighting Men, This Is America, Why We Fight* and *Private Snafu* series, as well as hundreds of other government titles. These include flag-waving World War II morale boosters narrated by Orson Welles or Katharine Hepburn, instructional cartoons (produced by Walt Disney and Warner Brothers), manners and hygiene shorts (the classic *Blondes Prefer Gentlemen* and the anti-LSD film, *Trip to Where?*); civil defense tutorials (*Duck and Cover*) and anti-Soviet propaganda (*Red Nightmare* and *The Big Lie*).

The Film Wha? Collection. Culled from its collection, Streamline maintains an extensive variety of clips that defy belief and description: 300-lb. country singers dancing on their heads; Johnny, the Philip Morris mascot, claiming that doctors endorse cigarettes because they are "easy on the throat"; Ethel Barrymore undressing for her husband; and "Fred Mertz" in a music video.

Great Hollywood stunts. Death-defying stunts culled from Streamline's collection of "B" Westerns, serials, short subjects and action features. Stunts include cars driving over cliffs, horses trampling cowboys and men clinging to airplanes.

Hollywood Babylon. Bloopers, outtakes, behind-the-scenes footage and other rare gems depicting the silent and golden ages of Hollywood. Features footage of major Hollywood premieres, awards ceremonies, stars at home and at play, discarded footage, and other seldom-seen materials.

Hollywood's golden age. Collection of feature films, short subjects, cartoons and related titles featuring some of the best and worst moments from Hollywood, with special emphasis on the years 1931-49. Titles run the gamut from Academy Award-winning features and Saturday matinee serials to low budget "B" Westerns and "Poverty Row" melodramas.

The News 12 Collection (1986-present; over 600 VHS videotapes). Extensive collection of contemporary video news footage; holdings increase on a daily basis. Collection covers all aspects of contemporary suburban and urban life and issues as shot and reported by News 12 Long Island, the award-winning 24-hour all-news channel produced by Cablevision Systems, one of the largest multiple system operators in the U.S.

The Plainview Collection. From *Cleanliness Brings Health* to *The Last Date,* The Plainview collection comprises Streamline's library of educational films (1930s-70s). As entertaining today as they might have been boring back in grade school, these films offer guidance (generally demonstrated by horrific-looking adolescents and teens) on virtually every aspect of life, from the proper way to cross the street to the right way to change a pair of underwear.

The silent years. Streamline's silent collection covers the entire silent era, including material on every major star, feature and director. Cornerstone of the collection is a remarkable library of silent comedies featuring the works of Chaplin, Keaton, the Tons of Fun, Billy Bevan, Mack Sennett and many others.
Size & Elements: Film: 35mm (a few negatives and release prints); 16mm (over 5 million feet, 8,000 titles; release prints). Videotape: 1" and 3/4" (masters); VHS (over 600 videotapes; viewing copies, matching 1" and 3/4" masters). Viewing copies on 3/4" and VHS videotape are available for all film titles.
Cataloging: Computerized cataloging for staff use only (printouts available to clients); shot lists; research library.
Access: Available for duplication and reuse. Research fees charged. Research requests accepted by telephone and in person (by appointment only). Viewing copies of selected material can be provided to clients.
Rights: Full rights held to some material. Some rights held to some material. Much material in the public domain. Additional clearances may be necessary in

some cases if material is to be reused.
Licensing: Available for licensing and reuse, subject to restrictions. Usage fees charged depending on intended markets and production media. Fees computed on amount of footage actually used in final cut. Minimum project fees (nonrefundable) charged upon shipment of broadcast-quality film or videotape masters. Discounts for quantity usage negotiable. Clients responsible for all videotape transfer, laboratory, messenger and shipping costs.
Restrictions: Clients must indemnify and hold library harmless from any and all claims, losses, demands and liabilities arising out of client's use of footage. Some material for reference and research use only; any reuse would require clearance from copyright holder.
Viewing Facilities: Film and videotape.
Duplication Facilities: Film (film-to-videotape transfers using Elmo system); videotape (3/4" and VHS).

NEW YORK METRO

STUDENT STRUGGLE FOR SOVIET JEWRY PROJECT EYEWITNESS
210 West 91st Street
New York, NY 10024
(212) 799-8900
Fax: (212) 799-8890

Glenn Richter (National Coordinator)

Contact: Glenn Richter
Services: Association. Videotapes available for duplication and possibly reuse.
Description: Interviews with Jews formerly in the Soviet Union, Americans who have visited Soviet Jewish "refuseniks" and Jews within the U.S.S.R. Also held are copies of television specials and news broadcasts relating to Soviet Jews and pro-Jewish demonstrations in the West.
Size & Elements: Videotape: VHS (over 25 videotapes).
Cataloging: None specified.
Access: Available for duplication. Research requests accepted by mail, telephone and in person (by appointment only). Research fees not charged.
Rights: Some rights held to some material.
Licensing: Apply for information. Usage fees not charged.
Restrictions: None specified.
Viewing Facilities: None.
Duplication Facilities: Videotape (VHS).

NEW YORK METRO

TAMIMENT LIBRARY/WAGNER LABOR ARCHIVES NEW YORK UNIVERSITY
Bobst Library
70 Washington Square South
New York, NY 10012
(212) 998-2630

Debra Bernhardt (Archivist)

Contact: Erika Gottfried
Services: Educational institution; library. Film and videotape collection open to the public. Materials available for research, duplication and reuse, subject to restrictions.
Description: Labor and radical movements in 20th century America, primarily New York City. Anarchism, civil rights, communism, socialism, the Spanish Civil War, unemployment in the 1930s, trade unions and women's issues are the primary issues addressed.

Titles include: *Crime to Fit the Punishment* (1982), documenting the making of the labor film *Salt of the Earth* during the McCarthy era; *The Emerging Woman* (1974); *Artists at Work: A Film on the New Deal Art Project* (1981); *Charge and Countercharge* (1969), with documentary footage on the Army-McCarthy hearings of 1954; *Blue-Collar Trap* (1972); *Citizen: The Political Life of Allard K. Lowenstein* (1983); *Great Weirton Steal* (1984); *Harvest of Shame* (1960), a documentary on migrant farm workers narrated by Edward R. Murrow; *Eugene Debs and the American Movement* (1978); *Farewell Etaoin Shrdlu,* on the transition from linotypes to phototypesetting at *The New York Times; Great Sit-down Strike* (1976), on the United Auto Workers' strike at General Motors (1936-37) which resulted in union recognition; *Red Nightmare* (1965); *Resurgence: The Movement for Equality vs. the KKK* (1982); *The Life and Times of Rosie the Riveter* (1980); *Molders of Troy* (1980); *Trials of Alger Hiss* (1981); *Union Maids* (1977); *Weavers:*

Wasn't That A Time (1981); *Song of the Canary* (1979), focusing on occupational health hazards; *The Wobblies* (1979), covering the history of the Industrial Workers of the World (1905 through World War I); *Mass Tribute to Buenaventura Durruti; Tomorrow is Another Day: History of the Seafarer's International Union;* and *LBJ Meets the AFL-CIO.*

Also holds commercial films and videotapes about labor or radical issues (e.g., *The Grapes of Wrath* and *On the Waterfront*).

Transport Workers Union Collection. Extensive footage of picket lines, demonstrations, conventions and social outings, all in the New York City area (1939-67).
Size & Elements: Film: 16mm (300 titles, 500 cans; originals and release prints). Videotape: 2" and 1/2" (300 videotapes; masters and viewing copies).
Cataloging: Published catalogs.
Access: Available to the public for research and duplication, with permission of copyright holder. Research fees not charged. Research requests accepted by mail, telephone and in person (walk-in).
Rights: Apply for information. Additional clearances may be necessary in some cases if material is to be reused.
Licensing: Available for reuse, subject to restrictions. Usage fees include cost of duplication.
Restrictions: Must have permission of copyright holder to duplicate. The commercial films are available for viewing only in the Avery Fisher Media Center of New York University's main library.
Viewing Facilities: Videotape (by appointment only).
Duplication Facilities: None.

NEW YORK METRO

TELLTALES ASSOCIATES INC.
1230 Park Avenue, Suite PHB
New York, NY 10128
(212) 249-8308
(401) 846-0073 (Newport, Rhode Island office)

Fred Cushing (Director)
Caterine Milinaire (Director)

Contact: Fred Cushing
Services: Videotape stock footage sales library. Custom shooting services available.
Description: Contemporary videotape footage, including: endangered species (lemurs, oryx, Dama gazelles and cranes); seasonal celebrations in the U.S., Europe and the Caribbean (New Year, carnivals, solstices and Halloween); motorless flight (kites and hang gliders in California and Elmira, New York); and Newport, Rhode Island, including aerial views of coastline and bridge, sailing and the town.
Size & Elements: Videotape: 3/4" (amount unspecified).
Cataloging: General listing available; logs (staff use only).
Access: Available for duplication and reuse. Research services available. Research fees charged. Research requests accepted by mail and telephone.
Rights: Full rights held to all material.
Licensing: Available for licensing and reuse. License fees charged.
Restrictions: None specified.
Viewing Facilities: Videotape (off-premises).
Duplication Facilities: Videotape (1" at outside facility; 3/4" in-house).

NEW YORK METRO

TWYLA THARP DANCE FOUNDATION
890 Broadway, 3rd Floor
New York, NY 10003
(212) 475-7788
Fax: (212) 254-5938

Sharon Luckman (Executive Director)

Contact: Sharon Luckman
Services: Foundation. Private videotape collection for in-house use only.
Description: Twyla Tharp Dance Company documentation of dance creation, choreography, studio rehearsals, on-stage and televised performances (1965-present).
Size & Elements: Videotape: 2" and 1" (20 videotapes; masters); 1/2" open reel (700 videotapes; masters).

Cataloging: Card catalogs; shot lists.
Access: For in-house use only.
Rights: Full rights held to some material. Some rights held to some material.
Licensing: Not presently available for licensing or reuse.
Restrictions: Policies on licensing and reuse not yet established. Access to collection very limited.
Viewing Facilities: None.
Duplication Facilities: None.

NEW YORK METRO

THIRD WORLD NEWSREEL
355 West 38th Street, 5th Floor
New York, NY 10018
(212) 947-9277

Ada G. Griffin (Director of Distribution)

Contact: Ada G. Griffin
Services: Film and videotape producer and distributor; film and videotape archive; media arts organization. Material available for licensing and reuse, subject to restrictions.
Description: "Third World Newsreel was conceived out of ideals that flourished when decades of historical upheaval reached a major peak in the late 1960s. At the height of the Vietnam conflict, hundreds of artists and activists were compelled to document the national events or concerns that were either being distorted or ignored by the mass media. In December 1967, a group met in New York to organize a network of filmmakers to record some of the major events of the time. Calling itself Newsreel, the founding collective began to produce large numbers of short black and white documentaries quickly and inexpensively. Their efforts to jar public awareness and to distribute the programs to the widest audience possible helped organizers and activities in their consciousness-raising activities, providing an alternative media. Newsreel filmmakers conveyed a sense of immediacy and experimentation through their work. Within two years of its founding, a dozen other Newsreels had been formed in places like Boston, Ann Arbor, and Washington, D.C. New York Newsreel (now Third World Newsreel) and San Francisco (now California Newsreel [q.v.]) are the last existing organizations that emerged from the original network.

"By 1971, New York Newsreel had begun to change. Slowly, the political consciousness-raising focus began to shift toward expanding the pool of skilled filmmakers and broadening their film constituency. Women and people of color who had been recruited into Newsreel began to assert their opinions; they demanded access to equipment and training. They reached out to community-based audiences. They also strongly influenced the decisions about how the collective should operate and about the subject matter for new films. In 1973, with few members and none of the original founders remaining, an African American, Latino and Asian caucus was convened to evaluate Newsreel's commitment to the larger scope of national and world issues, [and] the New York Newsreel chapter began its seventh year as Third World Newsreel."

Circulating collection now includes 150 titles.

Africa and the Middle East. Titles include: *Nazareth in August* (Norman Cowie, Ahmed Damian and Dan Walworth), a documentary on Palestinian Arabs within the State of Israel and their efforts as Israeli citizens to gain equal rights; *Beirut: On a Clear Day You Can See Peace* (Grassroots International Women for Peace in Lebanon); *Cancer of Betrayal* (Facts Africa), a record of the last speech by Amilcar Cabral, the leader of the movement to free Guinea-Bissau from Portuguese colonialism; and *Namibia: Independence Now!*, filmed inside nurseries, schools, medical training centers and SWAPO-organized communities in Angola and Zambia.

Latin America and the Caribbean. Programs relating to the Nicaraguan and Cuban revolutions, women organizing in Brazil, and the "Americanization" of Mexico, Guyana and Venezuela. Sample titles include: *Atencingo* (Eduardo Maldonado and the Grupo Testimonio Mexico), inspired by the 40-year struggle of the peasants of Mexico's Pueblo region; *Chronicle of Hope: Nicaragua* (Allan Siegel and Third World Newsreel), a privileged look into the lives and hearts of both North Americans and Nicaraguans as they labor to achieve a more just world; and *My Life, Our Struggle (Minha Vida, Nossa Luta)* (Suzana Amaral and TV Cultura 2), in which a group of poor women on the outskirts of Sao Paulo lead a community effort to achieve basic necessities.

Asia. The Vietnam war is the central focus of the films in this section, with several titles made by Vietnamese film units during the war. Titles include: *Seventy-Nine Springtimes of Ho Chi Minh* (Santiago Alvarez), an impressionist biography on Vietnam's leader using still photographs, newsreel footage and Ho's poetry; *U.S. Techniques and Genocide in Vietnam* (Vietnamese People's

Army Films), describes the use of elaborate U.S. weapons against civilian targets in Vietnam; and *Homes Apart: The Two Koreas* (Orinne J. T. Takagi and Christine Choy), explores the situations of Korean families separated since the Korean War.

Europe. Films focusing on Portugal, Ireland, England and the Basque region. Titles include: *Paris in the Month of May* (Chris Marker), on the 1968 student/worker uprisings in France that nearly succeeded in toppling the DeGaulle government; *Scenes of the Class Struggle in Portugal* (Robert Kramer and Phillip Spinelli), an eyewitness account of the political transformation of Portugal during the mid-1970s; and *Going, Going, Gone* (Hugh MacConville, Sinn Fein), presenting the argument for increased control by Irish people over Ireland's natural resources.

Cultural expression. Films and videotapes examining popular art forms such as music, theater, poetry and dance, within the context of history, culture and social concerns. Titles include: *Chinatown 2-Step* (Eddie Wong, Visual Communications), is a fresh, lively view of the Chinese American middle class; *Cruisin' J-Town* (Duane Kubo), a spirited profile of the popular jazz fusion band Hiroshima in its early days (late 1970s); *Percussions, Impression and Reality* (Allan Siegel), the first comprehensive U.S. film on the origins and growth of traditional Puerto Rican music; and *Sweet Sugar Rage* (Honor Ford-Smith and Harclyde Walcott), on Sistren Theatre Collective, a popular Jamaican women's troupe who uses improvisation and theater as a consciousness-raising tool among rural and urban audiences in Jamaica.

Issues and organizing. Documentaries that grapple with issues and problems within the United States and Canada. Titles include: *Adopted Son: The Death of Vincent Chin* (Christine Choy and Renée Tajima), tells the story of a death that shook the nation and led to the first federal civil rights trial involving discrimination against Asian Americans; *Omai Fa'atasi: Samoa Mo Samoa* (Visual Communications), examines the realities facing teenagers whose parents immigrated to southern California from the Pacific U.S. territory of Samoa in the early 1950s and 1960s; *People's Firehouse #1* (Paul Schneider), in which Polish Americans in Brooklyn protested the closing of their local firehouse, occupied it and won; *Update: Bernadette Powell*, videotaped by an all-woman film crew at the Bedford Hills (N.Y.) Women's Correctional Facility, interviews a woman convicted of murder based on the misconception that survivors of long-term battering enjoy physical abuse; *Flo and Charlie* (Molly Smolett), a docudrama on the plight of the homeless, taking the viewer through the streets that are home to hundreds of thousands of children and adults; *Between Two Worlds: The Hmong Shaman in America* (Taggart Siegel and Dwight Conquergood), on the 60,000 Hmong refugees transplanted from agrarian mountain villages in northern Laos to the U.S.; *Race Against Prime Time* (David Shulman), utilizing news footage and interviews to examine how news coverage of Miami riots was constructed; and *Inside Women Inside* (Christine Choy and Cynthia Maurizio), exposing the personal degradation that women prisoners experience on a daily basis.

Drama, animation and experimental works. Sample titles include: *After the Earthquake (Despues del Terremoto)* (Lourdes Portillo and Nina Serrano), the first dramatic film to be made about the lives of Nicaraguans who came to the United States to flee the violence of the Somoza regime, prior to the 1979 revolution; *Gaman...To Endure* (Bob Miyamoto), combines the drawings of Betty Chen and the music of Nobuko Miyamoto to tell the story of the incarceration of 110,000 Japanese Americans in concentration camps during World War II; *Killer Of Sheep* (Charles Burnett), a moving portrait of a young Black man employed in a Los Angeles slaughterhouse, whose grueling work infects his whole life, including his relationships with his wife, children and friends; and *Reassemblage* (Trinh T. Minh-ha), challenging conventional anthro-documentary approaches to cinematic consideration of non-Western cultures.

Newsreel films. Produced within the first years of Newsreel's formation, these films reflect an aesthetic of urgency and commitment characteristic of the 1960s. Sample titles are: *Amerikka* (1969), documenting the escalation of the antiwar protest movement; *Bobby Seale* (1969), in which the Black Panther Party Chairman talks about his treatment as a political prisoner; *The Case Against Lincoln Center* (1968), on the "redevelopment" and gentrification of Manhattan's West Side, displacing more than 20,000 Latino families; and *Makeout* (1972), showing a young couple necking in a car, as we hear the young woman's stream-of-consciousness thoughts. Other titles include *Boston Draft Resistance Group* (1968); *Chicago Convention Challenge* (1968); *Black Panther* (1968); *Columbia Revolt* (1968); *The Haight* (1968); *I. S. 201* (1968); *Isle of Youth* (1968); *Jeanette Rankin Brigade* (1968); *Up Against The Wall Miss America* (1968); *Yippie* (1968); *Community Control* (1969); *High School Rising* (1969); *People's Park* (1969); *People's War* (1969); *Pig Power* (1969); *R.O.T.C.* (1969); *Riot Control Weapons* (1969); *San Francisco State: On Strike* (1969); *She's Beautiful When She's Angry* (1969); *Wreck of the New York Subway* (1969); *Fuera Yanqui* (1970); *Lincoln Hospital* (1970); *El Pueblo Se*

Levanta (1970); *Wilmington* (1970); *My Country Occupied* (1971); and *The Women's Film* (1971).
Size & Elements: Film: 16mm (120 titles, 350 cans; release prints). Videotape: 3/4", VHS, Betamax I and II (34 titles originally produced on videotape; viewing copies of all materials) (154 titles total).
Cataloging: Card catalogs; published catalogs.
Access: Open to the public. Collection is maintained primarily for rental and purchase. Available for licensing and reuse. Research fees not charged.
Rights: Full rights held to some material. Some rights held to all material.
Licensing: Available for licensing and reuse, subject to restrictions.
Restrictions: Requests for licensing and reuse considered on a case-by-case basis.
Viewing Facilities: Film (screening room); videotape (VHS and Betamax).
Duplication Facilities: None.

NEW YORK METRO

THOROUGHBRED RACING ASSOCIATIONS
3000 Marcus Avenue, Suite 2W4
Lake Success, NY 11042
(516) 328-2660
Fax: (516) 328-8137

Lillian McKee (Film Librarian)

Contact: Lillian McKee
Services: Association. Circulating film library maintained primarily for rental and purchase.
Description: Films supplied by TRA member racetracks. Titles include: *Ak-Sar-Ben* (Ak-Sar-Ben); *Champions of 1962 through 1966* (TRA), including sequences filmed at Kentucky and California breeding farms, slow motion scenes of several leading jockeys in action and featured horses Kelso, Cicada, Never Bend, Smart Deb, Jaipur and Primonetta; *A Day in the Life of Longacres; First at the Finish* (produced by Hialeah Park); *Greentree Thoroughbreds* (J. H. Whitney); *The King, A Queen and The Prince,* a review of the brilliant racing season of 1969 at Santa Anita Park, including the riding comeback of Bill Shoemaker, racing exploits of the filly Dark Mirage, Stakes conquests of Majestic Prince in the Santa Anita Derby and other events; *Laffit Pincay Jr.: The Cool Latin* (Joe Burnham); *Donald Pierce: Journeyman Jockey* (Hollywood Park); *Two-Year-Olds of 1966* (TRA); *Triple Crown Champions* (TRA); and *Birth of a Foal.*
Size & Elements: Film: 16mm (approx. 30 films, 12,024 feet).
Cataloging: Printed list.
Access: Maintained for rental and purchase. Rental fees charged. Requests accepted by mail and telephone.
Rights: No rights held to any material. Additional clearances necessary if material is to be reused.
Licensing: Apply for information.
Restrictions: Restrictions may apply to licensing and reuse.
Viewing Facilities: None.
Duplication Facilities: None.

NEW YORK METRO

TIMESTEPS PRODUCTIONS, INC.
2 Glenside
West Orange, NJ 07052
(201) 669-1930

Marilyn Petrokubi (President)

Contact: Marilyn Petrokubi
Services: Film and videotape producer. Open to researchers, scholars and the public. Material available for duplication and reuse. Research services available.
Description: Historical subjects (1895-1959) include: accidents, airplanes, ambulances, Americana, automobiles, bands, Alexander Graham Bell, bicycles, breadlines, business, carriages, cheering, children, churches, coal, Calvin Coolidge, cowboys, crowds, dams, dancing, demolition, the Depression, disasters, diving, doctors, earthquakes, Thomas A. Edison, Dwight D. Eisenhower, Ellis Island, employees, factories, families, farms, fashion, fireworks, fishing, floods, football, foundries, funerals, gardening, gas stations, ghettos, Samuel Gompers, graduation, the handicapped, Herbert Hoover, hospitals, houses, immigrants, industry, the Korean War, Charles A. Lindbergh, manufacturing, men, military, motion pictures, Benito Mussolini,

New York City, offices, parades, parks, pedestrians, picnics, Prohibition, radio, raw materials, recreation, the Red Cross, refineries, Will Rogers, Eleanor Roosevelt, Franklin D. Roosevelt, Babe Ruth, schools, smoking, sports, the Stock Exchange, stores, street scenes, suffragettes, sweatshops, swimming, William Howard Taft, telephones, theaters, transportation, trolleys, V-J Day, Washington, D.C., women, World War I, World War II and the Wright Brothers.
Size & Elements: Videotape: 1" and 3/4" (masters transferred from film originals); VHS (time-coded viewing copies) (12 hours total).
Cataloging: Computerized cataloging available to researchers.
Access: Open to researchers, scholars and the public (by appointment only). Available for duplication and reuse. Research requests accepted by telephone. A printout is made (at no charge) of relevant subjects and a VHS reference cassette with visible time code is produced for client (fees apply).
Rights: Full rights held to some material. Some material in the public domain.
Licensing: Available for licensing and reuse, subject to restrictions. License and usage fees charged.
Restrictions: Written permission required for reuse.
Viewing Facilities: Videotape (VHS).
Duplication Facilities: Videotape (VHS to VHS with visible time code).

NEW YORK METRO

TWENTIETH CENTURY-FOX MOVIETONEWS, INC.
460 West 54th Street
New York, NY 10019
(212) 556-2560
Fax: (212) 869-7840

Burton Stone (President/Los Angeles)
Stanley de Covnick (Director of Administration)
Harold Potter (Manager of Operations)
Richard Plagge (Manager, Library Services)
Merle Joffe (Administrative Assistant)
Evelyn Champion; Tom Rowan; Mark Burdi (Librarians)

Contact: Richard Plagge
Services: Film newsreel library; stock footage sales library.
Description: The 20th Century-Fox Library Collection spans the years from World War I to 1963. The collection consists of cut newsreel stories from the Movietone newsreels (1919-63) produced by 20th Century-Fox; as well as outtakes and other material not used in the newsreels. Also included in the collection are many theatrically released short subjects. In the Library as well are a number of special collections — some with material from World War I.
Movietonews newsreels. Between 1919 and 1963, 20th Century-Fox produced and released 4,578 biweekly newsreels (104 per year). The newsreels were edited in and released from the Fox headquarters, then as now located on West 54th Street in New York. The U.S. national edition, a Canadian edition, and a South American edition (in Spanish) were issued from the New York headquarters. During most of the years of its production, Movietonews had hundreds of cameramen distributed across the globe and is generally acknowledged to be one of the strongest newsreel collections as far as international material is concerned.
The library has preserved in its collection a large portion of all the newsreels produced. All the issues from 1934-63 exist in their entirety, 60% exist from the years 1928-34, and 33% from the years 1919-28. Most of the film is housed in vaults on the premises; another 10% is stored in vaults in Ogdensburg, New Jersey. The material in Ogdensburg is largely backup material, some short subjects and silent cut stories. Material is rarely pulled from the vaults in Ogdensburg not only because of the difficulty in accessing material in the hinterlands of New Jersey, but also because of the additional cataloging and preservation work generally required of film that has for so long been in deep cover. Researchers desiring material dating from the early silent era should be warned that this material has often suffered from significant shrinkage and deterioration. Thus, there may be some restrictions vis-a-vis screening and duplication of the older material.
Until 1952 production was exclusively in 35mm film, and newsreels were distributed theatrically throughout the United States. After 1952, production in 16mm commenced, largely intended for distribution to television news services. Occasionally a 16mm story was blown up to 35mm for inclusion in the weekly newsreel. Since 35mm production continued in tandem with 16mm production, researchers are advised to investigate both the 35mm and 16mm collections, which are indexed separately, when looking for events after 1952. The 16mm coverage was wire-service type coverage for television news

produced by Fox and distributed by other distributors and news services. Joint ventures existed with UPI, as well as with NBC (for whom Fox produced the *Camel News Caravan*).

The newsreels produced for theatrical release all had a "dramatic" structure. "Dark and light," or serious and lightweight stories were juxtaposed and counterbalanced in an overall package that aimed to entertain and uplift as much as to inform. Issues generally opened with a hard news item, often an international piece or one involving a major U.S. public figure, politician or celebrity. The next item might be a fashion story or perhaps society news. The reel would return to headline coverage of increasingly "softer" stories, interspersed with mini-documentaries — "Cameragraphs," or short comedies, "Newsettes." The reels generally concluded with sports coverage. This structure remained fairly consistent throughout the history of the newsreel until the 1950s when, in response to increasing competition from television news, the newsreels became somewhat more hard-news oriented.

The vast size and range of the collection defy any very concise précis of its strengths and weaknesses. With that understood, it may be worth a moment to highlight a few categories which in themselves fill more file drawers than can easily be thumbed through in a single sitting. The War Department files — Army and Naval — are quite extensive. Should your subject be tanks, troops or revolution, look under Army; should you have need of saboteurs, prison camps or the Madagascar War, look under Naval. Aviation is another massive card file. Everything from blimps to zeppelins, or from christenings to stunt flying can be found here. Another strength of the collection is its coverage of the civil rights movement. There is film of the early bus boycotts in Montgomery and Tallahassee, of civil disturbances during the school desegregation years in Little Rock and elsewhere and personalities from Martin Luther King, Jr. and Thurgood Marshall to Autherine Lucy and James Meredith. Fashions, fads and sports are also abundant categories.

One "interruption" in the newsreel collection should be noted. In 1980 Fox donated a portion of the collection to the University of South Carolina, Newsfilm Library, Instructional Services Center (q.v.). Presently housed there and available from them is all the material received and released from September 1942 through August 1944, and outtakes and unused stories dating from 1919 to May 1934. A total of seven million feet of film was donated. The material included in this donation was so designated because of its deteriorating condition. (Due to shortages of precious metals in World War II, film stock from this period has very little silver and presents special preservation problems.) The gift to the University included funds for the transfer of all this material to safety stock, which has been completed. Material is available from the University; hardcopy research can be done in the New York office; videotapes for screening can be assembled in South Carolina.

During 1951 and 1952 an extra 208 editions (an additional 2 per week), were produced. These volumes — 35 and 36 — highlighted international news events. References to these special supplemental editions can be found in the 35mm card file under the Location heading.

Short subject theatrical releases. A total of 578 short subject films were produced by 20th Century-Fox (1931-64) for release to theaters to precede feature films. Most shorts from 1931-52 are divided into two series: *Adventures of a Newsreel Cameraman* and *Magic Carpet. The Adventures of a Newsreel Cameraman* glamorized that profession with exhibitions of daredevil feats performed while in pursuit of the story, and with privileged views and breathtaking camera angles. Most shorts were produced independently of the newsreels and used original footage — as in *Manhattan Medley*, a photo essay of New York City. Occasionally a subject would come along which would draw "stock" footage from the newsreel collection — as in *Breath of Disaster.* The other series, *Magic Carpet,* was a kind of travelogue which incorporated aspects of a country or region's social history. All the shorts are 35mm. Between 1931 and 1952 most are black and white, although there are several Technicolor shorts. From 1952 to 1964, 124 shorts were produced in Cinemascope and color.

Special collections. A number of 35mm documentaries, most 90 min., and 208 special newsreel editions (1951-52). One of these documentaries is a symposium on the First World War: *The War to End All Wars* (90 min.), compiled from some 40,000 feet of uncataloged World War I film in the collection. Originally produced in 1934, it was re-edited in 1950. A script is available; the film is on safety stock.

Anatomy of Crime (90 min.) is a history of crime focusing on the Kefauver hearings of the 1950s; *Today's Teens* (1963) is a satirical symposium on the "teenage era" which begins with the teens represented as modern witches and goblins. *United We Stand* and *Why Korea* relate to the Korean War. *Farewell to Yesterday* (1954) chronicles the history of international relations between the Treaty of Versailles and the Korean War. The *Dance Reel* (30 min.) is a compilation of changing dance styles and fads (1910s-60s). *The Truman Years* is a symposium on President Truman. *Cry of the World* is a history of the

period between World Wars I and II. There are reels on World War I, women voters and personalities in the suffragette movement, the 1930s hunger marches, the well-known faces of organized crime, the peace rallies and the 1932 Geneva peace conference, India's Mohandas K. Gandhi, and Japanese troops in Manchuria.

Size & Elements: Film: 35mm and 16mm (65 million feet; nitrate and safety, positive and negative, black and white and color, silent and sound, cut newsreels and outtakes).

Most of the library's material consists of the newsreels — cut (i.e., edited) stories, outtakes and unused material. Cut stories and complete newsreels exist in both master positive and original negative; outtakes and unused material in original negative. Most of the pre-1950 material is on original nitrate stock. Whenever possible, original negative is screened and used for duplication, to protect the master positive. Material before 1928 is silent; more recent material has an optical soundtrack. While screening the negative film, customers will be listening to the soundtrack as reproduced from an optical negative and should be advised that it is often somewhat difficult to hear all the details and nuances.

Most of the theatrically released short subjects exist in positive master form; some negatives are held.

Cataloging: Separate card files exist for the 35mm and 16mm collections. The 35mm card file contains approximately 2.2 million cards divided into category listings: personalities (A-Z); geographic, the United States and international (alphabetically organized); miscellaneous listings (A-Z) (the Newsettes, among other stories, can be found here); and the specific subjects file. A summary of category listings for the 35mm card file follows the text of this listing. The collection is very amply cross-referenced; it is not unusual to find an item in ten or more different file drawers.

The 16mm collection is cataloged in a simpler fashion. Subjects in the 16mm collection are listed under personality (A-Z); general (alphabetical listing); and under location (United States and international).

Other useful finding aids for the collection are the weekly release or continuity sheets which, for every edition of the newsreel produced, list in order the various stories contained in that particular newsreel, describing them in some detail. Also available to researchers are the inventory sheets, known as the "turnover sheets." These sheets list all the negatives delivered to the library department by date, and show material used in a particular volume and issue, as distinct from unused material. Both of the above can be useful reference guides for research when searching an event or events with specific dates. It should be understood that in general the date listed on the subject index card is the date that the film was entered in the library and not the actual event date (although in some cases these may coincide). For example, a story from Cincinnati will usually have reached the library by the day after the event, but a story from Europe or the Pacific will probably have occurred several days prior to its entry. In a case where an actual date is unknown and not evident from other sources, cameraman's dope sheets are on file and can be consulted on a limited basis (librarian's time permitting).

A list of the theatrical short subjects is available.

Access: Open to the public. Available for licensing and reuse.

While the Movietonews staff cannot provide research, in certain cases a cursory check can be made if specific information is provided (e.g., exact date of event, location, personalities involved, etc.). Staff can refer customers to qualified and experienced film researchers. It is recommended that all footage requested to be viewed at the Movietonews facilities before ordering.

Before screening material from the collection, a letter on company stationery is required. The letter should indicate the type of company requesting the film, the intended use of the material, the title or working title of the project, the expected immediate usage or rights being requested, any other rights anticipated, and the estimated release date of the production.

An appointment must be made for screening. It is advisable to allow some time for preparation of the order if a large amount of material is to be screened. A library service fee for pulling, handling and screening film will be charged for each viewing order. Cancellations of screening time must be made 24 hours before the scheduled appointment. A fee will be charged for no-shows.

Rights: Movietonews makes no representations or warranties with respect to the footage furnished except that Movietonews produced and/or owns the same and has the right and capacity to enter into a licensing agreement. Client must obtain at its own expense all clearances, waivers and permissions that are needed in connection with its use of the footage and must indemnify and hold Movietonews harmless from any and all claims, losses, demands and liabilities arising out of the client's use of this material.

Licensing: Available for licensing and reuse, subject to restrictions. Movietonews material is furnished to the customer only for the contracted usage. A scratched workprint or viewing cassette with a visual time code or property identification should be ordered before production-quality material can be furnished. An agreement will be reached between the client and

Movietonews before any preprint (production-quality) material is furnished. A footage report must be furnished in writing to Movietonews after the editing has been done by the client. There is a minimum charge per cut or scene of 6.66 seconds.

A standard contract, specifying terms and conditions, is available. All footage is supplied on a nonexclusive basis. A current rate card is available on request. Usage fees and laboratory prices are subject to change without notice.
Restrictions: Library footage supplied by Movietonews may include the use of narration, music, titles and logos as well as the images. However, this usage must be in the same context as the original, e.g., narration must be used in whole sentences.
Viewing Facilities: Film (35mm and 16mm flatbed viewing machines).
Duplication Facilities: None. All material is duplicated by approved film laboratories or videotape facilities; orders are handled and billed through Movietonews.
Works in Progress: While 20th Century-Fox Movietonews was headquartered in New York, there were foreign bureaus in London, Paris, Coblenz (Germany) and Sydney (Australia). Each of these bureaus is presently an independent source for footage from the international editions of the newsreel. Currently under consideration is a plan to centralize information about each of these bureaus and their holdings. One plan under discussion involves having each bureau's card catalog accessible for research on microfiche or by computer. Another project under consideration is acquiring the news collections of two Fox-affiliated television stations, WTTG and WNYW-TV.

This article was written and researched by Lewanne Jones, a film researcher working in New York City.

Listing of Files for 35mm Card Index

Personalities (A-Z)
Geographic (United States, by state; International)
Miscellaneous Listings (general file, A-Z)

Specific Subject Files:
  Animals.
  Aviation — specific headings. Airfields, air mail, air maneuvers, air scenes, anti-aircraft, balloons, blimps, bombings, catapulting, christenings, dirigibles, flight, flying instruction, gliders, meets and exhibitions, parachute operations, passenger service, smokescreens, speed races, stunt flying, zeppelins.
  Aviation — general headings. Air disasters, bombs, falling planes, miscellaneous aviation, names of planes, rockets and missiles, takeoffs, types of planes.
  Beauties. Body parts. Boy Scouts (also *Girl Scouts*). *Bridges. Birthdays.*
  Buildings. Castles, cemetery/graves, cities/towns/villages, city halls, dams/levees, fountains, gardens/grounds/estates, halls/auditoriums, hospitals (including operations), hotels, memorials and monuments, museums/libraries, palaces, pools, prisons, religious buildings, ruins and excavations, stadiums/fields, statues/busts/tablets, theaters (including premieres), tunnels, Unknown Soldiers' tombs, parts of buildings, interiors of buildings, miscellaneous buildings.
  Celebrations. Armistice Day, Christmas, Easter, Memorial Day, New Years' Day, Thanksgiving, anniversary, balls, breakfasts, banquets, dinners, luncheons, barbecues and picnics, commemorations, dedications, unveilings, wreath-laying, cornerstone-laying, pageants, re-enactments, parties/tea/gardens, general celebrations, parades.
  Civil Strife. Demonstrations, strikes/riots.
  Commerce and industry. Buying/selling, fishing, handicraft and home industry, lumbering, manufacturing, marketing, office work, rebuilding, reconversion (postwar), shipping, miscellaneous.
  Concerts. Crime. Assassinations, kidnapping, murders, miscellaneous. *Crowds.*
  Disasters. Auto and cycle crashes, cyclones, earthquakes, explosions, fire, floods, hurricanes, injured, landslides and snowslides, marine disaster, mine disaster, refugees, rescue, salvaging, survivors, tornado, train wrecks, victims.
  Education. Colleges, degrees, hazing, reunions, schools, shows, student life, technical schools, universities, miscellaneous.
  Engineering and construction. Blasting/dynamiting, heavy machinery, mines and quarries, razing, repairing/salvaging, tools and devices, wells and gas.
  Entertainment. Acrobats, amusement parks, chorus girls, circuses, comedy, daredevils, magic, nightclubs and bars, productions, rodeo and dude ranches, side shows, stunts, miscellaneous.
  Exhibitions. Bird show, cat show, dog show, horse show, livestock and cattle, pet show, poultry show.

  Fashions. Fire department. Flags. Funerals. Guards, Changing of. Gambling.
  Geology. Beach, canals/locks, canyons/gorge, caves, deserts, earth, falls, forest/woods, geyser, glacier, harbors, islands, jungles, lakes, mountains, oceans and seas, prairies and plains, rapids, reefs, rocks, rivers, scenery, tides, valley, volcanoes, waterholes, wells/waves.
  Government. Courts, hearings, inaugurations, investigations, oaths, politics, trials, world government.
  Inventions.
  Mankind. Babies, boys, children, Indians, men, women/girls.
  Mankind/miscellaneous. Defense industry, girls, Marines, men/women, nurses, SPARS, WAAFS, WAVES, WRENS.
  Matrimony/divorce.
  Meetings. Conferences, conventions, peace negotiations, rallies, United Nations.
  Meteorology. Astrology, blizzards, clouds, dust, earth, eclipse (sun/moon), fog, ice, mist, moon, moonlight, mud, rain, rainbow, sandstorms, seasons, sea storms, snow, storms, sun, wind.
  Music and bands. Dancing, instruments, names of music, orchestra, parks, singing.
  Photography. Dawn, dusk, into camera, night, over camera, reverse motion, silhouette, slow motion, stop-motion, trick photography.
  Police. Radio and television (including reception). *Religion. Science.* Chemical, electrical, medical, radar. *Skylines. Sound. Speeches.*
  Sports. Animal races, archery, auto races, baseball, basketball, basket carrying, bicycle races, billiards, boat races, bobsled, bowling, boxing, bullfight, checkers, contests, corn husking, cricket, cross-country, fencing, fishing, football, general sports, golf, gymnastics, handball, hiking, hockey, hoop rolling, horse racing, horse riding (jumping, stables, trotting/pacing, misc. riding), horseshoe pitching, hunting, hurling, ice boating, kite flying, lacrosse, lumber sports, marathon running, marbles, motorcycles, mountain climbing, obstacle races, Olympic Games, ping-pong, polo, push ball, roller-skating, rolling pin, rugby, shooting, skiing, sleighing, sliding, snowshoeing, soap box derby, soccer, swimming, tennis, track and field, walking race, water polo, water sports (summer), wrestling.
  Streets/roads/highways/traffic.
  Transportation (rail) (including railroad yards).
  Transportation (water). Types of ships, names of ships, ship arrivals, crews and passengers, departures, convoys, harbor facilities, launchings, lifesaving, parts of ships, shipyards, wrecks, miscellaneous.
  Vehicles.
  War Department/Army. Artillery, cavalry, forts and camps, infantry, reviews, revolution, schools, tanks, troops, misc. army.
  War Department/Navy. Aircraft carriers, battleships, cruisers, destroyers, fleets, sailors, schools, submarines, transports, Coast Guard, Marines, miscellaneous Navy.
  Wars. African War, American-Japanese crisis, Baltic crisis, Belgium invaded, British-French crisis, China Civil War, Chinese-Japanese War, commandoes, Czech-German crisis, Denmark invasion, fortifications, German-Austrian situation, German-Russian War, German War, Greek-Italian War, India War, Italian-French War, Holland invaded, Korean War, Madagascar War, maneuvers, Pacific War, prison camps, saboteurs, veterans, war prisoners, miscellaneous war.

NEW YORK METRO

UJA FEDERATION
130 East 59th Street, Room 306
New York, NY 10022
(212) 836-1895

Contact: Alan Treitman (Coordinator of Audiovisual Services)
Services: Association. Film and videotape collection available for free loan, duplication and reuse on a case-by-case basis, subject to restrictions.
Description: Archival collection of films and videotapes (1950s-present) relating to fundraising; the development of Jewish leadership; social services in New York's Jewish community; and an information film on renovation in Tel Aviv, Israel. Recent films and videotapes (1985-present, approx. 15-20 titles) were produced by the United Jewish Appeal and are available for distribution.
Size & Elements: Film: 16mm. Videotape: 2", 1", 3/4" and VHS (masters and viewing copies). (200 titles total; most archival; approx. 15-20 "recent" titles).
Cataloging: Some title lists; collection is mostly uncataloged.
Access: Open to researchers, scholars and the public. Available for loan (in the case of recent titles), duplication and reuse, subject to clearance and approval. Research fees charged in some cases. Research requests accepted by mail and

telephone.

Rights: Full rights held to some material. No rights held to some material. Can refer requesters to original producers in cases where their approval is required.

Licensing: Available for licensing and reuse, subject to restrictions. License fees charged in some cases.

Restrictions: All requests for reuse must be in writing and are considered on a case-by-case basis, subject to clearance and approval.

Viewing Facilities: Film and videotape.

Duplication Facilities: Videotape.

NEW YORK METRO

UNICEF
DIVISION OF INFORMATION AND PUBLIC AFFAIRS
RADIO/TV/FILM UNIT
UNICEF House
3 United Nations Plaza
New York, NY 10017
(212) 326-7290
Fax: (212) 888-7465

Norman Alinea (Radio/TV/Film Unit)

Contact: Norman Alinea
Services: International organization. Film and videotape collection available for distribution, research, duplication and reuse, subject to restrictions.
Description: Films relating to child survival and development issues, suitable for information, advocacy, fundraising and training, for use with both adult and youth audiences. Themes include oral rehydration therapy, immunization, breast-feeding and social mobilization, water and sanitation, Africa, and childhood disabilities. Short documentary sequences are also available.

Extensive film and videotape footage library holds elements ranging from archival materials to current footage about UNICEF projects.

The UNICEF Video and Radio Feature Service distributes short documentary news items for broadcast. Items are concerned with social development issues, particularly problems and solutions that relate to children and mothers. Television and radio broadcasters may regularly review current and cataloged stories, each of which has an international sound track and accompanying script.

Organization supplies information, whenever possible, to documentary and broadcast news producers to help research or develop a project on issues of concern to the organization. In these circumstances, UNICEF enters into co-production agreements with radio and television stations.

Titles available: *Global Report: The Silent Emergency,* on the role of oral rehydration therapy, immunization, growth monitoring and breast-feeding in saving nearly half of the 15 million children who die each year from preventable diseases; *No More Salty Than Tears (Mit Søde Barn Jr 8),* a videotape produced by an all-woman crew, powerfully captures life in areas of Bangladesh which have not often been seen by outsiders; *The Bond,* a documentary on global co-operation between United Nations development organizations and the Arab Gulf Fund for United Nations Development in projects being carried out in Egypt, Nepal, Peru and Somalia; *Herbal Medicine: Fact or Fiction?* explores the possibility of more extensive research into and use of herbal cures which have been a part of many ancient cultures' traditions; *Wild Fruits* documents the lifestyle of a village of Montagnards or Indochinese "hill people"; *Children on the Front Line — Mozambique,* where a child dies every few minutes due to famine, disease and the effects of war; *Artists for Africa,* on a program challenging Africa's artists, writers and intellectuals to find new ways to achieve universal child immunization by 1990; *Week of Sweet Water,* on daily life in a village in drought-stricken Burkina Faso, focusing on a young mother's worries about the grain shortage and the impending circumcision of her daughter; *Cradle of Humanity,* an in-depth study of the African mother's special relationship to her young child; and *A Toy Is What You Make It,* in which Liv Ullmann shows how children in Kenya, Peru, Sri Lanka and Turkey display enormous creativity and skill in making their own toys from whatever material their environment offers.
Size & Elements: Film and videotape (formats unspecified; over 300 titles).
Cataloging: Published catalogs.
Access: Open to the public. Available for distribution, duplication and reuse. Research fees not charged. Research requests accepted by mail and telephone.
Rights: Full rights held to some material. Additional clearances are necessary in some cases if material is to be reused.
Licensing: Available for licensing and reuse, subject to restrictions. License fees not charged.
Restrictions: Material available without cost to broadcasters, UNICEF national

committees and non-governmental organizations for projects and programs of relevance and value to UNICEF's purposes and concerns.
Viewing Facilities: Videotape.
Duplication Facilities: Videotape (any international format and standard).
Related Materials: Audio library; short radio documentary news items available for broadcast.

NEW YORK METRO

UNITED NATIONS
VISUAL MATERIALS LIBRARY
United Nations Plaza, Room S-820
New York, NY 10017
(212) 963-7318

Completed productions available for rental from:
UNIVERSITY OF ILLINOIS — FILM CENTER
1325 South Oak Street
Champaign, IL 61820
(800) 367-3456
(800) 252-1357 (Illinois only)

Contacts: Michos Tzovaras (Film Librarian); Tracey Hicks; Pam Prout; Norma Taylor
Services: International organization; film and videotape distributor. Film and videotape archives open to researchers, scholars and documentary film and video producers. Various materials available for distribution, rental, purchase, research, duplication and reuse.
Description: *Archives.* Holds production outtakes and in-house archival material collected (1920s-present), including film relating to the League of Nations (1920-45) and the United Nations Relief and Rehabilitation Agency (UNRRA) (1945-46).

Completed productions. Films and videotapes available for rental and purchase. Subject headings include economic concerns, human settlements, natural resources and the environment, political affairs, social issues and United Nations history, organization and structure.

Titles include: *Let Them Come with Rain,* on the landlocked southern African country of Botswana, showing the efforts of the United Nations to harness the water of Lake Ngami and transport it across the Kalahari Desert; *A Tale of Three Cities,* examining urban development in Jakarta, Caracas and Stockholm, concluding that most cities of the world need accelerated development if they are to avoid big trouble before the year 2000; *Power to the People,* exploring the environmental impact of atomic energy, including radiation safety, thermal pollution and disposal of nuclear wastes. *You Have Struck a Rock!* recalls the occupation of the seat of the all-white South African government by 20,000 women in 1956, and recreates their campaign against apartheid and its laws. *Asia: Two-Thirds and Counting* compares the population control strategies of India, China and Japan.
Size & Elements: Film: 35mm and 16mm (approx. 20 million feet, approx. 700 to 800 completed films; positive and negative, reversal originals). Videotape: 2", 1" and 3/4" (amount unspecified).
Cataloging: Card catalogs; camera dope sheets; release sheets.
Access: Open to researchers, scholars and documentary film and video producers. Some material maintained for distribution and rental. Some material available for duplication and reuse. Research requests accepted by mail, telephone and in person (by appointment only).
Rights: Full rights held to some material. Some rights held to some material. Additional clearances may be necessary in some cases if material is to be reused.
Licensing: Stock footage available for nonexclusive licensing and reuse, subject to restrictions. License fees charged.
Restrictions: Reuse restricted to news and documentary programs concerning the United Nations and its activities; or international affairs.
Viewing Facilities: Film (35mm and 16mm Steenbecks); videotape (3/4").
Duplication Facilities: Videotape (1", 3/4" and VHS) (limited facilities).

NEW YORK METRO

U.S. COMMITTEE FOR UNICEF
331 East 38th Street
New York, NY 10016
(212) 686-5522
Fax: (212) 779-1679

Larry E. Bruce (President)

Contact: Heatherlyn V. Francis
Services: Fundraising organization. Film and videotape collection maintained for distribution and rental. Material available for duplication, licensing and reuse, subject to restrictions.
Description: Documentation (1946-present) of UNICEF's work in developing countries of Asia, Africa and Latin America.

Titles available: *Fortieth Anniversary Program* (1986); *Especially the Children*, narrated by Liv Ullmann, illustrates how UNICEF is working to provide many basic services in the countries of Egypt, Lebanon, India, Mali, Mexico, Nepal, Peru and the Philippines; *A Kind of Paradise*, filmed in Barbados, Haiti, Grenada, Jamaica, Dominica, Trinidad and Tobago, shows the continuing struggle of the people of the Caribbean; *A Day, A Life*, about an Angolan mother seeking to improve her life so that she may provide better care for her five children; *All Our Futures*, narrated by Peter Ustinov, traces UNICEF's history from a postwar emergency relief organization to its current status as an international development agency working in over 100 countries.

Energy: Two Ways of Life documents how the choice of available energy sources affects the daily lives of the children of two families: the Cheges of Nairobi, Kenya and the Daniels of Albany, New York; *Nepal: Land of the Gods*, on the development of basic health services in Nepal (1964-present); *Western Samoa: The Best of Both Worlds?*, on the changes occurring in this fertile and peaceful land, causing the inhabitants to be concerned that their children will be forced to choose between traditional village life and modern society; *Look to the Future*, in which nutrition workers Maria and Marirude teach women and children of Brazil's North East region to raise vegetables, rabbits, goats and sheep; and *Ethiopia: Parched Land and Promises*, on the launching of a major relief program.

Series programming. Various materials comprising the *A Good Idea Film* series are available on the topics of interdependence, urban affairs, energy, hunger, education, health care, water and sanitation, disabled children and nutrition.
Size & Elements: Film: 16mm. Videotape: 3/4". ("A large number of titles which increases each year.")
Cataloging: Published brochures.
Access: Available for distribution and rental. Material possibly available for duplication. Research requests not accepted. Inquiries accepted by mail and telephone.
Rights: Full rights held to some material (including the Fortieth Anniversary Program). Additional clearances may be necessary in some cases if material is to be reused.
Licensing: Available for licensing and reuse, subject to restrictions.
Restrictions: Requests for licensing and reuse considered on a case-by-case basis.
Viewing Facilities: None.
Duplication Facilities: None.

NEW YORK METRO

VEDO FILMS/NOVACOM VIDEO
85 Longview Road
Port Washington, NY 11050
(516) 883-7460

David Cole (Director)

Contacts: Robinson Kiles (Sales); Phillip Melhorn (Publicity)
Services: Film and videotape producer and distributor. Material available for rental and purchase.
Description: *Vedo Films*. Distributes educational films on Americana, ancient history, anthropology, archaeology, art history, classical studies, comparative religion, folk industries, folklore and tradition, folk music, language arts, outdoor sports and social studies.

Sample titles include: *The Old Amish Order*, describing the contemporary Amish lifestyle as a crystallized vestige of early American rural society; *The Etruscans*, documenting the inhabitants of ancient Etruria through imaginative cinematography, tomb paintings and sculpture; *The Hasidim*, examining the group structure and ethic through the eyes of a young leader, finding striking similarities to aspects of life in 18th-century America; *The Falcon Gentle*, beginning with a short history of falconry, then documenting in detail the training of the now-rare peregrine falcon; *Crystal Tipps and Alistair* (12 programs), a BBC children's production that is the longest running film series ever to be featured on the *Captain Kangaroo* television program.

Novacom Video. Distributes almost 300 videotapes on the performing arts, featuring live recordings of ballet, opera theater and musical performances. Includes nearly 130 videotapes on operatic subjects, with about 70 recordings

of live performances and productions highlighting the performances of particular artists. Over 50 videotaped recordings of classical music concerts include *The Huberman Festival*, a series by the Israel Philharmonic Orchestra with performers Pinchas Zuckerman, Isaac Stern, Itzhak Perlman, Shlomo Mintz, Henryk Szeryng, Ivy Gitlis and Ida Haendel; the *Sounds Magnificent Music Series*, performances by the Royal Philharmonic Orchestra; musical performances by many other orchestras and performers. There are approximately 60 videotapes on ballet productions and dance-related subjects (classical, modern and contemporary). Approximately 100 featured theatrical performances include a series of Shakespeare plays, many classic Broadway productions and modern or contemporary works, e.g., Athol Fugard's *Master Harold and the Boys*, and Kenneth Brown's *The Brig*.
Size & Elements: Film: 16mm (35 titles; 60,000 feet). Videotape: VHS and Betamax (approx. 400 titles total; each 60 to 90 min.).
Cataloging: Published catalogs.
Access: Maintained for rental and purchase rather than for research or reuse. Research requests not accepted.
Rights: Full rights held to some material.
Licensing: Available for licensing and reuse, subject to restrictions. License and usage fees charged in some cases.
Restrictions: All requests for duplication, licensing and reuse subject to acceptance, negotiation and approval.
Viewing Facilities: None.
Duplication Facilities: None.

NEW YORK METRO

VIACOM INTERNATIONAL, INC.
1211 Avenue of the Americas
New York, NY 10036
(212) 575-5175

Services: Television syndicator and distributor.

NEW YORK METRO

VIDEO CATALOGUE CO., INC.
333 West 52nd Street
New York, NY 10019
(212) 757-0555

Janet Pytowski (President)

Contact: Janet Pytowski
Services: Videotape producer and distributor. Material available for rental, distribution and licensing.
Description: Fashion news, fashion education and fashion history. Includes 46 newsreels (1950s-60s) featuring fashions, hats, hairdos and accessories. Contemporary material (1985-87) includes runway shows, fashion "concept" videotapes, career dressing, furs, evening wear, tuxedos, dresses, tailored suits and textiles. Also holds historical sports footage (1950s-60s), including baseball, track and field, basketball, tennis, and annual sports roundups.
Size & Elements: Videotape: 1", 3/4" and VHS (50 titles).
Cataloging: Published catalog.
Access: Maintained for distribution and rental rather than research or reuse. Research fees charged. Research requests accepted by mail, telephone and in person (walk-in and by appointment).
Rights: Full rights held to some material. Some material in the public domain.
Licensing: Available for rental, licensing and reuse. License fees charged.
Restrictions: None specified.
Viewing Facilities: Videotape (1", 3/4" and VHS).
Duplication Facilities: Videotape (1", 3/4" and VHS).

NEW YORK METRO

VIDEO MONITORING SERVICES OF AMERICA
330 West 42nd Street
New York, NY 10036
(212) 736-2010

Dewitt Mallary (Vice President, Advertising Services)

Contact: Edie Thomas (Manager of Client Services)
Services: Television monitoring service. Videotape library available to corporations for research, reference and internal analysis only. *Not a stock*

footage source.

Description: Retrieves information from television broadcasts; videotapes local newscasts throughout the United States; and maintains reference library of U.S. and international television commercials videotaped off-air (primarily 1980s). Commercials are categorized by product category and advertiser. Newscasts are retained for one month only. *Material is maintained for research and reference use only; any publication, rebroadcast or public display for profit is forbidden. Not a stock footage source.*

Media Scan monitors television commercials and generates activity reports for the use of advertising agencies.

Size & Elements: Videotape: 3/4" and 1/2" (150,000 television commercials).

Cataloging: Card catalogs (commercials are categorized by advertiser and product category); staff assistance required.

Access: Not open to the public. Available to corporate users (primarily advertisers and advertising agencies) for research, reference and internal analysis purposes only. Research fees charged (based on material supplied). Requests accepted by mail and telephone.

Rights: No rights held to any material.

Licensing: Not available for licensing or reuse.

Restrictions: Available to corporate users only. Material is maintained for research and reference use only; any publication, rebroadcast or public display for profit is forbidden. *Not a stock footage source.*

Viewing Facilities: None.

Duplication Facilities: Videotape (3/4" and 1/2").

Related Materials: Photo boards (descriptions of television commercials, including picture and audio).

NEW YORK METRO

VIDEO RESOURCES NEW YORK, INC.

220 West 71st Street
New York, NY 10023
(212) 724-7055

Ira H. Gallen (President and Executive Producer)

Contacts: Ira H. Gallen; John Gallagher (Producer)

Services: Film and videotape producer; production facility; private collection; stock footage sales library. Material available for purchase, research, licensing and reuse.

Description: Collects and distributes television shows (1950s-60s); television commercials, especially for toys and consumer products; silent and early sound films; cartoons; motion picture trailers; short subjects; and newsreels. Many videotapes are available for purchase.

Classic television shows. Programs include: *The Paul Winchell Show,* featuring the ventriloquist and his wooden dummy Jerry Mahoney; *The Howdy Doody Circus; The Rootie Kazootie Club; Lionel Club House; Ramar of the Jungle; The Colgate Comedy Hour,* with Abbott & Costello; *Texaco Star Theatre; Andy's Gang; The Buccaneers; Chance of a Lifetime* (1956); *Captain Midnight,* featuring original Ovaltine commercials; *Lost in Space,* including the pilot episode and the never-aired first show; *Kukla, Fran & Ollie; The Gumby Show; Amos 'n Andy; Captain Gallant of the Foreign Legion; Ding Dong School; Rocky Jones Space Ranger; Winky Dink and You; Time for Beany; Toast of the Town,* including an episode in which Ed Sullivan pays tribute to Walt Disney; *Captain Video and His Video Rangers; Watch Mr. Wizard; The Roy Rogers Show; Flash Gordon; Arthur Godfrey's Talent Scouts;* and many other programs.

Classic television commercials (8 programs). Commercials for consumer products (1950s-60s). Special programs are also available, featuring automobiles; dolls; food and supermarket products; toys; Old Gold, Newport, Kent and other cigarette brands; Lustre Creme; commercials with cats and dogs; beer commercials; medicine and health aids.

Toys. Commercials and promotional films from Ideal Toys, Hasbro, Milton Bradley, Playskool, View-Master, Coleco, Duncan Yo-Yos, American Character Toy Company, and Buddy-L.

Cartoons. Programs featuring Fleischer Superman cartoons; *Aesop's Fables; Popeye Classics;* Felix the Cat (silent films); Famous Studios cartoons; pioneer animation producers; Flip the Frog; Warner Bros. cartoons; Betty Boop; Koko the Clown; Paul Terry cartoons; and Private Snafu cartoons.

Silent classics. Features and short films directed by D. W. Griffith; silent comedies; silent classic features such as *The Iron Mask, The Last Laugh, Potemkin, Blind Husbands, Metropolis* and *Nosferatu;* trailers; Hollywood outtakes; bloopers; rare shorts; and Hollywood behind-the-scenes films.

Ronald Reagan. Ronnie Dearest: The Lost Episodes, a video montage produced by Ira Gallen, mixes Reagan's Hollywood movies, World War II

training films, television commercials, bloopers and outtakes into a new and funny storyline.

Size & Elements: Film: 35mm, 16mm, Super 8mm and 8mm (release prints, some originals). Videotape: 1" and 3/4" (masters and viewing copies). (Approx. 4,000 titles total).

Cataloging: Published catalog; research library.

Access: Open to researchers, scholars and the public. Available for purchase, duplication and reuse. Research fees charged in some cases. Research requests accepted by mail, telephone and in person (by appointment only).

Rights: Full rights held to some material. Some material in the public domain. Additional clearances may be necessary in some cases if material is to be reused.

Licensing: Available for licensing and reuse. License fees charged.

Restrictions: None specified.

Viewing Facilities: Film and videotape.

Duplication Facilities: Film (outside arrangements can be made); videotape.

Related Materials: Library of rare books and periodicals relating to silent films, early sound cinema, D. W. Griffith and television history. Collection of silent film posters, still photographs, cameras and toys.

NEW YORK METRO

VIDEOFASHION, INC.

1 West 37th Street, 5th Floor
New York, NY 10018
(212) 869-4666
Fax: (212) 869-8208
Telex: 225707 VIDMO UR

Nicholas Charney (President)

Contact: Anne V. Adami (Marketing)

Services: Videotape producer and distributor. Materials available for rental by subscription.

Description: *Videofashion Monthly.* A series of 12 separate half-hour programs produced annually: six covering the spring/summer fashion, season, six covering the autumn/winter season. Programs highlight the most important examples of women's fashion from more than 50 designer collections shown in Milan, London, Paris and New York.

Videofashion Men. A edited 30-minute video magazine program, produced four times annually. Features regular departments, e.g. Fashion News, Designer Profiles, Video *Cover* Portraits, Special Features, and "Must Buys."

Videofashion Specials. Monthly programs presenting dynamic and different views of fashion and lifestyles for all those who want to be well-informed about the fashion business.

Videofashion News. Twelve programs per year, each 30 min. Highlights of over 100 major designer collections from around the world.

Size & Elements: Videotape: format and amount unspecified.

Cataloging: Printed brochures; press releases.

Access: Available for distribution and rental. Subscription fees charged. Requests accepted by mail and telephone.

Rights: Some rights held to all material.

Licensing: Apply for information.

Restrictions: None specified.

Viewing Facilities: None.

Duplication Facilities: None.

NEW YORK METRO

VISNEWS INTERNATIONAL

630 Fifth Avenue, 7th Floor
New York, NY 10111
(212) 698-4500
Fax: (212) 698-4513
Telex: 239875 VISCUR

London office:
VISNEWS INTERNATIONAL
Cumberland Avenue
London NW10 7EH
England
(01) 965-7733
(01) 453-4366 (after hours)
Fax: (01) 965-0620
Telex: 22678

Pam Turner (Head of Library, London) (01-453-4338)
Susan Ponsonby (Research, London) (01-453-4363)
Brian Phillips (Senior Librarian, London) (01-453-4366)

Contact: Marcy Simon
Services: News organization; film and videotape stock footage sales library. Custom shooting, production and post-production services available.
Description: International newsreel and television newsfilm archives (1896-present). Owned by NBC, Reuters PLC, and the British Broadcasting Corporation. The New York office serves as an access point to the library, which is physically located in London. Holds the following collections:

Newsreel libraries. Newsreels owned and held by Visnews include *Gaumont Graphic* (1910-33); *Empire News Bulletin* (1926-30); *Gaumont British News* (1929-59); *Universal News* (1930-49); and *British Paramount News* (1931-57). Nitrate-era materials (1896-1951) are available on videotape; film elements are held at the National Film Archive and Imperial War Museum, both in London. Safety-era materials (post-1951) are held by Visnews.

Television newsfilm and videotape. Holds videotape (1980-present); earlier material generally on 16mm film. Library holdings increase by approximately 500,000 feet per year.

Bird collection. Social life and worldwide travel material (1930s, 16mm).
British Transport Stockshot Collection (35mm, color and black and white).
Heart of the Dragon Collection (16mm, 200 hours, color). On-location material originally shot for the *Heart of the Dragon* series on China.
The World of Islam (16mm, color).

Visnews is equipped to produce film and videotape productions anywhere in the world. Through Visnews Productions, they offer audiovisual consultancy, staff producers, directors, scriptwriters, editors and camerapersons. Satellite uplink services are also available.
Size & Elements: Film (35mm and 16mm); videotape (2" and 1"). Over 50 million feet of material is held in all formats.
Cataloging: Card and microfiche catalogs (cross-referenced). Detailed shot listings available for most items; these can help researchers avoid unnecessary viewing.
Access: Open to the public. Available for duplication, licensing and reuse. Research fees (for examining catalogs and documentation) not charged. Screening fees charged.
Rights: Full rights held to all material. Additional clearances may be necessary in some cases, depending on intended use.
Licensing: Available for licensing and reuse. License fees charged.
Restrictions: None specified.
Viewing Facilities: Film and videotape.
Duplication Facilities: Film and videotape (all standards and formats).

NEW YORK METRO

VISUAL INFORMATION SYSTEMS

One Harmon Plaza
Secaucus, NJ 07094
(201) 867-7600
Fax: (201) 867-2491

Jay Raeben (President)

Contact: Vince Corrado (Assistant Director)
Services: Videotape producer and distributor. Material available by subscription.
Description: Produces continuing medical education videotapes for use by hospital personnel. Videotapes are distributed to subscribers every two weeks; each program highlights a different medical topic. Categories of medical practice covered are adolescent medicine, drug abuse, emergency medicine and trauma, infectious parasitic disease, intensive care, legal medicine, musculoskeletal and connective tissue disorders, nephrology, nutritional and metabolic diseases, otolaryngology, practice management and medical economics, public health, and surgery (including general, abdominal, cardiovascular, orthopedic, neurologic, pediatric, plastic, and thoracic).

Sample titles include: *Snake and Spider Bites: Aggressive Management of Venom Injuries; The Asphyxiating Patient: How And Why I Intubate; Stasis Ulcers of the Ankle; Managing Pet-Related Disease; The Overgrown Infant: An American Problem; Fitting a Diaphragm — Are You Making Any Mistakes?;* and *Retinal Tears: A Prelude to Retinal Detachment?*
Size & Elements: Videotape: 2" and 1" (masters); 3/4" (viewing copies) (500 titles total).
Cataloging: Published catalogs.
Access: Open to the public. Maintained for subscription distribution. Material

possibly available for reuse in some cases. Research fees generally not charged. Research requests accepted by mail and telephone.
Rights: Full rights held to all material.
Licensing: Available for licensing and reuse, subject to restrictions.
Restrictions: Requests for research, licensing and reuse considered on a case-by-case basis and subject to acceptance and approval.
Viewing Facilities: Videotape (3/4").
Duplication Facilities: Videotape.

NEW YORK METRO

WEILL-LENYA RESEARCH CENTER
KURT WEILL FOUNDATION FOR MUSIC

7 East 20th Street
New York, NY 10003
(212) 260-1650
Fax: (212) 353-9663

David Farneth (Director and Archivist)

Contact: David Farneth
Services: Foundation; research library. Film and videotape material available for reuse, subject to restrictions.
Description: Materials pertaining to Kurt Weill and Lotte Lenya, including documentation of performances, commercial films, stage works, interviews, oral histories, promotional materials and documentaries.
Size & Elements: Film: 16mm (2 items). Videotape: 1" (10 videotapes); VHS (40 NTSC; 10 PAL). (50 titles total).
Cataloging: Computerized cataloging for staff use only; research library.
Access: Open to researchers and scholars only. Research fees not charged. Research requests accepted by mail, telephone and in person (by appointment only).
Rights: Some rights held to some material.
Licensing: Available for reuse, subject to restrictions. Usage fees charged.
Restrictions: All requests for reuse subject to copyright clearance.
Viewing Facilities: Videotape (VHS; NTSC, PAL and SECAM).
Duplication Facilities: Videotape (VHS; NTSC only).
Related Materials: Maintains biographical archives of scores, correspondence, still photographs, programs, clippings and books.

NEW YORK METRO

WINDSOR PRODUCTION CORPORATION

350 Fifth Avenue, Suite 8008
New York, NY 10118
(212) 714-2501
Fax: (212) 967-5746

Contact: Eric F. Saltzman
Services: Film and videotape distributor; stock footage sales library.
Description: Windsor owns rights to all RKO and RKO-Pathe short subjects (1930s-50s).

Comedies. Featuring such performers as Clark and McCullough, Leon Errol, and such stars-to-be as Lucille Ball.

News features. Period Americana. Examples include: *From Courtship to Courthouse,* based on the then-current statistics reporting that one in every four American marriages ended in divorce; a story on recent immigrants; *Airline Glamour Girls,* a feature on the first school for airline stewardesses; Hollywood stars christening boats and visits to various American cities such as the Mardi Gras in New Orleans.

Sports features. College football, basketball and baseball; extensive coverage of golf and tennis; bird hunting and fishing around the world; skiing in Sun Valley with celebrities; ice skating; and ice boating.
Size & Elements: Film and videotape (formats and amounts unspecified).
Cataloging: Title list.
Access: Available to the public for licensing and reuse. Research fees not charged. Research requests accepted by mail and telephone.
Rights: Full rights held to all material.
Licensing: Available for licensing. License fees charged.
Restrictions: None specified.
Viewing Facilities: None.
Duplication Facilities: None.

NEW YORK METRO

WNET/THIRTEEN
356 West 58th Street
New York, NY 10019
(212) 560-2000

Services: Public television producer and broadcaster.

NEW YORK METRO

WOMBAT FILM & VIDEO
(A Division of CorTech, Inc.)
250 West 57th Street, Suite 2421
New York, NY 10019
(212) 315-2502
Fax: (212) 582-0585

Gene Feldman (President)
Suzette Winter (Vice President)
Stephen Janson (Vice President, Marketing)

Contact: Stephen Janson
Services: Film and videotape producer and distributor. Material available for distribution, broadcast and purchase.
Description: Produces non-theatrical films for distribution through television, cable and homevideo markets around the world.

Recent productions include: *Danny,* a children's film; the PBS entertainment documentaries *Hollywood's Children, The Horror of it All* and *Ingrid,* a critically acclaimed biography of the late Ingrid Bergman and the HBO documentaries *Marilyn Monroe: Beyond the Legend* and *Steve McQueen: Man on the Edge.*

North American distributor of films from two overseas television networks, Channel Nine from Perth, Australia and Television New Zealand. These include a five-part nature series entitled *The Wonder of Western Australia,* a homevideo series on the America's Cup and *Wild South,* a 21-part wildlife series on the South Pacific.

Distributes films from the National Film Board of Canada, the Canadian Broadcasting Company, Granada Television International, the Arts Council of Great Britain, Arts International, the American Broadcasting Company, CBS News, the New Zealand National Film Unit, Film Australia, All-Media Enterprises and Wombat. New releases include: *The Titanic: A Question of Murder; Rembetika: The Blues of Greece; Behind the Veil: Nuns; Decade of Delay; Norman's New Garden; Herpes: 400,000 New Cases Each Year; Don't Mess With Bill; Haiku — Short Poetry of Japan; Harrison's Yukon; Woody Guthrie: Hard Travelin'; Captain Noah and His Floating Zoo; Picturing Derry;* and *Paucartambo — Inca River.*

Also currently distributes about 20 titles for the homevideo market under the name of Brighton Video.
Size & Elements: Film: 16mm (87 titles). Videotape: VHS (viewing copies).
Cataloging: Published catalog.
Access: Research requests accepted by mail and telephone.
Rights: Full rights held to some material.
Licensing: Apply for information.
Restrictions: None specified.
Viewing Facilities: None.
Duplication Facilities: None.

NEW YORK METRO

WOMEN MAKE MOVIES, INC.
225 Lafayette Street, Room 212
New York, NY 10012
(212) 925-0606

Contact: Michelle Materre
Services: Distributor. Film and videotape collection available for distribution and rental.
Description: Founded 1972. National nonprofit organization devoted to the distribution of media by and about women. Also provides technical assistance, hosts festivals, exhibitions and conferences in New York City and organizes national and international touring programs.

Video art. Titles include: *Portrait Of An Artist* (Robin Schanzenbach); *Travels In The Combat Zone, Three Story Suite, Skyfish, Electra Tries to Speak, Glass Curtain* (Doris Chase); *There Was An Unseen Cloud Moving*

(Leslie Thornton), an elliptical portrayal of the story and character of Isabelle Eberhardt, who lived and travelled through Algeria at the turn of the century dressed as a man, and died in a flash flood in the desert at age 27; *Womb With A View* (Sherry Millner), a humorous meditation on the personal and social contradictions of the artist's incipient motherhood.

Performers. Titles include: *Remembering Thelma* (Kathe Sandler); *Run, Sister, Run* (Margie Soo Hoo Lee), a behind-the-scenes look at a collaboration between a choreographer and a photographer; *...But Then, She's Betty Carter* (Michelle Parkerson).

Cinema studies and drama. Titles include: *Illusions* (Julie Dash), in which two Black women in wartime Hollywood are forced to come to grips with a society that perpetuates false images as the status quo; *The Gold Diggers* and *Thriller* (Sally Potter); *Damned If You Don't, The Ties That Bind, Gently Down The Stream* and *Cool Hands, Warm Heart* (Su Friedrich); *Far From Poland* (Jill Godmilow with Susan Delson, Mark Magill and Andrzej Tymowsky); *The Minders* (Judy Rymer), science fiction that evokes an unforgettable woman-ruled paradise.

Health, birth and parenting. Titles include: *Disabled Women's Theatre Project,* conveying absurd and painful moments in the lives of the disabled; *Prescription for Change* (Tami Gold and Lyn Goldfarb), a rare behind-the-scenes look at nursing; *Trick or Drink* (Vanalyne Greene), a reconstruction of a young girl's life with alcoholic parents; *Our Right To Abortion* (Lori Hiris); *Granny Midwives (Abuelitas de Ombligo)* (Rachel Feld and Jackie Reiter), a training program for midwives developed by the Nicaraguan Ministry of Health which acknowledges the importance of local folklore while teaching basic nutrition, hygiene and maternal health care; *In The Best Interests of the Children* (Frances Reid, Elizabeth Stevens and Cathy Zheutlin), the ground-breaking film exploring the issue of child custody by lesbian parents.

Sexuality. Titles include: *Susana* (Susana Muñoz Velarde), an autobiographical portrait of a young Argentine lesbian growing up in a homophobic environment; *Farewell To Charms* (Carla Pontiac), a clever satire poking fun at gender roles and stereotypes; *Veronica 4 Rose* (Melanie Chait), in which teenage girls from Newcastle, Liverpool and London talking about what it means to be young lesbians; *Dyke-Tactics, Double Strength* and *Women I Love* (Barbara Hammer).

Historical and social issues. Titles include: *She Even Chewed Tobacco* (Liz Stevens and Estelle Freedman), on Gold Rush women's history; *Witches, Dykes, Faggots and Poofters* (Digby Duncan).

International perspectives. Titles include: *Reassemblage* and *Naked Spaces: Living Is Round* (Trinh T. Minh-ha); *Selbe: One Among Many* (Safi Faye), shot in Senegal, showing how one woman's personal struggle reflects the broader issues facing women in many developing countries; *Bread and Dignity (Pan y Dignidad)* (Maria José Alvarez); Permissible Dreams (Attiat El-Abnoudi); and *After The Earthquake (Despues Del Terremoto)* (Lourdes Portillo and Nina Serrano). *A Man, When He Is A Man (El Hombre, Cuando Es El Hombre)* (Valeria Sarmiento), set in Costa Rica, illuminates the social traditions which nurture *machismo.*
Size & Elements: Film: 35mm and 16mm (approx. 60 titles). Videotape: 3/4" and VHS (approx. 40 titles; masters and viewing copies).
Cataloging: Published catalog.
Access: Maintained for distribution and rental. Available for in-house research. Research requests accepted by mail, telephone and in person.
Rights: Full rights held to some material. Rights to most material retained by filmmakers. Additional clearances are necessary in most cases if material is to be reused.
Licensing: Apply for information.
Restrictions: Reuse and licensing permitted only by consent of individual filmmakers.
Viewing Facilities: Film and videotape.
Duplication Facilities: None.

NEW YORK METRO

WORKING GROUP ON SOVIET TELEVISION
W. AVERELL HARRIMAN INSTITUTE FOR THE ADVANCED
STUDY OF THE SOVIET UNION
COLUMBIA UNIVERSITY
420 West 118th Street, Room 1211
New York, NY 10027
(212) 854-4623

John Copp (Coordinator, Working Group on Soviet Television)

Contacts: John Copp; Bruce Pannier (Assistant Coordinator)
Services: Educational institution; restricted videotape research collection. Not

open to the public; open only to scholars and researchers with specific qualifications. Material available for duplication and reuse, subject to restrictions.

Description: Videotapes recorded from Soviet television satellite signals originating in Moscow. The Institute began videotaping in August, 1984 and has been recording five hours per day since February 1986, including *Vremya*, the evening news, and other politically and economically relevant material. The Institute also records movies, gardening, military, art, literature and youth programs, serials, product commercials and public service announcements.

Research can only be done by students involved in the Working Group on Soviet Television. Soviet Teleradio is aware of WGST's videotaping activities, and may be contacted for studio-quality material. A subject breakdown of Soviet Teleradio's archives is available from WGST.

Size & Elements: Videotape: 3/4" (small amount; SECAM); VHS (7,000 hours; SECAM).

Cataloging: None specified.

Access: Open to qualified researchers and scholars only. All research can only be done by students involved in the Working Group on Soviet Television. Access fees and student research fees charged. Research requests accepted by mail and telephone.

Rights: Full rights held to some material. Additional clearances may be necessary in some cases if material is to be duplicated.

Licensing: Available for duplication and reuse, subject to restrictions.

Restrictions: Duplication and reuse subject to copyright and legal qualifications pertaining to Soviet rights and international law.

Viewing Facilities: Videotape (VHS; SECAM).

Duplication Facilities: Videotape.

NEW YORK METRO

WORLDWIDE TELEVISION NEWS

1995 Broadway, 11th Floor
New York, NY 10023
(212) 362-4440
Fax: (212) 496-1269
Telex: 237853

Vince O'Reilly (Library Manager)

Contacts: Vince O'Reilly; Harold Philips (Librarian)

Services: Worldwide news service; film and videotape stock footage sales library.

Description: Worldwide Television News (WTN) is a full-service stock footage library, based in New York and London, handling the film and videotape collections of United Press International (UPI) News Film (1963-67), UPITN (WTN) (1967-present) and British Pathé News (1896-1966). WTN, a functioning news gathering service with principal bureaus in every continent, feeds 24 hours a day to over 1,000 broadcasters, affiliates and cable network operators around the world, and adds material to its library on a daily basis. WTN is owned by ABC in America, ITN (Independent Television News) in Britain and the Nine Network in Australia.

WTN began as an association between UPI and Fox Movietone News in 1951. Between 1951 and September 30, 1963, UPI-Movietonews provided a daily newsclip service for local television stations in the United States. (This 16mm black and white newsfilm is now held by Twentieth Century-Fox Movietonews, Inc. [q.v.]). In October 1963, Movietonews ceased production of its daily service and UPI assumed responsibility for operation of the news gathering operation, picking up most of the staff.

In 1967, UPI joined forces with ITN in the United Kingdom, founding UPITN, and began servicing networks and stations overseas. The name was changed to Worldwide Television News in 1980.

WTN holds or represents various collections, including:

British Pathé News. Representative for stock footage sales in North America. A limited amount of material is held on videotape in the New York office, but the collection is physically located at Elstree Studios near London, England. British Pathé features weekly newsreel coverage of major events and features (1896-1966). Coverage is strongest for British and British Commonwealth news and features, but there is some coverage of United States events. A microfiche catalog is available for research in the New York office. The Pathé collection was the footage source for a series of yearly wrapups called the *Time to Remember* series. These are also available for stock footage sale. (Note: there is no connection between the different "Pathé" newsreel companies.)

UPI News Film and UPITN collection (1963 through mid-1980s). The UPITN collection covers U.S. and foreign news events and personalities until

approximately 1975-77, when U.S. coverage was phased out. From 1977, coverage is restricted to foreign events. Holds in-depth coverage of events in the United States until the mid-1970s; for example, the file on Selma, Alabama is five inches thick. The Vietnam war at home and abroad is also well covered, with several drawers of index cards describing footage of pro- and antiwar demonstrations in the United States and in foreign countries and battle coverage.

As a rule, stories originating in North or South America were covered by the U.S. bureau, and stories elsewhere by the British bureau. However, in the case of Vietnam, coverage was coordinated out of New York. The New York office, therefore, retains camera original and all the outtakes. The collection is also strong on coverage of the Middle East, Iran, South Africa and Israel. South African and Middle East coverage is strong in the early 1960s, when the situation there received far less attention from other news gathering services. During the days of the Iranian hostage crisis, as well, the UPITN cameras were among the last Western eyes to remain in the country.

As a general rule, the film in the UPITN collection resides in New York if shot in the United States. If shot elsewhere, the original will be at ITN in London. If the material was used by WTN, a copy will also be in the New York library.

WTN collection, feeds and packages. Coverage is worldwide and all-inclusive, including international affairs, conflicts and wars, famines, disasters, scientific and medical achievements, the art world, personalities, human interest stories and oddities. WTN supplies news stories to CNN, ABC, CBS and hundreds of stations and networks internationally.

Daily Satellite Service Europe (DSSE) (not held in New York; available through ITN in London). This "hard news" satellite feed from London for subscribers in Europe, the Middle East and Africa is transmitted at 1400 GMT.

Daily Satellite Service America (DSSA) (1980-present). "Hard news" feed transmitted from London at 2050 GMT (1950 in the summertime). Each feed comprises seven to ten stories, and is held in New York on 3/4" videotape. WTN New York combines the most important items from the DSSA with stories from North and Latin America and transmits the DSSP (Daily Satellite Service Pacific) feed via Los Angeles to Asia and Australasia.

In addition to the Daily Satellite Services described above, WTN compiles and dispatches four special packages every week as background material for ongoing stories:

General News Service (GNS) (3/4" videotape, each 60 min., comprising up to 20 current news stories, each containing an update plus background material). GNS packages (1984-present) are held in New York; earlier packages are held in London. GNS contains some stories originating in the U.S. not produced by WTN; these are not available for stock footage sale.

Features (3/4" videotape, each 60 min., comprising up to 30 short "soft news" stories). The mix of stories is broad and international, covering subject areas such as education, medicine, current affairs, general knowledge and human interest. Packages (ca. 1985-present) are held in New York; earlier packages are held in London. Contains some stories originating in the U.S., which are not available for stock footage sale.

Roving Report (produced weekly 1967-present, each 30 min.) is the world's longest-running current affairs program. Covering 4 to 6 international stories in depth, the Roving Report now incorporates footage from the MacNeil-Lehrer Report (PBS). Sample features include *The Martyrdom of Martin Luther King* (1968); *San Francisco: Will the Quake Come* (1969); *Women's Liberation: "Sisterhood Is Powerful"* (1970); *Ralph Nader: The Car Safety Debate* (1971); *The Jesus Movement* (1971); *Chile: Allende's Problems* (1973); *Bavaria: Rafting Down the Isar* (1974); *Punk Rock and the Elvis Legend* (1978); *Afghanistan: The Struggle Continues* (1980); *Reagan's "Backyard": The Grenada Invasion* (1983); and *Football Hooliganism* (1985). The New York office holds irregular issues from the period in which the *Report* was produced on film (1967-80); all videotape issues (1980-present) are held in New York. A published index to *Roving Report* issues is available.

Earthfile (1988-present, 3/4" videotape). A weekly package of environmentally oriented news stories. Most issues are held in New York.

In December, WTN provides a *Year End Review* (60 min.) of the world's top international news stories. Also available each December are individual stories in WTN's *Top 100 News Stories*.

WNEW-TV collection (1975-77). Television news coverage (primarily relating to the New York City metropolitan area) from an independent station. This collection contains the original coverage of a bank robbery and hostage situation in New York City which became the basis for the feature film *Dog Day Afternoon*.

Case of Cities (1970s-early 1980s, 30 compilations, each 30 min., 16mm color reversal; also available in 3/4" videotape transferred from film). Compilations of stock shots of international cities, produced by WTN. A videotape original update is planned.

Nix-Muchmore footage. 8mm films of the John F. Kennedy assassination.

All WTN's principal bureaus are capable of videotape editing in 1" or 3/4", standards conversion, duplication and satellite transmission. Bureaus in London and Frankfurt cover European, African and Russian news; New York and Washington handle the United States and Latin America; Cairo and Beirut cover the Middle East; Tel Aviv handles Israel and South Lebanon; Hong Kong controls the Far East, China and Japan; and Sydney covers Australasia. Five additional principal bureaus are located in Paris, Rome, Johannesburg, Tokyo and New Delhi.

Size & Elements: Film: 16mm (130,000 stories; color reversal and black and white negative). Videotape: 3/4" (approx. 7,000 videotapes). The New York library holds 130,000 film clips (cut stories); 4,000 videotapes from Latin America and the DSSA (Daily Satellite Service America) (1980-present, approx. 2,920 videotapes; each comprising 7 to 10 stories). The London library holds 350,000 stories.

All material 1963-80 is on 16mm film; for North American stories, black and white negative (1963-68) or color reversal (1968-80); for European stories, duplicate negative and fine grain master. Since 1980, WTN has originated all stories on videotape.

Cataloging: Material from the UPI News Film and UPITN collection can be accessed through a card catalog. The catalog is a "small entry" system, with most subjects filed under their own alphabetical listings. Bridges, for instance will be found under "B" and not under "S" for Structures with a subheading of Bridges. Personalities are filed in a separate section of the catalog.

WTN and ITN material (1980-present) is indexed on a computer located in London and can be accessed in New York. A printed catalog is available to access the Roving Report collection, containing a general index and special indexes covering countries and personalities.

A microfiche catalog of the British Pathé News collection is available in the New York office.

Access: Open to the public. Available for licensing and reuse, subject to restrictions. Research fees charged. Research requests accepted by mail, telephone and in person (by appointment only). It is advisable to make an initial call to one of the librarians to determine how the library can best serve the client's needs. If a large amount of material is being sought, generally a follow-up letter and search list would be the next step. The card catalog is available for use by clients (by appointment). Fees are not charged for client access to the card catalog; fees apply for librarian services and screening.

Researchers and clients should allow sufficient time for film and videotapes to be brought in from the WTN storage facility in Fort Lee, New Jersey.

Rights: Full rights held to all material.

Licensing: Available for licensing and reuse, subject to restrictions. License fees charged (fee schedule available).

Restrictions: Restrictions apply in some cases, depending on intended use. Additional clearances and permissions may be required for commercial use of material.

Viewing Facilities: Film (16mm); videotape (3/4").

Duplication Facilities: Videotape. Film-to-videotape transfers are made out-of-house.

NEW YORK METRO

XCHANGE TV
P.O. Box 586
New York, NY 10009
(212) 260-6565
(212) 420-9045

Contact: Martha Wallner
Services: Media organization; distributor; film and videotape archives.
Description: Collective seeking to democratize the use of media by facilitating the direct exchange of video programs between the peoples of Central and North America. Presents a weekly program on public access cable television in New York City, featuring the work of Central American and independent North American videomakers.

Holds videotapes and television programs produced by Nicaraguans for Nicaraguan audiences (1983-87, all subtitled or with English voiceover), including videotapes produced by Sistema Sandinista de Television; police shows; game shows; public service announcements; news; videotapes produced by the labor video unit Taller Popular de Video C.S.T.-A.T.C.; the Audiovisual Department of the Nicaraguan Ministry of the Interior and the Ministry of Agrarian Reform Communications Department.

Collection especially strong with regard to women's issues, containing programs ranging from documentaries to those in the style of soap operas.

Titles cover such issues as *machismo,* women's work, wife abuse, women's role in the Nicaraguan revolution, jurisprudence, the effect of the war on women and women in the marketplace.

Sample titles include: *A Cincuenta Años...Sandino Vive (Fifty Years Later...Sandino Lives),* on the history of Nicaragua's struggle for independence and a chronicle of U.S. intervention in Central America; *Las Mujeres (The Women),* an introduction to the revolution within the revolution, women's struggle for equal pay and against the "double day"; *Que Pasa con el Papel Higiénico? (What Happened to the Toilet Paper?),* an often humorous investigation into the shortage of toilet paper and the problems of distribution in Nicaragua's besieged economy; *La Dalia,* in which two women in an agricultural collective on the Honduran border describe their participation in the anti-contra militia; *Testimonios: Así Avanzamos (Testimony: And So We Proceed),* in which Nicaraguans describe the effects of the contra aggression on their lives; *Aqui En Este Esquina (Here On This Corner)* (1985), an excerpt from a weekly traveling game show featuring dance contests, arm wrestling and politically conscious quiz show questions; and *Nieve (Snow),* an excerpt from a Sandinista-style cop show, based on true stories of gold smuggling and a contra/U.S. attempt to implicate the Sandinistas in cocaine dealing.

Videotapes from this collection are also held at the Latin American Video Archives, School of Contemporary Arts, Ramapo College of New Jersey (q.v.).

Size & Elements: Videotape: 3/4" and VHS (5 hours, 11 titles; masters and viewing copies). All are subtitled or carry English voiceovers.

Cataloging: Published catalogs.

Access: Available for distribution, broadcast, cablecast and reuse, subject to restrictions. Research fees charged in some cases. Research requests accepted on a limited basis by mail and telephone. Videotapes can be previewed in New York City at an office location. Videotapes from this collection are also held at the Latin American Video Archives, School of Contemporary Arts, Ramapo College of New Jersey (q.v.).

Rights: Apply for information. Additional clearances may be necessary in some cases if material is to be reused.

Licensing: Available for licensing and reuse, subject to restrictions. License fees charged in some cases (including television broadcast).

Restrictions: Context of intended reuse must be approved before footage is supplied. Footage cannot be used for anti-Nicaraguan propaganda.

Viewing Facilities: Videotape (at office location).

Duplication Facilities: Videotape (3/4" and VHS).

NEW YORK METRO

XICOM, INC.
Sterling Forest
Tuxedo, NY 10987
(914) 351-4735
(800) 431-2395
Fax: (914) 351-4762

Edward Northrop (Chairman)

Contact: Paul Graham (Unit Production Manager)
Services: Videotape producer. Material available for duplication, licensing and reuse.
Description: Scenics of Orange County, New York, including waterfalls, tugboats on the Hudson River, a robin building a nest, sunrises, winter scenes (ice on trees) and fall foliage.
Size & Elements: Videotape: 3/4" (approx. 200 min.; masters) and VHS (viewing copies).
Cataloging: Staff assistance required.
Access: Available to the public for duplication and reuse. Research fees negotiable. Research requests accepted by mail, telephone and in person (by appointment only).
Rights: Full rights held to all material.
Licensing: Available for licensing. License fees charged.
Restrictions: None specified.
Viewing Facilities: Videotape (3/4" and VHS).
Duplication Facilities: Videotape (3/4" and VHS).

NEW YORK METRO

YIVO INSTITUTE FOR JEWISH RESEARCH
FILM ARCHIVES
1048 Fifth Avenue
New York, NY 10028
(212) 535-6700

Marek Web (Chief Archivist)

Contact: Roby Newman (Archivist)
Services: Research institute. Film and videotape collections available to the public for in-house use only; available for duplication and reuse on a case-by-case basis.
Description: Films and videotapes primarily relating to Jewish life in Eastern Europe, including approximately 20 hours of unique travel films made by U.S. filmmakers (most 10 minutes each) depicting Eastern Europe (1930s). Some American materials produced by the same filmmakers and a few films produced by Jewish organizations are also held.
Size & Elements: Film: 35mm, 16mm, Super 8mm and 8mm (originals). Videotape: 3/4" and 1/2" (viewing copies). (Approx. 30 hours total).
Cataloging: Brief descriptions of films, noting time and place, filmmaker and known persons in film.
Access: Open to the public. For in-house use only. Available for duplication and reuse on a case-by-case basis. Research fees charged in some cases. Research requests accepted by mail, telephone and in person (by appointment only).
Rights: Full rights held to all material. Additional clearances may be necessary in some cases if material is to be reused (donor restrictions apply in rare instances).
Licensing: Available for licensing and reuse, subject to restrictions. License fees charged.
Restrictions: Requests for licensing and reuse considered on a case-by-case basis.
Viewing Facilities: Videotape (3/4" and 1/2"); videodisc.
Duplication Facilities: None.
Related Materials: Videodisc containing 17,000 still photographs depicting Eastern European Jewish life, indexed by computer; Institute collections contain a total of 100,000 still photographs.

NEW YORK METRO

YUE-SAI KAN, INC.
60 Sutton Place South
New York, NY 10022
(212) 223-0278
Fax: (212) 644-9146

Yue-Sai Kan (Principal)

Contacts: Yue-Sai Kan; Jacqueline Brown
Services: Videotape producer. Stock footage material available for licensing and reuse.
Description: Travel and lifestyle stock footage (1986-87), specializing in Asia. Extensive footage of People's Republic of China, Malaysia, Thailand and Singapore. Other countries include: Japan, Brazil, Tonga, Sweden, Denmark, Italy, France, England, Egypt, Greece and the U.S.
General subjects cover lifestyles, peoples, sights, culture, various monarchs and heads of state, politics and business.
Size & Elements: Videotape: mostly Betacam (350 hours; originals).
Cataloging: Computerized cataloging for staff use only.
Access: Not open to the public. Available for reuse. Research requests accepted by telephone.
Rights: Full rights held to all material.
Licensing: Available for licensing. License fees charged.
Restrictions: None specified.
Viewing Facilities: Videotape.
Duplication Facilities: Videotape.

NEW YORK METRO

ZINC INSTITUTE/
LEAD INDUSTRIES ASSOCIATION
292 Madison Avenue
New York, NY 10017
(212) 578-4750
Fax: (212) 684-7714
Telex: (910) 240-7013

Contact: Jerome F. Smith (Director of Communications)
Services: Association. Videotape material available for research and reuse.
Description: Lead, zinc, metals and minerals; industrial applications.
Titles include: *Zinc Metallizing: Long-Lasting Protection for Steel*

Structures, demonstrating a process in which molten zinc is applied to steel via a handheld spray gun to inhibit rust, including an indoor demonstration and in-field applications; *Zinc Die Casting: The Friendly Clone,* showing how industrial designers can use the process to their advantage; *Lead in Motion,* showing mining, refining and marketing of lead; and *Sheet Lead Flat Roofs,* promoting sheet lead as an alternative to membrane and built-up roofs.
Size & Elements: Videotape: format unspecified (4 titles).
Cataloging: Videotape list.
Access: Available to the public for duplication. Requests accepted by mail.
Rights: Full rights held to all material.
Licensing: Apply for information. License fees not charged.
Restrictions: None specified.
Viewing Facilities: Videotape.
Duplication Facilities: Videotape (3/4" and VHS).

ROCKEFELLER ARCHIVE CENTER
Pocantico Hills
North Tarrytown, NY 10591
(914) 631-4505
Fax: (914) 631-6017

Darwin H. Stapleton (Director)

Contacts: Lee Hiltzik (Archivist); Emily Oakhill (Archivist); Harold Oakhill (Archivist); Thomas Rosenbaum (Archivist); Melissa Smith (Archivist); Erwin Levold (Archivist)
Services: Archives. Film and videotape material available to researchers and scholars only for duplication and reuse, subject to restrictions.
Description: *John C. Bugher Film Collection.* (21 16mm prints and one negative, silent and sound). John C. Bugher was a doctor of medicine and public health, staff member of the Rockefeller Foundation, and official of the U.S. Atomic Energy Commission. Films (1920s-30s) show Bugher's work with yellow fever in Africa, Albania, Sardinia, Terracina and Bogotá (Colombia) and with malaria in Greece and Bulgaria; villages, natives, dancers, religious rites and scenic views of West Africa; scenic views of Colombia and other areas of South America; and films relating to the Atomic Energy Commission (ca. 1950-60).
CIAA Film Collection. (63 films, 16mm, silent and sound). The office of the Coordinator of Inter-American Affairs (1940-46) was created to maintain cultural and commercial relations between North and South America. Holds English and Spanish films made to promote better understanding between the United States and Latin America by documenting the work of the CIAA. Films depict the culture, geography, history, economic conditions and urban and rural life of Argentina, Brazil, Bolivia, Chile, Colombia, Haiti, Mexico, the Pan-American Highway, Peru, Uruguay and Venezuela. Also holds a number of public health and sanitation films made by Walt Disney Studios for use in Latin America.
Harold P. Fabian Film Collection. (18 8mm silent prints). Executive and director of Snake River Land Company, Grand Teton Lodge and Transportation Company, Jackson Hole Wildlife Park, Inc. and Jackson Hole Preserve, Inc. Films of Yellowstone National Park, Jackson Hole, Cascade Canyon, Moose Church, a boat trip, a rodeo and trips east.
International Basic Economy Corporation Film Collection. (16 films, fourteen 16mm and two 35mm prints, silent and sound). The IBEC is a private company established in 1947 to enhance the economic and social growth of developing countries, especially in Latin America. English and Spanish language films made for the use of IBEC or documenting IBEC work in Latin America. These include films on diet in the tropics, methods of agricultural improvement, housing in Puerto Rico and milk production.
JDR 3rd Fund Film Collection. (One 16mm sound print). Founded in 1963 "to stimulate, encourage, promote and support activities important to human welfare."
Frederick Knipe Film Collection. (16 16mm silent prints). Staff member of the International Health Division of the Rockefeller Foundation. Films (ca. 1930s) showing the Tirana (Albania) River Project, scenic views and drainage projects in Sardinia and Bulgaria, mosquito campaigns in Madras (India), and a film on malaria control in war areas (1942-44).
John H. Knowles Film Collection. (One 16mm sound print). Physician and director of Massachusetts General Hospital and the Rockefeller Foundation. Collection holds his appearance on *Open Mind.*
Memorial Sloan-Kettering Cancer Center. (72 films, 16mm, silent and sound, print and negative). Established in 1884 as the New York Cancer Hospital, one of the first hospitals devoted entirely to the treatment and

research of cancer. Films relating to cancer, cancer research and treatment, work at MSKCC, birthday and holiday parties, visits with child and adult patients, and scenes of the hospital.

Rockefeller Family Film Collection. (126 films, 35mm and 16mm and one 28mm film, silent and sound, print and negative). Home movies and newsreel footage of members of the Rockefeller family and family interests, including the dedication of Peking Union Medical College (1921), the construction of Rockefeller Center (ca. 1930), oilfields at the town of Winkler, Grand Teton National Park, the restoration of Versailles and the 60th anniversary of Standard Oil Company.

The Rockefeller Foundation Film Collection. (41 films, 35mm and 16mm, silent and sound, print and negative). Established in 1913 "to promote the well-being of mankind throughout the world." Films made by the Rockefeller Foundation to document Foundation activities, especially in the fields of public health and agriculture. Titles include: *Unhooking the Hookworm* (1920); *Peking and Its Environs* (1920); *Dallas Symphony Orchestra Composers Performers Workshop* (1965); *Eight Month Experiment* (1933, original and work prints) showing a psychopathic hospital in Peking; *Harvest* about rice research (1961); *International Rice Research Institute* (1965); *One Tenth of Our Nation* (1940) made by the General Education Board, on Blacks in the American South; *Rice* (1963, with original and work prints); and *The Unconquered Plague* (1970) on schistosomiasis in the Caribbean.

The Rockefeller University Film Collection. (Several hundred 35mm and 16mm films, silent and sound, mostly prints). Established in 1901 as the Rockefeller Institute for Medical Research; the first institution in the U.S. devoted solely to biomedical research. Holdings include films belonging to University staff members showing experiments and laboratory work at the University; lecture films including Christmas lectures and other addresses at the University; and a 1932 interview with William H. Welch about the early days of the Johns Hopkins University School of Medicine. Staff members include Edward H. Ahrens, Stanford Moore, Edward L. Tatum, Leslie T. Webster and Paul A. Weiss.

Sleepy Hollow Restorations Film Collections. (6 films, 16mm prints and negatives). Organized in 1951 to preserve historic sites in the lower Hudson River Valley. Films describe the SHR historic sites Philipsburg Manor, Van Cortlandt Manor and Sunnyside.

Woodstock Foundation Film Collection. Ben Thresher's Mill (1980), a National Educational Television *Odyssey* series episode on a 19th century mill. Includes all film used in production, from filed shots to finished products. Long and short versions are held.

Size & Elements: Film: amount unspecified (mostly positive and negative, some workprints and outtakes). Videotape (format and amount unspecified).
Cataloging: Finding aids (in-house inventory).
Access: Open to researchers and scholars only for duplication and possibly reuse. Research fees not charged. Research requests accepted by mail, telephone and in person (walk-in and by appointment).
Rights: Full rights held to some material. Some rights held to some material. Additional clearances may be necessary in some cases if material is to be reused. Rights status of some material unknown.
Licensing: Apply for information. License fees generally not charged.
Restrictions: Contact Director for all requests concerning licensing and reuse.
Viewing Facilities: Film (35mm, 16mm prints and negatives); videotape (3/4" and Betamax). Arrangements can be made for other formats.
Duplication Facilities: None.

NEW YORK (Oceanside)

FOCUS
See **NEW YORK METRO**

NEW YORK (Owego)

EXPERIMENTAL TELEVISION CENTER
180 Front Street
Owego, NY 13827
(607) 687-1423

Ralph Hocking (Director)
Sherry Miller Hocking (Assistant Director)

Contacts: Ralph Hocking; Sherry Miller Hocking
Services: Nonprofit media organization; production facility. Videotape collection available for in-house viewing only by artists, students, curators and researchers.
Description: Founded in 1971 to support the development of video as a

contemporary visual art, the Center is one of only a few video facilities in the country offering a concentration in electronic image processing. Provides production, research and support programs for individual artists, arts and educational organizations and the interested public.

The primary goal of the research program is the design of video tools which provide artists with significant new methods of image formation. Over the years it has resulted in the construction of a number of new devices including a multi-channel colorizer, a frame buffer and the interface of the imaging system with the Amiga computer, utilizing custom software programmed by David Jones. The imaging system includes both analog and digital image generating, processing and control devices.

The residency program offers artists the opportunity to use analog and digital video tools in an environment which emphasizes aesthetic investigation and personal creative work. Participating artists have complete aesthetic and technical control over all aspects of the making process. All equipment is operated by the videomaker, and the Center's staff do not serve as production crew. Individuals retain all rights over materials produced during the residency but are required to donate a copy of completed work to the Center's archives.

Archives holds independently produced art works (1970-present) representing various stylistic and aesthetic concerns, ranging from explorations of new narrative and documentary forms to formalistic studies. The major emphasis is on electronic image processing. Much of the material was produced in whole or in part through the residency program. Artists represented include: David Blair, Peer Bode, Coleman and Powell, Shalom Gorewitz, Gary Hill, Sara Hornbacher, Shigeko Kubota, Matt Schlanger and Ren Weidenaar.
Size & Elements: Videotape: 3/4", VHS, Betamax and 1/2" open reel (approx. 450 videotapes; primarily viewing copies). 1/2" open reel videotapes are not available for viewing unless copied to another format.
Cataloging: Card catalogs.
Access: Open to researchers, artists and scholars by appointment only. Archives is maintained for educational purposes only; videotapes are not loaned, leased or duplicated without the consent of the maker.
Rights: No rights held to any material. All rights retained by artists.
Licensing: Not available for licensing or reuse.
Restrictions: Available for in-house viewing and research purposes only. 1/2" open reel tapes not available for viewing unless copied to other format.
Viewing Facilities: Videotape (3/4").
Duplication Facilities: None.

NEW YORK (Pearl River)

AFRICA INLAND MISSION
P.O. Box 178
Pearl River, NY 10965
(914) 735-4014
Telex: 137015

Street address: 135 West Crooked Hill Road

Dr. Ted Barnett (U.S. Director)

Contact: Dr. Ted Barnett
Services: Mission society. Film and videotape available for research and reuse, subject to approval.
Description: Mission's work in relation with the church in East Africa, in particular Zaire, Kenya, Uganda, Tanzania and Central African Republic (1950s-present). Collection holds 14 titles of archival interest; 10 others in current distribution. There is material that would be helpful in tribal studies.
Size & Elements: Film: format unspecified (24 titles, 68 cans). Videotape: VHS (7 titles).
Cataloging: Computerized cataloging.
Access: Available to the public by request only. Requests accepted by mail, telephone and in person (walk-in).
Rights: Full rights held to all material. Additional clearances may be necessary in some cases if material is to be reused.
Licensing: Contact the Director (Ext. 234) regarding reuse. License fees charged in some cases.
Restrictions: Reuse requires written permission of the Mission.
Viewing Facilities: Film and videotape.
Duplication Facilities: None.

NEW YORK (Plainview)

ISLAND VIDEO
See **NEW YORK METRO**

NEW YORK (Port Washington)

PORT WASHINGTON PUBLIC LIBRARY
and
VEDO FILMS/NOVACOM VIDEO
See **NEW YORK METRO**

NEW YORK (Rochester)

INTERNATIONAL MUSEUM OF PHOTOGRAPHY AT GEORGE EASTMAN HOUSE
900 East Avenue
Rochester, NY 14607
(716) 271-3361

Jan-Christopher Horak (Curator of Film)

Contact: Jan-Christopher Horak (for research inquiries); Edward Stratman (Assistant Curator of Film) (for stock footage inquiries); Paolo Usai (Assistant Curator)
Services: Museum; library; film archives. Material available for in-house research and scholarly use only, and in some cases for duplication, licensing and reuse, subject to clearances and restrictions.
Description: George Eastman House, one of the major film archives in the United States, holds 6,600 films (1895-present). It is one of three full members of the International Federation of Film Archives (FIAF) in the United States.

Preservation activities began in 1950, and are designed to supplement rather than duplicate the Museum of Modern Art's acquisitions policy. Popular entertainment films, as well as those chiefly of interest to historians and scholars, are preserved. Major titles saved include Fred Niblo's *Ben Hur* (1925) and *Phantom of the Opera* (1925); King Vidor's *The Crowd* (1927-28); *Hunchback of Notre Dame* (1923), with Lon Chaney; Josef von Sternberg's *Docks of New York* (1928); Merian C. Cooper and Ernest B. Schoedsack's *Grass* (1925); and Erich von Stroheim's *The Merry Widow* (1925). At present, holds 7.5 million feet of nitrate film still in need of preservation.

Archives emphasizes silent films from all countries and American films, both silent and sound. Among collections held are:
Metro-Goldwyn-Mayer Collection. Silent and sound films.
Cecil B. DeMille Estate Collection. The result of a joint preservation effort with Library of Congress.
Greta Garbo films. Complete except for two "lost" films: *The Divine Woman* and *The Two Kings.*
Early American silent films. Thomas H. Ince Productions, Edison Kinetoscopes, Vitagraph Company, Lubin Company and Pathé Company.
Early Westerns (1906-on). Hoot Gibson, Tom Mix, Tim McCoy, Yakima Canutt and Tex Ritter, with particular strengths in William S. Hart films and one and two-reelers (1911-15).
British films (1901-60). Highlights include "English primitive" films *The Soldier's Return* and *The Acrobatic Tramp* (both 1902) by J. H. Williamson; and Sheffield Photo Company's *Daring Daylight Burglary* (1903), a very early chase film.
French films (1901-60s). Strongest in 1930s-50s, including five Sacha Guitry films.
German films (silent era through 1950s). Includes films by F. W. Murnau and G. W. Pabst (including *Pandora's Box* and *Diary of a Lost Girl*, with Louise Brooks).
Italian films (1909-60s). Strong in 1940s films.
Japanese films. Small collection, including the first Japanese sound film shown in the United States, Naruse's *Kimiko* (1935).

Also held are numerous kinescopes of 1950s television programs and some Eastman Teaching Films (1920s-30s), including several made by independent filmmaker J. S. Watson, Jr.
Size & Elements: Film: various formats and elements (6,600 titles).
Cataloging: Inventory and descriptive computerized cataloging in process; research library.
Access: Open only to researchers, scholars and representatives of the media. For in-house use only. Available for duplication, licensing and reuse, subject to restrictions. Research fees not charged. Screening fees apply. Research requests accepted by mail and telephone.
Rights: No rights held to any material. Additional clearances may be necessary in some cases if material is to be reused.
Licensing: Available for licensing and reuse, subject to restrictions. License fees not charged; duplication fees apply.
Restrictions: Copyright restrictions exist for most material in collection. Prospective users wishing to copy material not already preserved must cover the cost of making preservation masters for the archives.
Viewing Facilities: Film (35mm and 16mm screening room and viewing tables). Screening fees apply.
Duplication Facilities: None.
Related Materials: One million motion picture stills from the silent and sound eras; research library; archives of still photography; motion picture equipment and apparatus collection (1880-present).
Publications: *Image,* a magazine of photography and films. Available with membership to IMP/GEH. An anthology of articles appearing in *Image* (1952-77), edited by Marshall Deutelbaum, is available.

NEW YORK (Rochester)

UNIVERSITY OF ROCHESTER
DANCE FILM ARCHIVE
Rochester, NY 14627
(716) 275-5236

John Mueller (Director)

Contact: John Mueller
Services: Archives; producer and distributor. Films available for rental and purchase.
Description: Films documenting dance works of great historic and artistic value, especially American modern dance. DFA's goal is not only to archive films, but to make valuable dance films available through distribution. Collection includes films produced by other sources and distributed by DFA, films in which DFA has had varying degrees of production participation (i.e., in shooting or in adding sound to silent footage) and films purchased from distributors and made available for rental.

Dancers, choreographers and performances featured: Fred Astaire's *Second Chorus;* Trisha Brown's *Water Motor;* Jane Comfort's *For The Spider Woman;* Merce Cunningham's *Walkaround Time* and *Westbeth;* Fanny Elssler's *The Cachucha;* Michel Fokine's *Dying Swan* and *Les Sylphides* (performed by Margot Fonteyn); Martha Graham's *Flute of Krishna;* many works by Doris Humphrey, including *Air For The G String, Day On Earth, Two Ecstatic Themes;* José Limon's *Emperor Jones* and *The Traitor;* Kei Takei's *Light;* and Twyla Tharp's *Sue's Leg.*

Archive also holds many documentaries, ballet study films and feature films.
Size & Elements: Film: format unspecified (92 titles).
Cataloging: Published catalogs.
Access: Available for rental and purchase. Rental fees charged. Requests accepted by mail.
Rights: Full rights held to some material. Some material in the public domain. Additional clearances may be necessary in some cases if material is to be reused.
Licensing: Material possibly available for reuse. Usage fees charged under some conditions.
Restrictions: Some restrictions may apply in cases where DFA holds no rights.
Viewing Facilities: Film and videotape.
Duplication Facilities: None.

NEW YORK (Rochester)

UNIVERSITY OF ROCHESTER LIBRARY
DEPARTMENT OF RARE BOOKS AND SPECIAL COLLECTIONS
Rochester, NY 14627
(716) 275-4477

Peter Dzwonkoski (Head, Department of Rare Books and Special Collections)

Contacts: Karl S. Kabelac (Manuscripts Librarian); Mary M. Huth (Assistant Department Head)
Services: University library. Film and videotape collection open to researchers and scholars only. Some materials unavailable at present.
Description: *University Archives* (1927-86). Approximately 160 films and 90 videotapes documenting official University events and ceremonies, talks and speeches of University officials and outside speakers, and footage of student activities. Cataloged by printed lists.
Kenneth B. Keating Collection. Approximately 50 films from Keating's half-hour weekly television program, produced during his tenures as New York State congressman (1947-59) and Senator (1959-65). Program features discussions of then-current issues with guests who were usually government officials. Also includes campaign films. Collection is in the process of being

identified and cataloged; *material is currently unavailable.*

Thomas E. Dewey Collection. Approximately 40 films. Includes campaign films, documentation of speeches and newsreels featuring Dewey as governor of New York State (1943-54) and Republican candidate for president in 1944 and 1948. Card catalogs available.
Size & Elements: Film: 16mm (approx. 700 titles; originals and positives). Videotape: format unspecified (approx. 90 videotapes; masters and viewing copies).
Cataloging: Printed lists for University Archives; computerized cataloging in process and available to researchers for the Keating Collection; card catalogs for the Dewey Collection.
Access: Open to researchers and scholars only. Keating Collection not yet open to the public. Research fees not charged. Research requests accepted by mail, telephone and, preferably, in person (by appointment only).
Rights: Rights status of material not known for Keating and Dewey Collections; full rights held to all material in University Archives.
Licensing: Apply for information.
Restrictions: Access and use of some collections restricted.
Viewing Facilities: Film and videotape (facilities available on campus).
Duplication Facilities: Film and videotape (facilities available on campus).

NEW YORK (Rochester)

VISUAL STUDIES WORKSHOP
31 Prince Street
Rochester, NY 14607
(716) 442-8676

Nathan Lyons (Director)

Contact: Robert Doyle (Media Program Coordinator)
Services: Educational institution. Videotape collection available for in-house use only; some videotapes available for rental.
Description: *Portable Channel Collection.* Independent videotapes (early 1970s through mid-1980s) originated by the Rochester media organization. The collection is presently uncataloged.

Also holds video work (early 1970s-present) encompassing all genres, including independent videotapes, documentaries, narratives, computer graphics and video art.
Size & Elements: Videotape: format and amount unspecified.
Cataloging: Card catalogs (for a portion of collection).
Access: For in-house use only. Some material available for rental. Research requests accepted by mail and telephone.
Rights: No rights held to any material.
Licensing: Apply for information.
Restrictions: None specified.
Viewing Facilities: Film (16mm, Super 8mm and 8mm); videotape (3/4", Video 8, VHS and Betamax).
Duplication Facilities: Film (Super 8mm to videotape); videotape (3/4", Video 8, VHS and Betamax).

NEW YORK (Schenectady)

RID (REMOVE INTOXICATED DRIVERS)
P.O. Box 520
Schenectady, NY 12301
(518) 372-9624

William Aiken (Vice President)

Contact: William Aiken
Services: Foundation. Film available for purchase and licensing, subject to clearance and approval.
Description: Distributes one award-winning public awareness film *Until I Get Caught* (1980, 60 min.), narrated by Dick Cavett. Originally produced by the Psychology Department at Cornell University, the film, currently entitled *Update '88*, presents the tragedy that befell two families and shows how a community can form a group to combat the menace of intoxicated drivers.
Size & Elements: Film: 16mm. Videotape: VHS. (1 title total).
Cataloging: Published brochure.
Access: Available to the public for purchase. Requests accepted by mail and telephone.
Rights: Full rights held to some material. Additional clearances may be necessary in some cases if material is to be reused.
Licensing: Available for licensing and reuse. License fees charged in some

cases.
Restrictions: None specified.
Viewing Facilities: None.
Duplication Facilities: None.
Distributor: For sales information, contact Kinetic, Inc., 255 Delaware Avenue, Suite 340, Buffalo, NY 14202; (716) 856-7631. In Canada: Kinetic, Inc., 408 Dundas Street East, Toronto, ON M5A 2A5; (416) 963-5979.

NEW YORK (Staten Island)

ISLAND CINEMA RESOURCES
See **NEW YORK METRO**

NEW YORK (Syosset)

NEMIROFF PRODUCTIONS, INC.
See **NEW YORK METRO**

NEW YORK (Syracuse)

EVERSON MUSEUM OF ART
401 Harrison Street
Syracuse, New York 13202
(315) 474-6064

Ronald A. Kuchta (Director)

Contact: Dominique Nahas (Curator)
Services: Museum. Videotape collection open to researchers and scholars for in-house use only.
Description: Pioneer experimental video art collection (produced late 1960s-early 1970s) acquired through the Museum's video art program. Some of the videotapes (including installation works) were commissioned specifically by the Museum.

Artists represented include: Vito Acconci, John Baldessari, Lynda Benglis, Norman Bluhm, Barbara Buckner, Chris Burden, Doug Davis, Juan Downey, Richard Foreman, Terry Fox, Frank Gillette, Joan Jonas, Les Levine, Linda Montano, Nam June Paik, Dan Sandin, Lillian Schwartz, Ken Knowlton, Keith Sonnier, Aldo Tambellini, Francesco Torres, Bill Viola, William Wegman and Lawrence Weiner.

Holds most videotapes from the *Everson Video Revue* (1979 exhibition). Curator Richard Simmons, in the exhibition catalog, described the *Revue:* "Each of these artists work out a personal dedication or passion, offering unique, often idiosyncratic individuality. The key to understanding this independence of action is to embrace the artists' purpose of expression, the discovery of new forms, new techniques, new themes and ways of presenting them, to break from traditions and pre-conceived notions of definition and experience."

Videotapes in the *Revue* include: *You Can't Lick Stamps in China* (Gregory Battcock and Nam June Paik, 1979); *Resorts of the Catskills* (John Margolies and Skip Blumberg, 1977); *Pictures of Lost, Astral Love, Blue House, Untitled (3), Nica Twice* and *Comtemplation* (Barbara Buckner, 1977); *Sharon* (Nancy Cain, 1977); *Merce by Merce by Paik* (Merce Cunningham and Nam June Paik, 1978); *By the Crimson Bands of Cyttorak* (Tom Defanti, 1978); *The Abandoned Shabono* (Juan Downey, 1978); *Chant A Capella* (Jean Dupuy and Davidson Gigliotti, 1978); *Dubs* (Ed Emshwiller, 1978); *Entropy, Order, Motive, Access* (Kit Fitzgerald and John Sanborn, 1978); *Out of the Body Travel* (Richard Foreman, 1977); *New Reel* (Hermine Freed, 1977); *Vito's Reef Part I* (Howard Fried (1977); *Harold's Bar Mitzvah* (Bart Friedman, 1977); *Shopping Bag Ladies* (John Giummo and Elizabeth Sweetnam, 1977); *Windows, Objects w/ Destinations* and *Picture Story* (Gary Hill, 1978); *I Want to Live in The Country (and Other Romances)* (Joan Jonas, 1977); *In the Pictures* (Gunilla and Philip Mallory Jones, 1977); *The Last Space Voyage of Wallace Ramsel* (John Keeler and Ruth Rotko, 1977); *Sirens* and *Ax* (Marlene and Paul Kos, 1977-78); *Always Late* (Mitchell Kriegman, 1978); *AlieNation* (Barbara Latham, John Manning and Edward Rankus, 1979); *A Picture is Worth 1,000 Words, Stamp of Approval* and *But This Idea* (Les Levine, 1976); *Pink Beans* (Eva Maier, 1978); *Arab/Angel, Aging, Van Gogh's Bedroom* and *Group Shot* (Christa Maiwald, 1977); *Mitchell's Death* (Linda Montano, 1977); *Stag Hotel* (James Morris, 1978); *Barricade To Blue* (Rita Myers, 1977); *Sometime in September, Because It's My Image/Watching the Leatherman* and *2+1+1* (John Orentlicher and Tom Sherman, 1978-79); *Sheridan Square* (Pocket Video, 1977); *Suzy Q, Repulsion/Obsession* and *Seduction* (Susan Russell, 1977); *Several Minutes of Several Days in the Hamptons* and *Some Scenes from Southern California* (Ira Schneider, 1976); *Electronic Masks*

(Barbara Sykes, 1978); *Happy Birthday America* (Video Repetorie, 1976); *The Space Between the Teeth* and *Truth Through Mass Individuation* (Bill Viola, 1977); *Selected Works: Reel #7* and *Anthology* (William Wegman, 1977-78); and *Red as Well as Green as Well as Blue* (Lawrence Weiner, 1976).

The video program was begun under Jim Harithas and David Ross (1971-73) and continued under Ron Kuchta and Richard Simmons (director and curator, respectively) (1974-78). The program was discontinued due to lack of financial support and has not been revived. The Everson worked closely with other museums (particularly the Whitney) and with organizations and community groups such as the Experimental Television Center in Binghamton and the Electron Movers in Providence, R.I., as well as with individual artists (who were commissioned to produce videotapes at the Everson) in order to introduce the community to the possibilities of experimental video.

Size & Elements: Videotape: 3/4" and 1/2" open reel (most of collection) (approx. 500 videotapes total).
Cataloging: Computerized cataloging (printout available to researchers).
Access: Open to researchers and scholars. For in-house use only. Research fees not charged. Research requests accepted by mail, telephone and in person (by appointment only).

Most of the collection exists only on 1/2" open reel videotape and is difficult to view due to the fragility of the original material. 1/2" open reel master videotapes must be transferred to 3/4" prior to viewing. Viewing arrangements must be made well in advance of appointment. (Negotiations are currently underway with the Newhouse Media Center at Syracuse University to transfer videotape materials for preservation purposes.)

Rights: Some rights held to some material. Rights retained by original artists.
Licensing: Not available for licensing or reuse.
Restrictions: For in-house viewing only. Licensing or reuse not permitted.
Viewing Facilities: Videotape (3/4"). 1/2" open reel viewing equipment is available at Syracuse University (advance arrangements required).
Duplication Facilities: None.
Publications: Published catalogs relating to specific exhibitions.

NEW YORK (Syracuse)

SYRACUSE ALTERNATIVE MEDIA NETWORK
P.O. Box 550
Syracuse, NY 13210
(315) 425-8806

Jim Dessauer (Coordinator)

Contact: Jim Dessauer
Services: Videotape producer and distributor. Footage available for licensing and reuse on a case-by-case basis, subject to restrictions.
Description: Documentary videotapes on Central America, Nicaragua, the arms race and women's issues.
Size & Elements: Videotape: 1" and 3/4" (21 videotapes; masters); 3/4" and 1/2" (viewing copies). Some videotapes have been transferred from films.
Cataloging: Published catalog.
Access: Available to the public for rental and purchase. Videotapes produced by SAMN available for reuse, subject to restrictions. Requests accepted by mail and telephone.
Rights: Full rights held to material produced by SAMN.
Licensing: Available for licensing and reuse, subject to restrictions.
Restrictions: Requests for licensing and reuse considered on a case-by-case basis.
Viewing Facilities: None.
Duplication Facilities: Videotape (3/4" and 1/2").

NEW YORK (Syracuse)

SYRACUSE UNIVERSITY
ART MEDIA STUDIES COLLECTION
222 Smith Hall
Syracuse, NY 13210
(315) 443-1033

John Orentlicher (Chairman)

Contact: John Orentlicher
Services: Educational institution; videotape archives. Except for student work, collection is for in-house use only. Certain materials available for duplication; others unavailable for duplication or distribution.
Description: *Student Collection.* Work by Art Media Studies graduate and undergraduate students (1978-present), including cable television shows.
Synapse Collection. Copies of completed and partially completed projects from the now defunct Synapse Video Center.
Artist Collection. Holds contemporary works donated by artists for in-house educational use only.
Size & Elements: Videotape: 3/4" (approx. 300 videotapes, each 60 min.; viewing copies).
Cataloging: Card catalogs; computerized cataloging in process.
Access: Available for in-house use only, except for student videotapes, which may be available for duplication or distribution. Research requests accepted by mail. The Artist and Synapse Collections are not available for duplication or distribution of any kind.
Rights: Some rights held to some material. Artists retain rights to videotapes they have produced.
Licensing: Only portions of collections available for duplication.
Restrictions: The Artist and Synapse Collections not available for duplication or distribution of any kind.
Viewing Facilities: Videotape (by special arrangement only).
Duplication Facilities: None.

NEW YORK (Tuckahoe)

CAMPUS FILM DISTRIBUTORS CORP.
24 Depot Square
Tuckahoe, NY 10707
(914) 961-1900
Fax: (914) 961-6733

Steve Campus (President)

Contact: Gertrude Weis (Secretary, Film Library)
Services: Film and videotape producer and distributor. Library maintained primarily for distribution and rental. Some material available for licensing and reuse, subject to approval.
Description: Early childhood education and special education; many films designed for educators, child psychology courses and training.
Foundations of Learning Series teaches the foundations of reading, writing, science and mathematics.
Training Films for Early Childhood series covers outdoor play, dramatic play, setting up a room and playing with blocks.
Children's Dramatic Play series relates to facilitating dramatic play, role enactment in play, concept instancing in role enactment, and hospital visits.
Play and Cultural Continuity Series covers Appalachian, Southern Black, Mexican American and Montana Indian children.
Special education. Includes mental retardation, preschool children with handicapping conditions, educating young multi-handicapped children, special needs of handicapped children, dance troupe of deaf youngsters at Lexington School for the Deaf in New York City, oral communication and integration of deaf children into hearing world, parent participation in education of handicapped children, therapeutic play for handicapped, retarded and institutionalized children and hospitalization anxieties.
Size & Elements: Film: 16mm (amount unspecified). Videotape: 3/4" and VHS.
Cataloging: Release sheets.
Access: Maintained for distribution and rental rather than research or reuse.
Rights: Full rights held to some material.
Licensing: Apply for information. License fees charged.
Restrictions: None specified.
Viewing Facilities: None.
Duplication Facilities: None.

NEW YORK (Tuxedo)

XICOM, INC.
See **NEW YORK METRO**

NEW YORK (Valhalla)

IBM CORPORATION
See **NEW YORK METRO**

NEW YORK (Westbury)

PAN AMERICAN AIRLINES FILM LIBRARY
See **NEW YORK METRO**

NEW YORK (White Plains)

MARCH OF DIMES BIRTH DEFECTS FOUNDATION
and
WILL ROGERS INSTITUTE
and
SOCIETY OF MOTION PICTURE AND TV ENGINEERS (SMPTE)
See **NEW YORK METRO**

NEW YORK (Woodstock)

MEDIA BUS
P.O. Box 718
Woodstock, NY 12498
(914) 679-7739

Bart Friedman (Director)

Contact: Bart Friedman
Services: Not-for-profit arts service organization. Not open to the public. Videotape and film collection available for duplication, licensing and reuse, subject to clearance, staff time and availability. *Staff limitations and condition of collection may limit ability to respond to outside requests.*
Description: Incorporated 1971. Holds videotapes (both edited work and raw, unedited footage) from several pioneer video groups and collectives including Videofreex; People's Video Theatre; TVTV (Top Value Television); Global Village; and the Raindance Foundation.

Much early material in the collection preserves the work of Videofreex (under whose name Media Bus first operated), a collective started in New York City in 1969 and relocated to Greene County (upstate New York) in 1971. Many of the videotapes produced 1971-78 were broadcast over a pirate television station in Woodstock. Subjects covered include social and political activism; crafts and folk arts; collective and communal life (urban and rural); early community television programs; and "process" video (work exploring the nature of the video medium).

Collection includes videotapes from visiting artists, many documentaries, and videotapes donated to Media Bus or bartered in exchange for goods and services. Documentary coverage includes material relating to the "Chicago 8" trial (1969), featuring footage shot in and around the city of Chicago and interviews with conspiracy defendants; material on the murder of Black Panther Fred Hampton in Chicago (1969); footage shot in around New Haven, Connecticut, at the trial of Black Panthers Bobby Seale and Ericka Huggins; and material from the early Women's Liberation movement, including footage of demonstrations and other activities. A documentary on the May Day actions in Washington (1971), collectively produced and edited by representatives from a dozen video production collectives, is also held. There is also a Super 8mm film shot on the 1969 Videofreex tour across the United States, sponsored by CBS.

TVTV material held includes raw footage shot at the 1972 Republican National Convention, some of which was later edited into *Four More Years* (1972). TVTV's completed videotapes are held by Electronic Arts Intermix (q.v.) and other collections.
Size & Elements: Film: Super 8mm (one reel). Videotape: 3/4" and Betamax I (3,000 videotapes); 1/2" open reel (approx. 1,000 videotapes). Collection includes masters, viewing copies and unedited footage, and is held in various locations. Most 1/2" open reel videotape has not been copied onto other formats.
Cataloging: Card catalogs (covering 600 videotapes); remainder of collection uncataloged. Staff assistance available in some cases.
Access: *Staff limitations and condition of collection may limit ability to respond to outside requests. All research requests are subject to acceptance and approval.* Not open to the public. For in-house use only. Available for duplication and reuse, subject to clearance, staff time and availability. Most 1/2" open reel material must be cleaned before viewing. Research fees not charged. Research requests accepted by mail and telephone. Prospective users are encouraged to call to discuss availability of material and coverage of events with staff.
Rights: Full rights held to most material. Rights to some material retained by artists or videomakers. Additional clearances may be necessary in some cases if material is to be reused.
Licensing: Available for licensing and reuse, subject to clearance, availability and restrictions. License fees charged.
Restrictions: *Staff limitations and condition of collection may limit ability to respond to outside requests. All research requests are subject to acceptance and approval.*

Viewing Facilities: Videotape (3/4" and 1/2" open reel).
Duplication Facilities: Videotape (3/4" and 1/2" open reel).

NORTH CAROLINA

NORTH CAROLINA (Belmont)

BELMONT ABBEY COLLEGE
VINCENT TAYLOR LIBRARY
Belmont, NC 28012
(704) 825-3711

Contact: Bertrand A. Pattison (Librarian) (704/825-7051)
Services: Educational institution. Videotape collection available primarily for research; reuse permitted by agreement only.
Description: Videotape series *Cathedral Cities of Great Britain* describes the origins, history, art and environments of various cathedral towns in England, Wales, and Scotland. Locations include York, Durham, Edinburgh, St. Andrews, Chester, St. Asaph, Lichfield, Canterbury, Rochester, Salisbury, Winchester, Chichester, Exeter, Lincoln, Ely, Norwich, Colchester, Coventry, Oxford, Gloucester, Worcester, Wells, Bath and Glastonbury.
Size & Elements: Videotape: format unspecified (1 series in 4 parts, each 30 min.).
Cataloging: Card catalogs.
Access: Open to researchers and scholars. Research fees not charged. Research requests accepted by mail.
Rights: Full rights held to all material.
Licensing: Apply for information. License fees usually not charged.
Restrictions: Requests for reuse subject to acceptance and approval.
Viewing Facilities: Videotape.
Duplication Facilities: None.

NORTH CAROLINA (Boone)

APPALACHIAN STATE UNIVERSITY
W. L. EURY APPALACHIAN COLLECTION
University Hall
Boone, NC 28608
(704) 262-4041

Eric J. Olson (Librarian)

Contact: Eric J. Olson
Services: University library. Film and videotape collection available for research and distribution.
Description: Extensive collection of films and videotapes on Appalachian culture, customs and industries (1941-present). Strengths of collection are religion, local and family history, folklore, folk music and fiction about the Southern mountains. Additional topics include: Annual Georgia State Bluegrass Festival, ASU campus scenes (1955), American Indian tribes, the Appalachian Trail, apple butter making, blacksmiths, Blue Ridge mountains, Daniel Boone, children's stories, coal mining and strip mining, cockfighting, crafts, dance, education, electricity, feuds, food preparation, Harlan County coal miners' strike, hog butchering and dressing, John F. Kennedy's visit to Appalachia during his Presidential campaign (1960), land conspiracy, midwifery, mountain culture, mountain people and isolationists, national parks, politics, poverty, quilting, religious practices and customs (ranging from snake and fire handling to exchanging flowers), steam railroad engines and storytelling. Of particular note are two videotapes, *They Shall Take Up Serpents* and *Fire and Serpent Handlers,* that portray fundamentalist snake-handling sects, showing segments of church services and the rituals of snake-handling. Many of the films are produced by Appalshop Films, Inc. (q.v.) although this collection holds material significantly earlier than the Appalshop collection.
Size & Elements: Film: 16mm (amount unspecified). Videotape: 3/4", VHS and other formats (150 hours).
Cataloging: Card catalogs. Published catalog, *Appalachian Regional Films,* available on request.
Access: Open to the public. For in-house use only. Requests accepted by mail, telephone and in person (walk-in).
Rights: Full rights held to some material. Some rights held to some material.
Licensing: Apply for information.
Restrictions: Films may not be shown where admission is charged or for commercial uses; television rights are retained by the distributors or producers

and approval for use on television or for videotaping must be obtained directly from these sources. Videotapes housed in Appalachian collection do not circulate without special permission.
Viewing Facilities: Film (16mm); videotape (3/4" and VHS).
Duplication Facilities: None.
Related Materials: Approximately 500 hours of audiotaped oral interviews; 600 music phonograph recordings.

NORTH CAROLINA (Chapel Hill)

UNIVERSITY OF NORTH CAROLINA — CHAPEL HILL
MANUSCRIPTS DEPARTMENT
CB #3926, Wilson Library
Chapel Hill, NC 27599
(919) 962-1345

David Moltke-Hansen (Director)

Contact: John E. White (Reference Assistant); Dr. Richard Shrader (Reference Archivist)
Services: University library. Videotape collection open to the public.
Description: Southern historical collection. Videotapes document the lives of U.S. Senator Samuel Ervin and Congressman Allard Lowenstein.
Size & Elements: Videotape: format unspecified (8 videotapes).
Cataloging: Card catalogs; published catalogs.
Access: Open to the public. Research requests accepted by mail, telephone and in person (walk-in).
Rights: Some rights held to some material. Additional clearances may be necessary if material is to be reused.
Licensing: Apply for information.
Restrictions: None specified.
Viewing Facilities: Videotape (facilities located in adjacent library).
Duplication Facilities: None.

NORTH CAROLINA (Charlotte)

ANALOGOUS PRODUCTIONS
5007 Farmland Road
Charlotte, NC 28226
(704) 366-9099

Michael Klatt (Executive Producer)

Contact: Michael Klatt
Services: Film and videotape archives; film and videotape producer; stock footage sales library.
Description: Stock footage (1920-65, mostly black and white), featuring newsreel-type coverage of historical events, personalities and sports.

Historical events. Includes world events; Prohibition; the Depression; illegal gambling; sports; transportation; military; stunts and oddities; baseball; beauty contests; dedications; world's fairs and expositions; floods, hurricanes; disasters; demonstrations of products and inventions; personalities in the news; locales; and fashion.

Demonstrations. Includes boxing bear; rocket and missile tests; frog jumping; helicopter crane; fire department drills; chorus line practice; bulletproof vest; robotized arms for handling radioactive material; watermelon eating; waiters race with serving trays; glassblowing; Alpine horn blowing; gondola racing; hula hoops; baby diapering; ground-to-air airplane refueling; auto safety glass; rocket sled; flying contraptions; diving bell; cannons test fired; dumbwaiter tested; boats; road grating; child lion tamer; elevator bridge; train-mounted snowplow; conventional airplanes; non-skid tires; police I.D. sketching methods; water cannon; folding automobile; tire changing; trick golf shots.

Institutions. Includes baseball opening days; changing of the guard at Buckingham Palace; running of the bulls in Pamplona; Moscow May Day parades; Texas cattle drives; political conventions; beauty contests; ship launchings; Munich Oktoberfest; Chinese New Year celebrations; baseball spring training; political campaigning; Mardi Gras; sandlot baseball; winter and summer Olympics; ocean liners; movie premieres; ticker tape parades; Kentucky Derby; World Series; Indianapolis 500; America's Cup; Heisman Trophy presentations; Boston Marathon; public works, dedications and ribbon cuttings; ships at sea; planes in formation; victory, sports and commemorative parades; strikes; royal weddings; religious services; dog shows; flower shows; ice shows; circuses; Congressional hearings; scrap metal drives; air shows; and car pooling.

Famous locales. Includes Buckingham Palace; Berlin Wall; Cape Canaveral; the White House; U.S. Capitol; U.S. Supreme Court; Yankee Stadium; Golden Gate Bridge; New York World's Fair; Harvard University; Alcatraz; United Nations; Niagara Falls; Panama Canal; Guantanamo Bay; Havana; Taj Mahal; Fifth Avenue (New York City); Los Angeles Coliseum; Indianapolis Motor Speedway; Expo '67; the Olympics; West Point; Annapolis; Churchill Downs; Air Force Academy; the Vatican; Times Square; London Bridge; Mont Blanc; Little League World Series; Coney Island; Tomb of the Unknown Soldier; Hoover Dam; Baseball Hall of Fame; Grand Coulee Dam; the Astrodome; Cannes Film Festival; St. Patrick's Cathedral; Red Square; Grauman's Chinese Theatre; Madison Square Garden; New York City harbor; 10 Downing Street; Pearl Harbor; the North Pole; Broadway; Boulder Dam; John F. Kennedy Memorial; St. Paul's Cathedral; Carnival (Rio de Janeiro); Bonneville Salt Flats; Wimbledon; Nuremberg; and Augusta National Golf Club.

Military. Includes world military events; maneuvers and drills; airplanes; ship launchings; submarines; rockets; missiles; World War II footage; aircraft carriers; motorcycle units; gas mask plant in Ohio; aircraft factory assembly lines; test flying; troops; phony UFO recovered by Air Force; invasions; Vietnam War; China; Korea; Japan; Germany; France; Sputnik launching; A-bomb test; H-bomb test.

Transportation. Includes arrival of *Normandie* in New York Harbor; Pan American clipper planes; airplane takeoffs and landings; "Tall" ships; *S. S. France* launched; Italian liner *Rex* sets transatlantic speed record; French and Japanese bullet trains; preview of 1946 cars; *Queen Mary;* dirigibles in flight and landing; George Washington Bridge expanded to two levels; dedication of Golden Gate Bridge; moving sidewalks installed in New Jersey shopping area; motorized scooters for long hospital corridors; Boeing 747 jet debut; *Morro Castle* burns and sinks off New Jersey coast; early autogyro tested; side-by-side bicycle demonstrated; Hovercraft demonstrated; *Graf Zeppelin;* Triborough Bridge opens in New York City; *African Comet* launched; catamaran car ferry testing; Chinese junks in harbor; horseless carriages on parade.

Human stunts and oddities. Includes airborne stunts; finger wrestling in Bavarian costume; motorcycles; Black child with bulging eyes on command; baby beauty contests; woman with collection of 26,000 spoons; armless harness racing trainer; hurdle racing in snow; ski jumping on grass hill; chariot races on beach; 3 1/2 year old child weighing 101 pounds; house painting competition; flagpole sitter; auto daredevils; demolition derbies; artist sculpts with salt; artist sculpts with wool; baby crawling race; man eats razor blades, light bulbs and tacks at dinner table; fire department water fight; fraternity pranks; parachutist dives off suspension bridge; Japanese children paint designs on bald heads; The Flying Wallendas; man paints women's bare backs; man buries himself in ice; woman freefalls 24,000 feet; one-legged man walks on hands down mountainside; Model T traverses rope bridge on rims; baby strongman; basket-carrying competition; man wallpapers house interior with labels; bathing beauties on rocking horses suspended over pool; skiers use toboggan slide; girls play "king of the mountain" on raft; mud fight on college campus; surfboard towed by glider; woman powders nose and applies makeup; bathing beauties frolic in ice factory to beat summer heat; "cavemen" play bridge with six-foot wooden cards; kid writes everything upside down; wedding held in rollercoaster; highwire acts.

Animal stunts and oddities. Includes horse with mustache; goat acrobatics; bull with unicorn horn; dog show for mutts; frog jumping; handles for carrying dogs; chimp feeds sea lions; chicken plays mechanical baseball game; dogs talk; deer eats at table and rides in car; pet lion taken shopping; cow milked on Park Avenue median; dog catches fish with paws out of stream; monkeys sent aloft in hot-air balloon; polar bears cool off with ice blocks in zoo; lion cubs pop balloons with claws; mail delivered by dog sled; birds build nests in chimneys; dog jumps into net from platform; chimp has birthday party; chicken raised in glass jar.

Sports. Includes Alpine skiing; auto racing; baseball; basketball; bicycle racing; billiards; bobsledding; bodybuilding; bowling; boxing; bullfighting; college football; crew; curling; distance running; diving; dog sledding; endurance swimming; equestrian; fencing; golf; gymnastics; harness racing; high jumping; hockey; horses; ice skating; indoor soccer; kayaking; Little League; lumberjacking; marathons; motocross; motorcycle racing; pole vaulting; polo; powerboats; rodeo; roller derby; sailing; ski jumping; soccer; steeplechasing; swimming; tennis; track and field; water skiing; wrestling; women in sports. Also holds particular sports events.

Personalities. Political, artistic, achievers, sports, military and celebrities.
Size & Elements: Videotape: 1" and 3/4" (over 70 hours; masters); VHS and Betamax (viewing copies available on request).
Cataloging: Published catalog; research library; cross-references computerized cataloging for staff use only.
Access: Available to the public for duplication, licensing and reuse. Screening

copies available. Research fees not charged. Research requests accepted by mail and telephone.
Rights: Material in the public domain.
Licensing: Available for licensing and reuse. License fees charged.
Restrictions: None specified.
Viewing Facilities: None specified; screening copies available.
Duplication Facilities: Videotape (any format, with time code). Duplication fees charged (credited toward order).
Representative: Bill Denahy, 3 River Road, Grandview, NY 10960.

NORTH CAROLINA (Charlotte)

WALTER J. KLEIN COMPANY, LTD.
Box 2087
Charlotte, NC 28247-2087
(704) 542-1403
Fax: (704) 542-0735

Street address: 6311 Carmel Road

Contact: Distribution Department
Services: Film and videotape producer and distributor. Material available to the public.
Description: Educational and instructional materials.
Titles include: *Consumers Want to Know About Diabetes; Engine Additives: Seeing is Believing; Garden; The Great American Tee Shirt; From Here To There*, on automobiles and child safety; *Homework is What We Do Best*, about real estate sales careers; *The Lives We Touch*, on the Reform Jewish movement in America; *The Magnificent Ingredient*, on soy sauce; *The Making of a Television Commercial; The National Skin Care Quiz; A New Leash on Life*, about pet care; *Pharmacy is My Tomorrow; The Right Move*, about family and possessions; *The Robotics Phenomenon; Secrets of the E.T.*, on electric typewriters; *The Standard of Perfection*, pertaining to dinnerware manufacturing; *What Americans Should Know About Asthma; What's an Ergonomic?; Which Vitamins?;* and *Wrinkles*, relating to the history of starch and other consumer products in the home.
Size & Elements: Film and videotape (approx. 50 titles total).
Cataloging: Published catalog.
Access: Open to the public. Requests accepted by mail and telephone.
Rights: Apply for information.
Licensing: Apply for information.
Restrictions: None specified.
Viewing Facilities: None.
Duplication Facilities: None.

NORTH CAROLINA (Durham)

AMERICAN DANCE FESTIVAL
P.O. Box 6097, College Station
Durham, NC 27708
(919) 684-6402

Street address: 804 Berkeley Street, Durham, NC 27705

Charles L. Reinhart (Director)

Contact: Don Anderson (Administrative Director)
Services: Modern dance institution. Film and videotape collection available to researchers and scholars only for distribution.
Description: Documentation of historical modern dance. Collection includes films (1934-present) of works performed at the American Dance Festival in New London, Conn. and Bennington, Vermont. Videotapes (1974-present) document performances, classes and other events at the American Dance Festival.
Size & Elements: Film: 16mm (over 75 films). Videotape: 3/4" and VHS ("several hundred" videotapes); and 1/2" open reel (amount unspecified).
Cataloging: Computerized cataloging for staff use only.
Access: Available to researchers and scholars only. Maintained for distribution and rental rather than for research or reuse. Research fees not charged.
Rights: Full rights held to some material. Some rights held to all material. Additional clearances may be necessary in some cases if material is to be reused.
Licensing: Apply for information. License fees charged in some cases.
Restrictions: Restrictions may apply in some cases.
Viewing Facilities: None.

Duplication Facilities: None.
Representative: John Mueller, Dance Film Archive, University of Rochester, Rochester, NY 14627; (716) 275-5236 or (716) 275-4292.

NORTH CAROLINA (Durham)

DUKE UNIVERSITY
WILLIAM R. PERKINS LIBRARY
MANUSCRIPT DEPARTMENT
Durham, NC 27706
(919) 684-3372
Fax: (919) 684-2855

Robert Byrd (Curator)

Contact: Linda McCurdy (Interim Assistant Curator for Reader Services)
Services: University library. Film and videotape collections available for research; some videotapes may be duplicated for educational or scholarly purposes. Commercial use contracts are possibly available.
Description: *Movies of Local People*, filmed and produced by H. Lee Waters, was a documentary film project showing community life and special events in 118 different towns in North Carolina, Virginia and Tennessee. Mr. Waters visited these towns from July 29, 1936 to July 21, 1942 (when his business of portrait photography was slow) and filmed people on the streets and at work. This was done on contract with downtown movie theaters which would then show his films as special attractions along with the regular feature.
The restoration project, being funded by Duke University and researched in conjunction with Mr. Waters, is aimed at locating the 252 films originally produced, now dispersed throughout these three states, and obtaining the original materials in exchange for providing viewing copies. Originals collected will be restored, preserved and used to create an archives which will be housed at Duke University. To date, approximately half of the unique camera originals have been located at various libraries, local historical societies and chambers of commerce.
The Socialist Party of America Collection (8 reels). Films featuring Eugene V. Debs, Norman M. Thomas, and Darlington Hoopes. Sample titles include: *Eugene Debs, Labor's Merlyn* (1934); *The Challenge of Young Socialists* (1939), documenting the Tenth National Convention of the Young People's Socialist League at Cleveland, Ohio during September 1-4, 1939; *1944 Socialist Convention*, in which Norman Thomas, the presidential nominee, and Darlington Hoopes, the vice presidential nominee, appear with their wives; the 1956 acceptance speech of Hoopes, presidential nominee of the Socialist Party (produced by CBS).
Duke University Living History Program. Videotaped oral histories pertaining to U.S. foreign relations and other subjects. Interviewees include George Agree, Ellsworth Bunker, Lucius D. Clay, Sherman Cooper, Angier Biddle Duke, J. W. Fulbright, W. Stanton Griffis, W. Averell Harriman, Charles H. Percy, George Pillsbury, J. B. Rhine, Dean Rusk, Ryoichi Sasakawa and Earl E. T. Smith.
Robert L. Eichelberger (12 films). Material relating to the U.S. military occupation of Japan. Includes military reviews in Japan; views of Eichelberger's official residence in Tokyo; Army football games (1948); feature films on the Eighth Army; scenes reflecting Japanese culture, such as pearl diving and a marriage ceremony; gatherings of officials in Tokyo; and a youth rally in Nuremberg, Germany (1936).
Carlyle Marney. Film of the Baptist theologian's trip to South America; two programs from the television series *Look Up and Live*.
J. Walter Thompson Company Archives. Videotapes (107 items, mostly 3/4") include case histories for the development of television commercials, public relations productions, company seminars, commercials, the company's fortieth anniversary celebration in Mexico, office parties, gatherings and training sessions. Videotapes were collected from domestic and international offices; some are in foreign languages.
Size & Elements: Film: primarily 16mm (amount unspecified). Videotape: 1", 3/4" and VHS (amounts unspecified).
Cataloging: Limited inventories and guides.
Access: Open to the public. Research fees not charged. Although staff does not perform research, outside researchers are welcomed. Research requests accepted by mail, telephone and in person.
Rights: Clearances may be necessary in some cases if material is to be reused. Copies of the *Living History Program* interviews are available for deposit in other institutions for educational or scholarly purposes (duplication fees charged). Rights to J. Walter Thompson Company archives may be held by the company or by advertisers; copyright restrictions may apply.
Licensing: Commercial use contracts possibly available (apply for

information).
Restrictions: Restrictions may apply. Material in the J. Walter Thompson Company archives may not be duplicated without the permission of the Secretary of J. Walter Thompson Company and/or the permission of the advertiser.
Viewing Facilities: Film and videotape.
Duplication Facilities: Film and videotape (at other Duke University facilities).

NORTH CAROLINA (Durham)

NATIONAL PRESS PHOTOGRAPHERS ASSOCIATION, INC.
3200 Croasdaile Drive, Suite 306
Durham, NC 27705
(919) 383-7246

Charles H. Cooper (Executive Director)

Contact: Charles H. Cooper
Services: Association. Films and videotapes available to members, nonmembers, press organizations and educational institutions.
Description: Films include: Television News Awards *News Clips* (1972-78), featuring the winners in all categories of the annual television news competitions; *Careers in Broadcast News,* for high-school and college career guidance classes and counselors; *On Seeing,* a discourse on how a news photographer covers assignments for *The Christian Science Monitor;* and *No More Me,* a documentary about a young mother's awareness of her impending death from cancer, produced from still photographs by free-lance photographer Charles O'Rear.

Videotapes available include: *Television News Clips* (1978-84); *Kennerly Interview,* an interview with David Hume Kennerly, President Ford's personal photographer; *Arthur Rothstein and the Dustbowl Revisited,* Arthur Rothstein revisiting Cimarron County, Oklahoma, where he photographed the Cobel family for the Farm Security Administration in the 1930s; and *The Numbers Game,* in which a staff photographer for the 1982 TV News Photography Station of the Year, WFAA-TV, Dallas, discusses the current state of television news. Also holds videotape (21 hours) recorded live at the 25th anniversary Television News Video Workshop in March 1985.

Includes lectures covering basic skills of television photography and photojournalism. Titles include: *Situation Ethics Panel Discussion for TV News Photographers; Shooting the Non-Visual Story; Being a Visual Storyteller; Art of TV Photography from a Helicopter; Video Mistakes You're Gonna Make and How to Hold a Camera Steady; Writing with a Camera; Working As a Network Freelancer;* and *The Art of Working with People in Television Feature Stories.*
Size & Elements: Film: 16mm (10 titles). Videotape: 3/4" (approx. 30 hours); VHS and Betamax (some titles).
Cataloging: Brochure; list.
Access: Lending library open to the public. Research requests accepted by mail and telephone.
Rights: Additional clearances may be necessary in some cases if material is to be reused.
Licensing: Apply for information.
Restrictions: None specified.
Viewing Facilities: None.
Duplication Facilities: None.
Related Materials: Audiotapes; slide/tape presentations.

NORTH CAROLINA (Gastonia)

SCHIELE MUSEUM OF NATURAL HISTORY AND PLANETARIUM, INC.
AUDIO VISUAL DIVISION
P.O. Box 953
Gastonia, NC 28053
(704) 866-6901

Richard Alan Stout (Executive Director)

Contact: Dennis M. Goff (Audio Visual Specialist)
Services: Museum. Videotape collection available to the public for duplication and reuse.
Description: Wildlife, natural outdoors, Boy Scouting (early 1940s-50s), travel through North America and some of South America.

Boy Scout films. Titles include: *Boy Scouts of Gastonia County: 1940s* and *Piedmont Camp: 1930s-50s,* documentaries showing Boy Scout camp

activities, narrated by Bud Schiele; *Jamboree #1,* including footage of Scouts learning about nature and dissecting frogs at the Piedmont Scout Camp; and *Jamboree #2: 1940s,* showing a Scout jamboree in Washington, D.C. (includes footage of the White House and National Archives).

Travel, nature and scenic films. Includes: *St. Lawrence: 1940s,* a film of maps showing the profile of the lakes and a boat trip on the St. Lawrence Power Project and the Long Sault Dam; *Canadian Rockies: 1950s,* mountains and parks of the Rockies, with footage of Mrs. Schiele feeding chipmunks and a dinosaur replica built at actual size; *Niagara Falls: 1940s,* taken from the *Maid of the Mist,* at the foot of the falls; *Indians: 1949,* a film about the Arizona and Seminole Indians showing strange shapes in wind-carved rocks and Indians weaving; *White Mountains of Quebec: 1940s,* including footage of a steam locomotive ride to the top of Mount Washington, waterfalls, rock formations and a trolley car; *Colorado — Switzerland of America: 1940s,* including footage of Buffalo Bill's tombstone, Pikes Peak, chipmunks and blue jays; *Mexico: 1930s,* including footage of U.S. Mail plane, a bullfight and horse-drawn carriages; *Charleston: Late 1930s,* historic Charleston, South Carolina, including footage of the Cooper River Bridge, Charleston City Hall, Fort Sumter and canoeing in the swamp; *Safety Parade: 1952,* a parade including the Boy Scouts, Miss Safety Queen 1952 and the Belmont High School Band; *New Mexico: 1940s,* including footage of a Mexican *fiesta* and parade; *Yellowstone: 1930s,* including footage of the Fountain Paint Pot, Old Faithful and the Twin Geysers; *California: 1940s,* including footage of the Golden Gate Bridge, Ramona's Marriage Place, boats and beach scenes; *National Park: 1940s,* on Wind Cave National Park, Devil's Tower National Monument and Bandelier National Monument Frijoles Canyon; *Central America: 1940s,* taken in the Caribbean and West Indies during a cruise; *Gaspé and Bonaventure: 1930s,* featuring ocean scenes; *Black Hills, South Dakota: Late 1940s,* showing the graves of Wild Bill Hickok and Calamity Jane, and the view from Harney Peak; *Utah and Bear River: 1950s,* travel by train through the scenic countryside in the fall, showing the Mormon Temple and Great Salt Lake; *Yellowstone Park: Late 1940s,* including footage of a grizzly bear, timber wolf and elk; *Salt Lake City: Late 1940s,* showing mountains, lakes and the copper mines; *Smoky Mountains: Early 1960s,* featuring hummingbirds, the making of molasses and trout fishing; *Birds "Nestbuilding": 1930s,* including hummingbirds, kingfishers and owls; *Hunting Dogs: Late 1930s,* including retrievers, poodles and bird dogs in action; *Montreal and Ottawa: 1950s,* including spring flowers and black bears; *Zuñi: 1950s,* on the Zuñi Tribe Indians; *Canadian Geese and Mallards; Hummingbirds; Mt. Desert Island,* scenes of sea gulls and the rocky coast; *Alaska: 1950s,* on Harbor Town and the railroad through the mountains; and *Florida: 1940s,* including rubber trees, alligators and Mrs. Schiele drinking from the Fountain of Youth.
Size & Elements: Videotape: VHS (60 videotapes, each 10 to 60 min.).
Cataloging: Shot lists.
Access: Open to the public. Available for duplication and reuse. Research fees charged. Requests accepted by mail, telephone and in person (walk-in).
Rights: Full rights held to some material.
Licensing: Apply for information.
Restrictions: None specified.
Viewing Facilities: Film and videotape.
Duplication Facilities: Videotape.

NORTH CAROLINA (Montreat)

OFFICE OF HISTORY (MONTREAT) OF THE PRESBYTERIAN STUDY CENTER
Box 849
Montreat, NC 28757
(704) 669-7061

Robert Benedetto (Director)

Contact: William B. Bynum (Archivist)
Services: Religious organization; archives. *Material is completely inaccessible to research or reuse of any kind at this time.*
Description: Formerly known as Historical Foundation of the Presbyterian and Reformed Churches, Library and Archives. Collection holds historical films on foreign mission work and more current educational films used within the Church to promote particular Church programs, all produced by the Presbyterian and Reformed Churches.

Archives plans to make the films accessible to the public in the future.
Size & Elements: Film: format unspecified (approx. 30 to 50 titles).
Cataloging: None specified.
Access: *Not open to the public at the present time. Research requests not accepted.*

NORTH CAROLINA (Raleigh)

Rights: Full rights held to all material.
Licensing: Material not available for duplication and reuse.
Restrictions: No reuse permitted.
Viewing Facilities: None.
Duplication Facilities: None.

NORTH CAROLINA (Raleigh)

ACID RAIN FOUNDATION, INC.
1509 Varsity Drive
Raleigh, NC 27606
(919) 737-3520
Fax: (919) 737-3593

Dr. Harriet Stubbs (Executive Director)

Contact: Administrative Assistant
Services: Foundation. Film collection primarily maintained for distribution.
Description: Films relating to acid rain and air pollution and associated scientific issues, sponsored by environmentalists and utility companies.
Size & Elements: Film: format unspecified (5 titles).
Cataloging: None specified.
Access: Maintained for distribution and rental rather than for research or reuse.
Rights: Full rights held to some material. No rights held to other material.
Licensing: Apply for information.
Restrictions: None specified.
Viewing Facilities: None.
Duplication Facilities: None.

NORTH CAROLINA (Raleigh)

NORTH CAROLINA DIVISION OF ARCHIVES AND HISTORY
ICONOGRAPHIC COLLECTION
109 East Jones Street
Raleigh, NC 27611
(919) 733-3952

Dr. William S. Price (Director)

Contact: Roger Jones (Iconographic Archivist)
Services: State government archival agency. Film collection available to researchers, scholars and the public for research and duplication.
Description: Collection focuses on North Carolina history and politics. Holds films transferred from The (North Carolina) Division of Historic Sites and Museums or acquired from other state agencies; some material was obtained from individuals either by purchase or donation.
Titles include: *American Governors Tour Russia* (1959), documenting the tour by eight U.S. governors including North Carolina Governor Luther Hodges; *Ready on the Home Front* (ca. 1943), describing how the public alert system was designed to work in the event of an enemy attack; *Interviews with the Sixth North Carolina Regiment,* interviews with the reactivated Sixth North Carolina Regiment of the Confederate Army; *First Pageant of the Lost Colony* (1934); *Tourism in North Carolina* (1966); *Target: Satisfaction* (ca. 1962), covering the process of production and manufacturing of tobacco into cigarettes; *Rugged Road to Salem* (1959), the history of the Moravian settlements of Wachovia and Salem, and a tour of the Old Salem restoration; *Tar Heel Family* (1954), on North Carolina's transition from an agrarian to an industrial economy; *The Lafayette Escadrille* (1916), on the World War I air corps and its American members; *High Tide at Gettysburg,* a dramatization of the battle of Gettysburg through the use of statues representing men locked in combat; *Display of an Ancient Anchor,* shots of an ancient anchor being unloaded and weighed; *Re-enactments of Battles* (1964), incorporating reenactments of Civil War battles, including the Battle of New Market, Virginia (May 15, 1864) and the Antietam Campaign at Sharpsburg, Maryland (September 1862), with the participation of the 6th North Carolina Regiment; *Impossible Not An American Word* (1979), chronicling the establishment of the Southern Power Company in 1904, and its subsequent growth into the present-day Duke Power Company, with scenes of construction and power plants in the Piedmont region; and *North Carolina Lighthouses* (1981), showing the Cape Hatteras and Cape Lookout lights.
Size & Elements: Film: format unspecified (73 reels).
Cataloging: Card catalogs.
Access: Open to researchers, scholars and the public for research and duplication, depending on condition of film. Research requests accepted by mail, telephone and in person (by appointment only), subject to case-by-case

evaluation.
Rights: Full rights held to all material.
Licensing: Apply for information.
Restrictions: Access to materials depends on condition of film.
Viewing Facilities: Film and videotape.
Duplication Facilities: None.

NORTH CAROLINA (Research Triangle Park)

AMERICAN SOCIAL HEALTH ASSOCIATION
P.O. Box 13827
Research Triangle Park, NC 27709
(919) 361-2742

Street address: 100 Capitola Drive, Durham, NC 27713

Alan Gross (Acting Executive Director)

Contact: Sandy Moy (Herpes Resource Center Coordinator)
Services: Association. Videotape available for purchase.
Description: Distributes one videotape about herpes: *Common Concerns, Common Sense* (27 min.), on coping with the disease.
Size & Elements: Videotape: 3/4", VHS and Betamax (1 title; viewing copies).
Cataloging: None.
Access: Available for purchase.
Rights: Apply for information.
Licensing: Apply for information.
Restrictions: None specified.
Viewing Facilities: None.
Duplication Facilities: None.

NORTH CAROLINA (Wilmington)

UNIVERSITY OF NORTH CAROLINA AT WILMINGTON
DEVRIES-BULLUCK COLLECTION
SPECIAL COLLECTIONS
WILLIAM MADISON RANDALL LIBRARY
MS #53
601 South College Road
Wilmington, NC 28403-3297
(919) 395-3760
(919) 395-3276

Lana D. Taylor (Special Collections Librarian)

Contacts: Lana D. Taylor; Sue Cody (Head of Reference)
Services: University library. Videotape collection open to the public for research.
Description: Collection recently donated. Contents (unverified) include advertising, political campaign promotions and spots, documentaries and miscellaneous material (1960s-87).
Size & Elements: Videotape: 2" (12 videotapes); Betamax (246 videotapes).
Cataloging: Material uncataloged at present.
Access: Open to the public. Research fees not charged. Research requests accepted by mail, telephone and in person (walk-in).
Rights: Rights status of material not known.
Licensing: Apply for information.
Restrictions: Apply for information.
Viewing Facilities: None.
Duplication Facilities: None.

NORTH CAROLINA (Winston-Salem)

R. J. REYNOLDS TOBACCO USA
401 North Main Street
Winston-Salem, NC 27102
(919) 741-5000
Fax: (919) 741-4238

Contacts: Seth Moskowitz (919/741-7698) (for *Tobaccoville*); Kay Young (919/741-7645) (for *World Tobacco Auctioneering Championship*); Jan Cousart (919/741-6995) (for *We Asked the People of South Africa*)
Services: Corporation; corporate archives.
Description: *Tobaccoville* is a videotape tour of the world's largest and most automated cigarette manufacturing facility. *1987 World Tobacco Auctioneering*

Championship is a videotape of the seventh annual contest highlighting the skills and talents of tobacco auctioneers, including interviews with champion John Kessler.
Size & Elements: Videotape: format unspecified (2 titles).
Cataloging: Apply for information.
Access: Apply for information.
Rights: Apply for information.
Licensing: Apply for information.
Restrictions: Apply for information.
Viewing Facilities: None.
Duplication Facilities: None.
Related Materials: *We Asked The People of South Africa,* a videotape of a multi-image slide show discussing why RJR Nabisco has chosen to maintain its operations in South Africa.

NORTH DAKOTA

NORTH DAKOTA (Bismarck)

STATE HISTORICAL SOCIETY OF NORTH DAKOTA
STATE ARCHIVES AND HISTORICAL RESEARCH LIBRARY
North Dakota Heritage Center
Bismarck, ND 58505-0179
(701) 224-2668

Gerald G. Newborg (State Archivist)

Contact: Gerald G. Newborg
Services: Historical society. Film and videotape collection available to the public for research, licensing and reuse.
Description: Television newsfilm footage covering politics, agriculture, recreation, and disasters (ca. 1953-80) from WDAY-TV, Fargo; KFYR-TV, Bismarck; KXJB-TV, West Fargo; KMOT-TV, Minot; KUMV-TV, Williston; and local programming from Prairie Public Television, Fargo.

Also holds commercial film and videotapes, the work of North Dakota filmmaker Frithjof Holmboe, and local educational programs (ca. 1915-87).
Size & Elements: Film: format unspecified (positive, negative, originals and release prints). Videotape: 3/4" and 1/2" (masters and viewing copies). (Approx. 2 million feet total).
Cataloging: Card catalogs; finding aids.
Access: Available to the public for research, licensing and reuse. Research fees not charged. Research requests accepted by mail, telephone and in person (walk-in and by appointment).
Rights: Full rights held to all material.
Licensing: Available for licensing and reuse. License fees not charged.
Restrictions: None specified.
Viewing Facilities: Film; videotape (3/4" and 1/2").
Duplication Facilities: Videotape (3/4" and 1/2").

NORTH DAKOTA (Fargo)

NORTHCOAST COMMUNICATION, INC.
1321 23rd Street South, Suite A
Fargo, ND 58103
(701) 237-9491

Virginia Gregg (President)

Contacts: Virginia Gregg; Neal Miller (Videographer)
Services: Videotape producer; communications consultant. Footage available for duplication, licensing and reuse. Designs and constructs promotional display systems. Custom shooting services provided on request.
Description: Agriculture, including footage of planting, harvesting, food processing, manufacturing, wheat, barley and potatoes; medicine, including new technology, heart scanners and brain monitors, surgery equipment, lab and dental equipment; geriatrics and nursing homes; stock car races; parades, fairs (state and county fairs) and air shows; National Steam Threshing reunion (old-fashioned harvesting); scenics of winter, summer, rivers, birds and squirrels; the Blue Angels precision flying team; community Christmas scenes; elementary school and classroom scenes; Centennial celebrations in North Dakota and Minnesota cities; and Bridal Fair footage.
Size & Elements: Videotape: 3/4" (approx. 50 hours; masters).
Cataloging: Computerized cataloging in process; will be available to researchers.

Access: Available to the public for duplication and reuse. Research fees negotiable. Research requests accepted by mail, telephone and in person (by appointment only).
Rights: Full rights held to all material. Additional clearances may be necessary in some cases if material is to be reused (e.g., Bridal Fair footage contains background music requiring clearance).
Licensing: Available for licensing, subject to restrictions. License fees charged.
Restrictions: Permission from client may be necessary to reuse specific material.
Viewing Facilities: Videotape (3/4" and VHS).
Duplication Facilities: Videotape (3/4", VHS and Betamax).

NORTH DAKOTA (Fargo)

BILL SNYDER FILMS, INC.
Box 2784
Fargo, ND 58103
(701) 293-3600

Street address: 1419 First Avenue

Ron Abrahamson (President)

Contact: Tom Tollefson (Production Director)
Services: Film and videotape producer; stock footage sales library.
Description: Begins 1957. Includes footage from industrial films; educational footage on agriculture; television commercials; North Dakota travel and tourism films; North Dakota scenics; National Parks; Minnesota lakes and farms; fishing; winter scenes; documentaries on transportation and worldwide use of North Dakota wheat; wildlife footage; ecology; giant flocks of geese, ducks and cranes.

Also holds a black and white release print of a film on small towns in North Dakota, dating back to 1916. The rights to this footage are jointly held with the North Dakota Historical Society.
Size & Elements: Film: 35mm (a small amount); 16mm (approx. 3 million feet, mostly Ektachrome Commercial [ECO] color reversal positive film). Videotape: 3/4" (amount unspecified). ECO was shot almost exclusively until 1981; the 3/4" videotape collection begins ca. 1983.
Cataloging: Card catalog (in process of computerization).
Access: Available to the public for reuse. Research fees charged in some cases, depending upon nature of request. Research requests accepted by mail and telephone.
Rights: Full rights held to all material, except to historical film of North Dakota towns, in which rights are jointly held with North Dakota Historical Society.
Licensing: License fees charged.
Restrictions: None specified.
Viewing Facilities: Film (Moviola flatbed); videotape (3/4").
Duplication Facilities: Videotape (3/4" and 1/2").

OHIO

OHIO (Akron)

ALL-AMERICAN SOAP BOX DERBY
P.O. Box 7233, Derby Downs
Akron, OH 44306
(216) 733-8723

Street address: 789 Derby Downs Drive

Jeffrey A. Iula (General Manager)

Contact: Jeffrey A. Iula
Services: Film library. Films available for rental.
Description: Five films relating to the Soap Box Derby. The earliest, *Official Pictures of the First All-American Soap Box Derby* (1934) contains scenes and commentary from the first Derby ever held, in Dayton, Ohio. Another film depicts the first race at Derby Downs (1936). Three other films (1968-present) discuss construction techniques, father and son companionship and the excitement and competitiveness of the sport.
Size & Elements: Film: 16mm (5 titles).
Cataloging: None specified.

Access: Available to the public for rental. Research fees charged. Requests accepted by mail and telephone.
Rights: Full rights held to some material.
Licensing: Apply for information.
Restrictions: None specified.
Viewing Facilities: None.
Duplication Facilities: None.

OHIO (Akron)

GOODYEAR TIRE AND RUBBER
GOODYEAR ARCHIVES
Department 798
1144 East Market Street
Akron, OH 44316
(216) 796-8928

Mary Manley (Community Relations Representative)

Contact: Mary Manley
Services: Corporation; corporate archives. Film collection available for in-house use only.
Description: Blimps and airships; Macy's Thanksgiving Day Parade in New York City, featuring oversized balloon figures; some automobile racing footage from the Indianapolis 500 (ca. 1960s).
Size & Elements: Film: 16mm (over 100 titles).
Cataloging: Material uncataloged.
Access: Not open to the public. For in-house use only. Collection is currently in process of being relocated. Research requests not accepted.
Rights: Full rights held to all material.
Licensing: Apply for information.
Restrictions: Access to and use of collection restricted.
Viewing Facilities: None.
Duplication Facilities: None.

OHIO (Akron)

THE UNIVERSITY OF AKRON
ARCHIVES OF THE HISTORY OF AMERICAN PSYCHOLOGY
Bierce Library
Akron, Ohio 44325
(216) 375-7285

John A. Popplestone, Ph.D. (Director)
Marion White McPherson (Associate Director)

Contact: John A. Popplestone
Services: Film archives. Material available for research and scholarly use. Some items available for duplication and reuse, subject to restrictions.
Description: Established 1965. Films come from many sources, although most are instructional or educational. There is a small collection of films which originated as laboratory materials, and some home movies of psychological conventions.
   Of note is the film *Function of the Brain* (USSR, 1932, directed by V. I. Pudovkin), available on loan to educational organizations in a 16mm English-language version. This film was prepared by and under the direction of Ivan Petrovich Pavlov and was projected by him at the 14th International Congress of Physiology in Rome in 1932. Known elsewhere as *Mechanics of the Brain,* it demonstrates Soviet experiments relating to conditioned and unconditioned reflexes, using dogs and children as subjects.
Size & Elements: Film: various formats (approx. 200 items).
Cataloging: Films are cataloged with other archival material, controlled by the surnames of people and the names of organizations. There is no catalog of films per se.
Access: Open to any qualified scholar. Some films have restrictions on viewing and/or duplication. Research fees not charged. Videotape or film copies of unrestricted material can be made for qualified users at their expense. Materials may be used only on premises, with the exception of *Function of the Brain.*
Rights: Full rights held to some material. Additional clearances may be necessary in some cases if material is to be reused.
Licensing: Available for licensing and reuse, subject to restrictions. License and usage fees not charged.
Restrictions: Copyright and/or privacy restrictions apply to some material.
Viewing Facilities: Film (projector). Other facilities can be arranged through the University.

Duplication Facilities: None.
Related Materials: Documents and other non-film archival materials held in Archives. This collection supports the Child Development Film Archives at the University of Akron (q.v.).

OHIO (Akron)

THE UNIVERSITY OF AKRON
CHILD DEVELOPMENT FILM ARCHIVES
Bierce Library
Akron, Ohio 44325
(216) 375-7285

John A. Popplestone, Ph.D. (Director)
Marion White McPherson (Associate Director)

Contact: John A. Popplestone
Services: Film archives. Material available for research and scholarly use. Some items available for duplication and reuse, subject to restrictions.
Description: Established 1976 at the University as an adjunct to the Archives of the History of American Psychology (q.v.). Contains films taken for a variety of research purposes. Largest collections were developed by Arnold Gesell and L. Joseph Stone. Also includes footage taken for Margaret Mahler and reels photographed by six additional cinematographers. Collection is expanding.
   16mm prints of certain film photographed for Arnold Gesell are available for loan at no cost except for handling charges. These depict the cinematographic techniques he used as well as illustrative scenes of bathing, feeding and mobility.
Size & Elements: Film: various formats (804,232 feet, approx. 3,500 individual films).
Cataloging: Inventory sheet available for each film. Footage portraying following topics can be identified: child[ren] — number, sex, age, ethnicity, amount and nature of clothing, biopathology and psychopathology, as well as film that focuses on human details rather than the body as a whole; adult[s] — number, sex, and interaction with child[ren]; animal[s] — number and species; specific activities of the child[ren] and adult[s]; the milieu — laboratory, schoolroom, museum, etc.; the equipment or laboratory appurtenances (e.g., activity crib, visual cliff, psychometric equipment); play materials and children's productions (e.g., drawings, paintings, block structures).
   Also specified are titles (if any); the purpose of the footage, the presence of sound; whether the pictures are chromatic or achromatic (color or black and white); the existence and location of relevant documents; ratings of visual and audio clarity; names of members of the cast and of institutions; length of the footage; its width, projection time; container labels and storage location.
Access: Open to any qualified scholar. For in-house use only, except for certain Arnold Gesell films, which are available for loan. Some films restricted from viewing and/or duplication. Researchers are provided with an opportunity to review all inventories and to identify films they wish to consult. These films are then projected for them. Research fees not charged. Videotape or film copies of unrestricted material can be made for qualified users at their expense.
Rights: Full rights held to some material. Additional clearances may be necessary in some cases if material is to be reused.
Licensing: Available for licensing and reuse, subject to restrictions. License and usage fees not charged.
Restrictions: Copyright and/or privacy restrictions apply to some material (e.g., film depicting juvenile psychiatric patients, etc.)
Viewing Facilities: Film (projector). Other facilities can be arranged through University.
Duplication Facilities: None.

OHIO (Beachwood)

VIDEO GENESIS, INC.
24000 Mercantile Road
Beachwood, OH 44122
(216) 464-3635
Fax: (216) 464-5630

Howard Schwartz (President)

Contacts: Bill Roth (Producer/Director); Gary Gottchaulk (Producer/ Director)
Services: Videotape producer; post production facility. Material available for duplication, licensing and reuse.
Description: Footage of Cleveland, the city, people, scenics, traffic and aerials;

steel manufacturing (rolling, forming, etc.); industry (chemical manufacturing); medical and health-related footage of hospitals, patients, doctors and surgery; wildlife and nature; ships in locks and ports; and traffic scenes with cars, trucks, semitrailers, off-road vehicles and snowmobiles.
Size & Elements: Videotape: 1", Betacam and 3/4" (masters); 3/4" and 1/2" (viewing copies). (Approximately 100 hours).
Cataloging: Computerized cataloging available for staff use only.
Access: Available to the public for duplication and reuse. Research requests accepted by mail, telephone and in person (by appointment only).
Rights: Full rights held to some material. Some rights held to all material. Additional clearances may be necessary in some cases if material is to be reused (client approval required in some cases).
Licensing: Available for licensing. License fees charged (fees negotiable).
Restrictions: None specified.
Viewing Facilities: Videotape (1", 3/4", Betacam and 1/2").
Duplication Facilities: Videotape (1", 3/4", Betacam and 1/2").

OHIO (Bowling Green)

BOWLING GREEN STATE UNIVERSITY CENTER FOR ARCHIVAL COLLECTIONS
Jerome Library
Bowling Green, OH 43403
(419) 372-2411

Paul D. Yon (Director)

Contact: Ann Bowers (Assistant Director)
Services: University archives. Film collection available for research purposes only.
Description: Labor history collection features films on Building Trade and Construction Workers Union, inter-union activities, CIO day camps and local Golden Gloves boxing.
Sam Pollack Collection. Named for the labor organizer, this collection contains film clips and newsreels from the early 1950s campaign against the Right-to-Work Amendment in Ohio.
Other footage covers the University's history, football and basketball films (1948-72) and University-produced programs for local public television.
Size & Elements: Film: 16mm and 8mm (600 titles; positive).
Cataloging: Inventory of films.
Access: Open to the public. Research fees charged. Research requests accepted by mail, telephone and in person.
Rights: Some rights held to some material. Some material in the public domain.
Licensing: Apply for information. License fees not charged.
Restrictions: Available for research use only.
Viewing Facilities: By arrangement only.
Duplication Facilities: None.

OHIO (Bryan)

NATIONAL REYE'S SYNDROME FOUNDATION
P.O. Box 829
Bryan, OH 43506
(419) 636-2679

Street address: 426 North Lewis

John E. Freudenberger (President)

Contact: Terri J. Freudenberger (Co-Founder)
Services: Nonprofit health agency; foundation. Films and videotapes available to the public for research, purchase and reuse.
Description: *Reye's Syndrome: Child Killer in Disguise* (1985, 26 min.) is a documentary designed to increase public awareness of the disease and its toll on children and their families. Experts on the disease speak about its symptoms, Senator Metzenbaum speaks on placing a mandatory warning on aspirin products and parents of victims relate their experiences with this serious disease. A public service announcement (PSA) (:30), featuring Dick Van Dyke (Honorary National Chairman) is also available.
Size & Elements: Film: 16mm (1 title; several PSAs). Videotape: 3/4" and VHS (1 title).
Cataloging: Dope sheets or release sheets.
Access: Available to the public for research, purchase and reuse. Requests accepted by mail and telephone.

Rights: Full rights held to all material.
Licensing: Available for licensing, subject to restrictions. License fees depend on nature of the project.
Restrictions: Requests for licensing considered on a case-by-case basis.
Viewing Facilities: None.
Duplication Facilities: None.

OHIO (Cincinnati)

ATAVISTIC VIDEO
2254 Francis Lane, Suite 4
Cincinnati, OH 45206-2731

Kurt Kellison (Owner)

Contact: Kurt Kellison
Services: Videotape producer and distributor. Videotapes available for purchase.
Description: Video documentation of underground U.S. rock band performances. Produced under the name of Industrial Domination Faction (IDF), the videotapes use layered images and inverted chromas to create visuals which complement the music.
Titles include: *Entropy Video Compilation; Killdozer — Live Video; Pussy Galore — Maximum Penetration Video; Savage Republic — Disarmament; Live Skull — Skullfuck; IDF Mortality Video Compilation; Big Black Live;* and *Sonic Youth Live.*
Size & Elements: Videotape: VHS (10 titles; viewing copies).
Cataloging: List of available videotapes.
Access: Available for purchase. Requests accepted by mail.
Rights: Full rights held to all material.
Licensing: Apply for information.
Restrictions: None specified.
Viewing Facilities: None.
Duplication Facilities: None.
Related Materials: LP recordings; holograms.

OHIO (Cincinnati)

THE CINCINNATI HISTORICAL SOCIETY
Eden Park
Cincinnati, OH 45202
(513) 241-4622

Gale E. Peterson (Director)

Contact: Linda Bailey (Assistant Librarian, Photographs)
Services: Historical society. Film and videotape archives available for research and reuse, subject to clearance and approval.
Description: News footage from local Cincinnati television stations WLWT, WCPO and WKRC (1960s-70s); most of the footage originally comes from WLWT. WLWT programs on videotape include *Midwestern Hayride, Paul Dixon, On the Money,* and early shows hosted by Phil Donahue; local news and entertainment; Cincinnati Reds baseball games; commercials and documentaries.
Footage dating back to the 1930s (approx. 100 miscellaneous reels of 16mm film) includes scenes of Cincinnati parks, amusements, parades, boats on the Ohio River, aviation, railroads, commercials, the zoo and several interviews. A few 8mm home movies are also held.
Recently produced videotapes document Historical Society projects or use images from its collection.
Size & Elements: Film: 16mm (9,000 cans; mostly positive, some negative); 8mm (a "few" home movies). Videotape: 2" (approx. 300 videotapes); VHS (approx. 50 videotapes).
Cataloging: Research library; most material uncataloged.
Access: Open to researchers (limited access). Research requests accepted on a case-by-case basis. Research fees charged.
Rights: Rights to television collections retained by stations. Additional clearances may be necessary in some cases if material is to be reused.
Licensing: Available for licensing and reuse, subject to restrictions. Fees depend on amount and use of material.
Restrictions: Licensing or reuse requires clearance and approval of television stations.
Viewing Facilities: Videotape (VHS).
Duplication Facilities: None.

OHIO (Cincinnati)

PROCTER & GAMBLE CO.
CORPORATE ARCHIVES
P.O. Box 599
Cincinnati, OH 45201
(513) 983-5443
Fax: (513) 983-2060
Telex: 4333037 PG GOA

Street address: One Procter & Gamble Plaza, Cincinnati, OH 45202

Ed Rider (Corporate Archivist)

Contact: Ed Rider
Services: Corporation; corporate archives. Film and videotape collection available to researchers and scholars only (with special permission).
Description: Corporate films (1925-present), including publicity films, television commercials for company products, company "videomagazine" program, executive speeches, television soap operas and company-related films (e.g., production events).
    Collection is especially strong in Procter & Gamble television commercials (1950s-80s).
Size & Elements: Film: 16mm (500 cans; positive, negative and originals). Videotape: 3/4" (160 videotapes; masters).
Cataloging: Computerized cataloging for staff use only.
Access: Open to researchers and scholars only (with special permission). Research fees not charged. Research requests accepted by mail, telephone and in person (by appointment only).
Rights: Full rights held to some material. Some rights held to some material. Additional clearances may be necessary in some cases if material is to be reused.
Licensing: Possibly available for licensing, subject to restrictions. License fees not charged.
Restrictions: Material released only pursuant to approved contract with Procter & Gamble.
Viewing Facilities: Film (available in neighboring building); videotape (3/4").
Duplication Facilities: Film (16mm to videotape); videotape (3/4" and 1/2").

OHIO (Cincinnati)

PUBLIC LIBRARY OF CINCINNATI AND HAMILTON COUNTY
FILMS AND RECORDING CENTER
800 Vine Street
Library Square
Cincinnati, OH 45202
(513) 369-6924

James R. Hunt (Librarian-Director)

Contact: Robert Hudzik (Head of Films and Recordings Center)
Services: Library. Film and videotape collection available to the public for a service charge. Material not available for licensing or reuse.
Description: Cincinnati history (the 1937 flood); Appalachian life in the city; art and artists; film history; animated films; documentaries on art, music, the English language, natural science and history; Shakespeare's plays; opera; children's films.
Size & Elements: Film: 16mm (2,600 titles, 3,400 cans; release prints). Videotape: VHS (1,400 videotapes; viewing copies).
Cataloging: Card catalogs; published catalogs.
Access: Available to library patrons for a service charge. In-depth research is not permitted (reference questions only).
Rights: Some rights held to some material.
Licensing: Not available for licensing or reuse.
Restrictions: Films and videotapes available for viewing only. Duplication of material not permitted.
Viewing Facilities: Staff use only.
Duplication Facilities: None.

OHIO (Cleveland)

WESTERN RESERVE HISTORICAL SOCIETY
10825 East Boulevard
Cleveland, OH 44106
(216) 721-5722

Dr. Theodore A. Sande (Executive Director)

Contact: Kermit J. Pike (Library Director)
Services: Historical society. Film and videotape archives open to researchers and scholars only. Material possibly available for reuse, subject to clearance and restrictions.
Description: Materials relating primarily to the history of Cleveland and northeastern Ohio. Film holdings (1916-present) and videotapes (early 1970s-present) touch upon local social services, politics, immigration, business and industry, ethnicity and aviation history (particularly the National Air Races). Holds productions of social welfare agencies, such as *Cleveland: City on Schedule* (produced by the Cleveland Development Fund, late 1950s); productions by the Welfare Federation of Cleveland and the Greater Cleveland Growth Association (formerly the Chamber of Commerce); industrials (especially productions of TRW, Inc.); recent productions by local television stations using historical footage or stills (three to four produced annually); and a collection of videotaped interviews (over 400 3/4" videotapes) with survivors of the Nazi Holocaust now residing in the greater Cleveland area.
Size & Elements: Film: primarily 16mm (amount unspecified; black and white, positive, originals). Videotape: various formats (amount unspecified; masters and viewing copies).
Cataloging: Accession records for staff use only.
Access: Open to researchers and scholars only. Admittance fee charged.
Rights: Some rights held to some material. Some material in the public domain. Additional clearances may be necessary in some cases if material is to be reused.
Licensing: Available for licensing, subject to restrictions. License fees charged.
Restrictions: Restrictions apply to some material, based on donor agreements.
Viewing Facilities: Videotape (3/4").
Duplication Facilities: None.
Related Materials: 150,000 prints and still photographs.

OHIO (Columbus)

NATIONAL BLACK PROGRAMMING CONSORTIUM, INC.
929 Harrison Avenue, Suite 104
Columbus, OH 43215
(614) 299-5355

Mable Haddock (Director)

Contact: Mable Haddock
Services: Distributor. Videotape material maintained for distribution and rental rather than for research and reuse.
Description: Black-oriented material, including documentaries, public affairs, history, information and biographies.
Size & Elements: Film and videotape: format unspecified (150 items, various lengths).
Cataloging: Computerized cataloging available for staff use only.
Access: Maintained for distribution and rental rather than for research or resale. Available for reuse and resale, subject to restrictions.
Rights: Full rights held to some material. Some rights held to some material. Additional clearances may be necessary in some cases if material is to be reused.
Licensing: Apply for information. License fees charged.
Restrictions: Limitations on some programs for commercial release.
Viewing Facilities: Videotape (3/4" and 1/2").
Duplication Facilities: Film and videotape.

OHIO (Columbus)

OHIO HISTORICAL SOCIETY
ARCHIVES/LIBRARY DIVISION
1985 Velma Avenue
Columbus, OH 43211
(614) 297-2510

William Myers (Acting Division Chief)

Contact: Research Services Department
Services: Historical society. Film and videotape collections open to the public; some material available for duplication and possibly reuse.
Description: Holds forty-seven collections focusing on Ohio history and self-image (1913-present; primarily from 1940s-80s). Particular strengths include

Ohio industry, politics and social issues. Many of the films are sponsored by major Ohio corporations.

Earliest films in the collections include: *Hiawatha* (Gaumont, 1913), a safety print from original nitrate film; *Boston to Boston, Tour of 1919* (Goodyear Tire and Rubber Co.); *Zane Grey home movies* (1920s); *Sesqui-Centennial Commemorative of the Rise and Fall of the Moravian Mission at Gnadenhutten, 1771-1782* (produced under the supervision of the Ohio State Archaeological and Historical Society and the Gnadenhutten Historical Society, Sept. 2-3, 1932); *Stolen Pig* and *Getting Square*, two silent comedies.

Armed services. Collections include: Ohio Adjutant General (USAF) Collection and the Ohio Office of Civil Defense Collection. Material includes: *Ohio Soldiers* (SOHIO, 1942); *Builders of Peace* (The National Guard Bureau, 1947); *Ohio National Guard Summer Training Exercises* (1951); and *Enola Gay*.

Arts and history. Material includes: *Unveiling of H. C. Christy's Painting of Treaty of Greenville* (1945); *A Pilgrimage to Mount Vernon* (1954); *Centennial* (1970); *Dedication of WPBO-TV* (1974); *Worthington: A Study in the Communication of History: Part 1 — The New Eden* and *Part 2 — Worthington: The Virtuous Society in Transition* (1976); *17th Star*, bicentennial television commercials; Ashland County and City bicentennial celebrations; *History Recovered: The Custer Battlefield Archaeological Survey of 1984*, narrated by Dick Cavett; *Almost Home*, from the Ohio in Our Times conference; *Thomas Corwin; The Great Black Swamp*, about the settlement of Northwest Ohio; and *The Island Called Ellis*.

Environmental. Collections include: Ohio Forestry Association and Ohio Dept. of Natural Resources — Youth Conservation Corps. Material includes: *Water: Pattern of Life; The First Job — Conservation* (The Davey Tree Expert Co. of Kent, Ohio, 1955), showing environmental efforts in the "Buckeye State"; *Ohio Topographical Conference* (1977).

Health, human services and sports. Collections include: Blue Cross of Central Ohio; Ohio High School Athletic Association Collection; American Red Cross (Franklin Co. Chapter) Collection; Adjutant General Disaster Services; and Volunteers of America. Material includes: *City of the Sick* (Division of Mental Hygiene, Ohio Dept. of Public Welfare, 1949); *Alcoholic Information Center Television Spot; Boss Ket: One Man Working with Others* (Charles F. Kettering Foundation, 1980); Columbus Colony for deaf residents (1980); and Harding Hospital and an interview with Dr. Harding (1980s).

Industry. Collections include: Youngstown Sheet & Tube Co.; Ohio Bell — Ohio Story Collection; Federal Glass Co.; and Ohio Manufacturers Association Collection. Titles include: *Curtiss Plant Under Construction and Airshow* (1942); *The Land of Can-Do* (City Savings and Loan Co., 1953); *The Devil to Pay* (National Association of Wholesalers, 1960); *Ohio Crude: Excitement of Ohio's Gas and Oil Booms* (1986); *The Fragile Art* (WBGU-TV, 1986), on the glass industry; *Federal Glass* promotion film; *Goodyear Wingfoot Express* (Goodyear Tire and Rubber Co.); *The Industrial Revolution in America; Leaders of American Industrialization;* and *Once in a Lifetime* (Hanna Coal Co.).

Ohio presents itself and scenic Ohio. Collections include: Ohio Dept. of Development — Ohio Development & Publicity Commission Collection; Ohio Dept. of Education — Ohio Travelog Collection; Standard Oil of Ohio — Ohio Heritage. Material includes: *Ohio Suggests an Auto Tour Television Spots* (1950s), produced for the Ohio Development and Publicity Commission; *Ohio State Fair* (1940); *Ohio Youth on Parade* (1953), filmed at the Ohio State Fair; *What Makes Ohio Run* (Ohio Dept. of Administrative Services, 1957); *Ohio State Fair Highlights* (1958); *Blueprint for Progress* (Ohio Dept. of Industrial and Economic Development); *Ohio — The Growth State* (Bureau of Employment Services, 1957-59); *Overture to Ohio* (Ohio Arts Council, 1967), giving a view of the arts in Ohio; *Land of Legend Festival* (1967); aerial views of the Ohio State Fair (1969); *Toward a Better Understanding* (Governor's Office, Dept. of Administrative Services and Dept. of Economic and Community Development, 1974); *The Golden Lamb Hotel*, part of the *On the Road to '76 Series* (CBS Evening News, 1976); *The Victorian House* (1976-77); a lecture on the architecture of Clintonville; and *Columbus Area Chamber of Commerce Television Spots.*

Religion. Material includes: *The Fight Against Black Monday* (Mahoning Valley Ecumenical Coalition, 1978); ecumenism in Franklin County (1967-82); and *Working for the Lord — American Religious Life in the 18th and 19th Centuries and its Impact on the 20th Century* (1986).

Social interest. Collections include: Ohio AFL-CIO Video Collection. Material includes: *Not With Empty Hands* (American Negro Emancipation Centennial Authority/Ohio Division, in conjunction with Karamu, 1963); *Prohibition: Can Morality be Legislated?;* and *The Rise of the American Labor Movement: Toil and Struggle.*

State politics. Collections include: Governor C. W. O'Neill Collection;

Congressman Clarence Brown Collection; Governor Michael V. DiSalle Collection; Governor John Bricker Collection; Ohio Dept. of Education — General Instruction Collection; Warren G. Harding Motion Picture Film Collection; Public Access Coalition Collection; and Ohio Bureau of Employment Services. Material includes: Rep. John Vorys on cutting foreign aid (1952); *Job Security, Housewives and Clergy Theme*, three spots produced by Citizens for the Defeat of State Issue 2 (1958); the swearing-in of Ohio Supreme Court Justice Thomas M. Herbert (1969); a portrait of Governor John Gilligan (1971); *Cable Task Force Meetings* (Office of Public Utilities, donor, 1975); *Ohio's School Finance Crisis* (1977); the funeral of George T. Harding III (1985); and *Buyer Beware* (ca. 1972), on consumer awareness.

Transportation. Collections include: Ohio State Highway Patrol; and Ohio D.O.T. (Civil Defense). Material includes: *Photologing — Downtown Columbus* (Ohio Dept. of Transportation and Technical Services, 1975); *Ohio — A Heritage of Total Transportation* (Dept. of Highways, 1971); *A Question of Dignity* and *On the Move* (both from the Brotherhood of Railway, Airline, and Steamship Clerks).

Women's studies. Collections include: Ohio Federation of Republican Women; and the Ohio Bureau of Employment Services/Women's Service Division. Material includes: several films from the League of Women Voters (1972); *Kill Only the Ivy-League of Women Voters* (1972), a mystery; and *Oh Dear! A History of Woman Suffrage in Ohio* (1978).

Television news collections. Includes material from: WBNS-TV, Columbus (1950-70); WLWC-TV, Columbus; WOSU-TV, Columbus.

Size & Elements: Film: 35mm (5 items); 28mm (1 item); 16mm (approx. 48 items; negatives, internegatives and release prints); 8mm (3 items). Videotape: 2" (1 item); 3/4" (6 items); VHS (52 items). (Approx. 91 titles total).

Cataloging: Card catalogs; accession list; research library.

Access: Open to the public. Available for duplication. Research fees not charged. Research requests accepted by mail and in person (by appointment only).

Rights: Some rights held to all material. Some material in the public domain (e.g., government-generated). Additional clearances may be necessary in some cases if material is to be reused.

Licensing: Apply for information. License fees charged for public use.

Restrictions: Restrictions apply to some material.

Viewing Facilities: Film and videotape.

Duplication Facilities: None.

OHIO (Columbus)

THE OHIO STATE UNIVERSITY
DEPARTMENT OF PHOTOGRAPHY AND CINEMA
156 West 19th Avenue
Columbus, OH 43210-1183
(614) 292-5966

Dr. Charles Harpole (Chairperson)

Contact: Tom Snider (Manager, Film Editing and Distribution)

Services: Educational institution; film and videotape producer and distributor; film and videotape archives. Materials available for rental, purchase, licensing and reuse.

Description: The Department has been producing instructional films and videotapes in cooperation with educational institutions, business and industrial organizations and government agencies since 1936. Unlike other university film distribution systems, the Department does not purchase films from commercial and independent producers, but distributes films and videotapes produced by the University for other educational departments and outside sponsors.

Subjects include communications, education, health and safety education, marching bands, music, sports (especially football), and historical coverage of medicine and dentistry. Most titles were produced prior to 1983.

Sample titles include: *Action of the Human Heart Valves* (1965); *Airborne Television — Profile of a School* (1962), on the educational experiment in which television programs were transmitted into schools from a cargo aircraft flying at 30,000 feet; *America, Let's Celebrate!* (1976), on the OSU Marching Band's performance at the Tournament of Roses Parade; *Artificial Insemination of Dairy Cattle* (1960); *A Better Way* (1986), a dramatic film on the identification and prevention of suicide among deaf adolescents; *Broad and High: A Return to the City* (1978), on the past, present and future of the city of Columbus; *Buckeye Ballad* (1948), a visit to familiar OSU campus scenes with musical narration; *The Communication Revolution* (1967), on the impact of the information explosion and the mass media on Western civilization, with Marshall McLuhan, Gilbert Seldes, Keith Tyler and Edgar Dale; *Cut-Ups*

(1965), a gentle spoof about operations, nurses and doctors, using time-lapse photography to show the preoperative, operative and postoperative procedures of a modern hospital staff; *Physical Diagnosis of the Ear, Nose and Throat* (1960); *Police Reporter* (1950), showing general reporting techniques and problems; *Signs, Signals and Pavement Markings* (1979); and *Strength Through Struggle: A History of Ohio Labor* (1976), illustrating highlights of Ohio labor history (1930-present). *Thanks, Coach* (1987) is a videotape about Woody Hayes' championship football season (1954) as head coach of the OSU Buckeyes. Other films include interviews with Frank Capra and George Stevens, Jr.

Size & Elements: Film: 16mm (2 million feet, 400 titles; positive and negative originals and release prints; edited films and outtakes). Videotape: format unspecified (over 50 videotapes, representing nonsponsored student projects 1981-present).

Cataloging: Card catalogs; published catalogs.

Access: Not open to the public. For in-house use only. Completed films available for rental and purchase. Stock footage available for licensing and reuse. Research fees charged. Research requests accepted by mail, telephone and in person (by appointment).

Rights: Full rights held to some material. Additional clearances may be necessary in some cases if material is to be reused.

Licensing: Available for licensing and reuse. License and usage fees charged (fee schedule available).

Restrictions: None specified.

Viewing Facilities: Film (projector and Steenbeck); videotape (3/4" and VHS).

Duplication Facilities: Film (16mm color reversal workprints; 16mm film-to-videotape transfers); videotape (3/4" and 1/2").

OHIO (Columbus)

ALAN TWYMAN PRESENTS
THE ROHAUER COLLECTION
592 South Grant Avenue
Columbus, OH 43206-1250
(614) 469-0720
Fax: (614) 469-1607
Telex: 4972630 RAYROH

Alan P. Twyman (Managing Director)

Contact: Alan P. Twyman

Services: Film and videotape distributor. Material available for rental, licensing and reuse on a case-by-case basis.

Description: Renowned collection of classic films (1896-1970). Collection was originally amassed by Raymond Rohauer, curator of the Huntington Hartford Gallery of the Museum of Modern Art (New York) in the late 1960s. Starting his collection as a youth, Mr. Rohauer went on to found the Hollywood Film Society, and later established partnerships with Buster Keaton, Mrs. Harry Langdon, Douglas Fairbanks, Jr. and others in order to restore and distribute features and short subjects unseen for many years.

Buster Keaton. Titles include: *One Week* (1920); *Our Hospitality* (1923); *Sherlock Jr.* (1924); *The Navigator* (1924); *Go West* (1925); *The General* (1926); and *Steamboat Bill Jr.* (1928).

Harold Lloyd. Titles include: *Swing Your Partner* (1918); *On the Fire* (1919); *Back to the Woods* (1919); and *Haunted Spooks* (1920).

Harry Langdon. Titles include: *Picking Peaches* (1924); *Three's a Crowd* (1927); *Tramp Tramp Tramp* (1926); *His First Flame* (1926); *Saturday Afternoon* (1926); and *The Chaser* (1928).

W. C. Fields. Titles include: *The Dentist* (1932); *The Fatal Glass of Beer* (1933); *Sally of the Sawdust* (1925); *The Pharmacist* (1933); *Down Memory Lane* (1949); *The Big Fibber* (1933); and *Bring 'Em Back Sober* (1932).

Robert Benchley shorts. Titles include: *The Treasurer's Report* (1928); *Sex Life of a Polyp* (1929); *How To Take a Vacation* (1941); and *The Man's Angle* (1942).

Douglas Fairbanks, Sr. Titles include: *The Mark of Zorro* (1920); *Three Musketeers* (1921); *Robin Hood* (1922); *The Thief of Bagdad* (1924); and *The Taming of the Shrew* (1929).

D. W. Griffith. Titles include: *The Lonedale Operator* (1911); *Judith of Bethulia* (1913); *D. W. Griffith — An Interview* (1930); *The Birth of a Nation* (1915, revised 1930); *Intolerance* (1916); *Broken Blossoms* (1919); *True Heart Susie* (1919); *Way Down East* (1920); and *Orphans of the Storm* (1921).

Erich von Stroheim. Titles include: *Blind Husbands* (1918); *Foolish Wives* (1921); and *The Merry-Go-Round* (1922).

Rudolph Valentino. Titles include: *Blood and Sand* (1922); *The Eagle* (1925); and *Son of the Sheik* (1926).

Lon Chaney. Titles include: *Oliver Twist* (1922); *The Phantom of the Opera* (1925); and *The Hunchback of Notre Dame* (1923).

Paul Robeson. Titles include: *Body and Soul* (1925); *The Emperor Jones* (1933); *Sanders of the River* (1935); and *Song of Freedom* (1936).

Alfred Hitchcock. Titles include: *The Pleasure Garden* (1925); and *Jamaica Inn* (1939).

Josef von Sternberg. Titles include: *Salvation Hunters* (1925); *The Blue Angel* (1930); and *Anatahan* (1953).

Busby Berkeley. Titles include: *Gold Diggers of 1933; 42nd Street* (1933); *Dames* (1935); and *Hollywood Hotel* (1937).

American classics. Titles include: *Salome* (1923); *The Cat and the Canary* (1927); *The Swan* (1925); *The Lottery Bride* (1930); *The Old Dark House* (1932); *White Zombie* (1932); *Puttin' On the Ritz* (1930); *The Southerner* (1945); *Forever and a Day* (1943); *Mourning Becomes Electra* (1947); *Sudden Fear* (1952); and *The Living Idol* (1957).

Foreign classics. Titles include: *Thunder Over Mexico* (1933); *Tristana* (1970); *Chac* (1975); *Le Golem* (1936); *Carmen* (1918); *The Cabinet of Dr. Caligari* (1919); *Siegfrieds Tod* (1923); *Orlacs Hände (The Hands of Orlac)* (1925); *Faust* (1926); *Das Tagebuch Einer Verlorenen (The Diary of a Lost Girl)* (1929); *M* (1931); *Vampyr* (1932); and *Olympia I & II* (1936-38).

British classics. Titles include: *The Lodger* (1932); *Fire Over England* (1936); *Dark Journey* (1937); *Ten Days In Paris* (1939); *Call of the Blood* (1948); *The Fake* (1951); *Hotel Sahara* (1951); *The Diamond* (1954); *No Road Back* (1957); *In the Wake of the Stranger* (1958); *Expresso Bongo* (1959); *The Day the Earth Caught Fire* (1961); and *Jigsaw* (1962).

Documentaries. Titles include: *The Scopes Trial* (1925); *White Flood* (1935); *The Quiet Mind* (1948); *Van Meegeren's Faked Vermeers* (1950); *Seven Years in Tibet* (1957); *The Truth About Houdini* (1970); and *Star of India* (1953).

Animated classics. Titles include: *Gertie the Dinosaur* (1909); *The Winged Scourge* (1943); *Defense Against Invasion* (1946); and *Out of the Inkwell* (1961).

Avant-garde. Includes films by Man Ray, Joseph Vogel, Luis Buñuel, Jean Epstein, Jean-Isidore Isou, Marc'o, Charles Vidor, Jules Schwerin and Herman G. Weinberg.

Also available are selected short subjects.

Size & Elements: Film: 35mm and 16mm (approx. 900 titles, 5,000 cans). Videotape (transfers from film) available upon request.

Cataloging: Published catalog.

Access: Available for rental, licensing and reuse. Research fees charged. Requests accepted by mail, telephone and in person (by appointment only).

Rights: Full rights held to some material. Some rights held to all material.

"While portions of the Collection once were licensed for rental through Audio Brandon Films, Macmillan Films, Twyman Films and Blackhawk, all such licenses to them and their licensees are expired and are now held exclusively by Alan Twyman Presents as agent and sole distributor for The Collection. All motion pictures copyrighted or proprietary to The Collection offered by any other distributors may now be assumed to be pirated copies.

"The Rohauer Collection is the successor in rights (in most cases, all rights throughout the world) to the listed motion pictures of Buster Keaton, D. W. Griffith, Douglas Fairbanks, Sr., Harry Langdon, the German classics, the films of Marcel Hellman, Herbert Wilcox, Pendennis Films, Ltd., the Paramount short film library and others. These exclusive licenses and contracts bring to the Collection original nitrates, camera negatives, prints and other materials unavailable elsewhere to assure you receive the best prints possible."

"Broadcast, cable, video and other rights are available."

Licensing: Available for licensing and reuse, subject to restrictions. License fees charged.

Restrictions: Restrictions vary depending on intended use. Requests for licensing and reuse considered on a case-by-case basis.

Viewing Facilities: Film (16mm); videotape (VHS and Betamax; PAL, SECAM and NTSC).

Duplication Facilities: None.

OHIO (Dayton)

WRIGHT BROTHERS COLLECTION
WRIGHT STATE UNIVERSITY LIBRARY
Dayton, OH 45435
(513) 873-2092

Robert H. Smith, Jr. (Head of Archives and Special Collections)

Contact: Dorothy Smith (Reference Archivist)

Services: University library. Film and videotape collection available for duplication and reuse.

Description: Aviation history, notably the lives and work of Wilbur Wright (1867-1912) and Orville Wright (1871-1948). Contents include: Wilbur Wright flying at Camp d'Auvours near LeMans, France; setting both altitude and distance world records (November 13 and December 31, 1908); Orville Wright flying at Fort Myer, Virginia, near Washington, D.C.; visitors witnessing flights include President Taft, Alice Roosevelt Longworth, Frank Lahm and Benjamin Foulouis (July 27-30, 1909); Wright Brothers at Huffman Prairie in Dayton, including the construction and dedication of Wright Field; *Wright's Time To Fly*, a series of interviews with the Wright family members (December 15, 1985); interview with Ivonette Wright Miller, 92 years old, last surviving person to fly with the Wright Brothers (April 30, 1987).

Size & Elements: Film: 35mm (700 feet; positive and negative); 16mm (700 feet; positive) (5 titles; 12 cans total). Videotape: 3/4" and 1/2" (5 videotapes; masters and viewing copies).

Cataloging: Computerized cataloging (staff use only); card catalogs.

Access: Open to the public. Available for duplication. Research fees not charged. Research requests accepted by mail, telephone and in person (walk-in).

Rights: Full rights held to all material.

Licensing: Available for licensing and reuse. License fees charged (one-time fee for unlimited use).

Restrictions: None specified.

Viewing Facilities: Videotape.

Duplication Facilities: Videotape (3/4" and 1/2").

OHIO (Dublin)

NATIONAL WATER WELL ASSOCIATION
6375 Riverside Drive
Dublin, OH 43017
(614) 761-1711
Fax: (614) 761-1711 (Ext. 549)
Telex: 241302

Jay Lehr (Executive Director)

Contact: Susan Foreman (Publications Manager)
Services: Association. Film and videotape material available to members and to the public for purchase and rental.
Description: Nonprofit, professional society and trade association represents all segments of the ground water industry. Its 13,000 members include most of the world's leading ground water scientists and engineers, water well drilling contractors, pump installation contractors, and manufacturers and suppliers of ground water-related products and services. It provides leadership and guidance for sound and beneficial scientific and economic development, use, protection and management of the world's underground water resources.

Titles available: *Cable Tool Well Construction*, a technical film on the percussion drilling method; *Ground Water: America's Buried Treasure*, emphasizing the dangers of ground water pollution caused by man-made problems (e.g., sanitary landfills, improperly installed septic tanks and chemical effluents); *Ground Water: America's Hidden Reservoir*, explaining the hydrological system and basic ground water terminology; *Ground Water: Part of the Hydrological Cycle*, an instructive film concerning the occurrence of ground water, movement and ground study methods; *How the Water Witch Drowns in a Dry Hole*, describing the basic physics of ground water occurrence and movement utilizing laboratory test procedures and time-lapse photography of hydraulic sand models; *Inflation File*, in which a "Maxwell Smart"-type detective investigates the causes of inflation; *Mud Rotary Well Construction*, a technical film on the rotary drilling process; *The Incredible Bread Machine*, a look at the controversy of government control and regulation versus private enterprise and free competition to determine product prices; *The Subject is Water*, explaining the functions of the U.S. Geological Survey; *The Water Well Industry: Past, Present and Future*; *To Water by Air*, describing the method of "prospecting" for ground water from the air; *Water for the Future: Your Choice*, discussing water wells as the key to healthy national growth; *Water on Demand*, showing basics of good well construction, development and screen selection to produce efficient and reliable water wells; and *Video Proceedings — First National Outdoor Action Conference on Aquifer Restoration, Ground Water Monitoring and Geophysical Methods, Las Vegas, Nevada, May 1987*, featuring six hours of presentations from the conference.

Size & Elements: Film: 16mm. Videotape: 3/4", VHS and Betamax. (14 titles total).

Cataloging: Published catalog available on request.

Access: Open to the public and to NWWA members. Maintained for

distribution and rental rather than for research or reuse. Requests accepted by mail and telephone (all orders must be prepaid).

Rights: Full rights held to some material. Some rights held to some material. Additional clearances may be necessary in some cases if material is to be reused.

Licensing: Apply for information. License fees charged.

Restrictions: None specified.

Viewing Facilities: None (special arrangements may be possible).

Duplication Facilities: None (outside arrangements can be made).

OHIO (Eastlake)

HI-TECH PRODUCTIONS
36 Admiral Drive
Eastlake, OH 44094
(216) 953-0077

Dave McClimans (Owner/Chief Engineer)

Contact: Dave McClimans
Services: Videotape producer; field and post-production facility. Videotape collection not available to the general public; material available to post-production facility clients and sponsors only.
Description: Client-sponsored footage of Cleveland and the Lake Erie shorefront area. Footage includes shots of pigeons, sunsets, sailboats, powerboats, boat races, museums, statues, town squares, people and downtown traffic.
Size & Elements: Videotape: 1", 3/4", VHS and Betamax (approx. 8 hours, 24 videotapes; masters and viewing copies).
Cataloging: Shot lists.
Access: Not open to the public. Available for reuse by post-production facility clients and sponsors only. Research requests not accepted.
Rights: Full rights held to all material.
Licensing: Available for reuse to clients and sponsors only.
Restrictions: Material not available to the general public for licensing or reuse.
Viewing Facilities: Videotape (1", 3/4", VHS and Betamax).
Duplication Facilities: Videotape (1", 3/4", VHS and Betamax).

OHIO (Kings Island)

COLLEGE FOOTBALL HALL OF FAME
5440 Kings Island Drive
Kings Island, OH 45034
(513) 398-5410

Dick Craig (General Manager)

Contact: Pat Harmon (Curator and Historian)
Services: Museum. Film collection available for research and reuse in nonprofit situations only.
Description: Highlights of college football (1925-present); predominantly East Coast teams.
Size & Elements: Film: 16mm (approx. 250 films).
Cataloging: List available.
Access: Not open to the public. Research fees not charged. Research requests accepted by mail, telephone and in person. Usage may be restricted.
Rights: Some rights held to some material. Additional clearances may be necessary in some cases if material is to be reused.
Licensing: Available for licensing and reuse in some cases, subject to restrictions. Fees may be charged, depending on usage.
Restrictions: Films may not be used for profit or resale.
Viewing Facilities: Museum theater.
Duplication Facilities: None.

OHIO (Mansfield)

HIGHWAY SAFETY FILMS, INC.
P.O. Box 3563
Mansfield, OH 44907
(419) 756-5593

Street address: 890 Hollywood Lane

Earl J. Deems (President)

Contact: Office staff
Services: Film producer and distributor. Film and videotape material available for purchase.
Description: "Agony, death and destruction are our three constant traveling companions. In spite of all the recent mechanical improvements, they will continue to ride with us every minute and every mile we're on the streets and highways until individual drivers become better informed, accept personal responsibility, and are motivated toward a drastic reduction in our present awesome price of mobility."

"These documentaries, shown by organizations throughout the world, have been universally acclaimed as the most effective driver education, crime prevention and training tools available....Realism, authenticity and adroit handling of the story line create the feeling in viewers that they were there when it happened. Crime, accidents and mangled bodies are no longer cold detached statistics. They are dramatically brought to life...and death...to become a vivid personal experience. Victims become the girl next door, the teenager across the street and the businessman down the block. The message is brought home...where it hurts enough to do something about it."

Traffic safety and driver education. Titles available include: *Signal 30*, an award-winning film geared to all persons who operate motor vehicles ("It is an ugly film. It is meant to be. It is designed to drive home to those who see it that an accident is not pretty."); *Mechanized Death*, a portrayal of unnecessary tragedies that occur on highways and streets; and *Wheels of Tragedy*, produced in conjunction with the Ohio State Highway Patrol, following two patrolmen on their regular tour of duty and witnesses traffic accident scenes.

Other titles include: *The Unteachables*, directed at younger motorists and exploring the three main causes of highway deaths; *The Third Killer* (the number one and two causes of death are heart disease and cancer — the third killer is traffic deaths), which includes actual accident scene footage requiring two years of shooting by cameramen on duty around the clock; *A Matter of Judgement*, a driver improvement film explaining operating procedures to be used while driving in city and highway road traffic and under different weather conditions; *Highways of Agony*, in which viewers become on-the-spot witnesses to a dramatic selection of highway tragedies shown in living "and dying" color; *Carrier or Killer*, a dramatic safety film made specifically for the trucking industry; *Go Sober and Safe*, demonstrating the degrees of impairment caused by consuming various amounts of alcoholic beverages (six skilled drivers are given driving tests after being served alcohol — supervised by the Ohio State Highway Patrol); *Drive and Survive*, revealing the four most important life-saving precautions all drivers should take to enhance their chance of survival on streets and highways; and *Options to Live*, emphasizing those options which will influence a more positive attitude toward safe driving.

Store and plant security. Titles available include: *The Shoplifter*, in which a convicted shoplifter displays stealing methods under actual conditions and explains how employees could have prevented the thefts; *You and the Bank Robber*, showing two actual bank robberies filmed by security cameras and instructing bank employees in preventative measures; *Plant Pilferage*, directed to industrial management, describing eight security steps in a successful pilferage prevention program; and *The Paper Hangers*, exploring check fraud (two former paperhangers discuss the most common errors practiced by businessmen and show frequently used check cashing techniques).

Special purpose. Titles available: *The Child Molester*, stressing the importance of alerting children about molesters and showing how the rules of safety and good conduct can be successfully and safely taught; *A Great and Honorable Duty*, outlining ethics and rules of conduct for police officers and illustrating some of the diverse challenges that they confront; *There's a Message in Every Bottle*, an objective film about alcohol and the teenager; and *Special Delivery*, dealing with pupil transportation and the responsibilities involved in building, servicing, maintaining, driving and riding on a school bus.
Size & Elements: Film: 16mm (19 titles). Videotape: 3/4", VHS and Betamax I and II (same 19 titles).
Cataloging: Published catalog.
Access: Primarily available for purchase to educational organizations, driver training programs, schools, banks, merchandisers and police agencies.
Rights: Full rights held to all material. All films are copyrighted and are for optical projection only.
Licensing: Most of the films may be televised; contact office for permission.
Restrictions: Some films are restricted for use and viewing by merchandisers and police only.
Viewing Facilities: None.
Duplication Facilities: None.

OHIO (Sandusky)

NATIONAL AERONAUTICS AND SPACE ADMINISTRATION (NASA)
LEWIS RESEARCH CENTER
AUDIOVISUAL LIBRARY
6100 Columbus Avenue
Sandusky, OH 44870
(419) 625-1123

Contact: Distribution Staff
Services: Government agency; film and videotape distributor. Films and videotapes available to television and cable television stations on a free-loan basis.
Description: NASA films and television programs on numerous subjects, including the history of space travel; the space shuttle; history and technology of rockets; early American manned space missions; astronauts, including Alan Shepard, John Glenn, Neil Armstrong, Buzz Aldrin and Michael Collins; Skylab, the first United States manned space station; women in NASA; the Voyager spacecraft and planetary exploration; research and communications satellites; the universe; space research; history of NASA; preparation for the lunar landing; the moon landing (1969); the history of aeronautics and flight; air crash research; extraterrestrial life; Mars, Jupiter and other planets; science fiction and science fact art; human factors considerations in space; the Gaia hypothesis for the origins of the universe; Halley's comet; Spacelab; the orbiting space telescope; weather satellites; Landsat satellite and mapping from space; meteorology; space research spinoffs into everyday life; and life sciences research.
Size & Elements: Film: 16mm (hundreds of titles; release prints). Videotape: 2", 1" and 3/4" (hundreds of titles; each 5 to 60 min.; broadcast masters).
Cataloging: Published catalog.
Access: Available to television and cable television stations in the United States for short-term free loan. Research fees not charged. Requests accepted by mail.
Rights: Material in the public domain. Additional clearances may be necessary in some cases if material is to be reused.
Licensing: Available for broadcast, cablecast and reuse, subject to restrictions.
Restrictions: Some material may carry restrictions. NASA material or the voices and likenesses of astronauts are not to be used for advertising purposes.
Viewing Facilities: None.
Duplication Facilities: None.

OHIO (Toledo)

UNIVERSITY OF TOLEDO
WARD M. CANADAY CENTER
UNIVERSITY ARCHIVES
WILLIAM S. CARLSON LIBRARY
2801 West Bancroft Street
Toledo, OH 43606
(419) 537-2170

Leslie Sheridan (Director of Libraries)

Contact: Barbara Floyd (University Archivist)
Services: University archives. Film and videotape collection open to the public, primarily for in-house use.
Description: Historical documentation of the University of Toledo. Includes film and videotape footage of the construction of the campus (1930); football and basketball films (1963-78); oral histories of University administrators; military training films used in World War II-era classes; and three films on the Democratic Party and election procedures (1952-55), concerning Toledo politician John P. Kelly.
Size & Elements: Film: format unspecified (16 titles, 228 cans; positive). Videotape: 2" and VHS (4 videotapes total).
Cataloging: Finding aids.
Access: Open to the public primarily for in-house research. Research fees not charged. Research requests accepted by mail, telephone and in person (walk-in).
Rights: Some rights held to some material.
Licensing: Apply for information. License fees charged in some cases.
Restrictions: None specified.
Viewing Facilities: Videotape (facilities available in Audiovisual Services Department).
Duplication Facilities: None.

OHIO (Wilmington)

**WILMINGTON COLLEGE PEACE RESOURCE CENTER
HIROSHIMA/NAGASAKI MEMORIAL COLLECTION**
Pyle Center Box 1183
Wilmington, OH 45177
(513) 382-5338

Street address: 51 College Street

Helen Redding (Director)

Contact: Helen Redding
Services: Educational institution; nonprofit resource center. Videotapes available for distribution.
Description: Resource materials relating to the atomic bombing of Hiroshima and Nagasaki and the furthering of global awareness of the implications of nuclear warfare.
Arms race. Titles include: *Reliability and Risk: Computers and Nuclear War,* offering a critical look at the reliability of computers in our nation's defense program with major emphasis on the proposed "Star Wars" system, communicating a clear message from the computing community that there is no technological fix to the threat of nuclear war; *The Wichita Conference On Issues Of Peace and War,* a series of conferences on five topics (*Thinking and Feeling in the Nuclear Age; The Economics of the Arms Race and Problems of Conversion; Foreign Policy and the Meaning of Defense; Prospects of Global Order;* and *Education for Peace and Disarmament*).
Atomic bombings. Titles include: *Decision to Drop the Bomb,* a documentary covering events from April 12 to August 6, 1945, probing events leading to the actual decision in a non-judgmental way; *Hiroshima: The People's Legacy* (produced by NHK-TV, Japan), a documentary about A-bomb survivors and the drawings they made at the request of NHK, encouraging many people who had never expressed their feelings about the event to record their memories on paper; *Hiroshima: Document of Atomic Bombing,* using film footage shot in Hiroshima by an official team of Japanese photographers immediately following the bombing.
Nonviolence. Titles include: *Destination Nicaragua* (1985), a documentary record of one group's participation in Witness for Peace; *Alternatives to Violence Video Forum,* documenting conferences in various U.S. cities; *The Arms Race Within: The Story of the Nuclear Train and the Agape Community,* revealing the existence of the Nuclear Train to a much wider audience.
Nuclear war. Titles include: *The Last Epidemic; Medical Consequences of Nuclear Weapons and Nuclear War* (1981), a symposium conducted by Physicians for Social Responsibility, detailing the almost unimaginable consequences of nuclear war; *Puhi Pau,* an eloquent, gentle Hawaiian mother points out the lush beauty of the islands and explains the possible results of a thermonuclear attack on Pearl Harbor.
Peacemaking. Titles include: *The March for Disarmament: June 12, 1982,* edited from more than 30 hours of videotape of that historic event; *No Frames, No Boundaries,* exploring the frames of reference and artificial man-made boundaries that exist between nations, and the interconnectedness of caring for the planet and each other.
Size & Elements: Film: 16mm (release prints). Videotape: 3/4" and VHS (viewing copies). (Approx. 80 titles total).
Cataloging: Published catalogs.
Access: Open to the public. Maintained for distribution and rental rather than for research or reuse. Research fees not charged. Research requests accepted by mail, telephone and in person (by appointment only).
Rights: No rights held to any material.
Licensing: Not available for licensing or reuse.
Restrictions: Material cannot be duplicated without additional clearances.
Viewing Facilities: Film (16mm) and videotape (by special arrangement on nearby campus).
Duplication Facilities: None.
Related Materials: Print materials, slide sets and audiotapes.

OKLAHOMA

OKLAHOMA (Claremore)

WILL ROGERS MEMORIAL
P.O. Box 157
Claremore, OK 74018
(918) 341-0719

Street address: 1720 Will Rogers Boulevard

Dr. Reba Collins (Director)

Contacts: Gregory Malak (Manager); Patricia Lowe (Librarian)
Services: State owned museum and memorial. Film and videotape collection open to researchers and scholars only.
Description: Film and videotape materials directly related to Will Rogers as either star or subject.
Size & Elements: Film: 16mm (218,309 feet, 70 titles). Videotape: 3/4" (79 videotapes, 3,578 min.).
Cataloging: Card catalogs; book catalog; research library.
Access: Open to researchers and scholars only. Research fees charged, except for nonprofit organizations. Research access subject to approval by management. Research requests accepted by mail, telephone and in person (walk-in).
Rights: Full rights held to some material. Additional clearances may be necessary in some cases if material is to be reused.
Licensing: Apply for information. Usage fees charged in some cases.
Restrictions: Requests for research and reuse subject to acceptance and approval.
Viewing Facilities: Videotape.
Duplication Facilities: None.

OKLAHOMA (Norman)

**POLITICAL COMMERCIAL ARCHIVE
POLITICAL COMMUNICATION CENTER
THE UNIVERSITY OF OKLAHOMA**
Department of Communication, Room 331
780 Van Vleet Oval
Norman, OK 73019
(405) 325-3111

Prof. Julian P. Kanter (Curator)
Dr. Lynda Kaid (Director, Political Communication Center)

Contact: Prof. Julian P. Kanter
Services: Archives. Film and videotape material available for research and reuse, subject to restrictions.
Description: Founded in 1956 by a private collector, Archive has been housed at University of Oklahoma since 1985.
Holds over 30,000 television commercials (1950-present), representing candidates running for offices ranging from the U.S. presidency to school boards throughout the U.S. Also contains commercials by political action committees, advertisements on public issues sponsored by corporations and special interest groups, and commercials done for elections in foreign countries. Many items in Archive are unique copies and are no longer available through any other source. Commercials vary in length from very short spots to 60 minute programs.
Size & Elements: Film: 16mm (5,600 titles, 200,000 feet). Videotape: 2", 1" and 3/4" (over 15,000 titles).
Cataloging: Looseleaf catalog. Computerized cataloging for staff use in progress; also available to researchers.
Access: Available to the public for research and duplication, within limits of staff and equipment necessary to process requests. Access generally available only to copies of materials, primarily on-site; no originals are available for routine usage. In unusual cases copies may be rented to off-site users on a cost-recovery basis. Research requests accepted by mail and telephone. Research fees charged in some cases.
Rights: Archive holds no rights to any material, providing only physical copies of materials and conveying no other rights to user. Commercial users must assume full responsibility for securing any necessary clearances or authorizations required for whatever use they make of the materials.
Licensing: Available for reuse, subject to restrictions. Usage fees charged for rebroadcast.
Restrictions: Users must agree to limit use of commercials provided to the specific purpose for which they were requested and guarantee not to use them in any other context or to make them available to any other person or entity. Users must provide assurances to Archive that materials will not be used in any unauthorized ways. "It is the express policy of the Archive that its materials will not be used in any way to bring disrespect, ridicule or misrepresentation to the candidates or producers of the commercials it preserves."
Viewing Facilities: Videotape (3/4" and VHS). Videotape copies of film, rather than film originals, are made available for viewing.
Duplication Facilities: Film (film-to-videotape transfers); videotape (3/4" and VHS). 2" to 3/4" duplication possibly available.
Related Materials: 14,000 radio commercials (1936-present).

OKLAHOMA (Norman)

UNIVERSITY OF OKLAHOMA
WESTERN HISTORY COLLECTIONS
630 Parrington Oval, Room 452
Norman, OK 73019
(405) 325-3641

Donald L. DeWitt (Curator)

Contact: John R. Lovett, Jr. (Photographic Archivist)
Services: University; special collection. Film and videotape collection open to the public primarily for in-house use.
Description: Films relating to regional subjects and the University of Oklahoma. Includes 150 sports films (predominantly 16mm, some 35mm) documenting the University athletic program, primarily football (1959-70); 160 Oklahoma-related feature films (16mm) from station KOCO-TV in Oklahoma City, many of which are historical in treatment and content; and 20 productions related to Native Americans, some commercially produced for educational use, others independently produced (1920-50).
Size & Elements: Film: 35mm and 16mm (330 items).
Cataloging: Computerized cataloging for staff use only. Materials are not precisely cataloged as to content.
Access: Open to the public. For in-house use only. Researchers should inquire well in advance to assure availability of materials. Research fees not charged. Research requests accepted by mail and telephone.
Rights: Some rights held to some material. Rights status of some material not known. Additional clearances may be necessary in some cases if material is to be reused.
Licensing: Apply for information. License fees charged in some cases.
Restrictions: None specified.
Viewing Facilities: Film and videotape (researchers must make advance arrangements to schedule viewing facilities).
Duplication Facilities: None.

OKLAHOMA (Oklahoma City)

AMERICAN CITIZENSHIP CENTER
Box 11000
Oklahoma City, OK 73136-1100
(405) 425-5040

Robert H. Rowland (President)

Contact: Cecilia Stoll (Administrative Assistant)
Services: Educational center. Film and videotape library intended primarily for use by high-school and college teachers.
Description: Located on the campus of Oklahoma Christian College, the Center holds films and videotapes produced in the 1970s on American patriotic themes.

Sample titles include: *The Truth About Communism; Spirit of Enterprise; Communism vs. Capitalism; America's Distribution of Wealth; The War We Are In; Communist Encirclement; Republic of Apathy; Beginning Plymouth Colony; Communism and Morals; The Two Berlins; Our Two Great Documents; The Structure of the American Way of Life; The Secret of American Production; Private Property; The Profit System;* and *The Fall of Nations.*

Adventures in Economics Series consists of color cartoons produced by Harding College for the National Education Program (a division of the American Citizenship Center). In *Make Mine Freedom*, "Dr. Utopia offers his patent medicine 'Dr. Utopia's Ism' for curing political ills. Those who take it soon find themselves living under totalitarian government." In *Albert in Blunderland*, "through the medium of a dream, Albert, an American worker is transported to Antrovia, a police state. Albert learns the real nature of a life in a police state with its political, economic and social impact." *The Devil and John Q* is "a discussion of the nature and dangers of inflation. In this film Lucifer joins forces with the international conspiracy of Communism in order to destroy the United States."
Size & Elements: Film: 16mm (approx. 30 to 40 titles). Videotape: format unspecified (10 titles).
Cataloging: Title list.
Access: Primarily intended for use by high-school and college teachers. Research fees not charged. Research requests accepted by mail and telephone.
Rights: Full rights held to some material. Rights to cartoons held by the National Education Program.

Licensing: Apply for information.
Restrictions: None specified.
Viewing Facilities: None.
Duplication Facilities: None.

OKLAHOMA (Oklahoma City)

OKLAHOMA DEPARTMENT OF LIBRARIES
AUDIO VISUAL CENTER
200 Northeast 18th Street
Oklahoma City, OK 73105
(405) 521-2502

Robert L. Clark, Jr. (Director)

Contact: Lana Cross (Coordinator of Audiovisual Services)
Services: State library. Film and videotape collection maintained for distribution to local libraries in Oklahoma. Material available directly to Oklahoma state agencies and to the public (through Oklahoma libraries).
Description: Holds films on early Oklahoma history and personalities, including: *The Run* (Movieland, 1962), produced by WKY-TV in its *Oklahoma Heritage Series,* using over 1,000 actual photographs to tell the story of the mad rush to claim free land in Indian Territory on April 22, 1889; *Tom Mix; Wiley Post;* and *Will Rogers* (Official Films, 1962), describing important events in the life of cowboy humorist Will Rogers and tracing his career as a journalist, actor, politician and wry critic of the national scene.

The remainder of the collection consists of commercially acquired material maintained for distribution to other state and local libraries.
Size & Elements: Film: 16mm (2,000 titles). Videotape: VHS (150 titles).
Cataloging: Card catalogs; published catalogs.
Access: Available to the public through Oklahoma public libraries and state agencies. Research fees not charged. Non-copyrighted videotape holdings available for duplication under certain circumstances (e.g., for workshops and meetings). Research requests accepted by mail, telephone and in person (by appointment only).
Rights: No rights held to any material. Copyright clearances may be necessary in some cases if material is to be reused.
Licensing: Material generally not available for licensing or reuse.
Restrictions: Apply for information.
Viewing Facilities: Film (16mm); videotape (VHS).
Duplication Facilities: Videotape.

OKLAHOMA (Tahlequah)

CHEROKEE NATION HISTORICAL SOCIETY, INC.
P.O. Box 515
Tsa-La-Gi
Tahlequah, OK 74465
(918) 456-6007

A. Eugene Hileman (Acting Executive Director)

Contact: Tom Mooney (Archivist)
Services: Historical society. Archival film and videotape materials available for limited research and lending at the local level. *The Society is currently organizing its moving image material in order to make it accessible for research. Since most material is uncataloged and inaccessible, they are not prepared to respond to most research requests at this time.*
Description: Holds documentation of Cherokee culture, history and government relations; footage of the annual outdoor drama, *Trail of Tears* and some local television news clips and public service announcements.

Society is the sole repository for videotapes produced by the Cherokee Nation Tribal Government in Oklahoma. These videotapes document governmental activities, including tribal meetings and council meetings.

The currently pending Lost Arts Project videotape series will document the making of traditional arts and crafts, such as *Blow Guns* and *The Making of Traditional Foods.*
Size & Elements: Film: 16mm. Videotape: 3/4" (currently being transferred to 1/2"). (Approx. 60 separate items).
Cataloging: Listings available.
Access: Open to the public on a limited basis. Research requests accepted in person, by appointment only. The Society is currently in the process of organizing its collection in order to make it accessible for research, but much material is presently uncataloged and inaccessible. They are not prepared to respond to research requests on a large scale at the present time.

Rights: Some rights held to some material. Additional clearances may be necessary in some cases if material is to be reused.
Licensing: Apply for information. License fees usually not charged.
Restrictions: None specified.
Viewing Facilities: Videotape (1/2").
Duplication Facilities: None.

OKLAHOMA (Tulsa)

ORAL ROBERTS UNIVERSITY
P.O. Box 2187
Tulsa, OK 74171
(918) 495-6750

Roger Rydin (Archivist)

Contact: Roger Rydin
Services: Educational institution. Film and videotape collection not open to the public; available for in-house use only.
Description: Religious broadcasts by Oral Roberts and others. Collection includes film and documentation of tent crusades (1950s-60s); and videotapes of religious television shows, basketball games, religious services, seminars, classes and talk shows (1973-present).
Size & Elements: Film: 35mm and 16mm (5,000 reels). Videotape: 2", 1", 3/4" and 1/2" (amount unspecified).
Cataloging: Card catalogs.
Access: Not open to the public. For in-house use only. Research requests not accepted.
Rights: Full rights held to all material.
Licensing: Apply for information.
Restrictions: Material not available to the public for research and reuse.
Viewing Facilities: None.
Duplication Facilities: Videotape.

OKLAHOMA (Tulsa)

STEGMAN PRODUCTIONS
1715 South Boston Avenue
Tulsa, OK 74119
(918) 585-8194

Rocky Stegman (Owner and President)

Contact: Loren Ashford (Editor and Cameraperson)
Services: Videotape producer. Material available for duplication, licensing and reuse.
Description: Office interiors, buildings, computers and office workers; oil fields and oil production; children (various activities and ages); church exteriors, interiors and some church services; driving (seasonal), shots of automobiles and point-of-view shots from cars; city skylines (e.g., New York City, San Francisco and Chicago) and small town scenes. A wide variety of generic footage is also available.
Size & Elements: Videotape: 3/4" (1,000 hours; masters); VHS, Betamax and 8mm (viewing copies).
Cataloging: Computerized cataloging primarily for staff use; possibly available to researchers on a case-by-case basis.
Access: Available to the public for duplication, licensing and reuse. Some material available for one-time use only.
Rights: Full rights held to all material. Additional clearances may be necessary in some cases if material is to be reused; client approval may be required.
Licensing: Available for licensing. License fees charged.
Restrictions: None specified.
Viewing Facilities: Videotape (3/4", 1/2" and 8mm).
Duplication Facilities: Videotape (VHS, Betamax and 8mm).

OREGON

OREGON (Beaverton)

MEDIA WEST, INC.
10255 Southwest Arctic Drive
Beaverton, OR 97005
(800) 888-8273
(503) 626-7002

Fax: (503) 626-7023

Brian D. Ratty (Corporate President)

Contact: Cheryl Baba (Sales and Marketing Coordinator, Home Video Division)
Services: Videotape producer and distributor. Videotapes available for purchase. Material possibly available for licensing and reuse, subject to restrictions.
Description: Distributes videotapes produced for the home market, including: *Puppy's First Year; Kittens to Cats; On Assignment: A Video Series for Photographers; Golf in the Desert*, on the great golf courses and romance of the Palm Springs area; *Perennial Gardening; HighTech Workout;* and *Fly Fishing New Zealand.*
Size & Elements: Videotape: VHS and Betamax (12 videotapes, each 30 to 90 min.).
Cataloging: Card catalogs; published catalog.
Access: Available to the public for purchase.
Rights: Full rights held to all material.
Licensing: Available for licensing, subject to restrictions. License fees charged in some cases.
Restrictions: All licensing and reuse permitted by contract only.
Viewing Facilities: None.
Duplication Facilities: Videotape.

OREGON (Corvallis)

OREGON STATE UNIVERSITY ARCHIVES
Corvallis, OR 97331
(503) 754-2165

Contact: Merv Mecklenburg
Services: University archives. Film and videotape collection available to the public, primarily for research and duplication, subject to restrictions.
Description: Oregon agriculture, history and collegiate sports. Holds materials mainly from the University's Department of Information (Sports Information), Division of Continuing Education, and Agricultural Communications.
  Department of Information. Sports films (1936-present), including football, basketball, baseball, women's sports, wrestling, gymnastics, track and field, volleyball, coaches and players.
  Division of Continuing Education. Films (1920s-present), including footage of: snow-covered Mt. Hood aerial; Crooked River gorge and bridge; a milking contest; Salem State Fair; 4-H Club work and summer school; a cakewalk; boys showing pigs; a meat-cutting demonstration; a good posture demonstration; a bee demonstration; Knute Rockne giving boys a football demonstration; National Dairy Champions show (1925); bulls; cows; the world champion butter cow; Guernseys (cows); parades; livestock shows; judging and auctioning off of prize beef; Babe Ruth in Portland gives demonstration using snowballs in place of baseballs; Oregon State University events; ROTC; Detroit Toledo & Ironton Railroad; 4-H demonstrations (boys' vegetable displays, girls box lunches, girls showing curtains, girls modeling dresses, pigs, shoe polishing, poultry, cattle, corn field and tomato plants); salmon poisoning; dog research studies; and sheep and dog autopsies.
  Agricultural Communications. Films (late 1950s-present) include: *Planting Commercial Orchard; The Oregon Purple Plum; Dwarf Fruit Trees; Lawn Fertilization and Weed Control; Fruit Tree, Mechanical Harvesting; Christmas Tree Production; Acres of Orchids; Commercial Horticulture — At Bedding Plants; Forest Tree Nurseries; Logging Operation, Douglas Fir; Utilizing Marginal Timber; Oregon Hardwood; OMARK Chipping Chain Saw; Ryegrass Seed Harvest; Wheat Marketing & Handling; Snap Beans Production and Processing; Brussel Sprouts; Rhubarb Harvesting and Processing; Garlic Production; Grape Harvesting, Wine Manufacturing; Blackberries; Field Burning; Forest Fire Control; Beef Production Testing; Livestock Handling Techniques; Goat Dairy; Farm Buildings; Drainage; Egg Production; Sheep Shearing and Wool; Mink Production; Rat Control, Rats in Town and Country; Honey Bee Management; Commercial Clam Harvest and Processing; Shrimp Industry; Otter Trawl Fishing; Flour Milling; Cheese Manufacturing and October Cheese Festival; Port of Portland; Migrant Education, New Settlers; Peace Corps Training at Oregon State; Saddle Leather and Donkeys; Land Use Planning, Oregon Coast; Wet Lands Research; Solid Waste Disposal; Oregon State Fair; Converting Farmland to Recreational Use; Auto Wrecking Industry; Gravel Mulch; Aluminum Foundry; 4-H Leadership; Sagebrush Removal and Range Improvement; Balloon Logging; Organic Foods and Farming; Oregon Apples and Pears; Pesticide Safety; Beer Testing in OSU*

Flavorium; Coddling Moth Pheromone Application; and *Acid Rain Research Chambers.*
Size & Elements: Film and videotape (formats and amounts unspecified).
Cataloging: Card catalogs; lists.
Access: Available to the public for research and duplication, unless restricted by condition. Research requests accepted by mail, telephone and in person (by appointment only).
Rights: Full rights held to all material.
Licensing: Apply for information. License fees not charged.
Restrictions: Some films may be restricted due to poor condition.
Viewing Facilities: Film and videotape (by appointment).
Duplication Facilities: Film and videotape.

OREGON (Eugene)

JULIA LESAGE
3480 Mill
Eugene, OR 97405
(503) 344-8129
(503) 686-4171

Contact: Julia Lesage
Services: Videotape producer and distributor. Videotapes available to the public for purchase.
Description: Documentary videotapes relating to Nicaragua.
   Titles include: *El Crucero* (1984), an in-depth picture of a Nicaraguan coffee plantation, organized in four "movements," each in a different documentary style, to capture different aspects of life and politics on that farm; *The School* (1985), a Nicaraguan man telling of his experiences with the unjust educational system during the Somoza era; *Wilfred's Park* (1985), on how the funeral of a child shot by Somoza's *guardia* became the occasion for the revolutionary uprising of the city of Estelí; *Troubadours* (1987), a collaborative videotape made with the Grupo Camayoc of Estelí, young Nicaraguan musicians; *Las Nicas* (1981-82), containing in-depth interviews with women in the Managua area; and *Home Life* (1984), showing the memories and day-to-day experiences of a Nicaraguan family, and the experience of North Americans in a revolutionary society.
Size & Elements: Videotape: 3/4", VHS and Betamax (7 videotapes; masters and viewing copies).
Cataloging: Published brochure.
Access: Available to the public for purchase. Footage available for duplication and reuse on a case-by-case basis. Requests accepted by mail and telephone.
Rights: Full rights held to all material.
Licensing: Available for licensing and reuse, subject to restrictions.
Restrictions: Requests for licensing and reuse considered on a case-by-case basis.
Viewing Facilities: None.
Duplication Facilities: Videotape (3/4", VHS and Betamax).
Distributors: Selected videotapes distributed by Facets Multimedia, Inc. (q.v.); Video Data Bank (q.v.); and Foreign Images (q.v.).

OREGON (Eugene)

UNIVERSITY OF OREGON LIBRARY
INSTRUCTIONAL MEDIA CENTER
Eugene, OR 97403
(503) 686-3091

Howard Lindstrom (Assistant Director, IMC)

Contacts: Howard Lindstrom; Lori Jirges (Film Programmer)
Services: University library. Collection of educational film and videotape materials not open to the public; maintained for in-house use only.
Description: Holds one film produced at the University of Oregon: *Ed's Coed* (1929, 115 min., 16mm, black and white, silent), a dramatic film produced by and about students at the University in 1929 ("good camera work").
   Library also holds various materials produced by outside sources and many foreign language videotapes.
Size & Elements: Film: 16mm (1,200 titles). Videotape: 3/4" and VHS (550 titles).
Cataloging: Card catalogs; published catalogs; computerized cataloging available to researchers.
Access: Not open to the public. Available to University students and faculty only. For in-house use only.
Rights: No rights held to any material.

Licensing: Apply for information.
Restrictions: None specified.
Viewing Facilities: Film (16mm and Super 8mm); videotape (3/4" and VHS).
Duplication Facilities: Videotape (3/4" and VHS).

OREGON (Forest Grove)

OREGON ELECTRIC RAILWAY HISTORICAL SOCIETY
HCR 71, Box 1318
Forest Grove, OR 97116
(503) 640-1434
(503) 357-3574

Greg Bonn (President)

Contact: Paul Class (Trustee)
Services: Historical society. Holds archival film and videotape collection.
Description: Footage of historic electric trolley cars and trolley buses in Portland, Oregon (1950-56). Tramway was a complete system that had retained all its original equipment, 1898-1940, and was abandoned in 1956.
Size & Elements: Film: 16mm (800 feet); 8mm (2,000 feet; color and black and white). Videotape: VHS (3 videotapes, 2 hours).
Cataloging: None specified.
Access: Apply for information.
Rights: Apply for information.
Licensing: Apply for information.
Restrictions: None specified.
Viewing Facilities: None.
Duplication Facilities: None.

OREGON (Jacksonville)

SOUTHERN OREGON HISTORICAL SOCIETY
P.O. Box 480
Jacksonville, OR 97530
(503) 899-1847 (Jacksonville)
(503) 826-4908 (White City)

Street addresses: 520 North 5th Street, Jacksonville, OR
Southern Oregon Archives, 320 Antelope Road, White City, OR

Samuel J. Wegner (Executive Director)

Contact: Paul A. Richardson (Librarian/Archivist)
Services: State historical society. Film collection open to the public for in-house use only.
Description: Newsfilm footage originally produced by the local television station KMED (Medford, Oregon) (ca. 1965-76). The film is physically located at the Southern Oregon Archives in White City.
Size & Elements: Film: 16mm (194 cubic feet, 1.5 million feet, approx. 7,500 reels).
Cataloging: Finding aids (transmittal forms).
Access: Open to the public. For in-house use only. Research fees charged for mail requests. Requests accepted by mail, telephone and in person (walk-in).
Rights: Full rights held to all material. Additional clearances (copyright) may be necessary in some cases if material is to be reused.
Licensing: Apply for information. License fees charged.
Restrictions: None specified.
Viewing Facilities: None.
Duplication Facilities: None.

OREGON (Portland)

EDUCATIONAL PRODUCTIONS
4925 Southwest Humphrey Park Crest
Portland, OR 97221
(503) 292-9234

Contact: Staff
Services: Videotape producer and distributor. Materials available to health care professionals for rental and purchase.
Description: Videotape training programs designed for health care professionals and educators. Major areas covered include AIDS, kidney failure and disease, patient transport, back injuries, and language acquisition for children.

Size & Elements: Videotape: 3/4", VHS, Betamax I, II and III (13 titles).
Cataloging: Brochures.
Access: Available to health care professionals for five-day rental, preview and purchase. Requests accepted by mail and telephone. Multiple program purchase discounts may apply.
Rights: Apply for information.
Licensing: Apply for information.
Restrictions: Apply for information.
Viewing Facilities: None.
Duplication Facilities: None.

OREGON (Portland)

THE MEDIA PROJECT
Box 2008
Portland, OR 97208
(503) 223-5335
Fax: (503) 225-0809

Street address: Union Station, Room 200

Sue Mach (Director)

Contact: Sue Mach
Services: Media organization; film and videotape distributor. Material available for purchase and rental; available for duplication and reuse in some cases, subject to clearance and approval.
Description: Nonprofit organization designed to stimulate public awareness of and support for the work of regional film and video artists. Created in 1974 by filmmakers and teachers, the Project arranges workshops and seminars, provides a clearinghouse for information, and exhibits film and videotape programs. Distributes films and videotapes produced in the Northwest by local artists, film and videomakers. All work has been acquired since 1974.

The Pacific Northwest. Historical films and videotapes include: *Freedom Frontier* (1976), on the history of Blacks in Oregon; *Let 'er Buck* (1976), on rodeos and rodeo cowboys, past and present; *Looking Backwards* (1921-25, assembled 1973), early footage from Oregon restored by Lew Cook, now in the collection of the Oregon Historical Society, Film Archives (q.v.); *Gone For a Better Deal* (1972), a profile of the 1960s "youth movement"; *They Knew You By Name* (1982), on the past and present of Portland's Skid Road; *Tamanawis Illahee* (1982), the story of the U.S. Northwest from the mid-18th to mid-19th century; and *They Hailed a Steamboat Anyplace* (1974), the history of the Willamette River and its steamboats.

The land. Titles include: *Land's Edge* (1974), a documentary of coastal life, filmed in the Newport, Oregon area and on a fishing boat; *Natural Timber Country* (1972), on the history of logging in the Pacific Northwest; and *The Earth is Our Home* (1980), a portrait of Paiute Indian ways of life and culture.

The people. Titles include: *The People Are Dancing Again* (1976), documenting the struggle of the Siletz Indian tribe to regain federal recognition; *The Old Believers* (1981), exploring the traditions and beliefs of 5,000 members of an "Old Believer" community (until 1666, members of the Russian Orthodox Church) in Woodburn, Oregon; *Roger Baldwin* (1978), is an intimate biography of the founder and former director of the American Civil Liberties Union; *Luther Metke at 94* (1980), based on the folk art, poetry and philosophy of Luther Metke — a homesteader, Spanish American War veteran, and labor organizer who has lived in the Cascade Mountains since 1907; *Thorne Family Film* (1977), about a family of Eastern Oregon's "wheat country," its descendants and their way of life.

Art and artisans. Titles include *Oregon Woodcarvers* (1980); *Claymation* (1978), a behind-the-scenes look at the work of the Will Vinton studio; *Fireworks* (1979), an aerial display of 200 shells, created by pyrotechnician John Sinclair; and *Northwest Visionaries* (1979), on the work of Mark Tobey, Kenneth Callahan, Morris Graves, Margaret Tomkins, Guy Anderson, Paul Horiuchi, Helmi Junoven and George Tsutakawa.

Asian studies. Titles include: *East of Occidental* (1986), on the saga of Seattle's Chinatown (now known as the International District) and a portrait of Chinese, Japanese and Filipino immigrants to the United States; *China: The Land and Its People,* a four-part series of documentaries presenting the history and culture of China from prehistory to present.

Women's lives. Titles include: *Some of These Days* (Elaine Velazquez, 1980), about four women grappling with the process of aging in America; *Footbinding* (1978), combining a reenactment of the ancient footbinding ritual with historical stills and contemporary documentary footage to provide a comprehensive view of the dynamics which force women to accept male-defined standards of beauty; *A Family Affair* (1981), a drama about a battered wife who decides the battering must end.

Contemporary culture. Titles include: *Chickens: A Process* (1973-80), showing the slaughtering and processing of chickens destined for our supermarket shelves; *Property* (Penny Allen and Eric Edwards, 1978), a dramatic feature concerning the youth subculture in Southwest Portland; *Nobody Lives Here* (1979), depicting the consciousness of the prisoner, with interviews filmed at Washington State Penitentiary; *Goose Hollow* (1982), examining a section of Portland and its neighborhood identity; *Savage* (1978), showing the smoke, sweat and ritual of live wrestling; *Gas City* (Jeff Meyer, 1978), a portrait of the subculture centered along neon-lit U.S. Highway 101.

Labor. Titles include: *Cuts* (1980), showing Pacific Northwest mill workers, especially shingle sawyers and their work; *Company Town* (1979), examining a community (Westfir, Oregon) after its lumber mill closed, and the attempt by mill workers to buy the mill and run it as a cooperative; *Making Bread* (1979), on the machinations of a bread factory; *Oregon Work* (1982), exploring creative solutions to recession through labor/industry cooperation, using the example of the owner of a small mill in Philomath, Oregon; *Hurt on the Job* (1979), featuring handicapped workers describing the dangers of their former jobs, how they were injured, the reaction of their employers and the processes they went through to receive workers' compensation.

Animation. Work by Jim Blashfield, Rose Bond, Ken Butler, Jules Engel, Bob Gardiner, John Haugse, Uli Kretzschmar, Roger Kukes, Ken O'Connell, Joanna Priestley, Will Vinton and R. Dennis Wiancko.

Experimental films. Films by Jim Blashfield, Paul Brekke, Laura DiTrapani, Janice Findley, David Joyce, Karl Krogstad, Ken Levine, Sharon Niemczyk, Philip Perkins and Patricia Quinn.
Size & Elements: Film: 16mm. Videotape: 3/4", VHS and Betamax. (Approx. 100 titles total).
Cataloging: Published catalogs.
Access: Available for rental and purchase, and for licensing and reuse in some cases, subject to restrictions.
Rights: Some rights held to all material. Rights to some material, including clip rights, retained by filmmakers. Additional clearances may be necessary in some cases if material is to be reused.
Licensing: Available for licensing and reuse in some cases, subject to restrictions. License fees charged.
Restrictions: Reuse of some material is restricted due to rights status.
Viewing Facilities: Film.
Duplication Facilities: Videotape (3/4" to 1/2).

OREGON (Portland)

ODYSSEY PRODUCTIONS, INC.
2800 Northwest Thurman Street
Portland, OR 97210
(503) 223-3480

Stephen R. Heiser (Director/President)

Contacts: Jim Salmon (Executive Producer); Carol Sherman (Producer)
Services: Film and videotape producer. Material available for licensing and reuse.
Description: Northwest scenics (coasts, forests, mountains and cities); timber (all aspects); high technology (manufacturing); and wildlife.
Size & Elements: Film: 16mm (100,000 feet). Videotape: 1" (masters); VHS (viewing copies).
Cataloging: Shot lists; dope sheets or release sheets.
Access: Available for licensing and reuse. Research fees charged. Research requests accepted by mail and telephone.
Rights: Full rights held to some material. Some rights held to some material.
Licensing: Available for licensing and reuse. License fees charged.
Restrictions: None specified.
Viewing Facilities: Film (16mm); videotape (VHS).
Duplication Facilities: None.

OREGON (Portland)

OREGON HISTORICAL SOCIETY
FILM ARCHIVES
1230 SW Park Avenue
Portland, OR 97205
(503) 222-1741

Thomas Vaughan (Executive Director, Oregon Historical Society)
William Tramposch (Executive Director, effective July 1, 1989)

OREGON (Portland)

Contacts: Michele Kribs (Film Preservationist); Mikki Tint (Film Cataloger)
Services: Historical society. Film and videotape collection available for duplication, subject to restrictions.
Description: Material relating to Oregon and the Pacific Northwest region (Washington, Idaho, northern California, British Columbia, Alaska, and Hawaii) (1902-82, most holdings span the period 1911-82). Most material is 16mm film, including both original footage, such as television newsfilm and home movies, and reductions of 35mm nitrate films, such as newsreels. Several collections from commercial filmmakers of the region are also held.

In 1956, OHS began to collect and preserve historic film footage. Local filmmaker Lewis Clark Cook served as a consultant to the film archives until his retirement in 1976 when he joined OHS staff as Film Archivist. From 1956 until his death in 1983, he brought to bear his vast knowledge of films and filmmakers in the acquisition and preservation of motion picture films relating to Oregon and the West. Mr. Cook designed and built two reduction printers (for transferring the image from inflammable 35mm nitrate film to 16mm safety film). One of these machines is still used by OHS Film Archives staff in their preservation work.

Holdings include over 10,000 titles on diverse subjects (early newsreels, family movies, commercial and industrial films, scenics and wildlife, and a host of segments and outtakes) produced by professional and amateur cameramen and women. Archives also preserves television news and documentary film (early 1960s-82), when videotape largely replaced the use of motion picture film.

KOIN Collection. Local television newsfilm dailies from a Portland station (1962-63, 1966-82). Since KOIN began in 1980 to originate news stories on videotape, the Society does not have film for every day in 1980-82. Indexed.

KATU Collection. Local television newsfilm dailies from a Portland station (1968-70). Unindexed. The KATU "generic film file" contains stock footage material from the 1970s, largely undated, and is inventoried.

Northwest Illustrated (1978-83). A "magazine show" produced by KOIN. The Society holds edited film and outtakes, but no videotape or narration. Inventoried.

Following is a brief subject summary of Archives holdings:

Alaska. Anchorage (1914); Bering Sea (1928); Childs Glacier; Eagle River; Eskimo life (1920s); Glacier Bay (1915); Juneau (1920s); King Island; mining; Nunivak Island; Petersburg; Point Barrow; ship salvage; wildlife.

California. Death Valley; Golden Gate Bridge (San Francisco); missions; San Francisco World's Fair (1939); San Diego; Tournament of Roses (Pasadena, 1924).

Hawaii. Honolulu (1914); Kilauea Volcano (1914); Mauna Loa Volcano (1942).

Montana. Glacier National Park (1926); McDonald Pass, Continental Divide; mining, Missouri River.

Oregon. Agriculture including cattle (1920s), fruit (1920s-70s), hops, sheep (1920s-60s), wheat (1920s); aviation (1905-40s) featuring Edith Foltz, Dorothy Hester, Charles Lindbergh and Tex Rankin; Baker (1957), Canyon City (1935); Celilo Indians (1920s-59); coast (1924-54); Columbia River (1914-59); Crater Lake (1920s-66); Eugene (1920s); fishing (1924-50s); governors of Oregon including Victor Atiyeh, Mark Hatfield, Robert Holmes, Tom McCall, I. L. Patterson, Walter Pierce, Elmo Smith, Bob Straub, Oswald West, James Withycombe; Grants Pass (1927); Heppner (1920s); Hydro power and dams; Indians (1913-31); industry including fishing, forestry, heavy equipment, papermaking, retail sales; logging (1915-60s); Medford (1920s); mining; Mt. Hood (1920s-50s); newsreels (1910s-30s); nuclear power plants; Oregon State University (1920s); Pendleton Round-Up (rodeo, 1911-44); Portland (1914-70s) including airports, Christmas flood, and the Junior Symphony; Portland mayors including George Baker, Neil Goldschmidt, Frank Ivancie, Dorothy McCullough Lee, and Terry Schrunk; Portland Rose Festival (1914-83); shipyards (1940-42); streetcars (1930s-50s); Steve Prefontaine (athlete, 1971-75); Salem (1917-75); Silverton (1926); sports; The Dalles (1920s); Three Sisters (1916); U.S. congressmen including Harris Ellsworth, Walter Norblad); U.S. presidents including Dwight Eisenhower, Warren Harding, Herbert Hoover, Richard Nixon, Franklin Roosevelt; U.S. senators including Mark Hatfield, Wayne Morse, Richard Neuberger; Vanport (1948); Willamette River pollution; World War I.

Washington. Fort Vancouver; Grays Harbor; Mt. Baker (1930s); Mt. Rainier (including climbs, 1920s); Olympia (1930s); Olympic Peninsula Loop; Seattle (1922-40); Tacoma (1922-50); Vancouver (airport).

Other U.S. states. Arizona (Grand Canyon); Depression (1930s); Florida (1936); Idaho (Hells Canyon, mining, Salmon River); Nevada; Wyoming (Yellowstone National Park, 1926-30s); Washington D.C. (aerials, 1922).

Other countries. Afghanistan (1934); Canada (Yukon River, 1928); England (London); Italy (1920s); Indonesia (Java); Mexico (bullfight, 1924); Morocco (1920s); Northern Europe (1920s); Panama Canal (1954); San Marino (1921); Spain (1920s); Yugoslavia (1920s).

Size & Elements: Approx. 10,000 titles in 10,000 cans are held. Film: 35mm (approx. 241,200 feet); 28mm (approx. 300 feet); 17.5 mm (approx. 500 feet); 16mm (approx. 6,800,000 feet); 9.5 mm (approx. 400 feet); 8mm and Super 8mm (approx. 2,500 feet). Majority of film holdings are camera originals and reversal positives. Videotape: 1" (approx. 160 videotapes); 2" (approx. 250 videotapes); 3/4" (approx. 130 videotapes); 1/2" (approx. 20 VHS and Betamax videotapes); 1/2" open reel (approx. 390 videotapes). Videotapes are generally second and third generation dubs. Plans are underway to produce videotape viewing copies of entire collection.
Cataloging: Computerized cataloging available to researchers; other finding aids available. An in-house book catalog is planned.
Access: Open to the public. For in-house use only. Available for duplication. Research requests accepted by mail, telephone and in person. Research fees charged only when OHS staff time is involved; patrons not charged to do their own research. No original footage is loaned; all viewing is done on premises.
Rights: Some rights held to all material. Additional clearances may be necessary in some cases if material is to be reused.
Licensing: Available for licensing and reuse, subject to restrictions. License and usage fees charged (price schedule available). Special fee schedule applies to technical services, research services and production use for and by television news media.
Restrictions: Usage fee clears one-time use only. Air credit to Oregon Historical Society Film Archives and collection name required. Requests for reuse or change in use must be submitted in writing to the Film Preservationist. A complimentary copy of any production using OHS footage on film or videotape should be deposited in OHS Film Archives.
Viewing Facilities: Film and videotape (3/4") (by appointment only).
Duplication Facilities: Film (film-to-videotape transfer facilities, 16mm to 3/4"); videotape (3/4" to 3/4"). Archives also performs preservation work on 35mm, 16mm, regular and Super 8mm films for other institutions and individuals. Fee schedule for copy footage and preservation work is available.

OREGON (Portland)

PORTLAND CABLE ACCESS TV
2766 Northeast Union Avenue
Portland, OR 97212
(503) 288-1515

Deborah M. Luppold (General Manager)

Contact: Staff
Services: Public access television facility. Videotape footage available for reuse on a case-by-case basis, subject to restrictions.
Description: Provides facilities for public access programming to the community. Programming five channels, it provides a viable means of airing non-commercial and independent television programs.

Library holds file footage from community-produced programs and footage of Pacific Northwest and Portland landmarks.
Size & Elements: Videotape: 3/4" (amount unspecified).
Cataloging: None specified.
Access: Available for reuse at request of individual producers. Research fees not charged. Research requests accepted by mail only.
Rights: No rights held to any material. Rights retained by individual producers.
Licensing: Available for reuse, subject to restrictions. Usage fees not charged. Duplication and raw stock fees charged.
Restrictions: Available for reuse on a case-by-case basis at request of individual producers only.
Viewing Facilities: Videotape.
Duplication Facilities: Film (16mm, Super 8mm); videotape (3/4" and VHS) (duplication and raw stock fees charged).

OREGON (Tillamook)

AMERICAN NEPAL EDUCATION FOUNDATION
2790 Cape Meares Loop
Tillamook, OR 97141
(503) 842-4024

Hugh B. Wood (Executive Director)

Contact: Hugh B. Wood
Services: Foundation. Videotapes available for duplication, licensing and reuse.

Description: Two color films made in Nepal (ca. 1956-58, each approx. 30 min.).
Size & Elements: Videotape: VHS (2 titles; transfers from film).
Cataloging: None specified.
Access: Available for duplication, licensing and reuse.
Rights: Full rights held to all material.
Licensing: Available for licensing and reuse. License fees not charged.
Restrictions: None specified.
Viewing Facilities: None.
Duplication Facilities: None.
Related Materials: Approx. 300 color slides; recordings of Nepalese and Indian music.

PENNSYLVANIA

PENNSYLVANIA (Berwyn)

SPORTSFILM
511 Old Lancaster Pike
Berwyn, PA 19312
(215) 296-7834

Contacts: Ron Kentres; Joy Will
Services: Film stock footage sales library.
Description: Coverage of all sports except professional football (1950-65); some college football footage (1965-present). Holds a number of sports program series, including:

Telesports Digest (1950-66, 855 weekly episodes; each 30 min.). A national sports wrapup program that was syndicated throughout the United States and abroad. Coverage ranges from professional to college and amateur sports, and includes scheduled and/or recurring events. Most material is in black and white. *Sports Spotlight* (1953 through mid-1957, 231 episodes, each 15 min.) is a condensation of *Telesports Digest.*

College Football's Greatest Games (1961-65, 104 programs; black and white and color). Highlights of major contests.

Night at the Races (ca. 1953-62, approx. 100 programs, each 15 min.). Programs sponsored by racetracks in New Jersey and elsewhere, containing footage of famous horses and other material of historic interest.

Touchdown (1950-72, 11 weekly episodes during college football seasons, each 30 min., plus one All-American show and year-end review). Wrapups of major college football game highlights.

Telesports Digest coverage includes many of the following sports:

Auto racing. Stories include: *Joie Chitwood's Daredevil Drivers* (1950); *12-Hour Endurance From Sebring* (1952); *Race Drivers Dodge Drifts* (1955); *Johnny Thompson Wins 100-mile Race* (1957); *Ill-fated Cuban Race Called After 6 Laps* (1958); *Parisian Hell Drivers* (1960); *Trenton Hosts Big Cars* (1963); *Art Arfons Breaks Speed Record* (1964); and *Mount Washington Road Race* (1966).

Baseball. Stories include: *Eddie Sawyer and Harry Wismer* (interviews) (1950); *It's Those Yanks Again* (1951); *Mid-Season Roundup* (1953); *Casey Stengel Interview — Walt Alston Interview* (1955); *Distaff World Series* (1956); *Milwaukee Braves Dump New York Yanks in 7th Game of the World Series* (1957); *Indians Invade Manhattan* (1960); *Home Run King — Roger Maris* (1961); *Dodgers Clash with Pirates* (1963); *Sandy Koufax* (1963); and *Giants Invade Pittsburgh* (1965).

College basketball. Stories include: *Mikvy-Wismer Interview* (1951); *Duquesne vs. Villanova* (1954); *Wilt the Stilt* (1955); *Utah Beats Brigham Young* (1958); *National Women's AAU Basketball* (1962); and *USA-Russia Basketball* (1965).

Professional basketball. Stories include: *Cousy Grooms Future Stars* (1959); *The San Francisco Warriors* (1963); and *Red Auerbach and His Boston Celtics* (1965).

Boating. Stories include: *Single Scull World Championship* (1950); *Women's College Rowing* (1952); *White Water Canoeists* (1955); *Adams Cup on Schuylkill* (1957); *Crazy Float Parade* (1959); *Salt Lake Regatta* (1960); *Yacht Race of Mackinac* (1962); and *Whaleboat Cup Race IRA Regatta* (1966).

Boxing. Stories include: *Tiberio Mitri Training* (1950); *Jersey Joe Walcott Visits Vets at Valley Forge Hospital* (1951); *Pep-Savoie Fight* (1952); *Rawlings-Zulueta Fight* (1953); *Pastrano-Labua* (1954); *Summerlin Takes Carter* (1956); *Sonny Liston KO's Wayne Bethea in 69 Seconds* (1958); *Flying Leather in Chicago* (1961); *Robinson-Graziano* (1966); and *Joe Frazier* (1966).

Golf. Stories include: *Personality in the News: Lloyd Mangrum* (1951); *Salute to Babe Zaharias* (1956); *Dallas Women's Open* (1957); *World's Richest Golf Tournament for Women* (1959); *Pro-Am Golf Tournament at Aronimink* (1962); *Sahara Invitational* (1964); and *Billy Casper Feature Story* (1966).

Gymnastics. Stories include: *Olympic Tryouts at Penn State* (1952); *Swedish Team Exhibition* (1955); *Finland's Gymnasts at Penn State* (1959); and *North American Gymnastic Stars* (1964).

Horse racing. Stories include: *Brooklyn Handicap* (1950); *Saranac Handicap* (1952); *Washington Park Futurity* (1953); *The Monmouth Handicap* (1956); *American Trotting* (1958); *The Kentucky Derby* (1960); *Italy's Famous Siena Palio* (1960); *The Gray Lag Handicap* (1962); and *Spicy Living Eyes Triple Crown* (1963).

Miscellaneous sports action. Coverage of archery, badminton, billiards, bowling, bullfighting, cricket, cross-country, curling, cycling, dog shows, dog sled racing, fencing, field hockey, fly casting, handball, horseshoes, jai alai, judo, karate, keg hurdling, lacrosse, marbles, model airplanes, pistols, power lifting, roller derby, roller skating, rugby, Scottish games, skeet shooting, skin diving, soaring, spearfishing, speed skating, squash, surfing, volleyball, water polo and weightlifting. There is also excellent coverage of miscellaneous stunts and oddities involving both animals and human beings.

Motorcycle races. Stories include: *Two-Wheel Gypsies* (1951); *Motorcycles on Ice* (1956); *Two-Wheel Tornadoes* (1962); and *Roger Kussmavl Wins the 1964 Jack Pine Motorcycle Run* (1964).

Soccer. Stories include: *English-American Soccer Exhibition* (1951); *Gaelic football* (1962); *Philadelphia Ukrainian Booters Face Detroit Scots* (1961); and *NCAA Soccer Tourney* (1964).

Swimming and diving. Stories include: *Lifeguard Sequence* (1951); *AAU Women's Synchronized Swim* (1952); *Underwater Swimming* (1954); *Florence Chadwick* (1954); *Ten-Year-Old Swims Lake Dallas* (1955); *Juniors Plunge For Title* (1959); *Water Sports in Hawaii* (1961); *25-Mile Ocean Swim* (1963); *26-Mile Ocean Swim* (1965); and *Senior Men's National Water Polo Championship* (1966).

Tennis. Stories include: *U.S. Girls Tennis Championship* (1950); *Veterans Top Tennis Tournament* (1955); *Gonzales and Trabert Duel in Pro Tennis* (1956); *Seixas Shines in Grass Court Tennis* (1956); *Mervin Rose Wins Dallas Tennis* (1957); *Pennsylvania Lawn Tennis Championships* (1962); *Merion Grass Court Wizards* (1963); and *U.S. Girls Singles* (1966).

Track and field. Stories include: *Penn Relays* (1950); *Mormon Meteor* (1951); *National Women's Pentathlon* (1951); *Heel and Toe Race* (1953); *Kansas Relays* (1955); *Sports Personalities — Karen Anderson* (1956); *Eastern Track Stars Meet at Villanova* (1958); *Paavo Kotila wins Boston Marathon* (1960); *Wilma Rudolph, Don Bragg, Parry O'Brien* (1961); *Russian-American Track* (1964); and *Jim Ryun Sets New World Record for Mile* (1966).

Winter sports. Stories include: *Summer Ski Jump* (1950); *Snow Kids Invade Yosemite* (1952); *Stanley Cup* (1953); *Ski Joring* (1954); *Snow Fun* (1955); *Web Foot Racers* (1956); *Best on Ice* (1956); *Figure Skating* (1957); *Mid-Summer Iceskating* (1958); *Baby Sitters Ski School* (1960); *New Wrinkle on the Ice* (1961); *World Amateur Hockey* (1962); *Bruins-Montréal Ice Hockey* (1963); *Sled Dog Championships* (1964); *Swiss Wonderland* (1965); and *Spring Skiing in the Rockies* (1966).

Wrestling. Stories include: *Blind Wrestlers* (1951); *Alligator Wrestling* (1954); *Joe Louis Wrestles Sky Lee* (1956); *Grunt and Groan Grapplers* (1957); *June Byers Defends Title* (1958); *Mat Monsters Meet* (1961); *Sammartino Beats Blassie* (1964); and *Swiss Wrestling* (1965).
Size & Elements: Film: 16mm (over 40 million feet; positive, negative, reversal, originals, release prints).
Cataloging: Published catalog.
Access: Available to the public for licensing and reuse. Research fees charged. Research requests accepted by mail, telephone and in person (by appointment only).
Rights: Full rights held to all material.
Licensing: Available for licensing. License fees charged.
Restrictions: None specified.
Viewing Facilities: Film (16mm).
Duplication Facilities: None (arrangements can be made).

PENNSYLVANIA (Carlisle Barracks)

U.S. ARMY MILITARY HISTORY INSTITUTE AUDIOVISUAL ARCHIVES
Carlisle Barracks, PA 17013-5008
(717) 245-4114
(717) 245-3434

Col. Rod Paschall (Director, USAMHI)

Contact: Geffery Hoskins (Audiovisual Archivist)

PENNSYLVANIA (Clarks Summit)

Services: Government agency. Material available for research and reuse, subject to clearance and approval.
Description: Military history, specifically relating to the U.S. Army (Civil War-present). Particular strengths include World War II material.
Size & Elements: Film: 16mm (400 titles, 300 presently cataloged; positives and originals). Videotape: format unspecified (200 videotapes; masters).
Cataloging: Card catalogs.
Access: For in-house use only. Open to researchers and scholars only by permission of Director. Research fees not charged. Research requests accepted by mail, telephone and in person (walk-in).
Rights: Full rights held to all material. Additional clearances may be necessary in some cases if material is to be reused.
Licensing: Available for licensing and reuse, subject to restrictions. Usage fees generally not charged.
Restrictions: Requests for licensing and reuse subject to clearance and approval. Reuse of some material may be restricted.
Viewing Facilities: Film and videotape (supervised by Audiovisual Archivist).
Duplication Facilities: None.

PENNSYLVANIA (Clarks Summit)

INTERNATIONAL SOCIETY FOR ANIMAL RIGHTS FILM LIBRARY
421 South State Street
Clarks Summit, PA 18411
(717) 586-2200

Helen Jones (President)

Contact: Pamela Zikoski (Film Librarian)
Services: Nonprofit corporation; videotape distributor. Material available primarily for rental.
Description: Seeks to publicize and prevent the abuse and exploitation of animals. Films and videotapes examine animal experimentation, the anti-vivisection movement, animal shelters, and vegetarianism as a way of life. One film, *Products of Pain: Inside the Gillette Animal Labs,* shows rabbits struggling in dermal toxicity tests, Draize tests in which products are tested by placing substances (e.g., ink and deodorant) in rabbits' eyes, and other instances of animal abuse in product testing.
Size & Elements: Film and videotape: formats unspecified (6 titles).
Cataloging: Published catalog.
Access: Available to the public for rental. Research fees not charged.
Rights: Apply for information.
Licensing: Apply for information.
Restrictions: None specified.
Viewing Facilities: None.
Duplication Facilities: None.

PENNSYLVANIA (Doylestown)

*TOUGH*LOVE
P.O. Box 1069
Doylestown, PA 18901
(215) 348-7090

Gwen Olitsky (Managing Director)

Contact: Gwen Olitsky
Services: Nonprofit self-help organization. Videotape material available for licensing and reuse.
Description: "*Tough*love is a self-help program for families and neighborhoods. It is a combination of philosophy and action which, together, can help families and neighborhoods to change....It is a crisis-intervention program, structuring group meetings to support parents and spouses in demanding responsible cooperation from out-of-control family members."

Subjects covered include: adolescent problems, family problems, drug and alcohol issues. Two titles available: *Tough*love (ABC-TV docudrama aired October 13, 1985; starring Lee Remick and Bruce Dern), the story of two *Tough*love Families and their experiences; and *Tough*love: That's the Spirit (commissioned by the Passionist Fathers for Channel 9, New York City), about a *Tough*love Group. Features group members, the priest who started the group, the founder of Toughlove (David York) and a *Tough*love Kid.
Size & Elements: Videotape: format unspecified (2 titles).
Cataloging: None specified.
Access: Available for licensing and reuse. Research fees not charged.

Rights: Full rights held to some material. Additional clearances may be necessary in some cases if material is to be reused.
Licensing: Available for licensing and reuse. License and usage fees not charged.
Restrictions: Apply for information.
Viewing Facilities: None.
Duplication Facilities: None.

PENNSYLVANIA (Elverson)

INTERNATIONAL AL JOLSON SOCIETY
12 Mauger Road
Elverson, PA 19520
(215) 286-5289

Harold Rhinehart (President)

Contact: Harold Rhinehart
Services: Historical society. Film collection available for rental and purchase to society members only.
Description: Feature films, short subjects and home movies of Al Jolson.

Titles include: *The Jazz Singer* (1927); *The Singing Fool* (1928); *Say it With Songs* (1929); *Mammy* (1930); *Big Boy* (1930); *Hallelujah I'm a Bum* (1933); *Wonder Bar* (1934); *Go Into Your Dance* (1935); *The Singing Kid* (1936); *Rose of Washington Square* (1939); *Hollywood Cavalcade* (cameo appearance, 1939); *The Jolson Story* (1946); and *Jolson Sings Again* (1949). *The Best of Jolson* includes screen tests and movie trailers. Also held are outtakes from *The Jolson Story* and *Jolson Sings Again;* songs (1927-47) in *Jolie Sings;* Jolson tribute videotape at his 100th birthday celebration, including interviews with colleagues, rare footage and visits to the Jolson house in Encino, California; clips from radio shows and the Clive Baldwin show, with an appearance by Mrs. Jolson; *Steppin' Out with Clive Baldwin*; a recreation of Kraft Music Hall starring Clive Baldwin as Al Jolson (1986); Clive Baldwin in concert; *The Real Al Jolson Story,* a documentary from Britain's ITV; and *The Al Jolson 100th Birthday Celebration.*
Size & Elements: Videotape: VHS and Betamax (25 titles).
Cataloging: Research library.
Access: Not open to the public. Material available for rental and purchase to society members only. Maintained for distribution and rental rather than for research or reuse. Requests accepted by mail, telephone and in person (by appointment only).
Rights: Some rights held to some material. Some material in public domain. Rights status of some material not known.
Licensing: Apply for information.
Restrictions: Videotapes available to society members only.
Viewing Facilities: None.
Duplication Facilities: Videotape.

PENNSYLVANIA (Grantham)

BRETHREN IN CHRIST CHURCH AND MESSIAH COLLEGE ARCHIVES
Messiah College
Grantham, PA 17027
(717) 766-2511 (Ext. 388)

Contact: E. Morris Sider (Archivist)
Services: Church archives. Film and videotape collection available for duplication and reuse, subject to restrictions.
Description: Holds promotional films relating to Messiah College history; films on its sponsoring denomination (Brethren in Christ Church), including a historical pageant performed on the 200th anniversary of the denomination (1978); and a series of historical-doctrinal films concerning the same denomination.
Size & Elements: Film: format unspecified (approx. 12,000 feet, 14 titles, 14 cans; primarily originals). Videotape: format unspecified (approx. 12 hours, 10 titles; masters and viewing copies).
Cataloging: Card catalogs.
Access: Available to the public. Research fees not charged. Research requests accepted by mail and telephone.
Rights: Full rights held to all material.
Licensing: Available for licensing, subject to restrictions.
Restrictions: Special permission necessary for licensing or reuse.
Viewing Facilities: Film and videotape (in College media center).
Duplication Facilities: Available at College media center.

PENNSYLVANIA (Harrisburg)

JOSH HOOPER PRODUCTIONS, INC.
405 Boas Street
Harrisburg, PA 17102
(717) 545-8888

Josh Hooper (Principal)

Contacts: Mary Hargreaves (Production Coordinator); Michael Endy (Director)
Services: Film and videotape producer. Material available for duplication, licensing and reuse. Custom shooting service provided on request.
Description: Health care and hospital footage, including in- and out-patients, doctors and hospital scenes; transportation and trucking footage, including highways, aerials, several kinds of trucks and and shots of moving vehicles. Also holds a wide variety of generic footage.
Size & Elements: Film: format unspecified ("very little"). Videotape: 1", Betacam and 3/4" (approx. 100 hours; masters); 3/4" and 1/2" (viewing copies).
Cataloging: Computerized cataloging for staff use only (collection partially cataloged); shot lists.
Access: Available to the public for duplication, licensing and reuse. Research fees charged (fees negotiable). Research requests accepted by mail, telephone and in person (by appointment only).
Rights: Full rights held to all material.
Licensing: Available for licensing. License fees charged.
Restrictions: None specified.
Viewing Facilities: Videotape (3/4" and 1/2").
Duplication Facilities: None (outside arrangements can be made).

PENNSYLVANIA (Harrisburg)

PENNSYLVANIA STATE ARCHIVES
3rd and Forster Streets
Harrisburg, PA 17108-1026
(717) 787-2701

Harry E. Whipkey (State Archivist)

Contact: Search Room reference desk
Services: Government agency. Film and videotape collection available to the public for research and reuse.
Description: Pennsylvania history, persons, places and events (ca. 1926-85).
Records of the Department of Labor and Industry. Films made during World War II, dealing with the role of women in the war effort and the use of railroads by the military. Titles include: *All Out For Victory; Glamour Girls of 1943; Women on the Warpath; Community at War; Railroaders Always; Women Power; Lifeline of the National Railroads;* and *Your Job Insurance,* explaining the procedures for obtaining workmen's compensation, with footage of President Roosevelt and Governor Earle.
Bureau of Public Education films. Intended to increase public awareness about socially disadvantaged and mentally and physically handicapped people. Holds training films for social workers; and *After Agnes: The Quiet Crisis,* concerning the Department of Welfare's response to Hurricane Agnes (1972).
Miscellaneous acquisitions. Includes *Pennsylvania State Police,* shown at the United States Sesquicentennial Exposition (1926), explaining the establishment and duties of the State Police and the true-life story of Trooper Frances Haley, killed in the line of duty. Films by Sherm Lutz (ca. 1935-55) trace his activities as a trainer for the Civilian Pilot Training Program at Boalsburg Air Field. Scenes show trainees checking planes and practicing takeoffs and landings. Also included are scenes at the State College Air Depot (ca. 1945-55) with footage of the landing of the first DC-3. *Village Life at Laurelton State Village* (ca. 1945-50) taken by Dr. Catherine Edgett, with scenes of the facility and patients receiving treatment. *Ike at Gettysburg* (June 1952, color) shows a reception given by Mr. and Mrs. Dwight Eisenhower at their Gettysburg farm; personalities include U.S. senators James Duff and M. Harvey Taylor, and Governor John Fine. *Left Bank, Right Bank,* produced by Pennsylvania State University (1976), concerns the voyage of the Bicentennial Raft on the Susquehanna.
Size & Elements: Film: 16mm (approx. 500 titles, approx. 500 cans; positive). Videotape: 1/2" (15 videotapes; viewing copies).
Cataloging: Published catalogs.
Access: Open to the public. Research fees not charged. Research requests accepted by mail, telephone and in person (by appointment only).
Rights: Material in the public domain.

Licensing: Available for reuse, subject to restrictions. Usage fees not charged.
Restrictions: Proper credit must be given to Archives when material is used.
Viewing Facilities: Film and videotape.
Duplication Facilities: None.

PENNSYLVANIA (Hershey)

HERSHEY FOODS CORPORATION
Corporate Administrative Center
14 East Chocolate Avenue
Hershey, PA 17033
(717) 534-7500
Fax: (717) 534-7896
Telex: 6711079 HERSH UW

Available for free loan from:
MODERN TALKING PICTURE SERVICE, INC. (q.v.)

Contact: Mike Kinney (Community Relations Representative)
Services: Corporation. Films available for free loan to the public, schools and organizations.
Description: Films on the Hershey Foods Corporation and their chocolate products.
Titles include: *A Great American Chocolate Story,* an educational behind-the-scenes look at the world of chocolate making, including cocoa bean and sugar cane farms in Central America, almond groves in California, peanut farms in Georgia, dairy farms in Pennsylvania and the Hershey factory (the world's largest chocolate factory); and *The Winning Spirit,* presenting Hershey's National Track & Field Youth Program for boys and girls from 9-14.
Size & Elements: Film: format unspecified (2 titles; release prints).
Cataloging: None specified.
Access: Available for free loan to the public, schools and organizations. Requests accepted by mail.
Rights: Full rights held to all material.
Licensing: Apply for information.
Restrictions: Apply for information.
Viewing Facilities: None.
Duplication Facilities: None.
Related Materials: Free educational material available with film loans.

PENNSYLVANIA (Jenkintown)

AMERICAN ANTI-VIVISECTION SOCIETY
Noble Plaza, Suite 204
801 Old York Road
Jenkintown, PA 19046
(215) 887-0816

William A. Cave (President)

Contacts: Bernard Unti (Assistant to the President); Peggy Eldon (Office Manager)
Services: Animal welfare society. One item available for purchase and reuse.
Description: *Suffer the Animals,* a documentary film prescribing viable alternatives to animal experimentation in the sciences. Numerous examples of various types of animal experimentation are intercut with scenes of laboratory workers showing alternatives. "During the time it takes to view this documentary, 8,000 animals have died as victims of research." The film presumes some knowledge of science.
Size & Elements: Film: 16mm (1 title). Videotape: 3/4" and VHS (1 title).
Cataloging: Release sheet.
Access: Available to the public for purchase and reuse. Research fees not charged. Requests accepted by mail, telephone and in person (walk-in).
Rights: Apply for information.
Licensing: Available for licensing and reuse. License fees charged. Film is available for purchase in 16mm or VHS videotape; also available in 3/4" videotape with broadcast rights.
Viewing Facilities: Videotape.
Duplication Facilities: None.

PENNSYLVANIA (Lancaster)

FRANKLIN & MARSHALL COLLEGE
SHADEK-FACKENTHAL LIBRARY
ARCHIVES AND SPECIAL COLLECTIONS DEPARTMENT

PENNSYLVANIA (Lancaster)

P.O. Box 3003
Lancaster, PA 17604-3003
(717) 291-4225

Charlotte B. Brown (College Archivist)

Contact: Charlotte B. Brown
Services: College archives. Some film and videotape material possibly available for reuse, subject to clearance and approval.
Description: *Franklin J. Schaffner Collection.* Includes film, videotape and manuscripts relating to the director's career (1949-82) and the making of his 12 Hollywood feature films: *The Stripper* (1963); *The Best Man* (1964); *The War Lord* (1965); *The Double Man* (1967); *Planet of the Apes* (1968); *Patton* (1970); *Nicholas and Alexandra* (1971); *Papillon* (1973); *Islands in the Stream* (1977); *The Boys from Brazil* (1978); *Sphinx* (1981); and *Yes, Giorgio* (1982). Prints of all films except *Yes, Giorgio* are held.

Franklin & Marshall College Collection (ca. 1925-present). Film and videotape materials include college football films, campus events, commencement footage, homecoming films and faculty-produced projects.
Size & Elements: Film and videotape: formats and amounts unspecified.
Cataloging: Inventories; lists; computerized cataloging (in progress).
Access: Available to the public. Research fees not charged. Research requests accepted by mail, telephone and in person.
Rights: Full rights held to some material. Some material in the public domain. Copyrights to some materials retained by original producers or distributors.
Licensing: Schaffner Collection not available for reuse. Other material may be available for licensing (apply for information). License and usage fees charged in some cases.
Restrictions: None specified.
Viewing Facilities: Film and videotape (at Instructional Media Services Center).
Duplication Facilities: Film and videotape (at IMS).
Related Materials: Pressbooks, screenplay typescripts, publicity posters, stills, reviews, interviews, shooting scripts, director's notes, advertising trailers, soundtracks, storyboards, video scripts and interviews.

PENNSYLVANIA (Lancaster)

LANCASTER MENNONITE HISTORICAL SOCIETY
2215 Millstream Road
Lancaster, PA 17602-1499
(717) 393-9745

Carolyn C. Wenger (Director)

Contact: Lloyd Zeager (Librarian)
Services: Historical society; library; museum. Videotape collection available for research and reuse in some cases.
Description: Videotapes relating to the historical background, religious thought, religious expression and culture of Mennonite-related groups originating in Pennsylvania (1900-present).
Size & Elements: Videotape: format unspecified (less than 50 titles).
Cataloging: Research library.
Access: Available to the public. Nominal research fees charged for non-members of Society. Research requests accepted by mail, telephone and in person (walk-in).
Rights: Full rights held to some material.
Licensing: Apply for information.
Restrictions: None specified.
Viewing Facilities: None.
Duplication Facilities: None.

PENNSYLVANIA (Oley)

BULLFROG FILMS, INC.
Oley, PA 19547
(215) 779-8226
(800) 543-3764

Contact: John Hoskyns-Abrahall
Services: Distributor. Films and videotapes available for rental, purchase and reuse, subject to restrictions.
Description: Educational programs on science, including ecology and environment, marine biology, forests, genetics, botany, animal studies, endangered species and the human body; energy (theory, policy, design and engineering); agriculture and gardening; social studies, including Native Americans, women's studies, future studies, peace and global issues, economics, government and citizen action, and waste management; arts and humanities, including music and ethics; home economics; health and education. Also distributes children's programming in similar areas, including the *OWL/TV* nature and science series (20 programs, each 29 min.) for children.

Science: the human body. Titles include: *Cell Wars* (1986), an introduction to immunology for intermediate students; and *Radiation: Impact on Life* (1982).

Science: ecology and environment. Titles include: *New Alchemy: A Rediscovery of Promise* (1983), a portrait of the pioneering appropriate technology group and its research in the areas of solar aquaculture, bioshelters, wind power and organic agriculture; *The Four Corners: A National Sacrifice Area?* (1983), on the hidden cost of uranium mining and milling, coal strip mining, and synthetic fuels development in the "Golden Circle of National Parks"; *In Our Own Backyards: Uranium Mining in the United States* (1981), on the environmental and health impacts of uranium mining and milling; *In Our Own Backyard: The First Love Canal* (1982), on the nation's first encounter with toxic waste; and *Something Nobody Else Has...The Story of Turtle Trapping in Louisiana* (1985).

Science: marine biology. Titles include: *The Northern Elephant Seal: Living on the Edge of Extinction* (1986); *Estuary* (1979); *Gulfstream* (1982); *The Great Horseshoe Crab Field Trip* (1982), using the crab to illustrate the scientific method and the way we all learn; and *Where the Bay Becomes the Sea* (1985), on the marine ecosystem where the Bay of Fundy meets the Atlantic Ocean.

Science: forests. Titles include: *Replanting the Tree of Life* (1987), designed to heighten awareness of the importance of trees; and *On the Edge of the Forest* (1977), with E. F. Schumacher, on the efficiency of the perfectly balanced forest ecosystem and its lessons for long-term human survival in our biosphere.

Science: genetics. Titles include: *Fragile Harvest* (1986), on the crisis in world agriculture created by genetic engineering and plant breeding; and *Lights Breaking: Ethical Questions About Genetic Engineering* (1985).

Energy: theory and policy. Titles include: *Energy and Morality* (1981), on the complex relationship of energy use to different value systems; *Toast* (1974), illustrating our underlying dependence on fossil fuels, using the production and distribution of bread as an example; *No Act of God* (1977), on the question of nuclear power and the breeder reactor; *Lovins on the Soft Path: An Energy Future with a Future* (1982), explaining the "soft path" policy that concentrates on efficiency and the appropriate use of renewable energy sources such as sun, wind and water; and *E. F. Schumacher — As If People Mattered* (1977).

Energy: design and engineering. Titles include: *Harness the Wind* (1978), a concise overview of the history and potential of wind power; *Kilowatts From Cowpies: The Methane Option* (1981), an overview of methane (biogas) as an energy resource; *A Portrait of Small Hydro* (1983), on entrepreneurs who have bought old New England dam sites and are rebuilding them for production of hydroelectric power; *The Solar Promise* (1979); *Design With the Sun* (1979); and *The Home Energy Conservation Series* (1980, 3 films, each 28 min.).

Agriculture. Titles include: *On American Soil* (1983), on the soil erosion problem; *Growing Pains: Rural America in the 1980s* (1985); and *Circle of Plenty* (1987), on biointensive agricultural techniques to improve the yield of home gardens; *Living the Good Life* (1977), looking at the home and daily lives of Helen and Scott Nearing, homesteaders since the Great Depression.

Gardening. Titles include: *The Close to Nature Garden* (1982); *Organic Gardening: Composting* (1972); and *Getting the Most from Your Garden: Raised Beds for High Yields* (1981).

Native Americans. Titles include: *Children of the Long-Beaked Bird* (1976), a portrait of a modern Native American family that erases the stereotypes made infamous by Westerns; *The Mystery of the Lost Red Paint People: The Discovery of a Prehistoric North American Sea Culture* (1987), on new archaeological discoveries around the periphery of the North Atlantic; and *The Sun Dagger* (1982), on the celestial calendar created by ancient North American Indians.

Peace and global issues. Titles include: *In the King of Prussia* (Emile de Antonio, 1982), a drama on the trial of the "Plowshares 8," peace activists who destroyed missile nosecones in a defense plant; and *Going Back: A Return to Vietnam* (1982), on a journey by the first American combat troops to return to Vietnam since the end of the war.

Government and citizen action. Titles include: *Downwind/Downstream: Threats to the Mountains and Waters of the American West* (1987), on the Colorado Rockies and the environmental effects of mining operations, acid rain and urbanization; *Neighbors: Conservation in a Changing Community* (1977), on Boston's South End; and *River Town* (1983), on the transformation of

Soldier's Grove (Wisconsin) from a flood-plagued community to the nation's first "solar town."

Waste management. Titles include *Recycling: Waste Into Wealth* (1984); and *Waste* (1984), connecting consumer habits with the waste disposal problem.

Ethics. Titles include: *Tools for Research: Questions About Animal Rights* (1983), which questions the use of animals in research, and attempts to answer many of the stock reasons given to justify this use.

Home economics. Titles include: *Rediscovering Herbs — Overview* (1981); *Culinary Herbs* (1981); *Stocking Up* (1982), on home food preservation; and *The Vegetarian World* (1983), an overview of the history and practices of vegetarianism worldwide.

Also distributes low-cost how-to videotapes on various subjects: massage; consumer education; energy conservation; home economics; financial management; knitting; woodworking; car care; breadmaking; and flower arrangement.

Size & Elements: Film: 16mm (approx. 120 titles). Videotape: 3/4", VHS and Betamax (approx. 160 titles).
Cataloging: Published catalog.
Access: Available for preview, rental and purchase. Requests accepted by mail and telephone.
Rights: No rights held to any material. All rights retained by filmmakers or original producers. Many titles may be licensed for television broadcast (apply for information and fees). Purchase price of materials includes cost of license permitting public performance.
Licensing: Available for television broadcast and other markets.
Restrictions: Purchase, rental or previewing of any Bullfrog film or videocassette does not include the right to duplicate, televise (either broadcast, cable or closed-circuit) in whole or in part, edit, adapt or alter the program in any way whatsoever, without prior written permission from Bullfrog Films.
Viewing Facilities: None.
Duplication Facilities: None.
Related Materials: Study guides for many programs.

PENNSYLVANIA (Perkasie)

PEARL S. BUCK FOUNDATION
Green Hills Farm
Perkasie, PA 18944
(215) 249-0100 (Pennsylvania)
(800) 242-2825 (outside Pennsylvania)
Fax: (215) 249-9657
Telex: 750416

Street address: 520 Dublin Road, Hilltown, PA 18927

Grace C. K. Sum (Executive Director)

Contact: Mark Viggiano (Director of Communications)
Services: Nonprofit foundation. Film and videotape collection available for duplication and reuse.
Description: Material relating to Amerasian children (fathered by American men and borne by Asian women). Includes information about Asia and Amerasian issues, in particular the abandonment of Amerasian children by their American fathers. Holdings include public service announcements, videotaped television broadcasts, special events at the Foundation and films made for the Foundation.
Size & Elements: Videotape: 3/4", VHS and Betamax (amount unspecified).
Cataloging: Film lists. Collection is presently being cataloged.
Access: Available to the public for duplication. Research fees not charged. Requests accepted by mail, telephone and in person (walk-in).
Rights: Rights status of material not known.
Licensing: Apply for information. License fees not charged.
Restrictions: None specified.
Viewing Facilities: None.
Duplication Facilities: None.

PENNSYLVANIA (Philadelphia)

ACADEMY OF NATURAL SCIENCES OF PHILADELPHIA
LIBRARY
MANUSCRIPT/ARCHIVES DEPARTMENT
19th and the Benjamin Franklin Parkway
Philadelphia, PA 19103
(215) 299-1040

Carol M. Spawn (Librarian of the Academy)

Contact: Carol M. Spawn
Services: Museum; library; science research academy. Open to the public. Films available for duplication.
Description: Film is a mixture of amateur and professional work (1910s-60s; post-World War II, mostly color); and predominantly the result of expeditions by Academy staff, trustees and associates to collect natural history specimens such as birds, insects, plants and mammals.

Individuals associated with the films include: Brooke Dolan II, Richard E. Bishop, Wharton Huber, George Vanderbilt and R.R.M. Carpenter. Locations comprise: Greenland; Labrador; Sumatra (a film by the Vanderbilt Expedition); Tibet (a film by Brooke Dolan II, 1942); North Africa; the Congo (a film by the Vanderbilt Expedition in search of lowland gorillas); Muscat, Oman; the American West; and Maryland's Eastern Shore.

North African and Arabian films were made during Carpenter expeditions in search of specimens for museum dioramas (ca. 1946). They include various landscapes and native life.
Size & Elements: Film: 35mm (mostly). Apply for more detailed information.
Cataloging: None specified.
Access: Open to the public. Available for duplication. Research fees charged for extensive staff assistance. Research requests accepted by mail and in person (walk-in, though appointments are preferred).
Rights: Full rights held to all material.
Licensing: Apply for information.
Restrictions: Each request evaluated on its merits; no fixed policy exists as the films differ so much in condition and content.
Viewing Facilities: Film and videotape (can be arranged with advance notice).
Duplication Facilities: None.

PENNSYLVANIA (Philadelphia)

GRAY PANTHERS
311 South Juniper, Suite 601
Philadelphia, PA 19107
(215) 545-6555

Margaret Kuhn (President)
Frances Humphreys (Executive Director)

Contact: Jean Hopper
Services: Political organization. Videotape collection primarily maintained for distribution to Gray Panthers chapters rather than for research or reuse.
Description: Interviews and public events featuring Maggie Kuhn and others speaking on issues relating to the concerns of the Gray Panthers, an organization with emphasis on the concerns of older adults. Items in the collection are videotaped off the air, recorded by members or from other sources.
Size & Elements: Videotape: VHS (approx. 45 videotapes).
Cataloging: A printed list is currently being compiled.
Access: Primarily maintained for distribution to Gray Panthers chapters. Available to individuals for rental in some cases. Rental fees charged. Requests accepted by mail, telephone and in person.
Rights: Rights status of material currently not known. Additional clearances may be necessary in some cases if material is to be reused.
Licensing: Apply for information.
Restrictions: Requests for licensing or reuse considered on a case-by-case basis. Reuse of material may be restricted.
Viewing Facilities: None.
Duplication Facilities: None.

PENNSYLVANIA (Philadelphia)

THE MEDICAL COLLEGE OF PENNSYLVANIA
ARCHIVES AND SPECIAL COLLECTIONS ON WOMEN IN MEDICINE
3300 Henry Avenue
Philadelphia, PA 19129
(215) 842-7124

Janet Miller (Director, Archivist)

Contact: Jill Gates Smith (Curator of Photographs)
Services: Educational institution; archives. Film and videotape collection open to the public; available for research, duplication and reuse in some cases.

Description: Archives focuses on the history of women in medicine and the 137-year history of the Medical College of Pennsylvania, the first women's medical college in the United States. All films (1929-71) have been transferred to videotape with the originals retained in storage. Events (1972-present) have been recorded on videotape.

Events documented include: ceremonies related to the expansion of the College; social events accompanying commencement; presentations at the College on topics of health economics, care of the elderly and maternal health care; and humorous sketches by faculty and students. Prominent physicians Catharine Macfarlane, Alma Dea Morani, Helen Taussig, and Katharine Boucot Sturgis are featured in formal and informal interviews and in televised segments of *NOVA* and *This Is Your Life*. Drs. Morani and Sturgis were the subjects of the videotape *Profiles in Medicine* (1985).

Titles include: *Pioneer Pacesetter — The Medical College of Pennsylvania; Woman's Medical College of Pennsylvania: Women Doctors Laud the TB Drive* (1952, silent); *Woman's Medical College of Pennsylvania: Face of Philadelphia* (1958); *Senior Party Films* (1965); *Women in the Medicine Course: Student Interviews* (1985); and *Health Economics and the Elderly* (1987).

Size & Elements: Film: 16mm (12 titles; varying lengths, all titles transferred to VHS videotape for viewing). Videotape: VHS (22 titles; includes film transfers).

Cataloging: Title list.

Access: Open to the public. Some material for in-house use only; some material available for duplication. Research fees not charged. Research requests accepted by mail, telephone and in person (appointments preferred).

Rights: Full rights held to some material. Some rights held to some material. Some material in the public domain. Additional clearances may be necessary in some cases if material is to be reused.

Licensing: Some material possibly available for licensing and reuse, subject to restrictions. License and usage fees determined on a case-by-case basis.

Restrictions: Some restrictions apply.

Viewing Facilities: Film and videotape (equipment may be reserved in the College Library).

Duplication Facilities: Videotape.

THE NEIGHBORHOOD FILM AND VIDEO PROJECT

3701 Chestnut Street
Philadelphia, PA 19104
(215) 895-6542
Fax: (215) 895-6562

Linda Blackaby (Director)

Contacts: Linda Blackaby

Services: Media arts center. Film and videotape collection available to researchers, scholars and the public, subject to restrictions.

Description: Presents exhibitions and provides services to the independent film and videotape community. Also serves as an information and access point for those interested in the work of Philadelphia independent film and videotape producers.

Collection contains works by Philadelphia-based independent film and videotape producers and a collection of films containing documentaries, feature films and short subjects, obtained through the closing of the National Film Board of Canada office in New York City.

Size & Elements: Film: 16mm (amount unspecified; release prints). Videotape: 3/4" and VHS (assorted viewing copies).

Cataloging: List of the National Film Board of Canada films.

Access: Open to researchers, scholars and the public, and those interested in learning more about the local Philadelphia independent scene. Screening fees charged in some cases. Research requests accepted by telephone and in person (by appointment only).

Rights: No rights held to any material; rights retained by original film and videomakers. Additional clearances will be necessary if material is to be reused.

Licensing: Not available for licensing through Project (license fees would be set by original producers).

Restrictions: Reuse only by permission of original producers.

Viewing Facilities: Film (16mm projectors and large auditorium); videotape (3/4" and VHS). Appointments for screening must be made in advance.

Duplication Facilities: Videotape (3/4" and VHS).

STAINED GLASS ASSOCIATION OF AMERICA

778 South 5th Street
Philadelphia, PA 19147
(215) 247-5721 (day)
(215) 625-9528 (evening)

Contact: Helene Weis (Chairperson, Audiovisual Aids Committee)

Services: Association. *Film and videotape collection presently not available for research or reuse.*

Description: Small collection of film and videotape pertaining to stained glass.

Titles include: *Stained Glass, Painting with Light; Polish Film; Kokomo Glass; Images in Stained Glass; Stained Glass Process; Stained Glass, a Timeless Art Form;* and *History of Stained Glass*.

Size & Elements: Film and videotape: formats unspecified (20 titles total).

Cataloging: None specified.

Access: Material not presently available due to restructuring; viewing copies of material being made.

Rights: Apply for information.

Licensing: Apply for information. Usage fees charged; not available for purchase.

Restrictions: Collection not presently available to the public. Material not for sale; available for rental only.

Viewing Facilities: None.

Duplication Facilities: None.

Related Materials: Large slide collection.

TEMPLE UNIVERSITY
URBAN ARCHIVES CENTER
PHOTOJOURNALISM COLLECTION
SAMUEL PALEY LIBRARY

Philadelphia, PA 19122
(215) 787-8608

Street address: 13th Street and Berks Mall

Fredric Miller (Curator, Urban Archives Center)
George D. Brightbill (Curator, Photojournalism Collection)

Contact: George D. Brightbill

Services: University library. Film and videotape collection open to the public; available for research, duplication and reuse, subject to access procedures and restrictions.

Description: *WPVI/WFIL-TV television newsfilm* (1947-83; 16mm, 10,000 cans, approx. 4 million feet; black and white and color, silent and sound). Film broadcast as part of Philadelphia local news programs on local ABC affiliate. Documents all areas of Philadelphia history and local events during this time period; includes some coverage of southern New Jersey and Delaware, and some national coverage. One or more cans per day is missing (1962-67 and 1969).

WPVI/WFIL-TV documentaries (16mm, 500 cans). Various titles produced for public affairs programs; other titles acquired for broadcast. Limited holdings; multiple copies of some programs. Inventory in preparation.

WPVI-TV videotape programs (2", 500 reels; 1", 50 reels). Various titles produced for public affairs programs; most are related to minority audiences. Inventory in preparation.

KYW-TV collection (1950s-60s). Some Philadelphia local television news material.

Size & Elements: Film: 16mm (approx. 15,000 cans; black and white and color, silent and sound, positive). Videotape: 2" (500 reels); 1" (50 reels).

Cataloging: Inventory of WPVI/WFIL-TV film can contents by day (Sept. 13, 1947-Feb. 25, 1950 and July 28, 1952-Jan. 21, 1962); assignment logs (1954-58, Aug. 21, 1967-October 5, 1972, Aug. 12, 1974-Feb. 2, 1975, and 1976-83); inventory of dates for which film cans are available. Inventory and index of documentaries and videotapes are in preparation.

Access: Open to the public, subject to use and fee restrictions. No research work can be undertaken for the public due to staff restrictions; however, staff can check inventory of can dates to determine whether can is available for a specific date and check card file or assignment logs to see whether subjects are covered by film. Staff cannot view film contents; public must appear in person to view footage. Research fees charged (fee per can which is pulled for public searching). Research requests accepted by telephone and in person (by appointment).

Rights: Most rights retained by WPVI-TV. Photojournalism collection has

right to allow educational use of materials; no "personal" reuse allowed by WPVI-TV.
Licensing: Available for licensing and reuse, subject to access procedures and restrictions. License fees not charged.
Restrictions: All requests for duplication and reuse subject to acceptance and approval by WPVI-TV.
Viewing Facilities: Film (very limited).
Duplication Facilities: None.

PENNSYLVANIA (Philadelphia)

UNIVERSITY OF PENNSYLVANIA ARCHIVES
North Arcade, Franklin Field
Philadelphia, PA 19104-6320
(215) 898-7024

Mark Frazier Lloyd (Director of Archives and Records Center)

Contact: Maryellen C. Kaminsky (Archival Specialist)
Services: University archives. Film collection open to the public for research and possibly reuse, subject to restrictions.
Description: Footage relevant to special events at the University (1940-70), including its Bicentennial (1940), Alumni Day celebrations and commencements.
Size & Elements: Film: 16mm (31 cubic feet).
Cataloging: Inventory lists.
Access: Open to the public. Available for research and reuse. Staff cannot provide research services. Research requests accepted by mail, telephone and in person (by appointment only).
Rights: Full rights held to all material.
Licensing: Available for licensing, subject to restrictions. License fees charged.
Restrictions: Productions reusing footage must include a credit line.
Viewing Facilities: Film (16mm; facilities located in Audiovisual Services Department on campus; fees apply).
Duplication Facilities: None (outside arrangements can be made; fees apply).

PENNSYLVANIA (Pittsburgh)

ASSOCIATION FOR CHILDREN & ADULTS WITH LEARNING DISABILITIES (ACLD)
4156 Library Road
Pittsburgh, PA 15234
(412) 341-1515

Jean Petersen (National Executive Director)

Contact: Jean Petersen
Services: Association. Film library available to the public for rental.
Description: Films concerning people of all ages with learning disabilities and related issues and concerns.

Topics include: behavior problems and teaching challenges, non-readers, the academic and social struggles of children and teenagers with learning disabilities, delinquency and learning disabilities, the juvenile justice system and college students with learning disabilities. *The Invisible Handicap* discusses the difficulties in defining the term and determining the causes of learning disabilities; *The ABC's of Teaching the Learning Disabled Student* is for teacher training.
Size & Elements: Film: format unspecified (13 titles).
Cataloging: Film list.
Access: Available to the public for rental.
Rights: Apply for information.
Licensing: Apply for information.
Restrictions: None specified.
Viewing Facilities: None.
Duplication Facilities: None.

PENNSYLVANIA (Pittsburgh)

BUHL SCIENCE CENTER
Allegheny Square
Pittsburgh, PA 15212
(412) 237-3300
Fax: (412) 237-3375

Al De Sena (Director)

Contact: Karen Altares (Exhibit Supervisor)
Services: Museum. Film collection available for research, duplication and reuse.
Description: Holds films on the sciences and human experience, originally produced for museum exhibitions. *Robots: In Man's Image,* shot entirely in Western Pennsylvania, illustrates the capabilities and limitations of robots. *The Last Time Around* documents people's remembrances of the 1910 visit of Halley's Comet. *Harold Cohen: Computer As Artist* was produced to accompany an exhibit.
Size & Elements: Film: 16mm (4 hours; release prints). Videotape: 3/4" (2 titles).
Cataloging: Release sheets.
Access: Available to the public for research and duplication. Research requests accepted by mail.
Rights: Full rights held to all material.
Licensing: Available for licensing. License fees charged.
Restrictions: None specified.
Viewing Facilities: None.
Duplication Facilities: None.

PENNSYLVANIA (Pittsburgh)

CARNEGIE DISTRICT FILM CENTER
Allegheny Square
Pittsburgh, PA 15212
(412) 321-1344

Darlene Casey (Unit Head)

Contact: Darlene Casey
Services: Public library. Film collection maintained for loan purposes only.
Description: General collection includes works by local Pittsburgh filmmakers, including: *Voices From a Steel Town; Skokie; Murray Avenue; Mrs. G.; Bird House;* and *Suicide Squeeze.* Subjects include the breakdown of the steel mills, Duquesne Light, and other regional topics.

Other films held comprise children's stories, travel, social issues, health, old-time comedies and experimental works. The videotape collection includes feature films, documentary television series and classical music programs.
Size & Elements: Film: 16mm (1,694 titles, 1,800 cans). Videotape: VHS (900 titles).
Cataloging: Published catalogs; computerized cataloging for staff use only.
Access: Open to the public. Research fees not charged. Research requests accepted.
Rights: Most, if not all, rights retained by original producer or distributor. Additional clearances may be necessary in some cases if material is to be reused.
Licensing: Available for licensing and reuse, subject to restrictions. License and usage fees not charged.
Restrictions: Material licensed for reuse by permission from film distributor only.
Viewing Facilities: Film.
Duplication Facilities: None.

PENNSYLVANIA (Pittsburgh)

UNIVERSITY OF PITTSBURGH
THE ARCHIVES OF INDUSTRIAL SOCIETY
363 Hillman Library
Pittsburgh, PA 15260
(412) 648-8198

Contact: Frank J. Kurtik (Associate Curator)
Services: University archives. Open to researchers and scholars only, subject to clearance. Films and videotapes possibly available for reuse.
Description: *Pitt Parade Film Collection.* Daily television magazine program (1949-59) highlighting local news events. *Pitt Parade* was aired for most of its existence by KDKA-TV (Pittsburgh), but was originally broadcast on WDTV and ended its run on WQED. Archives holds footage, scripts, and cross-reference and chronological card files.

A card from the chronological files for a typical day (September 15, 1952, Monday) reads as follows: "Weather — Rain; Billy Graham — Forbes Field; Radio-TV Exposition; Tuberculosis Workers meet; Blackridge Garden Club Flower show; Pittsburgh Festival Play subscription drive; St. John's Nurse

Graduation; Fantasy Fair — Arts & Crafts; Buhl Photographic Prints on Plant Life; Tennis — Tech."

A typical cross-reference file card (Civic Development) includes such stories as Pitt Point Park (3/27/49); Airport control tower (1/18/49); Man of the Year — Scaife (1/19/49); Mellon gift — underground garage (4/24/49); New type sidewalks (4/24/49); Aluminum light poles (5/4/49); Conemaugh Dam Day dinner (5/10/49); Mt. Washington hillside damage (5/27/49); Able youth test, Carnegie Tech (4/3/50); Nixon marquee (8/31/50); and Welcome Week canoeists (5/15/50).

Size & Elements: Film: 16mm (30 boxes, 30 cubic feet; in process of being transferred to 3/4" videotape).
Cataloging: Card catalogs; programs cataloged chronologically and by subject.
Access: Open to researchers and scholars only. Research and reuse subject to clearance by the Archives and KDKA-TV. Research requests accepted by mail and telephone. Materials possibly available for reuse in the future. For permission to research or reuse, contact John Kirch, KDKA-TV, One Gateway Center, Pittsburgh, PA 15222; (412) 392-2256.
Rights: Full rights retained by KDKA-TV.
Licensing: Apply for information.
Restrictions: Permission to research or reuse must be obtained from the Archives and KDKA-TV.
Viewing Facilities: None (arrangements can be made).
Duplication Facilities: None.

UNIVERSITY OF PITTSBURGH
UNIVERSITY CENTER FOR INSTRUCTIONAL RESOURCES
G20 Hillman Library
Pittsburgh, PA 15260
(412) 648-7231

Michael Arenth (Coordinator)

Contacts: Katie Berry (Audiovisual Specialist)
Services: University library. Educational film and videotape collection not open to the public. Material possibly available for reuse, subject to copyright clearance.
Description: Holds educational films and videotapes for in-house use and medical films made on campus as teaching support materials. Collection holds copies of *The Strike* (5 min.), a film on Black history that is difficult to locate elsewhere.

Sample titles from the general collection include: *Abortion: London's Dilemma; Cardiac Arrythmias; The Case of the Bermuda Triangle; Entuziazm: Simfoniia Donbassa* (Dziga Vertov, 1930); *Order From Chaos: The Surprising Consequences of Randomness; Raised in Anger: A Special Program On Child Abuse; Respiratory Failure: Diagnosis and Airway Care; Sanjo: Korean Improvisational Music; Sickness Strikes; The Slingerland Multi-Sensory Approach; Spend It All; To Move Is To Be Alive;* and *We Dig Coal: A Portrait of Three Women.*
Size & Elements: Film: format unspecified (2,000 titles). Videotape: 3/4" and VHS (500 videotapes).
Cataloging: Card catalogs; computerized cataloging for staff use only.
Access: Available to the public. Research requests accepted by mail, telephone and in person (walk-in).
Rights: Full rights held to some material. Additional clearances may be necessary in some cases if material is to be reused.
Licensing: Apply for information.
Restrictions: None specified.
Viewing Facilities: Film and videotape.
Duplication Facilities: Film and videotape.

WQED/PITTSBURGH
4802 Fifth Avenue
Pittsburgh, PA 15213
(412) 622-1300
Fax: (412) 622-1488

Sam Silberman (Director of Programming)

Contact: Victoria Smith (Legal Department)
Services: Film and videotape producer; educational television broadcaster. Material available to researchers and scholars only. Footage possibly available for reuse.
Description: WQED has produced footage for its own broadcasts and National Geographic specials. Although WQED owns rights to the footage, it has consigned it to various other organizations for stock footage sale, including National Geographic Society Stock Footage Library (q.v.). WQED can be contacted for information and further clearances regarding materials owned by, but not housed with them.

Materials produced include: a Norman Rockwell special (approx. 40,000 feet); *A Day in the Life of America* (48 hours); *Planet Earth* (200,000 feet); and *The Infinite Voyage* series (500,000 feet). The station has also produced two hours of scientifically accurate special effects.
Size & Elements: Film: 35mm (2 hours); 16mm (approx. 850,000 feet). Videotape: 1" (amount unspecified).
Cataloging: None specified.
Access: Available to researchers and scholars only. Research requests accepted by mail and telephone.
Rights: Full rights held to some material. Some rights held to all material. Additional clearances may be necessary in some cases if material is to be reused.
Licensing: Apply for information. License fees charged.
Restrictions: None specified.
Viewing Facilities: None.
Duplication Facilities: None.

UNGER COMPUTER GRAPHICS
1313 Good Street
Reading, PA 19602
(215) 374-4679

Marianne Unger (Owner)

Contact: Marianne Unger
Services: Computer graphics design studio. Videotape material available for purchase, licensing and reuse.
Description: Computer-generated backgrounds available for use in productions ranging from community broadcasts to commercials.

Unlimited original custom artwork (e.g., maps, charts, graphs, textures, animated artwork and logos) is available. Sports images available include: basketball, football, hockey, baseball, bowling, golf, tennis, cross-country and downhill skiing, ski jump, bobsled, ice, figure and speed skating, luge, general sports and sports spotlights. Graphic backgrounds available include: grids, color, gradations, embossed effects, fireworks, woodgrain and other textures, original artwork and animated effects.

Five volumes (each 20 min.) of background images are available: Volume I (33 graphics), Volume II (18 graphics), Volume III (21 graphics), and Volume IV and V (20 graphics each).
Size & Elements: Videotape: 3/4" or 1/2" demonstration videotape available.
Cataloging: Release sheets.
Access: Available for purchase, licensing and reuse.
Rights: Full rights held to some material.
Licensing: One-time licensing agreement available for background images. License fees charged.
Restrictions: Apply for information.
Viewing Facilities: None.
Duplication Facilities: None.

NON-CIRCUMCISION EDUCATIONAL FOUNDATION
P.O. Box 5
Richboro, PA 18954
(215) 357-2792

James E. Peron, M.E. (Medical Research Writer, Lecturer, Founder and Executive Director)

Contact: James E. Peron
Services: Nonprofit foundation; educational institute. Maintains research library containing film and videotape. Available for distribution and rental to those actively engaged in childbirth, newborn care and research.
Description: The Foundation, a spinoff of the Childbirth Education Foundation, was established to address the "abuse" of routine neo-natal circumcision as practiced in the U.S. In addition, the Foundation desires to

present a public media rebuttal to the well-established and defined "health fallacies" of routine neo-natal circumcision.

Has the largest research library and perhaps the only film and videotape collection available on the subject of circumcision in the U.S. Library covers all aspects of circumcision, including historical, medical, cultural, complications, risks, physiological and psychological consequences and stress factors to the infant.

Also affiliated with PRI Films, distributors of medical and childbirth education films. PRI can provide films and videotapes on specific childbirth education concerns (apply for information).
Size & Elements: Film: 16mm. Videotape (format and amount unspecified).
Cataloging: Computerized cataloging available to researchers; research library.
Access: Available for distribution and rental to those actively engaged in childbirth, newborn care and research. Rental and shipping fees charged. Research fees not charged. Research requests accepted by mail and telephone.
Rights: Full rights held to some material. Additional clearances may be necessary in some cases if material is to be reused.
Licensing: Apply for information.
Restrictions: Restrictions apply in some cases.
Viewing Facilities: Film and videotape.
Duplication Facilities: Videotape.
Related Materials: Print material and publications.

PENNSYLVANIA (Spring House)

CREATIVE VENTURE FILMS
P.O. Box 235
Spring House, PA 19477
(215) 643-4177

Street address: 809 North Bethlehem Pike

Forney W. Miller (Owner)

Contacts: Forney W. Miller; Lottie A. Connor (Office Manager)
Services: Film and videotape producer and distributor. Available for rental, purchase, preview and reuse, subject to restrictions.
Description: A licensee of General Electric Educational Films, Creative Venture Films primarily holds contemporary and historical films from General Electric.

General Electric Historical Films. Original films accompanied by authentic music soundtracks. *The Home Electrical* (1915, 8 min., black and white, soundtrack added) was produced by the General Electric Photographic Section. Provides a look at an all-electric home of the time, replete with vacuum system and the electric cigar-lighter. The proud homeowner takes a passerby on a tour of his home. While the men chat and enjoy electrically lighted cigars, the housewife electrically heats a bottle for the baby and the maid prepares dinner by electricity. The film concludes romantically as husband and wife warm themselves in front of an electric heater. In *King of the Rails* (1915, 12 min., black and white, soundtrack added), pioneering industrial filmmakers tell the epic story of the evolution of transportation and the electrification of the railways. After an early documentary look at locomotive manufacturing, the camera takes the viewer on a cross-country ride atop the King of the Rails. This motion picture short was previewed in 1915 at the Mark Strand Theater, New York City. *Back to the Farm* (1915, 17 min, black and white, soundtrack added) was produced by General Electric Company and the California Power Company when few farms had electricity. Mr. Power, the electrical salesman, shows Mr. Work, the farmer, how electricity can turn everyday drudgery into easy work and happiness. At the end, Mr. Work's son, who was seeking his fortune in the city, returns to the farm in time to meet his father driving an electric truck filled with newly purchased electrical devices.

General Electric Educational Films. Titles include: *Principles of Electricity* (hosted by "Benjamin Franklin"; Spanish-language version available); *Fundamentals of AC/DC Generation; Lightning; A Is For Atom; How a Boiling Water Reactor Operates; Properties of Light; Sight, Light and Color;* and *Magnetism at Work.*

Other titles include: *What's It Like to be an Engineer?; What's It Like to Work with Computers?; The Techniques of Fighting Fires;* and *Fire Fighting and Electrical Hazards.*
Size & Elements: Film: 16mm. Videotape: 3/4", VHS and Betamax. (16 titles total).
Cataloging: Published brochures.
Access: Available for rental, purchase, preview and reuse. Preview service limited to potential purchasers. Orders and inquiries accepted by mail.
Rights: Full rights held to some material. Additional clearances may be

necessary in some cases if material is to be reused.
Licensing: Television networks and professional media organizations may license portions of films by paying a per-foot royalty. Apply for price quotations on special use privileges.
Restrictions: All films distributed are copyrighted; all rights to duplicate are reserved. Apply for information regarding conditions and requirements for broadcast use and videotaping privileges.
Viewing Facilities: Film and videotape.
Duplication Facilities: None.
Related Materials: Study guides available.

PENNSYLVANIA (Strasburg)

RAILROAD MUSEUM OF PENNSYLVANIA
P.O. Box 15
Strasburg, PA 17579
(717) 687-8628

Street address: Route 741 East

Robert Emerson (Director)

Contact: Benjamin F. G. Kline, Jr. (Acting Curator)
Services: Government agency; museum. Film collection available to researchers and scholars for in-house research. Not open to the public; material not available for loan, duplication and reuse.
Description: Films pertaining to railroads. Some films were originally produced under the sponsorship of railroad companies for public exhibition or employee training; others were obtained from commercial sources. Most films have been reviewed and repaired.

Sample titles include: *Above All Keep Your Head; Barney Oldfield: Race For Life* (1913); *Chicago Union Station* (1969); *Choo-Choo Swing; Dining Car Fragments* (1959); *Dow Chemical* (1966); *Don't Be A Sitting Duck; Escape From Limbo; Get A Grip On Yourself; A Girl and Her Trust* (1912); *A Gray Day For O'Grady; Home Railroad Movies* (8mm); *Ichabod, The Man Without A Head; The Last Run of The Shay* (1964); *Let's Keep It Moving* (Conrail, 1980); *Mainline USA* (1957); *New Age of Railroads* (1957); *News Highlights of 1961; No Witness; Oh My Aching Back; Penn Center Publicity* (1953); *Penn Station N.Y.* (1959); *Penn Station Ticket Sales* (1957); *PRR Wreck Scenes; The Right To Compete; Road To The Future* (1960); *Science Rides The High Iron* (1953); *When Steam Was King; The Voice of The Book; Wheels Of Steel* (1950); *You and Office Safety;* and *You Can Take It With You.*
Size & Elements: Film: 16mm (46 titles); Super 8mm (2 titles); regular 8mm (4 titles).
Cataloging: Computerized cataloging maintained primarily for staff use; available to researchers on a select basis.
Access: Not open to the public. Open to researchers and scholars. For in-house use only. Films are available by advance request, if made prior to visit. Use permitted for specific purposes only. Research fees not charged. Research requests accepted on a limited basis and by appointment only.
Rights: No rights held to any material. Rights status of material not known.
Licensing: Not available for licensing or reuse.
Restrictions: Not available for duplication, licensing or reuse, due to lack of proper viewing facilities, small staff and clearance problems.
Viewing Facilities: None.
Duplication Facilities: None.

PENNSYLVANIA (Upper Darby)

LANDMARK STOCK FOOTAGE CO.
207 South State Road
Upper Darby, PA 19082
(215) 352-7023
Fax: (215) 352-6225

Michael Davis (President)

Contacts: Don Creamer (General Manager); Michael Davis
Services: Film and videotape producer; stock footage sales library. Custom shooting services available.
Description: Stock footage of Philadelphia and vicinity, including historical buildings and landmarks; images that clearly identify the city; and quick shots of people involved in recreational and "slice of life" activities. New material is constantly being added to library, including footage of landmarks in other U.S. cities. Can shoot footage to order in 35mm, 16mm and any videotape format.

PENNSYLVANIA (Valley Forge)

Philadelphia footage includes: Philadelphia skyline from Camden, South Philadelphia, the Art Museum, West River Drive, Belmont Plateau and South Street; the Sports Complex; the Art Museum facade from the Central Courtyard; Head House Square; Benjamin Franklin Bridge with tall ships; the Art Museum from General Wayne Statue; Independence Hall from Independence Square and Independence Mall; Carpenter's Hall from Chestnut Street and Walnut Street; the Art Museum and Water Works; Boat House Row; and City Hall from Logan Circle.
Size & Elements: Film: 35mm and 16mm (approx. 10 hours; original negative and workprint). Videotape: 3/4" and VHS (demonstration reel available). Footage can be supplied as a film print or on 1", 3/4" or VHS videotape.
Cataloging: Staff assistance required; shot list of Philadelphia-related footage available (will be updated to include other material); brochure.
Access: Available to the public for duplication and reuse. Research, screening and shipping fees charged. Research requests accepted by telephone.
Rights: Full rights held to all material.
Licensing: Available for licensing and reuse. License fees charged.
Restrictions: None specified.
Viewing Facilities: Film (16mm flatbed); videotape (3/4" and VHS). Viewing fees charged.
Duplication Facilities: Film (16mm to 3/4" or VHS videotape); videotape (3/4" and VHS). In-house film-to-videotape transfers are reference-quality only; outside arrangements made for broadcast-quality transfers.

PENNSYLVANIA (Valley Forge)

AMERICAN BAPTIST FILMS/VIDEO
P.O. Box 851
Valley Forge, PA 19482-0851
(215) 768-2306

Ronald Schlosser (Director)

Contact: Ronald Schlosser
Services: Library; archives. Some films and videotapes available for distribution and rental; other material possibly available for research and reuse.
Description: Religious films on missionary work, educational programs, Bible stories and social issues (late 1940s-early 1970s).
Approximately twelve historic films from the 1960s are held in the archives. Items include: *Mississippi Kyrie,* concerning the Delta ministry; *Beggar at the Gates; Amnesty or Exile,* about the Vietnam era; *A Time for Burning;* and videotapes about the sanctuary movement and ordaining homosexual ministers.
There is more recent material in current distribution (apply for information).
Size & Elements: Film: 16mm (approx. 12 films). Videotape: format and amount unspecified.
Cataloging: Published catalog (for material in current distribution only).
Access: Maintained for distribution and rental rather than research or reuse. Researchers cannot be accommodated unless they request a specific title.
Rights: No rights held to any material.
Licensing: Apply for information. License fees not charged.
Restrictions: Licensing and reuse subject to clearance and approval.
Viewing Facilities: None.
Duplication Facilities: None.

PENNSYLVANIA (Williamsport)

LITTLE LEAGUE BASEBALL MUSEUM
Box 3485
Williamsport, PA 17701
(717) 326-3607
Fax: (717) 326-1074

Marc G. Pompeo (Curator)
David L. Fogel (Business Manager)

Contact: Marc G. Pompeo; Cynthia L. Stearns
Services: Museum. Film and videotape collection open to researchers and scholars only on a case-by-case basis. Material available for duplication, licensing and reuse, subject to approval and certain restrictions.
Description: Little League World Series championship games (historical); and some recent semifinals. Documentary and educational material relating to Little League baseball is also available. A museum display uses the Laserdisc format.
Size & Elements: Film: 16mm (100 cans). Videotape: Betacam (75

videotapes), 3/4" (50 videotapes) and VHS (20 videotapes). Videodisc: Laserdiscs (6 discs). Some viewing copies are available.
Cataloging: Finding aids.
Access: Open to researchers and scholars only on a case-by-case basis. Research requests accepted by mail, telephone and in person (by appointment only). Available for duplication and reuse, subject to approval and certain restrictions.
Rights: Full rights held to all material.
Licensing: Available for licensing and reuse, subject to restrictions. License fees charged in some cases. Footage is sometimes sold or licensed through representatives.
Restrictions: Requests for research, licensing and reuse considered on a case-by-case basis.
Viewing Facilities: Film and videotape.
Duplication Facilities: None.
Representative: Apply for information.

PUERTO RICO

PUERTO RICO (Hato Rey)

WIPR-TV
Box 909
Hato Rey, PR 00919
(809) 766-0505

Contact: Elmiro Torres (Filmoteca/Film Library)
Services: Government-owned television station. Film and videotape collection possibly available for reuse, subject to restrictions.
Description: Recent history and culture of Puerto Rico.
Size & Elements: Film: 16mm (amount unspecified). Videotape (format and amount unspecified).
Cataloging: Card catalogs.
Access: Open to requesters with a legitimate interest. Research requests accepted in person (by appointment only).
Rights: Full rights held to all material.
Licensing: Available for licensing, subject to restrictions. License fees charged in most cases.
Restrictions: Requests for research, licensing and reuse are considered on a case-by-case basis; policies vary according to nature of request and intended use.
Viewing Facilities: Film and videotape (by special arrangement).
Duplication Facilities: Videotape (by special arrangement; copies can be provided in any format).

PUERTO RICO (San Juan)

ARCHIVO DE IMAGENES EN MOVIMIENTO
INSTITUTE OF PUERTO RICAN CULTURE
P.O. Box 4184
San Juan, PR 00905
(809) 722-2113

Street address: Avenida Ponce de León

Contacts: Tito Rosario Albert; Inez Mongil Echandi
Services: Government agency; film and videotape archives. Material available to the public for research and duplication, subject to restrictions.
Description: Holds materials in a variety of subject areas, including newsreels (1954-present); social problems; public health; education; economics and economic development; and feature films.
La Division de la Educación de la Comunidad (Division of Community Education) films (ca. 1940s-50s, approx. 25-30 titles; negatives and prints). Films, primarily dramas, relating to social problems in Puerto Rico. Among the makers of these films was Jack Delano, formerly a photographer for the U.S. Farm Security Administration.
Fomento (Economic Development Agency) films (ca. 1950s-60s). Films relating to economic development efforts.
Also holds two commercial feature films (ca. 1950s) produced in Puerto Rico, and soap operas produced under the direction of the territorial government.
Size & Elements: Film: format unspecified (approx. 350 films; positive and negative). Videotape: 3/4" (masters); 1/2" (viewing copies). (Approx. 300 videotapes total). Plans are to transfer most films to videotape for viewing

purposes.
Cataloging: Card catalogs; published catalogs; computerized cataloging in progress (to be made available to researchers).
Access: Open to the public after March, 1989. Available for duplication. Research fees not charged. Research requests accepted by mail and in person (by appointment only).
Rights: Full rights held to all material.
Licensing: Available for licensing and reuse, subject to restrictions. License fees charged in some cases.
Restrictions: Research requests accepted after March 1989.
Viewing Facilities: Videotape.
Duplication Facilities: Videotape.

PUERTO RICO (San Juan)

BACARDI CORPORATION
G.P.O. Box 3549
San Juan, PR 00936
(809) 788-1500
Telex: 3453049

Manuel Luis del Valle (President)

Contacts: Adelina Silver (Public Relations Director); Mario S. Belaval (Vice President)
Services: Corporation; corporate archives. Material available for research and duplication.
Description: Bacardi Rum Troubadours Contest.
Size & Elements: Videotape: format unspecified (18 videotapes).
Cataloging: None specified.
Access: For in-house use only. Material available for research and duplication. Research requests accepted by mail.
Rights: Full rights held to all material.
Licensing: Apply for information. License fees not charged.
Restrictions: None specified.
Viewing Facilities: Videotape.
Duplication Facilities: Videotape (VHS).

PUERTO RICO (San Juan)

CENTRO PARA EL DESARROLLO Y MEJORAMIENTO DE LA ENSEÑANZA (CEDME)
(CENTER FOR THE DEVELOPMENT AND IMPROVEMENT OF TEACHING)
UNIVERSIDAD DE PUERTO RICO
Box 21305, U.P.R. Station
San Juan, PR 00931
(809) 761-8640

Street address: Edificio Monserrate, Avenida Ponce de León, Esq. Pastrana, Rio Piedras

Prof. Rafael Gracia (Director)

Contacts: Prof. Rafael Gracia; Ana Fabregas
Services: Distributor. Film collection available for rental only.
Description: General educational film collection. Subject areas include business administration, social sciences, law, education, physics, geography, health, literature, mathematics, the natural sciences and art.
Size & Elements: Film: 16mm (approx. 800 titles; release prints).
Cataloging: Card catalogs; published catalog (available for purchase).
Access: Available to the public for rental.
Rights: No rights held to any material. Rights retained by original producers.
Licensing: Not available for licensing or reuse.
Restrictions: For rental only; not available for licensing or reuse.
Viewing Facilities: Film.
Duplication Facilities: None.

PUERTO RICO (San Juan)

FILMOTECA LUIS MUÑOZ MARIN
P.O. Box 2367
San Juan, PR 00936
(809) 755-7979

Contacts: Inez Mongil; Tito Rosario Albert; Luis Molina
Services: Foundation; film and videotape archives. Material available to researchers and scholars for in-house use only.
Description: Material relating to the history of Puerto Rico (1916-present) and to the life and career of Luis Muñoz Marin. Footage includes the funeral of Muñoz Rivera, the first Governor of Puerto Rico (1916); and newsreels and material relating to the Popular Democratic Party (1940s-50s).
Size & Elements: Film: 16mm (70 films; 10 hours of stock footage). Videotape: format unspecified (80 videotapes; viewing copies).
Cataloging: Published catalogs; computerized cataloging available to researchers.
Access: Open to researchers and scholars only. For in-house use only.
Rights: No rights held to any material.
Licensing: Not available for licensing or reuse.
Restrictions: Collection available for in-house research only.
Viewing Facilities: Videotape.
Duplication Facilities: None.

RHODE ISLAND

RHODE ISLAND (Kingston)

UNIVERSITY OF RHODE ISLAND
UNIVERSITY LIBRARY
SPECIAL COLLECTIONS
Kingston, RI 02881
(401) 792-2594

David C. Maslyn (Head)

Contacts: David C. Maslyn; Kevin Logan (Records Analyst)
Services: University library. Film collection available to the public for research.
Description: *Sports films* (1,400 reels). Material covers Rhode Island football and basketball (1933-80). Football contests include Massachusetts, Connecticut, Vermont, Maine and New Hampshire; basketball include DePaul, St. John's, St. Joseph's and Providence.
Other University-produced films. Titles include: *The Kids Must Eat; This Is Working For; URI: The People's University; Centennial Year: University of Maine; Turkey Bowl 1973; Aspects of Aging/Adventure of Learning; Education With Pleasure: URI Life in the Mid-1950s; Class of 1929 Reunion; Situation Desperate: Report on Crisis at URI; Siberia; Frank Newman: Inauguration Celebration and Interviews; Disasters: Greenhouse Fire/Endeavor Runs Aground; R/V Endeavor: Sea Trials at Sturgeon Bay, Wisconsin;* and *Alton Jones Campus: Nettie Marie Jones, 1965.*
Holds informational films from the 1940s released by the U.S. Department of Agriculture, Department of Defense, Treasury Department and other agencies. Titles include: *Bonds of Victory; Canning the Victory Crop; Dehydration; Factory Farmers; Farm Offensive; Freedom and Famine; Peace Comes To America; President's Famine Emergency Committee; Wartime Farming in the Cornbelt; USO Military and the 1940s; Talking of Tomorrow;* and *Highways for the Telephone.*
Claiborne Pell Collection. Campaign films produced for his senatorial races in 1960, 1966 and 1972 (access restricted).
Size & Elements: Film: 16mm (65 titles).
Cataloging: Printed lists.
Access: Open to the public. Research fees not charged. Research requests accepted by mail and in person (walk-in).
Rights: Full rights held to some material.
Licensing: Apply for information.
Restrictions: None specified.
Viewing Facilities: None.
Duplication Facilities: None.

RHODE ISLAND (Providence)

INSTITUTE FOR LABOR STUDIES AND RESEARCH
1570 Westminster Street
Providence, RI 02909
(401) 331-4900

Charles Schwartz (Director)

Contact: Charles Schwartz

RHODE ISLAND (Providence)

Services: Nonprofit adult and labor education institution; videotape producer. Videotapes available for rental and purchase only.
Description: Produces *Rhode Island LaborVision* (1985-present). This series (each program 60 min.) features films and videotapes from outside sources, as well as Institute productions.

Institute productions all relate to labor issues, including labor history (oral histories and speeches); labor-oriented music (performances of Joe Glazer and others); AFL-CIO conventions; labor relations experts; labor-oriented events; and unions. Most productions contain interviews and documentary footage.

Maintains a small library of labor-related videotapes produced by other organizations and producers; these materials are available only for loan.
Size & Elements: Videotape: 3/4" (approx. 10 hours; masters and viewing copies); VHS (viewing copies).
Cataloging: List of videotapes available for loan and purchase.
Access: Available to the public for loan and purchase. Some materials available for in-house research and viewing only. Research fees not charged. Research requests accepted by mail and telephone.
Rights: Full rights held to Institute productions. No rights held to outside productions. Additional clearances may be necessary in some cases (interviews, etc.) if material is to be reused.
Licensing: Not available for licensing or reuse.
Restrictions: Material not available for licensing or reuse.
Viewing Facilities: Videotape (3/4" and 1/2").
Duplication Facilities: Videotape (3/4" and 1/2").

RHODE ISLAND (Providence)

RHODE ISLAND HISTORICAL SOCIETY
GRAPHICS DEPARTMENT
121 Hope Street
Providence, RI 02906
(401) 331-8575

Albert P. Klyberg (Executive Director)

Contact: Denise J. Bastien (Graphics Curator)
Services: Historical society. Film collection available to researchers and scholars for research purposes only. *Material not presently available for duplication or reuse.*
Description: Holds television newsfilm footage from WJAR-TV (Providence, 1952-78); WPRI-TV (Providence, 1962-78); and WTEV (New Bedford, Mass., now WLNE; material undated, possibly 1970s). Includes some documentaries from WJAR and WPRI which are cataloged by date and subject.

Also holds Rhode Island-produced feature films (1903-15); early amateur footage of Newport (1900-15), showing aristocracy, casinos and beach life (approx. 8 films); and the Havemeyer films, depicting the social elite of Newport.
Size & Elements: Film: 16mm (amount unspecified; positive, black and white and color, sound).
Cataloging: Computerized database planned for newsfilm collection. WPRI newsfilm is currently uncataloged. WJAR newsfilm is partially accessible by daily logbooks with keys to story titles, and is boxed and dated according to week of production.
Access: Open to researchers and scholars for research purposes only. Material presently unavailable for duplication or reuse. Research fees generally not charged; fees charged for mail requests. Research requests accepted by mail, telephone and in person (by appointment only).
Rights: No rights held to any material in the newsfilm collection. Rights retained by television stations.
Licensing: Available for licensing and reuse, subject to restrictions. License fees charged.
Restrictions: Television stations retain all rights to newsfilm collections.
Viewing Facilities: Film (Moviscop hand viewer); videotape (3/4" facilities planned).
Duplication Facilities: None.
Related Materials: Still photographs.

SOUTH CAROLINA

SOUTH CAROLINA (Charleston)

THE CITADEL
THE MILITARY COLLEGE OF SOUTH CAROLINA
ARCHIVES/MUSEUM

Charleston, SC 29409
(803) 792-6846

Contact: Jane Yates (Archivist)
Services: Military college; archives. Films held primarily for research purposes; possibly available for reuse, subject to restrictions.
Description: World War II military history.

World War II Combat Films. The *Why We Fight* series (5 films) was produced by the U.S. War Department to acquaint members of the Army with the causes and events leading up to the United States' entry into World War II and the principles for which they were fighting. Also held are Armed Forces Information Films and Training Films (12 films, 1940s-50s), which illustrate combat strategy and procedures using World War II battle footage.

General Mark W. Clark. Films (1942-83) consist of newsreels and interviews pertaining to Clark's role as Commander of Fifth Army in Italy during World War II and Commander-in-Chief, Far East Command, Korea in 1953.

The Citadel, The Military College of South Carolina. Recruiting films and footage of specific cadet and college events (1938-85).
Size & Elements: Film: format unspecified (positives). Videotape: format unspecified (viewing copies). (115 titles total).
Cataloging: Card catalogs.
Access: Available to researchers and scholars. For in-house use only. Research fees not charged. Research requests accepted by mail and in person (by appointment only).
Rights: Full rights held to some material. Additional clearances may be necessary in some cases if material is to be reused.
Licensing: Possibly available for licensing and reuse, subject to restrictions. License and usage fees not charged.
Restrictions: Permission of The Citadel, the U.S. Defense Department, or television networks may be required for reuse.
Viewing Facilities: Film and videotape (in museum).
Duplication Facilities: None.

SOUTH CAROLINA (Columbia)

SOUTH CAROLINA ARTS COMMISSION MEDIA ARTS CENTER
1800 Gervais Street
Columbia, SC 29201-3585
(803) 734-8696

Michael Fleishman (Director, Media Arts Center)
Susan Leonard (Exhibitions Director)

Contact: Susan Leonard
Services: Government agency; media organization. Open to the public. Film and videotape collection available to the public for rental.
Description: State agency promoting the visual, literary, performing and media arts in South Carolina. Supports media artists and media arts in the Southeastern United States, including Alabama, Florida, Kentucky, Louisiana, Mississippi, North Carolina, South Carolina, Tennessee and Virginia.

Independently produced films by artists and documentarians are offered in thematic packages: *The Personal Cinema* (4 programs), old and new experimental films; *Animation* (3 programs); *Documentary* (3 programs); *Southern Snapshots* (10 films), on Southerners and the South; *New Films from the New South,* avant-garde films; *Dance* (2 programs); *Dreams, Tales and Legends* (3 programs); *Humor, Parody and Satire* (4 programs), on the technical and theoretical aspects of filmmaking; *A Southern Film Experience* (30 min.), a documentary on filmmaking in the Southeast; and six programs for children.
Size & Elements: Film: 16mm (128 titles; viewing copies). Videotape: 3/4" and VHS (amount unspecified; viewing copies).
Cataloging: Published catalogs.
Access: Open to the public. Films and videotapes available for rental. Requests accepted by mail, telephone and in person (walk-in). Handling fees charged.
Rights: Some rights held to all material. Additional clearances may be necessary in some cases if material is to be reused.
Licensing: Apply for information.
Restrictions: None specified.
Viewing Facilities: Film and videotape.
Duplication Facilities: None.

SOUTH CAROLINA (Columbia)

SOUTH CAROLINA HUMANITIES RESOURCE CENTER
1610 Oak Street

Columbia, SC 29204
(803) 771-8864

Dr. Randy L. Akers (Executive Director)

Contact: Marilyn Jersild; Dr. Lois Shell
Services: Film and videotape distributor. Materials available to the public for free loan and distribution.
Description: Holds productions that have been partially funded by the Humanities Resource Center in South Carolina. Producers include local television stations, museums, libraries, colleges, historical societies, special councils and foundations, artists' groups and individuals. Subjects cover local history, society, race, community, industry, religion, women's issues, archaeology, Native Americans in South Carolina, with a few items on international subjects.

Sample titles include: *Long Shadows,* a documentary exploring the ways in which the echoes of the Civil War are still felt in American society; *Gullah Tales,* a fable that acquaints the audience with "Gullah," a language comprised of several different tongues including African, Scottish and Cockney, set in plantation days on the South Carolina coast; *Roanoak,* the story of the earliest contacts of Native American tribes on the southeastern coast with English explorers; *Southern Focus: People Who Take Up Serpents,* on an Appalachian snake-handling religion; *Everything Change Up Now,* on the study of the changing land uses of coastal South Carolina and its Sea Islands; *You Got To Move,* a documentary following people from Southern communities and their involvement in social change; *A Night in Tunisia,* a portrait of jazz great "Dizzy" Gillespie and his contribution to American jazz music through the introduction of the "bebop" style; *Ralph McGill and His Times,* on the life of journalist Ralph McGill, perhaps the most prominent and influential Southern white opponent of racial segregation; and *One-Third of A Nation, The Depression in the South,* a photographic history of the impact of the Great Depression on the lives of South Carolinians.
Size & Elements: Film: 16mm (2 titles, 4 films). Videotape: 3/4" and VHS (45 videotapes; viewing copies).
Cataloging: Published catalogs.
Access: Available to the public for distribution and free loan. Center's supply of materials and staff time is limited. Research fees not charged. Research requests accepted by mail and telephone.
Rights: No rights held to any material. Center will help to direct requests for reuse to the appropriate source.
Licensing: Apply for information.
Restrictions: None specified.
Viewing Facilities: Videotape.
Duplication Facilities: None.

SOUTH CAROLINA (Columbia)

UNIVERSITY OF SOUTH CAROLINA
NEWSFILM LIBRARY
INSTRUCTIONAL SERVICES CENTER
Columbia, SC 29208
(803) 777-6841

Glenn R. Smith (Division Director for Media Services, ISC)

Contacts: Andrew Murdoch (Researcher and Film Specialist); Don McCallister (Researcher)
Services: University library; special collection. Film material available for research, licensing and reuse.
Description: *Fox Movietone Collection.* Donated in 1980 by Twentieth Century-Fox Movietonews, Inc. (q.v.). Currently 15% of donation has been received, totaling approximately ten million feet of film (50% safety film, 50% nitrate). (Between 40 and 50 million feet remain in New York and New Jersey, stored by Twentieth Century-Fox.) Safety film (newsreels dating from September 1942 through August 1944); has been cataloged by computer and transferred to videotape. Outtakes and unused stories from the newsreels (1919 through May 1934), all nitrate, are currently stored in bunkers at Fort Jackson, S.C. Conversion of nitrate film to safety film has been impeded by prohibitive costs; various fundraising campaigns are underway. In the meantime, the film is safely stored in an air-conditioned, dehumidified facility. Outtakes for the period 1932-34 have been cataloged and converted to safety film.

Subjects covered include aviation history, World War II-era footage, fashion, humor, the arts, personalities (politicians, movie stars, etc.), accidents and disasters, and presidents.

For more information on this collection, see Twentieth Century-Fox

Movietonews, Inc.

WIS-TV Newsfilm. Local newsfilm from the NBC affiliate in Columbia, S.C. (1955 to mid-1970s). Detailed coverage of people and events in South Carolina.

Feltner Collection. Four million feet (50% safety, 50% nitrate) of stock footage (1920s-40s), donated by a private collector, comprises newsreel footage and other stories, much of it currently under copyright. 50% of collection is roughly cataloged; details of contents are currently not known.
Size & Elements: Film: 35mm (14 million feet; black and white; positive, negative, reversal, originals and release prints). Videotape: Betamax (viewing copies of a large portion of Movietone footage).
Cataloging: Card catalogs; computerized cataloging for staff use only; shot lists; dope sheets; release sheets.
Access: Available for scholarly research, licensing and reuse. Research fees not charged. Research requests accepted by mail, telephone and in person (by appointment only).
Rights: Full rights held to most material. Rights status of some material is not known.
Licensing: Available for licensing and reuse. License fees charged.
Restrictions: None specified.
Viewing Facilities: Videotape.
Duplication Facilities: Videotape (Rank Cintel film-to-videotape transfer: 1", 3/4", VHS and Betamax).

SOUTH CAROLINA (Greenville)

FRIENDS OF FREE CHINA
c/o Film Booking Office
Attention: Jack E. Buttram
38 Valerie Drive
Greenville, SC 29615
(803) 288-6651

Jack E. Buttram (President)

Contact: Jack E. Buttram
Services: Association; corporation. Films and videotapes available for rental and purchase.
Description: Material relating to China, including Taiwan, Hong Kong and the mainland. Consists of scenes of streets, lifestyle, transportation, scenics and student groups touring Taiwan.

Titles include: *China's Pearl of Freedom,* "a revealing comparison of Freedom vs. Communist suppression in China"; *Lesson From China,* including historical footage of General Chiang Kai-shek, Japan's war in China and World War II, as well as contemporary Hong Kong and the People's Republic of China; and *China Tomorrow,* filmed on location in the Republic of China (Taiwan).
Size & Elements: Film: 16mm (3 titles, approx. 5,000-7,000 feet; original negative, workprints and release prints). Videotape: format unspecified (3 titles).
Cataloging: Some shot lists; release sheets.
Access: Available for rental and purchase. Research fees charged. Requests accepted by mail, telephone and in person (walk-in).
Rights: Full rights held to all material.
Licensing: Available for licensing. License fees charged in some cases.
Restrictions: None specified.
Viewing Facilities: Film (16mm projector); videotape.
Duplication Facilities: Videotape (VHS).

SOUTH CAROLINA (Hilton Head Island)

TRI-COMM PRODUCTIONS
11 Palmetto Parkway
Hilton Head, SC 29938
(803) 681-5000
Fax: (803) 681-2945

William Robinson (President)

Contacts: Tracey Greene (Producer); William Robinson
Services: Videotape producer. Material available for duplication, licensing and reuse on a case-by-case basis.
Description: Southeastern U.S.; scenics of the coastal Carolinas, including sunsets, palmetto trees, beaches, marshes, wildlife and shrimp boats; activities at pools, Jacuzzis and golf courses in resort areas, including South Carolina,

SOUTH CAROLINA (Myrtle Beach)

Santa Fe (New Mexico), the Napa Valley (California), Scottsdale (Arizona), and Sacramento (California); aerial footage of resort areas; and airplanes (commercial footage shot for various companies).
Size & Elements: Videotape: 1" (approx. 50 hours; masters). Viewing copies available in any videotape format.
Cataloging: Staff assistance required.
Access: Available to the public for duplication, licensing and reuse. Research fees charged (fees negotiable). Research requests accepted by mail, telephone and in person (by appointment only).
Rights: Full rights held to some material. Some rights held to all material. Additional clearances may be necessary in some cases if material is to be reused (client approval required in some cases).
Licensing: Available for licensing and reuse, subject to restrictions. License fees charged.
Restrictions: Requests for licensing and reuse considered on a case-by-case basis.
Viewing Facilities: Videotape (3/4" and 1/2").
Duplication Facilities: Videotape (3/4" and 1/2").

SOUTH CAROLINA (Myrtle Beach)

ENCORE VIDEO PRODUCTIONS, INC.
811 Main Street
Myrtle Beach, SC 29577
(803) 448-9900
Fax: (803) 448-9235

Rick Dickinson (President)

Contacts: Frank Payne (Vice President); Rick Dickinson
Services: Videotape producer. Material available for duplication, licensing and reuse.
Description: Beach and ocean scenes; recreational activities, including vacations, tennis, surfing, fishing, swimming, boating, NASCAR racing, auto racing, jet skiing, water skiing, hang-gliding, golfing and baseball; scenics, including sunsets and aerials of ocean, beach and resort areas; industrial manufacturing (especially electronics); fireworks; amusement park rides (day and night); ballroom dancing; stage performances of rock and country groups (signed clearances on file); military and civilian aircraft in flight and undergoing maintenance.
Size & Elements: Videotape: 1", Betacam and 3/4" (over 400 hours; masters).
Cataloging: Computerized cataloging available for staff use only.
Access: Available to the public for duplication and reuse. Research fees charged (fees negotiable). Research requests accepted by mail, telephone and in person (by appointment only).
Rights: Full rights held to all material.
Licensing: Available for licensing. License fees charged.
Restrictions: None specified.
Viewing Facilities: Videotape (1", Betacam and 3/4").
Duplication Facilities: Videotape (1", Betacam and 3/4").

SOUTH CAROLINA (Rock Hill)

WINTHROP COLLEGE
IDA JANE DACUS LIBRARY
ARCHIVES
Rock Hill, SC 29733
(803) 323-2131 (Ext. 28)

Ron Chepesiuk (Head)

Contact: Ron Chepesiuk
Services: College library; film archives.
Description: Historical material depicting scenes of student activities at Winthrop College (1920s-30s).
Size & Elements: Film: 35mm (4,000 feet); 16mm (1,000 feet). (20 titles, 30 cans total). Videotape: format unspecified (60 videotapes).
Cataloging: Card catalogs; finding aids.
Access: Open to the public. Research fees not charged. Research requests accepted by mail, telephone and in person (walk-in and by appointment).
Rights: Full rights held to all material.
Licensing: Apply for information.
Restrictions: None specified.
Viewing Facilities: Film and videotape.
Duplication Facilities: None.

SOUTH DAKOTA

SOUTH DAKOTA (Pierre)

SOUTH DAKOTA STATE LIBRARY
FILM LIBRARY
800 Governors Drive
Pierre, SD 57501-2294
(605) 773-3131
Fax: (605) 773-4950

Jane Kolbe (State Librarian)

Contact: Dorothy M. Liegl (Deputy State Librarian)
Services: Library. Films and videotapes available to the public for free loan. Material not available for research, licensing or reuse.
Description: Lending library serving all persons in South Dakota. Materials are collected for all viewer audiences. Collection concentrates on educational and feature films; also holds films about the region, many produced by state agencies and South Dakota filmmakers. Some of the films produced by state agencies are rare; many are out of print.

Titles of special interest relating to South Dakota and the region include: *Charley Kills Enemy* (1974), showing the procedures and philosophy of a Sioux Indian medicine man, and footage of actual ceremonies; *Country School Legacy: Humanities of the Frontier* (1981), a nostalgic and contemporary look at the country school in the Northern Plains and Mountain States; *The Ingalls of DeSmet* (1978), visiting people who knew the Ingalls family (the family of noted author Laura Ingalls Wilder) when they lived in DeSmet; *Lakota Quillwork Art and Legend* (1985), Flossie New Holy Bear Robe and Alice New Holy Blue Legs demonstrating the process of quilling from catching the porcupine to making different products; *Lucy Swan* (1973), telling the story of an old Sioux woman and her many years of living in Central and Western South Dakota; *Oscar Howe: The Sioux Painter* (1973), explaining his art and the origin of the ancient Sioux designs he uses; *Prairie Killers* (1970), focusing on the critical place prairie dogs occupy in the ecological chain of life on the plains; *Rapid City Disaster* (1972), showing the damage done by the 1972 flood; *Sioux Nationalism* (1983), focusing on the deteriorating relationships between Indians and Whites in the 19th century; *Steve Charging Eagle: Family Man* (1966), documenting the bi-cultural life of a Sioux Indian living on the Cheyenne Reservation; and *Tahtonka: Plains Indians Buffalo Culture*, showing the importance of the buffalo in Indian culture, and how the Indians suffered starvation and disease as the herds diminished.

Small Towns: A Closer Look series (ca. 1970s, produced by KUSD-TV) profiles the South Dakota towns of Faulkton, Freeman, Gary, Keystone, Lemmon, Mobridge, Philip and Sisseton. Includes interviews with residents, reporters and local historians.

South Dakota Hall of Fame Shorts/South Dakota Personalities series (47 videotapes) profiles men and women noted for civic, business, religious and cultural leadership.
Size & Elements: Film: 16mm (3,586 titles, 4,692 prints, 5,110 reels). Videotape: mostly VHS (2,448 videotapes).
Cataloging: Published catalogs.
Access: Open to the public. Materials available for free loan to any citizen of South Dakota or any library located in South Dakota, subject to restrictions on specific titles. Requests accepted by mail and in person.
Rights: Some rights held to some material. No rights held to most material. Additional clearances may be necessary in some cases if material is to be reused.
Licensing: Apply for information.
Restrictions: None specified.
Viewing Facilities: Film (16mm); videotape (3/4" and VHS).
Duplication Facilities: Videotape (3/4" and VHS).

SOUTH DAKOTA (Sioux Falls)

SIOUXLAND HERITAGE MUSEUMS
200 West Sixth Street
Sioux Falls, SD 57102
(605) 335-4210

Mary Allman (Director)

Contact: John E. Rychtarik (Curator of Collections)
Services: Museum. Videotape collection currently inaccessible to the public.
Description: *George B. German Music Archives Collection.* Includes

documentation of and interviews with South Dakota "cowboy artists" and the Sioux River Folk Festival (1982), featuring bluegrass bands.

Due to inadequate cataloging, the collection is currently closed; however, there are plans to make the collection accessible to the public in the future.
Size & Elements: Videotape: 3/4" and VHS (approx. 30 videotapes).
Cataloging: Currently working on relocating and recataloging collection.
Access: Collection currently inaccessible. Inquiries accepted by mail.
Rights: Full rights held to all material.
Licensing: Material currently not available for licensing.
Restrictions: Collection currently not accessible for viewing or reuse of any kind.
Viewing Facilities: None.
Duplication Facilities: None.

TENNESSEE

TENNESSEE (Johnson City)

JAMES AGEE FILM PROJECT
316-1/2 East Main Street
Johnson City, TN 37601
(615) 926-8637

Film available for rental from:
JAMES AGEE FILM PROJECT LIBRARY
Box 315
Franklin Lakes, NJ 07417
(201) 891-8240

Ross Spears (Director, Filmmaker and Producer)

Contact: Dale Moore (Marketing Director)
Services: Documentary film producer. Films available for rental and purchase.
Description: Films include: *Agee,* a biography of the writer, incorporating interviews with John Huston, Walker Evans and Father Flye; *The Electric Valley,* about the Tennessee Valley Authority and its mission to tame the forces of nature, create cheap energy and produce a lasting prosperity in the Depression-wracked Tennessee Valley; *Long Shadows,* a feature-length documentary exploring the ways in which the echoes of the American Civil War can still be felt in society, featuring Robert Penn Warren, Studs Terkel, Jimmy Carter, Robert Coles, Tom Wicker, Albert Murray, John Hope Franklin, Virginius Dabney and C. Vann Woodward, as well as weekend soldiers, blues singers, battlefield guides, relic collectors, West Pointers, Vietnam veterans, old movie stars and civil rights activists; *An Afternoon with Father Flye,* with interviews James Agee's friend and mentor.
Size & Elements: Film: 16mm (4 titles).
Cataloging: Published catalogs.
Access: Available to the public for viewing, rental and purchase. Requests accepted by mail and telephone.
Rights: Full rights held to all material.
Licensing: Apply for information. License fees charged.
Restrictions: None specified.
Viewing Facilities: None.
Duplication Facilities: None.

TENNESSEE (Johnson City)

EAST TENNESSEE STATE UNIVERSITY
ARCHIVES OF APPALACHIA
THE SHERROD LIBRARY
Box 22450A
Johnson City, TN 37614-0002
(615) 929-4338

Dr. Fred P. Borchuck (Acting Director)

Contacts: Marie Tedesco (Public Services Archivist); Norma Thomas (Technical Services Archivist)
Services: Educational institution; videotape archives. Open to the public.
Description: Archives serves as a repository for documentation relating to political, social, cultural, historical, economic and environmental issues of Central South Appalachia. Strengths include: Appalachian customs and folkways; regional lifestyles; traditional country music; folk songs; folktales and storytelling; traditional arts and crafts; and religious practices.

Broadside TV, Inc. Collection. Consists of videotapes donated by Broadside Television, Inc., a now-defunct experimental videotape production and cable television facility located in Johnson City, Tennessee. Contains documentaries made by local producers (mid-1970s) concerning Central Southern Appalachia, dealing with topics such as regional politics, environmental issues, economic development, traditional arts and crafts, and religion. Also covers: midwifery; stories of boxcar travels in the 1930s; racism; Hyden mine disaster; coal mining, union organizing and strikes; *I Would Have Gone Back,* about a Vietnam veteran and his desertion from the Army, discussing the complexities of mountain people and the military; a tour of Jonesboro, the capital of the lost state of Franklin and the oldest town in Tennessee; *Fiddlin' Powers Family,* about the first Southern Appalachian musicians to make commercial recordings in the 1920s; the Ralph Stanley Memorial Bluegrass Festival; an Indian wedding ceremony; Jonesboro Storytelling workshop and festival; and Cherokee-Choctaw Indians.
WSJK-TV Collection (12 videotapes). Consists of local programming acquired from the now-defunct television station. Covers historical and literary subjects, including a series about the Overmountain Victory March, the Tilson Mill and Cherokee Indians. Also contains interviews with Appalachian authors, including Sherwood Anderson, Jesse Stuart, John Fox, and Thomas Wolfe's brother, Fred Wolfe.
Burton-Manning Videotape Collection. Largely consists of audiotapes documenting the oral traditions, music and folklore of the region. Videotapes in this collection feature various activities and events, including: tossing the caber; dancing competition; drum and pipe competition; tuning a bagpipe; archery; Scottish sheepdogs at work; and corn liquor still operations.
Size & Elements: Videotape: 3/4" (72 videotapes and 158 transfers from 1/2" open reel); 1/2" open reel (600 reels) (696 videotapes total).
Cataloging: Published catalog; computerized cataloging available to researchers.
Access: Open to the public. Research fees not charged. Requests accepted by mail, telephone and in person (by appointment and walk-in).
Rights: Full rights held to some material. Additional clearances may be necessary in some cases if material is to be reused.
Licensing: Apply for information. License and usage fees not charged.
Restrictions: Permission to duplicate needed for some materials.
Viewing Facilities: Videotape (3/4").
Duplication Facilities: None.
Related Materials: Personal papers and institutional records (2,500 linear feet); Appalachian vertical files containing news clippings, pamphlets, speeches and copies of periodical articles; Appalachian Photographic Archive containing prints, negatives and slides; audiotapes held in the Burton-Manning Oral History Project and Charles Gunter Collection; and 78 rpm phonograph records of country music.

TENNESSEE (Jonesborough)

NATIONAL ASSOCIATION FOR THE PRESERVATION AND PERPETUATION OF STORYTELLING (NAPPS)
P.O. Box 309
Jonesborough, TN 37659
(615) 753-2171

Street address: 116 West Main Street

Jimmy Neil Smith (Director)

Contacts: Jimmy Neil Smith
Services: Private nonprofit corporation. Videotapes available to the public for rental and purchase.
Description: Material relating to storytelling, primarily from National Storytelling Festivals (mid-1970s to present). Festivals feature performances by many professional storytellers from throughout the English-speaking world.
Titles include: *By Word of Mouth,* a documentary about storytelling and the 10th Annual National Storytelling Festival (1982); *American Storytelling Series* (8 volumes, H. W. Wilson Company), including the stories "Why The Dog Has A Cold Wet Nose" and "The Crack of Dawn"; *A Master Class in Storytelling* and *Six Stories About Little Heroes* (Vineyard Video), stories told by Jay O'Callahan; *Tell Me A Story* (Kartes Video Productions), a collection for children featuring some of America's foremost storytellers; and two videotapes by storyteller, educator and curriculum developer Lynn Rubright.
Size & Elements: Videotape: VHS and Betamax (approx. 200 hours).
Cataloging: Published catalog.
Access: Open to the public. Research fees not charged. Research requests not accepted. Orders accepted by mail and telephone.

Rights: Some rights held to some material.
Licensing: Apply for information.
Restrictions: None specified.
Viewing Facilities: Videotape (limited facilities).
Duplication Facilities: None.
Related Materials: Approximately 200 audiotapes.
Publications: *The National Storytelling Journal,* a quarterly magazine; *The Yarnspinner,* a monthly newsletter.

TENNESSEE (Knoxville)

TENNESSEE VALLEY AUTHORITY
MEDIA RELATIONS
400 West Summit Hill Drive
EPC-47
Knoxville, TN 37902
(615) 632-8023

William S. Lee (Manager, Media Relations)

Contact: William S. Lee
Services: Government agency. Stock footage available for media use, subject to restrictions.
Description: Provides videotape stock footage to the broadcast news media upon request. Subjects include aerials of TVA facilities, dams and steam plants.
Size & Elements: Videotape: 3/4" (over 1,000 videotapes).
Cataloging: Logs.
Access: Not open to the public. Film library available to the public. Stock footage available only to the broadcast news media. Research fees not charged. Research requests accepted by telephone.
Rights: Full rights held to all material.
Licensing: Apply for information. License fees not charged.
Restrictions: Stock footage available for use by the broadcast news media only.
Viewing Facilities: None.
Duplication Facilities: Videotape (3/4" and 1/2").

TENNESSEE (Memphis)

CENTER FOR SOUTHERN FOLKLORE
P.O. Box 40105
Memphis, TN 38174-0105
(901) 726-4205

Street address: 1216 Peabody Avenue

Judy Peiser (Executive Director, Artistic Development)

Contacts: Judy Peiser; Harry Gammerdinger
Services: Private nonprofit cultural center; film and videotape producer and distributor. Material possibly available for reuse, subject to clearance.
Description: Historical film footage (1939-59; 16mm, 170 rolls, color and black and white) of Memphis' Black community shot by Reverend L. O. Taylor, a Baptist minister and social philosopher. Material covers everyday life and special events in the Memphis Black community, including Baptist conventions, baptisms, high-school football games, the Cotton Maker's Jubilee Parade, the Negro Chamber of Commerce, Black-owned businesses, and portraits of celebrities such as Joe Lewis and W. C. Handy.

Other material produced by the Center covers such topics as contemporary folklife (1968-present), urban folklore, Memphis and Southern Judaica, folk arts and crafts, Black social history, Beale Street, Black religion, mid-South (Delta region) cultures, blues, gospel, storytelling, photography, filmmaking and festivals. Sample titles include: *Made in Mississippi: Black Folk Art and Crafts; It's Grits; Fannie Bell Chapman: Gospel Singer; I Ain't Lying: Folktales from Mississippi;* and *DuCote de Memphis.*

Additional material includes Chesterfield television commercials (35mm film) made with Black professionals; miscellaneous historical films; videotape documentation of events, such as stage shows and festivals, produced by the Center.
Size & Elements: Film: 35 and 16mm (approx. 50,000 feet; color and black and white). Videotape: format unspecified (approx. 10-15 hours).
Cataloging: Research library; dope sheets or release sheets.
Access: Open to the public by appointment. Research fees charged. Research requests accepted by mail, telephone and in person (by appointment only).
Rights: Full rights held to most material. Additional clearances may be

necessary in some cases if material is to be reused.
Licensing: Available for licensing and reuse, subject to clearance. License fees charged in some cases, depending on project.
Restrictions: None specified.
Viewing Facilities: Film (by appointment).
Duplication Facilities: Film and videotape duplication at local laboratory; fee for services apply.
Related Materials: Still photograph archives and vintage audio recordings (100 78 rpm home-cut recordings).
Publications: *American Folklore Films and Videotapes: An Index* (1976). Catalog of films and videotapes relating to folklore of the United States, including information on distributors and collections.

TENNESSEE (Memphis)

LUNAR PRODUCTIONS
51 North Cooper
Memphis, TN 38104
(901) 722-8571
Fax: (901) 276-2407

Geordy Wells (President)

Contact: Patricia Warren (Production Manager)
Services: Videotape producer. Collection maintained primarily for use by clients of facility.
Description: Memphis area scenics, including people and street scenes; generic footage of flags, crowds and more (1980-present).
Size & Elements: Videotape: Betacam ("thousands").
Cataloging: Computerized cataloging for staff use only (in process).
Access: Not open to the public. Collection maintained primarily for use by clients of facility.
Rights: Full rights held to all material.
Licensing: Material generally not available for licensing. License fees charged in some cases (for clients).
Restrictions: Collection maintained for use by clients at the facility.
Viewing Facilities: Videotape (for clients only).
Duplication Facilities: Videotape (3/4", VHS and Betamax).

TENNESSEE (Memphis)

MEMPHIS PINK PALACE MUSEUM AND LIBRARY
3050 Central Avenue
Memphis, TN 38111
(901) 454-5600
Fax: (901) 454-5620

Coralu Buddenbohm (Librarian)

Contact: Coralu Buddenbohm
Services: Museum; library. Film and videotape collection maintained primarily for in-house use.
Description: The "Pink Palace" was a private home (constructed of pink marble) acquired by the City of Memphis in 1926 to house the Museum's collections. The material in the Library focuses on Memphis and Pink Palace history. Additional acquired materials on zoology, botany, geology, paleontology and anthropology.
Size & Elements: Film: 16mm (28 titles); 8mm (200 film loops). Videotape: format unspecified (7 videotapes).
Cataloging: Card catalogs.
Access: Generally not open to the public. Materials for in-house use only. Research fees not charged. Research requests accepted on a case-by-case basis.
Rights: Rights status of material not known.
Licensing: Apply for information.
Restrictions: Research and access restrictions apply.
Viewing Facilities: Film viewing equipment used for classes only.
Duplication Facilities: None.

TENNESSEE (Memphis)

MEMPHIS-SHELBY COUNTY PUBLIC LIBRARY AND
INFORMATION CENTER
COMMUNITY INFORMATION CHANNEL
1850 Peabody Avenue
Memphis, TN 38104

(901) 725-8839

David Carter (Acting Department Head)

Contact: David Carter
Services: Library. Videotape collection open to the public for on-premises use only; not available for duplication or reuse.
Description: The Community Information Channel is a service of the Memphis and Shelby County Public Library and Information Center, which provides informational programming of community interest to Memphis-area cable television viewers.

Holds off-air videotape recordings of news broadcasts carried by Memphis television station WMC-TV (June 17, 1985-present). Coverage includes all local area news stories and events.
Size & Elements: Videotape: VHS (approx. 180 videotapes, each 5 hours).
Cataloging: Card catalogs filed by subjects and names; logs of each broadcast; and other finding aids.
Access: Open to the public. For on-premises use only. Not available for duplication. Research fees not charged. Research requests not accepted.
Rights: No rights held to any material. All rights retained by WMC-TV.
Licensing: Not available for licensing or reuse.
Restrictions: Maintained for research purposes only; not available for duplication or reuse.
Viewing Facilities: Videotape (VHS).
Duplication Facilities: None.

TENNESSEE (Memphis)

MEMPHIS STATE UNIVERSITY LIBRARIES
SPECIAL COLLECTIONS
MISSISSIPPI VALLEY COLLECTION
Memphis, TN 38152
(901) 454-2210

Michelle Fagan (Curator, Special Collections)

Contact: Michelle Fagan
Services: Educational institution. Film and videotape library open to the public; available for duplication and reuse, subject to restrictions.
Description: Footage relating to the Memphis sanitation workers strike and the assassination of Dr. Martin Luther King, Jr. (1968). Collection includes film footage from Memphis local television news and network news, both aired and unaired (February-April 1968); also held are several "anniversary" programs produced in later years.

Sanitation workers strike. Coverage of union leaders; workers; the mayor; several civil rights organizations; citizens involvement; meetings; speeches; sidewalk demonstrations; trash piling up on streets; picketing, riots and their aftermath in downtown Memphis; the arrival of National Guard troops; garbage trucks with police escorts; Memphis placed under curfew; Larry Payne's funeral; arrests and mass marches throughout the city.

Personalities highlighted include: Mayor Loeb; Governor Ellington; Charles Blackburn (head of Sanitation Department); Rev. Samuel Kyles; Roy Wilkins and Maxine Smith (NAACP); Rev. James Lawson; Bayard Rustin; Councilman Fred Davis; Dr. Ralph Abernathy; Rev. Jesse Jackson; and Dr. Martin Luther King, Jr. There is coverage of Dr. King's press conferences, several interviews and his last speech at Mason Temple in Memphis.

Assassination of Dr. Martin Luther King, Jr. (April 4, 1968). Includes coverage of the emergency situation in Memphis; shots of the Lorraine Motel and hospital emergency room; memorial march (April 8th) with Mrs. Coretta King; church services and memorials held for Dr. King; and interviews with Dr. King's friends, family and followers.

Follow-up programs include: *The War on Poverty: The Memphis Front* (1969); *Summer Rerun* (1969); and *Tribute to Dr. King and the Sanitation Workers* (1973). Also holds 20 interviews conducted with community leaders on the third anniversary of Dr. King's death (1971).
Size & Elements: Film: format unspecified (approx. 125 reels). Videotape (format and amount unspecified).
Cataloging: Card catalogs; printed lists; finding aids.
Access: Open to the public for duplication and reuse. Research fees not charged. Research request accepted by telephone and in person (walk-in).
Rights: Some rights held to some material. Some material donated from local news stations, who retain rights. Additional clearances may be necessary in some cases if material is to be reused.
Licensing: Available for licensing and reuse, subject to restrictions. License and usage fees not charged.

Restrictions: Duplication and reuse subject to permission of copyright holder.
Viewing Facilities: Film and videotape.
Duplication Facilities: Videotape.

TENNESSEE (Memphis)

PRODUCERS' SERVICE
3535 Park Avenue
Memphis, TN 38111
(901) 458-2578

Brian Frase; Joe Holmes (Owners)

Contact: Lee Hamilton (Production Manager)
Services: Videotape producer. Videotape collection available to the public for duplication, licensing and reuse.
Description: Extensive videotape footage of Memphis, Phoenix and Nashville, including lifestyles, landmarks, entertainment, scenics, people, panoramas, rivers, sunsets, sunrises and aerial views. Footage was produced for commercial clients (clearance required in some cases). Also holds extensive generic footage of fireworks.
Size & Elements: Videotape: 1" and Betacam (30 hours; masters).
Cataloging: Computerized cataloging for staff use only.
Access: Available to the public for duplication, licensing and reuse. Research fees not charged. Research requests accepted by telephone and in person (by appointment only).
Rights: Full rights held to some material. Some rights held to all material. Additional clearances will be necessary in some cases if material is to be reused.
Licensing: Available for licensing and reuse, subject to restrictions. License and usage fees charged.
Restrictions: Clearance from commercial clients necessary in some cases if material is to be reused.
Viewing Facilities: Videotape (1", Betacam, 3/4", VHS and Betamax).
Duplication Facilities: Videotape (1", Betacam, 3/4", VHS and Betamax).

TENNESSEE (Nashville)

AMERICAN ASSOCIATION FOR STATE & LOCAL HISTORY
172 Second Avenue North, Suite 102
Nashville, TN 37201
(615) 255-2971

Dr. Larry E. Tise (Director)

Contact: Bob Summer (Marketing Manager)
Services: Association. Collection of videotape programs available primarily to local history museums and organizations for purchase.
Description: Topics covered include: preservation techniques (ornamental wrought iron, slate roofs, ornamental plaster, ornamental painting and stained glass); current work in local history and priorities for scholarly study and public programs; museum marketing and promotion; writing, designing and producing museum labels; interpretive exhibit design; basic deterioration and preventive measures for museum collections; interpretation of history through pictorial documents, written documents and three-dimensional objects and the work of the oral historian.
Size & Elements: Videotape: 3/4", VHS and Betamax (21 titles total, each 20 to 25 min.)
Cataloging: Published catalog; publication list.
Access: Available primarily to local history museums and organizations for purchase. Research requests not accepted.
Rights: Full rights held to all material.
Licensing: Videotapes available for purchase only.
Restrictions: Footage from videotapes may not be reused without permission.
Viewing Facilities: None.
Duplication Facilities: None.

TENNESSEE (Nashville)

CASCOM
707 Eighteenth Avenue South
Nashville, TN 37203
(615) 329-4112
Fax: (615) 321-8512
Telex: 558649

Dennis Kostyk (President)

Contact: Timothy J. McGuire
Services: Syndicator of animated video graphic effects. Library available to broadcasters and producers on a subscription basis.
Description: Syndicator of animated video graphic effects, special effects and background elements to broadcast and nonbroadcast markets. Distributes the *Select Effects Library* (6 volumes containing over 2,000 effects) and ten other syndicated products, including station image graphics, television news graphics, thematic sales tags and movie-packaging graphics.
Size & Elements: Videotape: 1", Betacam and 3/4" (masters); 3/4" and VHS (demonstration videotapes). MII, Betacam SP and digital component videotape formats are available at an additional charge.
Cataloging: Published catalogs; sales promotion material.
Access: Available to the public for duplication, reuse and resale. Broadcast licenses are generally exclusive within a given market area. Annual subscription fee for nonbroadcast users permits access to effects library. Research requests accepted by mail and telephone.
Rights: Full rights held to all material.
Licensing: Available for syndication and licensing, subject to restrictions. License fees charged. Annual subscription fee for nonbroadcast users permits access to effects library.
Restrictions: Broadcast licenses are generally exclusive within a given market area.
Viewing Facilities: None.
Duplication Facilities: Videotape (1", Betacam and 3/4").

COUNTRY MUSIC FOUNDATION, INC.

4 Music Square East
Nashville, TN 37203
(615) 256-1639
Fax: (615) 255-2245

William J. Ivey (Executive Director)

Contact: Charlie Seemann (Deputy Director of Collections and Research)
Services: Cultural research foundation. Films and videotapes available for licensing and reuse, subject to approval and restrictions.
Description: Historical and current materials concerning country music, including Western movies, kinescopes of television shows, documentary footage, award programs, interviews and performances.

Television variety shows (1950s-60s). Titles include: *Ozark U.S.A.; Town & Country Time, Country Style U.S.A.; Stars of the Grand Old Opry; Pet Milk-Grand Old Opry Show, Purina-Grand Ole Opry Show;* and *National Life-Grand Old Opry Show.*

Feature films. Includes: Gene Autry and Tex Ritter cowboy movies; Snader Telescriptions (rights owned by Pathé Pictures, Inc. [q.v.]); and *The Singing Brakeman,* a short with Jimmie Rogers (Columbia Pictures, 1929).

Award shows. Includes footage from the Country Music Association, the Academy of Country Music, Music City News and the NARAS Grammys.

Documentaries. Material focusing on Nashville and the country music scene.

The Foundation is currently expanding its activities into the area of Southern folk culture; materials in this area may be available in the future (apply for information).
Size & Elements: Film: 35mm (15 titles); 16mm (980 titles); 8mm (5 titles) (films are mostly release prints with a few positive originals). Videotape: 2" (211 titles); 1" Type A (47 titles); 3/4" (361 titles); VHS (79 titles); Betamax (37 titles); 1/2" open reel (9 titles).
Cataloging: Research library; card catalogs.
Access: Available to the public. Research requests accepted by mail, telephone and in person (by appointment only). Research fees charged.
Rights: No rights held to any material.
Licensing: Available for licensing and reuse, subject to restrictions. Additional clearances may be necessary in some cases if material is to be reused.
Restrictions: Copyright restrictions may apply.
Viewing Facilities: Film (16mm projector); videotape (3/4", VHS and Betamax).
Duplication Facilities: Videotape (1/2" formats only).
Related Materials: Extensive audio materials available.

DCI VIDEO RESOURCES

1600 Hayes Street, Suite 300
Nashville, TN 37203
(615) 327-3061
Fax: (615) 329-2513

Gil Gilliam (Production Manager)

Contact: Gil Gilliam
Services: Videotape producer. Videotape collection available to the public for duplication, licensing and reuse.
Description: Footage on medical and surgical subjects, including organ donors, organ transplants, dialysis and heart surgery (1980-present).
Size & Elements: Videotape: 3/4" (several hundred hours; masters) (viewing copies available in all formats).
Cataloging: Staff assistance required.
Access: Available to the public for duplication, licensing and reuse. Research fees negotiable. Research requests accepted by telephone and in person (by appointment only).
Rights: Full rights held to most material. Some rights held to all material. Additional clearances may be necessary in some cases if material is to be reused.
Licensing: Available for licensing and reuse, subject to restrictions. License fees charged.
Restrictions: Requests for licensing considered on a case-by-case basis.
Viewing Facilities: Videotape (3/4", VHS and Betamax).
Duplication Facilities: Videotape (1", 3/4", VHS and Betamax).

DISCIPLES OF CHRIST HISTORICAL SOCIETY

1101 19th Avenue South
Nashville, TN 37212
(615) 327-1444

James M. Seale (President)

Contact: David I. McWhirter (Director of Library and Archives)
Services: Religious historical society. Films and videotapes available for in-house use by members only.
Description: Holdings relate to the Campbell-Stone Movement, an American religious movement started at the beginning of the 19th century, now comprised of the Christian Church (Disciples of Christ), the Christian Churches and Churches of Christ, and the non-instrumental churches of Christ.

Titles include: *Challenges: The History of the Restoration Movement in Texas; Women Go Forth With Vision; Ingila of the Congo,* in which a boy in the Congo is brought under the training and guidance of the missionaries; and various documentaries about missions in Africa, India, and the movement in the U.S. Little historical material is held.
Size & Elements: Film: 16mm (70 titles, 70 cans). Videotape: VHS (100 titles).
Cataloging: Card catalogs.
Access: Open to members. For in-house use only. Membership fees charged. Research requests accepted by mail, telephone and in person (walk-in).
Rights: Some rights held to all material. Additional clearances may be necessary in some cases if material is to be reused.
Licensing: Apply for information.
Restrictions: Available for in-house use by members only.
Viewing Facilities: Film (16mm projector).
Duplication Facilities: None.

DISCIPLESHIP RESOURCES

P.O. Box 840
Nashville, TN 37202
(615) 340-7068
Fax: (615) 340-7006

Street address: 1908 Grand Avenue

David L. Hazelwood (Executive Secretary)

Contact: Customer Services, P.O. Box 189, Nashville, TN 37202
Services: Nonprofit religious organization; videotape distributor. Videotapes

primarily for purchase by direct mail.
Description: Serves as the nonprofit publishing unit of the General Board of Discipleship, The United Methodist Church. Videotapes available include religious programs, concentrating on Christian education, evangelism, youth ministries, Christian stewardship, and preaching. *The Wesley Family Video Series,* with Dr. James S. Barrett, a well-known Wesley scholar, explores the Wesley family, its times and theology. Other titles include: *You Can't Do That in Church!; Preaching Christian Stewardship;* and *We Can Communicate! Asian-American Youth and Parents.*
Size & Elements: Videotape: VHS (27 titles, each 30 min.).
Cataloging: Published catalog.
Access: Available to the public for purchase by direct mail. Research requests not accepted.
Rights: Full rights held to some material. Some rights held to some material. Additional clearances may be necessary in some cases if material is to be reused.
Licensing: Apply for information.
Restrictions: Material may not be reused without permission.
Viewing Facilities: None.
Duplication Facilities: None.

TENNESSEE (Nashville)

JIM REEVES MUSEUM
1023 Joyce Lane
Nashville, TN 37216
(615) 226-2065

Mary Reeves (Owner/Director)

Contact: Mary Reeves
Services: Museum. Open to the public. Small film and videotape collection generally maintained for distribution and rental. Material possibly available for licensing and reuse, subject to restrictions.
Description: One feature-length film and several videotapes pertaining to the late country and western singing star, Jim Reeves. Includes a one-minute clip of a Jim Reeves recording session (the only one in existence); a feature-length film, *Kimberly Jim* (1963, South Africa); and videotaped copies of several television show appearances by Reeves including *The Dick Clark Show, The Ed Sullivan Show* and *Ozark Jubilee.*

Museum plans to expand videotape holdings. Currently in preparation for exhibition and purchase is a 1962 pilot for a television series starring Reeves.
Size & Elements: Film: 16mm (1 title). Videotape: VHS (amount unspecified).
Cataloging: None specified.
Access: Open to the public. Collection generally maintained for distribution and rental. Material possibly available for reuse, in some cases. Research requests accepted by mail, telephone and in person (walk-in).
Rights: Full rights held to all material.
Licensing: Available for licensing and reuse, subject to restrictions. License and usage fees charged.
Restrictions: Requests for licensing or reuse will be considered on a case-by-case basis.
Viewing Facilities: Videotape.
Duplication Facilities: None (outside arrangements can be made).

TENNESSEE (Nashville)

SOUTHERN BAPTIST HISTORICAL LIBRARY AND ARCHIVES
HISTORICAL COMMISSION, SBC
901 Commerce Street, Suite 400
Nashville, TN 37203-3620
(615) 244-0344

Dr. Lynn E. May, Jr. (Executive Director, Historical Commission, SBC)

Contacts: Bill Sumners (Archivist); Pat Brown (Librarian)
Services: Library. Film and videotape collection open to the public. Available for licensing and reuse, subject to acceptance and approval.
Description: Established in 1938 as part of the Southern Baptist Historical Society. Operated by the Historical Commission of the Southern Baptist Convention, Library is the world center for the study of Baptist history, and serves as the central depository and archives of the Southern Baptist Convention.

Collection (1922-present) contains films and videotapes related to Baptist history and lifestyle, focusing on the past ten years, including a major portion of materials produced by Southern Baptist Convention Agencies; videotape documentation of conferences and conventions of Baptist organizations, including proceedings of the Convention (1979-present); and a small amount of footage on local church activities.
Size & Elements: Film: 16mm (88 titles; primarily release prints). Videotape: 3/4" (208 videotapes); VHS (178 videotapes) (masters and viewing copies from Baptist agencies, the Foreign Mission Board and the Home Mission Board).
Cataloging: Card catalogs.
Access: Open to the public. Available for duplication, subject to restrictions. Research fees not charged. Research requests accepted by mail, telephone and in person (walk-in).
Rights: Full rights held to some material.
Licensing: Available for licensing and reuse, subject to restrictions. License fees charged for profit-making organizations.
Restrictions: Duplication, licensing and reuse subject to acceptance and approval.
Viewing Facilities: Film (16mm; viewing room); videotape (VHS; viewing room).
Duplication Facilities: Videotape (VHS).
Related Materials: Audio recordings of oral history interviews, sermons and music; still photograph collection containing some 6,000 images of Baptist leaders, pastors, missionaries, buildings and events.

TENNESSEE (Nashville)

TENNESSEE STATE LIBRARY AND ARCHIVES
403 Seventh Avenue North
Nashville, TN 37219
(615) 741-2451

Fran Schell (Reference Librarian)

Contact: Fran Schell
Services: State library; film archives. Maintains film collection.
Description: Films relating to conservation and various issues of concern to the state of Tennessee.

Conservation Department of Tennessee films. Includes: *Bledsoe County; Cherokee Indians; Chucalissa Indians* and *Chucalissa Indian Crafts; Conservation in Tennessee; Duck Hunt at Reelfoot Lake; Fishing Tennessee Lakes; Geese; Geology and Mining; Helping Our Bobwhites; Hiwassie Geese; Indian Summer in the Smokies; Pipeline to the Clouds; Rhododendron on Roane Mountain; The Sportsman's Dollar; Stream Survey; Taking Conservation to the Schools; Trees on the Warpath; United Nations Visit to Tennessee; Waterfowl Management; Where Indeed?; Wild Ducks in Sanctuary; Wildflower Pilgrimage; Tennessee: Nature's Partner; Reactor, Rockwood Area;* and *Yarnspinning.*

Interviews. Subjects include: Frank Clement; Jane Daniels (an interview on Black history); Alexander Heard, the Governor's Conference on Libraries; Hicks interview with the Scopes trial judge; Jackson Arts Council; James Robinson; interviews with legislators (1977-78), including Harper Brewer, Thomas S. Burnett, Bob Davis, Leonard Dunavant, Tom Jensen, Ned R. McWherter, Shelby Rhinehart, C. B. Robinson, Paul Scruggs, Jim White and John Wilder; and Richard Fulton (speech).

Miscellaneous footage. Items include: *1948 Duck River Flood; Planting Pine Trees; Autumn Colors; Oneida and Western Railroad; Roane Mountain; Sage Brush Fire;* and *Presidential Visit to Small Towns.*
Size & Elements: Film: 16mm (approx. 90 titles).
Cataloging: Title list.
Access: Research requests accepted by mail and telephone.
Rights: Apply for information.
Licensing: Apply for information.
Restrictions: None specified.
Viewing Facilities: None.
Duplication Facilities: None.

TENNESSEE (Nashville)

VANDERBILT UNIVERSITY
TELEVISION NEWS ARCHIVE
Jean and Alexander Heard Library
Nashville, TN 37240-0007
(615) 322-2927

Street address: 419 21st Avenue South

TENNESSEE (Summertown)

Scarlett Graham (Director)

Contacts: John Lynch; Jacklyn Freeman (Administrative Assistant).
Services: University library; videotape archives. Material available for research and loan; not available for reuse.
Description: Established August 5, 1968 to document on videotape the otherwise ephemeral phenomenon of television news. Prior to this, nowhere was television news consistently recorded and retained for research and study. The Archive remains unique in routinely recording, indexing and making available for study the most widely viewed national television newscasts. Also lends videotapes of news coverage for research, reference and study.

Network evening newscasts. Network evening newscasts comprise the core of the collection. These are videotaped off the air as broadcast in Nashville, Tennessee and supplemented, since 1978, by videotapes of broadcasts as are aired on weekends in Washington, D.C. (but not in Nashville). The weekend broadcasts are recorded for the Archive by the Gelman Library of George Washington University.

Prior to May 1, 1979, the Archive's videotapes of the broadcasts were in black and white; from May 1, 1979-present, in color. Each videotape is continuously marked at the top of the image with information identifying the network, the date and the time. The time code numbers change at ten-second intervals. This information corresponds with the listings in the *Television News Index and Abstracts.*

Special newcasts. Supplementing the evening newscasts are approximately 3,600 hours of videotapes of special newscasts. These cover presidential speeches and press conferences, political conventions, election nights, presidential and vice-presidential debates, coverage of domestic and international crises and a variety of documentaries elaborating on subjects reported on the evening news. About 200 hours of special newscasts are added to the collection each year.
Size & Elements: Videotape: 3/4", Betamax and VHS (viewing and loan copies). At least 10 hours of news videotapes are added each week to the existing collection of over 13,000 hours.
Cataloging: *Television News Index and Abstracts.* Published by the Archive and also functioning as its collection guide, this monthly publication consists of descriptive abstracts of items in the evening news collection only, presented in the format of the broadcast according to network, date and time of each item. For each month there is a subject and name index to the abstracts. The names of each person who speaks on screen and those prominently mentioned in each report are included in the abstract and indexed. The range of subjects is as broad as those of most standard indexes, and is cross-referenced. The monthly indexes are cumulated each year for an annual index, specifying the months when the entries appear. Plans are to move the published index to an on-line environment.
Access: Available to the public for research and loan. Videotapes may be viewed at the Archive during business hours. Duplicates may be borrowed from the Archive. Staff can duplicate individual items drawn from varied broadcasts (fees apply) at the instruction of the user, based on information from the *Index/Abstracts.* To remove the Archive from judgmental determinations, the Archive urges users to base their orders on information from the *Index/Abstracts.* For a fee, the Archive will provide limited reference service, but cannot undertake extensive research. Research requests accepted by mail and telephone.

Orders are generally filled within a few weeks. Rush orders for up to an hour of videotape can generally be filled by the end of the business day following receipt of the request. Such orders are charged at double the normal rates. The borrower agrees to pay for raw videotape replacement when any videotape is damaged or lost during the course of a loan. Loans are normally for 90 days.

The Archive is primarily maintained and organized as a research collection. Typical users are academics: professors, teachers and students. Academic rates set for those users also apply to public service or tax-exempt users, as well as to members of the Archive.

The Archive offers one service exclusively to members. The Archive will compile television coverage on a specific current topic on an ongoing basis, only to members. For example, coverage of the 1984 presidential campaign was compiled as it occurred. A member may request continuous compilation of news coverage of an issue or item of the member's choosing. The Archive will ship such a standing order monthly.

Members will receive a subscription to the *Index/Abstracts.* When the Index becomes available on-line, it is anticipated that access to members will be provided at special rates.
Rights: No rights held to any material. Rights retained by television networks. Public Law 94-553 includes provisions effective January 1, 1978 regarding copyright in audiovisual works and the archiving of television news broadcasts.

Some of the materials in the collection contain notice of copyright. Users should be guided by the provisions of the statute in using materials from the Archive.
Licensing: Not available for licensing or reuse.
Restrictions: Material under copyright restriction. The Archive only lends videotapes; nothing is available for purchase.
Viewing Facilities: Videotape.
Duplication Facilities: Videotape (3/4", VHS and Betamax).
Publication: *Television News Index and Abstracts,* a monthly guide to the evening news collection.

TENNESSEE (Summertown)

VIDEO FARM
12, The Farm
Summertown, TN 38483
(615) 964-2519

Ina May Gaskin (Director)

Contact: Ina May Gaskin
Services: Videotape producer and distributor. Films and videotapes available for nonprofit educational use.
Description: Videotapes produced at The Farm on the subject of natural childbirth. *The Breech Birth and Shoulder Dystocia* and *A Natural Delivery of Vertex Twins* are designed as teaching aids for midwives, obstetricians and gynecologists, medical students, nurses and childbirth educators. Programs are now being prepared showing other obstetrical techniques.
Size & Elements: Film: 16mm (1 title; release prints). Videotape: 3/4", Betamax and VHS (2 titles; viewing copies).
Cataloging: Printed brochure.
Access: Available for rental and purchase. Requests accepted by mail and telephone.
Rights: Some rights held to all material.
Licensing: Apply for information.
Restrictions: None specified.
Viewing Facilities: None.
Duplication Facilities: None.

TEXAS

TEXAS (Abilene)

**ABILENE CHRISTIAN UNIVERSITY
BROWN LIBRARY**
ACU Station Box 8177
Abilene, TX 79699
(915) 674-2344
Fax: (915) 674-2202

Street address: 1600 Campus Court

Marsha Harper (Director)

Contacts: Marsha Harper; Erma Jean Loveland (Special Services Librarian); Kenneth Gunselman (Media Librarian)
Services: Academic library. Maintains archival film and television collection. Material available for research and reuse, subject to restrictions.
Description: Christianity, Church of Christ and some World War II-era educational films.

Herald of Truth Archives. Holds a nearly complete series of films and radio programs produced by the *Herald of Truth* television ministry, a weekly evangelistic program which began radio broadcasts in 1952 and television broadcasts in 1954, operated under the auspices of the Highland Church of Christ in Abilene, Texas.
Size & Elements: Film: 16mm (approx. 1,700 titles; release prints). Videotape: format unspecified (313 videotapes; viewing copies).
Cataloging: Card catalogs; index.
Access: Open to the public. Interlibrary loan fees apply. Requests accepted by mail, telephone and in person (walk-in and by appointment).
Rights: Full rights held to some material. Some rights held to some material. Some material in the public domain.
Licensing: Available for licensing and reuse, subject to restrictions. License and usage fees charged in some cases.

Restrictions: Requests for licensing and reuse considered on a case-by-case basis.
Viewing Facilities: Film and videotape.
Duplication Facilities: None.
Related Materials: Scripts and other materials made available with *Herald of Truth* programs.

TEXAS (Arlington)

ARIES PRODUCTIONS
1110 Avenue H East, Suite 200
Arlington, TX 76011
(817) 640-9955
Fax: (817) 649-2529

Wynn Winberg (President)

Contact: Joe Wilson (Vice President)
Services: Videotape producer. Material available for duplication and reuse. Custom shooting service provided on request.
Description: Dallas/Fort Worth area, the Southwestern U.S. and Mexico (scenics, skylines, landscapes, cityscapes, country and desolate rural settings).
Size & Elements: Videotape: 1" and Betacam ("growing collection").
Cataloging: Computerized cataloging available for staff use only.
Access: Available to the public for duplication and reuse. Research fees charged (fees negotiable). Research requests accepted by mail, telephone and in person (by appointment only).
Rights: Full rights held to all material.
Licensing: Available for licensing, subject to restrictions. License fees charged.
Restrictions: Some limitations may apply.
Viewing Facilities: Videotape (all formats).
Duplication Facilities: Videotape (all formats).

TEXAS (Arlington)

ASSOCIATION FOR RETARDED CITIZENS
National Headquarters
2501 Avenue J
Arlington, TX 76006
(817) 640-0204

Alan Abeson (Executive Director)

Contacts: Liz Moore (Director of Communications); Ann Balson (Administrative Secretary of Department of Research and Program Services)
Services: Association. Videotapes available to the public for distribution.
Description: Collection pertains to the employment of mentally retarded adults. *A New Horizon* documents the story of Shirley Jennings, who learned to use a computer and operate various electrical devices after 42 years of total physical dependence on others. *It's Just Good Business* (Quaker Oats Company) describes an example of a work enclave model of supported employment for mentally retarded adults.
Size & Elements: Videotape: 3/4", VHS and Betamax (2 titles).
Cataloging: Release sheets.
Access: Available to the public for distribution.
Rights: Full rights held to some material. Additional clearances may be necessary in some cases if material is to be reused.
Licensing: Apply for information. License fees not charged.
Restrictions: None specified.
Viewing Facilities: Videotape (3/4" and 1/2").
Duplication Facilities: None.

TEXAS (Austin)

ALTERNATIVE INFORMATION NETWORK
P.O. Box 7279
Austin, TX 78712
(512) 474-2107

Frank Morrow (Producer)

Contact: Frank Morrow
Services: Nonprofit, educational media organization; producer of public access television programs. Programs available on videotape for public access

cablecast or purchase.
Description: *Alternative Views* is a public affairs cable television program presenting subjects and sources which are ignored or distorted by the conventional media. The program, appearing since 1978 on Austin Community Television (ACTV), is now carried in 260 different cities. Programs feature documentary footage, news gathered from a broad range of sources, and special expert or experienced guests. The program also shows documentaries by independent producers.

Interviews with nationally known peace and justice activists include: Helen Caldicott, Ramsey Clark, Charlie Clements, John Henry Faulk, Congressman Henry B. Gonzalez, Jim Hightower, Sonia Johnson, Bishop Leroy Matthiessen, Dr. Benjamin Spock and John Stockwell. Interviews with local activists include: Janis Heine (American Friends Service Committee & Casa Marianella); Gara LaMarche and Jim Harrington (Texas Civil Liberties Union); Paul Hernandez (EACEDC); and Barry George (Bikes Not Bombs).

Sample titles for sale from the first ten seasons of programming include: *The World Power Structure: The Bilderbergers and the Trilateral Commission; John Stockwell and the CIA; Gary Shaw and the Kennedy Assassination; Sunbelt Snowjob: The Selling of the Southwest; Nuclear Energy: Debate and Discussion; Agribusiness and the Death of the Family Farm; "Whatever Happened To...?": Greg Calvert, SDS, and the New Left; Mexico: An Impending Revolution?; A Conversation with Ralph Yarborough; Marx and "Socialism" Today: The Promise Betrayed?; A Conversation with Edward Dmytryk; A Conversation with George Wald; Iran, Civil Liberties, and the CIA; The Ku Klux Klan; Big Oil, Bad Oil; Pornography, Rape and Violence Toward Women; Nagasaki: A Survivor's Story; Inside Saudi Arabia; Repression in Argentina; Genocide in East Timor; Registering Opposition; Creeping McCarthyism: The McKinnon and Kelleher Cases; Inside Jamaica and Grenada with John Stockwell; A Conversation with Madalyn Murray O'Hair; Hollywood Films Today; An English Lesson: Austerity for the U.S.; Texas Farmworkers Revisited; The New Counterinsurgency; The FBI on Trial; CIA Update; Nicaragua Revisited; Stokely Carmichael Speaks Out!; Legalized Murder, Klan-Nazi Style; Ben Sargent: The Populist Cartoonist; Cointelpro Lives!: The Peltier Case;* and *Covert Action.*
Size & Elements: Videotape: 3/4" (over 340 programs, each 60 min.; viewing copies).
Cataloging: Published catalogs.
Access: Available for reuse. Programs are mailed to public access and educational organizations for cablecast on public access channels. Research requests accepted in person (by appointment only).
Rights: Full rights held to some material. Some rights held to all material. Additional clearances may be necessary in some cases if material is to be reused.
Licensing: Available for licensing. License fees charged in some cases.
Restrictions: None specified.
Viewing Facilities: Videotape (available at ACTV).
Duplication Facilities: Videotape (available at ACTV).

TEXAS (Austin)

LYNDON BAINES JOHNSON LIBRARY
2313 Red River Street
Austin, TX 78705
(512) 482-5137
Fax: (512) 478-9104

Harry J. Middleton (Director)

Contacts: Philip Scott (Audiovisual Archivist); Tina Houston (Chief of Archives)
Services: Presidential library. Material available for research and duplication, subject to copyright restrictions.
Description: Presidential library administered by the National Archives and Records Administration. Holds film and videotape relating to the activities of Lyndon B. Johnson as president of the U.S., and members of his family.

Government departments and agencies producing films. Atomic Energy Commission (35 titles); Agency for International Development (2 titles); Department of Agriculture (22 titles); Air Force (28 titles); Army (15 titles); Civil Defense (3 titles); Civil Service (6 titles); Coast Guard (3 titles); Commerce (34 titles); Department of Defense (56 titles); Equal Employment Opportunity Commission (1 title); Federal Aviation Administration (5 titles); General Services Administration (1 title); Health, Education and Welfare (34 titles); Housing and Urban Development (8 titles); Interior (6 titles); Justice (1 title); Marines (9 titles); National Aeronautics and Space Administration (61 titles); National Archives and Records Service (1 title); National Education

Agency (1 title); Navy (5 titles); Navy: White House Photographic Unit (83 titles, 611 rolls of outtakes); Office of Economic Opportunity (33 titles); President's Council on Aging (6 titles); President's Committee on Consumer Interests (3 titles); Post Office (4 titles); Senate (1 title); Small Business Administration (17 titles); Department of State (6 titles); Tennessee Valley Authority (3 titles); Treasury (11 titles); U.S. Information Agency (106 titles); Veterans Administration (29 titles).

Films given to President Johnson and to the Library. Assorted productions, mostly made during the Johnson administration by diverse individuals and organizations (225 titles).

Films produced by or commissioned for the Library. Some completed productions, some uncut footage, some sync sound, all color. Includes films done for exhibits at the Library, coverage of special events sponsored by the Library, and limited coverage of Mrs. Johnson's activities. Limited footage of President Johnson. Begins May 22, 1971. Special items include a short orientation film about the Library done by the staff; a biography (55 min.) of the former president; and coverage of a Cabinet meeting held in December, 1968 (100 titles total).

Democratic National Committee. Mostly television campaign commercials for Democratic presidential candidates (1960 and 1964) with a few spots from the 1950s. Includes a large number of short television spots and longer special broadcasts (79 titles, black and white).

Foreign governments. Primarily films about President Johnson's visits abroad, produced by the host countries and sent to him as gifts (19 titles).

Television networks. Primarily coverage of President Johnson's activities, including special broadcasts. The bulk of the collection is 134 titles from CBS, including black and white kinescopes of some of the post-presidential interviews with Walter Cronkite. Collection also includes coverage of the 1961 and 1965 inaugurals, and of President Johnson's funeral. CBS (134 titles); ABC (17 titles); NBC (20 titles); NET (2 titles).

Drew Pearson. Columnist Drew Pearson's television reports from the 1950s (450 feet each, 82 titles, black and white). Collection not yet open for research.

WHCA (White House Communications Agency) 1" videotape series. Recorded from direct feeds from the White House or off the air by the White House Communications Agency. Includes television appearances by President Johnson; special news broadcasts; and news interview program. Beginning April 1, 1968, also includes daily morning and evening news programs, network and local. The bulk of the collection is from 1968 (recorded from July 3, 1966 to January 20, 1969). Duplication restricted on copyrighted materials (3,163 videotapes).

LBJ Library videotape series. Expanding series of coverage of special events sponsored by the Library, including the appearances of guest speakers and symposia, dating from May 22, 1971 (529 videotapes, 3/4"; color, black and white).

Walt W. Rostow. Videotapes (124) of Rostow's lectures (1969, 1971-72 and 1976-78).

Size & Elements: Film: format unspecified (1 million feet, 1,200 titles). Videotape: mostly 1" Ampex Type A (4,000 videotapes, each 60 min.); remainder 3/4" videotapes.

Cataloging: Card catalogs; finding aids; list.

Access: Open to the public. Available for duplication, subject to copyright restrictions. Research fees not charged. Duplication fees charged. Research requests accepted by mail, telephone and in person (appointments preferred, not required).

Rights: Material, except for copyrighted items, is in the public domain.

Licensing: Available for reuse, subject to restrictions. Usage fees not charged.

Restrictions: Copyrights to some material retained by original producers.

Viewing Facilities: Film (16mm Steenbeck flatbed editing table); videotape (3/4").

Duplication Facilities: Videotape (3/4" to 3/4", Betamax and VHS).

Related Materials: Numerous audiotape recordings.

TEXAS STATE LIBRARY
ARCHIVES DIVISION
P.O. Box 12927
Austin, TX 78711
(512) 463-5480

Street address: 1201 Brazos, Austin, TX 78701

Christopher LaPlante (State Archivist)

Contacts: John Anderson (Photograph Archivist); Michael Green (Reference Archivist)

Services: State archives; film and videotape collection. Access to most material is extremely limited.

Description: Earliest dated footage (1941) documents the inauguration of Texas Governor W. Lee O'Daniel. The latest accessions are videotapes (1987). All material relates to the state of Texas, the activities of Texas government or Texans in general.

Size & Elements: Film: 35mm and 16mm. Videotape: 3/4", VHS and 1/2" open reel (23 cubic feet total).

Cataloging: Finding aids.

Access: Access to most items is extremely limited. A duplicate, copy print, internegative or other copy must be generated before most materials can be viewed or further reproduced. Research fees not charged. Research requests accepted by mail, telephone and in person (by appointment only).

Rights: Some material in the public domain. Additional clearances are necessary in most cases if material is to be reused.

Licensing: Available for licensing and reuse, subject to restrictions.

Restrictions: All requests for research and reuse subject to acceptance and approval. Reuse or broadcast of many items necessitates obtaining permission from the producers or copyright holders. Copyright research and compliance with all applicable copyright laws is the responsibility of user or researcher.

Viewing Facilities: Videotape (3/4").

Duplication Facilities: None.

UNIVERSITY OF TEXAS AT AUSTIN
EUGENE C. BARKER TEXAS HISTORY CENTER
Sid Richardson Hall 2.109
Austin, TX 78713-7330
(512) 471-5961

Dr. Don E. Carleton (Director)

Contacts: Lawrence A. Landis (Photographs Archivist); John Wheat (Sound Archivist); Ralph Elder (Head of Public Services)

Services: Historical society. Film and videotape collection open to the public for in-house use; and reuse, subject to restrictions. Temporary loans are available by appointment only.

Description: Holds materials acquired as part of manuscript collections that document Texas social history. Also holds completed productions incorporating Barker Center photographic resources. Holdings relate to the petroleum industry; Texas music and musicians; Texas folklife; Black Texans; westward expansion; the political careers of Ralph W. Yarborough and others; the University of Texas at Austin, Ala.; Coushatta Indians and Jewish culture in Texas.

Jesse Holman Jones Papers (2 films). *Dedication of the San Jacinto Battlefield Monument* (1936) and *Shoeshine Boy* (1954), with Jones, Fred Heyne and Oscar Holcomb.

Olin Culberson Papers (6 reels). Political advertisements for a member of the Texas Railroad Commission, produced by KRLR-TV of Dallas.

Ralph W. Yarborough Papers (35mm and 16mm film, 169 reels; 2" videotape, 40 reels). The political career of the former Texas Senator. Currently restricted.

Texas Jewish Historical Society Records (4 videotapes). Includes *A Well Kept Secret* (1986), an interview with Natalie Ornish by Dr. Walker Railey about Jewish pioneers on the Texas frontier, and footage of annual meetings.

Almetris Marsh Duren Videotapes (1983, 3 videotapes). Documentation of desegregation at the University of Texas at Austin as described by Duren, student advisor and housemother for the University's first black students.

Claude Mathews Collection. Over 40 videotapes and an edited documentary relating to Kenneth Threadgill and the musical life of Threadgill's Restaurant.

Austin City Limits Videotapes (5 videotapes). Broadcast recordings of the television program featuring Texas music. Includes the Squeezebox special, West Texas singers and songwriters, country music legends, Roy Orbison and others.

Also held is an interview with record producer Huey Meaux, known as the "Crazy Cajun"; and an interview with Lavada Durst ("Dr. Hepcat"), Austin's first black disc jockey.

Size & Elements: Film: 35mm (17 reels); 16mm (174 reels) (positive and negative). Videotape: 2" (106 videotapes; masters); VHS and Betamax (81 videotapes; masters and viewing copies).

Cataloging: Printed lists.

Access: Open to the public. For in-house use only. Temporary loan is possible (by appointment only). Material possibly available for reuse. Research fees not charged. Research not performed by Barker Center staff. Research requests accepted in person (walk-in).
Rights: Some rights held to some material. Rights status of some material not known. Very little footage is in the public domain.
Licensing: Available for reuse, subject to restrictions. Usage fees not charged, although the Barker Center requires a gratis copy of any production reusing its footage.
Restrictions: All research requests subject to restrictions, acceptance and approval.
Viewing Facilities: Film (available elsewhere on campus); videotape (VHS; other formats may be viewed elsewhere on campus).
Duplication Facilities: Videotape (at the UT Fine Arts Library).
Related Materials: Manuscripts collections, maps, microfilm, sound recordings, and photographs, including the Jimmie A. Dodd Photographic Archive, the Joseph F. Taulman Photographic Collection, and hundreds of images depicting persons, places and subjects relating to Texas.

TEXAS (Austin)

UNIVERSITY OF TEXAS AT AUSTIN
NETTIE LEE BENSON LATIN AMERICAN COLLECTION
General Libraries
Sid Richardson Hall 1.109
Austin, TX 78713-7330
(512) 471-3818

Laura Gutiérrez-Witt (Head Librarian)

Contact: Laura Gutiérrez-Witt
Services: University library. Film and videotape holdings maintained for in-house research use only.
Description: *Individually acquired material (not part of archival collections).* Materials from various sources and producers include: *Tejas Chicanas: Natives, Pioneers, Feminists* (1978), a talk held at the Chicano History Conference, University of Texas; *Inez García,* who was charged with the murder of Miguel Jiménez, her alleged rapist, on March 19, 1974, in Soledad, California; *A Thirst In the Garden,* examining conditions in the Rio Grande Valley *colonias,* the rural slums where Mexican American farmworkers cannot get uncontaminated drinking water; *Nuestra día,* a program aired on WFAA-TV (Dallas), presents a dramatic sketch on the social dilemma of having a "low-rider" car; *The Men of Company E,* a reunion of Mexican American Army veterans from El Paso who served together in World War II; and *Valentín Durán,* an interview with a 92-year-old Texan Chicano whose father settled in Dripping Springs in 1852 after leaving Mexico at age 12. *The Raza Unida Party* is a film documentary on the state of the political party in late 1975.
Culture and the arts. Titles include: *Dále kranque: Chicano Music and Art in South Texas,* the story of six Chicano musicians and artists; *Folk Dances and Quinceañera,* viewing forms of celebration often associated with Hispanics; *Reforma o...,* a program on Austin-based Chicano musicians exploring a synthesis of many musical styles accompanied by visual imagery; *Inès Tovar,* a reading by the poet and discussion of her life, background and the perspectives provided by her Nez Percé mother and Chicano father; *George Cisneros and Mel Casas,* a two-part film on the music of Cisneros with the James Clouser Dancers and on painter Mel Casas' show at the Houston Contemporary Arts Museum; *Freddy Fender,* a film documentary on the Chicano musician, his hometown and 1950s music.
José Angel Gutiérrez Papers (4 videotapes). Includes: *The Schools of Cristal* and *Cuba.*
Felipe Ortego Y Gasca Papers (7 videotapes). Includes: *The 53rd Annual LULAC Convention; What Is Color?; Presentation on Developing Programs for the Spanish Community; John Gray; Bob Like; Underemployment in Hispanic Communities.*
Domingo Reyes Papers (23 videotapes). Includes: *Video National Conference on Christians and Jews; Pilot Spots on Chicanitos — Public Service Announcements;* interviews with Ana Gómez, Anthony Quinn, Armando Rodríguez, Fernando de Baca, Chris Alderete, Dr. Daniel Valdéz (publisher of *La Luz*) and Gilbert Pompa; *Accent on the Barrio — Training and Employment Program;* and *Justicia,* including rare footage of Rubén Salazar and the Chicano Riots of 1972.
Julian Samora Papers (1 videotape). An address by Cesar Chávez at Notre Dame University (April 1979).
League of United Latin American Citizens (LULAC) Records (1 film, 5 videotapes). Titles include: *This Is My Family; 1982 LULAC National Convention; LULAC District VIII Convention;* and *LULAC Public Service Announcements.*
Joseph G. Moore Collection (44 cans of film). Shot in Jamaica by CBS professionals in 1957 under the direction of Joseph G. Moore, based on field work for his doctoral dissertation. Includes: religious cults in Jamaica; *Cumina at Cecil; Cumina at Seaforth, 1958; Revival Zion, Morant Bay Market Shops; Revival at Miller's Hill; Lamp Unto My Feet* (CBS broadcast); *Revival Zion at Kingston; Cumina: Start of Dance and Possessions; Revival Over Graves;* and many other types of footage.
In The Name Of The People (19 videotapes). Feature film intimately portraying the Salvadoran Revolution and its participants. Shot in the liberated zone of Guazapa, film shows the interrelationship between armed combatants and the peasant population.
La Raza Unida Party Records (1970-1980; 1 videotape and 23 motion pictures). Records of various events in the history of the Party.
Size & Elements: Film: format unspecified (68 cans). Videotape: format unspecified (121 videocassettes, 26 videotapes).
Cataloging: Card catalogs; inventories.
Access: Open to the public. For in-house use only. Research fees not charged. Research requests accepted by mail, telephone and in person (walk-in).
Rights: No rights held to any material.
Licensing: Material not available for reuse.
Restrictions: Material for research use only.
Viewing Facilities: None.
Duplication Facilities: None.

TEXAS (Austin)

THE UNIVERSITY OF TEXAS AT AUSTIN
PETROLEUM EXTENSION SERVICE
Balcones Research Center, Box 413
10100 Burnet Road
Austin, TX 78758-4497
(512) 471-3163
Telex: 767161

Contact: Staff
Services: University; continuing education service; film and videotape producer and distributor. Material available to the public for purchase.
Description: Industrial, technical and training materials for the petroleum industry.
Petroleum Stock Footage (1980, 12 min., 400 feet). Consists of footage from PETEX movies edited and printed as a B-wind (camera-wind) roll with no sound track (also available as a CRI). Purchaser may use this footage in motion picture or videotape productions without copyright infringement.
Other petroleum industry education and training productions include: *Geology: Perspective for Petroleum; Man Management and Rig Management; Moving Oil,* documenting the operation of a crude oil pipeline company from the wellhead to the products terminal; shows functions of the gauger, operations coordinator, terminal supervisor, and other pipeline employees as oil and products move through the pipeline; and *Makin' Hole in the Eighties,* a dramatic introduction to the modern drilling industry from seismic exploration to action on the rig floor. Other titles include: *Primary Cementing; Drilling Mud: Under Pressure; No Fishing This Year: Care and Handling of Drill Pipe, Drill Collars, and Tool Joints; Laying Down Pipe; Swivels, Blocks, Rotaries; F-FA Mud Pumps; Oilwell Blowouts: An Introduction; Acidizing: Freedom to Flow; Hydraulic Fracturing; Producing Oil,* showing the process of well to pipeline; *Kimray Glycol Pump Series; Treating Crude-Oil Emulsions; Abandon Ship* (Texaco, Inc.), covering the recommended step-by-step procedures for evacuating marine tanker vessels; *The Hidden Frontier: The Story of Deepwater Drilling; Helicopter Operations; Offshore Rescue;* and *Simultaneous Drilling and Production.*
Size & Elements: Film: 16mm (33 titles, also available in videotape). Videotape: 3/4", VHS, Betamax I and Betamax II (19 titles; NTSC, PAL and SECAM conversions available at additional charge).
Cataloging: Published catalogs.
Access: Available to the public for purchase. Requests accepted by mail and telephone.
Rights: All audiovisual materials distributed by PETEX are copyrighted.
Licensing: Apply for information. License fees charged.
Restrictions: Reproduction or alteration of any program without the express written consent of PETEX is strictly prohibited. A "copyright" (license) fee is charged for the use of PETEX materials.
Viewing Facilities: None.
Duplication Facilities: None.

Related Materials: Videotape transfers of slide programs available. Scripts, workbooks and instructor's guides available for some programs.
Distributor: Some titles are produced by Filmwest Associates in Canada. Canadian orders must be directed to Filmwest Associates, P.O. Box 11028, Edmonton, AB T5J 3K3; (403) 488-9178, Telex: 037-3787.

TEXAS (Austin)

UNIVERSITY OF TEXAS AT AUSTIN
HARRY RANSOM HUMANITIES RESEARCH CENTER
PHOTOGRAPHY COLLECTION
P.O. Drawer 7219
Austin, TX 78713-7219
(512) 471-9124

Street address: 21st and Guadalupe

Roy Flukinger (Curator)

Contact: Carey Thorton (Research Associate)
Services: Research library. Film and videotape collection available for duplication and reuse on a case-by-case basis, subject to restrictions.
Description: *Norman Bel Geddes Collection* (16mm, approx. 300 items). Subjects include the New York World's Fair (1939-40); home movies and studio research films. Titles include *Praying Mantis* and *Nude Woman, Slowly Dancing.*
  Mike Wallace Interviews (1957-59, approx. 60 kinescopes, some soundtracks and audiotape). Interviews with famous personalities.
  Why We Fight series (16mm, 10 titles). Titles include *The Battle of Russia; Desert Victory; The Battle of Britain; The Battle of China; Prelude to War; Divide and Conquer; Attack: Battle of New Britain; The Stilwell Road; The Nazis Strike;* and *War Comes to America.*
  Edward Larocque Tinker Collection. Includes Spanish and English versions of *The Gaucho* series: *The Gaucho of Salta; The Llanero; The Argentine Gaucho Today; The Gaucho of Corrientes;* and *The Gaucho of Pampas.*
  Erle Stanley Gardner Collection (16mm, 36 items). Home movies of his travels, activities on his ranch, etc.
  Alfred A. Knopf Collection (16mm, approx. 50 items). Films relating to authors, including home movies and some documentaries on their work.
  Klerekopfer Collection (16mm, 60 items). Documentaries relating to Alaska.
  Miscellaneous materials (16mm and 8mm, 35mm). Includes *Cavalcade of Texas.* Also holds a number of videotape copies of programs which have made use of footage from the Photography Collection.
Size & Elements: Film: 35mm, 16mm and 8mm (mostly 16mm, approx. 500 cans; positive, negative and originals, silent and sound, some three-strip color). Videotape: 3/4" (20 videotapes; masters and viewing copies).
Cataloging: Lists.
Access: Open to the public. Some material available for duplication. Research fees not charged. Research requests accepted by mail, telephone and in person (walk-in). Viewing of material is subject to condition of film or videotape, and is available only by special permission.
Rights: Some rights held to some material. Additional clearances may be necessary in some cases if material is to be reused.
Licensing: Available for licensing and reuse, subject to restrictions. License fees charged (waived for nonprofit institutions).
Restrictions: Some material subject to copyright and/or donor restrictions, depending on proposed use and user.
Viewing Facilities: Film (16mm); videotape (3/4"). Viewing of material is subject to condition of film or videotape, and is available only by special permission.
Duplication Facilities: None.
Related Materials: Manuscripts, photographs and other materials within individual collections.

TEXAS (Austin)

UNIVERSITY OF TEXAS AT AUSTIN
HARRY RANSOM HUMANITIES RESEARCH CENTER
THEATRE ARTS COLLECTIONS
P.O. Box 7219
Austin, TX 78713
(512) 471-9122

Dr. William H. Crain (Curator)

Contacts: Dr. Charles Bell (Assistant Curator); Prentiss L. Moore (Research Associate, in charge of photoduplication)
Services: Research library. Film and videotape collection open to the public. Material available for duplication, licensing and reuse, subject to restrictions.
Description: Major holdings include the Selznick Archive (685 cans of film footage) and the Perry Mason series (570 cans, each 1,000 feet).
Size & Elements: Film: format unspecified (1,250 cans, 300 titles). Videotape: 3/4" (100 videotapes, 50 titles).
Cataloging: Card catalogs; research library.
Access: Open to the public. Possibly available for duplication. If research is extensive, research assistants may be hired. Research requests accepted by mail, telephone and in person (walk-in).
Rights: Full rights held to some material. Some rights held to all material. Additional clearances may be necessary in some cases if material is to be reused.
Licensing: Possibly available for licensing and reuse, subject to restrictions. License and usage fees charged.
Restrictions: Duplicate materials must be returned to Center; extra duplicates must be made for the film archives at customer's expense.
Viewing Facilities: None.
Duplication Facilities: None (all duplication by outside arrangement and only under restricted terms).
Related Materials: Rare books, documents, archives, iconography and photography.

TEXAS (Bonham)

THE SAM RAYBURN LIBRARY
P.O. Box 309
Bonham, TX 75418
(214) 583-2455

Street address: 800 West Sam Rayburn Drive

H. G. Dulaney (Library Director)

Contact: H. G. Dulaney
Services: Library. Film collection available to researchers, scholars and the public.
Description: Films relating to the life and career of Sam Rayburn, beginning with his membership in the Texas State House of Representatives (1907) through his record-breaking tenure of office as Speaker of the U.S. House of Representatives that terminated with his death on November 16, 1961. Most films were donated by television stations after being broadcast.
  Titles include: *Sam Rayburn Parade* (1940); *Groundbreaking for The Sam Rayburn Library* (1955); *Mr. Rayburn's Visit to the Arlington Grade School* (1957); *Sam Rayburn Funeral* (1961); *Tribute to Mr. Sam; The Honorable Sam Rayburn, The Speaker of the House of Representatives* (CBS, February 1961); *Tour of the House of Representatives with Sam Rayburn and Joe Martin,* featuring Edward R. Murrow; *Tour of Mr. Sam's Home and Washington, D.C. in the 1930s; Appearance of Sam Rayburn and Highlights of 1956 Democratic Convention; Presidential Inauguration of John F. Kennedy* (1961); and an interview with Rayburn at the Library (KRLD News).
Size & Elements: Film: format unspecified (46 items).
Cataloging: Title list.
Access: Open to researchers, scholars and the public. Research fees not charged. Research requests accepted in person (walk-in).
Rights: Some rights held to some material. Rights status of some material not known. Most material was first broadcast on network television. Additional clearances may be necessary in some cases if material is to be reused.
Licensing: Apply for information. License fees not charged.
Restrictions: None specified.
Viewing Facilities: Film.
Duplication Facilities: None.
Related Materials: Books, mementos and personal papers.

TEXAS (Canyon)

PANHANDLE-PLAINS HISTORICAL MUSEUM
RESEARCH CENTER
Box 967
Canyon, TX 79016
(806) 656-2244

Street address: 2401 4th Avenue

Claire R. Kuehn (Archivist/Librarian)

Contact: Claire R. Kuehn
Services: Museum archives. Film and videotape collection available to the public for in-house research and duplication; possibly available for reuse.
Description: Material relating to the Texas Panhandle and its citizens. Collection includes: commercial films (1912-41); ranching in the Texas Panhandle (1916-59), including cowboys roping, branding and cattle (longhorns); Palo Duro Canyon (1930s); West Texas State University (1929-34); the oil boom in Borger, Texas (1926); Amarillo, Texas (1927, 1930s, and the snowstorm of 1983-84); soil erosion in the Texas Panhandle and South Plains (1949-51); Texas history; material on the Panhandle-Plains Historical Museum; documentaries for use in Museum education programs.

Also holds *Lone Star* (8-part series), a documentary television series produced by public television station KEDT-TV (Corpus Christi). Topics covered: Texas, Indians, filibusters, missions, explorers, revolution, Davy Crockett, the Republic, cotton, football, Lyndon B. Johnson and multinational oil companies.
Size & Elements: Film: 16mm (50,300 feet, 237 titles, 562 cans). Videotape: 3/4" (103 videotapes, each 20 min.); VHS (105 titles); Betamax (5 titles, 2 hours).
Cataloging: Card catalogs.
Access: Open to the public. For in-house use only. Possibly available for duplication. Research fees charged. Research requests accepted by mail, telephone and in person (walk-in).
Rights: Full rights held to some material.
Licensing: Some material possibly available for reuse. Usage fees charged (fees determined on an individual basis).
Restrictions: None specified.
Viewing Facilities: Film (16mm); videotape (VHS).
Duplication Facilities: None.

TEXAS (College Station)

TEXAS A&M UNIVERSITY UNIVERSITY ARCHIVES

College Station, TX 77843-5000
(409) 845-1815

Charles R. Schultz (University Archivist)

Contacts: Charles R. Schultz; David L. Chapman (Associate Archivist)
Services: University library. Film and videotape collection open to the public. Material available for duplication and possibly reuse, subject to restrictions.
Description: *Texas A&M football.* Comprises the bulk of the film collection, including game films, offense and defense films (1936-85). Includes a small amount of University basketball film, football videotapes, and videotape transfers from film footage of half-time performances of the University band (1938-39).

Dan Smoot Collection. Approximately 800 weekly television programs (each 15 min.) with Dan Smoot, broadcast from Dallas, Texas (1955-71). Features conservative political commentary.

General University footage. A small collection, including promotional films (1960-76) and footage of the inauguration of Jarvis Miller as president of Texas A&M University (1977).
Size & Elements: Film: format unspecified (1 million feet, 3,300 cans; originals and release prints). Videotape: 3/4" and VHS (18 videotapes; masters and viewing copies).
Cataloging: Inventory of football films; printed list of Dan Smoot programs.
Access: Open to the public. Available for research, duplication and possibly reuse. Research fees not charged. Research requests accepted by mail, telephone and in person (walk-in).
Rights: Some rights held to some material. Additional clearances may be necessary in some cases if material is to be reused.
Licensing: Available for licensing and reuse, subject to restrictions. License and usage fees not charged.
Restrictions: Duplication and reuse of football films is controlled by the Athletic Department. All requests for reuse subject to acceptance and approval.
Viewing Facilities: Film and videotape (facilities located in Library).
Duplication Facilities: Film and videotape (facilities located in Library).

TEXAS (Dallas)

AMERICAN HEART ASSOCIATION

National Center
7320 Greenville Avenue
Dallas, TX 75231
(214) 373-6300
Fax: (214) 706-1551

Contact: Linda Hood
Services: Nonprofit voluntary health organization. Films and videotapes available for public education and community programs through National Center and local chapters.
Description: Audiovisual materials cover the following subjects: cardiopulmonary resuscitation and emergency care, congenital heart defects, exercise, the heart at work, high blood pressure, nutrition, patient education, physiology, prevention, professional education, research, risk factors, smoking, strokes and youth messages.

In addition to current audiovisual material, AHA holds historical and archival footage. It is currently in the process of being cataloged by an outside firm and will be available in the future (apply for information).
Size & Elements: Film: 16mm. Videotape: 3/4" and 1/2". (Amounts unspecified).
Cataloging: Published audiovisual materials catalog.
Access: Available for public education and community programs from National Center and local chapters. Requests accepted by telephone.
Rights: All material is copyrighted. Additional clearances from original producers are necessary in some cases if material is to be reused.
Licensing: Apply for information.
Restrictions: Requests for duplication and/or reuse will be considered on a case-by-case basis.
Viewing Facilities: None.
Duplication Facilities: None.

TEXAS (Dallas)

CABLE ACCESS OF DALLAS

1253 Roundtable
Dallas, TX 75247
(214) 631-8004

Michael Bradley (Executive Director)

Contact: Mike Johnson; Michael Bradley
Services: Public access television facility; archive library. Videotape collection available for viewing, duplication and reuse; subject to clearance and restrictions.
Description: Holds community access sampler videotapes (1981-88) and Dallas community-produced videotapes covering such subjects as ethnic problems, cultural events, entertainment, politics, women's issues and religion (1981-86, mostly 1987-88, new programs added regularly).

Additional topics include: the arts in Dallas; peace news and disarmament issues; interviews with nationally noted authors; musicians (bluegrass, new age, rock and roll); tax information from certified public accountants; comedy; medical and health programs; educational programs from Dallas Independent School District; and municipal programs from City of Dallas Cable Communications.
Size & Elements: Videotapes: primarily 3/4"; some VHS (approx. 50 programs in archive library; varying lengths).
Cataloging: Computerized cataloging available for staff use only.
Access: Open to the public by appointment only. Material available for viewing or duplication.
Rights: Full rights held to some material produced by Cable Access. Some rights held to all material. Additional clearances will be necessary in some cases if material is to be reused.
Licensing: Apply for information. Usage fees charged in some cases, depending on the program.
Restrictions: Clearances must be obtained regarding any reuse.
Viewing Facilities: Videotape (by appointment only).
Duplication Facilities: Videotape (hourly duplication fee charged).

TEXAS (Dallas)

DR PEPPER COMPANY

Walnut Glen Tower
8144 Walnut Hill Lane
Dallas, TX 75231-8144

TEXAS (Dallas)

(214) 360-7000
Fax: (214) 360-7980

Contact: Harry Ellis (Company Historian) (214/360-7558)
Services: Corporation; corporate archives. Film and videotape collection currently unavailable to the public for viewing, research or distribution.
Description: History of the Dr Pepper Company and its soft drink products, including Dr Pepper and 7-Up.
Size & Elements: Film and videotape (formats and amounts unspecified).
Cataloging: Collection uncataloged at present; plans are to complete cataloging and make material available.
Access: Collection currently unavailable for viewing, research or distribution.
Rights: Apply for information.
Licensing: Apply for information.
Restrictions: Apply for information.
Viewing Facilities: None.
Duplication Facilities: None.
Related Materials: *Dr Pepper: King of Beverages,* a published hardbound book on the corporate history of Dr Pepper Company and its soft drink.

TEXAS (Dallas)

THE IMAGE BANK, TEXAS
1336 Conant Street
Dallas, TX 75207
(214) 631-3808
Fax: (214) 951-0278

Contacts: Rex Jobe; Lynn Martin (Manager)
Territory: Arkansas, Louisiana, New Mexico, Oklahoma and Texas.
Services: Exclusive marketing agent for Film Search, Inc. (q.v.).

TEXAS (Dallas)

OCTOBER PRODUCTIONS
4232 Herschel Avenue, Suite 208
Dallas, TX 75219
(214) 559-3439

Contact: Robert W. Tranchin
Services: Film and videotape producer. Material available for duplication and reuse.
Description: Footage of Texas oil wells, both historical (1900-40) and modern (1980s); Texas oilmen, including interviews (1980s); Texas landscapes; and a documentary, *Wildcatter: A Story of Texas Oil* (60 min., 1" master videotape transferred from film).
Size & Elements: Film: 16mm (40,000 feet; negative). Videotape: 1" (1 title).
Cataloging: None specified.
Access: Available for duplication and reuse. Research requests accepted by mail, telephone and in person.
Rights: Full rights held to some material. Some material in the public domain. Additional clearances may be necessary in some cases if material is to be reused. Rights status of some material not known.
Licensing: Possibly available for reuse. Usage fees charged.
Restrictions: None specified.
Viewing Facilities: Film (16mm); videotape (3/4" and VHS).
Duplication Facilities: None.

TEXAS (Dallas)

THE SALVATION ARMY
OFFICE OF MEDIA MINISTRIES
P.O. Box 2608
Dallas, TX 75221
(214) 353-2731

Street address: 6500 Harry Hines Boulevard, Dallas, TX 75235

Ian T. Adnams (Director)

Contact: David Vineyard (Senior Editor)
Services: Nonprofit organization. Videotape collection for in-house use only; available for licensing and reuse, subject to restrictions.
Description: Historical and current stock footage (unedited) of Salvation Army work in the U.S. and around the world.

Size & Elements: Videotape: 1", 3/4" and 1/2" (over 1,000 unedited videotapes).
Cataloging: Computerized cataloging for staff use only; shot lists.
Access: For in-house research use only. Available for reuse, subject to restrictions. Research fees charged. Research requests accepted by mail, telephone and in person (by appointment only).
Rights: Full rights held to some material. Additional clearances may be necessary in some cases if the material is to be reused.
Licensing: Available for licensing and reuse, subject to restrictions. License and usage fees charged.
Restrictions: Credit must be given to The Salvation Army. Additional copyright clearances may be necessary.
Viewing Facilities: Videotape (1", 3/4" and 1/2").
Duplication Facilities: Videotape (1", 3/4" and 1/2").

TEXAS (Dallas)

SOUTHWEST FILM/VIDEO ARCHIVES
SOUTHERN METHODIST UNIVERSITY
P.O. Box 4194
Dallas, TX 75275
(214) 373-3665

Street address: 3108 Fondren Drive, Suite 11

Dr. G. William Jones (Director)

Contacts: Lee Atwell (Archivist); Marica Chacona (Administrative Coordinator)
Services: Educational institution; film and videotape archives; stock footage sales library.
Description: Begun in 1970 with proceeds from the first USA Film Festival, the Archives is located in the Meadows School of the Arts at SMU. Numerous special collections are held, many evolving from regional and ethnic considerations. Strengths include: Western stock shots; feature films made for Black audiences (1935-50); and U.S. features and short subjects (1915-49) in the public domain.
  Atlanta Cinema Showcase Collection (21 items, 16mm film). Interviews with leading artists from the television program *Cinema Showcase,* shown on PBS in the early 1970s. Interviews are interspersed with clips from the artists' films. Several of those interviewed have already retired or died, leaving these interviews as a sort of "last testament."
  Gene Autry Film Collection (50 films, 35mm safety film; and over 1 million feet of 35mm stock shots, 1930s-50s, comprising 1,500 reels, some on nitrate). Official depository of the last remaining 35mm theatrical prints of Gene Autry features and a large collection of stock shots used in the production of his Westerns. Collection illuminates the origin and growth of the "singing cowboy" genre of "B" Western films, which document cowboy lore and Western balladry. Most material in this collection is represented for stock footage sale by Archive Film Productions, Inc./Stock Footage Library (q.v.).
  The Belo Newsfilm Collection (over 2 million feet, 16mm film, 1960-75, color and black and white). Contains daily newsfilm coverage from WFAA-TV (Dallas), covering Dallas, the Metroplex and the Southwestern U.S. Included are the assassinations of John F. Kennedy and Lee Harvey Oswald, civil rights marches, original footage by correspondents in Vietnam and Cambodia, trial coverage and personal interest stories.
  Benchmarks of Animation Art: 1909-1979 (248 items, 35mm and 16mm film). Contains animated films from all countries and decades, beginning with *Gertie, the Trained Dinosaur* (1909).
  The Ingmar Bergman Collection (8 films, 16mm; 4 hours of videotaped seminars). Archives contains copies of Bergman films and videotaped seminars of on-campus appearances by Bergman; and transcripts of conversations between Bergman and film, theater and dance students. Seminar videotapes have been edited as programs suitable for public television broadcast, or on cassette to classes and individuals.
  The Burke/Jones Filmclip Collection (over 200 videotapes, 3/4"). Comprises a collection of clips from feature films released since the mid-1970s. The sample clips were obtained and used in reviews by two professors who appeared on television as film critics. Material is copyrighted and cannot be shown in classrooms, but is available for students and instructors to view individually in the Archives' offices.
  Chantillis/Johnson Comic Film Collection (1905-75, 233 films, 16mm). Material donated by William Johnson and Peter Chantillis, two collectors of comedy films. Films range from slapstick to sophisticated comedies of manners.

The Dallas Power and Light Contemporary History Collection (1966-76, 80 films, 16mm). Collection of *Screen News Digests* (produced by Hearst Metrotone News) comprising monthly compilations of major news events sold to businesses across the nation for public relations purposes. In Dallas, the Dallas Power and Light Company was the local sponsor. After the program ended, the accumulated films were warehoused and eventually donated to the Archives.

The Howard/National Center for Experiments in Television (NCET) Collection (approx. 40 videotapes and 16mm films). Contains documents and videotapes of Brice Howard's work with NCET in San Francisco. After a varied career in network and educational television, Howard became the first director of NCET, a project funded by the Corporation for Public Broadcasting and the National Endowment for the Arts.

The International Non-Fiction Film Collection (1895-1965, over 250 films, 16mm). Collection covers the history of documentary film, containing the non-fiction and documentary films of John Grierson (England), Robert Flaherty (U.S.), their protegees and others.

The Kogan 9.5mm Collection (30 films, 9.5mm). A rare collection of 9.5mm films found in Brazil and donated to the Archives by Alex Kogan, a film collector and distributor from New York City. This unusual format was issued by Pathé Frères in France (1920s) for home use. Collection may hold some unique prints.

The Ginger Rogers Collection (25 feature films, 35mm nitrate stock; housed at Library of Congress). Consists of the actress's personal collection of 35mm prints of films in which she appeared. The nitrate films were donated to the Archives in 1967 and are now on deposit in the Library of Congress, Motion Picture, Broadcasting and Recorded Sound Division (q.v.), where they have been preserved on safety stock. In many cases, these prints represent more complete versions of the films than those held in studio archives.

Roosth Nitrate Film Collection (70 feature films, 35mm nitrate stock). Studio-produced and independent features, including romances, comedies and war stories. These nitrate films await restoration and preservation. Some of these films are unique copies.

The Saul/Love "War on Poverty" Collection (60 films, 16mm). Contains the works of two Washington filmmakers hired by the government in 1986 to document the War On Poverty, the VISTA job program and Operation Headstart.

Shinoda/Aoki Japanese Film Collection (19 films, 35mm and 16mm). Collection documents pre-World War II and postwar Japanese cinema, and changes in its style and content. Some material in the collection was added by film and television producer Yoichi Aoki and director Masahiro Shinoda.

The Tyler, Texas, Black Film Collection (108 titles, 35mm, 16mm and videotape). A unique collection of feature films, independent films, short subjects and newsreels produced, written and directed by Blacks for exclusively Black audiences (ca. 1910-1950s). Approximately 30 films were retrieved from an old warehouse in Tyler, Texas in 1983; many are the last or best remaining prints in existence. Most films in the collection are distributed through Phoenix Films and Video (q.v.).

The World War II Collection (116 films, 16mm). Collection of newsreels, documentaries, training films and propaganda films produced before, during and after the war, providing an exhaustive survey of every aspect of the conflict.

Size & Elements: Film: 35mm (1.5 million feet, 1,700 titles); 16mm (600,000 feet, 200 titles) (originals and release prints, positives and negatives). Videotape: 3/4" (100 videotapes, each 60 to 90 min.; masters); 1/2" (viewing copies).

Cataloging: Shot lists; computerized cataloging available to researchers; research library.

Access: Available for duplication. Research fees charged. Research requests accepted by mail, telephone and in person (by appointment only).

Rights: Full rights held to some material. Some material in the public domain.

Licensing: Available for licensing and reuse, subject to restrictions. License and usage fees charged.

Restrictions: Archives prefers to deal with educational and documentary filmmakers.

Viewing Facilities: Film (16mm; 35mm planned); videotape (3/4" and 1/2") (by appointment only).

Duplication Facilities: None.

Related Materials: *The Stills Collection* contains over 2,000 8x10 motion picture stills; *The Howard/N.C.E.T Collection* includes memos, documents and letters; *The Gatzke Antique Projector Collection* consists of 23 film projectors dating from 1905-40; *The Kogan 9.5mm Collection* includes a Pathé "Baby" 9.5mm projector; *Cinematheque/Film Festival Oral History Collection* contains over 400 hours of audiotaped interviews and on-stage discussions that followed the annual U.S.A. Film Festivals (1970-81).

AMERICAN AIRLINES
CORPORATE COMMUNICATIONS
P.O. Box 619616
Dallas/Fort Worth Airport, TX 75261-9616
(817) 355-1593
Fax: (817) 355-3816

Street address: 4200 American Boulevard, Fort Worth, TX 76155

Dan White (Manager, Corporate Communications)

Contacts: Edward Martelle (Writer/Editor) (817/355-1853); Kurt Wallace (Producer/Photographer) (817/355-1589)

Services: Corporate archives. Promotional videotape materials available primarily for distribution, rental and possibly for reuse, subject to approval.

Description: Airline operations, history and travelogues. Includes footage of airplanes, ramp operations, terminal activity, reservation systems, system operations and maintenance. Videotape travelogues of the airline's destinations include scenes from the U.S., Europe, Japan, Mexico and the Caribbean.

Historical material shows pre-DC-3 aircraft; footage (1930s-40s, black and white) encouraging passengers to fly and comparing airplanes to railroad trains; and commercials (1960s-70s). Other material held includes sales and training videotapes, and an employee magazine program.

Size & Elements: Videotape: Betacam (1,400 videotapes).

Cataloging: Computerized cataloging for staff use only.

Access: Available for distribution rather than for research or reuse. Research requests accepted by mail.

Rights: Full rights held to all materials. Additional clearances may be necessary in some cases if material is to be reused.

Licensing: Apply for information. License fees charged.

Restrictions: Requests for licensing and reuse subject to acceptance and approval.

Viewing Facilities: Videotape.

Duplication Facilities: Videotape (in-house; outside duplication can be arranged).

TEXAS WOMAN'S UNIVERSITY
BLAGG-HUEY LIBRARY
SPECIAL COLLECTIONS
P.O. Box 23715, TWU Station
Denton, TX 76204
(817) 898-3751

Metta Nicewarner (Head of Special Collections)

Contact: Metta Nicewarner

Services: Library. Videotape collection available to the public for research and interlibrary loan. Material possibly available for reuse, subject to clearance and approval.

Description: Texan women who have gained recognition in the arts, education, business, civic causes, medicine and politics; Texas history, including footage on the Texas Sesquicentennial wagon train.

Texas Women's Hall of Fame series features such women as Grace Cartwright (agriculture and ranching); Jenny Lind Porter (literary arts); Lydia Mendoza (performing arts); Edna Gardner Whyte (business and finance); Willie Lee Glass (civic leadership); Liz Carpenter (communications); Maria Elena Flood (education); Louise B. Raggio (legal); Dr. Benjy Brooks (health professions); Ann Richards (public service); Dr. Patricia Buffler (science and technology); and Helen Farabee (volunteerism).

Other videotapes include: *The Inauguration of Shirley Sears Chater as the Eighth President of the Texas Woman's University* (1987); a television interview with Sarah Weddington (1986-87); *Texas Women: A Celebration of History* (1983); an interview with Dr. Mary Evelyn Blagg Huey, president of TWU (1984); *TWU Anti-Merger Rally Clips* (1986); and *Voices of the Texas Woman's University* (1987).

Size & Elements: Videotape: 3/4" and VHS (16 videotapes, 954 min. total; masters and viewing copies).

Cataloging: Card catalogs; computerized cataloging available to researchers.

Access: Open to the public for research and viewing (in Media Services Department). Viewing copies may be borrowed on interlibrary loan. Vault masters for in-house use only. Research fees not charged. Research requests

accepted by mail, telephone and in person (walk-in).
Rights: Full rights held to some material. Additional clearances necessary in some cases if material is to be reused.
Licensing: Apply for information. Usage fees not charged.
Restrictions: None specified.
Viewing Facilities: Film and videotape (in Media Services Department).
Duplication Facilities: Film (film to VHS); videotape (VHS).

TEXAS (Denton)

UNIVERSITY OF NORTH TEXAS
DIVISION OF RADIO/TV/FILM
P.O. Box 13108
Denton, TX 76203-3108
(817) 565-2537

Street address: Building, Speech and Drama, Room 120

Dr. John B. Kuiper (Chairman, Division of RTVF)

Contacts: Dr. John B. Kuiper; Donald L. Staples (Professor, RTVF)
Services: Educational institution. Film and videotape collection open to researchers and scholars only.
Description: Television documentaries and educational programs (ca. 1960s); corporate films distributed by Association Films, Inc. (ca. 1960s); informational television programs produced for the University of North Texas (1986-present, produced by the Division of RTVF); and videotape programs produced for the Center of Texas Studies, University of North Texas (1987-present).

Subjects covered include: American culture (1960s, 25 films); foreign countries (18 films); American law (1960s, 12 films); health, medicine and biology (11 films); English language (7 films); religion (7 films); the arts (6 films); American business (1960s, 5 films); Negroes and blacks (5 films); campus uprisings (5 films); psychology (5 films); and University life (1980s, 250 films).
Size & Elements: Film: 16mm (180,000 feet, approx. 200 titles, approx. 400 cans; positive and release prints, black and white). Videotape: 3/4" (approx. 260 items; masters).
Cataloging: Card catalogs.
Access: Open to researchers and scholars only. Research fees not charged. Research requests accepted in person (by appointment only).
Rights: Some rights held to some material. Rights status of some material not known.
Licensing: Apply for information. License and usage fees charged in some cases, depending on intended use and rights to specific titles.
Restrictions: None specified.
Viewing Facilities: Film (Moviola and projection); videotape (off-line editing deck).
Duplication Facilities: None.

TEXAS (El Paso)

EL PASO COMMUNITY COLLEGE
P.O. Box 20500
El Paso, TX 79998
(915) 594-2000

Street address: Valle Verde Campus, 919 Hunter, El Paso, TX 79915

Carroll Nardone (Mass Communications Instructor)
Luis Chaparro (Learning Center Director)

Contacts: Carroll Nardone; Luis Chaparro
Services: Community college. Film and videotape collection currently uncataloged.
Description: Holds television newsfilm collection from a local CBS affiliate station (1970-81). Collection includes El Paso local news, border news coverage, stories on U.S.-Mexico relations, news stories concerning the Judge John Wood murder and other features.
Size & Elements: Film: format and amount unspecified (positive). Videotape: 3/4" (amount unspecified; masters).
Cataloging: Collection uncataloged at present.
Access: Apply for information.
Rights: Full rights held to all material.
Licensing: Apply for information.

Restrictions: None specified.
Viewing Facilities: None.
Duplication Facilities: None.
Related Materials: Film scripts available.

TEXAS (Fort Sam Houston)

ACADEMY OF HEALTH SCIENCES, UNITED STATES ARMY HEALTH SCIENCES MEDIA DIVISION
Attn: HSHA-SMD
Fort Sam Houston, TX 78234-6100
(512) 221-7845
AUTOVON: 471-7845

Contact: Ruth Mazurek
Services: Government agency; videotape distributor. Material available to health agencies for nonprofit use, subject to restrictions.
Description: Educational support and training materials for Army Medical Department personnel.

Continuing medical education. Approximately 2,000 programs supporting continuing education of professional medical personnel. Sample titles include: *Management of Heart Wounds; Emergency Airway; Immediate Care of the Injured Hand; Facial Nerve Paralysis; Intraocular Foreign Bodies; Near Drowning; Trauma and the Child; Penetrating Wounds of the Neck; Painless Wound Closure; Management of Pregnant Patients with Heart Valve Prosthesis; Nutritional Problems in Returning POWs; Creeping Eruption; Use of Living Related Donors with Familial Disease; Reversal of Rejection; Burn Seminar: From the Patient's Viewpoint; Irradiation and Preservation of Food for the Armed Services; The Male Cancer Patient — A Poignant View; New Concepts of the Mechanism of Blood Flow; Neglect in Men (Patients with Right Hemisphere Lesion); Violence As A Human Problem;* and *Sexual Abuse: An Old Family Tradition.*

Medical training and instruction (I). Nearly 1,000 titles to support training and instruction of paramedical personnel. Sample titles include: *Performance Counseling No Knows; Occupational Vision; Management of the Bad Trip; Emergency Splinting of a Horse; Fresh Fruits and Vegetables — Inspecting for Defects: Carrots; The Feeling of Rejection (Brief Enactment of Various Phenomena of the Feeling of Rejection); Flossing; Panama: Equal Health for All — An Approach to Decentralized Medicine; Privacy Act; Cliff Dwellers and the Ute Mountain Indians of Colorado; Making an Occupied Bed; Sonic Energy Cleaner; Inspection of Shell Eggs;* and *Elimination Procedures and Considerations.*

Medical training and instruction (II). Nearly 400 titles to support continuing education of professional medical personnel and training instruction of paramedical personnel. Sample titles include: *Global Medicine and Medical Intelligence; Managing Your Hand Receipts; Aging and Vitality — The Rectangularization of Life; Threat Briefing; Women in the Military: A Pictorial History; Survival During Captivity; Success Stories — Wellness Conference — Fort Meade; Assembly and Application of Entrainment Masks; Army Nurse Corps Experiences as Prisoners of War During World War II;* and *Smoking Cessation.*
Size & Elements: Videotape: 3/4" and VHS (approx. 3,000 titles; viewing copies).
Cataloging: Published catalogs.
Access: Available for distribution. Available for duplication by health agencies for nonprofit use. Duplication fees not charged. Requests accepted by mail and telephone.
Rights: Apply for information.
Licensing: Apply for information.
Restrictions: Copies of these programs may not be cut or otherwise modified without prior approval. Since programs are duplicated free of charge, programs are not to be reproduced by recipients. Playback of programs with the HSMD closed circuit cable system may be scheduled by submission of AHS F/L 191 in duplicate at least 10 days prior to showing date.
Viewing Facilities: None.
Duplication Facilities: None.

TEXAS (Fort Worth)

AMON CARTER MUSEUM
P.O. Box 2365
Fort Worth, TX 76113-2365
(817) 738-1933

Street address: 3501 Camp Bowie Boulevard

Contact: Mary Lampe (Audiovisual Coordinator)
Services: Museum; film and videotape producer and distributor.
Description: Has produced two educational composite videotape programs about artists represented in its collection and art techniques. Composite I (6 short programs): *Carlotta Corpron: Designer With Light; The Graphic Techniques of Mary Cassatt; Lost Wax Bronze Casting; Charles M. Russell: Paper Talk; Carleton Watkins;* and *Wet-Plate Photography.* Composite II (4 short programs): *How to Identify an Etching; What is a Lithograph?; Art of the Woodcut* and *"To Order."*
   Two films produced by the museum are: *Laura Gilpin: An Enduring Grace;* and *Water Garden,* on Fort Worth's public water garden park, including footage of the architect Philip Johnson.
Size & Elements: Film: 16mm (2 titles). Videotape: 3/4" and 1/2" (12 titles total).
Cataloging: Published lists.
Access: Composite videotapes in VHS format available to schools, museums and other educational organizations for a three-day loan period. 3/4" videotapes and films available to the public for rental and purchase.
Rights: Full rights held to all material.
Licensing: Apply for information.
Restrictions: None specified.
Viewing Facilities: Film (16mm); videotape.
Duplication Facilities: None.

TEXAS (Houston)

BAILEY PRODUCTIONS, INC.
931 Yale
Houston, TX 77008
(713) 864-2671

James Bailey (President)
Kenneth Bailey (Executive Vice President)

Contact: Billy Stewart (Production Coordinator)
Services: Film and videotape producer. Some material available for stock footage sales.
Description: Producer of corporate, industrial and educational films in the Houston area (1923-present), Texas, Israel, Brooklyn and other locations. Finished productions include *Romancing the Seed* and *For the Love of Roses,* both produced for the Brooklyn Botanic Garden (q.v.). Although this material is in some cases available for stock footage, it is largely uncataloged.
Size & Elements: Film: 16mm ("3 rooms full"). Videotape: 3/4" (amount unspecified).
Cataloging: None.
Access: Stock footage material available for reuse. Completed productions are maintained for distribution rather than for research or reuse. In-house viewing available for researchers. Research fees charged on an hourly basis. Research requests accepted by mail and telephone.
Rights: Full rights held to all stock footage. Full rights held to some finished productions.
Licensing: Some material available for licensing and reuse. License or usage fees charged.
Restrictions: None specified.
Viewing Facilities: Film (16mm); videotape (3/4").
Duplication Facilities: None (outside arrangements can be made).
Related Materials: Collection of 300,000 still photographs relating to Houston (some dating back to the 1930s).

TEXAS (Houston)

CONTINENTAL AIRLINES
2929 Allen Parkway, Suite 903
Houston, TX 77019
(713) 630-5316
Fax: (713) 639-2087

Contact: Tom Lambert (Video Specialist)
Services: Corporate videotape library. Material available for reuse, subject to restrictions.
Description: Continental Airlines aircraft, employees and facilities. Library includes a wide range of aircraft shots, airport passenger and work areas, and reservation offices. There are also commercials, advertising, employee meetings and interviews.
Size & Elements: Videotape: 3/4" (over 300 videotapes).

Cataloging: Shot lists.
Access: Not open to the public. Research requests may be accepted (apply for information).
Rights: Full rights held to all material.
Licensing: Apply for information.
Restrictions: Requests for licensing and reuse subject to clearance and approval.
Viewing Facilities: None.
Duplication Facilities: None.

TEXAS (Houston)

FIRST GROUP COMMUNICATIONS, INC.
11000 Ranchstone Drive
Houston, TX 77064
(713) 955-9300

Dal Knight (President)

Contacts: Dal Knight; Duke Newton
Services: Videotape producer. Material available for duplication and licensing, reuse.
Description: "One of the world's largest collections of oilfield footage." Footage relates to the petroleum industry, including offshore rigs in Texas, California, North Sea, Gulf of Mexico, Newfoundland and Alaska; drilling operations (offshore and onshore); maritime operations involving offshore rigs (drill ships and rigs moving); oil and gas production field footage in Texas, Oklahoma, California, Louisiana, Kansas, New Mexico, Utah and Wyoming; lease operations; pipeline operations (mainly in Kansas and Oklahoma); generic footage of refinery and chemical plants. Aerial and on-board footage is held in all subject areas.
Size & Elements: Videotape: 2", 1" and 3/4" (masters and viewing copies); VHS and Betamax (viewing copies). ("Hundreds" of videotapes total).
Cataloging: Computerized cataloging for staff use only.
Access: Available to the public for duplication and reuse. Research fees charged (fees negotiable). Research requests accepted by mail, telephone and in person (by appointment only).
Rights: Full rights held to all material.
Licensing: Available for licensing. License fees charged.
Restrictions: None specified.
Viewing Facilities: Videotape (3/4", VHS and Betamax).
Duplication Facilities: Videotape (3/4", VHS and Betamax).

TEXAS (Houston)

HOUSTON ACADEMY OF MEDICINE/
TEXAS MEDICAL CENTER LIBRARY
HISTORICAL RESEARCH CENTER
1133 M. D. Anderson Boulevard
Houston, TX 77030
(713) 797-1230 (Ext. 139)
Fax: (713) 790-7056

Elizabeth Borst White (Director)

Contact: Elizabeth Borst White
Services: Library. Film and videotape collection open to researchers and scholars for in-house use only.
Description: *NASA Space-Life Sciences Archive.* Film, videotapes and audiotapes (1965-75).
   Texas Heart Institute Film Collection. Cardiovascular surgery (1960-80), including the work of Drs. Cooley, Hallman, Norman, and Sandiford.
   Texas Medical Center. Videotaped interviews with founders (1970s) and some archival film (1950s-60s).
Size & Elements: Film: format unspecified (approx. 150 cans). Videotape: format unspecified (approx. 150 videotapes).
Cataloging: Card catalogs; computerized cataloging available to researchers; other finding aids.
Access: Open to researchers and scholars. For in-house use only. Research assistance available for Library cardholders only. Research requests accepted by telephone and in person (by appointment only).
Rights: Some rights held to some material. Additional clearances may be necessary in some cases if material is to be reused.
Licensing: Apply for information.
Restrictions: None specified.

TEXAS (Houston)

Viewing Facilities: None.
Duplication Facilities: None.

TEXAS (Houston)

NATIONAL AERONAUTICS AND SPACE ADMINISTRATION (NASA)
JOHNSON SPACE CENTER
FILM AND VIDEO DISTRIBUTION LIBRARY

1020 Bay Area Boulevard, Suite 102
Houston, TX 77058
(713) 486-9606

William W. Robbins (Audiovisual Manager, Office of Public Affairs, Media Services Branch)

Contact: Distribution Staff
Services: Government agency; film and videotape distributor. Material available for free loan, purchase, duplication and reuse, subject to restrictions.
Description: Films and videotapes relating to research and development, aeronautics and the manned spaceflight program. Library distributes numerous completed productions, many of which are not available from other NASA Regional Film Libraries. Stock footage is available through NASA, Johnson Space Center, Stock Film Library (q.v.).

Subject areas include: the space station program; the space shuttle program, including mission films, post-flight press conferences, mission video highlights (original videotape recordings of the important visual events of each mission including launch, onboard crew activities and landing), profiles of the shuttle and astronaut training; the Apollo-Soyuz mission; the Skylab program; the Apollo project, including the moon landing (Apollo 11); the Gemini and Mercury projects; earth views; the moon; the universe; the solar system; life sciences; satellites; LANDSAT and remote sensing; aeronautics; the history of NASA; the history of flight; biology and exobiology; civilian spinoffs of space technology; computers; NASA facilities; life support facilities; education; careers in research; and the Voyager program. Also distributes the *Aeronautics and Space Reports* series.

Sample titles include: *Space Station Assembly Flights MB 1–MB 8* (1987), using color computer animation to depict how the future space station will be assembled in eight space shuttle flights; *Building Towards New Heights* (1987), showcasing the on-orbit work accomplished by NASA astronauts in the Skylab and Space Shuttle programs; *Opportunities in Zero-Gravity* (1976), surveying the characteristics of the weightless environment and depicting mobility, mass transfer and handling of small parts; *Apollo 11: For All Mankind* (1969), showing the launch, lunar orbit, first moon landing, moon walk, rendezvous, recovery and return to Houston; *Earth Views from Shuttle Flights* (1986); *Earth Passes from Low Orbit* (1986); *I Will See Such Things* (1986), on Voyager II's passage by the planet Uranus, analyzing the images of its atmosphere, moons and rings; *Space Shuttle Challenger Accident Investigation* (1987), a history of the 51-L Space Shuttle Mission (January 28, 1987) documenting the findings of a task force investigating the tragic accident; *SMS Tour* (1987), on the Johnson Space Center's Shuttle Mission Simulators, the primary training facility for shuttle crews; and *Uranus and Satellites Rotation Movie: November 6-7, 1985* (1986).
Size & Elements: Film: 16mm (release prints). Videotape: 3/4" and VHS (masters and viewing copies). (374 titles total).
Cataloging: Published catalog.
Access: Available to the public for free loan, non-sponsored public affairs and sustained television broadcasts. Some titles available for purchase from Johnson Space Center, Media Services Branch or from NARA, National Audiovisual Center (q.v.). Research and rental fees not charged. Requests accepted by mail and telephone.
Rights: Material in the public domain.
Licensing: Available for reuse, subject to restrictions. Usage fees not charged.
Restrictions: Material cannot be used for advertising or commercial use in such a way as to indicate or imply endorsement by NASA. Footage featuring recognizable astronauts may not be used for advertising or promotional purposes.
Viewing Facilities: None.
Duplication Facilities: None.
Related Materials: Slides and still photographs.

TEXAS (Houston)

NATIONAL AERONAUTICS AND SPACE ADMINISTRATION (NASA)

JOHNSON SPACE CENTER
STOCK FILM LIBRARY

Media Services Branch/AP3
Houston, TX 77058
(713) 483-5111

William W. Robbins (Audiovisual Manager, Office of Public Affairs, Media Services Branch)

Contact: William W. Robbins
Services: Government agency. Film and videotape footage available for duplication and reuse, subject to restrictions.
Description: Footage relating to NASA's manned spaceflight programs (1958-present). Holds all photography shot in space and on the ground relating to the program, including astronaut and crew training, launches, landings (including moon landings), vehicle manufacturing and extravehicular activity (EVA). Projects covered include Mercury, Gemini, Apollo, Skylab, Apollo-Soyuz and the space shuttle. This is the repository for all original footage relating to these programs. Coverage is on 16mm film (1958-late 1970s); footage from late 1970s-present, including all coverage of space shuttle missions, is on videotape.

Completed NASA productions are available for rental from NASA Regional Film Libraries, including NASA, Johnson Space Center, Film and Video Distribution Library (q.v.); and in some cases for purchase from NARA, National Audiovisual Center (q.v.).
Size & Elements: Film: 16mm (approx. 6 million feet; originals and screening prints). Videotape: 1" (amount unspecified; masters); 3/4" (viewing copies of most material).
Cataloging: Computerized cataloging (electronic database) for staff use only. Footage can be retrieved by subject. Staff can process inquiries for outside researchers.
Access: Open to the public. Available for duplication and reuse. Research fees not charged. Research requests accepted by mail, telephone and in person (walk-in).
Rights: Material is in the public domain.
Licensing: Available for reuse, subject to restrictions. Usage fees not charged.
Restrictions: Material cannot be used for advertising or commercial use in such a way as to indicate or imply endorsement by NASA. Footage featuring recognizable astronauts may not be used for advertising or promotional purposes.
Viewing Facilities: Film and videotape.
Duplication Facilities: For internal use only. Outside requests fulfilled by commercial contractor laboratory located in Dallas, Texas. 1" videotape reproduction to any format and standard desired by requesters is available at cost. "Tab-to-tab" reproduction (reproduction of partial sections of reels or items) is permitted.
Related Materials: Slides and still photographs.

TEXAS (Houston)

SHELL OIL COMPANY

One Shell Plaza
Houston, TX 77001
(713) 241-6161

Films available only from:
MODERN TALKING PICTURE SERVICE, INC. (q.v.)

Contact: Ralph Pursche (Public Affairs Administrator, Shell Oil) (713/241-6698)
Services: Corporation. Film and videotape material available for rental and purchase through distributor.
Description: Crude and refined oil, natural gas and chemicals.

General interest programs include: *Oil*, a brief overview of the oil and chemical industries; *Oil Well*, showing what goes on in an oil well and drilling techniques; *Story in the Rocks*, a general-interest introduction to paleontology; *This Land*, giving insight into the ways geologists have been able to reconstruct and make sense of events that occurred beyond the reach of human history; and *Undersea Oasis*, exploring the undersea environment as a "living laboratory" for scientists.

Technical programs include: *Dynamic Continents*, computer animation depicting the movement of the continents over the last 550 million years; *Bahaman Tidal Flats*, depicting sedimentary processes and the criteria for recognition of humid tidal flats; *Carbonate Sands*, featuring the concepts relating to the origin and recognition of some important types of carbonate sand bodies from the Great Bahama Bank and South Florida; *Carbonate Sedimentation, South Florida Shelf Margin,* illustrating various sediments and sedimentary environments across the Florida reef tract; *Pennsylvanian Shallow Water Clastic Sediments of Western Arkansas and Eastern Oklahoma,* describing the "meandering stream" model of clastic sedimentation; *The Book Cliffs Field Trip,* featuring deltaic facies and their relationship with the natural resources and scenery of Eastern Utah; and *The Seismic Story,* showing typical seismic crew operations.

Size & Elements: Film: 16mm. Videotape: 3/4" and VHS. (Amounts unspecified).
Cataloging: Printed brochure (available on request).
Access: All access to films is through Modern Talking Picture Service, Inc. (q.v.). Material recommended for use by high schools, colleges and universities, and scientific business adult groups and organizations.
Rights: Copyright on programs listed retained by Shell Oil Co.
Licensing: Apply for information.
Restrictions: Written permission must be obtained regarding any reuse of material.
Viewing Facilities: None.
Duplication Facilities: None.

TEXAS (Houston)

SOUTHWEST ALTERNATE MEDIA PROJECT (SWAMP)
1519 West Main
Houston, TX 77006
(713) 522-8592

Edward T. Hugetz (Executive Director)
Tom Sims (Director of Operations)
Marian Luntz (Director of Exhibitions)
Deborah Leveranz (Director of Children's Programs)

Contacts: Tom Sims; Marian Luntz; Deborah Leveranz; Katie Cokinos
Services: Media organization. Videotape collection open to members, researchers and scholars for in-house use only.
Description: Media arts center for Texas, Oklahoma, Arkansas, Nebraska, Kansas and Missouri. Serves artists and organizations active in media education, production and exhibition. Coproduces *The Territory,* the longest-running public television showcase of independent media art in the U.S.

Holds an extensive videotape archives of works by Southwest independent videomakers. Most videotapes were produced in the Southwest and Midwest regions of the U.S.
Size & Elements: Videotape: 3/4" (amount unspecified).
Cataloging: None specified.
Access: Open to SWAMP members, programmers, festival directors, researchers, scholars and writers. For in-house use only. Research fees not charged. Research requests accepted by mail and in person (by appointment only).
Rights: No rights held to any material. Rights retained by original videomakers or producers.
Licensing: Not available for licensing or reuse. Can assist in contacting artists or videomakers to secure clearances.
Restrictions: Collection for in-house use only; not available for licensing or reuse.
Viewing Facilities: Videotape (3/4", VHS and Betamax).
Duplication Facilities: Videotape (3/4"; for preview only).
Related Materials: Resource Center holds publications, periodicals and program schedules from media arts centers throughout the U.S. and abroad.
Publications: *The Southwest Media Review,* a journal analyzing issues and ideas related to film, video and photography.

TEXAS (Hurst)

MOTHERS AGAINST DRUNK DRIVING (MADD)
669 Airport Freeway, Suite 310
Hurst, TX 76053
(817) 268-6233
Fax: (817) 268-6827

Robert J. King (Executive Director)
Micky Sadoff (National President)
Rob Beck (Chairman, Board of Directors)

Contact: Public Affairs Department

Services: Nonprofit public service organization. Videotapes available for purchase and loan.
Description: Holds one title, *Only You Share My Pain* (MADD, 1985, narrated by Rita Moreno), in which "alcohol-related crash victims candidly share their pain and feelings so that you, too, can understand the consequences of drunk driving...and learn how to most effectively help those who must endure the nightmare." Videotape material from other sources is available for loan to MADD chapter representatives, the media and the public. Various public service announcements (PSAs) are also available on videotape.
Size & Elements: Videotape: 3/4", Betamax II and 1/2" (1 title, 14 PSAs).
Cataloging: Lists and brochures.
Access: One title available to the public for purchase; PSAs available to the media for loan. Requests accepted by mail.
Rights: Full rights held to some material.
Licensing: Apply for information.
Restrictions: None specified.
Viewing Facilities: None.
Duplication Facilities: None.
Related Materials: Radio PSAs available.

TEXAS (Irving)

BOY SCOUTS OF AMERICA AUDIOVISUAL SERVICE
S-316
1325 Walnut Hill Lane
Irving, TX 75038-3096
(214) 580-2598
Fax: (214) 580-2502

John Johnson (Director, Audiovisual Service)

Contact: Caryl Adams (Audiovisual Coordinator)
Services: Educational institution; film and videotape producer and distributor. Films and videotapes available to Scout groups and the public for purchase.
Description: Scout leader training, leadership skills, outdoor skills, outdoor activities promotion, fundraising, and volunteer recruiting.

Titles available include: *Our Very Best* (1984), a recruiting film showing parents how a Cub Scout pack operates and the importance of good Cub Scout leaders; *Magic Balloon* (1985), an enjoyable adventure film about Cub Scouts; *My Son, The Scout* (1985), on Boy Scouting in the Jewish community; *Exploring Tomorrow Today* (1981), narrated by Charlton Heston, on today's Explorer program and what it can offer young adults in careers for tomorrow; *The Surprising Resource* (1983), designed to help professionals tell educators and volunteers in elementary and middle schools how Scouting can work for them; *A Bridge To Faith* (1983), in which evangelist Billy Graham "brings a stirring message of faith and a dramatic call for Scouting"; *Herbie* (1984), showing the importance of *Boys' Life* magazine to Scouts; *An American Passage* (1983), using scenic footage to show how the outdoors is enjoyed by young people through the Scouting program; *Coming On Strong* (1973), telling the story of "Philmont country" (the famed Scout and Explorer adventure base) and promoting Scout attendance; and *Winter Camping.*

Some outtake footage is also held. Other titles and out-of-date materials are held by the National Boy Scouts of America Museum, Murray State University (q.v.).
Size & Elements: Film: 16mm (8 titles). Videotape: VHS (37 titles).
Cataloging: Published catalog; collection only partially cataloged.
Access: Available to Scout organizations and the public for purchase. Research requests accepted by mail, telephone and in person (by appointment only).
Rights: Full rights held to some material. Some rights held to some material.
Licensing: Apply for information.
Restrictions: Commercial use not permitted.
Viewing Facilities: Film (16mm); videotape.
Duplication Facilities: Videotape (VHS).
Representatives: Contact any local Scout Council.
Related Materials: 35mm slides, filmstrips and audiotapes.

TEXAS (League City)

NATIONAL ASSOCIATION OF CONSERVATION DISTRICTS
CONSERVATION DISTRICTS FOUNDATION
WATERS DAVIS CONSERVATION FILM SERVICE LIBRARY
P.O. Box 776
League City, TX 77573-0776
(713) 332-3404

TEXAS (Liberty)

Street address: 404 East Main Street

Ron Francis (Manager, NACD Service Department)
Dana Farver (Librarian)

Contacts: Manager or Librarian
Services: Association; educational institution; film and videotape archives; foundation; library. Material available for rental and purchase rather than for research or reuse. Films and videotapes available to any organization or individual interested in fostering conservation education.
Description: The Conservation Districts Foundation is the educational adjunct of the National Association of Conservation Districts. It operates the Waters Davis Conservation Library and the Conservation Film Service. Library covers practical aspects of land use planning, soil and water conservation, conservation education, pollution abatement, recreation and resource management.

Titles include: *America's Wetlands* (U.S. Fish and Wildlife Service and the Environmental Protection Agency, 1982), covering swamps and wetlands from the Atchafalaya River Swamp in Lower Louisiana to Alaska's arctic tundra; *Cleaning Up* (Chemical Manufacturers Association, 1985), examining the urgent task of cleaning up hazardous waste sites in America; *Conservation: The Texas Approach* (Texas Soil and Water Conservation Districts, 1984), discussing the problems and solutions involved in preserving Texas' natural resources; *Field Trip to the Farm* (produced by a Salt Lake City television station, 1986), a visit to the Dale Bateman dairy farm near Salt Lake; *Hurricane — The Story of Alicia* (NOAA and the Federal Emergency Management Agency, 1984), tracking Alicia from its tame beginnings in the gulf of Mexico to its violent landfall at Galveston, Texas (1983); *The Mississippi River: America's Lifeline* (Freshwater Foundation, 1984), tracing the river from Canada to the Louisiana deltas and the Gulf of Mexico; *On American Soil* (Conservation Foundation, 1983), discussing the nature and extent of the soil erosion problem; *Once the Fire is Out...What Next?* (U.S. Forest Service, 1981), detailing the complex task of restoring fire-scarred areas, including land inspection, seeding, fertilization and terracing; *The Plow That Broke the Plains* (USDA, 1936), depicting the social and economic history of the Great Plains from the settlement of the prairies by cattlemen and farmers, through the World War I "boom," to drought and depression; *The Public Eye Is Watching* (Oklahoma Conservation Commission, 1983), a training film for conservation district boards; *Range Management* (Society for Range Management and Old West Regional Commission, 1977), an educational portrayal of the history of settlement, management problems and proper use of rangelands; *The River* (USDA, 1939), a documentary showing the effects of the Mississippi River on nature, and the effects of man on the river; and *There's More to Mining* (Interstate Mining Compact Commission, 1975), on the coal mining industry and preserving the environment at a coal site.

Other topics include: awards programs, careers in resource conservation, conservation education, conservation tillage, dam safety, energy resources, food efficiency, forest conservation, groundwater education, history of the conservation movement, mulch tillage, natural resources, pollution, soil conservation and erosion, storm water management, strip mining erosion, watershed management, water conservation and quality, wildlife resources and urban planning.
Size & Elements: Film: 16mm (60 titles). Videotape: 3/4", VHS and Betamax II (8 titles).
Cataloging: Published catalog.
Access: Available for rental and purchase; selected titles available for free loan. Films and videotapes available to any organization or individual interested in fostering conservation education. Research fees not charged. Research requests accepted by mail and telephone.
Rights: Full rights held to all material.
Licensing: Apply for information. License fees charged.
Restrictions: None specified.
Viewing Facilities: Film and videotape.
Duplication Facilities: None.
Related Materials: Slide sets and pamphlets.

TEXAS (Liberty)

SAM HOUSTON REGIONAL LIBRARY AND RESEARCH CENTER
Box 310
FM RD 1011
Liberty, Texas 77575
(409) 336-7097

Robert L. Schaadt (Director, Archivist)
Contact: Robert L. Schaadt

Services: Archives; research center. Film and videotape collection open to the public for in-house use only. Some materials possibly available for duplication and reuse.
Description: Holds collections pertaining to Southeast Texas history.

Ellen Virginia Daniel Collection. Representing the Daniel and Partlow families, the family of former Texas Governor Price Daniel. Films of family activities and boating on the Trinity River (ca. 1930s).

Sallie and Nadine Woods Collection. Archives of the Liberty Muscular Dystrophy Research Foundation (the first national foundation for muscular dystrophy research) containing films of activities, local events and public service announcements featuring Roy Rogers, former Texas Governor Price Daniel and other well-known personalities.

Videotapes produced by Glen Ely. Includes: *Southeast Texas Diary* (1985) produced for KBMT-TV (Beaumont, Texas), on historical subjects in Southeast Texas; *Road to Revolution,* on the Texas Revolution of 1836; and *Big Bend National Park.*
Size & Elements: Film: 16mm (33 titles); Super 8mm (13 titles). Videotape: format unspecified (4 titles).
Cataloging: Card catalogs; research library.
Access: Open to the public. For in-house use only. Available for duplication. Research fees not charged. Research requests accepted by mail, telephone and in person.
Rights: Full rights held to some material. Additional clearances may be necessary in some cases if material is to be reused. Some titles are copyrighted.
Licensing: Apply for information.
Restrictions: Copyrights apply to some material.
Viewing Facilities: None (outside arrangements can be made).
Duplication Facilities: None (outside arrangements can be made).

TEXAS (Longview)

LeTOURNEAU COLLEGE ARCHIVES
P.O. Box 7001
Longview, TX 75606
(214) 753-0231 (Ext. 231)

Dr. Paul Gray (Director of Library Services)

Contacts: Dr. Paul Gray (Director of Library Services); Louise Dick
Services: Educational institution; film archives. Material available for research, duplication, licensing and reuse, subject to restrictions.
Description: Material documenting the history, operations and products of the R. G. LeTourneau Company, manufacturer of large-scale earthmoving and construction equipment.
Size & Elements: Film: 35mm (4 cans); 16mm (715 cans); 8mm and 8mm cartridge (526 cans) (1245 titles total).
Cataloging: Finding aids.
Access: Open to researchers and scholars only. Research can be contracted out through the LeTourneau College Research Institute. Research requests accepted by mail, telephone and in person (walk-in and by appointment).
Rights: Full rights held to all material.
Licensing: Apply for information. License fees charged in some cases.
Restrictions: Requests for licensing and reuse considered on a case-by-case basis.
Viewing Facilities: Film.
Duplication Facilities: None.

TEXAS (Lubbock)

TEXAS TECH UNIVERSITY
SOUTHWEST COLLECTION
P.O. Box 4090
Lubbock, TX 79409
(806) 742-3749

David Murrah (Director of the Southwest Collection)

Contacts: Cindy Martin (Assistant Director); Robert Clark (Archival Assistant)
Services: University archives; manuscript repository. Extensive film collection used mainly for research. Material available for licensing and reuse, subject to restrictions.
Description: Collections held are particularly strong in politics and Texas political figures, such as Lyndon B. Johnson, Preston Smith and Waggoner Carr; as well as ranching, agriculture and the oil industry. They reflect the

504

history of Lubbock, Texas Tech University, West Texas, and, with the *Texas In Review Series*, all of Texas in the 1950s. The two local television newsfilm collections and the *Texas in Review Series* provide useful documents for social historians.

Preston Smith Films. Political films and commercial spots (ca. 1950s-70s, strongest in the 1960s) relating to the career of Preston Smith, former Texas Lieutenant Governor and Governor (ca. 1960s). Film: 16mm (approx. 40 films, 20,000 feet; black and white and color, sound and silent).

KLBK-TV (previously KDUB Films) *Collection.* Local television newsfilm from Lubbock, Texas (ca. 1955-68). Film: 16mm (approx. 130,377 feet; black and white, sound and silent). Videotape reference copies are available for some of this material, as well as an index for parts of the collection.

KAMC-TV Collection. Local television newsfilm from Lubbock, Texas (ca. 1977-80). Videotape: 3/4" (approx. 380 videotapes, each 45 min.; color, sound and silent). Reference copies are available for some of this material, as well as an index for parts of the collection.

Texas in Review Series. Television shows produced by Humble Oil (1954-58, each 30 min.). Each weekly episode features approximately five to six stories on Texas communities, events and personalities. Film: 16mm (98 films; approx. 117,600 feet; black and white, sound).

KTXT-TV Collection. Films from Texas Tech University television station (PBS affiliate) (ca. 1960s-70s). Most of these films are either local or educational in nature. Film: mostly 16mm (262 films; approx. 157,200 feet; color and black and white, sound and silent). Videotape (2").

West Texas Chamber of Commerce Films. Films relating to small West Texas town (ca. 1920s-30s). Film: 16mm (31 films; approx. 12,400 feet; black and white, silent). The condition of this film is very poor and use is restricted.

Marshall Formby Films. Campaign promotionals prepared for Formby's 1962 bid for the Governorship of Texas. Film (approx. 10 films; 1,000 feet).

Gordon McLendon Films. McLendon was a pioneer and innovator in radio broadcasting. He invented the "Top 40" radio format and broadcast play-by-play recreations of baseball games and also founded many radio stations throughout Texas, especially in the Dallas area. The collection consists of McLendon's political advertisements, speeches, and *Fatal Friday*, concerning the assassination of President John F. Kennedy. Film: 35mm and 16mm (24 items; approx. 24,000 feet); and videotape.

G. M. Kintz Films. These films (ca. 1928-31, some undated) demonstrate early oil drilling techniques. Kintz was the Subdistrict Manager for the Bureau of Mines, United States Department of Interior, in Dallas, Texas. Film: 16mm (14 films, approx. 5,600 feet; black and white, silent).

D. O. Wiley Films. Texas Tech University half-time shows and parades with visiting bands, including Hardin-Simmons Cowboy Band (1947-53, also undated). Also includes Sun Bowl Parade, El Paso, Texas (1948). Wiley was band director at Hardin-Simmons and Texas Tech University. Film: 16mm (13 films; approx. 3,900 feet).

Watson-Grappe Films. Four short films (ca. 1930s-40s): *A Fishing Trip to The Big Bend; Oil Derrick and Rodeo; Farm Scene and Football Scene* and *St. Helena Canyon Trip 1932.* Film: 16mm (4 films, approx. 400 feet; black and white and color).

Elmer Tarbox Films. Primarily athletic films (1937-62, also undated) including films of several Texas Tech University games in the 1930s. Film: 16mm and 8mm (approx. 10 films, 3,000 feet; black and white and color).

Clifford B. Jones Films. Primarily home movies (ca. 1920s-40s) shot by Clifford B. Jones while on vacation. Includes: a Los Angeles rodeo (1930s); a trip to Alaska and fishing trips. Film: 16mm (approx. 18 films, 5,400 feet; black and white, silent).

Thurber, Texas Films. Three films: *Thurber: Wonder City of the West* (ca. 1924); *Making Vitrified Brick* (ca. 1924), *Making Vitrified Brick* (ca. 1930). Although Thurber, Texas is now a ghost town, in 1900 it was the largest town between Fort Worth and El Paso, Texas. These films include shots of the coal mining and brickmaking town, as well as the process of making bricks and laying down brick streets. Film: 16mm (one film, approx. 800 feet; black and white, silent). Videotape reference copy is available.

Waggoner Carr films. Political films relating to Carr's career in Texas politics (1960-66 and undated). Film: various formats (approx. 51 films, 15,300 feet).

General. Various films, comprising a wide array of subject matter, dates, format types, condition and accessibility. Includes: *Renderbrook-Spade Ranch* (post-1965, 16mm, 1,200 feet, black and white, silent); *U-Lazy-S Ranch* (1928, 16mm, 400 feet, black and white, silent); *Lampassas, Texas Flood* (undated, 8mm, 400 feet); *Stamford, Texas Rodeo* (undated, 16mm, 1,600 feet, black and white, silent); *Frank Reeves* (ca. 1942, 16mm, 100 feet, black and white, silent, consists of chuck wagon scenes); *Santa Fe Railroad, Mile Post 100* (ca. 1960s, 16mm, 1,100 feet, color, sound); *Snake Hunt* (undated, 16mm, 400 feet, color, silent, concerns rattlesnake hunting); *Sweetwater, Texas* (1924, 635 feet); *J.*

Evetts Haley Discusses Charles Coodnight (1980, videotape); *JA Ranch Show, People Place* (1979, videotape); *Matador Ranch Scenes* and interviews with John and Helen Stevens; and also a reference copy of *Faces of Amarillo 1887-1987* (series produced by Amarillo College and the Amarillo PBS station). This series covers the history of Amarillo, Texas and is divided by subject (8 items).

Size & Elements: Film: 35mm and 16mm (approx. 502,812 feet, 793 cans; mostly 16mm original positives). Videotapes: 3/4" (380 masters, each 45 min.; 20 reference copies, each 60 min.); 1/2" (11 master videotapes, various lengths; 130 reference copies, each 60 min.).

Cataloging: Finding aids (film lists, index for newsfilm and inventories).

Access: Open to researchers, scholars and the public. Available for duplication. Research fees not charged. Research requests accepted by mail, telephone and in person (walk-in).

Rights: Full rights held to some material (includes materials generated by Texas Tech University). Some material in the public domain. Additional clearances may be necessary in some cases if material is to be reused (e.g., in cases where the donor of material is still living). Rights status of some material not known; some of the collections are currently being researched.

Licensing: Available for licensing in some cases, subject to restrictions.

Restrictions: Licensing and reuse depends on rights status of material.

Viewing Facilities: Film (manual film editor); videotape (3/4" and 1/2").

Duplication Facilities: Film (16mm to 3/4" and 1/2" videotape); videotape (3/4" to 1/2").

TEXAS (Richardson)

C. L. CARTER, JR. & ASSOCIATES, INC.
434 Banc Texas Building
P.O. Box 835001
Richardson, TX 75083
(214) 234-3296

Dr. C. L. Carter, Jr., P.E. (Vice President, Quality Assurance and Human Resource Consulting Services)

Contacts: G. M. Carter (President); Dr. C. L. Carter, Jr.

Services: Management and personnel consultants; corporate archives. Films available for rental and purchase.

Description: Films for management training and development cover these topics quality, reliability, safety, training, productivity, product liability and prevention of problems.

Sample titles include: *Product Liability Prevention; Don't Push Your Luck; How to Buy Quality Products; Reliable Soldering; This Sport Called Safety; Product Liability; The Goal Setters*, showing highly motivated pilots who race old fighter planes; and *Sport Snafus*, "funny 'Bloopers' that you see from time to time in baseball and football."

Size & Elements: Film: format unspecified (10 titles). Videotape: format unspecified (1 title).

Cataloging: Published catalogs.

Access: Maintained primarily for distribution and rental rather than for research and reuse. Research fees charged. Research requests accepted by mail.

Rights: Full rights held to some material.

Licensing: Apply for information.

Restrictions: Reuse of material may be restricted.

Viewing Facilities: None.

Duplication Facilities: None.

TEXAS (San Antonio)

HAYES PRODUCTIONS, INC.
4754 Shavano Oak, Suite 104
San Antonio, TX 78249
(512) 493-3551

Bill M. Hayes (President)

Contact: John M. Witherspoon (Vice President Marketing/Creative Services)

Services: Film and videotape producer; stock footage sales library.

Description: HayeStock Stock Video Tape Library is particularly strong in footage of San Antonio and South Texas, including twenty years of regional footage, scenery, events, festivals and local customs (1968-present); and food shots.

San Antonio. San Antonio Spurs; opening ceremonies of the San Jose Mission; downtown aerials; U.S., Texas and Mexico flags; Texas Folklife Festival; fireworks; wildflowers; Starving Artists Show in La Villita/River

Walk; women's soccer; Charros; Charro Queen; Mexican dancers; river parade (night); zoo; sunken gardens; Spanish Governor's Palace; the Alamo; Museum of Art (interior and exterior); Randolph Air Show (Thunderbirds, planes on ground); San Antonio Symphony; Christmas lights on San Antonio River Walk; space shuttle; oil well in sunset (pumper); Paseo del Alamo; fiesta daytime and nighttime parades at Alamo Plaza; Retamo Polo Center; modern pentathlon (including equestrian jumping event); night in Old San Antonio; bands and dancers at Arneson River Theatre; dancers in Juarez Plaza; El Curo; Steve's Homestead Interiors; King William Street; Espada Dam (picnic); El Mercado (shoppers and band); tennis at McFarlan Tennis Center; Brackenridge Park; carriages; trolley; Institute of Texan Cultures; Buckhorn Hall of Horns; Ranger Museum Statues; skyride; La Margarita Restaurant; Brackenridge stables; La Villita; San Fernando Cathedral; quadrangle at Fort Sam Houston; McNay Art Institute; botanical center; deer; and a parachute team.

Food shots. Extensive food shots, including: slicing a tomato; all types of foods photographed on a counter; butter melting on a dinner roll and on corn on the cob; tossed salad with pouring dressing; milk pouring into a glass; cracking egg; slicing bananas and other foods; pouring cherries into pie crust; foods on barbecue grill; breaking open a head of lettuce; party tray of hors d'oeuvres (ham and cheese); bacon frying on griddle; sausage on a stick on barbecue grill; and grilled wiener in hot dog bun (applying mustard).

Miscellaneous. Animation (marquees, special effects, outer space, grids, stars); apparel; automotive; children; cityscapes (buildings, corporate, architectural, residential); financial; food and beverages; fuel and energy; home furnishings, media and entertainment; personal and home products; political; pets and animals; recreational, travel and transportation; scenics (beaches and sunsets); titles and credits (days of week and sale graphics).
Size & Elements: Film and videotape (all elements).
Cataloging: Shot lists; research library.
Access: Available for duplication, licensing and reuse. Research fees charged (applicable to license fees). Research requests accepted by telephone.
Rights: Full rights held to all material.
Licensing: Available for licensing and reuse, subject to restrictions. License fees charged.
Restrictions: Some restrictions may apply to licensing and reuse.
Viewing Facilities: Film and videotape.
Duplication Facilities: Videotape.

TEXAS (San Antonio)

SAN ANTONIO CONSERVATION SOCIETY FOUNDATION LIBRARY
107 King William Street
San Antonio, TX 78204
(512) 224-6163

Marianna C. Jones (Librarian)

Contact: Marianna C. Jones
Services: Historic preservation organization. Maintains film and videotape collection.
Description: Videotape footage of the moving of the Fairmount Hotel (March, 1986), the largest building ever moved on pneumatic wheels (as listed in the *Guinness Book of World Records*). Also holds film and videotape footage of San Antonio's river walk.
Size & Elements: Film and videotape (formats and amounts unspecified).
Cataloging: None specified.
Access: Research fees not charged. Research requests accepted by mail, telephone and in person (walk-in).
Rights: Some rights held to some material. Additional clearances may be necessary in some cases if material is to be reused. Rights status of some material not known.
Licensing: Apply for information.
Restrictions: None specified.
Viewing Facilities: None.
Duplication Facilities: None.

TEXAS (San Antonio)

UNIVERSITY OF TEXAS
THE INSTITUTE OF TEXAN CULTURES AT SAN ANTONIO
P.O. Box 1226
San Antonio, TX 78294
(512) 226-7651
Fax: (512) 222-8564

John R. McGiffert (Interim Executive Director)

Contact: Ruth Silva (Ext. 259)
Services: Educational institution; historical society. Videotape holdings maintained for distribution and rental rather than for reuse.
Description: Videotapes relating to the cultural history of Texas. *Gonzales: Cradle of Texas Liberty* explores the long and picturesque history of Gonzales. In *The Kruger Family: Texas Immigrants,* the daughter of Russian Jewish immigrants tells the story of her parents' flight to the U.S. from Czarist Russia at the turn of the century. Historical photographs, drawings and poems written by her mother tell their story of immigration.
Size & Elements: Videotape: 3/4", VHS and Betamax (2 titles).
Cataloging: Published catalogs.
Access: Maintained for distribution and rental rather than for research or reuse. Research requests accepted by telephone and in person (by appointment only).
Rights: Full rights held to all material.
Licensing: Apply for information.
Restrictions: None specified.
Viewing Facilities: None.
Duplication Facilities: None.
Related Materials: Approximately 100,000 still photographs and negatives on Texas history; filmstrips, slide sets and audiotapes.

TEXAS (Temple)

SLAVONIC BENEVOLENT ORDER OF STATE OF TEXAS LIBRARY, ARCHIVES AND MUSEUM OF SPJST
P.O. Box 100
Temple, TX 76503
(817) 773-1575

Street address: 520 North Main

Howard Lesikar (President)

Contact: Thelma Bartosh (Curator and Librarian)
Services: Library; archives. Videotape collection available for loan.
Description: Repository of materials for the preservation of Czech language, culture and history. Titles include: *How to Play Taroks,* a Czech game; *How to Dance the Beseda,* a Czech folk dance; and *Czechs Within a Texas Checkerboard,* on the history of Texan Czechs.
Size & Elements: Videotape: format unspecified (3 titles).
Cataloging: Card catalogs.
Access: Available for loan. Rental fees charged. Research requests accepted by mail, telephone and in person (walk-in and by appointment).
Rights: Apply for information.
Licensing: Apply for information.
Restrictions: None specified.
Viewing Facilities: Film and videotape.
Duplication Facilities: None.

TEXAS (Texas City)

CONSTITUTIONAL RIGHTS FOUNDATION
National Headquarters
P.O. Box 2362
Texas City, TX 77592-2362

Dean Allen (National Director)

Contact: Sales Staff
Services: Foundation. Videotapes available to the public for purchase.
Description: *Tax Freedom* (2 parts) is a videotape presentation on federal income tax laws.

Part I "deals with what is wrong with our tax laws, and with the Taxpayers Bill of Rights (S. 1774) that will curb many of the abuses of the IRS." It is narrated by actor Chuck Connors and features President Ronald Reagan, Dr. Milton Friedman, Congressman Dick Armey, Senator Charles Grassley, Senator Phil Gramm and several other prominent experts from the fields of economics, politics and law.

Part II "deals with the income tax laws as they are now written and with how you can arrange your affairs now to legally avoid federal income taxes." This part features a lecture by Dean Allen speaking to a group of financial consultants and tax practitioners in Jackson, Miss. (1988).
Size & Elements: Videotape: VHS (1 title).

Cataloging: None specified.
Access: Available to the public for purchase. Research requests accepted; research fees charged.
Rights: Apply for information.
Licensing: Apply for information.
Restrictions: None specified.
Viewing Facilities: None.
Duplication Facilities: Videotape.

TEXAS (Waco)

BAYLOR UNIVERSITY
THE TEXAS COLLECTION
B.U. Box 7142
Waco, TX 76798
(817) 755-1268

Street address: Carroll Library Building, 5th and Speight

Kent Keeth (Director)

Contacts: Kent Keeth; Ellen K. Brown (Head of Historical Manuscripts)
Services: Library. Film and videotape collection open to the public for in-house use only.
Description: Athletic events, student activities, interviews with faculty and staff and special Baylor University productions. Includes the 1931 Baylor Band Members' Reunion, featuring interviews with band members from the late 1920s and early 1930s.

Interviews with Texas pastors, businessmen, oil tycoons, government officials, scholars, scientists, missionaries, sociologists, attorneys, farmers and civil servants.

The *Deep in the Heart of Texas* series includes close-ups of hummingbirds and clocks, shots of farm equipment, cemeteries, classic cars, old abandoned houses and fox hunts. There are discussions with an art restorer, chime maker, tool and die maker, spur maker, muzzleloader maker, catfish raiser, and the owner of Ann's Fashion Station (a combination gas station and dress shop).
Size & Elements: Film: format unspecified (positives; originals). Videotape: 3/4", VHS and Betamax (masters and viewing copies).
Cataloging: Finding aids.
Access: Open to the public. For in-house use only. Research fees not charged. Research requests accepted in person (by appointment only).
Rights: Full rights held to all material.
Licensing: Apply for information.
Restrictions: For in-house use only.
Viewing Facilities: Videotape (Betamax).
Duplication Facilities: None.

UTAH

UTAH (Salt Lake City)

CHURCH OF JESUS CHRIST OF LATTER-DAY SAINTS
HISTORICAL DEPARTMENT
50 East North Temple Street
Salt Lake City, UT 84150
(801) 240-2745
Fax: (801) 240-2033

Glen Rowe (Director, Library and Archives) (801/240-2787)

Contact: Glen Rowe. Media inquiries should be directed to Public Communications Department; (801) 240-2205.
Services: Church archives. Film and videotape material available for in-house use only; generally not available for reuse.
Description: Holds completed films and unedited footage pertaining to the history of the Mormons and the Church of Jesus Christ of Latter-Day Saints, featuring Church conferences and events. Some material has been used in church educational programs. Most holdings have not been analyzed for content.
Size & Elements: Film and videotape: formats unspecified (completed films and unedited footage).
Cataloging: Computerized cataloging for staff use only.
Access: For in-house use only.
Rights: Some rights held to some material.

Licensing: Material generally not available for reuse.
Restrictions: None specified.
Viewing Facilities: None.
Duplication Facilities: None.

UTAH (Salt Lake City)

UNIVERSITY OF UTAH
MARRIOTT LIBRARY
SPECIAL COLLECTIONS, MANUSCRIPTS DIVISION
Salt Lake City, UT 84112
(801) 581-8864

Dr. Gregory C. Thompson (Assistant Director)
Nancy V. Young (Manuscripts Librarian)

Contacts: Nancy V. Young; Karin Hardy (Manuscripts Division)
Services: University library. Film and videotape collection available to the public for in-house research. Material available for duplication and reuse, subject to restrictions.
Description: Films and videotapes produced by members of the University community, including student theses, research projects, documentation of lectures and university events; and some local television programming.

Native Americans. Sample items include: *American Indian Oral History*, Doris Duke's interviews with Native Americans (1960-68); *Standing Rock Indian Reservation* (1974, Frazier Gilbert), including six films (16mm) of *Ghost Dance,* four videotapes of *The Longest Walk* and ten videotapes of the *International Treaty Conference; The Blackfeet Medicine Lodge Ceremony Ritual and Dance: The Sun Dance* (Rosalie M. Jones); five home movies and informational films dealing with Southern Utah Navajo reservations (J. H. McGibbony).

Mormonism. Four videotapes concerning Sonia Johnson, the Equal Rights Amendment and the Church of Jesus Christ of Latter-Day Saints (1976-81); *The Mormon Meteor Does Its Thing* (J. H. McGibbony); and an 8mm film by Madeline R. McQuown dealing with the Church of Jesus Christ of Latter-Day Saints historical events.

Ethnic collections and Western history. Includes: *A Tapestry of Judaism* (21 videotapes produced and aired by KUED-TV, 1984) about Jewish residents of Utah; a number of videotapes covering the many conferences sponsored by the Institute of the American West.

Architecture and dance. Includes: a videotape production concerning architecture in Utah; *Ballet Archives* (30 films and 20 videotapes, 1965-present), on various ballets performed by Ballet West; and thesis films and videotapes.

Government and politics. Videotapes and films concerning the career of David S. King, U.S. congressman from Utah (1959-60, 1963-66); an interview with Governor Herbert B. Maw (1982); a film documenting the career of Reva Beck Bosone as Congresswoman and Salt Lake City's first woman judge; 54 films and three videotapes by Frank E. Moss on the Water Seminars at Vernal, Utah; six films on Ivy Baker Priest, U.S. Treasurer (1953-61) and California Treasurer (1966-74); two videotapes on Marriner S. Eccles, including his views of the Vietnam War and the Federal Reserve Board; 19 videotapes and 2 films relating to Dan Marriott, and Ted Wilson (1985).

University history and events. Includes: *Scenes Around the University* (1962-63); *Your State University* (1948); *Pioneer Memorial Theater Dedication* (1962); *University of Utah Telecourse Collection* (1973-74), comprised of 20 videotapes of philosophy lectures given by Dr. Charles H. Monson, Jr.
Size & Elements: Film: 16mm (amount unspecified). Videotape: format and amount unspecified.
Cataloging: Card catalogs; printed lists.
Access: Available to the public. For in-house use only. Possibly available for duplication, subject to clearance and approval. Research fees not charged. Research requests accepted by mail, telephone and in person (walk-in and by appointment).
Rights: Full rights held to some material. Some rights held to all material. Additional clearances may be necessary in some cases if material is to be reused.
Licensing: Available for licensing and reuse, subject to restrictions.
Restrictions: All requests subject to clearance and approval.
Viewing Facilities: Film and videotape (viewing facilities located in Audiovisual Department of Library).
Duplication Facilities: Film and videotape (duplication is handled by Instructional Media Services on campus).
Related Materials: Audio discs, audiocassettes and audiotapes.

UTAH MEDIA ARTS CENTER
20 South West Temple
Salt Lake City, UT 84101
(801) 534-1158

Alison A. Gregersen (Director)

Contact: Alison A. Gregersen
Services: Media organization. Film and videotape collection for in-house use only.
Description: Works by Utah film and videomakers (1970s-80s).
Size & Elements: Film: format unspecified (20 films). Videotape: format unspecified (45 videotapes).
Cataloging: None specified.
Access: For in-house use only.
Rights: Apply for information.
Licensing: Apply for information.
Restrictions: For in-house use only.
Viewing Facilities: Film and videotape.
Duplication Facilities: Videotape.

UTAH (Salt Lake City)

UTAH STATE ARCHIVES
Archives Building
State Capitol
Salt Lake City, UT 84114
(801) 538-3012

Jeff Johnson (Acting Archivist)

Contact: Terry Ellis (Patron Services Supervisor)
Services: State government agency; archives. Film collection open to the public for in-house use only. Material possibly available for licensing and reuse, subject to restrictions.
Description: Films relating to the state of Utah, including rodeos, parades and Bonneville Salt Flats racing. The *Centennial Commission Record Series* (1947), produced in five parts, celebrates Utah's centennial.
Size & Elements: Film: 16mm (5 reels, each 20 min.)
Cataloging: None specified.
Access: Open to the public. For in-house use only. Research fees not charged. Research requests accepted by mail and telephone.
Rights: Full rights held to all material.
Licensing: Available for licensing, subject to restrictions. License fees charged in some cases.
Restrictions: Requests for reuse considered on a case-by-case basis.
Viewing Facilities: Film.
Duplication Facilities: None.

UTAH (Salt Lake City)

UTAH STATE HISTORICAL SOCIETY
300 Rio Grande
Salt Lake City, UT 84101
(801) 533-5808

Max Evans (Director)

Contact: Gary Topping (Curator of Manuscripts)
Services: Historical society. Film collection available for research and possibly reuse.
Description: Historic river running trips on the Green, Colorado, San Juan and Salmon (Idaho) Rivers (ca. 1930-60). Highlights include: footage of Haldane "Buzz" Holmstrom's 1938 descent of the Colorado River, in which all rapids were run for the first time in a single trip; Dr. Russell G. Frazier, Bus Hatch and other members of the "Dusty Dozen" in Cataract and Grand Canyons (1930s); and Harry Aleson's upriver runs in the lower Grand Canyon (1940s) and early commercial trips in Glen Canyon (1950s) (the latter footage is historically important and visually appealing).
  Also holds extensive footage of early tourism in the national parks of southern Utah, including Zion and Bryce Canyon National Parks.
Size & Elements: Film: 16mm (50 cans, each approx. 30 min., color, positive; 80 cans, each approx. 15 min., black and white, positive).

Cataloging: Scene-by-scene lists; research library.
Access: Open to the public. Research fees not charged. Research requests accepted by mail, telephone and in person (walk-in).
Rights: Full rights held to some material.
Licensing: Possibly available for reuse. License fees charged in some cases (reuse for commercial purposes).
Restrictions: None specified.
Viewing Facilities: Film (16mm projector).
Duplication Facilities: None.

UTAH (Salt Lake City)

UTAH TRAVEL COUNCIL
Council Hall, Capitol Hill
Salt Lake City, UT 84114
(801) 538-1030
Fax: (801) 538-1399
TWX: (910) 250-2128

Jay C. Woolley (Director)

Contact: Joe Rutherford (Publicity Director)
Services: Government agency. Films and videotapes available for loan and reuse, subject to restrictions.
Description: Utah travel and tourism. Titles include: *Another Place, Another Time,* an overview of the state including national parks, monuments, historical and cultural attractions; *Impressions of Utah,* a general overview of state's scenic and recreational opportunities; *Greatest Snow on Earth,* on the breathtaking skiing available at Utah's resorts; *Fingerprints of Time,* a scenic tour of Utah's five national parks; and *From a Single Drop,* featuring Flaming Gorge and Lake Powell with a scenic overlook of their recreational opportunities.
Size & Elements: Film: 16mm (5 titles; release prints). Videotape: VHS (5 titles; viewing copies).
Cataloging: Printed list.
Access: Open to the public. Available for loan and possibly reuse. Research fees not charged. Research requests accepted by mail, telephone and in person (walk-in).
Rights: Full rights held to all material.
Licensing: Available for licensing, subject to restrictions. License fees not charged.
Restrictions: "Requests for film footage will be granted to those individuals and organizations which use them in a non-product, non-commercial fashion, subject to costs and protective procedures. Decisions for the use of the film footage will be made by the Director. Appeal of the Director's decision may be made to the Utah Travel Council Board of Commissioners."
Viewing Facilities: Videotape (VHS).
Duplication Facilities: None.

UTAH (Salt Lake City)

VIDEO WEST
5 Triad Center
Salt Lake City, UT 84110-1160
(801) 575-7400
Fax: (801) 575-7449

Al Henderson (Vice President and General Manager)

Contact: Jim Yorganson (Production Manager)
Services: Videotape producer; production facility. Material available for duplication, licensing and reuse, subject to restrictions.
Description: Utah scenics, including mountains, deserts, Great Salt Lake, winter snow scenes and holidays (e.g., Christmas); Utah sports including skiing and hiking. All footage is contemporary color material.
Size & Elements: Videotape: 1" (masters); 3/4", VHS and Betamax (viewing copies) (Approx. 5 to 10 hours total).
Cataloging: Shot lists.
Access: Available to the public for duplication, licensing and reuse. Research fees charged (on an hourly basis). Research requests accepted by telephone and in person (by appointment only).
Rights: Full rights held to all material.
Licensing: Available for licensing, subject to restrictions. License fees charged.
Restrictions: Requests for licensing considered on a case-by-case basis.

Viewing Facilities: Videotape (1", 3/4", VHS and Betamax).
Duplication Facilities: Videotape (1", 3/4", VHS and Betamax).

UTAH (Salt Lake City)

WEST STAR PRODUCTIONS
699 East South Temple Street, Suite 300
Salt Lake City, UT 84102
(801) 532-3909

R. Conrad Teichert (President)

Contact: R. Conrad Teichert
Services: Distributor; film and videotape producer; stock footage sales library.
Description: Subjects include: Western Americana, cowboys, ranches, Utah scenery and wildlife, horses, technical, high-speed and microscopic photography, children's and educational programming.
Size & Elements: Film: 16mm (100,000 feet, 36 titles; positive, negative, reversal, originals and release prints). Videotape: 1", 3/4" and VHS (some material available).
Cataloging: Computerized cataloging for staff use only.
Access: Available for duplication, licensing and reuse. Research fees not charged. Research requests accepted by mail and telephone.
Rights: Full rights held to all material.
Licensing: Available for licensing. License fees charged (rates negotiable).
Restrictions: None specified.
Viewing Facilities: Film (16mm); videotape (3/4" and 1/2").
Duplication Facilities: Film.

VERMONT

VERMONT (Burlington)

UNIVERSITY OF VERMONT
BAILEY/HOWE LIBRARY
SPECIAL COLLECTIONS
Burlington, VT 05401
(802) 656-2138

John Buechler (Director for Special Collections)

Contact: Connell B. Gallagher (University Archivist, Curator of Manuscripts)
Services: Film and videotape archives. Open to researchers, scholars and the public, primarily for in-house use. Material possibly available for duplication and licensing, subject to restrictions.
Description: Films made in or about Vermont. Includes two works by independent filmmaker Mack Derick from the 1930s: *The Vermont Special* (1935), produced by the State Development Department; and *Seeing Vermont with Dot and Glenn,* a comedy describing the state.

Also includes: a group of films by an unknown amateur filmmaker (1920s-30s) picturing a local flood in Vermont (1927), and footage of Vermont life and landscapes; some Vermont political campaigns and uncataloged footage relevant to state legislation; a series of films (currently being transferred to VHS videotape) documenting the "Youth Project" of Vermont, a "Great Society" project in which Black children from New York City were sent to Vermont in the summer of 1965.

Holds some programming (1960-80) from WCAX-TV (Burlington), a CBS affiliate. Includes portions of the *Evening News* and *You Can Quote Me,* a series of interviews with local politicians and artists. Also holds miscellaneous films by University film students, and material co-sponsored by the state and the University relating to the Vermont program on drunk driving, entitled *Crash Program.* Also two films, *Vermont Town Meeting* (eight hours of outtakes from a traditional New England town meeting) and *What If You Couldn't Read,* on the plight of illiterates in Vermont (with outtakes), both produced by amateur filmmaker Dorothy Todd (1970s).
Size & Elements: Film: 35mm and 16mm (approx. 75 titles, 100 cans). Videotape: 3/4" and VHS (approx. 50-60 videotapes).
Cataloging: Collection is uncataloged, with the exception of WCAX material (list).
Access: Open to researchers, scholars and the public. For in-house use only. Available for duplication and reuse in some cases. Research fees not charged. Research requests accepted by mail, telephone and in person (walk-in).
Rights: Full rights held to all material.
Licensing: Available for licensing and reuse, subject to restrictions. License

and usage fees charged in some cases.
Restrictions: Requests for reuse reviewed on a case-by-case basis, and are subject to acceptance and approval. The University usually requires a copy of final production.
Viewing Facilities: Film and videotape.
Duplication Facilities: Film and videotape.

VERMONT (Montpelier)

VERMONT HISTORICAL SOCIETY
109 State Street
Montpelier, VT 05602
(802) 828-2291

Michael Sherman (Director)

Contact: Michael Sherman
Services: Historical society; film and videotape archives. Available to researchers and scholars only. Material available for licensing and reuse, subject to restrictions.
Description: Vermont and Vermont-related subjects (1914-present). Subject categories cover: everyday commonplace events, including occupations and social occasions; seasonal activities such as skiing; farm chores and industrial processes; special recurring public events, including graduations, fairs, parades, church services, pageants and political rallies; private events and activities which reflect social life and customs in Vermont, such as birthday parties, weddings and family reunions; documentation of natural disasters, fires or other extraordinary events; town views and scenery shots which document a certain place and time; interpretive productions of people, places and events in Vermont. Also holds a few promotional and travel films. The archives is especially interested in films by independent producers and school groups, which might not otherwise be preserved.

Sample titles include: *Vermont Romance* (1916); *Lindbergh Day, Springfield, Vt.* (1927); *Skiing, Woodstock Area* (1954); *Pictures of Putney* (1953); *Timber is a Crop* (1942-45); *Winter Sports, Maple Corner* (1932); *Vermont Structural Steel Ads* (1950s); *The Price of Eggs* (1960s); *Marble, Today and Tomorrow* (1960s); *Summer Gardens and Fall Foliage in Old Vermont* (1949); *Betsy Ross Bread* (1952); *A Day in the Life of A Student Nurse* (1950); *Rutland Hospital* (1951); *Sketches of People* (1928); *Boy Scout Parade, Rutland* (1927); *Eastern States Exposition* (1928); *Knights of Birmingham Parade* (1921); *Frank Gauthier, Woodsplitter* (1971); *The Making of A Renaissance Book* (1960s); *Richford Train Wreck* (1942); *Grenville Dodge Centennial* (1951); *SS Ticonderoga and St. Johnsbury Fires* (1950s); *Champlain Bridge Trip* (1928); and *Industrial Vermont* (1935).

Calvin Coolidge films (1926-32). Titles include: *Brewer Home and Cemetery* (1926); *On Lynn Common* (1927); *Black Hills, S.D.* (1926-27); *Cedar Island* (1928); *Sapello Island, Georgia* (1928-29); *Swannanoa, Blue Ridge Mountains* (1928); *Hearst Ranch* (1929); *St. Petersburg, Florida* (1930); *Hoover Inauguration* (1929); *Yellowstone National Park* (1927); *Fishing on Cape Cod; Birds in Captivity;* and *At Home in Plymouth* (1932).
Size & Elements: Film: 16mm (70 titles, 27,000 feet; positive and negative copies of release prints); 8mm (1,000 feet). Videotape: 3/4" (15 hours; viewing copies); VHS (10 hours; viewing copies); 1/2" open reel (40 videotapes, each 30 min.; black and white, viewing copies).
Cataloging: Card catalogs; title list.
Access: Open to researchers, scholars and the public. Research fees not charged. Specific research requests accepted by mail, telephone and in person (by appointment only).
Rights: Full rights held to some material. Some rights held to some material. Additional clearances may be necessary in some cases if material is to be reused.
Licensing: Available for licensing and reuse, subject to restrictions.
Restrictions: Requests for licensing and reuse considered on a case-by-case basis, and are subject to acceptance and approval.
Viewing Facilities: Film (16mm projector and viewer); videotape (1/2" open reel).
Duplication Facilities: None.

VERMONT (Richmond)

ROZ PAYNE
P.O. Box 164
Richmond, VT 05477
(802) 434-3172

VERMONT (Saxtons River)

Contact: Roz Payne
Services: Film and still photograph collection. Material available for duplication, licensing and reuse.
Description: Political documentary film material (mid-1960s to early 1970s). Subjects covered include: high-school students; Black Panther Party; Bess Myerson's "Another Mother for Peace" speech; the 1968 Democratic Convention in Chicago; Yippies; anti-Vietnam War demonstrations, including Washington, D.C. (1969); People's Park, Berkeley, Calif. (1969); the Columbia University student strike (1968); the strike against Standard Oil Company in Richmond, Calif. (1969); the Venceremos Brigade in Cuba (1970); draft resistance; underground newspapers, including the preparation of *The Rat* for the Chicago Democratic Convention; the United Farm Workers; civil rights activism in Mississippi (1964); films produced in North Vietnam; women's liberation; a children's animated film on the People's Republic of China; and extensive coverage of Grenada prior to United States military involvement.
Size & Elements: Film: 16mm (amount unspecified).
Cataloging: Logs available for some material; staff assistance required. Some material currently being transferred to reference videotapes.
Access: Available for duplication, licensing and reuse. Research services available. Research fees charged. Research requests accepted by mail and telephone.
Rights: Full rights held to some material.
Licensing: Available for licensing and reuse. License fees charged.
Restrictions: None specified.
Viewing Facilities: Videotape (off-premises).
Duplication Facilities: None.
Related Materials: Still photographs covering many similar subjects.

VERMONT (Saxtons River)

CAMPBELL FILMS, INC.
P.O. Box 307
Cory Hill
Saxtons River, VT 05154
(802) 869-2547

Contact: Liz Chromec (Film Librarian)
Services: Distributor. Films available primarily to schools for rental.
Description: Educational films about handicapped people, careers working with the handicapped and health issues.
Special education. Titles include: *Physical Education For Blind Children; The Shape of a Leaf,* on art education for retarded children; *Oh Yes, These Are Very Special Children,* about introducing dance to retarded children; and *Stuttering,* in which stutterers explain problems they encounter.
Health and guidance. Titles include: *Worth Waiting For,* about teenagers and marriage; *When I'm Old Enough, Goodbye,* urging students to stay in school; *Drugs and the Nervous System;* and *To Plan Your Family.*
Elementary education. Titles include: *The Activity Oriented Classroom,* on an unusual approach to early elementary education.
General. Titles include: *Green Up,* showing the first time an entire state cooperated to clean up trash; and *The Flavor of Vermont,* the story of maple sugaring in Vermont.
Size & Elements: Film: 16mm (17 titles).
Cataloging: Printed list available upon request.
Access: Available primarily to schools for two-day rental. Requests accepted by mail and telephone.
Rights: Apply for information.
Licensing: Apply for information.
Restrictions: None specified.
Viewing Facilities: None.
Duplication Facilities: None.

VERMONT (Shelburne)

AMERICAN MORGAN HORSE ASSOCIATION, INC.
P.O. Box 960
Shelburne, VT 05482
(802) 985-4944

Street address: 3 Bostwick Road

Georgine Winslett (Executive Director)

Contact: Georgine Winslett
Services: Association. Films and videotapes available to the public for rental and purchase.
Description: History of the Morgan horse, including training; judging at horse shows; the Morgan's depiction in art through the centuries; and the history of the breed.
Video Encyclopedia of Horsemanship. Volumes in the series include: *Basic Training for Driving; Basic Training for Saddle; Advanced Classical Driving; Training the Western Pleasure Horse;* and *Western Equitation.*
Other titles include: *The Artist's Horse,* showing the Morgan as the breed exemplifying the classic "upheaded" horse depicted by the great masters of European art; *The Morgan Horse: Pride and Product of America,* a brief history of the breed and the many uses of the modern Morgan; *Morgans, For the Sport of It,* featuring New York's finest Morgans in dressage, combined training, competitive trail, combined driving and reining, with historical segments of the Morgan's use in early America; *Saddle Seat Equitation,* Helen Crabtree demonstrating her championship style of equitation; *All American Morgan Horse Show,* highlights of the competition at the 44th Annual New England Morgan Horse Show; and *A Winning Breed,* detailing the finer points of the Morgan horse.
Size & Elements: Videotape: 3/4", VHS and Betamax (11 titles; viewing copies).
Cataloging: None specified.
Access: Available to the public for rental and purchase. Research fees charged depending upon intended use. Research requests accepted by mail, telephone and in person (walk-in).
Rights: Rights status of material not known.
Licensing: Apply for information. License fees charged in some cases.
Restrictions: None specified.
Viewing Facilities: Videotape (VHS in Archive Library).
Duplication Facilities: None.
Related Materials: Library collection of *The Morgan Horse Magazine* (1960-present); still photograph archives of famous Morgans.

U.S. VIRGIN ISLANDS

VIRGIN ISLANDS (St. Thomas)

MOUNTAIN VIDEO ASSOCIATES
P.O. Box 4036
St. Thomas, VI 00801
(809) 776-8613

Frank Hurt (Manager/Owner)

Contact: Christine Lauterborn (Producer/Director)
Services: Videotape producer; stock footage sales library.
Description: Tropical beauty shots of the U.S. and British Virgin Islands (autumn 1985-present). Includes islands, beaches, sailing, West Indian peoples, carnivals, cruise ships, resort hotels, iguanas, mongoose, tropical vegetation, Virgin Islands National Park, sugar plantation ruins, architecture dating back to 17th century, seaplanes, sailboarding, ferry boats and underwater shots.
Size & Elements: Videotape: 3/4" (30 hours; mostly masters).
Cataloging: Shot lists.
Access: Available for duplication.
Rights: Full rights held to all material.
Licensing: Available for licensing and reuse. License fees charged (fee schedule available).
Restrictions: None specified.
Viewing Facilities: Videotape (3/4" and 1/2").
Duplication Facilities: Videotape (3/4" to 3/4").

VIRGIN ISLANDS (St. Thomas)

WTJX-TV (CHANNEL 12)
P.O. Box 7879
St. Thomas, VI 00801
(809) 774-6255

Calvin F. Bastian (General Manager)

Contact: Bill Arnet (Production Manager)
Services: Television broadcaster; videotape producer. Stock footage library available for reuse.
Description: Materials produced and held in library include:
Cultural affairs programming. Includes: a half-hour weekly show, *Getting*

510

Together, with Marielu Burnette and guests discussing social issues; *Carnival,* parades recorded in St. Thomas and St. Croix over several years; theatrical productions, including *Marie La Veau* (Derek Wolcott), *Up Mountain One Time* (Willie Wilson) and *Bonfire War; Virgin Island Storytellers,* featuring children's stories as told by local storytellers; *Poets in Paradise,* poems written by local poets; assorted music programs; *Undah De Taman Tree,* a series of children's programs using puppets; and other programs such as senior citizens' programming and a Dutch-Creole language special.

Public affairs programming. Includes: Addie Ottley's *Face to Face,* a live, one-hour phone-in program dealing with current issues; assorted governmental functions, such as inaugurations, State of the Territory addresses, press conferences, Offshore Territories conferences, Transfer Day ceremonies and Status hearings; and *History of the Virgin Islands,* a series of 14 lessons (each 30 min.) produced with the College of the Virgin Islands.
Size & Elements: Videotape: IVC, 1", 3/4" and VHS (approx. 125 hours).
Cataloging: Computerized cataloging for staff use only.
Access: Available for reuse. Research fees not charged, but staff time is limited. Research requests accepted by mail and telephone.
Rights: Full rights held to all material.
Licensing: Available for licensing and reuse.
Restrictions: None specified.
Viewing Facilities: Videotape (1", 3/4" and VHS).
Duplication Facilities: Videotape.

VIRGINIA

VIRGINIA (Alexandria)

AMERICAN ASSOCIATION FOR COUNSELING AND DEVELOPMENT
and
AMERICAN DIABETES ASSOCIATION
and
AMERICAN PHYSICAL THERAPY ASSOCIATION
and
AMERICAN TRUCKING ASSOCIATION
and
DEVELOPMENT COMMUNICATIONS INC.
and
FUTURE FARMERS OF AMERICA
and
NATIONAL ASSOCIATION OF CONVENIENCE STORES
and
NATIONAL CONSERVATIVE FOUNDATION
and
NATIONAL SCHOOL BOARDS ASSOCIATION
and
PUBLIC BROADCASTING SYSTEM (PBS) PROGRAM DATA & ANALYSIS
and
UNITED WAY OF AMERICA ARCHIVES
See **DISTRICT OF COLUMBIA METRO**

VIRGINIA (Arlington)

AMERICAN DEFENSE PREPAREDNESS ASSOCIATION
and
HIGH FRONTIER
and
INSURANCE INSTITUTE FOR HIGHWAY SAFETY LIBRARY
and
THE NATURE CONSERVANCY
and
THE WASHINGTON BROADCAST VIDEO LIBRARY CREATIVE VIDEO OF WASHINGTON, INC.
See **DISTRICT OF COLUMBIA METRO**

VIRGINIA (Boston)

AMERICAN SECURITY COUNCIL FOUNDATION
Route 522 North
Boston, VA 22713
(703) 547-1776

John M. Fisher (Chairman and Chief Executive Officer)

Contact: Film Coordinator
Services: Foundation. Film and videotape library available for rental and purchase. Material possibly available for reuse, subject to restrictions.
Description: Foundation is the educational secretariat of the American Security Council, a nonprofit organization supporting a strong defense, and the educational arm of the Coalition For Peace Through Strength.

Holds four documentary films (each 26 min.) focusing on issues of national security. Particular focus is placed upon Central American conflicts and the "realities of illegal drug traffic financing Marxist revolution in Central America"; the dangers of the nuclear freeze movement; nuclear weapons and strategic balance between the U.S. and U.S.S.R. *Countdown for America* (1982), narrated by Charlton Heston, has been updated by a new film, *Peace Through Strength* (1984) which incorporates new facts and figures. Both films show Soviet weaponry and troops. *Attack on the Americas* (1982), updated in 1985 by *Crisis in the Americas,* shows actual footage of the El Salvador elections, Grenada invasion and the contras in Nicaragua. The films were endorsed by President Reagan and assorted Congressmen and Senators.
Size & Elements: Film: 16mm (4 titles). Videotape: VHS and Betamax (4 films).
Cataloging: Film brochures.
Access: Available for rental, purchase and broadcast, subject to restrictions. Research requests accepted by mail, telephone and in person.
Rights: Full rights held to all material.
Licensing: Apply for information. License fees charged in some cases. Foundation will loan the films for screenings in schools.
Restrictions: Available for duplication and reuse only upon approval of Foundation.
Viewing Facilities: None.
Duplication Facilities: None.

VIRGINIA (Delaplane)

DAVENPORT FILMS
R.R. 1, Box 527
Routes 688 and 711
Delaplane, VA 22025
(703) 592-3701

Tom Davenport; Mimi Davenport

Contact: B. J. Williams (Distribution Manager)
Services: Film producer and distributor. Films available for rental and purchase; videotapes available for purchase only.
Description: American folk culture, American studies and other topics.
From the Brothers Grimm: American Versions of Folktale Classics. Titles include: *Bearskin, or The Man Who Didn't Wash For Seven Years,* a tale of endurance and transformation set after the end of the Civil War; *Jack and the Dentist's Daughter* (based on Grimm's *The Master Thief*), a tale set in small-town America during the 1930s, telling the comical story about a clever hero who wins his true love; and *Hansel & Gretel: An Appalachian Version.*
The American Traditional Culture Series. Titles include: *A Singing Stream: A Black Family Chronicle,* with gospel music performances; *Being a Joines: A Life in the Brushy Mountains,* on John E. "Frail" Joines, a master traditional tale-teller; *Born For Hard Luck: Peg Leg Sam Jackson,* a film portrait of one of the last and greatest of the medicine-show entertainers; and *The Shakers.*
Other films include: *It Ain't City Music; The Upperville Show,* a humorous documentary about wealthy Virginia society at the oldest horse show in the U.S.; *Thoughts on Fox Hunting;* and *T'ai Chi Ch'uan,* Chinese martial arts performed by Zen Master Nan Huai-Chin (filmed in Taiwan).
Size & Elements: Film: 16mm. Videotape: 3/4", VHS and Betamax. (17 titles total).
Cataloging: Brochures.
Access: Maintained for distribution and rental rather than for research or reuse. Preview service limited to 16mm purchase consideration. Videotape copies are for purchase only and for school and library use, subject to copyright restrictions.
Rights: Full rights held to all material.
Licensing: Apply for information.
Restrictions: Material protected by copyright.
Viewing Facilities: None.
Duplication Facilities: None.

VIRGINIA (Dumfries)

COAL EMPLOYMENT PROJECT
16221 Sunny Knoll Court
Dumfries, VA 22026
(703) 670-3416

Betty Jean Hall (Director)

Contact: Jeri McLaughlin (Administrative Assistant)
Services: Nonprofit public interest and legal organization; videotape producer and distributor. Material available for rental and possibly for reuse, subject to restrictions.
Description: Predominantly original footage relating to civil rights and women's issues in the coal industry, particularly sexual harassment, discrimination, the women's movement and history. Also documented is the history of coal mining, especially women in mining.
Size & Elements: Videotape: 3/4" and 1/2" (200 videotapes, various lengths).
Cataloging: Cataloging presently in progress. A typed list by subject will be available at a later date.
Access: Available primarily for rental. Rental fees charged. Requests accepted by mail and telephone.
Rights: Some rights held to all material.
Licensing: Apply for information.
Restrictions: Requests for reuse subject to approval.
Viewing Facilities: None.
Duplication Facilities: None.

VIRGINIA (Fairfax)

GEORGE MASON UNIVERSITY
SPECIAL COLLECTIONS AND ARCHIVES
FENWICK LIBRARY
See **DISTRICT OF COLUMBIA METRO**

VIRGINIA (Falls Church)

AMERICAN RED CROSS
AUDIOVISUAL DEPARTMENT
FRANK STANTON PRODUCTION CENTER
and
STUART FINLEY, INC.
and
R5/S8 PRESENTS
See **DISTRICT OF COLUMBIA METRO**

VIRGINIA (Ft. Eustis)

UNITED STATES ARMY TRANSPORTATION MUSEUM
Building 300, Besson Hall
Attn: ATZF-PTM
Ft. Eustis, VA 23604-5260
(804) 878-1115

Barbara Bower (Director)

Contact: Ruth Shepard (Library Technician) (804/878-1183)
Services: Museum. Film and videotape collection open to researchers and scholars only.
Description: Army transportation (1956-present), including aviation, marine, land and experimental vehicles.
Size & Elements: Film: 16mm (290 titles, 290 cans; positive). Videotape: 3/4" (29 videotapes; viewing copies).
Cataloging: Card catalogs.
Access: Open to researchers and scholars. For in-house use only (due to fragile condition of film). Research fees not charged. Research requests accepted by mail, telephone and in person (walk-in).
Rights: Full rights held to some material. Additional clearances may be necessary in some cases if material is to be reused. Apply for information through the Public Affairs Office.
Licensing: Handled through the Public Affairs Office.
Restrictions: Reuse restricted and permitted on a case-by-case basis.
Viewing Facilities: Videotape (limited access).
Duplication Facilities: None.

VIRGINIA (Great Falls)

INDUSTRIAL DESIGNERS SOCIETY OF AMERICA
1142-E Walker Road
Great Falls, VA 22066
(703) 759-0100
Fax: (703) 759-7679

Contact: Denise Piastrelli-Kocan
Services: Professional organization. Two videotapes available for purchase.
Description: *Marker Rendering* demonstrates different illustration techniques, including the use of color pencils, pastels and marker spray attachments and the various illustration properties of paper. *Marker Blending and Image Editing Techniques* demonstrates how to dissolve and blend colored pencil and pastel enrichments and how to create watercolor-like washes with custom-mixed colors.
Size & Elements: Videotape: VHS and Betamax (2 titles).
Cataloging: Published catalog.
Access: Available to the public for purchase. Orders must be prepaid.
Rights: Apply for information.
Licensing: Apply for information.
Restrictions: None specified.
Viewing Facilities: None.
Duplication Facilities: None.

VIRGINIA (Hampton)

NATIONAL AERONAUTICS AND SPACE ADMINISTRATION (NASA)
LANGLEY RESEARCH CENTER
REGIONAL FILM LIBRARY
MS-185
Hampton, VA 23665-5225
(804) 865-2634

Contact: Staff
Services: Government agency; circulating film and videotape library. Films and videotapes available for loan.
Description: Films and videotapes describing NASA research and development programs and achievements in space and aeronautics. Programs offered are similar to those available from other NASA Regional Film Libraries (q.v.).
Size & Elements: Film: 16mm. Videotape: 3/4". (Hundreds of titles total).
Cataloging: Published catalog.
Access: Available for loan to educational, civil, industrial, professional, youth and similar groups, and for unsponsored public service telecasts. Research and rental fees not charged. Requests accepted by mail.
Rights: Material is in the public domain. Additional clearances may be necessary in some cases if material is to be reused.
Licensing: Available for reuse, subject to restrictions.
Restrictions: Film material or footage of recognizable astronauts may not be reused for commercial purposes.
Viewing Facilities: None.
Duplication Facilities: None.

VIRGINIA (Lexington)

GEORGE C. MARSHALL RESEARCH LIBRARY
P.O. Box 1600
Lexington, VA 24450
(703) 463-7103

Street address: VMI Parade

Gordon R. Beyer (President)

Contact: John N. Jacob (Archivist/Librarian)
Services: Library. Film collection open to the public and available for reuse, subject to restrictions.
Description: Donated film collection relating to postwar Germany and the Marshall Plan (covering the years 1943-50, 1961-64 and 1976). Includes: George C. Marshall as Army Chief of Staff, Secretary of State and Secretary of Defense; postwar Germany; the *Marshall Plan in Action* series; and the *Why We Fight* series.
Size & Elements: Film: 35mm (a few titles); 16mm (majority of collection, 58

titles, 84 cans).
Cataloging: List of films by accession number. Films currently "loosely" cataloged. Contact Archivist/Librarian for information.
Access: Open to the public. Research fees not charged. Research requests accepted by mail, telephone and in person (walk-in).
Rights: No rights held to any material. Some rights may be retained by original producers. Some material in the public domain. Additional clearances may be necessary in some cases if material is to be reused.
Licensing: Available for licensing and reuse in some cases. License and usage fees not charged.
Restrictions: None specified.
Viewing Facilities: Film; videotape (VHS).
Duplication Facilities: None.

VIRGINIA (Lynchburg)

LIBERTY BROADCASTING NETWORK
2220 Langhorne Plaza
Lynchburg, VA 24514
(804) 582-2607
Fax: (804) 237-2768

Jerry Whitehurst (Program Director) (804/528-4112)

Contact: Dan Bathurst (Production Manager) (804/239-9281)
Services: Religious broadcaster and program producer. Videotape programs possibly available for licensing and reuse, subject to restrictions.
Description: "Inspirational" programs, including: *The Pastor's Study; Old Time Gospel Hour* (featuring the Rev. Jerry Falwell); *The Pastor's Bible Class; Thomas Road Baptist Church;* and specials.
Size & Elements: Videotape: 1" (masters); 3/4" (viewing copies).
Cataloging: Finding aids; show list.
Access: Open to researchers, scholars and the public. Research fees charged in some cases. Research requests accepted by mail and telephone.
Rights: Full rights held to all material.
Licensing: Available for licensing and reuse, subject to restrictions. License fees charged.
Restrictions: Material used mainly for LBN broadcasts; requests for reuse considered on a case-by-case basis.
Viewing Facilities: Videotape (3/4").
Duplication Facilities: None (outside arrangements made).

VIRGINIA (McLean)

NATIONAL GLASS ASSOCIATION
VIDEO GLASS
NGA MEMBER SERVICES
See **DISTRICT OF COLUMBIA METRO**

VIRGINIA (Newport News)

THE MARINERS' MUSEUM
One Museum Drive
Newport News, VA 23606
(804) 595-0368

Contact: Tamra L. Priddy (Photographic Services Coordinator)
Services: Museum. Film collection available to the public for rental. Archival film collection unavailable for viewing.
Description: Films (covering the period 1928-present) relating to ships, exploration and the sea.

Subject categories include: exploitation of the sea, including commercial fishing, shipping, port operations, Indian culture and tall ships; shipbuilding, including sailing vessels, power, nuclear and man-powered; exploration; sea power in the American Revolution, the Civil War and World War II; voyages; disasters at sea; boat races; marine and earth sciences; life at sea; safety at sea; the merchant marine; marine art; museum operations; historical events; river activities; and marine studies.

Sample titles include: *Billy Moore: Chesapeake Boatbuilder* (1980), depicting the construction of a traditional Chesapeake Bay deadrise oyster boat; *I Christen Thee* (1976), showing the preparation for the actual launching of the nuclear cruiser *U.S.S. Mississippi; Assault on Antarctica*, on the U.S. Navy operations base; *Old Ironsides* (1957), on the history of the *U.S.S. Constitution; J Boats "37"* (1937), on the "J" class sloops and their competition for the America's Cup; *Sailing the Square-Rigger, Dar Pomorza* (1930), showing

cadet life aboard the Polish school ship; *Warm Welcome* (1953), on the tumultuous welcome given the *S.S. United States* when it arrived in Southampton, England, after breaking the transatlantic speed record; and *Watermen of the Chesapeake* (1965), on the Chesapeake Bay fishing industry and its economic importance to the nation.

The archival collection contains films which are in poor condition and unavailable for viewing. Videotapes are also held, but are not available for public use.
Size & Elements: Film: 16mm (approx. 140 titles; release prints). Videotape: format and amount unspecified (viewing copies).
Cataloging: Film list.
Access: Films available to the public for rental. Videotapes available for staff use only. Rental requests accepted by mail and telephone. Shipping fees charged; films may be borrowed without charge if picked up at the Museum.
Rights: Full rights held to *Billy Moore: Chesapeake Boatbuilder*. Additional clearances may be necessary if material is to be reused.
Licensing: Available for licensing and reuse, subject to restrictions. License fees charged under some conditions.
Restrictions: Requests for reuse considered on a case-by-case basis. Archival film collection unavailable for viewing.
Viewing Facilities: None.
Duplication Facilities: None.
Related Materials: Models of some ships and boats featured in the films are on display at the Museum.

VIRGINIA (Norfolk)

THE COUSTEAU SOCIETY, INC.
930 West 21st Street
Norfolk, VA 23517
(804) 627-1144
Fax: (804) 627-7547
Telex: 6974570 COUSTEAUNFK

Jacques-Yves Cousteau (President and Chairman of the Board)

Contact: Sandra Bond (Supervisor, Research and Communications)
Services: Nonprofit, membership-supported environmental and scientific research organization; producer of films, videotapes, and television programs for research and educational purposes. Films and videotapes available for purchase.
Description: Captain Jacques-Yves Cousteau's extensive voyages and research in marine ecosystems are documented in films and television programs (mainly produced 1960s-80s). Theatrical films include 20 short documentaries (produced 1942-56), including *The Silent World; The Golden Fish; World Without Sun;* and *Voyage to the Edge of the World.*

The explorer's television career was inaugurated in 1966 with a National Geographic/CBS Special, *The World of Jacques-Yves Cousteau*, followed by *The Undersea World of Jacques Cousteau* series, beginning in 1968. Series titles include: *Sharks; The Savage World of the Coral Jungle; Search in the Deep; Whales; The Unexpected Voyage of Pepito and Cristobal; Sunken Treasure; The Legend of Lake Titicaca; The Desert Whales; The Night of the Squid; The Return of the Sea Elephant; Those Incredible Diving Machines; The Water Planet; The Tragedy of the Red Salmon; Lagoon of Lost Ships; The Dragons of Galapagos; Secrets of the Sunken Caves; The Unsinkable Sea Otter!; Octopus, Octopus; The Forgotten Mermaids; A Sound of Dolphins; The Smile of the Walrus; 500 Million Years Beneath the Sea; Hippo!; The Singing Whale; South to Fire and Ice; The Flight of Penguins; Beneath the Frozen World; Blizzard at Hope Bay; Life at the End of the World; Beavers of the North Country; The Coral Divers of Corsica; The Sleeping Sharks of Yucatan; The Sea Birds of Isabela; Mysteries of the Hidden Reefs; The Fish That Swallowed Jonah;* and *The Incredible March of the Spiny Lobsters.*

Oasis in Space series (1977) includes: *What Price Progress?; Grain of Conscience; Troubled Waters; Population Time Bomb; The Power Game; Visions of Tomorrow.*

Cousteau Odyssey series (1970s) includes: *Calypso's Search for the Britannic; Diving for Roman Plunder; Calypso's Search for Atlantis; Blind Prophets of Easter Island; Time Bomb at Fifty Fathoms; Mediterranean: Cradle or Coffin?; The Nile; Lost Relics of the Sea; Clipperton: The Island Time Forgot; Warm-Blooded Sea;* and *Mammals of the Deep.*

Amazon series (1984) includes: *Journey to a Thousand Rivers; The New El Dorado: Shadows in the Wilderness; River of Gold; River of the Future: Legacy of a Lost World; Blueprints for Amazonia;* and *Snowstorm in the Jungle.*

Rediscovery of the World series (1986) includes: *Haiti: Waters of Sorrow;*

Cuba: Waters of Destiny; Cape Horn: Waters of the Wind; Sea of Cortez: Legacy of Cortez; Marquesas Islands: Mountains from the Sea; and *Channel Islands: At the Edge of a Human Tide.*

A documentary on the career of Jacques Cousteau, *The First Seventy-Five Years,* is also available.

Size & Elements: Film: 16mm. Videotape: 3/4", VHS and Betamax. (Approx. 80 titles total).
Cataloging: Lists.
Access: Available to the public for purchase only. Available for in-house research only. Research fees may be charged in some cases. Research requests accepted by mail.
Rights: Some rights held to some material. Additional clearances may be necessary in some cases if material is to be reused.
Licensing: Possibly available for licensing and reuse; subject to restrictions.
Restrictions: Restrictions may apply, depending on material requested and intended purpose.
Viewing Facilities: Film and videotape.
Duplication Facilities: Videotape (very limited).
Distributors: Apply for information regarding educational and home video distributors.

VIRGINIA (Norfolk)

THE GENERAL DOUGLAS MACARTHUR MEMORIAL
MacArthur Square
Norfolk, VA 23510
(804) 441-2965
(804) 441-2966
(804) 441-2967
(804) 441-2968

Lyman H. Hammond, Jr. (Director)

Contacts: Edward J. Boone, Jr. (Archivist); Joseph Judge (Curator); Jeffrey Acosta (Assistant Archivist)
Services: Museum; library. Film and videotape collection open to researchers, scholars and the public for educational purposes, and for duplication, licensing and reuse, subject to restrictions.
Description: Films and videotapes relating to the life of General of the Army Douglas MacArthur (1880-1964). Most concern four major historical events in which MacArthur was involved: World War II (Pacific Theater, 1941-45); his tenure as the Supreme Allied Commander of the Pacific during the occupation of Japan (1946-51); his command of United Nations forces in Korea (1950-51); and his return to the United States, retirement and death (1951-64). A few films document MacArthur's early career (1903-41) and life in Japan following World War II. Several films contain interviews, with his widow (Mrs. Jean Faircloth MacArthur) and with other men and women who served with him. All films were produced 1942-87; most originally produced in 16mm, recently transferred to various videotape formats. Pre-1941 footage is largely based on still photographs.

Many titles were produced by newsreel companies and television networks, who retain rights.

Sample titles include: *A Soldier Comes Home: General MacArthur's Return to the United States* (NBC); *The Ambassador Hotel and the American Legion Honors General Douglas MacArthur on His 75th Birthday* (1955, 48 min.); *The Big Picture: The MacArthur Story* (U.S. Army Pictorial Center); *Bonus Army Riots in Washington, D.C., July 1932* (Universal and Paramount Newsreels); *Crusade in the Pacific: The Surrender and Occupation of Japan* (March of Time TV); *Surrender of Japan* (Movietone News); *Journey's End: Farewell, General MacArthur* (U.S. Army); *Korea's Tribute to General MacArthur* and *Korea's Friend: General Douglas MacArthur* (National Film Production Center, Republic of Korea); *Outcry of the Korean Race* (Korean Independence Producing Corp.); *General of the Army Douglas MacArthur 1880-1964* (General Douglas MacArthur Foundation); *The Old Soldier: Duty-Honor-Country* (Hearst Metrotone News, 1964); *General MacArthur's Departure from Japan* (U.S. Army Colonel Neiswender); *New York City's Parade for General MacArthur* (photographer unknown); *General MacArthur's Arrival in San Francisco* (Richfield Television Corp., 1951); *General MacArthur's Speech Before Congress* (NBC, 65 min.); *President Syngman Rhee's Arrival in Tokyo, Japan* (photographer unknown, color); *Tokyo 1945-1951* (Tokyo Metropolitan Office); and *Inside Occupied Japan* (Robert Carlisle, color, 60 min.).
Size & Elements: Film: 35mm (2 titles); 16mm (40 titles); 8mm (3 titles) (positives, originals and release prints). Videotape: 3/4" (amount unspecified; masters and viewing copies); VHS (33 titles; masters and viewing copies);

Betamax (2 titles; masters and viewing copies).
Cataloging: Printed list; descriptive inventory of collection.
Access: Open to researchers, scholars and the public. For in-house use only. Research fees not charged. Research requests accepted by mail, telephone and in person (walk-in).
Rights: Full rights held to some material. Rights to some material retained by original producers. Additional clearances may be necessary in some cases if material is to be duplicated or reused.
Licensing: Apply for information. Films can be duplicated (at cost) with written permission of copyright owner, if any. License and usage fees charged.
Restrictions: Duplication and reuse subject to permission of copyright owner, if any.
Viewing Facilities: Film; videotape (VHS).
Duplication Facilities: None.

VIRGINIA (Quantico)

MULTI-MEDIA PRE-ACCESSION POINT
CG MCCDC
Training and Education Center
Code TE32TSP
Quantico, VA 22134-5001
(703) 640-3373

John Willever (Multi-Media Specialist)

Contacts: John Willever; Ted Patton (Multi-Media Specialist)
Services: Government agency. Film and videotape collection available to the public for reuse, subject to restrictions.
Description: U.S. Marine Corps footage (pre-1956).

The MMPAP is charged with screening and evaluating material prior to its inclusion in the U.S. Department of Defense Motion Media Records Center (q.v.) at Norton AFB, Calif. All Marine Corps footage (1956-present) is held at Norton in master or original form; some recent material is held in duplicate form at MMPAP (see below). All pre-1956 Marine Corps footage is, however, held at MMPAP after its deaccessioning by the National Archives.

Collection includes footage from the World War II period (including a substantial amount of material from the Pacific Campaign); Korean War; Marine Corps involvement in Grenada, Lebanon and Vietnam; combat maneuvers, peacetime maneuvers; ceremonies and personalities. Also available is original coverage, on VHS videotape, of events such as Liberty Weekend in New York City.
Size & Elements: Film: 35mm (2,000 rolls; currently inaccessible); 16mm (2,000 rolls). Videotape: 3/4" (small amount; transfers from film); VHS (small amount; masters).
Cataloging: Card catalogs; research library.
Access: Available to the public for reuse. Research fees not charged. Research requests accepted by mail and telephone. Due to limited staffing, outside researchers are requested to do own research at MMPAP, using index cards there and cross-referenced index, still located at the National Archives and Records Administration (q.v.). Only 16mm film is accessible at this time.
Rights: Material in the public domain.
Licensing: Available for reuse, subject to restrictions. Usage fees not charged (duplication fees charged).
Restrictions: All requests subject to approval by the Marine Corps Public Affairs Office (see U.S. Department of Defense, Motion Media Records Center). 35mm material currently inaccessible.
Viewing Facilities: Film (16mm); videotape (3/4" and VHS).
Duplication Facilities: None.

VIRGINIA (Reston)

AMERICAN ALLIANCE FOR HEALTH, PHYSICAL EDUCATION, RECREATION AND DANCE ARCHIVES
and
BRICK INSTITUTE OF AMERICA
and
COUNCIL FOR EXCEPTIONAL CHILDREN
and
FUTURE HOMEMAKERS OF AMERICA, INC.
and
NATIONAL ASSOCIATION FOR SPORT & PHYSICAL EDUCATION
and
NATIONAL ASSOCIATION OF SECONDARY SCHOOL PRINCIPALS
and

NATIONAL DANCE ASSOCIATION
See **DISTRICT OF COLUMBIA METRO**

VIRGINIA (Richmond)

GROSVENOR USA
8503 Patterson Avenue, Suite 10
Richmond, VA 23229
(804) 741-7129

J. Terence Blair (Director)

Contact: J. Terence Blair
Services: Political and religious organization. Film and videotape available primarily for distribution.
Description: The ideas and activities of the Moral Re-Armament movement (1937-present).
Documentaries. Titles include: *Dawn in Zimbabwe/The Future We Long For,* on reconciliation within and between the races in this southern African country as it emerged from civil war to independence; *The Courage to Change,* stories of people, Black and White, in Richmond, Virginia, who have pioneered a new approach to building a united community; *Les Dennison,* an interview with the militant Marxist shop steward from Coventry, England, who, accepting a challenge to listen to his inner voice, found a more fundamental revolution; *A Man for All People,* on the life of Dr. William Nkomo, first Black doctor in Johannesburg and great leader of his people; and *One Word of Truth,* a film dramatization of Alexander Solzhenitsyn's Nobel Prize lecture. Other documentaries cover Moral Re-Armament themes. Other related films cover: Irene Laure, French resistance leader and Secretary General of the Socialist Women in France; an inner city school in northern England; and South African farmers.
Features. Titles include: *Freedom,* written by Africans and shot in Nigeria, dealing with political jealousies, ideological intrigue, and the motives driving men who shape the future of the continent; *Men of Brazil,* a true story of how peace and democracy came to one of the toughest waterfronts in the world, reenacted by the port workers of Rio de Janeiro and their families, expressing the hopes and longings of the ordinary people of Latin America; and *Poor Man Rich Man* asking how St. Francis of Assisi would have lived in and coped with today's world?
As We Want the World to Live. Half-hour community access cable television interviews by Michael Henderson, exploring what Moral Re-Armament means to men and women in many walks of life.
Size & Elements: Film: 16mm (approx. 50 titles). Videotape: VHS (approx. 80 titles).
Cataloging: Published catalog.
Access: Available to the public for rental and purchase. Rental fees charged. Requests accepted by mail and telephone.
Rights: Full rights held to all material.
Licensing: Apply for information.
Restrictions: Restrictions may apply depending on use, requests subject to approval.
Viewing Facilities: None.
Duplication Facilities: None.

VIRGINIA (Richmond)

VIRGINIA DIVISION OF TOURISM
202 North Ninth Street, Suite 500
Richmond, VA 23219
(804) 786-2051
Fax: (804) 786-1919
Telex: 828323

Patrick A. McMahon (Director)

Contact: Pamela Jewell (Audiovisual Services Manager)
Services: Government agency. Films and videotapes available for free loan to qualified organizations and the media. Research requests not accepted.
Description: Travel in Virginia. Films feature historic attractions, natural wonders, scenic beauty, lifestyles and recreational opportunities.
Titles include: *George Mason: Conservative Revolutionary; George Washington's Mount Vernon; Luray Caverns in Virginia's Shenandoah Valley; Norfolk-By-The-Sea; The Old Country: This Side of the Atlantic; The Virginia Peninsula: Virginia's New Vacationland; Music of Williamsburg; Voyage of the Godspeed;* and *The Parkway Promise.*

Size & Elements: Film: 16mm (20 titles). Videotape: 3/4" and VHS (13 titles).
Cataloging: Published catalog.
Access: Maintained for free loan to organizations in the travel industry, adult groups and broadcast media organizations. Research requests not accepted.
Rights: Full rights held to some material. Additional clearances from individual sponsors will be necessary in some cases if material is to be reused.
Licensing: Apply for information.
Restrictions: To duplicate specific footage, sponsor must be contacted. Films and videotapes generally not available for commercial reuse or excerpting.
Viewing Facilities: None.
Duplication Facilities: None.

VIRGINIA (Rosslyn)

INTER-AMERICAN FOUNDATION
See **DISTRICT OF COLUMBIA METRO**

VIRGINIA (Stafford)

AMERICAN LIFE LEAGUE
P.O. Box 1350
Stafford, VA 22554
(703) 659-4171
Fax: (703) 659-2586

Street address: 188 Onville Road

Judith A. Brown (President)

Contacts: Scarlett Clark (Office Manager); James F. Kappus (Vice President)
Services: Association; videotape producer. Videotape material available for reuse, subject to restrictions.
Description: Collection focuses on "life issues," such as abortion, euthanasia, school-based clinics and newborn "at risk" cases (e.g., "Baby Doe" cases).
Historical. Television coverage of pro-life and pro-family events; television news and talk show interviews with pro-life personalities.
In production. Series of four to six new productions on the American Life League and individual pro-life issues. The first series pertains to school-based health and birth control clinics.
Size & Elements: Videotape: 1", 3/4", VHS and Betamax (amount unspecified).
Cataloging: None specified.
Access: Available for reuse by permission only. Research fees charged (cost recovery only). Research requests accepted by mail.
Rights: Full rights held to some material.
Licensing: Apply for information. License fees charged for commercial use.
Restrictions: Requests for reuse subject to acceptance and approval.
Viewing Facilities: Videotape (limited).
Duplication Facilities: None.

VIRGINIA (Staunton)

WOODROW WILSON BIRTHPLACE FOUNDATION, INC.
P.O. Box 24
Staunton, VA 24401
(703) 885-0897

Street address: 20 North Coalter Street

Dr. Katharine L. Brown (Executive Director)

Contact: Dr. Katharine L. Brown
Services: Museum. Film collection open to researchers and scholars only.
Description: Holds a small research collection of films on the life and times of Woodrow Wilson.
Size & Elements: Film: format unspecified (5 titles, 10 cans; positives).
Cataloging: Card catalog.
Access: Open to researchers and scholars only. For in-house use only. Research requests accepted by mail, telephone and in person (by appointment only).
Rights: Apply for information.
Licensing: Apply for information.
Restrictions: None specified.
Viewing Facilities: Film can be screened in museum auditorium.
Duplication Facilities: None.

VIRGINIA (Virginia Beach)

CBN PUBLISHING
CBN Center
Virginia Beach, VA 23463
(804) 424-7777

Peter Bradley (President)

Contact: George Lutz (Product Development Manager)
Services: Film and videotape producer. Films available for purchase.
Description: Films on religious topics, produced by the publishing division of the Christian Broadcasting Network (CBN). Available items include: the *Operation Good Shepherd* series on prayer, Bible study, and faith, including lessons by Pat Robertson; animated Bible stories for children, including the *Flying House* and *Superbook* series, in which "children of all ages will enjoy traveling back to Biblical times with the animated characters of Chris, Joy and their toy robot, Gizmo"; and an *Alternative Creation/Life Science* series for children.
Size & Elements: Videotape: format unspecified (4 program series).
Cataloging: Published catalogs available.
Access: Videotapes available for purchase.
Rights: Full rights held to all material.
Licensing: Not available for licensing or reuse.
Restrictions: Not available for licensing or reuse.
Viewing Facilities: None.
Duplication Facilities: None.

VIRGINIA (Williamsburg)

METRO COMMUNICATIONS, INC.
P.O. Box FL
Williamsburg, VA 23187
(804) 253-0050
Fax: (804) 253-8558

Street address: 424 Duke of Gloucester Street

J. Scott Wheeler (President)
Lizabeth A. Rutgers (Vice President)

Contacts: Ruth Twiggs; Bill Wagner; Lizabeth A. Rutgers; J. Scott Wheeler
Services: Videotape producer; stock footage sales library.
Description: Footage includes: recreation, including tennis, golf, bike riding, pool, swimming and surfing; nature (flowers, hills, sunrise, deer and squirrels); lifestyles, including parties, relaxing on decks, sailing, yachting, eating in restaurants, at home and bringing in mail; light industry, including manufacturing of boxes, plastic cups and auto assembly; technology (computers and space); aerials of Virginia, and North Carolina; products (still life, with minimal human interaction); entertainment, including music, dance and drama; medicine (operations and seeing patients); science (lab work and field testing); military (aircraft, personnel and weapons); business management, including meetings, conferences and working at desks; education (classroom environment); tourism, including Colonial Williamsburg, Busch Gardens, Water Country, Yorktown, Jamestown, Virginia Beach, Monticello, Outer Banks of North Carolina, Wright Brothers, lighthouses, boats, sailing and fishing; and architecture (exteriors of buildings, interiors of spaces).
Size & Elements: Videotape (format and amount unspecified).
Cataloging: Computerized cataloging for staff use only.
Access: Available to the public for duplication, licensing and reuse. Research fees charged in some cases, depending on situation. Research requests accepted by mail and telephone.
Rights: Full rights held to some material.
Licensing: Available for licensing and reuse, subject to restrictions. License and usage fees charged.
Restrictions: Restrictions to be determined (apply for information).
Viewing Facilities: Videotape.
Duplication Facilities: Videotape.

WASHINGTON

WASHINGTON (Bellingham)

CENTER FOR PACIFIC NORTHWEST STUDIES

WESTERN WASHINGTON UNIVERSITY
Bellingham, WA 98225
(206) 676-3125
(206) 647-4776

Dr. James W. Scott (Director)

Contacts: Dr. James W. Scott (206/647-4776); James D. Moore (Regional State Archivist) (206/676-3125)
Services: University research center. Film collection open to the public; for in-house use only.
Description: Holds collection of 16mm films presented to the Center by KVOS Television (Bellingham, Wash.). The collection is exclusively documentary film covering many local and regional topics of political, economic and cultural interest (1960s-early 1970s). Topics relate to northwest Washington State and the Lower Mainland of British Columbia (1960s-early 1970s). Many of the films were prepared by Jack Webster of Vancouver, B.C. and Al Swift, then Public Affairs Director at KVOS, now a U.S. Congressman.
Titles include: *The Operators; Pension for a Hero; A Case of Terror; Yanks and Canadian Labor; North Pacific Salmon Treaty; Case of Bogus Barrister; Where is David Loveday?; Profile of Billy James Hargis; Wot! No Fingerprints; Uncomfortable Pew — Berton/Green; Mohawk Princess; This Hour Has 30 Minutes; Rebel in Kilts — Farley Mort; Snob Mob; Girls, Glitter & Gracie; God, Allah and Ju Ju; Castro Revisited; The First R; Potpourri: Bells & Whidbey Naval Station; Color of Black: Farmer; Place Called Home; Bellingham Technical School; He Would Be Dead Now* (outtakes); *Junk Mail; Western's Fourth R; Century 21 Interviews; European Common Market and You; Alaska Earthquake; Mr. Justice Douglas; World of Dick Gregory; Julian Bond Interview;* and *Christmas Concert — Sehome High.*
Size & Elements: Film: 16mm (69 titles, most 15 to 30 min. in length; positive).
Cataloging: Finding aids (inventory).
Access: Open to the public. For in-house use only. Research fees not charged. Research requests accepted by mail, telephone and in person (by appointment only).
Rights: Full rights held to all material.
Licensing: Available for licensing. License fees not charged.
Restrictions: None specified.
Viewing Facilities: Film (available on campus by arrangement).
Duplication Facilities: None.

WASHINGTON (Everett)

EVERETT PUBLIC LIBRARY
NORTHWEST HISTORY COLLECTION
2702 Hoyt
Everett, WA 98201
(206) 259-8857

Contacts: David Dilgard (Regional History Specialist); Margaret Riddle (Regional History Specialist)
Services: Library. Historical collection containing film footage. Open to the public.
Description: Pacific Northwest history, labor history, logging industry, plywood mills and home movies.
Specific footage includes: Everett Labor Day Parade (1916) preceding waterfront violence (original footage held by American Film Institute); Puget Sound powder plant explosion (1930); Robinson Manufacturing Company footage of labor violence, county fairs, and home movies (1930s, shot by Tom Robinson); footage of Coach Enoch Bagshaw, who took the University of Washington football team to the Rose Bowl; home movies of Governor Roland Hartley welcoming Queen Marie of Romania with Sam Hill (1926); University of Washington football (1926); *Life in Everett* (1946, color), a promotional film; Everett Parks Department footage (4 reels, black and white) containing WPA footage of the building of Legion Park (1930s) and footage of Park development (1930s-50s).
Size & Elements: Film: 35mm and 16mm (amount unspecified).
Cataloging: None specified.
Access: Open to the public. Research requests accepted by mail and telephone.
Rights: Full rights held to some material.
Licensing: Apply for information. License fees not charged.
Restrictions: None specified.
Viewing Facilities: Film.
Duplication Facilities: None (outside arrangements can be made).

WASHINGTON (Olympia)

WASHINGTON STATE ARCHIVES
P.O. Box 9000
Olympia, WA 98504
(206) 586-1492

Street address: 12th and Washington Streets

Sidney F. McAlpin (State Archivist)

Contact: David W. Hastings (Chief of Archives)
Services: State government agency and archives. Film collection open to the public.
Description: Promotional films for Washington State, containing scenic views of the state (1960s), including *Washington Wonderland;* governors' speeches (1960s-70s); and training films for government employees (1960s-70s).
Size & Elements: Film: 16mm (100 titles, 100 cans; release prints).
Cataloging: Computerized cataloging available to researchers. Complete inventory not available until spring 1989.
Access: Available to the public. Research fees charged (per hour). Research requests accepted by mail, telephone and in person (walk-in).
Rights: Material in the public domain.
Licensing: Apply for information. Usage fees not charged.
Restrictions: None specified.
Viewing Facilities: Film.
Duplication Facilities: None.

WASHINGTON (Richland)

VTR PRODUCTIONS
1780 Fowler, Suite A
Richland, WA 99352
(509) 783-5426

Gary Kuster (President)

Contact: Dean Martin (Production Manager)
Services: Videotape producer. Footage available to the public for duplication, licensing and reuse, subject to restrictions.
Description: Agriculture and industry of southeastern Washington State. Agricultural material includes the harvesting, planting and processing of cherries, peaches, pears, potatoes, peas, wheat and various other crops. Industrial and manufacturing footage includes generic shots of welding and parts-making.
Size & Elements: Videotape: 3/4" (approx. 12 hours; masters). Viewing copies and copies with visible time code can be made.
Cataloging: Shot lists (indexed).
Access: Available to the public for duplication and reuse by application only (negotiable).
Rights: Full rights held to some material. Some rights held to all material.
Licensing: Available for licensing, subject to restrictions. License fees charged.
Restrictions: All requests for licensing and reuse must be made by application and will be considered on a case-by-case basis.
Viewing Facilities: Videotape (3/4" and VHS).
Duplication Facilities: Videotape.

WASHINGTON (Seattle)

AMERICAN MOTION PICTURES
7023 15th Avenue Northwest
Seattle, WA 98117
(206) 789-8273
Fax: (206) 782-0551

Conrad W. Denke (President)

Contact: Angela Hendee (Stock Footage Librarian)
Services: Videotape stock footage sales library. Undertakes custom shooting assignments; research services and video post-production facility also available.
Description: Videotape footage from many producers and camerapeople in the Northwestern United States.
Collection includes: airplanes, animals, antique automobiles, autumn, Ballard Locks, Bangor (Trident nuclear) submarine base, baseball, bears, bicycle races, bicycle riding, birds, Blue Angels (U.S. Navy precision flight team), buck, bullhorn sheep, chain saw contests, Chief Sealth's grave, discus throwing, elderly group playing instruments, elk, esquire horses, fall foliage, farms, ferries, flowers, goats, Golden Gardens Park, Green Lake, hang-gliding, high jump, high-school bands, high-school football, hockey, hurdles, hydroplane crowds, Indians, javelin throwing, joggers, Lake Crescent, logging festival, loons, marathon runners, military vessels, milk carton battleships, the moon, moose, Mt. Rainier (Washington), NOAA boats, Olympic mountains, Oregon Coast, owls, parades, pigeons, Pike Place Market (Seattle), Port of Seattle, Puget Sound, racquetball, rivers, rodeo, roller-skating, sailboats, San Juan Islands (Washington), Scandinavian festival, sea gulls, seals, Seattle harbor tour boats, Seattle skyline, Seattle Space Needle, Seattle waterfront, Silverdale parade, skiing, skin divers, Snoqualmie Falls (Washington), sports, sunsets (foggy and clear), Suquamish Indians, swimming, Tacoma (Washington) Grand Prix, tennis, track, traffic, trains, tugboats, U.S. Marines, U.S.S. Missouri, U.S.S. Ohio, walkers, Washington State Capitol (Olympia), water, waterfalls, weight lifters and windsurfers.

Represents footage from the following sources: *East/West Pictures* (skiing); *Video Tech* (sports); *Sharp Hartwig* (Port of Seattle); *Brian Moratti* (sailboats, Ballard Locks); *High Sierra Productions* (wildlife, Oregon Coast, Snoqualmie Falls, train, antique cars); *John Fluke Manufacturing* (electronics); *Dan Gadd, Photographer* (Seattle sights, Columbia Center); *Stillwater Productions* (animals); *Alaska Video Productions* (Alaska scenery, fishing, bears); *Pacific Communications* (Washington state capitol building, Puget Sound); *Media Arts Marine Enterprises* (skin divers); *Videocast* (Golden Hinde ship, packaging company); *Tacoma Municipal Television* (Tacoma Grand Prix); *Dave Gray Productions* (autumn, flowers).
Size & Elements: Videotape: 1" (masters); 3/4" (time-coded viewing copies) (amount unspecified).
Cataloging: Shot lists and logs available for some material; computerized cataloging for staff use only.
Access: Research fees charged. Research requests accepted by mail, telephone and in person (walk-in and by appointment). Demonstration videotapes (with visible time code) can be compiled at a charge for customers who cannot come to office to view material.
Rights: Holds non-exclusive rights to sell all material in library.
Licensing: Available for licensing and reuse. Library usage fees charged depending on intended market of production. Footage from AMP in-house stock library (not from outside producers) available at special discounted per-shot rate for AMP editing customers only.
Restrictions: All material available for reuse unless specifically restricted by original producer.
Viewing Facilities: Videotape (3/4" edit suite).
Duplication Facilities: Videotape.

WASHINGTON (Seattle)

BOEING HISTORICAL ARCHIVES
Boeing 1R-24
P.O. Box 3707
Seattle, WA 98124-2207
(206) 655-4586

Street address: 7755 East Marginal Way South, Seattle, WA 98108

Dr. Paul G. Spitzer (Corporate Historian)

Contact: Marilyn Phipps
Services: Corporation; corporate archives. *Not open to the public at this time. Currently being processed for preservation and not available for viewing.*
Description: Films (post-World War II) of The Boeing Company's products (mainly aircraft), manufacturing and facilities. Produced primarily for technical and marketing purposes.
Size & Elements: Film: format unspecified (500,000 feet, 1,000 titles, 1,000 cans). Videotape: VHS (30 videotapes).
Cataloging: Finding aids (list by title).
Access: Not open to the public. Presently maintained for preservation purposes only. Research requests not accepted at this time.
Rights: Full rights held to all material.
Licensing: Not available at this time.
Restrictions: Material is currently not available for viewing or reuse.
Viewing Facilities: Film editing facility (viewing not available at this time).
Duplication Facilities: Available in-house (not located in Archives).

WASHINGTON (Seattle)

HISTORICAL SOCIETY OF SEATTLE AND KING COUNTY
SOPHIE FRYE BASS COLLECTION OF NORTHWEST AMERICANA
MUSEUM OF HISTORY AND INDUSTRY
2700 24th Avenue East
Seattle, WA 98112
(206) 324-1125

Rick Caldwell (Librarian)

Contact: Rick Caldwell
Services: Historical society. Film collection for in-house use only (limited access).
Description: Home movies from Seattle and the Northwest (1920s-40s); footage of the Century 21 World's Fair (1962), produced by the Fair's Public Relations Department; and "a few dozen" videotapes of oral histories (interviews with business and labor leaders). Pending funding, plans are to transfer films to videotape.
Size & Elements: Film: 35mm and 16mm ("a drawerful"). Videotape: assorted formats (amount unspecified).
Cataloging: Printed inventory.
Access: Open to the public. For in-house use only. Most of the films are in fragile condition. All requests for access are considered on an individual basis. Films are available for viewing only in videotape form; in order to view any films, researcher must pay cost of having film transferred to videotape at an outside facility. The videotape transfer becomes the property of the Society and can only be viewed in-house. Research fees not charged. Research requests accepted by mail and telephone.
Rights: Full rights held to all material.
Licensing: Available for licensing, subject to restrictions. License fees generally not charged.
Restrictions: Requests for licensing and reuse subject to acceptance and approval.
Viewing Facilities: Videotape.
Duplication Facilities: None.

WASHINGTON (Seattle)

STEVE MARTS PRODUCTIONS
6345 39th Avenue, SW
Seattle, WA 98136
(206) 932-6490

Contacts: Steve Marts; Sally Marts
Services: Cinematographer; stock footage sales library. Material available for duplication, licensing and reuse through authorized representative.
Description: Footage of mountainscapes and climbing; rural America; oceanscapes and coastline; logging (6,000 feet); giant suns (300mm to 1300mm); moons (crescent to full, with or without clouds, and time-lapse); harvesting combines; Oregon waterfalls; Japan (rural and urban, seascapes, misty mountains, temples and shrines; 21 rolls).
   Also holds approximately nine completed films. Titles include: *Fair Weather; Reckon With The Wind* (sailing); *Man of Wheat; Land of Gold;* and *Spoke Song.*
Size & Elements: Film: 16mm (amount unspecified; negative held by Steve Marts, workprints available through Film Search, Inc.).
Cataloging: Staff assistance required.
Access: Available to the public (locally). Available for duplication and reuse. Research requests accepted by mail and telephone.
Rights: Full rights held to all material.
Licensing: Available for licensing in the Northwest United States. Film Search, Inc. represents library for stock footage sales elsewhere. License fees charged.
Restrictions: Talent releases not available for some material.
Viewing Facilities: None.
Duplication Facilities: None (outside arrangements can be made).
Representative: Film Search, Inc. (q.v.).

WASHINGTON (Seattle)

911 CONTEMPORARY ARTS CENTER
1331 3rd Avenue, Suite 518
Seattle, WA 98101
(206) 682-6552

Susan Sagawa (Director)

Contact: Alan Pruzan (Media Arts Director)
Services: Media arts organization. Videotape collection open to the public for research and viewing.
Description: Video artworks and documentaries, with special emphasis on work by Northwest (mainly Seattle) videomakers.
   Artists featured in collection include: Vito Acconci, Michael Agat, Jane Alsen, Judy Altman, John Anderson, Ant Farm, Jules Backus, Rachael Brumer, Barbara Buckner, Ralph Busch, Peter Campus, Bruce Cannon, Peggy Case, Carl Chew, Sheryl Clark, Sally J. Cloniger, Kate Craig, Susan Davis, Randy Day, Paul Dougherty, Louise Durkee, Mark Dworkin, Bradley Eros, Sandra Eshleman, Kit Fitzgerald, Howard Fried, David Gigliotti, Pat Graney, Vanalyne Green, Guy Guillet, Randy Hayes, Gary Hill, Kathleen Hunt, Joan Jonas, Diane Katsiaficas, David P. Kerr, Kinetics Co., Mitchell Kriegman, Tony Labat, Alan Lande, Mark Larson, Ken LeBack, Paul Lenti, Christa Maiwald, Pier Marton, Bebe Miller, Heather Oaksen, Dennis Oppenheimer, Seth Otth, Tony Oursler, Nam June Paik, Bev Rackoff, Bill Ritchie, Willard Rosenquist, Nori Sato, Ilene Segalove, Maury Sheridan, Barbara Smith, J. B. Smith, Sue Stewart, John Sturgeon, Christin Swenson, Suzanne Tedesko, Steina and Woody Vasulka, Bill Viola, William Wegman, Erik Whimyre, Robin White and Lory Wilson.
Size & Elements: Videotape: 3/4" (190 videotapes); VHS (15 videotapes; viewing copies).
Cataloging: Published catalog.
Access: Open to the public. Research fees not charged. Research requests accepted in person (by appointment only).
Rights: Most rights retained by artists.
Licensing: Apply for information.
Restrictions: Apply for information.
Viewing Facilities: Videotape (editing suite).
Duplication Facilities: None.

WASHINGTON (Seattle)

NORDIC HERITAGE MUSEUM
3014 Northwest 67th Street
Seattle, WA 98117
(206) 789-5707

Marianne Forssblad (Director)

Contacts: Marianne Forssblad; Janet Baisinger (Curator)
Services: Museum. Moving image collection available to the public.
Description: Small collection relating to Nordic history. *Creative Finn* shows Finnish life in greater Seattle (1920s-present). Also available is pre-1920 footage of the Norwegian *Syttende Mai* (Constitution Day) parade.
Size & Elements: Formats unspecified (2 items total).
Cataloging: None specified.
Access: Research requests accepted in person (by appointment only).
Rights: Full rights held to all material.
Licensing: Apply for information.
Restrictions: None specified.
Viewing Facilities: None.
Duplication Facilities: None.

WASHINGTON (Seattle)

OFFSHORE PRODUCTIONS
617 East Thomas Street
Seattle, WA 98102
(206) 323-3040
Telex: 499 6860 OFFPROD

Dick Enersen (President and Founder)

Contact: Dick Enersen
Services: Film and videotape producer and distributor. Material available for licensing and reuse.
Description: Formed after the 1970 America's Cup race, Offshore has since been producing and distributing films and videotapes on maritime subjects, including sailing, racing, cruising grounds, the America's Cup and Olympic sailing.
   Sample titles include: *America's Cup '77,* highlights of the 1977 America's Cup in Newport; *Big Boats,* five "maxis" racing on San Francisco Bay; *The*

Congressional Cup, its history from the perspective of the 20th Anniversary regatta; *Freedom* (1980), a sailor's eye view of the 1980 America's Cup summer; *Gleam,* a restored prewar 12-meter yacht; *The Star Class,* the history of the International Star Class; and *Wavesailing Women,* outstanding sailboarders jumping waves in Hawaii.
Size & Elements: Film: 16mm (150,000 feet; color negative). Videotape: 1", 3/4" and VHS. (Approx. 100 titles total.)
Cataloging: Published catalogs.
Access: Open to researchers, scholars and the public. Available for licensing and reuse. Research fees not charged. Research requests accepted by mail and telephone.
Rights: Full rights held to all material. Additional clearances may be necessary in some cases if material is to be reused.
Licensing: Available for licensing and reuse, subject to restrictions. License and usage fees charged (fees vary with intended use; negotiable).
Restrictions: Requests for licensing and reuse considered on a case-by-case basis.
Viewing Facilities: Film and videotape.
Duplication Facilities: Videotape (3/4" and VHS).

WASHINGTON (Seattle)

PAINT BOX BACKGROUNDS
1921 Minor
Seattle, WA 98101
(206) 623-3444
Fax: (206) 340-1548

Mike Daigle (President)

Contacts: Ron Randall; Terri Williams
Services: Production facility. Videotape collection available to the public for licensing and reuse.
Description: Compilation of Quantel Paint Box backgrounds intended for use in titles and related bumpers. The collection is strong in patterns that can be used to echo certain themes, such as textures, paint spatters, lines, patterns, mosaics, and limited themes.
Size & Elements: Videotape: 1", 3/4" and Betamax (180 titles; masters and viewing copies).
Cataloging: None specified.
Access: Available to the public for reuse.
Rights: Full rights held to all material.
Licensing: Available for licensing. License fees charged.
Restrictions: None specified.
Viewing Facilities: Videotape.
Duplication Facilities: None.

WASHINGTON (Seattle)

RATIONAL ISLAND PUBLISHERS
P.O. Box 2081, Main Office Station
Seattle, WA 98111
(206) 284-0311

Street address: 719 Second Avenue North, Seattle WA 98109

Gordon Jackins (President)

Contacts: Katie Kauffman (Editor); Ann Steele (Editor)
Services: Corporation; corporate archives. Videotape collection maintained for distribution and rental rather than for research or reuse.
Description: "Re-evaluation Counseling views all human beings as inherently intelligent and good. It assumes that it is natural for a human to think well, to act wisely and successfully, to enjoy life and to have good relations with other humans."
Materials concern the theory and practice of Re-evaluation Counseling, talks and demonstrations. Videotapes cover a wide range of topics and emotional climates. Sample titles include: *A Jewish Commitment Against Isolation; The Human Side of Human Beings: An Introduction to Re-evaluation Counseling; How Parents Can Counsel Their Children; Discharging the Patterns of White Racism; Counseling on Sexist Oppression; A Rational Policy on Sexuality; Counseling on the Patterns of Homosexual Oppression; Counseling on Physical Hurts;* and *The Oppression of Physically Different Peoples.*
Size & Elements: Videotape: VHS and Betamax (25 titles; NTSC, PAL, and

SECAM; 13 in color, 12 in black and white).
Cataloging: Published catalogs.
Access: Open to the public. Maintained for distribution and rental rather than for research or reuse.
Rights: Full rights held to all material.
Licensing: Apply for information.
Restrictions: None specified.
Viewing Facilities: None.
Duplication Facilities: None.

WASHINGTON (Seattle)

SEATTLE PUBLIC LIBRARY
MEDIA AND PROGRAM SERVICES DEPARTMENT
1000 4th Avenue
Seattle, WA 98104
(206) 386-4636

Ray Serebrin (Managing Librarian)

Contacts: Ruth Webb (Librarian); Library staff
Services: Library. Film and videotape collection open to library cardholders.
Description: Holds a large collection of commercially acquired materials of general interest.
Also holds approx. 10 to 15 films and 30 to 40 videotapes made by local producers. Items include: *What Is This Thing Called Sludge?* and a videotape on backyard water (both by Seattle METRO); *Seattle Moves the Mountains* and *Picture of a Young City* (both by the Seattle Engineering Department); a film on the making of the Seattle Space Needle; other locally produced items on local issues; experimental and artistic materials.
Size & Elements: Film: 16mm (1,700 titles; release prints). Videotape: VHS (4,450 videotapes; viewing copies); Betamax (50 videotapes; viewing copies).
Cataloging: Published catalog (available for purchase); computerized cataloging available to researchers; other finding aids.
Access: Open to the public. Access to library materials available only to those holding Seattle Public Library cards. Research fees not charged. Research requests accepted by telephone and in person (walk-in).
Rights: Some rights held to some material. Additional clearances are necessary if material is to be reused.
Licensing: Apply for information. Can direct requester to original producer when information is available.
Restrictions: All requests for licensing and reuse subject to additional clearances.
Viewing Facilities: Videotape (3 carrels).
Duplication Facilities: None.

WASHINGTON (Seattle)

TELEMATION PRODUCTIONS
1200 Stewart Street
Seattle, WA 98101
(206) 623-5934
Fax: (206) 682-0353

Jim Hartzer (President)
Lance Kyde (General Manager)

Contacts: Lance Kyde; Claudia Mirchel (Seattle-King County Convention and Visitors Bureau; Seattle Information) (contact for *Washington State Location Reel*)
Services: Videotape producer. Some footage available to the public for duplication and reuse.
Description: *Washington State Location Reel* (5 min.; index reel 22 min.). Comprises scenic footage showing locations throughout Washington state, including rain forests; beaches; desert (Eastern Washington); mountains; and cityscapes, including Seattle. Footage for the *Location Reel* was collected from independent producers around the state.
Also holds material relating to the city of Seattle, including scenics, skylines and the Space Needle.
Size & Elements: Videotape: 1" (amount unspecified; masters); 3/4" and VHS (viewing copies).
Cataloging: Shots are numbered and indexed on index reel.
Access: Seattle footage available to the public for duplication and reuse. *Washington State Location Reel* is available to location scouts and researchers only. Research fees not charged. Research requests accepted by mail and

telephone.

Rights: Full rights held to all Seattle material. For information regarding reuse of footage contained on *Washington State Location Reel*, contact Claudia Mirchel.

Licensing: Some material available for licensing and reuse. License fees charged.

Restrictions: Apply for information.

Viewing Facilities: Videotape.

Duplication Facilities: Videotape.

WASHINGTON (Seattle)

UNIVERSITY OF WASHINGTON
EDUCATIONAL MEDIA COLLECTION
INSTRUCTIONAL MEDIA SERVICES
DG-10
23 Kane Hall
Seattle, WA 98195
(206) 543-9906

Leon W. Hevly (Director)

Contacts: Mary E. Nelson (Manager, Educational Media Collection); L. Donald Bartholomew (Reference and Cataloging)

Services: University media center. One film available for purchase.

Description: *The Tacoma Narrows Bridge Failure* (1964, revised 1988, 22 min., color), filmed by F. B. Farquharson, Professor of Civil Engineering and Director of the Engineering Department Station, University of Washington. The Tacoma Narrows Bridge was opened to traffic on July 1, 1940 and collapsed in a storm under the action of a wind of approximately 42 mph on November 7, 1940. The film presents footage showing construction and opening day ceremonies. During the four months of active life of this structure, it was under constant observation and motion pictures were taken to document the various modes of motion. Extensive footage, color and black and white, shows the collapse of the bridge from different angles. Experiments with a three-dimensional dynamic model conducted by the Structural Research Laboratory, Civil Engineering Department, University of Washington are shown. The experiments demonstrate the same erratic motions found in the span.

Size & Elements: Film: 16mm (1 title; release prints). Videotape: 3/4" and VHS (viewing copies).

Cataloging: Printed description.

Access: Available for purchase. Research requests accepted by mail and telephone.

Rights: Some rights held to material. Additional clearances may be necessary if material is to be reused.

Licensing: Apply for information.

Restrictions: Apply for information.

Viewing Facilities: None.

Duplication Facilities: None.

WASHINGTON (Seattle)

UNIVERSITY OF WASHINGTON PRESS
MULTIMEDIA DIVISION
P.O. Box 50096
Seattle, WA 98145-5096
(206) 543-4050
Fax: (206) 543-3932

Street address: 4045 Brooklyn Avenue NE, Seattle, WA 98105

Donald R. Ellegood (Director)

Contact: Juanita B. Pike (Multimedia Division Manager)

Services: University film and videotape producer and distributor. Material available for duplication and licensing, subject to restrictions.

Description: Materials cover such subject areas as the health sciences, anthropology, archaeology, ethnomusicology, music and glaciology.

Highlights include: *Avalanche Dynamics*, illustrating dry snow avalanches in motion; *The Kwakiutl of British Columbia*, a documentary by Franz Boas made during the winter of 1930-31 at Fort Rupert on Vancouver Island, which includes scenes depicting traditional dances, crafts, games, oratory and the actions of a shaman; and *In the Land of the War Canoes*, a saga of Kwakiutl Indian life on the Northwest Coast of America, filmed by Edward Curtis in the summer of 1914 in Kwakiutl villages on Vancouver Island. This film was shown theatrically under its original title *In the Land of the Head Hunters* in Seattle and New York (1914-15) and then lapsed into obscurity.

Additional titles on science and health-related issues include: *Congenital Malformations of the Heart*, a three-part series using cinemicrography of the growing chick embryo to illustrate early development of the primitive cardiac tube; *Consequences: Spinal Cord Injury*, in which young people with spinal injuries "tell it like it is"; *Observations of Living Primordial Germ Cells in the Mouse*, in which germ cells originate in the yolk sac and migrate to the genital ridges by their own ameboid movement; and *Ovulation and Egg Transport in Mammals*, designed for use by students in biology, medicine and other health professions, illustrating the phenomena of ovulation and egg transport in the mammal using the rabbit and cat as subjects.

In *Phasemicroscopy of Normal Living Blood*, the living blood leukocytes are shown in various stages of activity from the nonmotile state, as observed immediately after the preparation is made, to the most active state of motility. *Sperm Maturation in the Male Reproductive Tract* shows the gradual attainment of motility as spermatozoa pass from the seminiferous tubules through the ductuli efferentes, the epididymis and finally enter the ductus deferens. *Wheelin' Steel* captures the action and emotion of the 25th National Wheelchair Games over five days of intense competition in track and field, weightlifting, swimming, archery, table tennis and slalom, and many other events.

Size & Elements: Film: 16mm (release prints). Videotape: 3/4" and VHS (viewing copies). (Approx. 60 titles total).

Cataloging: Published catalog.

Access: Maintained for distribution and rental rather than for research or reuse. Research requests accepted by mail and telephone.

Rights: Full rights held to some material. Some rights held to all material. Additional clearances may be necessary in some cases if material is to be reused.

Licensing: Available for licensing and reuse, subject to restrictions. License fees charged.

Restrictions: All requests for licensing and reuse subject to acceptance and approval.

Viewing Facilities: None.

Duplication Facilities: None.

WASHINGTON (Seattle)

VIDEO SHORTS
958 North Motor Place
Seattle, WA 98103
(206) 547-8530

B. Parker Lindner (Project Director)

Contact: B. Parker Lindner

Services: Video art festival. Compilations of annual winners available for rental and purchase.

Description: Seattle-based national video festival devoted solely to short works.

Video Shorts Four, a compilation of annual winners, includes: *Elephant Bath* (Tony Silvers Films); *Keyboard Dance* (Ye Sook Ree); *Emergency Exit* (Joanne Kelly); and *Pumpkin Madness* (David Gray).

Video Shorts Five. Includes: *Black/White Jokes* (Dave Kerr), traveling salesman jokes with a Zen twist; *Army Arrangement* (Dan Dinello), a musical commentary on Fela Anikulapo Kuti; *Mr. President* (Jill Kroesen), a satirical videotape on the Presidency, with animated graphic commentary; *Grass* or *When the Rain Falls On the Water Does the Fish Get Any Wetter?* (Janice Tanaka), on man's evolution from communicator to omnipotent destroyer; and *Pop Up* (Maggie Annerino), a pop culture music video based on six ethnic jump rope rhythms.

There are seven collections of *Video Shorts*, each comprised of ten short titles.

Size & Elements: Videotape: 1" (masters); 3/4", Betamax and VHS (7 collections, approx. 70 titles total; masters and viewing copies).

Cataloging: Published brochures; programs; release sheets.

Access: Available for rental and purchase.

Rights: Full rights held to some material. Additional clearances will be necessary in some cases if material is to be reused.

Licensing: Apply for information. License fees charged in most cases.

Restrictions: None specified.

Viewing Facilities: None.

Duplication Facilities: None.

WASHINGTON (Spokane)

EASTERN WASHINGTON STATE HISTORICAL SOCIETY RESEARCH LIBRARY

West 2316 First Avenue
Spokane, WA 99204
(509) 456-3931
SCAN 545-3931

Glenn Mason (Director); Doug Olson (Librarian)

Contacts: Doug Olson; Ed Nolan (Archivist)
Services: Historical society. Archival films and videotapes available for research, licensing and reuse, subject to restrictions.
Description: Newsfilm footage on the history of Spokane and the Inland Empire (30 16mm films; 20 8mm films); and 20 16mm Civil Defense films (ca. 1950-55). Television newsfilm footage includes material from Spokane ABC affiliate KXLY-TV (1967-77, approx. 100,000 feet, 604 reels, organized chronologically) and footage from Spokane CBS affiliate KREM-TV (ca. 1973-77, 5,133 feet, 33 reels; with brief descriptions of contents, sound, color, date, etc.).
Videotape collection includes material produced by KHQ-TV and others. Topics include: Expo '74; Natatorium Park; Indian peoples, including *Contrary Warriors: The Story of the Crow Tribe* and *Echoes of Yesterday*, depicting the removal of Indian graves prior to the building of Lake Roosevelt; construction of the Chronicle Building (1927); and President Jimmy Carter's trip to Spokane.
Wallace Gamble archival film footage (ca. 1940s) includes: *Heron Rapids, Passing Parade; Early Stages of Grand Coulee Dam; Spokane Early Scenery and Parades; Mt. Spokane; Last Clearwater Log Drive;* and *Glacier Park, ca. 1942*.
U.S. Dept. of Interior, Bureau of Reclamation footage includes: *Columbia Frontier; Great River; Water in the West;* and *...of Time and a River*. Also held is *Hydro: The Story of Columbia River Power* (Bonneville Power Administration).
Size & Elements: Film: 16mm (50 films, approx. 105,000 feet) and 8mm (20 films). Videotape: 3/4" (51 videotapes); VHS (14 videotapes).
Cataloging: Lists; accession records; research library.
Access: Open to the public. Archival materials for in-house use only, but duplication is permitted. Research fees not charged. Research requests accepted by mail, telephone and in person (by appointment only).
Rights: Full rights held to all material.
Licensing: Available for licensing and reuse, subject to restrictions. License fees generally not charged.
Restrictions: Requests for licensing and reuse subject to clearance and approval.
Viewing Facilities: Film and videotape.
Duplication Facilities: None.

WASHINGTON (Tacoma)

WASHINGTON STATE HISTORICAL SOCIETY

315 North Stadium Way
Tacoma, WA 98406
(206) 593-2830

David Nicandri (Director)

Contact: Elaine Miller (Assistant Librarian, Photographs)
Services: Historical society; film archives. Open to the public by special arrangement.
Description: Historical film relevant to Tacoma and Washington state.
Historical events. Includes: *Ezra Meeker,* showing an early pioneer driving an ox team through Tacoma (pre-1913) on the banks of the Platte River, dismounting wagon, removing wheels and rowing flatbed across the river; *Picnic at Spanaway* (1918); *Construction of the 14th South Street Bridge, Tacoma* (1927); *Lindbergh Reception to Seattle* (1931); *Great Northern Railroad,* the view from a train window going from Chicago to Seattle on the "New Empire Builder"; home movies of Ruth Entz on a summer trip in Alaska (1950s); *Where the Strawberry Tree Blooms,* observing flora and fauna; *Civic Tacoma* and *Industrial Tacoma.*
Personalities. Includes *James Wehn,* showing the Seattle sculptor at work in his studio, surrounded by his sculptures of Isaac Stevens, Indian chiefs, Clarence Bagley, Asa Mercer, George Washington and John Muir.
KTNT television news footage (1964-71). Local Tacoma television news

footage. Collection is comprised of 70 archival storage boxes of 16mm film, currently uncataloged.
Size & Elements: Film: 16mm (17 titles, 70 archival storage boxes; originals and release prints).
Cataloging: Partial cataloging; printed list.
Access: Open to the public by special arrangement.
Rights: Full rights held to some material.
Licensing: Available for licensing and reuse, subject to restrictions. License and usage fees charged.
Restrictions: Requests for licensing and reuse subject to clearance, acceptance and approval.
Viewing Facilities: None.
Duplication Facilities: None.

WASHINGTON (Toppenish)

YAKIMA INDIAN NATION CULTURAL CENTER

P.O. Box 151
Toppenish, WA 98948
(509) 865-2800

Brycene Neaman (Museum Coordinator)

Contact: Brycene Neaman
Services: Museum; videotape archives. Material available for research and loan on a restricted basis due to limited staffing.
Description: Holds footage featuring various aspects of contemporary Yakima reservation life, including meetings, storytellers videotaped in their homes, oral histories, social programs and powwows (produced 1981-85).
Two videotapes produced by the Yakima Television Program, and currently available for loan, are *Mother Nature Is Our Teacher,* on the significance of nature in traditional Yakima thought and lifestyle, and the importance of preserving Yakima oral tradition and the Yakima language; and *The Yakima Time Ball,* showing the Yakima women's tradition of keeping a record of the events of their lives by knotting a long string, and then using this ball of string as a storytelling device for recounting their life stories.
Size & Elements: Videotape: 3/4" (100 videotapes; masters); VHS (viewing copies).
Cataloging: List; brochure.
Access: Available to the public. Currently transferring 3/4" videotape to VHS in order that the material can be viewed at the Museum. Research requests accepted by mail and telephone.
Rights: Full rights held to all material.
Licensing: Apply for information.
Restrictions: Archives limited in staffing and facilities. Requests considered on a case-by-case basis and subject to approval.
Viewing Facilities: Videotape (VHS).
Duplication Facilities: None.

WASHINGTON (Yakima)

YAKIMA TELEVISION PROGRAM

715 North Fourth Avenue
Yakima, WA 98902
(509) 457-4036

Robert Swanson (Video Producer)

Contact: Robert Swanson
Services: Media organization; public access television facility. Material available for licensing, subject to restrictions.
Description: Produces programming for community access cable television in the city of Yakima. Produced by and for the Yakima Nation, the programming is designed to break Native American stereotypes.
Productions include: music videos (2 videotapes, each 3 min.); a series on aerobic exercise (9 programs); a series on the legends of the Yakima Nation as told in stories by tribal members, made for school and museum audiences (2 programs); a series on the most important aspects of traditional Yakima lifestyle, made for museum audiences; *The Challenge of Spilyay,* the story of the mythical character Coyote; *Mother Nature is Our Teacher; Yakima Timeball,* about the tradition among Yakima women of recording the events of their lives by marking a string with knots and beads, and unwinding the string ball to tell a story; *Celilo Falls,* reporting on the effects of the construction of the Dalles Dam, and the consequent inundation of the former site of an important Native American trading post dating from before the time of Lewis

and Clark; a series of Yakima Indian profiles, including a family group which performs traditional drumming; oral histories of Yakima people; and a work in progress on the 50th year of one of the larger local powwows.

Size & Elements: Videotape (format and amount unspecified).

Cataloging: None specified.

Access: Apply for information.

Rights: Full rights held to all material.

Licensing: Available for licensing and reuse, subject to restrictions. License fees charged in some cases.

Restrictions: Requests for viewing, licensing and reuse subject to acceptance and approval.

Viewing Facilities: None.

Duplication Facilities: None.

WEST VIRGINIA

WEST VIRGINIA (Beckley)

U.S. DEPARTMENT OF LABOR
MINE SAFETY AND HEALTH ADMINISTRATION
NATIONAL MINE HEALTH AND SAFETY ACADEMY
P.O. Box 1166
Beckley, WV 25802-1166
(304) 255-0451
Fax: (304) 255-0451 (Ext. 299)

Street address: Airport Road

Contact: Mary Lord

Services: Government agency; film and videotape producer. Films and videotapes available for rental. Bureau of Mines Motion Picture Film Library distributes copies of its 16mm films on a free-loan basis.

Description: Holds over 80 films produced by the Bureau of Mines (27 films), the Mining Safety and Health Administration, or the Mining Enforcement and Safety Administration. Materials promote the health and safety of those who work in the mining industry, focusing on the following topics: safety and inspection procedures, accident prevention, investigations, industrial hygiene, mine emergency procedures, mining technology and mine management.

Titles include: *The Air We Breathe in Industrial Environments; Assume Nothing: Accident Investigation in Coal Mines; Barriers to the Prevention of Ground Fall Accidents; Cabs and Canopies for Your Safety;* and *Coal Dust: Hazards and Controls.*

First Aid Series includes: *Artificial Respiration; Burns and Scalds; Control of Bleeding; Fractures and Dislocations; Open and Closed Wounds;* and *Shock.* Related titles include: *Mine Rescue Contest Training; Open-Pit Mining Hazards; Plain Talk About A Serious Problem...Silicosis; Protection Against Radioactivity in Uranium Mines; Think Quicksand: Safety Around Bins and Hoppers;* and *Underground Coal Mine Blasting.*

Size & Elements: Film: 16mm. Videotape: 3/4", VHS and Betamax. (80 titles total).

Cataloging: Published catalog of training products for the mining industry.

Access: Maintained for distribution and rental rather than for research or reuse. Inquiries accepted by mail and telephone.

Rights: Full rights held to some material.

Licensing: Apply for information.

Restrictions: Apply for information.

Viewing Facilities: None.

Duplication Facilities: None.

Related Materials: Slide shows; latent image exercises; various print materials.

Distributor: For free loan of 16mm films produced by the Bureau of Mines, contact: U.S. Department of Interior — Bureau of Mines, Motion Picture Film Library, P.O. Box 18070, Cochrans Mill Road, Pittsburgh, PA 15236-0000; (412) 892-6845 (Commercial); (412) 723-6845 (FTS).

WEST VIRGINIA (Charleston)

WEST VIRGINIA DEPARTMENT OF CULTURE AND HISTORY
ARCHIVES DIVISION
Capitol Complex
Charleston, WV 25305
(304) 348-0230

Fredrick Armstrong (Associate Director, Archives Division)

Contact: Richard Fauss (Film Archivist)

Services: State archives. Film and videotape collection available for duplication and reuse, subject to restrictions.

Description: Materials significant to the historical and cultural heritage of West Virginia, including documentaries, industrial films, home movies and an extensive television newsfilm footage collection.

The Harry Brawley Collection of Broadcast Media. Named after the founder of home education shows *Radio Classroom* and *Television Classroom* (early 1950s), who was one of those responsible for the initiation of educational radio and television broadcasting in the state. Comprised of newsfilm donations from four West Virginia television stations:

WTRF-TV, Wheeling. 17,000 stories, with scripts (1955 to mid-1980). Covers visits to Wheeling by Harry S Truman, John F. Kennedy, Lyndon B. Johnson, Everett Dirksen and West Virginia notables. Other topics include: Wheeling Suspension Bridge; West Virginia Independence Hall; Marx Toy Company; other industrial and labor activities; civic and sports events; disasters; and coverage of the State Correctional Facility at Moundsville.

WSAZ-TV, Charleston. Over 19,000 stories, most concentrating on the Charleston-Kanawha Valley. Many of the stories deal with state and municipal government in the period which saw the Buffalo Creek flood, the "black lung" movement, Arnold Miller's term as President of the United Mine Workers of America and environmental challenges confronting the Valley's major chemical industries.

WCHS-TV, Charleston. 5,000 stories providing other views of the events documented by WSAZ-TV's crews, in addition to many community vignettes.

WVVA, Bluefield. Approximately 9,000 stories (1978-82) on events and issues in southern West Virginia, notably the coal industry.

Size & Elements: Film: 16mm (industrials, documentaries and home movies, 100 titles; television news footage, 2.5 million feet); 8mm (amount unspecified). Videotape: 3/4" (West Virginia Cultural Heritage, 200 hours; television news footage, 200 hours; masters and viewing copies).

Cataloging: Card catalogs; story lists.

Access: General collection open to the public. Available for duplication. Research fees not charged at the present time. Research requests accepted by mail and in person (by appointment only).

Access to the Harry Brawley Collection of Broadcast Media requires advance notice. Extensive card research should be conducted by the patron with staff supervision. At least two days' notice is required for film viewing; a greater period is required for extensive requests. This is necessary because film must be transferred to videotape before viewing in order to protect the original film. Duplication of film or videotape will be arranged by the Archives at an approved facility, with researchers responsible for all direct and indirect costs of videotapes, duplication, mailing and insurance.

Rights: Full rights held to some material.

Licensing: Available for duplication, licensing and reuse, subject to restrictions. License and usage fees not charged.

Restrictions: During the current period of processing the Collection, each request will be reviewed by the staff to see if the material can be located and made available without undue interference with processing activities.

Viewing Facilities: Videotape.

Duplication Facilities: Film (through approved laboratory); Videotape (through an approved lab or by special arrangement with one of the local television stations).

Related Materials: Television news scripts.

WEST VIRGINIA (Charleston)

WEST VIRGINIA STATE LIBRARY COMMISSION
FILM SERVICES DEPARTMENT
Cultural Center
Charleston, WV 25305
(304) 348-3976
(304) 348-3977

Stephen L. Fesenmaier (Department Head, Film Services)

Contacts: Stephen L. Fesenmaier; Frani Fesenmaier (Assistant Department Head)

Services: Government agency; film and videotape lending library. Material available on a free-loan basis to West Virginia citizens through the local public library system.

Description: Primarily holds commercially acquired films and videotapes. Collection is especially strong in the areas of feature films (800 titles); Appalachia (100 titles); Black history and culture (100 titles); women's issues (50 titles) and astronomy (10 titles). Holds one archival film about Charleston,

West Virginia (1932).
Size & Elements: Film: 16mm (4,400 films). Videotape: 3/4" and VHS (100 titles).
Cataloging: Published catalogs.
Access: Available to the public. Research requests accepted by mail. Most material available on a free-loan basis to West Virginia citizens through the local public library system.
Rights: Archival material is in the public domain.
Licensing: Apply for information.
Restrictions: None specified.
Viewing Facilities: Film (16mm); videotape (3/4" and VHS).
Duplication Facilities: None.

WEST VIRGINIA (Harpers Ferry)

U.S. NATIONAL PARK SERVICE HISTORY COLLECTION
HARPERS FERRY CENTER LIBRARY
Harpers Ferry, WV 25425
(304) 535-6371

David Nathanson (Chief Librarian and Supervisor)

Contact: David Nathanson (Special Collections Librarian, Museum Curator and Archivist)
Services: Government agency. Film and videotape collection available to the public. Material possibly available for reuse.
Description: Films (1930s-80s) from various sources, including the Civilian Conservation Corps (CCC) and the National Park Service. Coverage includes Bicentennial events (1976) and Liberty Weekend (1986). Some of these films are unique to this collection.

Also holds Horace Marsden Albright home movies (1924-31; transferred to videotape). Subjects include: the Gallup Intertribal ceremony in New Mexico (1931); the Old West, featuring Mt. Rainier, Mesa Verde, Canyon de Chelly; eastern sites, including Wakefield, Plymouth and Acadia; a trip to Alaska; and California, Yellowstone and Yosemite.
Size & Elements: Film: 16mm (100 items; originals and release prints). Videotape: VHS (viewing copies).
Cataloging: Film list.
Access: Open to the public. Available for nonprofit licensing and reuse on a case-by-case basis. Research fees not charged. Research requests accepted by mail and telephone.
Rights: Full rights held to some material. Some material in the public domain.
Licensing: Available for licensing and reuse, subject to restrictions. License and usage fees not charged.
Restrictions: Material available for nonprofit reuse only. Requests considered on a case-by-case basis.
Viewing Facilities: Film and videotape.
Duplication Facilities: None.

WEST VIRGINIA (Huntington)

MARSHALL UNIVERSITY
SPECIAL COLLECTIONS
JAMES E. MORROW LIBRARY
Huntington, WV 25701
(304) 696-2343
(304) 696-2344

Lisle G. Brown (Curator)

Contacts: Lisle G. Brown; Cora Teel (Archivist)
Services: University library. Film and videotape collection available for reuse.
Description: WSAZ-TV newsfilm archives, containing film and videotape from the station's news department (1953-82). WSAZ-TV covers the regional area known as the Tri-State: Huntington (West Virginia), Ashland (Kentucky) and Ironton (Ohio). The film held is not the actual on-air news broadcast, but the news clips used during the broadcast. Covers newsworthy events in the region (e.g., interviews, crime, politics, education and natural disasters); sports events are not covered. Each year, the station retires one year's worth of film or videotape which is added to the newsfilm archive in the Morrow Library's Special Collections department.
Size & Elements: Film: 16mm (approx. 1,600 cans; black and white and color, silent and sound, optical and magnetic tracks). Videotape: 3/4" (350 videotapes).
Cataloging: Card catalogs indexed by subject (except for 1974, when the

station kept no index).
Access: Open to the public. Research fees not charged. Research requests accepted by telephone and in person.
Rights: Full rights held to all material.
Licensing: Available for licensing and reuse. License and usage fees not charged.
Restrictions: None specified.
Viewing Facilities: Film (16mm sound projector); videotape (3/4").
Duplication Facilities: None.
Related Materials: News scripts.

WEST VIRGINIA (Morgantown)

WEST VIRGINIA UNIVERSITY
WEST VIRGINIA AND REGIONAL HISTORY COLLECTION
Colson Hall
Morgantown, WV 26506
(304) 293-3536

George Parkinson (Curator)

Contact: John Cuthbert (Associate Curator)
Services: Educational institution. Film and videotape collection available to the public for research, duplication and reuse, subject to restrictions.
Description: Regional history collection (1920-present), concentrating on University history; University athletics; regional history; folklore studies; folk music; the coal industry; and labor history.
Size & Elements: Film: format unspecified (130,000 feet, 800 titles, 1,000 cans). Videotape: VHS and Betamax (20 titles).
Cataloging: Card catalogs.
Access: Open to the public. Available for duplication. Research fees not charged. Research requests accepted by mail, telephone and in person (walk-in and by appointment).
Rights: Rights status of material not specified. Additional clearances may be necessary in some cases if material is to be reused.
Licensing: Available for licensing and reuse, subject to restrictions. License fees charged in some cases (for-profit uses).
Restrictions: Requests for licensing and reuse reviewed on a case-by-case basis.
Viewing Facilities: Film and videotape.
Duplication Facilities: Film and videotape.

WISCONSIN

WISCONSIN (Baraboo)

CIRCUS WORLD MUSEUM LIBRARY & RESEARCH CENTER
426 Water Street
Baraboo, WI 53913
(608) 356-8341

Street address: 415 Lynn Street

Robert L. Parkinson (Research Center Director)

Contact: William McCarthy (Researcher)
Services: Library; museum. Circulating film collection; material available for rental and for reuse in some cases, subject to restrictions.
Description: Circus films (1904-60; majority of collection post-1930). Mostly amateur footage, including scenes of circus loading and unloading, set-up and performance, trains coming into station, unloading in rail yard, wagons, setting up tents on lot and midway and parades.

Performance footage includes a wide variety of acts including aerials and wild animal acts, elephants, polar bears, cats, side shows (including fat lady and magician) and clowns, in particular Emmett Kelly. Also covered are Clyde Beatty's animal act, Jorgen Christiansen's 24-horse liberty act and Tim McCoy's Wild West show. Circuses represented include: Ringling Bros. Barnum & Bailey, Sparks Circus, Cole Bros. Circus, Hagenbeck-Wallace Circus, Arthur Bros. Circus, Christy Bros. Circus, Dailey Bros. Circus, Barnes Circus, Sells-Floto Circus, Cristiani Bros. Circus, Wallace Bros. Circus and Milwaukee Circus.

Earliest film (from 1904) documents the Barnum & Bailey Circus street parade in Waterloo, Iowa; it shows almost the entire parade with two hemispheres and a 40-horse team leading off and followed by cages, tableaus,

Continental band, chariots, elephants, camels and an organ wagon.
Size & Elements: Film: 16mm (150,000 feet).
Cataloging: Card catalog; film lists.
Access: Open to researchers and scholars. Research requests accepted by mail and in person (by appointment only). First hour of research free; fee charged for each additional hour, plus copying charges. Materials generally not available for reuse, although circulating materials are sometimes available on a rental basis. Allow six weeks advance notice; limit of two films per order, unless otherwise arranged with Museum Director.
Rights: Full rights held to most material, with some exceptions.
Licensing: Available for licensing and reuse, subject to restrictions. License and usage fees charged.
Restrictions: Must apply for permission regarding reuse.
Viewing Facilities: Film (advance appointment required).
Duplication Facilities: None.
Related Materials: 80,000 still photographs (mostly prints); card catalog of hundreds of thousands of circus employees.

WISCONSIN (Cudahy)

ALOIS F. DETTLAFF, SR.
3849 East Cudahy Avenue
Cudahy, WI 53110
(414) 481-1170

Contact: Alois F. Dettlaff, Sr.
Services: Private collection. Material available for reuse, subject to restrictions.
Description: Alois Dettlaff, Sr. has been collecting film since 1928, starting at the age of seven. Unique or very rare titles in his collection include: Thomas Edison's *Frankenstein* (1910), a unique film for which the American Film Institute honored Dettlaff in 1986; *Robin Hood* (Eclair, 1912), which he supplied for a 50th anniversary tribute to Robin Hood, as played by Errol Flynn; *If We Lived on the Moon* (1919) and *Hello Mars, Earth Calling* (1920), with animation by Max Fleischer; the first Jesse James film by Famous Players-Lasky; the first *Fall of the Alamo*; *Minnie's Yoo-Hoo* (1929), a unique copy of the first Mickey Mouse film; a preview of the first German talking film; and Thomas Edison's 1895 22mm film with three images per frame, designed to be run through the projector three times.
   Early film titles include: *Broadway Billy; Comrades; Divine Sinner;* and *She Played and Payed.* Thomas Edison films from the 1920s include: *May and December; Moonlight;* and *The Life of Thomas Edison.* Additional films include: *Helen's Babies* (Pathé); *Just Lucky; Taking the Count* (with Ben Turpin); previews of *Springtime in the Rockies;* and *Jezebel.*
   Also holds short subjects, newsreels and previews of coming attractions.
Size & Elements: Film: 70mm; 35mm (silent and sound); 28mm (silent); 16mm (silent and sound); 9.5mm (silent); Super 8mm (silent and sound); regular 8mm (1 million feet total, all formats).
Cataloging: None.
Access: Generally not open to the public. Research requests accepted by telephone.
Rights: Full rights held to some material. Some material in the public domain. Rights status of some material not known. Additional clearances may be necessary in some cases if material is to be reused.
Licensing: Some material available for licensing and reuse, subject to restrictions.
Restrictions: Requests for research, licensing and reuse considered on a case-by-case basis.
Viewing Facilities: None.
Duplication Facilities: None.

WISCONSIN (Green Bay)

DURANT FAMILY REGISTRY
2700 Timber Lane
Green Bay, WI 54303-5899
(414) 499-8797 (evenings only)

Jeff Gillis (President)

Contact: Jeff Gillis
Services: Antique car club. One film available for research only.
Description: Film combining two pieces of original footage shot in 1924 and 1930 in the Toronto factory of Durant Motors, showing the production and assembly of automobiles from those years.
Size & Elements: Film: 16mm (600 feet). Videotape: viewing copy of same.

Access: Not open to the public. Open to researchers and scholars. For in-house use only.
Rights: No rights held to any material.
Licensing: Not available for licensing or reuse.
Restrictions: Material is privately held and cannot be released for duplication or reuse, nor can it be loaned or otherwise made available for public distribution. Available for in-house screening and for research purposes only.
Viewing Facilities: Film (16mm); videotape.
Duplication Facilities: None.

WISCONSIN (Green Bay)

NEVILLE PUBLIC MUSEUM
210 Museum Place
Green Bay, WI 54303
(414) 436-3767

Ann Koski (Director)

Contact: Di L. Adams (Registrar, Collections Manager)
Services: Museum. Film collection maintained for archival purposes; currently not accessible to the public for research or reuse.
Description: Newsfilm from three local Green Bay television stations: WBAY (1957-74), WLUK (1971-80) and WFRV (1968-80).
Size & Elements: Film: 16mm (3.5 million feet, 7,000 cans).
Cataloging: Presently not cataloged, inventoried or indexed.
Access: Currently not accessible to the public for research or reuse.
Rights: Apply for information.
Licensing: Currently not accessible for reuse.
Restrictions: Collection maintained for archival purposes; not accessible to the public for research or reuse.
Viewing Facilities: None.
Duplication Facilities: None.

WISCONSIN (Green Bay)

UNIVERSITY OF WISCONSIN — GREEN BAY
CENTER FOR T.V. PRODUCTION
2420 Nicolet Drive
Green Bay, WI 54311-7001
(414) 465-2500

Larry Long (Associate Director for Television)

Contact: Joseph H. Gaunt (Manager, Administrative Services)
Services: Educational institution; film and videotape producer. Material available to the public for duplication, licensing and reuse.
Description: Green Bay, Wisconsin aerials and scenics; Northeastern Wisconsin scenics, primarily water (waterfalls, rivers, white water, Lake Michigan and Green Bay); Menominee and Oneida Indian reservations, ceremonies and dances; industrials (papermaking and shipbuilding); ethnic and folklore (Swiss dancers); footage of parties with teenagers, contemporary cars, swimming and beer parties; underwater footage, including small shipwrecks in Lake Michigan and Green Bay; "ultralight" footage (specially designed aircraft); wildlife, especially waterfowl; contemporary mining (gold, lead and zinc); ecological footage; drunk driving, featuring the legal process, sobriety test, trial and jail; historical re-creations and authentic events, often featuring children; and associated generic footage.
Size & Elements: Film: 16mm (color, originals). Videotape: 1" and 3/4" (masters). (Approx. 100 items total).
Cataloging: Program titles in film and videotape library.
Access: Available to the public for duplication and reuse. Research fees charged (fees negotiable). Research requests accepted by telephone.
Rights: Full rights held to all material. Additional clearances may be necessary in some cases if material is to be reused.
Licensing: Available for licensing. License fees charged.
Restrictions: None specified.
Viewing Facilities: Film (16mm); videotape (all formats).
Duplication Facilities: Film and videotape (all formats).

WISCONSIN (Greendale)

AMERICAN BOWLING CONGRESS FILM LIBRARY
5301 South 76th Street
Greendale, WI 53129-0500

(414) 421-6400
Fax: (414) 421-1194
Telex: 821-965

Roger H. Tessman (Executive Secretary/Treasurer)

Contact: Chris Lemke (Education Department, Head Secretary)
Services: Nonprofit association. Videotapes available to the public for free loan, purchase and duplication.
Description: Educational, instructional and entertainment films and videotapes relating to the sport of bowling.

Titles include: *Fantastic Masters*, 1983 ABC Tournament at Niagara Falls; *Showcase of the Stars*, 1981 ABC Tournament in Memphis, Tenn.; *Behind the Line*, describing ABC services, showing a test facility and bowling equipment manufacturing plants; *High Rollers*, 1977 ABC Masters; *One of a Kind*, 1974 ABC Masters; *What More Could You Ask For?*; *7th World Bowling Championships*; *7th FIQ World Bowling Championships*; *Bowling's Magic Moments*, 1965 ABC Tournament; *The Masters Touch*; *Shooting Stars*, 1966 ABC Masters; *Battle of the Ages*, 1968 ABC Masters; *One in a Million*, 1969 ABC Masters; *Bowling: The Right Approach*, basic instruction and common sense adjustments; *They Continue to Serve: The BVL Fund Story*, programs funded by the BVL fund for hospitalized veterans; and *Down the Center Aisle*, competition in the ABC Championships Tournament and an overview of ABC Convention and Hall of Fame induction ceremonies.
Size & Elements: Film: various formats (22 titles). Videotape: 1/2" (6 titles; viewing copies).
Cataloging: Brochure.
Access: Available to the public for free loan, purchase and duplication. Requests accepted by mail, telephone and in person (walk-in).
Rights: Copyright may be released when requested.
Licensing: Apply for information. License and usage fees not charged.
Restrictions: None specified.
Viewing Facilities: None.
Duplication Facilities: None.

WISCONSIN (Madison)

AMERICAN INSTITUTE OF THE HISTORY OF PHARMACY
Pharmacy Building
425 North Charter Street
Madison, WI 53706-1508
(608) 262-5378

Gregory J. Higby (Director)

Contact: Gregory J. Higby
Services: Historical society. Films and videotapes available to researchers and scholars only.
Description: History of pharmacy and drug compounding. May hold the only copies of certain titles.

Titles include: *Hand Processes for Making Drug Products* (ca. 1950); *Techniques of Weighing*; *Design for Life*; *150th Anniversary of USP*; *Filling a Collapsible Tube*; *Making Pills by Hand*; *State Historical Society of Wisconsin Pharmacy Museum* (ca. 1950); *Lititz Pharmacopoeia Marker Dedication* (July, 1976); *An Extra Measure of Care*; *Treatment of Acute Drug Overdose* (Eli Lilly Co., ca. 1973); *Life & Contribution of Takeru Higuchi* (1981); and *A Proud Profession*.
Size & Elements: Film: 16mm (15 reels; positive); 8mm (200 feet). Videotape: 3/4" (2 videotapes); VHS (1 videotape). (17 titles total).
Cataloging: Card catalogs.
Access: Available to researchers and scholars only. Research fees charged. Research requests accepted in person (by appointment only).
Rights: No rights held to any material. Can help locate rights holders if necessary.
Licensing: Apply for information. Usage fees not charged.
Restrictions: None specified.
Viewing Facilities: Film (16mm); videotape (in nearby facility; by appointment only).
Duplication Facilities: None.

WISCONSIN (Madison)

STATE HISTORICAL SOCIETY OF WISCONSIN
VISUAL AND SOUND ARCHIVES
816 State Street
Madison, WI 53706
(608) 262-9581

Nicholas Muller III (Director)

Contact: George Talbot (Curator) (608/262-2283)
Services: Historical society; film and videotape archives. Material available for licensing and reuse, subject to restrictions.
Description: *Labor history.* Substantial collection (150-200 titles) of films relating to the labor movement, created mostly by or for unions representing textile workers, packinghouse workers, steel workers, etc. Although many of these films were in wide distribution in the 1950s, in some cases the Archives now holds the only known prints in existence. In general, rights are held by the respective unions. (Please note: Wisconsin labor unions are currently developing their own archives, increasing the number of possible sources for labor union footage.)

Mass communications history. The largest state collection of television news footage, and some documentaries. Although collecting interests overlap somewhat with the Wisconsin Center for Film and Theater Research, the Society generally covers news and public affairs, while the Center covers entertainment. News coverage extends from 1955-77, with one weekly news magazine running to 1983. Mostly Wisconsin news is held, including the WHA (Madison) kinescopes (1950s-60s) and the KETC/St. Louis (Mo.) news footage (late 1950s to early 1960s). Also holds large collections from Madison television stations WKOW, WMTV, WISC, and smaller amounts of material from other television news sources.

Social action. A smaller collection which includes civil rights footage to which rights are held, and a film produced by James Farmer (rights status unknown).

Various films produced in Wisconsin. Includes many films produced or collected by Wisconsin state agencies; industrial films; various university productions (1930s-present) on conservation; home movies (1930s-50s, approx. 15,000 feet). In addition, the Archives has a long-standing interest in the documentation of family and community life, and holds a number of small town promotional films. The Archives has recently acquired 50 cubic feet of industrial film shot by WSAU-TV (Wausau, Wis.).
Size & Elements: Film: 16mm and 8mm (approx. 2,000 titles; originals and release prints). Videotape: 2", 3/4" and VHS (small amounts).
Cataloging: Card catalogs (main access point is by title).
Access: Open to the public. Available for reuse, subject to restrictions. Staff will conduct up to one hour of research, subject to written request; research fees charged for additional time. Research requests accepted by mail and telephone.
Rights: Full rights held to some material. Some rights held to some material. Some material in the public domain. Rights status of some material not known. Additional clearances may be necessary in some cases if material is to be reused.
Licensing: Available for licensing and reuse, subject to restrictions. License and usage fees charged in some cases.
Restrictions: Requests for licensing and reuse considered on a case-by-case basis. Users must sign an indemnification agreement regarding all issues of copyright.
Viewing Facilities: Film.
Duplication Facilities: None.

WISCONSIN (Madison)

UNIVERSITY OF WISCONSIN — EXTENSION
BUREAU OF AUDIOVISUAL INSTRUCTION
P.O. Box 2093
Madison, WI 53701-2093
(800) 362-6888
(608) 262-3902 (Wisconsin only)

Street address: 1327 University Avenue, Madison, WI 53715-2499

Bruce E. Dewey (Director)
Stephen A. Stuelke (Assistant Director)

Contacts: Linda DeMars (Program Assistant); Carol A. Woods (Program Assistant); Booking Department
Services: University library. Film and videotape collection available to the public for rental.
Description: Has produced over 200 films and videotapes on subjects relevant to University studies. Also maintains a distribution library containing over

8,000 titles by outside producers, covering a wide variety of subject areas.

Some University productions include: *The Divine Athlete* (Toronto Dance Theatre), an assemblage of rehearsals for a performance at Green Bay (1984); *Testing — None of the Above,* in which a school counselor's dreams dramatize the basic misconceptions and the problems of norm-referenced standardized testing; *Turbines, Turmoil and Tears,* on labor and the rise of labor unions during the late 1800s and early 1900s, including archival footage of the Allis-Chalmers strike in 1941; *Hoof Care in Dairy Cattle,* in three parts; *Facts About Food Irradiation,* discussing its effects; *Taking a Look at Taking Care,* introducing the 4-H health curriculum and explaining how health relates to emotional and spiritual needs; *Managua: One Year Later,* showing the recovery from the earthquake of December 23, 1972 and visiting several recovery projects that received funds from Wisconsin citizens through the "Partners of the Americas" program.

Logging in Wisconsin About 1938 contrasts the days of horses, trains and handsaws with today's Caterpillars, trucks and power-cutting equipment; *Wedding of the Goddess* pictures the annual 19-day Chittirai festival in the South Indian city of Madurai; *Cheesemaking, From the Feel of the Curd to the Tang on the Tongue* describes Swiss cheesemaking traditions and principles, as practiced in Green County, Wisconsin; *Infant Neurodevelopment Examination* shows normal responses of a one-month-old infant to different stimuli; *Story of Two Creeks* reports on geologic research conducted at a site on the Wisconsin shore of Lake Michigan, investigating the history and effects of glacial and interglacial periods; *Village Man, City Man* documents a young mill worker's life in an industrial section of Delhi and his visit to his village home; *Bolivia: Frontier Settlement of Japanese From Overseas* and *Indians from Highlands,* covering two colonization projects.

Size & Elements: Film: 16mm. Videotape: VHS. (8,000 titles total).
Cataloging: Published catalogs.
Access: Open to the public. Maintained for distribution and rental rather than research or reuse. Requests accepted by mail and telephone.
Rights: Full rights held to some material. Additional clearances may be necessary in some cases if material is to be reused.
Licensing: Apply for information.
Restrictions: Apply for information.
Viewing Facilities: Film (16mm; projection facilities offered free of charge; no appointment necessary).
Duplication Facilities: Videotape (VHS).

WISCONSIN (Madison)

WISCONSIN CENTER FOR FILM AND THEATER RESEARCH FILM AND PHOTO ARCHIVE
412 State Historical Society of Wisconsin
816 State Street
Madison, WI 53706
(608) 262-0585

Administrative offices:
6040 Vilas Communication Hall
821 University Avenue
University of Wisconsin — Madison
Madison, WI 53706
(608) 262-9706

Professor Donald Crafton (Director)
Maxine Fleckner Ducey (Archivist)

Contact: Maxine Fleckner Ducey
Services: Film and videotape archives; study center. Open to researchers and scholars for in-house viewing only. Material not available for licensing or reuse.
Description: The Center is co-sponsored by the University of Wisconsin — Madison and the State Historical Society of Wisconsin. Founded in 1960, it receives an operating budget from the University through the Department of Communication Arts. The Historical Society provides a home for the collections, archival storage and processing facilities, a reading room and screening room, and extensive, relevant documentation in its own collections. Over 200 collections from outstanding playwrights, television and motion picture writers, producers, motion picture companies, actors, designers and directors are preserved for scholarly research.
The United Artists Collection. Acquired by United Artists from Warner Bros., RKO and Monogram and donated to the Center. Includes: the Warner Bros. collection (over 800 features), a virtually complete record of the studio's output (1931-49), including pre-colorized versions of *Yankee Doodle Dandy,*

The Maltese Falcon and *Casablanca,* 300 cartoons from the popular *Looney Tunes* and *Merrie Melodies* series, some 1,500 *Vitaphone* short subjects and comprehensive documentation on these Warner productions; 700 films from RKO, constituting nearly all the features produced by this company (1930s-40s); and the Monogram Collection (approx. 200 films), typical of small, low-budget productions during the same period.
History of Cinema. Over 8,000 features, shorts and documentaries (1890s-1980s), including films by D. W. Griffith, Erich von Stroheim, Robert Flaherty, Luis Buñuel, Ladislas Starevich, Alfred Hitchcock, Jean Renoir, François Truffaut and many others.
Independent filmmakers. Holds the collections of Shirley Clarke (including such works as *Portrait of Jason* and *The Connection*), with video works and outtakes from feature films; Emile deAntonio (*Point of Order* and *In the Year of the Pig*), with stock footage, outtakes and soundtracks used in the production of his films; Doris Chase; and the Amos Vogel *Cinema 16* series, chronicling the early development of avant-garde filmmaking in the U.S. during the 1950s-60s. Also holds the Third World Newsreel collection, containing films relating to political and social issues (beginning 1968). Feature films and short subjects are also included in the collections of Gilbert Cates, Walter Mirisch, Kirk Douglas, Lionel Rogosin, Walter Wanger, Dore Schary and the American Film Institute.
Also holds the David Shepard Collection (180 films) and 35mm prints of 270 Soviet features and documentaries produced (1950s-70s). This represents the largest archival collection of postwar Soviet films in the United States, and includes the works of such directors as Andrei Tarkovsky and Sergei Paradjanov.
Television. Provides primary source material necessary for the assessment of the impact of television. Holdings include:
The Ziv Television Library (1948-62, 38 series, over 2,000 programs). Popular dramatic programs produced for first-run syndicated use, including every episode of *Boston Blackie, I Led Three Lives, Mr. District Attorney, Highway Patrol,* and *Bat Masterson.* Scripts, manuscript material and still photographs are available for many series.
Television documentary. Documentation, musical scores and release prints (13 episodes) for *Victory at Sea* (NBC, 1952), produced by Richard Hanser, Donald Hyatt, Isaac Kleinerman and Henry Solomon; research material, scripts, publicity and release prints (34 episodes) for *Project XX,* produced by the same team; the Kleinerman and Burton Benjamin collections, documenting their work on *The 20th Century* and *The 21st Century* for CBS, holding over 200 release prints from these series; and the collections of Ernest Pendrell (ABC) and Perry Wolff (CBS), with scripts and release prints of many documentaries.
Dramatic and episodic television. Includes: *The Defenders* (260 episodes; films and scripts), contributed by Reginald Rose; the Nat Hiken collection, containing over 140 films from *You'll Never Get Rich* and *Car 54, Where Are You?; Bonanza,* contributed by NBC; *Wichita Town,* in the Walter Mirisch collection; prints of many Ed Sullivan variety programs; episodes from *The Mary Tyler Moore Show, Rhoda, Bob Newhart* and other series, contributed by MTM Enterprises; and the Fred Coe collection, with scripts, production information and original kinescopes from anthology dramas, including *Philco Television Playhouse, Goodyear Playhouse, Playhouse 90, Playwrights '56* and *Producers' Showcase.* 35mm broadcast prints, donated by Paramount Television, include complete or near-complete runs of series such as *Mork and Mindy, Taxi, Happy Days, Laverne and Shirley, Mannix, Mission Impossible, The Brady Bunch* and *Love American Style.* Various collections also hold films and kinescopes of episodes from television series, including *Studio One, Electric Showcase, Person to Person, Camera Three, Omnibus, Climax* and *The Martha Raye Show.*
Size & Elements: Film: 35mm and 16mm (18,958,000 feet, 14,000 titles, 40,000 cans; primarily reference prints). Preprint material is held for the Ziv Television Collection. Videotape: 2" (masters); 3/4" (viewing copies); and 1/2" open reel (1,500 videotapes total).
Cataloging: Card catalogs; finding aids (main access point is by title).
Access: Open to researchers and scholars only (Monday-Friday, 1 pm-5 pm). Research fees charged for off-site research only. Research requests accepted by mail, telephone and in person (by appointment only). All films, videotapes and viewing equipment must be reserved in advance.
Rights: No rights held to any material.
Licensing: Not available for licensing or reuse.
Restrictions: Not available for duplication, licensing or reuse of any kind.
Viewing Facilities: Film (35mm and 16mm Steenbecks); videotape (3/4"). Reservations for viewing required.
Duplication Facilities: None.
Related Materials: Two million still photographs; several hundred manuscript collections from individuals and organizations involved in the production of

motion pictures, television and theater, including manuscripts and files donated by Warner Bros., United Artists Corporation, Marc Blitzstein, Paddy Chayefsky, Kirk Douglas, Edith Head, six members of the Hollywood Ten, Lunt and Fontanne, Fredric March, NBC, Dore Schary, Walter Wanger and others; over 7,000 film and television scripts.

WISCONSIN (Manitowoc)

MANITOWOC MARITIME MUSEUM
75 Maritime Drive
Manitowoc, WI 54220
(414) 684-0218

Burt Logan (Director)

Contact: Joan Kloster (Registrar)
Services: Museum. Films and videotapes available for educational loan or in-house research by members.
Description: Maritime history; Great Lakes maritime history, specifically western shore; commercial fishing; World War II; submarine construction on the Great Lakes during World War II; commercial shipbuilding and yachting. Covers period from late 1800s to mid-1900s.

Materials available particularly for classroom or institutional use include: *The Manitowoc War Effort,* documenting the World War II shipbuilding program at Manitowoc, Wisconsin. The film shows scenes at the Burger Boat Company and the Manitowoc Shipbuilding Company. Includes landing craft, minesweepers and submarines. *The Silent Service* is a Navy recruitment film, accurately depicting life on board a World War II submarine during war patrol. The operation of a submarine, battle stations, and an attack on an enemy vessel are shown. *The Christmas Tree Ship* covers the sinking of the *Rouse Simmons,* better known as the "Christmas Tree Ship," on November 23, 1912, approximately nine miles northeast of Two Rivers, Wisconsin. She had carried Christmas trees to Chicago for 28 years. For years after she sank, fishermen got their nets tangled in the trees on the wreck. The film documents the discovery of the wreck in 1969.

The Erie L. Hackley documents the survey and attempt to raise the *Erie L. Hackley* in 1981 from Green Bay, where she sank in 1903 with the loss of 11 lives. *The Shipbuilders* examines the shipbuilding industry in Sturgeon Bay, Wisconsin. Covers the Bay Shipbuilding Corp., a wholly owned subsidiary of the Manitowoc Company, Inc.; Peterson Builders, Inc.; and the Palmer Johnson Company. *The Mystery Ship* documents the raising of the *Alvin Clark,* a wooden sailing vessel that sank in Green Bay in 1864. The ship was raised in 1969 and is now docked at Menominee.
Size & Elements: Film: 16mm and 8mm (7,200 feet, 10 titles). Videotape: 3/4" and 1/2" (7 videotapes). Some films exist in the collection as both master and duplicate. Copies only are available for viewing.
Cataloging: Research library.
Access: Open to researchers and scholars only. For in-house use only. Research available to members only. Research fees not charged; facility access is included in membership benefits. Materials available for classroom or institutional loan. Research requests accepted by mail, telephone and in person (by appointment only).
Rights: Full rights held to all material.
Licensing: Apply for information.
Restrictions: No copying of materials permitted without clearance. Credit must be given to the Museum. The Museum reserves the right to refuse to lend any material due to its condition.
Viewing Facilities: Prior notice required for any in-house viewing or loan of material.
Duplication Facilities: None.

WISCONSIN (Milwaukee)

KALMBACH PUBLISHING CO.
1027 North Seventh Street
Milwaukee, WI 53233-1471
(414) 272-2060
Fax: (414) 272-3509

Contact: Distribution Staff
Services: Hobbyist publishing company; videotape producer and distributor. Videotapes available to the public for purchase.
Description: Trains and model railroads. Videotapes produced by Kalmbach include: *Building Model Railroad Scenery with the Experts; Building Model Railroad Wood Structures; Weathering Railroad Models with Malcolm*

Furlow; Airbrushing for Model Railroaders; The Basics of Model Railroading; Building Reliable Model Railroad Track; The Basics of Model Railroad Wiring; First Generation Diesels: A Search for the Survivors; and *Flying Radio Control Models.*

Sample titles by other producers include: *Aboard the Santa Fe Chief; Ace of Black Diamonds; Alcos, Iron Ore, and More; Cajon Pass-Tehachapi Loop; California Zephyr; Diesels on the Union Pacific; A Forties Memory; Juniata's Jewel; The Last Steamers of the Colorado & Southern; Nickel Plate Story; Norfolk & Western Class J; SD40-2's In the Canadian Rockies; The Steam Locomotive; Streamliners of Yesteryear;* and *Union Pacific's Steam Express.*
Size & Elements: Videotape: VHS and Betamax (approx. 75 titles).
Cataloging: Published catalogs; brochures.
Access: Available to the public for purchase. Requests accepted by mail.
Rights: Apply for information.
Licensing: Apply for information.
Restrictions: None specified.
Viewing Facilities: None.
Duplication Facilities: None.

WISCONSIN (Milwaukee)

LEMORANDE PRODUCTION COMPANY
207 East Michigan Avenue
Milwaukee, WI 53202
(414) 271-3358

Bill Lemorande (Chief Official)

Contact: Bill Lemorande
Services: Film and videotape producer. Footage available for licensing and reuse.
Description: Factories and manufacturing; Midwestern landscapes and cityscapes; hospital scenes; commercial outtakes. Athletic footage includes children's basketball, women's aerobics, men's racquetball, diving and gymnastics (balance beam).
Size & Elements: Film: 16mm (approx. 2-3 hours, 30-40 cans). Videotape: 1" (5 videotapes, each 60 min.; masters); 3/4" (20 videotapes, each 20 min.; masters). Viewing copies available in any format.
Cataloging: Staff assistance required.
Access: Available to the public for duplication and reuse. Research and duplication fees charged. Research requests accepted by mail and telephone.
Rights: Full rights held to all material. Additional clearances (on-camera talent) may be necessary in some cases if material is to be reused.
Licensing: Available for licensing and reuse. License fees charged.
Restrictions: None specified.
Viewing Facilities: Videotape (3/4" and 1/2").
Duplication Facilities: None.

WISCONSIN (Milwaukee)

MARQUETTE UNIVERSITY
DEPARTMENT OF SPECIAL COLLECTIONS AND UNIVERSITY ARCHIVES
MEMORIAL LIBRARY
1415 West Wisconsin Avenue
Milwaukee, WI 53233
(414) 224-7256
Fax: (414) 224-1578

Charles B. Elston (Archivist)

Contacts: Charles B. Elston; Phillip M. Runkel (Assistant Archivist); Mark Thiel (Assistant Archivist)
Services: University library. Film and videotape collections open to the public.
Description: *Don McNeill Collection (1948-55).* Includes 110 reels of 16mm black and white kinescopes of *Breakfast Club* simulcasts (1948-55) and *Don McNeill's TV Club* (1950-51). Guests featured include: Arthur Lake (Dagwood Bumstead) (11/22/50); Aunt Fanny (Fran Allison) (3/21/51); Boris Karloff (4/11/51); Jack Dempsey and Joe Louis (5/9/51); and the McNeill family (6/20/51). Also holds other television shows (ca. 1950-60), including *I've Got A Secret, Person to Person* and *This is Your Life,* all featuring McNeill.

Dorothy Day — Catholic Worker Collection. Videotapes of television programs on Dorothy Day and the Catholic Worker movement, videotaped talks by Day and Frank Cordaro, and videotapes of televised interviews of Fritz Eichenberg (1962-82). Titles include: *A Work of Mercy; Radical Nonviolence;*

Guardian Angels; and *Dorothy Day: Laborer of Love.*

   President's Committee on Employment of the Handicapped Archives. Promotional films and television spots (1951-76). Sample titles include: *Louise Lake: Handicapped American of the Year* (1957); *Wheelchair Wheel; Small Town Barriers; John Winters,* a one-armed toll collector on the Garden State Parkway, New Jersey; and *Ike* (1959), a one-minute television spot.

   WISN-TV (Channel 12) Collection. Small collection of late 1950s Milwaukee local television news footage.

   Miscellaneous holdings in the University Archives include a large number of basketball and football films, and unprocessed films and videotapes in the Clement J. Zablocki Papers.
Size & Elements: Film: 16mm (approx. 160 titles; positive and originals). Videotape: 3/4", VHS and 1/2" open reel (16 items total, 7 hours; masters and viewing copies).
Cataloging: Card catalogs; finding aids (inventories).
Access: Open to the public. Research fees not charged. Research requests accepted by mail, telephone and in person (walk-in and by appointment).
Rights: Some rights held to some material (three titles). No rights held to other material.
Licensing: Apply for information. License fees not charged.
Restrictions: None specified.
Viewing Facilities: Videotape (3/4" and VHS available in Library).
Duplication Facilities: None.

WISCONSIN (Milwaukee)

MARX PRODUCTION CENTER
3100 West Vera Avenue
Milwaukee, WI 53209
(414) 351-5060
Fax: (414) 351-4652

Bob Marx (President)

Contact: Tom Deming (Vice President)
Services: Videotape producer. Material available for duplication and reuse, subject to restrictions.
Description: Industrials, including footage of heavy equipment, milling machines, assembly lines, generic exterior and interior shots of plants; floral scenes, including home floral, the plant industry and garden centers; cosmetic application (originally shot for commercials) showing a woman shampooing and applying makeup.
Size & Elements: Videotape: 1" and Betacam (approx. 40-50 hours; masters).
Cataloging: Shot lists; staff assistance required.
Access: Available for duplication and reuse. Research fees charged. Research requests accepted by mail and telephone.
Rights: Full rights held to some material. Some rights held to all material. Additional clearances may be necessary in some cases if material is to be reused (client permission required for some material).
Licensing: Some material available for licensing and reuse, subject to restrictions. License and usage fees charged.
Restrictions: Permission from client who originally commissioned material may be necessary for reuse in some cases.
Viewing Facilities: Videotape (2", 1", Betacam and 1/2").
Duplication Facilities: Videotape (2", 1", Betacam and 1/2").

WISCONSIN (Milwaukee)

MILWAUKEE ACCESS TELECOMMUNICATIONS AUTHORITY
1610 North Second Street
Milwaukee, WI 53212
(414) 225-3560

Clifford Hall (Executive Director)

Contact: Kathy Lacy (Traffic Operator)
Services: Public access television facility. Videotapes available for duplication and reuse, subject to restrictions.
Description: Programs produced for local cablecast, covering: Milwaukee community issues (83 programs); senior citizens (9 local programs); educational and children (55 programs); entertainment, music, comedy, and variety (184 programs); government and political issues (28 programs); holidays, Christmas choirs and festivals (39 programs); informational, talk shows and interviews (184 programs); ethnic events (28 programs); performing arts (74 programs); religion, choir groups and church services (81 programs);

sports (20 programs); documentaries and interviews (7 programs); and youth (teenage programs done by and for youth, featuring local and national talent (40 programs).
Size & Elements: Videotape: 3/4" (over 1,000 videotapes, each 1 to 60 min.; viewing copies).
Cataloging: Computerized cataloging for staff use only.
Access: Available for duplication, subject to restrictions. Research requests accepted by mail.
Rights: Some rights held to all material. Additional clearances may be necessary in some cases if material is to be reused.
Licensing: Available for reuse, subject to restrictions. Duplication and shipping fees charged.
Restrictions: Requests for reuse subject to clearance and approval.
Viewing Facilities: Videotape (3/4" and 1/2").
Duplication Facilities: Videotape (3/4" and 1/2").

WISCONSIN (Milwaukee)

NATIONAL FUNERAL DIRECTORS ASSOCIATION
11121 West Oklahoma Avenue
Milwaukee, WI 53227
(414) 541-2500
Fax: (414) 541-1909

Bob Harden (Executive Director)

Contact: Kathy Walczak (Learning Resource Center)
Services: Association. Film and videotape material available to the public, researchers and scholars, and to NFDA members. Maintained for distribution rather than for research and reuse.
Description: Professional association established in 1882, providing professional education to funeral directors and consumers. With over 15,000 members, it is the largest professional organization of funeral directors in the world. Professional and consumer resources and audiovisual programs offered include films, videotapes and audiotapes on a variety of subjects. Material is geared towards funeral service directors, and in some cases is ideal for presentation to school and civic groups.

   Learning Resource Center material. Titles include: *The NFDA Embalming Short-Course for Experienced Practitioners,* a color videotape demonstrating effective embalming techniques (including multi-site injection and effective uses of the trocar); NFDA's *Tribute to Military-Mortuary Affairs,* paying tribute to the Graves Registration/Memorial Affairs personnel; *Hospice and the Funeral Director,* providing a comprehensive description of the funeral director's role in the hospice-care setting; *Funeral Service: A Healing Profession,* explaining the value of the funeral and is designed for use on local community access cable television stations; *A Natural Part of Life,* ideal for conveying to families the role of the funeral director, the need and value of the funeral service, and how families react to and confront death; and *When A Child Dies.*

   Videotapes from Batesville Management Services. Titles include: *Funeral Service in the 1980s — Serving People, Serving Needs,* a community education film that depicts funeral service today; *Why Study Death?,* the real story of a death education class as conducted by a funeral director; *Suicide; Talking about Death with Children,* created to explain to the child what death means, why it happens, what happens to the body, and why we have a funeral; *Living — When A Loved One Has Died,* suggesting ways to cope with the feelings of depression, guilt and anger so one can work toward a new life; *Widows and Widowers: Problems and Adjustments,* based on an actual research study examining the problems faced by widows and widowers during their first critical year of bereavement; and *Sudden Infant Death: The Promise Unfulfilled,* examining the SIDS phenomenon and discussing its effects.
Size & Elements: Film: 16mm. Videotape: VHS. (Approx. 15 to 20 titles total).
Cataloging: Published catalog.
Access: Open to researchers, scholars, the public, and members of the NFDA. Maintained for distribution rather than for research or reuse. Research fees not charged. Purchase requests accepted by mail and telephone.
Rights: Full rights held to some material. NFDA has specifically compiled videotapes for media use and educational presentations. There are usually no clearance problems with this material. Some of the other films and videotapes may require additional clearances depending on intended use of group or individual.
Licensing: Apply for information.
Restrictions: Apply for information.
Viewing Facilities: None.

Duplication Facilities: None.
Related Materials: Consumer education pamphlets available: *Anatomical Gifts; Cremation; Easing the Burden — Prearranging Your Funeral; Embalming; Funerals Are For the Living; Funeral Etiquette; Suicide; A Way To Remember — Choosing A Funeral Ceremony; What Are My Options? — A Guide to Final Disposition;* and *When A Co-Worker Has Died.* Pre-need audiocassettes available on related subjects.

WISCONSIN (Milwaukee)

WTMJ INC.
720 East Capitol Drive
Milwaukee, WI 53201
(414) 223-5383
(414) 332-9611
Fax: (414) 223-5298

Tom Luljak (News Director)

Contact: Wayne Will (Senior Tape Editor)
Services: Television broadcaster; film and videotape archives. Not open to the public. Very limited access for news organizations and researchers. Material not available for commercial reuse or rebroadcast.
Description: Television news coverage (1950-present). Holds an extensive range of Milwaukee news stories, as well as some national and international news.
Size & Elements: Film: 16mm (1 million feet; negative and positive, prints and originals, black and white and color, optical and magnetic sound). Videotape: 3/4" (2,000 hours).
Cataloging: Card catalogs; show rundowns; shot lists; dope sheets; research library.
Access: Not open to the public. Very limited access for news organizations and researchers. Research requests accepted by mail.
Rights: Full rights held to all material. Additional clearances may be necessary in some cases if material is to be reused.
Licensing: Available for licensing, subject to restrictions.
Restrictions: Requests for licensing and reuse considered on a case-by-case basis and subject to clearance and approval. Material not available for commercial purposes or for rebroadcast.
Viewing Facilities: Film and videotape.
Duplication Facilities: Film (film-to-videotape transfers); videotape (3/4").

WISCONSIN (Oshkosh)

EXPERIMENTAL AIRCRAFT ASSOCIATION
Wittman Airfield
Oshkosh, WI 54903-3086
(414) 426-4800
Fax: (414) 426-4828

Contact: Joan Philippi Seybold (Marketing and Communications) (Ext. 3067)
Services: Association; film and videotape producer. Material maintained primarily for distribution and purchase. Some material possibly available for reuse in nonprofit situations.
Description: Aviation footage (World War II-present). Subjects include experimental aircraft, airplanes, Voyager, aeronautics, World War II, Kitty Hawk, the Wright Brothers, aerobatics, Pearl Harbor, the Air Force and helicopters.
World War II and war documentaries. Historic aviation films include World War II footage drawn from the collection of Morton Lester. The *Aviation in the News* series is a collection of wartime news reports as they originally appeared (1942-45) in United News, the U.S. government-funded newsreel chronicle of World War II, originally produced for overseas audiences. *1942* features the Flying Tigers, Midway, North Africa, and the Air Cadets. *1943* includes Guadalcanal, gliders, Italy and General Douglas MacArthur. *1944* covers the D-Day Invasion, Saipan, China and Berlin. *1945* focuses on battles in the Philippines, Dresden, Okinawa and Tokyo. Other titles include: *Fighter Aces of World War II, War Hawks; The Mosquito Story; The Top Aces; P-51 Fighter Movie; Battle Hell Vietnam; Hell Over Korea; Attack-Pacific!; Battle of Britain; Thunderbolt* (color World War II documentary); *From Pearl Harbor to Tokyo; The B-17 Story; B-24 at War; Flying the Bombers; Bombers Over North Africa; World War II Flight Training; Combat Camera Unit* (May, 1945); and *Attack Carrier.* Other military films include: *MiG 29 Fulcrums,* a "sneak peek" at the famous Russian fighter, filmed secretly at a Finnish air show; *Chopper Pilot; The Story of the Helicopter;* and

Thunderbirds/Blue Angels.
Technical and mechanical videotapes. How-to videotapes on aircraft design, building and restoration. Complete flight training programs. Study guides for FAA examinations. Sample titles include: *The Wonderful World of Floats; Basic Aircraft Welding and Woodworking;* and *How to Fly Holding Patterns.*
Size & Elements: Videotape: VHS, Betamax and 8mm (approx. 70 videotapes).
Cataloging: Published catalogs.
Access: Available to the public for purchase. Research requests accepted by mail and telephone.
Rights: Full rights held to some material.
Licensing: Available for licensing and reuse, subject to restrictions.
Restrictions: Footage is available for nonprofit reuse only; no commercial use permitted.
Viewing Facilities: None.
Duplication Facilities: Videotape.

WYOMING

WYOMING (Cheyenne)

WYOMING STATE HISTORICAL SOCIETY
Executive Headquarters
Barrett Building
Cheyenne, WY 82002
(307) 777-7015

David Kathka, Ph.D. (Executive Secretary)

Contact: Judy West (State Coordinator)
Services: Historical society. One film available to the public for free loan.
Description: *Wyoming From the Beginning* (28 min.) is a film panorama of Wyoming's history and folklore. The film is an overview of the history of Wyoming from prehistoric times to statehood in 1890. Starting with the pictographs of prehistoric man, the film moves to 1743, when the French Canadian de la Verendrye brothers came to the area, and goes on to depict the era of mountain men, immigrants, Pony Express, railroad construction and expansion, establishment of the territory, womens' suffrage, Yellowstone Park, and the development of the cattle industry.
Size & Elements: Film: 16mm (1 title).
Cataloging: None specified.
Access: Open to the public. Videotape available for free loan.
Rights: Full rights held to all material.
Licensing: Apply for information. License fees not charged.
Restrictions: None specified.
Viewing Facilities: None.
Duplication Facilities: None.

WYOMING (Cody)

BUFFALO BILL HISTORICAL CENTER
HAROLD McCRACKEN RESEARCH LIBRARY
P.O. Box 1000
Cody, WY 82414
(307) 587-4771

Street address: 720 Sheridan

Peter H. Hassrick (Director)

Contact: Christina Stopka (Librarian/Archivist)
Services: Museum. Film and videotape archives available to researchers and scholars only.
Description: Majority of archival holdings are historical footage (ca. 1900-13) relating to William F. "Buffalo Bill" Cody and the Wild West Show, including original show footage and modern commentary. Other footage includes: *Cowboy Fun* in the rain; Mexican rope tricks; *Stampede; Yellowstone National Park; Porcupine; Branding; Sheep Dip* and original footage by photographer Charles Belden on ranch life (late 1920s-30s, 19 min.). Other films cover such topics as: General Custer; animals; the Indian Wars; Battle of Wounded Knee; and cavalry maneuvers. There is also footage of Cody, Wyoming and the surrounding area, including early parades and other events.
Western feature films held in the museum's collection include classics

WYOMING (Laramie)

starring Tom Mix, William S. Hart, Gene Autry, Roy Rogers, Audie Murphy, Lash LaRue, John Wayne and more.

Videotape documentaries, many produced for television, cover topics relating to the history of Wyoming and Colonel Cody.
Size & Elements: Film: 16mm (42 reels); 8mm (1 title). Videotape: 3/4" (15 titles); VHS (10 titles).
Cataloging: Film lists; research library.
Access: Open to researchers and scholars only. Research fees charged in some cases, depending on use. Research requests accepted by mail, telephone and in person (by appointment only).
Rights: Full rights held to some material. Some rights held to some material. Some material in the public domain. Rights status of some material not known.
Licensing: Available for licensing and reuse, subject to restrictions. License and usage fees charged in some cases.
Restrictions: Requests for viewing and reuse of material subject to case-by-case consideration (due to the rarity of some archival footage).
Viewing Facilities: None.
Duplication Facilities: None.

WYOMING (Laramie)

UNIVERSITY OF WYOMING
AMERICAN HERITAGE CENTER
P.O. Box 3924
University Station
Laramie, WY 82071
(307) 766-6385

Emmet D. Chisum (Research Historian)

Contact: Emmet D. Chisum
Services: Educational institution. Film collection open to researchers and scholars only. Material available for duplication and reuse, subject to restrictions.
Description: Film collections donated or loaned by approximately 150 individuals, accompanying their personal papers and manuscript collections. Donors include: Carroll Baker, Anne Baxter, Jack Benny, Robert Bloch, Skip Blumberg, Harry Joe Brown II, Niven Busch, Albert Glasser, Jack Glenn, Victor Gruen, A. Handley, Fay and Michael Kanin, Stan Lee, Warren Lewis, Helen Ives Lovelock, Jack Oakie, James Petrie, Richard de Rochemont, Jay Sandrich, William Self, Oliver Unger, Dick Van Dyke, Montgomery Ward, Mort Weisinger, Robert Wynn and Albert Zugsmith.
Size & Elements: Film (format and amount unspecified).
Cataloging: Currently cataloged only by donor name, not by film title.
Access: Open to researchers and scholars only. Research requests accepted by mail and telephone.
Rights: Full rights held to some material. Additional clearances necessary in some cases if material is to be reused.
Licensing: Available for duplication, licensing and reuse, subject to restrictions.
Restrictions: All research requests subject to acceptance and approval. Reuse of material subject to copyright and donor restrictions.
Viewing Facilities: None (facilities planned).
Duplication Facilities: None.

WYOMING (Riverton)

INTERNATIONAL AVIATION PUBLISHERS, INC.
P.O. Box 36
Riverton, WY 82501-0036
(800) 443-9250

Street address: 1000 College View Drive

Jerry L. Williams (President)

Contacts: Norma Franklin (Administrative Assistant); Jim Williams (Publisher's Representative)
Services: Film and videotape producer and distributor. Material maintained for distribution and rental rather than for research or reuse.
Description: Basic aviation maintenance training films and FAA instructional films. *Integrated Training Programs, Aviation Technician Training Series* and *Practical Projects* series are aimed at aviation and pilot training schools, and offer instruction in basic aviation maintenance knowledge. There are also supplementary training aids covering mathematics, physics, basic electricity,

aircraft and aircraft maintenance.
FAA Film Reproductions are also used for this purpose and cover a wide range of topics on maintenance and aviation safety. Topics include: air traffic control, history of flying machines, wind shears, skyfarming, aerobatic flying skills, airports, aircraft noise problems, microwave landing systems, hypoxia, disorientation, safe altitude warning, radar contact, low frequency navigation, density altitude and meteorology.
Size & Elements: Videotape: 3/4", VHS and Betamax (approx. 36 titles).
Cataloging: Published catalogs.
Access: Maintained for distribution and rental rather than for research or reuse.
Rights: Full rights held to all material. Additional clearances may be necessary in some cases if material is to be reused.
Licensing: Apply for information.
Restrictions: Material available for educational purposes only. Requests to duplicate material must be received in writing.
Viewing Facilities: None.
Duplication Facilities: None.
Distributors: Network of distributors (apply for information).

CANADA/ALBERTA

ALBERTA (Calgary)

EM/MEDIA ARCHIVES
1014 Macleod Trail, SE
Calgary, AB T2G 2M7
(403) 263-2833

Grant Poier (Administrator)

Contacts: Grant Poier; Patti Mertz (Production Manager)
Services: Nonprofit media center. Videotape archives open to the public for in-house use only; collection available for rental, broadcast and cablecast.
Description: Videotapes by artists working in and visiting Calgary (1978-present). Includes documentation of events, performances, exhibitions and single-channel video works. Material covers a broad range from experimental to documentary.
Experimental work by Calgary artists. Work reflects the individual interests of the artists. Some common themes are examination of physical and psychological environments; studies in the constructs of identity; and the effect of the media on the individual and society. Generally these works are non-narrative.
Documentary. Documentation of artistic activities such as performances, installations and other temporary exhibitions; and documentary videotapes on various subjects.
Size & Elements: Videotape: 3/4" (120 titles, each 4 to 60 min.; submasters and viewing copies).
Cataloging: Title listing; computerized database system planned.
Access: Open to the public. For in-house use only. Research fees not charged. Research requests accepted by mail and in person (walk-in and by appointment). Available for rental, broadcast and cablecast (apply for conditions and fees).
Rights: Some rights held to some material. Most rights retained by individual artists. Additional clearances may be necessary in some cases if material is to be reused.
Licensing: Apply for information.
Restrictions: None specified.
Viewing Facilities: Videotape (3/4" and VHS).
Duplication Facilities: Videotape (3/4" and VHS).
Related Materials: Audiotapes by artists, produced at EM/Media.

ALBERTA (Calgary)

GLENBOW MUSEUM
ARCHIVES
130 9th Avenue, SE
Calgary, AB T2G 0P3
(403) 264-8300
Fax: (403) 265-9769
Telex: 03-825571

Duncan Cameron (Director)

Contact: Glenn Myhr

Services: Museum. Film and videotape collection open to the public; some footage available for duplication and reuse, subject to restrictions.
Description: Regions covered (1917-78) include Canada (Alberta, Calgary, Saskatchewan, Northwest Territory and Yukon) and the U.S. (Alaska, Florida and Wyoming).

Subjects include: agriculture; archaeology (Buffalo jump dig); aviation, Bible camps; Calgary; Canadian Youth Hostel Association; charitable organizations (United Way); coal industry; Eskimos; Glenbow Museum; historical events; Hutterites; Indians (arts and crafts, ceremonies and way of life); military training; mountain sheep; Northwest Mounted Police; personalities (A.C. Leighton [artist] and Jimmy Simpson); petroleum industry; pioneer life; politicians (Robert Stanfield [PC Party] and Robert Thompson [Social Credit]); power development (Calgary Power Company); provincial parks (Kananaskis); rodeos; Royal tour (1951); Shriners (Florida); and sports (skiing).

Agriculture. Films (1930s-70s) relating to various topics, include: agricultural machinery; production of sugar beets; honeybees; milk; grain; hogs; cattle and poultry; weed and insect control; irrigation; cooperative associations (Alberta Wheat Pool Saskatchewan Wheat Pool, and United Grain Growers); and 4-H Clubs.

Aviation. Films (1928-30s) relating to bush pilots and Northern mail service; Calgary Air Show; and Trans-Canada Air Pageant.

Indian ceremonies. Films (1946-60s) include: Blood Indian Sun Dance; Blackfoot Medicine Pipe Dance; and Blackfoot Holy Hand Game.

Petroleum industry. Films (1920s-60s) include: oil exploration and drilling in the Yukon, Northwest Territories, Northern Alberta and Turner Valley, Alberta; and well fire at Atlantic #3 (Leduc, Alberta).

Rodeos. Films (1919-40) include: Calgary Stampede footage (rodeo events, chuck wagon racing and parades); *Calgary Stampede* (feature film starring Hoot Gibson); and Cheyenne rodeo.

Feature films include: *Back to God's Country* (1919); *Calgary Stampede* (1925); *Feathered Braves* (1926); *Nanook of the North* (1920); and *Until They Get Me* (1917).
Size & Elements: Film: 35mm (3,000 feet); 16mm (145,000 feet); 8mm (2,000 feet) (300 titles and 390 cans total). Videotape: 1/2" (6 videotapes, each 30 min.).
Cataloging: Rough draft of catalog available.
Access: Open to the public. Some footage available for in-house duplication. Research fees not charged. Research requests accepted by mail, telephone and in person (walk-in).
Rights: Full rights held to some material. Some rights held to some material. Additional clearances may be necessary in some cases if material is to be reused. Rights status of some material not known.
Licensing: Available for licensing and reuse, subject to restrictions. Usage fees charged; fees determined by nature of usage (no formal price schedule).
Restrictions: Requests for licensing and reuse subject to acceptance and approval. Restrictions may apply where full rights are not held.
Viewing Facilities: Film (16mm) (by appointment only); videotape.
Duplication Facilities: Film (16mm to 3/4" or 1/2" videotape).

ALBERTA (Calgary)

SUICIDE INFORMATION AND EDUCATION CENTRE
1615 10th Avenue, SW, Suite 201
Calgary, AB T3C 0J7
(403) 245-3900

G. G. Harrington (Director)

Contact: Karen Kiddey
Services: Government agency and library. Film and videotape available for research and loan; not available for duplication or reuse.
Description: Collection of films and videotapes on suicidal behavior, counseling and prevention, teenage suicide, bereavement, families with histories of suicide, suicidal depression and other subjects.
Size & Elements: Film: 16mm (5 titles; color). Videotape: 3/4" and VHS (13 titles).
Cataloging: Title list; computerized cataloging available to researchers.
Access: Open to the public. Available for rental for research, education and training purposes only. Research fees not charged. Rental requests accepted by mail, telephone and in person.
Rights: Some rights held to some material.
Licensing: Rights are largely retained by original media producers.
Restrictions: Not available for duplication or reuse. Some titles available only for training programs.

Viewing Facilities: Film (16mm); videotape (3/4" and VHS).
Duplication Facilities: None.

ALBERTA (Edmonton)

PROVINCIAL ARCHIVES OF ALBERTA
12845 102 Avenue
Edmonton, AB T5N 0M6
(403) 427-1750

Brian Speirs (Provincial Archivist)

Contacts: Brock Silversides (Senior Archivist; Audiovisual and Technical Services); Marlena Wyman (Archivist; Audiovisual and Technical Services)
Services: Government agency. Film and videotape collection open to the public. Material available for duplication and reuse, subject to restrictions.
Description: Films produced by or for the Government of Alberta; and broadcast archives containing material generated by Alberta radio and television stations. Materials are grouped by collection. Collections exceeding five moving image items include:

Alberta Public Affairs Bureau Collection (Province of Alberta) (1950s-60s, 12 films, 330 min. total). Titles include: *Alberta Food Products; Trout Fishing, Jasper; Holiday Activities in Rocky Mountains; Vacation in Calgary and Rocky Mountains; Provincial Government Programs; Skiing in Banff and Jasper National Parks; Fishing in Alberta; Winter Activities in Alberta;* and *Fundamental Hockey Skills, University of Alberta.*

Alberta School Broadcasts Collection (Department of Education) (1967-79, 144 videotapes, 70 hours total). Elementary school subjects. Sample titles include: *Lay of the Land; Community Helpers; Ears, Eyes and Nose Against the World; Alberta at Work; Peoples of Alberta; Focus on Wildlife; Sex N' Stuff; Alberta's Changing Environment; Canada's Endangered Species; Movement Colours the World; Art Galleries and Museums; Survival in the Wilderness;* and *Pow Wow.*

Alberta School Broadcasts Collection (Department of Education) (1950-73, 67 films, 31 hours total). Elementary school subjects. Sample titles include: *Pulp and Paper; In the Mountains,* on Banff; *Columbia Ice Fields; Lethbridge; Tar Sands, Fort McMurray; Alberta's Tourist Industry; Ukrainian Settlers; Peace River — W. A. Bennett Dam; Bill Before the House,* on the Alberta Legislature; *Alberta Manufacturing; Muskeg Swamps; Dying Coal Industry, Nordegg, Alberta;* and *Centennial Voyageur Canoe Race.*

Alberta's 75th Anniversary Commission Collection (Province of Alberta) (1980, 26 films, 32 videotapes). Historical recreations and dramatizations pertaining to Alberta's history.

Alberta Social Credit League Collection (1954, 51 films, 787 min. total). Speeches made by Social Credit politicians. Includes: speeches by Premier E. Manning; election addresses; a CBC-TV documentary about Premier E. Manning; *A Visit with Social Credit Premier Harry Strom; Alberta Together,* a campaign film with Premier Harry Strom; and *Social Credit Leadership Convention — Red Deer.*

Alfred Blyth Collection I (1939-50s, 18 films, 197 min. total). Scenic travel footage by an Edmonton photographer and cinematographer. Titles include: *Vacation: Edmonton to Florida; Vacation: Edmonton to California; Sunland Biscuit Company Limited, Edmonton; Calgary Stampede; Re-enactment of Reverend Rundle's arrival in Edmonton; New York footage; 49th Battalion in training; Autumn in the Rockies;* and *Québec City footage.*

Alfred Blyth Collection II (1940s-50s, 9 films, 75 min. total). Industrial and recreation footage. Titles include: *Canadian Bedding Company Limited, Edmonton; Ride 'Em Cowboy, Calgary Stampede; Events at Edmonton Gardens; Winter activities, Alberta; Calgary Stampede;* and *Poultry Industry, Alberta Poultry Producers Limited.*

The Leigh Brintnell/Stan McMillan Collection (1928-40, 10 reels, 2 hours total). Early northern prairie aviation. Items include: *Prairie Air Mail/Cleveland Air Races; Aviation at Fort McMurry/Bear Lake; Great Bear Lake Picnic; McKenzie Trip; Epic Plane Journey of 4,000 Miles;* and *Canadian Pacific Airlines.*

CBC-TV Collection (1940-84, 1417 cans, 478 hours total). News clips and documentaries on Alberta history, music and personalities.

CFRN Collection (1975-81, with a few items from 1935, 639 reels, 182 hours total). Provincial footage; news; airchecks; documentaries; and stock shots from the Edmonton affiliate of CTV. News and airchecks include: daily news highlights (January 1969-October 1970); Western Canada News Round-Ups (January-July 1969); year-end news summaries (1956-64); and airchecks (1958-60). Documentaries include: original footage, final programs and outtakes (1950-79), including the 1978 Commonwealth Games. Stock shots (1935, 1950s, 1975-81) cover communities in Alberta, personalities and a subject file including strikes, official openings, buildings, and other similar categories.

CITV Collection (1975-83, 177 films, 45 hours total). Local footage from an Edmonton television station, including commercials, news, sports, telecast film clips and documentaries. Titles and subjects include: *Fort McMurray;* City of Edmonton and Klondike Days promotions; *Snow Fighters,* on aspects of snow removal and road maintenance and repair undertaken by the city; *Orphans of Mount Yamnuska,* a feature length film; *Operation Morning Light,* on clean-up operations of Kosmos 954 Satellite which crashed in the Northwest Territories; footage relating to the construction and operation of the Edmonton LRT system; and material on the 1976 Federal Progressive Conservative Leadership Contest.

Department of Agriculture (Province of Alberta) (1920s-30s, 26 films, 148 min. total). Titles include: *Manufacture of Paper, Palmer-New York; Dairy Production, Edmonton; Raising Poultry; Growing/Marketing Potatoes; Bar U Ranch, Southern Alberta; Fur Farming, Edmonton District; Olds Agriculture College; Growing Registered Seed; Weeds of Alberta; Wildlife of Alberta; Alberta Government Buildings, Edmonton and Fort Saskatchewan; Household Hints;* and *Farming in Central Alberta, Ukrainian District.*

Department of Agriculture (Province of Alberta) (1963-81, 24 films, 600 min. total). Educational presentations on subjects related to agriculture. Titles include: *Sheep Shearing/Using Wool; More From the Land; Nutrition/Balanced Diet; Man's Dependence on Agriculture; Cattle Breed Importations; Alberta Food Products; Future of Grain Industry — Alberta Wheat Pool; Agricultural Spraying;* and *Horse Training, Cochrane, Alberta.*

Department of Agriculture (Province of Alberta) (1964-72, 19 films, 712 min. total). Produced by the CBC and government agencies. Titles include: *Farm Buildings in the Prairie Provinces; Farm Homes; Family Farm Management; Marketing Hogs and Cereal Grains; Swine Production; Soil Management; Designing the Shelterbelt; Farm Paying Practices; Sanitary Milk Production; Irrigation, Lethbridge; No Hoof — No Horse;* and *How to Sell Grain.*

Edmonton Commercial Graduates Basketball Club (1930s-40s, 11 films, 61 min. total). Activities and some game footage of Edmonton Graduates. Items include: *28 Graduates on way to 1936 Berlin Olympics; Parade and Royal Visit 1939; Graduates Vacationing at Cameron Falls; Graduates Banquet; Game footage, Graduates vs. Queen Anne Candies;* and *Highland Games, Edmonton.*

Ernest E. Poole Foundation Collection (1925-40s, 13 films, 67 min. total). Early construction activity. Items include: *Construction on Calgary-Banff highway; Edmonton Royal Visit; Construction sites; Winter Activities, Edmonton and Banff; Pile Driving; Opening of General Motors Plant, Regina; Signing of Natural Resources Agreement, Regina; Road construction near Regina; Poole family; Bricklaying;* and *Aerial footage of Medicine Hat.*

Thames Television (1972, 11 films, 77 min. total). British views of Alberta recreation and lifestyle. Titles include: *Trip on Air Canada; Heritage Park; Drumheller; Calgary Stampede; Cindy Rocket; 4-H Clubs; Native Life; Cadet Camp, Banff; The Rockies; Cutting Horses;* and *Klondyke Days.*

Size & Elements: Film: format unspecified (approx. 2,800 cans; positive, negative, reversal and originals). Videotape: 3/4" (amount unspecified; viewing copies).
Cataloging: Card catalogs; synopses.
Access: Open to the public. Some material available for duplication. Research fees not charged. Research requests accepted only in person (walk-in).
Rights: Full rights held to some material. Additional clearances may be necessary in some cases if material is to be reused.
Licensing: Available for licensing and reuse, subject to restrictions. License and usage fees not charged.
Restrictions: Various restrictions apply to certain collections (apply for information).
Viewing Facilities: Film (2 Cinescans, 2 Steenbecks); videotape (3/4").
Duplication Facilities: None.

ALBERTA (Edmonton)

UNIVERSITY OF ALBERTA
BOREAL INSTITUTE FOR NORTHERN STUDIES LIBRARY
CW 401 Biological Sciences Building
Edmonton, AB T6G 2E9
(403) 432-4409
Fax: (403) 492-1153
Telex: 037-2179

Mrs. G. A. Cooke (Head Librarian)

Contact: Elaine Simpson
Services: Research center. Film and videotape library available for research purposes.
Description: Contemporary documentaries (1940s-80s) relating to Arctic regions and native peoples. Topics include: the building of the Alaska highway, regional mythology, Atlantic Richfield's oil drilling, oil pipelines and offshore drilling, whaling, moose, seals, caribou, trapping, anthropological studies, Eskimo villages, ecology, fishing, the aurora borealis and the Aleut language.
Size & Elements: Film: format unspecified (30 titles). Videotape: format unspecified (18 titles).
Cataloging: Computerized cataloging available to researchers. Research library.
Access: Open to the public. Research fees not charged. Research requests accepted by mail and telephone.
Rights: Some rights held to some material.
Licensing: Apply for information. License fees not charged.
Restrictions: None specified.
Viewing Facilities: None.
Duplication Facilities: None.

ALBERTA (Edmonton)

UNIVERSITY OF ALBERTA
FACULTY OF EXTENSION
EDUCATIONAL MEDIA SERVICES
132 Corbett Hall
82nd Avenue and 112th Street
Edmonton, AB T6G 2G4
(403) 432-5041

Jim Shaw (Professor)

Contact: Clare Osterman (Operations Supervisor)
Services: University media services; film collection.
Description: Locally produced films, including: *Behavior of the Barren Ground Cariboo; Churchill Tribute; Soils of Alberta; Royal Visit of 1939; Banff to Lake Louise; Jasper National Park; Age of the Beaver;* and *We Just Take It All For Granted.*
Size & Elements: Film: 16mm (52 titles).
Cataloging: Printed list.
Access: Apply for information.
Rights: Full rights held to some material.
Licensing: Apply for information.
Restrictions: None specified.
Viewing Facilities: None.
Duplication Facilities: None.

CANADA/BRITISH COLUMBIA

BRITISH COLUMBIA (Burnaby)

INDEPENDENT MEDIA COMMUNICATIONS
301 North Grosvenor Avenue
Burnaby, BC V5B 1J3
(604) 298-6397

Michael Burri (Executive Director)

Contact: Michael Burri
Services: Film and videotape producer and distributor. Collection available to the public for duplication, licensing and reuse, subject to restrictions. Custom shooting services and location finding services available.
Description: Color footage of Canada, specifically Alberta and British Columbia, including various travel destinations such as cities, towns, resorts and national parks. Also holds footage of special events (fairs, sports, media events, and public events of all types); scenics; national parks; nature; and all parts of Canada, particularly Western Canada.

Also distributes full-length feature films, half-hour news programs, two-hour documentaries and self-help shows. Provides custom shooting services and location finding services. Also involved in development of the Sony high-definition television system (HDTV).
Size & Elements: Videotape: HDTV (high-definition television), D2 (digital), 1", MII, 3/4", VHS and Betamax.
Cataloging: Computerized cataloging for staff use only.

Access: Available to the public for duplication and reuse. Research fees charged. Research requests accepted by mail and telephone.
Rights: Full rights held to all material.
Licensing: Available for licensing, subject to restrictions. License fees charged (rates negotiable).
Restrictions: Some material not available for general release.
Viewing Facilities: Videotape (3/4" and VHS).
Duplication Facilities: None.
Related Materials: 100,000 35mm slides.

BRITISH COLUMBIA (Vancouver)

CANADIAN FILMMAKERS DISTRIBUTION WEST
Pacific Cine Centre
1131 Howe Street, Suite 100
Vancouver, BC V6Z 2L7
(604) 684-3014

Contact: Sylvia Jonescu-Lisitza
Services: Distributor. Films and videotapes available to the public for rental and purchase.
Description: Nonprofit organization operating as a collective and the largest distributor of independently produced Canadian films in Western Canada representing more than 200 filmmakers from British Columbia and throughout the country. Beginning in 1979 as a branch of the Toronto-based Canadian Filmmakers' Distribution Centre in 1979, the Vancouver office became an independent operation in 1982. The major purpose of the CFDW is to provide a viable channel for the distribution of films which are not generally regarded as commercially oriented. Collection consists of a varied body of work embracing a wide spectrum of the film arts, presenting film users with an alternative to mainstream cinema.

Categories include: animation; art and artists; British Columbia; environment; fiction; the individual and society; Canadian history; community studies; consumerism; war and peace; world cultures; sports and recreation.

Animation. Films by Jonathan Amitay, Jim Anderson, Cliff Baldwin, Jim Bescott, Dave Burgess, M. Marilyn Cherenko, Dan Collins, Richard Dudley, Sylvie Fefer, Eileen Hoeter, Bill Horne, Dave Horne, Mal Hoskin, Steve Insley, Kirk Johns, Jim Kalnin, Dorothy Kaminski, Tami Knight, Ted Laturnus, Gordon Lawson, Kathy Li, Ken Lidster, Bill Maylone, Kevin McCracken, Shelley McIntosh, Mark Murphy, John Paizs, Howard Pedlar, Peter von Puttkamer, Martin Rose, Al Sens, Keith Slade, John Straiton, Wendy Tilby, Carol Trepanier and Ken Wallace.

Art and artists. Titles include: *Celebration of the Raven* (Ken Kuramoto), on Bill Reid, Haida artist; *George Norris in Depth* (Noel Archambault), on the British Columbia sculptor; *Granny's Quilts* (Zale and Laara Dalen); *Ranch* (Steven DeNure), on the Alan Wood Ranch Project, a massive environmental art piece built in the Rockies; and *Shades of Red* (David Rimmer and Paula Ross).

British Columbia. Titles include *Canneries* (Bonnie Devlin, Steven Insley and Tracey Jeffrey), an historical exploration of the salmon canning industry in British Columbia; *Cowboys Don't Cry* (Barbara Willis Sweete), on a young woman filmmaker and her cowboy grandfather; *For Twenty Cents a Day* (Jim Monro and Eileen Bostwick), on the struggles of migrant workers during the Great Depression; *Foundry* (Myrna Cobb and Deborah Mason); *In the Daytime* (Stanley Fox and Peter Varley, 1950; restored by Dennis Duffy, 1986), an impressionistic record of Vancouver city life on a summer day in 1949; *A Living Celebration* (Nathan Enns), on Stanley Park; *Ninstints: Shadow Keepers of the Past,* the story of an abandoned Haida village on Anthony Island; and *Potlatch: A Strict Law Bids Us Dance* (Dennis Wheeler/U'Mista Cultural Society), on the history of the potlatch among the Kwakiutl Indians.

Environment. Titles include: *Ecology in Action* (Northern Lights Films), a history of the international Greenpeace movement; *Greenpeace: Voyages to Save the Whales* (Michael Chechik, Ron Precious and Fred Easton); *Kangaroos Under Fire* (Northern Lights Films); *Rites of Spring* (Michael Chechik), on the annual seal hunt off the Labrador coast; and *Slaves of the Harvest* (Northern Lights Films), on the slaughter of Pacific fur seals on the Pribilof Islands of Alaska.

Experimental. Films and videotapes by Jim Anderson, Gamma Bak, Raphael Bendahan, Marcella Bienvenue, Byron Black, Tom Braidwood, Peter Bryant, Robert Carney, Doug Chomyn, Steven DeNure, Jamie Dunnison, Bruce Elder, Ellie Epp, Chris Gallagher, Rob Groeneboer, Patricia Gruben, Sturla Gunnarsson, Rick Hancox, Scott Haynes, Maria Insell, Nicholas Kendall, Terry Kerr, Gordon Kidd, Fumio Kiyooka, Michael McGarry, Carolyn McLuskie, Lorne Marin, Richard Martin, Midi Onodera, Richard Patton, Al Razutis, David Rimmer, Randy Rotheisler, Michael Snow, Veronika

Soul, Kirk Tougas, Gord Verheul, Jana Veverka, Joe Vizmeg and Bruce Worrall.

The individual and society. Titles include: *The Bridal Shower* (Sandy Wilson), on the "collecting" ritual that reveals the games behind the gifts; *Inside/Out* (Peter Smilsky), on an inmate theater company at a Canadian federal prison preparing to stage the Joe Orton play *Loot;* and *White Lake, or The Making of Canadians* (Colin Browne), an experimental documentary on landscape, narrative and the invention of memory.
Size & Elements: Film: 16mm (approx. 400 titles). Videotape: format unspecified (approx. 50 titles).
Cataloging: Published catalog.
Access: Available to the public for rental and purchase. Requests accepted by mail and telephone.
Rights: Rights retained by original producers.
Licensing: Available for licensing and reuse, subject to clearance and restrictions. Written permission must be obtained.
Restrictions: Motion pictures are protected by copyright and the purchase of a film only includes the right to unlimited screenings of the film by a direct projection method in a non-commercial setting, but does not entail the right to distribute, sell, lease, duplicate, or televise the film, in whole or in part. Permission for any other use must be obtained in writing from the office of CFDW.
Viewing Facilities: None.
Duplication Facilities: None.
Representatives: Some titles available through Atlantic Independent Media (q.v.) and Canadian Filmmakers Distribution Centre (CFMDC) (q.v.).

BRITISH COLUMBIA (Vancouver)

GOETHE INSTITUTE VANCOUVER
944 West 8th Avenue
Vancouver, BC V5Z 1E5
(604) 732-3966
Fax: (604) 732-5062

Otfried Zimmermann (Director)

Contact: Helga Opsetmoen (Librarian)
Services: Educational institution; cultural institute; library. Videotape collection available primarily for teaching and research purposes.
Description: Documentaries on contemporary West Germany, its art and literature.
Size & Elements: Videotape: VHS (approx. 200 videotapes; viewing copies).
Cataloging: Card catalogs; published catalog.
Access: Open to the public for in-house viewing and free loan (to non-commercial users) (shipping fees charged). Research fees not charged. Research requests accepted by mail, telephone and in person (walk-in).
Rights: Full rights held to some material.
Licensing: Apply for information.
Restrictions: Copyright restrictions apply. Loaned only for non-commercial use.
Viewing Facilities: Videotape (by appointment only).
Duplication Facilities: None.

BRITISH COLUMBIA (Vancouver)

HOT SHOTS COMMERCIAL PRODUCTIONS INC.
1020 Mainland Street, Suite 100
Vancouver, BC V6B 2T4
(604) 662-7852
Fax: (604) 681-3299

Contact: Michael Terry (Production Coordinator)
Services: Film and videotape producer. Material available to the public for duplication, licensing and reuse.
Description: British Columbia-related subjects, including industrial and agricultural footage; wheat, fruit and fish harvesting; and aerial footage of Vancouver, glaciers, snow-capped mountains and the rugged British Columbia coastline. Licensor of *Our British Columbia,* a motion picture that played at the 1986 World Exposition.
Size & Elements: Film: 35mm and 16mm (amount unspecified). Videotape: 1" (amount unspecified; masters, transfers from film) and 3/4" (viewing copies).
Cataloging: Shot lists; computerized cataloging in progress.
Access: Available to the public for duplication and reuse. Research fees charged. Research requests accepted by mail and telephone.

CANADA/BRITISH COLUMBIA (Vancouver)

Rights: Full rights held to all material.
Licensing: Available for licensing and reuse. License fees charged.
Restrictions: None specified.
Viewing Facilities: Videotape (all formats)
Duplication Facilities: Videotape (all formats).

BRITISH COLUMBIA (Vancouver)

IDERA FILMS
2524 Cypress Street
Vancouver, BC V6J 3N2
(604) 738-8815

Contacts: Pat Dalgleish (Resource Center Manager); Carol Rublack (Films Officer)
Services: Resource center; film and videotape distributor. Materials available to the public for rental, purchase and broadcast in Canada only. Some material available for licensing and reuse.
Description: IDERA Films is the audiovisual resource library of the International Development Education Resource Association (IDERA), a nonprofit educational society established in 1974. IDERA's mandate is to provide educational resources to Canadians on international issues and concerns.

Films and videotapes (produced in many countries) relate to international development issues and are especially concerned with Third World countries.

Global development. Films and videotapes on banking, agribusiness and the pharmaceutical industry; and films produced by Habitat (United Nations Centre for Human Settlements).

Regional development. Films on Asia; the South Pacific region; Micronesia; the Philippines; Malaysia; Cambodia; India; Latin America; Central America; the Caribbean; Guatemala; Nicaragua; Honduras; El Salvador; Dominica; Puerto Rico; Jamaica; Cuba; Grenada; Chile; Peru; Bolivia; Brazil; South Africa; Zimbabwe; Tanzania; Namibia; and the Middle East.

Organizing for change. Films on economics; labor; the changing workplace; new technology; occupational health and safety; labor history; labor organizing; unemployment; indigenous peoples; women; the media; peace and disarmament; nuclear power; and community development.
Size & Elements: Film: 35mm and 16mm (approx. 275 titles, mostly 16mm; release prints). Videotape: 3/4" and VHS (some titles).
Cataloging: Published catalogs; release sheets.
Access: Open to the public. Available for rental, preview-for-purchase, purchase and broadcast in Canada only. Some material available for duplication and reuse. Research fees not charged. Research requests accepted by telephone and in person (by appointment only).
Rights: Full rights held to some material. Some rights held to all material. Additional clearances may be necessary in some cases if material is to be reused; IDERA will handle any necessary clearances.
Licensing: Available for licensing and reuse in some cases. License fees charged.
Restrictions: Available for rental, purchase and broadcast in Canada only.
Viewing Facilities: Film (16mm projector); videotape (3/4" and VHS).
Duplication Facilities: Videotape (3/4" and VHS).

BRITISH COLUMBIA (Vancouver)

PACIFIC CINÉMATHÈQUE PACIFIQUE
THE WESTERN CANADA FILM ARCHIVES COLLECTION
1131 Howe Street, Suite 200
Vancouver, BC V6Z 2L7
(604) 688-8202

Contact: Diedra McDevitt
Services: Film archives. Collection open to researchers and scholars for in-house use only.
Description: Films made in Canada, including independent documentary and experimental productions, collections donated by the National Film Board of Canada and by various Canadian libraries.

Sample titles and filmmakers represented: *1967-1969* (compiled 1971, Al Razutis); *The Bridal Shower* (1971) and *Growing Up At Paradise* (1977) (Sandy Wilson); *Brotherhood* (1970) and *Cinetude* (1969) (Al Sens); *Collected Films of Bryan R. Small* (Bryan R. Small); *Daylight Savings* (1976, Richard Bruce); *Do It With Joy* (1977, Nicholas Kendall); *Evolution at Brackendale* (1977, Claudine Viallon); *Gandy Dance* (1973) and *Granny's Quilts* (1974) (Zale Dalen); *Give That Person There A Camera* (1977, Richard Martin);

Greenpeace: Voyages To Save The Whales (1977, Michael Chechik); *The Inquiry Film* (1977, Jesse Nishihata); *Know Place* (1967, Sylvia Spring and Dave Rimmer); *Loin du Quebec (Far From Quebec)* (1971, Kirk Tougas); *Masks* (1972, Judith Eglington); *October Alms* (1978, Kalli Paakspuu); *Om Ma Ni Pad Me Hum* (1976, Byron Black); *The Paper Bag Catholix* (1975, Harry Kemball); *Passage* (1978-79, Sturla Gunnarson); *Potlatch... A Strict Law Bids Us Dance* (1975, Denis Wheeler); *Superfool* (1968), *Nitobe* (1969), *Shall We Gather At The River* (1970) (Tom Shandel); *Self-Portrait* (1976) (Gordon Kidd); *Synchronicity* (1974) (The Tunda Co-op); *Those Born at Massett: A Haida Stonemoving and Feast* (1978, Eileen Stearns); *Trapline* (1975, Ellie Epp); *Where Timber Wolves Call* (1974, Mike Collier); *Wind From the West* (1973, Tom Braidwood); *Woven In Time* (1977, Evelyn Roth); *Processed Gello* (1977, Pete Lipskis); *The Rules of Bowls* (1972, Doug White); and *Spartree* (1971, Phil Borsos).
Size & Elements: Film: format unspecified (approx. 200 titles). Videotape (format and amount unspecified).
Cataloging: Computerized list.
Access: Open to researchers and scholars only. Primarily for in-house use. Research requests accepted by mail and telephone.
Rights: Some rights held to some material. Additional clearances are necessary if material is to be reused.
Licensing: Apply for information.
Restrictions: Additional clearances are necessary in all cases if material is to be reused.
Viewing Facilities: Film.
Duplication Facilities: None.

BRITISH COLUMBIA (Vancouver)

VIDEO IN
(SATELLITE VIDEO EXCHANGE SOCIETY)
1102 Homer Street
Vancouver, BC V6B 2X6
(604) 688-4336

Contact: Karen Knights (Programmer); Cornelia Wyngaarden
Services: Media organization; library; film and videotape producer; film and videotape archives; educational institution; distributor. Videotape collection available for in-house viewing and distribution. Production and post-production services available to independent producers.
Description: Since 1973, SVES continues to integrate and facilitate noncommercial productions from around the world. A nonprofit organization dedicated to presenting and furthering the alternative uses of video, the SVES serves as an umbrella organization for a variety of services and special projects.

The international videotape library holds noncommercial videotape productions including video art, documentaries and experimental videotapes (1968-present). While the majority of the collection was produced by Canadian artists, work from the U.S. and other countries is represented. Virtually all important video artists are represented.

Special collections include: Vancouver Status of Women, Burnaby Art Gallery Video Collection, Metro Media and October Show collections.

Subject areas represented in collection include: biographies, education, labor, sexual awareness, drugs, handicapped lifestyles, adolescence, social awareness, ethnic cultures, native peoples, ecology, shelter technology, political theory, community politics, national politics, international politics, feminism, law, media, art theory, video art, multichannel video and installations, synaesthetic video, performance art, other visual arts, drama, music, dance, theater and literature.

Artists and producers represented in distribution collection include: Robert Adrian, Amelia Productions, Ric Amis, Neil Armstrong, Byron Ayanoglu, Anna Banana, Byron Black, Gabor Body, Lorna Boschman, Luc Bourdon, Gary Bourgeois, Dean Brousseau, Hank Bull, Mike Cady, Melodie Calvert, Canadian Shadow Players, Monty Cantsin, Doris Chase, Elizabeth Chitty, Teri Chmilar, Kate Craig, Arturo Cubacub, Gina Daniels, Nancy Davis, Janet Densmore, Sara Diamond, Daniel Dion, Downtown Community Television Center, Margaret Dragu, Lee Eisler, Teri Ewasiuk, Fraser Finlayson, Vera Frenkel, William Gaglione, John Galloway, Francois Girard, Michael Goldberg, Nelson Gray, John Greyson, Julie Harrison, Andy Harvey, Mona Hatoum, Bernar Hebert, High Hopes Media, Patrick Hughes, Hummer TV (Deanne Taylor, Jennifer Dean and Janet Burke), Nora Hutchinson, Mako Idemitsu, Joolz, Gerry Kisil, Richard Layzell, Paula Levine, Jorge Lozano, Mary Ann Lui, Tanya Mars, Marshalore, Steve McCaffery, Laurie McDonald, Robert McGinley, Eric Metcalfe, Edward Mowbray, Caroline Murray-Crick, Kou Nakajima, Marlin Oliveros, Michel Ouelette, Andrew James Paterson, Jan Peacock, Philippe Poloni, Popular Projects Society, Shawn Preus, Anne

Ramsden, Randy & Berenicci, Al Razutis, Jeanette Reinhardt, Clive Robertson, Ulrike Rosenbach, Donald Ellis Rothenberg, Marty St. James, Jay Samwald, Joe Sarahan, Jayce Salloum, Joyan Saunders, Lydia Schouten, James Seligman, Steve Smith, Valerie Soe, Speak Out Productions, Janice Starko, Lisa Steele, Barbara Steinman, Suite Five Video Productions, Ruth Taylor, Kim Tomczak, Vincent Trasov, Richard Truhlar, Ruby Truly, Keiko Tsuno, Vaerkstedet Vaerst, Elizabeth Vander Zaag, Mark Verabioff, Rodney Werden, Anne Wilson, Paul Wong, Joan Woodward, Cornelia Wyngaarden, Keigo Yamamoto, Bruce & Norman Yonemoto and Ivo Zanatta.

Size & Elements: Videotape: 3/4", VHS, Betamax and 1/2" open reel (approx. 2,000 titles; viewing copies).
Cataloging: Published catalogs; computerized cataloging for staff use only; research library.
Access: Open to the public. For in-house use only. Available for distribution, rental and purchase. Research fees not charged. Research requests accepted by mail, telephone and in person (walk-in).
Rights: Some rights held to all material. Most rights retained by artists or producers. Additional clearances may be necessary in some cases if material is to be reused.
Licensing: Available for licensing and reuse, subject to restrictions. License fees charged in some cases.
Restrictions: Permission for reuse must be obtained from artists or producers. Various restrictions apply, depending on specific production and intended use.
Viewing Facilities: Videotape (3/4", VHS, Betamax and 1/2" open reel; NTSC and PAL).
Duplication Facilities: Videotape (3/4", VHS, Betamax and 1/2" open reel).
Publications: *Video Guide,* published six times a year as a venue to promote and discuss independent video production.
Related Materials: Library and study center also holds a collection of print material relating to video and media.

BRITISH COLUMBIA (Vancouver)

WESTERN FRONT SOCIETY
WESTERN FRONT VIDEO
303 East 8th Avenue
Vancouver, BC V5T 1S1
(604) 876-9343

Kate Craig (Video Co-ordinator)

Contact: Kate Craig
Services: Educational institution; library; film and videotape producer; film and videotape archives. Material available for research, rental, purchase and reuse, subject to restrictions.
Description: Founded 1973 partly to facilitate the increasing demands being made by artists for production and performance-oriented activity. The first videotapes documented literary readings, music concerts and performances. In 1977 the Western Front began commissioning video works by artists, and has invited artists from Canada, the U.S., Europe and Japan to participate in this program.
Special productions. Works by Dana Atchley, Marcella Bienvenue, Susan Britton, Norbert Brunner, Hank Bull, Colin Campbell, Cioni Carpi, Elizabeth Chitty, Marie Chouinard, Norman Cohn, Kate Craig, Tom Dean, Margaret Dragu, Don Druick, Jane Ellison, Gathie Falk, Robert Filliou, Kenneth Fletcher, Vera Frenkel, General Idea, Jochen Gerz, Nora Hutchinson, Sanja Ivekovic, Glenn Lewis, Chip Lord, Marshalore, Dalibor Martinis, Fabio Mauri, Eric Metcalfe, Ian Murray, Kou Nakajima, David Alan Ostrem, Andrew James Paterson, Patricia Plattner, Randy & Berenicci, Patrick Ready, Clive Robertson, Tom Sherman, Lisa Steele, Kim Tomczak, Liz Vander Zaag, Klaus vom Bruch and Paul Wong.
Performance documents. Performances by Anna Banana, Bruce Barber, Hank Bull, Cabaret Voltaire, Jane Ellison, Fern Friedman, William Gaglione, Tom Graff, Terri Hanlon, Mike Haslam, Deborah Hay, The Kipper Kids, Robert Kleyn, Jill Kroesen, Eric Metcalfe, Alzek Misheff, Mondo Arte Cabaret, Randy & Berenicci, Deborah Slater, Michael Smith and Robert Young.
Music documents. Performances by Martin Bartlett, CCMC, Eugene Chadbourne, Doug Collinge, Ted Dawson, Don Druick, Larry Dubin, J. Jasmine, Katrina Krimsky, Steve Lacy, Lubomyr Melnyk, Al Neil, Evan Parker, David Rosenboom, Rova Saxophone Quartet, Dan Scheidt and Greg Simpson.
Literary documents. Readings by Kathy Acker, Robert Amos, Robert Amussen, Sonja Arntzen, John Bentley Mays, Bill Bisset, William Burroughs, Nancy Cole, Victor Coleman, Gerry Gilbert, Joan Haggarty, Jorj Heyman,

Dick Higgins, Monica Holden-Lawrence, Sherril Jaffe, Stephanie Judy, Lionel Kearns, Bill Little, Steve McCaffery, Daphne Marlett, Susan Musgrave and Opal L. Nations.
Size & Elements: Videotape: 3/4" (250 titles; masters).
Cataloging: Card catalogs; published catalogs; research library.
Access: Open to the public. Available for research, rental and purchase. Research fees not charged; Society membership required for researchers. Research requests accepted by mail, telephone and in person (walk-in and by appointment).
Rights: Some rights held to all material.
Licensing: Available for licensing and reuse, subject to restrictions. License fees charged.
Restrictions: Restrictions apply to most titles.
Viewing Facilities: Videotape (3/4").
Duplication Facilities: Videotape (3/4", 8mm, VHS and Betamax).
Representative: Video Out, 1102 Homer St., Vancouver, BC V6B 2X6; (604) 688-4336.

BRITISH COLUMBIA (Vancouver)

WOMEN IN FOCUS
204-456 West Broadway
Vancouver, BC V5Y 1R3
(604) 872-2250

Margot Butler (Director)

Contact: Zainub Verjee (Distribution Manager)
Services: Arts institution; media arts center; film and videotape producer; distributor.
Description: One of three nonprofit feminist arts centers in Canada devoted to women's cultural production in the film, videotape and visual arts disciplines. Provides facilities and workshops for the production of new works by women. Accepts works for exhibition, sales and rental distribution.
Art. Titles include: *Margaret Atwood: An Interview; Comptines* and *Pense à ton désir* (Diane Poitras); *Cows* (Alexis Krasilovsky); *The Flow of Appearances* (Tess Payne); *Lee à Two Rivers* (Nicole Benoit); and *Wallflower Order* (Marion Barling).
Bodies. Titles include: *Fashion as a Social Control* (Women in Focus); *Saying Goodbye* (Kate White); *This Isn't Wonderland* (Helen Doyle and Nicole Giguère); and *We Will Not Be Beaten* (Carl Greenwald and Mary Tiseo).
Economics. Titles include: *The Fleck Women* (Kem Murch); *The Gloria Tapes* (Lisa Steele); *No Small Change: The Story of the Eaton's Strike* (Emma Productions); and *Yes We Can!* (Vidéo Femmes).
Feminism. Titles include: *The Absence of Us* (Pamela Pike); *Brides Burning* (Gwyneth Baines); *Concerned Aboriginal Women* (Amelia Productions); *Chaperons Rouges (Little Red Riding Hood)* (La Femme Et Le Film and Le Groupe Intervention Vidéo); *Heroics: A Quest* and *The Influences of My Mother* (Sara Diamond); and *Rethinking Rape* (Jeanne LePage).
History. Titles include: *Caroline Herschel: Astronomer 1750-1848* (Women in Focus); *Daughters of the Nile* (Hillie Molenaar and Joop van Wijk); *Remember the Witches* (Laurie Meeker); *Tatyana Mamonova: Russian Feminist* (Amelia Productions); and *The Women's Suffrage Movement in Canada* (Women in Focus).
Archives. Holds rare videotape works which are flawed either by poor technical quality or presentation, outdated information, etc. Titles include: *Del Martin and Phyllis Lyon* (Women in Focus); *Euguelionne* (Meredith Bell and Yves Thibault); *Leaving For The Sea (Partir pour la mer)* (Catherine Brunelle); *Mary Daly Presents Gyn/Ecology* (Carolyn Shrewsbury); *Message from Women in Japan* (Women and Video-Japan); *The Miniature Theatre: Notes From An Unknown Source: A Science Fiction* (Nancy Nicol); and *Women Within Two Cultures* (Women in Focus).
Size & Elements: Film: 16mm (20 titles; release prints). Videotape: 3/4" and VHS (over 100 titles; viewing copies).
Cataloging: Published catalog.
Access: Open to the public for regular screenings. Material available for rental and purchase. Research requests accepted by mail, telephone and in person (walk-in and by appointment). Membership required for research.
Rights: Full rights held to some material. Additional clearances are necessary in some cases if material is to be reused.
Licensing: Some material possibly available for reuse, subject to restrictions.
Restrictions: Licensing and reuse permitted by permission of producers only.
Viewing Facilities: Film (16mm); videotape (3/4" and VHS).
Duplication Facilities: Videotape (3/4" and VHS).

CANADA/BRITISH COLUMBIA (Victoria)

BRITISH COLUMBIA (Victoria)

IMPACT AUDIO VISUAL
18-A Bastion Square
Victoria, BC V8W 1H9
(604) 382-0919
Fax: (604) 382-4236

Robert Montgomery (President)

Contact: Donna Mills (Office Manager)
Services: Film and videotape producer. Material available for duplication and reuse.
Description: Large variety of coastal scenes, including British Columbia and Victoria (waves, sunsets and ferries); footage gathered from over two years of videotaping in India, including scenics, people and activities; NASA footage, including space stations, satellites and views of Earth; special effects, including kinescope imagery, liquid imagery, footage of Paul Horn and David Bowie concert tours; fashions and flowers; laser feedback; Japan scenics; Amiga computer graphics and digital effects.
Size & Elements: Film: 16mm and 8mm (positives). Videotape: 3/4" and 1/2" (masters). (Approx. 500 hours total).
Cataloging: Catalog for staff use only; finding aids.
Access: Available to the public for duplication and reuse. Research fees charged (fees negotiable). Research requests accepted by mail and telephone.
Rights: Full rights held to some material. Some rights held to all material.
Licensing: Available for licensing and reuse. License and usage fees charged.
Restrictions: None specified.
Viewing Facilities: Film (16mm); videotape (3/4" and 1/2").
Duplication Facilities: Film (film to videotape); videotape (3/4" and 1/2").
Related Materials: Large quantity of photographic stills (35mm), slides and audiotapes.

BRITISH COLUMBIA (Victoria)

PROVINCIAL ARCHIVES OF BRITISH COLUMBIA
SOUND AND MOVING IMAGE DIVISION
655 Belleville Street
Victoria, BC V8V 1X4
(604) 387-6748
Fax: (604) 387-2072

Derek Reimer (Head, Sound and Moving Image Division)

Contacts: Derek Reimer; Sheila Norton; Allen Specht
Services: Film and videotape archives. Collection open to the public for in-house research. Material available for duplication and reuse.
Description: British Columbia, including its history, resources, industries, scenery and people. Collection holds film and videotape material produced by or for the Government of British Columbia, as well as various corporate, private, institutional and amateur productions. Bulk of the collection dates from the 1930s to the present, with some items from the 1910s and 1920s.
Industrial films. Films produced by and about important British Columbia corporations, including B.C. Hydro, B.C. Packers and Okanagan Helicopters.
Historical footage. Extensive historical footage, including logging and saw milling; fishing and fish processing; aviation (particularly helicopters); mining industry; travel and leisure activities such as skiing, camping and automobile travel; coastal steamers; railroads; street railroads; construction projects (particularly hydroelectric power projects); television news (mostly B.C. in the 1970s); animals (wild animal stock footage); Vancouver; Alaska Highway; British Royal Family visiting B.C.; national and provincial parks; Native Americans; mountains and mountain scenery.
CBC Vancouver television film. Holds most pre-1966 television film productions of CBC Vancouver (approx. 300 titles).
Size & Elements: Film: 16mm, Super 8mm and regular 8mm (mostly 16mm, approx. 4 million feet, 1,800 titles, 4,500 cans). Videotape: 2", 1", 3/4", VHS and Betamax (approx. 1,000 videotapes).
Cataloging: Card catalogs; inventories and lists.
Access: Open to the public. For in-house research. Available for duplication and reuse. Research fees not charged. Research requests accepted by mail, telephone and in person (walk-in and by appointment).
Rights: Full rights held to some material. Some rights held to some material. Some material in the public domain. Additional clearances may be necessary in some cases if material is to be reused. Rights status of some material not known.

Licensing: Available for licensing and reuse. License and usage fees not charged.
Restrictions: None specified.
Viewing Facilities: Film (flatbed and hand viewers); videotape (3/4" and VHS).
Duplication Facilities: Videotape (3/4" and VHS).
Publications: *Camera West: British Columbia on Film 1941-1965* (by Dennis J. Duff and published by the Provincial Archives), documents 1,082 films or film collections shot in British Columbia (1941-65) and identifies more than 70 institutions which hold British Columbia films.

CANADA/MANITOBA

MANITOBA (Winnipeg)

MANITOBA INDIAN CULTURAL EDUCATION CENTRE
119 Sutherland Avenue
Winnipeg, MB R2K 1Y6
(204) 942-0228

Dennis Daniels (Executive Director)

Contacts: Violet Chalmers (Film); Leonard McPherson (Videotape)
Services: Educational institution. Film and videotape material open to the public and available for duplication.
Description: Manitoba and Manitoba Indians, including arts and crafts, history and heritage, hunting, fishing and trapping, music and dances, political issues and traditions.
Some films in the People's Library include: *Porcupine Quill Work,* profiling Bernadette Pangawish (an Odawa Indian from Wikwemikong Reserve), who has been decorating items with porcupine quills for over fifty years; *Birch Bark Bitting by Angelique Mirasty,* on a Cree Indian who lives on Amisk Lake, who may be the only person living that is bitting bark in this unique way, taking designs from nature, using bees, butterflies and flowers to form intricately exquisite patterns; and *Wahbung (Our Tomorrows),* filmed by the Manitoba Indian Brotherhood, on the 1971 Indian Days Celebration at the Lower Fort Garry in commemoration of the signing of the treaties in 1871.
Some videotape productions in circulation include: *Tribal Councils of Manitoba,* an examination into the various members and operations of Manitoba's Tribal Councils; *Selkirk and Peguis Pow-Wows,* showing dance competitions at these two powwows; *Picking Seneca Root and Wecase (Indian Medicines),* tips on growing and using seneca and wecase; *Power to the People,* a study of the impact of environmental changes caused by hydro being implemented on northern reserves; *Northern Sun Farm (Survival Farm),* teaching mixed farming, alternative technology and child care to young couples on a co-op farm project; *Indian Family Centre,* a brief history and current look at the Centre and its activities; *Native Clan,* on the Halfway House for ex-inmates; *T.A.R.R. (Treaty and Land Claims),* in which the Treaty and Aboriginal Rights and Research Group talks about helping to settle unfulfilled treaties; *Band Operated Businesses,* looking at businesses run by the Roseau River, Fisher River and Norway House Bands; *Cultural Centres in Manitoba,* examining various cultural centres in Manitoba; *Youth Court,* a dramatization of a trial of young offenders; *New Student in the City,* on the lives of two students as they leave their reserves for better education in Winnipeg; *Native Women at Work,* on the difficulties of getting work; *Indian Self Government,* in which Leroy Little Bear presents good arguments in favor of Native self-government; *Metis Tour Guide,* in which Ray St. Germain traces the history of the Metis in Manitoba; *Music of the Indian and Metis,* on the music and dances of Indian and the Metis; *Native Culture,* Phil Lane talking about the proud heritage he feels all Natives should share; *Pastimes Past,* examining various Native games; *Playing the Moccasin Game,* instruction on playing the moccasin game; and *Native Handicrafts,* on various handicrafts, including beading, hair tufting and making ash hoops.
Size & Elements: Film: 16mm (47 titles, 47 cans). Videotape: 3/4", VHS and Betamax (24 titles).
Cataloging: Card catalogs; research library.
Access: Open to the public. Available for duplication. Research requests accepted by mail, telephone and in person (walk-in).
Rights: Full rights held to some material (produced by the Centre). Additional clearances may be necessary in some cases if material is to be reused (for other productions).
Licensing: Apply for information. Fees generally not charged if on-screen credit is given.
Restrictions: None specified.

536

Viewing Facilities: Film and videotape.
Duplication Facilities: Videotape.

MANITOBA (Winnipeg)

PROVINCIAL ARCHIVES OF MANITOBA
MOVING IMAGES AND SOUND DIVISION
Manitoba Archives Building
200 Vaughan Street
Winnipeg, MB R3C 1T5
(204) 945-3738

Peter Bower (Provincial Archivist)

Contact: Gilbert Comeault (Archivist)
Services: Government archives. Film and videotape collection open to the public. Material available for reuse in some cases.
Description: Films and videotapes, primarily produced by government agencies, nonprofit organizations and independent producers.

Subject areas include: ethnic culture, Native American culture, labor, the arts, experimental films, political life, remote communities in Northern Manitoba, women, religious life and organizations, cooperatives, lobbying issues and the military. Also holds coverage of the Winnipeg *Bombers* football team (beginning 1949), comprising about 35% of the total collection.

A videotape oral history project is currently being planned as an extension of their substantial oral history audiotape collection.
Size & Elements: Film: 16mm (amount unspecified). Videotape: 3/4", 1/2" and 1/2" open reel (409 videotapes).
Cataloging: Materials cataloged by provenance only, with no details on subject, title, producer, etc.
Access: Open to the public. Available for reuse in some cases. Research fees not charged. Research requests accepted by mail and telephone.
Rights: Full rights held to some material. Additional clearances may be necessary in some cases if material is to be reused. Archives can assist in tracing source and/or owner of material.
Licensing: Apply for information.
Restrictions: Apply for information.
Viewing Facilities: Film (16mm); videotape (3/4", 1/2" and 1/2" open reel).
Duplication Facilities: None.
Related Materials: Substantial collection of oral history audiotapes.

MANITOBA (Winnipeg)

UNIVERSITY OF MANITOBA LIBRARIES
DEPARTMENT OF ARCHIVES AND SPECIAL COLLECTIONS
Elizabeth Dafoe Library, Room 331
Winnipeg, MB R3T 2N2
(204) 474-6350
Fax: (204) 275-2597

Dr. Richard E. Bennett (University Archivist and Head, Department of Archives and Special Collections)

Contact: Richard E. Bennett
Services: University library. Film and videotape collection open to the public for in-house use only. Material available for duplication and possibly reuse.
Description: Documentation of University events (1940s-80s), including: student activities, athletic and sporting events; University ceremonies and openings; installation of University presidents; and promotion of the *Winnipeg Tribune Collection.* Also holds productions by student cinematographers.
Size & Elements: Film: 16mm (35 titles, 89 cans). Videotape: 3/4", VHS and Betamax (10 videotapes, 5 hours; viewing copies; color and sound).
Cataloging: Card catalogs; register.
Access: Open to the public. For in-house use only. Possibly available for duplication. Research fees not charged. Research requests accepted by mail, telephone and in person (walk-in).
Rights: Full rights held to some material. Some rights held to all material. Additional clearances may be necessary in some cases if material is to be reused.
Licensing: Apply for information. License fees charged in some cases.
Restrictions: Some restrictions may apply.
Viewing Facilities: Film and videotape (by special arrangement).
Duplication Facilities: Film and videotape (facilities located at the Instructional Media Center); fees apply.

MANITOBA (Winnipeg)

VIDEO POOL, INC.
300-100 Arthur Street
Winnipeg, MB R3B 1H3
(204) 949-9134

Gerry Kisil (Director)

Contact: Gerry Kisil; Tanis Kyle (Distribution Manager)
Services: Distributor; media arts center. Videotape collection available for in-house viewing, rental and purchase. Production and post-production services available to members.
Description: Founded in 1981 and incorporated in 1983. An artist-run, nonprofit, video and audio production and distribution center distributing the most comprehensive collection of independently produced video art work from Canada's prairie region. Many works come from groups such as WAIV (Women Artists in Video) and initiatives such as the + and = Projects (video by painters and sculptors, respectively).

Sample titles include: *Geography Is Destiny* (Rhonda Abrams); *Quackery* (Rosalie Bellefontaine); *Anita* and *Christina/Phillipe* (Per Brask); *Banff People* (Clancy Dennehy), a portrait of contemporary life in Banff; *When They First* (Nida Home Doherty); *Technodisiac* (Michael Drabot), on romantic love and sexuality as seen through the media landscape of high-technology leisure products; six videotapes by Wendy Geller, including *Seven, Domestic Bliss, Six, Learning About Feminine Sexuality, The Miss Teen Canada Pageant 1983* and *48 Hour Beauty Blitz; Omerta* (John Gurdebeke); *Herr Puntila: A Long Time Ago Brecht Once Had a Dream* (Grant Guy); *A Manitoba Salute to Giorgio Di Chirico* (Allan Hessler, installation); *Core* (Vern Hume), on the impact of a major urban renewal project in downtown Winnipeg; *Boom Town* (Vern Hume), on a woman's move to Calgary to find work as an unskilled laborer during Alberta's boom years; *Buck* (Vern Hume and Leila Sujir), on the personal history of a retired ranchhand, William Drummond; *A Pack of Lies* and *The Inspection* (Colleen Kerr); *Home Street* (Gerry Kisil), on the breakdown of the traditional family unit; *Dating and Mate Selection* (Gerry Kisil), on the ritualism and victimization of dating and mate selection; *Missing: The American Family* (Michael Klein, installation); *Framing the Perfect You* (Tanis Kyle); *Blinds and the Portable Window* and *Peeping Tommies* (Grace Martini); *Say It* and *The Measure of Success* (Cherie Moses and Coleen Finlayson); *Placing the Talent* (Cherie Moses); *Girl Talk* (Bev Nicol), on sexual harassment of high-school students; *Armour For Living* (Susan Peterson); *To Whom It May Concern* (Al Poruchnyk); *Los Ballet* and *Anarchist Weekly* (Al Rushton); *Motel* (Donnelly Smallwood); *Harvest of Dreams* (Janice Starko), on the first generation of Ukrainian pioneers who founded the "Edna/Star" settlement; *Pompidoleum* (Ryan Takatsu), a multi-layered ambient videotape about the Centre Pompidou, Paris; and *A Short Tape About Short People* (Diane Whitehouse).
Size & Elements: Videotape: 3/4" (168 videotapes; submasters and viewing copies).
Cataloging: Published catalog.
Access: Available for in-house viewing, rental and purchase. Rental and purchase requests accepted by mail and telephone; viewing requests accepted in person (by appointment only).
Rights: Full rights held to all material.
Licensing: Apply for information.
Restrictions: None specified.
Viewing Facilities: Videotape (3/4" and VHS).
Duplication Facilities: Videotape (3/4" and VHS).

CANADA/NEW BRUNSWICK

NEW BRUNSWICK (Moncton)

UNIVERSITÉ DE MONCTON
CENTRE D'ÉTUDES ACADIENNES
Moncton, NB E1A 3E9
(506) 858-4085

Ronald Le Blanc (Directeur)

Contact: R. Gilles Le Blanc (Archiviste)
Services: University. Videotape collection open to the public for research.
Description: Material relevant to New Brunswick, including unionization of workers in agriculture, fisheries, mining and the logging industry; activities of

workers (e.g., lobster, crab, cod and herring fishermen); and materials relating to social and economic development, including interviews with welfare recipients, women's rights issues, farmers' and fishermen's cooperatives, education, bilingualism, day care, community gardens, industrial health hazards and religion.

Titles include: *Loggers Camp; Family and Community Gardens: St. Wilfred, NB; Fisherwomen in the Northeast; Women's Faces* (oral histories); *Collèges et Universités Francophones; Romeo Le Blanc, Minister of Fisheries in Canada.*

Size & Elements: Videotape: VHS (36 videotapes, each 120 min.).
Cataloging: Computerized cataloging available to researchers.
Access: Open to the public. Available for duplication. Research fees not charged. Research requests accepted by mail, telephone and in person (walk-in).
Rights: Full rights held to all material.
Licensing: Apply for information. License fees charged.
Restrictions: Some restrictions may apply.
Viewing Facilities: Videotape (VHS).
Duplication Facilities: Videotape (VHS).

CANADA/NEWFOUNDLAND

NEWFOUNDLAND (St. John's)

NEWFOUNDLAND INDEPENDENT FILMMAKERS COOPERATIVE
40 Kings Road
St. John's, NF A1C 3P5
(709) 753-6121

Elizabeth Hagen (Coordinator)

Contact: Elizabeth Hagen
Services: Production facility for filmmaker members. Maintains film collection of members' works.
Description: Films by individual filmmakers who are members of NIFCO. Includes dramatic shorts, comedies, experimental films, features and documentaries relating to Newfoundland.
Size & Elements: Film: 16mm (50 titles; positive, negative and release prints).
Cataloging: Card catalog.
Access: Open to the public, researchers and scholars. Maintained for distribution (non-exclusive). Research fees not charged. Research requests accepted by mail, telephone and in person (walk-in, but an appointment is preferred).
Rights: Rights retained by filmmakers. Additional clearances will be necessary if material is to be reused.
Licensing: Apply for information. License and usage fees determined by filmmakers.
Restrictions: Requests for licensing and reuse subject to permission of filmmakers.
Viewing Facilities: Film (small screening room).
Duplication Facilities: None.

NEWFOUNDLAND (St. John's)

PROVINCIAL ARCHIVES OF NEWFOUNDLAND AND LABRADOR
Colonial Building
Military Road
St. John's, NF A1C 2C9
(709) 753-9390

David J. Davis (Provincial Archivist)

Contact: Ann Devlin-Fischer (Head, Still and Moving Image Collection)
Services: Film archives; research collection. Some material possibly available for duplication and reuse in some cases. *Staff has limited ability to service requests and duplication facilities are difficult to arrange.*
Description: *Canadian Broadcasting Company (CBC) films.* Approximately 6,000 titles are on deposit. Programs produced for broadcast (1962-present), including documentaries, newsreel footage, variety programs, specials and other material produced for Newfoundland television. CBC retains rights to all of these materials.

Atlantic Films Collection. Approximately 1,000 cans of film independently produced for the government (1952-78) relating to tourism, propaganda, post-Confederation (after 1949) programs, health, education, highway construction,

film trailers, local advertising and news footage. This collection will be receiving 180 cans of film shot by the Lieutenant Governor of Newfoundland (1940s-50s) documenting early aviation in Newfoundland and at the Botwood aviation station, a stopover point for North American and transatlantic flights. Archives holds rights to these films.

Newfoundland Historical Film Collection. Contains 100 films (originally nitrate) (1904 to mid-1940s), including footage from World War I and footage of the riot at the Colonial Building (1932). Also included are films made by Varick Frissell in Newfoundland (1920s-30s) (originals and copies are held either at National Archives of Canada or Library of Congress). Titles include: *Lore of Labrador; Great Arctic Seal Hunt* (1928); and *The Viking* (1931), the last film made before Frissell died in the explosion of the ship *The Viking*, onboard which this film was made. Archives holds rights to these films.
Size & Elements: Film: 35mm, 16mm and Super 8mm (over 7,000 cans). Videotape: 3/4" and VHS (approx. 40 videotapes; masters and viewing copies).
Cataloging: Work currently in progress on a filmography of moving image collections in Newfoundland.
Access: Open to the public. Available for duplication. Research fees generally not charged. Research requests accepted by mail, telephone and in person (by appointment only). *Staff has a very limited ability to service research requests.*
Rights: Full rights held to some material. Additional clearances may be necessary in some cases if material is to be reused.
Licensing: Apply for information.
Restrictions: Due to limited staffing, requests will be handled whenever possible, but access to material for research and reuse cannot be guaranteed.
Viewing Facilities: Film (Steenbeck); videotape (VHS).
Duplication Facilities: Duplication possibly available through the Division of Educational Technology at Memorial University. Limited duplication facilities can, however, prevent availability for duplication or reuse in some cases.
Related Materials: Extensive collection of still photographs.

CANADA/NORTHWEST TERRITORIES

NORTHWEST TERRITORIES (Inuvik)

INUVIK RESEARCH CENTRE
P.O. Box 1430
Inuvik, NT X0E 0T0
(403) 979-3838

John D. Ostrick (Manager)

Contact: John Ostrick
Services: Government agency. Open to the public.
Description: Arctic history and exploration (1890-present); strong in Western Arctic research, including geography, geology, construction, anthropology, archaeology and Northern wildlife. Some material was shot at the Centre.
Size & Elements: Film: 16mm (63 titles, 63 cans, each 30 min.; originals).
Cataloging: Card catalogs; research library.
Access: Open to the public. Research fees not charged. Research requests accepted by mail.
Rights: No rights held to any material.
Licensing: Apply for information. Usage fees not charged.
Restrictions: None specified.
Viewing Facilities: Film (16mm).
Duplication Facilities: None.

NORTHWEST TERRITORIES (Yellowknife)

NORTHWEST TERRITORIES ARCHIVES
PRINCE OF WALES NORTHERN HERITAGE CENTER
GOVERNMENT OF THE NORTHWEST TERRITORIES
Yellowknife, NT X1A 2L9
(403) 873-7698
Fax: (403) 873-0205

D. Richard Valpy (Territorial Archivist)

Contact: Janet Pennington (Archival Assistant)
Services: Government agency. Film and videotape material available to the public.
Description: Films and videotapes relating to the Northwest Territories, including: Arctic, Inuit and Eskimo peoples; Baffin Island; Barrenland, Keewatin District; Central Arctic; Mackenzie Delta. Also holds material on

Mackenzie River, Mackenzie Valley, Yellowknife, Great Slave Lake, Loucheux Slavery and Dogrib.

Titles include: *Arctic Patrol 1928-29; Cameron Falls; Canada Summer Games 1970; Caribou Carnival 1982; Igloo Dwellers 1928; Energy From the Arctic; Eskimo Visitors to Ottawa in 1967; Fisheries of the Great Slave Lake; Forest Fires* (February 5, 1981); *Ice Collecting; Here North; North, The Man and the Land; Panning Falls; Prohibition of the North; Scout Jamboree* (April 29, 1974); and *You Can't Grow Potatoes Like These.*
Size & Elements: Film: 16mm (110,630 feet); 8mm (2,325 feet) (76 titles, 236 cans total). Videotape: 3/4" and Betamax (27,000 feet, 28 titles total).
Cataloging: Card catalogs.
Access: Open to the public. Research requests accepted by mail, telephone and in person (walk-in).
Rights: Additional clearances may be necessary in some cases if material is to be reused.
Licensing: Apply for information. License or usage fees not charged.
Restrictions: None specified.
Viewing Facilities: Videotape (3/4").
Duplication Facilities: None.

CANADA/NOVA SCOTIA

NOVA SCOTIA (Halifax)

ATLANTIC INDEPENDENT MEDIA
P.O. Box 1647, Station M
Halifax, NS B3J 2Z1
(902) 422-5929

Street address: 1574 Argyle Street, 3rd Floor, Halifax, NS B3J 2B3

Bonnie Baker (Managing Director)

Contact: Bonnie Baker
Services: Distributor; nonprofit cooperative. Films and videotapes available to the public for rental and purchase.
Description: Formerly known as Canadian Filmmakers' Distribution Atlantic. The only distributor of independently produced Canadian films and videotapes based in Atlantic Canada. Collection represents more than 40 film and videotape producers. "In addition to developing and expanding the market for independent productions, especially those made in Atlantic Canada, it is the aim of CFDA to stimulate public awareness and appreciation of films and videos that do not comfortably fit the definitions of conventional or 'mainstream' cinema." Collection represents a variety of subjects and cinematic forms including feature length and short dramatics, animation, experimental, documentaries and uniquely east coast comedies.

Categories include: animation; the arts; drama; environment; experimental; humor; social commentary; community studies; Atlantic Canada studies; and recreation and leisure.

Film and videomakers represented include: Atlantic Filmmakers' Cooperative, Chris Aikenhead, Marusia Bocuirkiw, John Brett, Dean Brosseau, Linda Busby, Peggy Campbell, David Coole, Richard Cotter, Andy Dowen, John Doyle, Eric Emery, Willa Egrmajer, Floyd Gillis, Justin Hall, Claire Henry, Anthony Jackson, Michael Jones, Lulu Keating, Tom Lackey, Neal Livingston, Ramona Macdonald, Liz MacDougall, Bill MacGillivray, Michael Macintyre, Arthur Makosinski, Heather Macleod, James MacSwain, Rod Malay, Nigel Markham, Kevin Mathews, Debbie McGee, Tony Merzetti, Marion Mertens, Paul Mitcheltree, Doug Mulhall, Pam Murphy, Sarah Newman, Derek Norman, Elaine Pain, Harold Pearse, Ken Pittman, David Pope, Douglas Pope, Paul Pope, Popular Projects Society, Doug Porter, Lionel Simmons, Sharon Smith, Barbara Sternberg, Chris Straetling, David Ward, Glenn Walton, Sean Whalen, Women And Video Exploration and Christine Wong.
Size & Elements: Film: 16mm (approx. 116 titles). Videotape: 3/4" (some titles; masters and viewing copies); VHS (approx. 45 titles; viewing copies).
Cataloging: Published catalogs.
Access: Available to the public for rental and purchase. Requests accepted by mail and telephone.
Rights: Rights retained by original producers.
Licensing: Possibly available for licensing and reuse, subject to clearance and restrictions. Written permission must be obtained.
Restrictions: Motion pictures are protected by copyright and the purchase of a film only includes the right to unlimited screenings of the film by a direct projection method in a non-commercial setting, but does not entail the right to

distribute, sell, lease, duplicate, or televise the film, in whole or in part. Permission for any other use must be obtained in writing from the office of CFDA.
Viewing Facilities: None.
Duplication Facilities: None.
Representatives: Some titles available through Canadian Filmmakers Distribution Centre (q.v.) and Canadian Filmmakers Distribution West (q.v.).

NOVA SCOTIA (Halifax)

CENTRE FOR ART TAPES
2156 Brunswick Street
Halifax, NS B3K 2Y8
(902) 429-7299

Gordon Laurin (Managing Director)
Liz MacDougal (Production Coordinator)

Contacts: Gordon Laurin; Liz MacDougal
Services: Media organization. Videotape collection open to the public; available for duplication and reuse, subject to artists' approval.
Description: Nonprofit community access organization providing audio and videotape equipment, facilities and services to independent producers, artists, community groups and other organizations. Offers workshops, project consultation and production services, and provides a forum for the presentation of video exhibitions and in-house screenings.

Videotape archives (1979-present) holds work produced at the Centre; documentation of performances, lectures and readings; early social documentaries, especially relating to feminism, maritime issues and the Atlantic region of Canada; video art; "small-scale" commercial work; and the *Video Theatre* collection, consisting of early documentaries and documentation projects from a now-defunct production center.

Some material held in the archives is distributed by Atlantic Independent Media (q.v.).
Size & Elements: Videotape: 3/4" (approx. 150 videotapes; most 20 min.); 1/2" open reel (a few videotapes; black and white).
Cataloging: Card catalogs; computerized cataloging (Macintosh) in progress (to be available to researchers).
Access: Open to the public. Available for duplication and reuse, subject to artists' approval. Research fees not charged. Research requests accepted in person (by appointment only).
Rights: Full rights held to some material. Some rights held to some material. Rights to some material retained by artists or original producers. Additional clearances will be necessary in some cases if material is to be reused.
Licensing: Available for licensing and reuse, subject to restrictions. License fees not charged.
Restrictions: All reuse subject to approval of artist or original producer.
Viewing Facilities: Videotape (two viewing rooms).
Duplication Facilities: Videotape (3/4" and 1/2").
Related Materials: Audiotape archives.

NOVA SCOTIA (Halifax)

STUDIO EAST LTD.
5151 Terminal Road, Suite 702
Halifax, NS B3J 1A1
(902) 421-1164
Fax: (902) 422-2369

Andrew Cochran (President)

Contact: John H. Beanlands (Production Manager)
Services: Film and videotape producer. Footage available for licensing and reuse. Custom shooting services available.
Description: Stock footage of Nova Scotia and Prince Edward Island, including resources, scenics, industry and other subjects. Arrangements can be made to shoot footage professionally and furnish it at stock shot prices if the shot needed is not readily available.
Size & Elements: Videotape: 1" (approx. 55 hours; masters); Betacam (masters and viewing copies); 3/4", VHS and Betamax (viewing copies).
Cataloging: Computerized cataloging for staff use only.
Access: Research fees charged. Research requests accepted by mail, telephone and in person (walk-in and by appointment).
Rights: Full rights held to all material.
Licensing: Available for licensing and reuse. License fees charged. Rates vary

with specific footage being licensed and intended use.
Restrictions: None specified.
Viewing Facilities: Videotape (VHS and Betamax).
Duplication Facilities: Videotape (1", Betacam SP, VHS and Betamax).

NOVA SCOTIA (Sydney)

CANADIAN COAST GUARD COLLEGE LIBRARY
P.O. Box 4500
Sydney, NS B1P 6L1
(902) 564-3660
Telex: 01935185

Street address: 1190 Westmount Road

David MacSween (Librarian)

Contact: Louise McKenna (Assistant Librarian)
Services: Government agency library. Film and videotape collection available for research and free loan.
Description: Professional and pleasure navigation, sailing, marine engineering, seamanship, mechanical and electrical technology.
Size & Elements: Film: 16mm (150 titles; 160 cans). Videotape: 3/4", Betamax and VHS (300 videotapes; masters).
Cataloging: Card catalogs; published catalogs.
Access: Available to the public. For use of Transport Canada employees through library network. Research requests accepted through libraries; available through interlibrary loan.
Rights: No rights held to any material.
Licensing: Apply for information. Usage fees not charged.
Restrictions: None specified.
Viewing Facilities: Film (16mm); videotape.
Duplication Facilities: None.

NOVA SCOTIA (Sydney)

UNIVERSITY COLLEGE OF CAPE BRETON
BEATON INSTITUTE
P.O. Box 5300
Sydney, NS B1P 6L2
(902) 539-5300 (Ext. 346)

Street address: Glace Bay-Sydney Highway

Contact: Douglas MacPhee (Sound Archivist)
Services: University archives. Special section contains the videotape and audiotape collection, which is open to the public.
Description: Holdings relate to the Cape Breton area and local activities, including Scottish music performers, concerts, ethnic functions, ceremonies, installations, retirements and oral histories.
   Selected titles include: *Acadians in New Waterford; Cape Breton Italian Cultural Association; Multiculturalism; The Irish Benevolent Society; St. Mary's Polish Church, Sydney* (with interior shots); *Pierogi Making; Jewish Culture and Religion; Cape Breton Gaelic Society; Sts. Anargyroi Church/Greek Easter; St. Philip's African Orthodox Church; Holy Ghost Ukrainian Church; Herbal Medicine and Micmac Traditions; Divali Festival* (Hindu); *West Indian; Micmac Christmas Traditions: Mi'kmawey School; Halifax Public Gardens: Lake Ainslie Views; Lebanese Dancing; Decorating Ukrainian Easter Eggs; Acadian Micarme; Group of Seven, UCCB Art Gallery; Land and Sea: Can Steel Survive in Sydney?; Land and Sea: Oil and the Northwest Passage; Early Mining in Cape Breton; Micmac Chanting and Language Class; History of the Beaton Institute; Irish Benevolent Society's Weekend of Multiculturalism; Les Trois Pignons (The Three Gables); Moses Coady; Recollections: Parade of Sail; How Kids See Oil; Land and Sea: Oil Means Trouble; St. Ann's Mission* (Micmac); and *Whitney Pier Street Scenes.*
Size & Elements: Videotape: 3/4", VHS and 8mm (approx. 100 titles).
Cataloging: Card catalogs; release sheets.
Access: Open to the public. Research requests accepted by mail, telephone and in person (walk-in).
Rights: Some rights held to some material. Additional clearances may be necessary in some cases if material is to be reused.
Licensing: Apply for information.
Restrictions: None specified.
Viewing Facilities: Videotape (3/4").
Duplication Facilities: None.

ONTARIO (Don Mills)

ONTARIO FILM INSTITUTE
(incorporating ONTARIO FILM THEATRE and ONTARIO FILM ARCHIVE)
770 Don Mills Road
Don Mills, ON M3C 1T3
(416) 429-4100
Fax: (416) 429-2934
Telex: 06-218892 ONTSCICEN TOR

Gerald Pratley (Director)

Contact: Gerald Pratley
Services: Government agency; film and videotape archives; library. Film and videotape collection available to researchers, scholars and the public for in-house use only. Some material possibly available for duplication.
Description: In addition to an extensive feature film collection on VHS videotape, the Institute holds a variety of other materials.
   Province of Ontario motion pictures. Titles include: *Hello Toronto* (1948); *Ontario Day — Osaka* (1970); *Let's Go Fishing in the Northland* (1973); *St. Marie Among the Hurons* (1975); *Minawanamut* (1975); *Our Man in Muskoka* (1973); *North of Superior* (1974); *Black Creek Pioneer Village* (1970); *Spinning and Weaving* (1975); *L'Ontario Aux Mille Facettes* (1980); *Has Anybody Here Seen Canada?* (1979), part of *Dreamland*, a history of Canadian film; and *Big Thunder* (1980).
   Newsreel footage. Subjects include: *Visit of King George IV and Queen Elizabeth to Canada and U.S.* (1939); *Princess Elizabeth and Prince Philip's Wedding* (1949); *King and Queen Return, Bastille Day, Earthquake in Chile, Sub Disaster* and *China's Floods* (1938); *Tokyo: End of the Road* (1945); *Victory Joy Sweeps Continent (N.Y. City, Washington, Truman, Montréal, Toronto, Ottawa*, and *McKenzie King, Earl of Athlone)* (1945); *Radar: the Hidden Weapon* and *The Atomic Bomb!* (1945); *Holland: Vacation after Victory (Canadian troops relax)* (1945); *Ottawa: New Parliament Convenes (McKenzie King, Earl of Athlone)* (1945); *Portrait of Peace (Japan Surrenders, McArthur Signs Peace Treaty on the USS Missouri; Educational Course Trailer for Canadian Soldiers* (1945); *Nylons Are Back in N.Y.C.!, Argentina Report, Youth Takes to Wings (Gliding in Ottawa)* and *Return to Singapore (Mountbatten)* (1946); and many other newsreel items from Fox Movietone, Warner-Pathé, *MGM-News of the Day, News Parade* and Paramount.
   Also holds a variety of short documentary and fiction films.
Size & Elements: Film: 35mm and 16mm (200 titles). Videotape: VHS (1,100 videotapes; viewing copies).
Cataloging: Card catalogs; research library.
Access: Available to researchers, scholars and the public. For in-house use only. Some material available for duplication. Research requests accepted by mail, telephone and in person (by appointment only).
Rights: Some rights held to some material. Additional clearances may be necessary in some cases if material is to be reused. Rights status of some material not known.
Licensing: Apply for information.
Restrictions: None specified.
Viewing Facilities: Film (35mm and 16mm); videotape (VHS).
Duplication Facilities: None.
Related Materials: Books and files on motion pictures, related subjects and biographies (70,000); books on cinema (12,000); posters (4,000); soundtrack recordings (3,500) and still photographs (5,000).

ONTARIO (Guelph)

ED VIDEO MEDIA ARTS CENTRE
16A Wyndham Street North
Guelph, ON N1H 4E5
(519) 836-9811

Nancy Hallas (Director); Kevin Hogg (Technical Director)

Contact: Kevin Hogg
Services: Media arts production facility; media arts center; public access television facility; videotape archives. Collection available for research, distribution and rental for programming or exhibition, subject to restrictions.
Description: Founded 1974. Holds materials produced by local video artists through the Centre and the works of international artists who have visited the

Centre. The collection holds the work of 300-400 artists and is maintained for use as a research library and as a resource for programming and exhibition materials.

Provides 24-hour access to production facility for artists. Nonprofit and community groups receive technical instruction. Provides programming materials for local cable station Cable 8.
Size & Elements: Videotape: 3/4", VHS, Betamax and 1/2" open reel (approx. 500 videotapes total).
Cataloging: Computerized cataloging in progress.
Access: Open to researchers, scholars and the public. Maintained primarily for exhibition and cablecast. Research requests accepted by mail, telephone and in person (by appointment). Apply for information regarding research fees; membership is encouraged.
Rights: No rights held to any material. Rights retained by videomakers. Additional clearances are necessary if material is to be reused.
Licensing: Apply for information.
Restrictions: All requests for reuse subject to acceptance and approval.
Viewing Facilities: Videotape (3/4", VHS, Betamax and 1/2" open reel).
Duplication Facilities: Videotape.
Distributor: Approximately 5-10% of material distributed by V/Tape (q.v.).

ONTARIO (Kingston)

KINGSTON ARTISTS' ASSOCIATION, INC.
21A Queen Street
Kingston, ON K7K 1A1
(613) 542-7692

Chris Johnson (Artistic Director)

Contacts: Chris Johnson; Laura Cyr (Administrative Director)
Services: Association; corporate archives; film and videotape producer. Videotape collection available to the public for rental and broadcast.
Description: Video art (some titles available for broadcast); documentation of gallery exhibitions; and interviews with artists.
Size & Elements: Videotape: 1/2" (amount unspecified; edited and unedited).
Cataloging: Computerized cataloging for staff use only.
Access: Open to the public. Available for duplication, rental and broadcast. Research requests accepted by mail.
Rights: Full rights held to all material.
Licensing: Apply for information.
Restrictions: None specified.
Viewing Facilities: None.
Duplication Facilities: Videotape (1/2").

ONTARIO (Midland)

HURONIA HISTORICAL PARKS
P.O. Box 160
Midland, ON L4R 4K8
(705) 526-4980
(705) 526-7838 (office)
Fax: (705) 526-9193

Contact: Sandra Saddy
Services: Government agency; library. Film and videotape collection open to the public for in-house use only.
Description: Holds films and videotapes relating to two historic sites: Sainte Marie Among the Hurons, a 17th-century Jesuit mission designed as a retreat for itinerant missionaries and a refuge for Christian Wendat Indians; and the Historic Naval and Military Establishments, a full scale replica of a combined British naval dockyard and military garrison. Materials include documentation of on-site performances, promotional materials and recreations of historical events.

Other materials on similar subjects have been obtained from the National Film Board of Canada and from TV Ontario.
Size & Elements: Film: 16mm (2 titles; 2 cans). Videotape: 3/4" and VHS (80 videotapes).
Cataloging: Card catalogs; published catalog may be available in future.
Access: Open to the public. For in-house use only. Research fees not charged. Research requests accepted by telephone and in person (by appointment only).
Rights: Full rights to in-house productions are held by the Canadian Government. Additional clearances will be necessary if material is to be reused.
Licensing: Apply for information.
Restrictions: Additional clearances will be necessary if material is to be reused.
Viewing Facilities: Videotape (VHS).
Duplication Facilities: None.

ONTARIO (North York)

UNITED NATIONS CENTRE FOR HUMAN SETTLEMENTS (HABITAT)
Faculty of Environmental Studies
York University
4700 Keele Street
North York, ON M3J 1P3
(416) 736-5377
Telex: 06-218486 UNHABITAT TOR

Yvo DeBoer (Human Settlements Information Adviser)

Contact: Phyllis Eleazar
Services: United Nations agency. Film and videotape collection available to the public for loan, purchase and excerpting.
Description: International agency established to study, inform, educate and promote action towards improving the quality of life in human settlements around the world. Most films were produced specifically for the 1976 U.N. Conference on Human Settlements and address a wide range of human habitat problems in both industrialized and developing nations.

Issues include: how people live; land settlement; urban rehabilitation; alternate sources of energy; traffic and transportation; water supply; recreation; shelters; clean water; sanitation; infrastructure; land use; upgrading of slum and squatter settlements; indigenous construction materials; education and vocational training; research; planning and conserving the environment; sites and services.

Sample titles include: *Action in Rural Living Areas* (1976), showing government organization of Uruguayan agricultural communities to improve living conditions and increase food production; *The Ancient Eyes of Nepal Look to the Future* (1976), on the Katmandu Valley Plan's labor-intensive projects to improve sanitation and restore historic monuments; *As Good As New* (1976), on a British project to upgrade streets of small row housing in Britain's industrial towns; *Bardo* (1976), on upgrading "spontaneous" settlements in Abidjan, Ivory Coast, and integrating them into the city; *Beyond Family Planning* (1976), appraising Singapore's booming population problem and indicating that unprecedented social organization plus more concentrated use of industrial and commercial space are necessities; *Cairo As None Has Seen* (1976), a frank visual appraisal of the problems besetting the Egyptian capital; *Children* (1979), with compelling impressions of what it is like to be a child in today's world; *Citizen Involvement* (1976), showing community and grassroots organizations in Seattle, Arkansas and Philadelphia; and *Development of the City of Vilnus* (1976), an example of successful planning of a new residential district in the Byelorussian S.S.R.

Development Without Tears? (1979) contains interviews with development experts from Africa, Asia and Latin America, who stress the importance of political action in overcoming the enormous obstacles to material progress in developing countries; *Exploding Cities* (1979) views problems caused by rural to urban migration, discussing housing problems and solutions ranging from aided self-help to high technology; *The Fight for a Shelter* (1976), from Colombia, examines spontaneous settlements and their positive aspects, such as community participation; *Habitat and Urban Environment* (1976) deals with urban overcrowding in Morocco; *Houses and People* (1976), a Danish film questioning the desirability of housing families in high-rise apartment blocks; *The Key* (1976), produced by the Palestine Liberation Organization, on the plight of Palestinian refugees; *Land Policy* (1976), on the value of municipal control of land use and the importance of involving citizens in development planning in Sweden; *Managua Earthquake* (1976), on reconstruction planning and progress after the 1973 earthquake; *Old Land — New Land* (1976), on land reclamation in the Netherlands; *The Over-Crowded Capital* (1976), on urban congestion in Tokyo, Japan; *Resettlement of Illegal Squatters in Port Sudan Town* (1976); *A Roof for Everyone* (1976), on housing and infrastructure development in Kinshasa, Zaire; *To Build Better, More Quickly, More Cheaply* (1976), on prefabricated building techniques in France; *Traffic in Tokyo* (1976); and *Water: The Hazardous Necessity* (1979), on water-borne tropical diseases in Africa and the economic and social conditions which allow them to flourish.

Many films are available in Arabic, Chinese, English, French, Russian and Spanish; not all are available in every language.
Size & Elements: Film: 16mm (190 titles, approx. 650 cans). Videotape: 3/4" (211 videotapes; masters and viewing copies).

Cataloging: Published catalog with supplements.
Access: Most films available to the public for loan, purchase and "excerpting." Handling fees charged. Research requests accepted by mail and telephone.
Rights: Full rights held to some material. Additional clearances may be necessary in some cases if material is to be reused. The United Nations holds worldwide television, theatrical, non-theatrical, commercial and non-commercial rights.
Licensing: Available for excerpting (apply for information). License fees charged.
Restrictions: None specified.
Viewing Facilities: Videotape (3/4"). Material available for viewing at York University, at the University of Illinois Film Center (see below), and at UNCHS, DC2, Room 946, 2 United Nations Plaza, New York, NY 10017.
Duplication Facilities: None.
Distributors: Some titles distributed by the University of Illinois Film Center, 1325 South Oak Street, Champaign, IL 61820.

ONTARIO (North York)

YORK UNIVERSITY FILM LIBRARY
Scott Library, Room 114
4700 Keele Street
North York, ON M3J 1P3
(416) 736-5508

Kathryn Elder (Film and Video Librarian)

Contact: Kathryn Elder
Services: University library; film archives. Film and videotape material available to the public for in-house use only; not available for licensing or reuse.
Description: World War II propaganda from American, British and Canadian sources, comprised of donated materials and selected acquisitions; materials donated by Labatt Breweries of Canada, featuring sports coverage (1960-75, 350 titles); materials on modern and contemporary Canadian dance held on deposit for the Dance in Canada Association, in addition to selected acquisitions.

Also holds a collection of educational support materials that specialize in the social sciences and the humanities.
Size & Elements: Film: format unspecified (1,774 titles). Videotape: 3/4" (1,374 videotapes).
Cataloging: Published catalog; microfiche cataloging for staff use only.
Access: Available to the public. For in-house use only. Research fees not charged. Research requests accepted by mail, telephone and in person (walk-in).
Rights: No rights held to any material.
Licensing: Not available for licensing or reuse.
Restrictions: Not available for licensing or reuse.
Viewing Facilities: Videotape (3/4" and VHS).
Duplication Facilities: None.

ONTARIO (Ottawa)

CANADIAN FILM INSTITUTE FILM LIBRARY
150 Rideau Street
Ottawa, ON K1N 5X6
(613) 232-6727
Fax: (613) 232-6315

Available for rental from:
LM MEDIA MARKETING SERVICES, LTD.
115 Torbay Road, Unit 9
Markham, ON L3R 2M9
(416) 475-3750
Fax: (416) 475-3756

Frank Taylor (Director, Canadian Film Institute)

Contact: Brian Wilson
Services: Film and videotape archives; rental library. Material available for rental (restricted to nonprofit educational use).
Description: Distributes films and videotapes not otherwise available through Canada's private sector distributors. Special areas of focus of the collection include the sciences, the visual and performing arts and cinema studies. Both French and English-language materials are held.

With the assistance of the Canada Institute for Scientific and Technical Information, new science films are added each year; among them are 300 films deposited by the Scientific Council of the Embassy of France in Canada. Through the cooperation of the National Archives of Canada, projection prints of several rare Canadian film study classics are now available.

Sources that have deposited film and videotape materials with the collection are: L'Ambassade de France; Animal Defence League of Canada; Australian High Commission; Bell Canada Film Services; Boy Scouts of Canada; British High Commission; Caltec Petroleum Inc.; Canada Mortgage and Housing Corporation; Canadian Centre for Films on Art; Canadian Institute of Mining and Metallurgy; Embassy of West Germany; Embassy of the Netherlands; Dance Canada; Dorothy MacPherson; Department of Energy; Mines and Resources (Canada); Department of Energy (United States); Department of Health and Welfare (Canada); Department of National Defence (Canada); National Arts Centre; National Gallery of Canada; NASA; National Capital Commission; National Research Council of Canada; Royal Architectural Institute of Canada; Royal College of Physicians and Surgeons; Royal Norwegian Embassy; Royal Swedish Embassy; UNESCO; and United States International Communications Agency.
Size & Elements: Film: 16mm (release prints). Videotape: format unspecified (viewing copies) (6,000 titles total).
Cataloging: Published catalog.
Access: Open to the public. Available for rental for nonprofit educational use only. Research and rental requests accepted by mail and telephone.
Rights: No rights held to any material. Some material in the public domain. Additional clearances may be necessary in some cases if material is to be reused.
Licensing: Possibly available for licensing and reuse, subject to additional clearances.
Restrictions: Material is for distribution for nonprofit educational use; not for commercial use. Material cannot be reused without additional clearances.
Viewing Facilities: None.
Duplication Facilities: None.

ONTARIO (Ottawa)

CARLETON PRODUCTIONS INCORPORATED
1500 Merivale Road
Ottawa, ON K2E 6Z5
(613) 224-1313 (business)
Fax: (613) 224-7998
Telex: 053-4292

Wayne Hicks (Vice President, General Manager)

Contacts: Anna Baker (Production Coordinator); Carolin McRae (Production Coordinator); Dianne Van Velthoven (Producer, Account Executive)
Services: Film and videotape producer. Material available for duplication, licensing and reuse.
Description: Science and technology; communications; industry; transport; general places; environment; people; finance; sports; disasters; demonstrations and hearings; energy; defense; labor; medicine; education; entertainment; ceremonies and awards; leisure and recreation; holidays; history and politics, including world, U.S., federal (Canada), provincial (Ontario) and local (Ottawa and Ottawa Valley, Hull, Gloucester and Nepean).
Size & Elements: Videotape: 3/4" (560 videotapes, each 60 min.).
Cataloging: Card catalogs; shot lists.
Access: Available for duplication, licensing and reuse. Research fees charged (hourly). Research requests accepted by mail and telephone.
Rights: Full rights held to all material.
Licensing: Available for licensing. License fees charged.
Restrictions: None specified.
Viewing Facilities: Film and videotape.
Duplication Facilities: Film and videotape.

ONTARIO (Ottawa)

CRAWLEY FILMS, LTD.
19 Fairmont Avenue
Ottawa, ON K1Y 1X4
(613) 728-3513
Fax: (613) 728-6455

William Stevens, Jr. (Chief Executive Officer)

Contact: William O'Farrell (Vice President, Production)
Services: Documentary film producer. Film available for research, licensing and reuse, subject to restrictions.
Description: The Crawley Collection consists of documentary films (1939-75) relating to Canada, Canadian culture, corporations and institutions. All material is now held at the National Archives of Canada, Moving Image and Sound Archives (q.v.). The films were produced for a variety of sponsors, including government departments, tourist organizations, sports teams and organizations, pulp and paper companies, power companies, beer and liquor companies, soft drinks companies, medical and dental organizations, associations, Air Canada, Canadian Pacific Air and Hotels, and others.
Size & Elements: Film: primarily 16mm (approx. 6-8 million feet, approx. 3,000 titles, 15,000 cans).
Cataloging: Card catalogs.
Access: Open to researchers. Research requests accepted by mail and telephone. Research fees charged in some cases. For further information, see National Archives of Canada.
Rights: Rights status of materials varies.
Licensing: Available for licensing and reuse in some cases.
Restrictions: Restrictions vary on a case-by-case basis.
Viewing Facilities: Film and videotape (limited facilities).
Duplication Facilities: Film and videotape.

ONTARIO (Ottawa)

INUIT BROADCASTING CORPORATION
251 Laurier West, Suite 703
Ottawa, ON K1P 5J6
(613) 235-1892
Fax: (613) 230-8824

Doug Saunders (President)

Contact: Jerry Giberson (Director of Network Operations)
Services: Public television network. Videotape material available for duplication, licensing and reuse, subject to restrictions.
Description: Holds television programs produced by the IBC (1982-present). Produces five hours of programming per week for 40 weeks each year, all in Inuktitut, the Inuit language. Programs include drama, documentaries, news, current affairs, entertainment and children's programs, all aimed at an Inuit audience. Approximately one-third of programming is studio-based; the remainder is documentary or field production.

News and public affairs programming includes coverage of local politics, territorial issues and international affairs of interest to Arctic audiences. Documentaries relate to the Inuit way of life, Inuit history and culture, and to the Arctic landscape.

Although the production center and the bulk of the videotape library is located in the Arctic, researchers should contact the Ottawa office for information regarding access to and reuse of footage.
Size & Elements: Videotape: 3/4" (over 1,000 hours).
Cataloging: Title list (staff use only).
Access: Open to the public. Available for duplication and reuse. Research fees not charged. Research requests accepted by mail and telephone.
Rights: Full rights held to all material.
Licensing: Available for licensing and reuse, subject to restrictions. License fees charged.
Restrictions: Images of a dead person may not be shown until one year has passed since their death.
Viewing Facilities: Videotape (3/4" and VHS).
Duplication Facilities: Videotape (3/4", VHS and Betamax; for educational and research use only, outside arrangements made for commercial duplication).

ONTARIO (Ottawa)

NATIONAL ARCHIVES OF CANADA
MOVING IMAGE AND SOUND ARCHIVES (MISA)
395 Wellington Street
Ottawa, ON K1A 0N3
(613) 995-1311

Street address: 344 Wellington Street, Room 1014

Jana Vosikovska (Acting Director)

Andris Kesteris (Acting Chief, Public Service and Access Development Section) (613/996-4144)
Sylvie Robitaille (Acting Chief, Audiovisual Public Service Unit) (613/995-1312)

Contacts: Andris Kesteris; Sylvie Robitaille (for inquiries relating to moving image and recorded sound materials holdings)
Services: Government agency; film and videotape materials available to researchers and scholars for research and reuse, subject to restrictions.
Description: *Brief History.* Canadian libraries, museums and archives now recognize the value of moving images and sound documents as historical, cultural and social records in their own right. This has not always been the case, however, and because of the lack of concern for Canada's film heritage, more than half of the films produced in Canada between 1890 and 1950 have been lost. The existing films from this period were deteriorating rapidly before corrective action was initiated. Similarly, lack of concern over preserving past broadcast production, partly due to the small appreciation of its potential historical value and partly for reasons of economy in space and finance, has meant that only a small proportion of the broadcasting record has been preserved in archives.

The advent of television, progress in radio and sound technology, and the growth of the Canadian film industry in recent years kindled a general interest in moving image and sound documents. Broadcasting networks reassessed the value of past programs, at least to the point of recognizing them as production resources, if not as historical documents. The Public Archives of Canada too became active in preserving what was left of the audiovisual production of former years and attempted to replace missing documents, where possible, with duplicates secured elsewhere. The first step towards the creation of an organization that would realize this goal and prevent further loss was taken in 1968 when a sound archives was established.

In 1967, as if to underscore the urgency of immediate action, a disastrous fire near Montreal, fed by extremely flammable nitrate stock, destroyed millions of feet of film. This led the Federal Cabinet in 1969 to authorize the Public Archives to begin collecting the unstable nitrate film that remained in the country and to print as much footage as possible onto safety stock. As a result, by the end of 1972 almost 5,000 hours of nitrate film and numerous 16mm films needing restoration had been collected. A 1972 amendment to this National Film Policy launched a study to look into the formation of a film archives and in November of that year the National Film Archives Committee was set up and began work on the study.

In the meantime, the sound and film sections of the Archives were grouped together in 1973 as a separate division, the National Film Archives Division. After consultation with the Canadian Broadcasting Corporation, the National Film Board, and Cinémathèque québecoise, among others, the National Film Archives Committee recommended the establishment of the National Film Archives, a move which became official in 1976. Four years later, the National Film Archives became known as the National Film, Television and Sound Archives (NFTSA). Pursuant to national legislation in 1986, Public Archives Canada became the National Archives of Canada, and the NFTSA assumed its present title of Moving Image and Sound Archives (MISA).

Methods of selection and acquisition. Given the large numbers of potentially valuable documents, it became clear that uncontrolled acquisition would soon outstrip the facilities of the new Division. Fortunately, the MISA is able to control indiscriminate collecting by requiring that only those documents of enduring historical, cultural or social value to Canadians need be considered for acquisition. Specific criteria enable collection development personnel to be even more rigorous in their evaluation of promising deposits. It was also decided at the outset that rare documents should be prized more highly than easily available items or those already preserved in other archives. In addition, such factors as the amount of Canadian content, Canadian authorship, informational and evidential value, craftsmanship and the importance of the subject matter in relation to historical, cultural and social considerations, all have direct bearing on whether or not a collection becomes part of the MISA's holdings. Archivists also pay special attention to documents covering Canadian achievements that have been largely ignored or forgotten, such as the development of the film and broadcast industries, the opening of the Canadian frontier and the careers of influential Canadians.

This entry contains descriptions of subject areas that are accessible in the card catalogs of the Collection. Headed by a general subject category, each description refers to blocks of audiovisual documents which relate to a subject area. The range of dates following the subject category indicates the dates of the oldest and the most recent documents referred to in the description. The number of hours in each heading represents the approximate total of all documents (including both sound recordings and moving image materials) accessible under the heading and related references.

Since names of depositors are also used as collection names, the list of depositors following each Guide entry will facilitate references to the majority of collections mentioned in the *Inventory of Collections* and the card catalogs.

The descriptions and running times that follow may, in some cases, refer to sound recordings as well as motion picture and videotape materials.

Canada and abroad (1898-1970s, 650 hours). Most documents filmed or recorded on location reveal a great deal about the background of the country in which they are set.

Those documents set in the Arctic, for example, are typically works in which the land seems to dominate whatever theme is being explored, and they show, perhaps more than anywhere else in Canada, the adaptation of human existence to a harsh environment. Films and audiotapes center on people struggling for survival in isolated communities, or record the experiences of men who explored the icy reaches of the Polar region. Of particular interest are numerous documents on the Inuit, the missionaries and on individuals such as Stefansson, Larsen, Lawrence, Bernier, Finnie and others who travelled throughout the far North to open up new land, strengthen Canadian sovereignty, search for natural resources or to supply distant outposts.

To a lesser extent, the character of the Canadian landscape is depicted in documents showing other regions of the country and their farmland, forestland, coastal regions, prairies and mountain country. These aspects of the country are particularly well displayed in numerous travelogues produced to attract tourists by showing the most inviting attributes of the country.

Audiovisual documents pertaining to cities and towns also reveal a great deal about the areas in which they are set. Ottawa-Hull, the provincial capitals, Montreal, Vancouver, Calgary and many other centers are represented in the Collection by visual documents. Items set in Toronto, particularly those made as segments of popular television series, contribute valuable insights into a cross-section of the Canadian urban landscape. Some smaller centers are also well represented in the MISA Collection, including anniversary celebrations in Newcastle, Ontario and Swift Current, Saskatchewan; parades on Orono, Ontario and Les Éboulements, Quebec; and life in fishing villages in Nova Scotia and Newfoundland.

Background scenery and the accounts and commentaries relating to it are also useful in comparing different localities. In documents showing voyages to the Polar regions, for example, the Russian and Greenland Arctic landscapes may be compared, and valuable insights can be gleaned through studies carried out in Antarctica by the Byrd Expedition, the Scott Antarctic Expedition, the British Antarctic Expedition of 1898-1900 and the British Commonwealth Trans-Antarctic Expedition of 1955-58.

Here again, travelogues and documentaries provide uncluttered views of countries, even when they are made by amateur photographers. The MISA has a number of these films, dating back to the early 1920s, including those shot in the Americas, Europe, Scandinavia, the Mediterranean, the Near and Far East and Africa. Although scenes depicting cities and towns can be found intercut with much of the material in the Collection, many documentaries, especially those portraying the larger center, offer in-depth studies of urban landscapes. An example of this type of film is the 250-hour Habitat Collection deposited by the United Nations' Center for Human Settlement.

Collections include: Alberta Educational Communications Corporation; Aluminum Company of Canada; Associated Screen News; Bibliothèque municipale de Hull; British Columbia Planetarium; CBOT-TV (Ottawa); CJOC-TV (Lethbridge); CKY (Winnipeg); Canada, Canada Mortgage and Housing Corporation; Canada, Canadian Government Exhibition Commission; Canada, Canadian Government Travel Bureau; Canada, Fisheries and Oceans; Canada, Manpower and Immigration; Canada, National Museums; Canada, National Parks; Canada, Public Archives Records Centres; Canada, Transport Canada; Canada, Urban Affairs; Canadian Broadcasting Corporation; Canadian Film Institute; Canadian National Railways; Canadian Pacific Railway; Canadian Wildlife Service; Collège de Lévis; Edison, Thomas A.; Ford Foundation; Glenbow-Alberta Institute; Graphic Consultants; Imperial Oil Limited; Manitoba Provincial Archives; National Film Board; Ontario Science Centre; Polish Archives; Post, George; Les productions Via le Monde; Saskatchewan Archives; TV Ontario; and Yukon Archives.

Communication and the media (1896-1970s, 45,000 hours). This category covers documents which relate to the exchange of information through radio, television, film and newspapers. Documents on the development of the telephone are also included, as well as the broader subject of telecommunications.

Proceedings of conventions, speeches and comments by various groups and societies in the communications field have been recorded and deposited with the MISA. For instance, the MISA holdings contain about 170 hours of videotape on hearings by the Canadian Radio-Television and Telecommunications Commission concerning pay television.

Film has been accepted as a medium of communication and as a recorder of events since the turn of the century. For this and other reasons it has become an archival medium in its own right. The MISA holds an extensive collection of fiction features and shorts (over 4,500 hours) and an even larger collection of non-fiction films (5,500 hours). As with radio and television programming, fiction films in the Collection cover most of the genres produced, including comedy, drama, musicals, detective stories, westerns and horror films. The non-fiction film collection consists mainly of documentaries, news films and some educational films. In addition, the Archives holds excerpts from various productions which illustrate comments by film historians or provide samples of items in archival collections or of producers' outputs.

Also covers interviews with people involved with the cinema, including historians, filmmakers and technicians. As John Grierson, Stuart Legg, Roy Tash, Gordon Sparling and many others talk about their own films, careers and the film business in general, they chart the progress of the cinema, assess its impact on popular culture and recall the activities of institutions and companies such as the Canadian Government Motion Picture Bureau, National Film Board, Canadian Film Institute, Associated Screen News and Crawley Films. These holdings are complemented by an extensive library of books on the cinema and by the MISA Collection of film and television periodicals. A number of collections of private papers offer valuable insights into the industry and into the careers of the depositors.

The technical side of motion pictures is covered by filmed visits to movie studios and a document on the nature of nitrate film stock, for example. Lastly, the circumstances surrounding the unearthing and restoration of the Dawson City Museum Collection are outlined in the television program *Hour Long* by MISA's Director, Sam Kula.

With constant progress in satellite technology, the availability of audiovisual documentation on satellite communication is continually growing. Thanks to Bell Canada, Telesat Canada and the Canadian Broadcasting Corporation, the Archives has several documents on the Anik satellites and on Telstar. Other items deal with microwave communication, some of which are part of the 250 hour-long Bell Canada Collection of documentaries, compilations and news items relating to all aspects of telephone company management.

Collections include: Association coopérative de productions audio-visuelles; Association for Canadian Theatre History; Association for the Study of Canadian Radio and Television; Astral-Bellevue Pathé; Astral Films; Blackhawk Films; Bossin, Hy; British Broadcasting Corporation; British Film Institute; Bundesstaatliche Hauptstelle Fur Lichtbild und Bilungsfilm; Burg Productions; CBOT-TV (Ottawa); CFTO-TV (Toronto); Canada, External Affairs; Canada, National Film Board; Canada, Privy Council Office; Canada, Public Archives; Canada, Royal Commission on Newspapers; Canadian Association of Broadcasters; Canadian Broadcasting League; Canadian Film Group; Canadian Film Institute; Canadian Speech Association; Cinak; Cinema Canada; Cinepix Inc.; Clearwater Films; Columbia Pictures of Canada; Crawley Films; Criterion Pictures Corporation; Dawson City Museum; De Mohrenschildt, Walter; Desmarais, Marie; Faroun Films; Film House; Graphic Consultants; Institut d'histoire de l'Amérique française; Jon Slan Productions; Motion Magazine; Niagara College of Applied Arts and Technology; Ontario Film Institute; Les Productions mutuelles; Les Productions Pierre Lamy; Les Productions Prisma; Quadrant Films; Radio Bureau of Canada; Radiodiffusion-télévision française; Rainforest Productions; Sefel Pictures International; Sonneborn, Jon; Stern, Seymour; TV Ontario; Twentieth Century-Fox; United Artists; and Universal Films (Canada).

The economy, Canadian industries and natural resources (1900-70s, 2,500 hours). By the end of the 1930s, Canada was on the verge of economic recovery; some adventurous Canadians tried their hand at running small businesses. Recordings and interviews provide insights into the involvement of individuals and families in private enterprise. Audiovisual documentaries also record industrial progress on a countrywide scale in construction, food production, manufacturing, technological development, industrial standards and allied fields. One example of these is the 900 hours of sound and moving image documents dealing with farm management, processes and techniques. On the same subject, MISA holdings contain numerous audiovisual documents on country and farm life, cattle raising, wheat farming on the Prairies and on the studies of government committees on grain handling and transportation and on beef marketing.

The Canadian economy depends largely too on the exploitation of its abundant natural resources, and this is reflected in many archival documents. Sound and moving image documents record many discussions on energy sources, such as those from the Royal Commission on Energy, Public Petroleum Association of Canada, Canadian Council of Professional Engineers and the Canadian Broadcasting Corporation. Numerous documents focus on specific resources: hydroelectric power, for example, is covered in films on the construction of dams, power stations and power grids. Other documents deal with the oil and gas industries.

The development of underground resources, including mining and ore processing, is revealed in several documentaries covering such topics as asbestos production in the 1920s, prospecting for gold, the Klondike Gold Rush, nickel mining and even aquamining on the Famine River in Quebec.

On the subject of aboveground resources, the MISA holds a number of films on the exploitation of forests for papermaking and lumber. Canadian wildlife is also well covered in documents deposited by the CBC, the Canadian Wildlife Service and others. There are some items on the hunting and trapping of birds and fur-bearing animals, including those relating to contemporary issues, such as seal hunting in the Frissel classic film *The Viking* and *Les Phoques de banquises;* and whaling along the northwest coast and in the far north. The fishing industry is covered in a number of moving image documents, including those in the Millar Collection, in which the lives of fishermen are studied; while films in the Fisheries and Oceans Collection portray the arduous occupation of deepsea fishing.

Paralleling the exploitation of natural resources is the obligation to conserve those resources against depletion and to protect the environment. These issues concerning natural resources are stressed in the CBC programs *A Place for Everything* and *This Land,* and in the Canadian Film Institute film *Conservation Road.* Problems in ecology and resource conservation are also studied in documents relating to the Mackenzie Valley Pipeline Inquiry and to reforestation of woodlands, wildlife conservation and fish restocking programs.

Collections include: Associated Screen News; British Columbia Department of Agriculture; Canada, Agriculture; Canada, Energy, Mines and Resources; Canada, Fisheries; Canada, Food Prices Review Board; Canada, Indian Affairs and Northern Development; Canada, Mackenzie Valley Pipeline Inquiry; Canada, National Parks; Canada, Regional Economic Expansion; Canada, Royal Commission on Corporate Concentration; Canada, Royal Commission on Energy; Canada, Royal Commission on Grain Handling and Transportation; Canada, Royal Commission of Inquiry into the Marketing of Beef; Canadian Bankers Association; Canadian Film Institute; Canadian Wildlife Service; Edison, Thomas A.; Graphic Consultants; National Film Board; New Brunswick Provincial Archives; Newfoundland and Labrador Government; Ontario Film Institute; Saskatchewan Archives; and Western Development Museum.

History and related disciplines (1920s-70s, 2,500 hours). Contains documents on labor history, social history and the history of urban centers and the various regions of Canada. Other documents recall the lives and careers of people engaged in occupations such as prospecting, transport, photography, filmmaking and broadcasting. Canadian history is presented in contemporary documentaries about historic events and in dramatic productions set in colonial times. The National Film Board's contribution to MISA holdings contains several documentaries and docudramas relating to these topics.

A number of documents also cover historic events in other countries. Post-Victorian England and prewar France are brought to life in a few films. Other documents look at the evolution of the British Empire and Commonwealth and at early and contemporary American history.

The period covering World War I and World War II also received much attention by contemporary documentary producers. Their historical films chronicled the changing social and political scenes and hinted at approaching conflict. The events of the wars themselves are considered in films such as *Lest We Forget, The Canadian Army Newsreels, Canada at War* and in the propaganda documentaries made during the war by the National Film Board.

In the field of the preservation of historical records themselves, the MISA has acquired a number of documents relating to conservation work on manuscripts, broadcast documents, sound recordings, photographs, theater accessories, films and videotapes.

Collections include: Association for Canadian Theatre History; Bibliothèque municipale de Hull; CBOT-TV (Ottawa); Canada, National Defence (Directorate of History); Canada, National Library; Canada, Public Archives; Canada, Public Service Commission; Canada, Regional Economic Expansion; Canada, Secretary of State; Canada, Transport Department; Canadian Broadcasting Corporation; Canadian Ethnological Association; Canadian Film Institute; Canadian Historical Association; Canadian Medical Association; Canadian Serbian Club; Canadian Theatre Centre; Canadian Union of Public Employees; Columbia Records; Conseil québécois pour la diffusion du cinéma; Hannah Institute for the History of Medicine; Historic Society of Gatineau; Insight Productions; Institut d'histoire de l'Amérique française; Institute for Canadian Studies; International Council of Archives; Latent Images; Maher and Hurley Associates; National Film Board; Ontario Archives; Ontario Historical Association; Ontario Institute for Studies in Education; Ontario Woodsworth Memorial Foundation; Pan American Institute of Geography and History; Polish Archives; Saskatchewan Archives; See, Hear, Now; Société d'études et de relations publiques; Société historique de l'Ouest du Québec; Society for the Study of Architecture; Thunder Bay Labour History Project; Time Inc.; TV Ontario; United States, National Archives and Records Administration; Vancouver Archives; and World Book Company.

Justice and law enforcement (1910-70s, 1,200 hours). Documents on justice and law enforcement cover a variety of subjects related to human and civil rights, court cases, police activities and correctional institutions.

Collection contains a number of sound and moving image documents depicting efforts by women to gain voting rights and to secure equality in society. Available are documents on the history of women in Ontario, Nellie McClung and her work in the Suffragette Movement, women in the arts, the labor force, the military, industry and politics. Another collection consists of two films deposited by the French network of the CBC: *Nous les femmes,* an account of the development of the status of women in Quebec to 1979; and *Femmes d'aujourd'hui.* In the context of civil rights is the CBC series *Ombudsman.*

Holds numerous documents relating to justice provide material on court cases, capital punishment, prison sentences and on the law in general. Legal cases are dramatized in the series *A Case for the Courts* and *Famous Canadian Trials,* broadcast on television and radio.

A number of documents relate to international crime and racial violence abroad. Political extremism in Canada is the subject matter of a series of documents on the October Crisis of 1970 deposited by the Canadian Radio-Television and Telecommunications Commission.

Holdings also contain various fictional police adventures, the most frequently dramatized being films and serials such as *The Trail of the Royal Mounted, Sergeant Preston of the Yukon,* and *Cameron of the Royal Mounted.* More recent examples are those from the television series *RCMP.* In the non-fiction category, the Archives holds soundtracks for audiovisual teaching aids on the opening of the Canadian West and the history of the RCMP. The CBC series *Toronto File* looks at police work in the City of Toronto, while a National Film Board docudrama examines the operation of Canadian correctional institutions and the problem of prison custody and rehabilitation.

Collections include: Blackhawk Films; Brian Nolan Agency; British Film Institute; Canada, Indian Affairs and Northern Development; Canada, International Women's Year Secretariat; Canada, Public Service Commission; Canadian Broadcasting Corporation; Canadian Citizenship Council; Canadian Federation of University Women; Canadian Film Institute; Columbia Pictures Television Productions; Crawley Films; Latent Images; Montréal Council of Women; National Film Board; Ontario Institute for Studies in Education; Queen's University; See, Hear, Now; Supreme Court of the Northwest Territories; and Women's Liberal Federation of Canada.

Labor and labor unions (1910-70s, 500 hours). Holds audiovisual documents relating to the labor movement focus on three main topics: the labor movement in general, trade unions and strikes. The first, running about 340 hours, consists mainly of sound recordings and a few films covering a variety of subjects on the labor scene in the United States and Canada, including: the views of the members of the Canadian Union of Public Employees; retired longshoremen recounting their experiences on the Vancouver waterfront; and former union officials discuss working conditions during the early years of this century. In other collections, experts in the field discuss wage and price controls in the 1970s, seasonal employment, labor-management relations, safety and the employment of handicapped people.

Some research material looks at labor unions and working conditions from management's point of view. Films on the importance of attending union meetings, on the negotiation process and on union management have been deposited by the National Film Board and other institutions.

Strikes are also an important facet of the labor movement. Several sound and moving image documents in the Collection deal directly with various strikes, such as those involving the United Steel Workers and General Motors in the United States; and local unions in Stratford, Ontario in the 1930s.

Also contains several references to the related issue of unemployment. Footage on the Great Depression plays a prominent part in the Collection, and other instances of unemployment due to strikes, shutdowns and layoffs are also documented. Finally, a few titles deal with ways the unemployed react to the lack of work, including marches to provincial capitals and Ottawa, and participation in employment programs and work camps.

Collections include: Canada, Labour Department; Canada, Manpower and Immigration; Canadian Broadcasting Corporation; Canadian Labour Congress; Canadian Union of Public Employees; International Union of Mine, Mill and Smelter Workers; Jewish Labour Committee of Canada; Ontario Federation of Labour; Ontario Woodsworth Memorial Foundation; Perth County Archives; Public Service Alliance of Canada; Thunder Bay Labour History Project; United Electrical Workers; United Steel Workers of America; and University of New Brunswick.

Literature (1930s-70s). A small number of films and television programs offer readings of the works of William Shakespeare, William Cowper, Gwendolyn Brooks, James Jones and Kathleen Raine.

Researchers can also obtain moving image documents on the study of Canadian literature, including the role and influence of literature in the development of Canadian culture.

The role of the National Library of Canada as the main depository for Canadian literature is also covered by moving image documents on its history, activities and development.

Collections include: Canadian Broadcasting Corporation; Canadian Film Institute; and TV Ontario.

Medicine and related sciences (1930s-70s, 400 hours). Contains a selection of audiovisual documents relating to medicine and associated sciences. The field of mental health is covered in over a dozen films dealing with psychiatry, psychology, deviant behavior, treatment and rehabilitation. The most extensive collection, in terms of numbers of hours, deals with cancer research (170 hours) and general health care (40 hours). Also included are over 30 hours of interviews and programs on famous doctors and specialists in various branches of medicine, as well as capsule biographies of men who made Canadian medical history. In addition, the Archives holds films depicting diseases and their prevention; and a small number of programs from the CBC series *Checkup,* on preventive medicine.

Among topics considered are natural childbirth, emergency first aid in a nuclear attack, rehabilitation of war veterans and handicapped people, the use of photography in medicine and a variety of other medical subjects. Nursing personnel and the history of the Ottawa Civic Hospital are the topics of a number of documents deposited by that hospital. The staff and the hospital of the Grenfell Mission are also featured in films deposited by the International Grenfell Association.

Collections include: Canada, National Health and Welfare; Canada, Veterans Affairs; Canadian Film Institute; Canadian Lung Association; Canadian Medical Association; Canadian Mental Health Association; Canadian Psychiatric Association; Emergency Measures Organization; Hannah Institute for the History of Medicine; and National Film Board.

Science (1913-80, 800 hours). Archival holdings on scientific subjects consist of moving image documents dating back a number of years. The earliest science film in the collection (1913) is an educational film on the electrolysis of metals. Other documents, produced between 1916-19, and during the 1920s-30s, portray various experiments in physics, electronics, aerodynamics and other fields. Later offerings made to educate, as well as to entertain, are available thanks to the CBC Television Network, whose extensive deposits contain several programs from the series *Two for Physics; Live and Learn; Science Series; Man at the Centre; The Nature of Things;* and several programs made for young children.

Documents on various scientific topics, many relating to research, were deposited by several collectors and institutions; there are also over 80 hours of filmed records on research projects and experiments carried out by the Defence Research Board.

Collections include: Associated Screen News; British Broadcasting Corporation; Canada, National Museum of Science and Technology; Canada, National Research Council; Canada, Veterans Affairs; Canadian Broadcasting Corporation; Canadian Film Institute; Emergency Measures Organization; Ontario Science Centre; and Provincial Archives of Alberta.

The peoples of Canada (1910-70s, 9,500 hours). Represents the cultural aspects of the different peoples of Canada.

Numerous films and sound recordings depict the ways and customs of various Indian tribes and of the Inuit during the past seven decades, made on location from British Columbia to Newfoundland and throughout the Northwest Territories. A few documents look at the descendants of Western Indians and at their homes in Northern Manitoba and Saskatchewan. One film in particular, *Nanook of the North,* eloquently portrays the way of life of the Inuit in the 1920s.

The themes of a number of items on Indians and the Inuit relate to their art, songs, stories, dances and artifacts, and through these arts to different aspects of their cultures. Moving image and sound sequences of ceremonies show how the arts are used to express the traditions and beliefs of their origins and of the spirit world. Songs, stories and dances, such as the Inuit drum dance, are the vehicles of this expression.

The coming of the European settlers set in motion other trends which were portrayed in native arts and ceremonies, and later, in expression of thoughts and beliefs acquired directly from them. Holds various documents showing this process, including films on Bishop Marsh's voyages throughout the Arctic; a short fiction piece about a Christian Inuit girl; recollections by Dr. Maurice Haycock regarding his experiences with the Inuit; and interviews with Superintendent Henry Larsen on Inuit culture and various religious missions.

The influence of white settlement made itself felt in ways other than belief and religion, sometimes to the relative advantage of the native peoples. The documents deposited by the Anglican Provincial Synod of British Columbia portray the voyages of the hospital ship *Columbia* along the Pacific Coast and the work done by mission personnel among the Indians. Similarly, the work of the Grenfell Mission in Labrador is revealed in sound recordings and films deposited by the Mission. The MISA has over 150 hours of sound recordings and a few films documenting various disputes over treaties and reserves, social and economic problems and questions over aboriginal rights and land claims.

No description of the Collection would be complete without reference to Archibald Belaney, an Englishman who chose to live as an Indian under the name of Grey Owl. The Archives holds a small numbers of films and sound recordings on his life and the family of beavers which he befriended and cared for. Grey Owl's widow, Gertrude Bernard, also known as Anahareo, reminisces about her husband and his family history, his sculpting, prospecting and about their life together.

Also contributing material on the musical expression of the various cultures are the music, dance and variety programs referred to under the category of *The Performing Arts* described below. The artistic expressions of cultural identities, however, are not necessarily the only definitive statements on culture. Also revealing are the reflections on ways of life, customs and beliefs. These can be found in many documents cataloged under *The Peoples of Canada* and in references to the media and oral history under the headings of *Communication and the Media* and *History and Related Disciplines.* For example, television and radio non-fiction programs about everyday life, documents on journalism and literature, and oral history interviews reveal much about English Canadian and French Canadian cultures, and broaden our knowledge of Canadian ethnic groups.

Films and sound recordings relating to the latter look at the composition of ethnic communities in Canada and North America and their origins. Canadians from various backgrounds talk about migration from their former countries and about their experiences in the new world. Immigration itself is a subject for study in a number of documents, some dealing with immigration in relation to quotas and others with the need for skilled workers.

Numerous documents reveal details about the values, customs and traditions of Canadian life in general and the unique contributions of the English and French-speaking peoples who founded the country. The efforts of French Canada to check the erosion of traditional cultural patterns are well documented. Over 700 hours of sound and videotapes also record speeches, discussions and interviews concerning the work of the Task Force on Canadian Unity, the Royal Commission of Inquiry into Bilingualism and Biculturalism, the Commissioner of Official Languages and others.

Many documents portray the observance of national holidays, festivals and fairs, including the Canadian National Exhibition in Toronto. The event with the most coverage in terms of audiovisual documentation is Montreal's Worlds Fair, Expo 67 and the celebrations held throughout Canada to honor the 100th anniversary of Confederation.

Collections include: Alliance canadienne; Associated Screen News; Canada, Canadian Centre for Folk Culture; Canada, Canadian Radio-Television and Telecommunications Commission; Canada, Commissioner of Official Languages; Canada, Federal Cultural Policy Review Committee; Canada, Indian Affairs and Northern Development; Canada, Inuit Land Use and Occupancy Project; Canada, Manpower and Immigration; Canada, National Museums; Canada, National Parks; Canada, Public Service Commission; Canada, Royal Commission of Inquiry into Bilingualism and Biculturalism; Canada, Task Force on Canadian Unity; Canadian Broadcasting Corporation; Canadian Ethnology Association; Canadian Film Institute; Canadian Hadassah-Wizo; Canadian Jewish Congress; Canadian National Railways; Canadian Wildlife Service; Carleton Productions; Congress of Italian Canadians; Federation of Pakistani Canadians; Finnish Organization of Canada; Fort McLeod Historical Association; Glenbow-Alberta Institute; Global TV Network; International Film Seminar; Japanese-Canadian Citizens Association; Jewish Public Library; Maltese-Canadian Society of Toronto; National Film Board; Native Council of Canada; North American Indian Films; Ontario Archives; Ottawa Historical Association; Ottawa Jewish Community Council; Royal Society of Canada; Slovak World Congress; Supreme Court of the Northwest Territories; TV Ontario; Ukrainian National Youth Federation; and United Council of Filipinos.

The performing arts (1888-1970s, 12,000 hours). Consists of a sizeable collection of films, videotapes and sound recordings on music, drama, variety programs and folk songs. There are over 2,500 hours of television and radio programs, many deposited by the French and English networks of the CBC, featuring concerts and classical music performed by orchestras and individual musicians, as well as ballet and opera. Much of this collection consists of ballet music from the series *Dance in Canada.*

The most extensive collection of documents concerns the popular music of the last four decades, including: CBC videotapes of jazz performed by Phil Nimmons, Cal Jackson, Guido Basso and Peter Appleyard, among others; 78 hours of television programs featuring rock and roll and popular music performed by David Clayton-Thomas, Doug Riley, Lucio Agostini, Ricky Hyslop and other Canadian musicians; and a variety of television and radio specials with singers, including Joan Fairfax, Sylvia Murphy, Robert Goulet, Henri Deyglun, Joyce Sullivan, Wally Koster, Juliette and Ginette Rino.

The MISA's holdings contain a fairly extensive collection of country and western music in which names such as Gordie Tapp, Tommy Hunter, Tommy Common, Ronnie Prophet and Cliff McKay are prominent. In the field of non-traditional folk music, a fairly substantial collection spotlights Oscar Brand, Gordon Lightfoot, Judy Collins, Chad Mitchell and others from the CBC Television series *Let's Sing Out.*

Holds a small selection of traditional folk music documents deposited by several individuals and cultural organizations, including songs, music and dancing by Finnish, Latvian, German and Ukrainian groups, some of which were performed in folk festivals.

Television, particularly the CBC network, has also contributed a number of variety programs offering a wide range of entertainment. Accounting for 300 hours of viewing time, these include renditions of classical music, song and dance acts and comedy skits performed by entertainers such as Wayne and Shuster, Tommy Ambrose, Billy O'Connor, Lorne Michaels and Hart Pomeranz. *Talent Caravan* and *Music Canada,* two of the better talent shows, are also included in this category.

Radio and television variety shows produced for children and young people figure prominently in the MISA catalog of musical programs. These shows, totalling about 300 hours, are made up of nursery rhymes, cartoons, pop songs and stories. *Nursery School; Sing Ring Around; Maggie Muggins;* and *Time of Your Life* are some of the series included, as well as *Friendly Giant; Howdy Doody; Razzle Dazzle;* and *Uncle Chichimus.*

Complementing the large collection of musical performances are several documentaries and programs on performing arts personalities. Their careers and art are discussed on television programs including *90 Minutes Live; In Person; À la carte;* and *Portrait.* Other documentaries look at composers such as J. S. Bach and Arnold Schoenberg; country and western music and singers; the Viennese lieder singer Emmy Heim; vocalists Eva Gauthier, Emma Albani and Sarah Fischer; and violinist Kathleen Parlow.

A number of television programs and sound documents explore the theater and the theatrical professions.

Audiovisual documents showing performances by actors account for large segments of MISA holdings relating to the performing arts. About 3,500 hours of contemporary and classical productions were entrusted to the Archives by the television and radio networks of the CBC. A further 4,500 hours of documents have been deposited by numerous collectors and institutions and consist of an estimated 3,000 fiction features. Performances and acting styles are also fully documented in the extensive collection of books, periodicals and other texts located in the MISA library.

Collections include: Association coopérative de productions audio-visuelles; Astral-Bellevue Pathé; Astral Films; Blackhawk Films; Burg Productions; CBOT-TV (Ottawa) CFCF-TV (Montréal); Canada, National Arts Centre; Canada, National Film Board; Canada, National Library; Canadian Film Institute; Canadian Jewish Congress; Cinak; Cinepix Inc.; Clearwater Films; Columbia Pictures of Canada; Criterion Pictures Corporation; Dawson City Museum; De Mohrenschildt, Walter; Desmarais, Marie; Faroun Films; Film House; Graphic Consultants; Jon Slan Productions; Ontario Film Institute; Les Productions mutuelles; Les Productions Pierre Lamy; Les Productions Prisma; Quadrant Films; Quinn Laboratories; Rainforest Productions; Sefel Pictures International; Sonneborn, Jon; TV Ontario; Twentieth Century-Fox; United Artists; and Universal Films (Canada).

Politics, government and public administration (1888-present, 25,000 hours). The material concerning political subjects, events and personalities deposited with the MISA by Canadian political parties and those groups, associations and individuals involved with Canadian politics has enabled the National Archives to build a substantial collection of records of speeches; lectures; oral history accounts; interviews; documentaries on political figures; and accounts of national conventions, campaigns and general elections.

Holds many moving image and sound documents of interviews, speeches and appearances by heads of government, including Sir Wilfrid Laurier, R. B. Bennett, William Aberhart, Mackenzie King, Maurice Duplessis, John Diefenbaker and Pierre Trudeau. Various government figures, as well as people from the media and the academic world, also appear in films and sound recordings which look at the careers of well-known politicians and examine their governments, accomplishments and their impact on Canadian society and on world affairs.

Also holds a number of documents on the various people who have held the post of Governor General. The symbolic nature of the Governor General's duties figures importantly in discussions on the structure and principles of the Canadian federal system.

In addition to the fact that the Governor General represents the Crown in Canada and that the Canadian parliamentary system owes much to the "Mother of Parliaments" in Britain, relations between the two countries have been strengthened by the visits of the British Royal family over the years. Beginning early in this century Royal visits to Canada became increasingly frequent, and the Archives holds a number of documents reporting on those of the Prince of Wales and other members of the Royal family. It was not until 1939, though, that filmmakers had the opportunity of capturing a fullscale Royal visit, an accomplishment which continued with all subsequent visits to both Canada and the United States, and many of these documents, including some sequences shot by amateur cameramen, are stored in MISA vaults. Supplementing these are documents on the activities of the Royal family in Great Britain.

In many respects, it would be difficult to refer to politicians and political systems without seriously considering their underlying ideologies. Many of the documents in this collection look at the movements of liberalism, conservatism and socialism in the context of Canadian politics, and at other political ideologies which transcend international boundaries.

Canada's involvement in international affairs has provided opportunities for filmmakers and broadcasters to cover and report on many world events. Examples of their work have been deposited with the MISA and include documents on visits by United States presidents, French heads of state, British prime ministers, ambassadors and dignitaries from various countries, as well as the record of visits abroad by Canadian dignitaries. The United Nations and its organizations are the subject of many audiovisual documents recording their efforts to maintain peace among member countries, to protect human rights and to see to the welfare of much of the world's population. In the arena of international affairs, Canada has played a major role in international development and in the defense of the North Atlantic community, a fact in evidence in several documents. Canadian relations with the United States are also explored in a number of films and sound recordings.

Searches under the general category of "Government" will also turn up documents relating to municipal government.

Collections include: Canada, Centennial Commission; Canada, National Film Board; Canadian Banker's Association; Canadian Broadcasting Corporation; Canadian Film Institute; Canadian Zionist Federation; Canadians for Responsible Government; Czechoslovak Embassy; Economic Council of Canada; House of Commons; Liberal Party; New Democratic Party; Ontario Institute for Studies in Education; Progressive Conservative Party; Social Credit Party; Société d'études et de relations publiques; Standard Broadcast News; United Nations; United States, National Archives and Records Service; Université St-Paul; University of New Brunswick; and Various Inquiries and Royal Commissions.

Religion and the supernatural (1930s-70s, 350 hours). Consists of audiovisual documents on religion and related subjects, largely television and radio programs transferred from the CBC. An additional 150 hours of sound tapes and films have also come from both individual and corporate depositors.

A considerable portion of this material deals with general religious topics and feature well-known personalities. Contains television programs from the CBC series *Church Services, Ferment, Heritage, Horizon, Man Alive* and *Would You Believe.* Included in these are religious dramas, panel discussions and stories on Christianity and personal beliefs relating to faith, religion and the Church in general. The Collection also contains a number of television programs and other documents on various denominations and other subjects, such as the history of the Christian Church in Canada, the Hutterites of Alberta, and the survival of Christianity in the modern world.

The rituals practiced by the Jewish, Mennonite, Buddhist and Catholic faiths provide the themes for several documents.

Places of worship provide the background to religious services and may be seen in many moving image documents.

Although few documents look at the supernatural in a context other than that of religion, the MISA has 10 hours from the CBC dramatic series *The Unforseen,* a series dealing with the occult; and a series of documentaries on such subjects as fakirism, spell-casting, sorcery and astrology.

Collections include: Bellevue Pathé; Canada, National Library; Canadian Banker's Association; Conrad Grebel College; and Crossroads Christian Communications Inc.

Sports (1898-1980s, 1,700 hours). A considerable number of sports items deposited in the Collection have come from radio and television networks. There are also numerous deposits from individual sports-minded collectors.

While the majority of material deals with a particular sport, there is a lengthy series of recorded interviews and films dealing with physical education in Canada. Other instances where a number of sports are included in a single series of documents are those involving national and international games. The MISA has moving image and sound documents for every Olympic Games, for example, from Berlin (1936) to Montréal (1976), the latter being covered in over 500 hours of videotape. Available too are 165 hours of moving image documents of various Canada Games, as well as British Empire and Commonwealth Games, Pan American Games and meets of the Canadian Intercollegiate Athletic Union.

The three popular spectator sports in Canada (ice hockey, North American football and baseball) are well represented in the MISA Collection. There are over 250 hours of documents on hockey (1898-present) and depicting virtually a complete history of the sport. One film features the history of the Stanley Cup; while famous players are interviewed and shown in action, and experts provide game analysis and predictions in others. Many regular season and playoff games involving National Hockey League teams, amateur teams and even neighborhood teams have been recorded.

Football is equally well represented in the MISA Collection. Deposited almost entirely by the CBC, this collection runs 200 hours and covers selected games from the first Grey Cup game in 1909 to the Canadian Football League games, playoffs and college games of more recent years.

About 105 hours of audiovisual documents focus on baseball. Shown are World Series games from the NBC Television Network; and regular major league games, including those featuring the Montréal Expos and the Toronto Blue Jays.

Among the roughly two dozen remaining sports listed in the MISA catalogs are skiing, horseback riding and horse racing, golf, boxing, fishing and curling. Important to note among these are: a short clip on skiing in Montréal shot by Thomas Edison (1902), documents on equestrian events, including the Queen's Plate and the Calgary Stampede, the Canadian Open, the Master's Golf Championship and the Canadian Professional Golfing Association tournaments of the late 1960s. Finally, a series of short excerpts in the Maheux-Hill Collection, entitled *Greatest Fights of the Century*, star great boxers of the past. Other sports cataloged under this heading include motoring and car racing, skating, bowling, boat racing and wrestling.

Collections include: Associated Screen News; Bellevue Pathé; CBOT-TV (Ottawa); CFCF-TV (Montréal); CJOH-TV (Ottawa); CTV Network; Canada, National Health and Welfare; Canada, Veterans Affairs; Canada's Aviation Hall of Fame; Canadian Broadcasting Corporation; Canadian Film Institute; Canadian Football League; Canadian Red Cross; Comité organisateur des jeux Olympiques; Edison, Thomas A.; Hockey Night in Canada; McFarlane, Brian; National Film Board; Olympiad XII; Ontario Film Institute; Royal Canadian Yacht Club; and Vancouver Archives.

Transportation (1910-70s, 900 hours). Researchers consulting the MISA catalog under this category will find references to documents on air, water and ground transportation, some dating back to the early years of the century. Although most collections cover only one type of transportation, a few refer to all three, such as the 100-hour-long collection deposited by the Royal Commission of Inquiry into Newfoundland Transportation.

Holdings on air transportation cover various aspects of aeronautics and of aviation as a mode of transport, an industry and a sport. The evolution of aviation is the subject of a number of historical documentaries, including the film series *Powered Flight — The Story of the Century*. Other documents focus on significant events in the history of aviation: the flights of the Wright Brothers and of the *Silver Dart*, the 1926 Trans-Canada flight and Charles Lindbergh's epic crossing of the Atlantic.

An aspect of aviation which is unique to Canada is that of the group of men known as "bush pilots." Documents referring to the exploits of such pioneer aviators as Roy Maxwell, Doc Oakes, Punch Dickens and others are all available at the Archives. Films and sound recordings documenting the growth of commercial airlines, from the "bush lines" operated by these men to the major airlines of today, are also preserved, thanks to Air Canada, CP Air and others.

Another area of interest, perhaps originating in the experiences of long-distance flyers and bush pilots, is the growth of aviation as a sport and hobby. Some archival audiovisual documents focus on the activities of "Sunday flyers" in their light planes, airplane racers, and on those who fly restored antique airplanes. One series of films of special interest to aviation enthusiasts is a collection deposited by Lloyd Shales with footage of air shows featuring restored First World War aircraft and other planes dating back to the 1920s-30s.

Scenes of men attempting to fly in strange contraptions form part of many historical documents on aviation in the holdings of the Archives. Perhaps not so unusual as these, but equally as interesting, were the attempts of lighter-than-air enthusiasts to launch an industry based on the hot air balloon and the dirigible. A few film clips show the early successes these men had with the

German Zeppelins, Britain's R-100 and other airships. The era ended quite suddenly with the tragic explosion of the *Hindenburg* at Lakehurst, New Jersey, but the lighter-than-air craft was not forgotten, as evidenced by a few post-1937 documents on blimps and balloons.

The aircraft manufacturing industry is also represented by a significant number of documents including the Avro Collection, which contains film records on the development of the CF-100, the Arrow, and prototypes such as the Jetliner and Avrocar. Other collections contain documents on the construction of the Bolingbroke and Lancaster bombers, and on de Havilland Aircraft of Canada. Films and sound recordings on the test pilots who flew these aircraft are also part of the collection.

A few documents touch on topics closely related to air transportation. These include film footage on airports, and on meteorology and aerology, sciences which have an important bearing on flight safety.

In comparison to air transportation, there are relatively few documents on water transportation in the Collection. Some examples include film sequences on the passenger liner *Titanic* and other ships, and documentary clips on racing schooners such as the *Bluenose*. Documentaries dating back to the 1930s show CPR cruise ships sailing along the coast of British Columbia, and barges and supply ships in northern waters. Canal and seaway transportation, including the network of lighthouses along the St. Lawrence, are shown in a few moving image sequences and sound recordings. A collection deposited by Transport Canada covers the role played by Coast Guard vessels and icebreakers.

Scenes of harbors form part of many of the documents already mentioned, but a few items focus specifically on them. Holdings also contain a few newsreels of shipwrecks and moving image treatments recreating the sinking of the *Titanic*.

Railway and highway transportation are perhaps better represented. The MISA vaults contain several sound and moving image documents relating to railways dating from 1910. These include items on railroad construction and rolling stock; interviews with personnel; and holdings on street "railroads" — the street cars of the Toronto, Ottawa and Quebec City Transport Commissions.

The history of railroading is remembered in sequences on the Royal Scott locomotive and in filmed records of the "Fair of the Iron Horse" at the Baltimore and Ohio Railroad Pageant of 1927.

Under highway transport, the subjects best covered in the Collection are road and bridge construction and highways. Two moving image documents in particular focus on the Alaska Highway. Motor sports, racing and car rallying are fairly popular subjects, and the MISA holds a number of related films, including a cross-Canada tour in Ford automobiles in 1925; and an antique car tour of Canada in 1971.

Documents on automobile manufacturing show how far automotive technology has progressed since the first films were made on the subject in the 1920s.

Automobile safety is the subject of a small number of documents, one of which was made in the 1930s and deposited by the Society for Crippled Civilians. Another, deposited by the Craven Foundation, was made in the 1970s.

Collections include: Air Canada; Annis, Air Marshall C. L.; Beaudoin, Ted; Bellevue Pathé; British Columbia Provincial Archives; Browne, Cecil; CBOT-TV (Ottawa); Canada, Indian Affairs and Northern Development; Canada, National Museum of Science and Technology; Canada, Trade and Commerce; Canada, Transport Canada; Canada's Aviation Hall of Fame; Canadian Broadcasting Corporation; Canadian National Railways; Crawley Films; Ford Foundation; Manitoba Provincial Archives; National Film Board; Ontario Film Institute; and Toronto Transit Commission.

The visual arts (1930s-80s, 360 hours). Covers two categories: those concentrating on actual works of art; and those focusing on artists and other individuals involved in the arts.

A number of films and videotapes on paintings, sculpture, architecture, photography, folk arts and handicrafts are available. The CBC series *The Lively Arts* and other documents portraying collections and individual works may be of interest to researchers. Analysis and criticism on works of art may be found in such film series as *L'Art et son secret*, featuring the French academician René Huyghe.

Contains filmed and sound documentaries about many artists, including Emily Carr, Jack Chambers, Lawren Harris and the primitive painters of Charlevoix County, Quebec. Among architects, Walter Gropius is the subject of a CBC program in the series *Creative Persons*. The MISA's holdings also contain a moving image document on the National Gallery of Canada.

Collections include: CBOT-TV (Ottawa); Canada, National Film Board; Canadian Craft Council; and Canadian Film Institute.

War and the military (1899-present, 1,800 hours). Extensive collection of documents on various wars and armed conflicts, including profiles on the men and women who took part in them and the impact of war on the country's civilian population.

The earliest subject covered by moving image records in the Collection is the War of 1812, the topic of a CBC telecast. The Boer War is also documented by a short film clip showing troops embarking for South Africa.

For more recent conflicts, the number of documents available for research increases rapidly. Of the several documents showing actual fighting in World War I, most prominent is the epic documentary *Lest We Forget,* which depicts the role of the Canadian Expeditionary Force. The armed forces of Great Britain, the United States, France and Germany are featured in numerous film clips taken from newsreels and a few documentaries. A significant amount of film footage shows German air ace Baron Von Richtofen and the men of his "Flying Circus," English aircraft and naval vessels, trench warfare and battlefields. Documents also reveal life behind the front lines and on the homefront.

As the fledgling Royal Canadian Air Force began to grow after World War I, cameramen began to shoot documentary footage on the Force's personnel, bases and aircraft. A few examples of these films are preserved by the MISA, along with some documentaries from the period on other branches of the armed forces. Memories of World War I lingered on during the 1920s-30s. Films of overgrown battlefields and trenches and of the unveiling of the Vimy Ridge Monument in 1936 attest to this. Also dating from the period between the wars are documents depicting Hitler's rise to power, the growth of the Nazi movement, preparation for war and the growth of a new German army. Perhaps foreshadowing World War II, events such as the Spanish Civil War and the Sino-Japanese conflict are also recalled in a small number of documentaries in MISA's holdings, some featuring Canadian participants such as Dr. Norman Bethune.

Coverage of World War II was extensive, and numerous films and sound documents have been deposited with the National Archives. The activities of both Allied and enemy forces are depicted in most of the major campaigns and theaters of the war, including the Battle of Britain; the Dieppe Raid; the invasions of Sicily, Italy and Normandy; the liberation of Northern Europe and France; and the crossing of the Rhine. Documentaries and news clips depict Russian defeats and victories on the Eastern Front, and follow American advances in the South Pacific to the conclusion of the war.

Other aspects of the war are revealed in various documents. For example, the Archives has much of the background footage — 35 hours of outtakes and source material — that was produced during the making of the CBC television program *A Man Called Intrepid.*

The main sources of much of this war footage are the collection of National Film Board wartime documentaries deposited by the Academy of Motion Picture Arts and Sciences; documents donated by National Defence; the *Canada at War* series; the Canadian Army Newsreels; and many other documentaries made by the National Film Board, the Canadian Army Film Unit, Fox News and Paramount News.

Some films and sound recordings cover particular regiments and corps such as Princess Patricia's Canadian Light Infantry, the Queen's Own Rifles, the Corps of Signals, the Medical Corps and a few others.

The life of civilian populations during wartime is also covered in films and sound documents on the men and women who contributed to their country's war effort by working in factories, on farms or in home defense. The resistance of the British during the Battle of Britain in World War II is well represented, as is the participation of Canadians at home, which is shown in many news items and documentary clips from the National Film Board. Other documents covering both World Wars show victory bond campaigns, recruiting drives and civil defense activities. There are also several documents which relate to the way wars affect social values, and how propaganda influences the people of a country.

During the postwar period, new tensions developed between the Western allies and the USSR, leading to the creation of the "Cold War" between the West and the Soviet bloc. Symbolic of this period were the Berlin Wall and the Berlin airlift, about which there are several documents in the MISA Collection. Perhaps better represented are films and sound documents on the Korean War, one of which portrays René Levesque as a war correspondent for the French service of the CBC. Other material shows United Nations peacekeeping forces dispatched to many troubled areas in the world during the 1950s and 1960s. One document includes an interview with officers of Canada's Royal 22nd Regiment, which served with other UN forces in Cyprus. The activities of the North Atlantic Treaty Organization were also the subject of many television news programs and documentaries, a number of which are deposited at the MISA. More recently, a great many film and sound documentaries were generated by those covering the Vietnam War, and many of the programs produced in Canada have been deposited with the Archives.

Not all of the documents in this collection concern the waging of war,

however, and there are many references in it to peacekeeping efforts and treaties, including the Versailles Treaty of 1919; the development of the League of Nations (1920s-30s), the work for peace of the United Nations after World War II, and on the initiatives of those who have advocated nuclear disarmament.

Collections include: British Columbia Provincial Archives; CJOH-TV (Ottawa); Canada, External Affairs; Canada, Manpower and Immigration; Canada, National Defence; Canada, National Museum of Science and Technology; Canada, Trade and Commerce; Canada, Transport; Canada, Veterans Affairs; Canadian Broadcasting Corporation; Canadian Film Institute; Dawson City Museum; Emergency Measures Organization; Fox News; Graphic Consultants; McNaughton, Gen. A. G. L.; National Film Board; Pearson, Lester B.; Polish Veterans Association; Rigby, J. P.; Shales, Lloyd; Sise, Hazen; Stevenson, William; and United States, National Archives and Records Service.

Youth and education (1920s-70s, 500 hours). Material relating to the upbringing of children, their adolescence and their formal education at primary, secondary and university levels. Some television programs also look at various types of adult education.

Contains a number of documents showing the growth of children from infancy to young adulthood, particularly their psychological development, their ability to communicate and their adaptation to society's values. Some examples include: films on the famous Dionne quintuplets; documentaries on the work of the Toronto Children's Aid Society and on Jean Vanier's work with retarded children; and on the activities of the Ottawa Boys' and Girls' Club.

Topics relating to teenagers have provided the subject matter for a number of CBC television programs stored in the MISA Collection. These programs explore the thoughts and impressions of adolescents on their relations with the adult world, the social and sexual pressures exerted on them, their prospects for careers and other factors affecting their outlook and conduct.

Numerous documents on schools are available, some dating back to the 1930s, including primary schools in Great Britain and in Canada. These documents cover a variety of subjects including health, motivation and discipline and school curricula. Other documents look at the separate school system, high schools and vocational schools.

A considerable part of the Collection covers college and university education, from the viewpoints of both the institutions and the student population. Among these are documents on the University of Toronto and Queen's University, and on the history and activities of the Conseil des universités au Québec.

The concept of adult education has been of some interest to television and film producers, and the Archives has acquired a number of documents relating to it. Examples include documents on the return of veterans to universities after World War II, and the *University-of-the-Air* series of educational programs. Other educational programs shown on television include consumer education shows, such as the series *From Now On; Making Ends Meet;* and *Market Place,* aired by the CBC.

Collections include: Alberta Educational Communications; Aluminum Company of Canada; Associated Screen News; Bellevue Pathé; Canadian Association of University Teachers; Canadian Film Institute; Canadian Girls in Training; Canadian National Railways; Children's Aid Society; Commission on Relations between Universities and Governments; Council of Universities; Graphic Consultants; Health League of Canada; Insight Productions; National Film Board; Ontario Medical Association; Ottawa Boys' and Girls' Club; Religious Television Associates; and Queen's University.

Size & Elements: Film: all formats and elements (25,000 hours total). Television programs: film and videotape, all formats and elements (45,000 hours total). Over 36,000 hours of moving image preservation elements are held. All videotape reference copies are held in 3/4" or VHS formats.

Cataloging: The MISA produces finding aids to establish physical and intellectual control over the holdings. These take the form of inventories relating primarily to entire collections and catalog cards on individual items.

Documentation and Public Service staff rely to some degree on inventories to bring to the attention of researchers the content of collections of personal papers, production documentation and the memorabilia of well-known film and broadcast personalities. Collections Development and Media Cataloguing produce inventories of moving image and sound collections; 230 inventories are available. The efforts of these two sections have resulted in the publication of the first edition of the *Inventory of the Collections of the National Film, Television and Sound Archives.*

Although cards are used to update the inventory of collections, their main use is for cataloging individual items. The first series of item catalog cards are the Preliminary Data Cards (PDCs), produced by Technical Operations, to record physical data and match titles to shelf numbers. These are filed in the Public Service title index pending in-depth cataloging and serve as means of access, through titles only, to about 60 per cent of the holdings. The second series, produced by Media Cataloguing, brings together physical data and subject content in formal catalog entries filed in the title index, where they replace PDCs, in an extensive subject index and in indexes for added entries. Based on recommendations outlined in the *Anglo American Cataloguing Rules,* the data displayed on these cards can easily be converted to an automated system designed to accept the CANMARC Communication Format for audiovisual documents.

Catalog cards are also used by Documentation and Public Service staff to assist in finding information on subjects pertaining to the cinema or to broadcasting. Filed under titles, cards record original, version and alternate titles, credits, current distributors and references to trade publications containing reviews or other articles. Additional references also point to support material such as posters, scripts and still photos.

Since 1986, the MISA uses a MINISIS-based computer system for control of its holdings.

Access: Open to researchers, scholars and members of the public engaged in *bona fide* research projects. Research and screening fees not charged. Researchers are advised to contact the Public Service and Access Development Section by mail or telephone before visiting in person. Once they are registered, researchers are free to consult the catalogs and indexes by themselves, or with the help of trained research personnel. If required, copies of selected catalog cards can be provided for study. Staff members provide assistance in identifying and tracking down necessary documentation from the collections and in putting moving image and sound documents on appropriate viewers for researchers wishing to study them in depth. The Archives can also provide researchers with prints, videotapes or audiotapes of selected documents (on request) if this is not prohibited by copyright and/or donor restrictions.

Rights: No rights held to majority of material; rights retained by original producers. Some material (approx. one-third of collection) in the public domain.

Licensing: Available for reuse, subject to restrictions.

Restrictions: Most material subject to copyright and/or donor restrictions. Duplication is restricted to "physical entities" only (i.e., one full reel of film or videotape); partial sections of reels cannot be copied.

Viewing Facilities: Film (35mm and 16mm flatbeds and projection room); videotape (3/4" and VHS; NTSC, PAL and SECAM).

Duplication Facilities: Film (in-house laboratory for nitrate and 28mm preservation only; external laboratories are used for all outside orders); videotape (2", 1", 3/4", VHS, Betamax and 1/2" open reel to 3/4" and VHS).

Related Materials: Sound recordings, books, periodicals, posters, still photographs, manuscripts, press clippings, publicity material, catalogs and other documentation.

Publications: The following publications can be obtained free of charge, subject to availability, from the Publications Division of the National Archives of Canada.

Bibliography: FIAF Members' Publications. Ottawa, 1982.
General Guide Series 1983: National Film, Television and Sound Archives. Ottawa, 1983.
Inventory of Main Holdings — Sound Archives. Ottawa, 1979 (out of print).
Inventory of the Collections of the National Film, Television and Sound Archives. Ottawa, 1983.
National Film, Television and Sound Archives. Ottawa, 1981.
Periodical Holdings. Ottawa, 1982.
Sound Archives — Guide to Procedures. Ottawa, 1979 (out of print).

The information contained in this entry is largely drawn from *General Guide Series 1983 — The National Film, Television and Sound Archives,* Ottawa: National Archives of Canada, 1983. Copyright 1983, Minister of Supply and Services Canada. Reprinted by permission.

ONTARIO (Ottawa)

NATIONAL LIBRARY OF CANADA
MUSIC DIVISION
395 Wellington Street
Ottawa, ON K1A 0N4
(613) 996-7467
Fax: (613) 996-4424

S. Timothy Maloney (Chief, Music Division)

Contact: Dr. Stephen C. Willis (Head, Manuscripts Collection)
Services: Library. Open to the public. Videotape holdings maintained

primarily for archival and research purposes.

Description: *Glenn Gould Collection.* Approximately 150 videotape items from the pianist's personal collection, including television broadcasts of Gould's performances; materials that Gould videotaped from television; and videotapes given to him by friends. Also holds videotapes documenting his virtuoso piano performances (1950s-80s), produced mostly by the Canadian Broadcasting Corporation, American and European television networks.

Size & Elements: Videotape: 3/4" and 1/2" (150 videotapes total).

Cataloging: Computerized cataloging available to researchers.

Access: Open to the public. Research fees not charged. Research requests accepted by mail, telephone and in person (by appointment only).

Rights: No rights held to any material. Additional clearances may be necessary if material is to be reused. Library can direct researchers to sources for clearance. Some rights may be retained by the Gould Estate.

Licensing: Not available through Library (apply for source information).

Restrictions: Apply for information.

Viewing Facilities: Videotape.

Duplication Facilities: Videotape.

ONTARIO (Ottawa)

S.A.W. VIDEO CO-OP
130 Sparks Street, 2nd Floor
Ottawa, ON K1P 5B6
(613) 238-7648

Angèle Gagnon (Coordinator)

Contact: Angèle Gagnon
Services: Artist-run video access center; production and post-production facility. Videotape collection available to the public for in-house viewing. Material possibly available for duplication and reuse.

Description: Administered by S.A.W. Gallery (Ottawa). Provides production and post-production facilities to artists. Videotape collection includes works produced and/or post-produced at facility and recent works by artist members. Materials include documentaries, dramas and narratives produced in or relating to the Ottawa-Hull area.

Size & Elements: Videotape: 3/4" (50 videotapes; masters [few] and viewing copies).

Cataloging: None.

Access: Open to the public. For in-house viewing. Material possibly available for duplication and reuse. Research requests accepted by mail, telephone and in person (by appointment only). Minimal hourly screening fee charged.

Rights: All rights retained by original producers.

Licensing: Can refer requester to original producer for permission.

Restrictions: Some restrictions may apply regarding reuse.

Viewing Facilities: Videotape (3/4" and VHS).

Duplication Facilities: Videotape (3/4" and VHS).

ONTARIO (Peterborough)

TRENT INSTITUTE FOR THE STUDY OF POPULAR CULTURE
TRENT UNIVERSITY
Box 189 PRC
Peterborough, ON K9J 7B8
(705) 748-1768

Prof. Andrew Wernick (Director)

Contact: Staff
Services: Research institute. Videotape collection available to researchers and scholars for in-house use only.

Description: "The Institute [started 1987] is designed to advance research and education in the areas of mass media and popular culture, and a large part of its work involves the development of a comprehensive archive of mainstream Canadian and American media materials. As well as providing a resource of services to students, researchers and the wider community, the archive is designed to support the Institute's own central project: cross-media examination of how popular culture has developed in North America between 1945 and the present day."

Archives is organized into two main collections: "Mainstream North American" (i.e., Canadian-consumed) and "Canadian" (i.e., Canadian-produced or created). These, in turn, are divided into three separate sections: Print, Audio and Audio-Visual. Each section is designed to track the development of major media forms, particularly since 1945.

Holds representative samples of "mainstream" postwar television programs, ranging from music video and documentary to newscasts, advertising and situation comedies. Institute plans to assemble a representative collection of the top ten Nielsen-rated shows in Canada and the U.S. for each year since the early 1950s.

Size & Elements: Videotape: VHS (over 800 programs). Collection rapidly increasing in size.

Cataloging: Computerized cataloging in progress (MARC-compatible cataloging using DBase III Plus).

Access: Open to researchers and scholars only. For in-house use only. Available for reuse, subject to copyright clearance. Research fees not charged. Research requests accepted by mail and telephone. Institute contemplates setting up a membership structure in which members will have free access to materials; a charge would apply to use of collection by nonmembers.

Rights: No rights held to any material. Rights retained by original producers or broadcasters. Additional clearances may be necessary in some cases if material is to be reused.

Licensing: Available for reuse, subject to restrictions. Usage fees charged.

Restrictions: All materials subject to copyright clearance.

Viewing Facilities: Videotape (VHS).

Duplication Facilities: Videotape (VHS).

Related Materials: Print Archive is composed of mass-market magazines; advertising slides; and "paraliterature," including *Harlequin Romances,* comics, department store catalogs and radio and television guides. Audio Archive contains "top twenty" pop songs (1950s-present); 19,000 audiotapes of postwar original Canadian music; 78 rpm records, including CBC Radio's back catalog of pre-1955 incidental music.

ONTARIO (Toronto)

A SPACE
183 Bathurst Street, Suite 301
Toronto, ON M5T 2R7
(416) 364-3227

Betty Julian (Administrative Coordinator)
Hamish Buchanan (Acting Programming Coordinator)

Contacts: Betty Julian; Hamish Buchanan
Services: Artist-run gallery. Videotape collection open to gallery members and the general public for in-house viewing only.
Description: Videotapes produced by artists.
Size & Elements: Videotape (format and amount unspecified).
Cataloging: Published catalogs.
Access: Open to gallery members and the public (appointments required). Research fees not charged. Research requests accepted in person (by appointment only).
Rights: Full rights held to all material.
Licensing: Not available for licensing or reuse.
Restrictions: None specified.
Viewing Facilities: Videotape (screening room available when current show does not require use of space).
Duplication Facilities: None.

ONTARIO (Toronto)

ADDICTION RESEARCH FOUNDATION OF ONTARIO LIBRARY
33 Russell Street
Toronto, ON M5S 2S1
(416) 595-6144

Margy Chan (Manager, Library Services)

Contacts: Film Desk (for loans); David Britnell, A-V Productions (416/595-6066; for sales, licensing and reuse)
Services: Foundation; videotape producer and distributor. Some videotapes available for purchase, licensing and reuse; outside productions for distribution and research only.
Description: Foundation is an agency of the Province of Ontario that operates specialized research, educational, clinical, and community-service development programs throughout the province. Produces and distributes educational materials (for children and adults) relating to addiction, alcoholism, drug dependency and substance abuse.

Children's videotapes produced by the foundation include: *The Dr. Cooper Series,* classroom-tested children's puppet shows on tobacco, alcohol, and marijuana use; *Nothing to Sniff At: Inhalants and Their Dangers; Leave It Alone: Dangerous Substances Around the Home; Me & My Friends & Our Booze;* and *The Score on Cannabis.*

Videotape programs for adults include: *Alcohol Roulette; Play Your Hand; Fetal Alcohol Syndrome (FAS); A Fighting Chance; Ah! Relief: Responsible Drug Use; Communication Skills: A Demonstration Tape* (for addiction counselors); *The Bottom Line: Women and Alcohol; Moderation at All Times; Women & Their Use of Mood-Altering Drugs; The Immigrant Experience; Caffeine; Behavioral Management of Intoxicated and Disruptive Patients; It All Adds Up; Measure for Measure: Alcohol Conversions; Tobacco: The Complete Story; Stress & Relaxation; Gluing It Together;* and *Drugs and You.*

Films (acquired from commercial producers and distributors) cover alcoholism, drunk driving, teenage drug use, rehabilitation, families of alcoholics, cocaine, tranquilizers, marijuana, Valium, heroin, barbiturates, LSD, amphetamines, tobacco, drug counseling, drugs and pregnancy.

A few titles are available in French, Spanish, Italian and Portuguese.
Size & Elements: Film: format unspecified (approx. 200 titles). Videotape: 3/4", VHS and Betamax (approx. 30 titles).
Cataloging: Published catalogs.
Access: Available to Ontario residents for free loan. Foundation-produced materials available for purchase, distribution and research. Research fees not charged. Research requests accepted by mail, telephone and in person (walk-in).
Rights: Full rights held to all Foundation-produced videotapes. Rights to films retained by original producers. Additional clearances from production companies may be necessary if film material is to be reused (Foundation can provide references).
Licensing: Videotapes possibly available for licensing and reuse, subject to restrictions.
Restrictions: Requests for licensing and reuse considered on a case-by-case basis (contact David Britnell, A-V Productions, 416/595-6066, for information).
Viewing Facilities: Film (16mm); videotape (3/4").
Duplication Facilities: None.

ONTARIO (Toronto)

AIDS COMMITTEE OF TORONTO
P.O. Box 55, Station F
Toronto, ON M4Y 2L4
(416) 926-0063

Street address: 464 Yonge Street

Stephen Manning (Executive Director)

Contacts: Ed Jackson (Coordinator, Education Department); Janet Shusterman (Education Department); John Dunham (Coordinator, Resource Centre)
Services: Nonprofit foundation. Videotape collection maintained primarily for educational workshops.
Description: Community-based organization of volunteers (founded summer, 1983) working to confront AIDS through prevention, support and education. Collection provides AIDS-related information intended for educational purposes, and includes 22 (VHS) Shanti Project videotapes. Videotapes often accompany speakers at educational workshops.
Size & Elements: Videotape: 3/4" (3 videotapes); VHS (36 videotapes); and Betamax (12 videotapes) (all viewing copies).
Cataloging: Research library; card catalogs; in-house cataloging.
Access: Available for educational workshops and for in-house viewing by staff and researchers in some cases. Research fees not charged. Research requests accepted by mail, telephone and in person (by appointment only).
Rights: Apply for information.
Licensing: Material not available for licensing or reuse
Restrictions: For in-house viewing only. Material not available for licensing or reuse.
Viewing Facilities: Videotape (VHS).
Duplication Facilities: None.

ONTARIO (Toronto)

ARCHIVES OF ONTARIO
AUDIO-VISUAL COLLECTION
77 Grenville Street
Queen's Park

Toronto, ON M7A 2R9
(416) 965-4030
(416) 965-4039
Fax: (416) 324-3600

Richard Lochead (Archivist, Moving Image and Sound)
Ian E. Wilson (Archivist of Ontario)

Contact: Richard Lochead
Services: Government archives. Film and videotape material available to the public for research and reuse, subject to restrictions.
Description: Holds 265 separate collections of audiovisual materials, most of which do not include moving image material. Key collections containing film and/or videotape include:

Albert J. Kinsey Home Movies (collection 15) (16mm, 16 reels). Includes 1939 royal visit to Toronto and Ottawa; V-E Day in Toronto; Center Island at Toronto; Ice Follies and Toronto Granite Club Skating Carnival (both 1945).

Ontario Department of Public Works Collection (collection 67) (28mm, 6 reels; 16mm, 5 reels). Contains 28mm motion picture film produced by the Ontario Government Motion Picture Bureau (1926), unrelated to Ontario history.

Royal Commission on Electric Power Planning hearings (collection 80) (1/2" open-reel videotape, 333 reels). Commission proceedings (October 1975-August 1976).

Norman S. Bell Home Movie Collection (collection 96) (16mm, 21 reels). Includes movies of a Northern trip by bush aircraft (July 1929); the Grand Falls Power project, New Brunswick (1926-27); trips to California (1928) and the West Indies; and footage of the return to Montreal of the Black Watch after World War II.

Thor Hansen Films (collection 101) (16mm, 2 reels). Footage on Canadian crafts and art, particularly as used in office building decoration, in Toronto (Gulf Oil Building), Vancouver and Montreal; and National Gallery craft show. Footage of Toronto, including downtown; Lakeshore Boulevard near C.N.E. (Canadian National Exhibition); skyline from harbor islands; new subway; rail yards; and streets as seen from skyscrapers.

Mike Solski/Mine Mill Union, Local 598 Films (collection 102) (16mm, 7 reels). Films relating to the Sudbury, Ontario local union, including television news footage, union promotional films, and *Salt of the Earth*.

Ministry of Agriculture & Food, Communications Branch, Motion Picture Production Elements (collection 106) (16mm, 1,855 reels, 492,705 feet). Motion picture film production elements (1947-77), with topics covering many areas of interest to the agricultural sector, including: home economics, farm and crop management, plowing matches, the Royal Winter Fair, agricultural conferences, new equipment and techniques, agricultural education and the province's Colleges of Agricultural Technology.

Ontario Athletic Commission Films (collection 109) (28mm, 13 reels). Training and informational films (1920-47).

Royal Commission on Violence in the Communications Industry (collection 112) (videotape, 39 reels). Hearings, sample television programming (particularly newscasts), and CBC and CTV television presentations relative to the subject.

Ontario Ministry of Citizenship and Culture, Newcomer Services, Instructional Videotapes (collection 113) (1" videotape, 13 reels). Immigrant orientation in Portuguese, Spanish, Greek and Italian languages (1972-74).

Ontario Educational Communications Authority/TV Ontario Sample (collection 115). Television programming and production (1976-80). (3/4" videotape, 39 reels). Special debate of the Ontario Legislature on the eve of the Quebec referendum on separation, May 5-9, 1980. Samples of television shows from TV Ontario.

C. Ewart McLaughlin Home Movie Collection (collection 128) (16mm, 72 reels; 3/4" videotape viewing copies available). Home movies (1925-67) of Clarence Ewart McLaughlin, grandson of Robert McLaughlin, founder of the McLaughlin Carriage Company and the McLaughlin Motor Car Company (McLaughlin Buick), the forerunner of General Motors of Canada. Illustrates a wealthy lifestyle at Oshawa, Muskoka and Tyrone, with trips to the Mediterranean (1926); California via the Welland Canal (1927); South America (1931); and Bermuda (1932-38 and 1952).

Videotapes produced by Ontario Government Ministries (collection 144) (3/4" and Betamax, 130 min.). From the Ministry of Agriculture and Food, Ministry of Citizenship and Culture, Ministry of the Environment, and the Ministry of Government Services.

Murray Watts Collection (collection 157) (16mm, 18 reels; 8mm, 2 reels). Home movie style footage by Watts of his activities: in the Ungava Peninsula of Quebec with nickel and asbestos discoveries; in Northern Baffin Island, with the "iron mountain" and Baffinland Iron Mines properties; at Coppermine River, Northwest Territories, working on copper and base metal discoveries; and at Lost River, Alaska, attempting to resurrect an old mine. Also, *Hourglass — Murray Watts* (1970), a biographical production by the CBC.

MacDonald-Spector (Trotskyist) Collection (collection 163) (16mm, 15 reels). Films on antiwar demonstrations at Ottawa, women's liberation and miscellaneous subjects.

J. J. Taylor & Sons, Boatbuilders (collection 197) (16mm, 2 reels; 3/4" videotape viewing copies also available). Home movies (ca. 1944-54) of construction, launchings and trials of "Taylorcraft" pleasure craft, RCMP patrol craft and mine sweepers for the Canadian Navy, at the Toronto waterfront yard of J. J. Taylor & Sons, Boatbuilders.

Miscellaneous Motion Picture Films (collection 226) (35mm and 16mm, 6 reels). Safety-stock duplicates of nitrate-stock films donated to the Archives in 1975. Includes (tentatively identified): a visit with Ontario Premier George S. Henry at his farm (undated); a romantic adventure silent movie presentation, set in the 1890s and involving railway trains and an excursion steamer (undated); the visit of the Prince of Wales to Cobalt and Timmins, October 16, 1919; and parade and training exercises by the 118th Battalion, Kitchener-Waterloo (ca. 1917).

Canadian Association for Adult Education, Television Broadcast Kinescopes (1955-66) (collection 239) (16mm, 193 reels). *Citizens Forum* (1955-65), 144 reels; and *The Sixties* (1963-66), 39 reels.

Department of Trade & Development/Ministry of Industry & Tourism Circulation Films (1961-79) (collection 240) (16mm, 116 reels). Mainly release prints of tourism promotion and trade films.

Northern Motion Picture Film Laboratories Collection (1950s-82) (collection 241) (35mm and 16mm, 222 reels). Film production elements accumulated by Northern Motion Picture Film Labs, Toronto, and deposited (after selection) in the Archives at the dissolution of the business in 1984. Films are on a variety of subjects and produced by many filmmakers. Only films relating to Ontario were selected for this collection; others were sent to Manitoba and Quebec.

Tourism Marketing Films (collection 243) (16mm, 13 reels). Archival copies of tourism promotional films produced (1964-76) for the Ministry of Tourism & Recreation. Includes films about Algoma, Thunder Bay, boating, Niagara, Ontario Place and Toronto.

Electronic Hansard, 2nd Session, 33rd Parliament of Ontario (1986) (collection 257) (VHS videotape, 60 reels). Test recordings of the Ontario Legislature in preparation for the installation of full television recording facilities, April-July 1986. Includes the visit to the Ontario Legislature by South African Archbishop Desmond Tutu.

Several collections contain TV Ontario sample productions and programming.
Size & Elements: Film: 35mm, 28mm, 16mm, Super 8mm and 8mm (amount unspecified). Videotape: all formats (amounts unspecified).
Cataloging: Card catalog; printed catalog and holdings list of audiovisual collection; shot lists available for some productions.
Access: Open to the public. Research fees not charged. Research requests accepted by mail, telephone and in person (walk-in).
Rights: Full rights held to some material. Some material in the public domain.
Licensing: Available for licensing and reuse, subject to restrictions. License and usage fees not charged.
Restrictions: Donor or copyright restrictions apply to some material.
Viewing Facilities: Film (35mm, 16mm, super 8mm and 8mm); videotape (3/4", VHS, Betamax and 1/2" EIAJ open reel).
Duplication Facilities: Film (16mm to videotape transfers); videotape (3/4", VHS and Betamax).

ONTARIO (Toronto)

ART GALLERY OF ONTARIO
EDWARD P. TAYLOR AUDIO-VISUAL CENTRE
317 Dundas Street West
Toronto, ON M5T 1G4
(416) 977-0414
Fax: (416) 979-6646

Catherine Jonasson (Head, Film and Video)
Margaret Brennan (Head, Edward P. Taylor Audio-Visual Centre)

Contacts: Henry Dunsmore (Head, Media Productions); Margaret Brennan
Services: Art gallery; film and videotape producer. Material available for research and in some cases for licensing and reuse, subject to restrictions.
Description: The Audio-Visual Centre holds documentary films and videotapes (most produced at the Gallery) relating to exhibitions and interviews

with contemporary Canadian artists and art historians; as well as some material on conservation techniques. Also holds episodes of the public television show *Spectrum* (produced by the Media Productions department), which airs eight times a year and features interviews with artists currently showing at the gallery.

Artists represented in the videotape collection include: John Brown, Jack Bush, A. J. Casson, Judy Chicago, Moira Clark, Alex Colville, Graham Coughtry, Ken Danby, Paterson Ewen, Oliver Girling, Will Gorlitz, Richard Hamilton, David Hockney, Nancy Johnson, Joan Krawczyk, Annette Mangaard, Sandra Meigs, John Meredith, Henry Moore, Kazuo Nakamura, Dennis Oppenheim, Christopher Pratt, Reinhard Reitzenstein, Lupe Rodriguez, William Ronald, Michael Snow, Harold Town, George Trakas, Robert Ian Wallace, Joyce Wieland, Shirley Wiitasalo and R. York Wilson.

The Media Productions department maintains a library of outtakes for archival and research purposes, which can be accessed by contacting them directly.

Size & Elements: Film: 16mm (3 titles; 90 min. total). Videotape: 3/4" and Betacam (35 titles, approx. 15 hours; masters and viewing copies).
Cataloging: Card catalogs.
Access: Audio-Visual Centre open to the public. Material for in-house use only. Footage held by the Media Productions department is accessible by appointment to qualified researchers and scholars. Research fees charged. Research requests accepted by mail, telephone and in person (by appointment).
Rights: Full rights held to some material. Additional clearances are necessary if material is to be duplicated or reused; copyrights held by artists.
Licensing: Available for licensing with the approval of a Gallery representative. License or usage fees charged in some cases (determined by the relevance of project to Gallery mandate).
Restrictions: Requests for duplication or reuse are subject to acceptance and approval.
Viewing Facilities: Film (16mm) (by appointment and with special permission only); videotape (3/4" and VHS).
Duplication Facilities: Videotape (3/4" and VHS).

ONTARIO (Toronto)

ART METROPOLE

788 King Street West
Toronto, ON M5V 1N6
(416) 367-2304

Allan MacKay (Director)

Contact: Allan MacKay
Services: Arts organization; videotape distributor. Videotape collection available for research, rental and purchase.
Description: Artist-run center which exhibits, collects, distributes and publishes information on contemporary art. Collection (1960-present) is comprised of artists' work based on multiple format media (e.g., videotapes, audiotapes, records, artist's books, conceptual pieces and "multiples"). Philosophically interested in making artists' multiples available to a broad public at a low cost.

Includes contemporary videotapes emphasizing North American and European video works. The videotapes examine a wide range of subject matter and ideas, using many different styles of constructing visual images and sounds. Some of the works deal with issues such as sexuality, memory, relationships and technology, while others have more formal or ambiguous qualities investigating the nature of artmaking and mediamaking itself.

Works by noted artists include: Dana Atchley and Eric Metcalfe, producing fantasy narratives and detective thrillers; Helen Doyle, examining feminist and social issues; the infamous group *General Idea*, who create productions relating to the mass media and artists, the spectacle and the position of the artist in the 1980s; Noel Harding's videotapes and installations exploring personal notions of illusion and reality, subjective understanding and public perspective; Les Levine, using advertising and television as the raw materials and targets of his work, examining the notion of the programmability of individuals; Ardele Lister's storytelling videotapes, taking a look at a modern-day hell, family needs and relations; Ian Murray, fascinated with the alteration and manipulation of popular forms and mass media products; Jan Peacock's narratives, often from autobiographical sources, which expose and question the values by which we construct reality; Rodney Werden, whose videotapes relating to issues of gender roles and sexual identity lay the groundwork for an exploration of the fiction of artistic subjectivity; and Paul Wong's works, which explore the artist's position in relation to prevailing cultural standards on both the behavioral and sociological levels.

Size & Elements: Videotape: 3/4" (NTSC and PAL); VHS and Betamax (over 600 titles total).
Cataloging: Published distribution catalogs. Computerized cataloging for in-house and research purposes.
Access: Available for rental and purchase. For in-house viewing only. Open to researchers and scholars only.
Rights: Rights to all materials retained by artists.
Licensing: Not available for licensing or reuse.
Restrictions: Artists must be contacted directly for permission to reuse material.
Viewing Facilities: Videotape (NTSC and PAL).
Duplication Facilities: None.
Related Materials: Records and books produced by artists.
Publications: Publications relating to individual artists; *Video by Artists 1* and *2*, an authoritative anthology of international video writings and projects, collecting many diverse and revisionist viewpoints.

ONTARIO (Toronto)

ARTS TELEVISION CENTRE

142 George Street
Toronto, ON M5A 2M6
(416) 869-1589

Lawrence Adams (Director)

Contact: Lawrence Adams
Services: Media arts center; film and videotape producer; archives. Videotape collection available for in-house viewing (on request), duplication and reuse, subject to restrictions.
Description: Established 1974. Produces arts-oriented videotapes; promotes artists, performers and dancers; and operates a rental studio and video dubbing service.

Archives holds material relating to art and artists, performance and dance (1970s to early 1980s). Some artists' videotapes are held.
Size & Elements: Videotape: 1" and 3/4" (masters); 3/4" (viewing copies). (Approx. 350 hours total).
Cataloging: Handwritten lists (75% of collection cataloged).
Access: Open by request for videotape viewing. For in-house use only. Most material available for duplication and reuse. Research or screening fees not charged. Research requests accepted by mail, telephone and in person (appointments required).
Rights: Full rights held to some material (approx. 80%). Additional clearances may be necessary in some cases if material is to be reused.
Licensing: Available for licensing and reuse, subject to restrictions. License fees charged.
Restrictions: Some material restricted by artists or videomakers; certain material carries other restrictions.
Viewing Facilities: Videotape (3/4", VHS and 1/2" open reel) (by appointment only).
Duplication Facilities: Videotape (3/4", VHS and 1/2" open reel).

ONTARIO (Toronto)

CANADIAN BROADCASTING CORPORATION STOCK SHOT RESEARCH AND SALES

P.O. Box 500, Terminal A
Toronto, ON M5W 1E6
(416) 975-7608
Fax: (416) 975-2857

Anne Kelly (Supervisor of Stock Shots)

Contact: Anne Kelly
Services: Film and videotape stock footage sales library.
Description: Stock footage (1940s-present) from many cultures and countries around the world, depicting various aspects of social and daily life, nature, the arts, architecture and history. New footage is constantly being added to the collection. All footage has been evaluated to eliminate political or controversial subject matter. A very general listing of worldwide subjects covered includes, but is not limited to:

Canada. History, geography and culture; urban affairs and development. Especially strong in Ontario history and culture.

Asia. China, including industry; diplomatic visits and banquets; the Forbidden City; caves and statuary; Suchow gardens; people living along the

Suchow River; families washing clothes in the river; people riding bicycles; clotheslines in city streets; markets. There is also footage of Japan, Vietnam, Malaysia, Singapore, India, Bangladesh, Nepal and the Himalayas.

Mideast. Iran, Lebanon (pre-civil war), Yemen, Saudi Arabia, Israel, Jordan, Iraq (including footage of Kurds and schoolgirls dancing).

Soviet Union. Covers many areas, including Soviet Georgia, Moscow and Leningrad.

Europe. Greece, Yugoslavia, Turkey, Prague, Italy, Germany, West and East Berlin, France, Scandinavia, Belgium, Holland, Spain, Portugal, British Isles and Ireland.

Southern Hemisphere. Australia, New Zealand, South American flora and fauna, Ecuador, Chile, Galapagos Islands, Brazil, Venezuela and Colombia.

Central and North America. Panama, Mexico, United States and Canada.

Size & Elements: Film: 16mm (approx. 10 million feet). Videotape: Betacam (small amount; masters); 3/4" and VHS (viewing copies).

Cataloging: Computerized cataloging available to researchers; printouts of shot lists relating to particular footage requests can be furnished.

Access: Open to the public. Available for reuse. Research fees charged. Research requests accepted by mail and telephone.

Rights: Full rights held to all material.

Licensing: Available for licensing and reuse. License fees charged.

Restrictions: None specified.

Viewing Facilities: Videotape (3/4" and VHS).

Duplication Facilities: None (outside arrangements can be made).

ONTARIO (Toronto)

CANADIAN FILMMAKERS DISTRIBUTION CENTRE (CFMDC)

67A Portland Street
Toronto, ON M5V 2M9
(416) 593-1808

Ross Turnbull (Director)

Contact: Staff

Services: Distributor. Films and videotapes available to the public for rental and purchase.

Description: Founded in 1967 (and formally incorporated as a nonprofit organization in 1972) to promote the work of independent filmmakers across Canada, and to gain for them a financial return from the exhibition and sale of their films.

From an initial collection of fourteen short films, holdings have grown to over 1,000 titles by approximately 400 artists. 85% of the films in distribution are Canadian, the remainder being the work of experimental filmmakers from the United States, France, Britain and Australia. Major genres include: animation; documentary, including films on the arts, Canadian history, environment and nature, the individual and society, sociology and community studies, sports, recreation, travel, technology and media; drama; and experimental.

Canadian Filmmakers Distribution West (q.v.) (founded 1979) and Atlantic Independent Media (q.v.) (founded 1985) grew out of the need for increased regional distribution. Both have pledged to work cooperatively with the CFMDC to promote the films of Canada's independent filmmakers, and to distribute some of the same titles.

Animation. Sample titles from the extensive collection include: *Nukie's Lullaby* (Jonathan Amitay); *Bridging the Gap* and *Pursuit/Flight* (Marilyn Cherenko); *Steam Ballet, Animals in Motion, Eurynome* and *MM Myth Myth — A Collage* (John Straiton); *The Amazing Colossal Man* and *Yellow Ball Cache* (Yellow Ball Workshop).

Documentary (arts). Sample titles include: *Artist on Fire: The Work of Joyce Wieland* (Kay Armatage); *Jill Johnston: October 1975* (Kay Armatage and Lydia Wazana); seven films directed by Les Blank and others; *Nuclear Follies* (Michael Chechik), a satirical review of life in the atomic age, employing a collage of footage from the 1940s-50s; *Ranch: The Alan Wood Ranch Project* (Steve DeNure and Christopher Lowry), on a massive environmental art piece built in the foothills of the Rockies; *Bo Diddley's Back in Town* (Ian Mackenzie Ewing), the record of a Toronto concert and life outside the concert hall; *SPECTRUMSPECTRUMSPECTRUM* (Karen Firus), a human color wheel celebrating the spectrum of natural colors; *Linking Arms* (John Gareau), on the creation of Colette Whiten's sculpture linking five men in hardened plaster; *Mashiko Village Pottery, Japan 1937* (restored by Marty Gross), on ceramic manufacture and the centuries-old pottery-making cycle; *Divine Solitude* (Jean-Marc Larivière), a performance film featuring dancer-choreographer Nana Gleason; *John Nesbitt — Sculptor* (Neal Livingston); *Looking for Martin Lavut* (Al Maciulis), on the Canadian motion picture

director; *The Art of Haiti* (Mark Mamalakis); *Marcia Resnick's Bad Boys* (Ron Mann and Elliott Lefko), featuring photographs and anecdotes that explore the myth of malehood; *Sons of Captain Poetry*, on the Canadian poet b. p. nichol and *The Clinton Special: A Film About the Farm Show*, on the Theatre Passe Muraille Company and its play based on the farming community of Clinton, Ontario (Michael Ondaatje); *Threading Through Time* (Gloria Rosenberg), on quilt artistry; *Snowscreen: The Art of Michael Snow* (Rob Shoub); *A Film About Joyce Wieland* (Judy Steed); and *The Journals of Susanna Moodie* (Marie Waisberg), a dramatic interpretation of Margaret Atwood's poems.

Documentary (Canadian history). Titles include: *Chinese Cafes in Rural Saskatchewan* (Tony Chan), on the experiences of Chinese immigrants; *Chinese Canadians: A Search for Identity* (Allan Cheng), a history from 1858 on; *Countdown Canada* (Robert Fothergill), an actuality-style documentary of the last hours of Canada's independent existence before it joins the U.S.; *Dene Nation* (Rene Fumoleau), on the Dene people's decision to declare themselves a nation in 1978; *The Georgetown Boys* (Dorothy Manoukian), on the resettlement of Armenian Christian orphans in 1915, following the massacres and deportations in the Ottoman Empire; *Frozen Caution* (Elizabeth C. Moes), on the Temagami Indians and their fight for recognition of their aboriginal rights; *Harvest of Dreams* (Janice Starko), the story of early Ukrainian pioneers in Canada; and *Spadina* (David Troster), a portrait of the once-thriving but now dwindling Jewish community of Toronto's Spadina Avenue.

Documentary (environment and nature). Titles include: *The Nuclear Path* (Chris Aikenhead and Doug Mulhall); *Of Moose and Man* (Alistair Brown Associates); *The Rites of Spring* (Michael Chechik), on the annual seal hunt off the Labrador coast; *Greenpeace: Voyages to Save the Whales* (Michael Chechik, Ron Precious and Fred Easton); *Canary in a Coal Mine* (Greg Darling), on pollution in the Niagara River; *Whalewatch* (Brian Lewis); *Budworks* (Neal Livingston), on aerial insecticide spraying of forests; *Water Power* (Neal Livingston), on its history; *The Solar Frontier* (Frances and Peter Mellon), on the merits of residential solar heating in the snowbelt; and *Nahanni: Two Weeks of the River* (Jane Thompson), the story of six young men who canoed the legendary river in the Northwest Territories.

Documentary (the individual and society). Titles include: *Citizen of What Country* (Tony Bannon, Gregg Borland, J. T. Doran and Bob O. Lehmann, 1970), a cinema-verité record of a young American deserter making his way to Toronto; *A Kid From the Suburbs* (Alan Doucette), on one man's battle with AIDS; *A Moffie Called Simon* (John Greyson), on the case of Simon Nkodi, an imprisoned Black gay activist and student leader in South Africa; *Las Aradas* (Janis Lundman), on the Salvadorean Army massacre of a refugee camp in 1980; *Jim and Ernie* (Craig Philp), about a homosexual couple who have been together for 26 years; *In Exile* (Anton Wagner and Marvin Bernstein, 1972), on the lives of and assimilation problems faced by the approximately 75,000 American war resisters in Canada in the early 1970s; and *Theatre for Strangers* (Janet Walczewski), about a female stripper in Toronto.

Sociology and community studies. Titles include: *Rubblewomen (Trummerfrauen)* (Gamma Bak, Bryan Sutton and Ian Doncaster), a subjective approach to women's history in the workforce and an eyewitness report of the postwar cleanup of Berlin by its women workers; eight films by Les Blank and collaborators; and *The Last Pogo Movie* (Colin Brunton, 1979), on Toronto's punk music scene. Four films by Janis Cole and Holly Dale, including *Cream Soda* (1976), on the massage parlors of downtown Toronto; *Minimum Charge No Cover* (1976), on prostitution, homosexuals, transsexuals and transvestites; *Thin Line* (1977), on inmates of an Ontario maximum-security mental health center; and *P4W (Prison for Women)* (1972), on the invisible and complex community of incarcerated women.

Other titles include: *Keltie's Beard: A Woman's Story* (Sara Halprin); *For a Woman in El Salvador, Speaking* (Sara Halprin); *Re-Entry Women* (Sara Halprin), the story of six women reentering the workforce (age 30-60); *Celso and Cora: A Manila Story* (Gary Kildea), a feature-length documentary about a young couple living in a squatter settlement in the Philippine capital; *Downside Adjustments* (Emil Kolompar and Mary Jane Gomes), on the social impact of high technology, focusing on Windsor, Ontario; *This Film is About Rape* (Bonnie Kreps); *Body, Mind and Spirit* (Paul McLean), on naturopathic medicine; *Unstable Elements: Atomic Stories 1939-1985* (Andy Metcalfe and Newsreel Collective), combining documentary and fiction to trace the history of nuclear Britain and analyze the tunnel vision of the atomic scientist; *Not Dead Yet* (Edward Mowbray and Ruth Taylor, 1984), on a year in the life of Toronto's punk community; *Mondo Punk* (Suzanne Naughton, 1978); *Kadloona: Changing the Inuit* (Chuck Rosenberg), on the pressures steering Inuit children away from a traditional lifestyle; *No Sad Songs* (Nick Sheehan, 1985), the director's cut of the first Canadian film on AIDS; and *Namibia: Tell the World* (Colin Thomas and Newsreel Collective, 1985), on South Africa's occupation of Namibia.

Technology and media. Titles include: *Cooperage* (Phil Borsos), an

554

account of a barrel factory operating since 1895; *Spartree* (Phil Borsos), on heavy timber logging; *Lumen* (Gord Kilner), contrasting the handcrafting of neon lights with the mechanized making of light bulbs; *Eyes See, Ears Hear* (Donald Snowden, Memorial University), an anthropological documentary on the use of videotape recorders and television as an educational tool in an Indian village; *Red Rocket* (Colin Strayer), on the streetcar of the future as designed in 1929; and *The Big Adventure* (Colin Strayer), a time-lapse subway ride under Toronto.

Drama. Numerous titles (1964-86).

Experimental. Films and videotapes by Blaine Allan, Jim Anderson, Kay Armatage, Bruce Baillie, Freude Bartlett, Renny Bartlett, Richard Bartlett, Scott Bartlett, Warren Bass, Raphael Bendahan, David Bennell, James Benning, John Bertram, David Bienstock, Marcella Bienvenue, Tom Braidwood, Stan Brakhage, Robert Breer, Carl Brown, Amnon Buchbinder, Robert Carney, Mike Cartmell, Jack Chambers, Tom Chomont, Doug Chomyn, Shirley Clarke, Robert Cowan, Kim Cross, Greg Curnoe, Martha Davis, Richard Davis, Walter Delorey, Steve DeNure, Martin Devenyi, Keewatin Dewdney, Dave Douglas, Peter Dudar, Timothy Dugdale, Bruce Elder, Keith Elliott, Ed Emshwiller, Ellie Epp, Betty Ferguson, Robert Fothergill, Hollis Frampton, Su Friedrich, John Gagne, Charles Gagnon, Chris Gallagher, Cindy Gawel, Ernie Gehr, Barry Gerson, Vincent Grenier, George Griffin, Anna Gronau, Patricia Gruben, Walter Gutman, Howard Guttenplan, Rick Hancox, Scott Haynes, Michael Hoare, Dana Hodgson, Philip Hoffman, Mike Hoolboom, Leo Hunnako, Jim Irons, Ken Jacobs, Patrick Jenkins, Henry Jesionka, Larry Kardish, Nick Kendall, Michael Kennedy, Robert Kennedy, Richard Kerr, Gordon Kidd, Fumiko Kiyooka, Christine Koenigs, George Kuchar, Jean Claude Labrecque, Owen Land (George Landow), Kathleen Laughlin, Standish Lawder, Neal Livingston, Keith Lock, Rose Lowder, Andrew Lugg, Janis Lundman, Annette Mangaard, Lorne Marin, Richard Martin, Josephine Massarella, Bruce McDonald, Paul McGowan, Gary McLaren, Ross McLaren, Suzanne McLaren, Carolyn McLuskie, Sandra Meigs, Jonas Mekas, Peter Melnychuk, Marie Menken, Peter Mettler, Adrienne Mitchell, Arvind Narale, Gunvor Nelson, Micheline Noel, Derek Norman, Midi Onodera, Linda Outcault, Gerald Packer, Joseph Paitouski, Jean-Pol Passet, Daniel Pellerin, Peter Piotrowski, Jonathan Pollard, Gary Popovich, Psychomedia, Yvonne Rainer, Richard Raxlen, Robert Rayher, Al Razutis, David Rimmer, Keith Rodan, Peter Rose, Michael Rouse, Steven Sanguedolce, the Sargent Family, George Semsel, Paul Sharits, Guy Sherwin, Richard Shoichet, Lois Siegel, Joel Singer, Jim Smith, Stephen Smith, Michael Snow, Veronika Soul, Judy Steed, Barbara Sternberg, Igor Tertysznyj, Tom Thibault, Kirk Tougas, Lois Tupper, Denis Vachon, John Vainstein, Marco Vais, Jana Veverka, Janko Virant, Lawrence Weiner, Chris Welsby, Joyce Wieland, Paul Winkler, Wyndham Wise, Cal Woodruff, Lenni Workman and Caroline Wuschke.

Size & Elements: Film: 16mm (over 1,000 titles). Videotape: 3/4" and VHS (amount unspecified).

Cataloging: Published catalog.

Access: Available to the public for rental and purchase. Requests accepted by mail and telephone.

Rights: Rights retained by original producers.

Licensing: Possibly available for licensing and reuse, subject to clearance. Written permission must be obtained.

Restrictions: "Motion pictures are protected by copyright and the purchase of a film only includes the right to unlimited screenings of the film by a direct projection method in a non-commercial setting, but does not entail the right to distribute, sell, lease, duplicate, or televise the film, in whole or in part." Permission for any other use must be obtained in writing from the office of CFMDC.

Viewing Facilities: None.

Duplication Facilities: None.

Representatives: Some titles available through Atlantic Independent Media (q.v.) and Canadian Filmmakers Distribution West (q.v.).

ONTARIO (Toronto)

CANADIAN GAY ARCHIVES
Box 639, Station A
Toronto, ON M5W 1G2
(416) 921-6310

Harold Averill (President)

Contact: Harold Averill
Services: Incorporated charitable organization. Film and videotape collection open to the public for in-house use only. Some material restricted to *bona fide*

researchers. Material not available for licensing or reuse. A limited portion of the collection is cleared for duplication.

Description: Chartered to collect, preserve and arrange information and materials in any medium by and about gay men and lesbians, with primary emphasis on material produced in or concerning Canada. Holds mostly completed films and videotapes, although some unedited footage and outtakes are also retained.

Videotape materials include: various instructional programs; several television programs produced by Gayblevision in Vancouver, B.C. (1980-81); promotional videotapes produced by the Lesbian and Gay Pride Day Committee of Toronto (1981-86, outtakes and final edit versions); videotapes produced for broadcast on *Out of the Closet* (1977), a television program produced by gays in Ottawa; *Coming Out* (Mariposa Film Group); *No Sad Songs*, on AIDS; a videotape version of the independent feature film *I Heard the Mermaids Singing;* and erotica.

Size & Elements: Film: 16mm and 8mm (amount unspecified; originals and release prints). Videotape: VHS and Betamax (amount unspecified; masters and viewing copies).

Cataloging: Inventory in process.

Access: Open to the public. For in-house use only. Available for duplication, subject to restrictions. Some material restricted to use by *bona fide* researchers by donor request. Research fees not charged. Research requests accepted in person (walk-in: Tuesdays, Wednesdays and Thursdays, 7:30 pm–10 pm; and by appointment).

Rights: No rights held to any material. Additional clearances will be necessary if material is to be reused.

Licensing: Not available for licensing or reuse.

Restrictions: Some items carry donor restrictions limiting use to *bona fide* researchers. Most material not cleared for duplication. Footage not available for licensing or reuse.

Viewing Facilities: Film (8mm projector); videotape (Betamax).

Duplication Facilities: None (outside duplication can be arranged on a cost-recovery basis if material is cleared for duplication).

ONTARIO (Toronto)

JACK CHISHOLM FILM PRODUCTIONS, LTD.
229 Niagara Street
Toronto, ON M6J 2L5
(416) 366-4933

Mary DiTursi (President)

Contact: Margaret Baker (Library Manager)
Services: Film and videotape stock footage sales library.
Description: Historical events (1896-present); footage from early features, documentaries, industrial and educational films; Canadian scenics and aerials (35mm color negative); wildlife and nature, including animals, insects, flowers and birds; travel footage, including establishing shots of major international locations.

Subjects represented include: cities, disasters, education, history, industry, medicine, health, wars, leisure and recreational activities, arts and entertainment, social and political issues, sports (winter and summer), transportation, communications, stunts and personalities.

Also represents other producers, including National Film Board of Canada.
Size & Elements: Film: 35mm (color negative); 16mm (black and white, color negative and reversal). Videotape: 1", Betacam and 3/4" (over 7,000 hours).
Cataloging: Computerized cataloging for staff use only. Footage listed by subject, location, source, format and date.
Access: Available to the public. Research requests accepted by mail, telephone and in person (by appointment only). Research fees charged.
Rights: Full rights held to most material. Additional clearances may be necessary in some cases if material is to be reused.
Licensing: Available for licensing and reuse. Fees charged based on actual footage used and market requirements.
Restrictions: Minimum sales restrictions apply.
Viewing Facilities: Film and videotape. Library will assemble preview reel and send to producer; fees charged.
Duplication Facilities: Videotape (3/4" and 1/2").

ONTARIO (Toronto)

CITYPULSE LIBRARY
299 Queen Street West
Toronto, ON M5V 2Z5
(416) 591-5757
Fax: (416) 591-7791

Bill Patrick (News Director)

Contact: Denise Korol (Department Head, News Library)
Services: Television broadcaster. Videotape collection available for in-house use only.
Description: Airchecks of news programs broadcast over CITY-TV (Toronto), including local news stories and generic visuals of Toronto. One year's worth of airchecks is held.
Size & Elements: Videotape: format unspecified (1 year of news airchecks, 1,000 stock videotapes, each 60 min.).
Cataloging: Card catalogs.
Access: For in-house use only. Research requests accepted by telephone.
Rights: Additional clearances may be necessary in some cases if material is to be reused.
Licensing: Apply for information.
Restrictions: None specified.
Viewing Facilities: Videotape.
Duplication Facilities: Videotape.

ONTARIO (Toronto)

CTV TELEVISION NETWORK
CTV NEWS ARCHIVES
42 Charles Street East
Toronto, ON M4Y 1T5
(416) 928-6245
Fax: (416) 928-0907
Telex: 06 22734

Street address: 45 Charles Street East, 6th Floor

Peter Jermyn (Supervisor, News Archives)

Contacts: Lisa George; Lin Baier; Phil Williams; Crista Mechlinski; Dorothy Madill (Librarians)
Services: Television broadcaster; news archives. Film and videotape, including some stock footage, available for licensing and reuse, subject to restrictions.
Description: News and documentary programs (1966-present), including Canadian and worldwide coverage. Includes footage from China and the Middle East (from CTV's news bureaus in China and Jerusalem) and Vietnam (1966 through the end of the war). Other material includes Canadian scenics, general news and stock footage, such as war and disaster shots.
Size & Elements: Film: 16mm (amount unspecified; mostly reversal, some negative). Videotape: 2"; 1" (archive copies); Betacam and 3/4" (amount unspecified).
Cataloging: Card catalogs; computerized cataloging for staff use only.
Access: Available for reuse. For in-house use only. Research requests accepted by mail and telephone. Screening fees charged; no search fees charged.
Rights: Full rights held to some material.
Licensing: Available for licensing and reuse, subject to restrictions.
Restrictions: Reuse of news material subject to clearance and approval.
Viewing Facilities: Film (16mm); videotape (3/4").
Duplication Facilities: Film (telecine); videotape (2", 1", 3/4", VHS and Betamax).

ONTARIO (Toronto)

DEC FILM & VIDEO
394 Euclid Avenue
Toronto, Ontario M6G 2S9
(416) 925-9338

Contact: Peter Steven (Co-Director)
Services: Film and videotape distribution collective. Materials available for rental (in Canada only) and in some cases for purchase. Some material available for licensing and reuse.
Description: Founded in 1971 to provide alternative information about the Third World, with emphasis on materials from the Third World itself, news arising from popular struggles and Canadian social issues. Distributes films and videotapes (late 1960s-present) relating to social and political issues, concentrating on the Third World.

Africa. Films on South Africa, Zimbabwe, Mozambique, Tanzania, Guinea-Bissau, Angola and Senegal. Titles include: *Maids and Madams* (1985), on the painful relations between Black maids and White "madams" (employers) in South Africa today; *You Have Struck a Rock* (1981), on women's resistance to the "pass" laws in South Africa; *Grandfather, Your Right Foot Is Missing* (1984), about the destruction of a Cape Town neighborhood carried out as part of the Group Areas Act; *Bound to Strike Back* (1987), explaining the philosophies and strategies of anti-apartheid organizations, including the African National Congress, the United Democratic Front and the Congress of South African Trade Unions; and *Nelson Mandela* (1980). *Roots of Hunger, Roots of Change* (1985) examines the causes of hunger, looking beyond drought as its only cause.

Asia. Films on China, Vietnam, Japan, Papua New Guinea, the Philippines, India and Thailand. Titles include: *Small Happiness: Women of a Chinese Village, All Under Heaven* and *To Taste a Hundred Herbs* (Carma Hinton and Richard Gordon), about women, life, history and medicine in Long Bow village; *First Contact* (1983), on an unexpected 1930s confrontation between White goldseekers and isolated Stone Age people in New Guinea, and a visit to the same valley 50 years later; *Bombay: Our City* (1985), on slum dwellers' battle for survival; and *Ecocide: A Strategy of War* (1983), documenting the ecological effects of the war in Indochina; and a number of films relating to the Vietnam War.

Caribbean. Films from Cuba, Grenada, Haiti, Jamaica and Puerto Rico. Titles include: *Portrait of Teresa* (1979), on the *macho* heritage that persists in revolutionary Cuba; *Grenada: The Future Coming Toward Us* (1983), on Grenada's history and the revolutionary government of the late Maurice Bishop; and *Sweet Sugar Rage* (Sistren Collective, 1986), documenting a drama workshop for Jamaican women workers on a sugar estate.

Central America. Films on the guerrilla war in El Salvador; numerous films and videotapes on the Nicaraguan revolution; *Under the Gun: Democracy in Guatemala* (1988), examining history and current issues; and *Honduras: America's New Policeman* (1983), on internal conditions in Honduras and the role it has been called on to play in area conflicts.

South America. Films and videotapes on Argentina, Chile, Peru, Brazil, Uruguay, Bolivia, Colombia, Ecuador, Guyana and Venezuela. Titles include:

Sweet Country (1986), on Chile since 1970; *Missing Children* (1985), on the efforts of Argentine grandmothers to locate their grandchildren who were victims of the "dirty war" in Argentina; *Chile: I Don't Take Your Name in Vain* (1984), filmed clandestinely by Chileans in Chile, chronicling the emergence of mass opposition to the military dictatorship during 1983; and *In the Sky's Wild Noise* (1983), an extended interview with the late Walter Rodney, covering Guyana's history and the present crisis.

Middle East. Films on Israel, Palestine and South Yemen. Titles include: *Gaza Ghetto* (1985), about three generations of a Palestinian family living in the Jabalia refugee camp; and *On Our Land* (1983), looking at Palestinians living in Israel.

Culture. Titles include: *Black Wax* (1983), about poet and songwriter Gil Scott-Heron; *Mingus* (1966); *Painters Painting* (Emile de Antonio, 1972); *A Crime to Fit the Punishment* (1983), on the making of *Salt of the Earth* and the attempts to prevent its production; and *John Heartfield: Photomonteur* (1976).

Economics. Global Assembly Line (1986), showing the international division of labor and its effects on workers around the world; *Downside Adjustments* (1983), on the social costs of high technology in Windsor, Ont., Canada's automotive capital; *The History Book* (1974), nine animated films about the history of Western civilization from the Middle Ages to the present; and *Five Billion People* (1980), 13 films exploring our economic system.

Native people (North America). Films and videotapes on Native Americans in the United States and Canada. Includes *Lac La Croix* (1988), on the lives, activities and struggles of Ojibway Indians living on a reserve.

Race relations and immigration. Titles include: *Dread Beat An' Blood* (1978), on Black poet Linton Kwesi Johnson; *Blacks Britannica* (1978), an analysis of racism in Britain; *Electric Boogie* (1984), about breakdancing in New York; *Working Side By Side: Labour vs. Racism in the 1950s* (1985), on labor activism against racial intolerance in Canada; *Displaced View* (1988), a personal search for identity by a third-generation Japanese Canadian; and *Under the Table* (1984), looking at Latin American illegal immigrants in Canada.

Gays and lesbians. Titles include: *Silent Pioneers* (1985), about older gays and lesbians; *Orientations* (1985), looking at gay people of Asian backgrounds; *Track Two* (1983), showing Toronto's gay community and its struggles; *Just Because of Who We Are* (1986), examining the neglected issue of violence against lesbians; and *Witches and Faggots — Dykes and Poofters* (1979), on lesbian and gay activism in Australia.

Peace and disarmament. Titles include: *The Journey* (Peter Watkins, 1988, 14-1/2 hours); *Dark Circle* (1983), a contemporary portrait of the nuclear age; *The War At Home* (1980), on the Vietnam antiwar movement in Madison, Wisconsin; and *Stronger Than Before* (1985), looking at women's involvement in the peace movement.

Environment. Films on hazardous waste dumps, occupational health and safety, nuclear power and alternative energy.

Social and historical movements. Titles include: *The Wobblies* (1979), the history of the Industrial Workers of the World; *Poletown Lives!* (1983), about the destruction of a Detroit neighborhood to build a Cadillac plant; *The Ballad of Hard Times* (1983), examining the Great Depression of the 1930s and its repercussions in Quebec and Canada; *Not Crazy Like You Think* (1983), showing a dozen past or present psychiatric patients and how they interpret their own experiences; *The Animals Film* (1983), the first documentary on society's mass exploitation of animals; and *Hurry Tomorrow* (Kevin Rafferty, 1975), a cinema-verité exposé on the forced drugging of mental patients in state institutions; and numerous films by Newsreel (U.S.).

Women's movement. Titles include: *Born in Flames* (Lizzie Borden, 1983); *Carry Greenham Home* (1983), about the women's peace camp at Greenham Common, England; *Waking Up to Rape* (1986); *Breaking Out* (1985), a composite portrait of a women living through the economic and emotional devastation of marriage breakdown; *We Will Not Be Beaten* (1981); *Our Marilyn* (1987), comparing Marilyn Monroe to Marilyn Bell, an Ontario teenager who, in 1954, swam across Lake Ontario in the middle of the night, and probing the cultural differences and prevailing attitudes represented by these two cultural icons named Marilyn; *Our Choice: A Tape About Teenage Mothers* (1984); *The Struggle for Choice* (1987), a five-part videotape series that chronicles the movement and strategies of abortion rights groups in Canada since 1969; and *The Clean Sweep* (1978), examining *macho* sexual stereotypes in Quebec.

Women and work. Titles include: *Quel Numéro/What Number? The Electronic Sweatshop* (1985), showing the other side of the "computer revolution," as told by the women who do not control the new machines — secretaries, telephone operators, cashiers and postal workers; *A Wives' Tale* (1980), on the role of a women's support committee in a strike against INCO in Sudbury, Ont.; *With Babies and Banners* (1978), on the Women's Emergency Brigade and its actions during the 1936-37 sitdown strike at General Motors;

Proud Women, Strong Steps (1988), showing stresses faced by immigrant women and women of color in Canada; and *The Life and Times of Rosie the Riveter* (1980), looking at women workers during World War II.

Labor issues. Titles include: *To Pick Is Not To Choose* (1985), about farmworkers in Ontario; *Myth of the Careless Worker* (1984), an Australian videotape dispelling the myth that industrial accidents are simply caused by careless workers; and *Up From the Bargain Basement* (1979), on today's unorganized service sector workforce.

Films of Emile de Antonio. Titles include: *In the Year of the Pig* (1969), looking at the history of Vietnam; *Millhouse: A White Comedy* (1971), on Richard Nixon; *Underground* (1976), about the history and program of the Weather Underground Organization; *Rush to Judgment: The Assassination of John F. Kennedy* (1967), an indictment of the Warren Commission's findings, produced with Mark Lane; *Painters Painting* (1972); and *America Is Hard to See* (1970), an account of Eugene McCarthy's 1968 bid for the Democratic presidential nomination.

Size & Elements: Film: 16mm. Videotape: 1" (masters); 3/4" (masters and viewing copies); VHS (viewing copies). (Approx. 350 titles total).

Cataloging: Published catalogs.

Access: Open to the public. Available for rental in Canada (not in the United States); broadcast and purchase (in many cases). Footage available for licensing and reuse in some cases, depending upon specific rights situation. Research fees charged in some cases. Research requests accepted by mail, telephone and in person (walk-in and by appointment).

Rights: Full rights held to some material. Distribution rights held to all material. Additional clearances may be necessary in some cases if material is to be reused and may be obtained through DEC.

Licensing: Available for licensing and reuse in some cases. License fees charged.

Restrictions: None specified.

Viewing Facilities: Film (16mm projector); videotape (3/4" and VHS).

Duplication Facilities: None.

ONTARIO (Toronto)

FABULOUS FOOTAGE INC.
12 Mercer Street
Toronto, ON M5V 1H3
(416) 591-6955
Fax: (416) 591-1666

Dan Garson (President)

Contacts: Patricia Harvey Leitch; Robert MacLeod

Services: Film and videotape stock footage sales library; custom shooting services available.

Description: Film and videotape covering animation, sports, Olympics (1904-88), industrials, leisure, wildlife (nature films of animals indigenous to Canada), time-lapse cinematography, aerials, archival/historical (Ontario scenes, 1920s-40s), newsreels, agriculture, scenics (contemporary views of Canadian cities and points of interest), establishing shots of cities, landscapes, landmarks, foreign locations, manufacturing, energy and electricity, marine life, defense, nature, business, culture, transportation, natural phenomena, technology, space, World War I and World War II, features, science, entertainment and monsters.

Also holds unique collections of IMAX format footage, home movies, classic features and their outtakes.

Size & Elements: Film: IMAX (amount unspecified); 35mm (amount unspecified; original negative and positive elements). Videotape: 1" and other formats (1,800 hours; masters and time-coded screening videotapes; many film-to-videotape transfers).

Cataloging: Computerized cataloging for staff use only (in progress).

Access: Open to researchers. Research requests accepted by mail and telephone. Videotapes or workprints of requested material can be made or a screening can be set up by appointment. A brochure outlining services and charges is available upon request.

Rights: Full rights held to all material.

Licensing: Available for licensing. License fees charged (rates depend on usage and source).

Restrictions: None specified.

Viewing Facilities: Film (35mm and 16mm flatbeds); videotape (3/4", VHS and Betamax).

Duplication Facilities: Film (reference quality film-to-videotape transfers); videotape (3/4", VHS and Betamax).

ONTARIO (Toronto)

GOETHE INSTITUTE TORONTO
LIBRARY
1067 Yonge Street
Toronto, ON M4W 2L2
(416) 924-3327
Fax: (416) 924-0589

Dr. R. Lübbren (Director)

Contact: Ulla Habekost (Librarian)
Services: Educational institution; library. Film and videotape collection maintained primarily for educational and research purposes. Available to the public for in-house viewing and free loan.
Description: Feature and documentary films (in German and English) related to German language, life and culture, past and present.
Size & Elements: Film: 16mm (202 titles). Videotape: 3/4" and VHS (169 videotapes; NTSC and PAL, viewing copies).
Cataloging: Printed lists.
Access: Open to the public. For in-house viewing only. Available for free loan. Research fees not charged. Research requests accepted by mail, telephone and in person (walk-in).
Rights: No rights held to any material (Institute can refer inquirers to original source).
Licensing: Apply for information.
Restrictions: Copyright restrictions apply. Loaned only for non-commercial use.
Viewing Facilities: Film and videotape.
Duplication Facilities: None.

ONTARIO (Toronto)

THE IMAGE BANK, TORONTO
550 Queen Street East, Suite 300
Toronto, ON M5A 1V2
(416) 362-6931
Fax: (416) 362-4144

Contact: Julie Kovacs
Territory: Canada.
Services: Exclusive marketing agent for Film Search, Inc. (q.v.).

ONTARIO (Toronto)

IMPERIAL OIL LIMITED
111 St. Clair Avenue West
Toronto, ON M5W 1K3
(416) 968-4920

Contact: Linda Scott (Coordinator, Audio-Visual Resource Centre)
Services: Corporate archives. Completed film and videotape productions available for distribution and rental; stock footage possibly available for reuse.
Description: Holds material relating to the oil industry, including generic footage of oil refining, marketing (e.g., service stations), tankers, distribution terminals, employees, office technology and data centers.
    Archival film footage includes television advertising (1950s) and historic topics such as early exploration. Energy-related films, available for rental and purchase, include: *Refinery; The Frontier Below;* and *Issungnak: Oil Beneath the Beaufort Sea.* Canadiana include contemporary and historic films, including *Underground East,* a documentary record of the building of the world's longest oil pipeline halfway across Canada in 150 days; *A Mile Below the Wheat,* the dramatic story of the discovery of oil at Leduc, Alberta in 1947; and *The Loon's Necklace* (1948), the Indian legend of how the loon acquired the white stripes around its neck.
    Imperial Oil also commissioned *The Newcomers,* a series of television movies marking the company's centennial (1980). Series dramatizes the histories of Canada's various peoples, and is available on 16mm film, 3/4" and 1/2" videotape.
Size & Elements: Film: 16mm (approx. 25 films). Videotape: Betacam (100 videotapes).
Cataloging: Brochures; computerized cataloging for staff use only.
Access: Available to the public for rental and purchase. Requests accepted by mail and telephone.
Rights: Full rights held to all material.

Licensing: Possibly available for licensing and reuse. Videotapes stored at a post-production facility that can provide footage to client's specifications. License fees generally not charged. Duplication costs apply.
Restrictions: None specified.
Viewing Facilities: None.
Duplication Facilities: None (outside arrangements can be made).
Distributor: Films available for rental and purchase from L. M. Media Marketing Services, Ltd., 115 Torbay Road, Unit 9, Markham, Ontario L3R 2M9, (416) 475-3750; 9575 Cote de Liesse, Dorval, Quebec, H9P 1A3, (514) 631-9010; and 2168 Willingdon Ave., Burnaby, B.C. V5C 5Z9, (604) 294-6231.

ONTARIO (Toronto)

IMS CREATIVE COMMUNICATIONS
Medical Sciences Building
University of Toronto
1 King's College Circle
Toronto, ON M5S 1A8
(416) 978-6302
Fax: (416) 978-7552

Liivi Kask-Ruona (Director)

Contact: Bridget Hough (Television Producer)
Services: Educational institution. Produces and distributes videotape and some film materials; available for licensing and reuse, subject to restrictions.
Description: Medical education. Primary areas include: surgery, anatomy, physiology, embryology, pediatrics and oncology (no microscopic or endoscopic footage). Topics include: anesthesia, anatomy, biosafety, dermatology, health administration, hematology, immunology, medicine, neurology, nursing, nutrition, obstetrics and gynecology, occupational medicine, orthopedics, otolaryngology, paramedical, patient education, pediatrics, pharmacology, physiology, psychiatry, radiology, rehabilitation medicine, speech pathology, surgery and urology.
    Sample titles include: *Blood Cell Formation; Dissections of the Brain (The Cerebral Hemisphere: Fibre Bundles of the White Matter; The Lateral Ventricle, Hippocampus, Fornix, Corpus Striatium and Internal Capsule; etc.); The Placenta and Foetal Membranes; Surface Anatomy of the Head, Neck and Face; Acne; Immunoelectrophoresis; Delirium; Huntington's Chorea; Living with a Colostomy; Urodynamic Investigation of Lower Urinary Tract Problems in Women; The Assessment of a Child With Cerebral Palsy; Ultrasound; The Knee; The Hip; The Spine; Occupational Therapy: Treatments; Going Home After Your Bypass; Animal Models for Analgesia Research; Physiology of Vision; Normal Microcirculation of the Mammalian Liver; Transsexualism;* and *Radiology of the Gastrointestinal Tract.*
Size & Elements: Film: 16mm (amount unspecified). Videotape: 1" (viewing copies); Betacam (8 hours; masters; also viewing copies); 3/4" (4 hours; masters and viewing copies); VHS and Betamax (viewing copies).
Cataloging: Published catalogs; production files; shot lists.
Access: Open to the public. Available for rental and purchase. For rental and purchase in Canada, contact representative; outside Canada, contact IMS. For other film or stock footage inquiries contact IMS. Research fees charged. Research requests accepted by mail, telephone and in person (by appointment only).
Rights: Full rights held to some material. Some rights held to some material. Additional clearances (from patients whose faces are visible) may be necessary if material is to be reused.
Licensing: Available for licensing, subject to restrictions. License fees charged.
Restrictions: Restrictions may apply, depending on the program and confidentiality.
Viewing Facilities: Videotape (3/4" and 1/2").
Duplication Facilities: Videotape (1", 3/4" and 1/2").
Representatives: For sale: In Canada, contact: City Films Distribution, Ltd., 542 Gordon Baker Road, Willowdale, ON M2H 3B4; (416) 499-1400. Outside Canada, contact: Stella Hawke at IMS Creative Communications. Some materials distributed outside Canada by The Altschul Group (q.v.).

ONTARIO (Toronto)

MOLSTAR COMMUNICATIONS
250 Bloor Street East, Suite 805
Toronto, ON M4W 3P6
(416) 922-2443

Donald R. Thompson (Senior Vice President/General Manager)

Contact: Frank Selke
Services: Corporation; corporate archives; stock footage sales library. Material available for licensing and reuse, subject to restrictions.
Description: Holds collection of hockey films (late 1890s-present) from the National Hockey League and other sources; and television kinescopes (most transferred to 1" or 3/4" videotape).
Size & Elements: Film: 16mm (1.5 million feet). Videotape: 1" and 3/4" (amount unspecified).
Cataloging: None specified.
Access: Not open to the public. Research fees charged. Research requests accepted by mail and telephone.
Rights: Full rights held to all material.
Licensing: Available for licensing and reuse, subject to restrictions. License and usage fees charged.
Restrictions: Requests for licensing and reuse considered on a case-by-case basis; subject to acceptance and approval.
Viewing Facilities: None.
Duplication Facilities: Videotape.

ONTARIO (Toronto)

TRINITY SQUARE VIDEO
172 John Street, 4th Floor
Toronto, ON M5T 1X5
(416) 593-1332

Gwen MacGreggor (Administrative Director)

Contact: Pat Jeffries (Publicist)
Services: Media organization; videotape production and post-production facility. Videotape collection open to the public for viewing.
Description: Production and post-production facility open to any nonprofit producer. Videotape collection covers a broad range of genres and subject matter (1978-present). Collection comprises donated videotapes containing historical material on the organization itself, documentation of civil action groups (e.g., race relations groups and a women's union), art videotapes and other work done at TSV. Since 1981, approximately ten artists' videotapes per year have been purchased for the collection.
Size & Elements: Videotape: 3/4", VHS and Betamax (263 titles; masters and viewing copies).
Cataloging: Card catalogs; computerized cataloging available to researchers and scholars.
Access: Videotape collection open to the public for viewing. Fees charged for use of collection. Research requests not accepted.
Rights: Full rights held to some material. Some rights held to all material. Rights to most material retained by artists or producers. Additional clearances will be necessary if material is to be reused.
Licensing: Apply for information. License fees charged in some cases.
Restrictions: Requests for reuse must be negotiated with individual producers.
Viewing Facilities: Videotape (3/4", VHS and Betamax).
Duplication Facilities: Videotape (3/4", VHS and Betamax).

ONTARIO (Toronto)

TV ONTARIO
Box 200, Station Q
Toronto, ON M4T 2T1
(416) 484-2600
Fax: (416) 484-2725
Telex: 06-23547

Street address: 2180 Yonge Street

Contacts: Jessie Bédard (Film and Stock Shot Researcher); Geoffrey Hopkinson (Coordinator, Film & Stock Shot Research)
Services: Educational institution; film and videotape producer; television broadcaster; stock footage sales library.
Description: Producer and vendor of educational television programs, producing and coproducing an average of 450 hours of news programs annually. Programs cover business and industry, the arts, sciences, public affairs, social issues, drama, dance, music, sports, history, geography, technology and many other subjects. Stock footage (1980-present) covers numerous subjects, including:

Activities (summer). Windsurfing, swimming, sailing, canoeing, camping, white-water rafting, scuba diving, sculling, surfing, kayaking, boating and fishing.

Activities (winter). Carnivals, skiing, skating, snowmobiling, clowns, bed racing, Ice Capade-type show, horse and sleigh rides, children sliding, dog sled rides, sleigh hockey, campfire and roast.

Africa. Includes: Ghana; Togo; Dahomey; Niger; Nigeria; traditions of the Maghreb (Bedouins); Algeria; Morocco; Tunisia; the Sahara Desert; the Mourides (Black Muslims); Dakar, Senegal; veiled Arab women; mosques; schools; markets; a tin mine; street vendors; people in traditional costume; playing drums; ritual dances; playing music in the streets; snake charmers; making clay pots; mud houses, some with painted designs; dye vats and fabric dyeing; archaeological digs; textile factory; and irrigation.

Agriculture. Subjects include: farms; barns; silos; grain elevators; domestic animals; dairies and milk processing; harvesting; crops, including wheat, strawberries, raspberries, grapes (vineyard), tomatoes, carrots, asparagus, cucumbers, red and green peppers, cabbage, corn, potatoes, cantaloupe, pumpkin and herbs; maple syrup running; and gardening.

Aircraft. Includes: various airplanes, jets (with vapor trails), helicopters and water bombers.

Airports. Includes: Lester B. Pearson Airport (Toronto); immigration and customs; Dorval (Montreal); Buffalo airport; runways; wind socks; various airplanes and jets; aircraft interiors; control tower and workers; security controllers and radars; unloading luggage from airplane and interior of luggage conveyors; passengers bring greeted; and aircraft hangar.

Animals. Domestic animals include: cows, pigs, chickens, sheep, horses, rabbits and cattle (branding). Pets include: dogs, cats and birds. Birds include goldfinches, macaws, doves, sea gulls, pigeons, pelicans, budgies, cockatoos, pink flamingos, peacocks, owls, snowy white owls, mallard ducks, swans, cranes, sandpipers, great blue herons, hawks, Canadian geese and baby cedar waxwings in nest. Other animals include skunks, raccoons, turtles, frogs, buffalo, yaks, goats, boa constrictors, camels, iguanas, sea lions, deer, orangutans, leopards, tigers, polar bears, seals, reindeer and musk oxen.

Architecture. Victorian and modern buildings.

Arctic. Yukon and Northwest Territories; Tuktoyaktuk; Dawson City; Inuvik; Whitehorse; Yellowknife; Fort Simpson; Baffin Island; Beaufort Sea; Mackenzie River and area; oil exploration; dog sled racing; casino; arts and crafts; drum dance; Inuit skinning caribou; furs drying; Arctic cotton; vegetation; train and tourists; steamboat; icebergs; glacier; Native people in traditional costumes; hunting and fishing; mountains; Ski-Doos; surveyors; and scenics.

Arts and crafts. Wood carving; ice sculptures; batik; dollmaking; clay and pottery (Native Indian and African); quilt making; quill work (Native Indian); soapstone carving; ink print; Inuit tapestry; weaving; stalls with various displays, including jewelry and pottery.

Auctions. Cattle, auctioneers, grain and the Ontario Food Terminal.

Awards. Includes athletic awards, and college and university graduations.

Banking. People using "Instant Teller" machines; closeups of money machines.

Beaches. Shot in Toronto, California and Daytona (Florida). Includes sunbathers, children playing in sand, windsurfing, surfing, swimming, fishing, jogging, walking along the boardwalk, sunsets, cliffs and waves.

Bee farm. Bees, beekeeper and honey.

Boats and ships. Includes tankers, tugboats, barges, oil freighters, icebreaker, yacht, houseboat, ferry, paddle boat, drill ships, fishing boats, canoes, speedboats, sailboats and hovercraft.

California. Beaches; sea coast; surfing; sunbathing; Scripps Institute of Oceanography.

Careers for youth. Includes engineering, drafting, electrician, various technicians, tool and die, cook, waiter, baker, machinist, welder and fitter, cabinetmaker, computer programmer, sheet metal worker, heavy equipment operator, appliance repair, industrial woodwork, hotel management, nutritionist/dietitian, X-ray technician, fashion designer, critical care attendant, paramedics, ship master; fish and wildlife technician.

Charlottetown, P.E.I. Harbor and street scenes.

Children. In school, at day care, on the playground, and various summer and winter activities.

Christmas. Window displays, decorated trees, toyland and children, decorations being made and on display, shoppers, Santa Claus and children, creches and poinsettias.

Churches and cathedrals. Interiors and exteriors; architecture; Masses being celebrated; and weddings.

Circus. Includes clowns, acrobats, jugglers and spectators.

Communications. Footage of satellite dishes.

Competitions. Includes Special Olympics; Masters' Games, featuring swimming, hockey, weightlifting, marathon, orienteering, fencing, tennis, squash, running, basketball, 500-meter geriatric race, registration, scorekeeping, and various track and field; Winter Carnival, including speed skating, snowmobile race, snowshoe race, and bed racing; and seniors' ballroom dancing.

Computers. Includes the manufacturing of Apple Macintosh computers; CAD/CAM; various in-office settings; at home and in school; video games and arcades; mainframes; and microchips.

Construction. Includes highrises and skyscrapers, houses and energy-efficient houses and log cabins.

Crowds. At outdoor concerts, rally, parades, festivals, sports events, streeters, subway, ceremonies and circus.

Customs. Airports; Canada/U.S. border.

Dance. Includes amateur dance (ballet and jazz); seniors' ballroom dancing; and traditional dance, featuring Irish, Scottish, Filipino, Ukrainian, Korean, Indian powwow and Inuit drum dance.

Drugstores. Various cold and allergy remedies; prescription counters.

Eclipses. An annular eclipse of the sun shot at Greensboro, N.C.

Energy. Oil and gas exploration; rigs, drill ships and oil pumps; coal mining; tar sands; nuclear power plants; radio dispatch center; reactors and fusion power; solar energy, including heliostats, collectors and windmills; hydroelectric power, including generators, pylons, hydro towers and dams; and various heavy equipment.

Eyeglasses. Production and preparation.

Fashion. Designing, cutting patterns and fabric, sewing and a fashion show (1800s-style).

Festivals (outdoor). Franco-Ontarian Festival (Ottawa); Northwind Folk Festival (Toronto Island); Indigenous Festival (Laplanders, East Indians, Aborigines, South American Indians, Canadian and American Indians); Festival of Thanksgiving — Indian Pow Wow; Winter Carnival; fireworks display with balloons in the sky, people eating and listening to music, stalls with crafts displayed and children with painted faces; and Kiwanis Music Festival.

Fish. Species include: walleye, pike, trout, bass, salmon, perch, crappies, minnows, goldfish, tropical fish and eels.

Fishing. Sportsmen, women and children; fishing equipment.

Fitness and sports. Children in schools; seniors exercising; fitness club; tai chi chuan; swimming; hockey; jogging; badminton; cycling; basketball; tennis.

Florida. Daytona Beach; Walt Disney World.

Flowers and plants. Wildflowers; water lilies; lily pads; bulrushes; roses; dandelions; daisies; greenhouses; gardens; and tropical.

Food. Displays in pastry and delicatessen sections of food markets; fast-food outlets; supermarkets; St. Lawrence Market; Ontario Food Terminal; restaurant; cafeteria; lunch truck.

Forest fire. Helicopter and heliotorch; water bomber; Fire Control Training Centre; water pump and hose; and firefighters.

Forests. Aerials; pines; poplars; birches, aspens; boreal forest floor; seedlings and saplings; moss and lichen; scarred area; cutting down trees with axe and chainsaw; and heavy equipment.

Games. Youth playing Trivial Pursuit; seniors playing bingo; checkers; ping-pong; pool; cards; video games; pinball.

Handicapped people. Work environment; footage of Special Olympics.

Homes. Cities; suburbs; small towns; country; apartment buildings; townhouses; moving into houses; Florida beach house.

Industries, factories and manufacturing plants. Water filtration plant; prefabricated houses; automobile plants in Canada, including General Motors, Chrysler and Ford; the Nissan plant in Japan; General Electric (Erie, Pa.); paper mill; lumber and timber mill; plastic milk jug factory; textile and garment factory; phonograph record manufacturing (masters and album covers); milk processing; doughnut factory; tomato canning; fish packing; Stelco (Hamilton, Ont.).; garbage recycling plant; various heavy equipment; nuclear plant; Apple Macintosh assembly; making cheese; and flour mill.

Insects. Red ants; fly; spiderweb; ladybug; bees; black butterfly; cockroaches.

Japan. Niigata harbor; Akihabara market; Keggon Falls; Shinatitoku Maru (ship); Japanese music; spa; and rice fields.

Lobsters. Traps; packing in crates.

London, England. Big Ben; Parliament Buildings; Buckingham Palace; monuments and statues; Trafalgar Square; the Changing of the Guard; Covent Garden; British Museum; Albert Hall; East Anglia University; pubs (exteriors); outdoor cafes; crowds of pedestrians; traffic; double-decker buses; bobbies; horse guards in Hyde Park; Tower of London; Canada House; St. Paul's Cathedral; Stock Exchange (exterior); and National Gallery.

Magazines. Closeups of covers and articles; pornographic magazine covers.

Malls. Eaton Centre (Toronto); Woodbine Centre (kids' rides); Promenade.

Medical/hospital. Operating room, equipment and operation; testing flu virus; forensic laboratory; autopsy room; 911 emergency ambulance dispatch center; critical care attendants and paramedics; dissecting brain; medical equipment; nursery and babies.

Mexico. Mayan ruins and pyramids.

Middle East. Arabs; Jews; Christians; Turks; Judaism; Christianity; Islam; culture; architecture; desert region; Jerusalem; the ancient city of Petra; kibbutzim; bar mitzvahs; Istanbul; the Bosphorus; Turkey; the festival of the Kurban Bayram; a Muslim family.

Military academy. Kingston, Ontario, including cadets (male and female); exercising, fencing and hockey; obstacle course; firing range; practicing war maneuvers; helicopter; mess hall; and drills.

Mining. Coal; gold; tin; nickel; lead and zinc; explosions (rock blasting); heavy equipment; slag pouring.

Mountains. Himalayas; Rockies; Arctic; Boulder, Colo.

New York City. Central Park; Columbus Circle; Empire State Building; The Dakota (apartment house); busy streets; pedestrians.

Newspapers. Production of Toronto Star and small town papers; office interiors.

Observatories. Dunlop Observatory (Toronto); planetarium projectors; telescope.

Ottawa. Parliament buildings; street scenes; outdoor festival; aerials of the city and Rideau Canal in winter; Byward Market.

Pakistan. Village and family life.

Parades. Mounties (Toronto); Masters' Games (athletes) (Toronto); Halloween (New York City); Disney (Florida); Legion (Picton).

Paris, France. Right and Left Banks; L'Arc de Triomphe; Paris National Bank; Les Halles; Chartres; gendarme; pedestrians; traffic; fountains; statues; and cafes.

Petroglyphs. Peterborough, Ontario Indian burial ground.

Police. Cruiser; directing traffic; water patrol; digital radar system; writing out tickets; checking road at accident site; breathalyzer machine demonstration; jail cell door sliding open and closed; mug shots being taken; Canadian Mounties; London bobbies; Paris gendarmes.

Pollution. Water pollution tests; filtration plants; sewage; landfill; industries polluting air; billowing black smoke.

Rabies. Veterinarian inoculating pets, raccoons and skunks; swabbing ducks; preparing bait in lab.

Radio stations and recording studios. Engineers and equipment.

San Francisco. Golden Gate Bridge; skyline; Telegraph Hill; Russian Hill; Chinatown; Silicon Valley; cable cars.

Scenics. Various scenes shot in all Canadian provinces; sunrises and sunsets.

Schools and youth. University of Toronto; Queen's University (Kingston); McMaster University; initiation day; graduation; international students; punks; high-school students doing experiments in laboratory and outdoors, at computers and in classrooms; performing art school, with scenes of music, art, dance and theater; training for National Ballet of Canada; Alfred College (agricultural).

Scotland. Pipe bands and Falkland castle.

Signs. Street signs; restaurant, pubs, shops and fast food; help wanted; real estate; automobile dealers; banks; Visa, MasterCard and American Express; No Smoking; No Drinking; Prevent Forest Fires; no swimming; no dogs allowed except on leash; various billboards.

Stores and shops. Includes toys, pets, jewelry, beauty salon, records, clocks, videos, books, clothing, telephones, television and radio, supermarket, drug, hardware, bakery and health food.

Stress. Tranquillity tank; biofeedback.

Thailand. Village, family and school life.

Theater. Amateur plays; audience; people in lobby; ticket counter; seniors acting.

Toronto. Skyline; Ontario Place; Canadian National Exhibition; Children's Village; harbor and waterfront; City Hall; The Peace Garden; Queen's Park; Canada's Wonderland (rides); Chinatown; St. Lawrence Market; Ontario Food Terminal; CN Tower; Canadian flag; Tour of the Universe (ride simulator); Allen Gardens; Don Valley Parkway/Gardner Expressway and traffic; Cineplex; subway and crowds; street scenes; shops and fast-food outlets; shopping malls; beach; streetcars; Mounted Police; firemen and trucks; Toronto Island and ferry boat; Toronto Stock Exchange; Ontario Lottery Prize office; Art Gallery of Ontario; Ontario Science Centre.

Trains. Freight, passenger and steam.

Trucks. Trucks; transport company; truck at customs inspection station; flatbed truck moving house; weigh stations.

Vancouver, B.C. Skyline; World Trade Pavilion; Expo '87; Rockies.

Washington, D.C. Jefferson Memorial; Washington Monument; White House; Capitol Hill; Union Station.

Water. Lakes; streams; waterfalls; aerial and ground shots of Niagara Falls; oceans; swamps; marsh; ponds.

Weather station. Tower; weathervane; interiors.

Wedding. Church ceremony; reception.

Winter. Icicles; ice sculptures; icebergs; glaciers; snow; snowmaking.

Size & Elements: Film: format and amount unspecified. Videotape: 1", Betacam, 3/4", VHS and Betamax (amount unspecified). Library is constantly being updated in both film and videotape.

Cataloging: Card catalogs; published catalog.

Access: Open to the public. For in-house use. Available for duplication, licensing and reuse. Research fees charged. Research requests accepted by mail and telephone.

Rights: Full rights held to some material. Some rights held to some material. No rights held to some programs. Additional clearances (e.g., for talent and music) may be necessary in some cases if material is to be reused.

Licensing: Available for licensing and reuse. License and usage fees charged (rate sheet available).

Restrictions: Rights to some completed programs are not held by TV Ontario.

Viewing Facilities: Film (16mm Steenbecks); videotape (3/4", VHS and Betamax).

Duplication Facilities: Film (outside laboratories used); videotape (telecine).

ONTARIO (Toronto)

UNIVERSITY OF TORONTO
AUDIOVISUAL LIBRARY
9 King's College Circle
Toronto, ON M5S 1A5
(416) 978-6520 (Audio Visual Library Information Area)
(416) 978-6049 (Media Centre — Distribution)

Liz Avison (Audiovisual Librarian)
Michael Edmunds (Director, Media Centre)

Contacts: Audio Visual Library Information Area; Media Centre — Distribution

Services: University audiovisual library. Film and videotape material available for in-house research. Film and videotape producer (Media Centre); material available for reuse and broadcast. Only Media Centre-produced titles are available for duplication.

Description: The Media Centre produces programming (primarily on videotape) for the University and for distribution, including major series in medieval studies, labor relations and Canadian history.

Medieval studies. Programs include: *Vulcan's Net: Passion and Punishment,* the story of Paolo and Francesca, Dante's condemned lovers and its archetype, the adultery of Venus and Mars; *The Toronto Passion Play,* based on the two-part passion play segment from the medieval manuscript called the *Ludus Coventriae; The Medieval Universe: The Planets,* using passages from Chaucer, illustrations and paintings of the period to outline the medieval conceptions of the seven heavenly bodies which were counted as planets; *Le Roman de la Rose,* retelling the 13th-century French poem using 15th-century illustrations; *The Wonders of the East,* exploring the Anglo-Saxon conception of world geography (ca. 1000 A.D.); and *The York Cycle Pageant,* last performed in its entirety in 1569, tracing Biblical history from Creation to the Last Judgment.

The Bible and literature. Consists of a 30-part series of lectures and seminars by Professor Northrop Frye, illuminating such topics as: *Images of Paradise: Trees and Water; The Great Whore and the Forgiven Harlot; Leviathan, Dragons and the Anti-Christ; Genesis: The Creation of the Sexes; Revelation: Removing the Veil;* and *Revelation: After the Ego Disappears.*

Canadian history. Includes: *The Splendid Dream: Canadian Labour and the Left 1867-1976* (4 parts), using archival footage, examining the generations of labor reformers and radicals who built Canada's trade union movement; *Bread and Roses: The Struggle of Canadian Working Women,* using rare photographs and footage to present the experience of working women and trace the changing focus of the women's movement in seeking workplace reforms; *Truant Officer,* dramatizing the trials and tribulations of John Wilkinson, Toronto's first truant officer in 1872; and *The Last Buffalo Hunter,* examining the life of Norbert Welsh, a Metis living in the Canadian prairies, beginning with his 18th birthday in 1863.

Science. Programs include: *The Art of Sewage Treatment,* examining this aspect of urban infrastructure, over 2,000 years old; *The Bread We Live By,* presenting the history of breadmaking, including a time-lapse sequence

showing the development of a fungal colony over a five-day period; *The Moulds We Live With,* looking at the influence of this four hundred million-year-old life form on our daily lives; and *Sorting Out Sorting,* using computer animation to demonstrate nine computer sorting techniques.

History. Titles include: *The Country Curate,* a program based on the diaries of the Reverend Francis Kilverts, with colorful vignettes of the Victorian village world in which he lived; *Voices From The Ranks,* based on the memoirs of several common soldiers, recreates the adventures and hardships of life in Queen Victoria's military service; *The Railwaymen,* with period photographs highlighting the personal stories of an engineer, a navvy, an signal master and others, as the social consequences of Victorian technology are explored.

Industrial relations. Developed at the Centre for Industrial Relations at the University. Programs include: *The Grievance Arbitration Process, The Collective Bargaining Process* and *Anatomy of a Strike.*

The Media Centre Collection. Includes a wide range of materials. Sample titles: *On Campus with Marshall McLuhan; Harold Innis: The Philosophical Historian; Meeting Freire; Learning Through Play; The Well-Being of the Elderly; The ABC's of Canadian Family Life; Performer, Researcher, Organizer: Teaching Roles in Higher Education; The Conduct of a Civil Action; Crown Wardship Order; The Oboe; Lady Soul and the Devil's Burning Throne: The Golden Age of Melodrama; Les Visages de la littérature Canadienne-Française; The Discovery Series,* exploring a variety of research projects from literature to nutritional science; *In The Name Of The Cities,* a six-program series emphasizing ecological concerns in some of the most important cities in northern Italy.

The Audio Visual Library holds viewing copies of the above materials for in-house use; a curriculum support collection for the humanities, social, physical and applied sciences; and productions of the Faculty of Medicine's Instructional Media Services (IMS Creative Communications [q.v.]).

Size & Elements: Film: 16mm and Super 8mm. Videotape: 3/4" and VHS. (Over 200 Media Centre programs and approx. 3,000 titles in the Audio Visual Library).

Cataloging: Published catalogs; filmographies; computerized cataloging for staff use only.

Access: Audio Visual Library open to the public. For in-house use only. Media Centre materials available for rental, reuse or broadcast. Research fees not charged. Research requests accepted in person (by appointment only).

Rights: Some rights held to some material (Media Centre productions). Except for University productions, all Audio Visual Library materials are from commercial sources. Additional clearances may be necessary in some cases if material is to be reused.

Licensing: Media Centre material possibly available for licensing, subject to restrictions. License fees charged.

Restrictions: All requests for research and reuse subject to acceptance and approval.

Viewing Facilities: Film (4 screening rooms available for group viewing); videotape (pending availability of viewing carrels; no reservations).

Duplication Facilities: Videotape (3/4", VHS and Betamax). Only Media Centre titles may be duplicated.

ONTARIO (Toronto)

UNIVERSITY OF TORONTO
UNIVERSITY ARCHIVES
Fisher Library
120 St. George Street
Toronto, ON M5S 1A5
(416) 978-2277

Kent Haworth (Archivist)

Contact: Harold A. Averill (Assistant University Archivist)

Services: University archives. Film and videotape collection available to researchers, scholars and the public for in-house research only.

Description: Material pertaining to the history and activities of the University. Includes: approximately 70 to 80 football films (1950s-60s); approximately 50 promotional films about the University filmed by Sir Arthur Chetwynd, a football coach at the University (1950s-60s) who later became a filmmaker in Hollywood and England; documentation of various historical events, including the visit of King George and Queen Elizabeth to the University (1939); the awarding of an honorary degree to Dwight D. Eisenhower (1946); and various technical and research materials (e.g., films on mining and forestry).

Also holds a few campus-produced videotapes, primarily documentation of formal events.

Size & Elements: Film: 16mm (130 reels). Videotape: VHS (viewing copies, transfers from film).
Cataloging: None.
Access: Available to researchers, scholars and the public. For in-house research only. There are necessary limitations on viewing because the film is uncataloged and in fragile condition. Research requests accepted by mail and telephone.
Rights: Full rights held to all material.
Licensing: Requests for licensing and reuse considered on a case-by-case basis.
Restrictions: All research requests subject to acceptance and approval.
Viewing Facilities: Film (16mm; due to fragile condition, film can only be viewed on hand-cranked equipment; videotape (VHS).
Duplication Facilities: Videotape (VHS; facilities located elsewhere on campus).

ONTARIO (Toronto)

V/TAPE
183 Bathurst Street, 1st Floor
Toronto, ON M5T 2R7
(416) 863-9897

Brendan Cotter; Lisa Steele; Kim Tomczak (Co-ordinators)

Contacts: Brendan Cotter; Kim Tomczak
Services: Media organization; videotape archives; distributor. Videotapes available to the public for rental, purchase and reuse.
Description: Lists, catalogs, archives and distributes videotapes by artists and independent producers from around the world. The videotape collection and archives contains video art, educational productions and documentaries, a portion of which is available for distribution. Approximately 80% of collection originated in Canada; also holds work from the U.S., England, Japan, Italy and other countries. The collection contains work from the earliest period of Canadian independent video production (1970-71) to the present, with the majority of works from 1983-88.

V/tape is a non-curatorial service and is also non-exclusive. As such, they do not express a curatorial opinion as to the quality of individual works, but rather provide substantial information so that curators, educators and video programmers can make informed decisions as to the videotapes selected. Consultant services for video programmers are also offered.

Subject areas include: art and culture; business and industry; children; communities; documentaries; economics and finance; education; environment and energy; experimental video; fiction; gays; health; history; interpersonal relationships; labor unions; lesbians; the media; men; minorities; music; politics and government; philosophy and religion; rural issues; sexuality; social change; sports and recreation; urban issues; women; and work.
Size & Elements: Videotape: 3/4", Video 8, VHS and Betamax (620 titles).
Cataloging: Published catalogs; computerized cataloging available to researchers. Each videotape listing in database includes a full description of the videotape, technical information and distribution availability. Data can be cross-referenced by artist's name, title, subject heading, date, length, location and other information.
Access: Open to the public. Available for rental, purchase and reuse. Research fees charged. Research requests accepted by mail, telephone and in person (walk-in).
Rights: Full rights held to some material; some rights held to all material. Rights to most material retained by artists or original producers.
Licensing: Available for licensing and reuse. License fees charged.
Restrictions: None specified.
Viewing Facilities: Videotape (3/4" [NTSC, PAL and SECAM], Video 8, VHS and Betamax; by appointment).
Duplication Facilities: None.
Related Materials: Artist/producer files, containing reviews, press releases, photographs, videographies and resumes; and print archives, with international distribution catalogs, national and international exhibition catalogs and publications relating to video.
Publications: *Catalogue of Catalogues* (two volumes), containing a comprehensive list of independently produced videotapes available from various Canadian distributors.

ONTARIO (Waterloo)

THE SEAGRAM MUSEUM
57 Erb Street West

Waterloo, ON N2L 6C2
(519) 885-1857
Fax: (519) 746-1673

Spence Skelton (Director)

Contacts: David Nasby (Associate Director); Sandra Lowman (Archivist/Librarian)
Services: Museum. Film and videotape collection open to researchers and scholars only; available for reuse, subject to restrictions.
Description: Holds films (1930-86) and videotapes (1980-present). Primary topics include: sports events sponsored by beverage alcohol producers (Seagram and others); the production and marketing of beverage alcohol worldwide; cooperage; glassmaking and bottle manufacturing.

Titles include: *Golf on the Gold Trail* (1948), featuring scenes from the 1948 Canadian Open Gold Championship, Vancouver; similar films covering Canadian Opens (1949-69); *The Happiest Summer* (1969), on the Montreal Expos baseball team; *Who Does Your Father Work For?* (1971), on the philosophy of Samuel Bronfman; *Crown Royal Story* (ca. 1960), featuring the introduction of Crown Royal by Edgar Bronfman; *The Seagram Touch of Hospitality* (ca. 1965); *In the American Grain,* on the history of distilled spirits manufacturing in the U.S.; *Selling in the Liquor Industry; Mr. Samuel Bronfman — Funeral* (1971); *Bartender's Film: The Art of Mixing Drinks* (1973); *How to Remember Names and Faces* (ca. 1938), a sales training film; *Billets to Barrels,* on barrel manufacturing; *Usher's Green Stripe Races* (1931), on a snowshoe marathon in Quebec; *The Birth of a Building* (1957), on the construction of the Seagram Building, a 38-story bronze skyscraper in New York City; *Cane to Fame* (1976), on the story of rum and production of Captain Morgan rums; *Don't Put All Your Eggs In One Basket* (1968), on activities at Trelawney Estates, Jamaica; *Spirit of the Land* (1980), the story of the making of Canadian whiskey; and *Spirit of Scotland* (1986), on the production of Scotch whiskey.
Size & Elements: Film: 16mm (101 titles; release prints). Videotape: 3/4", VHS and Betamax (25 titles; masters and viewing copies).
Cataloging: Card catalogs; title lists; computerized cataloging for staff use only.
Access: Open to researchers and scholars only. Research fees charged. Research requests accepted by mail, telephone and in person (by appointment only).
Rights: Full rights held to some material. Additional clearances may be necessary in some cases if material is to be reused.
Licensing: Available for licensing and reuse. License and usage fees not charged.
Restrictions: Reuse requires credit acknowledgement. Use of worn or brittle films is restricted.
Viewing Facilities: Film (theater); videotape (library).
Duplication Facilities: None.

ONTARIO (Waterloo)

UNIVERSITY OF WATERLOO
AUDIO-VISUAL CENTRE
MEDIA LIBRARY
200 University Avenue West
Waterloo, ON N2L 3G1
(519) 888-4070
Fax: (519) 888-6197

W. Mark Ritchie (Media Librarian)

Contact: W. Mark Ritchie
Services: University media center; film and videotape producer. Collection open to researchers and scholars only. Some material possibly available for licensing and reuse, subject to clearance and restrictions.
Description: In addition to a wide variety of commercially acquired productions, the Media Library holds material produced by or relating to the University.

International. Includes: *Malaysia* (CBC; outtakes), five films covering government, rural development, people, exports, modernization, tin production, the Army, schooling and the Monarchy (all 1960-61); *Mercenaries — Costa Pinto; Imperatives For Growth In The Global Economy,* a lecture by N. A. Palkhivala.

Mathematics and engineering. Includes: *Graph Theory As I Have Known It; Angles And Cutting Planes: Freehand Sketching for Engineers; High Pressure Water Jet Cutter,* describing this implement developed at the

University; *Line In Space: Double Auxiliary Views*, orthographic views are shown, including the back view of the line; and *Photographic Study of Unsteady Flow Phenomena In Rotating Impeller Passages*, a high-speed film.

Literature and the humanities. Includes: *Anthem For Doomed Youth*, a detailed analysis of the sonnet by Wilfred Owen; *Creative Clothing/Body Sculpture Pageant*, a fashion show of designs using such materials as cotton, computer tape, wool, barbed wire, silk, eggs, balsa wood, Plexiglas, crêpe and even plastic-coated anchovies; *Dances And Masks At The Tudor Court*, demonstrating such Elizabethan dances as Sweet Kate, Branle, Allemande, Canary and Morris; *George Orwell: The Crystal Spirit*, using a combination of narration, mime and acting to bring to life Orwell's biography; *The Gothic Cathedral*, discussing protection against the weather and the increasing need for sunlight in the evolution of Gothic architecture up until the 16th century; *Man Makes Clothes*, discussing the history of clothing and the evolution of fashion; and *The Rape Of The Lock*, lectures by Prof. W. K. Thomas.

Science, medicine and health. Includes: *Extraocular Muscles*, explaining the concepts of synergism, antagonism and yoke muscles; *Smoking Prevention*, a five-part series including perspectives on mass media, parental pressure, peer pressure and thiocyanate analysis; *Some Contributions To Running Water Research; Sordaria; Spectronic 20: How To Use The Spectrometer; Spectacle Frame Fitting Adjustments;* and *Volumetric Analysis.*

University history and events. Includes: *A General Meeting With The President*, presenting the 1979 meeting between Dr. B. C. Matthews and University faculty and staff, at which he announced his resignation; *The Grand Tour*, an aerial view surveying the University of Waterloo campus; *A New President for the University of Guelph; A Testimonial Dinner In Honour Of The Rev. Dr. Cornelius Siegfried; Women and Books*, showing many of the holdings of the Doris Lewis Rare Books Room on the history of women's rights; and *Watmedia: May 1979*, program examining the Waterloo Media Cataloging System.

Local and University news on commercial television. Includes: *Big Sisters Bus Push; Bio-Conversion; Boiling Water Problems; Cardboard Food; Circadian Rhythms; Conflict Analysis; Dr. Pei — Microwave Cooking; End Of An Era: Goodbye; Eye Research; Femmes Engineering; Garbage Food; Hewlett-Packard To Build On Campus; Hunger Project; Industrial Innovation Centre; IBM Involvement at Waterloo; Murray Moo Young; Ontario Engineering Design Competition; Plastic Concrete; Religion and Sexuality; '57 Chevy; Theatre Posters With Earl Stieler; Video VDT's;* and *West Montrose Dam.*

Hagey Lecture Series. Comprised of 17 lectures including: *The African Origins of Mankind: Current Evidence — Richard Leakey*, in which Dr. Leakey states that paleontology provides no proof that violent acts in man can be found prior to 50,000 or 40,000 B.C.; *Beyond Realism: The Cult Of Beauty — Sir Ernst Gombrich*, discussing Plato, Christianity and the demise of classical beauty in the Romantic Period; *The Evolution of Peace*, a lecture by Dr. Elisa Boulding, who theorizes that prehistoric humanity was probably peaceful and states that violence occurs when people don't know how else to react; *The Writing Of Novels — Answers — Margaret Atwood.*

Size & Elements: Film: 35mm (10 titles); 16mm (1,141 titles) (positives, originals and release prints). Videotape: 3/4", VHS and 8mm (1,899 titles; masters and viewing copies).
Cataloging: Published catalog; computerized cataloging available to researchers.
Access: Available to researchers and scholars only. Research fees not charged. Research requests accepted by mail and in person (by appointment only).
Rights: Some rights held to some material. Copyright clearance may be necessary in some cases if material is to be reused.
Licensing: Some material available for licensing and reuse, subject to restrictions. License and usage fees not charged.
Restrictions: All requests for reuse subject to acceptance, approval and copyright clearance.
Viewing Facilities: Film (small preview room accommodating ten people); videotape (study carrels equipped for videotape playback).
Duplication Facilities: Videotape (3/4", VHS and 8mm).

CANADA/QUEBEC

QUEBEC (Hull)

CANADIAN MUSEUM OF CIVILIZATION
MÉDIATHÈQUE
P.O. Box 3100, Station B
Hull, PQ J8X 4H2
(819) 953-6456

Street address: 100 Laurier Street

Jacques Cinq-Mars (Chief, Médiathèque)

Contact: Staff
Services: Museum. Film collection partially accessible to the public on a case-by-case basis. *Access policies currently under review and may change as a result of ongoing reorganization.*
Description: The Museum of Civilization, formerly known as the National Museum of Man, is currently closed; a new building is due to open June 29, 1989. Consequently, many Museum services are deferred, curtailed or temporarily unavailable as the institution's resources are directed toward the reorganization.

The Médiathèque includes the film collection, a photograph collection and a library. Primary areas covered by the film collection include visual anthropology, ethnography, archaeology and history (generally 1920s-present; some older films held). Most items relate to North America.
Size & Elements: Film: 16mm (over 500 films; release prints); 8mm (a few films). Originals, when they exist, are held at the National Archives of Canada, Moving Image and Sound Archives (q.v.).
Cataloging: Cataloging and organization of collection in progress.
Access: Open to the public. Access, research and loan policies currently under review due to reorganization. It is planned to restrict film collection to internal use, to transfer most films to 3/4" videotape and to loan videotape (rather than film). Use of older material is restricted; more recent media-oriented films are loaned out for educational purposes (in some cases). Collection will also be used in the Museum's outreach program, administered by the Educational Cultural Affairs Dept.
Rights: Full rights held to some material. No rights held to most material. Rights to some films held jointly with other organizations (e.g., National Film Board of Canada). Additional clearances may be necessary in some cases if material is to be reused.
Licensing: Available for licensing and reuse on a case-by-case basis, subject to restrictions. License and usage fees charged in some cases.
Restrictions: Access, research and loan policies currently under review due to reorganization. Most material carries copyright restrictions.
Viewing Facilities: Film and videotape (group viewing facilities).
Duplication Facilities: Film (16mm to 3/4" videotape).

QUEBEC (Montreal)

BELL CANADA
HISTORICAL DEPARTMENT
1050 Beaver Hall Hill, Room 820
Montréal, PQ H2Z 1S4
(514) 870-7088

Stephanie Sykes (Director, Historical Dept./Information Resource Centre)

Contacts: Lise Noel (Manager, Historical Records); Catherine Lowe (Manager, Historical Research).
Services: Corporation; corporate archives. Film and videotape collection open to researchers, scholars and the public for research and duplication.
Description: Business archives of Bell Canada, its related companies and subsidiaries, including: Bell Canada Enterprises, Northern Telecom and Bell-Northern Research. The collection of historical material relating to telecommunications in Canada includes a large number of films, videotapes, sound recordings and photographs documenting the evolution of the company, its subsidiaries and the products and services of Bell Canada (e.g., advertisements, promotional projects, and the safety and training of employees).

Most films are currently deposited with the National Archives of Canada, Moving Image and Sound Archives (q.v.) by agreement between Bell Canada and the National Archives. The remainder of the collection is either stored at corporate storage facilities or in the viewing studio at Bell, where the collection is currently being reorganized and indexed.

Films are in both English and French. Sample titles include: *L'ABC du téléphone; Amperes Volts and Ohms; Anik; The Animated Network (Le réseau animé); Bell System Defensive Driving Course; Communications: The Wired World; Genesis of the Transistor; Her City; Intelsat IV — Canadian Visitors; Northern Telecom — The Innovators; One Canadian Company; A Phone for the Halversens; Power From the Cold; The Story of Syncom II; [Une téléphoniste de l'Assistance-annuaire];* and *Your Voice and the Telephone.*
Size & Elements: Film: format unspecified (approx. 2,500 films). Videotape: format unspecified (approx. 600 videotapes).

Cataloging: Card catalogs; other finding aids; computerized cataloging for staff use only.
Access: Open to researchers, scholars and the public. For in-house use only. Available for duplication. Research fees not charged. Research requests accepted by mail, telephone and in person (walk-in).
Rights: Apply for information.
Licensing: License and usage fees not charged.
Restrictions: None specified.
Viewing Facilities: Film (16mm projector).
Duplication Facilities: None.
Related Materials: Still photographs and sound recordings.

QUEBEC (Montreal)

BIBLIOTHÈQUE MUNICIPALE DE MONTRÉAL CINÉMATHÈQUE
880, rue Roy est, Suite 200
Montréal, PQ H2L 1E6
(514) 872-6579

Lise Depatie-Bourassa (Chief, Audiovisual Services)

Contact: Cinémathèque (514/872-3680)
Services: Library. Film and videotape materials available to the public for research (in-house viewing) and free loan.
Description: Municipal library of Montreal whose film department (Cinémathèque) (established 1947) oversees "the acquisition, treatment, conservation and [promotion] of audiovisual resources for the library system." Holds films and videotapes covering a wide range of subjects and from a variety of sources. Types of films include documentaries; archival films; experimental films; animation; films on contemporary problems; entertainment films; and silent and comic classics.

Film subject categories include: animation; architecture; silent films of Charlie Chaplin, Laurel and Hardy, and Buster Keaton; music; painting; sculpture; journalism; biographies; comedy films, including Abbott and Costello and The Little Rascals; children's films; travel and adventure films from Africa, North and South America, Asia, Europe, Antarctica and the Arctic; history; language; literature; philosophy; religion; science; social studies; and sports. Also holds 300 films deposited by four foreign consulates: Belgium, Israel, Switzerland and the Netherlands.

The videotape collection was established in 1981 and is mostly comprised of titles transferred from film. Also held are some educational broadcasts from Radio-Québec and documentaries from Radio-Canada.

Videotape subject categories include: arts; folklore; fiction; history; geography; language; literature; medicine and science; music; social studies; sports; technology; and zoology.
Size & Elements: Film: 35mm and 16mm (7,000 titles). Videotape: 3/4" (5,500 videotapes).
Cataloging: Card catalogs; published catalogs (in French only).
Access: Open to the public. Some material, including the videotape collection, for in-house viewing only. Research fees not charged. Research requests accepted by mail, telephone and in person (walk-in).
Rights: Rights retained by original producers.
Licensing: Apply for information.
Restrictions: None specified.
Viewing Facilities: Film; videotape (3/4").
Duplication Facilities: None.

QUEBEC (Montreal)

CANADIAN OLYMPIC ASSOCIATION/ ASSOCIATION OLYMPIQUE CANADIENNE
2380 Avenue Pierre Dupuy
Olympic House, Cité du Havre
Montréal, PQ H3C 3R4
(514) 861-3371
Fax: (514) 861-2896
Telex: 0524858

A. A. Crowell (Executive Director)

Contact: Sylvia Doucette (Information Centre Coordinator)
Services: Nonprofit association. Film and videotape available for research or rental; reuse subject to clearance and approval.
Description: Historical material relating to the Olympic Games. Includes documentation of the 1936 Olympics (Berlin), including footage linking classical Greek civilization to Berlin, opening ceremonies, Hitler's declaration, the release of thousands of pigeons, militaristic music and the triumph of sprinter Jesse Owens. Other Olympic Games footage covers Mexico City (1968), Melbourne (1956) and Moscow (1980).

Also holds material on the Pan-American Games, the Olympic movement and amateur sports.
Size & Elements: Film: 16mm (25 titles in English, 10 in French; release prints). Videotape: VHS (12 titles).
Cataloging: Research library; published catalogs; computerized cataloging available to researchers.
Access: Available primarily for rental. Research requests are accepted by mail, telephone and in person.
Rights: Some rights held to all material. Additional clearances may be necessary in some cases if material is to be reused.
Licensing: Apply for information. License and usage fees charged in some cases
Restrictions: Reuse subject to clearance and approval.
Viewing Facilities: Videotape (VHS).
Duplication Facilities: None.
Distributor: Films distributed by City Films (Toronto, Ontario).

QUEBEC (Montreal)

CINÉMATHÈQUE QUÉBECOISE
335, boulevard de Maisonneuve est
Montréal, PQ H2X 1K1
(514) 842-9763
Fax: (514) 842-1816

Robert Daudelin (Curator)

Contacts: Pierre Jutras (Quebec and Canadian Cinema); Pierre Véronneau (Publications and Collection of Old Apparatus); Louise Beaudet (Animation); Gisèle Côté (Film Collection); Alain Gauthier (Stills and Posters Collection)
Services: Museum. Film and videotape archives available to researchers and scholars only. Material not available for duplication.
Description: Created in 1963 to promote cinema, and to acquire, conserve and exhibit films for historical, pedagogical and artistic purposes. Includes a renowned collection of early animation with many rare and unique prints (4,000 titles), including such works as *Neighbors* (1952, Norman McLaren), *Rhinocéros* (1963, Jan Lenica) and the *Felix the Cat* cartoons of Otto Messmer and Pat Sullivan. Strong in Canadian films, particularly the works of current filmmakers in the Montreal area. Also holds a collection of international films, strong in French-language films of the 1940s-60s.

The Videothèque, organized within the Library in 1986, holds features, documentaries and animation (400 titles in all), which can be viewed in private screenings for the purposes of scholarly cinema studies research only.

Filmmakers, distributors, producers and individuals are invited to deposit films and printed documents which will be properly preserved in the vaults of the Cinémathèque.
Size & Elements: Film: format unspecified (20,000 titles). Videotape: format unspecified (400 titles).
Cataloging: None specified.
Access: Available to researchers and scholars only. Research requests accepted by mail.
Rights: No rights held to any material.
Licensing: Not available for licensing or reuse.
Restrictions: Material not available for duplication or reuse of any kind.
Viewing Facilities: Film and videotape.
Duplication Facilities: None.
Related Materials: Print materials, still photographs, antique cameras and projectors, and movie posters.

QUEBEC (Montreal)

DISADA PRODUCTIONS' WALT DISNEY MEMORIAL LIBRARY
5788 Notre Dame de Grace
Montréal, PQ H4A 1M4
(514) 489-0527

Peter Adamakos (Curator)

Contact: Peter Adamakos
Services: Private collection. Film and videotape material available primarily for research purposes.

Description: Historical collection, including animated cartoons on film and videotape, relating especially to Walt Disney and the work of the Disney studio (from the silent era to the present).
Size & Elements: Film: all formats (300,000 feet, 1,000 titles, 1,000 cans). Videotape: 1", 3/4" and VHS (500 videotapes; viewing copies).
Cataloging: Research library; card catalogs.
Access: Open to researchers and scholars only. Research fees charged in some cases. Research requests accepted by mail, telephone and in person (by appointment only).
Rights: Some rights held to some material.
Licensing: Not available for licensing.
Restrictions: Licensing and reuse restricted.
Viewing Facilities: Film (16mm); videotape (VHS).
Duplication Facilities: None.
Related Materials: Original animation artwork (drawings, cels, backgrounds, model sheets, layouts and storyboards) from studios around the world; books, magazines, clippings, files, publicity posters, stills, lobby cards and advertising material (1920s-present).

QUEBEC (Montreal)

GROUPE INTERVENTION VIDEO
3575 Boulevard St. Laurent, Suite 421
Montréal, PQ H2X 2T7
(514) 499-9840

Linda Peers (President)

Contacts: Nancy Marcotte (Coordinator); Gillian Robinson (English Distribution)
Services: Media organization; videotape producer and distributor. Material available for rental and purchase.
Description: Nonprofit women's collective producing and distributing progressive videotapes since 1975 on women's issues, including rape, abortion, sexuality, communication, and Third World women.

Titles available in French and English include: *Still Sane*, depicting a woman committed to a psychiatric institution in the 1970s for being a lesbian; *Rock and Romance*, on the representation of women in music videos; *Comptines*, showing women in the streets of Belfast marking the death of the ninth IRA hunger striker; *Lee à Two Rivers*, a woman's search for a unified self via experimental photography; and *Femme instinct*, a dance performance.

Titles available in English include: *Travel in the Combat Zone*, the poet Jessica Hagedorn's view of city living in a man's world; *Stronger than Before*, documenting the attempt by one hundred Toronto women to conduct a citizens' arrest of Litton Industries management for conspiracy to commit mass murder by means of missile guidance systems and microwave ovens; and *You're What?! A Story of Teenage Pregnancy*.

Titles available in French include: *Statistiques vitales* (Martha Rosler); *Reportage Bresil: 1*, on a women's police station in Sao Paulo dealing exclusively with violence against women; *Bertioga '85*, the third feminist Latina-american conference in Brazil; *Qu'est-ce que t'as fait pour souper?*, an experiment in living with non-sexist values; *On ne voulait pas des Miracles*, three general strikes (1937, 1940 and 1983) by seamstresses in Montreal; *Les sages femmes de Jalapa*, midwives in post-revolutionary Nicaragua; *Histoire des luttes feministes au Québec*; *As-tu des Bibittes*, on racism; *Memoire d'Octobre*, on the repression of the Québecois people during the events of October 1970; *Un enfant*, on Down's syndrome; and *Gus est encore dans l'armée*, on the masculine condition.
Size & Elements: Videotape: 3/4" and VHS (French-language titles: 23 videotapes on women; 8 videotapes on various topics; 3 experimental videotapes. English-language titles: approx. 20 videotapes).
Cataloging: Published catalogs.
Access: Available to the public for rental and purchase. Requests accepted by mail, telephone and in person (walk-in and by appointment). Rental fees charged per day (negotiable, based on profit or nonprofit status and the nature of project). If videotape is being rented for a profit-making project in a store or at a festival, rates will be set according to specific agreements.
Rights: Full rights held to some material. Some rights held to some material. Additional clearances may be necessary in some cases if material is to be reused.
Licensing: Apply for information.
Restrictions: Copyright restrictions apply. Buyers are forbidden to redistribute, sublet, lend or exchange videotapes outside the boundary of their organization. Renters promise to show videotape only at the places, times and circumstances specified in the contract; and promise not to sublet, lend,

exchange, copy, cut or edit videotape. Unless otherwise stated, transmission by cable, closed circuit or broadcast television is also prohibited.
Viewing Facilities: Videotape (3/4" and VHS).
Duplication Facilities: None.

QUEBEC (Montreal)

MUSÉE D'ART CONTEMPORAIN DE MONTRÉAL
Cité du Havre
Montréal, PQ H3C 3R4
(514) 873-2878

Marcel Brisebois (Director)
Manon Blanchette (Conservatrice en chef)

Contacts: Michelle Gauthier (Responsable du Centre de Documentation; for film collection only); Paulette Gagnon (Conservatrice, responsable de la collection permanente); Monique Gauthier (Archiviste des collections)
Services: Museum. Film and videotape collection open to researchers, scholars and the public for viewing only.
Description: Dedicated to the acquisition of significant contemporary works of art from Québecois, Canadian and international artists. Began to collect video art in 1979, and now holds over 60 videotapes, including work by Julien Poulin, Pierre Falardeau, Marshalore, Yves Chaput, Eric Metcalfe, Nan Hoover, Robert Filiou, Fabio Mauri, Dara Birnbaum and Nam June Paik. Also holds a collection of documentary and archival films which are not part of the permanent collections and presently uncataloged.
Size & Elements: Film: format and amount unspecified. Videotape: 3/4" and 1/2" (over 60 videotapes).
Cataloging: Card catalogs; computerized cataloging for staff use only; research library.
Access: Open to researchers, scholars and the public by appointment only. Research requests accepted by mail and telephone.
Rights: Some rights held to some material.
Licensing: Apply for information.
Restrictions: None specified.
Viewing Facilities: Videotape (by appointment only).
Duplication Facilities: None.

QUEBEC (Montreal)

NATIONAL FILM BOARD OF CANADA
AUDIOVISUAL COLLECTIONS
C.P. 6100, Station A
Montréal, PQ H3C 3H5
(514) 283-9437
(514) 283-9170 (Stockshot Library)

Street address: 3155 Côte de Liesse, St-Laurent, PQ H4N 2N4

United States contact:
NATIONAL FILM BOARD OF CANADA
1251 Avenue of the Americas, 16th Floor
New York, NY 10020-1173
(212) 586-5131
Attn: Rachelle Cournoyer

Contact: Mary Jane Terrell; John Rowe
Services: Government agency; film and videotape producer; film and videotape archives; stock footage sales library. Open to the public. Material in Stock Shot Library available for licensing and reuse. Completed productions distributed through NFB in Canada and commercial distributors around the world.
Description: The Audiovisual Collections department manages the production, distribution and circulation of NFB materials. Various services include:

The Stock Shot Library Unit. Views, selects and catalogs outtakes from NFB productions and makes the shots accessible to filmmakers by entering them into the library system. Collection (1900-80, over 20 million feet) includes footage relating to World War I, World War II and newsreels; the arts and music; cityscapes; Canadian landscapes; geography and travel; Canadian history; medicine and health sciences; multiculturalism; the natural sciences (biology, ecology, conservation, technology and applied sciences); social sciences (family, gerontology and the handicapped); sports and leisure; Olympics; domestic and wild animals; women; work and labor relations.

The Preview Library Vaults. Responsible for storage of materials including test prints, preview prints, archival prints, festival prints, negatives, stock shots, printing materials, cutting copies, filmstrips and slides. The Preview Library is also responsible for distribution of archival films to the public. The Vaults are located at three locations within NFB headquarters. The Printing Material Inventory Vaults store the original production negative, the master print and duplicate negative materials.

The Archives Special Project. Involves the preparation and transfer of films completed between 1958-79, which are then sent to the National Archives of Canada, Moving Image and Sound Archives (q.v.).

In addition to its stock shot collection, NFB maintains an active film and videotape distribution operation in Canada. Films are also available through commercial film distributors around the world.

Size & Elements: Film: 35mm (5,252 titles); 16mm (14,217 titles) (Stockshot Library contains over 20 million feet of 35mm and 16mm outtakes). Videotapes: format unspecified (4,756 items).

Cataloging: Card catalogs (for Stock Shot Library); published catalogs; research library.

Access: Open to the public. Stock shots available for licensing and reuse. Completed productions maintained for distribution and rental rather than for research or reuse. Research fees charged. Research requests accepted by mail, telephone and in person (walk-in and by appointment).

Rights: Full rights held to some material. Additional clearances may be necessary in some cases if material is to be reused.

Licensing: Some material available for licensing and reuse, subject to restrictions. License fees charged.

Restrictions: Shots in which professional actors appear are not available for stock footage sale in cases where the NFB does not have the required rights.

Viewing Facilities: Film and videotape (for viewing of stock footage).

Duplication Facilities: Film and videotape.

Related Materials: The Photothèque Unit contains photographs from NFB productions, maintains an inventory of such photographs and sells copies for other uses (e.g., in the production of information sheets, newspaper publicity, posters, catalogs, various NFB reports and publications).

QUEBEC (Montreal)

P.R.I.M. (PRODUCTIONS RÉALISATIONS INDÉPENDANTES DE MONTRÉAL)
3981 St.-Laurent, Suite 310
Montréal, PQ H2W 1Y5
(514) 849-5065

Guilhemme Saulnier (General Director)

Contacts: Michel Giroux (Access Coordinator); Jean Décarie (Technical Director)

Services: Media organization. Videotape collection available to the public for rental and purchase.

Description: Nonprofit artist-run organization concerned with assisting artists and independent producers in the production and post-production of their work. Also promotes works produced at P.R.I.M. and presents international video productions to local audiences. Coordinates video events, e.g., festivals, exchanges with other video organizations, curatorial work for galleries and museums, presentations in schools and collaborations with social and cultural groups. Distribution of works by P.R.I.M. members, Canadian and international artists commenced in 1984.

Holdings include video art, documentation of performances and exhibitions and technical experimentation with the medium for use in multi-media contexts (1972-present); most produced in Montreal and Quebec. Artists and titles include: *Couleur*, an installation and *Le Train* (François Girard); *La La La Human Sex Duo No. 1* (Bernar Hébert); *Machine/Machines* (Pierre Zovilé); *Ne retenez pas votre souffle* (Luc Bourdon and Louis Bronsard); *Interrupted Attempt, The Observer, Rejuvenation and Light Rail* (Grant Poier); *Vacation/Vacance* (Hum Sujir); *Voices, Sound, Track* (Rob Miltorp); *Rumble Sphynx* (Clark-Hamilton); *High Riders* (John Will); *Façade* (Collen Kerr); *Stupid Video* (Nelson Henricks); *Système des Beaux-Arts* (Daniel Pilon and Philippe Poloni); *La Loggia*, an installation by Francine Chaîné; *Insanity Training Department Meats Art* (D.E.I.T.); and *It's Always Movement?!*

Also holds works by Julie Bellemare, Hugo Brochu, Susana Cabrera, Joceline Chabot, Marie-José Gaulin, Nina Gauvin, La Toan Vinh, Sylvie Phaneuf, Robin Rousseau, Gabrielle Schloesser and Réal Tougas.

Size & Elements: Videotape: 3/4" (203 videotapes, 290 titles; masters, produced 1981-88); 1/2" open reel (100 reels, 200 titles; masters, produced 1971-82). Viewing copies available in 3/4" and VHS.

Cataloging: Shot lists; publicity materials.

Access: Open to the public. Available for research, rental and purchase. Rental fees charged. Research fees not charged. Research requests accepted by telephone and in person (walk-in).

Rights: Some rights held to some material.

Licensing: Apply for information. License and usage fees charged in some cases.

Restrictions: Apply for information.

Viewing Facilities: Videotape.

Duplication Facilities: Videotape.

QUEBEC (Montreal)

SOCIÉTÉ DE RADIO-TÉLÉVISION DE QUÉBEC (RADIO QUÉBEC)
800 Fullum Street
Montréal, PQ H2K 3L7
(514) 521-2424

Contacts: André Beaudet (Head of Public Relations [Ext. 2204]; for general information); Roger Cartier (Marketing Department; for distribution and sales of television series and single programs); Michel Boisvert (Film Library; for information about and access to stock footage)

Services: Television broadcaster. Programs and stock footage available for licensing and reuse.

Description: Programs produced for Radio Québec (1968-present). Most holdings are documentaries, with an emphasis on daily life and culture in Quebec. Several feature films of historical interest are held. Retired materials are transferred to the Archives Nationales du Québec, Archives Audiovisuelles (q.v.). A catalog of titles in current distribution may be obtained from the Marketing Department. Material from 1968-78 is held in 35mm; post-1978 material is held in videotape form.

Size & Elements: Film: 35mm (approx. 3 million feet). Videotape: 1" and 3/4". (Approx. 30,000 titles total; originals held for most titles).

Cataloging: Cataloging in process.

Access: Available for duplication and reuse. Research and screening fees charged.

Rights: Full rights held to some material. Additional clearances may be necessary in some cases if material is to be reused.

Licensing: Available for licensing and reuse. License fees charged.

Restrictions: Apply for information.

Viewing Facilities: Videotape (3/4"; viewing fees apply).

Duplication Facilities: Outside arrangements made in most cases.

QUEBEC (Montreal)

LE VIDÉOGRAPHE INC.
4550 rue Garnier
Montréal, PQ H2J 3S7
(514) 521-2116

Suzie Beaulieu (Responsable Section Internationale)

Contacts: Michel Hudon (Sales and Rental); Alexandre Nagy (Production); Suzie Beaulieu; Lise Lachapelle (Distribution); Luc Bourdon (Diffusion)

Services: Videotape producer and distributor; media arts center; archives. Videotapes available to the public for rental and purchase.

Description: Nonprofit organization (founded 1971) dedicated to the production and distribution of independent video art and documentary works produced by Quebec artists. Most videotapes in the collection are Québecois and Canadian in origin.

Subjects include labor and unionization, housing, the media, women, politics, health, international development, sexuality, art and artists, education, children and childhood, and history.

Titles include: *Les P'tits Nègres de la Great Lakes* (1974, Marie Chamberland, Pierre Joyal and Richard Proulx), with interviews in which workers at the Great Lakes Carbon Corporation Ltd. plant and residents of Berthier denounce working conditions and environmental hazards at the factory; *Que Pasa En El Barrio?* (1983, Andréas Tanzler), on a densely populated and underprivileged community in Mexico threatened by speculators and the formation of the *Union de vecinos*, the union of the neighbors; *Les Seins de Louise* (1972, Lise Noiseux-Labrecque), a humorous exploration of cultural attitudes focusing on breasts — their size, beauty and importance for a women's self-image and self-esteem; *Manufactured Romance* (1982-85, Anne Ramsden), looking at the media from a feminist point of view; *Poudrière Salvadorienne* (1982, Danielle Lacourse and Yvan Patry), made by one of the rare foreign production crews on hand in El Salvador during the bloody events of the 1982 elections, presenting the principal players: the large families of the coffee planters, the army and security forces, the American government, the Church and the guerrillas; *Temps Guay* (1977, Simone Trudeau), with testimony of women who have been incarcerated at the Tanguay Institute in Montreal; *T'en Sais Rien de Mes Rêves* (1984, Jean-Guy Michaud), following the lives of three 18-year-olds; and *L'incident Jones* (1986, Marc Paradis), a short videotape in three acts telling the story of an encounter.

Vidéo International, a part of Le Vidéographe, Inc., has produced over 40 works relating to Third World and multicultural issues. Video International focuses on videotaping the activities of Quebec and Canadian-based overseas non-governmental organizations, and producing documents on the international situation and organizations involved with international cooperation.
Size & Elements: Videotape: 3/4", VHS and Betamax (900 titles).
Cataloging: Published catalogs; brochures.
Access: Available to the public for research, rental and purchase. Research fees not charged. Research requests accepted by mail and telephone.
Rights: Full rights held to all material. Additional clearances may be necessary in some cases if material is to be reused.
Licensing: Possibly available for reuse, subject to restrictions. License and usage fees charged in some cases.
Restrictions: Some restrictions may apply.
Viewing Facilities: Videotape (3/4" and VHS; NTSC, PAL and SECAM).
Duplication Facilities: Videotape.

QUEBEC (Quebec)

ASSOCIATION COOPÉRATIVE OBSCURE
729 Côte d'Abraham
Québec, PQ G1R 1A2
(418) 529-3775

Gilles Arteau (President)

Contact: Louis Ouellet (Coordinateur)
Services: Videotape producer and distributor. Material available for research and reuse, subject to restrictions.
Description: Experimental and art videotapes produced by the members of OBSCURE. For three years, OBSCURE has offered its membership the opportunity to produce a videotape segment to be presented as part of an exhibition entitled *One Minute Video.*

They are the sole Canadian distributor of six videotapes conceived and directed (1966-86) by Samuel Beckett, intended to explain the essential aspects of his language.

Also distributes ten videotapes by Steina and Woody Vasulka, including: *The West* (1983); *The Commission* (1983); *Artifacts* (1980); *Art of Memory* (1987); *In Search for the Castle* (1981); *Progeny* (1981); *Cantaloup* (1980); *Urban Episode* (1980); *Summer Salt* (1982); *Selected Treecuts* (1980); and *Bad* (1979).

Also holds videotape documentation of all OBSCURE activities (50 unedited videotapes).
Size & Elements: Videotape: 3/4" and 1/2" (approx. 70 videotapes).
Cataloging: Printed list of videotapes available for distribution; shot lists.
Access: Available to the public for distribution. Archival material available to researchers and scholars only. Research fees charged. Research requests accepted by mail and telephone.
Rights: Full rights held to some material. Some rights held to other material.
Licensing: Available for reuse. License fees charged (individually negotiated, depending on intended use).
Restrictions: None specified.
Viewing Facilities: Film (16mm projector); videotape (3/4", VHS and Betamax).
Duplication Facilities: Videotape (3/4", VHS and Betamax).

QUEBEC (Quebec)

UNIVERSITÉ LAVAL
CINÉMATHÈQUE
Pavillon Jean-Charles-Bonenfant
Québec, PQ G1K 7P4
(418) 656-3252

Agathe Garon (Chief, Cinémathèque and Special Collections)

Contact: Agathe Garon
Services: University library. Film and videotape collection open to the public

for loan and possibly reuse, subject to restrictions.
Description: Feature-length fiction films. Documentaries on various subjects, including agriculture, cattle breeding, communications, earth sciences, economics, energy, environment, food industries, fine arts and literature, international relations and cooperation, human sciences, industry and technology, languages, labor, law, life sciences, media, management, medicine and health, politics and society, pure sciences, sports, teaching sciences, transportation, tourism and urban studies. Also holds approximately 30 experimental films by cinema students.

About 60% of these films and videotapes are in French; 40% in English.
Size & Elements: Film: 16mm, Super 8mm and 8mm (approx. 4,800 titles). Videotape: 3/4" and VHS (1,090 titles).
Cataloging: Computerized cataloging (microfiche) available to researchers.
Access: Open to the public. Research fees not charged. Research requests accepted by mail, telephone and in person (by appointment only).
Rights: Some rights held to some material. Some material in the public domain. Additional clearances may be necessary in some cases if material is to be reused.
Licensing: Available for licensing and reuse, subject to restrictions. License and usage fees charged.
Restrictions: Some restrictions may apply.
Viewing Facilities: Film; videotape (3/4" and VHS).
Duplication Facilities: Videotape (3/4" and VHS).

QUEBEC (Quebec)

VIDÉO FEMMES
56 Rue St.-Pierre, Suite 203
Québec, PQ G1K 4A1
(418) 692-3090
Fax: (418) 692-4250

Contact: Nicole Bonenfant (Distribution)
Services: Videotape producer and distributor. Material available to the public for distribution and rental.
Description: Has provided production and distribution services for over 50 independent video productions (1974-present). Works primarily in the field of women's communication, producing and distributing works with a feminist viewpoint. Also distributes over 60 national and international productions by outside producers.

Topics cover art and creativity, history, health, childbirth, abortion, sexuality, mental health, aging, sexism, social issues, education, family, social conditions affecting women, male-female relations, labor, working conditions, trade unions, non-traditional jobs and issues of violence, primarily concerning sexual abuse and rape.

Recent titles include: *Histoire Infâme* (Nicole Giguère), a brief musical history of women; *Respectrum Prologue* (Sylvy Gagné), a philosophical and personal vision denouncing the sad reality of war; and *Qui est Alice Guy?* (Nicole-Lise Bernheim), a documentary biography on cinematic pioneer Alice Guy-Blaché.

Some productions are currently available in English, including: *Breaking Silence,* on incest; *Psychiatry is gonna die,* the 10th international conference on human rights and psychiatric oppression in Toronto in 1982; and *Conference Internationale des femmes: Nairobi 1985.*

Vidéo Femmes sponsors an annual film and video festival featuring recent local and international productions by women.
Size & Elements: Videotape: 3/4", VHS and Betamax (142 titles total; masters and viewing copies; some PAL and SECAM viewing copies).
Cataloging: Published catalogs.
Access: Open to the public. Maintained for distribution and rental rather than for research and reuse. Research requests accepted in person (by appointment).
Rights: Full rights held to all material.
Licensing: Possibly available for licensing and reuse. License and usage fees charged.
Restrictions: Some restrictions may apply.
Viewing Facilities: Film (16mm); videotape (3/4", VHS and Betamax).
Duplication Facilities: Videotape (3/4", VHS and Betamax).

QUEBEC (Ste-Foy)

ARCHIVES NATIONALES DU QUÉBEC
ARCHIVES AUDIOVISUELLES
C. P. 10450
Ste-Foy, PQ G1V 4N1
(418) 643-1904

CANADA/QUEBEC (Ste-Foy)

Street address: 1210, Avenue du Séminaire

Yvan Dussault (Conservateur adjoint du Centre d'archives de Québec)

Contacts: Antoine Pelletier; Jacqueline Lévesque; Richard Gagnon
Services: Government agency. Film and videotape collection available to the public for research and reuse.
Description: Film and videotape relating to Quebec (1930-85). Strengths include history, geography, culture, agriculture, forestry and language. Holds original production materials from Radio-Télévision Québec (1920s-present).
Size & Elements: Film: 35mm (100,000 feet); 16mm (5 million feet) (6,000 titles, 15,000 cans total). Videotape: 2", 1", 3/4", VHS and 1/2" open reel (500 videotapes total).
Cataloging: None specified.
Access: Open to the public. Research fees not charged. Research requests accepted in person (walk-in).
Rights: Full rights held to Government-produced material. Additional clearances may be necessary in some cases if material is to be reused.
Licensing: Available for licensing and reuse, subject to restrictions.
Restrictions: Some restrictions may apply.
Viewing Facilities: Film (16mm, on request); videotape.
Duplication Facilities: Film (16mm to videotape); videotape.

QUEBEC (Ste-Foy)

UNIVERSITÉ LAVAL
SERVICE DES RESSOURCES PÉDAGOGIQUES
Pavillon De Koninck
Ste-Foy, PQ G1K 7P4
(418) 656-2218
(418) 656-4337

Daniel Guay (Chef, Opérations Centralisées)

Contact: Maryse Thivierge (Consultation production audiovisuelle) (418/656-4337)
Services: University instructional media center; videotape producer. Collection is open to the public for distribution and purchase.
Description: *Educational materials.* Produced in response to the specific needs of the University curriculum. Sample titles include: *Vieux Québec: Un Monument Vivant,* exploring three centuries of architecture in Quebec; *La Maison Michel Sarrazin,* a documentary videotape on an institution for terminally ill cancer patients, the only one of its kind in Canada; and *Musique de l'Amerique Latine,* on music of the Andes, the Plains and the coastal regions.
    Televised courses. Sample courses include: *Initiation à l'Économie Politique; Santé et Sécurité au Travail;* and *Histoire de la Littérature Biblique.*
    Interviews and conferences. Sample titles include: *La Maisonnée et les Systèmes Cagnatiques* and *L'Appropriation Sociale de la Logique,* lectures by Claude Lévi-Strauss; *L'Animation et la Diffusion au Musée,* a lecture by Danielle Giraudy; *Les rockers de Paris,* a lecture by Marie-Michèle Roué; *Les Kyakas de l'Angola,* a lecture by Mesquitela Lima; *La Liberté de la Presse au Québec,* an interview with Nicole Duplé; *Regard sur l'Astronomie,* an interview with Serge Pineault; *Feminisme de Recherche Universitaire,* an interview with Huguette Dagenais; *Le Français au Québec et Nos Mots,* an interview with Claude Poirier; *Les Mouvements Réligieux au Québec,* an interview with Jacques Zylberberg; and *Le Développement de la Personne Humaine,* a lecture by René Dubos.
Size & Elements: Videotape: 3/4", VHS and Betamax (375 titles; each 30 to 60 min.).
Cataloging: Card catalogs; published catalogs.
Access: Open to the public. Available for distribution and purchase. Research fees not charged. Preview fees charged in some cases (applicable to eventual purchase of videotape). Research requests accepted by mail and in person (walk-in).
Rights: Full rights held to all material.
Licensing: Apply for information.
Restrictions: None specified.
Viewing Facilities: Film and videotape.
Duplication Facilities: None.
Distributor: (For purchase) Roch Deblois, Presses Université Laval, Pavillon Pouliot, Ste-Foy, PQ G1K 7P4; (418/656-2320).

CANADA/SASKATCHEWAN

SASKATCHEWAN (Regina)

UNIVERSITY OF REGINA
SASKATCHEWAN ARCHIVES BOARD
Regina, SK S4S 0A2
(306) 787-3381

Saskatoon Office:
Murray Memorial Building
University of Saskatchewan
Saskatoon, SK
(306) 933-5832

Trevor J. D. Powell (Provincial Archivist)

Contact: Krzysztof Gebhard (Head, Sound and Moving Image Section)
Services: Provincial archives. Film and videotape collection available to the public for in-house use only. Material possibly available for duplication, subject to restrictions.
Description: Official repository for all documents created by the Saskatchewan government, comprising approximately 50-60% of total collection. Archives also collects and preserves material from corporate bodies, private organizations and individuals. Includes film and television materials of historical interest. Majority of the collection is from the 1950s-60s, with some material from the 1940s. Archives' goal is to preserve motion pictures not only as works of art, but also as a sounding line measuring trends, tastes and political conditions.
    Saskatchewan provincial government agencies. Films created by the Departments of Education, Agriculture, Tourism, Health and others (1940-85).
    Saskatchewan cinematographers. Items produced by Dick Bird, Laurence and Evelyn Cherry, Bob Long and others (1922-75).
    Lumby Films (Saskatoon). Various production elements from their films (1972-78).
    Broadcast Archives. Holds television newsfilm from CFQC Saskatoon and CKCK Regina (1958-78) and a selection of CBC-TV programming, including news, in Saskatchewan. Daily off-air videotape recordings of the evening news are held for CKCK Regina (1983-present); CBKT Regina (1984-present); CBKT Saskatoon (1986-present); and STV Regina (1987-present).
    Miscellaneous. Films produced in Saskatchewan by amateur and professional filmmakers (1922-present).
    Sample titles include: *Saskatchewan Furs: From Marsh to Market* (ca. 1940s); *Forage Crops* (1959); *Vitamin "A" for Cattle* (1961); *In Search of Utopia: The Doukhobors* (1978); *Royal Canadian Mounted Police Sunset Ceremony* (1971); *Buena Vista Park* (1929); *Combining and Hauling Grain* (1937); *Saskatoon Dam Construction* (1939); *Neepahquay-Simoowin: The Sundance* (1977); *Sanctuary: The Qu'Appelle Valley* (1970); *The Saskatchewan Museum of Natural History* (1967); *My Paddle's Keen and Bright* (ca. 1970s); and *Our School: The Wilderness* (1972).
Size & Elements: Film: 16mm (3,000 hours, 4,000 cans; originals, negatives and answer prints) (95% of film collection is 16mm; approx. 15% of film has been transferred to videotape for viewing purposes). Videotape: 1", Betacam, 3/4", VHS and 1/2" open reel (3,000 hours; masters and viewing copies).
Cataloging: Card catalogs; shot lists (if available); dope sheets or release sheets. Preliminary film catalog in progress.
Access: Open to the public. For in-house use only. Possibly available for duplication. Research fees not charged. Research requests accepted by mail, telephone and in person (walk-in and by appointment).
Rights: Full rights held to some material. Some rights held to some material. Rights status of some material not known. Government-produced material in the public domain. Additional clearances may be necessary in some cases if material is to be reused.
Licensing: Available for licensing and reuse, subject to restrictions. License and usage fees not charged.
Restrictions: Some restrictions apply to specific items.
Viewing Facilities: Film (16mm; hand-operated viewer); videotape (3/4" and VHS).
Duplication Facilities: Film (film-to-videotape transfer only); videotape: 3/4" and VHS.
Related Materials: Television news transcripts; extensive audiotape oral history collection; radio programming (1970s-present).

SASKATCHEWAN (Saskatoon)

**SASKATCHEWAN INDIAN CULTURAL CENTRE
LIBRARY & INFORMATION SERVICES**
R.R. No. 5, Group Box 150
Saskatoon, SK S7K 3J8
(306) 244-1146

Street address: 120-33 Street E

Barbara Blyth (Director, Library & Information Services)

Contact: Carol Lafond (Library Technician)
Services: Library. Film and videotape collection open to the public for in-house research and viewing.
Description: Indians (Canadian, North and South American), nature, geography, drug and alcohol abuse and treatment, and driving safety.
Titles include: *Age of the Buffalo; The Alaskan Eskimo Way of Life; An Eagle Must Fly; The Ecstasy of Rita Joe; History of Alcohol: S.I.C.C.; Ice People; Indian Artists of the Southwest; Lakota Quillwork: Arts and Legends; Look What We've Done to this Land; Requiem to a People; The Nature of Things; Windwalker; Sioux Legends; Alcohol: Pink Elephant; Along the Whoop Up Trail; Drivin' and Drinkin'; Geronimo's Children; He Comes Without Calling; Mexican Indian Legends; A Moon Mask; Native American Myths; Our Dear Sisters; The Sacred Circle;* and *Yesterday — Today — The Netsiluk Eskimo.*
Size & Elements: Film: format unspecified (over 350 titles; originals). Videotape: VHS (approx. 70 titles).
Cataloging: Published catalogs; computerized cataloging for staff use only.
Access: Available to the public for research and viewing. Research fees charged in some cases. Research requests accepted by mail, telephone and in person (walk-in and by appointment).
Rights: Full rights held to some material.
Licensing: Apply for information. License fees not charged.
Restrictions: None specified.
Viewing Facilities: Film and videotape.
Duplication Facilities: Videotape.

CANADA/YUKON TERRITORY

YUKON TERRITORY (Whitehorse)

TOURISM YUKON
Box 2703
Whitehorse, YT Y1A 2C6
(403) 667-5400

Kevin Schackell (Publicity Officer)

Contact: Kevin Schackell
Services: Government agency. One film available for rental and free loan.
Description: *Yukon, Canada's Last Frontier* (1986) is designed to promote tourism in the Yukon Territory. The film won an award for best cinematography at the Czech Tour Film Festival, and is available in German, French and Japanese.
Size & Elements: Film: 16mm. Videotape: 3/4". (1 title total).
Cataloging: None.
Access: Available for rental and free loan to qualified users for promotional purposes. Available in the U.S. through Karol Media, 22 Riverview Drive, Wayne NJ 07470-3191; (201) 628-9111 and distributed free to television stations. Requests accepted by mail and telephone.
Rights: Full rights held to some material. Additional clearances may be necessary in some cases if material is to be reused.
Licensing: Apply for information. License fees charged.
Restrictions: None specified.
Viewing Facilities: None.
Duplication Facilities: None.

YUKON TERRITORY (Whitehorse)

YUKON ARCHIVES
P.O. Box 2703
Whitehorse, YK Y1A 2C6
(403) 667-5321
Telex: 0368260

Street address: 2nd Avenue and Hawkins Street

Miriam McTiernan (Director of Libraries and Archives)

Contacts: Lesley Buchan (Accessions Archivist); Diane Chisholm (Assistant Territorial Archivist)
Services: Territorial archives. Film and videotape collection available to the public. Maintained as an in-house research facility. Much of the material not available for reuse of any kind. Restricted ability to handle research requests due to limited staffing.
Description: Acquires, preserves and maintains for research use many documentary sources related to Yukon history, culture and development. Spanning 1899-present, the majority of films cover the 1940s-70s. Includes professionally produced promotional and documentary films as well as home movies and videotapes.
Subjects relating to the Yukon cover Gold Rush scenes, Alaska Highway and Canal Project construction, Yukon communities, people, social activities such as the Rendezvous Festival and the Dawson Festivals, sports, mining, railway travel, sternwheelers, early aviation, commercial travelogues and documentaries describing the geography, culture and peoples of the Territory. Also holds some excellent footage of Yukon native people and culture, Royal Canadian Mounted Police activity, Kluane National Park, the Beaufort Sea Region, Herschel Island and mountaineering in the Yukon. Also held is footage of neighboring areas of Alaska, the Northwest Territories and Northern British Columbia.
About half of 16mm films and all 8mm films are home movies, shot by such well-known Yukoners as George Black, Emil J. Forrest, G. I. Cameron, Bill Hare and Al Wright, often of value for the view they provide into the lives of the filmmakers themselves. Home movie footage comprises the sole portion of the collection to which the Archives holds originals and rights.
Videotapes circulate as part of the Yukon Government's Audiovisual Unit, traveling to communities outside of Whitehorse.
Size & Elements: Film: 16mm (142 titles, 71,000 feet; originals and release prints) and 8mm (17 titles, 6,000 feet; originals). (159 cans total). Videotape: VHS (104 videotapes; masters, viewing copies and circulating copies).
Cataloging: Published catalogs; technical worksheets.
Access: Open to the public. Maintained primarily for in-house use. Videotapes circulate as part of Yukon Government's traveling Audiovisual Unit. Research fees not charged. Research requests accepted by mail and in person (*not by telephone*).
Rights: Some rights held to some material (home movies). Additional clearances from donors are often necessary if material is to be reused.
Licensing: Available for licensing and reuse, subject to restrictions. License and usage fees charged in some cases.
Restrictions: Duplication, licensing or reuse of any kind subject to donor restrictions.
Viewing Facilities: Film (16mm and 8mm projectors); videotape (VHS and Betamax I).
Duplication Facilities: Videotape (by special arrangement).
Related Materials: Sound recordings.

MEXICO

Researched and written by Lorena Parlee with the aid of Irma Avila

Introduction

This is a selected list of public and private film and videotape collections in Mexico City that are particularly rich in materials about Mexico and other Latin American nations. A few general suggestions are included to expedite requests for films, videotapes and stock footage.

Most Mexican archives and collections require a written request addressed to the director or owner detailing the materials needed, the type of production, the intended use and market, and your time frame. (For government archives, it is important to include the title "Director" as the individual may change with a change in administration.) A copy of this letter should be sent to the contact person (when different from the director or owner), informing him or her that you have requested this material. Once the director gives approval, the contact person will handle all the details of your request.

Initial telephone calls can be made to the contact person for information about the collection, but detailed research will not be done until you have obtained the approval of the director. While most archives and collections have staff who speak English, you will probably receive faster replies if you send a Spanish translation along with your letter. It is also a good idea to have someone who speaks Spanish help you with the initial telephone calls. Hours vary.

Many of the archives and collections permit you to send in your own researcher after you have made initial contact. All have viewing facilities, and many will send you 1/2" videotape viewing copies of materials.

The television broadcasting stations generally prefer that you make all requests by telephone or telex directly to the contact persons, as their staff does not have time to handle letters.

While not all collections are completely cataloged, the staff and personnel are generally very helpful and knowledgeable about the collections. They are often overworked and understaffed, so allow sufficient time to handle your requests.

Lorena Parlee is an award-winning independent film and video producer, writer, researcher, and Latin American historian specializing in Mexico and the Southwest.

Irma Avila is a producer and writer with TV-UNAM in Mexico City.

MEXICO, D.F.

ARCHIVO FOTOGRAFICO Y CINEMATOGRAFICO ABITIA
Medellin 193
C.P. 06760 México, D.F.
564-18-92

Jesús Abítia Pedrozo (Proprietario/Owner)

Contacts: Jesús Abítia Pedrozo; Fernando Del Moral Gonzalez
Services: Private film archives. Film footage available for duplication and reuse.
Description: Major collection relating to the Mexican Revolution (1913-24), containing unique material, filmed by one of Mexico's first documentary cameramen, Jesús H. Abítia. As official cameraman for General Alvaro Obregón, Abítia shot footage of the Mexican Revolution (1913-17) and major events during Obregón's presidency (1920-24). Also includes footage of the inauguration of President Plutarco Elías Calles (1924).

Epopoyas de la Revolución Mexicana/Epochs of the Mexican Revolution (1960), held at the Archive, is a compilation film that includes footage of the Revolution (1913-17).
Size & Elements: Film: 35mm (3,300 meters/10,800 feet, 2 titles; additional unedited footage, 11 cans; positive master); 16mm (viewing copies).
Cataloging: Finding aids; staff assistance available.
Access: Available for reuse. Research fees charged (determined by type of project and intended use). Research and footage requests accepted by mail and in person (by appointment only). All duplication requests handled through Archive.
Rights: Full rights held to all material.
Licensing: Available for licensing and reuse. License fees charged in some cases, depending upon intended market for production.
Restrictions: Requests for reuse subject to acceptance and approval.
Viewing Facilities: Film (35mm and 16mm).
Duplication Facilities: None.
Related Materials: Over 2,000 still photographs (1913-24) relating to the Mexican Revolution and the presidency of Alvaro Obregón (available for duplication and reuse).

MEXICO, D.F.

ARCHIVO HISTORICO CINEMATOGRAFICO
Prado Norte 450
Lomas de Chapultepec
C.P. 11000 México, D.F.
520-50-18
540-07-37

Octavio Moreno Toscano (Director)

Contact: Octavio Moreno Toscano
Services: Private film archives. Completed films and stock footage available for reuse.
Description: One of the major Mexican archives of early non-fiction film (1897-1930) consisting of films shot and collected by Salvador Toscano (1872-1947), cinematographer and pioneer of Mexican cinema.

Particularly strong in footage of Mexico City at the turn of the century, including daily life, President Porfirio Díaz and his government, and Mexico's

bicentennial independence celebration (1910). Extensive coverage of the Mexican Revolution (1910-17), including: major battles; Pancho Villa, Venustiano Carranza, Alvaro Obregón, Emiliano Zapata, Pascual Orozco and Victoriano Huerta; the U.S. invasion of Veracruz (1914); and activities of the general populace during the Revolution. Special strengths include Mexican urban and rural life in the 1920s; the aftermath of the revolution; and the presidencies of Carranza, Obregón and Plutarco Elías Calles.

Memorias de un mexicano (Memories of a Mexican) (1950) is a feature-length compilation film by Salvador's son, Carmen Toscano. Includes footage from the Archives on the revolution and its aftermath (1906-30).

Testimonios (1986), is a six-hour television compilation series, produced on videotape for IMEVISION (Instituto Mexicano de Televisión) on the Mexican Revolution and its aftermath. A one-hour version with English or French narration is available for purchase.
Size & Elements: Film: 35mm (2,802,000 feet, 2 completed titles and additional unedited footage; nitrate and safety negatives and positive master); 16mm (viewing copies). Videotape: 1" (masters); 3/4" (viewing copies) (primarily film transfers, 10% of collection).
Cataloging: Shot lists available for staff use.
Access: Open to researchers and scholars by appointment only. Available for duplication and reuse. Research fees charged. Research requests accepted by mail and in person (by appointment only). All duplication requests handled through Archive.
Rights: Full rights held to all material.
Licensing: Available for licensing and reuse. License fees charged, depending upon use and intended market.
Restrictions: Requests for reuse subject to written acceptance and approval. Material cannot be used for promotion of commercial products.
Viewing Facilities: Film (35mm); videotape (3/4").
Duplication Facilities: None.
Related Materials: Collection of vintage cameras and projectors (1900-20).

MEXICO, D.F.

CANAL 11
Instituto Politécnico Nacional
Secretaría de Educación Pública
Carpio 475
Casco de Santo Tomas
C.P. 11340 México, D.F.
541-33-40
541-18-50
Telex: 1777554 TV 11 MEX

Dr. Jorge Velasco (Director General)

Contact: Manuel Mendez (Jefe de la Division de Continuidad)
Services: Educational institution; television broadcaster. Programs and stock footage available for duplication and reuse. Camera crews and equipment available for rental if program being produced is educationally or culturally related.
Description: Canal 11 of the Instituto Politécnico Nacional (National Polytechnic Institute) was formed by the University in 1960 to help disseminate popular education and culture in Mexico. Produces educational and cultural television programs, broadcasting 16 hours a day in México, D.F. and the states of Hidalgo, México, Morelos and Veracruz.

Programs include: educational instruction; news coverage of Mexico, Central and South America; interview programs that present alternative views and opinions; coverage of amateur sports events; entertainment programs; and a wide variety of programs related to Mexican music, art, literature, theater and film. The Canal 11 archives encompass programs produced 1980-present, although some material from earlier periods is available. Due to limited resources, videotapes are often reused, and it is not always possible to preserve and archive programs and stock footage.
Size & Elements: Videotape: 2", 1" and 3/4" (2,000 hours; masters).
Cataloging: Cataloging in progress; staff assistance available.
Access: Programs and stock footage available for duplication and reuse. Research fees not charged. Requests accepted by mail; address requests to the Director of Canal 11, specifying needs and intended use.
Rights: Some rights held to some material. Staff can assist in obtaining additional rights clearances for materials held in the archives.
Licensing: Available for duplication, licensing and reuse. License fees charged, depending upon use.
Restrictions: Some restrictions apply. Requests for reuse subject to acceptance and approval.

Viewing Facilities: Videotape (3/4").
Duplication Facilities: Videotape (1", 3/4" and Betamax).

MEXICO, D.F.

CINETECA NACIONAL
Avenida México-Coyoacán 389
Colonia Xoco
C.P. 03330 México, D.F.
688-88-24
688-88-14

Lic. Fernando Macotela (Director de Cinematografía)

Contacts: Luz Fernandez de Alba (Subdirectora Cineteca Nacional); Cristina Felix (Jefe del Departamento de Documentación e Investigación); Mario Aguiñaga (Jefe del Departamento de Programación y Publicaciones); Salvador Alvarez (Jefe del Departamento de Control de Acervo)
Services: National film archives. Depository for feature films produced in Mexico. Selected materials available for duplication, reuse and resale; restricted to cultural uses. Feature-length fiction films distributed outside of Mexico by Azteca Films (q.v.) in Los Angeles.
Description: The Cineteca Nacional was created by the Mexican government in 1974 under the auspices of the Secretaría de Gobernación to collect, restore, preserve and exhibit Mexican films. The Cineteca is a member of the International Federation of Film Archives. The Mexican government first began organizing a national film archive in 1938 under the auspices of the Secretaría de Educación Pública, and later, under the Secretaría de Gobernación. In March 1982 a fire destroyed much of the Cineteca's film collection (6,506 films) and almost all documents (9,278 books and magazines and 2,300 scripts). Since then, there has been a major effort to rebuild the archives. Private collectors, film producers and archives from around the world have donated Mexican films to the collection.

Currently, the Cineteca holds 3,196 film titles. About half are Mexican feature-length films produced after 1960, primarily those produced after 1970; some titles date from the 1940s. The Cineteca has also transferred nitrate films previously held by the Archivo General de la Nación (National Archives) to 35mm safety film. Other titles held are foreign feature-length films for exhibition in Mexico.

The Cineteca also holds some shorts, newsreels and documentary films, most produced after 1970.

Operates a circulating library of classic Mexican and foreign feature and short films, available for rental by educational and cultural institutions.
Size & Elements: Film: 35mm (17,690,000 feet, 3,196 titles, 13,337 cans); 16mm (900,000 feet) (80% positive, 20% negative). Videotape: Betamax (3,140 titles).
Cataloging: Title lists available. Many collections have been cataloged by subject matter and personalities. Card catalog available for research in Cineteca research library. Staff assistance also available.
Access: Films in circulating library available for rental by educational and cultural institutions. Some material available for duplication and reuse. Research fees not charged. Research requests accepted by mail and in person (by appointment only).
Rights: Some rights held to some materials. Staff can assist in contacting producers who hold rights to the films deposited in the Cineteca.
Licensing: Some materials available for duplication and reuse. Usage fees not charged for cultural institutions within Mexico.
Restrictions: All requests subject to approval. Films rented to other archives and cultural institutions only.
Viewing Facilities: Film (35mm and 16mm).
Duplication Facilities: None.
Related Materials: Maintains a research library which includes posters, stills, lobby cards, unpublished screenplays, film files, film reviews, and film-related books and periodicals (1920s-present). The research library is open to researchers and scholars, and maintains an extensive reference service.

Research activities are supported and results published by the Cineteca, including: filmographies of Mexican cinema; scripts from newsreel collections, such as Cine Verde (1953-73); and logs of collections held by the Cineteca, such as the Miguel Alemán collection.

Also has four theaters and presents a minimum of 13 showings daily of films in its collection. In addition, the Cineteca spnsors film forums and film cycles for Mexican and foreign films and filmmakers.

The Cineteca maintains a bookstore for its publications and other books and periodicals about cinema, film-related topics and communications. The galleries of the Cineteca present exhibitions of posters and stills.

Publications: The Cineteca Nacional publishes books and monographs dealing with Mexican cinema, filmmakers, and actors and actresses, including the multi-volume works *Filmografía mexicana de medio y largo metrajes* and *Cuadernos de la Cineteca Nacional. Testimonios para la historia del cine mexicano.*

The Cineteca has an annual publication, *Memoria,* detailing its acquisitions and activities, including films exhibited during the year.
Representative: Azteca Films (q.v.) in Los Angeles is the foreign distributor of many films held by the Cineteca.

MEXICO, D.F.

FILMOTECA DE LA UNAM
San Idelfonso 43
Centro
C.P. 06020 Mexico, D.F.
522-40-97 (Ext. 243 or 244)
522-40-19 (Ext. 243 or 244)
522-41-50
522-41-91
522-46-65 (Director)
Telex: UNAME FILMOTECA 1777429

Professor Carlos Gonzales Morantes (Director de Actividades Cinematográficas de la UNAM)

Contact: Francisco Gaytan Fernandez (Curador de la Filmoteca)
Services: Government archives holding Mexico's major collection of fiction and non-fiction films. Film and videotape material available for research, duplication and reuse; some restrictions apply.
Description: Founded in 1960 under the auspices of the Universidad Nacional Autónoma de México (UNAM), the Filmoteca is Mexico's largest film archives, encompassing over 9,000 titles (fiction and non-fiction, 1896-present); the majority unavailable elsewhere. The Filmoteca has been active in locating, purchasing, preserving and restoring Mexico's cinematographic works for over 25 years.

The Filmoteca has Mexico's most comprehensive collection of silent fiction and non-fiction films, consisting of over 100 titles and thousands of fragments of works by Mexican cinematographers, and additional works by non-Mexicans.

The Paper Print collection includes short films and fragments of films of the Spanish-American-Cuban War (1898), by Thomas Edison and other early cinematographers.

Early non-fiction films highlight life in Mexico City and rural Mexico from 1896, when the earliest films were produced in Mexico; the political and social activities of Porfirio Diaz and his government; Mexico's bicentennial celebration in 1910; and the beginnings of the Mexican Revolution.

The collection is particularly strong in non-fiction films of the Mexican Revolution (1910-17), and includes footage by Mexican cinematographers Jesús Abítia, Enrique Rosas, the Alva brothers, and by other unidentified Mexican and U.S. cinematographers.

Holdings are also strong in silent newsreels and documentaries for theatrical release by Mexican cinematographers and by Pathé News, covering events and depicting life in Mexico (1917-31).

The Filmoteca holds the most important collection of Mexico's silent fiction films; feature-length and short films from 1896 until 1931, when sound was introduced into Mexican cinema. It has preserved such classics of Mexican silent cinema as *Santa* (1918, fragments; *Aniversario de la muerte de la suegra* (1912); *Tepeyac* (1918); *El puño de hierro* (1927); *El tren fantasma* (1928); and many others. It also holds some primitive French, Italian, and U.S. fiction and non-fiction films.

A major collection consists of the 35mm original negatives of Mexican sound newsreels produced for theatrical release (1940-74), including *Noticiero Mexicano* (EMA-España, México, Argentina) (1940-55); *El Mundo al Instante* (complete collection, 1950-74); *Cine Mundial;* and *Cinescopio*. Mexican newsreels covered important persons and events of the period; sports and cultural activities; and also included commercials, many for products of foreign companies. The sound newsreel collection also holds earlier Mexican and German newsreels from the 1930s.

Holds over 900 titles of Mexican feature-length fiction films (produced 1930-50); over half of these have been transferred to safety film. Many of these films are unavailable elsewhere and include classics of Mexican cinema. The collection also includes Spanish-language films produced in Hollywood in the 1930s; Argentine films (1940-60); more recent Mexican films (1950-70s); and some Uruguayan, Brazilian and Salvadoran films.

MEXICO

Other smaller collections consist of the documentary and fictional works of Michoacan filmmaker Garcia Urbizu (1920s); tourist and cultural films (1930-60, a few from the 1920s); promotional films of the Mexican government concerning the activities of the states of the Republic, including the series *Asi es México* (1940s); and home movies (1950s). Also held are 200 videotaped interviews with Mexican filmmakers.

Size & Elements: Film: 70mm, 35mm, 16mm and 9.5mm (over 9,000 titles and additional footage; 60% nitrate or safety negatives; 40% master positives). Videotape: 3/4" (400 titles, including 200 videotape transfers of films).

Cataloging: Published catalog of fiction film holdings available for public use and sale; card catalog and staff assistance available for other materials; computerized cataloging in progress.

Access: Open to researchers and scholars (by appointment only). Material available for duplication and reuse. Research fees charged. Research and footage requests accepted by mail, telephone and in person (by appointment only). Telephone requests must be followed by written request, which must include information on type of production, type of rights desired, and intended use of the material.

Rights: Some rights held to all material. Additional clearances may be necessary in some cases if material is to be reused.

Licensing: Available for duplication, reuse and resale. License fees charged, depending upon use and intended market for production.

Restrictions: Some restrictions apply to some materials.

Viewing Facilities: Film (35mm and 16mm); videotape (3/4").

Duplication Facilities: Film (black and white: 35mm and 16mm; color film contracted by archive to laboratory); videotape (all requests handled by contract through archives).

Related Materials: Production stills, scripts, posters, and some documents relating to film production in Mexico from the silent era to the 1970s.

Publications: *Pantalla,* a quarterly publication of the Dirección de Actividades Cinematográficas; *Veintecinco años de la Filmoteca de la UNAM (1960-1985),* a commemorative edition about the Filmoteca, including a list of the Mexican fiction films in its archives. Other books relating to film are published by UNAM.

MEXICO, D. F.

THE IMAGE BANK, MEXICO CITY
Oso. No. 41
Col. del Valle
Deleg. B. Juarez
03100 Mexico, D.F.
(905) 524-4644 (Where area code 905 is not valid, dial [52] plus [5].)
(905) 660-1528
(905) 534-6200
(905) 534-4581
Telex: 1760718

Contacts: Juan Carlos Pulido; Teresa Robert (Manager)
Territory: Mexico.
Services: Exclusive marketing agent for Film Search, Inc. (see Film Search, Inc., New York, N.Y.).

MEXICO, D.F.

IMAGEN Y SONIDO INDEPENDIENTE, S.A.
Saturnino Herron 35
Colonia San José Insurgentes
C.P. 03900 Mexico, D.F.
598-88-18
598-28-70

Eduardo Carrasco Z.
Hector Cervera G.

Contacts: Eduardo Carrasco Z.; Hector Cervera G.
Services: Film and videotape producer. Films, videotape programs and stock footage available for duplication, licensing and reuse.
Description: Independent production company producing non-fiction and narrative short subjects and feature-length films and videotapes for television and theatrical distribution (1976-present).

Holds documentaries on Mexico, Central America, Angola and Ethiopia; a weekly news interview program hosted by Luis Suarez (1977-85); several 10 and 13-week television series on Mexican and Latin American culture; a weekly series on science and technology (1980-82); a 38-week special on endangered species in Mexico; a weekly series on Mexican music concerts (1981-85); a 13-part series on history of Mexico through its music; a 35mm feature-length film, *Derrumbe* (1985), a fictional story of a security agent after the 1985 earthquake in Mexico; and industrials for governmental agencies and government-owned industries, such as PEMEX (Petroleos Mexicanos).

Stock footage relates to Afghanistan, Angola, Argentina, Belize, Brasil, Cambodia, Chile, Cuba, Ethiopia, Guatemala, Honduras, India, Mexico, Nicaragua, North Korea, Panama, the Soviet Union, Spain, Vietnam, Western Sahara; history; animal life; and personalities.

Size & Elements: Film: 35mm and 16mm (100 hours; 50% reversal; 50% negative). Videotape: 1" (200 hours); Betacam (amount unspecified); 3/4" (100 hours).

Cataloging: Published catalog available for completed programs and films; staff assistance available for stock shots.

Access: Open to researchers, scholars and the public (by appointment only). Available for duplication and reuse. Research fees not charged. Research requests accepted by mail, telephone and in person (by appointment only). Except for initial consultations, staff is unable to perform time-consuming research.

Rights: Full rights held to most material.

Licensing: Available for licensing and reuse. License fees determined by type of production and intended use and market.

Restrictions: Some restrictions apply.

Viewing Facilities: Film (16mm); videotape (3/4").

Duplication Facilities: Videotape (1", Betacam and 3/4").

MEXICO, D.F.

IMEVISION
Instituto Mexicano de Televisión
Periférico Sur 4121
Colonia Fuentes del Pedregal
C.P. 14141 México, D.F.
568-55-26
Telex: 1777642 TVNTME

Contacts: Ing. Fernando Rebollo Herrera (Subdirector de Videofilmotecas); Leonardo Cursio (Gerente de Contenidos)
Services: Government agency; videotape producer and broadcaster. Programs and stock footage available for duplication and reuse.
Description: Imevision (Instituto Mexicano de Televisión) was formed in 1968 to produce and develop programs for the government-owned television stations: Channel 13 (founded 1968), broadcasting nationally with programs designed for urban Mexico; Channel 22 (founded 1982), broadcasting Mexican and foreign films in the Federal District; and Channel 7 (founded 1986), broadcasting nationally with programs designed for rural Mexico.

The third largest television network broadcaster in Latin America, Imevision maintains an extensive film and videotape archives. In addition to programs produced by Imevision, collection includes over 18,000 rolls of Mexican newsreels (35mm) shown in Mexican theaters from 1950-68, including *Cine Verdad; Noticiero Mexicano* and *Noticiero Continental*. The newsreels contained news stories, coverage of political and special events, sports, culture and human interest stories gathered throughout the Mexican Republic.

Archives contains programs produced by Imevision (1968-present), including early 16mm productions (1968-73) by Canal 13 (Trecevision). Productions fall into five general categories: cultural, informational, entertainment, public service and educational; stressing Mexican culture, history, geography, personalities, national events, festivals, achievements, problems and Mexico in relation to other countries.

Collection is particularly strong in cultural programs, including productions and performances of music, dance, theater, art, literature, film and popular art; interview, biographical and documentary programs about Mexican musicians, artists, dancers, filmmakers, writers and poets. Also series on regional music, dance and traditions.

Dramatic series, comedies, children's programs, musicals, soap operas (1975-82), historical programs, specials, amateur sports events and news programs.

Children's programming includes instructional series on reading and writing, basic concepts of mathematics and science; fictional and animated films; theatrical works; puppet shows; national legends and stories; and children's talk shows and productions.

Historical programs about Mexico and Mexicans include a series of compilation films comprised of archival footage, documentaries, oral history interviews, dramatizations, and soap operas. A recent series, *Testimonios*

(1986) covers the Mexican Revolution of 1910-17.

News programs include daily news coverage, discussion programs analyzing events, all official activities of the president of Mexico, talk shows, round table discussions and documentaries. Other topics include women's roles in society, environmental issues, politics and amateur sports events.

Also included are instructional programs for adult literacy, agricultural practices, health and sanitation practices, regional customs and attractions.
Size & Elements: Film: 35mm (18,000 rolls); 16mm (amount unspecified). Videotape: 2" (22,500 videotapes); 1" (38,000 videotapes); 3/4" (over 150,000 videotapes).
Cataloging: Complete catalog of programs by title (published listing available); news programs by date; computerized subject list; staff assistance available.
Access: Open to researchers and scholars. Material available for duplication, reuse and resale. Research fees not charged. Research and footage requests accepted by mail, telephone, telex and in person (by appointment only). Except for initial consultations, staff is unable to perform time-consuming research requests, but outside researchers are welcomed.
Rights: Imevision holds all rights to about 60% of the material in its archives and partial rights for the remaining materials. Some additional clearances may be necessary (apply for information).
Licensing: Available for licensing and reuse. License fees charged depending upon intended use and market.
Restrictions: Requests for reuse subject to acceptance and approval.
Viewing Facilities: Film (16mm); videotape (1" and 3/4").
Duplication Facilities: Film (16mm, film-to-videotape transfers); videotape (1", 3/4", VHS and Betamax).

MEXICO, D.F.

INSTITUTO NACIONAL INDIGENISTA
ARCHIVO ETNOGRAFICO AUDIOVISUAL
Avenida Revolución 1227, 4º Piso
Colonia Alpes
C.P. 01010 México, D.F.
680-02-50
651-31-99 (Ext. 180)

Lic. Eduardo Ahued Ortega (Subdirector del Archivo Etnográfico Audiovisual del INI)

Contacts: Lic. Eduardo Ahued Ortega (Subdirector); Lic. Blanca Ornelas (Jefe de Oficina de Distribución)
Services: Government agency; film and videotape archives. Completed films, videotape programs, and stock footage available for duplication, research and reuse; subject to restrictions. Material cannot be used for commercial purposes.
Description: The Archivo Etnográfico Audiovisual of the Instituto Nacional Indigenista was created by the Mexican government in 1978 to promote and make known the cultural values of indigenous groups in Mexico. From 1978 to the present, the Archivo Etnográfico has systematically recorded and filmed the daily life and cultural manifestations of indigenous communities throughout Mexico. All projects involve close cooperation between filmmakers, anthropologists and community members.

Thirty-six ethnographic films have been completed to date, documenting the daily lives, cultures, ceremonies, dances, music and personal testamonies of the Mixe, Tepehuano, Totonaco, Mayo, Nahua, Tlapaneco, Zoque-Popoluca, Huichol, Pame, Otomíe, Chinanteco, Mazateco, Purépecha, Tepehua, Huasteco, Zapoteco, Tarahumara, Lacandón, Kikapú, Zoque and Xochimilcas. Footage also exists of other indigenous groups and of numerous multiethnic and mestizo ceremonies, such as El Día de los Muertos (Day of the Dead).
Size & Elements: Film: 35mm and 16mm (60,840 feet, 36 completed films; negative and positive masters and release prints; additional outtakes and unedited footage). Videotape: 3/4" (masters, edited titles and unedited footage).
Cataloging: Catalog of completed films and videotape programs available to public. All completed titles, outtakes and additional footage cataloged by subject, indigenous group, and stock shots; staff assistance available.
Access: Archive open to researchers and scholars (by appointment only). Material available for research and reuse. Requests for research and reuse of footage accepted by mail (address request to the Director of the Archive, stating the purpose and intended use of the material). Research fees not charged. Staff conducts all research and selects material for viewing. Requests also accepted by telephone and in person (by appointment only) if followed by a written request.
Rights: Full rights held to all material.
Licensing: Material available for duplication and reuse. License fees charged,

depending upon intended use.
Restrictions: Material can only be used for programs that promote the preservation and cultural values of indigenous groups, and cannot be used for advertising purposes. Permission of INI (including script approval) required for reuse of any material.
Viewing Facilities: Film (16mm); videotape (3/4").
Duplication Facilities: Videotape (3/4", VHS and Betamax). 1" videotape and film duplication handled by contract through the Archive.
Related Materials: Over 600 hours of original music of 48 indigenous groups from throughout Mexico, recorded on 1/4" audiotape. Listening facilities available for researchers and scholars. Available for reuse. Research requests accepted by mail through the director of the Archivo Etnográfico Audiovisual. For information, contact Jesus Herrera of the music department.

Thousands of still photographs (including 28,000 slides), of indigenous groups throughout Mexico. Some collections date back to the 1920s. Available for research, duplication and resale.

MEXICO, D.F.

LATINA, S.A. DE C.V.
Vicente García Torres 120
Colonia Barrio San Lucas
C.P. 04030 México, D.F.
689-13-37
549-72-25
549-77-24
Telex: (0230) 6503472147

Jorge Sanchez Sosa (Presidente)
Laura Ruiz G. (Gerente General)

Contact: Laura Ruiz G. (General Manager)
Services: Film and videotape distributor. Films available for rental and purchase. Staff can aid researchers in contacting filmmakers for footage and rights.
Description: International distributor of feature films by Mexico's foremost independent filmmakers (1965-present). Library includes feature-length fiction and non-fiction films, animated films, shorts and some television series.

Collection includes works by Paul Leduc, Felipe Cazals, Ariel Zuñiga, Hector Cervera, Oscar Mendez, Jose Luis Garcia Agraz, Alberto Cortes, Maria Novaro, Eduardo Carrasco, Raul Kamffer and Miguel Nicoechea, among others. Many of the films have received national and international awards. Documentaries about Argentina, El Salvador, Guatemala, India, Mexico, Nicaragua, Uruguay, Vietnam and a wide variety of ethnographic subjects; animated shorts on Mexican and Latin American history and politics. Television series include: *Los que hicieron nuestro cine* (61 videotape programs), on the history of Mexican film; and *De la vida de las mujeres* (25 videotape programs), on women in Mexican society.
Size & Elements: Film: 35mm and 16mm (positive, negative and release prints). Videotape: 1" and 3/4" (masters); VHS and Betamax (viewing copies). (100 titles total).
Cataloging: Catalog with description of all titles (available in English, French and Spanish).
Access: Maintained for distribution, rental and purchase outside Mexico. Staff can assist in contacting producers and production companies and in obtaining rights for clips or stock footage. Research fees charged. Requests for films and for other services accepted by mail, telephone, telex and in person (by appointment only).
Rights: Distribution rights held to all materials. Some clip or stock footage rights held.
Licensing: License fees charged (apply for rates).
Restrictions: Some restrictions may apply.
Viewing Facilities: Viewing copies of all materials available on VHS videotape.
Duplication Facilities: Film (all duplication handled by laboratories through distributor). Videotape (3/4", VHS and Betamax) (1" available through laboratory).

MEXICO, D.F.

NOTIMEX
Moreno 110 2º Piso
Colonia Del Valle
C.P. 03100 México, D.F.
687-05-00 (Exts. 201, 204, 217)

MEXICO

Telex: 01771162 or 01771084

Ing. Arturo Zamora B. (Jefe de Departamento T.V. NOTIMEX)

Contacts: Miguel A. Apeizaga P. (Productor T.V.); Carlos Ferreira H. (Continuista)
Services: Government agency; videotape producer; television broadcaster. Stock footage and edited news stories available for duplication and reuse. Offers program exchange with television stations outside Mexico.
Description: Notimex (Agencia Mexicana de Noticias) was formed in 1972 as the official news agency of the Mexican Government. Its newspaper, radio and television correspondents are located throughout Mexico and Latin America. Notimex produces videotape news stories and documentaries for government-owned television broadcasting stations and for other broadcasters in Mexico who wish to utilize them.

Archives include cut stories and stock footage of all official activities of Mexican presidents and of political developments in Mexico (1972-present); and in-depth coverage of rural and urban life throughout the Mexican Republic and the border areas, including the effects of U.S. immigration and economic policies on Mexico. Includes programs and footage from local television stations throughout Mexico. Extensive, in-depth coverage of political and cultural developments in Central America and the Caribbean (1980-present). Weekly cultural and political reports from South American television broadcasters.
Size & Elements: Film: 16mm (300 rolls, each 30 min.). Videotape: 3/4" (over 1,000 videotapes; masters).
Cataloging: Cataloged chronologically by news story; finding aids; staff assistance available.
Access: Archives open to researchers and scholars (by appointment only). Material available for duplication and reuse. Research fees not charged. Research and footage requests preferred by telephone, telex and in person (by appointment only). Must specify intended use for material.
Rights: Full rights held to all material.
Licensing: Available for licensing and reuse. License fees charged, depending upon material and intended use.
Restrictions: Requests for reuse subject to acceptance and approval.
Viewing Facilities: Videotape (3/4", VHS and Betamax); time-coded viewing copies available on request (fees charged).
Duplication Facilities: Videotape (3/4", VHS and Betamax).

MEXICO, D.F.

PROTELE, S.A.
Productora de Teleprogramas, S.A.
Doctor Rio de la Loza 196, 1° piso
Colonia Doctores
C.P. 06724 México, D.F.
761-40-66
761-56-61 (Director)
Fax: 5786108

C.P. Carlos Castro Acosta (Director General)

Contact: Sr. Oscar Gutierrez Centeno (Director de Ventas de Protele, S.A.)
Services: Represents all Televisa programs, except news and special events, for licensing and distribution within the Republic of Mexico. Duplicates all videotape formats. Subtitling service available in many languages and formats.
Description: Formed in 1965 by Televisa, S.A. to duplicate and preserve all programs produced for broadcast by Televisa. Programs held in Televisa's archives are available for duplication and reuse. Protele, S.A. licenses and distributes programs other than news and special events within Mexico. Licensing and distribution outside Mexico is handled by Protele, Inc. (q.v.) in Los Angeles. Televisa, S.A. (q.v.) licenses news and special events programs directly.

Programs represented by Protele include soap operas, comedies, dramatic series, variety shows, talk shows, and movies produced for television. Protele is also responsible for programming all Televisa broadcast stations and cable systems in the Republic of Mexico.
Size & Elements: Videotape: 2", 1", Betacam, 3/4" and Super VHS (500,000 titles; masters).
Cataloging: Computerized cataloging; staff assistance available.
Access: Available for duplication and reuse. Research fees not charged. Requests for programs and footage accepted by mail and fax.
Rights: Televisa holds all rights to most material in its archives. Additional clearances may be necessary in some cases if material is to be reused.

Licensing: Available for licensing and reuse. License fees charged, depending upon intended use.
Restrictions: Some restrictions apply to some materials.
Viewing Facilities: Videotape (2", 1" and 3/4").
Duplication Facilities: Film (35mm and 16mm; film-to-videotape transfers). Videotape (2", 1", Betacam, 3/4"; Super VHS and VHS). Standards conversions between NTSC, PAL and some types of SECAM. Subtitling service available in many languages and formats.

MEXICO, D.F.

REDES CINEVIDEO, S.A.
Prolongación Melchor Ocampo No. 660
Fraccionamento Pedregal de San Francisco
C.P. 04320 México, D.F.
554-92-34

Francis García (Producer)

Contact: Francis García
Services: Videotape producer. Videotape programs available for rental and purchase. Stock footage available for licensing and reuse.
Description: Independent videotape production company producing documentaries for Mexican television and independent distribution.

Programs and stock footage emphasize Mexican art, culture and customs. Includes interviews with prominent writers, artists and scientists of Mexico; popular art and culture; and indigenous customs, dances and ceremonies. Also documents ecological concerns throughout Mexico, including endangered species. Covers political issues in Mexico and exchanges material with correspondents throughout Latin America. Holds exclusive coverage of the presidential campaign of National Democratic Front leader Cuauhtémoc Cárdenas (1988).
Size & Elements: Videotape: 3/4" (50 hours; masters and viewing copies).
Cataloging: Published catalog of completed programs; finding aids; staff assistance available.
Access: Stock footage available for licensing and reuse; videotape programs available for rental and purchase. Research and footage requests accepted by mail (include information on the desired use, market, and on the nature of the production). Telephone requests accepted if followed by written request.
Rights: Full rights held to all materials.
Licensing: Available for licensing and reuse. Fees apply depending upon intended usage and market.
Restrictions: Any reuse of material requires prior approval.
Viewing Facilities: Videotape (3/4", VHS and Betamax).
Duplication Facilities: Videotape (3/4", VHS and Betamax).

MEXICO, D.F.

TELEVISA, S.A.
Dirección de Operaciones de Noticieros y Eventos
Avenida Chapultepec 28, 4° Piso
Colonia Doctores
C.P. 06724 México, D.F.
709-72-64
709-33-33 (Ext. 5764)
709-12-11
Fax: 7097776
Telex: 1772632 or 1760057

Javier Gonzalez (Director de Operaciones de Noticieros y Eventos)

Contacts: Javier Gonzalez; Ing. Manuel Ramirez; Lic. Alberto Sosa
Services: Television producer and broadcaster. Film and videotape material (news footage only) available for duplication and reuse through Televisa. Other television programs produced and broadcast by Televisa available for duplication and reuse through Protele, S.A. (q.v.). Some restrictions apply.
Description: Produces television programs and operates 40 local television stations and 83 cable systems throughout the Mexican Republic. Formed in 1965, Televisa is the largest television network broadcaster in Latin America. Maintains the largest television news archives in Latin America (1951-present), comprised of edited stories, outtakes and stock footage, including local coverage from affiliate stations; national and international political coverage; daily life and activities in Mexico; documentaries; special events (e.g., concerts, awards, visiting dignitaries in Mexico, contests and celebrations); regional, national and international sports events held in Mexico, including

World Cup Soccer, 1968 Olympics, and participation of Mexicans in regional and international sports events outside Mexico. Material from 1951-77 is on 16mm film; later material is on videotape.

Size & Elements: Film: 16mm (amount unspecified). Videotape: 2" (amount unspecified); 1" (30,737 titles in news archives; masters); Betacam (amount unspecified); 3/4" (35,400 titles in news archives; masters); Super VHS. Televisa archives contains approx. 500,000 titles total (masters).

Cataloging: Computerized catalog and shot lists; staff assistance available.

Access: Edited stories and stock footage available for duplication and reuse. Research fees charged. Research and footage requests preferred by telex, fax and telephone.

Rights: Full rights held to most material in the news and special events archive. Additional clearances may be necessary if some materials are to be reused.

Licensing: Available for licensing and reuse. License fees charged, depending upon intended use and market.

Restrictions: Some restrictions apply to some materials.

Viewing Facilities: Videotape (2", 1" and 3/4).

Duplication Facilities: Film (35mm and 16mm; transfers to videotape). Videotape (2", 1", Betacam, 3/4", Super VHS, and VHS). Standards conversions between NTSC, PAL and some types of SECAM are available.

Related Materials: A videotape containing information about facilities and contents of archives is available through Televisa's Departamento de Relaciones Públicas (Public Relations Department).

Representative: For Televisa programs other than news and special events contact Protele, S.A. (q.v.) in Mexico, D.F. (for use in Mexico) and Protele, Inc. (q.v.) in Los Angeles, California for use outside Mexico.

MEXICO, D.F.

TV-UNAM

Centro Cultural Universitario
Circuito Cultural Interior
Ciudad Universitaria
C.P. 04510 México, D.F.
573-85-69
Telex: 1777429 UNAMME

Sr. Héctor Covarrubias Vazquez (Director General de Television Universitaria)

Contacts: Sr. Fernando Chacón Torres (Subdirector de Producción); Lic. Pedro Javier Gutierrez (Jefe del Departamento de Producción); Lic. Luz María Graue Russek (Jefe del Departamento de Apoyo a Dependencias Universitarias)

Services: Educational institution; videotape producer. Programs and stock footage available for duplication and reuse.

Description: TV-UNAM was created in 1982 by the Universidad Nacional Autónoma de México (National University of Mexico) to produce programs in support of University teaching activities and to record University achievements and events. Shortly thereafter, TV-UNAM expanded to produce educational, cultural and informational programs for television broadcast throughout Mexico.

Collection is particularly strong in the areas of ecology, biological sciences, anthropology, literature, art and national culture from pre-Hispanic times to the present. Also strong in coverage of student movements throughout Mexico. About 15% of collection consists of programs produced 1982-85; and the remainder 1986-present.

Collection includes the series *Lo mejor de Presencia Universitaria,* discussions by the University community on relevant scientific, cultural, and research activities and how they relate to current events and national problems. Sample topics include: roundtable discussions on "Star Wars" and its implications for Mexico; contamination; events in other Latin American countries; employment problems and perspectives; archaeological finds; technological developments; mathematical and scientific discoveries and theories; Mexican art and literature; and architecture.

The on-going series *Desde la Universidad* consists of documentaries focusing on topics, activities and research at the University that affect the public interest. Includes programs on environmental issues facing Mexico City and Mexico as a nation; occupational health and safety; alternative energy sources; traditional and herbal medical practices; problems facing Mexican adolescents; industrialization of traditional industries in rural Mexico; implications of new biological and geological research; popular music, art and dance in Mexico; and migratory problems.

The ongoing series *Premios Universidad Nacional* features biographical sketches of University recipients of national and international awards and honors. In 1987, TV-UNAM produced a special series of five programs commemorating the 50 years of Radio UNAM.

The on-going documentary series *Prisma Universitario* shows part of the art, science, and technology world in historical perspective relevant to current events and activities. Covers diverse topics, including pre-Hispanic astronomy, urban music, popular poetry, children's games and toys, history of Mexican film, biographical sketches of educators, artists (including Mexican muralists), writers, musicians, alternative food and energy sources.

Videotapes for support of classroom instruction include programs on fieldwork throughout Mexico; documentaries about regions in Mexico and on events in other Latin American countries; and historical documentaries.

Size & Elements: Videotape: 3/4" (3,000 hours).

Cataloging: Computerized catalog; staff assistance available.

Access: Open to researchers and scholars (by appointment only). Programs and stock footage available for duplication, reuse and resale. Research fees charged. Research and footage requests accepted by mail and in person (by appointment only).

Rights: Full rights held to most material. Additional clearances may be necessary in some cases if material is to be reused. Staff assistance available.

Licensing: Available for licensing and reuse. License fees charged depending upon type of production and intended use.

Restrictions: Requests for reuse subject to acceptance and approval.

Viewing Facilities: Videotape (3/4").

Duplication Facilities: Videotape (3/4" and Betamax).

Publications: *Medios audiovisuales,* a quarterly publication on communications and television.

MEXICO, D.F.

ZAFRA, A.C.

Leonardo Da Vinci 82
Colonia Mixcoac
C.P. 03910 México, D.F.
563-25-93
563-07-09
Telex: Via New York (0230) 6503472147

Maria de la Luz Calzada (Directora)
Teresa Rodriguez (Directora)

Contacts: Maria de la Luz Calzada; Teresa Rodriguez

Services: Nonprofit organization; film producer and distributor. Some Mexican and Latin American films, film clips, and stock footage available for purchase outside Mexico, subject to restrictions.

Description: Zafra was organized in 1978 to aid independent filmmakers in Mexico and Latin America in distributing their feature-length and short films to non-commercial markets, and to promote these films among popular organizations, educational, cultural and nonprofit institutions, including community groups and labor unions in Mexico.

Collection is particularly strong in Mexican and Latin American documentaries. Today Zafra handles over 500 titles, including contemporary fiction films, documentaries and animated films from Mexico, Cuba, Brazil, El Salvador, Nicaragua and Guatemala. Also distributes some films by Sergei Eisenstein, Luis Buñuel, Paul Leduc and Miguel Littin; ethnographic films; classic Mexican films (1930s-40s); Soviet classics; and documentaries by U.S. independent filmmakers.

Size & Elements: Film: 16mm (over 100 titles; positive, negative, internegatives and release prints).

Cataloging: Published catalog (available on request); card catalog; staff assistance available.

Access: Open to researchers, scholars and the public. Collection maintained for rental to nonprofit organizations within Mexico, and for purchase outside Mexico. Staff can assist in contacting producers and production companies and in obtaining rights for clips or stock footage. Research fees charged. Requests for films and for other services accepted by mail, telephone, telex and in person.

Rights: Rights held in Mexico for non-commercial distribution and for purchase abroad. Some rights held to some material.

Licensing: Rental fees, licensing and usage fees charged depending upon nature of organization and intended use.

Restrictions: Some restrictions apply. Most films available for non-commercial use only.

Viewing Facilities: Film (16mm).

Duplication Facilities: Handled by distributor through laboratory.

BRITISH VIRGIN ISLANDS

BRITISH VIRGIN ISLANDS (Road Town, Tortola)

CARIBBEAN IMAGES, LTD.
P.O. Box 75
Road Town
Tortola, British Virgin Islands
(809) 495-2563
Fax: (809) 495-2541

U.S. mailing address: P.O. Box 4259, St. Thomas, VI 00801

David L. Mansfield (President)
Nan Wile (Production Coordinator)

Contacts: David L. Mansfield; Nan Wile
Services: Videotape producer; stock footage sales library.
Description: Specializing in underwater photography, the videotape library also includes Caribbean scenics, sailing, windsurfing, snorkeling, and wildlife. Other underwater footage includes shots of various fish, coral formations and general scuba diving from many parts of the world. Emphasizing ecology and conservation, other material covers dolphins, manatees (sea cows), sea horses, sharks, rays, underwater caves, submarines and more.
Size & Elements: Videotape: Betacam (amount unspecified).
Cataloging: Lists available.
Access: Available to the public for duplication and reuse. Research fees not charged. Research requests accepted by mail and telephone.
Rights: Full rights held to all material.
Licensing: Available for licensing, subject to restrictions. License fees charged.
Restrictions: Some restrictions may apply.
Viewing Facilities: Videotape (3/4" and 1/2").
Duplication Facilities: Videotape (for viewing: Betacam to 3/4" with time code; duplication fees charged); (for broadcast: Betacam to 1", Betacam and 3/4").
Related Materials: 35mm underwater still photographs.

CUBA

CUBA (Havana)

CINEMATECA DE CUBA
Calle 23 No. 1155
La Habana 4
Cuba
3-4719
30-50-41 (Ext. 341)
Telex: 511419 ICAIC CU

Services: Film archives.
Description: Founded in February 1960, the Cinemateca de Cuba (Cuban Film Archive) preserves Cuban films and a representative collection of Latin American and international films. Operates a film restoration laboratory. Exhibits a regular program of films from all countries and periods in the *Cine La Rampa*, its permanent screening room, as well as weekly screenings in 15 provincial capitals. Permanent member of FIAF (International Federation of Film Archives) and CLAIM (Coordinadora Latinoamericana de Archivos de Imágenes en Movimiento).
Size & Elements: Film: all formats (over 6,500 titles).
Cataloging: Apply for information.
Access: Apply for information.
Rights: Apply for information.
Licensing: Apply for information.
Restrictions: Apply for information.
Viewing Facilities: Film (theater on premises).
Duplication Facilities: Film (laboratory on premises; other facilities exist at ICAIC [Instituto Cubano del Cine]).
Related Materials: Books, periodicals, photographs, posters, promotional materials and equipment.
Publications: *Guía Temática del Cine Cubano (Producción ICAIC) 1959-1980* (1983), listing Cuban films, directors, production dates and brief synopses.

CUBA (Havana)

INSTITUTO CUBANO DE RADIO Y TELEVISION (ICRT)
CENTRO DE DOCUMENTACION DEL ICRT
(CUBAN INSTITUTE OF RADIO AND TELEVISION
CENTER FOR DOCUMENTATION AND INFORMATION)
Calle P y 23
Habana 4
Cuba
30-9656, 3-6048
Telex: 51 16 13 ICRT CU

Carlos Roberto Garcia (Director)
Alberto Martinez Martinez (Representative to FIAF and FIAT)

Contact: Alfredo Pereira (International Relations Department)
Services: Government agency; film and videotape archive. Material available for research, distribution, broadcast and reuse, subject to restrictions.
Description: The Center's parent organization is ICRT, a radio and television broadcaster, library and program distributor. The Center was established by the Cuban government in 1976 to organize moving image collections from Cuban television stations and to compile all information relating to television and its history.
Holds films (1920-present) and videotapes (1970-present). Special strengths of the archive include documentation of the history and development of Cuban television (1950-present) and the history of the Cuban revolution.
Television archives. Holds programs from the beginning of television broadcasting in Cuba (1950-present). Materials dating from before the revolution (pre-1959) originate mostly from other countries, and include serials, soap operas, cartoons, music programs, sports, fiction films and newsreels. Holdings include American programs aired in Cuba, such as *Bat Masterson* and *Highway Patrol*. All television programming prior to 1970 was originated on film and is held in film or kinescope form.
Materials (1959-present) emphasize Cuban productions, including children's programs, dramas, comedies, musicals, news and sports. The archives also hold news and sports programs acquired from other countries, including programs from other socialist countries, an abundance of dramatic, cultural and musical programs and soap operas from Mexico; and United Nations material. Due to the Latin American Film Festival which has been held in Havana (1978-present), and the inclusion of video exhibition beginning in 1986, Cuban TV has recently been acquiring programs produced by other television stations and independent producers from other Latin American countries, West Germany, Spain, Sweden, France and Italy.
The archive encompasses several distinct videotape and film libraries belonging to ICRT, all overseen by the Center.
Videotape libraries. Channel 6 (1" and 3/4" videotape). Channel 6 produces most Cuban entertainment programming. Library of entertainment programs, primarily produced in Cuba, including soap operas, musical programs, children's programs, movies, dance, game shows, cartoons and situation comedies; some holdings of programs received by exchange with other countries.
Channel 2. Channel 2 produces all news and sports coverage for Cuban television, whether national and international. Holds two videotape libraries. One includes news material produced for *Noticiero Nacional de TV (NTV)*, Cuba's primary evening news program aired nightly on channels 2 and 6; the other includes all other programming produced for channel 2, primarily sports but also documentary, musical and drama programs. Holds programming from Cuba and other countries.
Dirección de Video y Cinematografico. Videotape library held by division (founded 1970) responsible for purchasing and analyzing foreign-made films and videotapes for broadcast on Cuban television.
Film libraries. Estudios Cinematograficos (16mm, negatives and positives, color and black and white). Film library maintained by producer of 16mm documentaries, short films and cartoons for television broadcast. Holds all 16mm films produced at Cuban television studios. Programs include Cuban fiction television shows and "commentaries." A laboratory is maintained at the production facility.
Channel 2 (1920-present, mostly 16mm, color and black and white). Holds two separate film archives, presently housed in separate buildings. Holds many historic and newsworthy materials dating back to 1920. Television program materials (1950-68) are held in kinescope form.
Dirección de Video y Cinematografico. Film library holds copies of fiction films, cartoons and documentaries produced before and after the Cuban revolution. Many American feature films whch were shown before the

revolution are held, such as *Casablanca*.

Note: The Council of the State archives, not part of ICRT, holds moving image material relating to Fidel Castro. This material carries special restrictions; arrangements for research at this archives must be made separately with this organization.

Size & Elements: Film: 35mm and 16mm (amount unknown; original negatives, reversal originals, release prints, many 16mm kinescopes; 80% black and white, 20% color). Videotape: 2", 1" (NEC), 3/4" (amount unknown; masters and viewing copies).

Cataloging: Card catalog; computerized cataloging for staff use and for researchers is presently being established.

Access: Available for rental, broadcast, research, duplication and reuse, subject to restrictions. Research or consultation fees not charged. Requests accepted by mail, telephone and telex to the International Relations Department. Representative will then relay requests to the Center and arrange viewing appointments or meetings with individual archivists and historians connected with the Center.

Rights: Rights to all ICRT-produced materials held by ICRT; reuse must be cleared through INTER-TV (see below). Rights to materials from other Latin American and North American countries retained by individual governments and/or producers. Rights to coproductions shared by coproducing agencies. Additional clearances are necessary for reuse of any materials relating to Pres. Fidel Castro or the Cuban military.

Licensing: Available for rental, broadcast, licensing and reuse, subject to restrictions. Cuban materials must be licensed through INTER-TV, 19 y K, Vedado, Habana 4, Cuba; 32-1746, 32-7571, 32-7572; Telex 511600 TVC-CU (contact Mario Martinez). License fees charged (fees vary depending upon intended market for production, whether commercial or independent, and size of production budget). Clients are responsible for all duplication costs; prices are fixed according to the rates applying in other countries at the time of negotiation.

Restrictions: Reuse of Cuban materials requires clearance from INTER-TV, including a review of the proposed production or research project. Individual restrictions may apply to specific contracts.

Viewing Facilities: Film (35mm and 16mm screening rooms); videotape (3/4").

Duplication Facilities: Film (16mm, color and black and white); videotape (1" and 3/4").

Publications: *Video Latinoamericano,* a bimonthly bulletin, reviewing current national and international communications news and events.

Related Materials: Center maintains a library of books, publications and specialized magazines spanning the past 30 years, relating to the development of television throughout the world, particularly in Cuba and Latin America.

Research & Resources

This section lists individual researchers, research organizations and information resources. All information was supplied by the individuals and organizations themselves.

ALABAMA (Montgomery)

AEROFILM
P.O. Box 230035
Montgomery, AL 36123-0035
(205) 279-0182

Contact: Phil Stewart
Services: Film and video research.
Expertise & Interests: Aviation (1906-45). Has cataloged aviation material available in the Library of Congress and the National Archives.
Credits: *Aviation in the News* (6-hour newsreel footage compilation on World War II aviation; producer, director and researcher); research on film footage of the first German jet (ME-262); research for Atlantic Sound & Video Co.

CALIFORNIA (Berkeley)

MARK KITCHELL
KITCHELL FILMS
2600 10th Street
Berkeley, CA 94710
(415) 841-5050

Services: Film and video research.
Expertise & Interests: Footage relating to the 1960s, especially with regard to the San Francisco Bay Area.
Credits: *Berkeley in the 60's* (documentary film in progress; director).

CALIFORNIA (Los Angeles Metro)

WENDY BARTLETT BAILEY
14401 Villa Woods Place
Pacific Palisades, CA 90272
(213) 454-0351 (office)
(213) 454-4713 (home)

Services: Film and video research; film and video production.
Expertise & Interests: Space footage; footage (1950-65); aviation footage; *Greatest Headlines* series. Languages: French.
Credits: *Private Eyes Never Die* (Bruce Cohn Productions; stock footage researcher); *Unsolved Mysteries* (Cosgrove-Meurer Productions for NBC; segment producer); *Spacecamp* (ABC Motion Pictures; production supervisor and stock footage researcher); *That's Incredible!* (Alan Landsburg Productions; associate producer and film researcher); *Life's Most Embarrassing Moments* (Alan Landsburg Productions; segment producer and stock footage researcher); and others.

DEBORAH L. BOCK
415 San Vicente Boulevard, Apartment 11
Santa Monica, CA 90402
(213) 458-3455

Services: Film and video research; rights and clearances.
Expertise & Interests: Feature film clearances and newsreel research; history; art; social sciences. M.A. in Asian/Asian-American history.
Credits: *Murder or Mercy: Five American Families* (Dave Bell Associates for HBO; coordinating producer); *50 Years of Action!* (Directors Guild of America; associate producer); *The History of the Writers Guild* (Writers Guild of America West; associate producer); *Pearls* (PBS; producer); *Ripley's Believe It or Not!* (Columbia Pictures TV for ABC; film researcher); numerous freelance film and story research projects.

DREW BROWN
13030 Valleyheart Drive, Apartment 333
Studio City, CA 91604
(818) 905-1348

Services: Film and video research; film and video production; rights and clearances.
Expertise & Interests: General subjects; historical and entertainment footage; rights and clearances.
Credits: *Wilton North Report* (Fox Broadcasting; associate producer); *Isaac Asimov's Voyage to the Outer Planets* (Today Home Entertainment; producer and director); *Motown on Showtime* (Motown Productions; segment producer); *Return to the Titanic* (Westgate Productions; film research supervisor); *All Star Salute to Martin Luther King, Jr.* (Stevie Wonder Productions; film research supervisor); *USA for Africa — A Year of Giving* (Kragen Productions; film research supervisor); *Grammy Awards* (Pierre Cossette Productions; film research supervisor).

GREAT AMERICAN STOCK
420 Bond Street
Redlands, CA 92373
(714) 793-1903
Fax: (714) 793-9391 (by appointment only)

Contacts: Susan Haven Scheer (President); Dee Ann Dart
Services: Film and video research; film and video production; government/military liaison work.
Expertise & Interests: Military and aerospace material; historical newsreels; West Coast sources.
Credits: *The Nuclear Age* (WGBH; researcher); *The War in Korea* (BBC; researcher); *Dear America: Letters Home From Vietnam* (The Couturie Co.; researcher); *Vietnam: A Television History* (WGBH; researcher); *Reaching for the Skies* (aviation history series produced by John Gau Prods. for the BBC; researcher); *Vietnam: Lessons of a Lost War* (NBC; researcher).

MARIA GROUMBOS
4007 Ocean Front Walk
Marina Del Rey, CA 90292
(213) 301-9922

Services: Film and video research; technical consulting.
Expertise & Interests: Film-to-videotape mastering; digital sound and video mastering and duplication; location and technical evaluation of film and sound elements; computer colorization; post-production video coordination.
Credits: The Criterion Collection (40 laser videodiscs, including *2001: A Space Odyssey*, *Blade Runner*, *The Wizard of Oz*, and *West Side Story*; technical supervisor); Republic Pictures, Color Systems Technology, Time-Life Films, Home Box Office and American Film Technologies (technical consultant).

JAY R. HEIT
6181 Glen Oak
Los Angeles, CA 90068
(213) 467-3214

Services: Film and video research; film and video production.
Expertise & Interests: General subjects.
Credits: *Ripley's Believe It or Not!* (producer); *The Travel Channel* (producer); *Supercarrier* (stock footage coordinator); *Beverly Hills Cop I* and *II* (script researcher).

BRUCE HENSTELL
2617 Third Street
Santa Monica, CA 90405
(213) 392-2930

Services: Film, video and still photograph research; film and video production.
Expertise & Interests: Historical material, especially with regard to Southern California.
Credits: California Historical Society (former photographic librarian); Daily News, Special Collections, UCLA (director of research); KCET-TV (producer and correspondent); KCBS-TV (producer and writer); *Los Angeles History Series* (KCET-TV; consultant).

ALICE F. KUHNS
523 North Lucerne Boulevard
Los Angeles, CA 90004
(213) 466-3728

Services: Film and video research.
Expertise & Interests: Art; history; business.
Credits: *Pee Wee's Playhouse* (stock footage researcher); *Expo '88* (Panther Productions; stock footage researcher).

TRACEY LEIS
9022 Harratt Street, Apartment 5
West Hollywood, CA 90069
(213) 859-0659

Services: Film, video and still photograph research.
Expertise & Interests: Historical events; politics; current events; sports; health; San Francisco Bay Area.
Credits: *Secret Intelligence* (KCET for PBS; researcher and production assistant); *A Silent Cry* (Lifetime Cable; researcher).

LESLIE LEITNER
7219 Hampton, Apartment 19
Los Angeles, CA 90046
(213) 851-0583

Services: Film, video and still photograph research; post-production supervision.
Expertise & Interests: General topics.
Credits: *True Stories* (Pressman Films; photo and clip research coordinator); *A Year in the Life* (Universal Studios; post-production supervisor and footage researcher).

MILLER-GREGSON PRODUCTIONS
14827 Ventura Boulevard, Suite 207
Sherman Oaks, CA 91403
(818) 783-1445

4211 Laurel Canyon Boulevard, Apartment 306
Studio City, CA 91604
(818) 980-3562

Contact: Barbara Gregson
Services: Film, video and text research.
Expertise & Interests: Historical and current subjects. Has modem and CD-ROM drive.
Credits: *Around the World in 80 Days* (Harmony Gold; stock footage research); *Jackie Gleason: The Great One* (Viacom; director of research); *Mr. President* (Carson Productions; research); *L.A. Olympic Festival Bid Film* (David Wolper/Robert Guenette; director of film research); *The Witches of Eastwick* (Warner Bros.; film research); *Women of Valor* (InterPlanetary/Jeni Productions; film research); *To Heal a Nation* (Worldwide Media; film research); *Ripley's Believe It or Not!* (Columbia Pictures TV; film research); eight documentaries for HBO.

MICHAEL OCHS
MICHAEL OCHS ARCHIVES
524 Victoria Avenue
Venice, CA 90291
(213) 306-6111

Services: Music coordination; still photograph research. Operates still photograph archives containing pictures of musicians and music-related subjects.
Expertise & Interests: Music and musicians.
Credits: *Christine* (Columbia Pictures; music coordinator); *Losin' It* (Embassy Pictures; source music); *Liar's Moon* (Crown International; music director); *The Rose* (20th Century-Fox; set decorations).

BARRY M. PARKER
1155 Hacienda Place #310
West Hollywood, CA 90069
(213) 656-0719

Services: Film and video research.
Expertise & Interests: Historical research for miniseries, docudramas, documentaries and sports programming.
Credits: *The Wonder Years* (New World Television; video coordinator); *Robert Kennedy and His Times* (Columbia Pictures TV miniseries; film research); *Mussolini: The Untold Story* (Trian Productions; film research); *Homefront* (PBS; film research); *Hoover* (Finnegan Associates for Showtime; film research); *Wartime in Washington* (PBS).

THE ROGER RICHMAN AGENCY
9777 Wilshire Boulevard, Suite 815
Beverly Hills, CA 90212-1908
(213) 276-7000
Telex: 298793 RRA

Roger Richman (President)

Contact: Roger Richman
Services: Licensing agent. Represents celebrities and their estates for all licensing, conveying the "right of publicity" for advertising campaigns, merchandising, look-alike and sound-alike services, premiums and promotions. Exclusive licenses are available to use the names, voices, signatures and likenesses of internationally famous celebrities.
    Celebrities represented include: Edie Adams, Louis Armstrong, Clara Bow, Charlie Chaplin, Bing Crosby, Marlene Dietrich, Jimmy Durante, Albert Einstein, W. C. Fields, John Ford, Sigmund Freud, Clark Gable, John Garfield, Judy Garland, Betty Grable, Rita Hayworth, Al Jolson, Boris Karloff, Dorothy Lamour, Harold Lloyd, Carole Lombard, Sophia Loren, Bela Lugosi, The Marx Brothers, Marilyn Monroe, William Powell, Gloria Swanson, Jim Thorpe, Rudolph Valentino, Jack Webb, Mae West and Johnny Weismuller.

JEREMY ROSS
137 North Sycamore Avenue, Apartment 4
Los Angeles, CA 90036
(213) 931-7993

Services: Film, video and still image research; film and video production.
Expertise & Interests: Sports; aerials; time-lapse; National Archives; weather; World War II-era Germany; still photography; computer-enhanced films from satellite imagery.
Credits: *Spirit* (U.S. Information Agency; producer and researcher); *California Star Tours* (State of California; producer and researcher); *California Information Kiosk* (State of California; producer and researcher); *Pee Wee's Playhouse* (researcher).

PATRICIA RUSSELL
617 25th Street
Manhattan Beach, CA 90266
(213) 545-5469 (office)
(213) 545-8807 (home)

Services: Film, video and arts research; rights and clearances.
Expertise & Interests: Acquisition and rights negotiations; clearances; domestic and international experience.
Credits: *The West of the Imagination* (InCA for KERA-TV; art acquisition and business manager); *We the People* (InCA for KQED; archive researcher); assorted promos.

HOLLAND SUTTON
2342 20th Street
Santa Monica, CA 90405
(213) 452-1209

Services: Film, video and still photograph research; rights and clearances.
Expertise & Interests: Not specified.
Credits: *True Stories* (Pressman Films; photo researcher); *True Stories* (book; coordinator).

MICHAEL TOMPANE
3456 Greenfield Avenue
Los Angeles, CA 90034
(213) 559-4069

Services: Film and video research; film and video editing.
Expertise & Interests: Historical and newsreel footage; documentary and dramatic editing.
Credits: *Nitti: The Enforcer* (Leonard Hill Productions; editor and research supervisor); other credits available on request.

CYNDY TURNAGE
119 Brooks Avenue
Venice, CA 90291
(213) 399-2272

Services: Film, video, still photograph, library and public records research; writing consultant; film and video production.
Expertise & Interests: Film and television history, theory and production; local history; Los Angeles history; research interviews. MFA, Motion Pictures and Television, UCLA.
Credits: *Footage 89* (West Coast researcher); *California Gold: Stories of Two Women* (director and co-writer); *Brecht Meets HUAC* (play; co-writer and director); *Year One of the Empire* (play; assistant director); *Chicago*

Conspiracy Trial (play; assistant director); television miniseries on Nicaragua (Avnet-Kerner Company; researcher); *Controlling Interest* (California Newsreel; researcher).

JACQUI ZAMBRANO
21 Ozone Avenue
Venice, CA 90291
(213) 396-9757

Services: Film and video research; textual and library research for writers; writing; interviewing.
Expertise & Interests: General subjects; travel research; interviewing.
Credits: *Tour of Duty* (New World TV; staff researcher); Universal Pictures (Robert DeNiro feature film in progress; researcher); *Dian Fossey Movie of the Week* (Heritage Entertainment; researcher); *The Killing of America* (Toho Company; footage researcher).

CALIFORNIA (Oakland)

NATIONAL EDUCATIONAL VIDEO EXCHANGE
c/o Peralta Community College District
333 East Eighth Street
Oakland, CA 94606
(415) 466-7267
(415) 466-7268

Roger Ferragallo (Director of Telecommunications)

Contact: Roger Ferragallo
Services: Computerized database and information clearinghouse. Provides referrals to community colleges that have produced videotapes. Services available to the public. *Clearinghouse only; not a footage source.*
Description: Computerized database and information clearinghouse, identifying and cataloging non-commercial videotape materials produced by colleges and universities. Database includes single-concept serial instructional videotapes, telecourses, and generic videotapes suitable for ITFS and cablecasting on educational channels. The purpose of the Exchange is to facilitate the sharing of programs among users and producers of educational videotapes.
Size & Elements: Currently lists 3,200 videotapes; most are instructional. Approximately 20% are generic videotapes suitable for cablecasting.
Cataloging: Database maintained in DBase III programming language; published catalog (*1989 National Educational Video Exchange Directory*).
Access: Services available to the public. Research requests accepted by telephone.
Publications: *1989 National Educational Video Exchange Directory,* listing over 3,200 videotapes and their producers.

CALIFORNIA (Palo Alto)

PETER MARESCA
450 Monroe Drive
Palo Alto, CA 94306
(415) 941-1143

Services: Film and video research; film and video production; writing.
Expertise & Interests: Corporate video presentations; videodiscs; specializes in humorous and entertaining presentations.
Credits: *Lincoln Center for the Performing Arts 25th Anniversary Celebration* (writer and researcher); *Comedy Tonight* (syndicated television show; writer, segment producer and researcher); *True Stories* (researcher); Apple Computer videodiscs (producer); corporate presentations for Levi Strauss, Apple Computer, Hewlett-Packard, Shaklee Corporation and others.

CALIFORNIA (San Francisco)

SUSAN BELLOWS
581 Noe Street
San Francisco, CA 94114
(415) 552-8150

Services: Film and video research; film and video production.
Expertise & Interests: General subjects.
Credits: *The Blessings of Liberty* (ABC News; production assistant); *Racism 101* (Thomas Lennon Productions for PBS *Frontline*; associate producer);

Secret Intelligence (KCET for PBS; associate producer).

ALISON L. GIBSON
500 8th Street
San Francisco, CA 94103
(415) 553-2135
Fax: (415) 553-2241
Telex: UQ 9103726609 (KQED SFO)

Services: Film and video research; film and video production.
Expertise & Interests: Cultural programs (opera, symphony, ballet); historical; foreign languages; rights and clearances.
Credits: *Over Easy; Pavarotti Live in San Francisco; The San Francisco Symphony Opening Gala; Secrets of a Desert Sea; Untitled Work; A Piece of Cake; Comedy Tonight; Return of the Great Whales; The Animators; The Messiah; A.C.T.: The Training of an Actor; Superstitions; 1984 Opera in the Park; Lew Christiensen Biography; 1985 Chinese New Year's Parade; The Voice of Tango* (For all, production coordinator or associate producer; research/production of historical segments; footage researcher; rights and clearances).

R. C. RAACK
520 Connecticut Street
San Francisco, CA 94107
(415) 647-2096
(415) 881-3207

Services: Film and video research; film and video production.
Expertise & Interests: Historical. Foreign languages: French, Russian, Polish, German.
Credits: *Goodbye, Billy: America Goes to War, 1917-1918* (Cadre Films; producer and researcher); *The Frozen War: America Intervenes in Russia, 1918-1920* (Cadre Films; producer and researcher); *Storm of Fire: World War II and the Destruction of Dresden* (Cadre Films; producer, researcher and editor); *The Struggles for Poland* (Channel 4 UK; film consultant); *Der Letzte Tag (8 May 1945)* (ZDF West Germany; film consultant).

STIMULUS IMAGE RESEARCH
P.O. Box 11621
San Francisco, CA 94101
(415) 558-8339

Contact: Grant Johnson
Services: Film, video and computer graphics research; computer graphics and animation production.
Expertise & Interests: Computer graphics; LANDSAT imagery and image processing; computer-generated animation; government agencies (NASA, U.S. Geological Survey, Dept. of Defense, Defense Nuclear Agency, National Center for Atmospheric Research); space sciences; planetary exploration; earth sciences; geophysics.
Credits: La Musée de la Villette — La Cité des Sciences et de l'Industrie (France; researcher and supplier of material for exhibits on space exploration and earth sciences); National Geographic.

STOCK SEARCH/STOCK LOG
MEDIA MANAGEMENT SYSTEMS
1850 Union Street, Suite 267
San Francisco, CA 94123
(415) 883-8262
(415) 332-4172

Jackie Baldwin and Del Penny (Co-Owners)

Contacts: Jackie Baldwin; Del Penny
Services: Database of film and videotape stock footage and still photograph sources; audiovisual library organization service.
Description: Stock Search is a national computerized database clearinghouse offering instant search and retrieval for stock footage and still photographs. It contains listings of stock footage and stills available from thousands of established stock libraries, independent producers, corporations, universities and private collectors. The listings cover all subjects and time periods. Extensively researched specialty areas include: scenics (U.S. and worldwide); wildlife; sports; historical; and public domain. Clients are furnished with complete information about all sources, including licensing fees. Extended research is available upon request.

CALIFORNIA (San Rafael)

Stock Log is a complete audiovisual library organization service that categorizes and logs the contents of large and small libraries into searchable databases for instant retrieval. It also offers personnel training and continued maintenance and support.

CALIFORNIA (San Rafael)

HELEN WEISS
P.O. Box 1281
San Rafael, CA 94915
(415) 332-5947

Services: Film and video research; film and video production.
Expertise & Interests: Documentary producer and researcher for public television, educational, governmental and community cable programming. Has conducted on-site research at over 50 archives in the U.S., Canada, Hungary, Mexico, Colombia and the Soviet Union. B.A. in journalism and Spanish literature; M.A. in Third World history, with concentration in oral history. Languages: Spanish and Portuguese.
Credits: *The Dragon and the Eagle* (series for PBS); *Leo Szilard: Peace Provocateur in the Atomic Age* (PBS); *Kenya Safari: The Essence of Africa; Equality, Development and Peace: Visions From Nairobi;* various cable television news programs on environmental issues.

DISTRICT OF COLUMBIA METRO

EDDIE BECKER & KAREN GLYNN
1844 Mintwood Place, NW
Washington, DC 20009
(202) 332-1000

Services: Film and video research; documentation; photography.
Expertise & Interests: Historical; diplomatic; military; presidential; public domain footage.
Credits: *Frontline: Crisis in Central America* (WGBH; research and documentation); *De Peliculas* (Center for the Study of Filmed History; research and photography); *Korean War Series* (Thames Television; research and photography).

JOYCE COMPTON
1346 Rittenhouse Street, NW
Washington, DC 20011
(202) 726-1650

1274 First Avenue, Apartment 22
New York, NY 10021
(212) 744-0561

Services: Film and video research, editing and production.
Expertise & Interests: Fox Movietone News collection (including holdings in New York and South Carolina); historical subjects; women's sports.
Credits: *Lowell Thomas Remembers* (series of historical documentaries made from Fox Movietone footage; associate producer, researcher and editor); numerous television films, including *Blood Feud* and *Hoffa; Wall Street Week;* formerly archivist for Fox Movietone collection at University of South Carolina.

JOY CONLEY
MEDIA RESEARCH ASSOCIATES, INC.
502 Greenbrier Drive
Silver Spring, MD 20910
(301) 585-2400

Services: Film, video and still photograph research.
Expertise & Interests: General research topics; American and world history; public domain and commercial film and photograph sources.
Credits: *The Story of MIT's Radiation Laboratory* (WGBH, *NOVA*); *Why Hitler Lost* (Varied Directions); *The Modern Presidency* (documentary series for Simon & Schuster); *1964 in Review* (IBM Corp.); *Charlie Brown's History of America* (Mendelson Productions).

SALLY EVANS
2330 North Jackson Street
Arlington, VA 22201
(703) 527-3821

Services: Film, video and still photograph research.
Expertise & Interests: Public domain sources; collections and libraries throughout the U.S.; copyright research; rights negotiations. Thirteen years of experience at the National Archives, Library of Congress, Department of Defense and other Washington, D.C. sources.
Credits: *Munich 1938* (Brook Productions for Thames TV); *The Korean War* (series for Thames TV); *Frontline: In the Shadow of the Capitol* (WGBH); *The Nuclear Age: Proliferation* (WGBH); *Defense of the West* (series for ZDF West Germany); and *The A to Z of C&W* (series for Channel 4, London).

KATHARINE KING
871 Dolley Madison Boulevard
McLean, VA 22102
(703) 356-5439

Services: Film and video research; film and video production; writing.
Expertise & Interests: World War II; Vietnam War; women's aviation; pre-World War II newsreels; NASA footage; daring cameramen; floods and devastation. Foreign languages: French and Spanish.
Credits: *Cameramen Who Dared* (*National Geographic Explorer;* associate producer); *The Great Space Race* (Pacific Productions; researcher and writer); *Silver Wings and Santiago Blue* (King Productions; producer); *Memories of a Golden Age* (National Air & Space Museum; researcher); *The Johnstown Flood* (National Park Service; researcher).

LAURA A. KREISS
11323 Commonwealth Drive, Apartment 204
Rockville, MD 20852
(301) 468-6899

Services: Film, video and still photograph research.
Expertise & Interests: Washington, D.C.-area collections, including Smithsonian Institution; National Institutes of Health; national and international audiovisual archives; historical and contemporary photography process and formats.
Credits: Smithsonian Institution Photographic Survey Project (four years); National Institutes of Health (archivist).

BECKY LAUER
1771 N Street, NW
Washington, DC 20036
(202) 429-5374

Services: Film and video research; film and video production. Can assemble freelance production crews.
Expertise & Interests: News; history of broadcasting.
Credits: National Association of Broadcasters (associate producer).

JOSEF LUSTIG
4000 Tunlaw Road, NW
Washington, DC 20007
(301) 564-1585
Fax: (301) 530-7393

Services: Film and still photograph research.
Expertise & Interests: Modern history; Eastern and Central Europe; World War II; the Holocaust; Cold War; international relations; aviation; weapons; scientific advances; film history; travel. Languages: German, Russian, Czech, Serbo-Croatian, Polish, Italian, French and Spanish.
Credits: *My Dinner With Abbey* (Cohen-Katzman Productions; researcher); *Partisans of Vilna* (The Ciesla Foundation; researcher); *The Precious Legacy* (Philip Morris Inc.; assistant director); *Mafia on Trial* (WCVB-TV; researcher); *Chronicle of the Lodz Ghetto* (Jewish Heritage Writing Project and CPB; researcher); *The Global Rivals* (Antelope Films, Ltd. and WNET; researcher); *Arab and Jew* (Robert Gardner Associates; associate producer and researcher). Film and photo researcher for U.S. Holocaust Memorial Council, Washington, D.C. and Museum of Jewish Heritage, New York.

JENIFER MILLSTONE
Box 118
Garrett Park, MD 20896
(301) 933-4924
Telex: 4998104 TELLINK

Services: Film and video research; film and video production; editing; rights

and clearances.
Expertise & Interests: England; Israel; rights and clearances.
Credits: *Shattered Dreams* (Victor Productions, Ltd.; co-producer, editor and film researcher); *Courage Along the Divide* (Central TV, UK; associate producer and film researcher); *The World — A TV History* (associate producer); *Llamas Fair* (BBC Belfast; researcher); BBC Enterprises Film Library (sales executive); BBC and ITV (film editor for 10 years).

POLLY PETTIT
8005 Maple Avenue
Takoma Park, MD 20912
(301) 589-3025

Services: Film and video research.
Expertise & Interests: Historical footage in the public domain. Extensive experience with collections at the National Archives and Library of Congress.
Credits: *Who Cares For the Children, Knife Edge of Deterrence, Nuclear Legacy* and *Reunion* (KCTS/Seattle; researcher); *Globewatch* (University of North Carolina Public Television; researcher); NHK (many programs; researcher); *War and Remembrance* (ABC Circle Films; researcher).

DAVID PIERCE
P.O. Box 2748
Laurel, MD 20708
(301) 490-2364

Services: Copyright searches, registrations and renewals.
Expertise & Interests: Provides copyright searches, registration and renewal services for independent producers and distributors. Experienced in ownership and chain-of-title searches for features, documentaries and television shows.
Credits: Clients include the British Film Institute, Classic Movie Channel, Gene Autry Productions, Kino International, Michael Powell Productions and the Pacific Film Archive. Has performed copyright research for public domain footage and registrations for the *Happy Birthday Video* series (Kit Parker Films). Author of *Public Domain Motion Pictures 1950-1959* (Prelinger Associates, Inc.)

BONNIE G. ROWAN
1849 California Street, NW
Washington, DC 20009
(202) 265-1081

Services: Film and video research.
Expertise & Interests: National Archives holdings; embassy collections; public domain materials; historical footage; film history; U.S. Information Agency; Japan; Korea.
Credits: *Scholar's Guide to Washington, D.C. Film and Video Collections* (Smithsonian Institution Press; author); *Europe Since World War II* (Educational Audio Visual, Inc.; research); *Tennis History* (HBO; research); additional footage research for productions on Washington, D.C., Panama Canal, golf, Vietnam, anti-smoking, British literature and Black Americans.

RUTH SCHWARTZ
3632 Veazey Street, NW
Washington, DC 20008
(202) 363-1883

Services: Film and still photograph research.
Expertise & Interests: Historical; government and military; National Archives.
Credits: *To Bear Witness* (John J. Prescott & Associates; associate producer); *Windows on America* (John J. Prescott & Associates; producer).

THAXTON GREEN STUDIOS, INC.
P.O. Box 21068, Kalorama Station
Washington, DC 20009
(202) 232-0654

Contacts: David Thaxton; Kevin Green
Services: Historical documentary film and video research; film and video production.
Expertise & Interests: Extensive experience with feature film, newsreel and television archives; and private, commercial and public domain collections.
Credits: Recent research and production credits include *Reaching for the Skies* (BBC/CBS); *The Nuclear Age* (WGBH); *An Ocean Apart* (BBC/PBS); *Eyes on the Prize* (Blackside, Inc.); *Our World* (ABC News); *The American Experience* (WGBH); and *Frontline* (WGBH).

LEON A. WILLIAMS
6122 Sligo Mill Road, NE
Washington, DC 20011
(202) 723-3497

Services: Film, video, still photograph and audio research.
Expertise & Interests: Historical and contemporary materials held by the federal government and other resources in the Washington, D.C. area.
Credits: Thirty years' experience as government film librarian and freelance film researcher.

**KAREN WYATT
FILM AND PICTURE RESEARCH**
1155 Daleview Drive
McLean, VA 22102
(703) 448-5997
Fax: (703) 448-8332

Services: Film and picture research; rights and clearances.
Expertise & Interests: Special expertise in archival, historical, scientific, natural history and public domain footage. Extensive expertise in rights, clearances and copyright matters.
Credits: National Geographic Society educational films (over 20); *Osterreich II* (Portisch-Riff GmbH and ORF, 26 part series; researcher); *Die Welt der Jahrhundermitte* (ZDF, 13-part series; researcher); *Spaceflight* (Blaine Baggett Prods. for PBS, 4 parts; researcher). Consultant to *Smithsonian World* and National Geographic Educational Films in copyright and rights clearance matters.

FLORIDA (Miami)

PHOTONET
2655 LeJeune Road
Miami, FL 33134
(305) 444-0144
(800) 368-6638

Services: Communications and research network for the publishing and production industry. Connects over 30 major photographic agencies, several hundred professional photographers and stock footage sources throughout the United States and overseas by a computer network. Requests received by PHOTONET are transmitted by electronic mail to one or many sources as required. Requests may be submitted from personal computers, terminals or data terminals supplied by PHOTONET.

FLORIDA (Tampa)

SF.V INTERNATIONAL CORP.
7722 West Hiawatha Street
Tampa, FL 33615
(813) 884-5963

Contact: Mark Hallinan
Services: Film, video and still photograph research; stock footage sales library; custom shooting services; rights and clearances.
Expertise & Interests: General subjects. Can assemble custom catalog to client specifications. Catalog available.
Credits: Clients include Chiat-Day, Leo Burnett, Tracy-Locke, American Express, IBM and General Electric.

GEORGIA (Atlanta)

FRANCINE KAPLAN
2890 North Hills Drive, NE
Atlanta, GA 30305
(404) 233-4449

Services: Film and video research.
Expertise & Interests: Not specified.
Credits: *Ready For the Worst* (American National Red Cross; researcher); *Coca-Cola Centennial Celebration* (C. Henning Studios; researcher); *Energy: Progress Revisited, John R.: The Legend* and *Piedmont Park* (Vanderkloot

ILLINOIS (Chicago)

Film & TV; researcher); productions for U.S. Chamber of Commerce, United Steel Workers of America; Georgia Pacific; and C&P Telephone Company.

ILLINOIS (Chicago)

FILE TAPE COMPANY, INC.
210 East Pearson, Suite 14-C
Chicago, IL 60611
(800) 637-8273
(312) 649-0599 (Illinois only)

Contact: Susan Caraher (President)
Services: Film and video research. Crews available for custom shooting assignments.
Expertise & Interests: Historical and contemporary footage of news events and topical subjects, including personalities, disasters and scenics.
Credits: Numerous broadcast, corporate and industrial productions.

MASSACHUSETTS (Arlington)

FULCRUM MEDIA SERVICES
70 Grove Street
Arlington, MA 02174
(617) 648-0664
Fax: Can be received by appointment at above number.

Contact: Kenn Rabin
Services: Film and video research; archival coordination; archival consultation.
Expertise & Interests: Specializes in researching news and historical footage for historical documentaries. Consultation services include: budgeting advice for compilation documentaries; film versus tape concerns; developing IBM PC-based computer retrieval systems for documentary producers; negotiating rights fees with archives; editorial matters; and locating and duplicating vintage film and video material.
Credits: Archival film coordinator for *Eyes on the Prize; Frontline: Crisis in Central America; Vietnam: A Television History;* and *Through A Lens, Darkly.* Research for many network television documentaries.

MASSACHUSETTS (Boston)

RACHEL KING
7 Norway Street
Boston, MA 02115
(617) 267-0728

Services: Film and video research.
Expertise & Interests: General news; civil rights movement.
Credits: *The Unfinished Journey* (WBZ-TV; researcher); *World Monitor* (Christian Science Publishing; broadcast archivist).

MASSACHUSETTS (Cambridge)

DAN EISENBERG
36 Rice Street
Cambridge, MA 02140
(617) 491-2212

Services: Film and video research; editing.
Expertise & Interests: Early U.S. film; early European film; historical.
Credits: *Vietnam: A Television History* (WGBH; researcher and editor); *Frontline: Crisis in Central America* (WGBH; researcher and editor); *Eyes on the Prize* (Blackside, Inc.; editor).

MINNESOTA (Minneapolis)

TINSELTOWN TITLES
3405 45th Avenue South
Minneapolis, MN 55406-2924
(612) 729-4013

Contact: Ann McKee
Services: Film, video and print background research; bookseller.
Expertise & Interests: Short subjects; compiling encyclopedia on short subjects. Seller of used cinema books.
Credits: *Lindbergh Project* and *Minnesota Project* (Minnesota Historical

Society; researcher); CBS-Fox Video (motion picture trailers; researcher).

NEW JERSEY (Lindenwold)

KENT ST. JOHN
924 Linden Hill Apartments
Lindenwold, NJ 08021
(609) 627-0760

Services: Film and video research.
Expertise & Interests: Not specified.
Credits: *Atlantic City: The Ten-Year Gamble* (New Jersey Network; researcher); *Going Home Alone* (documentary on child care, New Jersey Network; researcher).

NEW MEXICO (Santa Fe)

RAY HEMENEZ
82H Calle Nopal
Santa Fe, NM 87501
(505) 982-4748

Services: Film and video research.
Expertise & Interests: Historical.
Credits: *Hoxsey: Quacks Who Cure Cancer?* (Realidad Productions; researcher); *Powaqqatsi* (North South Ltd.; researcher).

NEW YORK CITY METROPOLITAN AREA

LISA ALJIAN
1049 Briar Way
Fort Lee, NJ 07024
(201) 224-3141

Services: Licensing, contract and clearance negotiation; film and video research; stock footage consultation; library management.
Expertise & Interests: Sports libraries; European film libraries; baseball.
Credits: Former manager of Major League Baseball Productions' footage library.

DOROTHY ALLEYNE
2289 Fifth Avenue, Suite 10B
New York, NY 10037
(212) 690-1609

Services: Film and video research.
Expertise & Interests: Historical; sports; general topics.
Credits: *Preaching the Word* (WNET; film researcher); *Black Champions* (Miles Educational Films, Inc.; director of research); *Brown Sugar* (Roundhill Productions; researcher); *The Different Drummer* (Miles Film Productions; researcher); *I Remember Harlem* (I Remember Harlem, Inc.; researcher).

DIANE ALLFORD
21 St. Marks Place
Brooklyn, NY 11217
(718) 935-1286

Services: Film and still photograph research.
Expertise & Interests: Still photography; newsfilm; historical; contemporary; human interest; travel; Genigraphics; Black, Hispanic and Asian lifestyles; food.
Credits: Clients include *Forbes* Magazine, Ogilvy & Mather, Newspaper Advertising Bureau, Motivation Resources, The Kamber Group, *Medical Economics,* Interval International, and others.

PRUDENCE ARNDT
780 West End Avenue
New York, NY 10025
(212) 222-9290

Services: Film and video research; film and video production and direction.
Expertise & Interests: Historical; civil rights; current affairs. Languages: German.
Credits: *The Handmaid's Tale* (Daniel Wilson Productions, feature film; researcher and segment producer); *The Real Life of Ronald Reagan* (Martin

Smith Productions for PBS *Frontline;* director); *The Exiles* (WNET; researcher); *Eyes on the Prize* (Blackside, Inc.; associate producer); *An Empire of Reason* (Middlemarch Productions; researcher).

JESSICA BERMAN-BOGDAN
1033 Wilson Avenue
Teaneck, NJ 07666
(201) 836-7502

Services: Film, video and still photograph research.
Expertise & Interests: Entertainment specials; political documentaries; commercials; corporate and industrial films and videos; rights and clearances.
Credits: *Paul Robeson: Tribute to an Artist* (Janus Films; associate producer); *51st Annual Academy Awards Show* (film coordinator); numerous commercials. Film coordinator or researcher for the following entertainment and documentary specials and feature films: *Hollywood: The Gift of Laughter* (Jack Haley Jr./David Wolper); *Happy Birthday Hollywood* (Alexander Cohen/Jack Haley Jr.); *Minnelli on Minnelli* (Jack Haley, Jr.); *Ripley's Believe It or Not!* (Jack Haley/Rastar Productions); *Rolling Stone Magazine: 20 Years of Rock and Roll* and *Teenage America* (Malcolm Leo Productions); *1987 Rock and Roll Hall of Fame Awards* (MTV); *Bodywatching* (New Screen Concepts); *Television and the Presidency* (Ailes Communications); *That's Dancin'* (MGM); *This Is Elvis* (Warner Bros.); and others.

DIANE BEST
496 LaGuardia Place, Suite 131
New York, NY 10012
(718) 783-7285

Services: Film and video research; film and video production; rights and clearances.
Expertise & Interests: General subjects.
Credits: *Voices & Visions* (New York Center for Visual History for PBS; rights and clearances); John Wiley & Sons (educational videotape; producer).

PENELOPE BODRY-SANDERS
31 Greene Street
New York, NY 10013
(212) 219-1755

Services: Film and video research.
Expertise & Interests: Comprehensive knowledge of historical film material about Africa, covering people, animals and expeditions. Broad knowledge of expedition material and early ethnographic and zoological material.
Credits: *Twilight of the Gorilla* (American Adventure Productions; researcher); *Armchair Safaris* (EcoVentures; researcher); *In Brightest Africa* (Museum Television Workshop; consultant); *Cameramen Who Dared* (National Geographic; consultant). Researched, curated and wrote on over 300 titles in the American Museum of Natural History Film Archives.

ANNE BOHLEN
59 Franklin Street
New York, NY 10013
(212) 219-2767

Services: Film and video research; film production.
Expertise & Interests: Newsreels; National Archives.
Credits: *With Babies and Banners* (coproducer, production manager, archival research); *The Life and Times of Rosie the Riveter* (archival research); *Seeing Red* (archival research); *Reform on the River* (Cincinnati Historical Society; producer, director, archival research).

PETER BREGMAN
42 West 13th Street
New York, NY 10011
(212) 243-5083

Services: Film, videotape and still image research.
Expertise & Interests: Music; sports; historical footage.
Credits: Rock videos for Billy Joel, Todd Rundgren and Loverboy; *Vietnam: A Television History* (WGBH); *Remember When* and *Missing Persons* (HBO); *JFK* and *Organized Crime* (ABC *Close-Up*); *Austria 1* (ORF-Austrian TV); numerous television commercials for all major advertising agencies; many in-house and corporate films and videos.

KAREN E. BUTLER
321 Avenue C, Apartment 7D
New York, NY 10009
(212) 560-2860

Services: Film, video and still photograph research; rights and clearances; fee negotiations.
Expertise & Interests: History (world and American); Black history; dance; drama; natural history. Languages: French and Spanish. Experienced in international searches.
Credits: *The Mind* (BBC/PBS; associate producer and researcher); *Bill Moyers' Journal* (PBS; associate producer); *A Walk Through the 20th Century with Bill Moyers* (CEL; associate producer); *Up to the Minute* (CBS; associate producer).

BZ/RIGHTS & PERMISSIONS, INC.
145 West 86th Street
New York, NY 10024
(212) 580-0615
Fax: (212) 595-0626

Contact: Barbara Zimmerman (President)
Services: Rights and clearances. Obtains permission to use music, film and video clips, celebrity photos and testimonials, photographs, art, literature or other copyrighted works on behalf of users such as producers, advertising agencies and corporations.
Clients: Allstate, AT&T, American Express, Burson Marsteller, Doyle Dane Bernbach, Fallon McElligott, GTE, General Motors, Group W Cable, Illinois Power Company, Kentucky Fried Chicken, Maritz Communications, McDonald's, New York Telephone, Ogilvy & Mather, Procter & Gamble, Prudential, RCA, Southwestern Bell,, Wyse Advertising, Young & Rubicam.

CATHY CARAPELLA
10 Woodlot Road
Eastchester, NY 10709
(914) 699-7013
Fax: (914) 668-0769

Services: Film and video research; rights and clearances; budget planning.
Expertise & Interests: Post-production coordination; budget planning; music (performance footage).
Credits: *Today in Music History* (Man in the Moon Productions; associate producer); Showtime (special rights consultant); Chiat-Day Productions (special rights consultant).

JONI COHEN-ZLOTOWITZ
427A East 89th Street, Apartment 5
New York, NY 10128
(212) 348-3524

Services: Film and video research; rights and clearances negotiations.
Expertise & Interests: Has researched a wide variety of stock footage for broadcast, films and industrials. Coordinates film and tape elements for pre-production and post-production sessions.
Credits: *Saturday Night Live* (NBC; film researcher); CBS News Film and Videotape Archives (archivist).

JOYCE COMPTON
1274 First Avenue, Apartment 22
New York, NY 10021
(212) 744-0561

See **DISTRICT OF COLUMBIA METRO**

ELIZABETH COTNOIR
220 West 21st Street
New York, NY 10011
(212) 463-8906

Services: Film and video research; film and video production; rights and clearances.
Expertise & Interests: Historical footage; music.
Credits: *Michelob Presents Sunday Night* (Broadway Video for NBC; researcher and segment producer); corporate communications videos and presentations.

NANCY M. CRUMLEY
324 7th Avenue
Brooklyn, NY 11215
(718) 788-3306

Services: Film and video research; film and video production.
Expertise & Interests: General topics. Languages: French.
Credits: *Are We Winning, Mommy? America and the Cold War* (Cine Information; assistant producer); *The Faces of Frustration* (Jack Hilton Productions; film researcher); *Numismatic Fine Arts/Athena Fund II* (RKB Productions; film researcher and associate producer).

HILLARY DANN
51 Bank Street
New York, NY 10014
(212) 989-3378

Services: Film and video research; rights and clearances.
Expertise & Interests: Historical; nature and wildlife; medical. Languages: French.
Credits: Cousteau Society (several productions; researcher and contract administrator); *Are We Winning, Mommy?* (Cine Information; associate producer and archival film research coordinator); *In America* (Reeves Corporate Services; associate producer); several documentaries for PBS and cable television.

ANNE DERRY
115 South Street
New York, NY 10038
(212) 766-0053

Services: Film and video research; production; writing.
Expertise & Interests: Historical subjects.
Credits: *Our World* (Potter Productions for ABC News; producer, associate producer, researcher); *National Geographic Explorer* (producer, writer, researcher).

MARY DORE
253 West 16th Street, Apartment 3A
New York, NY 10011
(212) 929-0901

Services: Film and video research; film and video production and direction.
Expertise & Interests: Historical; American history (1930s-50s); European archives; popular culture.
Credits: *The Good Fight* (feature documentary aired on PBS; producer, director and film research); *The Comics* (Sphinx Productions; film research); *Journey to Birth* (March of Dimes; producer and film research); *Nova* (WGBH; film research); *Search for Mind* (WNET; film research).

MARGOT EDMAN
203 East 76th Street, Apartment 4B
New York, NY 10021
(212) 570-2648

Services: Film and video research; film and video production and direction.
Expertise & Interests: General subjects.
Credits: *Vietnam: A Television History* (PBS; film researcher); BBC (New York; field producer, director and film researcher); WGBH, *NOVA* (associate producer).

SUSAN EMERLING
244 East 7th Street, Apartment 18
New York, NY 10009
(212) 477-4191

Services: Film, video, still photograph and art reproduction research; rights and clearances.
Expertise & Interests: U.S. and foreign rights and clearances; copyright research at the Library of Congress; television commercials and public service announcements; historical; propaganda; feature film clips. Languages: French and Italian. Can provide Italian translation and interpreting.
Credits: *The Image and Its Power* (series for Institut National de la Communication Audiovisuelle; U.S. researcher and *documentaliste*); *Heaven* (Perpetual Productions for RCA Video; associate producer for clearances);

Jammin' Me (music video for MCA Records; research and clearances); *Constitution Film Series* (Agency for Instructional Technology; film and photo researcher).

WILLIAM K. EVERSON
118 West 79th Street
New York, NY 10024

Services: Historian. Available for special projects requiring consultation in European and American film history. Screenings of relevant motion pictures can be arranged.

RAYE FARR
25 East 83rd Street
New York, NY 10028
(212) 734-2088

Services: Archival film consultant.
Expertise & Interests: Historical subjects, especially European and Soviet history (1900-50) and World War II; European and American archives and collections; Chinese archives.
Credits: *World At War* (Thames Television; film research); *Hitler's Germany* (Thames Television; producer); *Struggles For Poland* (Channel 4 U.K./WNET; producer of one episode, *Poland's Jews*); *Vietnam: A Television History* (WGBH; film research); *China in Revolution* (Ambrica Productions; film research).

SUSAN GILBERT
33 Third Avenue, Apartment 12D1
New York, NY 10003
(212) 995-1058

Services: Film and video research.
Expertise & Interests: Historical and contemporary ethnographic footage.
Credits: Smithsonian Crossroads/Bering Strait video exhibit (Ted Timreck Productions; researcher).

ERIKA GOTTFRIED
313 Sackett Street
Brooklyn, NY 11231
(718) 852-5435

Services: Film, video and still photograph research; writing.
Expertise & Interests: Historical subjects; labor history; women's history; social issues.
Credits: Presently Curator of Nonprint Collections, Robert Wagner Labor Archives, New York University. *A Glory of Ghosts* (WNET; film and photograph researcher); *The Cancer War* and *Anarchism in America* (Pacific Street Film Projects; film and photograph researcher); *Man's Best Friends* (Frontline; film and photograph researcher); *Walking on the Moon* (Midwest Productions; film researcher).

VIRGINIA GRAY
125 West 12th Street
New York, NY 10011
(212) 675-1275

Services: Film and video research.
Expertise & Interests: Historical film; newsreels; television newsfilm and videotape; specials film and videotapes; feature films; nature films and videotapes.
Credits: CBS News; NBC News; ABC News; public television stations (WNET, WGBH, WQED, South Carolina ETV Network); advertising agencies; feature films.

LINDA GUTIERREZ
115 Perry Street, Apartment 5B
New York, NY 10014
(212) 675-2473

Calle Monjas 2, Apartment 3A
07470 Puerto Pollensa
Mallorca, Spain
34-71-71-47-70
34-71-53-28-13

Services: Film and video research.
Expertise & Interests: Research in London, Paris, Madrid and North American collections.
Credits: *Voices and Visions* (13-part series, New York Center for Visual History for PBS; research director and chief researcher).

DANA HEINZ
361 West Broadway
New York, NY 10013
(212) 431-3170
Fax: (212) 431-5754

Services: Film and video research; production management.
Expertise & Interests: Newsreels; music.
Credits: *John Hammond: On and Off the Record* (Holographic Films); *George Gershwin Remembered* (Archive Film Productions). Former manager of Archive Film Productions stock footage library.

CELESTE R. HOFFNAR
250 Mott Street
New York, NY 10012
(212) 633-2134
(212) 334-9254

Services: Film and video research; rights and clearances.
Expertise & Interests: General research and source information; television programs.
Credits: *Our World* (ABC News; research, rights and clearances); *Footage 89: North American Film & Video Sources* (Prelinger Associates, Inc.; co-editor, writer and researcher).

TESSA HORAN
3416 Park Avenue
Weehawken, NJ 07087
(201) 867-4941

Services: Film and video research; film and video production.
Expertise & Interests: Business; economy; real estate; environment; ecology.
Languages: French, Italian and Spanish.
Credits: CBS Evening News (researcher); Dokumenta Productions, Inc. (various business films); Infinity Productions (various children's films; associate producer and writer).

LEWANNE JONES
55 South 11th Street, 4th Floor
Brooklyn, NY 11211
(718) 387-6471

Services: Film and video research; film and video production.
Expertise & Interests: Historical; news and current affairs; Caribbean, Latin American and Third World subjects.
Credits: Recent credits include *Eyes on the Prize* (Blackside, Inc.; researcher); *The Nuclear Age* (WGBH; researcher).

NORMAN KAGAN
408 East 64th Street
New York, NY 10021
(212) 755-5147

Services: Film and video research; film and video producer.
Expertise & Interests: Science; medicine, high technology; social sciences; theatrical film and television.
Credits: *Science Screen Report* and *Screen News Digest* (Forman Productions; writer, producer and footage researcher); *Science Report* (U.S. Information Agency; writer, producer and footage researcher); *IT-KIT* (Instructavision for Silver Burdett Corporation; chief footage researcher).

BHUPENDER KAUL
234 East 5th Street
New York, NY 10003
(212) 475-0132

Services: Film and video research; rights and clearances.
Expertise & Interests: Historical, cultural, social and sports footage.
Credits: *One Hand Don't Clap* (Riverfilms; research director); *The Way We*

Footage 89: North American Film & Video Sources

Were: 1940-45 (CEL Communications; principal researcher); *Not Necessarily the News* (Second Line Search for Moffitt-Lee Productions; researcher); *Soul Gone Home* (Riverfilms; research director).

MARY LANCE
443 12th Street, Apartment 5A
Brooklyn, NY 11215
(718) 965-1419

Services: Archival film and video research; production and direction.
Expertise & Interests: General topics.
Credits: *The Last Emperor* (research); *Zelig* (research); PBS, independent and network documentaries and miniseries (research); *The Diego Rivera Film Project* (producer/director); *Artists at Work* (producer/director); *Northern Stars* (producer/director); *Truman: A Self-Portrait* (producer/director); and other documentaries on history and art.

PETRA LENT
106 MacDougal Street, Apartment 20
New York, NY 10012
(212) 505-7068

Services: Film, video and music research; rights and clearances.
Expertise & Interests: Historical stock footage. Languages: German (bilingual); French and Italian.
Credits: *Out of the Ashes* and *The Power of the Word* (*Heritage* series) (WNET; associate producer and stock footage researcher); *A.D.: Rome of the Emperors* (NBC; researcher); *Shadow of the Reich* (NBC; researcher); *Mussolini: Wolf of Rome* (NBC; associate producer/researcher).

VICKI GOLD LEVI
211 Central Park West
New York, NY 10024
(212) 724-1133

Services: Film, video and still photograph research; writing and consultation.
Expertise & Interests: General subjects; history of Atlantic City, N.J.; history of Times Square and 42nd Street, New York City.
Credits: *Atlantic City: 125 Years of Ocean Madness* (co-author). Other credits available on request.

ALAN F. LEWIS
3 Dover Court
Rockville Centre, NY 11570
(516) 763-1945

Services: Consultant in the establishment and operation of film and videotape archives and libraries.
Expertise & Interests: Public television programming; network news.
Credits: Founder and former director of the Public Television Archives; former director of the CBS News Film & Videotape Archives. *A Dream Called Public Television* (footage research); other documentaries using public television program materials.

MELISSE LEWIS
111 West 16th Street, Apartment 5F
New York, NY 10011
(212) 929-3502

Services: Film and video research; film and video production; post-production supervision.
Expertise & Interests: Production consulting, budgeting, rights and contracts negotiation, script development and footage research, all with union and nonunion, U.S. and European film and video crews. Languages: French and German.
Credits: *The Dead Come Home* (feature film; producer); *Boy (Go)* (Celluloid Records; producer); *Saturday Night Live* (NBC; research and production); ZDF, NDR and RAI (research and U.S. production manager); *Tales From the Darkside* (Laurel Entertainment; post-production supervisor); *Louisiana Low-Income Housing* (co-producer and director).

LINDA LILIENFELD
367 West 19th Street
New York, NY 10011
(212) 929-5672

Services: Film, video, still image and photography research.
Expertise & Interests: Science; history; the arts; rights and clearances.
Credits: *The Blessings of Liberty* (ABC News; archivist, film and still image research); *The Human Animal* (Multimedia Entertainment; archivist, film and still image research); Showtime/The Movie Channel on-air promotion spots (research); *The World of Tomorrow* and other documentary films for An American Portrait (film and picture research).

MARION LIPSCHUTZ
170 East 3rd Street, Apartment C
New York, NY 10009
(212) 260-1297
(914) 253-9229

Services: Film, video, still photograph, text and informational research; film and video production.
Expertise & Interests: New, unusual and low-cost sources; rights and clearances; interviewing.
Credits: Equinox Films (4 films on language); *The Entrepreneurs* (series for Concepts Unlimited; researcher and associate producer); *Everything About AIDS* (Concepts Unlimited for HBO; researcher and associate producer); *Smoking* (Concepts Unlimited for HBO; researcher).

MEDIA NETWORK
ALTERNATIVE MEDIA INFORMATION CENTER
121 Fulton Street, 5th Floor
New York, NY 10038
(212) 619-3455

Don Derosby (Director)

Contact: Kevin Duggan (Information Center Coordinator)
Services: Media information clearinghouse. Information and resource listings available to members.
Description: Media Network is the leading national organization supporting the use of alternative films and videotapes for grassroots organizing and education. Its programs include: a "media information clearinghouse" for social-issue films; and training and consulting for activist groups that want to use films as tools for social change. Media Network is a subscription membership organization, open to the public.
　　The Information Center recommends films, videotapes and slideshows on a wide range of issues. It also provides descriptions, running times, rental and sales costs and distributors' addresses. Using a computerized cross-referenced filing system with more than 200 topics, the Center has helped hundreds of organizations find titles suitable for their needs.
　　Provides detailed information about and distributes guides to films on urgent social issues, including: disarmament and the arms race; the environment, ecology and pollution; housing and homelessness; reproductive rights; women's rights; civil rights; minority and racial problems; migrant workers; gay and lesbian rights; the legal and judicial systems; rural and urban issues; international economics; immigration; education; ethnic culture and history; the role of the United States in Central America; apartheid and South Africa; and United States foreign and military policy.
Size & Elements: Does not maintain a film or videotape collection. Offers a computerized listing of over 3,000 titles of films and videotapes on a wide range of social issues.
Cataloging: Computerized listings, cross-referenced by title, subject and distributor availability. Listings also include descriptions, running times, rental and sales costs and distributors' addresses.
Access: Open to the public. Information services free to members; supplied at a nominal charge to non-members. Research requests accepted by mail and telephone (Tuesdays, Wednesdays and Thursdays; 1:00 pm-6:00 pm).
Rights: Not applicable. Contact distributor and producer of the film or videotape for information.
Licensing: Not applicable. Contact distributor and producer of the film or videotape for information.
Restrictions: Not applicable. Contact distributor and producer of the film or videotape for information.
Viewing Facilities: None.
Duplication Facilities: None.
Publications: *Media Guides,* providing detailed information about dozens of pre-screened films on selected topics. All guides include film titles; descriptions and evaluations; release date and running times; available formats; rental and purchase costs; distributor information; and tips on using films more effectively. All evaluations are based upon firsthand screenings by people

knowledgeable in the field. *Media Guides* include: *Guide to Films on Central America; Guide to Films on Apartheid and Southern Africa; Guide to Disarmament Media; Green Gems* (on environmental and energy issues); *Images of Color* (on issues facing Black, Latino, Asian and Native American communities); *Guide to Community Media; Reproductive Rights Film Guide; Guide to Films on Adoption;* and *Lights, Camera, Action: A Guide to Labor Related Media.*

Also publishes *Mediactive* (6 issues per year; free to members), a newsletter on alternative media use and production.

KATI MEISTER
81 Irving Place, Apartment 5E
New York, NY 10003
(212) 473-1443

Services: Film, video, still photograph and content research; rights and clearances; film and video production and direction.
Expertise & Interests: General subjects.
Credits: *Zelig* (Rollins & Joffe Productions; film research and rights and clearances); *Dear America: Letters Home From Vietnam* (HBO/Couturie Company/Vetco; supervisor of film research); *Saturday Night Live* (NBC/Broadway Video; film and video research, segment producer and rights and clearances); *Vietnam Requiem* (ABC News/Korty Films; film research); *NBC 60th Anniversary Show* (Alexander Cohen Productions; rights and clearances); *The Original Max Talking Headroom Show* (Cinemax; film research and rights and clearances); numerous HBO, PBS, cable and network specials, series and documentaries; television commercials and public service announcements.

ANDREW W. MILLSTEIN
53 Crosby Street, 3rd Floor East
New York, NY 10012
(212) 219-8075
Fax: (212) 966-7329

Services: Film and video research; film and video production.
Expertise & Interests: Historical footage; music; rights and clearances.
Credits: *Elvis '56* (Alan & Susan Raymond; researcher, associate producer and animation design).

SUSAN MORRIS
572 Grand Street, Apartment 1905-G
New York, NY 10002
(212) 995-5750

Services: Film and video research; film and video production.
Expertise & Interests: Historical topics; architecture; art.
Credits: *Pride of Place: Building the American Dream* (Malone-Gill Productions; director of research and production supervisor); *The Ten-Year Lunch: The Wit and Legend of the Algonquin Round Table* (Telltale Communications and Aviva Films for PBS; associate producer); Metropolitan Museum of Art, Office of Film and Television (research associate); and others.

CHASE MORRISON
625 Broadway, 10th Floor
New York, NY 10012
(212) 475-4401
Fax: (212) 475-4791

Services: Film and video research; rights and clearances; producers' agent.
Expertise & Interests: Public domain; serials; underlying music and literary rights; residuals and royalties; video rights; contract negotiations and drafting.
Credits: Represents, among others: *Natural States; Heifetz;* Merce Cunningham Dance Library; *She Must Be Seeing Things* (feature); *Because the Dawn* (feature); independent producers, advertising agencies, foreign and domestic television stations; video companies.

MRG PRODUCTION ASSOCIATES, INC.
2 Floyd Lane
Massapequa, NY 11762
(516) 489-1071
Fax: (516) 746-4733 (specify for MRG)

Contact: Michael Glaser (Producer and Director of Media Enterprises)
Services: Referral service for locating stock footage and custom field

production crews; clearance and contract negotiation; location services.
Expertise & Interests: Clearinghouse for film and videotape stock footage from many companies. Access to field production crews throughout the United States and in foreign countries.
Credits: Not specified.

NEWSREEL ACCESS SYSTEMS, INC.
150 East 58th Street, 35th Floor
New York, NY 10155
(212) 826-2800
(800) 242-2463

Sanford Fisher (Chairman and Chief Operating Officer)

Contact: Kris Zeronda
Services: Publisher of CineScan™ computer database containing over 130,000 descriptions of film and videotape footage. CineScan is available as a CD-ROM or can be searched by Newsreel Access Systems on a per project basis.
Description: CineScan is the first international computer database of its kind — a "yellow pages" of film and videotape containing over 130,000 detailed descriptions of footage compiled through years of painstaking research at archives all around the world. The available material spans everything from Thomas Edison's early experiments in film in 1894 to the major news events of 1987. CineScan is continuously being updated and expanded.

CineScan is published as a compact disc on which a vast amount of information can be stored and retrieved. This new technology is called Compact Disc-Read Only Memory, or CD-ROM. A number of different yearly subscription plans to the CineScan disc are available, some of which include CD-ROM hardware and software. Subscription rates vary depending on the size of the user organization and the number of individuals who will be utilizing the information contained within the CineScan database. Discounted rates can be arranged for nonprofit organizations and educational institutions.

CineScan on disc requires an IBM (or compatible) PC, XT, AT or 386 computer with at least one floppy disk drive (drive "A:"), a fixed-disk drive (drive "C:") with at least three megabytes of available storage space, 512K of random-access memory (RAM) and a printer. The computer must be running the MS-DOS or PC-DOS operating system, Version 2.0 or later. Also necessary is a CD-ROM drive, such as those made by Philips, Sony and Hitachi.

CineScan is also available for those companies, institutions or individuals who do not have access to a computer or whose film and videotape footage needs are not extensive. The NAS research staff is able to conduct the most complicated CineScan searches on a per project basis. Information can be provided to the user in a matter of seconds over the telephone and printouts can be available the next day.

Fees for over-the-telephone CineScan searches vary depending on how successful they prove to be. Fees are charged only if NAS is able to locate a CineScan catalog reference containing the search term(s) requested.

The CineScan database currently contains the following collections:
Universal Newsreels (1929-67). Held at the National Archives, Washington, D.C.
Hearst News of the Day (1919-67); *Hearst Farm Newsreel* (1958); and *This Week in Sports* (1954-63). Held at the UCLA Film and Television Archives, Los Angeles, Calif.
Hearst Telenews Weekly (1954-63); *Hearst Almanac* (1732-1960); *Hearst Reports* (various dates); *Time Out For Sports* (various dates); *Big Moments in Sports* (various dates); *Perspective on Greatness* (various dates); and *King Features Time Capsule* (various dates). Held by Hearst Metrotone News, New York, N.Y.
The March of Time (1935-50). Distributed by SFM Media Corp., New York, N.Y.
Paramount Newsreels (1927-57); *American Pathé News* (1932-57). Held by Sherman Grinberg Film Libraries, New York, N.Y. and Hollywood, Calif.
British Pathé News (1895-1970). Represented by Worldwide Television News, New York, N.Y.
Library of Congress Paper Print Collection. Washington, D.C.
NASA (Lyndon B. Johnson Space Center) Film/Video Distribution Library. Houston, Texas.
Archive Film Productions. New York, N.Y.
Halcyon Days Productions. New York, N.Y.
Worldwide Television News. New York, N.Y.

DEBORAH PAITCHEL
444 East 87th Street, Apartment 6E
New York, NY 10128
(212) 369-0354

Services: Film and video research; rights and clearances; music clearances; development and packaging.
Expertise & Interests: Lifestyles; archival; historical; current news footage; rock and roll; features; television shows.
Credits: *Lifestyles of the Rich and Famous* (TPE for Telerep; clearance coordinator); 3 Geraldo Rivera specials (researcher and associate producer); *1987 Emmy Awards* (Broadway Video for Fox Television; researcher).

LORENA M. PARLEE
c/o CINEQUEST
625 Broadway, 12th Floor
New York, NY 10012
(212) 777-6900 (Ext. 327)
Fax: (212) 979-8786

Services: Film and video research; film and video production.
Expertise & Interests: Historical films and newsreels; materials in Los Angeles, Mexico City and New York archives and television stations; Latin America; border areas; Latinos in the United States. Languages: Spanish (bilingual).
Credits: *The Wrath of Grapes* (United Farm Workers of America; director, producer and writer); *In the Name of the People* (Pan American Films; script consultant and researcher); *Ballad of an Unsung Hero* (KPBS-TV, San Diego; associate producer, writer and researcher); *Routes of Rhythm with Harry Belafonte* (Silver Star Productions; researcher); *The American Experience* (programs on Father Coughlin and Robert Moses for WGBH; researcher); *In the Shadow of the Law* (KPBS; researcher).

PERMISSIONS
125 West 92nd Street
New York, NY 10025
(212) 316-2390
Telex: 254-2438 MCI UW

Contact: Felice McGlincy
Services: Film and video research; rights and clearances.
Expertise & Interests: Historical research; general topics.
Credits: *In America* (20 episodes of entertainment clips, produced by Reeves Corporate Services; manager of rights and clearances); *U.S. Constitution with Bill Moyers* (Agency for Instructional Technology; head researcher); *The Health Century* (The Blackwell Corporation; researcher).

RICHARD PRELINGER
430 West 14th Street, Room 403
New York, NY 10014
(800) 243-2252
(212) 633-2134
Fax: (212) 691-8347

Services: Archival consultation; collection appraisal and evaluation.
Expertise & Interests: Organization, operation and appraisal of film and videotape archives and collections; marketing, publicity and promotion.
Credits: Has evaluated corporate and institutional moving image collections. Publisher and Editor of *Footage 89: North American Film & Video Sources*. Operates private film archives and stock footage sales library.

TERRI RANDALL
310 West 99th Street, Apartment 707
New York, NY 10025
(212) 749-9299

Services: Film and video research; film and video production.
Expertise & Interests: U.S. military history; arts; rights and clearances; medical subjects; NASA; U.S. space program.
Credits: *Wings Over Water: The History of Naval Aviation; Showdown on Tobacco Road; The Journey Back: Surviving Coma; Space Workers* (all for Varied Directions; producer and researcher).

DEBORAH RICHARDSON
70 East 96th Street, Apartment 7-D
New York, NY 10128
(212) 410-9118

Services: Film, video and still photograph research; film and video production; rights and clearances.

Expertise & Interests: Historical, including photographs and pre-motion picture images; feature film and television clips.
Credits: *That Memorable Year, 1963* (Media Access Corp.; producer); *Our World* (ABC News; associate producer); *JFK Remembered* (Obenhaus Films; researcher); *Murder: Live From Death Row* (Geraldo Rivera; associate producer); *Ogilvy and Mather* (various spots; film researcher).

DEBORAH RICKETTS
320 West 56th Street, Apt. 4E
New York, NY 10019
(212) 586-2272

c/o CINEQUEST
625 Broadway, 12th Floor
New York, NY 10012
(212) 777-6900 (Ext. 327)
Fax: (212) 979-8786

Services: Visual source and factual research for feature films.
Expertise & Interests: Historical, photographic and background research.
Credits: *We're No Angels* (Paramount Pictures; research coordinator); *Batman* (Warner Bros.; researcher and prop buyer); *CIA: A Forgotten History* (Oliver Stone/Hemdale Film Corp.; researcher); *Casualties of War* (Columbia Pictures; research coordinator and prop buyer); *Empire of the Sun* (Warner Bros.; researcher and prop buyer); *The Sicilian* (Gladden Entertainment; researcher); *The Fortunate Pilgrim* (NBC; researcher); *Year of the Dragon* (DEG; location assistant and researcher); *Harlem Shuffle* (Bakshi/Verges Productions; researcher).

ROGER RIFKIN
21 West 86th Street, Apartment 706
New York, NY 10024
(212) 362-7096

Services: Film, video and still photograph research.
Expertise & Interests: Film, television and theater history.
Credits: Phototeque (photo agency; assisted in research and purchase of film material and film stills).

RIGHTS CHASERS
35 West 90th Street
New York, NY 10024-1507
(212) 873-6390
Fax: (212) 362-8022

Contact: Ralph Berliner
Services: Rights and clearances.
Expertise & Interests: Clears film footage, music (sync and master use licenses), audio materials, theatrical rights and celebrity endorsements.
Credits: *This Week in Baseball* (Major League Baseball Productions); *Bette Midler's Mondo Beyondo* (Berner Schlamme Productions); McDonald's Corporation (corporate materials); Procter & Gamble (corporate materials); various producers of homevideos and commercials.

KAREN Y. ROSEN
131 East 17th Street, Apartment 5
New York, NY 10106
(212) 673-9659

Services: Film, video and historical research; rights and clearances.
Expertise & Interests: American history, film history. M.A. in Public History. Languages: French.
Credits: Janus Films (stock footage coordinator); *Generations* (Lifetime; stock footage coordinator).

SARALEE ROSEN
64 Thompson Street
New York, NY 10012
(212) 431-8012

Services: Film and video research.
Expertise & Interests: General subjects.
Credits: Former Director of Library Services at Film Search, Inc. Other credits available on request.

ROSEMARY ROTONDI
763 Washington Street, Apartment 16
New York, NY 10014
(212) 989-2025

Services: Visual and historical research for film and video projects; rights and clearances.
Expertise & Interests: Post-production supervision; videotape preservation.
Credits: *Ganapati: A Spirit in the Bush* (Daniel Reeves; visual researcher and post-production manager); *Sombra a Sombra* (Daniel Reeves; associate producer); Electronic Arts Intermix (preservation project coordinator).

STEVE RUGGI
415 West 118th Street, Apartment 23
New York, NY 10027
(212) 316-6773

Services: Film and video research; film and video production.
Expertise & Interests: Historical and/or arts and humanities-oriented projects.
Credits: *Easy Does It* [working title] (George T. Nierenberg Productions; associate producer and researcher); *Voices & Visions Series: Robert Lowell; Sylvia Plath; Marianne Moore; Elizabeth Bishop; T. S. Eliot; Wallace Stevens* (New York Center for Visual History; researcher).

SUSAN RYAN
200 East 26th Street, Apartment 5C
New York, NY 10010
(212) 683-2397

Services: Film, video and still photograph research.
Expertise & Interests: United Nations film library; television programs; rights and clearances. Languages: Spanish.
Credits: *The UN: Opportunity in Crisis* (Norwegian TV; primary researcher); *Frank Sinatra* (Antenne 2, France; researcher); *The Radio Priest* (WGBH; film researcher); *The Nuclear Age* (WGBH; researcher).

RICK SCHECKMAN
189-15 Radnor Road
Jamaica, NY 11423
(212) 664-5914 (office)
(718) 465-7164 (home)

Services: Film and video research; rights and clearances; contract negotiations; copyright research; segment production.
Expertise & Interests: Film historian and archivist; pre-1950 American film; newsreels; industrial and educational films. Extensive videotape edit room experience.
Credits: *Late Night With David Letterman* (NBC; film research and segment coordinator, 1982-present); JC Penney Corp. (film research consultant); *FDR: A One-Man Show* (Cinemax Comedy Experiment; graphics producer); *Action Family* (Cinemax; film segment coordinator).

SECOND LINE SEARCH
330 West 42nd Street, Room 2901
New York, NY 10036
(212) 594-5544
Fax: (212) 594-5213

Contacts: Rick Gell, Todd Pavlin
Services: Full service stock footage research company.
Expertise & Interests: Handles projects ranging from major advertising agency campaigns to corporate in-house productions and low-budget documentaries. Second Line is often brought into a project at the formative stage — acting as creative and financial consultants providing realistic budget estimates, production schedules and appropriate images. Specializes in clearing rock videos, feature films, television shows and other unusual sources for stock footage. Has ongoing working relationships with all major sports organizations and can navigate questions relating to sponsorship, trademark and logo usage. When research is initiated, can quickly access footage from around the world, saving the producer the time and difficulty of contacting many sources. Creates appropriate highlight reels, and once costs have been approved, handles all transfers, licensing and talent agreements, and provides the client with one consolidated bill.
Credits: *Not Necessarily the News* (Moffitt-Lee Productions for HBO; stock footage coordinators); numerous major advertising agencies.

Footage 89: North American Film & Video Sources

GAIL SEGAL
8 Harrison Street
New York, NY 10013
(212) 431-6485

Services: Film and video research; film and video production; rights and clearances.
Expertise & Interests: Historical; art history; rare manuscripts; biographical footage of literary figures, past and present.
Credits: *To Care* (Francis Thompson Inc.; associate producer); *The Shakespeare Hour* (WNET for PBS; associate producer); *Art of the Western World* (BBC and PBS; researcher); *William Blake: The Marriage of Heaven and Hell* (Media Group, Inc.; associate producer).

VIRGINIA (GINNY) SEIPT
112 West 74th Street
New York, NY 10023
(212) 873-0971

Services: Film, video and still image research; television production and direction.
Expertise & Interests: Historical; sports.
Credits: NBC Sports (producer and director); *NBC News Sunday Today* (feature producer).

SHEEN & ASSOCIATES
P.O. Box 275
New York, NY 10012
(212) 475-5281

Contact: Andrea Sheen
Services: Film and video research; rights and clearances.
Expertise & Interests: Historical subjects; entertainment industry; television news; analysis of existing programs with regard to clearances needed for homevideo release.
Credits: NBC News Archives (former manager); *NBC 60th Anniversary Special* (director of rights and clearances); *The NBC Story* (director of rights and clearances); *Television* (WNET; series consultant); *40th Annual Emmy Awards* (Lorne Michaels Productions; director of rights and clearances); PBS (rights and clearances).

DOUGLAS W. SMITH
246 Fifth Avenue, Apartment 1L
Brooklyn, NY 11215
(718) 857-0402

Services: Film and video research; film and video editing; post-production supervision.
Expertise & Interests: Historical footage. Languages: French and Spanish.
Credits: *Our World* (ABC News; associate producer and editor); *What Every Baby Knows* (New Screen Concepts; associate producer and editor); *3-2-1 Contact* (Children's Television Workshop; film and video editor); *Robert Moses* (Obenhaus Productions for WGBH; videotape editor).

LYRYSA SMITH
304 West 107th Street, Apartment 3B
New York, NY 10025
(212) 866-7258

Services: Film, video and still photograph research; production; rights and clearances.
Expertise & Interests: Unusual historical, biographical and cultural footage; historical and current news footage; rights and clearances; foreign countries.
Credits: *Senator Sam Ervin* (New Atlantic Productions; associate producer); *Our World* (ABC News; production associate); *45/85* (ABC News; researcher); *Inside the Cold War* (editorial and photo researcher); *Footage 89: North American Film & Video Sources* (writer).

BOB SUMMERS
430 West 14th Street, Room 402
New York, NY 10014
(212) 645-2112
Fax: (212) 691-8347
Services: Coordination of U.S. and overseas film and video research.
Expertise & Interests: Historical (pre-1970) subjects.

Credits: Recent list available on request.

CATHERINE TAYLOR
72 Seventh Avenue, Apartment 2R
Brooklyn, NY 11215
(718) 398-1336

Services: Film and video research; film and video production.
Expertise & Interests: Historical; arts and literature; human rights; music footage.
Credits: *The Exiles* (Richard Kaplan Productions and WNET; associate producer); George T. Nierenberg Productions (documentary for *The American Experience*, WGBH; researcher); *Premiere* magazine (researcher); The Human Rights Film Festival (New York, 1988; co-producer).

QUYNH THAI
12 Duffield Street
Brooklyn, NY 11201
(718) 855-8048

Services: Film and video research.
Expertise & Interests: Third World; Spanish-speaking; newsreels; contemporary society.
Credits: *Who Killed Vincent Chin?* (Film News Now Foundation; research assistant); *The Underclass* (HBO; assistant researcher).

TIMESTEPS PRODUCTIONS, INC.
2 Glenside
West Orange, NJ 07052
(201) 669-1930
Fax: (201) 731-8546

Services: Film and video research and production.
Expertise & Interests: Historical subjects.
Credits: Clients include AT&T, Johnson & Johnson, Jordan McGrath Case & Taylor and HBM Creamer.

DAWN VANDER VLOED
206 East 32nd Street, Apartment 1RW
New York, NY 10016
(212) 679-7663

Services: Film, video, still photograph and manuscript research.
Expertise & Interests: Historical subjects.
Credits: *The Beckett Project* (Global Village; associate producer and research coordinator).

PAMELA MASON WAGNER
304 West 102nd Street, Apartment 2A
New York, NY 10025
(212) 864-5187

Services: Film, video and still image research; film and video production.
Expertise & Interests: Fashion (historical and contemporary); aviation history; medical imaging systems; music, still image and fine arts rights and clearances. Languages: French.
Credits: *The Great Air Race of 1924* (David Grubin Productions for WGBH; coproducer and stock footage researcher); *Inside the Sexes* (New Screen Concepts for CBS; associate producer and medical photography researcher); *The Way We Wear* and *The Living Smithsonian* (David Grubin Productions for WETA/Smithsonian World; coproducer and director of stock footage research); *Bodywatching* (New Screen Concepts for CBS; associate producer).

ELLEN WEISSBROD
172 East 7th Street, Apartment 1B
New York, NY 10009
(212) 477-0237

Services: Film, video and still photograph research; film and video production.
Expertise & Interests: Commercials; arts; American history and politics.
Credits: *The Wonder Years* (New World TV for ABC; archival and commercial research); *This Honorable Court* (WETA; archival footage research); *Me and Him* (Constantin Films for Columbia Pictures; stock footage research); *America's Women* (Sagebrush Productions; archival researcher); *Elizabeth Bishop: One Art* (co-producer); *Strokes of Genius* (5 films on artists;

associate producer, photo and stock footage researcher).

MICHAEL WELDON
151 First Avenue, Department PV
New York, NY 10003
(212) 673-3823

Services: Film and video research and consulting.
Expertise & Interests: "Psychotronic" (horror, science fiction, exploitation, teen-oriented) films and videotapes.
Credits: *Heaven* (Perpetual Productions; research consultant); *Desperately Seeking Susan* (Orion Pictures; research consultant); *Psychotronic Video Magazine* (editor and publisher); *The Psychotronic Encyclopedia of Film* (Ballantine; author).

SUE WILLIAMS
2 Spring Street
New York, NY 10012
(212) 226-2560

Services: Film and video research and production.
Expertise & Interests: Foreign archives (e.g., United Kingdom, France, Cuba and China); rights and clearances.
Credits: *China in Revolution* (Ambrica Productions; producer and director); *Eyes on the Prize* (Blackside, Inc. for WGBH; researcher); *The Nuclear Age* (WGBH; researcher).

TEXAS (Austin)

KENT BENJAMIN
1613 Wheless Lane
Austin, TX 78723
(512) 459-3542 (home)
(512) 473-8995 (office)

Services: Film, video and music research and consultation.
Expertise & Interests: Music (primarily rock and roll); films and television appearances by rock and roll groups (1955-present); blues; rhythm and blues; copyright law. Maintains research files and personal reference film and video collection.
Credits: *The Many Faces of Ronnie Lane* (public access television; producer and writer); Video Festival of the South by Southwest (assistant director); Austin *Chronicle* (video editor and music writer, 1984-present).

TEXAS (Dallas)

ALAN GOVENAR
DOCUMENTARY ARTS, INC.
P.O. Box 140244
Dallas, TX 75214
(214) 824-3377

Services: Film, video, radio and music research and production; writing.
Expertise & Interests: Traditional music; new music.
Credits: *Deep Ellum Blues, Battle of the Guitars, Cigarette Blues* (with Les Blank), *Texas Style* (with Pacho Lane); *Black and White, White and Black* (with Pacho Lane) (producer, director and researcher for all); *Traditional Music in Texas* (39-part radio series; producer, writer and researcher); *New Music in America* (radio series; producer, writer and researcher); and *National Heritage Fellowship Recipients* (52-part radio series; producer, writer and researcher). Books include *Living Texas Blues* (1985); *Meeting the Blues* (1988); and *The Photography of Benny Joseph: The Early Years of Rhythm and Blues* (1989). Producer of Dallas Folk Festival.

TEXAS (San Antonio)

BARBARA STEELE HENDRICKS
3603 Invicta Drive
San Antonio, TX 78218
(512) 822-7456

Services: Film and video research; film and video production.
Expertise & Interests: Educational rights; industrial footage; scientific footage; esoteric and unusual footage.
Credits: *Introduction to Physical Science* (6 interactive videodiscs, River City

Productions; researcher); *Center for Entrepreneurial Development* (industrial video; writer, producer and director); *SMS* (scientific video; writer, producer and director); *Adrian the Explorer* (three educational videos; producer and director); *Portrait of Herman DeJori* (documentary; writer and producer).

WISCONSIN (Milwaukee)

RONNA BROMBERG-PACHEFSKY
2710 East Newton Avenue
Milwaukee, WI 53211
(414) 964-8224

Services: Film and video research; film and video production.
Expertise & Interests: General subjects.
Credits: *Treasures From the Past* (National Geographic; research assistant); *Spirit of Pittsburgh* (WQED/Pittsburgh; production associate and researcher).

ONTARIO (Ottawa)

ANDREA CROSS
368 Verdon Private
Ottawa, ON
(613) 526-4445

Services: Film and video research; film and video production; editing.
Expertise & Interests: Historical; sports; health; production coordination.
Credits: *Beyond the Printed Word...* (exhibition for the National Archives of Canada; coordinated production of 14 laserdiscs with archival film, television and radio clips); *Acid Rain: Requiem or Recovery?* (Crawley Films; assistant editor); *Labour of Love* (Primedia Productions; assistant director); *After the Wars* (Crawley Films; production assistant and researcher).

LAUREN WALKER
172 Primrose Avenue
Ottawa, ON K1R 6M6
(613) 236-8374

Services: Film, video, sound and still photograph research; film and video production; rights and clearances.
Expertise & Interests: Historical footage; World War II; newsreels; biographical and political research; natural sciences and environmental issues; copyright clearance.
Credits: *Beyond the Printed Word* (National Archives of Canada; researcher, writer and producer); *Patriotic Fever* (University of Ottawa; researcher and co-director); *National Archives of Canada* (data researcher/coordinator).

ONTARIO (Plantagenet)

PEGGY KELLY
Box 366
Plantagenet, ON K0B 1L0
(613) 673-4881

Services: Film, video and still photograph research; editing.
Expertise & Interests: Social history; ecology and environment; film history; current affairs; medical issues; women's movement; human rights. Languages: French.
Credits: Clients and employers include the National Archives of Canada, CJOH Television, Ontario Film Review Board, Canadian Broadcasting Corporation and Skyline Cablevision Ltd.

MEXICO (Mexico, D.F.)

FERNANDO DEL MORAL GONZALEZ
Apartado Postal M-9157
C.P. 06000
Mexico, D.F.
5-44-77-58

c/o **CINEQUEST**
625 Broadway, 12th Floor
New York, NY 10012
(212) 777-6900 (Ext. 327)
Fax: (212) 979-8786

UNITED KINGDOM

Services: Film research.
Expertise & Interests: Preservation and restoration of historical films.
Credits: *La Decena Trágica en México* (producer, researcher and preservationist); Archivo Fotografico y Cinematografico Abitia (curator and preservationist, 1988); Cineteca Nacional de Mexico (director of research, 1975-80; coordinator, 1980-82).

UNITED KINGDOM (London)

CORRINNE COLLETT
90A Leander Road
London SW 2 2LJ
United Kingdom
(01) 674-2707

Services: Film and video research.
Expertise & Interests: Pre-1960 film footage; library and archival management. Languages: German, Russian (some) and French (some).
Credits: Museum of Jewish Heritage (head of film research); John E. Allen, Inc. (librarian); researcher for Alvin H. Perlmutter, Inc., Rainbow Productions and Cine Information.

FILM RESEARCH & PRODUCTION SERVICES LIMITED
73 Newman Street
London W1P 3LA
United Kingdom
(01) 580-4882
(01) 580-4883
(01) 636-1140
Fax: (01) 436-4757

Contacts: Ian O'Brien; Amanda Dunne; David Collier; Gerard Wilkinson
Services: Film and video research. Represents owners of stock footage libraries for licensing and sales. Viewing facilities available.
Expertise & Interests: General subjects; worldwide archives and collections; rights and clearances.
Credits: Clients include: Paramount Pictures, Inc.; Channel 4 Television; Thames Television; J. Walter Thompson; Saatchi Saatchi Advertising; Young and Rubicam; Leo Burnett; McCann Erickson; Times Group Newspapers; Mirror Group Newspapers; Barclays Bank plc; Nicholas Laboratories plc; Central Electricity Generating Board.

SELINA MACNAIR
122A Endymion Road
London SW2 2BP
United Kingdom
(01) 674-7553

Services: Film, video, still image and music researcher; film and video production.
Expertise & Interests: U.S. social history and culture; East Coast (U.S.) archives.
Credits: *Master Smart Woman* (Jane Morrison Productions; picture researcher); *Twentieth Century Fads* (Kevin Rafferty Productions; associate producer, film and music research); *Corporate America* (Panoptic; film, music and informational research).

UNITED KINGDOM (Stafford)

ADRIAN WOOD
CRESWELL RESEARCH SERVICES
34 Creswell Grove
Eccleshall Road
Stafford ST18 9QP
United Kingdom
(44) (0785) 52710
Fax: (44) (0785) 59420

Services: Film and video research.
Expertise & Interests: Documentary films and series related to politics, crime, the motion picture industry and entertainers.
Credits: *Scandals* (Central TV; research and film research); *Richard Burton* (Isolde Films for Thames TV); *Spear of the Nation; For Valour; Crime Inc.; Israel: State of Insecurity;* and *The Troubles* (all Thames TV; film research).

Index

Cinematographer: Robin Lehman

The only *FILM* stock worth watching.

THE **IMAGE**BANK®

Headquarters:
111 Fifth Avenue, New York City 10003
(212) 529-6700   Telex: 429380 IMAGE   Fax: (212) 529-8886

The Image Bank & Film Search. Representing the finest Cinematographers in the world, throughout the world.

FILM SEARCH®
AN IMAGE BANK COMPANY
232 Madison Avenue,
New York City 10016
(212) 532-0600 Telex: 4973657
FILMS Fax: (212) 779-9732

9583 Alcott Avenue, #201
Los Angeles, CA 90035
(213) 550-1947

Atlanta (404) 233-9920   **Chicago** (312) 329-1817   **Dallas** (214) 631-3808   **Florida** (813) 566-3444
Los Angeles (213) 656-9003   **Minneapolis** (612) 332-8935   **Mexico City** (905) 524-4644/660-1528   **Naples, FL** (813) 566-3444
San Francisco (415) 788-2208 **San Juan** (809) 722-0165   **Toronto** (416) 362-6931   **Athens** (30) (1) 867-5386/6611
Barcelona (34) (3) 209-3544/3611   **Bogota** (57) (1) 257-9674   **Brussels** (32) (2) 735-6762   **Buenos Aires** (54) (1) 334-8121/4099
Capetown (27) (21) 24-4830   **Caracas** (58) (2) 92.86.19   **Helsinki** (358) (0) 17.40.66   **Hong Kong** (852) (5) 76.20.22
Johannesburg (27) (11) 642-5108/9   **London** (44) (1) 240-9621/7   **Madrid** (34) (1) 446-9061/9362   **Melbourne** (61) (3) 699-7833
Milan (39) (2) 86.93.964   **Montevideo** (598) (2) 95.73.04   **Munich** (49) (89) 470.20.68   **Oslo** (47) (2) 33.06.50
Paris (33) (1) 45.08.86.98   **Porto Alegre** (55) (512) 43-30-23   **Rio de Janeiro** (55) (21) 220-2129   **Santiago** (56) (2) 225-5189
Sao Paulo (55) (11) 852-3466   **Kuala Lumpur** (60) (3) 776-8136   **Seoul** (82) (2) 273.27.92   **Stockholm** (46) (8) 10.17.70
Sydney (61) (2) 927-158   **Tel Aviv** (972) (3) 662-588/664-308   **Tokyo** (81) (3) 573-4841   **Zurich** (41) (1) 69.11.60

How to Use This Index

This *Index* contains over 36,000 subject references derived from source listings in *Footage 89*. It directs the user to sources found in *Footage 89* containing the desired subject, topic, issue, personality or location. It also lists certain types of collections (e.g., stock footage sales libraries; presidential libraries) and genres (e.g., musical films and videotapes; safety films and videotapes).

This finding aid is exclusively derived from the contents of the individual listings themselves and is by no means a complete index to the holdings of sources listed. Since many larger collections (whether film archives, newsreel collections or stock footage libraries) defy brief description, they should be routinely consulted in the course of research.

Please note that this *Index* is intended as a research guide and is not a substitute for consulting the entries themselves.

Subject headings

The terms used in this *Index* are generally derived from the "Description" field of each source listing. The language used in that field was provided, for the most part, by the sources themselves. This has resulted in the use of differing indexing terms to describe similar footage. For example, manufacturing may be found under "Manufacturing," "Industry," "Factories," "Assembly lines," under all four headings, or under the names of specific industries.

Procedure

Look under the desired heading and note the sources listed beneath. Turn to the *Sources and Collections Index* (pages A-37 through A-81) and locate the page number where that source is found in the source listings (pages 1-577). Do not contact sources without first reading the entire entry. Pay special attention to policies on access, rights, licensing and restrictions.

If you wish to find additional information or sources for your research topic, try using a broader heading. For example, if you are looking for grasshoppers, check the specific heading "Grasshoppers" and read the suggested entries. If more sources are needed, check the broader heading "Insects" and then the still broader heading of "Nature." It is always advisable to consult the list of "General Film and Videotape Collections" (see below), as these sources often hold collections too comprehensive in scope to be adequately represented in this *Index*.

If no subject heading is located or very few sources are located for your topic, then look for alternative headings that may be used to describe the the same subject. Cross-references have often been included to supply additional leads.

Geographic locations

When checking specific geographic locations, it is important to know that a heading without a modification in parentheses generally refers to footage that is contemporary and/or of a scenic nature. If a heading is followed by "History and culture" in parentheses, it refers to any footage that is not contemporary. This may include scenics or footage that is "documentary" in nature (i.e., concerning the location, its people, history and culture). If a heading is followed by the modification "Contemporary issues," this refers to footage concerned with current topics, controversies or trends related to that location.

Some subjects combine several areas that are hard to define for the purpose of this *Index*. For example, footage appearing under the modification "History and culture" may also contain "scenics" of the area, or relate to "contemporary issues." To thoroughly research all aspects of a specific location, all above-mentioned modifications should be disregarded and all areas explored.

For footage relating to a specific region or continent (e.g., Africa, Southeast Asia or North America), check under the name of the region or continent as well as under the names of specific countries located within the area. For footage relating to regions of the United States, check under the names of individual states located in the region.

Celebrities and personalities

Celebrities are indexed as cited in the source listings, although presumably not every source reported every personality of whom they had footage. If a name is not shown, check under "Celebrities" and also under "Stock footage sales libraries" and "General film and videotape collections."

Directors, producers, filmmakers, video and performance artists are generally not indexed, unless a source holds actual footage showing that individual.

General film and videotape collections

These collections contain material on every conceivable subject and are often too comprehensive in scope to be completely represented in this *Index*. They should be routinely consulted in the course of research.

ABC News
Allen (John E.) Inc.
Archive Film Productions, Inc.
Britannica Films & Video
British Information Services, Radio & TV Division
CBS News Archives
CTV Television Network, CTV News Archives
Cable News Network Library
Cameo Film Library, Inc.
Canadian Broadcasting Corporation
Cannell (Stephen J.) Productions, Inc.
Chisholm (Jack) Film Productions, Ltd.
Cinenet (Cinema Network)

Columbia Pictures TV/Stock Film Library
Dreamlight Images, Inc.
Energy Productions
Film Bank
Film Search
Film/Audio Services, Inc.
Grinberg (Sherman) Film Libraries (East)
Grinberg (Sherman) Film Libraries (West)
Hearst Metrotone News
Independent Network News (INN)
Library of Congress, M/B/RS
Museum of Broadcasting
Museum of Modern Art, Department of Film
NBC News Video Archives
National Archives of Canada
National Archives, Motion Picture, Sound & Video Branch
National Archives, National Audiovisual Center
National Center for Film & Video Preservation
National Film Board of Canada
National Geographic Society, Stock Footage Library
Paramount Pictures Stock Film Library
Petrified Films, Inc.
Prelinger Associates, Inc.
Producers Library Service
Public Broadcasting System
Second Line Search
Spelling (Aaron) Productions
Stock House
TV Ontario
Televisa, S.A.
Twentieth Century-Fox Movietonews
U.S. Department of Defense, Motion Media Records Center
UCLA Film & Television Archive
Universal City Studios
Univ. of South Carolina, Newsfilm Library
Video Tape Library, Ltd.
Visnews International
WGBH Educational Foundation
Weintraub Screen Entertainment, Inc.
White Janssen, Inc.
Worldwide Television News

General examples

For footage about John F. Kennedy, check: (1) Kennedy, John Fitzgerald; (2) Presidents (U.S.); (3) Politics and government; (4) Political conventions; (5) Political campaigns; (6) Political campaign commercials; (7) Presidential elections (U.S.); (8) Stock footage sales libraries; (9) Television news; (10) General film and videotape collections

For footage about baseball, check: (1) Baseball, especially (Professional) and (Amateur); (2) Sports; (3) Athletes; (4) individual athletes by name; (5) Stock footage sales libraries; (6) General film and videotape collections

For footage on Three Mile Island: (1) Three Mile Island, Pa. (History); (2) Pennsylvania; (3) Nuclear energy and power; (4) Television news; (5) Stock footage sales libraries; (6) General film and videotape collections

ABBA (Musical group)
Archive Film Prods., Inc.
Clark (Dick) Media Archives, Inc.

AFL-CIO
See American Federation of Labor-
Congress of Industrial Organizations
(AFL-CIO)

AFSCME
See American Federation of State, County
and Municipal Employees (AFSCME)

AIDS
AIDS Committee of Toronto
AIDSFILMS
Adair Films
Amer. Correctional Assn.
Assn. of Independent Comm. Prod.
British Info. Svcs., Radio & TV Div.
Canadian Filmmakers Dist. Centre
Canadian Gay Archives
Centers for Disease Control
Churchill Films
Coronet/MTI Film & Video
Deep Dish TV
Educational Productions
Emory Medical Television Network
Filmakers Library
Films for the Humanities and Sciences
First Run/Icarus Films, Inc.
Focus Intl. Inc.
Gay Cable Network
Gay Men's Health Crisis
Keep the Faith, Inc.
Lambda Legal Defense & Education Fund
Los Angeles News Service
Ludlow (Fitz Hugh) Memorial Library
Multi-Focus, Inc.
Multi-Media Productions, Inc.
Narcotics Education, Inc.
New Day Films
New York Pub. Lib., Donnell Media Ctr.
O.D.N. Productions, Inc.
Petrified Films, Inc.
Polymorph Films, Inc.
Rogers (Will) Institute
Shanti Project
Smithsonian Inst., NMAH, Div. Med. Sci.
Southern Christian Leadership Conference
Univ. of West Fla., Hum. Res. Vid. Lib.
Video Data Bank

Aalto, Alvar
Southern Calif. Inst. of Architecture

Abbott and Costello
UCLA Film & Television Archive
Video Resources N.Y., Inc.

Abbott, Bud
Archive Film Prods., Inc.

Aberdeen, S. Dak. (History and culture)
Pennebaker Associates, Inc.

Abernathy, Ralph David Sr.
King (Dr. Martin Luther, Jr.) Ctr.
Memphis State Univ. Libraries

Abidjan, Ivory Coast (History and culture)
United Nations Ctr. for Human
Settlements

Able, John
Johns Hopkins Univ., School of Medicine

Aborigines
See Indigenous peoples

Abortion
ABC News
Baird (Bill) Inst.
CBS News Archives
Cambridge Documentary Films, Inc.
Cinema Guild
Fanlight Prods.
Groupe Intervention Video
Historical Health Film Coll.
Intermedia Arts Minnesota
Intl. Lutheran Layman's League
Multi-Focus, Inc.
Mus. & Hist. Div., City of Sacramento
New Day Films
Planned Parenthood Fed. of Amer.
Radcliffe Coll., Schlesinger Lib.
Univ. of Mich., Mich. Hist. Colls.
Vidéo Femmes

Abortion (Pro-choice)
Cinema Medica
DEC Film & Video
Natl. Abortion Rights Action League
Political Issue Archive
Radcliffe Coll., Schlesinger Lib.
Religious Coalition for Abortion Rights
Women Make Movies, Inc.

Abortion (Pro-life)
Amer. Life League
Amer. Portrait Films
Keep the Faith, Inc.
Moody Inst. of Science
Natl. Abortion Rights Action League
Natl. Right to Life Committee
Political Issue Archive
Pro-Life Action League
Talbert (Tom) Prods.

Abraham Lincoln Brigade
Brandeis Univ. Lib.
Cinema Guild
First Run/Icarus Films, Inc.
Intermedia Arts Minnesota
Southern Calif. Lib. for Soc. Stud. & Res.

Abrams, Elliott
Camino Film Projects

Abu Dhabi, United Arab Emirates (History and culture)
Middle East Institute

Abu Simbel, Egypt (History)
Natl. Archives (RG 59)

Abzug, Bella
Intermedia Arts Minnesota

Academy Awards
Academy Film Archive
Banks Film Library
Petrified Films, Inc.
Spalla (Rick) Video Prods.
Spectral Comms.
UCLA Film & Television Archive

Acadia National Park, Maine
Dobbs (Jeff) Prods.
Site Productions

Acapulco, Mexico
Petrified Films, Inc.
Preview Media
Source Stock Footage Lib., Inc.

Acapulco, Mexico (History and culture)
Petrified Films, Inc.

Accelerator pedals
See Automobiles (Gas pedals)

Accidents
Amer. Nuclear Society
CBS News Archives
Film Bank
Inst. of Makers of Explosives
Prelinger Assoc., Inc.
Pyramid Film and Video Corp.
Timesteps Prods., Inc.
Univ. of So. Carolina, Newsfilm Lib.
Zielinski Productions, Inc.
See also Aircraft (Accidents); Automobiles
(Accidents); Disasters; Railroads
(Accidents); Rescues; Shipwrecks;
Skiing (Snow) (Accidents)

Acconci, Vito
Blackwood Prods., Inc.
Electronic Arts Intermix
Southern Calif. Inst. of Architecture
Video Data Bank

Acheson, Dean
Natl. Archives (RG 59)

Acid rain
Acid Rain Foundation, Inc.
Bullfrog Films, Inc.
Direct Cinema Ltd.
Edison Electric Institute
Electric Power Research Institute
Film Bank
Filmfair Communications
New York State Dept. of Env. Cons.
Oregon State Univ., Archives
Richter Productions
See also Ecology; Pollution

Acid trips
Academy of Health Sciences, U.S. Army
Film Bank
MacDonald, J. Fred
Raindance Foundation
Streamline Film Archives
See also Drug culture

Acker, Kathy
Monday, Wednesday, Friday Video Club

Acne
Cinema Guild
Milady Publishing Corp.

Acoma Pueblo, N. Mex. (History and culture)
Wheelwright Mus. of the Amer. Indian

Acquired Immune Deficiency Syndrome
See AIDS

Acrobats
CBS News Archives
Film Bank
Fish Films, Inc.
Petrified Films, Inc.
TV Ontario
Twentieth Century-Fox Movietonews
See also Circuses

Actors and actresses
See Celebrities

Acupuncture and acupressure
Hartley Film Found., Inc.
Video-SIG
See also Medicine (China)

Adair, E. Ross
Indiana State Lib.

Adam, Helen
Giorno Poetry Systems Inst.

Adam, Margie
Intermedia Arts Minnesota

Adams, Ansel
Cantor (Arthur) Inc.
Port Washington Pub. Lib.

Adams, Brock
Natl. Archives (RG 398)

Adams County, Neb. (History and culture)
Adams County Hist. Soc.

Adams, Edie
Banks Film Library
Moviecraft, Inc.
Spalla (Rick) Video Prods.

Adams, Pepper
Rhapsody Films, Inc.

Adams, Samuel
Archive Film Prods., Inc.

Adato, Perry Miller
Port Washington Pub. Lib.

Addiction
Addiction Research Foundation of Ontario
See also Alcohol abuse; Alcoholism; Drug
abuse; Substance abuse; Twelve-step
programs

Adding machines
Energy Productions

Adenauer, Konrad
Smith (Margaret Chase) Lib. Ctr.

Adirondack Mountains, N.Y.
Florentine Films
Indiana State Comm. on Public Records
New York State Dept. of Econ. Devel.

Adirondack Mountains, N.Y. (History and culture)
Direct Cinema Ltd.
Film/Audio Services, Inc.
New York State Dept. of Env. Cons.
Omega Films
Prelinger Assoc., Inc.

Adler, Celia
Cantor (Arthur) Inc.

Adler, Stella
New York Pub. Lib., Perf. Arts Res. Ctr.,
Theatre on Film and Tape

Adobe huts
Petrified Films, Inc.

Adolescence
See Children; Teenagers

Adoption
CBS News Archives
Cambridge Documentary Films, Inc.
March of Time
Univ. of West Fla., Hum. Res. Vid. Lib.

Adventure
Beerger (Norman) Prods.
Coe Film Assoc., Inc.
Morcraft Films
Natl. Geographic Soc. Stock Footage Lib.
Preview Media
Sobek Productions
Spalla (Rick) Video Prods.
Streamline Film Archives

NOTE: Access policies, availability and restrictions vary for each source. Please read each entry in full. Always consult "General Film and Videotape Collections" (page 599); these comprehensive collections contain material on every conceivable subject.

Summit Films, Inc.
Video Yesteryear

Advertising
Adbank
Advertising Information Services, Inc.
American Airlines
Apertura
Archive Film Prods., Inc.
Brooklyn Coll., Diamant Mem. Lib.
Cambridge Documentary Films, Inc.
Center for Southern Folklore
Cinema Guild
Clio Awards
Coca-Cola Co., Archives Dept.
Continental Airlines
Duke Univ., Perkins Lib.
Electronic Arts Intermix
Encore Entertainment
Fairleigh Dickinson Univ. Lib.
Fashion Inst. of Design & Merchandising
Film Bank
Filmoteca de la UNAM
Gould (Bert)/bay area archive
Harvard Univ., Schl. of Educ., ACT Lib.
Illinois State Hist. Lib.
Imperial Oil Ltd.
Inst. of Outdoor Advertising
Intermedia Arts Minnesota
Intl. Air Check
Intl. Fashion Video Library
Latin Amer. Video Arch.
Lib. of Congress, M/B/RS
MacDonald, J. Fred
Miles Corporate Archive
Mus. of Adv. & Communications Design
Mus. of Broadcast Comms.
Narcotics Education, Inc.
Natl. Archives (RG 56)
Natl. Archives (RG 200)
New York State Dept. of Econ. Devel.
Paper Tiger TV
Petrified Films, Inc.
Phoenix Films and Video
Prelinger Assoc., Inc.
Procter & Gamble Co.
Prov. Arch. of Newfoundland & Labrador
Pyramid Film and Video Corp.
Saatchi & Saatchi DFS Compton
Smithsonian Inst., NMAH, Arch. Ctr.
Smithsonian Inst., NMAH, Div. Polit. Hist.
Spectacolor, Inc.
Streamline Film Archives
Studebaker Natl. Museum
TV Ontario
Trent Institute for Popular Culture
United Airlines, Creative Services
Univ. of Ill. Urbana-Champaign, Univ. Arch.
Univ. of Mich., Mich. Hist. Colls.
Univ. of N.C. Wilmington, Devries-Bulluck Coll.
Varied Directions, Inc.
Wolfson (Louis II) Media Hist. Ctr., Miami-Dade Pub. Lib.
See also Public service announcements; Signs (Advertising); Television commercials

Advertising (Outdoor)
Cambridge Documentary Films, Inc.
Dreamlight Images, Inc.
Fairleigh Dickinson Univ. Lib.
Film Bank
Inst. of Outdoor Advertising
Patrick Media Group
Petrified Films, Inc.
Prelinger Assoc., Inc.
TV Ontario
See also Signs (Advertising)

Aerial views
Airship Industries (USA), Inc.
Applegate Entertainment

Beerger (Norman) Prods.
Boston Stock Market
Brekke Television Prods.
Broad Street Prods.
CBS News Archives
Century Video Services, Inc.
Chicago Video Transfer
Chisholm (Jack) Film Productions
Cine-Mark
Cinema Arts Assoc.
Cinenet (Cinema Network)
Cineworks Prods. Inc.
Creative Video, Inc.
Crystal Pyramid Prods.
Development Communications, Inc.
Dobovan Productions, Inc.
Dorn (Larry) Associates
Dreamlight Images, Inc.
Elfstrom-Hilmer Prods.
Encore Video Prods., Inc.
Energy Productions
Fabulous Footage Inc.
Farkas Studios, Ltd.
Film Bank
First Group Comms., Inc.
Fish Films, Inc.
Hayes Prods., Inc.
Hooper (Josh) Prods., Inc.
Hot Shots Commercial Prods., Inc.
Image Bank/Film Search
Jalbert Productions
Jewell (Stuart) Productions
KD Enterprises Prods.
Kesser Stock Footage Library
Law (Lisa) Prods.
MVP Communications
MacGillivray Freeman Films
Metro Communications, Inc.
Missouri Hist. Soc.
Moving Media
NASA, Ames Res. Ctr., Dryden Fac.
NASA, Ames Res. Ctr., Imaging Tech. Branch
Natl. Archives (RG 18)
Network Productions
New Haven Colony Hist. Soc.
Newsreel Video Service
Nine Star Productions
Off-Broadway Video Prods.
Ohio Hist. Soc.
Omega Films
Oregon Hist. Soc.
Oregon State Univ., Archives
Orion Post Production
Petrified Films, Inc.
Postcards Unlimited
Prelinger Assoc., Inc.
Producers' Service
Prov. Arch. of Alberta
Renaissance Video Corp.
SF•V Intl.
Simon (Jeff) Productions
Source Stock Footage Lib., Inc.
Spectral Comms.
Stimulus
Stock Shots
Summit Films, Inc.
TV Ontario
TVA/Television Assoc.
Telltales Associates Inc.
Tennessee Valley Authority (TVA)
Tri-Comm Prods.
Unicorn Projects
Union Pacific Railroad
Univ. of Wis., Green Bay, Ctr. TV Prod.
Video Concepts, Inc.
Video Genesis, Inc.
Video Tape Library, Ltd.
Viz Wiz, Inc.
Washington Broadcast Video Lib.
Zielinski Productions, Inc.
See also specific geographic locations

Aerobatics
Experimental Aircraft Assn.

Film Bank
Intl. Aviation Publishers, Inc.
Mass. Inst. of Tech., MIT Museum
Video Tape Library, Ltd.
See also Aircraft (Stunts)

Aerobic exercise
Athletic Institute
Dreamlight Images, Inc.
Energy Productions
Film Bank
Intl. Dance Exercise Assn.
Lemorande Prod. Co.
Spectral Comms.
Video Tape Library, Ltd.
Yakima Television Program
See also Exercise; Joggers and jogging; Physical fitness

Aeronautical engineering
Northrop Univ., Amer. Hall of Aviation Hist.

Aeronautics
Amer. Arch. of the Factual Film
Experimental Aircraft Assn.
NASA, Ames Res. Ctr., Human Factors Res. Ctr.
NASA, Ames Res. Ctr., Regional Film Lib.
NASA, Goddard Space Flight Ctr.
NASA, Johnson Space Ctr., Film & Video Dist. Lib.
NASA, Langley Research Ctr.
NASA, Marshall Space Flight Ctr.
Natl. Archives of Canada
See also Aircraft; Aviation

Aeronautics (History of)
NASA, Lewis Research Center
Northrop Univ., Amer. Hall of Aviation Hist.

Afghanistan
Imagen y Sonido Independiente, S.A.

Afghanistan (Contemporary issues)
Film/Audio Services, Inc.
News On Film
Northstar Prods.

Afghanistan (History and culture)
British Info. Svcs., Radio & TV Div.
Downtown Community TV Ctr.
Film/Audio Services, Inc.
Lawren Prods., Inc.
Middle East Institute
Natl. Archives (RG 286)
Northstar Prods.
Oregon Hist. Soc.
Smithsonian Inst., Human Studies Film Arch.
Worldwide Television News

Africa
Di Sesso (Moe) Wild Life Film Lib.
Dorn (Larry) Associates
Film Bank
Film Search
Innerquest Communications Corp.
Summit Films, Inc.
World Monitor

Africa (Contemporary issues)
CARE
DEC Film & Video
Maryknoll Fathers & Brothers
Third World Newsreel

Africa (History and culture)
Africa Inland Mission
Allen (John E.) Inc.
Archive Film Prods., Inc.
Archives of the Mennonite Church
Atlantis Prods., Inc.

Benchmark Films, Inc.
Carousel Film & Video
DEC Film & Video
Disciples of Christ Hist. Soc.
Documentary Educational Resources
Duffy (Kevin) Prods.
Film/Audio Services, Inc.
Innerquest Communications Corp.
Interlock Media Associates
Intl. Film Foundation
Intl. Media Services, Inc.
Johnson (Martin & Osa) Safari Museum
Maryknoll Fathers & Brothers
Natl. Archives (RG 18)
Natl. Archives (RG 200)
Natl. Archives (RG 342)
Natl. Archives of Canada
Paulist Productions
Petrified Films, Inc.
Phoenix Films and Video
Prelinger Assoc., Inc.
Rockefeller Arch. Ctr.
Schomburg Ctr. for Res. in Black Culture
Schweitzer (Albert) Ctr.
Smithsonian Inst., Human Studies Film Arch.
TV Ontario
UNICEF, Div. Info. & Pub. Aff.
United Nations Ctr. for Human Settlements
Univ. of Mich., Mich. Hist. Colls.
Wheaton Coll., Billy Graham Ctr.
White Janssen, Inc.
World Monitor
Worldwide Television News

Afro-Brazilians
Benamou, Catherine/LAWAS

Agee, James
Agee (James) Film Project

Agency for International Development (U.S)
Natl. Archives (RG 286)
Natl. Archives (Stock Film Coll.)

Agent Orange
First Run/Icarus Films, Inc.
Green Mountain Post Films
Petrified Films, Inc.

Aging and gerontology
Amer. Foundation for the Blind
Carousel Film & Video
Cinema Guild
Coe Film Assoc., Inc.
Coronet/MTI Film & Video
Education Development Ctr., Inc.
Emory Medical Television Network
Film/Video Arts, Inc.
Filmakers Library
Films for the Humanities and Sciences
Focus Intl. Inc.
Hartley Film Found., Inc.
Intermedia Arts Minnesota
Intl. Lutheran Layman's League
Mass Media Ministries
Media Project
Milner-Fenwick, Inc.
Natl. Archives (RG 439)
Natl. Film Board of Canada
Phoenix Films and Video
Society for Nutrition Education
Univ. of Calif., Ext. Media Ctr.
Univ. of West Fla., Hum. Res. Vid. Lib.
Vidéo Femmes
See also Senior citizens and elderly

Agnew, Spiro Theodore
Archive Film Prods., Inc.

Agosta, Diana
Port Washington Pub. Lib.

Agree, George
Agricultural Workers Organizing
    Committee
Duke Univ., Perkins Lib.
Estuary Press

Agriculture
Ackerman-Black Prods., Inc.
Allen (John E.) Inc.
Alternative Information Network
Amer. Arch. of the Factual Film
Appalshop Films, Inc.
Archive Film Prods., Inc.
Archives Nationales du Québec
Archives of Ontario
Bishop Mus., Visual Coll.
Blue Sky Comms., Inc.
Board of Trade of the City of Chicago
Bullfrog Films, Inc.
Cable News Network Library
Cornell Univ., Media Services
Deep Dish TV
Dreamlight Images, Inc.
Energy Productions
Estuary Press
Fabulous Footage Inc.
Film Bank
Film/Audio Services, Inc.
Future Farmers of America
Glenbow Mus. Arch.
Grinberg (Sherman) Film Libraries (West)
Hot Shots Commercial Prods., Inc.
Imevision
Intermedia Arts Minnesota
Kentucky Dept. of Libraries & Archives
Michigan State Univ., Archives
Native Amer. Pub. Broad. Cons.
Natl. Archives (RG 16)
Natl. Archives (RG 33)
Natl. Archives (RG 48)
Natl. Archives (RG 75)
Natl. Archives (RG 96)
Natl. Archives (RG 103)
Natl. Archives (RG 145)
Natl. Archives (RG 200)
Natl. Archives (RG 242)
Natl. Archives (RG 286)
Natl. Archives (RG 310)
Natl. Archives of Canada
Natl. Archives/Natl. AV Ctr.
Natl. Cattlemen's Assn.
Natl. Dairy Council
Natl. Oceanic & Atmospheric Admin.
Northcoast Communication, Inc.
Oregon Hist. Soc.
Petrified Films, Inc.
Prelinger Assoc., Inc.
Prod. House, Inc., Motion Media Prods.
Prov. Arch. of Alberta
Rockefeller Arch. Ctr.
Snyder (Bill) Films, Inc.
Source Stock Footage Lib., Inc.
State Hist. Soc. of Iowa
State Hist. Soc. of North Dakota
TV Ontario
Texas Tech Univ., Southwest Coll.
Union Pacific Railroad
United Nations Ctr. for Human
    Settlements
Université de Moncton, Centre d'Études
    Acad.
Université Laval, Cinémathèque
Univ. of Calif., Davis, Shields Library
VTR Productions
Venard Films Ltd.
Video I-D, Inc.
White Janssen, Inc.
World Monitor
See also Crops; Farms and farming;
    Harvesting; specific crops

Agriculture (Soviet Union)
Natl. Coun. of Amer.-Sov. Friendship

Agriculture, Department of (U.S.)

Natl. Archives (RG 16)
Natl. Archives (RG 22)
Natl. Archives (RG 33)
Natl. Archives (Stock Film Coll.)

Air bags
See Automobiles (Seat belts and air bags)

Air Force (Canada)
Northstar Prods.
UDS Company

Air Force (Great Britain)
See Royal Air Force (RAF)

Air Force (U.S.)
CBS News Archives
Experimental Aircraft Assn.
March of Time
Military/Combat Stock Footage
Natl. Archives (RG 341)
Natl. Archives (RG 342)
Riccitelli (Bruce) Prods.
San Diego Aerospace Museum
Summit Films, Inc.
Sweet (Harry) Film Coll.
U.S. Dept. of Defense, Motion Media Rec.
    Ctr.
UDS Company
See also Air Force Academy (U.S.);
    Aircraft (Military); Korean War;
    Military; Thunderbirds (U.S. Air
    Force); Vietnam War; World War I;
    World War II; specific conflicts and
    wars

Air Force Academy (U.S.)
Analogous Productions
Natl. Archives (RG 342)
Summit Films, Inc.

Air mail
Allen (John E.) Inc.
Glenbow Museum
Natl. Archives (RG 28)
Natl. Archives (RG 178)
Natl. Archives (RG 342)
Petrified Films, Inc.
Twentieth Century-Fox Movietonews

Air Quality, National Commission on
Natl. Archives (RG 220)

Air races
Missouri Hist. Soc.
Natl. Archives (RG 111)
Natl. Archives (RG 342)
Natl. Archives of Canada
Petrified Films, Inc.
Prov. Arch. of Alberta
San Diego Aerospace Museum
Sonoma Video Productions
Twentieth Century-Fox Movietonews, Inc.
Western Reserve Hist. Soc.

Air raids
See Bombs and bombing

Air shows
Allen (John E.) Inc.
Analogous Productions
Energy Productions
Glenbow Mus. Arch.
Hayes Prods., Inc.
Jewell (Stuart) Prods.
Las Vegas News Bureau
MacGillivray Freeman Films
Missouri Hist. Soc.
Natl. Archives (RG 342)
Natl. Archives of Canada
Nei-Ali Prods.
Northcoast Communication, Inc.
Ohio Historical Soc.
Petrified Films, Inc.
Source Stock Footage Lib., Inc.

Twentieth Century-Fox Movietonews

Air traffic controllers
Bray Studios, Inc.
Dreamlight Images, Inc.
Energy Productions
TV Ontario

Aircraft
Airline Film & TV Promotions
Allen (John E.) Inc.
Amer. Airlines
Amer. Motion Pictures
Analogous Productions
Archive Film Prods., Inc.
Boeing Historical Archives
British Info. Svcs., Radio & TV Div.
Broad Street Prods.
CBS News Archives
Continental Airlines
Dorn (Larry) Associates
Encore Video Prods., Inc.
Energy Productions
Experimental Aircraft Assn.
FAA Technical Center
Film Bank
Film Education Institute
Fish Films, Inc.
Forsher (James) Prods. & Archives, Inc.
Glenbow Mus. Arch.
Grinberg (Sherman) Film Libraries (West)
Imageways, Inc.
Intl. Aviation Publishers, Inc.
Jewell (Stuart) Productions
Kesser Stock Footage Library
Link Flight Simulation Div.
NASA, Ames Res. Ctr., Dryden Fac.
NASA, Ames Res. Ctr., Imaging Tech.
    Branch
Natl. Archives (RG 342)
Nine Star Productions
Northrop Univ., Amer. Hall of Aviation
    Hist.
Pan American Airlines Film Lib.
Pennsylvania State Arch.
Petrified Films, Inc.
Prelinger Assoc., Inc.
Producers Library Service
Riccitelli (Bruce) Prods.
Rosebush Visions Corp.
Source Stock Footage Lib., Inc.
Stock House
Streamline Film Archives
TV Ontario
Timesteps Prods., Inc.
Tri-Comm Prods.
UDS Company
United Airlines, Creative Services
Univ. of Wis., Green Bay, Ctr. TV Prod.
Video Tape Library, Ltd.
World Monitor
See also Aerobatics; Aeronautics; Air
    Force; Air mail; Air races; Air shows;
    Airline operations; Airports; Aviation

Aircraft (Accidents)
Bray Studios, Inc.
Los Angeles News Service
Natl. Archives (RG 80)
Newsreel Video Service
Petrified Films, Inc.

Aircraft (Ambulance planes)
Petrified Films, Inc.

Aircraft (Amphibious)
Jewell (Stuart) Productions

Aircraft (Antique)
See Aircraft (Historical)

Aircraft (Autogiros)
Analogous Productions
Natl. Archives (RG 342)
Petrified Films, Inc.

Aircraft (Biplanes)
Film Bank
Film Education Institute
Petrified Films, Inc.
Prelinger Assoc., Inc.

Aircraft (Burning)
Natl. Fire Protection Assn.

Aircraft (Bush)
Archives of Ontario
Glenbow Mus. Arch.
Natl. Archives of Canada

Aircraft (Cargo)
Film Bank
Petrified Films, Inc.

Aircraft (Clipper)
Analogous Productions

Aircraft (Concorde)
See Aircraft (Supersonic)

Aircraft (Condor)
Natl. Archives (RG 200)

Aircraft (Control panels)
See Control panels

Aircraft (Crash tests)
Natl. Archives (RG 342)

Aircraft (Experimental)
Allen (John E.) Inc.
Experimental Aircraft Assn.
Jewell (Stuart) Productions
NASA, Ames Res. Ctr., Imaging Tech.
    Branch

NASA, Office of Comm.
Natl. Archives (RG 342)
Petrified Films, Inc.

Aircraft (Flying boats)
Prelinger Assoc., Inc.

Aircraft (Gliders)
CBS News Archives
Natl. Archives (RG 106)
Natl. Archives (RG 342)
Peak Productions, Inc.
Petrified Films, Inc.
Source Stock Footage Lib., Inc.
Sportsfilm
Twentieth Century-Fox Movietonews

Aircraft (Helicopters)
Analogous Productions
Archive Film Prods., Inc.
British Info. Svcs., Radio & TV Div.
CBS News Archives
Cinenet (Cinema Network)
Energy Productions
Experimental Aircraft Assn.
Film Bank
Forsher (James) Prods. & Archives, Inc.
Link Flight Simulation Div.
Mississippi Dept. of Arch. & Hist.
NASA, Ames Res. Ctr., Imaging Tech.
 Branch
Natl. Archives (RG 18)
Natl. Archives (RG 342)
Off-Broadway Video Prods.
Petrified Films, Inc.
Prelinger Assoc., Inc.
Producers Library Service
Prov. Arch. of British Columbia
Spectral Comms.
TV Ontario
Video Tape Library, Ltd.

Aircraft (Helicopters) (Accidents)
Los Angeles News Service

Aircraft (High-speed)
British Info. Svcs., Radio & TV Div.

Aircraft (Historical)
Airline Film & TV Promotions
Amer. Airlines
Archive Film Prods., Inc.
Boeing Historical Archives
Dorn (Larry) Associates
Dreamlight Images, Inc.
Experimental Aircraft Assn.
Film Bank
Glenbow Mus. Arch.
Intl. Aviation Publishers, Inc.
Jewell (Stuart) Productions
Mississippi Dept. of Arch. & Hist.
Missouri Hist. Soc.
Natl. Archives of Canada
Nei-Ali Prods.
Pan American Airlines Film Lib.
Petrified Films, Inc.
Prelinger Assoc., Inc.
Prov. Arch. of Newfoundland & Labrador

Aircraft (Hovercraft)
Analogous Productions
British Info. Svcs., Radio & TV Div.
TV Ontario

Aircraft (Jets)
Archive Film Prods., Inc.
Dreamlight Images, Inc.
Film Bank
Film Search
NASA, Ames Res. Ctr., Imaging Tech.
 Branch
Natl. Archives of Canada
Pan American Airlines Film Lib.
Petrified Films, Inc.
TV Ontario

Aircraft (Lighter-than-air)
Airship Industries (USA), Inc.
Allen (John E.) Inc.
Archive Film Prods., Inc.
CBS News Archives
Film Bank
Film Education Institute
Fish Films, Inc.
Goodyear Tire and Rubber
Grinberg (Sherman) Film Libraries (West)
Missouri Hist. Soc.
Natl. Archives (RG 18)
Natl. Archives (RG 24)
Natl. Archives (RG 80)
Natl. Archives (RG 111)
Natl. Archives (RG 342)
Natl. Archives of Canada
Petrified Films, Inc.
Spectral Comms.
Twentieth Century-Fox Movietonews
Video Tape Library, Ltd.

Aircraft (Military)
Allen (John E.) Inc.
Amer. Motion Pictures
Analogous Productions
British Info. Svcs., Radio & TV Div.
Cameo Film Library, Inc.
Development Communications, Inc.
Encore Video Prods., Inc.
Experimental Aircraft Assn.
Film Bank
Link Flight Simulation Div.
Metro Communications, Inc.
Military/Combat Stock Footage
NASA, Ames Res. Ctr., Imaging Tech.
 Branch
Natl. Archives (RG 18)
Natl. Archives (RG 80)
Natl. Archives (RG 111)
Natl. Archives (RG 178)
Natl. Archives (RG 342)
Natl. Archives of Canada
Petrified Films, Inc.
Prelinger Assoc., Inc.
Twentieth Century-Fox Movietonews
U.S. Army Transportation Museum
U.S. Dept. of Defense, Motion Media Rec.
 Ctr.
UDS Company
See also Air Force (U.S.); Navy (U.S.)

Aircraft (Model)
Petrified Films, Inc.
Prelinger Assoc., Inc.
Sportsfilm

Aircraft (Oddities)
Analogous Productions
Natl. Archives (RG 342)
Natl. Archives of Canada
Petrified Films, Inc.
See also Oddities

Aircraft (Production)
Analogous Productions
General Motors Corp.
Hagley Mus. and Lib.
Link Flight Simulation Div.
NASA, Ames Res. Ctr., Imaging Tech.
 Branch
Natl. Archives of Canada
Northrop Univ., Amer. Hall of Aviation
 Hist.
Petrified Films, Inc.
Prelinger Assoc., Inc.

Aircraft (Propeller)
CBS News Archives
Film Bank
Petrified Films, Inc.

Aircraft (Reconnaissance)
Petrified Films, Inc.

Aircraft (Research)
NASA, Ames Res. Ctr., Dryden Fac.
NASA, Ames Res. Ctr., Imaging Tech.
 Branch

Aircraft (Seaplanes)
Film Bank
Mountain Video Associates
Passage Home Communications
Petrified Films, Inc.

Aircraft (Snowplanes)
Jewell (Stuart) Productions

Aircraft (Stunts)
Amer. Motion Pictures
Cameo Film Library, Inc.
Film Bank
Grinberg (Sherman) Film Libraries (West)
Jewell (Stuart) Productions
Natl. Archives (RG 342)
Petrified Films, Inc.
Pyramid Film and Video Corp.
Twentieth Century-Fox Movietonews
See also Aerobatics; Blue Angels (U.S.
 Navy); Thunderbirds (U.S. Air Force)

Aircraft (Supersonic)
British Info. Svcs., Radio & TV Div.
Natl. Archives (RG 342)

Aircraft (Surveillance)
NASA, Ames Res. Ctr., Imaging Tech.
 Branch

Aircraft (Test flights)
See Aviation (Test flights)

Aircraft (Transport planes)
Petrified Films, Inc.

Aircraft (Triplanes)
Petrified Films, Inc.

Aircraft (Ultralight)
Dreamlight Images, Inc.
Peak Productions, Inc.
Sonoma Video Productions
Univ. of Wis., Green Bay, Ctr. TV Prod.

Aircraft (Vertical takeoff)
General Motors Corp.
NASA, Ames Res. Ctr., Imaging Tech.
 Branch

Aircraft (Water bombers)
TV Ontario

Aircraft carriers
See Ships (Aircraft carriers)

Airline operations
Amer. Airlines
Broad Street Prods.
California Newsreel
Continental Airlines
Dorn (Larry) Associates
Dreamlight Images, Inc.
Energy Productions
Film Bank
Kesser Stock Footage Library
Petrified Films, Inc.
Riccitelli (Bruce) Prods.
TV Ontario
United Airlines, Creative Services

Airplanes
See Aircraft

Airports
A.M. Stock Exchange
Airline Film & TV Promotions
British Info. Svcs., Radio & TV Div.
CBS News Archives
Continental Airlines

Dorn (Larry) Associates
Dreamlight Images, Inc.
Energy Productions
Farkas Studios, Ltd.
Film Bank
Intl. Aviation Publishers, Inc.
Kesser Stock Footage Library
Mississippi Dept. of Arch. & Hist.
Natl. Archives (RG 18)
Natl. Archives (RG 69)
Natl. Archives (RG 121)
Natl. Archives (RG 342)
Natl. Archives of Canada
Nine Star Productions
Oregon Hist. Soc.
Pennsylvania State Arch.
Petrified Films, Inc.
Port Authority of New York & New Jersey
Prelinger Assoc., Inc.
Pyramid Film and Video Corp.
Redden Archives
State Hist. Soc. of Iowa
Stock House
TV Ontario
Twentieth Century-Fox Movietonews
Wallen (Dick) Prods.
Washington Broadcast Video Lib.
World Monitor

Airships
See Aircraft (Lighter-than-air)

Ajanta, India
Petrified Films, Inc.

Akerman, Chantal
Video Data Bank

Akihabara, Tokyo
TV Ontario

Akiyoshi, Toshiko
Rhapsody Films, Inc.

Akron, Ohio (History and culture)
General Motors Corp.

Alabama
Energy Productions
Swedberg (Jack)

Alabama (History and culture)
Alabama State Dept. of Arch. & Hist.
Birmingham Pub. Lib., Media Svcs. Dept.
Estuary Press
Native Amer. Pub. Broad. Cons.
Petrified Films, Inc.
Prelinger Associates, Inc.
Univ. of Alabama, W.S. Hoole Spec. Coll.
Univ. of Tex. at Austin, Barker Tex. Hist.
 Ctr.
Worldwide Television News

Alamo, The (San Antonio, Tex.)
Hayes Prods., Inc.
Petrified Films, Inc.

Alas River, Indonesia
Sobek Productions

Alaska
Alaska Video Prods.
Beerger (Norman) Prods.
Bennett (Joel) Prods.
Bradley/McAfee Public Relations
Dreamlight Images, Inc.
First Group Comms., Inc.
Jewell (Stuart) Productions
Natl. Parks & Conservation Assn.
Nine Star Productions
Orion Post Production
Pacific Productions
Petrified Films, Inc.
Preview Media
Sonoma Video Productions

Source Stock Footage Lib., Inc.
Swedberg (Jack)
Visuart, Inc.

Alaska (History and culture)
Alaska Native Heritage Film Project
Alaska State Archives
Alaska Video Prods.
Archives of Ontario
Center for Pacific Northwest Studies
Documentary Educational Resources
Film/Audio Services, Inc.
Glenbow Mus. Arch.
Halcyon Days Prods.
KYUK-TV
Ketchikan (City of)
March of Time
Native Amer. Pub. Broad. Cons.
Natl. Archives (RG 18)
Natl. Archives (RG 22)
Natl. Archives (RG 48)
Natl. Archives (RG 69)
Natl. Archives (RG 75)
Natl. Archives (RG 77)
Natl. Archives (RG 200)
Oregon Hist. Soc.
Prelinger Assoc., Inc.
Schiele Museum
Sitka Natl. Hist. Park
Smithsonian Inst., Human Studies Film
   Arch.
Sobek Productions
U.S. Natl. Park Service Hist. Coll.
Univ. of Alaska, Fairbanks, Alaska Motion
   Picture Arch.
Univ. of Alaska, Fairbanks, Alaska Native
   Language Ctr.
Univ. of Alberta, Boreal Inst. for Northern
   Studies
Univ. of Tex. at Austin, Ransom Hum.
   Res. Ctr., Photo. Coll.
Washington State Hist. Soc.
Yukon Archives

Alaska Highway
Natl. Archives of Canada
Prov. Arch. of British Columbia
Univ. of Alberta, Boreal Inst. for Northern
   Studies
Yukon Archives

**Alaska Native Claims Settlement Act
   (1971)**
Natl. Archives (RG 75)
Sitka Natl. Hist. Park

Alaskan pipeline
See Pipelines

Albani, Emma
Natl. Archives of Canada

Albania (History and culture)
March of Time
Rockefeller Arch. Ctr.

Albany, N.Y.
New York State Dept. of Econ. Devel.

Albee, Edward
New York Pub. Lib., Perf. Arts Res. Ctr.,
   Theatre on Film and Tape

Albers, Josef
Camera Three Prods., Inc.
Mus. at Large, Ltd.

Albert, Eddie
MacDonald, J. Fred

Alberta

Departures, Inc.
Independent Media Communications
Preview Media
Prov. Arch. of Alberta
TV Ontario

Alberta (History and culture)
Glenbow Mus. Arch.
Imperial Oil Ltd.
Natl. Archives of Canada
Prov. Arch. of Alberta
Univ. of Alberta, Fac. of Ext.
Video Pool, Inc.

Albertson, Jack
Fund for Human Dignity, Inc.

Albright, Horace Marsden
U.S. Natl. Park Service Hist. Coll.

Albuquerque, N. Mex.
New Mexico State Records Ctr. & Arch.
Preview Media

Alcantara, Brazil
Brazilian-American Cultural Inst.

Alcatraz Island, Calif.
Film Bank
Petrified Films, Inc.

Alcohol abuse
AIMS Media
Addiction Research Foundation of Ontario
Alaska Native Heritage Film Project
Amer. Chemical Soc.
Amer. Hotel & Motel Assn.
Amer. Jail Assn.
Calif. Highway Patrol Acad. Media Center
Cambridge Documentary Films, Inc.
Center for Humanities, Inc.
Chicago Access Corp.
Coronet/MTI Film & Video
FMS Productions
GPN
Hazelden Found. Educ. Materials
Media Guild
Minn. Dept. of Public Safety Film Lib.
Motivational Media, Inc.
Narcotics Education, Inc.
Natl. Safety Council
PRIDE
Pyramid Film and Video Corp.
Salvation Army, Natl. Comm. Dept.
Saskatchewan Indian Cultural Ctr.
Signal Press
Toughlove
UCLA Behavioral Sci. Media Lab.
United Training Media
Univ. of West Fla., Hum. Res. Vid. Lib.
See also Alcoholism; Drug abuse; Drunk
   driving; Fetal alcohol syndrome;
   Substance abuse; Twelve-step
   programs

Alcoholics Anonymous
See Twelve-step programs

Alcoholism
Addiction Research Foundation of Ontario
Al-Anon Family Group Headquarters, Inc.
Cinema Guild
Educational Video Ctr.
FMS Productions
Hazelden Found. Educ. Materials
March of Time
Motivational Media, Inc.
Native Amer. Pub. Broad. Cons.
New Day Films
Phoenix Films and Video
Pyramid Film and Video Corp.

Sheen (Fulton J.) Comm. Ltd.
UCLA Behavioral Sci. Media Lab.
Univ. of Mich., Mich. Hist. Colls.
Women Make Movies, Inc.
See also Alcohol abuse

Alda, Alan
Spectral Comms.

Alderete, Chris
Univ. of Tex. at Austin, Benson Lat. Am.
   Coll.

Aldrin, Buzz
NASA, Lewis Research Center

**Aleutian Islands, Alaska (History and
   culture)**
Natl. Archives (RG 75)
Natl. Archives (RG 77)
Univ. of Alaska, Fairbanks, Alaska Motion
   Picture Arch.
Univ. of Alberta, Boreal Inst. for Northern
   Studies

Alexander, Jane
Christopher Closeup

Alexandra, Czarina
Archive Film Prods., Inc.

Alfonso, King
Archive Film Prods., Inc.
Natl. Archives (RG 24)

Algarin, Miguel
Giorno Poetry Systems Inst.

Algeria (History and culture)
Archive Film Prods., Inc.
March of Time
TV Ontario

Algoma, Ontario (History and culture)
Archives of Ontario

Ali, Muhammad
Archive Film Prods., Inc.

Alioto, Joseph
San Francisco Bay Area TV News Arch.

Allen, Fred
New York Pub. Lib., Perf. Arts Res. Ctr.,
   Theatre on Film and Tape

Allen, Gracie
Banks Film Library
New York Pub. Lib., Perf. Arts Res. Ctr.,
   Theatre on Film and Tape
Shokus Video

Allen, Steve
Baker (Fred) Film & Video Co.
Banks Film Library
Christopher Closeup
Natl. Archives (RG 29)
Shokus Video
Spectral Comms.
UCLA Film & Television Archive

Allende, Hortensia
Richter Productions

Allende, Salvador
Cinema Guild
New Time Films, Inc.
Worldwide Television News

Allergies
TV Ontario

Alligators
Dreamlight Images, Inc.
Energy Productions
Kesser Stock Footage Library
Minnesota Zoo
Orion Post Production
Petrified Films, Inc.

Allison, Fran
Marquette Univ., Spec. Coll.

Allport, Gordon
Inst. for Psychoanalysis

Allyson, June
Banks Film Library

Almarez, Carlos
Long Beach Mus. of Art

Almy, Max
Long Beach Mus. of Art
Video Data Bank

Alphabets and letters
Rosebush Visions Corp.

Alps
Dorn (Larry) Associates
Nemiroff Prods., Inc.
Petrified Films, Inc.

Alps (History and culture)
Petrified Films, Inc.

Alsace, France (History and culture)
Schweitzer (Albert) Ctr.

Alston, Walter
Sportsfilm

Altars
CBS News Archives
Petrified Films, Inc.
See also Churches; Religion

Aluminum
Aluminum Assn.
Archive Film Prods., Inc.
Film Bank
Natl. Archives (RG 70)
Oregon State Univ., Archives
Prelinger Assoc., Inc.

Alvarez, Augusto
Southern Calif. Inst. of Architecture

Alyea, Hubert N.
Amer. Chemical Soc.

Alzheimer's disease
Alzheimer's Disease & Rel. Disord. Assn.

Amarillo, Tex.
Dreamlight Images, Inc.

Amarillo, Tex. (History and culture)
Panhandle-Plains Hist. Museum
Texas Tech Univ., Southwest Coll.

Amazon basin, Brazil
Cousteau Society
Preview Media

**Amazon basin, Brazil (History and
   culture)**
Archive Film Prods., Inc.
Brazilian-American Cultural Inst.
Cinema Guild
Intl. Assn. of Independent Producers

NOTE: Access policies, availability and restrictions vary for each source. Please read each entry in full. Always consult "General Film and Videotape Collections" (page 599); these comprehensive collections contain material on every conceivable subject.

Smithsonian Inst., Human Studies Film
Arch.

Amazon River, Brazil-Peru
Cousteau Society
Petrified Films, Inc.

Ambient video
Stimulus

Ambrose, Tommy
Natl. Archives of Canada

Ambulances
CBS News Archives
Film Bank
Petrified Films, Inc.
Timesteps Prods., Inc.
Video Tape Library, Ltd.
See also Emergency medicine; Emergency
vehicles; Paramedics

Ameche, Don
Spectral Comms.
UCLA Film & Television Archive

Amerasians
Buck (Pearl S.) Foundation

America's Cup
America's Cup Org. Comm.
Analogous Productions
Lib. of Congress, M/B/RS
Mariners' Museum
Mystic Seaport Mus., Inc.
Offshore Productions
Wombat Film & Video

American Civil Liberties Union
Media Project

American Federation of Labor-
Congress of Industrial Organizations
(AFL-CIO)
Illinois State Hist. Lib.
Inst. for Labor Studies & Research
Labor Video Project
Natl. Archives (RG 200)
Ohio Hist. Soc.
Tamiment Lib./Wagner Labor Arch.
Wayne State Univ., Arch. Labor & Urb.
Aff.

American Federation of State, County
& Municipal Employees (AFSCME)
Smithsonian Inst., NMAH, Div. Polit.
Hist.

American Indian Movement
Chicago Comm. to Defend the Bill of
Rights
Cinema Guild
Intermedia Arts Minnesota
Natl. Archives (RG 200)

American Institute for Free Labor
Development (AIFLD)
Camino Film Projects

Americana
Allen (John E.) Inc.
Carousel Film & Video
Denver Pub. Lib., Western Hist. Dept.
Edwards, H.M.
Energy Productions
Film Search
Film/Audio Services, Inc.
Natl. Archives (RG 59)
Natl. Archives (RG 200)
Petrified Films, Inc.
Phoenix Films and Video
Postcards Associates
Prelinger Assoc., Inc.
Second Line Search
Stock Shots

Timesteps Prods., Inc.
Vedo Films/Novacom Video
Vermont Hist. Soc.
WQED/Pittsburgh
West Star Productions
White Janssen, Inc.
Windsor Prod. Corp.
See also Lifestyles

Amiens, France
Unicorn Projects

Amin Dada, Idi
Prestige Film Corp.

Amiotte, Arthur
Native Amer. Pub. Broad. Cons.

Amis, Kingsley
MacDonald, J. Fred

Amish people
See Religion (Amish)

Amnesty (Selective Service)
CBS News Archives
Intermedia Arts Minnesota

Amphibians
See Reptiles and amphibians

Amphibious vehicles
See Vehicles (Amphibious)

Amputees
See Disabled people

Amsterdam, Netherlands (History and
culture)
Petrified Films, Inc.

Amtrak
See Railroads (Amtrak)

Amusement parks
Allen (John E.) Inc.
Archive Film Prods., Inc.
Cinenet (Cinema Network)
Dreamlight Images, Inc.
Encore Video Prods., Inc.
Energy Productions
Film Bank
Forsher (James) Prods. & Archives, Inc.
Kesser Stock Footage Library
Petrified Films, Inc.
Postcards Unlimited
Prelinger Assoc., Inc.
Preview Media
Quinn (Bill) Prods.
Twentieth Century-Fox Movietonews
Video Tape Library, Ltd.
See also Bumper cars; Carousels; Penny
arcades; Point-of-view shots
(Amusement park rides); Roller
coasters; Wheels of fortune

Amusement parks (Indonesia)
Sheffield (Erin) Prods.

Anarchism
Cinema Guild
Intl. Women's Day Video Fest.
Taminent Lib./Wagner Labor Arch.

Anatomy
See Biology; Human body

Anaya, Herbert
Comm. in Sol. People of El Salvador

Anchorage, Alaska
Nine Star Productions
Preview Media

Anchorage, Alaska (History and
culture)
Oregon Hist. Soc.

Anchors
North Carolina Div. of Arch. & Hist.

Anderson, Eddie ("Rochester")
Natl. Archives/Natl. AV Ctr.
Shokus Video

Anderson, Guy
Media Project

Anderson, Karen
Sportsfilm

Anderson, Laurie
Blackwood Prods., Inc.
Monday, Wednesday, Friday Video Club
Video Data Bank

Anderson, Sherwood
East Tenn. State Univ., Arch. of
Appalachia

Andes Mountains (History and culture)
Archive Film Prods., Inc.

Ando, Tadao
Southern Calif. Inst. of Architecture

Andre, Carl
Albright-Knox Art Gallery
Blackwood Prods., Inc.
Video Data Bank

Andrew, Prince
Halcyon Days Prods.

Andrews, Dana
Banks Film Library

Andrews, Julie
Banks Film Library
Petrified Films, Inc.
Spectral Comms.
UCLA Film & Television Archive

Andrews Sisters, The
Archive Film Prods., Inc.

Andros Island, Bahamas
Passage Home Communications

Anemones
Moonlight Productions

Anesthesia
See Surgery

Angels
Film Bank
Prelinger Assoc., Inc.

Angkor Wat, Cambodia (History and
culture)
Hoover Institution

Angola (Contemporary issues)
DEC Film & Video
Third World Newsreel

Angola (History and culture)
California Newsreel
Imagen y Sonido Independiente, S.A.
U.S. Committee for UNICEF

Animal cruelty
See Animal rights and cruelty to animals

Animal races
Twentieth Century-Fox Movietonews

Animal rights and cruelty to animals

Amer. Anti-Vivisection Society
Amer. Fund For Alternatives to Animal
Res.
Animal Protection Institute of America
Animal Welfare Institute
Bullfrog Films, Inc.
Canadian Film Institute
DEC Film & Video
Focus on Animals
Friends of Animals
Intl. Soc. for Animal Rights
People for Ethical Treatment of Animals
Petrified Films, Inc.
Prelinger Assoc., Inc.
Pyramid Film and Video Corp.
See also Vivisection

Animals
Acad. of Nat. Sci. of Phila. Lib.
Allen (John E.) Inc.
Amer. Humane Assn.
Amer. Motion Pictures
Amer. Veterinary Medical Assn.
Animal Protection Institute of America
Archive Film Prods., Inc.
Benchmark Films, Inc.
Bennett (Joel) Prods.
Britannica Films & Video
Buffalo Bill Historical Center
Bullfrog Films, Inc.
CBS News Archives
Century Video Services, Inc.
Chisholm (Jack) Film Productions
Cineworks Prods. Inc.
Coe Film Assoc., Inc.
Columbia Pictures TV/Stock Film Library
Coronet/MTI Film & Video
Devillier Donegan Ent.
Di Sesso (Moe) Wild Life Film Lib.
Dobbs (Jeff) Prods.
Dreamlight Images, Inc.
Echo Film Prods., Inc.
Energy Productions
Fabulous Footage Inc.
Film Bank
Film Search
Forsher (James) Prods. & Archives, Inc.
Grinberg (Sherman) Film Libraries (East)
Grinberg (Sherman) Film Libraries (West)
Hayes Prods., Inc.
Hearst Metrotone News
Imagen y Sonido Independiente, S.A.
Innerquest Communications Corp.
Intl. Film Bureau, Inc.
Jewell (Stuart) Productions
Johnson (Martin & Osa) Safari Museum
Latham Foundation
Mass. Audubon Society
Miller (David Lee) Prods.
Minnesota Zoo
Moody Inst. of Science
Natl. Archives (RG 33)
Natl. Archives (RG 75)
Natl. Geographic Soc. Stock Footage Lib.
New York Zoological Society
Nine Star Productions
Palisades Wildlife Film Library
Petrified Films, Inc.
Phoenix Films and Video
Postcards Associates
Prelinger Assoc., Inc.
Prod. House, Inc., Motion Media Prods.
Producers Library Service
Prov. Arch. of British Columbia
Quinn (Bill) Prods.
Source Stock Footage Lib., Inc.
Spectral Comms.
TV Ontario
Twentieth Century-Fox Movietonews
Video Tape Library, Ltd.
Zielinski Productions, Inc.
See also Nature; Pets; Wildlife; Zoos;
specific animals

Animals (Endangered species)

Amer. Mus. Nat. Hist. Film Arch.
Animal Protection Institute of America
Bullfrog Films, Inc.
Ducks Unlimited, Inc.
Echo Film Prods., Inc.
Florentine Films
Focus on Animals
Imagen y Sonido Independiente, S.A.
Mass. Audubon Society
Nature Conservancy
New Jersey Network
New York Zoological Society
Pyramid Film and Video Corp.
Redes Cinevideo, S.A.
Smithsonian Inst., Off. of Telecomm.
Telltales Associates Inc.

Animals (Extinct species)
Amer. Mus. Nat. Hist. Film Arch.

Animals (In space)
NASA, Ames Res. Ctr., Imaging Tech. Branch

Animals (Oddities)
Analogous Productions
Film Bank
Hayes Prods., Inc.
Petrified Films, Inc.
See also Oddities

Animals (Performing)
Analogous Productions
Circus World Mus. Lib. & Res. Ctr.
Film Bank
Halcyon Days Prods.
Petrified Films, Inc.
Prelinger Assoc., Inc.
Shields Archival

Animation
ABC Distribution (Entertainment)
AIMS Media
Alan Twyman Presents
Amer. Federation of the Arts
Archive Film Prods., Inc.
Atlantic Independent Media
Belka Intl. Inc.
Bibliothèque Municipale de Montréal
Budget Films Inc.
CASCOM
CBS News Archives
CRM Films
Calif. Inst. of the Arts, Lib.
Canadian Filmmakers Dist. Centre
Canadian Filmmakers Dist. West
Canyon Cinema, Inc.
Carousel Film & Video
Cinema Guild
Cinémathèque québécoise
Coe Film Assoc., Inc.
Creative Film Society
DEC Film & Video
Dettlaff (Alois F. Sr.)
Disada Productions' Disney Mem. Lib.
Disney (Walt) Archives
Dreamlight Images, Inc.
Eden Entertainment, Inc.
Eisenhower (Dwight D.) Lib.
Em Gee Film Library
Encore Entertainment
Energy Productions
Fabulous Footage Inc.
Facets Multimedia, Inc.
Film Bank
Film Preservation Assoc.
Film Search
Film/Audio Services, Inc.
Film/Video Arts, Inc.
Filmack Studios
Filmtel Intl. Corp.

First Run/Icarus Films, Inc.
Fischinger, Elfriede
French Lib. in Boston
General Motors Corp.
German Language Video Ctr.
Goethe Institute Atlanta
Gould (Bert)/bay area archive
Handel Film Corp.
Hayes Prods., Inc.
Higgins (Alfred) Prods.
IFEX Films
Ideal Comms., Inc.
Imageways, Inc.
Imevision
Indiana Univ., Black Film Ctr./Arch.
Intermedia Arts Minnesota
Intl. Film Bureau, Inc.
Ivy Film
Jessiefilm
Kinsey Institute
Latina, S.A. de C.V.
Lib. of Congress, Amer. Folklife Ctr.
Lib. of Congress, M/B/RS
Lib. of Special Visual Effects
Mathematical Assn. of America
Media Project
Metropolitan Mus. of Art, Uris Ctr.
Moviecraft, Inc.
Mus. of Contemporary Art
Mus. of Mod. Art, Circulating Film Lib.
Mus. of Mod. Art, Dept. of Film
Narcotics Education, Inc.
Natl. Archives (RG 4)
Natl. Archives (RG 18)
Natl. Archives (RG 91)
Natl. Archives (RG 200)
Natl. Archives of Canada
Natl. Archives/Natl. AV Ctr.
Natl. Jewish Arch. of Broadcasting
Pacific Film Archive
Palladium Entertainment, Inc.
Parker (Kit) Films
Payne, Roz
Petrified Films, Inc.
Phoenix Films and Video
Picture Start, Inc.
Prelinger Assoc., Inc.
Pyramid Film and Video Corp.
SF•V Intl.
SIGGRAPH
San Diego State Univ., Spec. Coll.
San Francisco Acad. of Comic Art Lib.
Shell Oil Co.
Shokus Video
South Carolina Arts Comm. Media Arts Ctr.
Southwest Film/Video Archives, SMU
Spectacolor, Inc.
Starr, Cecile
Streamline Film Archives
Swank Motion Pictures, Inc.
Third World Newsreel
UCLA Film & Television Archive
UPA Prods. of America
Video Resources N.Y., Inc.
Weston Woods
Wisconsin Ctr. for Film & Theater Res.
Yale Film Study Ctr.
Z-Axis
Zafra, A.C.
See also Cartoons; Claymation; Computer graphics and animation

Animation (Computer)
See Computer graphics and animation

Animation (Slit-scan)
Film Bank
Lib. of Special Visual Effects

Animation (Stop-motion)

Prelinger Assoc., Inc.
Slingshot Prods.
Twentieth Century-Fox Movietonews

Animation (Wireframe)
Lib. of Special Visual Effects

Animation (Wirescan)
Film Bank

Animators
Camera Three Prods., Inc.

Anka, Paul
Banks Film Library

Ankara (Angora), Turkey (History and culture)
Armenian Film Foundation

Ankerberg, John
People for the American Way

Ann Arbor, Mich. (History and culture)
Petrified Films, Inc.

Ann-Margret
Banks Film Library
Petrified Films, Inc.
Spectral Comms.

Annapolis, Md. (History and culture)
Analogous Productions

Anniversaries
See Celebrations

Announcers
See Radio announcers

Anorexia
See Eating disorders

Ansara, Michael
Banks Film Library

Antarctic Ocean
Cousteau Society

Antarctica
Ocean Images

Antarctica (History and culture)
Allen (John E.) Inc.
Archive Film Prods., Inc.
Explorers Club
Mariners' Museum
NASA, Ames Res. Ctr., Imaging Tech. Branch
Natl. Archives (RG 126)
Natl. Archives (RG 200)
Natl. Archives (RG 307)
Natl. Archives (RG 342)
Natl. Archives (Stock Film Coll.)
Natl. Archives of Canada

Antelopes
Kesser Stock Footage Library
Minnesota Zoo
New Mexico State Records Ctr. & Arch.
Petrified Films, Inc.
Wings Wildlife Prods. Inc.

Antennas
Film Bank
Petrified Films, Inc.

Anthropological films and videotapes
Alaska Native Heritage Film Project
Allen (John E.) Inc.
Amer. Mus. Nat. Hist. Film Arch.

Anthropology Film Center Foundation
Appalshop Films, Inc.
Atlantis Prods., Inc.
Benchmark Films, Inc.
Bishop Mus., Visual Coll.
Brazilian-American Cultural Inst.
Canadian Filmmakers Dist. Centre
Canadian Mus. of Civilization
Canyon Cinema, Inc.
Cinema Guild
Coe Film Assoc., Inc.
Documentary Educational Resources
Duffy (Kevin) Productions
Education Development Ctr., Inc.
Film/Audio Services, Inc.
Filmakers Library
Innerquest Communications Corp.
Instituto Nacional Indigenista
Intl. Film Bureau, Inc.
Inuvik Research Ctr.
Johnson (Martin & Osa) Safari Museum
Ketchikan (City of)
Lib. of Congress, Amer. Folklife Ctr.
Lib. of Congress, M/B/RS
Manitoba Indian Cultural Centre
Native Amer. Pub. Broad. Cons.
Natl. Archives (RG 106)
Natl. Archives (RG 200)
Natl. Archives of Canada
Natl. Archives/Natl. AV Ctr.
Natl. Asian American Telecomm. Assn.
Natl. Geographic Soc. Stock Footage Lib.
Navajo Nation Library System
New Film Co., Inc.
New Zealand Embassy Film Lib.
Peralta Colleges TV
Petrified Films, Inc.
Phoenix Films and Video
Prelinger Assoc., Inc.
Prov. Arch. of Manitoba
Schomburg Ctr. for Res. in Black Culture
Singer-Sharrette Traditional Healing Films
Smithsonian Inst., Human Studies Film Arch.
Univ. of Alberta, Boreal Inst. for Northern Studies
Univ. of Calif., Ext. Media Ctr.
Univ. of Tex. at Austin, Benson Lat. Am. Coll.
Univ. of Wash. Press, Multimedia Div.
Vedo Films/Novacom Video
Wayne State Univ., Folklore Arch.
Wesleyan Univ., World Music Arch.
Western Kentucky Univ., Folklife Arch.
Wheelwright Mus. of the Amer. Indian
Yakima Indian Nation Cultural Ctr.
Yakima Television Program
Yukon Archives
Zafra, A.C.

Anti-ballistic missiles
See Missiles (Anti-ballistic)

Anti-communism
Amer. Citizenship Ctr.
Birch (John) Society
Forsher (James) Prods. & Archives, Inc.
Friends of Free China
Hoover Institution
Keep the Faith, Inc.
MacDonald, J. Fred
Mississippi Dept. of Arch. & Hist.
Natl. Archives (RG 59)
Natl. Archives/Natl. AV Ctr.
Paper Tiger TV
Parker (Kit) Films
Petrified Films, Inc.
Prelinger Assoc., Inc.
Sheen (Fulton J.) Comm. Ltd.

Anti-nuclear movement

NOTE: Access policies, availability and restrictions vary for each source. Please read each entry in full. Always consult "General Film and Videotape Collections" (page 599); these comprehensive collections contain material on every conceivable subject.

Anti-poverty programs
Bullfrog Films, Inc.
Cinema Guild
DEC Film & Video
Deep Dish TV
Estuary Press
Green Mountain Post Films
Intermedia Arts Minnesota
News On Film
Nuclear Free Zone Registry
Petrified Films, Inc.
Resource Ctr. for Nonviolence
Richter Productions
SANE/Freeze
Wilmington Coll. Peace Res. Ctr.

Anti-poverty programs
New Day Films
Southwest Film/Video Archives, SMU

Anti-Semitism
Alden Films
Amer. Zionist Youth Found.
Anti-Defamation League of B'nai B'rith
German Language Video Center
NSDAP/AO
Natl. Archives (RG 242)
Natl. Ctr. for Jewish Film
See also Holocaust; Jewish history and
culture; Prejudice

Anti-Vietnam War movement
See Vietnam antiwar movement

**Antigua and Barbuda (History and
culture)**
Natl. Archives (RG 48)

Antin, Eleanor
Video Data Bank

Antique airplanes
See Aircraft (Historical)

Antique automobiles
See Automobiles (Historical)

Antique shops
Stock House

Antiques
Video Tape Library, Ltd.

Ants
Dreamlight Images, Inc.
Film Bank
Petrified Films, Inc.
Prelinger Assoc., Inc.
Pyramid Film and Video Corp.
Wings Wildlife Prods. Inc.

Ants (Red)
TV Ontario

Apartheid
California Newsreel
DEC Film & Video
Film/Audio Services, Inc.
Filmakers Library
First Run/Icarus Films, Inc.
United Nations, Visual Materials Lib.
Villon Films
See also South Africa (Contemporary
issues); South Africa (History and
culture)

Apartments
Dorn (Larry) Associates
Film Bank
Petrified Films, Inc.
Spectral Comms.
TV Ontario

Apes
Coe Film Assoc., Inc.
Gorilla Foundation

Jewell (Stuart) Productions
Johnson (Martin & Osa) Safari Museum
Kesser Stock Footage Library
Minnesota Zoo
Petrified Films, Inc.

Aphids
Dreamlight Images, Inc.

Apollo Theatre (Harlem, N.Y.)
Pathé Pictures, Inc.

Appalachia (History and culture)
Agee (James) Film Project
Appalachian State Univ., Eury Coll.
Appalshop Films, Inc.
Blackwood (Christian) Prods., Inc.
Davenport Films
East Tenn. State Univ., Arch. of
Appalachia
Educational Video Ctr.
First Run/Icarus Films, Inc.
Flower Films & Video
Maryknoll Fathers & Brothers
Natl. Archives (RG 79)
Natl. Archives (RG 142)
Natl. Archives (RG 200)
New Time Films, Inc.
Univ. of Kentucky, AV Arch.
West Virginia State Lib. Comm.

Applause
Film Bank
Petrified Films, Inc.
See also Audiences; Spectators (Sports)

Apple picking
See Harvesting

Apples
Oregon State Univ., Archives

Appleyard, Peter
Natl. Archives of Canada

Appliances (Household)
Archive Film Prods., Inc.
CBS News Archives
Creative Venture Films
Encore Entertainment
Film Bank
General Motors Corp.
MacDonald, J. Fred
Moody Inst. of Science
Petrified Films, Inc.
Prelinger Assoc., Inc.

Aquariums
CBS News Archives
Latham Foundation
New York Zoological Society
Pyramid Film and Video Corp.
Spectral Comms.
Video Tape Library, Ltd.

Aqueducts
Calif. Dept. of Water Resources

Arab Americans
Amer.-Arab Anti-Discrimination Comm.
Middle East Institute

Arab people
Amer.-Arab Anti-Discrimination Comm.
Film Bank
Natl. Archives (RG 59)

Arab people (Depiction in the media)
Amer.-Arab Anti-Discrimination Comm.

Arabian horses
See Horses (Arabian)

Arafat, Yasir
Film Bank

Arbuckle, Fatty
Archive Film Prods., Inc.

Arbus, Diane
Camera Three Prods., Inc.
Port Washington Pub. Lib.

Arc de Triomphe (Paris)
Film Bank
Petrified Films, Inc.
TV Ontario

Arcades
Film Bank

Archaeology
Amer. Mus. Nat. Hist. Film Arch.
Amer. Zionist Youth Found.
Bullfrog Films, Inc.
CBS News Archives
Canadian Mus. of Civilization
Cinema Guild
Coe Film Assoc., Inc.
Film/Audio Services, Inc.
Glenbow Mus. Arch.
Intl. Film Bureau, Inc.
Inuvik Research Ctr.
KYUK-TV
Metropolitan Mus. of Art, Uris Ctr.
Natl. Archives (RG 106)
Natl. Archives (RG 229)
Natl. Archives (RG 307)
South Carolina Humanities Res. Ctr.
TV Ontario
TV-UNAM
Univ. of Calif., Ext. Media Ctr.
Univ. of Wash. Press, Multimedia Div.
Vedo Films/Novacom Video

**Archangel, U.S.S.R. (History and
culture)**
Univ. of Mich., Mich. Hist. Colls.

Archery
Athletic Institute
Dreamlight Images, Inc.
East Tenn. State Univ., Arch. of
Appalachia
Natl. Rifle Assn.
Prelinger Assoc., Inc.
Sportsfilm
Twentieth Century-Fox Movietonews

Archery (Instruction)
Natl. Assn. for Sport & Phys. Ed.

Architects
Amer. Inst. of Architects
Blackwood Prods., Inc.
Camera Three Prods., Inc.
Mus. of Contemporary Art
Petrified Films, Inc.
Southern Calif. Inst. of Architecture
Unicorn Projects

Architecture
Amer. Federation of the Arts
Amer. Institute of Architects
Atlantic Productions
Blackwood Prods., Inc.
Brick Institute of America
Canadian Broadcasting Corp.
Cantor (Arthur) Inc.
Channel L Working Group
Chicago Video Transfer
Coe Film Assoc., Inc.
Cranbrook Acad. of Arts
Devillier Donegan Ent.
Energy Productions
Film Bank
Film/Audio Services, Inc.
Films for the Humanities and Sciences
Intl. Film Bureau, Inc.
Mus. at Large, Ltd.
Natl. Archives of Canada

Natl. Geographic Soc. Stock Footage Lib.
New Jersey Network
Petrified Films, Inc.
Phoenix Films and Video
Postcards Associates
Prelinger Assoc., Inc.
Rosebush Visions Corp.
Site Productions
Southern Calif. Inst. of Architecture
TV Ontario
TV-UNAM
Unicorn Projects
Université Laval, Svc. des Res.
Pédagogiques
Univ. of Calif., Ext. Media Ctr.
Univ. of Minn. Libs., Manuscripts Div.
Univ. of Utah, Marriott Lib.
See also Buildings; Construction; Houses
and homes; Housing

Architecture (Art Deco)
Atlantic Productions
Spectral Comms.

Architecture (France)
Soc. for French Amer. Cult. Svcs. & Educ.
Aid

Architecture (Germany)
Goethe Institute Atlanta

Architecture (History)
Media Guild

Architecture (Islamic)
Middle East Institute

Architecture (Japan)
Southern Calif. Inst. of Architecture

Architecture (Landscape)
Landscape Architecture Found.

Architecture (Prehistoric)
Atlantic Productions

Architecture (Roman)
Film Bank

Architecture (Vernacular)
Southern Calif. Inst. of Architecture

Architecture (Victorian)
Atlantic Productions
Film Bank
Moving Media
New Jersey Network
Ohio Historical Soc.
TV Ontario

Arctic region
Alaska Video Prods.
Cousteau Society
Film Search
Natl. Assn. of Conservation Dists.
TV Ontario

Arctic region (History and culture)
Alaska Native Heritage Film Project
Allen (John E.) Inc.
Duffy (Kevin) Prods.
Explorers Club
Inuit Broadcasting Corp.
Inuvik Research Ctr.
Natl. Archives (RG 75)
Natl. Archives (RG 200)
Natl. Archives of Canada
Northstar Prods.
Northwest Territories Archives
Peary-MacMillan Arctic Museum
Petrified Films, Inc.
Prelinger Assoc., Inc.
Univ. of Alaska, Fairbanks, Alaska Motion
Picture Arch.

Univ. of Alberta, Boreal Inst. for Northern Studies

Ardoin, Alphonse
Tulane Univ., Amistad Res. Ctr.

Argentina
Imagen y Sonido Independiente, S.A.

Argentina (Contemporary issues)
Alternative Information Network
DEC Film & Video

Argentina (History and culture)
Allen (John E.) Inc.
Amnesty Intl. USA
Archive Film Prods., Inc.
Cinema Guild
DEC Film & Video
Documentary Educational Resources
Latina, S.A. de C.V.
March of Time
Natl. Archives (RG 59)
Petrified Films, Inc.
Prelinger Assoc., Inc.
Rockefeller Arch. Ctr.
Univ. of Tex. at Austin, Ransom Hum. Res. Ctr., Photo. Coll.

Aria, Arnulfo
Natl. Archives (RG 185)

Arithmetic
See Mathematics

Arizona
Beerger (Norman) Prods.
Cine-Mark
Creative Video, Inc.
Dorn (Larry) Assoc.
Dreamlight Images, Inc.
Energy Productions
Film Bank
Ideal Comms., Inc.
KD Enterprises Prods.
Oregon Hist. Soc.
Petrified Films, Inc.
Phoenix Videofilms/Karr Prods.
Preview Media
Producers' Service
Pyramid Film & Video Corp.
Sobek Prods.
Source Film & Tape Lib., Inc.
Southwest Prods., Inc.
Stimulus
Summit Films
Tri-Comm Prods.

Arizona (History and culture)
Archive Film Prods., Inc.
Arizona Hist. Soc.
Cine-Mark
MacDonald, J. Fred
Natl. Archives (RG 70)
Natl. Archives (RG 106)
Prelinger Assoc., Inc.
U.S. Natl. Park Service Hist. Coll.
Valley of the Sun Publishing

Arkansas
Arkansas Dept. of Parks & Tourism
Arkansas History Commission

Arkansas (History and culture)
Arkansas History Commission
Louisiana State Univ., Shreveport
United Nations Ctr. for Human Settlements

Arlen, Harold
Archive Film Prods., Inc.

Arlington National Cemetery (Washington, D.C.)
Petrified Films, Inc.

Arm wrestling
ABC Sports, Inc.

Armadillos
Wings Wildlife Prods. Inc.

Arman (artist)
Albright-Knox Art Gallery
Blackwood Prods., Inc.

Armenia (History and culture)
Armenian Film Foundation
Natl. Archives (RG 24)

Armenian Americans
Armenian Film Foundation

Armenian Canadians
Canadian Filmmakers Dist. Centre

Armey, Dick
Constitutional Rights Foundation

Armistice Day
See World War I (Armistice)

Armitage, Kenneth
Albright-Knox Art Gallery

Armories
CBS News Archives
Film Bank

Arms control
CBS News Archives
Cable Access of Dallas
Center for Defense Information
Cinema Guild
Idera Films
Maryknoll Fathers & Brothers
Natl. Archives (RG 200)
Natl. Archives (RG 330)
Natl. Archives of Canada
Syracuse Alternative Media Network

Arms control (Nuclear)
Amer. Security Council Foundation
Council for a Livable World Educ. Fund
DEC Film & Video
Educational Film & Video Project
Ideal Comms., Inc.
Inst. for Space & Security Studies
Ocean Earth Constr. and Dev. Corp.
Paulist Productions
People's Fund
Physicians for Social Responsibility
Public Interest Video Network
Resource Ctr. for Nonviolence
SANE/Freeze
Union of Concerned Scientists
Wilmington Coll. Peace Res. Ctr.
See also Anti-nuclear movement; Nuclear war; Nuclear weapons; Strategic Defense Initiative

Arms industry
March of Time
Natl. Archives (RG 24)
Natl. Archives (RG 111)
Natl. Archives (RG 242)

Armstrong, Louis
Banks Film Library
Chertok Assoc., Inc.

Armstrong, Neil
NASA, Lewis Research Center

Army (Canada)
Northstar Prods.

Army (Great Britain)
British Info. Svcs., Radio & TV Div.

Army (Soviet Union)
Prelinger Assoc., Inc.

Army (U.S.)
Academy of Health Sciences, U.S. Army
Archive Film Prods., Inc.
CBS News Archives
Citadel, The
Duke Univ., Perkins Lib.
Fish Films, Inc.
March of Time
Military/Combat Stock Footage
Natl. Archives (RG 111)
Natl. Archives (RG 338)
Natl. Archives/Natl. AV Ctr.
Twentieth Century-Fox Movietonews
U.S. Army Military Hist. Inst.
U.S. Army Transportation Museum
U.S. Dept. of Defense, Motion Media Rec. Ctr.
See also Battles; Korean War; Military; Military history; Military training; Military training films; Vietnam War; West Point, N.Y. (U.S. Military Academy); World War I; World War II; specific conflicts and wars

Army (U.S.) (Signal Corps)
Natl. Archives (RG 111)

Army (U.S.) (Women)
Natl. Archives (RG 342)

Army Air Corps (U.S.)
U.S. Dept. of Defense, Motion Media Rec. Ctr.

Army Air Forces (U.S.)
Natl. Archives (RG 18)

Arnaz, Desi
Banks Film Library
San Diego State Univ., Spec. Coll.
Shokus Video

Arnaz, Lucie
Shokus Video

Aronson, Boris
New York Pub. Lib., Perf. Arts Res. Ctr., Theatre on Film and Tape

Arp, Jean
Blackwood Prods., Inc.

Arquette, Rosanna
Spectral Comms.

Arrowhead, Lake (Calif.)
Petrified Films, Inc.

Arson and arsonists
Film Bank
March of Time
See also Crime and criminals; Fires

Art and artists
AIMS Media
Adair Films
Albright-Knox Art Gallery
Amer. Federation of the Arts
Amer. Zionist Youth Found.
Analogous Productions
Art Com/La Mamelle, Inc.
Art Gallery of Ontario

Artists' Television Project
Arts Television Centre
Asian American Resource Workshop
Atlantic Independent Media
Barr Films
Benchmark Films, Inc.
Blackwood (Christian) Prods., Inc.
Blackwood Prods., Inc.
Buhl Science Center
Bullfrog Films, Inc.
CBS News Archives
Cable News Network Library
Camera Three Prods., Inc.
Canadian Broadcasting Corp.
Canadian Film Institute
Canadian Filmmakers Dist. Centre
Canadian Filmmakers Dist. West
Cantor (Arthur) Inc.
Carousel Film & Video
Carter (Amon) Museum
Center for Humanities, Inc.
Center for New Television
Channel L Working Group
Chicago Video Transfer
Chisholm (Jack) Film Productions
Coe Film Assoc., Inc.
Corning Mus. of Glass
Coronet/MTI Film & Video
Cranbrook Acad. of Arts
DEC Film & Video
De Saisset Museum
EZTV
East Tenn. State Univ., Arch. of Appalachia
Electronic Arts Intermix
Em Gee Film Library
Energy Productions
Estate of Andy Warhol
Ethnic Folk Arts Center
Facets Multimedia, Inc.
Film Bank
Film Search
Filmakers Library
Films for the Humanities and Sciences
Films Incorporated
Franklin Furnace Archive, Inc.
GPN
Goethe Institute Chicago
Hallwalls Cont. Arts Ctr.
Hammer (Armand) Prods.
Handel Film Corp.
High Mus. of Art
Intermedia Arts Minnesota
Intl. Film Bureau, Inc.
Kartemquin Films
Kingston Artists' Assn., Inc.
Kitchen, The
Long Beach Mus. of Art
Media Project
Metropolitan Mus. of Art, Uris Ctr.
Mus. at Large, Ltd.
Mus. of Contemporary Art
Mus. of Mod. Art, Circulating Film Lib.
Mus. of Mod. Art, Dept. of Film
Mus. of Mod. Art of Latin America
Natl. Archives (RG 288)
Natl. Archives of Canada
Natl. Archives/Natl. AV Ctr.
Natl. Film Board of Canada
Ohio Historical Soc.
Petrified Films, Inc.
Phoenix Films and Video
Plains Art Mus. Lib.
Postcards Associates
Prov. Arch. of Manitoba
Pyramid Film and Video Corp.
Radcliffe Coll., Schlesinger Lib.
Smithsonian Inst., Off. of Telecomm.
Southwest Film/Video Archives, SMU
TV Ontario
Tamarelle's Intl. Films, Ltd.

NOTE: Access policies, availability and restrictions vary for each source. Please read each entry in full. Always consult "General Film and Videotape Collections" (page 599); these comprehensive collections contain material on every conceivable subject.

Tucson Community Cable Corp.
Université Laval, Cinémathèque
Univ. of Calif., Ext. Media Ctr.
Univ. of So. Carolina, Newsfilm Lib.
Univ. of Tex. at Austin, Benson Lat. Am.
 Coll.
V/tape
Video Data Bank
Vidéo Femmes
Video In
Video-SIG
Vidéographe Inc., Le
Walker Art Ctr.
Washington State Hist. Soc.
Women in Focus
World Monitor
Worldwide Television News
See also Art history; Crafts; Experimental
 films and videotapes; Folk art;
 Independent films and videotapes;
 Performance art; specific artists

Art and artists (African)
Camera Three Prods., Inc.
Cinema Guild
Schomburg Ctr. for Res. in Black Culture
TV Ontario

Art and artists (Asian)
Rainbow Video Prods.
Smithsonian Inst., Freer Gallery of Art

Art and artists (Aztec)
Mus. of Mod. Art of Latin America

Art and artists (Black American)
Pyramid Film and Video Corp.

Art and artists (Canadian)
Archives of Ontario

Art and artists (Caribbean)
Mus. of Mod. Art of Latin America

Art and artists (Computer)
Buhl Science Center
See also Computer graphics and animation

Art and artists ("Cowboy")
Siouxland Heritage Museum

Art and artists (German)
German Info. Ctr., Film Lib.
Goethe House, New York
Goethe Institute Atlanta
Goethe Institute Chicago
Goethe Institute Los Angeles
Goethe Institute San Francisco
Goethe Institute Vancouver

Art and artists (Graffiti)
New Day Films

Art and artists (Haitian)
Canadian Filmmakers Dist. Centre

Art and artists (Inuit)
Natl. Archives of Canada

Art and artists (Japanese)
Blackwood (Christian) Prods., Inc.
Blackwood Prods., Inc.
Japan Society, Inc. Film Center
Santa Barbara Mus. of Art

Art and artists (Latin American)
Mus. of Mod. Art of Latin America

Art and artists (Mexican)
Canal 11
Imevision
Redes Cinevideo, S.A.
TV-UNAM

Art and artists (Native American)

Echo Film Prods., Inc.
Native Amer. Pub. Broad. Cons.
Natl. Archives of Canada
Plains Art Mus. Lib.
Saskatchewan Indian Cultural Ctr.
South Dakota State Lib.
TV Ontario
See also Crafts (Native American); Native
 Americans

Art and artists (Prehistoric)
High Mus. of Art
New Film Co., Inc.

Art and artists (Public art)
Paper Tiger TV
Spectacolor, Inc.

Art and artists (Restoration)
Baylor Univ., Texas Coll.
Smithsonian Inst., Freer Gallery of Art

Art and artists (Ritual)
Samaya Foundation

Art and artists (Russian)
Smithsonian Inst., Off. of Telecomm.

Art and artists (Technique)
Carter (Amon) Museum
Corning Mus. of Glass
Industrial Designers Soc. of America
Metropolitan Mus. of Art, Uris Ctr.
Morris Video
Mus. of Contemporary Art
Soc. for French Amer. Cult. Svcs. & Educ.
 Aid

Art and artists (Teotihuacán)
Mus. of Mod. Art of Latin America

Art and artists (Women)
Amer. Federation of the Arts

Art galleries
Film Bank
Petrified Films, Inc.

Art history
Amer. Fed. of the Arts
Art Gallery of Ontario
Blackwood Prods., Inc.
Camera Three Prods., Inc.
Center for Humanities, Inc.
Creative Film Society
Handel Film Corp.
High Mus. of Art
Intl. Film Bureau, Inc.
Italian Cultural Institute
Metropolitan Mus. of Art, Uris Ctr.
Mus. of Contemporary Art
Natl. Gallery of Art
Pyramid Film and Video Corp.
Smithsonian Inst., Off. of Telecomm.
Soc. for French Amer. Cult. Svcs. & Educ.
 Aid
Univ. of Arizona, Film Coll.
Univ. of Waterloo, A-V Centre
Vedo Films/Novacom Video
Voyager Co.
Wesleyan Cinema Archives

Arthritis
Amer. Assn. of Retired Persons
Emory Medical Television Network

Artificial insemination
Ohio State Univ., Dept. of Photog. &
 Cinema

Artificial intelligence
See Computers

Artisans
Amer. Soc. Hist. Proj. Film Lib.

Artists
See Art and artists; specific artists

Arts and Crafts movement
Cranbrook Acad. of Arts

Artschwager, Richard
Albright-Knox Art Gallery

Aruba, Netherlands Antilles
Creative Video, Inc.

Asbestos
Archives of Ontario
Asbestos Victims of America
Natl. Archives (RG 70)
Natl. Archives of Canada
Prelinger Assoc., Inc.
Richter Productions
Univ. of Calif., Berkeley, Labor
 Occupational Health Prog.

Ashe, Arthur
U.S. Tennis Assn.

Asher, Betty
Video Data Bank

Ashland, Ky. (History and culture)
Marshall Univ., Spec. Coll.

Ashley, Robert
Port Washington Pub. Lib.

Ashtrays
Film Bank

Asia
Canadian Broadcasting Corp.
East-West Center
Farkas Studios, Ltd.
Film Bank
Film Search
United Airlines, Creative Services
World Monitor
Yue-Sai Kan, Inc.

Asia (Contemporary issues)
Maryknoll Fathers & Brothers

Asia (History and culture)
Allen (John E.) Inc.
Archive Film Prods., Inc.
Canadian Broadcasting Corp.
DEC Film & Video
Devillier Donegan Ent.
First Run/Icarus Films, Inc.
GPN
Halcyon Days Prods.
Idera Films
Intl. Film Bureau, Inc.
Maryknoll Fathers & Brothers
Media Project
Natl. Archives (RG 107)
Natl. Archives (RG 200)
Oakland Public Lib., Asian Branch Lib.
Petrified Films, Inc.
Prelinger Assoc., Inc.
Rainbow Video Prods.
Smithsonian Inst., Human Studies Film
 Arch.
Univ. of Hawaii at Manoa, Wong Ctr.
World Monitor
Worldwide Television News

Asian Americans
Anti-Defamation League of B'nai B'rith
Asian American Resource Workshop
Asian Cine-Vision
Natl. Asian American Telecomm. Assn.
Oakland Public Lib., Asian Branch Lib.
Third World Newsreel
Visual Communications
See also Chinese Americans; Japanese
 Americans

**Asian Americans (Depiction in the
 media)**
Asian American Resource Workshop
Asian Cine-Vision
Natl. Asian American Telecomm. Assn.

Asner, Ed
Spectral Comms.

Asparagus
TV Ontario

Aspen, Colo.
Aspen Historical Society
Moving Media
Preview Media
Summit Films, Inc.

Aspen, Colo. (History and culture)
Aspen Historical Society
Petrified Films, Inc.

Aspens
Summit Films, Inc.
TV Ontario

Assassinations
Archive Film Prods., Inc.
Calif. State Archives
Chicago Comm. to Defend the Bill of
 Rights
DEC Film & Video
Grinberg (Sherman) Film Libraries (East)
Kennedy (John F.) Library
MacDonald, J. Fred
Memphis State Univ. Libraries
Mus. & Hist. Div., City of Sacramento
Natl. Archives (RG 200)
Natl. Archives (RG 233)
Natl. Archives (RG 272)
San Francisco Bay Area TV News Arch.
Southwest Film/Video Archives, SMU
Texas Tech Univ., Southwest Coll.
Twentieth Century-Fox Movietonews
Univ. of Georgia, WSB TV News Film
 Arch.
Worldwide Television News

Assembly lines
Amer. Truck Historical Society
Broad Street Prods.
Energy Productions
Film Bank
Film Search
Forsher (James) Prods. & Archives, Inc.
Marx Production Center
Metro Communications, Inc.
Petrified Films, Inc.
Smithsonian Inst., NMAH, Div. Eng. &
 Ind.
See also Automobiles (Assembly lines);
 Factories; Industry; Manufacturing

Assembly lines (Automobiles)
See Automobiles (Assembly lines)

Asta Marias (Flowers)
Energy Productions

Astaire, Fred
Archive Film Prods., Inc.
Banks Film Library
UCLA Film & Television Archive

Astin, Patty Duke
Spectral Comms.

Astor, John Jacob
Archive Film Prods., Inc.

Astrology
Natl. Archives of Canada
Twentieth Century-Fox Movietonews
Video-SIG
Wishing Well Distribution

Astronauts
See Space program (U.S.)

Astronomy
AIMS Media
CBS News Archives
California Inst. of Tech., Inst. Arch.
Center for Humanities, Inc.
Films for the Humanities and Sciences
GPN
Harvard-Smithsonian Ctr. for Astrophysics
Natl. Archives (RG 78)
Natl. Archives (RG 307)
Natl. Science Foundation
Petrified Films, Inc.
SF•V Intl.
Univ. of Calif., Ext. Media Ctr.
See also Observatories; Space

Astronomy (Pre-Hispanic)
TV-UNAM

Astrophysics
Harvard-Smithsonian Ctr. for Astrophysics

Aswan Dam, Egypt
British Info. Svcs., Radio & TV Div.

Aswan Dam, Egypt (History)
Intl. Film Foundation

Ataturk, Kemal
Film/Audio Services, Inc.
Intl. Film Foundation
March of Time

Atchafalaya River Swamp, La. (History and culture)
Natl. Assn. of Conservation Dists.

Atget, Eugene
Port Washington Pub. Lib.

Atheism
Alternative Information Network

Athens, Greece
Preview Media

Athens, Greece (History and culture)
Petrified Films, Inc.

Athfield, Ian
Southern Calif. Inst. of Architecture

Athletes
Analogous Productions
Archive Film Prods., Inc.
Boston College, Univ. Arch.
Cappy Productions, Inc.
Charisma Prods., Ltd./Visual Motion
Fellowship of Christian Athletes
Film Bank
Film Education Institute
Film Search
Golden Gaters Prods.
Grinberg (Sherman) Film Libraries (West)
Jalbert Productions
Lemorande Prod. Co.
MTV Networks
McDonald's Corp.
NBA Entertainment, Inc.
NFL Films, Inc.
Natl. Wheelchair Athletic Assn.
Network Productions
Petrified Films, Inc.
Shields Archival
See also Olympics; Sports; specific athletes and sports

Athletes (Black)

Miles Educ. Film Prods.
Pyramid Film and Video Corp.

Athletes (Olympic)
See Olympics

Atkinson, Brooks
New York Pub. Lib., Perf. Arts Res. Ctr., Theatre on Film and Tape

Atlanta
Creative Video, Inc.
Energy Productions
Omega Films
Preview Media
Wallen (Dick) Prods.

Atlanta (History and culture)
Atlanta Hist. Soc.
Natl. Archives (RG 200)
Petrified Films, Inc.
Prelinger Assoc., Inc.
Southern Christian Leadership Conference
UCLA Film & Television Archive
Univ. of Georgia, WSB TV News Film Arch.

Atlantic City, N.J.
Dreamlight Images, Inc.
Film Bank
Preview Media

Atlantic City, N.J. (History and culture)
Archive Film Prods., Inc.
Levi, Vicki Gold
Miss America Pageant
New Jersey Network
Petrified Films, Inc.

Atlantic Ocean
Bullfrog Films, Inc.
Intl. Media Svcs., Inc.
Orion Post Production
Petrified Films, Inc.

Atlantic Ocean (History)
Natl. Archives (RG 18)

Atlantis
Cousteau Society

Atomic bombs
Analogous Productions
Archive Film Prods., Inc.
Dreamlight Images, Inc.
Energy Productions
Film Bank
Fish Films, Inc.
Hearst Metrotone News
Hoover Institution
Las Vegas News Bureau
MacDonald, J. Fred
Natl. Archives (RG 18)
Natl. Archives (RG 77)
Natl. Archives (RG 111)
Natl. Archives (RG 200)
Natl. Archives (RG 304)
Natl. Archives (RG 342)
Natl. Archives (RG 397)
Natl. Assn. of Radiation Survivors
New Mexico State Records Ctr. & Arch.
Petrified Films, Inc.
Prelinger Assoc., Inc.
Pyramid Film and Video Corp.
Rosebush Visions Corp.
SF•V Intl.
U.S. Defense Nuclear Agency
Univ. of Mich., Mich. Hist. Colls.
Wilmington Coll. Peace Res. Ctr.
See also Hiroshima, Japan (History and culture); Manhattan Project; Nagasaki,

Japan (History and culture); Nuclear war; Nuclear weapons

Atomic energy
See Nuclear energy and power

Atomic Energy Commission (U.S.)
Natl. Archives (RG 326)
Natl. Archives (RG 434)
Natl. Archives (Stock Film Coll.)
Rockefeller Arch. Ctr.

Atomic scientists
See Scientists (Atomic)

Atomic weapons
See Nuclear weapons

Atoms
Charisma Prods., Ltd./Visual Motion
Prelinger Assoc., Inc.
Rosebush Visions Corp.

Atwood, Frank Jarvis
Tucson Community Cable Corp.

Atwood, Margaret
Univ. of Waterloo, A-V Centre
Women in Focus

Auberjonois, René
Spectral Comms.

Auctions and auctioneering
Blue Sky Communications Inc.
CBS News Archives
Film Bank
Oregon State Univ., Archives
Petrified Films, Inc.
Reynolds (R.J.) Tobacco USA
TV Ontario

Audiences
Allen (John E.) Inc.
CBS News Archives
Cameo Film Library, Inc.
Dreamlight Images, Inc.
Film Bank
Fish Films, Inc.
Natl. Archives (RG 342)
Petrified Films, Inc.
Prelinger Assoc., Inc.
Spectral Comms.
TV Ontario
See also Spectators (Sports)

Audiences (Animal)
Petrified Films, Inc.

Auditoriums
Film Bank
Petrified Films, Inc.
Twentieth Century-Fox Movietonews
See also Theaters

Audubon, John James
Mass. Audubon Society

Auerbach, Red
Sportsfilm

Aurangabad, India (History and culture)
Petrified Films, Inc.

Aurora borealis
Univ. of Alberta, Boreal Inst. for Northern Studies

Austin, Tracy
U.S. Tennis Assn.

Australia
America's Cup Organizing Comm.
British Info. Svcs., Radio & TV Div.
Canadian Broadcasting Corp.
Farkas Studios, Ltd.
Pan American Airlines Film Lib.
Petrified Films, Inc.

Australia (History and culture)
Archive Film Prods., Inc.
DEC Film & Video
Devillier Donegan Ent.
Farkas Studios, Ltd.
Film/Audio Services, Inc.
Icarus Films Intl., Inc.
March of Time
Southern Calif. Inst. of Architecture
Worldwide Television News

Austria
Departures, Inc.
Goal Prods., Tourn. of Roses Film Lib.

Austria (History and culture)
Archive Film Prods., Inc.
Film/Audio Services, Inc.
Footage Inc.
Natl. Archives (RG 200)
Natl. Archives (RG 306)
Natl. Archives, Natl. AV Ctr.
Northstar Prods.
Twentieth Century-Fox Movietonews •

Autism
UCLA Behavioral Sci. Media Lab.

Autogiros
See Aircraft (Autogiros)

Automation
CBS News Archives
Film Bank
Natl. Archives (RG 378)
Prelinger Assoc., Inc.
Reynolds (R.J.) Tobacco USA
Society of Manufacturing Engineers
See also Assembly lines; Computers; Industry; Manufacturing; Robots and robotics

Automobiles
Allen (John E.) Inc.
Analogous Productions
Archive Film Prods., Inc.
CBS News Archives
Dreamlight Images, Inc.
Energy Productions
Film Bank
Fish Films, Inc.
Forsher (James) Prods. & Archives, Inc.
General Motors Corp.
Grinberg (Sherman) Film Libraries (West)
Halicki (H.B.) Productions
Hayes Prods., Inc.
Moody Inst. of Science
Petrified Films, Inc.
Prelinger Assoc., Inc.
Producers Library Service
Rosebush Visions Corp.
Slingshot Prods.
Spectral Comms.
Sports Car Club of America
Stegman Productions
Timesteps Prods., Inc.
U.S. Dept. of Transportation, Natl. Hwy. Traffic Safety Admin.
Univ. of Wis., Green Bay, Ctr. TV Prod.
Video Genesis, Inc.
Video Resources N.Y., Inc.
Video Tape Library, Ltd.
White Janssen, Inc.

NOTE: Access policies, availability and restrictions vary for each source. Please read each entry in full. Always consult "General Film and Videotape Collections" (page 599); these comprehensive collections contain material on every conceivable subject.

See also Car culture; Car washes;
   Demolition derbies; Driver education;
   Driving; Drunk driving; Traffic

Automobiles (Accidents)
Amer. Automobile Assn., FTS
Amer. Soc. of Clin. Path. Press
Cannell (Stephen J.) Productions, Inc.
Center for Auto Safety
Dreamlight Images, Inc.
Film Bank
General Motors Corp.
Highway Safety Films, Inc.
Insurance Inst. for Highway Safety
Los Angeles News Service
Natl. Archives (RG 416)
Newsreel Video Service
Off-Broadway Video Prods.
Petrified Films, Inc.
Prelinger Assoc., Inc.
Spectral Comms.
TV Ontario
Twentieth Century-Fox Movietonews
U.S. Dept. of Transportation, Natl. Hwy.
   Traffic Safety Admin.

Automobiles (Assembly lines)
Applegate Entertainment
Energy Productions
General Motors Corp.
Metro Communications, Inc.
Motor Vehicle Manufacturers Assn.
Natl. Archives (RG 25)
Natl. Archives (RG 70)
Natl. Archives (RG 200)
Pennebaker Associates, Inc.
Petrified Films, Inc.
Prelinger Assoc., Inc.
See also Assembly lines; Automobiles
   (Production); Workers (Automobile)

Automobiles (Auburn-Duesenberg)
Auburn-Cord-Duesenberg Museum
Indiana State Lib.
Indiana Univ. Folklore Arch.

Automobiles (Avanti)
Studebaker Natl. Museum

Automobiles (Buick)
General Motors Corp.
Perry (Merle G.) Arch.
Petrified Films, Inc.

Automobiles (Cadillac)
Petrified Films, Inc.

Automobiles (Chevrolet)
Archive Film Prods., Inc.
MacDonald, J. Fred
Petrified Films, Inc.
Prelinger Assoc., Inc.

Automobiles (Chrysler)
Archive Film Prods., Inc.
Chrysler Motors Corp.
Petrified Films, Inc.
Prelinger Assoc., Inc.
White Janssen, Inc.

Automobiles (Compact)
Prelinger Assoc., Inc.

Automobiles (Convertibles)
Archive Film Prods., Inc.
Petrified Films, Inc.

Automobiles (Corvair)
Petrified Films, Inc.
Prelinger Assoc., Inc.

Automobiles (Corvette)
MacDonald, J. Fred
Petrified Films, Inc.
Prelinger Assoc., Inc.

Automobiles (Dealerships)
Petrified Films, Inc.
Spectral Comms.
TV Ontario

Automobiles (DeLorean)
Pennebaker Associates, Inc.

Automobiles (Design and styling)
General Motors Corp.
Motor Vehicle Manufacturers Assn.
Pennebaker Associates, Inc.
Petrified Films, Inc.
Prelinger Assoc., Inc.

Automobiles (DeSoto)
White Janssen, Inc.

Automobiles (Dodge)
Petrified Films, Inc.
Prelinger Assoc., Inc.

Automobiles (Drag racing)
Diamond P. Sports
Film Bank
Fish Films, Inc.
Petrified Films, Inc.
Prelinger Assoc., Inc.
Sports Car Club of America
Wallen (Dick) Prods.
See also Automobiles (Hot rods);
   Automobiles (Racing)

Automobiles (Durant)
Durant Family Registry

Automobiles (Edsel)
Ford (Henry) Museum
Petrified Films, Inc.

Automobiles (Electric)
Edison Electric Institute
Electric Auto Assn.

Automobiles (Electronics)
Inst. of Electrical & Electronics Eng.

Automobiles (Engineering)
MVP Communications

Automobiles (Experimental)
Petrified Films, Inc.

Automobiles (Folding)
Analogous Productions

Automobiles (Ford)
Archive Film Prods., Inc.
Ford (Henry) Museum
Natl. Archives (RG 25)
Natl. Archives (RG 200)
Natl. Archives of Canada
Petrified Films, Inc.
Prelinger Assoc., Inc.

Automobiles (Ford Futura)
White Janssen, Inc.

Automobiles (France)
Soc. for French Amer. Cult. Svcs. & Educ.
   Aid

Automobiles (Gas pedals)
Petrified Films, Inc.
White Janssen, Inc.

Automobiles (General Motors)
General Motors Corp.
Perry (Merle G.) Arch.
Prelinger Assoc., Inc.

Automobiles (Glass)
Analogous Productions
Natl. Glass Assn.
See also Automobiles (Windshields)

Automobiles (Historical)
Amer. Motion Pictures
Baylor Univ., Texas Coll.
Dreamlight Images, Inc.
Natl. Archives of Canada
Source Stock Footage Lib., Inc.
White Janssen, Inc.

Automobiles (Hot rods)
Archive Film Prods., Inc.
Film Bank
Fish Films, Inc.
Petrified Films, Inc.

Automobiles (Industry)
DEC Film & Video
Forsher (James) Prods. & Archives, Inc.
Motor Vehicle Manufacturers Assn.
Prelinger Assoc., Inc.
Richter Productions

Automobiles (Interiors)
Film Bank

Automobiles (Jeeps)
CBS News Archives
Cannell (Stephen J.) Productions, Inc.
Chrysler Motors Corp.
Film Bank
Forsher (James) Prods. & Archives, Inc.
Insurance Inst. for Highway Safety
Natl. Archives/Natl. AV Ctr.
Peak Productions, Inc.
Petrified Films, Inc.

Automobiles (La Salle)
Petrified Films, Inc.

Automobiles (Limousines)
Cannell (Stephen J.) Productions, Inc.
Film Bank
Petrified Films, Inc.
Spectral Comms.

Automobiles (Lincoln)
Ford (Henry) Museum

Automobiles (Lincoln Continental)
Ford (Henry) Museum

Automobiles ("Low-rider")
Univ. of Tex. at Austin, Benson Lat. Am.
   Coll.

Automobiles (Maintenance)
Bullfrog Films, Inc.
Carousel Film & Video
Film Bank
Natl. Archives (RG 70)
Petrified Films, Inc.

Automobiles (Mercedes-Benz)
Film Bank

Automobiles (Miniature)
Grinberg (Sherman) Film Libraries (West)

Automobiles (Nash)
Petrified Films, Inc.
Prelinger Assoc., Inc.

Automobiles (Natural gas-powered)
Natl. Archives (RG 269)

Automobiles (Nissan)
Nissan Motor Corp. of the U.S.

Automobiles (Oldsmobile)
Archive Film Prods., Inc.
Petrified Films, Inc.
Prelinger Assoc., Inc.

Automobiles (Packard)
Petrified Films, Inc.

Automobiles (Parts)
Film Bank
Petrified Films, Inc.
White Janssen, Inc.

Automobiles (Plant openings)
Prov. Arch. of Alberta

Automobiles (Police cars)
See Police cars

Automobiles (Pontiac)
Petrified Films, Inc.
Prelinger Assoc., Inc.

Automobiles (Production)
Allen (John E.) Inc.
Durant Family Registry
Energy Productions
Film Bank
General Motors Corp.
MVP Communications
Motor Vehicle Manufacturers Assn.
Natl. Archives (RG 25)
Natl. Archives (RG 70)
Natl. Archives (RG 200)
Natl. Archives of Canada
Petrified Films, Inc.
Prelinger Assoc., Inc.
Robotic Industries Assn.
TV Ontario
See also Assembly lines; Automobiles
   (Assembly lines)

Automobiles (Production) (Japan)
TV Ontario

Automobiles (Racing)
ABC Sports, Inc.
Allen (John E.) Inc.
Analogous Productions
Auburn-Cord-Duesenberg Museum
Chrysler Motors Corp.
Diamond P. Sports
Edwards, H.M.
Encore Video Prods., Inc.
Film Bank
Film Search
Freewheelin' Films, Ltd.
Grinberg (Sherman) Film Libraries (West)
Indianapolis Motor Speedway Corp.
Intl. Media Services, Inc.
Las Vegas News Bureau
Lib. of Congress, M/B/RS
MVP Communications
Mass. Inst. of Tech., MIT Museum
NASCAR Video
Natl. Archives of Canada
Nissan Motor Corp. of the U.S.
Petrified Films, Inc.
Rainbow Video Prods.
Second Line Search
Spectral Comms.
Sports Car Club of America
Sportsfilm
Studebaker Natl. Museum
Summit Films, Inc.
Twentieth Century-Fox Movietonews
Univ. of Notre Dame, Joyce Sports Coll.
Utah State Archives
Video Tape Library, Ltd.
Volkswagen of America, Inc.
Wallen (Dick) Prods.
See also Automobiles (Drag racing);
   Automobiles (Hot rods)

Automobiles (Racing) (Grand Prix)
Amer. Motion Pictures
Film Bank
Network Productions
Petrified Films, Inc.
Sports Car Club of America

Automobiles (Racing) (Indianapolis 500)
Analogous Productions

Archive Film Prods., Inc.
Goodyear Tire and Rubber
Indiana State Lib.
Indianapolis Motor Speedway Corp.
Second Line Search
Sports Car Club of America
Wallen (Dick) Prods.

Automobiles (Racing) (Midget)
Petrified Films, Inc.

Automobiles (Racing) (Stock car)
Channell One Video
Diamond P. Sports
Encore Video Prods., Inc.
Film Bank
Grinberg (Sherman) Film Libraries (West)
NASCAR Video
Northcoast Communication, Inc.
Spalla (Rick) Video Prods.
Sports Car Club of America
Wallen (Dick) Prods.

Automobiles (Rallies)
Natl. Archives of Canada

Automobiles (Rambler)
White Janssen, Inc.

Automobiles (Repair)
See Automobiles (Maintenance)

Automobiles (Rolls Royce)
Petrified Films, Inc.

Automobiles (Safety)
MacDonald, J. Fred
New Jersey Network
Worldwide Television News
See also Automobiles (Seat belts and air bags)

Automobiles (Safety testing)
Calif. Dept. of Transportation
General Motors Corp.
Insurance Inst. for Highway Safety
Natl. Archives (RG 416)
Prelinger Assoc., Inc.
U.S. Dept. of Transportation, Natl. Hwy. Traffic Safety Admin.

Automobiles (Sales)
General Motors Corp.
Petrified Films, Inc.
Prelinger Assoc., Inc.

Automobiles (Seat belts and air bags)
Insurance Inst. for Highway Safety
Motor Vehicle Manufacturers Assn.
Natl. Archives (RG 416)
Prelinger Assoc., Inc.
Rogers (Will) Institute
U.S. Dept. of Transportation, Natl. Hwy. Traffic Safety Admin.

Automobiles (Showrooms)
Petrified Films, Inc.
Prelinger Assoc., Inc.

Automobiles (Solar-powered)
Electric Auto Assn.
Film/Audio Services, Inc.
General Motors Corp.
Northstar Prods.

Automobiles (Speedometers)
Petrified Films, Inc.
White Janssen, Inc.

Automobiles (Sports cars)
Petrified Films, Inc.

Spectral Comms.
Sports Car Club of America, Inc.

Automobiles (Studebaker)
Petrified Films, Inc.
Studebaker Natl. Museum

Automobiles (Stunts)
Cannell (Stephen J.) Productions, Inc.
Forsher (James) Prods. & Archives, Inc.
Grinberg (Sherman) Film Libraries (West)
Halicki (H.B.) Productions
Petrified Films, Inc.
Prelinger Assoc., Inc.
Sportsfilm

Automobiles (Stutz)
Petrified Films, Inc.

Automobiles (Taillights)
White Janssen, Inc.

Automobiles (Television commercials)
Brooklyn Coll., Diamant Mem. Lib.
Ford (Henry) Museum
MacDonald, J. Fred
Movietime, Inc. Archives
Prelinger Assoc., Inc.
Studebaker Natl. Museum
Video Resources N.Y., Inc.
White Janssen, Inc.
See also Television commercials

Automobiles (Testing)
Motor Vehicle Manufacturers Assn.

Automobiles (Three-wheeled)
White Janssen, Inc.

Automobiles (Thunderbird)
Ford (Henry) Museum
Petrified Films, Inc.
White Janssen, Inc.

Automobiles (Tires)
Analogous Productions
CBS News Archives
Film Bank
Prelinger Assoc., Inc.
Rosebush Visions Corp.
Tire Industry Safety Council

Automobiles (Used car lots)
Petrified Films, Inc.

Automobiles (Volkswagen)
Archive Film Prods., Inc.
Petrified Films, Inc.
Volkswagen of America, Inc.

Automobiles (Windshields)
Corning Mus. of Glass
Film Bank
Natl. Glass Assn.
Prelinger Assoc., Inc.
See also Automobiles (Glass)

Automobiles (Wrecking)
Oregon State Univ., Archives
See also Demolition

Autopsies
Film Bank
TV Ontario
Washington Univ., Brown Schl. of Soc. Work

Autopsies (Animal)
Oregon State Univ., Archives

Autry, Gene

Archive Film Prods., Inc.
Banks Film Library
Flying A Pictures Inc.
Southwest Film/Video Archives, SMU

Avalanches
Archive Film Prods., Inc.
CBS News Archives
Film Bank
Petrified Films, Inc.
Twentieth Century-Fox Movietonews
Univ. of Wash. Press, Multimedia Div.

Avalon, Frankie
Banks Film Library
Spalla (Rick) Video Prods.

Avalos, David
Paper Tiger TV

Avant-garde films and videotapes
See Experimental films and videotapes

Avery, Milton
Albright-Knox Art Gallery

Aviation
Allen (John E.) Inc.
Archive Film Prods., Inc.
Bray Studios, Inc.
Chiappetta Prods., Inc.
Em Gee Film Library
FAA Technical Center
Film Bank
Glenbow Mus. Arch.
Grinberg (Sherman) Film Libraries (West)
Hearst Metrotone News
Intl. Aviation Publishers, Inc.
Link Flight Simulation Div.
Los Angeles News Service
Military/Combat Stock Footage
Nassau County Museum
Natl. Archives (RG 200)
Natl. Archives of Canada
Natl. Archives/Natl. AV Ctr.
Pan American Airlines Film Lib.
Petrified Films, Inc.
Prov. Arch. of British Columbia
Redden Archives
San Diego Aerospace Museum
Smithsonian Inst., Natl. Air & Space Museum
Twentieth Century-Fox Movietonews
UDS Company
See also Aeronautics; Air Force; Air mail; Air races; Air shows; Air traffic controllers; Aircraft; Airline operations; Airports; Battles (Air); Point-of-view shots (Airplanes); World War I; World War II

Aviation (Barnstorming)
Allen (John E.) Inc.
Film Education Institute
Grinberg (Sherman) Film Libraries (West)
Petrified Films, Inc.

Aviation (History)
Bray Studios, Inc.
Connecticut State Library
Experimental Aircraft Assn.
FAA Technical Center
Film Preservation Assoc.
Military/Combat Stock Footage
NASA, Johnson Space Ctr., Film & Video Dist. Lib.
NASA, Lewis Research Center
Nassau County Museum
Natl. Archives (RG 24)
Natl. Archives (RG 106)

Natl. Archives (RG 111)
Natl. Archives (RG 200)
Natl. Archives (RG 306)
Natl. Archives (RG 342)
Natl. Archives of Canada
Northrop Univ., Amer. Hall of Aviation Hist.
Oregon Hist. Soc.
Pan American Airlines Film Lib.
Petrified Films, Inc.
Prov. Arch. of Alberta
Prov. Arch. of Newfoundland & Labrador
Redden Archives
San Diego Aerospace Museum
Smithsonian Inst., Natl. Air & Space Museum
U.S. Dept. of Defense, Motion Media Rec. Ctr.
UDS Company
Univ. of Alaska, Fairbanks, Alaska Motion Picture Arch.
Univ. of So. Carolina, Newsfilm Lib.
Western Reserve Hist. Soc.
Wright Brothers Coll.
Yukon Archives

Aviation (Military)
Natl. Archives (RG 127)
Petrified Films, Inc.
Redden Archives
U.S. Dept. of Defense, Motion Media Rec. Ctr.
See also Aircraft (Military)

Aviation (Naval)
Film Bank

Aviation (Prairie)
Prov. Arch. of Alberta

Aviation (Test flights)
Analogous Productions
Hagley Mus. and Lib.
NASA, Ames Res. Ctr., Dryden Fac.
NASA, Ames Res. Ctr., Imaging Tech. Branch
Natl. Archives of Canada

Aviation (Transatlantic flights)
Film Bank
Natl. Archives (RG 24)
Natl. Archives (RG 106)
Natl. Archives (RG 111)
Natl. Archives (RG 200)
Natl. Archives of Canada
Petrified Films, Inc.
Prelinger Assoc., Inc.
Prov. Arch. of Newfoundland & Labrador

Avionics
FAA Technical Center

Avocets
Wings Wildlife Prods. Inc.

Award ceremonies
Analogous Productions
Banks Film Library
CBS News Archives
Country Music Foundation, Inc.
Film Bank
Historic Thoroughbred Colls., Inc.
Intl. Dance Exercise Assn.
Intl. Fashion Video Library
New York Pub. Lib., Perf. Arts Res. Ctr., Theatre on Film and Tape
Petrified Films, Inc.
Prelinger Assoc., Inc.
Spectral Comms.
TV Ontario
UCLA Film & Television Archive

NOTE: Access policies, availability and restrictions vary for each source. Please read each entry in full. Always consult "General Film and Videotape Collections" (page 599); these comprehensive collections contain material on every conceivable subject.

See also Academy Awards

Awash River, Ethiopia
Sobek Productions

Aycock, Alice
Blackwood Prods., Inc.
Mus. of Contemporary Art
Video Data Bank
Walker Art Ctr.

Ayers Rock (Uluru), Australia
Petrified Films, Inc.

Ayers Rock (Uluru), Australia (History and culture)
Devillier Donegan Enterprises

Aznavour, Charles
Blackwood (Christian) Prods., Inc.

BMX racing
Film Bank

Babashoff, Shirley
U.S. Olympic Committee

Babbitt, Bruce
Natl. Assn. for the Advancement of
Colored People

Babies
Analogous Productions
Appalshop Films, Inc.
Archive Film Prods., Inc.
CBS News Archives
Churchill Films
Cinema Medica
File Tape Co.
Film Bank
Fish Films, Inc.
High/Scope Educ. Res. Found.
Inst. for Psychoanalysis
March of Time
Milner-Fenwick, Inc.
Petrified Films, Inc.
Polymorph Films, Inc.
Prelinger Assoc., Inc.
Stock Shots
TV Ontario
Twentieth Century-Fox Movietonews
Univ. of Wisconsin — Extension
See also Breast-feeding; Childbirth;
Children; Parents and parenting

Babies (New Year's)
New York Hosp.-Cornell Med. Ctr., Arch.

Babilonia, Tai
U.S. Olympic Comm.

Baboons
Dreamlight Images, Inc.
Jewell (Stuart) Productions
Univ. of Calif., Ext. Media Ctr.

Baby boom (U.S., 1940s-50s)
Archive Film Prods., Inc.
Petrified Films, Inc.
Prelinger Assoc., Inc.
Streamline Film Archives
Twentieth Century-Fox Movietonews
See also Lifestyles (U.S.) (1940s);
Lifestyles (U.S.) (1950s)

Babysitting
Prelinger Assoc., Inc.

Baca, Fernando de
Univ. of Tex. at Austin, Benson Lat. Am.
Coll.

Bacall, Lauren
Petrified Films, Inc.

Bacharach, Burt
Spectral Comms.

Backgrounds
Lib. of Special Visual Effects
Petrified Films, Inc.
Rosebush Visions Corp.
Unger Computer Graphics
See also Computer graphics and
animation; Process plates

Backpacking
See Hiking

Backstage scenes
Film Bank
Petrified Films, Inc.
Prelinger Assoc., Inc.

Backus, Jim
Banks Film Library

Backyards
Petrified Films, Inc.
Prelinger Assoc., Inc.

Bacolod Island, Philippines
Farkas Studios, Ltd.

Bacon, Francis
Amer. Federation of the Arts
Blackwood Prods., Inc.
Giorno Poetry Systems Inst.

Bacteria
British Info. Svcs., Radio & TV Div.
Film Bank
Historical Health Film Coll.
Petrified Films, Inc.

Badlands National Park, S. Dak.
Solaris Dance/Theatre/Video

Badminton
Athletic Institute
Film Bank
Sportsfilm
TV Ontario

Badminton (Instruction)
Natl. Assn. for Sport & Phys. Ed.

Baer, Max
Archive Film Prods., Inc.
Grinberg (Sherman) Film Libraries (West)

Baez, Joan
Creative Film Society
Estuary Press
Law (Lisa) Prods.
New Film Co., Inc.
United Farm Workers of America (UFW)
Villon Films

Baffin Island, Northwest Territories
TV Ontario

**Baffin Island, Northwest Territories
(History and culture)**
Archives of Ontario
Northwest Territories Archives
Peary-MacMillan Arctic Museum

Bagels
Ergo Media

Bagpipes
East Tenn. State Univ., Arch. of
Appalachia
TV Ontario

Baha'i religion
See Religion (Baha'i)

Bahamas

Creative Video, Inc.
Kesser Stock Footage Library
MacGillivray Freeman Films
Passage Home Communications
Preview Media

Bailey, F. Lee
Daphne Productions, Inc.

Bain, Barbara
Spectral Comms.

Bain, Myrna
Paper Tiger TV
Video Data Bank

**Bainbridge Island, Wash. (History and
culture)**
Plains Art Mus. Lib.

Baja California, Mexico
Jewell (Stuart) Productions
Preview Media

Baker, Anita
Spectral Comms.

Baker, Bonnie
Pathé Pictures, Inc.

Baker, Carroll
Univ. of Wyoming, Amer. Heritage Ctr.

Baker, Howard
Natl. Assn. for the Advancement of
Colored People

Baker, Josephine
Archive Film Prods., Inc.

Bakeries and baking industry
Amer. Bakers Assn.
Amer. Inst. of Baking
Dreamlight Images, Inc.
Film Bank
Media Project
Petrified Films, Inc.
Prelinger Assoc., Inc.
TV Ontario

Bakersfield, Calif. (History and culture)
Petrified Films, Inc.

**Bakery, Confectionery and Tobacco
Workers Union**
Univ. of Maryland, McKeldin Lib.

Baking
See Bakeries and baking industry

Bakker, Jim and Tammy
People for the American Way

Bald heads
See Heads (Bald)

Baldessari, John
Albright-Knox Art Gallery
Video Data Bank

Baldwin, Clive
Intl. Al Jolson Soc.

Baldwin, James
Schomburg Ctr. for Res. in Black Culture

Baldwin, Raymond
Connecticut State Library

Baldwin, Roger
Media Project

Balfour, Arthur J.
Natl. Archives (RG 59)

Bali, Indonesia
Farkas Studios, Ltd.
Sonoma Video Productions

Bali, Indonesia (History and culture)
Archive Film Prods., Inc.
Documentary Educational Resources
Film/Audio Services, Inc.
Lib. of Congress, M/B/RS
Petrified Films, Inc.

Ball, George
Natl. Archives (RG 59)

Ball, Lucille
Banks Film Library
Daphne Productions, Inc.
San Diego State Univ., Spec. Coll.
Shokus Video
UCLA Film & Television Archive
Windsor Prod. Corp.

Ballet
See Dance and dancing (Ballet)

Ballooning
Allen (John E.) Inc.
Dreamlight Images, Inc.
Energy Productions
Film Bank
Forsher (James) Prods. & Archives, Inc.
Goal Prods., Tourn. of Roses Film Lib.
Grinberg (Sherman) Film Libraries (West)
MacGillivray Freeman Films
Merkel Films
Natl. Archives (RG 342)
Peak Productions, Inc.
Petrified Films, Inc.
Photo-Chuting Enterprises
Pyramid Film and Video Corp.
Quinn (Bill) Prods.
Source Stock Footage Lib., Inc.
Sports Cinematography Group
Summit Films, Inc.
Twentieth Century-Fox Movietonews

Balloons
Archive Film Prods., Inc.
CBS News Archives
Energy Productions
Source Stock Footage Lib., Inc.
Spectral Comms.
TV Ontario

Balloons (Observation)
Petrified Films, Inc.

Ballroom dancing
See Dance and dancing (Ballroom)

Ballrooms
Film Bank

Baltic States investigation (1953-54)
Natl. Archives (RG 233)

Baltimore
Dreamlight Images, Inc.
Energy Productions
Preview Media
Unicorn Projects

Baltimore (History and culture)
MacDonald, J. Fred
Natl. Assn. for the Advancement of
Colored People
Petrified Films, Inc.
Prelinger Assoc., Inc.
Unicorn Projects
Univ. of Baltimore, Abell TV Arch.

Bamboo
Jewell (Stuart) Productions

Bananarama (Rock and roll band)
Spectral Comms.

Bananas
Film Bank

Bancroft, Anne
Spectral Comms.
Univ. of Mich., Mich. Hist. Colls.

Bandits
See Crime and criminals

Bangkok, Thailand
Farkas Studios, Ltd.

Bangkok, Thailand (History and culture)
Petrified Films, Inc.

Bangladesh
Canadian Broadcasting Corp.
East-West Center

Bangladesh (History and culture)
Arch. of the Mennonite Church
Johns Hopkins Univ./Population Comm. Svcs.
Middle East Institute
UNICEF, Div. Info. & Pub. Aff.

Bangor, Maine (History and culture)
Bangor Historical Society
Northeast Historic Film

Banham, Reyner
Southern Calif. Inst. of Architecture

Bankhead, Tallulah
Las Vegas News Bureau

Banking machines (ATMs)
TV Ontario

Banks and banking industry
Archive Film Prods., Inc.
Broad Street Prods.
CBS News Archives
Film Bank
Idera Films
Inst. of Financial Education
Petrified Films, Inc.
Prelinger Assoc., Inc.
TV Ontario
United Training Media
See also Financial industry

Banners
Film Bank
Prelinger Assoc., Inc.
See also Signs

Banquets
CBS News Archives
Film Bank
Fish Films, Inc.
Twentieth Century-Fox Movietonews

Bañuelos, Romana
Univ. of Tex. at Austin, Benson Lat. Am. Coll.

Baptists
See Religion (Baptist)

Bar mitzvahs
Magnes (Judah L.) Museum
TV Ontario

Baraka, Amiri
Giorno Poetry Systems Inst.

Baranceanu, Belle
De Saisset Museum

Barbados
Preview Media

Barbados (History and culture)
Mus. of Mod. Art of Latin America
U.S. Committee for UNICEF

Barbecues
Film Bank
Hayes Prods., Inc.
Lib. of Congress, Amer. Folklife Ctr.
Omega Films
Petrified Films, Inc.
Twentieth Century-Fox Movietonews

Barber, John
MacDonald, J. Fred

Barbers and barbershops
Film Bank
Petrified Films, Inc.
Prelinger Assoc., Inc.

Barbershop music
See Music (Barbershop)

Barcelona, Spain
Preview Media

Barfield, Owen
Wheaton Coll., Wade Ctr.

Barg, Barbara
Video Data Bank

Barges
See Boats and boating (Barges)

Barkers (Amusement parks)
Petrified Films, Inc.

Barkley, Alben W.
MacDonald, J. Fred

Barksdale Air Force Base, La.
Louisiana State Univ., Shreveport

Barlett, Bonnie
Spectral Comms.

Barley
British Info. Svcs., Radio & TV Div.
Northcoast Communication, Inc.

Barnes, Edward Larrabee
Unicorn Projects

Barnouw, Erik
Port Washington Pub. Lib.

Barns
Film Bank
Natl. Archives (RG 96)
Petrified Films, Inc.
TV Ontario
See also Farms and farming

Barnstorming
See Aviation (Barnstorming)

Barracudas
Marineland of Florida

Barrels
CBS News Archives

Film Bank

Barrels (Production)
Canadian Filmmakers Dist. Centre
Seagram Museum

Barrett, Rona
Spectral Comms.

Barricades
CBS News Archives
Film Bank

Barrios
Petrified Films, Inc.

Barrow, Alaska
Alaska Video Prods.

Barrow, Clyde
Natl. Archives (RG 21)

Barrymore, Ethel
Film/Audio Services, Inc.
Frontline Video, Inc.
Streamline Film Archives

Barrymore, John
Archive Film Prods., Inc.

Bars
CBS News Archives
Farkas Studios, Ltd.
Film Bank
Petrified Films, Inc.
Twentieth Century-Fox Movietonews
See also Bartenders; Discotheques; Nightclubs

Bars (Prison)
Petrified Films, Inc.
See also Prisons and prisoners

Bartenders
Petrified Films, Inc.
Seagram Museum

Bartlett, Jennifer
Long Beach Mus. of Art
Video Data Bank
Walker Art Ctr.

Baseball
Allen (John E.) Inc.
Amer. Motion Pictures
Analogous Productions
Archive Film Prods., Inc.
Athletic Institute
Chicago Access Corp.
Encore Video Prods., Inc.
Energy Productions
Film Bank
Fish Films, Inc.
Forsher (James) Prods. & Archives, Inc.
Kesser Stock Footage Library
Petrified Films, Inc.
Second Line Search
Source Stock Footage Lib., Inc.
Spalla (Rick) Video Prods.
Twentieth Century-Fox Movietonews
UCLA Film & Television Archive

Baseball (College)
NCAA Productions
Oregon State Univ., Archives
Windsor Prod. Corp.

Baseball (High school)
Eastern Kentucky Univ.
Petrified Films, Inc.

Baseball (Instruction)
NCAA Productions
Natl. Assn. for Sport & Phys. Ed.

Baseball (Little League)
ABC Sports, Inc.
Analogous Productions
Little League Baseball Museum
Petrified Films, Inc.

Baseball (Minor league)
4•6•8 Prods., Inc.

Baseball (Professional)
Cincinnati Hist. Soc.
Film Search
Grinberg (Sherman) Film Libraries (West)
Natl. Archives of Canada
Phoenix Communications Group, Inc.
Seagram Museum
Sports Mus. of New England
Sportsfilm

Baseball (Sandlot)
Analogous Productions
Petrified Films, Inc.
Prelinger Assoc., Inc.

Baseball Hall of Fame
Analogous Productions

Baselitz, George
Blackwood Prods., Inc.

Basie, Count
Archive Film Prods., Inc.
Chertok Assoc., Inc.
Pathé Pictures, Inc.
Rhapsody Films, Inc.

Basketball
Analogous Productions
Athletic Institute
Film Bank
Grinberg (Sherman) Film Libraries (West)
Northeast Historic Film
Prov. Arch. of Alberta
Second Line Search
Spalla (Rick) Video Prods.
TV Ontario
Twentieth Century-Fox Movietonews
U.S. Olympic Comm.
Univ. of Notre Dame, Joyce Sports Coll.
Video Tape Library, Ltd.
Zielinski Productions, Inc.

Basketball (Amateur)
Naismith Mem. Basketball Hall of Fame

Basketball (Children's)
Lemorande Prod. Co.

Basketball (College)
Auburn University Archives
Bowling Green State Univ., Ctr. Arch. Coll.
DePauw University, Archives
Louisiana State Univ. Libs., Spec. Coll.
Marquette Univ., Spec. Coll.
NCAA Productions
Northern Ill. Univ., Reg. Hist. Ctr.
Oregon State Univ., Archives
Petrified Films, Inc.
Roberts (Oral) Univ.
Sportsfilm
Texas A&M Univ., Univ. Arch.
Univ. of Kansas
Univ. of Rhode Island, Univ. Lib.
Univ. of Toledo, Univ. Arch.
Windsor Prod. Corp.

NOTE: Access policies, availability and restrictions vary for each source. Please read each entry in full. Always consult "General Film and Videotape Collections" (page 599); these comprehensive collections contain material on every conceivable subject.

Basketball (Girl's)
Eastern Kentucky Univ.

Basketball (High school)
Eastern Kentucky Univ.
Petrified Films, Inc.

Basketball (Instruction)
NCAA Productions
Naismith Mem. Basketball Hall of Fame
Natl. Assn. for Sport & Phys. Ed.

Basketball (International)
Naismith Mem. Basketball Hall of Fame

Basketball (Olympic)
Naismith Mem. Basketball Hall of Fame

Basketball (Professional)
Hayes Prods., Inc.
NBA Entertainment, Inc.
Naismith Mem. Basketball Hall of Fame
Sportsfilm
Univ. of Notre Dame, Joyce Sports Coll.

Basketball (Women's)
Sportsfilm

Basketball (Women's) (Instruction)
NCAA Productions

Basketmaking
Petrified Films, Inc.

Basques
First Run/Icarus Films, Inc.
Third World Newsreel

Basquiat, Jean-Michel
Monday, Wednesday, Friday Video Club

Bass (Fish)
New Film Co., Inc.
TV Ontario

Basso, Guido
Natl. Archives of Canada

Bates, Daisy
Natl. Assn. for the Advancement of
  Colored People

Bathing beauties
Allen (John E.) Inc.
Analogous Productions
Archive Film Prods., Inc.
Fish Films, Inc.
Miss America Pageant
Petrified Films, Inc.
Prelinger Assoc., Inc.

Bathrick, Serafina
Paper Tiger TV

Bathrooms
Film Bank
Fish Films, Inc.
Petrified Films, Inc.
Prelinger Assoc., Inc.

Bathyspheres
New York Zoological Society

Batik
TV Ontario

Batista, Fulgencio
Archive Film Prods., Inc.

Baton Rouge, La.
Preview Media

Baton twirling
Intermedia Arts Minnesota

Bats (Mammal)
Jewell (Stuart) Productions
Petrified Films, Inc.

Battcock, Gregory
Video Data Bank

Battered women
See Domestic violence

Batteries (Flashlight)
Prelinger Assoc., Inc.

Battles
Archivo Historico Cinematografico
Columbia Pictures TV/Stock Film Library
Film Bank
Grinberg (Sherman) Film Libraries (West)
Military/Combat Stock Footage
NSDAP/AO
Natl. Archives (RG 18)
Natl. Archives (RG 59)
Natl. Archives (RG 80)
Natl. Archives (RG 111)
Natl. Archives (RG 127)
Natl. Archives (RG 342)
Natl. Archives of Canada
Natl. Archives/Natl. AV Ctr.
Petrified Films, Inc.
Prelinger Assoc., Inc.
U.S. Dept. of Defense, Motion Media Rec.
  Ctr.
See also Korean War; Military; Military
  history; Vietnam War; Wars; World
  War I; World War II; specific conflicts
  and wars

Battles (Air)
Natl. Archives (RG 200)
Natl. Archives/Natl. AV Ctr.
Petrified Films, Inc.
UDS Company

Battles (Amphibious)
Natl. Archives (RG 18)

Battles (Land)
Natl. Archives (RG 18)
Natl. Archives (RG 200)
Natl. Archives (RG 242)

Battles (Sea)
Natl. Archives (RG 18)
Natl. Archives (RG 242)

Baugh, Sammy
NFL Films, Inc.

Bavaria, Germany (History and culture)
Worldwide Television News

Baxter, Anne
Univ. of Wyoming, Amer. Heritage Ctr.

Bay of Pigs (1961)
Cinema Guild
Natl. Archives (RG 64)

Bayer, Herbert
Cantor (Arthur) Inc.

Bayous
Film Bank
Petrified Films, Inc.
Preview Media

Bazaars
Petrified Films, Inc.

Beach Boys, The
Clark (Dick) Media Archives, Inc.

Beach houses
Film Bank
TV Ontario

Beaches
Applegate Entertainment
Brekke Television Prods.
British Info. Svcs., Radio & TV Div.
CBS News Archives
Century Video Services, Inc.
Cinenet (Cinema Network)
Communications Concepts
Creative Video, Inc.
Dobovan Productions, Inc.
Dorn (Larry) Associates
Dreamlight Images, Inc.
Echo Film Prods., Inc.
Encore Video Prods., Inc.
Energy Productions
Farkas Studios, Ltd.
Film Bank
Forsher (James) Prods. & Archives, Inc.
Hayes Prods., Inc.
Island Video
Kesser Stock Footage Library
Long Island State Park Comm.
Mountain Video Associates
Natl. Archives (RG 26)
Peak Productions, Inc.
Petrified Films, Inc.
Quenzer Driscoll Dawson, Inc.
Quinn (Bill) Prods.
Rhode Island Hist. Soc.
Riccitelli (Bruce) Prods.
Site Productions
Slingshot Prods.
Source Stock Footage Lib., Inc.
Spectral Comms.
TV Ontario
Telemation Productions
Tri-Comm Prods.
Twentieth Century-Fox Movietonews
Video Tape Library, Ltd.
Zielinski Productions, Inc.
See also Bikinis; Oceans; Seascapes;
  Seashores; Sunbathing

Beale Air Force Base, Calif.
Sweet (Harry) Film Coll.

Beale Street (Memphis, Tenn.)
Center for Southern Folklore

Beamer, John V.
Indiana State Lib.

Bearden, Romare
Video Data Bank

Bears
Amer. Motion Pictures
Dreamlight Images, Inc.
Energy Productions
Film Bank
Jewell (Stuart) Productions
Kesser Stock Footage Library
Minnesota Zoo
Natl. Archives (RG 200)
Nine Star Productions
Petrified Films, Inc.
Wings Wildlife Prods. Inc.

Bears (Performing)
Petrified Films, Inc.

Beastie Boys (Rock and roll band)
Spectral Comms.

Beatles, The
Archive Film Prods., Inc.
Banks Film Library
Encore Entertainment
Film Bank
Petrified Films, Inc.
UCLA Film & Television Archive

Beatniks
CBS News Archives
Film Bank

Prelinger Assoc., Inc.

Beatty, Warren
Banks Film Library
Daphne Productions, Inc.

Beaufort Sea
TV Ontario

Beaufort Sea (History and culture)
Yukon Archives

Beauty contests
See Beauty pageants

Beauty culture
MacDonald, J. Fred
March of Time
Media Project
Milady Publishing Corp.
Parker (Kit) Films
Video Resources N.Y., Inc.

Beauty pageants
Allen (John E.) Inc.
Analogous Productions
Democracy in Communication
Hist. Soc. of Palm Beach County
Las Vegas News Bureau
Prelinger Assoc., Inc.
Spalla (Rick) Video Prods.
Twentieth Century-Fox Movietonews
UCLA Film & Television Archive
White Janssen, Inc.

Beauty pageants (Baby)
Analogous Productions

Beauty pageants (Miss America)
Archive Film Prods., Inc.
Miss America Pageant

Beauty parlors
See Hairdressers

Beauty shots
Alaska Video Prods.
Cinenet (Cinema Network)
Dobovan Productions, Inc.
Dreamlight Images, Inc.
Film Bank
Film Search
MVP Communications
MacGillivray Freeman Films
Marts (Steve) Productions
Mountain Video Associates
Network Productions
Pacific Focus Inc.
Petrified Films, Inc.
Port Authority of New York & New Jersey
Prelinger Assoc., Inc.
Preview Media
Quenzer Driscoll Dawson, Inc.
Renaissance Video Corp.
Rock Solid Prods.
Sullivan Video Services
Summit Films, Inc.
WETA-TV
See also Scenics

Beavers
Cousteau Society
Film Bank
Minnesota Zoo
New Mexico State Records Ctr. & Arch.
Swedberg, Jack

Bebop
See Dance and dancing (Bebop)

Bebop music
See Music (Bebop)

Beck, Aaron T.
Psychological and Educational Films

Beckel, George
Videobrary, Inc.

Becker, Boris
U.S. Tennis Assn.

Beckett, Samuel
Assn. Coopérative OBSCURE

Beckman, Arnold O.
Amer. Chemical Soc.

Beckmann, Hans
Goethe Institute Chicago

Bed racing
TV Ontario

Bedouins
TV Ontario

Bedrooms
Film Bank
Petrified Films, Inc.
Prelinger Assoc., Inc.

Bee Gees, The
Banks Film Library

Beebe, William
New York Zoological Society

Beeby, Thomas
Mus. of Contemporary Art

Beef
Film Bank
March of Time
Natl. Archives (RG 33)
Natl. Archives of Canada
Natl. Cattlemen's Assn.
Oregon State Univ., Archives
Varied Directions, Inc.
See also Butchers and butchering;
    Meatpacking

Beekeepers
TV Ontario

Beer
Farkas Studios, Ltd.
Film Bank
Oregon State Univ., Archives
Petrified Films, Inc.
Prelinger Assoc., Inc.
Video Resources N.Y., Inc.

Bees
Cinenet (Cinema Network)
Dreamlight Images, Inc.
Energy Productions
Film Bank
Glenbow Mus. Arch.
Latham Foundation
Moody Inst. of Science
Oregon State Univ., Archives
Petrified Films, Inc.
TV Ontario

Beetles
Film Bank
Prelinger Assoc., Inc.
Wings Wildlife Prods. Inc.

Beets (Sugar)
Natl. Archives (RG 310)

Beggars
CBS News Archives
Film Bank

Begley, Ed Jr.
Spectral Comms.

Behavior modification
Cinema Guild
Research Press
See also Psychology

Beijing
Farkas Studios, Ltd.
Sullivan Video Services

Beijing (History and culture)
Amer. Mus. Nat. Hist. Film Arch.
Film/Audio Services, Inc.
Hammer (Armand) Prods.
Lawren Prods., Inc.
Nan Hai (U.S.A.) Co., Inc.
Ocean Earth Constr. and Dev. Corp.
Rockefeller Arch. Ctr.

Beirut, Lebanon (History and culture)
New Time Films, Inc.
Ocean Earth Constr. and Dev. Corp.

Bejart, Maurice
Camera Three Prods., Inc.

Bel Geddes, Norman
Prelinger Assoc., Inc.
Univ. of Tex. at Austin, Ransom Hum.
    Res. Ctr., Photo. Coll.

Belafonte, Harry
Educational Film & Video Project

Belau
See Palau

Belaúnde, Fernandao
Univ. of Miami, Arch. & Spec. Coll.

Belem, Brazil
Brazilian-American Cultural Inst.

Belfast, Northern Ireland (History and culture)
Groupe Intervention Video
Pennebaker Associates, Inc.

Belgium
Canadian Broadcasting Corp.

Belgium (History and culture)
Archive Film Prods., Inc.
Bibliothèque Municipale de Montréal
March of Time
Natl. Archives (RG 24)
Natl. Archives (RG 28)
Natl. Archives/Natl. AV Ctr.
Petrified Films, Inc.
Twentieth Century-Fox Movietonews

Belize
Imagen y Sonido Independiente, S.A.
Passage Home Communications
Preview Media

Belize (History and culture)
Mus. of Mod. Art of Latin America

Bell, Alexander Graham
Timesteps Prods., Inc.

Bell, John Kim
Native Amer. Pub. Broad. Cons.

Bell Laboratories
AT&T Archives & Rec. Mgmt. Svcs.
Cinema Guild

Bell, Marilyn
DEC Film & Video

Bell towers
See Towers

Bellamy, Ralph
Spectral Comms.

Beller, Claude
Port Washington Pub. Lib.

Bellingham, Wash. (History and culture)
Ctr. for Pacific Northwest Studies

Bells
CBS News Archives
Film Bank
Petrified Films, Inc.

Bells (Church)
Petrified Films, Inc.

Bells (Prize-fight)
Petrified Films, Inc.

Belly dancing
See Dance and dancing (Belly dancing)

Belo Horizonte, Brazil
Brazilian-American Cultural Inst.

Belts (Industrial)
Natl. Industrial Belting Assn.

Belts (Leather)
Prelinger Assoc., Inc.

Beltsville, Md. (History and culture)
Natl. Archives (RG 33)

Belushi, Jim
Spectral Comms.

Ben-Gurion, David
Amer. Zionist Youth Found.

Benares, India
Petrified Films, Inc.

Benchley, Robert
Alan Twyman Presents
Em Gee Film Library

Bender, Gary
Fellowship of Christian Athletes

Benedek, Therese
Inst. for Psychoanalysis

Benes, Edward
Czechoslovak Heritage Mus. Lib. & Arch.
March of Time

Bengal, Bay of (Asia)
Petrified Films, Inc.

Benghazi, Libya (Contemporary issues)
Ocean Earth Constr. and Dev. Corp.

Benglis, Lynda
Blackwood Prods., Inc.
Walker Art Ctr.

Bengston, Billy Al
Video Data Bank

Benin (History and culture)
Singer-Sharrette Traditional Healing Films

Bennett, Floyd
Natl. Archives (RG 342)

Bennett, Michael
New York Pub. Lib., Perf. Arts Res. Ctr.,
    Theatre on Film and Tape

Bennett, R.B.
Natl. Archives of Canada

Bennett, Tony
Univision Television Network

Benny, Jack
Banks Film Library
Christopher Closeup
Film/Audio Services, Inc.
Las Vegas News Bureau
New York Pub. Lib., Perf. Arts Res. Ctr.,
    Theatre on Film and Tape
Shokus Video
UCLA Film & Television Archive
Univ. of Wyoming, Amer. Heritage Ctr.

Benson, George S.
MacDonald, J. Fred

Benson, William S.
Natl. Archives (RG 24)

Benton, Barbi
Spectral Comms.

Bergen, Candice
Banks Film Library

Bergen, Edgar
Banks Film Library
New York Pub. Lib., Perf. Arts Res. Ctr.,
    Theatre on Film and Tape

Bergen, Polly
Banks Film Library

Berger, Eddie
Intermedia Arts Minnesota

Bergman, Ingrid
Wombat Film & Video

Bergner, Elisabeth
Cantor (Arthur) Inc.

Bering Sea (History and culture)
Alaska Native Heritage Film Project
Oregon Hist. Soc.

Berkeley, Calif.
Film Bank
Unicorn Projects

Berkeley, Calif. (History and culture)
Estuary Press
Mus. & Hist. Div., City of Sacramento
Payne, Roz
Petrified Films, Inc.

Berle, Milton
Archive Film Prods., Inc.
Banks Film Library
Encore Entertainment
MacDonald, J. Fred
Shokus Video
Spectral Comms.
UCLA Film & Television Archive
Videobrary, Inc.

Smithsonian Inst., Human Studies Film
    Arch.
TV Ontario

NOTE: Access policies, availability and restrictions vary for each source. Please read each entry in full. Always consult "General Film and Videotape Collections" (page 599); these comprehensive collections contain material on every conceivable subject.

Berlin
Canadian Broadcasting Corp.

Berlin (History and culture)
Archive Film Prods., Inc.
Cantor (Arthur) Inc.
German Info. Ctr., Film Lib.
Goethe Institute Atlanta
Intl. Assn. of Independent Producers
Natl. Archives (RG 242)
Natl. Archives (RG 306)
Natl. Archives of Canada
Petrified Films, Inc.
RK Editions
Smith (Margaret Chase) Lib. Ctr.
UDS Company

Berlin airlift (1948)
Natl. Archives (RG 306)

Berlin, East (History and culture)
MacDonald, J. Fred
Natl. Archives (RG 59)

Berlin, Irving
Archive Film Prods., Inc.
Camera Three Prods., Inc.

Berlin Wall
Analogous Productions
Goethe Institute Atlanta
Natl. Archives of Canada
See also Cold War; Germany

Bermuda
Creative Video, Inc.
Preview Media

Bermuda (History and culture)
Archive Film Prods., Inc.
Archives of Ontario

Bermuda Triangle
Pyramid Film and Video Corp.

Bernard, John T.
Intermedia Arts Minnesota

Bernhardt, Sarah
Lib. of Congress, M/B/RS

Bernier, Joseph
Natl. Archives of Canada

Bernini, G.L.
Southern Calif. Inst. of Architecture

Bernstein, Leonard
MacDonald, J. Fred
Wesleyan Cinema Archives

Berries
Film Bank

Berrigan, Ted
Giorno Poetry Systems Inst.
Video Data Bank

Berry, Chuck
Pennebaker Associates, Inc.

Berry, Richard
Los Angeles Blues Archives

Bertoli, Alberto
Southern Calif. Inst. of Architecture

Bethe, Hans
Blackwood Prods., Inc.

Bethesda, Md. (History and culture)
Natl. Archives (RG 31)

Bethlehem
Film Bank

Bethune, Norman
Natl. Archives of Canada

Bethune, Thomas Greene
Tulane Univ., Amistad Res. Ctr.

Beuys, Joseph
Blackwood Prods., Inc.
Electronic Arts Intermix
Goethe Institute Atlanta
Goethe Institute Chicago
Target Video
Video Data Bank

Bevan, Aneurin
Smith (Margaret Chase) Lib. Ctr.

Bevan, Billy
Streamline Film Archives
Videobrary, Inc.

Beverage industry
Coca-Cola Co., Archives Dept.
Dr Pepper Co.

Beverage industry (Television commercials)
Brooklyn Coll., Diamant Mem. Lib.
Coca-Cola Co., Archives Dept.

Beverages
CBS News Archives
Hayes Prods., Inc.
Petrified Films, Inc.
Prelinger Assoc., Inc.

Beverages (Alcoholic)
Seagram Museum

Beverly Hills, Calif.
Film Bank
Spectral Comms.

Beverly Hills, Calif. (History and culture)
Petrified Films, Inc.

Beyer, Herbert
Cantor (Arthur) Inc.

Bhopal, India (Contemporary issues)
Courter Films & Assoc.

Bhutan (History and culture)
Devillier Donegan Ent.

Biafra, Jello
Target Video

Biberman, Edward
De Saisset Museum

Bible stories and study
Amer. Baptist Films/Video
CBN Publishing
Concordia Publishing House
Golden Gate Theological Seminary
 Library
Joyce Media, Inc.
Keep the Faith, Inc.
Mass Media Ministries
Moody Inst. of Science
Pyramid Film and Video Corp.
Univ. of Toronto, AV Lib.
See also Religion; Religious films and
 videotapes

Bibles
Petrified Films, Inc.

Bicentennial celebration (Mexico, 1910)
Archivo Historico Cinematografico
Filmoteca de la UNAM

Bicentennial celebration (U.S., 1976)

Cabscott Broadcast Prods.
Delaware State Div. of Hist. & Cult. Aff.
Natl. Archives (RG 200)
Natl. Archives (RG 452)
U.S. Natl. Park Service Hist. Coll.

Bicycles and bicycling
ABC Sports, Inc.
Amer. Motion Pictures
Analogous Productions
CBS News Archives
Chicago Video Transfer
Cineworks Prods. Inc.
Crystal Pyramid Prods.
Dreamlight Images, Inc.
Farkas Studios, Ltd.
Film Bank
Forsher (James) Prods. & Archives, Inc.
Golden Gaters Prods.
Metro Communications, Inc.
Northern Ill. Univ., Reg. Hist. Ctr.
Peak Productions, Inc.
Petrified Films, Inc.
Prelinger Assoc., Inc.
Pyramid Film and Video Corp.
Summit Films, Inc.
TV Ontario
Timesteps Prods., Inc.
U.S. Olympic Comm.
Video-SIG

Bicycles and bicycling (Racing)
Amer. Motion Pictures
Analogous Productions
Dreamlight Images, Inc.
Grinberg (Sherman) Film Libraries (West)
Twentieth Century-Fox Movietonews

Biden, Joseph
Guggenheim Productions, Inc.

Bien Hoa Air Force Base (Vietnam)
Natl. Archives (RG 342)

Big band music
See Music (Big band)

Big Ben (London)
British Info. Svcs., Radio & TV Div.
Dreamlight Images, Inc.
Film Bank
Petrified Films, Inc.
TV Ontario

Big Brother and the Holding Company
Pennebaker Associates, Inc.

Big Sur, Calif.
Energy Productions
Film Bank
Petrified Films, Inc.
Preview Media
Unicorn Projects

Bigfoot
Pyramid Film and Video Corp.

Biggs, Ronald
Villon Films

Bikel, Theodore
Anti-Defamation League of B'nai B'rith

Bikini Atoll, Marshall Islands (History and culture)
Natl. Archives (RG 434)
Petrified Films, Inc.
Univ. of Mich., Mich. Hist. Colls.

Bikinis
Energy Productions
Film Education Institute
Spectral Comms.
See also Beaches; Sunbathing; Swimsuits

Biko, Steven
Villon Films

Bilingualism
Université de Moncton, Centre d'Études
 Acad.

Bilingualism and Biculturalism, Royal Commission on
Natl. Archives of Canada

Bill of Rights (U.S.)
Prelinger Assoc., Inc.

Billboards
See Advertising (Outdoor)

Billiards
Analogous Productions
Athletic Institute
Metro Communications, Inc.
Petrified Films, Inc.
Prelinger Assoc., Inc.
Sportsfilm
TV Ontario
Twentieth Century-Fox Movietonews

Bingo
TV Ontario

Binoculars
Film Bank

Biobehavioral sciences
UCLA Behavioral Sci. Media Lab.

BioBio River, Chile
Sobek Productions

Biochemistry
Educational Images, Ltd.
Emory Medical Television Network

Bioengineering
Amer. Occupational Therapy Assn.

Biofeedback
Amer. Occupational Therapy Assn.
Cinema Guild
Hartley Film Found., Inc.
Intermedia Arts Minnesota
Mankind Research Found., Inc.
TV Ontario

Biological warfare
See Chemical and biological warfare

Biology
Altschul Group
Benchmark Films, Inc.
Britannica Films & Video
Center for Humanities, Inc.
Churchill Films
Cinema Guild
Coronet/MTI Film & Video
Emory Medical Television Network
Film Bank
Films for the Humanities and Sciences
Intellimation
Media Guild
NASA, Johnson Space Ctr., Film & Video
 Dist. Lib.
Nassau Comm. Coll. Lib.
Natl. Archives/Natl. AV Ctr.
Natl. Film Board of Canada
Phoenix Films and Video
Prelinger Assoc., Inc.
Rosebush Visions Corp.
TV-UNAM
Univ. of Calif., Ext. Media Ctr.

Biomedicine
Center for Biomedical Comms.
Inst. of Electrical & Electronics Eng.
Natl. Medical Historical Film Prog.

618

Rockefeller Arch. Ctr.

Biosciences
Los Alamos Natl. Lab.

Biotechnology
Mankind Research Found., Inc.

Biplanes
See Aircraft (Biplanes)

Birch trees
TV Ontario

Bird, Lance
Port Washington Pub. Lib.

Birds
Acad. of Nat. Sci. of Phila. Lib.
Amer. Motion Pictures
Amer. Veterinary Medical Assn.
Bennett (Joel) Prods.
British Info. Svcs., Radio & TV Div.
CBS News Archives
Chisholm (Jack) Film Productions
Cinema Arts Assoc.
Cinenet (Cinema Network)
Cineworks Prods. Inc.
Coronet/MTI Film & Video
Cousteau Society
Di Sesso (Moe) Wild Life Film Lib.
Dobbs (Jeff) Prods.
Dreamlight Images, Inc.
Echo Film Prods., Inc.
Energy Productions
Film Bank
Film/Audio Services, Inc.
Florentine Films
Grinberg (Sherman) Film Libraries (East)
Grinberg (Sherman) Film Libraries (West)
Indiana State Comm. on Public Records
Jewell (Stuart) Productions
KD Enterprises Prods.
Kesser Stock Footage Library
Mass. Audubon Society
Miller (David Lee) Prods.
Minnesota Zoo
Moody Inst. of Science
New Mexico State Records Ctr. & Arch.
Norsgaard, Campbell
Northcoast Communication, Inc.
Peak Productions, Inc.
Petrified Films, Inc.
Phoenix Films and Video
Prelinger Assoc., Inc.
Quenzer Driscoll Dawson, Inc.
Rosebush Visions Corp.
Snyder (Bill) Films, Inc.
Spectral Comms.
Summit Films, Inc.
Swedberg, Jack
TV Ontario
TV-3
Twentieth Century-Fox Movietonews
Video I-D, Inc.
White Janssen, Inc.
Wings Wildlife Prods. Inc.
See also Nature; Wildlife; specific birds

Birds (Performing)
Miller (David Lee) Prods.

Birds of paradise
Petrified Films, Inc.

Birds-of-paradise (Flower)
Kesser Stock Footage Library

Birkerts, Gunnar
Southern Calif. Inst. of Architecture

Birmingham, Ala. (History and culture)
Birmingham Pub. Lib., Dept. of Arch.
Birmingham Pub. Lib., Media Svcs. Dept.

Birnbaum, Dara
Long Beach Mus. of Art
Port Washington Pub. Lib.
Southern Calif. Inst. of Architecture
Video Data Bank

Birth
See Childbirth

Birth control
Baird (Bill) Inst.
CBS News Archives
Cambridge Documentary Films, Inc.
Churchill Films
Cinema Medica
Focus Intl. Inc.
Johns Hopkins Univ./Population Comm. Svcs.
Milner-Fenwick, Inc.
Natl. Abortion Rights Action League
Planned Parenthood Fed. of Amer.
Radcliffe Coll., Schlesinger Lib.
See also Condoms; Sex education

Birth defects
March of Dimes Birth Defects Found.
Polymorph Films, Inc.

Birthdays
Fish Films, Inc.
Petrified Films, Inc.
Prelinger Assoc., Inc.
Twentieth Century-Fox Movietonews
Vermont Hist. Soc.

Bisexuality
Focus Intl. Inc.
Multi-Focus, Inc.
See also Sexuality

Bishop, Elizabeth
Intellimation

Bishop, Joey
Banks Film Library
Encore Entertainment
Las Vegas News Bureau
Shokus Video

Bishop, Maurice
Cinema Guild
DEC Film & Video
New Time Films, Inc.

Bishop, Steven
Spectral Comms.

Bismarck, N. Dak. (History and culture)
State Hist. Soc. of North Dakota

Bison
See Buffaloes

Bixby, Bill
Banks Film Library

Black cinema
Black Filmmaker Foundation
Budget Films Inc.
Em Gee Film Library
Indiana Univ., Black Film Ctr./Arch.
Lib. of Congress, M/B/RS
Manhattan Movietime
Natl. Ctr. for Film & Video Preservation
Paper Tiger TV
Phoenix Films and Video
Southwest Film/Video Archives, SMU

See also Feature films and videotapes; Independent films and videotapes

Black Flag (Rock and roll band)
Target Video

Black, George
Yukon Archives

Black Hills, S. Dak.
Solaris Dance/Theatre/Video

Black Hills, S. Dak. (History and culture)
Native Amer. Pub. Broad. Cons.
Schiele Museum

Black history and culture
ARC Videodance Coll./Eye on Dance Coll.
Alabama State Dept. of Arch. & Hist.
Allen (John E.) Inc.
Amer. Assn. for Counseling & Development
Amer. Soc. Hist. Proj. Film Lib.
Anti-Defamation League of B'nai B'rith
Archive Film Prods., Inc.
Atlantis Prods., Inc.
Black Filmmaker Foundation
Blackwood (Christian) Prods., Inc.
Bronx County Hist. Soc.
Carousel Film & Video
Center for New Amer. Media
Center for Southern Folklore
Chicago Comm. to Defend the Bill of Rights
Cinema Guild
Coe Film Assoc., Inc.
Columbia Univ., Teachers College
DEC Film & Video
Davenport Films
Direct Cinema Ltd.
Educational Video Ctr.
Film Bank
Films for the Humanities and Sciences
Grinberg (Sherman) Film Libraries (East)
Handel Film Corp.
Hatch-Billops Collection, Inc.
Illinois State Hist. Lib.
Indiana Univ., Black Film Ctr./Arch.
Intermedia Arts Minnesota
King (Dr. Martin Luther, Jr.) Ctr.
Kino Intl. Corp.
Lib. of Congress, M/B/RS
MacDonald, J. Fred
March of Time
Mass Media Ministries
Media Bus
Media Project
Memphis State Univ. Libraries
Metropolitan Council for Educ. Opport.
Miles Educ. Film Prods.
Mississippi Dept. of Arch. & Hist.
Natl. Archives (RG 16)
Natl. Archives (RG 111)
Natl. Archives (RG 119)
Natl. Archives (RG 200)
Natl. Archives (RG 208)
Natl. Archives (RG 381)
Natl. Archives/Natl. AV Ctr.
Natl. Assn. for the Advancement of Colored People
Natl. Black Prog. Cons.
Natl. Railway Historical Soc.
New Day Films
New York Pub. Lib., Perf. Arts Res. Ctr., Theatre on Film and Tape
Ohio Hist. Soc.
Pathé Pictures, Inc.
Petrified Films, Inc.
Phoenix Films and Video

Prelinger Assoc., Inc.
Pyramid Film and Video Corp.
Randolph (A. Philip) Educ. Fund
Rockefeller Arch. Ctr.
Schomburg Ctr. for Res. in Black Culture
Southern Calif. Lib. for Soc. Stud. & Res.
Southern Christian Leadership Conference
Southwest Film/Video Archives, SMU
Tennessee State Lib. & Arch.
Third World Newsreel
Tulane Univ., Amistad Res. Ctr.
Twentieth Century-Fox Movietonews
Univ. of Alabama, W.S. Hoole Spec. Coll.
Univ. of Calif., Ext. Media Ctr.
Univ. of Georgia, WSB TV News Film Arch.
Univ. of Mich., Mich. Hist. Colls.
Univ. of Pittsburgh, Univ. Ctr. Inst. Res.
Univ. of Tex. at Austin, Barker Tex. Hist. Ctr.
Villon Films
West Virginia State Lib. Comm.
See also Black cinema; Black people (Depiction in the media); Civil rights; Civil rights movement; Military history (Black); Music (Black); Prejudice; Racial discrimination; Racial stereotypes; Racism; Workers (Black); World War II (U.S., Black people)

Black lung
West Virginia Dept. of Culture & Hist.

Black music
See Music (Black)

Black Panther Party
Chicago Comm. to Defend the Bill of Rights
Cinema Guild
MacDonald, J. Fred
Media Bus
Payne, Roz
Petrified Films, Inc.
San Francisco Bay Area TV News Arch.
Third World Newsreel

Black people (Depiction in the media)
California Newsreel
Center for Southern Folklore
MacDonald, J. Fred
Schomburg Ctr. for Res. in Black Culture

Blackberries
Oregon State Univ., Archives

Blackbirds
KD Enterprises Prods.
Wings Wildlife Prods. Inc.

Blacklisting
Shire Films

Blacksmiths and blacksmithing
Appalachian State Univ., Eury Coll.
Film Bank
Petrified Films, Inc.
Prelinger Assoc., Inc.
Wayne State Univ., Folklore Arch.

Blades, Ruben
Daphne Productions, Inc.
Spectral Comms.

Blair, N. John
Southern Calif. Inst. of Architecture

Blake, Eubie
Lib. of Congress, M/B/RS
Rutgers Univ., Inst. of Jazz Studies

NOTE: Access policies, availability and restrictions vary for each source. Please read each entry in full. Always consult "General Film and Videotape Collections" (page 599); these comprehensive collections contain material on every conceivable subject.

Blake, Peter
Unicorn Projects

Blanc, Mont (France-Italy)
Analogous Productions

Blank, Les
Port Washington Pub. Lib.

Blarney Castle (Ireland)
Petrified Films, Inc.

Blassie, Fred
Sportsfilm

Blasting
See Explosions

Blimps
See Aircraft (Lighter-than-air)

Blindness
Amer. Foundation for the Blind
CBS News Archives
Film Bank
Filmfair Communications
Lib. of Congress, M/B/RS
Mankind Research Found., Inc.
Missouri Hist. Soc.
Natl. Archives (RG 12)
Natl. Archives (RG 306)
Natl. Soc. to Prevent Blindness
Perkins School for the Blind
Pyramid Film and Video Corp.

Blitzstein, Marc
Camera Three Prods., Inc.

Blizzards
British Info. Svcs., Radio & TV Div.
Film Bank
Petrified Films, Inc.
Twentieth Century-Fox Movietonews
See also Snow; Storms; Weather

Bloch, Robert
Univ. of Wyoming, Amer. Heritage Ctr.

Blondie (Rock and roll band)
Blackwood (Christian) Prods., Inc.

Blood
Academy of Health Sciences, U.S. Army
Amer. Chemical Soc.
Amer. Red Cross
CBS News Archives
Dreamlight Images, Inc.
Film Bank
Moody Inst. of Science
Prelinger Assoc., Inc.
Rogers (Will) Institute
Univ. of Wash. Press, Multimedia Div.

Blood, Sweat and Tears (Rock and roll band)
Archive Film Prods., Inc.

Bloomstein, Charles
Randolph (A. Philip) Educ. Fund

Bloopers
Budget Films Inc.
Em Gee Film Library
Forsher (James) Prods. & Archives, Inc.
Miller (Warren) Productions, Inc.
Movietime, Inc. Archives
Streamline Film Archives
Video Resources N.Y., Inc.
See also Sports (Bloopers)

Blue Angels (U.S. Navy)
Amer. Motion Pictures
Northcoast Communication, Inc.
San Diego Aerospace Museum

Blue jays
Cinenet (Cinema Network)
Di Sesso (Moe) Wild Life Film Lib.
Film Bank
Petrified Films, Inc.

Blue Mountains, Australia
Petrified Films, Inc.

Blue Ridge Mountains (U.S.)
Appalachian State Univ., Eury Coll.
Preview Media

Bluebirds
KD Enterprises Prods.

Bluefield, W. Va. (History and culture)
West Virginia Dept. of Culture & Hist.

Bluegrass music
See Music (Bluegrass)

Blueprints
Rosebush Visions Corp.

Blumberg, Skip
Port Washington Pub. Lib.
Univ. of Wyoming, Amer. Heritage Ctr.

Bly, Robert
Intermedia Arts Minnesota

Boa constrictors
Minnesota Zoo
TV Ontario

Boardwalks
CBS News Archives
Prelinger Assoc., Inc.
TV Ontario

Boars
Archive Film Prods., Inc.

Boat people
Atlantis Prods., Inc.
Cinema Guild
Natl. Asian American Telecomm. Assn.
See also Refugees

Boatbuilding
New Jersey Network

Boats and boating
Analogous Productions
Archive Film Prods., Inc.
Archives of Ontario
CBS News Archives
Century Video Services, Inc.
Cinenet (Cinema Network)
Dobbs (Jeff) Prods.
Dreamlight Images, Inc.
Elfstrom-Hilmer Prods.
Encore Video Prods., Inc.
Energy Productions
Film Bank
Fish Films, Inc.
Grinberg (Sherman) Film Libraries (West)
Kesser Stock Footage Library
Metro Communications, Inc.
Morris Video
Mountain Video Associates
Mystic Seaport Mus., Inc.
Petrified Films, Inc.
Quenzer Driscoll Dawson, Inc.
Simon (Jeff) Productions
Site Productions
Sportsfilm
TV Ontario
Zielinski Productions, Inc.
See also Boat racing; Canoes and canoeing; Hydroplanes and hydroplane racing; Sailing; Ships; Yachts and yachting

Boats and boating (Barges)
Dreamlight Images, Inc.
Energy Productions
Natl. Archives of Canada
Petrified Films, Inc.
TV Ontario

Boats and boating (Catamarans)
Analogous Productions
Dreamlight Images, Inc.
Film Bank
Second Line Search

Boats and boating (Dhows)
Petrified Films, Inc.

Boats and boating (Dugouts)
Petrified Films, Inc.

Boats and boating (Exploding boats)
Dreamlight Images, Inc.

Boats and boating (Ferries)
Amer. Motion Pictures
Energy Productions
Film Bank
Impact Audio Visual
Mountain Video Associates
Petrified Films, Inc.
Port Authority of New York & New Jersey
San Francisco Maritime Natl. Hist. Park

Boats and boating (Fireboats)
Petrified Films, Inc.

Boats and boating (Fishing boats)
TV Ontario

Boats and boating (Fishing trawlers)
Film Bank

Boats and boating (Houseboats)
Preview Media
TV Ontario

Boats and boating (Hydrofoil)
Mystic Seaport Mus., Inc.

Boats and boating (Ice boats)
Film Bank
Mystic Seaport Mus., Inc.
Petrified Films, Inc.
Twentieth Century-Fox Movietonews
Windsor Prod. Corp.

Boats and boating (Ketches)
Nemiroff Prods., Inc.

Boats and boating (Lobster boats)
Petrified Films, Inc.

Boats and boating (Oyster boats)
Mariners' Museum

Boats and boating (Paddle-wheel boats)
Film Bank
Petrified Films, Inc.
TV Ontario

Boats and boating (Pleasure)
Energy Productions
Petrified Films, Inc.
Riccitelli (Bruce) Prods.

Boats and boating (Power boats)
Analogous Productions
Hi-Tech Productions
Sea TV
Second Line Search

Boats and boating (Racing)
CBS News Archives
Channell One Video
Diamond P. Sports
Film Bank

Boats and boating (Racing) (Sailboats)
America's Cup Org. Comm.
Offshore Productions

Boats and boating (Reed boats)
Film Search

Boats and boating (Riverboats)
Alaska Video Prods.
MacDonald, J. Fred
Petrified Films, Inc.

Boats and boating (Rowboats)
Film Bank
Petrified Films, Inc.

Boats and boating (Sailboats)
Amer. Motion Pictures
America's Cup Org. Comm.
Applegate Entertainment
Cinenet (Cinema Network)
Dreamlight Images, Inc.
Energy Productions
Fish Films, Inc.
Forsher (James) Prods. & Archives, Inc.
Omega Films
Sea TV
Spectral Comms.
See also Boat racing (Sailboats); Sailing; Yachts and yachting

Boats and boating (Shrimp boats)
Energy Productions
Petrified Films, Inc.
Tri-Comm Prods.

Boats and boating (Speedboats)
Energy Productions
Film Bank
Petrified Films, Inc.
Pyramid Film and Video Corp.
Spectral Comms.
TV Ontario
Univ. of Notre Dame, Joyce Sports Coll.

Boats and boating (Steamboats)
See Ships (Steamboats)

Boats and boating (Tugboats)
Amer. Motion Pictures
Archive Film Prods., Inc.
Film Bank
Missouri Hist. Soc.
Petrified Films, Inc.
TV Ontario
Xicom, Inc.

Boats and boating (Water taxis)
Petrified Films, Inc.

Bobbies
TV Ontario

Bobcats
Di Sesso (Moe) Wild Life Film Lib.

Bobsledding
Analogous Productions
Grinberg (Sherman) Film Libraries (West)
Jalbert Productions
Prelinger Assoc., Inc.
Twentieth Century-Fox Movietonews

Boccioni, Umberto
Blackwood Prods., Inc.

Boats and boating (Barges) — (continued under fourth column)
Grinberg (Sherman) Film Libraries (West)
Hi-Tech Productions
Mystic Seaport Mus., Inc.
Natl. Archives of Canada
Petrified Films, Inc.
Sea TV
Twentieth Century-Fox Movietonews
See also America's Cup; Yachts and yachting (Racing)

Boddy, William
Paper Tiger TV
Video Data Bank

Bodyboarding
Merkel Films

Bodybuilding
Analogous Productions
Apertura
Spalla (Rick) Video Prods.
Spectral Comms.
Video Tape Library, Ltd.
See also Weightlifting

Boer War (1899)
Natl. Archives of Canada

Bogart, Humphrey
Archive Film Prods., Inc.
Halcyon Days Prods.
Petrified Films, Inc.
UCLA Film & Television Archive

Bogor, Indonesia
Sheffield (Erin) Prods.

Bogota, Colombia (History and culture)
Johns Hopkins Univ./Population Comm. Svcs.
Rockefeller Arch. Ctr.

Bolivia (Contemporary issues)
DEC Film & Video
Oxfam America

Bolivia (History and culture)
Cinema Guild
DEC Film & Video
Democracy in Communication
Idera Films
Natl. Archives (RG 59)
Rockefeller Arch. Ctr.
Univ. of Wisconsin — Extension

Böll, Heinrich
Goethe Institute Atlanta

Bolotowsky, Ilya
Albright-Knox Art Gallery

Bomb damage
See Ruins

Bombay, India
Petrified Films, Inc.

Bombay, India (History and culture)
Petrified Films, Inc.

Bombs and bombing
CBS News Archives
Film Bank
Natl. Archives (RG 18)
Natl. Archives (RG 22)
Natl. Archives (RG 80)
Natl. Archives (RG 171)
Natl. Archives (RG 243)
Natl. Archives (RG 342)
Petrified Films, Inc.
Prelinger Assoc., Inc.
Twentieth Century-Fox Movietonews
UDS Company
See also Atomic bombs; Battles;
    Explosions; specific conflicts and wars

Bonaire, Netherlands Antilles
Passage Home Communications

Bond drives
Halcyon Days Prods.

MacDonald, J. Fred
Natl. Archives (RG 24)
Natl. Archives (RG 53)
Natl. Archives (RG 56)
Natl. Archives (RG 200)
Natl. Archives (RG 208)
Natl. Archives of Canada
Petrified Films, Inc.
Prelinger Assoc., Inc.

Bond, Julian
Center for Pacific Northwest Studies
Estuary Press
Southern Calif. Lib. for Soc. Stud. & Res.
Univ. of Georgia, WSB TV News Film Arch.

Bonder, Lisa
U.S. Tennis Assn.

Bonneville Power Administration
Eastern Washington State Hist. Soc.
Natl. Archives (RG 115)
Natl. Archives (RG 305)

Bono, Sonny
Banks Film Library

Bonsai treemaking
Brooklyn Botanic Garden
Rainbow Video Prods.

Bontoc Igorot people
Smithsonian Inst., Human Studies Film Arch.

Bonus Army (1932)
MacArthur (Gen. Douglas) Memorial
Petrified Films, Inc.

Boobies (Birds)
Wings Wildlife Prods. Inc.

Boogieboarding
Energy Productions
Film Bank
Second Line Search

Bookburning
Film Bank

Bookchin, Murray
Paper Tiger TV

Bookmaking
Natl. Archives (RG 149)

Bookmobiles
Kentucky Dept. of Libraries & Archives

Books
CBS News Archives
Film Bank
Petrified Films, Inc.

Bookstores
Petrified Films, Inc.
Stock House
TV Ontario

Boone, Daniel
Appalachian State Univ., Eury Coll.

Boone, Debby
Banks Film Library

Boone, Pat
Banks Film Library

Boot camp (U.S. Marines)
Petrified Films, Inc.

See also Marine Corps (U.S.)

Booth, Evangeline
Salvation Army Arch. & Rec. Ctr.

Booth, William
Salvation Army, Natl. Comm. Dept.
Wheaton Coll., Billy Graham Ctr.

Bootlegging
See Prohibition (1919-33)

Border Patrol (U.S.)
Prelinger Assoc., Inc.

Borders (Geographic)
CBS News Archives

Borders (U.S.-Canada)
TV Ontario

Borders (U.S.-Mexico)
Petrified Films, Inc.

Borge, Tomas
Richter Productions

Borger, Tex. (History and culture)
Panhandle-Plains Hist. Museum

Borgnine, Ernest
Banks Film Library

Bork, Robert H.
Amer. Political Science Assn.
Cable News Network Library
Purdue Univ., Pub. Aff. Video Arch.

Borneo, Indonesia
Jewell (Stuart) Productions

Borneo, Indonesia (History and culture)
Archive Film Prods., Inc.

Borneo, North
See Malaysia

Borofsky, Jonathan
Walker Art Ctr.

Borscht Belt
Ergo Media
Film/Audio Services, Inc.
Villon Films
See also Catskill Mountains, N.Y.

Bosone, Reva Beck
Univ. of Utah, Marriott Lib.

Bosphorus Strait (Turkey)
TV Ontario

Bosses
Petrified Films, Inc.

Boston
Boston Stock Market
Cine-Mark
Creative Video, Inc.
Energy Productions
Florentine Films
Site Productions
Stock House
Unicorn Projects
Video I-D, Inc.
Viz Wiz, Inc.

Boston (Contemporary issues)
Boston Community Access & Prog. Found.

Boston (History and culture)
Amer. Jewish Hist. Soc.
Archdiocese of Boston
Archive Film Prods., Inc.
Asian American Resource Workshop
Boston Stock Market
Boston Univ. Film Archive
Bullfrog Films, Inc.
Deep Dish TV
Lib. of Congress, M/B/RS
Metropolitan Council for Educ. Opport.
Native Amer. Pub. Broad. Cons.
Petrified Films, Inc.
Redden Archives

Bostrum, Trish
U.S. Tennis Assn.

Boswell, Connie
Pathé Pictures, Inc.

Botanical gardens
Brooklyn Botanic Garden
Petrified Films, Inc.

Botany
Bailey Productions, Inc.
Bullfrog Films, Inc.
Educational Images, Ltd.
Intl. Film Bureau, Inc.

Botswana (History and culture)
California Newsreel
Documentary Educational Resources
Natl. Archives (RG 362)
Smithsonian Inst., Human Studies Film Arch.
United Nations, Visual Materials Lib.

Botta, Mario
Southern Calif. Inst. of Architecture

Bottle bills
Political Issue Archive

Bottles (Production)
Energy Productions
Seagram Museum

Bottling
Film Bank

Bottling (Beer)
Petrified Films, Inc.

Bottling (Milk)
Prelinger Assoc., Inc.

Botwood, Newfoundland (History and culture)
Prov. Arch. of Newfoundland & Labrador

Boulder, Colo.
TV Ontario

Boulder Dam, Nev.
Analogous Productions

Boulder Dam, Nev. (History)
Petrified Films, Inc.

Boulding, Elisa
Univ. of Waterloo, A-V Centre

Boulez, Pierre
Camera Three Prods., Inc.

Bourdelle, Antoine
Blackwood Prods., Inc.

NOTE: Access policies, availability and restrictions vary for each source. Please read each entry in full. Always consult "General Film and Videotape Collections" (page 599); these comprehensive collections contain material on every conceivable subject.

Bourgeois, Louise
Blackwood Prods., Inc.
Video Data Bank

Bourke-White, Margaret
Intl. Center of Photography
Petrified Films, Inc.

Boutiques
Film Bank
Petrified Films, Inc.

Bow, Clara
Archive Film Prods., Inc.

Bowen, Otis Ray
Indiana State Lib.

Bowhunting
New York State Dept. of Env. Cons.

Bowie, David
Clark (Dick) Media Archives, Inc.
Daphne Productions, Inc.
Impact Audio Visual

Bowie, Nolan
Paper Tiger TV

Bowling
ABC Sports, Inc.
Amer. Bowling Cong. Film Lib.
Analogous Productions
Athletic Institute
Film Bank
MacDonald, J. Fred
Natl. Archives of Canada
Petrified Films, Inc.
Prelinger Assoc., Inc.
Sportsfilm
Twentieth Century-Fox Movietonews
Video Tape Library, Ltd.

Bowling (Instruction)
Amer. Bowling Cong. Film Lib.
Natl. Assn. for Sport & Phys. Ed.

Bowling (Lawn)
Petrified Films, Inc.

Bowman, Robert
Inst. for Space & Security Studies

Bowser, Pearl
Paper Tiger TV

Box offices
Petrified Films, Inc.
Prelinger Assoc., Inc.

Boxer Rebellion (1900)
Lib. of Congress, M/B/RS

Boxes
Rosebush Visions Corp.

Boxing
Allen (John E.) Inc.
Analogous Productions
Archive Film Prods., Inc.
Bowling Green State Univ., Ctr. Arch. Coll.
Charisma Prods., Ltd./Visual Motion Dreamlight Images, Inc.
Film Bank
Fish Films, Inc.
Golden Gaters Prods.
Grinberg (Sherman) Film Libraries (West)
Intermedia Arts Minnesota
Las Vegas News Bureau
March of Time
Natl. Archives (RG 21)
Natl. Archives of Canada
Network Productions
New Jersey Network

Parker (Kit) Films
Petrified Films, Inc.
Prelinger Assoc., Inc.
Pyramid Film and Video Corp.
Sportsfilm
Streamline Film Archives
Twentieth Century-Fox Movietonews
UCLA Film & Television Archive
U.S. Olympic Comm.
Univ. of Notre Dame, Joyce Sports Coll.
Video Tape Library, Ltd.

Boy Scouts and Scouting
Allen (John E.) Inc.
Boy Scouts of America, AV Svcs.
Canadian Film Institute
Kentucky Dept. of Libraries & Archives
March of Time
Natl. Archives (RG 22)
Natl. Archives (RG 79)
Natl. Mus. of the Boy Scouts of Amer.
Northwest Territories Archives
Petrified Films, Inc.
Prelinger Assoc., Inc.
Schiele Museum
State Hist. Soc. of Iowa
Twentieth Century-Fox Movietonews
Vermont Hist. Soc.

Boycotts
CBS News Archives
United Farm Workers of America (UFW)

Boyer, Charles
UCLA Film & Television Archive

Boyle, Richard
Spectral Comms.

Boys
Boys Club of America
Natl. Mus. of the Boy Scouts of Amer.
Prelinger Assoc., Inc.
Twentieth Century-Fox Movietonews

Boys Clubs
Boys Club of America
Natl. Archives of Canada

Bracken, Eddie
Banks Film Library

Bradbury, Ray
Spectral Comms.

Braddock, Pa. (History and culture)
New Day Films

Braden, Vic
U.S. Tennis Assn.

Braderman, Joan
Paper Tiger TV
Video Data Bank

Bradford, Bobby
Rhapsody Films, Inc.

Bradley, Bill
Naismith Mem. Basketball Hall of Fame

Bradley, Omar
Archive Film Prods., Inc.

Bradley, Tom
Spectral Comms.

Bradshaw, Terry
NFL Films, Inc.

Bragg, Don
Sportsfilm

Brain
Altschul Group

Cinema Guild
Intellimation
Prelinger Assoc., Inc.
Rosebush Visions Corp.
TV Ontario
UCLA Behavioral Sci. Media Lab.

Brakhage, Stan
Video Data Bank

Bramson, Phyllis
Video Data Bank

Branca, Glenn
Monday, Wednesday, Friday Video Club

Branch, Billy
Rhapsody Films, Inc.

Brancusi, Constantin
Amer. Federation of the Arts
Blackwood Prods., Inc.

Brand, Oscar
Natl. Archives of Canada

Brand, Sybil
Banks Film Library

Branham, William Marrion
Wheaton Coll., Billy Graham Ctr.

Brasilia, Brazil
Brazilian-American Cultural Inst.

Brass bands
See Music (Brass bands)

Brass industry
Applegate Entertainment
Cinema Guild
Prelinger Assoc., Inc.

Braun, Eva
German Language Video Center
Intl. Historic Films, Inc.
Natl. Archives (RG 242)

Braverman, Barry
Port Washington Pub. Lib.

Bravo, M. Alvarez
Long Beach Mus. of Art

Brawls
Allen (John E.) Inc.
Film Bank
Fish Films, Inc.
Petrified Films, Inc.
See also Fist fights

Brazil
Canadian Broadcasting Corp.
Film Bank
Film Search
Grinberg (Sherman) Film Libraries (West)
Imagen y Sonido Independiente, S.A.
Sonoma Video Productions
World Monitor
Yue-Sai Kan, Inc.

Brazil (Contemporary issues)
DEC Film & Video

Brazil (History and culture)
Allen (John E.) Inc.
Analogous Prods.
Archive Film Prods., Inc.
Benamou, Catherine/LAWAS
Brazilian-American Cultural Inst.
Cinema Guild
DEC Film & Video
Democracy in Communication
Documentary Educational Resources
Grosvenor USA

Idera Films
Intl. Assn. of Independent Producers
NASA, Ames Res. Ctr., Imaging Tech. Branch
Natl. Archives (RG 59)
Natl. Archives (RG 234)
Petrified Films, Inc.
Rockefeller Arch. Ctr.
Third World Newsreel
U.S. Committee for UNICEF
Univ. of Arizona, Film Coll.
World Monitor

Breadlines
Allen (John E.) Inc.
Film Bank
Petrified Films, Inc.
Southern Calif. Lib. for Soc. Stud. & Res.
Timesteps Prods., Inc.

Breadmaking
Amer. Bakers Assn.
Bullfrog Films, Inc.
Univ. of Toronto, AV Lib.
See also Bakeries and baking industry

Breakdancing
See Dance and dancing (Breakdancing)

Breakfasts
Twentieth Century-Fox Movietonews

Breast-feeding
Courter Films & Assoc.
La Leche League of New Mexico
Polymorph Films, Inc.
UNICEF, Div. Info. & Pub. Aff.
Altschul Group
See also Babies

Breathalyzer machines
TV Ontario
See also Drunk driving

Breeches buoys
Prelinger Assoc., Inc.

Bregman, Buddy
Banks Film Library

Brennan, Walter
Banks Film Library

Breslin, Jimmy
Daphne Productions, Inc.

Breuer, Marcel
Electronic Arts Intermix

Brewer, Jim
Rhapsody Films, Inc.

Brewer, Teresa
Pathé Pictures, Inc.

Breweries
Farkas Studios, Ltd.
Petrified Films, Inc.

Brice, Fanny
New York Pub. Lib., Perf. Arts Res. Ctr., Theatre on Film and Tape

Bricker, John
Ohio Historical Soc.

Bricks and bricklaying
Brick Institute of America
Connecticut Historical Society
Petrified Films, Inc.
Prov. Arch. of Alberta
Texas Tech Univ., Southwest Coll.

Brides
See Weddings

Bridges
Allen (John E.) Inc.
Analogous Productions
Assoc. Gen. Contractors of America
Bangor Historical Society
British Info. Svcs., Radio & TV Div.
CBS News Archives
Calif. Dept. of Transportation
Dreamlight Images, Inc.
Elfstrom-Hilmer Prods.
Energy Productions
Farkas Studios, Ltd.
Film Bank
Forsher (James) Prods. & Archives, Inc.
Landmark Stock Footage Co.
Long Island State Park Comm.
Louisiana Tech Univ., Eng. Film Res. Ctr.
Massachusetts Archives
Petrified Films, Inc.
Port Authority of New York & New Jersey
Prelinger Assoc., Inc.
Prod. House, Inc., Motion Media Prods.
Source Stock Footage Lib., Inc.
Telltales Associates Inc.
Twentieth Century-Fox Movietonews
Univ. of Wash., Educ. Media Coll.
West Virginia Dept. of Culture & Hist.
Worldwide Television News
See also specific bridges

Bridges (Construction)
Allen (John E.) Inc.
Labor Video Project
Louisiana Tech Univ., Eng. Film Res. Ctr.
Natl. Archives of Canada
Petrified Films, Inc.
Smithsonian Inst., NMAH, Div. Eng. &
   Ind.
Washington State Hist. Soc.
See also Construction

Bridges (Exploding)
Dreamlight Images, Inc.

Bridges, Harry
San Francisco Bay Area TV News Arch.
Southern Calif. Lib. for Soc. Stud. & Res.

Bridges, Jeff
Spectral Comms.

Bridges, Lloyd
Banks Film Library
UCLA Film & Television Archive

Brimsek, Frank
U.S. Hockey Hall of Fame

Brinegar, Claude S.
Natl. Archives (RG 406)

Brisbane, Australia
Petrified Films, Inc.

Bristlecone pines
Energy Productions

British Columbia
Departures, Inc.
Hot Shots Commercial Prods., Inc.
Impact Audio Visual
Independent Media Communications
Preview Media
TV Ontario

British Columbia (History and culture)
Archive Film Prods., Inc.
Canadian Filmmakers Dist. West
Ctr. for Pacific Northwest Studies
Natl. Archives of Canada
Prov. Arch. of British Columbia

Univ. of Calif., Berkeley, Labor
   Occupational Health Prog.
Univ. of Wash. Press, Multimedia Div.
Voyager Co.
Yukon Archives

British Commonwealth
See United Kingdom

British Honduras
See Honduras (British)

British Virgin Islands
See Virgin Islands (British)

Brittany, Morgan
Spectral Comms.

Broadway theater
See Theater (Broadway)

Brocka, Lino
Blackwood (Christian) Prods., Inc.

Broderick, Matthew
Spectral Comms.

Broncos
See Horses

Bronfman, Edgar
Seagram Museum

Bronfman, Samuel
Seagram Museum

Bronson, Charles
Spectral Comms.

Bronx, N.Y. (History and culture)
Bronx County Hist. Soc.
Educational Video Ctr.

Bronzemaking
Smithsonian Inst., Freer Gallery of Art

Brooke, Hilary
Shokus Video

Brooklyn Bridge
Energy Productions

Brooklyn Bridge (History and culture)
Direct Cinema Ltd.
Louisiana Tech Univ., Eng. Film Res. Ctr.
Petrified Films, Inc.

Brooklyn, N.Y.
Bailey Productions, Inc.

Brooklyn, N.Y. (History and culture)
Archive Film Prods., Inc.
Cinema Guild
Educational Video Ctr.
New Day Films
Petrified Films, Inc.
Prelinger Assoc., Inc.
Regional Plan Assn.
Smithsonian Inst., Human Studies Film
   Arch.
Third World Newsreel

Brooks
See Streams

Brooks, Joel
Spectral Comms.

Brooks, Louise
Cantor (Arthur) Inc.

Brooks, Mel
Spectral Comms.

Brooks, Robert
Natl. Archives/Natl. AV Ctr.

**Brotherhood of Railway, Airline &
   Steamship Clerks**
Ohio Hist. Soc.

Broward County, Fla.
Video Ventures Prods.

Browder, Earl
Southern Calif. Lib. for Soc. Stud. & Res.

Brown, Charles
Southern Calif. Blues Soc.

Brown, Clarence
Ohio Historical Soc.

Brown, Edmund G. ("Pat")
Banks Film Library
KCRA-TV
Mus. & Hist. Div., City of Sacramento

Brown, Edmund G. Jr. ("Jerry")
KCRA-TV
Mus. & Hist. Div., City of Sacramento

Brown, George Stanford
Spectral Comms.

Brown, Harry Joe II
Univ. of Wyoming, Amer. Heritage Ctr.

Brown, James
Banks Film Library
Clark (Dick) Media Archives, Inc.
Target Video

Brown, Jim
Port Washington Pub. Lib.

Brown, Joan
Video Data Bank

Brown, Joe E.
Banks Film Library
Goodwill Industries of Amer.

Brown, Les
Banks Film Library

Brown, Peter
Banks Film Library

Brown, Roger
Mus. of Contemporary Art
Video Data Bank

Brown, Trisha
Blackwood Prods., Inc.

Brown, Walter F.
Natl. Archives (RG 28)

Browne, Jackson
Green Mountain Post Films

Brownstones
Film Bank
Video Tape Library, Ltd.

Broyard, Anatole
Pennebaker Associates, Inc.

Brubeck, Dave
Christopher Closeup

Bruce, Donald C.
Indiana State Lib.

Bruce, Lenny
Baker (Fred) Film & Video Co.

Brunhild, Queen
Archive Film Prods., Inc.

Brush fires
See Fires (Brush)

Brussel sprouts
Oregon State Univ., Archives

Brussels, Belgium (History and culture)
Archive Film Prods., Inc.
Petrified Films, Inc.

Bruton, Helen and Margaret
De Saisset Museum

Bryan, William Jennings
Grinberg (Sherman) Film Libraries (West)

Bryant, Anita
Shokus Video

Bryant, Kelvin
Archive Film Prods., Inc.

Bryce Canyon National Park, Utah
Energy Productions
Petrified Films, Inc.
Source Stock Footage Lib., Inc.
Stimulus

**Bryce Canyon National Park, Utah
   (History and culture)**
Utah State Hist. Soc.

Brynner, Yul
Banks Film Library

Bubbles (Soap)
Dreamlight Images, Inc.

Buchanan, Nancy
Long Beach Mus. of Art

Buchwald, Art
Pennebaker Associates, Inc.

Buckingham Palace (London)
Analogous Productions
Petrified Films, Inc.
TV Ontario

Buckley, James
Saint John's Univ., Spec. Coll.

Buckner, Barbara
Port Washington Pub. Lib.

Buddhas
Jewell (Stuart) Productions
Petrified Films, Inc.

Buddhism
See Religion (Buddhism)

Budgies
Film Bank
TV Ontario

**Buenos Aires, Argentina (History and
   culture)**
Archive Film Prods., Inc.
Prelinger Assoc., Inc.

NOTE: Access policies, availability and restrictions vary for each source. Please read each entry in full. Always consult "General Film and Videotape Collections" (page 599); these comprehensive collections contain material on every conceivable subject.

Buffalo Bill
See Cody, William F. ("Buffalo Bill")

Buffalo Bob
Archive Film Prods., Inc.

Buffalo Creek flood
Appalshop Films, Inc.
West Virginia Dept. of Culture & Hist.

Buffalo, N.Y.
4•6•8 Prods., Inc.

Buffalo, N.Y. (History and culture)
Buffalo & Erie County Hist. Soc.
Petrified Films, Inc.
Prelinger Assoc., Inc.

Buffaloes
Allen (John E.) Inc.
Amer. Bison Assn.
Archive Film Prods., Inc.
Di Sesso (Moe) Wild Life Film Lib.
Energy Productions
Film Bank
Innerquest Communications Corp.
Jewell (Stuart) Productions
Minnesota Zoo
New Mexico State Records Ctr. & Arch.
Petrified Films, Inc.
South Dakota State Lib.
Spalla (Rick) Video Prods.
Summit Films, Inc.
TV Ontario

Buggies (Horse-drawn)
Film Bank
Forsher (James) Prods. & Archives, Inc.
Petrified Films, Inc.

Building Trade & Construction Workers Union
Bowling Green State Univ., Ctr. Arch. Coll.

Buildings
A.M. Stock Exchange
Assoc. Gen. Contractors of America
Atlantic Productions
Borough of Manhattan Comm. Coll.
Broad Street Prods.
CBS News Archives
Cannell (Stephen J.) Productions, Inc.
Chicago Video Transfer
Cinephile Amalgamated Pictures
Columbia Pictures TV/Stock Film Library
Cornell Univ., Media Services
Dorn (Larry) Associates
Energy Productions
Farkas Studios, Ltd.
Film Bank
Film/Audio Services, Inc.
Fish Films, Inc.
Grinberg (Sherman) Film Libraries (West)
Hayes Prods., Inc.
Jewell (Stuart) Productions
Landmark Stock Footage Co.
Metro Communications, Inc.
Mountain Video Associates
Natl. Archives (RG 69)
Peak Productions, Inc.
Petrified Films, Inc.
Port Authority of New York & New Jersey
Producers Library Service
Prov. Arch. of Alberta
Renaissance Video Corp.
Rosebush Visions Corp.
Stegman Productions
Stock House
TV Ontario
Twentieth Century-Fox Movietonews
Unicorn Projects
Video Tape Library, Ltd.
Wallen (Dick) Prods.
Zielinski Productions, Inc.

See also Architecture; Construction; Houses and homes; Housing; specific buildings

Buildings (Burning)
See Fires

Buildings (Collapsing)
Archive Film Prods., Inc.
Petrified Films, Inc.
Prelinger Assoc., Inc.

Buildings (Construction)
Cranbrook Acad. of Arts
Eastern Washington State Historical Soc.
Farkas Studios, Ltd.
Intl. Film Foundation
Natl. Archives (RG 28)
Natl. Archives (RG 31)
Natl. Archives (RG 121)
Petrified Films, Inc.
Prelinger Assoc., Inc.
Seagram Museum
Spectral Comms.
TV Ontario
See also Construction

Buildings (Deserted)
Film Bank

Buildings (Exploding)
Dreamlight Images, Inc.
Film Bank
Petrified Films, Inc.
See also Explosions

Buildings (Government)
Farkas Studios, Ltd.
Moser (Michael)/Media
Natl. Archives (RG 28)
Natl. Archives (RG 33)
Natl. Archives (RG 82)
Natl. Archives (RG 103)
Petrified Films, Inc.
Stock House
Washington Broadcast Video Lib.
See also City halls

Buildings (Interiors)
Metro Communications, Inc.
Petrified Films, Inc.
Stegman Productions
Twentieth Century-Fox Movietonews

Buildings (Moving)
Petrified Films, Inc.
San Antonio Conservation Soc. Found. Lib.

Buildings (Office)
A.M. Stock Exchange
Dreamlight Images, Inc.
Film Bank
Petrified Films, Inc.
Prelinger Assoc., Inc.
Stegman Productions
Stock House

Buildings (Religious)
Twentieth Century-Fox Movietonews

Buitrago, Ann Mari
Paper Tiger TV

Bukowski, Charles
Giorno Poetry Systems Inst.

Bulgaria (History and culture)
Mankind Research Found., Inc.
Rockefeller Arch. Ctr.

Bulimia
See Eating disorders

Bulldozers

Energy Productions
General Motors Corp.
Petrified Films, Inc.
See also Earthmoving equipment; Heavy equipment

Bulletproof vests
Analogous Productions

Bullfights
Analogous Productions
Archive Film Prods., Inc.
Energy Productions
Film Bank
Oregon Hist. Soc.
Petrified Films, Inc.
Source Stock Footage Lib., Inc.
Sportsfilm
Twentieth Century-Fox Movietonews

Bulls
Analogous Productions
Oregon State Univ., Archives
Petrified Films, Inc.
Summit Films, Inc.

Bulrushes
TV Ontario

Bumper cars
Petrified Films, Inc.
See also Amusement parks

Bums
Archive Film Prods., Inc.
Southern Calif. Lib. for Soc. Stud. & Res.

Bunker, Ellsworth
Duke Univ., Perkins Lib.

Bunker Hill (Los Angeles) (History and culture)
Petrified Films, Inc.

Bunkers
Petrified Films, Inc.

Bunraku Puppet Theater
See Theater (Bunraku Puppet)

Bunsen burners
Film Bank

Bunting, Basil
Camera Three Prods., Inc.

Buoys
CBS News Archives
Natl. Archives (RG 26)

Burckhardt, Rudy
Port Washington Pub. Lib.
Video Data Bank

Burden, Chris
Electronic Arts Intermix

Burdon, Eric and the Animals
Archive Film Prods., Inc.
Pennebaker Associates, Inc.

Bureau of
See the bureau's "subject" area (e.g., Bureau of Mines is found under Mines, Bureau of [U.S.])

Burglars
See Crimes and criminals

Burkhalter, Marianne
Southern Calif. Inst. of Architecture

Burkina Faso (Contemporary issues)
UNICEF, Div. Info. & Pub. Aff.

Burlesque
New York Pub. Lib., Perf. Arts Res. Ctr., Theatre on Film and Tape
Petrified Films, Inc.
Prelinger Assoc., Inc.
See also Striptease; Vaudeville

Burma (History and culture)
Archive Film Prods., Inc.
Devillier Donegan Ent.
Petrified Films, Inc.

Burma Road
Hearst Metrotone News

Burnett, Carol
UCLA Film & Television Archive

Burning ships
See Ships (Burning)

Burns
Academy of Health Sciences, U.S. Army
Film Bank
Prelinger Assoc., Inc.
Rogers (Will) Institute

Burns, Ed
Banks Film Library

Burns, George
Banks Film Library
Em Gee Film Library
Encore Entertainment
MacDonald, J. Fred
New York Pub. Lib., Perf. Arts Res. Ctr., Theatre on Film and Tape
Shokus Video
Spectral Comms.
UCLA Film & Television Archive

Burns, James
Southern Calif. Inst. of Architecture

Burr, Raymond
Banks Film Library

Burra, Edward
Amer. Federation of the Arts

Burros
Cinenet (Cinema Network)

Burroughs, William
Giorno Poetry Systems Inst.

Burstyn, Varda
Paper Tiger TV
Video Data Bank

Burton, Richard
Banks Film Library

Burton, Scott
Blackwood Prods., Inc.

Bus terminals
Film Bank
Petrified Films, Inc.
Port Authority of New York & New Jersey

Busch Gardens, Va.
Metro Communications, Inc.

Busch, Niven
Univ. of Wyoming, Amer. Heritage Ctr.

Buses
Amer. Public Transit Assn.
CBS News Archives
Dreamlight Images, Inc.
Film Bank
Forsher (James) Prods. & Archives, Inc.
Kesser Stock Footage Library
Motor Bus Society Library

Petrified Films, Inc.
Prelinger Assoc., Inc.
Redden Archives
Spectral Comms.
Video Tape Library, Ltd.

Buses (Double-decker)
Missouri Hist. Soc.
Petrified Films, Inc.
TV Ontario

Buses (School)
Film Bank
Petrified Films, Inc.
Prelinger Assoc., Inc.

Bush, George
U.S. Hockey Hall of Fame

Bush, George Herbert Walker
ABC News Interactive
Churchill (Winston) Memorial and Library

Bush planes
See Aircraft (Bush)

Bush, Prescott
Connecticut State Library

Bush Tetras (Rock and roll band)
Target Video

Bush, Vannevar
Mass. Inst. of Tech., MIT Museum

Bushman, Francis X.
Banks Film Library
Natl. Archives (RG 47)

Business
ABC Distribution (Education)
Altschul Group
Barr Films
Britannica Films & Video
Cable News Network Library
Carousel Film & Video
Cinema Guild
Direct Cinema Ltd.
Energy Productions
Filmfair Communications
GPN
Hagley Mus. & Lib.
Intl. Film Bureau, Inc.
Natl. Archives/Natl. AV Ctr.
Perlmutter (Alvin H.) Inc.
Phoenix Films and Video
Prelinger Assoc., Inc.
Spalla (Rick) Video Prods.
TV Ontario
Timesteps Prods., Inc.
V/tape
Video-SIG
Yue-Sai Kan, Inc.

Business (Japan)
Japan External Trade Organization

Business scenes
Boston Stock Market
Chicago Video Transfer
Dreamlight Images, Inc.
Energy Productions
Fabulous Footage Inc.
Metro Communications, Inc.
Petrified Films, Inc.
Prelinger Assoc., Inc.
Twentieth Century-Fox Movietonews
Video Tape Library, Ltd.
See also Corporate scenes

Busing

Univ. of Mich., Mich. Hist. Coll.

Butchers and butchering
Appalachian State Univ., Eury Coll.
Appalshop Films, Inc.
Film Bank
Lib. of Congress, Amer. Folklife Ctr.
Natl. Archives (RG 33)
Oregon State Univ., Archives
Petrified Films, Inc.

Butte, Mont. (History and culture)
Estuary Press

Butter
See Dairy industry

Butterflies
Dreamlight Images, Inc.
Energy Productions
Film Bank
Petrified Films, Inc.
Summit Films, Inc.
TV Ontario

Buttes
Jewell (Stuart) Productions

Button, John
Video Data Bank

Buttons
Rosebush Visions Corp.

Buttons, Red
Banks Film Library
Spectral Comms.

Buzz saws
Film Bank

Buzzards
Di Sesso (Moe) Wild Life Film Lib.
Petrified Films, Inc.

Byard, Jaki
Rhapsody Films, Inc.

Byelorussian SSR (History and culture)
United Nations Ctr. for Human
   Settlements

Byrd, Richard E.
Archive Film Prods., Inc.
Natl. Archives (RG 126)
Natl. Archives (RG 178)
Natl. Archives (RG 200)
Natl. Archives (RG 342)
Natl. Archives of Canada

Byrne, David
Monday, Wednesday, Friday Video Club

CAD/CAM
See Computers (CAD/CAM)

CAT scans
Amer. Journal of Nursing Co.
See also Technology (Medical);
   Tomography

CCC
See Civilian Conservation Corps (CCC)

CIA
See Central Intelligence Agency (CIA)

CIO
See Congress of Industrial Organizations
   (CIO)

CPR
See Cardiopulmonary resuscitation (CPR)

Cabaret Voltaire (Musical group)
Giorno Poetry Systems Inst.

Cabbage
TV Ontario

Cabbage loopers
Dreamlight Images, Inc.

Cabinetmakers
TV Ontario

Cabins
Energy Productions
Film Bank
Peak Productions, Inc.
Petrified Films, Inc.

Cable cars
CBS News Archives
Dreamlight Images, Inc.
Petrified Films, Inc.
Prelinger Assoc., Inc.

Cabo San Lucas, Mexico
Preview Media

Cabral, Amilcar
Third World Newsreel

Cabs
See Taxis

Cactuses
Dreamlight Images, Inc.
Energy Productions
Petrified Films, Inc.
Prelinger Assoc., Inc.
Source Stock Footage Lib., Inc.

Cadets
CBS News Archives
Citadel, The
Mariners' Museum
Petrified Films, Inc.
TV Ontario

Cadillac Ranch (Amarillo, Tex.)
Dreamlight Images, Inc.

Cadmus, Paul
Amer. Federation of the Arts

Caernarvon, Wales
Unicorn Projects

Caesar, Julius
Archive Film Prods., Inc.

Caesar, Sid
Banks Film Library
Spalla (Rick) Video Prods.
Spectral Comms.

Caesarian sections
See Childbirth (Caesarian)

Cafes
CBS News Archives
Film Bank
TV Ontario
See also Restaurants

Cafeterias
CBS News Archives
Film Bank
Petrified Films, Inc.
TV Ontario

See also Restaurants

Caffeine
Addiction Research Foundation of Ontario

Cage, John
Blackwood Prods., Inc.
Cunningham Dance Foundation
Giorno Poetry Systems Inst.
Intermedia Arts Minnesota
Video Data Bank
Walker Art Ctr.

Cage, Nicholas
Daphne Productions, Inc.

Cages
Film Bank

Cagney, James
Archive Film Prods., Inc.
Banks Film Library

Cahn, Anne
Inst. for Space & Security Studies

Cahn, Sammy
Banks Film Library

Cairo, Egypt
Preview Media

Cairo, Egypt (History and culture)
Lib. of Congress, M/B/RS
Petrified Films, Inc.
Prelinger Assoc., Inc.
United Nations Ctr. for Human
   Settlements

Cajun music
See Music (Cajun)

Cakewalking
See Dance and dancing (Cakewalk)

Calcutta, India
Petrified Films, Inc.

Calcutta, India (History and culture)
Petrified Films, Inc.

Calder, Alexander
Blackwood Prods., Inc.
Mus. at Large, Ltd.
Natl. Gallery of Art

Calderone, Mary S.
Radcliffe Coll., Schlesinger Lib.

Caldicott, Helen
Alternative Information Network
Cambridge Documentary Films, Inc.
Direct Cinema Ltd.
Green Mountain Post Films
Physicians for Social Responsibility
Resource Ctr. for Nonviolence

Calendars and calendar pages
CBS News Archives
Film Bank
Petrified Films, Inc.

Calett, Walter
Videobrary, Inc.

Calgary, Alberta
Departures, Inc.
Preview Media

Calgary, Alberta (History and culture)
Glenbow Mus. Arch.

NOTE: Access policies, availability and restrictions vary for each source. Please read each entry in full. Always consult "General Film and Videotape Collections" (page 599); these comprehensive collections contain material on every conceivable subject.

Natl. Archives of Canada
Prov. Arch. of Alberta

Calgary Stampede
Glenbow Mus.
Natl. Archives of Canada
Prov. Arch. of Alberta

Calhoun, Rory
Banks Film Library
Spalla (Rick) Video Prods.

California
Airline Film & TV Promotions
Airship Industries (USA), Inc.
Analogous Prods.
Applegate Entertainment
Beerger (Norman) Prods.
Broad Street Prods.
Cabscott Broadcast Prods.
Cannell (Stephen J.) Prods., Inc.
Channel Sea Television
Cinenet (Cinema Network)
Cinephile Amalgamated Pictures
Creative Video, Inc.
Crystal Pyramid Prods.
Dorn (Larry) Assoc.
Dreamlight Images, Inc.
Elfstrom-Hilmer Prods.
Energy Productions
Film Bank
Film Search, Inc.
First Group Comms., Inc.
Goal Prods., Tourn. of Roses Film Lib.
Gornick Film Productions
Jewell (Stuart) Prods.
Loma Linda Univ., Webb Lib.
Los Angeles Dept. of Water & Power
Media West, Inc.
Nature Conservancy
New Film Co., Inc.
Petrified Films, Inc.
Phoenix Videofilms/Karr Prods.
Postcards Unlimited
Preview Media
Prod. House Inc., Motion Media Prods.
Solaris Dance/Theatre/Video
Sonoma Video Productions
Source Film & Tape Lib., Inc.
Spalla (Rick) Video Prods.
Spectral Comms.
Stegman Prods.
Stimulus
Stock House
Stock Shots
Summit Films, Inc.
TV Ontario
TVA/Television Assoc.
Telltales Associates Inc.
Tri-Comm Prods.
Unicorn Projects
Wallen (Dick) Prods.

California (History and culture)
Allen (John E.) Inc.
Archive Film Prods., Inc.
Archives of Ontario
Armenian Film Foundation
Atlantis Prods., Inc.
Banks Film Library
Calif. Dept. of Transportation
Calif. Dept. of Water Resources
Calif. State Archives
Calif. State Univ., Northridge
Cinema Guild
Creative Film Society
Eden Entertainment, Inc.
Em Gee Film Library
Estuary Press
Film Bank
Fish Films, Inc.
Flower Films & Video
Footage, Inc.
Forsher (James) Prods. & Archives, Inc.
Frontline Video, Inc.

General Motors Corp.
Gould (Bert)/bay area archive
Grinberg (Sherman) Film Libraries (East)
Hoover Institution
Jessiefilm
KCRA-TV
Labor Video Project
Los Angeles City Archives
Los Angeles News Service
Louisiana Tech. Univ., Eng. Film Res. Ctr.
MacDonald, J. Fred
Mus. & Hist. Div., City of Sacramento
Natl. Archives (RG 46)
Natl. Archives (RG 200)
Natl. Archives (RG 381)
Natl. Asian American Telecomm. Assn.
Natl. Railway Historical Soc.
Natural Reflections Video
Nature Conservancy
Newsreel Video Service
Nuclear Free Zone Registry
Oregon Hist. Soc.
Pacific Film Archive
Patrick Media Group
Payne, Roz
Petrified Films, Inc.
Phoenix Videofilms/Karr Prods.
Prelinger Assoc., Inc.
Prov. Arch. of Alberta
Quest Prods., Inc.
San Francisco Bay Area TV News Arch.
San Francisco Natl. Maritime Hist. Park
San Jose Hist. Museum
Southern Calif. Inst. of Architecture
Southern Calif. Lib. for Soc. Stud. & Res.
Spalla (Rick) Video Prods.
Sweet (Harry) Film Coll.
U.S. Natl. Park Service Hist. Coll.
UCLA Behavioral Science Media Lab.
Unicorn Projects
United Farm Workers of America (UFW)
Univ. of Calif., Berkeley, Bancroft Lib.
Video Data Bank
Visual Communications
White Janssen, Inc.
Worldwide Television News

California Zephyr
See Railroads (California Zephyr)

Callahan, Harry
Amer. Federation of the Arts
Port Washington Pub. Lib.
Santa Barbara Mus. of Art

Callahan, Kenneth
Media Project

Calloway, Cab
Archive Film Prods., Inc.
First Run/Icarus Films, Inc.
Las Vegas News Bureau

Calvet, Corinne
Banks Film Library

Calvin, Melvin
Amer. Chemical Soc.

Calypso music
See Music (Calypso)

Camay, Piroshaw
Randolph (A. Philip) Educ. Fund

Cambodia
Imagen y Sonido Independiente, S.A.

Cambodia (History and culture)
Devillier Donegan Ent.
Downtown Community TV Ctr.
Idera Films
San Francisco Bay Area TV News Arch.
Southwest Film/Video Archives, SMU

Cambridge, Mass.
Summit Films, Inc.

Camden, N.J. (History and culture)
Prelinger Assoc., Inc.

Camellias
Energy Productions

Camels
Circus World Mus. Lib. & Res. Ctr.
Minnesota Zoo
Petrified Films, Inc.
TV Ontario

Camera, Dom Helder
United Farm Workers of America (UFW)

Cameramen
CBS News Archives

Cameras
CBS News Archives
Film Bank
Petrified Films, Inc.
Rosebush Visions Corp.

Cameron, G.I.
Yukon Archives

Camouflage
CBS News Archives

Campaign commercials
See Political campaign commercials

Campaigns
See Political campaigns

Campanella, Roy
Natl. Archives (RG 220)

Campbell, Glen
Clark (Dick) Media Archives, Inc.

Campbell, Joseph
Perlmutter (Alvin H.) Inc.

Campfires
TV Ontario

Campobello Island, Maine (History and culture)
Roosevelt (Franklin D.) Lib.

Camps and camping
Boy Scouts of America, AV Svcs.
CBS News Archives
Edwards, H.M.
Film Bank
Film/Audio Services, Inc.
Glenbow Mus. Arch.
Jewell (Stuart) Productions
Natl. Mus. of the Boy Scouts of Amer.
Petrified Films, Inc.
Preview Media
Prov. Arch. of British Columbia
Source Stock Footage Lib., Inc.
TV Ontario
See also Boy Scouts and Scouting

Campus life
Appalachian State Univ., Eury Coll.
Auburn University Archives
Baylor Univ., Texas Coll.
Cornell Univ., Media Services
DePauw University, Archives
Emporia State Univ., Spec. Coll.
Film Bank
Franklin & Marshall Coll.
Kartemquin Films
Mass. Inst. of Tech., MIT Museum
Northern Ill. Univ., Reg. Hist. Ctr.
Ohio State Univ., Dept. of Photog. & Cinema

Oregon State Univ., Archives
Petrified Films, Inc.
Prelinger Assoc., Inc.
Stanford Univ. Lib., Dept. of Spec. Coll. & Univ. Arch.
Twentieth Century-Fox Movietonews
Univ. of Calif., Davis, Shields Library
Univ. of Ill. Urbana-Champaign, Univ. Arch.
Univ. of Manitoba Lib., Arch. Spec. Coll.
Univ. of Mich., Mich. Hist. Colls.
Univ. of North Texas, Div. of Radio/TV/Film
Univ. of Oregon Lib., Inst. Media Ctr.
Univ. of Pa. Arch.
Univ. of Rhode Island, Univ. Lib.
Univ. of Rochester Lib., Rare Books & Spec. Coll.
Winthrop Coll., Dacus Lib.
See also Cheerleaders; Colleges and universities; Graduations; Sports (College)

Campus, Peter
Blackwood Prods., Inc.

Campus Unrest, President's Commission on
Natl. Archives (RG 220)

Canada
Bennett (Joel) Prods.
Canadian Broadcasting Corp.
Chisholm (Jack) Film Productions
Creative Video, Inc.
Departures, Inc.
Energy Productions
Fabulous Footage Inc.
File Tape Co.
Independent Media Communications
Intl. Assn. of Independent Producers
Northstar Prods.
Petrified Films, Inc.
Preview Media
Summit Films, Inc.
TV Ontario
Video I-D, Inc.
World Monitor

Canada (Contemporary issues)
DEC Film & Video
Third World Newsreel

Canada (History and culture)
Archive Film Prods., Inc.
Archives of Ontario
Atlantic Independent Media
Bibliothèque Municipale de Montréal
Bullfrog Films, Inc.
CTV Television Network
Canadian Broadcasting Corp.
Canadian Filmmakers Dist. Centre
Canadian Filmmakers Dist. West
Canadian Gay Archives
Carleton Prods. Inc.
Center for Pacific Northwest Studies
Centre for Art Tapes
Chisholm (Jack) Film Productions
Crawley Films, Ltd.
Film/Audio Services, Inc.
Glenbow Mus. Arch.
Huronia Historical Parks
Imperial Oil Ltd.
MacDonald, J. Fred
March of Time
Native Amer. Pub. Broad. Cons.
Natl. Archives (RG 111)
Natl. Archives (RG 326)
Natl. Archives of Canada
Natl. Film Board of Canada
Northstar Prods.
Oregon Hist. Soc.
Pacific Cinémathèque Pacifique
Petrified Films, Inc.
Prov. Arch. of British Columbia

Prov. Arch. of Manitoba
Prov. Arch. of Newfoundland & Labrador
TV Ontario
Univ. of Regina, Sask. Arch. Board
Univ. of Toronto, AV Lib.
Women in Focus
World Monitor
York Univ. Archives

Canadian Brass (Musical group)
Camera Three Prods., Inc.

Canadian history (Re-creations)
Natl. Archives of Canada
Prov. Arch. of Alberta

Canadian National Exhibition (CNE)
Natl. Archives of Canada

Canadian Rockies
See Rocky Mountains

Canadian Union of Public Employees
Natl. Archives of Canada

Canadian Unity, Task Force on
Natl. Archives of Canada

Canal Zone (History and culture)
Natl. Archives (RG 18)

Canals
Allen (John E.) Inc.
CBS News Archives
Farkas Studios, Ltd.
Film Bank
Natl. Archives of Canada
Petrified Films, Inc.
Twentieth Century-Fox Movietonews

Canandaigua, N.Y. (History and culture)
New York State Hist. Assn.

Canaries
Di Sesso (Moe) Wild Life Film Lib.

Canberra, Australia
Petrified Films, Inc.

Cancer
ABC Distribution (Education)
Academy of Health Sciences, U.S. Army
Amer. Cancer Soc., Inc.
Cambridge Documentary Films, Inc.
Cinema Guild
Focus Intl. Inc.
Halcyon Days Prods.
Historical Health Film Coll.
IEA Prods., Inc.
Intellimation
March of Time
Milner-Fenwick, Inc.
Narcotics Education, Inc.
Nassau Comm. Coll. Lib.
Natl. Archives (RG 90)
Natl. Archives (RG 307)
Natl. Archives of Canada
Natl. Press Photographers Assn., Inc.
New Time Films, Inc.
Rockefeller Arch. Ctr.
Varied Directions, Inc.

Cancer (Nutritional therapy)
Gerson Institute

Cancun, Mexico
Preview Media

Candles
Film Bank

Petrified Films, Inc.

Candy and candy bars
Hershey Foods Corp.
Parker (Kit) Films
Prelinger Assoc., Inc.

Canemaker, John
Port Washington Pub. Lib.

Canned Heat (Rock and roll band)
Pennebaker Associates, Inc.

Canneries
Canadian Filmmakers Dist. West
Canned Fruit Promotion Service
Film Bank
San Francisco Maritime Natl. Hist. Park

Cannes, France
Petrified Films, Inc.

Cannes, France (History and culture)
Petrified Films, Inc.

Cannibals
Archive Film Prods., Inc.
Jewell (Stuart) Productions
Zielinski Productions, Inc.

Canning (Preserving)
CBS News Archives
Natl. Archives (RG 33)
Petrified Films, Inc.
TV Ontario

Cannons
Analogous Productions
Film Bank
See also Weapons

Cannons (Water)
Analogous Productions

Canoes and canoeing
Beerger (Norman) Prods.
Chiappetta Prods., Inc.
Energy Productions
Film Bank
Ideal Comms., Inc.
Jalbert Productions
New Film Co., Inc.
New Jersey Network
North Country Media Group
Petrified Films, Inc.
Prelinger Assoc., Inc.
Source Stock Footage Lib., Inc.
TV Ontario
Video Tape Library, Ltd.

Canright, Sarah
Video Data Bank

Cans
Rosebush Visions Corp.

Cantaloupes
TV Ontario

Cantinas
Petrified Films, Inc.
See also Bars

Cantinflas, Mario Marino
Spectral Comms.

Canton, China
See Zhu Jiang, China

Cantor, Eddie
Banks Film Library

Natl. Archives (RG 47)
Natl. Archives/Natl. AV Ctr.
New York Pub. Lib., Perf. Arts Res. Ctr.,
    Theatre on Film and Tape
UCLA Film & Television Archive

Canutt, Yakima
Intl. Mus. of Photography

Canyon de Chelly, Ariz.
Energy Productions
Source Stock Footage Lib., Inc.

Canyon de Chelly, Ariz. (History and culture)
U.S. Natl. Park Service Hist. Coll.

Canyons
CBS News Archives
Cinenet (Cinema Network)
Dreamlight Images, Inc.
Film Bank
Film Search
Petrified Films, Inc.
Summit Films, Inc.
Twentieth Century-Fox Movietonews

Capa, Robert
Port Washington Pub. Lib.

Cape Breton Island, Nova Scotia (History and culture)
Univ. Coll. of Cape Breton, Beaton Inst.

Cape Canaveral, Fla. (History and culture)
Analogous Productions
Lib. of Congress, M/B/RS

Cape Cod, Mass.
Energy Productions
Preview Media
Site Productions

Cape Hatteras, N.C. (History and culture)
North Carolina Div. of Arch. & Hist.

Cape Horn, Chile
Cousteau Society

Cape Horn, Chile (History and culture)
Mystic Seaport Mus., Inc.

Cape Lookout, N.C. (History and culture)
North Carolina Div. of Arch. & Hist.

Cape Town, South Africa (History and culture)
DEC Film & Video

Capehart, Homer
Indiana State Lib.

Capital punishment
Amnesty Intl. USA
CBS News Archives
Cinema Guild
March of Time
Mass Media Ministries
Mus. & Hist. Div., City of Sacramento
Natl. Archives of Canada
See also Electric chairs; Executions

Capitol building (U.S.) (Washington, D.C.)
Analogous Productions
Dirksen (E. M.) Cong. Lead. Res. Ctr.
Harriman Communications Ctr.
Moser (Michael)/Media

Petrified Films, Inc.
Prelinger Assoc., Inc.
Washington Broadcast Video Lib.

Capitol buildings (State)
Amer. Motion Pictures
Cimarron Productions
Film Bank
Petrified Films, Inc.

Capitol Records Building (Los Angeles)
Dreamlight Images, Inc.
Energy Productions
Film Bank

Capra, Frank
Ohio State Univ., Dept. of Photog. & Cinema

Car culture
Allen (John E.) Inc.
MacDonald, J. Fred
Petrified Films, Inc.
Prelinger Assoc., Inc.
See also Automobiles

Car washes
Film Bank
Petrified Films, Inc.

Caracara
Di Sesso (Moe) Wild Life Film Lib.

Caracas, Venezuela
Kesser Stock Footage Library

Caracas, Venezuela (History and culture)
United Nations, Visual Materials Lib.

Caravans
CBS News Archives

Carbon monoxide
Natl. Archives (RG 70)

Carborundum
Natl. Archives (RG 70)

Cardenal, Ernesto
Film/Audio Services, Inc.

Cárdenas, Cuauhtémoc
Redes Cinevideo, S.A.

Cardew, Michael
Amer. Federation of the Arts

Cardin, Pierre
Cinema Guild

Cardiology
Altschul Group
Amer. Heart Assn.
Milner-Fenwick, Inc.
Nassau Comm. Coll. Lib.
See also Electrocardiography; Heart

Cardiopulmonary resuscitation (CPR)
AIMS Media
Alternative Information Network
Amer. Heart Assn.
Film Bank
Nassau Comm. Coll. Lib.
Pyramid Film and Video Corp.
See also First aid; Heart

Cards (Playing)
TV Ontario

NOTE: Access policies, availability and restrictions vary for each source. Please read each entry in full. Always consult "General Film and Videotape Collections" (page 599); these comprehensive collections contain material on every conceivable subject.

Careers
AIMS Media
Amer. Assn. for Counseling &
 Development
Amer. Cancer Soc., Inc.
Amer. Dental Assn.
Amer. Hotel & Motel Assn.
Amer. Nuclear Society
Amer. Physical Therapy Assn.
Amer. Soc. of Clin. Path. Press
Amer. Truck Historical Society
Assoc. Gen. Contractors of America
Barr Films
Carousel Film & Video
Center for Humanities, Inc.
Churchill Films
Cinema Guild
Coe Film Assoc., Inc.
Educational Images, Ltd.
Electronic Industries Assn.
Film Bank
Filmfair Communications
Future Farmers of America
GPN
German Info. Ctr., Film Lib.
Handel Film Corp.
Inst. of Financial Education
Intl. Film Bureau, Inc.
NASA, Johnson Space Ctr., Film & Video
 Dist. Lib.
Natl. Archives (RG 307)
Natl. Assn. of Conservation Dists.
Natl. Press Photographers Assn., Inc.
Phoenix Films and Video
Prelinger Assoc., Inc.
Salenger Films Inc.
TV Ontario
See also Workers; specific careers and
 occupations

Carey, Hugh
New York State Arch. & Rec. Admin.
Saint John's Univ., Spec. Coll.

Cargo planes
See Aircraft (Cargo)

Cargo ships
See Ships (Cargo)

Carhops
Petrified Films, Inc.

Caribbean region
Amer. Airlines
Caribbean Images, Ltd.
Creative Video, Inc.
Dorn (Larry) Associates
Energy Productions
Kesser Stock Footage Library
NBC News Video Archives
Orion Post Production
Pan American Airlines Film Lib.
Petrified Films, Inc.
Sea TV
Simon (Jeff) Productions
Sonoma Video Productions
Source Stock Footage Lib., Inc.
Telltales Associates Inc.
World Monitor
See also Tropical scenes; specific islands
 and nations

**Caribbean region (Contemporary
 issues)**
Third World Newsreel

Caribbean region (History and culture)
Archive Film Prods., Inc.
DEC Film & Video
Idera Films
Mus. of Mod. Art of Latin America
Natl. Archives (RG 18)
Natl. Archives (RG 127)
Notimex

Roosevelt (Franklin D.) Lib.
World Monitor

Caribou
Alaska Video Prods.
Jewell (Stuart) Productions
TV Ontario
Univ. of Alberta, Boreal Inst. for Northern
 Studies
Univ. of Alberta, Fac. of Ext.

Carlson, Cynthia
Albright-Knox Art Gallery
Video Data Bank

Carmel, Calif.
Film Bank
Petrified Films, Inc.
Postcards Unlimited

Carmel, Calif. (History and culture)
Petrified Films, Inc.

Carmichael, Hoagy
Banks Film Library

Carmichael, Stokely
Alternative Information Network
Film/Audio Services, Inc.
Villon Films

**Carnaby Street, London (History and
 culture)**
Spalla (Rick) Video Prods.

Carnegie, Andrew
Petrified Films, Inc.

**Carnegie Hall (New York City) (History
 and culture)**
Petrified Films, Inc.

Carnera, Primo
Archive Film Prods., Inc.
Grinberg (Sherman) Film Libraries (West)

Carnes, Kim
Spectral Comms.

Carnivals
Analogous Productions
CBS News Archives
Cinema Guild
Cinenet (Cinema Network)
Energy Productions
Film Bank
Film Education Institute
Mountain Video Associates
Petrified Films, Inc.
Source Stock Footage Lib., Inc.
Telltales Associates Inc.
WTJX-TV

Carnivals (Winter)
TV Ontario

Caro, Anthony
Albright-Knox Art Gallery
Blackwood Prods., Inc.

Caroline Islands (History and culture)
Smithsonian Inst., Human Studies Film
 Arch.

Carousels
CBS News Archives
Film Bank
Kesser Stock Footage Library
Petrified Films, Inc.
See also Amusement parks

Carpentry
CBS News Archives
Petrified Films, Inc.

Carpets
Film Bank

Carr, Emily
Natl. Archives of Canada

Carr, Vicki
Banks Film Library

Carr, Waggoner
Texas Tech Univ., Southwest Coll.

Carradine, David
Spectral Comms.

Carranza, Venustiano
Archivo Historico Cinematografico
Natl. Archives (RG 200)

Carriages
CBS News Archives
Hayes Prods., Inc.
Omega Films
Timesteps Prods., Inc.

Carroll, Diahann
Banks Film Library

Carroll, Gene
Inst. for Space & Security Studies

Carroll, Jim
Giorno Poetry Systems Inst.
Target Video

Carroll, Julian
Kentucky Dept. of Libraries & Archives

Carrots
Academy of Health Sciences, U.S. Army
TV Ontario

Cars
See Automobiles

Carson City, Nev. (History and culture)
Petrified Films, Inc.

Carson, Johnny
Carson Tonight Inc.
Clark (Dick) Media Archives, Inc.
Shokus Video
UCLA Film & Television Archive

Carter, Betty
Women Make Movies, Inc.

Carter, Elliott
Pennebaker Associates, Inc.

Carter, Helena Bonham
Spectral Comms.

Carter, Jack
Spectral Comms.

Carter, Jimmy
Agee (James) Film Project
Carter (Jimmy) Library
Eastern Washington State Historical Soc.
Emory Univ., Spec. Coll.
Natl. Archives (RG 185)
Natl. Archives (RG 220)
Natl. Archives (RG 398)
Natl. Archives (RG 441)
Pennebaker Associates, Inc.
Pyramid Film and Video Corp.
UCLA Film & Television Archive
Univ. of Georgia, WSB TV News Film
 Arch.

Carter, John
Rhapsody Films, Inc.

Carter, Sara and Maybelle

Cinema Guild

Cartography
Natl. Archives (RG 24)
Prelinger Assoc., Inc.
See also Maps

Cartooning
Camera Three Prods., Inc.

Cartoons
Alan Twyman Presents
Amer. Citizenship Ctr.
Archive Film Prods., Inc.
Belka Intl. Inc.
Budget Films Inc.
Cinémathèque Québecoise
DeFlores, Bob
Dettlaff (Alois F.) Sr.
Disada Productions' Disney Mem. Lib.
Disney (Walt) Archives
Eisenhower (Dwight D.) Lib.
Em Gee Film Library
Encore Entertainment
Film Bank
Film Search
Filmtel Intl. Corp.
Fish Films, Inc.
French Lib. in Boston
German Language Video Ctr.
Imageways, Inc.
Instituto Cubano de Radio y Television
Kinsey Institute
Lib. of Congress, M/B/RS
MacDonald, J. Fred
Moviecraft, Inc.
Movietime, Inc. Archives
Narcotics Education, Inc.
Natl. Archives (RG 4)
Natl. Archives of Canada
Natl. Archives/Natl. AV Ctr.
Palladium Entertainment, Inc.
Prelinger Assoc., Inc.
Producers Library Service
Quest Productions Inc.
Rosebush Visions Corp.
San Diego State Univ., Spec. Coll.
San Francisco Acad. of Comic Art Lib.
Shields Archival
Shokus Video
Southwest Film/Video Archives, SMU
Streamline Film Archives
Swank Motion Pictures, Inc.
UCLA Film & Television Archive
UPA Prods. of America
Video Resources N.Y., Inc.
Video Yesteryear
Video-SIG
Wisconsin Ctr. for Film & Theater Res.
See also Animation

Cartoons (Political)
Mus. of Contemporary Art

Caruso, Enrico
Petrified Films, Inc.

Carvings (Erotic)
Petrified Films, Inc.

Casals, Rosie
U.S. Tennis Assn.

**Cascade Canyon, Wyo. (History and
 culture)**
Rockefeller Arch. Ctr.

Cascade Range, Wash.
Petrified Films, Inc.

Casey, William J.
Churchill (Winston) Memorial and Library

Cash registers
Film Bank

Cash Valley, Utah (History and culture)
MacDonald, J. Fred

Casinos
Broad Street Prods.
CBS News Archives
Creative Video, Inc.
Film Bank
Film Search
Kesser Stock Footage Library
Las Vegas News Bureau
Network Productions
Peak Productions, Inc.
Petrified Films, Inc.
Rhode Island Hist. Soc.
TV Ontario
Video Tape Library, Ltd.
See also Gambling; Las Vegas

Casinos (Signs)
See Signs (Casino)

Casper, Billy
Sportsfilm

Cass County Boys
Pathé Pictures, Inc.

Cassatt, Mary
Amer. Federation of the Arts

Cassavetes, John
UCLA Film & Television Archive

Cassidy, Jack
Banks Film Library

Castelli, Leo
Albright-Knox Art Gallery
Blackwood Prods., Inc.

Castles
Archive Film Prods., Inc.
British Info. Svcs., Radio & TV Div.
CBS News Archives
Dorn (Larry) Associates
Film Bank
Film/Audio Services, Inc.
Petrified Films, Inc.
Twentieth Century-Fox Movietonews
Unicorn Projects
Video Tape Library, Ltd.

Castro, Fidel
Archive Film Prods., Inc.
Banks Film Library
Center for Cuban Studies
Center for Pacific Northwest Studies
Cinema Guild
Downtown Community TV Ctr.
Film/Audio Services, Inc.
Halcyon Days Prods.
Instituto Cubano de Radio y Television
New Time Films, Inc.
Petrified Films, Inc.

Catacombs
Film Bank

Catamarans
See Boats and boating (Catamarans)

Caterpillars
Dreamlight Images, Inc.

Cathedrals
Belmont Abbey College
CBS News Archives
Film Bank
Film/Audio Services, Inc.
Hayes Prods., Inc.

TV Ontario
Unicorn Projects
Video Tape Library, Ltd.

Catholic Workers Movement
Marquette Univ., Spec. Coll.

Catholicism
See Religion (Catholicism)

Cats
Amer. Veterinary Medical Assn.
Archive Film Prods., Inc.
Film Bank
Film Search
Gorilla Foundation
Mass. Inst. of Tech., MIT Museum
Media West, Inc.
Petrified Films, Inc.
TV Ontario
Twentieth Century-Fox Movietonews
Video Resources N.Y., Inc.

Catskill Mountains, N.Y.
New York State Dept. of Econ. Devel.
Villon Films

Catskill Mountains, N.Y. (History and culture)
Ergo Media
Film/Audio Services, Inc.
Natl. Archives (RG 131)
Villon Films
See also Borscht Belt

Cattails
Film Bank

Cattell, Raymond
Inst. for Psychoanalysis

Cattle
Allen (John E.) Inc.
Archive Film Prods., Inc.
Blue Sky Comms., Inc.
British Info. Svcs., Radio & TV Div.
Cornell Univ., Media Services
Dreamlight Images, Inc.
Energy Productions
Film Bank
Glenbow Mus. Arch.
Lib. of Congress, Amer. Folklife Ctr.
Natl. Archives of Canada
Natl. Cattlemen's Assn.
Oregon Hist. Soc.
Oregon State Univ., Archives
Panhandle-Plains Hist. Mus.
Petrified Films, Inc.
Source Stock Footage Lib., Inc.
Université Laval, Cinémathèque
Univ. of Wisconsin — Extension

Cattle branding
Lib. of Congress, Amer. Folklife Ctr.
Peak Productions, Inc.
TV Ontario

Cattle drives
Analogous Productions
Film Bank
Fish Films, Inc.
Lib. of Congress, Amer. Folklife Ctr.
Petrified Films, Inc.

Cavalry
Archive Film Prods., Inc.
Buffalo Bill Historical Center
Film Bank
Twentieth Century-Fox Movietonews
See also Westerns

Cavellini
Target Video

Cavemen
Archive Film Prods., Inc.
Petrified Films, Inc.

Caves
CBS News Archives
Canadian Broadcasting Corp.
Forsher (James) Prods. & Archives, Inc.
Jewell (Stuart) Productions
Source Stock Footage Lib., Inc.
Twentieth Century-Fox Movietonews

Cavett, Dick
Daphne Prods., Inc.
Film Bank

Cawley, Evonne Goolagong
U.S. Tennis Assn.

Cayce, Edgar
Hartley Film Found., Inc.

Cayman Islands
Passage Home Comms.

Cedar Breaks, Utah
Petrified Films, Inc.

Cedar Rapids, Iowa (History and culture)
State Hist. Soc. of Iowa

Cedar trees
New Jersey Network

Celebrations
Allen (John E.) Inc.
CBS News Archives
Eisenhower (Dwight D.) Library
Energy Productions
Film Bank
Fish Films, Inc.
Natl. Archives (RG 24)
Natl. Archives (RG 59)
Natl. Archives (RG 80)
Natl. Archives (RG 111)
Natl. Archives (RG 200)
Natl. Archives (RG 342)
Northcoast Communication, Inc.
Petrified Films, Inc.
Televisa, S.A.
Twentieth Century-Fox Movietonews
Univ. of Pa. Arch.
See also Birthdays; Christmas; Easter;
   Holidays; Weddings

Celebrities
Allen (John E.) Inc.
Analogous Productions
Archive Film Prods., Inc.
Banks Film Library
Boston Univ., Dept. of Spec. Coll.
Camera Three Prods., Inc.
Cantor (Arthur) Inc.
Chisholm (Jack) Film Prods., Ltd.
Daphne Productions, Inc.
DeFlores, Bob
Em Gee Film Library
Film/Audio Services, Inc.
Footage Inc.
Forsher (James) Prods. & Arch. Inc.
Halcyon Days Prods.
Imagen y Sonido Independiente, S.A.
Imageways, Inc.
Imevision
Instant Replay, Inc.
Las Vegas News Bureau
Los Angeles News Service

MTV Networks
Monday, Wednesday, Friday Video Club
Network Productions
Petrified Films, Inc.
Playboy Programs, Inc.
Shields Archival
Shokus Video
Spalla (Rick) Video Prods.
Spectral Comms.
Streamline Film Archives
Twentieth Century-Fox Movietonews
UCLA Film & Television Archive
Univ. of So. Carolina, Newsfilm Lib.
Univision Television Network
White Janssen, Inc.
Windsor Prod. Corp.
Worldwide Television News

Celebrities (Black)
Center for Southern Folklore

Cellars
CBS News Archives
Petrified Films, Inc.

Cellars (Wine)
Film Bank

Cells (Biology)
Amer. Cancer Soc., Inc.
Dreamlight Images, Inc.
Educational Images, Ltd.
Energy Productions
Film Bank
Prelinger Assoc., Inc.
Pyramid Film and Video Corp.
Rosebush Visions Corp.
Univ. of Wash. Press, Multimedia Div.

Cement
Natl. Archives (RG 70)
See also Concrete

Cemeteries and graves
Apertura
Archive Film Prods., Inc.
CBS News Archives
Farkas Studios, Ltd.
Film Bank
Jewell (Stuart) Productions
New Jersey Network
Petrified Films, Inc.
Source Stock Footage Lib., Inc.
Twentieth Century-Fox Movietonews
See also Funerals; Mausoleums;
   Memorials; Tombs

Cemeteries and graves (Exploding)
Dreamlight Images, Inc.

Cemeteries and graves (Military)
Natl. Archives (RG 59)

Censorship
Forsher (James) Prods. & Archives, Inc.
Mass Media Ministries
Natl. Archives (RG 334)
Playboy Programs, Inc.
See also Bookburning

Census
CBS News Archives
Natl. Archives (RG 29)

Census, Bureau of the (U.S.)
Natl. Archives (RG 29)

Centipedes
Wings Wildlife Prods. Inc.

NOTE: Access policies, availability and restrictions vary for each source. Please read each entry in full. Always consult "General Film and Videotape Collections" (page 599); these comprehensive collections contain material on every conceivable subject.

Central African Republic (History and culture)
Africa Inland Mission

Central America
Canadian Broadcasting Corp.
Pan American Airlines Film Lib.
World Monitor
See also Latin America

Central America (Contemporary issues)
Camino Film Projects
Committee for Labor Access
Comm. in Sol. People of El Salvador
DEC Film & Video
Deep Dish TV
Educational Film & Video Project
Film/Audio Services, Inc.
First Run/Icarus Films, Inc.
Icarus-Tamouz Media, Inc.
Oxfam America
Public Interest Video Network
Skylight Pictures

Central America (History and culture)
Allen (John E.) Inc.
Archive Film Prods., Inc.
Baker (Fred) Film & Video Co.
Canal 11
DEC Film & Video
Downtown Community TV Ctr.
El Salvador Media Project
Film/Audio Services, Inc.
Icarus-Tamouz Media, Inc.
Idera Films
Imagen y Sonido Independiente, S.A.
Natl. Archives (RG 185)
Northstar Prods.
Notimex
Petrified Films, Inc.
Prelinger Assoc., Inc.
Schiele Mus.
Skylight Pictures
Smithsonian Inst., Human Studies Film Arch.
Syracuse Alternative Media Network
World Monitor

Central City, Colo.
Summit Films, Inc.

Central Intelligence Agency (CIA) (U.S.)
Alternative Information Network
Carousel Film & Video
Center for Cuban Studies
Chicago Comm. to Defend the Bill of Rights
Labor Video Project
Natl. Archives (RG 263)
New Time Films, Inc.
Nuclear Free Zone Registry
Paper Tiger TV

Central Park (New York City)
Petrified Films, Inc.
TV Ontario

Centre D'Art et Culture Georges Pompidou (Paris)
Camera Three Prods., Inc.
Cantor (Arthur) Inc.
New Day Films

Ceramics (Production)
Petrified Films, Inc.

Cereals
Prelinger Assoc., Inc.

Ceremonies
Allen (John E.) Inc.
Amer. Bowling Cong. Film Lib.
Banks Film Library
CBS News Archives
Canadian Olympic Assn.

Carleton Productions Inc.
Cinema Guild
Connecticut State Library
DePauw University, Archives
German Info. Ctr., Film Lib.
Hayes Prods., Inc.
Illinois State Hist. Lib.
Instituto Nacional Indigenista
Kennedy (John F.) Library
Magnes (Judah L.) Museum
Medical College of Pa., Arch. & Spec. Coll. Women in Medicine
Multi-Media Pre-Accession Point
Native Amer. Pub. Broad. Cons.
Natl. Archives (RG 12)
Natl. Archives (RG 24)
Natl. Archives (RG 59)
Natl. Archives (RG 64)
Natl. Archives (RG 75)
Natl. Archives (RG 80)
Natl. Archives (RG 82)
Natl. Archives (RG 111)
Natl. Archives (RG 128)
Natl. Archives (RG 200)
Natl. Archives (RG 207)
Natl. Archives (RG 274)
Natl. Archives (RG 330)
Natl. Archives (RG 342)
New York City Dept. of Rec. & Info. Svcs.
Petrified Films, Inc.
Redes Cinevideo, S.A.
Samaya Foundation
Smith College, Arch.
Smithsonian Inst., Human Studies Film Arch.
Spalla (Rick) Video Prods.
TV Ontario
U.S. Hockey Hall of Fame
U.S. Natl. Park Service Hist. Coll.
Univ. Coll. of Cape Breton, Beaton Inst.
Univ. of Manitoba Lib., Arch. Spec. Coll.
Univ. of Rochester Lib., Rare Books & Spec. Coll.
Univ. of Wash., Educ. Media Coll.
Wheelwright Mus. of the American Indian
See also Dedications; Funerals; Graduations; Religion; Rituals; Ships (Launchings); Tea ceremonies; Weddings

Césaire, Aimé
Benamou, Catherine/LAWAS

César
Blackwood Prods., Inc.

Ceylon
See Sri Lanka

Ch'i Kung (Qigong)
Wayfarer Publications

Chacon, Bobby
Downtown Community TV Ctr.

Chadwick, Lynn
Albright-Knox Art Gallery

Chaikin, Joseph
Cantor (Arthur) Inc.

Chains
CBS News Archives

Chainsaws
Oregon State Univ., Archives
TV Ontario

Chairs
Film Bank

Challenger (Space shuttle)
See Space shuttle (Challenger accident)

Chamberlain, George E.
Natl. Archives (RG 4)

Chamberlain, John
Blackwood Prods., Inc.

Chamberlain, Neville
Halcyon Days Prods.

Chamberlain, Wilt
Sportsfilm

Chamberlin, Clarence
Natl. Archives (RG 178)

Chambers, Jack
Natl. Archives of Canada

Champagne
Film Bank

Champagne (Corks popping)
Energy Productions

Champlain, Lake (Canada-U.S.)
New York State Dept. of Econ. Devel.

Chance, James
Target Video

Chandigarh, India (History and culture)
Southern Calif. Inst. of Architecture

Chandler, Jeff
Banks Film Library

Chaney, Lon
Alan Twyman Presents

Chaney, Lon Jr.
UCLA Film & Television Archive

Chaney, William M.
Indiana State Lib.

Changing of the guard
See Guard (Changing of the)

Channel Islands, United Kingdom
Cousteau Society
Gornick Film Productions

Channeling
Wishing Well Distribution

Chanukah
Amer. Zionist Youth Found.

Chaplin, Charles
Archive Film Prods., Inc.
Em Gee Film Library
Film/Audio Services, Inc.
Forsher (James) Prods. & Arch. Inc.
Mus. of Mod. Art, Circulating Film Lib.
Natl. Archives (RG 200)
Petrified Films, Inc.
Streamline Film Archives
Videobrary, Inc.

Chapman, Oscar L.
Natl. Archives (RG 48)

Chariots and chariot races
Analogous Productions
Archive Film Prods., Inc.
Circus World Mus. Lib. & Res. Ctr.

Charismatic religion
See Religion (Charismatic)

Charisse, Cyd
Banks Film Library
Spectral Comms.

Charlemagne

German Info. Ctr., Film Lib.

Charles, Ezzard
Grinberg (Sherman) Film Libraries (West)

Charles, Prince
Halcyon Days Prods.

Charleston (Dance)
See Dance and dancing (Charleston)

Charleston, S.C.
Creative Video, Inc.
Preview Media

Charleston, S.C. (History and culture)
First Run/Icarus Films, Inc.
Schiele Mus.

Charleston, W. Va. (History and culture)
West Virginia Dept. of Culture & Hist.
West Virginia State Lib. Comm.

Charlevoix County, Quebec (History and culture)
Natl. Archives of Canada

Charlottetown, Prince Edward Island
TV Ontario

Charney, Melvin
Mus. of Contemporary Art

Chartres, France
TV Ontario
Unicorn Projects

Charts
CBS News Archives
Rosebush Visions Corp.

Chase, Charley
Film Preservation Assoc.

Chase, Chevy
Spectral Comms.

Chase, Doris
Port Washington Pub. Lib.

Chase, Louisa
Video Data Bank

Chase scenes
Archive Film Prods., Inc.
Film Bank
Fish Films, Inc.
Halicki (H.B.) Productions
Petrified Films, Inc.

Chateaus
Petrified Films, Inc.

Chatham, Rhys
Monday, Wednesday, Friday Video Club

Chautauqua, N.Y.
New York State Dept. of Econ. Devel.

Chávez, Cesar
San Francisco Bay Area TV News Arch.
United Farm Workers of America (UFW)
Univ. of Tex. at Austin, Benson Lat. Am. Coll.

Cheating (Students)
Prelinger Assoc., Inc.

Checker, Chubby
Banks Film Library

Checkers
Film Bank
TV Ontario

Twentieth Century-Fox Movietonews

Cheerleaders
Archive Film Prods., Inc.
Athletic Institute
CBS News Archives
Film Bank
MacDonald, J. Fred
Nemiroff Prods., Inc.
Petrified Films, Inc.
Prelinger Assoc., Inc.
Timesteps Prods., Inc.

Cheese and cheesemaking
Oregon State Univ., Archives
Petrified Films, Inc.
Prelinger Assoc., Inc.
TV Ontario
Univ. of Wisconsin — Extension

Cheetahs
Di Sesso (Moe) Wild Life Film Lib.
Dreamlight Images, Inc.
Film Bank

Chefs
Petrified Films, Inc.

Chemical and biological warfare
MacDonald, J. Fred
Natl. Archives (RG 171)
Natl. Archives (RG 227)
Natl. Archives (RG 263)
Prelinger Assoc., Inc.
See also Agent Orange; Gas masks

Chemical fertilizer (Production)
Petrified Films, Inc.

Chemical industry
First Group Comms., Inc.
Prelinger Assoc., Inc.
Shell Oil Co.
Video Genesis, Inc.

Chemistry
Amer. Chemical Soc.
CBS News Archives
Center for Humanities, Inc.
Coronet/MTI Film & Video
Educational Images, Ltd.
Film Bank
Films for the Humanities and Sciences
Intl. Film Bureau, Inc.
Los Alamos Natl. Lab.
Media Guild
Natl. Archives/Natl. AV Ctr.
Prelinger Assoc., Inc.
Richter Productions
Screen Presentations, Inc.
Univ. of Calif., Ext. Media Ctr.

Cher
Banks Film Library
Daphne Productions, Inc.

Chernobyl, U.S.S.R. (Contemporary issues)
Devillier Donegan Ent.
Electric Power Research Inst.
Ocean Earth Constr. and Dev. Corp.

Cherries
VTR Productions

Cherry blossoms
Film Bank
Harriman Communications Ctr.

Chesapeake Bay, Md.-Va.
KD Enterprises Prods.

Preview Media

Chesapeake Bay, Md.-Va. (History and culture)
Mariners' Museum
Northstar Prods.

Chesse, Ralph
De Saisset Museum

Chesterton, G.K.
Wheaton Coll., Wade Ctr.

Chevalier, Maurice
Banks Film Library
UCLA Film & Television Archive

Chevrotain
Minnesota Zoo

Chewing gum
Jewell (Stuart) Productions

Chia, Sandro
Blackwood Prods., Inc.

Chiang Kai-Shek
Archive Film Prods., Inc.
Friends of Free China
Natl. Archives (RG 342)

Chiang Kai-Shek (Madame)
Natl. Archives (RG 59)

Chicago
Chicago A/V Studios
Chicago Video Transfer
Cine-Mark
Departures, Inc.
Dreamlight Images, Inc.
Energy Productions
File Tape Co.
Film Bank
Kesser Stock Footage Library
Preview Media
Renaissance Video Corp.
Stegman Productions
Stock House
Unicorn Projects
Video I-D, Inc.

Chicago (History and culture)
Allen (John E.) Inc.
Archive Film Prods., Inc.
Chicago Historical Society
Cinema Medica
Committee for Labor Access
Evangelical Covenant Church of Amer.
Flower Films & Video
Grinberg (Sherman) Film Libraries (East)
Illinois State Hist. Lib.
Intl. Historic Films, Inc.
Kartemquin Films
MacDonald, J. Fred
Mus. of Broadcast Comms.
Mus. of Contemporary Art
Natl. Archives (RG 12)
Natl. Archives (RG 46)
Natl. Archives (RG 267)
Natl. Archives/Natl. AV Ctr.
Natl. Railway Historical Soc.
Payne, Roz
Petrified Films, Inc.
Prelinger Assoc., Inc.
Quest Prods., Inc.
Southern Calif. Lib. for Soc. Stud. & Res.
Univ. of Ill. Urbana-Champaign, Univ. Arch.

Chicago 8 trial (1969)
Media Bus

Chicago, Judy
Amer. Federation of the Arts
Intermedia Arts Minnesota
Video Data Bank

Chicago Memorial Day massacre (1937)
Grinberg (Sherman) Film Libraries (East)
Southern Calif. Lib. for Soc. Stud. & Res.

Chichen Itza, Mexico
Summit Films, Inc.

Chickens
Analogous Productions
Flower Films & Video
Latham Foundation
Media Project
Petrified Films, Inc.
Prelinger Assoc., Inc.
TV Ontario
See also Poultry industry

Chieftains, The (Musical group)
Camera Three Prods., Inc.

Child abuse
Altschul Group
Cambridge Documentary Films, Inc.
Cinema Guild
Coronet/MTI Film & Video
Council for Exceptional Children
FMS Productions
Filmfair Communications
Intl. Lutheran Layman's League
Lawren Prods., Inc.
Mass Media Ministries
Natl. Coun. of Juv. & Fam. Court Judges
Natl. Ctr. Missing & Exploited Children
O.D.N. Productions, Inc.
Psychological and Educational Films

Child care
Natl. Archives (RG 33)
See also Babysitting; Day care

Child development and psychology
Altschul Group
Campus Film Distributors Corp.
Carousel Film & Video
Coronet/MTI Film & Video
Lawren Prods., Inc.
March of Time
New York Pub. Lib., Early Childhood Res. & Info. Ctr.
Univ. of Akron, Child Develop. Film Arch.
Univ. of Kansas
See also Pediatrics

Child, Julia
Radcliffe Coll., Schlesinger Lib.
WGBH Educational Foundation

Child labor
March of Time

Child molestation
Highway Safety Films, Inc.
KYUK-TV
See also Child abuse

Child psychology
See Child development and psychology

Childbirth
Churchill Films
Cinema Medica
Coronet/MTI Film & Video
Courter Films & Assoc.
Education Development Ctr., Inc.
Film Bank

Films for the Humanities and Sciences
Focus Intl. Inc.
Historical Health Film Coll.
Inst. for Psychoanalysis
Kartemquin Films
La Leche League of New Mexico
Multi-Focus, Inc.
Natl. Archives (RG 12)
Natl. Archives of Canada
Natl. Library of Medicine
Petrified Films, Inc.
Phoenix Films and Video
Polymorph Films, Inc.
Prelinger Assoc., Inc.
Video Farm
Vidéo Femmes

Childbirth (Caesarian)
Courter Films & Assoc.
Prelinger Assoc., Inc.

Childbirth (Emergency)
Media Guild

Childbirth (Premature)
New York Hosp.-Cornell Med. Ctr., Arch.

Children
ABC Distribution (Education)
Alaska Video Prods.
Amer. Assn. for Counseling & Development
Archive Film Prods., Inc.
CBS News Archives
Canyon Cinema, Inc.
Coronet/MTI Film & Video
Dreamlight Images, Inc.
Education Development Ctr., Inc.
Educational Productions
Fanlight Prods.
Film Bank
Film Search
Fish Films, Inc.
Grinberg (Sherman) Film Libraries (West)
Harvard Univ., Schl. of Educ., ACT Lib.
Hayes Prods., Inc.
Hearst Metrotone News
High/Scope Educ. Res. Found.
Inst. for Psychoanalysis
Intermedia Arts Minnesota
March of Time
Mass Media Ministries
Natl. Archives (RG 69)
Natl. Archives (RG 102)
Natl. Archives of Canada
Natl. Assn. of Secondary Schl. Principals
Petrified Films, Inc.
Prelinger Assoc., Inc.
Producers Library Service
Simon & Goodman Picture Co.
Spectral Comms.
Stegman Productions
TV Ontario
Timesteps Prods., Inc.
Twentieth Century-Fox Movietonews
U.S. Committee for UNICEF
UNICEF, Div. Info. & Pub. Aff.
Univ. of West Fla., Hum. Res. Vid. Lib.
Univ. of Wis., Green Bay, Ctr. TV Prod.
V/tape
Video In
Vidéographe Inc., Le
Washington Univ., Brown Schl. of Soc. Work

Children (Appalachian)
Campus Film Distributors Corp.

Children (Asia)
Pyramid Film and Video Corp.

NOTE: Access policies, availability and restrictions vary for each source. Please read each entry in full. Always consult "General Film and Videotape Collections" (page 599); these comprehensive collections contain material on every conceivable subject.

Children (Black)
Campus Film Distributors Corp.
Univ. of Vermont, Bailey/Howe Lib.

Children (Bush)
Petrified Films, Inc.

Children (International)
Films for the Humanities and Sciences

Children (Japan)
Asia Society
Farkas Studios, Ltd.

Children (Latchkey)
Filmfair Comms.

Children (Mexican American)
Campus Film Distributors Corp.

Children (Middle East)
Pyramid Film and Video Corp.

Children (Missing)
Natl. Ctr. Missing & Exploited Children

Children (Native American)
Campus Film Distributors Corp.

Children (Soviet Union)
Educational Film & Video Project
Estuary Press

Children's Bureau (U.S.)
Natl. Archives (RG 102)

Children's films and videotapes
Bullfrog Films, Inc.
Carousel Film & Video
Churchill Films
Facets Multimedia, Inc.
Goethe Institute Atlanta
Instituto Cubano de Radio y Television
Ivy Film
MacDonald, J. Fred
Mass Media Ministries
Media Guild
Moody Inst. of Science
Natl. Archives of Canada
Palisades Wildlife Film Lib.
Phoenix Films and Video
Tamarelle's Intl. Films, Ltd.
Video-SIG
WTJX-TV
West Star Prods.
Weston Woods
See also Television (Children's programming)

Children's television programming
See Television (Children's programming)

Childs, Lucinda
Blackwood Prods., Inc.

Chile
Canadian Broadcasting Corp.
Cousteau Society
Imagen y Sonido Independiente, S.A.
Preview Media
Sobek Prods.
World Monitor

Chile (Contemporary issues)
DEC Film & Video
Film/Audio Services, Inc.
Icarus-Tamouz Media, Inc.

Chile (History and culture)
Allen (John E.) Inc.
Archive Film Prods., Inc.
Cinema Guild
DEC Film & Video
Democracy in Communication
Film/Audio Services, Inc.

Icarus Films Intl., Inc.
Icarus-Tamouz Media, Inc.
Idera Films
New Time Films, Inc.
Rockefeller Arch. Ctr.
Sobek Productions
World Monitor
Worldwide Television News

Chiloquin, Edison
Native Amer. Pub. Broad. Cons.

Chime making
Baylor Univ., Texas Coll.

Chimneys
CBS News Archives

Chimpanzees
Analogous Productions
Petrified Films, Inc.
Prelinger Assoc., Inc.
Wings Wildlife Prods. Inc.

China, People's Republic of
Canadian Broadcasting Corp.
Energy Productions
Farkas Studios, Ltd.
Film Bank
Friends of Free China
Hammer (Armand) Prods.
Prelinger Assoc., Inc.
Preview Media
Sobek Productions
Sonoma Video Productions
Source Stock Footage Lib., Inc.
Sullivan Video Services
Yue-Sai Kan, Inc.

China, People's Republic of (Contemporary issues)
Film/Audio Services, Inc.

China, People's Republic of (History and culture)
Allen (John E.) Inc.
Amer. Mus. Nat. Hist. Film Arch.
Analogous Productions
Archive Film Prods., Inc.
CTV Television Network
Cambridge Documentary Films, Inc.
Canadian Broadcasting Corp.
Carousel Film & Video
DEC Film & Video
Devillier Donegan Ent.
Documentary Educational Resources
East-West Center
Film/Audio Services, Inc.
Friends of Free China
Hammer (Armand) Prods.
Hansen, Jack
Hearst Metrotone News
Hoover Institution
Intl. Film Foundation
March of Time
Maryknoll Fathers & Brothers
Media Project
Nan Hai (U.S.A.) Co., Inc.
Natl. Archives (RG 18)
Natl. Archives (RG 170)
Natl. Archives (RG 200)
Natl. Archives (RG 226)
Natl. Archives (RG 242)
Natl. Archives/Natl. AV Ctr.
Natl. Ctr. for Jewish Film
New Day Films
Northern Ill. Univ., Reg. Hist. Ctr.
Oakland Public Lib., Asian Branch Lib.
Payne, Roz
Perlmutter (Alvin H.) Inc.
Rainbow Video Prods.
Southern Calif. Lib. for Soc. Stud. & Res.
Twentieth Century-Fox Movietonews
United Nations, Visual Materials Lib.
Univ. of Calif., Ext. Media Ctr.

Univ. of Mich., Mich. Hist. Colls.
Univ. of Tex. at Austin, Ransom Hum.
  Res. Ctr., Photo. Coll.
Villon Films
Visnews Intl.
Worldwide Television News

China-Japan War
Natl. Archives (RG 200)

China Sea
Petrified Films, Inc.

Chinatowns
Downtown Community TV Ctr.
Elfstrom-Hilmer Prods.
Film Bank
Media Project
Petrified Films, Inc.
Prelinger Assoc., Inc.
Spectral Comms.
TV Ontario

Chinatowns (History and culture)
Asian American Resource Workshop
Natl. Asian American Telecomm. Assn.
New York Chinatown History Project

Chinese Americans
Nan Hai (U.S.A.) Co., Inc.
Natl. Asian American Telecomm. Assn.
See also Asian Americans; Chinatowns

Chinese Americans (History and culture)
Asian American Resource Workshop
New York Chinatown History Project
Third World Newsreel
Canadian Filmmakers Dist. Centre

Chinese calligraphy
Apertura

Chinese New Year's
See New Year's (Chinese)

Chipmunks
Energy Productions
Film Bank
Petrified Films, Inc.

Chisholm, Shirley
Daphne Productions, Inc.

Chitwood, Joie
Prelinger Assoc., Inc.
Sportsfilm

Chlamydia
See Sexually transmitted diseases (STDs)

Chocolate
Hershey Foods Corp.

Choirs
See Music (Choral)

Cholesterol
Natl. Dairy Council
Rogers (Will) Institute

Chomsky, Noam
Cambridge Documentary Films, Inc.
Paper Tiger TV

Chong, Rae Dawn
Daphne Productions, Inc.

Chorus girls and chorus lines
Analogous Productions
Archive Film Prods., Inc.
Fish Films, Inc.
Twentieth Century-Fox Movietonews
See also Radio City Music Hall

Chou En-lai
See Zhou En-lai

Choy, Christine
Video Data Bank

Christ of the Andes
Petrified Films, Inc.

Christenings
CBS News Archives
Spalla (Rick) Video Prods.

Christian, Bill
U.S. Hockey Hall of Fame

Christianity
See Religion (Christianity)

Christie, Al
Moviecraft, Inc.

Christmas
Archive Film Prods., Inc.
Banks Film Library
Budget Films Inc.
Coe Film Assoc., Inc.
Dreamlight Images, Inc.
Energy Productions
Film Bank
Fish Films, Inc.
Hayes Prods., Inc.
Milwaukee Access Telecomm. Auth.
Natl. Archives (RG 59)
New Jersey Network
Northcoast Communication, Inc.
Northeast Historic Film
Petrified Films, Inc.
Prelinger Assoc., Inc.
Simon & Goodman Picture Co.
TV Ontario
Twentieth Century-Fox Movietonews
Univ. of Ill. Urbana-Champaign, Univ. Arch.
Video West

Christmas trees
Charisma Prods., Ltd./Visual Motion
Oregon State Univ., Archives
Petrified Films, Inc.
TV Ontario

Christo
Blackwood (Christian) Prods., Inc.
Blackwood Prods., Inc.
Creative Film Society
Video Data Bank

Christy, June
Pathé Pictures, Inc.

Chuck wagons
Texas Tech Univ., Southwest Coll.

Church of Christ
See Religion (Church of Christ)

Churches
CBS News Archives
Dreamlight Images, Inc.
Farkas Studios, Ltd.
Film Bank
Jewell (Stuart) Productions
Lib. of Congress, Amer. Folklife Ctr.
Mass Media Ministries
Natl. Archives of Canada
Petrified Films, Inc.
Prelinger Assoc., Inc.
Stegman Productions
TV Ontario
Timesteps Prods., Inc.
Video Tape Library, Ltd.
See also Altars; Religion; Religious films and videotapes; Television (Religious)

Churchill, Winston Spencer
Archive Film Prods., Inc.
Churchill (Winston) Memorial and Library
Film Bank
Film Education Institute
Halcyon Days Prods.
Mass. Inst. of Tech., MIT Museum
Natl. Archives (RG 80)
Natl. Archives (RG 200)
Natl. Archives (RG 342)
Roosevelt (Franklin D.) Lib.
UCLA Film & Television Archive
Univ. of Ill. Urbana-Champaign, Univ. Arch.

Ciepinski, Waldemar
U.S. Olympic Committee

Cigarettes
Cinema Guild
Film Bank
Jessiefilm
MacDonald, J. Fred
North Carolina Div. of Arch. & Hist.
Prelinger Assoc., Inc.
Reynolds (R. J.) Tobacco USA
Streamline Film Archives
White Janssen, Inc.
See also Smokers and smoking; Tobacco; Tobacco industry

Cigarettes (Advertising)
Center for Southern Folklore
Narcotics Education, Inc.
See also Advertising; Cigarettes (Television commercials); Television commercials

Cigarettes (Anti/pro-smoking)
Amer. Cancer Soc., Inc.
Amer. Heart Assn.
Narcotics Education, Inc.
Political Issue Archive
Varied Directions, Inc.

Cigarettes (Television commercials)
Brooklyn Coll., Diamant Mem. Lib.
Prelinger Assoc., Inc.
Video Resources N.Y., Inc.
White Janssen, Inc.
See also Advertising; Cigarettes (Advertising); Television commercials

Cigars
Film Bank
Fish Films, Inc.
See also Smokers and smoking; Tobacco; Tobacco industry

Cimarron County, Okla. (History and culture)
Natl. Press Photographers Assn., Inc.

Cinchona trees
Natl. Archives (RG 234)

Cincinnati
Creative Video, Inc.
Energy Productions

Cincinnati (History and culture)
Cincinnati Hist. Soc.
Petrified Films, Inc.
Prelinger Assoc., Inc.
Pub. Lib. of Cincinnati & Hamilton Cty.

Circumcision
Courter Films & Assoc.
Non-Circumcision Educ. Found.

Circumcision (Female)

UNICEF, Div. Info. & Pub. Aff.

Circuses
Allen (John E.) Inc.
Analogous Productions
Appalshop Films, Inc.
Archive Film Prods., Inc.
CBS News Archives
Circus World Mus. Lib. & Res. Ctr.
Film Bank
Fulton County Hist. Soc., Inc.
Petrified Films, Inc.
Prelinger Assoc., Inc.
SF•V Intl.
TV Ontario
Twentieth Century-Fox Movietonews
See also Acrobats; Animals; Clowns

Citadel, The (Charleston, S.C.)
Citadel, The
Film Bank

Cities
Chisholm (Jack) Film Productions
Cinenet (Cinema Network)
Energy Productions
File Tape Co.
Film Bank
Fish Films, Inc.
Halicki (H.B.) Productions
Kesser Stock Footage Library
Northstar Prods.
Phoenix Films and Video
Second Line Search
Spectral Comms.
TV Ontario
Twentieth Century-Fox Movietonews
Video Tape Library, Ltd.
White Janssen, Inc.
See also Cityscapes; Skylines; Towns; specific cities

Cities (Africa)
Film Bank

Cities (Asia)
Petrified Films, Inc.

Cities (Canada)
Fabulous Footage Inc.
Independent Media Communications
Natl. Archives of Canada

Cities (Eastern Europe)
Intl. Historic Films, Inc.

Cities (Europe)
Applegate Entertainment

Cities (International)
Airline Film & TV Promotions
Chisholm (Jack) Film Productions
Dorn (Larry) Associates
Dreamlight Images, Inc.
Fabulous Footage Inc.
Film Bank
Film Search
Forsher (James) Prods. & Archives, Inc.
Producers Library Service
Shields Archival
Summit Films, Inc.
Worldwide Television News
Zielinski Productions, Inc.

Cities (Miniature)
Grinberg (Sherman) Film Libraries (West)

Cities (North America)
Cameo Film Library, Inc.
Simon (Jeff) Productions

Cities (U.S.)
Airline Film & TV Promotions
Amer. Motion Pictures
Boston Stock Market
Broad Street Prods.
Cabscott Broadcast Prods.
Cinema Arts Assoc.
Creative Video, Inc.
Departures, Inc.
Dreamlight Images, Inc.
Energy Productions
Film Bank
Film Search
Forsher (James) Prods. & Archives, Inc.
Landmark Stock Footage Co.
Lemorande Prod. Co.
MacGillivray Freeman Films
Natl. Archives (RG 200)
Nine Star Productions
Odyssey Prods., Inc.
Postcards Unlimited
Prelinger Assoc., Inc.
Producers Library Service
Rock Solid Prods.
Shields Archival
Stegman Productions
Stock House
United Airlines, Creative Services
Wallen (Dick) Prods.
Windsor Prod. Corp.
Zielinski Productions, Inc.

Citizen action
Bullfrog Films, Inc.
Ideal Comms., Inc.

Citizens' Councils
Citizens' Councils of America
Mississippi Dept. of Arch. & Hist.

Citizenship
Barr Films
Britannica Films & Video
CBS News Archives
Natl. Archives (RG 200)
Prelinger Assoc., Inc.
See also Civics

City halls
DeSaisset Museum
Film Bank
Landmark Stock Footage Co.
Petrified Films, Inc.
Prelinger Assoc., Inc.
Schiele Museum
Twentieth Century-Fox Movietonews
See also Buildings (Government)

City lights
Film Bank

City planning
See Urban planning

Cityscapes
Aries Prods.
Energy Productions
Film Bank
Film Search
Hayes Prods., Inc.
Lemorande Prod. Co.
Simon & Goodman Picture Co.
Site Productions
Slingshot Prods.
Telemation Productions
See also Cities; Skylines

Civics
Barr Films
Handel Film Corp.
MacDonald, J. Fred

Natl. Archives (RG 200)
Natl. Archives/Natl. AV Ctr.
Prelinger Assoc., Inc.
See also Citizenship

Civil defense
CBS News Archives
Delaware State Div. of Hist. & Cultural Aff.
Eastern Washington State Historical Soc.
Halcyon Days Prods.
MacDonald, J. Fred
Minn. Dept. of Public Safety Film Lib.
Natl. Archives (RG 171)
Natl. Archives (RG 304)
Natl. Archives (RG 306)
Natl. Archives (RG 311)
Natl. Archives (RG 397)
Natl. Archives of Canada
New Haven Colony Hist. Soc.
New Mexico State Records Ctr. & Arch.
North Carolina Div. of Arch. & Hist.
Northeast Historic Film
Ohio Historical Soc.
Petrified Films, Inc.
Prelinger Assoc., Inc.
Streamline Film Archives

Civil Defense and Mobilization, Office of (U.S.)
Natl. Archives (RG 304)

Civil Defense, Office of (U.S.)
Natl. Archives (RG 397)

Civil disobedience
Green Mountain Post Films
Natl. Archives (RG 200)
Petrified Films, Inc.
See also Demonstrations (Political)

Civil disorders
See Riots

Civil engineering
Assoc. Gen. Contractors of America
Louisiana Tech Univ., Eng. Film Res. Ctr.
Mass. Inst. of Tech., MIT Museum
Port Authority of New York & New Jersey
Smithsonian Inst., NMAH, Div. Eng. & Ind.
Univ. of Minn. Libs., Manuscripts Div.
Univ. of Wash., Educ. Media Coll.
See also Engineering

Civil liberties
Alternative Information Network
Intermedia Arts Minnesota
Natl. Archives/Natl. AV Ctr.
People for the American Way
Richter Productions

Civil rights
ABC News
Asian American Resource Workshop
Cambridge Documentary Films, Inc.
Coal Employment Project
Intermedia Arts Minnesota
Lambda Legal Defense & Education Fund
March of Time
Natl. Archives (RG 174)
Natl. Archives (RG 200)
Natl. Archives of Canada
New Jersey Network
Third World Newsreel
Univ. of Ill. Urbana-Champaign, Univ. Arch.
See also Black history and culture; Gay and lesbian issues

NOTE: Access policies, availability and restrictions vary for each source. Please read each entry in full. Always consult "General Film and Videotape Collections" (page 599); these comprehensive collections contain material on every conceivable subject.

Civil rights movement
Alabama State Dept. of Arch. & Hist.
Birmingham Pub. Lib., Media Svcs. Dept.
CBS News Archives
Estuary Press
Forsher (James) Prods. & Archives, Inc.
Hoover Institution
Kartemquin Films
King (Dr. Martin Luther, Jr.) Ctr.
MacDonald, J. Fred
McDonald's Corp.
Memphis State Univ. Libraries
Miles Educ. Film Prods.
Mississippi Dept. of Arch. & Hist.
Natl. Archives (RG 64)
Natl. Assn. for the Advancement of
     Colored People
New Time Films, Inc.
Payne, Roz
Petrified Films, Inc.
Randolph (A. Philip) Educ. Fund
Southern Calif. Lib. for Soc. Stud. & Res.
Southern Christian Leadership Conference
Southwest Film/Video Archives, SMU
State Hist. Soc. of Wisconsin
Taminent Lib./Wagner Labor Arch.
Tulane Univ., Amistad Res. Ctr.
Twentieth Century-Fox Movietonews
UCLA Film & Television Archive
Univ. of Georgia, WSB TV News Film
     Arch.
Univ. of Mich., Mich. Hist. Colls.
Univ. of Tex. at Austin, Barker Tex. Hist.
     Ctr.
Worldwide Television News

Civil service (U.S.)
Archive Film Prods., Inc.

Civil Service Commission (U.S.)
Natl. Archives (RG 146)

Civil War (U.S.)
Agee (James) Film Project
Amer. Soc. Hist. Proj. Film Lib.
Atlanta Hist. Soc.
Film Bank
Fish Films, Inc.
Louisiana State Univ. Libs., Spec. Coll.
North Carolina Div. of Arch. & Hist.
Petrified Films, Inc.
Prelinger Assoc., Inc.
Producers Library Service
South Carolina Humanities Res. Ctr.
U.S. Army Military Hist. Inst.

Civil War (U.S.) (Naval activities)
Mariners' Mus.

Civilian Conservation Corps (CCC)
March of Time
Natl. Archives (RG 35)
Natl. Archives (RG 48)
Natl. Archives (RG 69)
Natl. Assn. of CCC Alumni
Petrified Films, Inc.
U.S. Natl. Park Service Hist. Coll.

Civilian Defense, Office of (U.S.)
Natl. Archives (RG 171)

Clair, René
Parker (Kit) Films

Clams
Jewell (Stuart) Productions
Oregon State Univ., Archives

Clapping
See Applause

Clark and McCullough
Windsor Prod. Corp.

Clark, Champ

Clark, Dick
Daphne Productions, Inc.
Spectral Comms.

Clark, Joe
Northstar Prods.

Clark, Mark W.
Citadel, The

Clark, Ramsey
Alternative Information Network

Clash, The (Rock and roll band)
Target Video

Classrooms
CBS News Archives
Cornell Univ., Media Services
Film Bank
Northcoast Communication, Inc.
Prelinger Assoc., Inc.
TV Ontario
Villon Films
See also Colleges and universities;
     Schools; Teachers and teaching

Claudel, Paul
Soc. for French Amer. Cult. Svcs. & Educ.
     Aid

Claws
Film Bank

Clay
Natl. Archives (RG 70)
TV Ontario

Clay, Lucius D.
Duke Univ., Perkins Lib.

Claymation
Film Bank
Media Project
Pyramid Film and Video Corp.

Clayton, Buck
Rhapsody Films, Inc.

Clayton, Jan
MacDonald, J. Fred

Clayton-Thomas, David
Natl. Archives of Canada

Clearwater, Fla. (History and culture)
Swain (Hack) Prods., Inc.

Cleary, Bill
U.S. Hockey Hall of Fame

Cleaver, Eldridge
Pennebaker Associates, Inc.

Cleese, John
Daphne Productions, Inc.
Video Arts Inc.

Clemente, Francesco
Blackwood Prods., Inc.

Clements, Charlie
Alternative Information Network
Film/Audio Services, Inc.
First Run/Icarus Films, Inc.
Northstar Prods.
Skylight Pictures

Cleopatra
Archive Film Prods., Inc.

Clergy
CBS News Archives

Natl. Archives (RG 4)

Petrified Films, Inc.

Cleveland
Hi-Tech Productions
Video Genesis, Inc.

Cleveland (History and culture)
Petrified Films, Inc.
Prelinger Assoc., Inc.
Western Reserve Hist. Soc.

Cliburn, Van
Banks Film Library

Cliff divers
See Diving (Cliff)

Cliff dwellings
Film Bank

Cliffs
British Info. Svcs., Radio & TV Div.
CBS News Archives
Film Bank
TV Ontario
Video Tape Library, Ltd.
Wings Wildlife Prods., Inc.

Cline, Paul
Southern Calif. Lib. for Soc. Stud. & Res.

Clinics
Historical Health Film Coll.

Clinton, Ontario (History and culture)
Canadian Filmmakers Dist. Centre

Clipper planes
See Aircraft (Clipper)

Clocks and watches
CBS News Archives
Dreamlight Images, Inc.
Energy Productions
Film Bank
Filmack Studios
Fish Films, Inc.
Natl. Archives (RG 70)
Petrified Films, Inc.
Prelinger Assoc., Inc.

Clocks and watches (Exploding)
Cinema Arts Assoc.

Close, Chuck
Blackwood Prods., Inc.
Mus. of Contemporary Art
Video Data Bank

Clothing
CBS News Archives
Intl. Fashion Video Library
Petrified Films, Inc.
Prelinger Assoc., Inc.
See also Costumes (Historical); Fashions
     and fashion industry

Clothing stores
TV Ontario

Clouds
Beerger (Norman) Prods.
CBS News Archives
Cinenet (Cinema Network)
Dreamlight Images, Inc.
Echo Film Prods., Inc.
Energy Productions
Film Bank
Film Search
Fish Films, Inc.
Grinberg (Sherman) Film Libraries (West)
Image Bank
Jewell (Stuart) Productions
MacGillivray Freeman Films
Moody Inst. of Science

Moving Media
Petrified Films, Inc.
Rosebush Visions Corp.
Slingshot Prods.
Source Stock Footage Lib., Inc.
Spectral Comms.
Summit Films, Inc.
Twentieth Century-Fox Movietonews
See also Skies

Clough, Charles
Albright-Knox Art Gallery

Clover, Elzada Urseba
Univ. of Mich., Mich. Hist. Colls.

Clowler, Jerry
Film Bank

Clowns
CBS News Archives
Cinenet (Cinema Network)
Circus World Mus. Lib. & Res. Ctr.
Film Bank
Fish Films, Inc.
Palisades Wildlife Film Library
Petrified Films, Inc.
TV Ontario
Univ. of Southern Calif., Film & Video
     Dist. Ctr.
See also Circuses

Clyde, Andy
Videobrary, Inc.

Coachella Valley, Calif.
Nature Conservancy

Coaches and coaching
Archive Film Prods., Inc.
Athletic Institute
Charisma Prods., Ltd./Visual Motion
Dreamlight Images, Inc.
Fellowship of Christian Athletes
Film Bank
Oregon State Univ., Archives

Coal and coal industry
Archive Film Prods., Inc.
CBS News Archives
Electric Power Research Institute
Film Bank
Glenbow Mus. Arch.
March of Time
Richter Productions
Timesteps Prods., Inc.
West Virginia Dept. of Culture & Hist.
West Virginia Univ.
See also Energy; Mines, Bureau of (U.S.);
     Mining (Coal); Workers (Coal)

Coast Guard (Canada)
Natl. Archives of Canada

Coast Guard (U.S.)
CBS News Archives
March of Time
Natl. Archives (RG 18)
Natl. Archives (RG 26)
Natl. Archives (RG 178)
Natl. Archives (Stock Film Coll.)
Twentieth Century-Fox Movietonews

**Coast Guard (U.S.) (Rest and
     recreation)**
Natl. Archives (RG 26)

Coast Guard Academy (U.S.)
Natl. Archives (RG 26)

Coastlines
Beerger (Norman) Prods.
British Info. Svcs., Radio & TV Div.
CBS News Archives
Cineworks Prods. Inc.

Creative Video, Inc.
Dobbs (Jeff) Prods.
Dreamlight Images, Inc.
Echo Film Prods., Inc.
Energy Productions
Film Bank
Hot Shots Commercial Prods., Inc.
Impact Audio Visual
Jewell (Stuart) Productions
MVP Communications
MacGillivray Freeman Films
Marts (Steve) Productions
Nei-Ali Prods.
Odyssey Prods., Inc.
Petrified Films, Inc.
Spectral Comms.
TV Ontario
Telltales Associates Inc.
Tri-Comm Prods.

Coate, Roland
Southern Calif. Inst. of Architecture

Coatimundi
Wings Wildlife Prods. Inc.

Cobalt, Ontario (History and culture)
Archives of Ontario

Cobb, Ty
Grinberg (Sherman) Film Libraries (West)

Cobras
Petrified Films, Inc.
Wings Wildlife Prods. Inc.

Coburn, James
Spectral Comms.

Coca, Imogene
Banks Film Library

Coca-Cola
Archive Film Prods., Inc.
Coca-Cola Co., Archives Dept.
Farkas Studios, Ltd.
Prelinger Assoc., Inc.

Cocaine
Addiction Research Foundation of Ontario
Fish Films, Inc.
Hazelden Found. Educ. Materials
Narcotics Education, Inc.
New Jersey Network
Pyramid Film and Video Corp.
Signal Press
United Training Media
See also Crack (Cocaine); Drug abuse

Cochise County, Ariz.
Preview Media

Cockatoos
TV Ontario
Wings Wildlife Prods. Inc.

Cockcroft, Eva
Paper Tiger TV
Video Data Bank

Cocker, Joe
Clark (Dick) Media Archives, Inc.

Cockfighting
Appalachian State Univ., Eury Coll.
Appalshop Films, Inc.

Cockroaches
Prelinger Assoc., Inc.
TV Ontario

Cocktail lounges
Petrified Films, Inc.

Coconuts
Cinenet (Cinema Network)
Film Search
Petrified Films, Inc.

Cocoons
Dreamlight Images, Inc.

Cody, "Iron Eyes"
Spectral Comms.

Cody, William F. ("Buffalo Bill")
Archive Film Prods., Inc.
Buffalo Bill Historical Center
Grinberg (Sherman) Film Libraries (West)
Natl. Archives/Natl. AV Ctr.
Petrified Films, Inc.

Cody, Wyo. (History and culture)
Buffalo Bill Historical Center

Coe, David Allen
Daphne Productions, Inc.

Coe, Sue
First Run/Icarus Films, Inc.

Coffee
Film Bank
Prelinger Assoc., Inc.

Coffee industry
Ackerman-Black Prods., Inc.
British Info. Svcs., Radio & TV Div.
Petrified Films, Inc.
Prelinger Assoc., Inc.

Coffee plantations
Foreign Images
Lesage, Julia

Coffee shops
See Restaurants (Coffee shops)

Coffins
CBS News Archives
Film Bank
See also Funerals; Morticians and mortuaries

Cohen, Mickey
Banks Film Library

Cohen, Stuart
Mus. of Contemporary Art

Coins
CBS News Archives
Natl. Archives (RG 104)
See also Money

Cointelpro
Alternative Information Network

Colbert, Claudette
UCLA Film & Television Archive

Colby, William
Educational Film & Video Project

Cold War
Amer. Portrait, An
Churchill (Winston) Memorial and Library
Cinema Guild
First Run/Icarus Films, Inc.
Forsher (James) Prods. & Archives, Inc.
Hoover Institution
Intl. Historic Films, Inc.

MacDonald, J. Fred
March of Time
Natl. Archives of Canada
Petrified Films, Inc.
Prelinger Assoc., Inc.
Quest Productions Inc.
Streamline Film Archives
Univ. of Mich., Mich. Hist. Colls.
See also Anti-communism; Berlin Wall; United States-Soviet relations

Colds (Illness)
Handel Film Corp.
TV Ontario

Cole, Cozy
Rhapsody Films, Inc.

Cole, Nat King
Archive Film Prods., Inc.
Banks Film Library
Chertok Assoc., Inc.
Pathé Pictures, Inc.
UCLA Film & Television Archive

Coleman, A.D.
Video Data Bank

Coleman, Mary S.
Univ. of Mich., Mich. Hist. Colls.

Coleman, William
Natl. Archives (RG 406)

Coles, Robert
Agee (James) Film Project

Colette
Soc. for French Amer. Cult. Svcs. & Educ. Aid

Collection plates
Petrified Films, Inc.

Colleges and universities (Footage of)
Allen (John E.) Inc.
Analogous Productions
Archive Film Prods., Inc.
Auburn University Archives
Baylor Univ., Texas Coll.
Borough of Manhattan Comm. Coll.
Boston College, Univ. Arch.
Bowling Green State Univ., Ctr. Arch. Coll.
Brethren in Christ Church & Messiah Coll., Arch.
CBS News Archives
California Inst. of Tech., Inst. Arch.
Citadel, The
City Univ. of N.Y., City Coll. Arch.
Cornell Univ., Media Services
DePauw University, Archives
Emory Univ., Spec. Coll.
Emporia State Univ., Spec. Coll.
Film Bank
Forsher (James) Prods. & Archives, Inc.
Franklin & Marshall Coll.
Georgetown Univ., Spec. Coll. Div.
Illinois State Hist. Lib.
Kartemquin Films
Loma Linda Univ., Webb Lib.
Louisiana State Univ. Libs., Spec. Coll.
Mass. Inst. of Tech., MIT Museum
Medical College of Pa., Arch. & Spec. Coll. Women in Medicine
Michigan State Univ., Archives
Missouri Hist. Soc.
Natl. Archives of Canada
Northern Ill. Univ., Reg. Hist. Ctr.
Occidental College Library
Oregon Hist. Soc.

Oregon State Univ., Archives
Panhandle-Plains Hist. Museum
Petrified Films, Inc.
Prelinger Assoc., Inc.
Roberts (Oral) Univ.
Smith College, Arch.
Source Stock Footage Lib., Inc.
Stanford Univ. Lib., Dept. of Spec. Coll. & Univ. Arch.
State Hist. Soc. of Iowa
TV Ontario
Texas A&M Univ., Univ. Arch.
Texas Tech Univ., Southwest Coll.
Texas Woman's Univ.
Twentieth Century-Fox Movietonews
Univ. of Alabama, W.S. Hoole Spec. Colls.
Univ. of Calif., Berkeley, Bancroft Lib.
Univ. of Calif., Davis, Shields Library
Univ. of Chicago Lib., Dept. Spec. Coll.
Univ. of Colo., Boulder, Western Hist. Coll.
Univ. of Kentucky, AV Arch.
Univ. of Manitoba Lib., Arch. Spec. Coll.
Univ. of Mass., Union Video Ctr.
Univ. of Miami, Arch. & Spec. Coll.
Univ. of North Texas, Div. Radio/TV/Film
Univ. of Okla., Western Hist. Colls.
Univ. of Oregon Lib., Inst. Media Ctr.
Univ. of Pa. Arch.
Univ. of Rhode Island, Univ. Lib.
Univ. of Rochester Lib., Rare Books & Spec. Coll.
Univ. of Tex. at Austin, Barker Tex. Hist. Ctr.
Univ. of Toledo, Univ. Arch.
Univ. of Toronto, Univ. Arch.
Univ. of Utah, Marriott Lib.
Univ. of Waterloo, A-V Centre
Villon Films
Wayne State Univ., Arch. Labor & Urb. Aff.
West Virginia Univ.
White Star Prof. Film Svcs., Inc.
Winthrop Coll., Dacus Lib.
Yale Film Study Ctr.
See also Campus life

Collins, Joan
Banks Film Library
Spectral Comms.

Collins, Judy
Natl. Archives of Canada

Collins, Michael
NASA, Lewis Research Center

Collins, Monty
Videobrary, Inc.

Collins, Phil
Archive Film Prods., Inc.

Colombia
Canadian Broadcasting Corp.
Hammer (Armand) Prods.

Colombia (Contemporary issues)
DEC Film & Video

Colombia (History and culture)
Archive Film Prods., Inc.
Cinema Guild
DEC Film & Video
Documentary Educational Resources
Hammer (Armand) Prods.
Intl. Assn. of Independent Producers
Natl. Archives (RG 70)
Rockefeller Arch. Ctr.

NOTE: Access policies, availability and restrictions vary for each source. Please read each entry in full. Always consult "General Film and Videotape Collections" (page 599); these comprehensive collections contain material on every conceivable subject.

United Nations Ctr. for Human
 Settlements

Colombian Americans
New Jersey Network

Color
Prelinger Assoc., Inc.

Colorado
Aitken (Len) Productions, Inc.
Aspen Historical Society
Cimarron Productions
Colorado Historical Society
Film Bank
Moving Media
Preview Media
Source Stock Footage Lib., Inc.
Summit Films, Inc.
Volkswagen of America, Inc.

Colorado (History and culture)
Aspen Historical Society
Colorado Historical Society
Datura Productions
Denver Pub. Lib., Western Hist. Dept.
Natl. Archives (RG 70)
Natl. Archives (RG 106)
New Haven Colony Hist. Soc.
Petrified Films, Inc.
Schiele Museum
U.S. Natl. Park Service Hist. Coll.
Univ. of Colo., Boulder, Western Hist.
 Coll.

Colorado River
Energy Productions
Jewell (Stuart) Productions
Petrified Films, Inc.
Preview Media
Pyramid Film and Video Corp.
Sobek Productions
Source Stock Footage Lib., Inc.
Spalla (Rick) Video Prods.

Colorado River (History and culture)
Utah State Hist. Soc.

Colorado River Canyon (History and culture)
Univ. of Mich., Mich. Hist. Colls.

Colorado Springs, Colo. (History and culture)
Petrified Films, Inc.
Summit Films, Inc.

Colson, Charles
Moody Inst. of Science

Coltrane, John
Chertok Assoc., Inc.

Columbia (Space shuttle)
See Space shuttle

Columbia River, Wash.-Oreg.
Natl. Archives (RG 115)

Columbus, Ohio (History and culture)
Ohio Hist. Soc.
Ohio State Univ., Dept. of Photog. &
 Cinema

Comaneci, Nadia
U.S. Olympic Comm.

Comas
Varied Directions, Inc.

Comedians
Art Com/La Mamelle, Inc.
Charisma Prods., Ltd./Visual Motion
Film Bank
March of Time

New York Pub. Lib., Perf. Arts Res. Ctr.,
 Theatre on Film and Tape
Pathé Pictures, Inc.
Petrified Films, Inc.

Comedy
Allen (John E.) Inc.
Archive Film Prods., Inc.
Boston Stock Market
Budget Films Inc.
Cable Access of Dallas
Canyon Cinema, Inc.
Center for New Television
Coe Film Assoc., Inc.
Creative Film Society
Deep Dish TV
DeFlores, Bob
Electronic Arts Intermix
Em Gee Film Library
Facets Multimedia, Inc.
Film Bank
Film Education Institute
Film Preservation Assoc.
Forsher (James) Prods. & Archives, Inc.
German Language Video Ctr.
Grinberg (Sherman) Film Libraries (West)
Imageways, Inc.
Instituto Cubano de Radio y Television
Intermedia Arts Minnesota
Ivy Film
Jessiefilm
Killiam Shows, Inc.
Lib. of Congress, M/B/RS
MacDonald, J. Fred
Morcraft Films
Moviecraft, Inc.
Natl. Archives of Canada
Picture Start, Inc.
Postcards Associates
Prelinger Assoc., Inc.
Producers Library Service
Pyramid Film and Video Corp.
Southwest Film/Video Archives, SMU
Swank Motion Pictures, Inc.
Twentieth Century-Fox Movietonews
UCLA Film & Television Archive
Univ. of So. Carolina, Newsfilm Lib.
Video Tape Library, Ltd.
Video Yesteryear
Video-SIG
Videobrary, Inc.
Windsor Prod. Corp.

Comets
Buhl Science Center
CBS News Archives
NASA, Office of Comm.
Natl. Science Foundation
Petrified Films, Inc.

Comets (Halley's)
Beerger (Norman) Prods.
Buhl Science Center
NASA, Lewis Research Center
NASA, Office of Comm.
Rosebush Visions Corp.

Comets (Kohoutek)
NASA, Office of Comm.
Natl. Science Foundation

Commerce, Dept. of (U.S.)
Natl. Archives (RG 277)
Natl. Archives (Stock Film Coll.)

Commodities exchanges
Board of Trade of the City of Chicago

Common Market
CBS News Archives

Common, Tommy
Natl. Archives of Canada

Commonwealth Games

Prov. Arch. of Alberta

Communes
Media Bus

Communication satellites
See Satellites

Communications
Carleton Prods. Inc.
Center for Humanities, Inc.
Chisholm (Jack) Film Productions
Fish Films, Inc.
GPN
Ideal Comms., Inc.
Inst. of Electrical & Electronics Eng.
Natl. Archives of Canada
Ohio State Univ., Dept. of Photog. &
 Cinema
Petrified Films, Inc.
Prelinger Assoc., Inc.
Rosebush Visions Corp.
TV Ontario
Université Laval, Cinémathèque

Communications industry
Cinema Guild
Paper Tiger TV
Video Data Bank

Communism
Allen (John E.) Inc.
Americas in Transition/Fossil Films
CBS News Archives
Carousel Film & Video
Communist Party USA
Hoover Institution
Intl. Historic Films, Inc.
Natl. Archives (RG 200)
New Day Films
Taminent Lib./Wagner Labor Arch.
See also Anti-communism

Communist Party (U.S.)
Communist Party USA
New Day Films
Southern Calif. Lib. for Soc. Stud. & Res.
Taminent Lib./Wagner Labor Arch.
See also Left-wing politics

Commuters
CBS News Archives

Como, Perry
MacDonald, J. Fred
Shokus Video

Compact cars
See Automobiles (Compact)

Computer graphics and animation
CASCOM
Charisma Prods., Ltd./Visual Motion
Dreamlight Images, Inc.
Editel/Boston
Energy Productions
Film Bank
Harvard-Smithsonian Ctr. for Astrophysics
Hayes Prods., Inc.
Impact Audio Visual
Instant Replay, Inc.
Inter Video/TTI
Lib. of Special Visual Effects
Mass. Inst. of Tech., MIT Museum
NASA, Ames Res. Ctr., Imaging Tech.
 Branch
NASA, Johnson Space Ctr. Film & Video
 Dist. Ctr.
Renaissance Video Corp.
Rosebush Visions Corp.
SIGGRAPH
Stimulus
Unger Computer Graphics
Univ. of Toronto, AV Lib.
Video Data Bank

Video Tape Library, Ltd.
Visual Studies Workshop
Voyager Co.
Z-Axis

Computer industry
Computer Television Group, Inc.

Computer operators
Applegate Entertainment
Cimarron Productions
Kesser Stock Footage Library
TV Ontario

Computer printouts
Film Bank

Computer programmers
TV Ontario

Computer screens
Rosebush Visions Corp.

Computer security
Coronet/MTI Film & Video

Computer software
Belove, Laiserin & Walsh
Computer Television Group, Inc.

Computer terrain modeling
Stimulus

Computers
AIMS Media
Amer. Hotel & Motel Assn.
Applegate Entertainment
Archive Film Prods., Inc.
BNA Communications, Inc.
Britannica Films & Video
British Info. Svcs., Radio & TV Div.
CBS News Archives
California Newsreel
Carousel Film & Video
Center for Humanities, Inc.
Churchill Films
Cinema Guild
Computer Museum
Computer Television Group, Inc.
Coronet/MTI Film & Video
Creative Venture Films
DEC Film & Video
Dreamlight Images, Inc.
Educational Film & Video Project
Film Bank
Films Incorporated
GPN
Hewlett-Packard Co.
IBM Corporation
Ideal Comms., Inc.
Inst. of Electrical & Electronics Eng.
Intellimation
Interlock Media Associates
Kesser Stock Footage Library
Los Alamos Natl. Lab.
Media Guild
Metro Communications, Inc.
NASA, Johnson Space Ctr., Film & Video
 Dist. Ctr.
Natl. Archives/Natl. AV Ctr.
Perlmutter (Alvin H.) Inc.
Petrified Films, Inc.
Prelinger Assoc., Inc.
Raindance Foundation
Rosebush Visions Corp.
Society of Manufacturing Engineers
Spectral Comms.
Stegman Productions
Stock Shots
United Training Media
Univ. of Toronto, AV Lib.
Video Tape Library, Ltd.
Wilmington Coll. Peace Res. Ctr.
World Monitor
Zielinski Productions, Inc.

Computers (CAD/CAM)
General Motors Corp.
Society of Manufacturing Engineers
TV Ontario

Computers (History)
Computer Museum
MacDonald, J. Fred
Mass. Inst. of Tech., MIT Museum

Computers (Production)
TV Ontario

Concentration camps
Center for Holocaust Studies
Cinema Guild
First Run/Icarus Films, Inc.
Hoover Institution
Natl. Archives (RG 18)
Natl. Archives (RG 238)
Natl. Archives (RG 342)
Natl. Archives/Natl. AV Ctr.
Natl. Ctr. for Jewish Film
Soc. for French Amer. Cult. Svcs. & Educ.
    Aid
Wiesenthal (Simon) Ctr.
See also Holocaust

Concert halls
Petrified Films, Inc.

Concerts
Archive Film Prods., Inc.
Baker (Fred) Film & Video Co.
Banks Film Library
CBS News Archives
Canadian Filmmakers Dist. Centre
Country Music Foundation, Inc.
Dance Theater Workshop
Dreamlight Images, Inc.
Encore Video Prods., Inc.
Ethnic Folk Arts Center
Forsher (James) Prods. & Archives, Inc.
Green Mountain Post Films
Imagen y Sonido Independiente, S.A.
Impact Audio Visual
Instant Replay, Inc.
Kansas City Film Archive
Law (Lisa) Prods.
MTV Networks
Natl. Archives (RG 274)
Natl. Archives of Canada
Natl. Lib. of Canada, Music Div.
New Film Co., Inc.
Peak Productions, Inc.
Pennebaker Associates, Inc.
Petrified Films, Inc.
Rhapsody Films, Inc.
Southern Calif. Blues Soc.
Spectral Comms.
Sullivan Video Services
Summit Films, Inc.
TV Ontario
Teatro Campesino, El
Televisa, S.A.
Twentieth Century-Fox Movietonews
UPA Prods. of America
Univ. Coll. of Cape Breton, Beaton Inst.
Univ. of Mississippi, Blues Arch.
Univ. of Tex. at Austin, Barker Tex. Hist.
    Ctr.
Vedo Films/Novacom Video
Zielinski Productions, Inc.
See also Music

Concord, Mich. (History and culture)
Univ. of Mich., Mich. Hist. Colls.

Concorde
See Aircraft (Supersonic)

Concrete
Amer. Concrete Inst.
Energy Productions
Louisiana Tech Univ., Eng. Film Res. Ctr.
Prelinger Assoc., Inc.
See also Cement

Condominiums
Film Bank
Peak Productions, Inc.
Spectral Comms.

Condoms
AIDSFILMS
Focus Intl. Inc.
Johns Hopkins Univ./Population Comm.
    Svcs.
See also Birth control; Sex education

Condor planes
See Aircraft (Condor)

Condors
Coe Film Assoc., Inc.

Conductors
Film Bank

Coney Island, N.Y.
Petrified Films, Inc.

**Coney Island, N.Y. (History and
    culture)**
Analogous Productions
Prelinger Assoc., Inc.

Confederation Centennial (Canada)
Natl. Archives of Canada

Conferences
Allen (John E.) Inc.
CBS News Archives
Metro Communications, Inc.
Twentieth Century-Fox Movietonews
See also Meetings

Confessionals
Petrified Films, Inc.

Confetti
CBS News Archives
Petrified Films, Inc.

Conflict resolution
Barr Films

Congo
See Zaire

**Congo River, Africa (History and
    culture)**
Solaris Dance/Theatre/Video

Congress (U.S.)
Archive Film Prods., Inc.
C-SPAN (Cable Satellite Public Affairs
    Network)
CBS News Archives
Intellimation
March of Time
Purdue Univ., Pub. Aff. Video Arch.
WETA-TV
See also House of Representatives (U.S.);
    Senate (U.S)

**Congress of Industrial Organizations
    (CIO)**
Bowling Green State Univ., Ctr. Arch.
    Coll.
MacDonald, J. Fred
March of Time

Connecticut
Energy Productions
Norsgaard, Campbell
Preview Media
Wallen (Dick) Prods.

Connecticut (History and culture)
Archive Film Prods., Inc.
Cinema Guild
Connecticut Historical Society
Connecticut State Library
MacDonald, J. Fred
Media Bus
Native Amer. Pub. Broad. Cons.
New Haven Colony Hist. Soc.
Petrified Films, Inc.
Regional Plan Assn.
Univ. of Miss., Ctr. for Study of Southern
    Culture

Conner, Dennis
America's Cup Organizing Comm.

Conner, Lois
Port Washington Pub. Lib.

Connery, Sean
Banks Film Library

Connors, Jimmy
U.S. Tennis Assn.

Consciousness research
Hartley Film Found., Inc.

Conservation
CBS News Archives
Cinema Guild
Ducks Unlimited, Inc.
Echo Film Prods., Inc.
Environmental Action Coalition
Mass. Audubon Society
Natl. Archives (RG 48)
Natl. Archives (RG 96)
Natl. Archives (RG 200)
Natl. Archives of Canada
Natl. Assn. of Conservation Dists.
Natl. Film Board of Canada
Natl. Parks & Conservation Assn.
Nature Conservancy
Northstar Prods.
Ohio Historical Soc.
State Hist. Soc. of Wisconsin
Tennessee State Lib. & Arch.
Univ. of Calif., Berkeley, Bancroft Lib.
Univ. of Mich., Mich. Hist. Colls.
See also Ecology; Energy; Pollution;
    Toxic waste

Conservation (Architectural)
See Historic preservation

Conservation (Coal)
Natl. Archives (RG 223)

Conservation (Energy)
AIMS Media
Carousel Film & Video
Edison Electric Institute
Finley (Stuart) Inc.
Inst. for Local Self-Reliance
Los Angeles Dept. of Water & Power

Conservation (Farmland)
Natl. Archives (RG 145)

Conservation (Forest)
North Central Forest Exp. Sta.

Conservation (Fuel)
MacDonald, J. Fred

Conservation (History of)
Natl. Assn. of Conservation Dists.

Conservation (Marine)
Caribbean Images, Ltd.
Natl. Oceanic & Atmospheric Admin.

Conservation (Soil)
Finley (Stuart) Inc.
Natl. Archives (RG 33)
Natl. Assn. of Conservation Dists.
State Hist. Soc. of Iowa

Conservation (War)
Natl. Archives (RG 171)
Natl. Archives (RG 208)
See also World War I (Canada,
    Homefront); World War I (U.S.,
    Homefront); World War II (Canada,
    Homefront); World War II (U.S.,
    Homefront)

Conservation (Water)
Bullfrog Films, Inc.
Calif. Dept. of Water Resources
Finley (Stuart) Inc.
Los Angeles Dept. of Water & Power
Natl. Archives (RG 75)
Natl. Assn. of Conservation Dists.

Conservation (Wetlands)
Ducks Unlimited, Ltd.

Conservation (Wildlife)
Natl. Archives (RG 33)

Conservatism (Canada)
Natl. Archives of Canada

Constantinople
See Istanbul, Turkey

Constitution (U.S.)
Amer. Political Science Assn.
Intellimation
League of Women Voters of the U.S.
MacDonald, J. Fred
Mason (George) Univ. Spec. Coll. & Arch.
Natl. Archives (RG 64)
Perlmutter (Alvin H.) Inc.
Prelinger Assoc., Inc.

Constitution (U.S.S.R.)
Mariners' Museum

Constitution Hall (Philadelphia)
Petrified Films, Inc.

Construction
Allen (John E.) Inc.
Assoc. Gen. Contractors of America
Banks Film Library
Broad Street Prods.
CBS News Archives
Calif. Dept. of Transportation
Calif. Dept. of Water Resources
Cranbrook Acad. of Arts
Crystal Pyramid Prods.
Development Communications, Inc.
Dreamlight Images, Inc.
Energy Productions
Farkas Studios, Ltd.
Film Bank
General Motors Corp.
Gypsum Assn.
Hammer (Armand) Prods.
Inuvik Research Ctr.
Kentucky Dept. of Libraries & Archives
Kesser Stock Footage Library
Labor Video Project
LeTourneau College Archives

NOTE: Access policies, availability and restrictions vary for each source. Please read each entry in full. Always consult "General Film and Videotape Collections" (page 599); these comprehensive collections contain material on every conceivable subject.

Loma Linda Univ., Webb Lib.
Louisiana Tech Univ., Eng. Film Res. Ctr.
Massachusetts Archives
Missouri Hist. Soc.
Natl. Archives (RG 28)
Natl. Archives (RG 31)
Natl. Archives (RG 59)
Natl. Archives (RG 69)
Natl. Archives (RG 77)
Natl. Archives (RG 96)
Natl. Archives (RG 121)
Natl. Archives (RG 200)
Natl. Archives (RG 207)
Natl. Archives (RG 238)
Natl. Archives (RG 342)
Natl. Archives of Canada
Navajo Tribe, Off. Broadcast Svcs.
Nine Star Productions
North Carolina Div. of Arch. & Hist.
Ohio Hist. Soc.
Peak Productions, Inc.
Petrified Films, Inc.
Port Authority of New York & New Jersey
Prelinger Assoc., Inc.
Prov. Arch. of Alberta
Prov. Arch. of British Columbia
Prov. Arch. of Newfoundland & Labrador
San Jose Hist. Mus.
Smithsonian Inst., NMAH, Div. Eng. & Ind.
Stock Shots
Sweet (Harry) Film Coll.
TV Ontario
Twentieth Century-Fox Movietonews
Univ. of Alberta, Boreal Inst. for Northern Studies
Univ. of Mich., Mich. Hist. Colls.
Univ. of Toledo, Univ. Arch.
Washington State Hist. Soc.
White Star Prof. Film Svcs., Inc.
Yukon Archives
See also Bridges (Construction); Buildings (Construction); Dams (Construction); Highways (Construction); Houses and homes (Construction); Streets and roads (Construction)

Construction industry
Assoc. Gen. Contractors of America

Consulates
See Embassies

Consumer education
Altschul Group
Barr Films
Carousel Film & Video
GPN
Intermedia Arts Minnesota
Morris Video
Natl. Archives (RG 12)
Natl. Archives (RG 16)
Natl. Archives (RG 88)
Natl. Archives (RG 188)
New York Pub. Lib., Rare Books & Manuscripts Div.
Ohio Hist. Soc.
Perlmutter (Alvin H.) Inc.
Phoenix Films and Video
Prelinger Assoc., Inc.
Richter Productions

Consumer movement
Consumers Union of the U.S.
Perlmutter (Alvin H.) Inc.

Consumerism
Bullfrog Films, Inc.
Canadian Filmmakers Dist. West
Cinema Guild
Coe Film Assoc., Inc.
Coronet/MTI Film & Video
Higgins (Alfred) Prods.
Natl. Archives (RG 200)
Natl. Archives of Canada

Petrified Films, Inc.
Prelinger Assoc., Inc.

Consumers (Japan)
Japan External Trade Organization

Contests
CBS News Archives
Film Bank
Petrified Films, Inc.
Twentieth Century-Fox Movietonews

Continental Divide
Film Bank

Contortions (Rock and roll band)
Target Video

Contraceptives
See Birth control

Contracts
Prelinger Assoc., Inc.

Control panels
Energy Productions
Film Bank
Link Flight Simulation Div.
NASA, Ames Res. Ctr., Imaging Tech. Branch

Convenience stores
Natl. Assn. of Convenience Stores

Conventions
Allen (John E.) Inc.
CBS News Archives
Film Bank
Inst. for Labor Studies & Research
Spectral Comms.
Tamiment Lib./Wagner Labor Arch.
Twentieth Century-Fox Movietonews
Univ. of Maryland, McKeldin Lib.
See also Political conventions

Convents
CBS News Archives
Petrified Films, Inc.

Convertibles
See Automobiles (Convertibles)

Conveyor belts
CBS News Archives
Energy Productions
Film Bank
Natl. Industrial Belting Assn.
Petrified Films, Inc.

Conway, Wales
Unicorn Projects

Coogan, Jackie
Banks Film Library

Cook Islands, New Zealand
Hawaii Public Broadcasting Authority

Cook, Joe
Videobrary, Inc.

Cook, Lia
Video Data Bank

Cook, Peter
Southern Calif. Inst. of Architecture

Cooke, Ray
Videobrary, Inc.

Cookeville, Tenn. (History and culture)
Western Kentucky Univ., Folklife Arch.

Cooking
Armenian Film Foundation

CBS News Archives
Dreamlight Images, Inc.
Farkas Studios, Ltd.
Film Bank
Morris Video
Natl. Oceanic & Atmospheric Admin.
Prelinger Assoc., Inc.
Radcliffe Coll., Schlesinger Lib.

Cooking (Instruction)
Charisma Prods., Ltd./Visual Motion
Culinary Inst. of America
Peralta Colleges TV
Soc. for French Amer. Cult. Svcs. & Educ. Aid
WGBH Educational Foundation

Cooks
TV Ontario

Cooley, Denton A.
Houston Acad. of Medicine

Coolgardie, Australia
Petrified Films, Inc.

Coolidge, Calvin
Archive Film Prods., Inc.
Lib. of Congress, M/B/RS
Natl. Archives (RG 33)
Natl. Archives (RG 59)
Natl. Archives (RG 130)
Natl. Archives (RG 200)
Prelinger Assoc., Inc.
Timesteps Prods., Inc.
Vermont Hist. Soc.

Cooper, Alice
Pennebaker Associates, Inc.

Cooper, Gary
Banks Film Library
UCLA Film & Television Archive

Cooper, Jackie
Banks Film Library

Cooper, Sherman
Duke Univ., Perkins Lib.

Cooperatives (Agricultural)
Natl. Archives (RG 33)
Natl. Archives (RG 96)
Université de Moncton, Centre d'Études Acad.
Univ. of Mich., Mich. Hist. Colls.

Cooperatives (Electrical)
Natl. Archives/Natl. AV Ctr.

Cooperatives (Fishing)
Natl. Archives (RG 22)
Université de Moncton, Centre d'Études Acad.

Cooperatives (Industrial)
Natl. Archives (RG 96)

Coots
Wings Wildlife Prods. Inc.

Copper
Archives of Ontario
Energy Productions
Natl. Archives (RG 70)
Prelinger Assoc., Inc.
Seagram Museum
Source Stock Footage Lib., Inc.
See also Mining (Copper)

Coral and coral reefs
Caribbean Images, Ltd.
Cousteau Society
Dreamlight Images, Inc.
Kesser Stock Footage Library

Marineland of Florida
Moonlight Productions
Passage Home Communications

Coral Gables, Fla. (History and culture)
Prelinger Assoc., Inc.

Corcoran, Lynn
Port Washington Pub. Lib.

Cord, Alex
Spectral Comms.

Cordaro, Frank
Marquette Univ., Spec. Coll.

Corman, Roger
Blackwood (Christian) Prods., Inc.
Blackwood Prods., Inc.

Corn
Energy Productions
Native Amer. Pub. Broad. Cons.
Oregon State Univ., Archives
Petrified Films, Inc.
TV Ontario
Twentieth Century-Fox Movietonews
Video I-D, Inc.

Cornell, Joseph
Amer. Federation of the Arts

Coronations
CBS News Archives
Film Search
March of Time
See also Royal Family (Great Britain); Royalty

Coroners
Film Bank
See also Autopsies

Corporate archives
AT&T Archives & Rec. Mgmt. Svcs.
Airship Industries (USA), Inc.
Amer. Airlines
Amer. Stock Exchange
Anheuser-Busch Cos., Inc.
Arch. of the Mennonite Church
Bacardi Corporation
Bell Canada
Boeing Historical Archives
Carter (C. L.) Jr. & Assoc., Inc.
Chrysler Motors Corp.
Coca-Cola Co., Archives Dept.
Continental Airlines
Disney (Walt) Archives
Dorn (Larry) Associates
Dr Pepper Co.
Duke Univ., Perkins Lib.
Ford (Henry) Mus.
General Mills, Inc.
General Motors Corp.
Goodyear Tire and Rubber
Hagley Mus. and Lib.
Hammer (Armand) Prods.
Hewlett-Packard Co.
IBM Corporation
Imperial Oil Ltd.
Indianapolis Motor Speedway Corp.
Lilly (Eli) and Co.
Marineland of Florida
Miles Corporate Archive
Molstar Comm.
New York Stock Exchange
Nissan Motor Corp. of the U.S.
Procter & Gamble Co.
Rational Island Publishers
Reynolds (R. J.) Tobacco USA
Saatchi & Saatchi DFS Compton
Sarnoff (David) Res. Ctr. Lib.
Stock House
Titan Sports, Inc.
United Airlines, Creative Services

Volkswagen of America, Inc.

Corporate scenes
Cineworks Prods. Inc.
Petrified Films, Inc.
Sullivan Video Services
See also Business scenes; Offices;
   Workers (Office); Workers (White-
   collar)

Corpses
See Autopsies; Death scenes; Morgues

Corrals
CBS News Archives
Petrified Films, Inc.

Corrections
See Prisons and prisoners

Corsica Island, France
Cousteau Society

Cortez, Jayne
Giorno Poetry Systems Inst.

Cosby, Bill
King (Dr. Martin Luther, Jr.) Ctr.
Pyramid Film and Video Corp.

Cosell, Howard
Moving Media

Cosmetics
CBS News Archives
Film Bank
Marx Production Center
See also Beauty culture

Cosmetology
Milady Publishing Corp.

Costa del Sol, Spain
Preview Media

Costa Rica
Preview Media
World Monitor

Costa Rica (History and culture)
Film/Audio Services, Inc.
Footage Inc.
Johns Hopkins Univ./Population Comm.
   Svcs.
Northstar Prods.
Prelinger Assoc., Inc.
Women Make Movies, Inc.
World Monitor

Costa, Teresa
Paper Tiger TV

Costakis, George
Mus. of Contemporary Art

Costello, Lou
Archive Film Prods., Inc.

Costume balls and parties
Banks Film Library
Petrified Films, Inc.

Costumes
CBS News Archives
Petrified Films, Inc.

Costumes (Historical)
Fashion Inst. of Design & Merchandising
Intl. Fashion Video Library
Petrified Films, Inc.
TV Ontario

Video Catalogue Co., Inc.

Côte d'Azur, France
Petrified Films, Inc.

Cottages
Film Bank

Cotten, Elizabeth
Schomburg Ctr. for Res. in Black Culture

Cotton
Center for Southern Folklore
Johns Hopkins Univ., School of Medicine
March of Time
Petrified Films, Inc.
See also Cotton gins; Workers (Cotton)

Cotton (Arctic)
TV Ontario

Cotton candy
Energy Productions
Petrified Films, Inc.
Prelinger Assoc., Inc.

Cotton gins
General Motors Corp.
See also Cotton

Cougars
Echo Film Prods., Inc.
Film Bank
Wings Wildlife Prods. Inc.

Coughlin, Charles E.
March of Time

Counseling
Academy of Health Sciences, U.S. Army
Altschul Group
Amer. Assn. for Counseling &
   Development
Coe Film Assoc., Inc.
IEA Productions, Inc.
Media Guild
Natl. Assn. of Secondary Schl. Principals
Pyramid Film and Video Corp.
Rational Island Publishers
Shanti Project
Suicide Information & Education Ctr.

Countdowns
Fish Films, Inc.

Counterculture (U.S.)
Cinema Guild
Clark (Dick) Media Archives, Inc.
Law (Lisa) Prods.
MacDonald, J. Fred
Media Bus
Media Project
Petrified Films, Inc.
Raindance Foundation
UCLA Behavioral Sci. Media Lab.
Video Tape Library, Ltd.
White Janssen, Inc.
See also Hippies; Love-ins

Counterfeiting (Money)
Inst. of Financial Education
Natl. Archives (RG 87)

Country and western music
See Music (Country and western)

Country clubs
Las Vegas News Bureau
Sea TV

Country Joe and the Fish

Pennebaker Associates, Inc.

Countrysides
Applegate Entertainment
Boston Stock Market
British Info. Svcs., Radio & TV Div.
Dorn (Larry) Associates
Film Bank
Petrified Films, Inc.

County fairs
See Fairs and expositions

Couples
Film Bank

Courthouses
CBS News Archives
Film Bank
Petrified Films, Inc.

Courtrooms
CBS News Archives
Connecticut State Library
Film Bank
Fish Films, Inc.
Forsher (James) Prods. & Archives, Inc.
Twentieth Century-Fox Movietonews
See also Courthouses; Crime and
   criminals; Judges; Lawyers; Murder
   and murderers; Trials

Cousteau, Jacques-Yves
Cousteau Society
Wesleyan Cinema Archives

Cousy, Bob
Wesleyan Cinema Archives

Covered wagons
Archive Film Prods., Inc.
See also Westerns

Coward, Noel
Camera Three Prods., Inc.

Cowboys
Allen (John E.) Inc.
Archive Film Prods., Inc.
Buffalo Bill Historical Center
CBS News Archives
Cinenet (Cinema Network)
Country Music Foundation, Inc.
Dreamlight Images, Inc.
Film Bank
Fish Films, Inc.
Freewheelin' Films, Ltd.
Lib. of Congress, Amer. Folklife Ctr.
Lib. of Congress, M/B/RS
Media Project
Moving Media
Panhandle-Plains Hist. Museum
Petrified Films, Inc.
Prelinger Assoc., Inc.
Prov. Arch. of Alberta
Sheffield (Erin) Prods.
Source Stock Footage Lib., Inc.
Southwest Film/Video Archives, SMU
Streamline Film Archives
Summit Films, Inc.
Timesteps Prods., Inc.
Univ. of Arizona, Film Coll.
West Star Productions
See also Ranches; Rodeos; Westerns

Cowboys (Black)
Anti-Defamation League of B'nai B'rith

Cowboys (Brazil)
Cinema Guild

Cows
Analogous Productions
Dreamlight Images, Inc.
Film Bank
Lib. of Congress, Amer. Folklife Ctr.
Natl. Archives (RG 16)
Natl. Dairy Council
Oregon State Univ., Archives
Petrified Films, Inc.
Prelinger Assoc., Inc.
TV Ontario

Cox, Ronny
Spectral Comms.

Cox, Wally
General Motors Corp.

Coyotes
Di Sesso (Moe) Wild Life Film Lib.
Energy Productions
Film Bank
Jewell (Stuart) Productions
New Mexico State Records Ctr. & Arch.
Petrified Films, Inc.
Summit Films, Inc.
Wings Wildlife Prods. Inc.

Cozumel, Mexico
Passage Home Communications

Crabs
Bullfrog Films, Inc.
Cinenet (Cinema Network)
Petrified Films, Inc.
Wings Wildlife Prods. Inc.

Crack (Cocaine)
Hazelden Found. Educ. Materials
Narcotics Education, Inc.
Rogers (Will) Institute
See also Cocaine; Drug abuse

Crafts
Amer. Craft Council
CBS News Archives
Coe Film Assoc., Inc.
Manitoba Indian Cultural Centre
Media Bus
Media Guild
Media Project
Morris Video
Phoenix Films and Video
Source Stock Footage Lib., Inc.
See also Art and artists; Folk art

Crafts (African)
TV Ontario

Crafts (Alaskan)
KYUK-TV

Crafts (Appalachian)
Appalshop Films, Inc.
East Tenn. State Univ., Arch. of
   Appalachia

Crafts (Asian)
Rainbow Video Prods.

Crafts (Canadian)
Archives of Ontario

Crafts (Javanese)
Sheffield (Erin) Prods.

Crafts (Latin American)
Mus. of Mod. Art of Latin America

Crafts (Native American)
Akwesasne Library Cultural Ctr.

NOTE: Access policies, availability and restrictions vary for each source. Please read each entry in full. Always consult "General Film and Videotape Collections" (page 599); these comprehensive collections contain material on every conceivable subject.

Cherokee Nation Hist. Soc., Inc.
Echo Film Prods., Inc.
Jewell (Stuart) Productions
Native Amer. Pub. Broad. Cons.
Petrified Films, Inc.
Sitka Natl. Hist. Park
South Dakota State Lib.
TV Ontario
Tennessee State Lib. & Arch.
Univ. of Wash. Press, Multimedia Div.
Wheelwright Mus. of the Amer. Indian

Crafts (Thai)
Jewell (Stuart) Productions

Crafts (Traditional)
Amer. Craft Council
Appalshop Films, Inc.
Bur. of Florida Folklife Progs.
Cherokee Nation Hist. Soc., Inc.
KYUK-TV
Native Amer. Pub. Broad. Cons.
Ozark Folk Center

Cramps (Rock and roll band)
Target Video

Cranberries
New Jersey Network

Crane, Hart
Intellimation

Crane, Henry Hitt
Univ. of Mich., Mich. Hist. Colls.

Cranes (Birds)
Echo Film Prods., Inc.
Educational Film & Video Project
Film Bank
Kesser Stock Footage Library
Mass. Audubon Society
Snyder (Bill) Films, Inc.
TV Ontario
Telltales Associates Inc.
Wings Wildlife Prods. Inc.

Cranes (Construction)
CBS News Archives
Film Bank
Petrified Films, Inc.
See also Heavy equipment

Cranston, Alan
Southern Calif. Lib. for Soc. Stud. & Res.
Spectral Comms.

Crap games
Petrified Films, Inc.
See also Gambling

Crappies
TV Ontario

Crash tests
See Automobiles (Safety testing)

Crashes
See Accidents

Crater Lake, Oreg.
Oregon Hist. Soc.

Crater Lake, Oreg. (History and culture)
Prelinger Assoc., Inc.

Craters
Echo Film Prods., Inc.

Crawford, Cheryl
New York Pub. Lib., Perf. Arts Res. Ctr.,
    Theatre on Film and Tape

Crawford, Joan

Archive Film Prods., Inc.
Las Vegas News Bureau

Crawford, Percy
Wheaton Coll., Billy Graham Ctr.

Crayton, Pee Wee
Southern Calif. Blues Soc.

Creationism
CBN Publishing
See also Evolution

Creativity
Psychological and Educational Films

Creches
TV Ontario

Creedence Clearwater Revival
Archive Film Prods., Inc.

Creeks
See Streams

Creeley, Robert
Giorno Poetry Systems Inst.

Crenna, Richard
Spectral Comms.

Creole music
See Music (Creole)

Crested Butte, Colo.
Summit Films, Inc.

Crevier, Tanya
Fellowship of Christian Athletes

Crew (Instruction)
NCAA Productions

Cricket
Kesser Stock Footage Library
Petrified Films, Inc.
Sportsfilm
Twentieth Century-Fox Movietonews
Wings Wildlife Prods. Inc.

Crime and criminals
ABC Distribution (Education)
Amer. Hotel & Motel Assn.
Archive Film Prods., Inc.
CBS News Archives
Cable News Network Library
Cinema Guild
Coronet/MTI Film & Video
Film Bank
Fish Films, Inc.
Hearst Metrotone News
Highway Safety Films, Inc.
Inst. of Financial Education
MacDonald, J. Fred
March of Time
Mass Media Ministries
Minn. Citizens Counc. on Crime & Justice
Minn. Dept. of Public Safety Film Lib.
Natl. Archives (RG 21)
Natl. Archives (RG 65)
Natl. Archives (RG 129)
Natl. Archives of Canada
Natl. Assn. of Convenience Stores
Natl. Crime Prevention Council
Petrified Films, Inc.
Phoenix Films and Video
Prelinger Assoc., Inc.
Quest Productions Inc.
Twentieth Century-Fox Movietonews
United Training Media
Worldwide Television News
See also Arson and arsonists; Kidnapping;
    Murder and murderers; Rape

Crime and criminals (Organized crime)

CBS News Archives

Crime prevention
AIMS Media
Coronet/MTI Film & Video
Minn. Citizens Counc. on Crime & Justice
Minn. Dept. of Public Safety Film Lib.
Natl. Crime Prevention Council

Crimean War (1853)
UCLA Film & Television Archive

Cripple Creek, Colo. (History and culture)
Univ. of Colo., Boulder, Western Hist.
    Coll.

Crisp, Quentin
Daphne Productions, Inc.

Criss, Sonny
Rhapsody Films, Inc.

Criswell, Ronnie
Appalshop Films, Inc.

Crocodiles
Jewell (Stuart) Productions
Petrified Films, Inc.
Summit Films, Inc.

Cronin, Isaac
Video Data Bank

Cronkite, Walter
Daphne Productions, Inc.

Cronyn, Hume
Northeast Historic Film

Crooked River, Oreg.
Oregon State Univ., Archives

Crop dusting
Petrified Films, Inc.

Crops
British Info. Svcs., Radio & TV Div.
CBS News Archives
Cornell Univ., Media Services
Energy Productions
Film Bank
TV Ontario
VTR Productions
See also Agriculture; Farms and farming;
    Harvesting; specific crops

Crosby, Bing
Banks Film Library
Grinberg (Sherman) Film Libraries (East)
Petrified Films, Inc.
UCLA Film & Television Archive
Videobrary, Inc.

Crosby, Cathy Lee
Spectral Comms.

Crosby, Gary
Banks Film Library

Cross-country running
See Running (Cross-country)

Crosses
CBS News Archives
Petrified Films, Inc.

Crow Agency, Mont. (History and culture)
Smithsonian Inst., Human Studies Film
    Arch.

Crowds
British Info. Svcs., Radio & TV Div.
CBS News Archives

Cinema Arts Associates
Cinenet (Cinema Network)
Dreamlight Images, Inc.
Energy Productions
Film Bank
Film Search
Lunar Productions
Minnesota Zoo
Petrified Films, Inc.
Source Stock Footage Lib., Inc.
Spectral Comms.
TV Ontario
Timesteps Prods., Inc.
Twentieth Century-Fox Movietonews
Video Tape Library, Ltd.
Zielinski Productions, Inc.
See also Audiences; Spectators (Sports)

Crows
Di Sesso (Moe) Wild Life Film Lib.
Petrified Films, Inc.

Cruikshank, Sally
Port Washington Pub. Lib.

Cruises and cruise ships
See Ships (Cruise)

Crying
See Weeping

Cryonics
Cinema Guild

Crypts
Petrified Films, Inc.

Crystal, Billy
Spectral Comms.

Crystal City, Tex. (History and culture)
Natl. Archives (RG 85)

Crystals
Dreamlight Images, Inc.
Energy Productions
Video-SIG

Cuba
Analogous Productions
Cousteau Society
Imagen y Sonido Independiente, S.A.
Petrified Films, Inc.

Cuba (History and culture)
Archive Film Prods., Inc.
Center for Cuban Studies
Cinema Guild
Cinemateca de Cuba
DEC Film & Video
Downtown Community TV Ctr.
Film/Audio Services, Inc.
Hoover Institution
Idera Films
Instituto Cubano de Radio y Television
Intl. Assn. of Independent Producers
Natl. Archives (RG 64)
Natl. Archives (RG 200)
Natl. Archives (RG 291)
Natl. Archives (RG 381)
Natl. Archives/Natl. AV Ctr.
Payne, Roz
Petrified Films, Inc.
Third World Newsreel
Univ. of Miami, Arch. & Spec. Coll.
Univ. of Mich., Mich. Hist. Colls.
Villon Films
See also Bay of Pigs (1961); Castro, Fidel;
    Cuban missile crisis (1962); United
    States-Cuba relations

Cuban Americans
Flower Films & Video
Univ. of Miami, Arch. & Spec. Coll.

Cuban missile crisis (1962)
Natl. Archives (RG 64)
Natl. Archives (RG 381)
Petrified Films, Inc.
UCLA Film & Television Archive

Cucumbers
TV Ontario

Cukor, George
Natl. Archives (RG 47)

Culinary education
See Cooking (Instruction)

Cullen, Bill
Encore Entertainment

Cullen, Ed
Port Washington Pub. Lib.

Culp, Robert
UCLA Film & Television Archive

Culpepper, Emily
Cambridge Documentary Films, Inc.

Cult of the Orisha
Cinema Guild

Cults
Cult Awareness Network
Electronic Arts Intermix
FOCUS
Graduate Theological Union Lib.
Keep the Faith, Inc.
MacDonald, J. Fred
Prestige Film Corp.
Spectral Comms.
Univ. of Tex. at Austin, Benson Lat. Am. Coll.
Video Tape Library, Ltd.

Cumming, Robert
Video Data Bank

Cummings, Bob
Banks Film Library

Cunningham, Glen
Natl. Archives (RG 220)

Cunningham, Imogen
Amer. Federation of the Arts

Cunningham, Merce
Amer. Federation of the Arts
Cunningham Dance Foundation
Pennebaker Associates, Inc.
Walker Art Ctr.

Cuomo, Mario
Natl. Assn. for the Advancement of Colored People

Curacao, Netherlands Antilles
Kesser Stock Footage Library

Curie, Marie
Forsher (James) Prods. & Archives, Inc.
Petrified Films, Inc.

Curley, James Michael
Massachusetts Archives
WGBH Educational Foundation

Curling
Analogous Productions
Natl. Archives of Canada
Sportsfilm

Current issues
See Social and political issues

Curtis, George
Amer. Federation of the Arts

Curtis, Jackie
Giorno Poetry Systems Inst.

Curtis, Tony
Banks Film Library
Spalla (Rick) Video Prods.
UCLA Film & Television Archive

Curtis, William
Southern Calif. Inst. of Architecture

Custer, Gen. George
Buffalo Bill Historical Center
Montana Dept. of Commerce

Custodians
Film Bank

Customs (Import and export)
CBS News Archives
Petrified Films, Inc.
TV Ontario

Cyclamates
New York Pub. Lib., Rare Books & Manuscripts Div.

Cyclones
See Tornadoes

Cypress trees
Historic New Orleans Collection

Cyprus (History and culture)
Natl. Archives of Canada

Cystic fibrosis
Cystic Fibrosis Found.
UCLA Behavioral Sci. Media Lab.

Cytology
Educational Images, Ltd.

Czech Americans
Slavonic Benev. Order. of State of Texas

Czechoslovakia
Canadian Broadcasting Corp.
Pan American Airlines Film Lib.

Czechoslovakia (History and culture)
Archive Film Prods., Inc.
Czechoslovak Heritage Mus. Lib. & Arch.
Hoover Institution
March of Time
Natl. Archives/Natl. AV Ctr.
Slavonic Benev. Order. of State of Texas
Twentieth Century-Fox Movietonews

DEW Line
Northstar Prods.

DNA
Fanlight Prods.

DNA (Rock and roll band)
Target Video

Dabney, Virginius
Agee (James) Film Project

Dada
Amer. Federation of the Arts
Blackwood Prods., Inc.

Dade County, Fla.
Video Ventures Prods.

Dade County, Fla. (History and culture)
Univ. of Miami, Arch. & Spec. Coll.

Dafoe, Willem
Spectral Comms.

Dagenais, Huguette
Université Laval, Svc. des Res. Pédagogiques

D'Agostino, Peter
Port Washington Pub. Lib.

Dahomey
See Benin

Dailey, Dan
Spalla (Rick) Video Prods.

Dairy industry
Natl. Archives (RG 16)
Natl. Assn. of Conservation Dists.
Natl. Dairy Council
New Zealand Embassy Film Lib.
Oregon State Univ., Archives
Petrified Films, Inc.
Prelinger Assoc., Inc.
Prov. Arch. of Alberta
TV Ontario
See also Cows; Farms and farming; Milk

Daisies
Film Bank
Petrified Films, Inc.

Dakar, Senegal (History and culture)
TV Ontario

Dalai Lama
Office of Tibet

Dale, Edgar
Ohio State Univ., Dept. of Photog. & Cinema

Dali, Salvador
Creative Film Society
Daphne Productions, Inc.
Petrified Films, Inc.

Dalin, Marcel
Videobrary, Inc.

Dallas
Cable Access of Dallas
Creative Video, Inc.
Dreamlight Images, Inc.
Kesser Stock Footage Library
Postcards Unlimited
Preview Media

Dallas (History and culture)
Archive Film Prods., Inc.
MacDonald, J. Fred
Petrified Films, Inc.
Southwest Film/Video Archives, SMU

Dallas/Fort Worth, Tex.
Aries Prods.

Dallas/Fort Worth, Tex. (History and culture)
Southwest Film/Video Archives, SMU

Daly City, Calif.
Unicorn Projects

Daly City, Calif. (History and culture)
Petrified Films, Inc.

Daly, John
General Motors Corp.

Daly, Mary
Cambridge Documentary Films, Inc.
Women in Focus

Daly, Tyne
Spectral Comms.

Damascus, Syria (History and culture)
Archive Film Prods., Inc.

Damone, Vic
Banks Film Library

Dams
Aitken (Len) Productions, Inc.
Allen (John E.) Inc.
Archive Film Prods., Inc.
Beerger (Norman) Prods.
CBS News Archives
Dreamlight Images, Inc.
Eastern Washington State Historical Soc.
Echo Film Prods., Inc.
Energy Productions
Film Bank
Natl. Archives (RG 142)
Natl. Archives of Canada
Natl. Assn. of Conservation Dists.
Oregon Hist. Soc.
Petrified Films, Inc.
Source Stock Footage Lib., Inc.
Spectral Comms.
Sweet (Harry) Film Coll.
TV Ontario
Tennessee Valley Authority (TVA)
Timesteps Prods., Inc.
Twentieth Century-Fox Movietonews
Univ. of Minn. Libs., Manuscripts Div.

Dams (Construction)
Allen (John E.) Inc.
Calif. Dept. of Water Resources
Intl. Film Foundation
Natl. Archives (RG 69)
Natl. Archives of Canada
Petrified Films, Inc.
See also Construction

Dance and dancing
ARC Videodance Coll./Eye on Dance Coll.
Amer. Alliance for Health, Phys. Ed., Rec. & Dance Arch.
Archive Film Prods., Inc.
Arts Television Centre
Athletic Institute
Blackwood Prods., Inc.
CBS News Archives
Calif. Inst. of the Arts, Lib.
Canyon Cinema, Inc.
Channel L Working Group
Chicago Pub. Lib., Visual & Perf. Arts
Coe Film Assoc., Inc.
Corinth Films/Corinth Video
Cunningham Dance Foundation
Dance Theater of Harlem
Dance Theater Workshop
Dreamlight Images, Inc.
EZTV
Electronic Arts Intermix
Em Gee Film Library
Energy Productions
Facets Multimedia, Inc.
Film Bank
Film Search
Fish Films, Inc.
Forsher (James) Prods. & Archives, Inc.

NOTE: Access policies, availability and restrictions vary for each source. Please read each entry in full. Always consult "General Film and Videotape Collections" (page 599); these comprehensive collections contain material on every conceivable subject.

Groupe Intervention Video
House Found. for the Arts
Intermedia Arts Minnesota
Intl. Film Bureau, Inc.
Juilliard Schl., Wallace Lib.
Kansas City Film Archive
Media Guild
Metro Communications, Inc.
Natl. Dance Assn.
New American Makers
New York Pub. Lib., Perf. Arts Res. Ctr.,
    Dance Coll.
Petrified Films, Inc.
Phoenix Films and Video
Prelinger Assoc., Inc.
Pyramid Film and Video Corp.
Solaris Dance/Theatre/Video
South Carolina Arts Comm. Media Arts
    Ctr.
Spectral Comms.
TV Ontario
Tharp (Twyla) Dance Foundation
Timesteps Prods., Inc.
Twentieth Century-Fox Movietonews
Univ. of Calif., Ext. Media Ctr.
Univ. of Rochester, Dance Film Arch.
Video In
Video Tape Library, Ltd.
White Janssen, Inc.
Zielinski Productions, Inc.

Dance and dancing (African)
Innerquest Communications Corp.
Petrified Films, Inc.
Prelinger Assoc., Inc.
Smithsonian Inst., Human Studies Film
    Arch.

Dance and dancing (Australian)
Wesleyan Univ., World Music Arch.

Dance and dancing (Austrian)
White Janssen, Inc.

Dance and dancing (Avant-garde)
Kitchen, The
Twin Cities Public Television (KTCA)

Dance and dancing (Balinese)
Petrified Films, Inc.
Rainbow Video Prods.
Wesleyan Univ., World Music Arch.

Dance and dancing (Ballet)
Allen (John E.) Inc.
Blackwood (Christian) Prods., Inc.
Cantor (Arthur) Inc.
Center for Cuban Studies
Chicago Pub. Lib., Visual & Perf. Arts
Corinth Films/Corinth Video
Energy Productions
Natl. Archives of Canada
New York Pub. Lib., Perf. Arts Res. Ctr.,
    Dance Coll.
Pennebaker Associates, Inc.
Prelinger Assoc., Inc.
Pyramid Film and Video Corp.
Solaris Dance/Theatre/Video
TV Ontario
Univ. of Rochester, Dance Film Arch.
Univ. of Utah, Marriott Lib.
Vedo Films/Novacom Video

Dance and dancing (Ballroom)
Encore Video Prods., Inc.
Fish Films, Inc.
TV Ontario

Dance and dancing (Bar girls)
Farkas Studios, Ltd.

Dance and dancing (Barroom)
Petrified Films, Inc.

Dance and dancing (Bebop)

Rhapsody Films, Inc.

Dance and dancing (Belly dancing)
Spalla (Rick) Video Prods.
Spectral Comms.

Dance and dancing (Black)
Schomburg Ctr. for Res. in Black Culture

Dance and dancing (Brazilian)
Brazilian-American Cultural Inst.

Dance and dancing (Breakdancing)
DEC Film & Video

Dance and dancing (Cakewalk)
Allen (John E.) Inc.
Oregon State Univ., Archives

Dance and dancing (Cambodian Palace)
Camera Three Prods., Inc.

Dance and dancing (Canadian)
Canadian Film Institute
Natl. Archives of Canada
York Univ. Archives

Dance and dancing (Caribbean)
Mus. of Mod. Art of Latin America

Dance and dancing (Charleston)
Archive Film Prods., Inc.
Petrified Films, Inc.

Dance and dancing (Chinese)
Petrified Films, Inc.
Rainbow Video Prods.

Dance and dancing (Classical)
Vedo Films/Novacom Video

Dance and dancing (Clog)
Western Kentucky Univ., Folklife Arch.

Dance and dancing (Contests)
Fish Films, Inc.
Petrified Films, Inc.
TV Ontario

Dance and dancing (Country swing)
Petrified Films, Inc.

Dance and dancing (Cuban)
Center for Cuban Studies

Dance and dancing (Czech)
Slavonic Benev. Order. of State of Texas

Dance and dancing (Discotheques)
See Discotheques

Dance and dancing (Elizabethan)
Univ. of Waterloo, A-V Centre

Dance and dancing (Eskimo)
Alaska Native Heritage Film Project
KYUK-TV

Dance and dancing (Ethnic)
Camera Three Prods., Inc.

Dance and dancing (Exotic)
See Striptease

Dance and dancing (Filipino)
TV Ontario

Dance and dancing (Finnish)
Natl. Archives of Canada

Dance and dancing (Flamenco)
Petrified Films, Inc.

Dance and dancing (Folk)
Natl. Archives of Canada

Prelinger Assoc., Inc.
Univ. of Tex. at Austin, Benson Lat. Am.
    Coll.
See also Folk culture

Dance and dancing (Foxtrot)
Petrified Films, Inc.

Dance and dancing (French)
Soc. for French Amer. Cult. Svcs. & Educ.
    Aid

Dance and dancing (German)
Goethe Institute Atlanta
Goethe Institute Los Angeles
Goethe Institute San Francisco
Natl. Archives of Canada

Dance and dancing (Go-go)
Petrified Films, Inc.

Dance and dancing (Greek)
White Janssen, Inc.

Dance and dancing (Hawaiian)
White Janssen, Inc.

Dance and dancing (Hindu)
Petrified Films, Inc.

Dance and dancing (Hula)
Ackerman-Black Prods., Inc.
Bishop Mus., Visual Coll.
Dobovan Productions, Inc.
Dreamlight Images, Inc.
East-West Center
Petrified Films, Inc.

Dance and dancing (Indian)
Films of India

Dance and dancing (Indonesia)
Farkas Studios, Ltd.

Dance and dancing (Instruction)
Clark (Dick) Media Archives, Inc.
Cunningham Dance Foundation

Dance and dancing (International)
Film Education Institute
White Janssen, Inc.

Dance and dancing (Inuit)
Natl. Archives of Canada
TV Ontario

Dance and dancing (Irish)
TV Ontario
Petrified Films, Inc.

Dance and dancing (Japanese)
Rainbow Video Prods.

Dance and dancing (Jazz)
Chicago Pub. Lib., Visual & Perf. Arts
TV Ontario

Dance and dancing (Jitterbug)
Allen (John E.) Inc.
Archive Film Prods., Inc.
Film Education Institute
Fish Films, Inc.
Petrified Films, Inc.

Dance and dancing (Korean)
Rainbow Video Prods.
TV Ontario

Dance and dancing (Kurdish)
Canadian Broadcasting Corp.

Dance and dancing (Latin)
Prelinger Assoc., Inc.

Dance and dancing (Latvian)

Natl. Archives of Canada

Dance and dancing (Lebanese)
Univ. Coll. of Cape Breton, Beaton Inst.

Dance and dancing (Lindy hop)
Archive Film Prods., Inc.

Dance and dancing (Marathon)
Film Education Institute
Petrified Films, Inc.

Dance and dancing (Masai)
Wings Wildlife Prods. Inc.

Dance and dancing (Mexican)
Hayes Prods., Inc.
Imevision
Redes Cinevideo, S.A.

Dance and dancing (Modern)
Amer. Dance Festival
Blackwood (Christian) Prods., Inc.
Blackwood Prods., Inc.
Camera Three Prods., Inc.
Chicago Pub. Lib., Visual & Perf. Arts
Intermedia Arts Minnesota
New York Pub. Lib., Perf. Arts Res. Ctr.,
    Dance Coll.
Schomburg Ctr. for Res. in Black Culture
Univ. of Rochester, Dance Film Arch.
Vedo Films/Novacom Video
Wesleyan Cinema Archives
York Univ. Archives

Dance and dancing (Native American)
Cinema Guild
Energy Productions
Instituto Nacional Indigenista
Natl. Archives (RG 75)
Natl. Archives of Canada
New Mexico State Records Ctr. & Arch.
North Country Media Group
Petrified Films, Inc.
Prelinger Assoc., Inc.
Sheffield (Erin) Prods.
TV Ontario
Univ. of Utah, Marriott Lib.
Univ. of Wash. Press, Multimedia Div.
Univ. of Wis., Green Bay, Ctr. TV Prod.
Wings Wildlife Prods. Inc.

Dance and dancing (Nepalese)
White Janssen, Inc.

Dance and dancing (New Guinean)
Kinsey Institute

Dance and dancing (Nightclub)
Petrified Films, Inc.
See also Nightclubs

Dance and dancing (Nightclub adagio)
Allen (John E.) Inc.

Dance and dancing (Peruvian)
White Janssen, Inc.

Dance and dancing (Philippine)
Prelinger Assoc., Inc.

Dance and dancing (Polka)
Flower Films & Video

Dance and dancing (Popular)
Clark (Dick) Media Archives, Inc.

Dance and dancing (Portuguese)
White Janssen, Inc.

Dance and dancing (Proms)
See Proms

Dance and dancing (Ritual)
Country Dance & Song Society of
America
Petrified Films, Inc.
TV Ontario

Dance and dancing (Rumba)
Center for Cuban Studies

Dance and dancing (Scottish)
TV Ontario

Dance and dancing ("Shouter" churches)
Smithsonian Inst., Human Studies Film
Arch.

Dance and dancing (Social)
Schomburg Ctr. for Res. in Black Culture

Dance and dancing (Soviet Union)
Natl. Coun. of Amer.-Sov. Friendship

Dance and dancing (Square)
Archive Film Prods., Inc.
Country Dance & Song Society of
America
Petrified Films, Inc.
Source Stock Footage Lib., Inc.
Western Kentucky Univ., Folklife Arch.

Dance and dancing (Street)
Petrified Films, Inc.

Dance and dancing (Swiss)
Univ. of Wis., Green Bay, Ctr. TV Prod.

Dance and dancing (Tap)
Blackwood (Christian) Prods., Inc.
Blackwood Prods., Inc.
Camera Three Prods., Inc.
Chertok Associates Inc.
Chicago Pub. Lib., Visual & Perf. Arts
Direct Cinema Ltd.
Schomburg Ctr. for Res. in Black Culture
Wesleyan Cinema Archives

Dance and dancing (Thai)
Petrified Films, Inc.
Rainbow Video Prods.
White Janssen, Inc.

Dance and dancing (Third World)
ARC Videodance Coll./Eye on Dance
Coll.

Dance and dancing (Tibetan)
Office of Tibet
Petrified Films, Inc.
Samaya Foundation

Dance and dancing (Traditional)
Alaska Native Heritage Film Project
Allen (John E.) Inc.
Chicago Pub. Lib., Visual & Perf. Arts
Country Dance & Song Society of
America
East-West Center
Ethnic Folk Arts Center
TV Ontario
Wesleyan Univ., World Music Arch.

Dance and dancing (Twist)
Archive Film Prods., Inc.
Halcyon Days Prods.
Petrified Films, Inc.

Dance and dancing (Ukrainian)
Natl. Archives of Canada
TV Ontario

Dance and dancing (Uzbek)
Wesleyan Univ., World Music Arch.

Dance and dancing (Vanuatu, New Hebrides)
Smithsonian Inst., Human Studies Film
Arch.

Dance and dancing (Voodoo)
Archive Film Prods., Inc.
Energy Productions

Dance and dancing (Watusi, The)
Petrified Films, Inc.

Dance and dancing (Yugoslavian)
White Janssen, Inc.

Dandelions
Dreamlight Images, Inc.
Film Bank
See also Weeds

Dangerfield, Rodney
Banks Film Library
Spectral Comms.

Daniel, Price
Houston (Sam) Regional Lib. & Res. Ctr.
MacDonald, J. Fred

Daniels, Josephus
Natl. Archives (RG 24)

Daniels, William
Spectral Comms.

Danson, Ted
Spectral Comms.

Danysh, Joseph
De Saisset Museum

Dar es Salaam, Tanzania
Summit Films, Inc.

Darcy, Sam
Southern Calif. Lib. for Soc. Stud. & Res.

Daredevils
Archive Film Prods., Inc.
Film Bank
Film Search
Grinberg (Sherman) Film Libraries (West)
Navajo Tribe, Off. Broadcast Svcs.
Petrified Films, Inc.
SF•V Intl.
Spalla (Rick) Video Prods.
Twentieth Century-Fox Movietonews
See also Stunts

Darin, Bobby
Banks Film Library

Darmstadt, Germany (History and culture)
Petrified Films, Inc.

Darnell, Linda
Banks Film Library

Darrow, Clarence
Archive Film Prods., Inc.

Dating
MacDonald, J. Fred
Multi-Media Productions, Inc.
Picture Start, Inc.
Prelinger Assoc., Inc.

Davies, Marion

Archive Film Prods., Inc.

Davila, Bill
Spectral Comms.

Davis, Angela
Communist Party USA
Petrified Films, Inc.

Davis, Bette
Banks Film Library
Film Bank
Spectral Comms.

Davis, Billy
Appalshop Films, Inc.

Davis, Brad
Video Data Bank

Davis, Fred
Memphis State Univ. Libraries

Davis, John-John
U.S. Olympic Committee

Davis, Martha
Pathé Pictures, Inc.

Davis, Miles
Archive Film Prods., Inc.
Chertok Assoc., Inc.

Davis, Ossie
Villon Films

Davis, Ron
Blackwood Prods., Inc.

Davis, Sammy Jr.
Banks Film Library
Daphne Productions, Inc.
Las Vegas News Bureau
Pennebaker Associates, Inc.

Davis, Thulani
Paper Tiger TV

Dawson City, Yukon Territory
TV Ontario

Dawson City, Yukon Territory (History and culture)
Yukon Archives

Day care
Broad Street Prods.
TV Ontario
See also Babysitting; Child care

Day, Dennis
Shokus Video

Day, Doris
Banks Film Library
Halcyon Days Prods.

Day, Dorothy
Marquette Univ., Spec. Coll.

Day of the Dead (Mexico)
Instituto Nacional Indigenista

Dayton, June
Videobrary, Inc.

Dayton, Ohio (History and culture)
All-American Soap Box Derby
Petrified Films, Inc.
Prelinger Assoc., Inc.

Daytona Beach, Fla.
Postcards Unlimited
TV Ontario

Daytona Beach, Fla. (History and culture)
Archive Film Prods., Inc.

De Baca, Fernando
Univ. of Tex. at Austin, Benson Lat. Am.
Coll.

DeCarava, Roy
Port Washington Pub. Lib.

DeCordova, Frederick
Spectral Comms.

DeForest, Lee
Archive Film Prods., Inc.

DeGaulle, Charles
Film Education Institute
Halcyon Days Prods.
Natl. Archives (RG 200)
Univ. of Ill. Urbana-Champaign, Univ.
Arch.

DeKalb, Ill. (History and culture)
Northern Ill. Univ., Reg. Hist. Ctr.

De Kooning, Willem
Blackwood Prods., Inc.
Direct Cinema Ltd.
Mus. at Large, Ltd.

DeLorean, John
Daphne Productions, Inc.
Pennebaker Associates, Inc.

DeMarco, Antonio
Spectral Comms.

DeMille, Cecil B.
Archive Film Prods., Inc.
Natl. Archives (RG 47)

DeMilt, Charles
New York Pub. Lib., Perf. Arts Res. Ctr.,
Theatre on Film and Tape

DePalma, Brian
Daphne Productions, Inc.

de Rochemont, Richard
Univ. of Wyoming, Amer. Heritage Ctr.

de Rothschild, Philippe
Soc. for French Amer. Cult. Svcs. & Educ.
Aid

De Smet, S. Dak. (History and culture)
South Dakota State Lib.

De Valera, Eamon
March of Time

DeVincent, George
Port Washington Pub. Lib.

DeVito, Danny
Spectral Comms.

Dead Boys (Rock and roll band)
Blackwood (Christian) Prods., Inc.
Target Video

Dead Kennedys (Rock and roll band)
Target Video

NOTE: Access policies, availability and restrictions vary for each source. Please read each entry in full. Always consult "General Film and Videotape Collections" (page 599); these comprehensive collections contain material on every conceivable subject.

Dead Sea Scrolls
Pyramid Film and Video Corp.

Deaf-blindness
Amer. Foundation for the Blind
Perkins School for the Blind

Deafness
Amer. Foundation for the Blind
Bell (Alexander Graham) Assn.
Camera Three Prods., Inc.
Joyce Media, Inc.
Kentucky School for the Deaf
Nassau Comm. Coll. Lib.
Ohio Historical Soc.
Ohio State Univ., Dept. of Photog. &
    Cinema

Death and dying
Amer. Journal of Nursing Co.
Boston Family Inst.
Carousel Film & Video
Churchill Films
Concordia Publishing House
Coronet/MTI Film & Video
Fanlight Prods.
Film Bank
Film/Video Arts, Inc.
Filmakers Library
Hartley Film Found., Inc.
Historical Health Film Coll.
Inst. for Psychoanalysis
Lawren Prods., Inc.
Mass Media Ministries
Native Amer. Pub. Broad. Cons.
Natl. Funeral Directors Assn.
Natl. Press Photographers Assn., Inc.
Natl. Sudden Infant Death Syndrome
    Found.
Northern Ill. Univ., Reg. Hist. Ctr.
Paulist Productions
Phoenix Films and Video
Polymorph Films, Inc.
Prelinger Assoc., Inc.
Research Press
Smithsonian Inst., NMAH, Div. Med. Sci.
Université Laval, Svc. des Res.
    Pédagogiques

Death scenes
Film Bank
Fish Films, Inc.
Highway Safety Films, Inc.

Death Valley, Calif.
Beerger (Norman) Prods.
Energy Productions
Oregon Hist. Soc.
Petrified Films, Inc.

Debs, Eugene Victor
Cambridge Documentary Films, Inc.
Duke Univ., Perkins Lib.

Debutantes
Archive Film Prods., Inc.

Decathlon
U.S. Olympic Comm.

Declaration of Independence (U.S.)
Natl. Archives (RG 64)
Prelinger Assoc., Inc.

Decomposition
Dreamlight Images, Inc.

Decorations
CBS News Archives
Petrified Films, Inc.

Decorations (Holiday)
Film Bank

Dedications

Analogous Productions
Farkas Studios, Ltd.
Los Angeles Dept. of Water & Power
Natl. Archives of Canada
New York City Dept. of Rec. & Info.
    Svcs.
New York State Arch. & Rec. Admin.
Ohio Historical Soc.
Roosevelt (Franklin D.) Lib.
Twentieth Century-Fox Movietonews
Univ. of Utah, Marriott Lib.

Dedications (Airports)
Natl. Archives (RG 121)
Natl. Archives (RG 342)
Wright Brothers Coll.

Dedications (Buildings)
General Motors Corp.
Natl. Archives (RG 28)
Natl. Archives (RG 82)
Natl. Assn. for the Advancement of
    Colored People

Dedications (Memorials)
Amer. Legion
Churchill (Winston) Memorial and Library
Natl. Archives (RG 117)

Dedications (Monuments)
Natl. Archives (RG 24)
Univ. of Tex. at Austin, Barker Tex. Hist.
    Ctr.

Dee, Ruby
Villon Films

Dee, Sandra
Banks Film Library
Petrified Films, Inc.

Deer
Analogous Productions
Di Sesso (Moe) Wild Life Film Lib.
Dreamlight Images, Inc.
Echo Film Prods., Inc.
Energy Productions
Film Bank
Indiana State Comm. on Public Records
Metro Communications, Inc.
New Mexico State Records Ctr. & Arch.
North Country Media Group
Peak Productions, Inc.
Petrified Films, Inc.
Prelinger Assoc., Inc.
Source Stock Footage Lib., Inc.
Summit Films, Inc.
Swedberg (Jack)
TV Ontario
Woods N' Water Television Series

Defense Atomic Support Agency (U.S.)
Natl. Archives (RG 374)

Defense Production Act of 1950
Natl. Archives (RG 48)

Defense, Dept. of (U.S.)
Natl. Archives (RG 330)
U.S. Dept. of Defense, Motion Media Rec.
    Ctr.

Degas, Edgar
Blackwood Prods., Inc.

Delano, California (History and culture)
Estuary Press
United Farm Workers of America (UFW)

Delaunay, Sonia
Albright-Knox Art Gallery

Delaware (History and culture)
Delaware State Div. of Hist. & Cult. Aff.

Delhi, India
Petrified Films, Inc.

Delhi, India (History and culture)
Archive Film Prods., Inc.
Univ. of Wisconsin — Extension

Delia B (Ship)
Natl. Archives (RG 59)

Delicatessens
Petrified Films, Inc.

Della Francesca, Piero
Amer. Federation of the Arts

Delmarva Peninsula (Del.-Md.-Va.)
Preview Media

Del Moral, Enrique
Southern Calif. Inst. of Architecture

Deltas
Film Bank

Democratic Party
Harriman Comm. Ctr.
Johnson (Lyndon Baines) Library
MacDonald, J. Fred
Natl. Archives (RG 200)
Purdue Univ., Public Affairs Video Arch.
Roosevelt (Franklin D.) Lib.
Univ. of Toledo, Univ. Arch.

Demolition
CBS News Archives
Dreamlight Images, Inc.
Film Bank
Film Search
Petrified Films, Inc.
Stock House
Timesteps Prods., Inc.

Demolition derbies
Analogous Productions
Petrified Films, Inc.
Wallen (Dick) Prods.

Demonstrations (Political)
Alabama State Dept. of Arch. & Hist.
Allen (John E.) Inc.
Archives of Ontario
Baird (Bill) Inst.
CBS News Archives
Camino Film Projects
Carleton Prods. Inc.
Communist Party USA
Creative Film Society
Estuary Press
Film Bank
Film/Audio Services, Inc.
Fish Films, Inc.
Hearst Metrotone News
Homosexual Info. Ctr.
Intl. Gay and Lesbian Archives
King (Dr. Martin Luther, Jr.) Ctr.
Labor Video Project
MacDonald, J. Fred
Media Bus
Memphis State Univ. Libraries
Mus. & Hist. Div., City of Sacramento
Natl. Abortion Rights Action League
Natl. Archives (RG 185)
Natl. Archives (RG 200)
Natl. Archives (RG 220)
Natl. Archives of Canada
Natl. Right to Life Committee
News On Film
Office of the Gay & Lesbian March on
    Wash.
Payne, Roz
People's Fund
Petrified Films, Inc.
Pro-Life Action League
Public Interest Video Network

Raindance Foundation
Richter Productions
San Francisco Bay Area TV News Arch.
Smithsonian Inst., NMAH, Div. Polit.
    Hist.
Southern Calif. Lib. for Soc. Stud. & Res.
Southwest Film/Video Archives, SMU
State Hist. Soc. of Iowa
Student Struggle for Soviet Jewry
Taminent Lib./Wagner Labor Arch.
Third World Newsreel
Twentieth Century-Fox Movietonews
Univ. of Mich., Mich. Hist. Coll.
Wilmington Coll. Peace Res. Ctr.
See also Civil disobedience

Dempsey, Jack
Grinberg (Sherman) Film Libraries (West)
Marquette Univ., Spec. Coll.
Natl. Archives (RG 21)

Deneuve, Catherine
Spectral Comms.

Denmark
Pyramid Film and Video Corp.
Yue-Sai Kan, Inc.

Denmark (History and culture)
Archive Film Prods., Inc.
Natl. Archives/Natl. AV Ctr.
Twentieth Century-Fox Movietonews

Dentists and dentistry
Academy of Health Sciences, U.S. Army
Altschul Group
Amer. Dental Assn.
CBS News Archives
Historical Health Film Coll.
Milner-Fenwick, Inc.
Nassau Comm. Coll. Lib.
Natl. Archives/Natl. AV Ctr.
Northcoast Communication, Inc.
Ohio State Univ., Dept. of Photog. &
    Cinema
Petrified Films, Inc.
Prelinger Assoc., Inc.
Univ. of Southern Calif., Film & Video
    Dist. Ctr.

Denver
Cimarron Productions
Cinenet (Cinema Network)
Film Bank
Summit Films, Inc.

Denver (History and culture)
Colorado Historical Society
Datura Productions
Denver Pub. Lib., Western Hist. Dept.
Petrified Films, Inc.

Department of
See the department's "subject" area
    (e.g., Department of Education is found
    under Education, Department of [U.S.])

Department stores
Petrified Films, Inc.
Prelinger Assoc., Inc.

Department stores (Japan)
Japan External Trade Organization

Depo Provera
Intl. Women's Day Video Fest.

Deportations
CBS News Archives

Depression (1930s)
Allen (John E.) Inc.
Analogous Productions
Archive Film Prods., Inc.
Canadian Filmmakers Dist. West

DEC Film & Video
Direct Cinema Ltd.
East Tenn. State Univ., Arch. of
    Appalachia
Film Bank
Forsher (James) Prods. & Archives, Inc.
MacDonald, J. Fred
March of Time
Miles Educ. Film Prods.
Natl. Archives (RG 130)
Natl. Archives of Canada
Oregon Hist. Soc.
Petrified Films, Inc.
Prelinger Assoc., Inc.
South Carolina Humanities Res. Ctr.
Southern Calif. Lib. for Soc. Stud. & Res.
Tamiment Lib./Wagner Labor Arch.
Timesteps Prods., Inc.
Twentieth Century-Fox Movietonews

Dermatology
Emory Medical Television Network
IMS Creative Communications

Derricks
See Oil industry

Des Moines, Iowa
Wallen (Dick) Prods.

Desert rats
Petrified Films, Inc.

Deserts
Aitken (Len) Productions, Inc.
British Info. Svcs., Radio & TV Div.
CBS News Archives
Cinenet (Cinema Network)
Creative Video, Inc.
Dorn (Larry) Associates
Dreamlight Images, Inc.
Echo Film Prods., Inc.
Energy Productions
Film Bank
Film Search
Forsher (James) Prods. & Archives, Inc.
Grinberg (Sherman) Film Libraries (West)
Image Bank
Jewell (Stuart) Productions
New Mexico State Records Ctr. & Arch.
Petrified Films, Inc.
Preview Media
SF•V Intl.
Source Stock Footage Lib., Inc.
Spectral Comms.
Summit Films, Inc.
TV Ontario
Telemation Productions
Twentieth Century-Fox Movietonews
Video Tape Library, Ltd.
Video West

Design
See Industrial design

Detectives
Archive Film Prods., Inc.
CBS News Archives
Prelinger Assoc., Inc.
See also Police

Detergents
Prelinger Assoc., Inc.

Detroit
Dreamlight Images, Inc.
Energy Productions
Film Bank

Detroit (History and culture)
Archive Film Prods., Inc.

Cranbrook Acad. of Arts
DEC Film & Video
General Motors Corp.
MacDonald, J. Fred
Natl. Archives (RG 200)
Natl. Railway Historical Soc.
New Day Films
Petrified Films, Inc.
Prelinger Assoc., Inc.
Univ. of Mich., Mich. Hist. Colls.
Wayne State Univ., Arch. Labor & Urb.
    Aff.
Wayne State Univ., Folklore Arch.

Deukmejian, George
KCRA-TV
Spectral Comms.

Devane, William
Spectral Comms.

Developing countries
See Third World

Developmentally disabled
Altschul Group
Apertura
Assn. for Retarded Citizens
Birmingham Pub. Lib., Media Svcs. Dept.
Campbell Films, Inc.
Council for Exceptional Children
Finley (Stuart) Inc.
Goodwill Industries of America
Green Mountain Post Films
Latham Foundation
Lawren Prods., Inc.
New Day Films
Phoenix Films and Video
Research Press
Special Olympics Intl.
Univ. of West Fla., Hum. Res. Vid. Lib.

Devil's Island (History and culture)
March of Time

Devilbiss, Connie
Port Washington Pub. Lib.

Devine, Andy
Shokus Video

Devito, Cara
Port Washington Pub. Lib.

Devlin, Bernadette
Intermedia Arts Minnesota

Devo (Rock and roll band)
Target Video

Dew drops
Dreamlight Images, Inc.
Film Bank

Dewdney, Christopher
Giorno Poetry Systems Inst.

Dewey, George
Lib. of Congress, M/B/RS

Dewey, John
Archive Film Prods., Inc.

Dewey, Thomas E.
MacDonald, J. Fred
New York State Arch. & Rec. Admin.
Roosevelt (Franklin D.) Lib.
Univ. of Rochester Lib., Rare Books &
    Spec. Coll.

Deyglun, Henri

Natl. Archives of Canada

Deyneka, Peter Sr.
Wheaton Coll., Billy Graham Ctr.

Diabetes
Altschul Group
Amer. Diabetes Assn.
Emory Medical Television Network
Miles Corporate Archive
Milner-Fenwick, Inc.
Polymorph Films, Inc.
Pyramid Film and Video Corp.
Washington Univ., Brown Schl. of Soc.
    Work

**Diablo Canyon, Calif. (History and
culture)**
Petrified Films, Inc.

Diagrams
Rosebush Visions Corp.

Diamond Head, Hawaii
Petrified Films, Inc.

Diamonds
Petrified Films, Inc.
Rosebush Visions Corp.

Diapers
Analogous Productions

Diatoms
Dreamlight Images, Inc.

Díaz, Porfirio
Archivo Historico Cinematografico
Filmoteca de la UNAM

Di Biumo, Giuseppe Panza
Long Beach Mus. of Art

Dickens, Punch
Natl. Archives of Canada

Dickies (Rock and roll band)
Target Video

Dickinson, Angie
Banks Film Library
Daphne Productions, Inc.
Spectral Comms.

Dickinson, Emily
Intellimation

Dictators
Allen (John E.) Inc.

Diddley, Bo
Canadian Filmmakers Dist. Centre
Pennebaker Associates, Inc.
Southern Calif. Blues Soc.

Didrickson, Babe
Film Education Institute

Diefenbaker, John
Natl. Archives of Canada

Dienes, Sari
Amer. Federation of the Arts

Dieting
CBS News Archives
Milner-Fenwick, Inc.
Prelinger Assoc., Inc.

Dietitians
TV Ontario

Dietrich, Frank
Video Data Bank

Dietrich, Marlene
Archive Film Prods., Inc.
Las Vegas News Bureau
Natl. Archives/Natl. AV Ctr.
UCLA Film & Television Archive

Dietz, Donald
Port Washington Pub. Lib.

Digestive system
Milner-Fenwick, Inc.

Dignitaries (Visits to U.S.)
Natl. Archives (RG 24)
Natl. Archives (RG 59)
Natl. Archives (RG 119)
Natl. Archives (RG 200)
Natl. Archives (RG 306)
See also Diplomats; Royalty

Dignitaries (Visits to Mexico)
Televisa, S.A.

Dikes
Petrified Films, Inc.

Diller, Phyllis
Spalla (Rick) Video Prods.
Spectral Comms.

Dillinger, John
Archive Film Prods., Inc.

Dillon, C. Douglas
Natl. Archives (RG 59)

Dillon, S.C. (History and culture)
Petrified Films, Inc.

Dils (Rock and roll band)
Target Video

DiMaggio, Joe
Archive Film Prods., Inc.
Grinberg (Sherman) Film Libraries (West)

Dine, Jim
Albright-Knox Art Gallery
Blackwood Prods., Inc.
Video Data Bank
Walker Art Ctr.

Diners
See Restaurants (Diners)

Dining rooms and halls
Film Bank
Petrified Films, Inc.

**Dinkelsbühl, Germany (History and
culture)**
German Info. Ctr., Film Lib.

Dinners
Twentieth Century-Fox Movietonews

Dinners (Testimonial)
Banks Film Library

Dinnerware
Prelinger Assoc., Inc.

Dinosaurs
Amer. Mus. Nat. Hist. Film Arch.
Film Bank
Fish Films, Inc.
Forsher (James) Prods. & Archives, Inc.
Pyramid Film and Video Corp.

NOTE: Access policies, availability and restrictions vary for each source. Please read each entry in full. Always consult "General Film and Videotape Collections" (page 599); these comprehensive collections contain material on every conceivable subject.

Dionne quintuplets
See Quintuplets (Dionne)

Diphtheria
Historical Health Film Coll.

Diplomats
Allen (John E.) Inc.
CBS News Archives
See also Embassies

DiPrima, Diane
Giorno Poetry Systems Inst.

Dire Straits (Rock and roll band)
Clark (Dick) Media Archives, Inc.

Dirigibles
See Aircraft (Lighter-than-air)

Dirksen, Everett McKinley
Dirksen (E.M.) Cong. Lead. Res. Ctr.
West Virginia Dept. of Culture & Hist.

Disabled children
Broad Street Prods.
Lawren Prods., Inc.
U.S. Committee for UNICEF
UNICEF, Div. Info. & Pub. Aff.

Disabled people
Amer. Occupational Therapy Assn.
Amer. Public Transit Assn.
Amer. Red Cross
CBS News Archives
Campbell Films, Inc.
Campus Film Distributors Corp.
Carousel Film & Video
Channel L Working Group
Coe Film Assoc., Inc.
Coronet/MTI Film & Video
Direct Cinema Limited
Film Bank
Films for the Humanities and Sciences
Focus Intl. Inc.
Fund for Human Dignity, Inc.
Goodwill Industries of Amer.
Inst. for Psychoanalysis
Intermedia Arts Minnesota
Intl. Ctr. for the Disabled
Landscape Architecture Found.
Latham Foundation
Marquette Univ., Spec. Coll.
Mass Media Ministries
Multi-Focus, Inc.
Natl. Archives (RG 12)
Natl. Archives (RG 58)
Natl. Archives (RG 220)
Natl. Archives of Canada
Natl. Easter Seal Society
Natl. Film Board of Canada
Rehab. Inst. of Chicago
TV Ontario
Timesteps Prods., Inc.
Univ. of Southern Calif., Film & Video
    Dist. Ctr.
Univ. of West Fla., Hum. Res. Vid. Lib.
Video In
Washington Univ., Brown Schl. of Soc.
    Work
Women Make Movies, Inc.
World Wide Pictures, Inc.
See also Blindness; Deafness

Disabled people and sports
Amer. Cancer Soc., Inc.
Amer. Foundation for the Blind
Athletic Institute
Natl. Wheelchair Athletic Assn.
Peak Productions, Inc.
Pyramid Film and Video Corp.
Special Olympics Intl.
Spectral Comms.
TV Ontario
Univ. of Wash. Press, Multimedia Div.

DiSalle, Michael V.
Ohio Historical Soc.

Disarmament
See Arms control

Disaster planning
Amer. Nuclear Society
Edison Electric Institute
Institute of Makers of Explosives
Natl. Archives (RG 235)
Natl. Archives (RG 311)

Disasters
Amer. Red Cross
Analogous Productions
Archive Film Prods., Inc.
Assoc. Gen. Contractors of America
CBS News Archives
CTV Television Network
Cable News Network Library
Carleton Prods. Inc.
Chisholm (Jack) Film Productions
Em Gee Film Library
Film Bank
Forsher (James) Prods. & Archives, Inc.
Grinberg (Sherman) Film Libraries (West)
Halcyon Days Prods.
Hearst Metrotone News
Los Angeles News Service
March of Time
Mariners' Museum
Minn. Dept. of Public Safety Film Lib.
Natl. Archives (RG 26)
Natl. Archives (RG 70)
Natl. Archives (RG 80)
Natl. Archives (RG 111)
Natl. Archives (RG 200)
Natl. Archives (RG 255)
Natl. Archives (RG 311)
Natl. Archives (RG 342)
Natl. Fire Protection Assn.
Natl. Oceanic & Atmospheric Admin.
Petrified Films, Inc.
Prelinger Assoc., Inc.
SF•V Intl.
Salvation Army, Natl. Comm. Dept.
Shields Archival
State Hist. Soc. of North Dakota
Timesteps Prods., Inc.
Twentieth Century-Fox Movietonews
Univ. of Ill. Urbana-Champaign, Univ.
    Arch.
Univ. of So. Carolina, Newsfilm Lib.
Univ. of Wash., Educ. Media Coll.
Vermont Hist. Soc.
Video Tape Library, Ltd.
West Virginia Dept. of Culture & Hist.
Worldwide Television News
See also Accidents; Earthquakes; Fires;
    Floods; Hurricanes; Tornadoes;
    Volcanoes

Disciples of Christ
See Religion (Disciples of Christ)

Discotheques
Film Bank
Kesser Stock Footage Library
MacDonald, J. Fred
Petrified Films, Inc.
See also Bars; Nightclubs

Diseases
Amer. Cancer Soc., Inc.
CBS News Archives
Centers for Disease Control
Emory Medical Television Network
Films for the Humanities and Sciences
Milner-Fenwick, Inc.
Narcotics Education, Inc.
Nassau Comm. Coll. Lib.
Natl. Archives (RG 90)
Natl. Archives (RG 100)
Natl. Archives (RG 102)

Natl. Archives of Canada
Natl. Kidney Foundation, Inc.
Prelinger Assoc., Inc.
South Dakota State Lib.
United Nations Ctr. for Human
    Settlements
Visual Information Systems
See also Health; Health education;
    Medicine; Patient education films and
    videotapes; specific diseases

Dishwashers
Petrified Films, Inc.

Disney, Walt
Archive Film Prods., Inc.
Disada Productions' Disney Mem. Lib.
MacDonald, J. Fred
Video Resources N.Y., Inc.

Disney World, Florida
TV Ontario

Disneyland, Calif.
Energy Productions
Source Stock Footage Lib., Inc.

Displaced persons
See Refugees

Displays (Data)
Inter Video/TTI

Di Suvero, Mark
Amer. Federation of the Arts
Blackwood Prods., Inc.

Ditchdiggers
Petrified Films, Inc.

Diving
ABC Sports, Inc.
Analogous Productions
Archive Film Prods., Inc.
Athletic Institute
British Info. Svcs., Radio & TV Div.
CBS News Archives
Energy Productions
Film Bank
Intl. Swimming Hall of Fame
Kesser Stock Footage Library
Lemorande Prod. Co.
Second Line Search
Sportsfilm
Timesteps Prods., Inc.
Video Tape Library, Ltd.

Diving (Cliff)
Energy Productions
Petrified Films, Inc.
Source Film & Tape Lib., Inc.

Diving (College)
NCAA Productions

Diving (Deep sea)
See Skin diving

Diving (High)
Petrified Films, Inc.

Diving (Instruction)
NCAA Productions

Diving machines
Cousteau Society
See also Bathyspheres

Divorce
Amer. Assn. for Counseling &
    Development
CBS News Archives
Coronet/MTI Film & Video
DEC Film & Video
March of Time

Mass Media Ministries
New Day Films
Prelinger Assoc., Inc.
Twentieth Century-Fox Movietonews
Washington Univ., Brown Schl. of Soc.
    Work
Windsor Prod. Corp.

Dixieland music
See Music (Dixieland jazz)

Dixon, Joseph M.
Natl. Archives (RG 75)

Dixon-Hinson, Mary Alice
Southern Calif. Inst. of Architecture

Djerassi, Carl
Amer. Chemical Soc.

Dmytryk, Edward
Alternative Information Network

Dobbs, Ben
Southern Calif. Lib. for Soc. Stud. & Res.

Docks
See Harbors

Doctors
Blue Sky Comms., Inc.
CBS News Archives
Cabscott Broadcast Prods.
Cambridge Documentary Films, Inc.
Center for Biomedical Comms.
Emory Medical Television Network
Film Bank
Hooper (Josh) Prods., Inc.
Johns Hopkins Univ., School of Medicine
MacDonald, J. Fred
March of Time
Medical College of Pa.
Metro Communications, Inc.
Natl. Archives of Canada
Ohio State Univ., Dept. of Photog. &
    Cinema
Petrified Films, Inc.
Prelinger Assoc., Inc.
Timesteps Prods., Inc.
UCLA Behavioral Sci. Media Lab.
Video Genesis, Inc.

Doctors (Women)
Fanlight Prods.
Historical Health Film Coll.
Medical College of Pa., Arch. & Spec.
    Coll. Women in Medicine

Doe, John (Musician)
Target Video

Dog food
Film Bank
Prelinger Assoc., Inc.

Dog grooming salons
Petrified Films, Inc.

Dog racing
Kesser Stock Footage Library
Source Stock Footage Lib., Inc.

Dog shows
Amer. Kennel Club Lib.
Analogous Productions
Sportsfilm
Twentieth Century-Fox Movietonews

Dog sledding
Alaska Video Prods.
Analogous Productions
Chiappetta Prods.
Dobbs (Jeff) Prods.
Film Bank
KYUK-TV

646

Petrified Films, Inc.
Prelinger Assoc., Inc.
Sportsfilm
Summit Films, Inc.
TV Ontario
Univ. of Alaska, Fairbanks, Alaska Motion
　Picture Arch.
Visuart, Inc.

Dog weight pull competitions
Peak Productions, Inc.

Dogfights
See World War I (Dogfights)

**Dogrib, Northwest Territories (History
　and culture)**
Northwest Territories Archives

Dogs
Amer. Kennel Club Lib.
Amer. Veterinary Medical Assn.
Analogous Productions
Ducks Unlimited, Inc.
Energy Productions
Film Bank
Film Search
Fish Films, Inc.
Forsher (James) Prods. & Archives, Inc.
March of Time
Media West, Inc.
New York Pub. Lib., Rare Books &
　Manuscripts Div.
Northern Ill. Univ., Reg. Hist. Ctr.
Oregon State Univ., Archives
Petrified Films, Inc.
Prelinger Assoc., Inc.
TV Ontario
Video I-D, Inc.
Video Resources N.Y., Inc.

Dogs (Performing)
Petrified Films, Inc.
Prelinger Assoc., Inc.
See also Animals (Performing)

Dogs (Police)
Handel Film Corp.

Doherty, William
Camino Film Projects

D'Olivo, Marcelo
Southern Calif. Inst. of Architecture

Dollmaking
Rainbow Video Prods.
TV Ontario

Dolls
Film Bank
Video Resources N.Y., Inc.

Dolls (Kachina)
Native Amer. Pub. Broad. Cons.

Dolphins
Animal Welfare Institute
Caribbean Images, Ltd.
Cousteau Society
Dreamlight Images, Inc.
Latham Foundation
Marineland of Florida
Minnesota Zoo
Moonlight Productions
Ocean Images
Petrified Films, Inc.

Domestic violence
DEC Film & Video
FMS Productions

Groupe Intervention Video
Intermedia Arts Minnesota
Intl. Women's Day Video Fest.
March of Dimes Birth Defects Found.
Media Project
New Day Films
New Jersey Network
New Orleans Video Access Ctr.
O.D.N. Productions, Inc.
Third World Newsreel
Women in Focus
Xchange TV

Domingo, Placido
Spectral Comms.

Dominica (History and culture)
Idera Films
U.S. Committee for UNICEF

Dominican Republic
Preview Media

**Dominican Republic (Contemporary
　issues)**
Icarus-Tamouz Media, Inc.

**Dominican Republic (History and
　culture)**
Archive Film Prods., Inc.
Film/Audio Services, Inc.
Icarus-Tamouz Media, Inc.
Mus. of Mod. Art of Latin America
Natl. Archives (RG 200)

Don Juan
Archive Film Prods., Inc.

Donahue, Phil
Cincinnati Hist. Soc.
Daphne Productions, Inc.
Spectral Comms.

Donahue, Troy
Banks Film Library

Donaldson, Sam
Daphne Productions, Inc.

Donegan, Lonnie
Archive Film Prods., Inc.

Donkeys
Film Bank
Petrified Films, Inc.

Donlevy, Brian
UCLA Film & Television Archive

**Donner Lake, Calif. (History and
　culture)**
Petrified Films, Inc.

**Donner Pass, Calif. (History and
　culture)**
Petrified Films, Inc.

Dooley, Thomas A.
Univ. of Missouri-St. Louis

Doolittle, Jimmy
Film Education Institute

Doorknobs
Petrified Films, Inc.

Doormen
CBS News Archives

Doors
CBS News Archives

Doors (Glass)
Natl. Glass Assn.

Doors (Slamming)
Film Bank

Doors, The (Rock and roll band)
Clark (Dick) Media Archives, Inc.

Dopsie, Rockin'
Los Angeles Blues Archives
Tulane Univ., Amistad Res. Ctr.

Dorazio, Piero
Albright-Knox Art Gallery

Dorsey, Tommy and Jimmy
Archive Film Prods., Inc.
MacDonald, J. Fred

Double-decker buses
See Buses (Double-decker)

Double-Dutch
Varied Directions, Inc.

Doughnut dunking
Film Bank

Doughnut making
TV Ontario

Douglas, Eric
Spectral Comms.

Douglas, Kirk
Banks Film Library
Spectral Comms.

Douglas, William O.
Banks Film Library
California Inst. of Tech., Inst. Arch.
Center for Pacific Northwest Studies

Douglass, Frederick
Pyramid Film and Video Corp.

Dover (Cliffs of)
Archive Film Prods., Inc.
Petrified Films, Inc.

Doves
Di Sesso (Moe) Wild Life Film Lib.
Indiana State Comm. on Public Records
Petrified Films, Inc.
TV Ontario
Wings Wildlife Prods. Inc.

Dowdey, Kathleen
Port Washington Pub. Lib.

Down's syndrome
Direct Cinema Limited
Groupe Intervention Video

Downes, Rackstraw
Video Data Bank

Downey, Morton Sr.
MacDonald, J. Fred

Downs, Amy
Monday, Wednesday, Friday Video Club

Downs, Hugh
Christopher Closeup
Daphne Productions, Inc.
Shokus Video

Dowsing
Film Bank

Singer-Sharrette Traditional Healing Films

Dracula
Archive Film Prods., Inc.

Draft (Military)
See Selective Service System (U.S.)

Draft resistance
See Vietnam antiwar movement

Draftspersons
Petrified Films, Inc.
TV Ontario

Drag racing
See Automobiles (Drag racing)

Dragonflies
Dreamlight Images, Inc.
Film Bank

Dragons
Petrified Films, Inc.

Dragons (Chinese)
Film Bank
Petrified Films, Inc.

Dreams
Jung (C.G.) Foundation
Native Amer. Pub. Broad. Cons.

**Dresden, East Germany (History and
　culture)**
Archive Film Prods., Inc.

Dreyfuss, Richard
Spectral Comms.

Drinking
CBS News Archives
Film Bank
White Janssen, Inc.

Drisch, Russell
Port Washington Pub. Lib.

Drive-in restaurants
See Restaurants (Drive-ins)

Drive-in theaters
See Theaters (Drive-in)

Driver education
AIMS Media
Amer. Automobile Assn., FTS
Amer. Driver & Traffic Safety Educ. Assn.
Bell Canada
Calif. Highway Patrol Acad. Media Center
GPN
General Motors Corp.
Highway Safety Films, Inc.
Intl. Film Bureau, Inc.
MacDonald, J. Fred
March of Time
Minn. Dept. of Public Safety Film Lib.
Natl. Archives (RG 70)
Natl. Safety Council
Ohio State Univ., Dept. of Photog. &
　Cinema
Prelinger Assoc., Inc.
Saskatchewan Indian Cultural Ctr.
Streamline Film Archives
Tire Industry Safety Council
See also Drunk driving; Safety films and
　videotapes

Driveways
Petrified Films, Inc.

NOTE: Access policies, availability and restrictions vary for each source. Please read each entry in full. Always consult "General Film and Videotape Collections" (page 599); these comprehensive collections contain material on every conceivable subject.

Driving
Cinenet (Cinema Network)
Dreamlight Images, Inc.
Fish Films, Inc.
General Motors Corp.
Petrified Films, Inc.
Prelinger Assoc., Inc.
Stegman Productions
Volkswagen of America, Inc.
White Janssen, Inc.
See also Automobiles; Driver education;
Drunk driving

Driving (Point-of-view shots)
See Point-of-view shots (Driving)

Droughts
CARE
Calif. Dept. of Water Resources
Documentary Educational Resources
Finley (Stuart) Inc.
Natl. Archives (RG 69)
Natl. Archives (RG 96)
San Francisco Bay Area TV News Arch.
UNICEF, Div. Info. & Pub. Aff.
World Monitor

Drug abuse
ABC News
AIMS Media
Addiction Research Foundation of Ontario
Amer. Chemical Soc.
Apertura
Archive Film Prods., Inc.
Athletic Institute
Boston Comm. Access & Prog. Found.
CBS News Archives
Calif. Highway Patrol Acad. Media Center
Center for Humanities, Inc.
Channel L Working Group
Chicago Access Corp.
Cinema Guild
Coronet/MTI Film & Video
FMS Productions
Filmfair Communications
GPN
Hazelden Found. Educ. Materials
Historical Health Film Coll.
Mass Media Ministries
McDonald's Corp.
Media Guild
Minn. Dept. of Public Safety Film Lib.
Motivational Media, Inc.
Multi-Media Productions, Inc.
Narcotics Education, Inc.
Natl. Archives (RG 90)
Natl. Archives (RG 170)
Natl. Safety Council
PRIDE
Phoenix Films and Video
Prelinger Assoc., Inc.
Pyramid Film and Video Corp.
Rogers (Will) Institute
San Francisco Bay Area TV News Arch.
Saskatchewan Indian Cultural Ctr.
Signal Press
Smithsonian Inst., NMAH, Div. Med. Sci.
Toughlove
U.S. Tennis Assn.
United Training Media
Univ. of West Fla., Hum. Res. Vid. Lib.
Visual Information Systems
See also Addiction; Cocaine; Crack
(Cocaine); Drug culture; Narcotics;
Opium; Substance abuse; Twelve-step
programs

Drug culture
Film/Video Arts, Inc.
Fish Films, Inc.
Ludlow (Fitz Hugh) Memorial Library
MacDonald, J. Fred
Petrified Films, Inc.
Prelinger Assoc., Inc.
See also Acid trips

Drug stores
Film Bank
Petrified Films, Inc.
Prelinger Assoc., Inc.
TV Ontario

Drummond, Bulldog
Archive Film Prods., Inc.

Drums
Film Bank
Fish Films, Inc.
See also Music

Drunk driving
AIMS Media
Addiction Research Foundation of Ontario
Amer. Automobile Assn., FTS
General Motors Corp.
Highway Safety Films, Inc.
Mothers Against Drunk Driving
Motor Vehicle Manufacturers Assn.
Narcotics Education, Inc.
Natl. Archives (RG 416)
Natl. Safety Council
PRIDE
Prelinger Assoc., Inc.
RID (Remove Intoxicated Drivers)
Rogers (Will) Institute
UCLA Behavioral Sci. Media Lab.
Univ. of Vermont, Bailey/Howe Lib.
Univ. of Wis., Green Bay, Ctr. TV Prod.
Varied Directions, Inc.
See also Breathalyzer machines; Driver
education

Dry, Carolyn
Southern Calif. Inst. of Architecture

Dry cleaners
Petrified Films, Inc.

Dryers
MacDonald, J. Fred
Prelinger Assoc., Inc.

Drysdale, Don
Banks Film Library

Dublin, Ireland
Preview Media

Dublin, Ireland (History and culture)
Archive Film Prods., Inc.

Dubois, Diane
Videobrary, Inc.

Dubos, René
Université Laval, Svc. des Res.
Pédagogiques

Duchamp, Marcel
Amer. Federation of the Arts
Blackwood Prods., Inc.
Electronic Arts Intermix

Duchamp-Villon, Raymond
Blackwood Prods., Inc.

Ducks
Cinenet (Cinema Network)
Di Sesso (Moe) Wild Life Film Lib.
Ducks Unlimited, Inc.
Film Bank
KD Enterprises Prods.
March of Time
Minnesota Zoo
New Mexico State Records Ctr. & Arch.
Petrified Films, Inc.
Snyder (Bill) Films, Inc.
TV Ontario
Video I-D, Inc.
Wings Wildlife Prods. Inc.

Dude ranches
Moving Media
Petrified Films, Inc.
Preview Media
Twentieth Century-Fox Movietonews

Duff, James
Pennsylvania State Arch.

Dukakis, Michael
Daphne Productions, Inc.

Duke, Angier Biddle
Duke Univ., Perkins Lib.

Duke, Patty
Banks Film Library

Dulcimers
Appalshop Films, Inc.

Dulles, John Foster
Natl. Archives (RG 200)
Univ. of Ill. Urbana-Champaign, Univ.
Arch.

Duluth, Minn. (History and culture)
Petrified Films, Inc.

Dumbwaiters
Analogous Productions

Dumont, Nat
Banks Film Library

Dump trucks
See Trucks (Dump)

Dumps
Finley (Stuart) Inc.
Northern Ill. Univ., Reg. Hist. Ctr.

Dune buggies
Film Bank
Petrified Films, Inc.
Pyramid Film and Video Corp.

Dunes (Sand)
See Sand dunes

Dunham, Katherine
Schomburg Ctr. for Res. in Black Culture

Dunn, David
Southern Calif. Inst. of Architecture

Dunn, Douglass
Blackwood Prods., Inc.

Dunne, Irene
Christopher Closeup

Dunning, George
Camera Three Prods., Inc.

Duplé, Nicole
Université Laval, Svc. des Res.
Pédagogiques

Duplessis, Maurice
Natl. Archives of Canada

Durante, Jimmy
Banks Film Library
Halcyon Days Prods.
Natl. Archives/Natl. AV Ctr.
Parker (Kit) Films
Shokus Video

Dürer, Albrecht
Goethe Institute Atlanta

Durham, Eddie
Rhapsody Films, Inc.

Durocher, Leo
Banks Film Library

Durst, Lavada
Univ. of Tex. at Austin, Barker Tex. Hist.
Ctr.

Duryea, Dan
Banks Film Library

Dust
Twentieth Century-Fox Movietonews

Dust Bowl (1930s)
Film Bank
March of Time
Natl. Archives (RG 96)
Natl. Archives (RG 145)
Natl. Archives/Natl. AV Ctr.
Prelinger Assoc., Inc.

Dust storms
See Storms (Dust)

Dutch East Indies
See Indonesia

Duvalier, François ("Papa Doc")
Film/Audio Services, Inc.
Northstar Prods.

Duvall, Shelly
Spectral Comms.

Dyer, Alexander B.
Natl. Archives (RG 24)

Dylan, Bob
Pennebaker Associates, Inc.

Dynamite
Energy Productions
Natl. Archives (RG 70)
Source Stock Footage Lib., Inc.
See also Explosions; Explosives

Dyslexia
March of Dimes Birth Defects Found.

Dystonia
UCLA Behavioral Sci. Media Lab.

ESP (Extrasensory perception)
Cinema Guild

Eagles
Charisma Prods., Ltd./Visual Motion
Di Sesso (Moe) Wild Life Film Lib.
Dobbs (Jeff) Prods.
Echo Film Prods., Inc.
Energy Productions
Film Search
Indiana State Comm. on Public Records
Mass. Audubon Society
New Film Co., Inc.
North Country Media Group
Orion Post Production
Petrified Films, Inc.
Summit Films, Inc.
Swedberg (Jack)
Video I-D, Inc.
Wings Wildlife Prods. Inc.

Eames, Charles and Ray
Southern Calif. Inst. of Architecture

Earhart, Amelia
Archive Film Prods., Inc.
Film Education Institute
Forsher (James) Prods. & Archives, Inc.
Natl. Archives (RG 28)
Petrified Films, Inc.
Prelinger Assoc., Inc.
Pyramid Film and Video Corp.

Ears
Prelinger Assoc., Inc.

Earth (Planet)
Archive Film Prods., Inc.
CBS News Archives
Charisma Prods., Ltd./Visual Motion
Dreamlight Images, Inc.
Energy Productions
Film Bank
Impact Audio Visual
Intl. Telecommunications Satellite Org.
Kesser Stock Footage Library
Media Guild
NASA, Johnson Space Ctr., Film & Video
  Dist. Lib.
Natl. Archives (RG 307)
Petrified Films, Inc.
Prelinger Assoc., Inc.
Rosebush Visions Corp.
Second Line Search
Twentieth Century-Fox Movietonews
WQED/Pittsburgh

Earth sciences
Britannica Films & Video
Center for Humanities, Inc.
Coronet/MTI Film & Video
Educational Images, Ltd.
Los Alamos Natl. Lab.
Mariners' Museum
Media Guild
Natl. Science Foundation
Phoenix Films and Video
Université Laval, Cinémathèque

Earthmoving equipment
Film Bank
LeTourneau College Archives
See also Bulldozers; Heavy equipment

Earthquakes
Allen (John E.) Inc.
Archive Film Prods., Inc.
CBS News Archives
Cinema Guild
Film Bank
Grinberg (Sherman) Film Libraries (East)
Grinberg (Sherman) Film Libraries (West)
Los Angeles Dept. of Water & Power
Timesteps Prods., Inc.
Twentieth Century-Fox Movietonews
Video Tape Library, Ltd.
Worldwide Television News
See also Disasters

Earthquakes (Alaska)
Center for Pacific Northwest Studies

Earthquakes (Chile)
Ontario Film Institute

Earthquakes (Coalinga, Calif., 1983)
Los Angeles News Service

Earthquakes (Friuli, Italy, 1976)
Italian Cultural Institute

Earthquakes (Guatemala)
Jewell (Stuart) Productions

Earthquakes (Guatemala, 1976)
Salvation Army, Natl. Comm. Dept.

Earthquakes (Japan, 1923)
Allen (John E.) Inc.

Earthquakes (Los Angeles, 1933)
Grinberg (Sherman) Film Libraries (East)

Earthquakes (Mexico, 1985)

Imagen y Sonido Independiente, S.A.
Salvation Army, Natl. Comm. Dept.

Earthquakes (Mexico, 1987)
Northstar Prods.

Earthquakes (Nicaragua, 1972)
United Nations Ctr. for Human
  Settlements
Univ. of Wisconsin — Extension

Earthquakes (San Francisco, 1906)
Allen (John E.) Inc.
Film Education Institute
Forsher (James) Prods. & Archives, Inc.
Grinberg (Sherman) Film Libraries (West)

East Africa (History and culture)
Johnson (Martin & Osa) Safari Museum
Natl. Archives (RG 200)

East Berlin
See Berlin, East

East Indians
TV Ontario

East Los Angeles
Spectral Comms.

East Los Angeles (History and culture)
Cinema Guild
Creative Film Society
Petrified Films, Inc.

East River (New York City)
Petrified Films, Inc.

East Timor (Contemporary issues)
Alternative Information Network

Easter
Petrified Films, Inc.
St. Augustine Hist. Soc.
Twentieth Century-Fox Movietonews

Easter Island
Cousteau Society
Film Bank

Easter Island (History and culture)
Mus. of Mod. Art of Latin America

Easter lilies
Energy Productions

Easter parades
See Parades (Easter)

Eastern Europe (History and culture)
Film/Audio Services, Inc.
Intl. Historic Films, Inc.
North Central Forest Exp. Sta.
Yivo Inst. for Jewish Research

Eastman, George
Archive Film Prods., Inc.
Hearst Metrotone News

Eastwood, Clint
Banks Film Library
Spectral Comms.
Mus. of Mod. Art, Dept. of Film

Easy Aces, The
Videobrary, Inc.

Eating
Applegate Entertainment
CBS News Archives
Dreamlight Images, Inc.

Energy Productions
Film Bank
Film Education Institute
Fish Films, Inc.
Metro Communications, Inc.
Petrified Films, Inc.
Prelinger Assoc., Inc.
TV Ontario

Eating disorders
Amer. Anorexia/Bulimia Assn. Inc.
Boston Family Inst.
Cambridge Documentary Films, Inc.
Fanlight Prods.
Hazelden Found. Educ. Materials
Narcotics Education, Inc.
Research Press

Eatman, Irv
Archive Film Prods., Inc.

Eber, Jose
Spectral Comms.

Ebsen, Buddy
Banks Film Library

Eccles, Marriner S.
Univ. of Utah, Marriott Lib.

Eclipses
CBS News Archives
Film Bank
Natl. Archives (RG 78)
Natl. Archives (RG 434)
TV Ontario
Twentieth Century-Fox Movietonews

Ecology
ABC News
AIMS Media
Acid Rain Foundation, Inc.
Apertura
Appalshop Films, Inc.
Archives of Ontario
Barr Films
Bennett (Joel) Prods.
Bullfrog Films, Inc.
CBS News Archives
Calif. Dept. of Water Resources
Canadian Filmmakers Dist. Centre
Canadian Filmmakers Dist. West
Canyon Cinema, Inc.
Caribbean Images, Ltd.
Carleton Prods. Inc.
Carousel Film & Video
Center for Humanities, Inc.
Cinema Guild
Coe Film Assoc., Inc.
Coronet/MTI Film & Video
Cousteau Society
Ducks Unlimited, Inc.
Educational Film & Video Project
Educational Images, Ltd.
Em Gee Film Library
Environmental Action Coalition
Estuary Press
Film/Audio Services, Inc.
Films for the Humanities and Sciences
Finley (Stuart) Inc.
Florentine Films
GPN
Greenpeace, U.S.A.
Higgins (Alfred) Prods.
Imevision
Interlock Media Associates
Intl. Film Bureau, Inc.
Los Angeles Dept. of Water & Power
Mass. Audubon Society
Media Guild
Natl. Archives (RG 151)

Natl. Archives (RG 267)
Natl. Archives (RG 412)
Natl. Archives of Canada
Natl. Film Board of Canada
Natl. Science Foundation
Nature Conservancy
New Film Co., Inc.
New York State Dept. of Env. Cons.
Northstar Prods.
Palisades Wildlife Film Library
Phoenix Films and Video
Public Interest Video Network
Pyramid Film and Video Corp.
Raindance Foundation
Redes Cinevideo, S.A.
Richter Productions
Snyder (Bill) Films, Inc.
Soc. for French Amer. Cult. Svcs. & Educ.
  Aid
Southern Calif. Inst. of Architecture
TV-UNAM
Université Laval, Cinémathèque
Univ. of Alberta, Boreal Inst. for Northern
  Studies
Univ. of Calif., Berkeley, Bancroft Lib.
Univ. of Calif., Ext. Media Ctr.
Univ. of Wis., Green Bay, Ctr. TV Prod.
V/tape
Video In
WQED/Pittsburgh
World Monitor
Worldwide Television News
See also Acid rain; Animals (Endangered
  species); Conservation; Pollution;
  Toxic waste

Economic development
Archivo de Imagenes en Movimiento
Cinema Guild
Inst. for Local Self-Reliance
Natl. Archives (RG 59)

Economic development (Third World)
California Newsreel
Idera Films
Inter-American Foundation
Oxfam America

Economic Opportunity, Office of (U.S.)
Natl. Archives (RG 381)

Economics
AIMS Media
Alternative Information Network
Amer. Citizenship Ctr.
Archivo de Imagenes en Movimiento
Barr Films
Britannica Films & Video
Bullfrog Films, Inc.
CBS News Archives
California Newsreel
Carousel Film & Video
Cinema Guild
Committee to Restore the Constitution
DEC Film & Video
Films for the Humanities and Sciences
First Run/Icarus Films, Inc.
GPN
General Motors Corp.
Hoover Institution
Idera Films
Intermedia Arts Minnesota
Media Guild
Natl. Archives/Natl. AV Ctr.
Phoenix Films and Video
Prelinger Assoc., Inc.
Richter Productions
U.S. Chamber of Commerce
Université Laval, Cinémathèque
V/tape
Video-Documentary Clearinghouse

NOTE: Access policies, availability and restrictions vary for each source. Please read each entry in full. Always consult "General Film and Videotape Collections" (page 599); these comprehensive collections contain material on every conceivable subject.

Video-SIG
Wayne State Univ., Arch. Labor & Urb.
   Aff.
World Monitor

Ecorse, Mich. (History and culture)
Univ. of Mich., Mich. Hist. Colls.

Ecuador
Canadian Broadcasting Corp.
Film Bank
Kesser Stock Footage Library

Ecuador (Contemporary issues)
DEC Film & Video

Ecuador (History and culture)
Archive Film Prods., Inc.
DEC Film & Video
Intl. Assn. of Independent Producers
Natl. Archives (RG 59)
Natl. Archives (RG 286)

Eddy, Nelson
Archive Film Prods., Inc.

Edelson, Mary Beth
Albright-Knox Art Gallery

Eden, Barbara
Spectral Comms.

Ederle, Gertrude
Grinberg (Sherman) Film Libraries (West)

Edgerton, Harold E.
Mass. Inst. of Tech., MIT Museum

Edinburgh, Scotland (History and culture)
Archive Film Prods., Inc.

Edison, Sweet
Rhapsody Films, Inc.

Edison, Thomas Alva
Archive Film Prods., Inc.
Edison Natl. Historic Site
Forsher (James) Prods. & Archives, Inc.
Grinberg (Sherman) Film Libraries (West)
Handel Film Corp.
Hearst Metrotone News
Natl. Archives/Natl. AV Ctr.
Petrified Films, Inc.
Prelinger Assoc., Inc.
Timesteps Prods., Inc.

Edmonton, Alberta (History and culture)
Prov. Arch. of Alberta

Edsall, John T.
Amer. Chemical Soc.

Education
Amer. ORT Federation
Anti-Defamation League of B'nai B'rith
Appalachian State Univ., Eury Coll.
Appalshop Films, Inc.
Archivo de Imagenes en Movimiento
Birch (John) Society
Bullfrog Films, Inc.
Cable News Network Library
Campbell Films, Inc.
Campus Film Distributors Corp.
Carleton Prods. Inc.
Carousel Film & Video
Chisholm (Jack) Film Productions
Coe Film Assoc., Inc.
East-West Center
Education Development Ctr., Inc.
Educators for Social Responsibility
Estuary Press
German Info. Ctr., Film Lib.
High/Scope Educ. Res. Found.

Hoover Institution
Inst. of Electrical & Electronics Eng.
Intermedia Arts Minnesota
Intl. Women's Day Video Fest.
KYUK-TV
Kartemquin Films
Kentucky Dept. of Libraries & Archives
MALDEF
Mankind Research Found., Inc.
March of Time
Maryknoll Fathers & Brothers
Media Guild
Metropolitan Council for Educ. Opport.
Native Amer. Pub. Broad. Cons.
Natl. Archives (RG 12)
Natl. Archives (RG 33)
Natl. Archives (RG 69)
Natl. Archives (RG 75)
Natl. Archives (RG 80)
Natl. Archives (RG 111)
Natl. Archives (RG 200)
Natl. Archives (RG 208)
Natl. Archives (RG 235)
Natl. Archives (RG 286)
Natl. Archives of Canada
Natl. Archives/Natl. AV Ctr.
Natl. Assn. of Secondary Schl. Principals
Natl. Catholic Educational Assn.
Natl. Science Foundation
Ohio State Univ., Dept. of Photog. &
   Cinema
Perkins School for the Blind
Phoenix Films and Video
Prelinger Assoc., Inc.
Prov. Arch. of Newfoundland & Labrador
Psychological and Educational Films
Radcliffe Coll., Schlesinger Lib.
Research Press
Twentieth Century-Fox Movietonews
U.S. Committee for UNICEF
Université de Moncton, Centre d'Études
   Acad.
V/tape
Vidéo Femmes
Video In
Video-SIG
Vidéographe Inc., Le
Villon Films
White Star Prof. Film Svcs., Inc.
World Monitor
Worldwide Television News
See also Classrooms; Colleges and
   universities; High schools; Schools;
   Students; Teachers and teaching

Education (Bilingual)
MALDEF

Education (Catholic)
Natl. Catholic Educational Assn.

Education (Christian)
Mass Media Ministries

Education (Germany)
Goethe Institute Atlanta

Education (Medical)
Natl. Archives (RG 80)
Natl. Library of Medicine

Education (Soviet Union)
Educational Film & Video Project
MacDonald, J. Fred

Education, Department of (U.S.)
Natl. Archives (RG 12)
Natl. Archives (RG 441)

Education, Office of (U.S.)
Natl. Archives (RG 12)

Educational films and videotapes
AIMS Media
Abilene Christian University

Allen (John E.) Inc.
Altschul Group
Amer. Alliance for Health, Phys. Ed., Rec.
   & Dance Arch.
Amer. Arch. of the Factual Film
Amer. Bakers Assn.
Amer. Chemical Soc.
Amer. Dental Assn.
Amer. Truck Historical Society
Archive Film Prods., Inc.
Asia Society
Athletic Institute
Bailey Productions, Inc.
Barr Films
Benchmark Films, Inc.
Britannica Films & Video
Bullfrog Films, Inc.
Canadian Film Institute
Canal 11
Canyon Cinema, Inc.
Carousel Film & Video
Center for Humanities, Inc.
Centro Para el Desarrollo y Mejoramiento
   de la Enseñanza
Children's Television Workshop
Chisholm (Jack) Film Productions
Churchill Films
Colorado Historical Society
Columbia Univ., Teachers College
Coronet/MTI Film & Video
Creative Venture Films
Educational Images, Ltd.
Educators for Social Responsibility
Emporia State Univ., Spec. Coll.
Film Bank
Filmfair Communications
Films for the Humanities and Sciences
Films Incorporated
Finley (Stuart) Inc.
Fish Films, Inc.
Folger Shakespeare Library
French Lib. in Boston
Future Farmers of America
GPN
Handel Film Corp.
Hazelden Found. Educ. Materials
Hearst Metrotone News
Hershey Foods Corp.
Higgins (Alfred) Prods.
High/Scope Educ. Res. Found.
Imageways, Inc.
Indiana Univ., Audio-Visual Center
Inst. of Electrical & Electronics Eng.
Intellimation
Intl. Fashion Video Library
Intl. Film Bureau, Inc.
Intl. Mus. of Photography
Klein (Walter J.) Co., Ltd.
Lib. of Congress, M/B/RS
MacDonald, J. Fred
McDonald's Corp.
Massachusetts Archives
Mathematical Assn. of America
Media Guild
Modern Talking Picture Service
Motor Vehicle Manufacturers Assn.
Moviecraft, Inc.
Movietime, Inc. Archives
Multi-Focus, Inc.
Narcotics Education, Inc.
Natl. Archives (RG 33)
Natl. Archives (RG 69)
Natl. Archives (RG 90)
Natl. Archives (RG 111)
Natl. Archives (RG 170)
Natl. Archives (RG 200)
Natl. Archives (RG 242)
Natl. Archives of Canada
Natl. Archives/Natl. AV Ctr.
Natl. Assn. for Sport & Phys. Ed.
Natl. Dairy Council
Natl. Dance Assn.
Natl. Geographic Soc. Stock Footage Lib.
Natl. Science Foundation
New Mexico State Records Ctr. & Arch.

New York City Dept. of Rec. & Info.
   Svcs.
Ohio State Univ., Dept. of Photog. &
   Cinema
Peralta Colleges TV
Petrified Films, Inc.
Phoenix Films and Video
Physicians for Social Responsibility
Prelinger Assoc., Inc.
Prov. Arch. of Alberta
Rudra Press
Snyder (Bill) Films, Inc.
Society for Nutrition Education
Society of Manufacturing Engineers
Streamline Film Archives
TV-UNAM
Trans-World Films, Inc.
U.S. Chamber of Commerce
Union Pacific Railroad
Université Laval, Cinémathèque
Université Laval, Svc. des Res.
   Pédagogiques
Univ. of Akron, Arch. of Hist. of Amer.
   Psychol.
Univ. of Arizona, Film Coll.
Univ. of Calif., Ext. Media Ctr.
Univ. of Hawaii at Manoa, Wong Ctr.
Univ. of Kansas
Univ. of Pittsburgh, Univ. Ctr. Inst. Res.
Video-SIG
Voyager Co.
WGBH Educational Foundation
Wayfarer Publications
YMCA of the U.S.A. Archives
See also Training films and videotapes

Educational television
See Television (Educational)

Edward VIII
UCLA Film & Television Archive

Edwards Air Force Base, Calif.
Los Angeles News Service

Edwards, Blake
Spectral Comms.

Edwards, Harry
Pyramid Film and Video Corp.

Edwards, Teddy
Rhapsody Films, Inc.

Edwards, Vincent
Banks Film Library

Eels
Dreamlight Images, Inc.
Summit Films, Inc.
TV Ontario

Effigies
CBS News Archives

Eggs
Academy of Health Sciences, U.S. Army
Oregon State Univ., Archives
Wings Wildlife Prods. Inc.

Egrets
Archive Film Prods., Inc.
Kesser Stock Footage Library
Minnesota Zoo

Egypt
British Info. Svcs., Radio & TV Div.
Cousteau Society
Energy Productions
Film Bank
Film Search
Jewell (Stuart) Productions
Preview Media
Rosebush Visions Corp.
Source Stock Footage Lib., Inc.

650

Unicorn Projects
World Monitor
Yue-Sai Kan, Inc.

Egypt (History and culture)
Allen (John E.) Inc.
Archive Film Prods., Inc.
Film/Audio Services, Inc.
Films for the Humanities and Sciences
Intl. Film Bureau, Inc.
Intl. Film Foundation
Johns Hopkins Univ./Population Comm.
　　Svcs.
Lib. of Congress, M/B/RS
Middle East Institute
Natl. Archives (RG 59)
Natl. Archives (RG 170)
Northstar Prods.
Petrified Films, Inc.
Prelinger Assoc., Inc.
U.S. Committee for UNICEF
UNICEF, Div. Info. & Pub. Aff.
United Nations Ctr. for Human
　　Settlements
Villon Films
World Monitor

Egyptian Sinai
Preview Media

Eichelberger, Robert L.
Duke Univ., Perkins Lib.

Eichenberg, Fritz
Marquette Univ., Spec. Coll.

Eichmann, Adolf
Natl. Jewish Arch. of Broadcasting

Eiffel Tower (Paris)
Archive Film Prods., Inc.
Film Bank

Eiffel Tower (Paris) (History and culture)
Petrified Films, Inc.

Einstein, Albert
Archive Film Prods., Inc.
Blackwood Prods., Inc.
California Inst. of Tech., Inst. Arch.
Forsher (James) Prods. & Archives, Inc.
Goethe Institute Atlanta

Eisenhower, Dwight David
Archive Film Prods., Inc.
Banks Film Library
Eisenhower (Dwight D.) Library
Film Bank
Halcyon Days Prods.
Hearst Metrotone News
Illinois State Hist. Lib.
Kennedy (John F.) Library
MacDonald, J. Fred
Natl. Archives (RG 12)
Natl. Archives (RG 59)
Natl. Archives (RG 111)
Natl. Archives (RG 200)
Natl. Archives (RG 220)
Natl. Archives (RG 342)
Oregon Hist. Soc.
Pennsylvania State Archives
Petrified Films, Inc.
Prelinger Assoc., Inc.
Timesteps Prods., Inc.
Univ. of Ill. Urbana-Champaign, Univ.
　　Arch.
Univ. of Toronto, Univ. Arch.
White Janssen, Inc.

Eisenhower, Mamie Doud

Pennsylvania State Archives

Eisenhower, Milton
Eisenhower (Dwight D.) Library

Eisenstaedt, Alfred
Amer. Federation of the Arts

Eisler, Edwin
Inst. for Psychoanalysis

Eisner, Thomas
Film/Audio Services, Inc.
Florentine Films

Ekstein, Rudolf
Inst. for Psychoanalysis

El Paso, Tex. (History and culture)
El Paso Community College
Petrified Films, Inc.

El Salvador
World Monitor

El Salvador (Contemporary issues)
Amer. Security Council Foundation
Camino Film Projects
Cinema Guild
Comm. in Sol. People of El Salvador
DEC Film & Video
Deep Dish TV
El Salvador Media Project
First Run/Icarus Films, Inc.
New York City Labor Film Club
News On Film
Northstar Prods.
Oxfam America
Skylight Pictures

El Salvador (History and culture)
Baker (Fred) Film & Video Co.
Camino Film Projects
Canadian Filmmakers Dist. Centre
DEC Film & Video
Democracy in Communication
El Salvador Media Project
First Run/Icarus Films, Inc.
Idera Films
Johns Hopkins Univ./Population Comm.
　　Svcs.
Labor Video Project
Latina, S.A. de C.V.
Maryknoll Fathers & Brothers
Natl. Archives (RG 59)
New Time Films, Inc.
Northstar Prods.
Univ. of Tex. at Austin, Benson Lat. Am.
　　Coll.
Vidéographe Inc., Le
World Monitor

Elder, J.D.
Schomburg Ctr. for Res. in Black Culture

Eldridge, Roy
Rhapsody Films, Inc.

Elections
Archive Film Prods., Inc.
C-SPAN (Cable Satellite Public Affairs
　　Network)
CBS News Archives
See also Political campaign commercials;
　　Political campaigns; Political
　　conventions; Politics and government;
　　Presidential elections (U.S.); Voting

Electric chairs
Archive Film Prods., Inc.
See also Capital punishment; Executions

Electrical engineering
Hewlett-Packard Co.
Inst. of Electrical & Electronics Eng.

Electricians
TV Ontario

Electricity
Amer. Nuclear Society
Appalachian State Univ., Eury Coll.
Baltimore Mus. of Industry
British Info. Svcs., Radio & TV Div.
CBS News Archives
Creative Venture Films
Eastern Washington State Historical Soc.
Edison Electric Institute
Electric Power Research Institute
Fabulous Footage Inc.
Fish Films, Inc.
Inst. of Electrical & Electronics Eng.
Natl. Archives (RG 16)
Natl. Archives (RG 43)
Natl. Archives (RG 70)
Natl. Archives (RG 142)
Natl. Archives (RG 305)
Natl. Archives of Canada
Natl. Archives/Natl. AV Ctr.
North Carolina Div. of Arch. & Hist.
Petrified Films, Inc.
Prelinger Assoc., Inc.
TV Ontario
U.S. Council for Energy Awareness
See also Energy; Power plants

Electrocardiography (EKG)
Northcoast Communication, Inc.
See also Technology (Medical)

Electrodynamics
Prelinger Assoc., Inc.

Electroencephalography (EEG)
Film Bank
Northcoast Communication, Inc.
See also Technology (Medical)

Electronic instruments
Hewlett-Packard Co.

Electronics
Antique Wireless Assn., Inc.
CBS News Archives
Inst. of Electrical & Electronics Eng.
Natl. Archives of Canada
Natl. Archives/Natl. AV Ctr.
Prelinger Assoc., Inc.

Electronics (Consumer)
Electronic Industries Assn.

Electronics (Production)
Petrified Films, Inc.

Electronics industry
California Newsreel
Cineworks Prods. Inc.
Encore Video Prods., Inc.
Northstar Prods.

Electronics stores
TV Ontario

Electrotechnology
Inst. of Electrical & Electronics Eng.

Elephant seals
Bullfrog Films, Inc.
Moonlight Productions

Elephants
Archive Film Prods., Inc.

British Info. Svcs., Radio & TV Div.
Circus World Mus. Lib. & Res. Ctr.
Devillier Donegan Ent.
Di Sesso (Moe) Wild Life Film Lib.
Dreamlight Images, Inc.
Film Bank
Innerquest Communications Corp.
Jewell (Stuart) Productions
Johnson (Martin & Osa) Safari Museum
Kesser Stock Footage Library
Miller (David Lee) Prods.
Petrified Films, Inc.
Prelinger Assoc., Inc.
Quinn (Bill) Prods.
Summit Films, Inc.
Wings Wildlife Prods. Inc.

Elevators
CBS News Archives
Dreamlight Images, Inc.
Film Bank
Fish Films, Inc.
Petrified Films, Inc.
Prelinger Assoc., Inc.

Elías Calles, Plutarco
Archivo Fotografico y Cinematografico
　　Abítia
Archivo Historico Cinematografico

Eliot, T.S.
Intellimation

Elizabeth I, Queen
Archive Film Prods., Inc.

Elizabeth II, Queen
Archive Film Prods., Inc.
Banks Film Library
Film Bank
Halcyon Days Prods.
Natl. Archives (RG 119)
Petrified Films, Inc.
Purdue Univ., Public Affairs Video Arch.
Univ. of Ill. Urbana-Champaign, Univ.
　　Arch.
Univ. of Toronto, Univ. Arch.

Elizabeth, N.J.
Port Authority of New York & New Jersey

Elk
Amer. Motion Pictures
Cinenet (Cinema Network)
Di Sesso (Moe) Wild Life Film Lib.
Dreamlight Images, Inc.
Echo Film Prods., Inc.
Energy Productions
Film Bank
Jewell (Stuart) Productions
Minnesota Zoo
New Mexico State Records Ctr. & Arch.
North Country Media Group
Peak Productions, Inc.
Petrified Films, Inc.
Source Stock Footage Lib., Inc.
Summit Films, Inc.

**Ellesmere Island, Northwest Territories
　(History and culture)**
Peary-MacMillan Arctic Museum

Ellington, Duke
Archive Film Prods., Inc.
Chertok Assoc., Inc.
Pathé Pictures, Inc.
Petrified Films, Inc.

Ellis Island, N.Y.
New Jersey Network
Petrified Films, Inc.

NOTE: Access policies, availability and restrictions vary for each source. Please read each entry in full. Always consult "General Film and Videotape Collections" (page 599); these comprehensive collections contain material on every conceivable subject.

Ellis Island, N.Y. (History and culture)
Allen (John E.) Inc.
Fish Films, Inc.
House Found. for the Arts
Lib. of Congress, M/B/RS
Natl. Ctr. for Jewish Film
Petrified Films, Inc.
Timesteps Prods., Inc.

Ellis, Albert
Psychological and Educational Films

Ellis, Perry
Daphne Productions, Inc.

Ellora Caves, India
Petrified Films, Inc.

Ellsberg, Daniel
Ideal Comms., Inc.

Ellsworth, Lincoln
Natl. Archives (RG 200)

Elman, Mischa
Archive Film Prods., Inc.

Elmira, N.Y.
Telltales Associates Inc.

Elmslie, Kenward
Giorno Poetry Systems Inst.

Elves
Film Bank

Em, David
Long Beach Mus. of Art

Embalming
Natl. Funeral Directors Assn.

Embassies
Archive Film Prods., Inc.
CBS News Archives
Petrified Films, Inc.
See also Diplomats

Embry, Queen Sylvia
Rhapsody Films, Inc.

Embryology
IMS Creative Communications
Nassau Comm. Coll. Lib.

Embryos
Film Bank

Emergency management
See Disaster planning

Emergency medicine
Academy of Health Sciences, U.S. Army
Amer. Heart Assn.
Amer. Red Cross
Calif. Highway Patrol Acad. Media Center
Film Bank
Films for the Humanities and Sciences
IMS Creative Communications
Newsreel Video Service
Petrified Films, Inc.
Prelinger Assoc., Inc.
Visual Information Systems
See also Ambulances; Paramedics;
   Vehicles (Emergency)

Emerson, Faye
Shokus Video

Emotions
Petrified Films, Inc.
Prelinger Assoc., Inc.

Emphysema
Narcotics Education, Inc.

Empire State Building (New York City)
TV Ontario
Unicorn Projects

Empire State Building (New York City)
   (History and culture)
Archive Film Prods., Inc.
Dreamlight Images, Inc.
Energy Productions
Petrified Films, Inc.
Prelinger Assoc., Inc.

Employment of the Handicapped,
   President's Committee on
Natl. Archives (RG 220)

Emshwiller, Ed
Port Washington Pub. Lib.

Emu
Farkas Studios, Ltd.

Endangered species
See Animals (Endangered species)

Endocrinology
Nassau Comm. Coll. Lib.

Endoscopy
Nassau Comm. Coll. Lib.

Enemas
Nassau Comm. Coll. Lib.

Energy
AIMS Media
Agee (James) Film Project
Amer. Nuclear Society
Barr Films
Blackwood Prods., Inc.
Bullfrog Films, Inc.
CBS News Archives
Calif. Dept. of Transportation
Carleton Prods. Inc.
Center for Humanities, Inc.
Cinema Guild
Coronet/MTI Film & Video
Eastern Washington State Historical Soc.
Echo Film Prods., Inc.
Edison Electric Institute
Electric Power Research Institute
Fabulous Footage Inc.
Film Bank
Finley (Stuart) Inc.
General Motors Corp.
Glenbow Mus. Arch.
Green Mountain Post Films
Hayes Prods., Inc.
Hoover Institution
Imperial Oil Ltd.
Inst. for Local Self-Reliance
Inst. of Electrical & Electronics Eng.
Intermedia Arts Minnesota
Los Angeles Dept. of Water & Power
Mass. Audubon Society
Media Guild
Moody Inst. of Science
Natl. Archives (RG 16)
Natl. Archives (RG 43)
Natl. Archives (RG 70)
Natl. Archives (RG 115)
Natl. Archives (RG 305)
Natl. Assn. of Conservation Dists.
Natl. Science Foundation
Pennebaker Associates, Inc.
Phoenix Films and Video
Prelinger Assoc., Inc.
Public Interest Video Network
Source Stock Footage Lib., Inc.
Stanford Univ. Lib., Dept. of Spec. Coll.
   & Univ. Arch.
TV Ontario
U.S. Committee for UNICEF
Université Laval, Cinémathèque
V/tape

See also Coal and coal industry;
   Conservation (Energy); Electricity;
   Natural gas; Nuclear energy and power;
   Oil industry; Power plants

Energy (Alternative)
Bullfrog Films, Inc.
Calif. Dept. of Transportation
DEC Film & Video
Inst. of Electrical & Electronics Eng.
TV-UNAM
United Nations Ctr. for Human
   Settlements
Video Tape Library, Ltd.

Energy (Japan)
Japan External Trade Organization

Energy (Solar)
Canadian Filmmakers Dist. Centre
Cinema Guild
Electric Auto Assn.
Film Bank
Film/Audio Services, Inc.
Finley (Stuart) Inc.
Green Mountain Post Films
Handel Film Corp.
Northstar Prods.
Quest Productions, Inc.
Southern Calif. Inst. of Architecture
TV Ontario

Energy (Tidal power)
Cinema Guild

Energy (Wind)
Video Tape Library, Ltd.

Energy, Department of (U.S.)
Natl. Archives (RG 434)
Natl. Archives (Stock Film Coll.)

Engineering
Calif. Dept. of Transportation
Engineering Societies Lib.
Film Bank
Inst. of Electrical & Electronics Eng.
Los Alamos Natl. Lab.
Louisiana Tech Univ., Eng. Film Res. Ctr.
Natl. Archives (RG 48)
Natl. Archives/Natl. AV Ctr.
Natl. Science Foundation
Prelinger Assoc., Inc.
Smithsonian Inst., NMAH, Div. Eng. &
   Ind.
TV Ontario
Twentieth Century-Fox Movietonews
Univ. of Minn. Libs., Manuscripts Div.
Univ. of Wash., Educ. Media Coll.
Univ. of Waterloo, A-V Centre
See also Aeronautical engineering; Civil
   engineering; Electrical engineering

Engineering management
Stanley Consultants

Engines
CBS News Archives

Engines (Diesel)
General Motors Corp.

Engines (Internal combustion)
Natl. Archives (RG 70)
Prelinger Assoc., Inc.

Engines (Jet)
Prelinger Assoc., Inc.

Engines (Steam turbine)
Natl. Archives (RG 178)

Engines (Turbo-prop)
Prelinger Assoc., Inc.

Engines (V-8)
Prelinger Assoc., Inc.

England
See United Kingdom

Englewood, Colo. (History and culture)
New Haven Colony Hist. Soc.

English as a Second Language (ESL)
Borough of Manhattan Comm. Coll.

English Canadians
Natl. Archives of Canada

English Channel (History and culture)
Archive Film Prods., Inc.

Eno, Brian
Monday, Wednesday, Friday Video Club
Video Data Bank

Enola Gay
Ohio Historical Soc.

Entertainment industry
Cable News Network Library
Carleton Prods. Inc.
Charisma Prods., Ltd./Visual Motion
Creative Video, Inc.
Eden Entertainment, Inc.
Hearst Metrotone News
Las Vegas News Bureau
MTV Networks
March of Time
Petrified Films, Inc.
Spalla (Rick) Video Prods.
Twentieth Century-Fox Movietonews
See also Celebrities; Hollywood; Motion
   pictures (Industry); World War II (U.S.,
   Entertainment industry)

Entomology
Educational Images, Ltd.

Environment
See Ecology

Environmental Protection Agency (U.S.)
Natl. Archives (RG 412)
Natl. Archives (Stock Film Coll.)

Environmental studies
Intl. Film Bureau, Inc.

Epidemics
Amer. Red Cross
Historical Health Film Coll.

Episcopalians
See Religion (Episcopalian)

Epstein, Jacob
Blackwood Prods., Inc.

Epstein, Mitch
Port Washington Pub. Lib.

Equal Rights Amendment (ERA)
Smithsonian Inst., NMAH, Div. Polit.
   Hist.
Univ. of Utah, Marriott Lib.

Equestrian sports
ABC Sports, Inc.
Amer. Morgan Horse Assn., Inc.
Amer. Saddlebred Horse Assn.
Edwards, H. M.
Intl. Arabian Horse Assn.
Kesser Stock Footage Library
Natl. Archives of Canada
Petrified Films, Inc.
Southwest Prods., Inc.
U.S. Olympic Comm.
White Janssen, Inc.

See also Horse racing; Horse shows;
   Horses

Erhard, Ludwig
Archive Film Prods., Inc.

Erie Canal, N.Y.
New York State Dept. of Econ. Devel.

Erie, Lake (Canada-U.S.)
Hi-Tech Productions

Erie, Pa. (History and culture)
TV Ontario

Erikson, Erik
Inst. for Psychoanalysis

Ernst, Max
Blackwood Prods., Inc.

Erosion
Bullfrog Films, Inc.
Finley (Stuart) Inc.
Natl. Archives (RG 35)
Natl. Archives (RG 96)
Natl. Assn. of Conservation Dists.
Panhandle-Plains Hist. Museum

Erotic dancers (Male)
Crystal Pyramid Prods.

Erotica
Canadian Gay Archives
Canyon Cinema, Inc.
Dreamlight Images, Inc.
Em Gee Film Library
Femme Distribution, Inc.
Focus Intl. Inc.
Kinsey Institute
Multi-Focus, Inc.
Petrified Films, Inc.
Playboy Programs, Inc.
See also Pornography

Errol, Leon
Videobrary, Inc.
Windsor Prod. Corp.

Erskine, Ralph
Blackwood Prods., Inc.

Ervin, Samuel
Univ. of N.C.-Chapel Hill, Manuscripts
   Dept.

Erving, Julius ("Dr. J.")
Daphne Productions, Inc.
Natl. Assn. for the Advancement of
   Colored People

Erwin, Stu
Moviecraft, Inc.

Escalators
CBS News Archives
Energy Productions
Film Bank

Eskimos
See Native Americans (Eskimos)

Espinal, Luis
Democracy in Communication

Espionage
See Spies

Esposito, Phil
Archive Film Prods., Inc.

Establishing shots
Airline Film & TV Promotions
Boston Stock Market
Chisholm (Jack) Film Productions
Cinenet (Cinema Network)
Cinephile Amalgamated Pictures
Dreamlight Images, Inc.
Fabulous Footage Inc.
Film Bank
Moving Media
Petrified Films, Inc.
Producers Library Service
Spectral Comms.
Summit Films, Inc.
Wallen (Dick) Prods.
White Janssen, Inc.

Estabrook, Ronald W.
Amer. Chemical Soc.

Estes, Richard
Albright-Knox Art Gallery

Estuaries
Bullfrog Films, Inc.
Natl. Oceanic & Atmospheric Admin.
Petrified Films, Inc.

Ethics
Bullfrog Films, Inc.
Fanlight Prods.
Intellimation
Mass Media Ministries
Media Guild

Ethics (Medical)
Emory Medical Television Network

Ethiopia
Imagen y Sonido Independiente, S.A.
World Monitor

Ethiopia (Contemporary issues)
CARE

Ethiopia (History and culture)
Explorers Club
Film/Audio Services, Inc.
Imagen y Sonido Independiente, S.A.
March of Time
Maryknoll Fathers & Brothers
Natl. Archives (RG 286)
Northstar Prods.
Paulist Productions
Sobek Productions
U.S. Committee for UNICEF
World Monitor

Ethnographic films and videotapes
   See Anthropological films and
   videotapes

Etiquette
Film Bank
Prelinger Assoc., Inc.
Streamline Film Archives

Etruscans
Vedo Films/Novacom Video

Eugenics
Historical Health Film Coll.

**Euphrates River, Asia (History and
   culture)**
Ocean Earth Constr. and Dev. Corp.

Europe
Amer. Airlines
Canadian Broadcasting Corp.
Creative Video, Inc.

File Tape Co.
Film Bank
Film Search
Pan American Airlines Film Lib.
Petrified Films, Inc.
Stimulus
Summit Films, Inc.
Telltales Associates Inc.
World Monitor

Europe (History and culture)
American Portrait, An
Archive Film Prods., Inc.
Beerger (Norman) Prods.
Cantor (Arthur) Inc.
Ergo Media
Film Bank
Footage Inc.
General Motors Corp.
Halcyon Days Prods.
Icarus Films Intl., Inc.
Intl. Film Bureau, Inc.
Israel Broadcasting Service
March of Time
Natl. Archives (RG 18)
Natl. Archives (RG 59)
Natl. Archives (RG 107)
Natl. Archives (RG 117)
Natl. Archives (RG 208)
Natl. Archives (RG 306)
Natl. Archives (RG 342)
Natl. Archives of Canada
Oregon Hist. Soc.
Petrified Films, Inc.
Phoenix Films and Video
Prelinger Assoc., Inc.
Schweitzer (Albert) Ctr.
Smithsonian Inst., Human Studies Film
   Arch.
World Monitor
Worldwide Television News

European Common Market
Center for Pacific Northwest Studies

Euthanasia
Amer. Life League
Hartley Film Found., Inc.
Intl. Lutheran Layman's League
Mus. & Hist. Div., City of Sacramento
Natl. Right to Life Committee

Evangelical Covenant Church of Christ
See Religion (Evangelical Covenant
   Church)

Evangelicalism
See Religion (Evangelicalism)

Evans, Bill
Rhapsody Films, Inc.

Evans, Dale
Archive Film Prods., Inc.

Evans, Dame Edith
Cantor (Arthur) Inc.
New York Pub. Lib., Perf. Arts Res. Ctr.,
   Theatre on Film and Tape

Evans, Linda
Film Bank
Spectral Comms.

Evans, Minnie
Amer. Federation of the Arts

Evans, Walker
Agee (James) Film Project

Everest, Mount (Tibet-Nepal)

Film Bank
Petrified Films, Inc.

**Everest, Mount (Tibet-Nepal) (History
   and culture)**
Archive Film Prods., Inc.

Everglades, Fla.
Film Bank
Grinberg (Sherman) Film Libraries (West)
Moody Inst. of Science

Everly Brothers (Don and Phil)
Archive Film Prods., Inc.
Spectral Comms.

Evers, Medgar
Archive Film Prods., Inc.

Evers, Myrlie
Natl. Assn. for the Advancement of
   Colored People

Evert-Lloyd, Chris
U.S. Tennis Assn.

Everyday life
See Lifestyles

Evictions
CBS News Archives
Film Bank

Evolution
Educational Images, Ltd.
See also Creationism

Ewen, Stuart
Paper Tiger TV

Ewing, Lauren
Video Data Bank

Excavations
CBS News Archives
Spectral Comms.
Twentieth Century-Fox Movietonews

Executions
CBS News Archives
Film Bank
See also Capital punishment; Electric
   chairs

Exel, Prince
Natl. Archives (RG 24)

Exercise
Amer. Heart Assn.
Athletic Institute
Broad Street Prods.
Coronet/MTI Film & Video
Dreamlight Images, Inc.
Intl. Dance Exercise Assn.
Media West, Inc.
Narcotics Education, Inc.
Perlmutter (Alvin H.) Inc.
Prelinger Assoc., Inc.
Rudra Press
Spectral Comms.
TV Ontario
Video Tape Library, Ltd.
Video-SIG
Wayfarer Publications
See also Aerobic exercise; Joggers and
   jogging; Physical fitness

Exercise bicycles
Dreamlight Images, Inc.

NOTE: Access policies, availability and restrictions vary for each source. Please read each entry in full. Always consult "General Film and
Videotape Collections" (page 599); these comprehensive collections contain material on every conceivable subject.

Exotic dancing
See Striptease

Expeditions
Acad. of Nat. Sci. of Phila. Lib.
Allen (John E.) Inc.
Amer. Mus. Nat. Hist. Film Arch.
CBS News Archives
Cousteau Society
Explorers Club
Grinberg (Sherman) Film Libraries (West)
Intl. Assn. of Independent Producers
Jewell (Stuart) Productions
Johnson (Martin & Osa) Safari Museum
Lib. of Congress, Amer. Folklife Ctr.
Marineland of Florida
Metropolitan Mus. of Art, Uris Ctr.
Natl. Archives (RG 48)
Natl. Archives (RG 75)
Natl. Archives (RG 78)
Natl. Archives (RG 126)
Natl. Archives (RG 200)
Natl. Archives (RG 342)
Natl. Archives of Canada
Natl. Geographic Soc. Stock Footage Lib.
New York Zoological Society
Peary-MacMillan Arctic Museum
Petrified Films, Inc.
Prelinger Assoc., Inc.
Smithsonian Inst., Human Studies Film Arch.
Spalla (Rick) Video Prods.
State Hist. Soc. of Iowa
Wheaton Coll., Billy Graham Ctr.
See also Explorers and exploration

Experimental films and videotapes
A Space
Alan Twyman Presents
Amer. Federation of the Arts
Anoka County Comm. Workshop, Inc.
Anthology Film Archives
Art Com/La Mamelle, Inc.
Art Metropole
Artists' Television Project
Arts Television Centre
Assoc. Coopérative Obscure
Atlantic Independent Media
Bay Area Video Coalition
Bibliothèque Municipale de Montréal
Calif. Inst. of the Arts, Lib.
Canadian Filmmakers Dist. Centre
Canadian Filmmakers Dist. West
Canyon Cinema, Inc.
Carnegie District Film Ctr.
Castelli/Sonnabend Tapes & Films
Center for Creative Photography
Center for New Television
Centre for Art Tapes
Channel L Working Group
Chautauqua-Cattaraugus Library System
Contemporary Art Television (CAT) Fund
Creative Film Society
Cunningham Dance Foundation
De Saisset Museum
Downtown Community TV Ctr.
EM/Media Archives
EZTV
Ed Video Media Arts Centre
Electronic Arts Intermix
Em Gee Film Library
Estate of Andy Warhol
Everson Mus. of Art
Experimental Intermedia Foundation
Experimental Television Ctr.
Facets Multimedia, Inc.
Film Arts Foundation
Film-Makers' Cooperative
Film/Video Arts, Inc.
First Run/Icarus Films, Inc.
Fischinger, Elfriede
Foreign Images
Image Film & Video Coll.
Intermedia Arts Minnesota
Island Cinema Resources

Kingston Artists' Assn., Inc.
Kinsey Institute
Kitchen, The
Latin Amer. Video Arch.
Locus Communications
Long Beach Mus. of Art
Los Angeles Contemporary Exhibitions
Media Bus
Media Project
Monday, Wednesday, Friday Video Club
Musée d'Art Contemporain de Montréal
Mus. of Mod. Art, Circulating Film Lib.
Mus. of Mod. Art, Dept. of Film
Natl. Endow. for the Arts, Media Arts Prog.
New American Makers
New Langton Arts
New York Pub. Lib., Donnell Media Ctr.
New York State Council on the Arts
Newfoundland Independent Filmmakers Coop.
911 Contemporary Arts Ctr.
P.R.I.M.
Pacific Cinémathèque Pacifique
Pacific Film Archive
Phoenix Films and Video
Picture Start, Inc.
Plains Art Mus. Lib.
Port Washington Pub. Lib.
Prov. Arch. of Manitoba
Raindance Foundation
Real Art Ways
Rosebush Visions Corp.
S.A.W. Video Co-op
Samaya Foundation
School of the Art Inst. of Chicago, Flaxman Mem. Lib.
South Carolina Arts Comm. Media Arts Ctr.
Southwest Alternate Media Project
Southwest Film/Video Archives, SMU
Squeaky Wheel
Starr, Cecile
State Hist. Soc. of Iowa
Syracuse Univ., Art Media Studies Coll.
Trinity Square Video
Twin Cities Public Television (KTCA)
Université Laval, Cinémathèque
Univ. of Tampa, Kelce Lib.
V/tape
Video Data Bank
Video In
Video Pool, Inc.
Video Shorts
Video-SIG
Vidéographe Inc., Le
Visual Studies Workshop
Voyager Co.
Walker Art Ctr.
Western Front Society
Wisconsin Ctr. for Film & Theater Res.
Women in Focus
Women Make Movies, Inc.
See also Independent films and videotapes

Experiments
See Science experiments

Expert systems
See Computers

Exploitation films and videotapes
Em Gee Film Library
Gordon Films, Inc.
Hurlock Cine-World, Inc.
Ludlow (Fitz Hugh) Memorial Library
Producers Library Service
UCLA Film & Television Archive

Explorers and exploration
Allen (John E.) Inc.
Amer. Mus. Nat. Hist. Film Arch.
Archive Film Prods., Inc.
Australian Info. Serv.
CBS News Archives

California Inst. of Tech., Jet Propulsion Laboratory
Explorers Club
Inuvik Research Ctr.
Johnson (Martin & Osa) Safari Museum
MacDonald, J. Fred
Mariners' Museum
NASA, Office of Comm.
Natl. Archives (RG 126)
Natl. Archives (RG 200)
Natl. Archives (RG 342)
Natl. Archives of Canada
Natl. Geographic Soc. Stock Footage Lib.
Peary-Macmillan Arctic Museum
Petrified Films, Inc.
Univ. of Alaska, Fairbanks, Alaska Motion Picture Arch.
Video Tape Library, Ltd.
See also Expeditions

Explorers and exploration (Women)
Univ. of Mich., Mich. Hist. Colls.

Explosions
Archive Film Prods., Inc.
CBS News Archives
Charisma Prods., Ltd./Visual Motion
Dreamlight Images, Inc.
Energy Productions
Everett Pub. Lib., N.W. Hist. Coll.
Film Bank
Fish Films, Inc.
Grinberg (Sherman) Film Libraries (West)
Halicki (H.B.) Productions
Lib. of Special Visual Effects
Natl. Archives (RG 70)
Natl. Archives (RG 200)
Natl. Archives (RG 226)
Natl. Archives (RG 227)
Natl. Archives (RG 304)
Natl. Archives (RG 397)
Petrified Films, Inc.
Prelinger Assoc., Inc.
Rosebush Visions Corp.
Source Stock Footage Lib., Inc.
TV Ontario
Twentieth Century-Fox Movietonews
Video Tape Library, Ltd.
See also Bombs and bombing; Buildings (Exploding); Dynamite; Explosives

Explosives
Crystal Pyramid Prods.
Inst. of Makers of Explosives
See also Dynamite; Explosions

Expo '67
See World's Fairs (Montreal, 1967)

Expo '87
See World's Fairs (Vancouver, 1987)

Expositions
See Fairs and expositions

Extraterrestrial life
NASA, Lewis Research Center

Eyes
Altschul Group
Charisma Prods., Ltd./Visual Motion
Corning Mus. of Glass
Film Bank
Fish Films, Inc.
Motion Picture Services
Natl. Soc. to Prevent Blindness
Petrified Films, Inc.
Prelinger Assoc., Inc.
Rosebush Visions Corp.
White Janssen, Inc.

FAA
See Federal Aviation Administration (FAA)

FBI
See Federal Bureau of Investigation (FBI)

FCC
See Federal Communications Commission (FCC)

Fabian
Banks Film Library
Spalla (Rick) Video Prods.

Faces
CBS News Archives
Film Bank
Petrified Films, Inc.

Factories
Amer. Truck Historical Society
Analogous Productions
Archive Film Prods., Inc.
British Info. Svcs., Radio & TV Div.
CBS News Archives
Canadian Filmmakers Dist. Centre
Dreamlight Images, Inc.
Energy Productions
Farkas Studios, Ltd.
Film Bank
Film Search
Gypsum Assn.
Hershey Foods Corp.
Intl. Assn. of Independent Producers
Intl. Film Foundation
Kesser Stock Footage Library
Lemorande Prod. Co.
Natl. Dairy Council
New York State Dept. of Econ. Devel.
Petrified Films, Inc.
Prelinger Assoc., Inc.
Reynolds (R.J.) Tobacco USA
Riccitelli (Bruce) Prods.
Smithsonian Inst., NMAH, Div. Eng. & Ind.
Spectral Comms.
TV Ontario
Timesteps Prods., Inc.
Univ. of Mich., Mich. Hist. Colls.
Video Tape Library, Ltd.
See also Assembly lines; Automobiles (Assembly lines); Industry; Manufacturing

Fads
ABC News
Analogous Productions
Archive Film Prods., Inc.
Film Bank
Film Education Institute
Halcyon Days Prods.
Las Vegas News Bureau
Petrified Films, Inc.
Twentieth Century-Fox Movietonews

Fahlen, Charles
Blackwood Prods., Inc.

Fairbanks, Alaska (History and culture)
Alaska Video Prods.

Fairbanks, Douglas
Alan Twyman Presents
Archive Film Prods., Inc.
Film/Audio Services, Inc.
Mus. of Mod. Art, Dept. of Film
Petrified Films, Inc.

Fairchild, Morgan
Spectral Comms.

Fairfax, Joan
Natl. Archives of Canada

Fairfield County, Conn. (History and culture)
Regional Plan Assn.

Fairies
Film Bank

Fairs and expositions
Allen (John E.) Inc.
Analogous Productions
Archives of Ontario
CBS News Archives
Everett Pub. Lib., N.W. Hist. Coll.
Film Bank
General Motors Corp.
Illinois State Hist. Lib.
Independent Media Communications
Intl. Assn. of Fairs & Expositions
Kentucky Dept. of Libraries & Archives
Lib. of Congress, M/B/RS
Natl. Archives of Canada
Northcoast Communication, Inc.
Ohio Historical Soc.
Oregon State Univ., Archives
Petrified Films, Inc.
Vermont Hist. Soc.
White Janssen, Inc.
See also World's Fairs

Fairweather, Paul
Long Beach Mus. of Art

Fairy tales
Archive Film Prods., Inc.
Benchmark Films, Inc.
Coe Film Assoc., Inc.
Coronet/MTI Film & Video
Davenport Films
Film Bank
Phoenix Films and Video

Faith healing
See Healing (Faith)

Faithfull, Marianne
Archive Film Prods., Inc.

Falcons and falconry
Echo Film Prods., Inc.
New Jersey Network
Vedo Films/Novacom Video

Falicoff, Waquidi
Southern Calif. Inst. of Architecture

Falk, Peter
Banks Film Library

Falkland Islands
British Info. Svcs., Radio & TV Div.

Falkland Islands (History and culture)
Ocean Earth Constr. and Dev. Corp.

Fall (Season)
Amer. Motion Pictures
Cineworks Prods. Inc.
Dreamlight Images, Inc.
Energy Productions
Film Bank
4•6•8 Prods., Inc.
Intl. Film Bureau, Inc.
Jewell (Stuart) Productions
Moving Media
North Country Media Group
Source Stock Footage Lib., Inc.
Summit Films, Inc.
White Star Prof. Film Svcs., Inc.
See also Foliage (Fall)

Fall foliage
See Foliage (Fall)

Fallout shelters
Amer. Portrait, An

MacDonald, J. Fred
Petrified Films, Inc.

Falwell, Jerry
Liberty Broadcasting Network
People for the American Way

Families
ABC Distribution (Education)
Amer. Assn. for Counseling &
  Development
Amer. Soc. Hist. Proj. Film Lib.
Appalachian State Univ., Eury Coll.
Boston Family Inst.
CBS News Archives
Carousel Film & Video
Coe Film Assoc., Inc.
Coronet/MTI Film & Video
Film Bank
Film Education Institute
Films for the Humanities and Sciences
GPN
Kartemquin Films
Lawren Prods., Inc.
Mass Media Ministries
Media Guild
Moody Inst. of Science
Multi-Media Productions, Inc.
Native Amer. Pub. Broad. Cons.
Natl. Archives (RG 220)
Natl. Film Board of Canada
New Day Films
Ozark Folk Center
Petrified Films, Inc.
Phoenix Films and Video
Prelinger Assoc., Inc.
Radcliffe Coll., Schlesinger Lib.
Shields Archival
Timesteps Prods., Inc.
Toughlove
U.S. Committee for UNICEF
Video Pool, Inc.
Wheelwright Mus. of the Amer. Indian

Families (Hispanic)
MALDEF

Families (Japan)
Japan Society, Inc. Film Center

Families, White House Conference on
Natl. Archives (RG 220)

Family therapy
Boston Family Inst.
IEA Productions, Inc.

Famine River, Quebec (History and culture)
Natl. Archives of Canada

Famines
CARE
CBS News Archives
Icarus Films Intl., Inc.
March of Time
Maryknoll Fathers & Brothers
Paulist Productions
UNICEF, Div. Info. & Pub. Aff.
World Monitor
Worldwide Television News

Fans (Celebrity)
Banks Film Library
Las Vegas News Bureau
Petrified Films, Inc.

Far East
British Info. Svcs., Radio & TV Div.

Far East (History and culture)

Archive Film Prods., Inc.
Natl. Archives of Canada

Farenthold, Frances ("Sissy")
Radcliffe Coll., Schlesinger Lib.

Fargo, N. Dak. (History and culture)
State Hist. Soc. of North Dakota

Farley, James A.
Natl. Archives (RG 28)

Farlow, Talmage
Rhapsody Films, Inc.

Farm Credit Administration (U.S.)
Natl. Archives (RG 103)

Farm Security Administration (U.S.)
Natl. Archives (RG 96)
Natl. Press Photographers Assn., Inc.

Farmer, Frances
DePauw University, Archives

Farmers Home Administration (U.S.)
Natl. Archives (RG 96)

Farmersville, Calif. (History and culture)
Natl. Archives (RG 381)

Farms and farming
Alternative Information Network
Amer. Motion Pictures
Amer. Soc. Hist. Proj. Film Lib.
Appalshop Films, Inc.
Archive Film Prods., Inc.
Archives of Ontario
British Info. Svcs., Radio & TV Div.
CBS News Archives
Cimarron Productions
Cinema Guild
Cinenet (Cinema Network)
Cornell Univ., Media Services
Creative Venture Films
Creative Video, Inc.
Deep Dish TV
Dreamlight Images, Inc.
Echo Film Prods., Inc.
Energy Productions
Farkas Studios, Ltd.
Film Bank
Film Search
Forsher (James) Prods. & Archives, Inc.
Glenbow Mus. Arch.
Hearst Metrotone News
Hershey Foods Corp.
Intl. Film Foundation
Kentucky Dept. of Libraries & Archives
March of Time
Natl. Archives (RG 4)
Natl. Archives (RG 16)
Natl. Archives (RG 31)
Natl. Archives (RG 33)
Natl. Archives (RG 96)
Natl. Archives (RG 145)
Natl. Archives (RG 208)
Natl. Archives (RG 306)
Natl. Archives of Canada
Natl. Archives/Natl. AV Ctr.
Natl. Assn. of Conservation Dists.
Natl. Dairy Council
New Jersey Network
North Country Media Group
Northcoast Communication, Inc.
Oregon State Univ., Archives
Petrified Films, Inc.
Prelinger Assoc., Inc.
Prov. Arch. of Alberta
Pyramid Film and Video Corp.

Snyder (Bill) Films, Inc.
Source Stock Footage Lib., Inc.
Spectral Comms.
State Hist. Soc. of Iowa
TV Ontario
Texas Tech Univ., Southwest Coll.
Timesteps Prods., Inc.
Université de Moncton, Centre d'Études
  Acad.
Univ. of Mich., Mich. Hist. Colls.
Vermont Hist. Soc.
Video I-D, Inc.
Video Tape Library, Ltd.
Video Ventures Prods.
White Janssen, Inc.
See also Agriculture; Barns; Crops; Dairy
  industry; Harvesting; Workers
  (Agricultural); Workers (Farm);
  Workers (Migrant)

Farms and farming (Black farmers)
Estuary Press

Farms and farming (Egypt)
Energy Prods.

Farms and farming (Japan)
Japan Society, Inc. Film Center

Farms and farming (Mexico)
Energy Prods.

Farms and farming (Tenant)
Southern Calif. Lib. for Soc. Stud. & Res.

Farrell, Mike
Fund for Human Dignity, Inc.
Spectral Comms.

Farris, Christine King
King (Dr. Martin Luther, Jr.) Ctr.

Fascell, Dante
Univ. of Miami, Arch. & Spec. Coll.

Fascism
Freedom Information Service
MacDonald, J. Fred
March of Time
Natl. Archives/Natl. AV Ctr.
Prelinger Assoc., Inc.

Fashion models
See Models (Fashion)

Fashion shows
Film Bank
Peak Productions, Inc.
Petrified Films, Inc.
TV Ontario

Fashion videos
Intl. Fashion Video Library
Video Catalogue Co., Inc.
Videofashion, Inc.

Fashions and fashion industry
Analogous Productions
Archive Film Prods., Inc.
Broad Street Prods.
CBS News Archives
Fashion Inst. of Design & Merchandising
Film Bank
Film Education Institute
Film Search
Fish Films, Inc.
Grinberg (Sherman) Film Libraries (East)
Grinberg (Sherman) Film Libraries (West)
Halcyon Days Prods.
Impact Audio Visual
Intl. Fashion Video Library

NOTE: Access policies, availability and restrictions vary for each source. Please read each entry in full. Always consult "General Film and Videotape Collections" (page 599); these comprehensive collections contain material on every conceivable subject.

MacDonald, J. Fred
March of Time
Prelinger Assoc., Inc.
Spalla (Rick) Video Prods.
TV Ontario
Timesteps Prods., Inc.
Twentieth Century-Fox Movietonews
Univ. of Ill. Urbana-Champaign, Univ.
    Arch.
Univ. of So. Carolina, Newsfilm Lib.
Univ. of Waterloo, A-V Centre
Video Catalogue Co., Inc.
Videofashion, Inc.
White Janssen, Inc.
Women in Focus
See also Clothing; Costumes (Historical)

Fashions and fashion industry (France)
Soc. for French Amer. Cult. Svcs. & Educ.
    Aid

Fast-food restaurants
See Restaurants (Fast-food)

Fatepur Sikri, India
Petrified Films, Inc.

Father Divine
March of Time

Faubus, Orval
Univ. of Ill. Urbana-Champaign, Univ.
    Arch.

Faulk, John Henry
Alternative Information Network

Faulkton, S. Dak. (History and culture)
South Dakota State Lib.

Favro, Diane
Southern Calif. Inst. of Architecture

Faye, Alice
UCLA Film & Television Archive

Faye, Joey
New York Pub. Lib., Perf. Arts Res. Ctr.,
    Theatre on Film and Tape

Fayol, Henri
Salenger Films Inc.

Fear (Emotion)
Blackwood (Christian) Prods.
Prelinger Assoc., Inc.

Feature films and videotapes
ABC Video Enterprises
Alan Twyman Presents
Amer. Science Fiction Assn.
Archive Film Prods., Inc.
Archivo de Imagenes en Movimiento
Azteca Films
Blackwood (Christian) Prods., Inc.
Cinema Arts Assoc.
Cineteca Nacional
Cinémathèque québécoise
Circle Releasing Corp.
Clip Joint For Film
Coe Film Assoc., Inc.
Corinth Films/Corinth Video
Country Music Foundation, Inc.
Creative Film Society
Disney (Walt) Archives
Dreamlight Images, Inc.
Dube (Jackson) (JED Prods.) Corp.
East West Classics
Em Gee Film Library
Fabulous Footage Inc.
Facets Multimedia, Inc.
Film Search
Film/Audio Services, Inc.
Filmoteca de la UNAM
Films Incorporated

Footage Inc.
Franklin & Marshall Coll.
French Lib. in Boston
German Language Video Center
Goethe Institute Chicago
Goethe Institute Toronto
Gordon Films, Inc.
Hurlock Cine-World, Inc.
IFEX Films
Imagen y Sonido Independiente, S.A.
Imageways, Inc.
Independent Media Communications
Indiana Univ., Black Film Ctr./Arch.
Interama
Intl. Al Jolson Society
Intl. Mus. of Photography
Italian Cultural Institute
Ivy Film
Janus Films
Killiam Shows, Inc.
Kino Intl. Corp.
Latina, S.A. de C.V.
Lib. of Congress, M/B/RS
Manhattan Movietime
Moviecraft, Inc.
Mus. of Mod. Art, Dept. of Film
Natl. Archives (RG 200)
Natl. Archives of Canada
Natl. Ctr. for Film & Video Preservation
Natl. Ctr. for Jewish Film
New York Pub. Lib., Perf. Arts Res. Ctr.,
    Theatre on Film and Tape
New Yorker Films
Northeast Historic Film
Ontario Film Institute
Pacific Film Archive
Palladium Entertainment, Inc.
Parker (Kit) Films
Prestige Film Corp.
Producers Library Service
R5/S8 Presents
SF•V Intl.
Shields Archival
Streamline Film Archives
Swank Motion Pctures, Inc.
Tamarelle's Intl. Films, Ltd.
Trans-World Films, Inc.
UCLA Film & Television Archive
UDS Company
UPA Prods. of America
Video Resources N.Y., Inc.
Video Yesteryear
Videobrary, Inc.
Voyager Co.
Walker Art Ctr.
Weintraub Screen Entertainment, Inc.
Williams (Wade) Prods.
Wisconsin Ctr. for Film & Theater Res.
Yale Film Study Ctr.

**Feature films and videotapes (Public
    domain)**
Archive Film Prods., Inc.
Budget Films Inc.
DeFlores, Bob
Eden Entertainment, Inc.
Imageways, Inc.
Jessiefilm
Kehr (Timothy D.) Advertising
MacDonald, J. Fred
Manhattan Movietime
Morcraft Films
Movietime, Inc. Archives
Parker (Kit) Films
Petrified Films, Inc.
Producers Library Service
Southwest Film/Video Archives, SMU
Stavis, Gene
Streamline Film Archives
Video-SIG

Federal Art Project (U.S.)
Natl. Archives (RG 69)

**Federal Aviation Administration (FAA)
    (U.S.)**
FAA Technical Center
Natl. Archives (RG 237)
Natl. Archives (Stock Film Coll.)

**Federal Bureau of Investigation (FBI)
    (U.S)**
Alternative Information Network
Chicago Comm. to Defend the Bill of
    Rights
Film Bank
Intermedia Arts Minnesota
March of Time
Mus. & Hist. Div., City of Sacramento
Natl. Archives (RG 26)
Natl. Archives (RG 65)
Petrified Films, Inc.

**Federal Civil Defense Administration
    (U.S)**
Natl. Archives (RG 304)

**Federal Communications Commission
    (FCC) (U.S.)**
Natl. Archives (RG 173)

**Federal Emergency Management
    Agency (FEMA) (U.S.)**
Natl. Archives (RG 311)

**Federal Emergency Relief
    Administration (U.S.)**
Natl. Archives (RG 33)

Federal Highway Administration (U.S.)
Natl. Archives (RG 406)
Natl. Archives (Stock Film Coll.)

Federal Housing Administration (U.S.)
Natl. Archives (RG 31)

**Federal Reserve Building (Washington,
    D.C.)**
Natl. Archives (RG 82)

Federal Reserve System (U.S.)
Natl. Archives (RG 82)

Federal Theater Project (U.S.)
Natl. Archives (RG 69)

Federal Works Agency (U.S.)
Natl. Archives (RG 48)

Feet
CBS News Archives
Film Bank
Petrified Films, Inc.
Prelinger Assoc., Inc.
Rosebush Visions Corp.

Feinstein, Dianne
San Francisco Bay Area TV News Arch.

Feitelson, Lorser
De Saisset Museum

Feld, Eliot
Blackwood (Christian) Prods., Inc.
Blackwood Prods., Inc.

Fellini, Federico
Daphne Productions, Inc.

Fellman, Sandi
Port Washington Pub. Lib.

Fellows, Jay
Southern Calif. Inst. of Architecture

Feminism
See Women's history; Women's issues

Fences

CBS News Archives

Fencing (Sport)
Analogous Productions
Dreamlight Images, Inc.
Prelinger Assoc., Inc.
Sportsfilm
TV Ontario
Twentieth Century-Fox Movietonews

Fencing (Sport) (Instruction)
NCAA Productions

Fender, Freddy
Univ. of Tex. at Austin, Benson Lat. Am.
    Coll.

Ferber, Herbert
Albright-Knox Art Gallery
Blackwood Prods., Inc.

Ferns
Dreamlight Images, Inc.
Film Bank

Ferraro, John
Spectral Comms.

Ferrer, Jose
Banks Film Library

Ferrer, Mel
Banks Film Library

Ferries
See Boats and boating (Ferries)

Ferris wheels
Energy Productions
Film Bank
Kesser Stock Footage Library
Petrified Films, Inc.
See also Amusement parks

Ferry, Nancy W.
Psychological and Educational Films

Festivals
CBS News Archives
Energy Productions
Film Bank
Natl. Archives of Canada
See also Film festivals; Music festivals

Festivals (Canada) (Outdoor)
TV Ontario

Festivals (Folk)
Natl. Archives of Canada

Festivals (Food)
Spectral Comms.

Festivals (Germany)
Goethe Institute Atlanta

Festivals (Hong Kong)
Farkas Studios, Ltd.

Festivals (India)
Univ. of Wisconsin — Extension

Festivals (Logging)
Amer. Motion Pictures

Festivals (Mexico)
Imevision

Festivals (Oktoberfest)
Analogous Productions

Festivals (Rose)
Oregon Hist. Soc.

Festivals (Scandinavian)
Amer. Motion Pictures

Festivals (St. Augustine, Fla.)
St. Augustine Hist. Soc.

Festivals (Storytelling)
Natl. Assn. for the Pres. & Perpetuation of Storytelling

Festivals (Street)
Spectral Comms.

Festivals (Texas)
Hayes Prods., Inc.

Festivals (Tulip)
Petrified Films, Inc.

Festivals (Yukon Territory)
Yukon Archives

Fetal alcohol syndrome
Addiction Research Foundation of Ontario
March of Dimes Birth Defects Found.
Rogers (Will) Institute
Signal Press
See also Alcohol abuse; Women and health

Fetchit, Stepin
Archive Film Prods., Inc.

Fetuses
Film Bank

Fiber optics
Hewlett-Packard Co.
Inst. of Electrical & Electronics Eng.

Field hockey
Sportsfilm

Field hockey (Instruction)
Natl. Assn. for Sport & Phys. Ed.

Field, Connie
Port Washington Pub. Lib.

Field, Sally
Spectral Comms.

Fields, W.C.
Alan Twyman Presents
Archive Film Prods., Inc.
Em Gee Film Library
Grinberg (Sherman) Film Libraries (East)
UCLA Film & Television Archive

Fierstein, Harvey
Gay Cable Network

Fiestas
Hayes Prods., Inc.

Fiji
Preview Media

Fiji (History and culture)
Archive Film Prods., Inc.
Film/Audio Services, Inc.

Filipino Americans
Natl. Asian American Telecomm. Assn.
Visual Communications

Film festivals
Analogous Productions

Financial industry
Amer. Stock Exchange
Board of Trade of the City of Chicago
Broad Street Prods.
California Newsreel
Carleton Prods. Inc.
Hayes Prods., Inc.
Merrill Lynch Pierce Fenner & Smith
Perlmutter (Alvin H.) Inc.
Petrified Films, Inc.
Video-Documentary Clearinghouse
See also Banks and banking industry;
    Stock exchanges; Stock market

Finches
Wings Wildlife Prods. Inc.

Fine, John
Pennsylvania State Arch.

Finger Lakes, N.Y.
New York State Dept. of Econ. Devel.

Finger wrestling
Analogous Productions

Fingerprints and fingerprinting
CBS News Archives
Petrified Films, Inc.

Finish lines
Film Bank

Finkelstein, Fred
Port Washington Pub. Lib.

Finland
Northstar Prods.

Finland (History and culture)
Allen (John E.) Inc.
Archive Film Prods., Inc.
March of Time
Natl. Archives (RG 96)
Natl. Archives (RG 111)
Northstar Prods.
Singer-Sharrette Traditional Healing Films

Finnie, Richard S.
Natl. Archives of Canada

Finnish Americans
Nordic Heritage Museum
Wayne State Univ., Folklore Arch.

Fire drills
CBS News Archives

Fire engines
See Firefighters and firefighting

Fire escapes
CBS News Archives
Film Bank

Fire extinguishers
CBS News Archives
Fire Prev. Through Films, Inc.
Prelinger Assoc., Inc.

Fire hoses
See Firefighters and firefighting

Fire hydrants
CBS News Archives
Film Bank

Fire Island, N.Y.
Island Video

Fire safety
Amer. Plywood Assn., Inc.
Coronet/MTI Film & Video
Fire Prev. Through Films, Inc.
Gypsum Assn.
Indiana State Comm. on Public Records
Inst. of Makers of Explosives
Minn. Dept. of Public Safety Film Lib.
Natl. Archives (RG 33)
Natl. Archives (RG 70)
Natl. Fire Protection Assn.
Natl. Safety Council
Prelinger Assoc., Inc.
Pyramid Film and Video Corp.

Fire stations
Film Bank
Petrified Films, Inc.

Fire trucks
Film Bank
Petrified Films, Inc.

Firearms
See Guns and rifles

Fireballs
Film Bank

Fireboats
See Boats and boating (Fireboats)

Firecrackers
See Fireworks

Firefighters and firefighting
Analogous Productions
CBS News Archives
Courter Films & Assoc.
Creative Venture Films
Film Bank
Fire Prev. Through Films, Inc.
Grinberg (Sherman) Film Libraries (West)
March of Time
Natl. Archives (RG 26)
Natl. Archives (RG 171)
Newsreel Video Service
Off-Broadway Video Prods.
Petrified Films, Inc.
Prelinger Assoc., Inc.
Spectral Comms.
TV Ontario
Twentieth Century-Fox Movietonews
Video Tape Library, Ltd.

Firefighters and firefighting (Historical)
Fire Mus. of Maryland

Fires
Archive Film Prods., Inc.
British Info. Svcs., Radio & TV Div.
CBS News Archives
Connecticut Historical Society
Courter Films & Assoc.
Dreamlight Images, Inc.
Energy Productions
Film Bank
Fire Prev. Through Films, Inc.
Fish Films, Inc.
Grinberg (Sherman) Film Libraries (West)
Gypsum Assn.
Inst. of Makers of Explosives
Lib. of Congress, M/B/RS
Los Angeles News Service
Natl. Fire Protection Assn.
Newsreel Video Service
Petrified Films, Inc.
Spectral Comms.
Twentieth Century-Fox Movietonews
Univ. of Ill. Urbana-Champaign, Univ. Arch.
Vermont Hist. Soc.
Zielinski Productions, Inc.
See also Disasters; Fire safety; Flames

Fires (Automobiles)
Energy Productions

Fires (Brush)
Newsreel Video Service
Petrified Films, Inc.
Spectral Comms.
Tennessee State Lib. & Arch.

Fires (Forest)
Film Bank
Grinberg (Sherman) Film Libraries (West)
Indiana State Comm. on Public Records
Natl. Assn. of Conservation Dists.
Northwest Territories Arch.
Oregon State Univ., Archives
Petrified Films, Inc.
TV Ontario

Fires (Hydrogen)
Courter Films & Assoc.

Fires (Mine)
Natl. Archives (RG 70)

Fires (Oil)
Glenbow Mus. Arch.
Grinberg (Sherman) Film Libraries (West)
Natl. Archives (RG 70)
Petrified Films, Inc.

Fires (Paramount Studios, 1967)
Spalla (Rick) Video Prods.

Fires (Prairie)
Petrified Films, Inc.

Fires (Ships)
See Ships (Burning)

Firestone, Robert W.
Psychological and Educational Films

Firewalkers
Film Education Institute
Pyramid Film and Video Corp.

Fireworks
Archive Film Prods., Inc.
British Info. Svcs., Radio & TV Div.
Broad Street Prods.
CBS News Archives
Cabscott Broadcast Prods.
Cinenet (Cinema Network)
Dreamlight Images, Inc.
Encore Video Prods., Inc.
Energy Productions
Farkas Studios, Ltd.
Film Bank
Fish Films, Inc.
Hayes Prods., Inc.
Lib. of Special Visual Effects
MacGillivray Freeman Films
Media Project
Petrified Films, Inc.
Producers' Service
Rosebush Visions Corp.
SF•V Intl.
Source Stock Footage Lib., Inc.
Spectral Comms.
Stock House
Sullivan Video Services
Timesteps Prods., Inc.
Video Tape Library, Ltd.

First aid
AIMS Media
CBS News Archives
Center for Humanities, Inc.
Churchill Films
Coronet/MTI Film & Video

NOTE: Access policies, availability and restrictions vary for each source. Please read each entry in full. Always consult "General Film and Videotape Collections" (page 599); these comprehensive collections contain material on every conceivable subject.

Intl. Film Bureau, Inc.
Natl. Archives (RG 24)
Natl. Archives (RG 70)
Natl. Archives of Canada
New York State Dept. of Env. Cons.
Prelinger Assoc., Inc.
U.S. Dept. of Labor, Mine Safety & Health
  Admin.
See also Cardiopulmonary resuscitation
  (CPR)

Firsts
Film Bank

Firsts (Medical)
Johns Hopkins Univ., School of Medicine

Fischer, Sarah
Natl. Archives of Canada

Fischl, Eric
Mus. of Contemporary Art
Video Data Bank

Fish
British Info. Svcs., Radio & TV Div.
CBS News Archives
Calif. Dept. of Water Resources
Caribbean Images, Ltd.
Cinenet (Cinema Network)
Echo Film Prods., Inc.
Energy Productions
Film Bank
Grinberg (Sherman) Film Libraries (East)
Indiana State Comm. on Public Records
Intl. Game Fish Assn.
Kesser Stock Footage Library
March of Time
Marineland of Florida
Miller (David Lee) Prods.
Minnesota Zoo
Moonlight Productions
Natl. Archives (RG 22)
Natl. Archives (RG 115)
Natl. Oceanic & Atmospheric Admin.
New Mexico State Records Ctr. & Arch.
New York Zoological Society
Passage Home Communications
Petrified Films, Inc.
Summit Films, Inc.
See also Marine life; Underwater footage;
  specific fish

Fish and Wildlife Service (U.S.)
Natl. Archives (RG 22)
Natl. Archives (Stock Film Coll.)

Fish and wildlife technicians
TV Ontario

Fish markets
Energy Productions

Fisher (Animal)
Minnesota Zoo

Fisher, Eddie
Archive Film Prods., Inc.
Banks Film Library
MacDonald, J. Fred

Fisher, M.F.K.
Radcliffe Coll., Schlesinger Lib.

Fisheries
See Fishing industry

Fishermen and fishing
Ackerman-Black Prods., Inc.
Alaska Video Prods.
Archive Film Prods., Inc.
Beerger (Norman) Prods.
Bur. of Florida Folklife Progs.
CBS News Archives
Chiappetta Prods., Inc.

Dreamlight Images, Inc.
Echo Film Prods., Inc.
Encore Video Prods., Inc.
Energy Productions
Film Bank
Indiana State Comm. on Public Records
Intl. Game Fish Assn.
Jewell (Stuart) Productions
Kentucky Dept. of Libraries & Archives
Kesser Stock Footage Library
MacDonald, J. Fred
Media West, Inc.
Metro Communications, Inc.
Natl. Archives (RG 130)
Natl. Archives of Canada
Natl. Oceanic & Atmospheric Admin.
Natl. Rifle Assn.
New Mexico State Records Ctr. & Arch.
New York State Dept. of Env. Cons.
North Country Media Group
Northeast Historic Film
Omega Films
Ontario Film Institute
Oregon Hist. Soc.
Peak Productions, Inc.
Petrified Films, Inc.
Prelinger Assoc., Inc.
Preview Media
Prov. Arch. of Alberta
Prov. Arch. of British Columbia
Pyramid Film and Video Corp.
Riccitelli (Bruce) Prods.
Site Productions
Snyder (Bill) Films, Inc.
Sonoma Video Productions
Source Stock Footage Lib., Inc.
Spalla (Rick) Video Prods.
Spectral Comms.
Sportsfilm
Summit Films, Inc.
TV Ontario
Texas Tech Univ., Southwest Coll.
Timesteps Prods., Inc.
Twentieth Century-Fox Movietonews
Univ. of Alberta, Boreal Inst. for Northern
  Studies
Video I-D, Inc.
Visuart, Inc.
Windsor Prod. Corp.

Fishermen and fishing (Fly-fishing)
North Country Media Group
Sonoma Video Prods.

Fishing industry
Baylor Univ., Texas Coll.
Canadian Filmmakers Dist. West
Dreamlight Images, Inc.
Film Bank
Hot Shots Commercial Prods., Inc.
KYUK-TV
Manitowoc Maritime Museum
March of Time
Mariners' Museum
Media Project
Natl. Archives (RG 22)
Natl. Archives (RG 242)
Natl. Archives of Canada
Natl. Oceanic & Atmospheric Admin.
New Mexico State Records Ctr. & Arch.
Nine Star Productions
Ocean Earth Constr. and Dev. Corp.
Oregon State Univ., Archives
Prelinger Assoc., Inc.
San Francisco Maritime Natl. Hist. Park
Université de Moncton, Centre d'Études
  Acad.

Fishing trawlers
See Boats and boating (Fishing trawlers)

Fishing villages
Petrified Films, Inc.

Fishman, Louise

Video Data Bank

Fisk Jubilee Singers
Schomburg Ctr. for Res. in Black Culture

Fist fights
Archive Film Prods., Inc.
Dreamlight Images, Inc.
Fish Films, Inc.
See also Brawls

Fitch, James Marston
Unicorn Projects

Fitch, John T.
Mass. Inst. of Tech., MIT Museum

Fitness
See Physical fitness

Fitzgerald, Ella
Archive Film Prods., Inc.
Banks Film Library
Chertok Assoc., Inc.
Schomburg Ctr. for Res. in Black Culture
UCLA Film & Television Archive

Fitzpatrick (Cartoonist)
MacDonald, J. Fred

Flack, Audrey
Video Data Bank

Flagpole sitting
Analogous Productions
Petrified Films, Inc.
See also Fads

Flags
CBS News Archives
Film Bank
Hayes Prods., Inc.
Lunar Productions
Twentieth Century-Fox Movietonews

Flags (Canada)
TV Ontario

Flags (International)
Petrified Films, Inc.

Flags (Mexico)
Hayes Prods., Inc.

Flags (U.S.)
Amer. Legion
Dreamlight Images, Inc.
Energy Productions
Fish Films, Inc.
Hayes Prods., Inc.
Petrified Films, Inc.
Prelinger Assoc., Inc.

Flaherty, Robert J.
Natl. Archives/Natl. AV Ctr.

Flamenco dancing
See Dance and dancing (Flamenco)

Flames
Film Bank
Fish Films, Inc.
Newsreel Video Service
Petrified Films, Inc.
Rosebush Visions Corp.
See also Fires

Flaming Gorge, Utah
Utah Travel Council

Flamingos
Energy Productions
Film Bank
Jewell (Stuart) Prods.
Kesser Stock Footage Library

Minnesota Zoo
Petrified Films, Inc.
Rosebush Visions Corp.
Summit Films, Inc.

Flamingos (Pink)
TV Ontario

Flanagan, Tommy
Rhapsody Films, Inc.

Flappers
Allen (John E.) Inc.
Archive Film Prods., Inc.
Forsher (James) Prods. & Archives, Inc.
Grinberg (Sherman) Film Libraries (West)

Flare guns
Film Bank

Flavin, Dan
Blackwood Prods., Inc.

Flea markets
Appalshop Films, Inc.

Fleetwood Mac
Archive Film Prods., Inc.

Fleischer, Dave
Natl. Archives (RG 47)

Fleischner, Richard
Blackwood Prods., Inc.

Fleming, Peggy
Jalbert Productions

Flemming, Rhonda
Banks Film Library

Flies (House)
Film Bank
Hagley Mus. and Lib.
TV Ontario

Flight attendants
Archive Film Prods., Inc.
Committee for Labor Access
Windsor Prod. Corp.
Prelinger Assoc., Inc.

Flight simulation
Link Flight Simulation Div.
NASA, Ames Res. Ctr., Imaging Tech.
  Branch
NASA, Office of Comm.
Prelinger Assoc., Inc.

Flight tests
See Aircraft (Flight tests)

Flint, Mich. (History and culture)
General Motors Corp.
New Day Films
Perry (Merle G.) Arch.
Petrified Films, Inc.
Prelinger Assoc., Inc.

Floats (Parade)
CBS News Archives
Petrified Films, Inc.
White Janssen, Inc.
See also Parades

Flood control
Natl. Archives (RG 142)

Flood, Edward
Video Data Bank

Floods
Allen (John E.) Inc.
Analogous Productions
Appalshop Films, Inc.

Archive Film Prods., Inc.
Bullfrog Films, Inc.
Colorado Historical Society
Dreamlight Images, Inc.
Estuary Press
Film Bank
Finley (Stuart) Inc.
Forsher (James) Prods. & Archives, Inc.
Grinberg (Sherman) Film Libraries (West)
Hearst Metrotone News
Indiana State Comm. on Public Records
Indiana State Lib.
Kentucky Dept. of Libraries & Archives
Massachusetts Archives
Missouri Hist. Soc.
Mus. & Hist. Div., City of Sacramento
Natl. Archives (RG 18)
Natl. Archives (RG 69)
Natl. Archives (RG 96)
Natl. Archives (RG 115)
Natl. Archives (RG 304)
Natl. Archives (RG 397)
Natl. Archives/Natl. AV Ctr.
Natl. Oceanic & Atmospheric Admin.
Oregon Hist. Soc.
Petrified Films, Inc.
Prelinger Assoc., Inc.
Pub. Lib. of Cincinnati & Hamilton Cty.
South Dakota State Lib.
Sweet (Harry) Film Coll.
Texas Tech Univ., Southwest Coll.
Timesteps Prods., Inc.
Twentieth Century-Fox Movietonews
Univ. of Vermont, Bailey/Howe Lib.
West Virginia Dept. of Culture & Hist.
See also Disasters

Floor hockey
See Hockey (Floor)

Flora and fauna
Brazilian-American Cultural Inst.
Canadian Broadcasting Corp.
Film Bank
KD Enterprises Prods.
Navajo Tribe, Off. Broadcast Svcs.
Peary-MacMillan Arctic Museum
Prelinger Assoc., Inc.
Schweitzer (Albert) Ctr.
Washington State Hist. Soc.
See also Flowers; Foliage; Nature;
   Wildlife

Florence, Italy
Preview Media
Quest Productions Inc.

Florence, Italy (History and culture)
Archive Film Prods., Inc.

Flores Sea, Indonesia
Source Stock Footage Lib., Inc.

Florida
Airline Film & TV Promotions
Atlantic Productions
Century Video Services, Inc.
Cine-Mark
Communications Concepts
Creative Video, Inc.
Energy Prods.
Florida State Archives
Grinberg (Sherman) Film Libraries (West)
Kesser Stock Footage Library
Marineland of Florida
Moody Inst. of Science
Orion Post Production
Passage Home Communications
Petrified Films, Inc.
Postcards Unlimited
Preview Media

Sea TV
Shell Oil Co.
Simon (Jeff) Productions
Sonoma Video Productions
Spalla (Rick) Video Prods.
Video I-D, Inc.
Video Management Systems
Video Ventures Prods.
Villon Films
Wallen (Dick) Prods.

Florida (History and culture)
Analogous Prods.
Archive Film Prods., Inc.
Bur. of Florida Folklife Progs.
Film/Audio Services, Inc.
Florida State Archives
Glenbow Mus. Arch.
Hist. Soc. of Palm Beach County
Lib. of Congress, M/B/RS
March of Time
Oregon Hist. Soc.
Petrified Films, Inc.
Prelinger Assoc., Inc.
Prestige Film Corp.
Prov. Arch. of Alberta
Schiele Museum
St. Augustine Hist. Soc.
Swain (Hack) Prods., Inc.
United Farm Workers of America (UFW)
Univ. of Miami, Arch. & Spec. Coll.
Wolfson (Louis II) Media Hist. Ctr.,
   Miami-Dade Pub. Lib.

Florida Keys
Video I-D, Inc.

Florists
Petrified Films, Inc.

Flory, Paul J.
Amer. Chemical Soc.

Flour
Oregon State Univ., Archives

Flower arrangement
Bullfrog Films, Inc.

Flower shows
Analogous Productions

Flowers
Ackerman-Black Prods., Inc.
Amer. Motion Pictures
Bailey Productions, Inc.
Brooklyn Botanic Garden
CBS News Archives
Chisholm (Jack) Film Productions
Cinenet (Cinema Network)
Dobovan Productions, Inc.
Dreamlight Images, Inc.
Echo Film Prods., Inc.
Energy Productions
Film Bank
Film Search
Image Bank
Impact Audio Visual
Jewell (Stuart) Productions
Kesser Stock Footage Library
Marx Production Center
Metro Communications, Inc.
New Mexico State Records Ctr. & Arch.
Petrified Films, Inc.
Quenzer Driscoll Dawson, Inc.
Source Stock Footage Lib., Inc.
Spectral Comms.
Swedberg (Jack)
TV Ontario
TV-3
Video Tape Library, Ltd.

Wings Wildlife Prods. Inc.

Floyd, Pretty Boy
Archive Film Prods., Inc.

Flu
Historical Health Film Coll.

Fluid mechanics
Engineering Societies Lib.

Fluoridation
Amer. Dental Assn.

Flutie, Doug
Archive Film Prods., Inc.
Boston Coll., Univ. Arch.

Fly-fishing
See Fishermen and fishing (Fly-fishing)

Flye, Father
Agee (James) Film Project

Flying boats
See Aircraft (Flying boats)

Flying Lizards (Rock and roll band)
Target Video

Flying saucers
See Unidentified flying objects (UFOs)

Flying Wallendas
Analogous Productions

Flynn, Errol
Archive Film Prods., Inc.
Banks Film Library

Flynn, Rita
Videobrary, Inc.

Fo, Dario
Richter Productions

Foch, Ferdinand
Natl. Archives (RG 24)
Natl. Archives (RG 75)

Fog
CBS News Archives
Charisma Prods., Ltd./Visual Motion
Cinenet (Cinema Network)
Dreamlight Images, Inc.
Energy Productions
Film Bank
Image Bank
Twentieth Century-Fox Movietonews

Foliage
Charisma Prods., Ltd./Visual Motion
Cineworks Prods. Inc.
Dreamlight Images, Inc.
Energy Productions
Film Bank
Video Tape Library, Ltd.
See also Flowers; Forests; Nature; Plants;
   Trees

Foliage (Fall)
Amer. Motion Pictures
Cinenet (Cinema Network)
Dreamlight Images, Inc.
Echo Film Prods., Inc.
Energy Productions
Film Bank
Moving Media
Preview Media
Site Productions
Source Stock Footage Lib., Inc.

Vermont Hist. Soc.
Xicom, Inc.
See also Fall (Season)

Foliage (Tropical)
Kesser Stock Footage Library

Folk art
Appalshop Films, Inc.
Bur. of Florida Folklife Progs.
Center for Southern Folklore
Corning Mus. of Glass
East-West Center
Ethnic Folk Arts Center
Film Bank
Filmfair Communications
High Mus. of Art
Media Bus
Media Project
Natl. Archives of Canada
Natl. Coun. of Amer.-Sov. Friendship
See also Crafts; Folk culture

Folk art (Black)
Schomburg Ctr. for Res. in Black Culture
Univ. of Miss., Ctr. for Study of Southern
   Culture

Folk culture
Appalshop Films, Inc.
Bur. of Florida Folklife Progs.
Country Music Foundation, Inc.
Davenport Films
Documentary Educational Resources
East-West Center
Indiana Univ. Folklore Arch.
Lib. of Congress, Amer. Folklife Ctr.
Ozark Folk Center
Postcards Associates
Pyramid Film and Video Corp.
Univ. of Tex. at Austin, Barker Tex. Hist.
   Ctr.
Vedo Films/Novacom Video
Western Kentucky Univ., Folklife Arch.
See also Crafts; Dance and dancing; Folk
   art; Folklore

Folk dancing
See Dance and dancing (Folk)

Folk festivals
See Festivals (Folk)

Folk music
See Music (Folk)

Folkers, Karl
Amer. Chemical Soc.

Folklore
Alaska Native Heritage Film Project
Amer. Zionist Youth Found.
Appalachian State Univ., Eury Coll.
Center for Southern Folklore
Churchill Films
Coronet/MTI Film & Video
Davenport Films
Documentary Educational Resources
East Tenn. State Univ., Arch. of
   Appalachia
Farkas Studios, Ltd.
Films for the Humanities and Sciences
Indiana Univ. Folklore Arch.
Intermedia Arts Minnesota
Native Amer. Pub. Broad. Cons.
Ozark Folk Center
Postcards Associates
Univ. of Alabama, W.S. Hoole Spec. Coll.
Univ. of Alberta, Boreal Inst. for Northern
   Studies

NOTE: Access policies, availability and restrictions vary for each source. Please read each entry in full. Always consult "General Film and Videotape Collections" (page 599); these comprehensive collections contain material on every conceivable subject.

Univ. of Miss., Ctr. for Study of Southern
   Culture
Univ. of Wis., Green Bay, Ctr. TV Prod.
Vedo Films/Novacom Video
Wayne State Univ., Folklore Arch.
West Virginia Univ.
Western Kentucky Univ., Folklife Arch.
Women Make Movies, Inc.
Wyoming State Historical Society

Foltz, Edith
Oregon Hist. Soc.

Fon, Ree Woo
Blackwood Prods., Inc.

Fonda, Henry
Archive Film Prods., Inc.
Banks Film Library
UCLA Film & Television Archive

Fonda, Jane
Banks Film Library
Daphne Productions, Inc.
Film Bank
Intl. Dance Exercise Assn.
Spectral Comms.

Fonda, Peter
Banks Film Library

Fontaine, Frank
Pathé Pictures, Inc.

Fontaine, Joan
Banks Film Library

Fontenot, Canray
Tulane Univ., Amistad Res. Ctr.

Food
Amer. Bakers Assn.
Appalachian State Univ., Eury Coll.
Archives of Ontario
CBS News Archives
Center for New Amer. Media
Dreamlight Images, Inc.
Energy Productions
Ergo Media
Film Bank
Film Search
General Motors Corp.
Handel Film Corp.
Hayes Prods., Inc.
Intermedia Arts Minnesota
Native Amer. Pub. Broad. Cons.
Natl. Archives (RG 4)
New Time Films, Inc.
Oxfam America
Petrified Films, Inc.
Prelinger Assoc., Inc.
TV Ontario
See also Cooking; Eating; Food industry;
   Food service industry; Restaurants;
   specific foods

Food (Decomposing)
Dreamlight Images, Inc.

Food (Packaging)
Prelinger Assoc., Inc.

Food Administration (U.S.)
Natl. Archives (RG 4)

Food and Drug Administration (U.S.)
Natl. Archives (RG 88)
Natl. Library of Medicine

Food industry
Amer. Inst. of Baking
Canned Fruit Promotion Service
March of Time
Natl. Archives of Canada
Natl. Cattlemen's Assn.

Northcoast Communication, Inc.
Petrified Films, Inc.
Université Laval, Cinémathèque
See also Food; Food service industry;
   Restaurants

**Food, Nutrition and Health, White
House Conference on**
Natl. Archives (RG 381)

Food preservation
Bullfrog Films, Inc.
Hearst Metrotone News

Food service industry
Amer. Hotel & Motel Assn.
Applegate Entertainment
Culinary Inst. of America
Icarus Films Intl., Inc.
Natl. Assn. of Convenience Stores
Natl. Restaurant Assn.
Petrified Films, Inc.

Fools
Petrified Films, Inc.

Football
Amateur Athletic Foundation
Archive Film Prods., Inc.
Athletic Institute
Duke Univ., Perkins Lib.
Film Bank
Forsher (James) Prods. & Archives, Inc.
Freewheelin' Films, Ltd.
Grinberg (Sherman) Film Libraries (West)
Kesser Stock Footage Library
Oregon State Univ., Archives
Petrified Films, Inc.
Pyramid Film and Video Corp.
Second Line Search
Spalla (Rick) Video Prods.
Texas Tech Univ., Southwest Coll.
Timesteps Prods., Inc.
Twentieth Century-Fox Movietonews
Video Tape Library, Ltd.
White Janssen, Inc.
Zielinski Productions, Inc.

Football (Australian rules)
Farkas Studios, Ltd.
Petrified Films, Inc.

Football (Canadian)
Prov. Arch. of Manitoba

Football (College)
ABC Sports, Inc.
Allen (John E.) Inc.
Analogous Productions
Auburn University Archives
Boston College, Univ. Arch.
Bowling Green State Univ., Ctr. Arch.
   Coll.
College Football Hall of Fame
Connecticut Historical Society
Cornell Univ., Media Services
DePauw University, Archives
Eastern Kentucky Univ.
Everett Pub. Lib., N.W. Hist. Coll.
Franklin & Marshall Coll.
Goal Prod., Tourn. of Roses Film Lib.
Golden Gaters Prods.
Grinberg (Sherman) Film Libraries (West)
Marquette Univ., Spec. Coll.
Michigan State Univ., Archives
NCAA Productions
Natl. Archives (RG 111)
Northern Ill. Univ., Reg. Hist. Ctr.
Ohio State Univ., Dept. of Photog. &
   Cinema
Oregon State Univ., Archives
Petrified Films, Inc.
Sportsfilm
Texas A&M Univ., Univ. Arch.

Univ. of Colo., Boulder, Western Hist.
   Coll.
Univ. of Kansas
Univ. of Mich., Mich. Hist. Colls.
Univ. of Okla., Western Hist. Colls.
Univ. of Rhode Island, Univ. Lib.
Univ. of Toledo, Univ. Arch.
Univ. of Toronto, Univ. Arch.
Windsor Prod. Corp.

Football (High school)
Amer. Motion Pictures
Center for Southern Folklore
Central New England Film Arch.
Eastern Kentucky Univ.
Grinberg (Sherman) Film Libraries (West)
Nemiroff Prods., Inc.
Petrified Films, Inc.

Football (Instruction)
NCAA Productions
NFL Films, Inc.

Football (Mud)
Channell One Video

Football (North American)
Natl. Archives of Canada

Football (Professional)
Allen (John E.) Inc.
Archive Film Prods., Inc.
4•6•8 Prods., Inc.
Golden Gaters Prods.
Grinberg (Sherman) Film Libraries (West)
March of Time
NFL Films, Inc.
Sports Mus. of New England
Video Tape Library, Ltd.

Footbinding
Media Project

Footprints
Banks Film Library
Dreamlight Images, Inc.
Petrified Films, Inc.
Spalla (Rick) Video Prods.

Footwear
See Shoes

Ford (Henry) Family
Natl. Archives (RG 200)

Ford (Henry) Museum
Natl. Archives (RG 200)

Ford, Betty
Spectral Comms.

Ford, Gerald R.
Amer. Enterprise Institute
Archive Film Prods., Inc.
Daphne Productions, Inc.
Ford (Gerald R.) Library

Ford, Glenn
Banks Film Library

Ford, Henry
Hearst Metrotone News
Natl. Archives (RG 200)
Natl. Archives/Natl. AV Ctr.
Prelinger Assoc., Inc.

Ford, Hermine
Video Data Bank

Ford, Leighton
Wheaton Coll., Billy Graham Ctr.

Ford Motor Company
Natl. Archives (RG 200)

Ford, Tennessee Ernie
Pathé Pictures, Inc.
Shokus Video

Ford, Whitey
Daphne Productions, Inc.

Foreign language instruction
Britannica Films & Video
Coe Film Assoc., Inc.
Facets Multimedia, Inc.
Films Incorporated
Films for the Humanities and Sciences
French Lib. in Boston
GPN
Goethe House, New York
Goethe Institute Atlanta
Goethe Institute Chicago
Goethe Institute Los Angeles
Goethe Institute San Francisco
Handel Film Corp.
Intellimation
Intl. Film Bureau, Inc.
Italian Cultural Institute
Media Guild
Natl. Archives/Natl. AV Ctr.
Peralta Colleges TV
Soc. for French Amer. Cult. Svcs. & Educ.
   Aid

Foreign Legion
Fish Films, Inc.

Foreign relations (U.S.)
Duke Univ., Perkins Lib.
Educational Film & Video Project
Ideal Comms., Inc.
Illinois State Hist. Lib.
Myrin Institute
Natl. Archives (RG 59)
Natl. Archives (RG 174)
Natl. Archives (RG 200)
Natl. Archives (RG 306)
Natl. Archives (RG 330)
Richter Productions
Univ. of Mich., Mich. Hist. Colls.
Vietnam Veterans Against the War
Villon Films
See also Social and political issues; United
   States-China relations; United States-
   Cuba relations; United States-Japan
   relations; United States-Latin America
   relations; United States-Mexico
   relations; United States-Soviet
   relations; United States-Third World
   relations

Foreign Service (U.S.)
Natl. Archives (RG 59)

Foreigner (Rock and roll band)
Clark (Dick) Media Archives, Inc.

Forest fires
See Fires (Forest)

Forest rangers
CBS News Archives

Forest Service (U.S.)
Natl. Archives (RG 33)

Forestry
Arch. Nationales du Québec
British Info. Svcs., Radio & TV Div.
Echo Film Prods., Inc.
Estuary Press
GPN
Indiana State Comm. on Public Records
Natl. Archives (RG 33)
Natl. Archives/Natl. AV Ctr.
Natl. Assn. of Conservation Dists.
North Central Forest Exp. Sta.
Oregon Hist. Soc.
Petrified Films, Inc.

Richter Productions
TV Ontario
Univ. of Toronto, Univ. Arch.
See also Logging industry

Forests
Bullfrog Films, Inc.
CBS News Archives
Cinenet (Cinema Network)
Dreamlight Images, Inc.
Energy Productions
Film Bank
Forsher (James) Prods. & Archives, Inc.
Moving Media
Natl. Archives of Canada
Natl. Science Foundation
Nature Conservancy
Nei-Ali Prods.
Odyssey Prods., Inc.
Prelinger Assoc., Inc.
Second Line Search
Source Stock Footage Lib., Inc.
Southwest Prods., Inc.
Spectral Comms.
TV Ontario
TVA/Television Assoc.
Twentieth Century-Fox Movietonews
Video Tape Library, Ltd.
See also Logging industry; Trees

Forgery
Highway Safety Films, Inc.
Inst. of Financial Education

Forges
Apertura
Petrified Films, Inc.

Forklifts
Film Bank
Gypsum Assn.
See also Heavy equipment

Formosa
See Taiwan

Forrest, Emil J.
Yukon Archives

Forrest, Helen
Archive Film Prods., Inc.

Forsberg, Randall
Ideal Comms., Inc.

Forster, Kurt
Southern Calif. Inst. of Architecture

Forsyth County, Ga. (History and culture)
King (Dr. Martin Luther, Jr.) Ctr.
Southern Christian Leadership Conference

Forsythe, John
Prelinger Assoc., Inc.
Spectral Comms.

Fort Bragg, N.C. (History and culture)
Connecticut State Lib.

Fort Dix, N.J. (History and culture)
Petrified Films, Inc.

Fort Jackson, S.C. (History and culture)
Natl. Archives (RG 48)

Fort, Joel
Psychological and Educational Films

Fort Lauderdale, Fla.
Kesser Stock Footage Library

Video Ventures Prods.

Fort Lauderdale, Fla. (History and culture)
Petrified Films, Inc.

Fort McMurray, Alberta (History and culture)
Prov. Arch. of Alberta

Fort Saskatchewan, Alberta (History and culture)
Prov. Arch. of Alberta

Fort Simpson, Northwest Territories
TV Ontario

Fort Worth, Tex.
Creative Video, Inc.
Dreamlight Images, Inc.

Fort Worth, Tex. (History and culture)
MacDonald, J. Fred
Petrified Films, Inc.

Forts
Atlantic Productions
CBS News Archives
Film Bank
Petrified Films, Inc.
Twentieth Century-Fox Movietonews
Video Tape Library, Ltd.

Fortune tellers
CBS News Archives

Fosse, Bob
Daphne Productions, Inc.

Fossils
CBS News Archives
Spectral Comms.

Foster care
Washington Univ., Brown Schl. of Soc. Work

Foster, Hal
Southern Calif. Inst. of Architecture

Foster, William Z.
Southern Calif. Lib. for Soc. Stud. & Res.

Foucault, Michel
Long Beach Mus. of Art
Video Data Bank

Foulkes, Llyn
Video Data Bank

Foulouis, Benjamin
Wright State Univ. Lib.

Foundries
Petrified Films, Inc.
Prelinger Assoc., Inc.
Timesteps Prods., Inc.
CBS News Archives
Energy Productions
Film Bank
Spectral Comms.
TV Ontario
Twentieth Century-Fox Movietonews
See also Metals and metallurgy

Four Tops
Clark (Dick) Media Archives, Inc.

Four-H Clubs
Glenbow Mus. Arch.
Hearst Metrotone News

Natl. Archives (RG 200)
Oregon State Univ., Archives
Prov. Arch. of Alberta
Univ. of Wisconsin — Extension

Four-dimensional space (Animation)
Rosebush Visions Corp.

Fox hunting
See Hunting and trapping

Fox, John
East Tenn. State Univ., Arch. of Appalachia

Fox, Michael J.
Spectral Comms.

Fox, Silas Fowler
Wheaton Coll., Billy Graham Ctr.

Foxes
Di Sesso (Moe) Wild Life Film Lib.
Minnesota Zoo
New Jersey Network
Petrified Films, Inc.
Wings Wildlife Prods. Inc.

Foxtrot dancing
See Dance and dancing (Foxtrot)

Foxx, Jimmy
Grinberg (Sherman) Film Libraries (West)

Foxx, Redd
Daphne Productions, Inc.

Fractals
Rosebush Visions Corp.

Frampton, Hollis
Video Data Bank

France
Archive Film Prods., Inc.
Beerger (Norman) Prods.
Canadian Broadcasting Corp.
Cousteau Society
Creative Video, Inc.
Dorn (Larry) Associates
Dreamlight Images, Inc.
Film Bank
Goal Prods., Tourn. of Roses Film Lib.
Grinberg (Sherman) Film Libraries (West)
Kesser Stock Footage Library
Pan American Airlines Film Lib.
Petrified Films, Inc.
Preview Media
Stimulus
Summit Films, Inc.
Unicorn Projects
World Monitor
Yue-Sai Kan, Inc.

France (History and culture)
Allen (John E.) Inc.
Analogous Productions
Archive Film Prods., Inc.
Cantor (Arthur) Inc.
Film Search, Inc.
Films for the Humanities and Sciences
French Lib. in Boston
Hoover Institution
March of Time
Natl. Archives (RG 4)
Natl. Archives (RG 18)
Natl. Archives (RG 24)
Natl. Archives (RG 28)
Natl. Archives (RG 111)
Natl. Archives (RG 208)
Natl. Archives (RG 242)

Natl. Archives (RG 326)
Natl. Archives (RG 342)
Natl. Archives of Canada
Natl. Archives/Natl. AV Ctr.
Petrified Films, Inc.
Prelinger Assoc., Inc.
Rockefeller Arch. Ctr.
Roosevelt (Franklin D.) Lib.
Schweitzer (Albert) Ctr.
Soc. for French Amer. Cult. Svcs. & Educ. Aid
Third World Newsreel
Twentieth Century-Fox Movietonews
United Nations Ctr. for Human Settlements
Voyager Co.
Wiesenthal (Simon) Ctr.
World Monitor

Franciosa, Tony
Banks Film Library

Francis, Sam
Blackwood Prods., Inc.

Franco, Debra
Port Washington Pub. Lib.

Franco, Francisco
Halcyon Days Prods.
March of Time
Smith (Margaret Chase) Lib. Ctr.

Franconia, Germany (History and culture)
German Info. Ctr., Film Lib.

Frank, Richard
Spectral Comms.

Frank, Robert
Giorno Poetry Systems Inst.

Frankenthaler, Helen
Albright-Knox Art Gallery
Amer. Federation of the Arts
Blackwood Prods., Inc.

Frankfort, Ky. (History and culture)
Kentucky Dept. of Libraries & Archives

Frankfurt, Germany (History and culture)
Archive Film Prods., Inc.
Petrified Films, Inc.

Frankl, Victor
Graduate Theological Union Lib.
Psychological and Educational Films

Franklin, Aretha
Clark (Dick) Media Archives, Inc.

Franklin, Benjamin
Archive Film Prods., Inc.
Petrified Films, Inc.
Prelinger Assoc., Inc.
Pyramid Film and Video Corp.

Franklin, John Hope
Agee (James) Film Project

Franz Josef, Emperor
Petrified Films, Inc.

Frasconi, Antonio
Amer. Federation of the Arts

Fraternities
Analogous Productions
Petrified Films, Inc.

NOTE: Access policies, availability and restrictions vary for each source. Please read each entry in full. Always consult "General Film and Videotape Collections" (page 599); these comprehensive collections contain material on every conceivable subject.

See also Campus life

Fratianne, Linda
U.S. Olympic Committee

Frazier, Joe
Sportsfilm

Freberg, Stan
Banks Film Library

Free enterprise
General Motors Corp.
Prelinger Assoc., Inc.
U.S. Chamber of Commerce
See also Economics

Free Speech Movement (Berkeley, 1964)
Estuary Press
KCRA-TV
Mus. & Hist. Div., City of Sacramento

Freedman, Jill
Port Washington Pub. Lib.

Freeman, Orville
Univ. of Ill. Urbana-Champaign, Univ.
   Arch.

Freeman, Roland
Port Washington Pub. Lib.

Freeman, S. Dak. (History and culture)
South Dakota State Lib.

Freeways
See Highways

Freezers
Petrified Films, Inc.

Freight trains
See Railroads (Freight)

Freighters
See Ships (Freighters)

Fremantle, Australia
Petrified Films, Inc.

French Americans
Assoc. Canado-Américaine

French Canadians
Natl. Archives of Canada

Frescoes
Petrified Films, Inc.

Fresno, Calif. (History and culture)
Armenian Film Foundation

Freud, Anna
Inst. for Psychoanalysis

Freud, Sigmund
Inst. for Psychoanalysis

Fridley, Minn. (History and culture)
Anoka County Comm. Workshop, Inc.

Friedan, Betty
Radcliffe Coll., Schlesinger Lib.
Univ. of Mich., Mich. Hist. Colls.

Friedman, Benno
Video Data Bank

Friedman, Milton
Constitutional Rights Foundation

Fries, Charles
Spectral Comms.

Frisbees

Film Bank
Pyramid Film and Video Corp.
Video Tape Library, Ltd.

Frogs
Analogous Productions
Dreamlight Images, Inc.
Film Bank
Petrified Films, Inc.
TV Ontario
Wings Wildlife Prods. Inc.

Frost, Robert
Intellimation

Fruit
Academy of Health Sciences, U.S. Army
Canned Fruit Promotion Service
Energy Productions
Hot Shots Commercial Prods., Inc.
Oregon Hist. Soc.
Oregon State Univ., Archives
Petrified Films, Inc.

Fruit and vegetable stands
Energy Productions

Frye, Northrop
Univ. of Toronto, AV Lib.
Film/Audio Services, Inc.
Richter Productions

Fugard, Athol
Film/Audio Services, Inc.
Villon Films

Fujimoto, Shun
U.S. Olympic Committee

Fujimoto, Yoshiko
Amer. Federation of the Arts

Fulbright, J. William
Duke Univ., Perkins Lib.

Fuller, R. Buckminster
Cantor (Arthur) Inc.
Fuller (Buckminster) Institute
Long Beach Mus. of Art
Mass. Inst. of Tech., MIT Museum
Pyramid Film and Video Corp.
Raindance Foundation
Southern Calif. Inst. of Architecture
Video Data Bank

Fuller, Samuel
Blackwood (Christian) Prods., Inc.

Fundraising
Boy Scouts of America
March of Dimes Birth Defects Found.
UJA Federation

**Fundy, Bay of, Canada (History and
   culture)**
Bullfrog Films, Inc.

Funeral industry
Natl. Funeral Directors Assn.
See also Funerals; Morticians and
   mortuaries

Funerals
Appalshop Films, Inc.
CBS News Archives
Film Bank
Filmoteca Luis Muñoz Marin
Fish Films, Inc.
Lib. of Congress, M/B/RS
Memphis State Univ. Libraries
Natl. Archives (RG 111)
Natl. Archives (RG 200)
Natl. Archives (RG 342)
Natl. Funeral Directors Assn.
Ohio Historical Soc.

Petrified Films, Inc.
Prelinger Assoc., Inc.
Timesteps Prods., Inc.
Tulane Univ., Hogan Jazz Archive
Twentieth Century-Fox Movietonews
See also Cemeteries and graves; Coffins;
   Hearses; Mausoleums; Morticians and
   mortuaries; Tombs

Fungi
British Info. Svcs., Radio & TV Div.
Film Bank

Funston, Frederick
Natl. Archives (RG 200)

Fur industry
Canadian Filmmakers Dist. West
Focus on Animals
Friends of Animals
Native Amer. Pub. Broad. Cons.
Natl. Archives (RG 26)
Natl. Archives of Canada
Oregon State Univ., Archives
Prov. Arch. of Alberta
TV Ontario
See also Furs

Furnaces
CBS News Archives

Furnaces (Blast)
Prelinger Assoc., Inc.
See also Steel industry

Furness, Betty
Archive Film Prods., Inc.
MacDonald, J. Fred
Natl. Archives (RG 88)

Furnishings (Home)
CBS News Archives

Furniss, Bruce
U.S. Olympic Committee

Furniture
Petrified Films, Inc.
Prelinger Assoc., Inc.

Furniture (Production)
Univ. of Mich., Mich. Hist. Colls.

Furniture stores
Petrified Films, Inc.

Furs
CBS News Archives
Intl. Fashion Video Library
New York Pub. Lib., Rare Books &
   Manuscripts Div.
Video Catalogue Co., Inc.
See also Fur industry

Futurism
Bullfrog Films, Inc.
General Motors Corp.
Prelinger Assoc., Inc.
Studebaker Natl. Museum

Gabin, Jean
Camera Three Prods., Inc.

Gable, Clark
Banks Film Library
UCLA Film & Television Archive

Gabo, Naum
Blackwood Prods., Inc.

Gabon (History and culture)
Schweitzer (Albert) Ctr.

Gabor, Eva
Banks Film Library

Spectral Comms.

Gabor, Zsa Zsa
Archive Film Prods., Inc.
Banks Film Library
Spalla (Rick) Video Prods.

Gadgets and gizmos
Grinberg (Sherman) Film Libraries (West)
Northeast Historic Film
Petrified Films, Inc.

Galapagos Islands, Ecuador
Canadian Broadcasting Corp.
Cousteau Society
Preview Media

Galas, Diamanda
Giorno Poetry Systems Inst.

Galaxies
Dorn (Larry) Associates
Film Bank
Rosebush Visions Corp.
See also Space; Starfields

Galbraith, John Kenneth
Cinema Guild

Gale, Max
Spectral Comms.

Galloway, Kit
Southern Calif. Inst. of Architecture

Galveston, Tex. (History and culture)
Natl. Assn. of Conservation Dists.
Natl. Oceanic & Atmospheric Admin.

Galway, James
Camera Three Prods., Inc.

Gambia
British Info. Svcs., Radio & TV Div.

Gambling
Allen (John E.) Inc.
Analogous Productions
Archive Film Prods., Inc.
Broad Street Prods.
CBS News Archives
Film Bank
Fish Films, Inc.
March of Time
Narcotics Education, Inc.
Petrified Films, Inc.
Twentieth Century-Fox Movietonews
See also Casinos

Games
CBS News Archives
Energy Productions
Film Bank
Slavonic Benev. Order of State of Texas
TV Ontario

Games (Board)
TV Ontario

Games (Scottish)
Sportsfilm

Gamma rays
Smithsonian Inst., Off. of Telecomm.

Gance, Abel
Parker (Kit) Films

Gandhi, Indira
Petrified Films, Inc.

Gandhi, Mohandas K. ("Mahatma")
Archive Film Prods., Inc.
Film Education Institute
Films of India

Halcyon Days Prods.
Hearst Metrotone News
Twentieth Century-Fox Movietonews

Gang of Four (Rock and roll band)
Target Video

Ganges River, Bangladesh-India
British Info. Svcs., Radio & TV Div.
Petrified Films, Inc.

Gangs
Cinema Guild
Newsreel Video Service
Quest Productions Inc.
See also Crime and criminals; Juvenile
delinquents

Gangs (Motorcycle)
Villon Films

Gangsters
Allen (John E.) Inc.
Archive Film Prods., Inc.
Film Bank
Petrified Films, Inc.
See also Crime and criminals

Garage attendants
Petrified Films, Inc.

Garages
CBS News Archives
Petrified Films, Inc.
Prelinger Assoc., Inc.

Garbage
TV Ontario
See also Waste management

Garbo, Greta
Archive Film Prods., Inc.
Intl. Mus. of Photography

García, Inez
Univ. of Tex. at Austin, Benson Lat. Am.
Coll.

García Márquez, Gabriel
Richter Productions

Garcia Villas, Marianella
New Time Films, Inc.

Garden centers
Marx Production Center

Gardena, Calif. (History and culture)
Petrified Films, Inc.

Gardenias
Petrified Films, Inc.

Gardens and gardening
Bailey Productions, Inc.
Brooklyn Botanic Garden
Bullfrog Films, Inc.
CBS News Archives
Carter (Amon) Museum
Film Bank
Landscape Architecture Found.
Marx Production Center
Media West, Inc.
Petrified Films, Inc.
TV Ontario
Timesteps Prods., Inc.
Twentieth Century-Fox Movietonews
WGBH Educational Foundation

**Gardens and gardening (Sunken
gardens)**

Hayes Prods., Inc.

Gardner, Ava
Banks Film Library

Gardner, Erle Stanley
Univ. of Tex. at Austin, Ransom Hum.
Res. Ctr., Photo. Coll.

Gardner, Randy
U.S. Olympic Comm.

Garfield, Allen
Spectral Comms.

Gargoyles
Film Bank

Garibaldis (Fish)
Moonlight Productions

Garland, Judy
Banks Film Library
Las Vegas News Bureau
Natl. Archives/Natl. AV Ctr.
UCLA Film & Television Archive

Garlic
Flower Films & Video
Oregon State Univ., Archives

Garment industry
Cinema Guild
TV Ontario
See also Fashion industry

Garment industry (Hong Kong)
Northstar Prods.

Garner, James
Banks Film Library

Garr, Teri
Spectral Comms.

Garroway, Dave
Shokus Video

Garson, Greer
Banks Film Library

Garwin, Dick
Inst. for Space & Security Studies

Gary, Ind. (History and culture)
Indiana Univ. Folklore Arch.
Indiana Univ. Northwest Lib.

Gary, S. Dak. (History and culture)
South Dakota State Lib.

Gas masks
Analogous Productions
Film Bank
Natl. Archives (RG 227)

Gas pedals
See Automobiles (Gas pedals)

Gas stations
Allen (John E.) Inc.
Baylor Univ., Texas Coll.
CBS News Archives
Film Bank
Fish Films, Inc.
Natl. Archives (RG 59)
Petrified Films, Inc.
Prelinger Assoc., Inc.
Timesteps Prods., Inc.
White Janssen, Inc.

Gases
Film Bank

Gasohol
Calif. Dept. of Transportation
North Country Media Group

Gasoline
CBS News Archives
Prelinger Assoc., Inc.

Gastroenterology
Milner-Fenwick, Inc.

Gates, Bill
Computer Television Group, Inc.

Gateway Arch (St. Louis)
Dreamlight Images, Inc.
Energy Productions

Gauchos
Brazilian-American Cultural Inst.
Sheffield (Erin) Prods.
Univ. of Tex. at Austin, Ransom Hum.
Res. Ctr., Photo. Coll.

Gauthier, Eva
Natl. Archives of Canada

Gay and lesbian issues
Adair Films
Amer. Baptist Films/Video
Boston Comm. Access & Prog. Found.
Cambridge Documentary Films, Inc.
Canadian Filmmakers Dist. Centre
Canadian Gay Archives
Cinema Guild
DEC Film & Video
Direct Cinema Ltd.
Exodus Trust Archives of Erotology
Fanlight Prods.
First Run/Icarus Films, Inc.
Focus Intl. Inc.
Fund for Human Dignity, Inc.
Gay Cable Network
Gay Media Task Force
Gay Men's Health Crisis
Groupe Intervention Video
Homosexual Information Center
Intermedia Arts Minnesota
Intl. Gay and Lesbian Archives
Intl. Women's Day Video Fest.
Kinsey Institute
Labor Video Project
Lambda Legal Defense & Education Fund
Multi-Focus, Inc.
Office of the Gay & Lesbian March on
Wash.
One, Inc.
Petrified Films, Inc.
Political Issue Archive
Rational Island Publishers
San Francisco Bay Area TV News Arch.
V/tape
Women Make Movies, Inc.

**Gay and lesbian people (Depiction in the
media)**
Gay Media Task Force

Gaye, Marvin
Clark (Dick) Media Archives, Inc.
UPA Prods. of America

Gaylor, Noel
Educational Film & Video Project
Physicians for Social Responsibility

Gaza Strip (History and culture)
Natl. Archives (RG 59)

Gazelles
Dreamlight Images, Inc.
Jewell (Stuart) Productions
Petrified Films, Inc.
Summit Films, Inc.
Telltales Associates Inc.

Geese
Cinenet (Cinema Network)
Dreamlight Images, Inc.
Ducks Unlimited, Inc.
Echo Film Prods., Inc.
Film Bank
KD Enterprises Prods.
Minnesota Zoo
Petrified Films, Inc.
Snyder (Bill) Films, Inc.
TV Ontario
Wings Wildlife Prods. Inc.

Gehrig, Lou
Grinberg (Sherman) Film Libraries (West)

Gehry, Frank
Blackwood Prods., Inc.
Southern Calif. Inst. of Architecture

Geiger counters
Petrified Films, Inc.

Geiger, H. Jack
Physicians for Social Responsibility

Gellhorn, Martha
Villon Films

Gems
Dreamlight Images, Inc.
See also Jewels and jewelry

Gender
See Sex roles; Sexuality

General Accounting Office (U.S.)
Natl. Archives (RG 217)

General equivalency degrees (GED)
Peralta Colleges TV

General Services Administration (U.S.)
Natl. Archives (RG 269)

General film and videotape collections
ABC News
Allen (John E.) Inc.
Archive Film Prods., Inc.
Britannica Films & Video
British Info. Svcs., Radio & TV Div.
CBS News Archives
CTV Television Network, CTV News
Arch.
Cable News Network Library
Cameo Film Library, Inc.
Canadian Broadcasting Corp.
Cannell (Stephen J.) Productions, Inc.
Chisholm (Jack) Film Prods., Ltd.
Cinenet (Cinema Network)
Columbia Pictures TV/Stock Film Library
Dreamlight Images, Inc.
Energy Productions
Film Bank
Film Search
Film/Audio Services, Inc.
Grinberg (Sherman) Film Libraries (East)
Grinberg (Sherman) Film Libraries (West)
Hearst Metrotone News
Independent Network News (INN)
Lib. of Congress, M/B/RS
Mus. of Broadcasting
Mus. of Mod. Art, Dept. of Film
NBC News Video Archives

NOTE: Access policies, availability and restrictions vary for each source. Please read each entry in full. Always consult "General Film and
Videotape Collections" (page 599); these comprehensive collections contain material on every conceivable subject.

Natl. Archives of Canada
Natl. Archives/Motion Picture, Sound & Video Branch
Natl. Archives/Natl. AV Ctr.
Natl. Ctr. for Film & Video Preservation
Natl. Film Board of Canada
Natl. Geographic Soc. Stock Footage Lib.
Paramount Pictures Stock Film Lib.
Petrified Films, Inc.
Prelinger Assoc., Inc.
Producers Library Service
Public Broadcasting System
Second Line Search
Spelling (Aaron) Productions
Stock House
TV Ontario
Televisa, S.A.
Twentieth Century-Fox Movietonews
U.S. Dept. of Defense, Motion Media Rec. Ctr.
UCLA Film & Television Archive
Universal City Studios
Univ. of So. Carolina, Newsfilm Lib.
Video Tape Library, Ltd.
Visnews Intl.
WGBH Educational Foundation
Weintraub Screen Entertainment, Inc.
White Janssen, Inc.
Worldwide Television News

Generation gap
MacDonald, J. Fred
Prelinger Assoc., Inc.
See also Counterculture (U.S.)

Generators
CBS News Archives
Film Bank

Genesee County, Mich. (History and culture)
Perry (Merle G.) Arch.

Genet, Jean
Film/Audio Services, Inc.
Villon Films

Genetic engineering
Bullfrog Films, Inc.

Genetics
British Info. Svcs., Radio & TV Div.
Bullfrog Films, Inc.
Cinema Guild
Educational Images, Ltd.
Emory Medical Television Network
March of Dimes Birth Defects Found.
Milner-Fenwick, Inc.

Geneva, Switzerland (History and culture)
Archive Film Prods., Inc.

Geneva, Utah (History and culture)
Petrified Films, Inc.

Genies
Prelinger Assoc., Inc.

Gentrification
Channel L Working Group
Cinema Guild
Deep Dish TV
Kartemquin Films
Third World Newsreel

Geography
AIMS Media
Barr Films
Beerger (Norman) Prods.
Britannica Films & Video
Coe Film Assoc., Inc.
Coronet/MTI Film & Video
GPN
Handel Film Corp.

Intl. Film Bureau, Inc.
Inuvik Research Ctr.
Natl. Archives (RG 200)
Natl. Archives (RG 226)
Natl. Archives/Natl. AV Ctr.
Natl. Film Board of Canada
Natl. Geographic Soc. Stock Footage Lib.
Phoenix Films and Video
Prelinger Assoc., Inc.
Pyramid Film and Video Corp.
Rosebush Visions Corp.
TV Ontario
Univ. of Toronto, AV Lib.
Video-SIG

Geological Survey (U.S.)
Natl. Archives (RG 48)

Geology
Amer. Mus. Nat. Hist. Film Arch.
Educational Images, Ltd.
Films for the Humanities and Sciences
Higgins (Alfred) Prods.
Inuvik Research Ctr.
Natl. Archives (RG 48)
Natl. Archives (RG 307)
Nature Conservancy
Phoenix Films and Video
Shell Oil Co.
Twentieth Century-Fox Movietonews
Univ. of Wisconsin — Extension

Geometric shapes and forms
Rosebush Visions Corp.

Geometry
Intl. Film Bureau, Inc.

George V, King
Natl. Archives (RG 24)

George VI, King
Natl. Archives (RG 119)
Roosevelt (Franklin D.) Lib.
Univ. of Toronto, Univ. Arch.

George, Phyllis
Miss America Pageant

George Washington Bridge (New York City)
Analogous Productions
New York State Dept. of Econ. Devel.
Petrified Films, Inc.

Georgetown, D.C.
Washington Broadcast Video Lib.

Georgia
Creative Video, Inc.
Energy Prods.
Omega Films
Preview Media
Unicorn Projects
Video I-D, Inc.
Wallen (Dick) Prods.

Georgia (History and culture)
Atlanta Hist. Soc.
Emory Univ., Spec. Coll.
Estuary Press
King (Dr. Martin Luther, Jr.) Ctr.
Natl. Archives (RG 200)
Ocean Earth Constr. and Dev. Corp.
Petrified Films, Inc.
Roosevelt (Franklin D.) Lib.
Smithsonian Inst., Human Studies Film Arch.
Southern Christian Leadership Conference
Univ. of Georgia, WSB TV News Film Arch.

Georgian, S.S.R.
Canadian Broadcasting Corp.

Geothermal energy
See Energy

Gerenuks
Dreamlight Images, Inc.

German Americans
Blackwood Prods., Inc.

German-American Vocational League
Natl. Archives (RG 131)

Germany
Canadian Broadcasting Corp.
Creative Video, Inc.
Pan American Airlines Film Lib.
Sonoma Video Productions
Stimulus
World Monitor

Germany (East)
Canadian Broadcasting Corp.

Germany (History and culture)
Allen (John E.) Inc.
Analogous Productions
Archive Film Prods., Inc.
Film/Audio Services, Inc.
Films for the Humanities and Sciences
Footage Inc.
German Info. Ctr., Film Lib.
Goethe House, New York
Goethe Institute Atlanta
Goethe Institute Chicago
Goethe Institute Los Angeles
Goethe Institute San Francisco
Goethe Institute Toronto
Goethe Institute Vancouver
March of Time
Natl. Archives (RG 111)
Petrified Films, Inc.
Twentieth Century-Fox Movietonews
Univ. of Tex. at Austin, Ransom Hum. Res. Ctr., Photo. Coll.
Video Yesteryear
Villon Films
World Monitor
Worldwide Television News

Germany (1914-18)
Allen (John E.) Inc.
Natl. Archives (RG 24)
Natl. Archives (RG 200)
Natl. Archives (RG 242)
Natl. Archives of Canada

Germany (1919-33)
Allen (John E.) Inc.
B'nai B'rith Intl. Headquarters
Cantor (Arthur) Inc.
Natl. Archives (RG 131)

Germany (1933-45)
Archive Film Prods., Inc.
Duke Univ., Perkins Lib.
German Language Video Ctr.
Hoover Institution
Intl. Film Foundation
Intl. Historic Films, Inc.
March of Time
Marshall (George C.) Res. Lib.
Moviecraft, Inc.
Natl. Archives (RG 200)
Natl. Archives (RG 238)
Natl. Archives (RG 242)
Natl. Archives (RG 243)
Natl. Archives (RG 342)
Natl. Archives of Canada
Natl. Archives/Natl. AV Ctr.
Petrified Films, Inc.
Prelinger Assoc., Inc.
UCLA Film and Television Archive
UDS Company

Germany (1946-present)

Archive Film Prods., Inc.
March of Time
Marshall (George C.) Res. Lib.
Natl. Archives (RG 18)
Natl. Archives (RG 59)
Natl. Archives (RG 111)
Natl. Archives (RG 306)
Natl. Archives (RG 342)
Natl. Archives of Canada
Prelinger Assoc., Inc.

Germs
Prelinger Assoc., Inc.

Gerontology
See Aging and gerontology

Gershwin, George
Archive Film Prods., Inc.

Gerulaitis, Vitas
Moving Media

Gesell, Arnold
March of Time
Univ. of Akron, Child Develop. Film Arch.

Gettysburg, Pa. (History and culture)
Pennsylvania State Arch.

Getz, Stan
Baker (Fred) Film & Video Co.
Daphne Productions, Inc.

Geysers
Dreamlight Images, Inc.
Energy Productions
Jewell (Stuart) Productions
Twentieth Century-Fox Movietonews
Video Tape Library, Ltd.

Ghana
British Info. Svcs., Radio & TV Div.

Ghana (History and culture)
Singer-Sharrette Traditional Healing Films
Smithsonian Inst., Human Studies Film Arch.
TV Ontario

Ghettos
Archive Film Prods., Inc.
CBS News Archives
Timesteps Prods., Inc.

Ghost towns
See Towns (Ghost)

Ghosts
Fish Films, Inc.
SF•V Intl.

Giacometti, Alberto
Amer. Federation of the Arts
Blackwood Prods., Inc.

Giardello, Joey
New Jersey Network

Gibbons
Minnesota Zoo

Gibbs, Michelle
Paper Tiger TV

Gibraltar, United Kingdom (History and culture)
Archive Film Prods., Inc.
March of Time

Gibson, Hoot
Archive Film Prods., Inc.
Intl. Mus. of Photography

Gila monsters
Wings Wildlife Prods. Inc.

Gilbert and George
Blackwood Prods., Inc.

Gilbert, Billy
Videobrary, Inc.

Gill, Merton
Inst. for Psychoanalysis

Gillespie, Dizzy
Chertok Assoc., Inc.
Rhapsody Films, Inc.
South Carolina Humanities Res. Ctr.

Gilliam, Sam
Video Data Bank

Gilligan, John
Ohio Historical Soc.

Gilpin, Laura
Port Washington Pub. Lib.

Ginnevar, Charles
Long Beach Mus. of Art

Ginsberg, Allen
Giorno Poetry Systems Inst.
San Francisco Bay Area TV News Arch.
Video Data Bank
Villon Films

Ginseng
Nan Hai (U.S.A.) Co., Inc.

Giorno, John
Giorno Poetry Systems Inst.
Monday, Wednesday, Friday Video Club
Video Data Bank

Giovanni, Nikki
Icarus Films Intl., Inc.

Giraffes
Archive Film Prods., Inc.
Di Sesso (Moe) Wild Life Film Lib.
Dreamlight Images, Inc.
Jewell (Stuart) Productions
Miller (David Lee) Prods.
Petrified Films, Inc.
Quinn (Bill) Prods.
Summit Films, Inc.
Wings Wildlife Prods. Inc.

Giraudy, Danielle
Université Laval, Svc. des Res.
   Pédagogiques

Girl Scouts
Allen (John E.) Inc.
Archive Film Prods., Inc.
Girl Scouts of the U.S.A.
Low (J.G.) Girl Scout Natl. Ctr.
Twentieth Century-Fox Movietonews

Gish, Dorothy
UCLA Film & Television Archive

Gish, Lillian
Archive Film Prods., Inc.
Daphne Productions, Inc.
UCLA Film & Television Archive

Giza, Egypt
Petrified Films, Inc.
Rosebush Visions Corp.

Gizmos
See Gadgets and gizmos

Glacier Bay, Alaska (History and culture)
Oregon Hist. Soc.

Glacier National Park, Mont.
Montana Dept. of Commerce
North Country Media Group

Glaciers
Archive Film Prods., Inc.
CBS News Archives
Cinenet (Cinema Network)
Film Bank
Hot Shots Commercial Prods., Inc.
Jewell (Stuart) Productions
Nine Star Productions
North Country Media Group
Petrified Films, Inc.
Source Stock Footage Lib., Inc.
TV Ontario
Twentieth Century-Fox Movietonews
Univ. of Wash. Press, Multimedia Div.
Video Tape Library, Ltd.
Visuart, Inc.

Gladiolas
Petrified Films, Inc.

Glance, Harvey
U.S. Olympic Committee

Glaser, Joe
Inst. for Labor Studies & Research

Glass
CBS News Archives
Corning Mus. of Glass
See also Glassblowing; Glassmaking;
   Stained glass

Glass (Automobile)
See Automobiles (Glass)

Glass (Safety)
Hearst Metrotone News
Natl. Archives (RG 70)

Glass industry
Natl. Glass Assn.
Ohio Historical Soc.

Glass, Philip
Blackwood Prods., Inc.

Glass tubes
Petrified Films, Inc.

Glassblowing
Analogous Productions
Corning Mus. of Glass
Film Bank

Glasser, Albert
Univ. of Wyoming, Western Heritage Ctr.

Glasses (Drinking)
Film Bank

Glasses (Eye)
Corning Mus. of Glass
Prelinger Assoc., Inc.
TV Ontario

Glassmaking
Amer. Craft Council
Corning Mus. of Glass
Prelinger Assoc., Inc.
Seagram Museum

Glaucoma
Nassau Comm. Coll. Lib.
Natl. Soc. to Prevent Blindness

Gleason, Jackie
Banks Film Library
MacDonald, J. Fred

Gleaves, Albert
Natl. Archives (RG 24)

Glen Canyon, Utah
Utah State Hist. Soc.

Glenn, Jack
Univ. of Wyoming, Western Heritage Ctr.

Glenn, John H.
Film Education Institute
Lib. of Congress, M/B/RS
NASA, Lewis Research Center
Natl. Archives (RG 200)

Gless, Sharon
Spectral Comms.

Glick, John
Amer. Federation of the Arts

Glider planes
See Aircraft (Gliders)

Globes
CBS News Archives
Charisma Prods., Ltd./Visual Motion
Petrified Films, Inc.
Prelinger Assoc., Inc.

Gloucester, Ontario
Carleton Prods. Inc.

Go-go dancing
See Dance and dancing (Go-go)

Go-Gos (Rock and roll band)
Target Video

Goats
Amer. Motion Pictures
Amer. Veterinary Medical Assn.
Dreamlight Images, Inc.
Film Bank
Minnesota Zoo
Oregon State Univ., Archives
Petrified Films, Inc.
TV Ontario

Gobi Desert, China-Mongolia
Amer. Mus. Nat. Hist. Film Arch.

Godard, Jean-Luc
Daphne Productions, Inc.
Pennebaker Associates, Inc.
Walker Art Ctr.

Goddard, Paulette
Archive Film Prods., Inc.

Goddard, Robert H.
Hearst Metrotone News
Natl. Archives (RG 200)

Goddard Space Flight Center
Natl. Archives (RG 255)

Godfrey, Arthur
Encore Entertainment
MacDonald, J. Fred
Natl. Archives (RG 56)
Shokus Video
Video Resources N.Y., Inc.

Godiva, Lady
Archive Film Prods., Inc.

Goering, Hermann
Prelinger Assoc., Inc.

Gofman, John
Green Mountain Post Films

Gold
Colorado Historical Society
Film Bank
Jewell (Stuart) Productions
Natl. Archives of Canada
Source Stock Footage Lib., Inc.
See also Mining (Gold)

Gold panning
Dreamlight Images, Inc.
Petrified Films, Inc.

Gold Rush
Archive Film Prods., Inc.
Natl. Archives of Canada
Natural Reflections Video
Women Make Movies, Inc.
Yukon Archives

Gold, Tami
Paper Tiger TV

Goldberg, Arthur
Natl. Archives (RG 59)
Natl. Archives (RG 174)

Goldberg, Rube
Prelinger Assoc., Inc.

Goldberg, Whoopi
Daphne Productions, Inc.
Spectral Comms.

Golden Gate (San Francisco)
Petrified Films, Inc.

Golden Gate Bridge (San Francisco)
Elfstrom-Hilmer Prods.
Energy Productions
Film Search
Source Stock Footage Lib., Inc.
TV Ontario

Golden Gate Bridge (San Francisco) (History and culture)
Analogous Productions
Labor Video Project
Louisiana Tech Univ., Eng. Film Res. Ctr.
Oregon Hist. Soc.
Petrified Films, Inc.
Prelinger Assoc., Inc.

Golden Gate International Exposition
See World's Fairs (San Francisco 1939-40)

Golden Gate Park (San Francisco)
Petrified Films, Inc.
Unicorn Projects

Goldfinches
TV Ontario

Goldfish
TV Ontario

Goldstein, Marna
Video Data Bank

Goldwater, Barry
Banks Film Library
Mus. & Hist. Div., City of Sacramento

NOTE: Access policies, availability and restrictions vary for each source. Please read each entry in full. Always consult "General Film and Videotape Collections" (page 599); these comprehensive collections contain material on every conceivable subject.

Goldwyn, Samuel Jr.
Spectral Comms.

Golf
ABC Sports, Inc.
Allen (John E.) Inc.
Analogous Productions
Archive Film Prods., Inc.
Athletic Institute
Brekke Television Prods.
Creative Video, Inc.
Encore Video Prods., Inc.
Energy Productions
Farkas Studios, Ltd.
Film Bank
Fish Films, Inc.
Kesser Stock Footage Library
March of Dimes Birth Defects Found.
Metro Communications, Inc.
Natl. Archives of Canada
Network Productions
Nightingale-Conant Corp.
North Country Media Group
Peak Productions, Inc.
Petrified Films, Inc.
Rosebush Visions Corp.
Seagram Museum
Second Line Search
Source Stock Footage Lib., Inc.
Spalla (Rick) Video Prods.
Sportsfilm
Summit Films, Inc.
Twentieth Century-Fox Movietonews
U.S. Golf Assn.
Univ. of Notre Dame, Joyce Sports Coll.
Windsor Prod. Corp.

Golf (College)
NCAA Productions

Golf (Instruction)
NCAA Productions
Natl. Assn. for Sport & Phys. Ed.

Golf (Professional)
Emory Univ., Spec. Coll.
Film Search
Natl. Archives of Canada
U.S. Golf Assn.

Golf (Trick)
Analogous Productions

Golf courses
Cinenet (Cinema Network)
Media West, Inc.
Petrified Films, Inc.
Tri-Comm Prods.

Golub, Leon
Mus. of Contemporary Art
Video Data Bank

Gombrich, Ernst
Univ. of Waterloo, A-V Centre

Gómez, Ana
Univ. of Tex. at Austin, Benson Lat. Am.
   Coll.

Gompers, Samuel
Timesteps Prods., Inc.

Gondolas
Analogous Productions
Petrified Films, Inc.

Gonzales, Julio
Blackwood Prods., Inc.

Gonzales, Teodoro
Southern Calif. Inst. of Architecture

Gonzales, Tex. (History and culture)
Univ. of Texas, Inst. of Texan Cultures

Goodell, Charles Ellsworth
New York Pub. Lib., Rare Books &
   Manuscripts Div.

Goodman, Benny
Chertok Assoc., Inc.
Daphne Productions, Inc.
Petrified Films, Inc.

Gophers
Wings Wildlife Prods. Inc.

Gorchov, Rob
Video Data Bank

Gordon, David
Blackwood Prods., Inc.

Gordon, Flash
Archive Film Prods., Inc.

Gordon, Peter
Target Video

Gordon, Richard
Port Washington Pub. Lib.

Gore, Albert Jr.
Guggenheim Productions, Inc.
Natl. Assn. for the Advancement of
   Colored People

Gorges
Film Bank
Video Tape Library, Ltd.

Gorillas
See Apes

Gorky, Arshile
Blackwood Prods., Inc.
Direct Cinema Ltd.

Gorky, Maxim
Film/Audio Services, Inc.
Intl. Film Foundation

Gorme, Eydie
Banks Film Library

Gorshin, Frank
Banks Film Library

Goshawks
KD Enterprises Prods.

Gospel music
See Music (Gospel)

Gossett, Louis Jr.
Spectral Comms.

Gottlieb, Adolph
Blackwood Prods., Inc.

Gould, Glenn
Natl. Lib. of Canada, Music Div.

Goulet, Robert
Banks Film Library
Natl. Archives of Canada
Spectral Comms.

Gouletas, Evangeline
New York State Arch. & Rec. Admin.
Saint John's Univ., Spec. Coll.

Government
See Politics and government

Government buildings
See Buildings (Government)

Government Printing Office (U.S.)
Natl. Archives (RG 149)

Grable, Betty
Archive Film Prods., Inc.
UCLA Film & Television Archive

Grace, Princess
Petrified Films, Inc.

Graceland (Memphis, Tenn.)
Dreamlight Images, Inc.

Graduations
CBS News Archives
Cornell Univ., Media Services
Franklin & Marshall Coll.
Petrified Films, Inc.
TV Ontario
Timesteps Prods., Inc.
Univ. of Pa. Arch.
Vermont Hist. Soc.
See also Campus life; Colleges and
   universities

Graffiti
Dreamlight Images, Inc.
Film Bank
Icarus Films Intl., Inc.
New Day Films
New Jersey Network

Graham, Bill
Cinema Guild

Graham, Martha
Amer. Federation of the Arts

Graham, Otto
NFL Films, Inc.

Graham, William Franklin Jr. ("Billy")
Boy Scouts of America, AV Svcs.
MacDonald, J. Fred
Univ. of Pittsburgh, Arch. of Indust. Soc.
Wheaton Coll., Billy Graham Ctr.
World Wide Pictures, Inc.

Grain
British Info. Svcs., Radio & TV Div.
Energy Productions
Glenbow Mus. Arch.
Petrified Films, Inc.
See also Wheat

Grain (Sprouting)
Energy Productions

Grain (Waves of)
Radio City Music Hall Prods.
See also Wheatfields

Grain elevators
Petrified Films, Inc.
TV Ontario

Gramm, Phil
Constitutional Rights Foundation

Granada, Spain
Preview Media

Grand Canyon, Ariz.
Cine-Mark
Dorn (Larry) Associates
Dreamlight Images, Inc.
KD Enterprises Prods.
Oregon Hist. Soc.
Petrified Films, Inc.
Phoenix Videofilms/Karr Prods.
Pyramid Film and Video Corp.
Sobek Productions
Source Stock Footage Lib., Inc.
Summit Films, Inc.

**Grand Canyon, Ariz. (History and
   culture)**
Prelinger Assoc., Inc.

Utah State Hist. Soc.

Grand Canyon National Park, Ariz.
Beerger (Norman) Prods.
Energy Productions
Natl. Archives (RG 70)
Preview Media
Stimulus

Grand Cayman, Cayman Islands
Passage Home Communications

**Grand Central Terminal (New York
   City)**
Energy Productions

**Grand Central Terminal (New York
   City) (History and culture)**
Archive Film Prods., Inc.
Petrified Films, Inc.

Grand Coulee Dam, Wash.
Analogous Productions

Grand juries
Cinema Guild

Grand Old Opry (Nashville, Tenn.)
Country Music Foundation, Inc.

Grand Prix automobile racing
See Automobiles (Racing) (Grand Prix)

Grand Teton National Park, Wyo.
Energy Productions

**Grand Teton National Park, Wyo.
   (History and culture)**
Rockefeller Arch. Ctr.

Grand Tetons, Wyo.
Beerger (Norman) Prods.
Petrified Films, Inc.
Summit Films, Inc.

Grandmothers
Native Amer. Pub. Broad. Cons.
Prelinger Assoc., Inc.

Grange, Harold ("Red")
Grinberg (Sherman) Film Libraries (West)

Granite
Natl. Archives (RG 70)

Grant, Cary
Banks Film Library

Grant, Johnny
Banks Film Library
Spectral Comms.

Grant's Tomb (New York City)
Petrified Films, Inc.

Grantsmanship
GPN

Grapes
Film Bank
Oregon State Univ., Archives
Petrified Films, Inc.
TV Ontario
United Farm Workers of America (UFW)
Film Bank
Rosebush Visions Corp.

Grass
Film Bank

Grasshoppers
Dreamlight Images, Inc.
Film Bank

666

Grassley, Charles
Constitutional Rights Foundation

Grasso, Ella T.
Connecticut State Library

Grateful Dead
Petrified Films, Inc.

Grauman's Chinese Theatre (Hollywood)
Analogous Productions
Archive Film Prods., Inc.
Banks Film Library
Dreamlight Images, Inc.
Petrified Films, Inc.

Graves
See Cemeteries and graves

Graves, Michael
Southern Calif. Inst. of Architecture

Graves, Morris
Media Project

Graves, Nancy
Albright-Knox Art Gallery
Blackwood Prods., Inc.
Santa Barbara Mus. of Art
Video Data Bank
Walker Art Ctr.

Graves, Peter
Banks Film Library

Gravestone rubbing
New Jersey Network

Gray, Spalding
New York Pub. Lib., Perf. Arts Res. Ctr.,
    Theatre on Film and Tape

Graziano, Rocky
New Jersey Network

Great Barrier Reef, Australia
Petrified Films, Inc.

Great Britain
See United Kingdom

Great Lakes (Canada-U.S.)
Manitowoc Maritime Museum
Video I-D, Inc.

Great Lakes (Canada-U.S.) (History and culture)
Natl. Archives (RG 178)

Great Lakes Naval Training Center
Natl. Archives (RG 24)

Great Salt Lake, Utah
Video West

Great Slave Lake, Northwest Territories
Northwest Territories Archives

Great Smoky Mountains (N.C.-Tenn.)
Preview Media

Great Wall of China
Farkas Studios, Ltd.
Sullivan Video Services

Grebes
Wings Wildlife Prods. Inc.

Greco-Bulgar incident (1925)
Natl. Archives (RG 200)

Greece
Canadian Broadcasting Corp.
Petrified Films, Inc.
Preview Media
Yue-Sai Kan, Inc.

Greece (History and culture)
Archive Film Prods., Inc.
Hellenic College
Intl. Film Bureau, Inc.
March of Time
Natl. Archives (RG 24)
Natl. Archives (RG 59)
Natl. Archives (RG 200)
Natl. Archives (RG 242)
Natl. Ctr. for Jewish Film
Petrified Films, Inc.
Prelinger Assoc., Inc.
Rockefeller Arch. Ctr.
Twentieth Century-Fox Movietonews

Greek Orthodox religion
See Religion (Greek Orthodox)

Green, Aaron
Unicorn Projects

Green, Alan
Albright-Knox Art Gallery

Green Bay, Wis.
Univ. of Wis., Green Bay, Ctr. TV Prod.

Green Bay, Wis. (History and culture)
Native Amer. Pub. Broad. Cons.
Neville Pub. Museum

Green beans
Energy Productions

Green peppers
TV Ontario

Green River, Utah (History and culture)
Utah State Hist. Soc.

Greenbelt, Md. (History and culture)
Prelinger Assoc., Inc.

Greenberg, Clement
Blackwood Prods., Inc.

Greene, Lorne
Banks Film Library

Greenfield Village (Dearborn, Mich.)
Natl. Archives (RG 200)

Greenham Common, England (History and culture)
DEC Film & Video

Greenhouse effect
Natl. Oceanic & Atmospheric Admin.

Greenhouses
CBS News Archives
Film Bank

Greenland (History and culture)
Acad. of Nat. Sci. of Phila. Lib.
Duffy (Kevin) Prods.
Natl. Archives (RG 200)
Peary-MacMillan Arctic Museum

Greenpeace
Canadian Filmmakers Dist. Centre
Canadian Filmmakers Dist. West
Film Bank
Focus on Animals
Greenpeace, U.S.A.

Pyramid Film and Video Corp.
U.S. Council for Energy Awareness

Greensboro, N.C.
TV Ontario

Greenwich, N.J. (History and culture)
New Jersey Network

Greenwich Village, N.Y. (History and culture)
Petrified Films, Inc.

Greenwood, Charlotte
Videobrary, Inc.

Greenwood, Miss. (History and culture)
Mississippi Dept. of Arch. & Hist.

Greer, Germaine
Pennebaker Associates, Inc.

Greeting cards
Film Bank

Greeting cards (Production)
Petrified Films, Inc.

Gregory, Cynthia
Daphne Productions, Inc.

Gregory, Dick
Center for Pacific Northwest Studies
Green Mountain Post Films
King (Dr. Martin Luther, Jr.) Ctr.
Natl. Assn. for the Advancement of
    Colored People

Gremp, David
Mus. of Contemporary Art

Grenada
Northstar Prods.
Sea TV

Grenada (Contemporary issues)
Alternative Information Network
Amer. Security Council Foundation

Grenada (History and culture)
Cinema Guild
DEC Film & Video
Film/Audio Services, Inc.
Idera Films
Military/Combat Stock Footage
Multi-Media Pre-Accession Point
Mus. of Mod. Art of Latin America
New Time Films, Inc.
Payne, Roz
U.S. Committee for UNICEF
Worldwide Television News

Grenadines
Preview Media

Grey jays
Cinenet (Cinema Network)

Grey Owl (Archibald Belaney)
Natl. Archives of Canada

Grey, Zane
Ohio Historical Soc.

Grids
Rosebush Visions Corp.

Griffin, Merv
Spectral Comms.

Griffis, W. Stanton

Duke Univ., Perkins Lib.

Griffith, Andy
Encore Entertainment
Shokus Video

Griffith, D.W.
Alan Twyman Presents
Archive Film Prods., Inc.

Griffiths, Martha Wright
Univ. of Mich., Mich. Hist. Colls.

Grimes, Lucia Voorhees
Univ. of Mich., Mich. Hist. Colls.

Grimsby, Roger
Daphne Productions, Inc.

Griots
See Black history and culture

Gripsholm (S.S.)
Natl. Archives (RG 59)

Grocery stores
See Supermarkets

Grodin, Charles
Spectral Comms.

Gronk
Video Data Bank

Grooming
Fish Films, Inc.
Prelinger Assoc., Inc.

Grooms
See Weddings

Gropius, Walter
Goethe Institute Chicago
Natl. Archives of Canada

Grossman, Nancy
Video Data Bank

Grossman, Tatyana
Camera Three Prods., Inc.

Grotowski, Jerzy
Camera Three Prods., Inc.

Grottos
Film Bank

Group therapy
See Psychoanalysis and psychotherapy
    (Group therapy)

Grouse
Petrified Films, Inc.
Summit Films, Inc.

Groves, Leslie
Film Bank

Grozza, Lou ("The Toe")
MacDonald, J. Fred

Gruen, Victor
Univ. of Wyoming, Western Heritage Ctr.

Guadalajara, Mexico
Preview Media

Guam (History and culture)
March of Time

NOTE: Access policies, availability and restrictions vary for each source. Please read each entry in full. Always consult "General Film and Videotape Collections" (page 599); these comprehensive collections contain material on every conceivable subject.

Guanaja, Honduras
Passage Home Communications

Guanajuato, Mexico
Source Stock Footage Lib., Inc.

Guantanamo Bay, Cuba
Analogous Productions

Guard (Changing of the)
Petrified Films, Inc.
TV Ontario
Twentieth Century-Fox Movietonews

Guards
CBS News Archives
Film Bank

Guarnieri, Johnny
Rhapsody Films, Inc.

Guatemala
British Info. Svcs., Radio & TV Div.
Imagen y Sonido Independiente, S.A.
Jewell (Stuart) Productions
Northstar Prods.
Source Stock Footage Lib., Inc.

Guatemala (Contemporary issues)
DEC Film & Video
Film/Audio Services, Inc.
Icarus-Tamouz Media, Inc.
Oxfam America
Skylight Pictures

Guatemala (History and culture)
Anthropology Film Ctr. Foundation
Archive Film Prods., Inc.
DEC Film & Video
Documentary Educational Resources
Film/Audio Services, Inc.
Icarus Films Intl., Inc.
Icarus-Tamouz Media, Inc.
Idera Films
Latina, S.A. de C.V.
Mus. of Mod. Art of Latin America
Natl. Archives (RG 234)
Salvation Army, Natl. Comm. Dept.
Southern Calif. Inst. of Architecture

Guaymas, Mexico
Source Stock Footage Lib., Inc.

Guerrero, Raúl
Long Beach Mus. of Art

Guevara, Ernesto ("Che")
Center for Cuban Studies

Guidance
Altschul Group
Britannica Films & Video
Campbell Films, Inc.
Churchill Films
Phoenix Films and Video

Guides (Outfitters)
North Country Media Group

Guides (Tourism)
CBS News Archives

Guinea-Bissau (Contemporary issues)
DEC Film & Video

Guinea-Bissau (History and culture)
Third World Newsreel

Guitars
Archive Film Prods., Inc.

Gujerat, India (History and culture)
Smithsonian Inst., Human Studies Film Arch.

Gulf of Mexico
Century Video Services, Inc.
First Group Comms., Inc.
Orion Post Production

Gullahs
South Carolina Humanities Res. Ctr.

Gulliver
Archive Film Prods., Inc.

Gulmarg, Kashmir, India
Petrified Films, Inc.

Gun control
Foundation for Handgun Education
Political Issue Archive

Gunfights
See Shootouts

Gunnison, Colo.
Summit Films, Inc.

Guns and rifles
CBS News Archives
Coronet/MTI Film & Video
Film Bank
Foundation for Handgun Education
Natl. Archives (RG 111)
Natl. Rifle Assn.
New York State Dept. of Env. Cons.
Petrified Films, Inc.
See also Pistol shooting (Sport); Rifle ranges; Shootouts; Weapons

Gunshots
Film Bank
Prelinger Assoc., Inc.

Gunsmithing
Baylor Univ., Texas Coll.

Guppies
Film Bank

Guston, Philip
Blackwood Prods., Inc.

Guthrie, Arlo
Christopher Closeup

Guthrie, Janet
Indiana State Lib.

Guthrie, Woody
Wombat Film & Video

Guy, Buddy
Rhapsody Films, Inc.

Guyana (Contemporary issues)
DEC Film & Video

Guyana (History and culture)
DEC Film & Video
Singer-Sharrette Traditional Healing Films
Third World Newsreel

Gwathmey, Charles
Southern Calif. Inst. of Architecture

/Gwi San people
Smithsonian Inst., Human Studies Film Arch.

Gymnasiums
CBS News Archives
Film Bank
Petrified Films, Inc.
ABC Sports, Inc.
Analogous Productions
Athletic Institute
Dreamlight Images, Inc.
Energy Productions

Film Bank
Lemorande Prod. Co.
Natl. Dance Assn.
Pyramid Film and Video Corp.
Sportsfilm
Twentieth Century-Fox Movietonews
Video Tape Library, Ltd.

Gymnastics (College)
NCAA Productions
Oregon State Univ., Archives

Gymnastics (Instruction)
NCAA Productions
Natl. Assn. for Sport & Phys. Ed.

Gyms
See Gymnasiums

Gynecology
See Obstetrics and gynecology

Gypsies
Archive Film Prods., Inc.

Gypsum
Gypsum Assn.

Gysin, Brion
Giorno Poetry Systems Inst.

HUAC
See House Un-American Activities Committee (HUAC)

Haacke, Hans
Video Data Bank

Haas, Philip
Metropolitan Mus. of Art, Uris Ctr.

Haberdasheries
Petrified Films, Inc.

Hackensack River Valley, N.J. (History and culture)
New Jersey Network

Hacket, Bobby
Rhapsody Films, Inc.

Hackett, Buddy
Banks Film Library

Hadid, Zaha
Southern Calif. Inst. of Architecture

Hadrian's Wall, England
British Info. Svcs., Radio & TV Div.

Hagen, Jean
Shokus Video

Haggerty, Dan
Spectral Comms.
Videobrary, Inc.

Hagman, Larry
Anti-Defamation League of B'nai B'rith

Hague, The, Netherlands (History and culture)
Archive Film Prods., Inc.

Hahn, Betty
Port Washington Pub. Lib.

Haight-Ashbury, San Francisco (History and culture)
Petrified Films, Inc.
UCLA Behavioral Sci. Media Lab.
White Janssen, Inc.

Haile Selassie
Film Search

March of Time

Hair and hairdos
CBS News Archives
Milady Publishing Corp.
Petrified Films, Inc.
Video Catalogue Co., Inc.
See also Beauty culture

Hair dryers
Petrified Films, Inc.
Prelinger Assoc., Inc.

Hairdos
See Hair and hairdos

Hairdressers
Petrified Films, Inc.
TV Ontario
Univ. of Calif., Berkeley, Labor Occupational Health Prog.

Haiti
Cousteau Society
Renaissance Video Corp.
World Monitor

Haiti (History and culture)
Cinema Guild
DEC Film & Video
Film/Audio Services, Inc.
Mus. of Mod. Art of Latin America
Northstar Prods.
Rockefeller Arch. Ctr.
Schomburg Ctr. for Res. in Black Culture
Schweitzer (Albert) Ctr.
U.S. Committee for UNICEF
Video Mgmt. Systems
White Janssen, Inc.
World Monitor

Hale, Alan
Spectral Comms.

Haleakula, Hawaii
Energy Productions

Haley, Alex
Natl. Assn. for the Advancement of Colored People

Haley, Jack Jr.
Banks Film Library
Spectral Comms.

Hall, Gus
Banks Film Library
Communist Party USA

Hall, Michael
Amer. Federation of the Arts

Hall, Susan
Video Data Bank

Halleck, Dee Dee
Port Washington Pub. Lib.

Halley's Comet
See Comets (Halley's)

Hallinan, Vincent
Southern Calif. Lib. for Soc. Stud. & Res.

Halloween
Natl. Crime Prevention Council
Petrified Films, Inc.
Preview Media
TV Ontario
Telltales Associates Inc.

Halls
Twentieth Century-Fox Movietonews

Hallucinations
Dreamlight Images, Inc.
See also Acid trips

Halprin, Lawrence
Landscape Architecture Found.
Southern Calif. Inst. of Architecture

Halsey, Brett
Banks Film Library

Halsey, William F.
Natl. Archives (RG 200)

Hamburger stands
See Restaurants (Hamburger stands)

Hamburgers
Film Bank
MacDonald, J. Fred
Oxfam America

Hamer, Fannie Lou
Estuary Press
Southern Calif. Lib. for Soc. Stud. & Res.

Hamer, Rusty
Shokus Video

Hamill, Dorothy
U.S. Olympic Comm.

Hamilton, George
Banks Film Library

Hamilton, Lloyd
Videobrary, Inc.

Hamilton, Ontario (History and culture)
MacDonald, J. Fred

Hamilton, Richard
Amer. Federation of the Arts

Hamilton, Scott
Jalbert Productions

Hammer, Armand
Hammer (Armand) Prods.
Spectral Comms.

Hammett, Louis P.
Amer. Chemical Soc.

Hamnett, Katherine
Film Bank

Hampton, Fred
Chicago Comm. to Defend the Bill of
    Rights
Media Bus

Hampton, Lionel
Chertok Assoc., Inc.
Pathé Pictures, Inc.

Hamptons, Long Island, N.Y.
Island Video

Hamrol, Lloyd
Blackwood Prods., Inc.

Hancock, Herbie
Spectral Comms.

Handbags
Prelinger Assoc., Inc.

Handball
Sportsfilm
Twentieth Century-Fox Movietonews

Handcars
Film Bank

Handicapped people
See Disabled people

Handicrafts
See Crafts

Handley, A.
Univ. of Wyoming, Western Heritage Ctr.

Handley, Harold
Indiana State Lib.

Handprints
See Footprints

Hands
CBS News Archives
Film Bank
Natl. Archives/Natl. AV Ctr.
Petrified Films, Inc.
Prelinger Assoc., Inc.
Rosebush Visions Corp.

Hands Across America (1986)
Film Bank
Maryknoll Fathers & Brothers
Spectral Comms.

Handy, W. C.
Center for Southern Folklore

Hang-gliding
Aitken (Len) Productions, Inc.
Amer. Motion Pictures
British Info. Svcs., Radio & TV Div.
Dreamlight Images, Inc.
Encore Video Prods., Inc.
Energy Productions
Film Bank
Jalbert Productions
MacGillivray Freeman Films
Merkel Films
Photo-Chuting Enterprises
Pyramid Film and Video Corp.
Second Line Search
Summit Films, Inc.
Telltales Associates Inc.
Video Tape Library, Ltd.

Hanks, Tom
Daphne Productions, Inc.
Spectral Comms.

Hansom cabs
CBS News Archives

Happiness (Emotion)
March of Time

Harbin, China
Farkas Studios, Ltd.

Harbin, China (History and culture)
Film/Audio Services, Inc.

Harbord, James G.
Armenian Film Foundation

Harbors
Allen (John E.) Inc.
Amer. Motion Pictures
Analogous Productions
CBS News Archives
Cannell (Stephen J.) Productions, Inc.
Dreamlight Images, Inc.
Farkas Studios, Ltd.
Film Bank
Forsher (James) Prods. & Archives, Inc.

Natl. Archives (RG 24)
Natl. Archives (RG 26)
Natl. Archives (RG 59)
Natl. Archives (RG 111)
Natl. Archives of Canada
Omega Films
Petrified Films, Inc.
Port Authority of New York & New Jersey
Riccitelli (Bruce) Prods.
Spectral Comms.
Stock House
TV Ontario
Twentieth Century-Fox Movietonews
Video Genesis, Inc.
See also Boats and boating; Shipping;
    Ships

Hard Rock Cafes
Broad Street Prods.

Hardin, Ty
Banks Film Library

Harding, Florence Kling
Natl. Archives (RG 24)

Harding, Noel
Long Beach Mus. of Art

Harding, Warren Gamaliel
Natl. Archives (RG 24)
Ohio Historical Soc.
Oregon Hist. Soc.
Prelinger Assoc., Inc.

Hardware stores
TV Ontario

Hardwick, Elizabeth
Pennebaker Associates, Inc.

Hardy, Oliver
Archive Film Prods., Inc.
Natl. Archives (RG 16)

Hare, Bill
Yukon Archives

Hare, David
Blackwood Prods., Inc.

Hargis, Billy James
Ctr. for Pacific Northwest Studies

Hargitay, Mickey
Banks Film Library

**Harlan County, Ky. (History and
    culture)**
Appalachian State Univ., Eury Coll.
Prestige Film Corp.
Univ. of Kentucky, AV Arch.

Harlem, N.Y.
New York State Dept. of Econ. Devel.
Simon & Goodman Picture Co.

Harlem, N.Y. (History and culture)
Allen (John E.) Inc.
Archive Film Prods., Inc.
Blackwood (Christian) Prods., Inc.
First Run/Icarus Films, Inc.
March of Time
Miles Educ. Film Prods.
Pathé Pictures, Inc.
Petrified Films, Inc.
Schomburg Ctr. for Res. in Black Culture

Harriman, W. Averell
Duke Univ., Perkins Lib.
Natl. Archives (RG 59)

Univ. of Ill. Urbana-Champaign, Univ.
    Arch.

Harrington, Donald
Randolph (A. Philip) Educ. Fund

Harris, Barry
Rhapsody Films, Inc.

Harris, Lawren
Natl. Archives of Canada

Harris, Patricia Roberts
Unicorn Projects

Harrisburg, Pa. (History and culture)
Center for Public Dialogue
Petrified Films, Inc.

Harrison, Anna J.
Amer. Chemical Soc.

Harrison, Benjamin
Indiana State Lib.

Harrison, George
Daphne Productions, Inc.

Harrison, Joan
Port Washington Pub. Lib.

Harrison, William Henry
Petrified Films, Inc.

Harry, Debbie
Monday, Wednesday, Friday Video Club

Hart, Gary
Guggenheim Productions, Inc.
Natl. Archives (RG 220)

Hart, Philip Aloysius
Univ. of Mich., Mich. Hist. Colls.

Hart, William S.
Archive Film Prods., Inc.
Intl. Mus. of Photography

Hartebeest
Summit Films, Inc.

Hartford, Conn.
Energy Productions
Wallen (Dick) Prods.

Hartford, Conn. (History and culture)
Connecticut Historical Society
Petrified Films, Inc.

Hartigan, Grace
Albright-Knox Art Gallery

Hartley, Mariette
Spectral Comms.

Hartung, Hans
Albright-Knox Art Gallery

Harvesting
Blue Sky Comms., Inc.
British Info. Svcs., Radio & TV Div.
Cinenet (Cinema Network)
Cornell Univ., Media Services
Dreamlight Images, Inc.
Energy Productions
Film Bank
Marts (Steve) Productions
Natl. Archives (RG 310)
North Country Media Group
Northcoast Communication, Inc.
Oregon State Univ., Archives

NOTE: Access policies, availability and restrictions vary for each source. Please read each entry in full. Always consult "General Film and
Videotape Collections" (page 599); these comprehensive collections contain material on every conceivable subject.

Petrified Films, Inc.
TV Ontario
VTR Productions
Video I-D, Inc.
See also Agriculture; Crops; Farms and
farming

Hasegawa, Itsuko
Southern Calif. Inst. of Architecture

Hashey, Jan
Video Data Bank

Hatfield, Ken
Fellowship of Christian Athletes

Hatfield, Mark
Oregon Hist. Soc.

Hats
Petrified Films, Inc.
Video Catalogue Co., Inc.

Haunted houses
Archive Film Prods., Inc.
Petrified Films, Inc.

Hauptmann, Bruno Richard
March of Time

Havana
Analogous Productions

Havana (History and culture)
Archive Film Prods., Inc.
Downtown Community TV Ctr.
Petrified Films, Inc.

Havasu Falls, Ariz.
Source Stock Footage Lib., Inc.

Hawaii
Ackerman-Black Prods., Inc.
Airline Film & TV Promotions
America's Cup Organizing Comm.
Bishop Mus., Visual Coll.
Brekke Television Prods.
Channel Sea Television
Cine-Mark
Cinenet (Cinema Network)
Creative Video, Inc.
Departures, Inc.
Dobovan Productions, Inc.
Dreamlight Images, Inc.
Echo Film Prods., Inc.
Energy Productions
Film Bank
Hawaii Public Broadcasting Authority
Jewell (Stuart) Productions
MacGillivray Freeman Films
New Film Co., Inc.
North Country Media Group
Pacific Focus Inc.
Pacific Productions
Passage Home Communications
Postcards Unlimited
Preview Media
Quenzer Driscoll Dawson, Inc.
Rainbow Video Prods.
Sonoma Video Productions
Stimulus
Summit Films, Inc.
TV-3
United Airlines, Creative Services
Video Concepts, Inc.
Wallen (Dick) Prods.
Warner (Dane) Photography

Hawaii (Contemporary issues)
People's Fund

Hawaii (History and culture)
Ackerman-Black Prods., Inc.
Archive Film Prods., Inc.
Bishop Mus., Visual Coll.

East-West Center
Halcyon Days Prods.
Hawaii Public Broadcasting Authority
Johns Hopkins Univ./Population Comm.
Svcs.
March of Time
Natl. Archives (RG 48)
Natl. Archives (RG 200)
Natl. Archives (RG 220)
Oregon Hist. Soc.
Pacific Productions
People's Fund
Petrified Films, Inc.
Prelinger Assoc., Inc.
Univ. of Hawaii at Manoa, Wong Ctr.

Hawes, Hampton
Rhapsody Films, Inc.

Hawkins, Coleman
Chertok Assoc., Inc.
Rhapsody Films, Inc.

Hawkins, W. Lincoln
Amer. Chemical Soc.

Hawks
Di Sesso (Moe) Wild Life Film Lib.
Echo Film Prods., Inc.
Energy Productions
Film Bank
KD Enterprises Prods.
Minnesota Zoo
Petrified Films, Inc.
Summit Films, Inc.
TV Ontario
Wings Wildlife Prods. Inc.

Hawley, Christine
Southern Calif. Inst. of Architecture

Hawn, Goldie
Spectral Comms.

Hay and haystacks
Energy Productions
Lib. of Congress, Amer. Folklife Ctr.
North Country Media Group
Petrified Films, Inc.

Hayden, Tom
Pennebaker Associates, Inc.
Petrified Films, Inc.
Southern Calif. Inst. of Architecture

Hayes, Helen
Daphne Productions, Inc.

Hayes, Woody
Ohio State Univ., Dept. of Photog. &
Cinema

Haymarket affair (1886)
Committee for Labor Access

Hays, Will H.
Indiana State Lib.

Hayward, Susan
Banks Film Library

Hayworth, Rita
Banks Film Library

Hazardous materials
Courter Films & Assoc.

Hazardous waste
See Toxic waste

Head, Edith
Blackwood (Christian) Prods., Inc.

Headhunters
White Janssen, Inc.

Headlines
See Newspapers (Headlines)

Headphones
Film Bank

Heads
Rosebush Visions Corp.

Heads (Bald)
Analogous Productions
Petrified Films, Inc.
Postcards Associates

Healey, Dorothy
Southern Calif. Lib. for Soc. Stud. & Res.

Healing
Documentary Educational Resources
Hartley Film Found., Inc.
Mass Media Ministries
Singer-Sharrette Traditional Healing Films
Smithsonian Inst., Human Studies Film
Arch.
Valley of the Sun
Wheaton Coll., Billy Graham Ctr.
Wheelwright Mus. of the Amer. Indian
See also Medicine (Traditional)

Healing (Faith)
Historical Health Film Coll.
Social Psychiatry Res. Inst.
Univ. of Miss., Ctr. for Study of Southern
Culture

Health
ABC Distribution (Education)
AIMS Media
Allen (John E.) Inc.
Amer. Alliance for Health, Phys. Ed., Rec.
& Dance Arch.
Amer. Assn. of Retired Persons
Amer. Dental Assn.
Amer. Medical Assn.
Amer. Nuclear Society
Amer. Red Cross
Barr Films
Bullfrog Films, Inc.
Cable Access of Dallas
Cable News Network Library
Carousel Film & Video
Center for Humanities, Inc.
Centers for Disease Control
Chisholm (Jack) Film Productions, Ltd.
Churchill Films
Cinema Guild
Coe Film Assoc., Inc.
Coronet/MTI Film & Video
Education Development Ctr., Inc.
Estuary Press
Filmakers Library
Films for the Humanities and Sciences
GPN
Gay Men's Health Crisis
Handel Film Corp.
Hartley Film Found., Inc.
Historical Health Film Coll.
Hooper (Josh) Prods., Inc.
Imevision
Intermedia Arts Minnesota
Intl. Film Bureau, Inc.
KYUK-TV
Los Angeles Dept. of Water & Power
March of Time
Maryknoll Fathers & Brothers
Media Guild
Milner-Fenwick, Inc.
Morris Video
Native Amer. Pub. Broad. Cons.
Natl. Archives (RG 16)
Natl. Archives (RG 75)
Natl. Archives (RG 102)
Natl. Archives (RG 200)
Natl. Archives (RG 235)
Natl. Archives/Natl. AV Ctr.

Natl. Library of Medicine
Natl. Safety Council
New Mexico State Records Ctr. & Arch.
New York Hosp.-Cornell Med. Ctr., Arch.
Phoenix Films and Video
Prelinger Assoc., Inc.
Prov. Arch. of Newfoundland & Labrador
Pyramid Film and Video Corp.
Radcliffe Coll., Schlesinger Lib.
Tucson Community Cable Corp.
Université Laval, Cinémathèque
Univ. of Calif., Ext. Media Ctr.
Univ. of Waterloo, A-V Centre
Univ. of Wisconsin — Extension
V/tape
Video-SIG
Visual Information Systems
See also Diseases; Health care; Health
education; Medical films and
videotapes; Medical footage; Medicine;
Patient education films and videotapes;
Patients; Women and health

Health care
Center for Biomedical Comms.
Downtown Community TV Ctr.
IMS Creative Communications
Native Amer. Pub. Broad. Cons.
Natl. Archives of Canada
New Orleans Video Access Ctr.
U.S. Committee for UNICEF
Washington Univ., Brown Schl. of Soc.
Work
Wayne State Univ., Dir. Educ. in Nursing
See also Medicine; Workers (Health care)

Health care (Nicaragua)
Women Make Movies, Inc.

Health care (Soviet Union)
Estuary Press

Health clubs
TV Ontario

Health economics
Medical College of Pa., Arch. & Spec.
Coll. Women in Medicine

Health education
Altschul Group
Alzheimer's Disease & Rel. Disord. Assn.
Amer. Cancer Soc., Inc.
Amer. Correctional Assn.
Amer. Dental Assn.
Amer. Diabetes Assn.
Amer. Heart Assn.
Amer. Journal of Nursing Co.
Amer. Medical Assn.
Britannica Films & Video
Centers for Disease Control
Churchill Films
Cystic Fibrosis Foundation
Emory Medical Television Network
Film Bank
Filmfair Communications
Films for the Humanities and Sciences
Hartley Film Found., Inc.
Higgins (Alfred) Prods.
Klein (Walter J.) Co., Ltd.
La Leche League of New Mexico Film
Depot
Lawren Prods., Inc.
Leukemia Soc. of Amer.
March of Dimes Birth Defects Found.
Media Guild
Miles Corporate Archive
Milner-Fenwick, Inc.
Narcotics Education, Inc.
Nassau Comm. Coll. Lib.
Natl. Archives (RG 90)
Natl. Dairy Council
Natl. Kidney Foundation, Inc.
Natl. Safety Council
Natl. Soc. to Prevent Blindness

Ohio State Univ., Dept. of Photog. & Cinema
Perlmutter (Alvin H.) Inc.
Planned Parenthood Fed. of Amer.
Polymorph Films, Inc.
Prelinger Assoc., Inc.
Pyramid Film and Video Corp.
Rogers (Will) Institute
Soc. for Nutrition Education
Streamline Film Archives
Varied Directions, Inc.
Wayfarer Publications
See also Health; Patient education films and videotapes

Health, Education & Welfare, Dept. of (U.S.)
Natl. Archives (RG 235)
Natl. Archives (Stock Film Coll.)

Health food and health food stores
TV Ontario
Video Tape Library, Ltd.

Health sciences
Natl. Film Board of Canada
Univ. of Wash. Press, Multimedia Div.

Hearses
CBS News Archives
Petrified Films, Inc.
See also Funerals

Hearst, Patricia
KCRA-TV
Mus. & Hist. Div., City of Sacramento
San Francisco Bay Area TV News Arch.

Hearst, William Randolph
Forsher (James) Prods. & Archives, Inc.

Heart
Amer. Heart Assn.
Center for Biomedical Comms.
Film Bank
Emory Medical Television Network
Milner-Fenwick, Inc.
Ohio State Univ., Dept. of Photog. & Cinema
Perlmutter (Alvin H.) Inc.
Prelinger Assoc., Inc.
Pyramid Film and Video Corp.
Rosebush Visions Corp.
Univ. of Wash. Press, Multimedia Div.

Heart (Rock and roll band)
Blackwood (Christian) Prods., Inc.

Heart monitors
Energy Productions
See also Electroencephalography (EEG); Technology (Medical)

Heart transplants
See Transplants (Organ)

Heartfield, John
Amer. Federation of the Arts
DEC Film & Video

Hearts (Candy)
Energy Productions

Heaven
Prelinger Assoc., Inc.
See also Angels

Heavy equipment
Energy Productions
LeTourneau College Archives
Marx Production Center

Oregon Hist. Soc.
Petrified Films, Inc.
TV Ontario
Twentieth Century-Fox Movietonews
Univ. of Wisconsin — Extension
See also Bulldozers; Cranes (Construction); Earthmoving equipment

Hecker, Zvi
Southern Calif. Inst. of Architecture

Hedren, Tippi
Banks Film Library

Heflin, Van
Banks Film Library

Hefner, Hugh
Banks Film Library
Spectral Comms.

Heiden, Eric
Jalbert Productions
U.S. Olympic Comm.

Heights, Dorothy
Natl. Assn. for the Advancement of Colored People

Heim, Emmy
Natl. Archives of Canada

Heineken, Robert
Video Data Bank

Heizer, Michael
Blackwood Prods., Inc.

Held, Al
Blackwood Prods., Inc.

Helicopters
See Aircraft (Helicopters)

Hell's Kitchen, N.Y. (History and culture)
Prelinger Assoc., Inc.

Hellman, Lillian
San Francisco Bay Area TV News Arch.

Hells Canyon, Idaho (History and culture)
Oregon Hist. Soc.

Helms, Jesse
Keep the Faith, Inc.

Hematology
IMS Creative Communications
Nassau Comm. Coll. Lib.

Henderson, Tex. (History and culture)
Petrified Films, Inc.

Hendrix, Jimi
Clark (Dick) Media Archives, Inc.
Daphne Productions, Inc.
Pennebaker Associates, Inc.

Henie, Sonja
Archive Film Prods., Inc.
Film Education Institute

Henning, Doug
Christopher Closeup

Henninger, Manfred
Film/Audio Services, Inc.

Henry, George S.
Archives of Ontario

Henry, Prince (Prussia)
Lib. of Congress, M/B/RS

Hentoff, Nat
Baker (Fred) Film & Video Co.

Hepburn, Audrey
Banks Film Library
Petrified Films, Inc.

Hepworth, Barbara
Amer. Federation of the Arts
Blackwood Prods., Inc.

Herbs
Brooklyn Botanic Garden
Bullfrog Films, Inc.
TV Ontario

Heredity
Prelinger Assoc., Inc.

Herman's Hermits
Archive Film Prods., Inc.
Spalla (Rick) Video Prods.

Hermann, Joel Wm.
Long Beach Mus. of Art

Hernandez, Augustin
Southern Calif. Inst. of Architecture

Hernandez, Keith
Daphne Productions, Inc.

Heroes (Decorated)
Film Bank
Petrified Films, Inc.

Heroin
Addiction Research Foundation of Ontario
Monday, Wednesday, Friday Video Club
Signal Press

Herons
Film Bank
New Zealand Embassy Film Lib.
TV Ontario
Wings Wildlife Prods. Inc.

Herpes
Amer. Social Health Assn.
Emory Medical Television Network
Wombat Film & Video

Herrick, Myron T.
Natl. Archives (RG 24)

Herrmann, Bernard
Camera Three Prods., Inc.

Herron, Jason
De Saisset Museum

Herschel, Caroline
Women in Focus

Herschel Island, Yukon Territory (History and culture)
Yukon Archives

Hershey, Lewis B.
Natl. Archives (RG 147)

Herter, Christian
Natl. Archives (RG 59)

Herzog, Werner

Flower Films & Video

Hess, Karl
Direct Cinema Ltd.

Hesse, Eva
Blackwood Prods., Inc.

Hesseman, Howard
Spectral Comms.

Hester, Dorothy
Oregon Hist. Soc.

Heston, Charlton
Banks Film Library
Daphne Productions, Inc.
Film Bank
Goodwill Industries of Amer.
Natl. Archives (RG 56)
Spalla (Rick) Video Prods.
Spectral Comms.
UCLA Film & Television Archive

Hibbing, Minn. (History and culture)
Petrified Films, Inc.

Hickman, Dwayne
Banks Film Library
Shokus Video

High blood pressure
See Hypertension

High schools
Film Bank
Natl. Archives of Canada
Petrified Films, Inc.
Prelinger Assoc., Inc.
TV Ontario
See also Education; Schools; Students

High technology
See Technology (High)

High-speed cinematography
Cinenet (Cinema Network)
Dreamlight Images, Inc.
Energy Productions
Mass. Inst. of Tech., MIT Museum
Moody Inst. of Science
Nemiroff Prods., Inc.
Univ. of Waterloo, A-V Centre
West Star Productions

Hightower, Jim
Alternative Information Network

Highway beautification
Calif. Dept. of Transportation

Highway safety
See Driver education

Highway Traffic Safety Administration, National (NHTSA)
Natl. Archives (RG 416)
U.S. Dept. of Transportation, Natl. Hwy. Traffic Safety Admin.

Highways
Archive Film Prods., Inc.
Assoc. Gen. Contractors of America
Calif. Dept. of Transportation
Dreamlight Images, Inc.
Energy Productions
Film Bank
General Motors Corp.
Hooper (Josh) Prods., Inc.
Illinois State Hist. Lib.
Image Bank

NOTE: Access policies, availability and restrictions vary for each source. Please read each entry in full. Always consult "General Film and Videotape Collections" (page 599); these comprehensive collections contain material on every conceivable subject.

Long Island State Park Comm.
Louisiana Tech Univ., Eng. Film Res. Ctr.
Natl. Archives (RG 33)
Natl. Archives of Canada
Nei-Ali Prods.
New Mexico State Records Ctr. & Arch.
New York State Arch. & Rec. Admin.
Petrified Films, Inc.
Postcards Associates
Prelinger Assoc., Inc.
Riccitelli (Bruce) Prods.
Source Stock Footage Lib., Inc.
Spectral Comms.
Transportation Research Board
Twentieth Century-Fox Movietonews
Video Tape Library, Ltd.
See also Streets and roads; Traffic

Highways (Construction)
Assoc. Gen. Contractors of America
General Motors Corp.
Missouri Hist. Soc.
Natl. Archives of Canada
Petrified Films, Inc.
Prelinger Assoc., Inc.
Prov. Arch. of Alberta
Prov. Arch. of Newfoundland & Labrador
San Jose Hist. Museum
White Star Prof. Film Svcs., Inc.
Yukon Archives
See also Construction; Streets and roads
  (Construction)

Highwire acts
See Circuses

Higuchi, Takeru
Amer. Inst. of the Hist. of Pharmacy

Hiking
Energy Productions
Film Bank
Moving Media
Peak Productions, Inc.
Prelinger Assoc., Inc.
Source Stock Footage Lib., Inc.
Summit Films, Inc.
Twentieth Century-Fox Movietonews
Video West

Hildebrand, Joel
Amer. Chemical Soc.

Hilgard, Ernest R.
Inst. for Psychoanalysis

Hill, Blind Jo
Los Angeles Blues Archives

Hill, Gary
Giorno Poetry Systems Inst.
Long Beach Mus. of Art
Video Data Bank

Hill, James
Video Data Bank

Hill, Norman
Randolph (A. Philip) Educ. Fund

Hillary, Sir Edmund
MacDonald, J. Fred
New Zealand Embassy Film Lib.

Hillbillies (Depiction in the media)
Appalshop Films, Inc.

Hills
Film Bank
MacGillivray Freeman Films
Metro Communications, Inc.

Hilton, Conrad
Banks Film Library

Hilton Head Island, S.C.
Creative Video, Inc.
Preview Media

Himalaya Mountains (Asia)
Amer. Mus. Nat. Hist. Film Arch.
Canadian Broadcasting Corp.
Petrified Films, Inc.
TV Ontario

Himes, Chester
Camera Three Prods., Inc.

Hindenburg (Zeppelin)
Archive Film Prods., Inc.
Film Bank
Grinberg (Sherman) Film Libraries (West)
Natl. Archives (RG 111)
Natl. Archives (RG 342)
Petrified Films, Inc.
See also Aircraft (Lighter-than-air)

Hindu dance
See Dance and dancing (Hindu)

Hine, Lewis
Cinema Guild

Hinton, Milt
Rhapsody Films, Inc.

Hippies
Archive Film Prods., Inc.
CBS News Archives
Clark (Dick) Media Archives, Inc.
Film Bank
Law (Lisa) Prods.
MacDonald, J. Fred
Parker (Kit) Films
Petrified Films, Inc.
White Janssen, Inc.
See also Acid trips; Counterculture (U.S.);
  Love-ins

Hippopotamuses
Cousteau Society
Di Sesso (Moe) Wild Life Film Lib.
Dreamlight Images, Inc.
Miller (David Lee) Prods.
Petrified Films, Inc.
Summit Films, Inc.
Wings Wildlife Prods. Inc.

Hirohito, Emperor
Archive Film Prods., Inc.
Hearst Metrotone News

Hiroshima, Japan (History and culture)
Archive Film Prods., Inc.
Council for a Livable World Educ. Fund
Educational Film & Video Project
First Run/Icarus Films, Inc.
Hoover Institution
Natl. Archives (RG 18)
Natl. Archives (RG 342)
Natl. Asian American Telecomm. Assn.
Petrified Films, Inc.
U.S. Defense Nuclear Agency
Wilmington Coll. Peace Res. Ctr.

Hirschfeld, Al
New York Pub. Lib., Perf. Arts Res. Ctr.,
  Theatre on Film and Tape

Hispanics
Anthropology Film Center Foundation
Anti-Defamation League of B'nai B'rith
Cinema Guild
Kartemquin Films
MALDEF
New York Pub. Lib., Perf. Arts Res. Ctr.,
  Theatre on Film and Tape
Saint Paul Pub. Lib., Film & Video Ctr.
Univ. of Calif., Ext. Media Ctr.
Univision Television Network

Hispanics (Depiction in the media)
MALDEF

Hiss, Alger
Direct Cinema Ltd.

Histology
Educational Images, Ltd.

Historic preservation
Amer. Assn. for State & Local Hist.
Apertura
San Antonio Conservation Soc. Found.
  Lib.
Unicorn Projects
Univ. of Waterloo, A-V Centre

History
AIMS Media
Britannica Films & Video
Carleton Prods. Inc.
Center for Humanities, Inc.
Cinema Guild
Coe Film Assoc., Inc.
Coronet/MTI Film & Video
Films for the Humanities and Sciences
GPN
Natl. Archives (RG 200)
Natl. Archives/Natl. AV Ctr.
Natl. Geographic Soc. Stock Footage Lib.
Peralta Colleges TV
Richter Productions
Vedo Films/Novacom Video
Vidéo Femmes
Vidéographe Inc., Le

Hitchcock, Alfred
Banks Film Library
Daphne Productions, Inc.
Encore Entertainment
MacDonald, J. Fred

Hitchcock, Henry Russell
Unicorn Projects

Hitler, Adolf
Archive Film Prods., Inc.
Canadian Olympic Assn.
Film Bank
Film/Audio Services, Inc.
German Language Video Center
Hearst Metrotone News
Hoover Institution
Intl. Film Foundation
Intl. Historic Films, Inc.
March of Time
NSDAP/AO
Natl. Archives (RG 131)
Natl. Archives of Canada
Petrified Films, Inc.
Video Tape Library, Ltd.
See also Germany; Holocaust; Nazis;
  World War II

Hitler, Adolf (Assassination attempts)
Natl. Archives (RG 238)

Hitler Youth
Natl. Archives (RG 242)

**Ho Chi Minh City, Vietnam (History
  and culture)**
Raindance Foundation
White Janssen, Inc.

Hobbies
All-American Soap Box Derby
CBS News Archives
General Motors Corp.
Hobby Industries of America
Kalmbach Publishing Co.
Morris Video
Prelinger Assoc., Inc.
Spalla (Rick) Video Prods.
See also specific hobbies

Hoboes
CBS News Archives

Hoboken, N.J. (History and culture)
Downtown Community TV Ctr.
New Jersey Network

Hockey
Amer. Motion Pictures
Analogous Productions
Archive Film Prods., Inc.
Athletic Institute
Charisma Prods., Ltd./Visual Motion
Film Bank
Jalbert Productions
Molstar Comm.
Natl. Archives of Canada
Petrified Films, Inc.
Second Line Search
TV Ontario
Twentieth Century-Fox Movietonews
U.S. Hockey Hall of Fame
U.S. Olympic Comm.

Hockey (College)
NCAA Productions

Hockey (Floor)
Athletic Institute

Hockey (Instruction)
NCAA Productions

Hockey (Professional)
Film Search
4•6•8 Prods., Inc.
Molstar Comm.
Natl. Archives of Canada
Phoenix Communications Group, Inc.
Sports Mus. of New England

Hockey (Sleigh)
TV Ontario

Hockney, David
Blackwood (Christian) Prods., Inc.
Blackwood Prods., Inc.
Daphne Productions, Inc.
Metropolitan Mus. of Art, Uris Ctr.
Walker Art Ctr.

Hodges, Luther
Illinois State Hist. Lib.
North Carolina Div. of Arch. & Hist.

Hoff, Philip
Apertura

Hoffa, Jimmy
Banks Film Library
Daphne Productions, Inc.
Univ. of Ill. Urbana-Champaign, Univ.
  Arch.

Hoffman, Abbie
Daphne Productions, Inc.
Film/Audio Services, Inc.
Petrified Films, Inc.
Raindance Foundation
Villon Films

Hoffman, Anna Rosenberg
Radcliffe Coll., Schlesinger Lib.

Hoffman, Roald
Amer. Chemical Soc.

Hofmann, Hans
Blackwood Prods., Inc.

Hogs
Cornell Univ., Media Services
Glenbow Mus. Arch.
Petrified Films, Inc.
Prov. Arch. of Alberta

Holden, William
Christopher Closeup

Holiday, Billie
Baker (Fred) Film & Video Co.
Chertok Assoc., Inc.

Holidays
Allen (John E.) Inc.
Amer. Zionist Youth Found.
Barr Films
Carleton Prods. Inc.
Coe Film Assoc., Inc.
Coronet/MTI Film & Video
Energy Productions
Ergo Media
Films for the Humanities and Sciences
Milwaukee Access Telecomm. Auth.
Natl. Archives of Canada
Petrified Films, Inc.
Phoenix Films and Video
Telltales Associates Inc.
Univ. of Ill. Urbana-Champaign, Univ. Arch.
Video West
See also Celebrations; specific holidays

Holidays (Mexico)
Echo Film Prods., Inc.

Holistic health
See Medicine (Alternative)

Holland
See Netherlands

Holland, Mich. (History and culture)
Petrified Films, Inc.

Hollein, Hans
Southern Calif. Inst. of Architecture

Holliday, Polly
Christopher Closeup

Hollings, Ernest O.
Guggenheim Productions, Inc.

Hollis, Douglas
Albright-Knox Art Gallery
Video Data Bank

Holloman, Earl
Spectral Comms.

Holly, Buddy
Clark (Dick) Media Archives, Inc.

Hollywood
Banks Film Library
Broad Street Prods.
Creative Video, Inc.
Dreamlight Images, Inc.
Em Gee Film Library
Film Bank
Fish Films, Inc.
Forsher (James) Prods. & Archives, Inc.
Preview Media
Spalla (Rick) Video Prods.
Spectral Comms.
See also Entertainment industry

Hollywood (History and culture)
Allen (John E.) Inc.
Archive Film Prods., Inc.
Banks Film Library
Eden Entertainment, Inc.
Footage Inc.
Jessiefilm
Natl. Archives (RG 200)
Petrified Films, Inc.

Southern Calif. Lib. for Soc. Stud. & Res.

Hollywood (Sign)
Dreamlight Images, Inc.
Energy Productions
Film Bank

Hollywood Fats
Los Angeles Blues Archives

Hollywood Ten (1947)
Shire Films

Holm, Celeste
Daphne Productions, Inc.

Holm, Elinor
Grinberg (Sherman) Film Libraries (West)

Holman, Bob
Video Data Bank

Holmes, Sherlock
Archive Film Prods., Inc.

Holocaust
Amer. Zionist Youth Found.
Anti-Defamation League of B'nai B'rith
Carousel Film & Video
Center for Holocaust Studies
Christopher Closeup
Cinema Guild
Documentary Educational Resources
Emory Univ., Spec. Coll.
Ergo Media
Film Bank
Finley (Stuart) Inc.
First Run/Icarus Films, Inc.
Freedom Information Service
Goethe Institute Atlanta
Holocaust Center of Northern California
Holocaust Survivors Mem. Found.
Hoover Institution
Intermedia Arts Minnesota
Israel Broadcasting Service
Magnes (Judah L.) Museum
Mass Media Ministries
Mus. of Jewish Heritage
Natl. Archives (RG 18)
Natl. Archives (RG 238)
Natl. Archives (RG 342)
Natl. Archives/Natl. AV Ctr.
Natl. Ctr. for Jewish Film
Natl. Jewish Arch. of Broadcasting
Western Reserve Hist. Soc.
Wiesenthal (Simon) Ctr.
World Wide Pictures, Inc.
See also Concentration camps; Jewish history and culture; World War II

Holocaust ("Revisionist history")
Inst. for Historical Review

Holography
SIGGRAPH

Holovak, Mike
Boston Coll., Univ. Arch.

Holt, Nancy
Amer. Federation of the Arts

Holtzman, Elizabeth
Radcliffe Coll., Schlesinger Lib.

Home economics
Altschul Group
Archives of Ontario
Bullfrog Films, Inc.
Coronet/MTI Film & Video
Natl. Archives (RG 33)

Prelinger Assoc., Inc.
Radcliffe Coll., Schlesinger Lib.

Home improvement
Natl. Archives (RG 31)
Natl. Archives (RG 33)
Natl. Assn. of Home Builders
Prelinger Assoc., Inc.

Home movies
Academy Film Archive
Allen (John E.) Inc.
Amer. Truck Historical Society
Archives of Ontario
Boston Univ., Dept. of Spec. Coll.
Chicago Historical Society
Cincinnati Hist. Soc.
Circus World Mus. Lib. & Res. Ctr.
Connecticut Historical Society
Eisenhower (Dwight D.) Library
Everett Pub. Lib., Northwest Hist. Coll.
Fabulous Footage Inc.
Film Bank
Film/Audio Services, Inc.
Filmoteca de la UNAM
Halcyon Days Prods.
Hist. Soc. of Seattle & King County
Hoover (Herbert) Presidential Library
Houston (Sam) Regional Library
Indiana State Lib.
Intl. Al Jolson Society
KYUK-TV
Kinsey Institute
Mystic Seaport Mus., Inc.
Natl. Archives (RG 200)
Natl. Archives (RG 242)
Natl. Archives of Canada
New York Chinatown History Project
New York Pub. Lib., Perf. Arts Res. Ctr., Theatre on Film and Tape
Northeast Historic Film
Ohio Historical Soc.
Oregon Hist. Soc.
Petrified Films, Inc.
Prelinger Assoc., Inc.
Rockefeller Arch. Ctr.
Roosevelt (Franklin D.) Lib.
San Diego State Univ., Spec. Coll.
San Francisco Maritime Natl. Hist. Park
San Jose Hist. Museum
Schiele Museum
Smith College, Arch.
State Hist. Soc. of Iowa
State Hist. Soc. of Wisconsin
Streamline Film Archives
Texas Tech Univ., Southwest Coll.
Twain (Mark) Memorial
U.S. Natl. Park Service Hist. Coll.
Univ. of Akron, Arch. of Hist. of Amer. Psychol.
Univ. of Alaska, Fairbanks, Alaska Motion Picture Arch.
Univ. of Mich., Mich. Hist. Colls.
Univ. of Tex. at Austin, Ransom Hum. Res. Ctr., Photo. Coll.
Univ. of Utah, Marriott Lib.
Washington State Hist. Soc.
West Virginia Dept. of Culture & Hist.
Wheaton Coll., Billy Graham Ctr.
Wiesenthal (Simon) Ctr.
Yukon Archives

Homecomings
Emporia State Univ., Spec. Coll.
Franklin & Marshall Coll.
Northern Ill. Univ., Reg. Hist. Ctr.
See also Campus life; Colleges and universities

Homefront

See World War I (Canada, Homefront); World War II (U.S.); World War II (Canada, Homefront); World War II (U.S., Homefront)

Homelessness
Channel L Working Group
Committee for Labor Access
Downtown Community TV Ctr.
Educational Video Ctr.
Film Bank
Labor Video Project
MALDEF
Maryknoll Fathers & Brothers
New Jersey Network
Petrified Films, Inc.
Third World Newsreel
World Monitor

Homeopathy
See Medicine (Homeopathy)

Homes
See Houses and homes; Housing

Homestead, Pa. (History and culture)
Prelinger Assoc., Inc.

Homing pigeons
See Pigeons (Homing)

Homosexuality
See Gay and lesbian issues

Honduras
Imagen y Sonido Independiente, S.A.
Passage Home Communications

Honduras (British) (History and culture)
Film/Audio Services, Inc.
Villon Films

Honduras (Contemporary issues)
Committee for Labor Access
DEC Film & Video
Film/Audio Services, Inc.
Northstar Prods.
Skylight Pictures

Honduras (History and culture)
DEC Film & Video
Film/Audio Services, Inc.
Idera Films
Mus. of Mod. Art of Latin America
Natl. Archives (RG 106)

Honey
TV Ontario

Honeymoons
Preview Media

Hong Kong
Beerger (Norman) Prods.
British Info. Svcs., Radio & TV Div.
Creative Video, Inc.
Farkas Studios, Ltd.
Film Search
Friends of Free China
Northstar Prods.
Pan American Airlines Film Lib.
Petrified Films, Inc.
Preview Media
Sonoma Video Productions

Hong Kong (History and culture)
Devillier Donegan Ent.
Film/Audio Services, Inc.
Natl. Archives (RG 200)
Petrified Films, Inc.

NOTE: Access policies, availability and restrictions vary for each source. Please read each entry in full. Always consult "General Film and Videotape Collections" (page 599); these comprehensive collections contain material on every conceivable subject.

Salvation Army, Natl. Comm. Dept.

Honolulu
Cine-Mark
Departures, Inc.
Dobovan Productions, Inc.
Film Bank
Preview Media
Wallen (Dick) Prods.

Honolulu (History and culture)
Oregon Hist. Soc.
Petrified Films, Inc.

Hood, Mount (Oreg.)
Oregon State Univ., Archives

Hookahs
Petrified Films, Inc.

Hooker, Evelyn
One, Inc.

Hooks, Benjamin L.
Natl. Assn. for the Advancement of
    Colored People

Hoop rolling
Twentieth Century-Fox Movietonews

Hoopes, Darlington
Duke Univ., Perkins Lib.

Hoover Dam, Ariz.-Nev.
Analogous Productions
Beerger (Norman) Prods.
Cinenet (Cinema Network)
Las Vegas News Bureau
Network Productions

Hoover Dam, Ariz.-Nev. (History)
Louisiana Tech Univ., Eng. Film Res. Ctr.

Hoover, Herbert Clark
Archive Film Prods., Inc.
Hoover (Herbert) Presidential Library
Hoover Institution
Natl. Archives (RG 4)
Natl. Archives (RG 28)
Natl. Archives (RG 33)
Natl. Archives (RG 130)
Oregon Hist. Soc.
Petrified Films, Inc.
Prelinger Assoc., Inc.
State Hist. Soc. of Iowa
Timesteps Prods., Inc.

Hoover, J. Edgar
Archive Film Prods., Inc.
Chicago Comm. to Defend the Bill of
    Rights
Petrified Films, Inc.

Hoovervilles
Allen (John E.) Inc.
Petrified Films, Inc.
Southern Calif. Lib. for Soc. Stud. & Res.

Hooves
Film Bank

Hope, Bob
Banks Film Library
Christopher Closeup
Clark (Dick) Media Archives, Inc.
Daphne Productions, Inc.
Film/Audio Services, Inc.
Grinberg (Sherman) Film Libraries (East)
Las Vegas News Bureau
Natl. Archives/Natl. AV Ctr.
Petrified Films, Inc.
Shokus Video
Spectral Comms.
UCLA Film & Television Archive
Videobrary, Inc.

Hope diamond
Colorado Historical Society

Hopkins, Lightnin'
Rhapsody Films, Inc.

Hopkins, Miriam
UCLA Film & Television Archive

Hopper, Edward
Amer. Federation of the Arts

Hopper, Hedda
Banks Film Library

Hops
Oregon Hist. Soc.

Horiuchi, Paul
Media Project

Horn, Paul
Impact Audio Visual

Hornbills
Minnesota Zoo

Horne, Lena
Banks Film Library
Daphne Productions, Inc.
Natl. Archives/Natl. AV Ctr.
UCLA Film & Television Archive

Horns (Alpine)
Analogous Productions

Hornsby, Bruce
Spectral Comms.

Hornsby, Rogers
Grinberg (Sherman) Film Libraries (West)

Horror (Emotion)
Petrified Films, Inc.

Horror films and videotapes
Archive Film Prods., Inc.
Budget Films Inc.
Em Gee Film Library
Gordon Films, Inc.
Hurlock Cine-World, Inc.
Imageways, Inc.
Morcraft Films
Moviecraft, Inc.
Streamline Film Archives
Swank Motion Pictures, Inc.
Video Yesteryear
Williams (Wade) Prods.

Horse racing
Allen (John E.) Inc.
Analogous Productions
Arabian Horse Trust
Archive Film Prods., Inc.
CBS News Archives
Energy Productions
Farkas Studios, Ltd.
Fish Films, Inc.
Golden Gaters Prods.
Grinberg (Sherman) Film Libraries (West)
Historic Thoroughbred Colls., Inc.
Intl. Arabian Horse Assn.
Kesser Stock Footage Library
Miller (Warren) Productions, Inc.
Natl. Archives of Canada
Petrified Films, Inc.
Source Stock Footage Lib., Inc.
Sportsfilm
Thoroughbred Racing Assns.
Trotting Horse Museum
Twentieth Century-Fox Movietonews
Univ. of Notre Dame, Joyce Sports Coll.
Video Tape Library, Ltd.

Horse racing (Kentucky Derby)

Analogous Productions
Historic Thoroughbred Colls., Inc.
Sportsfilm
UCLA Film & Television Archive

Horse shows
Amer. Morgan Horse Assn.
Petrified Films, Inc.
Southwest Prods., Inc.
Twentieth Century-Fox Movietonews
Video Tape Library, Ltd.

Horses
ABC Sports, Inc.
Amer. Motion Pictures
Amer. Saddlebred Horse Assn.
Amer. Veterinary Medical Assn.
Analogous Productions
Arabian Horse Owners Foundation
Archive Film Prods., Inc.
Charisma Prods., Ltd./Visual Motion
Cinenet (Cinema Network)
Creative Video, Inc.
Davenport Films
Dreamlight Images, Inc.
Echo Film Prods., Inc.
Edwards, H.M.
Energy Productions
Film Bank
Forsher (James) Prods. & Archives, Inc.
Hayes Prods., Inc.
Historic Thoroughbred Colls., Inc.
Kesser Stock Footage Library
Latham Foundation
Minnesota Zoo
Morris Video
Moving Media
Natl. Archives of Canada
North Country Media Group
Omega Films
Peak Productions, Inc.
Petrified Films, Inc.
Prelinger Assoc., Inc.
Preview Media
Prov. Arch. of Alberta
Source Stock Footage Lib., Inc.
Summit Films, Inc.
TV Ontario
Twentieth Century-Fox Movietonews
Video Tape Library, Ltd.
West Star Productions
White Janssen, Inc.
See also Equestrian sports

Horses (Appaloosa)
Appaloosa Horse Club, Inc.

Horses (Arabian)
Arabian Horse Owners Foundation
Arabian Horse Trust
Hammer (Armand) Prods.
Intl. Arabian Horse Assn.
Southwest Prods., Inc.
Video Ventures Prods.

Horses (Clydesdale)
Anheuser-Busch Cos., Inc.
Freewheelin' Films, Ltd.

Horses (Morgan)
Amer. Morgan Horse Assn.

Horses (Wild)
Petrified Films, Inc.

Horses and buggies
See Buggies (Horse-drawn)

Horseshoes
Peak Productions, Inc.
Sportsfilm
Twentieth Century-Fox Movietonews

Horticulture
Intl. Film Bureau, Inc.

See also Agriculture

Horton, Rick
Port Washington Pub. Lib.

Hospices
Lawren Prods., Inc.
Natl. Funeral Directors Assn.

Hospitals
Altschul Group
Analogous Productions
Archive Film Prods., Inc.
Blue Sky Comms., Inc.
British Info. Svcs., Radio & TV Div.
CBS News Archives
Center for Biomedical Comms.
Emory Medical Television Network
Energy Productions
Estuary Press
Film Bank
Fish Films, Inc.
Forsher (James) Prods. & Archives, Inc.
Hooper (Josh) Prods., Inc.
Johns Hopkins Univ., School of Medicine
Lemorande Prod. Co.
Natl. Archives of Canada
New York Hosp.-Cornell Med. Ctr., Arch.
Ohio State Univ., Dept. of Photog. &
    Cinema
Petrified Films, Inc.
Polymorph Films, Inc.
Prelinger Assoc., Inc.
Pyramid Film and Video Corp.
Rockefeller Arch. Ctr.
Silver Image
Stock House
Stock Shots
TV Ontario
Timesteps Prods., Inc.
Twentieth Century-Fox Movietonews
United Training Media
Video Genesis, Inc.

Hospitals (Historical)
Johns Hopkins Univ., School of Medicine

Hot dog stands
See Restaurants (Hot dog stands)

Hot dogs
Prelinger Assoc., Inc.

Hot rods
See Automobiles (Hot rods)

Hotels and motels
Ackerman-Black Prods., Inc.
Amer. Hotel & Motel Assn.
Atlantic Productions
Brekke Television Prods.
CBS News Archives
Creative Video, Inc.
Dorn (Larry) Associates
Farkas Studios, Ltd.
Film Bank
Fish Films, Inc.
Las Vegas News Bureau
Network Productions
New Orleans Video Access Ctr.
Petrified Films, Inc.
Preview Media
Stock House
Summit Films, Inc.
TV Ontario
Twentieth Century-Fox Movietonews
White Janssen, Inc.

Houdini, Harry
Archive Film Prods., Inc.

Hourglasses
Petrified Films, Inc.

House of Lords (U.K.)
Purdue Univ., Public Affairs Video Arch.

House of Representatives (U.S.)
C-SPAN (Cable Satellite Public Affairs Network)
Natl. Archives (RG 200)
Natl. Archives (RG 233)
Purdue Univ., Pub. Aff. Video Arch.
U.S. House of Representatives
See also Congress (U.S.)

House Un-American Activities Committee (HUAC)
Chicago Comm. to Defend the Bill of Rights
Film Bank
MacDonald, J. Fred

Houseboats
See Boats and boating (Houseboats)

Household appliances
See Appliances (Household)

Housekeeping
See Housework

Houses and homes
Broad Street Prods.
CBS News Archives
Century Video Services, Inc.
Cinephile Amalgamated Pictures
Creative Venture Films
Film Bank
Forsher (James) Prods. & Archives, Inc.
General Motors Corp.
Kesser Stock Footage Library
Lawren Prods., Inc.
March of Time
Natl. Archives (RG 31)
Peak Productions, Inc.
Petrified Films, Inc.
Prelinger Assoc., Inc.
Producers Library Service
Spectral Comms.
Stock House
TV Ontario
Timesteps Prods., Inc.
Univ. of Alaska, Fairbanks, Alaska Motion Picture Arch.
Univ. of Minn. Libs., Manuscripts Div.
Video Tape Library, Ltd.
See also Housing

Houses and homes (Abandoned)
Baylor Univ., Texas Coll.

Houses and homes (Celebrity)
Shokus Video

Houses and homes (Construction)
Allen (John E.) Inc.
Natl. Archives (RG 31)
TV Ontario

Houses and homes (Haunted)
See Haunted houses

Houses and homes (Row)
Energy Productions

Housewares
Film Bank
Prelinger Assoc., Inc.

Housewives
Creative Venture Films
General Motors Corp.
New Day Films
Petrified Films, Inc.

Prelinger Assoc., Inc.

Housewives (Japan)
Japan External Trade Organization

Housework
Film Bank
Natl. Archives (RG 33)
Prelinger Assoc., Inc.

Housing
Archive Film Prods., Inc.
Deep Dish TV
Downtown Community TV Ctr.
Intermedia Arts Minnesota
Latin Amer. Video Arch.
Natl. Archives (RG 31)
Natl. Archives (RG 96)
Natl. Archives (RG 207)
Natl. Archives (RG 208)
Natl. Archives (RG 242)
Natl. Archives (RG 252)
New Orleans Video Access Ctr.
Regional Plan Assn.
United Nations Ctr. for Human Settlements
United Nations, Visual Materials Lib.
Vidéographe Inc., Le
See also Houses and homes

Housing (Chile)
Democracy in Communication

Housing (Public)
Missouri Hist. Soc.
Natl. Archives (RG 31)
Unicorn Projects

Housing (Puerto Rico)
Rockefeller Arch. Ctr.

Housing (Soviet Union)
Estuary Press

Housing (Tract)
Unicorn Projects

Housing and Urban Development, Dept. of (U.S.)
Natl. Archives (RG 207)

Housing industry
March of Time
Natl. Assn. of Home Builders
Prelinger Assoc., Inc.
Twentieth Century-Fox Movietonews

Housing projects
Natl. Archives (RG 48)
Petrified Films, Inc.
Southern Calif. Lib. for Soc. Stud. & Res.

Houston
Bailey Productions, Inc.
Dreamlight Images, Inc.
Energy Productions

Houston (History and culture)
Archive Film Prods., Inc.
Petrified Films, Inc.

Houston, Joe
Southern Calif. Blues Soc.

How-to films and videotapes
Bullfrog Films, Inc.
Coe Film Assoc., Inc.
Hobby Industries of America
Industrial Designers Soc. of America
Intl. Fashion Video Library
Kalmbach Publishing Co.

Morris Video
Natl. Rifle Assn.
Peralta Colleges TV
Valley of the Sun Publishing
Video-SIG
Wishing Well Distribution
Woods N' Water Television Series
See also Educational films and videotapes;
Training films and videotapes

Howard, Coy
Southern Calif. Inst. of Architecture

Howard, Roy
General Motors Corp.

Howard, Tom
Videobrary, Inc.

Howard, Willie
Videobrary, Inc.

Howdy Doody
Archive Film Prods., Inc.
Moviecraft, Inc.

Howe, Lyman H.
Cinema Guild

Howe, Oscar
Native Amer. Pub. Broad. Cons.

Howland, Rebecca
Monday, Wednesday, Friday Video Club

Hoyland, John
Albright-Knox Art Gallery

Hubbell, Carl
Grinberg (Sherman) Film Libraries (West)

Hubley, Faith
Port Washington Pub. Lib.

Hudson River, N.Y.
New York State Dept. of Econ. Devel.
Petrified Films, Inc.
Xicom, Inc.

Hudson River, N.Y. (History and culture)
Port Authority of New York & New Jersey

Hudson River Valley, N.Y.
New York State Dept. of Econ. Devel.

Hudson River Valley, N.Y. (History and culture)
Rockefeller Arch. Ctr.

Hudson, Rock
Banks Film Library
Halcyon Days Prods.
Los Angeles News Service
Natl. Archives (RG 56)
Petrified Films, Inc.

Huerta, Victoriano
Archivo Historico Cinematografico
Natl. Archives (RG 200)

Huffman, Kathy Rae
Long Beach Mus. of Art

Hufsteder, Shirley
Natl. Archives (RG 441)

Huggins, Ericka
Media Bus

Hughes, Howard

Archive Film Prods., Inc.
Beerger (Norman) Prods.
Forsher (James) Prods. & Archives, Inc.

Hughes, Langston
Intellimation

Hula dancing
See Dance and dancing (Hula)

Hula hoops
Analogous Productions
Archive Film Prods., Inc.
CBS News Archives
Film Bank
Halcyon Days Prods.
Petrified Films, Inc.

Hull, Cordell
Archive Film Prods., Inc.
Natl. Archives (RG 47)

Hull, Jim
Southern Calif. Inst. of Architecture

Hull, Quebec
Carleton Prods. Inc.

Human body
Bullfrog Films, Inc.
CBS News Archives
Coronet/MTI Film & Video
Educational Images, Ltd.
Emory Medical Television Network
Film Bank
Focus Intl. Inc.
IMS Creative Communications
Multi-Focus, Inc.
Nassau Comm. Coll. Lib.
Petrified Films, Inc.
Rosebush Visions Corp.
Twentieth Century-Fox Movietonews
See also Biology; specific body parts

Human factors research and engineering
NASA, Ames Res. Ctr., Human Factors Res. Ctr.
Southern Calif. Inst. of Architecture

Human flies
Film Education Institute
Grinberg (Sherman) Film Libraries (West)
Streamline Film Archives

Human potential movement
Cinema Guild

Human reproduction
See Reproduction (Human)

Human rights
Amnesty Intl. USA
CBS News Archives
Camino Film Projects
Channel L Working Group
Comm. in Sol. People of El Salvador
Facets Multimedia, Inc.
Freedom Information Service
Icarus-Tamouz Media, Inc.
Interlock Media Associates
Maryknoll Fathers & Brothers
Natl. Archives of Canada
New Time Films, Inc.
Vidéo Femmes
See also Civil liberties; Civil rights; Civil rights movement; Gay and lesbian issues

Human-animal communication
Gorilla Foundation

NOTE: Access policies, availability and restrictions vary for each source. Please read each entry in full. Always consult "General Film and Videotape Collections" (page 599); these comprehensive collections contain material on every conceivable subject.

Latham Foundation

Human-machine interaction
NASA, Ames Res. Ctr., Human Factors
Res. Ctr.

Human-powered vehicles
See Vehicles (Human-powered)

Hummingbirds
Di Sesso (Moe) Wild Life Film Lib.
Dreamlight Images, Inc.
Film Bank
Hagley Mus. and Lib.
Jewell (Stuart) Productions
Mass. Inst. of Tech., MIT Museum
Petrified Films, Inc.
Summit Films, Inc.
Wings Wildlife Prods. Inc.

Humor
See Comedy

Humphrey, Hubert Horatio
Archive Film Prods., Inc.
Boston Univ. Film Archive
MacDonald, J. Fred
Minnesota Hist. Soc.
Natl. Archives (RG 56)
Natl. Archives (RG 174)
Natl. Archives (RG 255)

Hunchbacks
Archive Film Prods., Inc.

Hungary (History and culture)
Archive Film Prods., Inc.
Natl. Archives (RG 242)

Hunger
CARE
Carousel Film & Video
DEC Film & Video
Downtown Community TV Ctr.
Interfaith Action for Economic Justice
Intl. Lutheran Layman's League
Maryknoll Fathers & Brothers
Mass Media Ministries
Natl. Archives/Natl. AV Ctr.
New Time Films, Inc.
Oxfam America
Population Reference Bureau, Inc.
Richter Productions
U.S. Committee for UNICEF

Hunt, Richard
Video Data Bank

Hunter, Alberta
Camera Three Prods., Inc.

Hunter, Jeffrey
Banks Film Library

Hunter, Tommy
Natl. Archives of Canada

Hunting and trapping
Alaska Native Heritage Film Project
Alaska Video Prods.
Animal Welfare Institute
Chiappetta Prods., Inc.
Davenport Films
Ducks Unlimited, Inc.
Echo Film Prods., Inc.
Film Bank
Focus on Animals
Friends of Animals
Grinberg (Sherman) Film Libraries (East)
Grinberg (Sherman) Film Libraries (West)
Indiana State Comm. on Public Records
KYUK-TV
Native Amer. Pub. Broad. Cons.
Natl. Archives (RG 200)
Natl. Archives of Canada

Natl. Rifle Assn.
New Jersey Network
New Mexico State Records Ctr. & Arch.
New York State Dept. of Env. Cons.
Petrified Films, Inc.
Prelinger Assoc., Inc.
Spalla (Rick) Video Prods.
TV Ontario
Twentieth Century-Fox Movietonews
Univ. of Alaska, Fairbanks, Alaska Motion
Picture Arch.
Univ. of Alberta, Boreal Inst. for Northern
Studies
Video I-D, Inc.
Windsor Prod. Corp.
Woods N' Water Television Series
See also Seal hunting

Huntington, W. Va. (History & culture)
Marshall Univ., Spec. Coll.

Hurley, Robert
Connecticut State Library

Hurling
Twentieth Century-Fox Movietonews

Hurricanes
Allen (John E.) Inc.
Analogous Productions
Archive Film Prods., Inc.
Connecticut Historical Society
Film Bank
Grinberg (Sherman) Film Libraries (West)
Hist. Soc. of Palm Beach County
Natl. Archives (RG 69)
Natl. Archives (RG 342)
Natl. Assn. of Conservation Dists.
Natl. Oceanic & Atmospheric Admin.
Pennsylvania State Arch.
Petrified Films, Inc.
Pyramid Film and Video Corp.
Twentieth Century-Fox Movietonews
See also Meteorology; Storms; Tornadoes;
Weather

Hurt, John
Spectral Comms.

Hüsker Du (Rock and roll band)
Giorno Poetry Systems Inst.
Target Video

Hussein, King
Illinois State Hist. Lib.

Hussein, Saddam
Film Bank

Huston, Angelica
Spectral Comms.

Huston, John
Agee (James) Film Project
Blackwood (Christian) Prods., Inc.
Daphne Productions, Inc.
Gray City Inc.
Spectral Comms.

Hutterites
Arch. of the Mennonite Church
Glenbow Mus. Arch.
Natl. Archives of Canada

Hutto, J.B.
Rhapsody Films, Inc.

Hutton, Barbara
Archive Film Prods., Inc.

Hutton, Betty
Natl. Archives/Natl. AV Ctr.

Hutton, Lauren
Giorno Poetry Systems Inst.

Hyacinths
Kesser Stock Footage Library

Hyde Park, N.Y. (History and culture)
Roosevelt (Franklin D.) Lib.

Hydrofoils
See Boats and boating (Hydrofoils)

Hydroplanes and hydroplane racing
Amer. Motion Pictures
Diamond P. Sports
Freewheelin' Films, Ltd.
Network Productions
Petrified Films, Inc.
Spalla (Rick) Video Prods.

Hyenas
Di Sesso (Moe) Wild Life Film Lib.
Film Bank
Petrified Films, Inc.
Wings Wildlife Prods. Inc.

Hygiene
See Personal hygiene

Hylan, John F.
Natl. Archives (RG 24)

Hyperspace
Film Bank

Hypertension
Amer. Heart Assn.
Amer. Red Cross
Emory Medical Television Network
Hartley Film Found., Inc.
New Orleans Video Access Ctr.
Pyramid Film and Video Corp.
Rogers (Will) Institute

Hypnosis
Erickson (Milton H.) Foundation, Inc.
Hartley Film Found., Inc.
Pyramid Film and Video Corp.
Social Psychiatry Res. Inst.
Valley of the Sun Publishing

Hyslop, Ricky
Natl. Archives of Canada

ILGWU
See International Ladies' Garment
Workers' Union (ILGWU)

IMAX format footage
Fabulous Footage Inc.
Natl. Archives (RG 151)

IRS
See Internal Revenue Service (U.S.)

Ibadan, Nigeria (History and culture)
Archive Film Prods., Inc.

Ice
CBS News Archives
Dreamlight Images, Inc.
Energy Productions
Film Bank
Image Bank
Nine Star Productions
Twentieth Century-Fox Movietonews
Xicom, Inc.

Ice climbing
Alaska Video Prods.

Ice cream
Archive Film Prods., Inc.
Prelinger Assoc., Inc.

Ice cutting and harvesting
Bangor Historical Society
Northeast Historic Film

Ice fields
Natl. Archives (RG 75)

Ice floes
British Info. Svcs., Radio & TV Div.
Film Bank
Petrified Films, Inc.

Ice sculptures
TV Ontario

Ice shows
Analogous Productions
Petrified Films, Inc.
TV Ontario

Ice skating
See Skating (Ice)

Icebergs
Archive Film Prods., Inc.
Dreamlight Images, Inc.
Jewell (Stuart) Productions
Natl. Archives (RG 26)
Petrified Films, Inc.
TV Ontario

Icebreakers
See Ships (Icebreakers)

Iceland
Beerger (Norman) Prods.

Iceland (History and culture)
Peary-MacMillan Arctic Museum

Icicles
Energy Productions
Film Bank
Summit Films, Inc.
TV Ontario

Idaho
Echo Film Prods., Inc.
Nez Percé Natl. Hist. Park
Preview Media

Idaho (History and culture)
Idaho State Library
Nature Conservancy
Oregon Hist. Soc.
Utah State Hist. Soc.

Idiot savants
UCLA Behavioral Sci. Media Lab.

Ifagao people
Smithsonian Inst., Human Studies Film
Arch.

Iggy Pop
Target Video

Iglesias, Julio
Spectral Comms.

Igloos
Archive Film Prods., Inc.
Film Bank
Petrified Films, Inc.

Iguanas
Mountain Video Associates
TV Ontario

Iguacu Cataracts, Brazil
Brazilian-American Cultural Inst.

Illinois
Chicago A/V Studios
Chicago Video Transfer
Cine-Mark
Departures, Inc.
Dreamlight Images, Inc.
Energy Prods.

File Tape Co.
Film Bank
Kesser Stock Footage Lib.
Preview Media
Renaissance Video Corp.
Stegman Prods.
Stock House
Unicorn Projects
Video I-D, Inc.

Illinois (History and culture)
Allen (John E.) Inc.
Archive Film Prods., Inc.
Chicago Historical Society
Cinema Medica
Committee for Labor Access
Evangelical Covenant Church of Amer.
Flower Films & Video
Grinberg (Sherman) Film Libraries (East)
Illinois State Hist. Lib.
Intl. Historic Films
Kartemquin Films
MacDonald, J. Fred
Mus. of Broadcast Communications
Mus. of Contemporary Art
Natl. Archives (RG 12)
Natl. Archives (RG 46)
Natl. Archives (RG 70)
Natl. Archives (RG 267)
Natl. Archives/Natl. AV Ctr.
Natl. Railway Hist. Soc.
New Day Films
Northern Ill. Univ. Reg. Hist. Ctr.
Payne, Roz
Petrified Films, Inc.
Prelinger Assoc., Inc.
Quest Prods., Inc.
Southern Calif. Lib. for Soc. Stud. & Res.
Univ. of Ill. Urbana-Champaign, Univ. Arch.

Illiteracy
See Literacy

Iltis, Hugh
Film/Audio Services, Inc.
Florentine Films

Image processing
SIGGRAPH

Immigrants and immigration
Addiction Research Foundation of Ontario
Allen (John E.) Inc.
Amer. Soc. Hist. Proj. Film Lib.
Amer. Zionist Youth Found.
Anti-Defamation League of B'nai B'rith
Archive Film Prods., Inc.
Archives of Ontario
Armenian Film Foundation
Asian American Resource Workshop
CBS News Archives
Canadian Filmmakers Dist. Centre
Cinema Guild
DEC Film & Video
Deep Dish TV
Downtown Community TV Ctr.
East-West Center
El Paso Community College
Estuary Press
Evangelical Covenant Church of Amer.
Fish Films, Inc.
Historical Health Film Coll.
House Found. for the Arts
Intermedia Arts Minnesota
Labor Video Project
Latin Amer. Video Arch.
Lib. of Congress, M/B/RS
MALDEF
March of Time
Media Project

Mus. of Jewish Heritage
Native Amer. Pub. Broad. Cons.
Natl. Archives (RG 131)
Natl. Archives of Canada
Natl. Archives/Natl. AV Ctr.
Natl. Asian American Telecomm. Assn.
Natl. Ctr. for Jewish Film
New Day Films
New Jersey Network
Notimex
Prelinger Assoc., Inc.
Richter Productions
Slavonic Benev. Order of State of Texas
TV Ontario
TV-UNAM
Third World Newsreel
Timesteps Prods., Inc.
Tucson Community Cable Corp.
Univ. of Texas, Inst. of Texan Cultures
Video Data Bank
Visual Communications
Western Reserve Hist. Soc.
Windsor Prod. Corp.
World Monitor

Immigration and Naturalization Service (U.S.)
Natl. Archives (RG 85)

Immortality
Pyramid Film and Video Corp.

Immunization
Historical Health Film Coll.
Rogers (Will) Institute
UNICEF, Div. Info. & Pub. Aff.

Immunology
Altschul Group
Bullfrog Films, Inc.
Emory Medical Television Network
IMS Creative Communications

Impalas
Kesser Stock Footage Library

Impeachment (Presidential)
Natl. Archives (RG 200)

Imperial Valley, Calif. (History and culture)
United Farm Workers of America (UFW)

Impresarios
Archive Film Prods., Inc.

Inaugurations
CBS News Archives
Film Bank
Indiana Hist. Soc., Smith Memorial Lib.
Kentucky Dept. of Libraries & Archives
New York State Arch. & Rec. Admin.
Twentieth Century-Fox Movietonews
WTJX-TV

Inaugurations (Presidential) (U.S.)
Banks Film Library
Eisenhower (Dwight D.) Library
Film Education Institute
Hearst Metrotone News
Johnson (Lyndon Baines) Lib.
MacDonald, J. Fred
Natl. Archives (RG 24)
Natl. Archives (RG 111)
Natl. Archives (RG 119)
Natl. Archives (RG 128)
Natl. Archives (RG 200)
Natl. Archives (RG 274)
Natl. Archives (RG 330)
Natl. Archives (RG 342)
Roosevelt (Franklin D.) Lib.

UCLA Film & Television Archive
Univ. of Ill. Urbana-Champaign, Univ. Arch.
White Janssen, Inc.

Inaugurations (Presidential, Mexico)
Archivo Fotografico y Cinematografico Abítia

Inaugurations (Presidential, Panama)
Natl. Archives (RG 185)

Ince, Thomas
Archive Film Prods., Inc.

Incest
FMS Productions
Multi-Focus, Inc.
Planned Parenthood Fed. of Amer.
Univ. of West Fla., Hum. Res. Vid. Lib.

Incubators (Baby)
CBS News Archives
Energy Productions
Prelinger Assoc., Inc.

Independence Day (Liberty Weekend, 1986) (U.S.)
Energy Productions
Grinberg (Sherman) Film Libraries (East)
Multi-Media Pre-Accession Point
Simon (Jeff) Productions
U.S. Natl. Park Service Hist. Coll.

Independence Day (U.S.)
Dreamlight Images, Inc.
Moving Media
Natl. Archives (RG 59)
Natl. Archives (RG 200)
Petrified Films, Inc.

Independence Hall (Philadelphia)
Petrified Films, Inc.

Independent films and videotapes
Anthology Film Archives
Asian Cine-Vision
Atlantic Independent Media
Bay Area Video Coalition
Black Filmmaker Foundation
Canadian Filmmakers Dist. Centre
Canadian Filmmakers Dist. West
Canyon Cinema, Inc.
Carnegie District Film Ctr.
Center for New Television
Chautauqua-Cattaraugus Library System
Cinecom Entertainment Group
Contemporary Art Television (CAT) Fund
Creative Film Society
Downtown Community TV Ctr.
EZTV
Ed Video Media Arts Centre
Facets Multimedia, Inc.
Film Arts Foundation
Film-Makers' Cooperative
First Run/Icarus Films, Inc.
Image Film & Video Coll.
Indiana Univ., Audio-Visual Center
Intl. Women's Day Video Fest.
Kino Intl. Corp.
Latina, S.A. de C.V.
Media Project
Monday, Wednesday, Friday Video Club
Mus. of Mod. Art, Circulating Film Lib.
Mus. of Mod. Art, Dept. of Film
Museum of the American Indian
Natl. Endow. for the Arts, Media Arts Prog.
Neighborhood Film and Video Project
New Time Films, Inc.
New York State Council on the Arts

Newfoundland Independent Filmmakers Coop
911 Contemporary Arts Ctr.
Northeast Historic Film
Pacific Cinémathèque Pacifique
Parker (Kit) Films
Picture Start, Inc.
School of the Art Inst. of Chicago, Flaxman Lib.
South Carolina Arts Comm. Media Arts Ctr.
Southwest Alternate Media Project
Univ. of Kentucky, AV Arch.
Univ. of Southern Calif., Film & Video Dist. Ctr.
Utah Media Arts Center
Vidéo Femmes
Vidéographe Inc., Le
Visual Studies Workshop
Walker Art Ctr.
Wisconsin Ctr. for Film & Theater Res.
Women Make Movies, Inc.
Women in Focus
Yale Film Study Ctr.
Zafra, A.C.
See also Experimental films and videotapes

India
British Info. Svcs., Radio & TV Div.
Canadian Broadcasting Corp.
Energy Productions
Film Search
Grinberg (Sherman) Film Libraries (West)
Imagen y Sonido Independiente, S.A.
Impact Audio Visual
Jewell (Stuart) Productions
Pan American Airlines Film Lib.
Petrified Films, Inc.
Smithsonian Inst., Human Studies Film Arch.

India (Contemporary issues)
Courter Films & Assoc.
DEC Film & Video

India (History and culture)
Allen (John E.) Inc.
Archive Film Prods., Inc.
Cantor (Arthur) Inc.
DEC Film & Video
Devillier Donegan Ent.
Disciples of Christ Hist. Soc.
Duffy (Kevin) Prods.
Film/Audio Services, Inc.
Films of India
Idera Films
Latina, S.A. de C.V.
Magnes (Judah L.) Museum
March of Time
Media Guild
Natl. Archives (RG 18)
Natl. Archives (RG 200)
Natl. Archives (RG 208)
Natl. Archives (RG 286)
Natl. Archives (RG 326)
Natl. Archives (RG 362)
Oakland Public Lib., Asian Branch Lib.
Petrified Films, Inc.
Rockefeller Arch. Ctr.
Singer-Sharrette Traditional Healing Films
Smithsonian Inst., Human Studies Film Arch.
Southern Calif. Inst. of Architecture
Twentieth Century-Fox Movietonews
U.S. Committee for UNICEF
United Nations, Visual Materials Lib.
Univ. of Wisconsin — Extension
Wheaton Coll., Billy Graham Ctr.
White Janssen, Inc.

NOTE: Access policies, availability and restrictions vary for each source. Please read each entry in full. Always consult "General Film and Videotape Collections" (page 599); these comprehensive collections contain material on every conceivable subject.

India Gate (Bombay, India)
Petrified Films, Inc.

Indian Affairs, Bureau of (U.S.)
Natl. Archives (RG 75)

Indian Affairs, Office of (U.S.)
Natl. Archives (RG 48)

Indian Ocean
Petrified Films, Inc.

Indian Ocean (History and culture)
Natl. Archives (RG 59)

Indiana
Energy Prods.
Preview Media
Video Management Systems

Indiana (History and culture)
Auburn-Cord-Duesenberg Museum
Ball State Univ., Middletown Coll.
Fulton County Hist. Soc., Inc.
Indiana Hist. Soc., Smith Memorial Lib.
Indiana State Comm. on Public Records
Indiana State Lib.
Indiana Univ. Folklore Arch.
Indiana Univ. Northwest Lib.
Natl. Archives (RG 91)
Natl. Archives/Natl. AV Ctr.
Petrified Films, Inc.
Prelinger Assoc., Inc.

Indiana, Robert
Cantor (Arthur) Inc.

Indianapolis
Energy Productions
Video Mgmt. Systems

Indianapolis (History and culture)
DePauw University, Archives
Indiana Hist. Soc., Smith Memorial Lib.

Indianapolis 500
See Automobiles (Racing) (Indianapolis 500)

Indians
See Native Americans

Indigenous peoples
Acad. of Nat. Sci. of Phila. Lib.
Archive Film Prods., Inc.
Documentary Educational Resources
Film Bank
Film Search
Fish Films, Inc.
Idera Films
Interlock Media Associates
Jewell (Stuart) Productions
Native Amer. Pub. Broad. Cons.
Natl. Archives (RG 18)
Natl. Archives (RG 75)
Natl. Archives (RG 234)
Natl. Geographic Soc. Stock Footage Lib.
Petrified Films, Inc.
Sobek Productions
TV Ontario
United Nations Ctr. for Human Settlements
Video In
White Janssen, Inc.
Women in Focus
Yukon Archives
Zielinski Productions, Inc.
See also Native Americans

Indigenous peoples (Africa)
Africa Inland Mission
Duffy (Kevin) Productions
Innerquest Communications Corp.
Johnson (Martin & Osa) Safari Museum
Petrified Films, Inc.

Indigenous peoples (Alaska)
Intl. Women's Day Video Fest.
Sitka Natl. Hist. Park
See also Native Americans

Indigenous peoples (Arctic)
Univ. of Alberta, Boreal Inst. for Northern Studies

Indigenous peoples (Australia)
Devillier Donegan Ent.
Icarus Films Intl., Inc.
Smithsonian Inst., Human Studies Film Arch.
TV Ontario

Indigenous peoples (Hawaii)
Natl. Archives (RG 220)

Indigenous peoples (Mexico)
Instituto Nacional Indigenista
Redes Cinevideo, S.A.
Smithsonian Inst., Human Studies Film Arch.
See also Native Americans

Indigenous peoples (North America)
Alaska Native Heritage Film Project
Ketchikan (City of)
Natl. Archives of Canada
See also Native Americans

Indigenous peoples (Peru)
Cinema Guild
See also Native Americans

Indochina (History and culture)
Allen (John E.) Inc.
DEC Film & Video
Natl. Archives (RG 286)

Indonesia
Farkas Studios, Ltd.
Image Bank/Film Search
Jewell (Stuart) Prods.
Sheffield (Erin) Prods.
Simon & Goodman Picture Co.
Sonoma Video Prods.
Source Film & Tape Lib.

Indonesia (History and culture)
Archive Film Prods., Inc.
Documentary Educational Resources
Film/Audio Services, Inc.
Johns Hopkins Univ./Population Comm. Svcs.
Lib. of Congress, M/B/RS
March of Time
Natl. Archives (RG 286)
Natl. Archives (RG 362)
Northstar Prods.
Oregon Hist. Soc.
Petrified Films, Inc.
Sobek Productions
United Nations, Visual Materials Lib.

Indoor Life (Musical group)
Target Video

Industrial arts
Natl. Archives/Natl. AV Ctr.

Industrial design
Cranbrook Acad. of Arts
Media Guild
Petrified Films, Inc.
Prelinger Assoc., Inc.
Univ. of Tex. at Austin, Ransom Hum. Res. Ctr., Photo. Coll.

Industrial films and videotapes

Smithsonian Inst., Human Studies Film Arch.
Summit Films, Inc.

AT&T Archives & Rec. Mgmt. Svcs.
Amer. Arch. of the Factual Film
Amer. Inst. of Baking
Amer. Inst. of the Hist. of Pharmacy
Archive Film Prods., Inc.
Auburn-Cord-Duesenberg Museum
Bailey Prods., Inc.
Baltimore Mus. of Industry
Chicago Historical Society
Chisholm (Jack) Film Productions
Echo Film Prods., Inc.
Edison Natl. Historic Site
Fabulous Footage Inc.
Fish Films, Inc.
General Motors Corp.
Grinberg (Sherman) Film Libraries (West)
Hagley Mus. & Lib.
Halcyon Days Prods.
Imagen y Sonido Independiente, S.A.
Imageways, Inc.
Indiana Univ. Northwest Lib.
LeTourneau College Archives
Mass. Inst. of Tech., MIT Museum, Hart Nautical Coll.
Modern Talking Picture Service
Moviecraft, Inc.
Natl. Archives of Canada
Natl. Assn. of Home Builders
Natl. Railway Historical Soc.
Northeast Historic Film
Northrop Univ., Amer. Hall of Aviation Hist.
Ohio Hist. Soc.
Oregon Hist. Soc.
Prelinger Assoc., Inc.
Prov. Arch. of British Columbia
Railroad Mus. of Pennsylvania
Read (Brooks) & Assoc.
Smithsonian Inst., NMAH, Arch. Ctr.
Snyder (Bill) Films, Inc.
Source Stock Footage Lib., Inc.
State Hist. Soc. of Wisconsin
Streamline Film Archives
Studebaker Natl. Museum
Union Pacific Railroad
Voyager Co.
West Virginia Dept. of Culture & Hist.
Western Reserve Hist. Soc.
White Janssen, Inc.
Zinc Inst./Lead Industries Assn.
See also Sponsored films and videotapes

Industrial relations
Richter Productions
See also Management and management training

Industrial Workers of the World (IWW)
DEC Film & Video
First Run/Icarus Films, Inc.

Industry
Allen (John E.) Inc.
Aluminum Assn.
Appalshop Films, Inc.
Archive Film Prods., Inc.
Baltimore Mus. of Industry
British Info. Svcs., Radio & TV Div.
Broad Street Prods.
CBS News Archives
Cable News Network Library
Carleton Prods. Inc.
Carousel Film & Video
Chisholm (Jack) Film Productions
Cineworks Prods. Inc.
Creative Video, Inc.
Dreamlight Images, Inc.
Energy Productions
Film Bank
Film Search
Forsher (James) Prods. & Archives, Inc.
4•6•8 Prods., Inc.
German Info. Ctr., Film Lib.
Grinberg (Sherman) Film Libraries (West)
Hagley Mus. & Lib.

Hot Shots Commercial Prods., Inc.
Lemorande Prod. Co.
Natl. Archives (RG 200)
Natl. Archives (RG 208)
Natl. Archives (RG 306)
Natl. Archives (RG 378)
Natl. Archives of Canada
Nine Star Prods.
North Country Media Group
Northstar Prods.
Ohio Historical Soc.
Phoenix Films and Video
Prelinger Assoc., Inc.
Producers Library Service
Prov. Arch. of British Columbia
Rosebush Visions Corp.
Shields Archival
Spalla (Rick) Video Prods.
Stock House
Studio East Ltd.
TV Ontario
Timesteps Prods., Inc.
Twentieth Century-Fox Movietonews
Université Laval, Cinémathèque
Univ. of Calif., Berkeley, Bancroft Lib.
V/tape
VTR Productions
Video Genesis, Inc.
Video I-D, Inc.
Western Reserve Hist. Soc.
See also Factories; Manufacturing; specific industries

Industry (Heavy)
Hammer (Armand) Prods.
Source Stock Footage Lib., Inc.

Industry (History of)
Smithsonian Inst., NMAH, Div. Eng. & Ind.

Industry (Light)
Cineworks Prods. Inc.
Film Search
Metro Communications, Inc.

Infertility
Polymorph Films, Inc.

Inflation
CBS News Archives

Information technology
Natl. Archives (RG 307)

Infrared cinematography
Film Bank
Prelinger Assoc., Inc.

Infrastructure
Assoc. Gen. Contractors of America
Bronx County Hist. Soc.
Development Communications, Inc.
Ocean Earth Constr. and Dev. Corp.
Port Authority of New York & New Jersey
United Nations Ctr. for Human Settlements
Univ. of Toronto, AV Lib.
See also Bridges; Highways; Sewers; Streets and roads

Ingersoll, Richard
Southern Calif. Inst. of Architecture

Inglewood, Calif. (History and culture)
General Motors Corp.

Ingram, James
Spectral Comms.

Ingram, Rex
Archive Film Prods., Inc.
Natl. Archives (RG 47)

Inhelder, Barbel
Inst. for Psychoanalysis

Injuries
Academy of Health Sciences, U.S. Army
Amer. Occupational Therapy Assn.
Film Bank
Twentieth Century-Fox Movietonews

Ink Spots, The
Archive Film Prods., Inc.

Innis, Harold
Univ. of Toronto, AV Lib.

Inoculations
CBS News Archives

Inoue, Manji
Amer. Federation of the Arts

Inouye, Daniel
Daphne Productions, Inc.

Insecticides
See Pest control; Pesticides

Insects
Acad. of Nat. Sci. of Phila. Lib.
Archive Film Prods., Inc.
British Info. Svcs., Radio & TV Div.
CBS News Archives
Chisholm (Jack) Film Productions
Coronet/MTI Film & Video
Dreamlight Images, Inc.
Energy Productions
Film Bank
Glenbow Mus. Arch.
Grinberg (Sherman) Film Libraries (East)
Historical Health Film Coll.
Indiana State Comm. on Public Records
March of Time
Minnesota Zoo
Moody Inst. of Science
Natl. Archives (RG 7)
Norsgaard, Campbell
Petrified Films, Inc.
Prelinger Assoc., Inc.
TV Ontario
Wings Wildlife Prods. Inc.

Insomnia
Prelinger Assoc., Inc.
UCLA Behavioral Sci. Media Lab.
See also Sleep

Instructional films and videotapes
See Educational films and videotapes;
How-to films and videotapes; Training
films and videotapes

Insurance
CBS News Archives
Historical Health Film Coll.
Prelinger Assoc., Inc.

Insurance (National health)
Natl. Archives (RG 200)

Integration
See Civil rights movement

Inter-American Affairs, Office of (U.S.)
Natl. Archives (RG 229)

Interactive light
Film Bank

Interactive videodiscs
ABC News Interactive
BNA Communications, Inc.

Voyager Co.

Interactivity
SIGGRAPH

Interior decorating
Prelinger Assoc., Inc.

Interior design
Peralta Colleges TV

Interior, Department of the (U.S.)
Natl. Archives (RG 48)
Natl. Archives (Stock Film Coll.)

**Interlochen, Michigan (History and
culture)**
Univ. of Mich., Mich. Hist. Colls.

Internal Revenue Service (U.S.)
Natl. Archives (RG 58)

**International Brotherhood of
Teamsters, Chauffeurs,
Warehousemen and Helpers of
America**
Intermedia Arts Minnesota

**International Cooperation
Administration**
Natl. Archives (RG 286)

International Geophysical Year
CBS News Archives
Natl. Archives (RG 342)

**International Ladies' Garment
Workers' Union (ILGWU)**
Univ. of Missouri-St. Louis

**International Longshoremen's &
Warehousemen's Union (ILWU)**
Southern Calif. Lib. for Soc. Stud. & Res.

**International Women's Year
Commission**
Natl. Archives (RG 220)

Inuvik, Northwest Territories
TV Ontario

Inventions
Allen (John E.) Inc.
Analogous Productions
Archive Film Prods., Inc.
CBS News Archives
Grinberg (Sherman) Film Libraries (West)
Imageways, Inc.
Twentieth Century-Fox Movietonews

Iowa
Wallen (Dick) Prods.

Iowa (History and culture)
MacDonald, J. Fred
State Hist. Soc. of Iowa

Iowa City, Iowa (History and culture)
State Hist. Soc. of Iowa

Iowa Federation of Labor
State Hist. Soc. of Iowa

Ipanema, Brazil (History and culture)
Archive Film Prods., Inc.

Iran
Canadian Broadcasting Corp.
Film Bank
World Monitor

Iran (Contemporary issues)
Amnesty Intl. USA
Natl. Archives (RG 46)

Iran (History and culture)
Archive Film Prods., Inc.
Downtown Community TV Ctr.
Film/Audio Services, Inc.
First Run/Icarus Films, Inc.
Intl. Film Foundation
March of Time
Middle East Institute
NBC News Video Archives
Smithsonian Inst., Human Studies Film
Arch.
White Janssen, Inc.
World Monitor
Worldwide Television News

Iran hostage crisis
Hearst Metrotone News
NBC News Video Archives
Worldwide Television News

Iran-Contra hearings
Natl. Archives (RG 46)

Iran-Iraq War
Ocean Earth Constr. and Dev. Corp.

Iraq
Canadian Broadcasting Corp.
Film Bank
World Monitor

Iraq (History and culture)
Archive Film Prods., Inc.
World Monitor

Ireland
Canadian Broadcasting Corp.
Dorn (Larry) Associates
Film Bank
Petrified Films, Inc.
Preview Media
Sullivan Video Services

Ireland (History and culture)
ABC Distribution (Education)
Archive Film Prods., Inc.
Hoover Institution
March of Time
Petrified Films, Inc.
Third World Newsreel
White Janssen, Inc.

Ireland, John
Archive Film Prods., Inc.

Iris (Camera)
Film Bank

Irises (Flower)
Petrified Films, Inc.

Irish Canadians
Univ. Coll. of Cape Breton, Beaton Inst.

Irish jigs
See Dance and dancing (Irish)

Irish Republican movement
Groupe Intervention Video
Hoover Institution
Intl. Women's Day Video Fest.

Iron
Natl. Archives (RG 70)
Prelinger Assoc., Inc.
See also Mining (Iron)

Iron Curtain
Goethe Institute Atlanta
MacDonald, J. Fred
See also Cold War

Iron lungs
Johns Hopkins Univ., School of Medicine

Irons (Appliance)
MacDonald, J. Fred
Petrified Films, Inc.
Prelinger Assoc., Inc.

Ironside, Harry
Wheaton Coll., Billy Graham Ctr.

Ironton, Ohio (History and culture)
Marshall Univ., Spec. Coll.

Irradiation (Food)
Academy of Health Sciences, U.S. Army
U.S. Council for Energy Awareness
Univ. of Wisconsin — Extension

Irrigation
CBS News Archives
Calif. Dept. of Water Resources
Dreamlight Images, Inc.
Energy Productions
Glenbow Mus. Arch.
Interlock Media Associates
Natl. Archives (RG 75)
Petrified Films, Inc.
TV Ontario
Univ. of Arizona, Film Coll.

Irving, John
Daphne Productions, Inc.

Irwin, Robert
Blackwood Prods., Inc.
Video Data Bank

**Isar River, Germany (History and
culture)**
Worldwide Television News

Isham, Sheila
Albright-Knox Art Gallery

Isherwood, Christopher
Cantor (Arthur) Inc.
Daphne Productions, Inc.
One, Inc.

Islam
See Religion (Islam)

Islands
CBS News Archives
Dorn (Larry) Associates
Film Bank
Mountain Video Associates
Pacific Focus Inc.
Passage Home Communications
Twentieth Century-Fox Movietonews
Video Tape Library, Ltd.
Zielinski Productions, Inc.
See also Tropical scenes; specific islands

Isolation tanks
TV Ontario

Isozaki, Arata
Blackwood Prods., Inc.

Israel
Bailey Productions, Inc.
Beerger (Norman) Prods.
Canadian Broadcasting Corp.
Creative Video, Inc.

NOTE: Access policies, availability and restrictions vary for each source. Please read each entry in full. Always consult "General Film and Videotape Collections" (page 599); these comprehensive collections contain material on every conceivable subject.

Film Bank
Israel Broadcasting Service
Preview Media
World Monitor
See also Middle East; Palestine

Israel (Contemporary issues)
Alden Films
Amer. Zionist Youth Found.
Anti-Defamation League of B'nai B'rith
DEC Film & Video
First Run/Icarus Films, Inc.
Icarus-Tamouz Media, Inc.
Israel Broadcasting Service
Labor Video Project
Third World Newsreel

Israel (History and culture)
Alden Films
Amer. Zionist Youth Found.
American ORT Federation
Archive Film Prods., Inc.
B'nai B'rith Intl. Headquarters
Bibliothèque Municipale de Montréal
DEC Film & Video
Devillier Donegan Ent.
Ergo Media
Film/Audio Services, Inc.
First Run/Icarus Films, Inc.
Intl. Film Foundation
Israel Broadcasting Service
Mus. of Jewish Heritage
Natl. Archives (RG 59)
Natl. Ctr. for Jewish Film
Northstar Prods.
Roosevelt (Franklin D.) Lib.
Singer-Sharrette Traditional Healing Films
Southern Calif. Lib. for Soc. Stud. & Res.
UJA Federation
White Janssen, Inc.
World Monitor
Worldwide Television News

Istanbul, Turkey
TV Ontario

Istanbul, Turkey (History and culture)
Archive Film Prods., Inc.
Armenian Film Foundation
Hellenic College

Italian Americans
Anti-Defamation League of B'nai B'rith
New Jersey Network
Smithsonian Inst., Human Studies Film
  Arch.

Italo-Ethiopian conflict (1936)
Natl. Archives (RG 111)
Natl. Archives (RG 200)
Natl. Archives (RG 242)

Italy
Beerger (Norman) Prods.
Cameo Film Library, Inc.
Canadian Broadcasting Corp.
Departures, Inc.
Dreamlight Images, Inc.
Film Bank
Pan American Airlines Film Lib.
Petrified Films, Inc.
Preview Media
Quest Prods., Inc.
Yue-Sai Kan, Inc.

Italy (History and culture)
Allen (John E.) Inc.
Archive Film Prods., Inc.
Citadel, The
Hoover Institution
Intl. Film Bureau, Inc.
Italian Cultural Institute
March of Time
Natl. Archives (RG 59)
Natl. Archives (RG 111)

Natl. Archives (RG 292)
Natl. Archives (RG 326)
Natl. Archives of Canada
Natl. Archives/Natl. AV Ctr.
Oregon Hist. Soc.
Petrified Films, Inc.
Prelinger Assoc., Inc.
Rockefeller Arch. Ctr.
Twentieth Century-Fox Movietonews
Univ. of Arizona, Film Lib.

Itatani, Michiko
Mus. of Contemporary Art

Ito, Miyoko
Video Data Bank

Itter, Diane
Video Data Bank

Ivens, Joris
Villon Films

Ivory Coast (History and culture)
United Nations Ctr. for Human
  Settlements

Iwo Jima
Dreamlight Images, Inc.

Iwo Jima (History and culture)
Archive Film Prods., Inc.

Iwo Jima Memorial (Washington, D.C.)
Energy Productions
Petrified Films, Inc.

Ixtapa-Zihuatanejo, Mexico
Preview Media

Izenour, Steve
Southern Calif. Inst. of Architecture

Jackals
Di Sesso (Moe) Wild Life Film Lib.
Wings Wildlife Prods. Inc.

Jackson, Cal
Natl. Archives of Canada

Jackson Hole, Wyo.
Preview Media

**Jackson Hole, Wyo. (History and
culture)**
Rockefeller Arch. Ctr.

Jackson, J.B.
Southern Calif. Inst. of Architecture

Jackson, Janet
Spectral Comms.

Jackson, Jesse
Boston College, Univ. Arch.
Daphne Productions, Inc.
King (Dr. Martin Luther, Jr.) Ctr.
Memphis State Univ. Libraries
Natl. Assn. for the Advancement of
  Colored People
News On Film

Jackson, John
Rhapsody Films, Inc.

Jackson, Kenneth T.
Bronx County Hist. Soc.

Jackson, Mahalia
Archive Film Prods., Inc.
Schwerin, Jules

Jackson, Maynard
Univ. of Georgia, WSB TV News Film
  Arch.

Jackson, Michael
Los Angeles News Service
Spectral Comms.

Jackson, Sherry
Banks Film Library
Shokus Video

Jackson, William Henry
Blackwood Prods., Inc.

Jacksons
Clark (Dick) Media Archives, Inc.

Jacksonville, Fla.
Energy Productions

Jacob, John
Natl. Assn. for the Advancement of
  Colored People

Jacobi, Lotte
Port Washington Pub. Lib.

Jacobs, Paul
New Time Films, Inc.

Jacquette, Yvonne
Amer. Federation of the Arts
Video Data Bank

Jacuzzis
Tri-Comm Prods.

Jaeger, Andrea
U.S. Tennis Assn.

Jaffe, Sam
Banks Film Library

Jagger, Bianca
Daphne Productions, Inc.

Jagger, Dean
Banks Film Library

Jaguars
Petrified Films, Inc.

Jai alai
Kesser Stock Footage Library
Petrified Films, Inc.
Sportsfilm

Jailbreaks
Mississippi Dept. of Arch. & Hist.

Jails
See Prisons and prisoners

Jainism
See Religion (Jainism)

Jaipur (Rajastan, India)
Petrified Films, Inc.

Jakarta, Indonesia
Sheffield (Erin) Prods.

Jakarta, Indonesia (History and culture)
United Nations, Visual Materials Lib.

Jam, Jimmy
Spectral Comms.

Jam, The (Rock and roll band)
Target Video

Jamaica
Creative Video, Inc.
Departures, Inc.
Northstar Prods.
Preview Media
Seagram Museum
World Monitor

Jamaica (Contemporary issues)
Alternative Information Network

Jamaica (History and culture)
DEC Film & Video
Film/Audio Services, Inc.
Idera Films
Inter-American Foundation
Johns Hopkins Univ./Population Comm.
  Svcs.
Mus. of Mod. Art of Latin America
Schomburg Ctr. for Res. in Black Culture
Smithsonian Inst., Human Studies Film
  Arch.
Third World Newsreel
U.S. Committee for UNICEF
Univ. of Tex. at Austin, Benson Lat. Am.
  Coll.
Villon Films
World Monitor

Jamestown, N.Y. (History and culture)
Chautauqua-Cattaraugus Library System

Jamestown, Va.
Metro Communications, Inc.

Jamestown, Va. (History and culture)
Archive Film Prods., Inc.

Janesville, Wis. (History and culture)
Prelinger Assoc., Inc.

Jannings, Emil
Archive Film Prods., Inc.

Janssen, David
Banks Film Library

Japan
Amer. Airlines
Bennett (Joel) Prods.
British Info. Svcs., Radio & TV Div.
Canadian Broadcasting Corp.
Consulate General of Japan
Dreamlight Images, Inc.
Farkas Studios, Ltd.
Film Bank
Impact Audio Visual
Japan External Trade Organization
Japan Society, Inc. Film Center
Marts (Steve) Productions
Pacific Productions
Pan American Airlines Film Lib.
Petrified Films, Inc.
Source Film & Tape Lib., Inc.
Summit Films, Inc.
TV Ontario
World Monitor
Yue-Sai Kan, Inc.

Japan (Foreign trade)
Japan External Trade Organization

Japan (History and culture)
Allen (John E.) Inc.
Alternative Information Network
Analogous Productions
Archive Film Prods., Inc.
Benamou, Catherine/LAWAS
Council for a Livable World Educ. Fund
DEC Film & Video
Devillier Donegan Ent.
Duke Univ., Perkins Lib.
East-West Center
Educational Film & Video Project
Film Bank
Film/Audio Services, Inc.
First Run/Icarus Films, Inc.
Footage Inc.
Hansen, Jack
Hoover Institution
Intl. Film Foundation
Japan Natl. Tourist Organization
Japan Society, Inc. Film Center

MacArthur (Gen. Douglas) Memorial
March of Time
Natl. Archives (RG 18)
Natl. Archives (RG 22)
Natl. Archives (RG 59)
Natl. Archives (RG 80)
Natl. Archives (RG 111)
Natl. Archives (RG 131)
Natl. Archives (RG 200)
Natl. Archives (RG 226)
Natl. Archives (RG 238)
Natl. Archives (RG 242)
Natl. Archives (RG 342)
Natl. Archives/Natl. AV Ctr.
Natl. Asian Telecomm. Assn.
Natural Reflections Video
Oakland Public Lib., Asian Branch Lib.
Pacific Productions
Perlmutter (Alvin H.) Inc.
Petrified Films, Inc.
Roosevelt (Franklin D.) Lib.
Samaya Foundation
Smithsonian Inst., Human Studies Film Arch.
Southern Calif. Inst. of Architecture
Twentieth Century-Fox Movietonews
UCLA Film & Television Archive
UDS Company
United Nations Ctr. for Human Settlements
United Nations, Visual Materials Lib.
White Janssen, Inc.
Wilmington Coll. Peace Res. Ctr.
World Monitor
Worldwide Television News

Japan (Industry and technology)
California Newsreel
Devillier Donegan Ent.
East-West Center
Japan External Trade Organization
Salenger Films Inc.
TV Ontario

Japan-China War (1930s)
Friends of Free China
Hoover Institution
March of Time
Natl. Archives (RG 242)
Natl. Archives of Canada
Southern Calif. Lib. for Soc. Stud. & Res.
Twentieth Century-Fox Movietonews

Japanese Americans
Anti-Defamation League of B'nai B'rith
Asian American Resource Workshop
First Run/Icarus Films, Inc.
Natl. Archives (RG 111)
Natl. Archives (RG 210)
Natl. Asian American Telecomm. Assn.
New Jersey Network
Oakland Public Lib., Asian Branch Lib.
Visual Communications

Japanese Americans (World War II internment)
Anti-Defamation League of B'nai B'rith
Asian American Resource Workshop
Downtown Community TV Ctr.
Intl. Historic Films, Inc.
Natl. Archives (RG 85)
Natl. Archives (RG 208)
Natl. Archives (RG 210)
Natl. Archives (RG 220)
Natl. Archives/Natl. AV Ctr.
Plains Art Mus. Lib.
Third World Newsreel

Japanese Canadians
DEC Film & Video

Jarmusch, Jim
Giorno Poetry Systems Inst.

Java, Indonesia
Sheffield (Erin) Prods.

Java, Indonesia (History and culture)
Johns Hopkins Univ./Population Comm. Svcs.
Oregon Hist. Soc.

Javelina
Energy Productions

Jazz Age (1920s)
Allen (John E.) Inc.

Jazz music
See Music (Jazz)

Jeepneys
Farkas Studios, Ltd.

Jeeps
See Automobiles (Jeeps)

Jefferson Airplane (Rock and roll band)
Pennebaker Associates, Inc.

Jefferson, Joseph
Lib. of Congress, M/B/RS

Jefferson, Thomas
Archive Film Prods., Inc.
Pyramid Film and Video Corp.

Jeffersonville, Ind. (History and culture)
Natl. Archives (RG 91)

Jeffries, Herb
Pathé Pictures, Inc.

Jekyll, Dr. (and Mr. Hyde)
Archive Film Prods., Inc.

Jellyfish
Dreamlight Images, Inc.
Marineland of Florida
Moonlight Productions

Jencks, Charles
Southern Calif. Inst. of Architecture

Jenner, Bruce
McDonald's Corp.
U.S. Olympic Comm.

Jennings, Al
Lib. of Congress, M/B/RS

Jensen, Alfred
Albright-Knox Art Gallery
Electronic Arts Intermix

Jerde, Jon A.
Southern Calif. Inst. of Architecture

Jeremiah, Maryalyce
Fellowship of Christian Athletes

Jersey City, N.J.
Port Authority of New York & New Jersey

Jerusalem
Film Bank
TV Ontario

Jerusalem (Contemporary issues)
Middle East Institute

Jerusalem (History and culture)

Amer. Zionist Youth Found.
Archive Film Prods., Inc.
Atlantis Prods., Inc.
Hellenic College
Israel Broadcasting Service
Natl. Archives (RG 59)
Natl. Ctr. for Jewish Film

Jessel, George
Banks Film Library

Jesus Christ
Archive Film Prods., Inc.

Jet engines
See Engines (Jet)

Jet skiing
Encore Entertainment
Film Bank
Kesser Stock Footage Library
Second Line Search
Spectral Comms.
Video Tape Library, Ltd.

Jethro Tull (Rock and roll band)
Archive Film Prods., Inc.

Jets
See Aircraft (Jets)

Jewelers
Prelinger Assoc., Inc.

Jewelry stores
Petrified Films, Inc.
TV Ontario

Jewels and jewelry
Archive Film Prods., Inc.
CBS News Archives
Film Bank
Petrified Films, Inc.
Prelinger Assoc., Inc.
Rosebush Visions Corp.

Jewish history and culture
Alden Films
Amer. Jewish Hist. Soc.
Amer. Zionist Youth Found.
Anti-Defamation League of B'nai B'rith
Archive Film Prods., Inc.
B'nai B'rith Intl. Headquarters
Bund Arch. of the Jewish Labor Movement
Cantor (Arthur) Inc.
Center for Holocaust Studies
Center for Southern Folklore
Direct Cinema Ltd.
Documentary Educational Resources
Ergo Media
First Run/Icarus Films, Inc.
Icarus Films Intl., Inc.
Intermedia Arts Minnesota
Israel Broadcasting Service
Kino Intl. Corp.
Magnes (Judah L.) Mus.
Middle East Institute
Mus. of Jewish Heritage
Natl. Archives (RG 200)
Natl. Archives of Canada
Natl. Ctr. for Jewish Film
Natl. Jewish Arch. of Broadcasting
New Day Films
New York Pub. Lib., Perf. Arts Res. Ctr., Theatre on Film and Tape
92nd Street YM & YWHA Assn. Archives
Phoenix Films and Video
Prestige Film Corp.
RK Editions
TV Ontario

UJA Federation
Univ. of Southern Calif., Film & Video Dist. Ctr.
Univ. of Texas, Inst. of Texan Cultures
Vedo Films/Novacom Video
Yivo Inst. for Jewish Research
See also Anti-Semitism; Holocaust

Jewish history and culture (Canada)
Canadian Filmmakers Dist. Centre
Univ. Coll. of Cape Breton, Beaton Inst.

Jewish history and culture (China)
Natl. Ctr. for Jewish Film

Jewish history and culture (Cuba)
Univ. of Miami, Arch. & Spec. Coll.

Jewish history and culture (Ethiopia)
Ergo Media

Jewish history and culture (Europe)
Natl. Ctr. for Jewish Film

Jewish history and culture (Germany)
B'nai B'rith Intl. Headquarters
Blackwood Prods., Inc.
Cantor (Arthur) Inc.
German Info. Ctr., Film Lib.
Intl. Film Foundation

Jewish history and culture (Greece)
Natl. Ctr. for Jewish Film

Jewish history and culture (Hungary)
Natl. Ctr. for Jewish Film

Jewish history and culture (Morocco)
First Run/Icarus Films, Inc.
Natl. Ctr. for Jewish Film

Jewish history and culture (Poland)
Intl. Film Foundation
Natl. Ctr. for Jewish Film

Jewish history and culture (Soviet Union)
Anti-Defamation League of B'nai B'rith
Birch (John) Society
Hoover Institution
Natl. Ctr. for Jewish Film
Student Struggle for Soviet Jewry

Jewish history and culture (Texas)
Univ. of Tex. at Austin, Barker Tex. Hist. Ctr.

Jewish history and culture (U.S.)
Amer. Jewish Hist. Soc.
Natl. Ctr. for Jewish Film

Jewish history and culture (Utah)
Univ. of Utah, Marriott Lib.

Jewish history and culture (Yemen)
Natl. Ctr. for Jewish Film

Jewish-Christian relations
Anti-Defamation League of B'nai B'rith

Jie people
Smithsonian Inst., Human Studies Film Arch.

Jigsaw puzzles
Petrified Films, Inc.

Jitterbugging
See Dance and dancing (Jitterbugging)

NOTE: Access policies, availability and restrictions vary for each source. Please read each entry in full. Always consult "General Film and Videotape Collections" (page 599); these comprehensive collections contain material on every conceivable subject.

Jobs, Steven
Computer Television Group, Inc.

Jockeys
See Horse racing

Joggers and jogging
Amer. Motion Pictures
Archive Film Prods., Inc.
Cinema Arts Assoc.
Dreamlight Images, Inc.
Film Bank
TV Ontario
Video Tape Library, Ltd.

Johansen, David
Giorno Poetry Systems Inst.

John Paul II, Pope
Dreamlight Images, Inc.
Natl. Catholic Educational Assn.

John XXIII, Pope
Univ. of Ill. Urbana-Champaign, Univ.
Arch.

Johns, Jasper
Blackwood Prods., Inc.
Cunningham Dance Foundation

Johnson, Bill
Jalbert Productions

Johnson, Irving
Mystic Seaport Mus., Inc.

Johnson, Jack
Grinberg (Sherman) Film Libraries (West)
Lib. of Congress, M/B/RS

Johnson, Lady Bird
Banks Film Library
Johnson (Lyndon Baines) Library
Natl. Archives (RG 381)
White Janssen, Inc.

Johnson, Linton Kwesi
Amer. Federation of the Arts
DEC Film & Video

Johnson, Luci Baines
White Janssen, Inc.

Johnson, Lyndon Baines
Archive Film Prods., Inc.
Banks Film Library
Boston Univ. Film Archive
Cinema Arts Assoc.
Film Bank
Film Education Institute
Halcyon Days Prods.
Johnson (Lyndon Baines) Library
Las Vegas News Bureau
Lib. of Congress, M/B/RS
MacDonald, J. Fred
Massachusetts Archives
Mus. & Hist. Div., City of Sacramento
Natl. Archives (RG 128)
Natl. Archives (RG 174)
Natl. Archives (RG 207)
Natl. Archives (RG 274)
Panhandle-Plains Hist. Museum
Petrified Films, Inc.
Texas Tech Univ., Southwest Coll.
Univ. of Ill. Urbana-Champaign, Univ.
Arch.
West Virginia Dept. of Culture & Hist.
White Janssen, Inc.

Johnson, Martin and Osa
Archive Film Prods., Inc.
Johnson (Martin & Osa) Safari Museum
Prelinger Assoc., Inc.

Johnson, Philip

Amer. Institute of Architects
Camera Three Prods., Inc.
Carter (Amon) Museum
Southern Calif. Inst. of Architecture

Johnson, Sonia
Alternative Information Network

Johnson, Tom
Port Washington Pub. Lib.

Johnson, Van
Archive Film Prods., Inc.
Banks Film Library

Johnston, Jill
Canadian Filmmakers Dist. Centre
Pennebaker Associates, Inc.

Joint Chiefs of Staff (U.S.)
Natl. Archives (RG 218)

Jolson, Al
Archive Film Prods., Inc.
Intl. Al Jolson Society

Jones, Allen
Albright-Knox Art Gallery
Blackwood (Christian) Prods., Inc.
Blackwood Prods., Inc.

Jones Beach, N.Y.
Island Video

Jones Beach, N.Y. (History and culture)
Archive Film Prods., Inc.

Jones, Bobby
Film Education Institute

Jones, Buck
UCLA Film & Television Archive

Jones, Carolyn
Banks Film Library

Jones, Elvin
Rhapsody Films, Inc.

Jones, Ernest
Inst. for Psychoanalysis

Jones, Floyd
Rhapsody Films, Inc.

Jones, Jack
Banks Film Library

Jones, Jim
Univ. of Southern Calif., Film & Video
Dist. Ctr.

Jones, Jo
Rhapsody Films, Inc.

Jones, John Paul
Long Beach Mus. of Art

Jones, LeRoi
Pennebaker Associates, Inc.

Jones, Rhodessa
Video Data Bank

Jones, Shirley
Banks Film Library
Spectral Comms.

Jones, Spike
Banks Film Library
Shokus Video

Jonesboro, Tenn. (History and culture)
East Tenn. State Univ., Arch. of
Appalachia

Joplin, Janis
Archive Film Prods., Inc.
Pennebaker Associates, Inc.

Joplin, Scott
Camera Three Prods., Inc.

Jordan
Canadian Broadcasting Corp.

Jordan (History and culture)
Film/Audio Services, Inc.
Villon Films

Jordan, Clifford
Rhapsody Films, Inc.

Jordan, Louis
Archive Film Prods., Inc.

Jordan, Vernon
Randolph (A. Philip) Educ. Fund

Jorgensen, Christine
Las Vegas News Bureau

Josephson, Kenneth
Mus. of Contemporary Art

Joshua Tree Desert, Calif.
Energy Productions

Joshua Tree National Forest, Calif.
Film Bank

Joshua trees
Energy Productions
Petrified Films, Inc.

Jotter, Lois
Univ. of Mich., Mich. Hist. Colls.

Journalism
Accuracy in Media, Inc.
Carousel Film & Video
GPN
Intermedia Arts Minnesota
Prelinger Assoc., Inc.
See also Newspapers; Offices
(Newspaper); Photojournalism; World
War II (U.S., War correspondents)

Journalism (History of)
MacDonald, J. Fred

Juarez, Mexico (History and culture)
Archive Film Prods., Inc.

Judd, Donald
Blackwood Prods., Inc.

Judges
Archive Film Prods., Inc.

Judo
Sportsfilm

Jugglers
Film Bank
Petrified Films, Inc.
TV Ontario

Juilliard School (New York City)
Blackwood (Christian) Prods.
Juilliard Schl., Wallace Lib.
Pyramid Film and Video Corp.

Juke boxes
Fish Films, Inc.
Petrified Films, Inc.

Juke joints
Petrified Films, Inc.

Juliana, Princess

Archive Film Prods., Inc.

Juliana, Queen
Archive Film Prods., Inc.

Jump ropes
Film Bank

Juneau, Alaska (History and culture)
Oregon Hist. Soc.

Jung, Carl Gustav
Inst. for Psychoanalysis
Jung (C.G.) Foundation

Jungles
Archive Film Prods., Inc.
British Info. Svcs., Radio & TV Div.
CBS News Archives
Cinema Guild
Democracy in Communication
Dreamlight Images, Inc.
Energy Productions
Film Bank
Flower Films & Video
Forsher (James) Prods. & Archives, Inc.
Intl. Assn. of Independent Producers
Jewell (Stuart) Productions
Johnson (Martin & Osa) Safari Museum
Petrified Films, Inc.
Source Stock Footage Lib., Inc.
Spalla (Rick) Video Prods.
Twentieth Century-Fox Movietonews
Video Tape Library, Ltd.
White Janssen, Inc.

Junkyards
CBS News Archives
Petrified Films, Inc.

Junoven, Helmi
Media Project

Jupiter
Beerger (Norman) Prods., Inc.
NASA, Lewis Research Center
Rosebush Visions Corp.

Jussim, Estelle
Video Data Bank

Justice, Department of (U.S.)
Natl. Archives (RG 60)

Juvenile delinquents
Archive Film Prods., Inc.
Cinema Guild
Educational Video Ctr.
Fish Films, Inc.
Lawren Prods., Inc.
MacDonald, J. Fred
Manitoba Indian Cultural Centre
March of Time
Minn. Citizens Counc. on Crime & Justice
Petrified Films, Inc.
Prelinger Assoc., Inc.
Pyramid Film and Video Corp.

Kaanapali, Hawaii
Preview Media

Kabbala
Video-SIG

Kabuki theater
See Theater (Kabuki)

Kahlo, Frida
Hoover Institution

Kahn, Herb
Southern Calif. Inst. of Architecture

Kahn, Louis I.
Mus. at Large, Ltd.

Southern Calif. Inst. of Architecture

Kahn, Tom
Labor Video Project

Kaiser, Henry J.
Natl. Archives (RG 178)

Kalahari Desert, Botswana-Namibia (History and culture)
Documentary Educational Resources
United Nations, Visual Materials Lib.

Kalgoorlie, Australia
Petrified Films, Inc.

Kalinga people
Smithsonian Inst., Human Studies Film Arch.

Kampuchea (Contemporary issues)
Oxfam America

Kampuchea (History and culture)
First Run/Icarus Films, Inc.

Kangaroos
Archive Film Prods., Inc.
Farkas Studios, Ltd.
Petrified Films, Inc.

Kanin, Fay
Univ. of Wyoming, Western Heritage Ctr.

Kanin, Garson
New York Pub. Lib., Perf. Arts Res. Ctr., Theatre on Film and Tape

Kanin, Michael
Univ. of Wyoming, Amer. Heritage Ctr.

Kansas
First Group Comms., Inc.

Kansas (History and culture)
Archive Film Prods., Inc.
Kansas State Historical Society
MacDonald, J. Fred
Prelinger Assoc., Inc.
Southern Calif. Lib. for Soc. Stud. & Res.

Kansas City, Mo.
Film Bank

Kansas City, Mo. (History and culture)
Amer. Truck Historical Soc.
Petrified Films, Inc.
Prelinger Assoc., Inc.

Kapoor, Anish
Albright-Knox Art Gallery

Kappe, Raymond
Southern Calif. Inst. of Architecture

Kaprow, Allan
Video Data Bank

Karate
Asian American Resource Workshop
Crystal Pyramid Prods.
Film Bank
Network Productions
Pyramid Film and Video Corp.
Sportsfilm

Kariba Dam, Zambia-Zimbabwe
British Info. Svcs., Radio & TV Div.

Karlen, John
Spectral Comms.

Karloff, Boris
Archive Film Prods., Inc.
Marquette Univ., Spec. Coll.

Karras, Alex
Spectral Comms.

Kashmir, India
British Info. Svcs., Radio & TV Div.
Petrified Films, Inc.

Kassler, Charles
De Saisset Museum

Kasten, Barbara
Port Washington Pub. Lib.

Katmai National Monument, Alaska (History and culture)
Natl. Archives (RG 48)

Katmandu, Nepal
British Info. Svcs., Radio & TV Div.
Film Bank
Film Search

Katydids
Dreamlight Images, Inc.

Katz, Alex
Amer. Federation of the Arts
Video Data Bank

Katzenberg, Jeff
Spectral Comms.

Kauai, Hawaii
Cinenet (Cinema Network)
Energy Productions
Passage Home Communications
Warner (Dane) Photography

Kaufman, David E.
Natl. Archives (RG 59)

Kaufman, Jane
Video Data Bank

Kayaking
Aitken (Len) Productions, Inc.
Analogous Productions
Echo Film Prods., Inc.
Film Bank
Jalbert Productions
Merkel Films
Moving Media
Petrified Films, Inc.
Second Line Search
Sports Cinematography Group
Summit Films, Inc.
TV Ontario

Kaye, Danny
MacDonald, J. Fred
Shokus Video
UCLA Film & Television Archive

Kaye, Lenny
Giorno Poetry Systems Inst.
Target Video

Keach, Stacy
Spectral Comms.

Keating, Kenneth B.
Univ. of Rochester Lib., Rare Books & Spec. Coll.

Keaton, Buster
Alan Twyman Presents
Archive Film Prods., Inc.

Banks Film Library
Camera Three Prods., Inc.
Em Gee Film Library
Film Bank
Film/Audio Services, Inc.
Petrified Films, Inc.
Shokus Video
Streamline Film Archives

Keewatin District, Northwest Territories
Northwest Territories Archives

Kefauver, Estes
Illinois State Hist. Lib.
UCLA Film & Television Archive

Kefauver hearings (1951)
Twentieth Century-Fox Movietonews

Keg hurdling
Sportsfilm

Keller, Helen
Amer. Foundation for the Blind
Archive Film Prods., Inc.
Hearst Metrotone News
Lib. of Congress, M/B/RS
Perkins School for the Blind

Keller, Kent
Illinois State Hist. Lib.

Kellerman, Sally
Spectral Comms.

Kellog, Ken
Southern Calif. Inst. of Architecture

Kelly, Ellsworth
Blackwood Prods., Inc.

Kelly, Emmett
Archive Film Prods., Inc.
Circus World Mus. Lib. & Res. Ctr.

Kelly, Gene
Banks Film Library
Spectral Comms.
Wesleyan Cinema Archives

Kelly, Grace
Archive Film Prods., Inc.
Banks Film Library

Kelly, Jim
Archive Film Prods., Inc.

Kelly, "Machine Gun"
Natl. Archives (RG 21)

Kelp
Gornick Film Prods.
Moonlight Productions
Ocean Earth Constr. and Dev. Corp.
Passage Home Communications

Kelton, Pert
Videobrary, Inc.

Kenai Peninsula, Alaska
Preview Media

Kendo
Camera Three Prods., Inc.

Kennan, George
Blackwood Prods., Inc.
Educational Film & Video Project
Quest Productions Inc.

Kennedy, Edgar
Videobrary, Inc.

Kennedy, Edward Moore
Daphne Productions, Inc.
Guggenheim Productions, Inc.
Kennedy (John F.) Library
King (Dr. Martin Luther, Jr.) Ctr.
Massachusetts Archives
Smithsonian Inst., NMAH, Div. Polit. Hist.

Kennedy Family
Cinema Guild
Halcyon Days Prods.
Kennedy (John F.) Library

Kennedy, George
Spectral Comms.

Kennedy, Jane
Spectral Comms.

Kennedy, John Fitzgerald
Alternative Information Network
Appalachian State Univ., Eury Coll.
Archive Film Prods., Inc.
Banks Film Library
Cinema Arts Assoc.
DEC Film & Video
Direct Cinema Ltd.
Film Bank
Film Education Institute
Forsher (James) Prods. & Archives, Inc.
German Info. Ctr., Film Lib.
Guggenheim Productions, Inc.
Halcyon Days Prods.
Hearst Metrotone News
Illinois State Hist. Lib.
Kennedy (John F.) Library
Lib. of Congress, M/B/RS
MacDonald, J. Fred
Massachusetts Archives
Natl. Archives (RG 174)
Natl. Archives (RG 200)
Natl. Archives (RG 233)
Natl. Archives (RG 272)
Natl. Archives (RG 330)
Natl. Archives (RG 342)
New York Pub. Lib., Rare Books & Manuscripts Div.
Petrified Films, Inc.
Prelinger Assoc., Inc.
Roosevelt (Franklin D.) Lib.
Southwest Film/Video Archives, SMU
Texas Tech Univ., Southwest Coll.
UCLA Film & Television Archive
Univ. of Georgia, WSB TV News Film Arch.
West Virginia Dept. of Culture & Hist.
Worldwide Television News

Kennedy (John F.) Memorial (Washington, D.C.)
Analogous Productions

Kennedy, Joseph Jr.
United Farm Workers of America (UFW)

Kennedy, Joseph P.
March of Time

Kennedy, Joseph III
Daphne Productions, Inc.

Kennedy, Moorhead
Myrin Institute

Kennedy, Robert Francis
Archive Film Prods., Inc.
Banks Film Library

NOTE: Access policies, availability and restrictions vary for each source. Please read each entry in full. Always consult "General Film and Videotape Collections" (page 599); these comprehensive collections contain material on every conceivable subject.

Calif. State Archives
Direct Cinema Ltd.
Guggenheim Productions, Inc.
Kennedy (John F.) Library
Mus. & Hist. Div., City of Sacramento
Natl. Archives (RG 381)
Pennebaker Associates, Inc.
Petrified Films, Inc.
Read (Brooks) & Assoc.
United Farm Workers of America (UFW)
Univ. of Ill. Urbana-Champaign, Univ.
Arch.

Kennedy, Rose
Daphne Productions, Inc.

Kennedy Space Center (Houston, Tex.)
Communications Concepts

Kennerly, David Hume
Natl. Press Photographers Assn., Inc.

Kennon, Paul
Southern Calif. Inst. of Architecture

Kent State University (May 1-4, 1970)
Natl. Archives (RG 220)

Kentucky
Omega Films

Kentucky (History and culture)
Appalachian State Univ., Eury Coll.
Appalshop Films, Inc.
Archive Film Prods., Inc.
Blackwood Prods., Inc.
Kentucky Dept. of Libraries & Archives
Marshall Univ., Spec. Coll.
Petrified Films, Inc.
Prestige Film Corp.
Univ. of Kentucky, AV Arch.
Western Kentucky Univ., Folklife Arch.

Kentucky Derby
See Horse racing (Kentucky Derby)

Kenya
Film Search
Summit Films, Inc.

Kenya (Current issues)
CARE

Kenya (History and culture)
Africa Inland Mission
Johns Hopkins Univ./Population Comm.
Svcs.
Johnson (Martin & Osa) Safari Museum
Maryknoll Fathers & Brothers
Singer-Sharrette Traditional Healing Films
U.S. Committee for UNICEF
UNICEF, Div. Info. & Pub. Aff.
Univ. of Arizona, Film Coll.

Kern County, Calif. (History and culture)
Southern Calif. Lib. for Soc. Stud. & Res.

Kerner, Otto
Univ. of Ill. Urbana-Champaign, Univ.
Arch.

Kerr, Deborah
Banks Film Library

Kertesz, Andre
Camera Three Prods., Inc.
Plains Art Mus. Lib.

Kessler, Jon
Mus. of Contemporary Art

Ketches
See Boats and boating (Ketches)

Ketchikan, Alaska
Alaska Video Prods.

Kettering, Charles F.
Ohio Historical Soc.

Key Largo, Fla.
Passage Home Communications

Key West, Fla.
Petrified Films, Inc.
Preview Media
Video Ventures Prods.

Key West, Fla. (History and culture)
Petrified Films, Inc.

Keyboards
Archive Film Prods., Inc.
Dreamlight Images, Inc.
Film Bank

Keystone Kops
Archive Film Prods., Inc.
Petrified Films, Inc.

Keystone, S. Dak. (History and culture)
South Dakota State Lib.

Khajaraho, India
Petrified Films, Inc.

Khalili, Nader
Southern Calif. Inst. of Architecture

Khrushchev, Nikita S.
Archive Film Prods., Inc.
Halcyon Days Prods.
Illinois State Hist. Lib.
Natl. Archives (RG 59)
Natl. Archives (RG 64)
Natl. Archives (RG 200)

Kibbutzim
TV Ontario

Kick boxing
Network Productions

Kidd, Billy
Channell One Video

Kidnapping
Natl. Archives (RG 21)
Natl. Archives (RG 106)
Twentieth Century-Fox Movietonews
See also Crimes and criminals

Kidney dialysis
DCI Video Resources
Natl. Kidney Found., Inc.

Kidneys
Educational Productions
Natl. Kidney Foundation, Inc.
Pyramid Film and Video Corp.
Visual Information Systems

Kienholz, Edward
Blackwood Prods., Inc.

Kijowicz, Miroslaw
Port Washington Pub. Lib.

Kikuyu people
Johnson (Martin & Osa) Safari Museum

Kilgore, Thomas
Randolph (A. Philip) Educ. Fund

Kilimanjaro, Tanzania
Summit Films, Inc.

Killian, James Rhyne
Mass. Inst. of Tech., MIT Museum

Killing Joke (Rock and roll band)
Target Video

Killy, Jean-Claude
Jalbert Productions
Soc. for French Amer. Cult. Svcs. & Educ.
Aid

Kim, Nelli
U.S. Olympic Committee

Kindergartens
Petrified Films, Inc.

King, Albert
De Saisset Museum

King, B.B.
Daphne Productions, Inc.
Univ. of Miss., Ctr. for Study of Southern
Culture

King, Bernice
King (Dr. Martin Luther, Jr.) Ctr.

King, Billie Jean
Daphne Productions, Inc.
U.S. Tennis Assn.

King, Coretta Scott
King (Dr. Martin Luther, Jr.) Ctr.
Memphis State Univ. Libraries
Natl. Assn. for the Advancement of
Colored People
Spectral Comms.
United Farm Workers of America (UFW)

King, David S.
Univ. of Utah, Marriott Lib.

King, Kenneth
Blackwood Prods., Inc.

King, Mackenzie
Natl. Archives of Canada

King, Martin Luther Jr.
Archive Film Prods., Inc.
Banks Film Library
Chicago Comm. to Defend the Bill of
Rights
Film Bank
King (Dr. Martin Luther, Jr.) Ctr.
Lib. of Congress, M/B/RS
MacDonald, J. Fred
McDonald's Corp.
Memphis State Univ. Libraries
Natl. Archives (RG 233)
Natl. Assn. for the Advancement of
Colored People
Petrified Films, Inc.
Twentieth Century-Fox Movietonews
Univ. of Calif., Ext. Media Ctr.
Univ. of Georgia, WSB TV News Film
Arch.
Worldwide Television News

King, Phillip
Albright-Knox Art Gallery

King snakes
Wings Wildlife Prods. Inc.

King, Stephen
Daphne Productions, Inc.

King, Ynestra
Paper Tiger TV

Kingston, Jamaica (History and culture)
Inter-American Foundation

Kingston, Ontario
TV Ontario

Kinoy, Peter
Port Washington Pub. Lib.

Kinsey, Alfred Charles
Kinsey Institute

Kinshasa, Zaire (History and culture)
United Nations Ctr. for Human
Settlements

Kipper Kids
Monday, Wednesday, Friday Video Club

Kirkland, Lane
Randolph (A. Philip) Educ. Fund

Kirkpatrick, Jeanne
Amer. Enterprise Institute

Kirlian electrophotography
Mankind Research Found., Inc.

Kirov, U.S.S.R. (Contemporary issues)
Ocean Earth Constr. and Dev. Corp.

Kirrane, John
U.S. Hockey Hall of Fame

Kissing
Archive Film Prods., Inc.
CBS News Archives
Film Bank
Fish Films, Inc.
Petrified Films, Inc.
Prelinger Assoc., Inc.

Kissinger, Henry
Amer. Enterprise Institute
Daphne Productions, Inc.

Kitaj, R.B.
Amer. Federation of the Arts

Kitchens
Archive Film Prods., Inc.
Film Bank
General Motors Corp.
Petrified Films, Inc.
Prelinger Assoc., Inc.

Kitchens (Chinese)
Film Bank

Kites
CBS News Archives
Film Bank
Quinn (Bill) Prods.
Telltales Associates Inc.
Twentieth Century-Fox Movietonews

Kitt, Eartha
Banks Film Library
Daphne Productions, Inc.

Kitt Peak, Ariz.
Source Stock Footage Lib., Inc.

Kittens
See Cats

Kiwi fruit
New Zealand Embassy Film Lib.

Klammer, Franz
Jalbert Productions

Klein, Franz
Blackwood Prods., Inc.

Klein, Robert
Daphne Productions, Inc.

Klein, Yves
Blackwood Prods., Inc.

Klieg lights
Petrified Films, Inc.

Klondike Gold Rush
See Gold Rush

Kluane National Park, Yukon Territory
Yukon Archives

Knievel, Evel
Daphne Productions, Inc.

Knight, Goodwin
Banks Film Library
Mus. & Hist. Div., City of Sacramento

Knights
Archive Film Prods., Inc.

Knitting
Bullfrog Films, Inc.

Knives
Prelinger Assoc., Inc.

Knodel, Gerhardt
Amer. Federation of the Arts
Video Data Bank

Knopf, Alfred A.
Univ. of Tex. at Austin, Ransom Hum.
Res. Ctr., Photo. Coll.

Knotts, Don
Banks Film Library
Shokus Video

Knoxville, Tenn.
Preview Media

Koala bears
Farkas Studios, Ltd.
Petrified Films, Inc.

Koch, Bill
Aitken (Len) Prods.
Jalbert Productions
U.S. Olympic Committee

Koch, Edward I.
Daphne Productions, Inc.

Kodascopes
Forsher (James) Prods. & Archives, Inc.
Yale Film Study Ctr.

Koestler, Arthur
Cantor (Arthur) Inc.

Koetter, Fred
Southern Calif. Inst. of Architecture

Kohl, Helmut
Natl. Archives (RG 306)

Kohner, Susan
Banks Film Library

Kohoutek (Comet)
See Comets (Kohoutek)

Koi
Cinenet (Cinema Network)

Kollek, Teddy
Amer. Zionist Youth Found.

Kollwitz, Käthe
Cantor (Arthur) Inc.
Goethe Institute Chicago

Kolthoff, Izaak
Amer. Chemical Soc.

Komar and Melamid
High Mus. of Art

Komodo dragons
Amer. Mus. Nat. Hist. Film Arch.
Sheffield (Erin) Prods.

Kona, Hawaii
Cinenet (Cinema Network)

Kona Coast, Hawaii
Preview Media

Koolhaas, Rem
Southern Calif. Inst. of Architecture

Koop, C. Everett
Amer. Portrait Films
Natl. Assn. for the Advancement of
Colored People

Koppel, Ted
Daphne Productions, Inc.

Kopu, U.S.S.R. (Contemporary issues)
Ocean Earth Constr. and Dev. Corp.

Korbut, Olga
U.S. Olympic Comm.

Korea
World Monitor

Korea (History and culture)
Pacific Productions
Third World Newsreel
World Monitor

Korea (Pre-1945) (History and culture)
Film/Audio Services, Inc.

Korea, North
Imagen y Sonido Independiente, S.A.

Korea, North (History and culture)
Natl. Archives (RG 242)

Korea, South
Farkas Studios, Ltd.
Intl. Assn. of Independent Producers
Pacific Productions

Korea, South (History and culture)
Devillier Donegan Ent.
East-West Center
Film/Audio Services, Inc.
Johns Hopkins Univ./Population Comm.
Svcs.
Korean Cultural Service

Korean War
Analogous Productions
Archive Film Prods., Inc.
Citadel, The
Forsher (James) Prods. & Archives, Inc.
Halcyon Days Prods.
MacArthur (Gen. Douglas) Memorial
MacDonald, J. Fred
Military/Combat Stock Footage
Natl. Archives (RG 56)
Natl. Archives (RG 59)
Natl. Archives (RG 80)
Natl. Archives (RG 111)
Natl. Archives (RG 263)
Natl. Archives (RG 277)
Natl. Archives (RG 342)
Natl. Archives (RG 428)
Natl. Archives of Canada

Northstar Prods.
Petrified Films, Inc.
Producers Library Service
Southern Calif. Lib. for Soc. Stud. & Res.
Streamline Film Archives
Timesteps Prods., Inc.
Twentieth Century-Fox Movietonews
U.S. Dept. of Defense, Motion Media Rec.
Ctr.
Villon Films

Korean War (Ford Motor Co.)
Natl. Archives (RG 200)

Korean War (Marines, U.S.)
Multi-Media Pre-Accession Point

Korean War (Prisoners of war)
Natl. Archives (RG 242)
Natl. Archives (RG 389)

Korean War (Truce signing)
Natl. Archives (RG 342)

Kormann, Peter
U.S. Olympic Committee

Koster, Wally
Natl. Archives of Canada

Kosuth, Joseph
Blackwood Prods., Inc.

Koufax, Sandy
Sportsfilm

Kouprey
New York Zoological Society

Kovacs, Ernie
Banks Film Library
MacDonald, J. Fred
Moviecraft, Inc.
New Jersey Network
Shokus Video
UCLA Film & Television Archive

Kovel, Joel
Paper Tiger TV

Kovel, Molly
Paper Tiger TV

**Kowloon, Hong Kong (History and
culture)**
Petrified Films, Inc.

Kramer, Margia
Port Washington Pub. Lib.

Kramer, Stanley
Banks Film Library

Krasner, Lee
Albright-Knox Art Gallery
Amer. Federation of the Arts
Blackwood Prods., Inc.
Video Data Bank

Krassner, Paul
Baker (Fred) Film & Video Co.

Kremlin (Moscow) (History and culture)
Archive Film Prods., Inc.

Krieger, Danny
Los Angeles Blues Archives

Krishnamurti
Graduate Theological Union Lib.
Krishnamurti Foundation of America

Kristofferson, Kris
Spectral Comms.

Kruger, Barbara
Video Data Bank

Krupp Family
Natl. Archives (RG 238)

Ku Klux Klan
Allen (John E.) Inc.
Alternative Information Network
Anti-Defamation League of B'nai B'rith
Archive Film Prods., Inc.
Carousel Film & Video
Deep Dish TV
Film Bank
First Run/Icarus Films, Inc.
Forsher (James) Prods. & Archives, Inc.
Indiana State Lib.
Northstar Prods.
Skylight Pictures
Univ. of Georgia, WSB TV News Film
Arch.

Kuala Lumpur, Malaysia
Farkas Studios, Ltd.

Kubelka, Peter
Video Data Bank

Kubler-Ross, Elizabeth
Inst. for Psychoanalysis

Kubota, Shigeko
Port Washington Pub. Lib.
Video Data Bank

Kubrick, Stanley
UCLA Film & Television Archive

Kuchar, George
Picture Start, Inc.

Kuhlman, Kathryn
Daphne Productions, Inc.
Wheaton Coll., Billy Graham Ctr.

Kuhn, Maggie
Gray Panthers

!Kung people
Documentary Educ. Resources
Smithsonian Inst., Human Studies Film
Arch.

Kupferberg, Tuli
Paper Tiger TV

Kurdish people
Canadian Broadcasting Corp.

Kuwait
Middle East Institute

Kwan, Paul
Video Data Bank

Ky, Nguyen Cao
Archive Film Prods., Inc.
White Janssen, Inc.

Kyles, Samuel
Memphis State Univ. Libraries

L'Enfant, Pierre
Petrified Films, Inc.

LSD
See Acid trips; Counterculture (U.S.);
Drug culture

NOTE: Access policies, availability and restrictions vary for each source. Please read each entry in full. Always consult "General Film and Videotape Collections" (page 599); these comprehensive collections contain material on every conceivable subject.

La Belle, Patti
Clark (Dick) Media Archives, Inc.

La Jolla, Calif.
Petrified Films, Inc.

La Paz, Bolivia (History and culture)
Natl. Archives (RG 59)

La Raza Unida (Partido Nacional)
Partido Nacional La Raza Unida
Univ. of Tex. at Austin, Benson Lat. Am. Coll.

Labor history
Allen (John E.) Inc.
Amer. Soc. Hist. Proj. Film Lib.
Analogous Productions
Appalachian State Univ., Eury Coll.
Appalshop Films, Inc.
Archive Film Prods., Inc.
Archives of Ontario
Ball State Univ., Middletown Coll.
Bowling Green State Univ., Ctr. Arch. Coll.
CBS News Archives
California Newsreel
California State Univ., Northridge
Cambridge Documentary Films, Inc.
Cinema Guild
Committee for Labor Access
Communist Party USA
DEC Film & Video
Deep Dish TV
Downtown Community TV Ctr.
East Tenn. State Univ., Arch. of Appalachia
Estuary Press
Everett Pub. Lib., Northwest Hist. Coll.
First Run/Icarus Films, Inc.
General Motors Corp.
Grinberg (Sherman) Film Libraries (East)
Idera Films
Illinois Labor History Society
Illinois State Hist. Lib.
Indiana Univ., Northwest Lib.
Inst. for Labor Studies & Research
Intermedia Arts Minnesota
KCRA-TV
Kartemquin Films
Labor Inst. of Public Affairs
Labor Video Project
MacDonald, J. Fred
March of Time
Media Project
Mus. & Hist. Div., City of Sacramento
Natl. Archives (RG 46)
Natl. Archives (RG 86)
Natl. Archives (RG 174)
Natl. Archives (RG 200)
Natl. Archives (RG 277)
Natl. Archives of Canada
Natl. Film Board of Canada
New Day Films
New York City Labor Film Club
Ohio Historical Soc.
Ohio State Univ., Dept. of Photog. & Cinema
Prelinger Assoc., Inc.
Prov. Arch. of Alberta
Prov. Arch. of Manitoba
Radcliffe Coll., Schlesinger Lib.
Roosevelt (Franklin D.) Lib.
Smithsonian Inst., NMAH, Div. Polit. Hist.
Southern Calif. Lib. for Soc. Stud. & Res.
State Hist. Soc. of Iowa
State Hist. Soc. of Wisconsin
Tamiment Lib./Wagner Labor Arch.
Twentieth Century-Fox Movietonews
United Farm Workers of America (UFW)
Université de Moncton, Centre d'Études Acad.
Université Laval, Cinémathèque

Univ. of Calif., Berkeley, Labor Occupational Health Prog.
Univ. of Kentucky, AV Arch.
Univ. of Maryland, McKeldin Lib.
Univ. of Missouri-St. Louis
Univ. of Toronto, AV Lib.
Univ. of Wisconsin — Extension
Vidéo Femmes
Vidéographe Inc., Le
Wayne State Univ., Arch. Labor & Urb. Aff.
West Virginia Dept. of Culture & Hist.
West Virginia Univ.
See also Demonstrations (Political); Labor issues; Strikes; Workers; specific labor unions

Labor issues
BNA Communications, Inc.
California Newsreel
Carleton Prods. Inc.
Center for Pacific Northwest Studies
Chicago Access Corp.
Committee for Labor Access
DEC Film & Video
Deep Dish TV
First Run/Icarus Films, Inc.
Idera Films
Inst. for Labor Studies & Research
Intermedia Arts Minnesota
Kartemquin Films
Labor Inst. of Public Affairs
Labor Video Project
Latin Amer. Video Arch.
Media Project
Natl. Archives (RG 200)
Natl. Archives (RG 208)
New Day Films
New York City Labor Film Club
Richter Productions
Univ. of Calif., Berkeley, Labor Occupational Health Prog.
V/tape
Video In

Labor Relations Board, National (U.S.)
Natl. Archives (RG 25)

Labor Statistics, Bureau of (U.S.)
Natl. Archives (RG 100)

Labor, Department of (U.S.)
Natl. Archives (RG 174)

Laboratories
AT&T Archives & Rec. Mgmt. Svcs.
Animal Welfare Institute
Broad Street Prods.
CBS News Archives
Centers for Disease Control
Farkas Studios, Ltd.
Film Bank
Fire Prev. Through Films, Inc.
Mass. Inst. of Tech., MIT Museum
Metro Communications, Inc.
Northcoast Communication, Inc.
Petrified Films, Inc.
Prelinger Assoc., Inc.
TV Ontario
Video Tape Library, Ltd.
See also Scientists

Laboratories (High-voltage)
Film Bank

Laboratories (Marine)
Film Bank

Labrador, Newfoundland
Alaska Video Prods.

Labrador, Newfoundland (History and culture)
Acad. of Nat. Sci. of Phila. Lib.
Canadian Filmmakers Dist. Centre

Natl. Archives of Canada
Peary-MacMillan Arctic Museum
Prov. Arch. of Newfoundland & Labrador

Labrot, Syl
Video Data Bank

Lacrosse
Petrified Films, Inc.
Sportsfilm
Twentieth Century-Fox Movietonews

Lacrosse (College)
NCAA Productions

Lacrosse (Instruction)
NCAA Productions

Lacy, Steve
Rhapsody Films, Inc.

Ladd, Alan
UCLA Film & Television Archive

Ladybugs
Dreamlight Images, Inc.
TV Ontario

Lafayette, La. (History and culture)
Tulane Univ., Amistad Res. Ctr.

Lagoons
Video Tape Library, Ltd.

Lagos, Nigeria (History and culture)
Singer-Sharrette Traditional Healing Films

LaGuardia, Fiorello
Archive Film Prods., Inc.
March of Time
Natl. Archives (RG 342)

Laguna Beach, Calif. (History and culture)
Petrified Films, Inc.

Lahaina, Hawaii
Preview Media

LaHaye, Tim
Family Life Seminars

Lahm, Frank
Wright State Univ. Lib.

Lahr, Bert
Moviecraft, Inc.

Laine, Frankie
Shokus Video

Laing, R.D.
Camera Three Prods., Inc.
Villon Films

Laire, Judson
Shokus Video

Lake, Arthur
Marquette Univ., Spec. Coll.

Lakes
Aitken (Len) Productions, Inc.
Amer. Motion Pictures
Archive Film Prods., Inc.
CBS News Archives
Cinenet (Cinema Network)
Dorn (Larry) Associates
Energy Productions
Film Bank
Film Search
Jewell (Stuart) Productions
Kesser Stock Footage Library
Peak Productions, Inc.
Petrified Films, Inc.

Prelinger Assoc., Inc.
Second Line Search
Snyder (Bill) Films, Inc.
Source Stock Footage Lib., Inc.
Summit Films, Inc.
TV Ontario
Twentieth Century-Fox Movietonews
Univ. of Wis., Green Bay, Ctr. TV Prod.
Wings Wildlife Prods. Inc.
See also specific lakes (e.g., Lake Tahoe is found under Tahoe, Lake [Calif.-Nev.])

LaLanne, Jack
MacDonald, J. Fred

Lamarr, Hedy
Natl. Archives/Natl. AV Ctr.

Lambaréné, Gabon (History and culture)
Schweitzer (Albert) Ctr.

Lambert, Dave
Pennebaker Associates, Inc.

Lambs
British Info. Svcs., Radio & TV Div.

Lamm, Richard
Graduate Theological Union Lib.

Lamps
CBS News Archives

Lamu, Colo.
Summit Films, Inc.

Lanais
Petrified Films, Inc.

Lancashire, England (History and culture)
Archive Film Prods., Inc.

Lancaster, Burt
Banks Film Library
Spectral Comms.

Land Management, Bureau of (U.S.)
Natl. Archives (RG 49)

Land mines
Prelinger Assoc., Inc.

Land use
Natl. Assn. of Conservation Dists.
United Nations Ctr. for Human Settlements

Land use planning
Oregon State Univ., Archives

Landfills
TV Ontario

Landis, Kenesaw Mountain
Grinberg (Sherman) Film Libraries (West)

Landmarks
Ackerman-Black Prods., Inc.
Atlantic Productions
Broad Street Prods.
Chicago A/V Studios
Cinephile Amalgamated Pictures
Dreamlight Images, Inc.
Energy Productions
Fabulous Footage Inc.
Farkas Studios, Ltd.
Film Bank
Film Search
Fish Films, Inc.
4•6•8 Prods., Inc.
Harriman Communications Ctr.
Island Video
Landmark Stock Footage Co.

MacGillivray Freeman Films
Moser (Michael)/Media
Natl. Archives (RG 48)
Natl. Archives (RG 103)
Natl. Archives (RG 111)
Northern Ill. Univ., Reg. Hist. Ctr.
Northstar Prods.
Petrified Films, Inc.
Portland Cable Access TV
Prelinger Assoc., Inc.
Producers' Service
Renaissance Video Corp.
Rock Solid Prods.
Site Productions
Southwest Prods., Inc.
TV Ontario
Viz Wiz, Inc.
Wallen (Dick) Prods.
Washington Broadcast Video Lib.
Zielinski Productions, Inc.

Landon, Alfred M.
MacDonald, J. Fred
Natl. Archives (RG 47)

Landry, Tom
Film Bank

Landsailing
Video Tape Library, Ltd.

Landscapes
Acad. of Nat. Sci. of Phila. Lib.
Archive Film Prods., Inc.
Aries Prods.
Cinema Arts Assoc.
Cinenet (Cinema Network)
Crystal Pyramid Prods.
Di Sesso (Moe) Wild Life Film Lib.
Dorn (Larry) Associates
Dreamlight Images, Inc.
Echo Film Prods., Inc.
Energy Productions
Fabulous Footage Inc.
Film Bank
Film/Audio Services, Inc.
Lemorande Prod. Co.
MVP Communications
Metro Communications, Inc.
October Productions
Petrified Films, Inc.
Prelinger Assoc., Inc.
Simon & Goodman Picture Co.
Slingshot Prods.
Summit Films, Inc.
TVA/Television Assoc.
Union Pacific Railroad
See also Cityscapes; Rural scenes;
  Seascapes

Landslides
Twentieth Century-Fox Movietonews

Lane, Mark
DEC Film & Video

Langdon, Harry
Alan Twyman Presents
Archive Film Prods., Inc.
Em Gee Film Library
Moviecraft, Inc.
Videobrary, Inc.

Lange, Dorothea
San Francisco Bay Area TV News Arch.

Lange, Hope
Banks Film Library

Langford, Francis
Film/Audio Services, Inc.

Language arts
AIMS Media
Altschul Group
Barr Films
Britannica Films & Video
Carousel Film & Video
Center for Humanities, Inc.
Churchill Films
Coronet/MTI Film & Video
Direct Cinema Ltd.
Filmfair Comms.
GPN
Handel Film Corp.
Higgins (Alfred) Prods.
Media Guild
Phoenix Films and Video
Prelinger Assoc., Inc.
Pyramid Film and Video Corp.
Univ. of Calif., Ext. Media Ctr.
Vedo Films/Novacom Video

Lansbury, Angela
Anti-Defamation League of B'nai B'rith
Petrified Films, Inc.
Spectral Comms.

Lansing, Mich.
White Star Prof. Film Svcs., Inc.

Lansing, Mich. (History and culture)
Amer. Truck Historical Soc.

Lansing, Robert
Natl. Archives (RG 24)

Lantana
Film Bank

Lanyon, Ellen
Video Data Bank

Laon, France
Unicorn Projects

Laos (History and culture)
Univ. of Missouri-St. Louis

Laotian Americans
New Day Films
Third World Newsreel

Laplanders
TV Ontario

Larroquette, John
Spectral Comms.

Larsen, Henry
Natl. Archives of Canada

Lartigue, Jacques-Henri
Port Washington Pub. Lib.
Soc. for French Amer. Cult. Svcs. & Educ.
  Aid

Larvae
Dreamlight Images, Inc.

Las Vegas, Nev.
Airline Film & TV Promotions
Beerger (Norman) Prods.
Cinenet (Cinema Network)
Departures, Inc.
Energy Productions
Film Bank
Film Search
Network Productions
Peak Productions, Inc.
Postcards Unlimited
Preview Media
Source Stock Footage Lib., Inc.

Wallen (Dick) Prods.

Las Vegas, Nev. (History and culture)
Las Vegas News Bureau
Petrified Films, Inc.
Spalla (Rick) Video Prods.

Laser effects
Impact Audio Visual
Z-Axis

Lasers
British Info. Svcs., Radio & TV Div.
Film Bank
Louisiana Tech Univ., Eng. Film Res. Ctr.
Society of Manufacturing Engineers

Lassaw, Ibram
Albright-Knox Art Gallery
Blackwood Prods., Inc.

Lasser, Louise
Daphne Productions, Inc.
Shokus Video

Latin America
See entries listed below; Central America;
  South America

Latin America (Contemporary issues)
Amer. Security Council Foundation
Americas in Transition/Fossil Films
Cinema Guild
Democracy in Communication
Icarus-Tamouz Media, Inc.
Intermedia Arts Minnesota
Maryknoll Fathers & Brothers
Natl. Archives (RG 46)
Third World Newsreel

Latin America (History and culture)
Cinema Guild
Democracy in Communication
Films for the Humanities and Sciences
First Run/Icarus Films, Inc.
Icarus-Tamouz Media, Inc.
Idera Films
Imagen y Sonido Independiente, S.A.
Latin Amer. Video Arch.
Latina, S.A. de C.V.
March of Time
Maryknoll Fathers & Brothers
Mus. of Mod. Art of Latin America
Natl. Archives (RG 59)
Natl. Archives (RG 185)
Natl. Archives (RG 207)
Natl. Archives (RG 229)
Phoenix Films and Video
Prelinger Assoc., Inc.
Redes Cinevideo, S.A.
TV-UNAM
Worldwide Television News
Zafra, A.C.
See also United States-Latin America
  relations

Latinos
Deep Dish TV

Latinos (Depiction in the media)
New Jersey Network

Latvia (History and culture)
Hoover Institution

Laughter
Petrified Films, Inc.

Laughton, Charles
Banks Film Library

Launchings
See Ships (Launchings)

Laundries and laundromats
CBS News Archives
Petrified Films, Inc.

Laundry rooms
Petrified Films, Inc.

Laurel and Hardy
Em Gee Film Library
Film Preservation Assoc.

Laurel, Miss. (History and culture)
Skylight Pictures

Laurel, Stan
Archive Film Prods., Inc.
Natl. Archives (RG 16)

Laurence, Baby
Rhapsody Films, Inc.

Laurens, Henry
Blackwood Prods., Inc.

Laurier, Sir Wilfrid
Natl. Archives of Canada

Lava
See Volcanoes

Laval, Pierre
March of Time

Lavender flowers
Film Bank

Laver, Rod
U.S. Tennis Assn.

Lavut, Martin
Canadian Filmmakers Dist. Centre

Law
CBS News Archives
GPN
Université Laval, Cinémathèque
Video In

Law (Labor)
Natl. Archives (RG 174)

Lawford, Peter
Las Vegas News Bureau

Lawn bowling
Petrified Films, Inc.

Lawn mowers
Petrified Films, Inc.
Prelinger Assoc., Inc.
White Janssen, Inc.

Lawrence, Jacob
Tulane Univ., Amistad Res. Ctr.

Lawrence Livermore Laboratory (Calif.)
Calif. Highway Patrol Acad. Media Center

Lawson, James
Memphis State Univ. Libraries

Lawson, Thomas
Video Data Bank

Lawyers
Archive Film Prods., Inc.
Cabscott Broadcast Prods.

NOTE: Access policies, availability and restrictions vary for each source. Please read each entry in full. Always consult "General Film and Videotape Collections" (page 599); these comprehensive collections contain material on every conceivable subject.

Lazarus, Arnold
Psychological and Educational Films

Le Corbusier
Southern Calif. Inst. of Architecture

Lead
Natl. Archives (RG 70)
Zinc Inst./Lead Industries Assn.
See also Mining (Lead)

Leadville, Colorado
Summit Films, Inc.

Leaf, Caroline
Port Washington Pub. Lib.

Leaf, June
Video Data Bank

League of Nations
March of Time
Natl. Archives (RG 24)
Natl. Archives (RG 200)
Natl. Archives of Canada
United Nations, Visual Materials Lib.
See also United Nations

Leakey, Richard
Univ. of Waterloo, A-V Centre

Leander, Zarah
Blackwood (Christian) Prods., Inc.

Leaning Tower of Pisa (Italy)
Archive Film Prods., Inc.

Lear, Norman
Daphne Productions, Inc.

Learning disabilities
Assn. for Children & Adults with Learning
  Disabilities

Leary, Timothy
Cinema Guild
Pennebaker Associates, Inc.

Leather
Oregon State Univ., Archives
Prelinger Assoc., Inc.
U.S. Hide, Skin & Leather Assn.

Leaves
See Foliage

Lebanon
Canadian Broadcasting Corp.

Lebanon (Contemporary issues)
Icarus-Tamouz Media, Inc.

Lebanon (History and culture)
Film/Audio Services, Inc.
Intl. Film Foundation
Military/Combat Stock Footage
New Time Films, Inc.
Ocean Earth Constr. and Dev. Corp.
U.S. Committee for UNICEF
Worldwide Television News

Lebanon (Marines, U.S.)
Multi-Media Pre-Accession Point

Led Zeppelin
Clark (Dick) Media Archives, Inc.

Ledbetter, Huddie ("Leadbelly")
March of Time

Lederer, Francis
Cantor (Arthur) Inc.

Leduc, Alberta (History and culture)
Imperial Oil Ltd.

Lee, Fran
New York Pub. Lib., Rare Books &
  Manuscripts Div.

Lee, John Marshall
Educational Film & Video Project

Lee, Peggy
Archive Film Prods., Inc.
Banks Film Library
Pathé Pictures, Inc.

Lee, Stan
Univ. of Wyoming, Amer. Heritage Ctr.

Left-wing politics
Allen (John E.) Inc.
Alternative Information Network
Archives of Ontario
Bund Arch. of the Jewish Labor
  Movement
Cambridge Documentary Films, Inc.
Communist Party USA
Estuary Press
First Run/Icarus Films, Inc.
Hoover Institution
MacDonald, J. Fred
New Day Films
Prelinger Assoc., Inc.
Southern Calif. Lib. for Soc. Stud. & Res.
Taminent Lib./Wagner Labor Arch.
Third World Newsreel
Univ. of Toronto, AV Lib.

LeGallienne, Eva
New York Pub. Lib., Perf. Arts Res. Ctr.,
  Theatre on Film and Tape

Legoretta, Ricardo
Southern Calif. Inst. of Architecture

Lehmbruck, Wilhelm
Blackwood Prods., Inc.

Leigh, Janet
Banks Film Library

Leipzig, Arthur
Port Washington Pub. Lib.

Leisure
Atlantic Independent Media
Carleton Prods. Inc.
Chisholm (Jack) Film Productions
Fabulous Footage Inc.
Film Bank
Film Education Institute
Film Search
Kesser Stock Footage Library
March of Time
Metro Communications, Inc.
Natl. Film Board of Canada
Prelinger Assoc., Inc.
Prov. Arch. of British Columbia
Video-SIG

LeMay, Curtis
March of Time

Lemmon, Jack
Banks Film Library
Daphne Productions, Inc.

Lemmon, S. Dak. (History and culture)
South Dakota State Lib.

Lemons
Prelinger Assoc., Inc.

Lemurs
Telltales Associates Inc.

Lendl, Ivan
U.S. Tennis Assn.

Lenin, Vladimir Ilyich
Archive Film Prods., Inc.
Grinberg (Sherman) Film Libraries (West)
Hoover Institution
Natl. Archives (RG 242)
Natl. Coun. of Amer.-Sov. Friendship, Inc.

Leningrad, U.S.S.R.
Canadian Broadcasting Corp.

**Leningrad, U.S.S.R. (History and
  culture)**
Archive Film Prods., Inc.
Hoover Institution
Prelinger Assoc., Inc.

Lennon, John
Daphne Productions, Inc.

Lennon Sisters, The
Banks Film Library

Lenoir, J.B.
Rhapsody Films, Inc.

Lenya, Lotte
Weill-Lenya Res. Ctr.

Leonard Crow Dog
Cinema Guild

Leonard, Justin W.
Univ. of Mich., Mich. Hist. Colls.

Leonard, Sugar Ray
U.S. Olympic Comm.

Leopards
Archive Film Prods., Inc.
Coe Film Assoc., Inc.
Di Sesso (Moe) Wild Life Film Lib.
Petrified Films, Inc.
Summit Films, Inc.
TV Ontario
Wings Wildlife Prods. Inc.

Leopold, King
Archive Film Prods., Inc.

Leprosy
British Info. Svcs., Radio & TV Div.

Lerner, Alan Jay
Camera Three Prods., Inc.

**Les Éboulements, Quebec (History and
  culture)**
Natl. Archives of Canada

Lesbian issues
See Gay and lesbian issues

Letelier, Orlando
Chicago Comm. to Defend the Bill of
  Rights

Leukemia
Leukemia Soc. of Amer.

Levees
CBS News Archives

Lever, Asbury F.
Natl. Archives (RG 4)

Levesque, René
Natl. Archives of Canada

Lévi-Strauss, Claude
Université Laval, Svc. des Res.
  Pédagogiques

Levine, Joseph E.
Banks Film Library

Levine, Les
Long Beach Mus. of Art
Video Data Bank

Levittown, N.Y. (History and culture)
Petrified Films, Inc.
Prelinger Assoc., Inc.

Levittown, Pa. (History and culture)
Prelinger Assoc., Inc.

Lewis, C.S.
Wheaton Coll., Wade Ctr.

Lewis, Chris
U.S. Tennis Assn.

Lewis, Jerry
Banks Film Library
Clark (Dick) Media Archives, Inc.
MacDonald, J. Fred
Petrified Films, Inc.
Spalla (Rick) Video Prods.
UCLA Film & Television Archive

Lewis, Jerry Lee
Pennebaker Associates, Inc.

Lewis, Joe
Center for Southern Folklore

Lewis, Joe E.
Banks Film Library

Lewis, John
King (Dr. Martin Luther, Jr.) Ctr.
Randolph (A. Philip) Educ. Fund

Lewis, John L.
March of Time

Lewis, Johnnie
Rhapsody Films, Inc.

Lewis, Robert Q.
Shokus Video

Lewis, Shari
Spectral Comms.

Lewis, Terry
Spectral Comms.

Lewis, Warren
Univ. of Wyoming, Amer. Heritage Ctr.

Lewis, Warren K.
Mass. Inst. of Tech., MIT Museum

Lewitt, Sol
Mus. of Contemporary Art
Video Data Bank

Lexington, Ky. (History and culture)
Petrified Films, Inc.

Liberace
Banks Film Library
Encore Entertainment
Las Vegas News Bureau
Spalla (Rick) Video Prods.

Liberalism (Canada)
Natl. Archives of Canada

Libertarian issues
Constitutional Revival
Freeland Press
Libertarian Party

Liberty Bell (Philadelphia)
Petrified Films, Inc.

Liberty Loan drives
See Bond drives

Liberty Weekend, 1986
See Independence Day (Liberty Weekend, 1986) (U.S.)

Libraries and librarians
CBS News Archives
Film Bank
Petrified Films, Inc.
Prelinger Assoc., Inc.
Twentieth Century-Fox Movietonews

Library science
Natl. Archives/Natl. AV Ctr.
Prelinger Assoc., Inc.

Library skills
AIMS Media
Barr Films
Center for Humanities, Inc.

Libya
World Monitor

Libya (Contemporary issues)
Ocean Earth Constr. and Dev. Corp.

Libya (History and culture)
Middle East Institute
Natl. Archives (RG 286)
World Monitor

Lice
Prelinger Assoc., Inc.

License plates
Dreamlight Images, Inc.
Film Bank

Lichen
TV Ontario

Lichtenstein, Roy
Albright-Knox Art Gallery
Amer. Federation of the Arts
Blackwood Prods., Inc.

Liddy, G. Gordon
Daphne Productions, Inc.

Lieberman, Harry
Amer. Federation of the Arts

Liechtenstein (History and culture)
Intl. Assn. of Independent Producers

Life preservers
CBS News Archives

Life sciences
AIMS Media
Britannica Films & Video
Center for Humanities, Inc.
Coronet/MTI Film & Video
Media Guild
NASA, Ames Res. Ctr., Imaging Tech. Branch
NASA, Johnson Space Ctr., Film & Video Dist. Lib.
NASA, Lewis Research Center
Natl. Archives (RG 90)
Université Laval, Cinémathèque

Lifeguards
Archive Film Prods., Inc.
CBS News Archives
Forsher (James) Prods. & Archives, Inc.
Spectral Comms.

Lifestyles
Coe Film Assoc., Inc.
Dreamlight Images, Inc.

Film Bank
Film Education Institute
Moody Inst. of Science
Preview Media
Producers' Service

Lifestyles (Hong Kong)
Friends of Free China

Lifestyles (International)
Canadian Broadcasting Corp.
Yue-Sai Kan, Inc.

Lifestyles (Japan)
Asia Society

Lifestyles (Native American)
Navajo Tribe, Off. Broadcast Svcs.

Lifestyles (Quebec)
Société de Radio-Télévision de Québec

Lifestyles (Taiwan)
Friends of Free China

Lifestyles (U.S.)
Allen (John E.) Inc.
Amer. Arch. of the Factual Film
Archive Film Prods., Inc.
Film Search
Metro Communications, Inc.
Natl. Archives (RG 306)
UCLA Film & Television Archive
WQED/Pittsburgh
White Janssen, Inc.
Yue-Sai Kan, Inc.
See also Americana

Lifestyles (U.S.) (1910s)
Natl. Archives (RG 200)
Natl. Archives/Natl. AV Ctr.
Petrified Films, Inc.

Lifestyles (U.S.) (1920s)
Natl. Archives (RG 200)
Petrified Films, Inc.
Univ. of So. Carolina, Newsfilm Lib.

Lifestyles (U.S.) (1930s)
Amer. Portrait, An
Natl. Archives (RG 200)
Petrified Films, Inc.
Postcards Associates
Prelinger Assoc., Inc.
Univ. of So. Carolina, Newsfilm Lib.
Windsor Prod. Corp.

Lifestyles (U.S.) (1940s)
Amer. Portrait, An
Intl. Film Foundation
Natl. Archives (RG 59)
Petrified Films, Inc.
Postcards Associates
Prelinger Assoc., Inc.
Producers Library Service
Univ. of So. Carolina, Newsfilm Lib.
Windsor Prod. Corp.

Lifestyles (U.S.) (1950s)
Amer. Portrait, An
Fish Films, Inc.
Intl. Film Foundation
MacDonald, J. Fred
Natl. Archives (RG 59)
Petrified Films, Inc.
Prelinger Assoc., Inc.
Producers Library Service
White Janssen, Inc.
Windsor Prod. Corp.

Lifestyles (U.S.) (1950s) (Black)

Allen (John E.) Inc.

Lifestyles (U.S.) (1960s)
Amer. Portrait, An
Clark (Dick) Media Archives, Inc.
Film/Audio Services, Inc.
Fish Films, Inc.
MacDonald, J. Fred
Petrified Films, Inc.
Prelinger Assoc., Inc.

Lifestyles (U.S.) (1980s)
Ball State Univ., Middletown Coll.

Light bulbs
Canadian Filmmakers Dist. Centre

Light bulbs (Exploding)
Dreamlight Images, Inc.

Light switches
Petrified Films, Inc.

Lighter-than-air craft
See Aircraft (Lighter-than-air)

Lightfoot, Gordon
Natl. Archives of Canada

Lighthouses
Archive Film Prods., Inc.
CBS News Archives
Cinenet (Cinema Network)
Dreamlight Images, Inc.
Film Bank
Metro Communications, Inc.
Natl. Archives (RG 26)
Natl. Archives of Canada
North Carolina Div. of Arch. & Hist.
Petrified Films, Inc.
Riccitelli (Bruce) Prods.
Site Productions
Video Tape Library, Ltd.

Lightning
Archive Film Prods., Inc.
CBS News Archives
Cinenet (Cinema Network)
Dreamlight Images, Inc.
Energy Productions
Film Bank
Fish Films, Inc.
Grinberg (Sherman) Film Libraries (West)
Image Bank
Moving Media
Petrified Films, Inc.
Radio City Music Hall Prods.
SF•V Intl.
Source Stock Footage Lib., Inc.
Spectral Comms.

Lights
CBS News Archives
Film Bank

Lilacs
Film Bank

Lily pads
TV Ontario

Lima, Mesquitela
Université Laval, Svc. des Res. Pédagogiques

Lima, Peru (History and culture)
Archive Film Prods., Inc.

Limestone
Natl. Archives (RG 70)

Limousines
See Automobiles (Limousines)

Lincoln, Abraham
Archive Film Prods., Inc.
Film Bank
Hearst Metrotone News
Illinois State Hist. Lib.
Prelinger Assoc., Inc.

Lincoln (Abraham) Brigade
See Abraham Lincoln Brigade

Lincoln Center (New York City)
Film Bank
Petrified Films, Inc.

Lincoln, Elmo
Fulton County Hist. Soc., Inc.

Lincoln Memorial (Washington, D.C.)
Film Bank
Petrified Films, Inc.

Lincoln, Neb. (History and culture)
Nebraska State Hist. Soc.

Lindbergh, Charles Augustus
Archive Film Prods., Inc.
Film Bank
Film Education Institute
Forsher (James) Prods. & Archives, Inc.
Hearst Metrotone News
Missouri Hist. Soc.
Natl. Archives (RG 106)
Natl. Archives (RG 111)
Natl. Archives (RG 342)
Natl. Archives of Canada
Natl. Railway Historical Soc.
Oregon Hist. Soc.
Prelinger Assoc., Inc.
San Diego Aerospace Museum
Timesteps Prods., Inc.
Vermont Hist. Soc.
Washington State Hist. Soc.

Linderman, Earl
Plains Art Mus. Lib.

Lindner, Richard
Blackwood (Christian) Prods., Inc.

Lindy hop
See Dance and dancing (Lindy hop)

Linguistics
Center for New Amer. Media
Finley (Stuart) Inc.

Linkletter, Art
Banks Film Library
MacDonald, J. Fred
Shokus Video

Linnets
Di Sesso (Moe) Wild Life Film Lib.

Lions
Analogous Productions
Archive Film Prods., Inc.
Di Sesso (Moe) Wild Life Film Lib.
Dreamlight Images, Inc.
Film Bank
Jewell (Stuart) Productions
Kesser Stock Footage Library
Petrified Films, Inc.
Summit Films, Inc.
Wings Wildlife Prods. Inc.

Lippard, Lucy
Paper Tiger TV

NOTE: Access policies, availability and restrictions vary for each source. Please read each entry in full. Always consult "General Film and Videotape Collections" (page 599); these comprehensive collections contain material on every conceivable subject.

Video Data Bank

Lips
Rosebush Visions Corp.

Lipschitz, Jacques
Blackwood Prods., Inc.

Lipscomb, Maurice
Amer. Federation of the Arts

Liquor
Film Bank
Petrified Films, Inc.
Seagram Museum

Liquor stores
Petrified Films, Inc.

Lisbon, Portugal (History and culture)
Archive Film Prods., Inc.

Liston, Sonny
Las Vegas News Bureau
Sportsfilm

Literacy
Adair Films
Borough of Manhattan Comm. Coll.
CBS News Archives
Educational Video Ctr.
Imevision
Natl. Archives (RG 12)
Prelinger Assoc., Inc.
Univ. of Vermont, Bailey/Howe Lib.

Literature
Coe Film Assoc., Inc.
Coronet/MTI Film & Video
Films Incorporated
Intermedia Arts Minnesota
Intl. Film Bureau, Inc.
Media Guild
Natl. Archives of Canada
Prelinger Assoc., Inc.
Pyramid Film and Video Corp.
Université Laval, Cinémathèque
Univ. of Calif., Ext. Media Ctr.
Univ. of Waterloo, A-V Centre
Video In

Literature (American)
Center for Humanities, Inc.
Films for the Humanities and Sciences

Literature (English)
Center for Humanities, Inc.
Films for the Humanities and Sciences

Literature (German)
Goethe House, New York
Goethe Institute Atlanta
Goethe Institute Los Angeles
Goethe Institute San Francisco
Goethe Institute Vancouver

Literature (Mexican)
Canal 11
Imevision
TV-UNAM

Lithgow, John
Spectral Comms.

Lithuania (History and culture)
Balzekas Mus. of Lithuanian Culture

Little Big Horn, Battle of (1876)
Montana Dept. of Commerce
Pyramid Film and Video Corp.

Little Cayman, Cayman Islands
Passage Home Communications

Little Italy, N.Y. (History and culture)

Petrified Films, Inc.
Prelinger Assoc., Inc.

Little League baseball
See Baseball (Little League)

Little Lulu
Film Bank

Little Richard (Richard Penniman)
Newsreel Video Service
Pennebaker Associates, Inc.

Liverpool, England (History and culture)
Archive Film Prods., Inc.

Livestock
Archive Film Prods., Inc.

Livestock shows
Oregon State Univ., Archives
Twentieth Century-Fox Movietonews

Livingstone, Joan
Video Data Bank

Lizards
Di Sesso (Moe) Wild Life Film Lib.
Energy Productions
Film Bank
Kesser Stock Footage Library
Nature Conservancy
Petrified Films, Inc.
Wings Wildlife Prods. Inc.

Llamas
Amer. Veterinary Medical Assn.
Moving Media

Lloyd, Harold
Alan Twyman Presents
Archive Film Prods., Inc.
Em Gee Film Library
Natl. Archives (RG 47)

Lobbying
Ideal Comms., Inc.

Lobstermen and lobstering
Site Productions
TV Ontario
Wesleyan Cinema Archives

Lobsters
Cousteau Society
Film Bank
TV Ontario

Local history
Adams County Hist. Soc.
Alabama State Dept. of Arch. & Hist.
Amer. Assn. for State & Local Hist.
Appalshop Films, Inc.
Archdiocese of Boston
Aspen Historical Society
Atlanta Hist. Soc.
Bangor Historical Society
Baylor Univ., Texas Coll.
Birmingham Pub. Lib., Dept. of Arch.
Birmingham Pub. Lib., Media Svcs. Dept.
Boston Community Access & Prog. Found.
Boston Univ. Film Archive
Bronx County Hist. Soc.
Buffalo & Erie County Hist. Soc.
Buffalo Bill Historical Center
Bur. of Florida Folklife Progs.
CITY Pulse Library
Calif. State Archives
California State Univ., Northridge
Center for Pacific Northwest Studies
Center for Southern Folklore
Central New England Film Arch.
Chautauqua-Cattaraugus Library System

Chicago Historical Society
Cincinnati Hist. Soc.
Colorado Historical Society
Connecticut Historical Society
Connecticut State Library
Datura Productions
DePauw University, Archives
Delaware State Div. of Hist. & Cult. Aff.
Denver Pub. Lib., Western Hist. Dept.
Duke Univ., Perkins Lib.
Eastern Washington State Historical Soc.
El Paso Community College
Evangelical Covenant Church of Amer.
Everett Pub. Lib., Northwest Hist. Coll.
Fulton County Hist. Soc., Inc.
GRTV — Archives
Historic New Orleans Coll.
Historical Soc. of Seattle & King County
Houston (Sam) Regional Library
Illinois State Hist. Lib.
Independent Network News (INN)
Indiana Hist. Soc., Smith Memorial Lib.
Indiana State Lib.
Indiana Univ. Folklore Arch.
Indiana Univ. Northwest Lib.
Intermedia Arts Minnesota
Inuit Broadcasting Corp.
KCRA-TV
KYUK-TV
Kansas State Historical Society
Kentucky Dept. of Libraries & Archives
Las Vegas News Bureau
Los Alamos County Hist. Mus. Arch.
Louisiana State Univ., Shreveport
MacDonald, J. Fred
Manitowoc Maritime Museum
Marquette Univ., Spec. Coll.
Marshall Univ., Spec. Coll.
Memphis Pink Palace Mus. and Lib.
Memphis State Univ. Libraries
Memphis-Shelby Cty. Pub. Lib. & Info. Ctr.
Milwaukee Access Telecomm. Auth.
Minnesota Hist. Soc.
Mississippi Dept. of Arch. & Hist.
Missouri Hist. Soc.
Montgomery Community Television, Inc.
Mus. & Hist. Div., City of Sacramento
Mus. of Broadcast Comms.
Nantucket Hist. Assn.
Natl. Archives of Canada
Navajo Tribe, Off. Broadcast Svcs.
Nebraska State Hist. Soc.
Neville Pub. Museum
New Jersey Historical Society
New Mexico State Records Ctr. & Arch.
New Orleans Pub. Lib., La. Div.
New York Chinatown History Project
New York City Dept. of Rec. & Info. Svcs.
Newsreel Video Service
Northeast Historic Film
Northern Ill. Univ., Reg. Hist. Ctr.
Ohio Historical Soc.
Oregon Hist. Soc.
Ozark Folk Center
Panhandle-Plains Hist. Museum
Pennsylvania State Arch.
Perry (Merle G.) Arch.
Prov. Arch. of Newfoundland & Labrador
Pub. Lib. of Cincinnati & Hamilton Cty.
Read (Brooks) & Assoc.
Rhode Island Hist. Soc.
St. Augustine Hist. Soc.
Saint Paul Pub. Lib., Film & Video Ctr.
San Jose State Univ. Museum
South Carolina Humanities Res. Ctr.
South Dakota State Lib.
Southern Oregon Hist. Soc.
Southwest Film/Video Archives, SMU
State Hist. Soc. of Iowa
State Hist. Soc. of North Dakota
State Hist. Soc. of Wisconsin
Sweet (Harry) Film Coll.
Temple Univ., Urban Arch. Ctr.

Texas Tech Univ., Southwest Coll.
Tulane Univ., Amistad Res. Ctr.
Univ. Coll. of Cape Breton, Beaton Inst.
Univ. of Alabama, W.S. Hoole Spec. Coll.
Univ. of Baltimore, Abell TV Arch.
Univ. of Kentucky, AV Arch.
Univ. of Miami, Arch. & Spec. Coll.
Univ. of Mich., Mich. Hist. Colls.
Univ. of Pittsburgh, Arch. of Indust. Soc.
Univ. of Regina, Sask. Arch. Board
Univ. of Utah, Marriott Lib.
Univ. of Vermont, Bailey/Howe Lib.
Utah State Archives
Vermont Hist. Soc.
WETA-TV
WTMJ-TV
Washington State Hist. Soc.
West Virginia Dept. of Culture & Hist.
West Virginia Univ.
Western Reserve Hist. Soc.
Wolfson (Louis II) Media Hist. Ctr., Miami-Dade Pub. Lib.
Worldwide Television News
Wyoming State Historical Society
Yukon Archives

Locker rooms
Archive Film Prods., Inc.

Lockwood, Robert
Rhapsody Films, Inc.

Locomotives
See Railroads (Locomotives)

Lodges
Film Bank

Loewe, Frederick
Camera Three Prods., Inc.

Loewy, Raymond
Studebaker Natl. Museum
Univ. of Tex. at Austin, Ransom Hum. Res. Ctr., Photo. Coll.

Lofts
Film Bank

Log cabins (Construction)
TV Ontario

Log rolling
Archive Film Prods., Inc.
Film Bank
See also Lumber sports

Logan, John Juice
Los Angeles Blues Archives

Logging industry
Amer. Pulpwood Assn., Inc.
Analogous Productions
Apertura
British Info. Svcs., Radio & TV Div.
CBS News Archives
Eastern Washington State Historical Soc.
Everett Pub. Lib., Northwest Hist. Coll.
Film/Audio Services, Inc.
Florentine Films
Marts (Steve) Productions
Native Amer. Pub. Broad. Cons.
Natl. Archives (RG 33)
Natl. Archives of Canada
Northeast Historic Film
Odyssey Prods., Inc.
Oregon Hist. Soc.
Oregon State Univ., Archives
Petrified Films, Inc.
Prelinger Assoc., Inc.
Prov. Arch. of British Columbia
San Francisco Maritime Natl. Hist. Park
Twentieth Century-Fox Movietonews
Université de Moncton, Centre d'Études Acad.

Univ. of Calif., Berkeley, Labor
    Occupational Health Prog.
Univ. of Wisconsin — Extension
See also Forestry

**Loire River, France (History and
    culture)**
Petrified Films, Inc.
Voyager Co.

Lollobrigida, Gina
Banks Film Library
Daphne Productions, Inc.

Loma Linda, Calif.
Loma Linda Univ., Webb Lib.

Lombard, Carole
Archive Film Prods., Inc.

Lombardi, Vince
Dartnell
NFL Films, Inc.

London
Analogous Prods.
British Info. Svcs., Radio & TV Div.
Creative Video, Inc.
Dreamlight Images, Inc.
Film Bank
Kesser Stock Footage Library
Preview Media
Source Stock Footage Lib., Inc.
Stock House
TV Ontario
Video Ventures Prods.

London (History and culture)
Archive Film Prods., Inc.
Natl. Archives (RG 24)
Natl. Archives (RG 171)
Natl. Archives (RG 200)
Oregon Hist. Soc.
Petrified Films, Inc.
Purdue Univ., Public Affairs Video Arch.
Spalla (Rick) Video Prods.

London Bridge
Analogous Productions
Dreamlight Images, Inc.
Energy Productions

London, Julie
Archive Film Prods., Inc.

Loneliness
Univ. of West Fla., Hum. Res. Vid. Lib.

Long Beach, Calif.
Film Bank
Preview Media

Long Beach, Calif. (History and culture)
Petrified Films, Inc.

Long, Earl K.
Louisiana State Univ. Libs., Spec. Coll.

Long, Harold
Univ. of Miami, Arch. & Spec. Coll.

Long, Huey P.
March of Time

Long Island, N.Y.
Island Video
New York State Dept. of Econ. Devel.

Long Island, N.Y. (History and culture)
Streamline Film Archives

Long, Russell B.
Louisiana State Univ. Libs., Spec. Coll.

Long, Shelley
Spectral Comms.

Longworth, Alice Roosevelt
Wright Brothers Coll.

Loons (Bird)
Amer. Motion Pictures
Imperial Oil Ltd.
Minnesota Zoo
Video I-D, Inc.

Lopez, Trini
Banks Film Library
Daphne Productions, Inc.

Lopresti, Sam
U.S. Hockey Hall of Fame

Lord, Chip
Paper Tiger TV
Video Data Bank

Lordstown, Ohio (History and culture)
General Motors Corp.

Loren, Sophia
Banks Film Library
Daphne Productions, Inc.

Lorenz, Konrad
Inst. for Psychoanalysis

Lorrain, Claude
Amer. Federation of the Arts

Lorre, Peter
Banks Film Library
UCLA Film & Television Archive

Lortel, Lucille
New York Pub. Lib., Perf. Arts Res. Ctr.,
    Theatre on Film and Tape

Los Alamos, N. Mex.
Film Bank

**Los Alamos, N. Mex. (History and
    culture)**
Los Alamos County Hist. Mus. Arch.

Los Angeles
Airline Film & TV Promotions
Airship Industries (USA), Inc.
Applegate Entertainment
Cannell (Stephen J.) Productions, Inc.
Cinephile Amalgamated Pictures
Creative Video, Inc.
Dorn (Larry) Associates
Dreamlight Images, Inc.
Energy Productions
Film Bank
Postcards Unlimited
Preview Media
Spectral Comms.
Stock House
Unicorn Projects

Los Angeles (History and culture)
Allen (John E.) Inc.
Archive Film Prods., Inc.
Banks Film Library
California State Univ., Northridge
Creative Film Society
Film Bank
Grinberg (Sherman) Film Libraries (East)
Los Angeles City Archives
Los Angeles Dept. of Water & Power

Los Angeles News Service
Newsreel Video Service
Patrick Media Group
Petrified Films, Inc.
Prelinger Assoc., Inc.
Southern Calif. Inst. of Architecture
Southern Calif. Lib. for Soc. Stud. & Res.
Spalla (Rick) Video Prods.

Lost River, Alaska (History and culture)
Archives of Ontario

Lotteries
World Monitor

Loud Family
Daphne Productions, Inc.

Loudspeakers
Film Bank
Petrified Films, Inc.

Louganis, Greg
Second Line Search

Louis, Joe
Archive Film Prods., Inc.
Marquette Univ., Spec. Coll.

Louis, Morris
Blackwood Prods., Inc.

Louis, Murray
Blackwood (Christian) Prods., Inc.

Louise, Tina
Spalla (Rick) Video Prods.

Louisiana
Bullfrog Films, Inc.
Departures, Inc.
Energy Prods.
Film Bank
First Group Comms., Inc.
New Orleans Pub. Lib., La. Div.
Preview Media
Video I-D, Inc.

Louisiana (History and culture)
Center for New American Media
Cinema Guild
Historic New Orleans Collection
Louisiana State Univ. Libs., Spec. Coll.
Louisiana State Univ., Shreveport
New Orleans Pub. Lib., La. Div.
New Orleans Video Access Ctr.
Petrified Films, Inc.
Prelinger Assoc., Inc.
Read (Brooks) & Assoc.
Tulane Univ., Amistad Res. Ctr.

**Louisiana Purchase Exposition (St.
    Louis, 1904)**
Lib. of Congress, M/B/RS

Louisville, Ky.
Omega Films

Louisville, Ky. (History and culture)
Kentucky Dept. of Libraries & Archives
Univ. of Kentucky, AV Arch.

Lounge Lizards (Musical group)
Target Video

Love birds
Petrified Films, Inc.

Love scenes
Fish Films, Inc.

Love-ins
Clark (Dick) Media Archives, Inc.
Film Bank
Petrified Films, Inc.
See also Counterculture (U.S.); Hippies

Lovejoy, Sam
Green Mountain Post Films

Lovelock, Helen Ives
Univ. of Wyoming, Amer. Heritage Ctr.

Lovins, Amory
Green Mountain Post Films

"Low Rider" cars
See Automobiles ("Low Rider")

Lowe, Edmund
UCLA Film & Television Archive

Lowell, Mass. (History and culture)
Amer. Soc. Hist. Proj. Film Lib.

Lowell, Robert
Intellimation

Lowen, Alexander
Psychological and Educational Films

Lowenstein, Allard K.
Cinema Guild
Univ. of N.C.-Chapel Hill, Manuscripts
    Dept.

**Lower East Side, N.Y. (History and
    culture)**
Cinema Guild
Deep Dish TV
Educational Video Ctr.
Film/Video Arts, Inc.
Lib. of Congress, M/B/RS
Monday, Wednesday, Friday Video Club
Petrified Films, Inc.

Lowery, Joseph
Natl. Assn. for the Advancement of
    Colored People

Lubbock, Tex. (History and culture)
Texas Tech Univ., Southwest Coll.

Lucas, George
Direct Cinema Limited

Lucas, Scott
Illinois State Hist. Lib.

Lucier, Mary
Port Washington Pub. Lib.

Lucy, Autherine
Twentieth Century-Fox Movietonews

Luff, DeWitt
Randolph (A. Philip) Educ. Fund

Luge racing
Jalbert Productions
Petrified Films, Inc.
Summit Films, Inc.

Lumber sports
Twentieth Century-Fox Movietonews
See also Log rolling

Lumberjacks
See Logging industry

Lumberyards
Petrified Films, Inc.

NOTE: Access policies, availability and restrictions vary for each source. Please read each entry in full. Always consult "General Film and Videotape Collections" (page 599); these comprehensive collections contain material on every conceivable subject.

Lumet, Sidney
Daphne Productions, Inc.

Lunch hours
Film Bank

Lunch, Lydia
Target Video

Lunch trucks
TV Ontario

Luncheons
Twentieth Century-Fox Movietonews

Lundeberg, Helen
De Saisset Museum

Lungs
Rosebush Visions Corp.

Lupertz, Markus
Blackwood Prods., Inc.

Lupino, Ida
Videobrary, Inc.

Luther, Martin
Concordia Publishing House
Goethe Institute Atlanta

Lutherans
See Religion (Lutherans)

Luxor Temple, Egypt
Unicorn Projects

Luxury
Source Stock Footage Lib., Inc.

Luzon, Philippines (History and culture)
Smithsonian Inst., Human Studies Film
   Arch.

Lydon, Johnny
Target Video

Lymon, Frankie
Cinema Guild

Lynch, David
Spectral Comms.

Lynx
Minnesota Zoo

Lynyrd Skynyrd
Clark (Dick) Media Archives, Inc.

Lyon, France (History and culture)
Archive Film Prods., Inc.

Lyons, Nathan
Video Data Bank

Lytton, Bart
Banks Film Library

MacArthur, Douglas
Archive Film Prods., Inc.
Experimental Aircraft Assn.
Film Bank
Hearst Metrotone News
MacArthur (Gen. Douglas) Memorial
March of Time
Petrified Films, Inc.

MacArthur, Jean Faircloth
MacArthur (Gen. Douglas) Memorial

McAuliffe, Christa
NASA, Office of Comm.

McCafferty, Jay
Long Beach Mus. of Art

McCann, Les
Rhapsody Films, Inc.

McCarthy, Charlie
Archive Film Prods., Inc.
New York Pub. Lib., Perf. Arts Res. Ctr.,
   Theatre on Film and Tape

McCarthy, Eugene J.
DEC Film & Video
Georgetown Univ., Spec. Coll. Div.
Southern Calif. Lib. for Soc. Stud. & Res.

McCarthy, Joseph
Archive Film Prods., Inc.
Film Bank
Forsher (James) Prods. & Arch. Inc.
Halcyon Days Prods.
UCLA Film & Television Archive

McCarthy, Joseph (Hearings, 1954)
Cambridge Documentary Films, Inc.
Taminent Lib./Wagner Labor Arch.

McCarthyism
Cinema Guild

McCartney, Bill
Fellowship of Christian Athletes

McClellan Air Force Base, Calif.
Sweet (Harry) Film Coll.

McClung, Nellie
Natl. Archives of Canada

McClure, Michael
Giorno Poetry Systems Inst.

McCoo, Marilyn
Spectral Comms.

McCormick, Carlo
Monday, Wednesday, Friday Video Club

McCoy, Tim
Intl. Mus. of Photography

McCrea, Joel
Banks Film Library
UCLA Film & Television Archive

McCune, Hank
Encore Entertainment

MacDonald, Jeannette
UCLA Film & Television Archive

McDonald, Larry
Birch (John) Society

McDowall, Roddy
Banks Film Library
Spectral Comms.

McDowell, Elliott
Port Washington Pub. Lib.

McDowell, Malcolm
Spectral Comms.

McEnroe, John
Moving Media
U.S. Tennis Assn.

McEvilley, Thomas
Southern Calif. Inst. of Architecture

McFerran, Bobby
Spectral Comms.

McGavin, Darren
Banks Film Library

McGee, Fibber and Molly

Archive Film Prods., Inc.
New York Pub. Lib., Perf. Arts Res. Ctr.,
   Theatre on Film and Tape

McGill, Ralph
South Carolina Humanities Res. Ctr.

McGovern, Elizabeth
Spectral Comms.

McGovern, George
Daphne Productions, Inc.
Guggenheim Productions, Inc.
Kennedy (John F.) Library
United Farm Workers of America (UFW)

MacGowran, Jack
New York Pub. Lib., Perf. Arts Res. Ctr.,
   Theatre on Film and Tape

McGraw, John
Grinberg (Sherman) Film Libraries (West)

McGregor, Douglas
Salenger Films Inc.

McGuire, Jean
Metropolitan Council for Educ.
   Opportunity

McIntire, Mark
Spectral Comms.

McKay, Cliff
Natl. Archives of Canada

McKeesport, Pa. (History and culture)
Center for Public Dialogue

McKenzie, Scott
Pennebaker Associates, Inc.

McKeon, Nancy
Spectral Comms.

McKinley, Mount (Alaska)
Beerger (Norman) Prods.

**McKinley, Mount (Alaska) (History and
   culture)**
Natl. Archives (RG 79)

McKinley, William
Archive Film Prods., Inc.
Film Education Institute
Lib. of Congress, M/B/RS

McKinnon, Edna R.
Radcliffe Coll., Schlesinger Lib.

MacLaine, Shirley
Banks Film Library
Spectral Comms.

McLaren, Norman
Camera Three Prods., Inc.

McLaughlin, Clarence Ewart
Archives of Ontario

McLaughlin, Robert
Archives of Ontario

McLaurin, Charles
Estuary Press

McLean, Evelyn Walsh
Colorado Historical Society

McLean, Helen
Inst. for Psychoanalysis

McLean, Jackie
Rhapsody Films, Inc.

MacLeay, Scott
Port Washington Pub. Lib.

McLuhan, Marshall
Cinema Guild
MacDonald, J. Fred
Ohio State Univ., Dept. of Photog. &
   Cinema
Univ. of Toronto, AV Lib.

McMahon, Ed
Spectral Comms.

MacMillan, Andrew
Southern Calif. Inst. of Architecture

McMillan, Donald
Natl. Archives (RG 200)

MacMurray, Fred
Banks Film Library
Spectral Comms.

McNamara, Robert
Educational Film & Video Project
Ideal Comms., Inc.
Intellimation

McNeill, Don
Marquette Univ., Spec. Coll.

McNichol, Kristy
Spectral Comms.

McPhee, Colin
Blackwood Prods., Inc.

McPherson, Aimee Semple
Wheaton Coll., Billy Graham Ctr.

McQueen, Steve
Banks Film Library
Petrified Films, Inc.
Wombat Film & Video

McShann, Jay
Rhapsody Films, Inc.

MacWeeny, Alen
Port Washington Pub. Lib.

Macadamia nuts
Ackerman-Black Prods., Inc.

Macaques
Minnesota Zoo

Macaws
Di Sesso (Moe) Wild Life Film Lib.
Energy Productions
Miller (David Lee) Prods.
TV Ontario

Macfarlane, Catherine
Medical College of Pa., Arch. & Spec.
   Coll. Women in Medicine

Machine shops
Prelinger Assoc., Inc.

Machine vision
Robotic Industries Assn.
Society of Manufacturing Engineers

Machinery
Archives of Ontario
CBS News Archives
Film Bank
Marx Production Center
Prelinger Assoc., Inc.
Riccitelli (Bruce) Prods.
Smithsonian Inst., NMAH, Arch. Ctr.

Machinery (Agricultural)
Cornell Univ., Media Services

692

Dreamlight Images, Inc.
Glenbow Mus. Arch.
Natl. Archives (RG 33)

Machinery (Naval)
Natl. Archives (RG 24)

Machines (Office)
Energy Prods.
Petrified Films, Inc.
Prelinger Assoc., Inc.

Machinists
Petrified Films, Inc.
TV Ontario

Mack, Connie
Grinberg (Sherman) Film Libraries (West)

Mack, Heinz
Blackwood Prods., Inc.

Mack, Ted
Moviecraft, Inc.

Mackenzie River, Canada
TV Ontario

Mackenzie Valley, Northwest Territories (History and culture)
Northwest Territories Archives

Mackinac Island, Mich.
Preview Media

Mackintosh, Charles R.
Southern Calif. Inst. of Architecture

Macoska, Jill
Paper Tiger TV

Macrophages
Film Bank

Mad scientists
See Scientists (Mad)

Madagascar (History and culture)
Twentieth Century-Fox Movietonews, Inc.

Madison, Ind. (History and culture)
Natl. Archives/Natl. AV Ctr.

Madison Square Garden (New York City) (History and culture)
Analogous Productions

Madison, Wis. (History and culture)
DEC Film & Video
First Run/Icarus Films, Inc.
State Hist. Soc. of Wisconsin

Madonna (Singer)
Los Angeles News Service

Madras, India (History and culture)
Rockefeller Arch. Ctr.

Madrid, Miguel de la
Film/Audio Services, Inc.
Northstar Prods.

Madrid, Spain
Preview Media

Madrid, Spain (History and culture)
Archive Film Prods., Inc.

Magasich, John
U.S. Hockey Hall of Fame

Magazines
CBS News Archives
Petrified Films, Inc.
Prelinger Assoc., Inc.
TV Ontario

Magazines (Pornographic)
TV Ontario

Magdoff, Harry
Paper Tiger TV

Maggots
Dreamlight Images, Inc.
Energy Productions

Magic carpets
Prelinger Assoc., Inc.

Magicians and magic tricks
CBS News Archives
Film Bank
Palisades Wildlife Film Library
Petrified Films, Inc.
Prelinger Assoc., Inc.
Twentieth Century-Fox Movietonews

Maginot Line (France-Germany border)
March of Time

Magnesium
Natl. Archives (RG 70)

Magnets and magnetism
Archive Film Prods., Inc.
CBS News Archives
Prelinger Assoc., Inc.

Magnolia trees
Film Bank

Magritte, René
Amer. Federation of the Arts

Magsaysay, Ramon
Smith (Margaret Chase) Lib. Ctr.

Mahre, Phil
U.S. Olympic Committee

Maids
Film Bank
See also Workers (Domestic)

Mail and mail carriers
Archive Film Prods., Inc.
CBS News Archives
Film Bank
Natl. Archives (RG 28)
Petrified Films, Inc.
Prelinger Assoc., Inc.
See also Post Office Department (U.S.);
Post offices; Postal Service (U.S.)

Mailer, Norman
Daphne Productions, Inc.
Pennebaker Associates, Inc.

Maillol, Aristide
Blackwood Prods., Inc.

Maimonides, Moses
Anti-Defamation League of B'nai B'rith

Maine
Cineworks Prods. Inc.
Dobbs (Jeff) Prods.
Dreamlight Images, Inc.
Petrified Films, Inc.
Site Productions

Maine (Battleship)
Natl. Archives (RG 18)

Maine (History and culture)
Bangor Hist. Soc.
New Film Co., Inc.
Northeast Historic Film
Roosevelt (Franklin D.) Lib.

Majorettes
See Marching bands

Makarova, Natalia
Daphne Productions, Inc.

Makavejev, Dusan
Walker Art Ctr.

Malacca, Malaysia
Farkas Studios, Ltd.

Malaria
Historical Health Film Coll.
Natl. Archives (RG 90)
New Mexico State Records Ctr. & Arch.
Prelinger Assoc., Inc.
Rockefeller Arch. Ctr.

Malaysia
Canadian Broadcasting Corp.
Farkas Studios, Ltd.
Intl. Assn. of Independent Producers
Yue-Sai Kan, Inc.

Malaysia (History and culture)
Film/Audio Services, Inc.
Idera Films
Johnson (Martin & Osa) Safari Museum
Petrified Films, Inc.
Univ. of Waterloo, A-V Centre

Malcolm X
Carousel Film & Video

Malden, Karl
Spectral Comms.

Maleeva, Manuela
U.S. Tennis Assn.

Malevich, Kasimir
Amer. Federation of the Arts

Mali (History and culture)
U.S. Committee for UNICEF

Malibu, Calif. (History and culture)
Frontline Video, Inc.

Mallard ducks
Indiana State Comm. on Public Records
Petrified Films, Inc.

Malle, Louis
Daphne Productions, Inc.

Mallory-Jones, Phillip
Port Washington Pub. Lib.

Malls
Film Bank

Malone, Dorothy
Banks Film Library

Malt shops
Petrified Films, Inc.

Malta (History and culture)
Prelinger Assoc., Inc.

Mamas and the Papas, The (Rock and roll band)
Pennebaker Associates, Inc.

Mamonova, Tatyana
Women in Focus

Management and management training
AMA Film/Video
Amer. Journal of Nursing Co.
BNA Communications, Inc.
Barr Films
CRM Films L.P.
Carter (C. L., Jr.) & Assoc., Inc.
Cinema Guild
Coe Film Assoc., Inc.
Coronet/MTI Film & Video
Dartnell
Films Incorporated
GPN
Intl. Film Bureau, Inc.
Natl. Assn. of Convenience Stores
Nightingale-Conant Corp.
Phoenix Films and Video
Prelinger Assoc., Inc.
Salenger Films Inc.
United Training Media
Université Laval, Cinémathèque
Univ. of Texas at Austin, Petrol. Ext. Svc.
Video Arts Inc.
Video-Documentary Clearinghouse

Managua, Nicaragua (History and culture)
First Run/Icarus Films, Inc.
Lesage, Julia
United Nations Ctr. for Human Settlements
Univ. of Wisconsin — Extension

Manatee County, Fla. (History and culture)
Swain (Hack) Prods., Inc.

Manatees
Caribbean Images, Ltd.
Echo Film Prods., Inc.
Passage Home Communications
Video Mgmt. Systems

Manaus, Brazil
Brazilian-American Cultural Inst.

Manchuria (History and culture)
Archive Film Prods., Inc.
Natl. Archives/Natl. AV Ctr.

Manchuria (Japanese occupation)
Twentieth Century-Fox Movietonews

Mancini, Henry
Spectral Comms.

Mandalas
Petrified Films, Inc.

Mandel, Howie
Spectral Comms.

Mandel, Mike
Video Data Bank

Mandela, Nelson
California Newsreel
DEC Film & Video
Film/Audio Services, Inc.
New Time Films, Inc.
Villon Films

Mandela, Winnie
California Newsreel

NOTE: Access policies, availability and restrictions vary for each source. Please read each entry in full. Always consult "General Film and Videotape Collections" (page 599); these comprehensive collections contain material on every conceivable subject.

Film/Audio Services, Inc.
Villon Films

Mandlikova, Hana
U.S. Tennis Assn.

Mangold, Robert
Albright-Knox Art Gallery

Mangrum, Lloyd
Sportsfilm

Manhattan Project
Amer. Chemical Soc.
Hoover Institution
Los Alamos County Hist. Mus. Arch.
March of Time
Natl. Archives (RG 18)
Natl. Archives (RG 77)
See also Atomic bombs

Maniacs
Archive Film Prods., Inc.

Manicures
Milady Publishing Corp.
Petrified Films, Inc.

Manila, Philippines
Farkas Studios, Ltd.

Manila, Philippines (History and culture)
Petrified Films, Inc.

Manilatown, San Francisco (History and culture)
Natl. Asian American Telecomm. Assn.

Manilow, Barry
Univision Television Network

Manitoba
TV Ontario

Manitoba (History and culture)
Manitoba Indian Cultural Centre
Natl. Archives of Canada
Prov. Arch. of Manitoba
Video Pool, Inc.

Manitowoc, Wis. (History and culture)
Manitowoc Maritime Museum

Manley, Michael
Schomburg Ctr. for Res. in Black Culture

Manne, Shelly
Rhapsody Films, Inc.

Mannequins
Film Bank

Manning, E.
Prov. Arch. of Alberta

Mansfield, Jayne
Archive Film Prods., Inc.
Banks Film Library
Petrified Films, Inc.
Spalla (Rick) Video Prods.

Mansion, Gracie
Monday, Wednesday, Friday Video Club

Mansions
Film Bank
Petrified Films, Inc.

Manson, Charles
Target Video

Manta rays
Dreamlight Images, Inc.
Moonlight Productions

Mantegna, Andrea
Amer. Federation of the Arts

Mantle, Mickey
Daphne Productions, Inc.
Wesleyan Cinema Archives

Manufacturing
Allen (John E.) Inc.
Applegate Entertainment
Archive Film Prods., Inc.
Banks Film Library
Boston Stock Market
Chicago Video Transfer
Corning Mus. of Glass
Encore Video Prods., Inc.
Fabulous Footage Inc.
Film Bank
4•6•8 Prods., Inc.
Hagley Mus. and Lib.
Lemorande Prod. Co.
Marx Production Center
NASA, Johnson Space Ctr., Stock Film Lib.
Natl. Archives (RG 24)
Natl. Archives (RG 70)
Natl. Archives (RG 178)
Natl. Archives (RG 200)
Natl. Archives of Canada
Northcoast Communication, Inc.
Ohio Hist. Soc.
Petrified Films, Inc.
Prelinger Assoc., Inc.
Reynolds (R.J.) Tobacco USA
Rosebush Visions Corp.
Smithsonian Inst., NMAH, Div. Eng. & Ind.
Society of Manufacturing Engineers
Sullivan Video Services
TV Ontario
Timesteps Prods., Inc.
Twentieth Century-Fox Movietonews
VTR Productions
Video Genesis, Inc.
Videotroupe
World Monitor
See also Assembly lines; Factories; Industry

Mao Tse-tung
See Mao Zedong

Mao Zedong
March of Time
Natl. Archives (RG 226)

Maori
New Zealand Embassy Film Lib.

Maple sugaring
Campbell Films, Inc.

Maple syrup
Petrified Films, Inc.
TV Ontario

Maps
Archive Film Prods., Inc.
CBS News Archives
Handel Film Corp.
Prelinger Assoc., Inc.
Rosebush Visions Corp.
Schiele Museum

Marathon dancing
See Dance and dancing (Marathon)

Marathon running
See Running (Marathon)

Marbles
Sportsfilm
Twentieth Century-Fox Movietonews

Marcantonio, Vito

New York Pub. Lib., Rare Books & Manuscripts Div.

March birds
KD Enterprises Prods.

Marches (Political)
See Demonstrations (Political)

Marching bands
Amer. Motion Pictures
Baylor Univ., Texas Coll.
Central New England Film Arch.
Eastern Kentucky Univ.
Emporia State Univ., Spec. Coll.
Film Bank
Louisiana State Univ. Libs., Spec. Coll.
Nemiroff Prods., Inc.
New Jersey Network
Northern Ill. Univ., Reg. Hist. Ctr.
Ohio State Univ., Dept. of Photog. & Cinema
Petrified Films, Inc.
Texas Tech Univ., Southwest Coll.
Timesteps Prods., Inc.
Univ. of Calif., Davis, Shields Library
Univ. of Ill. Urbana-Champaign, Univ. Arch.

Marciano, Rocky
Grinberg (Sherman) Film Libraries (West)

Marcos, Ferdinand
Banks Film Library

Marcos Island, Fla.
Preview Media

Marcuse, Herbert
Villon Films

Marden, Brice
Amer. Federation of the Arts

Mardi Gras
Windsor Prod. Corp.

Mardi Gras (History and culture)
Analogous Productions
Center for New Amer. Media
Historic New Orleans Collection
New Orleans Pub. Lib., La. Div.
Pennebaker Associates, Inc.
Petrified Films, Inc.

Maricopa Mountains, Ariz.
Petrified Films, Inc.

Marie, Queen (Romania)
Everett Pub. Lib., N.W. Hist. Coll.
Archive Film Prods., Inc.

Marijuana
Addiction Research Foundation of Ontario
Fish Films, Inc.
Intermedia Arts Minnesota
Narcotics Education, Inc.
Petrified Films, Inc.
Prelinger Assoc., Inc.
Signal Press
See also Drug abuse; Drug culture

Marin, Cheech
Spectral Comms.

Marin Headlands, Calif.
Petrified Films, Inc.

Marinas
Cannell (Stephen J.) Productions, Inc.
Elfstrom-Hilmer Prods.
Energy Productions
Film Bank
Petrified Films, Inc.

Marine biology
Bullfrog Films, Inc.
Coronet/MTI Film & Video
Gornick Film Productions
Phoenix Films and Video

Marine Corps (U.S.)
Amer. Motion Pictures
Archive Film Prods., Inc.
CBS News Archives
MacDonald, J. Fred
March of Time
Military/Combat Stock Footage
Multi-Media Pre-Accession Point
Natl. Archives (RG 24)
Natl. Archives (RG 127)
Natl. Archives (RG 200)
Petrified Films, Inc.
Twentieth Century-Fox Movietonews
U.S. Dept. of Defense, Motion Media Rec. Ctr.
See also Korean War; Military; Navy (U.S.); Vietnam War; World War I; World War II; specific conflicts and wars

Marine life
Caribbean Images, Ltd.
Century Video Services, Inc.
Cousteau Society
Dreamlight Images, Inc.
Echo Film Prods., Inc.
Educational Images, Ltd.
Energy Productions
Fabulous Footage Inc.
Film Bank
Film Search
Gornick Film Productions
Marineland of Florida
Moonlight Productions
Natl. Archives (RG 40)
Natl. Geographic Soc. Stock Footage Lib.
Natl. Oceanic & Atmospheric Admin.
Ocean Images
Passage Home Communications
Shell Oil Co.
See also Fish; Underwater footage; specific forms and species of underwater life

Marine sciences
Mariners' Museum

Marino, Dan
NFL Films, Inc.

Marionettes
See Puppets

Maris, Roger
Sportsfilm

Maritime Commission (U.S.)
Natl. Archives (RG 178)

Maritime history
Battleship Cove
Manitowoc Maritime Museum
Mariners' Museum
Mystic Seaport Mus., Inc.
Nantucket Hist. Assn.
Natl. Archives (RG 178)
Peary-MacMillan Arctic Museum
San Francisco Maritime Natl. Hist. Park
See also Boats and boating; Marine Corps (U.S.); Merchant marine; Navy; Ships

Maritime Provinces, Canada (History and culture)
Northeast Historic Film

Mariucci, John
U.S. Hockey Hall of Fame

694

Mark, Herman
Amer. Chemical Soc.

Market County, Mich. (History and culture)
Wayne State Univ., Folklore Arch.

Marketing
Film Search
Video-Documentary Clearinghouse

Markets
CBS News Archives
Energy Productions
Petrified Films, Inc.
Prelinger Assoc., Inc.
TV Ontario
See also Stores

Marlins
Film Bank

Marquees
CBS News Archives
Film Bank
Lib. of Special Visual Effects
Petrified Films, Inc.
Prelinger Assoc., Inc.
Spectacolor, Inc.

Marquees (Animated)
Hayes Prods., Inc.

Marquesas Islands
Cousteau Society

Marriage
Amer. Assn. for Counseling &
  Development
Campbell Films, Inc.
Concordia Publishing House
MacDonald, J. Fred
March of Time
Mass Media Ministries
New Day Films
Prelinger Assoc., Inc.
Research Press
White Janssen, Inc.
See also Weddings

Marriott, Dan
Univ. of Utah, Marriott Lib.

Mars
CBS News Archives
NASA, Lewis Research Center

Marseilles, France (History and culture)
Archive Film Prods., Inc.

Marsh, Stanley III
Long Beach Mus. of Art
Video Data Bank

Marshall, George C.
Marshall (George C.) Res. Lib.

Marshall Islands (History and culture)
Natl. Archives (RG 434)
Petrified Films, Inc.
Univ. of Mich., Mich. Hist. Colls.

Marshall, Penny
Spectral Comms.

Marshall Plan
Amer. Arch. of the Factual Film
German Info. Ctr., Film Lib.
Marshall (George C.) Res. Lib.
Natl. Archives (RG 59)
Natl. Archives (RG 306)

Marshall, Thurgood
Twentieth Century-Fox Movietonews

Marshes
See Swamps; Wetlands

Martha's Vineyard, Mass.
Site Productions

Martial arts
Camera Three Prods., Inc.
Charisma Prods., Ltd./Visual Motion
Crystal Pyramid Prods.
Davenport Films
Film Bank
Nan Hai (U.S.A.) Co., Inc.
Network Prods.
Pyramid Film and Video Corp.
Sportsfilm
Video Tape Library, Ltd.
Wayfarer Publications

Martians
Pyramid Film and Video Corp.

Martin, Agnes
Video Data Bank

Martin, Dean
Banks Film Library
Las Vegas News Bureau
Natl. Archives (RG 56)
Spalla (Rick) Video Prods.
UCLA Film & Television Archive

Martin, Freddy
Banks Film Library

Martin, Pamela Sue
Spectral Comms.

Martin, Pepper
Grinberg (Sherman) Film Libraries (West)

Martin, Tony
Banks Film Library
Spectral Comms.

Martinez, Maria
Amer. Federation of the Arts

Martinique
Kesser Stock Footage Library

Martinis
White Janssen, Inc.

Maruyama, Kinya
Southern Calif. Inst. of Architecture

Marvel, Carl S.
Amer. Chemical Soc.

Marvin, Lee
Banks Film Library
Daphne Productions, Inc.
Spalla (Rick) Video Prods.
UCLA Film & Television Archive

Marx Brothers
Archive Film Prods., Inc.
UCLA Film & Television Archive

Marx, Groucho
Banks Film Library
Daphne Productions, Inc.
New York Pub. Lib., Perf. Arts Res. Ctr.,
  Theatre on Film and Tape
Shokus Video
Smithsonian Inst., NMAH, Arch. Ctr.

Marx, Harpo
Banks Film Library

Marx, Roberto Burle
Landscape Architecture Found.

Mary, Queen
Archive Film Prods., Inc.

Maryland
Dreamlight Images, Inc.
Energy Prods.
Preview Media
Unicorn Projects

Maryland (History and culture)
Acad. of Nat. Sci. of Phila. Lib.
Analogous Prods.
MacDonald, J. Fred
Montgomery Community Television, Inc.
Natl. Archives (RG 33)
Natl. Archives (RG 79)
Natl. Assn. for the Advancement of
  Colored People
Petrified Films, Inc.
Prelinger Assoc., Inc.
Unicorn Projects
Univ. of Baltimore, Abell TV Arch.

Masai people
Documentary Educational Resources
Innerquest Communications Corp.
Johnson (Martin & Osa) Safari Museum
New York Zoological Society
Summit Films, Inc.

Masaryk, Jan
Czechoslovak Heritage Mus. Lib. & Arch.

Mascots
CBS News Archives

Masekela, Hugh
Pennebaker Associates, Inc.

Masks
CBS News Archives
KYUK-TV

Masks (Egyptian)
Rosebush Visions Corp.

Maslow, Abraham
Inst. for Psychoanalysis
Psychological and Educational Films
Salenger Films Inc.

Mass transit
Amer. Public Transit Assn.
British Info. Svcs., Radio & TV Div.
Cinema Guild
Film Bank
Lib. of Congress, M/B/RS
Port Authority of New York & New Jersey
Prelinger Assoc., Inc.
Prov. Arch. of Alberta
Stock Shots
See also Buses; Subways

Massachusetts
Boston Stock Market
Cine-Mark
Energy Prods.
Florentine Films
Preview Media
Site Productions
Stock House
Swedberg (Jack)
Unicorn Projects
Video I-D, Inc.
Viz Wiz, Inc.

Massachusetts (Contemporary issues)
Boston Community Access & Prog.
  Found.

Massachusetts (History and culture)
Amer. Jewish Hist. Soc.
Amer. Soc. Hist. Proj. Film Lib.
Archdiocese of Boston
Archive Film Prods., Inc.
Asian American Resource Workshop
Boston Stock Market
Boston Univ., Film Arch.
Bullfrog Films, Inc.
Central New England Film Arch.
Deep Dish TV
Green Mountain Post Films
Interlock Media Associates
Lib. of Congress, M/B/RS
Mass Inst. of Tech., MIT Museum, Hart
  Nautical Coll.
Massachusetts Archives
Metropolitan Council for Educ.
  Opportunity
Nantucket Hist. Assn.
Native Amer. Pub. Broad. Cons.
Natl. Archives (RG 378)
Petrified Films, Inc.
Redden Archives
Rhode Island Hist. Soc.

Massage
Bullfrog Films, Inc.
Crystal Pyramid Prods.
Dreamlight Images, Inc.
Multi-Focus, Inc.

Massage parlors
Canadian Filmmakers Dist. Centre

Masters and Johnson
Cinema Guild

Mastroianni, Marcello
Petrified Films, Inc.

Masturbation
Focus Intl., Inc.
Kinsey Institute
Multi-Focus, Inc.
See also Sex education; Sexuality

Matadors
See Bullfights

Maternity wards
Petrified Films, Inc.

Mathematicians
Film Bank

Mathematics
AIMS Media
Altschul Group
Barr Films
Britannica Films & Video
Center for Humanities, Inc.
Churchill Films
Coe Film Assoc., Inc.
Coronet/MTI Film & Video
GPN
Handel Film Corp.
Hewlett-Packard Co.
Higgins (Alfred) Prods.
Imevision
Intellimation
Intl. Film Bureau, Inc.
Los Alamos Natl. Lab.
Mathematical Assn. of America
Media Guild
Natl. Archives/Natl. AV Ctr.
Pyramid Film and Video Corp.

NOTE: Access policies, availability and restrictions vary for each source. Please read each entry in full. Always consult "General Film and Videotape Collections" (page 599); these comprehensive collections contain material on every conceivable subject.

Univ. of Waterloo, A-V Centre
Video-SIG

Mather Air Force Base, Calif.
Sweet (Harry) Film Coll.

Mathews, Carole
Videobrary, Inc.

Mathewson, Christy
Grinberg (Sherman) Film Libraries (West)

Mathis, Johnny
Banks Film Library

Matisse, Henri
Amer. Federation of the Arts
Blackwood Prods., Inc.

Matlin, Marlee
Spectral Comms.

Matta-Clark, Gordon
Blackwood Prods., Inc.

Matte shots
Film Bank
Petrified Films, Inc.
See also Process plates

Mattelart, Michele
Paper Tiger TV

Matterhorn, Switzerland
Petrified Films, Inc.

Mattson, Miss. (History and culture)
Mississippi Dept. of Arch. & Hist.

Maui, Hawaii
Cinenet (Cinema Network)
Energy Productions
Passage Home Communications
Preview Media
Video Concepts, Inc.

Mauna Kea, Hawaii
Dobovan Productions, Inc.

Mausoleums
Farkas Studios, Ltd.
Petrified Films, Inc.

Maw, Herbert B.
Univ. of Utah, Marriott Lib.

Maxwell, Roy
Natl. Archives of Canada

May Day
Analogous Productions
Univ. of Missouri, St. Louis

May Day (Soviet Union)
Natl. Archives (RG 342)
Petrified Films, Inc.

May, Elaine
Wesleyan Cinema Archives

May, Gisela
Camera Three Prods., Inc.

May, Rollo
Amer. Assn. for Counseling &
Development
Psychological and Educational Films

Mayall, Maggie
Los Angeles Blues Archives

Maybeck, Bernard
Unicorn Projects

Maynard, Ken

UCLA Film & Television Archive

Maypoles
CBS News Archives

Mays, Willie
Banks Film Library
White Janssen, Inc.

Mazatlan, Mexico
Preview Media

Mazatlan, Mexico (History and culture)
Petrified Films, Inc.

Mbogate people
Smithsonian Inst., Human Studies Film
Arch.

Mead, Lake (Nev.-Ariz.)
Network Productions
Petrified Films, Inc.

Mead, Margaret
Daphne Productions, Inc.
East-West Center

Meader, George
Univ. of Mich., Mich. Hist. Colls.

Meadowlark Lemon
Film Bank

Meadows
Cinenet (Cinema Network)
Petrified Films, Inc.

Meadows, Audrey
Banks Film Library

Meat Puppets (Rock and roll band)
Target Video

Meatpacking
Baltimore Mus. of Industry
See also Beef; Butchers and butchering;
Workers (Packinghouse)

Meaux, Huey
Univ. of Tex. at Austin, Barker Tex. Hist.
Ctr.

**Mecca, Saudi Arabia (History and
culture)**
Archive Film Prods., Inc.

Mecham, Evan
Tucson Community Cable Corp.

Mechanics
Petrified Films, Inc.

Medford, Oregon (History and culture)
Southern Oregon Hist. Soc.

Medicaid
CBS News Archives

Medical centers
See Hospitals

Medical films and videotapes
Academy of Health Sciences, U.S. Army
Altschul Group
Amer. Dental Assn.
Amer. Soc. of Clin. Path. Press
Calif. Coll. of Podiatric Medicine
Cinema Medica
Educational Productions
Emory Medical Television Network
IMS Creative Communications
Johns Hopkins Univ./Population Comm.
Svcs.
Johns Hopkins Univ., School of Medicine
Nassau Comm. Coll. Lib.

New York Hosp.-Cornell Med. Ctr., Arch.
Ohio State Univ., Dept. of Photog. &
Cinema
Prelinger Assoc., Inc.
Rockefeller Arch. Ctr.
Smithsonian Inst., NMAH, Arch. Ctr.
Streamline Film Archives
Video Farm
Visual Information Systems
See also Health; Health education;
Medical footage; Medicine; Patient
education films and videotapes

Medical footage
Allen (John E.) Inc.
Blue Sky Comms., Inc.
Boston Stock Market
Center for Biomedical Comms.
DCI Video Resources
Film Bank
Fish Films, Inc.
Intl. Media Services, Inc.
Johns Hopkins Univ., School of Medicine
Metro Communications, Inc.
Schweitzer (Albert) Ctr.
Source Stock Footage Lib., Inc.
Stock Shots
TV Ontario
Twentieth Century-Fox Movietonews
Video Genesis, Inc.
White Star Prof. Film Svcs., Inc.
See also Medicine

Medicare
CBS News Archives
Perlmutter (Alvin H.) Inc.

Medicine
Academy of Health Sciences, U.S. Army
Altschul Group
Amer. Medical Assn.
Amer. Osteopathic Assn.
Archive Film Prods., Inc.
CBS News Archives
Cable News Network Library
Canadian Film Institute
Carleton Prods. Inc.
Carousel Film & Video
Centers for Disease Control
Chisholm (Jack) Film Productions
Cinema Guild
Creative Video, Inc.
Emory Medical Television Network
File Tape Co.
Film Bank
GPN
Historical Health Film Coll.
Houston Acad. of Medicine
IMS Creative Communications
Medical College of Pa., Arch. & Spec.
Coll. Women in Medicine
Metro Communications, Inc.
Nassau Comm. Coll. Lib.
Natl. Archives (RG 80)
Natl. Archives (RG 111)
Natl. Archives (RG 286)
Natl. Archives (RG 306)
Natl. Archives of Canada
Natl. Archives/Natl. AV Ctr.
Natl. Film Board of Canada
Natl. Library of Medicine
Northcoast Communication, Inc.
Ohio State Univ., Dept. of Photog. &
Cinema
Prelinger Assoc., Inc.
Radcliffe Coll., Schlesinger Lib.
Rockefeller Arch. Ctr.
Screen Presentations, Inc.
Université Laval, Cinémathèque
Univ. of Calif., Ext. Media Ctr.
Univ. of Waterloo, A-V Centre
Video Resources N.Y., Inc.
Worldwide Television News
See also Ambulances; Biology; Diseases;
Doctors; Health; Health care; Health

education; Hospitals; Human body;
Medical films and videotapes; Medical
footage; Medicine; Nurses and nursing;
Patient education films and videotapes;
Patients; Public health; Surgery;
Technology (Medical); Transplants
(Organ); Women and health; Workers
(Health); Workers (Health care);
specific medical disciplines

Medicine (Alternative)
Cinema Medica
Hartley Film Found., Inc.
Video-SIG

Medicine (China)
Cambridge Documentary Films, Inc.
DEC Film & Video
New Day Films
See also Acupuncture and acupressure

Medicine (Herbal)
TV-UNAM

Medicine (History)
Emory Medical Television Network

Medicine (Homeopathy)
Smithsonian Inst., NMAH, Div. Med. Sci.
Video-SIG

Medicine (Legal)
Visual Information Systems

Medicine (Naturopathy)
Canadian Filmmakers Dist. Centre

Medicine (Nuclear)
Amer. Nuclear Society
Natl. Archives (RG 434)
Prelinger Assoc., Inc.

Medicine (Occupational)
IMS Creative Communications

Medicine (Soviet Union)
Natl. Coun. of Amer.-Sov. Friendship

Medicine (Sports)
Athletic Institute
Emory Medical Television Network
Films for the Humanities and Sciences

Medicine (Tibetan)
Office of Tibet

Medicine (Traditional)
Appalshop Films, Inc.
Cinema Guild
DEC Film & Video
Devillier Donegan Ent.
Documentary Educational Resources
Intl. Women's Day Video Fest.
Manitoba Indian Cultural Centre
Native Amer. Pub. Broad. Cons.
Singer-Sharrette Traditional Healing Films
Smithsonian Inst., Human Studies Film
Arch.
Solaris Dance/Theatre/Video
South Dakota State Lib.
TV-UNAM
UNICEF, Div. Info. & Pub. Aff.
Wheelwright Mus. of the Amer. Indian
See also Healing

**Medicine Hat, Alberta (History and
culture)**
Prov. Arch. of Alberta

Medicine men
See Medicine (Traditional)

Medicine shows
Davenport Films

Medieval studies
Univ. of Toronto, AV Lib.

Meditation
Cinema Guild
Hartley Film Found., Inc.
Krishnamurti Foundation of America
Valley of the Sun Publishing
Varied Directions, Inc.

Mediterranean Sea
Cousteau Society
Petrified Films, Inc.

**Mediterranean Sea (History and
  culture)**
Natl. Archives of Canada

Meese, Edwin
Natl. Archives (RG 60)

Meetings
Film Bank
General Motors Corp.
Metro Communications, Inc.
Twentieth Century-Fox Movietonews
Video Tape Library, Ltd.
See also Conferences

Megaphones
Petrified Films, Inc.

Mehta, Zubin
Anti-Defamation League of B'nai B'rith

Meichenbaum, Donald
Psychological and Educational Films

Meier, Richard
Blackwood Prods., Inc.

Mekas, Jonas
Monday, Wednesday, Friday Video Club
Video Data Bank

Melanesian people
Smithsonian Inst., Human Studies Film
  Arch.

Melbourne, Australia
Farkas Studios, Ltd.
Petrified Films, Inc.

Méliès, Georges
Archive Film Prods., Inc.

Memorial Day (U.S.)
Twentieth Century-Fox Movietonews

Memorial Day Massacre (1937)
Grinberg (Sherman) Film Libraries (East)

Memorials
Energy Productions
Farkas Studios, Ltd.
Natl. Archives (RG 75)
Natl. Archives of Canada
Northstar Prods.
Petrified Films, Inc.
Twentieth Century-Fox Movietonews
Washington Broadcast Video Lib.
See also Monuments

Memphis, Tenn.
Dreamlight Images, Inc.
Energy Productions
Lunar Productions
Producers' Service

Memphis, Tenn. (History and culture)
Center for Southern Folklore

Memphis Pink Palace Mus. and Lib.
Memphis State Univ. Libraries
Memphis-Shelby Cty. Pub. Lib. & Info.
  Ctr.
Southern Christian Leadership Conference

Mendelowitz, Daniel
De Saisset Museum

Mendes-France, Pierre
Smith (Margaret Chase) Lib. Ctr.

Mendieta, Ana
Video Data Bank

Mendocino County, Calif.
Preview Media

Mennonites
See Religion (Mennonites)

Menominee, Wis.
Univ. of Wis., Green Bay, Ctr. TV Prod.

Menstruation
Film Bank
Prelinger Assoc., Inc.
See also Obstetrics and gynecology; Sex
  education

Mental health
AIMS Media
Barr Films
Carousel Film & Video
Churchill Films
Cinema Guild
DEC Film & Video
Fanlight Prods.
Hazelden Found. Educ. Materials
Historical Health Film Coll.
Inst. for Psychoanalysis
March of Time
Nassau Comm. Coll. Lib.
Natl. Archives of Canada
Natl. Archives/Natl. AV Ctr.
Pennsylvania State Arch.
Phoenix Films and Video
Prelinger Assoc., Inc.
Rockefeller Arch. Ctr.
Schweitzer (Albert) Ctr.
Singer-Sharrette Traditional Healing Films
Social Psychiatry Res. Inst.
UCLA Behavioral Sci. Media Lab.
Univ. of Calif., Ext. Media Ctr.
Univ. of West Fla., Hum. Res. Vid. Lib.
Vidéo Femmes
Washington Univ., Brown Schl. of Soc.
  Work
See also Mental institutions; Psychiatry
  and psychiatrists; Psychoanalysis and
  psychotherapy; Psychology

Mental hospitals
See Mental institutions

Mental illness
See Mental health

Mental institutions
Natl. Library of Medicine
Schweitzer (Albert) Ctr.
See also Sanitariums

Mentally retarded
See Developmentally disabled

Mer de Glace, France
Petrified Films, Inc.

Mercenaries
Cinema Guild

Univ. of Waterloo, A-V Centre

Mercer, Asa
Washington State Hist. Soc.

Merchant marine (U.S.)
Mariners' Museum
Natl. Archives (RG 178)

Mercury (Planet)
California Inst. of Tech., Jet Propulsion
  Laboratory

Meredith, James
Twentieth Century-Fox Movietonews

Mergers and acquisitions
World Monitor

Mermaids
Film Bank

Merman, Ethel
Banks Film Library
Daphne Productions, Inc.

Merry-go-rounds
See Carousels

**Mesa Verde National Park, Colo.
  (History and culture)**
U.S. Natl. Park Service Hist. Coll.

Mess halls
TV Ontario

Metals and metallurgy
Aluminum Assn.
CBS News Archives
Canadian Film Institute
Natl. Archives (RG 70)
Natl. Archives (RG 291)
Natl. Archives of Canada
Prelinger Assoc., Inc.
Source Stock Footage Lib., Inc.
Zinc Inst./Lead Industries Assn.
See also Foundries; Mining (Metals);
  Workers (Sheet metal); specific metals

Metalsmithing
Film Bank

Meteorites
Charisma Prods., Ltd./Visual Motion
Harvard-Smithsonian Ctr. for Astrophysics

Meteorology
Edison Electric Institute
Educational Images, Ltd.
Intl. Aviation Publishers, Inc.
NASA, Lewis Research Center
Natl. Archives (RG 26)
Natl. Archives (RG 33)
Natl. Archives of Canada
Natl. Oceanic & Atmospheric Admin.
Natl. Science Foundation
Twentieth Century-Fox Movietonews
See also Weather

Methane
Bullfrog Films, Inc.

Methodists
See Religion (Methodists)

Metke, Luther
Media Project

Metzner, Sheila
Port Washington Pub. Lib.

Mexican Americans
Atlantis Prods., Inc.
Cinema Guild
Creative Film Society
Denver Pub. Lib., Western Hist. Dept.
Estuary Press
MALDEF
Natl. Archives (RG 381)
Partido Nacional La Raza Unida
Quest Productions Inc.
Teatro Campesino, El
United Farm Workers of America (UFW)
Univ. of Tex. at Austin, Benson Lat. Am.
  Coll.
Video Data Bank

Mexican Revolution
See Revolutions (Mexico)

Mexico
Amer. Airlines
Aries Prods.
Canadian Broadcasting Corp.
Cousteau Society
Echo Film Prods., Inc.
Energy Productions
Film Bank
Imagen y Sonido Independiente, S.A.
Pan American Airlines Film Lib.
Passage Home Comms.
Petrified Films, Inc.
Preview Media
Sonoma Video Productions
Source Stock Footage Lib., Inc.
Summit Films, Inc.
TV Ontario
U.S. Committee for UNICEF
World Monitor

Mexico (Contemporary issues)
Alternative Information Network
Film/Audio Services, Inc.

Mexico (History and culture)
Allen (John E.) Inc.
Archive Film Prods., Inc.
Archivo Fotografico y Cinematografico
  Abítia
Archivo Historico Cinematografico
Canal 11
Cinema Guild
Cineteca Nacional
Documentary Educational Resources
East-West Center
Film/Audio Services, Inc.
Filmoteca de la UNAM
Footage Inc.
Hammer (Armand) Prods.
Hoover Institution
IFEX Films
Imagen y Sonido Independiente, S.A.
Imevision
Instituto Nacional Indigenista
Inter-American Foundation
Intl. Assn. of Independent Producers
Intl. Film Foundation
Johns Hopkins Univ./Population Comm.
  Svcs.
Latina, S.A. de C.V.
Lib. of Congress, M/B/RS
March of Time
Natl. Archives (RG 59)
Natl. Archives (RG 106)
Natl. Archives (RG 111)
Natl. Archives (RG 200)
Natl. Archives (RG 362)
Northstar Prods.
Notimex
Oregon Hist. Soc.
Petrified Films, Inc.
Redes Cinevideo, S.A.

NOTE: Access policies, availability and restrictions vary for each source. Please read each entry in full. Always consult "General Film and
Videotape Collections" (page 599); these comprehensive collections contain material on every conceivable subject.

Rockefeller Arch. Ctr.
Salvation Army, Natl. Comm. Dept.
Schiele Museum
Schweitzer (Albert) Ctr.
Singer-Sharrette Traditional Healing Films
Smithsonian Inst., Human Studies Film Arch.
Spalla (Rick) Video Prods.
TV-UNAM
Televisa, S.A.
Third World Newsreel
Vidéographe Inc., Le
White Janssen, Inc.
World Monitor
Zafra, A.C.

Mexico City
Preview Media
Source Stock Footage Lib., Inc.

Mexico City (History and culture)
Archivo Historico Cinematografico
Filmoteca de la UNAM
Hammer (Armand) Prods.
Petrified Films, Inc.
TV-UNAM

Meyer, Kurt
Southern Calif. Inst. of Architecture

Miami
Airline Film & TV Promotions
Creative Video, Inc.
Energy Productions
Kesser Stock Footage Library
Petrified Films, Inc.
Video Ventures Prods.
Villon Films
Wallen (Dick) Prods.

Miami (History and culture)
Petrified Films, Inc.
Prelinger Assoc., Inc.
Univ. of Miami, Arch. & Spec. Coll.

Miami Beach, Fla.
Kesser Stock Footage Library
Preview Media

Miami Beach, Fla. (History and culture)
Petrified Films, Inc.
Prelinger Assoc., Inc.
Prestige Film Corp.

Mice
Wings Wildlife Prods. Inc.

Michaels, Lorne
Natl. Archives of Canada

Michals, Duane
Amer. Federation of the Arts

Micheaux, Oscar
Paper Tiger TV

Michels, Doug
Southern Calif. Inst. of Architecture

Michelson, Albert A.
Cinema Guild

Michelson, Annette
Video Data Bank

Michigan
Dreamlight Images, Inc.
Energy Prods.
Film Bank
Preview Media
White Star Prof. Film Svcs., Inc.

Michigan (History and culture)
Amer. Truck Historical Soc.
Archive Film Prods., Inc.

Cranbrook Acad. of Arts
DEC Film & Video
General Motors Corp.
MacDonald, J. Fred
Natl. Archives (RG 200)
Natl. Railway Hist. Soc.
New Day Films
Perry (Merle G.) Arch.
Petrified Films, Inc.
Prelinger Assoc., Inc.
Univ. of Mich., Mich. Hist. Colls.
Wayne State Univ., Arch. Labor & Urb. Aff.
Wayne State Univ., Folklore Arch.

Michigan, Lake
Chicago Video Transfer
Univ. of Wis., Green Bay, Ctr. TV Prod.

Michigan, Lake (History and culture)
Univ. of Wisconsin — Extension

Microbiology
Emory Medical Television Network

Microchips
TV Ontario

Microcinematography
Dreamlight Images, Inc.
Energy Productions
Film Bank
Grinberg (Sherman) Film Libraries (West)
Historical Health Film Coll.
Petrified Films, Inc.
West Star Productions

Microcinematography (Medical)
Film Bank

Micronesia
Passage Home Communications

Micronesia (History and culture)
Devillier Donegan Ent.
Idera Films
Natl. Archives (RG 234)
Smithsonian Inst., Human Studies Film Arch.

Microphones
Petrified Films, Inc.

Microphotography
Benchmark Films, Inc.
Prelinger Assoc., Inc.
Univ. of Wash. Press, Multimedia Div.
See also Microcinematography

Microscopes
Film Bank
Petrified Films, Inc.

Middle East
British Info. Svcs., Radio & TV Div.
Film Bank
Film Search
Intl. Film Foundation
TV Ontario
World Monitor
See also Israel; Palestine

Middle East (Contemporary issues)
Amer. Zionist Youth Found.
Amer.-Arab Anti-Discrimination Comm.
Anti-Defamation League of B'nai B'rith
Atlantis Prods., Inc.
DEC Film & Video
Icarus-Tamouz Media, Inc.
Middle East Institute
Natl. Archives (RG 200)
Third World Newsreel

Middle East (History and culture)
Amer. Zionist Youth Found.

Amer.-Arab Anti-Discrimination Comm.
Archive Film Prods., Inc.
Atlantis Prods., Inc.
CTV Television Network
Cinema Guild
DEC Film & Video
Film/Audio Services, Inc.
First Run/Icarus Films, Inc.
Grinberg (Sherman) Film Libraries (West)
Hellenic College
Ideal Comms., Inc.
Idera Films
Israel Broadcasting Serv.
Middle East Institute
Myrin Institute
Natl. Archives (RG 59)
Natl. Ctr. for Jewish Film
Northstar Prods.
Phoenix Films and Video
Prelinger Assoc., Inc.
UCLA Film & Television Archive
Villon Films
World Monitor
Worldwide Television News

Midgets
CBS News Archives
Petrified Films, Inc.

Midler, Bette
Spectral Comms.

Midwifery
Appalachian State Univ., Eury Coll.
Appalshop Films, Inc.
Cinema Medica
East Tenn. State Univ., Arch. of Appalachia
Groupe Intervention Video
New Day Films
Univ. of Alabama, W.S. Hoole Spec. Coll.
Women Make Movies, Inc.

Migrants and migration
Canadian Filmmakers Dist. West
Icarus-Tamouz Media, Inc.
Inter-American Foundation
Johns Hopkins Univ./Population Comm. Svcs.
KYUK-TV
See also Workers (Migrant)

Milan, Italy (History and culture)
Archive Film Prods., Inc.

Miles, William
Port Washington Pub. Lib.

Milford, Mich. (History and culture)
Petrified Films, Inc.

Milhaud, Darius
San Francisco Bay Area TV News Arch.

Mili, Gjon
Port Washington Pub. Lib.

Military
Allen (John E.) Inc.
Analogous Productions
CBS News Archives
Cable News Network Library
Carleton Productions Inc.
Cinema Guild
Development Communications, Inc.
Fabulous Footage Inc.
Film Bank
Film/Audio Services, Inc.
Great American Stock
Ideal Comms., Inc.
Metro Communications, Inc.
Natl. Archives (RG 226)
Natl. Archives/Natl. AV Ctr.
Producers Library Service
Prov. Arch. of Manitoba

Riccitelli (Bruce) Prods.
SF•V Intl.
Screen Presentations, Inc.
Timesteps Prods., Inc.
Twentieth Century-Fox Movietonews
See also Air Force; Aircraft (Military); Army; Aviation (Military); Battles; Korean War; Marine Corps; Military history; Military training; Military training films; Missiles; Navy; Nuclear weapons; Vehicles (Military); Vietnam War; Wars; World War I; World War II; specific conflicts and wars

Military (Canada)
Glenbow Mus. Arch.
Natl. Archives of Canada

Military (Israel)
White Janssen, Inc.

Military (Soviet Union)
Ideal Comms., Inc.

Military (Taiwan)
Farkas Studios, Ltd.

Military academies
CBS News Archives
Citadel, The
TV Ontario
See also Air Force Academy (U.S.); Naval Academy (U.S.); West Point, N.Y. (U.S. Military Academy)

Military bases
Natl. Archives (RG 77)

Military equipment
U.S. Dept. of Defense, Motion Media Rec. Ctr.

Military history
Allen (John E.) Inc.
Citadel, The
Films for the Humanities and Sciences
Ideal Comms., Inc.
Intl. Historic Films, Inc.
Manitowoc Maritime Museum
March of Time
Military/Combat Stock Footage
Movietime, Inc. Archives
Multi-Media Pre-Accession Point
Natl. Archives (RG 107)
Natl. Archives (RG 111)
Natl. Archives (RG 127)
Natl. Archives (RG 200)
Natl. Archives/Natl. AV Ctr.
U.S. Army Military Hist. Inst.
U.S. Dept. of Defense, Motion Media Rec. Ctr.
See also Military

Military history (Black)
MacDonald, J. Fred
Miles Educ. Film Prods.
Natl. Archives (RG 16)
See also Black history and culture

Military ships
See Ships (Military)

Military spending
Center for Defense Information

Military training
Development Communications, Inc.
Natl. Archives (RG 24)
Natl. Archives (RG 26)
Natl. Archives (RG 200)
Natl. Archives (RG 208)
Prov. Arch. of Alberta

Military training films
Citadel, The

MacDonald, J. Fred
Military/Combat Stock Footage
Movietime, Inc. Archives
Natl. Archives (RG 18)
Natl. Archives (RG 80)
Natl. Archives (RG 111)
Natl. Archives (RG 127)
Natl. Archives (RG 342)
Petrified Films, Inc.
Prelinger Assoc., Inc.
Southwest Film/Video Archives, SMU
Streamline Film Archives
U.S. Dept. of Defense, Motion Media Rec. Ctr.
U.S. Marine Corps, Hist. Ctr. Lib.
Univ. of Toledo, Univ. Arch.
Video Resources N.Y., Inc.

Military vehicles
See Vehicles (Military)

Milk
Glenbow Mus. Arch.
Johns Hopkins Univ., School of Medicine
Natl. Dairy Council
Prelinger Assoc., Inc.
TV Ontario
See also Dairy industry

Milk drops
Mass. Inst. of Tech., MIT Museum

Milk, Harvey
San Francisco Bay Area TV News Arch.

Milkmen
Petrified Films, Inc.

Mill Valley, Calif. (History and culture)
Nuclear Free Zone Registry

Milland, Ray
Encore Entertainment
UCLA Film & Television Archive
Videobrary, Inc.

Miller, Ann
Banks Film Library
New York Pub. Lib., Perf. Arts Res. Ctr.,
    Theatre on Film and Tape

Miller, Arnold
West Virginia Dept. of Culture & Hist.

Miller, Arthur
Daphne Productions, Inc.
Inst. for Psychoanalysis
New York Pub. Lib., Perf. Arts Res. Ctr.,
    Theatre on Film and Tape

Miller, Henry
Cantor (Arthur) Inc.

Miller, Kid Punch
Rhapsody Films, Inc.

Miller, Marc Crispin
Paper Tiger TV

Miller, Melissa
Albright-Knox Art Gallery

Miller, Steve
Clark (Dick) Media Archives, Inc.

Millipedes
Dreamlight Images, Inc.
Wings Wildlife Prods. Inc.

Mills
Appalshop Films, Inc.

Energy Productions
Rockefeller Arch. Ctr.

Mills (Flour)
TV Ontario

Mills (Grain)
Film Bank

Mills (Lumber)
Petrified Films, Inc.
TV Ontario
Univ. of Calif., Berkeley, Labor
    Occupational Health Prog.

Mills (Paper)
Petrified Films, Inc.
TV Ontario

Mills (Plywood)
Everett Pub. Lib., N.W. Hist. Coll.

Mills (Sash and door)
Petrified Films, Inc.

Mills (Sawmills)
General Motors Corp.
Prov. Arch. of British Columbia

Mills (Steel)
Petrified Films, Inc.
See also Steel industry; Workers (Steel)

Mills (Textile)
Amer. Soc. Hist. Proj. Film Lib.

Mills (Turbine-powered)
Apertura

Mills (Water)
Petrified Films, Inc.

Millsap, Ronnie
Spectral Comms.

Milton, Ted
Giorno Poetry Systems, Inc.

Milwaukee, Wis. (History and culture)
Marquette Univ., Spec. Coll.
WTMJ-TV

Mimes
New York Pub. Lib., Perf. Arts Res. Ctr.,
    Theatre on Film and Tape
Palisades Wildlife Film Library
Pyramid Film and Video Corp.
Soc. for French Amer. Cult. Svcs. & Educ.
    Aid

Mind readers
Fish Films, Inc.

Mine detectors
CBS News Archives

Mine laying
Natl. Archives (RG 24)

Mine, Mill and Smelter Workers Union
Estuary Press

Mineo, Sal
Banks Film Library

Mineral baths
Video Tape Library, Ltd.

Minerals
British Info. Svcs., Radio & TV Div.
CBS News Archives

Natl. Archives (RG 229)
Zinc Inst./Lead Industries Assn.

Mines, Bureau of (U.S.)
Natl. Archives (RG 48)
Natl. Archives (RG 70)
Natl. Archives (RG 111)

Mingus, Charles
DEC Film & Video

Mini-malls
Spectral Comms.

Miniatures
Grinberg (Sherman) Film Libraries (West)
Paramount Pictures Stock Film Lib.

Mining
Allen (John E.) Inc.
British Info. Svcs., Radio & TV Div.
CBS News Archives
Canadian Film Institute
Energy Productions
Film Bank
Forsher (James) Prods. & Archives, Inc.
Intl. Film Foundation
Natl. Archives (RG 48)
Natl. Archives (RG 70)
Natl. Archives of Canada
Oregon Hist. Soc.
Prelinger Assoc., Inc.
Prov. Arch. of British Columbia
Source Stock Footage Lib., Inc.
Twentieth Century-Fox Movietonews
U.S. Dept. of Labor, Mine Safety & Health
    Admin.
Université de Moncton, Centre d'Études
    Acad.
Univ. of Alaska, Fairbanks, Alaska Motion
    Picture Arch.
Univ. of Toronto, Univ. Arch.
Wayne State Univ., Folklore Arch.
Yukon Archives
See also Workers (Mine)

Mining (Accidents)
East Tenn. State Univ., Arch. of
    Appalachia

Mining (Bolivia)
Cinema Guild

Mining (Coal)
Appalachian State Univ., Eury Coll.
Appalshop Films, Inc.
Coal Employment Project
East Tenn. State Univ., Arch. of
    Appalachia
Film Bank
First Run/Icarus Films, Inc.
Maryknoll Fathers & Brothers
Natl. Archives (RG 70)
Natl. Archives (RG 223)
Natl. Assn. of Conservation Dists.
Petrified Films, Inc.
Prelinger Assoc., Inc.
Prestige Film Corp.
Smithsonian Inst., Human Studies Film
    Arch.
Source Stock Footage Lib., Inc.
TV Ontario
Texas Tech Univ., Southwest Coll.
U.S. Dept. of Labor, Mine Safety & Health
    Admin.
Univ. of Alabama, W.S. Hoole Library
Univ. of Colo., Boulder, Western Hist.
    Coll.
See also Coal and coal industry

Mining (Copper)

Petrified Films, Inc.
See also Copper

Mining (Gold)
Democracy in Communication
Downtown Community TV Ctr.
Film Bank
Petrified Films, Inc.
TV Ontario
Univ. of Calif., Ext. Media Ctr.
Univ. of Colo., Boulder, Western Hist.
    Coll.
Univ. of Wis., Green Bay, Ctr. TV Prod.
See also Gold

Mining (Gypsum)
Gypsum Assn.

Mining (Iron)
Archive Film Prods., Inc.
Iron Range Res. Ctr.
Petrified Films, Inc.
See also Iron

Mining (Lead)
TV Ontario
Univ. of Wis., Green Bay, Ctr. TV Prod.
See also Lead

Mining (Metals)
Archives of Ontario
Natl. Archives (RG 70)
See also Metals and metallurgy

Mining (Nickel)
Natl. Archives of Canada
TV Ontario

Mining (Strip)
Appalachian State Univ., Eury Coll.
Appalshop Films, Inc.
Bullfrog Films, Inc.
Film Bank
Kentucky Dept. of Libraries & Archives
Natl. Assn. of Conservation Dists.
Petrified Films, Inc.

Mining (Tin)
TV Ontario

Mining (Uranium)
Archive Film Prods., Inc.
Bullfrog Films, Inc.
Finley (Stuart) Inc.
U.S. Dept. of Labor, Mine Safety & Health
    Admin.
See also Uranium

Mining (Zinc)
TV Ontario
Univ. of Wis., Green Bay, Ctr. TV Prod.
See also Zinc

Mining towns
See Towns (Mining)

Miniskirts
Petrified Films, Inc.

Mink
Oregon State Univ., Archives

Minneapolis
Applegate Entertainment
Energy Productions

Minneapolis (History and culture)
Intermedia Arts Minnesota
Minnesota Hist. Soc.
Petrified Films, Inc.

NOTE: Access policies, availability and restrictions vary for each source. Please read each entry in full. Always consult "General Film and Videotape Collections" (page 599); these comprehensive collections contain material on every conceivable subject.

Minnelli, Lee
Spectral Comms.

Minnelli, Liza
UCLA Film & Television Archive

Minnelli, Vincente
Banks Film Library

Minnesota
Energy Prods.
Ideal Comms., Inc.
Northcoast Communication, Inc.
Prelinger Assoc., Inc.
Preview Media
Snyder (Bill) Films, Inc.
Video I-D, Inc.

Minnesota (History and culture)
Anoka County Comm. Workshop, Inc.
Archive Film Prods., Inc.
Footage Inc.
Intermedia Arts Minnesota
Iron Range Res. Ctr.
Minnesota Hist. Soc.
Petrified Films, Inc.
Prelinger Assoc., Inc.
St. Paul Pub. Lib., Film & Video Ctr.

Minnie Mouse
Spectral Comms.

Minnows
Film Bank
TV Ontario

Minot, N. Dak. (History and culture)
State Hist. Soc. of North Dakota

Minsky, Morton
New York Pub. Lib., Perf. Arts Res. Ctr.,
  Theatre on Film and Tape

Mint, Bureau of the (U.S.)
Natl. Archives (RG 104)

Minutemen (Rock and roll band)
Target Video

Miranda, Carmen
Archive Film Prods., Inc.

Miró, Joan
Blackwood Prods., Inc.
Natl. Gallery of Art

Mirror Lake, Calif.
Petrified Films, Inc.

Mirrors
Natl. Glass Assn.

Miss America pageants
See Beauty pageants (Miss America)

Miss, Mary
Blackwood Prods., Inc.
Southern Calif. Inst. of Architecture
Video Data Bank

Missile bases (Soviet Union)
Ocean Earth Constr. and Dev. Corp.

Missiles
Analogous Productions
Archive Film Prods., Inc.
British Info. Svcs., Radio & TV Div.
CBS News Archives
Film Bank
Hagley Mus. and Lib.
Natl. Archives (RG 218)
Natl. Archives (RG 342)
Petrified Films, Inc.
Twentieth Century-Fox Movietonews
U.S. Defense Nuclear Agency

World Monitor

Missiles (Anti-ballistic)
Grinberg (Sherman) Film Libraries (East)
U.S. Dept. of Defense, Motion Media Rec.
  Ctr.

Missionaries
Africa Inland Mission
Amer. Baptist Films/Video
Arch. of the Mennonite Church
Disciples of Christ Hist. Soc.
Evangelical Lutheran Church in America
Hoover Institution
Loma Linda Univ., Webb Lib.
Maryknoll Fathers & Brothers
Mennonite Library and Archives
Natl. Archives of Canada
Off. of History (Montreal) of the
  Presbyterian Study Ctr.
United Methodist Churches
Univ. of Alaska, Fairbanks, Alaska Motion
  Picture Arch.
Univ. of Missouri, St. Louis
Wheaton Coll., Billy Graham Ctr.
White Janssen, Inc.

Missions
Oregon Hist. Soc.
Petrified Films, Inc.

Mississippi
Center for Southern Folklore
Film Bank

Mississippi (History and culture)
Archive Film Prods., Inc.
Estuary Press
Mississippi Dept. of Arch. & Hist.
New Time Films, Inc.
Payne, Roz
Univ. of Miss., Ctr. for Study of Southern
  Culture

Mississippi (U.S.S.)
Mariners' Museum

Mississippi Delta (History and culture)
Ocean Earth Constr. and Dev. Corp.

Mississippi River
Petrified Films, Inc.
Preview Media
State Hist. Soc. of Iowa

Mississippi River (History and culture)
Kentucky Dept. of Libraries & Archives
MacDonald, J. Fred
Missouri Hist. Soc.
Natl. Archives (RG 91)
Natl. Archives (RG 96)
Natl. Archives/Natl. AV Ctr.
Natl. Assn. of Conservation Dists.

Missouri
Dreamlight Images, Inc.
Energy Prods.
File Tape Co.
Film Bank

Missouri (History and culture)
Amer. Truck Historical Soc.
Missouri Hist. Soc.
Natl. Archives (RG 131)
Petrified Films, Inc.
Prelinger Assoc., Inc.
Skylight Pictures
State Hist. Soc. of Wisconsin
Unicorn Projects

Missouri (U.S.S.)
Natl. Archives (RG 80)

Missouri River
State Hist. Soc. of Iowa

Mist
Film Bank
Marts (Steve) Prods.
Twentieth Century-Fox Movietonews

Mister Ed
Spalla (Rick) Video Prods.

Mitchell, Billy
Natl. Archives (RG 342)

Mitchell, Chad
Natl. Archives of Canada

Mitchell, Edgar D.
Hartley Film Found., Inc.

Mitchell, Joan
Blackwood Prods., Inc.
Video Data Bank

Mitchell, Margarette
Port Washington Pub. Lib.

Mitchum, Robert
Banks Film Library

Mix, Tom
Archive Film Prods., Inc.
Em Gee Film Library
Intl. Mus. of Photography

Miyake, Riichi
Southern Calif. Inst. of Architecture

Mobile, Ala.
Energy Productions

Mobley, Mary Ann
Miss America Pageant

Mobridge, S. Dak. (History and culture)
South Dakota State Lib.

Mobsters
See Gangsters

Mockingbirds
Wings Wildlife Prods. Inc.

Model airplanes
See Aircraft (Model)

Model, Lisette
Port Washington Pub. Lib.

Model railroads
See Railroads (Model)

Model ships
See Ships (Model)

Models (Fashion)
Broad Street Prods.
CBS News Archives
Film Bank
March of Time
Petrified Films, Inc.
Prelinger Assoc., Inc.
White Janssen, Inc.

Modern Jazz Quartet
Camera Three Prods., Inc.

Moellenhoff, Fritz
Inst. for Psychoanalysis

Moholy-Nagy, Laszlo
Goethe Institute Chicago

Moire patterns
Film Bank

**Mojave Desert, Calif.-Nev. (History and
  culture)**

Mist

New Film Co., Inc.
Petrified Films, Inc.

Molds
Dreamlight Images, Inc.
Univ. of Toronto, AV Lib.

Molecules
Rosebush Visions Corp.

Moles
Wings Wildlife Prods. Inc.

Molotov, Vyacheslav M.
Natl. Archives (RG 342)

Monaco
Petrified Films, Inc.

Monaco (History and culture)
Petrified Films, Inc.

Monasteries
CBS News Archives
Film Bank

Monasteries (Buddhist)
Petrified Films, Inc.
See also Religion (Buddhism)

Mondale, Walter F.
Guggenheim Productions, Inc.
Natl. Archives (RG 185)

Monet, Claude
Amer. Federation of the Arts

Money
Archive Film Prods., Inc.
CBS News Archives
Dreamlight Images, Inc.
Film Bank
Natl. Archives (RG 87)
Natl. Archives (RG 104)
Prelinger Assoc., Inc.

Mongolia
Prelinger Assoc., Inc.

Mongolia (History and culture)
Amer. Mus. Nat. Hist. Film Arch.

Mongooses
Mountain Video Associates

Monitor (U.S.S.)
Natl. Oceanic & Atmospheric Admin.

Monk, Meredith
Blackwood Prods., Inc.
House Found. for the Arts
Video Data Bank

Monkeys
Analogous Productions
Di Sesso (Moe) Wild Life Film Lib.
Film Bank
Kesser Stock Footage Library
Minnesota Zoo
Petrified Films, Inc.
Prelinger Assoc., Inc.
Summit Films, Inc.

Monks
Jewell (Stuart) Productions
Petrified Films, Inc.

Monks (Buddhist)
Farkas Studios, Ltd.
See also Religion (Buddhism)

**Monongahela River (Penn.-W. Va.)
  (History and culture)**
Kentucky Dept. of Libraries & Archives

Monroe Doctrine
Prelinger Assoc., Inc.

Monroe, Marilyn
Archive Film Prods., Inc.
Banks Film Library
DEC Film & Video
Halcyon Days Prods.
UCLA Film & Television Archive
Wombat Film & Video

Monroe, Robert
Port Washington Pub. Lib.

Monsters
Archive Film Prods., Inc.
Fabulous Footage Inc.
Film Bank
Fish Films, Inc.
Pyramid Film and Video Corp.
See also Science fiction

Montages
Film Bank
Petrified Films, Inc.

Montagnard people (History and culture)
UNICEF, Div. Info. & Pub. Aff.

Montagu, Ashley
Psychological and Educational Films

Montalban, Ricardo
Spectral Comms.

Montana
Montana Dept. of Commerce
North Country Media Group

Montana (History and culture)
Archive Film Prods., Inc.
Estuary Press
Montana Dept. of Commerce
North Country Media Group
Oregon Hist. Soc.
Singer-Sharrette Traditional Healing Films
Smithsonian Inst., Human Studies Film Arch.

Montana, Joe
NFL Films, Inc.

Montand, Yves
Banks Film Library

Montano, Linda
Video Data Bank

Monterey, Calif.
Petrified Films, Inc.
Postcards Unlimited
Preview Media

Monterey, Calif. (History and culture)
Natl. Asian American Telecomm. Assn.
Petrified Films, Inc.

Montevideo, Uruguay (History and culture)
Archive Film Prods., Inc.

Montezuma Castle National Monument, Arizona
Source Stock Footage Lib., Inc.

Montgomery, Ala. (History and culture)
Petrified Films, Inc.

Montgomery, Jim
U.S. Olympic Committee

Montgomery, Little Brother
Rhapsody Films, Inc.

Montgomery, Robert
UCLA Film & Television Archive

Monticello (Charlottesville, Va.)
Metro Communications, Inc.

Montoya, Coco
Los Angeles Blues Archives

Montreal
Departures, Inc.

Montreal (History and culture)
Archives of Ontario
Groupe Intervention Video
Natl. Archives of Canada
Schiele Museum
Société de Radio-Télévision de Québec

Monument Valley, Ariz.-Utah
Energy Productions
Phoenix Videofilms/Karr Prods.
Source Stock Footage Lib., Inc.
Spalla (Rick) Video Prods.

Monuments
CBS News Archives
Creative Video, Inc.
Development Communications, Inc.
Energy Productions
Film Bank
Harriman Communications Ctr.
Intl. Film Foundation
Moser (Michael)/Media
Natl. Archives (RG 24)
Natl. Archives (RG 48)
Natl. Archives (RG 117)
Northstar Prods.
Petrified Films, Inc.
TV Ontario
Twentieth Century-Fox Movietonews
Univ. of Tex. at Austin, Barker Tex. Hist. Ctr.
Washington Broadcast Video Lib.
See also Landmarks

Moody, Blair
Univ. of Mich., Mich. Hist. Colls.

Moomaw, Donn
Fellowship of Christian Athletes

Moon
See Moons

Moon landing
Film Bank
Film Education Institute
Kesser Stock Footage Library
NASA, Johnson Space Ctr., Film & Video Dist. Lib.
NASA, Johnson Space Ctr., Stock Film Lib.
NASA, Lewis Research Center
NASA, Office of Comm.
Prelinger Assoc., Inc.
Weintraub Screen Entertainment, Inc.
See also Space; Space program (U.S.)

Moon, Sun Myung
Graduate Theological Union Lib.

Mooney, Tom
Southern Calif. Lib. for Soc. Stud. & Res.

Moonies
See Religion (Unification Church)

Moonlight
CBS News Archives
Twentieth Century-Fox Movietonews

Moons
Amer. Motion Pictures
CBS News Archives
Cinenet (Cinema Network)
Dreamlight Images, Inc.
Energy Productions
Film Bank
Film Search
Finley (Stuart) Inc.
Fish Films, Inc.
Halicki (H.B.) Productions
Marts (Steve) Productions
Moving Media
NASA, Johnson Space Ctr., Film & Video Dist. Lib.
Petrified Films, Inc.
Source Stock Footage Lib., Inc.
Stock House
Twentieth Century-Fox Movietonews
Video Tape Library, Ltd.
Wings Wildlife Prods. Inc.
See also Space

Moonshining
Appalshop Films, Inc.

Moore, Archie
Natl. Archives (RG 47)

Moore, Charles
Southern Calif. Inst. of Architecture

Moore, Dudley
Spectral Comms.

Moore, Garry
MacDonald, J. Fred
Shokus Video

Moore, Henry
Albright-Knox Art Gallery
Amer. Federation of the Arts
Blackwood Prods., Inc.
Camera Three Prods., Inc.
Schweitzer (Albert) Ctr.

Moore, Marianne
Intellimation

Moore, Mary Tyler
Daphne Productions, Inc.
MacDonald, J. Fred
Shokus Video
UCLA Film & Television Archive
Wisconsin Ctr. for Film & Theater Res.

Moore, Roger
Daphne Productions, Inc.

Moore, Stefan
Port Washington Pub. Lib.

Moorehead, Agnes
Daphne Productions, Inc.

Moose
Amer. Motion Pictures
Di Sesso (Moe) Wild Life Film Lib.
Dreamlight Images, Inc.
Echo Film Prods., Inc.
Energy Productions
Minnesota Zoo
Nine Star Productions
North Country Media Group
Univ. of Alberta, Boreal Inst. for Northern Studies

Mopeds
Handel Film Corp.

Moral Majority
Cambridge Documentary Films, Inc.

Morani, Alma Dea
Medical College of Pa., Arch. & Spec. Coll. Women in Medicine

Moravians
North Carolina Div. of Arch. & Hist.

Moray eels
Petrified Films, Inc.

Morellet, François
Albright-Knox Art Gallery

Morgan, Barbara
Amer. Federation of the Arts
Port Washington Pub. Lib.

Morgan horses
See Horses (Morgan)

Morgan, J.P.
Archive Film Prods., Inc.

Morgenthau, Henry
MacDonald, J. Fred

Morgues
Stock House

Morial, Ernest N. ("Dutch")
New Orleans Pub. Lib., La. Div.

Morisseau, Carole
Amer. Federation of the Arts

Mormons
See Religion (Mormons)

Mornings
Prelinger Assoc., Inc.

Morocco (History and culture)
Archive Film Prods., Inc.
First Run/Icarus Films, Inc.
March of Time
Middle East Institute
Natl. Ctr. for Jewish Film
Oregon Hist. Soc.
Roosevelt (Franklin D.) Lib.
TV Ontario
United Nations Ctr. for Human Settlements

Morris, Robert
Blackwood Prods., Inc.

Morro Castle (Ship)
Analogous Productions
Grinberg (Sherman) Film Libraries (West)

Morse, Wayne
Oregon Hist. Soc.

Morticians and mortuaries
Archive Film Prods., Inc.
Film Bank
Prelinger Assoc., Inc.
See also Funeral industry

Morton, Ree
Blackwood Prods., Inc.
Video Data Bank

Mosaics
Petrified Films, Inc.

NOTE: Access policies, availability and restrictions vary for each source. Please read each entry in full. Always consult "General Film and Videotape Collections" (page 599); these comprehensive collections contain material on every conceivable subject.

Moscone, George
San Francisco Bay Area TV News Arch.

Moscow
Canadian Broadcasting Corp.
Film Bank

Moscow (History and culture)
Analogous Productions
Archive Film Prods., Inc.
Estuary Press
Hoover Institution
Mankind Research Found., Inc.
March of Time
Natl. Archives (RG 342)
Natl. Coun. of Amer.-Sov. Friendship
Pennebaker Associates, Inc.

Moses
Anti-Defamation League of B'nai B'rith

Moses, Bob
Estuary Press

Moses, Grandma
Schweitzer (Albert) Ctr.

Moses, Robert
Bronx County Hist. Soc.
New York Pub. Lib., Rare Books &
    Manuscripts Div.
Prelinger Assoc., Inc.

Mosley, Snub
Rhapsody Films, Inc.

Mosques
British Info. Svcs., Radio & TV Div.
CBS News Archives
Film Bank
Petrified Films, Inc.
TV Ontario

Mosquitoes
Dreamlight Images, Inc.
Finley (Stuart) Inc.
Petrified Films, Inc.
Rockefeller Arch. Ctr.

Moss
TV Ontario

Motels
See Hotels and motels

Mother's Finest (Rock and roll band)
Blackwood (Christian) Prods., Inc.

Mothers
Prelinger Assoc., Inc.
U.S. Committee for UNICEF
UNICEF, Div. Info. & Pub. Aff.

Motherwell, Robert
Albright-Knox Art Gallery
Blackwood Prods., Inc.

Motion graphics
Lib. of Special Visual Effects

Motion picture music
See Music (Motion picture)

Motion picture theaters
See Theaters (Motion picture)

Motion picture trailers
See Trailers (Motion picture)

Motion pictures
See entries listed below; Black cinema;
    Experimental films and videotapes;
    Feature films and videotapes;
    Independent films and videotapes;
    Musical films and videotapes

Motion pictures (Early) (Pre-1915)
Academy Film Archive
Allen (John E.) Inc.
Amer. Federation of the Arts
Archive Film Prods., Inc.
Archivo Fotografico y Cinematografico
    Abítia
Archivo Historico Cinematografico
Dettlaff, Alois F. Sr.
Edison Natl. Historic Site
Em Gee Film Library
Film Bank
Filmoteca de la UNAM
Forsher (James) Prods. & Archives, Inc.
Gould (Bert)/bay area archive
Intl. Mus. of Photography
Lib. of Congress, M/B/RS
Morcraft Films
Mus. of Mod. Art, Circulating Film Lib.
Mus. of Mod. Art, Dept. of Film
Natl. Archives (RG 21)
Natl. Archives (RG 200)
Natl. Archives of Canada
Natl. Archives/Natl. AV Ctr.
Natl. Ctr. for Film & Video Preservation
Pacific Film Archive
Parker (Kit) Films
Prelinger Assoc., Inc.
Streamline Film Archives
UCLA Film & Television Archive
Wisconsin Ctr. for Film & Theater Res.

Motion pictures (Equipment)
Film Bank
Petrified Films, Inc.

**Motion pictures (Equipment) (Test
films)**
Soc. of Motion Picture & TV Engineers

**Motion pictures (Film) (Nitrate burn
tests)**
Natl. Archives (RG 64)

Motion pictures (History of)
Academy Film Archive
Allen (John E.) Inc.
Archive Film Prods., Inc.
Budget Films Inc.
Dettlaff, Alois F. Sr.
Films Incorporated
First Run/Icarus Films, Inc.
Gould (Bert)/bay area archive
Imageways, Inc.
Intl. Mus. of Photography
Killiam Shows, Inc.
Lib. of Congress, M/B/RS
March of Time
Mus. of Mod. Art, Circulating Film Lib.
Mus. of Mod. Art, Dept. of Film
Natl. Archives/Natl. AV Ctr.
Natl. Ctr. for Film & Video Preservation
UCLA Film & Television Archive
Wisconsin Ctr. for Film & Theater Res.

Motion pictures (History of) (Mexico)
Latina, S.A. de C.V.
TV-UNAM

Motion pictures (India, production)
Petrified Films, Inc.

Motion pictures (Industry)
Academy Film Archive
Broad Street Prods.
Cinema Guild
March of Time
Natl. Archives (RG 200)
Prelinger Assoc., Inc.
Southern Calif. Lib. for Soc. Stud. & Res.
Streamline Film Archives
Timesteps Prods., Inc.
See also Celebrities; Entertainment
    industry; Hollywood

Motion pictures (Paper prints)
Filmoteca de la UNAM
Lib. of Congress, M/B/RS
UCLA Film & Television Archive

Motion pictures (Premieres)
Analogous Productions
Archive Film Prods., Inc.
Atlanta Hist. Soc.
Banks Film Library
Forsher (James) Prods. & Arch. Inc.
Grinberg (Sherman) Film Libraries (East)
Petrified Films, Inc.
Prelinger Assoc., Inc.
Spectral Comms.
Twentieth Century-Fox Movietonews
UCLA Film & Television Archive

Motion pictures (Production)
AIMS Media
Allen (John E.) Inc.
Blackwood (Christian) Prods., Inc.
Broad Street Prods.
Film Bank
Gray City Inc.
Intl. Film Bureau, Inc.
Natl. Archives (RG 33)
Natl. Archives of Canada
Petrified Films, Inc.
Pyramid Film and Video Corp.
Video Resources N.Y., Inc.

Motion pictures (Projectors)
Film Bank
Petrified Films, Inc.
Prelinger Assoc., Inc.
Rosebush Visions Corp.

Motion pictures (Restoration)
Natl. Archives of Canada

Motion pictures (Studios)
Dreamlight Images, Inc.
Petrified Films, Inc.
Spalla (Rick) Video Prods.
See also **Hollywood**

Motion pictures (Stunts)
Petrified Films, Inc.
See also Stunts

Motion pictures (Technique)
Pyramid Film and Video Corp.

Motion pictures (Trailers)
See Trailers (Motion picture)

Motivational research
MacDonald, J. Fred

Motocross racing
Analogous Productions
Diamond P. Sports
Film Bank
Nemiroff Prods., Inc.
Video Tape Library, Ltd.

Motorcades
CBS News Archives

Motorcycles and motorcycling
Archive Film Prods., Inc.
CBS News Archives
Diamond P. Sports
Intl. Women's Day Video Fest.
Merkel Films
Petrified Films, Inc.
Prelinger Assoc., Inc.
Pyramid Film and Video Corp.
Twentieth Century-Fox Movietonews

**Motorcycles and motorcycling (Dirt
racing)**
Petrified Films, Inc.

Motorcycles and motorcycling (Racing)
Analogous Productions
Rainbow Video Prods.
Spalla (Rick) Video Prods.
Sportsfilm

Motorcycles and motorcycling (Stunts)
Forsher (James) Prods. & Archives, Inc.
Petrified Films, Inc.
See also Stunts

Mount Desert Island, Maine
Dobbs (Jeff) Prods.

**Mount Palomar Observatory (Calif.)
    (History and culture)**
Petrified Films, Inc.

**Mount Rainier National Park, Wash.
    (History and culture)**
Natl. Archives (RG 28)
U.S. Natl. Park Service Hist. Coll.

Mountain biking
Moving Media

Mountain climbing
Amer. Alpine Club
Aspen Historical Society
Jewell (Stuart) Productions
Nine Star Productions
Oregon Hist. Soc.
Petrified Films, Inc.
Phoenix Films and Video
Pyramid Film and Video Corp.
Summit Films, Inc.
Twentieth Century-Fox Movietonews
Yukon Archives

Mountain lions
Petrified Films, Inc.

Mountains
Alaska Video Prods.
Amer. Motion Pictures
Aspen Historical Society
CBS News Archives
Cimarron Productions
Cinenet (Cinema Network)
Creative Video, Inc.
Crystal Pyramid Prods.
Dobovan Productions, Inc.
Dreamlight Images, Inc.
Echo Film Prods., Inc.
Energy Productions
Film Bank
Film Search
Forsher (James) Prods. & Archives, Inc.
Hot Shots Commercial Prods., Inc.
Jewell (Stuart) Productions
Marts (Steve) Productions
Moving Media
Network Productions
Odyssey Prods., Inc.
Omega Films
Peak Productions, Inc.
Petrified Films, Inc.
Prelinger Assoc., Inc.
Preview Media
Prov. Arch. of British Columbia
Quenzer Driscoll Dawson, Inc.
Second Line Search
Source Stock Footage Lib., Inc.
Spectral Comms.
Summit Films, Inc.
TV Ontario
TV-3
Telemation Productions
Twentieth Century-Fox Movietonews
Video Tape Library, Ltd.
Video West
Yukon Archives
See also specific mountains (e.g., Mount
    Rainer is found under Rainier, Mount
    [Wash.]).

Mounties
See Royal Canadian Mounted Police
(RCMP)

Movies
See Motion pictures

Moving sidewalks
See Sidewalks (Moving)

Moyers, Bill
Perlmutter (Alvin H.) Inc.

Mozambique
World Monitor

Mozambique (Contemporary issues)
DEC Film & Video
First Run/Icarus Films, Inc.
UNICEF, Div. Info. & Pub. Aff.

Mozambique (History and culture)
California Newsreel
Singer-Sharrette Traditional Healing Films
World Monitor

Mroczynski, Claus
Port Washington Pub. Lib.

Mud
Twentieth Century-Fox Movietonews

Mud baths
Video Tape Library, Ltd.

Mud fights
Analogous Productions

Mud houses
TV Ontario

Mueller, Cookie
Monday, Wednesday, Friday Video Club

Mueller, Peter
U.S. Olympic Committee

Muezzin
Petrified Films, Inc.

Mug shots
TV Ontario

Muggeridge, Malcolm
Baker (Fred) Film & Video Co.
Smith (Margaret Chase) Lib. Ctr.

Muggings
Prelinger Assoc., Inc.

Muhammad, Wallace
Schomburg Ctr. for Res. in Black Culture

Muir, John
Washington State Hist. Soc.

Muir Woods, Calif.
Elfstrom-Hilmer Prods.

Mules
Petrified Films, Inc.

Mulligan, Gerry
Archive Film Prods., Inc.

Mulroney, Brian
Film/Audio Services, Inc.
Northstar Prods.

Multi-image presentations
Assn. for Multi-Image Intl., Inc.

Multicultural music
See Music (Multicultural)

Multinational corporations
Appalshop Films, Inc.
CARE
California Newsreel
Cinema Guild
Labor Inst. of Public Affairs
Richter Productions

Multnomah Falls, Oreg.
Petrified Films, Inc.

Mumford, Lewis
Film/Audio Services, Inc.
Unicorn Projects

Mummies
Unicorn Projects

Muncie, Ind. (History and culture)
Ball State Univ., Middletown Coll.
Petrified Films, Inc.

Muni, Paul
Cantor (Arthur) Inc.

Munich, Germany (History and culture)
Analogous Productions
Petrified Films, Inc.

Muñoz Marin, Luis
Filmoteca Luis Muñoz Marin

Muntadas, Antonio
Long Beach Mus. of Art
Video Data Bank

Muntjacs
Minnesota Zoo

Murals
Film Bank
Kartemquin Films

Murder and murderers
Archive Film Prods., Inc.
El Paso Community College
Quest Prods., Inc.
Twentieth Century-Fox Movietonews
See also Crime and criminals

Murmansk, U.S.S.R. (Contemporary issues)
Ocean Earth Constr. and Dev. Corp.

Murphy, Eddie
Daphne Productions, Inc.
Spectral Comms.

Murphy, Frank
Univ. of Mich., Mich. Hist. Colls.

Murphy, Gardner
Inst. for Psychoanalysis

Murphy, George
Banks Film Library

Murphy, Sylvia
Natl. Archives of Canada

Murray, Albert
Agee (James) Film Project

Murray, Elizabeth
Blackwood Prods., Inc.
Video Data Bank

Murray, Henry
Inst. for Psychoanalysis

Murray, Pauli
Radcliffe Coll., Schlesinger Lib.

Murray, Sunny
Rhapsody Films, Inc.

Murrow, Edward R.
MacDonald, J. Fred

Muscat, Oman (History and culture)
Acad. of Nat. Sci. of Phila. Lib.

Muscle Beach contests
Petrified Films, Inc.

Muscles
Prelinger Assoc., Inc.

Muscular dystrophy
Houston (Sam) Regional Library

Museology
Amer. Assn. for State & Local Hist.
Amer. Mus. Nat. Hist. Film Arch.
Natl. Archives (RG 106)

Museums
Amer. Assn. for State & Local Hist.
CBS News Archives
De Saisset Museum
Dreamlight Images, Inc.
Energy Productions
Film Bank
Grapevine Prods., Ltd.
Hammer (Armand) Prods.
Hayes Prods., Inc.
Hi-Tech Productions
High Mus. of Art
Intl. Film Foundation
Mus. at Large, Ltd.
Petrified Films, Inc.
Postcards Associates
Smithsonian Inst., Hirshhorn Mus. Lib.
Soc. for French Amer. Cult. Svcs. & Educ.
Aid
Source Stock Footage Lib., Inc.
Spectral Comms.
TV Ontario
Twentieth Century-Fox Movietonews
Video Tape Library, Ltd.
Voyager Co.

Museums (Germany)
Goethe Institute Atlanta

Mushrooms
Dreamlight Images, Inc.
Energy Productions
Film Bank

Music
AIMS Media
ARC Videodance Coll./Eye on Dance
Coll.
Anoka County Comm. Workshop, Inc.
Archive Film Prods., Inc.
Barr Films
Bullfrog Films, Inc.
CBS News Archives
Canyon Cinema, Inc.
Carousel Film & Video
Churchill Films
Coe Film Assoc., Inc.
Coronet/MTI Film & Video
Dance Theater Workshop
Electronic Arts Intermix
Facets Multimedia, Inc.
Film Bank
Film/Audio Services, Inc.

Films Incorporated
Films for the Humanities and Sciences
Flower Films & Video
GPN
Giorno Poetry Systems Inst.
House Found. for the Arts
Intermedia Arts Minnesota
Intl. Film Bureau, Inc.
Latin Amer. Video Arch.
Media Guild
Metro Communications, Inc.
Milwaukee Access Telecomm. Auth.
Morris Video
92nd Street YM & YWHA Assn. Archives
Natl. Film Board of Canada
Ohio State Univ., Dept. of Photog. &
Cinema
Peralta Colleges TV
Petrified Films, Inc.
Picture Start, Inc.
TV Ontario
Tamarelle's Intl. Films, Ltd.
Twentieth Century-Fox Movietonews
Univ. of Calif., Ext. Media Ctr.
Univ. of Mich., Mich. Hist. Colls.
Univ. of Wash. Press, Multimedia Div.
V/tape
Video In
Video-SIG
White Janssen, Inc.
See also Concerts; Musical instruments;
Musicians; Orchestras; specific musical
groups, instruments and musicians

Music (Afghan)
Wesleyan Univ., World Music Arch.

Music (African)
East-West Center
Petrified Films, Inc.

Music (Afro-Asian)
Asian American Resource Workshop

Music (Afro-Brazilian)
Democracy in Communication

Music (Afro-Caribbean)
Wesleyan Univ., World Music Arch.

Music (Andean)
Université Laval, Svc. des Res.
Pédagogiques

Music (Appalachian)
Appalachian State Univ., Eury Coll.
Appalshop Films, Inc.
East Tenn. State Univ., Arch. of
Appalachia

Music (Asian)
Blackwood Prods., Inc.

Music (Asian American)
Asian American Resource Workshop

Music (Austrian)
Northstar Prods.

Music (Avant-garde)
Kitchen, The
Western Front Society

Music (Balinese)
Petrified Films, Inc.

Music (Barbershop)
Northern Ill. Univ., Reg. Hist. Ctr.

Music (Bebop)
Forsher (James) Prods. & Archives, Inc.

NOTE: Access policies, availability and restrictions vary for each source. Please read each entry in full. Always consult "General Film and Videotape Collections" (page 599); these comprehensive collections contain material on every conceivable subject.

Rhapsody Films, Inc.

Music (Big band)
Archive Film Prods., Inc.
Chertok Associates Inc.
DeFlores, Bob
Em Gee Film Library
Pathé Pictures, Inc.
Petrified Films, Inc.

Music (Black)
Applegate Entertainment
Chertok Associates Inc.
Cinema Guild
Clark (Dick) Media Archives, Inc.
Los Angeles Blues Archives
Pathé Pictures, Inc.
Picture Start, Inc.
Rhapsody Films, Inc.
Schomburg Ctr. for Res. in Black Culture
Southern Calif. Blues Soc.
Univ. of Alabama, W.S. Hoole Spec. Coll.
Univ. of Miss., Blues Arch.
Univ. of Miss., Ctr. for Study of Southern
  Culture
Western Kentucky Univ., Folklife Arch.

Music (Bluegrass)
Appalachian State Univ., Eury Coll.
Cable Access of Dallas
Charisma Prods., Ltd./Visual Motion
Indiana State Lib.
Peak Productions, Inc.
Siouxland Heritage Museum
Summit Films, Inc.

Music (Blues)
Archive Film Prods., Inc.
Center for Southern Folklore
Chertok Associates Inc.
Chicago Pub. Lib., Visual & Perf. Arts
Cinema Guild
Flower Films & Video
Forsher (James) Prods. & Archives, Inc.
Los Angeles Blues Archives
March of Time
Rhapsody Films, Inc.
Southern Calif. Blues Soc.
Univ. of Miss., Blues Arch.

Music (Brass bands)
Petrified Films, Inc.

Music (Burlesque)
New York Pub. Lib., Perf. Arts Res. Ctr.,
  Theatre on Film and Tape

Music (Cajun)
Flower Films & Video

Music (Calypso)
Petrified Films, Inc.

Music (Canadian)
Natl. Archives of Canada

Music (Caribbean)
Mus. of Mod. Art of Latin America

Music (Chinese)
Asian American Resource Workshop

Music (Choral)
Milwaukee Access Telecomm. Auth.
Natl. Archives (RG 59)
New Jersey Network

Music (Classical)
Metropolitan Opera House
Natl. Archives of Canada
Natl. Lib. of Canada, Music Div.
Prelinger Assoc., Inc.
Research Video
Schweitzer (Albert) Ctr.
Sullivan Video Services

Vedo Films/Novacom Video
WGBH Educational Foundation
Wesleyan Cinema Archives

Music (Country and western)
Archive Film Prods., Inc.
Clark (Dick) Media Archives, Inc.
Country Music Foundation, Inc.
Encore Video Prods., Inc.
Natl. Archives of Canada
Northern Ill. Univ., Reg. Hist. Ctr.
Pathé Pictures, Inc.
Petrified Films, Inc.
Reeves (Jim) Museum
Southwest Film/Video Archives, SMU
Univ. of Tex. at Austin, Barker Tex. Hist.
  Ctr.

Music (Creole)
Flower Films & Video

Music (Cuban)
Center for Cuban Studies
New Jersey Network
Univ. of Miami, Arch. & Spec. Coll.

Music (Dixieland jazz)
Northern Ill. Univ., Reg. Hist. Ctr.

Music (Electronic)
Pyramid Film and Video Corp.

Music (Eskimo)
Alaska Native Heritage Film Project

Music (Experimental)
Experimental Intermedia Foundation
Target Video

Music (Finnish)
Natl. Archives of Canada

Music (Folk)
Archive Film Prods., Inc.
Charisma Prods., Ltd./Visual Motion
Lawren Prods., Inc.
Natl. Archives of Canada
Pathé Pictures, Inc.
Research Video
Vedo Films/Novacom Video
Wayne State Univ., Folklore Arch.
West Virginia Univ.

Music (French)
Soc. for French Amer. Cult. Svcs. & Educ.
  Aid

Music (German)
Goethe Institute Atlanta
Goethe Institute San Francisco
Natl. Archives of Canada

Music (Gospel)
Applegate Entertainment
Center for Southern Folklore
Davenport Films
Univ. of Miss., Blues Arch.
Western Kentucky Univ., Folklife Arch.

Music (Hawaiian)
Hawaii Public Broadcasting Authority

Music (Indian)
Films of India
Wesleyan Univ., World Music Arch.

Music (Indonesian)
Petrified Films, Inc.

Music (Inuit)
Natl. Archives of Canada

Music (Japanese)
Petrified Films, Inc.
TV Ontario

Music (Javanese)
Wesleyan Univ., World Music Arch.

Music (Jazz)
Archive Film Prods., Inc.
Baker (Fred) Film & Video Co.
Center for Southern Folklore
Chertok Associates Inc.
DeFlores, Bob
Direct Cinema Ltd.
Flower Films & Video
Footage Inc.
Forsher (James) Prods. & Archives, Inc.
Icarus Films Intl., Inc.
Island Records, Inc.
Kansas City Film Archive
Lib. of Congress, M/B/RS
Natl. Archives of Canada
New Jersey Network
New Orleans Video Access Ctr.
Pathé Pictures, Inc.
Peak Productions, Inc.
Petrified Films, Inc.
Phoenix Films and Video
Research Video
Rhapsody Films, Inc.
Rutgers Univ., Inst. of Jazz Studies
Schomburg Ctr. for Res. in Black Culture
Soc. for French Amer. Cult. Svcs. & Educ.
  Aid
South Carolina Humanities Res. Ctr.
Spectral Comms.
Third World Newsreel
Tucson Community Cable Corp.
Tulane Univ., Amistad Res. Ctr.
Tulane Univ., Hogan Jazz Archive

Music (Klezmer)
Ethnic Folk Arts Center
First Run/Icarus Films, Inc.

Music (Latin)
Petrified Films, Inc.

Music (Latvian)
Natl. Archives of Canada

Music (Mexican)
Canal 11
Imagen y Sonido Independiente, S.A.
Imevision
Petrified Films, Inc.
TV-UNAM

Music (Mexican American)
Univ. of Tex. at Austin, Benson Lat. Am.
  Coll.

Music (Motion picture)
Blackwood (Christian) Prods., Inc.

Music (Multicultural)
Archive of Contemp. Music
Univ. of Wash. Press, Multimedia Div.
Wesleyan Univ., World Music Arch.

Music (Native American)
Manitoba Indian Cultural Centre
Native Amer. Pub. Broad. Cons.
Natl. Archives of Canada
Wesleyan Univ., World Music Arch.

Music (New Age)
Cable Access of Dallas
Valley of the Sun Publishing
Wishing Well Distribution

Music (New Orleans)
Center for New Amer. Media
Flower Films & Video
Tulane Univ., Hogan Jazz Archive

Music (New wave)
Target Video

Music (Nicaraguan)
Lesage, Julia

Music (Oceania)
Lib. of Congress, Amer. Folklife Ctr.

Music (Polka)
Pathé Pictures, Inc.

Music (Popular)
Arch. of Contemp. Music
Arizona State Univ., Wayne King Coll.
Benamou, Catherine/LAWAS
Chertok Associates Inc.
Clark (Dick) Media Archives, Inc.
Island Records, Inc.
Karnbach, James
Natl. Archives of Canada
Pathé Pictures, Inc.
Research Video

Music (Puerto Rican)
Third World Newsreel

Music (Punk)
Canadian Filmmakers Dist. Centre
Target Video
Worldwide Television News

Music (Reggae)
Camera Three Prods., Inc.
Intl. Women's Day Video Fest.
R5/S8 Presents

Music (Rhythm and blues)
Chertok Associates Inc.
Clark (Dick) Media Archives, Inc.
Island Records, Inc.
Pathé Pictures, Inc.
Phoenix Films and Video
Univ. of Miss., Blues Arch.

Music (Rock and roll)
Archive Film Prods., Inc.
Archive of Contemp. Music
Atavistic Video
Banks Film Library
Belka Intl. Inc.
Blackwood (Christian) Prods., Inc.
Cable Access of Dallas
Chertok Associates Inc.
Cinema Guild
Clark (Dick) Media Archives, Inc.
Em Gee Film Library
Encore Video Prods., Inc.
Fish Films, Inc.
Forsher (James) Prods. & Archives, Inc.
Impact Audio Visual
Island Records, Inc.
Karnbach, James
Law (Lisa) Prods.
Los Angeles Blues Archives
MTV Networks
Monday, Wednesday, Friday Video Club
Movietime, Inc. Archives
Natl. Archives of Canada
Pennebaker Associates, Inc.
Petrified Films, Inc.
Research Video
Soc. for French Amer. Cult. Svcs. & Educ.
  Aid
Spalla (Rick) Video Prods.
Spectral Comms.
Sullivan Video Services
Target Video
Tucson Community Cable Corp.

Music (Scottish)
Univ. Coll. of Cape Breton, Beaton Inst.

Music (Serbo)
Ethnic Folk Arts Center

Music (Soul)
Clark (Dick) Media Archives, Inc.

704

UPA Prods. of America

Music (Southeast Asia)
Lib. of Congress, Amer. Folklife Ctr.

Music (Soviet Union)
Belka Intl. Inc.
Natl. Archives (RG 242)

Music (Swing)
Archive Film Prods., Inc.
Forsher (James) Prods. & Archives, Inc.
March of Time
Rhapsody Films, Inc.

Music (Tex-Mex)
Flower Films & Video

Music (Texan)
Univ. of Tex. at Austin, Barker Tex. Hist.
Ctr.

Music (Tibetan)
Petrified Films, Inc.

Music (Traditional)
Appalachian State Univ., Eury Coll.
Appalshop Films, Inc.
Cinema Guild
Ethnic Folk Arts Center
Indiana Univ. Folklore Arch.
Native Amer. Pub. Broad. Cons.
Ozark Folk Center
TV Ontario
Wesleyan Univ., World Music Arch.
Western Kentucky Univ., Folklife Arch.
Yakima Television Program

Music (Ukrainian)
Natl. Archives of Canada

Music (Work chants)
Univ. of Miss., Ctr. for Study of Southern
Culture

Music (Zydeco)
Flower Films & Video
Tulane Univ., Amistad Res. Ctr.

Music festivals
Law (Lisa) Prods.
New Film Co., Inc.
Peak Productions, Inc.
Siouxland Heritage Museum
TV Ontario

Music festivals (Bluegrass)
East Tenn. State Univ., Arch. of
Appalachia

Music festivals (Monterey Pop, 1967)
Pennebaker Associates, Inc.

Music festivals (Woodstock, 1969)
Law (Lisa) Prods.
MacDonald, J. Fred
New Film Co., Inc.
Raindance Foundation

Music videos
Archive of Contemp. Music
Atavistic Video
Clark (Dick) Media Archives, Inc.
Democracy in Communication
Film Bank
Groupe Intervention Video
Image Film & Video Coll.
Instant Replay, Inc.
Intl. Fashion Video Library
Island Records, Inc.
Monday, Wednesday, Friday Video Club

Picture Start, Inc.
Streamline Film Archives
Target Video
Titan Sports, Inc.
Trent Institute for Popular Culture

Musical films and videotapes
Budget Films Inc.
Country Music Foundation, Inc.
DeFlores, Bob
Em Gee Film Library
Facets Multimedia, Inc.
Footage Inc.
Lib. of Congress, M/B/RS
MacDonald, J. Fred
Morcraft Films
Prelinger Assoc., Inc.
Streamline Film Archives
Video Yesteryear

Musical instruments
Film Bank
Petrified Films, Inc.
Twentieth Century-Fox Movietonews
See also Music; specific instruments

Musical instruments (Early)
Films for the Humanities & Sciences

Musical instruments (Manufacturing)
Japan External Trade Organization

Musical notes
Charisma Prods., Ltd./Visual Motion

Musical theater
See Theater (Musical)

Musicians
Archive Film Prods., Inc.
Film Bank
Fish Films, Inc.
MTV Networks
Petrified Films, Inc.
Research Video
See also Music; specific musicians and
musical groups

Musk oxen
Minnesota Zoo
Nine Star Productions
TV Ontario

Muskoka, Ontario (History and culture)
Archives of Ontario

Muslims
See Religion (Islam)

Mussolini, Benito
Archive Film Prods., Inc.
Forsher (James) Prods. & Archives, Inc.
Intl. Historic Films, Inc.
Petrified Films, Inc.
Timesteps Prods., Inc.

Muybridge, Eadweard
Blackwood Prods., Inc.

Muzzle flashes
Film Bank

My Lai massacre
Richter Productions

Myers, Joan
Port Washington Pub. Lib.

Myers, William I.
Natl. Archives (RG 103)

Myerson, Bess
Payne, Roz

Mylar
Prelinger Assoc., Inc.

Myna birds
Cinenet (Cinema Network)

Myrtle Beach, S.C.
Creative Video, Inc.

Mysticism
Hartley Film Found., Inc.

Mythology
Akwesasne Library Cultural Ctr.
Center for Humanities, Inc.
Films for the Humanities and Sciences
Hartley Film Found., Inc.
Jung (C.G.) Foundation
Postcards Associates

NABET
See National Association of Broadcast &
Electronic Technicians (NABET)

NASA
See National Aeronautics and Space
Administration (NASA)

NATO
See North Atlantic Treaty Organization
(NATO)

NORAD
See North American Air Defense
Command (NORAD)

NOW
See National Organization for Women
(NOW)

NRA
See National Recovery Administration
(NRA)

N!ai people
Documentary Educ. Resources

Nabor, John
U.S. Olympic Committee

Nader, Ralph
MacDonald, J. Fred
Natl. Archives (RG 217)
Worldwide Television News

Nagasaki, Japan (History and culture)
Alternative Information Network
Archive Film Prods., Inc.
Council for a Livable World Educ. Fund
First Run/Icarus Films, Inc.
Hoover Institution
Natl. Archives (RG 18)
Natl. Archives (RG 342)
Petrified Films, Inc.
U.S. Defense Nuclear Agency
Wilmington Coll. Peace Res. Ctr.

Nagin, Lake (Kashmir, India)
Petrified Films, Inc.

Nairobi, Kenya
Summit Films, Inc.

Nairobi, Kenya (History and culture)
U.S. Committee for UNICEF

Najibullah, Mohammed
Film/Audio Services, Inc.

Namath, Joe
Archive Film Prods., Inc.
NFL Films, Inc.

Namibia (Contemporary issues)
Canadian Filmmakers Dist. Centre
Third World Newsreel

Namibia (History and culture)
California Newsreel
Documentary Educational Resources
Idera Films
Smithsonian Inst., Human Studies Film
Arch.

Nanking, China (History and culture)
Natl. Archives (RG 200)

Nannies
Petrified Films, Inc.

Nantucket Island, Mass.
Site Productions

**Nantucket Island, Mass.(History and
culture)**
Nantucket Hist. Assn.

Napa County, Calif.
Preview Media

Napa Valley, Calif.
Elfstrom-Hilmer Prods.
Tri-Comm Prods.

Napali Coast, Hawaii
TV-3

Napalm
Petrified Films, Inc.

Naples, Fla.
Preview Media

Naples, Italy (History and culture)
Archive Film Prods., Inc.
Prelinger Assoc., Inc.

Napoleon
Archive Film Prods., Inc.

Narcotics
Ludlow (Fitz Hugh) Memorial Library
March of Time
Nassau Comm. Coll. Lib.
Natl. Archives (RG 170)
See also Drug abuse; Drug culture;
Substance abuse; specific drugs

**Narcotics and Dangerous Drugs, Bureau
of (U.S.)**
Natl. Archives (RG 170)

Narita, Katsuhiku
Blackwood Prods., Inc.

Nash, David
Amer. Federation of the Arts

Nash, Paul
Amer. Federation of the Arts

Nash, Roderick
Film/Audio Services, Inc.
Florentine Films

Nashville, Tenn.
Departures, Inc.
Dreamlight Images, Inc.
Energy Productions
Omega Films

NOTE: Access policies, availability and restrictions vary for each source. Please read each entry in full. Always consult "General Film and Videotape Collections" (page 599); these comprehensive collections contain material on every conceivable subject.

Preview Media
Producers' Service

Nashville, Tenn. (History and culture)
Country Music Foundation, Inc.

Nassau, Bahamas
Kesser Stock Footage Library

Nassau County, N.Y. (History and culture)
Nassau County Museum

Nasser, Gamal Abdel
Smith (Margaret Chase) Lib. Ctr.

Nastase, Ilie
U.S. Tennis Assn.

Natchez, Miss. (History and culture)
Mississippi Dept. of Arch. & Hist.

Nathanson, Bernard
Moody Inst. of Science

National Aeronautics and Space Administration (NASA)
NASA, Ames Res. Ctr., Dryden Fac.
NASA, Ames Res. Ctr., Human Factors Res. Ctr.
NASA, Ames Res. Ctr., Imaging Tech. Branch
NASA, Ames Res. Ctr., Regional Film Lib.
NASA, Goddard Space Ctr.
NASA, Johnson Space Ctr., Film & Video Dist. Lib.
NASA, Johnson Space Ctr., Stock Film Lib.
NASA, Langley Research Ctr.
NASA, Lewis Research Center
NASA, Marshall Space Flight Ctr.
NASA, Office of Comm.
Natl. Archives (RG 255)
Natl. Archives (Stock Film Coll.)
See also Space Program (U.S.)

National Archives and Records Service (U.S.)
Natl. Archives (RG 64)

National Archives Council (U.S.)
Natl. Archives (RG 64)

National Association of Broadcast & Electronic Technicians (NABET)
Committee for Labor Access

National Commission
See the commission's "subject" area (e.g., National Commission on Air Quality is found under Air Quality, National Commission on)

National Democratic Front (Mexico)
Redes Cinevideo, S.A.

National forests (U.S.)
Natl. Archives (RG 33)

National Foundation on the Arts and Humanities (U.S.)
Natl. Archives (RG 288)

National Gallery of Canada
Natl. Archives of Canada

National Guard (U.S.)
Archive Film Prods., Inc.
Committee for Labor Access
Ohio Historical Soc.

National Organization for Women (NOW)
Natl. Organization for Women

Radcliffe Coll., Schlesinger Lib.
Spectral Comms.

National parks (Canada)
Bennett (Joel) Prods.
Independent Media Communications
Prov. Arch. of Alberta
Prov. Arch. of British Columbia
Yukon Archives

National parks (U.S.)
Allen (John E.) Inc.
Appalachian State Univ., Eury Coll.
Beerger (Norman) Prods.
Bennett (Joel) Prods.
Buffalo Bill Historical Center
Colorado Historical Society
Dobbs (Jeff) Prods.
Dreamlight Images, Inc.
Eastern Washington State Historical Soc.
Echo Film Prods., Inc.
Energy Productions
Film Bank
Florentine Films
Jewell (Stuart) Productions
MacGillivray Freeman Films
Mountain Video Associates
Natl. Archives (RG 28)
Natl. Archives (RG 33)
Natl. Archives (RG 48)
Natl. Archives (RG 70)
Natl. Archives (RG 79)
Natl. Archives (RG 200)
Natl. Parks & Conservation Assn.
Oregon Hist. Soc.
Petrified Films, Inc.
Preview Media
Schiele Museum
Snyder (Bill) Films, Inc.
Sonoma Video Productions
Stimulus
U.S. Natl. Park Service Hist. Coll.
Utah State Hist. Soc.
Utah Travel Council
White Janssen, Inc.
See also Parks; specific parks

National Recovery Administration (NRA)
MacDonald, J. Fred
March of Time
Natl. Archives (RG 9)

National security (U.S.)
Amer. Security Council Foundation
Center for Defense Information
Inst. for Space & Security Studies

Native Americans
Akwesasne Library Cultural Ctr.
Amer. Motion Pictures
Anthropology Film Center Foundation
Anti-Defamation League of B'nai B'rith
Appalachian State Univ., Eury Coll.
Archive Film Prods., Inc.
Atlantis Prods., Inc.
Buffalo Bill Historical Center
Bullfrog Films, Inc.
Cherokee Nation Hist. Soc., Inc.
Cinema Guild
Colorado Historical Society
Coronet/MTI Film & Video
DEC Film & Video
Democracy in Communication
Denver Pub. Lib., Western Hist. Dept.
Downtown Community TV Ctr.
Dreamlight Images, Inc.
Eastern Washington State Historical Soc.
Echo Film Prods., Inc.
Energy Productions
Film Bank
Film/Audio Services, Inc.
Filmfair Communications
Films for the Humanities and Sciences
Fish Films, Inc.

Freewheelin' Films, Ltd.
Fulton County Hist. Soc., Inc.
GPN
Glenbow Mus. Arch.
Handel Film Corp.
Intermedia Arts Minnesota
Ketchikan (City of)
Latin Amer. Video Arch.
Lib. of Congress, Amer. Folklife Ctr.
Manitoba Indian Cultural Centre
Mariners' Museum
Minnesota Hist. Soc.
Montana Dept. of Commerce
Mus. & Hist. Div., City of Sacramento
Museum of the American Indian
Native Amer. Pub. Broad. Cons.
Natl. Archives (RG 48)
Natl. Archives (RG 75)
Natl. Archives (RG 200)
Natl. Archives (RG 378)
Natl. Archives (RG 381)
Natl. Archives of Canada
Navajo Nation Library System
Navajo Tribe, Off. Broadcast Svcs.
New Film Co., Inc.
New Jersey Network
New Mexico State Records Ctr. & Arch.
New Time Films, Inc.
North Country Media Group
Oregon Hist. Soc.
Panhandle-Plains Hist. Museum
Prov. Arch. of British Columbia
Prov. Arch. of Manitoba
Pyramid Film and Video Corp.
San Diego State Univ., Spec. Coll.
Saskatchewan Indian Cultural Ctr.
Schiele Museum
Sheffield (Erin) Prods.
Smithsonian Inst., Human Studies Film Arch.
Source Stock Footage Lib., Inc.
South Carolina Humanities Res. Ctr.
Southwest Prods., Inc.
Stimulus
TV Ontario
Twentieth Century-Fox Movietonews
U.S. Natl. Park Service Hist. Coll.
Univ. of Calif., Ext. Media Ctr.
Univ. of Okla., Western Hist. Colls.
Univ. of Southern Calif., Film & Video Dist. Ctr.
Univ. of Utah, Marriott Lib.
Univ. of Wash. Press, Multimedia Div.
Univ. of West Fla., Hum. Res. Vid. Lib.
Univ. of Wis., Green Bay, Ctr. TV Prod.
Villon Films
Washington State Hist. Soc.
Wheelwright Mus. of the Amer. Indian
White Janssen, Inc.
Yakima Indian Nation Cultural Ctr.
Yakima Television Program
See also American Indian Movement

Native Americans (Aleuts)
Alaska Video Prods.

Native Americans (Amazon)
Benamou, Catherine/LAWAS
Petrified Films, Inc.

Native Americans (Anasazi)
Native Amer. Pub. Broad. Cons.

Native Americans (Apache)
Energy Productions

Native Americans (Arizona)
Schiele Museum

Native Americans (Athabaskan)
Native Amer. Pub. Broad. Cons.
New Day Films

Native Americans (Aztec)
Films for the Humanities and Sciences

Native Americans (Blackfoot)
North Country Media Group

Native Americans (Carib)
Cinema Guild

Native Americans (Celilo)
Oregon Hist. Soc.

Native Americans (Cherokee)
Cherokee Nation Hist. Soc., Inc.
Native Amer. Pub. Broad. Cons.
Tennessee State Lib. & Arch.

Native Americans (Cherokee-Choctaw)
East Tenn. State Univ., Arch. of Appalachia

Native Americans (Chinanteco)
Instituto Nacional Indigenista

Native Americans (Chippewa)
Intermedia Arts Minnesota
Smithsonian Inst., Human Studies Film Arch.

Native Americans (Chucalissa)
Tennessee State Lib. & Arch.

Native Americans (Contemporary issues)
Cinema Guild
DEC Film & Video
Manitoba Indian Cultural Centre
Native Amer. Pub. Broad. Cons.

Native Americans (Coushatta)
Native Amer. Pub. Broad. Cons.
Univ. of Tex. at Austin, Barker Tex. Hist. Ctr.

Native Americans (Cree)
Akwesasne Lib. Cultural Ctr.
Manitoba Indian Cultural Centre
Native Amer. Pub. Broad. Cons.

Native Americans (Creek)
Native Amer. Pub. Broad. Cons.

Native Americans (Crow)
Eastern Washington State Historical Soc.
Native Amer. Pub. Broadcasting Cons.
Natl. Archives (RG 75)
North Country Media Group
Smithsonian Inst., Human Studies Film Arch.
Villon Films

Native Americans (Dene)
Canadian Filmmakers Dist. Centre

Native Americans (Dineh)
Native Amer. Pub. Broad. Cons.

Native Americans (Eskimo)
Alaska Native Heritage Film Project
Alaska Video Prods.
Archive Film Prods., Inc.
Bradley/McAfee Public Relations
Glenbow Mus. Arch.
KYUK-TV
Ketchikan (City of)
Natl. Archives (RG 75)
Northwest Territories Archives
Oregon Hist. Soc.
Petrified Films, Inc.
Prelinger Assoc., Inc.
Saskatchewan Indian Cultural Ctr.
Smithsonian Inst., Human Studies Film Arch.
Univ. of Alaska, Fairbanks, Alaska Motion Picture Arch.
Univ. of Alaska, Fairbanks, Alaska Native Language Ctr.

Univ. of Alberta, Boreal Inst. for Northern Studies

Native Americans (Great Plains)
Natl. Archives (RG 106)

Native Americans (Hopi)
Energy Productions
Native Amer. Pub. Broad. Cons.
Natl. Archives (RG 75)
Natl. Archives (RG 200)
New Day Films
Petrified Films, Inc.
Smithsonian Inst., Human Studies Film Arch.

Native Americans (Huasteco)
Instituto Nacional Indigenista

Native Americans (Huichol)
Instituto Nacional Indigenista
Smithsonian Inst., Human Studies Film Arch.

Native Americans (Hupa)
Smithsonian Inst., Human Studies Film Arch.

Native Americans (Incas)
Univ. of Arizona, Film Coll.
Natl. Archives (RG 229)

Native Americans (Inuit)
Alaska Video Prods.
Canadian Filmmakers Dist. Centre
Inuit Broadcasting Corp.
Natl. Archives of Canada
Northwest Territories Archives
Peary-MacMillan Arctic Museum
TV Ontario

Native Americans (Iroquois)
Akwesasne Library Cultural Ctr.
Natl. Archives (RG 75)

Native Americans (Kamaiuras)
Brazilian-American Cultural Inst.

Native Americans (Karuk)
Smithsonian Inst., Human Studies Film Arch.

Native Americans (Kikapú)
Instituto Nacional Indigenista

Native Americans (Kwakiutl)
Canadian Filmmakers Dist. West
Univ. of Wash. Press, Multimedia Div.

Native Americans (Lacandón)
Instituto Nacional Indigenista

Native Americans (Lakota Sioux)
Solaris Dance/Theatre/Video

Native Americans (Manitoba)
Manitoba Indian Cultural Centre

Native Americans (Mayans)
Anthropology Film Ctr. Foundation
Hartley Film Found., Inc.
Jewell (Stuart) Productions
Smithsonian Inst., Human Studies Film Arch.
Univ. of Calif., Ext. Media Ctr.

Native Americans (Mayo)
Instituto Nacional Indigenista

Native Americans (Mazateco)
Instituto Nacional Indigenista

Native Americans (Menominee)
Native Amer. Pub. Broad. Cons.
Univ. of West Fla., Hum. Res. Vid. Lib.

Native Americans (Mexican Indians)
Film/Audio Services, Inc.

Native Americans (Micmac)
Univ. Coll. of Cape Breton, Beaton Inst.

Native Americans (Miskito)
Icarus Films Intl., Inc.

Native Americans (Mixe)
Instituto Nacional Indigenista

Native Americans (Mohawk)
Akwesasne Library Cultural Ctr.
Natl. Archives (RG 75)

Native Americans (Mohegan)
Native Amer. Pub. Broad. Cons.

Native Americans (Nahua)
Instituto Nacional Indigenista

Native Americans (Narragansett)
Native Amer. Pub. Broad. Cons.

Native Americans (Navajo)
Archive Film Prods., Inc.
Energy Productions
Native Amer. Pub. Broad. Cons.
Natl. Archives (RG 75)
Navajo Nation Library System
Navajo Tribe, Off. Broadcast Svcs.
Petrified Films, Inc.
Smithsonian Inst., Human Studies Film Arch.
Univ. of Utah, Marriott Lib.
Villon Films
Wheelwright Mus. of the Amer. Indian

Native Americans (Nez Perce)
Appaloosa Horse Club, Inc.

Native Americans (Oglala Sioux)
Downtown Community TV Ctr.
Intermedia Arts Minnesota

Native Americans (Ojibwa)
DEC Film & Video
Intermedia Arts Minnesota
Video Yesteryear

Native Americans (Omaha)
Native Amer. Pub. Broad. Cons.

Native Americans (Oneida)
Native Amer. Pub. Broad. Cons.

Native Americans (Otomíe)
Instituto Nacional Indigenista

Native Americans (Paiute)
Media Project
Native Amer. Pub. Broad. Cons.

Native Americans (Pame)
Instituto Nacional Indigenista

Native Americans (Passamaquoddy)
Northeast Historic Film

Native Americans (Paugausett)
Native Amer. Pub. Broad. Cons.

Native Americans (Pawnee)
Native Amer. Pub. Broad. Cons.

Native Americans (Penobscot)

Northeast Historic Film

Native Americans (Pequot)
Native Amer. Pub. Broad. Cons.

Native Americans (Potawatomi)
Fulton County Hist. Soc., Inc.

Native Americans (Pueblo)
Anthropology Film Ctr. Foundation
Native Amer. Pub. Broad. Cons.
Natl. Archives (RG 75)
Natl. Archives (RG 200)
New Film Co., Inc.
Petrified Films, Inc.

Native Americans (Purépecha)
Instituto Nacional Indigenista

Native Americans (Q'eros)
Cinema Guild

Native Americans (Quechua)
Films for the Humanities and Sciences

Native Americans (San Carlos)
Natl. Archives (RG 378)

Native Americans (Schaghticoke)
Native Amer. Pub. Broad. Cons.

Native Americans (Seminole)
Bur. of Florida Folklife Progs.
Native Amer. Pub. Broad. Cons.
Schiele Museum

Native Americans (Shoshone)
Cinema Guild

Native Americans (Shuar)
Cinema Guild

Native Americans (Siletz)
Media Project

Native Americans (Sioux)
Cinema Guild
Native Amer. Pub. Broad. Cons.
Petrified Films, Inc.
Saskatchewan Indian Cultural Ctr.
Smithsonian Inst., Human Studies Film Arch.
South Dakota State Lib.

Native Americans (Suquamish)
Amer. Motion Pictures

Native Americans (Tarahumara)
Instituto Nacional Indigenista

Native Americans (Temagami)
Canadian Filmmakers Dist. Centre

Native Americans (Tepehua)
Instituto Nacional Indigenista

Native Americans (Tepehuano)
Instituto Nacional Indigenista

Native Americans (Tlapaneco)
Instituto Nacional Indigenista

Native Americans (Tlingit)
Native Amer. Pub. Broad. Cons.
Sitka Natl. Hist. Park

Native Americans (Totonaco)
Instituto Nacional Indigenista

Native Americans (Ute Mountain)
Academy of Health Sciences, U.S. Army

Native Americans (Wampanoag)
Native Amer. Pub. Broad. Cons.
Petrified Films, Inc.

Native Americans (Wendat)
Huronia Historical Parks

Native Americans (Winnebago)
Native Amer. Pub. Broad. Cons.

Native Americans (Xingu)
Democracy in Communication

Native Americans (Xochimilcas)
Instituto Nacional Indigenista

Native Americans (Yakima)
Yakima Indian Nation Cultural Ctr.
Yakima Television Program

Native Americans (Yanomamo)
Documentary Educational Resources
Smithsonian Inst., Human Studies Film Arch.

Native Americans (Yaqui)
Petrified Films, Inc.

Native Americans (Yurok)
Smithsonian Inst., Human Studies Film Arch.

Native Americans (Zapoteco)
Instituto Nacional Indigenista

Native Americans (Zoque)
Instituto Nacional Indigenista

Native Americans (Zoque-Popoluca)
Instituto Nacional Indigenista

Native Americans (Zuñi)
Natl. Archives (RG 75)
Petrified Films, Inc.
Schiele Museum
Smithsonian Inst., Human Studies Film Arch.

Natives
See Indigenous peoples

Natural gas
British Info. Svcs., Radio & TV Div.
CBS News Archives
Edison Electric Institute
Finley (Stuart) Inc.
First Group Comms., Inc.
Natl. Archives (RG 269)
Natl. Archives of Canada
Ohio Hist. Soc.
Pennebaker Associates, Inc.
Prelinger Assoc., Inc.
Shell Oil Co.
Twentieth Century-Fox Movietonews

Natural history
AIMS Media
Acad. of Nat. Sci. of Phila. Lib.
Amer. Mus. Nat. Hist. Film Arch.
Bennett (Joel) Prods.
Bishop Mus., Visual Coll.
Educational Images, Ltd.
Grinberg (Sherman) Film Libraries (East)
Grinberg (Sherman) Film Libraries (West)
Jewell (Stuart) Productions
Johnson (Martin & Osa) Safari Museum
Mass. Audubon Society
Prelinger Assoc., Inc.

Natural sciences
Natl. Archives (RG 242)

NOTE: Access policies, availability and restrictions vary for each source. Please read each entry in full. Always consult "General Film and Videotape Collections" (page 599); these comprehensive collections contain material on every conceivable subject.

Natl. Film Board of Canada
Pyramid Film and Video Corp.

Naturalization
CBS News Archives

Nature
Allen (John E.) Inc.
Beerger (Norman) Prods.
Bennett (Joel) Prods.
Britannica Films & Video
Canadian Broadcasting Corp.
Chisholm (Jack) Film Productions
Coe Film Assoc., Inc.
Cousteau Society
Dreamlight Images, Inc.
Echo Film Prods., Inc.
Energy Productions
Fabulous Footage Inc.
Facets Multimedia, Inc.
Film Bank
Filmfair Communications
Grinberg (Sherman) Film Libraries (East)
Grinberg (Sherman) Film Libraries (West)
Ideal Comms., Inc.
Independent Media Communications
Innerquest Communications Corp.
Mass. Audubon Society
Metro Communications, Inc.
Minnesota Zoo
Mountain Video Associates
Natl. Archives (RG 200)
Natl. Geographic Soc. Stock Footage Lib.
New Jersey Network
New York State Dept. of Env. Cons.
New Zealand Embassy Film Lib.
Norsgaard, Campbell
Peary-MacMillan Arctic Museum
Saskatchewan Indian Cultural Ctr.
Schiele Museum
Simon (Jeff) Productions
Sitka Natl. Hist. Park
Stock Shots
Streamline Film Archives
Summit Films, Inc.
TV-3
Video Genesis, Inc.
Video I-D, Inc.
WQED/Pittsburgh
White Janssen, Inc.
Zielinski Productions, Inc.
See also Animals; Wildlife

Naturopathy
See Medicine (Naturopathy)

Naugatuck Valley, Conn. (History and culture)
Cinema Guild

Naumann, Bruce
Blackwood Prods., Inc.

Naval Academy (U.S.)
Natl. Archives (RG 24)

Naval bases
Ocean Earth Constr. and Dev. Corp.

Naval Observatory (U.S.)
Natl. Archives (RG 78)

Naval science
Natl. Archives/Natl. AV Ctr.

Navratilova, Martina
U.S. Tennis Assn.

Navy (Great Britain)
British Info. Svcs., Radio & TV Div.
Natl. Archives (RG 24)

Navy (Italy)
Natl. Archives (RG 24)

Navy (Soviet Union)
Villon Films

Navy (Turkey)
Natl. Archives (RG 24)

Navy (U.S.)
Archive Film Prods., Inc.
Battleship Cove
CBS News Archives
Film Bank
Manitowoc Maritime Museum
March of Time
Military/Combat Stock Footage
Natl. Archives (RG 24)
Natl. Archives (RG 38)
Natl. Archives (RG 80)
Natl. Archives (RG 111)
Natl. Archives (RG 428)
Natl. Archives/Natl. AV Ctr.
Twentieth Century-Fox Movietonews
U.S. Dept. of Defense, Motion Media Rec. Ctr.
Villon Films
See also Blue Angels (U.S. Navy); Korean War; Military; Naval Academy (U.S.); Ships (Military); Submarines; World War I; World War II; specific conflicts and wars

Navy (U.S.) (Rest and recreation)
Natl. Archives (RG 24)

Navy, Department of the (U.S.)
Natl. Archives (RG 80)

Nazimova, Alla
Archive Film Prods., Inc.

Nazis
Archive Film Prods., Inc.
Film Bank
Intl. Film Foundation
NSDAP/AO
Natl. Archives of Canada
See also Germany; Hitler, Adolf; Holocaust; World War II

Nazis (South America)
Natl. Archives (RG 59)

Nazis (U.S.)
Freedom Information Service
German Language Video Center
Icarus Films Intl., Inc.
Intl. Historic Films, Inc.
Natl. Archives (RG 131)
New Day Films

Neal, Patricia
Daphne Productions, Inc.

Neal, Wes
Fellowship of Christian Athletes

Near East (History and culture)
Natl. Archives (RG 111)
Natl. Archives of Canada

Nearing, Helen and Scott
Bullfrog Films, Inc.

Nebraska
Film Bank

Nebraska (History and culture)
Adams County Hist. Soc.
Native Amer. Pub. Broad. Cons.
Nebraska State Hist. Soc.

Nebulae
Dreamlight Images, Inc.

Neel, Alice
Amer. Federation of the Arts

New Day Films
Video Data Bank

Negrito Pygmies
Smithsonian Inst., Human Studies Film Arch.

Nehru, Jawaharlal
Archive Film Prods., Inc.
Halcyon Days Prods.
March of Time
Film Education Institute
Smith (Margaret Chase) Lib. Ctr.

Neier, Aryeh
Camino Film Projects

Nellis Air Force Base, Nev.
Las Vegas News Bureau

Nelson, Cindy
U.S. Olympic Committee

Nelson, David
Banks Film Library

Nelson, Ricky
Archive Film Prods., Inc.

Nelson, Sarah
Green Mountain Post Films

Nemerov, Howard
Washington Univ., Olin Library

Neon
Dreamlight Images, Inc.
Energy Productions
Petrified Films, Inc.
Spectral Comms.
Univ. of Southern Calif., Film & Video Dist. Ctr.

Nepal
British Info. Svcs., Radio & TV Div.
Canadian Broadcasting Corp.
Film Bank
Film Search, Inc.
Jewell (Stuart) Productions
Petrified Films, Inc.

Nepal (History and culture)
Amer. Nepal Education Foundation
Archive Film Prods., Inc.
Petrified Films, Inc.
Southern Calif. Inst. of Architecture
U.S. Committee for UNICEF
UNICEF, Div. Info. & Pub. Aff.
United Nations Ctr. for Human Settlements

Nepean, Ontario
Carleton Prods. Inc.

Neptune, King
Archive Film Prods., Inc.

Nerds
Fish Films, Inc.
Petrified Films, Inc.
Prelinger Assoc., Inc.

Nero
Archive Film Prods., Inc.

Neruda, Pablo
Cinema Guild

Nesbitt, John
Canadian Filmmakers Dist. Centre

Nests
Film Bank
TV Ontario

Netherlands
Canadian Broadcasting Corp.

Netherlands (History and culture)
Archive Film Prods., Inc.
Bibliothèque Municipale de Montréal
Natl. Archives (RG 24)
Natl. Archives (RG 28)
Natl. Archives (RG 59)
Natl. Archives (RG 200)
Natl. Archives/Natl. AV Ctr.
Petrified Films, Inc.
Twentieth Century-Fox Movietonews
United Nations Ctr. for Human Settlements

Netherlands Antilles
Creative Video
Kesser Stock Footage Lib.
Passage Home Comms.
Preview Media

Nettles, Bea
Port Washington Pub. Lib.

Neuberger, Richard
Oregon Hist. Soc.

Neumayer, Fritz
Southern Calif. Inst. of Architecture

Neurology
IMS Creative Communications
Nassau Comm. Coll. Lib.

Neurosurgery
Nassau Comm. Coll. Lib.

Nevada
Airline Film & TV Promotions
Beerger (Norman) Prods.
Departures, Inc.
Energy Prods.
Film Bank
Film Search
Network Productions
Peak Prods., Inc.
Postcards Unlimited
Preview Media
Source Film & Tape Lib., Inc.

Nevada (History and culture)
Archive Film Prods., Inc.
First Run/Icarus Films, Inc.
Las Vegas News Bureau
Lib. of Congress, Amer. Folklife Ctr.
Oregon Hist. Soc.
Petrified Films, Inc.
Spalla (Rick) Video Prods.

Nevelson, Louise
Amer. Federation of the Arts
Blackwood Prods., Inc.
High Mus. of Art
Video Data Bank

New Age films and videotapes
Hartley Film Found., Inc.
Rudra Press
Valley of the Sun Publishing
Video-SIG
Wishing Well Distribution

New Age music
See Music (New Age)

New Bedford, Mass. (History and culture)
Natl. Archives (RG 378)
Rhode Island Hist. Soc.

New Britain, Conn. (History and culture)
New Haven Colony Hist. Soc.

New Brunswick
TV Ontario

New Brunswick (History and culture)
Université de Moncton, Centre d'Études
Acad.

New Castle, Pa. (History and culture)
Center for Public Dialogue

New Deal (1930s)
MacDonald, J. Fred
Prelinger Assoc., Inc.

New Delhi, India
Petrified Films, Inc.

New Delhi, India (History and culture)
Cantor (Arthur) Inc.

New Guinea (History and culture)
Lib. of Congress, M/B/RS
Sobek Productions
White Janssen, Inc.

New Hampshire
Apertura
Cineworks Prods. Inc.

New Hampshire (History and culture)
Apertura
Green Mountain Post Films

New, Harry S.
Natl. Archives (RG 28)

New Haven, Conn. (History and culture)
MacDonald, J. Fred
Media Bus
Univ. of Miss., Ctr. for Study of Southern
Culture

New Hebrides
See Vanuatu

New Jersey
Dreamlight Images, Inc.
Film Bank
Intl. Media Services, Inc.
Port Authority of New York & New Jersey
Preview Media
Riccitelli (Bruce) Prods.
Swedberg, Jack

New Jersey (History and culture)
Archive Film Prods., Inc.
Cinema Guild
Downtown Community TV Ctr.
Levi, Vicki Gold
Miss America Pageant
New Jersey Historical Society
New Jersey Network
Petrified Films, Inc.
Prelinger Assoc., Inc.
Regional Plan Assn.
United Farm Workers of America (UFW)

New Mexico
Cine-Mark
Film Bank
First Group Comms., Inc.
New Mexico State Records Ctr. & Arch.
Preview Media
Southwest Prods., Inc.
Summit Films, Inc.
Tri-Comm Prods.

New Mexico (History and culture)
Film Bank
Los Alamos County Hist. Mus. Arch.
Natl. Archives (RG 106)

New Film Co., Inc.
New Mexico State Records Ctr. & Arch.
Petrified Films, Inc.
Schiele Museum
Summit Films, Inc.
Tri-Comm Prods.
U.S. Natl. Park Service Hist. Coll.
Wheelwright Mus. of the Amer. Indian

New Orleans
Departures, Inc.
Energy Productions
Film Bank
New Orleans Pub. Lib., La. Div.
Preview Media
Windsor Prod. Corp.

New Orleans (Contemporary issues)
New Orleans Video Access Ctr.

New Orleans (History and culture)
Analogous Prods.
Center for New Amer. Media
Historic New Orleans Collection
New Orleans Pub. Lib., La. Div.
New Orleans Video Access Ctr.
Pennebaker Assoc., Inc.
Petrified Films, Inc.
Prelinger Assoc., Inc.
Tulane Univ., Amistad Res. Ctr.

New Year's (Chinese)
Analogous Productions
Petrified Films, Inc.

New Year's Eve
Clark (Dick) Media Archives, Inc.
Fish Films, Inc.
Petrified Films, Inc.
Telltales Associates Inc.
Twentieth Century-Fox Movietonews

New York (City)
Airline Film & TV Promotions
Airship Industries (USA), Inc.
Borough of Manhattan Comm. Coll.
Broad Street Prods.
Cabscott Broadcast Prods.
Cameo Film Library, Inc.
Cinema Arts Assoc.
Creative Video, Inc.
Dorn (Larry) Associates
Dreamlight Images, Inc.
Energy Productions
File Tape Co.
Film Bank
Fish Films, Inc.
Grinberg (Sherman) Film Libraries (West)
Kesser Stock Footage Library
Natl. Railway Historical Soc.
New York State Dept. of Econ. Devel.
Petrified Films, Inc.
Port Authority of New York & New Jersey
Preview Media
Riccitelli (Bruce) Prods.
Simon & Goodman Picture Co.
Source Stock Footage Lib., Inc.
Spectacolor, Inc.
Stegman Productions
Stock House
TV Ontario
Timesteps Prods., Inc.
Unicorn Projects
Wallen (Dick) Prods.

New York (City) (Contemporary issues)
Channel L Working Group

New York (City) (History and culture)
Allen (John E.) Inc.

Amer. Alliance for Health, Phys. Ed., Rec.
& Dance Arch.
Amer. Soc. Hist. Proj. Film Lib.
Analogous Productions
Archive Film Prods., Inc.
Bailey Prods., Inc.
Blackwood (Christian) Prods., Inc.
Boston Stock Market
Bronx County Hist. Soc.
Cantor (Arthur) Inc.
Cinema Guild
Deep Dish TV
Direct Cinema Ltd.
Downtown Community TV Ctr.
Educational Video Ctr.
Ergo Media
Film Search
Film/Video Arts, Inc.
First Run/Icarus, Inc.
Icarus Films Intl., Inc.
Independent Network News (INN)
Lib. of Congress, M/B/RS
Louisiana Tech. Univ., Eng. Film Res.
MacDonald, J. Fred
March of Time
Miles Educ. Film Prods.
Monday, Wednesday, Friday Video Club
Natl. Archives (RG 24)
Natl. Archives (RG 200)
Natl. Archives (RG 342)
New Day Films
New York Chinatown History Project
New York City Dept. of Rec. & Info.
Svcs.
New York City Labor Film Club
New York Pub. Lib., Rare Books &
Manuscripts Div.
Omega Films
Pathé Pictures, Inc.
Pennebaker Associates, Inc.
Petrified Films, Inc.
Port Authority of New York & New Jersey
Prelinger Assoc., Inc.
Regional Plan Assn.
Rosebush Visions Corp.
Schomburg Ctr. for Res. in Black Culture
Smithsonian Inst., Human Studies Film
Arch.
Taminent Lib./Wagner Labor Arch.
Third World Newsreel
Twentieth Century-Fox Movietonews
UJA Federation
Unicorn Projects
Worldwide Television News

New York (State)
Analogous Prods.
Film Bank
Florentine Films
4•6•8 Prods., Inc.
Island Video
MacGillivray Freeman Films
New York State Dept. of Econ. Devel.
Preview Media
Rockefeller Arch. Ctr.
Villon Films
Xicom, Inc.

New York (State) (History and culture)
Archive Film Prods., Inc.
Buffalo & Erie County Hist. Soc.
Chautauqua-Cattaraugus Lib. Syst.
Cinema Guild
Film/Audio Services
Finley (Stuart) Inc.
Long Island State Park Comm.
Nassau County Museum
New York Pub. Lib., Rare Books &
Manuscripts Div.
New York State Arch. & Rec. Admin.
New York State Dept. of Econ. Devel.

New York State Dept. of Env. Cons.
New York State Hist. Assn.
Omega Films
Petrified Films, Inc.
Prelinger Assoc., Inc.
Roosevelt (Franklin D.) Lib.
Saint John's Univ., Spec. Coll.
Schiele Museum
Streamline Film Arch.
United Farm Workers of America (UFW)
Villon Films

New York Stock Exchange
See Stock exchanges

New Zealand
Canadian Broadcasting Corp.
Film Bank
Hawaii Public Broadcasting Authority
Media West, Inc.
New Zealand Embassy Film Lib.
Pan American Airlines Film Lib.
Preview Media
Source Stock Footage Lib., Inc.

New Zealand (History and culture)
New Zealand Embassy Film Lib.
Nuclear Free Zone Registry
Worldwide Television News

Newark, N.J.
Port Authority of New York & New Jersey

Newark, N.J. (History and culture)
New Jersey Network
Prelinger Assoc., Inc.

**Newcastle, Ontario (History and
culture)**
Natl. Archives of Canada

Newcombe, John
U.S. Tennis Assn.

Newfoundland
Alaska Video Prods.
First Group Comms., Inc.
TV Ontario

Newfoundland (History and culture)
Acad. of Nat. Sci. of Phila. Lib.
Canadian Filmmakers Dist. Ctr.
Natl. Archives of Canada
Newfoundland Independent Filmmakers
Coop.
Peary-MacMillan Arctic Museum
Prov. Arch. of Newfoundland & Labrador

**Newfoundland Transportation, Royal
Commission on**
Natl. Archives of Canada

Newhart, Bob
Spectral Comms.
Wisconsin Ctr. for Film & Theater Res.

**Newhaven, England (History and
culture)**
Petrified Films, Inc.

Newman, Barnett
Blackwood Prods., Inc.

Newman, Edwin
Daphne Productions, Inc.

Newman, Joe
Rhapsody Films, Inc.

Newman, Paul
Archive Film Prods., Inc.

NOTE: Access policies, availability and restrictions vary for each source. Please read each entry in full. Always consult "General Film and
Videotape Collections" (page 599); these comprehensive collections contain material on every conceivable subject.

Banks Film Library
Nissan Motor Corp. of the U.S.
UCLA Film & Television Archive

Newport Beach, Calif. (History and culture)
Petrified Films, Inc.

Newport, Oreg. (History and culture)
Media Project

Newport, R.I.
Preview Media
Telltales Associates Inc.

Newport, R.I. (History and culture)
Rhode Island Hist. Soc.

Newsboys
Petrified Films, Inc.
Prelinger Assoc., Inc.

Newspapers
Allen (John E.) Inc.
Archive Film Prods., Inc.
CBS News Archives
Film Bank
Fish Films, Inc.
March of Time
Petrified Films, Inc.
Prelinger Assoc., Inc.
TV Ontario
White Janssen, Inc.

Newspapers (Headlines)
Allen (John E.) Inc.
Film Bank
Petrified Films, Inc.

Newsprint (Production)
Petrified Films, Inc.

Newsreels
Allen (John E.) Inc.
Archive Film Prods., Inc.
Archivo de Imagenes en Movimiento
Blackwood (Christian) Prods., Inc.
Boston Stock Market
Budget Films Inc.
Chertok Associates Inc.
Cinema Arts Assoc.
Cineteca Nacional
Colorado Historical Society
DeFlores, Bob
Dettlaff, Alois F. Sr.
Edison Natl. Historic Site
Em Gee Film Library
Emory Univ., Spec. Coll.
Experimental Aircraft Assn.
Fabulous Footage Inc.
Film Education Institute
Film Preservation Assoc.
Film Search
Film/Audio Services, Inc.
Filmoteca de la UNAM
Filmoteca Luis Muñoz Marin
Fish Films, Inc.
Ford (Henry) Museum
Forsher (James) Prods. & Archives, Inc.
German Info. Ctr., Film Lib.
Gould (Bert)/bay area archive
Great American Stock
Grinberg (Sherman) Film Libraries (East)
Grinberg (Sherman) Film Libraries (West)
Halcyon Days Prods.
Hawaii Public Broadcasting Authority
Hearst Metrotone News
Historic Thoroughbred Colls., Inc.
Hoover (Herbert) Presidential Library
Hoover Institution
Imageways, Inc.
Indiana State Lib.
Indiana Univ., Black Film Ctr./Arch.
Instituto Cubano de Radio y Television
Intl. Assn. of Independent Producers

Intl. Historic Films, Inc.
Ivy Film
Killiam Shows, Inc.
Lib. of Congress, M/B/RS
MacArthur (Gen. Douglas) Memorial
MacDonald, J. Fred
March of Time
Miss America Pageant
Morcraft Films
Moviecraft, Inc.
Movietime, Inc. Archives
Mus. of Jewish Heritage
Mystic Seaport Mus., Inc.
Natl. Archives (RG 24)
Natl. Archives (RG 46)
Natl. Archives (RG 47)
Natl. Archives (RG 59)
Natl. Archives (RG 111)
Natl. Archives (RG 200)
Natl. Archives (RG 208)
Natl. Archives (RG 242)
Natl. Archives (RG 306)
Natl. Archives (RG 428)
Natl. Archives of Canada
Natl. Ctr. for Film & Video Preservation
Natl. Film Board of Canada
Northeast Historic Film
Northrop Univ., Amer. Hall of Aviation Hist.
Ontario Film Institute
Oregon Hist. Soc.
Parker (Kit) Films
Petrified Films, Inc.
Prelinger Assoc., Inc.
Producers Library Service
Prov. Arch. of Newfoundland & Labrador
Read (Brooks) & Assoc.
Roosevelt (Franklin D.) Lib.
San Jose Hist. Museum
Second Line Search
Southwest Film/Video Archives, SMU
Spalla (Rick) Video Prods.
Stock Shots
Streamline Film Archives
Trotting Horse Museum
Truman (Harry S) Library
Twentieth Century-Fox Movietonews
UCLA Film & Television Archive
Univ. of Ill. Urbana-Champaign, Univ. Arch.
Univ. of Rochester Lib., Rare Books & Spec. Coll.
Univ. of So. Carolina, Newsfilm Lib.
Video Catalogue Co., Inc.
Video Resources N.Y., Inc.
Video Yesteryear
Visnews Intl.
Weintraub Screen Entertainment, Inc.
Wiesenthal (Simon) Ctr.
Worldwide Television News

Newsreels (Allied Powers)
Intl. Historic Films, Inc.

Newsreels (Canada)
Natl. Archives of Canada
Natl. Film Board of Canada
Twentieth Century-Fox Movietonews

Newsreels (Cuba)
Instituto Cubano de Radio y Television

Newsreels (Eastern Europe)
Intl. Historic Films, Inc.

Newsreels (France)
Natl. Archives (RG 208)

Newsreels (Germany)
Filmoteca de la UNAM
Hoover Institution
Intl. Historic Films, Inc.
Lib. of Congress, M/B/RS
Mus. of Contemporary Art
NSDAP/AO

Natl. Archives (RG 200)
Natl. Archives (RG 242)
Natl. Archives (RG 306)
UCLA Film & Television Archive
Video Yesteryear
Wiesenthal (Simon) Ctr.

Newsreels (India)
Natl. Archives (RG 208)

Newsreels (Italy)
Lib. of Congress, M/B/RS
Natl. Archives (RG 242)

Newsreels (Japan)
Lib. of Congress, M/B/RS
Natl. Archives (RG 242)
UCLA Film & Television Archive

Newsreels (Latvia)
Hoover Institution

Newsreels (Mexico)
Filmoteca de la UNAM
Imevision

Newsreels (South America)
Twentieth Century-Fox Movietonews

Newsreels (Spanish-language)
Filmoteca de la UNAM

Newsreels (U.S.S.R.)
Intl. Historic Films, Inc.
Natl. Archives (RG 208)
Natl. Archives (RG 242)
UCLA Film & Television Archive

Newsreels (United Kingdom)
Natl. Archives (RG 208)
UCLA Film & Television Archive
Visnews Intl.
Worldwide Television News

Newsstands
Petrified Films, Inc.

Newton-John, Olivia
Spectral Comms.

Nez Percé National Historical Park (Idaho)
Nez Percé Natl. Hist. Park

Ngami, Lake (Botswana) (History and culture)
United Nations, Visual Materials Lib.

Ngas people
Smithsonian Inst., Human Studies Film Arch.

Niagara Falls
Analogous Productions
Film Bank
Florentine Films
MacGillivray Freeman Films
Preview Media
TV Ontario

Niagara Falls (History and culture)
Archive Film Prods., Inc.
Film/Audio Services, Inc.
Petrified Films, Inc.
Schiele Museum

Niagara Frontier Area, N.Y.
New York State Dept. of Econ. Devel.

Niagara, Ontario (History and culture)
Archives of Ontario

Nicaragua
Imagen y Sonido Independiente, S.A.
Rock Solid Prods.

World Monitor

Nicaragua (Contemporary issues)
Alternative Information Network
Amer. Security Council Foundation
Cinema Guild
DEC Film & Video
Deep Dish TV
Educational Film & Video Project
Film/Audio Services, Inc.
First Run/Icarus Films, Inc.
Intl. Freedom Foundation
Natl. Archives (RG 46)
Northstar Prods.
Skylight Pictures
Third World Newsreel
Vietnam Veterans Against the War
Wilmington Coll. Peace Res. Ctr.
Women Make Movies, Inc.
Xchange TV

Nicaragua (History and culture)
Baker (Fred) Film & Video Co.
DEC Film & Video
Democracy in Communication
Downtown Community TV Ctr.
First Run/Icarus Films, Inc.
Foreign Images
Groupe Intervention Video
Icarus Films Intl., Inc.
Idera Films
Latina, S.A. de C.V.
Lesage, Julia
New Time Films, Inc.
Paper Tiger TV
Spalla (Rick) Video Prods.
Syracuse Alternative Media Network
Third World Newsreel
United Nations Ctr. for Human Settlements
Univ. of Wisconsin — Extension
World Monitor
Xchange TV

Nice, France (History and culture)
Archive Film Prods., Inc.

Nichol, b.p.
Canadian Filmmakers Dist. Centre

Nicholas II, Czar of Russia
Grinberg (Sherman) Film Libraries (West)
Hoover Institution
Petrified Films, Inc.

Nichols, Mike
Wesleyan Cinema Archives

Nickel
Archives of Ontario
Natl. Archives (RG 70)

Nicklaus, Jack
Archive Film Prods., Inc.

Nicks, Stevie
Spectral Comms.

Nielsen, Brigitte
Los Angeles News Service
Spectral Comms.

Niger (Contemporary issues)
Oxfam America

Niger (History and culture)
Documentary Educational Resources
TV Ontario

Nigeria (History and culture)
Archive Film Prods., Inc.
Documentary Educational Resources
Hoover Institution
Singer-Sharrette Traditional Healing Films

Smithsonian Inst., Human Studies Film Arch.
TV Ontario

Nightclubs
Allen (John E.) Inc.
Archive Film Prods., Inc.
Charisma Prods., Ltd./Visual Motion Film Bank
First Run/Icarus Films, Inc.
Fish Films, Inc.
Forsher (James) Prods. & Archives, Inc.
Las Vegas News Bureau
MacDonald, J. Fred
March of Time
Petrified Films, Inc.
Twentieth Century-Fox Movietonews
Video Tape Library, Ltd.
See also Bars; Discotheques

Nightclubs (Saigon)
White Janssen, Inc.

Niigata, Japan
TV Ontario

Nikolais, Alwin
Blackwood (Christian) Prods., Inc.

Nile River, Egypt
Cousteau Society
Jewell (Stuart) Productions
Petrified Films, Inc.

Nile River, Egypt (History and culture)
Intl. Film Foundation
Preview Media

Nimmons, Phil
Natl. Archives of Canada

Nin, Anais
Camera Three Prods., Inc.
Cantor (Arthur) Inc.

Nine to Five (Organization)
Radcliffe Coll., Schlesinger Lib.

Nisei
See Japanese Americans

Niven, David
Banks Film Library

Nixon, Agnes
Daphne Productions, Inc.

Nixon, Julie
Villon Films

Nixon, Patricia
Natl. Archives/Nixon Presidential Materials Proj.

Nixon, Richard Milhous
Appalshop Films, Inc.
Archive Film Prods., Inc.
Banks Film Library
DEC Film & Video
Grinberg (Sherman) Film Libraries (West)
Halcyon Days Prods.
Indiana Hist. Soc., Smith Memorial Lib.
Las Vegas News Bureau
MacDonald, J. Fred
Mus. & Hist. Div., City of Sacramento
Natl. Archives (RG 128)
Natl. Archives (RG 200)
Natl. Archives (RG 255)
Natl. Archives (RG 274)
Natl. Archives (RG 342)

Natl. Archives/Nixon Presidential Materials Proj.
Oregon Hist. Soc.
Parker (Kit) Films
Petrified Films, Inc.
Pyramid Film and Video Corp.
Quest Productions Inc.
Shokus Video
Univ. of Ill. Urbana-Champaign, Univ. Arch.
Video Yesteryear
Villon Films

Nixon-Khrushchev debate
Natl. Archives (RG 64)
Petrified Films, Inc.

Nkodi, Simon
Canadian Filmmakers Dist. Centre

Noggle, Anne
Port Washington Pub. Lib.

Noguchi, Isamu
Albright-Knox Art Gallery
Blackwood Prods., Inc.
Camera Three Prods., Inc.
Walker Art Ctr.

Noguchi, Thomas
Daphne Productions, Inc.

Noise
CBS News Archives

Noland, Kenneth
Blackwood Prods., Inc.

Noland, Lloyd
Birmingham Pub. Lib., Media Svcs. Dept.

Nomads
Petrified Films, Inc.

Nonviolence
See Pacifism

Nordic history and culture
Nordic Heritage Museum

Nördlingen, Germany (History and culture)
German Info. Ctr., Film Lib.

Norfolk, Va. (History and culture)
MacDonald, J. Fred

Normand, Mabel
Archive Film Prods., Inc.

Normandie (S.S.)
Analogous Productions
Grinberg (Sherman) Film Libraries (West)

Normandy, France (History and culture)
Archive Film Prods., Inc.

North Africa (History and culture)
Acad. of Nat. Sci. of Phila. Lib.
Hoover Institution
Natl. Archives (RG 226)
Natl. Archives (RG 242)
Natl. Archives (RG 306)

North American Air Defense Command (NORAD)
Northstar Prods.

North Atlantic Treaty Organization (NATO)

Natl. Archives (RG 286)
Natl. Archives of Canada

North Carolina
Metro Communications, Inc.
TV Ontario
Tri-Comm Prods.

North Carolina (History and culture)
Amer. Truck Historical Soc.
Connecticut State Lib.
Duke Univ., Perkins Lib.
North Carolina Div. of Arch. & Hist.
Petrified Films, Inc.
Skylight Pictures

North Dakota
Northcoast Communication, Inc.
Snyder (Bill) Films, Inc.

North Dakota (History and culture)
Snyder (Bill) Films, Inc.
State Hist. Soc. of North Dakota

North, Jay
Shokus Video

North Korea
See Korea, North

North, Oliver
Intl. Freedom Foundation

North Pole
Analogous Productions
Film Bank

North Pole (History and culture)
Natl. Archives (RG 64)
Natl. Archives (RG 342)

North Richmond, Calif. (History and culture)
MacDonald, J. Fred

North Sea
First Group Comms., Inc.

North Sea (History)
Hammer (Armand) Prods.

North Slope, Alaska
Source Stock Footage Lib., Inc.

Northern Ireland (History and culture)
Archive Film Prods., Inc.
Pennebaker Assoc., Inc.

Northwest Mounted Police (Canada)
Glenbow Mus. Arch.

Northwest Territories
Alaska Video Prods.
TV Ontario

Northwest Territories (History and culture)
Archives of Ontario
Canadian Filmmakers Dist. Centre
Glenbow Mus. Arch.
Natl. Archives of Canada
New Film Co., Inc.
Northwest Territories Archives
Peary-Macmillan Arctic Museum
Yukon Archives

Norway
British Info. Svcs., Radio & TV Div.
Preview Media

Norway (History and culture)

Archive Film Prods., Inc.
Film/Audio Services, Inc.
March of Time
Natl. Archives/Natl. AV Ctr.
Prelinger Assoc., Inc.
Villon Films
White Janssen, Inc.

Norwegian Americans
Intermedia Arts Minnesota

Notre Dame de Paris
Petrified Films, Inc.
Unicorn Projects

Nova Scotia
Studio East Ltd.
TV Ontario

Nova Scotia (History and culture)
MacDonald, J. Fred
Natl. Archives of Canada
Univ. Coll. of Cape Breton, Beaton Inst.

Novak, Barbara
Video Data Bank

Novak, Kim
Archive Film Prods., Inc.
Banks Film Library

Novas
Dreamlight Images, Inc.

Nuclear disarmament
See Arms control (Nuclear)

Nuclear energy and power
Alternative Information Network
Amer. Nuclear Society
British Info. Svcs., Radio & TV Div.
Bullfrog Films, Inc.
CBS News Archives
Calif. Highway Patrol Acad. Media Center
DEC Film & Video
Edison Electric Institute
Electric Power Research Institute
Energy Productions
Film Bank
Film/Audio Services, Inc.
Finley (Stuart) Inc.
Green Mountain Post Films
Greenpeace, U.S.A.
Hearst Metrotone News
Hoover (Herbert) Presidential Library
Hoover Institution
Idera Films
Illinois State Hist. Lib.
Indiana Univ. Northwest Lib.
Intermedia Arts Minnesota
Los Alamos Natl. Laboratory
Los Angeles Dept. of Water & Power
March of Time
Natl. Archives (RG 200)
Natl. Archives (RG 306)
Natl. Archives (RG 326)
Natl. Archives (RG 434)
Natl. Archives/Natl. AV Ctr.
Natl. Coun. of Amer.-Sov. Friendship
New York State Dept. of Env. Cons.
Northstar Prods.
Oregon Hist. Soc.
Petrified Films, Inc.
Political Issue Archive
Prelinger Assoc., Inc.
Public Interest Video Network
Richter Productions
Safe Energy Communication Council
State Hist. Soc. of Iowa
TV Ontario
U.S. Council for Energy Awareness

NOTE: Access policies, availability and restrictions vary for each source. Please read each entry in full. Always consult "General Film and Videotape Collections" (page 599); these comprehensive collections contain material on every conceivable subject.

U.S. Defense Nuclear Agency
United Nations, Visual Materials Lib.
Villon Films
World Monitor
See also Anti-nuclear movement; Energy

Nuclear medicine
See Medicine (Nuclear)

Nuclear radiation
See Radiation (Nuclear)

Nuclear war
Adair Films
Direct Cinema Ltd.
Educational Film & Video Project
MacDonald, J. Fred
Mass Media Ministries
Natl. Archives (RG 311)
Natl. Archives of Canada
Physicians for Social Responsibility
Public Interest Video Network
Resource Ctr. for Nonviolence
Union of Concerned Scientists
Wilmington Coll. Peace Res. Ctr.

Nuclear weapons
Alaska Native Heritage Film Project
Amer. Assn. for Counseling &
  Development
Cambridge Documentary Films, Inc.
Center for Defense Information
Council for a Livable World Educ. Fund
DEC Film & Video
Educational Film & Video Project
Educators for Social Responsibility
Inst. for Space & Security Studies
Intellimation
March of Time
Natl. Archives (RG 200)
Natl. Archives (RG 374)
Nuclear Free Zone Registry
Petrified Films, Inc.
Physicians for Social Responsibility
Political Issue Archive
Prelinger Assoc., Inc.
Richter Productions
Roosevelt Ctr. for American Policy
  Studies
SANE/Freeze
U.S. Defense Nuclear Agency
See also Anti-nuclear movement

Nudism
CBS News Archives
Elysium Archives & Research Center
Kinsey Institute

N/um Tchai people
Documentary Educ. Resources

Numbers
Rosebush Visions Corp.

Nunn, Sam
Ideal Comms., Inc.

Nuns
Archive Film Prods., Inc.
CBS News Archives
Petrified Films, Inc.

**Nuremberg, Germany (History and
  culture)**
Analogous Productions
Archive Film Prods., Inc.

Nuremberg trials
See World War II (Nuremberg trials)

Nureyev, Rudolf
Cunningham Dance Foundation
Daphne Productions, Inc.
New York Pub. Lib., Perf. Arts Res. Ctr.,
  Dance Coll.

Nurseries
CBS News Archives
Film Bank
Stock Shots
TV Ontario

Nursery schools
Petrified Films, Inc.

Nurses and nursing
Altschul Group
Amer. Journal of Nursing Co.
Amer. Nurses' Assn.
CBS News Archives
Carousel Film & Video
Center for Biomedical Comms.
Dartnell
Emory Medical Television Network
Fanlight Prods.
Film Bank
Film/Audio Services, Inc.
Florentine Films
Historical Health Film Coll.
IMS Creative Communications
MacDonald, J. Fred
Milner-Fenwick, Inc.
Nassau Comm. Coll. Lib.
Natl. Archives (RG 306)
Natl. Archives of Canada
New Mexico State Records Ctr. & Arch.
New York City Labor Film Club
New York Hosp.-Cornell Med. Ctr., Arch.
Perlmutter (Alvin H.) Inc.
Petrified Films, Inc.
Prelinger Assoc., Inc.
Twentieth Century-Fox Movietonews
UCLA Behavioral Sci. Media Lab.
Univ. of Calif., Berkeley, Labor
  Occupational Health Prog.
Wayne State Univ., Dir. Educ. in Nursing
Women Make Movies, Inc.

Nursing homes
Broad Street Prods.
CBS News Archives
Fanlight Prods.
Northcoast Communication, Inc.
State Hist. Soc. of Iowa

Nutrition
AIMS Media
Academy of Health Sciences, U.S. Army
Altschul Group
Amer. Bakers Assn.
Amer. Cancer Soc., Inc.
Amer. Heart Assn.
Athletic Institute
Barr Films
Center for Humanities, Inc.
Charisma Prods., Ltd./Visual Motion
Churchill Films
Cinema Guild
Cinema Medica
Coronet/MTI Film & Video
Films for the Humanities and Sciences
GPN
Handel Film Corp.
Higgins (Alfred) Prods.
IMS Creative Communications
KYUK-TV
La Leche League of New Mexico
March of Dimes Birth Defects Found.
McDonald's Corp.
Nassau Comm. Coll. Lib.
Natl. Archives (RG 33)
Natl. Archives (RG 307)
Natl. Archives (RG 381)
Natl. Dairy Council
Perlmutter (Alvin H.) Inc.
Phoenix Films and Video
Prelinger Assoc., Inc.
Prov. Arch. of Alberta
Pyramid Film and Video Corp.
Rogers (Will) Institute
Society for Nutrition Education

U.S. Committee for UNICEF
Univ. of West Fla., Hum. Res. Vid. Lib.
Women Make Movies, Inc.

Nutritionists
TV Ontario

Nylon, Judy
Target Video

Nylon stockings
Prelinger Assoc., Inc.

OSS
See Strategic Services, Office of (OSS)

OWI
See War Information, Office of (OWI)

O'Banion, Nance
Video Data Bank

O'Brian, Hugh
Spectral Comms.

O'Brien, Edmond
Archive Film Prods., Inc.

O'Brien, Margaret
Archive Film Prods., Inc.

O'Brien, Parry
Sportsfilm

O'Brien, Pat
Banks Film Library
UCLA Film & Television Archive

O'Connell, Cardinal
Archive Film Prods., Inc.

O'Connor, Billy
Natl. Archives of Canada

O'Connor, Carroll
Anti-Defamation League of B'nai B'rith
Spectral Comms.

O'Connor, Donald
Archive Film Prods., Inc.

O'Connor, Francis
De Saisset Museum

O'Daniel, W. Lee
MacDonald, J. Fred
Texas State Lib., Arch. Div.

O'Donnel, Hugh J.
Indiana State Lib.

O'Hair, Madalyn Murray
Alternative Information Network

O'Hanlon, Richard and Anne
De Saisset Museum

O'Hara, Maureen
Banks Film Library

O'Keeffe, Georgia
Amer. Federation of the Arts
Plains Art Mus. Lib.

O'Malley, Walter
Banks Film Library

O'Neill, C.W.
Ohio Historical Soc.

O'Neill, Tip
WGBH Educational Foundation

O'Sullivan, T.H.
Blackwood Prods., Inc.

Oahu, Hawaii
Preview Media

Oahu, Hawaii (History and culture)
Petrified Films, Inc.

**Oak Creek Canyon, Ariz. (History and
  culture)**
Petrified Films, Inc.

Oak Park, Ill.
Unicorn Projects

Oak Ridge, Tenn. (History and culture)
Petrified Films, Inc.

Oakes, Doc
Natl. Archives of Canada

Oakie, Jack
Banks Film Library
Univ. of Wyoming, Amer. Heritage Ctr.

Oakland, Calif. (History and culture)
Creative Film Society
Estuary Press
Prelinger Assoc., Inc.
Quest Prods., Inc.

Oakley, Annie
Archive Film Prods., Inc.

Oates, Joyce Carol
Daphne Productions, Inc.

Oaths
Twentieth Century-Fox Movietonews

Oberon, Merle
Archive Film Prods., Inc.
Banks Film Library

Obesity
Cinema Guild

Obregón, Alvaro
Archivo Fotografico y Cinematografico
  Abítia
Archivo Historico Cinematografico

Observatories
CBS News Archives
California Inst. of Tech., Inst. Arch.
Cinenet (Cinema Network)
Film Bank
Harvard-Smithsonian Ctr. for Astrophysics
Petrified Films, Inc.
Prelinger Assoc., Inc.
Spectral Comms.
TV Ontario
See also Telescopes

Obstacle courses
TV Ontario

Obstacle races
Twentieth Century-Fox Movietonews

Obstetrics and gynecology
Altschul Group
Cambridge Documentary Films, Inc.
Cinema Medica
Film Bank
IMS Creative Communications
Milner-Fenwick, Inc.
Nassau Comm. Coll. Lib.
Natl. Archives (RG 12)
Petrified Films, Inc.
Polymorph Films, Inc.
Prelinger Assoc., Inc.
Singer-Sharrette Traditional Healing Films
Video Farm
Visual Information Systems
See also Childbirth; Pregnancy

712

Occult
See Supernatural

Occupational health and safety
AIMS Media
Aluminum Assn.
Amer. Pulpwood Assn., Inc.
Asbestos Victims of America
Assoc. Gen. Contractors of America
BNA Communications, Inc.
California Newsreel
Computer & Business Equip. Mfrs. Assn.
DEC Film & Video
Estuary Press
Green Mountain Post Films
Idera Films
Labor Inst. of Public Affairs
Media Project
Natl. Archives (RG 70)
Natl. Archives (RG 100)
Natl. Safety Council
New Day Films
Richter Productions
Salenger Films Inc.
TV-UNAM
U.S. Dept. of Labor, Mine Safety & Health Admin.
United Farm Workers of America (UFW)
Université de Moncton, Centre d'Études Acad.
Univ. of Calif., Berkeley, Labor Occupational Health Prog.
Vidéographe Inc., Le

Occupational medicine
See Medicine (Occupational)

Occupational therapy
Amer. Occupational Therapy Assn.

Ocean liners
See Ships (Ocean liners)

Ocean Park, Santa Monica, Calif. (History and culture)
Petrified Films, Inc.

Oceania (History and culture)
Lib. of Congress, Amer. Folklife Ctr.
Smithsonian Inst., Human Studies Film Arch.

Oceanography
Amer. Mus. Nat. Hist. Film Arch.
Natl. Archives (RG 307)
Natl. Science Foundation
New York Zoological Society

Oceans
British Info. Svcs., Radio & TV Div.
CBS News Archives
Cinema Guild
Cinenet (Cinema Network)
Cousteau Society
Crystal Pyramid Prods.
Dreamlight Images, Inc.
Echo Film Prods., Inc.
Elfstrom-Hilmer Prods.
Encore Video Prods., Inc.
Energy Productions
Film Bank
Film Search
Forsher (James) Prods. & Archives, Inc.
Great Waves/Delaney Films
Greenpeace, U.S.A.
Intl. Film Bureau, Inc.
Kesser Stock Footage Library
MacGillivray Freeman Films
Marineland of Florida
Marts (Steve) Productions
Merkel Films

NASA, Office of Comm.
Natl. Archives (RG 26)
Natl. Oceanic & Atmospheric Admin.
Natl. Science Foundation
Nei-Ali Prods.
Petrified Films, Inc.
Quenzer Driscoll Dawson, Inc.
Riccitelli (Bruce) Prods.
Source Stock Footage Lib., Inc.
Spectral Comms.
Sullivan Video Services
Summit Films, Inc.
TV Ontario
TV-3
Twentieth Century-Fox Movietonews
Wings Wildlife Prods., Inc.
See also Beaches; Seascapes; Waves; specific oceans

Oceanscapes
See Seascapes

Ochs, Phil
MacDonald, J. Fred

Ockenga, Starr
Port Washington Pub. Lib.

Octopuses
Archive Film Prods., Inc.
Cousteau Society
Marineland of Florida
Moonlight Productions
Petrified Films, Inc.

Oddities
Analogous Productions
CBS News Archives
Film Bank
Film Education Institute
Grinberg (Sherman) Film Libraries (West)
Halcyon Days Prods.
Hearst Metrotone News
MacDonald, J. Fred
Petrified Films, Inc.
Postcards Associates
Prelinger Assoc., Inc.
Shields Archival
Source Stock Footage Lib., Inc.
Spalla (Rick) Video Prods.
Streamline Film Archives
Twentieth Century-Fox Movietonews
Univ. of So. Carolina, Newsfilm Lib.
White Janssen, Inc.
Worldwide Television News
See also Aircraft (Oddities); Animals (Oddities)

Odessa, Poland (History and culture)
Archive Film Prods., Inc.

Oeschlin, Werner
Southern Calif. Inst. of Architecture

Off-Broadway theater
See Theater (Off-Broadway)

Office of
See the agency's "subject" area (e.g., Office of Civil Defense is found under Civil Defense, Office of [U.S.])

Office technology
See Technology (Office)

Offices
Applegate Entertainment
CBS News Archives
Film Bank
Fish Films, Inc.
4•6•8 Prods., Inc.

Petrified Films, Inc.
Prelinger Assoc., Inc.
Stegman Productions
Stock House
TV Ontario
Timesteps Prods., Inc.
Twentieth Century-Fox Movietonews
Video Tape Library, Ltd.
See also Workers (Office); Workers (White-collar)

Offices (Newspaper)
Petrified Films, Inc.
Prelinger Assoc., Inc.
TV Ontario

Official Languages, Commissioner of
Natl. Archives of Canada

Officials (Competition)
Film Bank

Offs (Rock and roll band)
Target Video

Ohio
Creative Video, Inc.
Energy Prods.
Hi-Tech Prods.
Ohio Historical Soc.
Video Genesis, Inc.

Ohio (History and culture)
All-American Soap Box Derby
Archive Film Prods., Inc.
Cincinnati Hist. Soc.
Cinema Guild
General Motors Corp.
Marshall Univ., Spec. Coll.
Natl. Archives/Natl. AV Ctr.
Ohio Historical Soc.
Ohio State Univ., Dept. of Photog. & Cinema
Petrified Films, Inc.
Prelinger Assoc., Inc.
Pub. Lib. of Cincinnati & Hamilton Cty.
Univ. of Toledo, Univ. Arch.
Western Reserve Hist. Soc.

Ohio River (Ohio-Ky.) (History and culture)
Kentucky Dept. of Libraries & Archives

Ohio River Valley (Ohio-Ky.) (History and culture)
Finley (Stuart) Inc.

Oil fires
See Fires (Oil)

Oil industry
Alaska Video Prods.
Alternative Information Network
Archive Film Prods., Inc.
British Info. Svcs., Radio & TV Div.
Broad Street Prods.
CBS News Archives
Cabscott Broadcast Prods.
Canadian Film Institute
Dreamlight Images, Inc.
Energy Productions
Farkas Studios, Ltd.
Film Bank
First Group Comms., Inc.
Fish Films, Inc.
Glenbow Mus. Arch.
Hammer (Armand) Prods.
Imperial Oil Ltd.
Natl. Archives (RG 70)
Natl. Archives (RG 331)
Natl. Archives of Canada

New Film Co., Inc.
Nine Star Productions
Northstar Prods.
October Productions
Panhandle-Plains Hist. Museum
Petrified Films, Inc.
Political Issue Archive
Riccitelli (Bruce) Prods.
Rockefeller Arch. Ctr.
Shell Oil Co.
Source Stock Footage Lib., Inc.
Spectral Comms.
Stegman Productions
Summit Films, Inc.
TV Ontario
Texas Tech Univ., Southwest Coll.
Timesteps Prods., Inc.
Twentieth Century-Fox Movietonews
Univ. of Alberta, Boreal Inst. for Northern Studies
Univ. of Tex. at Austin, Barker Tex. Hist. Ctr.
Univ. of Tex. at Austin, Petrol. Ext. Svc.
White Janssen, Inc.
World Monitor

Oil tanker ships
See Ships (Oil tankers)

Oklahoma
Energy Prods.
First Group Comms., Inc.

Oklahoma (History and culture)
Archive Film Prods., Inc.
Natl. Press Photographers Assn., Inc.
Oklahoma Dept. of Libraries
Petrified Films, Inc.
Univ. of Okla., Western Hist. Colls.

Oklahoma City
Energy Productions

Okra
Energy Productions

Oktoberfests
See Festivals (Oktoberfest)

Oland, Warner
Archive Film Prods., Inc.

Old Faithful (Yellowstone National Park)
Film Bank
Jewell (Stuart) Productions
Source Stock Footage Lib., Inc.

Old Faithful (Yellowstone National Park) (History and culture)
Archive Film Prods., Inc.

Old Sturbridge Village, Mass.
Unicorn Projects

Oldenburg, Claes
Blackwood Prods., Inc.
Walker Art Ctr.

Oleszko, Pat
Blackwood Prods., Inc.
Video Data Bank

Olgas Range, Australia
Petrified Films, Inc.

Olitsky, Jules
Blackwood Prods., Inc.

Olivier, Laurence
Archive Film Prods., Inc.

NOTE: Access policies, availability and restrictions vary for each source. Please read each entry in full. Always consult "General Film and Videotape Collections" (page 599); these comprehensive collections contain material on every conceivable subject.

Daphne Productions, Inc.

Oliviera, Nathan
Albright-Knox Art Gallery

Ollman, Arthur
Port Washington Pub. Lib.

Olsen, Ole
Archive Film Prods., Inc.

Olson, Charles
San Francisco Bay Area TV News Arch.

Olson, Culbert
Southern Calif. Lib. for Soc. Stud. & Res.

Olympia, Wash. (History and culture)
Oregon Hist. Soc.

Olympic National Park, Wash.
Amer. Motion Pictures
Energy Productions
Petrified Films, Inc.

Olympics
ABC Sports, Inc.
Allen (John E.) Inc.
Amateur Athletic Foundation
Analogous Productions
Archive Film Prods., Inc.
Canadian Olympic Assn.
Fabulous Footage Inc.
Film Bank
Fish Films, Inc.
McDonald's Corp.
Natl. Archives (RG 111)
Natl. Archives of Canada
Second Line Search
Twentieth Century-Fox Movietonews
U.S. Olympic Comm.
Zielinski Productions, Inc.

Olympics (Berlin, 1936)
Canadian Olympic Assn.
Hoover Institution
Natl. Archives (RG 242)
Natl. Archives of Canada
Prelinger Assoc., Inc.
Prov. Arch. of Alberta

Olympics (Calgary, 1988)
Cappy Productions, Inc.

Olympics (Grenoble, 1968)
U.S. Olympic Comm.

Olympics (History)
U.S. Olympic Comm.

Olympics (Innsbruck, 1976)
U.S. Olympic Comm.

Olympics (Lake Placid, 1980)
Freewheelin' Films, Ltd.
New York State Arch. & Rec. Admin.
New York State Dept. of Econ. Devel.
U.S. Olympic Comm.

Olympics (Los Angeles, 1932)
Petrified Films, Inc.
Southern Calif. Lib. for Soc. Stud. & Res.

Olympics (Los Angeles, 1984)
Cappy Productions, Inc.
U.S. Olympic Comm.

Olympics (Melbourne, 1956)
Canadian Olympic Assn.

Olympics (Mexico City, 1968)
Canadian Olympic Assn.
Televisa, S.A.

Olympics (Montreal, 1976)

Natl. Archives of Canada
U.S. Olympic Comm.

Olympics (Moscow, 1980)
Canadian Olympic Assn.

Olympics (Munich, 1972)
U.S. Olympic Comm.

Olympics (Oslo, 1952)
Natl. Archives (RG 342)

Olympics (Sapporo, 1972)
U.S. Olympic Comm.

Olympics (Summer)
Analogous Productions

Olympics (Tokyo, 1964)
R5/S8 Presents

Olympics (Torch runners)
Applegate Entertainment

Olympics (Winter)
Analogous Productions
Jalbert Productions

Omaha, Nebr.
Film Bank

Oman (History and culture)
Acad. of Nat. Sci. of Phila. Lib.

Omo River, Ethiopia (History and culture)
Sobek Productions

"On the air" signs
See Signs ("On the air")

Onassis, Jacqueline Kennedy
Halcyon Days Prods.
MacDonald, J. Fred

Oncology
IMS Creative Communications

Ondaatje, Michael
Giorno Poetry Systems Inst.

Oneida, Wis.
Univ. of Wis., Green Bay, Ctr. TV Prod.

Ono, Yoko
Daphne Productions, Inc.

Ontario
Carleton Prods., Inc.
Departures, Inc.
Film Bank
4•6•8 Prods., Inc.
Natl. Arch. of Canada
Preview Media
TV Ontario

Ontario (History and culture)
Archives of Ontario
CITY Pulse Library
Canadian Broadcasting Corp.
Canadian Filmmakers Dist. Centre
DEC Film & Video
Fabulous Footage Inc.
First Run/Icarus Films, Inc.
Groupe Intervention Video
Huronia Hist. Parks
MacDonald, J. Fred
Natl. Arch. of Canada
Natl. Archives (RG 200)
Ontario Film Institute
Petrified Films, Inc.
Schiele Museum

Ontario Place (Toronto)
Archives of Ontario

TV Ontario

Opera
Blackwood Prods., Inc.
Cantor (Arthur) Inc.
Corinth Films/Corinth Video
Facets Multimedia, Inc.
Films Incorporated
House Found. for the Arts
Lib. of Congress, M/B/RS
March of Time
Metropolitan Opera House
Phoenix Films and Video
Research Video
Tamarelle's Intl. Films, Ltd.
Vedo Films/Novacom Video

Opera (Chinese)
Nan Hai (U.S.A.) Co., Inc.

Opera houses
Petrified Films, Inc.

Operating rooms
Amer. Journal of Nursing Co.
Center for Biomedical Comms.
Film Bank
Petrified Films, Inc.
Stock Shots
TV Ontario
See also Medical footage; Surgery

Operation Headstart
Southwest Film/Video Archives, SMU

Operation Sail (1976)
Allen (John E.) Inc.

Ophthalmology
Altschul Group
Emory Medical Television Network
Milner-Fenwick, Inc.
Nassau Comm. Coll. Lib.

Ophüls, Marcel
WGBH Educational Foundation

Opium
Natl. Archives (RG 170)
See also Narcotics

Opossums
Di Sesso (Moe) Wild Life Film Lib.

Oppenheim, Dennis
Blackwood Prods., Inc.
Video Data Bank

Oppenheimer, J. Robert
Archive Film Prods., Inc.
Film Bank
Los Alamos County Hist. Mus. Arch.
Pyramid Film and Video Corp.

Oral history
Agee (James) Film Project
Amer. Assn. for State & Local Hist.
Appalshop Films, Inc.
Arizona Hist. Soc.
B'nai B'rith Intl. Headquarters
Baylor Univ., Texas Coll.
Brandeis Univ. Lib.
Buhl Science Center
Central New England Film Arch.
Duke Univ., Perkins Lib.
Emory Univ., Spec. Coll.
Filmoteca de la UNAM
First Run/Icarus Films, Inc.
Flower Films & Video
Georgetown Univ., Spec. Coll. Div.
Hawaii Public Broadcasting Authority
Hist. Soc. of Seattle & King County
Imevision
Indiana Univ. Folklore Arch.
Indiana Univ. Northwest Lib.

Inst. for Labor Studies & Research
Intl. Gay & Lesbian Arch.
Intl. Women's Day Video Fest.
Labor Video Project
MacArthur (Gen. Douglas) Memorial
Mass. Inst. of Tech., MIT Museum
Memphis State Univ. Libraries
Nantucket Hist. Assn.
Natl. Archives of Canada
New Day Films
North Carolina Div. of Arch. & Hist.
Northern Ill. Univ., Reg. Hist. Ctr.
One, Inc.
Ozark Folk Center
Schomburg Ctr. for Res. in Black Culture
Siouxland Heritage Museum
State Hist. Soc. of Iowa
Tulane Univ., Amistad Res. Ctr.
Univ. Coll. of Cape Breton, Beaton Inst.
Université de Moncton, Centre d'Études Acad.
Univ. of Alabama, W.S. Hoole Spec. Coll.
Univ. of Miami, Arch. & Spec. Coll.
Univ. of Miss., Ctr. for Study of Southern Culture
Univ. of Southern Calif., Film & Video Dist. Ctr.
Univ. of Tex. at Austin, Barker Tex. Hist. Ctr.
Univ. of Tex. at Austin, Benson Lat. Am. Coll.
Univ. of Toledo, Univ. Arch.
Univ. of Utah, Marriott Lib.
Wayne State Univ., Folklore Arch.
Weill-Lenya Res. Ctr.
Western Kentucky Univ., Folklife Arch.
Western Reserve Hist. Soc.
Wheaton Coll., Wade Ctr.
Wright Brothers Coll.
Yakima Indian Nation Cultural Ctr.
Yakima Television Program

Oral hygiene
See Dentists and dentistry

Oral rehydration therapy
UNICEF, Div. Info. & Pub. Aff.

Orange County, New York
Xicom, Inc.

Oranges and orange groves
Film Bank
Petrified Films, Inc.

Orangutans
Johnson (Martin & Osa) Safari Museum
Kesser Stock Footage Library
Petrified Films, Inc.
Sobek Productions
TV Ontario

Orbison, Roy
Univ. of Tex. at Austin, Barker Tex. Hist. Ctr.

Orchards
CBS News Archives
Dreamlight Images, Inc.
Petrified Films, Inc.

Orchestras
Archive Film Prods., Inc.
Film Bank
Fish Films, Inc.
Hayes Prods., Inc.
Rockefeller Arch. Ctr.
Sullivan Video Services
Twentieth Century-Fox Movietonews
Vedo Films/Novacom Video
Video Tape Library, Ltd.
See also Concerts; Music

Orchids
Kesser Stock Footage Library

Oregon State Univ., Archives
Petrified Films, Inc.

Oregon
Amer. Motion Pictures
Dreamlight Images, Inc.
Film Bank
Jewell (Stuart) Productions
Marts (Steve) Prods.
Oregon Hist. Soc.
Petrified Films, Inc.
Portland Cable Access TV
Preview Media
Sobek Prods.
Stock Shots

Oregon (History and culture)
Archive Film Prods., Inc.
MacDonald, J. Fred
Media Project
Natl. Archives (RG 49)
Oregon Electric Railway Hist. Soc.
Oregon Hist. Soc.
Sobek Productions

Oregon Trail
Jewell (Stuart) Productions

Organ transplants
See Transplants (Organ)

Organized crime
See Crime and criminals (Organized crime)

Orienteering
TV Ontario

Orioles
Di Sesso (Moe) Wild Life Film Lib.

Orlando, Fla.
Creative Video, Inc.
Postcards Unlimited
Preview Media

Orono, Ontario (History and culture)
Natl. Archives of Canada

Orozco, Pascual
Archivo Historico Cinematografico
Natl. Archives (RG 200)

Orphanages
CBS News Archives
Petrified Films, Inc.

Orphans
Archive Film Prods., Inc.

Ortega, Daniel
Film/Audio Services, Inc.

Orthopedics
Emory Medical Television Network
IMS Creative Communications
Milner-Fenwick, Inc.
Nassau Comm. Coll. Lib.

Oryx
Telltales Associates Inc.

Osborn, Stella (Brunt)
Univ. of Mich., Mich. Hist. Colls.

Osborne, Tom
Fellowship of Christian Athletes

Oscilloscopes
Hewlett-Packard Co.

Oshawa, Ontario (History and culture)
Archives of Ontario

Oslo, Norway (History and culture)
Archive Film Prods., Inc.

Ospreys
Echo Film Prods., Inc.
Orion Post Production
Summit Films, Inc.
Wings Wildlife Prods. Inc.

Osteopathy
Amer. Osteopathic Assn.

Osteoporosis
Natl. Dairy Council

Ostriches
Miller (David Lee) Prods.
Petrified Films, Inc.
Wings Wildlife Prods. Inc.

Oswald, Lee Harvey
Archive Film Prods., Inc.
Southwest Film/Video Archives, SMU

Oswald, Marina
Daphne Productions, Inc.

Otis, Johnny
Los Angeles Blues Archives

Otolaryngology
IMS Creative Communications
Milner-Fenwick, Inc.
Ohio State Univ., Dept. of Photog. & Cinema
Visual Information Systems

Otorhinolaryngology
Nassau Comm. Coll. Lib.

Ottawa, Ontario
Carleton Prods. Inc.
Departures, Inc.
TV Ontario

Ottawa, Ontario (History and culture)
Archive Film Prods., Inc.
Archives of Ontario
Natl. Archives of Canada
Schiele Museum

Otters
Dreamlight Images, Inc.
Minnesota Zoo

Otto (Archduke)
March of Time

Our Gang
Film Preservation Assoc.
Videobrary, Inc.

Ouray, Colo.
Summit Films, Inc.

Outer space
See Space

Outfitters
See Guides (Outfitters)

Ouzels
Summit Films, Inc.
Wings Wildlife Prods. Inc.

Ovens
Prelinger Assoc., Inc.

Owen, Maureen
Video Data Bank

Owens, Craig
Video Data Bank

Owens, Jesse
Archive Film Prods., Inc.
Canadian Olympic Assn.
Jessiefilm
Prelinger Assoc., Inc.
U.S. Olympic Comm.

Owens, Nathaniel
Unicorn Projects

Owls
Amer. Motion Pictures
Di Sesso (Moe) Wild Life Film Lib.
Echo Film Prods., Inc.
Energy Productions
Film Bank
Minnesota Zoo
Petrified Films, Inc.
TV Ontario
Wings Wildlife Prods. Inc.

Ox wagon trains
Wings Wildlife Prods. Inc.

Oxen
Energy Productions
Petrified Films, Inc.

Oxford, England (History and culture)
Intl. Film Foundation

Oxyacetylene torches
Natl. Archives (RG 70)

Oystering
Mystic Seaport Museum, Inc.

Oysters
Film Bank

Ozark Mountains
Preview Media

Ozark Mountains (History and culture)
Ozark Folk Center

Ozone
NASA, Ames Res. Ctr., Imaging Tech. Branch

Paar, Jack
Daphne Productions, Inc.
Encore Entertainment
MacDonald, J. Fred
Moviecraft, Inc.

Pacemakers
Lawren Prods., Inc.
See also Heart

Pacific Basin region (History and culture)
East-West Center

Pacific Islands
Hawaii Public Broadcasting Authority
Pacific Productions

Pacific Islands (History and culture)
East-West Center
Johnson (Martin & Osa) Safari Museum
March of Time
Univ. of Hawaii at Manoa, Wong Ctr.

Pacific Ocean

Orion Post Production
Petrified Films, Inc.

Pacific Ocean (History and culture)
Natl. Archives (RG 18)

Pacifism
CBS News Archives
Creative Film Society
Films of India
Marquette Univ., Spec. Coll.
Petrified Films, Inc.
Resource Ctr. for Nonviolence
Univ. of Mich., Mich. Hist. Colls.

Paddy fields
See Rice paddies

Paderewski, Jan Ignace
Archive Film Prods., Inc.

Padre Island, Tex.
Preview Media

Page, Patti
Archive Film Prods., Inc.
MacDonald, J. Fred

Pageants
Brethren in Christ Church & Messiah Coll., Arch.
CBS News Archives
Twentieth Century-Fox Movietonews
See also Beauty pageants

Pagodas
Farkas Studios, Ltd.
Petrified Films, Inc.

Pahlavi, Mohammad Reza (Shah)
Halcyon Days Prods.
Grinberg (Sherman) Film Libraries (West)
Petrified Films, Inc.

Paik, Nam June
Long Beach Mus. of Art
Port Washington Pub. Lib.

Pain
Amer. Journal of Nursing Co.
Milner-Fenwick, Inc.

Paint
Prelinger Assoc., Inc.

Paint (Production)
Petrified Films, Inc.

Paint stores
Film Bank

Paintings
See Art and artists

Pakistan
Hammer (Armand) Prods.
Pan American Airlines Film Lib.
TV Ontario

Pakistan (History and culture)
Hammer (Armand) Prods.
Johns Hopkins Univ./Population Comm. Svcs.

Palaces
CBS News Archives
Echo Film Prods., Inc.
Hayes Prods., Inc.
Intl. Film Foundation
Petrified Films, Inc.
Twentieth Century-Fox Movietonews

NOTE: Access policies, availability and restrictions vary for each source. Please read each entry in full. Always consult "General Film and Videotape Collections" (page 599); these comprehensive collections contain material on every conceivable subject.

Palance, Jack
Banks Film Library

Palau
Passage Home Communications

Palau (History and culture)
Cinema Guild
Nuclear Free Zone Registry

Paleontology
Amer. Mus. Nat. Hist. Film Arch.
Media Guild
Shell Oil Co.
Univ. of Waterloo, A-V Centre

Palestine (Contemporary issues)
DEC Film & Video
Palestinian Cong. of North Amer.
Third World Newsreel
See also Israel; Middle East

Palestine (History and culture)
Amer.-Arab Anti-Discrimination Comm.
DEC Film & Video
First Run/Icarus Films, Inc.
March of Time
Monday, Wednesday, Friday Video Club
Natl. Archives (RG 59)
United Nations Ctr. for Human
    Settlements
Villon Films
See also Israel; Middle East

Pallas, Jim
Amer. Federation of the Arts

**Palm Beach County, Fla. (History and
    culture)**
Hist. Soc. of Palm Beach County

Palm Beach, Fla.
Passage Home Communications
Sea TV
Video Ventures Prods.

Palm Beach, Fla. (History and culture)
Petrified Films, Inc.

Palm Springs, Calif.
Creative Video, Inc.
Media West, Inc.
Preview Media

**Palm Springs, Calif. (History and
    culture)**
Petrified Films, Inc.

Palm trees
Brekke Television Prods.
Cinenet (Cinema Network)
Dreamlight Images, Inc.
Energy Productions
Fish Films, Inc.
Image Bank
Peak Productions, Inc.
Petrified Films, Inc.
Spectral Comms.

Palmdale, Calif. (History and culture)
Petrified Films, Inc.

Palmetto trees
Tri-Comm Prods.

Palo Alto, Calif.
Unicorn Projects

**Palo Duro Canyon, Tex. (History and
    culture)**
Panhandle-Plains Hist. Museum

**Pamlico Sound, Ga. (History and
    culture)**
Ocean Earth Constr. and Dev. Corp.

Pamphlets
Petrified Films, Inc.

Pamplona, Spain (History and culture)
Analogous Productions

Pan American Highway
Intl. Assn. of Independent Producers
Jewell (Stuart) Productions
Rockefeller Arch. Ctr.

**Pan-American Exposition (Buffalo,
    1901)**
Allen (John E.) Inc.
Film Bank
Lib. of Congress, M/B/RS

Pan-American Games
Canadian Olympic Assn.
U.S. Olympic Committee

**Pan-Pacific Exposition (San Francisco,
    1915)**
Pacific Film Archive

Panama
Canadian Broadcasting Corp.
Imagen y Sonido Independiente, S.A.

Panama (History and culture)
Academy of Health Sciences, U.S. Army
Democracy in Communication
March of Time
Natl. Archives (RG 59)
Natl. Archives (RG 185)

Panama Canal
Preview Media

Panama Canal (History and culture)
Analogous Productions
Archive Film Prods., Inc.
Cinema Guild
Natl. Archives (RG 18)
Natl. Archives (RG 59)
Natl. Archives (RG 111)
Natl. Archives (RG 185)
Oregon Hist. Soc.

Pandas
Hearst Metrotone News
Hoover Institution
Minnesota Zoo
New York Zoological Society
Petrified Films, Inc.

Panov, Valery and Galina
Villon Films

Panthers
Petrified Films, Inc.

Papanicolaou, George
New York Hosp.-Cornell Med. Ctr., Arch.

Paparazzi
Petrified Films, Inc.

Paper prints
See Motion pictures (Paper prints)

Paper products (Manufacturing)
Metro Communications, Inc.

Papermaking
Film Bank
Natl. Archives of Canada
Oregon Hist. Soc.
Prelinger Assoc., Inc.
Prov. Arch. of Alberta
Univ. of Wis., Green Bay, Ctr. TV Prod.

Papp, Joseph
New York Pub. Lib., Perf. Arts Res. Ctr.,
    Theatre on Film and Tape

**Papua New Guinea (History and
    culture)**
DEC Film & Video
Documentary Educational Resources

Parachuting
Analogous Productions
CBS News Archives
Energy Productions
Film Bank
Natl. Archives (RG 111)
Natl. Archives (RG 342)
Petrified Films, Inc.
Photo-Chuting Enterprises
Source Stock Footage Lib., Inc.
Summit Films, Inc.
Twentieth Century-Fox Movietonews
Video Tape Library, Ltd.
See also Skydiving

Parade floats
See Floats (Parade)

Parades
Allen (John E.) Inc.
Amer. Motion Pictures
Analogous Productions
Archive Film Prods., Inc.
Buffalo Bill Historical Center
CBS News Archives
Center for Southern Folklore
Circus World Mus. Lib. & Res. Ctr.
Energy Productions
Exodus Trust Archives of Erotology
Film Bank
Fish Films, Inc.
Glenbow Mus. Arch.
Goal Prod., Tourn. of Roses Film Lib.
Goodyear Tire and Rubber
Illinois State Hist. Lib.
Kentucky Dept. of Libraries & Archives
Las Vegas News Bureau
MacArthur (Gen. Douglas) Memorial
Miss America Pageant
Missouri Hist. Soc.
Natl. Archives (RG 24)
Natl. Archives (RG 111)
Natl. Archives (RG 200)
Natl. Archives (RG 274)
Natl. Archives (RG 330)
Natl. Archives of Canada
New York City Dept. of Rec. & Info.
    Svcs.
Nordic Heritage Museum
Northcoast Communication, Inc.
Northern Ill. Univ., Reg. Hist. Ctr.
Ohio State Univ., Dept. of Photog. &
    Cinema
Oregon State Univ., Archives
Petrified Films, Inc.
Prelinger Assoc., Inc.
Rainbow Video Prods.
SF•V Intl.
Schiele Museum
Sheffield (Erin) Prods.
TV Ontario
Texas Tech Univ., Southwest Coll.
Timesteps Prods., Inc.
Tulane Univ., Hogan Jazz Archive
Twentieth Century-Fox Movietonews
Univ. of Ill. Urbana-Champaign, Univ.
    Arch.
Utah State Archives
Video Tape Library, Ltd.
WTJX-TV
White Janssen, Inc.
See also Floats (Parades)

Parades (Easter)
Archive Film Prods., Inc.
Banks Film Library
Grinberg (Sherman) Film Libraries (West)
Petrified Films, Inc.

Parades (Ticker tape)

**Papua New Guinea (History and
    culture)** ...

Analogous Productions
Film Bank
Petrified Films, Inc.

Paraguay (History and culture)
Natl. Archives (RG 286)

Paramedics
Film Bank
IMS Creative Communications
Newsreel Video Service
Spectral Comms.
TV Ontario
See also Emergency medicine

Paramilitary groups (U.S.)
Hoover Institution

Parapsychology
Hartley Film Found., Inc.

Parasailing
Dreamlight Images, Inc.
Energy Productions
Source Stock Footage Lib., Inc.

Paratroopers
CBS News Archives
Spalla (Rick) Video Prods.

Parents and parenting
Altschul Group
Cambridge Documentary Films, Inc.
Courter Films & Assoc.
Education Development Ctr., Inc.
GPN
La Leche League of New Mexico
Lawren Prods., Inc.
Milner-Fenwick, Inc.
Natl. Archives (RG 33)
Natl. Archives (RG 102)
Natl. Archives (RG 306)
Natl. Archives of Canada
Natl. Assn. of Secondary Schl. Principals
New Day Films
New Orleans Video Access Ctr.
New York Pub. Lib., Early Childhood Res.
    & Info. Ctr.
Petrified Films, Inc.
Phoenix Films and Video
Polymorph Films, Inc.
Prelinger Assoc., Inc.
Sheen (Fulton J.) Comm. Ltd.
Toughlove
Univ. of Calif., Ext. Media Ctr.

Parícutin, Mexico (History and culture)
Natl. Archives (RG 200)

Paris
Beerger (Norman) Prods.
Creative Video, Inc.
Dreamlight Images, Inc.
Film Bank
Grinberg (Sherman) Film Libraries (West)
Kesser Stock Footage Library
Summit Films, Inc.
TV Ontario

Paris (History and culture)
Archive Film Prods., Inc.
Film Search
Petrified Films, Inc.
Soc. for French Amer. Cult. Svcs. & Educ.
    Aid
Third World Newsreel
Wiesenthal (Simon) Ctr.

Paris Peace Conference (World War I)
See World War I (Paris Peace Conference)

Park City, Utah
Source Stock Footage Lib., Inc.

Park Service, National (U.S.)
Natl. Archives (RG 48)
Natl. Archives (RG 79)

Parker, Bill
Video Data Bank

Parker, Bonnie
Archive Film Prods., Inc.
Natl. Archives (RG 21)

Parker, Charlie
Baker (Fred) Film & Video Co.
Chertok Assoc., Inc.

Parker, Fess
Banks Film Library

Parker, Olivia
Port Washington Pub. Lib.

Parker, Tom ("Colonel")
Banks Film Library

Parking lots
Baltimore Mus. of Industry
CBS News Archives
Film Bank
Petrified Films, Inc.

Parking meters
Prelinger Assoc., Inc.

Parks
Amer. Motion Pictures
CBS News Archives
Chicago Video Transfer
Elfstrom-Hilmer Prods.
Energy Productions
Everett Pub. Lib., Northwest Hist. Coll.
Film Bank
Glenbow Mus. Arch.
Indiana State Comm. on Public Records
Intl. Film Foundation
Long Island State Park Comm.
Natl. Archives (RG 69)
Network Productions
Petrified Films, Inc.
Prelinger Assoc., Inc.
Spectral Comms.
Stock House
Timesteps Prods., Inc.
Twentieth Century-Fox Movietonews
See also National parks; specific parks

Parks, Rosa
Natl. Assn. for the Advancement of
Colored People

Parliaments
CBS News Archives
TV Ontario

Parliaments (Ontario)
TV Ontario

Parliaments (Ontario) (History)
Archives of Ontario

Parliaments (U.K.)
Film Bank
Purdue Univ., Public Affairs Video Arch.

Parlow, Kathleen
Natl. Archives of Canada

Parrots
Di Sesso (Moe) Wild Life Film Lib.
Film Bank
Minnesota Zoo

Parsons, Betty
Video Data Bank

Parsons, Louella O.
Archive Film Prods., Inc.
Banks Film Library

Parties
Banks Film Library
CBS News Archives
Eisenhower (Dwight D.) Library
Film Bank
Fish Films, Inc.
Metro Communications, Inc.
Spectral Comms.
Twentieth Century-Fox Movietonews
Univ. of Wis., Green Bay, Ctr. TV Prod.

Pasadena, Calif. (History and culture)
Petrified Films, Inc.
Unicorn Projects

Paschke, Ed
Mus. of Contemporary Art
Video Data Bank

Pashtoon Nomads
Smithsonian Inst., Human Studies Film
Arch.

Passengers
Film Bank

Passover
Natl. Ctr. for Jewish Film

Pastures
CBS News Archives
Film Bank
Petrified Films, Inc.
Video Ventures Prods.

Pathology
Amer. Soc. of Clin. Path. Press
Emory Medical Television Network
Film Bank
Nassau Comm. Coll. Lib.

Patient education films and videotapes
Altschul Group
Amer. Dental Assn.
Amer. Heart Assn.
Amer. Journal of Nursing Co.
Amer. Soc. of Plastic & Recon. Surgeons
IMS Creative Communications
Milner-Fenwick, Inc.
Natl. Kidney Foundation, Inc.
Pyramid Film and Video Corp.
Rehab. Inst. of Chicago

Patients (Medical)
Blue Sky Comms., Inc.
Center for Biomedical Comms.
Dartnell
Film Bank
Fire Prev. Through Films, Inc.
Hooper (Josh) Prods., Inc.
Metro Communications, Inc.
Petrified Films, Inc.
Prelinger Assoc., Inc.
Rockefeller Arch. Ctr.
UCLA Behavioral Sci. Media Lab.
Video Genesis, Inc.
Wayne State Univ., Dir. Educ. in Nursing

Patios
Film Bank

Patriotism (U.S.)
Allen (John E.) Inc.
Amer. Citizenship Ctr.

Amer. Legion
Birch (John) Society
MacDonald, J. Fred
Natl. Archives (RG 24)
Streamline Film Archives

Patti, Sandi
Spectral Comms.

Paul, Les
Direct Cinema Ltd.

Pauline, Mark
Target Video

Pauling, Linus
Richter Productions

Pavlov, Ivan Petrovich
Film/Audio Services, Inc.
Intl. Film Foundation
Univ. of Akron, Arch. of Hist. of Amer.
Psychol.

Pawn shops
Petrified Films, Inc.

Payton, Walter
Nightingale-Conant Corp.

Pea pods
Energy Productions

Peace
Alternative Information Network
Bullfrog Films, Inc.
Canadian Filmmakers Dist. West
DEC Film & Video
Deep Dish TV
GRTV — Archives
Idera Films
Inst. for Space & Security Studies
Maryknoll Fathers & Brothers
Mass Media Ministries
Natl. Archives (RG 200)
Nuclear Free Zone Registry
Prelinger Assoc., Inc.
Richter Productions
SANE/Freeze
Southern Calif. Lib. for Soc. Stud. & Res.
Univ. of Waterloo, A-V Centre
Wilmington Coll. Peace Res. Ctr.
World Monitor

Peace Corps (U.S.)
Natl. Archives (RG 362)
Oregon State Univ., Archives
Peace Corps

Peaches
Petrified Films, Inc.
VTR Productions

Peacocks
Forsher (James) Prods. & Archives, Inc.
Latham Foundation
TV Ontario

Peanuts
Petrified Films, Inc.

Pearl Harbor, Hawaii
Analogous Productions
Film Bank

**Pearl Harbor, Hawaii (History and
culture)**
Amer. Portrait, An
Experimental Aircraft Assn.
Grinberg (Sherman) Film Libraries (East)
Hawaii Public Broadcasting Authority

Natl. Archives (RG 226)
Natl. Archives (RG 342)
Natl. Archives/Natl. AV Ctr.
Petrified Films, Inc.
Prelinger Assoc., Inc.

Pearls
Film Bank
Natl. Archives (RG 22)

Pearlstein, Philip
Creative Film Society
Video Data Bank

Pears
Oregon State Univ., Archives
VTR Productions

Pearson, Drew
Johnson (Lyndon Baines) Library

Pearson, Paul David
Southern Calif. Inst. of Architecture

Peas
VTR Productions

Peasants
Cinema Guild

Pebbles
Film Bank

Peck, Gregory
Banks Film Library
Spectral Comms.

Pedestrians
Film Bank
Prelinger Assoc., Inc.
TV Ontario
Timesteps Prods., Inc.

Pediatrics
Altschul Group
Amer. Journal of Nursing Co.
Emory Medical Television Network
IMS Creative Communications
Milner-Fenwick, Inc.
Nassau Comm. Coll. Lib.

Pedicabs
CBS News Archives

Peep shows
Lib. of Congress, M/B/RS
See also Pornography

Peking
See Beijing

Pelicans
Jewell (Stuart) Productions
Kesser Stock Footage Library
TV Ontario

Pell, Claiborne
Univ. of Rhode Island, Univ. Lib.

Pelli, Cesar
Mus. of Contemporary Art

Peltier, Leonard
Alternative Information Network
Intermedia Arts Minnesota

Penang, Malaysia
Farkas Studios, Ltd.

Pencil sharpeners
Prelinger Assoc., Inc.

NOTE: Access policies, availability and restrictions vary for each source. Please read each entry in full. Always consult "General Film and Videotape Collections" (page 599); these comprehensive collections contain material on every conceivable subject.

Pendulums
Prelinger Assoc., Inc.

Penguins
Cousteau Society
Film Bank
Kesser Stock Footage Library
Marineland of Florida
Petrified Films, Inc.

Penicillin
Amer. Chemical Soc.

Penn, Sean
Los Angeles News Service

Pennsylvania
Cabscott Broadcast Prods.
Dreamlight Images, Inc.
Energy Prods.
Kesser Stock Footage Lib.
Landmark Stock Footage Co.
Preview Media
Riccitelli (Bruce) Prods.
Unicorn Projects
Wallen (Dick) Prods.

Pennsylvania (History and culture)
Archive Film Prods., Inc.
California Newsreel
Carnegie District Film Ctr.
Center for Public Dialogue
Documentary Educ. Resources
Finley (Stuart) Inc.
Icarus Films Intl., Inc.
Natl. Archives (RG 24)
Natl. Archives (RG 378)
Natl. Library of Medicine
New Day Films
Pennsylvania State Arch.
Petrified Films, Inc.
Prelinger Assoc., Inc.
Smithsonian Inst., Human Studies Film
  Arch.
TV Ontario
Temple Univ., Urban Arch. Ctr.
United Nations Ctr. for Human
  Settlements
Univ. of Pittsburgh, Arch. of Indust. Soc.

Pennsylvania Dutch country
Preview Media

Penny arcades
Petrified Films, Inc.

Penshurst, Wales
Unicorn Projects

**Pension Policy, President's Committee
  on**
Natl. Archives (RG 220)

Pentagon, The (Washington, D.C.)
Carousel Film & Video
Natl. Archives (RG 121)

Pentathlons
Hayes Prods., Inc.

Pentecostal
See Religion (Pentecostal)

People and products
Film Bank
Petrified Films, Inc.
Prelinger Assoc., Inc.
See also Product shots

Peoria, Ill.
Video I-D, Inc.

Peoria, Ill. (History and culture)
Illinois State Hist. Lib.

Pep, Willy
New Jersey Network

Peppard, George
Banks Film Library

Pepper fields
Petrified Films, Inc.

Peppers
Energy Productions

Perception
Prelinger Assoc., Inc.

Perch
TV Ontario

Percy, Charles H.
Duke Univ., Perkins Lib.

Perez, Richie
Paper Tiger TV

Perez-Gomez, Alberto
Southern Calif. Inst. of Architecture

Performance art
Art Com/La Mamelle, Inc.
Artists' Television Project
Arts Television Centre
Center for New Television
Dance Theater Workshop
De Saisset Museum
EM/Media Archives
EZTV
Electronic Arts Intermix
Experimental Intermedia Foundation
Film Bank
Franklin Furnace Archive, Inc.
Giorno Poetry Systems Inst.
Hallwalls Cont. Arts Ctr.
House Found. for the Arts
Kitchen, The
New American Makers
New Langton Arts
P. R. I. M.
Real Art Ways
Survival Research Laboratories
Target Video
Twin Cities Public Television (KTCA)
Video In
Walker Art Ctr.
Western Front Society

Performing animals
See Animals (Performing)

Perfume
CBS News Archives

Perkins, Anthony
Spectral Comms.

Perlman, Rhea
Spectral Comms.

Perls, Frederick
Psychological and Educational Films

Peron, Eva
Film Education Institute

Peron, Juan
Archive Film Prods., Inc.
Film Education Institute

Pershing, Gen. John J.
Archive Film Prods., Inc.
Natl. Archives (RG 24)
Natl. Archives (RG 200)
Natl. Archives (RG 342)

Persian Gulf (Contemporary issues)
Center for Defense Information

Personal hygiene
Churchill Films
Film Bank
Natl. Archives (RG 90)
Prelinger Assoc., Inc.
Streamline Film Archives

Personalities
See Celebrities

Perth, Australia
Farkas Studios, Ltd.
Petrified Films, Inc.

Peru
Film Search
Hammer (Armand) Prods.
Preview Media

Peru (Contemporary issues)
DEC Film & Video
Icarus-Tamouz Media, Inc.
Oxfam America

Peru (History and culture)
Archive Film Prods., Inc.
DEC Film & Video
Democracy in Communication
Film/Audio Services, Inc.
Hammer (Armand) Prods.
Idera Films
Inter-American Foundation
Intl. Film Foundation
Rockefeller Arch. Ctr.
Schweitzer (Albert) Ctr.
U.S. Committee for UNICEF
UNICEF, Div. Info. & Pub. Aff.
Univ. of Arizona, Film Lib.

Pest control
Natl. Archives (RG 22)
Natl. Archives (RG 33)

Pesticides
Canadian Filmmakers Dist. Centre
Cinema Guild
Intermedia Arts Minnesota
Natl. Archives (RG 7)
Natl. Archives (RG 16)
Natl. Archives (RG 227)
Petrified Films, Inc.
Prelinger Assoc., Inc.
Richter Productions
United Farm Workers of America (UFW)

Pet shops
Petrified Films, Inc.
TV Ontario

Pet shows
Pennebaker Associates, Inc.
Twentieth Century-Fox Movietonews

Peterborough, Ontario
TV Ontario

Peters, Bernadette
Spectral Comms.

Peters, Tom
Ideal Comms., Inc.

**Petersburg, Alaska (History and
  culture)**
Oregon Hist. Soc.

Petra, Jordan
TV Ontario

Petra, Jordan (History and culture)
Villon Films

Petri dishes
Film Bank

Petrie, James
Univ. of Wyoming, Amer. Heritage Ctr.

Petrified Forest, Ariz.
Petrified Films, Inc.

Petrochemical industry
Farkas Studios, Ltd.
Richter Productions

Petroglyphs
TV Ontario

Petroleum industry
See Oil industry; Petrochemical industry

Pets
AIMS Media
Amer. Humane Assn.
Amer. Veterinary Medical Assn.
Analogous Productions
Animal Protection Institute of America
Film Search
Focus on Animals
Hayes Prods., Inc.
Latham Foundation
Petrified Films, Inc.
Phoenix Films and Video
SF•V Intl.
TV Ontario
See also Cats; Dogs

Petting
Prelinger Assoc., Inc.

Pettit, Philippe
Navajo Tribe, Off. Broadcast Svcs.

Pettus, Terry
Intermedia Arts Minnesota

Petty, Tom
Spectral Comms.

Pevsner, Antoine
Blackwood Prods., Inc.

Pews
Petrified Films, Inc.

Peyote
Smithsonian Inst., Human Studies Film
  Arch.

Pfaff, Judy
Albright-Knox Art Gallery

Pharmaceutical industry
Amer. Inst. of the Hist. of Pharmacy
Idera Films
Intl. Media Services, Inc.
Miles Corporate Archive
See also Drug stores; Pharmacology

Pharmacies
See Drug stores

Pharmacology
Amer. Inst. of the Hist. of Pharmacy
Emory Medical Television Network
IMS Creative Communications
Nassau Comm. Coll. Lib.

Pharmacy
Amer. Assn. of Retired Persons

Pheasants
Indiana State Comm. on Public Records
New Mexico State Records Ctr. & Arch.
New Zealand Embassy Film Lib.
Petrified Films, Inc.

Philadelphia
Cabscott Broadcast Prods.
Dreamlight Images, Inc.

Landmark Stock Footage Co.
Preview Media
Wallen (Dick) Prods.

Philadelphia (History and culture)
Archive Film Prods., Inc.
Icarus Films Intl., Inc.
Petrified Films, Inc.
Prelinger Assoc., Inc.
Temple Univ., Urban Arch. Ctr.
United Nations Ctr. for Human
    Settlements

Philadelphia Mint
Natl. Archives (RG 104)

**Philadelphia, Miss. (History and
    culture)**
MacDonald, J. Fred

Philanthropy
Natl. Archives (RG 200)
Prelinger Assoc., Inc.

Philip, Prince
Spalla (Rick) Video Prods.

Philip, S. Dak. (History and culture)
South Dakota State Lib.

Philippines
Farkas Studios, Ltd.
Pan American Airlines Film Lib.
People's Fund
World Monitor

Philippines (Contemporary issues)
Icarus-Tamouz Media, Inc.

Philippines (History and culture)
Blackwood (Christian) Prods., Inc.
Canadian Filmmakers Dist. Centre
DEC Film & Video
Film/Audio Services, Inc.
Flower Films & Video
Hansen, Jack
Icarus Films Intl., Inc.
Icarus-Tamouz Media, Inc.
Idera Films
Johns Hopkins Univ./Population Comm.
    Svcs.
Lib. of Congress, M/B/RS
March of Time
Natl. Archives (RG 200)
Natl. Archives (RG 242)
Natl. Archives (RG 331)
Natl. Archives/Natl. AV Ctr.
Oakland Public Lib., Asian Branch Lib.
Petrified Films, Inc.
Singer-Sharrette Traditional Healing Films
Smithsonian Inst., Human Studies Film
    Arch.
U.S. Committee for UNICEF
Univ. of Mich., Mich. Hist. Colls.
White Janssen, Inc.
World Monitor

**Philipsburg Manor, N.Y. (History and
    culture)**
Rockefeller Arch. Ctr.

Phillips, Tom
Amer. Federation of the Arts

Philomath, Oreg. (History and culture)
Media Project

Philosophers and philosophy
Long Beach Mus. of Art
Phoenix Films and Video

Soc. for French Amer. Cult. Svcs. & Educ.
    Aid
Univ. of Calif., Ext. Media Ctr.
V/tape

Phoenix, Ariz.
Creative Video, Inc.
Preview Media
Producers' Service

Phoenix, Ariz. (History and culture)
MacDonald, J. Fred
Prelinger Assoc., Inc.

Phonographs and phonograph records
Film Bank
Fish Films, Inc.
Petrified Films, Inc.
Prelinger Assoc., Inc.
See also Recording industry

**Phonographs and phonograph records
    (Manufacturing)**
Prelinger Assoc., Inc.
TV Ontario

Photochemistry
Media Guild

Photocopy machines
Petrified Films, Inc.

Photocopy machines (Production)
Applegate Entertainment

Photographers and photography
Blackwood Prods., Inc.
CBS News Archives
Camera Three Prods., Inc.
Cantor (Arthur) Inc.
Carousel Film & Video
Center for Creative Photography
Center for Humanities, Inc.
Center for Southern Folklore
Cinema Guild
Coronet/MTI Film & Video
Creative Film Society
Fish Films, Inc.
GPN
Hearst Metrotone News
Intl. Center of Photography
Media West, Inc.
Mus. at Large, Ltd.
Natl. Archives of Canada
Passage Home Communications
Petrified Films, Inc.
Phoenix Films and Video
Port Washington Pub. Lib.
Prelinger Assoc., Inc.
Pyramid Film and Video Corp.
Ski TV Prods., Inc./Channel 24
Soc. for French Amer. Cult. Svcs. & Educ.
    Aid
Twentieth Century-Fox Movietonews

Photojournalism
Natl. Press Photographers Assn., Inc.

Photosynthesis
Amer. Chemical Soc.

Physical education
AIMS Media
Amer. Alliance for Health, Phys. Ed., Rec.
    & Dance Arch.
Barr Films
Finley (Stuart) Inc.
GPN
Natl. Archives of Canada
Natl. Assn. for Sport & Phys. Ed.
Phoenix Films and Video

Physical fitness
Athletic Institute
Coronet/MTI Film & Video
Films for the Humanities and Sciences
Intl. Dance Exercise Assn.
McDonald's Corp.
Narcotics Education, Inc.
Prelinger Assoc., Inc.
Rogers (Will) Institute
TV Ontario
United Training Media
See also Aerobic exercise; Exercise

Physical sciences
AIMS Media
Britannica Films & Video
Center for Humanities, Inc.
Cinema Guild
Coronet/MTI Film & Video
Nassau Comm. Coll. Lib.
Natl. Archives (RG 69)
Natl. Archives (RG 307)
Natl. Archives/Natl. AV Ctr.
Prelinger Assoc., Inc.
Pyramid Film and Video Corp.
Univ. of Calif., Ext. Media Ctr.

Physical therapy
Amer. Physical Therapy Assn.
Blue Sky Comms., Inc.

Physics
Center for Humanities, Inc.
Cinema Guild
Creative Venture Films
Educational Images, Ltd.
Films for the Humanities and Sciences
Intl. Film Bureau, Inc.
Los Alamos Natl. Lab.
Media Guild
Natl. Archives of Canada
Natl. Archives/Natl. AV Ctr.
Natl. Science Foundation
Prelinger Assoc., Inc.
Univ. of Calif., Ext. Media Ctr.

Physics (Nuclear)
Amer. Nuclear Society

Physiology
Amer. Heart Assn.
Center for Humanities, Inc.
Churchill Films
Coronet/MTI Film & Video
Educational Images, Ltd.
Focus Intl. Inc.
Historical Health Film Coll.
IMS Creative Communications
Intl. Film Bureau, Inc.
Multi-Focus, Inc.
Pyramid Film and Video Corp.

Piaget, Jean
Inst. for Psychoanalysis

Piano players
Fish Films, Inc.

Piano stores
Petrified Films, Inc.

Pianos
See Keyboards

Picasso, Pablo
Amer. Federation of the Arts
Blackwood Prods., Inc.
Creative Film Society
Natl. Gallery of Art
Prestige Film Corp.

Piccadilly Circus (London)
Dreamlight Images, Inc.
Film Bank
Petrified Films, Inc.

**Piccadilly Circus (London) (History and
    culture)**
Archive Film Prods., Inc.

Pickens, Slim
Archive Film Prods., Inc.

Pickford, Mary
Banks Film Library
Film/Audio Services, Inc.
Petrified Films, Inc.

Picnics
CBS News Archives
Dreamlight Images, Inc.
Forsher (James) Prods. & Archives, Inc.
Hayes Prods., Inc.
Petrified Films, Inc.
Timesteps Prods., Inc.
Twentieth Century-Fox Movietonews

Picon, Molly
Cantor (Arthur) Inc.

Picos, Corey
Second Line Search

Pie fights
Fish Films, Inc.

Piene, Otto
Blackwood Prods., Inc.

Piers
See Harbors

Pigeons
Amer. Motion Pictures
Di Sesso (Moe) Wild Life Film Lib.
Film Bank
Hi-Tech Productions
Petrified Films, Inc.
TV Ontario

Pigeons (Homing)
UDS Company

Pigs
Amer. Veterinary Medical Assn.
Oregon State Univ., Archives
Petrified Films, Inc.
Prelinger Assoc., Inc.
TV Ontario

Pike
TV Ontario

Pike's Peak, Colo.
Summit Films, Inc.
Volkswagen of America, Inc.

Pilgrimages
CBS News Archives

Pilgrims
Archive Film Prods., Inc.
Petrified Films, Inc.
Prelinger Assoc., Inc.

Pills
Amer. Inst. of the Hist. of Pharmacy
Film Bank
See also Drug stores; Pharmaceutical
    industry; Pharmacology

NOTE: Access policies, availability and restrictions vary for each source. Please read each entry in full. Always consult "General Film and Videotape Collections" (page 599); these comprehensive collections contain material on every conceivable subject.

Pillsbury, George
Duke Univ., Perkins Lib.

Pilots
See Aircraft; Aviation

Pilsudski, J.
Pilsudski (J.) Inst. of Amer.

Pin-ups
Archive Film Prods., Inc.

Pinball
TV Ontario

Pinderhughes, John
Port Washington Pub. Lib.

Pine cones
Film Bank

Pine trees
Energy Productions
TV Ontario

Pineapples
Bishop Mus., Visual Coll.
Dreamlight Images, Inc.
Petrified Films, Inc.

Pineault, Serge
Université Laval, Svc. des Res.
Pédagogiques

Pinelands National Reserve, N.J.
New Jersey Network

Ping-pong
Film Bank
TV Ontario
Twentieth Century-Fox Movietonews

Pinochet, Augusto
Cinema Guild

Pinza, Ezio
MacDonald, J. Fred

Pioneers
Archive Film Prods., Inc.
Film Bank
Glenbow Mus. Arch.
Washington State Hist. Soc.

Pipe (Corrugated) (Production)
Petrified Films, Inc.

Pipe organs
New Jersey Network

Pipelines
Alaska Video Prods.
Dreamlight Images, Inc.
Energy Productions
First Group Comms., Inc.
Hammer (Armand) Prods.
Imperial Oil Ltd.
Petrified Films, Inc.
Prelinger Assoc., Inc.
Summit Films, Inc.
Univ. of Alberta, Boreal Inst. for Northern
Studies
Univ. of Tex. at Austin, Petrol. Ext. Svc.

Piscopo, Joe
Spectral Comms.

Pistol shooting (Sport)
Dreamlight Images, Inc.
Sportsfilm

Pit blasts
Energy Productions

Pittsburgh

Energy Productions
Kesser Stock Footage Library
Unicorn Projects

Pittsburgh (History and culture)
Archive Film Prods., Inc.
California Newsreel
Carnegie District Film Ctr.
Center for Public Dialogue
Documentary Educational Resources
Natl. Archives (RG 24)
New Day Films
Petrified Films, Inc.
Prelinger Assoc., Inc.
Univ. of Pittsburgh, Arch. of Indust. Soc.

Pius XII, Pope
Archive Film Prods., Inc.
March of Time
Univ. of Ill. Urbana-Champaign, Univ.
Arch.

Pixar image computer
SIGGRAPH

Pizzas
Film Bank

Planes
See Aircraft

Planetariums
CBS News Archives
TV Ontario

Planets
CBS News Archives
California Inst. of Tech., Jet Propulsion
Laboratory
Charisma Prods., Ltd./Visual Motion
Dreamlight Images, Inc.
Film Bank
NASA, Lewis Research Center
NASA, Office of Comm.
Rosebush Visions Corp.
Video Tape Library, Ltd.
See also Solar system; Space; specific
planets

Plantations
Mississippi Dept. of Arch. & Hist.
Mountain Video Associates
Natl. Archives (RG 234)
Prelinger Assoc., Inc.
Preview Media

Plants
Acad. of Nat. Sci. of Phila. Lib.
Britannica Films & Video
CBS News Archives
Cinenet (Cinema Network)
Coronet/MTI Film & Video
Dreamlight Images, Inc.
Energy Productions
Film Bank
Image Bank
Jewell (Stuart) Productions
Kesser Stock Footage Library
Moody Inst. of Science
Natl. Archives (RG 33)
Oregon State Univ., Archives
Postcards Associates
TV Ontario
See also Flowers; Nature; specific plants

Plants (Carnivorous)
Dreamlight Images, Inc.

Plants (Hothouse)
Petrified Films, Inc.

**Plaquemines Parish, La. (History and
culture)**
Cinema Guild

Plaques
CBS News Archives

Plastics
Prelinger Assoc., Inc.

Plastics industry
Hagley Mus. and Lib.
Metro Communications, Inc.
Prelinger Assoc., Inc.
Riccitelli (Bruce) Prods.
TV Ontario

Plate tectonics
Natl. Oceanic & Atmospheric Admin.

Plates (Food)
Film Bank

Plath, Sylvia
Camera Three Prods., Inc.
Intellimation

Playgrounds
Amer. Alliance for Health, Phys. Ed., Rec.
& Dance Arch.
CBS News Archives
Film Bank
TV Ontario

Plazas
Petrified Films, Inc.

Pleshette, Suzanne
Banks Film Library

Plexiglas
Prelinger Assoc., Inc.

Plossu, Bernard
Port Washington Pub. Lib.

Plows and plowing
CBS News Archives
Energy Productions
Farkas Studios, Ltd.
Natl. Archives (RG 96)
See also Farms and farming

Plumbers
Petrified Films, Inc.

Plums
Oregon State Univ., Archives

Plutonium
Amer. Chemical Soc.
Petrified Films, Inc.

Plymire, Victor Guy
Wheaton Coll., Billy Graham Ctr.

Pocahontas
Archive Film Prods., Inc.

Pocock, Philip
Port Washington Pub. Lib.

Pocono Mountains (Pa.)
New Jersey Network
Preview Media

Podiatry
Calif. College of Podiatric Medicine

Poe, Edgar Allan
Bronx County Hist. Soc.
Handel Film Corp.

Poetry
Carousel Film & Video
Coe Film Assoc., Inc.
Coronet/MTI Film & Video
DEC Film & Video
EZTV

Giorno Poetry Systems Inst.
Imevision
Intellimation
92nd Street YM & YWHA Assn. Archives
Phoenix Films and Video
Prestige Film Corp.
Univ. of Calif., Davis, Shields Library
Video Data Bank
WTJX-TV

Poff, Richard H.
Natl. Archives (RG 200)

Poinsettias
TV Ontario

**Point Barrow, Alaska (History and
culture)**
Oregon Hist. Soc.
Smithsonian Inst., Human Studies Film
Arch.

Point 4 Program (U.S.) (1949)
Natl. Archives (RG 59)

Point Lobos, Calif.
Energy Productions

Point-of-view shots
Cinenet (Cinema Network)
Dorn (Larry) Associates
Dreamlight Images, Inc.
Echo Film Prods., Inc.
Energy Productions
Film Bank
Petrified Films, Inc.
Second Line Search
Zielinski Productions, Inc.

Point-of-view shots (Airplanes)
Dreamlight Images, Inc.
Energy Productions
Petrified Films, Inc.

**Point-of-view shots (Amusement park
rides)**
Dreamlight Images, Inc.
Energy Productions
Petrified Films, Inc.
Quinn (Bill) Prods.

**Point-of-view shots (Automobiles
racing)**
Petrified Films, Inc.

Point-of-view shots (Ballooning)
Peak Productions, Inc.

Point-of-view shots (Boats)
Dreamlight Images, Inc.
Energy Productions
Petrified Films, Inc.

Point-of-view shots (Driving)
Cinenet (Cinema Network)
Dreamlight Images, Inc.
Energy Productions
Halicki (H.B.) Prods.
MacGillivray Freeman Films
Petrified Films, Inc.
Stegman Productions

Point-of-view shots (Elevators)
Petrified Films, Inc.

Point-of-view shots (Flying)
Dreamlight Images, Inc.
Energy Productions

Point-of-view shots (Gliders)
Peak Productions, Inc.

Point-of-view shots (Gondolas)
Petrified Films, Inc.

Point of view shots (Hang-gliding)
Dreamlight Images, Inc.
Energy Productions
Summit Films, Inc.

Point-of-view shots (Helicopters)
Echo Film Prods., Inc.

Point-of-view shots (Kayaking)
Summit Films, Inc.

Point-of-view shots (Overhead)
Film Bank

Point-of-view shots (Parasails)
Energy Productions

Point-of-view shots (Phonograph styli)
Prelinger Assoc., Inc.

Point-of-view shots (Rafting)
Energy Productions
Natural Reflections Video

Point-of-view shots (Railroads)
Energy Productions
Petrified Films, Inc.

Point-of-view shots (Sailing)
Energy Productions

Point-of-view shots (Skiing)
Energy Productions
Summit Films, Inc.

Point-of-view shots (Space shuttle)
Energy Productions

Point-of-view shots (Stagecoaches)
Petrified Films, Inc.

Point-of-view shots (Subways)
Energy Productions

Point-of-view shots (Trucks)
Energy Productions

Point-of-view shots (Ultralights)
Peak Productions, Inc.

Poipu, Hawaii
Preview Media

Poirier, Claude
Université Laval, Svc. des Res.
  Pédagogiques

Poker
Petrified Films, Inc.

Poland
Film Bank

Poland (History and culture)
Allen (John E.) Inc.
Archive Film Prods., Inc.
Bund Arch. of the Jewish Labor
  Movement
Film/Audio Services, Inc.
Finley (Stuart) Inc.
Hoover Institution
Intl. Film Foundation
March of Time
Mariners' Museum
Natl. Archives (RG 28)
Natl. Archives (RG 226)
Natl. Archives (RG 342)
Natl. Archives/Natl. AV Ctr.
Natl. Ctr. for Jewish Film
Pilsudski (J.) Inst. of Amer.
Prestige Film Corp.

Southern Calif. Lib. for Soc. Stud. & Res.

Polanski, Roman
Daphne Productions, Inc.

Polar bears
Analogous Productions
Circus World Mus. Lib. & Res. Ctr.
Dreamlight Images, Inc.
Miller (David Lee) Prods.
Petrified Films, Inc.
TV Ontario

Polar sciences
Natl. Archives (RG 77)
Natl. Archives (RG 342)
Natl. Science Foundation

Pole vaulting
See Track and field

Police
Analogous Productions
Archive Film Prods., Inc.
CBS News Archives
Cinema Guild
Coronet/MTI Film & Video
Film Bank
Fish Films, Inc.
Forsher (James) Prods. & Archives, Inc.
Grinberg (Sherman) Film Libraries (West)
Highway Safety Films, Inc.
Icarus Films Intl., Inc.
Los Angeles News Service
March of Time
Monday, Wednesday, Friday Video Club
Natl. Archives of Canada
New York City Dept. of Rec. & Info.
  Svcs.
Newsreel Video Service
Off-Broadway Video Prods.
Pennebaker Associates, Inc.
Pennsylvania State Arch.
Petrified Films, Inc.
Prelinger Assoc., Inc.
Prestige Film Corp.
Producers Library Service
Spectral Comms.
TV Ontario
Twentieth Century-Fox Movietonews
Video Tape Library, Ltd.
White Star Prof. Film Svcs., Inc.
See also Detectives

Police (Horseback)
Petrified Films, Inc.

Police (London)
TV Ontario

Police (Motorcycle)
Petrified Films, Inc.

Police (Nicaragua)
Xchange TV

Police (Oddities)
Petrified Films, Inc.

Police (Paris)
TV Ontario

Police (Training)
Calif. Highway Patrol Acad. Media Center
Coronet/MTI Film & Video

Police (Water patrol)
TV Ontario

Police cars
Columbia Pictures TV/Stock Film Library

Film Bank
Petrified Films, Inc.

Police stations
Film Bank
Forsher (James) Prods. & Archives, Inc.
Petrified Films, Inc.
Stock House

Police-community relations
Coronet/MTI Film & Video
Natl. Archives (RG 381)

Policeband, Boris
Monday, Wednesday, Friday Video Club

Polio
Hearst Metrotone News
Historical Health Film Coll.
March of Dimes Birth Defects Found.

Polish Americans
Flower Films & Video
Pilsudski (J.) Inst. of Amer.

Polish Canadians
Univ. Coll. of Cape Breton, Beaton Inst.

Political campaign commercials
Adbank
Apertura
Aristotle Industries
Eisenhower (Dwight D.) Library
Georgetown Univ., Spec. Coll. Div.
Guggenheim Productions, Inc.
Illinois State Hist. Lib.
Johnson (Lyndon Baines) Library
Kennedy (John F.) Library
MacDonald, J. Fred
Mus. of Broadcasting
Ohio Historical Soc.
Political Commercial Archive
Prelinger Assoc., Inc.
Read (Brooks) & Assoc.
Saint John's Univ., Spec. Coll.
Smith (Margaret Chase) Lib. Ctr.
Smithsonian Inst., NMAH, Div. Polit.
  Hist.
State Hist. Soc. of Iowa
Texas Tech Univ., Southwest Coll.
UCLA Film & Television Archive
Univ. of Maryland, McKeldin Lib.
Univ. of Mich., Mich. Hist. Colls.
Univ. of Missouri-St. Louis
Univ. of N.C. Wilmington, Devries-
  Bulluck Coll.
Univ. of Tex. at Austin, Barker Tex. Hist.
  Ctr.

Political campaigns
ABC News Interactive
Analogous Productions
Appalachian State Univ., Eury Coll.
C-SPAN (Cable Satellite Public Affairs
  Network)
CBS News Archives
Calif. State Archives
Duke Univ., Perkins Lib.
Eisenhower (Dwight D.) Library
Hearst Metrotone News
Illinois State Hist. Lib.
Kennedy (John F.) Library
MacDonald, J. Fred
Mus. & Hist. Div., City of Sacramento
New York Pub. Lib., Rare Books &
  Manuscripts Div.
News on Film
Roosevelt (Franklin D.) Lib.
Saint John's Univ., Spec. Coll.
Truman (Harry S) Library
UCLA Film & Television Archive

Univ. of Missouri-St. Louis
Univ. of Rhode Island, Univ. Lib.
Univ. of Rochester Lib., Rare Books &
  Spec. Coll.
Univ. of Vermont, Bailey/Howe Lib.
See also Elections; Presidential elections
  (U.S.)

Political conventions
Allen (John E.) Inc.
Analogous Productions
Boston Stock Market
C-SPAN (Cable Satellite Public Affairs
  Network)
CBS News Archives
Mus. & Hist. Div., City of Sacramento
Natl. Archives (RG 200)
Petrified Films, Inc.
Purdue Univ., Public Affairs Video Arch.

**Political conventions (Communist
  Party)**
Communist Party USA

Political conventions (Democratic)
Roosevelt (Franklin D.) Lib.

Political conventions (Democratic, 1956)
MacDonald, J. Fred

Political conventions (Democratic, 1968)
MacDonald, J. Fred
Payne, Roz

Political conventions (Democratic, 1972)
Electronic Arts Intermix
Illinois State Hist. Lib.

Political conventions (Democratic, 1976)
Natl. Archives (RG 200)

Political conventions (Democratic, 1980)
Natl. Archives (RG 200)

Political conventions (Democratic, 1984)
Gay Cable Network
Harriman Communications Ctr.
Natl. Archives (RG 200)

Political conventions (Democratic, 1988)
Harriman Communications Ctr.

Political conventions (Prohibition Party)
Univ. of Mich., Mich. Hist. Colls.

Political conventions (Republican)
Indiana Hist. Soc., Smith Memorial Lib.
Republican Natl. Committee

Political conventions (Republican, 1932)
Natl. Archives (RG 130)

Political conventions (Republican, 1952)
Eisenhower (Dwight D.) Library

Political conventions (Republican, 1956)
Eisenhower (Dwight D.) Library
MacDonald, J. Fred

Political conventions (Republican, 1964)
Estuary Press

Political conventions (Republican, 1972)
Electronic Arts Intermix
Media Bus

Political conventions (Republican, 1976)
Natl. Archives (RG 200)

Political conventions (Republican, 1980)
Natl. Archives (RG 200)

NOTE: Access policies, availability and restrictions vary for each source. Please read each entry in full. Always consult "General Film and Videotape Collections" (page 599); these comprehensive collections contain material on every conceivable subject.

Political conventions (Republican, 1984)
Gay Cable Network
Natl. Archives (RG 200)

Political conventions (Socialist Party)
Duke Univ., Perkins Lib.

Political demonstrations
See Demonstrations (Political)

Political science
Alternative Information Network
Amer. Political Science Assn.
Carousel Film & Video
Center for Humanities, Inc.
Cinema Guild
Dirksen (E.M.) Cong. Lead. Res. Ctr.
Hoover Institution
League of Women Voters of the U.S.
Mason (George) Univ. Spec. Coll. & Arch.
Prelinger Assoc., Inc.
Richter Productions

Politicians
Allen (John E.) Inc.
Appalshop Films, Inc.
Boston Univ. Film Arch.
Cable News Network Library
Film Bank
Film/Audio Services, Inc.
Forsher (James) Prods. & Archives, Inc.
4•6•8 Prods., Inc.
Halcyon Days Prods.
Hearst Metrotone News
MacDonald, J. Fred
Mus. & Hist. Div., City of Sacramento
Natl. Archives of Canada
New York City Dept. of Rec. & Info. Svcs.
News On Film
Northstar Prods.
Petrified Films, Inc.
Pyramid Film and Video Corp.
Spalla (Rick) Video Prods.
St. John's Univ., Spec. Coll.
Univ. of Maryland, McKeldin Lib.
Univ. of South Carolina, Newsfilm Lib.
WETA-TV
Worldwide Television News

Politics and government
ABC Distribution (Education)
ABC News
Allen (John E.) Inc.
Archive Film Prods., Inc.
Britannica Films & Video
Bullfrog Films, Inc.
C-SPAN (Cable Satellite Public Affairs Network)
Cable News Network Library
Carousel Film & Video
Channel L Working Group
Coe Film Assoc., Inc.
Coronet/MTI Film & Video
Em Gee Film Library
Film Bank
Film/Audio Services, Inc.
Florida State Archives
Hearst Metrotone News
Imevision
Indiana Hist. Soc., Smith Memorial Lib.
Intellimation
Intermedia Arts Minnesota
Latin Amer. Video Arch.
March of Time
Massachusetts Archives
Milwaukee Access Telecommunications Auth.
Mus. & Hist. Div., City of Sacramento
Natl. Archives of Canada
Petrified Films, Inc.
Radcliffe Coll., Schlesinger Lib.
SF•V Intl.
State Hist. Soc. of North Dakota
Televisa, S.A.

Texas Tech Univ., Southwest Coll.
Twentieth Century-Fox Movietonews
U.S. Conference of Mayors
UCLA Film & Television Archive
Université Laval, Cinémathèque
Univ. of Ill. Urbana-Champaign, Univ. Arch.
V/tape
WETA-TV
Western Reserve Hist. Soc.
World Monitor
Worldwide Television News
Yue-Sai Kan, Inc.

Polk County, Fla. (History and culture)
Swain (Hack) Prods., Inc.

Polka
See Dance and dancing (Polka)

Polka music
See Music (Polka)

Pollock, Jackson
Blackwood Prods., Inc.
Direct Cinema Ltd.
Mus. at Large, Ltd.

Pollution
British Info. Svcs., Radio & TV Div.
CBS News Archives
Dreamlight Images, Inc.
Energy Productions
Environmental Action Coalition
Indiana State Comm. on Public Records
Intermedia Arts Minnesota
Natl. Archives (RG 412)
Natl. Archives/Natl. AV Ctr.
Natl. Assn. of Conservation Dists.
Public Interest Video Network
Source Stock Footage Lib., Inc.
TV Ontario
TV-UNAM
Video Tape Library, Ltd.
World Monitor
See also Acid rain; Conservation; Ecology; Smog; Toxic waste

Pollution (Air)
Acid Rain Foundation, Inc.
Cinema Guild
Dreamlight Images, Inc.
Electric Power Research Institute
Energy Productions
General Motors Corp.
Mass. Audubon Society
NASA, Ames Res. Ctr., Imaging Tech. Branch
Natl. Archives (RG 220)
New York State Dept. of Env. Cons.
Richter Productions
TV Ontario
Transportation Research Board

Pollution (Noise)
Cinema Guild
New York Pub. Lib., Rare Books & Manuscripts Div.
Transportation Research Board

Pollution (Thermal)
United Nations, Visual Materials Lib.

Pollution (Water)
Assoc. Gen. Contractors of America
Canadian Filmmakers Dist. Centre
Cinema Guild
Energy Productions
Estuary Press
Finley (Stuart) Inc.
Indiana State Comm. on Public Records
Mass. Audubon Society
Moonlight Productions
Natl. Water Well Assn.
New Day Films

Ocean Earth Constr. and Dev. Corp.
Oregon Hist. Soc.
Richter Productions
San Francisco Bay Area TV News Arch.
Soc. for French Amer. Cult. Svcs. & Educ. Aid
TV Ontario

Polo
Analogous Productions
Archive Film Prods., Inc.
Charisma Prods., Ltd./Visual Motion
Film Bank
Kesser Stock Footage Library
Petrified Films, Inc.
Sea TV
Twentieth Century-Fox Movietonews

Polonsky, Rolanda
Amer. Federation of the Arts

Polyarny, U.S.S.R. (Contemporary issues)
Ocean Earth Constr. and Dev. Corp.

Polynesia (History and culture)
Petrified Films, Inc.

Polyvinyl chloride (PVC)
Public Interest Video Network

Pom-pom girls
See Cheerleaders

Pomeranz, Hart
Natl. Archives of Canada

Pomeroy, Wardell
Daphne Productions, Inc.

Pomona, Calif. (History and culture)
Petrified Films, Inc.

Pompa, Gilbert
Univ. of Tex. at Austin, Benson Lat. Am. Coll.

Pompeii
Cinema Guild

Ponape, Micronesia
Passage Home Communications

Ponchartrain, Lake (Louisiana) (History)
Prelinger Assoc., Inc.

Ponds
CBS News Archives
Energy Productions
Film Bank
Image Bank
TV Ontario

Ponies
See Horses

Pons, Lily
Archive Film Prods., Inc.

Pontiac, Mich. (History and culture)
Petrified Films, Inc.

Pontius Pilate
Concordia Publishing House

Pony Express
Petrified Films, Inc.

Poodles
Petrified Films, Inc.

Pool (Billiards)
See Billiards

Pools
See Swimming pools

Pooper scooper law
New York Pub. Lib., Rare Books & Manuscripts Div.

Popes
Archdiocese of Boston
Archive Film Prods., Inc.
Film Bank
March of Time
Petrified Films, Inc.
Univ. of Ill. Urbana-Champaign, Univ. Arch.
See also Religion (Catholic); specific popes

Poplar trees
TV Ontario

Poppies
Energy Productions
Film Bank
Natl. Archives (RG 170)
Petrified Films, Inc.

Popular culture
See Lifestyles

Popular culture (Critical perspectives on)
Deep Dish TV
Paper Tiger TV
Trent Institute for Popular Culture

Popular music
See Music (Popular)

Population control
Cousteau Society
Johns Hopkins Univ./Population Comm. Svcs.
Population Reference Bureau, Inc.
United Nations, Visual Materials Lib.

Population explosion
Cinema Guild

Porcupines
Buffalo Bill Historical Center
Minnesota Zoo
Natl. Archives (RG 22)
South Dakota State Lib.

Pornography
CBS News Archives
Cambridge Documentary Films, Inc.
Citizens for Decency Through Law
Intermedia Arts Minnesota
Intl. Gay and Lesbian Archives
Kinsey Institute
Morality in Media
Natl. Archives (RG 60)
See also Erotica; Peep shows

Pornography (Theaters)
Film Bank

Pornography, U.S. Commission on
Citizens for Decency Through Law
Natl. Archives (RG 60)

Porpoises
See Dolphins

Port of Spain, Trinidad (History and culture)
Petrified Films, Inc.

Port-au-Prince, Haiti (History and culture)
Video Mgmt. Systems

Porter, Edwin S.
First Run/Icarus Films, Inc.

Portland, Maine (History and culture)
Northeast Historic Film

Portland, Oreg.
Dreamlight Images, Inc.
Portland Cable Access TV
Stock Shots

Portland, Oreg. (History and culture)
MacDonald, J. Fred
Media Project
Oregon Electric Railway Hist. Soc.
Oregon Hist. Soc.
Oregon State Univ., Archives

Porto Alegre, Brazil (History and culture)
Democracy in Communication

Portraits
CBS News Archives
Film Bank

Ports
See Harbors

Portugal
Canadian Broadcasting Corp.

Portugal (History and culture)
Archive Film Prods., Inc.
March of Time
Third World Newsreel

Post Office Department (U.S.)
Film/Audio Services, Inc.
March of Time
Natl. Archives (RG 28)
Petrified Films, Inc.
Prelinger Assoc., Inc.
See also Mail and mail carriers; Postal Service (U.S.)

Post offices
CBS News Archives
Dreamlight Images, Inc.
Natl. Archives (RG 28)
Petrified Films, Inc.
See also Mail and mail carriers; Postal Service (U.S.)

Post, Wiley
Natl. Archives (RG 342)

Post-Vietnam syndrome
See Veterans (Vietnam)

Postage stamps
See Stamps (Postage)

Postal Service (U.S.)
Natl. Archives (Stock Film Coll.)
See also Mail and mail carriers; Post Office Department (U.S.); Post offices

Posters
Petrified Films, Inc.

Posture
Oregon State Univ., Archives

Potatoes
Northcoast Communication, Inc.
Prov. Arch. of Alberta
TV Ontario
VTR Productions

Potlatches

Canadian Filmmakers Dist. West

Potomac River, Md.-Va.
Finley (Stuart) Inc.
Petrified Films, Inc.

Potomac River, Md.-Va. (History)
Finley (Stuart) Inc.

Potter, Charles E.
Univ. of Mich., Mich. Hist. Colls.

Pottery
New Mexico State Records Ctr. & Arch.
Petrified Films, Inc.
TV Ontario

Poultry
Glenbow Mus. Arch.
Natl. Archives (RG 306)
Oregon State Univ., Archives
Prov. Arch. of Alberta
Twentieth Century-Fox Movietonews
See also Chickens; Farms and farming

Poultry industry
Paper Tiger TV

Poussin, Nicolas
Amer. Federation of the Arts

Poverty
Appalachian State Univ., Eury Coll.
CBS News Archives
Carousel Film & Video
Cinema Guild
Democracy in Communication
Documentary Educational Resources
Educational Video Ctr.
Estuary Press
First Run/Icarus Films, Inc.
Interfaith Action for Economic Justice
Latin Amer. Video Arch.
MALDEF
Mass Media Ministries
Media Project
Natl. Archives (RG 200)
Natl. Archives (RG 207)
Natl. Archives (RG 381)
New Day Films
Regional Plan Assn.
Southern Christian Leadership Conference
Southwest Film/Video Archives, SMU
World Monitor

Powell, Bernadette
Third World Newsreel

Powell, Dick
Banks Film Library
Encore Entertainment
MacDonald, J. Fred
Shokus Video

Powell, Lake (Utah)
Energy Productions
Preview Media
Source Stock Footage Lib., Inc.
Utah Travel Council

Powell, Michael
Walker Art Ctr.

Powell, Paul
Illinois State Hist. Lib.

Power lines
Film Bank

Power plants
Amer. Nuclear Society

Archives of Ontario
British Info. Svcs., Radio & TV Div.
Bullfrog Films, Inc.
CBS News Archives
Calif. Dept. of Water Resources
Echo Film Prods., Inc.
Edison Electric Institute
Electric Power Research Institute
Energy Productions
Film Bank
Film/Audio Services, Inc.
Indiana Univ. Northwest Lib.
Long Island State Park Comm.
Natl. Archives (RG 43)
Natl. Archives (RG 115)
Natl. Archives (RG 142)
Natl. Archives (RG 305)
Natl. Archives of Canada
North Carolina Div. of Arch. & Hist.
Oregon Hist. Soc.
Petrified Films, Inc.
Prelinger Assoc., Inc.
Richter Productions
Source Stock Footage Lib., Inc.
TV Ontario
Tennessee Valley Authority (TVA)
U.S. Council for Energy Awareness
See also Energy; Nuclear energy and power

Power, Tyrone
UCLA Film & Television Archive

Powers, Francis Gary
Villon Films

Powers, Stefanie
Spectral Comms.

Powwows
Intermedia Arts Minnesota
Manitoba Indian Cultural Centre
TV Ontario
Yakima Indian Nation Cult. Ctr.
Yakima Television Program
See also Native Americans

Prague, Czechoslovakia
Canadian Broadcasting Corp.

Prague, Czechoslovakia (History and culture)
Archive Film Prods., Inc.

Prairie chickens
New Mexico State Records Ctr. & Arch.

Prairie dogs
Energy Productions
Film Bank
Minnesota Zoo
Natl. Archives (RG 22)
South Dakota State Lib.

Prairies
CBS News Archives
Petrified Films, Inc.
Source Stock Footage Lib., Inc.
Twentieth Century-Fox Movietonews

Praying
Film Search
Petrified Films, Inc.
See also Religion

Praying mantises
Dreamlight Images, Inc.

Prefabrication (Housing)
TV Ontario

United Nations Ctr. for Human Settlements

Pregnancy
Addiction Research Foundation of Ontario
CBS News Archives
Cinema Medica
Emory Medical Television Network
Film Bank
Films for the Humanities and Sciences
Intellimation
Intermedia Arts Minnesota
Johns Hopkins Univ./Population Comm. Svcs.
La Leche League of New Mexico
March of Dimes Birth Defects Found.
Medical College of Pa., Arch. & Spec. Coll. Women in Medicine
Multi-Focus, Inc.
Nassau Comm. Coll. Lib.
Natl. Archives (RG 102)
Natl. Archives/Natl. AV Ctr.
New York Hosp.-Cornell Med. Ctr., Arch.
Petrified Films, Inc.
Polymorph Films, Inc.
Pyramid Film and Video Corp.
Society for Nutrition Education
Stock Shots
See also Babies; Childbirth; Midwifery; Obstetrics and gynecology; Teenage pregnancy; Women and health

Prehistoric art
See Art and artists (Prehistoric)

Preibisius, Hilda
De Saisset Museum

Prejudice
AIMS Media
Anti-Defamation League of B'nai B'rith
Cambridge Documentary Films, Inc.
Carousel Film & Video
Intl. Lutheran Layman's League
Mass Media Ministries
Motivational Media, Inc.
Phoenix Film and Video
Pyramid Film & Video Corp.
Video Arts, Inc.
See also Anti-Semitism; Racism; Sexism

Premieres
See Motion pictures (Premieres)

Preminger, Otto
Banks Film Library

Presbyterian and Reformed Churches
See Religion (Presbyterian and Reformed Churches)

Presidential elections (U.S.)
ABC News Interactive
C-SPAN (Cable Satellite Public Affairs Network)
DEC Film & Video
Eisenhower (Dwight D.) Library
Georgetown Univ., Spec. Coll. Div.
Hearst Metrotone News
Johnson (Lyndon Baines) Library
Kennedy (John F.) Library
Labor Video Project
March of Time
Mus. & Hist. Div., City of Sacramento
Pennebaker Associates, Inc.
Purdue Univ., Pub. Aff. Video Arch.
Roosevelt (Franklin D.) Lib.
Smith (Margaret Chase) Lib. Ctr.
Southern Calif. Lib. for Soc. Stud. & Res.
Truman (Harry S) Library
UCLA Film & Television Archive

NOTE: Access policies, availability and restrictions vary for each source. Please read each entry in full. Always consult "General Film and Videotape Collections" (page 599); these comprehensive collections contain material on every conceivable subject.

Univ. of Rochester Lib., Rare Books &
  Spec. Coll.
Vanderbilt Univ., TV News Arch.
See also Elections

Presidential libraries
Carter (Jimmy) Library
Ford (Gerald R.) Library
Hoover (Herbert) Presidential Lib.
Johnson (Lyndon Baines) Lib.
Kennedy (John F.) Library
Natl. Archives/Nixon Presidential
  Materials Proj.
Roosevelt (Franklin D.) Lib.
Truman (Harry S) Library

Presidents (Latin America)
Film Bank
Natl. Archives (RG 59)
Natl. Archives (RG 185)
Univ. of Miami, Arch. & Spec. Coll.

Presidents (Mexico)
Archivo Historico Cinematografico
Imevision
Notimex

Presidents (U.S.)
Allen (John E.) Inc.
Archive Film Prods., Inc.
Carter (Jimmy) Library
Cinema Arts Assoc.
Eisenhower (Dwight D.) Library
Film Bank
Film Education Institute
Fish Films, Inc.
Ford (Gerald R.) Library
Halcyon Days Prods.
Handel Film Corp.
Hoover (Herbert) Presidential Library
Johnson (Lyndon Baines) Library
Kennedy (John F.) Library
Lib. of Congress, M/B/RS
March of Time
Natl. Archives (RG 24)
Natl. Archives (RG 33)
Natl. Archives (RG 48)
Natl. Archives (RG 59)
Natl. Archives (RG 80)
Natl. Archives (RG 82)
Natl. Archives (RG 111)
Natl. Archives (RG 119)
Natl. Archives (RG 128)
Natl. Archives (RG 130)
Natl. Archives (RG 174)
Natl. Archives (RG 185)
Natl. Archives (RG 200)
Natl. Archives (RG 220)
Natl. Archives (RG 255)
Natl. Archives (RG 272)
Natl. Archives (RG 274)
Natl. Archives (RG 306)
Natl. Archives (RG 330)
Natl. Archives (RG 342)
Natl. Archives (RG 398)
Natl. Archives/Nixon Presidential
  Materials Proj.
Natl. Archives of Canada
Oregon Hist. Soc.
Petrified Films, Inc.
Prelinger Assoc., Inc.
Republican Natl. Committee
Truman (Harry S) Library
UCLA Film & Television Archive
Univ. of So. Carolina, Newsfilm Lib.
West Virginia Dept. of Culture & Hist.

President's Commission
See the commission's "subject" area (e.g.,
  President's Commission on Campus
  Unrest is found under Campus Unrest,
  President's Commission on)

President's Committee

See the committee's "subject" area (e.g.,
  President's Committee on Pension
  Policy is found under Pension Policy,
  President's Committee on)

Presley, Elvis
Archive Film Prods., Inc.
Banks Film Library
Film Bank
Halcyon Days Prods.
Las Vegas News Bureau
Natl. Archives (RG 56)
Picture Start, Inc.
Twentieth Century-Fox Movietonews

Presser, Jacob
Documentary Educ. Resources

Price Administration, Office of (U.S.)
Natl. Archives (RG 188)
Natl. Archives (RG 200)

Price, Vincent
UCLA Film & Television Archive

Priest, Ivy Baker
Univ. of Utah, Marriott Lib.

Priests
See Clergy

Primal therapy
Cinema Guild

Primitive motion pictures
See Motion pictures (Early)

Prince Edward Island
Studio East Ltd.

Prince, Richard
Video Data Bank

Princes and princesses
See Royalty

Princeton, Mich. (History and culture)
Wayne State Univ., Folklore Arch.

**Princeton, West Virginia (History and
  culture)**
Finley (Stuart) Inc.

Printing (History of)
MacDonald, J. Fred

Printing presses
Petrified Films, Inc.
Prelinger Assoc., Inc.

Printing presses (Gutenberg)
Petrified Films, Inc.

Printing presses (Newspaper)
Petrified Films, Inc.

Prisbrey, Tressa
Amer. Federation of the Arts

Prison camps
Twentieth Century-Fox Movietonews

Prisoners of war (POWs)
Academy of Health Sciences, U.S. Army
Film Bank
MacDonald, J. Fred
Red Badge of Courage, Inc.
Twentieth Century-Fox Movietonews
See also Korean War (Prisoners of war);
  World War I (Prisoners of war); World
  War II (Prisoners of war)

Prisons and prisoners
Amer. Correctional Assn.
Amer. Jail Assn.

Analogous Productions
Apertura
Archive Film Prods., Inc.
CBS News Archives
Cambridge Documentary Films, Inc.
Canadian Filmmakers Dist. Centre
Carousel Film & Video
Cinema Guild
Colorado Historical Society
Film Bank
First Run/Icarus Films, Inc.
Icarus Films Intl., Inc.
Intermedia Arts Minnesota
March of Time
Media Project
Mus. & Hist. Div., City of Sacramento
Natl. Archives of Canada
Petrified Films, Inc.
Prelinger Assoc., Inc.
Pyramid Film and Video Corp.
Radcliffe Coll., Schlesinger Lib.
Stock House
TV Ontario
Third World Newsreel
Twentieth Century-Fox Movietonews
Video Tape Library, Ltd.
West Virginia Dept. of Culture & Hist.
See also Women (Prisoners)

Prisons, Bureau of (U.S.)
Natl. Archives (RG 129)

Privacy
Academy of Health Sciences, U.S. Army
Cinema Guild
Intellimation

Process plates
Dorn (Larry) Associates
Grinberg (Sherman) Film Libraries (West)
Petrified Films, Inc.
Stock House
See also Backgrounds

Processions
Petrified Films, Inc.

Prochnow, Jurgen
Spectral Comms.

Product shots
Film Bank
Hayes Prods., Inc.
Metro Communications, Inc.
Petrified Films, Inc.
Prelinger Assoc., Inc.
Rosebush Visions Corp.
White Star Prof. Film Svcs., Inc.

Progressive Party
Southern Calif. Lib. for Soc. Stud. & Res.

Prohibition (1919-1933)
Allen (John E.) Inc.
Analogous Productions
Archive Film Prods., Inc.
Film Bank
Ohio Historical Soc.
Petrified Films, Inc.
Timesteps Prods., Inc.

Prohibition Party
Univ. of Mich., Mich. Hist. Colls.

Projectors (Motion picture)
See Motion pictures (Projectors)

Proms
MacDonald, J. Fred
Petrified Films, Inc.
Prelinger Assoc., Inc.

Propaganda and propaganda films
Film Bank
German Language Video Center

Halcyon Days Prods.
Hoover Institution
Intl. Historic Films, Inc.
Latin Amer. Video Arch.
Lib. of Congress, M/B/RS
MacDonald, J. Fred
March of Time
Morcraft Films
Moviecraft, Inc.
Mus. of Contemporary Art
NSDAP/AO
Natl. Archives (RG 28)
Natl. Archives (RG 200)
Natl. Archives (RG 208)
Natl. Archives (RG 229)
Natl. Archives (RG 242)
Natl. Archives (RG 263)
Natl. Archives of Canada
Natl. Ctr. for Jewish Film
Pacific Film Archive
Parker (Kit) Films
Petrified Films, Inc.
Prelinger Assoc., Inc.
Quest Productions Inc.
Southwest Film/Video Archives, SMU
Streamline Film Archives
Video Yesteryear
York Univ. Archives

Propeller airplanes
See Aircraft (Propeller)

Prophet, Ronnie
Natl. Archives of Canada

Prophets
CBS News Archives

Prospectors
Natl. Archives of Canada
Petrified Films, Inc.

Prostitution
Canadian Filmmakers Dist. Centre
Educational Video Ctr.
Film Bank
First Run/Icarus Films, Inc.
Historical Health Film Coll.
Multi-Focus, Inc.

Protozoa
Petrified Films, Inc.

Providence, R.I.
Villon Films

Providence, R.I. (History and culture)
Prelinger Assoc., Inc.
Rhode Island Hist. Soc.

Provincetown, Mass.
Site Productions

Provine, Dorothy
Banks Film Library

Prowse, Juliet
Banks Film Library

Prudhoe Bay, Alaska
Alaska Video Prods.

Pryor, Richard
Spectral Comms.

Psychiatry and psychiatrists
Amer. Psychiatric Assn.
Emory Medical Television Network
Film Bank
Historical Health Film Coll.
IMS Creative Communications
Inst. for Psychoanalysis
Nassau Comm. Coll. Lib.
Natl. Archives of Canada
Natl. Library of Medicine

Social Psychiatry Res. Inst.
UCLA Behavioral Sci. Media Lab.
Vidéo Femmes

Psychic TV (Rock and roll band)
Giorno Poetry Systems Inst.

Psychics
Pyramid Film and Video Corp.
Valley of the Sun Publishing
Wishing Well Distribution

Psychoanalysis and psychotherapy
Erickson (Milton H.) Foundation, Inc.
IEA Productions, Inc.
Inst. for Psychoanalysis
Psychological and Educational Films

Psychoanalysis and psychotherapy (Group therapy)
Psychological and Educational Films

Psychokinesis
Cinema Guild

Psychological warfare
CBS News Archives
Prelinger Assoc., Inc.

Psychology
Academy of Health Sciences, U.S. Army
Amer. Assn. for Counseling & Development
Barr Films
Boston Family Inst.
Cinema Guild
Coe Film Assoc., Inc.
Columbia Univ., Teachers College
Films for the Humanities and Sciences
GPN
Inst. for Psychoanalysis
Intermedia Arts Minnesota
Jung (C.G.) Foundation
Natl. Archives of Canada
Natl. Archives/Natl. AV Ctr.
Peralta Colleges TV
Phoenix Films and Video
Prelinger Assoc., Inc.
Psychological and Educational Films
Pyramid Film and Video Corp.
Research Press
UCLA Behavioral Sci. Media Lab.
Univ. of Akron, Arch. of Hist. of Amer. Psychol.
Univ. of Akron, Child Develop. Film Arch.
Univ. of Calif., Ext. Media Ctr.
Univ. of Kansas

Psychology (Sports)
Athletic Institute

Psychotherapy
See Psychoanalysis and psychotherapy

Pu Yi (Wang Xui Shan)
Nan Hai (U.S.A.) Co., Inc.

Public Buildings Administration (U.S.)
Natl. Archives (RG 48)

Public Health Service (U.S.)
Natl. Archives (RG 90)

Public Image Ltd. (Rock and roll band)
Target Video

Public Information, U.S. Committee on
Natl. Archives (RG 200)

Public Roads, Bureau of (U.S.)

Natl. Archives (RG 33)

Public administration
Richter Productions

Public domain films
See Feature films and videotapes (Public domain)

Public health
Amer. Journal of Nursing Co.
Archivo de Imagenes en Movimiento
Emory Medical Television Network
Historical Health Film Coll.
Nassau Comm. Coll. Lib.
Natl. Library of Medicine
Northern Ill. Univ., Reg. Hist. Ctr.
Rockefeller Arch. Ctr.
Visual Information Systems

Public housing
See Housing (Public)

Public lands
Natl. Archives (RG 49)

Public relations
General Motors Corp.
March of Time
Natl. Assn. of Secondary Schl. Principals
Prelinger Assoc., Inc.
Wolfson (Louis II) Media Hist. Ctr., Miami-Dade Pub. Lib.

Public service announcements (PSAs)
Adbank
Al-Anon Family Group Headquarters, Inc.
Amer. Automobile Assn., FTS
Amer. Cancer Soc., Inc.
Amer. Chemical Soc.
Amer. Nuclear Society
Animal Welfare Institute
Anti-Defamation League of B'nai B'rith
Apertura
Arch. of the Mennonite Church
Assn. of Independent Comm. Prod.
Bay Area Video Coalition
Buck (Pearl S.) Foundation
Cherokee Nation Hist. Soc., Inc.
Cystic Fibrosis Found.
Fund for Human Dignity, Inc.
Halcyon Days Prods.
Houston (Sam) Regional Library
Image Film & Video Coll.
Indiana State Comm. on Public Records
Kennedy (John F.) Library
Lambda Legal Defense & Education Fund
Leukemia Soc. of Amer.
MacDonald, J. Fred
Marquette Univ., Spec. Coll.
Mothers Against Drunk Driving
Motor Vehicle Manufacturers Assn.
Natl. Archives (RG 47)
Natl. Archives (RG 56)
Natl. Archives (RG 88)
Natl. Archives (RG 220)
Natl. Archives (RG 311)
Natl. Archives (RG 412)
Natl. Crime Prevention Council
Natl. Jewish Arch. of Broadcasting
Natl. Reye's Syndrome Found.
Natl. School Boards Assn.
Natl. Sudden Infant Death Syndrome Found.
New Orleans Pub. Lib., La. Div.
New Orleans Video Access Ctr.
People for Ethical Treatment of Animals
Rogers (Will) Institute
Salvation Army, Natl. Comm. Dept.
Smithsonian Inst., NMAH, Div. Polit. Hist.

Special Olympics Intl.
United Way of America
Univ. of Ill. Urbana-Champaign, Univ. Arch.
Univ. of Tex. at Austin, Benson Lat. Am. Coll.
Xchange TV

Public speaking
Prelinger Assoc., Inc.

Public utilities
Intermedia Arts Minnesota

Public works
Analogous Productions
Calif. Dept. of Transportation
Los Angeles City Archives
Massachusetts Archives
Nassau County Museum
Natl. Archives (RG 39)
Natl. Archives (RG 69)
Transportation Research Board

Publishing (Desktop)
Computer Television Group, Inc.

Pubs (Britain)
TV Ontario
Villon Films

Puddles
Film Bank

Puerto Ricans (New York City)
Bronx County Hist. Soc.
Cinema Guild

Puerto Rico
Kesser Stock Footage Library
Preview Media

Puerto Rico (History and culture)
Archivo de Imagenes en Movimiento
Cinema Guild
DEC Film & Video
Filmoteca Luis Muñoz Marin
Idera Films
Mus. of Mod. Art of Latin America
Roosevelt (Franklin D.) Lib.
WIPR-TV

Puerto Vallarta, Mexico
Preview Media

Puffins
Coe Film Assoc., Inc.
Dobbs (Jeff) Prods.
Wings Wildlife Prods. Inc.

Puget Sound, Wash.
Amer. Motion Pictures

Pukeko, New Zealand
New Zealand Embassy Film Lib.

Pullman porters
See Railroads (Pullman porters)

Pulpits
Petrified Films, Inc.

Pumas
Minnesota Zoo
Petrified Films, Inc.

Pumpkins
Petrified Films, Inc.
TV Ontario

Punk music

See Music (Punk)

Punks
Dreamlight Images, Inc.
Film Bank
TV Ontario
Video Tape Library, Ltd.

Puppets
CBS News Archives
Camera Three Prods., Inc.
Chicago Historical Society
Film Bank
Filmfair Communications
Fish Films, Inc.
French Lib. in Boston
German Language Video Ctr.
Imevision
MacDonald, J. Fred
Native Amer. Pub. Broad. Cons.
New York Pub. Lib., Perf. Arts Res. Ctr., Theatre on Film and Tape
Petrified Films, Inc.
Prelinger Assoc., Inc.
Pyramid Film and Video Corp.
Univision Television Network

Puppies
See Dogs

Purcell, Rosamond
Port Washington Pub. Lib.

Purcell, Sarah
Spectral Comms.

Pure Food and Drug Act (U.S.)
Natl. Archives (RG 33)

Puryear, Martin
Video Data Bank

Pushcarts
Lib. of Congress, M/B/RS

Putnam, George
Banks Film Library

Pygmies
Duffy (Kevin) Productions
Innerquest Communications Corp.
Johnson (Martin & Osa) Safari Museum
Smithsonian Inst., Human Studies Film Arch.

Pyle, Ernie
New Mexico State Records Ctr. & Arch.

Pylons
TV Ontario

Pyramids
Archive Film Prods., Inc.
CBS News Archives
Energy Productions
Film Bank
Film/Audio Services, Inc.
Jewell (Stuart) Productions
Petrified Films, Inc.
Rosebush Visions Corp.
Source Stock Footage Lib., Inc.
Unicorn Projects

Pyramids (Mexico)
TV Ontario

Pythons
Minnesota Zoo
Petrified Films, Inc.

NOTE: Access policies, availability and restrictions vary for each source. Please read each entry in full. Always consult "General Film and Videotape Collections" (page 599); these comprehensive collections contain material on every conceivable subject.

Quabbin Valley, Mass.
Florentine Films

Quackery
Amer. Cancer Soc., Inc.
Historical Health Film Coll.

Quail
Indiana State Comm. on Public Records
Wings Wildlife Prods. Inc.

Quarries
Archive Film Prods., Inc.
CBS News Archives
Film Bank
Massachusetts Archives
Natl. Archives (RG 70)
Twentieth Century-Fox Movietonews

Quebec
Carleton Prods., Inc.
Departures, Inc.
TV Ontario

Quebec (History and culture)
Archive Film Prods., Inc.
Archives Nationales du Québec
Archives of Ontario
Bibliothèque Municipale de Montréal
DEC Film & Video
Groupe Intervention Video
Natl. Archives of Canada
Schiele Museum
Université Laval, Svc. des Res.
　Pédagogiques
Vidéographe Inc., Le

Quebec City, Quebec (History and culture)
Natl. Archives of Canada
Prov. Arch. of Alberta

Queen Elizabeth (S.S.)
Petrified Films, Inc.

Queen Mary (S.S.)
Analogous Productions
Petrified Films, Inc.

Question marks
Prelinger Assoc., Inc.

Queues
CBS News Archives
See also Breadlines

Quicksand
Archive Film Prods., Inc.

Quill pens
Petrified Films, Inc.

Quilling
South Dakota State Lib.
TV Ontario

Quilting
Appalachian State Univ., Eury Coll.
Appalshop Films, Inc.
New Day Films
Pyramid Film and Video Corp.
TV Ontario

Quincy Market (Boston)
Unicorn Projects

Quinine
Natl. Archives (RG 234)

Quinn, Anthony
Daphne Productions, Inc.
Spectral Comms.
Univ. of Tex. at Austin, Benson Lat. Am.
　Coll.

Quintuplets
Archive Film Prods., Inc.

Quintuplets (Dionne)
General Motors Corp.
Natl. Archives (RG 178)
Natl. Archives of Canada

Quintuplets (Fischer)
Pennebaker Associates, Inc.

Quito, Ecuador
Kesser Stock Footage Library

Quonset huts
Prelinger Assoc., Inc.

RIO
Natl. Archives (RG 286)

ROTC (Reserve Officer Training Corps)
DePauw University, Archives
Natl. Archives (RG 111)
Oregon State Univ., Archives

Rabbis
Petrified Films, Inc.
See also Clergy; Jewish history and culture

Rabbits
Di Sesso (Moe) Wild Life Film Lib.
Energy Productions
Petrified Films, Inc.
Prelinger Assoc., Inc.
TV Ontario
Wings Wildlife Prods. Inc.

Rabies
TV Ontario

Rabinowitz, Sherrie
Southern Calif. Inst. of Architecture

Raccoons
Di Sesso (Moe) Wild Life Film Lib.
Dreamlight Images, Inc.
Energy Productions
TV Ontario
Wings Wildlife Prods. Inc.

Racetracks (Horse)
See Horse racing

Racewalking
Summit Films, Inc.
Twentieth Century-Fox Movietonews

Racial discrimination
Asian American Resource Workshop
CBS News Archives
King (Dr. Martin Luther, Jr.) Ctr.
MALDEF
March of Time
Natl. Archives (RG 174)
Natl. Archives (RG 207)

Racial stereotypes
Amer.-Arab Anti-Discrimination Comm.
Asian American Resource Workshop
California Newsreel
Icarus Films Intl., Inc.
MALDEF
Petrified Films, Inc.
Pyramid Film and Video Corp.

Racing ("Geriatric race")
TV Ontario

Racism
Cinema Guild
DEC Film & Video
Deep Dish TV
East Tenn. State Univ., Arch. of
　Appalachia

First Run/Icarus Films, Inc.
Groupe Intervention Video
Kartemquin Films
Latin Amer. Video Arch.
MacDonald, J. Fred
Natl. Archives (RG 200)
Natl. Archives (RG 381)
Phoenix Films and Video
Rational Island Publishers
South Carolina Humanities Res. Ctr.
See also Black history and culture;
　Prejudice; Racial discrimination; Racial
　stereotypes

Racquetball
Amer. Motion Pictures
Athletic Institute
Film Bank
Lemorande Prod. Co.
Pyramid Film and Video Corp.

Radar
Bray Studios, Inc.
CBS News Archives
FAA Technical Center
Natl. Archives (RG 218)
Natl. Archives (RG 227)
Natl. Archives (RG 342)
Petrified Films, Inc.
Prelinger Assoc., Inc.
TV Ontario
Twentieth Century-Fox Movietonews

Radar (Police)
TV Ontario

Radar dishes
Film Bank
Zielinski Productions, Inc.

Radar screens
Film Bank
Inter Video/TTI
Petrified Films, Inc.

Radar towers
Film Bank

Radburn, N.J. (History and culture)
Prelinger Assoc., Inc.

Rader, Daniel Paul
Wheaton Coll., Billy Graham Ctr.

Radiation
Amer. Nuclear Society
Bullfrog Films, Inc.
CBS News Archives
Educational Images, Ltd.
Green Mountain Post Films
Petrified Films, Inc.
Prelinger Assoc., Inc.

Radiation (Electromagnetic)
Electric Power Research Institute

Radiation (Non-ionizing)
Computer & Business Equip. Mfrs. Assn.

Radiation (Nuclear)
Minn. Dept. of Public Safety Film Lib.
Natl. Archives (RG 311)
Natl. Archives (RG 434)
Petrified Films, Inc.
U.S. Council for Energy Awareness
U.S. Defense Nuclear Agency

Radiation hazards
Courter Films & Assoc.
Natl. Archives (RG 88)
U.S. Dept. of Labor, Mine Safety & Health
　Admin.

Radio
Archive Film Prods., Inc.

CBS News Archives
MacDonald, J. Fred
Natl. Archives (RG 218)
Prelinger Assoc., Inc.
Timesteps Prods., Inc.
Twentieth Century-Fox Movietonews
See also Radios

Radio (History of)
Antique Wireless Assn., Inc.
MacDonald, J. Fred

Radio announcers
Film Bank
Fish Films, Inc.
Petrified Films, Inc.

Radio broadcasting
Film Bank
MacDonald, J. Fred
March of Time
Natl. Archives (RG 173)
Natl. Archives (RG 200)
Petrified Films, Inc.
Prelinger Assoc., Inc.
Streamline Film Archives
TV Ontario

Radio City Music Hall (New York City)
Dreamlight Images, Inc.

Radio City Music Hall (New York City) (History)
Petrified Films, Inc.
Radio City Music Hall Prods.

Radio dispatch centers
TV Ontario

Radio engineers
TV Ontario

Radio stations
Film Bank
Petrified Films, Inc.
TV Ontario

Radio telescopes
See Telescopes (Radio)

Radio towers
Petrified Films, Inc.

Radio waves
Natl. Archives (RG 18)
Prelinger Assoc., Inc.

Radiology
IMS Creative Communications
Nassau Comm. Coll. Lib.

Radios
Film Bank
Petrified Films, Inc.
Prelinger Assoc., Inc.

Radishes
Jewell (Stuart) Productions

Rafferty, Kevin
Port Washington Pub. Lib.

Raft, George
Banks Film Library

Rafting
CBS News Archives
Dreamlight Images, Inc.
Energy Productions
Film Bank
Jewell (Stuart) Productions
Merkel Films
Moving Media
Natural Reflections Video
North Country Media Group

726

Peak Productions, Inc.
Preview Media
Sobek Productions
Source Stock Footage Lib., Inc.
Spalla (Rick) Video Prods.
Stimulus
Summit Films, Inc.
TV Ontario
Video Tape Library, Ltd.
Worldwide Television News
See also White water

Railbirds
New Jersey Network

Railroad stations
Film Bank
Petrified Films, Inc.
Port Authority of New York & New Jersey
Spectral Comms.

Railroad tracks
Film Bank
Petrified Films, Inc.

Railroads
Allen (John E.) Inc.
Amer. Airlines
Amer. Motion Pictures
Archive Film Prods., Inc.
Bay Area Electric Railroad Assn., Inc.
CBS News Archives
Calif. State Railroad Mus. Lib.
Cinenet (Cinema Network)
Colorado Historical Society
Creative Venture Films
Dorn (Larry) Associates
Dreamlight Images, Inc.
Em Gee Film Library
Energy Productions
Farkas Studios, Ltd.
Film Bank
Fish Films, Inc.
Grinberg (Sherman) Film Libraries (West)
Jewell (Stuart) Productions
Kalmbach Publishing Co.
Kansas State Historical Society
Lib. of Congress, M/B/RS
March of Time
Natl. Archives (RG 48)
Natl. Archives of Canada
Natl. Railway Historical Soc.
Nine Star Productions
Oregon State Univ., Archives
Pennsylvania State Arch.
Petrified Films, Inc.
Port Authority of New York & New Jersey
Prelinger Assoc., Inc.
Producers Library Service
Prov. Arch. of British Columbia
Railroad Mus. of Pa.
State Hist. Soc. of Iowa
Stock House
Twentieth Century-Fox Movietonews
Union Pacific Railroad
Univ. of Alaska, Fairbanks, Alaska Motion Picture Arch.
Video Tape Library, Ltd.
Washington State Hist. Soc.
Yukon Archives

Railroads (Accidents)
Film Bank
Petrified Films, Inc.
Prelinger Assoc., Inc.
Twentieth Century-Fox Movietonews
Vermont Hist. Soc.

Railroads (Adirondack Mountains, N.Y.)
New York State Dept. of Econ. Devel.

Railroads (Amtrak)
Peak Productions, Inc.
Preview Media

Railroads (California Zephyr)
Archive Film Prods., Inc.
Hogg, John F.

Railroads (China)
Preview Media

Railroads (Coal trains)
Film Bank

Railroads (Cog)
Farkas Studios, Ltd.
Summit Films, Inc.

Railroads (Construction)
Allen (John E.) Inc.
Massachusetts Archives
Natl. Archives of Canada
Wyoming State Hist. Soc.

Railroads (Diesel)
British Info. Svcs., Radio & TV Div.
Petrified Films, Inc.

Railroads (Diesel-electric)
General Motors Corp.

Railroads (Electric)
British Info. Svcs., Radio & TV Div.
Petrified Films, Inc.

Railroads (Elevated)
CBS News Archives
Petrified Films, Inc.

Railroads (Exploding)
Dreamlight Images, Inc.

Railroads (Freight)
Petrified Films, Inc.
Prelinger Assoc., Inc.
TV Ontario

Railroads (High-speed)
Analogous Productions
British Info. Svcs., Radio & TV Div.
Farkas Studios, Ltd.
Film Search

Railroads (Historical)
Dorn (Larry) Associates
Hogg, John F.
Mississippi Dept. of Arch. & Hist.
Natl. Railway Historical Soc.
Oregon Electric Railway Hist. Soc.
Petrified Films, Inc.
Railroad Mus. of Pa.

Railroads (History)
Bay Area Electric Railroad Assn., Inc.
Calif. State Railroad Mus. Lib.
Film Preservation Assoc.
General Motors Corp.
Natl. Archives of Canada
Union Pacific Railroad

Railroads (Japan)
Japan External Trade Organization

Railroads (Locomotives)
General Motors Corp.

Railroads (Miniature)
Spectral Comms.

Railroads (Model)
Film Bank

Kalmbach Publishing Co.

Railroads (Narrow-Gauge)
Summit Films, Inc.

Railroads (Passenger)
Petrified Films, Inc.
Prelinger Assoc., Inc.
TV Ontario

Railroads (Pullman porters)
Hogg, John F.
Illinois Labor Hist. Soc.
Natl. Railway Historical Soc.
New Day Films
See also Workers (Railroads)

Railroads (Snowplows)
Analogous Productions

Railroads (Steam)
Allen (John E.) Inc.
Appalachian State Univ., Eury Coll.
Film Bank
Jewell (Stuart) Productions
Natl. Railway Historical Soc.
Petrified Films, Inc.
Prelinger Assoc., Inc.
TV Ontario
Union Pacific Railroad

Railroads (Wrecks)
See Railroads (Accidents)

Rain
Charisma Prods., Ltd./Visual Motion
Dreamlight Images, Inc.
Energy Productions
Film Bank
Fish Films, Inc.
Petrified Films, Inc.
Source Stock Footage Lib., Inc.
Spectral Comms.
Twentieth Century-Fox Movietonews
Video Tape Library, Ltd.
See also Lightning; Storms; Weather

Rain forests
Dreamlight Images, Inc.
Duffy (Kevin) Productions
Educational Film & Video Project
Interlock Media Associates
Petrified Films, Inc.
Solaris Dance/Theatre/Video
Telemation Productions
Video Tape Library, Ltd.

Rainbow Bridge National Monument, Utah
Source Stock Footage Lib., Inc.

Rainbows
Cinenet (Cinema Network)
Dreamlight Images, Inc.
Energy Productions
Film Bank
Image Bank
Moving Media
Petrified Films, Inc.
Source Stock Footage Lib., Inc.
Twentieth Century-Fox Movietonews
Video Tape Library, Ltd.

Rainer, Yvonne
Video Data Bank

Rainier, Mount (Wash.)
Summit Films, Inc.
Amer. Motion Pictures
Beerger (Norman) Prods.

Rainier, Mount (Wash.) (History and culture)
Oregon Hist. Soc.

Rainier, Prince
Banks Film Library
Petrified Films, Inc.

Rainmakers
Film Bank

Rame, Franca
Richter Productions

Ramey, Gene
Rhapsody Films, Inc.

Ramones
Target Video

Ramsey, William
Ideal Comms., Inc.

Ranches
Buffalo Bill Historical Center
CBS News Archives
Film Bank
Lib. of Congress, Amer. Folklife Ctr.
Panhandle-Plains Hist. Museum
Peak Productions, Inc.
Texas Tech Univ., Southwest Coll.
West Star Productions

Ranches (Cattle)
Petrified Films, Inc.

Rand, Sally
Archive Film Prods., Inc.

Randall, Tony
Banks Film Library

Randolph, John
Spectral Comms.

Randolph, Leo
U.S. Olympic Committee

Rankin, Jeannette
Radcliffe Coll., Schlesinger Lib.

Rankin, Scott
Long Beach Mus. of Art

Rankin, Tex
Oregon Hist. Soc.

Ranucci, Karen
Port Washington Pub. Lib.

Rape
ABC Distribution (Education)
Alternative Information Network
Cambridge Documentary Films, Inc.
Canadian Filmmakers Dist. Centre
Cinema Guild
Coronet/MTI Film & Video
DEC Film & Video
Groupe Intervention Video
Mus. & Hist. Div., City of Sacramento
Natl. Crime Prevention Council
O.D.N. Productions, Inc.
Univ. of Tex. at Austin, Benson Lat. Am. Coll.
Vidéo Femmes
Women in Focus

Rapids
Beerger (Norman) Prods.
CBS News Archives

NOTE: Access policies, availability and restrictions vary for each source. Please read each entry in full. Always consult "General Film and Videotape Collections" (page 599); these comprehensive collections contain material on every conceivable subject.

Energy Productions
Film Bank
Twentieth Century-Fox Movietonews
See also Rafting; White water

Raspberries
TV Ontario

Rastafarians
Smithsonian Inst., Human Studies Film Arch.

Raster scan graphics
Energy Productions

Rathbone, Basil
Archive Film Prods., Inc.

Rats
Natl. Archives (RG 22)
Oregon State Univ., Archives
Petrified Films, Inc.
Prelinger Assoc., Inc.
Wings Wildlife Prods. Inc.

Rattlesnakes
Di Sesso (Moe) Wild Life Film Lib.
Film Bank
Minnesota Zoo
New Mexico State Records Ctr. & Arch.
Petrified Films, Inc.
Wings Wildlife Prods. Inc.

Rauschenberg, Robert
Blackwood Prods., Inc.
Cunningham Dance Foundation

Raven, Arlene
Video Data Bank

Ravens
Di Sesso (Moe) Wild Life Film Lib.
Minnesota Zoo
Wings Wildlife Prods. Inc.

Ravines
Image Bank

Ray, Man
Blackwood Prods., Inc.

Rayburn, Sam
Rayburn (Sam) Library

Raye, Martha
Banks Film Library
UCLA Film & Television Archive
Wisconsin Ctr. for Film & Theater Res.

Raymond, Gene
Goodwill Industries of Amer.

Razors (Electric)
Petrified Films, Inc.

Reaction shots
Petrified Films, Inc.

Reagan, Nancy Davis
Banks Film Library

Reagan, Ronald Wilson
Amer. Enterprise Institute
Archive Film Prods., Inc.
Banks Film Library
Constitutional Rights Foundation
Cystic Fibrosis Found.
Daphne Productions, Inc.
Film/Audio Services, Inc.
Grinberg (Sherman) Film Libraries (East)
Halcyon Days Prods.
Hearst Metrotone News
Intl. Historic Films, Inc.
KCRA-TV
Mus. & Hist. Div., City of Sacramento

Natl. Archives (RG 128)
Natl. Archives (RG 220)
Natl. Archives (RG 306)
Northstar Prods.
Petrified Films, Inc.
UCLA Film & Television Archive
United Farm Workers of America (UFW)
Video Resources N.Y., Inc.

Realtors
Petrified Films, Inc.

Reapportionment
CBS News Archives

Reasoner, Harry
Daphne Productions, Inc.
MacDonald, J. Fred

Recife, Brazil
Brazilian-American Cultural Inst.

Reclamation, Bureau of (U.S.)
Natl. Archives (RG 48)
Natl. Archives (RG 115)

Reconstruction Finance Corporation (U.S.)
Natl. Archives (RG 234)

Record stores
TV Ontario

Recording engineers
TV Ontario

Recording industry
March of Time
Prelinger Assoc., Inc.

Recording studios
Spectral Comms.
TV Ontario

Recreation
Alaska Video Prods.
Amer. Alliance for Health, Phys. Ed., Rec. & Dance Arch.
Atlantic Independent Media
Canadian Filmmakers Dist. West
Carleton Prods. Inc.
Chiappetta Prods., Inc.
Chicago Video Transfer
Chisholm (Jack) Film Productions
Cineworks Prods. Inc.
Echo Film Prods., Inc.
Encore Video Prods., Inc.
Farkas Studios, Ltd.
Film Bank
Film/Audio Services, Inc.
Grinberg (Sherman) Film Libraries (West)
Hayes Prods., Inc.
Intl. Film Bureau, Inc.
Landmark Stock Footage Co.
March of Time
Metro Communications, Inc.
Morris Video
Moving Media
Natl. Archives (RG 111)
Natl. Archives (RG 200)
Natl. Archives/Natl. AV Ctr.
Natl. Geographic Soc. Stock Footage Lib.
North Country Media Group
Peak Productions, Inc.
Petrified Films, Inc.
Phoenix Films and Video
Phoenix Videofilms/Karr Prods.
Postcards Unlimited
Prelinger Assoc., Inc.
Ski TV Prods., Inc./Channel 24
State Hist. Soc. of North Dakota
Timesteps Prods., Inc.
United Nations Ctr. for Human Settlements
V/tape

Recreational vehicles (RVs)
Preview Media
Spalla (Rick) Video Prods.
Video Tape Library, Ltd.

Recycling
Aluminum Assn.
Bullfrog Films, Inc.
Environmental Action Coalition
Filmfair Communications
Finley (Stuart) Inc.
Political Issue Archive
TV Ontario

Red Cross
Amer. Red Cross
Historical Health Film Coll.
Natl. Archives (RG 18)
Natl. Archives (RG 24)
Natl. Archives (RG 59)
Natl. Archives (RG 111)
Natl. Archives (RG 200)
Schweitzer (Albert) Ctr.
Timesteps Prods., Inc.

Red Elk, Herman
Native Amer. Pub. Broad. Cons.

Red peppers
TV Ontario

Red Sea (History and culture)
Archive Film Prods., Inc.

Red Square (Moscow) (History and culture)
Analogous Productions

Redding, Otis
Archive Film Prods., Inc.
Clark (Dick) Media Archives, Inc.
Pennebaker Associates, Inc.

Reddy, Helen
Spectral Comms.

Redmond, Jim
Channell One Video

Redon, Odilon
Amer. Federation of the Arts

Redwoods
Estuary Press
Film Bank

Reed, Donna
Banks Film Library

Reeds
Film Bank

Reefs
Cousteau Society
Twentieth Century-Fox Movietonews
See also Coral and coral reefs

Reese, Della
Archive Film Prods., Inc.

Reeve, Christopher
Spectral Comms.

Reeves, Dan
Port Washington Pub. Lib.

Reeves, Jim
Reeves (Jim) Museum

Referees
Dreamlight Images, Inc.

Refineries
See Oil industry

Reflections
Energy Productions
Film Bank

Refrigerators
General Motors Corp.
Petrified Films, Inc.
Prelinger Assoc., Inc.

Refugees
CARE
CBS News Archives
Camino Film Projects
DEC Film & Video
Deep Dish TV
Democracy in Communication
Film/Audio Services, Inc.
Hoover Institution
Icarus-Tamouz Media, Inc.
Intl. Freedom Foundation
MacDonald, J. Fred
March of Time
Maryknoll Fathers & Brothers
Natl. Archives (RG 24)
Natl. Archives (RG 59)
Natl. Archives (RG 200)
Natl. Archives/Natl. AV Ctr.
Natl. Asian American Telecomm. Assn.
New Day Films
New Time Films, Inc.
Salvation Army, Natl. Comm. Dept.
Third World Newsreel
Twentieth Century-Fox Movietonews
United Nations Ctr. for Human Settlements
White Janssen, Inc.
World Monitor
See also Boat people

Regattas
See Boats and boating (Racing); Yachts and yachting (Racing)

Reggae music
See Music (Reggae)

Regina, Saskatchewan (History and culture)
Prov. Arch. of Alberta
Univ. of Regina, Sask. Arch. Board

Rehabilitation
Amer. Foundation for the Blind
IMS Creative Communications
Intl. Ctr. for the Disabled
Nassau Comm. Coll. Lib.
Rehab. Inst. of Chicago

Reindeer
Archive Film Prods., Inc.
Coe Film Assoc., Inc.
Hoover Institution
Minnesota Zoo
Natl. Archives (RG 75)
Petrified Films, Inc.
TV Ontario
Visuart, Inc.

Reinhardt, Ad
Blackwood Prods., Inc.

Relaxation
Addiction Research Foundation of Ontario
Hartley Film Found., Inc.
Prelinger Assoc., Inc.
Research Press
See also Stress

Relief organizations
CARE
Catholic Relief Services
Natl. Archives/Natl. AV Ctr.
U.S. Committee for UNICEF

Religion
ABC News
Amer. Zionist Youth Found.
Analogous Productions
Appalachian State Univ., Eury Coll.
Archive Film Prods., Inc.
CBS News Archives
Cable Access of Dallas
Cable News Network Library
Canyon Cinema, Inc.
Coe Film Assoc., Inc.
Devillier Donegan Ent.
Dreamlight Images, Inc.
Film Bank
Film/Audio Services, Inc.
Filmakers Library
Graduate Theological Union Lib.
Intermedia Arts Minnesota
Intl. Film Foundation
Maryknoll Fathers & Brothers
Milwaukee Access Telecomm. Auth.
Natl. Archives of Canada
Petrified Films, Inc.
Phoenix Films and Video
Pyramid Film and Video Corp.
South Carolina Humanities Res. Ctr.
Tucson Community Cable Corp.
Twentieth Century-Fox Movietonews
Université de Moncton, Centre d'Études
    Acad.
Univ. of Tex. at Austin, Benson Lat. Am.
    Coll.
V/tape
Vedo Films/Novacom Video
Video-SIG
WGBH Educational Foundation
See also Bible stories and study;
    Cathedrals; Ceremonies; Churches;
    Clergy; Healing; Jewish history and
    culture; Mosques; Religious films and
    videotapes; Television (Religious);
    Temples

Religion (African-based)
Schomburg Ctr. for Res. in Black Culture

Religion (Amish)
Mennonite Library and Archives
Petrified Films, Inc.
Preview Media
Vedo Films/Novacom Video

Religion (Appalachian)
East Tenn. State Univ., Arch. of
    Appalachia

Religion (Baha'i)
Hartley Film Found., Inc.
Petrified Films, Inc.

Religion (Baptist)
Amer. Baptist Films/Video
Appalshop Films, Inc.
Center for Southern Folklore
Golden Gate Theological Seminary
    Library
Liberty Broadcasting Network
Petrified Films, Inc.

Religion (Black)
Center for Southern Folklore
Miles Educ. Film Prods.
Univ. of Miss., Ctr. for Study of Southern
    Cult.

Religion (Brethren in Christ Church)
Brethren in Christ Church & Messiah
    Coll., Arch.

Religion (Buddhism)
Archive Film Prods., Inc.

Hartley Film Found., Inc.
Japan Society, Inc. Film Center
Natl. Archives of Canada
Petrified Films, Inc.

Religion (Catholicism)
Archdiocese of Boston
California Newsreel
Keep the Faith, Inc.
Natl. Archives of Canada
Paulist Prods.
Petrified Films, Inc.

Religion (Charismatic)
Mass Media Ministries
Wheaton Coll., Billy Graham Ctr.

Religion (Christianity)
Abilene Christian University
Middle East Institute
Myrin Institute
Natl. Archives of Canada
TV Ontario

Religion (Church of Christ)
Abilene Christian University

Religion (Disciples of Christ)
Disciples of Christ Hist. Soc.

Religion (Eastern)
Krishnamurti Foundation of America

Religion (Episcopalian)
Petrified Films, Inc.

Religion (Evangelical Covenant Church)
Evangelical Covenant Church of Amer.

Religion (Evangelicalism)
Abilene Christian Univ., Brown Lib.
Loma Linda Univ., Webb Lib.
Roberts (Oral) Univ.
Wheaton Coll., Billy Graham Ctr.

Religion (Greek Orthodox)
Hellenic College
Petrified Films, Inc.

Religion (Hinduism)
Hartley Film Found., Inc.
Petrified Films, Inc.
Singer-Sharrette Traditional Healing Films

Religion (India)
Duffy (Kevin) Prods.

Religion (Islam)
Amer.-Arab Anti-Discrimination Comm.
Chicago Access Corp.
Films for the Humanities and Sciences
Hartley Film Found., Inc.
Middle East Institute
Natl. Coun. of Amer.-Sov. Friendship, Inc.
Petrified Films, Inc.
TV Ontario
Visnews Intl.

Religion (Jainism)
Hartley Film Found., Inc.

Religion (Jewish)
See Jewish history and culture

Religion (Lutheran)
Concordia Publishing House
Evangelical Lutheran Church in America
Intl. Lutheran Layman's League

Religion (Mennonite)
Arch. of the Mennonite Church

Lancaster Mennonite Hist. Soc.
Mennonite Library and Archives
Natl. Archives of Canada

Religion (Methodist)
DePauw University, Archives
United Methodist Churches

Religion (Mormonism)
Church of Jesus Christ of LDS
Filmakers Library
March of Time
Univ. of Utah, Marriott Lib.

Religion (Pentecostal)
Indiana Univ. Folklore Arch.

**Religion (Presbyterian & Reformed
    Churches)**
Off. of Hist. (Montreal) of the Presbyterian
    Study Ctr.

Religion (RLDS)
Reorg. Church of Jesus Christ of LDS

Religion (Russian Orthodox)
Media Project
Petrified Films, Inc.

Religion (Shakers)
Davenport Films

Religion (Shintoism)
Japan Society, Inc. Film Center

Religion ("Shouter" churches)
Smithsonian Inst., Human Studies Film
    Arch.

Religion (Snake handlers)
Appalachian State Univ., Eury Coll.
South Carolina Humanities Res. Ctr.

Religion (Southern Baptist)
Southern Baptist Hist. Lib. & Arch.

Religion (Soviet Union)
Hoover Institution

Religion (Sufism)
Hartley Film Found., Inc.

Religion (Taoism)
Hartley Film Found., Inc.

Religion (Tibetan Buddhism)
Smithsonian Inst., Human Studies Film
    Arch.

Religion (Unification Church)
Pyramid Film and Video Corp.

Religion (United Methodist)
Discipleship Resources

Religion (Zen Buddhism)
Camera Three Prods., Inc.
Davenport Films
Hartley Film Found., Inc.

Religious films and videotapes
Abilene Christian University
Amer. Baptist Films/Video
Arch. of the Mennonite Church
Brethren in Christ Church & Messiah
    Coll., Arch.
Budget Films Inc.
CBN Publishing
Concordia Publishing House
Disciples of Christ Hist. Soc.
Discipleship Resources

Evangelical Lutheran Church in America
Fellowship of Christian Athletes
Golden Gate Theological Seminary
    Library
Hellenic College
Intl. Lutheran Layman's League
Keep the Faith, Inc.
Lancaster Mennonite Hist. Soc.
Loma Linda Univ., Webb Lib.
Mass Media Ministries
Moody Inst. of Science
Myrin Institute
Natl. Catholic Educational Assn.
Natl. Jewish Arch. of Broadcasting
Prelinger Assoc., Inc.
Pyramid Film and Video Corp.
Reorg. Church of Jesus Christ of LDS
Sheen (Fulton J.) Comm. Ltd.
United Methodist Churches
Wheaton Coll., Billy Graham Ctr.
World Wide Pictures, Inc.
See also Bible stories and study; Religion;
    Television (Religious)

Religious television
See Television (Religious)

Rembrandt van Rijn
Amer. Federation of the Arts

Remick, Lee
Banks Film Library

Remote sensing
NASA, Johnson Space Ctr., Film & Video
    Dist. Lib.
NASA, Office of Comm.
Ocean Earth Constr. and Dev. Corp.
Stimulus

Remotely piloted vehicles
See Vehicles (Remotely piloted)

Rennels, Sig
Blackwood Prods., Inc.

Reno, Nev.
Film Bank
Postcards Unlimited
Preview Media

Reno, Nev. (History and culture)
Petrified Films, Inc.

Renoir, Auguste
Archive Film Prods., Inc.

Rent control
CBS News Archives

**Reorganized Church of Jesus Christ of
    Latter-Day Saints (RLDS)**
See Religion (RLDS)

Reporters
CBS News Archives
Petrified Films, Inc.
See also Journalism; Newspapers;
    Television news

Reproduction (Animal)
Energy Productions
Univ. of Wash. Press, Multimedia Div.

Reproduction (Human)
Emory Medical Television Network
Focus Intl., Inc.
Historical Health Film Coll.
Mass Media Ministries
Prelinger Assoc., Inc.
Pyramid Film and Video Corp.

NOTE: Access policies, availability and restrictions vary for each source. Please read each entry in full. Always consult "General Film and Videotape Collections" (page 599); these comprehensive collections contain material on every conceivable subject.

See also Childbirth; Pregnancy; Sex education

Reptiles and amphibians
Dreamlight Images, Inc.
Echo Film Prods., Inc.
Energy Productions
Film Bank
Latham Foundation
Miller (David Lee) Prods.
Petrified Films, Inc.
Wings Wildlife Prods. Inc.

Republican Party
Eisenhower (Dwight D.) Library
Estuary Press
Hoover Institution
Indiana Hist. Soc., Smith Memorial Lib.
MacDonald, J. Fred
March of Time
Media Bus
Natl. Archives (RG 130)
Natl. Archives (RG 200)
Prelinger Assoc., Inc.
Purdue Univ., Public Affairs Video Arch.
Republican Natl. Committee
Smithsonian Inst., NMAH, Div. Polit. Hist.

Rescues
CBS News Archives
Film Bank
Fire Prev. Through Films, Inc.
Los Angeles News Service
Natl. Archives (RG 24)
Natl. Archives (RG 26)
Natl. Archives (RG 70)
Natl. Archives (RG 171)
Natl. Archives (RG 178)
Natl. Archives (RG 342)
Natl. Archives (RG 428)
Newsreel Video Service
Petrified Films, Inc.
Twentieth Century-Fox Movietonews
U.S. Dept. of Labor, Mine Safety & Health Admin.
Video Tape Library, Ltd.

Reservoirs
Aitken (Len) Productions, Inc.
CBS News Archives
Florentine Films

Resnick, Marcia
Video Data Bank

Resorts
Atlantic Productions
CBS News Archives
Cineworks Prods. Inc.
Communications Concepts
Creative Video, Inc.
Encore Video Prods., Inc.
Energy Productions
Ergo Media
Film Bank
Independent Media Communications
Las Vegas News Bureau
Mountain Video Associates
Network Productions
Petrified Films, Inc.
Ski TV Prods., Inc./Channel 24
Summit Films, Inc.
Tri-Comm Prods.
Utah Travel Council

Respiratory diseases
Milner-Fenwick, Inc.

Respiratory distress syndrome
March of Dimes Birth Defects Found.

Restaurants
Applegate Entertainment
Brekke Television Prods.

Broad Street Prods.
CBS News Archives
Century Video Services, Inc.
Creative Video, Inc.
Dreamlight Images, Inc.
Energy Productions
Film Bank
Fish Films, Inc.
Forsher (James) Prods. & Archives, Inc.
Hayes Prods., Inc.
Kesser Stock Footage Library
Metro Communications, Inc.
Natl. Restaurant Assn.
Peak Productions, Inc.
Petrified Films, Inc.
Prelinger Assoc., Inc.
Spectral Comms.
Stock House
TV Ontario
Video Tape Library, Ltd.

Restaurants (Coffee shops)
Film Bank
Petrified Films, Inc.

Restaurants (Diners)
Film Bank
Fish Films, Inc.
Petrified Films, Inc.
White Janssen, Inc.

Restaurants (Drive-ins)
Natl. Archives (RG 59)
Petrified Films, Inc.

Restaurants (Fast-food)
Film Bank
Film Search
Icarus Films Intl., Inc.
MacDonald, J. Fred
TV Ontario

Restaurants (Hamburger stands)
Film Bank

Restaurants (Hot dog stands)
Dreamlight Images, Inc.

Retail industry
Boston Stock Market

Retarded people
See Developmentally disabled

Retirement
Natl. Archives (RG 439)
Univ. of Mich., Mich. Hist. Colls.
See also Senior citizens and elderly

Rettig, Tommy
MacDonald, J. Fred

Retton, Mary Lou
McDonald's Corp.

Reunions
CBS News Archives
Mass. Inst. of Tech., MIT Museum
New Day Films
Twentieth Century-Fox Movietonews
Univ. of Rhode Island, Univ. Lib.
Vermont Hist. Soc.

Reuther, Walter P.
United Farm Workers of America (UFW)
Univ. of Mich., Mich. Hist. Colls.

Revere, Paul
Archive Film Prods., Inc.

Reverse-motion cinematography
Twentieth Century-Fox Movietonews, Inc.

Revolutionary War (U.S.)
Amer. Soc. Hist. Proj. Film Lib.

New Jersey Network
Petrified Films, Inc.
Prelinger Assoc., Inc.

Revolutionary War (U.S.) (Naval activities)
Mariners' Museum

Revolutions
Archive Film Prods., Inc.
CBS News Archives
New Time Films, Inc.
Southern Calif. Lib. for Soc. Stud. & Res.
Twentieth Century-Fox Movietonews

Revolutions (Latin America)
Amer. Security Council Foundation
Americas in Transition/Fossil Films
DEC Film & Video
Natl. Archives (RG 200)
New Time Films, Inc.
Petrified Films, Inc.
Third World Newsreel
Univ. of Tex. at Austin, Benson Lat. Am. Coll.
Xchange TV

Revolutions (Mexico)
Archivo Fotografico y Cinematografico Abítia
Archivo Historico Cinematografico
Cinema Guild
Filmoteca de la UNAM
Imevision
Natl. Archives (RG 200)

Revolutions (Soviet Union)
Archive Film Prods., Inc.
Hoover Institution

Revolving doors
Energy Productions

Reye's syndrome
Natl. Reye's Syndrome Found.

Reynolds, Burt
Banks Film Library

Reynolds, Debbie
Banks Film Library

Reynolds, Malvina
Amer. Federation of the Arts
New Day Films

Rhee, Syngman
MacArthur (Gen. Douglas) Memorial
Natl. Archives (RG 342)

Rheims, France
Unicorn Projects

Rheumatology
Milner-Fenwick, Inc.

Rhine, J.B.
Duke Univ., Perkins Lib.

Rhine River (Europe)
Petrified Films, Inc.
Preview Media

Rhinoceros
Di Sesso (Moe) Wild Life Film Lib.
Film Bank
Innerquest Communications Corp.
Johnson (Martin & Osa) Safari Museum
Miller (David Lee) Prods.
Petrified Films, Inc.
Prelinger Assoc., Inc.
Quinn (Bill) Prods.
Summit Films, Inc.
Wings Wildlife Prods. Inc.

Rhode Island
Prelinger Assoc., Inc.
Preview Media
Telltales Assoc., Inc.
Villon Films

Rhode Island (History and culture)
Native Amer. Pub. Broad. Cons.
Rhode Island Hist. Soc.

Rhône River, France-Switzerland
Petrified Films, Inc.

Rhubarb
Oregon State Univ., Archives

Rhythm and blues
See Music (Rhythm and blues)

Ribbons
Rosebush Visions Corp.

Riboud, Marc
Port Washington Pub. Lib.

Rice
Farkas Studios, Ltd.
Jewell (Stuart) Productions
Petrified Films, Inc.
Rockefeller Arch. Ctr.

Rice paddies
British Info. Svcs., Radio & TV Div.
Petrified Films, Inc.
Sheffield (Erin) Prods.
TV Ontario

Richard, Cliff
Archive Film Prods., Inc.

Richardson, H.H.
Unicorn Projects

Richardson, Sly
Spectral Comms.

Richier, Germaine
Blackwood Prods., Inc.

Richmond, Calif. (History and culture)
Payne, Roz

Richmond, Va.
Energy Productions

Richmond, Va. (History and culture)
Petrified Films, Inc.

Richter, Hans
Camera Three Prods., Inc.

Rickenbacker, Edward V. ("Eddie")
Archive Film Prods., Inc.
Natl. Archives (RG 342)

Rickey, George
Blackwood Prods., Inc.

Rickles, Don
Banks Film Library
MacDonald, J. Fred
Spectral Comms.

Rickshaws
CBS News Archives
Petrified Films, Inc.

Ricoeur, Paul
Churchill (Winston) Memorial and Library

Riefenstahl, Leni
Camera Three Prods., Inc.

Rietveld, Rijk
Southern Calif. Inst. of Architecture

Rifle ranges
Dreamlight Images, Inc.
Petrified Films, Inc.
TV Ontario
See also Guns and rifles

Right-to-work laws
Bowling Green State Univ., Ctr. Arch.
Coll.

Right-wing politics
Alternative Information Network
Birch (John) Society
Cambridge Documentary Films, Inc.
Citizens' Councils of America
Constitutional Rights Foundation
Family Life Seminars
Hoover Institution
MacDonald, J. Fred
March of Time
Mississippi Dept. of Arch. & Hist.
New Time Films, Inc.
Quest Productions Inc.
Univ. of Mich., Mich. Hist. Colls.

Riley, Bridget
Albright-Knox Art Gallery
Amer. Federation of the Arts

Riley, Doug
Natl. Archives of Canada

Ringtail cats
Di Sesso (Moe) Wild Life Film Lib.

Ringwald, Molly
Spectral Comms.

Rino, Juliette and Ginette
Natl. Archives of Canada

Rio de Janeiro, Brazil
Brazilian-American Cultural Inst.
Film Bank
Grinberg (Sherman) Film Libraries (West)

Rio de Janeiro, Brazil (History and culture)
Analogous Productions
Archive Film Prods., Inc.
Intl. Assn. of Independent Producers
Petrified Films, Inc.

Rio Grande (Mexico-U.S.)
Petrified Films, Inc.

Rio Grande Valley (History and culture)
Univ. of Tex. at Austin, Benson Lat. Am.
Coll.

Riots
Archive Film Prods., Inc.
CBS News Archives
Estuary Press
Film Bank
Grinberg (Sherman) Film Libraries (East)
Memphis State Univ. Libraries
Mus. & Hist. Div., City of Sacramento
Natl. Archives (RG 185)
Petrified Films, Inc.
Quest Productions Inc.
Twentieth Century-Fox Movietonews
Univ. of Tex. at Austin, Benson Lat. Am.
Coll.
World Monitor

Ripplof, Frank
Gay Cable Network

Ripps, Rodney
Video Data Bank

Rites
White Janssen, Inc.

Ritter, John
Spectral Comms.

Ritter, Tex
Intl. Mus. of Photography
Pathé Pictures, Inc.
UCLA Film & Television Archive

Rituals
Energy Productions
Film Bank
Film Search
Film/Audio Services, Inc.
Jewell (Stuart) Productions
Natl. Archives of Canada
Petrified Films, Inc.
Samaya Foundation
Univ. of Arizona, Film Lib.
Valley of the Sun Publ.
White Janssen, Inc.

Rivera, Diego
Hoover Institution

Riverboats
See Boats and boating (Riverboats)

Rivers
Aitken (Len) Productions, Inc.
Amer. Motion Pictures
British Info. Svcs., Radio & TV Div.
CBS News Archives
Communications Concepts
Dreamlight Images, Inc.
Echo Film Prods., Inc.
Energy Productions
Farkas Studios, Ltd.
Film Bank
Film Search
Forsher (James) Prods. & Archives, Inc.
Jewell (Stuart) Productions
KD Enterprises Prods.
Mariners' Museum
Natl. Archives (RG 96)
Natl. Archives (RG 111)
Natl. Assn. of Conservation Dists.
Natural Reflections Video
Nature Conservancy
Northcoast Communication, Inc.
Petrified Films, Inc.
Prelinger Assoc., Inc.
Producers' Service
Second Line Search
Summit Films, Inc.
Twentieth Century-Fox Movietonews
Univ. of Wis., Green Bay, Ctr. TV Prod.
Video Tape Library, Ltd.
See also specific rivers

Rivers, Larry
Blackwood Prods., Inc.

Riverside Park, New York City (History)
Archive Film Prods., Inc.

Riviera (Italy-France)
Petrified Films, Inc.

Riviera (Italy-France) (History and culture)
Archive Film Prods., Inc.

Roach, Hal
Em Gee Film Library

Road signs
See Signs (Road)

Roadrunners
Cinenet (Cinema Network)
Wings Wildlife Prods. Inc.

Roads
See Streets and roads

Roadside attractions
Allen (John E.) Inc.
Petrified Films, Inc.
Postcards Associates

Robbe-Grillet, Alain
Albright-Knox Art Gallery

Robbery
See Crime and criminals

Robbins, Le Roy
De Saisset Museum

Roberts, Dave
U.S. Olympic Committee

Roberts, Lillian
Schomburg Ctr. for Res. in Black Culture

Roberts, Oral
Roberts (Oral) Univ.

Robertson, Cliff
Banks Film Library
UCLA Film & Television Archive

Robertson, Pat
People for the American Way

Robeson, Paul
Alan Twyman Presents
Southern Calif. Lib. for Soc. Stud. & Res.

Robins
Di Sesso (Moe) Wild Life Film Lib.
Film Bank
Xicom, Inc.

Robinson, Bill ("Bojangles")
Archive Film Prods., Inc.

Robinson, Earl
Southern Calif. Lib. for Soc. Stud. & Res.

Robinson, Edward G.
Banks Film Library

Robinson, Jackie
MacDonald, J. Fred

Robinson, Smokey
Clark (Dick) Media Archives, Inc.

Robinson, Sugar Ray
Banks Film Library
Natl. Archives (RG 29)
Spectral Comms.
Wesleyan Cinema Archives

Robots and robotics
Analogous Productions
Archive Film Prods., Inc.
Assn. for Unmanned Vehicle Systems
Buhl Science Center
CBS News Archives
Cinema Guild
Film Bank
Film Search
Fish Films, Inc.
General Motors Corp.
Inst. of Electrical & Electronics Eng.
Motor Vehicle Manufacturers Assn.
Petrified Films, Inc.

Prelinger Assoc., Inc.
Robotic Industries Assn.
Rosebush Visions Corp.
SF•V Intl.
Soc. for French Amer. Cult. Svcs. & Educ.
Aid
Society of Manufacturing Engineers
Video Tape Library, Ltd.

Robots and robotics (Japan)
Japan External Trade Organization

Roche, Jim
Blackwood Prods., Inc.

Roche, Kevin
Unicorn Projects

Rochester
See Anderson, Eddie ("Rochester")

Rochester, Mich. (History and culture)
Petrified Films, Inc.

Rochester, N.Y. (History and culture)
Petrified Films, Inc.
Prelinger Assoc., Inc.

Rock and roll music
See Music (Rock and roll)

Rock climbing
Aitken (Len) Productions, Inc.
Alaska Video Prods.
Amer. Alpine Club
Channell One Video
Dobbs (Jeff) Prods.
Film Bank
Moving Media
Second Line Search
Sports Cinematography Group

Rock formations
Film Bank

Rock, Monte III
Pennebaker Associates, Inc.

Rockburne, Dorothea
Blackwood Prods., Inc.

Rockefeller Center (New York City) (History)
March of Time
Petrified Films, Inc.
Rockefeller Arch. Ctr.

Rockefeller Family
March of Time
Rockefeller Arch. Ctr.

Rockefeller, Michael
Pyramid Film and Video Corp.

Rockefeller, Nelson Aldrich
MacDonald, J. Fred
New York State Arch. & Rec. Admin.
Univ. of Ill. Urbana-Champaign, Univ.
Arch.

Rocker, Lee
Spectral Comms.

Rockets
Analogous Productions
Archive Film Prods., Inc.
British Info. Svcs., Radio & TV Div.
CBS News Archives
Communications Concepts
Film Bank
Fish Films, Inc.

NOTE: Access policies, availability and restrictions vary for each source. Please read each entry in full. Always consult "General Film and Videotape Collections" (page 599); these comprehensive collections contain material on every conceivable subject.

Grinberg (Sherman) Film Libraries (West)
Kesser Stock Footage Library
NASA, Lewis Research Center
NASA, Office of Comm.
Natl. Archives (RG 200)
Natl. Archives (RG 227)
Natl. Archives (RG 242)
Natl. Archives (RG 342)
Petrified Films, Inc.
Prelinger Assoc., Inc.
Twentieth Century-Fox Movietonews
U.S. Defense Nuclear Agency
Universal City Studios
See also Space; Space program (U.S.);
   Spacecraft and spaceships

Rockettes
See Chorus girls and chorus lines; Radio
   City Music Hall

Rockne, Knute
Archive Film Prods., Inc.
Film Education Institute
Forsher (James) Prods. & Archives, Inc.
Grinberg (Sherman) Film Libraries (West)
Oregon State Univ., Archives

Rocks
Twentieth Century-Fox Movietonews

Rockville, Md. (History and culture)
Montgomery Community Television, Inc.

Rockwell, Norman
WQED/Pittsburgh

Rocky Flats, Colo. (History and culture)
Petrified Films, Inc.

Rocky Mountain National Park, Colo.
   (History and culture)
Natl. Archives (RG 70)

Rocky Mountains
Cimarron Productions
Departures, Inc.
Petrified Films, Inc.
Prov. Arch. of Alberta
TV Ontario

Rocky Mountains (History and culture)
Bullfrog Films, Inc.
Prov. Arch. of Alberta
Schiele Museum

Rodents
Film Bank
See also Mice; Rats

Rodeos
ABC Sports, Inc.
Allen (John E.) Inc.
Amer. Motion Pictures
Analogous Productions
Archive Film Prods., Inc.
CBS News Archives
Cinenet (Cinema Network)
Echo Film Prods., Inc.
Energy Productions
Film Bank
Footage Inc.
Freewheelin' Films, Ltd.
Glenbow Mus. Arch.
Golden Gaters Prods.
Indiana State Comm. on Public Records
Lib. of Congress, Amer. Folklife Ctr.
Media Project
Native Amer. Pub. Broad. Cons.
Network Productions
New Mexico State Records Ctr. & Arch.
North Country Media Group
Oregon Hist. Soc.
Petrified Films, Inc.
Rockefeller Arch. Ctr.
Second Line Search

Source Stock Footage Lib., Inc.
Summit Films, Inc.
Texas Tech Univ., Southwest Coll.
Twentieth Century-Fox Movietonews
Utah State Archives
Video Tape Library, Ltd.
White Janssen, Inc.

Rodeos (Ski)
Peak Productions, Inc.

Rodgers, Reginald
Green Mountain Post Films

Rodin, Auguste
Blackwood Prods., Inc.

Rodman, Hugh
Natl. Archives (RG 24)

Rodney, Red
Rhapsody Films, Inc.

Rodney, Walter
DEC Film & Video

Rodríguez, Armando
Univ. of Tex. at Austin, Benson Lat. Am.
   Coll.

Rodriguez, Chi Chi
Natl. Archives (RG 29)

Roebling, N.J. (History and culture)
New Jersey Network

Rogers, Buddy
Banks Film Library

Rogers, Carl
Amer. Assn. for Counseling &
   Development
Psychological and Educational Films
Salenger Films Inc.

Rogers, Edith Nourse
Radcliffe Coll., Schlesinger Lib.

Rogers, Ginger
Banks Film Library
Daphne Productions, Inc.
Southwest Film/Video Archives, SMU

Rogers, Jimmie
Country Music Foundation, Inc.

Rogers, Kenny
Spectral Comms.

Rogers, Roy
Banks Film Library
Em Gee Film Library
Encore Entertainment
Houston (Sam) Regional Library
Shokus Video
UPA Prods. of America
Video Resources N.Y., Inc.

Rogers, Wayne
Spectral Comms.

Rogers, Will
Archive Film Prods., Inc.
Em Gee Film Library
Rogers (Will) Memorial
Timesteps Prods., Inc.

Rogoff, Caryn
Port Washington Pub. Lib.

Rogovin, Milton
Albright-Knox Art Gallery

Rogue River, Oregon
Sobek Productions

Roller coasters
Analogous Productions
Dreamlight Images, Inc.
Energy Productions
Film Bank
Nemiroff Prods., Inc.
Petrified Films, Inc.
Prelinger Assoc., Inc.
See also Amusement parks

Roller derby
Analogous Productions
MacDonald, J. Fred
Sportsfilm

Roller-skating
Amer. Motion Pictures
Archive Film Prods., Inc.
Cinema Arts Assoc.
Dreamlight Images, Inc.
Film Bank
Fish Films, Inc.
Forsher (James) Prods. & Archives, Inc.
Pyramid Film and Video Corp.
Sportsfilm
Twentieth Century-Fox Movietonews
Video Tape Library, Ltd.

Rolling Stones, The
Archive Film Prods., Inc.
Clark (Dick) Media Archives, Inc.
Daphne Productions, Inc.
UPA Prods. of America

Rollins, Sonny
Rhapsody Films, Inc.

Romance
SF•V Intl.

Rome
Beerger (Norman) Prods.
Cameo Film Library, Inc.
Dreamlight Images, Inc.
Preview Media

Rome (History and culture)
Archive Film Prods., Inc.
Intl. Film Bureau, Inc.
Petrified Films, Inc.

Romero, Cesar
Banks Film Library
Spectral Comms.

Romney, George Wilcken
Univ. of Mich., Mich. Hist. Colls.

Ronettes, The
Clark (Dick) Media Archives, Inc.
UPA Prods. of America

Ronne, Finne
Natl. Archives (RG 342)

Ronstadt, Linda
Clark (Dick) Media Archives, Inc.
Daphne Productions, Inc.

Rooley, Anthony
Amer. Federation of the Arts

Rooms
Rosebush Visions Corp.

Rooney, Mickey
Banks Film Library
New York Pub. Lib., Perf. Arts Res. Ctr.,
   Theatre on Film and Tape
UCLA Film & Television Archive

Roosevelt, Eleanor
Banks Film Library
Lib. of Congress, M/B/RS
Roosevelt (Franklin D.) Lib.

Smith (Margaret Chase) Lib. Ctr.
Timesteps Prods., Inc.

Roosevelt, Franklin Delano
Archive Film Prods., Inc.
Cinema Arts Assoc.
Film Bank
Film Education Institute
Forsher (James) Prods. & Archives, Inc.
Hearst Metrotone News
Intl. Historic Films, Inc.
Kennedy (John F.) Library
MacDonald, J. Fred
Natl. Archives (RG 28)
Natl. Archives (RG 39)
Natl. Archives (RG 47)
Natl. Archives (RG 70)
Natl. Archives (RG 80)
Natl. Archives (RG 82)
Natl. Archives (RG 103)
Natl. Archives (RG 111)
Natl. Archives (RG 119)
Natl. Archives (RG 121)
Natl. Archives (RG 178)
Natl. Archives (RG 200)
Natl. Archives (RG 208)
Natl. Archives (RG 233)
Natl. Archives (RG 342)
Oregon Hist. Soc.
Pennsylvania State Arch.
Petrified Films, Inc.
Prelinger Assoc., Inc.
Roosevelt (Franklin D.) Lib.
Southern Calif. Lib. for Soc. Stud. & Res.
Timesteps Prods., Inc.

Roosevelt, James
Banks Film Library

Roosevelt, N.J. (History and culture)
Cinema Guild

Roosevelt, Theodore
Archive Film Prods., Inc.
Film Bank
Film Education Institute
Forsher (James) Prods. & Archives, Inc.
Grinberg (Sherman) Film Libraries (West)
Halcyon Days Prods.
Lib. of Congress, M/B/RS
Natl. Archives (RG 342)
Petrified Films, Inc.
Prelinger Assoc., Inc.
Pyramid Film and Video Corp.

Roosters
Petrified Films, Inc.

Rope climbing
Dreamlight Images, Inc.

Rope tricks
Buffalo Bill Historical Center
Petrified Films, Inc.
Sheffield (Erin) Prods.

Rose Bowl and **Rose Parade**
See Tournament of Roses

Rosenberg, Ethel and Julius
First Run/Icarus Films, Inc.
Halcyon Days Prods.
Natl. Archives (RG 200)

Rosenberg, Harold
Blackwood Prods., Inc.

Rosenblum, Walter and Naomi
Port Washington Pub. Lib.

Rosenquist, James
Albright-Knox Art Gallery
Plains Art Mus. Lib.

Roses
Brooklyn Botanic Garden
Energy Productions
Film Bank
Image Bank
Petrified Films, Inc.

Rosewall, Ken
U.S. Tennis Assn.

Rosin, Carol
Inst. for Space & Security Studies

Rosler, Martha
Paper Tiger TV
Video Data Bank

Ross, Betsy
Petrified Films, Inc.

Ross, Helen
Inst. for Psychoanalysis

Ross, Lanny
Pathé Pictures, Inc.

Rosso, Medardo
Blackwood Prods., Inc.

Rostow, Walt Whitman
Johnson (Lyndon Baines) Library

Roszak, Theodore
Blackwood Prods., Inc.

Rothblatt, Abe
Blackwood Prods., Inc.

Rothenberg, Susan
Blackwood Prods., Inc.
Video Data Bank

Rothenburg, Germany (History and culture)
German Info. Ctr., Film Lib.

Rothko, Mark
Blackwood Prods., Inc.

Rothschild, Amalie
Port Washington Pub. Lib.

Rothstein, Arthur
Natl. Press Photographers Assn., Inc.

Rotterdam, Netherlands (History and culture)
Archive Film Prods., Inc.

Roué, Marie-Michèle
Université Laval, Svc. des Res. Pédagogiques

Roulette
Film Bank
Petrified Films, Inc.
See also Gambling

Rowan, Carl
Natl. Assn. for the Advancement of Colored People

Rowbotham, Sheila
Paper Tiger TV

Rowing
Analogous Productions
Athletic Institute
Dreamlight Images, Inc.
Sportsfilm
U.S. Olympic Comm.

Royal Air Force (RAF)
British Info. Svcs., Radio & TV Div.
March of Time
Petrified Films, Inc.
UDS Company

Royal Canadian Air Force (RCAF)
Natl. Archives of Canada

Royal Canadian Mounted Police (RCMP)
Natl. Archives of Canada
TV Ontario
Yukon Archives

Royal Commission
See the commission's "subject" area (e.g., Royal Commission on Bilingualism and Biculturalism is found under Bilingualism and Biculturalism, Royal Commission on)

Royal Family (Great Britain)
Film Bank
Hearst Metrotone News
Natl. Archives of Canada
Prov. Arch. of Alberta
Prov. Arch. of British Columbia
See also Coronations; Royalty; specific individuals

Royalton, Ill. (History and culture)
Natl. Archives (RG 70)

Royalty
Allen (John E.) Inc.
Analogous Productions
Archive Film Prods., Inc.
Archives of Ontario
Film Bank
Fish Films, Inc.
Glenbow Mus. Arch.
Natl. Archives (RG 24)
Natl. Archives (RG 119)
Prelinger Assoc., Inc.
Spalla (Rick) Video Prods.
Univ. of Alberta, Fac. of Ext.
Yue-Sai Kan, Inc.
See also Coronations; Royal Family (Great Britain); specific individuals

Rozier, Mike
Archive Film Prods., Inc.

Rubber
CBS News Archives
Farkas Studios, Ltd.

Rubber industry
Mississippi Dept. of Arch. & Hist.
Natl. Archives (RG 234)
Ohio Hist. Soc.

Rubdowns
See Massage

Rubin, Jerry
Film/Audio Services, Inc.
MacDonald, J. Fred
Petrified Films, Inc.
Villon Films

Rudner, Sara
Blackwood Prods., Inc.

Rudolph (the Red-Nosed Reindeer)
Film Bank
Prelinger Assoc., Inc.

Rudolph, Wilma
Sportsfilm

Rugby
Moving Media
New Zealand Embassy Film Lib.
Sportsfilm
Twentieth Century-Fox Movietonews
Video Tape Library, Ltd.

Rugs
CBS News Archives
Petrified Films, Inc.

Ruins
Energy Productions
Film Bank
Mountain Video Associates
New Film Co., Inc.
Petrified Films, Inc.
Twentieth Century-Fox Movietonews

Ruins (Ancient)
CBS News Archives

Ruins (Mayan)
TV Ontario

Ruins (War)
CBS News Archives
Natl. Archives/Natl. AV Ctr.

Rukeyser, Muriel
New Day Films

Ruleville, Miss. (History and culture)
Mississippi Dept. of Arch. & Hist.

Rum
Seagram Museum

Rumania
Pan American Airlines Film Lib.

Rumania (History and culture)
Natl. Archives (RG 226)

Rumba
See Dance and dancing (Rumba)

Runaways
Filmfair Communications

Runge, Fritz
Southern Calif. Inst. of Architecture

Running
Athletic Institute
Chicago Video Transfer
Dreamlight Images, Inc.
Film Bank
Peak Productions, Inc.
Summit Films, Inc.
See also Olympics; Sports; Track and field

Running (Cross-country)
Dreamlight Images, Inc.
Sportsfilm
Twentieth Century-Fox Movietonews

Running (Marathon)
Amer. Motion Pictures
Analogous Productions
Archive Film Prods., Inc.
Dreamlight Images, Inc.
Spectral Comms.
Sports Mus. of New England
TV Ontario
Twentieth Century-Fox Movietonews

Rural Electrification Administration (U.S.)
Natl. Archives (RG 16)
Natl. Archives/Natl. AV Ctr.

Rural scenes
Allen (John E.) Inc.
Aries Prods.
Dreamlight Images, Inc.
Energy Productions
Farkas Studios, Ltd.
Film Bank
Film Search
Florentine Films
Forsher (James) Prods. & Arch. Inc.
Hearst Metrotone News
Intl. Film Foundation
Marts (Steve) Productions
Natl. Archives/Natl. AV Ctr.
New Jersey Network
Petrified Films, Inc.
Prelinger Assoc., Inc.
Riccitelli (Bruce) Prods.
White Janssen, Inc.

Rural Settlement Administration (U.S.)
Natl. Archives (RG 96)

Ruscha, Ed
Blackwood Prods., Inc.

Rush, Barbara
Banks Film Library

Rush, Ed
Fellowship of Christian Athletes

Rushmore, Mount (S. Dak.)
Film Bank
Petrified Films, Inc.

Rusk, Dean
Duke Univ., Perkins Lib.
Natl. Archives (RG 59)

Russell, A.J.
Blackwood Prods., Inc.

Russell, Jane
Natl. Archives (RG 47)

Russell, Kevin
Spectral Comms.

Russell, Kurt
Spectral Comms.

Russell, Lillian
Grinberg (Sherman) Film Libraries (West)
Petrified Films, Inc.

Russell, Rosalind
Banks Film Library

Russia
See Soviet Union

Russian Orthodox Church
See Religion (Russian Orthodox)

Russian music
See Music (Soviet Union)

Russo-Finnish War
Natl. Archives (RG 200)

Russo-Japanese War
Lib. of Congress, M/B/RS

Rust
Dreamlight Images, Inc.

Rust, Matthias
Belka Intl. Inc.

NOTE: Access policies, availability and restrictions vary for each source. Please read each entry in full. Always consult "General Film and Videotape Collections" (page 599); these comprehensive collections contain material on every conceivable subject.

Rustin, Bayard
Memphis State Univ. Libraries
Randolph (A. Philip) Educ. Fund

Rustlers
Archive Film Prods., Inc.

Ruth, George Herman ("Babe")
Archive Film Prods., Inc.
Film Education Institute
Forsher (James) Prods. & Archives, Inc.
Grinberg (Sherman) Film Libraries (West)
Hearst Metrotone News
Oregon State Univ., Archives
Petrified Films, Inc.
Timesteps Prods., Inc.

Ryan, Amy
Albright-Knox Art Gallery

Ryan, Robert
UCLA Film & Television Archive

Ryman, Robert
Blackwood Prods., Inc.
Video Data Bank

Ryukyu Islands, Japan (History and culture)
Natl. Archives (RG 80)

Ryun, Jim
Sportsfilm

SEATO
See South Eastern Atlantic Treaty Organization (SEATO)

SIDS
See Sudden Infant Death Syndrome (SIDS)

SNCC
See Student Non-Violent Coordinating Committee (SNCC)

SPARS
Twentieth Century-Fox Movietonews

SWAT operations
Newsreel Video Service

Saar, Betye
Amer. Federation of the Arts

Saarinen, Eliel
Cranbrook Acad. of Arts

Saba (Netherlands Antilles)
Passage Home Communications

Sabah, Malaysia (History and culture)
Film/Audio Services, Inc.

Sabotage
CBS News Archives
March of Time
Natl. Archives (RG 18)
Natl. Archives (RG 226)
Northeast Historic Film
Twentieth Century-Fox Movietonews

Sacco-Vanzetti case
Natl. Archives (RG 200)

Sacramento, Calif.
Energy Productions
Tri-Comm Prods.

Sacramento, Calif. (History and culture)
Estuary Press
KCRA-TV
Mus. & Hist. Div., City of Sacramento
Petrified Films, Inc.

Sacramento Valley, Calif. (History and culture)
Mus. & Hist. Div., City of Sacramento
Sweet (Harry) Film Coll.

Sadat, Anwar
Halcyon Days Prods.

Safaris
Footage Inc.
Grinberg (Sherman) Film Libraries (West)
Jewell (Stuart) Productions
Johnson (Martin & Osa) Safari Museum
Prelinger Assoc., Inc.

Safety belts
See Automobiles (Seat belts and air bags)

Safety films and videotapes
ABC Distribution (Education)
AIMS Media
Aluminum Assn.
Amer. Arch. of the Factual Film
Amer. Automobile Assn., FTS
Amer. Driver & Traffic Safety Educ. Assn.
Amer. Hotel & Motel Assn.
Amer. Medical Assn.
Amer. Nuclear Society
Amer. Public Transit Assn.
Amer. Pulpwood Assn., Inc.
Amer. Red Cross
Amer. Truck Historical Society
Amer. Trucking Assn.
Asbestos Victims of America
Assoc. Gen. Contractors of America
Barr Films
Bell Canada
British Info. Svcs., Radio & TV Div.
Calif. Highway Patrol Acad. Media Center
Carter (C.L.) Jr. & Assoc., Inc.
Center for Humanities, Inc.
Chrysler Motors Corp.
Churchill Films
Coe Film Assoc., Inc.
Connecticut State Library
Coronet/MTI Film & Video
Courter Films & Assoc.
Filmfair Communications
Fire Prev. Through Films, Inc.
Foundation for Handgun Education
GPN
General Motors Corp.
Gypsum Assn.
Handel Film Corp.
Hewlett-Packard Co.
Higgins (Alfred) Prods.
Highway Safety Films, Inc.
Historical Health Film Coll.
Indiana State Comm. on Public Records
Inst. of Makers of Explosives
Insurance Inst. for Highway Safety
Intl. Film Bureau, Inc.
Kentucky Dept. of Libraries & Archives
Klein (Walter J.) Co., Ltd.
Los Angeles Dept. of Water & Power
McDonald's Corp.
Media Guild
Miles Corporate Archive
Minn. Dept. of Public Safety Film Lib.
Modern Talking Picture Service
Motion Picture Services
Motor Vehicle Manufacturers Assn.
Movietime, Inc. Archives
Natl. Archives (RG 70)
Natl. Archives (RG 100)
Natl. Archives (RG 434)
Natl. Archives of Canada
Natl. Archives/Natl. AV Ctr.
Natl. Assn. of Conservation Dists.
Natl. Crime Prevention Council
Natl. Dance Assn.
Natl. Fire Protection Assn.
Natl. Glass Assn.
Natl. Oceanic & Atmospheric Admin.
Natl. Railway Historical Soc.
Natl. Rifle Assn.
Natl. Safety Council
Natl. Soc. to Prevent Blindness
New York State Dept. of Env. Cons.
Ohio State Univ., Dept. of Photog. & Cinema
Phoenix Films and Video
Polymorph Films, Inc.
Prelinger Assoc., Inc.
Pyramid Film and Video Corp.
U.S. Dept. of Labor, Mine Safety & Health Admin.
Union Pacific Railroad
Univ. of Calif., Ext. Media Ctr.
Univ. of Tex. at Austin, Petrol. Ext. Svc.
See also Driver education; Fire safety

Safety patrols
Prelinger Assoc., Inc.

Safety testing (Automobiles)
See Automobiles (Safety testing)

Sagan, Carl
Educational Film & Video Project
Inst. for Space & Security Studies

Sage, Kay
Amer. Federation of the Arts

Sagebrush
Film Bank
Oregon State Univ., Archives
Petrified Films, Inc.

Sager, Carole Bayer
Spectral Comms.

Sahara Desert, Africa
Documentary Educational Resources
Petrified Films, Inc.

Sahara Desert, Africa (History and culture)
Archive Film Prods., Inc.
TV Ontario

Sahl, Mort
Baker (Fred) Film & Video Co.
Spalla (Rick) Video Prods.

Saigon, Vietnam
See Ho Chi Minh City, Vietnam

Sailboarding
Merkel Films
Mountain Video Associates
Offshore Productions

Sailboat racing
See Boats and boating (Racing) (Sailboats)

Sailboats
See Boats and boating (Sailboats)

Sailing
Allen (John E.) Inc.
Analogous Productions
Archive Film Prods., Inc.
Brekke Television Prods.
Canadian Coast Guard College Library
Caribbean Images, Ltd.
Creative Video, Inc.
Dreamlight Images, Inc.
Elfstrom-Hilmer Prods.
Energy Productions
Film Bank
Grinberg (Sherman) Film Libraries (West)
MacGillivray Freeman Films
Metro Communications, Inc.
Mountain Video Associates
Mystic Seaport Mus., Inc.
Nemiroff Prods., Inc.
New Film Co., Inc.
North Country Media Group

Offshore Productions
Passage Home Comms.
Peak Productions, Inc.
Sea TV
Simon (Jeff) Productions
Site Productions
Source Stock Footage Lib., Inc.
Spectral Comms.
Sports Cinematography Group
TV Ontario
Telltales Associates Inc.
See also Boats and boating; Ships; Yachts and yachting

Sailors
Film Bank
Petrified Films, Inc.
Twentieth Century-Fox Movietonews

Sailplaning
Crystal Pyramid Prods.
MacGillivray Freeman Films

Saint Augustine, Fla.
Preview Media

Saint Augustine, Fla. (History and culture)
Petrified Films, Inc.
St. Augustine Hist. Soc.

Saint Bernard Parish, La. (History and culture)
Cinema Guild

Saint Croix, V.I. (History and culture)
Natl. Archives (RG 48)
WTJX-TV

Saint Denis, France
Unicorn Projects

Saint Helens, Mount (Wash.)
Beerger (Norman) Prods.
NASA, Office of Comm.

St John, Jill
Spectral Comms.

Saint Johns, Antigua (History and culture)
Natl. Archives (RG 48)

Saint Lawrence Island, Alaska (History and culture)
Alaska Native Heritage Film Project

Saint Lawrence River, Quebec (History)
Schiele Museum

Saint Lawrence Seaway
New York State Arch. & Rec. Admin.
New York State Dept. of Econ. Devel.

Saint Lawrence Seaway (History)
March of Time
Natl. Archives of Canada

Saint Louis
Dreamlight Images, Inc.
Energy Productions
File Tape Co.

Saint Louis (History and culture)
Lib. of Congress, M/B/RS
Missouri Hist. Soc.
Natl. Archives (RG 131)
Petrified Films, Inc.
Prelinger Assoc., Inc.
State Hist. Soc. of Wisconsin
Unicorn Projects

Saint Lucia
Creative Video, Inc.
Preview Media

Saint Lucia (History and culture)
Mus. of Mod. Art of Latin America

Saint Moritz, Switzerland
Preview Media

Saint Patrick's Cathedral (New York City)
Analogous Productions

Saint Paul, Minn.
Energy Productions
Preview Media

Saint Paul, Minn. (History and culture)
Intermedia Arts Minnesota
Petrified Films, Inc.
Prelinger Assoc., Inc.
Saint Paul Pub. Lib., Film & Video Ctr.

Saint Paul's Cathedral (London)
Analogous Productions

Saint Petersburg, Fla.
Energy Productions
Preview Media

Saint Petersburg, Russia
See Leningrad

Saint Phalle, Niki de
Cantor (Arthur) Inc.

Saint Thomas, V.I.
Kesser Stock Footage Library
Ski TV Prods., Inc.

Saint Thomas, V.I. (History and culture)
Natl. Archives (RG 48)
WTJX-TV

Saint Vincent and the Grenadines
Preview Media

Sainte Marie Among the Hurons, Ontario (History and culture)
Huronia Historical Parks

Saionji (Prince Kimmochi)
March of Time

Salamanders
Wings Wildlife Prods. Inc.

Salazar, Rubén
Univ. of Tex. at Austin, Benson Lat. Am. Coll.

Salem, Mass.
Preview Media

Salem, N.C. (History and culture)
North Carolina Div. of Arch. & Hist.

Salem, Oreg. (History and culture)
Oregon Hist. Soc.

Sales training
AMA Film/Video
BNA Communications, Inc.
Barr Films
CRM Films
Dartnell
Films Incorporated
General Motors Corp.
Natl. Assn. of Home Builders
Perlmutter (Alvin H.) Inc.
Prelinger Assoc., Inc.
Salenger Films Inc.
Seagram Museum

Video Arts Inc.

Salespeople
Dartnell
Petrified Films, Inc.
Prelinger Assoc., Inc.

Salinger, Pierre
Banks Film Library

Salk, Lee
Daphne Productions, Inc.

Salle, David
Blackwood Prods., Inc.

Salmon
Calif. Dept. of Water Resources
Cousteau Society
Echo Film Prods., Inc.
Film Bank
March of Time
Moonlight Productions
Natl. Oceanic & Atmospheric Admin.
Oregon State Univ., Archives
Prelinger Assoc., Inc.
TV Ontario
Wings Wildlife Prods. Inc.

Salmon River, Idaho (History and culture)
Utah State Hist. Soc.

Salomon, Haym
Amer. Jewish Hist. Soc.

Saloons
Dreamlight Images, Inc.
Grinberg (Sherman) Film Libraries (West)
Petrified Films, Inc.

Salt
Prelinger Assoc., Inc.

Salt Lake City (History and culture)
Petrified Films, Inc.
Schiele Museum

Salton Sea, Calif.
Petrified Films, Inc.

Salvador, Brazil
Brazilian-American Cultural Inst.

Salvaging
CBS News Archives

Salvation Army
Natl. Archives (RG 53)
Salvation Army Arch. & Rec. Ctr.
Salvation Army, Natl. Comm. Dept.
Salvation Army, Off. of Media Ministries
Wheaton Coll., Billy Graham Ctr.

Salzburg, Austria (History and culture)
Petrified Films, Inc.

Samburu people
Johnson (Martin & Osa) Safari Museum

Sammartino, Bruno
Sportsfilm

Samoa (History and culture)
Film/Audio Services, Inc.
Maryknoll Fathers & Brothers
Natl. Archives (RG 78)

Samoa, Western (History and culture)
U.S. Committee for UNICEF

Samoan Americans
Third World Newsreel

Sams, Emma
Spectral Comms.

Samu, Charles
Port Washington Pub. Lib.

San (Bushmen)
Documentary Educational Resources

San Andreas Fault, Calif.
TVA/Television Assoc.

San Antonio, Tex.
Hayes Prods., Inc.
Preview Media

San Antonio, Tex. (History and culture)
Hayes Prods., Inc.
Petrified Films, Inc.
San Antonio Conservation Soc. Found. Lib.

San Diego, Calif.
Crystal Pyramid Prods.
Dorn (Larry) Associates
Petrified Films, Inc.
Postcards Unlimited
Preview Media
Stock House
Stock Shots

San Diego, Calif. (History and culture)
Oregon Hist. Soc.
Petrified Films, Inc.
Video Data Bank

San Fernando Valley, Calif. (History and culture)
Prelinger Assoc., Inc.

San Francisco
Airline Film & TV Promotions
Airship Industries (USA), Inc.
Analogous Prods.
Cinephile Amalgamated Pictures
Creative Video, Inc.
Dorn (Larry) Associates
Dreamlight Images, Inc.
Elfstrom-Hilmer Prods.
Energy Productions
Film Bank
Film Search
New Film Co., Inc.
Petrified Films, Inc.
Postcards Unlimited
Preview Media
Prod. House, Inc., Motion Media Prods.
Source Stock Footage Lib., Inc.
Spectral Comms.
Stegman Productions
Stock House
Stock Shots
Summit Films, Inc.
TV Ontario
Unicorn Projects
Wallen (Dick) Prods.

San Francisco (History and culture)
Archive Film Prods., Inc.
Cinema Guild
Gould (Bert)/bay area archive
Labor Video Project
Louisiana Tech. Univ., Eng. Film Res. Ctr.
MacDonald, J. Fred
Natl. Archives (RG 46)
Natl. Asian American Telecomm. Assn.
Oregon Hist. Soc.
Pacific Film Archive

Patrick Media Group
Petrified Films, Inc.
Prelinger Assoc., Inc.
San Francisco Maritime Natl. Hist. Park
Southern Calif. Lib. for Soc. Stud. & Res.
UCLA Behavioral Sci. Media Lab.
Unicorn Projects
White Janssen, Inc.
Worldwide Television News

San Francisco Bay (Contemporary issues)
Ocean Earth Constr. and Dev. Corp.

San Francisco Bay Area
Petrified Films, Inc.
Prod. House, Inc., Motion Media Prods.
TVA/Television Assoc.

San Francisco Bay Area (History and culture)
Estuary Press
Gould (Bert)/bay area archive
Labor Video Project
Mus. & Hist. Div., City of Sacramento
Natl. Railway Historical Soc.
Petrified Films, Inc.
San Francisco Bay Area TV News Arch.

San Francisco Mime Troupe
First Run/Icarus Films, Inc.
Intermedia Arts Minnesota

San Joaquin Valley, Calif. (History and culture)
United Farm Workers of America (UFW)

San Jose, Calif.
Stock Shots

San Jose, Calif. (History and culture)
San Jose Hist. Museum

San José, Costa Rica (History and culture)
Northstar Prods.

San Juan Capistrano, Calif.
Petrified Films, Inc.

San Juan Capistrano, Calif. (History and culture)
Petrified Films, Inc.

San Juan Islands, Wash.
Amer. Motion Pictures
Preview Media

San Juan River, Utah
Sobek Productions

San Juan River, Utah (History and culture)
Utah State Hist. Soc.

San Luis Obispo, Calif. (History and culture)
Petrified Films, Inc.

San Marino (History and culture)
Oregon Hist. Soc.

San Pedro, Calif. (History and culture)
Petrified Films, Inc.

San Quentin Prison (Calif.)
Petrified Films, Inc.

San Salvador, El Salvador (History and culture)
Camino Film Projects

NOTE: Access policies, availability and restrictions vary for each source. Please read each entry in full. Always consult "General Film and Videotape Collections" (page 599); these comprehensive collections contain material on every conceivable subject.

Natl. Archives (RG 59)

San Simeon, Calif.
Petrified Films, Inc.
Preview Media

San Xavier, Ariz.
Source Stock Footage Lib., Inc.

Sanborn, John
Port Washington Pub. Lib.

Sanchez, Sonia
Intermedia Arts Minnesota

Sanctuary movement
Amer. Baptist Films/Video
Educational Film & Video Project

Sand
TV Ontario

Sand castles
Film Bank
Petrified Films, Inc.

Sand dunes
Dreamlight Images, Inc.
Echo Film Prods., Inc.
Energy Productions
Film Bank
New Mexico State Records Ctr. & Arch.
Petrified Films, Inc.
Video Tape Library, Ltd.

Sandbags
Film Bank
Petrified Films, Inc.

Sandboxes
Petrified Films, Inc.

Sandburg, Carl
Banks Film Library
Illinois State Hist. Lib.

Sanders, Ed
Giorno Poetry Systems Inst.

Sanders, Ricky
Archive Film Prods., Inc.

Sandin, Dan
Video Data Bank

Sandlin, Martha
Port Washington Pub. Lib.

Sandoval, Arturo
Video Data Bank

Sandpipers
Film Bank
TV Ontario

Sandrich, Jay
Univ. of Wyoming, Amer. Heritage Ctr.

Sands, Tommy
Banks Film Library
Las Vegas News Bureau

Sandstone
Natl. Archives (RG 70)

Sandstorms
See Storms (Sand)

Sanger, Margaret
Planned Parenthood Federation of Amer.

Sanitariums
CBS News Archives
Historical Health Film Coll.
Petrified Films, Inc.

Sanitariums (Tuberculosis)
Natl. Library of Medicine

Sanitation
Amer. Inst. of Baking
CBS News Archives
Historical Health Film Coll.
Imevision
Natl. Archives (RG 200)
Rockefeller Arch. Ctr.
U.S. Committee for UNICEF
UNICEF, Div. Info. & Pub. Aff.
United Nations Ctr. for Human
  Settlements

Santa Ana, Calif. (History and culture)
Petrified Films, Inc.

Santa Barbara, Calif.
Applegate Entertainment
Petrified Films, Inc.
Preview Media

Santa Barbara, Calif. (History and culture)
Petrified Films, Inc.

Santa Catalina Island
Preview Media

Santa Catalina Island (History and culture)
Petrified Films, Inc.

Santa Clara Valley, Calif. (History and culture)
San Jose Hist. Museum

Santa Claus
Archive Film Prods., Inc.
Film Bank
Petrified Films, Inc.
TV Ontario
See also Christmas

Santa Cruz Island, Calif. (History and culture)
Nature Conservancy

Santa Cruz Trail, N. Mex. (History and culture)
Prelinger Assoc., Inc.

Santa Fe, N. Mex.
New Mexico State Records Ctr. & Arch.
Preview Media
Summit Films, Inc.
Tri-Comm Prods.

Santa Fe, N. Mex. (History and culture)
Petrified Films, Inc.

Santa Monica, Calif.
Petrified Films, Inc.
Spectral Comms.

Santa Monica, Calif. (History and culture)
Petrified Films, Inc.

Santiago, Chile (History and culture)
Archive Film Prods., Inc.

Sao Lius, Brazil
Brazilian-American Cultural Inst.

Sao Paulo, Brazil
Brazilian-American Cultural Inst.
Film Search

Sapporo, Japan
Summit Films, Inc.

Sarasota, Fla. (History and culture)
Swain (Hack) Prods., Inc.

Sardinia, Italy (History and culture)
Rockefeller Arch. Ctr.

Sarnath, India
Petrified Films, Inc.

Sasakawa, Ryoichi
Duke Univ., Perkins Lib.
King (Dr. Martin Luther, Jr.) Ctr.

Saskatchewan (History and culture)
Canadian Filmmakers Dist. Centre
Glenbow Mus. Arch.
Natl. Archives of Canada
Prov. Arch. of Alberta
Univ. of Regina, Sask. Arch. Board

Saskatoon, Sask. (History and culture)
Univ. of Regina, Sask. Arch. Board

Satanism
MacDonald, J. Fred

Satellite dishes
Broad Street Prods.
Intl. Telecommunications Satellite Org.
TV Ontario

Satellite imagery
Ocean Earth Constr. and Dev. Corp.
Stimulus

Satellites
CBS News Archives
Film Bank
Impact Audio Visual
Intl. Telecommunications Satellite Org.
NASA, Lewis Research Center
NASA, Office of Comm.
Natl. Archives (RG 255)
Natl. Archives (RG 342)
Natl. Archives of Canada
Prelinger Assoc., Inc.
Rosebush Visions Corp.
U.S. Dept. of Defense, Motion Media Rec.
  Ctr.
Video Tape Library, Ltd.
See also Space; Space program (U.S.)

Satellites (ERTS)
NASA, Office of Comm.

Satellites (Echo)
Natl. Archives (RG 255)

Satellites (Environmental)
Natl. Oceanic & Atmospheric Admin.

Satellites (INTELSAT)
Bell Canada
Intl. Telecommunications Satellite Org.
Natl. Archives (RG 255)

Satellites (LANDSAT)
NASA, Johnson Space Ctr., Film & Video
  Dist. Lib.
NASA, Lewis Research Center
NASA, Office of Comm.

Satellites (LANDSAT imagery)
Stimulus

Satellites (RELAY)
Natl. Archives (RG 255)

Satellites (SYNCOM)
Natl. Archives (RG 255)

Satellites (Sputnik)
Analogous Productions
Film Bank

Satellites (TELSTAR)
Natl. Archives (RG 255)

Satellites (Weather)
NASA, Lewis Res. Ctr.

Saturn
Beerger (Norman) Prods., Inc.
Rosebush Visions Corp.

Saudi Arabia
Canadian Broadcasting Corp.

Saudi Arabia (Contemporary issues)
Alternative Information Network

Saudi Arabia (History and culture)
Archive Film Prods., Inc.
Middle East Institute

Saulsbury, Willard
Natl. Archives (RG 4)

Sausalito, Calif. (History and culture)
Petrified Films, Inc.

Savalas, Telly
Banks Film Library

Savannah, Ga.
Creative Video, Inc.
Preview Media
Unicorn Projects

Savannah, Ga. (History and culture)
Petrified Films, Inc.

Savings Bonds (U.S.)
Natl. Archives (RG 56)

Sawmills
See Mills (Sawmills)

Saws
CBS News Archives

Sawyer, Eddie
Sportsfilm

Saxon, John
Banks Film Library

Saxophones
Archive Film Prods., Inc.

Sayers, Dorothy L.
Wheaton Coll., Wade Ctr.

Scaffolds
CBS News Archives
Film Bank

Scala, Gia
Banks Film Library

Scandinavia
Bennett (Joel) Prods.
Canadian Broadcasting Corp.

Scandinavia (History and culture)
Natl. Archives of Canada

Scandinavian Americans
Univ. of Mich., Mich. Hist. Colls.

Scenics
Ackerman-Black Prods., Inc.
Aries Prods.
Beerger (Norman) Prods.
Bishop Mus., Visual Coll.
Boston Stock Market
Bradley/McAfee Public Relations
Bransby (John) Prods., Ltd.
Brekke Television Prods.
CBS News Archives
CTV Television Network
Cameo Film Library, Inc.
Cannell (Stephen J.) Prods.

Caribbean Images, Ltd.
Century Video Services, Inc.
Channel Sea Television
Channell One Video
Chisholm (Jack) Film Productions
Cine-Mark
Cineworks Prods. Inc.
Columbia Pictures TV/Stock Film Library
Creative Video, Inc.
Di Sesso (Moe) Wild Life Film Lib.
Dittrich (Scott) Films
Dobbs (Jeff) Prods.
Dobovan Productions, Inc.
Dorn (Larry) Associates
Dreamlight Images, Inc.
Echo Film Prods., Inc.
Elfstrom-Hilmer Prods.
Encore Video Prods., Inc.
Energy Productions
Fabulous Footage Inc.
Film Bank
Film Search
Film/Audio Services, Inc.
Florentine Films
4•6•8 Prods., Inc.
Friends of Free China
Grinberg (Sherman) Film Libraries (West)
Hawaii Public Broadcasting Authority
Hayes Prods., Inc.
Impact Audio Visual
Independent Media Communications
Indiana State Comm. on Public Records
Intl. Media Services, Inc.
Jalbert Productions
Jewell (Stuart) Productions
Loma Linda Univ., Webb Lib.
Los Angeles News Service
Lunar Productions
MVP Communications
MacGillivray Freeman Films
Marts (Steve) Productions
Metro Communications, Inc.
Miller (Warren) Productions, Inc.
Moving Media
Navajo Tribe, Off. Broadcast Svcs.
Nei-Ali Prods.
Network Productions
New York Zoological Society
Nine Star Productions
Northcoast Communication, Inc.
Northstar Prods.
Ocean Images
Odyssey Prods., Inc.
Palisades Wildlife Film Library
Petrified Films, Inc.
Phoenix Videofilms/Karr Prods.
Postcards Associates
Postcards Unlimited
Prelinger Assoc., Inc.
Preview Media
Producers Library Service
Producers' Service
Production House, Inc., Motion Media
    Prods.
Prov. Arch. of Alberta
Prov. Arch. of British Columbia
Quenzer Driscoll Dawson, Inc.
Rainbow Video Prods.
Renaissance Video Corp.
Rock Solid Prods.
Sea TV
Simon & Goodman Picture Co.
Site Productions
Snyder (Bill) Films, Inc.
Source Stock Footage Lib., Inc.
Southwest Prods., Inc.
Stimulus
Stock House
Stock Shots
Studio East Ltd.
Sullivan Video Services

Summit Films, Inc.
TV Ontario
TV-3
TVA/Television Assoc.
Telemation Productions
Tri-Comm Prods.
Twentieth Century-Fox Movietonews
Univ. of Wis., Green Bay, Ctr. TV Prod.
Video Genesis, Inc.
Video I-D, Inc.
Video Ventures Prods.
Video West
Virginia Div. of Tourism
Viz Wiz, Inc.
WETA-TV
Warner (Dane) Photography
Washington State Archives
West Star Productions
White Janssen, Inc.
World Monitor
Xicom, Inc.
Zielinski Productions, Inc.
See also Beauty shots

Schaffner, Franklin J.
Franklin & Marshall Coll.

Schapiro, Meyer
Blackwood Prods., Inc.

Schapiro, Miriam
Video Data Bank

Scheider, Roy
Spectral Comms.

Schenectady, N.Y. (History and culture)
Petrified Films, Inc.

Schidor, Dieter
Gay Cable Network

Schiller, Herb
Paper Tiger TV
Video Data Bank

Schistosomiasis
Rockefeller Arch. Ctr.

Schjeldahl, Peter
Video Data Bank

Schlafly, Phyllis
Smithsonian Inst., NMAH, Div. Polit.
    Hist.

Schlieren cinematography
Prelinger Assoc., Inc.

Schmeling, Max
Archive Film Prods., Inc.

Schnabel, Julian
Blackwood Prods., Inc.

Schnier, Jacques
De Saisset Museum

Schoenberg, Arnold
Natl. Archives of Canada
Schoenberg (Arnold) Inst. Arch.

Schöffer, Nicolas
Albright-Knox Art Gallery

Scholder, Fritz
Plains Art Mus. Lib.

School boards
Natl. School Boards Assn.
Prelinger Assoc., Inc.

School buses
See Buses (School)

Schools
A.M. Stock Exchange
Amer. Institute of Architects
Appalshop Films, Inc.
CBS News Archives
Connecticut Historical Society
Film Bank
Fish Films, Inc.
Forsher (James) Prods. & Archives, Inc.
Intl. Film Foundation
Metro Communications, Inc.
Natl. Assn. of Secondary Schl. Principals
New Mexico State Records Ctr. & Arch.
Northcoast Communication, Inc.
Perkins School for the Blind
Petrified Films, Inc.
Prelinger Assoc., Inc.
South Dakota State Lib.
State Hist. Soc. of Iowa
Stock House
TV Ontario
Timesteps Prods., Inc.
Twentieth Century-Fox Movietonews
Villon Films
White Janssen, Inc.
See also Campus life; Classrooms;
    Colleges and universities; Education;
    High schools; Students; Teachers and
    teaching

Schools (Africa)
TV Ontario

Schools (Integration)
Metropolitan Council for Educ. Opport.

Schools (Secondary)
Natl. Assn. of Secondary Schl. Principals

Schools (Soviet Union)
Educators for Social Responsibility

Schools (Summer)
Oregon State Univ., Archives

Schools (Technical)
Twentieth Century-Fox Movietonews

Schooners
See Ships (Schooners)

Schorr, Daniel
Natl. Archives (RG 200)

Schroeder, Patricia
Ideal Comms., Inc.

Schultz, Victoria
Port Washington Pub. Lib.

Schumacher, E.F.
Bullfrog Films, Inc.
Intermedia Arts Minnesota

**Schuylkill County, Pa. (History and
    culture)**
Smithsonian Inst., Human Studies Film
    Arch.

Schwartz, Maurice
Cantor (Arthur) Inc.

Schwarzenegger, Arnold
Spectral Comms.

Schweiker, Richard
MacDonald, J. Fred

Schweitzer, Albert
Schweitzer (Albert) Ctr.

Schygulla, Hanna
Video Data Bank

Science
AIMS Media
Altschul Group
Amer. Chemical Soc.
Archive Film Prods., Inc.
Barr Films
Benchmark Films, Inc.
Britannica Films & Video
British Info. Svcs., Radio & TV Div.
Buhl Science Center
Bullfrog Films, Inc.
CBS News Archives
California Inst. of Tech., Jet Propulsion
    Laboratory
Canadian Film Institute
Carleton Prods. Inc.
Carousel Film & Video
Center for Humanities, Inc.
Children's Mus. Res. Ctr.
Churchill Films
Coe Film Assoc., Inc.
Dreamlight Images, Inc.
Educational Images, Ltd.
Energy Productions
Fabulous Footage Inc.
Film Bank
Filmfair Communications
Films for the Humanities and Sciences
Finley (Stuart) Inc.
GPN
Goethe Institute Atlanta
Grinberg (Sherman) Film Libraries (East)
Handel Film Corp.
Hearst Metrotone News
Higgins (Alfred) Prods.
Houston Acad. of Medicine
Imevision
Intl. Film Bureau
Mass. Inst. of Tech., MIT Museum
Media Guild
Metro Communications, Inc.
Moody Inst. of Science
Natl. Archives (RG 69)
Natl. Archives (RG 307)
Natl. Archives of Canada
Natl. Archives/Natl. AV Ctr.
Natl. Geographic Soc. Stock Footage Lib.
Natl. Science Foundation
Petrified Films, Inc.
Prelinger Assoc., Inc.
Pyramid Film and Video Corp.
SF•V Intl.
Stock Shots
TV Ontario
TV-UNAM
Twentieth Century-Fox Movietonews
Union of Concerned Scientists
Université Laval, Cinémathèque
Univ. of Southern Calif., Film & Video
    Dist. Ctr.
Univ. of Waterloo, A-V Centre
WGBH Educational Foundation
Worldwide Television News
See also specific sciences

Science experiments
CBS News Archives
Film Bank
Films for the Humanities and Sciences
Metro Communications, Inc.
Natl. Archives of Canada
Natl. Library of Medicine
Petrified Films, Inc.
Prelinger Assoc., Inc.
Rockefeller Arch. Ctr.

NOTE: Access policies, availability and restrictions vary for each source. Please read each entry in full. Always consult "General Film and Videotape Collections" (page 599); these comprehensive collections contain material on every conceivable subject.

Science fairs
Energy Productions

Science fiction
Amer. Science Fiction Assn.
Archive Film Prods., Inc.
CBS News Archives
Coe Film Assoc., Inc.
Em Gee Film Library
Facets Multimedia, Inc.
Film Bank
Film/Video Arts, Inc.
Fish Films, Inc.
Gordon Films, Inc.
Grinberg (Sherman) Film Libraries (West)
Hurlock Cine-World, Inc.
Imageways, Inc.
Morcraft Films
Moviecraft, Inc.
NASA, Lewis Research Center
Prelinger Assoc., Inc.
Streamline Film Archives
UPA Prods. of America
Univ. of Southern Calif., Film & Video
   Dist. Ctr.
Video Yesteryear
Williams (Wade) Prods.

Science Foundation, National (U.S.)
Natl. Archives (RG 307)
Natl. Archives (Stock Film Coll.)

Scientific management
California Newsreel
Salenger Films, Inc.

Scientists
Amer. Chemical Soc.
Amer. Mus. Nat. Hist. Film Arch.
Amer. Nuclear Society
California Inst. of Tech., Inst. Arch.
Inst. of Electrical & Electronics Eng.
March of Time
Mass. Inst. of Tech., MIT Museum
Natl. Archives (RG 200)
Natl. Science Foundation
Petrified Films, Inc.
Prelinger Assoc., Inc.
Univ. of Calif., Ext. Media Ctr.

Scientists (Atomic)
Amer. Nuclear Soc.
Canadian Filmmakers Dist. Centre
Natl. Archives (RG 18)
See also Atomic bombs; Manhattan
   Project; Nuclear energy and power

Scientists (Computer)
Ideal Comms., Inc.

Scientists (Mad)
Film Bank
Petrified Films, Inc.

Scientists (Mexico)
Redes Cinevideo, S.A.

Scientology
Graduate Theological Union Lib.

Scooters
Analogous Productions

Scopes ("Monkey") Trial
Tennessee State Lib. & Arch.

Scoreboards
Film Bank
Petrified Films, Inc.

Scorekeeping
TV Ontario

Scorpions
Energy Productions

Film Bank
Wings Wildlife Prods. Inc.

Scorsese, Martin
Daphne Productions, Inc.

Scotland
British Info. Svcs., Radio & TV Div.
Dorn (Larry) Associates
TV Ontario

Scotland (History and culture)
Archive Film Prods., Inc.
Intl. Film Foundation
Natl. Archives (RG 96)

Scotland Yard (London)
March of Time
Petrified Films, Inc.

Scott, George C.
Petrified Films, Inc.

Scott-Heron, Gil
DEC Film & Video

Scott, Robert F.
Natl. Archives of Canada

Scott, William
Albright-Knox Art Gallery

Scott, Zachary
MacDonald, J. Fred

Scottsdale, Ariz.
Preview Media
Tri-Comm Prods.

Scouting (Boy Scouts)
See Boy Scouts and Scouting

Scranton, Pa. (History and culture)
Center for Public Dialogue
Petrified Films, Inc.

Scrap metal drives
Analogous Productions

Screen tests
Academy Film Archive
Em Gee Film Library
Intl. Al Jolson Society

Scuba diving
Caribbean Images, Ltd.
Creative Video, Inc.
Film Bank
Natl. Oceanic & Atmospheric Admin.
Passage Home Communications
TV Ontario
Zielinski Productions, Inc.
See also Skin diving

Scuba diving (Lessons)
Energy Productions

Sculley, John
Computer Television Group, Inc.

Sculling
Film Bank
Sportsfilm
TV Ontario

Sculptors and sculpture
See Art and artists

Sea animals
See Marine life

Sea creatures
See Marine life

Sea cucumbers

Moonlight Productions

Sea elephants
Cousteau Society

Sea gulls
Amer. Motion Pictures
British Info. Svcs., Radio & TV Div.
Di Sesso (Moe) Wild Life Film Lib.
Energy Productions
Film Bank
Kesser Stock Footage Library
MacGillivray Freeman Films
Petrified Films, Inc.
Summit Films, Inc.
TV Ontario

Sea horses
Caribbean Images, Ltd.
Petrified Films, Inc.

Sea lions
Dreamlight Images, Inc.
Moonlight Productions
Summit Films, Inc.
TV Ontario

Sea mammals
See Marine life

Sea otters
Cousteau Society
Moonlight Productions
Wings Wildlife Prods. Inc.

Sea plants
Energy Productions

Sea turtles
Marineland of Florida
Orion Post Production
Petrified Films, Inc.
Summit Films, Inc.

Seaborg, Glenn T.
Amer. Chemical Soc.

Seabrook, N.H. (History and culture)
Green Mountain Post Films

Seabrook, N.J. (History and culture)
New Jersey Network

Seal hunting
Canadian Filmmakers Dist. Centre
Canadian Filmmakers Dist. West
Friends of Animals
Natl. Archives of Canada
Prov. Arch. of Newfoundland & Labrador

Seale, Bobby
Media Bus
Third World Newsreel
Villon Films

Seals
Amer. Motion Pictures
Cinema Arts Assoc.
Coe Film Assoc., Inc.
Dreamlight Images, Inc.
Film Bank
Friends of Animals
Kesser Stock Footage Library
Moonlight Productions
Natl. Archives of Canada
Petrified Films, Inc.
Prov. Arch. of Newfoundland & Labrador
TV Ontario
Univ. of Alberta, Boreal Inst. for Northern
   Studies

Seals, Son
Rhapsody Films, Inc.

Seaman, Barbara

Radcliffe Coll., Schlesinger Lib.

Seamstresses
Groupe Intervention Video
Petrified Films, Inc.

Seaplanes
See Aircraft (Seaplanes)

Searchlights
Charisma Prods., Ltd./Visual Motion
Film Bank
Petrified Films, Inc.
Prelinger Assoc., Inc.

Seascapes
Amer. Motion Pictures
Dreamlight Images, Inc.
Energy Productions
Film Bank
Great Waves/Delaney Films
Jewell (Stuart) Productions
Marts (Steve) Prods.
See also Beaches; Oceans

Seashores
Film Bank
Pyramid Film and Video Corp.
Quinn (Bill) Prods.
Sea TV
See also Beaches

Seasickness
Film Bank

Seasons
See Fall; Spring; Summer; Winter

Seat belts
See Automobiles (Seat belts and air bags)

Seattle
Amer. Motion Pictures
Dreamlight Images, Inc.
Energy Productions
Hist. Soc. of Seattle & King County
Preview Media
Telemation Productions

Seattle (History and culture)
Amer. Truck Historical Soc.
Media Project
Natl. Asian American Telecomm. Assn.
Nordic Heritage Museum
Oregon Hist. Soc.
Patrick Media Group
Petrified Films, Inc.
Seattle Public Library
United Nations Ctr. for Human
   Settlements
Washington State Hist. Soc.

Sebastian, Ellen
Video Data Bank

Secret Service (U.S.)
March of Time
Natl. Archives (RG 87)

Secretaries
Fish Films, Inc.
Petrified Films, Inc.
Prelinger Assoc., Inc.
See also Offices; Workers (Office);
   Workers (White-collar)

Sedimentation
Shell Oil Co.

Sedona, Ariz.
Film Bank
Source Stock Footage Lib., Inc.

Sedona, Ariz. (History and culture)
Valley of the Sun Publishing

Seeds
Brooklyn Botanic Garden
Dreamlight Images, Inc.
Film Bank
Moody Inst. of Science
Natl. Archives (RG 33)
Oregon State Univ., Archives
Prelinger Assoc., Inc.
Prov. Arch. of Alberta

Seeger, Pete
Daphne Productions, Inc.
Green Mountain Post Films
MacDonald, J. Fred
Schwerin, Jules

Segal, George
Albright-Knox Art Gallery
Blackwood Prods., Inc.

Segalove, Ilene
Long Beach Mus. of Art

Seger, Bob
Spectral Comms.

Seidenbaum, Art
Banks Film Library

Seigel, Judy
Port Washington Pub. Lib.

Seine River, France
Beerger (Norman) Prods.
Petrified Films, Inc.

Sekine, Nobuo
Blackwood Prods., Inc.

Seldes, George
Picture Start, Inc.
Villon Films

Seldes, Gilbert
Ohio State Univ., Dept. of Photog. &
  Cinema

Selective Service System (U.S.)
CBS News Archives
Natl. Archives (RG 147)

Self, William
Univ. of Wyoming, Amer. Heritage Ctr.

Self-defense
Crystal Pyramid Prods.
Kartemquin Films

Self-esteem
Coronet/MTI Film & Video

Selleck, Tom
Spectral Comms.

Selma, Ala. (History and culture)
Petrified Films, Inc.
Worldwide Television News

Selznick, David O.
Univ. of Tex. at Austin, Ransom Hum.
  Res. Ctr., Theatre Arts Coll.

Semantics
GPN

Semmel, Joan
Long Beach Mus. of Art

Semon, Larry
Archive Film Prods., Inc.

Senate (U.S.)
Archive Film Prods., Inc.
C-SPAN (Cable Satellite Public Affairs
  Network)
Natl. Archives (RG 46)
Natl. Archives (RG 200)
Purdue Univ., Pub. Aff. Video Arch.
See also Congress (U.S.); House of
  Representatives (U.S.)

Senegal (Contemporary issues)
DEC Film & Video
Oxfam America

Senegal (History and culture)
TV Ontario

Senior citizens and elderly
Amer. Assn. of Retired Persons
Amer. Occupational Therapy Assn.
Appalshop Films, Inc.
Broad Street Prods.
Chicago Access Corp.
Churchill Films
Deep Dish TV
Echo Film Prods., Inc.
Fund for Human Dignity, Inc.
Gray Panthers
Kartemquin Films
March of Time
Medical College of Pa., Arch. & Spec.
  Coll. Women in Medicine
Milwaukee Access Telecomm. Auth.
Natl. Archives (RG 47)
Natl. Archives (RG 58)
Natl. Archives (RG 174)
New Film Co., Inc.
Northcoast Communication, Inc.
Ski TV Prods., Inc./Channel 24
TV Ontario
Univ. of West Fla., Hum. Res. Vid. Lib.
See also Aging and gerontology;
  Retirement

Sennett, Mack
Archive Film Prods., Inc.
Em Gee Film Library
Streamline Film Archives

Seoul, South Korea
Farkas Studios, Ltd.

**Seoul, South Korea (History and
  culture)**
Petrified Films, Inc.

Sequoias
Beerger (Norman) Prods.
Energy Productions
Film Bank

Serban, Andre
Camera Three Prods., Inc.

Serbian Americans
Flower Films & Video

Serials
Archive Film Prods., Inc.
Budget Films Inc.
Creative Film Society
Em Gee Film Library
Forsher (James) Prods. & Archives, Inc.
Ivy Film
Moviecraft, Inc.
Streamline Film Archives
Video Yesteryear

Serling, Rod
Daphne Productions, Inc.
Natl. Archives (RG 47)

Serra, Richard
Blackwood Prods., Inc.
Paper Tiger TV
Video Data Bank

Service stations (Automobile)
See Gas stations

Sete Quedas, Brazil
Brazilian-American Cultural Inst.

Setzer, Brian
Spectral Comms.

**Severomorsk, U.S.S.R. (Contemporary
  issues)**
Ocean Earth Constr. and Dev. Corp.

Seville, Spain
Preview Media

Sewers
CBS News Archives
Finley (Stuart) Inc.
TV Ontario

Sewing
CBS News Archives
Charisma Prods., Ltd./Visual Motion
Film Bank
Natl. Archives (RG 33)
Prelinger Assoc., Inc.
TV Ontario

Sewing machines
Petrified Films, Inc.
Prelinger Assoc., Inc.

Sex education
AIMS Media
Altschul Group
CBS News Archives
Campbell Films, Inc.
Carousel Film & Video
Center for Humanities, Inc.
Center for Marital and Sexual Studies
Churchill Films
Cinema Guild
Concordia Publishing House
Coronet/MTI Film & Video
Films for the Humanities and Sciences
Focus Intl. Inc.
GPN
Higgins (Alfred) Prods.
Historical Health Film Coll.
Intl. Film Bureau, Inc.
Kinsey Institute
Multi-Focus, Inc.
Natl. Archives (RG 90)
Phoenix Films and Video
Prelinger Assoc., Inc.
Prov. Arch. of Alberta
Univ. of Calif., Ext. Media Ctr.

Sex Pistols (Rock and roll band)
Target Video

Sex roles
Appalshop Films, Inc.
Blackwood (Christian) Prods., Inc.
Blackwood Prods., Inc.
Cambridge Documentary Films, Inc.
Cinema Verite Intl.
DEC Film & Video
Direct Cinema Ltd.
Focus Intl. Inc.
General Motors Corp.
Groupe Intervention Video
Historical Health Film Coll.
Inst. for Psychoanalysis
MacDonald, J. Fred

March of Time
Mass Media Ministries
Multi-Focus, Inc.
New Day Films
Petrified Films, Inc.
Prelinger Assoc., Inc.
Univ. of West Fla., Hum. Res. Vid. Lib.
Washington Univ., Brown Schl. of Soc.
  Work
Women Make Movies, Inc.
See also Sexuality

Sex therapy
Kinsey Institute
Multi-Focus, Inc.

Sexism
Amer. Jail Assn.
Cambridge Documentary Films, Inc.
New Day Films
Rational Island Publishers
Third World Newsreel
Vidéo Femmes
See also Women (Depiction in the media);
  Women's issues

Sexual abuse
Academy of Health Sciences, U.S. Army
Amer. Assn. for Counseling &
  Development
Cambridge Documentary Films, Inc.
Council for Exceptional Children
Focus Intl. Inc.
O.D.N. Productions, Inc.
Varied Directions, Inc.
Vidéo Femmes
Washington Univ., Brown Schl. of Soc.
  Work

Sexual counseling
Milner-Fenwick, Inc.

Sexual harassment
Coal Employment Project
United Training Media
Video Pool, Inc.

Sexuality
Center for Marital and Sexual Studies
Cinema Guild
Concordia Publishing House
Coronet/MTI Film & Video
Emory Medical Television Network
Exodus Trust Archives of Erotology
Film/Video Arts, Inc.
Filmakers Library
Focus Intl. Inc.
Groupe Intervention Video
Historical Health Film Coll.
IMS Creative Communications
Intermedia Arts Minnesota
Johns Hopkins Univ./Population Comm.
  Svcs.
Kinsey Institute
MacDonald, J. Fred
Milner-Fenwick, Inc.
Multi-Focus, Inc.
Multi-Media Productions, Inc.
Planned Parenthood Fed. of Amer.
Playboy Programs, Inc.
Rational Island Publishers
Social Psychiatry Res. Inst.
Third World Newsreel
Univ. of West Fla., Hum. Res. Vid. Lib.
V/tape
Vidéo Femmes
Video In
Video Pool, Inc.
Vidéographe Inc., Le
Wayne State Univ., Dir. Educ. in Nursing

NOTE: Access policies, availability and restrictions vary for each source. Please read each entry in full. Always consult "General Film and Videotape Collections" (page 599); these comprehensive collections contain material on every conceivable subject.

See also Birth control; Bisexuality; Gay and lesbian issues; Sex education; Sex roles; Sex therapy; Transsexualism; Transvestism

Sexually transmitted diseases (STDs)
Centers for Disease Control
Churchill Films
Emory Medical Television Network
Focus Intl. Inc.
Historical Health Film Coll.
MacDonald, J. Fred
Milner-Fenwick, Inc.
Natl. Archives (RG 90)
Natl. Archives (RG 200)
New York Pub. Lib., Donnell Media Ctr.
Prelinger Assoc., Inc.
Producers Library Service
Wombat Film & Video
See also AIDS

Seychelles
British Info. Svcs., Radio & TV Div.

Seymour, Jane
Spectral Comms.

Shabelle River, Somalia (History and culture)
Interlock Media Associates

Shackleton, Sir Ernest
Natl. Archives (RG 200)

Shakers (Religion)
See Religion (Shakers)

Shakertown, Ky. (History and culture)
Kentucky Dept. of Libraries & Archives

Shakespeare, William
Folger Shakespeare Library

Sham 69 (Rock and roll band)
Target Video

Shamans
Singer-Sharrette Traditional Healing Films
Univ. of Wash. Press, Multimedia Div.

Shange, Ntozake
Giorno Poetry Systems Inst.

Shanghai, China
Farkas Studios, Ltd.

Shanghai, China (History and culture)
Film/Audio Services, Inc.
Hoover Institution
Natl. Archives (RG 59)
Natl. Archives (RG 200)

Shankar, Ravi
Camera Three Prods., Inc.
Daphne Productions, Inc.
Pennebaker Associates, Inc.

Shanty towns
Petrified Films, Inc.

Shapiro, Joel
Blackwood Prods., Inc.
Video Data Bank

Shapiro, Louis B.
Inst. for Psychoanalysis

Sharecroppers
Hearst Metrotone News

Sharks
Beerger (Norman) Prods.
Caribbean Images, Ltd.
Cousteau Society
Dreamlight Images, Inc.

Energy Productions
Film Search
Moonlight Productions
Ocean Images
Passage Home Communications
Petrified Films, Inc.
Spalla (Rick) Video Prods.
Summit Films, Inc.
Video Tape Library, Ltd.

Sharp, Gene
Resource Ctr. for Nonviolence

Sharp, Willoughby
Electronic Arts Intermix
Monday, Wednesday, Friday Video Club

Shatner, William
Spectral Comms.

Shaw, Woody
Rhapsody Films, Inc.

Sheedy, Ally
Spectral Comms.

Sheen, Fulton J.
MacDonald, J. Fred
Sheen (Fulton J.) Comm. Ltd.

Sheen, Martin
Banks Film Library

Sheep
Amer. Motion Pictures
Amer. Veterinary Medical Assn.
British Info. Svcs., Radio & TV Div.
Buffalo Bill Historical Center
Di Sesso (Moe) Wild Life Film Lib.
Dreamlight Images, Inc.
Echo Film Prods., Inc.
Energy Productions
Film Bank
Glenbow Mus. Arch.
New Mexico State Records Ctr. & Arch.
Oregon Hist. Soc.
Oregon State Univ., Archives
Petrified Films, Inc.
Prov. Arch. of Alberta
Source Stock Footage Lib., Inc.
TV Ontario

Sheepdogs
East Tenn. State Univ., Arch. of Appalachia

Shelter technology
Video In

Shelton, George
Videobrary, Inc.

Shenandoah (Dirigible)
Natl. Archives (RG 80)

Shenandoah National Park, Va. (History)
Natl. Archives (RG 70)

Shepard, Alan
NASA, Lewis Research Center
Univ. of Georgia, WSB TV News Film Arch.

Shepherd, Cybill
Spectral Comms.

Shepherds
CBS News Archives
Petrified Films, Inc.

Sherman, Cindy
Video Data Bank

Sherpas

Petrified Films, Inc.

Shields, Alan
Walker Art Ctr.

Shifrin, Avraham
Birch (John) Society

Shining Path guerrilla movement (Peru)
Icarus-Tamouz Media, Inc.

Shintoism
See Religion (Shintoism)

Ship masters
TV Ontario

Shipbuilding
Allen (John E.) Inc.
Archives of Ontario
Battleship Cove
CBS News Archives
Manitowoc Maritime Museum
Mariners' Museum
Mass. Inst. of Tech., MIT Museum, Hart Nautical Coll.
Mystic Seaport Museum, Inc.
Natl. Archives (RG 267)
Univ. of Wis., Green Bay, Ctr. TV Prod.

Shipping
Allen (John E.) Inc.
British Info. Svcs., Radio & TV Div.
Film Bank
Kesser Stock Footage Library
Mariners' Museum
Natl. Archives (RG 178)
Nine Star Productions
Port Authority of New York & New Jersey
Riccitelli (Bruce) Prods.
Twentieth Century-Fox Movietonews
See also Harbors; Ships

Shippingport, Pa. (History and culture)
Petrified Films, Inc.

Ships
Allen (John E.) Inc.
Analogous Productions
Archive Film Prods., Inc.
Archives of Ontario
CBS News Archives
Dreamlight Images, Inc.
Film Bank
Grinberg (Sherman) Film Libraries (West)
Intl. Media Services, Inc.
March of Time
Natl. Archives (RG 24)
Natl. Archives (RG 26)
Natl. Archives (RG 59)
Natl. Archives (RG 75)
Natl. Archives (RG 178)
Ocean Images
Producers Library Service
San Francisco Maritime Natl. Hist. Park
Source Stock Footage Lib., Inc.
Stock Shots
Twentieth Century-Fox Movietonews
Video Genesis, Inc.
See also Boats and boating; Harbors; Sailing; Shipbuilding; Shipping; Shipwrecks; Shipyards; Submarines; Yachts and yachting

Ships (Accidents)
See Shipwrecks

Ships (Aircraft carriers)
Petrified Films, Inc.
See also Ships (Military)

Ships (Automobile carriers)
Spectral Comms.

Ships (Burning)

Analogous Productions
Natl. Archives (RG 24)
Petrified Films, Inc.

Ships (Cargo)
Film Bank

Ships (Clipper)
Film Bank

Ships (Container)
Energy Productions

Ships (Cruise)
Cineworks Prods. Inc.
Creative Video, Inc.
Dreamlight Images, Inc.
Energy Productions
Film Bank
Kesser Stock Footage Library
Mountain Video Associates
Natl. Archives of Canada
Orion Post Production
Petrified Films, Inc.
Prelinger Assoc., Inc.
Preview Media
SF•V Intl.
Sullivan Video Services

Ships (Drill ships)
TV Ontario

Ships (Freighters)
Dreamlight Images, Inc.
Energy Productions
Film Bank
Natl. Archives (RG 59)
Petrified Films, Inc.
Riccitelli (Bruce) Prods.
TV Ontario

Ships (Icebreakers)
Natl. Archives (RG 26)
Natl. Archives of Canada
TV Ontario

Ships (Launchings)
Analogous Productions
Archives of Ontario
Battleship Cove
Mariners' Museum
Natl. Archives (RG 24)
Natl. Archives (RG 91)
Natl. Archives (RG 178)
Natl. Archives (RG 428)
Petrified Films, Inc.
Twentieth Century-Fox Movietonews
Windsor Prod. Corp.

Ships (Merchant)
Natl. Archives (RG 178)

Ships (Military)
Amer. Motion Pictures
Battleship Cove
Development Communications, Inc.
Film Bank
Forsher (James) Prods. & Archives, Inc.
Manitowoc Maritime Museum
Natl. Archives (RG 24)
Natl. Archives (RG 70)
Natl. Archives (RG 80)
Natl. Archives (RG 178)
Natl. Archives (RG 428)
Petrified Films, Inc.
Twentieth Century-Fox Movietonews
U.S. Dept. of Defense, Motion Media Rec. Ctr.
See also Navy; Submarines; specific conflicts and wars

Ships (Models)
Mystic Seaport Mus., Inc.
Sullivan Video Services

Ships (Nuclear)
Mariners' Museum

Ships (Ocean liners)
Analogous Productions
Dreamlight Images, Inc.
Petrified Films, Inc.

Ships (Oil tankers)
Energy Productions
Imperial Oil Ltd.
Petrified Films, Inc.
TV Ontario
Univ. of Tex. at Austin, Petrol. Ext. Svc.

Ships (Outrigger)
Petrified Films, Inc.

Ships (Packet boats)
Natl. Archives (RG 91)

Ships (Pirate)
Petrified Films, Inc.

Ships (Racing schooners)
Natl. Archives of Canada

Ships (Sailing ships)
Allen (John E.) Inc.
San Francisco Maritime Natl. Hist. Park

Ships (Schooners)
Mystic Seaport Mus., Inc.
Petrified Films, Inc.

Ships (Sinking)
See Shipwrecks

Ships (Square riggers)
Petrified Films, Inc.

Ships (Steamboats)
Film Bank
Media Project
Missouri Hist. Soc.

Ships (Steamships)
Fish Films, Inc.
Natl. Archives (RG 178)
Prov. Arch. of British Columbia

Ships (Sternwheelers)
Yukon Archives

Ships (Tall ships)
Energy Productions
Intl. Media Services, Inc.
Landmark Stock Footage Co.
Mariners' Museum
Natl. Archives (RG 200)
Site Productions
Sullivan Video Services

Ships (Tuna clippers)
Petrified Films, Inc.

Ships (Windjammers)
Site Productions

Shipwrecks
Analogous Productions
Cousteau Society
Dreamlight Images, Inc.
Film Bank
Gornick Film Productions
Kesser Stock Footage Library
Manitowoc Maritime Museum
Natl. Archives (RG 26)
Natl. Archives of Canada
Natl. Oceanic & Atmospheric Admin.
Ocean Images

Oregon Hist. Soc.
Petrified Films, Inc.
Twentieth Century-Fox Movietonews
Univ. of Wis., Green Bay, Ctr. TV Prod.

Shipyards
Farkas Studios, Ltd.
Film Bank
Mass. Inst. of Tech., MIT Museum, Hart
    Nautical Coll.
Natl. Archives (RG 24)
Oregon Hist. Soc.
Twentieth Century-Fox Movietonews

Shoe polishing
Oregon State Univ., Archives

Shoe stores
Petrified Films, Inc.

Shoemaker, Willie
Banks Film Library
Thoroughbred Racing Assns.

Shoemaking
Smithsonian Inst., NMAH, Arch. Ctr.

Shoes
Film Bank
Intl. Fashion Video Library
Prelinger Assoc., Inc.
Rosebush Visions Corp.

Shooting
See Guns and rifles

Shootouts
Allen (John E.) Inc.
Film Bank
Fish Films, Inc.

Shoplifting
Coronet/MTI Film & Video
Highway Safety Films, Inc.
Minn. Citizens Coun. on Crime & Justice
Minn. Dept. of Public Safety Film Lib.

Shopping
Creative Video, Inc.
Film Bank
Prelinger Assoc., Inc.
TV Ontario

Shopping arcades
Farkas Studios, Ltd.

Shopping malls
Broad Street Prods.
Film Bank
Petrified Films, Inc.
Stock House
TV Ontario

Shops
See Stores

Shore, Dinah
Banks Film Library
Daphne Productions, Inc.
MacDonald, J. Fred
Natl. Archives/Natl. AV Ctr.
Shokus Video

Shore, Susan
Long Beach Mus. of Art

Shorelines
See Coastlines

Shorter, Frank
U.S. Olympic Committee

Shostrom, Everett L.
Psychological and Educational Films

"Shouter" churches
See Religion ("Shouter" churches)

Shovels
CBS News Archives

Showgirls
See Chorus girls and chorus lines

Showrooms
Petrified Films, Inc.

Shreveport, La. (History and culture)
Louisiana State Univ., Shreveport

Shrews
Mass. Audubon Society
Wings Wildlife Prods. Inc.

Shrimp
Bur. of Florida Folklife Progs.
Farkas Studios, Ltd.
Oregon State Univ., Archives

Shriners
Glenbow Mus. Arch.

Shrines
CBS News Archives
Marts (Steve) Prods.
Petrified Films, Inc.

Shriver, Maria
Spectral Comms.

Shyness
Prelinger Assoc., Inc.

Siam
See Thailand

Siamese twins
Johns Hopkins Univ., School of Medicine

Siberia, U.S.S.R. (History and culture)
Archive Film Prods., Inc.
Natl. Archives (RG 75)
Natl. Coun. of Amer.-Sov. Friendship

Sicily, Italy (History and culture)
Natl. Archives (RG 59)
Univ. of Arizona, Film Coll.

Side shows
Circus World Mus. Lib. & Res. Ctr.
Prelinger Assoc., Inc.
Twentieth Century-Fox Movietonews

Sidewalks (Moving)
Analogous Productions

Siegel, Bernie
Hartley Film Found., Inc.
Varied Directions, Inc.

Siegfried
Spectral Comms.

Sierra Nevada, Calif.
Film Bank
Petrified Films, Inc.

Sigler, Hollis
Video Data Bank

Sign language
Gorilla Foundation
Joyce Media, Inc.

Kentucky School for the Deaf
Natl. Archives (RG 106)

Signal Corps
See Army (U.S.) (Signal Corps)

Signoret, Simone
Banks Film Library

Signs
CBS News Archives
Film Bank
Landscape Architecture Found.
Spectral Comms.
TV Ontario
Wallen (Dick) Prods.

Signs (Advertising)
Film Bank
Fish Films, Inc.
Inst. of Outdoor Advertising
Postcards Associates
See also Advertising (Outdoor)

Signs (Casino)
Peak Productions, Inc.

Signs (Neon)
Film Bank
Petrified Films, Inc.
See also Neon

Signs ("On the air")
Petrified Films, Inc.

Signs (Road)
Petrified Films, Inc.
Prelinger Assoc., Inc.
White Janssen, Inc.

Signs (Street)
TV Ontario

Sikorsky, Igor
Archive Film Prods., Inc.
Natl. Archives (RG 342)

Siles, Hernando
Natl. Archives (RG 59)

Silhouettes
Energy Productions
Film Bank
Fish Films, Inc.
Twentieth Century-Fox Movietonews

Silicon Valley, Calif.
Stock Shots
TV Ontario

Silicosis
Estuary Press
Natl. Archives (RG 100)
U.S. Dept. of Labor, Mine Safety & Health
    Admin.

Silk
Soc. for French Amer. Cult. Svcs. & Educ.
    Aid

Silver
Natl. Archives (RG 70)
Prelinger Assoc., Inc.

Silver Bullet Band
Spectral Comms.

Silvers, Phil
Banks Film Library
MacDonald, J. Fred
Shokus Video

NOTE: Access policies, availability and restrictions vary for each source. Please read each entry in full. Always consult "General Film and Videotape Collections" (page 599); these comprehensive collections contain material on every conceivable subject.

Silversmithing
Film Bank
Native Amer. Pub. Broad. Cons.

Silverware
See Housewares

Silvetti, Jorge
Southern Calif. Inst. of Architecture

Simmons, Laurie
Video Data Bank

Simon, Neil
New York Pub. Lib., Perf. Arts Res. Ctr.,
Theatre on Film and Tape

Simon, Paul
Spectral Comms.

Simonds, Charles
Amer. Federation of the Arts
Video Data Bank
Walker Art Ctr.

Simpson, O.J.
Pyramid Film and Video Corp.

Simpson, Silvia Salazar
Long Beach Mus. of Art

Sims, William S.
Natl. Archives (RG 24)

Sims, Zoot
Rhapsody Films, Inc.

Simulators
See Flight simulation

Sinai, Mount
Jewell (Stuart) Productions

Sinatra, Frank
Archive Film Prods., Inc.
Banks Film Library
Grinberg (Sherman) Film Libraries (East)
Las Vegas News Bureau
Petrified Films, Inc.
Spalla (Rick) Video Prods.
UCLA Film & Television Archive

Sinatra, Nancy
Banks Film Library
Las Vegas News Bureau
Spalla (Rick) Video Prods.

Singapore
British Info. Svcs., Radio & TV Div.
Canadian Broadcasting Corp.
Creative Video, Inc.
Farkas Studios, Ltd.
Petrified Films, Inc.
Preview Media
Sonoma Video Productions
Yue-Sai Kan, Inc.

Singapore (History and culture)
Archive Film Prods., Inc.
Film/Audio Services, Inc.
Petrified Films, Inc.
United Nations Ctr. for Human
Settlements

Singing Hills, Calif.
Petrified Films, Inc.

Sino-Japanese conflict
See China-Japan War

**Siouxsie and the Banshees (Rock and
roll band)**
Target Video

Sirens (Air raid)

Petrified Films, Inc.

Sirens (Prison)
Petrified Films, Inc.

Sirtre, Libya (Contemporary issues)
Ocean Earth Constr. and Dev. Corp.

Sischy, Ingrid
Video Data Bank

Siskind, Aaron
Amer. Federation of the Arts

Sisseton, S. Dak. (History and culture)
South Dakota State Lib.

Sit-ins
See Demonstrations (Political)

Sitka, Alaska (History and culture)
Sitka Natl. Hist. Park

Skate (U.S.S.)
Natl. Archives (RG 64)

Skateboarding
Dittrich (Scott) Films
Dreamlight Images, Inc.
Film Bank
MacGillivray Freeman Films
Merkel Films
Pyramid Film and Video Corp.
Video Tape Library, Ltd.

Skating (Ice)
Analogous Productions
Archive Film Prods., Inc.
Archives of Ontario
Athletic Institute
Film Bank
Jalbert Productions
Natl. Archives of Canada
Petrified Films, Inc.
Sportsfilm
Summit Films, Inc.
TV Ontario
U.S. Olympic Comm.
Video Tape Library, Ltd.
Windsor Prod. Corp.

Skating (Roller)
See Roller-skating

Skating (Speed)
Sportsfilm
TV Ontario

Skeet shooting
Sportsfilm

Skeletons
Rosebush Visions Corp.

Skelton, Red
Banks Film Library
Encore Entertainment
Natl. Archives/Natl. AV Ctr.
Shokus Video
Spectral Comms.
UCLA Film & Television Archive

Ski flying
Video Tape Library, Ltd.

Ski lifts
Film Bank

Ski-Doos
TV Ontario

Skid rows
Media Project
New Orleans Video Access Ctr.
Petrified Films, Inc.

Skies
Cinenet (Cinema Network)
Energy Prods.
Film Bank
Radio City Music Hall Prods.
See also Clouds

Skiing
ABC Sports, Inc.
Aitken (Len) Productions, Inc.
Amer. Motion Pictures
Archive Film Prods., Inc.
Film Search
Fish Films, Inc.
Glenbow Mus. Arch.
Natl. Archives of Canada
Prov. Arch. of British Columbia

Skiing (Cross-country)
Aitken (Len) Prods.
Athletic Institute
Dobbs (Jeff) Prods.
Energy Productions
New Jersey Network
Sports Cinematography Group
Summit Films, Inc.
U.S. Olympic Committee

Skiing (Snow)
Analogous Productions
Apertura
Aspen Historical Society
Athletic Institute
Channell One Video
Chiappetta Prods., Inc.
Cineworks Prods. Inc.
Dreamlight Images, Inc.
Echo Film Prods., Inc.
Energy Productions
Film Bank
Freewheelin' Films, Ltd.
Frontline Video, Inc.
Golden Gaters Prods.
Grinberg (Sherman) Film Libraries (West)
Jalbert Productions
Jewell (Stuart) Productions
Miller (Warren) Productions, Inc.
Moving Media
Nemiroff Prods., Inc.
Network Productions
Nine Star Productions
North Country Media Group
Omega Films
Peak Productions, Inc.
Petrified Films, Inc.
Prelinger Assoc., Inc.
Preview Media
Prov. Arch. of Alberta
Pyramid Film and Video Corp.
Ski TV Prods., Inc./Channel 24
Source Stock Footage Lib., Inc.
Sports Cinematography Group
Sportsfilm
Summit Films, Inc.
TV Ontario
Twentieth Century-Fox Movietonews
U.S. Olympic Comm.
Utah Travel Council
Vermont Hist. Soc.
Video West
Windsor Prod. Corp.

Skiing (Snow) (Accidents)
Peak Productions, Inc.

Skiing (Water)
Aitken (Len) Productions, Inc.
Analogous Productions
Cineworks Prods. Inc.
Dreamlight Images, Inc.
Echo Film Prods., Inc.
Encore Video Prods., Inc.
Energy Productions
Film Bank
Grinberg (Sherman) Film Libraries (West)

Kesser Stock Footage Library
MacGillivray Freeman Films
Merkel Films
Network Productions
North Country Media Group
Petrified Films, Inc.
Second Line Search
Source Stock Footage Lib., Inc.
Sports Cinematography Group
Video Tape Library, Ltd.

Skimboarding
Merkel Films

Skin
Milady Publishing Corp.
Rosebush Visions Corp.

Skin diving
Ackerman-Black Prods., Inc.
Amer. Motion Pictures
Dreamlight Images, Inc.
Kesser Stock Footage Library
Moonlight Productions
Ocean Images
Sportsfilm
See also Scuba diving; Snorkeling

Skinks
Wings Wildlife Prods. Inc.

Skinner, B.F.
Amer. Assn. for Counseling &
Development
Inst. for Psychoanalysis
Psychological and Educational Films
Research Press

Skokie, Ill. (History and culture)
New Day Films

Skulnik, Menasha
Cantor (Arthur) Inc.

Skunks
Minnesota Zoo
Petrified Films, Inc.
TV Ontario
Wings Wildlife Prods. Inc.

Skydiving
CBS News Archives
Film Bank
Photo-Chuting Enterprises
Pyramid Film and Video Corp.
Spectral Comms.
Sports Cinematography Group
See also Parachuting

Skylab
See Space program (U.S.)

Skylines
Amer. Motion Pictures
Archives of Ontario
Aries Prods.
Borough of Manhattan Comm. Coll.
CBS News Archives
Cinephile Amalgamated Pictures
Creative Video, Inc.
Dreamlight Images, Inc.
Elfstrom-Hilmer Prods.
Energy Productions
Farkas Studios, Ltd.
Film Bank
Film Search
Jalbert Productions
Kesser Stock Footage Library
Landmark Stock Footage Co.
Petrified Films, Inc.
Port Authority of New York & New Jersey
Prelinger Assoc., Inc.
Source Stock Footage Lib., Inc.
Spectral Comms.
Stegman Productions

TV Ontario
Telemation Productions
Twentieth Century-Fox Movietonews
Video I-D, Inc.
See also Cityscapes

Skyscrapers
Allen (John E.) Inc.
Archive Film Prods., Inc.
Archives of Ontario
Cinema Guild
Energy Productions
Film Bank
Petrified Films, Inc.
Seagram Museum
Southern Calif. Lib. for Soc. Stud. & Res.
Spectral Comms.
TV Ontario

Skywriting
CBS News Archives
Film Bank
Prelinger Assoc., Inc.

Slapstick
Allen (John E.) Inc.
Archive Film Prods., Inc.
Film Education Institute
Fish Films, Inc.
Producers Library Service
Southwest Film/Video Archives, SMU

Slaughter, Enos
Grinberg (Sherman) Film Libraries (West)

Slaves
Amer. Soc. Hist. Proj. Film Lib.
Archive Film Prods., Inc.
Film Bank

Slavin, Neal
Video Data Bank

Sled dog racing
See Dog sledding

Sledding
CBS News Archives
Film Bank
TV Ontario

Sleep
Film Bank
Film Education Institute
Prelinger Assoc., Inc.
See also Insomnia

Sleighs
Film Bank
TV Ontario

Slick, Grace
Spectral Comms.

Sligh, Charles Robert Jr.
Univ. of Mich., Mich. Hist. Colls.

Sloan, Alfred P. Jr.
General Motors Corp.
Mass. Inst. of Tech., MIT Museum

Slot machines
Film Bank
Petrified Films, Inc.

Sloths
Petrified Films, Inc.

Slow-motion cinematography
Echo Film Prods., Inc.
Film Bank

Film Search
Mass. Inst. of Tech., MIT Museum
Natl. Archives (RG 304)
Prelinger Assoc., Inc.
Summit Films, Inc.
Twentieth Century-Fox Movietonews

Slums
CBS News Archives
Cinema Medica
Educational Video Ctr.
Emory Univ., Spec. Coll.
Natl. Archives (RG 12)
Natl. Archives (RG 69)
Natl. Archives/Natl. AV Ctr.
Petrified Films, Inc.
Southern Calif. Lib. for Soc. Stud. & Res.
United Nations Ctr. for Human Settlements
Univ. of Tex. at Austin, Benson Lat. Am. Coll.
See also Tenements

Sly and the Family Stone
Daphne Productions, Inc.

Small Business, White House Conference on
Natl. Archives (RG 220)

Small, Glen
Southern Calif. Inst. of Architecture

Smelling
Film Bank

Smelters
See Metals and metallurgy

Smigly-Rydz, Edward
Intl. Film Foundation

Smith, Alfred E.
Hearst Metrotone News

Smith and Dale (Comedians)
New York Pub. Lib., Perf. Arts Res. Ctr., Theatre on Film and Tape

Smith, Ansel Brooks
Univ. of Mich., Mich. Hist. Colls.

Smith, Bessie
Archive Film Prods., Inc.
Cinema Guild

Smith, Buffalo Bob
Daphne Productions, Inc.

Smith, David
Blackwood Prods., Inc.
Natl. Gallery of Art

Smith, Dean
Naismith Mem. Basketball Hall of Fame

Smith, Earl E.T.
Duke Univ., Perkins Lib.

Smith, Gerald L.K.
March of Time
Univ. of Mich., Mich. Hist. Colls.

Smith, Ian
Citizens' Councils of America

Smith, Keely
Banks Film Library

Smith, Keith
Video Data Bank

Smith, Kevon
Spectral Comms.

Smith, Margaret Chase
Smith (Margaret Chase) Lib. Ctr.

Smith, Maxine
Memphis State Univ. Libraries

Smith, Michael
Monday, Wednesday, Friday Video Club

Smith, Patti
Giorno Poetry Systems Inst.

Smith, Preston
Texas Tech Univ., Southwest Coll.

Smith, Ralph T.
Illinois State Hist. Lib.

Smith, Sam
Amer. Federation of the Arts

Smith, Stan
U.S. Tennis Assn.

Smith, Tony
Albright-Knox Art Gallery
Blackwood Prods., Inc.

Smithson, Robert
Amer. Federation of the Arts
Blackwood Prods., Inc.

Smithsonian Institution (Washington, D.C.)
Natl. Archives (RG 106)
Smithsonian Institution, Off. Telecomm.

Smog
Dreamlight Images, Inc.
Film Bank
Spectral Comms.
See also Pollution (Air)

Smoke
CBS News Archives
Film Bank
Petrified Films, Inc.
TV Ontario

Smoke signals
Petrified Films, Inc.

Smokers and smoking
CBS News Archives
Fish Films, Inc.
Historical Health Film Coll.
Prelinger Assoc., Inc.
Pyramid Film and Video Corp.
Timesteps Prods., Inc.
See also Cigarettes; Cigars; Tobacco

Smokescreens
Twentieth Century-Fox Movietonews

Smokestacks
Energy Productions
Film Bank

Smoky Mountains, Idaho (History and culture)
Schiele Museum

Smoot, Dan
Texas A&M Univ., Univ. Arch.

Smothers Brothers
Halcyon Days Prods.
MacDonald, J. Fred

UCLA Film & Television Archive

Smuggling
Natl. Archives (RG 26)

Snails
Film Bank

Snake charmers
Petrified Films, Inc.
Prelinger Assoc., Inc.
TV Ontario

Snake handlers
See Religion (Snake handlers)

Snake River Canyon, Idaho (History and culture)
Nature Conservancy

Snakes
Di Sesso (Moe) Wild Life Film Lib.
Energy Productions
Film Bank
Miller (David Lee) Prods.
Minnesota Zoo
Prelinger Assoc., Inc.
Texas Tech Univ., Southwest Coll.
Video Tape Library, Ltd.
Wings Wildlife Prods. Inc.

Sneezing
Prelinger Assoc., Inc.

Snelson, Kenneth
Albright-Knox Art Gallery

Snider, Jenny
Video Data Bank

Snorkeling
Ackerman-Black Prods., Inc.
Brekke Television Prods.
Caribbean Images, Ltd.
Film Bank
See also Skin diving

Snow
British Info. Svcs., Radio & TV Div.
CBS News Archives
Dreamlight Images, Inc.
Echo Film Prods., Inc.
Energy Productions
Film Bank
Jewell (Stuart) Productions
MacGillivray Freeman Films
Miller (Warren) Prods., Inc.
Montana Dept. of Commerce
Moving Media
Petrified Films, Inc.
Prov. Arch. of Alberta
Source Stock Footage Lib., Inc.
Summit Films, Inc.
Twentieth Century-Fox Movietonews
Utah Travel Council
Video Tape Library, Ltd.
Video West
Washington Broadcast Video Lib.
See also Blizzards; Storms; Winter

Snow (Television)
Film Bank

Snow (Thawing)
Film Bank

Snow, Michael
Amer. Federation of the Arts
Canadian Filmmakers Dist. Centre

Snow shakes
Film Bank

Snowballs
Oregon State Univ., Archives

Snowboarding
Dittrich (Scott) Films
Merkel Films
Miller (Warren) Productions, Inc.
Summit Films, Inc.

Snowflakes
Charisma Prods., Ltd./Visual Motion

Snowmaking
TV Ontario

Snowmen
Film Bank

Snowmobiling
CBS News Archives
Chiappetta Prods., Inc.
Dreamlight Images, Inc.
Energy Productions
Pyramid Film and Video Corp.
Sports Cinematography Group
Summit Films, Inc.
TV Ontario
Video Genesis, Inc.

Snowplanes
See Aircraft (Snowplanes)

Snowplows
Analogous Productions
Petrified Films, Inc.

Snowshoeing
Native Amer. Pub. Broad. Cons.
Seagram Museum
TV Ontario
Twentieth Century-Fox Movietonews

Snowslides
Twentieth Century-Fox Movietonews
See also Avalanches

Snowstorms
See Storms (Snow)

Snowy Mountains, Australia
Petrified Films, Inc.

Snyder, Alvin
Univ. of Miami, Arch. & Spec. Coll.

Snyder, Gary
Giorno Poetry Systems Inst.

Soap Box Derby
All-American Soap Box Derby
Film Bank
General Motors Corp.
Petrified Films, Inc.
Prelinger Assoc., Inc.
Twentieth Century-Fox Movietonews
Univ. of Mich., Mich. Hist. Colls.

Soapstone carving
TV Ontario

Soccer
Analogous Productions
Archive Film Prods., Inc.
Athletic Institute
Charisma Prods., Ltd./Visual Motion
Dreamlight Images, Inc.
Film Bank
Freewheelin' Films, Ltd.
Kesser Stock Footage Library
Sportsfilm
Televisa, S.A.
Twentieth Century-Fox Movietonews

U.S. Soccer Federation

Soccer (College)
NCAA Productions

Soccer (Instruction)
NCAA Productions
Natl. Assn. for Sport & Phys. Ed.

Soccer (Women's)
Hayes Prods., Inc.

Social and political issues
ABC Distribution (Education)
ABC News
Adair Films
Alternative Information Network
Amer. Enterprise Institute
Anti-Defamation League of B'nai B'rith
Appalshop Films, Inc.
Archivo de Imagenes en Movimiento
Blackwood Prods., Inc.
Boston Comm. Access & Prog. Found.
Cable News Network Library
Cambridge Documentary Films, Inc.
Center for Defense Information
Channel L Working Group
Chicago Access Corp.
Chisholm (Jack) Film Productions
DEC Film & Video
Deep Dish TV
Downtown Community TV Ctr.
Educational Film & Video Project
Educators for Social Responsibility
Film/Audio Services, Inc.
Filmakers Library
First Run/Icarus Films, Inc.
Intellimation
Intermedia Arts Minnesota
Latin Amer. Video Arch.
Media Bus
Media Guild
Milwaukee Access Telecomm. Auth.
Mus. & Hist. Div., City of Sacramento
Natl. Archives (RG 200)
Natl. Archives of Canada
New Day Films
New Time Films, Inc.
Northstar Prods.
Paper Tiger TV
People's Fund
Political Issue Archive
Richter Productions
San Francisco Bay Area TV News Arch.
Skylight Pictures
TV Ontario
TV-UNAM
Third World Newsreel
Trinity Square Video
UCLA Film & Television Archive
United Nations, Visual Materials Lib.
Univ. of Calif., Ext. Media Ctr.
Vidéo Femmes
Video In
Villon Films
WGBH Educational Foundation
WTJX-TV
Wisconsin Ctr. for Film & Theater Res.
World Monitor
Worldwide Television News
Zafra, A.C.
Zipporah Films

Social Credit League (Canada)
Prov. Arch. of Alberta

Social guidance
Archive Film Prods., Inc.
Imageways
MacDonald, J. Fred
Prelinger Assoc., Inc.
Streamline Film Archives

Social mores
Amer. Arch. of the Factual Film

Prelinger Assoc., Inc.

Social sciences
Intellimation
Intl. Film Bureau, Inc.
Natl. Film Board of Canada
Pyramid Film and Video Corp.

Social security (Soviet Union)
Natl. Council of Amer.-Soviet Friendship, Inc.

Social Security (U.S.)
CBS News Archives
Natl. Archives (RG 47)
Natl. Archives (RG 200)
Natl. Archives (RG 208)

Social Security Administration (U.S.)
Natl. Archives (RG 47)

Social services
Research Press
Univ. of West Fla., Hum. Res. Vid. Lib.

Social studies
AIMS Media
Altschul Group
Barr Films
Bullfrog Films, Inc.
Carousel Film & Video
Center for Humanities, Inc.
Churchill Films
Cinema Guild
Coe Film Assoc., Inc.
Coronet/MTI Film & Video
Filmfair Communications
Films for the Humanities and Sciences
GPN
Handel Film Corp.
Higgins (Alfred) Prods.
Media Guild
Natl. Archives (RG 200)
Phoenix Films and Video
Prelinger Assoc., Inc.
Vedo Films/Novacom Video

Social work
Univ. of West Fla., Hum. Res. Vid. Lib.
Washington Univ., Brown Schl. of Soc. Work

Socialism
Alternative Information Network
Cambridge Documentary Films, Inc.
Duke Univ., Perkins Lib.
Estuary Press
Taminent Lib./Wagner Labor Arch.
See also Communism; Left-wing politics

Socialism (Canada)
Natl. Archives of Canada

Sociobiology
Cinema Guild

Sociology
Ball State Univ., Middletown Coll.
Benchmark Films, Inc.
Carousel Film & Video
GPN
Natl. Archives/Natl. AV Ctr.
Peralta Colleges TV
Phoenix Films and Video
Pyramid Film and Video Corp.
Soc. for French Amer. Cult. Svcs. & Educ. Aid

Softball
Athletic Institute

Softball (Instruction)
NCAA Productions
Natl. Assn. for Sport & Phys. Ed.

Soil
Bullfrog Films, Inc.
Natl. Archives (RG 33)
Natl. Assn. of Conservation Dists.

Sokolow, Anna
Amer. Federation of the Arts
New Day Films

Solar energy
See Energy (Solar)

Solar flares
Film Bank

Solar system
California Inst. of Tech., Jet Propulsion Laboratory
Intl. Film Bureau, Inc.
NASA, Office of Comm.
Rosebush Visions Corp.
See also Planets; Space

Solar-powered automobiles
See Automobiles (Solar-powered)

Soldering
Hewlett-Packard Co.

Soldier's Grove, Wis. (History and culture)
Bullfrog Films, Inc.

Soldiers
Archive Film Prods., Inc.
Deep Dish TV
Film Bank
Petrified Films, Inc.
See also Military

Soleri, Paolo
Camera Three Prods., Inc.
Cinema Guild
Unicorn Projects

Solomon Islands (History and culture)
Johnson (Martin & Osa) Safari Museum

Solstices
Telltales Associates Inc.

Solzhenitsyn, Aleksandr I.
Hoover Institution

Somack, Jack
Shokus Video

Somalia (Contemporary issues)
CARE

Somalia (History and culture)
Interlock Media Associates
UNICEF, Div. Info. & Pub. Aff.

Somersaults
Energy Productions

Somerville, Mass. (History and culture)
Deep Dish TV

Sommer, Elke
Spalla (Rick) Video Prods.

Sondheim, Stephen
Camera Three Prods., Inc.

Sonfist, Alan
Albright-Knox Art Gallery

Sonic booms
MacDonald, J. Fred

Sonic Youth (Rock and roll band)
Atavistic Video
Target Video

Sonny and Cher
Spalla (Rick) Video Prods.

Sonora, Calif. (History and culture)
Petrified Films, Inc.

Sonoran Desert, Ariz.-Calif.
Grapevine Prods., Ltd.

Sons of the Pioneers, The (Musical group)
Archive Film Prods., Inc.

Sorce, Wayne
Port Washington Pub. Lib.

Sorcery
Natl. Archives of Canada

Sorensen, Vibeke
Long Beach Mus. of Art

Sostre, Martin
Cinema Guild

Soul music
See Music (Soul)

Soul, Veronica
Port Washington Pub. Lib.

Sound
Prelinger Assoc., Inc.

Soundies
Chertok Associates Inc.
Jessiefilm
Petrified Films, Inc.
Prelinger Assoc., Inc.
Streamline Film Archives

Soup
Prelinger Assoc., Inc.

Soup lines
See Breadlines

Sousa, John Philip
Natl. Archives (RG 24)

South Africa
Film Bank

South Africa (Contemporary issues)
ARC Videodance Coll./Eye on Dance Coll.
Committee for Labor Access
DEC Film & Video
Grosvenor USA
Intl. Freedom Foundation
Labor Video Project
Oxfam America

South Africa (History and culture)
California Newsreel
Canadian Filmmakers Dist. Centre
DEC Film & Video
Devillier Donegan Ent.
Film/Audio Services, Inc.
First Run/Icarus Films, Inc.
Idera Films
Natl. Archives of Canada
Schomburg Ctr. for Res. in Black Culture
United Nations, Visual Materials Lib.
Villon Films
Worldwide Television News

South America
Film Search
Pan American Airlines Film Lib.
Simon (Jeff) Productions

World Monitor
See also Latin America

South America (Contemporary issues)
DEC Film & Video
Film/Audio Services, Inc.

South America (History and culture)
Allen (John E.) Inc.
Archive Film Prods., Inc.
Archives of Ontario
Canal 11
DEC Film & Video
Film/Audio Services, Inc.
Intl. Assn. of Independent Producers
Intl. Film Foundation
Media Guild
Natl. Archives (RG 18)
Natl. Archives (RG 59)
Natl. Archives (RG 306)
Natl. Archives of Canada
Notimex
Petrified Films, Inc.
Phoenix Films and Video
Rockefeller Arch. Ctr.
Smithsonian Inst., Human Studies Film Arch.
White Janssen, Inc.
World Monitor

South Bronx, N.Y. (History and culture)
Ergo Media

South Carolina
Creative Video, Inc.
Preview Media
Tri-Comm Prods.

South Carolina (History and culture)
First Run/Icarus Films, Inc.
Petrified Films, Inc.
Schiele Museum
South Carolina Humanities Res. Ctr.
Univ. of So. Carolina, Newsfilm Lib.

South Dakota (History and culture)
Downtown Community TV Ctr.
Native Amer. Pub. Broad. Cons.
Pennebaker Assoc., Inc.
Prelinger Assoc., Inc.
San Diego Aerospace Museum
Schiele Museum
Siouxland Heritage Museum
South Dakota State Lib.

South Eastern Atlantic Treaty Organization (SEATO)
Natl. Archives (RG 286)

South Korea
See Korea, South

South Mountain, Pa. (History and culture)
Natl. Library of Medicine

South Pacific
Creative Video, Inc.
Film Bank
Jewell (Stuart) Productions
Pan American Airlines Film Lib.
Petrified Films, Inc.
Sonoma Video Productions

South Pacific (History and culture)
Allen (John E.) Inc.
Archive Film Prods., Inc.
Film/Audio Services, Inc.
Idera Films
Intl. Film Foundation
Johnson (Martin & Osa) Safari Museum

South Pole
Explorers Club
Natl. Archives (RG 200)

South Yemen (Contemporary issues)
DEC Film & Video

South Yemen (History and culture)
DEC Film & Video

Southeast Asia (History and culture)
Downtown Community TV Ctr.
Lib. of Congress, Amer. Folklife Ctr.
Richter Productions

Southern Africa (Contemporary issues)
Film/Audio Services, Inc.
First Run/Icarus Films, Inc.

Southern Africa (History and culture)
California Newsreel
Film/Audio Services, Inc.
Villon Films
See also South Africa

Southern, Terry
Giorno Poetry Systems Inst.

Southside Johnny & the Asbury Jukes
Blackwood (Christian) Prods., Inc.

Souvenirs
Postcards Associates

Soviet Union
Canadian Broadcasting Corp.
Film Bank
Film/Audio Services, Inc.
Hammer (Armand) Prods.
Imagen y Sonido Independiente, S.A.
Pan American Airlines Film Lib.

Soviet Union (Contemporary issues)
Devillier Donegan Ent.
Educational Film & Video Project
Ocean Earth Constr. and Dev. Corp.

Soviet Union (History and culture)
Allen (John E.) Inc.
Analogous Prods.
Archive Film Prods., Inc.
Devillier Donegan Ent.
Estuary Press
File Tape Co.
Film/Audio Services, Inc.
Films for the Humanities and Sciences
Grinberg (Sherman) Film Libraries (West)
Hoover Institution
IFEX Films
Intl. Assn. of Independent Producers
Intl. Film Foundation
Intl. Historic Films, Inc.
Mankind Research Found., Inc.
March of Time
Military/Combat Stock Footage
Natl. Archives (RG 75)
Natl. Archives (RG 96)
Natl. Archives (RG 111)
Natl. Archives (RG 200)
Natl. Archives (RG 207)
Natl. Archives (RG 208)
Natl. Archives (RG 242)
Natl. Archives (RG 306)
Natl. Archives (RG 326)
Natl. Archives (RG 342)
Natl. Archives of Canada
Natl. Archives/Natl. AV Ctr.
Natl. Ctr. for Jewish Film
Natl. Coun. of Amer.-Sov. Friendship, Inc.
North Carolina Div. of Arch. & Hist.
North Central Forest Exp. Sta.

Pennebaker Assoc., Inc.
Petrified Films, Inc.
Pilsudski (J.) Inst. of Amer.
Prelinger Assoc., Inc.
Screen Presentations, Inc.
Twentieth Century-Fox Movietonews, Inc.
UCLA Film & Television Archive
United Nations Ctr. for Human Settlements
Univ. of Mich., Mich. Hist. Colls.
Univ. of Tex. at Austin, Ransom Hum. Res. Ctr., Photo. Coll.
Video Tape Library, Ltd.
Working Group on Soviet TV
Worldwide Television News
See also Cold War; United States-Soviet relations

Soybeans
Amer. Soybean Assn.
Blue Sky Comms., Inc.
Video I-D, Inc.

Space
AIMS Media
Archive Film Prods., Inc.
Beerger (Norman) Prods.
Boston Stock Market
CBS News Archives
California Inst. of Tech., Jet Propulsion Laboratory
Cinema Guild
Coronet/MTI Film & Video
Creative Video, Inc.
Dreamlight Images, Inc.
Energy Productions
Fabulous Footage Inc.
Film Bank
Film Education Institute
Fish Films, Inc.
Great American Stock
Grinberg (Sherman) Film Libraries (West)
Hayes Prods., Inc.
Hearst Metrotone News
Houston Acad. of Medicine
Impact Audio Visual
Inst. for Space & Security Studies
Intermedia Arts Minnesota
Kesser Stock Footage Library
Lib. of Congress, M/B/RS
Link Flight Simulation Div.
Metro Communications, Inc.
Multi-Media Productions, Inc.
NASA, Ames Res. Ctr., Regional Film Lib.
NASA, Goddard Space Flight Ctr.
NASA, Johnson Space Ctr., Film & Video Dist. Lib.
NASA, Johnson Space Ctr., Stock Film Lib.
NASA, Langley Research Ctr.
NASA, Lewis Research Ctr.
NASA, Marshall Space Flight Ctr.
NASA, Office of Comm.
Natl. Archives (RG 200)
Natl. Archives (RG 255)
Natl. Archives (RG 342)
Natl. Archives (RG 434)
Natl. Archives (Stock Film Coll.)
Natl. Archives/Natl. AV Ctr.
Natl. Science Foundation
Petrified Films, Inc.
Prelinger Assoc., Inc.
Pyramid Film and Video Corp.
Rosebush Visions Corp.
Silver Image
Smithsonian Inst., Natl. Air & Space Museum
Video Tape Library, Ltd.
Video-SIG
World Monitor

NOTE: Access policies, availability and restrictions vary for each source. Please read each entry in full. Always consult "General Film and Videotape Collections" (page 599); these comprehensive collections contain material on every conceivable subject.

See also Astronomy; Galaxies; Moon
   landing; Moons; Planets; Rockets;
   Satellites; Solar System; Space
   program (U.S.); Space shuttle; Space
   stations; Spacecraft and spaceships;
   Starfields; Stars; Unidentified flying
   objects

Space Needle (Seattle)
Energy Productions
Telemation Productions

Space Needle (Seattle) (Construction)
Seattle Public Library

Space program (U.S.)
Beerger (Norman) Prods.
Boston Stock Market
California Inst. of Tech., Jet Propulsion
   Laboratory
Communications Concepts
Film Bank
Halcyon Days Prods.
Impact Audio Visual
Kesser Stock Footage Library
Link Flight Simulation Div.
NASA, Ames Res. Ctr., Dryden Flight
   Res. Fac.
NASA, Ames Res. Ctr., Imaging Tech.
   Branch
NASA, Ames Res. Ctr., Regional Film
   Lib.
NASA, Goddard Space Flight Ctr.
NASA, Johnson Space Ctr., Film & Video
   Dist. Lib.
NASA, Johnson Space Ctr., Stock Film
   Lib.
NASA, Langley Research Ctr.
NASA, Lewis Research Ctr.
NASA, Marshall Space Flight Ctr.
NASA, Office of Comm.
Natl. Archives (RG 200)
Natl. Archives (RG 255)
Natl. Archives (Stock Film Coll.)
Prelinger Assoc., Inc.
Second Line Search
Smithsonian Inst., Natl. Air & Space
   Museum
U.S. Dept. of Defense, Motion Media Rec.
   Ctr.
Univ. of Georgia, WSB TV News Film
   Arch.
World Monitor

Space shuttle
Communications Concepts
Energy Productions
Film Bank
Hayes Prods., Inc.
Kesser Stock Footage Library
Link Flight Simulation Div.
NASA, Ames Res. Ctr., Dryden Flight
   Res. Fac.
NASA, Ames Res. Ctr., Imaging Tech.
   Branch
NASA, Johnson Space Ctr., Film & Video
   Dist. Lib.
NASA, Johnson Space Ctr., Stock Film
   Lib.
NASA, Lewis Research Ctr.
NASA, Office of Comm.
Natl. Archives (RG 220)
Natl. Archives (RG 306)
Prelinger Assoc., Inc.
Smithsonian Inst., Natl. Air & Space
   Museum
Source Stock Footage Lib., Inc.

Space shuttle (Challenger accident)
NASA, Johnson Space Ctr., Film & Video
   Dist. Lib.
Natl. Archives (RG 220)

Space shuttle (Columbia)
Natl. Archives (RG 306)

**Space Shuttle, President's Commission
on**
Natl. Archives (RG 220)

Space stations
Impact Audio Visual
See also Space program (U.S.)

Spacecraft and spaceships
Archive Film Prods., Inc.
Film Bank
Film Search
Lib. of Special Visual Effects
NASA, Ames Res. Ctr., Imaging Tech.
   Branch
Petrified Films, Inc.
Universal City Studios
See also Rockets; Space; Space program
   (U.S.); Unidentified flying objects

Spacek, Sissy
Spectral Comms.

Spada
Monday, Wednesday, Friday Video Club

Spain
Canadian Broadcasting Corp.
Film Bank
Imagen y Sonido Independiente, S.A.
Pan American Airlines Film Lib.
Preview Media

Spain (History and culture)
Allen (John E.) Inc.
Analogous Prods.
Archive Film Prods., Inc.
Documentary Educational Resources
Films for the Humanities and Sciences
Hoover Institution
Oregon Hist. Soc.
Petrified Films, Inc.
Shire Films
Third World Newsreel
White Janssen, Inc.

Spanish Civil War
Brandeis Univ. Lib.
Cinema Guild
First Run/Icarus Films, Inc.
Intl. Women's Day Video Fest.
March of Time
Natl. Archives (RG 111)
Natl. Archives of Canada
Shire Films
Southern Calif. Lib. for Soc. Stud. & Res.
Taminent Lib./Wagner Labor Arch.
Twentieth Century-Fox Movietonews, Inc.
See also Abraham Lincoln Brigade

Spanish-American War
Film Education Institute
Filmoteca de la UNAM
Lib. of Congress, M/B/RS
Media Project

Spann, Otis
Rhapsody Films, Inc.

Spark plugs
Natl. Archives (RG 70)
Prelinger Assoc., Inc.

Sparks
Film Bank

Spas
Creative Video, Inc.
Preview Media

Spas (Japan)
TV Ontario

Speakeasies
Allen (John E.) Inc.

See also Prohibition

Speaker, Tris
Grinberg (Sherman) Film Libraries (West)

Spearfishing
Sportsfilm

Special effects
CASCOM
CBS News Archives
Charisma Prods., Ltd./Visual Motion
Dreamlight Images, Inc.
Editel/Boston
Energy Productions
Film Bank
Hayes Prods., Inc.
Impact Audio Visual
Lib. of Special Visual Effects
MacDonald, J. Fred
Paint Box Backgrounds
Radio City Music Hall Prods.
Slingshot Prods.
Spalla (Rick) Video Prods.
Twentieth Century-Fox Movietonews
Universal City Studios
WQED/Pittsburgh
Z-Axis
See also specific special effects

Special Olympics
ABC Sports, Inc.
Special Olympics Intl.
See also Disabled people and sports

Speckled Red
Rhapsody Films, Inc.

Spectators (Sports)
Amer. Motion Pictures
Archive Film Prods., Inc.
Dreamlight Images, Inc.
Energy Productions
Film Bank
Stock House
Goal Prods., Tourn. of Roses Film Lib.
Zielinski Productions, Inc.
See also Audiences

Speech pathology
IMS Creative Communications

Speechways
Center for New Amer. Media

Speed skating
See Skating (Speed)

Speedboats
See Boats and boating (Speedboats)

Speedometers
See Automobiles (Speedometers)

Spelling, Aaron
Spectral Comms.

Sperm
Prelinger Assoc., Inc.
Univ. of Wash. Press, Multimedia Div.
See also Reproduction (Human); Sex
   education

Spero, Nancy
Video Data Bank

Spheres
Rosebush Visions Corp.

Sphinx
Energy Productions
Jewell (Stuart) Productions
Petrified Films, Inc.
Unicorn Projects

Spices
Petrified Films, Inc.

Spider webs
Film Bank
TV Ontario
Video Tape Library, Ltd.

Spiders
Cinenet (Cinema Network)
Dreamlight Images, Inc.
Energy Productions
Film Bank
Jewell (Stuart) Productions
MacDonald, J. Fred
Petrified Films, Inc.
Wings Wildlife Prods. Inc.

Spiegel, John
Inst. for Psychoanalysis

Spielberg, Steven
Daphne Productions, Inc.
Spectral Comms.

Spies
Archive Film Prods., Inc.
CBS News Archives
Link Flight Simulation Div.
MacDonald, J. Fred
Natl. Archives (RG 18)
Natl. Archives (RG 26)
Natl. Archives (RG 59)
Natl. Archives (RG 200)
Natl. Archives (RG 226)
Villon Films

Spillane, Mickey
Daphne Productions, Inc.

Spinal cord injuries
Rehab. Inst. of Chicago

Spine
Pyramid Film and Video Corp.

Spinks, Leon
U.S. Olympic Comm.

Spinks, Michael
U.S. Olympic Comm.

Spock, Dr. Benjamin
Alternative Information Network
Green Mountain Post Films
MacDonald, J. Fred

Spoerri, Daniel
Blackwood Prods., Inc.

Spokane, Wash. (History and culture)
Eastern Washington State Historical Soc.
Petrified Films, Inc.

Spoleto Festival (Spoleto, Italy)
Blackwood (Christian) Prods., Inc.
Blackwood Prods., Inc.

Sponsored films and videotapes
Amer. Arch. of the Factual Film
Amer. Nuclear Society
Amer. Truck Historical Society
Amer. Veterinary Medical Assn.
Archive Film Prods., Inc.
Assn. for Multi-Image Intl., Inc.
Auburn-Cord-Duesenberg Museum
Audience Planners, Inc.
Bailey Productions, Inc.
Canadian Film Institute
Cine-Mark
Coca-Cola Co., Archives Dept.
Colorado Historical Society
Crawley Films, Ltd.
Creative Venture Films
Delaware State Div. of Hist. & Cult. Aff.

Echo Film Prods., Inc.
Filmoteca de la UNAM
Florida State Archives
Ford (Henry) Museum
Grinberg (Sherman) Film Libraries (West)
Hershey Foods Corp.
Imperial Oil Ltd.
Indiana State Comm. on Public Records
Klein (Walter J.) Co., Ltd.
Modern Talking Picture Service
Natl. Archives (RG 200)
Natl. Railway Historical Soc.
Ohio Historical Soc.
Perry (Merle G.) Arch.
Prelinger Assoc., Inc.
Procter & Gamble Co.
Prov. Arch. of Newfoundland & Labrador
Railroad Mus. of Pa.
Schweitzer (Albert) Ctr.
Studebaker Natl. Mus.
Univ. of North Texas, Div. of
    Radio/TV/Film
Venard Films Ltd.
Voyager Co.
See also Industrial films and videotapes

Sporting goods stores
Petrified Films, Inc.

Sports
ABC Distribution (Education)
ABC Sports, Inc.
Aitken (Len) Productions, Inc.
Alaska Video Prods.
Allen (John E.) Inc.
Amateur Athletic Foundation
Amer. Motion Pictures
Analogous Productions
Archive Film Prods., Inc.
Archives of Ontario
Aspen Photo & Film Agency
Athletic Institute
Boys Club of America
Budget Films Inc.
CBS News Archives
Canadian Filmmakers Dist. West
Canadian Olympic Assn.
Cappy Productions, Inc.
Carleton Prods. Inc.
Charisma Prods., Ltd./Visual Motion
Coe Film Assoc., Inc.
DeFlores, Bob
Dittrich (Scott) Films
Dorn (Larry) Associates
Dreamlight Images, Inc.
Edwards, H.M.
Em Gee Film Library
Energy Productions
Fabulous Footage Inc.
Film Bank
Film Education Institute
Film Search
Films for the Humanities and Sciences
Freewheelin' Films, Ltd.
Glenbow Mus. Arch.
Golden Gaters Prods.
Grinberg (Sherman) Film Libraries (East)
Grinberg (Sherman) Film Libraries (West)
Halcyon Days Prods.
Hearst Metrotone News
Independent Media Communications
Instituto Cubano de Radio y Televisión
Jalbert Productions
Kesser Stock Footage Library
Lemorande Prod. Co.
MacDonald, J. Fred
MacGillivray Freeman Films
Metro Communications, Inc.
Miller (Warren) Productions, Inc.
Milwaukee Access Telecomm. Auth.
Morris Video

NBC TV Network, Enterprises Dept.
NFL Films, Inc.
Natl. Archives (RG 111)
Natl. Archives (RG 200)
Natl. Archives (RG 306)
Natl. Archives of Canada
Natl. Film Board of Canada
Natl. Rifle Assn.
Network Productions
Nine Star Productions
Oregon Hist. Soc.
Petrified Films, Inc.
Phoenix Films and Video
Prelinger Assoc., Inc.
Preview Media
Producers Library Service
Pyramid Film and Video Corp.
Rainbow Video Prods.
SF•V Intl.
Seagram Museum
Second Line Search
Spalla (Rick) Video Prods.
Special Olympics Intl.
Spectral Comms.
Sports Mus. of New England
Sportsfilm
State Hist. Soc. of Iowa
Stock House
Stock Shots
Streamline Film Archives
Summit Films, Inc.
TV Ontario
Texas Tech Univ., Southwest Coll.
Timesteps Prods., Inc.
Twentieth Century-Fox Movietonews
UCLA Film & Television Archive
U.S. Golf Assn.
U.S. Soccer Federation
U.S. Tennis Assn.
United Training Media
Université Laval, Cinémathèque
Univ. of Ill. Urbana-Champaign, Univ.
    Arch.
Univ. of Notre Dame, Joyce Sports Coll.
V/tape
Vedo Films/Novacom Video
Video Tape Library, Ltd.
Video West
Video-SIG
White Janssen, Inc.
Windsor Prod. Corp.
York Univ. Archives
Zielinski Productions, Inc.
See also Athletes; Olympics; specific
    athletes and sports

Sports (Amateur)
Amateur Athletic Union
Petrified Films, Inc.
Prelinger Assoc., Inc.

Sports (Australia)
Petrified Films, Inc.

Sports (Beach)
Film Bank

Sports (Bloopers)
Carter (C.L.) Jr. & Assoc., Inc.
Miller (Warren) Productions, Inc.
NFL Films, Inc.
Pyramid Film and Video Corp.
United Training Media
Zielinski Productions, Inc.
See also Bloopers

Sports (Children's)
Zielinski Productions, Inc.

Sports (College)
Auburn University Archives

Baylor Univ., Texas Coll.
Eastern Kentucky Univ.
Michigan State Univ., Archives
NCAA Productions
Occidental College Library
Ohio State Univ., Dept. of Photog. &
    Cinema
Oregon State Univ., Archives
Sports Mus. of New England
Stanford Univ. Lib., Dept. of Spec. Coll.
    & Univ. Arch.
Univ. of Ill. Urbana-Champaign, Univ.
    Arch.
Univ. of Manitoba Lib., Arch. Spec. Coll.
Univ. of Notre Dame, Joyce Sports Coll.
Univ. of Okla., Western Hist. Colls.
Univ. of Rhode Island, Univ. Lib.
West Virginia Univ.
Zielinski Productions, Inc.

Sports (Computer graphics)
Unger Computer Graphics

Sports (France)
Soc. for French Amer. Cult. Svcs. & Educ.
    Aid

Sports (Germany)
German Info. Ctr., Film Lib.
Goethe Institute Atlanta

Sports (Great Britain)
Zielinski Prods., Inc.

Sports (High-school)
Eastern Kentucky Univ.
Zielinski Productions, Inc.

Sports (Humor)
Miller (Warren) Productions, Inc.

Sports (Instruction)
Video-SIG

Sports (Intercollegiate)
Northern Ill. Univ., Reg. Hist. Ctr.

Sports (Mexico)
Canal 11
Imevision
Televisa, S.A.

Sports (Oddities)
Petrified Films, Inc.
See also Oddities

Sports (Outdoor)
Moving Media

Sports (Professional)
Allen (John E.) Inc.
Creative Video, Inc.
Film Bank
Film Search
SF•V Intl.
Second Line Search
Sports Mus. of New England
Univ. of Notre Dame, Joyce Sports Coll.
Zielinski Productions, Inc.

Sports (Soviet Union)
Natl. Coun. of Amer.-Sov. Friendship.

Sports (Summer)
Chisholm (Jack) Film Productions
Moving Media
Peak Productions, Inc.
TV Ontario
U.S. Olympic Comm.

Sports (Water)

Creative Video, Inc.
Grinberg (Sherman) Film Libraries (West)
Intl. Swimming Hall of Fame
Merkel Films
Moving Media
Omega Films
Petrified Films, Inc.
Quinn (Bill) Prods.
Second Line Search
Simon (Jeff) Productions
Video Tape Library, Ltd.

Sports (Winter)
Chisholm (Jack) Film Productions
Energy Productions
Jalbert Productions
Jewell (Stuart) Productions
Miller (Warren) Productions, Inc.
Moving Media
Peak Productions, Inc.
Petrified Films, Inc.
Sportsfilm
TV Ontario
U.S. Olympic Comm.
Visuart, Inc.

Sports (Women's)
Analogous Productions
Film Bank
Oregon State Univ., Archives
Zielinski Productions, Inc.

Sports cars
See Automobiles (Sports cars)

Sports medicine
See Medicine (Sports)

Sports psychology
See Psychology (Sports)

Spring (Season)
Cineworks Prods. Inc.
Dreamlight Images, Inc.
Energy Productions
Film Bank
4•6•8 Prods., Inc.
Intl. Film Bureau, Inc.
Preview Media
Pyramid Film and Video Corp.
Source Stock Footage Lib., Inc.
Summit Films, Inc.
White Star Prof. Film Svcs., Inc.

Springfield, Mass. (History and culture)
Florentine Films

Springs
Film Bank

Sprinklers
CBS News Archives
Prelinger Assoc., Inc.

Spruce Goose (Airplane)
Beerger (Norman) Prods.

Sputnik
See Satellites (Sputnik)

Square dancing
See Dances and dancing (Square)

Square riggers
See Ships (Square riggers)

Squares
CBS News Archives
Film Bank

NOTE: Access policies, availability and restrictions vary for each source. Please read each entry in full. Always consult "General Film and Videotape Collections" (page 599); these comprehensive collections contain material on every conceivable subject.

Squash (Sport)
Sportsfilm
TV Ontario

Squash (Vegetable)
White Janssen, Inc.

Squatters
Canadian Filmmakers Dist. Centre
Cinema Guild
United Nations Ctr. for Human
Settlements

Squid
Cousteau Society
Moonlight Productions
Petrified Films, Inc.

Squirrels
Cinema Arts Assoc.
Cinenet (Cinema Network)
Di Sesso (Moe) Wild Life Film Lib.
Film Bank
Metro Communications, Inc.
Northcoast Communication, Inc.
Petrified Films, Inc.
Wings Wildlife Prods. Inc.

Sri Lanka (Contemporary issues)
Amnesty Intl. USA
Oxfam America

Sri Lanka (History and culture)
Archive Film Prods., Inc.
Explorers Club
First Run/Icarus Films, Inc.
UNICEF, Div. Info. & Pub. Aff.

Srinagar, Kashmir, India
Petrified Films, Inc.

St.
Entries beginning with St. are alphabetized
as though spelled Saint

Stables
CBS News Archives
Film Bank
See also Horses

Stack, Robert
Banks Film Library
Spalla (Rick) Video Prods.
Spectral Comms.

Stackhouse, Robert
Video Data Bank

Stadiums
Analogous Productions
Archive Film Prods., Inc.
CBS News Archives
Dreamlight Images, Inc.
Energy Productions
Film Bank
Forsher (James) Prods. & Archives, Inc.
Petrified Films, Inc.
Prelinger Assoc., Inc.
Stock House
Twentieth Century-Fox Movietonews
Video Tape Library, Ltd.

Stag films
See Pornography

Stagecoaches
Archive Film Prods., Inc.
Petrified Films, Inc.
See also Westerns

Stained glass
Film Bank
Petrified Films, Inc.
Stained Glass Assn. of Amer.
Unicorn Projects

Stairways
CBS News Archives
Film Bank

Stalin, Josef
Archive Film Prods., Inc.
Halcyon Days Prods.
Natl. Archives (RG 342)
Petrified Films, Inc.

Stalingrad
See Volgograd, U.S.S.R.

Stallone, Sylvester
Los Angeles News Service
Spectral Comms.

Stampedes
Archive Film Prods., Inc.
Fish Films, Inc.
Petrified Films, Inc.

Stamps (Postage)
CBS News Archives
Natl. Archives (RG 28)

Stamps (Trading)
Prelinger Assoc., Inc.

Stanton, Harry Dean
Spectral Comms.

Stanwyck, Barbara
Banks Film Library
Encore Entertainment
Halcyon Days Prods.
UCLA Film & Television Archive

Star Wars
See Strategic Defense Initiative (Star
Wars)

Starbursts
Charisma Prods., Ltd./Visual Motion
Z-Axis

Starfields
Charisma Prods., Ltd./Visual Motion
Dreamlight Images, Inc.
Editel/Boston
Energy Productions
Film Bank
Lib. of Special Visual Effects
Petrified Films, Inc.
Rosebush Visions Corp.
Z-Axis
See also Space

Starfish
Moonlight Productions

Stars
Cinenet (Cinema Network)
Dorn (Larry) Associates
Dreamlight Images, Inc.
Energy Productions
Film Bank
Prelinger Assoc., Inc.
See also Space

Stars of David
Petrified Films, Inc.

Starting lines
Film Bank

State fairs
See Fairs and expositions

State, Department of (U.S.)
Natl. Archives (RG 59)
Natl. Archives (Stock Film Coll.)

Statistics
Media Guild

Statue of Liberty (New York City)
Dreamlight Images, Inc.
Energy Productions
Film Bank
Film Search
Fish Films, Inc.
New York State Dept. of Econ. Devel.
Petrified Films, Inc.
Port Authority of New York & New Jersey

Statues
Atlantic Productions
CBS News Archives
Film Bank
Hi-Tech Productions
Petrified Films, Inc.
TV Ontario
Twentieth Century-Fox Movietonews
Video Tape Library, Ltd.

Staubach, Roger
NFL Films, Inc.

Stealing
See Crime and criminals; Shoplifting

Steam baths
Petrified Films, Inc.

Steamboats
See Ships (Steamboats)

Steckel, Ed
Fellowship of Christian Athletes

Steel industry
Amer. Iron & Steel Institute
British Info. Svcs., Radio & TV Div.
California Newsreel
Carnegie District Film Ctr.
Film Bank
Film Search
First Run/Icarus Films, Inc.
Forsher (James) Prods. & Archives, Inc.
Indiana Univ. Northwest Lib.
Motion Picture Services
Natl. Archives (RG 70)
Natl. Archives (RG 238)
Natl. Archives (RG 277)
Natl. Archives/Natl. AV Ctr.
New Jersey Network
Petrified Films, Inc.
Prelinger Assoc., Inc.
Richter Productions
Smithsonian Inst., NMAH, Div. Eng. &
Ind.
Univ. of Calif., Berkeley, Labor
Occupational Health Prog.
Univ. of Mich., Mich. Hist. Colls.
Video Genesis, Inc.
See also Mills (Steel); Workers (Steel)

Steele, Bob
UCLA Film & Television Archive

Stefansson, Vilhjalmur
Natl. Archives of Canada

Stegner, Wallace
Film/Audio Services, Inc.
Florentine Films

Steinem, Gloria
Daphne Productions, Inc.

Steir, Pat
Video Data Bank

Stella, Frank
Albright-Knox Art Gallery
Blackwood Prods., Inc.
Walker Art Ctr.

Stengel, Casey
Banks Film Library

Sportsfilm

Stepfamilies
Stepfamily Foundation, Inc.

Steppenwolf (Rock and roll band)
Clark (Dick) Media Archives, Inc.

Stereophonic sound
Prelinger Assoc., Inc.

Stereos
Archive Film Prods., Inc.

Sterilization
Cinema Guild

Sternwheelers
See Ships (Sternwheelers)

Stevedores
Petrified Films, Inc.
See also Shipping

Stevens, April
Spalla (Rick) Video Prods.

Stevens, Connie
Banks Film Library

Stevens, George Jr.
Ohio State Univ., Dept. of Photog. &
Cinema

Stevens, Inger
Banks Film Library

Stevens, John Paul
Illinois State Hist. Lib.

Stevens, Wallace
Intellimation

Stevenson, Adlai
Illinois State Hist. Lib.
Kennedy (John F.) Library
MacDonald, J. Fred
UCLA Film & Television Archive
Univ. of Ill. Urbana-Champaign, Univ.
Arch.
Univ. of Mich., Mich. Hist. Colls.

Stewardesses
See Flight attendants

Stewart, Jimmy
Banks Film Library
Halcyon Days Prods.
Natl. Archives (RG 56)
Spectral Comms.

Stewart, Michael
Monday, Wednesday, Friday Video Club

Stickball
Spalla (Rick) Video Prods.

Stieglitz, Alfred
Amer. Federation of the Arts
Mus. at Large, Ltd.

Still, Clyfford
Blackwood Prods., Inc.

Still, James
Appalshop Films, Inc.

Stills (Corn liquor)
East Tenn. State Univ., Arch. of
Appalachia

Stinkbugs
Wings Wildlife Prods. Inc.

Stirling, James
Amer. Federation of the Arts
Blackwood Prods., Inc.

Stock car racing
See Automobiles (Racing) (Stock car)

Stock exchanges
Amer. Stock Exchange
Broad Street Prods.
CBS News Archives
Chicago Video Transfer
Dreamlight Images, Inc.
Film Bank
Merrill Lynch Pierce Fenner & Smith
New York Stock Exchange
Petrified Films, Inc.
Prelinger Assoc., Inc.
TV Ontario
Timesteps Prods., Inc.
Video Tape Library, Ltd.
See also Financial industry; Stock market;
  Wall Street, N.Y.

Stock footage sales libraries
A.M. Stock Exchange
Ackerman-Black Prods., Inc.
Airline Film & TV Promotions
Alaska Video Prods.
Allen (John E.) Inc.
Amer. Motion Pictures
Amer. Portrait, An
Analogous Productions
Archive Film Prods., Inc.
Aspen Photo & Film Agency
Banks Film Library
Beerger (Norman) Prods.
Boston Stock Market
Bransby (John) Prods., Ltd.
Brekke Television Prods.
Britannica Films & Video
Broad Street Prods.
Budget Films Inc.
CBS News Archives
CTV Television Network
Cable News Network Library
Cameo Film Library, Inc.
Canadian Broadcasting Corp.
Cannell (Stephen J.) Productions, Inc.
Caribbean Images, Ltd.
Channel Sea Television
Chertok Associates Inc.
Chiappetta Prods., Inc.
Chicago A/V Studios
Chisholm (Jack) Film Productions
Cimarron Productions
Cine-Mark
Cinenet (Cinema Network)
Cinephile Amalgamated Pictures
Clark (Dick) Media Archives, Inc.
Clip Joint For Film
Coe Film Assoc., Inc.
Columbia Pictures TV/Stock Film Library
Creative Video, Inc.
Departures, Inc.
Di Sesso (Moe) Wild Life Film Lib.
Diamond P. Sports
Dittrich (Scott) Films
Dobbs (Jeff) Prods.
Dobovan Productions, Inc.
Dorn (Larry) Associates
Dreamlight Images, Inc.
Duffy (Kevin) Productions
Echo Film Prods., Inc.
Eden Entertainment, Inc.
Edwards, H.M.
Em Gee Film Library
Encore Entertainment
Energy Productions
Fabulous Footage Inc.
File Tape Co.

Film Bank
Film Education Institute
Film Preservation Assoc.
Film Search
Film/Audio Services, Inc.
Finley (Stuart) Inc.
Fish Films, Inc.
Flying A Pictures Inc.
Footage Inc.
Forsher (James) Prods. & Archives, Inc.
Goal Prods., Tourn. of Roses Film Lib.
Gould (Bert)/bay area archive
Great Waves/Delaney Films
Grinberg (Sherman) Film Libraries (East)
Grinberg (Sherman) Film Libraries (West)
Halcyon Days Prods.
Halicki (H.B.) Productions
Hayes Prods., Inc.
Hearst Metrotone News
Imageways, Inc.
Innerquest Communications Corp.
Inter Video/TTI
Intl. Historic Films, Inc.
Jalbert Productions
Jessiefilm
Jewell (Stuart) Productions
KD Enterprises Prods.
Kesser Stock Footage Library
Killiam Shows, Inc.
Landmark Stock Footage Co.
MacDonald, J. Fred
MacGillivray Freeman Films
Marts (Steve) Productions
Merkel Films
Metro Communications, Inc.
Military/Combat Stock Footage
Miller (Warren) Productions, Inc.
Minnesota Zoo
Molstar Comm.
Monday, Wednesday, Friday Video Club
Moonlight Productions
Mountain Video Associates
Moviecraft, Inc.
Moving Media
Mystic Seaport Mus., Inc.
NBA Entertainment, Inc.
NBC News Video Archives
NFL Films, Inc.
Natl. Ctr. for Jewish Film
Natl. Film Board of Canada
Natl. Geographic Soc. Stock Footage Lib.
Network Productions
New Jersey Network
News On Film
Nine Star Productions
Ocean Images
Omega Films
Orion Post Production
Palisades Wildlife Film Library
Paramount Pictures Stock Film Lib.
Pathé Pictures, Inc.
Petrified Films, Inc.
Phoenix Communications Group, Inc.
Postcards Associates
Prelinger Assoc., Inc.
Producers Library Service
Pyramid Film and Video Corp.
Quenzer Driscoll Dawson, Inc.
Research Video
Rosebush Visions Corp.
SF•V Intl.
Second Line Search
Shields Archival
Simon (Jeff) Productions
Snyder (Bill) Films, Inc.
Sobek Productions
Source Stock Footage Lib., Inc.
Southwest Film/Video Archives, SMU
Spalla (Rick) Video Prods.
Spelling (Aaron) Productions
Sportsfilm

Stavis, Gene
Stock House
Stock Shots
Streamline Film Archives
Summit Films, Inc.
TV Ontario
TV-3
Telltales Associates Inc.
Timesteps Prods., Inc.
Twentieth Century-Fox Movietonews
U.S. Dept. of Defense, Motion Media Rec.
  Ctr.
Universal City Studios
Video Concepts, Inc.
Video Resources N.Y., Inc.
Video Tape Library, Ltd.
Video Yesteryear
Visnews Intl.
Visuart, Inc.
Wallen (Dick) Prods.
Warner (Dane) Photography
Weintraub Screen Entertainment, Inc.
West Star Productions
White Janssen, Inc.
White Star Prof. Film Svcs., Inc.
Williams (Wade) Prods.
Windsor Prod. Corp.
Wings Wildlife Prods. Inc.
Worldwide Television News
Zielinski Productions, Inc.

Stock market
CBS News Archives
Energy Productions
Farkas Studios, Ltd.
Perlmutter (Alvin H.) Inc.
Petrified Films, Inc.

See also Financial industry; Stock
  exchanges; Wall Street, N.Y.

**Stockholm, Sweden (History and
  culture)**
Petrified Films, Inc.
United Nations, Visual Materials Lib.

Stockton, Calif. (History and culture)
Natl. Archives (RG 46)

Stockwell, John
Alternative Information Network
New Time Films, Inc.
Nuclear Free Zone Registry

Stockyards
CBS News Archives
Energy Productions
Petrified Films, Inc.

Stokowski, Leopold
Archive Film Prods., Inc.

Stone, L. Joseph
Univ. of Akron, Child Develop. Film
  Arch.

Stone, Oliver
Spectral Comms.

Stonehenge, England
Film Bank

Stones, Dwight
U.S. Olympic Committee

NOTE: Access policies, availability and restrictions vary for each source. Please read each entry in full. Always consult "General Film and Videotape Collections" (page 599); these comprehensive collections contain material on every conceivable subject.

Stoney, George
Port Washington Pub. Lib.

Stoopnagle and Budd (Comedians)
Videobrary, Inc.

Stop-motion cinematography
See Animation (Stop-motion)

Storage depots
CBS News Archives

Storch, Larry
Spectral Comms.

Storefronts
Film Bank

Stores
Broad Street Prods.
CBS News Archives
Farkas Studios, Ltd.
Petrified Films, Inc.
TV Ontario
Timesteps Prods., Inc.
See also Markets; specific kinds of stores

Stores (China)
Farkas Studios, Ltd.

Storks
Film Bank
Jewell (Stuart) Productions
Miller (David Lee) Prods.

Storm, Gale
MacDonald, J. Fred
Pathé Pictures, Inc.
Prelinger Assoc., Inc.

Storms
Alaska Native Heritage Film Project
CBS News Archives
Cinenet (Cinema Network)
Dreamlight Images, Inc.
Energy Productions
Film Bank
Grinberg (Sherman) Film Libraries (West)
Hearst Metrotone News
Merkel Films
Moving Media
Panhandle-Plains Hist. Museum
Petrified Films, Inc.
Twentieth Century-Fox Movietonews
See also Blizzards; Disasters; Hurricanes;
   Lightning; Meteorology; Tornadoes;
   Weather

Storms (Dust)
Petrified Films, Inc.

Storms (Sand)
Jewell (Stuart) Productions
Twentieth Century-Fox Movietonews

Storms (Snow)
Allen (John E.) Inc.
Jewell (Stuart) Productions
State Hist. Soc. of Iowa

Storytelling
Adair Films
Appalachian State Univ., Eury Coll.
Appalshop Films, Inc.
Center for Southern Folklore
Davenport Films
East Tenn. State Univ., Arch. of
   Appalachia
Native Amer. Pub. Broad. Cons.
Natl. Assn. for the Pres. & Perpetuation of
   Storytelling
WTJX-TV
Yakima Indian Nation Cult. Ctr.
Yakima Television Program

Stoves
CBS News Archives
Petrified Films, Inc.
Prelinger Assoc., Inc.

Stowaways
CBS News Archives

Stranglers (Rock and roll band)
Target Video

Strategic Air Command (SAC)
March of Time

Strategic Defense Initiative (Star Wars)
Amer. Defense Preparedness Assn.
Center for Defense Information
Cinema Guild
Committee for Labor Access
Educational Film & Video Project
High Frontier
Inst. for Space & Security Studies
Interlock Media Associates
League of Women Voters of the U.S.
Physicians for Social Responsibility
TV-UNAM
Union of Concerned Scientists
Wilmington Coll. Peace Res. Ctr.

Strategic Services, Office of (OSS) (U.S.)
Natl. Archives (RG 59)
Natl. Archives (RG 226)
Villon Films

Stratford, Ontario (History and culture)
Natl. Archives of Canada

Stratton, William G.
Illinois State Hist. Lib.

Stravinsky, Igor
Pennebaker Associates, Inc.

Strawberries
Energy Productions
TV Ontario

Streams
CBS News Archives
Cinenet (Cinema Network)
Echo Film Prods., Inc.
Film Bank
Kesser Stock Footage Library
Peak Productions, Inc.
Source Stock Footage Lib., Inc.
Summit Films, Inc.
TV Ontario

Street peddlers
Petrified Films, Inc.
Prelinger Assoc., Inc.

Street performers
Simon & Goodman Picture Co.

Streetcars
CBS News Archives
Film Bank
Missouri Hist. Soc.
Oregon Hist. Soc.
Petrified Films, Inc.
Prelinger Assoc., Inc.
See also Trolleys

Streetman, Evon
Video Data Bank

Streets and roads
Applegate Entertainment
Broad Street Prods.
CBS News Archives
Cabscott Broadcast Prods.
Cameo Film Library, Inc.
Crystal Pyramid Prods.
Energy Productions

Farkas Studios, Ltd.
Film Bank
Friends of Free China
Grinberg (Sherman) Film Libraries (West)
Hammer (Armand) Prods.
Image Bank
Jewell (Stuart) Productions
Lib. of Congress, M/B/RS
Los Angeles City Archives
Lunar Productions
MacGillivray Freeman Films
Moving Media
Natl. Archives (RG 69)
Patrick Media Group
Petrified Films, Inc.
Prelinger Assoc., Inc.
Preview Media
Renaissance Video Corp.
Simon & Goodman Picture Co.
Spectral Comms.
Timesteps Prods., Inc.
Twentieth Century-Fox Movietonews
Zielinski Productions, Inc.
See also Highways; Traffic

Streets and roads (Construction)
MacDonald, J. Fred
Massachusetts Archives
Natl. Archives (RG 69)
Natl. Archives of Canada
Petrified Films, Inc.
Prelinger Assoc., Inc.
Prov. Arch. of Alberta
See also Construction; Highways
   (Construction)

Streisand, Barbra
Spectral Comms.

Stress
Addiction Research Foundation of Ontario
Amer. Assn. for Counseling & Devel.
Barr Films
Churchill Films
Cinema Guild
Coronet/MTI Film & Video
Hartley Film Found., Inc.
Intellimation
Intl. Ctr. for the Disabled
Narcotics Education, Inc.
Natl. Safety Council
Prelinger Assoc., Inc.
Rogers (Will) Institute
TV Ontario
United Training Media
Univ. of West Fla., Hum. Res. Vid. Lib.
See also Relaxation

Strikes
Allen (John E.) Inc.
Amer. Soc. Hist. Proj. Film Lib.
Analogous Productions
Appalchian State Univ., Eury Coll.
Appalshop Films, Inc.
Archive Film Prods., Inc.
CBS News Archives
Calif. Newsreel
Calif. State Univ., Northridge, Urban
   Arch.
Cinema Guild
Committee for Labor Access
Communist Party USA
DEC Film & Video
East Tenn. State Univ., Arch. of
   Appalachia
Estuary Press
First Run/Icarus Films, Inc.
Grinberg (Sherman) Film Libraries (East)
Groupe Intervention Video
Illinois Labor Hist. Soc.
Intermedia Arts Minnesota
March of Time
Memphis State Univ. Libraries
Natl. Archives (RG 46)
Natl. Archives (RG 277)

Natl. Archives of Canada
New Day Films
New York City Labor Film Club
Payne, Roz
Petrified Films, Inc.
Prelinger Assoc., Inc.
Prov. Arch. of Alberta
Skylight Pictures
Southern Calif. Lib. for Soc. Stud. & Res.
Spectral Comms.
Taminent Lib./Wagner Labor Arch.
Third World Newsreel
Twentieth Century-Fox Movietonews
Univ. of Toronto, AV Lib.
Univ. of Wisconsin — Extension
Video Tape Library, Ltd.
Women in Focus
See also Labor history

Strip mining
See Mining (Strip)

Striptease
Canadian Filmmakers Dist. Centre
Exotic Dancers League of North America
Fish Films, Inc.
Frontline Video, Inc.
Villon Films

Striptease joints
Petrified Films, Inc.

Strom, Harry
Prov. Arch. of Alberta

Strupp, Hans
Psychological and Educational Films

Struthers, Sally
Spectral Comms.

Stuart, Jesse
East Tenn. State Univ., Arch. of
   Appalachia

Stuart, Michelle
Video Data Bank

**Student Non-Violent Coordinating
   Committee (SNCC)**
Estuary Press
Southern Calif. Lib. for Soc. Stud. & Res.

Students
Anti-Defamation League of B'nai Brith
Archive Film Prods., Inc.
Auburn University Archives
CBS News Archives
Film Bank
Future Farmers of America
German Info. Ctr.
Kartemquin Films
Mass. Inst. of Tech., MIT Museum
Natl. Archives (RG 59)
Natl. Archives (RG 119)
Natl. Assn. of Secondary Schl. Principals
Petrified Films, Inc.
Prelinger Assoc., Inc.
TV Ontario
Third World Newsreel
See also Campus life; Colleges and
   universities; Education; Schools

Study skills
AIMS Media
Barr Films
Center for Humanities, Inc.
Coronet/MTI Film & Video
GPN
Higgins (Alfred) Prods.
Prelinger Assoc., Inc.

Stunt aircraft
See Aircraft (Stunt)

750

Stunt driving
See Automobiles (Stunts)

Stunts
Analogous Productions
Archive Film Prods., Inc.
CBS News Archives
Chisholm (Jack) Film Productions
Columbia Pictures TV/Stock Film Library
Film Bank
Film Search
Forsher (James) Prods. & Archives, Inc.
Grinberg (Sherman) Film Libraries (West)
Las Vegas News Bureau
Petrified Films, Inc.
Prelinger Assoc., Inc.
Spalla (Rick) Video Prods.
Streamline Film Archives
Twentieth Century-Fox Movietonews
See also Aircraft (Stunts); Automobiles
(Stunts); Daredevils; Motion pictures
(Stunts); Motorcycling (Stunts)

Sturgeon Bay, Wis. (History and culture)
Manitowoc Maritime Museum

Sturgeon, John
Video Data Bank

Sturgis, Katharine Boucot
Medical College of Pa., Arch. & Spec.
Coll. Women in Medicine

Stuttering
Campbell Films, Inc.

Stuyvesant, Peter
Prelinger Assoc., Inc.

Suarez, Luis
Imagen y Sonido Independiente, S.A.

Submarines
Amer. Motion Pictures
Analogous Productions
Archive Film Prods., Inc.
British Info. Svcs., Radio & TV Div.
Caribbean Images, Ltd.
Film Bank
General Motors Corp.
Manitowoc Maritime Museum
Natl. Archives (RG 24)
Natl. Archives (RG 26)
Natl. Archives (RG 59)
Natl. Archives (RG 64)
Natl. Archives (RG 80)
Natl. Archives (RG 111)
Natl. Archives (RG 428)
Twentieth Century-Fox Movietonews

Submarines (Nuclear) (Soviet Union)
Ocean Earth Constr. and Dev. Corp.

Subsistence lifestyles (Alaska)
Alaska Native Heritage Film Project
KYUK-TV

Substance abuse
ABC Distribution (Education)
AIMS Media
Addiction Research Foundation of Ontario
Carousel Film & Video
Churchill Films
Coronet/MTI Film & Video
Emory Medical Television Network
Films for the Humanities and Sciences
Hazelden Found. Educ. Materials
Signal Press
United Training Media

See also Alcohol abuse; Alcoholism; Drug
abuse; Twelve-step programs; specific
drugs

Suburbia
Broad Street Prods.
Cinenet (Cinema Network)
Development Communications, Inc.
Downtown Community TV Ctr.
Dreamlight Images, Inc.
Energy Productions
Film Bank
Missouri Hist. Soc.
New Jersey Network
Petrified Films, Inc.
Prelinger Assoc., Inc.
Regional Plan Assn.
Source Stock Footage Lib., Inc.
Streamline Film Archives
TVA/Television Assoc.
Unicorn Projects

Subways
Archives of Ontario
British Info. Svcs., Radio & TV Div.
CBS News Archives
Canadian Filmmakers Dist. Centre
Dreamlight Images, Inc.
Energy Productions
Farkas Studios, Ltd.
Film Bank
Film Search
Icarus Films Intl., Inc.
Natl. Archives (RG 398)
Natl. Coun. of Amer.-Sov. Friendship
Natl. Railway Historical Soc.
New York State Dept. of Econ. Devel.
Port Authority of New York & New Jersey
TV Ontario

Success
Nightingale-Conant Corp.

Sudan (History and culture)
Natl. Archives (RG 286)

Sudbury, Ontario (History and culture)
DEC Film & Video

Sudden Infant Death Syndrome (SIDS)
Natl. Funeral Directors Assn.
Natl. Sudden Infant Death Syndrome
Found.
Washington Univ., Brown Schl. of Soc.
Work

Suffragettes and suffrage movement
Allen (John E.) Inc.
Archive Film Prods., Inc.
Grinberg (Sherman) Film Libraries (West)
Mass. Inst. of Tech., MIT Museum
Natl. Archives of Canada
Ohio Hist. Soc.
Parker (Kit) Films
Radcliffe Coll., Schlesinger Lib.
Timesteps Prods., Inc.
Twentieth Century-Fox Movietonews
Univ. of Mich., Mich. Hist. Colls.
Women in Focus
See also Women's history

Sufism
See Religion (Sufism)

Sugar and sugar industry
Ackerman-Black Prods., Inc.
Bishop Mus., Visual Coll.
Cinema Guild
Farkas Studios, Ltd.
Icarus Films Intl., Inc.
Icarus-Tamouz Media, Inc.

Narcotics Education, Inc.
Natl. Archives (RG 48)
Natl. Archives (RG 310)
New York Hosp.-Cornell Med. Ctr., Arch.
Petrified Films, Inc.
Pyramid Film and Video Corp.

Sugar beets
Glenbow Mus. Arch.

Suicide
Amer. Assn. for Counseling &
Development
Amer. Jail Assn.
Boston Family Inst.
CBS News Archives
Cinema Guild
Coronet/MTI Film & Video
Educational Video Ctr.
Filmfair Communications
Intl. Lutheran Layman's League
Lawren Prods., Inc.
Mass Media Ministries
Media Guild
Multi-Media Productions, Inc.
Natl. Funeral Directors Assn.
Ohio State Univ., Dept. of Photog. &
Cinema
Suicide Information & Education Centre
UCLA Behavioral Sci. Media Lab.

Sukarno
Film/Audio Services, Inc.
Northstar Prods.

Sulfur
Natl. Archives (RG 70)

Sullivan, Anne
Amer. Foundation for the Blind
Lib. of Congress, M/B/RS
Perkins School for the Blind

Sullivan, Ed
MacDonald, J. Fred
Shokus Video
Video Resources N.Y., Inc.
Wisconsin Ctr. for Film & Theater Res.

Sullivan, Joyce
Natl. Archives of Canada

Sullivan, Leon
MacDonald, J. Fred

Sullivan, Louis
Amer. Federation of the Arts
Unicorn Projects

Sulphur
Film Bank

Sultan, Donald
Mus. of Contemporary Art

Sultan, Larry
Video Data Bank

Sumatra, Indonesia (History and culture)
Acad. of Nat. Sci. of Phila. Lib.

Summer
Cineworks Prods. Inc.
Departures, Inc.
Dreamlight Images, Inc.
Echo Film Prods., Inc.
Film Bank
4•6•8 Prods., Inc.
Intl. Film Bureau, Inc.
Jalbert Productions

Jewell (Stuart) Productions
Nine Star Productions
North Country Media Group
Northcoast Communication, Inc.
Northeast Historic Film
Petrified Films, Inc.
Ski TV Prods., Inc./Channel 24
Summit Films, Inc.
TV Ontario
White Star Prof. Film Svcs., Inc.

Summer, Robert
Unicorn Projects

Sun Ra
Rhapsody Films, Inc.

Sun Valley, Idaho
Preview Media

Sun Yat-sen
Hoover Institution

Sunbathing
Cinenet (Cinema Network)
Dreamlight Images, Inc.
Energy Productions
Film Bank
Petrified Films, Inc.
TV Ontario
See also Beaches; Bikinis

Sunday, William Ashley ("Billy")
Wheaton Coll., Billy Graham Ctr.

Sundials
CBS News Archives
Petrified Films, Inc.

Sunflowers
Petrified Films, Inc.

Sunglasses
Petrified Films, Inc.

Sunnyland Slim
Rhapsody Films, Inc.

Sunnyside, N.Y. (History and culture)
Rockefeller Arch. Ctr.

Sunrises and sunsets
Ackerman-Black Prods., Inc.
Amer. Motion Pictures
Broad Street Prods.
CBS News Archives
Charisma Prods., Ltd./Visual Motion
Cinenet (Cinema Network)
Creative Video, Inc.
Di Sesso (Moe) Wild Life Film Lib.
Dorn (Larry) Associates
Dreamlight Images, Inc.
Echo Film Prods., Inc.
Encore Video Prods., Inc.
Energy Productions
Film Bank
Film Search
Hayes Prods., Inc.
Hi-Tech Productions
Impact Audio Visual
Jewell (Stuart) Productions
Kesser Stock Footage Library
Lib. of Special Visual Effects
MacGillivray Freeman Films
Merkel Films
Metro Communications, Inc.
Moving Media
Peak Productions, Inc.
Petrified Films, Inc.
Producers' Service
Source Stock Footage Lib., Inc.

NOTE: Access policies, availability and restrictions vary for each source. Please read each entry in full. Always consult "General Film and Videotape Collections" (page 599); these comprehensive collections contain material on every conceivable subject.

Southwest Prods., Inc.
Spectral Comms.
TV Ontario
Tri-Comm Prods.
Twentieth Century-Fox Movietonews
Wings Wildlife Prods. Inc.
Xicom, Inc.
Zielinski Productions, Inc.

Suns
CBS News Archives
Charisma Prods., Ltd./Visual Motion
Cinenet (Cinema Network)
Dreamlight Images, Inc.
Energy Productions
Film Bank
Film Search
Grinberg (Sherman) Film Libraries (West)
Halicki (H.B.) Productions
Jewell (Stuart) Productions
Marts (Steve) Productions
Moody Inst. of Science
Petrified Films, Inc.
Prelinger Assoc., Inc.
Source Stock Footage Lib., Inc.
Stock House
Twentieth Century-Fox Movietonews

Sunset Strip, Los Angeles
Patrick Media Group

Sunset Strip, Los Angeles (History and culture)
Petrified Films, Inc.
Spalla (Rick) Video Prods.

Sunspots
Film Bank

Superconductors
Cinema Guild

Supermarkets
Film Bank
Natl. Archives (RG 59)
Petrified Films, Inc.
Prelinger Assoc., Inc.
TV Ontario
See also Markets; Stores

Supernatural
Intl. Lutheran Layman's League
MacDonald, J. Fred
Natl. Archives of Canada
Phoenix Films and Video
Singer-Sharrette Traditional Healing Films

Supersonic jets
See Aircraft (Supersonic)

Supreme Court (U.S.)
Analogous Productions
Center for Pacific Northwest Studies
Film Bank
March of Time
Natl. Archives (RG 267)
Petrified Films, Inc.
Purdue Univ., Pub. Aff. Video Arch.

Supremes, The
Clark (Dick) Media Archives, Inc.
Daphne Productions, Inc.
UPA Prods. of America

Surf
See Waves

Surfing
ABC Sports, Inc.
Ackerman-Black Prods., Inc.
Archive Film Prods., Inc.
Bishop Mus., Visual Coll.
Brekke Television Prods.
Cinenet (Cinema Network)
Dittrich (Scott) Films

Dobovan Productions, Inc.
Dreamlight Images, Inc.
Echo Film Prods., Inc.
Encore Video Prods., Inc.
Energy Productions
Farkas Studios, Ltd.
Film Bank
Film Search
Fish Films, Inc.
Frontline Video, Inc.
Great Waves/Delaney Films
Grinberg (Sherman) Film Libraries (West)
Kesser Stock Footage Library
MacGillivray Freeman Films
Merkel Films
Metro Communications, Inc.
Petrified Films, Inc.
Prelinger Assoc., Inc.
Pyramid Film and Video Corp.
Quenzer Driscoll Dawson, Inc.
Second Line Search
Source Stock Footage Lib., Inc.
Spectral Comms.
Sports Cinematography Group
Sportsfilm
Summit Films, Inc.
TV Ontario
Video Tape Library, Ltd.

Surgery
Altschul Group
Amer. Journal of Nursing Co.
Amer. Veterinary Medical Assn.
Blue Sky Comms., Inc.
CBS News Archives
Calif. College of Podiatric Medicine
Center for Biomedical Comms.
DCI Video Resources
Emory Medical Television Network
Energy Productions
Film Bank
Historical Health Film Coll.
IMS Creative Communications
Johns Hopkins Univ., School of Medicine
March of Time
Metro Communications, Inc.
Milner-Fenwick, Inc.
Nassau Comm. Coll. Lib.
Natl. Archives/Natl. AV Ctr.
Ohio State Univ., Dept. of Photog. & Cinema
Petrified Films, Inc.
TV Ontario
Twentieth Century-Fox Movietonews
Video Genesis, Inc.
Visual Information Systems
See also Medical footage; Medicine

Surgery (Abdominal)
Visual Information Systems

Surgery (Cardiovascular)
Houston Acad. of Medicine
Visual Information Systems

Surgery (Cosmetic)
Amer. Soc. of Plastic & Recon. Surgeons

Surgery (Eye)
Natl. Soc. to Prevent Blindness

Surgery (Heart)
Center for Biomedical Comms.
DCI Video Resources

Surgery (Kidney)
Natl. Kidney Foundation, Inc.

Surgery (Neurologic)
Emory Medical Television Network
Nassau Comm. Coll. Lib.
Visual Information Systems

Surgery (Orthopedic)
Visual Information Systems

Surgery (Pediatric)
Visual Information Systems

Surgery (Plastic)
Amer. Soc. of Plastic & Recon. Surgeons
Social Psychiatry Res. Inst.

Surgery (Psychic)
Singer-Sharrette Traditional Healing Films

Surgery (Reconstructive)
Amer. Soc. of Plastic & Recon. Surgeons
Films for the Humanities and Sciences

Surgery (Thoracic)
Visual Information Systems

Surgical equipment
Northcoast Communication, Inc.

Surls, James
Blackwood Prods., Inc.

Surrealism
Amer. Federation of the Arts
Canyon Cinema, Inc.
Em Gee Film Library
Energy Productions
Mus. of Mod. Art, Circulating Film Lib.
Prelinger Assoc., Inc.

Surrenders
See World War I (Armistice); World War II (Germany, Surrender); World War II (Japan, Surrender)

Surveillance
CBS News Archives
Chicago Comm. to Defend the Bill of Rights
Freedom Information Service
MacDonald, J. Fred
Mus. & Hist. Div., City of Sacramento
Perlmutter (Alvin H.) Inc.

Surveyors and surveying
CBS News Archives
Petrified Films, Inc.
TV Ontario

Survival Research Laboratories (SRL)
Monday, Wednesday, Friday Video Club
Survival Research Laboratories
Target Video

Susanville, Calif. (History and culture)
Petrified Films, Inc.

Sushi and sushi bars
Film Bank

Sussex, England (History and culture)
Unicorn Projects

Susskind, David
Daphne Productions, Inc.

Susso, Pappa
Schomburg Ctr. for Res. in Black Culture

Sutherland, Donald
Daphne Productions, Inc.

Sutherland, Graham
Albright-Knox Art Gallery

Svengali
Archive Film Prods., Inc.

Swaggart, Jimmy
People for the American Way

Swainson, John Burley
Univ. of Mich., Mich. Hist. Colls.

Swallows
Mass. Audubon Society
New Zealand Embassy Film Lib.

Swamp buggies
Diamond P. Sports

Swamps
CBS News Archives
Film Bank
Natl. Archives (RG 40)
Natl. Assn. of Conservation Dists.
Petrified Films, Inc.
Read (Brooks) & Assoc.
TV Ontario
Tri-Comm Prods.
Wings Wildlife Prods., Inc.
See also Wetlands

Swans
Energy Productions
Farkas Studios, Ltd.
Giorno Poetry Systems Inst.
Minnesota Zoo
Petrified Films, Inc.
TV Ontario

Swanson, Gloria
Archive Film Prods., Inc.
Banks Film Library
Daphne Productions, Inc.

Swayze, John Cameron
Shokus Video

Swaziland
Hammer (Armand) Prods.

Swaziland (History and culture)
Smithsonian Inst., Human Studies Film Arch.

Sweatshops
Prelinger Assoc., Inc.
Timesteps Prods., Inc.

Sweden
Yue-Sai Kan, Inc.

Sweden (History and culture)
Archive Film Prods., Inc.
Footage Inc.
March of Time
Natl. Archives (RG 96)
Petrified Films, Inc.
United Nations Ctr. for Human Settlements
United Nations, Visual Materials Lib.

Swedish Americans
Evangelical Covenant Church of Amer.

Sweetwater, Tex. (History and culture)
Texas Tech Univ., Southwest Coll.

Swift Current, Sask. (History and culture)
Natl. Archives of Canada

Swigget, Gene
De Saisset Museum

Swimming
ABC Sports, Inc.
Amer. Motion Pictures
Analogous Productions
Archive Film Prods., Inc.
Athletic Institute
Dreamlight Images, Inc.
Encore Video Prods., Inc.
Energy Productions
Film Bank
Fish Films, Inc.
Grinberg (Sherman) Film Libraries (West)
Intl. Swimming Hall of Fame

Jessiefilm
Metro Communications, Inc.
Natl. Archives (RG 18)
Natl. Archives (RG 306)
Omega Films
Petrified Films, Inc.
Prelinger Assoc., Inc.
Second Line Search
Source Stock Footage Lib., Inc.
Spectral Comms.
Sportsfilm
Summit Films, Inc.
TV Ontario
Timesteps Prods., Inc.
Twentieth Century-Fox Movietonews
U.S. Olympic Comm.
Univ. of Wis., Green Bay, Ctr. TV Prod.
Video Tape Library, Ltd.

Swimming (College)
NCAA Productions

Swimming (High school)
Eastern Kentucky Univ.

Swimming (Instruction)
NCAA Productions

Swimming pools
CBS News Archives
Film Bank
Petrified Films, Inc.
Tri-Comm Prods.
Twentieth Century-Fox Movietonews

Swimsuits
Petrified Films, Inc.

Swing music
See Music (Swing)

Swiss Alps
See Alps

Switchboard operators
See Telephones (Switchboards and switchboard operators)

Switzerland
Bibliothèque Municipale de Montréal
Dorn (Larry) Associates
Goal Prods., Tourn. of Roses Film Lib.
Petrified Films, Inc.
Preview Media

Switzerland (History and culture)
Archive Film Prods., Inc.
Archives of the Mennonite Church
Petrified Films, Inc.
White Janssen, Inc.

Switzgable, Meg
Port Washington Pub. Lib.

Swordfish
Archive Film Prods., Inc.
Mystic Seaport Mus., Inc.

Swords
Film Bank
Rainbow Video Prods.

Sydney, Australia
Petrified Films, Inc.

Sydney, Australia (History and culture)
Farkas Studios, Ltd.

Sykes, Barbara
Long Beach Mus. of Art

Sylacauga, Ala. (History and culture)
Prelinger Assoc., Inc.

Symbionese Liberation Army (SLA)
KCRA-TV
Mus. & Hist. Div., City of Sacramento
San Francisco Bay Area TV News Arch.

Symphonies
See Orchestras

Symptoms (Rock and roll band)
Target Video

Synagogues
CBS News Archives
Petrified Films, Inc.

Synthetics
Prelinger Assoc., Inc.

Syphilis
See Sexually transmitted diseases (STDs)

Syria (History and culture)
Archive Film Prods., Inc.
Film/Audio Services, Inc.
Northstar Prods.

Szent-Gyorgyi, Albert
Cinema Guild

T'singtao, China (History and culture)
Hansen, Jack

Tacoma Narrows Bridge (Tacoma, Wash.)
Louisiana Tech Univ., Eng. Film Res. Ctr.
Univ. of Wash., Educ. Media Coll.

Tacoma, Wash.
Amer. Motion Pictures
Energy Productions

Tacoma, Wash. (History and culture)
Oregon Hist. Soc.
Washington State Hist. Soc.

Tadpoles
Wings Wildlife Prods. Inc.

Taft, William Howard
Archive Film Prods., Inc.
Natl. Archives (RG 75)
Natl. Archives (RG 111)
Natl. Archives (RG 200)
Prelinger Assoc., Inc.
Timesteps Prods., Inc.
Wright Brothers Coll.

Tahiti
Film Search
Hawaii Public Broadcasting Authority
MacGillivray Freeman Films
Preview Media

Tahiti (History and culture)
Archive Film Prods., Inc.

Tahoe, Lake (Calif.-Nev.)
Energy Productions
KD Enterprises Prods.
Petrified Films, Inc.
Postcards Unlimited
Preview Media
Source Stock Footage Lib., Inc.

Tai chi chuan
TV Ontario
Wayfarer Publications

Taillights
See Automobiles (Taillights)

Tailors
Petrified Films, Inc.

Taipei, Taiwan
Farkas Studios, Ltd.

Taiwan
Farkas Studios, Ltd.
Friends of Free China
Preview Media
See also China, People's Republic of

Taiwan (History and culture)
Archive Film Prods., Inc.
Asian American Resource Workshop
Film/Audio Services, Inc.
March of Time

Taj Mahal (India)
Analogous Productions
Jewell (Stuart) Productions
Petrified Films, Inc.

Taj Mahal (India) (History and culture)
Archive Film Prods., Inc.

Taj Mahal (Singer)
United Farm Workers of America (UFW)

Tajima, Renee
Paper Tiger TV

Takai, George
Spectral Comms.

Takamatzu, Jiro
Blackwood Prods., Inc.

Takeyama, Minoru
Southern Calif. Inst. of Architecture

Talk shows
Black Filmmaker Foundation
Daphne Productions, Inc.
Estate of Andy Warhol
Imevision
Joyce Media, Inc.
Milwaukee Access Telecomm. Auth.
Monday, Wednesday, Friday Video Club
Natl. Archives (RG 174)
Natl. Archives (RG 200)
Pro-Life Action League
Protele, S.A.

Talking Heads (Rock and roll band)
Target Video

Tall ships
See Ships (Tall ships)

Tampa, Fla.
Creative Video, Inc.
Energy Productions
Preview Media

Tank shots
Film Bank

Tanker ships
See Ships (Oil tankers)

Tanks (Military)
British Info. Svcs., Radio & TV Div.
CBS News Archives
Colorado Historical Society
Film Bank
Forsher (James) Prods. & Archives, Inc.
Link Flight Simulation Div.

See also Vehicles (Military)

Tanks (Storage)
CBS News Archives

Tanna Island, Vanuatu (History and culture)
Smithsonian Inst., Human Studies Film Arch.

Tannenbaum, Marc
Randolph (A. Philip) Educ. Fund

Tanning (Hides)
U.S. Hide, Skin & Leather Assn.

Tanning tanks
Film Bank

Tanzania
Summit Films, Inc.

Tanzania (Contemporary issues)
DEC Film & Video

Tanzania (History and culture)
Africa Inland Mission
Idera Films
Johnson (Martin & Osa) Safari Museum
Maryknoll Fathers & Brothers
Univ. of Arizona, Film Coll.

Taoism
See Religion (Taoism)

Taos, N. Mex.
New Mexico State Records Ctr. & Arch.
Preview Media
Summit Films, Inc.

Tap dancing
See Dance and dancing (Tap)

Tape recorders
Petrified Films, Inc.

Tapestries
Schweitzer (Albert) Ctr.

Tapirs
Kesser Stock Footage Library

Tapp, Gordie
Natl. Archives of Canada

Tar sands
TV Ontario

Tarahumara
UCLA Behavioral Sci. Media Lab.

Tarantulas
Energy Productions
Miller (David Lee) Prods.
Minnesota Zoo
Petrified Films, Inc.
Wings Wildlife Prods. Inc.

Tarkenton, Fran
Daphne Productions, Inc.
NFL Films, Inc.

Tarpon
Film Bank

Tarrytown, N.Y. (History and culture)
Prelinger Assoc., Inc.

Tarzan
Archive Film Prods., Inc.
Fulton County Hist. Soc., Inc.

NOTE: Access policies, availability and restrictions vary for each source. Please read each entry in full. Always consult "General Film and Videotape Collections" (page 599); these comprehensive collections contain material on every conceivable subject.

Tate, Buddy
Rhapsody Films, Inc.

Tatlin, Vladimir
Blackwood Prods., Inc.

Tattoos and tattooing
Film/Audio Services, Inc.
Flower Films & Video

Tatum, Art
Chertok Assoc., Inc.
Petrified Films, Inc.

Taussig, Helen
Medical College of Pa., Arch. & Spec.
　Coll. Women in Medicine

Taut, Bruno
Southern Calif. Inst. of Architecture

Taxation
Apertura
CBS News Archives
Center for Public Dialogue
Constitutional Revival
Constitutional Rights Foundation
Natl. Archives (RG 58)
Natl. Archives (RG 200)
Political Issue Archive
Prelinger Assoc., Inc.
U.S. Conference of Mayors

Taxco, Mexico
Source Stock Footage Lib., Inc.

Taxis
CBS News Archives
Film Bank
Petrified Films, Inc.
Stock House
Wallen (Dick) Prods.

Taylor, Elizabeth
Archive Film Prods., Inc.
Banks Film Library
Halcyon Days Prods.
Petrified Films, Inc.

Taylor, Frederick Winslow
California Newsreel
Salenger Films Inc.

Taylor, Herbert John
Wheaton Coll., Billy Graham Ctr.

Taylor, M. Harvey
Pennsylvania State Arch.

Taylor, Rod
Banks Film Library

Taylor, Sam
Los Angeles Blues Archives

Taylor, Susan
Schomburg Ctr. for Res. in Black Culture

Tea ceremonies
Rainbow Video Prods.
Wesleyan Univ., World Music Arch.

Teach-ins
CBS News Archives
See also Demonstrations (Political)

Teachers and teaching
Intl. Film Bureau, Inc.
Lawren Prods., Inc.
March of Time
Natl. Archives (RG 306)
Natl. Assn. of Secondary Schl. Principals
Petrified Films, Inc.
Prelinger Assoc., Inc.

See also Classrooms; Colleges and
　universities; Education; High schools;
　Schools; Students

Teaff, Grant
Fellowship of Christian Athletes

Teamsters
See International Brotherhood of
　Teamsters, Chauffeurs, Warehousemen
　and Helpers of America

Tear gas
Film Bank
Petrified Films, Inc.

Teatro Campesino, El
Teatro Campesino, El
United Farm Workers of America (UFW)

Technicians
Film Bank
Fish Films, Inc.
Petrified Films, Inc.
TV Ontario

Technicolor (History of)
Academy Film Arch.
Prelinger Assoc., Inc.

Technology
Bullfrog Films, Inc.
Cable News Network Library
Canadian Filmmakers Dist. Centre
Carleton Prods. Inc.
Carousel Film & Video
Cinema Guild
Educational Images, Ltd.
Fabulous Footage Inc.
Film Bank
Film Search
Hagley Mus. & Lib.
Halcyon Days Prods.
Idera Films
Imageways, Inc.
Intl. Film Bureau, Inc.
Kesser Stock Footage Library
Mass. Inst. of Tech., MIT Museum
Media Guild
Metro Communications, Inc.
Military/Combat Stock Footage
NASA, Office of Comm.
Natl. Archives (RG 242)
Natl. Archives (RG 307)
Natl. Archives of Canada
Natl. Film Board of Canada
Northcoast Communication, Inc.
Prelinger Assoc., Inc.
Robotic Industries Assn.
Soc. for French Amer. Cult. Svcs. & Educ.
　Aid
TV Ontario
TV-UNAM
Union of Concerned Scientists
Université Laval, Cinémathèque
World Monitor
See also Computers; Robots and robotics

Technology (Agricultural)
Univ. of Calif., Davis, Shields Library
See also Agriculture; Farms and farming

Technology (High)
Applegate Entertainment
Boston Stock Market
Canadian Filmmakers Dist. Centre
Computer Museum
Film Search
General Motors Corp.
Hewlett-Packard Co.
IBM Corporation
Ideal Comms., Inc.
Inst. of Electrical & Electronics Eng.
Kesser Stock Footage Library
Link Flight Simulation Div.

Metro Communications, Inc.
Odyssey Prods., Inc.
Spectral Comms.
Stock Shots
Sullivan Video Services
TV Ontario
Video Tape Library, Ltd.
Videotroupe
Zielinski Productions, Inc.
See also Computers; Robots and robotics

Technology (Medical)
Energy Productions
Film Bank
Hewlett-Packard Co.
Johns Hopkins Univ., School of Medicine
Natl. Library of Medicine
Northcoast Communication, Inc.
Rosebush Visions Corp.
TV Ontario

Technology (Office)
Imperial Oil Ltd.

Teddy bears
Film Bank

**Teenage Jesus and the Jerks (Rock and
　roll band)**
Target Video

Teenage pregnancy
Cambridge Documentary Films, Inc.
Courter Films & Assoc.
DEC Film & Video
First Run/Icarus Films, Inc.
Groupe Intervention Video
Higgins (Alfred) Prods.
Intermedia Arts Minnesota
March of Dimes Birth Defects Found.
Natl. Abortion Rights Action League
O.D.N. Productions, Inc.
Planned Parenthood Fed. of Amer.
Polymorph Films, Inc.
Pyramid Film and Video Corp.

Teenagers
Addiction Research Foundation of Ontario
Amer. Assn. for Counseling &
　Development
Apertura
Archive Film Prods., Inc.
CBS News Archives
Campbell Films, Inc.
Chicago Access Corp.
Clark (Dick) Media Archives, Inc.
Coe Film Assoc., Inc.
Coronet/MTI Film & Video
Education Development Ctr., Inc.
Film Bank
Film/Video Arts, Inc.
First Run/Icarus Films, Inc.
Insurance Inst. for Highway Safety
Intermedia Arts Minnesota
Intl. Lutheran Layman's League
MacDonald, J. Fred
March of Time
Mass Media Ministries
Multi-Media Productions, Inc.
Narcotics Education, Inc.
Natl. Archives (RG 378)
Natl. Archives of Canada
Natl. Assn. of Secondary Schl. Principals
New Day Films
New Jersey Network
Petrified Films, Inc.
Planned Parenthood Fed. of Amer.
Prelinger Assoc., Inc.
Spalla (Rick) Video Prods.
Streamline Film Archives
Third World Newsreel
Toughlove
Univ. of Wis., Green Bay, Ctr. TV Prod.
Video In
World Wide Pictures, Inc.

See also Lifestyles; Youth

Teenagers (Japan)
Asia Society

Teenagers (U.S., 1950s)
Archive Film Prods., Inc.
Clark (Dick) Media Archives, Inc.
MacDonald, J. Fred
Petrified Films, Inc.
Prelinger Assoc., Inc.
Streamline Film Archives

Teenagers (U.S., 1960s)
Clark (Dick) Media Archives, Inc.
Petrified Films, Inc.
Twentieth Century-Fox Movietonews

Teepees
Petrified Films, Inc.

Teeth
Amer. Dental Assn.
Film Bank
Prelinger Assoc., Inc.
Pyramid Film and Video Corp.
See also Dentists and dentistry

Tel Aviv, Israel (History and culture)
UJA Federation

Tele-evangelism
See Television (Religious)

Telecommunications
AT&T Archives & Rec. Mgmt. Svcs.
Cinema Guild
East-West Center
Film Bank
Intl. Telecommunications Satellite Org.
Natl. Archives of Canada
Prelinger Assoc., Inc.
Silver Image

Telecommunications (Canada)
Bell Canada

Telecommunications (History)
Antique Wireless Assn., Inc.

Telecommunications industry
New Jersey Network

Telegraphy
Archive Film Prods., Inc.
Broad Street Prods.
CBS News Archives
Petrified Films, Inc.
Prelinger Assoc., Inc.

Telemarketing
United Training Media

Telepathy
Fish Films, Inc.

Telephone poles
See Telephones (Poles and wires)

Telephones
AT&T Archives & Rec. Mgmt. Svcs.
Allen (John E.) Inc.
Archive Film Prods., Inc.
Bell Canada
CBS News Archives
Cimarron Productions
Dreamlight Images, Inc.
Fish Films, Inc.
MacDonald, J. Fred
Natl. Archives (RG 179)
Natl. Archives (RG 200)
Petrified Films, Inc.
Prelinger Assoc., Inc.
Rosebush Visions Corp.
Salenger Films Inc.

Timesteps Prods., Inc.
Video Tape Library, Ltd.

Telephones (Booths)
Petrified Films, Inc.

Telephones (Dialing)
Petrified Films, Inc.

Telephones (Factories)
Farkas Studios, Ltd.
Prelinger Assoc., Inc.

Telephones (Operators)
Fish Films, Inc.
Prelinger Assoc., Inc.

Telephones (Poles and wires)
Dreamlight Images, Inc.
Film Bank
Petrified Films, Inc.
Prelinger Assoc., Inc.

**Telephones (Switchboards and
switchboard operators)**
Film Bank
Petrified Films, Inc.
Prelinger Assoc., Inc.

Telephones (Switching exchanges)
Rosebush Visions Corp.

Telescopes
British Info. Svcs., Radio & TV Div.
CBS News Archives
California Inst. of Tech., Inst. Arch.
Energy Productions
Harvard-Smithsonian Ctr. for Astrophysics
Petrified Films, Inc.
TV Ontario
Univ. of Arizona, Film Coll.
See also Observatories

Telescopes (Radio)
Source Stock Footage Lib., Inc.

Teletype machines
CBS News Archives
Petrified Films, Inc.

Television
Allen (John E.) Inc.
Archive Film Prods., Inc.
CBS News Archives
Dreamlight Images, Inc.
Energy Productions
Film Bank
Latin Amer. Video Arch.
Natl. Archives (RG 307)
Petrified Films, Inc.
Prelinger Assoc., Inc.
Twentieth Century-Fox Movietonews

Television (Advocacy)
Political Issue Archive

Television (Airborne)
Ohio State Univ., Dept. of Photog. &
Cinema

Television (Australia)
Wombat Film & Video

Television (Child-produced)
Deep Dish TV
Milwaukee Access Telecomm. Auth.

Television (Children's programming)
ABC Distribution (Education)
ABC Video Enterprises
Children's Television Workshop

Coe Film Assoc., Inc.
Filmtel Intl. Corp.
Harvard Univ., Schl. of Educ., ACT Lib.
Imevision
Milwaukee Access Telecomm. Auth.
Mus. of Broadcast Comms.
Mus. of Broadcasting
Natl. Archives of Canada
Natl. Endow. for the Arts, Media Arts
Prog.
Univision Television Network
WGBH Educational Foundation
See also Children's films and videotapes

Television (China)
Nan Hai (U.S.A.) Co., Inc.

Television (Cuba)
Instituto Cubano de Radio y Television

Television (Educational)
Auburn University Archives
Indiana Univ., Audio-Visual Center
Lib. of Congress, M/B/RS
MacDonald, J. Fred
Public Broadcasting System
State Hist. Soc. of North Dakota

Television (France)
Soc. for French Amer. Cult. Svcs. & Educ.
Aid

Television (Great Britain)
BBC/Lionheart Television
Devillier Donegan Ent.
MacDonald, J. Fred
Wombat Film & Video

Television (History of)
MacDonald, J. Fred
Mus. of Broadcasting
Prelinger Assoc., Inc.
Sarnoff (David) Res. Ctr. Lib.

Television (History of) (International)
MacDonald, J. Fred

Television (Japan)
Devillier Donegan Ent.
East-West Center

Television (Latin America)
Democracy in Communication

Television (Mexico)
Canal 11
Imagen y Sonido Independiente, S.A.
Imevision
Latina, S.A. de C.V.
Protele, S.A.
Redes Cinevideo, S.A.
TV-UNAM

Television (New Zealand)
Wombat Film & Video

Television (Nicaragua)
Video Data Bank
Xchange TV

Television (Production)
Film Bank
Prelinger Assoc., Inc.

Television (Religious)
Abilene Christian University
Christopher Closeup
Intl. Lutheran Layman's League
Liberty Broadcasting Network
MacDonald, J. Fred
Paulist Productions

People for the American Way
Reorg. Church of Jesus Christ of LDS
Roberts (Oral) Univ.
Sheen (Fulton J.) Comm. Ltd.
United Methodist Churches
Wheaton Coll., Billy Graham Ctr.

Television (Soviet Union)
Belka Intl. Inc.
Working Group on Soviet TV

**Television (Spanish-language
programming)**
Archivo Historico Cinematografico
Canal 11
Imagen y Sonido Independiente, S.A.
Imevision
Latina, S.A. de C.V.
Protele, S.A.
Redes Cinevideo, S.A.
TV-UNAM
Titan Sports, Inc.
Univision Television Network

Television (Violence)
Harvard Univ., Schl. of Educ., ACT Lib.

Television antennas
See Antennas

Television archives
ABC News
Advertising Information Services, Inc.
Arch. Nationales du Québec
C-SPAN (Cable Satellite Public Affairs
Network)
CBS News Archives
CTV Television Network
Cable News Network Library
Clio Awards
Encore Entertainment
Instituto Cubano de Radio y Television
Intl. Air Check
Lib. of Congress, M/B/RS
Mus. of Broadcast Comms.
Mus. of Broadcasting
NBC News Video Archives
Natl. Archives of Canada
Natl. Conservative Foundation
Natl. Ctr. for Film & Video Preservation
Natl. Jewish Arch. of Broadcasting
Peabody (George Foster) Collection
Public Broadcasting System
Purdue Univ., Pub. Aff. Video Arch.
UCLA Film & Television Archive
Vanderbilt University, TV News Arch.
WGBH Educational Foundation
Wisconsin Ctr. for Film & Theater Res.
Wolfson (Louis II) Media Hist. Ctr.

Television broadcasting
Streamline Film Archives

Television cameras
Film Bank
Petrified Films, Inc.
Prelinger Assoc., Inc.

Television campaign commercials
See Political campaign commercials

Television commercials
Adbank
Advertising Information Services, Inc.
American Airlines
Anheuser-Busch Cos., Inc.
Apertura
Archive Film Prods., Inc.
Brekke Television Prods.
Brooklyn Coll., Diamant Mem. Lib.
Center for Southern Folklore

Cincinnati Hist. Soc.
Clio Awards
Coca-Cola Co., Archives Dept.
Continental Airlines
Duke Univ., Perkins Lib.
Electronic Arts Intermix
Encore Entertainment
Fashion Inst. of Design & Merchandising
Film Bank
Ford (Henry) Museum
General Mills, Inc.
Halcyon Days Prods.
Harvard Univ., Schl. of Educ., ACT Lib.
IBM Corporation
Imperial Oil Ltd.
Intl. Air Check
Intl. Assn. of Fairs & Expositions
Intl. Fashion Video Library
Island Video
MacDonald, J. Fred
Miles Corporate Archive
Movietime, Inc. Archives
Mus. of Adv. & Communications Design
Mus. of Broadcast Comms.
Mus. of Broadcasting
Natl. Archives (RG 207)
Natl. Jewish Arch. of Broadcasting
Natl. Right to Life Committee
New York State Dept. of Econ. Devel.
Ohio Historical Soc.
Perlmutter (Alvin H.) Inc.
Petrified Films, Inc.
Political Commercial Archive
Political Issue Archive
Prelinger Assoc., Inc.
Procter & Gamble Co.
Radio City Music Hall Prods.
Read (Brooks) & Assoc.
Saatchi & Saatchi DFS Compton
Safe Energy Communication Council
Shields Archival
Shokus Video
Smithsonian Inst., NMAH, Arch. Ctr.
Smithsonian Inst., NMAH, Div. Polit.
Hist.
Snyder (Bill) Films, Inc.
Streamline Film Archives
Studebaker Natl. Museum
United Airlines, Creative Services
Video Monitoring Svcs. of America
Video Resources N.Y., Inc.
See also Advertising; Automobiles
(Television commercials); Cigarettes
(Television commercials); Political
campaign commercials; Public service
announcements (PSAs)

Television commercials (Blacks in)
Schomburg Ctr. for Res. in Black Culture

Television engineering
Soc. of Motion Picture & TV Engineers

Television news
ABC Distribution (Education)
ABC News
CBS News Archives
CONUS Communications
CTV Television Network
Cable News Network Library
Carter (Jimmy) Library
Dupont (Alfred I.) Survey & Awards
Eisenhower (Dwight D.) Library
Ford (Gerald R.) Library
Instant Replay, Inc.
Johnson (Lyndon Baines) Lib.
Kennedy (John F.) Library
Lib. of Congress, M/B/RS
MacDonald, J. Fred
Mus. of Broadcasting
NBC News Video Archives

NOTE: Access policies, availability and restrictions vary for each source. Please read each entry in full. Always consult "General Film and Videotape Collections" (page 599); these comprehensive collections contain material on every conceivable subject.

Natl. Archives (RG 200)
Natl. Archives (RG 306)
Natl. Archives (RG 330)
Natl. Archives (RG 342)
Natl. Archives/Nixon Presidential
  Materials Proj.
Natl. Conservative Foundation
Natl. Jewish Arch. of Broadcasting
Natl. Press Photographers Assn., Inc.
Prov. Arch. of Newfoundland & Labrador
Roosevelt (Franklin D.) Lib.
Sullivan Video Services
Trent Institute for Popular Culture
Univ. of Ill. Urbana-Champaign, Univ.
  Arch.
Univision Television Network
Visnews Intl.
WETA-TV
Worldwide Television News

Television news (Cuba)
Instituto Cubano de Radio y Television

Television news (International)
Grinberg (Sherman) Film Libraries (East)
Hearst Metrotone News
World Monitor

Television news (Local)
Local television news collections are listed
by station call letters in the "Sources
and Collections Index" in front of book
Bangor Historical Society
Birmingham Pub. Lib., Dept. of Arch.
Boston Community Access & Prog.
  Found.
Boston Univ. Film Archive
Buffalo & Erie County Hist. Soc.
CITY Pulse Library
Cable News Network Library
Ctr. for Pacific Northwest Studies
Chicago Historical Society
Cincinnati Hist. Soc.
Datura Productions
Eastern Washington State Historical Soc.
El Paso Community College
Independent Network News (INN)
Indiana Hist. Soc., Smith Memorial Lib.
Indiana State Lib.
Inuit Broadcasting Corp.
KCRA-TV
Kansas State Historical Society
Los Angeles News Service
Louisiana State Univ., Shreveport
MacDonald, J. Fred
Marquette Univ., Spec. Coll.
Marshall Univ., Spec. Coll.
Memphis State Univ. Libraries
Memphis-Shelby Cty. Pub. Lib. & Info.
  Ctr.
Mississippi Dept. of Arch. & Hist.
Mus. & Hist. Div., City of Sacramento
Mus. of Broadcast Comms.
Natl. Archives (RG 200)
Navajo Tribe, Off. Broadcast Svcs.
Nebraska State Hist. Soc.
Neville Pub. Museum
New Mexico State Records Ctr. & Arch.
New Orleans Pub. Lib., La. Div.
Newsreel Video Service
Northeast Historic Film
Ohio Historical Soc.
Oregon Hist. Soc.
Perry (Merle G.) Arch.
Prov. Arch. of Alberta
Prov. Arch. of British Columbia
Read (Brooks) & Assoc.
Rhode Island Hist. Soc.
San Francisco Bay Area TV News Arch.
San Jose Hist. Museum
Southern Oregon Hist. Soc.
Southwest Film/Video Archives, SMU
Spalla (Rick) Video Prods.
State Hist. Soc. of Iowa
State Hist. Soc. of North Dakota

State Hist. Soc. of Wisconsin
Streamline Film Archives
Sweet (Harry) Film Coll.
Temple Univ., Urban Arch. Ctr.
Texas Tech Univ., Southwest Coll.
Univ. of Baltimore, Abell TV Arch.
Univ. of Georgia, WSB TV News Film
  Arch.
Univ. of Ill. Urbana-Champaign, Univ.
  Arch.
Univ. of Kentucky, AV Arch.
Univ. of Pittsburgh, Arch. of Indust. Soc.
Univ. of Regina, Sask. Arch. Board
Univ. of So. Carolina, Newsfilm Lib.
Univ. of Vermont, Bailey/Howe Lib.
Video Monitoring Svcs. of America
WIPR-TV
WTMJ-TV
Washington State Hist. Soc.
Wayne State Univ., Arch. Labor & Urb.
  Aff.
West Virginia Dept. of Culture & Hist.
Wolfson (Louis II) Media Hist. Ctr.,
  Miami-Dade Pub. Lib.
Worldwide Television News

Television news (Mexico)
Imevision
Notimex
Televisa, S.A.

Television news (National)
C-SPAN (Cable Satellite Public Affairs
  Network)
Independent Network News (INN)
Memphis State Univ. Libraries
Natl. Archives (RG 200)
Purdue Univ., Pub. Aff. Video Arch.
Vanderbilt University, TV News Arch.

Television news (Soviet Union)
Belka Intl. Inc.
Working Group on Soviet TV

Television programs
See also "Television Series Index" (pages
  779-787) for specific series titles
ABC Distribution (Education)
ABC Video Enterprises
Archive Film Prods., Inc.
Archives of Ontario
Arizona State Univ., Wayne King Coll.
Art Gallery of Ontario
Ball State Univ., Middletown Coll.
Battleship Cove
C-SPAN (Cable Satellite Public Affairs
  Network)
CBS Entertainment
Camera Three Prods., Inc.
Canadian Gay Archives
Carson Tonight Inc.
Carter (Jimmy) Library
Channell One Video
Chicago Historical Society
Children's Television Workshop
Cincinnati Hist. Soc.
Citizens' Councils of America
Clark (Dick) Media Archives, Inc.
Clip Joint For Film
Colorado Historical Society
Computer Television Group, Inc.
Connecticut State Library
Country Music Foundation, Inc.
Datura Productions
Devillier Donegan Ent.
Dirksen (E.M.) Cong. Lead. Res. Ctr.
Dupont (Alfred I.) Survey & Awards
Eisenhower (Dwight D.) Library
Encore Entertainment
Facets Multimedia, Inc.
Film Bank
Film Search
Ford (Gerald R.) Library
Fremantle Intl.
Frontline Video, Inc.

Gay Cable Network
Gay Men's Health Crisis
Grinberg (Sherman) Film Libraries (East)
Hagley Mus. and Lib.
Hoover (Herbert) Presidential Lib.
Imageways, Inc.
Indiana Univ., Audio-Visual Center
Inst. for Labor Studies & Research
Instant Replay, Inc.
Intellimation
Intl. Gay and Lesbian Archives
Intl. Mus. of Photography
Inuit Broadcasting Corp.
Island Video
Johnson (Lyndon Baines) Library
KCRA-TV
Kehr (Timothy D.) Advertising
Kennedy (John F.) Library
MacDonald, J. Fred
Marquette Univ., Spec. Coll.
Milner-Fenwick, Inc.
Mississippi Dept. of Arch. & Hist.
Morcraft Films
Morgan (Jess S.) & Co., Inc.
Moviecraft, Inc.
Movietime, Inc. Archives
Mus. of Broadcasting
NBC TV Network, Enterprises Dept.
Natl. Archives (RG 12)
Natl. Archives (RG 16)
Natl. Archives (RG 64)
Natl. Archives (RG 116)
Natl. Archives (RG 146)
Natl. Archives (RG 174)
Natl. Archives (RG 311)
Natl. Archives (RG 330)
Natl. Archives/Nixon Presidential
  Materials Proj.
Natl. Endow. for the Arts, Media Arts
  Prog.
Natl. Jewish Arch. of Broadcasting
New York City Dept. of Rec. & Info.
  Svcs.
New York Pub. Lib., Perf. Arts Res. Ctr.,
  Theatre on Film and Tape
New York Pub. Lib., Rare Books &
  Manuscripts Div.
New York State Arch. & Rec. Admin.
Ohio Historical Soc.
Palladium Entertainment, Inc.
Pathé Pictures, Inc.
Perlmutter (Alvin H.) Inc.
Playboy Programs, Inc.
Procter & Gamble Co.
Prov. Arch. of Alberta
Prov. Arch. of British Columbia
Prov. Arch. of Newfoundland & Labrador
Radio City Music Hall Prods.
Rayburn (Sam) Library
Roosevelt (Franklin D.) Lib.
San Diego State Univ., Spec. Coll.
Schomburg Ctr. for Res. in Black Culture
Sheen (Fulton J.) Comm. Ltd.
Shields Archival
Shokus Video
Smith (Margaret Chase) Lib. Ctr.
Sports Mus. of New England
State Hist. Soc. of Wisconsin
Streamline Film Archives
Student Struggle for Soviet Jewry
TV Collector
TV Ontario
Texas A&M Univ., Univ. Arch.
Trent Institute for Popular Culture
Trotting Horse Museum
Truman (Harry S) Library
Twin Cities Public Television (KTCA)
UPA Prods. of America
Univ. of Rochester Lib., Rare Books &
  Spec. Coll.
Univ. of Tex. at Austin, Barker Tex. Hist.
  Ctr.
Univ. of Tex. at Austin, Ransom Hum.
  Res. Ctr., Theatre Arts Coll.
Univision Television Network

Video Resources N.Y., Inc.
Video Yesteryear
Video-SIG
Videobrary, Inc.
WTJX-TV
Weintraub Screen Entertainment, Inc.
Wesleyan Cinema Archives
Wheaton Coll., Billy Graham Ctr.
Williams (Wade) Prods.
Windsor Productions
Wombat Film & Video
Woods N' Water Television Series
Yale Film Study Ctr.

Television repair shops
Film Bank

Television screens
Fish Films, Inc.

Television sets
Archive Film Prods., Inc.
Energy Productions
Fish Films, Inc.
Petrified Films, Inc.
Prelinger Assoc., Inc.

Television sets (Exploding)
Petrified Films, Inc.

Television sets (Production)
Prelinger Assoc., Inc.

Television snow
See Snow (Television)

Television stations
Film Bank
Prelinger Assoc., Inc.
MacDonald, J. Fred

Teller, Edward
Amer. Nuclear Society

Telluride, Colo.
Summit Films, Inc.

Temperance (Alcohol)
March of Time
Signal Press
Univ. of Mich., Mich. Hist. Colls.

Temple, Shirley
Archive Film Prods., Inc.
UCLA Film & Television Archive
Videobrary, Inc.

Temples
British Info. Svcs., Radio & TV Div.
CBS News Archives
Farkas Studios, Ltd.
Film Bank
Jewell (Stuart) Productions
Marts (Steve) Productions
Petrified Films, Inc.
Unicorn Projects

Temples (Japanese)
Dreamlight Images, Inc.
Japan Society, Inc. Film Center

Tempo, Nino
Spalla (Rick) Video Prods.

Tenant farmers
See Farms and farming (Tenant)

Tenants' rights
Channel L Working Group

Tenements
Archive Film Prods., Inc.
Film Bank
Petrified Films, Inc.
Stock House

See also Slums

Tennessee
Departures, Inc.
Dreamlight Images, Inc.
Energy Prods.
Lunar Prods.
Omega Films
Preview Media
Producers' Service

Tennessee (History and culture)
Archive Film Prods., Inc.
Center for Southern Folklore
Country Music Foundation, Inc.
Duke Univ., Perkins Lib.
East Tenn. State Univ., Arch. of
 Appalachia
Educational Video Ctr.
Memphis Pink Palace Mus. & Lib.
Memphis-Shelby Cty. Pub. Lib. & Info.
 Ctr.
Natl. Archives (RG 106)
Natl. Archives (RG 200)
Petrified Films, Inc.
Prelinger Assoc., Inc.
Southern Christian Leadership Conf.
Tennessee State Lib. & Arch.
Western Kentucky Univ., Folklife Arch.

Tennessee Valley Authority (TVA)
Agee (James) Film Project
March of Time
Natl. Archives (RG 48)
Natl. Archives (RG 142)
Natl. Archives/Natl. AV Ctr.
Prelinger Assoc., Inc.
Tennessee Valley Authority (TVA)

Tennis
Allen (John E.) Inc.
Amer. Motion Pictures
Analogous Productions
Archive Film Prods., Inc.
Athletic Institute
Brekke Television Prods.
Charisma Prods., Ltd./Visual Motion
Chicago Video Transfer
Creative Video, Inc.
Dreamlight Images, Inc.
Encore Video Prods., Inc.
Energy Productions
Film Bank
Hayes Prods., Inc.
Intl. Tennis Hall of Fame & Museum
Jalbert Productions
Kesser Stock Footage Library
Metro Communications, Inc.
Moving Media
Peak Productions, Inc.
Second Line Search
Source Stock Footage Lib., Inc.
Sportsfilm
Summit Films, Inc.
TV Ontario
Twentieth Century-Fox Movietonews
U.S. Tennis Assn.
Univ. of Notre Dame, Joyce Sports Coll.
Video Tape Library, Ltd.
Windsor Prod. Corp.

Tennis (Instruction)
NCAA Productions
Natl. Assn. for Sport & Phys. Ed.
U.S. Tennis Assn.

Tennis (Professional)
Film Search
Golden Gaters Prods.
U.S. Tennis Assn.

Tennis camps
Preview Media

Tents
CBS News Archives

Terkel, Studs
Agee (James) Film Project

Termites
Wings Wildlife Prods. Inc.

Terracina, Italy (History and culture)
Rockefeller Arch. Ctr.

Terrell, Steve
Videobrary, Inc.

Territories (U.S.)
Prelinger Assoc., Inc.

Terrorism
Anti-Defamation League of B'nai B'rith
Coronet/MTI Film & Video
Crystal Pyramid Prods.
Film Bank
Film/Audio Services, Inc.
Myrin Institute
Northstar Prods.
U.S. Defense Nuclear Agency
World Monitor

Terry, Sonny
Lawren Prods., Inc.

Tesla photography
Film Bank

Test films and videotapes
See Motion pictures (Equipment) (Test
 films)

Test flights
See Aircraft (Test flights)

Test pilots
See Aviation (Test pilots)

Test tubes
Prelinger Assoc., Inc.

Teton Mountains, Idaho-Wyo.
Source Stock Footage Lib., Inc.

Texas
Analogous Productions
Aries Prods.
Bailey Productions, Inc.
Cable Access of Dallas
Cine-Mark
Creative Video
Dreamlight Images, Inc.
Film Bank
First Group Comms., Inc.
Hayes Prods., Inc.
Kesser Stock Footage Library
October Productions
Postcards Unlimited
Preview Media
Univ. of North Texas, Div. of
 Radio/TV/Film

Texas (History and culture)
Archive Film Prods., Inc.
Baylor Univ., Texas Coll.
El Paso Comm. Coll.
Hayes Prods., Inc.
Houston (Sam) Regional Library
Louisiana State Univ., Shreveport
MacDonald, J. Fred
March of Time

Natl. Archives (RG 48)
Natl. Archives (RG 70)
Natl. Archives (RG 85)
Natl. Archives (RG 200)
Natl. Assn. of Conservation Dists.
Natl. Oceanic & Atmospheric Admin.
October Productions
Panhandle-Plains Hist. Museum
Petrified Films, Inc.
Prelinger Assoc., Inc.
San Antonio Conservation Soc. Found.
 Lib.
Slavonic Benev. Order. of State of Texas
Southwest Film/Video Archives, SMU
Texas State Lib., Arch. Div.
Texas Tech Univ., Southwest Coll.
Texas Woman's Univ.
Univ. of North Texas, Div. Radio/TV/Film
Univ. of Tex. at Austin, Barker Tex. Hist.
 Ctr.
Univ. of Tex. at Austin, Ransom Hum.
 Res. Ctr., Photo. Coll.
Univ. of Tex., Inst. of Texan Cultures

Texas City, Tex. (History and culture)
Natl. Archives (RG 200)

Textile industry
Amer. Textile Mfrs. Inst.
New Jersey Network
Petrified Films, Inc.
Prelinger Assoc., Inc.
TV Ontario
White Janssen, Inc.

Textiles
Prelinger Assoc., Inc.
TV Ontario

Thailand
Farkas Studios, Ltd.
Grinberg (Sherman) Film Libraries (West)
Jewell (Stuart) Productions
Pacific Productions
Yue-Sai Kan, Inc.

Thailand (History and culture)
DEC Film & Video
Film/Audio Services, Inc.
Johns Hopkins Univ./Population Comm.
 Svcs.
Natl. Archives (RG 286)
Petrified Films, Inc.
Salvation Army, Natl. Comm. Dept.
Singer-Sharrette Traditional Healing Films
Video Tape Library, Ltd.

Thalberg, Irving
Archive Film Prods., Inc.

Thames River, England
Petrified Films, Inc.

**Thames River, England (History and
 culture)**
Archive Film Prods., Inc.
Petrified Films, Inc.

Thanksgiving
Goodyear Tire & Rubber
Petrified Films, Inc.
Prelinger Assoc., Inc.
Twentieth Century-Fox Movietonews

Tharp, Twyla
Daphne Productions, Inc.
Tharp (Twyla) Dance Foundation

Thatcher, Margaret
Film/Audio Services, Inc.
Villon Films

Theater
Appalshop Films, Inc.
Blackwood (Christian) Prods., Inc.
Cantor (Arthur) Inc.
Channel L Working Group
Corinth Films/Corinth Video
Electronic Arts Intermix
Facets Multimedia, Inc.
GPN
Gay Cable Network
House Found. for the Arts
Intermedia Arts Minnesota
March of Time
Media Guild
New American Makers
New York Pub. Lib., Perf. Arts Res. Ctr.,
 Theatre on Film and Tape
Peralta Colleges TV
Univ. of Calif., Davis, Shields Library
Univ. of Calif., Ext. Media Ctr.
Univ. of Mich., Mich. Hist. Colls.
Vedo Films/Novacom Video
Video In

Theater (Alternative)
Cantor (Arthur) Inc.
New York Pub. Lib., Perf. Arts Res. Ctr.,
 Theatre on Film and Tape
Twin Cities Public Television (KTCA)
Univ. of Calif., Davis, Shields Library

Theater (Amateur)
TV Ontario

Theater (Broadway)
Analogous Productions
Archive Film Prods., Inc.
Charisma Prods., Ltd./Visual Motion
Creative Video, Inc.
Inst. of the Amer. Musical
March of Time
New York Pub. Lib., Perf. Arts Res. Ctr.,
 Theatre on Film and Tape

Theater (Bunraku puppets)
Camera Three Prods., Inc.

Theater (Deaf)
Camera Three Prods., Inc.

Theater (France)
Soc. for French Amer. Cult. Svcs. & Educ.
 Aid

Theater (Germany)
Goethe Institute Atlanta
Goethe Institute Los Angeles

Theater (India)
Smithsonian Inst., Human Studies Film
 Arch.

Theater (Kabuki)
Camera Three Prods., Inc.
Devillier Donegan Ent.

Theater (Mexican)
Canal 11
Imevision

Theater (Mexican American)
Teatro Campesino, El

Theater (Musical)
Inst. of the Amer. Musical
New York Pub. Lib., Perf. Arts Res. Ctr.,
 Theatre on Film and Tape
Research Video

Theater (Nigerian)
Camera Three Prods., Inc.

NOTE: Access policies, availability and restrictions vary for each source. Please read each entry in full. Always consult "General Film and Videotape Collections" (page 599); these comprehensive collections contain material on every conceivable subject.

Theater (Off-Broadway)
New York Pub. Lib., Perf. Arts Res. Ctr., Theatre on Film and Tape
Petrified Films, Inc.

Theater (Off-Off-Broadway)
New York Pub. Lib., Perf. Arts Res. Ctr., Theatre on Film and Tape

Theater (Regional)
New York Pub. Lib., Perf. Arts Res. Ctr., Theatre on Film and Tape

Theater (Shakespeare)
Folger Shakespeare Library

Theater (Soviet Union)
Natl. Coun. of Amer.-Sov. Friendship

Theater (Yiddish)
Cantor (Arthur) Inc.
Ergo Media
New York Pub. Lib., Perf. Arts Res. Ctr., Theatre on Film and Tape

Theater arts
Carousel Film & Video
GPN
Phoenix Films and Video

Theater screens
Petrified Films, Inc.

Theaters
Archive Film Prods., Inc.
Broad Street Prods.
CBS News Archives
Film Bank
Fish Films, Inc.
Forsher (James) Prods. & Archives, Inc.
March of Time
Petrified Films, Inc.
Saint Paul Pub. Lib., Film & Video Ctr.
Spectral Comms.
Timesteps Prods., Inc.
Twentieth Century-Fox Movietonews
White Janssen, Inc.

Theaters (Drive-in)
Film Bank
Petrified Films, Inc.

Theaters (Germany)
Goethe Institute Atlanta

Theaters (Motion picture)
Blackwood (Christian) Prods., Inc.
Petrified Films, Inc.
Prelinger Assoc., Inc.
Spectral Comms.
TV Ontario

Theme parks
Preview Media
See also Amusement parks

Theologians
Natl. Archives (RG 200)

Thermometers
CBS News Archives

Thicke, Alan
Spectral Comms.

Think tanks
Cinema Guild

Third World
Film Search
Public Interest Video Network

Third World (Contemporary issues)
Boston Comm. Access & Prog. Found.
DEC Film & Video

Deep Dish TV
Johns Hopkins Univ./Population Comm. Svcs.
Maryknoll Fathers & Brothers
Mass Media Ministries
New Time Films, Inc.
Oxfam America
Richter Productions

Third World (History and culture)
DEC Film & Video
Idera Films
Natl. Archives (RG 200)
New Day Films
Rockefeller Arch. Ctr.
United Nations Ctr. for Human Settlements
White Janssen, Inc.

Thomas, Betty
Spectral Comms.

Thomas, Danny
Banks Film Library
MacDonald, J. Fred
Natl. Archives (RG 47)
Shokus Video
Spectral Comms.

Thomas, James ("Son")
Univ. of Miss., Ctr. for Study of Southern Culture

Thomas, Lowell
New York Pub. Lib., Rare Books & Manuscripts Div.

Thomas, Marlo
Spectral Comms.

Thomas, Matthew
Long Beach Mus. of Art

Thomas, Norman M.
Duke Univ., Perkins Lib.

Thomas, Willie
Rhapsody Films, Inc.

Thompson, Bobby
Rhapsody Films, Inc.

Thompson, Polly
Amer. Foundation for the Blind

Thompson, Rewi
Southern Calif. Inst. of Architecture

Thornton, Big Mama
Southern Calif. Blues Soc.

Thousand Islands, N.Y.
New York State Dept. of Econ. Devel.

Threadgill, Kenneth
Univ. of Tex. at Austin, Barker Tex. Hist. Ctr.

Three Mile Island, Pa. (History)
Electric Power Research Institute
Natl. Archives (RG 220)
Petrified Films, Inc.
State Hist. Soc. of Iowa
U.S. Council for Energy Awareness

Three Mile Island, President's Commission Investigating the Accident at
Natl. Archives (RG 220)

Three Stooges
Archive Film Prods., Inc.
Banks Film Library
Film Bank
Moviecraft, Inc.

Shokus Video

Thunder Bay, Ontario (History and culture)
Archives of Ontario

Thunderbirds (U.S. Air Force)
Energy Productions
Hayes Prods., Inc.
Natl. Archives (RG 342)
San Diego Aerospace Museum

Tiber River, Italy
Petrified Films, Inc.

Tibet (History and culture)
Acad. of Nat. Sci. of Phila. Lib.
Office of Tibet
Wheaton Coll., Billy Graham Ctr.

Tibetan Buddhism
See Religion (Tibetan Buddhism)

Tice, George
Port Washington Pub. Lib.

Ticker tape machines
Petrified Films, Inc.

Ticker tape parades
See Parades (Ticker tape)

Ticket counters
TV Ontario

Tickets
CBS News Archives
Petrified Films, Inc.

Tidal power
See Energy (Tidal power)

Tidepools
Cinenet (Cinema Network)
Film Bank
Video Tape Library, Ltd.

Tides
Jewell (Stuart) Productions
Twentieth Century-Fox Movietonews

Tiflis, U.S.S.R. (History and culture)
Armenian Film Foundation

Tigerlilies
Energy Productions

Tigerman, Stanley
Mus. of Contemporary Art
Southern Calif. Inst. of Architecture

Tigers
British Info. Svcs., Radio & TV Div.
Devillier Donegan Ent.
Grinberg (Sherman) Film Libraries (West)
Kesser Stock Footage Library
Miller (David Lee) Prods.
Minnesota Zoo
Petrified Films, Inc.
TV Ontario

Tigris River, Asia (History and culture)
Ocean Earth Constr. and Dev. Corp.

Tijuana, Mexico
Petrified Films, Inc.

Tijuana, Mexico (History and culture)
Archive Film Prods., Inc.
Petrified Films, Inc.

Tilden, Bill
Archive Film Prods., Inc.
Film Education Institute

Time and motion study
Prelinger Assoc., Inc.

Time capsules
Las Vegas News Bureau
Northeast Historic Film
Petrified Films, Inc.

Time-lapse cinematography
Cinenet (Cinema Network)
Dreamlight Images, Inc.
Echo Film Prods., Inc.
Energy Productions
Fabulous Footage Inc.
Film Bank
Film Search
Finley (Stuart) Inc.
Grinberg (Sherman) Film Libraries (East)
Jewell (Stuart) Productions
MacGillivray Freeman Films
Moody Inst. of Science
Moving Media
Ohio State Univ., Dept. of Photog. & Cinema
Petrified Films, Inc.
Phoenix Films & Video
Pyramid Film and Video Corp.
SF•V Intl.
Second Line Search
Slingshot Prods.
Source Stock Footage Lib., Inc.
Summit Films, Inc.

Times Square (New York City)
Energy Productions
Film Bank
Fish Films, Inc.
Rosebush Visions Corp.
Spectacolor, Inc.

Times Square (New York City) (History and culture)
Analogous Productions
Archive Film Prods., Inc.
Petrified Films, Inc.
Prelinger Assoc., Inc.

Timmins, Ontario (History and culture)
Archives of Ontario

Tinguely, Jean
Blackwood Prods., Inc.
Pennebaker Associates, Inc.

Tiny Tim
Daphne Productions, Inc.

Tires
See Automobiles (Tires)

Tiriac, Ion
U.S. Tennis Assn.

Tishler, Max
Amer. Chemical Soc.

Tissue cultures
Film Bank

Titanic (S.S.)
Archive Film Prods., Inc.
Natl. Archives of Canada

Tito, Josip Broz
Film/Audio Services, Inc.
Halcyon Days Prods.
Intl. Film Foundation
March of Time

Toads
Dreamlight Images, Inc.

Toasters
Archive Film Prods., Inc.
Petrified Films, Inc.

Prelinger Assoc., Inc.

Tobacco
Addiction Research Foundation of Ontario
Appalshop Films, Inc.
Narcotics Education, Inc.
Petrified Films, Inc.
Pyramid Film and Video Corp.
Reynolds (R.J.) Tobacco USA
See also Cigarettes; Cigars; Smokers and
    smoking; Tobacco industry

Tobacco industry
North Carolina Div. of Arch. & Hist.
Reynolds (R.J.) Tobacco USA
Varied Directions, Inc.
White Janssen, Inc.

Tobacco industry (Brazil)
Cinema Guild

Tobago (History and culture)
U.S. Committee for UNICEF

Tobey, Mark
Media Project

Tobogganing
Petrified Films, Inc.

Tock's Island, N.J. (History and culture)
New Jersey Network

Todorovich, Miro
Amer. Nuclear Society

Toffler, Alvin
Cinema Guild

Togo (History and culture)
Intl. Women's Day Video Fest.
TV Ontario

Toilets
See Bathrooms

Tojo, Hideki
Petrified Films, Inc.

Tokelu people
New Zealand Embassy Film Lib.

Tokyo
Dreamlight Images, Inc.
Farkas Studios, Ltd.
Film Bank
Japan Society, Inc. Film Center
Petrified Films, Inc.
Source Stock Footage Lib., Inc.

Tokyo (History and culture)
Archive Film Prods., Inc.
March of Time
Petrified Films, Inc.
United Nations Ctr. for Human
    Settlements

Tokyo Rose
MacDonald, J. Fred

Toledo, Ohio (History and culture)
Univ. of Toledo, Univ. Arch.

Tolkien, J.R.R.
Wheaton Coll., Wade Ctr.

Tolstoy, Alexandria
Inst. for Psychoanalysis

Tolstoy, Leo
Archive Film Prods., Inc.

Hoover Institution

Tomatoes
Energy Productions
TV Ontario

Tomatoes (Canning)
TV Ontario

**Tomb of the Unknown Soldier (Arc de
    Triomphe, Paris)**
Petrified Films, Inc.

**Tomb of the Unknown Soldier
    (Washington, D.C.)**
Analogous Productions
Natl. Archives (RG 111)
Petrified Films, Inc.
Twentieth Century-Fox Movietonews

Tombs
CBS News Archives
Film Bank
Jewell (Stuart) Productions
Petrified Films, Inc.

Tombstones
See Cemeteries and graves

Tomkins, Margaret
Media Project

Tomlin, Lily
Spectral Comms.

Tomography
Rosebush Visions Corp.
See also CAT scans

Tonga
Yue-Sai Kan, Inc.

Tons of Fun (Comedians)
Streamline Film Archives

Tool and die making
Baylor Univ., Texas Coll.
TV Ontario

Tools
CBS News Archives
Intl. Film Bureau
Twentieth Century-Fox Movietonews

Topanga Canyon, Calif.
Petrified Films, Inc.

Topeka, Kans. (History and culture)
Kansas State Historical Society
MacDonald, J. Fred

Topo Gigio
Univision Television Network

Topology
Intl. Film Bureau, Inc.

Torches
CBS News Archives

Torme, Mel
Archive Film Prods., Inc.
Daphne Productions, Inc.
Pathé Pictures, Inc.

Tornadoes
Film Bank
MacDonald, J. Fred
Missouri Hist. Soc.
Natl. Oceanic & Atmospheric Admin.
Twentieth Century-Fox Movietonews

See also Disasters; Hurricanes;
    Meteorology; Storms; Weather

Toronto, Ontario
Departures, Inc.
Film Bank
Natl. Archives of Canada
Preview Media
TV Ontario

Toronto, Ontario (History and culture)
Archives of Ontario
CITY Pulse Library
Canadian Filmmakers Dist. Centre
DEC Film & Video
First Run/Icarus Films, Inc.
Groupe Intervention Video
Natl. Archives of Canada
Ontario Film Institute

Torpedoes
Natl. Archives (RG 24)
Natl. Archives (RG 200)

Torres, Augusto
Santa Barbara Mus. of Art

Tortoises
Energy Productions
Film Bank

Torture
Amnesty Intl. USA
New Time Films, Inc.

Toscanini, Arturo
Archive Film Prods., Inc.
Camera Three Prods., Inc.

Totem poles
Film Bank
Petrified Films, Inc.
Sitka Natl. Hist. Park

Touchdowns
Film Bank
See also Football

Touconettes
Di Sesso (Moe) Wild Life Film Lib.

Tourism and tourists
Ackerman-Black Prods., Inc.
Allen (John E.) Inc.
Archives of Ontario
Arkansas Dept. of Parks & Tourism
Arkansas History Commission
Bishop Mus., Visual Coll.
Bradley/McAfee Public Relations
Brekke Television Prods.
CBS News Archives
Center for Cuban Studies
Century Video Services, Inc.
Cine-Mark
Cineworks Prods. Inc.
Colorado Historical Society
Creative Video, Inc.
Devillier Donegan Ent.
Dobbs (Jeff) Prods.
Elfstrom-Hilmer Prods.
Energy Productions
Farkas Studios, Ltd.
Filmoteca de la UNAM
Florida State Archives
Illinois State Hist. Lib.
Japan Natl. Tourist Organization
Kentucky Dept. of Libraries & Archives
Las Vegas News Bureau
Metro Communications, Inc.
Montana Dept. of Commerce
Natl. Archives (RG 48)

Natl. Archives (RG 79)
Natl. Parks & Conservation Assn.
Navajo Nation Library System
New Mexico State Records Ctr. & Arch.
New York State Dept. of Econ. Devel.
New Zealand Embassy Film Lib.
North Carolina Div. of Arch. & Hist.
Northstar Prods.
Petrified Films, Inc.
Postcards Unlimited
Prelinger Assoc., Inc.
Prov. Arch. of Alberta
Prov. Arch. of Newfoundland & Labrador
Site Productions
Sonoma Video Productions
Spalla (Rick) Video Prods.
TV Ontario
Tourism Yukon
Université Laval, Cinémathèque
Utah State Hist. Soc.
Utah Travel Council
Virginia Div. of Tourism
Wallen (Dick) Prods.
Washington State Archives
See also Travel

Tournament of Roses
Everett Pub. Lib., N.W. Hist. Coll.
Goal Prod., Tourn. of Roses Film Lib.
Ohio State Univ., Dept. of Photog. &
    Cinema
Oregon Hist. Soc.
Petrified Films, Inc.
Univ. of Ill. Urbana-Champaign, Univ.
    Arch.
White Janssen, Inc.
Zielinski Productions, Inc.

Tower of London
Petrified Films, Inc.

Towers
CBS News Archives
Film Bank

Towers (Clock)
Dreamlight Images, Inc.

Town meetings
CBS News Archives
Univ. of Vermont, Bailey/Howe Lib.

Town squares
Cineworks Prods. Inc.
Hi-Tech Productions

Towns
Airline Film & TV Promotions
Allen (John E.) Inc.
British Info. Svcs., Radio & TV Div.
Cinenet (Cinema Network)
Film Bank
Film Search
Hearst Metrotone News
Independent Media Communications
Moving Media
Natl. Archives of Canada
Natl. Archives/Natl. AV Ctr.
Petrified Films, Inc.
Snyder (Bill) Films, Inc.
State Hist. Soc. of Wisconsin
Stegman Productions
Stock House
Summit Films, Inc.
TV Ontario
Telltales Associates Inc.
Texas Tech Univ., Southwest Coll.
Twentieth Century-Fox Movietonews
Vermont Hist. Soc.
White Janssen, Inc.
Wings Wildlife Prods. Inc.

NOTE: Access policies, availability and restrictions vary for each source. Please read each entry in full. Always consult "General Film and
Videotape Collections" (page 599); these comprehensive collections contain material on every conceivable subject.

See also Cities; specific towns

Towns (Desert)
Petrified Films, Inc.

Towns (Ghost)
Colorado Historical Society
KD Enterprises Prods.
Montana Dept. of Commerce
Petrified Films, Inc.
Summit Films, Inc.

Towns (Mining)
Natl. Archives (RG 70)
Petrified Films, Inc.
Summit Films, Inc.
Video Tape Library, Ltd.

Townsend, Dr. Francis
March of Time

Townsend, Robert
Spectral Comms.

Townshend, Peter
Cinema Guild

Toxic waste
Appalshop Films, Inc.
Bullfrog Films, Inc.
DEC Film & Video
Downtown Community TV Ctr.
Greenpeace, U.S.A.
Natl. Assn. of Conservation Dists.
Nuclear Free Zone Registry
Richter Productions
Southwest Prods., Inc.
State Hist. Soc. of Iowa
Video Tape Library, Ltd.
See also Ecology; Pollution

Toy stores
TV Ontario

Toynbee, Arnold Joseph
Smith (Margaret Chase) Lib. Ctr.

Toys
CBS News Archives
Film Bank
TV-UNAM
UNICEF, Div. Info. & Pub. Aff.
Video Resources N.Y., Inc.
West Virginia Dept. of Culture & Hist.

Track and field
Amer. Motion Pictures
Analogous Productions
Archive Film Prods., Inc.
Athletic Institute
Auburn University Archives
Dreamlight Images, Inc.
Jalbert Productions
NCAA Productions
Petrified Films, Inc.
Spalla (Rick) Video Prods.
Sportsfilm
TV Ontario
Twentieth Century-Fox Movietonews
U.S. Olympic Comm.
Video Tape Library, Ltd.

Track and field (College)
Oregon State Univ., Archives
Univ. of Kansas

Track and field (Instruction)
NCAA Productions
Natl. Assn. for Sport & Phys. Ed.

Tractor pulling
Cinenet (Cinema Network)
Diamond P. Sports

Tractor-trailers

Petrified Films, Inc.

Tractors
CBS News Archives
Dreamlight Images, Inc.
Energy Productions
Film Bank
Natl. Archives (RG 337)
Petrified Films, Inc.

Tracy, Dick
Archive Film Prods., Inc.

Tracy, Spencer
Halcyon Days Prods.
UCLA Film & Television Archive

Trading posts
Film Bank

Trading stamps
See Stamps (Trading)

Trafalgar Square, London
Film Bank
TV Ontario

Trafalgar Square, London (History and culture)
Archive Film Prods., Inc.
Petrified Films, Inc.

Traffic
Amer. Motion Pictures
British Info. Svcs., Radio & TV Div.
CBS News Archives
Cinenet (Cinema Network)
Dreamlight Images, Inc.
Energy Productions
Farkas Studios, Ltd.
Film Bank
Film Search
Fish Films, Inc.
Hi-Tech Productions
March of Time
Nei-Ali Prods.
Petrified Films, Inc.
Source Stock Footage Lib., Inc.
Spectral Comms.
State Hist. Soc. of Iowa
Stock Shots
Transportation Research Board
Twentieth Century-Fox Movietonews
United Nations Ctr. for Human
  Settlements
Video Genesis, Inc.
Video I-D, Inc.
Video Tape Library, Ltd.
See also Automobiles; Streets and roads;
  Highways

Traffic lights
Petrified Films, Inc.
Prelinger Assoc., Inc.

Traffic safety
See Driver education

Trailers (Motion picture)
Allen (John E.) Inc.
Archive Film Prods., Inc.
Budget Films Inc.
Cinema Arts Assoc.
Dettlaff, Alois F. Sr.
Em Gee Film Library
Encore Entertainment
Film Bank
Filmack Studios
Forsher (James) Prods. & Archives, Inc.
Intl. Al Jolson Society
Morcraft Films
Moviecraft, Inc.
Movietime, Inc. Archives
Prelinger Assoc., Inc.
Prov. Arch. of Newfoundland & Labrador

Streamline Film Archives
Trailers on Tape
Video Resources N.Y., Inc.
Williams (Wade) Prods.

Trailers and trailer courts
March of Time
Prelinger Assoc., Inc.

Training films and videotapes
AMA Film/Video
Academy of Health Sciences, U.S. Army
Altschul Group
Aluminum Assn.
Amateur Athletic Foundation
Amer. Airlines
Amer. Alliance for Health, Phys. Ed., Rec.
  & Dance Arch.
Amer. Bakers Assn.
Amer. Concrete Inst.
Amer. Correctional Assn.
Amer. Dental Assn.
Amer. Heart Assn.
Amer. Inst. of Baking
Amer. Jail Assn.
Amer. Public Transit Assn.
Amer. Pulpwood Assn., Inc.
Amer. Soc. of Clin. Path. Press
Amer. Trucking Assn.
Anheuser-Busch Cos., Inc.
Archives of Ontario
Assoc. Gen. Contractors of America
BNA Communications, Inc.
Belove, Laiserin & Walsh
Borough of Manhattan Comm. Coll.
Boston Family Inst.
Bray Studios, Inc.
CRM Films L.P.
Calif. Highway Patrol Acad. Media Center
Campus Film Distributors Corp.
Canadian Coast Guard College Library
Canadian Film Institute
Carousel Film & Video
Carter (C.L.) Jr. & Assoc., Inc.
Channel L Working Group
Coe Film Assoc., Inc.
Columbia Univ., Teachers College
Computer Television Group, Inc.
Coronet/MTI Film & Video
Council for Exceptional Children
Courter Films & Assoc.
Culinary Inst. of America
Cunningham Dance Foundation
Dartnell
Edison Electric Institute
Experimental Aircraft Assn.
FAA Technical Center
Films Incorporated
Gypsum Assn.
Hewlett-Packard Co.
High/Scope Educ. Res. Found.
Inst. of Financial Education
Intl. Aviation Publishers, Inc.
Lawren Prods., Inc.
Minn. Citizens Counc. on Crime & Justice
Minn. Dept. of Public Safety Film Lib.
Modern Talking Picture Service
Movietime, Inc. Archives
Natl. Archives (RG 29)
Natl. Archives (RG 70)
Natl. Archives (RG 75)
Natl. Archives (RG 171)
Natl. Archives (RG 178)
Natl. Archives (RG 179)
Natl. Archives (RG 306)
Natl. Archives (RG 334)
Natl. Archives (RG 374)
Natl. Assn. of Conservation Dists.
Natl. Assn. of Convenience Stores
Natl. Assn. of Home Builders
Natl. Assn. of Secondary Schl. Principals
Natl. Coun. of Juv. & Fam. Court Judges
Natl. Funeral Directors Assn.
Natl. Glass Assn.
Natl. Press Photographers Assn., Inc.

Natl. Railway Historical Soc.
Natl. Restaurant Assn.
Natl. School Boards Assn.
New York City Dept. of Rec. & Info.
  Svcs.
New York Hosp.-Cornell Med. Ctr., Arch.
Nissan Motor Corp. of the U.S.
Northrop Univ., Alumni Lib.
Pennsylvania State Arch.
Prelinger Assoc., Inc.
Railroad Mus. of Pa.
Read (Brooks) & Assoc.
Rehab. Inst. of Chicago
Research Press
Salenger Films Inc.
United Training Media
Univ. of Akron, Arch. of Hist. of Amer.
  Psychol.
Univ. of Tex. at Austin, Petrol. Ext. Svc.
Video Arts Inc.
Washington State Archives
Washington Univ., Brown Schl. of Soc.
  Work
Wayne State Univ., Dir. Educ. in Nursing
Women Make Movies, Inc.
See also Educational films and videotapes;
  How-to films and videotapes; Military
  training films

Trains
See Railroads

Trakas, George
Blackwood Prods., Inc.

Tramps
Film Bank

Trams
See Trolleys

Tranquilizers
Addiction Research Foundation of Ontario

Trans-Alaska pipeline
See Pipelines

Transatlantic flights
See Aviation (Transatlantic flights)

Transistors
Hewlett-Packard Co.

Transplants (Organ)
DCI Video Resources
Houston Acad. of Medicine
Johns Hopkins Univ., School of Medicine
Loma Linda Univ., Webb Lib.
Los Angeles News Service
Natl. Kidney Foundation, Inc.

Transport Workers Union
New York City Labor Film Club
Tamiment Lib./Wagner Labor Arch.

Transportation
Allen (John E.) Inc.
Analogous Productions
Calif. Dept. of Transportation
Carleton Prods. Inc.
Dreamlight Images, Inc.
Energy Productions
Film Search
Hayes Prods., Inc.
Hooper (Josh) Prods., Inc.
Moviecraft, Inc.
Natl. Archives (RG 242)
Natl. Archives of Canada
Natl. Geographic Soc. Stock Footage Lib.
Petrified Films, Inc.
Prelinger Assoc., Inc.
Regional Plan Assn.
Snyder (Bill) Films, Inc.
Timesteps Prods., Inc.
Transportation Research Board

Twentieth Century-Fox Movietonews
United Nations Ctr. for Human
    Settlements
Université Laval, Cinémathèque
Visnews Intl.
White Janssen, Inc.
See also specific forms of transportation

Transportation (Germany)
Goethe Institute Atlanta

Transportation (History of)
Amer. Public Transit Assn.
Creative Venture Films
Filmfair Communications

Transportation, Department of (U.S.)
Natl. Archives (RG 398)
Natl. Archives (Stock Film Coll.)

Transsexualism
Canadian Filmmakers Dist. Centre
Center for Marital and Sexual Studies
IMS Creative Communications
Kinsey Institute

Transvestism
Canadian Filmmakers Dist. Centre
Petrified Films, Inc.
Univ. of West Fla., Hum. Res. Vid. Lib.

Trapping
See Hunting and trapping

Trash
Campbell Films, Inc.
Memphis State Univ. Libraries

Travel
Amer. Mus. Nat. Hist. Film Arch.
Archives of Ontario
Beerger (Norman) Prods.
Budget Films Inc.
Coe Film Assoc., Inc.
Creative Video, Inc.
Departures, Inc.
Em Gee Film Library
Explorers Club
Facets Multimedia, Inc.
Film Education Institute
Film Search
Film/Audio Services, Inc.
German Language Video Ctr.
Hayes Prods., Inc.
Idaho State Library
Kentucky Dept. of Libraries & Archives
Kesser Stock Footage Library
March of Time
Moviecraft, Inc.
Natl. Archives (RG 131)
Natl. Archives (RG 242)
Natl. Film Board of Canada
Passage Home Communications
Petrified Films, Inc.
Preview Media
Prov. Arch. of British Columbia
Schiele Museum
Schomburg Ctr. for Res. in Black Culture
Second Line Search
Smithsonian Inst., Human Studies Film
    Arch.
Sonoma Video Productions
Spalla (Rick) Video Prods.
Tamarelle's Intl. Films, Ltd.
Utah Travel Council
Video-SIG
Visnews Intl.
White Janssen, Inc.
White Star Prof. Film Svcs., Inc.
Yivo Inst. for Jewish Research
Yue-Sai Kan, Inc.

See also Tourism and tourists; Travelogues

Travel agents
Film Bank

Travel Service (U.S.)
Natl. Archives (Stock Film Coll.)

Travelogues
Allen (John E.) Inc.
Amer. Airlines
Amer. Mus. Nat. Hist. Film Arch.
Archives of Ontario
Arkansas Dept. of Parks & Tourism
Arkansas History Commission
Calif. State Railroad Mus. Lib.
Chisholm (Jack) Film Productions
Chrysler Motors Corp.
Cine-Mark
Colorado Historical Society
Creative Video, Inc.
Delaware State Div. of Hist. & Cult. Aff.
Footage Inc.
Hogg, John F.
Indiana State Comm. on Public Records
Intl. Assn. of Independent Producers
Israel Broadcasting Service
Italian Cultural Institute
Jalbert Productions
Japan Natl. Tourist Organization
Jewell (Stuart) Productions
Las Vegas News Bureau
Nan Hai (U.S.A.) Co., Inc.
Natl. Archives (RG 200)
Natl. Archives of Canada
Natl. Council of Amer.-Soviet Friendship
Natl. Geographic Soc. Stock Footage Lib.
Natl. Parks & Conservation Assn.
Natl. Railway Historical Soc.
New Mexico State Records Ctr. & Arch.
Ohio Hist. Soc.
Prelinger Assoc., Inc.
Prov. Arch. of Alberta
Quenzer Driscoll Dawson, Inc.
Snyder (Bill) Films, Inc.
Sobek Productions
Streamline Film Archives
Studebaker Natl. Museum
Summit Films, Inc.
Tourism Yukon
Twentieth Century-Fox Movietonews
Virginia Div. of Tourism
Volkswagen of America, Inc.
Washington State Archives
Yukon Archives

Treadmills
Film Bank

Treasure (Underwater)
Ocean Images
SF•V Intl.

Treasury Department (U.S.)
March of Time
Natl. Archives (RG 39)
Natl. Archives (RG 53)
Natl. Archives (RG 56)

Treaties
CBS News Archives
Center for Pacific Northwest Studies
Natl. Archives (RG 306)

Tree houses
Film Bank

Trees
British Info. Svcs., Radio & TV Div.
Bullfrog Films, Inc.
CBS News Archives

Charisma Prods., Ltd./Visual Motion
Dreamlight Images, Inc.
Echo Film Prods., Inc.
Energy Productions
Film Bank
Indiana State Comm. on Public Records
Jewell (Stuart) Productions
Oregon State Univ., Archives
Petrified Films, Inc.
TV Ontario
See also Forests; specific trees

Treib, Marc
Southern Calif. Inst. of Architecture

Trelawney Estates, Jamaica
Seagram Museum

Trenton, N.J. (History and culture)
New Jersey Network

Trials
Archive Film Prods., Inc.
Film Bank
Natl. Jewish Arch. of Broadcasting
Southwest Film/Video Archives, SMU
Tucson Community Cable Corp.
Twentieth Century-Fox Movietonews
Univ. of Wis., Green Bay, Ctr. TV Prod.
See also Courtrooms

Trials (Canada)
Natl. Archives of Canada

Triathlons
Freewheelin' Films, Ltd.

Tribe, Lawrence
Amer. Enterprise Institute

Trilateral Commission
Alternative Information Network

Trilling, Diana
Pennebaker Associates, Inc.

Trinidad and Tobago
Petrified Films, Inc.

**Trinidad and Tobago (History and
culture)**
Petrified Films, Inc.
Prelinger Assoc., Inc.
U.S. Committee for UNICEF

Trinity Church (New York City)
Broad Street Prods.
Unicorn Projects

Trolleys
Archive Film Prods., Inc.
CBS News Archives
Dreamlight Images, Inc.
Farkas Studios, Ltd.
Film Bank
Hayes Prods., Inc.
Natl. Archives of Canada
Natl. Railway Historical Soc.
Oregon Electric Railway Hist. Soc.
Petrified Films, Inc.
Prelinger Assoc., Inc.
Prov. Arch. of British Columbia
San Francisco Maritime Natl. Hist. Park
Timesteps Prods., Inc.

Trophies
Petrified Films, Inc.

Tropical scenes
Ackerman-Black Prods., Inc.
Bishop Mus., Visual Coll.

Brekke Television Prods.
Caribbean Images, Ltd.
Channel Sea Television
Cinenet (Cinema Network)
Creative Video, Inc.
Dittrich (Scott) Films
Dobovan Productions, Inc.
Energy Productions
Film Bank
Forsher (James) Prods. & Arch. Inc.
Hawaii Public Broadcasting Authority
Intl. Assn. of Independent Producers
Mountain Video Associates
Pacific Focus Inc.
Passage Home Communications
Peak Productions, Inc.
Petrified Films, Inc.
Quenzer Driscoll Dawson, Inc.
Video Concepts, Inc.
Warner (Dane) Photography

Trotsky, Leon
Archive Film Prods., Inc.
Grinberg (Sherman) Film Libraries (West)
Hoover Institution

Trout
Cinenet (Cinema Network)
Echo Film Prods., Inc.
Film Bank
Indiana State Comm. on Public Records
New Mexico State Records Ctr. & Arch.
Summit Films, Inc.
TV Ontario

Truant officers
Univ. of Toronto, AV Lib.

Truck pulling
Diamond P. Sports

Truck stops
Film Bank

Trucks
Allen (John E.) Inc.
Amer. Truck Historical Society
Amer. Trucking Assn.
Archive Film Prods., Inc.
CBS News Archives
Dreamlight Images, Inc.
Energy Productions
Film Bank
General Motors Corp.
Hooper (Josh) Prods., Inc.
Petrified Films, Inc.
Prelinger Assoc., Inc.
Source Stock Footage Lib., Inc.
Studebaker Natl. Museum
TV Ontario
Video Genesis, Inc.

Trucks (Dump)
Energy Productions
Film Bank
Petrified Films, Inc.

Trucks (Monster)
Cinenet (Cinema Network)
Energy Productions

Trucks (Newspaper)
Petrified Films, Inc.
Prelinger Assoc., Inc.

Trucks (Sanitation)
Petrified Films, Inc.

Trudeau, Pierre
Natl. Archives of Canada

NOTE: Access policies, availability and restrictions vary for each source. Please read each entry in full. Always consult "General Film and Videotape Collections" (page 599); these comprehensive collections contain material on every conceivable subject.

Truffaut, François
Camera Three Prods., Inc.

Trujillo, Rafael Leonidas
Archive Film Prods., Inc.

Truk Island, Micronesia
Passage Home Communications

Truman, Harry S
Halcyon Days Prods.
Hearst Metrotone News
Illinois State Hist. Lib.
MacDonald, J. Fred
Natl. Archives (RG 48)
Natl. Archives (RG 80)
Natl. Archives (RG 111)
Natl. Archives (RG 200)
Natl. Archives (RG 342)
New York City Dept. of Rec. & Info.
  Svcs.
Petrified Films, Inc.
Prelinger Assoc., Inc.
Roosevelt (Franklin D.) Lib.
Truman (Harry S) Library
Twentieth Century-Fox Movietonews
Univ. of Ill. Urbana-Champaign, Univ.
  Arch.
West Virginia Dept. of Culture & Hist.

Trumpets
Film Bank

Tschumi, Bernard
Southern Calif. Inst. of Architecture

Tsipis, Kosta
Cambridge Documentary Films, Inc.

Tsutakawa, George
Media Project

Tuataras people
New Zealand Embassy Film Lib.

Tuberculosis
Natl. Library of Medicine

Tubing (sport)
Summit Films, Inc.

Tubman, Harriet
Pyramid Film and Video Corp.

Tucker, Marcia
Video Data Bank

Tucker, Sophie
Banks Film Library

Tucson, Ariz.
Energy Productions
Preview Media
Source Stock Footage Lib., Inc.

Tug-of-wars (Elephant)
Petrified Films, Inc.

Tug-of-wars (Native American)
Petrified Films, Inc.

Tugboats
See Boats and boating (Tugboats)

Tuhoe people
New Zealand Embassy Film Lib.

Tuktoyaktuk, Northwest Territories
TV Ontario

Tulips
Petrified Films, Inc.

Tulsa, Okla. (History and culture)
Petrified Films, Inc.

Tumbleweeds
Energy Productions
Film Bank
Petrified Films, Inc.

Tumors
Nassau Comm. Coll. Lib.

Tunisia (History and culture)
Archive Film Prods., Inc.
Johns Hopkins Univ./Population Comm.
  Svcs.
Middle East Institute
Prelinger Assoc., Inc.
TV Ontario

Tunnel vortexes
Film Bank

Tunnels
Archive Film Prods., Inc.
CBS News Archives
Film Bank
Image Bank
Natl. Archives (RG 200)
Petrified Films, Inc.
Port Authority of New York & New Jersey
Prelinger Assoc., Inc.
Twentieth Century-Fox Movietonews

Tunnels (Construction)
Natl. Archives (RG 77)
Natl. Archives (RG 200)
Port Authority of New York & New Jersey
Univ. of Mich., Mich. Hist. Colls.

Tunney, Gene
Grinberg (Sherman) Film Libraries (West)

Tupamaros (Uruguay)
Cinema Guild

Turbines
CBS News Archives

Turkana people
Smithsonian Inst., Human Studies Film
  Arch.

Turkey
British Info. Svcs., Radio & TV Div.
Canadian Broadcasting Corp.
Film Bank
Intl. Film Foundation

Turkey (History and culture)
Allen (John E.) Inc.
Archive Film Prods., Inc.
Armenian Film Foundation
Film/Audio Services, Inc.
March of Time
Natl. Archives (RG 24)
TV Ontario
UNICEF, Div. Info. & Pub. Aff.

Turkey callers
Woods N' Water Television Series

Turkeys
Film Bank
Hearst Metrotone News
Indiana State Comm. on Public Records
Woods N' Water Television Series

Turnbull, William
Albright-Knox Art Gallery

Turner, Big Joe
Southern Calif. Blues Soc.

Turner, Ike and Tina
Daphne Productions, Inc.

Turner, Joe
Pathé Pictures, Inc.

Rhapsody Films, Inc.

Turner, Joseph Mallard William
Amer. Federation of the Arts

Turner, Kathleen
Spectral Comms.

Turner, Lana
Natl. Archives/Natl. AV Ctr.

Turner, Ted
Spectral Comms.

Turner, Tina
Daphne Productions, Inc.
Spectral Comms.
UPA Prods. of America
Univision Television Network

Turnstiles
CBS News Archives

Turpin, Ben
Archive Film Prods., Inc.

Turtles
Bullfrog Films, Inc.
Echo Film Prods., Inc.
Jewell (Stuart) Productions
Summit Films, Inc.
TV Ontario

Tuscany, Italy (History and culture)
Archive Film Prods., Inc.

Tutankhamen, King
Jewell (Stuart) Productions
Middle East Institute
Unicorn Projects

Tutshenshini River, Alaska
Sobek Productions

Tuttle, Westle
Pathé Pictures, Inc.

Tutu, Desmond
Archives of Ontario
King (Dr. Martin Luther, Jr.) Ctr.
Schomburg Ctr. for Res. in Black Culture

Tuxedomoon (Rock and roll band)
Target Video

Tuxedos
Video Catalogue Co., Inc.

Twain, Mark
Twain (Mark) Memorial

Twelve-step programs
Al-Anon Family Group Headquarters, Inc.
Hazelden Found. Educ. Materials
Motivational Media, Inc.
Narcotics Education, Inc.

Twins
UCLA Behavioral Sci. Media Lab.
Video Farm

Twist, The
See Dance and dancing (Twist)

Tworkov, Jack
Blackwood Prods., Inc.
Electronic Arts Intermix
Video Data Bank

Tycoons
Archive Film Prods., Inc.

Tyler, Keith
Ohio State Univ., Dept. of Photog. &
  Cinema

Tynan, Kenneth
Baker (Fred) Film & Video Co.

Typesetting
Prelinger Assoc., Inc.

Typewriters and typists
Archive Film Prods., Inc.
CBS News Archives
Film Bank
Petrified Films, Inc.
Prelinger Assoc., Inc.

Typhoid
Historical Health Film Coll.

Typing classes
Film Bank

Tyrone, Ontario (History and culture)
Archives of Ontario

Tyson, Mike
Daphne Productions, Inc.

UAW
See United Automobile Workers (UAW)

UFOs
See Unidentified flying objects (UFOs)

UFW
See United Farm Workers of America
  (UFW)

UMWA
See United Mine Workers of America
  (UMWA)

UNESCO
Natl. Archives (RG 59)

USDA
See Agriculture, Department of (U.S.)

U-boats
Archive Film Prods., Inc.
Natl. Archives (RG 24)
See also Submarines

U-2 incident (1960)
Natl. Archives (RG 64)

Udaipur, India
Petrified Films, Inc.

Uecker, Gunther
Blackwood Prods., Inc.

Uelsmann, Jerry
Port Washington Pub. Lib.

Uganda (Contemporary issues)
Oxfam America

Uganda (History and culture)
Africa Inland Mission
Archive Film Prods., Inc.
Prestige Film Corp.
Salvation Army, Natl. Comm. Dept.
Smithsonian Inst., Human Studies Film
  Arch.

Uggams, Leslie
Archive Film Prods., Inc.

Ukeleles
Archive Film Prods., Inc.

Ukrainian Canadians
Canadian Filmmakers Dist. Centre

Ullmann, Liv
Daphne Productions, Inc.
Randolph (A. Philip) Educ. Fund

UNICEF, Div. Info. & Pub. Aff.

Ulster, Northern Ireland (History and culture)
Archive Film Prods., Inc.

Umbrellas
CBS News Archives
Energy Productions
Film Bank

Umpires
Archive Film Prods., Inc.
Athletic Institute

Underground films and videotapes
See Experimental films and videotapes

Underground press
Cinema Guild
Payne, Roz

Underground trains
See Subways

Undertakers
See Morticians and mortuaries

Underwater footage
Archive Film Prods., Inc.
Brekke Television Prods.
CBS News Archives
Caribbean Images, Ltd.
Cousteau Society
Creative Video, Inc.
Dreamlight Images, Inc.
Energy Productions
Film Bank
Film Search
Gornick Film Productions
Grinberg (Sherman) Film Libraries (West)
KD Enterprises Prods.
Kesser Stock Footage Library
Marineland of Florida
Mass. Inst. of Tech., MIT Museum
Moonlight Productions
Mountain Video Associates
NBC News Video Archives
Natl. Geographic Soc. Stock Footage Lib.
Natl. Oceanic & Atmospheric Admin.
Ocean Images
Passage Home Communications
Petrified Films, Inc.
SF•V Intl.
Simon (Jeff) Productions
Sonoma Video Productions
Source Stock Footage Lib., Inc.
Univ. of Wis., Green Bay, Ctr. TV Prod.
Video Concepts, Inc.
Video Mgmt. Systems
Video Tape Library, Ltd.
Zielinski Productions, Inc.
See also Marine life

Underwater treasure
See Treasure (Underwater)

Unemployment
Allen (John E.) Inc.
CBS News Archives
Film Bank
Idera Films
Labor Video Project
March of Time
Native Amer. Pub. Broad. Cons.
Natl. Archives (RG 29)
Natl. Archives (RG 47)
Natl. Archives (RG 119)
Natl. Archives (RG 378)
Natl. Archives of Canada
Natl. Archives/Natl. AV Ctr.

Petrified Films, Inc.
Taminent Lib./Wagner Labor Arch.

Unger, Oliver
Univ. of Wyoming, Amer. Heritage Ctr.

Ungers, O.M.
Blackwood Prods., Inc.

Unicorns
Forsher (James) Prods. & Archives, Inc.

Unicycles
Film Bank

Unidentified flying objects (UFOs)
Analogous Productions
CBS News Archives
Fry, Daniel W.
Natl. Archives (RG 341)
Petrified Films, Inc.
Pyramid Film and Video Corp.
See also Spacecraft and spaceships

Unification Church
See Religion (Unification Church)

Unions
See Labor history; Labor issues; Strikes; specific unions

Unitas, Johnny
Archive Film Prods., Inc.
NFL Films, Inc.
Wesleyan Cinema Archives

United Arab Emirates
British Info. Svcs., Radio & TV Div.

United Arab Emirates (History and culture)
Middle East Institute

United Automobile Workers (UAW)
General Motors Corp.
Smithsonian Inst., NMAH, Div. Polit. Hist.
Tamiment Lib./Wagner Labor Arch.
Wayne State Univ., Arch. Labor & Urb. Aff.

United Automobile Workers (UAW) (Canada)
Calif. Newsreel

United Electrical, Radio & Machine Workers of America (UE)
Natl. Archives of Canada
Prelinger Assoc., Inc.
Southern Calif. Lib. for Soc. Stud. & Res.

United Farm Workers of America (UFW)
Committee for Labor Access
Estuary Press
KCRA-TV
Mus. & Hist. Div., City of Sacramento
Payne, Roz
San Francisco Bay Area TV News Arch.
United Farm Workers of America (UFW)

United Kingdom
Beerger (Norman) Prods.
British Info. Svcs.
Canadian Broadcasting Corp.
Cousteau Society
Creative Video, Inc.
Dorn (Larry) Associates
Dreamlight Images, Inc.
Film Bank
Gornick Film Prods.

Kesser Stock Footage Lib.
Preview Media
Stock House
TV Ontario
Video Ventures Prods.
World Monitor
Yue-Sai Kan, Inc.

United Kingdom (Black people in)
DEC Film & Video

United Kingdom (History and culture)
Allen (John E.) Inc.
Archive Film Prods., Inc.
Belmont Abbey College
British Info. Svcs.
Churchill (Winston) Memorial and Library
Emory Univ., Spec. Coll.
Film/Audio Services, Inc.
Intl. Film Foundation
March of Time
Natl. Archives (RG 18)
Natl. Archives (RG 24)
Natl. Archives (RG 59)
Natl. Archives (RG 80)
Natl. Archives (RG 96)
Natl. Archives (RG 111)
Natl. Archives (RG 171)
Natl. Archives (RG 200)
Natl. Archives (RG 207)
Natl. Archives (RG 208)
Natl. Archives (RG 342)
Natl. Archives of Canada
Natl. Archives/Natl. AV Ctr.
Oregon Hist. Soc.
Petrified Films, Inc.
Purdue Univ., Public Affairs Video Arch.
Pyramid Film & Video Corp.
Roosevelt (Franklin D.) Library
Spalla (Rick) Video Prods.
Third World Newsreel
Twentieth Century-Fox Movietonews
UCLA Film & Television Archive
Unicorn Projects
United Nations Ctr. for Human Settlements
Univ. of Tex. at Austin, Ransom Hum. Res. Ctr., Photo. Coll.
Univ. of Toronto, AV Lib.
Villon Films
Visnews Intl.
World Monitor
Worldwide Television News

United Methodists
See Religion (United Methodist)

United Mine Workers of America (UMWA)
Appalshop Films, Inc.
West Virginia Dept. of Culture & Hist.

United Nations
Analogous Productions
Archive Film Prods., Inc.
CBS News Archives
Downtown Community TV Ctr.
Film Bank
Hoover Institution
MacArthur (Gen. Douglas) Memorial
MacDonald, J. Fred
Natl. Archives (RG 59)
Natl. Archives of Canada
New York City Dept. of Rec. & Info. Svcs.
Petrified Films, Inc.
Roosevelt (Franklin D.) Lib.
Tennessee State Lib. & Arch.
Twentieth Century-Fox Movietonews
UNICEF, Div. Info. & Pub. Aff.
United Nations, Visual Materials Lib.

Univ. of Mich., Mich. Hist. Colls.
See also League of Nations

United Nations Relief and Rehabilitation Agency (UNRRA)
United Nations, Visual Materials Lib.

United Packinghouse Workers of America
MacDonald, J. Fred
State Hist. Soc. of Iowa

United States history (Re-creations)
Film Bank
Lib. of Congress, M/B/RS
MacDonald, J. Fred
Natl. Archives (RG 18)
Natl. Archives (RG 59)
Natl. Archives (RG 116)
Natl. Archives (RG 178)
Natl. Archives/Natl. AV Ctr.
New Jersey Network
North Carolina Div. of Arch. & Hist.
Petrified Films, Inc.
Prelinger Assoc., Inc.
Producers Library Service
Southern Calif. Lib. for Soc. Stud. & Res.
Twentieth Century-Fox Movietonews
Univ. of Wis., Green Bay, Ctr. TV Prod.

United States Information Agency
Natl. Archives (RG 306)

United States-China relations
Southern Calif. Lib. for Soc. Stud. & Res.
Univ. of Mich., Mich. Hist. Colls.

United States-Cuba relations
Estuary Press
MacDonald, J. Fred
Natl. Archives (RG 64)
See also Bay of Pigs (1961); Cuba (History and culture); Cuban missile crisis (1962)

United States-Japan relations
Perlmutter (Alvin H.) Inc.

United States-Latin America relations
Americas in Transition/Fossil Films
Camino Film Projects
DEC Film & Video
Democracy in Communication
Hoover Institution
Natl. Archives (RG 229)
Rockefeller Arch. Ctr.

United States-Mexico relations
El Paso Community College
Notimex

United States-Soviet relations
Amer. Security Council Foundation
Center for Defense Information
Educators for Social Responsibility
Natl. Archives (RG 64)
Quest Productions Inc.
SANE/Freeze
See also Cold War; Soviet Union (History and culture)

United States-Third World relations
California Newsreel
Cambridge Documentary Films, Inc.
League of Women Voters of the U.S.

United Steel Workers
Natl. Archives of Canada

Unruh, Jesse
Calif. State Archives

NOTE: Access policies, availability and restrictions vary for each source. Please read each entry in full. Always consult "General Film and Videotape Collections" (page 599); these comprehensive collections contain material on every conceivable subject.

Upholstery
Prelinger Assoc., Inc.

Uranium
Amer. Nuclear Society
Finley (Stuart) Inc.
MacDonald, J. Fred
Petrified Films, Inc.
See also Mining (Uranium)

Uranus
NASA, Johnson Space Ctr., Film & Video
Dist. Lib.

Urban affairs
Intermedia Arts Minnesota
Kartemquin Films
U.S. Committee for UNICEF

Urban planning
Amer. Institute of Architects
Channel L Working Group
Finley (Stuart) Inc.
Natl. Archives (RG 200)
Natl. Archives (RG 207)
Natl. Assn. of Conservation Dists.
Petrified Films, Inc.
Prelinger Assoc., Inc.
Regional Plan Assn.
Southern Calif. Inst. of Architecture
Unicorn Projects
United Nations, Visual Materials Lib.

Urban planning (Germany)
German Info. Ctr.
Goethe Institute Atlanta

Urban renewal
KCRA-TV
MacDonald, J. Fred
Mus. & Hist. Div., City of Sacramento
Natl. Archives (RG 207)
Unicorn Projects
Video Pool, Inc.

Urban renewal (Great Britain)
Emory Univ., Spec. Coll.

Urban studies
Carousel Film & Video
Cinema Guild
Film/Audio Services, Inc.
Films for the Humanities and Sciences
Université Laval, Cinémathèque

Urbanism
Amer. Institute of Architects
Bronx County Hist. Soc.
MacDonald, J. Fred

Urology
IMS Creative Communications
Milner-Fenwick, Inc.
Nassau Comm. Coll. Lib.

Uruguay
Natl. Archives (RG 59)

Uruguay (Contemporary issues)
Cinema Guild
DEC Film & Video

Uruguay (History and culture)
Archive Film Prods., Inc.
DEC Film & Video
Democracy in Communication
Latina, S.A. de C.V.
Rockefeller Arch. Ctr.
United Nations Ctr. for Human
Settlements

Used car lots
See Automobiles (Used car lots)

Ustinov, Peter

Daphne Productions, Inc.
Wesleyan Cinema Archives

Utah
Energy Prods.
First Group Comms., Inc.
Petrified Films, Inc.
Preview Media
Shell Oil Co.
Sobek Productions
Source Film & Tape Lib., Inc.
Southwest Prods., Inc.
Stimulus
Utah Travel Council
Video West
West Star Productions

Utah (History and culture)
Archive Film Prods., Inc.
Petrified Films, Inc.
Schiele Museum
Sobek Productions
Univ. of Utah, Marriott Lib.
Utah State Archives
Utah State Hist. Soc.

VISTA
Natl. Archives (RG 362)
Southwest Film/Video Archives, SMU

V-E Day
See World War II (Canada, V-E Day);
World War II (U.S., V-E Day)

V-8 engines
See Engines (V-8)

V-J Day
See World War II (U.S., V-J Day)

Vaadia, Boaz
Amer. Federation of the Arts

Vacations
Cine-Mark
Encore Video Prods., Inc.
Film/Audio Services, Inc.
Indiana State Comm. on Public Records
Kesser Stock Footage Library
March of Time
Omega Films
Prelinger Assoc., Inc.
Preview Media
Prov. Arch. of Alberta
Roosevelt (Franklin D.) Lib.
Washington State Hist. Soc.

Vaccines
Hearst Metrotone News
March of Dimes Birth Defects Found.

Vacuum cleaners
Archive Film Prods., Inc.
Petrified Films, Inc.
Prelinger Assoc., Inc.

Vail, Colo.
Preview Media

Valdéz, Daniel
Univ. of Tex. at Austin, Benson Lat. Am.
Coll.

Valdéz, Luis
United Farm Workers of America (UFW)

Valentine's Day
Energy Productions

Valentines
Archive Film Prods., Inc.

Valentino, Rudolph
Alan Twyman Presents
Archive Film Prods., Inc.

Valenzuela, Fernando
Spectral Comms.

Valium
Addiction Research Foundation of Ontario

Vallee, Rudy
Archive Film Prods., Inc.
Natl. Archives (RG 47)

Valleys
CBS News Archives
Cinenet (Cinema Network)
Dobovan Productions, Inc.
Energy Productions
Film Bank
Twentieth Century-Fox Movietonews

Values clarification
Barr Films
Carousel Film & Video
Churchill Films
Intl. Film Bureau, Inc.
Phoenix Films & Video

Vampira
Las Vegas News Bureau

Vampires
Archive Film Prods., Inc.

Van Buren, Abigail ("Dear Abby")
Fund for Human Dignity, Inc.

Van Cortlandt Manor, N.Y. (History and culture)
Rockefeller Arch. Ctr.

Van der Rohe, Mies
Blackwood Prods., Inc.
German Info. Ctr., Film Lib.
Goethe Institute Atlanta
Southern Calif. Inst. of Architecture
Unicorn Projects

Van Dongen, Helen
Villon Films

Van Doren, Mamie
Archive Film Prods., Inc.
Banks Film Library

Van Dyke, Dick
Daphne Productions, Inc.
Shokus Video
Spectral Comms.
UCLA Film & Television Archive
Univ. of Wyoming, Amer. Heritage Ctr.

Van Dyke, Willard
Cinema Guild

Van Nuys, Dorothy
Archive Film Prods., Inc.

Van Patten, Dick
Shokus Video

Van Zandt, Steven
Spectral Comms.

Vance, Vivian
Shokus Video

Vancouver, British Columbia
Departures, Inc.
Hot Shots Commercial Prods., Inc.
Preview Media
TV Ontario

Vancouver, British Columbia (History and culture)
Archive Film Prods., Inc.
Natl. Archives of Canada
Prov. Arch. of British Columbia

Voyager Co.

Vancouver Island, British Columbia (History and culture)
Univ. of Wash. Press, Multimedia Div.

Vancouver, Wash. (History and culture)
Oregon Hist. Soc.

Vandenberg, Arthur Hendrick
Univ. of Mich., Mich. Hist. Colls.

Vanderbeek, Stan
Camera Three Prods., Inc.

Vanuatu (History and culture)
Johnson (Martin & Osa) Safari Museum
Smithsonian Inst., Human Studies Film
Arch.

Varanasi, India
Petrified Films, Inc.

Vasarely, Victor
Albright-Knox Art Gallery

Vasectomies
Multi-Focus, Inc.

Vatican City
Analogous Productions
Dreamlight Images, Inc.
Film Bank
Petrified Films, Inc.

Vatican City (History and culture)
Archive Film Prods., Inc.
March of Time
Petrified Films, Inc.

Vaudeville
Allen (John E.) Inc.
Archive Film Prods., Inc.
Lib. of Congress, M/B/RS
New York Pub. Lib., Perf. Arts Res. Ctr.,
Theatre on Film and Tape
Petrified Films, Inc.
See also Burlesque

Vaughan, Sarah
Archive Film Prods., Inc.
Chertok Assoc., Inc.
Pathé Pictures, Inc.

Veal
Amer. Veterinary Med. Assn.
Varied Directions, Inc.

Vegetable fields
Petrified Films, Inc.

Vegetables
Academy of Health Sciences, U.S. Army
Dreamlight Images, Inc.
Energy Productions
Oregon State Univ., Archives
Petrified Films, Inc.

Vegetarianism
Bullfrog Films, Inc.
Focus on Animals
Intl. Soc. for Animal Rights

Vehicles
Cannell (Stephen J.) Productions, Inc.
Film Bank
Grinberg (Sherman) Film Libraries (West)
Hooper (Josh) Prods., Inc.
Petrified Films, Inc.
Prelinger Assoc., Inc.
Twentieth Century-Fox Movietonews
Video Genesis, Inc.
See also Automobiles; Police cars; Trucks

Vehicles (Amphibious)
Natl. Archives (RG 227)
See also World War II (U.S., Amphibious
operations)

Vehicles (Emergency)
Petrified Films, Inc.
Spectral Comms.
Video Tape Library, Ltd.
See also Ambulances

Vehicles (Four-wheel drive)
Film Bank

Vehicles (Human-powered)
Intl. Human Powered Vehicle Assn.
Video Mgmt. Systems

Vehicles (Military)
Cannell (Stephen J.) Productions, Inc.
Petrified Films, Inc.
U.S. Army Transportation Museum
Video Tape Library, Ltd.
See also Tanks (Military)

Vehicles (Oddities)
Film Bank

Vehicles (Off-road)
Video Genesis, Inc.

Vehicles (Remotely piloted)
Assn. for Unmanned Vehicle Systems

Veins (Blood)
Film Bank

Velez, Edin
Port Washington Pub. Lib.

Velez, Lupe
Archive Film Prods., Inc.

Velez, Tony
Port Washington Pub. Lib.

Velikovsky, Immanuel
Camera Three Prods., Inc.

Venceremos Brigade
Payne, Roz

Vending machines
Petrified Films, Inc.
Prelinger Assoc., Inc.

Venezuela
Canadian Broadcasting Corp.
Kesser Stock Footage Lib.

Venezuela (Contemporary issues)
DEC Film & Video

Venezuela (History and culture)
Allen (John E.) Inc.
Archive Film Prods., Inc.
DEC Film & Video
Documentary Educational Resources
Film/Audio Services, Inc.
Rockefeller Arch. Ctr.
Third World Newsreel
United Nations, Visual Materials Lib.

Venice Beach, Calif.
Film Bank

Venice, Calif.
Film Bank
Source Stock Footage Lib., Inc.

Venice, Calif. (History and culture)

Petrified Films, Inc.

Venice, Fla. (History and culture)
Swain (Hack) Prods., Inc.

Venice, Italy
Preview Media

Venice, Italy (History and culture)
Archive Film Prods., Inc.
Petrified Films, Inc.

Venturi, Robert
Southern Calif. Inst. of Architecture

Venus
Rosebush Visions Corp.

Venus flytraps
Film Bank

Veracruz, Mexico (History and culture)
Archivo Historico Cinematografico

Vermont
Campbell Films, Inc.
Preview Media

Vermont (History and culture)
Apertura
Archive Film Prods., Inc.
Univ. of Vermont, Bailey/Howe Lib.
Vermont Hist. Soc.

Versailles, France (History and culture)
Archive Film Prods., Inc.
Natl. Archives (RG 24)
Rockefeller Arch. Ctr.
Soc. for French Amer. Cult. Svcs. & Educ.
Aid

Versailles, Treaty of (1919)
Natl. Archives (RG 111)
Natl. Archives of Canada

Vesey, Denmark
Pyramid Film and Video Corp.

Vesuvius, Mount (History and culture)
Archive Film Prods., Inc.
Prelinger Assoc., Inc.

Veterans
Amer. Legion
Archive Film Prods., Inc.
CBS News Archives
Chicago Access Corp.
Film/Audio Services, Inc.
GRTV — Archives
Natl. Archives (RG 15)
Natl. Archives (RG 252)
Natl. Archives (RG 306)
Natl. Archives of Canada
Twentieth Century-Fox Movietonews

Veterans (Black)
Cinema Guild
Vietnam Veterans Against the War

Veterans (Korean War)
Prelinger Assoc., Inc.

Veterans (Mexican American)
Univ. of Tex. at Austin, Benson Lat. Am.
Coll.

Veterans (Native American)
Vietnam Veterans Against the War

Veterans (Vietnam)
Cinema Guild

Committee for Labor Access
Daphne Productions, Inc.
East Tenn. State Univ., Arch. of
Appalachia
First Run/Icarus Films, Inc.
Green Mountain Post Films
Indiana Univ. Northwest Lib.
Northstar Prods.
Southern Calif. Lib. for Soc. Stud. & Res.
Vietnam Veterans Against the War
Vietnam Veterans of Amer.

Veterans (World War II)
Illinois State Hist. Lib.
March of Time
Prelinger Assoc., Inc.

Veterans Administration (U.S.)
Natl. Archives (RG 15)

Veterinary medicine
Amer. Veterinary Medical Assn.
Historical Health Film Coll.
Minnesota Zoo
TV Ontario

Vicious, Sid
Target Video

Vicksburg, Miss. (History and culture)
Univ. of Miss., Ctr. for Study of Southern
Culture

Victoria, British Columbia
Impact Audio Visual
Preview Media

**Victoria, British Columbia (History and
culture)**
Archive Film Prods., Inc.

Victoria Falls, Zimbabwe
British Info. Svcs., Radio & TV Div.

Victoria, Queen (Great Britain)
Weintraub Screen Entertainment, Inc.

Victoria, Queen (Spain)
Natl. Archives (RG 24)

Victoria Station (Bombay, India)
Petrified Films, Inc.

Victory
Analogous Productions
Film Bank

Victory gardens
See World War II (U.S., Victory gardens)

Victrolas
Petrified Films, Inc.

Vidal, Gore
Daphne Productions, Inc.

Video arcades
TV Ontario

Video art
See Experimental films and videotapes

**Video display terminals (VDTs) (Safety
issues)**
California Newsreel
Computer & Business Equip. Mfrs. Assn.
Natl. Safety Council

Video equipment
Broad Street Prods.

Video games
Spectral Comms.
TV Ontario
Video Tape Library, Ltd.

Video pixillation
Dreamlight Images, Inc.

Video playback scenes
Inter Video/TTI
Newsreel Video Service

Video production
GPN

Video stores
Broad Street Prods.
TV Ontario

Vidler, Anthony
Southern Calif. Inst. of Architecture

Vidor, King
Archive Film Prods., Inc.

Vietnam
Canadian Broadcasting Corp.
Film Bank
Imagen y Sonido Independiente, S.A.

Vietnam (Contemporary issues)
DEC Film & Video

Vietnam (History and culture)
Archive Film Prods., Inc.
Bullfrog Films, Inc.
California Newsreel
DEC Film & Video
Downtown Community TV Ctr.
Film/Audio Services, Inc.
Intl. Assn. of Independent Producers
Intl. Historic Films, Inc.
Johns Hopkins Univ./Population Comm.
Svcs.
Latina, S.A. de C.V.
Northstar Prods.
Oakland Public Lib., Asian Branch Lib.
Petrified Films, Inc.
Singer-Sharrette Traditional Healing Films
Third World Newsreel
Univ. of Mich., Mich. Hist. Colls.
White Janssen, Inc.

Vietnam antiwar movement
Archives of Ontario
Baker (Fred) Film & Video Co.
Canadian Filmmakers Dist. Centre
Creative Film Society
DEC Film & Video
Estuary Press
First Run/Icarus Films, Inc.
Kartemquin Films
MacDonald, J. Fred
Media Bus
Mus. & Hist. Div., City of Sacramento
Natl. Archives (RG 200)
Payne, Roz
People's Fund
Petrified Films, Inc.
Prestige Film Corp.
Third World Newsreel
Univ. of Mich., Mich. Hist. Colls.
Vietnam Veterans Against the War
Villon Films
Worldwide Television News
See also Demonstrations (Political)

**Vietnam Veterans Memorial
(Washington, D.C.)**
Petrified Films, Inc.

NOTE: Access policies, availability and restrictions vary for each source. Please read each entry in full. Always consult "General Film and
Videotape Collections" (page 599); these comprehensive collections contain material on every conceivable subject.

Vietnam War
Accuracy in Media, Inc.
Amer. Baptist Films/Video
Analogous Productions
CTV Television Network
Cinema Guild
DEC Film & Video
Farkas Studios, Ltd.
Film Bank
Film/Video Arts, Inc.
Films for the Humanities and Sciences
First Run/Icarus Films, Inc.
Florentine Films
Forsher (James) Prods. & Archives, Inc.
Green Mountain Post Films
Grinberg (Sherman) Film Libraries (East)
Halcyon Days Prods.
Hearst Metrotone News
Intermedia Arts Minnesota
Intl. Historic Films, Inc.
Kartemquin Films
Lib. of Congress, M/B/RS
MacDonald, J. Fred
Michigan State Univ., Archives
Military/Combat Stock Footage
Multi-Media Pre-Accession Point
NBC News Video Archives
Natl. Archives (RG 56)
Natl. Archives (RG 127)
Natl. Archives (RG 147)
Natl. Archives (RG 200)
Natl. Archives (RG 242)
Natl. Archives (RG 330)
Natl. Archives (RG 342)
Natl. Archives of Canada
Natl. Archives/Natl. AV Ctr.
Petrified Films, Inc.
Producers Library Service
Raindance Foundation
Richter Productions
Southern Calif. Lib. for Soc. Stud. & Res.
Southwest Film/Video Archives, SMU
State Hist. Soc. of Iowa
Streamline Film Archives
Third World Newsreel
U.S. Dept. of Defense, Motion Media Rec. Ctr.
U.S. Marine Corps, Hist. Ctr. Lib.
UCLA Film & Television Archive
Univ. of Mich., Mich. Hist. Colls.
Univ. of Utah, Marriott Lib.
Video Tape Library, Ltd.
WGBH Educational Foundation
White Janssen, Inc.
Worldwide Television News

Vietnamese Americans
Natl. Asian American Telecomm. Assn.

Viewscreens
Film Bank

Vilas, Guillermo
U.S. Tennis Assn.

Vilcabamba, Peru (History and culture)
Cinema Guild

Villa, Francisco ("Pancho")
Archive Film Prods., Inc.
Archivo Historico Cinematografico
Film Education Institute
Natl. Archives (RG 200)

Villages
CBS News Archives
Farkas Studios, Ltd.
Film Bank
Petrified Films, Inc.
Sheffield (Erin) Prods.
TV Ontario
Video Tape Library, Ltd.

Villains
Archive Film Prods., Inc.

Villas
Dorn (Larry) Associates
Video Tape Library, Ltd.

Vineyards
CBS News Archives
Film Bank
Goal Prods., Tourn. of Roses Film Lib.
Petrified Films, Inc.
Second Line Search
TV Ontario

Vinnegar, Leroy
Rhapsody Films, Inc.

Vinton, Will
Media Project

Viola, Bill
Long Beach Mus. of Art
Port Washington Pub. Lib.
Video Data Bank

Violence
Academy of Health Sciences, U.S. Army
Archives of Ontario
Cinema Guild
Everett Pub. Lib., N.W. Hist. Coll.
Mass Media Ministries
Natl. Archives (RG 200)
Natl. Archives of Canada
Quest Productions Inc.

Violence (Against women)
See Domestic violence; Rape; Sexual abuse; Women's issues

Violins and violinists
Film Bank
Moving Media

Viren, Lasse
U.S. Olympic Committee

Virgin Islands
Sea TV

Virgin Islands (British)
Mountain Video Associates
Passage Home Communications

Virgin Islands (U.S.)
Kesser Stock Footage Lib.
Mountain Video Associates
Ski TV Prods., Inc.

Virgin Islands (U.S.) (Contemporary issues)
WTJX-TV

Virgin Islands (U.S.) (History and culture)
Natl. Archives (RG 24)
Natl. Archives (RG 48)
Roosevelt (Franklin D.) Lib.
WTJX-TV

Virgin Islands National Park, St. Thomas
Mountain Video Associates

Virginia
Creative Video, Inc.
Energy Prods.
Metro Comms., Inc.
Preview Media
Swedberg, Jack
Virginia Div. of Tourism

Virginia (History and culture)
Archive Film Prods., Inc.
Davenport Films
Duke Univ., Perkins Lib.
Educational Video Ctr.
MacDonald, J. Fred

Natl. Archives (RG 70)
Natl. Archives (RG 79)
Petrified Films, Inc.

Virginia Barrier Islands, Va. (History and culture)
Nature Conservancy

Virginia Beach, Va.
Metro Communications, Inc.

Virginia City, Nev. (History and culture)
Petrified Films, Inc.

Viruses
Film Bank
Rosebush Visions Corp.

Visual effects
See Special effects

Vitamins
Amer. Chemical Soc.
Prelinger Assoc., Inc.

Vivisection
Amer. Anti-Vivisection Society
Amer. Fund Alternatives to Animal Res.
Amer. Veterinary Medical Assn.
Focus on Animals
Intl. Soc. for Animal Rights
People for Ethical Treatment of Animals
Petrified Films, Inc.
Pyramid Film and Video Corp.
See also Animal rights and cruelty to animals

Vladivostok, U.S.S.R. (History and culture)
Archive Film Prods., Inc.

Vocational education and training
AIMS Media
Amer. ORT Federation
Center for Humanities, Inc.
Coronet/MTI Film & Video
Inst. of Financial Education
Natl. Archives of Canada
Prelinger Assoc., Inc.
United Nations Ctr. for Human Settlements

Vogel, Amos
Port Washington Pub. Lib.

Vogel, Dorothy and Herbert
Video Data Bank

Voight, Jon
Spectral Comms.

Volcanoes
Ackerman-Black Prods., Inc.
Archive Film Prods., Inc.
Beerger (Norman) Prods.
Bishop Mus., Visual Coll.
Brekke Television Prods.
CBS News Archives
Dobovan Productions, Inc.
Dreamlight Images, Inc.
Energy Productions
Film Bank
Film Search
Fish Films, Inc.
Jewell (Stuart) Productions
Moonlight Productions
NASA, Office of Comm.
Natl. Archives (RG 48)
Natl. Archives (RG 111)
Natl. Archives (RG 200)
Oregon Hist. Soc.
Petrified Films, Inc.
Prelinger Assoc., Inc.
Producers Library Service

Quenzer Driscoll Dawson, Inc.
Twentieth Century-Fox Movietonews
Univ. of Arizona, Film Lib.
Video Tape Library, Ltd.

Volga River, U.S.S.R.
Petrified Films, Inc.

Volgograd, U.S.S.R. (History and culture)
Archive Film Prods., Inc.
Natl. Coun. of Amer.-Sov. Friendship

Volleyball
Archive Film Prods., Inc.
Athletic Institute
Energy Productions
Film Bank
Petrified Films, Inc.
Spectral Comms.
Sportsfilm
Video Tape Library, Ltd.

Volleyball (College)
NCAA Productions
Oregon State Univ., Archives

Volleyball (Instruction)
NCAA Productions
Natl. Assn. for Sport & Phys. Ed.

Volpe, John
Natl. Archives (RG 406)

Volta, Alessandro
Prelinger Assoc., Inc.

Volunteers
Natl. Archives (RG 362)
Peace Corps
Radcliffe Coll., Schlesinger Lib.

Volz, Hermann
De Saisset Museum

von Braun, Wernher
Daphne Productions, Inc.

von Eckhardt, Wolf
Unicorn Projects

von Hindenburg, Paul
Natl. Archives (RG 242)
Natl. Archives (RG 342)

von Richthofen, Baron
Natl. Archives of Canada

von Sternberg, Josef
Alan Twyman Presents
Archive Film Prods., Inc.

von Stroheim, Erich
Alan Twyman Presents
Archive Film Prods., Inc.

von Weizsacker, Richard
German Info. Ctr., Film Lib.

von Zell, Harry
Videobrary, Inc.

Vorys, John
Ohio Historical Soc.

Voter registration
Estuary Press
Project Vote!

Voting
Archive Film Prods., Inc.
CBS News Archives
Petrified Films, Inc.
See also Elections

Vultures
Archive Film Prods., Inc.
Miller (David Lee) Prods.
Wings Wildlife Prods. Inc.

WAAFS
Twentieth Century-Fox Movietonews

WAVES
Twentieth Century-Fox Movietonews

WRENS
Twentieth Century-Fox Movietonews

Wachovia, N.C. (History and culture)
North Carolina Div. of Arch. & Hist.

Wade, Virginia
U.S. Tennis Assn.

Wagner, Honus
Grinberg (Sherman) Film Libraries (West)

Wagner, Paul
Port Washington Pub. Lib.

Wagner, Robert
Banks Film Library
Film Bank
Spectral Comms.

Wagner, Robert F.
New York Pub. Lib., Rare Books &
    Manuscripts Div.

Waikiki Beach, Hawaii
Cinenet (Cinema Network)
Dobovan Productions, Inc.
Preview Media

Waikiki Beach, Hawaii (History and culture)
Archive Film Prods., Inc.
Petrified Films, Inc.

Waiters and waitresses
Analogous Productions
Archive Film Prods., Inc.
CBS News Archives
Film Bank
Natl. Restaurant Assn.
TV Ontario
See also Food service industry;
    Restaurants; Workers (Restaurant)

Waiting rooms (Hospital)
Petrified Films, Inc.

Waits, Tom
Giorno Poetry Systems Inst.

Walcott, Jersey Joe
Grinberg (Sherman) Film Libraries (West)
New Jersey Network
Sportsfilm

Wald, George
Alternative Information Network

Walden, Robert
Spectral Comms.

Waldman, Anne
Giorno Poetry Systems Inst.
Video Data Bank

Waldman, Wendy
Intermedia Arts Minnesota

Wales
Unicorn Projects

Waletzky, Josh
Port Washington Pub. Lib.

Walker, Herschel
Archive Film Prods., Inc.

Walker, Roger
Southern Calif. Inst. of Architecture

Walker, T-Bone
Film/Audio Services, Inc.

Walker, William
Spalla (Rick) Video Prods.

Walkie-talkies
Film Bank
Petrified Films, Inc.
Prelinger Assoc., Inc.

Walking
Amer. Motion Pictures
Cinenet (Cinema Network)
Film Bank
TV Ontario

Walking sticks (Insect)
Energy Productions

Wall Street, N.Y.
Broad Street Prods.
Cinema Arts Assoc.
Creative Video, Inc.
Energy Productions
Merrill Lynch Pierce Fenner & Smith
New York Stock Exchange
Prelinger Assoc., Inc.
See also Stock exchanges

Wall Street, N.Y. (History and culture)
Petrified Films, Inc.

Wallabies
Minnesota Zoo

Wallace, George Corley
Banks Film Library
Boston Univ. Film Archive
MacDonald, J. Fred
Univ. of Alabama, W.S. Hoole Spec. Coll.

Wallace, Henry A.
MacDonald, J. Fred
New York Pub. Lib., Rare Books &
    Manuscripts Div.

Wallace, Mike
Daphne Productions, Inc.
Univ. of Tex. at Austin, Ransom Hum.
    Res. Ctr., Photo. Coll.

Wallace, Sippie
Rhapsody Films, Inc.

Wallenberg, Raoul
Wiesenthal (Simon) Ctr.

Waller, Fats
Archive Film Prods., Inc.
Camera Three Prods., Inc.
Chertok Assoc., Inc.

Walleye
TV Ontario

Wallis, Alfred
Amer. Federation of the Arts

Walruses
Cousteau Society
Natl. Archives (RG 200)

Petrified Films, Inc.

Wapitis
Petrified Films, Inc.

War Department (U.S.)
Natl. Archives (RG 107)

War Information, Office of (OWI) (U.S.)
Natl. Archives (RG 59)
Natl. Archives (RG 208)

War of 1812
Natl. Archives of Canada

War on Poverty
See Anti-poverty programs

War Production Board (U.S.)
Natl. Archives (RG 179)

War Relocation Authority (U.S.)
Natl. Archives (RG 111)
Natl. Archives (RG 210)

War Risk Insurance, Bureau of (U.S.)
Natl. Archives (RG 15)

War Trade Board (U.S.)
Natl. Archives (RG 182)

Warblers
Mass. Audubon Society

Ward, Montgomery
Univ. of Wyoming, Amer. Heritage Ctr.

Wardens
CBS News Archives

Warehouses
CBS News Archives
Film Bank
Petrified Films, Inc.

Warhol, Andy
Blackwood Prods., Inc.
Estate of Andy Warhol

Warm Springs, Ga. (History and culture)
Roosevelt (Franklin D.) Lib.

Warner, Jack Jr.
MacDonald, J. Fred

Warner, Jack L.
Banks Film Library

Warren Commission (1963-64)
Natl. Archives (RG 272)

Warren County, Ky. (History and culture)
Western Kentucky Univ., Folklife Arch.

Warren, Earl
Mus. & Hist. Div., City of Sacramento
Rhapsody Films, Inc.

Warren, Robert Penn
Agee (James) Film Project
Appalshop Films, Inc.

Wars
ABC News
Amer. Zionist Youth Found.
Archive Film Prods., Inc.
British Info. Svcs., Radio & TV Div.
Budget Films Inc.

CBS News Archives
CTV Television Network
Canadian Filmmakers Dist. West
Chisholm (Jack) Film Productions
Educational Film & Video Project
Film Bank
Forsher (James) Prods. & Archives, Inc.
Grinberg (Sherman) Film Libraries (East)
Hearst Metrotone News
Hoover Institution
Imageways, Inc.
Intl. Historic Films, Inc.
Latin Amer. Video Arch.
March of Time
Natl. Archives (RG 127)
Natl. Archives (RG 242)
Natl. Archives of Canada
News On Film
Northstar Prods.
Petrified Films, Inc.
Quest Productions Inc.
Richter Productions
Shields Archival
Twentieth Century-Fox Movietonews
Video Tape Library, Ltd.
World Monitor
Worldwide Television News
See also Korean War; Military; Vietnam
    War; World War I; World War II;
    specific conflicts and wars

Warsaw, Poland
Film Bank

Warsaw, Poland (History and culture)
Archive Film Prods., Inc.
Film/Audio Services, Inc.
Natl. Ctr. for Jewish Film

Warsaw uprising (1944)
Hoover Institution

Wart hogs
Film Bank
Summit Films, Inc.
Wings Wildlife Prods. Inc.

Wartime Relocation and Internment of Civilians, U.S. Committee on
Natl. Archives (RG 220)

Washing machines
MacDonald, J. Fred
Petrified Films, Inc.
Prelinger Assoc., Inc.

Washington (State)
Amer. Motion Pictures
Dreamlight Images, Inc.
Eastern Washington State Historical Soc.
Energy Prods.
Petrified Films, Inc.
Plains Art Museum Lib.
Preview Media
Telemation Productions
Washington State Archives

Washington (State) (History and culture)
Amer. Truck Historical Society
Analogous Prods.
Ctr. for Pacific Northwest Studies
Everett Pub. Lib., Northwest Hist. Coll.
Hoover Institution
Media Project
Natl. Asian American Telecomm. Assn.
Nordic Heritage Museum
Oregon Hist. Soc.
Patrick Media Group
Petrified Films, Inc.
Seattle Public Library

NOTE: Access policies, availability and restrictions vary for each source. Please read each entry in full. Always consult "General Film and Videotape Collections" (page 599); these comprehensive collections contain material on every conceivable subject.

U.S. Natl. Park Service Hist. Coll.
United Nations Ctr. for Human
 Settlements
Univ. of Calif., Berkeley, Labor
 Occupational Health Prog.
VTR Productions
Washington State Archives
Washington State Hist. Soc.

Washington, D.C.
Airline Film & TV Promotions
Analogous Prods.
Broad Street Prods.
Cinema Arts Assoc.
Creative Video, Inc.
Development Communications, Inc.
Dreamlight Images, Inc.
Energy Productions
File Tape Co.
Film Bank
Harriman Communications Ctr.
Moser (Michael)/Media
Northstar Prods.
Petrified Films, Inc.
Prelinger Assoc., Inc.
Preview Media
Public Interest Video Network
Silver Image
Summit Films, Inc.
TV Ontario
Timesteps Prods., Inc.
Video I-D, Inc.
WETA-TV
Wallen (Dick) Prods.
Washington Broadcast Video Lib.

Washington, D.C. (History and culture)
Allen (John E.) Inc.
Archive Film Prods., Inc.
Dirksen (E.M.) Cong. Lead. Res. Ctr.
Finley (Stuart) Inc.
Natl. Archives (RG 24)
Natl. Archives (RG 28)
Natl. Archives (RG 33)
Natl. Archives (RG 82)
Natl. Archives (RG 103)
Natl. Archives (RG 106)
Natl. Archives (RG 200)
Natl. Archives (RG 381)
Natl. Archives (RG 398)
Ocean Earth Constr. and Dev. Corp.
Oregon Hist. Soc.
Payne, Roz
Petrified Films, Inc.
Prelinger Assoc., Inc.
Schiele Museum
WETA-TV

Washington, Dinah
Archive Film Prods., Inc.

Washington, George
Archive Film Prods., Inc.
Hearst Metrotone News
Prelinger Assoc., Inc.

Washington, Harold
Natl. Assn. for the Advancement of
 Colored People

Washington, Lake (Wash.)
Petrified Films, Inc.

Washington Monument (Washington, D.C.)
Dreamlight Images, Inc.
Film Bank
TV Ontario

Wasps
Energy Productions

Waste disposal
Amer. Nuclear Society
Oregon State Univ., Archives

Petrified Films, Inc.
U.S. Council for Energy Awareness

Waste management
Bullfrog Films, Inc.
Finley (Stuart) Inc.

Watches
See Clocks and watches

Water
Amer. Motion Pictures
Assoc. Gen. Contractors of America
British Info. Svcs., Radio & TV Div.
CBS News Archives
Calif. Dept. of Water Resources
Dreamlight Images, Inc.
Energy Productions
Film Bank
Film/Audio Services, Inc.
Finley (Stuart) Inc.
Interlock Media Associates
Kesser Stock Footage Library
Los Angeles Dept. of Water & Power
Mass. Audubon Society
Natl. Archives (RG 267)
Natl. Archives (RG 307)
Natl. Water Well Assn.
Public Interest Video Network
Rosebush Visions Corp.
Summit Films, Inc.
TV Ontario
U.S. Committee for UNICEF
UNICEF, Div. Info. & Pub. Aff.
United Nations Ctr. for Human
 Settlements
Univ. of Wis., Green Bay, Ctr. TV Prod.

Water (Drops)
Cinema Arts Assoc.
Dreamlight Images, Inc.
Film Bank

Water ballet
Energy Productions

Water bombers
See Aircraft (Water bombers)

Water buffalo
Film Bank
Petrified Films, Inc.

Water bugs
Wings Wildlife Prods. Inc.

Water filtration plants
TV Ontario

Water lilies
Petrified Films, Inc.
TV Ontario

Water mains
CBS News Archives

Water polo
Sportsfilm
Twentieth Century-Fox Movietonews
Video Tape Library, Ltd.

Water polo (Instruction)
NCAA Productions

Water skiing
See Skiing (Water)

Water slides
Cineworks Prods. Inc.

Water taxis
See Boats and boating (Water taxis)

Water towers
Film Bank

Water witches
See Dowsing

Water works
Univ. of Minn. Libs., Manuscripts Div.

Waterfalls
Ackerman-Black Prods., Inc.
Amer. Motion Pictures
Archive Film Prods., Inc.
CBS News Archives
Cinenet (Cinema Network)
Dobovan Productions, Inc.
Dreamlight Images, Inc.
Energy Productions
Film Bank
Grinberg (Sherman) Film Libraries (West)
Kesser Stock Footage Library
Marts (Steve) Productions
Omega Films
Petrified Films, Inc.
Quenzer Driscoll Dawson, Inc.
Summit Films, Inc.
TV Ontario
TV-3
Twentieth Century-Fox Movietonews
Univ. of Wis., Green Bay, Ctr. TV Prod.
Xicom, Inc.

Waterfowl
Ducks Unlimited, Inc.
Echo Film Prods., Inc.
KD Enterprises Prods.
Latham Foundation
Minnesota Zoo
Swedberg, Jack
Univ. of Wis., Green Bay, Ctr. TV Prod.

Waterfronts
Communications Concepts
Film Bank
Petrified Films, Inc.
See also Harbors

Watergate
CBS News Archives
Petrified Films, Inc.

Watergate hearings (1974)
Villon Films
WETA-TV

Waterholes
Jewell (Stuart) Productions
Twentieth Century-Fox Movietonews

Watermelons
Analogous Productions

Waters, John
Giorno Poetry Systems Inst.

Waters, Muddy
Archive Film Prods., Inc.
Rhapsody Films, Inc.

Waterways (U.S.)
Natl. Archives (RG 90)

Watkins, Carleton
Blackwood Prods., Inc.

Watsonville, Calif. (History and culture)
Labor Video Project

Watts, Alan
Hartley Film Found., Inc.

Watts, Calif. (History and culture)
Petrified Films, Inc.

Watts, Murray
Archives of Ontario

Watusi, The

See Dance and dancing (Watusi, The)

Watut River, Papau, New Guinea
Sobek Productions

Waves
Archive Film Prods., Inc.
Beerger (Norman) Prods.
CBS News Archives
Echo Film Prods., Inc.
Energy Productions
Film Bank
Film Search
Great Waves/Delaney Films
Impact Audio Visual
Jewell (Stuart) Productions
Kesser Stock Footage Library
MacGillivray Freeman Films
Merkel Films
Petrified Films, Inc.
Spectral Comms.
TV Ontario
Twentieth Century-Fox Movietonews
Video Tape Library, Ltd.
Wings Wildlife Prods. Inc.
See also Oceans

Waves (Human)
Film Bank

Waxwings
TV Ontario

Wayne and Shuster
Natl. Archives of Canada

Wayne, John
Archive Film Prods., Inc.
Banks Film Library
Camera Three Prods., Inc.
Navajo Tribe, Off. Broadcast Svcs.
UCLA Film & Television Archive
Videobrary, Inc.

Weapons
CBS News Archives
Crystal Pyramid Prods.
Development Communications, Inc.
Film Bank
Ideal Comms., Inc.
MacDonald, J. Fred
Mass. Inst. of Tech., MIT Museum
Metro Communications, Inc.
Military/Combat Stock Footage
Natl. Archives (RG 70)
Natl. Archives (RG 111)
Natl. Archives (RG 342)
See also Cannons; Guns and rifles;
 Missiles; Nuclear weapons

Weasels
Minnesota Zoo

Weather
AIMS Media
CBS News Archives
Cinema Guild
Film Bank
Grinberg (Sherman) Film Libraries (West)
Mystic Seaport Mus., Inc.
Natl. Oceanic & Atmospheric Admin.
Natl. Science Foundation
Petrified Films, Inc.
Spectral Comms.
See also Blizzards; Clouds; Lightning;
 Hurricanes; Meteorology; Rain; Snow;
 Storms; Tornadoes; Weather

Weather Bureau (U.S.)
Natl. Archives (RG 33)

Weather stations
TV Ontario

768

Weather Underground Organization
DEC Film & Video
First Run/Icarus Films, Inc.

Weathervanes
CBS News Archives
Film Bank
TV Ontario

Weaver, Dennis
Spectral Comms.

Weaver, Robert C.
Natl. Archives (RG 207)

Weaver, Sigourney
Spectral Comms.

Weavers and weaving
Film Bank
Petrified Films, Inc.
TV Ontario
Villon Films

Webb, Jack
Banks Film Library
Natl. Archives (RG 56)

Webber, Gordon
Univ. of Mich., Mich. Hist. Colls.

Webs
See Spider webs

Wedding chapels
Petrified Films, Inc.

Weddings
Analogous Productions
Applegate Entertainment
Archive Film Prods., Inc.
CBS News Archives
Film Bank
Film Education Institute
Los Angeles News Service
Pennebaker Associates, Inc.
Petrified Films, Inc.
Spalla (Rick) Video Prods.
TV Ontario
Twentieth Century-Fox Movietonews
Vermont Hist. Soc.
White Janssen, Inc.

Weddings (China)
Nan Hai (U.S.A.) Co., Inc.

Weddings (International)
Film Education Institute

Weddings (Native American)
East Tenn. State Univ., Arch. of
    Appalachia

Weeds
Film Bank
Oregon State Univ., Archives
Prov. Arch. of Alberta
See also Dandelions

Weeping
CBS News Archives
Petrified Films, Inc.

Weese, Harry
Unicorn Projects

Wegman, William
Video Data Bank

Weight control
See Dieting

Weightlifting
ABC Sports, Inc.
Amer. Motion Pictures
Dreamlight Images, Inc.
Film Bank
Prestige Film Corp.
Sportsfilm
TV Ontario
U.S. Olympic Comm.
Video Tape Library, Ltd.
See also Bodybuilding

Weill, Kurt
Weill-Lenya Res. Ctr.

Weinberger, Caspar L.
Churchill (Winston) Memorial and Library

Weisinger, Mort
Univ. of Wyoming, Amer. Heritage Ctr.

Weiskopf, Victor
Mass. Inst. of Tech., MIT Museum

Weisman, Fred and Marcia
Long Beach Mus. of Art
Video Data Bank

Weissmuller, Johnny
Archive Film Prods., Inc.
Banks Film Library
Film Education Institute
Grinberg (Sherman) Film Libraries (West)
Jessiefilm

Weitzmann, Chaim
Amer. Zionist Youth Found.

Welch, Raquel
Daphne Productions, Inc.

Welch, William
Johns Hopkins Univ., School of Medicine

Weld, Tuesday
Banks Film Library

Welders
Petrified Films, Inc.

Welding
British Info. Svcs., Radio & TV Div.
Dreamlight Images, Inc.
Energy Productions
Film Bank
Petrified Films, Inc.
Source Stock Footage Lib., Inc.
VTR Productions

Welfare
Intermedia Arts Minnesota
MALDEF
March of Time
Natl. Archives (RG 69)
Natl. Archives (RG 235)
Natl. Archives (RG 381)
New Mexico State Records Ctr. & Arch.
Université de Moncton, Centre d'Études
    Acad.

Welk, Lawrence
Banks Film Library
Camera Three Prods., Inc.
MacDonald, J. Fred

**Welland Canal, Ontario (History and
    culture)**
Archives of Ontario

Welles, Orson
Archive Film Prods., Inc.

Las Vegas News Bureau
Voyager Co.

Welles, Roger
Natl. Archives (RG 24)

Welles, Sumner
Natl. Archives (RG 59)

Welliver, Neil
Amer. Federation of the Arts

Wells
CBS News Archives
Natl. Water Well Assn.
Twentieth Century-Fox Movietonews

Wells, Dickie
Rhapsody Films, Inc.

Wells, Junior
Rhapsody Films, Inc.

Wells, Tracy
Spectral Comms.

Welsh, Bill
Spectral Comms.

Welsh, Matthew E.
Indiana State Lib.

Wertmuller, Lina
Daphne Productions, Inc.

Wessels, Glenn
De Saisset Museum

West, Adam
Spectral Comms.

West and Patricola
Videobrary, Inc.

West Africa (History and culture)
Documentary Educational Resources
Rockefeller Arch. Ctr.

West Bank
See Middle East

West, Dorothy
Radcliffe Coll., Schlesinger Lib.

**West Fargo, N. Dak. (History and
    culture)**
State Hist. Soc. of North Dakota

West Indies
British Info. Svcs., Radio & TV Div.
Mountain Video Associates

West Indies (History and culture)
Archives of Ontario

West, Mae
Archive Film Prods., Inc.
Las Vegas News Bureau
UCLA Film & Television Archive

West Palm Beach, Fla.
Preview Media

**West Point, N.Y. (U.S. Military
    Academy)**
Analogous Productions
Eisenhower (Dwight D.) Library
Natl. Archives (RG 111)

West Virginia (History and culture)
Appalshop Films, Inc.

Archive Film Prods., Inc.
Finley (Stuart) Inc.
Marshall Univ., Spec. Coll.
West Virginia Dept. of Culture & Hist.
West Virginia State Lib. Comm.

Westbrook, Mike
Amer. Federation of the Arts

**Westchester County, N.Y. (History and
    culture)**
Regional Plan Assn.

Western Sahara
Imagen y Sonido Independiente, S.A.

Western Sahara (History and culture)
First Run/Icarus Films, Inc.

Western Union offices
Broad Street Prods.

Westerns
Allen (John E.) Inc.
Archive Film Prods., Inc.
Buffalo Bill Historical Center
Country Music Foundation, Inc.
Dreamlight Images, Inc.
Em Gee Film Library
Film Bank
Fish Films, Inc.
Flying A Pictures Inc.
Footage Inc.
Grinberg (Sherman) Film Libraries (West)
Hurlock Cine-World, Inc.
Intl. Mus. of Photography
Lib. of Congress, M/B/RS
MacDonald, J. Fred
Morcraft Films
Moviecraft, Inc.
Petrified Films, Inc.
Producers Library Service
Southwest Film/Video Archives, SMU
Spalla (Rick) Video Prods.
Streamline Film Archives
UCLA Film & Television Archive
Video Yesteryear
See also Cowboys; Horses; Native
    Americans; Shootouts

Westminster Abbey, London
British Info. Svcs., Radio & TV Div.
Petrified Films, Inc.

**Westminster Abbey, London (History
    and culture)**
Archive Film Prods., Inc.

Westmoreland, William
Natl. Archives (RG 56)

Weston, Edward
Cinema Guild
San Francisco Bay Area TV News Arch.

Wetlands
Ducks Unlimited, Inc.
Echo Film Prods., Inc.
Natl. Assn. of Conservation Dists.
New Jersey Network
Oregon State Univ., Archives
See also Swamps

Whale watching
Site Productions

Whales
Alaska Native Heritage Film Project
Brekke Television Prods.
Channell One Video
Cousteau Society

NOTE: Access policies, availability and restrictions vary for each source. Please read each entry in full. Always consult "General Film and Videotape Collections" (page 599); these comprehensive collections contain material on every conceivable subject.

Dobovan Productions, Inc.
Dreamlight Images, Inc.
Film Bank
Film Search
Focus on Animals
Greenpeace, U.S.A.
Jewell (Stuart) Productions
Mass. Audubon Society
Minnesota Zoo
Moonlight Productions
Ocean Images
Petrified Films, Inc.
Preview Media
Pyramid Film and Video Corp.
Video Tape Library, Ltd.
Wings Wildlife Prods. Inc.

Whaling
Canadian Filmmakers Dist. Centre
Canadian Filmmakers Dist. West
Mystic Seaport Mus., Inc.
Native American Pub. Broad. Cons.
Natl. Archives (RG 26)
Natl. Archives (RG 200)
Natl. Archives of Canada
Petrified Films, Inc.
Univ. of Alberta, Boreal Inst. for Northern
   Studies

Wharton, Margaret
Mus. of Contemporary Art

Wheat
British Info. Svcs., Radio & TV Div.
Dreamlight Images, Inc.
Film Search
Hot Shots Commercial Prods., Inc.
Natl. Archives of Canada
North Country Media Group
Northcoast Communication, Inc.
Oregon Hist. Soc.
Oregon State Univ., Archives
Petrified Films, Inc.
Prov. Arch. of Alberta
Pyramid Film and Video Corp.
Snyder (Bill) Films, Inc.
TV Ontario
VTR Productions
See also Grain

Wheatfields
Archive Film Prods., Inc.
Film Bank
MacGillivray Freeman Films
See alao Grain (Waves of)

Wheelbarrows
CBS News Archives

Wheelchairs
Film Bank

Wheeling, W. Va. (History and culture)
West Virginia Dept. of Culture & Hist.

Wheelmaking
Prelinger Assoc., Inc.

Wheelock, Martha
Port Washington Pub. Lib.

Wheels
CBS News Archives

Wheels (Spinning)
Film Bank
Petrified Films, Inc.

Wheels of fortune
Petrified Films, Inc.
Prelinger Assoc., Inc.

Whippings
Film Bank

Whistleblowers
Ideal Comms., Inc.

Whistles
CBS News Archives

Whistles (Railroad)
Petrified Films, Inc.

Whitcomb, Edgar D.
Indiana State Lib.

White, Betty
Spectral Comms.

White House
Analogous Productions
Archive Film Prods., Inc.
CBS News Archives
Film Bank
MacDonald, J. Fred
Natl. Archives (RG 103)
Natl. Archives (RG 130)
TV Ontario
WETA-TV
Washington Broadcast Video Lib.

White House Conference
See the conference's "subject" area (e.g.,
   White House Conference on Small
   Business is found under Small
   Business, White House Conference on)

White, Pearl
Archive Film Prods., Inc.

White, Reggie
Archive Film Prods., Inc.

**White Sands National Monument,
   N. Mex.**
Stimulus

White water
Echo Film Prods., Inc.
Kesser Stock Footage Library
Natural Reflections Video
North Country Media Group
Sports Cinematography Group
TV Ontario
Univ. of Wis., Green Bay, Ctr. TV Prod.
Video Tape Library, Ltd.
See also Rafting; Rapids

Whitehorse, Yukon Territory
TV Ontario

**Whitehorse, Yukon Territory (History
   and culture)**
Alaska Video Prods.

Whiteman, Paul
Archive Film Prods., Inc.

Whitman, Charles S.
Natl. Archives (RG 24)

Whitman, Walt
Intellimation
New Jersey Network

Whitney, John
Camera Three Prods., Inc.

Who, The (Rock and roll band)
Archive Film Prods., Inc.
Clark (Dick) Media Archives, Inc.
Pennebaker Associates, Inc.

**Wichita Falls, Tex. (History and
   culture)**
Natl. Oceanic & Atmospheric Admin.

Wichita, Kans. (History and culture)
Archive Film Prods., Inc.

Wicker, Tom
Agee (James) Film Project

Widmark, Richard
Banks Film Library

Widows and widowers
Natl. Funeral Directors Assn.

Wieland, Joyce
Canadian Filmmakers Dist. Centre

Wild West shows
Allen (John E.) Inc.
Buffalo Bill Historical Center
Sheffield (Erin) Prods.

Wildebeests
Dreamlight Images, Inc.
Film Bank
Summit Films, Inc.

Wilder, Laura Ingalls
South Dakota State Lib.

Wilderness
Echo Film Prods., Inc.
Film Bank
North Country Media Group
Orion Post Production
Preview Media

Wildflowers
Hayes Prods., Inc.
Jewell (Stuart) Productions
Moving Media
North Country Media Group
Peak Productions, Inc.
Summit Films, Inc.
TV Ontario
White Janssen, Inc.

Wildlife
Alaska Video Prods.
Amer. Veterinary Medical Assn.
Animal Protection Institute of America
Aspen Photo & Film Agency
Bennett (Joel) Prods.
Caribbean Images, Ltd.
Cinema Arts Assoc.
Cineworks Prods. Inc.
Cousteau Society
Echo Film Prods., Inc.
Fabulous Footage Inc.
Film Bank
Film Search
Greenpeace, U.S.A.
Grinberg (Sherman) Film Libraries (East)
Grinberg (Sherman) Film Libraries (West)
Inuvik Research Ctr.
Jewell (Stuart) Productions
Kesser Stock Footage Library
Latham Foundation
Marineland of Florida
Metro Communications, Inc.
Natl. Assn. of Conservation Dists.
Natl. Geographic Soc. Stock Footage Lib.
Natural Reflections Video
New York State Dept. of Env. Cons.
New York Zoological Society
Orion Post Production
Peak Productions, Inc.
Petrified Films, Inc.
Prelinger Assoc., Inc.
Preview Media
SF•V Intl.
Schiele Museum
Sobek Productions
Sonoma Video Productions
Source Stock Footage Lib., Inc.
Swedberg (Jack)
Univ. of Wis., Green Bay, Ctr. TV Prod.
Video Genesis, Inc.
White Janssen, Inc.
White Star Prof. Film Svcs., Inc.

Wings Wildlife Prods. Inc.
World Monitor
See also Animals; Flora and fauna;
   Flowers; Nature; specific animals

Wildlife (Africa)
Di Sesso (Moe) Wild Life Film Lib.
Dreamlight Images, Inc.
Duffy (Kevin) Productions
Film Bank
Film Search
Focus on Animals
Innerquest Communications Corp.
Intl. Media Services, Inc.
Jewell (Stuart) Productions
Johnson (Martin & Osa) Safari Museum
New York Zoological Society
Petrified Films, Inc.
Summit Films, Inc.
Video Tape Library, Ltd.
Wings Wildlife Prods., Inc.

Wildlife (Antarctica)
New York Zoological Society

Wildlife (Arctic)
Duffy (Kevin) Productions
Film Search
Petrified Films, Inc.

Wildlife (Asia)
Duffy (Kevin) Productions
Film Search
Johnson (Martin & Osa) Safari Museum
New York Zoological Society

Wildlife (Australia)
Petrified Films, Inc.

Wildlife (Europe)
Film Search

Wildlife (North America)
Bradley/McAfee Public Relations
Chiappetta Prods., Inc.
Chisholm (Jack) Film Productions
Di Sesso (Moe) Wild Life Film Lib.
Ducks Unlimited, Inc.
Echo Film Prods., Inc.
Film Search
Idaho State Library
Indiana State Comm. on Public Records
KD Enterprises Prods.
Mass. Audubon Society
Natl. Archives (RG 33)
Natl. Archives (RG 115)
Natl. Archives (RG 267)
Natl. Archives of Canada
New Mexico State Records Ctr. & Arch.
New York Zoological Society
North Country Media Group
Odyssey Prods., Inc.
Oregon Hist. Soc.
Palisades Wildlife Film Library
Prov. Arch. of Alberta
Snyder (Bill) Films, Inc.
Swedberg (Jack)
Tri-Comm Prods.
Video I-D, Inc.
Visuart, Inc.
West Star Productions
Wings Wildlife Prods., Inc.

Wildlife (South America)
Film Search
New York Zoological Society

Wildlife (South Pacific)
Wombat Film & Video

Wiley, William T.
Long Beach Mus. of Art
Video Data Bank

Wilhelm, Franz
Grinberg (Sherman) Film Libraries (West)

Wilhelm, Kaiser
Archive Film Prods., Inc.
Grinberg (Sherman) Film Libraries (West)
Petrified Films, Inc.

Wilhelmina, Queen
Archive Film Prods., Inc.

Wilkes-Barre, Pa. (History and culture)
Natl. Archives (RG 378)

Wilkins, Roy
Memphis State Univ. Libraries

Willamette River, Oreg. (History and culture)
Media Project

Willard, J.E.
Grinberg (Sherman) Film Libraries (West)

Williams, Andy
Banks Film Library

Williams, Cara
Banks Film Library

Williams, Charles
Wheaton Coll., Wade Ctr.

Williams, Esther
Film Education Institute

Williams, Gerhard Mennen
Univ. of Mich., Mich. Hist. Colls.

Williams, Hosea
Univ. of Georgia, WSB TV News Film Arch.

Williams, Robert Franklin
Univ. of Mich., Mich. Hist. Colls.

Williams, T. Harry
Louisiana State Univ. Libs., Spec. Coll.

Williams, Ted
Grinberg (Sherman) Film Libraries (West)

Williams, Tennessee
Daphne Productions, Inc.

Williams, Tex
Pathé Pictures, Inc.

Williams, Vanessa
Miss America Pageant

Williams, William Carlos
Intellimation

Williamsburg, N.Y. (History and culture)
Cinema Guild

Williamsburg, Va.
Creative Video, Inc.
Metro Communications, Inc.
Preview Media

Williamsburg, Va. (History and culture)
Petrified Films, Inc.

Williamson, Judith
Paper Tiger TV

Willingboro Township, N.J. (History and culture)

New Jersey Network

Willis, Bruce
Spectral Comms.

Williston, N. Dak. (History and culture)
State Hist. Soc. of North Dakota

Willkie, Wendell A.
Natl. Archives (RG 200)
Prelinger Assoc., Inc.

Willows, Md. (History and culture)
Natl. Archives (RG 79)

Wills, Bob
Pathé Pictures, Inc.

Wills, Chill
Banks Film Library

Wilmington, N.C. (History and culture)
Petrified Films, Inc.

Wilson, Anne
Mus. of Contemporary Art

Wilson, Don
Shokus Video

Wilson, Malcolm
New York State Arch. & Rec. Admin.

Wilson, Ted
Univ. of Utah, Marriott Lib.

Wilson, Woodrow
Archive Film Prods., Inc.
Natl. Archives (RG 24)
Natl. Archives (RG 111)
Natl. Archives/Natl. AV Ctr.
Prelinger Assoc., Inc.
UCLA Film & Television Archive
Wilson (Woodrow) Birthplace Found.

Wimbledon, England (History and culture)
Archive Film Prods., Inc.

Winchell, Paul
Banks Film Library
Video Resources N.Y., Inc.

Winchell, Walter
Shokus Video

Wind generators
Source Stock Footage Lib., Inc.

Wind socks
Petrified Films, Inc.
TV Ontario

Wind tunnels
NASA, Ames Res. Ctr., Imaging Tech. Branch
NASA, Office of Comm.

Windjammers
See Ships (Windjammers)

Windmills
Archive Film Prods., Inc.
British Info. Svcs., Radio & TV Div.
CBS News Archives
Film Bank
Petrified Films, Inc.
TV Ontario

Windows
CBS News Archives

Film Bank
See also Automobiles (Windshields);
Stained glass

Winds
Grinberg (Sherman) Film Libraries (West)
Natl. Archives (RG 96)
Twentieth Century-Fox Movietonews

Windsailing
Video Tape Library, Ltd.

Windshields
See Automobiles (Windshields)

Windsor, Duke of
Roosevelt (Franklin D.) Lib.

Windsor, Ontario (History and culture)
Canadian Filmmakers Dist. Centre
DEC Film & Video
Natl. Archives (RG 200)
Petrified Films, Inc.

Windsurfing
Amer. Motion Pictures
Brekke Television Prods.
Caribbean Images, Ltd.
Century Video Services, Inc.
Creative Video, Inc.
Dittrich (Scott) Films
Dobovan Productions, Inc.
Dreamlight Images, Inc.
Echo Film Prods., Inc.
Energy Productions
Film Bank
Great Waves/Delaney Films
Grinberg (Sherman) Film Libraries (East)
Jalbert Productions
Kesser Stock Footage Library
Merkel Films
Miller (Warren) Productions, Inc.
North Country Media Group
Peak Productions, Inc.
Quinn (Bill) Prods.
Second Line Search
Sports Cinematography Group
Summit Films, Inc.
TV Ontario
Video Tape Library, Ltd.

Wine
Preview Media
Sonoma Video Productions
Univ. of Calif., Davis, Shields Library

Wine cellars
See Cellars (Wine)

Winemaking
Miller (Warren) Productions, Inc.
Oregon State Univ., Archives
Soc. for French Amer. Cult. Svcs. & Educ. Aid

Wineries
Goal Prods., Tourn. of Roses Film Lib.
Sonoma Video Productions

Winfrey, Oprah
Spectral Comms.

Winkler, Henry
Spectral Comms.

Winkler, Paul
Port Washington Pub. Lib.

Winsor, Jackie
Video Data Bank

Winston, Brian
Video Data Bank

Winston, Henry
Communist Party USA

Winter
Aitken (Len) Productions, Inc.
Charisma Prods., Ltd./Visual Motion
Cineworks Prods. Inc.
Departures, Inc.
Dreamlight Images, Inc.
Echo Film Prods., Inc.
Energy Productions
Film Bank
Filmfair Communications
4•6•8 Prods., Inc.
Intl. Film Bureau, Inc.
Jalbert Productions
Jewell (Stuart) Productions
Moving Media
Nine Star Productions
North Country Media Group
Northcoast Communication, Inc.
Northeast Historic Film
Petrified Films, Inc.
Preview Media
Ski TV Prods., Inc./Channel 24
Snyder (Bill) Films, Inc.
Summit Films, Inc.
TV Ontario
Video West
White Star Prof. Film Svcs., Inc.
Xicom, Inc.

Winter Haven, Fla. (History and culture)
Swain (Hack) Prods., Inc.

Winters, Jonathan
Banks Film Library
Natl. Archives (RG 47)

Winters, Shelley
Banks Film Library
Daphne Productions, Inc.

Winwood, Steve
Spectral Comms.

Wipes
Lib. of Special Visual Effects
Petrified Films, Inc.

Wire (Rock and roll band)
Target Video

Wiretapping
See Surveillance

Wirtz, Willard W.
Natl. Archives (RG 174)

Wisconsin
Florentine Films
Preview Media
Univ. of Wis., Green Bay, Ctr. TV Prod.

Wisconsin (History and culture)
Archive Film Prods., Inc.
Bullfrog Films, Inc.
DEC Film & Video
First Run/Icarus Films, Inc.
Manitowoc Maritime Museum
Marquette Univ., Spec. Coll.
Native Amer. Pub. Broad. Cons.
Neville Pub. Museum
Prelinger Assoc., Inc.
State Hist. Soc. of Wisconsin
Univ. of Wisconsin — Extension
WTMJ-TV

NOTE: Access policies, availability and restrictions vary for each source. Please read each entry in full. Always consult "General Film and Videotape Collections" (page 599); these comprehensive collections contain material on every conceivable subject.

Wise, Bob
Spectral Comms.

Wismer, Harry
Sportsfilm

Witches
Women in Focus
Women Make Movies, Inc.

With, Barb
Intermedia Arts Minnesota

Withers, Jane
Spectral Comms.

Wizards
Archive Film Prods., Inc.

Wobblies
See Industrial Workers of the World

Wohl, Ira
Port Washington Pub. Lib.

Wolfe, Fred
East Tenn. State Univ., Arch. of
 Appalachia

Wolfli, Adolf
Amer. Federation of the Arts

Wolman, Abel
Finley (Stuart) Inc.

Wolverines
Minnesota Zoo

Wolves
Di Sesso (Moe) Wild Life Film Lib.
Focus on Animals
Latham Foundation
Mass. Audubon Society
Petrified Films, Inc.
Wings Wildlife Prods. Inc.

Women
Anti-Defamation League of B'nai B'rith
Coe Film Assoc., Inc.
Film Bank
Film/Video Arts, Inc.
Hearst Metrotone News
Idera Films
NASA, Lewis Research Center
Natl. Film Board of Canada
Prelinger Assoc., Inc.
Sheen (Fulton J.) Comm. Ltd.
Timesteps Prods., Inc.
Twentieth Century-Fox Movietonews
V/tape
Women in Focus
Women Make Movies, Inc.
See also Women and health; Women's
 history; Women's issues

Women (Arab)
TV Ontario

Women (Artists)
Amer. Federation of the Arts

Women (Asian American)
Natl. Asian American Telecomm. Assn.

Women (Black)
Inter-American Foundation
Radcliffe Coll., Schlesinger Lib.
Villon Films

Women (Brazil)
Benamou, Catherine/LAWAS

Women (China)
Cambridge Documentary Films, Inc.
DEC Film & Video

New Day Films

Women (Depiction in the media)
Cambridge Documentary Films, Inc.
Groupe Intervention Video
Intl. Women's Day Video Fest.
Natl. Asian American Telecomm. Assn.
White Janssen, Inc.

Women (El Salvador)
El Salvador Media Project

Women (Hispanic)
MALDEF

Women (Israel)
Anti-Defamation League of B'nai B'rith

Women (Jamaica)
DEC Film & Video

Women (Japan)
Japan External Trade Organization
Women in Focus

Women (Latin America)
Cinema Guild
Third World Newsreel

Women (Lithuania)
Balzekas Mus. of Lithuanian Culture

Women (Mexico)
Democracy in Communication
Latina, S.A. de C.V.

Women (Military)
Academy of Health Sciences, U.S. Army
CBS News Archives
MacDonald, J. Fred
Natl. Archives of Canada
Twentieth Century-Fox Movietonews

Women (Native American)
Bur. of Florida Folklife Progs.
Manitoba Indian Cultural Centre
Native Amer. Pub. Broad. Cons.
South Dakota State Lib.
Univ. of West Fla., Hum. Res. Vid. Lib.
Yakima Indian Nation Cultural Ctr.
Yakima Television Program

Women (Nicaragua)
Lesage, Julia
Xchange TV

Women (Peru)
Democracy in Communication

Women (Prisoners)
First Run/Icarus Films, Inc.
Mus. & Hist. Div., City of Sacramento

Women (Scientists)
Natl. Science Foundation

Women (South Africa)
California Newsreel
United Nations, Visual Materials Lib.

Women (Soviet Union)
Estuary Press
Natl. Coun. of Amer.-Sov. Friendship

Women (Tanzania)
Maryknoll Fathers & Brothers

Women (Third World)
Groupe Intervention Video

Women (Workers)
See Workers (Women)

Women and health
Addiction Research Foundation of Ontario

Altschul Group
Amer. Cancer Soc., Inc.
Appalshop Films, Inc.
Bronx County Hist. Soc.
Cambridge Documentary Films, Inc.
Cinema Guild
Cinema Medica
Estuary Press
Gay Men's Health Crisis
Historical Health Film Coll.
Inst. for Psychoanalysis
Intl. Women's Day Video Fest.
Johns Hopkins Univ./Population Comm.
 Svcs.
Kinsey Institute
La Leche League of New Mexico
March of Dimes Birth Defects Found.
March of Time
Medical College of Pa., Arch. & Spec.
 Coll. Women in Medicine
Narcotics Education, Inc.
Nassau Comm. Coll. Lib.
Natl. Abortion Rights Action League
Natl. Archives (RG 12)
Natl. Archives (RG 102)
Natl. Archives/Natl. AV Ctr.
New Day Films
New York Hosp.-Cornell Med. Ctr., Arch.
Planned Parenthood Fed. of Amer.
Polymorph Films, Inc.
Prelinger Assoc., Inc.
Radcliffe Coll., Schlesinger Lib.
Social Psychiatry Res. Inst.
Society for Nutrition Education
Video Farm
Vidéo Femmes
Women in Focus
Women Make Movies, Inc.
See also Abortion; Midwifery; Obstetrics
 and gynecology; Pregnancy; Rape

Women's Bureau (U.S.)
Natl. Archives (RG 86)

Women's history
Amer. Soc. Hist. Proj. Film Lib.
Archives of Ontario
Canadian Filmmakers Dist. Centre
Centre for Art Tapes
Cinema Guild
DEC Film & Video
Estuary Press
Grinberg (Sherman) Film Libraries (West)
Hearst Metrotone News
MacDonald, J. Fred
March of Time
Mass. Inst. of Tech., MIT Museum
Media Bus
Media Project
Medical College of Pa., Arch. & Spec.
 Coll. Women in Medicine
Natl. Archives (RG 69)
Natl. Archives (RG 86)
Natl. Archives (RG 208)
Natl. Archives (RG 220)
Natl. Archives (RG 342)
Natl. Archives of Canada
Natl. Archives/Natl. AV Ctr.
Natl. Organization for Women
New Day Films
Nuclear Free Zone Registry
Ohio Historical Soc.
Parker (Kit) Films
Payne, Roz
Pennebaker Associates, Inc.
Pennsylvania State Arch.
Phoenix Films and Video
Prov. Arch. of Manitoba
Radcliffe Coll., Schlesinger Lib.
Taminent Lib./Wagner Labor Arch.
Texas Woman's Univ.
Trinity Square Video
Twentieth Century-Fox Movietonews
Univ. of Alabama, W.S. Hoole Spec. Coll.
Univ. of Maryland, McKeldin Lib.

Univ. of Mich., Mich. Hist. Colls.
Univ. of Missouri-St. Louis
Univ. of Toronto, AV Lib.
Univ. of Waterloo, A-V Centre
Vidéo Femmes
Women in Focus
Women Make Movies, Inc.
Worldwide Television News
See also Suffragettes and suffrage
 movement; Women; Workers (Women)

Women's issues
Alternative Information Network
Apertura
Boston Comm. Access & Prog. Found.
Bullfrog Films, Inc.
CBS News Archives
Cable Access of Dallas
Cambridge Documentary Films, Inc.
Canyon Cinema, Inc.
Carousel Film & Video
Channel L Working Group
Chicago Access Corp.
Cinema Guild
Cinema Verite Intl.
Coal Employment Project
DEC Film & Video
Deep Dish TV
Filmakers Library
Films for the Humanities and Sciences
First Run/Icarus Films, Inc.
Focus Intl. Inc.
Foreign Images
Groupe Intervention Video
Intermedia Arts Minnesota
Intl. Women's Day Video Fest.
Kartemquin Films
Latin Amer. Video Arch.
MALDEF
Multi-Focus, Inc.
Natl. Archives (RG 220)
Natl. Archives of Canada
Natl. Organization for Women
New Day Films
New Jersey Network
Paper Tiger TV
Phoenix Films and Video
Political Issue Archive
Prelinger Assoc., Inc.
Radcliffe Coll., Schlesinger Lib.
South Carolina Humanities Res. Ctr.
Syracuse Alternative Media Network
Taminent Lib./Wagner Labor Arch.
Université de Moncton, Centre d'Études
 Acad.
Univ. of Calif., Ext. Media Ctr.
Univ. of Waterloo, A-V Centre
Video Data Bank
Vidéo Femmes
Video In
Video Pool, Inc.
Vidéographe Inc., Le
Washington Univ., Brown Schl. of Soc.
 Work
West Virginia State Lib. Comm.
Women in Focus
Women Make Movies, Inc.
World Monitor
Xchange TV
See also Abortion; Domestic violence;
 Equal Rights Amendment (ERA);
 Rape; Sexism; Sexual abuse; Women
 and health

Women's movement
See Women's history; Women's issues

Women's studies
See Women's history; Women's issues

Woo, Michael
Spectral Comms.

Wood
Oregon State Univ., Archives

772

Wood, John
Video Data Bank

Wood, Natalie
Banks Film Library
Spalla (Rick) Video Prods.

Wood, Peggy
Shokus Video

Wood rings
Film Bank

Woodcarving
See Woodworking

Woodchucks
Di Sesso (Moe) Wild Life Film Lib.
Film Bank
Minnesota Zoo

Wooden, John
Naismith Mem. Basketball Hall of Fame

Woodpeckers
Energy Productions
Wings Wildlife Prods. Inc.

Woodruff, Judy
Future Homemakers of America, Inc.

Woodruff, Robert W.
Atlanta Hist. Soc.
Emory Univ., Spec. Coll.

Woods, Jane
Spectral Comms.

Woodstock Music Festival (1969)
See Music festivals (Woodstock, 1969)

Woodward, C. Vann
Agee (James) Film Project

Woodward, Joanne
Banks Film Library
UCLA Film & Television Archive

Woodworking
Bullfrog Films, Inc.
Dreamlight Images, Inc.
Petrified Films, Inc.
Prelinger Assoc., Inc.
TV Ontario

Wool
Film Bank
Natl. Archives (RG 103)
Oregon State Univ., Archives
Prov. Arch. of Alberta

Work chants
See Music (Work chants)

Worker's compensation
Pennsylvania State Arch.

Workers
Allen (John E.) Inc.
Amer. Soc. Hist. Proj. Film Lib.
CBS News Archives
Cabscott Broadcast Prods.
Crystal Pyramid Prods.
Dreamlight Images, Inc.
Echo Film Prods., Inc.
Energy Productions
Film Bank
Fish Films, Inc.
Grinberg (Sherman) Film Libraries (West)
Intl. Film Foundation
Maryknoll Fathers & Brothers

Natl. Archives (RG 200)
Natl. Archives of Canada
Natl. Film Board of Canada
Petrified Films, Inc.
Prelinger Assoc., Inc.
Riccitelli (Bruce) Prods.
Source Stock Footage Lib., Inc.
TV Ontario
Timesteps Prods., Inc.
V/tape
See also Labor history; Labor issues;
  specific occupations, industries and
  products

Workers (Agricultural)
Dreamlight Images, Inc.
Estuary Press
Film Bank
Inter-American Foundation
March of Time
Petrified Films, Inc.
Southern Calif. Lib. for Soc. Stud. & Res.
See also Agriculture; Farms and farming;
  Workers (Cotton); Workers (Farm);
  Workers (Migrant); Workers (Sugar)

Workers (Asian American)
Natl. Asian American Telecomm. Assn.
See also Asian Americans

Workers (Automobile)
California Newsreel
Cinema Guild
Prelinger Assoc., Inc.
Studebaker Natl. Museum
Univ. of Missouri-St. Louis
Wayne State Univ., Arch. Labor & Urb.
  Aff.
See also Automobiles (Assembly lines)

Workers (Black)
Allen (John E.) Inc.
Cinema Guild
Memphis State Univ. Libraries
Natl. Railway Historical Soc.
Petrified Films, Inc.
Prelinger Assoc., Inc.
Tulane Univ., Amistad Res. Ctr.
See also Black history and culture

Workers (Blue collar)
Energy Productions
See also Factories; Workers (Automobile);
  Workers (Factory)

Workers (Cannery)
Labor Video Project

Workers (Clerical)
Committee for Labor Access
Radcliffe Coll., Schlesinger Lib.
Univ. of Calif., Berkeley, Labor
  Occupational Health Prog.
Video Tape Library, Ltd.
See also Offices; Secretaries; Workers
  (Office)

Workers (Coal)
Energy Productions
First Run/Icarus Films, Inc.
See also Coal and coal industry; Mining
  (Coal); Workers (Mine)

Workers (Construction)
Petrified Films, Inc.
Spectral Comms.
Video Tape Library, Ltd.
See also Construction

Workers (Cotton)
Fish Films, Inc.

Oxfam America
Petrified Films, Inc.
Prelinger Assoc., Inc.
See also Cotton; Workers (Agricultural)

Workers (Domestic)
First Run/Icarus Films, Inc.
See also Maids; Workers (Household)

Workers (Factory)
Amer. Soc. Hist. Proj. Film Lib.
Dreamlight Images, Inc.
Energy Productions
Petrified Films, Inc.
See also Factories; Workers (Automobile);
  Workers (Blue collar)

Workers (Farm)
Alternative Information Network
Deep Dish TV
Downtown Community TV Ctr.
Prelinger Assoc., Inc.
United Farm Workers of America (UFW)
Univ. of Tex. at Austin, Benson Lat. Am.
  Coll.
See also Agriculture; Farms and farming;
  Workers (Agricultural); Workers
  (Migrant)

Workers (Fruit packers)
Film Bank

Workers (Garment)
Prelinger Assoc., Inc.

Workers (Health)
Altschul Group
Cabscott Broadcast Prods.
Center for Biomedical Comms.
Cimarron Productions
First Run/Icarus Films, Inc.
Labor Video Project
Petrified Films, Inc.
Univ. of Calif., Berkeley, Labor
  Occupational Health Prog.
See also Doctors; Medicine; Nurses and
  nursing

Workers (Health care)
Dartnell
TV Ontario
See also Health care

Workers (High technology)
California Newsreel
See also Technology (High)

Workers (Household)
Tulane Univ., Amistad Res. Ctr.
See also Maids; Workers (Domestic)

Workers (Immigrant)
Cinema Guild
See also Immigrants and immigration;
  Workers (Undocumented)

Workers (Industrial)
Energy Productions
See also Factories; Workers (Automobile);
  Workers (Factory)

Workers (Japan)
California Newsreel
See also Japan

Workers (Laboratory)
Petrified Films, Inc.
See also Laboratories

Workers (Laundry)
Prelinger Assoc., Inc.

See also Laundries and laundromats

Workers (Logging)
Petrified Films, Inc.
See also Logging industry

Workers (Longshore)
Labor Video Project
See also Shipping

Workers (Lumber mill)
Petrified Films, Inc.
See also Mills (Lumber)

Workers (Machinery)
Energy Productions
See also Machinery

Workers (Maritime)
Labor Video Project

Workers (Migrant)
Downtown Community TV Ctr.
Echo Film Prods., Inc.
Inter-American Foundation
Natl. Archives (RG 96)
Natl. Archives (RG 174)
Natl. Archives/Natl. AV Ctr.
Petrified Films, Inc.
United Farm Workers of America (UFW)
See also Workers (Agricultural)

Workers (Mill)
Media Project
See also Mills

Workers (Mine)
Appalshop Films, Inc.
Cinema Guild
Coal Employment Project
Estuary Press
Film Bank
Petrified Films, Inc.
See also Mining; Workers (Coal)

Workers (Motion picture production)
Petrified Films, Inc.
See also Motion pictures (Production)

Workers (Office)
Cimarron Productions
Dreamlight Images, Inc.
Energy Productions
Petrified Films, Inc.
Prelinger Assoc., Inc.
Stegman Productions
Twentieth Century-Fox Movietonews
See also Offices; Secretaries; Workers
  (Clerical)

Workers (Packinghouse)
State Hist. Soc. of Wisconsin
See also Meatpacking

Workers (Palestinian)
Labor Video Project

Workers (Postal)
Film Bank
Petrified Films, Inc.
See also Mail and mail carriers

Workers (Railroad)
Allen (John E.) Inc.
Hogg, John F.
Labor Video Project
Mississippi Dept. of Arch. & Hist.
Natl. Railway Historical Soc.
Petrified Films, Inc.
Prelinger Assoc., Inc.

NOTE: Access policies, availability and restrictions vary for each source. Please read each entry in full. Always consult "General Film and Videotape Collections" (page 599); these comprehensive collections contain material on every conceivable subject.

See also Railroads; Railroads (Pullman porters)

Workers (Refinery)
Energy Productions
See also Oil industry

Workers (Restaurant)
Natl. Restaurant Assn.
Petrified Films, Inc.
See also Restaurants; Waiters and waitresses

Workers (Sanitation)
Environmental Action Coalition
Memphis State Univ. Libraries

Workers (Sheet metal)
TV Ontario
See also Metals and metallurgy

Workers (Shipyard)
Labor Video Project
See also Shipyards

Workers (Steel)
Deep Dish TV
Indiana Univ. Folklore Arch.
Natl. Archives/Natl. AV Ctr.
Petrified Films, Inc.
State Hist. Soc. of Wisconsin
Univ. of Calif., Berkeley, Labor Occupational Health Prog.
See also Steel industry

Workers (Sugar)
Oxfam America
Petrified Films, Inc.
See also Sugar and sugar industry

Workers (Textile)
Prelinger Assoc., Inc.
State Hist. Soc. of Wisconsin
See also Textile industry

Workers (Transport)
Taminent Lib./Wagner Labor Arch.
See also Transportation

Workers (Undocumented)
Labor Video Project
See also Immigrants and immigration; Workers (Migrant)

Workers (White-collar)
Amer. Soc. Hist. Proj. Film Lib.
California Newsreel
Energy Productions
General Motors Corp.
Metro Communications, Inc.
New York City Labor Film Club
Prelinger Assoc., Inc.
Video Tape Library, Ltd.
See also Business scenes; Corporate scenes; Offices; Workers (Office)

Workers (Women)
ABC Distribution (Education)
Allen (John E.) Inc.
Appalshop Films, Inc.
California Newsreel
Canadian Filmmakers Dist. Centre
Coal Employment Project
DEC Film & Video
Deep Dish TV
First Run/Icarus Films, Inc.
Grinberg (Sherman) Film Libraries (West)
Inter-American Foundation
March of Time
Natl. Archives (RG 12)
Natl. Archives (RG 69)
Natl. Archives (RG 86)
Natl. Archives (RG 208)
Natl. Archives of Canada
Radcliffe Coll., Schlesinger Lib.

Univ. of Calif., Berkeley, Labor Occupational Health Prog.
Univ. of Toronto, AV Lib.
See also Women; Women's history; Women's issues

Workers (World War II)
See World War II (U.S., Homefront)

Workers' Alliance
March of Time

Works Progress Administration (WPA)
De Saisset Museum
Everett Pub. Lib., Northwest Hist. Coll.
March of Time
Natl. Archives (RG 69)
Natl. Archives/Natl. AV Ctr.
New Day Films
Parker (Kit) Films
Petrified Films, Inc.

World Trade Center (New York City)
Dreamlight Images, Inc.
Energy Productions
Petrified Films, Inc.
Port Authority of New York & New Jersey

World War I
Allen (John E.) Inc.
Archive Film Prods., Inc.
Em Gee Film Library
Fabulous Footage Inc.
Film Bank
Film Education Institute
Film/Audio Services, Inc.
Fish Films, Inc.
Forsher (James) Prods. & Archives, Inc.
Grinberg (Sherman) Film Libraries (West)
Military/Combat Stock Footage
Natl. Archives (RG 111)
Natl. Archives (RG 200)
Natl. Archives (RG 342)
Natl. Archives of Canada
Natl. Film Board of Canada
Oregon Hist. Soc.
Timesteps Prods., Inc.
Twentieth Century-Fox Movietonews
UCLA Film & Television Archive
Villon Films

World War I (Armistice)
Natl. Archives (RG 24)
Natl. Archives (RG 111)
Petrified Films, Inc.
Twentieth Century-Fox Movietonews

World War I (Atlantic Ocean)
Natl. Archives (RG 24)

World War I (Battles)
Natl. Archives of Canada
Petrified Films, Inc.

World War I (Belgium)
Natl. Archives (RG 24)

World War I (Canada)
Prov. Arch. of Newfoundland & Labrador

World War I (Canada, Canadian Expeditionary Forces)
Natl. Archives of Canada

World War I (Canada, Homefront)
Natl. Archives of Canada

World War I (Dogfights)
Petrified Films, Inc.

World War I (France)
Allen (John E.) Inc.
Natl. Archives (RG 4)
Natl. Archives (RG 24)

Natl. Archives (RG 111)
Natl. Archives (RG 342)
Natl. Archives of Canada

World War I (France, Lafayette Escadrille)
North Carolina Div. of Arch. & Hist.

World War I (Germany)
Allen (John E.) Inc.
Natl. Archives (RG 200)
Natl. Archives (RG 242)
Natl. Archives of Canada

World War I (Germany, Air Force)
Natl. Archives of Canada

World War I (Great Britain)
Natl. Archives (RG 111)
Natl. Archives of Canada
Pyramid Film & Video Corp.

World War I (Great Britain, Air Force)
Natl. Archives of Canada

World War I (Great Britain, Navy)
Natl. Archives of Canada

World War I (Italy)
Allen (John E.) Inc.
Natl. Archives (RG 111)

World War I (Near East)
Natl. Archives (RG 111)

World War I (Paris Peace Conference)
Natl. Archives (RG 200)

World War I (Prisoners of war)
Natl. Archives (RG 24)

World War I (Soviet Union)
Allen (John E.) Inc.
Natl. Archives (RG 111)

World War I (U.S.)
Hoover Institution
Natl. Archives (RG 53)
Natl. Archives (RG 111)
Natl. Archives of Canada

World War I (U.S., Aircraft)
Prelinger Assoc., Inc.

World War I (U.S., Army)
U.S. Army Military Hist. Inst.

World War I (U.S., Army Air Service)
Natl. Archives (RG 342)

World War I (U.S., Department of Agriculture)
Natl. Archives (RG 33)

World War I (U.S., Ford Motor Co.)
Natl. Archives (RG 200)

World War I (U.S., Homefront)
Natl. Archives (RG 111)

World War I (U.S., Naval aviation)
Natl. Archives (RG 24)

World War I (U.S., Navy)
Natl. Archives (RG 24)
Natl. Archives (RG 111)

World War I (U.S., Nurses)
Florentine Films

World War I (U.S., Production)
Natl. Archives (RG 111)

World War II
Amer. Arch. of the Factual Film

Analogous Productions
Archive Film Prods., Inc.
Churchill (Winston) Memorial & Library
Delaware State Div. of Hist. & Cult. Aff.
Denver Pub. Lib., Western Hist. Dept.
Eisenhower (Dwight D.) Library
Em Gee Film Library
Experimental Aircraft Assn.
Fabulous Footage Inc.
Film Bank
Film/Audio Services, Inc.
Films for the Humanities and Sciences
Fish Films, Inc.
Footage Inc.
Forsher (James) Prods. & Archives, Inc.
Grinberg (Sherman) Film Libraries (West)
Halcyon Days Prods.
Hansen, Jack
Holocaust Survivors Mem. Found.
Hoover Institution
Kansas State Historical Society
MacDonald, J. Fred
Manitowoc Maritime Museum
March of Time
Military/Combat Stock Footage
Morcraft Films
Moviecraft, Inc.
Movietime, Inc. Archives
Multi-Media Productions, Inc.
Mus. of Mod. Art, Circulating Film Lib.
Natl. Archives (RG 18)
Natl. Archives (RG 56)
Natl. Archives (RG 80)
Natl. Archives (RG 200)
Natl. Archives (RG 208)
Natl. Archives (RG 306)
Natl. Archives of Canada
Natl. Archives/Natl. AV Ctr.
Natl. Film Board of Canada
Petrified Films, Inc.
Producers Library Service
Roosevelt (Franklin D.) Lib.
Southwest Film/Video Archives, SMU
Streamline Film Archives
Timesteps Prods., Inc.
Twentieth Century-Fox Movietonews
UCLA Film & Television Archive
Univ. of So. Carolina, Newsfilm Lib.
Univ. of Tex. at Austin, Ransom Hum. Res. Ctr., Photo. Coll.
Video Resources N.Y., Inc.
Villon Films
Wiesenthal (Simon) Ctr.

World War II (Africa)
Natl. Archives (RG 342)

World War II (Aircraft)
Petrified Films, Inc.

World War II (Allied Powers)
Natl. Archives (RG 111)
Natl. Archives (RG 179)
Natl. Archives (RG 208)
Natl. Archives of Canada

World War II (Allied Powers, Summit conference)
Natl. Archives (RG 80)
Natl. Archives (RG 111)
Roosevelt (Franklin D.) Lib.

World War II (Allied Powers, Yalta conference)
Natl. Archives (RG 111)

World War II (Asia)
Halcyon Days Prods.
Natl. Archives (RG 107)
Prelinger Assoc., Inc.

World War II (Atrocities)
Natl. Archives (RG 18)
Natl. Archives (RG 238)
Natl. Archives (RG 338)

Prelinger Assoc., Inc.

World War II (Australia)
March of Time

World War II (Austria)
Natl. Archives/Natl. AV Ctr.
Northstar Prods.

World War II (Axis Powers)
Natl. Archives (RG 111)
Natl. Archives (RG 179)
Natl. Archives (RG 208)
Natl. Archives (RG 226)
Natl. Archives of Canada

World War II (Balkans)
Natl. Archives (RG 226)

World War II (Battles)
Moviecraft, Inc.
NSDAP/AO
Natl. Archives (RG 59)
Petrified Films, Inc.
Roosevelt (Franklin D.) Lib.
U.S. Dept. of Defense, Motion Media Rec. Ctr.

World War II (Belgium)
Natl. Archives (RG 28)
Natl. Archives/Natl. AV Ctr.

World War II (Black market)
MacDonald, J. Fred

World War II (Bulge, Battle of the)
Natl. Archives (RG 338)

World War II (Canada)
MacDonald, J. Fred
March of Time
York Univ. Archives

World War II (Canada, Corps of Signals)
Natl. Archives of Canada

World War II (Canada, Homefront)
Natl. Archives of Canada

World War II (Canada, Medical Corps)
Natl. Archives of Canada

World War II (Canada, Princess Patricia's Canadian Light Infantry)
Natl. Archives of Canada

World War II (Canada, V-E Day)
Archives of Ontario

World War II (Captured enemy footage)
Lib. of Congress, M/B/RS
Natl. Archives (RG 80)
Natl. Archives (RG 107)
Natl. Archives (RG 111)
Natl. Archives (RG 242)
Natl. Archives (RG 243)
Natl. Archives (RG 342)
Natl. Archives (RG 428)
Petrified Films, Inc.

World War II (China)
Friends of Free China
Hoover Institution
Natl. Archives (RG 226)
Natl. Archives/Natl. AV Ctr.
Univ. of Tex. at Austin, Ransom Hum. Res. Ctr., Photo. Coll.

World War II (China-Burma-India theater)
General Motors Corp.
Natl. Archives (RG 226)

World War II (Color footage)
Hansen, Jack
Natl. Archives (RG 18)
Natl. Archives (RG 242)
Natl. Archives/Natl. AV Ctr.
Petrified Films, Inc.
Prelinger Assoc., Inc.

World War II (Czechoslovakia)
Natl. Archives/Natl. AV Ctr.

World War II (Denmark)
Natl. Archives/Natl. AV Ctr.

World War II (Eastern Europe)
Intl. Historic Films, Inc.

World War II (Elbe River)
Natl. Archives (RG 242)

World War II (Eniwetok Island)
Natl. Archives (RG 80)

World War II (Espionage)
Natl. Archives (RG 18)

World War II (Europe)
Amer. Portrait, An
Beerger (Norman) Prods.
General Motors Corp.
Halcyon Days Prods.
Natl. Archives (RG 107)
Natl. Archives (RG 342)
Prelinger Assoc., Inc.

World War II (Europe, Jewish resistance)
Ergo Media
Icarus Films Intl., Inc.
Israel Broadcasting Service

World War II (Europe, Postwar occupation and reconstruction)
German Info. Ctr., Film Lib.
Intl. Film Foundation
Natl. Archives (RG 59)
Natl. Archives (RG 306)
Prelinger Assoc., Inc.

World War II (Europe, Resistance)
March of Time

World War II (France)
Hoover Institution
March of Time
Natl. Archives (RG 18)
Natl. Archives (RG 28)
Natl. Archives (RG 242)
Natl. Archives/Natl. AV Ctr.

World War II (France, Dieppe raid)
Natl. Archives of Canada

World War II (France, Liberation)
Natl. Archives of Canada

World War II (France, Normandy)
Natl. Archives/Natl. AV Ctr.
Natl. Archives of Canada

World War II (France, Paris)
Wiesenthal (Simon) Ctr.

World War II (Germany)
German Language Video Center
Intl. Historic Films, Inc.

March of Time
Moviecraft, Inc.
Natl. Archives (RG 18)
Natl. Archives (RG 238)
Natl. Archives (RG 242)
Natl. Archives (RG 243)
Natl. Archives (RG 342)
Prelinger Assoc., Inc.
UCLA Film & Television Archive
Univ. of Tex. in Austin, Ransom Hum. Res. Ctr., Photo. Coll.
Video Yesteryear

World War II (Germany, Berlin)
Natl. Archives (RG 242)
Petrified Films, Inc.
UDS Company

World War II (Germany, Dresden bombing)
Natl. Archives (RG 200)

World War II (Germany, Eichmann trial)
Natl. Jewish Arch. of Broadcasting

World War II (Germany, Nuremberg trials)
Film Bank
Halcyon Days Prods.
March of Time
Natl. Archives (RG 111)
Natl. Archives (RG 238)
Natl. Archives/Natl. AV Ctr.

World War II (Germany, Postwar occupation)
Natl. Archives (RG 18)

World War II (Germany, Rocket experiments)
Natl. Archives (RG 242)
Petrified Films, Inc.

World War II (Germany, Surrender)
Natl. Archives (RG 342)
Natl. Archives/Natl. AV Ctr.

World War II (Great Britain)
British Info. Svcs., Radio & TV Div.
March of Time
Natl. Archives (RG 80)
Natl. Archives (RG 208)
Natl. Archives (RG 342)
Natl. Archives/Natl. AV Ctr.
Roosevelt (Franklin D.) Lib.
UCLA Film & Television Archive

World War II (Great Britain, Battle of Britain)
Natl. Archives of Canada
Petrified Films, Inc.
Univ. of Tex. at Austin, Ransom Hum. Res. Ctr., Photo. Coll.

World War II (Great Britain, London)
Natl. Archives (RG 171)
Natl. Archives (RG 200)

World War II (Great Britain, Queen's Own Rifles)
Natl. Archives of Canada

World War II (Great Britain, Royal Air Force)
Petrified Films, Inc.

World War II (Greece)
Natl. Archives (RG 200)
Natl. Archives (RG 242)

World War II (Guam)
Natl. Archives (RG 80)

World War II (India)
March of Time

World War II (Indonesia, Banda Sea)
Hansen, Jack

World War II (Italy)
Citadel, The
Hoover Institution
Natl. Archives (RG 59)
Natl. Archives (RG 242)
Natl. Archives of Canada
Natl. Archives/Natl. AV Ctr.

World War II (Italy, Sicily)
Natl. Archives (RG 59)

World War II (Japan)
Duke Univ., Perkins Lib.
Hansen, Jack
Hoover Institution
March of Time
Natl. Archives (RG 80)
Natl. Archives (RG 226)
Natl. Archives (RG 238)
Natl. Archives (RG 342)
UCLA Film & Television Archive

World War II (Japan, Army Air Force)
UDS Company

World War II (Japan, Kamikaze attacks)
Archive Film Prods., Inc.
Natl. Archives (RG 80)
Petrified Films, Inc.

World War II (Japan, Okinawa)
Natl. Archives (RG 80)
Natural Reflections Video

World War II (Japan, Postwar occupation)
Duke Univ., Perkins Lib.
Natl. Archives (RG 18)
Natl. Archives (RG 80)
Natl. Archives (RG 342)

World War II (Japan, Surrender)
MacArthur (Gen. Douglas) Memorial
Natl. Archives (RG 80)
Natl. Archives (RG 200)
Natl. Archives (RG 342)

World War II (Japan, War crimes trials)
Natl. Archives (RG 111)
Natl. Archives (RG 238)

World War II (Latin America)
March of Time
Natl. Archives (RG 229)

World War II (Latvia)
Hoover Institution

World War II (Marianas, Battle of the)
Natl. Archives (RG 80)

World War II (Mediterranean)
March of Time

World War II (Midway, Battle of)
Natl. Archives (RG 80)
Natl. Archives/Natl. AV Ctr.

World War II (Naval activities)
Mariners' Museum

NOTE: Access policies, availability and restrictions vary for each source. Please read each entry in full. Always consult "General Film and Videotape Collections" (page 599); these comprehensive collections contain material on every conceivable subject.

World War II (Netherlands)
Natl. Archives (RG 28)
Natl. Archives (RG 200)
Natl. Archives/Natl. AV Ctr.

World War II (North Africa)
Hoover Institution
Natl. Archives (RG 226)
Natl. Archives (RG 242)

World War II (Northern Europe, Liberation)
Natl. Archives of Canada

World War II (Norway)
Natl. Archives/Natl. AV Ctr.
Villon Films

World War II (Pacific theater)
Amer. Portrait, An
Halcyon Days Prods.
MacArthur (Gen. Douglas) Memorial
March of Time
Multi-Media Pre-Accession Point
Natl. Archives (RG 80)
Natl. Archives (RG 242)
Natl. Archives (RG 331)
Natl. Archives (RG 342)
Natl. Archives/Natl. AV Ctr.
Petrified Films, Inc.
Roosevelt (Franklin D.) Lib.

World War II (Pearl Harbor)
Amer. Portrait, An
Experimental Aircraft Assn.
Grinberg (Sherman) Film Libraries (East)
Hawaii Public Broadcasting Authority
Natl. Archives (RG 226)
Natl. Archives (RG 342)
Natl. Archives/Natl. AV Ctr.
Petrified Films, Inc.
Prelinger Assoc., Inc.

World War II (Philippines)
Hansen, Jack
Natl. Archives (RG 242)
Natl. Archives (RG 331)

World War II (Philippines, Bataan)
Natl. Archives/Natl. AV Ctr.

World War II (Poland)
Film/Audio Services, Inc.
Finley (Stuart) Inc.
Natl. Archives (RG 28)
Natl. Archives (RG 226)
Natl. Archives (RG 342)
Natl. Archives/Natl. AV Ctr.

World War II (Poland, Warsaw)
Film/Audio Services, Inc.
Hoover Institution

World War II (Prisoners of war)
Academy of Health Sciences, U.S. Army
Natl. Archives (RG 18)
Natl. Archives (RG 59)
Natl. Archives (RG 80)
Natl. Archives (RG 226)
Natl. Archives (RG 242)
Natl. Archives (RG 331)
Natl. Archives (RG 338)
Natl. Archives (RG 342)

World War II (Propaganda)
MacDonald, J. Fred
Natl. Archives (RG 28)
Pacific Film Archive
Parker (Kit) Films
York Univ. Archives
See also Propaganda and propaganda films

World War II (Rumania)
Natl. Archives (RG 226)

World War II (Saipan)
Natl. Archives (RG 80)

World War II (Solomon Islands)
Natl. Archives (RG 80)

World War II (South Pacific)
Natl. Archives (RG 127)
Natl. Archives of Canada

World War II (Soviet Union)
Hoover Institution
Intl. Assn. of Independent Producers
Intl. Historic Films, Inc.
March of Time
Natl. Archives (RG 208)
Natl. Archives (RG 242)
Natl. Archives of Canada
Natl. Archives/Natl. AV Ctr.
Pilsudski (J.) Inst. of Amer.
Univ. of Tex. at Austin, Ransom Hum.
  Res. Ctr., Photo. Coll.

World War II (Soviet Union, Moscow)
Natl. Archives (RG 342)

World War II (U.S.)
Citadel, The
Hoover Institution
March of Time
Natl. Archives (RG 26)
Natl. Archives (RG 80)
Natl. Archives (RG 107)

World War II (U.S., Amphibious operations)
Natl. Archives (RG 18)
Natl. Archives (RG 26)
Natl. Archives (RG 428)
See also Vehicles (Amphibious)

World War II (U.S., Army)
Natl. Archives/Natl. AV Ctr.
U.S. Army Military Hist. Inst.
U.S. Dept. of Defense, Motion Media Rec.
  Ctr.
Univ. of Ill. Urbana-Champaign, Univ.
  Arch.

World War II (U.S., Army Air Corps)
Natl. Archives (RG 200)

World War II (U.S., Army Air Forces)
Petrified Films, Inc.
Natl. Archives (RG 18)
Natl. Archives (RG 342)
Natl. Archives/Natl. AV Ctr.
U.S. Dept. of Defense, Motion Media Rec.
  Ctr.

World War II (U.S., Army Nurse Corps)
Academy of Health Sciences, U.S. Army

World War II (U.S., Aviation)
Experimental Aircraft Assn.
Petrified Films, Inc.

World War II (U.S., Black people)
Natl. Archives (RG 111)
Natl. Archives (RG 200)
Natl. Archives (RG 208)
Natl. Archives/Natl. AV Ctr.

World War II (U.S., Coast Guard)
Natl. Archives (RG 26)
Natl. Archives (RG 200)

World War II (U.S., Department of Agriculture)
Natl. Archives (RG 33)

World War II (U.S., Entertainment industry)
Hoover Institution

March of Time
Natl. Archives (RG 18)
Natl. Archives (RG 111)
Natl. Archives/Natl. AV Ctr.

World War II (U.S., Ford Motor Co.)
Natl. Archives (RG 200)

World War II (U.S., Homefront)
DEC Film & Video
Film Bank
General Motors Corp.
MacDonald, J. Fred
March of Time
Natl. Archives (RG 59)
Natl. Archives (RG 111)
Natl. Archives (RG 171)
Natl. Archives (RG 179)
Natl. Archives (RG 188)
Natl. Archives (RG 200)
Natl. Archives (RG 208)
Natl. Archives (RG 223)
Natl. Archives/Natl. AV Ctr.
Pennsylvania State Arch.
Petrified Films, Inc.
Prelinger Assoc., Inc.
State Hist. Soc. of Iowa
North Carolina Div. of Arch. & Hist.

World War II (U.S., Japanese Americans)
Natl. Archives (RG 111)
Natl. Archives (RG 210)
See also Japanese Americans (World War II internment)

World War II (U.S., Marine Corps)
Multi-Media Pre-Accession Point
Natl. Archives (RG 127)
Natl. Archives (RG 200)

World War II (U.S., Materiel)
Petrified Films, Inc.

World War II (U.S., Merchant marine)
Natl. Archives (RG 178)

World War II (U.S., Native Americans)
Native Amer. Pub. Broad. Cons.

World War II (U.S., Naval aviation)
Natl. Archives (RG 428)

World War II (U.S., Navy)
Battleship Cove
Manitowoc Maritime Museum
Natl. Archives (RG 80)
Natl. Archives (RG 200)
Natl. Archives (RG 428)
Natl. Archives/Natl. AV Ctr.

World War II (U.S., Neutrality)
March of Time

World War II (U.S., Nurses)
MacDonald, J. Fred

World War II (U.S., Production)
Film Bank
General Motors Corp.
Manitowoc Maritime Museum
Natl. Archives (RG 111)
Natl. Archives (RG 178)
Natl. Archives (RG 179)
Prelinger Assoc., Inc.
Studebaker Natl. Museum

World War II (U.S., Reconversion)
March of Time
Prelinger Assoc., Inc.
Twentieth Century-Fox Movietonews

World War II (U.S., Rest and recreation)
Natl. Archives (RG 18)

World War II (U.S., V-E Day)
Film Bank
Natl. Archives (RG 18)
Petrified Films, Inc.

World War II (U.S., V-J Day)
Natl. Archives (RG 18)
Natl. Archives (RG 80)
Petrified Films, Inc.
Timesteps Prods., Inc.

World War II (U.S., Victory gardens)
Connecticut State Library
General Motors Corp.
Natl. Archives (RG 171)

World War II (U.S., War correspondents)
Natl. Archives (RG 18)

World War II (U.S., Weapons development)
Mass. Inst. of Tech., MIT Museum

World War II (U.S., Women)
DEC Film & Video
Natl. Archives (RG 208)
Natl. Archives (RG 342)
Pennsylvania State Arch.
State Hist. Soc. of Iowa

World War II (Yugoslavia)
Natl. Archives (RG 226)

World's Fairs
Allen (John E.) Inc.
Analogous Productions
Archive Film Prods., Inc.
Film/Audio Services, Inc.
See also Louisiana Purchase Exposition;
  Pan-American Exposition; Pan-Pacific
  Exposition

World's Fairs (Brussels, 1958)
Natl. Archives (RG 59)

World's Fairs (Chicago, 1933-34)
Allen (John E.) Inc.
Amer. Portrait, An
MacDonald, J. Fred
Petrified Films, Inc.
Southern Calif. Lib. for Soc. Stud. & Res.

World's Fairs (Montreal, 1967)
Analogous Productions
Natl. Archives of Canada

World's Fairs (New Orleans, 1984)
Louisiana State Off. of Sec. of State

World's Fairs (New York, 1939-40)
Allen (John E.) Inc.
Amer. Portrait, An
Analogous Productions
General Motors Corp.
Petrified Films, Inc.
Prelinger Assoc., Inc.
Sarnoff (David) Res. Ctr. Lib.
Streamline Film Archives
Univ. of Tex. at Austin, Ransom Hum.
  Res. Ctr., Photo. Coll.

World's Fairs (New York, 1964-65)
General Motors Corp.
MacDonald, J. Fred
New York Pub. Lib., Rare Books &
  Manuscripts Div.
Petrified Films, Inc.
Prelinger Assoc., Inc.
Streamline Film Archives

World's Fairs (San Antonio, 1968)
Natl. Archives (RG 43)

World's Fairs (San Francisco, 1939-40)
General Motors Corp.
Oregon Hist. Soc.
Petrified Films, Inc.
Prelinger Assoc., Inc.

World's Fairs (Seattle, 1962)
Center for Pacific Northwest Studies
Hist. Soc. of Seattle & King County
Natl. Archives (RG 43)
Prelinger Assoc., Inc.
Univ. of Mich., Mich. Hist. Colls.

World's Fairs (Spokane, 1974)
Eastern Washington State Historical Soc.
Natl. Archives (RG 151)

World's Fairs (Vancouver, 1987)
TV Ontario

Worms
Dreamlight Images, Inc.
Film Bank

Worry (Emotion)
Petrified Films, Inc.

Wounded Knee, S. Dak. (History and culture)
Buffalo Bill Historical Center
Cinema Guild
Intermedia Arts Minnesota
Natl. Archives (RG 200)

Wounds
Film Bank

Wozniak, Stephen
Computer Television Group, Inc.

Wreath-laying
Twentieth Century-Fox Movietonews

Wreaths
Film Bank

Wrecking
See Automobiles (Wrecking); Demolition

Wrecks (Underwater)
See Shipwrecks

Wrens
Wings Wildlife Prods. Inc.

Wrestling
Analogous Productions
Archive Film Prods., Inc.
Athletic Institute
Dreamlight Images, Inc.
Film Bank
Fish Films, Inc.
Media Project
Moviecraft, Inc.
Movietime, Inc. Archives
Natl. Archives of Canada
Sportsfilm
Titan Sports, Inc.
Twentieth Century-Fox Movietonews
Video Tape Library, Ltd.

Wrestling (College)
NCAA Productions
Oregon State Univ., Archives

Wrestling (High school)
Eastern Kentucky Univ.

Wrestling (Instruction)
NCAA Productions

Wright, Al
Yukon Archives

Wright, Frank Lloyd
Amer. Federation of the Arts
Unicorn Projects

Wright, Orville and Wilbur
Archive Film Prods., Inc.
Experimental Aircraft Assn.
Film Bank
Film Education Institute
Forsher (James) Prods. & Archives, Inc.
Grinberg (Sherman) Film Libraries (West)
Metro Communications, Inc.
Military/Combat Stock Footage
Natl. Archives (RG 342)
Natl. Archives of Canada
Petrified Films, Inc.
Smithsonian Inst., Natl. Air & Space Museum
Timesteps Prods., Inc.
Wright Brothers Coll.

Writing (History of)
Prelinger Assoc., Inc.

Writing (Instruction)
Intellimation

Wurlitzer, Rudy
Giorno Poetry Systems Inst.

Wyeth, Andrew
Creative Film Society

Wynn, Ed
Banks Film Library
Encore Entertainment
Shokus Video

Wynn, Keenan
Banks Film Library
Spalla (Rick) Video Prods.

Wynn, Robert
Univ. of Wyoming, Amer. Heritage Ctr.

Wyoming
Beerger (Norman) Prods.
Energy Prods.
Film Bank
First Group Comms., Inc.
Petrified Films, Inc.
Preview Media
Summit Films, Inc.

Wyoming (History and culture)
Buffalo Bill Historical Center
Glenbow Mus. Arch.
Oregon Hist. Soc.
Rockefeller Arch. Ctr.
Wyoming State Historical Society

X (Rock and roll band)
Target Video

XTC (Rock and roll band)
Target Video

X-ray machines
Johns Hopkins Univ., School of Medicine

X-ray technicians
Cimarron Productions
TV Ontario

X-rays
Archive Film Prods., Inc.
CBS News Archives
Film Bank

Historical Health Film Coll.
Petrified Films, Inc.
Prelinger Assoc., Inc.
Rosebush Visions Corp.
Wesleyan Cinema Archives

Xian, China
Farkas Studios, Ltd.

Xian, China (History and culture)
Film/Audio Services, Inc.

Xochimilco, Mexico
Source Stock Footage Lib., Inc.

Xochimilco, Mexico (History and culture)
Petrified Films, Inc.

Xylophones
Spectral Comms.

Yachts and yachting
America's Cup Org. Comm.
Analogous Productions
Archive Film Prods., Inc.
Broad Street Prods.
Channel Sea Television
Dreamlight Images, Inc.
Film Bank
Forsher (James) Prods. & Archives, Inc.
Manitowoc Maritime Museum
Metro Communications, Inc.
Mystic Seaport Mus., Inc.
Natl. Archives (RG 26)
Natl. Archives of Canada
Offshore Productions
Spectral Comms.
Sportsfilm
TV Ontario
U.S. Olympic Comm.

Yachts and yachting (Presidential)
Natl. Archives (RG 24)
Northstar Prods.
Roosevelt (Franklin D.) Lib.

Yachts and yachting (Racing)
America's Cup Org. Comm.
Mystic Seaport Mus., Inc.
Natl. Archives (RG 26)
Sportsfilm
See also America's Cup; Boats and boating (Racing); Sailing

Yaks
Petrified Films, Inc.
TV Ontario

Yalow, Rosalyn S.
Amer. Chemical Soc.

Yangtze River, China
Sobek Productions

Yarborough, Ralph W.
Univ. of Tex. at Austin, Barker Tex. Hist. Ctr.

Yarn spinning
Archive Film Prods., Inc.

Yazoo City, Miss.
Film Bank

Yeast
Archive Film Prods., Inc.

Yecuana Chaman people
Cinema Guild

Yellow fever
Historical Health Film Coll.
Rockefeller Arch. Ctr.

Yellowknife, Northwest Territories
TV Ontario

Yellowknife, Northwest Territories (History and culture)
Northwest Territories Archives

Yellowstone National Park, Idaho-Mont.-Wyo.
Beerger (Norman) Prods.
Dreamlight Images, Inc.
Energy Productions
Film Bank
Film Search
Montana Dept. of Commerce
North Country Media Group
Petrified Films, Inc.
Preview Media
Source Stock Footage Lib., Inc.
U.S. Natl. Park Service Hist. Coll.

Yellowstone National Park, Idaho-Mont.-Wyo. (History and culture)
Archive Film Prods., Inc.
Buffalo Bill Hist. Ctr.
Natl. Archives (RG 70)
Oregon Hist. Soc.
Rockefeller Arch. Ctr.
Roosevelt (Franklin D.) Lib.
Schiele Museum

Yemen
Canadian Broadcasting Co.

Yemen (History and culture)
Natl. Ctr. for Jewish Film

Yeoman, Bill
Fellowship of Christian Athletes

Yevtushenko, Yevgeny
IFEX Films

Yippies
Payne, Roz

Yo-yos
Archive Film Prods., Inc.
Film Bank
Petrified Films, Inc.
Video Resources N.Y., Inc.

Yoga
Hartley Film Found., Inc.
Peralta Colleges TV
Rudra Press
Video-SIG

Yonkers, N.Y. (History and culture)
Petrified Films, Inc.

York and King (Comedians)
Videobrary, Inc.

York, Dick
Prelinger Assoc., Inc.

York, Duke of
Archive Film Prods., Inc.

Yorktown, Va.
Metro Communications, Inc.

Yorty, Sam
Banks Film Library

NOTE: Access policies, availability and restrictions vary for each source. Please read each entry in full. Always consult "General Film and Videotape Collections" (page 599); these comprehensive collections contain material on every conceivable subject.

Television Series Index

This finding aid lists television series cited in the source listings only. It is not a definitive list of program owners or holders of rights. Please read entries in their entirety to ascertain specific policies relating to viewing, access, duplication, licensing and reuse.

THE VIDEO DATA BANK

- The largest distributor of the most comprehensive collections of experimental video works

- Interviews with contemporary artists, critics, photographers

- Works on feminist and contemporary political issues in 3/4" format

- Available for purchase in VHS format: **What Does *She* Want** and **Video Against AIDS**

- Call or write for catalogs and new listings or to book time in the screening room.

School of the Art Institute
of Chicago
280 South Columbus Drive
Chicago, Illinois 60603
(312) 443-3793

22 Warren Street
New York, NY 10007
(212) 233-3441

Glossary

A&B rolls Motion picture elements employing two rolls, one each for odd and even-numbered shots. Each roll of film, which can be either negative or positive, is of equal length; picture material on one roll corresponds to black (opaque) film leader on the other. When printed, images on the two rolls combine to produce a single roll of picture. A&B printing is used to permit fades, dissolves and "optical" effects without optical printing, and also prevents visible splices from appearing in the **release print.**

acetate-base Also known as **safety stock.** Film base material in general use (1951-present). A binder holds the film base to the emulsion, which incorporates the image. Unlike **nitrate-base,** which was in widespread use before 1951, acetate-base film will not burn rapidly and is not considered a fire hazard. Certain varieties of acetate base (such as diacetate) pose special preservation problems, even though they are not inflammable. See "Film and Videotape Preservation Factsheet" (page A-28) for further information.

actuality footage Footage depicting real life or actual events.

ADO Trademark of the Ampex Corporation. Abbreviation for *Ampex Digital Optics.* Electronic device for generating computerized video effects and distortions.

Agfacolor Color process originally developed in Germany (1930s) employing a single strip of film with three emulsion layers, each layer corresponding to a primary color. **Ansco Color,** introduced in the United States after World War II, was derived from this process.

aircheck Videotape or audiotape copy of a program, recorded off-air as broadcast.

anamorphic Image horizontally compressed by special lenses to fit the width of the film frame, then expanded during projection to its normal width and appearance. The vertical axis of the image is not distorted. Numerous anamorphic systems of cinematography have been developed; best-known are **CinemaScope,** SuperScope and Panavision.

Ansco color System of color cinematography originally invented in Germany (1930s) and marketed there as **Agfacolor.** After World War II, the system was imported into the U.S. to compete with the **Technicolor** process.

archives Institution involved in the storage and preservation of historically significant records. See **film archives.**

backing Original, first-generation or best available film **element.**

Betacam Broadcast-quality videotape format (introduced 1981) using 1/2" tape transported at a speed six times faster than that employed by consumer **Betamax** recorders. Chrominance and luminance (the two components of the video signal) are recorded separately, providing higher image quality and eliminating image artifacts.

Betacam SP Newer version of the **Betacam** system (developed 1985) utilizing metal particle videotape capable of recording higher video subcarrier frequencies, yielding improved picture resolution and dubbing capability.

Betamax I, II and **III** Industrial-quality and consumer videotape format using 1/2" videotape (introduced 1976 by Sony). Has lost market share to VHS, but still used widely throughout Latin America. **Betamax II** and **Betamax III** are similar formats operating at slower speeds.

broadcast quality Footage meeting technical standards for television broadcast or cablecast. Frequently, stock footage libraries decline to provide **broadcast quality** footage until all license fees are paid, preferring to provide footage with **visible time code.** Many provide **reference-quality film-to-videotape transfers,** which are economical to make but do not meet broadcast standards.

B-roll In broadcast journalism, footage or cutaways (usually silent or accompanied by natural sound) shot to accompany interviews or appearances of on-air talent.

burn-in See **visible time code.**

can A container for motion-picture film. In stating the size of a collection, it should be noted that the number of cans do not necessarily respond to the number of titles or completed productions; many titles may be held in multiple copies, and the elements for a given film may fill many cans.

CAV format Constant Angular Velocity laser videodisc format. Each side of a standard CAV disc contains up to 54,000 tracks, each representing one video frame (30 minutes playing time total). Because CAV discs reproduce exactly one frame per disc revolution, features such as freeze-frame, step-frame and slow motion are possible.

CinemaScope System of **anamorphic** cinematography developed originally (1953) for Twentieth Century-Fox. Many other anamorphic widescreen systems have since been introduced.

cinemacrography Also known as **macrocinematography.** Photography of small objects so as to magnify them, using special lenses (macro lenses) rather than microscopes.

cinemicrography Also known as **microcinematography.** Filming through microscopes or other magnifying devices.

clearances Permissions to use copyrighted or proprietary moving images, still photographs, music or literary works, likenesses of recognizable individuals, certain buildings and locations, and other images and sounds as required.

clip rights Rights to use excerpts or "clips" from completed films or videotapes.

CLV format Constant Linear Velocity laser videodisc format. Each side of a standard CLV disc holds up to 60 minutes playing time. Although CLV discs store twice as much program material as CAV discs, features such as freeze-frame, step-frame and slow motion are not generally supported.

composite print Print incorporating picture and soundtrack on the same strip of film. See also **release print.**

copyright Form of protection provided by the laws of the United States to the authors of "original works of authorship" including literary, dramatic, music, artistic and audiovisual works, whether published or unpublished. Copyright law generally gives the owner of copyright the exclusive right to do, and to authorize others to do, the following: *to reproduce the copyrighted work*; *to prepare derivative works* based upon the copyrighted work; *to distribute copies* of the copyrighted work to the public by sale or other transfer of ownership, or by rental, lease or lending; *to perform the copyrighted work publicly,* in the case of motion pictures and other audiovisual works, and *to display the copyrighted work publicly,* including the individual images of a motion picture or other audiovisual work. For more information on copyright, see Philip Miller's article, "Licensing Footage: Copyright and Other Legal Considerations" (page A-19) and "How to Investigate the Copyright Status of a Work" (page A-23).

custom shooting services Many producers and stock footage libraries will shoot specific footage to meet a client's request. In this way the client enjoys first use of the footage, which may then enter the library for subsequent sale to other users.

dailies Positive prints made from camera negatives and used to check the results of the preceding day's shooting. Also known as **rushes.**

DGA member Member of the Directors Guild of America.

distribution In *Footage 89,* used to denote the loan, rental, syndication and/or sale of films and videotapes.

D1 All-digital videotape system (introduced 1986). Used most widely in computerized graphics and animation applications, digital video permits many generations of editing and/or dubbing without loss of quality.

D2 Hybrid digital videotape system (introduced 1987), employing conventional analog video inputs and outputs while digitizing signals internally. D2 is less expensive than D1 and more easily integrated into existing videotape production systems.

dope sheet Reports, generally prepared by news or documentary camerapersons, describing footage that has been shot. Dope sheets frequently indicate which takes of a given scene are of superior quality, and may also describe conditions encountered on a shoot.

double-system sound Sound recorded on film or magnetic tape separately from the picture.

duplication In *Footage 89,* used to denote duplication of film or videotape material whether or not the material is actually licensed or reused. Many sources permit duplication of material (e.g., for academic, research or demonstration purposes) but prohibit **licensing** or **reuse.** Conversely, other sources (e.g., stock footage libraries) may furnish material for licensing or reuse while limiting or controlling duplication. With few exceptions, stock footage libraries require that all materials furnished to customers be returned upon the conclusion of their productions.

Eastmancolor Color negative film manufactured by Kodak (introduced 1951). Now the primary medium of origination for most North American motion pictures. Available in 35mm and 16mm. Until the 1980s, its color dyes were known for their impermanence, and many films originally shot in Eastmancolor have faded to a permanent reddish-magenta, especially in the case of release prints. A new dye-stable Eastmancolor film is now in use, however, and the life of Eastmancolor moving images is now claimed to be from 75 to 100 years, provided that specified temperature and humidity conditions are maintained.

ECO Ektachrome Commercial (color reversal) film manufactured by Kodak. Replaced **Kodachrome** in professional motion picture markets.

edited film In contrast to **unedited footage,** a completed, fully structured and cut production in final form.

EFP Electronic Field Production (videotape production outside a studio).

EIAJ Abbreviation for Electronic Industries Association of Japan, promulgator of various industry standards. In *Footage 89,* refers to one format for 1/2" open reel videotape which was standardized in the early 1960s and heavily used, due to its use by Sony in much of its 1/2" open reel equipment in the 1960s and 1970s.

8mm The narrowest-gauge motion picture film, containing 80 frames per foot, primarily used by amateur and home movie makers. Supplanted and largely replaced by **Super 8mm** in 1966.

8mm video Amateur videotape format introduced by Sony in 1984. Also known as **Video 8.** High-band Video 8 equipment, known as "High 8" and offering near-broadcast quality, was introduced in the United States in 1989.

Ektachrome Commercial (ECO) Color reversal film manufactured by Kodak. Replaced Kodachrome in professional motion picture markets.

element Film or videotape material available for duplication or use in a production.

ENG Electronic News Gathering (production of news material on videotape).

establishing shot Shot which establishes a location or mood, or fixes a sequence in a specific time or space (e.g., shots of a city skyline, landmark, or the exterior of a building).

Fairchild cassette Enclosure holding an endless loop of **Super 8mm** film which may be projected simply by insertion into a projector, avoiding threading and film handling.

film archives Institution involved in the storage and preservation of motion picture materials. The primary responsibility of a film archives is to preserve the materials in its custody.

filmstrip Also known as slidefilm. Strip containing a succession of images intended to be projected individually. May be synchronized with a phonograph record or audiotape. Filmstrips were popularized beginning in the 1910s and were often produced when the expense of motion picture production was unwarranted; they saw heavy use in schools and training situations.

film-to-videotape transfer Process of converting filmed images to videotape. Many stock footage libraries furnish **reference-quality** transfers (not suitable for broadcast) for demonstration purposes. **Broadcast-quality** transfers are performed using special equipment (e.g., **Rank Cintel**, Bosch).

film transfer See **film-to-videotape transfer.**

finding aid Lists, files, inventories, transcripts or other similar reference materials useful to researchers working with a particular collection.

fine grain, fine grain master or **fine grain master positive** High-definition positive black and white film **element** made from an original **negative.** Fine grain masters are used to make duplicate (or dupe) negatives, from which **release prints** are made, thus protecting **original negatives** from wear.

flatbed Film editing and viewing tables manufactured by **Steenbeck, Moviola** and Kem, among others. Silent or sound film and separate soundtracks rest on plates which run through the machine horizontally; the picture is viewed on a small screen. Generally, slow-motion and accelerated viewing speeds are provided.

flyby Footage shot from a moving aircraft, generally of a fixed or slower-moving subject.

format Film formats include **IMAX, 70mm, 35mm, 28mm,** 17.5mm, **16mm, 9.5mm, Super 8mm, 8mm,** and others. Videotape formats include **2", 1", Betacam, MII, 3/4", VHS, 1/2" open reel, VHS, Betamax I, II and III,** and others. See "Film and Videotape Preservation Factsheet" (page A-28) for additional information.

free loan Distribution for which no rental or distribution fee is charged. Shipping and handling fees, however, may apply.

Many films and videotapes sponsored by corporations and institutions are available for free loan through the organizations themselves or through distributors such as Modern Talking Picture Service and Audience Planners.

full rights All rights associated with the duplication, distribution, broadcast, exhibition, licensing and release of a film or videotape, including theatrical; non-theatrical; cable, broadcast and pay television; educational; and corporate (in-house).

gauge Width of film, commonly **70mm, 35mm, 28mm, 16mm, Super 8mm** and **8mm.** See "Film and Videotape Preservation Factsheet" (page A-28) for additional information.

1/2" open reel Also known as **reel-to-reel.** Videotape format introduced in the late 1960s. Its low cost and portability (as part of the "portapak," a portable camera/recorder combination) was a factor in the birth of the independent videomaking movement. Many videotapes in this format cannot be played without special treatment and are in need of immediate preservation. See "Old Open-Reel Videotape Restoration" (page A-31).

HDTV Abbreviation for High Definition Television, currently known also as Advanced Television (ATV). HDTV is not one system, but rather a term denoting some 30 proposals for advanced television systems, a handful of which have been demonstrated and are in use in Japan, Europe and the U.S. One or more proposals will presumably be adopted as new television standards. Though HDTV systems differ in technical detail, most employ twice as many horizontal resolution lines as ordinary television systems, transmit a wider-screen picture and attempt to achieve resolution and a "look" akin to theatrical motion pictures.

high-speed cinematography When footage shot at higher-than-normal speeds is viewed at normal speed, the action appears in slow motion. High-speed cinematography is also used in scientific research and in shooting miniatures or models.

homevideo Videotapes (generally VHS, Betamax or Video 8) produced for rental or sale to the general public.

IMAX Motion picture format designed for projection on very large screens. Using film measuring approx. 71mm by 53mm (approx. 10 times larger than 35mm) moving through the camera and projector horizontally, an image of extremely high resolution and visual presence is achieved.

indemnification Compensation for claims, losses, damages and liabilities that may be incurred as a result of footage licensing or reuse. Most newsreel, television and stock footage libraries, as well as many public institutions, require footage users to indemnify them, usually stipulating that any legal challenges will be resolved at the users' expense. See "Licensing Footage: Copyright and Other Legal Considerations" (page A-19).

internegative Negatives used for striking **release prints.** Depending on the nature of the duplication path, internegatives can be made either from positive or negative **originals.**

interpositive Color master positive printed from an original negative. Interpositives are used for making dupe negatives, which in turn are used for striking **release prints.**

ITFS Abbreviation for Instructional Television Fixed Service. System of microwave television transmission used by local and regional school systems to transmit educational programs.

IVC Abbreviation for International Video Corporation, manufacturer of videotape recording and playback equipment. In *Footage 89,* refers to an early 1" format not compatible with **1" Type A** or **1" Type C.**

kill fee Payment for footage which has been supplied by a source but not actually aired or used as originally planned. Many stock footage libraries charge customers a minimum license fee whenever master or **broadcast-quality** material is released; this fee becomes a kill fee if plans change and the material is not used for its intended purpose.

kinescope A film recording of a live television transmission or video program, photographed directly off a television screen. Prior to the invention of videotape in 1956, kinescopes were the only means of recording television programs for delay or rebroadcast, and were widely used to distribute programs to remote stations (not connected to networks by cable) and for delayed broadcast to various time zones. Today, various kinescope processes (some proprietary) are employed for videotape-to-film transfers.

Kinetoscope Viewing machine developed 1891 by Thomas A. Edison and W. K. L. Dickson. Motion pictures on short strips were viewed through a peephole; the machines were frequently coin-operated.

Kodachrome Color **reversal** film (16mm and 8mm) introduced in 1935. Known for its color fidelity and brilliance, Kodachrome has been a mainstay of amateurs and low-to-medium budget industrial and educational filmmakers, and is still in use.

Kodascope Series of 16mm motion pictures (features and short subjects of all kinds) distributed to the home market by Eastman Kodak Co., beginning in the 1920s. Kodascopes were introduced to distribute viewable product to the growing number of home projector owners.

laserdisc See videodisc.

license fees Fees charged by a holder of copyright and/or other rights for reuse of moving image material.

licensing In *Footage 89,* the **reuse** of moving image material as permitted by a holder of copyright and/or other rights to the material.

loan Distribution for which no charge is made.

macrocinematography See **cinemacrography.**

magnetic sound Sound recorded on magnetic media, including magnetic tape, magnetic film (generally 35mm or 16mm format) or a **magnetic track** on the same strand of film as the picture track.

magnetic track Magnetically recorded soundtrack placed on the same strand of film as the picture in the area normally used for optical soundtrack. Also known as mag stripe. Magnetic tracks are frequently found on 16mm newsfilm, which utilized them for direct sound recording.

MARC Abbreviation for MAchine Readable Cataloging.

master or **master element** The best-quality material (i.e., original or closest to the original) available for a given moving image sequence. Depending upon circumstances, this might be a film negative, a film positive or a videotape master.

microcinematography See **cinemicrography.**

MOS Silent.

motion media See **moving image.**

moving image Generic descriptive term encompassing motion picture film, videotape, videodisc, computer graphics, motion holography and other media. Sometimes known as **motion media.**

Moviola Trademark for a machine used to view film, usually during the editing process. *Upright Moviolas,* the original configuration, are still in widespread use, especially by feature and commercial editors. *Flatbed Moviolas,* in which rolls of film sit on horizontal circular plates, are frequently seen in editing rooms and stock footage libraries. Both permit multi-speed viewing and analysis of footage and magnetic soundtracks.

MII Broadcast-quality videotape format introduced by Panasonic in 1986. Currently in use by the NBC Television Network and many of its affiliates for location and studio production. Uses metal particle videotape to record at high video subcarrier frequencies, improving detail and resolution.

multistandard Equipment operating on more than one television standard.

newsfilm In *Footage 89,* denotes film shot by or for television stations or news organizations depicting news events. Newsfilm is distinct from newsreel film in that newsreel film was shot primarily for theatrical release.

newsreel Short films depicting news, sports, oddities and other general-interest stories, produced primarily for theatrical release. Newsreels date back to the beginnings of motion picture production in the late 1890s and flourished until competition from television news broadcasts forced them out of business in the 1950s and 1960s. Five major newsreels were produced in the United States. All were distributed through major studios: *Fox Movietone News,* released through Twentieth Century-Fox; *News of the Day* (also known as *Hearst Metrotone News*), released through MGM; *Paramount News; Universal Newsreel;* and *Warner-Pathé News,* released through Warner Bros. Numerous other newsreels were produced, including *The March of Time, All-American Newsreel* (intended for Black audiences) and *Kinograms.*

9.5mm Film format marketed primarily to amateurs and home users in Europe, introduced by Pathé Freres in 1923. 9.5mm film was perforated in the center of the strip between frames and used a large portion of the film area for picture information.

nitrate-base Film stock used for 35mm motion picture film prior to 1951. Nitrate-base film is inflammable; national and local fire codes restrict its storage to specially designed and located vaults. Nitrate-base film is also subject to deterioration, and all nitrate film must be considered endangered until copied (preserved) onto safety film stock. Though nitrate film was no longer produced after 1951, hundreds of millions of feet (including feature films, newsreels, documentaries and actuality footage) remain unpreserved at present. See "Film and Videotape Preservation Factsheet" (page A-28).

non-theatrical Distribution of motion pictures in educational, institutional and private situations.

NTSC Abbreviation for National Television Standards Committee. In 1941, the NTSC recommended the television standard which, with some revisions, currently governs broadcasting in the United States, Canada, parts of Latin America and Japan.

1" In *Footage 89,* generally refers to **1" Type C,** the predominant 1" videotape format in use throughout North America.

1" Type A Earliest 1" videotape standard, still in use in Europe and in some North American locations.

1" Type C Videotape format in general use throughout North America for broadcast and studio production.

optical sound System for the recording and reproduction of sound on film in which a soundtrack incorporating light patterns corresponds to electrical impulses that are converted into original sound. Release prints generally employ optical soundtracks running parallel to the visual track; soundtrack and picture are most often separated in preprint materials.

original Also known as **camera original.** First-generation (and highest quality) film element (the actual film used to photograph a subject).

outtake Material shot but not used in a completed film or videotape.

PAL Abbreviation for Phase Alternation by Line. Television standard used outside North America (including the United Kingdom, Germany, many other European countries and the People's Republic of China) employing 625 horizontal lines of resolution and 25 frames per second.

PAL-M Version of **PAL** used in Brazil.

preservation master Film element made for preservation purposes, usually one generation removed from an endangered element (e.g., a safety **fine grain master positive** printed from a nitrate negative).

preview The loan of a film or videotape in order to permit its evaluation for purchase. Most distributors permit bona fide potential purchasers to preview films for purchase, but do not allow previews-for-rental.

process plate Background shots, either stationary or moving, produced for rear projection behind live action as it is being photographed.

public domain Not subject to **copyright.** Public domain works may be freely reproduced and reused by anybody for any purpose. Works fall into the public domain in the United States for various reasons, including the expiration of their copyright, publication without proper copyright notice, or the failure to secure legal copyright. Works produced by the United States government are generally not subject to copyright law and, from the moment of their creation, are in the public domain. However, the determination of a work's status is often complicated, and many situations can restrict the reuse of public domain works. Works that are in the public domain in the United States may still be under copyright protection in other countries. Films or videotapes themselves in the public domain may incorporate copyrighted materials (e.g., music) and may be based in whole or in part on copyrighted source materials (e.g., books, stories or dramatic works). Finally, the public domain status of a work has no bearing on additional "bundled" rights (e.g., the right to reuse the likeness of an individual or the right to rebroadcast performances originally filmed or taped under a union contract). See also **third-party clearances.** For additional information, see "Licensing Footage: Copyright and Other Legal Considerations" (page A-19) and "How to Investigate the Copyright Status of a Work" (page A-23).

quadruplex or **quad** See **2".**

q.v. See the specified entry. From the Latin *quod vide* (which see).

Rank Cintel Broadcast-quality system for transferring film to videotape.

raw footage Unedited original footage not part of a completed film or videotape.

reel to reel See **1/2" open reel.**

reference cassette Videotapes supplied for reference, evaluation or screening purposes.

reference-quality Videotapes intended for reference, evaluation, screening or rough-cut editing rather than for duplication or broadcast.

regular 8mm Film gauge (80 frames per foot) used primarily by amateur filmmakers. Although the dimensions of the film itself are identical to Super 8mm, regular 8mm has larger perforations and a smaller image area.

release print A print (generally a **composite print,** with picture and soundtrack in sync) of a completed motion picture, intended for screening and distribution.

release sheet Promotional or descriptive material relating to a film or videotape, often prepared by a producer or distributor.

reuse In *Footage 89,* the use of moving image material by permission of its owner or custodian, who may or may not possess the copyright and/or other rights to the material; also, the use of public domain material, which is exempt from copyright considerations.

reversal Film which when developed yields a positive image.

runby Stationary shot of a moving vehicle or other subject.

rushes See **dailies.**

safety stock Film stock used for 35mm motion pictures (1951-present); 16mm (1920s-present) and for other gauges. Unlike **nitrate-base** film, safety film is not inflammable.

scratched workprint Workprint furnished by a stock footage library to a user and intentionally scratched lengthwise to prevent unauthorized use.

SECAM Acronym for *Sequential Couleur à Mémoire.* Line-sequential color television system originally introduced in France in 1962. Presently used as broadcast standard in France, the Soviet Union, parts of Eastern Europe, Africa and the Middle East.

70mm Film gauge generally used for release prints of large-budget feature films. Generally, 70mm prints are made from 65mm negatives or blown up from 35mm negatives.

show history Copy of a television program as broadcast.

16mm Film gauge (introduced 1923) widely used by educational, industrial, government, scientific and amateur filmmakers. Most non-theatrical film distribution, as well as most television newsfilm and documentary film production, has also used the 16mm format. 16mm runs 40 frames to the foot.

standards conversion The process of converting television or video transmissions and videotapes from one standard to another. Since three basic television standards (**NTSC, PAL** and **SECAM**) are in use throughout the world, and since equipment designed for one standard cannot reproduce video signals in another, the necessity for conversion arises. In the early days of international television, this was accomplished by simple means; a camera was trained on a monitor. Today, the quality of the process has greatly increased, but so has its cost. See **NTSC, PAL** and **SECAM.**

Steenbeck Trademark for a machine used to view film. Rolls of film and/or soundtracks sit on horizontal circular plates and can be viewed in or out of synchronization at various speeds. Steenbecks are frequently used in editing rooms and stock footage libraries.

stock footage sales library A corporation or organization that sells or supplies stock footage as one of its primary activities. In *Footage 89,* all stock footage is considered to be available for reuse.

stop-motion animation Technique in which the camera is started and stopped to allow for movement of the subject when the camera is not shooting, in order to produce an effect when the film is run continuously. Although **time-lapse cinematography** is technically one kind of stop-motion animation, the term is more often used to refer to a technique in which subjects are photographed in a still position and then moved slightly when the camera is stopped, as in the famous "marching cigarettes" television commercials.

Super 8mm Introduced in 1966 to replace regular **8mm** film. Used as a distribution medium for educational, scientific and training motion pictures in the 1960s and 1970s. Now largely used by amateurs and independent filmmakers. Though the dimensions of the film in both formats are identical, Super 8mm employs reduced-size perforations to permit an increase of 50% in image area. There are 72 frames to the foot. **Broadcast-quality film-to-videotape transfers** from Super 8mm are now possible on **telecine** machines equipped with the proper gate.

Super VHS or **S-VHS** Enhanced VHS format introduced 1986. By separating chrominance and luminance signals, S-VHS achieves better picture quality and has been promoted as a replacement for **3/4" U-Matic** in the industrial and "prosumer" (high-end consumer) markets. As of 1989, however, S-VHS has proven more appealing to consumers than to professional users.

syndication Distribution of television programs, series and packages to individual broadcasters and cablecasters.

syndicator Company involved in the distribution of television programs to individual broadcasters and cablecasters.

tab-to-tab reproduction Duplication of a section or sections of a film roll. The required section is marked by paper tabs or tape (known as a "tabbed section") or by string (a "corded section"). Many film archives, including the National Archives and Records Adminstration and the Library of Congress, forbid tab-to-tab reproduction; the major newsreel collections usually permit it. When transferring film to videotape, it is generally possible to supervise the transfer session and request the transfer of specific sections only.

talent release A legal form granting permission to reproduce or distribute the likeness or voice of an individual within a production.

Technicolor Trademark of the Technicolor Corporation. Designates various color processes, including two-color Technicolor, **three-strip Technicolor,** and IB (imbibition) Technicolor printing.

Technicolor cassette Enclosure holding an endless loop of Super 8mm film which may be projected simply by insertion into a projector, avoiding film handling and threading.

telecine Apparatus for transferring film to videotape. See **film-to-videotape transfer.**

telecourse Instructional television program, frequently presented as part of a series.

theatrical Distribution of motion pictures in theaters for public showings.

third-party clearances Clearances from recognizable individuals appearing in films or videotapes; from owners or proprietors of musical or literary copyrights on material included within a film or videotape; clearances from unions and guilds; and clearances from owners of recognizable properties or trademarks appearing in a film. Producers are required to secure third-party clearances in many situations, especially when a project is being prepared for broadcast or theatrical release.

35mm Standard film gauge for theatrical and commercial motion picture production; each foot contains 16 frames.

3/4" Videotape format (introduced 1969) now in general use throughout the world for broadcast, industrial production and **ENG.**

three-strip Technicolor Process (introduced 1932) utilizing a special camera that exposed three color separation negatives, recording red, green and blue respectively. Each negative strip was used to make a matrix; each matrix transferred dyes to the final release print.

time code System for numbering video frames in which a code denoting hours, minutes, seconds and frames is assigned to each frame. Time code information is generally stored in digital form on an unused audio track or an address track. In North America, SMPTE (Society of Motion Picture and Television Engineers) time code is standard; EBU (European Broadcasting Union) time code is used in Europe and generally throughout **PAL** standard countries.

time-coded window dub Videotape onto which visible time code numbers have been "burned in." Used for screening, logging purposes, rough editing, and to prevent videotaped footage from unauthorized use.

trailer Also known as "preview." A short film advertising a motion picture, usually containing excerpts from the film.

28mm Film gauge (now obsolete) used primarily in Canada for safety-base release prints.

2" The first videotape recording format (introduced 1956 by Ampex, generally replaced by 1" in the 1970s and 1980s), using reel-to-reel tape running at 15" per second. Also known as **quadruplex** or **quad** after the four heads on the scanning drum.

U-matic See **3/4".**

unedited footage Raw footage not incorporated into a completed film.

usage fees Also known as "access fees." In *Footage 89,* fees charged for the reuse of **public domain** or other material. Usage fees are charged by an entity not necessarily owning copyright to the material, in contrast to **license fees,** charged by copyright owners only.

VHS Consumer videotape format introduced 1977, now dominant throughout the world.

videodisc Medium capable of storing high-quality video, sound and data. Videodiscs employ an optical non-contact pickup system, permitting high-speed access to any information stored on the disc. Information is recorded on the disc in the form of tiny "pits" which are read by a laser beam. Videodiscs generally feature higher image quality than videotape and, because of their random-access capabilities, are an ideal storage medium for interactive programs.

Video 8 Amateur videotape format introduced by Sony. Also known as **8mm video.** Near-broadcast-quality Video 8 equipment was introduced in the United States in 1989.

viewing copy Videotape intended for viewing purposes rather than to generate new copies. Distinct from **master.**

visible time code Visible time code numbers "burned in" over a videotaped image. Used for viewing, logging, rough editing, and to protect footage from unauthorized use. Many stock footage libraries furnish videotapes with visible time code for demonstration purposes and supply master or broadcast-quality videotape only after license fees have been fully paid. Also known as **time-coded window dub.**

window dub See **visible time code.**

wireframe animation Animation (frequently created with the assistance of computer graphic systems) showing the outlines or contours of an object or figure.

workprint Positive film print made from camera original (negative or positive). Used for viewing and editing in place of the original, to which it is matched by edge or key numbers. Also denotes the assembly of picture and sound workprint produced in the editing process, which represents the sum of editing decisions for the entire film. Sometimes used in video production to denote window dubs or videotapes with visible time code which have been prepared for editing purposes.

TWO IMPORTANT FILM COMPILATIONS

❧ For five years, media archaeologist Richard Prelinger has been exploring the hidden layers of our recent past. ❧ What he has discovered will amaze you as much as it entertains you. ❧

TO NEW HORIZONS,

Ephemeral Films 1931 - 1945

Join Roll-Oh the robot, The Breakfast Pals and an army of marching tools on a ride through the futuristic dreams of pre-WWII America.
60 minutes.

Laserdisc or VHS tape $39.95

YOU CAN'T GET THERE FROM HERE,

Ephemeral Films 1946 - 1960

Come back to the age of Dick and Jane and see the movies made to ease Mom and Dad through their "wonderful new (post-war) world."
60 minutes

Laserdisc or VHS tape $39.95

The Voyager Company

1351 PACIFIC COAST HIGHWAY · SANTA MONICA, CALIFORNIA 90401
213.451.1383 · 800.446.2001 · CA ONLY 800.443.2001

The Voyager Company is a joint venture of Janus Films and Voyager Press